JAVA™

HOW TO PROGRAM

SIXTH EDITION

How To Program Series

Advanced Java™ 2 Platform How to Program

C How to Program, 4/E

C++ How to Program, 4/E

C# How to Program

e-Business and e-Commerce How to Program

Internet and World Wide Web How to Program, 3/E

Java How to Program, 6/E

Small Java™ How to Program, 6/E

Perl How to Program

Python How to Program

Visual C++® .NET How to Program

Visual Basic® 6 How to Program

Visual Basic® .NET How to Program, 2/E

Wireless Internet & Mobile Business How to Program

XML How to Program

Simply Series

Simply C++: An Application-Driven Tutorial Approach

Simply C#: An Application-Driven Tutorial Approach

Simply Java™ Programming: An Application-Driven Tutorial Approach

Simply Visual Basic® .NET: An Application Driven Tutorial Approach (Visual Studio .NET 2002 Edition)

Simply Visual Basic® .NET: An Application Driven Tutorial Approach (Visual Studio .NET 2003 Edition)

.NET How to Program Series

C# How to Program

Visual Basic® .NET How to Program, 2/E

Visual C++® .NET How to Program

For Managers Series

e-Business and e-Commerce for Managers

Visual Studio® Series

C# How to Program

Visual Basic® .NET How to Program, 2/E

Getting Started with Microsoft® Visual C++® 6 with an Introduction to MFC

Visual Basic® 6 How to Program

Also Available

e-books

Premium CourseCompass, WebCT and Blackboard Multimedia Cyber Classroom versions

Pearson Choices: SafariX

Multimedia Cyber Classroom and Web-Based Training Series

C++ Multimedia Cyber Classroom, 4/E

C# Multimedia Cyber Classroom

e-Business and e-Commerce Multimedia Cyber Classroom

Internet and World Wide Web Multimedia Cyber Classroom, 2/E

Java™ 2 Multimedia Cyber Classroom, 5/E

Perl Multimedia Cyber Classroom

Python Multimedia Cyber Classroom

Visual Basic® 6 Multimedia Cyber Classroom

Visual Basic® .NET Multimedia Cyber Classroom, 2/E

Wireless Internet & Mobile Business Programming Multimedia Cyber Classroom

XML Multimedia Cyber Classroom

The Complete Training Course Series

The Complete C++ Training Course, 4/E

The Complete C# Training Course

The Complete e-Business and e-Commerce Programming Training Course

The Complete Internet and World Wide Web Programming Training Course, 2/E

The Complete Java™ 2 Training Course, 5/E

The Complete Perl Training Course

The Complete Python Training Course

The Complete Visual Basic® 6 Training Course

The Complete Visual Basic® .NET Training Course, 2/E

The Complete Wireless Internet & Mobile Business Programming Training Course

The Complete XML Programming Training Course

To follow the Deitel publishing program, please register at:
www.deitel.com/newsletter/subscribe.html
for the free *DEITEL® BUZZ ONLINE* e-mail newsletter.

To communicate with the authors, send e-mail to:
   deitel@deitel.com

For information on corporate on-site seminars offered by Deitel & Associates, Inc. worldwide, visit:
   www.deitel.com or write to deitel@deitel.com

For continuing updates on Prentice Hall/Deitel publications visit:
   www.deitel.com,
   www.prenhall.com/deitel or
   www.InformIT.com/deitel

Library of Congress Cataloging-in-Publication Data
On file

Vice President and Editorial Director, ECS: *Marcia J. Horton*
Senior Acquisitions Editor: *Kate Hargett*
Associate Editor: *Jennifer Cappello*
Assistant Editor: *Sarah Parker*
Editorial Assistant: *Michael Giacobbe*
Vice President and Director of Production and Manufacturing, ESM: *David W. Riccardi*
Executive Managing Editor: *Vince O'Brien*
Managing Editor: *Tom Manshreck*
Production Editor: *John F. Lovell*
Production Editor, Media: *Bob Engelhardt*
Production Assistant: *Asha Rohra*
Director of Creative Services: *Paul Belfanti*
A/V Production Editor: *Xiaohong Zhu*
Art Studio: *Artworks, York, PA*
Art Director: *Geoffrey Cassar*
Cover Design: *Harvey M. Deitel, Shawn Murphy, Geoffrey Cassar*
Interior Design: *Harvey M. Deitel, Geoffrey Cassar*
Manufacturing Manager: *Trudy Pisciotti*
Manufacturing Buyer: *Lisa McDowell*
Marketing Manager: *Pamela Hersperger*
Marketing Assistant: *Barrie Reinhold*

© 2005 by Pearson Education, Inc.
Upper Saddle River, New Jersey 07458

Printed in the United States of America

10 9 8 7 6 5 4 3 2

ISBN 0-13-148398-6

Pearson Education Ltd., *London*
Pearson Education Australia Pty. Ltd., *Sydney*
Pearson Education Singapore, Pte. Ltd.
Pearson Education North Asia Ltd., *Hong Kong*
Pearson Education Canada, Inc., *Toronto*
Pearson Educacion de Mexico, S.A. de C.V.
Pearson Education–Japan, *Tokyo*
Pearson Education Malaysia, Pte. Ltd.
Pearson Education, Inc., *Upper Saddle River, New Jersey*

JAVA™

HOW TO PROGRAM

SIXTH EDITION

H. M. Deitel

Deitel & Associates, Inc.

P. J. Deitel

Deitel & Associates, Inc.

PEARSON
Prentice
Hall

Upper Saddle River, New Jersey 07458

Trademarks

In memory of Edsger W. Dijkstra:
We continue to learn from your writings every day.

Harvey M. Deitel and Paul J. Deitel

Contents

8   Classes and Objects: A Deeper Look   357

9   Object-Oriented Programming: Inheritance   415

12 Graphics and Java 2D™ 595

13 Exception Handling 638

20 Introduction to Java Applets 958

21 Multimedia: Applets and Applications 977

22 GUI Components: Part 2 1005

26 Servlets 1236

27 JavaServer Pages (JSP) 1280

Preface

"Live in fragments no longer, only connect."
—Edgar Morgan Foster

Welcome to Java and *Java How to Program, Sixth Edition*! At Deitel & Associates, we write computer science textbooks and professional books. This book was a joy to create. To start, we put the fifth edition of *Java How to Program* under the microscope:

- We audited the presentation against the most recent ACM/IEEE curriculum recommendations and the Computer Science Advanced Placement Examination.

- All of the chapters have been significantly updated and upgraded.

- We changed to an early classes and objects pedagogy. Now students build their first reusable classes starting in Chapter 3.

- All of the GUI and graphics in the early chapters has been replaced by carefully paced optional sections in Chapters 3–10 with two special exercise sections in Chapters 11 and 12. Instructors have a broad choice of the amount of GUI and graphics to cover—from none, to a 10-section introductory sequence, to a deep treatment in Chapters 11, 12 and 22.

- We updated our object-oriented presentation to use the latest version of the *UML (Unified Modeling Language)—UML™ 2.0*—the industry-standard graphical language for modeling object-oriented systems.

- We replaced the optional elevator simulator case study from the previous edition with a new optional OOD/UML automated teller machine (ATM) case study in Chapters 1–8 and 10. The new case study is much simpler and more attractive for first and second programming courses.

- Several multi-section object-oriented programming case studies have been added.

- We incorporated key new features of Sun Microsystems' latest release of Java— the *Java 2 Platform, Standard Edition version 5.0 (J2SE 5.0)*.

- The design of the book has been completely revised. This new design uses color, fonts and various design elements to enhance a student's learning experience.

All of this has been carefully scrutinized by a team of 37 distinguished academic and industry reviewers.

We believe that this book and its support materials have everything instructors and students need for an informative, interesting, challenging and entertaining Java educational experience. In this Preface, we overview various conventions used in the book, such as syntax coloring the code examples, "code washing" and code highlighting. We discuss the software bundled with the book as well as the comprehensive suite of educational materials that help instructors maximize their students' learning experience, including the *Instructor's*

Resource CD, PowerPoint® Slide lecture notes, lab manual, companion Web site, course management systems, SafariX (Pearson Education's WebBook publications) and more.

As you read this book, if you have questions, send an e-mail to deitel@deitel.com; we will respond promptly. Please visit our Web site, www.deitel.com, regularly and be sure to sign up for the free *Deitel® Buzz Online* e-mail newsletter at www.deitel.com/newsletter/subscribe.html. We use the Web site and the newsletter to keep our readers and industry clients informed of the latest news on Deitel publications and services. Please check the Web site occasionally for errata, updates regarding the Java software, free downloads and other resources.

Features in *Java How to Program, 6/e*

This new edition contains many new and enhanced features including:

Updated for the Java 2 Platform Standard Edition 5.0 (J2SE 5.0)

We updated entire text to reflect the latest release of J2SE 5.0. New topics include:

- obtaining formatted input with class Scanner
- displaying formatted output with the System.out object's printf method
- using enhanced for statements to process array elements and collections
- declaring methods with variable-length argument lists ("varargs")
- using enum classes that declare sets of constants
- importing the static members of one class for use in another
- converting primitive-type values to type-wrapper objects and vice versa using autoboxing and auto-unboxing, respectively
- using generics to create general models of methods and classes that can be declared once, but used with many different data types
- using the generics-enhanced data structures of the Collections API
- using the Concurrency API to implement multithreaded applications
- using JDBC RowSets to access data in a database

In addition, we carefully audited the manuscript against the *Java Language Specification* (available at java.sun.com/docs/books/jls/index.html). The programs you create as you study this text should work with any J2SE 5.0 compatible Java platform.

[*Note:* Sun Microsystems recently renamed J2SE from the **Java 2 Platform, Standard Edition 1.5.0** to the **Java 2 Platform, Standard Edition 5.0**. However, Sun decided not to replace all occurrences of 1.5.0 with 5.0 in the online Java documentation (available at java.sun.com/j2se/1.5.0/docs/api/index.html) and in the software installation directory (which is called jdk1.5.0). Sun's Web site accepts URLs that replace 1.5.0 with 5.0. For example, you can use the URL java.sun.com/j2se/5.0/docs/api/index.html to access the online documentation.]

New Interior Design

Working with the creative services team at Prentice Hall, we redesigned the interior styles for our *How to Program* Series. In response to reader requests, we now place the key terms and the index's page reference for each defining occurrence in blue, bold style text for easier reference. We emphasize on-screen components in the bold **Helvetica** font (e.g., the **File** menu) and emphasize Java program text in the Lucida font (for example, int x = 5).

Syntax Coloring

This book is presented in full color to show programs and their outputs as they typically appear on a computer screen. We syntax color all the Java code, as most Java integrated-development environments and code editors do. This greatly improves code readability—an especially important goal, given that this book contains 20,383 lines of code. Our syntax-coloring conventions are as follows:

```
comments appear in green
keywords appear in dark blue
errors and JSP scriptlet delimiters appear in red
constants and literal values appear in light blue
all other code appears in black
```

Code Highlighting

Extensive code highlighting makes it easy for readers to spot each program's featured segments and helps students review the material rapidly when preparing for exams or labs.

"Code Washing"

"Code washing" is our term for applying comments, using meaningful identifiers, applying uniform indentation conventions and using vertical spacing to highlight significant program units. This process results in programs that are easy to read and self-documenting. We have extensively "code washed" of all the source-code programs in the text and in the book's ancillaries. We have worked hard to make our code exemplary.

Early Classes and Objects Approach

Students are still introduced to the basic concepts and terminology of object technology in Chapter 1. In the previous edition, students began developing their customized classes and objects in Chapter 8, but in this edition, they start doing that in our completely new Chapter 3. Chapters 4–7 have been carefully rewritten from an "early classes and objects approach." For all intents and purposes, this new edition is object-oriented from the start and throughout the text. Moving the discussion of objects and classes to earlier chapters gets students "thinking about objects" immediately and mastering these concepts more thoroughly. Java is not trivial by any means, but it's fun to program with, and students can see immediate results. Students can get text-based and graphical programs running quickly by using Java's extensive class libraries of reusable components.

Carefully Tuned Treatment of Object-Oriented Programming in Chapters 8–10

We performed a high-precision upgrade of *Java How to Program, 5/e*. This edition is clearer and more accessible—especially if you are new to object-oriented programming (OOP). We completely rewrote the OOP chapters with an integrated case study in which we develop an employee payroll hierarchy, and we motivate interfaces with a payables hierarchy.

Case Studies

This book is loaded with case studies that span multiple sections and chapters. Often we build on a class introduced earlier in the book to demonstrate new programming concepts later in the book. Students learn the new concepts in the context of applications that they already know. These case studies include the development of the:

- GradeBook class in Chapters 3, 4, 5 and 7
- ATM application in the optional OOD/UML sections of Chapters 1–8 and 10
- polymorphic drawing program in the optional GUI and Graphics track in Chapters 3–12
- Time class in several sections of Chapter 8
- Employee payroll application in Chapter 9 and Chapter 10

Integrated *GradeBook* Case Study

To reinforce our early classes presentation, we present an integrated case study using classes and objects in Chapters 3–5 and 7. We incrementally build a GradeBook class that represents an instructor's grade book and performs various calculations based on a set of student grades—finding the average, finding the maximum and minimum, and printing a bar chart. Our goal is to familiarize students with the important concepts of objects and classes through a real-world example of a substantial class. We develop this class from the ground up, constructing methods from control statements and carefully developed algorithms, and adding instance variables and arrays as needed to enhance the functionality of the class.

GUI and Graphics Case Study (Optional)

The optional GUI and Graphics Case Study in Chapters 3–12 demonstrates techniques for adding visual elements to applications. It is designed for those who want to begin learning Java's powerful capabilities for creating graphical user interfaces (GUIs) and graphics. Each section introduces basic concepts and provides visual, graphical examples and complete source code. In the first few sections, we show how to create simple graphical applications. In the subsequent sections, we use the object-oriented programming concepts presented through Chapter 10 to create an application that draws a variety of shapes polymorphically. In Chapter 11, we add an event-driven GUI interface and in Chapter 12 we incorporate graphics features of Java 2D.

Unified Modeling Language (UML)—Using the UML 2.0 to Develop an Object-Oriented Design of an ATM

The Unified Modeling Language™ (UML) has become the preferred graphical modeling language for designing object-oriented systems. All the UML diagrams in the book comply with the new UML 2.0 specification. We use UML class diagrams to visually represent classes and their inheritance relationships, and we use UML activity diagrams to demonstrate the flow of control in each of Java's several control statements.

This *Sixth Edition* includes a new, optional (but highly recommended) case study on object-oriented design using the UML. The case study was reviewed by a distinguished team of OOD/UML academic and industry professionals, including leaders in the field from Rational (the creators of the UML and now a division of IBM) and the Object Management Group (responsible for maintaining and evolving the UML). In the case study, we design and fully implement the software for a simple automatic teller machine (ATM). The "Software Engineering Case Study" sections at the ends of Chapters 1–8 and 10 present a carefully paced introduction to object-oriented design using the UML. We introduce a concise, simplified subset of the UML 2.0, then guide the reader through a first design experience intended for the novice object-oriented designer/programmer. The case study is not an exercise; rather, it is an end-to-end learning experience that concludes with a detailed walkthrough of the complete Java code. The "Software Engineering Case Study" sections help students develop an object-oriented design to complement the object-oriented programming concepts they begin learning in Chapter 1 and implementing in Chapter 3. In the first of these sections at the end of Chapter 1, we introduce basic concepts and terminology of OOD. In the optional "Software Engineering Case Study" sections at the ends of Chapters 2–5, we consider more substantial issues, as we undertake a challenging problem with the techniques of OOD. We analyze a typical requirements document that specifies a system to be built, determine the objects needed to implement that system, determine the attributes these objects need to have, determine the behaviors these objects need to exhibit and specify how the objects must interact with one another to meet the system requirements. In Appendix J, we include a Java implementation of the object-oriented system that we designed in the earlier chapters. This case study will help prepare students for the kinds of substantial projects they will encounter in industry. We employ a carefully developed, incremental object-oriented design process to produce a UML model for our ATM system. From this design, we produce a substantial working Java implementation using key programming notions, including classes, objects, encapsulation, visibility, composition, inheritance and polymorphism.

Database and Web-Applications Development with JDBC, Servlets and JSP

Chapter 25, Accessing Databases with JDBC, demonstrates how to build data-driven applications with the JDBC™ API. Chapter 26, Servlets, and Chapter 27, JavaServer Pages (JSP), expand our treatment of Internet and Web programming topics, giving readers everything they need to develop their own Web-based applications. Readers will learn how to build so-called *n*-tier applications, in which the functionality provided by each tier can be distributed to separate computers across the Internet or executed on the same computer. In particular, we build a three-tier Web-based survey application and a three-tier Web-based guest-book application. Each application's information is stored in the application's data tier—in this book, a database implemented with MySQL (a trial version is on the CD that accompanies this book). The user enters requests and receives responses at each application's client tier, which is typically a computer running a Web browser such as Microsoft Internet Explorer or Netscape. Web browsers, of course, know how to communicate with Web sites throughout the Internet. The middle tier contains both a Web server and one or more application-specific servlets (Java programs that extend the server to handle requests from client browsers) or JavaServer Pages (an extension of servlets that simplifies handling requests and formatting responses to client browsers). We use Apache's Tomcat Web server for these examples. Tomcat, which is the reference implementation for the servlets and JavaServer Pages technologies, is included on the CD that accompanies this book and is available free for download from `www.apache.org`. Tomcat communicates with client Web browsers across the Internet using the HyperText Transfer Protocol (HTTP)—the foundation of the World Wide Web. We discuss the crucial role of the Web server in Web programming and provide extensive examples demonstrating interactions between a Web browser and a Web server.

Teaching Approach

Java How to Program, 6/e contains a rich collection of examples, exercises and projects drawn from many fields to provide the student with a chance to solve interesting real-world problems. The book concentrates on the principles of good software engineering and stresses program clarity. We avoid arcane terminology and syntax specifications in favor of teaching by example. Our code examples have been tested on popular Java platforms. We are educators who teach leading-edge topics in industry classrooms worldwide. Dr. Harvey M. Deitel has 20 years of college teaching experience and 15 years of industry teaching experience. Paul Deitel has 12 years of industry teaching experience and is one of the world's most experienced Java corporate trainers, having taught about 100 Java courses at all levels since 1996 to government, industry, military and academic clients of Deitel & Associates.

Learning Java via the LIVE-CODE Approach

Java How to Program, 6/e, is loaded with LIVE-CODE examples—each new concept is presented in the context of a complete working Java application that is immediately followed by one or more sample executions showing the program's inputs and outputs. This style exemplifies the way we teach and write about programming. We call this method of teaching and writing the LIVE-CODE Approach. *We use programming languages to teach programming languages.* Reading the examples in the text is much like typing and running them on a computer. We provide all the source code for the book's examples on the accompanying CD and at www.deitel.com—making it easy for students to run each example as they study it.

World Wide Web Access

All of the source-code examples for *Java How to Program, 6/e,* (and our other publications) are available on the Internet as downloads from the following Web sites:

```
www.deitel.com
www.prenhall.com/deitel
```

Registration is quick and easy, and the downloads are free. We suggest that students download all the examples, then run each program as they read the corresponding text discussions. Making changes to the examples and immediately seeing the effects of those changes is a great way to enhance your Java learning experience.

Objectives

Each chapter begins with a statement of objectives. This lets students know what to expect and gives them an opportunity, after reading the chapter, to determine if they have met these objectives. This is a confidence builder and a source of positive reinforcement.

Quotations

The learning objectives are followed by quotations. Some are humorous, philosophical or offer interesting insights. We hope that you will enjoy relating the quotations to the chapter material. Many of the quotations are worth a second look after reading the chapter.

Outline

The chapter outline helps students approach the material in a top-down fashion, so they can anticipate what is to come, and set a comfortable and effective learning pace.

20,383 Lines of Code in 256 Example Programs (with Program Outputs)

Our LIVE-CODE programs range in size from just a few lines of code to substantial examples containing hundreds of lines of code. Each program is followed by a window containing the outputs produced when the program is run, so students can confirm that the programs run as expected. Relating outputs to the program statements that produce them is an excellent way to learn and to reinforce concepts. Our programs demonstrate the diverse features of Java. The code is syntax colored, with Java keywords, comments and other program text each appearing in different colors. This facilitates reading the code—students will especially appreciate the syntax coloring when they read the larger programs.

816 Illustrations/Figures

An abundance of charts, tables, line drawings, programs and program outputs is included. We model the flow of control in control statements with UML activity diagrams. UML class diagrams model the fields, constructors and methods of classes. We use additional types of UML diagrams throughout our optional OOD/UML ATM case study.

481 Programming Tips

We include programming tips to help students focus on important aspects of program development. We highlight these tips in the form of *Good Programming Practices, Common Programming Errors, Error-Prevention Tips, Look-and-Feel Observations, Performance Tips, Portability Tips* and *Software Engineering Observations*. These tips and practices represent the best we have gleaned from a combined six decades of programming and teaching experience. One of our students—a mathematics major—told us that she feels this approach is like the highlighting of axioms, theorems and corollaries in mathematics books; it provides a basis on which to build good software.

Good Programming Practices

Good Programming Practices *are tips for writing clear programs. These techniques help students produce programs that are more readable, self-documenting and easier to maintain.*

Common Programming Errors

Students who are new to programming (or a programming language) tend to make certain errors frequently. Focusing on these Common Programming Errors *reduces the likelihood that students will make the same mistakes and shortens long lines outside instructors' offices during office hours!*

Error-Prevention Tips

When we first designed this "tip type," we thought we would use it strictly to tell people how to test and debug Java programs. In fact, many of the tips describe aspects of Java that reduce the likelihood of "bugs" and thus simplify the testing and debugging processes.

Look-and-Feel Observations

Look-and-Feel Observations *highlight graphical user interface conventions. These observations help students design their own graphical user interfaces in conformance with industry norms.*

Performance Tips

In our experience, teaching students to write clear and understandable programs is by far the most important goal for a first programming course. But students want to write the programs that run the fastest, use the least memory, require the smallest number of keystrokes, or dazzle other nifty ways. Students really care about performance. They want to know what they can to "turbo charge" their programs. So we highlight opportunities for improving program performance—making programs run faster or minimizing the amount of memory that they occupy.

Portability Tips

One of Java's "claims to fame" is "universal" portability, so some programmers assume that an application written in Java will automatically be "perfectly" portable across all Java platforms. Unfortunately, this is not always the case. We include Portability Tips *to help students write portable code and to provide insights on how Java achieves its high degree of portability.*

Software Engineering Observations

The object-oriented programming paradigm requires a complete rethinking about the way we build software. Java is an effective language for performing good software engineering. The Software Engineering Observations *highlight architectural and design issues that affect the construction of software systems, especially large-scale systems. Much of what the student learns here will be useful in upper-level courses and in industry as the student begins to work with large, complex, real-world systems.*

Wrap-Up Section

New in this edition, each chapter ends with a brief "wrap-up" section that recaps the topics that were presented. Each section also helps the student transition to the next chapter.

Summary (1,303 Summary Bullets)

Each chapter ends with additional pedagogical devices. We present a thorough, bullet-list-style summary of the chapter. On average, there are 45 summary bullets per chapter. This helps the students review and reinforce key concepts.

Terminology (2,388 Terms)

We include an alphabetized list of the important terms defined in each chapter—again, for further reinforcement. There is an average of 82 terms per chapter. Each term also appears in the index, and the defining occurrence of each term is highlighted in the index with a blue, bold page number so the student can locate the definitions of terms quickly.

701 Self-Review Exercises and Answers (Count Includes Separate Parts)

Extensive self-review exercises and answers are included for self-study. This gives the student a chance to build confidence with the material and prepare for the regular exercises. We encourage students to do all the self-review exercises and check their answers.

Exercises (Count Includes Separate Parts)

Each chapter concludes with a set of exercises, including simple recall of important terminology and concepts; writing individual Java statements; writing small portions of Java methods and classes; writing complete Java methods, classes, applications and applets; and major term projects. The large number of exercises across a wide variety of areas enables instructors to tailor their courses to the unique needs of their classes and to vary course assignments each semester. Instructors can use these exercises to form homework assignments, short quizzes and/or major examinations. The solutions for the vast majority of the exercises are included on the *Instructor's Resource CD (IRCD)*, which is *available only* to instructors through their Prentice Hall representatives. [**NOTE: Please do not write to us requesting the instructor's CD. Distribution of this ancillary is limited strictly to college professors teaching from the book. Instructors may obtain the solutions manual only from their Prentice Hall representatives.**] Students will have access to approximately half of the solutions in the book in the free, Web-based *Cyber Classroom* which will be available in Spring 2005. For more information about the availability of the *Cyber Classroom*, please visit `www.deitel.com` or sign up for the free *Deitel® Buzz Online* e-mail newsletter at `www.deitel.com/newsletter/subscribe.html`.

Approximately 7150 Index Entries
We have included an extensive index at the back of the book. This helps students find terms or concepts by keyword. The Index is useful to people reading the book for the first time and is especially useful to practicing programmers who use the book as a reference.

"Double Indexing" of Java LIVE-CODE Examples
Java How to Program, 6/e has 256 live-code examples and 874 exercises (including parts). We have double indexed each of the live-code examples and most of the more substantial exercises. For every source-code program in the book, we indexed the figure caption both alphabetically and as a subindex item under "Examples." This makes it easier to find examples using particular features. The more substantial exercises are also indexed both alphabetically and as subindex items under "Exercises."

Tour of the Book

In this section, we take a tour of the many capabilities of Java that we explore in *Java How to Program, 6/e*. Figure 1 illustrates the dependencies among the chapters. We recommend studying these topics in the order indicated by the arrows, though other orders are possible. This book is widely used in all levels of Java programming courses. Search the Web for "syllabus," "Java" and "Deitel" to find syllabi used with recent editions this book.

Chapter 1—Introduction to Computers, the Internet and the Web—discusses what computers are, how they work and how they are programmed. The chapter gives a brief history of the development of programming languages from machine languages, to assembly languages and to high-level languages. The origin of the Java programming language is discussed. The chapter includes an introduction to a typical Java programming environment. Chapter 1 walks readers through a "test drive" of a typical Java application. This chapter also introduces basic object technology concepts and terminology and the Unified Modeling Language.

Chapter 2—Introduction to Java Applications—provides a lightweight introduction to programming applications in the Java programming language. The chapter introduces nonprogrammers to basic programming concepts and constructs. The programs in this chapter illustrate how to display data on the screen and how to obtain data from the user at the keyboard. This chapter introduces J2SE 5.0's new `Scanner` class, which greatly simplifies obtaining user input. This chapter also introduces some of J2SE 5.0's new formatted output capabilities with method `System.out.printf`. Chapter 2 ends with detailed treatments of decision making and arithmetic operations.

Chapter 3—Introduction to Classes and Objects—introduces classes, objects, methods, constructors and instance variables using five simple real-world examples. The first four of these begin our **case study on developing a grade-book class** that instructors can use to maintain student test scores. The first example presents a `GradeBook` class with one method that simply displays a welcome message when it is called. We show how to create an object of that class and call the method so that it displays the welcome message. The second example modifies the first by allowing the method to receive a course name as

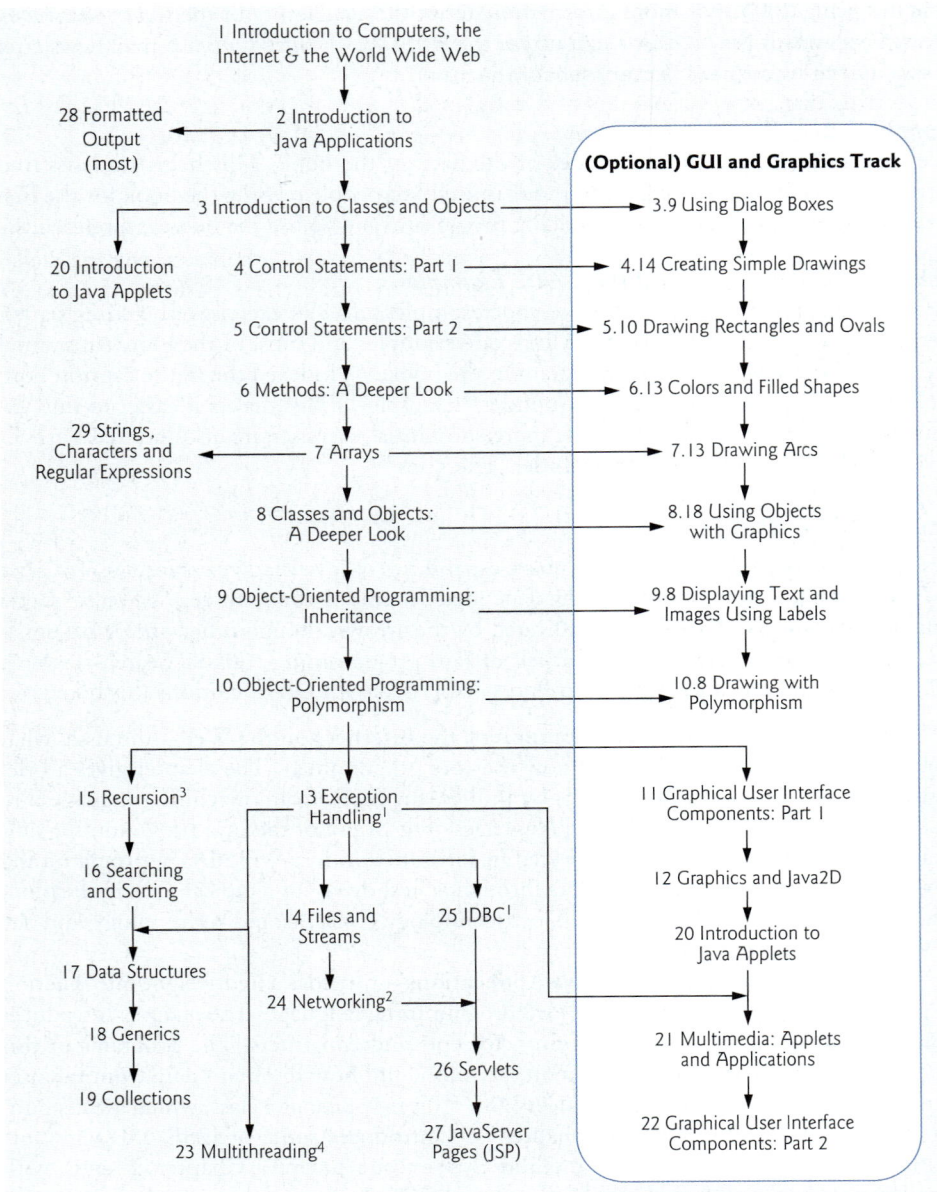

1. Dependent on Chapter 11 for GUI used in one example.
2. Dependent on Chapter 20 for one example that uses an applet. The two large case studies at the end of this chapter each depend on Chapter 22 for GUI and Chapter 23 for multithreading.
3. Dependent on Chapters 11 and 12 for GUI and graphics used in one example.
4. Dependent on Chapter 11 for GUI used in one example. Dependent on Chapters 18 and 19 for one example.

Fig. 1 | Flowchart illustrating the dependencies among chapters in *Java How to Program, 6/e*.

an argument and by displaying the name as part of the welcome message. The third example illustrates storing the course name in a GradeBook object. For this version of the class, we also show how to set the course name and obtain the course name using methods. The fourth example demonstrates how the data in a GradeBook object can be initialized when the object is created—the initialization is performed by the class's constructor. The last example introduces floating-point numbers in the context of a bank account class that maintains a customer's balance. The chapter describes how to declare a class and use it to create an object and then discusses how to declare methods in a class to implement the class's behaviors, how to declare instance variables in a class to implement the class's attributes and how to call an object's methods to make them perform their tasks. Chapter 3 explains the differences between instance variables of a class and local variables of a method, how to use a constructor to ensure that an object's data is initialized when the object is created, and the differences between primitive and reference types.

Chapter 4—**Control Statements: Part 1**—focuses on the program-development process. The chapter discusses how to take a problem statement and develop a working Java program from it, including performing intermediate steps in pseudocode. The chapter introduces some primitive types and simple control statements for decision making (if and if...else) and repetition (while). We examine counter-controlled and sentinel-controlled repetition using the **GradeBook class** from Chapter 3, and introduce Java's increment, decrement and assignment operators. The chapter includes **two enhanced versions of the GradeBook class**, each based on Chapter 3's final version. These versions each include a method that uses control statements to calculate the average of a set of student grades. In the first version, the method uses counter-controlled repetition to input 10 student grades from the user, then determines the average grade. In the second version, the method uses sentinel-controlled repetition to input an arbitrary number of grades from the user, then calculates the average of the grades that were entered. The chapter uses simple UML activity diagrams to show the flow of control through each of the control statements.

Chapter 5—**Control Statements: Part 2**—continues the discussions of Java control statements with examples of the for repetition statement, the do...while repetition statement, the switch selection statement, the break statement and the continue statement. We create an **enhanced version of class GradeBook** that uses a switch statement to count the number of A, B, C, D and F grade equivalents in a set of numeric grades entered by the user. This version uses sentinel-controlled repetition to input the grades. While reading the grades from the user, a method modifies instance variables that keep track of the sum of the grades entered and the number of grades entered, as well as the count of grades in each letter grade category. Other methods of the class then use these instance variables to perform the averaging calculation and display a summary report based on the grades entered. The chapter also discusses logical operators.

Chapter 6—**Methods: A Deeper Look**—takes a deeper look inside objects and their methods. We discuss class-library methods and examine more closely how students can build their own methods. We present our first example of a method with multiple parameters. A portion of the chapter focuses on developing a game playing application that uses random number generation to simulate the rolling of dice. This application divides its required work into small, reusable methods. The techniques presented in Chapter 6 are essential to the production of properly organized programs, especially the larger programs that system programmers and application programmers are likely to develop. The topic of method overloading (i.e., allowing multiple methods to have the same name provided they have different "signatures") is motivated and explained clearly. We introduce the method call stack to explain how Java is able to keep track of which method is currently executing, how local variables of methods are maintained in memory and how a method knows where to return after it completes execution. Additional chapter topics include static methods, static fields, class Math, enumerations and the scope of declarations.

Chapter 7—Arrays—explains how to process lists and tables of values. Arrays in Java are objects, further evidence of Java's commitment to almost 100% object orientation. We discuss the structuring data in arrays of data items of the same type. The chapter presents numerous examples of both one-dimensional arrays and two-dimensional arrays. The examples investigate common array manipulations, printing bar charts, passing arrays to methods and an introduction to the field of survey data analysis (with simple statistics). The chapter includes a case study that simulates the shuffling and dealing of playing cards in a game playing application. Also, the chapter includes the **final two GradeBook case study sections**, in which we use arrays to store student grades for the duration of a program's execution. Previous versions of the class process a set of grades entered by the user, but do not maintain the individual grade values in instance variables of the class. Thus, repeat calculations require the user to reenter the same grades. In this chapter, we use arrays to enable an object of the GradeBook class to maintain a set of grades in memory, thus eliminating the need to repeatedly input the same set of grades. The first version of the class in this chapter stores the grades in a one-dimensional array and can produce a report containing the average of the grades, the minimum and maximum grades and a bar chart representing the grade distribution. The second version of the class in this chapter (i.e., the final version in the case study) uses a two-dimensional array to store the grades of a number of students on multiple exams in a semester. This version can calculate each student's semester average, as well as the minimum and maximum grades across all grades received for the semester. The class also produces a bar chart displaying the overall grade distribution for the semester. This chapter introduces J2SE 5.0's new enhanced for statement to traverse the elements of an array. Variable-length argument lists (new in J2SE 5.0) are also demonstrated.

Chapter 8—Objects: A Deeper Look—begins a deeper discussion of objects and classes. The chapter represents a wonderful opportunity for teaching data abstraction the "right way"—through a language (Java) expressly devoted to implementing new types. Building on the concepts introduced in Chapters 3–7, the chapter focuses on the essence and terminology of classes and objects. In the context of the **Time class case study**, Chapter 8 discusses implementing Java classes, accessing class members, enforcing information hiding with access modifiers, separating interface from implementation, using access methods and utility methods and initializing objects with constructors. We discuss declaring and using constants, composition, the this reference, static class members and examples of popular abstract data types such as stacks and queues. We introduce the package statement and discuss how to create reusable packages, and present J2SE 5.0's new static import and enum capabilities. Java's enums are class types that can have methods, constructors and fields.

Chapter 9—Object-Oriented Programming: Inheritance—introduces one of the most fundamental capabilities of object-oriented programming languages—inheritance—which is a form of software reusability in which new classes are developed quickly and easily by absorbing the capabilities of existing classes and adding appropriate new capabilities. In the context of an `Employee hierarchy`, this substantially revised chapter presents a five-example sequence demonstrating `private` data, `protected` data and software reuse via inheritance. We begin by demonstrating a class with `private` instance variables and `public` methods to manipulate that data. Next, we implement a second class with additional capabilities. To do this, we duplicate much of the first example's code. The third example begins our discussion of inheritance and software reuse—we use the class from the first example as a superclass and inherit its data and functionality into a new subclass. This example introduces the inheritance mechanism and demonstrates that a subclass cannot access its superclass's `private` members directly. This motivates our fourth example, in which we introduce `protected` data in the superclass and demonstrate that the subclass can indeed access the `protected` data inherited from the superclass. The last example in the sequence demonstrates proper software engineering by defining the superclass's data as `private` and using the superclass's `public` methods (that were inherited by the subclass) to manipulate the superclass's `private` data in the subclass. The chapter discusses the notions of superclasses and subclasses, direct and indirect superclasses, use of constructors in superclasses and subclasses, and software engineering with inheritance. The chapter also compares inheritance (*is a* relationships) with composition (*has a* relationships).

Chapter 10—Object-Oriented Programming: Polymorphism—deals with another fundamental capability of object-oriented programming: polymorphic behavior. The completely revised Chapter 10 builds on the inheritance concepts presented in Chapter 9 and focuses on the relationships among classes in a class hierarchy, and the powerful processing capabilities that these relationships enable. A feature of this chapter is its two polymorphism case studies—a **payroll system using an abstract class `Employee`** and an **accounts payable system using an interface `Payable`**. Both case studies expand on the `Employee hierarchy` introduced in Chapter 9. The first case study processes an array of variables that contain references to `Employee` objects. All the objects referenced by the array elements have a common abstract superclass `Employee` containing the set of methods common to every class in the hierarchy. The case study demonstrates that when a method is invoked via a superclass reference, the subclass-specific version of that method is invoked. The case study also shows how a program that processes objects polymorphically can perform type-specific processing by determining the type of the object currently being processed via operator `instanceof`. This chapter distinguishes between abstract classes and concrete classes, and introduces interfaces—Java's replacement for the feature of C++ called multiple inheritance—in the context of the second payroll case study.

Chapter 11—Graphical User Interface Components: Part 1—introduces several of Java's Swing components for creating programs with user-friendly graphical user interfaces (GUIs). These platform-independent GUI components are written entirely in Java, providing them with great flexibility. Swing components can be customized to look like the computer platform on which the program executes, or they can use the standard Java look-and-feel to provide an identical user interface on all computer platforms. GUI development is a huge topic, so we divided it into two chapters. These chapters cover the material in sufficient depth to enable you to build rich user interfaces. The chapter illustrates GUI principles, the `javax.swing` hierarchy, labels, buttons, lists, textfields, combo boxes, checkboxes, radio buttons, panels, handling mouse events, handling keyboard events and layout managers used to position components. We present the powerful concept of nested classes that help hide implementation details. Then, the chapter demonstrates our first

GUI-based applications as part of a more complete introduction to event handling. In these examples, we use nested classes to define the event handlers for several GUI components.

Chapter 12—Graphics and Java 2D—presents Java's graphical capabilities. We discuss graphics contexts and graphics objects; drawing strings, characters and bytes; color and font control; screen manipulation; and paint modes and drawing lines, rectangles, rounded rectangles, three-dimensional rectangles, ovals, arcs and polygons. We introduce the Java 2D API, which provides powerful two-dimensional graphics capabilities. Figure 12.29 and Fig. 12.30 are examples of how easy it is to use the Java 2D API to create complex graphics effects such as textures and gradients.

Chapter 13—Exception Handling—is one of the most important chapters in the book from the standpoint of building "mission-critical" or "business-critical" applications. Programmers need to be concerned with, "What happens when the component I call on to do a job experiences difficulty? How will that component signal that it had a problem?" To use a Java component, you need to know not only how that component behaves when "things go well," but also what exceptions that component "throws" when "things go poorly." The chapter distinguishes between Exceptions and rather serious system Errors, and distinguishes further between checked Exceptions (which the compiler requires an application to catch or declare) and unchecked Exceptions (which an application is not required to catch or declare). The chapter discusses the elements of exception handling, including try blocks, catch blocks, finally blocks and the throw statement. The chapter also introduces Java's chained-exception facility. The material in this chapter is crucial to many of the examples in the remainder of the book.

Chapter 14—Files and Streams—deals with input/output that is accomplished through streams of data directed to and from files. The chapter begins with an introduction to the data hierarchy from bits, to bytes, to fields, to records, to files. Next, Java's view of files and streams is presented as well as the differences between text files and binary files. We show how programs pass data to secondary storage devices, like disks, and how programs retrieve data already stored on those devices. We demonstrate manipulating both sequential- and random-access files. We discuss class File which programs use to obtain information about files and directories. The chapter explains how objects can be input and output in their entirety by using object serialization. We also introduce the JFileChooser dialog, which enables users of a program to easily select files. Many of the stream processing techniques demonstrated in this chapter can also be used to create applications that communicate with one another across networks (Chapter 24), such as the Internet.

[Note: The next five chapters form the core of a nice Java-specific data structures course.]
Chapter 15—Recursion (New Chapter)—discusses recursive methods—i.e., methods that call themselves. We discuss the notions of base cases, recursion steps and infinite recursion. We present some popular recursion examples, including factorials, the Fibonacci series, string permutations, The Towers of Hanoi and fractals. We explain how recursion works "under the hood," including the order in which method activation records are pushed on or popped off the program execution stack. We compare and contrast recursive methods and iterative methods, and explain when to choose each. We introduce recursive backtracking. The chapter exercises include recursive approaches to: raising an integer to an integer power, visualizing recursion, greatest common divisor, palindromes, the Eight Queens problem (recursive backtracking), printing an array, minimum value in an array, star fractal, maze traversal (recursive backtracking), and generating mazes. The recursive

examples and exercises of Chapter 16 and Chapter 17 include merge sort, linear search, binary search, quicksort, binary tree insert, (preorder, inorder and postorder) binary tree traversals, and various linked list manipulations.

Chapter 16—Sorting and Searching (New Chapter)—discusses two of the most important classes of algorithms in Computer Science. We consider a variety of specific algorithms for each and compare them with regard to their memory consumption and processor consumption (introducing Big O notation, which indicates how hard an algorithm may have to work to solve a problem). Searching data involves determining whether a value (referred to as the search key) is present in the data and, if so, finding the value's location. In the examples and exercises of this chapter, we discuss a variety of searching algorithms, including: linear search, binary search, recursive linear search and recursive binary search; Chapter 17 discusses linear list search and the binary tree search; Chapter 19 discusses the `binarySearch` method of class `Collections`. Sorting places data in ascending or descending order based on one or more sort keys. Chapter 16 discusses through examples and exercises the selection sort, insertion sort, recursive merge sort, bubble sort, bucket sort and the recursive quicksort; Chapter 17 discusses the binary tree sort and Chapter 19 discusses the `sort` method of class `Collections` and the `SortedSet` collection. Chapter 16 also discusses the notion of loop invariants.

Chapter 17—Data Structures—discusses the techniques used to create and manipulate dynamic data structures, such as linked lists, stacks, queues and trees. For each type of data structure, we present examples with sample outputs. Although it is valuable to know how these classes are implemented, Java programmers will quickly discover that most of the data structures they need are available in class libraries, such as Java's own `java.util` that we discuss in Chapter 19. This chapter also introduces the J2SE 5.0's boxing capability, which simplifies converting between primitive-type values and type-wrapper objects. The chapter offers a rich selection of exercises, including a special section on building your own compiler that will enable you to compile high-level language programs into machine language code that will execute on the Simpletron simulator in the exercises of Chapter 7.

Chapter 18—Generics (New Chapter)—presents one of J2SE 5.0's new features: generics. The examples demonstrate generic methods and generic classes which enable programmers to specify, with a single method declaration, an entire range of related methods or, with a single class declaration, an entire range of related types, respectively. The chapter discusses how this new feature achieves legacy compatibility with earlier versions, such as through raw types. This chapter also introduces wildcards, a powerful generics concept that enables programmers to represent an "unknown type."

Chapter 19—Collections—discusses the `java.util` classes of the Java Collections Framework that provide predefined implementations of many of the data structures discussed in Chapter 17. Collections provide Java programmers with a standard set of data structures for storing and retrieving data and a standard set of algorithms (i.e., procedures) that allow programmers to manipulate the data (such as searching for particular data items and sorting data into ascending or descending order). The chapter examples demonstrate collections, such as linked lists, trees, maps and sets, and algorithms for searching, sorting, finding the maximum value, finding the minimum value and so on. We also demonstrate how generics are used in the collections API.

Chapter 20—Introduction to Applets—introduces Java applets, which are Java programs designed to be transported over the Internet and executed in Web browsers, such as Microsoft Internet Explorer, Netscape, Opera and Mozilla Firefox. The chapter shows several of the demonstration applets supplied with the JDK. We then write Java applets that perform tasks similar to the programs of Chapter 2, and we explain the similarities and differences between applets and applications. This chapter can be covered early in the book—after Chapter 3. Applets are GUIs and graphical, so for a deeper understanding of Chapter 20, cover it after Chapters 11 and 12 (these prerequisites are not absolutely necessary). The next chapter and Chapter 24 present additional interesting applets.

Chapter 21—Multimedia: Images, Animation and Audio—presents some of Java's capabilities that make programs come alive through multimedia. The chapter discusses images and image manipulation, audio, animation and video. We present an image-map application with the icons from the programming tips shown earlier in the Preface and that appear throughout the book. As the user moves the mouse pointer across the icons, the tip type is displayed. Once you have read this chapter, you will be eager to try out all these techniques, so we have included many exercises to challenge and entertain you.

Chapter 22—Graphical User Interface Components: Part 2—continues the Swing discussion started in Chapter 11. Through its programs, tables and line drawings, the chapter illustrates GUI design principles, sliders, windows, menus, pop-up menus, changing the look-and-feel, multiple-document interfaces, tabbed panes and using advanced layout managers.

Chapter 23—Multithreading—introduces Java's capabilities that enable programmers to implement applications that can perform tasks concurrently. We introduce threads, and present a thread state transition diagram. We overview thread priorities and thread scheduling. We then present a simple example that creates three threads. Next, we introduce the producer/consumer relationship in which a producer thread places data in a shared location and a consumer thread then reads that data. In this context, we use a sequence of examples to illustrate problems that may arise when multiple threads manipulate shared data. The first example demonstrates these problems. We then introduce features of J2SE 5.0's new concurrency API and use them to "synchronize" access to the shared data to ensure correct operation. Next, we enhance the example to use a shared circular buffer in which the producer can place up to three values before the consumer attempts to read a value. The last example in the sequence reimplements the circular buffer example using J2SE 5.0's `ArrayBlockingQueue` class, which automatically synchronizes access to its contents. This is significant, because programming concurrent applications is a difficult and error-prone undertaking. The last example in the chapter demonstrates the producer/consumer relationship using the pre-J2SE 5.0 synchronization techniques. Though we present several of J2SE 5.0's lower-level synchronization features in this chapter for those who are interested, the vast majority of programmers should use the predefined classes like `ArrayBlockingQueue` to provide synchronized access to data in multithreaded applications.

[Note: The next four chapters form the core of a nice introduction to distributed computing in Java.]

Chapter 24—Networking—focuses on Java programs that communicate over computer networks. This chapter presents Java's lowest-level networking capabilities. The chapter examples illustrate an applet interacting with the browser in which it executes, creating a mini Web browser, communicating between two Java programs using streams-based sockets and communicating between two Java programs using packets of data. A key feature of the chapter is the implementation of a collaborative client/server Tic-Tac-Toe game in which two clients play Tic-Tac-Toe against each other arbitrated by a multithreaded server—great stuff! The capstone example in the chapter is the `DeitelMessenger` case study, which simulates many of today's popular instant-messaging applications that enable computer users to communicate with friends, relatives and coworkers over the Internet. This 788-line, multithreaded, client/server case study uses most of the programming techniques presented up to this point in the book.

Chapter 25—Accessing Databases with JDBC™—discusses the JDBC API, which enables applications to access data in databases. Today's most popular database systems are relational databases. The examples in this chapter use the MySQL database management system (DBMS), which is included on the CD that accompanies the book. In the context of a database that contains information about many of our publications, this chapter introduces JDBC and uses it to connect to a MySQL database, then to manipulate its content. We discuss the Structured Query Language (SQL) and how it can be used to extract information from, insert information into and update data in a database. The examples enable you to obtain data from the database with SQL queries and display the data in a `JTable` GUI component. In addition, we discuss J2SE 5.0's `RowSets`, which simplify connecting to a database and accessing its data. In the next two chapters, we use the JDBC techniques in Chapter 25 to build data-driven three-tier Web applications.

Chapter 26—Servlets—discusses servlets—Java programs that extend the functionality of Web servers. Servlets are effective for developing Web-based solutions that interact with databases on behalf of clients, dynamically generate custom content to be displayed by browsers and maintain unique session information for each client. The Java Servlet API allows developers to add functionality to Web servers for handling client requests. Servlets are also reusable across Web servers and across platforms. This chapter demonstrates the Web's request/response mechanism (primarily with HTTP get and post requests), redirecting requests to other resources and interacting with databases through JDBC. The chapter features a three-tier client/server application that tracks users' responses to a survey. For readers not familiar with developing Web pages, the CD includes PDFs of three chapters from our book *Internet & World Wide Web How to Program, Third Edition*—Introduction to XHTML: Part 1, Introduction to XHTML: Part 2 and Cascading Style Sheets (CSS). These chapters are also useful in Chapter 27.

Chapter 27—JavaServer Pages (JSP)—introduces an extension of servlet technology called JavaServer Pages (JSP). JSPs enable delivery of dynamically generated Web content, and are frequently used by Web designers and others who are not familiar with Java programming. JSPs may contain Java code in the form of scriptlets. Each JSP is compiled into a Java servlet—this normally occurs the first time a JSP is requested by a client. Subsequent client requests are fulfilled by the compiled servlet. This chapter features a three-tier client/ server guest-book application that stores guest information in a database.

Chapter 28—Formatted Output (New Chapter)—presents the powerful formatting capabilities of `printf`, which is new to J2SE 5.0. We discuss `printf`'s capabilities such as rounding floating point values to a given number of decimal places, aligning columns of numbers, right justification and left justification, insertion of literal information, forcing a plus sign, printing leading zeros, using exponential notation, using octal and hexadecimal numbers, controlling field widths and precisions, and displaying dates and times in various formats. We also demonstrate formatting output with class `Formatter`.

Chapter 29—Strings, Characters and Regular Expressions—deals with processing words, sentences, characters and groups of characters. We present classes `String`, `String-Buffer`, `Character` and `StringTokenizer`. The chapter explores Java's API for regular expressions, which enables programs to search strings for sequences of characters that match specified patterns.

Appendix A—Operator Precedence Chart—lists each of the Java operators and indicates their relative precedence and associativity.

Appendix B—ASCII Character Set—lists the characters of the ASCII (American Standard Code for Information Interchange) character set and indicates the character code value for each. Java uses the Unicode character set with 16-bit characters for representing all of the characters in the world's "commercially significant" languages. Unicode includes ASCII as a subset.

Appendix C—Keywords and Reserved Words—lists all keywords and reserved words defined in the *Java Programming Language Specification*.

Appendix D—Primitive Types—lists all primitive types defined in the *Java Programming Language Specification*.

Appendix E (On CD)—Number Systems—discusses the binary (base 2), decimal (base 10), octal (base 8) and hexadecimal (base 16) number systems.

Appendix F (On CD)—Unicode®—discusses the Unicode character set, which enables Java to display information in many languages. The appendix provides a sample Java program that displays "Welcome to Unicode" in several languages—English, Chinese, Cyrillic, French, German, Japanese, Portuguese and Spanish.

Appendix G—Using the Java API Documentation—introduces the Java API documentation, which provides easy-to-use information on Java's built-in packages. **This appendix is important for Java novices**. You should search the Java API documentation regularly to learn more about the Java API classes used in this book and additional predefined classes—Java provides thousands of them that perform all kinds of useful tasks. Reusing these classes enables you to develop applications faster. The appendix discusses the information you can find, how this information is organized, and how to navigate the Java API documentation online, including viewing a package, a class and a method. The appendix also demonstrates how to find a particular package, class or method from the index page.

Appendix H (On CD)—Creating HTML Documentation with `javadoc`—introduces the `javadoc` documentation generation tool. Sun Microsystems uses the `javadoc` tool to produce the Java API documentation that is presented in Appendix G. The example takes the reader through the `javadoc` documentation process. First, we introduce the comment style and tags that `javadoc` recognizes and uses to create documentation. Next, we discuss the commands and options used to run the utility. Finally, we examine the source files `javadoc` uses and the HTML files `javadoc` creates.

Appendix I (On CD)—Bit Manipulation—discusses Java's bit-manipulation operators and class `Bitset`. It also includes an extensive discussion of bit-manipulation operators, such as bitwise AND, bitwise inclusive OR, bitwise exclusive OR, left shift, signed right shift, unsigned right shift and complement. The appendix also discusses class `BitSet`, which enables the creation of bit-array-like objects for setting and getting individual bit values.

Appendix J (On CD)—ATM Case Study Code—contains the implementation of our case study on object-oriented design with the UML. This appendix is discussed in the overview of the case study (presented shortly).

Appendix K (On CD)—Labeled **break and continue** Statements—introduces specialized versions of the break and continue statements presented in Chapter 5. These versions are for use with nested repetition statements.

Appendix L (On CD)—UML 2: Additional Diagram Types—Overviews the UML 2 diagram types that are not found in the OOD/UML Case Study.

Appendix M (On CD)—Design Patterns. In their book, *Design Patterns, Elements of Reusable Object-Oriented Software*, the "Gang of Four" (E. Gamma, R. Helm, R. Johnson, and J. Vlissides) described 23 design patterns that provide proven architectures for building object-oriented software systems. We briefly discuss 18 of their patterns—creational patterns address issues related to object creation; structural patterns organize classes and objects in a system; and behavioral patters offer strategies for modeling how objects collaborate with one another. We also discuss concurrency patterns, which are useful in multithreaded systems, and architectural patterns, which help designers assign functionality to subsystems. We mention how Java API packages take advantage of design patterns and explain how certain programs in this book use design patterns. Design patterns are used mostly in the J2EE (Java 2 Platform, Enterprise Edition) community, where systems tend to be large and complex.

Appendix N (On CD)—Using the Debugger—demonstrates key features of the J2SE Development Kit (JDK) version 5.0's built-in debugger, which allows a programmer to monitor the execution of applications to locate and remove logic errors. The appendix presents step-by-step instructions, so students learn how to use the debugger in a hands-on manner.

A Tour of the Optional Case Study on Object-Oriented Design with the UML

In this section we tour the book's optional case study of object-oriented design with the UML. This tour previews the contents of the nine "Software Engineering Case Study" sections (in Chapters 1–8 and 10). After completing this case study, the reader will be thoroughly familiar with an object-oriented design and implementation for a significant Java application.

The design presented in the ATM case study was developed at Deitel & Associates, Inc. and scrutinized by industry professionals. We crafted this design to meet the requirements of introductory course sequences. Surely real ATM systems used by banks around the world are based on more sophisticated designs that take into consideration many more issues than we have addressed here. Our primary goal throughout the design process, however, was to create a simple design that would be clear to OOD and UML novices, while still demonstrating key OOD concepts and the related UML modeling techniques.

Section 1.16—Software Engineering Case Study: Introduction to Object Technology and the UML—introduces the object-oriented design case study with the UML. The section introduces the basic concepts and terminology of object technology, including classes, objects, encapsulation, inheritance and polymorphism. We discuss the history of the UML. This is the only required section of the case study.

Section 2.9—(Optional) Software Engineering Case Study: Examining the Requirements—discusses a *requirements document* that specifies the requirements for a system that we will design and implement—the software for a simple automated teller machine (ATM). We investigate the structure and behavior of object-oriented systems in general. We discuss how the UML will facilitate the design process in subsequent "Software Engineering Case Study" sections by providing several additional types of diagrams to model our system. We include a list of URLs and book references on object-oriented design with the UML. We discuss the interaction between the ATM system specified by the requirements document and its user. Specifically, we investigate the scenarios that may occur between the user and the system itself—these are called *use cases*. We model these interactions, using *use case diagrams* of the UML.

Section 3.9—(Optional) Software Engineering Case Study: Identifying the Classes in the Requirements Documents—begins to design the ATM system. We identify its classes, or "building blocks," by extracting the nouns and noun phrases from the requirements document. We arrange these classes into a UML class diagram that describes the class structure of our simulation. The class diagram also describes relationships, known as *associations*, among classes.

Section 4.14—(Optional) Software Engineering Case Study: Identifying Class Attributes—focuses on the attributes of the classes discussed in Section 3.9. A class contains both *attributes* (data) and *operations* (behaviors). As we see in later sections, changes in an object's attributes often affect the object's behavior. To determine the attributes for the classes in our case study, we extract the adjectives describing the nouns and noun phrases (which defined our classes) from the requirements document, then place the attributes in the class diagram we created in Section 3.9.

Section 5.10—(Optional) Software Engineering Case Study: Identifying Objects' States and Activities—discusses how an object, at any given time, occupies a specific condition called a *state*. A *state transition* occurs when that object receives a message to change state. The UML provides the *state machine diagram*, which identifies the set of possible states that an object may occupy and models that object's state transitions. An object also has an *activity*—the work it performs in its lifetime. The UML provides the *activity diagram*—a flowchart that models an object's activity. In this section, we use both types of diagrams to begin modeling specific behavioral aspects of our ATM system, such as how the ATM carries out a withdrawal transaction and how the ATM responds when the user is authenticated.

Section 6.13—(Optional) Software Engineering Case Study: Identifying Class Operations—identifies the operations, or services, of our classes. We extract from the requirements document the verbs and verb phrases that specify the operations for each class. We then modify the class diagram of Section 3.9 to include each operation with its associated class. At this point in the case study, we will have gathered all information possible from the requirements document. However, as future chapters introduce such topics as inheritance, we will modify our classes and diagrams.

Section 7.10—(Optional) Software Engineering Case Study: Collaboration Among Objects—provides a "rough sketch" of the model for our ATM system. In this section, we see how it works. We investigate the behavior of the simulation by discussing *collaborations*—messages that objects send to each other to communicate. The class operations that we discovered in Section 6.13 turn out to be the collaborations among the objects in our system. We determine the collaborations, then collect them into a *communication diagram*—the UML diagram for modeling collaborations. This diagram reveals which objects collaborate and when. We present a communication diagram of the collaborations among objects to perform an ATM balance inquiry. We then present the UML *sequence diagram* for modeling interactions in a system. This diagram emphasizes the chronological ordering of messages. A sequence diagram models how objects in the system interact to carry out withdrawal and deposit transactions.

Section 8.19—(Optional) Software Engineering Case Study: Starting to Program the Classes of the ATM System—takes a break from designing the behavior of our system. We begin the implementation process to emphasize the material discussed in Chapter 8. Using the UML class diagram of Section 3.9 and the attributes and operations discussed in Section 4.14 and Section 6.13, we show how to implement a class in Java from a design. We do not implement all classes—because we have not completed the design process. Working from our UML diagrams, we create code for the `Withdrawal` class.

Section 10.8—(Optional) Software Engineering Case Study: Incorporating Inheritance into the ATM System—continues our discussion of object-oriented programming. We consider inheritance—classes sharing common characteristics may inherit attributes and operations from a "base" class. In this section, we investigate how our ATM system can benefit from using inheritance. We document our discoveries in a class diagram that models inheritance relationships—the UML refers to these relationships as *generalizations*. We modify the class diagram of Section 3.9 by using inheritance to group classes with similar characteristics. This section concludes the design of the model portion of our simulation. We implement this model as Java code in Appendix J.

Appendix J (On CD)—ATM Case Study Code—The majority of the case study involved designing the model (i.e., the data and logic) of the ATM system. In this appendix, we implement that model in Java. Using all the UML diagrams we created, we present the Java classes necessary to implement the model. We apply the concepts of object-oriented design with the UML and object-oriented programming in Java that you learned in the chapters. By the end of this appendix, students will have completed the design and implementation of a real-world system, and should now feel confident tackling larger systems, such as those that professional software engineers build.

Appendix L—UML 2 Additional Diagrams—Overviews the UML 2 diagram types not found in the OOD/UML Case Study.

A Tour of the Optional GUI and Graphics Case Study

In this section, we tour the book's optional 10-section case study on creating graphics and graphical user interfaces (GUIs) in Java. The goal of this case study is to create a polymorphic drawing application in which the user can select a shape to draw, select the characteristics of the shape (such as the color of the shape and whether it is filled with color or hollow) and use the mouse to draw the shape. This integrated case study builds gradually toward that goal, with the reader implementing polymorphic drawing in Chapter 10, adding an event-driven GUI in Chapter 11 and enhancing the drawing capabilities in Chapter 12 with Java 2D. This tour previews the topics covered in each section of the case study. After completing this case study, students will be able to create their own simple graphical applications.

Section 3.9—Using Dialog Boxes—introduces graphical user interfaces and demonstrates handling input and output with dialog boxes. We use predefined `JOptionPane` dialogs to display information and read text in an application.

Section 4.14—Creating Simple Drawings—introduces Java's graphics capabilities. First, we describe Java's coordinate system, then we cover drawing lines and creating a window that displays drawings.

Section 5.10—Rectangles and Ovals—explains how to use the graphics methods that draw rectangles and ovals.

Section 6.13—Colors and Filled Shapes—discusses how computers represent colors, how to use colors in graphics, and how to fill oval or rectangular regions with a solid color.

Section 7.13—Drawing Arcs—describes how Java specifies angles; then we demonstrate drawing arcs (i.e., sections of an oval) by defining an oval and angular positions along the oval.

Section 8.18—Using Objects with Graphics—describes how to use objects to represent shapes. We create classes to represent each shape type, store these objects in arrays and retrieve the shapes each time we need to draw them.

Section 9.8—Displaying Text and Images Using Labels—explores creating labels and attaching them to the application window. Applications use labels to display information to the user. Labels in Java can display text, an image or both.

Section 10.8—Drawing with Polymorphism—focuses on the common characteristics of the classes created in Section 8.18. In this section, we examine these similarities and redesign the individual shape classes so that they inherit their common functionality from a "base" class and can be processed polymorphically.

Exercise 11.18—Expanding the Interface—asks the reader to apply the event-driven GUI programming techniques they learn in Chapter 11. Readers create a GUI that allows users to select the shape to draw and its color, then draw the shape with a mouse. The application stores and manipulates shapes using the classes created in Section 10.8.

Exercise 12.31—Adding Java2D—asks the reader to use Java 2D's more elaborate two-dimensional drawing capabilities to create a robust drawing application in which users select a shape's line thickness and fill options (solid colors or gradients that transition between colors). To do this, the reader enhances the shape classes in Exercise 11.18 to store information about each shape's Java 2D features.

Software Included with *Java How to Program, 6/e*

A number of for-sale Java development tools are available, but you do not need any to get started with Java. We wrote *Java How to Program, 6/e* using only the new Java 2 Standard Edition Development Kit (JDK), version 5.0. The current JDK version can be downloaded from Sun's Java Web site `java.sun.com/j2se/downloads/index.html`. This site also contains the JDK documentation downloads.

The CD that accompanies *Java How to Program, 6/e*, contains several Java editors, including BlueJ Version 1.3.5, JCreator Lite Version 3.10 (Windows only), jEdit Version 4.1 and jGRASP Version 1.7.0. The CD also contains the NetBeans™ Version 3.6 Integrated Development Environment (IDE). Windows and Linux versions of MySQL® 4.0.20 and MySQL® Connector/J Version 3.0.14 are provided for the database processing performed in Chapters 25–27. Finally, Apache Tomcat Version 5.0.25 is provided for use with servlets and JavaServer Pages in Chapters 26–27. If you have questions about using this software, please read the documentation on the CD, or read our *Dive Into*™ Series publications, which are available with the resources for *Java How to Program, 6/e* at `www.deitel.com/books/downloads.html`. The free *Dive-Into*™ Series publications help students and instructors familiarize themselves with various Java development tools. These publications include: *Dive Into*™ *NetBeans*, *Dive Into*™ *Eclipse*, *Dive Into*™ *JBuilder*, *Dive Into*™ *jEdit*, *Dive Into*™ *jCreator*, *Dive Into*™ *jGRASP* and *Dive Into*™ *BlueJ*.

The CD also contains the book's examples and an HTML Web page with links to the Deitel & Associates, Inc. Web site and the Prentice Hall Web site. This Web page can be loaded to a Web browser to afford quick access to all the resources.

Teaching Resources for *Java How to Program, 6/e*

Java How to Program, 6/e, has extensive resources for instructors. The *Instructor's Resource CD (IRCD)* contains the *Solutions Manual* with solutions to the vast majority of the end-of-chapter exercises, a *Test Item File* of multiple-choice questions (approximately two per book section) and PowerPoint slides containing all the code and figures in the text, plus bulleted items that summarize the key points in the text. Instructors can customize the slides.

Prentice Hall's *Companion Web Site* (www.prenhall.com/deitel) for *Java How to Program, 6/e* offers resources for students and instructors. For instructors, the *Companion Web Site* offers a *Syllabus Manager*, which helps instructors plan courses interactively and create online syllabi.

Chapter-specific resources available for students on the *Companion Web Site* include:

- Chapter objectives
- Highlights (e.g., chapter summary)
- Outline
- Tips (e.g., *Common Programming Errors, Error-Prevention Tips, Good Programming Practices, Portability Tips, Performance Tips* and *Software Engineering Observations*)
- Online Study Guide—contains additional short-answer self-review exercises (e.g., true/false) with answers and provides immediate feedback to the student

Students can track their results and course performance on quizzes using the *Student Profile* feature, which records and manages all feedback and results from tests taken on the *Companion Web Site*. To access the *Companion Web Site*, visit www.prenhall.com/deitel.

Java in the Lab

Java in the Lab, Lab Manual to Accompany Java How to Program, 6/e (ISBN 0-13-149497-X) complements *Java How to Program, 6/e* and *Small Java How to Program 6/e* with hands-on lab assignments designed to reinforce students' understanding of lecture material. This lab manual is designed for closed laboratories—regularly scheduled classes supervised by an instructor. Closed laboratories provide an excellent learning environment, because students can use concepts presented in class to solve carefully designed lab problems. Instructors are better able to gauge the students' understanding of the material by monitoring the students' progress in lab. This lab manual also can be used for open laboratories, homework and for self-study. *Java How to Program, 6/e*, and the lab manual are available individually or together in a value pack (ISBN 0-13-167380-7).

Every chapter in the lab manual is divided into *Prelab Activities, Lab Exercises* and *Postlab Activities*. Each chapter contains objectives that introduce the lab's key topics and an assignment checklist that allows students to mark which exercises the instructor has assigned. The lab manual pages are perforated, so students can submit their answers (if required).

Solutions to the lab manual's *Prelab Activities, Lab Exercises* and *Postlab Activities* are available in electronic form. Instructors can obtain these materials from their regular Prentice Hall representatives; the solutions are not available to students.

Prelab Activities

Prelab Activities are intended to be completed by students after studying each chapter of *Java How to Program, 6/e*. *Prelab Activities* test students' understanding of the textbook material and prepare students for the programming exercises in the lab session. The exercises focus on important terminology and programming concepts and are effective for self-review. *Prelab Activities* include *Matching Exercises, Fill-in-the-Blank Exercises, Short-Answer Questions, Programming-Output Exercises* (determine what short code segments do without actually running the program) and *Correct-the-Code Exercises* (identify and correct all errors in short code segments).

Lab Exercises

The most important section in each chapter is the *Lab Exercises*. These teach students how to apply the material learned in *Java How to Program, 6/e*, and prepare them for writing Java programs. Each lab contains one or more lab exercises and a debugging problem. The *Lab Exercises* contain the following:

- *Lab Objectives* highlight specific concepts on which the lab exercise focuses.

- *Problem Descriptions* provide the details of the exercise and hints to help students implement the program.

- *Sample Outputs* illustrate the desired program behavior, which further clarifies the problem descriptions and aids the students with writing programs.

- *Program Templates* take complete Java programs and replace key lines of code with comments describing the missing code.

- *Problem-Solving Tips* highlight key issues that students need to consider when solving the lab exercises.

- *Follow-Up Questions and Activities* ask students to modify solutions to lab exercises, write new programs that are similar to their lab-exercise solutions or explain the implementation choices that were made when solving lab exercises.

- *Debugging Problems* consist of blocks of code that contain syntax errors and/or logic errors. These alert students to the types of errors they are likely to encounter while programming.

Postlab Activities

Professors typically assign *Postlab Activities* to reinforce key concepts or to provide students with more programming experience outside the lab. *Postlab Activities* test the students' understanding of the *Prelab* and *Lab Exercise* material, and ask students to apply their knowledge to creating programs from scratch. The section provides two types of programming activities: coding exercises and programming challenges. Coding exercises are short and serve as review after the *Prelab Activities* and *Lab Exercises* have been completed. The coding exercises ask students to write programs or program segments using key concepts from the textbook. *Programming Challenges* allow students to apply their knowledge to substantial programming exercises. Hints, sample outputs and pseudocode are provided to aid students with these problems. Students who successfully complete the *Programming Challenges* for a chapter have mastered the chapter material. Answers to the programming challenges are available at www.deitel.com/books/downloads.html.

OneKey, CourseCompassSM, WebCT™ and by Blackboard™

OneKey is Prentice Hall's exclusive new resource that gives instructors and students access to the best online teaching and learning tools through one convenient Web site. OneKey enables instructors to prepare their courses effectively, present their courses more dramatically and assess students easily. An abundance of searchable presentation material together with practice activities and test questions—all organized by chapter or topic—helps to simplify course preparation.

Selected content from the Deitels' introductory programming language *How to Program* series, including *Java How to Program, 6/e*, is available to integrate into various popular course management systems, including CourseCompass, Blackboard and WebCT. Course management systems help faculty create, manage and use sophisticated Web-based educational tools and programs. Instructors can save hours of inputting data by using Deitel course-management-systems content. [*Note:* The e-Book included with OneKey contains the entire text of *Java How to Program, 6/e*.]

Blackboard, CourseCompass and WebCT offer:

- **Features to create and customize an online course**, such as areas to post course information (e.g., policies, syllabi, announcements, assignments, grades, performance evaluations and progress tracking), class and student management tools, a gradebook, reporting tools, page tracking, a calendar and assignments.

- **Communication tools** to help create and maintain interpersonal relationships between students and instructors, including chat rooms, whiteboards, document sharing, bulletin boards and private e-mail.

- **Flexible testing tools** that allow an instructor to create online quizzes and tests from questions directly linked to the text, and that grade and track results effectively. All tests can be inputted into the gradebook for efficient course management. WebCT also allows instructors to administer timed online quizzes.

- **Support materials** for instructors are available in print and online formats.

In addition to the types of tools found in Blackboard and WebCT, CourseCompass from Prentice Hall includes:

- **CourseCompass course home page**, which makes the course as easy to navigate as a book. An expandable table of contents allows instructors to view course content at a glance and to link to any section.

- **Hosting on Prentice Hall's centralized servers**, which allows course administrators to avoid separate licensing fees or server-space issues. Access to Prentice Hall technical support is available.

- **"How Do I" online-support sections** are available for users who need help personalizing course sites, including step-by-step instructions for adding PowerPoint slides, video and more.

- **Instructor Quick Start Guide** helps instructors create online courses using a simple, step-by-step process.

To view free online demonstrations and learn more about these Course Management Systems, which support Deitel content, visit the following Web sites:

- Blackboard: www.blackboard.com and www.prenhall.com/blackboard

- WebCT: www.webct.com and www.prenhall.com/webct
- CourseCompass: www.coursecompass.com and www.prenhall.com/coursecompass

Java 2 Multimedia Cyber Classroom, 6/e Through OneKey

Java How to Program, 6/e and *Small Java How to Program, 6/e* will now include a free, Web-based interactive multimedia accompaniment to the book—*The Java 2 Multimedia Cyber Classroom, 6/e*—available in spring 2005 through OneKey. Our Web-based *Cyber Classroom* will include audio walkthroughs of code examples in the text, solutions to about half of the exercises in the book and more. For more information about the new Web-based *Cyber Classroom* and its availability through OneKey, please visit our Web site at www.deitel.com or sign up for the free *Deitel® Buzz Online* e-mail newsletter at www.deitel.com/newsletter/subscribe.html.

Students who use our *Cyber Classrooms* tell us that they like the interactivity and that the *Cyber Classroom* is a powerful reference tool. Professors tell us that their students enjoy using the *Cyber Classroom* and consequently spend more time on the courses, mastering more of the material than in textbook-only courses. For a complete list of our current CD-ROM-based *Cyber Classrooms*, see the *Deitel® Series* page at the beginning of this book, the product listing and ordering information at the end of this book, or visit www.deitel.com, www.prenhall.com/deitel or www.InformIT.com/deitel.

PearsonChoices

Today's students have increasing demands on their time and money, and they need to be resourceful about how, when and where they study. Pearson/Prentice Hall, a division of Pearson Education, has responded to that need by creating PearsonChoices to allow faculty and students to choose from a variety of textbook formats and prices.

Small Java How to Program 6/e

Small Java How to Program, 6/e is our new 10-chapter alternative print edition to *Java How to Program, 6/e*. *Small Java How to Program, 6/e* is focused on first-semester Computer Science (CS1) programming courses and is priced lower than our 29-chapter *Java How to Program, 6/e* and other competing texts in the CS1 market. The following is a chapter-level table of contents for the book. [*Note*: This book includes Chapters 1–10 of *Java How to Program, 6/e* and their corresponding optional GUI and graphics case study sections, but does not include the OOD/UML optional automated teller machine (ATM) case study.]

Chapters in Both Small Java How to Program, 6/e *and* Java How to Program, 6/e
Chapter 1—Introduction to Computers, the Internet and the Web
Chapter 2—Introduction to Java Applications
Chapter 3—Introduction to Classes and Objects
Chapter 4—Control Statements: Part 1
Chapter 5—Control Statements Part 2
Chapter 6—Methods: A Deeper Look
Chapter 7—Arrays
Chapter 8—Classes and Objects: A Deeper Look
Chapter 9—Object-Oriented Programming: Inheritance
Chapter 10—Object-Oriented Programming: Polymorphism

SafariX WebBooks

SafariX Textbooks Online is a new service for college students looking to save money on required or recommended textbooks for academic courses. This secure WebBooks platform creates a new option in the higher education market; an additional choice for students alongside conventional textbooks and online learning services. Pearson provides students with a WebBook at 50% of the cost of its conventional print equivalent.

SafariX WebBooks are viewed through a Web browser connected to the Internet. No special plug-ins are required and no applications need to be downloaded. Students simply log in, purchase access and begin studying. With SafariX Textbooks Online students can search the text, make notes online, print out reading assignments that incorporate their professors' lecture notes and bookmark important passages they want to review later. They can navigate easily to a page number, reading assignment, or chapter. The Table of Contents of each WebBook appears in the left hand column alongside the text.

We are pleased to offer students the *Java How to Program, 6/e* SafariX WebBook available for January 2005 classes. Visit www.pearsonchoices.com for more information. Other Deitel titles available as SafariX WebBooks include *Small Java How to Program, 6/e* and *Simply C++: An Application-Driven Tutorial Approach*. Visit www.safarix.com/tour.html for more information.

Computer Science AP Courses

Java How to Program, 6/e, is a suitable textbook for teaching AP Computer-Science classes and for preparing students to take the corresponding exams. While writing this book, we carefully reviewed the syllabi for the AP Computer Science A and AB exams, to ensure that *Java How to Program, 6/e*, covers the vast majority of the information required for the exams. Instructors and students interested in preparing for these exams should visit:

```
www.deitel.com/books/jHTP6/Java_AP_Exam.html
```

This site is dedicated to the use of *Java How to Program, 6/e*, in the Computer Science AP curriculum. We will update this site regularly with additional information about the exams. For detailed information on the Computer Science AP curriculum, please visit

```
apcentral.collegeboard.com
```

DEITEL® Buzz Online Free E-mail Newsletter

Our free e-mail newsletter, the *Deitel® Buzz Online*, includes commentary on industry trends and developments, links to free articles and resources from our published books and upcoming publications, product-release schedules, errata, challenges, anecdotes, information on our corporate instructor-led training courses and more. It's also our way to notify our readers proactively about issues related to *Java How to Program, 6/e*. To subscribe, visit

```
www.deitel.com/newsletter/subscribe.html
```

Acknowledgments

One of the great pleasures of writing a textbook is acknowledging the efforts of many people whose names may not appear on the cover, but whose hard work, cooperation, friendship and understanding were crucial to the production of the book. Many people at Deitel & Associates, Inc. devoted long hours to this project.

- Andrew B. Goldberg is a recent graduate of Amherst College, where he earned a degree in Computer Science. Andrew is a co-author with us of *Internet and World Wide Web How to Program, 3/e* and contributed to *Operating Systems, Third Edition*. Andrew's contributions to *Java How to Program, 6/e* included updating Chapters 3–10 based on the new early-classes presentation of the book and other content revisions. He co-designed and co-authored the new, optional OOD/UML ATM case study. He updated Appendix M, Design Patterns and co-authored Appendix L, UML 2: Additional Diagram Types and Appendix N, Using the Debugger.

- Jeff Listfield is a Computer Science graduate of Harvard College. Jeff co-authored *C# How to Program*, *C# A Programmer's Introduction*, *C# for Experienced Programmers* and *Simply Java Programming*. He has also contributed to *Perl How to Program* and *Operating Systems, Third Edition*. Jeff contributed to Chapter 11, GUI: Part 1; Chapter 16, Searching and Sorting; Chapter 22, GUI: Part 2; Chapter 23, Multithreading; Chapter 24, Networking; and Chapter 29, Strings, Characters and Regular Expressions.

- Su Zhang holds B.Sc. and a M.Sc. degrees in Computer Science from McGill University. She is co-author with us of *Java Web Services for Experienced Programmers* and *Simply Java Programming*. She has also contributed to other Deitel publications, including *Advanced Java 2 Platform How to Program*, *Python How to Program* and *Operating Systems, Third Edition*. Su contributed to the sections on the new features of J2SE 5.0 in Chapters 7 and 8. She contributed to Chapter 18, Generics; Chapter 19, Collections; Chapter 25, Manipulating Database with JDBC; Chapter 26, Servlets; Chapter 27, JavaServer Pages; Chapter 28, Formatted Output; Appendix F, Unicode®; Appendix G, Using Java API Documentation; Appendix H, Creating HTML Documentation with javadoc; and Appendix I, Bit Manipulation. Su also converted much of the code from *Java How to Program, 5/e* to J2SE 5.0.

- Cheryl Yaeger graduated from Boston University in three years with a bachelor's degree in Computer Science. Cheryl has co-authored various Deitel & Associates, Inc. publications, including *C# How to Program*, *C#: A Programmer's Introduction*, *C# for Experienced Programmers*, *Visual Basic .NET for Experienced Programmers*, *Simply Visual Basic .NET 2003* and *Simply C#*. Cheryl has also contributed to other Deitel & Associates publications including *Perl How to Program*, *Wireless Internet and Mobile Business How to Program*, *Internet and World Wide Web How to Program, 3/e*, *Visual Basic .NET How to Program, 2/e* and *Simply Java Programming*. Cheryl contributed to Chapter 12, Graphics; Chapter 13, Exceptions; Chapter 14, Files and Streams; Chapter 15, Recursion; and Chapter 21, Multimedia.

- Jing Hu, a participant in the Deitel & Associates, Inc. Summer Internship Program, is a sophomore at Cornell University studying Computer Science. He contributed to the new optional GUI and Graphics Case Study and the instructor's manual for Chapters 3–8. He also contributed to the sections on preconditions/postconditions, assertions, invariants, and the discussion of video in Chapter 21, Multimedia.

- Sin Han Lo, a participant in the Deitel & Associates, Inc. Summer Internship Program in 2003, is a recent graduate of Wellesley College where she studied Computer Science and Economics. She contributed to Chapter 15, Recursion, and designed the fractal example in that chapter.

- John Paul Casiello, a participant in the Deitel & Associates, Inc. Summer Internship Program in 2003, is a Computer Science student at Northeastern University. He contributed to Chapter 16, Searching and Sorting.

- Barbara Deitel, Chief Financial Officer at Deitel & Associates, Inc. researched the quotes at the beginning of each chapter and applied copyedits to the book.

- Abbey Deitel, President of Deitel & Associates, Inc., is an Industrial Management graduate of Carnegie Mellon University. She co-authored the Preface. She also suggested the theme and bug names for the cover of the book.

- Christi Kelsey, a Management Information Systems graduate of Purdue University, contributed to Chapter 1, the Preface and Appendix N, Using the Debugger. She edited the Index and paged the entire manuscript.

We are fortunate to have worked on this project with the talented and dedicated team of publishing professionals at Prentice Hall. We especially appreciate the extraordinary efforts of our Computer Science Editor, Kate Hargett and her boss and our mentor in publishing—Marcia Horton, Editorial Director of Prentice Hall's Engineering and Computer Science Division. Jennifer Cappello did an extraordinary job recruiting the review team and managing the review process. Vince O'Brien, Tom Manshreck and John Lovell did a marvelous job managing the production of the book. The talents of Carole Anson, Paul Belfanti and Geoffrey Cassar are evident in the re-design of the book's interior and the new cover art, and Sarah Parker managed the publication of the book's extensive ancillary package.

We sincerely appreciate the efforts of our fifth edition post-publication reviewers and our sixth edition reviewers:

Academic Reviewers
Karen Arlien, Bismarck State College
Ben Blake, Cleveland State University
Walt Bunch, Chapman University
Marita Ellixson, Eglin AFB/University of Arkansas
Ephrem Eyob, Virginia State University
Bjorn Foss, Florida Metropolitan University
Bill Freitas, The Lawrenceville School
Joe Kasprzyk, Salem State College
Brian Larson, Modesto Junior College
Roberto Lopez-Herrejon, University of Texas at Austin
Dean Mellas, Cerritos College
David Messier, Eastern University
Andy Novobilski, University of Tennessee, Chattanooga
Richard Ord, University of California, San Diego
Gavin Osborne, Saskatchewan Institute of Applied Science & Technology
Donna Reese, Mississippi State University
Craig Slinkman, University of Texas at Arlington

Sreedhar Thota, Western Iowa Tech Community College
Mahendran Velauthapillai, Georgetown University
Loran Walker, Lawrence Technological University
Stephen Weiss, University of North Carolina at Chapel Hill

Industry Reviewers
Butch Anton, Wi-Tech Consulting
Jonathan Bruce, Sun Microsystems, Inc. (JCP Specification Lead for JDBC)
Gilad Bracha, Sun Microsystems, Inc. (JCP Specification Lead for Generics)
Michael Develle, Independent Consultant
Jonathan Gadzik, Independent Consultant
Brian Goetz, Quiotix Corporation (JCP Concurrency Utilities Specification
    Expert Group Member)
Anne Horton, AT&T Bell Laboratories
James Huddleston, Independent Consultant
Peter Jones, Sun Microsystems, Inc.
Doug Kohlert, Sun Microsystems, Inc.
Earl LaBatt, Altaworks Corp./ University of New Hampshire
Paul Monday, Sun Microsystems, Inc.
Bill O'Farrell, IBM
Cameron Skinner, Embarcadero Technologies, Inc.
Brandon Taylor, Sun Microsystems, Inc.
Karen Tegtmeyer, Independent Consultant

OOD/UML Optional Case Study Reviewers
Sinan Si Alhir, Independent Consultant
Gene Ames, Star HRG
Jan Bergandy, University of Massachusetts at Dartmouth
Marita Ellixson, Eglin AFB/University of Arkansas
Jonathan Gadzik, Independent Consultant
Thomas Harder, ITT ESI, Inc.
James Huddleston, Independent Consultant
Terrell Hull, Independent Consultant
Kenneth Hussey, IBM
Joe Kasprzyk, Salem State College
Dan McCracken, City College of New York
Paul Monday, Sun Microsystems, Inc.
Davyd Norris, Rational Software
Cameron Skinner, Embarcadero Technologies, Inc.
Craig Slinkman, University of Texas at Arlington
Steve Tockey, Construx Software

Under a tight time schedule, they scrutinized every aspect of the text and made countless suggestions for improving the accuracy and completeness of the presentation.

Well, there you have it! Java is a powerful programming language that will help you write programs quickly and effectively. Java scales nicely into the realm of enterprise-systems development to help organizations build their critical information systems. As you read the book, we would sincerely appreciate your comments, criticisms, corrections and suggestions for improving the text. Please address all correspondence to:

deitel@deitel.com

We will respond promptly, and we will post corrections and clarifications on our Web site:

www.deitel.com

We hope you enjoy learning with *Java How to Program, Sixth Edition* as much as we enjoyed writing it!

Dr. Harvey M. Deitel
Paul J. Deitel

About the Authors

Dr. Harvey M. Deitel, Chairman and Chief Strategy Officer of Deitel & Associates, Inc., has 43 years experience in the computing field, including extensive industry and academic experience. Dr. Deitel earned B.S. and M.S. degrees from the Massachusetts Institute of Technology and a Ph.D. from Boston University. He worked on the pioneering virtual-memory operating-systems projects at IBM and MIT that developed techniques now widely implemented in systems such as UNIX, Linux and Windows XP. He has 20 years of college teaching experience, including earning tenure and serving as the Chairman of the Computer Science Department at Boston College before founding Deitel & Associates, Inc., with his son, Paul J. Deitel. He and Paul are the co-authors of several dozen books and multimedia packages and they are writing many more. With translations published in Japanese, German, Russian, Spanish, Traditional Chinese, Simplified Chinese, Korean, French, Polish, Italian, Portuguese, Greek, Urdu and Turkish, the Deitels' texts have earned international recognition. Dr. Deitel has delivered hundreds of professional seminars to major corporations, academic institutions, government organizations and the military.

Paul J. Deitel, CEO and Chief Technical Officer of Deitel & Associates, Inc., is a graduate of the MIT's Sloan School of Management, where he studied Information Technology. Through Deitel & Associates, Inc., he has delivered Java, C, C++, Internet and World Wide Web courses to industry clients, including IBM, Sun Microsystems, Dell, Lucent Technologies, Fidelity, NASA at the Kennedy Space Center, the National Severe Storm Laboratory, Compaq, White Sands Missile Range, Rogue Wave Software, Boeing, Stratus, Cambridge Technology Partners, Open Environment Corporation, One Wave, Hyperion Software, Adra Systems, Entergy, CableData Systems and many other organizations. Paul is one of the most experienced Java corporate trainers having taught about 100 professional Java training courses. He has also lectured on C++ and Java for the Boston Chapter of the Association for Computing Machinery. He and his father, Dr. Harvey M. Deitel, are the world's best-selling Computer Science textbook authors.

About Deitel & Associates, Inc.

Deitel & Associates, Inc., is an internationally recognized corporate training and content-creation organization specializing in computer programming languages, Internet/World Wide Web software technology and object technology education. The company provides instructor-led courses on major programming languages and platforms, such as Java, Advanced Java, C, C++, .NET programming languages, XML, Perl, Python; object technology; and Internet and World Wide Web programming. The founders of Deitel & Associates, Inc., are Dr. Harvey M. Deitel and Paul J. Deitel. The company's clients include many of the world's largest computer companies, government agencies, branches of the military and business organizations. Through its 28-year publishing partnership with Prentice Hall, Deitel & Associates, Inc. publishes leading-edge programming textbooks, professional books, interactive multimedia *Cyber Classrooms, Complete Training Courses,* Web-based training courses and course management systems e-content for popular CMSs such as WebCT, Blackboard and Pearson's CourseCompass. Deitel & Associates, Inc., and the authors can be reached via e-mail at:

    deitel@deitel.com

To learn more about Deitel & Associates, Inc., its publications and its worldwide *DIVE INTO*™ Series Corporate Training curriculum, see the last few pages of this book or visit:

    www.deitel.com

and subscribe to the free *Deitel*® *Buzz Online* e-mail newsletter at:

    www.deitel.com/newsletter/subscribe.html

Individuals wishing to purchase Deitel books, Cyber Classrooms, Complete Training Courses and Web-based training courses can do so through:

    www.deitel.com/books/index.html

Bulk orders by corporations and academic institutions should be placed directly with Prentice Hall. See the last few pages of this book for worldwide ordering details.

Before You Begin

Please follow the instructions in this section to ensure that Java is installed properly on your computer before you begin using this book.

Font and Naming Conventions

We use fonts to distinguish between on-screen components (such as menu names and menu items) and Java code or commands. Our convention is to emphasize on-screen components in a sans-serif bold **Helvetica** font (for example, **File** menu) and to emphasize Java code and commands in a sans-serif Lucida font (for example, System.out.println()).

Software and Other Resources on the CD That Accompanies *Java How to Program, Sixth Edition*

The CD that accompanies this book includes:

- BlueJ (version 1.3.5) for Windows/Linux
- jGRASP (version 1.7.0) and handbook, for Windows/Linux
- jEdit (version 4.1) for Windows/Linux
- JCreator LE (version 3.10) for Windows only
- NetBeans IDE (version 3.6) for Windows/Linux
- MySQL (version 4.0.20c) for Windows/Linux
- MySQL Connector/J (version 3.0.14) for Windows/Linux
- Apache Tomcat (version 5.0.25) for Windows/Linux

The examples in this book were developed with the Java 2 Platform, Standard Edition Development Kit (JDK) version 5.0. At the time of this printing the JDK 5.0 was still in its final beta version, so the JDK is not included on the CD that accompanies this book. You can download the latest version of JDK 5.0 and its documentation from

```
java.sun.com/j2se/5.0/download.jsp
```

When Sun releases the final version of JDK 5.0, it will be included on the CD in future prints. If you have any questions, please feel free to email us at deitel@deitel.com. We will respond promptly.

Hardware and Software Requirements to Run JDK 5.0

To install and run JDK 5.0, Sun recommends that PCs meet the following minimum requirements:

- 500 MHz, Pentium III processor

- 256 MB RAM
- 100 MB of available disk space

[*Note:* the JDK is available for Windows, Linux and Solaris Operating Systems.]

Copying and Organizing Files

All of the examples for *Java How To Program, Sixth Edition* are included on the CD that accompanies this textbook. Follow the steps in the next section, *Copying the Book Examples from the CD*, to copy the examples directory from the CD onto your hard drive. We suggest that you work from your hard drive rather than your CD drive for two reasons: The CD is read-only, so you cannot save your applications to the book's CD, and files can be accessed faster from a hard drive than from a CD. The examples from the book are also available for download from:

```
www.deitel.com
www.prenhall.com/deitel
```

Screen shots in the following section might differ slightly from what you see on your computer, depending on whether you are using Windows 2000 or Windows XP, or your version of Internet Explorer.

Copying the Book Examples from the CD

1. *Inserting the CD.* Insert the CD that accompanies *Java How To Program, Sixth Edition* into your computer's CD drive. The window displayed in Fig. 1 should appear. If the page appears, proceed to *Step 3* of this section. If the page does not appear, proceed to *Step 2*.

2. *Opening the CD directory using* **My Computer.** If the page shown in Fig. 1 does not appear, double click the **My Computer** icon on your desktop. In the **My Computer** window, double click your CD-ROM drive (Fig. 2) to access the CD's contents. Proceed to *Step 4*.

3. *Opening the CD-ROM directory.* If the page in Fig. 1 does appear, click the **Browse CD Contents** link (Fig. 1) to access the CD's contents.

4. *Copying the* **examples** *directory.* Right click the examples directory (Fig. 3), then select **Copy**. Next, go to **My Computer** and double click the **C:** drive. Select the **Edit** menu's **Paste** option to copy the directory and its contents from the CD to your **C:** drive. [*Note:* We save the examples to the **C:** drive and refer to this drive throughout the text. You may choose to save your files to a different drive based on your computer's set up, the setup in your school's lab or personal preferences. If you are working in a computer lab, please see your instructor for more information to confirm where the examples should be saved.]

The book example files you copied onto your computer from the CD are read-only. Next, you will remove the read-only property so you can modify and run the examples.

Changing the Read-Only Property of Files

1. *Opening the Properties dialog.* Right click the examples directory and select **Properties** from the menu. The **examples Properties** dialog appears (Fig. 4).

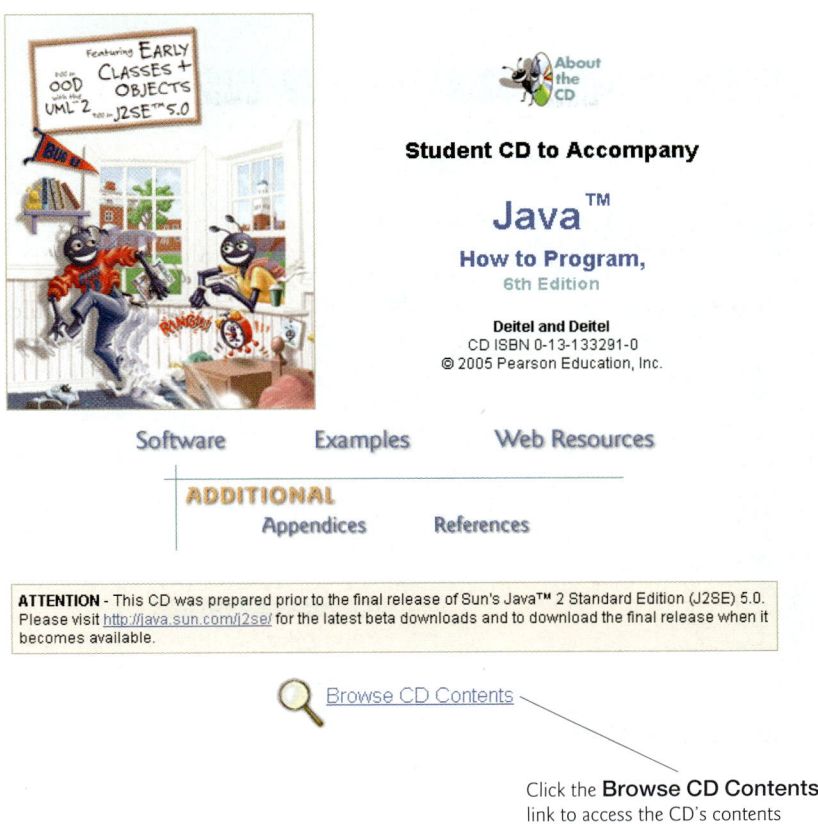

Fig. I | Welcome page for *Java How to Program* CD.

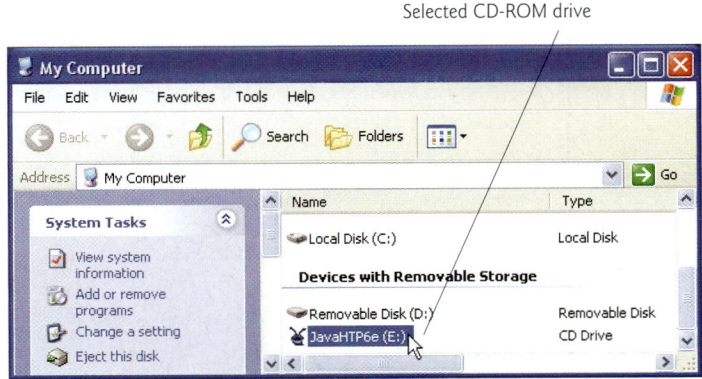

Fig.2 | Locating the CD-ROM drive.

Right click the
`examples` directory

Select **Copy**

Fig.3 | Copying the **examples** directory.

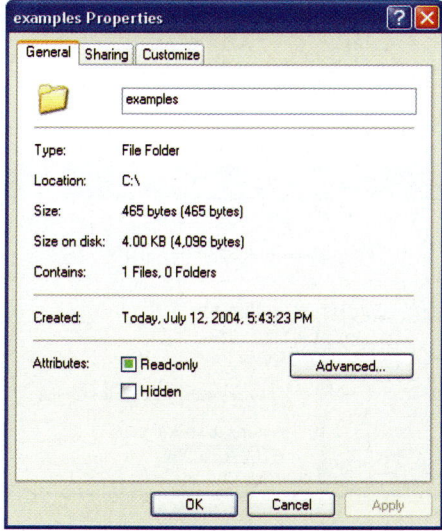

Fig.4 | **examples Properties** dialog.

2. *Changing the read-only property.* In the **Attributes** section of this dialog, click the box next to **Read-only** to remove the check mark (Fig. 5). Click **Apply** to apply the changes.

3. *Changing the property for all files.* Clicking **Apply** will display the **Confirm Attribute Changes** window (Fig. 6). In this window, click the radio button next to **Apply changes to this folder, subfolders and files** and click **OK** to remove the read-only property for all of the files and directories in the **examples** directory.

Before you can run the applications in *Java How To Program, Sixth Edition* or build your own applications, you must install the Java Development Kit (JDK) 5.0 or another Java development tool. The following section describes how to install JDK 5.0.

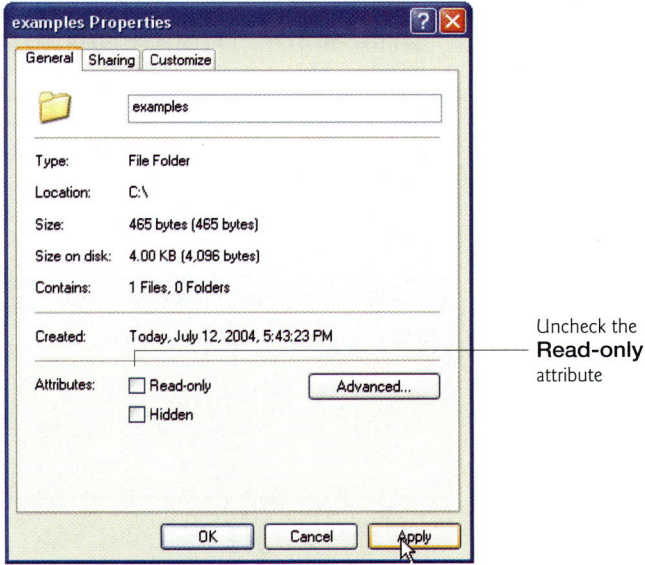

Uncheck the
Read-only
attribute

Fig.5 | Unchecking the **Read-only** check box.

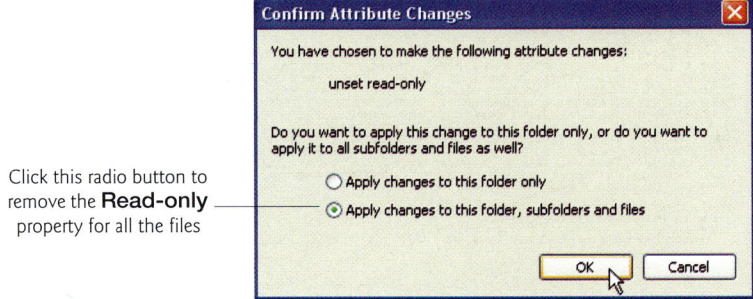

Click this radio button to
remove the **Read-only**
property for all the files

Fig.6 | Removing read-only for all the files in the **examples** directory.

Installing the J2SE Development Kit (JDK)

1. *Locating the JDK installer.* At the time of publication, the JDK 5.0 was still in beta releases and being updated frequently. As a result, the JDK installer might not be included on the CD that accompanies your book. If this is the case, you can download the most recent version of the installer from Sun's Web site. Go to java.sun.com/j2se/5.0/download.jsp and click the **DOWNLOAD** link in the **SDK** column. You must accept the license agreement before downloading. Once you accept the license agreement, you are directed to a download page, where you can select and download the installer for your computer platform. Save the installer on your hard disk and keep track of where you save it. The following steps show the installation procedure on the Windows platform.

2. *Starting installation of the JDK.* After either downloading the JDK installer or locating it on the CD that accompanies the book, double click the installer program to begin installing the JDK. The **InstallShield Wizard** window (Fig. 7) is displayed. Wait for the wizard to finish the configuration.

3. *Accepting the license agreement.* Carefully read the license agreement. Select **Yes** to agree to the terms (Fig. 8). [*Note:* If you choose not to accept the license agreement, the software will not install and you will not be able to execute or create Java applications.]

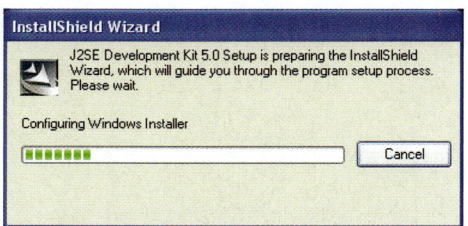

Fig.7 | **InstallShield Wizard** for the JDK.

Fig.8 | JDK license agreement.

4. *Choosing the installation directory for the JDK.* Select the directory in which you want the JDK to be installed (Fig. 9). If you change the default installation directory, be sure to write down the exact name and location of the directory you choose, as you will need this information later in the installation process. After selecting a directory, click the **Next >** button to install the development tool.

5. *Choosing the installation directory for the Java Runtime Environment (JRE).* Select the directory in which you want the JRE to be installed (Fig. 10). We recommend that you choose the default installation directory. After you have selected a directory, click the **Next >** button to install the JRE.

6. *Selecting browsers.* As part of the installation, you have the option of making the Java plug-in the default Java runtime environment for Java programs called applets that run in Web browsers (Fig. 11). After you select the desired browsers click the **Next >** button.

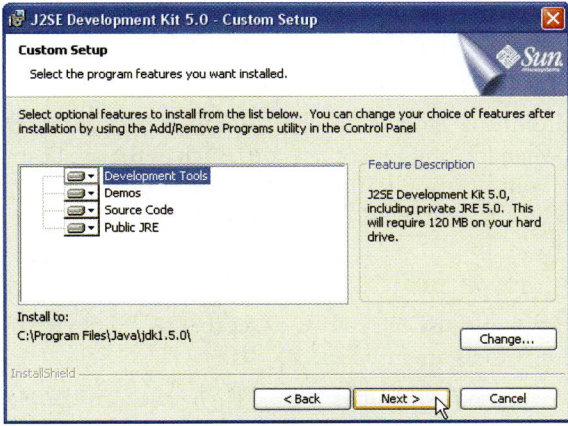

Fig.9 | Choosing the destination location.

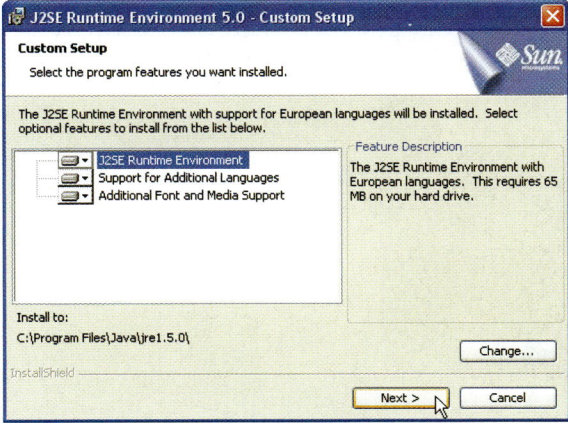

Fig.10 | Selecting the components of the JDK to install.

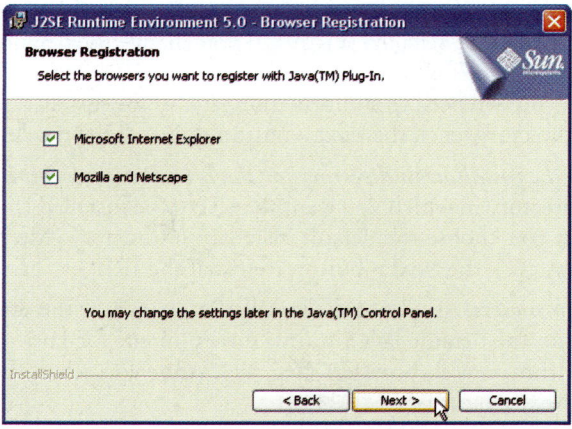

Fig. 11 | Selecting browsers.

7. *Finishing the installation.* The program will now install the JRE. Click the **Finish** button to complete the installation process (Fig. 12).

The PATH environment variable on your computer designates which directories the computer searches when looking for applications, such as the applications that enable you to compile and run your Java applications (called `javac.exe` and `java.exe`, respectively). You will now learn how to set the PATH environment variable on your computer.

Setting the PATH Variable

The last step before you can use the JDK is to set the PATH environment variable to indicate where the JDK's tools are installed.

1. *Opening the* **System Properties** *dialog.* Right click on the **My Computer** icon on your desktop and select **Properties** from the menu. The **System Properties** dialog (Fig. 13) appears. [*Note*: Your **System Properties** dialog may appear different than

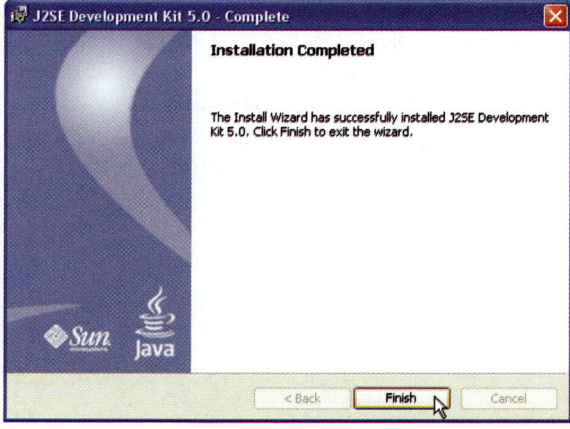

Fig. 12 | Completing the installation.

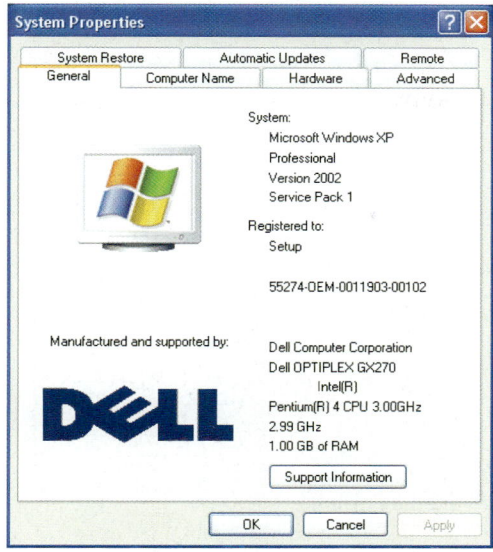

Fig. 13 | **System Properties** dialog.

the one shown in Fig. 13, depending on your version of Microsoft Windows. This particular dialog is from a computer running Microsoft Windows XP. Your dialog might include different information.]

2. *Opening the Environment Variables dialog.* Select the **Advanced** tab at the top of the **System Properties** dialog (Fig. 14). Click the **Environment Variables** button to display the **Environment Variables** dialog (Fig. 15).

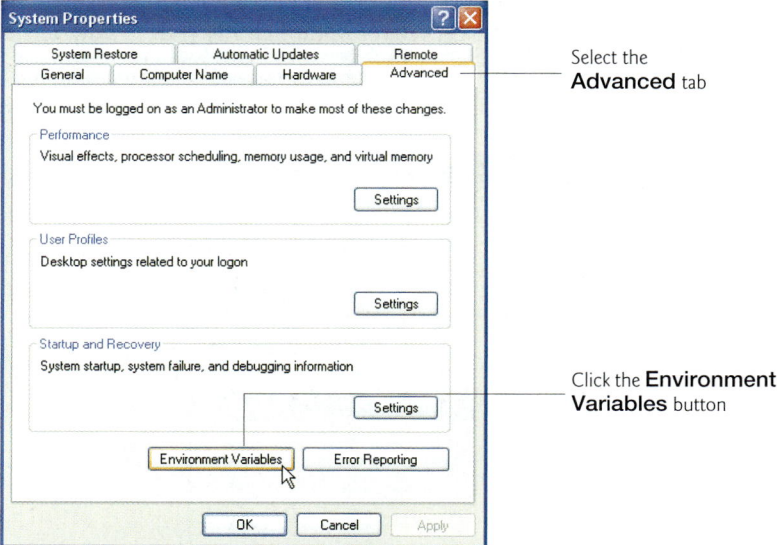

Select the **Advanced** tab

Click the **Environment Variables** button

Fig. 14 | **Advanced** tab of **System Properties** dialog.

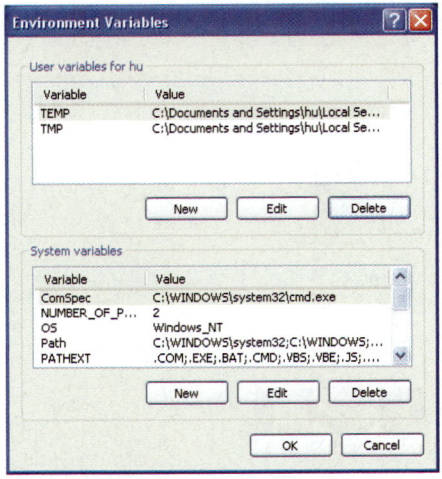

Fig. 15 | **Environment Variables** dialog.

3. *Editing the **PATH** variable.* Scroll down inside the **System variables** box to select the PATH variable. Click the **Edit** button. This will cause the **Edit System Variable** dialog to appear (Fig. 16).

4. *Changing the contents of the **PATH** variable.* Place the cursor inside the **Variable Value** field. Use the left-arrow key to move the cursor to the beginning of the list. At the beginning of the list, type the name of the directory in which you placed the JDK followed by \bin; (Fig. 17). If you chose the default installation directory in *Step 4* of *Installing the J2SE Development Kit (JDK)*, you will add C:\Program Files\Java\jdk1.5.0\bin; to the PATH variable. Click the **OK** button to complete the modification of the PATH variable. [*Note:* The default installation directory is named jdk1.5.0, even though the JDK is now version 5.0.]

You are now ready to being your Java studies with *Java How to Program*. We hope you enjoy the book! You can reach us easily at deitel@deitel.com. We will respond promptly.

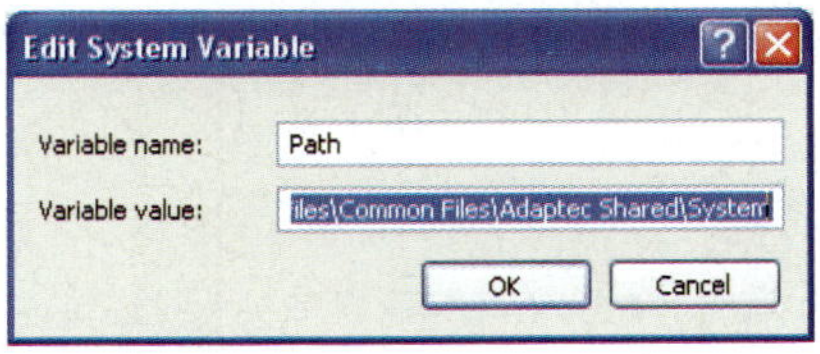

Fig. 16 | Edit **System Variable** dialog.

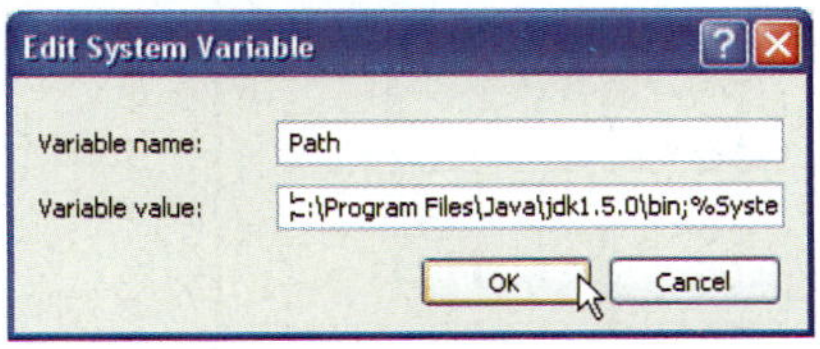

Fig. 17 | Editing the PATH variable.

Introduction to Computers, the Internet and the World Wide Web

OBJECTIVES

In this chapter you will learn:

- Basic hardware and software concepts.
- Basic object technology concepts, such as classes, objects, attributes, behaviors, encapsulation, inheritance and polymorphism.
- The different types of programming languages.
- Which programming languages are most widely used.
- A typical Java development environment.
- Java's role in developing distributed client/server applications for the Internet and the Web.
- The history of the industry-standard object-oriented design language, the UML.
- The history of the Internet and the World Wide Web.
- To test-drive Java applications.

1.1 Introduction

Welcome to Java! We have worked hard to create what we hope you will find to be an informative, entertaining and challenging learning experience. Java is a powerful computer programming language that is fun for novices and appropriate for experienced programmers to use in building substantial information systems. *Java How to Program, Sixth Edition*, is an effective learning tool for each of these audiences.

The core of the book emphasizes achieving program *clarity* through the proven techniques of object-oriented programming. Nonprogrammers will learn programming the right way from the beginning. The presentation is clear, straightforward and abundantly illustrated. It includes hundreds of working Java programs and shows the outputs produced when those programs are run on a computer. We teach Java features in the context of complete working Java programs—we call this the **live-code approach**. The example programs are included on the CD that accompanies this book, or you may download them from www.deitel.com or www.prenhall.com/deitel.

The early chapters introduce the fundamentals of computers, computer programming and the Java computer programming language, providing a solid foundation for the deeper treatment of Java in the later chapters. Experienced programmers tend to read the early chapters quickly and find the treatment of Java in the later chapters rigorous and challenging.

Most people are familiar with the exciting tasks computers perform. Using this textbook, you will learn how to command computers to perform those tasks. It is software (i.e., the instructions you write to command computers to perform **actions** and make **deci-**

sions) that controls computers (often referred to as hardware). Java, developed by Sun Microsystems, is one of today's most popular software development languages.

This book is based on Sun's **Java 2 Platform, Standard Edition (J2SE)**. Sun provides an implementation of this platform, called the **J2SE Development Kit (JDK)**, that includes the minimum set of tools you need to write software in Java. We used JDK version 5.0 to implement and test the programs in this book. When Sun makes the JDK available to publishers, it will be wrapped with the textbook on the accompanying CD. Sun updates the JDK on a regular basis to fix bugs. To download the most recent version of the JDK, visit `java.sun.com/j2se`.

Computer use is increasing in almost every field of endeavor. Computing costs have been decreasing dramatically due to rapid developments in both hardware and software technologies. Computers that might have filled large rooms and cost millions of dollars two decades ago can now be inscribed on silicon chips smaller than a fingernail, costing perhaps a few dollars each. Fortunately, silicon is one of the most abundant materials on earth—it is an ingredient in common sand. Silicon chip technology has made computing so economical that hundreds of millions of general-purpose computers are in use worldwide, helping people in business, industry and government, and in their personal lives. The number could easily double in the next few years.

Over the years, many programmers learned the programming methodology called structured programming. You will learn structured programming and an exciting newer methodology, **object-oriented programming**. Why do we teach both? Object orientation is the key programming methodology used by programmers today. You will create and work with many software **objects** in this text. But you will discover that their internal structure is often built using structured-programming techniques. Also, the logic of manipulating objects is occasionally expressed with structured programming.

Java has become the language of choice for implementing Internet-based applications and software for devices that communicate over a network. Before long the stereo and other devices in your home will be networked together by Java technology. Don't be surprised when your wireless devices, like cell phones, pagers and personal digital assistants (PDAs), begin to communicate over the so-called wireless Internet via the kind of Java-based networking applications that you will learn in this book and its companion, *Advanced Java 2 Platform How to Program*. According to Sun's Web site (`www.sun.com`), in 2003, over 267 million cell phones equipped with Java technology were shipped! Java has evolved rapidly into the large-scale applications arena. It is no longer used simply to make World Wide Web pages come alive—it has become the preferred language for meeting the enterprise-wide programming needs of many organizations.

Java has evolved so rapidly that this sixth edition of *Java How to Program* has been written just eight years after the first edition was published. This edition is based on the *Java 2 Platform, Standard Edition (J2SE) version 5.0*. Java has grown so large that it now has two other editions. The **Java 2 Platform, Enterprise Edition (J2EE)**, is geared toward developing large-scale, distributed networking applications and Web-based applications. The **Java 2 Platform, Micro Edition (J2ME)** is geared toward developing applications for small, memory-constrained devices, such as cell phones, pagers and PDAs. *Advanced Java 2 Platform How to Program* emphasizes developing applications with J2EE and provides coverage of several high-end topics from the J2SE. *Advanced Java 2 Platform How to Program* also includes substantial materials on J2ME and wireless-application development.

You are embarking on a challenging and rewarding path. As you proceed, if you would like to communicate with us, please send e-mail to

deitel@deitel.com

or browse our Web site at

www.deitel.com

We will respond promptly. To keep up to date with Java developments at Deitel & Associates, please register for our free e-mail newsletter, *The Deitel Buzz Online,* at

www.deitel.com/newsletter/subscribe.html

We hope that you will enjoy learning with *Java How to Program.*

1.2 What Is a Computer?

A computer is a device capable of performing computations and making logical decisions at speeds millions (even billions) of times faster than human beings can. For example, many of today's personal computers can perform a billion additions per second. A person operating a desk calculator could spend an entire lifetime performing calculations and still not complete as many calculations as a powerful personal computer can perform in one second. (Points to ponder: How would you know whether the person added the numbers correctly? How would you know whether the computer added the numbers correctly?) Today's fastest supercomputers can perform hundreds of billions of additions per second. And trillion-instructions-per-second computers are already functioning in research laboratories.

Computers process data under the control of sets of instructions called computer programs. These programs guide the computer through orderly sets of actions specified by people called computer programmers.

A computer consists of various devices referred to as hardware (e.g., the keyboard, screen, mouse, disks, memory, DVD, CD-ROM and processing units). The programs that run on a computer are referred to as software. Hardware costs have been declining dramatically in recent years, to the point that personal computers have become a commodity. Unfortunately, in the absence of significantly improved technology for software development, costs have been rising steadily as programmers develop ever more powerful and complex applications. In this book, you will learn proven methodologies that *can* reduce software development costs—object-oriented programming and (in our optional Software Engineering Case Study in Chapters 2–8 and 10) object-oriented design.

1.3 Computer Organization

Regardless of differences in physical appearance, virtually every computer may be envisioned as divided into six logical units or sections:

1. *Input unit.* This is the "receiving" section of the computer. It obtains information (data and computer programs) from input devices and places this information at the disposal of the other units so that it can be processed. Most information is entered into computers through keyboards and mouse devices. Information also can be entered in many other ways, including by speaking to your computer, by scanning images and by having your computer receive information from a network, such as the Internet.

2. *Output unit.* This is the "shipping" section of the computer. It takes information that the computer has processed and places it on various output devices to make the information available for use outside the computer. Most information output from computers today is displayed on screens, printed on paper or used to control other devices. Computers also can output their information to networks, such as the Internet.

3. *Memory unit.* This is the rapid-access, relatively low-capacity "warehouse" section of the computer. It retains information that has been entered through the input unit, so that it will be immediately available for processing when needed. The memory unit also retains processed information until it can be placed on output devices by the output unit. Information in the memory unit is typically lost when the computer's power is turned off. The memory unit is often called either memory or primary memory.

4. *Arithmetic and logic unit (ALU).* This is the "manufacturing" section of the computer. It is responsible for performing calculations, such as addition, subtraction, multiplication and division. It contains the decision mechanisms that allow the computer, for example, to compare two items from the memory unit to determine whether they are equal.

5. *Central processing unit (CPU).* This is the "administrative" section of the computer. It coordinates and supervises the operation of the other sections. The CPU tells the input unit when information should be read into the memory unit, tells the ALU when information from the memory unit should be used in calculations and tells the output unit when to send information from the memory unit to certain output devices. Many of today's computers have multiple CPUs and, hence, can perform many operations simultaneously—such computers are called multiprocessors.

6. *Secondary storage unit.* This is the long-term, high-capacity "warehousing" section of the computer. Programs or data not actively being used by the other units normally are placed on secondary storage devices (e.g., your hard drive) until they are again needed, possibly hours, days, months or even years later. Information in secondary storage takes much longer to access than information in primary memory, but the cost per unit of secondary storage is much less than that of primary memory. Examples of secondary storage devices include CDs and DVDs, which can hold up to hundreds of millions of characters and billions of characters, respectively.

1.4 Early Operating Systems

Early computers could perform only one job or task at a time. This is often called single-user batch processing. The computer runs a single program at a time while processing data in groups or batches. In these early systems, users generally submitted their jobs to a computer center on decks of punched cards and often had to wait hours or even days before printouts were returned to their desks.

Software systems called operating systems were developed to make using computers more convenient. Early operating systems smoothed and speeded up the transition between jobs, and hence increased the amount of work, or throughput, computers could process.

As computers became more powerful, it became evident that single-user batch processing was inefficient, because so much time was spent waiting for slow input/output devices to complete their tasks. It was thought that many jobs or tasks could *share* the resources of the computer to achieve better utilization. This is called multiprogramming. Multiprogramming involves the simultaneous operation of many jobs that are competing to share the computer's resources. With early multiprogramming operating systems, users still submitted jobs on decks of punched cards and waited hours or days for results.

In the 1960s, several groups in industry and the universities pioneered timesharing operating systems. Timesharing is a special case of multiprogramming in which users access the computer through terminals, typically devices with keyboards and screens. Dozens or even hundreds of users share the computer at once. The computer actually does not run them all simultaneously. Rather, it runs a small portion of one user's job, then moves on to service the next user, perhaps providing service to each user several times per second. Thus, the users' programs *appear* to be running simultaneously. An advantage of timesharing is that user requests receive almost immediate responses.

1.5 Personal, Distributed and Client/Server Computing

In 1977, Apple Computer popularized personal computing. Computers became so economical that people could buy them for their own personal or business use. In 1981, IBM, the world's largest computer vendor, introduced the IBM Personal Computer. This quickly legitimized personal computing in business, industry and government organizations.

These computers were "standalone" units—people transported disks back and forth between them to share information (often called "sneakernet"). Although early personal computers were not powerful enough to timeshare several users, these machines could be linked together in computer networks, sometimes over telephone lines and sometimes in local area networks (LANs) within an organization. This led to the phenomenon of distributed computing, in which an organization's computing, instead of being performed only at some central computer installation, is distributed over networks to the sites where the organization's work is performed. Personal computers were powerful enough to handle the computing requirements of individual users as well as the basic communications tasks of passing information between computers electronically.

Today's personal computers are as powerful as the million-dollar machines of just two decades ago. The most powerful desktop machines—called workstations—provide individual users with enormous capabilities. Information is shared easily across computer networks where computers called file servers offer a common data store that may be used by client computers distributed throughout the network, hence the term client/server computing. Java has become widely used for writing software for computer networking and for distributed client/server applications. Today's popular operating systems, such as UNIX, Linux, Apple Mac OS X (pronounced "O-S ten") and Microsoft Windows, provide the kinds of capabilities discussed in this section.

1.6 The Internet and the World Wide Web

The Internet—a global network of computers—was developed almost four decades ago with funding supplied by the U.S. Department of Defense. Originally designed to connect the main computer systems of about a dozen universities and research organizations, the Internet today is accessible by hundreds of millions of computers worldwide.

With the introduction of the World Wide Web—which allows computer users to locate and view multimedia-based documents on almost any subject over the Internet—the Internet has exploded into one of the world's premier communication mechanisms.

The Internet and the World Wide Web are surely among humankind's most important and profound creations. In the past, most computer applications ran on computers that were not connected to one another. Today's applications can be written to communicate among the world's hundreds of millions of computers. The Internet mixes computing and communications technologies. It makes our work easier. It makes information instantly and conveniently accessible worldwide. It enables individuals and local small businesses to get worldwide exposure. It is changing the way business is done. People can search for the best prices on virtually any product or service. Special-interest communities can stay in touch with one another. Researchers can be made instantly aware of the latest breakthroughs.

Java How to Program, 6/e, presents programming techniques that allow Java applications to use the Internet and the Web to interact with other applications. These capabilities, and those discussed in our companion book, *Advanced Java 2 Platform How to Program*, allow Java programmers to develop the kind of enterprise-level distributed applications that are used in industry today. Java applications can be written to execute on every major type of computer, greatly reducing the time and cost of systems development for corporations. If you are interested in developing applications to run over the Internet and the Web, learning Java may be the key to rewarding career opportunities for you.

1.7 Machine Languages, Assembly Languages and High-Level Languages

Programmers write instructions in various programming languages, some directly understandable by computers and others requiring intermediate translation steps. Hundreds of computer languages are in use today. These may be divided into three general types:

1. Machine languages
2. Assembly languages
3. High-level languages

Any computer can directly understand only its own machine language. Machine language is the "natural language" of a computer and as such is defined by its hardware design. Machine languages generally consist of strings of numbers (ultimately reduced to 1s and 0s) that instruct computers to perform their most elementary operations one at a time. Machine languages are machine dependent (i.e., a particular machine language can be used on only one type of computer). Such languages are cumbersome for humans, as illustrated by the following section of an early machine-language program that adds overtime pay to base pay and stores the result in gross pay:

```
+1300042774
+1400593419
+1200274027
```

Machine-language programming was simply too slow and tedious for most programmers. Instead of using the strings of numbers that computers could directly understand, programmers began using English-like abbreviations to represent elementary operations. These abbreviations formed the basis of assembly languages. Translator programs called assemblers were developed to convert early assembly-language programs to machine language at computer speeds. The following section of an assembly-language program also adds overtime pay to base pay and stores the result in gross pay:

```
load    basepay
add     overpay
store   grosspay
```

Although such code is clearer to humans, it is incomprehensible to computers until translated to machine language.

Computer usage increased rapidly with the advent of assembly languages, but programmers still had to use many instructions to accomplish even the simplest tasks. To speed the programming process, high-level languages were developed in which single statements could be written to accomplish substantial tasks. Translator programs called compilers convert high-level language programs into machine language. High-level languages allow programmers to write instructions that look almost like everyday English and contain commonly used mathematical notations. A payroll program written in a high-level language might contain a statement such as

```
grossPay = basePay + overTimePay
```

Obviously, high-level languages are preferable to machine and assembly language from the programmer's standpoint. C, C++, Microsoft's .NET languages (e.g., Visual Basic .NET, Visual C++ .NET and C#) and Java are among the most widely used high-level programming languages.

The process of compiling a high-level language program into machine language can take a considerable amount of computer time. Interpreter programs were developed to execute high-level language programs directly, although much more slowly. Interpreters are popular in program-development environments in which new features are being added and errors corrected. Once a program is fully developed, a compiled version can be produced to run most efficiently.

You now know that there are ultimately two ways to translate a high-level language program into a form that the computer understands—compilation and interpretation. As you will learn in Section 1.13, Java uses a clever mixture of these technologies.

1.8 History of C and C++

Java evolved from C++, which evolved from C, which evolved from BCPL and B. BCPL was developed in 1967 by Martin Richards as a language for writing operating systems software and compilers. Ken Thompson modeled many features in his language B after their counterparts in BCPL, using B to create early versions of the UNIX operating system at Bell Laboratories in 1970.

The C language was evolved from B by Dennis Ritchie at Bell Laboratories and was originally implemented in 1972. It initially became widely known as the development language of the UNIX operating system. Today, most of the code for general-purpose operating systems (e.g., those found in laptops, desktops, workstations and small servers) is written in C or C++.

C++, an extension of C, was developed by Bjarne Stroustrup in the early 1980s at Bell Laboratories (now part of Lucent). C++ provides a number of features that "spruce up" the

C language, but more important, it provides capabilities for object-oriented programming (discussed in more detail in Section 1.16 and throughout this book). C++ is a hybrid language—it is possible to program in either a C-like style, an object-oriented style or both.

A revolution is brewing in the software community. Building software quickly, correctly and economically remains an elusive goal at a time when demands for new and more powerful software are soaring. Objects, or more precisely—as we will see in Section 1.16—the classes objects come from, are essentially reusable software components. There are date objects, time objects, audio objects, automobile objects, people objects and so on. In fact, almost any noun can be represented as a software object in terms of attributes (e.g., name, color and size) and behaviors (e.g., calculating, moving and communicating). Software developers are discovering that using a modular, object-oriented design and implementation approach can make software-development groups much more productive than was possible with earlier popular programming techniques like structured programming. Object-oriented programs are often easier to understand, correct and modify. Java is the world's most widely used object-oriented programming language.

1.9 History of Java

The microprocessor revolution's most important contribution to date is that it made possible the development of personal computers, which now number in the hundreds of millions worldwide. Personal computers have profoundly affected people's lives and the ways organizations conduct and manage their business.

Microprocessors are having a profound impact in intelligent consumer-electronic devices. Recognizing this, Sun Microsystems in 1991 funded an internal corporate research project code-named Green, which resulted in the development of a C++-based language that its creator, James Gosling, called Oak after an oak tree outside his window at Sun. It was later discovered that there already was a computer language called Oak. When a group of Sun people visited a local coffee shop, the name Java was suggested, and it stuck.

The Green project ran into some difficulties. The marketplace for intelligent consumer-electronic devices was not developing in the early 1990s as quickly as Sun had anticipated. The project was in danger of being canceled. By sheer good fortune, the World Wide Web exploded in popularity in 1993, and Sun people saw the immediate potential of using Java to add dynamic content, such as interactivity and animations, to Web pages. This breathed new life into the project.

Sun formally announced Java at a major conference in May 1995. Java garnered the attention of the business community because of the phenomenal interest in the World Wide Web. Java is now used to develop large-scale enterprise applications, to enhance the functionality of Web servers (the computers that provide the content we see in our Web browsers), to provide applications for consumer devices (e.g., cell phones, pagers and personal digital assistants) and for many other purposes.

1.10 Java Class Libraries

Java programs consist of pieces called classes. Classes include pieces called methods that perform tasks and return information when they complete them. Programmers can create each piece they need to form Java programs. However, most Java programmers take advantage of the rich collections of existing classes in the Java class libraries, which are also known as the **Java APIs (Application Programming Interfaces)**. Thus, there are really two aspects to learning the Java "world." The first is the Java language itself, so that you can program your own classes, and the second is the classes in the extensive Java class libraries. Throughout this book, we discuss many library classes. Class libraries are provided primarily by compiler vendors, but many are supplied by independent software vendors (ISVs).

Software Engineering Observation 1.1

Use a building-block approach to create programs. Avoid reinventing the wheel—use existing pieces wherever possible. Called software reuse, *this practice is central to object-oriented programming.*

We include many tips such as these **Software Engineering Observations** throughout the book to explain concepts that affect and improve the overall architecture and quality of software systems. We also highlight other kinds of tips, including **Good Programming Practices** (to help you write programs that are clearer, more understandable, more maintainable and easier to test and **debug**—or remove programming errors), **Common Programming Errors** (problems to watch out for and avoid), **Performance Tips** (techniques for writing programs that run faster and use less memory), **Portability Tips** (techniques to help you write programs that can run, with little or no modification, on a variety of computers—these tips also include general observations about how Java achieves its high degree of portability), **Error-Prevention Tips** (techniques for removing bugs from your programs and, more important, techniques for writing bug-free programs in the first place) and **Look and Feel Observations** (techniques to help you design the "look" and "feel" of your applications' user interfaces for appearance and ease of use). Many of these are only guidelines. You will, no doubt, develop your own preferred programming style.

Software Engineering Observation 1.2

When programming in Java, you will typically use the following building blocks: Classes and methods from class libraries, classes and methods you create yourself and classes and methods that others create and make available to you.

The advantage of creating your own classes and methods is that you know exactly how they work and you can examine the Java code. The disadvantage is the time-consuming and potentially complex effort that is required.

Performance Tip 1.1

Using Java API classes and methods instead of writing your own versions can improve program performance, because they are carefully written to perform efficiently. This technique also shortens program development time.

Portability Tip 1.1

Using classes and methods from the Java API instead of writing your own improves program portability, because they are included in every Java implementation.

Software Engineering Observation 1.3

Extensive class libraries of reusable software components are available over the Internet and the Web, many at no charge.

To download the Java API documentation, go to the Sun Java site `java.sun.com/j2se/5.0/download.jsp`.

1.11 FORTRAN, COBOL, Pascal and Ada

Hundreds of high-level languages have been developed, but only a few have achieved broad acceptance. FORTRAN (FORmula TRANslator) was developed by IBM Corporation in the mid-1950s to be used for scientific and engineering applications that require complex mathematical computations. FORTRAN is still widely used, especially in engineering applications.

COBOL (COmmon Business Oriented Language) was developed in the late 1950s by computer manufacturers, the U.S. government and industrial computer users. COBOL is used for commercial applications that require precise and efficient manipulation of large amounts of data. Much business software is still programmed in COBOL.

During the 1960s, many large software-development efforts encountered severe difficulties. Software deliveries were typically late, costs greatly exceeded budgets and the finished products were unreliable. People began to realize that software development was a far more complex activity than they had imagined. Research in the 1960s resulted in the evolution of structured programming—a disciplined approach to writing programs that are clearer, easier to test and debug and easier to modify than large programs produced with previous techniques.

One of the more tangible results of this research was the development of the Pascal programming language by Professor Niklaus Wirth in 1971. Named after the seventeenth-century mathematician and philosopher Blaise Pascal, it was designed for teaching structured programming in academic environments and rapidly became the preferred programming language in most colleges. Pascal lacks many features needed to make it useful in commercial, industrial and government applications, so it has not been widely accepted in these environments.

The Ada programming language was developed under the sponsorship of the U.S. Department of Defense (DOD) during the 1970s and early 1980s. Hundreds of separate languages were being used to produce the DOD's massive command-and-control software systems. The DOD wanted a single language that would fill most of its needs. The Ada language was named after Lady Ada Lovelace, daughter of the poet Lord Byron. Lady Lovelace is credited with writing the world's first computer program in the early 1800s (for the Analytical Engine mechanical computing device designed by Charles Babbage). One important capability of Ada, called multitasking, allows programmers to specify that many activities are to occur in parallel. Java, through a technique called multithreading, also enables programmers to write programs with parallel activities.

1.12 BASIC, Visual Basic, Visual C++, C# and .NET

The BASIC (Beginner's All-Purpose Symbolic Instruction Code) programming language was developed in the mid-1960s at Dartmouth College as a means of writing simple programs. BASIC's primary purpose was to familiarize novices with programming techniques.

Microsoft's Visual Basic language was introduced in the early 1990s to simplify the development of Microsoft Windows applications and is one of the most popular programming languages in the world.

Microsoft's latest development tools are part of its corporate-wide strategy for integrating the Internet and the Web into computer applications. This strategy is implemented in Microsoft's .NET platform, which provides developers with the capabilities they need to create and run computer applications that can execute on computers distributed across the Internet. Microsoft's three primary programming languages are Visual Basic .NET (based on the original BASIC), Visual C++ .NET (based on C++) and C# (a new language based on C++ and Java that was developed expressly for the .NET platform). Developers using .NET can write software components in the language they are most familiar with and then form applications by combining those components with components written in any .NET language.

1.13 Typical Java Development Environment

We now explain the commonly used steps in creating and executing a Java application using a Java development environment (illustrated in Fig. 1.1).

Java programs normally go through five phases—*edit, compile, load, verify* and *execute*. We discuss these phases in the context of the *J2SE Development Kit (JDK) version 5.0* from Sun Microsystems, Inc., which will be wrapped with the book as an accompanying CD once Sun releases the final version of the JDK 5.0. If the CD for your book does not have the JDK on it, you can download both the JDK and its documentation now from `java.sun.com/j2se/5.0/download.jsp`. For help with the download, visit `servlet.java.sun.com/help/download`. *Carefully follow the installation instructions for the JDK provided on the CD (or at `java.sun.com/j2se/5.0/install.html`) to ensure that you set up your computer properly to compile and execute Java programs.* Complete installation instructions can also be found on Sun's Java Web site at

`java.sun.com/learning/new2java/index.html`

[*Note:* This Web site provides installation instructions for Windows, UNIX/Linux and Mac OS X. If you are not using one of these operating systems, refer to the manuals for your system's Java environment or ask your instructor how to accomplish these tasks based on your computer's operating system. In addition, please keep in mind that Web links occasionally break as companies evolve their Web sites. If you encounter a problem with this link or any other links referenced in this book, please check our Web site (`www.deitel.com`) for errata and please notify us by e-mail at `deitel@deitel.com`. We will respond promptly.]

Phase 1: Creating a Program

Phase 1 consists of editing a file with an editor program (normally known simply as an editor). You type a Java program (typically referred to as source code) using the editor, make any necessary corrections and save the program on a secondary storage device, such as your hard drive. Java source-code file names end with the .java extension, which indicates that a file contains Java source code. We assume that the reader knows how to edit a file.

Two editors widely used on UNIX/Linux systems are vi and emacs. On Windows, a simple editing program like Windows Notepad will suffice. Many freeware and shareware editors are also available for download from the Internet on sites like `www.download.com`.

For organizations that develop substantial information systems, integrated development environments (IDEs) are available from many major software suppliers, including Sun Microsystems. IDEs provide many tools that support the software development process, including editors for writing and editing programs and debuggers for locating logic errors in programs.

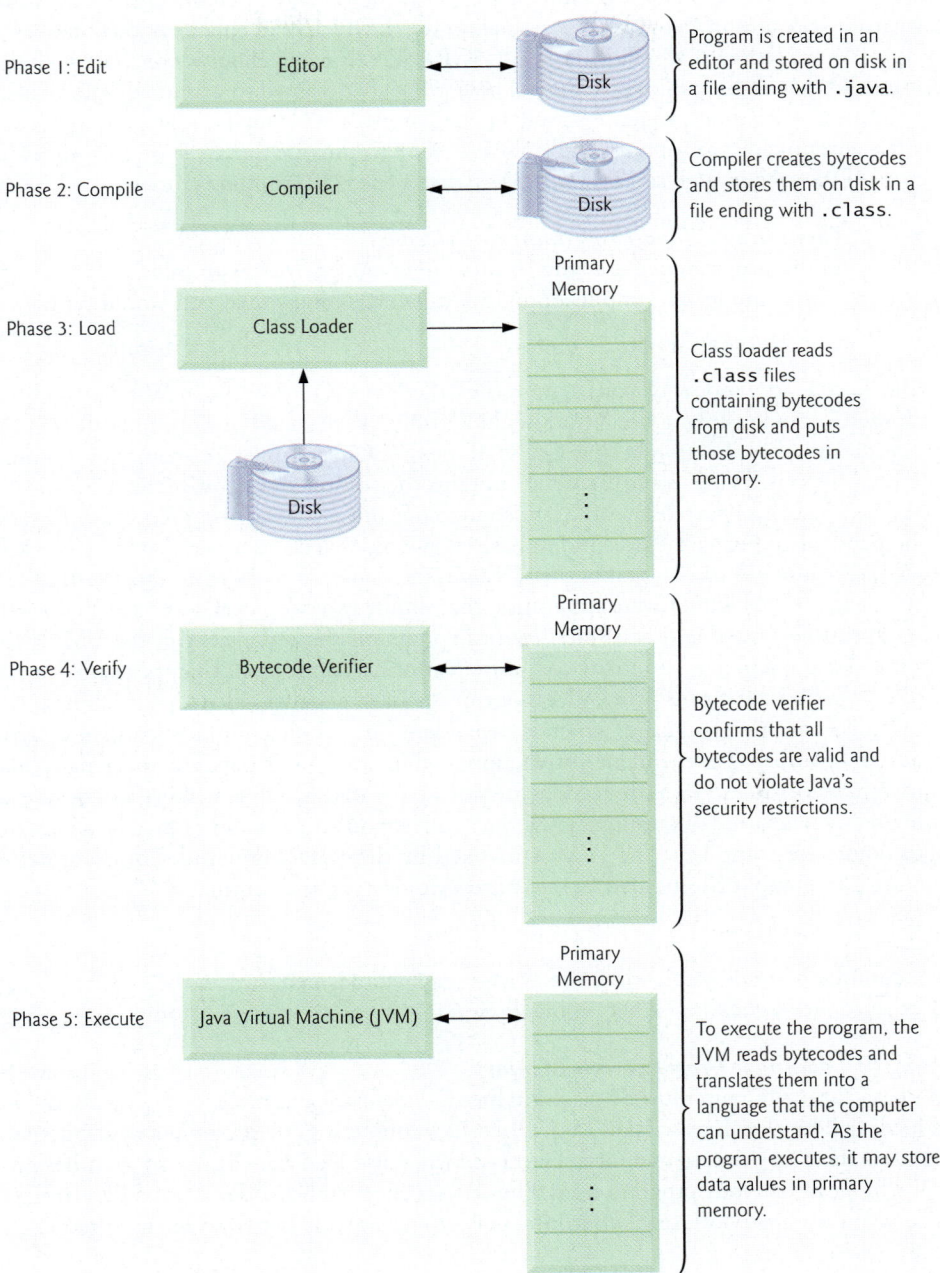

Fig. 1.1 | Typical Java development environment.

Several popular IDEs are NetBeans (`www.netbeans.org`), jEdit (`www.jedit.org`), Eclipse (`www.eclipse.org`), JBuilder (`www.borland.com`), JCreator (`www.jcreator.com`), BlueJ (`www.bluej.org`) and jGRASP (`www.jgrasp.org`). Sun Microsystems has the Sun Java Studio (`wwws.sun.com/software/sundev/jde/`), which is an enhanced version of Net-Beans. [*Note:* NetBeans v. 3.6, jEdit v. 4.1, jGRASP v. 1.7 and BlueJ v. 1.3.5 are included on the CD that accompanies this book. These IDEs are designed to execute on most major platforms. Our example programs should operate properly with any Java integrated development environment that supports the JDK 5.0. We also provide free *Dive Into*™ guides for various IDEs on our Web site at `www.deitel.com/books/jHTP6/index.html`.]

Phase 2: Compiling a Java Program into Bytecodes

In Phase 2, the programmer uses the command **javac** (the Java compiler) to compile a program. For example, to compile a program called `Welcome.java`, you would type

```
javac Welcome.java
```

in the command window of your system (i.e., the MS-DOS prompt in Windows 95/98/ ME, the Command Prompt in Windows NT/2000/XP, the shell prompt in UNIX/Linux or the Terminal application in Mac OS X). If the program compiles, the compiler produces a `.class` file called `Welcome.class` that contains the compiled version of the program.

The Java compiler translates the Java source code into bytecodes that represent the tasks to be performed during the execution phase (Phase 5). Bytecodes are executed by the Java Virtual Machine (JVM)—a part of the JDK and the foundation of the Java platform. A virtual machine (VM) is a software application that simulates a computer, but hides the underlying operating system and hardware from the programs that interact with the VM. If the same VM is implemented on many computer platforms, applications that it executes can be used on all those platforms. The JVM is one of the most widely used virtual machines.

Unlike machine language, which is dependent on specific computer hardware, bytecodes are platform-independent instructions—they are not dependent on a particular hardware platform. So Java's bytecodes are portable—that is, the same bytecodes can execute on any platform containing a JVM that understands the version of Java in which the bytecodes were compiled. The JVM is invoked by the **java** command. For example, to execute a Java application called `Welcome`, you would type the command

```
java Welcome
```

in a command window to invoke the JVM, which would then initiate the steps necessary to execute the application. This begins Phase 3.

Phase 3: Loading a Program into Memory

In Phase 3, the program must be placed in memory before it can execute—a process known as loading. The class loader takes the `.class` files containing the program's bytecodes and transfers them to primary memory. The class loader also loads any of the `.class` files provided by Java that your program uses. The `.class` files can be loaded from a disk on your system or over a network (e.g., your local college or company network, or the Internet).

Phase 4: Bytecode Verification

In Phase 4, as the classes are loaded, the bytecode verifier examines their bytecodes to ensure that they are valid and do not violate Java's security restrictions. Java enforces strong security, to make sure that Java programs arriving over the network do not damage your files or your system (as computer viruses and worms might).

Phase 5: Execution

In Phase 5, the JVM executes the program's bytecodes, thus performing the actions specified by the program. In early Java versions, the JVM was simply an interpreter for Java bytecodes. This caused most Java programs to execute slowly because the JVM would interpret and execute one bytecode at a time. Today's JVMs typically execute bytecodes using a combination of interpretation and so-called just-in-time (JIT) compilation. In this process, The JVM analyzes the bytecodes as they are interpreted, searching for hot spots—parts of the bytecodes that execute frequently. For these parts, a just-in-time (JIT) compiler—known as the Java HotSpot compiler—translates the bytecodes into the underlying computer's machine language. When the JVM encounters these compiled parts again, the faster machine-language code executes. Thus Java programs actually go through two compilation phases—one in which source code is translated into bytecodes (for portability across JVMs on different computer platforms) and a second in which, during execution, the bytecodes are translated into machine language for the actual computer on which the program executes.

Problems That May Occur at Execution Time

Programs might not work on the first try. Each of the preceding phases can fail because of various errors that we will discuss throughout this book. For example, an executing program might attempt to divide by zero (an illegal operation for whole-number arithmetic in Java). This would cause the Java program to display an error message. If this occurs, you would have to return to the edit phase, make the necessary corrections and proceed through the remaining phases again to determine that the corrections fix the problem(s). [*Note:* Most programs in Java input or output data. When we say that a program displays a message, we normally mean that it displays that message on your computer's screen. Messages and other data may be output to other devices, such as disks and hardcopy printers, or even to a network for transmission to other computers.]

Common Programming Error 1.1

Errors like division by zero occur as a program runs, so they are called runtime errors *or* execution-time errors. *Fatal runtime errors* cause programs to terminate immediately without having successfully performed their jobs. Nonfatal runtime errors *allow programs to run to completion, often producing incorrect results.*

1.14 Notes about Java and *Java How to Program, Sixth Edition*

Java is a powerful programming language. Experienced programmers sometimes take pride in creating weird, contorted, convoluted usage of a language. This is a poor programming practice. It makes programs more difficult to read, more likely to behave strangely, more difficult to test and debug, and more difficult to adapt to changing requirements. This book stresses *clarity*. The following is our first "good programming practice" tip.

Good Programming Practice 1.1

Write your Java programs in a simple and straightforward manner. This is sometimes referred to as KIS ("keep it simple"). Do not "stretch" the language by trying bizarre usages.

You have heard that Java is a portable language and that programs written in Java can run on many different computers. For programming in general, *portability is an elusive goal*. The ANSI C standard document (located at `www.ansi.org`), which describes the C programming language, contains a lengthy list of portability issues. In fact, whole books have been written to discuss portability, such as Rex Jaeschke's *Portability and the C Language*.

Portability Tip 1.2

Although it is easier to write portable programs in Java than in other programming languages, differences between compilers, JVMs and computers can make portability difficult to achieve. Simply writing programs in Java does not guarantee portability.

Error-Prevention Tip 1.1

Always test your Java programs on all systems on which you intend to run them, to ensure that they will work correctly for their intended audiences.

We have audited our presentation against Sun's current Java documentation for completeness and accuracy. However, Java is a rich language, and no textbook can cover every topic. A Web-based version of the Java API documentation can be found at `java.sun.com/j2se/5.0/docs/api/index.html` or you can download this documentation to your own computer from `java.sun.com/j2se/5.0/download.html`. For additional technical details on Java, visit `java.sun.com/reference/docs/index.html`. This site provides detailed information about many aspects of Java development, including all three Java platforms.

Good Programming Practice 1.2

Read the documentation for the version of Java you are using. Refer to it frequently to be sure you are aware of the rich collection of Java features and are using them correctly.

Good Programming Practice 1.3

Your computer and compiler are good teachers. If, after carefully reading your Java documentation manual, you are not sure how a feature of Java works, experiment and see what happens. Study each error or warning message you get when you compile your programs (called compile-time errors or compilation errors), and correct the programs to eliminate these messages.

Software Engineering Observation 1.4

The J2SE Development Kit comes with the Java source code. Some programmers like to read the source code for the Java API classes to determine how the classes work and to learn additional programming techniques.

1.15 Test-Driving a Java Application

In this section, you will run and interact with your first Java application. You will begin by running an ATM application that simulates the transactions that take place when using an ATM machine (e.g., withdrawing money, making deposits and checking account balances). You will learn how to build this application in the optional, object-oriented case study included in Chapters 1–8 and 10. Figure 1.10 at the end of this section suggests many additional interesting applications that you may also want to test-drive after completing the ATM test-drive.

In the following steps, you will run the application and perform various transactions. The elements and functionality you see in this application are typical of what you will learn to program in this book. [*Note:* We use fonts to distinguish between features you see on a screen (e.g., the **Command Prompt**) and elements that are not directly related to a screen. Our convention is to emphasize screen features like titles and menus (e.g., the **File** menu) in a semibold **sans-serif Helvetica** font and to emphasize non-screen elements, such as file names or input (e.g., `ProgramName.java`) in a `sans-serif Lucida` font. As you have already noticed, the defining occurrence of each term is set in blue, heavy bold. In the figures in this section, we highlight in yellow the user input required by each step and point out significant parts of the application with lines and text. To make these features more visible, we have modified the background color of the **Command Prompt** windows.]

1. *Checking your setup.* Read the *For Students and Instructors: Important Information Before You Begin* section to confirm that you have set up Java properly on your computer and that you have copied the book's examples to your hard drive.

2. *Locating the completed application.* Open a **Command Prompt** window. For readers using Windows 95, 98 or 2000, this can be done by selecting **Start > Programs > Accessories > Command Prompt**. For Windows XP users, select **Start > All Programs > Accessories > Command Prompt**. Change to your completed ATM application directory by typing `cd C:\examples\ch01\ATM` and then pressing *Enter* (Fig. 1.2). The command `cd` is used to change directories.

3. *Running the ATM application.* Now that you are in the directory that contains the ATM application, type the command `java ATMCaseStudy` (Fig. 1.3) and press *Enter*. Remember from the preceding section that the `java` command, followed by the name of the application's `.class` file (in this case, `ATMCaseStudy`), executes the application. It is not necessary to specify the `.class` extension when using the `java` command. [*Note:* Java commands are case sensitive. It is important to type the name of this application with a capital A, T and M in "ATM," a capital C in "Case" and a capital S in "Study." Otherwise, the application will not execute.]

4. *Entering an account number.* When the application first executes, it displays a `"Welcome!"` greeting and prompts you for an account number. Type `12345` at the `"Please enter your account number:"` prompt (Fig. 1.4) and press *Enter*.

Using the **cd** command to
change directories   File location of the ATM application

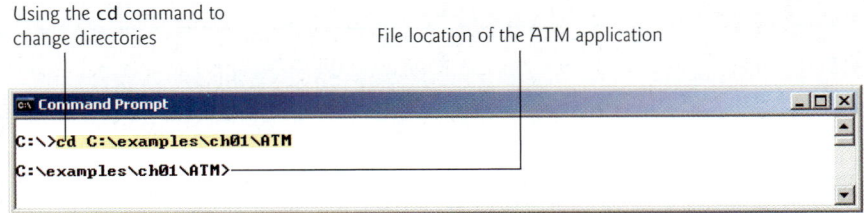

Fig. 1.2 | Opening a Windows XP **Command Prompt** and changing directories.

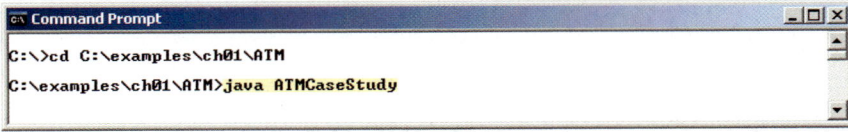

Fig. 1.3 | Using the `java` command to execute the ATM application.

ATM welcome message   Enter account number prompt

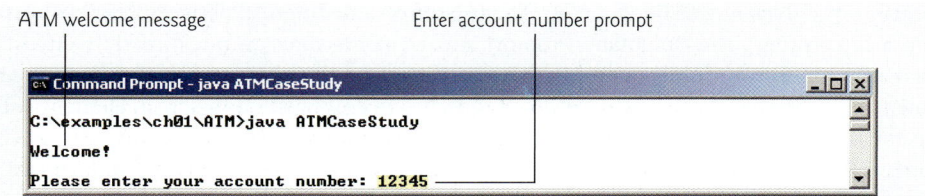

Fig. 1.4 | Prompting the user for an account number.

5. *Entering a PIN.* Once a valid account number is entered, the application displays the prompt "Enter your PIN:". Type "54321" as your valid PIN (Personal Identification Number) and press *Enter*. The ATM main menu containing a list of options will be displayed (Fig. 1.5).

6. *Viewing the account balance.* Select option 1, "View my balance", from the ATM menu. The application then displays two numbers—the Available balance ($1000.00) and the Total balance ($1,200.00). The available balance is the maximum amount of money in your account which is available for withdrawal at a given time. In some cases, certain funds, such as recent deposits, are not immediately available for the user to withdraw, so the available balance may be less than the total balance, as it is here. After the account balance information is shown, the application's main menu is displayed again (Fig. 1.6).

Enter valid PIN   ATM main menu

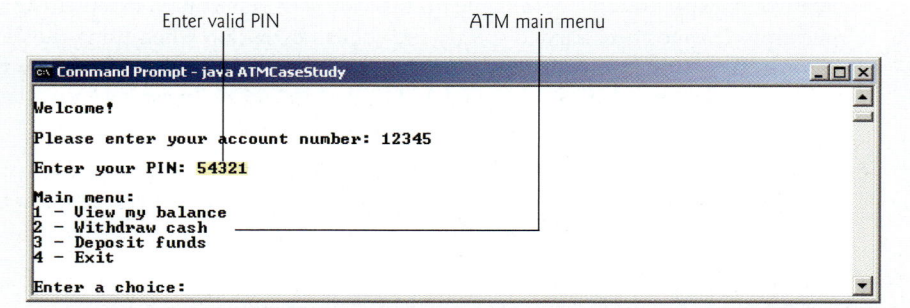

Fig. 1.5 | Entering a valid PIN number and displaying the ATM application's main menu.

Account balance information

```
c:\ Command Prompt - java ATMCaseStudy                              _ |□| x|
Enter a choice: 1

Balance Information:
 - Available balance: $1,000.00
 - Total balance:     $1,200.00

Main menu:
1 - View my balance
2 - Withdraw cash
3 - Deposit funds
4 - Exit

Enter a choice:
```

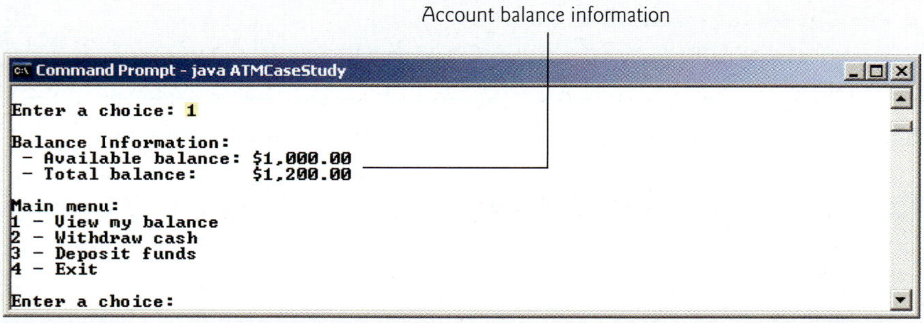

Fig. 1.6 | ATM application displaying user account balance information.

7. ***Withdrawing money from the account.*** Select option 2, "Withdraw cash", from the application menu. You are then presented (Fig. 1.7) with a list of dollar amounts (e.g., 20, 40, 60, 100 and 200). You are also given the option to cancel the transaction and return to the main menu. Withdraw $100 by selecting option 4. The application displays "Please take your cash now." and returns to the main menu. [*Note:* Unfortunately, this application only *simulates* the behavior of a real ATM and thus does not actually dispense money.]

8. ***Confirming that the account information has been updated.*** From the main menu, select option 1 again to view your current account balance. Note that both the available balance and the total balance have been updated to reflect your withdrawal transaction (Fig. 1.8).

9. ***Ending the transaction.*** To end your current ATM session, select option 4, "Exit" from the main menu. The ATM will exit the system and display a goodbye message to the user. The application will then return to its original prompt asking for the next user's account number (Fig. 1.9).

ATM withdrawal menu

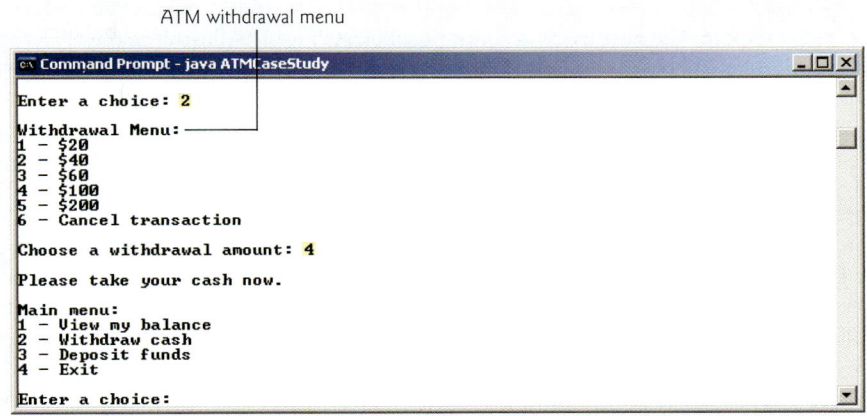

Fig. 1.7 | Withdrawing money from the account and returning to the main menu.

Confirming updated account balance
information after withdrawal transaction

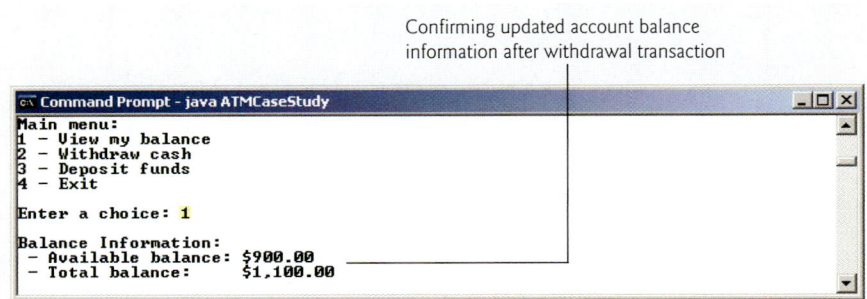

Fig. 1.8 | Checking new balance.

ATM goodbye message.   Account number prompt for next user

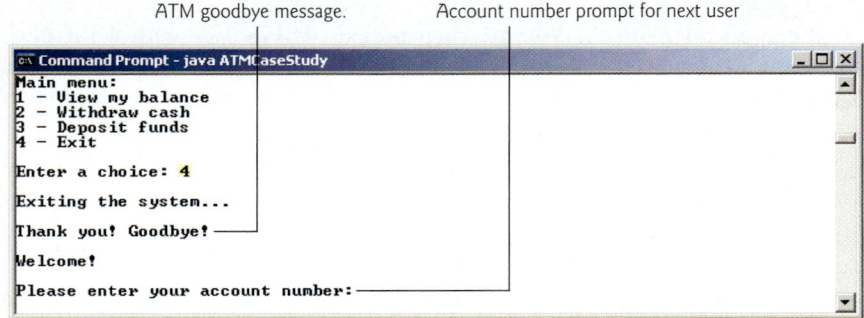

Fig. 1.9 | Ending an ATM transaction session.

10. *Exiting the ATM application and closing the* **Command Prompt** *window*. Most applications provide an option to exit and return to the **Command Prompt** directory from which the application was run. A real ATM does not provide a user with the option to turn off the ATM machine. Rather, when a user has completed all desired transactions and chooses the menu option to exit, the ATM resets itself and displays a prompt for the next user's account number. As Fig. 1.9 illustrates, the ATM application here behaves similarly. Choosing the menu option to exit ends only the current user's ATM session, not the entire ATM application. To actually exit the ATM application, click the close (**x**) button in the upper-right corner of the **Command Prompt** window. Closing the window causes the running application to terminate.

Additional Applications Found in **Java How to Program, 6/e**

We encourage you to practice running some of the Java applications featured in this textbook. Figure 1.10 lists a few of the hundreds of applications found in the examples and exercises in this text. Many of these programs simulate real-world applications and introduce the powerful and fun features of Java programming. Please feel free to run any or all of the programs listed to see some of the different types of applications you will learn how to build as you study the programming concepts in this textbook. The examples folder for Chapter 1 contains all the files required to run each application. You can do so by typing the commands listed in Fig. 1.10 in a **Command Prompt** window.

Application Name	Chapter Location	Commands to Run
Tic-Tac-Toe	Chapters 8 and 24	`cd C:\examples\ch01\Tic-Tac-Toe` `java TicTacToeTest`
Guessing Game	Chapter 11	`cd C:\examples\ch01\GuessGame` `java GuessGame`
Logo Animator	Chapter 21	`cd C:\examples\ch01\LogoAnimator` `java LogoAnimator`
Bouncing Ball	Chapter 23	`cd C:\examples\ch01\BouncingBall` `java BouncingBall`

Fig. 1.10 | Examples of additional Java applications found in *Java How to Program, 6/e*.

1.16 Software Engineering Case Study: Introduction to Object Technology and the UML (Required)

Now we begin our early introduction to object orientation, a natural way of thinking about the world and writing computer programs. Chapters 1–8 and 10 all end with a brief "Software Engineering Case Study" section in which we present a carefully paced introduction to object orientation. Our goal here is to help you develop an object-oriented way of thinking and to introduce you to the Unified Modeling Language™ (UML™)—a graphical language that allows people who design software systems to use an industry standard notation to represent them.

In this required section, we introduce object-oriented concepts and terminology. The optional sections in Chapters 2–8 and 10 present an object-oriented design and implementation of the software for a simple automated teller machine (ATM). The "Software Engineering Case Study" sections at the ends of Chapters 2–7

- analyze a typical requirements document that describes a software system (the ATM) to be built

- determine the objects required to implement that system

- determine the attributes the objects will have

- determine the behaviors these objects will exhibit

- specify how the objects interact with one another to meet the system requirements

The "Software Engineering Case Study" sections at the ends of Chapters 8 and 10 modify and enhance the design presented in Chapters 2–7. Appendix J contains a complete, working Java implementation of the object-oriented ATM system.

You will experience a solid introduction to object-oriented design with the UML. Also, you will sharpen your code-reading skills by touring the complete, carefully written and well-documented Java implementation of the ATM.

Basic Object Technology Concepts

We begin our introduction to object orientation with some key terminology. Everywhere you look in the real world you see objects—people, animals, plants, cars, planes, buildings, computers and so on. Humans think in terms of objects. Telephones, houses, traffic lights, microwave ovens and water coolers are just a few more objects we see around us every day. Computer programs, such as the Java programs you will read in this book and the ones you will write, can also be viewed as objects, composed of lots of interacting software objects.

We sometimes divide objects into two categories: animate and inanimate. Animate objects are "alive" in some sense—they move around and do things. Inanimate objects, on the other hand, do not move on their own. Objects of both types, however, have some things in common. They all have attributes (e.g., size, shape, color and weight), and they all exhibit behaviors (e.g., a ball rolls, bounces, inflates and deflates; a baby cries, sleeps, crawls, walks and blinks; a car accelerates, brakes and turns; a towel absorbs water). We will study the kinds of attributes and behaviors that software objects have.

Humans learn about existing objects by studying their attributes and observing their behaviors. Different objects can have similar attributes and can exhibit similar behaviors. Comparisons can be made, for example, between babies and adults and between humans and chimpanzees.

Object-oriented design (OOD) models software in terms similar to those that people use to describe real-world objects. It takes advantage of **class** relationships, where objects of a certain class, such as a class of vehicles, have the same characteristics—cars, trucks, little red wagons and roller skates have much in common. OOD also takes advantage of **inheritance** relationships, where new classes of objects are derived by absorbing characteristics of existing classes and adding unique characteristics of their own. An object of class "convertible" certainly has the characteristics of the more general class "automobile," but more specifically, the roof goes up and down.

Object-oriented design provides a natural and intuitive way to view the software design process—namely, modeling objects by their attributes and behaviors just as we describe real-world objects. OOD also models communication between objects. Just as people send messages to one another (e.g., a sergeant commands a soldier to stand at attention), objects also communicate via messages. A bank account object may receive a message to decrease its balance by a certain amount because the customer has withdrawn that amount of money.

OOD **encapsulates** (i.e., wraps) attributes and **operations** (behaviors) into objects—an object's attributes and operations are intimately tied together. Objects have the property of **information hiding**. This means that objects may know how to communicate with one another across well-defined **interfaces**, but normally they are not allowed to know how other objects are implemented—implementation details are hidden within the objects themselves. We can drive a car effectively, for instance, without knowing the details of how engines, transmissions, brakes and exhaust systems work internally—as long as we know how to use the accelerator pedal, the brake pedal, the wheel and so on. Information hiding, as we will see, is crucial to good software engineering.

Languages like Java are **object oriented**. Programming in such a language is called **object-oriented programming (OOP),** and it allows computer programmers to implement an object-oriented design as a working system. Languages like C, on the other hand, are **procedural,** so programming tends to be **action oriented**. In C, the unit of programming is the **function**. Groups of actions that perform some common task are formed into functions, and functions are grouped to form programs. In Java, the unit of programming is the class from which objects are eventually **instantiated** (created). Java classes contain **methods** (which implement operations and are similar to functions in C) as well as **fields** (which implement attributes).

Java programmers concentrate on creating classes. Each class contains fields and the set of methods that manipulate the fields and provide services to **clients** (i.e., other classes that use the class). The programmer uses existing classes as the building blocks for constructing new classes.

Classes are to objects as blueprints are to houses. Just as we can build many houses from one blueprint, we can instantiate (create) many objects from one class. You cannot cook meals in the kitchen of a blueprint; you can cook meals in the kitchen of a house.

Classes can have relationships with other classes. For example, in an object-oriented design of a bank, the "bank teller" class needs to relate to the "customer" class, the "cash drawer" class, the "safe" class, and so on. These relationships are called **associations**.

Packaging software as classes makes it possible for future software systems to **reuse** the classes. Groups of related classes are often packaged as reusable **components**. Just as realtors often say that the three most important factors affecting the price of real estate are "location, location and location," people in the software community often say that the three most important factors affecting the future of software development are "reuse, reuse and reuse." Reuse of existing classes when building new classes and programs saves time and effort. Reuse also helps programmers build more reliable and effective systems, because existing classes and components often have gone through extensive testing, debugging and performance tuning.

Indeed, with object technology, you can build much of the software you will need by combining classes, just as automobile manufacturers combine interchangeable parts. Each new class you create will have the potential to become a valuable software asset that you and other programmers can use to speed and enhance the quality of future software development efforts.

Introduction to Object-Oriented Analysis and Design (OOAD)

Soon you will be writing programs in Java. How will you create the code for your programs? Perhaps, like many beginning programmers, you will simply turn on your computer and start typing. This approach may work for small programs (like the ones we present in the early chapters of the book), but what if you were asked to create a software system to control thousands of automated teller machines for a major bank? Or suppose you were asked to work on a team of 1,000 software developers building the next U.S. air traffic control system. For projects so large and complex, you could not sit down and simply start writing programs.

To create the best solutions, you should follow a detailed process for analyzing your project's requirements (i.e., determining *what* the system is supposed to do) and developing a design that satisfies them (i.e., deciding *how* the system should do it). Ideally, you would go through this process and carefully review the design (or have your design reviewed by other software professionals) before writing any code. If this process involves analyzing and designing your system from an object-oriented point of view, it is called an object-oriented analysis and design (OOAD) process. Experienced programmers know that analysis and design can save many hours by helping them to avoid an ill-planned system-development approach that has to be abandoned part of the way through its implementation, possibly wasting considerable time, money and effort.

OOAD is the generic term for the process of analyzing a problem and developing an approach for solving it. Small problems like the ones discussed in these first few chapters do not require an exhaustive OOAD process. It may be sufficient to write pseudocode before we begin writing Java code—pseudocode is an informal means of expressing program logic. It is not actually a programming language, but we can use it as a kind of outline to guide us as we write our code. We introduce pseudocode in Chapter 4.

As problems and the groups of people solving them increase in size, the methods of OOAD become more appropriate than pseudocode. Ideally, a group should agree on a strictly defined process for solving its problem and a uniform way of communicating the results of that process to one another. Although many different OOAD processes exist, a single graphical language for communicating the results of *any* OOAD process has come into wide use. This language, known as the Unified Modeling Language (UML), was developed in the mid-1990s under the initial direction of three software methodologists: Grady Booch, James Rumbaugh and Ivar Jacobson.

History of the UML

In the 1980s, increasing numbers of organizations began using OOP to build their applications, and a need developed for a standard OOAD process. Many methodologists—including Booch, Rumbaugh and Jacobson—individually produced and promoted separate processes to satisfy this need. Each process had its own notation, or "language" (in the form of graphical diagrams), to convey the results of analysis and design.

By the early 1990s, different organizations, and even divisions within the same organization, were using their own unique processes and notations. At the same time, these organizations also wanted to use software tools that would support their particular processes. Software vendors found it difficult to provide tools for so many processes. Clearly, a standard notation and standard processes were needed.

In 1994, James Rumbaugh joined Grady Booch at Rational Software Corporation (now a division of IBM), and the two began working to unify their popular processes. They soon were joined by Ivar Jacobson. In 1996, the group released early versions of the UML to the software engineering community and requested feedback. Around the same time, an organization known as the Object Management Group™ (OMG™) invited submissions for a common modeling language. The OMG (www.omg.org) is a nonprofit organization that promotes the standardization of object-oriented technologies by issuing guidelines and specifications, such as the UML. Several corporations—among them HP, IBM, Microsoft, Oracle and Rational Software—had already recognized the need for a common modeling language. In response to the OMG's request for proposals, these companies formed UML Partners—the consortium that developed the UML version 1.1 and submitted it to the OMG. The OMG accepted the proposal and, in 1997, assumed responsibility for the continuing maintenance and revision of the UML. In March 2003, the OMG released UML version 1.5. The UML version 2 now under development marks the first major revision of the UML since the 1997 version 1.1 standard. Owing to the forthcoming adoption of UML 2 by the OMG and the fact that many books, modeling tools and industry experts are already using UML 2, we present UML 2 terminology and notation throughout this book.

What Is the UML?

The Unified Modeling Language is now the most widely used graphical representation scheme for modeling object-oriented systems. It has indeed unified the various popular notational schemes. Those who design systems use the language (in the form of diagrams) to model their systems.

An attractive feature of the UML is its flexibility. The UML is extensible (i.e., capable of being enhanced with new features) and is independent of any particular OOAD process. UML modelers are free to use various processes in designing systems, but all developers can now express their designs with one standard set of graphical notations.

The UML is a complex, feature-rich graphical language. In our "Software Engineering Case Study" sections, we present a simple, concise subset of these features. We then use this subset to guide you through a first design experience with the UML intended for novice object-oriented programmers in a first- or second-semester programming course.

Internet and Web UML Resources

For more information about the UML, refer to the following Web sites.

www.uml.org

This UML resource page from the Object Management Group (OMG) provides specification documents for the UML and other object-oriented technologies.

www.ibm.com/software/rational/uml
This is the UML resource page for IBM Rational—the successor to the Rational Software Corporation (the company that created the UML).

Recommended Readings

Many books on the UML have been published. The following recommended books provide information about object-oriented design with the UML.

Arlow, J., and I. Neustadt. *UML and the Unified Process: Practical Object-Oriented Analysis and Design*. London: Pearson Education Ltd., 2002.

Fowler, M. *UML Distilled, Third Edition: A Brief Guide to the Standard Object Modeling Language*. Boston: Addison-Wesley, 2004.

Reed, P. *Developing Applications with Java and UML*. Boston: Addison-Wesley, 2002.

Rumbaugh, J., I. Jacobson and G. Booch. *The Unified Modeling Language User Guide*. Reading, MA: Addison-Wesley, 1999.

For additional books on the UML, please refer to the recommended readings listed at the end of Section 2.9, or visit www.amazon.com or www.bn.com. IBM Rational, formerly Rational Software Corporation, also provides a recommended-reading list for UML books at www.ibm.com/software/rational/info/technical/books.jsp.

Section 1.16 Self-Review Exercises

1.1   List three examples of real-world objects that we did not mention. For each object, list several attributes and behaviors.

1.2   Pseudocode is _____.
a) another term for OOAD
b) a programming language used to display UML diagrams
c) an informal means of expressing program logic
d) a graphical representation scheme for modeling object-oriented systems

1.3   The UML is used primarily to _____.
a) test object-oriented systems
b) design object-oriented systems
c) implement object-oriented systems
d) Both a and b

Answers to Section 1.16 Self-Review Exercises

1.1   [*Note:* Answers may vary.] a) A television's attributes include the size of the screen, the number of colors it can display, its current channel and its current volume. A television turns on and off, changes channels, displays video and plays sounds. b) A coffee maker's attributes include the maximum volume of water it can hold, the time required to brew a pot of coffee and the temperature of the heating plate under the coffee pot. A coffee maker turns on and off, brews coffee and heats coffee. c) A turtle's attributes include its age, the size of its shell and its weight. A turtle walks, retreats into its shell, emerges from its shell and eats vegetation.

1.2   c.

1.3   b.

1.17 Wrap-Up

This chapter introduced basic hardware and software concepts, and basic object technology concepts, including classes, objects, attributes, behaviors, encapsulation, inheritance and polymorphism. We discussed the different types of programming languages and which programming languages are most widely used. You learned the steps for creating and executing a Java application using Sun's JDK 5.0. The chapter explored the history of the Internet and the World Wide Web and Java's role in developing distributed client/server applications for the Internet and the Web. You also learned about the history and purpose of the UML—the industry-standard graphical language for modeling software systems. Finally, you "test drove" a sample Java application similar to the types of applications you will learn to program in this book.

In the next chapter, you will create your first Java applications. You will see several examples that demonstrate how programs display messages and obtain information from the user for processing. We closely analyze and explain each example to help ease your way into Java programming.

1.18 Web Resources

This section provides many Web resources that will be useful to you as you learn Java. The sites include Java resources, Java development tools for students and professionals, and our own Web sites where you can find downloads and resources associated with this book. We also provide a link where you can subscribe to our free *Deitel Buzz Online* e-mail newsletter.

Deitel & Associates Web Sites

`www.deitel.com/books/jHTP6/index.html`
The Deitel & Associates home page for *Java How to Program, Sixth Edition*. Here you will find links to the book's examples (also included on the CD that accompanies the book) and other resources, such as our free *Dive Into*™ guides that help you get started with several Java integrated development environments (IDEs).

`www.deitel.com`
Please check the Deitel & Associates home page for updates, corrections and additional resources for all Deitel publications.

`www.deitel.com/newsletter/subscribe.html`

Please visit this site to subscribe to the free *Deitel Buzz Online* e-mail newsletter to follow the Deitel & Associates publishing program.

`www.prenhall.com/deitel`
Prentice Hall's home page for Deitel publications. Here you will find detailed product information, sample chapters and *Companion Web Sites* containing book- and chapter-specific resources for students and instructors.

Sun Microsystems Web Sites

`java.sun.com`
Sun's home page for Java technology. Here you will find downloads, reference guides for developers, community forums, online tutorials and many other valuable Java resources.

`java.sun.com/j2se`
The home page for the Java 2 Platform, Standard Edition.

`java.sun.com/j2se/5.0/download.jsp`
The download page for the Java 2 Platform, Standard Edition version 5.0 and its documentation. This development kit includes everything you need to compile and execute your Java applications. Please note that as Sun updates Java, the number 5.0 in the preceding URL will change. You can always go to `java.sun.com/j2se` to locate the most recent version of Java.

`java.sun.com/j2se/5.0/install.html`
Instructions for installing the JDK version 5.0 on Solaris, Windows and Linux platforms. Please check this site if you are having difficulty installing Java on your computer. Also please note that as Java is updated, 5.0 in the preceding URL will change. You can always go to `java.sun.com/j2se` to locate the most recent version of Java.

`java.sun.com/learning/new2java/index.html`
The "New to Java Center" on the Sun Microsystems Web site features online training resources to help you get started with Java programming.

`java.sun.com/j2se/5.0/docs/api/index.html`
This site provides the Java 2 Platform, Standard Edition version 5.0 API documentation. Refer to this site to learn about the Java class library's predefined classes and interfaces.

`java.sun.com/reference/docs/index.html`
Sun's documentation site for all Java technologies. Here you will find technical information on all Java technologies, including API (application programming interface) specifications for Java and related Sun technologies.

`java.sun.com/products/hotspot`
Visit the product information page for Sun's HotSpot virtual machine and compiler, a standard component of the Java 2 Runtime Environment and the JDK, for the latest information on high-speed Java program translation.

`developers.sun.com`
Sun's home page for Java developers provides downloads, APIs, code samples, articles with technical advice and other resources on the best Java development practices.

Editors and Integrated Development Environments

`www.download.com`
A site that contains freeware and shareware application downloads. In particular, several editors are available at this site that can be used to edit Java source code.

`www.eclipse.org`
The home page for the Eclipse development environment, which can be used to develop code in any programming language. You can download the environment and several Java plug-ins to use this environment to develop your Java programs.

`www.netbeans.org`
The home page for the NetBeans IDE, one of the most widely used, freely distributed Java development tools.

`borland.com/products/downloads/download_jbuilder.html`
Borland provides a free Foundation Edition version of its popular Java IDE JBuilder. The site also provides 30-day trial versions of the Enterprise and Developer editions.

`www.blueJ.org`
The home page for the BlueJ environment—a tool designed to help teach object-oriented Java to new programmers. BlueJ is available as a free download.

`www.jgrasp.org`
The home page for jGRASP provides downloads, documentation and tutorials for this tool that displays visual representations of Java programs to aid comprehension.

`www.jedit.org`
The home page for jEdit—a text editor for programmers that is written in Java.

`wwws.sun.com/software/sundev/jde/`
The home page for Sun Java Studio—the Sun Microsystems enhanced version of NetBeans.

`www.jcreator.com`
The home page for JCreator—a popular Java IDE. JCreator Lite Edition is available as a free download. A 30-day trial version of JCreator Pro Edition is also available.

Additional Java Resource Sites

`www.javalobby.org`
Provides up-to-date Java news, forums where developers can exchange tips and advice, and a comprehensive Java knowledge base organizing articles and downloads from across the Web.

`www.jguru.com`
Provides forums, downloads, articles, online courses and a large collection of Java FAQs (Frequently Asked Questions).

`www.javaworld.com`
Provides resources for Java developers, such as articles, indices of popular Java books, tips and FAQs.

`www.ftponline.com/javapro`
The home page for the JavaPro magazine features monthly articles, programming tips, book reviews and more.

`sys-con.com/java/`
The home page for the Java Developer's Journal from Sys-Con Media, provides articles, e-books and other Java resources.

Summary

- The various devices that comprise a computer system (e.g., the keyboard, screen, disks, memory and processing units) are referred to as hardware.
- The computer programs that run on a computer are referred to as software.
- Java is one of today's most popular software development languages. Java is a fully object-oriented language with strong support for proper software-engineering techniques.
- A computer is a device capable of performing computations and making logical decisions at speeds millions, even billions, of times faster than humans can.
- Computers process data under the control of sets of instructions called computer programs. Computer programs guide the computer through actions specified by computer programmers.
- The input unit is the "receiving" section of the computer. It obtains information from input devices and places it at the disposal of other units for processing.
- The output unit is the "shipping" section of the computer. It takes information processed by the computer and places it on output devices to make it available for use outside the computer.
- The memory unit is the rapid-access, relatively low-capacity "warehouse" section of the computer. It retains information that has been entered through the input unit, making it immediately available for processing when needed, and retains information that has already been processed until that information can be placed on output devices by the output unit.
- The arithmetic and logic unit (ALU) is the "manufacturing" section of the computer. It is responsible for performing calculations and making decisions.
- The central processing unit (CPU) is the "administrative" section of the computer. It coordinates and supervises the operation of the other sections.

- The secondary storage unit is the long-term, high-capacity "warehousing" section of the computer. Programs or data not being used by the other units are normally placed on secondary storage devices (e.g., disks) until they are needed, possibly hours, days, months or even years later.

- Software systems called operating systems were developed to help make it more convenient to use computers.

- Multiprogramming involves the sharing of a computer's resources among the jobs competing for its attention, so that the jobs appear to run simultaneously.

- With distributed computing, an organization's computing is distributed over networks to the sites where the work of the organization is performed.

- Java has become the language of choice for developing Internet-based applications.

- Any computer can directly understand only its own machine language. Machine languages generally consist of strings of numbers (ultimately reduced to 1s and 0s) that instruct computers to perform their most elementary operations one at a time.

- English-like abbreviations form the basis of assembly languages. Translator programs called assemblers convert assembly-language programs to machine language.

- Compilers translate high-level language programs into machine-language programs. High-level languages (like Java) contain English words and conventional mathematical notations.

- Interpreter programs directly execute high-level language programs, eliminating the need to compile them into machine language.

- Java is used to create Web pages with dynamic and interactive content, develop large-scale enterprise applications, enhance the functionality of Web servers, provide applications for consumer devices and more.

- Java programs consist of pieces called classes. Classes include pieces called methods that perform tasks and return information when they complete their tasks.

- C++ is an extension of C developed by Bjarne Stroustrup in the early 1980s at Bell Laboratories. C++ provides a number of features that "spruce up" the C language, but more important, it provides capabilities for object-oriented programming.

- FORTRAN (FORmula TRANslator) was developed by IBM Corporation in the mid-1950s for scientific and engineering applications that require complex mathematical computations.

- COBOL (COmmon Business Oriented Language) was developed in the late 1950s by a group of computer manufacturers and government and industrial computer users. COBOL is used primarily for commercial applications that require precise and efficient data manipulation.

- Ada was developed under the sponsorship of the United States Department of Defense (DOD) during the 1970s and early 1980s. One important capability of Ada is multitasking—this allows programmers to specify that many activities are to occur in parallel. The Ada language was named after Lady Ada Lovelace, daughter of the poet Lord Byron. Lady Lovelace is credited with writing the world's first computer program in the early 1800s.

- The BASIC (Beginner's All-Purpose Symbolic Instruction Code) programming language was developed in the mid-1960s at Dartmouth College as a language for writing simple programs. BASIC's primary purpose was to familiarize novices with programming techniques.

- Microsoft's Visual Basic was introduced in the early 1990s to simplify the process of developing Microsoft Windows applications.

- Microsoft has a corporate-wide strategy for integrating the Internet and the Web into computer applications. This strategy is implemented in Microsoft's .NET platform, which provides developers with the capabilities they need to create and run computer applications that can execute on computers distributed across the Internet.

- The .NET platform's three primary programming languages are Visual Basic .NET (based on the original BASIC), Visual C++ .NET (based on C++) and C# (a new language based on C++ and Java that was developed expressly for the .NET platform).

- Developers using .NET can write software components in the language they are most familiar with and then form applications by combining those components with components written in any .NET language.

- Java, through a technique called multithreading, enables programmers to write programs with parallel activities.

- Java programs normally go through five phases—*edit, compile, load, verify* and *execute*.

- Java source code file names end with the .java extension.

- The Java compiler (javac) translates a Java program into bytecodes—instructions understood by the Java Virtual Machine (JVM), which executes Java programs. If a program compiles correctly, the compiler produces a file with the .class extension. This is the file containing the bytecodes that are executed by the JVM.

- A Java program must be placed in memory before it can execute. This is done by the class loader, which takes the .class file (or files) containing the bytecodes and transfers it to memory. The .class file can be loaded from a disk on your system or over a network.

- Object orientation is a natural way of thinking about the world and of writing computer programs.

- The Unified Modeling Language (UML) is a graphical language that allows people who build systems to represent their object-oriented designs in a common notation.

- Object-oriented design (OOD) models software components in terms of real-world objects. It takes advantage of class relationships, where objects of a certain class have the same characteristics. It also takes advantage of inheritance relationships, where newly created classes of objects are derived by absorbing characteristics of existing classes and adding unique characteristics of their own. OOD encapsulates data (attributes) and functions (behavior) into objects—the data and functions of an object are intimately tied together.

- Objects have the property of information hiding—objects normally are not allowed to know how other objects are implemented.

- Object-oriented programming (OOP) allows programmers to implement object-oriented designs as working systems.

- In Java, the unit of programming is the class from which objects are eventually instantiated. Java programmers concentrate on creating their own classes and reusing existing classes. Each class contains data and functions that manipulate that data. Function components are called methods.

- An instance of a class is called an object.

- Classes can have relationships with other classes. These relationships are called associations.

- With object technology, programmers can build much of the software they will need by combining standardized, interchangeable parts called classes.

- The process of analyzing and designing a system from an object-oriented point of view is called object-oriented analysis and design (OOAD).

Terminology

Ada	assembly language
ALU (arithmetic and logic unit)	attribute
ANSI C	BASIC
arithmetic and logic unit (ALU)	behavior
assembler	bytecode

bytecode verifier
C
C#
C++
central processing unit (CPU)
class
.class file
class libraries
class loader
client/server computing
COBOL
compile phase
compiler
compile-time error
computer
computer program
computer programmer
CPU (central processing unit)
disk
distributed computing
dynamic content
edit phase
editor
encapsulation
execute phase
execution-time error
fatal runtime error
file server
FORTRAN
hardware
high-level language
HotSpot™ compiler
HTML (Hypertext Markup Language)
IDE (Integrated Development Environment)
information hiding
inheritance
input device
input unit
input/output (I/O)
Internet
interpreter
Java
Java API (Java Application Programming Interface)
.java file-name extension
Java 2 Platform Standard Edition (J2SE)
Java 2 Platform Enterprise Edition (J2EE)
Java 2 Platform Micro Edition (J2ME)
J2SE Development Kit (JDK)
java interpreter

Java Virtual Machine (JVM)
javac compiler
JIT (just-in-time) compiler
KIS (keep it simple)
LAN (local area network)
legacy systems
live-code approach
load phase
machine language
memory unit
method
Microsoft Internet Explorer Web browser
modeling
multiprocessor
multiprogramming
multithreading
.NET
nonfatal runtime error
object
object-oriented design (OOD)
object-oriented programming (OOP)
operating system
output device
output unit
Pascal
personal computing
platform
portability
primary memory
problem statement
procedural programming
programmer-defined type
pseudocode
requirements document
reusable componentry
runtime error
secondary storage unit
software
software reuse
structured programming
Sun Microsystems
throughput
timesharing
translation
translator program
Unified Modeling Language (UML)
verify phase
Visual Basic .NET
Visual C++ .NET
World Wide Web

Self-Review Exercises

1.1   Fill in the blanks in each of the following statements:
a) The company that popularized personal computing was _____.
b) The computer that made personal computing legitimate in business and industry was the _____.
c) Computers process data under the control of sets of instructions called _____.
d) The six key logical units of the computer are the _____, _____, _____, _____, _____ and _____.
e) The three classes of languages discussed in the chapter are _____, _____ and _____.
f) The programs that translate high-level language programs into machine language are called _____.
g) The _____ allows computer users to locate and view multimedia-based documents on almost any subject over the Internet.
h) _____ allows a Java program to perform multiple activities in parallel.

1.2   Fill in the blanks in each of the following sentences about the Java environment:
a) The _____ command from the J2SE Development Kit executes a Java application.
b) The _____ command from the J2SE Development Kit compiles a Java program.
c) A Java program file must end with the _____ file extension.
d) When a Java program is compiled, the file produced by the compiler ends with the _____ file extension.
e) The file produced by the Java compiler contains _____ that are executed by the Java Virtual Machine.

1.3   Fill in the blanks in each of the following statements (based on Section 1.16):
a) Objects have the property of _____—although objects may know how to communicate with one another across well-defined interfaces, they normally are not allowed to know how other objects are implemented.
b) Java programmers concentrate on creating _____, which contain fields and the set of methods that manipulate those fields and provide services to clients.
c) Classes can have relationships with other classes. These relationships are called _____.
d) The process of analyzing and designing a system from an object-oriented point of view is called _____.
e) OOD also takes advantage of _____ relationships, where new classes of objects are derived by absorbing characteristics of existing classes then adding unique characteristics of their own.
f) _____ is a graphical language that allows people who design software systems to use an industry standard notation to represent them.
g) The size, shape, color and weight of an object are considered _____ of the object.

Answers to Self-Review Exercises

1.1   a) Apple. b) IBM Personal Computer. c) programs. d) input unit, output unit, memory unit, arithmetic and logic unit, central processing unit, secondary storage unit. e) machine languages, assembly languages, high-level languages. f) compilers. g) World Wide Web. h) Multithreading.

1.2   a) `java`. b) `javac`. c) `.java`. d) `.class`. e) bytecodes.

1.3   a) information hiding. b) classes. c) associations. d) object-oriented analysis and design (OOAD). e) inheritance. f) The Unified Modeling Language (UML). g) attributes.

Exercises

1.4 Categorize each of the following items as either hardware or software:
a) CPU
b) Java compiler
c) JVM
d) input unit
e) editor

1.5 Fill in the blanks in each of the following statements:
a) The logical unit of the computer that receives information from outside the computer for use by the computer is the _____.
b) The process of instructing the computer to solve a problems is called _____.
c) _____ is a type of computer language that uses English-like abbreviations for machine-language instructions.
d) _____ is a logical unit of the computer that sends information which has already been processed by the computer to various devices so that it may be used outside the computer.
e) _____ and _____ are logical units of the computer that retain information.
f) _____ is a logical unit of the computer that performs calculations.
g) _____ is a logical unit of the computer that makes logical decisions.
h) _____ languages are most convenient to the programmer for writing programs quickly and easily.
i) The only language that a computer can directly understand is that computer's _____.
j) _____ is a logical unit of the computer that coordinates the activities of all the other logical units.

1.6 What is the difference between fatal errors and nonfatal errors? Why might you prefer to experience a fatal error rather than a nonfatal error?

1.7 Fill in the blanks in each of the following statements:
a) _____ is now used to develop large-scale enterprise applications, to enhance the functionality of Web servers, to provide applications for consumer devices and for many other purposes.
b) _____ was designed specifically for the .NET platform to enable programmers to migrate easily to .NET.
c) _____ initially became widely known as the development language of the UNIX operating system.
d) _____ was developed at Dartmouth College in the mid-1960s as a means of writing simple programs.
e) _____ was developed by IBM Corporation in the mid-1950s to be used for scientific and engineering applications that require complex mathematical computations.
f) _____ is used for commercial applications that require precise and efficient manipulation of large amounts of data.
g) _____ was developed by Bjarne Stroustrup in the early 1980s at Bell Laboratories (now part of Lucent).

1.8 Fill in the blanks in each of the following statements (based on Section 1.13):
a) Java programs normally go through five phases—_____, _____, _____, _____ and _____.
b) A(n) _____ provides many tools that support the software development process, such as editors for writing and editing programs, debuggers for locating logic errors in programs and many other features.

    c) The command java invokes the _____, which executes Java programs.

    d) A(n) _____ is a software application that simulates a computer, but hides the underlying operating system and hardware from the programs that interact with the VM.

    e) A(n) _____ program can run on multiple platforms.

    f) The _____ takes the .class files containing the program's bytecodes and transfers them to primary memory.

    g) The _____ examines bytecodes to ensure that they are valid.

1.9   Explain the two compilation phases of Java programs.

Introduction to Java Applications

What's in a name?
that which we call a rose
By any other name
would smell as sweet.
—William Shakespeare

When faced with a decision,
I always ask, "What would
be the most fun?"
—Peggy Walker

"Take some more tea," the
March Hare said to Alice,
very earnestly. "I've had
nothing yet, "Alice replied in
an offended tone: "so I can't
take more." "You mean you
can't take less," said the
Hatter: "it's very easy to take
more than nothing."
—Lewis Carroll

OBJECTIVES

In this chapter you will learn:

- To write simple Java applications.
- To use input and output statements.
- Java's primitive types.
- Basic memory concepts.
- To use arithmetic operators.
- The precedence of arithmetic operators.
- To write decision-making statements.
- To use relational and equality operators.

2.1 Introduction

We now introduce Java application programming which facilitates a disciplined approach to program design. Most of the Java programs you will study in this book process information and display results. We present six examples that demonstrate how your programs can display messages and how they can obtain information from the user for processing. We begin with several examples that simply display messages on the screen. We then demonstrate a program that obtains two numbers from a user, calculates their sum and displays the result. You will learn how to perform various arithmetic calculations and save their results for later use. Many programs contain logic that requires the program to make decisions. The last example in this chapter demonstrates decision-making fundamentals by showing you how to compare numbers then display messages based on the comparison results. For example, the program displays a message indicating that two numbers are equal only if they have the same value. We analyze each example one line at a time to help you ease your way into Java programming. To help you apply the skills you learn here, we provide many fun and challenging problems in the chapter's exercises.

2.2 First Program in Java: Printing a Line of Text

Every time you use a computer, you execute various applications that perform tasks for you. For example, your e-mail application helps you send and receive e-mail, and your Web browser lets you view Web pages from Web sites around the world. Computer programmers create such applications by writing **computer programs**.

A Java **application** is a computer program that executes when you use the java command to launch the Java Virtual Machine (JVM). Let us consider a simple application that displays a line of text. (Later in this section we will discuss how to compile and run an application.) The program and its output are shown in Fig. 2.1. The output appears in the light blue box at the end of the program. The program illustrates several important Java language features. Java uses notations that may look strange to nonprogrammers. In addition, for your convenience, each program we present in this book includes line numbers, which are not part of actual Java programs. We will soon see that line 9 does the real work of the program—namely, displaying the phrase `Welcome to Java Programming!` on the screen. We now consider each line of the program in order.

```
1   // Fig. 2.1: Welcome1.java
2   // Text-printing program.
3
4   public class Welcome1
5   {
6      // main method begins execution of Java application
7      public static void main( String args[] )
8      {
9         System.out.println( "Welcome to Java Programming!" );
10
11     } // end method main
12
13  } // end class Welcome1
```

```
Welcome to Java Programming!
```

Fig. 2.1 | Text-printing program.

Line 1

```
// Fig. 2.1: Welcome1.java
```

begins with //, indicating that the remainder of the line is a **comment**. Programmers insert comments to **document programs** and improve their readability. This helps other people to read and understand programs. The Java compiler ignores comments, so they do not cause the computer to perform any action when the program is run. We begin every program with a comment indicating the figure number and file name.

A comment that begins with // is called an **end-of-line** (or **single-line**) **comment**, because the comment terminates at the end of the line on which it appears. A // comment also can begin in the middle of a line and continue until the end of that line (as in lines 11 and 13).

Traditional comments (also called **multiple-line comments**), such as

```
/* This is a traditional
   comment. It can be
   split over many lines */
```

can be spread over several lines. This type of comment begins with the delimiter /* and ends with */. All text between the delimiters is ignored by the compiler. Java incorporated traditional comments and end-of-line comments from the C and C++ programming languages, respectively. In this book, we use end-of-line comments.

Java also provides **Javadoc comments** that are delimited by /** and */. As with traditional comments, all text between the Javadoc comment delimiters is ignored by the compiler. Javadoc comments enable programmers to embed program documentation directly in their programs. Such comments are the preferred Java commenting format in industry. The **javadoc** utility program (part of the J2SE Development Kit) reads Javadoc comments and uses them to prepare your program's documentation in HTML format. We demonstrate Javadoc comments and the javadoc utility in Appendix H. For complete information, visit Sun's **javadoc Tool Home Page** at java.sun.com/j2se/javadoc.

Common Programming Error 2.1

Forgetting one of the delimiters of a traditional or Javadoc comment is a syntax error. The syntax *of a programming language specifies the rules for creating a proper program in that language. A* syntax error *occurs when the compiler encounters code that violates Java's language rules (i.e., its syntax). In this case, the compiler does not produce a* .class *file. Instead, the compiler issues an error message to help the programmer identify and fix the incorrect code. Syntax errors are also called* compiler errors, compile-time errors *or* compilation errors, *because the compiler detects them during the compilation phase. You will be unable to execute your program until you correct all the syntax errors in it.*

Line 2

```
// Text-printing program.
```

is an end-of-line comment that describes the purpose of the program.

Good Programming Practice 2.1

Every program should begin with a comment that explains the purpose of the program, the author and the date and time the program was last modified. (We are not showing the author, date and time in this book's programs because this information would be redundant.)

Line 3 is simply a blank line. Programmers use blank lines and space characters to make programs easier to read. Together, blank lines, space characters and tab characters are known as white space. (Space characters and tabs are known specifically as white-space characters.) White space is ignored by the compiler. In this chapter and the next several chapters, we discuss conventions for using white space to enhance program readability.

Good Programming Practice 2.2

Use blank lines and space characters to enhance program readability.

Line 4

```
public class Welcome1
```

begins a class declaration for class Welcome1. Every program in Java consists of at least one class declaration that is defined by you—the programmer. These are known as program-mer-defined classes or user-defined classes. The **class** keyword introduces a class declaration in Java and is immediately followed by the class name (Welcome1). Keywords (sometimes called reserved words) are reserved for use by Java (we discuss the various keywords throughout the text) and are always spelled with all lowercase letters. The complete list of Java keywords is shown in Appendix C.

By convention, all class names in Java begin with a capital letter and capitalize the first letter of each word they include (e.g., SampleClassName). A Java class name is an identifier—a series of characters consisting of letters, digits, underscores (_) and dollar signs ($) that does not begin with a digit and does not contain spaces. Some valid identifiers are Welcome1, $value, _value, m_inputField1 and button7. The name 7button is not a valid identifier because it begins with a digit, and the name input field is not a valid identifier because it contains a space. Normally, an identifier that does not begin with a capital letter is not the name of a Java class. Java is case sensitive—that is, uppercase and lowercase letters are distinct, so a1 and A1 are different (but both valid) identifiers.

Good Programming Practice 2.3

By convention, always begin a class name's identifier with a capital letter and start each subsequent word in the identifier with a capital letter. Java programmers know that such identifiers normally represent Java classes, so naming your classes in this manner makes your programs more readable.

Common Programming Error 2.2

Java is case sensitive. Not using the proper uppercase and lowercase letters for an identifier normally causes a compilation error.

In Chapters 2–7, every class we define begins with the `public` keyword. For now, we will simply require this keyword. When you save your `public` class declaration in a file, the file name must be the class name followed by the "`.java`" file-name extension. For our application, the file name is `Welcome1.java`. You will learn more about `public` and non-`public` classes in Chapter 8.

Common Programming Error 2.3

It is an error for a `public` class to have a file name that is not identical to the class name (plus the `.java` extension) in terms of both spelling and capitalization.

Common Programming Error 2.4

It is an error not to end a file name with the `.java` extension for a file containing a class declaration. If that extension is missing, the Java compiler will not be able to compile the class declaration.

A left brace (at line 5 in this program), {, begins the body of every class declaration. A corresponding right brace (at line 13), }, must end each class declaration. Note that lines 6–11 are indented. This indentation is one of the spacing conventions mentioned earlier. We define each spacing convention as a Good Programming Practice.

Good Programming Practice 2.4

Whenever you type an opening left brace, {, in your program, immediately type the closing right brace, }, then reposition the cursor between the braces and indent to begin typing the body. This practice helps prevent errors due to missing braces.

Good Programming Practice 2.5

Indent the entire body of each class declaration one "level" of indentation between the left brace, {, and the right brace, }, that delimit the body of the class. This format emphasizes the class declaration's structure and makes it easier to read.

Good Programming Practice 2.6

Set a convention for the indent size you prefer, and then uniformly apply that convention. The Tab key may be used to create indents, but tab stops vary among text editors. We recommend using three spaces to form a level of indent.

Common Programming Error 2.5

It is a syntax error if braces do not occur in matching pairs.

Line 6

```
// main method begins execution of Java application
```

is an end-of-line comment indicating the purpose of lines 7–11 of the program. Line 7

```
public static void main( String args[] )
```

is the starting point of every Java application. The **parentheses** after the identifier main indicate that it is a program building block called a **method.** Java class declarations normally contain one or more methods. For a Java application, exactly one of the methods must be called main and must be defined as shown on line 7; otherwise, the JVM will not execute the application. Methods are able to perform tasks and return information when they complete their tasks. Keyword **void** indicates that this method will perform a task but will not return any information when it completes its task. Later, we will see that many methods return information when they complete their task. You will learn more about methods in Chapters 3 and 6. For now, simply mimic main's first line in your Java applications. In Line 7, the String args[] in parentheses is a required part of the method main's declaration. We discuss this in Chapter 7, Arrays.

The left brace, {, on line 8 begins the **body of the method declaration**. A corresponding right brace, }, must end the method declaration's body (line 11 of the program). Note that line 9 in the body of the method is indented between the braces.

Good Programming Practice 2.7

Indent the entire body of each method declaration one "level" of indentation between the left brace, {, and the right brace, }, that define the body of the method. This format makes the structure of the method stand out and makes the method declaration easier to read.

Line 9

```
System.out.println( "Welcome to Java Programming!" );
```

instructs the computer to **perform an action**—namely, to print the **string** of characters contained between the double quotation marks. A string is sometimes called a **character string**, a **message** or a **string literal**. We refer to characters between double quotation marks simply as **strings**. White-space characters in strings are not ignored by the compiler.

System.out is known as the **standard output object**. System.out allows Java applications to display sets of characters in the **command window** from which the Java application executes. In Microsoft Windows 95/98/ME, the command window is the **MS-DOS prompt**. In Microsoft Windows NT/2000/XP, the command window is the **Command Prompt**. In UNIX/Linux/Mac OS X, the command window is called a **terminal window** or a **shell**. Many programmers refer to the command window simply as the **command line**.

Method **System.out.println** displays (or **prints**) **a line** of text in the command window. The string in the parentheses on line 9 is the **argument** to the method. Method System.out.println performs its task by displaying (also called outputting) its argument in the command window. When System.out.println completes its task, it positions the **output cursor** (the location where the next character will be displayed) to the beginning of the next line in the command window. (This move of the cursor is similar to when a user presses the *Enter* key while typing in a text editor—the cursor appears at the beginning of the next line in the file.)

The entire line 9, including `System.out.println`, the argument `"Welcome to Java Programming!"` in the parentheses and the **semicolon** (`;`), is called a **statement**. Each statement ends with a semicolon. When the statement on line 9 of our program executes, it displays the message `Welcome to Java Programming!` in the command window. As we will see in subsequent programs, a method is typically composed of one or more statements that perform the method's task.

Common Programming Error 2.6

Omitting the semicolon at the end of a statement is a syntax error.

Error-Prevention Tip 2.1

When learning how to program, sometimes it is helpful to "break" a working program so you can familiarize yourself with the compiler's syntax-error messages. These messages do not always state the exact problem in the code. When you encounter such syntax-error messages in the future, you will have an idea of what caused the error. Try removing a semicolon or brace from the program of Fig. 2.1, then recompile the program to see the error messages generated by the omission.

Error-Prevention Tip 2.2

When the compiler reports a syntax error, the error may not be on the line number indicated by the error message. First, check the line for which the error was reported. If that line does not contain syntax errors, check several preceding lines.

Some programmers find it difficult when reading or writing a program to match the left and right braces (`{` and `}`) that delimit the body of a class declaration or a method declaration. For this reason, some programmers include an end-of-line comment after a closing right brace (`}`) that ends a method declaration and after a closing right brace that ends a class declaration. For example, line 11

```
} // end method main
```

specifies the closing right brace (`}`) of method `main`, and line 13

```
} // end class Welcome1
```

specifies the closing right brace (`}`) of class `Welcome1`. Each comment indicates the method or class that the right brace terminates.

Good Programming Practice 2.8

Following the closing right brace (`}`) of a method body or class declaration with an end-of-line comment indicating the method or class declaration to which the brace belongs improves program readability.

Compiling and Executing Your First Java Application

We are now ready to compile and execute our program. For this purpose, we assume you are using the Sun Microsystems' J2SE Development Kit. On the **Downloads** page at our Web site (`www.deitel.com`), we provide Deitel® *Dive Into*™ *Series* publications to help you begin using several popular Java development tools.

To prepare to compile the program, open a command window and change to the directory where the program is stored. Most operating systems use the command **cd** to **change directories**. For example,

```
cd c:\examples\ch02\fig02_01
```

changes to the `fig02_01` directory on Windows. The command

```
cd ~/examples/ch02/fig02_01
```

changes to the `fig02_01` directory on UNIX/Linux/Max OS X.

To compile the program, type

```
javac Welcome1.java
```

If the program contains no syntax errors, the preceding command creates a new file called `Welcome1.class` (known as the class file for `Welcome1`) containing the Java bytecodes that represent our application. When we use the `java` command to execute the application, these bytecodes will be executed by the JVM.

Error-Prevention Tip 2.3

When attempting to compile a program, if you receive a message such as "bad command or file-name," "`javac: command not found`" or "`'javac' is not recognized as an internal or external command, operable program or batch file`," then your Java software installation was not completed properly. If you are using the J2SE Development Kit, this indicates that the system's PATH environment variable was not set properly. Please review the J2SE Development Kit installation instructions at `java.sun.com/j2se/5.0/install.html` carefully. On some systems, after correcting the PATH, you may need to reboot your computer or open a new command window for these settings to take effect.

Error-Prevention Tip 2.4

The Java compiler generates syntax-error messages when the syntax of a program is incorrect. Each error message contains the file name and line number where the error occurred. For example, `Welcome1.java:6` indicates that an error occurred in the file `Welcome1.java` at line 6. The remainder of the error message provides information about the syntax error.

Error-Prevention Tip 2.5

The compiler error message "`Public class ClassName must be defined in a file called ClassName.java`" indicates that the file name does not exactly match the name of the public class in the file or that you typed the class name incorrectly when compiling the class.

Figure 2.2 shows the program of Fig. 2.1 executing in a Microsoft® Windows® XP **Command Prompt** window. To execute the program, type `java Welcome1`. This launches the JVM, which loads the "`.class`" file for class `Welcome1`. Note that the "`.class`" file-name extension is omitted from the preceding command; otherwise, the JVM will not execute the program. The JVM calls method `main`. Next, the statement at line 9 of `main` displays `"Welcome to Java Programming!"` [*Note:* Many environments show command prompts with black backgrounds and white text. We adjusted these settings in our environment to make our screen captures more readable.]

You type this command to execute
the application

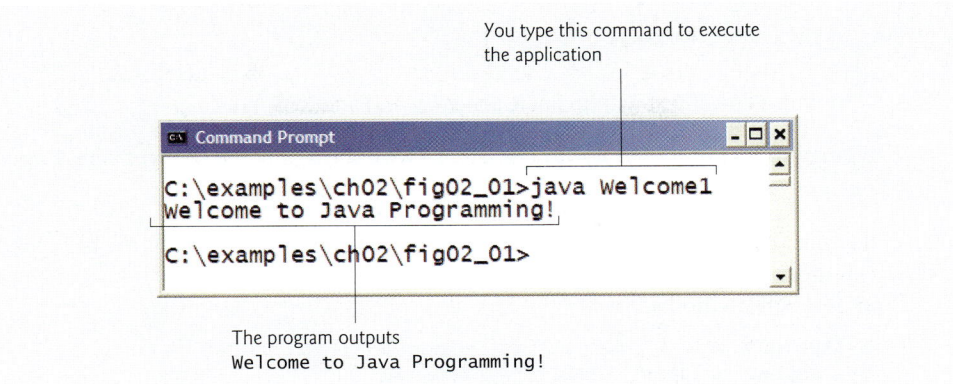

The program outputs
Welcome to Java Programming!

Fig. 2.2 | Executing Welcome1 in a Microsoft Windows XP **Command Prompt** window.

Error-Prevention Tip 2.6

*When attempting to run a Java program, if you receive a message such as "Exception in thread
"main" java.lang.NoClassDefFoundError: Welcome1," your CLASSPATH environment variable has not been set properly. Please review the J2SE Development Kit installation instructions
carefully. On some systems, you may need to reboot your computer or open a new command window after configuring the CLASSPATH.*

2.3 Modifying Our First Java Program

This section continues our introduction to Java programming with two examples that
modify the example in Fig. 2.1 to print text on one line by using multiple statements and
to print text on several lines by using a single statement.

Displaying a Single Line of Text with Multiple Statements

Welcome to Java Programming! can be displayed several ways. Class Welcome2, shown in
Fig. 2.3, uses two statements to produce the same output as that shown in Fig. 2.1. From
this point forward, we highlight the new and key features in each code listing, as shown in
lines 9–10 of this program.

```
1   // Fig. 2.3: Welcome2.java
2   // Printing a line of text with multiple statements.
3
4   public class Welcome2
5   {
6      // main method begins execution of Java application
7      public static void main( String args[] )
8      {
9         System.out.print( "Welcome to " );
10        System.out.println( "Java Programming!" );
11
12     } // end method main
13
14  } // end class Welcome2
```

Fig. 2.3 | Printing a line of text with multiple statements. (Part 1 of 2.)

```
Welcome to Java Programming!
```

Fig. 2.3 | Printing a line of text with multiple statements. (Part 2 of 2.)

The program is almost identical to Fig. 2.1, so we discuss only the changes here. Line 2

```
// Printing a line of text with multiple statements.
```

is an end-of-line comment stating the purpose of this program. Line 4 begins the Welcome2 class declaration.

Lines 9–10 of method main

```
System.out.print( "Welcome to " );
System.out.println( "Java Programming!" );
```

display one line of text in the command window. The first statement uses System.out's method print to display a string. Unlike println, after displaying its argument, print does not position the output cursor at the beginning of the next line in the command window—the next character the program displays will appear immediately after the last character that print displays. Thus, line 10 positions the first character in its argument (the letter "J") immediately after the last character that line 9 displays (the space character before the string's closing double-quote character). Each print or println statement resumes displaying characters from where the last print or println statement stopped displaying characters.

Displaying Multiple Lines of Text with a Single Statement
A single statement can display multiple lines by using newline characters, which indicate to System.out's print and println methods when they should position the output cursor at the beginning of the next line in the command window. Like blank lines, space characters and tab characters, newline characters are white-space characters. Figure 2.4 outputs four lines of text, using newline characters to determine when to begin each new line.

Most of the program is identical to those in Fig. 2.1 and Fig. 2.3, so we discuss only the changes here. Line 2

```
// Printing multiple lines of text with a single statement.
```

is a comment stating the purpose of this program. Line 4 begins the Welcome3 class declaration. Line 9

```
System.out.println( "Welcome\nto\nJava\nProgramming!" );
```

displays four separate lines of text in the command window. Normally, the characters in a string are displayed exactly as they appear in the double quotes. Note, however, that the two characters \ and n (repeated three times in the statement) do not appear on the screen. The **backslash** (\) is called an **escape character**. It indicates to System.out's print and println methods that a "special character" is to be output. When a backslash appears in a string of characters, Java combines the next character with the backslash to form an **escape sequence.** The escape sequence \n represents the newline character. When a newline character appears in a string being output with System.out, the newline character causes the screen's output cursor to move to the beginning of the next line in the command window. Figure 2.5 lists several common escape sequences and describes how they affect the display of characters in the command window.

```
 1   // Fig. 2.4: Welcome3.java
 2   // Printing multiple lines of text with a single statement.
 3
 4   public class Welcome3
 5   {
 6      // main method begins execution of Java application
 7      public static void main( String args[] )
 8      {
 9         System.out.println( "Welcome\nto\nJava\nProgramming!" );
10
11      } // end method main
12
13   } // end class Welcome3
```

```
Welcome
to
Java
Programming!
```

Fig. 2.4 | Printing multiple lines of text with a single statement.

Escape sequence	Description
\n	Newline. Position the screen cursor at the beginning of the next line.
\t	Horizontal tab. Move the screen cursor to the next tab stop.
\r	Carriage return. Position the screen cursor at the beginning of the current line—do not advance to the next line. Any characters output after the carriage return overwrite the characters previously output on that line.
\\	Backslash. Used to print a backslash character.
\"	Double quote. Used to print a double-quote character. For example,

```
            System.out.println( "\"in quotes\"" );
```

displays

```
        "in quotes"
```

Fig. 2.5 | Some common escape sequences.

2.4 Displaying Text with `printf`

A new feature of J2SE 5.0 is the `System.out.printf` method for displaying formatted data—the f in the name `printf` stands for "formatted." Figure 2.6 outputs the strings `"Welcome to"` and `"Java Programming!"` with `System.out.printf`.
    Lines 9–10

```
        System.out.printf( "%s\n%s\n",
            "Welcome to", "Java Programming!" );
```

```
 1   // Fig. 2.6: Welcome4.java
 2   // Printing multiple lines in a dialog box.
 3
 4   public class Welcome4
 5   {
 6      // main method begins execution of Java application
 7      public static void main( String args[] )
 8      {
 9         System.out.printf( "%s\n%s\n",
10            "Welcome to", "Java Programming!" );
11
12      } // end method main
13
14   } // end class Welcome4
```

```
Welcome to
Java Programming!
```

Fig. 2.6 | Displaying multiple lines with method `System.out.printf`.

call method `System.out.printf` to display the program's output. The method call specifies three arguments. When a method requires multiple arguments, the arguments are separated with commas (,)—this is known as a comma-separated list.

Good Programming Practice 2.9

Place a space after each comma (,) in an argument list to make programs more readable.

Remember that all statements in Java end with a semicolon (;). Therefore, lines 9–10 represent only one statement. Java allows large statements to be split over many lines. However, you cannot split a statement in the middle of an identifier or in the middle of a string.

Common Programming Error 2.7

Splitting a statement in the middle of an identifier or a string is a syntax error.

Method `printf`'s first argument is a format string that may consist of fixed text and format specifiers. Fixed text is output by `printf` just as it would be output by `print` or `println`. Each format specifier is a placeholder for a value and specifies the type of data to output. Format specifiers also may include optional formatting information.

Format specifiers begin with a percent sign (%) and are followed by a character that represents the data type. For example, the format specifier `%s` is a placeholder for a string. The format string in line 9 specifies that `printf` should output two strings and that each string should be followed by a newline character. At the first format specifier's position, `printf` substitutes the value of the first argument after the format string. At each subsequent format specifier's position, `printf` substitutes the value of the next argument in the argument list. So this example substitutes "Welcome to" for the first %s and "Java Programming!" for the second %s. The output shows that two lines of text were displayed.

We introduce various formatting features as they are needed in our examples. Chapter 28 presents the details of formatting output with `printf`.

2.5 Another Java Application: Adding Integers

Our next application reads (or inputs) two integers (whole numbers, like –22, 7, 0 and 1024) typed by a user at the keyboard, computes the sum of the values and displays the result. This program must keep track of the numbers supplied by the user for the calculation later in the program. Programs remember numbers and other data in the computer's memory and access that data through program elements called variables. The program of Fig. 2.7 demonstrates these concepts. In the sample output, we use highlighting to differentiate between the user's input and the program's output.

Lines 1–2

```java
// Fig. 2.7: Addition.java
// Addition program that displays the sum of two numbers.
```

state the figure number, file name and purpose of the program.

Line 3

```java
import java.util.Scanner; // program uses class Scanner
```

```java
1   // Fig. 2.7: Addition.java
2   // Addition program that displays the sum of two numbers.
3   import java.util.Scanner; // program uses class Scanner
4
5   public class Addition
6   {
7      // main method begins execution of Java application
8      public static void main( String args[] )
9      {
10        // create Scanner to obtain input from command window
11        Scanner input = new Scanner( System.in );
12
13        int number1; // first number to add
14        int number2; // second number to add
15        int sum; // sum of number1 and number2
16
17        System.out.print( "Enter first integer: " ); // prompt
18        number1 = input.nextInt(); // read first number from user
19
20        System.out.print( "Enter second integer: " ); // prompt
21        number2 = input.nextInt(); // read second number from user
22
23        sum = number1 + number2; // add numbers
24
25        System.out.printf( "Sum is %d\n", sum ); // display sum
26
27     } // end method main
28
29  } // end class Addition
```

```
Enter first integer: 45
Enter second integer: 72
Sum is 117
```

Fig. 2.7 | Addition program that displays the sum of two numbers.

is an **import declaration** that helps the compiler locate a class that is used in this program. A great strength of Java is its rich set of predefined classes that programmers can reuse rather than "reinventing the wheel." These classes are grouped into **packages**—named collections of classes. Collectively, Java's packages are referred to as the **Java class library**, or the **Java Application Programming Interface** (**Java API**). Programmers use `import` declarations to identify the predefined classes used in a Java program. The `import` declaration in line 3 indicates that this example uses Java's predefined `Scanner` class (discussed shortly) from package `java.util`. Then the compiler attempts to ensure that you use class `Scanner` correctly.

Common Programming Error 2.8

All `import` declarations must appear before the first class declaration in the file. Placing an import declaration inside a class declaration's body or after a class declaration is a syntax error.

Error-Prevention Tip 2.7

Forgetting to include an `import` declaration for a class used in your program typically results in a compilation error containing a message such as "`cannot resolve symbol`." When this occurs, check that you provided the proper `import` declarations and that the names in the `import` declarations are spelled correctly, including proper use of uppercase and lowercase letters.

Line 5

```
public class Addition
```

begins the declaration of class `Addition`. The file name for this `public` class must be `Addition.java`. Remember that the body of each class declaration starts with an opening left brace (line 6), {, and ends with a closing right brace (line 29), }.

The application begins execution with method `main` (lines 8–27). The left brace (line 9) marks the beginning of `main`'s body, and the corresponding right brace (line 27) marks the end of `main`'s body. Note that method `main` is indented one level in the body of class `Addition` and that the code in the body of `main` is indented another level for readability.

Line 11

```
Scanner input = new Scanner( System.in );
```

is a **variable declaration statement** (also called a **declaration**) that specifies the name and type of a variable (`input`) that is used in this program. A **variable** is a location in the computer's memory where a value can be stored for use later in a program. All variables must be declared with a **name** and a **type** before they can be used. A variable's name enables the program to access the value of the variable in memory. A variable's name can be any valid identifier. (See Section 2.2 for identifier naming requirements.) A variable's type specifies what kind of information is stored at that location in memory. Like other statements, declaration statements end with a semicolon (;).

The declaration in line 11 specifies that the variable named `input` is of type `Scanner`. A **Scanner** enables a program to read data (e.g., numbers) for use in a program. The data can come from many sources, such as a file on disk or the user at the keyboard. Before using a `Scanner`, the program must create it and specify the source of the data.

The equal sign (=) in line 11 indicates that `Scanner` variable `input` should be **initialized** (i.e., prepared for use in the program) in its declaration with the result of the expression `new Scanner( System.in )` to the right of the equal sign. This expression creates a `Scanner` object that reads data typed by the user at the keyboard. Recall that the standard output object, `System.out`, allows Java applications to display characters in the command window. Similarly, the standard input object, `System.in`, enables Java applications to read information typed by the user. So, line 11 creates a `Scanner` that enables the application to read information typed by the user at the keyboard.

The variable declaration statements at lines 13–15

```
int number1; // first number to add
int number2; // second number to add
int sum; // sum of number1 and number2
```

declare that variables `number1`, `number2` and `sum` are data of type `int`—these variables will hold integer values (whole numbers such as 7, –11, 0 and 31,914). These variables are not yet initialized. The range of values for an `int` is –2,147,483,648 to +2,147,483,647. We will soon discuss types `float` and `double`, for specifying real numbers, and type `char`, for specifying character data. Real numbers are numbers that contain decimal points, such as 3.4, 0.0 and –11.19. Variables of type `char` represent individual characters, such as an uppercase letter (e.g., A), a digit (e.g., 7), a special character (e.g., * or %) or an escape sequence (e.g., the newline character, \n). Types such as `int`, `float`, `double` and `char` are often called primitive types or built-in types. Primitive-type names are keywords and therefore must appear in all lowercase letters. Appendix D summarizes the characteristics of the eight primitive types (`boolean`, `byte`, `char`, `short`, `int`, `long`, `float` and `double`).

Variable declaration statements can be split over several lines, with the variable names separated by commas (i.e., a comma-separated list of variable names). Several variables of the same type may be declared in one declaration or in multiple declarations. For example, lines 13–15 can also be written as follows:

```
int number1, // first number to add
    number2, // second number to add
    sum; // sum of number1 and number2
```

Note that we used end-of-line comments in lines 13–15. This use of comments is a common programming practice for indicating the purpose of each variable in the program.

Good Programming Practice 2.10

Declare each variable on a separate line. This format allows a descriptive comment to be easily inserted next to each declaration.

Good Programming Practice 2.11

Choosing meaningful variable names helps a program to be self-documenting (i.e., one can understand the program simply by reading it rather than by reading manuals or viewing an excessive number of comments).

Good Programming Practice 2.12

By convention, variable-name identifiers begin with a lowercase letter, and every word in the name after the first word begins with a capital letter. For example, variable-name identifier `firstNumber` *has a capital N in its second word,* `Number`.

Line 17

```
System.out.print( "Enter first integer: " ); // prompt
```

uses `System.out.print` to display the message "`Enter first integer: `". This message is called a **prompt** because it directs the user to take a specific action. Recall from Section 2.2 that identifiers starting with capital letters represent class names. So, `System` is a class. Class `System` is part of package `java.lang`. Notice that class `System` is not imported with an `import` declaration at the beginning of the program.

Software Engineering Observation 2.1

By default, package `java.lang` is imported in every Java program; thus, `java.lang` is the only package in the Java API that does not require an `import` declaration.

Line 18

```
number1 = input.nextInt(); // read first number from user
```

uses `Scanner` object `input`'s `nextInt` method to obtain an integer from the user at the keyboard. At this point the program waits for the user to type the number and press the *Enter* key to submit the number to the program.

Technically, the user can type anything as the input value. Our program assumes that the user enters a valid integer value as requested. In this program, if the user types a non-integer value, a runtime logic error will occur and the program will terminate. Chapter 13, Exception Handling, discusses how to make your programs more robust by enabling them to handle such errors. This is also known as making your program **fault tolerant**.

In line 17, the result of the call to method `nextInt` (an `int` value) is placed in variable `number1` by using the **assignment operator**, `=`. The statement is read as "`number1` gets the value of `input.nextInt()`." Operator `=` is called a **binary operator** because it has two **operands**—`number1` and the result of the method call `input.nextInt()`. This statement is called an **assignment statement** because it is a statement that assigns a value to a variable. Everything to the right of the assignment operator, `=`, is always evaluated before the assignment is performed.

Good Programming Practice 2.13

Place spaces on either side of a binary operator to make it stand out and make the program more readable.

Line 20

```
System.out.print( "Enter second integer: " ); // prompt
```

prompts the user to input the second integer. Line 21

```
number2 = input.nextInt(); // read second number from user
```

reads the second integer and assigns it to variable `number2`.

Line 23

```
sum = number1 + number2; // add numbers
```

is an assignment statement that calculates the sum of the variables `number1` and `number2` and assigns the result to variable `sum` by using the assignment operator, `=`. The statement is read as "`sum` gets the value of `number1 + number2`." Most calculations are performed in assignment statements. When the program encounters the addition operation, it uses the values stored in the variables number1 and number2 to perform the calculation. In the preceding statement, the addition operator is a binary operator—its two operands are number1 and number2. Portions of statements that contain calculations are called expressions. In fact, an expression is any portion of a statement that has a value associated with it. For example, the value of the expression number1 + number2 is the sum of the numbers. Similarly, the value of the expression input.nextInt() is an integer typed by the user.

After the calculation has been performed, line 25

```
System.out.printf( "Sum is %d\n", sum ); // display sum
```

uses method System.out.printf to display the sum. The format specifier **%d** is a placeholder for an int value (in this case the value of sum)—the letter d stands for "decimal integer." Note that other than the %d format specifier, the remaining characters in the format string are all fixed text. So method printf displays "Sum is ", followed by the value of sum (in the position of the %d format specifier) and a newline.

Note that calculations can also be performed inside printf statements. We could have combined the statements at lines 23 and 25 into the statement

```
System.out.printf( "Sum is %d\n", ( number1 + number2 ) );
```

The parentheses around the expression number1 + number2 are not required—they are included to emphasize that the value of the expression is output in the position of the %d format specifier.

Java API Documentation

For each new Java API class we use, we indicate the package in which it is located. This package information is important because it helps you locate descriptions of each package and class in the Java API documentation. A Web-based version of this documentation can be found at

```
java.sun.com/j2se/5.0/docs/api/
```

Also, you can download this documentation to your own computer from

```
java.sun.com/j2se/5.0/download.jsp
```

The download is approximately 40 megabytes (MB) in size. Appendix G provides an overview of using the Java API documentation.

2.6 Memory Concepts

Variable names such as number1, number2 and sum actually correspond to locations in the computer's memory. Every variable has a name, a type, a size and a value.

In the addition program of Fig. 2.7, when the statement (line 18)

```
number1 = input.nextInt(); // read first number from user
```

executes, the number typed by the user is placed into a memory location to which the name number1 has been assigned by the compiler. Suppose that the user enters 45. The computer places that integer value into location number1, as shown in Fig. 2.8. Whenever a value is placed in a memory location, the value replaces the previous value in that location. The previous value is lost.

number1   45

Fig. 2.8 | Memory location showing the name and value of variable `number1`.

When the statement (line 21)

```
number2 = input.nextInt(); // read second number from user
```

executes, suppose that the user enters 72. The computer places that integer value into location `number2`. The memory now appears as shown in Fig. 2.9.

After the program of Fig. 2.7 obtains values for `number1` and `number2`, it adds the values and places the sum into variable `sum`. The statement (line 23)

```
sum = number1 + number2; // add numbers
```

performs the addition, then replaces `sum`'s previous value. After `sum` has been calculated, memory appears as shown in Fig. 2.10. Note that the values of `number1` and `number2` appear exactly as they did before they were used in the calculation of `sum`. These values were used, but not destroyed, as the computer performed the calculation. Thus, when a value is read from a memory location, the process is nondestructive.

2.7 Arithmetic

Most programs perform arithmetic calculations. The **arithmetic operators** are summarized in Fig. 2.11. Note the use of various special symbols not used in algebra. The **asterisk** (*) indicates multiplication, and the **percent sign** (%) is the **remainder operator** (called-**modulus** in some languages), which we will discuss shortly. The arithmetic operators in Fig. 2.11 are binary operators because they each operate on two operands. For example, the expression f + 7 contains the binary operator + and the two operands f and 7.

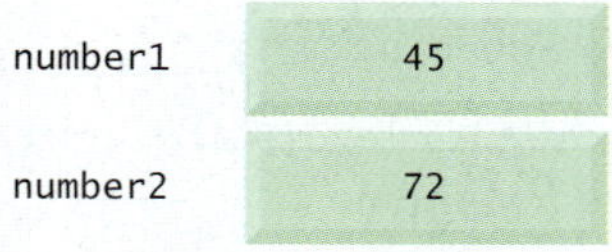

number1   45

number2   72

Fig. 2.9 | Memory locations after storing values for `number1` and `number2`.

number1   45

number2   72

sum   117

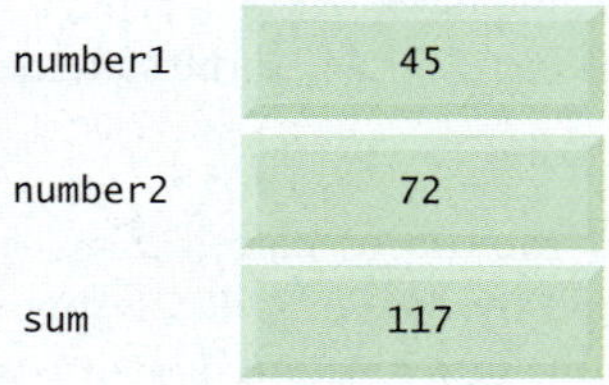

Fig. 2.10 | Memory locations after calculating and storing the sum of `number1` and `number2`.

Java operation	Arithmetic operator	Algebraic expression	Java expression
Addition	+	$f + 7$	f + 7
Subtraction	–	$p - c$	p - c
Multiplication	*	bm	b * m
Division	/	x / y or $\dfrac{x}{y}$ or $x \div y$	x / y
Remainder	%	$r \bmod s$	r % s

Fig. 2.11 | Arithmetic operators.

Integer division yields an integer quotient—for example, the expression 7 / 4 evaluates to 1, and the expression 17 / 5 evaluates to 3. Any fractional part in integer division is simply discarded (i.e., truncated)—no rounding occurs. Java provides the remainder operator, %, which yields the remainder after division. The expression x % y yields the remainder after x is divided by y. Thus, 7 % 4 yields 3, and 17 % 5 yields 2. This operator is most commonly used with integer operands, but can also be used with other arithmetic types. In this chapter's exercises and in later chapters, we consider several interesting applications of the remainder operator, such as determining whether one number is a multiple of another.

Arithmetic expressions in Java must be written in **straight-line form** to facilitate entering programs into the computer. Thus, expressions such as "a divided by b" must be written as a / b, so that all constants, variables and operators appear in a straight line. The following algebraic notation is generally not acceptable to compilers:

$$\frac{a}{b}$$

Parentheses are used to group terms in Java expressions in the same manner as in algebraic expressions. For example, to multiply a times the quantity b + c, we write

a * (b + c)

If an expression contains **nested parentheses**, such as

((a + b) * c)

the expression in the innermost set of parentheses (a + b in this case) is evaluated first.

Java applies the operators in arithmetic expressions in a precise sequence determined by the following **rules of operator precedence**, which are generally the same as those followed in algebra (Fig. 2.12):

1. Multiplication, division and remainder operations are applied first. If an expression contains several such operations, the operators are applied from left to right. Multiplication, division and remainder operators have the same level of precedence.

2. Addition and subtraction operations are applied next. If an expression contains several such operations, the operators are applied from left to right. Addition and subtraction operators have the same level of precedence.

Operator(s)	Operation(s)	Order of evaluation (precedence)
* / %	Multiplication Division Remainder	Evaluated first. If there are several operators of this type, they are evaluated from left to right.
+ -	Addition Subtraction	Evaluated next. If there are several operators of this type, they are evaluated from left to right.

Fig. 2.12 | Precedence of arithmetic operators.

These rules enable Java to apply operators in the correct order. When we say that operators are applied from left to right, we are referring to their associativity. You will see that some operators associate from right to left. Figure 2.12 summarizes these rules of operator precedence. The table will be expanded as additional Java operators are introduced. A complete precedence chart is included in Appendix A.

Now let us consider several expressions in light of the rules of operator precedence. Each example lists an algebraic expression and its Java equivalent. The following is an example of an arithmetic mean (average) of five terms:

Algebra: $m = \dfrac{a + b + c + d + e}{5}$

Java: m = (a + b + c + d + e) / 5;

The parentheses are required because division has higher precedence than addition. The entire quantity (a + b + c + d + e) is to be divided by 5. If the parentheses are erroneously omitted, we obtain a + b + c + d + e / 5, which evaluates as

$$a + b + c + d + \frac{e}{5}$$

The following is an example of the equation of a straight line:

Algebra: $y = mx + b$

Java: y = m * x + b;

No parentheses are required. The multiplication operator is applied first because multiplication has a higher precedence than addition. The assignment occurs last because it has a lower precedence than multiplication or addition.

The following example contains remainder (%), multiplication, division, addition and subtraction operations:

Algebra: $z = pr\,\%q + w/x - y$

Java: z = p * r % q + w / x - y;

(6) (1) (2) (4) (3) (5)

The circled numbers under the statement indicate the order in which Java applies the operators. The multiplication, remainder and division operations are evaluated first in left-to-right order (i.e., they associate from left to right), because they have higher precedence than addition and subtraction. The addition and subtraction operations are evaluated next. These operations are also applied from left to right.

To develop a better understanding of the rules of operator precedence, consider the evaluation of a second-degree polynomial ($y = ax^2 + bx + c$):

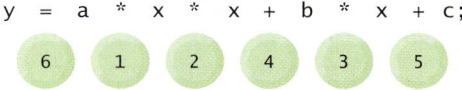

The circled numbers indicate the order in which Java applies the operators. The multiplication operations are evaluated first in left-to-right order (i.e., they associate from left to right), because they have higher precedence than addition. The addition operations are evaluated next and are applied from left to right. There is no arithmetic operator for exponentiation in Java, so x^2 is represented as x * x. Section 5.4 shows an alternative for performing exponentiation in Java.

Suppose that a, b, c and x in the preceding second-degree polynomial are initialized (given values) as follows: a = 2, b = 3, c = 7 and x = 5. Figure 2.13 illustrates the order in which the operators are applied.

As in algebra, it is acceptable to place unnecessary parentheses in an expression to make the expression clearer. These are called redundant parentheses. For example, the preceding assignment statement might be parenthesized as follows:

```
y = ( a * x * x ) + ( b * x ) + c;
```

Good Programming Practice 2.14

Using parentheses for complex arithmetic expressions, even when the parentheses are not necessary, can make the arithmetic expressions easier to read.

Step 1.   y = 2 * 5 * 5 + 3 * 5 + 7;   *(Leftmost multiplication)*
           2 * 5 is 10

Step 2.   y = 10 * 5 + 3 * 5 + 7;   *(Leftmost multiplication)*
           10 * 5 is 50

Step 3.   y = 50 + 3 * 5 + 7;   *(Multiplication before addition)*
                    3 * 5 is 15

Step 4.   y = 50 + 15 + 7;   *(Leftmost addition)*
           50 + 15 is 65

Step 5.   y = 65 + 7;   *(Last addition)*
           65 + 7 is 72

Step 6.   y = 72   *(Last operation—place 72 in y)*

Fig. 2.13 | Order in which a second-degree polynomial is evaluated.

2.8 Decision Making: Equality and Relational Operators

A condition is an expression that can be either true or false. This section introduces a simple version of Java's if statement that allows a program to make a decision based on the value of a condition. For example, the condition "grade is greater than or equal to 60" determines whether a student passed a test. If the condition in an if statement is true, the body of the if statement executes. If the condition is false, the body does not execute. We will see an example shortly.

Conditions in if statements can be formed by using the equality operators (== and !=) and relational operators (>, <, >= and <=) summarized in Fig. 2.14. Both equality operators have the same level of precedence, which is lower than that of the relational operators. The equality operators associate from left to right. The relational operators all have the same level of precedence and also associate from left to right.

The application of Fig. 2.15 uses six if statements to compare two integers input by the user. If the condition in any of these if statements is true, the assignment statement associated with that if statement executes. The program uses a Scanner to input the two integers from the user and store them in variables number1 and number2. Then the program compares the numbers and displays the results of the comparisons that are true.

The declaration of class Comparison begins at line 6

```
public class Comparison
```

The class's main method (lines 9–41) begins the execution of the program.
Line 12

```
Scanner input = new Scanner( System.in );
```

declares Scanner variable input and assigns it a Scanner that inputs data from the standard input (i.e., the keyboard).

Standard algebraic equality or relational operator	Java equality or relational operator	Sample Java condition	Meaning of Java condition
Equality operators			
=	==	x == y	x is equal to y
≠	!=	x != y	x is not equal to y
Relational operators			
>	>	x > y	x is greater than y
<	<	x < y	x is less than y
≥	>=	x >= y	x is greater than or equal to y
≤	<=	x <= y	x is less than or equal to y

Fig. 2.14 | Equality and relational operators.

```
1   // Fig. 2.15: Comparison.java
2   // Compare integers using if statements, relational operators
3   // and equality operators.
4   import java.util.Scanner; // program uses class Scanner
5
6   public class Comparison
7   {
8      // main method begins execution of Java application
9      public static void main( String args[] )
10     {
11        // create Scanner to obtain input from command window
12        Scanner input = new Scanner( System.in );
13
14        int number1; // first number to compare
15        int number2; // second number to compare
16
17        System.out.print( "Enter first integer: " ); // prompt
18        number1 = input.nextInt(); // read first number from user
19
20        System.out.print( "Enter second integer: " ); // prompt
21        number2 = input.nextInt(); // read second number from user
22
23        if ( number1 == number2 )
24           System.out.printf( "%d == %d\n", number1, number2 );
25
26        if ( number1 != number2 )
27           System.out.printf( "%d != %d\n", number1, number2 );
28
29        if ( number1 < number2 )
30           System.out.printf( "%d < %d\n", number1, number2 );
31
32        if ( number1 > number2 )
33           System.out.printf( "%d > %d\n", number1, number2 );
34
35        if ( number1 <= number2 )
36           System.out.printf( "%d <= %d\n", number1, number2 );
37
38        if ( number1 >= number2 )
39           System.out.printf( "%d >= %d\n", number1, number2 );
40
41     } // end method main
42
43  } // end class Comparison
```

```
Enter first integer: 777
Enter second integer: 777
777 == 777
777 <= 777
777 >= 777
```

Fig. 2.15 | Equality and relational operators. (Part 1 of 2.)

```
Enter first integer: 1000
Enter second integer: 2000
1000 != 2000
1000 < 2000
1000 <= 2000
```

```
Enter first integer: 2000
Enter second integer: 1000
2000 != 1000
2000 > 1000
2000 >= 1000
```

Fig. 2.15 | Equality and relational operators. (Part 2 of 2.)

Lines 14–15

```
int number1; // first number to compare
int number2; // second number to compare
```

declare the `int` variables used to store the values input from the user.

Lines 17–18

```
System.out.print( "Enter first integer: " ); // prompt
number1 = input.nextInt(); // read first number from user
```

prompt the user to enter the first integer and input the value, respectively. The input value is stored in variable `number1`.

Lines 20–21

```
System.out.print( "Enter second integer: " ); // prompt
number2 = input.nextInt(); // read second number from user
```

prompt the user to enter the second integer and input the value, respectively. The input value is stored in variable `number2`.

Lines 23–24

```
if ( number1 == number2 )
    System.out.printf( "%d == %d\n", number1, number2 );
```

declare an `if` statement that compares the values of the variables `number1` and `number2` to determine whether they are equal. An `if` statement always begins with keyword `if`, followed by a condition in parentheses. An `if` statement expects one statement in its body. The indentation of the body statement shown here is not required, but it improves the program's readability by emphasizing that the statement in line 24 is part of the `if` statement that begins on line 23. Line 24 executes only if the numbers stored in variables `number1` and `number2` are equal (i.e., the condition is true). The `if` statements at lines 26–27, 29–30, 32–33, 35–36 and 38–39 compare `number1` and `number2` with the operators `!=`, `<`, `>`, `<=` and `>=`, respectively. If the condition in any of the `if` statements is true, the corresponding body statement executes.

Common Programming Error 2.9

Forgetting the left and/or right parentheses for the condition in an if statement is a syntax error—the parentheses are required.

Common Programming Error 2.10

Confusing the equality operator, ==, with the assignment operator, =, can cause a logic error or a syntax error. The equality operator should be read as "is equal to," and the assignment operator should be read as "gets" or "gets the value of." To avoid confusion, some people read the equality operator as "double equals" or "equals equals."

Common Programming Error 2.11

It is a syntax error if the operators ==, !=, >= and <= contain spaces between their symbols, as in = =, ! =, > = and < =, respectively.

Common Programming Error 2.12

Reversing the operators !=, >= and <=, as in =!, => and =<, is a syntax error.

Good Programming Practice 2.15

Indent an if statement's body to make it stand out and to enhance program readability.

Good Programming Practice 2.16

Place only one statement per line in a program. This format enhances program readability.

Note that there is no semicolon (;) at the end of the first line of each if statement. Such a semicolon would result in a logic error at execution time. For example,

```
if ( number1 == number2 );  // logic error
   System.out.printf( "%d == %d\n", number1, number2 );
```

would actually be interpreted by Java as

```
if ( number1 == number2 )
   ; // empty statement

System.out.printf( "%d == %d\n", number1, number2 );
```

where the semicolon on the line by itself—called the empty statement—is the statement to execute if the condition in the if statement is true. When the empty statement executes, no task is performed in the program. The program then continues with the output statement, which always executes, regardless of whether the condition is true or false, because the output statement is not part of the if statement.

Common Programming Error 2.13

Placing a semicolon immediately after the right parenthesis of the condition in an if statement is normally a logic error.

Note the use of white space in Fig. 2.15. Recall that white-space characters, such as tabs, newlines and spaces, are normally ignored by the compiler. So statements may be split over several lines and may be spaced according to the programmer's preferences without affecting the meaning of a program. It is incorrect to split identifiers and strings. Ideally, statements should be kept small, but this is not always possible.

Good Programming Practice 2.17

A lengthy statement can be spread over several lines. If a single statement must be split across lines, choose breaking points that make sense, such as after a comma in a comma-separated list, or after an operator in a lengthy expression. If a statement is split across two or more lines, indent all subsequent lines until the end of the statement.

Figure 2.16 shows the precedence of the operators introduced in this chapter. The operators are shown from top to bottom in decreasing order of precedence. All these operators, with the exception of the assignment operator, =, associate from left to right. Addition is left associative, so an expression like x + y + z is evaluated as if it had been written as (x + y) + z. The assignment operator, =, associates from right to left, so an expression like x = y = 0 is evaluated as if it had been written as x = (y = 0), which, as we will soon see, first assigns the value 0 to variable y and then assigns the result of that assignment, 0, to x.

Good Programming Practice 2.18

Refer to the operator precedence chart (see the complete chart in Appendix A) when writing expressions containing many operators. Confirm that the operations in the expression are performed in the order you expect. If you are uncertain about the order of evaluation in a complex expression, use parentheses to force the order, exactly as you would do in algebraic expressions. Observe that some operators, such as assignment, =, associate from right to left rather than from left to right.

2.9 (Optional) Software Engineering Case Study: Examining the Requirements Document

Now we begin our optional object-oriented design and implementation case study. The "Software Engineering Case Study" sections at the ends of this and the next several chapters will ease you into object orientation by examining an automated teller machine (ATM) case study. This case study will provide you with a concise, carefully paced, complete design and implementation experience. In Chapters 3–8 and 10, we will perform the various steps of an object-oriented design (OOD) process using the UML while relating these steps to the object-oriented concepts discussed in the chapters. Appendix J implements the ATM using the techniques of object-oriented programming (OOP) in Java. We present the complete case-study solution. This is not an exercise; rather, it is an end-to-end learning experience that concludes with a detailed walkthrough of the Java code that implements our design. It will acquaint you with the kinds of substantial problems encountered in industry and their potential solutions. We hope you enjoy this learning experience.

Operators				Associativity	Type
*	/	%		left to right	multiplicative
+	-			left to right	additive
<	<=	>	>=	left to right	relational
==	!=			left to right	equality
=				right to left	assignment

Fig. 2.16 | Precedence and associativity of operations discussed.

We begin our design process by presenting a **requirements document** that specifies the overall purpose of the ATM system and *what* it must do. Throughout the case study, we refer to the requirements document to determine precisely what functionality the system must include.

Requirements Document

A local bank intends to install a new automated teller machine (ATM) to allow users (i.e., bank customers) to perform basic financial transactions (Fig. 2.17). Each user can have only one account at the bank. ATM users should be able to view their account balance, withdraw cash (i.e., take money out of an account) and deposit funds (i.e., place money into an account).

The user interface of the automated teller machine contains the following components:

- a screen that displays messages to the user
- a keypad that receives numeric input from the user
- a cash dispenser that dispenses cash to the user and
- a deposit slot that receives deposit envelopes from the user.

The cash dispenser begins each day loaded with 500 $20 bills. [*Note:* Due to the limited scope of this case study, certain elements of the ATM described here do not accurately mimic those of a real ATM. For example, a real ATM typically contains a device that reads a user's account number from an ATM card, whereas this ATM asks the user to type an account number on the keypad. A real ATM also usually prints a receipt at the end of a session, but all output from this ATM appears on the screen.]

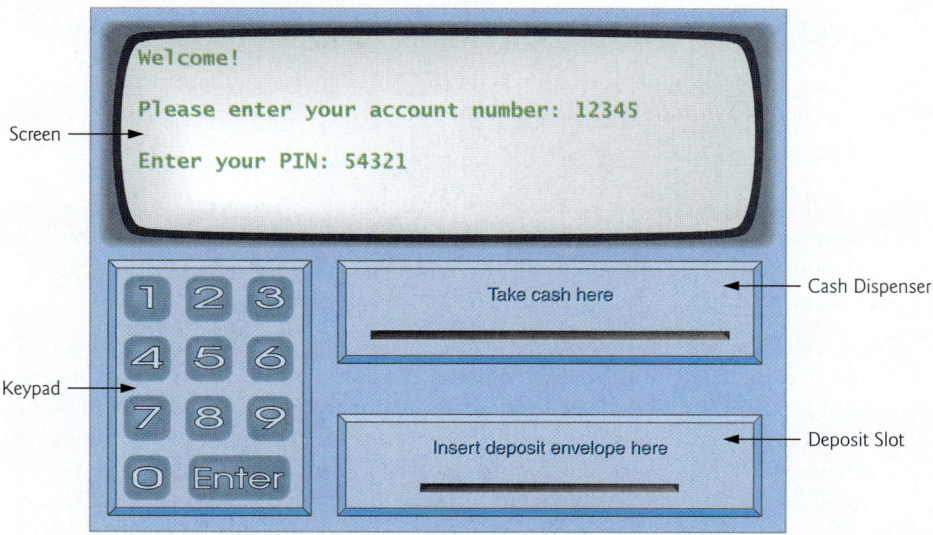

Fig. 2.17 | Automated teller machine user interface.

The bank wants you to develop software to perform the financial transactions initiated by bank customers through the ATM. The bank will integrate the software with the ATM's hardware at a later time. The software should encapsulate the functionality of the hardware devices (e.g., cash dispenser, deposit slot) within software components, but it need not concern itself with how these devices perform their duties. The ATM hardware has not been developed yet, so instead of writing your software to run on the ATM, you should develop a first version of the software to run on a personal computer. This version should use the computer's monitor to simulate the ATM's screen, and the computer's keyboard to simulate the ATM's keypad.

An ATM session consists of authenticating a user (i.e., proving the user's identity) based on an account number and personal identification number (PIN), followed by creating and executing financial transactions. To authenticate a user and perform transactions, the ATM must interact with the bank's account information database (i.e., an organized collection of data stored on a computer). For each bank account, the database stores an account number, a PIN and a balance indicating the amount of money in the account. [*Note:* We assume that the bank plans to build only one ATM, so we do not need to worry about multiple ATMs accessing this database at the same time. Furthermore, we assume that the bank does not make any changes to the information in the database while a user is accessing the ATM. Also, any business system like an ATM faces reasonably complicated security issues that go well beyond the scope of a first- or second-semester computer science course. We make the simplifying assumption, however, that the bank trusts the ATM to access and manipulate the information in the database without significant security measures.]

Upon first approaching the ATM (assuming no one is currently using it), the user should experience the following sequence of events (shown in Fig. 2.17):

1. The screen displays a welcome message and prompts the user to enter an account number.

2. The user inputs a five-digit account number using the keypad.

3. The screen prompts the user to enter the PIN (personal identification number) associated with the specified account number.

4. The user enters a five-digit PIN using the keypad.

5. If the user enters a valid account number and the correct PIN for that account, the screen displays the main menu (Fig. 2.18). If the user enters an invalid account number or an incorrect PIN, the screen displays an appropriate message, then the ATM returns to *Step 1* to restart the authentication process.

After the ATM authenticates the user, the main menu (Fig. 2.18) should contain a numbered option for each of the three types of transactions: balance inquiry (option 1), withdrawal (option 2) and deposit (option 3). The main menu also should contain an option to allow the user to exit the system (option 4). The user then chooses either to perform a transaction (by entering 1, 2 or 3) or to exit the system (by entering 4).

If the user enters 1 to make a balance inquiry, the screen displays the user's account balance. To do so, the ATM must retrieve the balance from the bank's database.

The following steps describe the actions that occur when the user enters 2 to make a withdrawal:

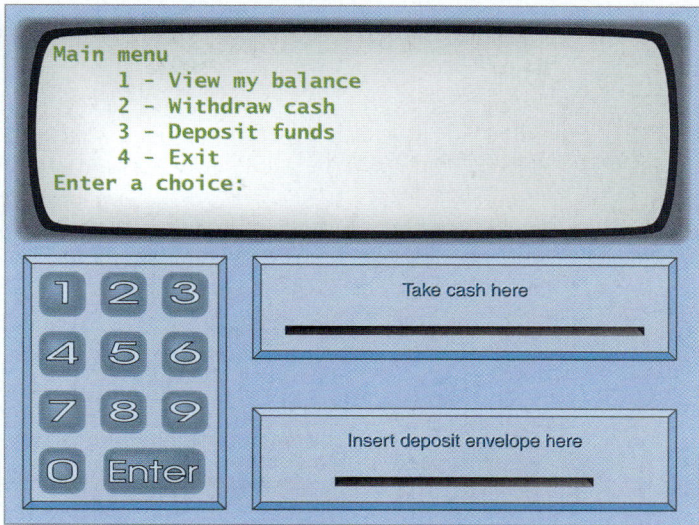

Fig. 2.18 | ATM main menu.

1. The screen displays a menu (shown in Fig. 2.19) containing standard withdrawal amounts: $20 (option 1), $40 (option 2), $60 (option 3), $100 (option 4) and $200 (option 5). The menu also contains an option to allow the user to cancel the transaction (option 6).

2. The user inputs a menu selection using the keypad.

3. If the withdrawal amount chosen is greater than the user's account balance, the screen displays a message stating this and telling the user to choose a smaller amount. The ATM then returns to *Step 1*. If the withdrawal amount chosen is less than or equal to the user's account balance (i.e., an acceptable amount), the ATM proceeds to *Step 4*. If the user chooses to cancel the transaction (option 6), the ATM displays the main menu and waits for user input.

4. If the cash dispenser contains enough cash to satisfy the request, the ATM proceeds to *Step 5*. Otherwise, the screen displays a message indicating the problem and telling the user to choose a smaller withdrawal amount. The ATM then returns to *Step 1*.

5. The ATM debits the withdrawal amount from the user's account in the bank's database (i.e., subtracts the withdrawal amount from the user's account balance).

6. The cash dispenser dispenses the desired amount of money to the user.

7. The screen displays a message reminding the user to take the money.

The following steps describe the actions that occur when the user enters 3 to make a deposit:

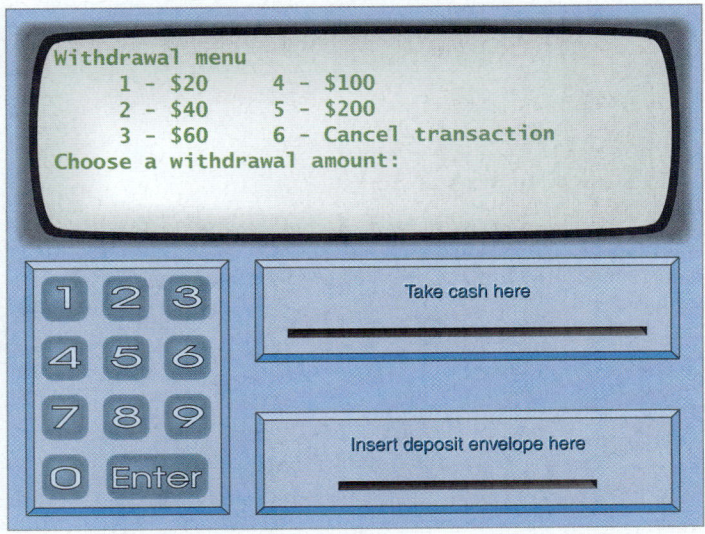

Fig. 2.19 | ATM withdrawal menu.

1. The screen prompts the user to enter a deposit amount or type 0 (zero) to cancel the transaction.

2. The user inputs a deposit amount or 0 using the keypad. [*Note:* The keypad does not contain a decimal point or a dollar sign, so the user cannot type a real dollar amount (e.g., $1.25). Instead, the user must enter a deposit amount as a number of cents (e.g., 125). The ATM then divides this number by 100 to obtain a number representing a dollar amount (e.g., 125 ÷ 100 = 1.25).]

3. If the user specifies a deposit amount, the ATM proceeds to *Step 4*. If the user chooses to cancel the transaction (by entering 0), the ATM displays the main menu and waits for user input.

4. The screen displays a message telling the user to insert a deposit envelope into the deposit slot.

5. If the deposit slot receives a deposit envelope within two minutes, the ATM credits the deposit amount to the user's account in the bank's database (i.e., adds the deposit amount to the user's account balance). [*Note:* This money is not immediately available for withdrawal. The bank first must physically verify the amount of cash in the deposit envelope, and any checks in the envelope must clear (i.e., money must be transferred from the check writer's account to the check recipient's account). When either of these events occur, the bank appropriately updates the user's balance stored in its database. This occurs independently of the ATM system.] If the deposit slot does not receive a deposit envelope within this time period, the screen displays a message that the system has canceled the transaction due to inactivity. The ATM then displays the main menu and waits for user input.

After the system successfully executes a transaction, the system should return to the main menu so that the user can perform additional transactions. If the user chooses to exit the system, the screen should display a thank you message, then display the welcome message for the next user.

Analyzing the ATM System

The preceding statement is a simplified example of a requirements document. Typically, such a document is the result of a detailed process of requirements gathering that might include interviews with possible users of the system and specialists in fields related to the system. For example, a systems analyst who is hired to prepare a requirements document for banking software (e.g., the ATM system described here) might interview financial experts to gain a better understanding of what the software must do. The analyst would use the information gained to compile a list of system requirements to guide systems designers as they design the system.

The process of requirements gathering is a key task of the first stage of the software life cycle. The software life cycle specifies the stages through which software goes from the time it is first conceived to the time it is retired from use. These stages typically include: analysis, design, implementation, testing and debugging, deployment, maintenance and retirement. Several software life cycle models exist, each with its own preferences and specifications for when and how often software engineers should perform each of these stages. Waterfall models perform each stage once in succession, whereas iterative models may repeat one or more stages several times throughout a product's life cycle.

The analysis stage of the software life cycle focuses on defining the problem to be solved. When designing any system, one must *solve the problem right*, but of equal importance, one must *solve the right problem*. Systems analysts collect the requirements that indicate the specific problem to solve. Our requirements document describes the requirements of our ATM system in sufficient detail that you do not need to go through an extensive analysis stage—it has been done for you.

To capture what a proposed system should do, developers often employ a technique known as use case modeling. This process identifies the use cases of the system, each of which represents a different capability that the system provides to its clients. For example, ATMs typically have several use cases, such as "View Account Balance," "Withdraw Cash," "Deposit Funds," "Transfer Funds Between Accounts" and "Buy Postage Stamps." The simplified ATM system we build in this case study allows only the first three use cases.

Each use case describes a typical scenario for which the user uses the system. You have already read descriptions of the ATM system's use cases in the requirements document; the lists of steps required to perform each transaction type (i.e., balance inquiry, withdrawal and deposit) actually described the three use cases of our ATM—"View Account Balance," "Withdraw Cash" and "Deposit Funds."

Use Case Diagrams

We now introduce the first of several UML diagrams in the case study. We create a use case diagram to model the interactions between a system's clients (in this case study, bank customers) and its use cases. The goal is to show the kinds of interactions users have with a system without providing the details—these are provided in other UML diagrams (which we present throughout this case study). Use case diagrams are often accompanied by informal text that describes the use cases in more detail—like the text that appears in the requirements document. Use case diagrams are produced during the analysis stage of the software life cycle. In larger systems, use case diagrams are indispensable tools that help system designers remain focused on satisfying the users' needs.

Figure 2.20 shows the use case diagram for our ATM system. The stick figure represents an **actor**, which defines the roles that an external entity—such as a person or another system—plays when interacting with the system. For our automated teller machine, the actor is a User who can view an account balance, withdraw cash and deposit funds from the ATM. The User is not an actual person, but instead comprises the roles that a real person—when playing the part of a User—can play while interacting with the ATM. Note that a use case diagram can include multiple actors. For example, the use case diagram for a real bank's ATM system might also include an actor named Administrator that refills the cash dispenser each day.

Our requirements document supplies the actors—"ATM users should be able to view their account balance, withdraw cash and deposit funds." Therefore, the actor in each of the three use cases is the user who interacts with the ATM. An external entity—a real person—plays the part of the user to perform financial transactions. Figure 2.20 shows one actor, whose name, User, appears below the actor in the diagram. The UML models each use case as an oval connected to an actor with a solid line.

Software engineers (more precisely, systems designers) must analyze the requirements document or a set of use cases and design the system before programmers implement it in a particular programming language. During the analysis stage, systems designers focus on understanding the requirements document to produce a high-level specification that describes *what* the system is supposed to do. The output of the design stage—a **design specification**—should specify clearly *how* the system should be constructed to satisfy these requirements. In the next several "Software Engineering Case Study" sections, we perform the steps of a simple object-oriented design (OOD) process on the ATM system to produce a design specification containing a collection of UML diagrams and supporting text. The UML is designed for use with any OOD process. Many such processes exist, the most well-known of which is the Rational Unified Process™ (RUP) developed by Rational Software Corporation. RUP is a rich process intended for designing "industrial strength" applications. For this case study, we present our own simplified design process, designed for students in first- and second-semester programming courses.

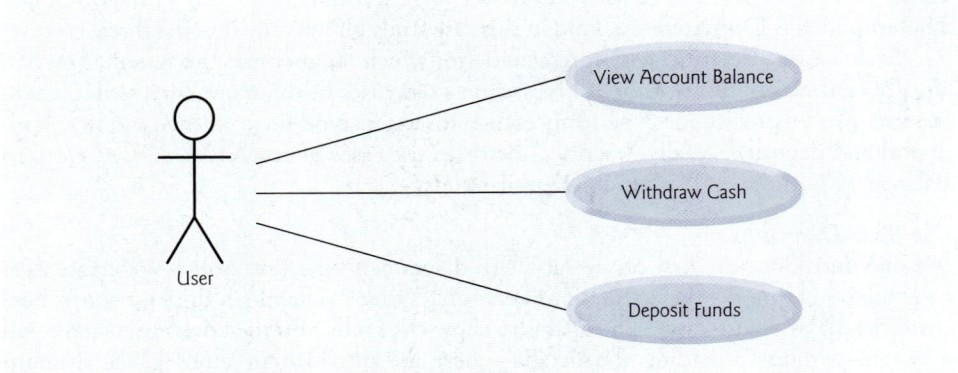

Fig. 2.20 | Use case diagram for the ATM system from the user's perspective.

Designing the ATM System

We now begin the design stage of our ATM system. A system is a set of components that interact to solve a problem. For example, to perform the ATM system's designated tasks, our ATM system has a user interface (Fig. 2.17), contains software that executes financial transactions and interacts with a database of bank-account information. System structure describes the system's objects and their interrelationships. System behavior describes how the system changes as its objects interact with one another. Every system has both structure and behavior—designers must specify both. There are several distinct types of system structures and behaviors. For example, the interactions among objects in the system differ from those between the user and the system, yet both constitute a portion of the system behavior.

The UML 2 specifies 13 diagram types for documenting the models of systems. Each models a distinct characteristic of a system's structure or behavior—six diagrams relate to system structure; the remaining seven relate to system behavior. We list here only the six types used in our case study—one of these (class diagrams) models system structure, whereas the remaining five model system behavior. We overview the remaining seven UML diagram types in Appendix L, UML 2: Additional Diagram Types.

1. **Use case diagrams**, such as the one in Fig. 2.20, model the interactions between a system and its external entities (actors) in terms of use cases (system capabilities, such as "View Account Balance," "Withdraw Cash" and "Deposit Funds").

2. **Class diagrams**, which you will study in Section 3.10, model the classes, or "building blocks," used in a system. Each noun or "thing" described in the requirements document is a candidate to be a class in the system (e.g., Account, Keypad). Class diagrams help us specify the structural relationships between parts of the system. For example, the ATM system class diagram will specify that the ATM is physically composed of a screen, a keypad, a cash dispenser and a deposit slot.

3. **State machine diagrams**, which you will study in Section 5.11, model the ways in which an object changes state. An object's state is indicated by the values of all the object's attributes at a given time. When an object changes state, that object may behave differently in the system. For example, after validating a user's PIN, the ATM transitions from the "user not authenticated" state to the "user authenticated" state, at which point the ATM allows the user to perform financial transactions (e.g., view account balance, withdraw cash, deposit funds).

4. **Activity diagrams**, which you will also study in Section 5.11, model an object's activity—the object's workflow (sequence of events) during program execution. An activity diagram models the actions the object performs and specifies the order in which the object performs these actions. For example, an activity diagram shows that the ATM must obtain the balance of the user's account (from the bank's account information database) before the screen can display the balance to the user.

5. **Communication diagrams** (called **collaboration diagrams** in earlier versions of the UML) model the interactions among objects in a system, with an emphasis on *what* interactions occur. You will learn in Section 7.14 that these diagrams show which objects must interact to perform an ATM transaction. For example, the ATM must communicate with the bank's account information database to retrieve an account balance.

6. **Sequence diagrams** also model the interactions among the objects in a system, but unlike communication diagrams, they emphasize *when* interactions occur. You will learn in Section 7.14 that these diagrams help show the order in which interactions occur in executing a financial transaction. For example, the screen prompts the user to enter a withdrawal amount before cash is dispensed.

In Section 3.10, we continue designing our ATM system by identifying the classes from the requirements document. We accomplish this by extracting key nouns and noun phrases from the requirements document. Using these classes, we develop our first draft of the class diagram that models the structure of our ATM system.

Internet and Web Resources
The following URLs provide information on object-oriented design with the UML.

www-306.ibm.com/software/rational/uml/
Lists frequently asked questions about the UML, provided by IBM Rational.

www.softdocwiz.com/Dictionary.htm
Hosts the Unified Modeling Language Dictionary, which lists and defines all terms used in the UML.

www-306.ibm.com/software/rational/offerings/design.html
Provides information about IBM Rational software available for designing systems. Provides downloads of 30-day trial versions of several products, such as IBM Rational Rose® XDE Developer.

www.embarcadero.com/products/describe/index.html
Provides a free 15-day license to download a trial version of Describe™—a UML modeling tool from Embarcadero Technologies®.

www.borland.com/together/index.html
Provides a free 30-day license to download a trial version of Borland® Together® Control-Center™—a software-development tool that supports the UML.

www.ilogix.com/rhapsody/rhapsody.cfm
Provides a free 30-day license to download a trial version of I-Logix Rhapsody®—a UML 2 based model-driven development environment.

argouml.tigris.org
Contains information and downloads for ArgoUML, a free open-source UML tool written in Java.

www.objectsbydesign.com/books/booklist.html
Lists books on the UML and object-oriented design.

www.objectsbydesign.com/tools/umltools_byCompany.html
Lists software tools that use the UML, such as IBM Rational Rose, Embarcadero Describe, Sparx Systems Enterprise Architect, I-Logix Rhapsody and Gentleware Poseidon for UML.

www.ootips.org/ood-principles.html
Provides answers to the question, "What Makes a Good Object-Oriented Design?"

www.parlezuml.com/tutorials/java/class/index_files/frame.htm
Provides a UML tutorial for Java developers that presents UML diagrams side by side with the Java code that implements them.

www.cetus-links.org/oo_uml.html
Introduces the UML and provides links to numerous UML resources.

www.agilemodeling.com/essays/umlDiagrams.htm
Provides in-depth descriptions and tutorials on each of the 13 UML 2 diagram types.

Recommended Readings
The following books provide information on object-oriented design with the UML.

Booch, G. *Object-Oriented Analysis and Design with Applications*. 3/e. Boston: Addison-Wesley, 2004.

Eriksson, H., et al. *UML 2 Toolkit*. New York: John Wiley, 2003.

Kruchten, P. *The Rational Unified Process: An Introduction*. Boston: Addison-Wesley, 2004.

Larman, C. *Applying UML and Patterns: An Introduction to Object-Oriented Analysis and Design*. 2nd ed. Upper Saddle River, NJ: Prentice Hall, 2002.

Roques, P. *UML in Practice: The Art of Modeling Software Systems Demonstrated Through Worked Examples and Solutions*. New York: John Wiley, 2004.

Rosenberg, D., and K. Scott. *Applying Use Case Driven Object Modeling with UML: An Annotated e-Commerce Example*. Reading, MA: Addison-Wesley, 2001.

Rumbaugh, J., I. Jacobson and G. Booch. *The Complete UML Training Course*. Upper Saddle River, NJ: Prentice Hall, 2000.

Rumbaugh, J., I. Jacobson and G. Booch. *The Unified Modeling Language Reference Manual*. Reading, MA: Addison-Wesley, 1999.

Rumbaugh, J., I. Jacobson and G. Booch. *The Unified Software Development Process*. Reading, MA: Addison-Wesley, 1999.

Software Engineering Case Study Self-Review Exercises

2.1   Suppose we enabled a user of our ATM system to transfer money between two bank accounts. Modify the use case diagram of Fig. 2.20 to reflect this change.

2.2   _____ model the interactions among objects in a system with an emphasis on *when* these interactions occur.
  a) Class diagrams
  b) Sequence diagrams
  c) Communication diagrams
  d) Activity diagrams

2.3   Which of the following choices lists stages of a typical software life cycle in sequential order?
  a) design, analysis, implementation, testing
  b) design, analysis, testing, implementation
  c) analysis, design, testing, implementation
  d) analysis, design, implementation, testing

Answers to Software Engineering Case Study Self-Review Exercises

2.1   Figure 2.21 contains a use case diagram for a modified version of our ATM system that also allows users to transfer money between accounts.

2.2   b.

2.3   d.

2.10 **Wrap-Up**

You learned many important features of Java in this chapter, including displaying data on the screen in a command prompt, inputting data from the keyboard, performing calculations and making decisions. The applications presented here were meant to introduce you to basic programming concepts. As you will see in Chapter 3, Java applications typically contain just a few lines of code in method `main`—these statements normally create the objects that perform the work of the application. In Chapter 3, you will learn how to implement your own classes and use objects of those classes in applications.

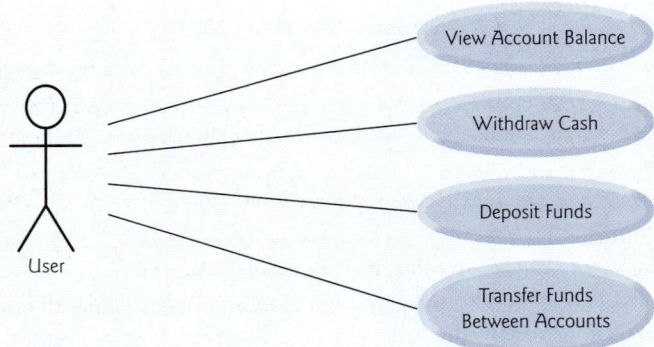

Fig. 2.21 | Use case diagram for a modified version of our ATM system that also allows users to transfer money between accounts.

Summary

- Computer programmers create applications by writing computer programs. A Java application is a computer program that executes when you use the `java` command to launch the JVM.
- Programmers insert comments to document programs and improve their readability. The Java compiler ignores comments.
- A comment that begins with `//` is called an end-of-line (or single-line) comment because the comment terminates at the end of the line on which it appears.
- Traditional (multiple-line) comments can be spread over several lines and are delimited by `/*` and `*/`. All text between the delimiters is ignored by the compiler.
- Javadoc comments are delimited by `/**` and `*/`. Javadoc comments enable programmers to embed program documentation directly in their programs. The `javadoc` utility program generates HTML documentation based on Javadoc comments.
- A programming language's syntax specifies the rules for creating a proper program in that language.
- A syntax error (also called a compiler error, compile-time error or compilation error) occurs when the compiler encounters code that violates Java's language rules.
- Programmers use blank lines and space characters to make programs easier to read. Together, blank lines, space characters and tab characters are known as white space. Space characters and tabs are known specifically as white-space characters. White space is ignored by the compiler.
- Every program in Java consists of at least one class declaration that is defined by the programmer (also known as a programmer-defined class or a user-defined class).
- Keywords are reserved for use by Java and are always spelled with all lowercase letters.
- Keyword `class` introduces a class declaration and is immediately followed by the class name.
- By convention, all class names in Java begin with a capital letter and capitalize the first letter of each word they include (e.g., `SampleClassName`).
- A Java class name is an identifier—a series of characters consisting of letters, digits, underscores (_) and dollar signs ($) that does not begin with a digit and does not contain spaces. Normally, an identifier that does not begin with a capital letter is not the name of a Java class.
- Java is case sensitive—that is, uppercase and lowercase letters are distinct.
- The body of every class declaration is delimited by braces, { and }.

- A `public` class declaration must be saved in a file with the same name as the class followed by the ".java" file-name extension.
- Method `main` is the starting point of every Java application and must begin with

      public static void main(String args[])

  otherwise, the JVM will not execute the application.
- Methods are able to perform tasks and return information when they complete their tasks. Keyword `void` indicates that a method will perform a task but will not return any information.
- Statements instruct the computer to perform actions.
- A sequence of characters in double quotation marks is called a string, a character string, a message or a string literal.
- `System.out`, the standard output object, allows Java applications to display characters in the command window.
- Method `System.out.println` displays its argument in the command window followed by a newline character to position the output cursor to the beginning of the next line.
- Every statement ends with a semicolon.
- Most operating systems use the command `cd` to change directories in the command window.
- You compile a program with the command `javac`. If the program contains no syntax errors, a class file containing the Java bytecodes that represent the application is created. These bytecodes are interpreted by the JVM when we execute the program.
- `System.out.print` displays its argument and positions the output cursor immediately after the last character displayed.
- A backslash (\) in a string is an escape character. It indicates that a "special character" is to be output. Java combines the next character with the backslash to form an escape sequence. The escape sequence \n represents the newline character, which positions the cursor on the next line.
- `System.out.printf` method (`f` means "formatted") displays formatted data.
- When a method requires multiple arguments, the arguments are separated with commas (,)—this is known as a comma-separated list.
- Method `printf`'s first argument is a format string that may consist of fixed text and format specifiers. Fixed text is output by `printf` just as it would be output by `print` or `println`. Each format specifier is a placeholder for a value and specifies the type of data to output.
- Format specifiers begin with a percent sign (%) and are followed by a character that represents the (-) data type. The format specifier `%s` is a placeholder for a string.
- At the first format specifier's position, `printf` substitutes the value of the first argument after the format string. At each subsequent format specifier's position, `printf` substitutes the value of the next argument in the argument list.
- Integers are whole numbers, like –22, 7, 0 and 1024.
- An `import` declaration helps the compiler locate a class that is used in a program.
- Java provides a rich set of predefined classes that programmers can reuse rather than "reinventing the wheel." These classes are grouped into packages—named collections of classes.
- Collectively, Java's packages are referred to as the Java class library, or the Java Application Programming Interface (Java API).
- A variable declaration statement specifies the name and type of a variable.
- A variable is a location in the computer's memory where a value can be stored for use later in a program. All variables must be declared with a name and a type before they can be used.

- A variable's name enables the program to access the value of the variable in memory. A variable name can be any valid identifier.
- Like other statements, variable declaration statements end with a semicolon (;).
- A Scanner (package java.util) enables a program to read data for use in a program. The data can come from many sources, such as a file on disk or the user at the keyboard. Before using a Scanner, the program must create it and specify the source of the data.
- Variables should be initialized to prepare them for use in a program.
- The expression new Scanner(System.in) creates a Scanner that reads from the keyboard. The standard input object, System.in, enables Java applications to read data typed by the user.
- Data type int is used to declare variables that will hold integer values. The range of values for an int is –2,147,483,648 to +2,147,483,647.
- Types float and double specify real numbers, and type char specifies character data. Real numbers are numbers that contain decimal points, such as 3.4, 0.0 and –11.19. Variables of type char data represent individual characters, such as an uppercase letter (e.g., A), a digit (e.g., 7), a special character (e.g., * or %) or an escape sequence (e.g., the newline character, \n).
- Types such as int, float, double and char are often called primitive types or built-in types. Primitive-type names are keywords; thus, they must appear in all lowercase letters.
- A prompt directs the user to take a specific action.
- Scanner method nextInt obtains an integer for use in a program.
- The assignment operator, =, enables the program to give a value to a variable. Operator = is called a binary operator because it has two operands. An assignment statement uses an assignment operator to assign a value to a variable.
- Portions of statements that have values are called expressions.
- The format specifier %d is a placeholder for an int value.
- Variable names correspond to locations in the computer's memory. Every variable has a name, a type, a size and a value.
- Whenever a value is placed in a memory location, the value replaces the previous value in that location. The previous value is lost.
- Most programs perform arithmetic calculations. The arithmetic operators are + (addition), - (subtraction, * (multiplication), / (division) and % (remainder).
- Integer division yields an integer quotient.
- The remainder operator, %, yields the remainder after division.
- Arithmetic expressions in Java must be written in straight-line form.
- If an expression contains nested parentheses, the innermost set of parentheses is evaluated first.
- Java applies the operators in arithmetic expressions in a precise sequence determined by the rules of operator precedence.
- When we say that operators are applied from left to right, we are referring to their associativity. Some operators associate from right to left.
- Redundant parentheses in an expression can make an expression clearer.
- A condition is an expression that can be either true or false. Java's if statement allows a program to make a decision based on the value of a condition.
- Conditions in if statements can be formed by using the equality (== and !=) and relational (>, <, >= and <=) operators.
- An if statement always begins with keyword if, followed by a condition in parentheses, and expects one statement in its body.
- The empty statement is a statement that does not perform a task.

Terminology

addition operator (+)
application
argument
arithmetic operators (*, /, %, + and -)
assignment operator (=)
assignment statement
associativity of operators
backslash (\) escape character
binary operator
body of a class declaration
body of a method declaration
built-in type
case sensitive
char primitive type
character string
class declaration
class file
.class file extension
class keyword
class name
comma (,)
comma-separated list
command line
Command Prompt
command window
comment
compilation error
compiler error
compile-time error
condition
%d format specifier
decision
division operator (/)
document a program
double primitive type
empty statement (;)
end-of-line comment (//)
equality operators
    == "is equal to"
    != "is not equal to"
escape character
escape sequence
false
fault tolerant
fixed text in a format string
float primitive type
format specifier
format string
identifier

if statement
import declaration
int (integer) primitive type
integer
integer division
Java API documentation
Java Application Programming Interface (API)
Java class library
.java file extension
java command
javadoc utility program
javadoc tool home page
java.lang package
Javadoc comment (/** */)
left brace ({)
literal
location of a variable
main method
memory location
message
method
modulus operator (%)
multiple-line comment (/* */)
MS-DOS prompt
multiplication operator (*)
name of a variable
nested parentheses
newline character (\n)
object
operand
operator
optional package
output cursor
package
parentheses ()
perform an action
precedence
primitive type
programmer-defined class
prompt
public keyword
redundant parentheses
relational operators
    < "is less than"
    <= "is less than or equal to"
    > "is greater than"
    >= "is greater than or equal to"
remainder operator (%)
reserved words

right brace (})	`System.in` (standard input) object
rules of operator precedence	`System.out` (standard output) object
%s format specifier	`System.out.print` method
Scanner class	`System.out.printf` method
self-documenting	`System.out.println` method
semicolon (;)	terminal window
shell	traditional comment (/* */)
single-line comment (//)	true
size of a variable	type of a variable
standard input object (`System.in`)	user-defined class
standard output object (`System.out`)	variable
statement	variable declaration
straight-line form	variable declaration statement
string	variable name
string literal	variable value
subtraction operator (-)	void keyword
syntax error	white space
System class	white-space characters

Self-Review Exercises

2.1 Fill in the blanks in each of the following statements:

a) A(n) _____ begins the body of every method, and a(n) _____ ends the body of every method.

b) Every statement ends with a(n) _____.

c) The _____ statement is used to make decisions.

d) _____ begins an end-of-line comment.

e) _____, _____, _____ and _____ are called white space.

f) _____ are reserved for use by Java.

g) Java applications begin execution at method _____.

h) Methods _____, _____ and _____ display information in the command window.

2.2 State whether each of the following is *true* or *false*. If *false*, explain why.

a) Comments cause the computer to print the text after the // on the screen when the program executes.

b) All variables must be given a type when they are declared.

c) Java considers the variables `number` and `NuMbEr` to be identical.

d) The remainder operator (%) can be used only with integer operands.

e) The arithmetic operators *, /, %, + and - all have the same level of precedence.

2.3 Write statements to accomplish each of the following tasks:

a) Declare variables `c`, `thisIsAVariable`, `q76354` and `number` to be of type `int`.

b) Prompt the user to enter an integer.

c) Input an integer and assign the result to int variable `value`. Assume Scanner variable `input` can be used to read a value from the keyboard.

d) If the variable `number` is not equal to 7, display `"The variable number is not equal to 7"`.

e) Print `"This is a Java program"` on one line in the command window.

f) Print `"This is a Java program"` on two lines in the command window. The first line should end with Java. Use method `System.out.println`.

g) Print `"This is a Java program"` on two lines in the command window. The first line should end with Java. Use method `System.out.printf` and two %s format specifiers.

2.4 Identify and correct the errors in each of the following statements:

a) `if ( c < 7 );`
   `    System.out.println( "c is less than 7" );`

b) `if ( c => 7 )`
   `    System.out.println( "c is equal to or greater than 7" );`

2.5 Write declarations, statements or comments that accomplish each of the following tasks:

a) State that a program will calculate the product of three integers.
b) Create a `Scanner` that reads values from the standard input.
c) Declare the variables x, y, z and `result` to be of type `int`.
d) Prompt the user to enter the first integer.
e) Read the first integer from the user and store it in the variable x.
f) Prompt the user to enter the second integer.
g) Read the second integer from the user and store it in the variable y.
h) Prompt the user to enter the third integer.
i) Read the third integer from the user and store it in the variable z.
j) Compute the product of the three integers contained in variables x, y and z, and assign the result to the variable `result`.
k) Display the message `"Product is"` followed by the value of the variable `result`.

2.6 Using the statements you wrote in Exercise 2.5, write a complete program that calculates and prints the product of three integers.

Answers to Self-Review Exercises

2.1 a) left brace (`{`), right brace (`}`). b) semicolon (`;`). c) `if`. d) `//`. e) Blank lines, space characters, newline characters and tab characters. f) Keywords. g) `main`. h) `System.out.print`, `System.out.println` and `System.out.printf`.

2.2 a) False. Comments do not cause any action to be performed when the program executes. They are used to document programs and improve their readability.
b) True.
c) False. Java is case sensitive, so these variables are distinct.
d) False. The remainder operator can also be used with noninteger operands in Java.
e) False. The operators *, / and % are on the same level of precedence, and the operators + and - are on a lower level of precedence.

2.3 a) `int c, thisIsAVariable, q76354, number;`
   or
   `int c;`
   `int thisIsAVariable;`
   `int q76354;`
   `int number;`
b) `System.out.print( "Enter an integer: " );`
c) `value = input.nextInt();`
d) `if ( number != 7 )`
   `    System.out.println( "The variable number is not equal to 7" );`
e) `System.out.println( "This is a Java program" );`
f) `System.out.println( "This is a Java\nprogram" );`
g) `System.out.printf( "%s\n%s\n", "This is a Java", "program" );`

2.4 The solutions to Self-Review Exercise 2.4 are as follows:
a) Error: Semicolon after the right parenthesis of the condition (c < 7) in the `if`. Correction: Remove the semicolon after the right parenthesis. [*Note*: As a result, the output statement will execute regardless of whether the condition in the `if` is true.]
b) Error: The relational operator => is incorrect. Correction: Change => to >=.

2.5   a) // Calculate the product of three integers
      b) `Scanner input = new Scanner( System.in );`
      c) `int x, y, z, result;`
        or
        `int x;`
        `int y;`
        `int z;`
        `int result;`
      d) `System.out.print( "Enter first integer: " );`
      e) `x = input.nextInt();`
      f) `System.out.print( "Enter second integer: " );`
      g) `y = input.nextInt();`
      h) `System.out.print( "Enter third integer: " );`
      i) `z = input.nextInt();`
      j) `result = x * y * z;`
      k) `System.out.printf( "Product is %d\n", result );`

2.6   The solution to Exercise 2.6 is as follows:

```
 1   // Ex. 2.6: Product.java
 2   // Calculate the product of three integers.
 3   import java.util.Scanner; // program uses Scanner
 4
 5   public class Product
 6   {
 7      public static void main( String args[] )
 8      {
 9         // create Scanner to obtain input from command window
10         Scanner input = new Scanner( System.in );
11
12         int x; // first number input by user
13         int y; // second number input by user
14         int z; // third number input by user
15         int result; // product of numbers
16
17         System.out.print( "Enter first integer: " ); // prompt for input
18         x = input.nextInt(); // read first integer
19
20         System.out.print( "Enter second integer: " ); // prompt for input
21         y = input.nextInt(); // read second integer
22
23         System.out.print( "Enter third integer: " ); // prompt for input
24         z = input.nextInt(); // read third integer
25
26         result = x * y * z; // calculate product of numbers
27
28         System.out.printf( "Product is %d\n", result );
29
30      } // end method main
31
32   } // end class Product
```

```
Enter first integer: 10
Enter second integer: 20
Enter third integer: 30
Product is 6000
```

Exercises

2.7 Fill in the blanks in each of the following statements:

a) _____ are used to document a program and improve its readability.

b) A decision can be made in a Java program with a(n) _____.

c) Calculations are normally performed by _____ statements.

d) The arithmetic operators with the same precedence as multiplication are _____ and _____.

e) When parentheses in an arithmetic expression are nested, the _____ set of parentheses is evaluated first.

f) A location in the computer's memory that may contain different values at various times throughout the execution of a program is called a(n) _____.

2.8 Write Java statements that accomplish each of the following tasks:

a) Display the message "Enter an integer: ", leaving the cursor on the same line.

b) Assign the product of variables b and c to variable a.

c) State that a program performs a sample payroll calculation (i.e., use text that helps to document a program).

2.9 State whether each of the following is *true* or *false*. If *false*, explain why.

a) Java operators are evaluated from left to right.

b) The following are all valid variable names: _under_bar_, m928134, t5, j7, her_sales$, his_$account_total, a, b$, c, z and z2.

c) A valid Java arithmetic expression with no parentheses is evaluated from left to right.

d) The following are all invalid variable names: 3g, 87, 67h2, h22 and 2h.

2.10 Assuming that x = 2 and y = 3, what does each of the following statements display?

a) `System.out.printf( "x = %d\n", x );`

b) `System.out.printf( "Value of %d + %d is %d\n", x, x, ( x + x ) );`

c) `System.out.printf( "x =" );`

d) `System.out.printf( "%d = %d\n", ( x + y ), ( y + x ) );`

2.11 Which of the following Java statements contain variables whose values are modified?

a) `p = i + j + k + 7;`

b) `System.out.println( "variables whose values are destroyed" );`

c) `System.out.println( "a = 5" );`

d) `value = input.nextInt();`

2.12 Given that $y = ax^3 + 7$, which of the following are correct Java statements for this equation?

a) `y = a * x * x * x + 7;`

b) `y = a * x * x * ( x + 7 );`

c) `y = ( a * x ) * x * ( x + 7 );`

d) `y = ( a * x ) * x * x + 7;`

e) `y = a * ( x * x * x ) + 7;`

f) `y = a * x * ( x * x + 7 );`

2.13 State the order of evaluation of the operators in each of the following Java statements, and show the value of x after each statement is performed:

```
a) x = 7 + 3 * 6 / 2 - 1;
b) x = 2 % 2 + 2 * 2 - 2 / 2;
c) x = ( 3 * 9 * ( 3 + ( 9 * 3 / ( 3 ) ) ) );
```

2.14   Write an application that displays the numbers 1 to 4 on the same line, with each pair of adjacent numbers separated by one space. Write the program using the following techniques:

a) Use one `System.out.println` statement.
b) Use four `System.out.print` statements.
c) Use one `System.out.printf` statement.

2.15   Write an application that asks the user to enter two integers, obtains them from the user and prints their sum, product, difference and quotient (division). Use the techniques shown in Fig. 2.7.

2.16   Write an application that asks the user to enter two integers, obtains them from the user and displays the larger number followed by the words "is larger". If the numbers are equal, print the message "These numbers are equal." Use the techniques shown in Fig. 2.15.

2.17   Write an application that inputs three integers from the user and displays the sum, average, product, smallest and largest of the numbers. Use the techniques shown in Fig. 2.15. [*Note*: The calculation of the average in this exercise should result in an integer representation of the average. So if the sum of the values is 7, the average should be 2, not 2.3333....]

2.18   Write an application that displays a box, an oval, an arrow and a diamond using asterisks (*), as follows:

```
*********        ***           *            *
*       *      *     *       ***          *   *
*       *     *       *     *****        *     *
*       *     *       *       *         *       *
*       *     *       *       *        *         *
*       *     *       *       *         *       *
*       *     *       *       *          *     *
*       *     *       *       *           *   *
*       *      *     *       *              *
*********        ***           *            *
```

2.19   What does the following code print?

```
System.out.println( "*\n**\n***\n****\n*****" );
```

2.20   What does the following code print?

```
System.out.println( "*" );
System.out.println( "***" );
System.out.println( "*****" );
System.out.println( "****" );
System.out.println( "**" );
```

2.21   What does the following code print?

```
System.out.print( "*" );
System.out.print( "***" );
System.out.print( "*****" );
System.out.print( "****" );
System.out.println( "**" );
```

2.22 What does the following code print?

```
System.out.print( "*" );
System.out.println( "***" );
System.out.println( "*****" );
System.out.print( "****" );
System.out.println( "**" );
```

2.23 What does the following code print?

```
System.out.printf( "%s\n%s\n%s\n", "*", "***", "*****" );
```

2.24 Write an application that reads five integers, determines and prints the largest and smallest integers in the group. Use only the programming techniques you learned in this chapter.

2.25 Write an application that reads an integer and determines and prints whether it is odd or even. [*Hint*: Use the remainder operator. An even number is a multiple of 2. Any multiple of 2 leaves a remainder of 0 when divided by 2.]

2.26 Write an application that reads two integers, determines whether the first is a multiple of the second and prints the result. [*Hint*: Use the remainder operator.]

2.27 Write an application that displays a checkerboard pattern, as follows:

```
* * * * * * * *
 * * * * * * * *
* * * * * * * *
 * * * * * * * *
* * * * * * * *
 * * * * * * * *
* * * * * * * *
 * * * * * * * *
```

2.28 Here's a peek ahead. In this chapter, you have learned about integers and the type `int`. Java can also represent floating-point numbers that contain decimal points, such as 3.14159. Write an application that inputs from the user the radius of a circle as an integer and prints the circle's diameter, circumference and area using the floating-point value 3.14159 for π. Use the techniques shown in Fig. 2.7. [*Note*: You may also use the predefined constant `Math.PI` for the value of π. This constant is more precise than the value 3.14159. Class `Math` is defined in package `java.lang`. Classes in that package are imported automatically, so you do not need to `import` class `Math` to use it.] Use the following formulas (*r* is the radius):

$$diameter = 2r$$
$$circumference = 2\pi r$$
$$area = \pi r^2$$

Do not store the results of each calculation in a variable. Rather, specify each calculation as the value that will be output in a `System.out.printf` statement. Note that the values produced by the circumference and area calculations are floating-point numbers. Such values can be output with the format specifier `%f` in a `System.out.printf` statement. You will learn more about floating-point numbers in Chapter 3.

2.29 Here's another peek ahead. In this chapter, you have learned about integers and the type `int`. Java can also represent uppercase letters, lowercase letters and a considerable variety of special symbols. Every character has a corresponding integer representation. The set of characters a computer uses and the corresponding integer representations for those characters is called that computer's character set. You can indicate a character value in a program simply by enclosing that character in single quotes, as in 'A'.

You can determine the integer equivalent of a character by preceding that character with (int), as in

```
(int) 'A'
```

This form is called a cast operator. (You will learn about cast operators in Chapter 4.) The following statement outputs a character and its integer equivalent:

```
System.out.printf(
    "The character %c has the value %d\n", 'A', ( (int) 'A' ) );
```

When the preceding statement executes, it displays the character A and the value 65 (from the so-called Unicode® character set) as part of the string. Note that the format specifier %c is a place-holder for a character (in this case, the character 'A').

Using statements similar to the one shown earlier in this exercise, write an application that displays the integer equivalents of some uppercase letters, lowercase letters, digits and special symbols. Display the integer equivalents of the following: A B C a b c 0 1 2 $ * + / and the blank character.

2.30   Write an application that inputs one number consisting of five digits from the user, separates the number into its individual digits and prints the digits separated from one another by three spaces each. For example, if the user types in the number 42339, the program should print

```
4   2   3   3   9
```

Assume that the user enters the correct number of digits. What happens when you execute the program and type a number with more than five digits? What happens when you execute the program and type a number with fewer than five digits? [*Hint*: It is possible to do this exercise with the techniques you learned in this chapter. You will need to use both division and remainder operations to "pick off" each digit.]

2.31   Using only the programming techniques you learned in this chapter, write an application that calculates the squares and cubes of the numbers from 0 to 10 and prints the resulting values in table format, as shown below. [*Note:* This program does not require any input from the user.]

```
number   square   cube
0        0        0
1        1        1
2        4        8
3        9        27
4        16       64
5        25       125
6        36       216
7        49       343
8        64       512
9        81       729
10       100      1000
```

2.32   Write a program that inputs five numbers and determines and prints the number of negative numbers input, the number of positive numbers input and the number of zeros input.

Introduction to Classes and Objects

OBJECTIVES

In this chapter you will learn:

- What classes, objects, methods and instance variables are.

- How to declare a class and use it to create an object.

- How to declare methods in a class to implement the class's behaviors.

- How to declare instance variables in a class to implement the class's attributes.

- How to call an object's method to make that method perform its task.

- The differences between instance variables of a class and local variables of a method.

- How to use a constructor to ensure that an object's data is initialized when the object is created.

- The differences between primitive and reference types.

3.1   Introduction

We introduced the basic terminology and concepts of object-oriented programming in Section 1.16. In Chapter 2, you began to use those concepts to create simple applications that displayed messages to the user, obtained information from the user, performed calculations and made decisions. One common feature of every application in Chapter 2 was that all the statements that performed tasks were located in method `main`. Typically, the applications you develop in this book will consist of two or more classes, each containing one or more methods. If you become part of a development team in industry, you might work on applications that contain hundreds, or even thousands, of classes. In this chapter, we present a simple framework for organizing object-oriented applications in Java.

First, we motivate the notion of classes with a real-world example. Then we present five complete working applications to demonstrate creating and using your own classes. The first four of these examples begin our case study on developing a grade-book class that instructors can use to maintain student test scores. This case study is enhanced over the next several chapters, culminating with the version presented in Chapter 7, Arrays. The last example in the chapter introduces floating-point numbers—that is, numbers containing decimal points, such as 0.0345, –7.23 and 100.7—in the context of a bank account class that maintains a customer's balance.

3.2   Classes, Objects, Methods and Instance Variables

Let's begin with a simple analogy to help you understand classes and their contents. Suppose you want to drive a car and make it go faster by pressing down on its accelerator pedal. What must happen before you can do this? Well, before you can drive a car, someone has to design the car. A car typically begins as engineering drawings, similar to the blueprints used to design a house. These engineering drawings include the design for an accelerator pedal to make the car go faster. The pedal "hides" the complex mechanisms that actually make the car go faster, just as the brake pedal "hides" the mechanisms that slow the car and the steering wheel "hides" the mechanisms that turn the car. This enables people with little or no knowledge of how engines work to drive a car easily.

Unfortunately, you cannot drive the engineering drawings of a car. Before you can drive a car, the car must be built from the engineering drawings that describe it. A completed car will have an actual accelerator pedal to make the car go faster, but even that's not enough—the car will not accelerate on its own, so the driver must press the accelerator pedal.

Now let's use our car example to introduce the key programming concepts of this section. Performing a task in a program requires a method. The method describes the mechanisms that actually perform its tasks. The method hides from its user the complex tasks that it performs, just as the accelerator pedal of a car hides from the driver the complex mechanisms of making the car go faster. In Java, we begin by creating a program unit called a class to house a method, just as a car's engineering drawings house the design of an accelerator pedal. In a class, you provide one or more methods that are designed to perform the class's tasks. For example, a class that represents a bank account might contain one method to deposit money to an account, another to withdraw money from an account and a third to inquire what the current balance is.

Just as you cannot drive an engineering drawing of a car, you cannot "drive" a class. Just as someone has to build a car from its engineering drawings before you can actually drive a car, you must build an object of a class before you can get a program to perform the tasks the class describes how to do. That is one reason Java is known as an object-oriented programming language.

When you drive a car, pressing its gas pedal sends a message to the car to perform a task—that is, make the car go faster. Similarly, you send messages to an object—each message is known as a method call and tells a method of the object to perform its task.

Thus far, we have used the car analogy to introduce classes, objects and methods. In addition to the capabilities a car provides, it also has many attributes, such as its color, the number of doors, the amount of gas in its tank, its current speed and its total miles driven (i.e., its odometer reading). Like the car's capabilities, these attributes are represented as part of a car's design in its engineering diagrams. As you drive a car, these attributes are always associated with the car. Every car maintains its own attributes. For example, each car knows how much gas is in its own gas tank, but not how much is in the tanks of other cars. Similarly, an object has attributes that are carried with the object as it is used in a program. These attributes are specified as part of the object's class. For example, a bank account object has a balance attribute that represents the amount of money in the account. Each bank account object knows the balance in the account it represents, but not the balances of the other accounts in the bank. Attributes are specified by the class's instance variables.

The remainder of this chapter presents examples that demonstrate the concepts we introduced in the context of the car analogy. The first four examples, summarized below, incrementally build a GradeBook class to demonstrate these concepts:

1. The first example presents a GradeBook class with one method that simply displays a welcome message when it is called. We then show how to create an object of that class and call the method so that it displays the welcome message.

2. The second example modifies the first by allowing the method to receive a course name as an argument and by displaying the name as part of the welcome message.

3. The third example shows how to store the course name in a GradeBook object. For this version of the class, we also show how to use methods to set the course name and obtain the course name.

4. The fourth example demonstrates how the data in a GradeBook object can be initialized when the object is created—the initialization is performed by the class's constructor.

The last example in the chapter presents an Account class that reinforces the concepts presented in the first four examples and introduces floating-point numbers—numbers containing decimal points, such as 0.0345, –7.23 and 100.7. For this purpose, we present an Account class that represents a bank account and maintains its balance as a floating-point number. The class contains two methods—one that credits a deposit to the account, thus increasing the balance, and another that retrieves the balance. The class's constructor allows the balance of each Account object to be initialized as the object is created. We create two Account objects and make deposits into each to show that each object maintains its own balance. The example also demonstrates how to input and display floating-point numbers.

3.3 Declaring a Class with a Method and Instantiating an Object of a Class

We begin with an example that consists of classes GradeBook (Fig. 3.1) and GradeBook-Test (Fig. 3.2). Class GradeBook (declared in file GradeBook.java) will be used to display a message on the screen (Fig. 3.2) welcoming the instructor to the grade-book application. Class GradeBookTest (declared in file GradeBookTest.java) is an application class in which the main method will use class GradeBook. Each class declaration that begins with keyword public must be stored in a file that has the same name as the class and ends with the .java file-name extension. Thus, classes GradeBook and GradeBookTest must be declared in separate files, because each class is declared public.

 Common Programming Error 3.1

Declaring more than one public class in the same file is a compilation error.

Class *GradeBook*

The GradeBook class declaration (Fig. 3.1) contains a displayMessage method (lines 7–10) that displays a message on the screen. Line 9 of the class performs the work of displaying the message. Recall that a class is like a blueprint—we'll need to make an object of this class and call its method to get line 9 to execute and display its message.

```
1   // Fig. 3.1: GradeBook.java
2   // Class declaration with one method.
3
4   public class GradeBook
5   {
6      // display a welcome message to the GradeBook user
7      public void displayMessage()
8      {
9         System.out.println( "Welcome to the Grade Book!" );
10     } // end method displayMessage
11
12  } // end class GradeBook
```

Fig. 3.1 | Class declaration with one method.

The class declaration begins at line 4. The keyword `public` is an **access modifier**. For now, we will simply declare every class `public`. Every class declaration contains keyword `class` followed immediately by the class's name. Every class's body is enclosed in a pair of left and right braces ({ and }), as in lines 5 and 12 of class `GradeBook`.

In Chapter 2, each class we declared had one method named `main`. Class `GradeBook` also has one method—`displayMessage` (lines 7–10). Recall that `main` is a special method that is always called automatically by the Java Virtual Machine (JVM) when you execute an application. Most methods do not get called automatically. As you will soon see, you must call method `displayMessage` to tell it to perform its task.

The method declaration begins with keyword `public` to indicate that the method is "available to the public"—that is, it can be called from outside the class declaration's body by methods of other classes. Keyword `void` indicates that this method will perform a task but will not return (i.e., give back) any information to its **calling method** when it completes its task. You have already used methods that return information—for example, in Chapter 2 you used `Scanner` method `nextInt` to input an integer typed by the user at the keyboard. When `nextInt` inputs a value, it returns that value for use in the program.

The name of the method, `displayMessage`, follows the return type. By convention, method names begin with a lowercase first letter and all subsequent words in the name begin with a capital letter. The parentheses after the method name indicate that this is a method. An empty set of parentheses, as shown in line 7, indicates that this method does not require additional information to perform its task. Line 7 is commonly referred to as the **method header**. Every method's body is delimited by left and right braces ({ and }), as in lines 8 and 10.

The body of a method contains statement(s) that perform the method's task. In this case, the method contains one statement (line 9) that displays the message `"Welcome to the Grade Book!"` followed by a newline in the command window. After this statement executes, the method has completed its task.

Next, we'd like to use class `GradeBook` in an application. As you learned in Chapter 2, method `main` begins the execution of every application. A class that contains method `main` is a Java application. Such a class is special because the JVM can use `main` to begin execution. Class `GradeBook` is not an application because it does not contain `main`. Therefore, if you try to execute `GradeBook` by typing `java GradeBook` in the command window, you will get the error message:

```
Exception in thread "main" java.lang.NoSuchMethodError: main
```

This was not a problem in Chapter 2, because every class you declared had a `main` method. To fix this problem for the `GradeBook`, we must either declare a separate class that contains a `main` method or place a `main` method in class `GradeBook`. To help you prepare for the larger programs you will encounter later in this book and in industry, we use a separate class (`GradeBookTest` in this example) containing method `main` to test each new class we create in this chapter.

Class *GradeBookTest*

The `GradeBookTest` class declaration (Fig. 3.2) contains the `main` method that will control our application's execution. Any class that contains `main` declared as shown on line 7 can be used to execute an application. This class declaration begins at line 4 and ends at line 16. The class contains only a `main` method, which is typical of many classes that begin an application's execution.

```
 1   // Fig. 3.2: GradeBookTest.java
 2   // Create a GradeBook object and call its displayMessage method.
 3
 4   public class GradeBookTest
 5   {
 6      // main method begins program execution
 7      public static void main( String args[] )
 8      {
 9         // create a GradeBook object and assign it to myGradeBook
10         GradeBook myGradeBook = new GradeBook();
11
12         // call myGradeBook's displayMessage method
13         myGradeBook.displayMessage();
14      } // end main
15
16   } // end class GradeBookTest
```

```
Welcome to the Grade Book!
```

Fig. 3.2 | Creating an object of class `GradeBook` and calling its `displayMessage` method.

Lines 7–14 declare method `main`. Recall from Chapter 2 that the `main` header must appear as shown in line 7; otherwise, the application will not execute. A key part of enabling the JVM to locate and call method `main` to begin the application's execution is the `static` keyword (line 7), which indicates that `main` is a `static` method. A `static` method is special because it can be called without first creating an object of the class in which the method is declared. We thoroughly explain `static` methods in Chapter 6, Methods: A Deeper Look.

In this application, we'd like to call class `GradeBook`'s `displayMessage` method to display the welcome message in the command window. Typically, you cannot call a method that belongs to another class until you create an object of that class, as shown in line 10. We begin by declaring variable `myGradeBook`. Note that the variable's type is `GradeBook`—the class we declared in Fig. 3.1. Each new class you create becomes a new type in Java that can be used to declare variables and create objects. Programmers can declare new class types as needed; this is one reason why Java is known as an **extensible language**.

Variable `myGradeBook` is initialized with the result of the **class instance creation expression** `new GradeBook()`. Keyword `new` creates a new object of the class specified to the right of the keyword (i.e., `GradeBook`). The parentheses to the right of the `GradeBook` are required. As you will learn in Section 3.7, those parentheses in combination with a class name represent a call to a constructor, which is similar to a method, but is used only at the time an object is created to initialize the object's data. In that section you will see that data can be placed in parentheses to specify initial values for the object's data. For now, we simply leave the parentheses empty.

Just as we can use object `System.out` to call methods `print`, `printf` and `println`, we can now use `myGradeBook` to call method `displayMessage`. Line 13 calls the method `displayMessage` (declared at lines 7–10 of Fig. 3.1) using variable `myGradeBook` followed by a **dot separator** (`.`), the method name `displayMessage` and an empty set of parentheses. This call causes the `displayMessage` method to perform its task. This method call differs from the method calls in Chapter 2 that displayed information in a command window—

each of those method calls provided arguments that specified the data to display. At the beginning of line 13, "myGradeBook." indicates that main should use the GradeBook object that was created on line 10. Line 7 of Fig. 3.1 indicates that method displayMessage has an empty parameter list—that is, displayMessage does not require additional information to perform its task. For this reason, the method call (line 13 of Fig. 3.2) specifies an empty set of parentheses after the method name to indicate that no arguments are being passed to method displayMessage. When method displayMessage completes its task, method main continues executing at line 14. This is the end of method main, so the program terminates.

Compiling an Application with Multiple Classes

You must compile the classes in Fig. 3.1 and Fig. 3.2 before you can execute the application. First, change to the directory that contains the application's source-code files. Next, type the command

```
javac GradeBook.java GradeBookTest.java
```

to compile both classes at once. If the directory containing the application includes only the files for this application, you can compile all the classes in the directory with the command

```
javac *.java
```

The asterisk (*) in *.java indicates that all files in the current directory that end with the file name extension ".java" should be compiled.

UML Class Diagram for Class GradeBook

Figure 3.3 presents a UML class diagram for class GradeBook of Fig. 3.1. Recall from Section 1.16 that the UML is a graphical language used by programmers to represent their object-oriented systems in a standardized manner. In the UML, each class is modeled in a class diagram as a rectangle with three compartments. The top compartment contains the name of the class centered horizontally in boldface type. The middle compartment contains the class's attributes, which correspond to instance variables in Java. In Fig. 3.3, the middle compartment is empty because the version of class GradeBook in Fig. 3.1 does not have any attributes. The bottom compartment contains the class's operations, which correspond to methods in Java. The UML models operations by listing the operation name followed by a set of parentheses. Class GradeBook has one method, displayMessage, so the bottom compartment of Fig. 3.3 lists one operation with this name. Method displayMessage does not require additional information to perform its tasks, so the parentheses following displayMessage in the class diagram are empty, just as they were in the method's declaration in line 7 of Fig. 3.1. The plus sign (+) in front of the operation name indicates that displayMessage is a public operation in the UML (i.e., a public method in Java). We will often use UML class diagrams to summarize a class's attributes and operations.

Fig. 3.3 | UML class diagram indicating that class GradeBook has a public displayMessage operation.

3.4 Declaring a Method with a Parameter

In our car analogy from Section 3.2, we discussed the fact that pressing a car's gas pedal sends a message to the car to perform a task—make the car go faster. But how fast should the car accelerate? As you know, the farther down you press the pedal, the faster the car accelerates. So the message to the car actually includes the task to perform and additional information that helps the car perform the task. This additional information is known as a parameter—the value of the parameter helps the car determine how fast to accelerate. Similarly, a method can require one or more parameters that represent additional information it needs to perform its task. A method call supplies values—called arguments—for each of the method's parameters. For example, the method System.out.println requires an argument that specifies the data to output in a command window. Similarly, to make a deposit into a bank account, a deposit method specifies a parameter that represents the deposit amount. When the deposit method is called, an argument value representing the deposit amount is assigned to the method's parameter. The method then makes a deposit of that amount.

Our next example declares class GradeBook (Fig. 3.4) with a displayMessage method that displays the course name as part of the welcome message. (See the sample execution in Fig. 3.5.) The new displayMessage method requires a parameter that represents the course name to output.

Before discussing the new features of class GradeBook, let's see how the new class is used from the main method of class GradeBookTest (Fig. 3.5). Line 12 creates a Scanner named input for reading the course name from the user. Line 15 creates an object of class GradeBook and assigns it to variable myGradeBook. Line 18 prompts the user to enter a course name. Line 19 reads the name from the user and assigns it to the nameOfCourse variable, using Scanner method nextLine to perform the input. The user types the course name and presses *Enter* to submit the course name to the program. Note that pressing *Enter* inserts a newline character at the end of the characters typed by the user. Method nextLine reads characters typed by the user until the newline character is encountered, then returns a String containing the characters up to, but not including, the newline. The newline character is discarded. Note that Scanner provides a similar method—next—that reads individual words. When the user presses *Enter* after typing input, method next reads characters until a white-space character (such as a space, tab or newline) is encountered,

```java
 1   // Fig. 3.4: GradeBook.java
 2   // Class declaration with a method that has a parameter.
 3
 4   public class GradeBook
 5   {
 6      // display a welcome message to the GradeBook user
 7      public void displayMessage( String courseName )
 8      {
 9         System.out.printf( "Welcome to the grade book for\n%s!\n",
10            courseName );
11      } // end method displayMessage
12
13   } // end class GradeBook
```

Fig. 3.4 | Class declaration with one method that has a parameter.

```java
1   // Fig. 3.5: GradeBookTest.java
2   // Create GradeBook object and pass a String to
3   // its displayMessage method.
4   import java.util.Scanner; // program uses Scanner
5
6   public class GradeBookTest
7   {
8      // main method begins program execution
9      public static void main( String args[] )
10     {
11         // create Scanner to obtain input from command window
12         Scanner input = new Scanner( System.in );
13
14         // create a GradeBook object and assign it to myGradeBook
15         GradeBook myGradeBook = new GradeBook();
16
17         // prompt for and input course name
18         System.out.println( "Please enter the course name:" );
19         String nameOfCourse = input.nextLine(); // read a line of text
20         System.out.println(); // outputs a blank line
21
22         // call myGradeBook's displayMessage method
23         // and pass nameOfCourse as an argument
24         myGradeBook.displayMessage( nameOfCourse );
25     } // end main
26
27  } // end class GradeBookTest
```

```
Please enter the course name:
CS101 Introduction to Java Programming

Welcome to the grade book for
CS101 Introduction to Java Programming!
```

Fig. 3.5 | Creating a GradeBook object and passing a String to its displayMessage method.

then returns a String containing the characters up to, but not including, the white-space character (which is discarded). All information after the first white-space character is not lost—it can be read by other statements that call the Scanner's methods later in the program.

Line 24 calls myGradeBooks's displayMessage method. The variable nameOfCourse in parentheses is the argument that is passed to method displayMessage so that the method can perform its task. The value of variable nameOfCourse in main becomes the value of method displayMessage's parameter courseName in line 7 of Fig. 3.4. When you execute this application, notice that method displayMessage outputs the name you type as part of the welcome message (Fig. 3.5).

Software Engineering Observation 3.1

Normally, objects are created with new. One exception is a string literal that is contained in quotes, such as "hello". String literals are references to String objects that are implicitly created by Java.

More on Arguments and Parameters

When you declare a method, you must specify in the method's declaration whether the method requires data to perform its task. To do so, you place additional information in the method's parameter list, which is located in the parentheses that follow the method name. The parameter list may contain any number of parameters, including none at all. Empty parentheses following the method name (as in Fig. 3.1, line 7) indicate that a method does not require any parameters. In Fig. 3.4, displayMessage's parameter list (line 7) declares that the method requires one parameter. Each parameter must specify a type and an identifier. In this case, the type String and the identifier courseName indicate that method displayMessage requires a String to perform its task. At the time the method is called, the argument value in the call is assigned to the corresponding parameter (in this case, courseName) in the method header. Then, the method body uses the parameter courseName to access the value. Lines 9–10 of Fig. 3.4 display parameter courseName's value, using the %s format specifier in printf's format string. Note that the parameter variable's name (Fig. 3.4, line 7) can be the same or different from the argument variable's name (Fig. 3.5, line 24).

A method can specify multiple parameters by separating each parameter from the next with a comma (we'll see an example of this in Chapter 6). The number of arguments in a method call must match the number of parameters in the parameter list of the called method's declaration. Also, the argument types in the method call must be consistent with the types of the corresponding parameters in the method's declaration. (As you will learn in subsequent chapters, an argument's type and its corresponding parameter's type are not always required to be identical.) In our example, the method call passes one argument of type String (nameOfCourse is declared as a String on line 19 of Fig. 3.5) and the method declaration specifies one parameter of type String (line 7 in Fig. 3.4). So the type of the argument in the method call exactly matches the type of the parameter in the method header.

Common Programming Error 3.2

A compilation error occurs if the number of arguments in a method call does not match the number of parameters in the method declaration.

Common Programming Error 3.3

A compilation error occurs if the types of the arguments in a method call are not consistent with the types of the corresponding parameters in the method declaration.

*Updated UML Class Diagram for Class **GradeBook***

The UML class diagram of Fig. 3.6 models class GradeBook of Fig. 3.4. Like Fig. 3.1, this GradeBook class contains public operation displayMessage. However, this version of dis-

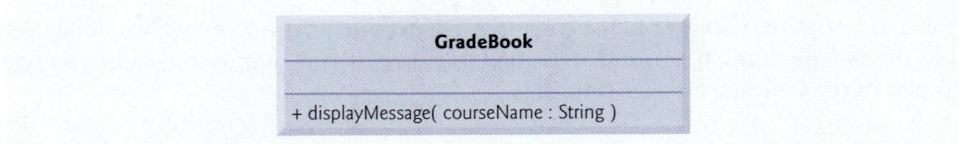

Fig. 3.6 | UML class diagram indicating that class GradeBook has a displayMessage operation with a courseName parameter of UML type String.

playMessage has a parameter. The UML models a parameter a bit differently from Java by listing the parameter name, followed by a colon and the parameter type in the parentheses following the operation name. The UML has its own data types similar to those of Java (but as you will see, not all the UML data types have the same names as the corresponding Java types). The UML type String does correspond to the Java type String. Method displayMessage of class GradeBook (Fig. 3.4) has a String parameter named courseName, so Fig. 3.6 lists courseName : String between the parentheses following displayMessage.

Notes on *import* Declarations

Notice the import declaration in Fig. 3.5 (line 4). This indicates to the compiler that the program uses class Scanner. Why do we need to import class Scanner, but not class System, String or class GradeBook? Most classes you will use in Java programs must be imported. Classes System and String are in package java.lang, which is implicitly imported into every Java program. Thus, all programs can use package java.lang's classes without explicitly importing them.

There is a special relationship between classes that are compiled in the same directory on disk, like classes GradeBook and GradeBookTest. By default, such classes are considered to be in the same package—known as the default package. Classes in the same package are implicitly imported into the source code files of other classes in the same package. Thus, an import declaration is not required when one class in a package uses another in the same package—such as when class GradeBookTest uses class GradeBook.

Actually, the import declaration at line 4 is not required if we always refer to class Scanner as java.util.Scanner, which includes the full package name and class name. This is known as the class's fully qualified class name. For example, line 12 could be written as

```
java.util.Scanner input = new java.util.Scanner( System.in );
```

Software Engineering Observation 3.2

The Java compiler does not require import declarations in a Java source code file if the fully qualified class name is specified every time a class name is used in the source code. But most Java programmers consider using fully qualified names to be cumbersome, and instead prefer to use import declarations.

3.5 Instance Variables, *set* Methods and *get* Methods

In Chapter 2, we declared all of an application's variables in the application's main method. Variables declared in the body of a particular method are known as local variables and can be used only in that method. When that method terminates, the values of its local variables are lost. Recall from Section 3.2 that an object has attributes that are carried with the object as it is used in a program. Such attributes exist before a method is called on an object and after the method completes execution.

A class normally consists of one or more methods that manipulate the attributes that belong to a particular object of the class. Attributes are represented as variables in a class declaration. Such variables are called fields and are declared inside a class declaration but outside the bodies of the class's method declarations. When each object of a class maintains its own copy of an attribute, the field that represents the attribute is also known as an instance variable—each object (instance) of the class has a separate instance of the variable in memory. The example in this section demonstrates a GradeBook class that contains a courseName instance variable to represent a particular GradeBook object's course name.

GradeBook Class with an Instance Variable, a set *Method and a* get *Method*

In our next application (Fig. 3.7–Fig. 3.8), class GradeBook (Fig. 3.7) maintains the course name as an instance variable so that it can be used or modified at any time during an application's execution. The class contains three methods—setCourseName, get-CourseName and displayMessage. Method setCourseName stores a course name in a GradeBook. Method getCourseName obtains a GradeBook's course name. Method displayMessage—which now specifies no parameters—still displays a welcome message that includes the course name. However, as you will see, the method now obtains the course name by calling another method in the same class—getCourseName.

A typical instructor teaches more than one course, each with its own course name. Line 7 declares that courseName is a variable of type String. Because the variable is declared in the body of the class (lines 6–30) but outside the bodies of the class's methods (lines 10–13, 16–19 and 22–28), line 7 is a declaration for an instance variable. Every instance (i.e., object) of class GradeBook contains one copy of each instance variable. For example, if there are two GradeBook objects, each object has its own copy of courseName

```java
1   // Fig. 3.7: GradeBook.java
2   // GradeBook class that contains a courseName instance variable
3   // and methods to set and get its value.
4
5   public class GradeBook
6   {
7      private String courseName; // course name for this GradeBook
8
9      // method to set the course name
10     public void setCourseName( String name )
11     {
12        courseName = name; // store the course name
13     } // end method setCourseName
14
15     // method to retrieve the course name
16     public String getCourseName()
17     {
18        return courseName;
19     } // end method getCourseName
20
21     // display a welcome message to the GradeBook user
22     public void displayMessage()
23     {
24        // this statement calls getCourseName to get the
25        // name of the course this GradeBook represents
26        System.out.printf( "Welcome to the grade book for\n%s!\n",
27           getCourseName() );
28     } // end method displayMessage
29
30  } // end class GradeBook
```

Fig. 3.7 | GradeBook class that contains a courseName instance variable.

(one per object). A benefit of making `courseName` an instance variable is that all the methods of the class (in this case, `GradeBook`) can manipulate any instance variables that appear in the class (in this case, `courseName`).

Access Modifiers **public** and **private**

Most instance variable declarations are preceded with the **private** keyword (as in line 7). Like `public`, keyword `private` is an access modifier. Variables or methods declared with access modifier `private` are accessible only to methods of the class in which they are declared. Thus, variable `courseName` can be used only in methods `setCourseName`, `get-CourseName` and `displayMessage` of (every object of) class `GradeBook`.

Software Engineering Observation 3.3

Precede every field and method declaration with an access modifier. As a rule of thumb, instance variables should be declared private *and methods should be declared* public. *(We will see that it is appropriate to declare certain methods* private, *if they will be accessed only by other methods of the class.)*

Good Programming Practice 3.1

We prefer to list the fields of a class first, so that, as you read the code, you see the names and types of the variables before you see them used in the methods of the class. It is possible to list the class's fields anywhere in the class outside its method declarations, but scattering them tends to lead to hard-to-read code.

Good Programming Practice 3.2

Place a blank line between method declarations to separate the methods and enhance program readability.

Declaring instance variables with access modifier `private` is known as **data hiding**. When a program creates (instantiates) an object of class `GradeBook`, variable `courseName` is encapsulated (hidden) in the object and can be accessed only by methods of the object's class. In class `GradeBook`, methods `setCourseName` and `getCourseName` manipulate the instance variable `courseName`.

Method `setCourseName` (lines 10–13) does not return any data when it completes its task, so its return type is `void`. The method receives one parameter—`name`—which represents the course name that will be passed to the method as an argument. Line 12 assigns `name` to instance variable `courseName`.

Method `getCourseName` (lines 16–19) returns a particular `GradeBook` object's `course-Name`. The method has an empty parameter list, so it does not require additional information to perform its task. The method specifies that it returns a `String`—this is known as the method's **return type**. When a method that specifies a return type is called and completes its task, the method returns a result to its calling method. For example, when you go to an automated teller machine (ATM) and request your account balance, you expect the ATM to give you back a value that represents your balance. Similarly, when a statement calls method `get-CourseName` on a `GradeBook` object, the statement expects to receive the `GradeBook`'s course name (in this case, a `String`, as specified in the method declaration's return type). If you have a method `square` that returns the square of its argument, you would expect the statement

```
int result = square( 2 );
```

to return 4 from method `square` and assign 4 to variable `result`. If you have a method max-imum that returns the largest of three integer arguments, you would expect the statement

```
int biggest = maximum( 27, 114, 51 );
```

to return 114 from method `maximum` and assign 114 to variable `biggest`.

Note that the statements at lines 12 and 18 each use `courseName` even though it was not declared in any of the methods. We can use `courseName` in the methods of class `GradeBook` because `courseName` is a field of the class. Also note that the order in which methods are declared in a class does not determine when they are called at execution time. So method `getCourseName` could be declared before method `setCourseName`.

Method `displayMessage` (lines 22–28) does not return any data when it completes its task, so its return type is `void`. The method does not receive parameters, so the parameter list is empty. Lines 26–27 output a welcome message that includes the value of instance variable `courseName`. Once again, we need to create an object of class `GradeBook` and call its methods before the welcome message can be displayed.

GradeBookTest *Class That Demonstrates Class* GradeBook

Class `GradeBookTest` (Fig. 3.8) creates one object of class `GradeBook` and demonstrates its methods. Line 11 creates a `Scanner` that will be used to obtain a course name from the user. Line 14 creates a `GradeBook` object and assigns it to local variable `myGradeBook` of type `GradeBook`. Lines 17–18 display the initial course name calling the object's `getCourseName` method. Note that the first line of the output shows the name "null." Unlike local variables, which are not automatically initialized, every field has a default initial value—a value provided by Java when the programmer does not specify the field's initial value. Thus, fields are not required to be explicitly initialized before they are used in a program—unless they must be initialized to values other than their default values. The default value for a field of type `String` (like `courseName` in this example) is `null`, which we say more about in Section 3.6.

Line 21 prompts the user to enter a course name. Local `String` variable `theName` (declared in line 22) is initialized with the course name entered by the user, which is returned by the call to the `nextLine` method of the `Scanner` object `input`. Line 23 calls object `myGradeBook`'s `setCourseName` method and supplies `theName` as the method's argument. When the method is called, the argument's value is assigned to parameter `name` (line 10, Fig. 3.7) of method `setCourseName` (lines 10–13, Fig. 3.7). Then the parameter's value is assigned to instance variable `courseName` (line 12, Fig. 3.7). Line 24 (Fig. 3.8) skips a line in the output, then line 27 calls object `myGradeBook`'s `displayMessage` method to display the welcome message containing the course name.

set *and* get *Methods*

A class's `private` fields can be manipulated only by methods of that class. So a client of an object—that is, any class that calls the object's methods—calls the class's `public` methods to manipulate the `private` fields of an object of the class. This is why the statements in method `main` (Fig. 3.8) call methods `setCourseName`, `getCourseName` and `displayMessage` on a `GradeBook` object. Classes often provide `public` methods to allow clients of the class to *set* (i.e., assign values to) or *get* (i.e., obtain the values of) `private` instance variables. The names of these methods need not begin with *set* or *get*, but this naming convention is highly recommended in Java and is required for special Java software components called JavaBeans that can simplify programming in many Java integrated development environments (IDEs). The

```
 1    // Fig. 3.8: GradeBookTest.java
 2    // Create and manipulate a GradeBook object.
 3    import java.util.Scanner; // program uses Scanner
 4
 5    public class GradeBookTest
 6    {
 7       // main method begins program execution
 8       public static void main( String args[] )
 9       {
10          // create Scanner to obtain input from command window
11          Scanner input = new Scanner( System.in );
12
13          // create a GradeBook object and assign it to myGradeBook
14          GradeBook myGradeBook = new GradeBook();
15
16          // display initial value of courseName
17          System.out.printf( "Initial course name is: %s\n\n",
18             myGradeBook.getCourseName() );
19
20          // prompt for and read course name
21          System.out.println( "Please enter the course name:" );
22          String theName = input.nextLine(); // read a line of text
23          myGradeBook.setCourseName( theName ); // set the course name
24          System.out.println(); // outputs a blank line
25
26          // display welcome message after specifying course name
27          myGradeBook.displayMessage();
28       } // end main
29
30    } // end class GradeBookTest
```

```
Initial course name is: null

Please enter the course name:
CS101 Introduction to Java Programming

Welcome to the grade book for
CS101 Introduction to Java Programming!
```

Fig. 3.8 | Creating and manipulating a GradeBook object.

method that *sets* instance variable courseName in this example is called setCourseName, and the method that *gets* the value of instance variable courseName is called getCourseName.

GradeBook's UML Class Diagram with an Instance Variable and* set *and* get *Methods
Figure 3.9 contains an updated UML class diagram for the version of class GradeBook in Fig. 3.7. This diagram models class GradeBook's instance variable courseName as an attribute in the middle compartment of the class. The UML represents instance variables as attributes by listing the attribute name, followed by a colon and the attribute type. The UML type of attribute courseName is String. Instance variable courseName is private in Java, so the class diagram lists a minus sign (–) in front of the corresponding attribute's name. Class GradeBook contains three public methods, so the class diagram lists three op-

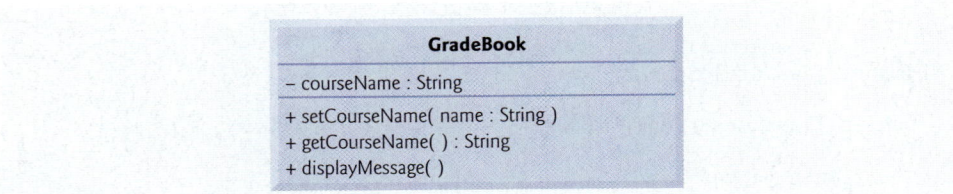

Fig. 3.9 | UML class diagram indicating that class `GradeBook` has a `courseName` attribute of UML type `String` and three operations—`setCourseName` (with a `name` parameter of UML type `String`), `getCourseName` (returns UML type `String`) and `displayMessage`.

erations in the third compartment. Recall that the plus (+) sign before each operation name indicates that the operation is `public`. Operation `setCourseName` has a `String` parameter called `name`. The UML indicates the return type of an operation by placing a colon and the return type after the parentheses following the operation name. Method `getCourseName` of class `GradeBook` (Fig. 3.7) has a `String` return type in Java, so the class diagram shows a `String` return type in the UML. Note that operations `setCourseName` and `displayMessage` do not return values (i.e., they return `void`), so the UML class diagram does not specify a return type after the parentheses of these operations.

3.6 Primitive Types vs. Reference Types

Data types in Java are divided into two categories—primitive types and reference types (sometimes called nonprimitive types). The primitive types are `boolean`, `byte`, `char`, `short`, `int`, `long`, `float` and `double`. All nonprimitive types are reference types, so classes, which specify the types of objects, are reference types.

A primitive-type variable can store exactly one value of its declared type at a time. For example, an `int` variable can store one whole number (such as 7) at a time. When another value is assigned to that variable, its initial value is replaced. Primitive-type instance variables are initialized by default—variables of types `byte`, `char`, `short`, `int`, `long`, `float` and `double` are initialized to 0, and variables of type `boolean` are initialized to `false`. Programmers can specify their own initial values for primitive-type variables. Recall that local variables are *not* initialized by default.

Programs use variables of reference types (normally called references) to store the locations of objects in the computer's memory. Such variables are said to refer to objects in the program. Objects that are referenced may each contain many instance variables and methods. Line 14 of Fig. 3.8 creates an object of class `GradeBook`, and the variable `myGradeBook` contains a reference to that `GradeBook` object. Reference type instance variables are initialized by default to the value `null`—a reserved word that represents a "reference to nothing." This is why the first call to `getCourseName` in Fig. 3.8 returned `null`—the value of `courseName` had not been set, so the default initial value `null` was returned. The complete list of reserved words and keywords is listed in Appendix C, Keywords and Reserved Words.

A reference to an object is required to invoke (i.e., call) the object's methods. In the application of Fig. 3.8, the statements in method `main` use the variable `myGradeBook` to send messages to the `GradeBook` object. These messages are calls to methods (like `setCourseName` and `getCourseName`) that enable the program to interact with the `GradeBook` objects. For example, the statement (in line 23)

```
myGradeBook.setCourseName( theName ); // set the course name
```

uses myGradeBook to send the setCourseName message to the GradeBook object. The message includes the argument that setCourseName requires to perform its task. The GradeBook object uses this information to set the courseName instance variable. Note that primitive-type variables do not refer to objects, so such variables cannot be used to invoke methods.

Software Engineering Observation 3.4

A variable's declared type (e.g., int, double or GradeBook) indicates whether the variable is of a primitive or a reference type. If a variable's type is not one of the eight primitive types, then it is a reference type. For example, Account account1 indicates that account1 is a reference to an Account object).

3.7 Initializing Objects with Constructors

As mentioned in Section 3.5, when an object of class GradeBook (Fig. 3.7) is created, its instance variable courseName is initialized to null by default. What if you want to provide a course name when you create a GradeBook object? Each class you declare can provide a constructor that can be used to initialize an object of a class when the object is created. In fact, Java requires a constructor call for every object that is created. Keyword new calls the class's constructor to perform the initialization. The constructor call is indicated by the class name followed by parentheses. For example, line 14 of Fig. 3.8 first uses new to create a GradeBook object. The empty parentheses after "new GradeBook" indicate a call to the class's constructor without arguments. By default, the compiler provides a default constructor with no parameters in any class that does not explicitly include a constructor.

When you declare a class, you can provide your own constructor to specify custom initialization for objects of your class. For example, a programmer might want to specify a course name for a GradeBook object when the object is created, as in

```
GradeBook myGradeBook =
    new GradeBook( "CS101 Introduction to Java Programming" );
```

In this case, the argument "CS101 Introduction to Java Programming" is passed to the GradeBook object's constructor and used to initialize the courseName. The preceding statement requires that the class provide a constructor with a String parameter. Figure 3.10 contains a modified GradeBook class with such a constructor.

```
1   // Fig. 3.10: GradeBook.java
2   // GradeBook class with a constructor to initialize the course name.
3
4   public class GradeBook
5   {
6      private String courseName; // course name for this GradeBook
7
8      // constructor initializes courseName with String supplied as argument
9      public GradeBook( String name )
10     {
11        courseName = name; // initializes courseName
12     } // end constructor
```

Fig. 3.10 | GradeBook class with a constructor that receives a course name. (Part 1 of 2.)

```
13
14      // method to set the course name
15      public void setCourseName( String name )
16      {
17         courseName = name; // store the course name
18      } // end method setCourseName
19
20      // method to retrieve the course name
21      public String getCourseName()
22      {
23         return courseName;
24      } // end method getCourseName
25
26      // display a welcome message to the GradeBook user
27      public void displayMessage()
28      {
29         // this statement calls getCourseName to get the
30         // name of the course this GradeBook represents
31         System.out.printf( "Welcome to the grade book for\n%s!\n",
32            getCourseName() );
33      } // end method displayMessage
34
35   } // end class GradeBook
```

Fig. 3.10 | GradeBook class with a constructor that receives a course name. (Part 2 of 2.)

Lines 9–12 declare the constructor for class GradeBook. A constructor must have the same name as its class. Like a method, a constructor specifies in its parameter list the data it requires to perform its task. When you create a new object, this data is placed in the parentheses that follow the class name. Line 9 indicates that class GradeBook's constructor has a parameter called name of type String. In line 11 of the constructor's body, the name passed to the constructor is assigned to instance variable courseName.

Figure 3.11 demonstrates initializing GradeBook objects using this constructor. Lines 11–12 create and initialize a GradeBook object. The constructor of class GradeBook is called with the argument "CS101 Introduction to Java Programming" to initialize the course name. The class instance creation expression to the right of = in lines 11–12 returns a reference to the new object, which is assigned to variable gradeBook1. Lines 13–14 repeat this process for another GradeBook object, this time passing the argument "CS102 Data Structures in Java" to initialize the course name for gradeBook2. Lines 17–20 use each object's getCourseName method to obtain the course names and show that they were indeed initialized when the objects were created. In the introduction to Section 3.5, you learned that each instance (i.e., object) of a class contains its own copy of the class's instance variables. The output confirms that each GradeBook maintains its own copy of instance variable courseName.

Like methods, constructors also can take arguments. However, an important difference between constructors and methods is that constructors cannot return values, so they cannot specify a return type (not even void). Normally, constructors are declared public. If a class does not include a constructor, the class's instance variables are initialized to their default values. If a programmer declares any constructors for a class, Java will not create a default constructor for that class.

```
1   // Fig. 3.11: GradeBookTest.java
2   // GradeBook constructor used to specify the course name at the
3   // time each GradeBook object is created.
4
5   public class GradeBookTest
6   {
7      // main method begins program execution
8      public static void main( String args[] )
9      {
10        // create GradeBook object
11        GradeBook gradeBook1 = new GradeBook(
12           "CS101 Introduction to Java Programming" );
13        GradeBook gradeBook2 = new GradeBook(
14           "CS102 Data Structures in Java" );
15
16        // display initial value of courseName for each GradeBook
17        System.out.printf( "gradeBook1 course name is: %s\n",
18           gradeBook1.getCourseName() );
19        System.out.printf( "gradeBook2 course name is: %s\n",
20           gradeBook2.getCourseName() );
21     } // end main
22
23  } // end class GradeBookTest
```

```
gradeBook1 course name is: CS101 Introduction to Java Programming
gradeBook2 course name is: CS102 Data Structures in Java
```

Fig. 3.11 | Constructor used to initialize `GradeBook` objects.

Error-Prevention Tip 3.1

Unless default initialization of your class's instance variables is acceptable, provide a constructor to ensure that your class's instance variables are properly initialized with meaningful values when each new object of your class is created.

Adding the Constructor to Class *GradeBook*'s UML Class Diagram

The UML class diagram of Fig. 3.12 models class `GradeBook` of Fig. 3.10, which has a constructor that has a `name` parameter of type `String`. Like operations, the UML models constructors in the third compartment of a class in a class diagram. To distinguish a constructor from a class's operations, the UML places the word "constructor" between

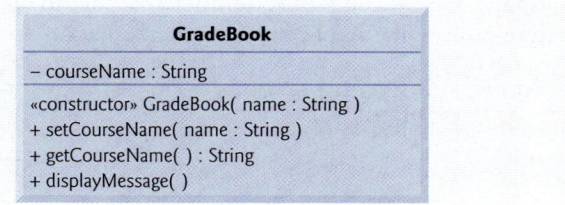

Fig. 3.12 | UML class diagram indicating that class `GradeBook` has a constructor that has a `name` parameter of UML type `String`.

guillemets (« and ») before the constructor's name. It is customary to list constructors before other operations in the third compartment.

3.8 Floating-Point Numbers and Type double

In our next application, we depart temporarily from our GradeBook case study to declare a class called Account that maintains the balance of a bank account. Most account balances are not whole numbers (e.g., 0, –22 and 1024). For this reason, class Account represents the account balance as a floating-point number (i.e., a number with a decimal point, such as 7.33, 0.0975 or 1000.12345). Java provides two primitive types for storing floating-point numbers in memory—float and double. The primary difference between them is that double variables can store numbers with larger magnitude and finer detail (i.e., more digits to the right of the decimal point—also known as the number's precision) than float variables.

Floating-Point Number Precision and Memory Requirements

Variables of type float represent single-precision floating-point numbers and have seven significant digits. Variables of type double represent double-precision floating-point numbers. These require twice as much memory as float variables and provide 15 significant digits—approximately double the precision of float variables. For the range of values required by most programs, variables of type float should suffice, but you can use double to "play it safe." In some applications, even variables of type double will be inadequate—such applications are beyond the scope of this book. Most programmers represent floating-point numbers with type double. In fact, Java treats all floating-point numbers you type in a program's source code (such as 7.33 and 0.0975) as double values by default. Such values in the source code are known as floating-point literals. See Appendix D, Primitive Types, for the ranges of values for floats and doubles.

Although floating-point numbers are not always 100% precise, they have numerous applications. For example, when we speak of a "normal" body temperature of 98.6, we do not need to be precise to a large number of digits. When we read the temperature on a thermometer as 98.6, it may actually be 98.5999473210643. Calling this number simply 98.6 is fine for most applications involving body temperatures. Due to the imprecise nature of floating-point numbers, type double is preferred over type float because double variables can represent floating-point numbers more accurately. For this reason, we use type double throughout the book.

Floating-point numbers also arise as a result of division. In conventional arithmetic, when we divide 10 by 3, the result is 3.3333333..., with the sequence of 3s repeating infinitely. The computer allocates only a fixed amount of space to hold such a value, so clearly the stored floating-point value can be only an approximation.

Common Programming Error 3.4

Using floating-point numbers in a manner that assumes they are represented precisely can lead to logic errors.

Account Class with an Instance Variable of Type double

Our next application (Fig. 3.13–Fig. 3.14) contains a class named Account (Fig. 3.13) that maintains the balance of a bank account. A typical bank services many accounts, each

```
 1   // Fig. 3.13: Account.java
 2   // Account class with a constructor to
 3   // initialize instance variable balance.
 4
 5   public class Account
 6   {
 7      private double balance; // instance variable that stores the balance
 8
 9      // constructor
10      public Account( double initialBalance )
11      {
12         // validate that initialBalance is greater than 0.0;
13         // if it is not, balance is initialized to the default value 0.0
14         if ( initialBalance > 0.0 )
15            balance = initialBalance;
16      } // end Account constructor
17
18      // credit (add) an amount to the account
19      public void credit( double amount )
20      {
21         balance = balance + amount; // add amount to balance
22      } // end method credit
23
24      // return the account balance
25      public double getBalance()
26      {
27         return balance; // gives the value of balance to the calling method
28      } // end method getBalance
29
30   } // end class Account
```

Fig. 3.13 | Account class with an instance variable of type `double`.

with its own balance, so line 7 declares an instance variable named `balance` of type `double`. Variable `balance` is an instance variable because it is declared in the body of the class (lines 6–30) but outside the class's method declarations (lines 10–16, 19–22 and 25–28). Every instance (i.e., object) of class `Account` contains its own copy of `balance`.

Class `Account` contains a constructor and two methods. Since it is common for someone opening an account to place money in the account immediately, the constructor (lines 10–16) receives a parameter `initialBalance` of type `double` that represents the account's starting balance. Lines 14–15 ensure that `initialBalance` is greater than `0.0`. If so, `initialBalance`'s value is assigned to instance variable `balance`. Otherwise, `balance` remains at `0.0`—its default initial value.

Method `credit` (lines 19–22) does not return any data when it completes its task, so its return type is `void`. The method receives one parameter named `amount`—a `double` value that will be added to the balance. Line 21 adds `amount` to the current value of `balance`, then assigns the result to `balance` (thus replacing the prior balance amount).

Method `getBalance` (lines 25–28) allows clients of the class (i.e., other classes that use this class) to obtain the value of a particular `Account` object's `balance`. The method specifies return type `double` and an empty parameter list.

Once again, note that the statements at lines 15, 21 and 27 use instance variable balance even though it was not declared in any of the methods. We can use balance in these methods because it is an instance variable of the class.

AccountTest *Class to Use Class* Account

Class AccountTest (Fig. 3.14) creates two Account objects (lines 10–11) and initializes them with 50.00 and -7.53, respectively. Lines 14–17 output the balance in each Account by calling the Account's getBalance method. When method getBalance is called for account1 from line 15, the value of account1's balance is returned from line 27 of Fig. 3.13 and displayed by the System.out.printf statement (Fig. 3.14, lines 14–15). Similarly, when method getBalance is called for account2 from line 17, the value of the account2's balance is returned from line 27 of Fig. 3.13 and displayed by the System.out.printf statement (Fig. 3.14, lines 16–17). Note that the balance of account2 is 0.00 because the constructor ensured that the account could not begin with a negative balance. The value is output by printf with the format specifier %.2f. The format specifier %f is used to output values of type float or double. The .2 between % and f represents the number of decimal places (2) that should be output to the right of the decimal point in the floating-point number—also known as the number's **precision**. Any floating point value output with %.2f will be rounded to the hundredths position—for example, 123.457 would be rounded to 123.46, and 27.333 would be rounded to 27.33.

```java
1   // Fig. 3.14: AccountTest.java
2   // Create and manipulate an Account object.
3   import java.util.Scanner;
4
5   public class AccountTest
6   {
7      // main method begins execution of Java application
8      public static void main( String args[] )
9      {
10        Account account1 = new Account( 50.00 ); // create Account object
11        Account account2 = new Account( -7.53 ); // create Account object
12
13        // display initial balance of each object
14        System.out.printf( "account1 balance: $%.2f\n",
15           account1.getBalance() );
16        System.out.printf( "account2 balance: $%.2f\n\n",
17           account2.getBalance() );
18
19        // create Scanner to obtain input from command window
20        Scanner input = new Scanner( System.in );
21        double depositAmount; // deposit amount read from user
22
23        System.out.print( "Enter deposit amount for account1: " ); // prompt
24        depositAmount = input.nextDouble(); // obtain user input
25        System.out.printf( "\nadding %.2f to account1 balance\n\n",
26           depositAmount );
27        account1.credit( depositAmount ); // add to account1 balance
28
```

Fig. 3.14 | Inputting and outputting floating-point numbers with Account objects. (Part 1 of 2.)

```
29          // display balances
30          System.out.printf( "account1 balance: $%.2f\n",
31             account1.getBalance() );
32          System.out.printf( "account2 balance: $%.2f\n\n",
33             account2.getBalance() );
34
35          System.out.print( "Enter deposit amount for account2: " ); // prompt
36          depositAmount = input.nextDouble(); // obtain user input
37          System.out.printf( "\nadding %.2f to account2 balance\n\n",
38             depositAmount );
39          account2.credit( depositAmount ); // add to account2 balance
40
41          // display balances
42          System.out.printf( "account1 balance: $%.2f\n",
43             account1.getBalance() );
44          System.out.printf( "account2 balance: $%.2f\n",
45             account2.getBalance() );
46       } // end main
47
48    } // end class AccountTest
```

```
account1 balance: $50.00
account2 balance: $0.00

Enter deposit amount for account1: 25.53

adding 25.53 to account1 balance

account1 balance: $75.53
account2 balance: $0.00

Enter deposit amount for account2: 123.45

adding 123.45 to account2 balance

account1 balance: $75.53
account2 balance: $123.45
```

Fig. 3.14 | Inputting and outputting floating-point numbers with Account objects. (Part 2 of 2.)

Line 20 creates a Scanner that will be used to obtain deposit amounts from a user. Line 21 declares local variable depositAmount to store each deposit amount entered by the user. Unlike the instance variable balance in class Account, local variable depositAmount in main is not initialized to 0.0 by default. However, this variable does not need to be initialized here because its value will be determined by the user's input.

Line 23 prompts the user to enter a deposit amount for account1. Line 24 obtains the input from the user by calling Scanner object input's **nextDouble** method, which returns a double value entered by the user. Lines 25–26 display the deposit amount. Line 27 calls object account1's credit method and supplies depositAmount as the method's argument. When the method is called, the argument's value is assigned to parameter amount (line 19 of Fig. 3.13) of method credit (lines 19–22 of Fig. 3.13), then method credit adds that value to the balance (line 21 of Fig. 3.13). Lines 30–33 (Fig. 3.14) output the balances of both Accounts again to show that only account1's balance changed.

Line 35 prompts the user to enter a deposit amount for account2. Line 36 obtains the input from the user by calling Scanner object input's nextDouble method. Lines 37–38 display the deposit amount. Line 39 calls object account2's credit method and supplies depositAmount as the method's argument, then method credit adds that value to the balance. Finally, lines 42–45 output the balances of both Accounts again to show that only account2's balance changed.

UML Class Diagram for Class *Account*

The UML class diagram in Fig. 3.15 models class Account of Fig. 3.13. The diagram models the private attribute balance of UML type Double to correspond to the class's instance variable balance of Java type double. The diagram models class Account's constructor with a parameter initialBalance of UML type Double in the third compartment of the class. The class's two public methods are modeled as operations in the third compartment as well. The diagram models operation credit with an amount parameter of UML type Double (because the corresponding method has an amount parameter of Java type double) and operation getBalance with a return type of Double (because the corresponding Java method returns a double value).

3.9 (Optional) GUI and Graphics Case Study: Using Dialog Boxes

Introduction

This case study is designed for those who want to begin learning Java's powerful capabilities for creating graphical user interfaces (GUIs) and graphics earlier in the book than the main discussions of these topics in Chapter 11, GUI Components: Part 1, Chapter 12, Graphics and Java2D, and Chapter 22, GUI Components: Part 2.

The GUI and Graphics Case Study appears in 10 brief sections (Fig. 3.16). Each section introduces a few basic concepts and provides visual, graphical examples and full source code. In the first few sections, you create your first graphical applications. In the following sections, you use the object-oriented programming concepts presented through Chapter 10 to create a drawing application that draws a variety of shapes. When we formally introduce GUIs in Chapter 11, we use the mouse to choose exactly which shapes to draw and where to draw them. In Chapter 12, we add capabilities of the Java 2D graphics API to draw the shapes with different line thicknesses and fills. We hope you will find this case study informative and entertaining.

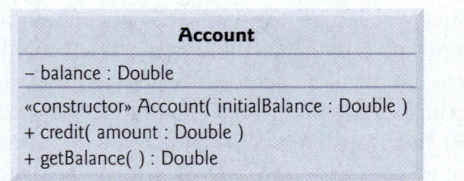

Fig. 3.15 | UML class diagram indicating that class Account has a private balance attribute of UML type Double, a constructor (with a parameter of UML type Double) and two public operations—credit (with an amount parameter of UML type Double) and getBalance (returns UML type Double).

Location	Title—Exercise(s)
Section 3.9	Using Dialog Boxes—Basic input and output with dialog boxes
Section 4.14	Creating Simple Drawings—Displaying and drawing lines on the screen
Section 5.10	Drawing Rectangles and Ovals—Using shapes to represent data
Section 6.13	Colors and Filled Shapes—Drawing a bull's-eye and random graphics
Section 7.13	Drawing Arcs—Drawing spirals with arcs
Section 8.18	Using Objects with Graphics—Storing shapes as objects
Section 9.8	Displaying Text and Images Using Labels—Providing status information
Section 10.8	Drawing with Polymorphism—Identifying the similarities between shapes
Exercise 11.18	Expanding the Interface—Using GUI components and event handling
Exercise 12.12	Adding Java 2D—Using the Java 2D API to enhance drawings

Fig. 3.16 | Summary of the GUI and Graphics Case Study in each chapter.

Displaying Text in a Dialog Box

Although the programs presented in this book thus far display output in the command window, many Java applications use windows or dialog boxes (also called dialogs) to display output. For example, World Wide Web browsers such as Netscape or Microsoft Internet Explorer display Web pages in their own windows. E-mail programs allow you to type and read messages in a window. Typically, dialog boxes are windows in which programs display important messages to the user of the program. Class `JOptionPane` provides prepackaged dialog boxes that enable programs to display windows containing messages to users—such windows are called message dialogs. Figure 3.17 displays the string `"Welcome\nto\nJava"` in a message dialog.

```
// Fig. 3.17: Dialog1.java
// Printing multiple lines in dialog box.
import javax.swing.JOptionPane; // import class JOptionPane

public class Dialog1
{
   public static void main( String args[] )
   {
      // display a dialog with the message
      JOptionPane.showMessageDialog( null, "Welcome\nto\nJava" );
   } // end main
} // end class Dialog1
```

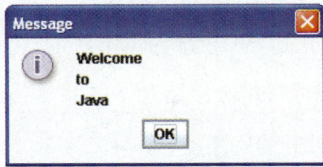

Fig. 3.17 | Using `JOptionPane` to display multiple lines in a dialog box.

Line 3 indicates that our program uses class JOptionPane from package `javax.swing`. This package contains many classes that help Java programmers create **graphical user interfaces** (**GUIs**) for applications. **GUI components** facilitate data entry by a program's user, and formatting or presenting data outputs to the user. In method main, line 10 calls method **showMessageDialog** of class JOptionPane to display a dialog box containing a message. The method requires two arguments. The first argument helps the Java application determine where to position the dialog box. When the first argument is null, the dialog box appears in the center of the computer screen. The second argument is the String to display in the dialog box.

Method showMessageDialog is a special method of class JOptionPane called a **static method**. Such methods often define frequently used tasks that do not explicitly require creating an object. For example, many programs display messages to users in dialog boxes. Rather than require programmers to create code that performs this task, the designers of Java's JOptionPane class declared a static method for this purpose. Now, with a simple method call, all programmers can make a program display a dialog box containing a message. A static method typically is called by using its class name followed by a dot (.) and the method name, as in

> *ClassName*.*methodName*(*arguments*)

Chapter 6, Methods: A Deeper Look will cover calling static methods in greater detail.

Entering Text in a Dialog Box

Our next application (Fig. 3.18) demonstrates input using dialogs. This program uses another predefined dialog box from class JOptionPane called an **input dialog** that allows the user to enter data for use in the program. The program asks for the user's name and responds with a greeting containing the name entered by the user.

```
1   // Fig. 3.18: NameDialog.java
2   // Basic input with a dialog box.
3   import javax.swing.JOptionPane;
4
5   public class NameDialog
6   {
7      public static void main( String args[] )
8      {
9         // prompt user to enter name
10        String name =
11           JOptionPane.showInputDialog( "What is your name?" );
12
13        // create the message
14        String message =
15           String.format( "Welcome, %s, to Java Programming!", name );
16
17        // display the message to welcome the user by name
18        JOptionPane.showMessageDialog( null, message );
19     } // end main
20  } // end class NameDialog
```

Fig. 3.18 | Obtaining user input from a dialog. (Part 1 of 2.)

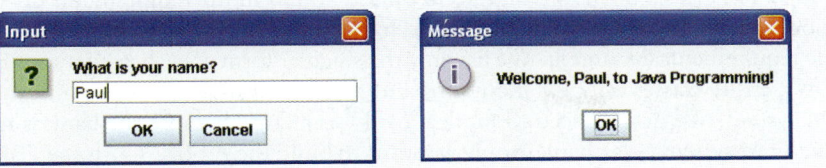

Fig. 3.18 | Obtaining user input from a dialog. (Part 2 of 2.)

Lines 10–11 use method `showInputDialog` of class JOptionPane to display a simple input dialog containing a prompt and a field for the user to enter text, known as a text field. The argument to `showInputDialog` is the prompt that indicates what the user should enter. The user types characters in the text field, then clicks the **OK** button or presses the *Enter* key to return the String to the program. Method `showInputDialog` returns a String containing the characters typed by the user, which we store in variable name. [*Note:* If you press the **Cancel** button in the dialog, the method returns null and the program displays the word "null" as the name.]

Lines 14–15 use `static` String method `format` to return a String containing a greeting with the name entered by the user. Method `format` is similar to method `System.out.printf`, except that `format` returns a formatted String rather than displaying it in a command window. Line 18 displays the greeting in a message dialog.

GUI and Graphics Case Study Exercise

3.1 Modify the addition program in Fig. 2.7 to use dialog-based input with JOptionPane instead of console-based input using Scanner. Since method `showInputDialog` only returns a String, you must convert the String the user enters to an int for use in calculations. Method `Integer.parseInt( String s )` takes a String argument representing an integer (e.g., the result of `JOptionPane.showInputDialog`) and returns the value as an int. If the String does not contain a valid integer, then the program will terminate with an error.

3.10 (Optional) Software Engineering Case Study: Identifying the Classes in a Requirements Document

Now we begin designing the ATM system that we introduced in Chapter 2. In this section, we identify the classes that are needed to build the ATM system by analyzing the nouns and noun phrases that appear in the requirements document. We introduce UML class diagrams to model the relationships between these classes. This is an important first step in defining the structure of our system.

Identifying the Classes in a System

We begin our OOD process by identifying the classes required to build the ATM system. We will eventually describe these classes using UML class diagrams and implement these classes in Java. First, we review the requirements document of Section 2.9 and identify key nouns and noun phrases to help us identify classes that comprise the ATM system. We may decide that some of these nouns and noun phrases are attributes of other classes in the system. We may also conclude that some of the nouns do not correspond to parts of the system and thus should not be modeled at all. Additional classes may become apparent to us as we proceed through the design process.

Figure 3.19 lists the nouns and noun phrases found in the requirements document in Section 2.9. We list them from left to right in the order in which we first encounter them in the requirements document. We list only the singular form of each noun or noun phrase.

We create classes only for the nouns and noun phrases that have significance in the ATM system. We do not need to model "bank" as a class, because the bank is not a part of the ATM system—the bank simply wants us to build the ATM. "Customer" and "user" also represent entities outside of the system—they are important because they interact with our ATM system, but we do not need to model them as classes in the ATM software. Recall that we modeled an ATM user (i.e., a bank customer) as the actor in the use case diagram of Fig. 2.20.

We do not model "$20 bill" or "deposit envelope" as classes. These are physical objects in the real world, but they are not part of what is being automated. We can adequately represent the presence of bills in the system using an attribute of the class that models the cash dispenser. (We assign attributes to classes in Section 4.15.) For example, the cash dispenser maintains a count of the number of bills it contains. The requirements document does not say anything about what the system should do with deposit envelopes after it receives them. We can assume that simply acknowledging the receipt of an envelope—an operation performed by the class that models the deposit slot—is sufficient to represent the presence of an envelope in the system. (We assign operations to classes in Section 6.14.)

In our simplified ATM system, representing various amounts of "money," including the "balance" of an account, as attributes of other classes seems most appropriate. Likewise, the nouns "account number" and "PIN" represent significant pieces of information in the ATM system. They are important attributes of a bank account. They do not, however, exhibit behaviors. Thus, we can most appropriately model them as attributes of an account class.

Though the requirements document frequently describes a "transaction" in a general sense, we do not model the broad notion of a financial transaction at this time. Instead, we model the three types of transactions (i.e., "balance inquiry," "withdrawal" and "deposit") as individual classes. These classes possess specific attributes needed for executing the transactions they represent. For example, a withdrawal needs to know the amount of money the user wants to withdraw. A balance inquiry, however, does not

Nouns and noun phrases in the requirements document		
bank	money / funds	account number
ATM	screen	PIN
user	keypad	bank database
customer	cash dispenser	balance inquiry
transaction	$20 bill / cash	withdrawal
account	deposit slot	deposit
balance	deposit envelope	

Fig. 3.19 | Nouns and noun phrases in the requirements document.

require any additional data. Furthermore, the three transaction classes exhibit unique behaviors. A withdrawal includes dispensing cash to the user, whereas a deposit involves receiving deposit envelopes from the user. [*Note:* In Section 10.9, we "factor out" common features of all transactions into a general "transaction" class using the object-oriented concept of inheritance.]

We determine the classes for our system based on the remaining nouns and noun phrases from Fig. 3.19. Each of these refers to one or more of the following:

- ATM
- screen
- keypad
- cash dispenser
- deposit slot
- account
- bank database
- balance inquiry
- withdrawal
- deposit

The elements of this list are likely to be classes we will need to implement our system.

We can now model the classes in our system based on the list we have created. We capitalize class names in the design process—a UML convention—as we will do when we write the actual Java code that implements our design. If the name of a class contains more than one word, we run the words together and capitalize each word (e.g., `MultipleWordName`). Using this convention, we create classes `ATM`, `Screen`, `Keypad`, `CashDispenser`, `DepositSlot`, `Account`, `BankDatabase`, `BalanceInquiry`, `Withdrawal` and `Deposit`. We construct our system using all of these classes as building blocks. Before we begin building the system, however, we must gain a better understanding of how the classes relate to one another.

Modeling Classes

The UML enables us to model, via **class diagrams**, the classes in the ATM system and their interrelationships. Figure 3.20 represents class `ATM`. In the UML, each class is modeled as a rectangle with three compartments. The top compartment contains the name of the class centered horizontally in boldface. The middle compartment contains the class's attributes. (We discuss attributes in Section 4.15 and Section 5.11.) The bottom compartment contains the class's operations (discussed in Section 6.14). In Fig. 3.20, the middle and bot-

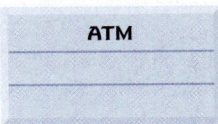

Fig. 3.20 | Representing a class in the UML using a class diagram.

tom compartments are empty because we have not yet determined this class's attributes and operations.

Class diagrams also show the relationships between the classes of the system. Figure 3.21 shows how our classes ATM and Withdrawal relate to one another. For the moment, we choose to model only this subset of classes for simplicity. We present a more complete class diagram later in this section. Notice that the rectangles representing classes in this diagram are not subdivided into compartments. The UML allows the suppression of class attributes and operations in this manner to create more readable diagrams, when appropriate. Such a diagram is said to be an elided diagram—one in which some information, such as the contents of the second and third compartments, is not modeled. We will place information in these compartments in Section 4.15 and Section 6.14.

In Fig. 3.21, the solid line that connects the two classes represents an association—a relationship between classes. The numbers near each end of the line are multiplicity values, which indicate how many objects of each class participate in the association. In this case, following the line from one end to the other reveals that, at any given moment, one ATM object participates in an association with either zero or one Withdrawal objects—zero if the current user is not currently performing a transaction or has requested a different type of transaction, and one if the user has requested a withdrawal. The UML can model many types of multiplicity. Figure 3.22 lists and explains the multiplicity types.

An association can be named. For example, the word Executes above the line connecting classes ATM and Withdrawal in Fig. 3.21 indicates the name of that association. This part of the diagram reads "one object of class ATM executes zero or one objects of class Withdrawal." Note that association names are directional, as indicated by the filled arrowhead—so it would be improper, for example, to read the preceding association from right to left as "zero or one objects of class Withdrawal execute one object of class ATM."

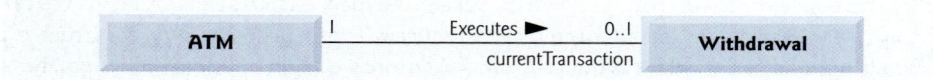

Fig. 3.21 | Class diagram showing an association among classes.

Symbol	Meaning
0	None
1	One
m	An integer value
0..1	Zero or one
m, n	*m* or *n*
m..n	At least *m*, but not more than *n*
*	Any non-negative integer (zero or more)
0..*	Zero or more (identical to *)
1..*	One or more

Fig. 3.22 | Multiplicity types.

The word `currentTransaction` at the `Withdrawal` end of the association line in Fig. 3.21 is a role name, which identifies the role the `Withdrawal` object plays in its relationship with the ATM. A role name adds meaning to an association between classes by identifying the role a class plays in the context of an association. A class can play several roles in the same system. For example, in a school personnel system, a person may play the role of "professor" when relating to students. The same person may take on the role of "colleague" when participating in a relationship with another professor, and "coach" when coaching student athletes. In Fig. 3.21, the role name `currentTransaction` indicates that the `Withdrawal` object participating in the `Executes` association with an object of class ATM represents the transaction currently being processed by the ATM. In other contexts, a `Withdrawal` object may take on other roles (e.g., the previous transaction). Notice that we do not specify a role name for the ATM end of the `Executes` association. Role names in class diagrams are often omitted when the meaning of an association is clear without them.

In addition to indicating simple relationships, associations can specify more complex relationships, such as objects of one class being composed of objects of other classes. Consider a real-world automated teller machine. What "pieces" does a manufacturer put together to build a working ATM? Our requirements document tells us that the ATM is composed of a screen, a keypad, a cash dispenser and a deposit slot.

In Fig. 3.23, the solid diamonds attached to the association lines of class ATM indicate that class ATM has a composition relationship with classes `Screen`, `Keypad`, `CashDispenser` and `DepositSlot`. Composition implies a whole/part relationship. The class that has the composition symbol (the solid diamond) on its end of the association line is the whole (in this case, ATM), and the classes on the other end of the association lines are the parts—in this case, classes `Screen`, `Keypad`, `CashDispenser` and `DepositSlot`. The compositions in Fig. 3.23 indicate that an object of class ATM is formed from one object of class `Screen`, one object of class `CashDispenser`, one object of class `Keypad` and one object of class `DepositSlot`. The ATM "has a" screen, a keypad, a cash dispenser and a deposit slot. The "has-a" relationship defines composition. (We will see in the "Software Engineering Case Study" section in Chapter 10 that the "is-a" relationship defines inheritance.)

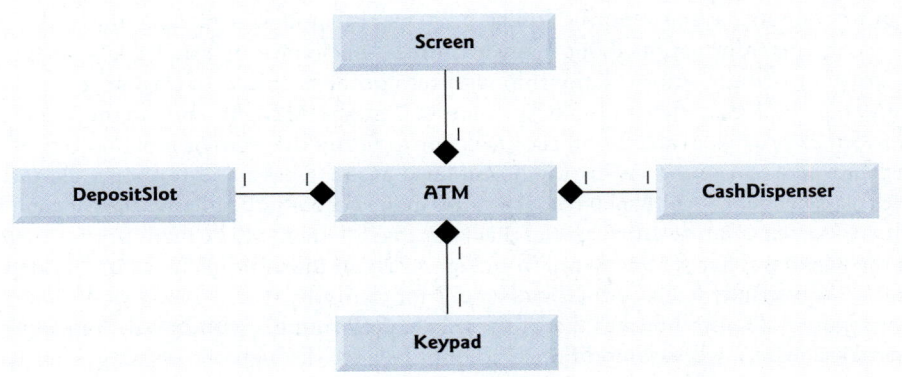

Fig. 3.23 | Class diagram showing composition relationships.

According to the UML specification (www.uml.org), composition relationships have the following properties:

1. Only one class in the relationship can represent the whole (i.e., the diamond can be placed on only one end of the association line). For example, either the screen is part of the ATM or the ATM is part of the screen, but the screen and the ATM cannot both represent the whole in the relationship.

2. The parts in the composition relationship exist only as long as the whole, and the whole is responsible for the creation and destruction of its parts. For example, the act of constructing an ATM includes manufacturing its parts. Furthermore, if the ATM is destroyed, its screen, keypad, cash dispenser and deposit slot are also destroyed.

3. A part may belong to only one whole at a time, although the part may be removed and attached to another whole, which then assumes responsibility for the part.

The solid diamonds in our class diagrams indicate composition relationships that fulfill these three properties. If a "has-a" relationship does not satisfy one or more of these criteria, the UML specifies that hollow diamonds be attached to the ends of association lines to indicate aggregation—a weaker form of composition. For example, a personal computer and a computer monitor participate in an aggregation relationship—the computer "has a" monitor, but the two parts can exist independently, and the same monitor can be attached to multiple computers at once, thus violating the second and third properties of composition.

Figure 3.24 shows a class diagram for the ATM system. This diagram models most of the classes that we identified earlier in this section, as well as the associations between them that we can infer from the requirements document. [*Note:* Classes BalanceInquiry and Deposit participate in associations similar to those of class Withdrawal, so we have chosen to omit them from this diagram to keep the diagram simple. In Chapter 10, we expand our class diagram to include all the classes in the ATM system.]

Figure 3.24 presents a graphical model of the structure of the ATM system. This class diagram includes classes BankDatabase and Account, and several associations that were not present in either Fig. 3.21 or Fig. 3.23. The class diagram shows that class ATM has a one-to-one relationship with class BankDatabase—one ATM object authenticates users against one BankDatabase object. In Fig. 3.24, we also model the fact that the bank's database contains information about many accounts—one object of class BankDatabase participates in a composition relationship with zero or more objects of class Account. Recall from Fig. 3.22 that the multiplicity value 0..* at the Account end of the association between class BankDatabase and class Account indicates that zero or more objects of class Account take part in the association. Class BankDatabase has a one-to-many relationship with class Account—the BankDatabase stores many Accounts. Similarly, class Account has a many-to-one relationship with class BankDatabase—there can be many Accounts stored in the BankDatabase. [*Note:* Recall from Fig. 3.22 that the multiplicity value * is identical to 0..*. We include 0..* in our class diagrams for clarity.]

Figure 3.24 also indicates that if the user is performing a withdrawal, "one object of class Withdrawal accesses/modifies an account balance through one object of class BankDatabase." We could have created an association directly between class Withdrawal and class Account. The requirements document, however, states that the "ATM must interact

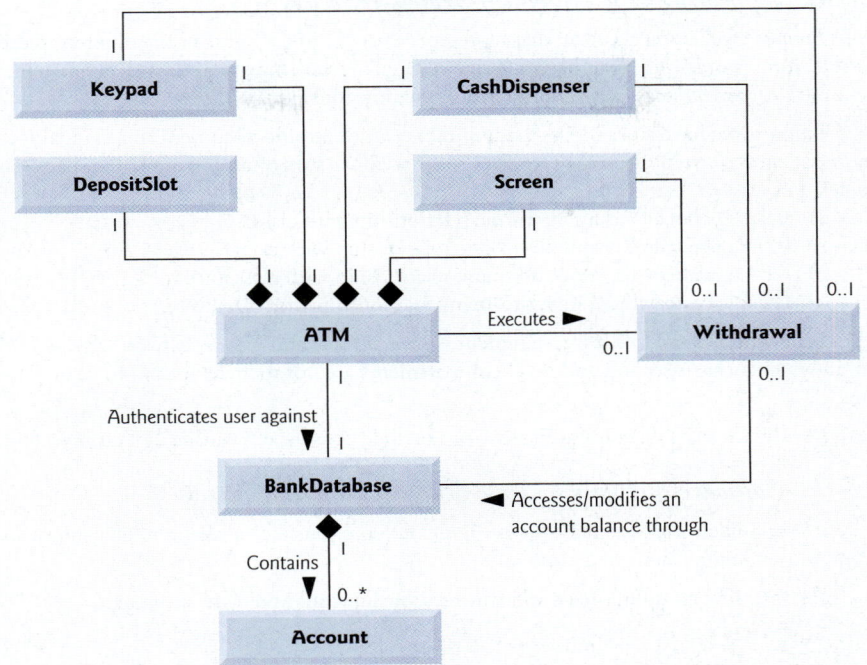

Fig. 3.24 | Class diagram for the ATM system model.

with the bank's account information database" to perform transactions. A bank account contains sensitive information, and systems engineers must always consider the security of personal data when designing a system. Thus, only the BankDatabase can access and manipulate an account directly. All other parts of the system must interact with the database to retrieve or update account information (e.g., an account balance).

The class diagram in Fig. 3.24 also models associations between class Withdrawal and classes Screen, CashDispenser and Keypad. A withdrawal transaction includes prompting the user to choose a withdrawal amount and receiving numeric input. These actions require the use of the screen and the keypad, respectively. Furthermore, dispensing cash to the user requires access to the cash dispenser.

Classes BalanceInquiry and Deposit, though not shown in Fig. 3.24, take part in several associations with the other classes of the ATM system. Like class Withdrawal, each of these classes associates with classes ATM and BankDatabase. An object of class Balance-Inquiry also associates with an object of class Screen to display the balance of an account to the user. Class Deposit associates with classes Screen, Keypad and DepositSlot. Like withdrawals, deposit transactions require use of the screen and the keypad to display prompts and receive input, respectively. To receive deposit envelopes, an object of class Deposit accesses the deposit slot.

We have now identified the classes in our ATM system (although we may discover others as we proceed with the design and implementation). In Section 4.15, we determine the attributes for each of these classes, and in Section 5.11, we use these attributes to examine how the system changes over time.

Software Engineering Case Study Self-Review Exercises

3.1 Suppose we have a class Car that represents a car. Think of some of the different pieces that a manufacturer would put together to produce a whole car. Create a class diagram (similar to Fig. 3.23) that models some of the composition relationships of class Car.

3.2 Suppose we have a class File that represents an electronic document in a standalone, non-networked computer represented by class Computer. What sort of association exists between class Computer and class File?
   a) Class Computer has a one-to-one relationship with class File.
   b) Class Computer has a many-to-one relationship with class File.
   c) Class Computer has a one-to-many relationship with class File.
   d) Class Computer has a many-to-many relationship with class File.

3.3 State whether the following statement is *true* or *false*, and if *false*, explain why: A UML diagram in which a class's second and third compartments are not modeled is said to be an elided diagram.

3.4 Modify the class diagram of Fig. 3.24 to include class Deposit instead of class Withdrawal.

Answers to Software Engineering Case Study Self-Review Exercises

3.1 [*Note:* Student answers may vary.] Figure 3.25 presents a class diagram that shows some of the composition relationships of a class Car.

3.2 c. [*Note:* In a computer network, this relationship could be many-to-many.]

3.3 True.

3.4 Figure 3.26 presents a class diagram for the ATM including class Deposit instead of class Withdrawal (as in Fig. 3.24). Note that Deposit does not access CashDispenser, but does access DepositSlot.

3.11 Wrap-Up

In this chapter, you learned the basic concepts of classes, objects, methods and instance variables—these will be used in most Java applications you create. In particular, you learned how to declare instance variables of a class to maintain data for each object of the class, and how to declare methods that operate on that data. You learned how to call a

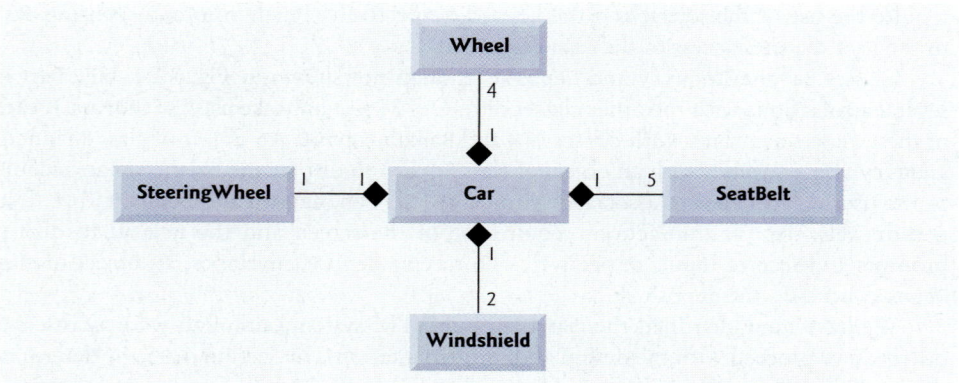

Fig. 3.25 | Class diagram showing composition relationships of a class Car.

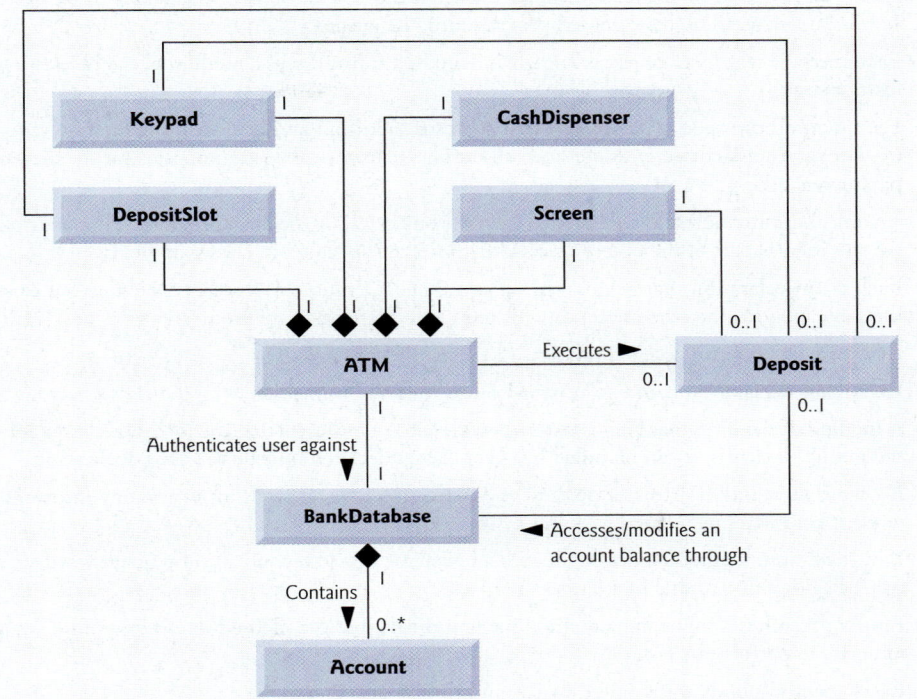

Fig. 3.26 | Class diagram for the ATM system model including class `Deposit`.

method to tell it to perform its task and how to pass information to methods as arguments. You learned the difference between a local variable of a method and an instance variable of a class and that only instance variables are initialized automatically. You also learned how to use a class's constructor to specify the initial values for an object's instance variables. Throughout the chapter, you saw how the UML can be used to create class diagrams that model the constructors, methods and attributes of classes. Finally, you learned about floating-point numbers—how to store them with variables of primitive type `double`, how to input them with a `Scanner` object and how to format them with `printf` and format specifier `%f` for display purposes. In the next chapter we begin our introduction to control statements, which specify the order in which a program's actions are performed. You will use these in your methods to specify how they should perform their tasks.

Summary

- Performing a task in a program requires a method. Inside the method you put the mechanisms that make the method do its tasks—that is, the method hides the implementation details of the tasks that it performs.
- The program unit that houses a method is called a class. A class may contain one or more methods that are designed to perform the class's tasks.
- A method can perform a task and return a result.

- A class can be used to create an instance of the class called an object. This is one of the reasons Java is known as an object-oriented programming language.

- Each message sent to an object is known as a method call and tells a method of the object to perform its task.

- Each method can specify parameters that represent additional information the method requires to perform its task correctly. A method call supplies values—called arguments—for the method's parameters.

- An object has attributes that are carried with the object as it is used in a program. These attributes are specified as part of the object's class. Attributes are specified in classes by fields.

- Each class declaration that begins with keyword public must be stored in a file that has exactly the same name as the class and ends with the .java file-name extension.

- Keyword public is an access modifier.

- Every class declaration contains keyword class followed immediately by the class's name.

- A method declaration that begins with keyword public indicates that the method is "available to the public"—that is, it can be called by other classes declared outside the class declaration.

- Keyword void indicates that a method will perform a task but will not return any information when it completes its task.

- By convention, method names begin with a lowercase first letter and all subsequent words in the name begin with a capital first letter.

- Empty parentheses following a method name indicate that the method does not require any parameters to perform its task.

- Every method's body is delimited by left and right braces ({ and }).

- The body of a method contains statements that perform the method's task. After the statements execute, the method has completed its task.

- When you attempt to execute a class, Java looks for the class's main method to begin execution.

- Any class that contains public static void main(String args[]) can be used to execute an application.

- Typically, you cannot call a method that belongs to another class until you create an object of that class.

- Class instance creation expressions beginning with keyword new create new objects.

- To call a method of an object, follow the variable name with a dot separator (.), the method name and a set of parentheses containing the method's arguments.

- Methods often require additional information to perform their tasks. Such additional information is provided to methods via arguments in method calls.

- Scanner method nextLine reads characters until a newline character is encountered, then returns the characters as a String.

- Scanner method next reads characters until any white-space character is encountered, then returns the characters as a String.

- A method that requires data to perform its task must specify this in its declaration by placing additional information in the method's parameter list.

- Each parameter must specify both a type and an identifier.

- At the time a method is called, its arguments are assigned to its parameters. Then the method body uses the parameter variables to access the argument values.

- A method can specify multiple parameters by separating each parameter from the next with a comma.

- The number of arguments in the method call must match the number of parameters in the method declaration's parameter list. Also, the argument types in the method call must be consistent with the types of the corresponding parameters in the method's declaration.

- Class `String` is in package `java.lang`, which is imported implicitly into all source-code files.

- There is a special relationship between classes that are compiled in the same directory on disk. By default, such classes are considered to be in the same package—known as the default package. Classes in the same package are implicitly imported into the source code files of other classes in the same package. Thus, an `import` declaration is not required when one class in a package uses another in the same package.

- An `import` declaration is not required if you always refer to a class with its fully qualified class name.

- Variables declared in the body of a particular method are known as local variables and can be used only in that method.

- A class normally consists of one or more methods that manipulate the attributes (data) that belong to a particular object of the class. Attributes are represented as fields in a class declaration. Such variables are called fields and are declared inside a class declaration but outside the bodies of the class's method declarations.

- When each object of a class maintains its own copy of an attribute, the field that represents the attribute is also known as an instance variable. Each object (instance) of the class has a separate instance of the variable in memory.

- Most instance variable declarations are preceded with the `private` access modifier. Variables or methods declared with access modifier `private` are accessible only to methods of the class in which they are declared.

- Declaring instance variables with access modifier `private` is known as data hiding.

- A benefit of fields is that all the methods of the class can use the fields. Another distinction between a field and a local variable is that a field has a default initial value provided by Java when the programmer does not specify the field's initial value, but a local variable does not.

- The default value for a field of type `String` is `null`.

- When a method that specifies a return type is called and completes its task, the method returns a result to its calling method.

- Classes often provide `public` methods to allow clients of the class to *set* or *get* `private` instance variables. The names of these methods need not begin with *set* or *get*, but this naming convention is highly recommended in Java and is required for special Java software components called Java-Beans.

- Types in Java are divided into two categories—primitive types and reference types (sometimes called nonprimitive types). The primitive types are `boolean`, `byte`, `char`, `short`, `int`, `long`, `float` and `double`. All other types are reference types, so classes, which specify the types of objects, are reference types.

- A primitive-type variable can store exactly one value of its declared type at a time.

- Primitive-type instance variables are initialized by default. Variables of types `byte`, `char`, `short`, `int`, `long`, `float` and `double` are initialized to 0. Variables of type `boolean` are initialized to `false`.

- Programs use variables of reference types (called references) to store the location of an object in the computer's memory. Such variables refer to objects in the program. The object that is referenced may contain many instance variables and methods.

- Reference-type fields are initialized by default to the value null.

- A reference to an object is required to invoke an object's instance methods. A primitive-type variable does not refer to an object and therefore cannot be used to invoke a method.

- A constructor can be used to initialize an object of a class when the object is created.

- Constructors can specify parameters but cannot specify return types.

- If no constructor is provided for a class, the compiler provides a default constructor with no parameters.

- A floating-point number is a number with a decimal point, such as 7.33, 0.0975 or 1000.12345. Java provides two primitive types for storing floating-point numbers in memory—float and double. The primary difference between these types is that double variables can store numbers with larger magnitude and finer detail (known as the number's precision) than float variables.

- Variables of type float represent single-precision floating-point numbers and have seven significant digits. Variables of type double represent double-precision floating-point numbers. These require twice as much memory as float variables and provide 15 significant digits—approximately double the precision of float variables.

- Floating-point values that appear in source code are known as floating-point literals and are type double by default.

- Scanner method nextDouble returns a double value.

- The format specifier %f is used to output values of type float or double. A precision can be specified between % and f to represent the number of decimal places that should be output to the right of the decimal point in the floating-point number.

- The default value for a field of type double is 0.0, and the default value for a field of type int is 0.

- In the UML, each class is modeled in a class diagram as a rectangle with three compartments. The top compartment contains the name of the class centered horizontally in boldface. The middle compartment contains the class's attributes, which correspond to fields in Java. The bottom compartment contains the class's operations, which correspond to methods and constructors in Java.

- The UML models operations by listing the operation name followed by a set of parentheses. A plus sign (+) in front of the operation name indicates that the operation is a public operation in the UML (i.e., a public method in Java).

- The UML models a parameter of an operation by listing the parameter name, followed by a colon and the parameter type between the parentheses following the operation name.

- The UML has its own data types similar to those of Java. Not all the UML data types have the same names as the corresponding Java types.

- The UML type String corresponds to the Java type String.

- The UML represents instance variables as attributes by listing the attribute name, followed by a colon and the attribute type.

- Private attributes are preceded by a minus sign (–) in the UML.

- The UML indicates the return type of an operation by placing a colon and the return type after the parentheses following the operation name.

- UML class diagrams do not specify return types for operations that do not return values.

- Like operations, the UML models constructors in the third compartment of a class diagram. To distinguish a constructor from a class's operations, the UML places the word "constructor" between guillemets (« and ») before the constructor's name.

Terminology

%f format specifier	.java file name extension
access modifier	local variable
attribute (UML)	message
calling method	method
class	method header
class declaration	new keyword
class instance	next method of class Scanner
class keyword	nextDouble method of class Scanner
class instance creation expression	nextLine method of class Scanner
client of an object or a class	nonprimitive types
compartment in a class diagram (UML)	null reserved word
constructor	object (or instance)
create an object	operation (UML)
data hiding	parameter
default constructor	parameter list
default package	precision of a floating-point value
default value	precision of a formatted floating-point number
dot (.) separator	private access modifier
double-precision floating-point number	public access modifier
double primitive type	public method
field	refer to an object
float primitive type	reference
floating-point number	reference type
get method	send a message
guillemets, « and » (UML)	*set* method
instance of a class (object)	single-precision floating-point number
instance variable	UML class diagram
instantiate (or create) an object	void keyword
invoke a method	

Self-Review Exercises

3.1   Fill in the blanks in each of the following:

   a) A house is to a blueprint as a(n) _____ is to a class.

   b) Each class declaration that begins with keyword _____ must be stored in a file that has exactly the same name as the class and ends with the .java file-name extension.

   c) Every class declaration contains keyword _____ followed immediately by the class's name.

   d) Keyword _____ creates an object of the class specified to the right of the keyword.

   e) Each parameter must specify both a(n) _____ and a(n) _____.

   f) By default, classes that are compiled in the same directory are considered to be in the same package—known as the _____.

   g) When each object of a class maintains its own copy of an attribute, the field that represents the attribute is also known as a(n) _____.

   h) Java provides two primitive types for storing floating-point numbers in memory— _____ and _____.

   i) Variables of type double represent _____ floating-point numbers.

   j) Scanner method _____ returns a double value.

   k) Keyword public is a(n) _____.

l) Return type _____ indicates that a method will perform a task but will not return any information when it completes its task.

m) Scanner method _____ reads characters until a newline character is encountered, then returns those characters as a String.

n) Class String is in package _____.

o) A(n) _____ is not required if you always refer to a class with its fully qualified class name.

p) A(n) _____ is a number with a decimal point, such as 7.33, 0.0975 or 1000.12345.

q) Variables of type float represent _____ floating-point numbers.

r) The format specifier _____ is used to output values of type float or double.

s) Types in Java are divided into two categories—_____ types and _____ types.

3.2   State whether each of the following is *true* or *false*. If *false*, explain why.

a) By convention, method names begin with an uppercase first letter and all subsequent words in the name begin with a capital first letter.

b) An import declaration is not required when one class in a package uses another in the same package.

c) Empty parentheses following a method name in a method declaration indicate that the method does not require any parameters to perform its task.

d) Variables or methods declared with access modifier private are accessible only to methods of the class in which they are declared.

e) A primitive-type variable can be used to invoke a method.

f) Variables declared in the body of a particular method are known as instance variables and can be used in all methods of the class.

g) Every method's body is delimited by left and right braces ({ and }).

h) Primitive-type local variables are initialized by default.

i) Reference-type instance variables are initialized by default to the value null.

j) Any class that contains public static void main(String args[]) can be used to execute an application.

k) The number of arguments in the method call must match the number of parameters in the method declaration's parameter list.

l) Floating-point values that appear in source code are known as floating-point literals and are type float by default.

3.3   What is the difference between a local variable and a field?

3.4   Explain the purpose of a method parameter. What is the difference between a parameter and an argument?

Answers to Self-Review Exercises

3.1   a) object. b) public. c) class. d) new. e) type, name. f) default package. g) instance variable. h) float, double. i) double-precision. j) nextDouble. k) access modifier. l) void. m) nextLine. n) java.lang. o) import declaration. p) floating-point number. q) single-precision. r) %f. s) primitive, reference.

3.2   a) False. By convention, method names begin with a lowercase first letter and all subsequent words in the name begin with a capital first letter. b) True. c) True. d) True. e) False. A primitive-type variable cannot be used to invoke a method—a reference to an object is required to invoke the object's methods. f) False. Such variables are called local variables and can be used only in the method in which they are declared. g) True. h) False. Primitive-type instance variables are initialized by default. i) True. j) True. k) True. l) False. Such literals are of type double by default.

3.3 A local variable is declared in the body of a method and can be used only from the point at which it is declared through the end of the method declaration. A field is declared in a class, but not in the body of any of the class's methods. Every object (instance) of a class has a separate copy of the class's fields. Also, fields are accessible to all methods of the class. (We will see an exception to this in Chapter 8, Classes and Objects: A Deeper Look.)

3.4 A parameter represents additional information that a method requires to perform its task. Each parameter required by a method is specified in the method's declaration. An argument is the actual value for a method parameter. When a method is called, the argument values are passed to the method so that it can perform its task.

Exercises

3.5 What is the purpose of keyword new? Explain what happens when this keyword is used in an application.

3.6 What is a default constructor? How are an object's instance variables initialized if a class has only a default constructor?

3.7 Explain the purpose of an instance variable.

3.8 Most classes need to be imported before they can be used in an application. Why is every application allowed to use classes System and String without first importing them?

3.9 Explain how a program could use class Scanner without importing the class from package java.util.

3.10 Explain why a class might provide a *set* method and a *get* method for an instance variable.

3.11 Modify class GradeBook (Fig. 3.10) as follows:
   a) Include a second String instance variable that represents the name of the course's instructor.
   b) Provide a *set* method to change the instructor's name and a *get* method to retrieve it.
   c) Modify the constructor to specify two parameters—one for the course name and one for the instructor's name.
   d) Modify method displayMessage such that it first outputs the welcome message and course name, then outputs "This course is presented by: " followed by the instructor's name.

Use your modified class in a test application that demonstrates the class's new capabilities.

3.12 Modify class Account (Fig. 3.13) to provide a method called debit that withdraws money from an Account. Ensure that the debit amount does not exceed the Account's balance. If it does, the balance should be left unchanged and the method should print a message indicating "Debit amount exceeded account balance." Modify class AccountTest (Fig. 3.14) to test method debit.

3.13 Create a class called Invoice that a hardware store might use to represent an invoice for an item sold at the store. An Invoice should include four pieces of information as instance variables—a part number (type String), a part description (type String), a quantity of the item being purchased (type int) and a price per item (double). Your class should have a constructor that initializes the four instance variables. Provide a *set* and a *get* method for each instance variable. In addition, provide a method named getInvoiceAmount that calculates the invoice amount (i.e., multiplies the quantity by the price per item), then returns the amount as a double value. If the quantity is not positive, it should be set to 0. If the price per item is not positive, it should be set to 0.0. Write a test application named InvoiceTest that demonstrates class Invoice's capabilities.

3.14 Create a class called Employee that includes three pieces of information as instance variables—a first name (type String), a last name (type String) and a monthly salary (double). Your class should have a constructor that initializes the three instance variables. Provide a *set* and a *get* method for each instance variable. If the monthly salary is not positive, set it to 0.0. Write a test application named EmployeeTest that demonstrates class Employee's capabilities. Create two Employee objects and display each object's *yearly* salary. Then give each Employee a 10% raise and display each Employee's yearly salary again.

3.15 Create a class called Date that includes three pieces of information as instance variables—a month (type int), a day (type int) and a year (type int). Your class should have a constructor that initializes the three instance variables and assumes that the values provided are correct. Provide a *set* and a *get* method for each instance variable. Provide a method displayDate that displays the month, day and year separated by forward slashes (/). Write a test application named DateTest that demonstrates class Date's capabilities.

4

Control Statements: Part 1

Let's all move one place on.
—Lewis Carroll

The wheel is come full circle.
—William Shakespeare

How many apples fell on Newton's head before he took the hint!
—Robert Frost

All the evolution we know of proceeds from the vague to the definite.
—Charles Sanders Peirce

OBJECTIVES

In this chapter you will learn:

- To use basic problem-solving techniques.

- To develop algorithms through the process of top-down, stepwise refinement.

- To use the `if` and `if`...`else` selection statements to choose among alternative actions.

- To use the `while` repetition statement to execute statements in a program repeatedly.

- To use counter-controlled repetition and sentinel-controlled repetition.

- To use the assignment, increment and decrement operators.

4.1 Introduction

Before writing a program to solve a problem, it is essential to have a thorough understanding of the problem and a carefully planned approach to solving it. When writing a program, it is also essential to understand the types of building blocks that are available and to employ proven program-construction techniques. In this chapter and in Chapter 5, Control Statements: Part 2, we discuss these issues in our presentation of the theory and principles of structured programming. The concepts presented here are crucial in building classes and manipulating objects.

In this chapter, we introduce Java's `if`, `if...else` and `while` statements, three of the building blocks that allow programmers to specify the logic required for methods to perform their tasks. We devote a portion of this chapter (and Chapters 5 and 7) to further developing the `GradeBook` class introduced in Chapter 3. In particular, we add a method to the `GradeBook` class that uses control statements to calculate the average of a set of student grades. Another example demonstrates additional ways to combine control statements to solve a similar problem. We introduce Java's compound assignment operators and explore Java's increment and decrement operators. These additional operators abbreviate and simplify many program statements. Finally, we present an overview of the primitive data types available to programmers.

4.2 Algorithms

Any computing problem can be solved by executing a series of actions in a specific order. A procedure for solving a problem in terms of

1. the **actions** to execute and

2. the **order** in which these actions execute

is called an algorithm. The following example demonstrates that correctly specifying the order in which the actions execute is important.

Consider the "rise-and-shine algorithm" followed by one executive for getting out of bed and going to work: (1) Get out of bed; (2) take off pajamas; (3) take a shower; (4) get dressed; (5) eat breakfast; (6) carpool to work. This routine gets the executive to work well prepared to make critical decisions. Suppose that the same steps are performed in a slightly different order: (1) Get out of bed; (2) take off pajamas; (3) get dressed; (4) take a shower; (5) eat break-fast; (6) carpool to work. In this case, our executive shows up for work soaking wet.

Specifying the order in which statements (actions) execute in a program is called program control. This chapter investigates program control using Java's control statements.

4.3 Pseudocode

Pseudocode is an informal language that helps programmers develop algorithms without having to worry about the strict details of Java language syntax. The pseudocode we present is particularly useful for developing algorithms that will be converted to structured portions of Java programs. Pseudocode is similar to everyday English—it is convenient and user friendly, but it is not an actual computer programming language.

Pseudocode does not execute on computers. Rather, it helps the programmer "think out" a program before attempting to write it in a programming language, such as Java. This chapter provides several examples of how to use pseudocode to develop Java programs.

The style of pseudocode we present consists purely of characters, so programmers can type pseudocode conveniently, using any text-editor program. A carefully prepared pseudocode program can easily be converted to a corresponding Java program. In many cases, this simply requires replacing pseudocode statements with Java equivalents.

Pseudocode normally describes only statements representing the actions that occur after a programmer converts a program from pseudocode to Java and the program is run on a computer. Such actions might include input, output or a calculation. We typically do not include variable declarations in our pseudocode. However, some programmers choose to list variables and mention their purposes at the beginning of their pseudocode.

4.4 Control Structures

Normally, statements in a program are executed one after the other in the order in which they are written. This process is called sequential execution. Various Java statements, which we will soon discuss, enable the programmer to specify that the next statement to execute is not necessarily the next one in sequence. This is called transfer of control.

During the 1960s, it became clear that the indiscriminate use of transfers of control was the root of much difficulty experienced by software development groups. The blame was pointed at the goto statement (used in most programming languages of the time), which allows the programmer to specify a transfer of control to one of a very wide range of possible destinations in a program. The notion of so-called structured programming became almost synonymous with "goto elimination." [*Note:* Java does not have a goto statement; however, the word goto is reserved by Java and should not be used as an identifier in programs.]

The research of Bohm and Jacopini[1] had demonstrated that programs could be written without any goto statements. The challenge of the era for programmers was to shift their styles to "goto-less programming." Not until the 1970s did programmers start taking structured programming seriously. The results were impressive. Software development groups reported shorter development times, more frequent on-time delivery of systems and more frequent within-budget completion of software projects. The key to these successes was that structured programs were clearer, easier to debug and modify, and more likely to be bug free in the first place.

Bohm and Jacopini's work demonstrated that all programs could be written in terms of only three control structures—the sequence structure, the selection structure and the repetition structure. The term "control structures" comes from the field of computer science. When we introduce Java's implementations of control structures, we will refer to them in the terminology of the *Java Language Specification* as "control statements."

Sequence Structure in Java

The sequence structure is built into Java. Unless directed otherwise, the computer executes Java statements one after the other in the order in which they are written, that is, in sequence. The activity diagram in Fig. 4.1 illustrates a typical sequence structure in which two calculations are performed in order. Java lets us have as many actions as we want in a sequence structure. As we will soon see, anywhere a single action may be placed, we may place several actions in sequence.

Activity diagrams are part of the UML. An activity diagram models the workflow (also called the activity) of a portion of a software system. Such workflows may include a portion of an algorithm, such as the sequence structure in Fig. 4.1. Activity diagrams are composed of special-purpose symbols, such as action-state symbols (rectangles with their left and right sides replaced with arcs curving outward), diamonds and small circles. These symbols are connected by transition arrows, which represent the flow of the activity, that is, the order in which the actions should occur

Like pseudocode, activity diagrams help programmers develop and represent algorithms, although many programmers prefer pseudocode. Activity diagrams clearly show how control structures operate.

Consider the activity diagram for the sequence structure in Fig. 4.1. It contains two action states that represent actions to perform. Each action state contains an action expression—for example, "add grade to total" or "add 1 to counter"—that specifies a particular action to perform. Other actions might include calculations or input/output operations. The arrows in the activity diagram represent transitions, which indicate the order in which the actions represented by the action states occur. The program that implements the activities illustrated by the diagram in Fig. 4.1 first adds grade to total, then adds 1 to counter.

The solid circle located at the top of the activity diagram represents the activity's initial state—the beginning of the workflow before the program performs the modeled actions. The solid circle surrounded by a hollow circle that appears at the bottom of the diagram represents the final state—the end of the workflow after the program performs its actions.

Figure 4.1 also includes rectangles with the upper-right corners folded over. These are UML notes (like comments in Java)—explanatory remarks that describe the purpose of symbols in the diagram. Figure 4.1 uses UML notes to show the Java code associated with each action state in the activity diagram. A dotted line connects each note with the ele-

---

1.   Bohm, C., and G. Jacopini, "Flow Diagrams, Turing Machines, and Languages with Only Two Formation Rules," *Communications of the ACM*, Vol. 9, No. 5, May 1966, pp. 336–371.

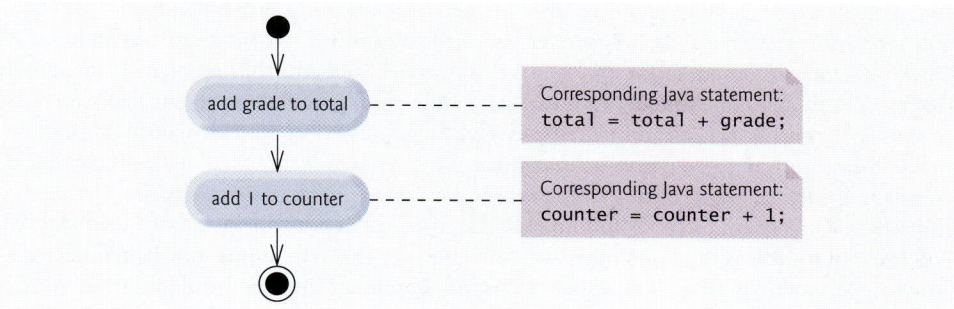

Fig. 4.1 | Sequence structure activity diagram.

ment that the note describes. Activity diagrams normally do not show the Java code that implements the activity. We use notes for this purpose here to illustrate how the diagram relates to Java code. For more information on the UML, see our optional case study, which appears in the Software Engineering Case Study sections at the ends of Chapters 1–8 and 10, or visit www.uml.org.

Selection Statements in Java

Java has three types of selection statements (discussed in this chapter and Chapter 5). The if statement either performs (selects) an action if a condition is true or skips the action, if the condition is false. The if...else statement performs an action if a condition is true and performs a different action if the condition is false. The switch statement (Chapter 5) performs one of many different actions, depending on the value of an expression.

The if statement is a **single-selection statement** because it selects or ignores a single action (or, as we will soon see, a single group of actions). The if...else statement is called a **double-selection statement** because it selects between two different actions (or groups of actions). The switch statement is called a **multiple-selection statement** because it selects among many different actions (or groups of actions).

Repetition Statements in Java

Java provides three repetition statements (also called **looping statements**) that enable programs to perform statements repeatedly as long as a condition (called the **loop-continuation condition**) remains true. The repetition statements are the while, do...while and for statements. (Chapter 5 presents the do...while and for statements.) The while and for statements perform the action (or group of actions) in their bodies zero or more times—if the loop-continuation condition is initially false, the action (or group of actions) will not execute. The do...while statement performs the action (or group of actions) in its body one or more times.

The words if, else, switch, while, do and for are Java keywords. Recall that keywords are used to implement various Java features, such as control statements. Keywords cannot be used as identifiers, such as variable names. A complete list of Java keywords appears in Appendix C.

Summary of Control Statements in Java

Java has only three kinds of control structures, which from this point forward we refer to as control statements: the sequence statement, selection statements (three types) and repetition statements (three types). Every program is formed by combining as many sequence, selection and repetition statements as is appropriate for the algorithm the program implements. As with the sequence statement in Fig. 4.1, we can model each control statement as an activity diagram. Each diagram contains an initial state and a final state that represent a control statement's entry point and exit point, respectively. **Single-entry/single-exit control statements** make it easy to build programs—the control statements are "attached" to one another by connecting the exit point of one to the entry point of the next. This procedure is similar to the way in which a child stacks building blocks, so we call it **control-statement stacking**. We will learn that there is only one other way in which control statements may be connected—**control-statement nesting**—in which a control statement appears inside another control statement. Thus, algorithms in Java programs are constructed from only three kinds of control statements, combined in only two ways. This is the essence of simplicity.

4.5 if Single-Selection Statement

Programs use selection statements to choose among alternative courses of action. For example, suppose that the passing grade on an exam is 60. The pseudocode statement

> *If student's grade is greater than or equal to 60*
> *Print "Passed"*

determines whether the condition "student's grade is greater than or equal to 60" is true or false. If the condition is true, "Passed" is printed, and the next pseudocode statement in order is "performed." (Remember that pseudocode is not a real programming language.) If the condition is false, the *Print* statement is ignored, and the next pseudocode statement in order is performed. The indentation of the second line of this selection statement is optional, but recommended, because it emphasizes the inherent structure of structured programs.

The preceding pseudocode *If* statement may be written in Java as

```
if ( studentGrade >= 60 )
    System.out.println( "Passed" );
```

Note that the Java code corresponds closely to the pseudocode. This is one of the properties of pseudocode that makes it such a useful program development tool.

Figure 4.2 illustrates the single-selection if statement. This activity diagram contains what is perhaps the most important symbol in an activity diagram—the diamond, or **decision symbol**, which indicates that a decision is to be made. The workflow will continue along a path determined by the symbol's associated **guard conditions**, which can be true or false. Each transition arrow emerging from a decision symbol has a guard condition (specified in square brackets next to the transition arrow). If a guard condition is true, the workflow enters the action state to which the transition arrow points. In Fig. 4.2, if the grade is greater than or equal to 60, the program prints "Passed," then transitions to the final state of this activity. If the grade is less than 60, the program immediately transitions to the final state without displaying a message.

The if statement is a single-entry/single-exit control statement. We will see that the activity diagrams for the remaining control statements also contain initial states, transition arrows, action states that indicate actions to perform, decision symbols (with associated guard conditions) that indicate decisions to be made and final states. This is consistent with the **action/decision model of programming** we have been emphasizing.

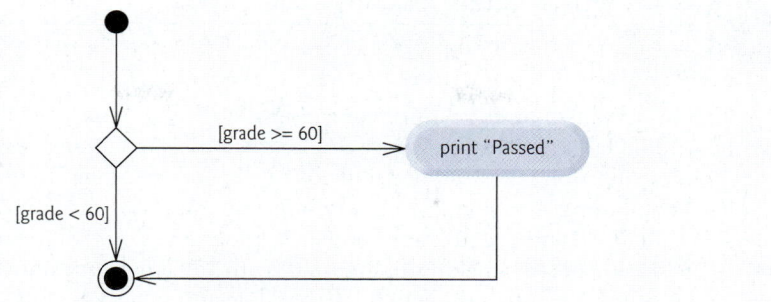

Fig. 4.2 | if single-selection statement UML activity diagram.

Envision seven bins, each containing only one type of Java control statement. The control statements are all empty. Your task is to assemble a program from as many of each type of control statement as the algorithm demands, combining the control statements in only two possible ways (stacking or nesting), then filling in the action states and decisions with action expressions and guard conditions appropriate for the algorithm. We will discuss the variety of ways in which actions and decisions can be written.

4.6 if...else Double-Selection Statement

The if single-selection statement performs an indicated action only when the condition is true; otherwise, the action is skipped. The if...else double-selection statement allows the programmer to specify an action to perform when the condition is true and a different action when the condition is false. For example, the pseudocode statement

> *If student's grade is greater than or equal to 60*
> > *Print "Passed"*
> *Else*
> > *Print "Failed"*

prints "Passed" if the student's grade is greater than or equal to 60, but prints "Failed" if it is less than 60. In either case, after printing occurs, the next pseudocode statement in sequence is "performed."

The preceding *If…Else* pseudocode statement can be written in Java as

```
if ( grade >= 60 )
    System.out.println( "Passed" );
else
    System.out.println( "Failed" );
```

Note that the body of the else is also indented. Whatever indentation convention you choose should be applied consistently throughout your programs. It is difficult to read programs that do not obey uniform spacing conventions.

Good Programming Practice 4.1

Indent both body statements of an if…else statement.

Good Programming Practice 4.2

If there are several levels of indentation, each level should be indented the same additional amount of space.

Figure 4.3 illustrates the flow of control in the if...else statement. Once again, the symbols in the UML activity diagram (besides the initial state, transition arrows and final state) represent action states and decisions. We continue to emphasize this action/decision model of computing. Imagine again a deep bin containing as many empty if...else statements as might be needed to build any Java program. Your job is to assemble these if...else statements (by stacking and nesting) with any other control statements required by the algorithm. You fill in the action states and decision symbols with action expressions and guard conditions appropriate to the algorithm you are developing.

Conditional Operator (?:)

Java provides the **conditional operator** (**?:**) that can be used in place of an if...else statement. This is Java's only **ternary operator**—this means that it takes three operands. Together, the operands and the ?: symbol form a **conditional expression.** The first operand (to the left of the ?) is a **boolean** expression (i.e., a condition that evaluates to a boolean value—**true** or **false**), the second operand (between the ? and :) is the value of the conditional expression if the boolean expression is true and the third operand (to the right of the :) is the value of the conditional expression if the boolean expression evaluates to false. For example, the statement

```
System.out.println( studentGrade >= 60 ? "Passed" : "Failed" );
```

prints the value of println's conditional-expression argument. The conditional expression in this statement evaluates to the string "Passed" if the boolean expression studentGrade >= 60 is true and evaluates to the string "Failed" if the boolean expression is false. Thus, this statement with the conditional operator performs essentially the same function as the if...else statement shown earlier in this section. The precedence of the conditional operator is low, so the entire conditional expression is normally placed in parentheses. We will see that conditional expressions can be used in some situations where if...else statements cannot.

Good Programming Practice 4.3

Conditional expressions are more difficult to read than if...else statements and should be used to replace only simple if...else statements that choose between two values.

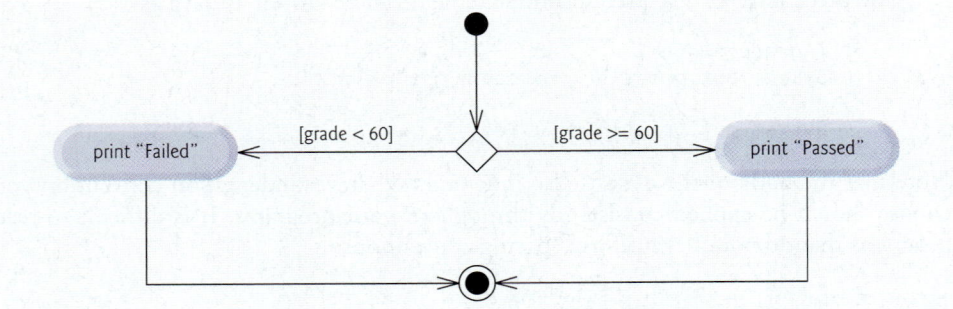

Fig. 4.3 | if...else double-selection statement UML activity diagram.

Nested if...else Statements

A program can test multiple cases by placing if...else statements inside other if...else statements to create **nested if...else statements**. For example, the following pseudocode represents a nested if...else that prints A for exam grades greater than or equal to 90, B for grades in the range 80 to 89, C for grades in the range 70 to 79, D for grades in the range 60 to 69 and F for all other grades:

> *If student's grade is greater than or equal to 90*
>   *Print "A"*
> *else*
>   *If student's grade is greater than or equal to 80*
>   *Print "B"*
>   *else*
>   *If student's grade is greater than or equal to 70*
>   *Print "C"*
>   *else*
>   *If student's grade is greater than or equal to 60*
>   *Print "D"*
>   *else*
>   *Print "F"*

This pseudocode may be written in Java as

```java
if ( studentGrade >= 90 )
   System.out.println( "A" );
else
   if ( studentGrade >= 80 )
      System.out.println( "B" );
   else
      if ( studentGrade >= 70 )
         System.out.println( "C" );
      else
         if ( studentGrade >= 60 )
            System.out.println( "D" );
         else
            System.out.println( "F" );
```

If studentGrade is greater than or equal to 90, the first four conditions will be true, but only the statement in the if-part of the first if...else statement will execute. After that statement executes, the else-part of the "outermost" if...else statement is skipped. Most Java programmers prefer to write the preceding if...else statement as

```java
if ( studentGrade >= 90 )
   System.out.println( "A" );
else if ( studentGrade >= 80 )
   System.out.println( "B" );
else if ( studentGrade >= 70 )
   System.out.println( "C" );
else if ( studentGrade >= 60 )
   System.out.println( "D" );
else
   System.out.println( "F" );
```

The two forms are identical except for the spacing and indentation, which the compiler ignores. The latter form is popular because it avoids deep indentation of the code to the right. Such indentation often leaves little room on a line of code, forcing lines to be split and decreasing program readability.

Dangling-*else* Problem

The Java compiler always associates an else with the immediately preceding if unless told to do otherwise by the placement of braces ({ and }). This behavior can lead to what is referred to as the **dangling-else problem**. For example,

```
if ( x > 5 )
   if ( y > 5 )
      System.out.println( "x and y are > 5" );
else
   System.out.println( "x is <= 5" );
```

appears to indicate that if x is greater than 5, the nested if statement determines whether y is also greater than 5. If so, the string "x and y are > 5" is output. Otherwise, it appears that if x is not greater than 5, the else part of the if...else outputs the string "x is <= 5".

Beware! This nested if...else statement does not execute as it appears. The compiler actually interprets the statement as

```
if ( x > 5 )
   if ( y > 5 )
      System.out.println( "x and y are > 5" );
   else
      System.out.println( "x is <= 5" );
```

in which the body of the first if is a nested if...else. The outer if statement tests whether x is greater than 5. If so, execution continues by testing whether y is also greater than 5. If the second condition is true, the proper string—"x and y are > 5"—is displayed. However, if the second condition is false, the string "x is <= 5" is displayed, even though we know that x is greater than 5.

To force the nested if...else statement to execute as it was originally intended, we must write it as follows:

```
if ( x > 5 )
{
   if ( y > 5 )
      System.out.println( "x and y are > 5" );
}
else
   System.out.println( "x is <= 5" );
```

The braces ({}) indicate to the compiler that the second if statement is in the body of the first if and that the else is associated with the first if. Exercise 4.27 and Exercise 4.28 investigate the dangling-else problem further.

Blocks

The if statement normally expects only one statement in its body. To include several statements in the body of an if (or the body of an else for an if...else statement), enclose the statements in braces ({ and }). A set of statements contained within a pair of braces is called a block. A block can be placed anywhere in a program that a single statement can be placed.

The following example includes a block in the else-part of an if...else statement:

```
if ( grade >= 60 )
    System.out.println( "Passed" );
else
{
    System.out.println( "Failed" );
    System.out.println( "You must take this course again." );
}
```

In this case, if grade is less than 60, the program executes both statements in the body of the else and prints

```
Failed.
You must take this course again.
```

Note the braces surrounding the two statements in the else clause. These braces are important. Without the braces, the statement

```
System.out.println( "You must take this course again." );
```

would be outside the body of the else-part of the if...else statement and would execute regardless of whether the grade was less than 60.

Syntax errors (e.g., when one brace in a block is left out of the program) are caught by the compiler. A logic error (e.g., when both braces in a block are left out of the program) has its effect at execution time. A fatal logic error causes a program to fail and terminate prematurely. A nonfatal logic error allows a program to continue executing, but causes the program to produce incorrect results.

Common Programming Error 4.1

Forgetting one or both of the braces that delimit a block can lead to syntax errors or logic errors in a program.

Good Programming Practice 4.4

Always using braces in an if...else (or other) statement helps prevent their accidental omission, especially when adding statements to the if-part or the else-part at a later time. To avoid omitting one or both of the braces, some programmers type the beginning and ending braces of blocks before typing the individual statements within the braces.

Just as a block can be placed anywhere a single statement can be placed, it is also possible to have an empty statement. Recall from Section 2.8 that the empty statement is represented by placing a semicolon (;) where a statement would normally be.

Common Programming Error 4.2

Placing a semicolon after the condition in an if or if...else statement leads to a logic error in single-selection if statements and a syntax error in double-selection if...else statements (when the if-part contains an actual body statement).

4.7 `while` Repetition Statement

A repetition statement (also called a looping statement or a loop) allows the programmer to specify that a program should repeat an action while some condition remains true. The pseudocode statement

> *While there are more items on my shopping list*
> *Purchase next item and cross it off my list*

describes the repetition that occurs during a shopping trip. The condition "there are more items on my shopping list" may be true or false. If it is true, then the action "Purchase next item and cross it off my list" is performed. This action will be performed repeatedly while the condition remains true. The statement(s) contained in the *While* repetition statement constitute the body of the *While* repetition statement, which may be a single statement or a block. Eventually, the condition will become false (when the last item on the shopping list has been purchased and crossed off the list). At this point, the repetition terminates, and the first statement after the repetition statement executes.

As an example of Java's `while` repetition statement, consider a program segment designed to find the first power of 3 larger than 100. Suppose that the `int` variable `product` is initialized to 3. When the following `while` statement finishes executing, `product` contains the result:

```
int product = 3;

while ( product <= 100 )
    product = 3 * product;
```

When this `while` statement begins execution, the value of variable `product` is 3. Each iteration of the `while` statement multiplies `product` by 3, so `product` takes on the values 9, 27, 81 and 243 successively. When variable `product` becomes 243, the `while` statement condition—product <= 100—becomes false. This terminates the repetition, so the final value of `product` is 243. At this point, program execution continues with the next statement after the `while` statement.

Common Programming Error 4.3

Not providing, in the body of a `while` *statement, an action that eventually causes the condition in the* `while` *to become false normally results in a logic error called an infinite loop, in which the loop never terminates.*

The UML activity diagram in Fig. 4.4 illustrates the flow of control that corresponds to the preceding `while` statement. Once again, the symbols in the diagram (besides the initial state, transition arrows, a final state and three notes) represent an action state and a decision. This diagram also introduces the UML's merge symbol. The UML represents both the merge symbol and the decision symbol as diamonds. The merge symbol joins two flows of activity into one. In this diagram, the merge symbol joins the transitions from the initial state and from the action state, so they both flow into the decision that determines whether the loop should begin (or continue) executing. The decision and merge symbols can be distinguished by the number of "incoming" and "outgoing" transition arrows. A decision symbol has one transition arrow pointing to the diamond and two or more transition arrows pointing out from the diamond to indicate possible transitions from that

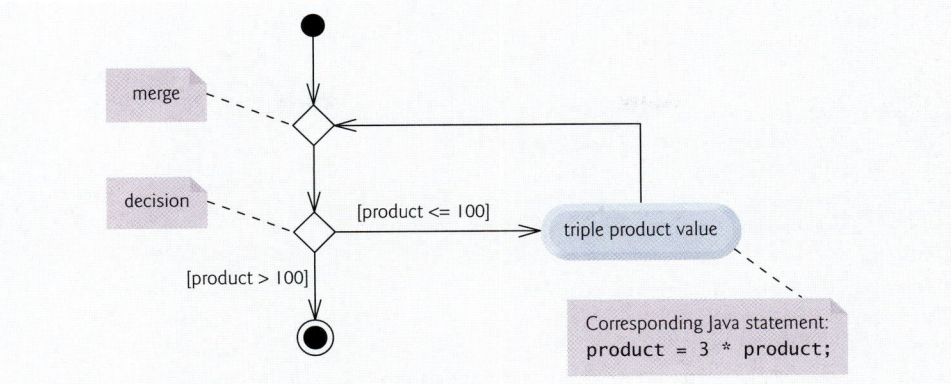

Fig. 4.4 | `while` repetition statement UML activity diagram.

point. In addition, each transition arrow pointing out of a decision symbol has a guard condition next to it. A merge symbol has two or more transition arrows pointing to the diamond and only one transition arrow pointing from the diamond, to indicate multiple activity flows merging to continue the activity. None of the transition arrows associated with a merge symbol have guard conditions.

Figure 4.4 clearly shows the repetition of the `while` statement discussed earlier in this section. The transition arrow emerging from the action state points back to the merge, from which program flow transitions back to the decision that is tested at the beginning of each iteration of the loop. The loop continues to execute until the guard condition `product > 100` becomes true. Then the `while` statement exits (reaches its final state), and control passes to the next statement in sequence in the program.

4.8 Formulating Algorithms: Counter-Controlled Repetition

To illustrate how algorithms are developed, we modify the `GradeBook` class of Chapter 3 to solve two variations of a problem that averages student grades. Consider the following problem statement:

> *A class of ten students took a quiz. The grades (integers in the range 0 to 100) for this quiz are available to you. Determine the class average on the quiz.*

The class average is equal to the sum of the grades divided by the number of students. The algorithm for solving this problem on a computer must input each grade, keep track of the total of all grades input, perform the averaging calculation and print the result.

Pseudocode Algorithm with Counter-Controlled Repetition

Let's use pseudocode to list the actions to execute and specify the order in which they should execute. We use counter-controlled repetition to input the grades one at a time. This technique uses a variable called a counter (or control variable) to control the number of times a set of statements will execute. Counter-controlled repetition is often called definite repetition, because the number of repetitions is known before the loop begins executing. In this example, repetition terminates when the counter exceeds 10. This section presents a fully developed pseudocode algorithm (Fig. 4.5) and a version of class Grade-

1	*Set total to zero*
2	*Set grade counter to one*
3	
4	*While grade counter is less than or equal to ten*
5	*Prompt the user to enter the next grade*
6	*Input the next grade*
7	*Add the grade into the total*
8	*Add one to the grade counter*
9	
10	*Set the class average to the total divided by ten*
11	*Print the class average*

Fig. 4.5 | Pseudocode algorithm that uses counter-controlled repetition to solve the class-average problem.

Book (Fig. 4.6) that implements the algorithm in a Java method. The section then presents an application (Fig. 4.7) that demonstrates the algorithm in action. In Section 4.9, we demonstrate how to use pseudocode to develop such an algorithm from scratch.

Software Engineering Observation 4.1

Experience has shown that the most difficult part of solving a problem on a computer is developing the algorithm for the solution. Once a correct algorithm has been specified, the process of producing a working Java program from the algorithm is normally straightforward.

Note the references in the algorithm of Fig. 4.5 to a total and a counter. A total is a variable used to accumulate the sum of several values. A counter is a variable used to count—in this case, the grade counter indicates which of the 10 grades is about to be entered by the user. Variables used to store totals are normally initialized to zero before being used in a program.

Implementing Counter-Controlled Repetition in Class *GradeBook*

Class GradeBook (Fig. 4.6) contains a constructor (lines 11–14) that assigns a value to the class's instance variable courseName (declared in line 8). Lines 17–20, 23–26 and 29–34 declare methods setCourseName, getCourseName and displayMessage, respectively. Lines 37–66 declare method determineClassAverage, which implements the class-averaging algorithm described by the pseudocode in Fig. 4.5.

Line 40 declares and initializes Scanner variable input, which is used to read values entered by the user. Lines 42–45 declare local variables total, gradeCounter, grade and average to be of type int. Variable grade stores the user input.

Note that the declarations (in lines 42–45) appear in the body of method determineClassAverage. Recall that variables declared in a method body are local variables and can be

```
1   // Fig. 4.6: GradeBook.java
2   // GradeBook class that solves class-average problem using
3   // counter-controlled repetition.
4   import java.util.Scanner; // program uses class Scanner
5
```

Fig. 4.6 | Counter-controlled repetition: Class-average problem. (Part 1 of 3.)

```
6   public class GradeBook
7   {
8      private String courseName; // name of course this GradeBook represents
9
10     // constructor initializes courseName
11     public GradeBook( String name )
12     {
13        courseName = name; // initializes courseName
14     } // end constructor
15
16     // method to set the course name
17     public void setCourseName( String name )
18     {
19        courseName = name; // store the course name
20     } // end method setCourseName
21
22     // method to retrieve the course name
23     public String getCourseName()
24     {
25        return courseName;
26     } // end method getCourseName
27
28     // display a welcome message to the GradeBook user
29     public void displayMessage()
30     {
31        // getCourseName gets the name of the course
32        System.out.printf( "Welcome to the grade book for\n%s!\n\n",
33           getCourseName() );
34     } // end method displayMessage
35
36     // determine class average based on 10 grades entered by user
37     public void determineClassAverage()
38     {
39        // create Scanner to obtain input from command window
40        Scanner input = new Scanner( System.in );
41
42        int total; // sum of grades entered by user
43        int gradeCounter; // number of the grade to be entered next
44        int grade; // grade value entered by user
45        int average; // average of grades
46
47        // initialization phase
48        total = 0; // initialize total
49        gradeCounter = 1; // initialize loop counter
50
51        // processing phase
52        while ( gradeCounter <= 10 ) // loop 10 times
53        {
54           System.out.print( "Enter grade: " ); // prompt
55           grade = input.nextInt(); // input next grade
56           total = total + grade; // add grade to total
57           gradeCounter = gradeCounter + 1; // increment counter by 1
58        } // end while
```

Fig. 4.6 | Counter-controlled repetition: Class-average problem. (Part 2 of 3.)

```
59
60          // termination phase
61          average = total / 10; // integer division yields integer result
62
63          // display total and average of grades
64          System.out.printf( "\nTotal of all 10 grades is %d\n", total );
65          System.out.printf( "Class average is %d\n", average );
66       } // end method determineClassAverage
67
68    } // end class GradeBook
```

Fig. 4.6 | Counter-controlled repetition: Class-average problem. (Part 3 of 3.)

used only from the line of their declaration in the method to the closing right brace (}) of the method declaration. A local variable's declaration must appear before the variable is used in that method. A local variable cannot be accessed outside the method in which it is declared.

In the versions of class GradeBook in this chapter, we simply read and process a set of grades. The averaging calculation is performed in method determineClassAverage using local variables—we do not preserve any information about student grades in instance variables of the class. In later versions of the class (in Chapter 7, Arrays), we maintain the grades in memory using an instance variable that refers to a data structure known as an array. This allows a GradeBook object to perform various calculations on the same set of grades without requiring the user to enter the grades multiple times.

Good Programming Practice 4.5

Separate declarations from other statements in methods with a blank line for readability.

The assignments (in lines 48–49) initialize total to 0 and gradeCounter to 1. Note that these initializations occur before the variables are used in calculations. Variables grade and average (for the user input and calculated average, respectively) need not be initialized here—their values will be assigned as they are input or calculated later in the method.

Common Programming Error 4.4

Using the value of a local variable before it is initialized results in a compilation error. All local variables must be initialized before their values are used in expressions.

Error-Prevention Tip 4.1

Initialize each counter and total, either in its declaration or in an assignment statement. Totals are normally initialized to 0. Counters are normally initialized to 0 or 1, depending on how they are used (we will show examples of when to use 0 and when to use 1).

Line 52 indicates that the while statement should continue looping (also called iterating) as long as the value of gradeCounter is less than or equal to 10. While this condition remains true, the while statement repeatedly executes the statements between the braces that delimit its body (lines 53–58).

Line 54 displays the prompt "Enter grade: " at the command line. Line 55 reads the grade entered by the user and assigns it to variable grade. Then line 56 adds the new grade entered by the user to the total and assigns the result to total, which replaces its previous value.

Line 57 adds 1 to grade Counter to indicate that the program has processed a grade and is ready to input the next grade from the user. Incrementing gradeCounter eventually causes gradeCounter to exceed 10. At that point the while loop terminates because its condition (line 52) becomes false.

When the loop terminates, line 61 performs the averaging calculation and assigns its result to the variable average. Line 64 uses System.out's printf method to display the text "Total of all 10 grades is " followed by variable total's value. Line 65 then uses printf to display the text "Class average is " followed by variable average's value. Method determineClassAverage returns control to the calling method (i.e., main in GradeBookTest of Fig. 4.7) after reaching line 66.

Class *GradeBookTest*

Class GradeBookTest (Fig. 4.7) creates an object of class GradeBook (Fig. 4.6) and demonstrates its capabilities. Lines 10–11 of Fig. 4.7 create a new GradeBook object and assign it to variable myGradeBook. The String in line 11 is passed to the GradeBook constructor (lines 11–14 of Fig. 4.6). Line 13 calls myGradeBook's displayMessage method to display a welcome message to the user. Line 14 then calls myGradeBook's determineClassAverage method to allow the user to enter 10 grades, for which the method then calculates and prints the average—the method performs the algorithm shown in Fig. 4.5.

Notes on Integer Division and Truncation

The averaging calculation performed by method determineClassAverage in response to the method call at line 14 in Fig. 4.7 produces an integer result. The program's output indicates that the sum of the grade values in the sample execution is 846, which, when divided by 10, should yield the floating-point number 84.6. However, the result of the calculation total / 10 (line 61 of Fig. 4.6) is the integer 84, because total and 10 are both integers. Dividing two integers results in integer division—any fractional part of the calculation is lost (i.e., truncated). We will see how to obtain a floating-point result from the averaging calculation in the next section.

```
1   // Fig. 4.7: GradeBookTest.java
2   // Create GradeBook object and invoke its determineClassAverage method.
3
4   public class GradeBookTest
5   {
6      public static void main( String args[] )
7      {
8         // create GradeBook object myGradeBook and
9         // pass course name to constructor
10        GradeBook myGradeBook = new GradeBook(
11           "CS101 Introduction to Java Programming" );
12
13        myGradeBook.displayMessage(); // display welcome message
14        myGradeBook.determineClassAverage(); // find average of 10 grades
15     } // end main
16
17  } // end class GradeBookTest
```

Fig. 4.7 | GradeBookTest class creates an object of class GradeBook (Fig. 4.6) and invokes its determineClassAverage method. (Part 1 of 2.)

```
Welcome to the grade book for
CS101 Introduction to Java Programming!

Enter grade: 67
Enter grade: 78
Enter grade: 89
Enter grade: 67
Enter grade: 87
Enter grade: 98
Enter grade: 93
Enter grade: 85
Enter grade: 82
Enter grade: 100

Total of all 10 grades is 846
Class average is 84
```

Fig. 4.7 | GradeBookTest class creates an object of class GradeBook (Fig. 4.6) and invokes its determineClassAverage method. (Part 2 of 2.)

Common Programming Error 4.5

Assuming that integer division rounds (rather than truncates) can lead to incorrect results. For example, 7 ÷ 4, which yields 1.75 in conventional arithmetic, truncates to 1 in integer arithmetic, rather than rounding to 2.

4.9 Formulating Algorithms: Sentinel-Controlled Repetition

Let us generalize Section 4.8's class-average problem. Consider the following problem:

> *Develop a class-averaging program that processes grades for an arbitrary number of students each time it is run.*

In the previous class-average example, the problem statement specified the number of students, so the number of grades (10) was known in advance. In this example, no indication is given of how many grades the user will enter during the program's execution. The program must process an arbitrary number of grades. How can it determine when to stop the input of grades? How will it know when to calculate and print the class average?

One way to solve this problem is to use a special value called a **sentinel value** (also called a **signal value**, a **dummy value** or a **flag value**) to indicate "end of data entry." The user enters grades until all legitimate grades have been entered. The user then types the sentinel value to indicate that no more grades will be entered. Sentinel-controlled repetition is often called **indefinite repetition** because the number of repetitions is not known before the loop begins executing.

Clearly, a sentinel value must be chosen that cannot be confused with an acceptable input value. Grades on a quiz are nonnegative integers, so –1 is an acceptable sentinel value for this problem. Thus, a run of the class-average program might process a stream of inputs such as 95, 96, 75, 74, 89 and –1. The program would then compute and print the class average for the grades 95, 96, 75, 74 and 89. Since –1 is the sentinel value, it should not enter into the averaging calculation.

Common Programming Error 4.6

Choosing a sentinel value that is also a legitimate data value is a logic error.

Developing the Pseudocode Algorithm with Top-Down, Stepwise Refinement: The Top and First Refinement

We approach the class-average program with a technique called top-down, stepwise refinement, which is essential to the development of well-structured programs. We begin with a pseudocode representation of the top—a single statement that conveys the overall function of the program:

Determine the class average for the quiz

The top is, in effect, a *complete* representation of a program. Unfortunately, the top rarely conveys sufficient detail from which to write a Java program. So we now begin the refinement process. We divide the top into a series of smaller tasks and list these in the order in which they will be performed. This results in the following first refinement:

Initialize variables
Input, sum and count the quiz grades
Calculate and print the class average

This refinement uses only the sequence structure—the steps listed should execute in order, one after the other.

Software Engineering Observation 4.2

Each refinement, as well as the top itself, is a complete specification of the algorithm—only the level of detail varies.

Software Engineering Observation 4.3

Many programs can be divided logically into three phases: an initialization phase that initializes the variables; a processing phase that inputs data values and adjusts program variables (e.g., counters and totals) accordingly; and a termination phase that calculates and outputs the final results.

Proceeding to the Second Refinement

The preceding *Software Engineering Observation* is often all you need for the first refinement in the top-down process. To proceed to the next level of refinement, that is, the second refinement, we commit to specific variables. In this example, we need a running total of the numbers, a count of how many numbers have been processed, a variable to receive the value of each grade as it is input by the user and a variable to hold the calculated average. The pseudocode statement

Initialize variables

can be refined as follows:

Initialize total to zero
Initialize counter to zero

Only the variables *total* and *counter* need to be initialized before they are used. The variables *average* and *grade* (for the calculated average and the user input, respectively) need not be initialized, because their values will be replaced as they are calculated or input.

The pseudocode statement

Input, sum and count the quiz grades

requires a repetition structure (i.e., a loop) that successively inputs each grade. We do not know in advance how many grades are to be processed, so we will use sentinel-controlled repetition. The user enters grades one at a time. After entering the last grade, the user enters the sentinel value. The program tests for the sentinel value after each grade is input and terminates the loop when the user enters the sentinel value. The second refinement of the preceding pseudocode statement is then

Prompt the user to enter the first grade
Input the first grade (possibly the sentinel)

While the user has not yet entered the sentinel
 Add this grade into the running total
 Add one to the grade counter
 Prompt the user to enter the next grade
 Input the next grade (possibly the sentinel)

In pseudocode, we do not use braces around the statements that form the body of the *While* structure. We simply indent the statements under the *While* to show that they belong to the *While*. Again, pseudocode is only an informal program-development aid.

The pseudocode statement

Calculate and print the class average

can be refined as follows:

If the counter is not equal to zero
 Set the average to the total divided by the counter
 Print the average
else
 Print "No grades were entered"

We are careful here to test for the possibility of division by zero—normally a logic error that, if undetected, would cause the program to fail or produce invalid output. The complete second refinement of the pseudocode for the class-average problem is shown in Fig. 4.8.

Error-Prevention Tip 4.2

When performing division by an expression whose value could be zero, explicitly test for this possibility and handle it appropriately in your program (e.g., by printing an error message) rather than allow the error to occur

```
1   Initialize total to zero
2   Initialize counter to zero
3
4   Prompt the user to enter the first grade
5   Input the first grade (possibly the sentinel)
6
```

Fig. 4.8 | Class-average problem pseudocode algorithm with sentinel-controlled repetition. (Part 1 of 2.)

```
7    While the user has not yet entered the sentinel
8        Add this grade into the running total
9        Add one to the grade counter
10       Prompt the user to enter the next grade
11       Input the next grade (possibly the sentinel)
12
13   If the counter is not equal to zero
14       Set the average to the total divided by the counter
15       Print the average
16   else
17       Print "No grades were entered"
```

Fig. 4.8 | Class-average problem pseudocode algorithm with sentinel-controlled repetition. (Part 2 of 2.)

In Fig. 4.5 and Fig. 4.8, we included some completely blank lines and indentation in the pseudocode to make it more readable. The blank lines separate the pseudocode algorithms into their various phases and set off control statements, and the indentation emphasizes the bodies of the control statements.

The pseudocode algorithm in Fig. 4.8 solves the more general class-averaging problem. This algorithm was developed after only two refinements. Sometimes more refinements are necessary.

Software Engineering Observation 4.4

Terminate the top-down, stepwise refinement process when you have specified the pseudocode algorithm in sufficient detail for you to convert the pseudocode to Java. Normally, implementing the Java program is then straightforward.

Software Engineering Observation 4.5

Some experienced programmers write programs without ever using program-development tools like pseudocode. They feel that their ultimate goal is to solve the problem on a computer and that writing pseudocode merely delays the production of final outputs. Although this method may work for simple and familiar problems, it can lead to serious errors and delays in large, complex projects.

Implementing Sentinel-Controlled Repetition in Class *GradeBook*

Figure 4.9 shows the Java class GradeBook containing method determineClassAverage that implements the pseudocode algorithm of Fig. 4.8. Although each grade is an integer, the averaging calculation is likely to produce a number with a decimal point—in other words, a real number or floating-point number. The type int cannot represent such a number, so this class uses type double to do so.

```java
1    // Fig. 4.9: GradeBook.java
2    // GradeBook class that solves class-average program using
3    // sentinel-controlled repetition.
4    import java.util.Scanner; // program uses class Scanner
5
```

Fig. 4.9 | Sentinel-controlled repetition: Class-average problem. (Part 1 of 3.)

```
6   public class GradeBook
7   {
8      private String courseName; // name of course this GradeBook represents
9
10     // constructor initializes courseName
11     public GradeBook( String name )
12     {
13        courseName = name; // initializes courseName
14     } // end constructor
15
16     // method to set the course name
17     public void setCourseName( String name )
18     {
19        courseName = name; // store the course name
20     } // end method setCourseName
21
22     // method to retrieve the course name
23     public String getCourseName()
24     {
25        return courseName;
26     } // end method getCourseName
27
28     // display a welcome message to the GradeBook user
29     public void displayMessage()
30     {
31        // getCourseName gets the name of the course
32        System.out.printf( "Welcome to the grade book for\n%s!\n\n",
33           getCourseName() );
34     } // end method displayMessage
35
36     // determine the average of an arbitrary number of grades
37     public void determineClassAverage()
38     {
39        // create Scanner to obtain input from command window
40        Scanner input = new Scanner( System.in );
41
42        int total; // sum of grades
43        int gradeCounter; // number of grades entered
44        int grade; // grade value
45        double average; // number with decimal point for average
46
47        // initialization phase
48        total = 0; // initialize total
49        gradeCounter = 0; // initialize loop counter
50
51        // processing phase
52        // prompt for input and read grade from user
53        System.out.print( "Enter grade or -1 to quit: " );
54        grade = input.nextInt();
55
56        // loop until sentinel value read from user
57        while ( grade != -1 )
58        {
```

Fig. 4.9 | Sentinel-controlled repetition: Class-average problem. (Part 2 of 3.)

```
59              total = total + grade; // add grade to total
60              gradeCounter = gradeCounter + 1; // increment counter
61
62              // prompt for input and read next grade from user
63              System.out.print( "Enter grade or -1 to quit: " );
64              grade = input.nextInt();
65          } // end while
66
67          // termination phase
68          // if user entered at least one grade...
69          if ( gradeCounter != 0 )
70          {
71              // calculate average of all grades entered
72              average = (double) total / gradeCounter;
73
74              // display total and average (with two digits of precision)
75              System.out.printf( "\nTotal of the %d grades entered is %d\n",
76                  gradeCounter, total );
77              System.out.printf( "Class average is %.2f\n", average );
78          } // end if
79          else // no grades were entered, so output appropriate message
80              System.out.println( "No grades were entered" );
81      } // end method determineClassAverage
82
83  } // end class GradeBook
```

Fig. 4.9 | Sentinel-controlled repetition: Class-average problem. (Part 3 of 3.)

In this example, we see that control statements may be stacked on top of one another (in sequence) just as a child stacks building blocks. The `while` statement (lines 57–65) is followed in sequence by an `if...else` statement (lines 69–80). Much of the code in this program is identical to the code in Fig. 4.6, so we concentrate on the new features and issues.

Line 45 declares `double` variable `average`. This variable allows us to store the calculated class average as a floating-point number. Line 49 initializes `gradeCounter` to 0, because no grades have been entered yet. Remember that this program uses sentinel-controlled repetition to input the grades from the user. To keep an accurate record of the number of grades entered, the program increments `gradeCounter` only when the user inputs a valid grade value.

Program Logic for Sentinel-Controlled Repetition vs. Counter-Controlled Repetition
Compare the program logic for sentinel-controlled repetition in this application with that for counter-controlled repetition in Fig. 4.6. In counter-controlled repetition, each iteration of the `while` statement (e.g., lines 52–58 of Fig. 4.6) reads a value from the user, for the specified number of iterations. In sentinel-controlled repetition, the program reads the first value (lines 53–54 of Fig. 4.9) before reaching the `while`. This value determines whether the program's flow of control should enter the body of the `while`. If the condition of the `while` is false, the user entered the sentinel value, so the body of the `while` does not execute (i.e., no grades were entered). If, on the other hand, the condition is true, the body begins execution, and the loop adds the `grade` value to the `total` (line 59). Then lines 63–64 in the loop's body input the next value from the user. Next, program control reaches

the closing right brace (}) of the body at line 65, so execution continues with the test of the `while`'s condition (line 57). The condition uses the most recent `grade` input by the user to determine whether the loop's body should execute again. Note that the value of variable `grade` is always input from the user immediately before the program tests the `while` condition. This allows the program to determine whether the value just input is the sentinel value *before* the program processes that value (i.e., adds it to the `total`). If the sentinel value is input, the loop terminates, and the program does not add –1 to the `total`.

Good Programming Practice 4.6

In a sentinel-controlled loop, the prompts requesting data entry should explicitly remind the user of the sentinel value.

After the loop terminates, the `if...else` statement at lines 69–80 executes. The condition at line 69 determines whether any grades were input. If none were input, the `else` part (lines 79–80) of the `if...else` statement executes and displays the message "No grades were entered" and the method returns control to the calling method.

Notice the `while` statement's block in Fig. 4.9 (lines 58–65). Without the braces, the loop would consider its body to be only the first statement, which adds the `grade` to the `total`. The last three statements in the block would fall outside the loop's body, causing the computer to interpret the code incorrectly as follows:

```java
while ( grade != -1 )
   total = total + grade; // add grade to total
gradeCounter = gradeCounter + 1; // increment counter

// prompt for input and read next grade from user
System.out.print( "Enter grade or -1 to quit: " );
grade = input.nextInt();
```

The preceding code would cause an infinite loop in the program if the user did not input the sentinel `-1` at line 54 (before the `while` statement).

Common Programming Error 4.7

Omitting the braces that delimit a block can lead to logic errors, such as infinite loops. To prevent this problem, some programmers enclose the body of every control statement in braces even if the body contains only a single statement.

Explicitly and Implicitly Converting Between Primitive Types

If at least one grade was entered, line 72 of Fig. 4.9 calculates the average of the grades. Recall from Fig. 4.6 that integer division yields an integer result. Even though variable `average` is declared as a `double` (line 45), the calculation

```java
average = total / gradeCounter;
```

loses the fractional part of the quotient before the result of the division is assigned to `average`. This occurs because `total` and `gradeCounter` are both integers and integer division yields an integer result. To perform a floating-point calculation with integer values, we must temporarily treat these values as floating-point numbers for use in the calculation. Java provides the **unary cast operator** to accomplish this task. Line 72 uses the `(double)` cast operator—a unary operator—to create a *temporary* floating-point copy of its operand `total` (which appears to the right of the operator). Using a cast operator in this manner is called **explicit conversion**. The value stored in `total` is still an integer.

The calculation now consists of a floating-point value (the temporary `double` version of `total`) divided by the integer `gradeCounter`. Java knows how to evaluate only arithmetic expressions in which the operands' types are identical. To ensure that the operands are of the same type, Java performs an operation called **promotion** (or **implicit conversion**) on selected operands. For example, in an expression containing values of the types `int` and `double`, the `int` values are **promoted** to `double` values for use in the expression. In this example, the value of `gradeCounter` is promoted to type `double`, then the floating-point division is performed and the result of the calculation is assigned to `average`. As long as the `(double)` cast operator is applied to any variable in the calculation, the calculation will yield a `double` result. Later in this chapter, we discuss all the primitive types. You will learn more about the promotion rules in Section 6.7.

Common Programming Error 4.8

The cast operator can be used to convert between primitive numeric types, such as `int` and `double`, and between related reference types (as we discuss in Chapter 10, Object-Oriented Programming: Polymorphism). Casting to the wrong type may cause compilation errors or runtime errors.

Cast operators are available for any type. The cast operator is formed by placing parentheses around the name of a type. The operator is a **unary operator** (i.e., an operator that takes only one operand). In Chapter 2, we studied the binary arithmetic operators. Java also supports unary versions of the plus (+) and minus (–) operators, so the programmer can write expressions like –7 or +5. Cast operators associate from right to left and have the same precedence as other unary operators, such as unary + and unary –. This precedence is one level higher than that of the **multiplicative operators** *, / and %. (See the operator precedence chart in Appendix A.) We indicate the cast operator with the notation (*type*) in our precedence charts, to indicate that any type name can be used to form a cast operator.

Line 77 outputs the class average using `System.out`'s `printf` method. In this example, we decided that we'd like to display the class average rounded to the nearest hundredth and output the average with exactly two digits to the right of the decimal point. The format specifier `%.2f` in `printf`'s format control string (line 77) indicates that variable `average`'s value should be displayed with two digits of precision to the right of the decimal point—indicated by `.2` in the format specifier. The three grades entered during the sample execution of class `GradeBookTest` (Fig. 4.10) total 257, which yields the average 85.666666…. Method `printf` uses the precision in the format specifier to round the value to the specified number of digits. In this program, the average is rounded to the hundredths position and the average is displayed as `85.67`.

```
1   // Fig. 4.10: GradeBookTest.java
2   // Create GradeBook object and invoke its determineClassAverage method.
3
4   public class GradeBookTest
5   {
6      public static void main( String args[] )
7      {
```

Fig. 4.10 | `GradeBookTest` class creates an object of class `GradeBook` (Fig. 4.9) and invokes its `determineClassAverage` method. (Part 1 of 2.)

```
 8          // create GradeBook object myGradeBook and
 9          // pass course name to constructor
10          GradeBook myGradeBook = new GradeBook(
11             "CS101 Introduction to Java Programming" );
12
13          myGradeBook.displayMessage(); // display welcome message
14          myGradeBook.determineClassAverage(); // find average of grades
15       } // end main
16
17    } // end class GradeBookTest
```

```
Welcome to the grade book for
CS101 Introduction to Java Programming!

Enter grade or -1 to quit: 97
Enter grade or -1 to quit: 88
Enter grade or -1 to quit: 72
Enter grade or -1 to quit: -1

Total of the 3 grades entered is 257
Class average is 85.67
```

Fig. 4.10 | GradeBookTest class creates an object of class GradeBook (Fig. 4.9) and invokes its determineClassAverage method. (Part 2 of 2.)

4.10 Formulating Algorithms: Nested Control Statements

For the next example, we once again formulate an algorithm by using pseudocode and top-down, stepwise refinement, and write a corresponding Java program. We have seen that control statements can be stacked on top of one another (in sequence) just as a child stacks building blocks. In this case study, we examine the only other structured way control statements can be connected, namely, by **nesting** one control statement within another.

Consider the following problem statement:

A college offers a course that prepares students for the state licensing exam for real estate brokers. Last year, ten of the students who completed this course took the exam. The college wants to know how well its students did on the exam. You have been asked to write a program to summarize the results. You have been given a list of these 10 students. Next to each name is written a 1 if the student passed the exam or a 2 if the student failed.

Your program should analyze the results of the exam as follows:

1. *Input each test result (i.e., a 1 or a 2). Display the message "Enter result" on the screen each time the program requests another test result.*

2. *Count the number of test results of each type.*

3. *Display a summary of the test results indicating the number of students who passed and the number who failed.*

4. *If more than eight students passed the exam, print the message "Raise tuition."*

After reading the problem statement carefully, we make the following observations:

1. The program must process test results for 10 students. A counter-controlled loop can be used because the number of test results is known in advance.

2. Each test result has a numeric value—either a 1 or a 2. Each time the program reads a test result, the program must determine whether the number is a 1 or a 2. We test for a 1 in our algorithm. If the number is not a 1, we assume that it is a 2. (Exercise 4.24 considers the consequences of this assumption.)

3. Two counters are used to keep track of the exam results—one to count the number of students who passed the exam and one to count the number of students who failed the exam.

4. After the program has processed all the results, it must decide whether more than eight students passed the exam.

Let us proceed with top-down, stepwise refinement. We begin with a pseudocode representation of the top:

Analyze exam results and decide whether tuition should be raised

Once again, the top is a *complete* representation of the program, but several refinements are likely to be needed before the pseudocode can evolve naturally into a Java program.

Our first refinement is

Initialize variables
Input the 10 exam results, and count passes and failures
Print a summary of the exam results and decide whether tuition should be raised

Here, too, even though we have a complete representation of the entire program, further refinement is necessary. We now commit to specific variables. Counters are needed to record the passes and failures, a counter will be used to control the looping process and a variable is needed to store the user input. The variable in which the user input will be stored is not initialized at the start of the algorithm, because its value is read from the user during each iteration of the loop.

The pseudocode statement

Initialize variables

can be refined as follows:

Initialize passes to zero
Initialize failures to zero
Initialize student counter to one

Notice that only the counters are initialized at the start of the algorithm.

The pseudocode statement

Input the 10 exam results, and count passes and failures

requires a loop that successively inputs the result of each exam. We know in advance that there are precisely 10 exam results, so counter-controlled looping is appropriate. Inside the loop (i.e., **nested** within the loop), a double-selection structure will determine whether each exam result is a pass or a failure and will increment the appropriate counter. The refinement of the preceding pseudocode statement is then

> *While student counter is less than or equal to 10*
>> *Prompt the user to enter the next exam result*
>> *Input the next exam result*
>>
>> *If the student passed*
>>> *Add one to passes*
>>
>> *Else*
>>> *Add one to failures*
>>
>> *Add one to student counter*

We use blank lines to isolate the *If...Else* control structure, which improves readability. The pseudocode statement

> *Print a summary of the exam results and decide whether tuition should be raised*

can be refined as follows:

> *Print the number of passes*
> *Print the number of failures*
>
> *If more than eight students passed*
>> *Print "Raise tuition"*

Complete Second Refinement of Pseudocode and Conversion to Class *Analysis*

The complete second refinement of the pseudocode appears in Fig. 4.11. Notice that blank lines are also used to set off the *While* structure for program readability. This pseudocode is now sufficiently refined for conversion to Java. The Java class that implements the pseudocode algorithm is shown in Fig. 4.12, and two sample executions appear in Fig. 4.13.

```
 1   Initialize passes to zero
 2   Initialize failures to zero
 3   Initialize student counter to one
 4
 5   While student counter is less than or equal to 10
 6       Prompt the user to enter the next exam result
 7       Input the next exam result
 8
 9       If the student passed
10           Add one to passes
11       Else
12           Add one to failures
13
14       Add one to student counter
15
16   Print the number of passes
17   Print the number of failures
18
19   If more than eight students passed
20       Print "Raise tuition"
```

Fig. 4.11 | Pseudocode for examination-results problem.

```java
 1   // Fig. 4.12: Analysis.java
 2   // Analysis of examination results.
 3   import java.util.Scanner; // class uses class Scanner
 4
 5   public class Analysis
 6   {
 7      public void processExamResults()
 8      {
 9         // create Scanner to obtain input from command window
10         Scanner input = new Scanner( System.in );
11
12         // initializing variables in declarations
13         int passes = 0; // number of passes
14         int failures = 0; // number of failures
15         int studentCounter = 1; // student counter
16         int result; // one exam result (obtains value from user)
17
18         // process 10 students using counter-controlled loop
19         while ( studentCounter <= 10 )
20         {
21            // prompt user for input and obtain value from user
22            System.out.print( "Enter result (1 = pass, 2 = fail): " );
23            result = input.nextInt();
24
25            // if...else nested in while
26            if ( result == 1 )            // if result 1,
27               passes = passes + 1;       // increment passes;
28            else                          // else result is not 1, so
29               failures = failures + 1; // increment failures
30
31            // increment studentCounter so loop eventually terminates
32            studentCounter = studentCounter + 1;
33         } // end while
34
35         // termination phase; prepare and display results
36         System.out.printf( "Passed: %d\nFailed: %d\n", passes, failures );
37
38         // determine whether more than 8 students passed
39         if ( passes > 8 )
40            System.out.println( "Raise Tuition" );
41      } // end method processExamResults
42
43   } // end class Analysis
```

Fig. 4.12 | Nested control structures: Examination-results problem.

Lines 13–16 of Fig. 4.12 declare the variables that method processExamResults of class Analysis uses to process the examination results. Several of these declarations use Java's ability to incorporate variable initialization into declarations (passes is assigned 0, failures is assigned 0 and studentCounter is assigned 1). Looping programs may require initialization at the beginning of each repetition—such reinitialization would normally be performed by assignment statements rather than in declarations.

The while statement (lines 19–33) loops 10 times. During each iteration, the loop inputs and processes one exam result. Notice that the if...else statement (lines 26–29) for processing each result is nested in the while statement. If the result is 1, the if...else statement increments passes; otherwise, it assumes the result is 2 and increments failures. Line 32 increments studentCounter before the loop condition is tested again at line 19. After 10 values have been input, the loop terminates and line 36 displays the number of passes and the number of failures. The if statement at lines 39–40 determines whether more than eight students passed the exam and, if so, outputs the message "Raise Tuition".

Error-Prevention Tip 4.3

Initializing local variables when they are declared helps the programmer avoid any compilation errors that might arise from attempts to use uninitialized data. While Java does not require that local variable initializations be incorporated into declarations, it does require that local variables be initialized before their values are used in an expression.

AnalysisTest Class That Demonstrates Class Analysis

Class AnalysisTest (Fig. 4.13) creates an Analysis object (line 8) and invokes the object's processExamResults method (line 9) to process a set of exam results entered by the user. Figure 4.13 shows the input and output from two sample executions of the program. During the first sample execution, the condition at line 39 of method processExamResults in Fig. 4.12 is true—more than eight students passed the exam, so the program outputs a message indicating that the tuition should be raised.

```java
1   // Fig. 4.13: AnalysisTest.java
2   // Test program for class Analysis.
3
4   public class AnalysisTest
5   {
6      public static void main( String args[] )
7      {
8         Analysis application = new Analysis(); // create Analysis object
9         application.processExamResults(); // call method to process results
10     } // end main
11
12  } // end class AnalysisTest
```

```
Enter result (1 = pass, 2 = fail): 1
Enter result (1 = pass, 2 = fail): 2
Enter result (1 = pass, 2 = fail): 1
Enter result (1 = pass, 2 = fail): 1
Enter result (1 = pass, 2 = fail): 1
Enter result (1 = pass, 2 = fail): 1
Enter result (1 = pass, 2 = fail): 1
Enter result (1 = pass, 2 = fail): 1
Enter result (1 = pass, 2 = fail): 1
Enter result (1 = pass, 2 = fail): 1
Passed: 9
Failed: 1
Raise Tuition
```

Fig. 4.13 | Test program for class Analysis (Fig. 4.12). (Part 1 of 2.)

```
Enter result (1 = pass, 2 = fail): 1
Enter result (1 = pass, 2 = fail): 2
Enter result (1 = pass, 2 = fail): 1
Enter result (1 = pass, 2 = fail): 2
Enter result (1 = pass, 2 = fail): 1
Enter result (1 = pass, 2 = fail): 2
Enter result (1 = pass, 2 = fail): 2
Enter result (1 = pass, 2 = fail): 1
Enter result (1 = pass, 2 = fail): 1
Enter result (1 = pass, 2 = fail): 1
Passed: 6
Failed: 4
```

Fig. 4.13 | Test program for class `Analysis` (Fig. 4.12). (Part 2 of 2.)

4.11 Compound Assignment Operators

Java provides several compound assignment operators for abbreviating assignment expressions. Any statement of the form

> *variable = variable operator expression;*

where *operator* is one of the binary operators +, -, *, / or % (or others we discuss later in the text) can be written in the form

> *variable operator= expression;*

For example, you can abbreviate the statement

> `c = c + 3;`

with the addition compound assignment operator, +=, as

> `c += 3;`

The += operator adds the value of the expression on the right of the operator to the value of the variable on the left of the operator and stores the result in the variable on the left of the operator. Thus, the assignment expression c += 3 adds 3 to c. Figure 4.14 shows the arithmetic compound assignment operators, sample expressions using the operators and explanations of what the operators do.

Assignment operator	Sample expression	Explanation	Assigns
Assume: int c = 3, d = 5, e = 4, f = 6, g = 12;			
+=	c += 7	c = c + 7	10 to c
-=	d -= 4	d = d - 4	1 to d
*=	e *= 5	e = e * 5	20 to e
/=	f /= 3	f = f / 3	2 to f
%=	g %= 9	g = g % 9	3 to g

Fig. 4.14 | Arithmetic compound assignment operators.

4.12 Increment and Decrement Operators

Java provides two unary operators for adding 1 to or subtracting 1 from the value of a numeric variable. These are the unary increment operator, ++, and the unary decrement operator, --, which are summarized in Fig. 4.15. A program can increment by 1 the value of a variable called c using the increment operator, ++, rather than the expression c = c + 1 or c += 1. An increment or decrement operator that is prefixed to (placed before) a variable is referred to as the prefix increment or prefix decrement operator, respectively. An increment or decrement operator that is postfixed to (placed after) a variable is referred to as the postfix increment or postfix decrement operator, respectively.

Using the prefix increment (or decrement) operator to add (or subtract) 1 from a variable is known as preincrementing (or predecrementing) the variable. Preincrementing (or predecrementing) a variable causes the variable to be incremented (decremented) by 1, and then the new value of the variable is used in the expression in which it appears. Using the postfix increment (or decrement) operator to add (or subtract) 1 from a variable is known as postincrementing (or postdecrementing) the variable. Postincrementing (or postdecrementing) the variable causes the current value of the variable to be used in the expression in which it appears, and then the variable's value is incremented (decremented) by 1.

Good Programming Practice 4.7

Unlike binary operators, the unary increment and decrement operators should be placed next to their operands, with no intervening spaces.

Figure 4.16 demonstrates the difference between the prefix increment and postfix increment versions of the ++ increment operator. The decrement operator (--) works similarly. Note that this example contains only one class, with method main performing all the class's work. In this chapter and in Chapter 3, you have seen examples consisting of two classes—one class containing methods that perform useful tasks and one containing method main, which creates an object of the other class and calls its methods. In this example, we simply want to show the mechanics of the ++ operator, so we use only one

Operator	Called	Sample expression	Explanation
++	prefix increment	++a	Increment a by 1, then use the new value of a in the expression in which a resides.
++	postfix increment	a++	Use the current value of a in the expression in which a resides, then increment a by 1.
--	prefix decrement	--b	Decrement b by 1, then use the new value of b in the expression in which b resides.
--	postfix decrement	b--	Use the current value of b in the expression in which b resides, then decrement b by 1.

Fig. 4.15 | Increment and decrement operators.

```
1   // Fig. 4.16: Increment.java
2   // Prefix increment and postfix increment operators.
3
4   public class Increment
5   {
6      public static void main( String args[] )
7      {
8         int c;
9
10        // demonstrate postfix increment operator
11        c = 5; // assign 5 to c
12        System.out.println( c );    // print 5
13        System.out.println( c++ ); // print 5 then postincrement
14        System.out.println( c );    // print 6
15
16        System.out.println(); // skip a line
17
18        // demonstrate prefix increment operator
19        c = 5; // assign 5 to c
20        System.out.println( c );    // print 5
21        System.out.println( ++c ); // preincrement then print 6
22        System.out.println( c );    // print 6
23
24     } // end main
25
26  } // end class Increment
```

```
5
5
6

5
6
6
```

Fig. 4.16 | Preincrementing and postincrementing.

class declaration containing method main. Occasionally, when it does not make sense to try to create a reusable class to demonstrate a simple concept, we will use a mechanical example contained entirely within the main method of a single class.

Line 11 initializes the variable c to 5, and line 12 outputs c's initial value. Line 13 outputs the value of the expression c++. This expression postincrements the variable c, so c's original value (5) is output, then c's value is incremented. Thus, line 13 outputs c's initial value (5) again. Line 14 outputs c's new value (6) to prove that the variable's value was indeed incremented in line 13.

Line 19 resets c's value to 5, and line 20 outputs c's value. Line 21 outputs the value of the expression ++c. This expression preincrements c, so its value is incremented, then the new value (6) is output. Line 22 outputs c's value again to show that the value of c is still 6 after line 21 executes.

The arithmetic compound assignment operators and the increment and decrement operators can be used to simplify program statements. For example, the three assignment statements in Fig. 4.12 (lines 27, 29 and 32)

```
passes = passes + 1;
failures = failures + 1;
studentCounter = studentCounter + 1;
```

can be written more concisely with compound assignment operators as

```
passes += 1;
failures += 1;
studentCounter += 1;
```

with prefix increment operators as

```
++passes;
++failures;
++studentCounter;
```

or with postfix increment operators as

```
passes++;
failures++;
studentCounter++;
```

When incrementing or decrementing a variable in a statement by itself, the prefix increment and postfix increment forms have the same effect, and the prefix decrement and postfix decrement forms have the same effect. It is only when a variable appears in the context of a larger expression that preincrementing and postincrementing the variable have different effects (and similarly for predecrementing and postdecrementing).

Common Programming Error 4.9

Attempting to use the increment or decrement operator on an expression other than one to which a value can be assigned is a syntax error. For example, writing ++(x + 1) is a syntax error because (x + 1) is not a variable.

Figure 4.17 shows the precedence and associativity of the operators we have introduced to this point. The operators are shown from top to bottom in decreasing order of precedence. The second column describes the associativity of the operators at each level of precedence. The conditional operator (?:); the unary operators increment (++), decrement (--), plus (+) and minus (-); the cast operators and the assignment operators =, +=, -=, *=, /= and %= associate from right to left. All the other operators in the operator precedence chart in Fig. 4.17 associate from left to right. The third column names the groups of operators.

4.13 Primitive Types

The table in Appendix D, Primitive Types, lists the eight primitive types in Java. Like its predecessor languages C and C++, Java requires all variables to have a type. For this reason, Java is referred to as a **strongly typed language**.

Operators					Associativity	Type
++	--				right to left	unary postfix
++	--	+	-	(*type*)	right to left	unary prefix
*	/	%			left to right	multiplicative
+	-				left to right	additive
<	<=	>	>=		left to right	relational
==	!=				left to right	equality
?:					right to left	conditional
=	+=	-=	*=	/= %=	right to left	assignment

Fig. 4.17 | Precedence and associativity of the operators discussed so far.

In C and C++, programmers frequently have to write separate versions of programs to support different computer platforms, because the primitive types are not guaranteed to be identical from computer to computer. For example, an int value on one machine might be represented by 16 bits (2 bytes) of memory, while an int value on another machine might be represented by 32 bits (4 bytes) of memory. In Java, int values are always 32 bits (4 bytes).

Portability Tip 4.1

Unlike C and C++, the primitive types in Java are portable across all computer platforms that support Java. Thanks to this and Java's many other portability features, a programmer can write a program once and be certain that it will execute on any computer platform that supports Java. This capability is sometimes referred to as WORA (Write Once, Run Anywhere).

Each type in Appendix D is listed with its size in bits (there are eight bits to a byte) and its range of values. Because the designers of Java want it to be maximally portable, they use internationally recognized standards for both character formats (Unicode; for more information, visit www.unicode.org) and floating-point numbers (IEEE 754; for more information, visit grouper.ieee.org/groups/754/).

Recall from Section 3.5 that variables of primitive types declared outside of a method as fields of a class are automatically assigned default values unless explicitly initialized. Instance variables of types char, byte, short, int, long, float and double are all given the value 0 by default. Instance variables of type boolean are given the value false by default. Similarly, reference type instance variables are initialized by default to the value null.

4.14 (Optional) GUI and Graphics Case Study: Creating Simple Drawings

One of Java's appealing features is its graphics support that enables programmers to visually enhance their applications. This section introduces one of Java's graphical capabilities—drawing lines. It also covers the basics of creating a window to display a drawing on the computer screen.

To begin drawing in Java, you must first understand Java's coordinate system (Fig. 4.18), a scheme for identifying every point on the screen. By default, the upper-left corner of a GUI component has the coordinates (0, 0). A coordinate pair is composed of an *x*-coordinate (the horizontal coordinate) and a *y*-coordinate (the vertical coordinate). The *x*-coordinate is the horizontal location moving from left to right. The *y*-coordinate is the vertical location moving top to bottom. The *x*-axis describes every horizontal coordinate, and the *y*-axis every vertical coordinate.

Coordinates are used to indicate where graphics should be displayed on a screen. Coordinate units are measured in pixels. A pixel is a display monitor's smallest unit of resolution. (The term pixel stands for "picture element.")

Our first drawing application simply draws two lines from the corners. Class DrawPanel (Fig. 4.19) performs the actual drawing, while class DrawPanelTest (Fig. 4.20) creates a window to display the drawing. In class DrawPanel, the import statements in lines 3–4 allow us to use class **Graphics** (from package java.awt), which provides various methods for drawing text and shapes onto the screen, and class **JPanel** (from package javax.swing), which provides an area on which we can draw.

Line 6 uses the keyword **extends** to indicate that class DrawPanel is an enhanced type of JPanel. The keyword extends represents a so-called inheritance relationship in which our new class DrawPanel begins with the existing members (data and methods) from class JPanel. The class from which DrawPanel inherits, JPanel, appears to the right of keyword extends. In this inheritance relationship, JPanel is called the superclass and DrawPanel is called the subclass. This results in a DrawPanel class that has the attributes (data) and behaviors (methods) of class JPanel as well as the new features we are adding in our Draw-Panel class declaration (specifically, the ability to draw two lines along the diagonals of the panel). Inheritance will be explained in more detail in Chapter 9.

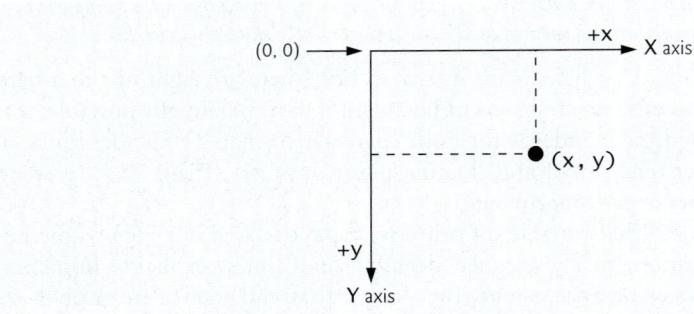

Fig. 4.18 | Java coordinate system. Units are measured in pixels.

```
1   // Fig. 4.19: DrawPanel.java
2   // Draws two crossing lines on a panel.
3   import java.awt.Graphics;
4   import javax.swing.JPanel;
5
```

Fig. 4.19 | Using drawLine to connect the corners of a panel. (Part 1 of 2.)

```
6  public class DrawPanel extends JPanel
7  {
8     // draws an X from the corners of the panel
9     public void paintComponent( Graphics g )
10    {
11       // call paintComponent to ensure the panel displays correctly
12       super.paintComponent( g );
13
14       int width = getWidth();   // total width
15       int height = getHeight(); // total height
16
17       // draw a line from the upper-left to the lower-right
18       g.drawLine( 0, 0, width, height );
19
20       // draw a line from the lower-left to the upper-right
21       g.drawLine( 0, height, width, 0 );
22    } // end method paintComponent
23 } // end class DrawPanel
```

Fig. 4.19 | Using drawLine to connect the corners of a panel. (Part 2 of 2.)

Every JPanel, including our DrawPanel, has a **paintComponent** method (lines 9–22), which the system automatically calls every time it needs to display the JPanel. Method paintComponent must be declared as shown on line 9—otherwise, the system will not call the method. This method is called when a JPanel is first displayed on the screen, when it is covered then uncovered by a window on the screen and when the window in which it appears is resized. Method paintComponent requires one argument, a Graphics object, that is provided for you by the system when it calls paintComponent.

The first statement in every paintComponent method you create should always be

```
super.paintComponent( g );
```

This will ensure that the panel is properly rendered on the screen before we begin drawing on it. Next, lines 14 and 15 call two methods that class DrawPanel inherits from class JPanel. Because DrawPanel extends JPanel, DrawPanel can use any public methods that are declared in JPanel. Methods **getWidth** and **getHeight** return the width and the height of the JPanel respectively. Lines 14–15 store these values in the local variables width and height. Finally, lines 18 and 21 use the Graphics reference g to call method **drawLine** to draw the two lines. Method drawLine draws a line between two points represented by its four arguments. The first two arguments are the x- and y-coordinates for one endpoint of the line, and the last two arguments are the coordinates for the other endpoint of the line. If you resize the window, the lines will scale accordingly because the arguments are based on the width and height of the panel. Note that resizing the window in this application causes the system to call paintComponent to redraw the DrawPanel's contents.

To display the DrawPanel on the screen, we must place it in a window. You create a window with an object of class **JFrame**. In DrawPanelTest.java (Fig. 4.20), line 3 imports class JFrame from package javax.swing. Line 10 in the main method of class DrawPanelTest creates an instance of class DrawPanel, which contains our drawing, and line 13 creates a new JFrame that can hold and display our panel. Line 16 calls method **setDefaultCloseOperation** with the argument **JFrame.EXIT_ON_CLOSE** to indicate that the

```
 1   // Fig. 4.20: DrawPanelTest.java
 2   // Application to display a DrawPanel.
 3   import javax.swing.JFrame;
 4
 5   public class DrawPanelTest
 6   {
 7      public static void main( String args[] )
 8      {
 9         // create a panel that contains our drawing
10         DrawPanel panel = new DrawPanel();
11
12         // create a new frame to hold the panel
13         JFrame application = new JFrame();
14
15         // set the frame to exit when it is closed
16         application.setDefaultCloseOperation( JFrame.EXIT_ON_CLOSE );
17
18         application.add( panel ); // add the panel to the frame
19         application.setSize( 250, 250 ); // set the size of the frame
20         application.setVisible( true ); // make the frame visible
21      } // end main
22   } // end class DrawPanelTest
```

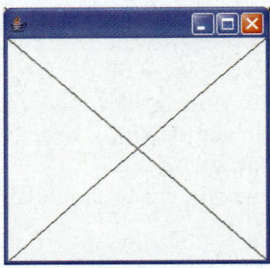 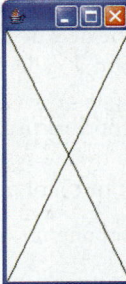

Fig. 4.20 | Creating JFrame to display DrawPanel.

application should terminate when the user closes the window. Line 18 uses JFrame's **add** method to attach the DrawPanel containing our drawing to the JFrame. Line 19 sets the size of the JFrame. Method **setSize** takes two parameters—the first parameter is the width of the JFrame, and the second is the height. Finally, line 20 displays the JFrame. When the JFrame is displayed, the DrawPanel's paintComponent method (lines 9–22 of Fig. 4.19) is called, and the two lines are drawn (see the sample outputs in Fig. 4.20). Try resizing the window to see that the lines always draw based on the window's current width and height.

For the next several GUI and graphics sections, there will be very few changes required in the main method. As we introduce additional drawing capabilities, most of the changes will come in the class that extends JPanel, since that is where the drawing takes place.

GUI and Graphics Case Study Exercises

4.1   Using loops and control statements to draw lines can lead to many interesting designs.
   a) Create the design in the left screen capture of Fig. 4.21. This design draws lines from the top-left corner, fanning out the lines until they cover the upper-left half of the panel.

One approach is to divide the width and height into an equal number of steps (we found 15 steps worked well). The first endpoint of a line will always be in the top-left corner (0, 0). The second endpoint can be found by starting at the bottom-left corner and moving up one vertical step and moving right one horizontal step. Draw a line between the two endpoints. Continue moving up and to the right one step to find each successive endpoint. The figure should scale accordingly as you resize the window.

b) Modify your answer in part (a) to have lines fan out from all four corners, as shown in the right screen capture of Fig. 4.21. Lines from opposite corners should intersect along the middle.

4.2 Figure 4.22 displays two additional designs created using `while` loops and `drawLine`.

a) Create the design in the left screen capture of Fig. 4.22. Begin by dividing each edge into an equal number of increments (we chose 15 again). The first line starts in the top-left corner and ends one step right on the bottom edge. For each successive line, move down one increment on the left edge and right one increment on the bottom edge. Continue drawing lines until you reach the bottom-right corner. The figure should scale as you resize the window so that the endpoints always touch the edges.

b) Modify your answer in part (a) to mirror the design in all four corners, as shown in the right screen capture of Fig. 4.22.

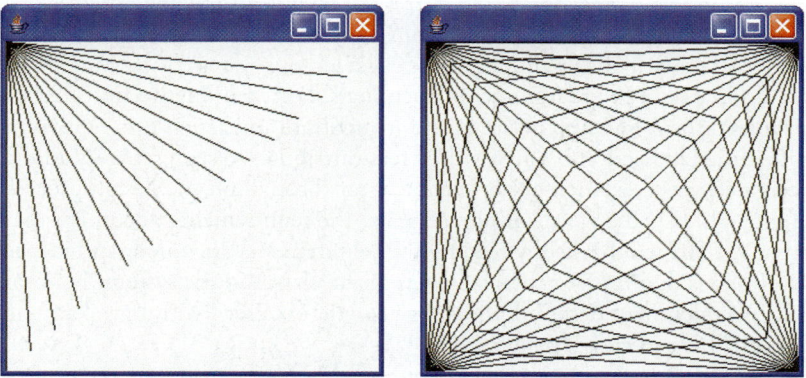

Fig. 4.21 | Lines fanning from a corner.

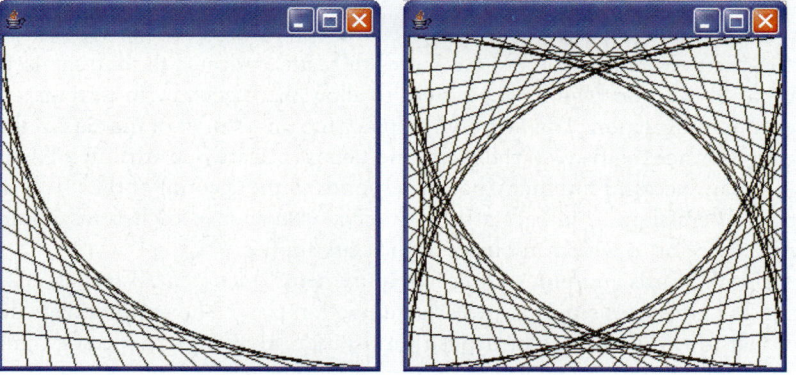

Fig. 4.22 | Line art with loops and `drawLine`.

4.15 (Optional) Software Engineering Case Study: Identifying Class Attributes

In Section 3.10, we began the first stage of an object-oriented design (OOD) for our ATM system—analyzing the requirements document and identifying the classes needed to implement the system. We listed the nouns and noun phrases in the requirements document and identified a separate class for each one that plays a significant role in the ATM system. We then modeled the classes and their relationships in a UML class diagram (Fig. 3.24). Classes have attributes (data) and operations (behaviors). Class attributes are implemented in Java programs as fields, and class operations are implemented as methods. In this section, we determine many of the attributes needed in the ATM system. In Chapter 5, we examine how these attributes represent an object's state. In Chapter 6, we determine class operations.

Identifying Attributes

Consider the attributes of some real-world objects: A person's attributes include height, weight and whether the person is left-handed, right-handed or ambidextrous. A radio's attributes include its station setting, its volume setting and its AM or FM setting. A car's attributes include its speedometer and odometer readings, the amount of gas in its tank and what gear it is in. A personal computer's attributes include its manufacturer (e.g., Dell, Sun, Apple or IBM), type of screen (e.g., LCD or CRT), main memory size and hard disk size.

We can identify many attributes of the classes in our system by looking for descriptive words and phrases in the requirements document. For each one we find that plays a significant role in the ATM system, we create an attribute and assign it to one or more of the classes identified in Section 3.10. We also create attributes to represent any additional data that a class may need, as such needs become clear throughout the design process.

Figure 4.23 lists the words or phrases from the requirements document that describe each class. We formed this list by reading the requirements document and identifying any words or phrases that refer to characteristics of the classes in the system. For example, the requirements document describes the steps taken to obtain a "withdrawal amount," so we list "amount" next to class Withdrawal.

Figure 4.23 leads us to create one attribute of class ATM. Class ATM maintains information about the state of the ATM. The phrase "user is authenticated" describes a state of the ATM (we introduce states in Section 5.11), so we include userAuthenticated as a **Boolean attribute** (i.e., an attribute that has a value of either true or false) in class ATM. Note that the Boolean attribute type in the UML is equivalent to the boolean type in Java. This attribute indicates whether the ATM has successfully authenticated the current user—userAuthenticated must be true for the system to allow the user to perform transactions and access account information. This attribute helps ensure the security of the data in the system.

Classes BalanceInquiry, Withdrawal and Deposit share one attribute. Each transaction involves an "account number" that corresponds to the account of the user making the transaction. We assign an integer attribute accountNumber to each transaction class to identify the account to which an object of the class applies.

Descriptive words and phrases in the requirements document also suggest some differences in the attributes required by each transaction class. The requirements document indicates that to withdraw cash or deposit funds, users must input a specific "amount" of money to be withdrawn or deposited, respectively. Thus, we assign to classes Withdrawal and Deposit an attribute amount to store the value supplied by the user. The amounts of

Class	Descriptive words and phrases
ATM	user is authenticated
BalanceInquiry	account number
Withdrawal	account number
	amount
Deposit	account number
	amount
BankDatabase	[no descriptive words or phrases]
Account	account number
	PIN
	balance
Screen	[no descriptive words or phrases]
Keypad	[no descriptive words or phrases]
CashDispenser	begins each day loaded with 500 $20 bills
DepositSlot	[no descriptive words or phrases]

Fig. 4.23 | Descriptive words and phrases from the ATM requirements.

money related to a withdrawal and a deposit are defining characteristics of these transactions that the system requires for these transactions to take place. Class BalanceInquiry, however, needs no additional data to perform its task—it requires only an account number to indicate the account whose balance should be retrieved.

Class Account has several attributes. The requirements document states that each bank account has an "account number" and "PIN," which the system uses for identifying accounts and authenticating users. We assign to class Account two integer attributes: accountNumber and pin. The requirements document also specifies that an account maintains a "balance" of the amount of money in the account and that money the user deposits does not become available for a withdrawal until the bank verifies the amount of cash in the deposit envelope, and any checks in the envelope clear. An account must still record the amount of money that a user deposits, however. Therefore, we decide that an account should represent a balance using two attributes: availableBalance and totalBalance. Attribute availableBalance tracks the amount of money that a user can withdraw from the account. Attribute totalBalance refers to the total amount of money that the user has "on deposit" (i.e., the amount of money available, plus the amount waiting to be verified or cleared). For example, suppose an ATM user deposits $50.00 into an empty account. The totalBalance attribute would increase to $50.00 to record the deposit, but the availableBalance would remain at $0. [*Note:* We assume that the bank updates the availableBalance attribute of an Account some length of time after the ATM transaction occurs, in response to confirming that $50 worth of cash or checks was found in the deposit envelope. We assume that this update occurs through a transaction that a bank employee performs using some piece of bank software other than the ATM. Thus, we do not discuss this transaction in our case study.]

Class `CashDispenser` has one attribute. The requirements document states that the cash dispenser "begins each day loaded with 500 $20 bills." The cash dispenser must keep track of the number of bills it contains to determine whether enough cash is on hand to satisfy withdrawal requests. We assign to class `CashDispenser` an integer attribute `count`, which is initially set to 500.

For real problems in industry, there is no guarantee that requirements documents will be rich enough and precise enough for the object-oriented systems designer to determine all the attributes or even all the classes. The need for additional classes, attributes and behaviors may become clear as the design process proceeds. As we progress through this case study, we too will continue to add, modify and delete information about the classes in our system.

Modeling Attributes

The class diagram in Fig. 4.24 lists some of the attributes for the classes in our system—the descriptive words and phrases in Fig. 4.23 lead us to identify these attributes. For simplicity, Fig. 4.24 does not show the associations among classes—we showed these in Fig. 3.24. This is a common practice of systems designers when designs are being developed. Recall from Section 3.10 that in the UML, a class's attributes are placed in the middle compartment of the class's rectangle. We list each attribute's name and type separated by a colon (:), followed in some cases by an equal sign (=) and an initial value.

Consider the `userAuthenticated` attribute of class `ATM`:

```
userAuthenticated : Boolean = false
```

This attribute declaration contains three pieces of information about the attribute. The attribute name is `userAuthenticated`. The attribute type is `Boolean`. In Java, an attribute can be represented by a primitive type, such as `boolean`, `int` or `double`, or a reference type like a class—as discussed in Chapter 3. We have chosen to model only primitive-type attributes in Fig. 4.24, however—we discuss the reasoning behind this decision below. [*Note:* The attribute types in Fig. 4.24 are in UML notation. We will associate the types `Boolean`, `Integer` and `Double` in the UML diagram with the primitive types `boolean`, `int` and `double` in Java, respectively.]

We can also indicate an initial value for an attribute. The `userAuthenticated` attribute in class `ATM` has an initial value of `false`. This indicates that the system initially does not consider the user to be authenticated. If an attribute has no initial value specified, only its name and type (separated by a colon) are shown. For example, the `accountNumber` attribute of class `BalanceInquiry` is an integer. Here we show no initial value, because the value of this attribute is a number that we do not yet know. This number will be determined at execution time based on the account number entered by the current ATM user.

Figure 4.24 does not include any attributes for classes `Screen`, `Keypad` and `DepositSlot`. These are important components of our system, for which our design process simply has not yet revealed any attributes. We may still discover some, however, in the remaining phases of design or when we implement these classes in Java. This is perfectly normal.

Software Engineering Observation 4.6

At early stages in the design process, classes often lack attributes (and operations). Such classes should not be eliminated, however, because attributes (and operations) may become evident in the later phases of design and implementation.

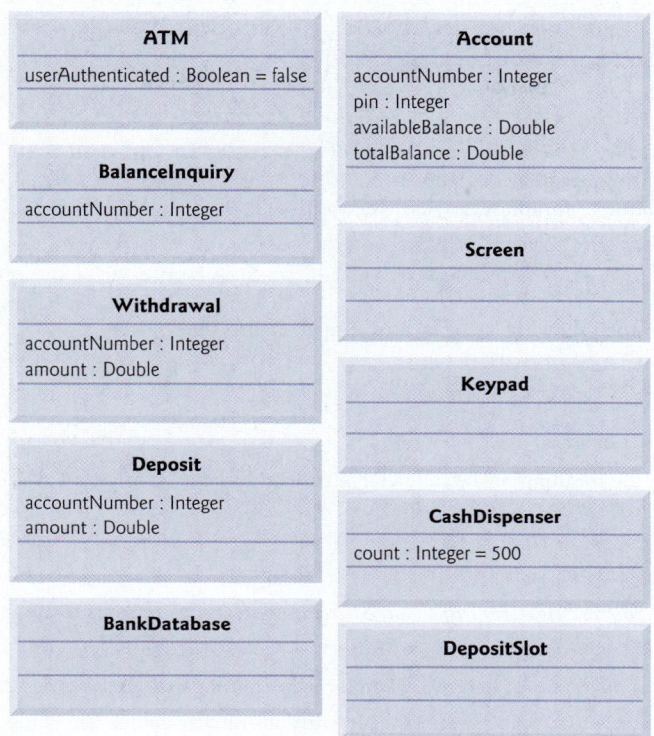

Fig. 4.24 | Classes with attributes.

Note that Fig. 4.24 also does not include attributes for class BankDatabase. Recall from Chapter 3 that in Java, attributes can be represented by either primitive types or reference types. We have chosen to include only primitive-type attributes in the class diagram in Fig. 4.24 (and in similar class diagrams throughout the case study). A reference-type attribute is modeled more clearly as an association (in particular, a composition) between the class holding the reference and the class of the object to which the reference points. For example, the class diagram in Fig. 3.24 indicates that class BankDatabase participates in a composition relationship with zero or more Account objects. From this composition, we can determine that when we implement the ATM system in Java, we will be required to create an attribute of class BankDatabase to hold references to zero or more Account objects. Similarly, we can determine reference-type attributes of class ATM that correspond to its composition relationships with classes Screen, Keypad, CashDispenser and DepositSlot. These composition-based attributes would be redundant if modeled in Fig. 4.24, because the compositions modeled in Fig. 3.24 already convey the fact that the database contains information about zero or more accounts and that an ATM is composed of a screen, keypad, cash dispenser and deposit slot. Software developers typically model these whole/part relationships as compositions rather than as attributes required to implement the relationships.

The class diagram in Fig. 4.24 provides a solid basis for the structure of our model, but the diagram is not complete. In Section 5.11, we identify the states and activities of the objects in the model, and in Section 6.14 we identify the operations that the objects perform. As we present more of the UML and object-oriented design, we will continue to strengthen the structure of our model.

Software Engineering Case Study Self-Review Exercises

4.1   We typically identify the attributes of the classes in our system by analyzing the _____ in the requirements document.
a) nouns and noun phrases
b) descriptive words and phrases
c) verbs and verb phrases
d) All of the above.

4.2   Which of the following is not an attribute of an airplane?
a) length
b) wingspan
c) fly
d) number of seats

4.3   Describe the meaning of the following attribute declaration of class `CashDispenser` in the class diagram in Fig. 4.24:

```
count : Integer = 500
```

Answers to Software Engineering Case Study Self-Review Exercises

4.1   b.

4.2   c. Fly is an operation or behavior of an airplane, not an attribute.

4.3   This indicates that `count` is an `Integer` with an initial value of 500. This attribute keeps track of the number of bills available in the `CashDispenser` at any given time.

4.16 Wrap-Up

This chapter presented basic problem-solving strategies that programmers use in building classes and developing methods for these classes. We demonstrated how to construct an algorithm (i.e., an approach to solving a problem), then how to refine the algorithm through several phases of pseudocode development, resulting in Java code that can be executed as part of a method. The chapter showed how to use top-down, stepwise refinement to plan out the specific actions that a method must perform and the order in which the method must perform these actions.

Only three types of control structures—sequence, selection and repetition—are needed to develop any problem-solving algorithm. Specifically, this chapter demonstrated the `if` single-selection statement, the `if...else` double-selection statement and the `while` repetition statement. These are some of the building blocks used to construct solutions to many problems. We used control-statement stacking to total and compute the average of a set of student grades with counter- and sentinel-controlled repetition, and we used control-statement nesting to analyze and make decisions based on a set of exam results. We introduced Java's compound assignment operators, as well as its increment and decrement operators. Finally, we discussed the primitive types available to Java programmers. In Chapter 5, Control Statements: Part 2, we continue our discussion of control statements, introducing the `for`, `do...while` and `switch` statements.

Summary

- An algorithm is a procedure for solving a problem in terms of the actions to execute and the order in which the actions execute.

- Specifying the order in which statements (actions) execute in a program is called program control.

- Pseudocode helps a programmer think out a program before attempting to write it in a programming language.

- Activity diagrams are part of the Unified Modeling Language (UML)—an industry standard for modeling software systems.

- An activity diagram models the workflow (also called the activity) of a software system.

- Activity diagrams are composed of special-purpose symbols, such as action-state symbols, diamonds and small circles. These symbols are connected by transition arrows that represent the flow of the activity.

- Like pseudocode, activity diagrams help programmers develop and represent algorithms.

- An action state is represented as a rectangle with its left and right sides replaced with arcs curving outward. The action expression appears inside the action state.

- The arrows in an activity diagram represent transitions, which indicate the order in which the actions represented by action states occur.

- The solid circle located at the top of an activity diagram represents the initial state—the beginning of the workflow before the program performs the modeled actions.

- The solid circle surrounded by a hollow circle that appears at the bottom of the activity diagram represents the final state—the end of the workflow after the program performs its actions.

- Rectangles with the upper-right corners folded over are called notes in the UML. Notes are explanatory remarks that describe the purpose of symbols in the diagram. A dotted line connects each note with the element that the note describes.

- A diamond or decision symbol in an activity diagram indicates that a decision is to be made. The workflow will continue along a path determined by the symbol's associated guard conditions, which can be true or false. Each transition arrow emerging from a decision symbol has a guard condition (specified in square brackets next to the transition arrow). If a guard condition is true, the workflow enters the action state to which the transition arrow points.

- A diamond in an activity diagram also represents the merge symbol, which joins two flows of activity into one. A merge symbol has two or more transition arrows pointing to the diamond and only one transition arrow pointing from the diamond, to indicate multiple activity flows merging to continue the activity.

- Top-down, stepwise refinement is a process for refining pseudocode by maintaining a complete representation of the program during each refinement.

- There are three types of control structures—sequence, selection and repetition.

- The sequence structure is built into Java—by default, statements execute in the order they appear.

- A selection structure chooses among alternative courses of action.

- The `if` single-selection statement either performs (selects) an action if a condition is true, or skips the action if the condition is false.

- The `if...else` double-selection statement performs (selects) an action if a condition is true and performs a different action if the condition is false.

- To include several statements in an `if`'s body (or the body of `else` for an `if...else` statement), enclose the statements in braces (`{` and `}`). A set of statements contained within a pair of braces is called a block. A block can be placed anywhere in a program that a single statement can be placed.

- An empty statement, indicating that no action is to be taken, is indicated by a semicolon (;).

- A repetition statement specifies that an action is to be repeated while some condition remains true.

- The format for the `while` repetition statement is

    > `while` (*condition*)
    >   *statement*

- Counter-controlled repetition is used when the number of repetitions is known before a loop begins executing.

- The unary cast operator `(double)` creates a temporary floating-point copy of its operand.

- Sentinel-controlled repetition is used when the number of repetitions is not known before a loop begins executing.

- A nested control statement appears in the body of another control statement.

- Java provides the arithmetic compound assignment operators +=, -=, *=, /= and %= for abbreviating assignment expressions.

- The increment operator, ++, and the decrement operator, --, increment or decrement a variable by 1, respectively. If the operator is prefixed to the variable, the variable is incremented or decremented by 1 first, and then its new value is used in the expression in which it appears. If the operator is postfixed to the variable, the variable is first used in the expression in which it appears, and then the variable's value is incremented or decremented by 1.

- The primitive types (`boolean`, `char`, `byte`, `short`, `int`, `long`, `float` and `double`) are portable across all computer platforms that support Java.

- Java is a strongly typed language—it requires all variables to have a type.

- Local variables are declared inside methods and are not assigned default values.

- Variables declared outside of methods as fields are assigned default values. Instance variables of types `char`, `byte`, `short`, `int`, `long`, `float` and `double` are all given the value 0 by default. Instance variables of type `boolean` are given the value `false` by default. Reference-type instance variables are initialized by default to the value `null`.

Terminology

-- operator
?: operator
++ operator
action
action/decision model of programming
action expression (in the UML)
action state (in the UML)
action-state symbol (in the UML)
activity (in the UML)
activity diagram (in the UML)
addition compound assignment operator (+=)
algorithm
arithmetic compound assignment operators:
    +=, -=, *=, /= and %=
block
`boolean` primitive type
body of a loop
cast operator, (*type*)

compound assignment operator
conditional expression
conditional operator (?:)
control statement
control-statement nesting
control-statement stacking
control variable
counter
counter-controlled repetition
creating an instance of a class
dangling-`else` problem
decision
decision symbol (in the UML)
decrement operator (--)
definite repetition
diamond (in the UML)
dotted line
double-selection statement

dummy value
explicit conversion
`false`
fatal logic error
final state (in the UML)
first refinement
flag value
`goto` statement
guard condition (in the UML)
`if` statement
`if...else` statement
implicit conversion
increment operator (++)
indefinite repetition
infinite loop
initial state (in the UML)
initialization
integer division
instantiate an object
iteration
logic error
loop
loop-continuation condition
loop counter
looping statement
merge symbol (in the UML)
multiple-selection statement
multiplicative operator
nested control statements
nested `if...else` statements
new keyword
nonfatal logic error
note (in the UML)
order in which actions should execute
postdecrement a variable
postfix decrement operator
postfix increment operator
postincrement a variable
predecrement a variable
prefix decrement operator

prefix increment operator
preincrement a variable
primitive types
procedure
program control
promotion
pseudocode
repetition
repetition structure
second refinement
selection structure
sentinel-controlled repetition
sentinel value
sequence structure
sequential execution
signal value
single-entry/single-exit control statements
single-selection statement
small circle (in the UML)
solid circle (in the UML)
solid circle surrounded by a hollow circle
   (in the UML)
stacked control statements
strongly typed language
structured programming
syntax error
ternary operator
top-down stepwise refinement
top
total
transfer of control
transition (in the UML)
transition arrow (in the UML)
`true`
truncate
unary cast operator
unary operator
`while` statement
WORA (write once, run anywhere)
workflow

Self-Review Exercises

4.1   Fill in the blanks in each of the following statements:
    a) All programs can be written in terms of three types of control structures: _____, _____ and _____.
    b) The _____ statement is used to execute one action when a condition is true and another when that condition is false.
    c) Repeating a set of instructions a specific number of times is called _____ repetition.

d) When it is not known in advance how many times a set of statements will be repeated, a(n) _____ value can be used to terminate the repetition.

e) The _____ structure is built into Java—by default, statements execute in the order they appear.

f) Instance variables of types `char`, `byte`, `short`, `int`, `long`, `float` and `double` are all given the value _____ by default.

g) Java is a _____ language—it requires all variables to have a type.

h) If the increment operator is _____ to a variable, the variable is incremented by 1 first, then its new value is used in the expression.

4.2   State whether each of the following is *true* or *false*. If *false*, explain why.

a) An algorithm is a procedure for solving a problem in terms of the actions to execute and the order in which these actions execute.

b) A set of statements contained within a pair of parentheses is called a block.

c) A selection statement specifies that an action is to be repeated while some condition remains true.

d) A nested control statement appears in the body of another control statement.

e) Java provides the arithmetic compound assignment operators +=, -=, *=, /= and %= for abbreviating assignment expressions.

f) The primitive types (`boolean`, `char`, `byte`, `short`, `int`, `long`, `float` and `double`) are portable across only Windows platforms.

g) Specifying the order in which statements (actions) execute in a program is called program control.

h) The unary cast operator (`double`) creates a temporary integer copy of its operand.

i) Instance variables of type `boolean` are given the value `true` by default.

j) Pseudocode helps a programmer think out a program before attempting to write it in a programming language.

4.3   Write four different Java statements that each add 1 to integer variable x.

4.4   Write Java statements to accomplish each of the following tasks:

a) Assign the sum of x and y to z, and increment x by 1 after the calculation. Use only one statement.

b) Test whether variable count is greater than 10. If it is, print "Count is greater than 10".

c) Decrement the variable x by 1, then subtract it from the variable total. Use only one statement.

d) Calculate the remainder after q is divided by divisor, and assign the result to q. Write this statement in two different ways.

4.5   Write a Java statement to accomplish each of the following tasks:

a) Declare variables sum and x to be of type int.

b) Assign 1 to variable x.

c) Assign 0 to variable sum.

d) Add variable x to variable sum, and assign the result to variable sum.

e) Print "The sum is: ", followed by the value of variable sum.

4.6   Combine the statements that you wrote in Exercise 4.5 into a Java application that calculates and prints the sum of the integers from 1 to 10. Use a `while` statement to loop through the calculation and increment statements. The loop should terminate when the value of x becomes 11.

4.7   Determine the value of the variables in the following statement after the calculation is performed. Assume that when the statement begins executing, all variables are type int and have the value 5.

```
product *= x++;
```

4.8   Identify and correct the errors in each of the following sets of code:

a) ```
while (c <= 5)
    {
        product *= c;

        ++c;
```

b) ```
if ( gender == 1 )
        System.out.println( "Woman" );
    else;
        System.out.println( "Man" );
```

4.9   What is wrong with the following while statement?

```
while ( z >= 0 )
    sum += z;
```

Answers to Self-Review Exercises

4.1   a) sequence, selection, repetition. b) if...else. c) counter-controlled (or definite). d) sentinel, signal, flag or dummy. e) sequence. f) 0 (zero). g) strongly typed. h) prefixed.

4.2   a) True. b) False. A set of statements contained within a pair of braces ({ and }) is called a block. c) False. A repetition statement specifies that an action is to be repeated while some condition remains true. d) True. e) True. f) False. The primitive types (boolean, char, byte, short, int, long, float and double) are portable across all computer platforms that support Java. g) True. h) False. The unary cast operator (double) creates a temporary floating-point copy of its operand. i) False. Instance variables of type boolean are given the value false by default. j) True.

4.3   ```
x = x + 1;
x += 1;
++x;
x++;
```

**4.4**   a) ```
z = x++ + y;
```
b) ```
if (count > 10)
        System.out.println("Count is greater than 10");
```
c) ```
total -= --x;
```
d) ```
q %= divisor;
q = q % divisor;
```

**4.5**   a) ```
int sum, x;
```
b) ```
x = 1;
```
c) ```
sum = 0;
```
d) ```
sum += x; or sum = sum + x;
```
e) ```
System.out.printf( "The sum is: %d\n", sum );
```

4.6   The program is as follows:

```
1   // Calculate the sum of the integers from 1 to 10
2   public class Calculate
3   {
4       public static void main( String args[] )
5       {
6           int sum;
7           int x;
8
```

```
 9          x = 1;    // initialize x to 1 for counting
10          sum = 0; // initialize sum to 0 for totaling
11
12          while ( x <= 10 ) // while x is less than or equal to 10
13          {
14             sum += x; // add x to sum
15             ++x; // increment x
16          } // end while
17
18          System.out.printf( "The sum is: %d\n", sum );
19       } // end main
20
21    } // end class Calculate
```

```
The sum is: 55
```

4.7   product = 25, x = 6

4.8   a) Error: The closing right brace of the while statement's body is missing.
              Correction: Add a closing right brace after the statement ++c;.
          b) Error: The semicolon after else results in a logic error. The second output statement
              will always be executed.
              Correction: Remove the semicolon after else.

4.9   The value of the variable z is never changed in the while statement. Therefore, if the loop-continuation condition (z >= 0) is true, an infinite loop is created. To prevent an infinite loop from occurring, z must be decremented so that it eventually becomes less than 0.

Exercises

4.10   Compare and contrast the if single-selection statement and the while repetition statement. How are these two statements similar? How are they different?

4.11   Explain what happens when a Java program attempts to divide one integer by another. What happens to the fractional part of the calculation? How can a programmer avoid that outcome?

4.12   Describe the two ways in which control statements can be combined.

4.13   What type of repetition would be appropriate for calculating the sum of the first 100 positive integers? What type of repetition would be appropriate for calculating the sum of an arbitrary number of positive integers? Briefly describe how each of these tasks could be performed.

4.14   What is the difference between preincrementing a variable and postincrementing a variable?

4.15   Identify and correct the errors in each of the following pieces of code. [*Note:* There may be more than one error in each piece of code.]

```
a)  if ( age >= 65 );
        System.out.println( "Age greater than or equal to 65" );
    else
        System.out.println( "Age is less than 65 )";
b)  int x = 1, total;
    while ( x <= 10 )
    {
        total += x;
        ++x;
    }
```

c) ```
while (x <= 100)
    total += x;
    ++x;
```
d) ```
while ( y > 0 )
{
    System.out.println( y );
    ++y;
```

4.16   What does the following program print?

```
1   public class Mystery
2   {
3      public static void main( String args[] )
4      {
5         int y;
6         int x = 1;
7         int total = 0;
8
9         while ( x <= 10 )
10        {
11           y = x * x;
12           System.out.println( y );
13           total += y;
14           ++x;
15        } // end while
16
17        System.out.printf( "Total is %d\n", total );
18     } // end main
19
20  } // end class Mystery
```

For Exercise 4.17 through Exercise 4.20, perform each of the following steps:
   a) Read the problem statement.
   b) Formulate the algorithm using pseudocode and top-down, stepwise refinement.
   c) Write a Java program.
   d) Test, debug and execute the Java program.
   e) Process three complete sets of data.

4.17   Drivers are concerned with the mileage their automobiles get. One driver has kept track of several tankfuls of gasoline by recording the miles driven and gallons used for each tankful. Develop a Java application that will input the miles driven and gallons used (both as integers) for each tankful. The program should calculate and display the miles per gallon obtained for each tankful and print the combined miles per gallon obtained for all tankfuls up to this point. All averaging calculations should produce floating-point results. Use class Scanner and sentinel-controlled repetition to obtain the data from the user.

4.18   Develop a Java application that will determine whether any of several department-store customers has exceeded the credit limit on a charge account. For each customer, the following facts are available:
   a) account number
   b) balance at the beginning of the month
   c) total of all items charged by the customer this month
   d) total of all credits applied to the customer's account this month
   e) allowed credit limit.

The program should input all these facts as integers, calculate the new balance (= *beginning balance* + *charges* − *credits*), display the new balance and determine whether the new balance exceeds the customer's credit limit. For those customers whose credit limit is exceeded, the program should display the message "Credit limit exceeded".

4.19 A large company pays its salespeople on a commission basis. The salespeople receive $200 per week plus 9% of their gross sales for that week. For example, a salesperson who sells $5,000 worth of merchandise in a week receives $200 plus 9% of $5,000, or a total of $650. You have been supplied with a list of the items sold by each salesperson. The values of these items are as follows:

Item	Value
1	239.99
2	129.75
3	99.95
4	350.89

Develop a Java application that inputs one salesperson's items sold for last week and calculates and displays that salesperson's earnings. There is no limit to the number of items that can be sold by a salesperson.

4.20 Develop a Java application that will determine the gross pay for each of three employees. The company pays straight time for the first 40 hours worked by each employee and time and a half for all hours worked in excess of 40 hours. You are given a list of the employees of the company, the number of hours each employee worked last week and the hourly rate of each employee. Your program should input this information for each employee and should determine and display the employee's gross pay. Use class Scanner to input the data.

4.21 The process of finding the largest value (i.e., the maximum of a group of values) is used frequently in computer applications. For example, a program that determines the winner of a sales contest would input the number of units sold by each salesperson. The salesperson who sells the most units wins the contest. Write a pseudocode program and then a Java application that inputs a series of 10 integers and determines and prints the largest integer. Your program should use at least the following three variables:
   a) counter: A counter to count to 10 (i.e., to keep track of how many numbers have been input and to determine when all 10 numbers have been processed).
   b) number: The integer most recently input by the user.
   c) largest: The largest number found so far.

4.22 Write a Java application that uses looping to print the following table of values:

N	10*N	100*N	1000*N
1	10	100	1000
2	20	200	2000
3	30	300	3000
4	40	400	4000
5	50	500	5000

4.23 Using an approach similar to that for Exercise 4.21, find the *two* largest values of the 10 values entered. [*Note*: You may input each number only once.]

4.24 Modify the program in Fig. 4.12 to validate its inputs. For any input, if the value entered is other than 1 or 2, keep looping until the user enters a correct value.

4.25 What does the following program print?

```
1   public class Mystery2
2   {
3      public static void main( String args[] )
4      {
5         int count = 1;
6
7         while ( count <= 10 )
8         {
9            System.out.println( count % 2 == 1 ? "****" : "++++++++" );
10           ++count;
11        } // end while
12     } // end main
13
14  } // end class Mystery2
```

4.26 What does the following program print?

```
1   public class Mystery3
2   {
3      public static void main( String args[] )
4      {
5         int row = 10;
6         int column;
7
8         while ( row >= 1 )
9         {
10           column = 1;
11
12           while ( column <= 10 )
13           {
14              System.out.print( row % 2 == 1 ? "<" : ">" );
15              ++column;
16           } // end while
17
18           --row;
19           System.out.println();
20        } // end while
21     } // end main
22
23  } // end class Mystery3
```

4.27 *(Dangling-else Problem)* Determine the output for each of the given sets of code when x is 9 and y is 11 and when x is 11 and y is 9. Note that the compiler ignores the indentation in a Java program. Also, the Java compiler always associates an else with the immediately preceding if unless told to do otherwise by the placement of braces ({}). On first glance, the programmer may not be sure which if an else matches—this situation is referred to as the "dangling-else problem." We have eliminated the indentation from the following code to make the problem more challenging. [*Hint*: Apply the indentation conventions you have learned.]

a)
```
if ( x < 10 )
if ( y > 10 )
System.out.println( "*****" );
else
System.out.println( "#####" );
System.out.println( "$$$$$" );
```
b)
```
if ( x < 10 )
{
if ( y > 10 )
System.out.println( "*****" );
}
else
{
System.out.println( "#####" );
System.out.println( "$$$$$" );
}
```

4.28 *(Another Dangling-else Problem)* Modify the given code to produce the output shown in each part of the problem. Use proper indentation techniques. Make no changes other than inserting braces and changing the indentation of the code. The compiler ignores indentation in a Java program. We have eliminated the indentation from the given code to make the problem more challenging. [*Note*: It is possible that no modification is necessary for some of the parts.]

```
if ( y == 8 )
if ( x == 5 )
System.out.println( "@@@@@" );
else
System.out.println( "#####" );
System.out.println( "$$$$$" );
System.out.println( "&&&&&" );
```

a) Assuming that x = 5 and y = 8, the following output is produced:

```
@@@@@
$$$$$
&&&&&
```

b) Assuming that x = 5 and y = 8, the following output is produced:

```
@@@@@
```

c) Assuming that x = 5 and y = 8, the following output is produced:

```
@@@@@
&&&&&
```

d) Assuming that x = 5 and y = 7, the following output is produced. [*Note*: The last three output statements after the else are all part of a block.]

```
#####
$$$$$
&&&&&
```

4.29 Write an application that prompts the user to enter the size of the side of a square, then displays a hollow square of that size made of asterisks. Your program should work for squares of all side lengths between 1 and 20.

4.30 *(Palindromes)* A palindrome is a sequence of characters that reads the same backward as forward. For example, each of the following five-digit integers is a palindrome: 12321, 55555, 45554 and 11611. Write an application that reads in a five-digit integer and determines whether it is a palindrome. If the number is not five digits long, display an error message and allow the user to enter a new value.

4.31 Write an application that inputs an integer containing only 0s and 1s (i.e., a binary integer) and prints its decimal equivalent. [*Hint*: Use the remainder and division operators to pick off the binary number's digits one at a time, from right to left. In the decimal number system, the rightmost digit has a positional value of 1 and the next digit to the left has a positional value of 10, then 100, then 1000, and so on. The decimal number 234 can be interpreted as 4 * 1 + 3 * 10 + 2 * 100. In the binary number system, the rightmost digit has a positional value of 1, the next digit to the left has a positional value of 2, then 4, then 8, and so on. The decimal equivalent of binary 1101 is 1 * 1 + 0 * 2 + 1 * 4 + 1 * 8, or 1 + 0 + 4 + 8 or, 13.]

4.32 Write an application that uses only the output statements

```
System.out.print( "* " );
System.out.print( " " );
System.out.println();
```

to display the checkerboard pattern that follows. Note that a `System.out.println` method call with no arguments causes the program to output a single newline character. [*Hint*: Repetition statements are required.]

```
* * * * * * * *
 * * * * * * * *
* * * * * * * *
 * * * * * * * *
* * * * * * * *
 * * * * * * * *
* * * * * * * *
 * * * * * * * *
```

4.33 Write an application that keeps displaying in the command window the multiples of the integer 2—namely, 2, 4, 8, 16, 32, 64, and so on. Your loop should not terminate (i.e., create an infinite loop). What happens when you run this program?

4.34 What is wrong with the following statement? Provide the correct statement to add one to the sum of x and y.

```
System.out.println( ++(x + y) );
```

4.35 Write an application that reads three nonzero values entered by the user and determines and prints whether they could represent the sides of a triangle.

4.36 Write an application that reads three nonzero integers and determines and prints whether they could represent the sides of a right triangle.

4.37 A company wants to transmit data over the telephone, but is concerned that its phones may be tapped. It has asked you to write a program that will encrypt the data so that it may be transmitted more securely. All the data is transmitted as four-digit integers. Your application should read a four-digit integer entered by the user and encrypt it as follows: Replace each digit with the result of adding 7 to the digit and getting the remainder after dividing the new value by 10. Then swap the first digit with the third, and swap the second digit with the fourth. Then print the encrypted integer. Write a separate application that inputs an encrypted four-digit integer and decrypts it to form the original number.

4.38   The factorial of a nonnegative integer n is written as $n!$ (pronounced "n factorial") and is defined as follows:

$$n! = n \cdot (n-1) \cdot (n-2) \cdot \ldots \cdot 1 \quad \text{(for values of } n \text{ greater than or equal to 1)}$$

and

$$n! = 1 \quad \text{(for } n = 0)$$

For example, $5! = 5 \cdot 4 \cdot 3 \cdot 2 \cdot 1$, which is 120.

a) Write an application that reads a nonnegative integer and computes and prints its factorial.

b) Write an application that estimates the value of the mathematical constant e by using the formula

$$e = 1 + \frac{1}{1!} + \frac{1}{2!} + \frac{1}{3!} + \ldots$$

c) Write an application that computes the value of e^x by using the formula

$$e^x = 1 + \frac{x}{1!} + \frac{x^2}{2!} + \frac{x^3}{3!} + \ldots$$

Control Statements: Part 2

Not everything that can be counted counts, and not every thing that counts can be counted.
—Albert Einstein

Who can control his fate?
—William Shakespeare

The used key is always bright.
—Benjamin Franklin

Intelligence ... is the faculty of making artificial objects, especially tools to make tools.
—Henri Bergson

Every advantage in the past is judged in the light of the final issue.
—Demosthenes

OBJECTIVES

In this chapter you will learn:

- The essentials of counter-controlled repetition.
- To use the `for` and `do...while` repetition statements to execute statements in a program repeatedly.
- To understand multiple selection using the `switch` selection statement.
- To use the `break` and `continue` program control statements to alter the flow of control.
- To use the logical operators to form complex conditional expressions in control statements.

5.1 Introduction

Chapter 4 began our introduction to the types of building blocks that are available for problem solving. We used those building blocks to employ proven program-construction techniques. In this chapter, we continue our presentation of the theory and principles of structured programming by introducing Java's remaining control statements. The control statements we study here and in Chapter 4 are helpful in building and manipulating objects.

In this chapter, we demonstrate Java's for, do...while and `switch` statements. Through a series of short examples using `while` and `for`, we explore the essentials of counter-controlled repetition. We devote a portion of the chapter (and Chapter 7) to expanding the GradeBook class presented in Chapters 3–4. In particular, we create a version of class GradeBook that uses a `switch` statement to count the number of A, B, C, D and F grade equivalents in a set of numeric grades entered by the user. We introduce the break and continue program control statements. We discuss Java's logical operators, which enable programmers to use more complex conditional expressions in control statements. Finally, we summarize Java's control statements and the proven problem-solving techniques presented in this chapter and Chapter 4.

5.2 Essentials of Counter-Controlled Repetition

This section uses the `while` repetition statement introduced in Chapter 4 to formalize the elements required to perform counter-controlled repetition. Counter-controlled repetition requires

1. a control variable (or loop counter)
2. the initial value of the control variable
3. the increment (or decrement) by which the control variable is modified each time through the loop (also known as each iteration of the loop)
4. the loop-continuation condition that determines whether looping should continue.

To see these elements of counter-controlled repetition, consider the application of Fig. 5.1, which uses a loop to display the numbers from 1 through 10. Note that Fig. 5.1 contains only one method, main, which does all of the class's work. For most applications in Chapters 3–4, we have encouraged the use of two separate files—one that declares a reusable class (e.g., Account) and one that instantiates one or more objects of that class (e.g., AccountTest) and demonstrates its (their) functionality. Occasionally, however, it is more appropriate simply to create one class whose main method concisely illustrates a basic concept. Throughout this chapter, we use several one-class examples like Fig. 5.1 to demonstrate the mechanics of Java's control statements.

In main of Fig. 5.1 (lines 6–17), the elements of counter-controlled repetition are defined in lines 8, 10 and 13. Line 8 declares the control variable (counter) as an int, reserves space for it in memory and sets its initial value to 1. Variable counter could also have been declared and initialized with the following local-variable declaration and assignment statements:

```
int counter; // declare counter
counter = 1; // initialize counter to 1
```

Line 12 in the while statement displays control variable counter's value during each iteration of the loop. Line 13 increments the control variable by 1 for each iteration of the loop. The loop-continuation condition in the while (line 10) tests whether the value of the control variable is less than or equal to 10 (the final value for which the condition is true). Note that the program performs the body of this while even when the control variable is 10. The loop terminates when the control variable exceeds 10 (i.e., counter becomes 11).

Common Programming Error 5.1

Because floating-point values may be approximate, controlling loops with floating-point variables may result in imprecise counter values and inaccurate termination tests.

```
1   // Fig. 5.1: WhileCounter.java
2   // Counter-controlled repetition with the while repetition statement.
3
4   public class WhileCounter
5   {
6      public static void main( String args[] )
7      {
8         int counter = 1; // declare and initialize control variable
9
10        while ( counter <= 10 ) // loop-continuation condition
11        {
12           System.out.printf( "%d   ", counter );
13           ++counter; // increment control variable by 1
14        } // end while
15
16        System.out.println(); // output a newline
17     } // end main
18  } // end class WhileCounter
```

```
1  2  3  4  5  6  7  8  9  10
```

Fig. 5.1 | Counter-controlled repetition with the while repetition statement.

Error-Prevention Tip 5.1

Control counting loops with integers.

Good Programming Practice 5.1

Place blank lines above and below repetition and selection control statements, and indent the statement bodies to enhance readability.

The program in Fig. 5.1 can be made more concise by initializing `counter` to 0 in line 8 and preincrementing `counter` in the `while` condition as follows:

```
while ( ++counter <= 10 ) // loop-continuation condition
   System.out.printf( "%d  ", counter );
```

This code saves a statement (and eliminates the need for braces around the loop's body), because the `while` condition performs the increment before testing the condition. (Recall from Section 4.12 that the precedence of `++` is higher than that of `<=`.) Coding in such a condensed fashion takes practice and might make code more difficult to read, debug, modify and maintain, and typically should be avoided.

Software Engineering Observation 5.1

"Keep it simple" remains good advice for most of the code you will write.

5.3 for Repetition Statement

Section 5.2 presented the essentials of counter-controlled repetition. The `while` statement can be used to implement any counter-controlled loop. Java also provides the `for` repetition statement, which specifies the counter-controlled-repetition details in a single line of code. Figure 5.2 reimplements the application in Fig. 5.1 using `for`.

```java
1   // Fig. 5.2: ForCounter.java
2   // Counter-controlled repetition with the for repetition statement.
3
4   public class ForCounter
5   {
6      public static void main( String args[] )
7      {
8         // for statement header includes initialization,
9         // loop-continuation condition and increment
10        for ( int counter = 1; counter <= 10; counter++ )
11           System.out.printf( "%d  ", counter );
12
13        System.out.println(); // output a newline
14     } // end main
15  } // end class ForCounter
```

```
1  2  3  4  5  6  7  8  9  10
```

Fig. 5.2 | Counter-controlled repetition with the `for` repetition statement.

The application's `main` method operates as follows: When the `for` statement (lines 10–11) begins executing, the control variable `counter` is declared and initialized to 1. (Recall from Section 5.2 that the first two elements of counter-controlled repetition are the control variable and its initial value.) Next, the program checks the loop-continuation condition, `counter <= 10`, which is between the two required semicolons. Because the initial value of `counter` is 1, the condition initially is true. Therefore, the body statement (line 11) displays control variable `counter`'s value, namely 1. After executing the loop's body, the program increments `counter` in the expression `counter++`, which appears to the right of the second semicolon. Then the loop-continuation test is performed again to determine whether the program should continue with the next iteration of the loop. At this point, the control variable value is 2, so the condition is still true (the final value is not exceeded)—thus, the program performs the body statement again (i.e., the next iteration of the loop). This process continues until the numbers 1 through 10 have been displayed and the `counter`'s value becomes 11, causing the loop-continuation test to fail and repetition to terminate (after 10 repetitions of the loop body at line 11). Then the program performs the first statement after the `for`—in this case, line 13.

Note that Fig. 5.2 uses (in line 10) the loop-continuation condition `counter <= 10`. If the programmer incorrectly specified `counter < 10` as the condition, the loop would iterate only nine times. This mistake is a common logic error called an **off-by-one error**.

Common Programming Error 5.2

Using an incorrect relational operator or an incorrect final value of a loop counter in the loop-continuation condition of a repetition statement can cause an off-by-one error.

Good Programming Practice 5.2

Using the final value in the condition of a `while` *or* `for` *statement and using the* `<=` *relational operator helps avoid off-by-one errors. For a loop that prints the values 1 to 10, the loop-continuation condition should be* `counter <= 10` *rather than* `counter < 10` *(which causes an off-by-one error) or* `counter < 11` *(which is correct). Many programmers prefer so-called zero-based counting, in which to count 10 times,* `counter` *would be initialized to zero and the loop-continuation test would be* `counter < 10`.

Figure 5.3 takes a closer look at the `for` statement in Fig. 5.2. The `for`'s first line (including the keyword `for` and everything in parentheses after `for`)—line 10 in Fig. 5.2—is sometimes called the **for statement header**, or simply the **for header**. Note that the `for` header "does it all"—it specifies each of the items needed for counter-controlled repetition with a control variable. If there is more than one statement in the body of the `for`, braces ({ and }) are required to define the body of the loop.

The general format of the `for` statement is

```
for ( initialization; loopContinuationCondition; increment )
    statement
```

where the *initialization* expression names the loop's control variable and provides its initial value, *loopContinuationCondition* is the condition that determines whether the loop should continue executing and *increment* modifies the control variable's value (possibly an increment or decrement), so that the loop-continuation condition eventually becomes false. The two semicolons in the `for` header are required.

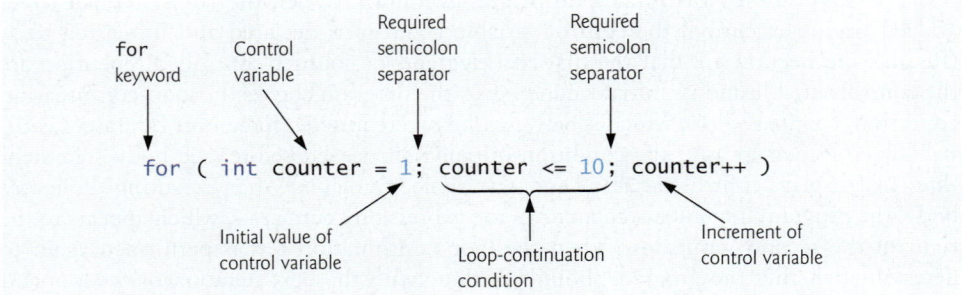

Fig. 5.3 | `for` statement header components.

Common Programming Error 5.3

Using commas instead of the two required semicolons in a `for` header is a syntax error.

In most cases, the `for` statement can be represented with an equivalent `while` statement as follows:

> *initialization*;
>
> `while` (*loopContinuationCondition*)
> {
>   *statement*
>   *increment*;
> }

In Section 5.7, we show a case in which a `for` statement cannot be represented with an equivalent `while` statement.

Typically, `for` statements are used for counter-controlled repetition and `while` statements are used for sentinel-controlled repetition. However, `while` and `for` can each be used for either repetition type.

If the *initialization* expression in the `for` header declares the control variable (i.e., the control variable's type is specified before the variable name, as in Fig. 5.2), the control variable can be used only in that `for` statement—it will not exist outside the `for` statement. This restricted use of the name of the control variable is known as the variable's scope. The scope of a variable defines where it can be used in a program. For example, a local variable can be used only in the method that declares the variable and only from the point of declaration through the end of the method. Scope is discussed in detail in Chapter 6, Methods: A Deeper Look.

Common Programming Error 5.4

When a `for` statement's control variable is declared in the initialization section of the `for`'s header, using the control variable after the `for`'s body is a compilation error.

All three expressions in a `for` header are optional. If the *loopContinuationCondition* is omitted, Java assumes that the loop-continuation condition is always true, thus creating an infinite loop. You might omit the *initialization* expression if the program initializes the control variable before the loop. You might omit the *increment* expression if the program calculates the increment with statements in the loop's body or if no increment is needed. The increment expression in a for acts as if it were a stand-alone statement at the end of the for's body. Therefore, the expressions

```
counter = counter + 1
counter += 1
++counter
counter++
```

are equivalent increment expressions in a for statement. Many programmers prefer counter++ because it is concise and because a for loop evaluates its increment expression after its body executes. Therefore, the postfix increment form seems more natural. In this case, the variable being incremented does not appear in a larger expression, so preincrementing and postincrementing actually have the same effect.

Performance Tip 5.1

There is a slight performance advantage to preincrementing, but if you choose to postincrement because it seems more natural (as in a for header), optimizing compilers will generate Java byte-code that uses the more efficient form anyway.

Good Programming Practice 5.3

In the most cases, preincrementing and postincrementing are both used to add 1 to a variable in a statement by itself. In these cases, the effect is exactly the same, except that preincrementing has a slight performance advantage. Given that the compiler typically optimizes your code to help you get the best performance, use the idiom with which you feel most comfortable in these situations.

Common Programming Error 5.5

Placing a semicolon immediately to the right of the right parenthesis of a for header makes that for's body an empty statement. This is normally a logic error.

Error-Prevention Tip 5.2

Infinite loops occur when the loop-continuation condition in a repetition statement never becomes false. To prevent this situation in a counter-controlled loop, ensure that the control variable is incremented (or decremented) during each iteration of the loop. In a sentinel-controlled loop, ensure that the sentinel value is eventually input.

The initialization, loop-continuation condition and increment portions of a for statement can contain arithmetic expressions. For example, assume that x = 2 and y = 10. If x and y are not modified in the body of the loop, the statement

```
for ( int j = x; j <= 4 * x * y; j += y / x )
```

is equivalent to the statement

```
for ( int j = 2; j <= 80; j += 5 )
```

The increment of a for statement may also be negative, in which case it is really a decrement, and the loop counts downward.

If the loop-continuation condition is initially false, the program does not execute the for statement's body. Instead, execution proceeds with the statement following the for.

Programs frequently display the control variable value or use it in calculations in the loop body, but this use is not required. The control variable is commonly used to control repetition without mentioning the control variable in the body of the for.

Error-Prevention Tip 5.3

Although the value of the control variable can be changed in the body of a for loop, avoid doing so, because this practice can lead to subtle errors.

The for statement's UML activity diagram is similar to that of the while statement (Fig. 4.4). Figure 5.4 shows the activity diagram of the for statement in Fig. 5.2. The diagram makes it clear that initialization occurs once before the loop-continuation test is evaluated the first time, and that incrementing occurs each time through the loop after the body statement executes.

5.4 Examples Using the for Statement

The following examples show techniques for varying the control variable in a for statement. In each case, we write the appropriate for header. Note the change in the relational operator for loops that decrement the control variable.

a) Vary the control variable from 1 to 100 in increments of 1.

```
for ( int i = 1; i <= 100; i++ )
```

b) Vary the control variable from 100 to 1 in decrements of 1.

```
for ( int i = 100; i >= 1; i-- )
```

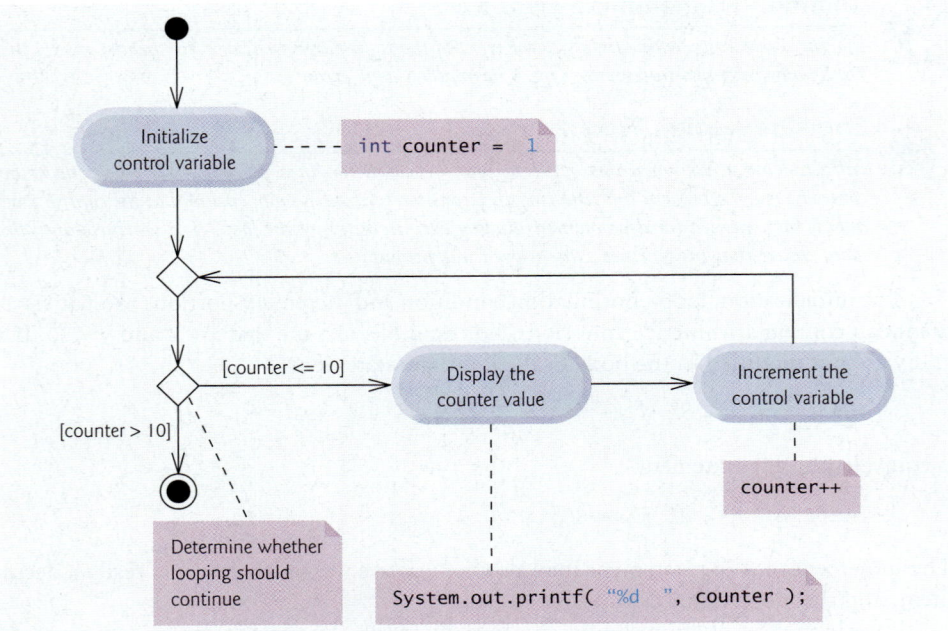

Fig. 5.4 | UML activity diagram for the for statement in Fig. 5.2.

c) Vary the control variable from 7 to 77 in increments of 7.

```
for ( int i = 7; i <= 77; i += 7 )
```

d) Vary the control variable from 20 to 2 in decrements of 2.

```
for ( int i = 20; i >= 2; i -= 2 )
```

e) Vary the control variable over the following sequence of values: 2, 5, 8, 11, 14, 17, 20.

```
for ( int i = 2; i <= 20; i += 3 )
```

f) Vary the control variable over the following sequence of values: 99, 88, 77, 66, 55, 44, 33, 22, 11, 0.

```
for ( int i = 99; i >= 0; i -= 11 )
```

Common Programming Error 5.6

Not using the proper relational operator in the loop-continuation condition of a loop that counts downward (e.g., using i <= 1 instead of i >= 1 in a loop counting down to 1) is usually a logic error.

Application: Summing the Even Integers from 2 to 20

We now consider two sample applications that demonstrate simple uses of **for**. The application in Fig. 5.5 uses a **for** statement to sum the even integers from 2 to 20 and store the result in an **int** variable called **total**.

The *initialization* and *increment* expressions can be comma-separated lists of expressions that enable the programmer to use multiple initialization expressions or multiple increment expressions. For example, the body of the **for** statement in lines 11–12 of Fig. 5.5 could be merged into the increment portion of the **for** header by using a comma as follows:

```
for ( int number = 2; number <= 20; total += number, number += 2 )
    ; // empty statement
```

```
 1   // Fig. 5.5: Sum.java
 2   // Summing integers with the for statement.
 3
 4   public class Sum
 5   {
 6      public static void main( String args[] )
 7      {
 8         int total = 0; // initialize total
 9
10         // total even integers from 2 through 20
11         for ( int number = 2; number <= 20; number += 2 )
12            total += number;
13
14         System.out.printf( "Sum is %d\n", total ); // display results
15      } // end main
16   } // end class Sum
```

```
Sum is 110
```

Fig. 5.5 | Summing integers with the **for** statement.

Good Programming Practice 5.4

Limit the size of control statement headers to a single line if possible.

Good Programming Practice 5.5

Place only expressions involving the control variables in the initialization and increment sections of a for statement. Manipulations of other variables should appear either before the loop (if they execute only once, like initialization statements) or in the body of the loop (if they execute once per iteration of the loop, like increment or decrement statements).

Application: Compound Interest Calculations

The next application uses the for statement to compute compound interest. Consider the following problem:

> *A person invests $1,000 in a savings account yielding 5% interest. Assuming that all the interest is left on deposit, calculate and print the amount of money in the account at the end of each year for 10 years. Use the following formula to determine the amounts:*
>
> $$a = p\,(1 + r)^n$$
>
> *where*
>
> > *p is the original amount invested (i.e., the principal)*
> > *r is the annual interest rate (e.g., use 0.05 for 5%)*
> > *n is the number of years*
> > *a is the amount on deposit at the end of the nth year.*

This problem involves a loop that performs the indicated calculation for each of the 10 years the money remains on deposit. The solution is the application shown in Fig. 5.6. Lines 8–10 in method main declare double variables amount, principal and rate, and initialize principal to 1000.0 and rate to 0.05. Java treats floating-point constants like 1000.0 and 0.05 as type double. Similarly, Java treats whole number constants like 7 and -22 as type int.

Line 13 outputs the headers for this application's two columns of output. The first column displays the year, and the second column displays the amount on deposit at the end of that year. Note that we use the format specifier %20s to output the String "Amount on Deposit". The integer 20 between the % and the conversion character s indicates that the value output should be displayed with a field width of 20—that is, printf displays the value with at least 20 character positions. If the value to be output is less than 20 character positions wide (17 characters in this example), the value is right justified in the field by default. If the year value to be output were more than four character positions wide, the field width would be extended to the right to accommodate the entire value—this would push the amount field to the right, upsetting the neat columns of our tabular output. To indicate that values should be output left justified, simply precede the field width with the minus sign (–) formatting flag.

The for statement (lines 16–23) executes its body 10 times, varying control variable year from 1 to 10 in increments of 1. This loop terminates when control variable year becomes 11. (Note that year represents *n* in the problem statement.)

Classes provide methods that perform common tasks on objects. In fact, most methods must be called on a specific object. For example, to output text in Fig. 5.6, line 13 calls method printf on the System.out object. Many classes also provide methods that perform

```
1   // Fig. 5.6: Interest.java
2   // Compound-interest calculations with for.
3
4   public class Interest
5   {
6      public static void main( String args[] )
7      {
8         double amount; // amount on deposit at end of each year
9         double principal = 1000.0; // initial amount before interest
10        double rate = 0.05; // interest rate
11
12        // display headers
13        System.out.printf( "%s%20s\n", "Year", "Amount on deposit" );
14
15        // calculate amount on deposit for each of ten years
16        for ( int year = 1; year <= 10; year++ )
17        {
18           // calculate new amount for specified year
19           amount = principal * Math.pow( 1.0 + rate, year );
20
21           // display the year and the amount
22           System.out.printf( "%4d%,20.2f\n", year, amount );
23        } // end for
24     } // end main
25  } // end class Interest
```

```
Year    Amount on deposit
  1             1,050.00
  2             1,102.50
  3             1,157.63
  4             1,215.51
  5             1,276.28
  6             1,340.10
  7             1,407.10
  8             1,477.46
  9             1,551.33
 10             1,628.89
```

Fig. 5.6 | Compound-interest calculations with for.

common tasks and do not require objects. Such methods are called **static methods**. For example, Java does not include an exponentiation operator, so the designers of Java's Math class defined static method pow for raising a value to a power. You can call a static method by specifying the class name followed by a dot (.) and the method name, as in

> *ClassName.methodName(arguments)*

In Chapter 6, you will learn how to implement static methods in your own classes.

We use static method pow of class Math to perform the compound interest calculation in Fig. 5.6. Math.pow(x, y) calculates the value of x raised to the yth power. The method receives two double arguments and returns a double value. Line 19 performs the calculation $a = p(1 + r)^n$, where a is amount, p is principal, r is rate and n is year.

After each calculation, line 22 outputs the year and the amount on deposit at the end of that year. The year is output in a field width of four characters (as specified by %4d). The amount is output as a floating-point number with the format specifier %,20.2f. The comma (,) formatting flag indicates that the floating-point value should be output with a thousands separator. The actual separator used is specific to the user's locale (i.e., country). For example, in the United States, the number will be output using commas to separate the thousands and a decimal point to separate the fractional part of the number, as in 1,234.45. The number 20 in the format specification indicates that the value should be output right justified in a field width of 20 characters. The .2 specifies the formatted number's precision—in this case, the number is rounded to the nearest hundredth and output with two digits to the right of the decimal point.

We declared variables amount, principal and rate to be of type double in this example. We are dealing with fractional parts of dollars and thus need a type that allows decimal points in its values. Unfortunately, floating-point numbers can cause trouble. Here is a simple explanation of what can go wrong when using double (or float) to represent dollar amounts (assuming that dollar amounts are displayed with two digits to the right of the decimal point): Two double dollar amounts stored in the machine could be 14.234 (which would normally be rounded to 14.23 for display purposes) and 18.673 (which would normally be rounded to 18.67 for display purposes). When these amounts are added, they produce the internal sum 32.907, which would normally be rounded to 32.91 for display purposes. Thus, your output could appear as

```
   14.23
+ 18.67
 -------
   32.91
```

but a person adding the individual numbers as displayed would expect the sum to be 32.90. You have been warned!

Good Programming Practice 5.6

Do not use variables of type double (or float) to perform precise monetary calculations. The imprecision of floating-point numbers can cause errors that will result in incorrect monetary values. In the exercises, we explore the use of integers to perform monetary calculations. [Note: Some third-party vendors provide for-sale class libraries that perform precise monetary calculations. In addition, the Java API provides class java.math.BigDecimal for performing calculations with arbitrary precision floating-point values.]

Note that the body of the for statement contains the calculation 1.0 + rate, which appears as an argument to the Math.pow method. In fact, this calculation produces the same result each time through the loop, so repeating the calculation every iteration of the loop is wasteful.

Performance Tip 5.2

In loops, avoid calculations for which the result never changes—such calculations should typically be placed before the loop. [Note: Many of today's sophisticated optimizing compilers will place such calculations outside loops in the compiled code.]

5.5 do...while Repetition Statement

The do...while repetition statement is similar to the while statement. In the while, the program tests the loop-continuation condition at the beginning of the loop, before executing the loop's body. If the condition is false, the body never executes. The do...while statement tests the loop-continuation condition *after* executing the loop's body; therefore, the body always executes at least once. When a do...while statement terminates, execution continues with the next statement in sequence. Figure 5.7 uses a do...while (lines 10–14) to output the numbers 1–10.

Line 8 declares and initializes control variable counter. Upon entering the do...while statement, line 12 outputs counter's value and line 13 increments counter. Then the program evaluates the loop-continuation test at the bottom of the loop (line 14). If the condition is true, the loop continues from the first body statement in the do...while (line 12). If the condition is false, the loop terminates and the program continues with the next statement after the loop.

Figure 5.8 contains the UML activity diagram for the do...while statement. This diagram makes it clear that the loop-continuation condition is not evaluated until after the loop performs the action state at least once. Compare this activity diagram with that of the while statement (Fig. 4.4). It is not necessary to use braces in the do...while repetition statement if there is only one statement in the body. However, most programmers include the braces, to avoid confusion between the while and do...while statements. For example,

```
while ( condition )
```

is normally the first line of a while statement. A do...while statement with no braces around a single-statement body appears as:

```
 1   // Fig. 5.7: DoWhileTest.java
 2   // do...while repetition statement.
 3
 4   public class DoWhileTest
 5   {
 6      public static void main( String args[] )
 7      {
 8         int counter = 1; // initialize counter
 9
10         do
11         {
12            System.out.printf( "%d  ", counter );
13            ++counter;
14         } while ( counter <= 10 ); // end do...while
15
16         System.out.println(); // outputs a newline
17      } // end main
18   } // end class DoWhileTest
```

```
1  2  3  4  5  6  7  8  9  10
```

Fig. 5.7 | do...while repetition statement.

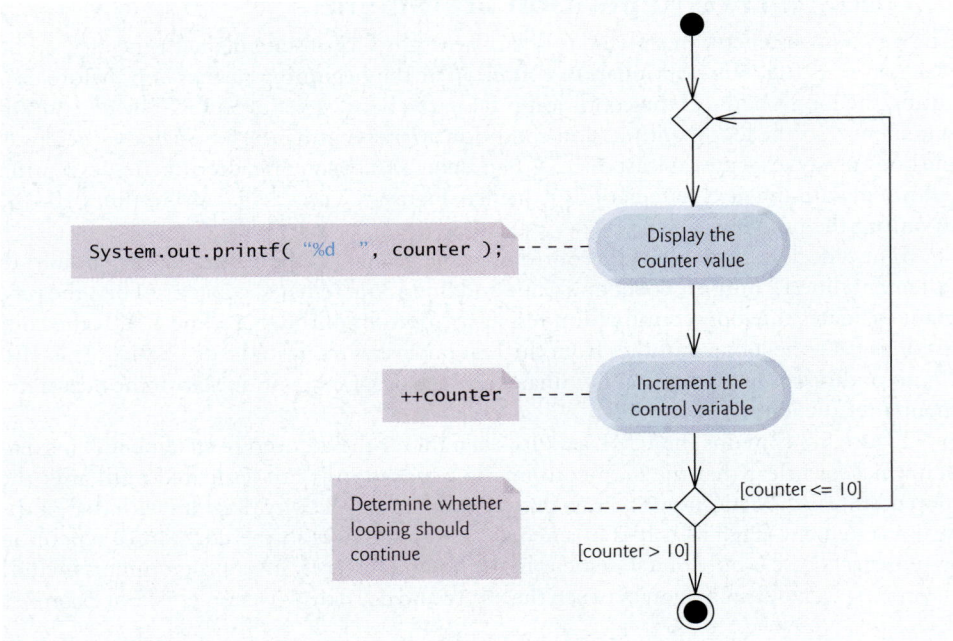

Fig. 5.8 | do...while repetition statement UML activity diagram.

```
do
    statement
while ( condition );
```

which can be confusing. A reader may misinterpret the last line—while(*condition*);— as a while statement containing an empty statement (the semicolon by itself). Thus, the do...while statement with one body statement is usually written as follows:

```
do
{
    statement
} while ( condition );
```

Good Programming Practice 5.7

Always include braces in a do...while statement, even if they are not necessary. This helps eliminate ambiguity between the while statement and a do...while statement containing only one statement.

5.6 switch Multiple-Selection Statement

We discussed the if single-selection statement and the if...else double-selectionstate-ment in Chapter 4. Java provides the switch multiple-selection statement to perform different actions based on the possible values of an integer variable or expression. Each action. is associated with the value of a constant integral expression (i.e., a constant value of type byte, short, int or char, but not long) that the variable or expression on which the switch is based may assume.

GradeBook Class with switch Statement to Count A, B, C, D and F Grades.
Figure 5.9 contains an enhanced version of the GradeBook class introduced in Chapter 3 and further developed in Chapter 4. The version of the class we now present not only calculates the average of a set of numeric grades entered by the user, but uses a switch statement to determine whether each grade is the equivalent of an A, B, C, D or F and to increment the appropriate grade counter. The class also displays a summary of the number of students who received each grade. Please refer to Fig. 5.10 for sample input and output of the GradeBook-Test application that uses class GradeBook to process a set of grades.

```java
 1   // Fig. 5.9: GradeBook.java
 2   // GradeBook class uses switch statement to count A, B, C, D and F grades.
 3   import java.util.Scanner; // program uses class Scanner
 4
 5   public class GradeBook
 6   {
 7      private String courseName; // name of course this GradeBook represents
 8      private int total; // sum of grades
 9      private int gradeCounter; // number of grades entered
10      private int aCount; // count of A grades
11      private int bCount; // count of B grades
12      private int cCount; // count of C grades
13      private int dCount; // count of D grades
14      private int fCount; // count of F grades
15
16      // constructor initializes courseName;
17      // int instance variables are initialized to 0 by default
18      public GradeBook( String name )
19      {
20         courseName = name; // initializes courseName
21      } // end constructor
22
23      // method to set the course name
24      public void setCourseName( String name )
25      {
26         courseName = name; // store the course name
27      } // end method setCourseName
28
29      // method to retrieve the course name
30      public String getCourseName()
31      {
32         return courseName;
33      } // end method getCourseName
34
35      // display a welcome message to the GradeBook user
36      public void displayMessage()
37      {
38         // getCourseName gets the name of the course
39         System.out.printf( "Welcome to the grade book for\n%s!\n\n",
40            getCourseName() );
41      } // end method displayMessage
42
```

Fig. 5.9 | GradeBook class uses switch statement to count A, B, C, D and F grades. (Part 1 of 3.)

```
43    // input arbitrary number of grades from user
44    public void inputGrades()
45    {
46       Scanner input = new Scanner( System.in );
47
48       int grade; // grade entered by user
49
50       System.out.printf( "%s\n%s\n   %s\n   %s\n",
51          "Enter the integer grades in the range 0-100.",
52          "Type the end-of-file indicator to terminate input:",
53          "On UNIX/Linux/Mac OS X type <ctrl> d then press Enter",
54          "On Windows type <ctrl> z then press Enter" );
55
56       // loop until user enters the end-of-file indicator
57       while ( input.hasNext() )
58       {
59          grade = input.nextInt(); // read grade
60          total += grade; // add grade to total
61          ++gradeCounter; // increment number of grades
62
63          // call method to increment appropriate counter
64          incrementLetterGradeCounter( grade );
65       } // end while
66    } // end method inputGrades
67
68    // add 1 to appropriate counter for specified grade
69    public void incrementLetterGradeCounter( int Grade )
70    {
71       // determine which grade was entered
72       switch ( grade / 10 )
73       {
74          case 9:  // grade was between 90
75          case 10: // and 100
76             ++aCount; // increment aCount
77             break; // necessary to exit switch
78
79          case 8: // grade was between 80 and 89
80             ++bCount; // increment bCount
81             break; // exit switch
82
83          case 7: // grade was between 70 and 79
84             ++cCount; // increment cCount
85             break; // exit switch
86
87          case 6: // grade was between 60 and 69
88             ++dCount; // increment dCount
89             break; // exit switch
90
91          default: // grade was less than 60
92             ++fCount; // increment fCount
93             break; // optional; will exit switch anyway
94       } // end switch
95    } // end method incrementLetterGradeCounter
```

Fig. 5.9 | GradeBook class uses switch statement to count A, B, C, D and F grades. (Part 2 of 3.)

```
96
97      // display a report based on the grades entered by user
98      public void displayGradeReport()
99      {
100         System.out.println( "\nGrade Report:" );
101
102         // if user entered at least one grade...
103         if ( gradeCounter != 0 )
104         {
105            // calculate average of all grades entered
106            double average = (double) total / gradeCounter;
107
108            // output summary of results
109            System.out.printf( "Total of the %d grades entered is %d\n",
110               gradeCounter, total );
111            System.out.printf( "Class average is %.2f\n", average );
112            System.out.printf( "%s\n%s%d\n%s%d\n%s%d\n%s%d\n%s%d\n",
113               "Number of students who received each grade:",
114               "A: ", aCount,    // display number of A grades
115               "B: ", bCount,    // display number of B grades
116               "C: ", cCount,    // display number of C grades
117               "D: ", dCount,    // display number of D grades
118               "F: ", fCount );  // display number of F grades
119         } // end if
120         else // no grades were entered, so output appropriate message
121            System.out.println( "No grades were entered" );
122      } // end method displayGradeReport
123   } // end class GradeBook
```

Fig. 5.9 | GradeBook class uses switch statement to count A, B, C, D and F grades. (Part 3 of 3.)

Like earlier versions of the class, class GradeBook (Fig. 5.9) declares instance variable courseName (line 7) and contains methods setCourseName (lines 24–27), getCourseName (lines 30–33) and displayMessage (lines 36–41), which set the course name, store the course name and display a welcome message to the user, respectively. The class also contains a constructor (lines 18–21) that initializes the course name.

Class GradeBook also declares instance variables total (line 8) and gradeCounter (line 9), which keep track of the sum of the grades entered by the user and the number of grades entered, respectively. Lines 10–14 declare counter variables for each grade category. Class GradeBook maintains total, gradeCounter and the five letter-grade counters as instance variables so that these variables can be used or modified in any of the class's methods. Note that the class's constructor (lines 18–21) sets only the course name, because the remaining seven instance variables are ints and are initialized to 0 by default.

Class GradeBook (Fig. 5.9) contains three additional methods—inputGrades, incrementLetterGradeCounter and displayGradeReport. Method inputGrades (lines 44–66) reads an arbitrary number of integer grades from the user using sentinel-controlled repetition and updates instance variables total and gradeCounter. Method inputGrades calls method incrementLetterGradeCounter (lines 69–95) to update the appropriate letter-grade counter for each grade entered. Class GradeBook also contains method displayGradeReport (lines 98–122), which outputs a report containing the total of all grades entered, the average of the grades and the number of students who received each letter grade. Let's examine these methods in more detail.

Line 48 in method `inputGrades` declares variable `grade`, which will store the user's input. Lines 50–54 prompt the user to enter integer grades and to type the end-of-file indicator to terminate the input. The **end-of-file indicator** is a system-dependent keystroke combination which the user enters to indicate that there is no more data to input. In Chapter 14, Files and Streams, we will see how the end-of-file indicator is used when a program reads its input from a file.

On UNIX/Linux/Mac OS X systems, end-of-file is entered by typing the sequence

    <ctrl> d

on a line by itself. This notation means to simultaneously press both the *ctrl* key and the *d* key. On Windows systems, end-of-file can be entered by typing

    <ctrl> z

[*Note:* On some systems, you must press *Enter* after typing the end-of-file key sequence. Also, Windows typically displays the characters ^Z on the screen when the end-of-file indicator is typed, as is shown in the output of Fig. 5.9.]

Portability Tip 5.1

The keystroke combinations for entering end-of-file are system dependent.

The `while` statement (lines 57–65) obtains the user input. The condition at line 57 calls `Scanner` method **hasNext** to determine whether there is more data to input. This method returns the `boolean` value `true` if there is more data; otherwise, it returns `false`. The returned value is then used as the condition in the `while` statement. As long as the end-of-file indicator has not been typed, method `hasNext` will return `true`.

Line 59 inputs a grade value from the user. Line 60 uses the `+=` operator to add `grade` to `total`. Line 61 increments `gradeCounter`. The class's `displayGradeReport` method uses these variables to compute the average of the grades. Line 64 calls the class's `incrementLetterGradeCounter` method (declared in lines 69–95) to increment the appropriate letter-grade counter based on the numeric grade entered.

Method `incrementLetterGradeCounter` contains a `switch` statement (lines 72–94) that determines which counter to increment. In this example, we assume that the user enters a valid grade in the range 0–100. A grade in the range 90–100 represents A, 80–89 represents B, 70–79 represents C, 60–69 represents D and 0–59 represents F. The `switch` statement consists of a block that contains a sequence of **case labels** and an optional **default case**. These are used in this example to determine which counter to increment based on the grade.

When the flow of control reaches the `switch`, the program evaluates the expression in the parentheses (`grade / 10`) following keyword `switch`. This is called the **controlling expression** of the `switch`. The program compares the value of the controlling expression (which must evaluate to an integral value of type `byte`, `char`, `short` or `int`) with each `case` label. The controlling expression in line 72 performs integer division, which truncates the fractional part of the result. Thus, when we divide any value for 0–100 by 10, the result is always a value from 0 to 10. We use several of these values in our `case` labels. For example, if the user enters the integer 85, the controlling expression evaluates to the `int` value 8. The switch compares 8 with each case. If a match occurs (case 8: at line 79), the program executes the statements for that case. For the integer 8, line 80 increments bCount, because a grade in the 80s is a B. The break statement (line 81) causes program control to proceed with the first statement after the switch—in this program, we reach the end of method incrementLetterGradeCounter's body, so control returns to line 65 in method inputGrades (the first line after the call to incrementLetterGradeCounter). This line marks the end of the body of the while loop that inputs grades (lines 57–65), so control flows to the while's condition (line 57) to determine whether the loop should continue executing.

The cases in our switch explicitly test for the values 10, 9, 8, 7 and 6. Note the cases at lines 74–75 that test for the values 9 and 10 (both of which represent the grade A). Listing cases consecutively in this manner with no statements between them enables the cases to perform the same set of statements—when the controlling expression evaluates to 9 or 10, the statements in lines 76–77 will execute. The switch statement does not provide a mechanism for testing ranges of values, so every value that must be tested should be listed in a separate case label. Note that each case can have multiple statements. The switch statement differs from other control statements in that it does not require braces around multiple statements in each case.

Without break statements, each time a match occurs in the switch, the statements for that case and subsequent cases execute until a break statement or the end of the switch is encountered. This is often referred to as "falling through" to the statements in subsequent cases. (This feature is perfect for writing a concise program that displays the iterative song "The Twelve Days of Christmas" in Exercise 5.29.)

 Common Programming Error 5.7

Forgetting a break *statement when one is needed in a* switch *is a logic error.*

If no match occurs between the controlling expression's value and a case label, the default case (lines 91–93) executes. We use the default case in this example to process all controlling-expression values that are less than 6, that is, all failing grades. If no match occurs and the switch does not contain a default case, program control simply continues with the first statement after the switch.

GradeBookTest *Class That Demonstrates Class* GradeBook

Class GradeBookTest (Fig. 5.10) creates a GradeBook object (lines 10–11). Line 13 invokes the object's displayMessage method to output a welcome message to the user. Line 14 invokes the object's inputGrades method to read a set of grades from the user and keep track of the sum of all the grades entered and the number of grades. Recall that method inputGrades also calls method incrementLetterGradeCounter to keep track of the number of students who received each letter grade. Line 15 invokes method displayGradeReport of class GradeBook, which outputs a report based on the grades entered (as in the input/output window in Fig. 5.10). Line 103 of class GradeBook (Fig. 5.9) determines whether the user entered at least one grade—this helps us avoid dividing by zero. If so, line 106 calculates the average of the grades. Lines 109–118 then output the total of all the grades, the class average and the number of students who received each letter grade. If no grades were entered, line 121 outputs an appropriate message. The output in Fig. 5.10 shows a sample grade report based on 10 grades.

```
1   // Fig. 5.10: GradeBookTest.java
2   // Create GradeBook object, input grades and display grade report.
3
4   public class GradeBookTest
5   {
6      public static void main( String args[] )
7      {
8         // create GradeBook object myGradeBook and
9         // pass course name to constructor
10        GradeBook myGradeBook = new GradeBook(
11           "CS101 Introduction to Java Programming" );
12
13        myGradeBook.displayMessage(); // display welcome message
14        myGradeBook.inputGrades(); // read grades from user
15        myGradeBook.displayGradeReport(); // display report based on grades
16     } // end main
17  } // end class GradeBookTest
```

```
Welcome to the grade book for
CS101 Introduction to Java Programming!

Enter the integer grades in the range 0-100.
Type the end-of-file indicator to terminate input:
   On UNIX/Linux/Mac OS X type <ctrl> d then press Enter
   On Windows type <ctrl> z then press Enter
99
92
45
57
63
71
76
85
90
100
^Z

Grade Report:
Total of the 10 grades entered is 778
Class average is 77.80
Number of students who received each grade:
A: 4
B: 1
C: 2
D: 1
F: 2
```

Fig. 5.10 | GradeBookTest creates a GradeBook object and invokes its methods.

Note that class GradeBookTest (Fig. 5.10) does not directly call GradeBook method incrementLetterGradeCounter (lines 69–95 of Fig. 5.9). This method is used exclusively by method inputGrades of class GradeBook to update the appropriate letter-grade counter as each new grade is entered by the user. Method incrementLetterGradeCounter exists solely to support the operations of class GradeBook's other methods and thus could be declared private. Recall from Chapter 3 that methods declared with access modifier private can be called only by other methods of the class in which the private methods are declared. Such methods are commonly referred to as **utility methods** or **helper methods** because they can be called only by other methods of that class and are used to support the operation of those methods.

switch Statement UML Activity Diagram

Figure 5.11 shows the UML activity diagram for the general switch statement. Most switch statements use a break in each case to terminate the switch statement after processing the case. Figure 5.11 emphasizes this by including break statements in the activity diagram. The diagram makes it clear that the break statement at the end of a case causes control to exit the switch statement immediately.

The break statement is not required for the switch's last case (or the default case, when it appears last), because execution continues with the next statement after the switch.

Software Engineering Observation 5.2

Provide a default case in switch statements. Including a default case focuses you on the need to process exceptional conditions.

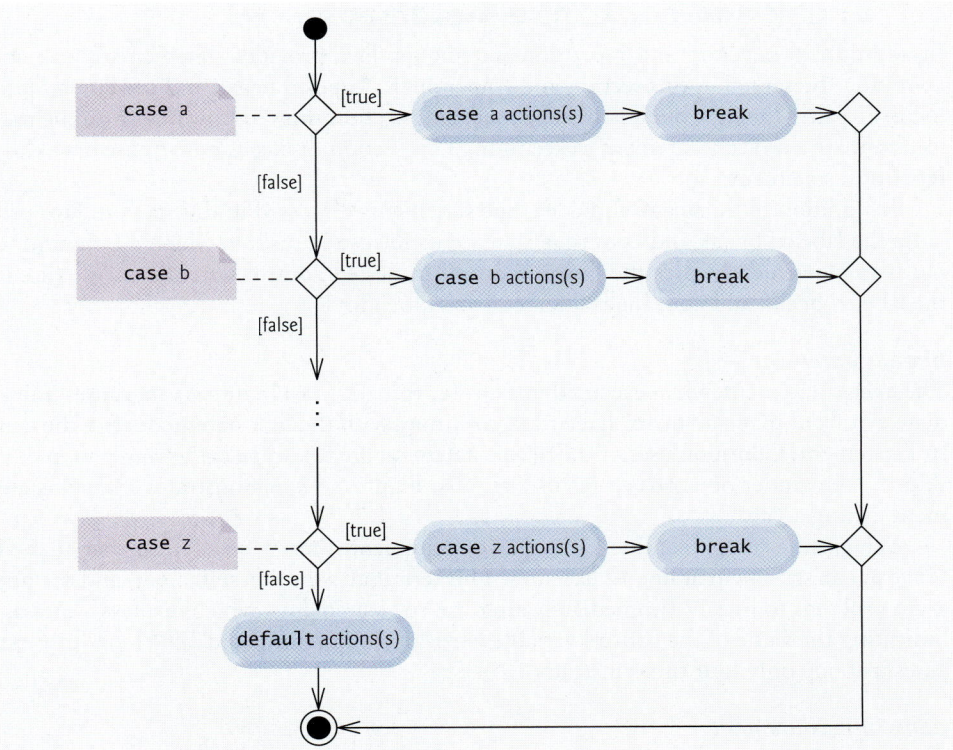

Fig. 5.11 | switch multiple-selection statement UML activity diagram with **break** statements.

Good Programming Practice 5.8

Although each `case` *and the* `default` *case in a* `switch` *can occur in any order, place the* `default` *case last. When the* `default` *case is listed last, the* `break` *for that case is not required. Some programmers include this* `break` *for clarity and symmetry with other cases.*

When using the `switch` statement, remember that the expression after each `case` can be only a constant integral expression—that is, any combination of integer constants that evaluates to a constant integer value (e.g., -7, 0 or 221). An integer constant is simply an integer value. In addition, you can use **character constants**—specific characters in single quotes, such as `'A'`, `'7'` or `'$'`—which represent the integer values of characters. (Appendix B, ASCII Character Set shows the integer values of the characters in the ASCII character set, which is a subset of the Unicode character set used by Java.)

The expression in each `case` also can be a **constant variable**—a variable that contains a value which does not change for the entire program. Such a variable is declared with keyword `final` (discussed in Chapter 6, Methods: A Deeper Look). J2SE 5.0 has a new feature called enumerations, which we also present in Chapter 6. Enumeration constants can also be used in `case` labels. In Chapter 10, Object-Oriented Programming: Polymorphism, we present a more elegant way to implement `switch` logic—we use a technique called polymorphism to create programs that are often clearer, easier to maintain and easier to extend than programs using `switch` logic.

5.7 break and continue Statements

In addition to selection and repetition statements, Java provides statements `break` and `continue` (presented in this section and Appendix K, Labeled `break` and `continue` Statements) to alter the flow of control. The preceding section showed how `break` can be used to terminate a `switch` statement's execution. This section discusses how to use `break` in a repetition statement.

In addition to the `break` and `continue` statements discussed in this section, Java provides the labeled `break` and `continue` statements for use in cases in which a programmer needs to conveniently alter the flow of control in nested control statements. We discuss the labeled `break` and `continue` statements in Appendix K.

break Statement

The `break` statement, when executed in a `while`, `for`, `do...while` or `switch`, causes immediate exit from that statement. Execution continues with the first statement after the control statement. Common uses of the `break` statement are to escape early from a loop or to skip the remainder of a `switch` (as in Fig. 5.9). Figure 5.12 demonstrates a `break` statement exiting a `for`.

When the `if` nested at line 11 in the `for` statement (lines 9–15) detects that `count` is 5, the `break` statement at line 12 executes. This terminates the `for` statement, and the program proceeds to line 17 (immediately after the `for` statement), which displays a message indicating the value of the control variable when the loop terminated. The loop fully executes its body only four times instead of 10.

continue Statement

The `continue` statement, when executed in a `while`, `for` or `do...while`, skips the remaining statements in the loop body and proceeds with the next iteration of the loop. In `while`

```
 1   // Fig. 5.12: BreakTest.java
 2   // break statement exiting a for statement.
 3   public class BreakTest
 4   {
 5      public static void main( String args[] )
 6      {
 7         int count; // control variable also used after loop terminates
 8
 9         for ( count = 1; count <= 10; count++ ) // loop 10 times
10         {
11            if ( count == 5 ) // if count is 5,
12               break;           // terminate loop
13
14            System.out.printf( "%d ", count );
15         } // end for
16
17         System.out.printf( "\nBroke out of loop at count = %d\n", count );
18      } // end main
19   } // end class BreakTest
```

```
1 2 3 4
Broke out of loop at count = 5
```

Fig. 5.12 | break statement exiting a for statement.

and do...while statements, the program evaluates the loop-continuation test immediately after the continue statement executes. In a for statement, the increment expression executes, then the program evaluates the loop-continuation test.

Figure 5.13 uses the continue statement in a for to skip the statement at line 12 when the nested if (line 9) determines that the value of count is 5. When the continue statement executes, program control continues with the increment of the control variable in the for statement (line 7).

```
 1   // Fig. 5.13: ContinueTest.java
 2   // continue statement terminating an iteration of a for statement.
 3   public class ContinueTest
 4   {
 5      public static void main( String args[] )
 6      {
 7         for ( int count = 1; count <= 10; count++ ) // loop 10 times
 8         {
 9            if ( count == 5 ) // if count is 5,
10               continue;        // skip remaining code in loop
11
12            System.out.printf( "%d ", count );
13         } // end for
14
15         System.out.println( "\nUsed continue to skip printing 5" );
16      } // end main
17   } // end class ContinueTest
```

Fig. 5.13 | continue statement terminating an iteration of a for statement. (Part 1 of 2.)

```
1 2 3 4 6 7 8 9 10
Used continue to skip printing 5
```

Fig. 5.13 | `continue` statement terminating an iteration of a `for` statement. (Part 2 of 2.)

In Section 5.3, we stated that `while` could be used in most cases in place of `for`. The one exception occurs when the increment expression in the `while` follows a `continue` statement. In this case, the increment does not execute before the program evaluates the repetition-continuation condition, so the `while` does not execute in the same manner as the `for`.

Software Engineering Observation 5.3

Some programmers feel that `break` and `continue` violate structured programming. Since the same effects are achievable with structured programming techniques, these programmers do not use `break` or `continue`.

Software Engineering Observation 5.4

There is a tension between achieving quality software engineering and achieving the best-performing software. Often, one of these goals is achieved at the expense of the other. For all but the most performance-intensive situations, apply the following rule of thumb: First, make your code simple and correct; then make it fast and small, but only if necessary.

5.8 Logical Operators

The `if`, `if...else`, `while`, `do...while` and `for` statements each require a condition to determine how to continue a program's flow of control. So far, we have studied only **simple conditions**, such as `count <= 10`, `number != sentinelValue` and `total > 1000`. Simple conditions are expressed in terms of the relational operators `>`, `<`, `>=` and `<=` and the equality operators `==` and `!=`, and each expression tests only one condition. To test multiple conditions in the process of making a decision, we performed these tests in separate statements or in nested `if` or `if...else` statements. Sometimes, control statements require more complex conditions to determine a program's flow of control.

Java provides **logical operators** to enable programmers to form more complex conditions by combining simple conditions. The logical operators are `&&` (conditional AND), `||` (conditional OR), `&` (boolean logical AND), `|` (boolean logical inclusive OR), `^` (boolean logical exclusive OR) and `!` (logical NOT).

Conditional AND (&&) Operator

Suppose that we wish to ensure at some point in a program that two conditions are *both* true before we choose a certain path of execution. In this case, we can use the **&& (conditional AND)** operator, as follows:

```
if ( gender == FEMALE && age >= 65 )
    ++seniorFemales;
```

This `if` statement contains two simple conditions. The condition `gender == FEMALE` compares variable `gender` to the constant `FEMALE`. This might be evaluated, for example, to determine whether a person is female. The condition age >= 65 might be evaluated to determine whether a person is a senior citizen. The if statement considers the combined condition

```
gender == FEMALE && age >= 65
```

which is true if and only if both simple conditions are true. If the combined condition is true, the if statement's body increments seniorFemales by 1. If either or both of the simple conditions are false, the program skips the increment. Some programmers find that the preceding combined condition is more readable when redundant parentheses are added, as in:

```
( gender == FEMALE ) && ( age >= 65 )
```

The table in Fig. 5.14 summarizes the && operator. The table shows all four possible combinations of false and true values for *expression1* and *expression2*. Such tables are called **truth tables**. Java evaluates to false or true all expressions that include relational operators, equality operators or logical operators.

Conditional OR (||) Operator

Now suppose that we wish to ensure that either *or* both of two conditions are true before we choose a certain path of execution. In this case, we use the || (**conditional OR**) operator, as in the following program segment:

```
if ( ( semesterAverage >= 90 ) || ( finalExam >= 90 ) )
    System.out.println ( "Student grade is A" );
```

This statement also contains two simple conditions. The condition semesterAverage >= 90 evaluates to determine whether the student deserves an A in the course because of a solid performance throughout the semester. The condition finalExam >= 90 evaluates to determine whether the student deserves an A in the course because of an outstanding performance on the final exam. The if statement then considers the combined condition

```
( semesterAverage >= 90 ) || ( finalExam >= 90 )
```

and awards the student an A if either or both of the simple conditions are true. The only time the message "Student grade is A" is *not* printed is when both of the simple conditions are false. Figure 5.15 is a truth table for operator conditional OR (||). Operator && has a higher precedence than operator ||. Both operators associate from left to right.

expression1	expression2	expression1 && expression2
false	false	false
false	true	false
true	false	false
true	true	true

Fig. 5.14 | && (conditional AND) operator truth table.

expression1	expression2	expression1 || expression2
false	false	false
false	true	true
true	false	true
true	true	true

Fig. 5.15 | \|\| (conditional OR) operator truth table.

Short-Circuit Evaluation of Complex Conditions

The parts of an expression containing && or \|\| operators are evaluated only until it is known whether the condition is true or false. Thus, evaluation of the expression

        (gender == FEMALE) && (age >= 65)

stops immediately if gender is not equal to FEMALE (i.e., the entire expression is false) and continues if gender *is* equal to FEMALE (i.e., the entire expression could still be true if the condition age >= 65 is true). This feature of conditional AND and conditional OR expressions is called short-circuit evaluation.

Common Programming Error 5.8

In expressions using operator &&, a condition—we will call this the dependent condition—may require another condition to be true for the evaluation of the dependent condition to be meaningful. In this case, the dependent condition should be placed after the other condition, or an error might occur. For example, in the expression (i != 0) && (10 / i == 2), the second condition must appear after the first condition, or a divide-by-zero error might occur.

Boolean Logical AND (&) and Boolean Logical OR (|) Operators

The boolean logical AND (&) and boolean logical inclusive OR (|) operators work identically to the && (conditional AND) and \|\| (conditional OR) operators, with one exception: The boolean logical operators always evaluate both of their operands (i.e., they do not perform short-circuit evaluation). Therefore, the expression

        (gender == 1) & (age >= 65)

evaluates age >= 65 regardless of whether gender is equal to 1. This is useful if the right operand of the boolean logical AND or boolean logical inclusive OR operator has a required side effect—a modification of a variable's value. For example, the expression

        (birthday == true) | (++age >= 65)

guarantees that the condition ++age >= 65 will be evaluated. Thus, the variable age is incremented in the preceding expression, regardless of whether the overall expression is true or false.

Error-Prevention Tip 5.4

For clarity, avoid expressions with side effects in conditions. The side effects may look clever, but they can make it harder to understand code and can lead to subtle logic errors.

Boolean Logical Exclusive OR (^)

A simple condition containing the boolean logical exclusive OR (^) operator is true *if and only if one of its operands is* true *and the other is* false. If both operands are true or both are false, the entire condition is false. Figure 5.16 is a truth table for the boolean logical exclusive OR operator (^). This operator is also guaranteed to evaluate both of its operands.

Logical Negation (!) Operator

The ! (logical NOT, also called logical negation or logical complement) operator enables a programmer to "reverse" the meaning of a condition. Unlike the logical operators &&, ||, &, | and ^, which are binary operators that combine two conditions, the logical negation operator is a unary operator that has only a single condition as an operand. The logical negation operator is placed before a condition to choose a path of execution if the original condition (without the logical negation operator) is false, as in the program segment

```
if ( ! ( grade == sentinelValue ) )
    System.out.printf( "The next grade is %d\n", grade );
```

which executes the printf call only if grade is not equal to sentinelValue. The parentheses around the condition grade == sentinelValue are needed because the logical negation operator has a higher precedence than the equality operator.

In most cases, the programmer can avoid using logical negation by expressing the condition differently with an appropriate relational or equality operator. For example, the previous statement may also be written as follows:

```
if ( grade != sentinelValue )
    System.out.printf( "The next grade is %d\n", grade );
```

This flexibility can help a programmer express a condition in a more convenient manner. Figure 5.17 is a truth table for the logical negation operator.

expression1	expression2	expression1 ^ expression2
false	false	false
false	true	true
true	false	true
true	true	false

Fig. 5.16 | ^ (boolean logical exclusive OR) operator truth table.

expression	!expression
false	true
true	false

Fig. 5.17 | ! (logical negation, or logical NOT) operator truth table.

Logical Operators Example

Figure 5.18 demonstrates the logical operators and boolean logical operators by producing their truth tables. The output shows the expression that was evaluated and the boolean result of that expression. The values of the boolean expressions are displayed with printf using the **%b format specifier**, which outputs the word "true" or the word "false" based on the expression's value. Lines 9–13 produce the truth table for &&. Lines 16–20 produce the truth table for ||. Lines 23–27 produce the truth table for &. Lines 30–35 produce the truth table for |. Lines 38–43 produce the truth table for ∧. Lines 46–47 produce the truth table for !.

Figure 5.19 shows the precedence and associativity of the Java operators introduced so far. The operators are shown from top to bottom in decreasing order of precedence.

```java
1   // Fig. 5.18: LogicalOperators.java
2   // Logical operators.
3
4   public class LogicalOperators
5   {
6      public static void main( String args[] )
7      {
8         // create truth table for && (conditional AND) operator
9         System.out.printf( "%s\n%s: %b\n%s: %b\n%s: %b\n%s: %b\n\n",
10           "Conditional AND (&&)", "false && false", ( false && false ),
11           "false && true", ( false && true ),
12           "true && false", ( true && false ),
13           "true && true", ( true && true ) );
14
15        // create truth table for || (conditional OR) operator
16        System.out.printf( "%s\n%s: %b\n%s: %b\n%s: %b\n%s: %b\n\n",
17           "Conditional OR (||)", "false || false", ( false || false ),
18           "false || true", ( false || true ),
19           "true || false", ( true || false ),
20           "true || true", ( true || true ) );
21
22        // create truth table for & (boolean logical AND) operator
23        System.out.printf( "%s\n%s: %b\n%s: %b\n%s: %b\n%s: %b\n\n",
24           "Boolean logical AND (&)", "false & false", ( false & false ),
25           "false & true", ( false & true ),
26           "true & false", ( true & false ),
27           "true & true", ( true & true ) );
28
29        // create truth table for | (boolean logical inclusive OR) operator
30        System.out.printf( "%s\n%s: %b\n%s: %b\n%s: %b\n%s: %b\n\n",
31           "Boolean logical inclusive OR (|)",
32           "false | false", ( false | false ),
33           "false | true", ( false | true ),
34           "true | false", ( true | false ),
35           "true | true", ( true | true ) );
36
37        // create truth table for ^ (boolean logical exclusive OR) operator
38        System.out.printf( "%s\n%s: %b\n%s: %b\n%s: %b\n%s: %b\n\n",
39           "Boolean logical exclusive OR (^)",
40           "false ^ false", ( false ^ false ),
```

Fig. 5.18 | Logical operators. (Part 1 of 2.)

```
41              "false ^ true", ( false ^ true ),
42              "true ^ false", ( true ^ false ),
43              "true ^ true", ( true ^ true ) );
44
45          // create truth table for ! (logical negation) operator
46          System.out.printf( "%s\n%s: %b\n%s: %b\n", "Logical NOT (!)",
47              "!false", ( !false ), "!true", ( !true ) );
48      } // end main
49  } // end class LogicalOperators
```

```
Conditional AND (&&)
false && false: false
false && true: false
true && false: false
true && true: true

Conditional OR (||)
false || false: false
false || true: true
true || false: true
true || true: true

Boolean logical AND (&)
false & false: false
false & true: false
true & false: false
true & true: true

Boolean logical inclusive OR (|)
false | false: false
false | true: true
true | false: true
true | true: true

Boolean logical exclusive OR (^)
false ^ false: false
false ^ true: true
true ^ false: true
true ^ true: false

Logical NOT (!)
!false: true
!true: false
```

Fig. 5.18 | Logical operators. (Part 2 of 2.)

Operators						Associativity	Type
++ --						right to left	unary postfix
++ - + - ! (*type*)						right to left	unary prefix
* / %						left to right	multiplicative

Fig. 5.19 | Precedence/associativity of the operators discussed so far. (Part 1 of 2.)

Operators						Associativity	Type
+	-					left to right	additive
<	<=	>	>=			left to right	relational
==	!=					left to right	equality
&						left to right	boolean logical AND
^						left to right	boolean logical exclusive OR
|						left to right	boolean logical inclusive OR
&&						left to right	conditional AND
||						left to right	conditional OR
?:						right to left	conditional
=	+=	-=	*=	/=	%=	right to left	assignment

Fig. 5.19 | Precedence/associativity of the operators discussed so far. (Part 2 of 2.)

5.9 Structured Programming Summary

Just as architects design buildings by employing the collective wisdom of their profession, so should programmers design programs. Our field is younger than architecture, and our collective wisdom is considerably sparser. We have learned that structured programming produces programs that are easier than unstructured programs to understand, test, debug, modify and even prove correct in a mathematical sense.

Figure 5.20 uses UML activity diagrams to summarize Java's control statements. The initial and final states indicate the single entry point and the single exit point of each control statement. Arbitrarily connecting individual symbols in an activity diagram can lead to unstructured programs. Therefore, the programming profession has chosen a limited set of control statements that can be combined in only two simple ways to build structured programs.

For simplicity, only single-entry/single-exit control statements are used—there is only one way to enter and only one way to exit each control statement. Connecting control statements in sequence to form structured programs is simple. The final state of one control statement is connected to the initial state of the next control statement—that is, the control statements are placed one after another in a program in sequence. We call this "control-statement stacking." The rules for forming structured programs also allow for control statements to be nested.

Figure 5.21 shows the rules for forming structured programs. The rules assume that action states may be used to indicate any action. The rules also assume that we begin with the simplest activity diagram (Fig. 5.22) consisting of only an initial state, an action state, a final state and transition arrows.

Applying the rules in Fig. 5.21 always results in a properly structured activity diagram with a neat, building-block appearance. For example, repeatedly applying rule 2 to the simplest activity diagram results in an activity diagram containing many action states in sequence (Fig. 5.23). Rule 2 generates a stack of control statements, so let us call rule 2 the stacking rule. [*Note:* The vertical dashed lines in Fig. 5.23 are not part of the UML. We use them to separate the four activity diagrams that demonstrate rule 2 of Fig. 5.21 being applied.]

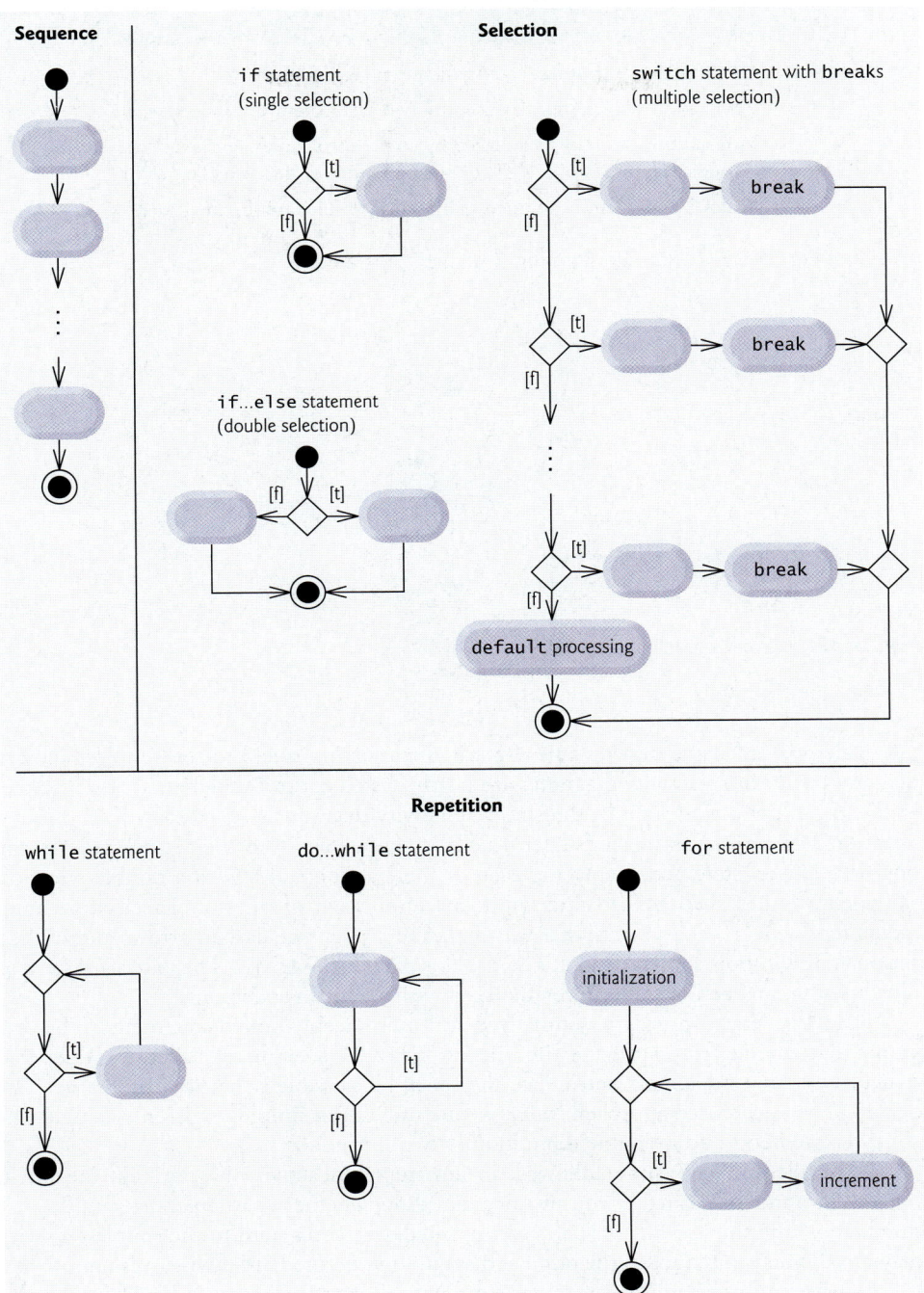

Fig. 5.20 | Java's single-entry/single-exit sequence, selection and repetition statements.

Rules for Forming Structured Programs
1   Begin with the simplest activity diagram (Fig. 5.22).
2   Any action state can be replaced by two action states in sequence.
3   Any action state can be replaced by any control statement (sequence of action states, `if`, `if...else`, `switch`, `while`, `do...while` or `for`).
4   Rules 2 and 3 can be applied as often as you like and in any order.

Fig. 5.21 | Rules for forming structured programs.

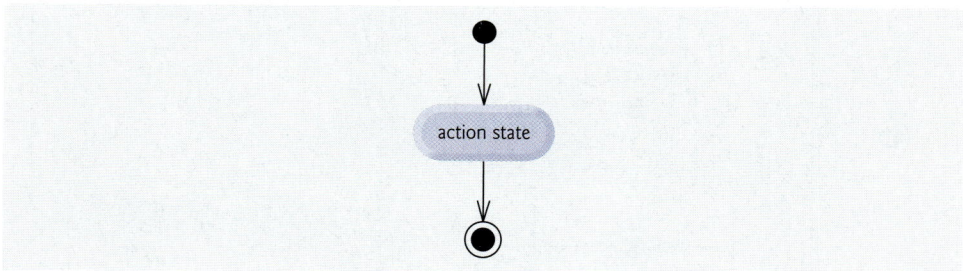

Fig. 5.22 | Simplest activity diagram.

Rule 3 is called the **nesting rule**. Repeatedly applying rule 3 to the simplest activity diagram results in an activity diagram with neatly nested control statements. For example, in Fig. 5.24, the action state in the simplest activity diagram is replaced with a double-selection (`if...else`) statement. Then rule 3 is applied again to the action states in the double-selection statement, replacing each of these action states with a double-selection statement. The dashed action-state symbols around each of the double-selection statements represent the action state that was replaced. [*Note:* The dashed arrows and dashed action state symbols shown in Fig. 5.24 are not part of the UML. They are used here to illustrate that any action state can be replaced with a control statement.]

Rule 4 generates larger, more involved and more deeply nested statements. The diagrams that emerge from applying the rules in Fig. 5.21 constitute the set of all possible structured activity diagrams and hence the set of all possible structured programs. The beauty of the structured approach is that we use only seven simple single-entry/single-exit control statements and assemble them in only two simple ways.

If the rules in Fig. 5.21 are followed, an "unstructured' activity diagram (like the one in Fig. 5.25) cannot be created. If you are uncertain about whether a particular diagram is structured, apply the rules of Fig. 5.21 in reverse to reduce the diagram to the simplest activity diagram. If you can reduce it, the original diagram is structured; otherwise, it is not.

Structured programming promotes simplicity. Bohm and Jacopini have given us the result that only three forms of control are needed to implement an algorithm:

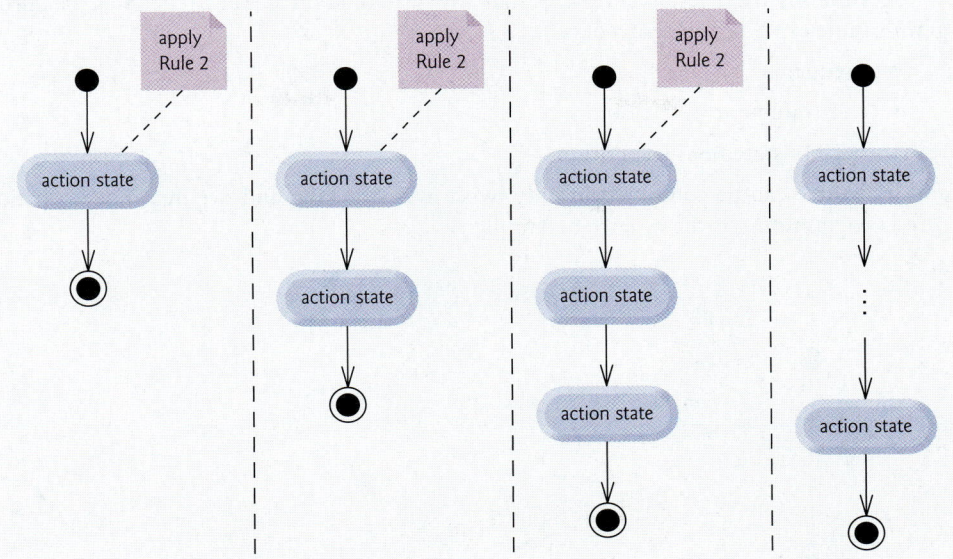

Fig. 5.23 | Repeatedly applying the stacking rule (rule 2) of Fig. 5.21 to the simplest activity diagram.

- Sequence
- Selection
- Repetition

The sequence structure is trivial. Simply list the statements to execute in the order in which they should execute. Selection is implemented in one of three ways:

- `if` statement (single selection)
- `if...else` statement (double selection)
- `switch` statement (multiple selection)

In fact, it is straightforward to prove that the simple `if` statement is sufficient to provide any form of selection—everything that can be done with the `if...else` statement and the `switch` statement can be implemented by combining `if` statements (although perhaps not as clearly and efficiently).

Repetition is implemented in one of three ways:

- `while` statement
- `do...while` statement
- `for` statement

It is straightforward to prove that the `while` statement is sufficient to provide any form of repetition. Everything that can be done with the `do...while` statement and the `for` statement can be done with the `while` statement (although perhaps not as conveniently).

Combining these results illustrates that any form of control ever needed in a Java program can be expressed in terms of

- sequence
- if statement (selection)
- while statement (repetition)

and that these can be combined in only two ways—stacking and nesting. indeed, structured programming is the essence of simplicity.

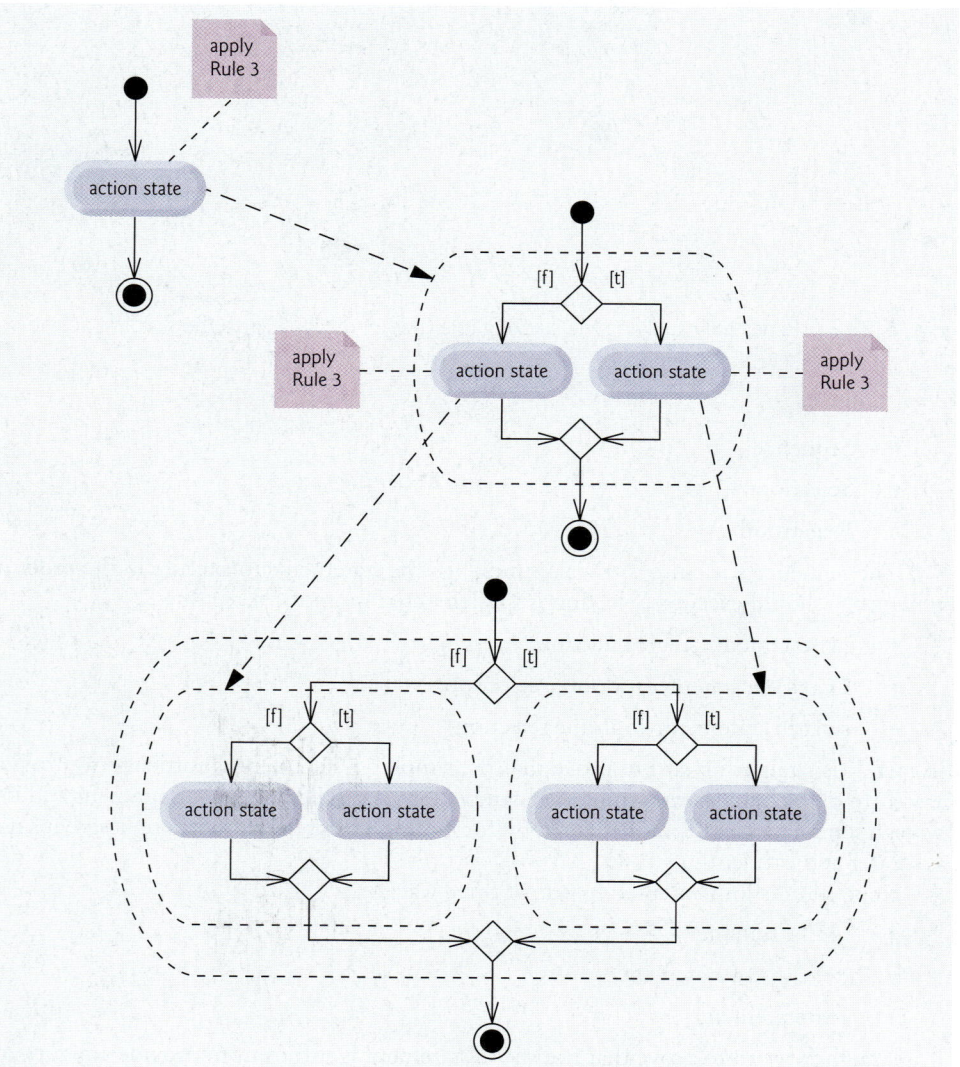

Fig. 5.24 | Repeatedly applying the nesting rule (rule 3) of Fig. 5.21 to the simplest activity diagram.

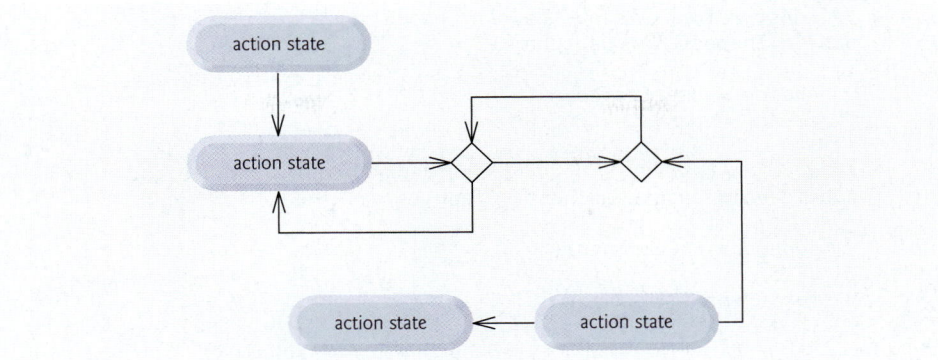

Fig. 5.25 | "Unstructured" activity diagram.

5.10 (Optional) GUI and Graphics Case Study: Drawing Rectangles and Ovals

This section introduces two other shapes you can draw using the graphics features in Java—rectangles and ovals. To draw rectangles and ovals, we call Graphics methods drawRect and drawOval, respectively, as demonstrated in Fig. 5.26.

Line 6 begins the class declaration for Shapes, which extends JPanel. Shapes contains one instance variable, choice, declared on line 8, that determines whether paint-Component should draw rectangles or ovals. The Shapes constructor at lines 11–14 initial-izes choice with the value passed in parameter userChoice.

Method paintComponent (lines 17–36) performs the actual drawing. Remember, the first statement in every paintComponent method should be a call to super.paintComponent, as in line 19. The for statement (lines 21–35) loops 10 times to draw 10 shapes. The switch statement (Lines 24–34) chooses between drawing rectangles and drawing ovals.

If choice is 1, then the program draws a rectangle. Lines 27–28 call Graphics method drawRect. Method drawRect requires four arguments. The first two arguments represent the x- and y-coordinates of the upper-left corner of the rectangle. The next two represent the width and the height of the rectangle. In this example, we start at a position 10 pixels down and 10 pixels right of the top-left corner, and every iteration of the loop moves the upper-left corner another 10 pixels down and to the right. The width and the height of the rectangle start at 50 pixels and increase by 10 pixels in each iteration.

```
1   // Fig. 5.26: Shapes.java
2   // Demonstrates drawing different shapes.
3   import java.awt.Graphics;
4   import javax.swing.JPanel;
5
6   public class Shapes extends JPanel
7   {
8      private int choice; // user's choice of which shape to draw
9
```

Fig. 5.26 | Drawing a cascade of shapes based on the user's choice. (Part 1 of 2.)

```
10        // constructor sets the user's choice
11        public Shapes( int userChoice )
12        {
13           choice = userChoice;
14        } // end Shapes constructor
15
16        // draws a cascade of shapes starting from the top left corner
17        public void paintComponent( Graphics g )
18        {
19           super.paintComponent( g );
20
21           for ( int i = 0; i < 10; i++ )
22           {
23              // pick the shape based on the user's choice
24              switch ( choice )
25              {
26                 case 1: // draw rectangles
27                    g.drawRect( 10 + i * 10, 10 + i * 10,
28                       50 + i * 10, 50 + i * 10 );
29                    break;
30                 case 2: // draw ovals
31                    g.drawOval( 10 + i * 10, 10 + i * 10,
32                       50 + i * 10, 50 + i * 10 );
33                    break;
34              } // end switch
35           } // end for
36        } // end method paintComponent
37     } // end class Shapes
```

Fig. 5.26 | Drawing a cascade of shapes based on the user's choice. (Part 2 of 2.)

If choice is 2, then the program performs a similar operation, drawing an oval instead of a rectangle. When drawing an oval, an imaginary rectangle called a **bounding rectangle** is created, and an oval that touches the midpoints of all four sides of the bounding rectangle is placed inside. Method drawOval (lines 31–32) requires the same four arguments as method drawRect. The arguments specify the position and size of the bounding rectangle for the oval. The values passed to drawOval in this example are exactly the same as the values passed to drawRect in lines 27–28. Since the width and height of the bounding rectangle are identical in this example, lines 27–28 draw a circle. You may modify the program to draw both rectangles and ovals to see how drawOval and drawRect are related.

Figure 5.27 is responsible for handling input from the user and creating a window to display the appropriate drawing based on the user's response. Line 3 imports JFrame to handle the display, and Line 4 imports JOptionPane to handle the input.

Lines 11–13 prompt the user with an input dialog and store the user's response in variable input. Line 15 uses Integer method parseInt to convert the String entered by the user to an int and stores the result in variable choice. An instance of class Shapes is created at line 18, with the user's choice passed to the constructor. Lines 20–25 perform the standard operations for creating and setting up a window—creating a frame, setting it to exit the application when closed, adding the drawing to the frame, setting the frame size and making it visible.

```java
1   // Fig. 5.27: ShapesTest.java
2   // Test application that displays class Shapes.
3   import javax.swing.JFrame;
4   import javax.swing.JOptionPane;
5
6   public class ShapesTest
7   {
8      public static void main( String args[] )
9      {
10        // obtain user's choice
11        String input = JOptionPane.showInputDialog(
12           "Enter 1 to draw rectangles\n" +
13           "Enter 2 to draw ovals" );
14
15        int choice = Integer.parseInt( input ); // convert input to int
16
17        // create the panel with the user's input
18        Shapes panel = new Shapes( choice );
19
20        JFrame application = new JFrame(); // creates a new JFrame
21
22        application.setDefaultCloseOperation( JFrame.EXIT_ON_CLOSE );
23        application.add( panel ); // add the panel to the frame
24        application.setSize( 300, 300 ); // set the desired size
25        application.setVisible( true ); // show the frame
26     } // end main
27  } // end class ShapesTest
```

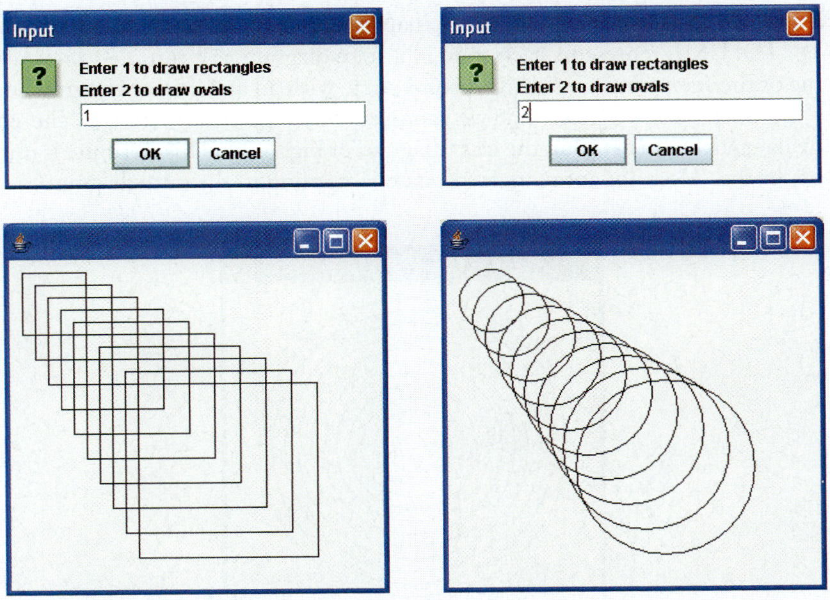

Fig. 5.27 | Obtaining user input and creating a JFrame to display Shapes.

GUI and Graphics Case Study Exercises

5.1 Draw 12 concentric circles in the center of a JPanel (Fig. 5.28). The innermost circle should have a radius of 10 pixels, and each successive circle should have a radius 10 pixels larger than the previous one. Begin by finding the center of the JPanel. To get the upper-left corner of a circle, move up one radius and to the left one radius from the center. The width and height of the bounding rectangle is the diameter of the circle (twice the radius).

5.2 Modify Exercise 5.16 from the end-of-chapter exercises to read input using dialogs and to display the bar chart using rectangles of varying lengths.

5.11 (Optional) Software Engineering Case Study: Identifying Objects' States and Activities

In Section 4.15, we identified many of the class attributes needed to implement the ATM system and added them to the class diagram in Fig. 4.24. In this section, we show how these attributes represent an object's state. We identify some key states that our objects may occupy and discuss how objects change state in response to various events occurring in the system. We also discuss the workflow, or *activities*, that objects perform in the ATM system. We present the activities of BalanceInquiry and Withdrawal transaction objects in this section.

State Machine Diagrams

Each object in a system goes through a series of states. An object's current state is indicated by the values of the object's attributes at a given time. **State machine diagrams** (commonly called **state diagrams**) model several states of an object and show under what circumstances the object changes state. Unlike the class diagrams presented in earlier case study sections, which focused primarily on the structure of the system, state diagrams model some of the behavior of the system.

Figure 5.29 is a simple state diagram that models some of the states of an object of class ATM. The UML represents each state in a state diagram as a **rounded rectangle** with the name of the state placed inside it. A **solid circle** with an attached stick arrowhead designates the **initial state**. Recall that we modeled this state information as the Boolean attribute userAuthenticated in the class diagram of Fig. 4.24. This attribute is initialized to false, or the "User not authenticated" state, according to the state diagram.

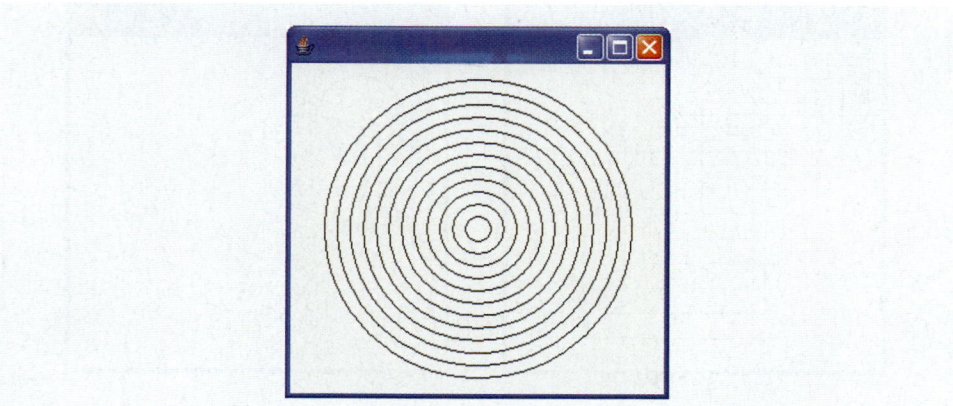

Fig. 5.28 | Drawing concentric circles.

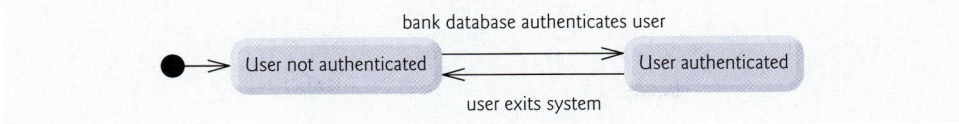

Fig. 5.29 | State diagram for the ATM object.

The arrows with stick arrowheads indicate **transitions** between states. An object can transition from one state to another in response to various events that occur in the system. The name or description of the event that causes a transition is written near the line that corresponds to the transition. For example, the ATM object changes from the "User not authenticated" state to the "User authenticated" state after the database authenticates the user. Recall from the requirements document that the database authenticates a user by comparing the account number and PIN entered by the user with those of an account in the database. If the database indicates that the user has entered a valid account number and the correct PIN, the ATM object transitions to the "User authenticated" state and changes its userAuthenticated attribute to a value of true. When the user exits the system by choosing the "exit" option from the main menu, the ATM object returns to the "User not authenticated" state.

> ### Software Engineering Observation 5.5
>
> *Software designers do not generally create state diagrams showing every possible state and state transition for all attributes—there are simply too many of them. State diagrams typically show only key states and state transitions.*

Activity Diagrams

Like a state diagram, an **activity diagram** models aspects of system behavior. Unlike a state diagram, an activity diagram models an object's **workflow** (sequence of events) during program execution. An activity diagram models the **actions** the object will perform and in what order. The activity diagram in Fig. 5.30 models the actions involved in executing a balance-inquiry transaction. We assume that a BalanceInquiry object has already been initialized and assigned a valid account number (that of the current user), so the object knows which balance to retrieve. The diagram includes the actions that occur after the user selects a balance inquiry from the main menu and before the ATM returns the user to the main menu—a BalanceInquiry object does not perform or initiate these actions, so we do not model them here. The diagram begins with retrieving the balance of the account from the database. Next, the BalanceInquiry displays the balance on the screen. This action completes the execution of the transaction. Recall that we have chosen to represent an account balance as both the availableBalance and totalBalance attributes of class Account, so the actions modeled in Fig. 5.30 refer to the retrieval and display of both balance attributes.

The UML represents an action in an activity diagram as an action state modeled by a rectangle with its left and right sides replaced by arcs curving outward. Each action state contains an action expression—for example, "get balance of account from database"—that specifies an action to be performed. An arrow with a stick arrowhead connects two action states, indicating the order in which the actions represented by the action states occur. The solid circle (at the top of Fig. 5.30) represents the activity's initial state—the beginning of the workflow before the object performs the modeled actions. In this case, the transaction

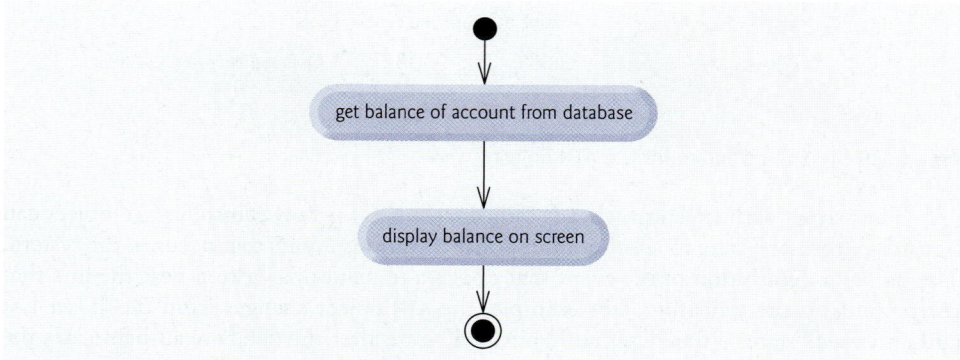

Fig. 5.30 | Activity diagram for a `BalanceInquiry` object.

first executes the "get balance of account from database" action expression. The transaction then displays both balances on the screen. The solid circle enclosed in an open circle (at the bottom of Fig. 5.30) represents the final state—the end of the workflow after the object performs the modeled actions. We used UML activity diagrams to illustrate the flow of control for the control statements presented in Chapters 4–5.

Figure 5.31 shows an activity diagram for a withdrawal transaction. We assume that a `Withdrawal` object has been assigned a valid account number. We do not model the user selecting a withdrawal from the main menu or the ATM returning the user to the main menu because these are not actions performed by a `Withdrawal` object. The transaction first displays a menu of standard withdrawal amounts (shown in Fig. 2.19) and an option to cancel the transaction. The transaction then receives a menu selection from the user. The activity flow now arrives at a decision (a fork indicated by the small diamond symbol). [*Note:* A decision was known as a branch in earlier versions of the UML.] This point determines the next action based on the associated guard condition (in square brackets next to the transition), which states that the transition occurs if this condition is met. If the user cancels the transaction by choosing the "cancel" option from the menu, the activity flow immediately skips to the final state. Note the merge (indicated by the small diamond symbol) where the cancellation flow of activity joins the main flow of activity before reaching the activity's final state. If the user selects a withdrawal amount from the menu, `Withdrawal` sets `amount` (an attribute originally modeled in Fig. 4.24) to the value chosen by the user.

After setting the withdrawal amount, the transaction retrieves the available balance of the user's account (i.e., the `availableBalance` attribute of the user's `Account` object) from the database. The activity flow then arrives at another decision. If the requested withdrawal amount exceeds the user's available balance, the system displays an appropriate error message informing the user of the problem, then returns to the beginning of the activity diagram and prompts the user to input a new amount. If the requested withdrawal amount is less than or equal to the user's available balance, the transaction proceeds. The transaction next tests whether the cash dispenser has enough cash remaining to satisfy the withdrawal request. If it does not, the transaction displays an appropriate error message, then returns to the beginning of the activity diagram and prompts the user to choose a new amount. If sufficient cash is available, the transaction interacts with the database to debit the withdrawal amount from the user's account (i.e., subtract the amount from both the

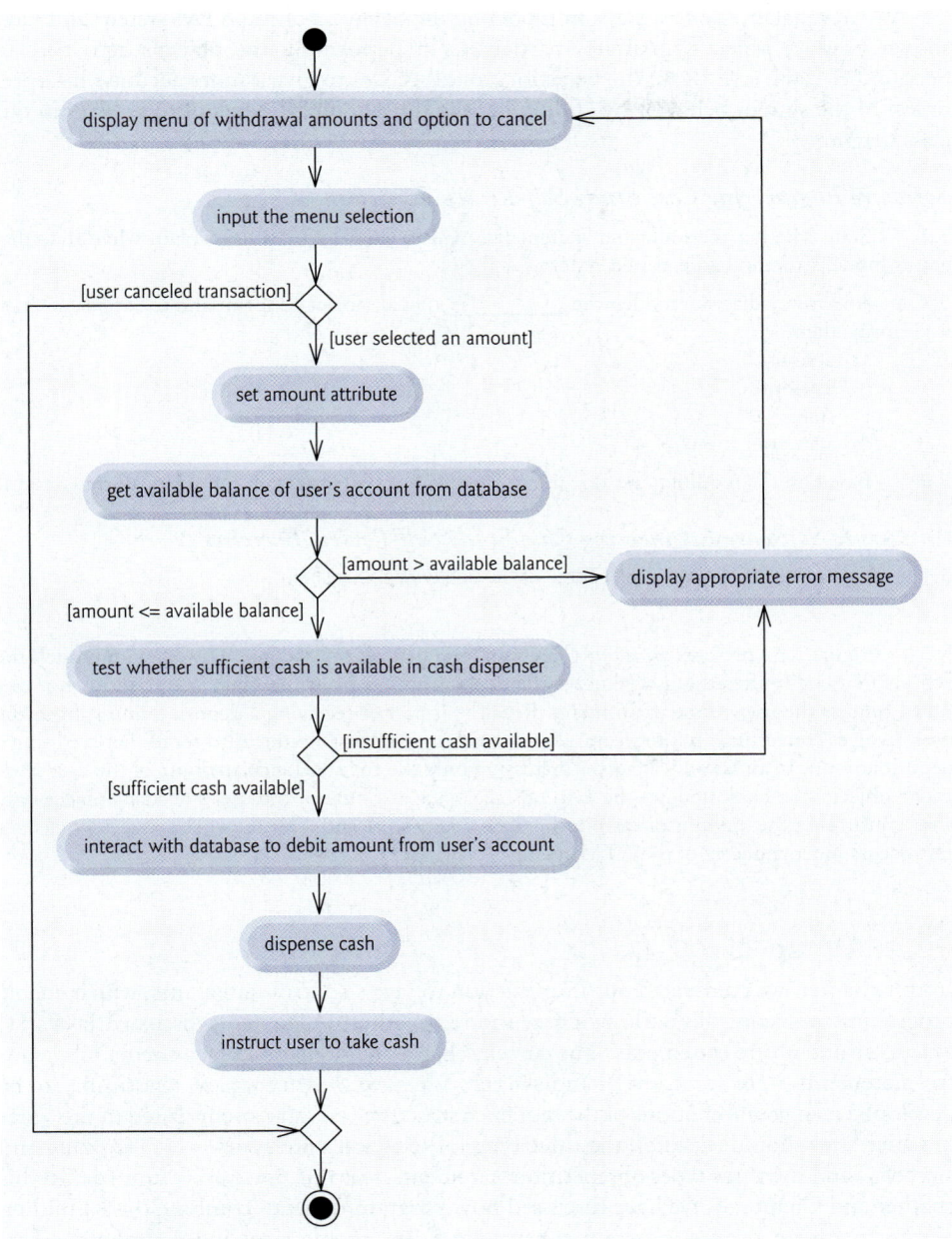

Fig. 5.31 | Activity diagram for a withdrawal transaction.

availableBalance and totalBalance attributes of the user's Account object). The transaction then dispenses the desired amount of cash and instructs the user to take the cash that is dispensed. Finally, the main flow of activity merges with the cancellation flow of activity before reaching the final state.

We have taken the first steps in modeling the behavior of the ATM system and have shown how an object's attributes participate in performing the object's activities. In Section 6.14, we investigate the behaviors for all classes to give a more accurate interpretation of the system behavior by "filling in" the third compartments of the classes in our class diagram.

Software Engineering Case Study Self-Review Exercises

5.1 State whether the following statement is *true* or *false*, and if *false*, explain why: State diagrams model structural aspects of a system.

5.2 An activity diagram models the _____ that an object performs and the order in which it performs them.
   a) actions
   b) attributes
   c) states
   d) state transitions

5.3 Based on the requirements document, create an activity diagram for a deposit transaction.

Answers to Software Engineering Case Study Self-Review Exercises

5.1 False. State diagrams model some of the behavior of a system.

5.2 a.

5.3 Figure 5.32 presents an activity diagram for a deposit transaction. The diagram models the actions that occur after the user chooses the deposit option from the main menu and before the ATM returns the user to the main menu. Recall that part of receiving a deposit amount from the user involves converting an integer number of cents to a dollar amount. Also recall that crediting a deposit amount to an account involves increasing only the totalBalance attribute of the user's Account object. The bank updates the availableBalance attribute of the user's Account object only after confirming the amount of cash in the deposit envelope and after the enclosed checks clear—this occurs independently of the ATM system.

5.12 Wrap-Up

In this chapter, we completed our introduction to Java's control statements, which enable programmers to control the flow of execution in methods. Chapter 4 discussed Java's if, if...else and while statements. The current chapter demonstrated Java's remaining control statements—for, do...while and switch. We have shown that any algorithm can be developed using combinations of the sequence structure (i.e., statements listed in the order in which they should execute), the three types of selection statements—if, if...else and switch—and the three types of repetition statements—while, do...while and for. In this chapter and Chapter 4, we have discussed how programmers can combine these building blocks to utilize proven program-construction and problem-solving techniques. This chapter also introduced Java's logical operators, which enable programmers to use more complex conditional expressions in control statements.

In Chapter 3, we introduced the basic concepts of objects, classes and methods. Chapter 4 and this chapter provided a thorough introduction to the types of control statements that programmers use to specify program logic in methods. In Chapter 6, we examine methods in greater depth.

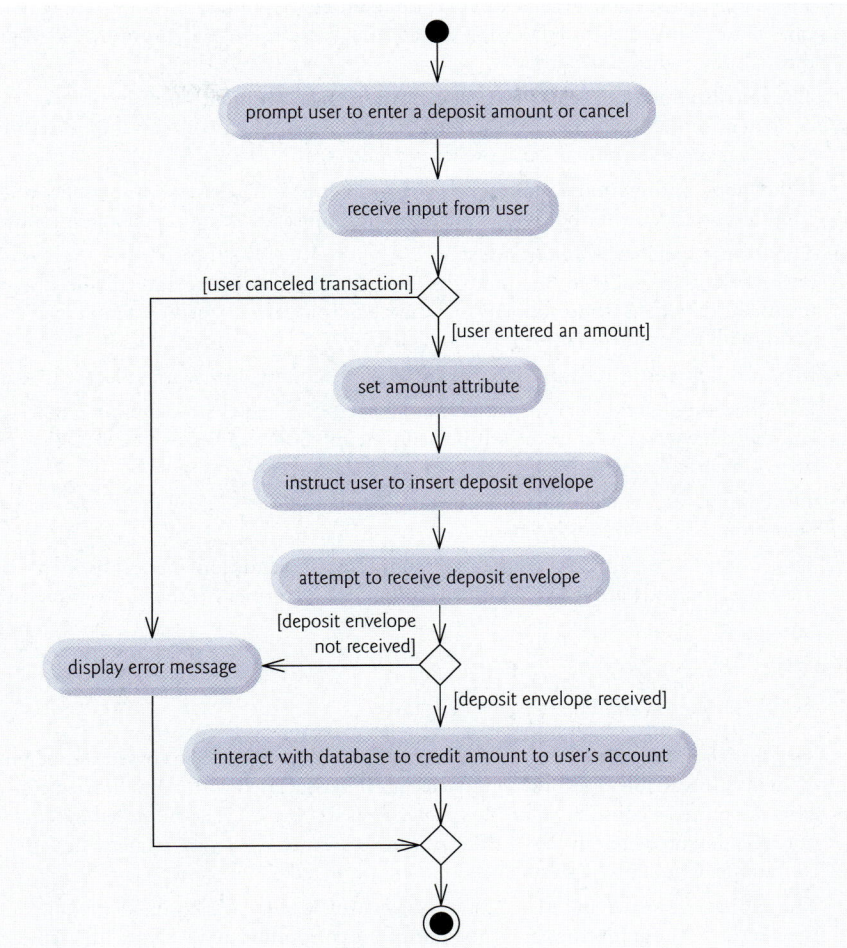

Fig. 5.32 | Activity diagram for a deposit transaction.

Summary

- The for repetition statement specifies the details of counter-controlled-repetition. The general format of the for statement is

  for (*initialization*; *loopContinuationCondition*; *increment*)
      statement

  where the *initialization* expression names the loop's control variable and provides its initial value, *loopContinuationCondition* is the condition that determines whether the loop should continue executing and *increment* modifies the control variable's value, so that the loop-continuation condition eventually becomes false.

- Typically, for statements are used for counter-controlled repetition and while statements are used for sentinel-controlled repetition.

- The scope of a variable defines where it can be used in a program. For example, a local variable can be used only in the method that declares the variable and only from the point of declaration through the end of the method.

- The initialization, loop-continuation condition and increment portions of a `for` statement can contain arithmetic expressions. The increment of a `for` statement may also be negative, in which case it is really a decrement, and the loop counts downward.

- If the loop-continuation condition in a `for` header is initially `false`, the program does not execute the `for` statement's body. Instead, execution proceeds with the statement following the `for`.

- The format specifier `%20s` outputs a `String` with a field width of 20 (i.e., at least 20 character positions). If the value to be output is less than 20 character positions wide, the value is right justified in the field by default. A value can be output left justified by simply preceding the field width with the minus sign (–) formatting flag.

- Methods that perform common tasks and do not require objects are called `static` methods.

- Java does not include an exponentiation operator. Instead, `Math.pow(x, y)` can be used to calculate the value of x raised to the yth power. The method receives two `double` arguments and returns a `double` value.

- The comma (`,`) formatting flag in a format specifier (e.g., `%,20.2f`) indicates that a value should be output with a thousands separator.

- The `do...while` statement tests the loop-continuation condition *after* executing the loop's body; therefore, the body always executes at least once. The format for the `do...while` statement is

```
do
{
    statement
} while ( condition );
```

- The `switch` multiple-selection statement performs different actions based on the possible values of an integer variable or expression. Each action is associated with the value of a constant integral expression (i.e., a constant value of type `byte`, `short`, `int` or `char`, but not `long`) that the variable or expression on which the `switch` is based may assume. The `switch` statement consists of a block containing a sequence of `case` labels and an optional `default` case.

- The expression in parentheses following keyword `switch` is called the controlling expression of the `switch`. A program compares the value of the controlling expression with each `case` label, and if a match occurs, the program executes the statements for that `case`.

- The `switch` statement does not provide a mechanism for testing ranges of values, so every value that must be tested should be listed in a separate `case` label.

- Listing cases consecutively with no statements between them enables those cases to perform the same set of statements.

- Each `case` can have multiple statements. The `switch` statement differs from other control statements in that it does not require braces around multiple statements in each `case`.

- Most `switch` statements use a `break` in each `case` to terminate the `switch` statement after processing the `case`.

- The end-of-file indicator is a system-dependent keystroke combination which indicates that there is no more data to input.

- `Scanner` method `hasNext` determines whether there is more data to input. This method returns the `boolean` value `true` if there is more data; otherwise, it returns `false`.

- The `break` statement, when executed in one of the repetition statements, causes immediate exit from that statement. Execution continues with the first statement after the control statement.

- The continue statement, when executed in a while, for or do...while, skips the remaining statements in the loop body and proceeds with the next iteration of the loop.
- Logical operators enable programmers to form complex conditions by combining simple conditions. The logical operators are && (conditional AND), || (conditional OR), & (boolean logical AND), | (boolean logical inclusive OR), ∧ (boolean logical exclusive OR) and ! (logical NOT).
- The && (conditional AND) operator can be used to ensure that two conditions are *both* true before choosing a certain path of execution.
- The || (conditional OR) operator can be used to ensure that either *or* both of two conditions are true before choosing a certain path of execution.
- The parts of an expression containing && or || operators are evaluated only until it is known whether the condition is true or false. This feature of conditional AND and conditional OR expressions is called short-circuit evaluation.
- The boolean logical AND (&) and boolean logical inclusive OR (|) operators work identically to the && (conditional AND) and || (conditional OR) operators, with one exception: The boolean logical operators always evaluate both of their operands (i.e., they do not perform short-circuit evaluation).
- A simple condition containing the boolean logical exclusive OR (∧) operator is true if and only if one of its operands is true and the other is false. If both operands are true or both are false, the entire condition is false.
- The ! (logical NOT, also called logical negation or logical complement) operator enables a programmer to "reverse" the meaning of a condition. The logical negation operator is placed before a condition to choose a path of execution if the original condition (without the logical negation operator) is false. In most cases, the programmer can avoid using logical negation by expressing the condition differently with an appropriate relational or equality operator.
- Unlike the logical operators &&, ||, &, | and ∧, which are binary operators that combine two conditions, the logical negation operator is a unary operator that has only a single condition as an operand.
- The %b format specifier causes the value of a boolean expression to be output as the word "true" or the word "false" based on the expression's value.
- Any form of control ever needed in a Java program can be expressed in terms of sequence, selection and repetition statements, and these can be combined in only two ways—stacking and nesting.

Terminology

!, logical not operator
&, boolean logical AND operator
&&, conditional AND operator
|, boolean logical OR operator
||, conditional OR operator
∧, boolean logical exclusive OR operator
boolean logical AND (&)
boolean logical exclusive OR (∧)
boolean logical inclusive OR (|)
break statement
case label
character constant
conditional AND (&&)
conditional OR (||)

constant integral expression
constant variable
continue statement
control variable
controlling expression of a switch
decrement a control variable
default case in switch
do...while repetition statement
final keyword
for header
for repetition statement
for statement header
increment a control variable
initial value

iteration of a loop
logical complement (!)
logical negation (!)
logical operators
loop-continuation condition
multiple selection
nested control statements
nesting rule
off-by-one error
repetition statement

scope of a variable
short-circuit evaluation
side effect
simple condition
single-entry/single-exit control statements
stacked control statements
stacking rule
static method
switch selection statement
truth table

Self-Review Exercises

5.1   Fill in the blanks in each of the following statements:
a) Typically, _____ statements are used for counter-controlled repetition and _____ statements are used for sentinel-controlled repetition.
b) The do...while statement tests the loop-continuation condition _____ executing the loop's body; therefore, the body always executes at least once.
c) The _____ statement selects among multiple actions based on the possible values of an integer variable or expression.
d) The _____ statement, when executed in a repetition statement, skips the remaining statements in the loop body and proceeds with the next iteration of the loop.
e) The _____ operator can be used to ensure that two conditions are *both* true before choosing a certain path of execution.
f) If the loop-continuation condition in a for header is initially _____, the program does not execute the for statement's body.
g) Methods that perform common tasks and do not require objects are called _____ methods.

5.2   State whether each of the following is *true* or *false*. If *false*, explain why.
a) The default case is required in the switch selection statement.
b) The break statement is required in the last case of a switch selection statement.
c) The expression ((x > y) && (a < b)) is true if either x > y is true or a < b is true.
d) An expression containing the || operator is true if either or both of its operands are true.
e) The comma (,) formatting flag in a format specifier (e.g., %,20.2f) indicates that a value should be output with a thousands separator.
f) To test for a range of values in a switch statement, use a hyphen (–) between the start and end values of the range in a case label.
g) Listing cases consecutively with no statements between them enables the cases to perform the same set of statements.

5.3   Write a Java statement or a set of Java statements to accomplish each of the following tasks:
a) Sum the odd integers between 1 and 99, using a for statement. Assume that the integer variables sum and count have been declared.
b) Calculate the value of 2.5 raised to the power of 3, using the pow method.
c) Print the integers from 1 to 20, using a while loop and the counter variable i. Assume that the variable i has been declared, but not initialized. Print only five integers per line. [*Hint*: Use the calculation i % 5. When the value of this expression is 0, print a newline character; otherwise, print a tab character. Assume that this code is an application. Use the System.out.println() method to output the newline character, and use the System.out.print('\t') method to output the tab character.]
d) Repeat part (c), using a for statement.

5.4   Find the error in each of the following code segments, and explain how to correct it:
a) `i = 1;`

```
while ( i <= 10 );
   i++;

}
```
b) `for ( k = 0.1; k != 1.0; k += 0.1 )`
```
   System.out.println( k );
```
c) `switch ( n )`
```
{
   case 1:
      System.out.println( "The number is 1" );
   case 2:
      System.out.println( "The number is 2" );
      break;
   default:
      System.out.println( "The number is not 1 or 2" );
      break;
}
```
d) The following code should print the values 1 to 10:
`n = 1;`

```
while ( n < 10 )
   System.out.println( n++ );
```

Answers to Self-Review Exercises

5.1   a) `for`, `while`.   b) after.   c) `switch`.   d) `continue`.   e) `&&` (conditional AND).   f) `false`.
g) `static`.

5.2   a) False. The `default` case is optional. If no default action is needed, then there is no need
for a `default` case. b) False. The `break` statement is used to exit the `switch` statement. The `break`
statement is not required for the last case in a `switch` statement. c) False. Both of the relational expressions must be true for the entire expression to be true when using the `&&` operator. d) True.
e) True. f) False. The `switch` statement does not provide a mechanism for testing ranges of values,
so every value that must be tested should be listed in a separate case label. g) True.

5.3   a) `sum = 0;`
```
   for ( count = 1; count <= 99; count += 2 )
      sum += count;
```
b) `double result = Math.pow( 2.5, 3 );`
c) `i = 1;`

```
while ( i <= 20 )
{
   System.out.print( i );

   if ( i % 5 == 0 )
      System.out.println();
   else
      System.out.print( '\t' );

   ++i;
}
```
d) `for ( i = 1; i <= 20; i++ )`
```
{
```

```
System.out.print( i );

if ( i % 5 == 0 )
    System.out.println();
else
    System.out.print( '\t' );
}
```

5.4 a) Error: The semicolon after the `while` header causes an infinite loop, and there is a missing left brace.
Correction: Replace the semicolon by a {, or remove both the ; and the }.

b) Error: Using a floating-point number to control a `for` statement may not work, because floating-point numbers are represented only approximately by most computers.
Correction: Use an integer, and perform the proper calculation in order to get the values you desire:

```
for ( k = 1; k != 10; k++ )
    System.out.println( (double) k / 10 );
```

c) Error: The missing code is the `break` statement in the statements for the first case.
Correction: Add a `break` statement at the end of the statements for the first case. Note that this omission is not necessarily an error if the programmer wants the statement of case 2: to execute every time the case 1: statement executes.

d) Error: An improper relational operator is used in the `while` repetition-continuation condition.
Correction: Use <= rather than <, or change 10 to 11.

Exercises

5.5 Describe the four basic elements of counter-controlled repetition.

5.6 Compare and contrast the `while` and `for` repetition statements.

5.7 Discuss a situation in which it would be more appropriate to use a `do...while` statement than a `while` statement. Explain why.

5.8 Compare and contrast the `break` and `continue` statements.

5.9 Find and correct the error(s) in each of the following segments of code:
a) `for ( i = 100, i >= 1, i++ )`
```
    System.out.println( i );
```
b) The following code should print whether integer `value` is odd or even:

```
switch ( value % 2 )
{
    case 0:
        System.out.println( "Even integer" );

    case 1:
        System.out.println( "Odd integer" );
}
```

c) The following code should output the odd integers from 19 to 1:

```
for ( i = 19; i >= 1; i += 2 )
    System.out.println( i );
```

d) The following code should output the even integers from 2 to 100:

```
counter = 2;

do
{
    System.out.println( counter );
    counter += 2;
} While ( counter < 100 );
```

5.10 What does the following program do?

```
 1  public class Printing
 2  {
 3     public static void main( String args[] )
 4     {
 5        for ( int i = 1; i <= 10; i++ )
 6        {
 7           for ( int j = 1; j <= 5; j++ )
 8              System.out.print( '@' );
 9
10           System.out.println();
11        } // end outer for
12     } // end main
13  } // end class Printing
```

5.11 Write an application that finds the smallest of several integers. Assume that the first value read specifies the number of values to input from the user.

5.12 Write an application that calculates the product of the odd integers from 1 to 15.

5.13 *Factorials* are used frequently in probability problems. The factorial of a positive integer *n* (written *n!* and pronounced "*n* factorial") is equal to the product of the positive integers from 1 to *n*. Write an application that evaluates the factorials of the integers from 1 to 5. Display the results in tabular format. What difficulty might prevent you from calculating the factorial of 20?

5.14 Modify the compound-interest application of Fig. 5.6 to repeat its steps for interest rates of 5, 6, 7, 8, 9 and 10%. Use a for loop to vary the interest rate.

5.15 Write an application that displays the following patterns separately, one below the other. Use for loops to generate the patterns. All asterisks (*) should be printed by a single statement of the form System.out.print('*'); which causes the asterisks to print side by side. A statement of the form System.out.println(); can be used to move to the next line. A statement of the form System.out.print(' '); can be used to display a space for the last two patterns. There should be no other output statements in the program. [*Hint:* The last two patterns require that each line begin with an appropriate number of blank spaces.]

```
(a)              (b)              (c)              (d)
*                **********       **********               *
**               *********        *********               **
***              ********         ********                ***
****             *******          *******                 ****
*****            ******           ******                  *****
******           *****            *****                   ******
*******          ****             ****                    *******
********          ***              ***                    ********
*********         **               **                     *********
**********        *                *                      **********
```

5.16 One interesting application of computers is to display graphs and bar charts. Write an application that reads five numbers between 1 and 30. For each number that is read, your program should display the same number of adjacent asterisks. For example, if your program reads the number 7, it should display *******.

5.17 A mail-order house sells five products whose retail prices are as follows: Product 1, $2.98; product 2, $4.50; product 3, $9.98; product 4, $4.49 and product 5, $6.87. Write an application that reads a series of pairs of numbers as follows:

a) product number
b) quantity sold

Your program should use a switch statement to determine the retail price for each product. It should calculate and display the total retail value of all products sold. Use a sentinel-controlled loop to determine when the program should stop looping and display the final results.

5.18 Modify the application in Fig. 5.6 to use only integers to calculate the compound interest. [*Hint*: Treat all monetary amounts as integral numbers of pennies. Then break the result into its dollars and cents portions by using the division and remainder operations, respectively. Insert a period between the dollars and the cents portions.]

5.19 Assume that i = 1, j = 2, k = 3 and m = 2. What does each of the following statements print?

a) `System.out.println( i == 1 );`
b) `System.out.println( j == 3 );`
c) `System.out.println( ( i >= 1 ) && ( j < 4 ) );`
d) `System.out.println( ( m <= 99 ) & ( k < m ) );`
e) `System.out.println( ( j >= i ) || ( k == m ) );`
f) `System.out.println( ( k + m < j ) | ( 3 - j >= k ) );`
g) `System.out.println( !( k > m ) );`

5.20 Calculate the value of π from the infinite series

$$\pi = 4 - \frac{4}{3} + \frac{4}{5} - \frac{4}{7} + \frac{4}{9} - \frac{4}{11} + \cdots$$

Print a table that shows the value of π approximated by computing one term of this series, by two terms, by three terms, and so on. How many terms of this series do you have to use before you first get 3.14? 3.141? 3.1415? 3.14159?

5.21 (*Pythagorean Triples*) A right triangle can have sides whose lengths are all integers. The set of three integer values for the lengths of the sides of a right triangle is called a Pythagorean triple. The lengths of the three sides must satisfy the relationship that the sum of the squares of two of the sides is equal to the square of the hypotenuse. Write an application to find all Pythagorean triples for side1, side2 and the hypotenuse, all no larger than 500. Use a triple-nested for loop that tries all possibilities. This method is an example of "brute-force" computing. You will learn in more advanced computer science courses that there are large numbers of interesting problems for which there is no known algorithmic approach other than using sheer brute force.

5.22 Modify Exercise 5.15 to combine your code from the four separate triangles of asterisks such that all four patterns print side by side. Make clever use of nested for loops.

5.23 (*De Morgan's Laws*) In this chapter, we have discussed the logical operators &&, &, ||, |, ^ and !. De Morgan's Laws can sometimes make it more convenient for us to express a logical expression. These laws state that the expression !(*condition1* && *condition2*) is logically equivalent to the expression (!*condition1* || !*condition2*). Also, the expression !(*condition1* || *condition2*) is logically equivalent to the expression (!*condition1* && !*condition2*). Use De Morgan's Laws to write equivalent expressions for each of the following, then write an application to show that both the original expression and the new expression in each case produce the same value:

a) !(x < 5) && !(y >= 7)
b) !(a == b) || !(g != 5)
c) !((x <= 8) && (y > 4))
d) !((i > 4) || (j <= 6))

5.24 Write an application that prints the following diamond shape. You may use output statements that print a single asterisk (*), a single space or a single newline character. Maximize your use of repetition (with nested for statements), and minimize the number of output statements.

```
    *
   ***
  *****
 *******
*********
 *******
  *****
   ***
    *
```

5.25 Modify the application you wrote in Exercise 5.24 to read an odd number in the range 1 to 19 to specify the number of rows in the diamond. Your program should then display a diamond of the appropriate size.

5.26 A criticism of the break statement and the continue statement is that each is unstructured. Actually, break statements and continue statements can always be replaced by structured statements, although doing so can be awkward. Describe in general how you would remove any break statement from a loop in a program and replace that statement with some structured equivalent. [*Hint*: The break statement exits a loop from the body of the loop. The other way to exit is by failing the loop-continuation test. Consider using in the loop-continuation test a second test that indicates "early exit because of a 'break' condition."] Use the technique you develop here to remove the break statement from the application in Fig. 5.12.

5.27 What does the following program segment do?

```
for ( i = 1; i <= 5; i++ )
{
    for ( j = 1; j <= 3; j++ )
    {
        for ( k = 1; k <= 4; k++ )
            System.out.print( '*' );

        System.out.println();
    } // end inner for

    System.out.println();
} // end outer for
```

5.28 Describe in general how you would remove any continue statement from a loop in a program and replace it with some structured equivalent. Use the technique you develop here to remove the continue statement from the program in Fig. 5.13.

5.29 (*"The Twelve Days of Christmas" Song*) Write an application that uses repetition and switch statements to print the song "The Twelve Days of Christmas." One switch statement should be used to print the day (i.e., "First," "Second," etc.). A separate switch statement should be used to print the remainder of each verse. Visit the Web site www.12days.com/library/carols/12daysofxmas.htm for the complete lyrics of the song.

6

Methods:
A Deeper Look

OBJECTIVES

In this chapter you will learn:

- How **static** methods and fields are associated with an entire class rather than specific instances of the class.

- To use common **Math** methods available in the Java API.

- To understand the mechanisms for passing information between methods.

- How the method call/return mechanism is supported by the method call stack and activation records.

- How packages group related classes.

- How to use random-number generation to implement game-playing applications.

- To understand how the visibility of declarations is limited to specific regions of programs.

- What method overloading is and how to create overloaded methods.

6.1 Introduction

Most computer programs that solve real-world problems are much larger than the programs presented in the first few chapters of this book. Experience has shown that the best way to develop and maintain a large program is to construct it from small, simple pieces, or modules. This technique is called divide and conquer. We introduced methods in Chapter 3. In Chapter 6, we study methods in more depth. We emphasize how to declare and use methods to facilitate the design, implementation, operation and maintenance of large programs.

You will see that it is possible for certain methods, called static methods, to be called without the need for an object of the class to exist. You will learn how to declare a method with more than one parameter. You will also learn how Java is able to keep track of which method is currently executing, how local variables of methods are maintained in memory and how a method knows where to return after it completes execution.

We will take a brief diversion into simulation techniques with random-number generation and develop a version of the casino dice game called craps that will use most of the programming techniques you have used to this point in the book. In addition, you will learn two techniques for declaring values that cannot change (i.e., constants) in your programs.

Many of the classes you will use or create while developing applications will have more than one method of the same name. This technique, called overloading, is used by programmers to implement methods that perform similar tasks for arguments of different types or possibly for different numbers of arguments.

6.2 Program Modules in Java

Three kinds of modules exist in Java—methods, classes and packages. Java programs are written by combining new methods and classes that the programmer writes with predefined methods and classes available in the Java Application Programming Interface (also referred to as the Java API or Java class library) and in various other class libraries. Related classes are typically grouped into packages so that they can be imported into programs and reused. You will learn how to group your own classes into packages in Chapter 8. The Java API provides a rich collection of predefined classes that contain methods for performing common mathematical calculations, string manipulations, character manipulations, input/output operations, database operations, networking operations, file processing, error checking and many other useful operations. The Java API classes are part of the J2SE Development Kit (JDK) 5.0.

Good Programming Practice 6.1

Familiarize yourself with the rich collection of classes and methods provided by the Java API (java.sun.com/j2se/5.0/docs/api/index.html). In Section 6.8, we present an overview of several common packages. In Appendix G, we explain how to navigate the Java API documentation.

Software Engineering Observation 6.1

Don't try to reinvent the wheel. When possible, reuse Java API classes and methods. This reduces program development time and avoids introducing programming errors.

Methods (called functions or procedures in other programming languages) allow the programmer to modularize a program by separating its tasks into self-contained units. You have declared methods in every program you have written. These methods are sometimes referred to as programmer-declared methods. The actual statements in the method bodies are written only once, reused from perhaps several locations in a program and are hidden from other methods.

There are several motivations for modularizing a program by means of methods. One is the divide-and-conquer approach, which makes program development more manageable by constructing programs from small, simple pieces. Another is software reusability—using existing methods as building blocks to create new programs. Often, you can create programs mostly from standardized methods rather than by building customized code. For example, in earlier programs, we did not have to define how to read data values from the keyboard—Java provides these capabilities in class Scanner. A third motivation is to avoid repeating code. Dividing a program into meaningful methods makes the program easier to debug and maintain.

Software Engineering Observation 6.2

To promote software reusability, every method should be limited to performing a single, well-defined task, and the name of the method should express that task effectively. Such methods make programs easier to write, debug, maintain and modify.

Error-Prevention Tip 6.1

A small method that performs one task is easier to test and debug than a larger method that performs many tasks.

> **Software Engineering Observation 6.3**
>
> *If you cannot choose a concise name that expresses a method's task, your method might be attempting to perform too many diverse tasks. It is usually best to break such a method into several smaller method declarations.*

As you know, a method is invoked by a method call, and when the called method completes its task, it either returns a result or simply control to the caller. An analogy to this program structure is the hierarchical form of management (Figure 6.1). A boss (the caller) asks a worker (the called method) to perform a task and report back (i.e., return) the results after completing the task. The boss method does not know how the worker method performs its designated tasks. The worker may also call other worker methods, unbeknownst to the boss. This "hiding" of implementation details promotes good software engineering. Figure 6.1 shows the boss method communicating with several worker methods in a hierarchical manner. The boss method divides the responsibilities among the various worker methods. Note that worker1 acts as a "boss method" to worker4 and worker5.

6.3 static Methods, static Fields and Class Math

As you know, every class provides methods that perform common tasks on objects of the class. For example, to input data from the keyboard, you have called methods on a Scanner object that was initialized in its constructor to obtain input from the standard input stream (System.in). As you will learn in Chapter 14, Files and Streams, you can initialize a Scanner to obtain input from other sources, such as a file on disk. One program could have a Scanner object that inputs information from the standard input stream and a second Scanner that inputs information from a file. Each input method called on the standard input stream Scanner would obtain input from the keyboard, and each input method called on the file Scanner would obtain input from the specified file on disk.

Although most methods execute in response to method calls on specific objects, this is not always the case. Sometimes a method performs a task that does not depend on the contents of any object. Such a method applies to the class in which it is declared as a whole and is known as a static method or a class method. It is not uncommon for a class to contain a group of convenient static methods to perform common tasks. For example, recall that we used static method pow of class Math to raise a value to a power in Fig. 5.6.

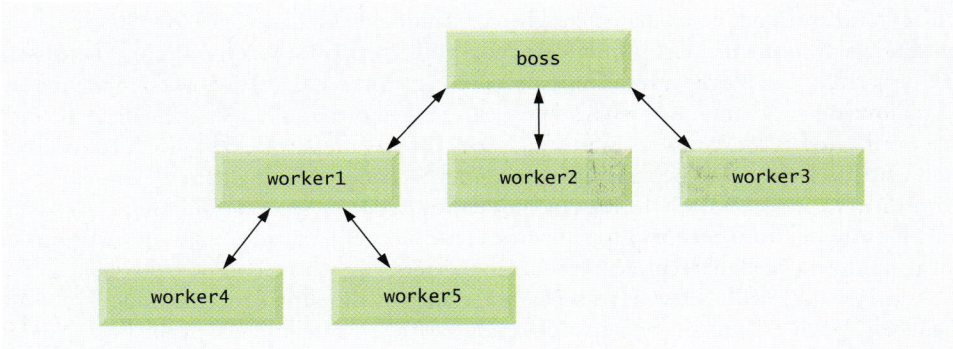

Fig. 6.1 | Hierarchical boss-method/worker-method relationship.

To declare a method as `static`, place the keyword `static` before the return type in the method's declaration. You can call any `static` method by specifying the name of the class in which the method is declared, followed by a dot (.) and the method name, as in

> *ClassName*.*methodName*(*arguments*)

We use various `Math` class methods here to present the concept of `static` methods. Class `Math` provides a collection of methods that enable you to perform common mathematical calculations. For example, you can calculate the square root of `900.0` with the `static` method call

```
Math.sqrt( 900.0 )
```

The preceding expression evaluates to `30.0`. Method `sqrt` takes an argument of type `double` and returns a result of type `double`. To output the value of the preceding method call in the command window, you might write the statement

```
System.out.println( Math.sqrt( 900.0 ) );
```

In this statement, the value that `sqrt` returns becomes the argument to method `println`. Note that there was no need to create a `Math` object before calling method `sqrt`. Also note that *all* `Math` class methods are `static`—therefore, each is called by preceding the name of the method with the class name `Math` and a dot (.) separator.

 Software Engineering Observation 6.4

Class `Math` is part of the `java.lang` package, which is implicitly imported by the compiler, so it is not necessary to import class `Math` to use its methods.

Method arguments may be constants, variables or expressions. If `c = 13.0, d = 3.0` and `f = 4.0`, then the statement

```
System.out.println( Math.sqrt( c + d * f ) );
```

calculates and prints the square root of `13.0 + 3.0 * 4.0 = 25.0`—namely, `5.0`. Figure 6.2 summarizes several `Math` class methods. In the figure, *x* and *y* are of type `double`.

Math Class Constants PI and E

Class `Math` also declares two fields that represent commonly used mathematical constants: `Math.PI` and `Math.E`. The constant `Math.PI` (3.14159265358979323846) is the ratio of a circle's circumference to its diameter. The constant `Math.E` (2.7182818284590452354) is the base value for natural logarithms (calculated with `static` `Math` method `log`). These fields are declared in class `Math` with the modifiers `public`, `final` and `static`. Making them `public` allows other programmers to use these fields in their own classes. Any field declared with keyword **`final`** is constant—its value cannot be changed after the field is initialized. Both `PI` and `E` are declared `final` because their values never change. Making these fields `static` allows them to be accessed via the class name `Math` and a dot (.) separator, just like class `Math`'s methods. Recall from Section 3.5 that when each object of a class maintains its own copy of an attribute, the field that represents the attribute is also known as an instance variable—each object (instance) of the class has a separate instance of the variable in memory. There are fields for which each object of a class does not have a separate instance of the field. That is the case with `static` fields, which are also known as **class variables**. When objects of a class containing `static` fields are created, all the objects of that class share one copy of the class's

Method	Description	Example
abs(x)	absolute value of x	abs(23.7) is 23.7 abs(0.0) is 0.0 abs(-23.7) is 23.7
ceil(x)	rounds x to the smallest integer not less than x	ceil(9.2) is 10.0 ceil(-9.8) is -9.0
cos(x)	trigonometric cosine of x (x in radians)	cos(0.0) is 1.0
exp(x)	exponential method e^x	exp(1.0) is 2.71828 exp(2.0) is 7.38906
floor(x)	rounds x to the largest integer not greater than x	floor(9.2) is 9.0 floor(-9.8) is -10.0
log(x)	natural logarithm of x (base e)	log(Math.E) is 1.0 log(Math.E * Math.E) is 2.0
max(x, y)	larger value of x and y	max(2.3, 12.7) is 12.7 max(-2.3, -12.7) is -2.3
min(x, y)	smaller value of x and y	min(2.3, 12.7) is 2.3 min(-2.3, -12.7) is -12.7
pow(x, y)	x raised to the power y (i.e., x^y)	pow(2.0, 7.0) is 128.0 pow(9.0, 0.5) is 3.0
sin(x)	trigonometric sine of x (x in radians)	sin(0.0) is 0.0
sqrt(x)	square root of x	sqrt(900.0) is 30.0
tan(x)	trigonometric tangent of x (x in radians)	tan(0.0) is 0.0

Fig. 6.2 | Math class methods.

static fields. Together the class variables and instance variables represent the fields of a class. You will learn more about static fields in Section 8.11.

Why Is Method main Declared static?

Why must main be declared static? When you execute the Java Virtual Machine (JVM) with the java command, the JVM attempts to invoke the main method of the class you specify—when no objects of the class have been created. Declaring main as static allows the JVM to invoke main without creating an instance of the class. Method main is usually declared with the header:

```
public static void main( String args[] )
```

When you execute your application, you specify its class name as an argument to the command java, as in

```
java ClassName argument1 argument2 ...
```

The JVM loads the class specified by *ClassName* and uses that class name to invoke method main. In the preceding command, *ClassName* is a **command-line argument** to the JVM that tells it which class to execute. Following the *ClassName*, you can also specify a list of `Strings` (separated by spaces) as command-line arguments that the JVM will pass to your application. Such arguments might be used to specify options (e.g., a file name) to run the application. As you will learn in Chapter 7, Arrays, your application can access those command-line arguments and use them to customize the application.

Additional Comments about Method `main`

In earlier chapters, every application had one class that contained only `main` and possibly a second class that was used by `main` to create and manipulate objects. Actually, any class can contain a `main` method. In fact, each of our two-class examples could have been implemented as one class. For example, in the application in Fig. 5.9 and Fig. 5.10, method `main` (lines 6–16 of Fig. 5.10) could have been taken as is and placed in class `GradeBook` (Fig. 5.9). You would then execute the application by typing the command `java Grade-Book` in the command window—the application results would be identical to those of the two-class version. You can place a `main` method in every class you declare. The JVM invokes the `main` method only in the class used to execute the application. Some programmers take advantage of this to build a small test program into each class they declare.

6.4 Declaring Methods with Multiple Parameters

Chapters 3–5 presented classes containing simple methods that had at most one parameter. Methods often require more than one piece of information to perform their tasks. We now consider how programmers write their own methods with multiple parameters.

The application in Fig. 6.3 and Fig. 6.4 uses a programmer-declared method called `maximum` to determine and return the largest of three `double` values that are input by the user. When the application begins execution, class `MaximumFinderTest`'s `main` method (lines 7–11 of Fig. 6.4) creates one object of class `MaximumFinder` (line 9) and calls the object's `determineMaximum` method (line 10) to produce the program's output. In class `MaximumFinder` (Fig. 6.3), lines 14–18 of method `determineMaximum` prompt the user to enter three `double` values and read them from the user. Line 21 calls method `maximum` (declared in lines 28–41) to determine the largest of the three `double` values passed as arguments to the method. When method `maximum` returns the result to line 21, the program assigns `maximum`'s return value to local variable `result`. Then line 24 outputs the maximum value. At the end of this section, we'll discuss the use of operator + in line 24.

Consider the declaration of method `maximum` (lines 28–41). Line 28 indicates that the method returns a `double` value, that the method's name is `maximum` and that the method requires three `double` parameters (x, y and z) to accomplish its task. When a method has more than one parameter, the parameters are specified as a comma-separated list. When `maximum` is called from line 21, the parameter x is initialized with the value of the argument `number1`, the parameter y is initialized with the value of the argument `number2` and the parameter z is initialized with the value of the argument `number3`. There must be one argument in the method call for each parameter (sometimes called a formal parameter) in the method declaration. Also, each argument must be consistent with the type of the corresponding parameter. For example, a parameter of type `double` can receive values like 7.35, 22 or –0.03456, but not `Strings` like `"hello"`. Section 6.7 discusses the argument types that can be provided in a method call for each parameter of a primitive type.

```
1   // Fig. 6.3: MaximumFinder.java
2   // Programmer-declared method maximum.
3   import java.util.Scanner;
4
5   public class MaximumFinder
6   {
7      // obtain three floating-point values and locate the maximum value
8      public void determineMaximum()
9      {
10        // create Scanner for input from command window
11        Scanner input = new Scanner( System.in );
12
13        // obtain user input
14        System.out.print(
15           "Enter three floating-point values separated by spaces: " );
16        double number1 = input.nextDouble(); // read first double
17        double number2 = input.nextDouble(); // read second double
18        double number3 = input.nextDouble(); // read third double
19
20        // determine the maximum value
21        double result = maximum( number1, number2, number3 );
22
23        // display maximum value
24        System.out.println( "Maximum is: " + result );
25     } // end method determineMaximum
26
27     // returns the maximum of its three double parameters
28     public double maximum( double x, double y, double z )
29     {
30        double maximumValue = x; // assume x is the largest to start
31
32        // determine whether y is greater than maximumValue
33        if ( y > maximumValue )
34           maximumValue = y;
35
36        // determine whether z is greater than maximumValue
37        if ( z > maximumValue )
38           maximumValue = z;
39
40        return maximumValue;
41     } // end method maximum
42  } // end class MaximumFinder
```

Fig. 6.3 | Programmer-declared method `maximum` that has three `double` parameters.

To determine the maximum value, we begin with the assumption that parameter x contains the largest value, so line 30 declares local variable maximumValue and initializes it with the value of parameter x. Of course, it is possible that parameter y or z contains the actual largest value, so we must compare each of these values with maximumValue. The if statement at lines 33–34 determines whether y is greater than maximumValue. If so, line 34 assigns y to maximumValue. The if statement at lines 37–38 determines whether z is greater than maximumValue. If so, line 38 assigns z to maximumValue. At this point the largest of the three values resides in maximumValue, so line 40 returns that value to line 21. When program con-

```
1   // Fig. 6.4: MaximumFinderTest.java
2   // Application to test class MaximumFinder.
3
4   public class MaximumFinderTest
5   {
6      // application starting point
7      public static void main( String args[] )
8      {
9         MaximumFinder maximumFinder = new MaximumFinder();
10        maximumFinder.determineMaximum();
11     } // end main
12  } // end class MaximumFinderTest
```

```
Enter three floating-point values separated by spaces: 9.35 2.74 5.1
Maximum is: 9.35
```

```
Enter three floating-point values separated by spaces: 5.8 12.45 8.32
Maximum is: 12.45
```

```
Enter three floating-point values separated by spaces: 6.46 4.12 10.54
Maximum is: 10.54
```

Fig. 6.4 | Application to test class `MaximumFinder`.

trol returns to the point in the program where `maximum` was called, `maximum`'s parameters x, y and z no longer exist in memory. Note that methods can return at most one value, but the returned value could be a reference to an object that contains many values.

Note that `result` is a local variable in `determineMaximum` because it is declared in the block that represents the method's body. Variables should be declared as fields of a class only if they are required for use in more than one method of the class or if the program should save their values between calls to the class's methods.

Common Programming Error 6.1

Declaring method parameters of the same type as `float x, y` instead of `float x, float y` is a syntax error—a type is required for each parameter in the parameter list.

Software Engineering Observation 6.5

A method that has many parameters may be performing too many tasks. Consider dividing the method into smaller methods that perform the separate tasks. As a guideline, try to fit the method header on one line if possible.

Implementing Method `maximum` by Reusing Method `Math.max`

Recall from Fig. 6.2 that class `Math` has a `max` method that can determine the larger of two values. The entire body of our maximum method could also be implemented with two calls to `Math.max`, as follows:

```
return Math.max( x, Math.max( y, z ) );
```

The first call to `Math.max` specifies arguments x and `Math.max( y, z )`. Before any method can be called, all its arguments must be evaluated to determine their values. If an argument is a method call, the method call must be performed to determine its return value. So, in the preceding statement, `Math.max( y, z )` is evaluated first to determine the maximum of y and z. Then the result is passed as the second argument to the other call to `Math.max`, which returns the larger of its two arguments. Using `Math.max` in this manner is a good example of software reuse—we find the largest of three values by reusing `Math.max`, which finds the largest of two values. Note how concise this code is compared to lines 30–40 of Fig. 6.3.

Assembling Strings with String Concatenation

Java allows `String` objects to be created by assembling smaller strings into larger strings using operator + (or the compound assignment operator +=). This is known as string concatenation. When both operands of operator + are `String` objects, operator + creates a new `String` object in which the characters of the right operand are placed at the end of those in the left operand. For example, the expression `"hello " + "there"` creates the `String` `"hello there"`.

In line 24 of Fig. 6.3, the expression `"Maximum is: " + result` uses operator + with operands of types `String` and `double`. Every primitive value and object in Java has a `String` representation. When one of the + operator's operands is a `String`, the other is converted to a `String`, then the two are concatenated. In line 24, the `double` value is converted to its `String` representation and placed at the end of the `String` `"Maximum is: "`. If there are any trailing zeros in a `double` value, these will be discarded when the number is converted to a `String`. Thus, the number 9.3500 would be represented as 9.35 in the resulting `String`.

For primitive values used in string concatenation, the primitive values are converted to `Strings`. If a `boolean` is concatenated with a `String`, the `boolean` is converted to the `String` `"true"` or `"false"`. All objects have a method named `toString` that returns a `String` representation of the object. When an object is concatenated with a `String`, the object's `toString` method is implicitly called to obtain the `String` representation of the object. You will learn more about method `toString` in Chapter 7, Arrays.

When a large `String` literal is typed into a program's source code, programmers sometimes prefer to break that `String` into several smaller `Strings` and place them on multiple lines of code for readability. In this case, the `Strings` can be reassembled using concatenation. We discuss the details of `Strings` in Chapter 29, Strings, Characters and Regular Expressions.

Common Programming Error 6.2

It is a syntax error to break a `String` literal across multiple lines in a program. If a `String` does not fit on one line, split the `String` into several smaller `Strings` and use concatenation to form the desired `String`.

Common Programming Error 6.3

Confusing the + operator used for string concatenation with the + operator used for addition can lead to strange results. Java evaluates the operands of an operator from left to right. For example, if integer variable y has the value 5, the expression "y + 2 = " + y + 2 results in the string "y + 2 = 52", not "y + 2 = 7", because first the value of y (5) is concatenated with the string "y + 2 = ", then the value 2 is concatenated with the new larger string "y + 2 = 5". The expression "y + 2 = " + (y + 2) produces the desired result "y + 2 = 7".

6.5 Notes on Declaring and Using Methods

There are three ways to call a method:

1. Using a method name by itself to call another method of the same class—such as `maximum( number1, number2, number3 )` in line 21 of Fig. 6.3.

2. Using a variable that contains a reference to an object, followed by a dot (.) and the method name to call a method of the referenced object—such as the method call in line 10 of Fig. 6.4, `maximumFinder.determineMaximum()`, which calls a method of class `MaximumFinder` from the `main` method of `MaximumFinderTest`.

3. Using the class name and a dot (.) to call a `static` method of a class—such as `Math.sqrt( 900.0 )` in Section 6.3.

Note that a `static` method can call only other `static` methods of the same class directly (i.e., using the method name by itself) and can manipulate only `static` fields in the same class directly. To access the class's non-`static` members, a `static` method must use a reference to an object of the class. Recall that `static` methods relate to a class as a whole, whereas non-`static` methods are associated with a specific instance (object) of the class and may manipulate the instance variables of that object. Many objects of a class, each with its own copies of the instance variables, may exist at the same time. Suppose a `static` method were to invoke a non-`static` method directly. How would the method know which object's instance variables to manipulate? What would happen if no objects of the class existed at the time the non-`static` method was invoked? Clearly, such a situation would be problematic. Thus, Java does not allow a `static` method to access non-`static` members of the same class directly.

There are three ways to return control to the statement that calls a method. If the method does not return a result, control returns when the program flow reaches the method-ending right brace or when the statement

```
return;
```

is executed. If the method returns a result, the statement

```
return expression;
```

evaluates the *expression*, then returns the result to the caller.

Common Programming Error 6.4

Declaring a method outside the body of a class declaration or inside the body of another method is a syntax error.

Common Programming Error 6.5

Omitting the return-value-type *in a method declaration is a syntax error.*

Common Programming Error 6.6

Placing a semicolon after the right parenthesis enclosing the parameter list of a method declaration is a syntax error.

Common Programming Error 6.7

Redeclaring a method parameter as a local variable in the method's body is a compilation error.

Common Programming Error 6.8

Forgetting to return a value from a method that should return a value is a compilation error. If a return value type other than void *is specified, the method must contain a* return *statement that returns a value consistent with the method's* return-value-type. *Returning a value from a method whose return type has been declared* void *is a compilation error.*

6.6 Method Call Stack and Activation Records

To understand how Java performs method calls, we first need to consider a data structure (i.e., collection of related data items) known as a stack. Students can think of a stack as analogous to a pile of dishes. When a dish is placed on the pile, it is normally placed at the top (referred to as pushing the dish onto the stack). Similarly, when a dish is removed from the pile, it is always removed from the top (referred to as popping the dish off the stack). Stacks are known as last-in, first-out (LIFO) data structures—the last item pushed (inserted) on the stack is the first item popped (removed) from the stack.

When a program calls a method, the called method must know how to return to its caller, so the return address of the calling method is pushed onto the program execution stack (sometimes referred to as the method call stack). If a series of method calls occurs, the successive return addresses are pushed onto the stack in last-in, first-out order so that each method can return to its caller.

The program execution stack also contains the memory for the local variables used in each invocation of a method during a program's execution. This data, stored as a portion of the program execution stack, is known as the activation record or stack frame of the method call. When a method call is made, the activation record for that method call is pushed onto the program execution stack. When the method returns to its caller, the activation record for this method call is popped off the stack and those local variables are no longer known to the program. If a local variable holding a reference to an object is the only variable in the program with a reference to that object, when the activation record containing that local variable is popped off the stack, the object can no longer be accessed by the program and will eventually be deleted from memory by the JVM during "garbage collection." We'll discuss garbage collection in Section 8.10.

Of course, the amount of memory in a computer is finite, so only a certain amount of memory can be used to store activation records on the program execution stack. If more method calls occur than can have their activation records stored on the program execution stack, an error known as a stack overflow occurs.

6.7 Argument Promotion and Casting

Another important feature of method calls is argument promotion—converting an argument's value to the type that the method expects to receive in its corresponding parameter. For example, a program can call Math method sqrt with an integer argument even though the method expects to receive a double argument (but, as we will soon see, not vice versa). The statement

```
System.out.println( Math.sqrt( 4 ) );
```

correctly evaluates Math.sqrt(4) and prints the value 2.0. The method declaration's parameter list causes Java to convert the int value 4 to the double value 4.0 before passing the value to sqrt. Attempting these conversions may lead to compilation errors if Java's *promotion rules* are not satisfied. The promotion rules specify which conversions are allowed, that is, which conversions can be performed without losing data. In the sqrt example above, an int is converted to a double without changing its value. However, converting a double to an int truncates the fractional part of the double value—thus, part of the value is lost. Converting large integer types to small integer types (e.g., long to int) may also result in changed values.

The promotion rules apply to expressions containing values of two or more primitive types and to primitive-type values passed as arguments to methods. Each value is promoted to the "highest" type in the expression. (Actually, the expression uses a temporary copy of each value—the types of the original values remain unchanged.) Figure 6.5 lists the primitive types and the types to which each can be promoted. Note that the valid promotions for a given type are always to a type higher in the table. For example, an int can be promoted to the higher types long, float and double.

Converting values to types lower in the table of Fig. 6.5 will result in different values if the lower type cannot represent the value of the higher type (e.g., the int value 2000000 cannot be represented as a short, and any floating-point number with digits after its decimal point cannot be represented in an integer type such as long, int or short). Therefore, in cases where information may be lost due to conversion, the Java compiler requires the programmer to use a cast operator (introduced in Section 4.9) to explicitly force the conversion to occur—otherwise a compilation error occurs. This enables the programmer to "take control" from the compiler. The programmer essentially says, "I know this conversion might cause loss of information, but for my purposes here, that's fine." Suppose method square calculates the square of an integer and thus requires an int argument. To call square with a double argument named doubleValue, we would be required to write the method call as square((int) doubleValue). This method call explicitly casts (converts) the value of doubleValue to an integer for use in method square. Thus, if doubleValue's value is 4.5, the method receives the value 4 and returns 16, not 20.25.

Type	Valid promotions
double	None
float	double
long	float or double
int	long, float or double
char	int, long, float or double
short	int, long, float or double (but not char)
byte	short, int, long, float or double (but not char)
boolean	None (boolean values are not considered to be numbers in Java)

Fig. 6.5 | Promotions allowed for primitive types.

Common Programming Error 6.9

Converting a primitive-type value to another primitive type may change the value if the new type is not a valid promotion. For example, converting a floating-point value to an integral value may introduce truncation errors (loss of the fractional part) into the result.

6.8 Java API Packages

As we have seen, Java contains many predefined classes that are grouped into categories of related classes called packages. Together, we refer to these packages as the Java Application Programming Interface (Java API), or the Java class library.

Throughout the text, `import` declarations specify the classes required to compile a Java program. For example, a program includes the declaration

```
import java.util.Scanner;
```

to specify that the program uses class `Scanner` from the `java.util` package. This allows programmers to use the simple class name `Scanner`, rather than the fully qualified class name `java.util.Scanner`, in the code. A great strength of Java is the large number of classes in the packages of the Java API. Some key Java API packages are described in Fig. 6.6, which represents only a small portion of the reusable components in the Java API. When learning Java, spend a portion of your time browsing the packages and classes in the Java API documentation (`java.sun.com/j2se/5.0/docs/api/index.html`).

The set of packages available in the J2SE Development Kit (JDK) is quite large. In addition to the packages summarized in Fig. 6.6, the JDK includes packages for complex graphics, advanced graphical user interfaces, printing, advanced networking, security, database processing, multimedia, accessibility (for people with disabilities) and many other capabilities. For an overview of the packages in the JDK 5.0, visit

```
java.sun.com/j2se/5.0/docs/api/overview-summary.html
```

Many other packages are also available for download at `java.sun.com`.

Package	Description
`java.applet`	The Java Applet Package contains a class and several interfaces required to create Java applets—programs that execute in Web browsers. (Applets are discussed in Chapter 20, Introduction to Java Applets; interfaces are discussed in Chapter 10, Object-Oriented Programming: Polymorphism.)
`java.awt`	The Java Abstract Window Toolkit Package contains the classes and interfaces required to create and manipulate GUIs in Java 1.0 and 1.1. In current versions of Java, the Swing GUI components of the `javax.swing` packages are often used instead. (Some elements of the `java.awt` package are discussed in Chapter 11, GUI Components: Part 1, Chapter 12, Graphics and Java2D, and Chapter 22, GUI Components: Part 2.)

Fig. 6.6 | Java API packages (a subset). (Part 1 of 2.)

Package	Description
`java.awt.event`	The Java Abstract Window Toolkit Event Package contains classes and interfaces that enable event handling for GUI components in both the `java.awt` and `javax.swing` packages. (You will learn more about this package in Chapter 11, GUI Components: Part 1 and Chapter 22, GUI Components: Part 2.)
`java.io`	The Java Input/Output Package contains classes and interfaces that enable programs to input and output data. (You will learn more about this package in Chapter 14, Files and Streams.)
`java.lang`	The Java Language Package contains classes and interfaces (discussed throughout this text) that are required by many Java programs. This package is imported by the compiler into all programs, so the programmer does not need to do so.
`java.net`	The Java Networking Package contains classes and interfaces that enable programs to communicate via computer networks like the Internet. (You will learn more about this in Chapter 24, Networking.)
`java.text`	The Java Text Package contains classes and interfaces that enable programs to manipulate numbers, dates, characters and strings. The package provides internationalization capabilities that enable a program to be customized to a specific locale (e.g., a program may display strings in different languages, based on the user's country).
`java.util`	The Java Utilities Package contains utility classes and interfaces that enable such actions as date and time manipulations, random-number processing (class `Random`), the storing and processing of large amounts of data and the breaking of strings into smaller pieces called tokens (class `StringTokenizer`). (You will learn more about the features of this package in Chapter 19, Collections.)
`javax.swing`	The Java Swing GUI Components Package contains classes and interfaces for Java's Swing GUI components that provide support for portable GUIs. (You will learn more about this package in Chapter 11, GUI Components: Part 1 and Chapter 22, GUI Components: Part 2.)
`javax.swing.event`	The Java Swing Event Package contains classes and interfaces that enable event handling (e.g., responding to button clicks) for GUI components in package `javax.swing`. (You will learn more about this package in Chapter 11, GUI Components: Part 1 and Chapter 22, GUI Components: Part 2.)

Fig. 6.6 | Java API packages (a subset). (Part 2 of 2.)

You can locate additional information about a predefined Java class's methods in the Java API documentation at `java.sun.com/j2se/5.0/docs/api/index.html`. When you visit this site, click the **Index** link to see an alphabetical listing of all the classes and methods in the Java API. Locate the class name and click its link to see the online description of the class. Click the **METHOD** link to see a table of the class's methods. Each `static` method will be listed with the word "static" preceding the method's return type. For a more detailed overview of navigating the Java API documentation, see Appendix G, Using the Java API Documentation.

Good Programming Practice 6.2

The online Java API documentation is easy to search and provides many details about each class. As you learn a class in this book, you should get in the habit of looking at the class in the online documentation for additional information.

6.9 Case Study: Random-Number Generation

We now take a brief and, hopefully, entertaining diversion into a popular type of programming application—simulation and game playing. In this and the next section, we develop a nicely structured game-playing program with multiple methods. The program uses most of the control statements presented thus far in the book and introduces several new programming concepts.

There is something in the air of a casino that invigorates people—from the high rollers at the plush mahogany-and-felt craps tables to the quarter poppers at the one-armed bandits. It is the element of chance, the possibility that luck will convert a pocketful of money into a mountain of wealth. The element of chance can be introduced in a program via an object of class Random (package java.util) or via the static method random of class Math. Objects of class Random can produce random boolean, byte, float, double, int, long and Gaussian values, whereas Math method random can produce only double values in the range $0.0 \le x < 1.0$, where x is the value returned by method random. In the next several examples, we use objects of class Random to produce random values.

A new random-number generator object can be created as follows:

```
Random randomNumbers = new Random();
```

The random-number generator object can then be used to generate random boolean, byte, float, double, int, long and Gaussian values—we discuss only random int values here. For more information on the Random class, see java.sun.com/j2se/5.0/docs/api/java/util/Random.html.

Consider the following statement:

```
int randomValue = randomNumbers.nextInt();
```

Method nextInt of class Random generates a random int value in the range –2,147,483,648 to +2,147,483,647. If the nextInt method truly produces values at random, then every value in that range should have an equal chance (or probability) of being chosen each time method nextInt is called. The values returned by nextInt are actually pseudorandom numbers—a sequence of values produced by a complex mathematical calculation. The calculation uses the current time of day (which, of course, changes constantly) to seed the random-number generator such that each execution of a program yields a different sequence of random values.

The range of values produced directly by method nextInt often differs from the range of values required in a particular Java application. For example, a program that simulates coin tossing might require only 0 for "heads" and 1 for "tails." A program that simulates the rolling of a six-sided die might require random integers in the range 1–6. A program that randomly predicts the next type of spaceship (out of four possibilities) that will fly across the horizon in a video game might require random integers in the range 1–4. For cases like these, class Random provides another version of method nextInt that receives an int argument and returns a value from 0 up to, but not including, the argument's value. For example, to simulate coin tossing, you might use the statement

```
int randomValue = randomNumbers.nextInt( 2 );
```

which returns 0 or 1.

Rolling a Six-Sided Die

To demonstrate random numbers, let us develop a program that simulates 20 rolls of a six-sided die and displays the value of each roll. We begin by using nextInt to produce random values in the range 0–5, as follows:

```
face = randomNumbers.nextInt( 6 );
```

The argument 6—called the **scaling factor**—represents the number of unique values that nextInt should produce (in this case six—0, 1, 2, 3, 4 and 5). This manipulation is called **scaling** the range of values produced by Random method nextInt.

A six-sided die has the numbers 1–6 on its faces, not 0–5. So we **shift** the range of numbers produced by adding a **shifting value**—in this case 1—to our previous result, as in

```
face = 1 + randomNumbers.nextInt( 6 );
```

The shifting value (1) specifies the first value in the desired set of random integers. The preceding statement assigns face a random integer in the range 1–6.

Figure 6.7 shows two sample outputs which confirm that the results of the preceding calculation are integers in the range 1–6, and that each run of the program can produce a different sequence of random numbers. Line 3 imports class Random from the java.util package. Line 9 creates the Random object randomNumbers to produce random values. Line 16 executes 20 times in a loop to roll the die. The if statement (lines 21–22) in the loop starts a new line of output after every five numbers, so the results can be presented on multiple lines.

Rolling a Six-Sided Die 6000 Times

To show that the numbers produced by nextInt occur with approximately equal likelihood, let us simulate 6000 rolls of a die with the application in Fig. 6.8. Each integer from 1 to 6 should appear approximately 1000 times.

As the two sample outputs show, scaling and shifting the values produced by method nextInt enables the program to realistically simulate rolling a six-sided die. The application uses nested control statements (the switch is nested inside the for) to determine the number of times each side of the die occurred. The for statement (lines 21–47) iterates 6000 times. During each iteration, line 23 produces a random value from 1 to 6. That value is then used as the controlling expression (line 26) of the switch statement (lines 26–46). Based on the face value, the switch statement increments one of the six counter variables during each iteration of the loop. (When we study arrays in Chapter 7, we will show an elegant way to replace the entire switch statement in this program with a single statement!) Note that the switch statement has no default case because we have a case for every possible die value that the expression in line 23 could produce. Run the program several times, and observe the results. As you will see, every time you execute this program, it produces different results.

```java
 1   // Fig. 6.7: RandomIntegers.java
 2   // Shifted and scaled random integers.
 3   import java.util.Random; // program uses class Random
 4
 5   public class RandomIntegers
 6   {
 7      public static void main( String args[] )
 8      {
 9         Random randomNumbers = new Random(); // random number generator
10         int face; // stores each random integer generated
11
12         // loop 20 times
13         for ( int counter = 1; counter <= 20; counter++ )
14         {
15            // pick random integer from 1 to 6
16            face = 1 + randomNumbers.nextInt( 6 );
17
18            System.out.printf( "%d  ", face ); // display generated value
19
20            // if counter is divisible by 5, start a new line of output
21            if ( counter % 5 == 0 )
22               System.out.println();
23         } // end for
24      } // end main
25   } // end class RandomIntegers
```

```
1  5  3  6  2
5  2  6  5  2
4  4  4  2  6
3  1  6  2  2
```

```
6  5  4  2  6
1  2  5  1  3
6  3  2  2  1
6  4  2  6  4
```

Fig. 6.7 | Shifted and scaled random integers.

```java
 1   // Fig. 6.8: RollDie.java
 2   // Roll a six-sided die 6000 times.
 3   import java.util.Random;
 4
 5   public class RollDie
 6   {
 7      public static void main( String args[] )
 8      {
 9         Random randomNumbers = new Random(); // random number generator
10
11         int frequency1 = 0; // maintains count of 1s rolled
```

Fig. 6.8 | Rolling a six-sided die 6000 times. (Part 1 of 3.)

```
12        int frequency2 = 0; // count of 2s rolled
13        int frequency3 = 0; // count of 3s rolled
14        int frequency4 = 0; // count of 4s rolled
15        int frequency5 = 0; // count of 5s rolled
16        int frequency6 = 0; // count of 6s rolled
17
18        int face; // stores most recently rolled value
19
20        // summarize results of 6000 rolls of a die
21        for ( int roll = 1; roll <= 6000; roll++ )
22        {
23           face = 1 + randomNumbers.nextInt( 6 ); // number from 1 to 6
24
25           // determine roll value 1-6 and increment appropriate counter
26           switch ( face )
27           {
28              case 1:
29                 ++frequency1; // increment the 1s counter
30                 break;
31              case 2:
32                 ++frequency2; // increment the 2s counter
33                 break;
34              case 3:
35                 ++frequency3; // increment the 3s counter
36                 break;
37              case 4:
38                 ++frequency4; // increment the 4s counter
39                 break;
40              case 5:
41                 ++frequency5; // increment the 5s counter
42                 break;
43              case 6:
44                 ++frequency6; // increment the 6s counter
45                 break; // optional at end of switch
46           } // end switch
47        } // end for
48
49        System.out.println( "Face\tFrequency" ); // output headers
50        System.out.printf( "1\t%d\n2\t%d\n3\t%d\n4\t%d\n5\t%d\n6\t%d\n",
51           frequency1, frequency2, frequency3, frequency4,
52           frequency5, frequency6 );
53     } // end main
54  } // end class RollDie
```

```
Face    Frequency
1       982
2       1001
3       1015
4       1005
5       1009
6       988
```

Fig. 6.8 | Rolling a six-sided die 6000 times. (Part 2 of 3.)

Face	Frequency
1	1029
2	994
3	1017
4	1007
5	972
6	981

Fig. 6.8 | Rolling a six-sided die 6000 times. (Part 3 of 3.)

6.9.1 Generalized Scaling and Shifting of Random Numbers

Previously, we demonstrated the statement

```
face = 1 + randomNumbers.nextInt( 6 );
```

which simulates the rolling of a six-sided die. This statement always assigns to variable face an integer in the range 1 ≤ face ≤ 6. The width of this range (i.e., the number of consecutive integers in the range) is 6, and the starting number in the range is 1. Referring to the preceding statement, we see that the width of the range is determined by the number 6 that is passed as an argument to Random method nextInt, and the starting number of the range is the number 1 that is added to randomNumberGenerator.nextInt(6). We can generalize this result as

```
number = shiftingValue + randomNumbers.nextInt( scalingFactor );
```

where *shiftingValue* specifies the first number in the desired range of consecutive integers and *scalingFactor* specifies how many numbers are in the range.

It is also possible to choose integers at random from sets of values other than ranges of consecutive integers. For example, to obtain a random value from the sequence 2, 5, 8, 11 and 14, you could use the statement

```
number = 2 + 3 * randomNumbers.nextInt( 5 );
```

In this case, randomNumberGenerator.nextInt(5) produces values in the range 0–4. Each value produced is multiplied by 3 to produce a number in the sequence 0, 3, 6, 9 and 12. We then add 2 to that value to shift the range of values and obtain a value from the sequence 2, 5, 8, 11 and 14. We can generalize this result as

```
number = shiftingValue +
    differenceBetweenValues * randomNumbers.nextInt( scalingFactor );
```

where *shiftingValue* specifies the first number in the desired range of values, *differenceBetweenValues* represents the difference between consecutive numbers in the sequence and *scalingFactor* specifies how many numbers are in the range.

6.9.2 Random-Number Repeatability for Testing and Debugging

As we mentioned earlier in Section 6.9, the methods of class Random actually generate pseudorandom numbers based on complex mathematical calculations. Repeatedly calling any of Random's methods produces a sequence of numbers that appears to be random. The calculation that produces the pseudorandom numbers uses the time of day as a **seed value** to change the sequence's starting point. Each new `Random` object seeds itself with a value based on the computer system's clock at the time the object is created, enabling each execution of a program to produce a different sequence of random numbers.

When debugging an application, it is sometimes useful to repeat the exact same sequence of pseudorandom numbers during each execution of the program. This repeatability enables you to prove that your application is working for a specific sequence of random numbers before you test the program with different sequences of random numbers. When repeatability is important, you can create a `Random` object as follows:

```
Random randomNumbers = new Random( seedValue );
```

The `seedValue` argument (type `long`) seeds the random-number calculation. If the same `seedValue` is used every time, the `Random` object produces the same sequence of random numbers. You can set a `Random` object's seed at any time during program execution by calling the object's `setSeed` method, as in

```
randomNumbers.setSeed( seedValue );
```

Error-Prevention Tip 6.2

While a program is under development, create the `Random` object with a specific seed value to produce a repeatable sequence of random numbers each time the program executes. If a logic error occurs, fix the error and test the program again with the same seed value—this allows you to reconstruct the same sequence of random numbers that caused the error. Once the logic errors have been removed, create the `Random` object without using a seed value, causing the `Random` object to generate a new sequence of random numbers each time the program executes.

6.10 Case Study: A Game of Chance (Introducing Enumerations)

A popular game of chance is a dice game known as "craps," which is played in casinos and back alleys throughout the world. The rules of the game are straightforward:

> *You roll two dice. Each die has six faces, which contain one, two, three, four, five and six spots, respectively. After the dice have come to rest, the sum of the spots on the two upward faces is calculated. If the sum is 7 or 11 on the first throw, you win. If the sum is 2, 3 or 12 on the first throw (called "craps"), you lose (i.e., the "house" wins). If the sum is 4, 5, 6, 8, 9 or 10 on the first throw, that sum becomes your "point." To win, you must continue rolling the dice until you "make your point" (i.e., roll that same point value). You lose by rolling a 7 before making the point.*

The application in Fig. 6.9 and Fig. 6.10 simulates the game of craps, using methods to define the logic of the game. In the `main` method of class `CrapsTest` (Fig. 6.10), line 8 creates an object of class `Craps` (Fig. 6.9) and line 9 calls its `play` method to start the game. The `play` method (Fig. 6.9, lines 21–65) calls the `rollDice` method (Fig. 6.9, lines 68–81) as necessary to roll the two dice and compute their sum. Four sample outputs in Fig. 6.10 show winning on the first roll, losing on the first roll, winning on a subsequent roll and losing on a subsequent roll, respectively.

Let's discuss the declaration of class `Craps` in Fig. 6.9. In the rules of the game, the player must roll two dice on the first roll, and must do the same on all subsequent rolls.

We declare method `rollDice` (lines 68–81) to roll the dice and compute and print their sum. Method `rollDice` is declared once, but it is called from two places (lines 26 and 50) in method `play`, which contains the logic for one complete game of craps. Method `roll-Dice` takes no arguments, so it has an empty parameter list. Each time it is called, `rollDice` returns the sum of the dice, so the return type `int` is indicated in the method header (line 68). Although lines 71 and 72 look the same (except for the die names), they do not necessarily produce the same result. Each of these statements produces a random value in the range 1–6. Note that `randomNumbers` (used in lines 71–72) is not declared in the method. Rather it is declared as a `private` instance variable of the class and initialized in line 8. This enables us to create one Random object that is reused in each call to `rollDice`.

```java
1   // Fig. 6.9: Craps.java
2   // Craps class simulates the dice game craps.
3   import java.util.Random;
4
5   public class Craps
6   {
7      // create random number generator for use in method rollDice
8      private Random randomNumbers = new Random();
9
10     // enumeration with constants that represent the game status
11     private enum Status { CONTINUE, WON, LOST };
12
13     // constants that represent common rolls of the dice
14     private final static int SNAKE_EYES = 2;
15     private final static int TREY = 3;
16     private final static int SEVEN = 7;
17     private final static int YO_LEVEN = 11;
18     private final static int BOX_CARS = 12;
19
20     // plays one game of craps
21     public void play()
22     {
23        int myPoint = 0; // point if no win or loss on first roll
24        Status gameStatus; // can contain CONTINUE, WON or LOST
25
26        int sumOfDice = rollDice(); // first roll of the dice
27
28        // determine game status and point based on first roll
29        switch ( sumOfDice )
30        {
31           case SEVEN: // win with 7 on first roll
32           case YO_LEVEN: // win with 11 on first roll
33              gameStatus = Status.WON;
34              break;
35           case SNAKE_EYES: // lose with 2 on first roll
36           case TREY: // lose with 3 on first roll
37           case BOX_CARS: // lose with 12 on first roll
38              gameStatus = Status.LOST;
39              break;
```

Fig. 6.9 | Craps class simulates the dice game craps. (Part 1 of 2.)

```
40          default: // did not win or lose, so remember point
41              gameStatus = Status.CONTINUE; // game is not over
42              myPoint = sumOfDice; // remember the point
43              System.out.printf( "Point is %d\n", myPoint );
44              break; // optional at end of switch
45          } // end switch
46
47          // while game is not complete
48          while ( gameStatus == Status.CONTINUE ) // not WON or LOST
49          {
50              sumOfDice = rollDice(); // roll dice again
51
52              // determine game status
53              if ( sumOfDice == myPoint ) // win by making point
54                  gameStatus = Status.WON;
55              else
56                  if ( sumOfDice == SEVEN ) // lose by rolling 7 before point
57                      gameStatus = Status.LOST;
58          } // end while
59
60          // display won or lost message
61          if ( gameStatus == Status.WON )
62              System.out.println( "Player wins" );
63          else
64              System.out.println( "Player loses" );
65      } // end method play
66
67      // roll dice, calculate sum and display results
68      public int rollDice()
69      {
70          // pick random die values
71          int die1 = 1 + randomNumbers.nextInt( 6 ); // first die roll
72          int die2 = 1 + randomNumbers.nextInt( 6 ); // second die roll
73
74          int sum = die1 + die2; // sum of die values
75
76          // display results of this roll
77          System.out.printf( "Player rolled %d + %d = %d\n",
78              die1, die2, sum );
79
80          return sum; // return sum of dice
81      } // end method rollDice
82  } // end class Craps
```

Fig. 6.9 | Craps class simulates the dice game craps. (Part 2 of 2.)

The game is reasonably involved. The player may win or lose on the first roll, or may win or lose on any subsequent roll. Method play (lines 21–65) uses local variable myPoint (line 23) to store the "point" if the player does not win or lose on the first roll, local variable gameStatus (line 24) to keep track of the overall game status and local variable sumOfDice (line 26) to maintain the sum of the dice for the most recent roll. Note that myPoint is initialized to 0 to ensure that the application will compile. If you do not initialize myPoint, the compiler issues an error, because myPoint is not assigned a value in every branch of the switch

```java
 1    // Fig. 6.10: CrapsTest.java
 2    // Application to test class Craps.
 3
 4    public class CrapsTest
 5    {
 6       public static void main( String args[] )
 7       {
 8          Craps game = new Craps();
 9          game.play(); // play one game of craps
10       } // end main
11    } // end class CrapsTest
```

```
Player rolled 5 + 6 = 11
Player wins
```

```
Player rolled 1 + 2 = 3
Player loses
```

```
Player rolled 5 + 4 = 9
Point is 9
Player rolled 2 + 2 = 4
Player rolled 2 + 6 = 8
Player rolled 4 + 2 = 6
Player rolled 3 + 6 = 9
Player wins
```

```
Player rolled 2 + 6 = 8
Point is 8
Player rolled 5 + 1 = 6
Player rolled 2 + 1 = 3
Player rolled 1 + 6 = 7
Player loses
```

Fig. 6.10 | Application to test class Craps.

statement, and thus the program could try to use myPoint before it is assigned a value. By contrast, gameStatus does not require initialization because it *is* assigned a value in every branch of the switch statement—thus, it is guaranteed to be initialized before it is used.

Note that local variable gameStatus is declared to be of a new type called Status, which we declared at line 11. Type Status is declared as a private member of class Craps, because Status will be used only in that class. Status is a programmer-declared type called an **enumeration**, which, in its simplest form, declares a set of constants represented by identifiers. An enumeration is a special kind of class that is introduced by the keyword **enum** (new to J2SE 5.0) and a type name (in this case, Status). As with any class, braces ({ and }) delimit the body of an enum declaration. Inside the braces is a comma-separated list of **enumeration constants**, each representing a unique value. The identifiers in an enum must be unique. (You will learn more about enumerations in Chapter 8.)

Good Programming Practice 6.3

Use only uppercase letters in the names of constants. This makes the constants stand out in a program and reminds the programmer that enumeration constants are not variables.

Variables of type `Status` can be assigned only one of the three constants declared in the enumeration or a compilation error will occur. When the game is won, the program sets local variable `gameStatus` to `Status.WON` (lines 33 and 54). When the game is lost, the program sets local variable `gameStatus` to `Status.LOST` (lines 38 and 57). Otherwise, the program sets local variable `gameStatus` to `Status.CONTINUE` (line 41) to indicate that the dice must be rolled again.

Good Programming Practice 6.4

Using enumeration constants (like `Status.WON`, `Status.LOST` and `Status.CONTINUE`) rather than literal integer values (such as 0, 1 and 2) can make programs easier to read and maintain.

Line 26 in method `play` calls `rollDice`, which picks two random values from 1 to 6, displays the value of the first die, the value of the second die and the sum of the dice, and returns the sum of the dice. Method `play` next enters the `switch` statement at lines 29–45, which uses the `sumOfDice` value from line 26 to determine whether the game has been won or lost, or whether it should continue with another roll. The sums of the dice that would result in a win or loss on the first roll are declared as `public final static int` constants in lines 14–18. These are used in the cases of the `switch` statement. The identifier names use casino parlance for these sums. Note that these constants, like `enum` constants, are declared with all capital letters by convention, to make them stand out in the program. Lines 31–34 determine whether the player won on the first roll with SEVEN (7) or YO_LEVEN (11). Lines 35–39 determine whether the player lost on the first roll with SNAKE_EYES (2), TREY (3), or BOX_CARS (12). After the first roll, if the game is not over, the `default` case (lines 40–44) saves `sumOfDice` in `myPoint` (line 42) and displays the point (line 43).

If we are still trying to "make our point" (i.e., the game is continuing from a prior roll), the loop in lines 48–58 executes. Line 50 rolls the dice again. In line 53, if `sumOfDice` matches `myPoint`, line 54 sets `gameStatus` to `Status.WON`, then the loop terminates because the game is complete. In line 56, if `sumOfDice` is equal to SEVEN (7), line 57 sets `gameStatus` to `Status.LOST`, and the loop terminates because the game is complete. When the game completes, lines 61–64 display a message indicating whether the player won or lost and the program terminates.

Note the use of the various program-control mechanisms we have discussed. The `Craps` class uses three methods—`main`, `play` (called from `main`) and `rollDice` (called twice from `play`)—and the `switch`, `while`, `if...else` and nested `if` control statements. Note also the use of multiple `case` labels in the `switch` statement to execute the same statements for sums of SEVEN and YO_LEVEN (lines 31–32) and for sums of SNAKE_EYES, TREY and BOX_CARS (lines 35–37).

You might be wondering why we declared the sums of the dice as `public final static int` constants rather than as `enum` constants. The answer lies in the fact that the program must compare `int sumOfDice` (line 26) to these constants to determine the outcome of each roll. Suppose we were to declare `enum Sum` containing constants (e.g., `Sum.SNAKE_EYES`) representing the five sums used in the game, then use these constants in place of the `final` variables in the cases of the `switch` statement (lines 29–45). Doing so would prevent us from using `sumOfDice` as the `switch` statement's controlling expression—Java does not allow an `int` to be compared to an enumeration constant. To achieve the same functionality as the current program, we would have to use a variable `currentSum` of type `Sum` as the `switch`'s controlling expression. Unfortunately, Java does not provide an easy way to convert an `int` value to a particular `enum` constant. To translate an `int` into an `enum` constant would require a separate `switch` statement. Clearly this would be cumbersome and not improve the readability of the program (thus defeating the purpose of using an `enum`), so we are better off using `public final static int` constants to represent the sums of the dice.

6.11 Scope of Declarations

You have seen declarations of various Java entities, such as classes, methods, variables and parameters. Declarations introduce names that can be used to refer to such Java entities. The scope of a declaration is the portion of the program that can refer to the declared entity by its name. Such an entity is said to be "in scope" for that portion of the program. This section introduces several important scope issues. (For more scope information, see the *Java Language Specification, Section 6.3: Scope of a Declaration*, at `java.sun.com/docs/books/jls/second_edition/html/names.doc.html#103228`.)

The basic scope rules are as follows:

1. The scope of a parameter declaration is the body of the method in which the declaration appears.

2. The scope of a local-variable declaration is from the point at which the declaration appears to the end of that block.

3. The scope of a local-variable declaration that appears in the initialization section of a `for` statement's header is the body of the `for` statement and the other expressions in the header.

4. The scope of a method or field of a class is the entire body of the class. This enables non-`static` methods of a class to use the class's fields and other methods.

Any block may contain variable declarations. If a local variable or parameter in a method has the same name as a field, the field is "hidden" until the block terminates execution—this is called shadowing. In Chapter 8, we discuss how to access shadowed fields.

Common Programming Error 6.10

A compilation error occurs when a local variable is declared more than once in a method.

Error-Prevention Tip 6.3

Use different names for fields and local variables to help prevent subtle logic errors that occur when a method is called and a local variable of the method shadows a field of the same name in the class.

The application in Fig. 6.11 and Fig. 6.12 demonstrates scoping issues with fields and local variables. When the application begins execution, class `ScopeTest`'s `main` method (Fig. 6.12, lines 7–11) creates an object of class `Scope` (line 9) and calls the object's `begin` method (line 10) to produce the program's output (shown in Fig. 6.12).

```
 1   // Fig. 6.11: Scope.java
 2   // Scope class demonstrates field and local variable scopes.
 3
 4   public class Scope
 5   {
 6      // field that is accessible to all methods of this class
 7      private int x = 1;
 8
 9      // method begin creates and initializes local variable x
10      // and calls methods useLocalVariable and useField
11      public void begin()
12      {
13         int x = 5; // method's local variable x shadows field x
14
15         System.out.printf( "local x in method begin is %d\n", x );
16
17         useLocalVariable(); // useLocalVariable has local x
18         useField(); // useField uses class Scope's field x
19         useLocalVariable(); // useLocalVariable reinitializes local x
20         useField(); // class Scope's field x retains its value
21
22         System.out.printf( "\nlocal x in method begin is %d\n", x );
23      } // end method begin
24
25      // create and initialize local variable x during each call
26      public void useLocalVariable()
27      {
28         int x = 25; // initialized each time useLocalVariable is called
29
30         System.out.printf(
31            "\nlocal x on entering method useLocalVariable is %d\n", x );
32         ++x; // modifies this method's local variable x
33         System.out.printf(
34            "local x before exiting method useLocalVariable is %d\n", x );
35      } // end method useLocalVariable
36
37      // modify class Scope's field x during each call
38      public void useField()
39      {
40         System.out.printf(
41            "\nfield x on entering method useField is %d\n", x );
42         x *= 10; // modifies class Scope's field x
43         System.out.printf(
44            "field x before exiting method useField is %d\n", x );
45      } // end method useField
46   } // end class Scope
```

Fig. 6.11 | Scope class demonstrating scopes of a field and local variables.

In class Scope, line 7 declares and initializes the field x to 1. This field is shadowed (hidden) in any block (or method) that declares a local variable named x. Method begin (lines 11–23) declares a local variable x (line 13) and initializes it to 5. This local variable's value is output to show that the field x (whose value is 1) is shadowed in method begin. The program declares two other methods—useLocalVariable (lines 26–35) and use-

```
 1   // Fig. 6.12: ScopeTest.java
 2   // Application to test class Scope.
 3
 4   public class ScopeTest
 5   {
 6      // application starting point
 7      public static void main( String args[] )
 8      {
 9         Scope testScope = new Scope();
10         testScope.begin();
11      } // end main
12   } // end class ScopeTest
```

```
local x in method begin is 5

local x on entering method useLocalVariable is 25
local x before exiting method useLocalVariable is 26

field x on entering method useField is 1
field x before exiting method useField is 10

local x on entering method useLocalVariable is 25
local x before exiting method useLocalVariable is 26

field x on entering method useField is 10
field x before exiting method useField is 100

local x in method begin is 5
```

Fig. 6.12 | Application to test class Scope.

Field (lines 38–45)—that each take no arguments and do not return results. Method begin calls each method twice (lines 17–20). Method useLocalVariable declares local variable x (line 28). When useLocalVariable is first called (line 17), it creates local variable x and initializes it to 25 (line 28), outputs the value of x (lines 30–31), increments x (line 32) and outputs the value of x again (lines 33–34). When uselLocalVariable is called a second time (line 19), it re-creates local variable x and re-initializes it to 25, so the output of each useLocalVariable call is identical.

Method useField does not declare any local variables. Therefore, when it refers to x, field x (line 7) of the class is used. When method useField is first called (line 18), it outputs the value (1) of field x (lines 40–41), multiplies the field x by 10 (line 42) and outputs the value (10) of field x again (lines 43–44) before returning. The next time method useField is called (line 20), the field has its modified value, 10, so the method outputs 10, then 100. Finally, in method begin, the program outputs the value of local variable x again (line 22) to show that none of the method calls modified begin's local variable x, because the methods all referred to variables named x in other scopes.

6.12 Method Overloading

Methods of the same name can be declared in the same class, as long as they have different sets of parameters (determined by the number, types and order of the parameters)—this is called **method overloading**. When an overloaded method is called, the Java compiler selects the appropriate method by examining the number, types and order of the arguments in the call. Method overloading is commonly used to create several methods with the same name that perform the same or similar tasks, but on different types or different numbers of arguments. For example, Math methods abs, min and max (summarized in Section 6.3) are overloaded with four versions each:

1. One with two double parameters.

2. One with two float parameters.

3. One with two int parameters.

4. One with two long parameters.

Our next example demonstrates declaring and invoking overloaded methods. You will see examples of overloaded constructors in Chapter 8.

Declaring Overloaded Methods

In our class MethodOverload (Fig. 6.13), we include two overloaded versions of a method called square—one that calculates the square of an int (and returns an int) and one that calculates the square of a double (and returns a double). Although these methods have the same name and similar parameter lists and bodies, you can think of them simply as *different* methods. It may help to think of the method names as "square of int" and "square of double," respectively. When the application begins execution, class MethodOverloadTest's main method (Fig. 6.14, lines 6–10) creates an object of class MethodOverload (line 8) and calls the object's method testOverloadedMethods (line 9) to produce the program's output (Fig. 6.14).

```
1   // Fig. 6.13: MethodOverload.java
2   // Overloaded method declarations.
3
4   public class MethodOverload
5   {
6      // test overloaded square methods
7      public void testOverloadedMethods()
8      {
9         System.out.printf( "Square of integer 7 is %d\n", square( 7 ) );
10        System.out.printf( "Square of double 7.5 is %f\n", square( 7.5 ) );
11     } // end method testOverloadedMethods
12
13     // square method with int argument
14     public int square( int intValue )
15     {
16        System.out.printf( "\nCalled square with int argument: %d\n",
17           intValue );
18        return intValue * intValue;
19     } // end method square with int argument
20
```

Fig. 6.13 | Overloaded method declarations. (Part 1 of 2.)

```
21        // square method with double argument
22        public double square( double doubleValue )
23        {
24           System.out.printf( "\nCalled square with double argument: %f\n",
25              doubleValue );
26           return doubleValue * doubleValue;
27        } // end method square with double argument
28   } // end class MethodOverload
```

Fig. 6.13 | Overloaded method declarations. (Part 2 of 2.)

```
1    // Fig. 6.14: MethodOverloadTest.java
2    // Application to test class MethodOverload.
3
4    public class MethodOverloadTest
5    {
6       public static void main( String args[] )
7       {
8          MethodOverload methodOverload = new MethodOverload();
9          methodOverload.testOverloadedMethods();
10      } // end main
11   } // end class MethodOverloadTest
```

```
Called square with int argument: 7
Square of integer 7 is 49

Called square with double argument: 7.500000
Square of double 7.5 is 56.250000
```

Fig. 6.14 | Overloaded method declarations.

In Fig. 6.13, line 9 invokes method square with the argument 7. Literal integer values are treated as type int, so the method call on line 9 invokes the version of square at lines 14–19 that specifies an int parameter. Similarly, line 10 invokes method square with the argument 7.5. Literal floating-point values are treated as type double, so the method call on line 10 invokes the version of square at lines 22–27 that specifies a double parameter. Each method first outputs a line of text to prove that the proper method was called in each case. In line 10, note that the argument value and return value are displayed with the format specifier %f and that we did not specify a precision in either case. By default, floating-point values are displayed with six digits of precision if the precision is not specified in the format specifier.

Distinguishing Between Overloaded Methods

The compiler distinguishes overloaded methods by their signature—a combination of the method's name and the number, types and order of its parameters. If the compiler looked only at method names during compilation, the code in Fig. 6.13 would be ambiguous— the compiler would not know how to distinguish between the two square methods (lines 14–19 and 22–27). Internally, the compiler uses longer method names that include the original method name, the types of each parameter and the exact order of the parameters to determine whether the methods in a class are unique in that class.

For example, in Fig. 6.13, the compiler might use the logical name "square of `int`" for the `square` method that specifies an `int` parameter and "square of `double`" for the `square` method that specifies a `double` parameter (the actual names the compiler uses are messier). If `method1`'s declaration begins as

```
void method1( int a, float b )
```

then the compiler might use the logical name "`method1` of `int` and `float`." If the parameters are specified as

```
void method1( float a, int b )
```

then the compiler might use the logical name "`method1` of `float` and `int`." Note that the order of the parameter types is important—the compiler considers the preceding two `method1` headers to be distinct.

Return Types of Overloaded Methods

In discussing the logical names of methods used by the compiler, we did not mention the return types of the methods. This is because method *calls* cannot be distinguished by return type. The program in Fig. 6.15 illustrates the compiler errors generated when two methods have the same signature and different return types. Overloaded methods can have different return types if the methods have different parameter lists. Also, overloaded methods need not have the same number of parameters.

```java
1   // Fig. 6.15: MethodOverloadError.java
2   // Overloaded methods with identical signatures
3   // cause compilation errors, even if return types are different.
4
5   public class MethodOverloadError
6   {
7      // declaration of method square with int argument
8      public int square( int x )
9      {
10         return x * x;
11     }
12
13     // second declaration of method square with int argument
14     // causes compilation error even though return types are different
15     public double square( int y )
16     {
17        return y * y;
18     }
19  } // end class MethodOverloadError
```

```
MethodOverloadError.java:15: square(int) is already defined in
MethodOverloadError
   public double square( int y )
                 ^
1 error
```

Fig. 6.15 | Overloaded method declarations with identical signatures cause compilation errors, even if the return types are different.

Common Programming Error 6.11

Declaring overloaded methods with identical parameter lists is a compilation error regardless of whether the return types are different.

6.13 (Optional) GUI and Graphics Case Study: Colors and Filled Shapes

Although you can create many interesting designs with just lines and basic shapes, class Graphics provides many more capabilities. The next two features we introduce are colors and filled shapes. Adding color brings another dimension to the drawings a user sees on the computer screen. Filled shapes fill entire regions with solid colors, rather than just drawing outlines.

Colors displayed on computer screens are defined by their red, green, and blue components. These components, called RGB values, have integer values from 0 to 255. The higher the value of a particular component, the brighter the particular shade will be in the final color. Java uses class **Color** in package java.awt to represent colors using their RGB values. For convenience, the Color object contains 13 predefined static Color objects—Color.BLACK, Color.BLUE, Color.CYAN, Color.DARK_GRAY, Color.GRAY, Color.GREEN, Color.LIGHT_GRAY, Color.MAGENTA, Color.ORANGE, Color.PINK, Color.RED, Color.WHITE and Color.YELLOW. Class Color also contains a constructor of the form:

```
public Color( int r, int g, int b )
```

so you can create custom colors by specifying values for the individual red, green and blue components of a color.

Filled rectangles and filled ovals are drawn using Graphics methods **fillRect** and **fillOval**, respectively. These two methods have the same parameters as their unfilled counterparts drawRect and drawOval; the first two parameters are the coordinates for the upper-left corner of the shape, while the next two parameters determine its width and height. The example in Fig. 6.16 and Fig. 6.17 demonstrates colors and filled shapes by drawing and displaying a yellow smiley face on the screen.

The import statements in lines 3–5 of Fig. 6.16 import Color, Graphics and JPanel. Class DrawSmiley uses class Color to specify drawing colors and class Graphics to draw. Class JPanel again provides the area in which we draw. Line 14 in method paintComponent uses Graphics method **setColor** to set the current drawing color to Color.YELLOW. Method setColor requires one argument, the Color to set as the drawing color. In this case, we use the predefined object Color.YELLOW. Line 15 draws a circle with diameter 200 to represent the face—when the width and height arguments are identical, method fillOval draws a circle. Next, line 18 sets the color to Color.Black, and lines 19–20 draw the eyes. Line 23 draws the mouth as an oval, but this is not quite what we want. To create a happy face, we will "touch up" the mouth. Line 26 sets the color to Color.YELLOW, so any shapes we draw will blend in with the face. Line 27 draws a rectangle that is half the mouth's height. This "erases" the top half of the mouth, leaving just the bottom half. To create a better smile, line 28 draws another oval to slightly cover the upper portion of the mouth. Class DrawSmileyTest (Fig. 6.17) creates and displays a JFrame containing the drawing, resulting in the system calling method paintComponent to draw the smiley face.

```java
1   // Fig. 6.16: DrawSmiley.java
2   // Demonstrates filled shapes.
3   import java.awt.Color;
4   import java.awt.Graphics;
5   import javax.swing.JPanel;
6
7   public class DrawSmiley extends JPanel
8   {
9      public void paintComponent( Graphics g )
10     {
11        super.paintComponent( g );
12
13        // draw the face
14        g.setColor( Color.YELLOW );
15        g.fillOval( 10, 10, 200, 200 );
16
17        // draw the eyes
18        g.setColor( Color.BLACK );
19        g.fillOval( 55, 65, 30, 30 );
20        g.fillOval( 135, 65, 30, 30 );
21
22        // draw the mouth
23        g.fillOval( 50, 110, 120, 60 );
24
25        // "touch up" the mouth into a smile
26        g.setColor( Color.YELLOW );
27        g.fillRect( 50, 110, 120, 30 );
28        g.fillOval( 50, 120, 120, 40 );
29     } // end method paintComponent
30  } // end class DrawSmiley
```

Fig. 6.16 | Drawing a smiley face using colors and filled shapes.

```java
1   // Fig. 6.17: DrawSmileyTest.java
2   // Test application that displays a smiley face.
3   import javax.swing.JFrame;
4
5   public class DrawSmileyTest
6   {
7      public static void main( String args[] )
8      {
9         DrawSmiley panel = new DrawSmiley();
10        JFrame application = new JFrame();
11
12        application.setDefaultCloseOperation( JFrame.EXIT_ON_CLOSE );
13        application.add( panel );
14        application.setSize( 230, 250 );
15        application.setVisible( true );
16     } // end main
17  } // end class DrawSmileyTest
```

Fig. 6.17 | Creating JFrame to display a smiley face. (Part 1 of 2.)

Fig. 6.17 | Creating `JFrame` to display a smiley face. (Part 2 of 2.)

GUI and Graphics Case Study Exercises

6.1   Using method `fillOval`, draw a bull's-eye that alternates between two random colors, as in Fig. 6.18. Use the constructor `Color( int r, int g, int b )` with random arguments to generate random colors.

6.2   Create a program that draws 10 random filled shapes in random colors and positions (Fig. 6.19). Method `paintComponent` should contain a loop that iterates 10 times. In each iteration, the loop should determine whether to draw a filled rectangle or an oval, create a random color and choose coordinates and dimensions at random. The coordinates should be chosen based on the panel's width and height. Lengths of sides should be limited to half the width or height of the window. What happens each time `paintComponent` is called (i.e., the window is resized, uncovered, etc.)? We will resolve this issue in Chapter 8.

6.14 (Optional) Software Engineering Case Study: Identifying Class Operations

In the "Software Engineering Case Study" sections at the ends of Chapters 3, 4 and 5, we performed the first few steps in the object-oriented design of our ATM system. In Chapter 3, we identified the classes that we will need to implement and created our first class diagram. In Chapter 4, we described some attributes of our classes. In Chapter 5, we examined objects' states and modeled objects' state transitions and activities. In this section, we determine some of the class operations (or behaviors) needed to implement the ATM system.

Fig. 6.18 | A bull's-eye with two alternating, random colors.

Fig. 6.19 | Randomly generated shapes.

Identifying Operations

An operation is a service that objects of a class provide to clients (users) of the class. Consider the operations of some real-world objects. A radio's operations include setting its station and volume (typically invoked by a person adjusting the radio's controls). A car's operations include accelerating (invoked by the driver pressing the accelerator pedal), decelerating (invoked by the driver pressing the brake pedal or releasing the gas pedal), turning and shifting gears. Software objects can offer operations as well—for example, a software graphics object might offer operations for drawing a circle, drawing a line, drawing a square and the like. A spreadsheet software object might offer operations like printing the spreadsheet, totaling the elements in a row or column and graphing information in the spreadsheet as a bar chart or pie chart.

We can derive many of the operations of each class by examining the key verbs and verb phrases in the requirements document. We then relate each of these to particular classes in our system (Fig. 6.20). The verb phrases in Fig. 6.20 help us determine the operations of each class.

Modeling Operations

To identify operations, we examine the verb phrases listed for each class in Fig. 6.20. The "executes financial transactions" phrase associated with class ATM implies that class ATM instructs transactions to execute. Therefore, classes BalanceInquiry, Withdrawal and Deposit each need an operation to provide this service to the ATM. We place this operation (which we have named execute) in the third compartment of the three transaction classes in the updated class diagram of Fig. 6.21. During an ATM session, the ATM object will invoke the execute operation of each transaction object to tell it to execute.

Class	Verbs and verb phrases
ATM	executes financial transactions
BalanceInquiry	[none in the requirements document]
Withdrawal	[none in the requirements document]
Deposit	[none in the requirements document]
BankDatabase	authenticates a user, retrieves an account balance, credits a deposit amount to an account, debits a withdrawal amount from an account
Account	retrieves an account balance, credits a deposit amount to an account, debits a withdrawal amount from an account
Screen	displays a message to the user
Keypad	receives numeric input from the user
CashDispenser	dispenses cash, indicates whether it contains enough cash to satisfy a withdrawal request
DepositSlot	receives a deposit envelope

Fig. 6.20 | Verbs and verb phrases for each class in the ATM system.

The UML represents operations (which are implemented as methods in Java) by listing the operation name, followed by a comma-separated list of parameters in parentheses, a colon and the return type:

operationName(parameter1 , parameter2 , ... , parameterN) : return type

Each parameter in the comma-separated parameter list consists of a parameter name, followed by a colon and the parameter type:

parameterName : parameterType

For the moment, we do not list the parameters of our operations—we will identify and model the parameters of some of the operations shortly. For some of the operations, we do not yet know the return types, so we also omit them from the diagram. These omissions are perfectly normal at this point. As our design and implementation proceed, we will add the remaining return types.

Figure 6.20 lists the phrase "authenticates a user" next to class BankDatabase—the database is the object that contains the account information necessary to determine whether the account number and PIN entered by a user match those of an account held at the bank. Therefore, class BankDatabase needs an operation that provides an authentication service to the ATM. We place the operation authenticateUser in the third compartment of class BankDatabase (Fig. 6.21). However, an object of class Account, not class BankDatabase, stores the account number and PIN that must be accessed to authenticate a user, so class Account must provide a service to validate a PIN obtained through user input against a PIN stored in an Account object. Therefore, we add a validatePIN operation to class Account. Note that we specify a return type of Boolean for the authenticateUser and validatePIN operations. Each operation returns a value indi-

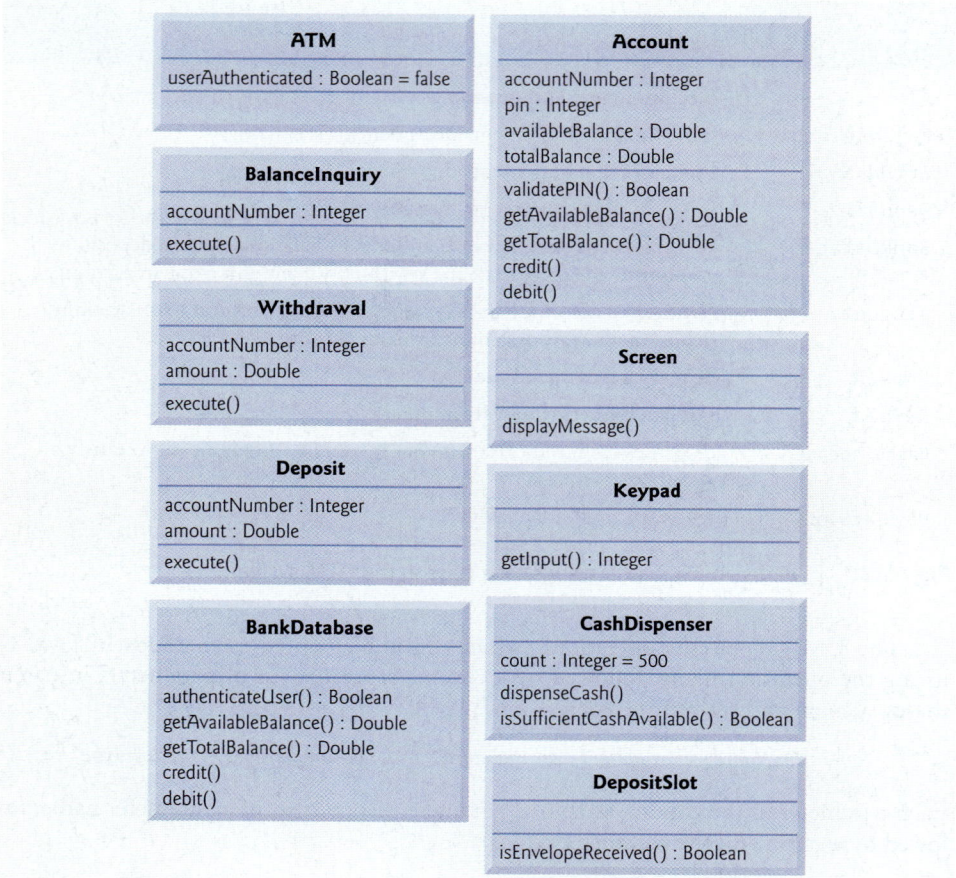

Fig. 6.21 | Classes in the ATM system with attributes and operations.

cating either that the operation was successful in performing its task (i.e., a return value of true) or that it was not (i.e., a return value of false).

Figure 6.20 lists several additional verb phrases for class BankDatabase: "retrieves an account balance," "credits a deposit amount to an account" and "debits a withdrawal amount from an account." Like "authenticates a user," these remaining phrases refer to services that the database must provide to the ATM, because the database holds all the account data used to authenticate a user and perform ATM transactions. However, objects of class Account actually perform the operations to which these phrases refer. Thus, we assign an operation to both class BankDatabase and class Account to correspond to each of these phrases. Recall from Section 3.10 that, because a bank account contains sensitive information, we do not allow the ATM to access accounts directly. The database acts as an intermediary between the ATM and the account data, thus preventing unauthorized access. As we will see in Section 7.14, class ATM invokes the operations of class BankDatabase, each of which in turn invokes the operation with the same name in class Account.

The phrase "retrieves an account balance" suggests that classes BankDatabase and Account each need a getBalance operation. However, recall that we created two attributes in class Account to represent a balance—availableBalance and totalBalance. A balance inquiry requires access to both balance attributes so that it can display them to the user, but a withdrawal needs to check only the value of availableBalance. To allow objects in the system to obtain each balance attribute individually, we add operations getAvailableBalance and getTotalBalance to the third compartment of classes Bank-Database and Account (Fig. 6.21). We specify a return type of Double for these operations because the balance attributes which they retrieve are of type Double.

The phrases "credits a deposit amount to an account" and "debits a withdrawal amount from an account" indicate that classes BankDatabase and Account must perform operations to update an account during a deposit and withdrawal, respectively. We there-fore assign credit and debit operations to classes BankDatabase and Account. You may recall that crediting an account (as in a deposit) adds an amount only to the totalBalance attribute. Debiting an account (as in a withdrawal), on the other hand, subtracts the amount from both balance attributes. We hide these implementation details inside class Account. This is a good example of encapsulation and information hiding.

If this were a real ATM system, classes BankDatabase and Account would also provide a set of operations to allow another banking system to update a user's account balance after either confirming or rejecting all or part of a deposit. Operation confirmDepositAmount, for example, would add an amount to the availableBalance attribute, thus making deposited funds available for withdrawal. Operation rejectDepositAmount would sub-tract an amount from the totalBalance attribute to indicate that a specified amount, which had recently been deposited through the ATM and added to the totalBalance, was not found in the deposit envelope. The bank would invoke this operation after deter-mining either that the user failed to include the correct amount of cash or that any checks did not clear (i.e, they "bounced"). While adding these operations would make our system more complete, we do not include them in our class diagrams or our implementation because they are beyond the scope of the case study.

Class Screen "displays a message to the user" at various times in an ATM session. All visual output occurs through the screen of the ATM. The requirements document describes many types of messages (e.g., a welcome message, an error message, a thank you message) that the screen displays to the user. The requirements document also indicates that the screen displays prompts and menus to the user. However, a prompt is really just a message describing what the user should input next, and a menu is essentially a type of prompt consisting of a series of messages (i.e., menu options) displayed consecutively. Therefore, rather than assign class Screen an individual operation to display each type of message, prompt and menu, we simply create one operation that can display any message specified by a parameter. We place this operation (displayMessage) in the third compart-ment of class Screen in our class diagram (Fig. 6.21). Note that we do not worry about the parameter of this operation at this time—we model the parameter later in this section.

From the phrase "receives numeric input from the user" listed by class Keypad in Fig. 6.20, we conclude that class Keypad should perform a getInput operation. Because the ATM's keypad, unlike a computer keyboard, contains only the numbers 0–9, we specify that this operation returns an integer value. Recall from the requirements docu-ment that in different situations the user may be required to enter a different type of number (e.g., an account number, a PIN, the number of a menu option, a deposit amount as a number of cents). Class `Keypad` simply obtains a numeric value for a client of the class—it does not determine whether the value meets any specific criteria. Any class that uses this operation must verify that the user entered an appropriate number in a given situation, then respond accordingly (i.e., display an error message via class `Screen`). [*Note:* When we implement the system, we simulate the ATM's keypad with a computer keyboard, and for simplicity we assume that the user does not enter non-numeric input using keys on the computer keyboard that do not appear on the ATM's keypad.]

Figure 6.20 lists "dispenses cash" for class `CashDispenser`. Therefore, we create operation `dispenseCash` and list it under class `CashDispenser` in Fig. 6.21. Class `CashDispenser` also "indicates whether it contains enough cash to satisfy a withdrawal request." Thus, we include `isSufficientCashAvailable`, an operation that returns a value of UML type `Boolean`, in class `CashDispenser`. Figure 6.20 also lists "receives a deposit envelope" for class `DepositSlot`. The deposit slot must indicate whether it received an envelope, so we place an operation `isEnvelopeReceived`, which returns a `Boolean` value, in the third compartment of class `DepositSlot`. [*Note:* A real hardware deposit slot would most likely send the ATM a signal to indicate that an envelope was received. We simulate this behavior, however, with an operation in class `DepositSlot` that class `ATM` can invoke to find out whether the deposit slot received an envelope.]

We do not list any operations for class `ATM` at this time. We are not yet aware of any services that class `ATM` provides to other classes in the system. When we implement the system with Java code, however, operations of this class, and additional operations of the other classes in the system, may emerge.

Identifying and Modeling Operation Parameters

So far, we have not been concerned with the parameters of our operations—we have attempted to gain only a basic understanding of the operations of each class. Let's now take a closer look at some operation parameters. We identify an operation's parameters by examining what data the operation requires to perform its assigned task.

Consider the `authenticateUser` operation of class `BankDatabase`. To authenticate a user, this operation must know the account number and PIN supplied by the user. Thus we specify that operation `authenticateUser` takes integer parameters `userAccountNumber` and `userPIN`, which the operation must compare to the account number and PIN of an `Account` object in the database. We prefix these parameter names with "user" to avoid confusion between the operation's parameter names and the attribute names that belong to class `Account`. We list these parameters in the class diagram in Fig. 6.22 that models only class `BankDatabase`. [*Note:* It is perfectly normal to model only one class in a class diagram. In this case, we are most concerned with examining the parameters of this one class in particular, so we omit the other classes. In class diagrams later in the case study, in which parameters are no longer the focus of our attention, we omit these parameters to save space. Remember, however, that the operations listed in these diagrams still have parameters.]

Recall that the UML models each parameter in an operation's comma-separated parameter list by listing the parameter name, followed by a colon and the parameter type (in UML notation). Figure 6.22 thus specifies that operation `authenticateUser` takes two parameters—`userAccountNumber` and `userPIN`, both of type `Integer`. When we implement the system in Java, we will represent these parameters with `int` values.

BankDatabase
authenticateUser(userAccountNumber : Integer : userPIN : Integer) : Boolean getAvailableBalance(userAccountNumber : Integer) : Double getTotalBalance(userAccountNumber : Integer) : Double credit(userAccountNumber : Integer, amount : Double) debit(userAccountNumber : Integer, amount : Double)

Fig. 6.22 | Class `BankDatabase` with operation parameters.

Class `BankDatabase` operations `getAvailableBalance`, `getTotalBalance`, `credit` and `debit` also each require a `userAccountNumber` parameter to identify the account to which the database must apply the operations, so we include these parameters in the class diagram of Fig. 6.22. In addition, operations `credit` and `debit` each require a `Double` parameter `amount` to specify the amount of money to be credited or debited, respectively.

The class diagram in Fig. 6.23 models the parameters of class `Account`'s operations. Operation `validatePIN` requires only a `userPIN` parameter, which contains the user-specified PIN to be compared with the PIN associated with the account. Like their counterparts in class `BankDatabase`, operations `credit` and `debit` in class `Account` each require a `Double` parameter `amount` that indicates the amount of money involved in the operation. Operations `getAvailableBalance` and `getTotalBalance` in class `Account` require no additional data to perform their tasks. Note that class `Account`'s operations do not require an account number parameter to distinguish between `Accounts`, because these operations can be invoked only on a specific `Account` object.

Figure 6.24 models class `Screen` with a parameter specified for operation `displayMessage`. This operation requires only a `String` parameter `message` that indicates the text to be displayed. Recall that the parameter types listed in our class diagrams are in UML notation, so the `String` type listed in Fig. 6.24 refers to the UML type. When we implement the system in Java, we will in fact use the Java class `String` to represent this parameter.

The class diagram in Fig. 6.25 specifies that operation `dispenseCash` of class `CashDispenser` takes a `Double` parameter `amount` to indicate the amount of cash (in dollars) to be dispensed. Operation `isSufficientCashAvailable` also takes a `Double` parameter `amount` to indicate the amount of cash in question.

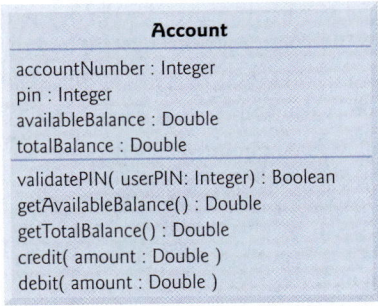

Account
accountNumber : Integer pin : Integer availableBalance : Double totalBalance : Double
validatePIN(userPIN: Integer) : Boolean getAvailableBalance() : Double getTotalBalance() : Double credit(amount : Double) debit(amount : Double)

Fig. 6.23 | Class `Account` with operation parameters.

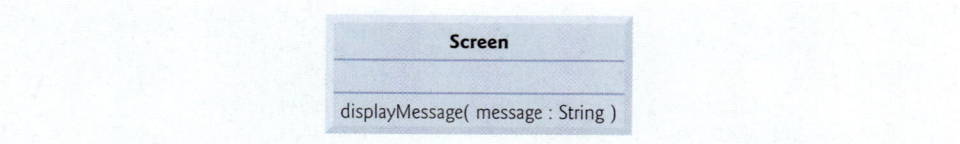

Fig. 6.24 | Class Screen with operation parameters.

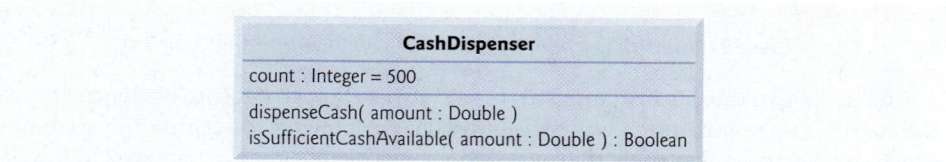

Fig. 6.25 | Class CashDispenser with operation parameters.

Note that we do not discuss parameters for operation execute of classes BalanceInquiry, Withdrawal and Deposit, operation getInput of class Keypad and operation isEnvelopeReceived of class DepositSlot. At this point in our design process, we cannot determine whether these operations require additional data to perform their tasks, so we leave their parameter lists empty. As we progress through the case study, we may decide to add parameters to these operations.

In this section, we have determined many of the operations performed by the classes in the ATM system. We have identified the parameters and return types of some of the operations. As we continue our design process, the number of operations belonging to each class may vary—we might find that new operations are needed or that some current operations are unnecessary—and we might determine that some of our class operations need additional parameters and different return types.

Software Engineering Case Study Self-Review Exercises

6.1 Which of the following is not a behavior?
  a) reading data from a file
  b) printing output
  c) text output
  d) obtaining input from the user

6.2 If you were to add to the ATM system an operation that returns the amount attribute of class Withdrawal, how and where would you specify this operation in the class diagram of Fig. 6.21?

6.3 Describe the meaning of the following operation listing that might appear in a class diagram for an object-oriented design of a calculator:

```
add( x : Integer, y : Integer ) : Integer
```

Answers to Software Engineering Case Study Self-Review Exercises

6.1 c.

6.2 To specify an operation that retrieves the amount attribute of class Withdrawal, the following operation listing would be placed in the operation (i.e., third) compartment of class Withdrawal:

```
getAmount( ) : Double
```

6.3 This operation listing indicates an operation named add that takes integers x and y as parameters and returns an integer value.

6.15 Wrap-Up

In this chapter, you learned more about the details of method declarations. You also learned the difference between non-static and static methods and how to call static methods by preceding the method name with the name of the class in which it appears and a dot (.). You learned how to use operator + to perform string concatenations. You learned how to declare named constants using both enum types and public final static variables. You saw how to use class Random to generate sets of random numbers that can be used for simulations. You also learned about the scope of fields and local variables in a class. Finally, you learned that multiple methods in one class can be overloaded by providing methods with the same name and different signatures. Such methods can be used to perform the same or similar tasks using different types or different numbers of parameters.

In Chapter 7, you will learn how to maintain lists and tables of data in arrays. You will see a more elegant implementation of the application that rolls a die 6000 times and two enhanced versions of our GradeBook case study that you studied in Chapters 3–5. You will also learn how to access an application's command-line arguments that are passed to method main when an application begins execution.

Summary

- Experience has shown that the best way to develop and maintain a large program is to construct it from small, simple pieces, or modules. This technique is called divide and conquer.
- There are three kinds of modules in Java—methods, classes and packages. Methods are declared within classes. Classes are typically grouped into packages so that they can be imported into programs and reused.
- Methods allow the programmer to modularize a program by separating its tasks into self-contained units. The statements in a method are written only once and hidden from other methods.
- Using existing methods as building blocks to create new programs is a form of software reusability that allows programmers to avoid repeating code within a program.
- A method call specifies the name of the method to call and provides the arguments that the called method requires to perform its task. When the method call completes, the method returns either a result or simply control to its caller.
- A class may contain static methods to perform common tasks that do not require an object of the class. Any data a static method might require to perform its tasks can be sent to the method as arguments in a method call. A static method is called by specifying the name of the class in which the method is declared followed by a dot (.) and the method name, as in

  ClassName.*methodName*(*arguments*)

- Method arguments may be constants, variables or expressions.
- Class Math provides static methods for performing common mathematical calculations. Class Math declares two fields that represent commonly used mathematical constants: Math.PI and Math.E. The constant Math.PI (3.14159265358979323846) is the ratio of a circle's circumference to its diameter. The constant Math.E (2.7182818284590452354) is the base value for natural logarithms (calculated with static Math method log).

- `Math.PI` and `Math.E` are declared with the modifiers `public`, `final` and `static`. Making them `public` allows other programmers to use these fields in their own classes. Any field declared with keyword `final` is constant—its value cannot be changed after the field is initialized. Both `PI` and `E` are declared `final` because their values never change. Making these fields `static` allows them to be accessed via the class name `Math` and a dot (`.`) separator, just like class `Math`'s methods.

- When objects of a class containing `static` fields (class variables) are created, all the objects of that class share one copy of the class's `static` fields. Together the class variables and instance variables represent the fields of a class. You will learn more about `static` fields in Section 8.11.

- When you execute the Java Virtual Machine (JVM) with the `java` command, the JVM attempts to invoke the `main` method of the class you specify. The JVM loads the class specified by *Class-Name* and uses that class name to invoke method `main`. You can specify an optional list of `String`s (separated by spaces) as command-line arguments that the JVM will pass to your application.

- You can place a `main` method in every class you declare—only the `main` method in the class you use to execute the application will be called. Some programmers take advantage of this to build a small test program into each class they declare.

- When a method is called, the program makes a copy of the method's argument values and assigns them to the method's corresponding parameters, which are created and initialized when the method is called. When program control returns to the point in the program where the method was called, the method's parameters are removed from memory.

- A method can return at most one value, but the returned value could be a reference to an object that contains many values.

- Variables should be declared as fields of a class only if they are required for use in more than one method of the class or if the program should save their values between calls to the class's methods.

- There are three ways to call a method—using a method name by itself to call another method of the same class; using a variable that contains a reference to an object, followed by a dot (`.`) and the method name to call a method of the referenced object; and using the class name and a dot (`.`) to call a `static` method of a class.

- There are three ways to return control to a statement that calls a method. If the method does not return a result, control returns when the program flow reaches the method-ending right brace or when the statement

  ```
  return;
  ```

  is executed. If the method returns a result, the statement

  ```
  return expression;
  ```

  evaluates the *expression*, then immediately returns the resulting value to the caller.

- When a method has more than one parameter, the parameters are specified as a comma-separated list. There must be one argument in the method call for each parameter in the method declaration. Also, each argument must be consistent with the type of the corresponding parameter. If a method does not accept arguments, the parameter list is empty.

- `String`s can be concatenated using operator `+`, which places the characters of the right operand at the end of those in the left operand.

- Every primitive value and object in Java has a `String` representation. When an object is concatenated with a `String`, the object is converted to a `String`, then the two `String`s are concatenated.

- For primitive values used in string concatenation, the JVM handles the conversion of the primitive values to `String`s. If a `boolean` is concatenated with a `String`, the word `"true"` or the word "false" is used to represent the boolean value. If there are any trailing zeros in a floating-point value, these will be discarded when the number is concatenated to a String.

- All objects in Java have a special method named toString that returns a String representation of the object's contents. When an object is concatenated with a String, the JVM implicitly calls the object's toString method to obtain the string representation of the object.

- When a large String literal is typed into a program's source code, programmers sometimes break that String into several smaller Strings and place them on multiple lines of code for readability, then reassemble the Strings using concatenation.

- Stacks are known as last-in, first-out (LIFO) data structures—the last item pushed (inserted) on the stack is the first item popped (removed) from the stack.

- A called method must know how to return to its caller, so the return address of the calling method is pushed onto the program execution stack when the method is called. If a series of method calls occurs, the successive return addresses are pushed onto the stack in last-in, first-out order so that the last method to execute will be the first to return to its caller.

- The program execution stack contains the memory for the local variables used in each invocation of a method during a program's execution. This data is known as the activation record or stack frame of the method call. When a method call is made, the activation record for that method call is pushed onto the program execution stack. When the method returns to its caller, the activation record for this method call is popped off the stack and those local variables are no longer known to the program. If a local variable holding a reference to an object is the only variable in the program with a reference to that object, when the activation record containing that local variable is popped off the stack, the object can no longer be accessed by the program and will eventually be deleted from memory by the JVM during "garbage collection."

- The amount of memory in a computer is finite, so only a certain amount of memory can be used to store activation records on the program execution stack. If there are more method calls than can have their activation records stored on the program execution stack, an error known as a stack overflow occurs. The application will compile correctly, but its execution causes a stack overflow.

- An important feature of method calls is argument promotion—converting an argument's value to the type that the method expects to receive in its corresponding parameter.

- A set of promotion rules apply to expressions containing values of two or more primitive types and to primitive-type values passed as arguments to methods. Each value is promoted to the "highest" type in the expression. In cases where information may be lost due to conversion, the Java compiler requires the programmer to use a cast operator to explicitly force the conversion to occur.

- Objects of class Random (package java.util) can produce random int, long, float or double values. Math method random can produce double values in the range $0.0 \le x < 1.0$, where x is the value returned by method random.

- Random method nextInt generates a random int value in the range −2,147,483,648 to +2,147,483,647. The values returned by nextInt are actually pseudorandom numbers—a sequence of values produced by a complex mathematical calculation. That calculation uses the current time of day to seed the random-number generator such that each execution of a program yields a different sequence of random values.

- Class Random provides another version of method nextInt that receives an int argument and returns a value from 0 up to, but not including, the argument's value.

- Random numbers in a range can be generated with

      number = *shiftingValue* + randomNumbers.nextInt(*scalingFactor*);

   where *shiftingValue* specifies the first number in the desired range of consecutive integers, and *scalingFactor* specifies how many numbers are in the range.

- Random numbers can be chosen from nonconsecutive integer ranges, as in

      number = *shiftingValue* +
          differenceBetweenValues * randomNumbers.nextInt(*scalingFactor*);

  where *shiftingValue* specifies the first number in the range of values, *differenceBetweenValues* represents the difference between consecutive numbers in the sequence and *scalingFactor* specifies how many numbers are in the range.

- For debugging, it is sometimes useful to repeat the same sequence of pseudorandom numbers during each program execution to prove that your application is working for a specific sequence of random numbers before testing the program with different sequences of random numbers. When repeatability is important, you can create a Random object by passing a long integer value to the constructor. If the same seed is used every time the program executes, the Random object produces the same sequence of random numbers. You can also set a Random object's seed at any time by calling the object's setSeed method.

- An enumeration is introduced by the keyword enum (new to J2SE 5.0) and a type name. As with any class, braces ({ and }) delimit the body of an enum declaration. Inside the braces is a comma-separated list of enumeration constants, each representing a unique value. The identifiers in an enum must be unique. Variables of an enum type can be assigned only constants of that enum type.

- Constants can also be declared as public final static variables. Such constants are declared with all capital letters by convention to make them stand out in the program.

- Scope is the portion of the program in which an entity, such as a variable or a method, can be referred to by its name. Such an entity is said to be "in scope" for that portion of the program.

- The scope of a parameter declaration is the body of the method in which the declaration appears.

- The scope of a local-variable declaration is from the point at which the declaration appears to the end of that block.

- The scope of a label in a labeled break or continue statement is the labeled statement's body.

- The scope of a local-variable declaration that appears in the initialization section of a for statement's header is the body of the for statement and the other expressions in the header.

- The scope of a method or field of a class is the entire body of the class. This enables a class's methods to use simple names to call the class's other methods and to access the class's fields.

- Any block may contain variable declarations. If a local variable or parameter in a method has the same name as a field, the field is shadowed until the block terminates execution.

- Java allows several methods of the same name to be declared in a class, as long as the methods have different sets of parameters (determined by the number, order and types of the parameters). This technique is called method overloading.

- Overloaded methods are distinguished by their signatures—combinations of the methods' names and the number, types and order of their parameters. Methods cannot be distinguished by return type.

Terminology

activation record	comma-separated list of parameters
application programming interface	command-line argument
argument promotion	divide-and-conquer approach
block	element of chance
class variable	enum keyword
class method	enumeration

enumeration constant
`final` keyword
formal parameter
function
"hidden" fields
hide implementation details
hierarchical boss method/worker method
    relationship
invoke a method
Java API documentation
Java Application Programming Interface (API)
last-in, first-out (LIFO) data structure
local variable
make your point (game of craps)
method call
method call stack
method declaration
method overloading
modularizing a program with methods
module
`nextInt` method of `Random`
overload method
package
parameter
parameter list
popping (from a stack)

primitive type promotions
procedure
program execution stack
programmer-declared method
promotion rules
pushing (onto a stack)
pseudorandom number
`Random class`
random method of `Math`
random numbers
`return` keyword
reusable software components
scaling factor (random numbers)
scope of a declaration
seed value (random numbers)
`setSeed` method of `Random`
shadow a field
shift a range (random numbers)
shifting value (random numbers)
signature of a method
simulation
software reuse
stack
stack frame
stack overflow
string concatenation

Self-Review Exercises

6.1   Fill in the blanks in each of the following statements:

a) A method is invoked with a(n) _____.

b) A variable known only within the method in which it is declared is called a(n) _____.

c) The _____ statement in a called method can be used to pass the value of an expression back to the calling method.

d) The keyword _____ indicates that a method does not return a value.

e) Data can be added or removed only from the _____ of a stack.

f) Stacks are known as _____ data structures—the last item pushed (inserted) on the stack is the first item popped (removed) from the stack.

g) The three ways to return control from a called method to a caller are _____, _____ and _____.

h) An object of class _____ produces random numbers.

i) The program execution stack contains the memory for local variables on each invocation of a method during a program's execution. This data, stored as a portion of the program execution stack, is known as the _____ or _____ of the method call.

j) If there are more method calls than can be stored on the program execution stack, an error known as a(n) _____ occurs.

k) The _____ of a declaration is the portion of a program that can refer to the entity in the declaration by name.

l) In Java, it is possible to have several methods with the same name that each operate on different types or numbers of arguments. This feature is called method _____.

m) The program execution stack is also referred to as the _____ stack.

6.2 For the class `Craps` in Fig. 6.9, state the scope of each of the following entities:
a) the variable `randomNumbers`.
b) the variable `die1`.
c) the method `rollDice`.
d) the method `play`.
e) the variable `sumOfDice`.

6.3 Write an application that tests whether the examples of the `Math` class method calls shown in Fig. 6.2 actually produce the indicated results.

6.4 Give the method header for each of the following methods:
a) Method `hypotenuse`, which takes two double-precision, floating-point arguments `side1` and `side2` and returns a double-precision, floating-point result.
b) Method `smallest`, which takes three integers x, y and z and returns an integer.
c) Method `instructions`, which does not take any arguments and does not return a value. [*Note*: Such methods are commonly used to display instructions to a user.]
d) Method `intToFloat`, which takes an integer argument `number` and returns a floating-point result.

6.5 Find the error in each of the following program segments. Explain how to correct the error.
a)
```
int g()
{
    System.out.println( "Inside method g" );
    int h()
    {
        System.out.println( "Inside method h" );
    }
}
```
b)
```
int sum( int x, int y )
{
    int result;
    result = x + y;
}
```
c)
```
void f( float a );
{
    float a;
    System.out.println( a );
}
```
d)
```
void product()
{
    int a = 6, b = 5, c = 4, result;
    result = a * b * c;
    System.out.printf( "Result is %d\n", result );
    return result;
}
```

6.6 Write a complete Java application to prompt the user for the `double` radius of a sphere, and call method `sphereVolume` to calculate and display the volume of the sphere. Use the following statement to calculate the volume:

```
double volume = ( 4.0 / 3.0 ) * Math.PI * Math.pow( radius, 3 )
```

Answers to Self-Review Exercises

6.1   a) method call. b) local variable. c) return. d) void. e) top. f) last-in, first-out (LIFO).
g) return; or return *expression*; or encountering the closing right brace of a method. h) Random.
i) activation record, stack frame. j) stack overflow. k) scope. l) overloading. m) method call.

6.2   a) class body. b) block that defines method rollDice's body. c) class body. d) class body.
e) block that defines method play's body.

6.3   The following solution demonstrates the Math class methods in Fig. 6.2:

```
1   // Exercise 6.3: MathTest.java
2   // Testing the Math class methods.
3
4   public class MathTest
5   {
6      public static void main( String args[] )
7      {
8         System.out.printf( "Math.abs( 23.7 ) = %f\n", Math.abs( 23.7 ) );
9         System.out.printf( "Math.abs( 0.0 ) = %f\n", Math.abs( 0.0 ) );
10        System.out.printf( "Math.abs( -23.7 ) = %f\n", Math.abs( -23.7 ) );
11        System.out.printf( "Math.ceil( 9.2 ) = %f\n", Math.ceil( 9.2 ) );
12        System.out.printf( "Math.ceil( -9.8 ) = %f\n", Math.ceil( -9.8 ) );
13        System.out.printf( "Math.cos( 0.0 ) = %f\n", Math.cos( 0.0 ) );
14        System.out.printf( "Math.exp( 1.0 ) = %f\n", Math.exp( 1.0 ) );
15        System.out.printf( "Math.exp( 2.0 ) = %f\n", Math.exp( 2.0 ) );
16        System.out.printf( "Math.floor( 9.2 ) = %f\n", Math.floor( 9.2 ) );
17        System.out.printf( "Math.floor( -9.8 ) = %f\n",
18           Math.floor( -9.8 ) );
19        System.out.printf( "Math.log( Math.E ) = %f\n",
20           Math.log( Math.E ) );
21        System.out.printf( "Math.log( Math.E * Math.E ) = %f\n",
22           Math.log( Math.E * Math.E ) );
23        System.out.printf( "Math.max( 2.3, 12.7 ) = %f\n",
24           Math.max( 2.3, 12.7 ) );
25        System.out.printf( "Math.max( -2.3, -12.7 ) = %f\n",
26           Math.max( -2.3, -12.7 ) );
27        System.out.printf( "Math.min( 2.3, 12.7 ) = %f\n",
28           Math.min( 2.3, 12.7 ) );
29        System.out.printf( "Math.min( -2.3, -12.7 ) = %f\n",
30           Math.min( -2.3, -12.7 ) );
31        System.out.printf( "Math.pow( 2.0, 7.0 ) = %f\n",
32           Math.pow( 2.0, 7.0 ) );
33        System.out.printf( "Math.pow( 9.0, 0.5 ) = %f\n",
34           Math.pow( 9.0, 0.5 ) );
35        System.out.printf( "Math.sin( 0.0 ) = %f\n", Math.sin( 0.0 ) );
36        System.out.printf( "Math.sqrt( 900.0 ) = %f\n",
37           Math.sqrt( 900.0 ) );
38        System.out.printf( "Math.sqrt( 9.0 ) = %f\n", Math.sqrt( 9.0 ) );
39        System.out.printf( "Math.tan( 0.0 ) = %f\n", Math.tan( 0.0 ) );
40      } // end main
41   } // end class MathTest
```

```
Math.abs( 23.7 ) = 23.700000
Math.abs( 0.0 ) = 0.000000
Math.abs( -23.7 ) = 23.700000
Math.ceil( 9.2 ) = 10.000000
Math.ceil( -9.8 ) = -9.000000
Math.cos( 0.0 ) = 1.000000
Math.exp( 1.0 ) = 2.718282
Math.exp( 2.0 ) = 7.389056
Math.floor( 9.2 ) = 9.000000
Math.floor( -9.8 ) = -10.000000
Math.log( Math.E ) = 1.000000
Math.log( Math.E * Math.E ) = 2.000000
Math.max( 2.3, 12.7 ) = 12.700000
Math.max( -2.3, -12.7 ) = -2.300000
Math.min( 2.3, 12.7 ) = 2.300000
Math.min( -2.3, -12.7 ) = -12.700000
Math.pow( 2.0, 7.0 ) = 128.000000
Math.pow( 9.0, 0.5 ) = 3.000000
Math.sin( 0.0 ) = 0.000000
Math.sqrt( 900.0 ) = 30.000000
Math.sqrt( 9.0 ) = 3.000000
Math.tan( 0.0 ) = 0.000000
```

6.4 a) `double hypotenuse( double side1, double side2 )`
      b) `int smallest( int x, int y, int z )`
      c) `void instructions()`
      d) `float intToFloat( int number )`

6.5 a) Error: Method h is declared within method g.
       Correction: Move the declaration of h outside the declaration of g.
      b) Error: The method is supposed to return an integer, but does not.
       Correction: Delete the variable `result`, and place the statement
           `return x + y;`
       in the method, or add the following statement at the end of the method body:
           `return result;`
      c) Error: The semicolon after the right parenthesis of the parameter list is incorrect, and
       the parameter a should not be redeclared in the method.
       Correction: Delete the semicolon after the right parenthesis of the parameter list, and
       delete the declaration `float a;`.
      d) Error: The method returns a value when it is not supposed to.
       Correction: Change the return type from `void` to `int`.

6.6   The following solution calculates the volume of a sphere, using the radius entered by the user:

```
 1   // Exercise 6.6: Sphere.java
 2   // Calculate the volume of a sphere.
 3   import java.util.Scanner;
 4
 5   public class Sphere
 6   {
 7      // obtain radius from user and display volume of sphere
 8      public void determineSphereVolume()
 9      {
```

```
10          Scanner input = new Scanner( System.in );
11
12          System.out.print( "Enter radius of sphere: " );
13          double radius = input.nextDouble();
14
15          System.out.printf( "Volume is %f\n", sphereVolume( radius ) );
16       } // end method determineSphereVolume
17
18       // calculate and return sphere volume
19       public double sphereVolume( double radius )
20       {
21          double volume = ( 4.0 / 3.0 ) * Math.PI * Math.pow( radius, 3 );
22          return volume;
23       } // end method sphereVolume
24    } // end class Sphere
```

```
1    // Exercise 6.6: SphereTest.java
2    // Calculate the volume of a sphere.
3
4    public class SphereTest
5    {
6       // application starting point
7       public static void main( String args[] )
8       {
9          Sphere mySphere = new Sphere();
10          mySphere.determineSphereVolume();
11       } // end main
12    } // end class SphereTest
```

```
Enter radius of sphere: 4
Volume is 268.082573
```

Exercises

6.7   What is the value of x after each of the following statements is executed?

    a) x = Math.abs(7.5);
    b) x = Math.floor(7.5);
    c) x = Math.abs(0.0);
    d) x = Math.ceil(0.0);
    e) x = Math.abs(-6.4);
    f) x = Math.ceil(-6.4);
    g) x = Math.ceil(-Math.abs(-8 + Math.floor(-5.5)));

6.8   A parking garage charges a $2.00 minimum fee to park for up to three hours. The garage charges an additional $0.50 per hour for each hour *or part thereof* in excess of three hours. The maximum charge for any given 24-hour period is $10.00. Assume that no car parks for longer than 24 hours at a time. Write an application that calculates and displays the parking charges for each customer who parked in the garage yesterday. You should enter the hours parked for each customer. The program should display the charge for the current customer and should calculate and display the running total of yesterday's receipts. The program should use the method calculateCharges to determine the charge for each customer.

6.9   An application of method `Math.floor` is rounding a value to the nearest integer. The statement

```
y = Math.floor( x + 0.5 );
```

will round the number x to the nearest integer and assign the result to y. Write an application that reads `double` values and uses the preceding statement to round each of the numbers to the nearest integer. For each number processed, display both the original number and the rounded number.

6.10   `Math.floor` may be used to round a number to a specific decimal place. The statement

```
y = Math.floor( x * 10 + 0.5 ) / 10;
```

rounds x to the tenths position (i.e., the first position to the right of the decimal point). The statement

```
y = Math.floor( x * 100 + 0.5 ) / 100;
```

rounds x to the hundredths position (i.e., the second position to the right of the decimal point). Write an application that defines four methods for rounding a number x in various ways:
   a)   `roundToInteger( number )`
   b)   `roundToTenths( number )`
   c)   `roundToHundredths( number )`
   d)   `roundToThousandths( number )`

For each value read, your program should display the original value, the number rounded to the nearest integer, the number rounded to the nearest tenth, the number rounded to the nearest hundredth and the number rounded to the nearest thousandth.

6.11   Answer each of the following questions:
   a)   What does it mean to choose numbers "at random?"
   b)   Why is the `Math.random` method useful for simulating games of chance?
   c)   Why is it often necessary to scale or shift the values produced by a `Random` object?
   d)   Why is computerized simulation of real-world situations a useful technique?

6.12   Write statements that assign random integers to the variable *n* in the following ranges:
   a) $1 \leq n \leq 2$
   b) $1 \leq n \leq 100$
   c) $0 \leq n \leq 9$
   d) $1000 \leq n \leq 1112$
   e) $-1 \leq n \leq 1$
   f) $-3 \leq n \leq 11$

6.13   For each of the following sets of integers, write a single statement that will display a number at random from the set:
   a)   2, 4, 6, 8, 10.
   b)   3, 5, 7, 9, 11.
   c)   6, 10, 14, 18, 22.

6.14   Write a method `integerPower( base, exponent )` that returns the value of

$$base^{\,exponent}$$

For example, `integerPower( 3, 4 )` calculates 3^4 (or 3 * 3 * 3 * 3). Assume that `exponent` is a positive, nonzero integer and that `base` is an integer. Method `integerPower` should use a `for` or `while` loop to control the calculation. Do not use any math-library methods. Incorporate this method into an application that reads integer values for `base` and `exponent` and performs the calculation with the `integerPower` method.

6.15   Define a method `hypotenuse` that calculates the length of the hypotenuse of a right triangle when the lengths of the other two sides are given. (Use the sample data in Fig. 6.26.) The method

Triangle	Side 1	Side 2
1	3.0	4.0
2	5.0	12.0
3	8.0	15.0

Fig. 6.26 | Values for the sides of triangles in Exercise 6.15.

should take two arguments of type `double` and return the hypotenuse as a `double`. Incorporate this method into an application that reads values for `side1` and `side2` and performs the calculation with the `hypotenuse` method. Determine the length of the hypotenuse for each of the triangles in Fig. 6.26.

6.16   Write a method `multiple` that determines, for a pair of integers, whether the second integer is a multiple of the first. The method should take two integer arguments and return `true` if the second is a multiple of the first and `false` otherwise. Incorporate this method into an application that inputs a series of pairs of integers (one pair at a time) and determines whether the second value in each pair is a multiple of the first.

6.17   Write a method `isEven` that uses the remainder operator (%) to determine whether an integer is even. The method should take an integer argument and return `true` if the integer is even and `false` otherwise. Incorporate this method into an application that inputs a sequence of integers (one at a time) and determines whether each is even or odd.

6.18   Write a method `squareOfAsterisks` that displays a solid square (the same number of rows and columns) of asterisks whose side is specified in integer parameter `side`. For example, if `side` is 4, the method should display

```
****
****
****
****
```

Incorporate this method into an application that reads an integer value for `side` from the user and outputs the asterisks with the `squareOfAsterisks` method.

6.19   Modify the method created in Exercise 6.18 to form the square out of whatever character is contained in character parameter `fillCharacter`. Thus, if `side` is 5 and `fillCharacter` is "#", the method should display

```
#####
#####
#####
#####
#####
```

6.20   Write an application that prompts the user for the radius of a circle and uses a method called `circleArea` to calculate the area of the circle.

6.21   Write program segments that accomplish each of the following tasks:
  a) Calculate the integer part of the quotient when integer a is divided by integer b.
  b) Calculate the integer remainder when integer a is divided by integer b.
  c) Use the program pieces developed in parts (a) and (b) to write a method `displayDigits` that receives an integer between 1 and 99999 and displays it as a sequence of digits, separating each pair of digits by two spaces. For example, the integer 4562 should appear as

```
4  5  6  2
```

    d) Incorporate the method developed in part (c) into an application that inputs an integer and calls `displayDigits` by passing the method the integer entered. Display the results.

6.22 Implement the following integer methods:

    a) Method `celsius` returns the Celsius equivalent of a Fahrenheit temperature, using the calculation

```
C = 5.0 / 9.0 * ( F - 32 );
```

    b) Method `fahrenheit` returns the Fahrenheit equivalent of a Celsius temperature, using the calculation

```
F = 9.0 / 5.0 * C + 32;
```

    c) Use the methods from parts (a) and (b) to write an application that enables the user either to enter a Fahrenheit temperature and display the Celsius equivalent or to enter a Celsius temperature and display the Fahrenheit equivalent.

6.23 Write a method `minimum3` that returns the smallest of three floating-point numbers. Use the `Math.min` method to implement `minimum3`. Incorporate the method into an application that reads three values from the user, determines the smallest value and displays the result.

6.24 An integer number is said to be a *perfect number* if its factors, including 1 (but not the number itself), sum to the number. For example, 6 is a perfect number, because 6 = 1 + 2 + 3. Write a method `perfect` that determines whether parameter `number` is a perfect number. Use this method in an application that determines and displays all the perfect numbers between 1 and 1000. Display the factors of each perfect number to confirm that the number is indeed perfect. Challenge the computing power of your computer by testing numbers much larger than 1000. Display the results.

6.25 An integer is said to be *prime* if it is divisible by only 1 and itself. For example, 2, 3, 5 and 7 are prime, but 4, 6, 8 and 9 are not.

    a) Write a method that determines whether a number is prime.

    b) Use this method in an application that determines and displays all the prime numbers less than 10,000. How many numbers up to 10,000 do you have to test to ensure that you have found all the primes?

    c) Initially, you might think that $n/2$ is the upper limit for which you must test to see whether a number is prime, but you need only go as high as the square root of n. Why? Rewrite the program, and run it both ways. Estimate the performance improvement.

6.26 Write a method that takes an integer value and returns the number with its digits reversed. For example, given the number 7631, the method should return 1367. Incorporate the method into an application that reads a value from the user and displays the result.

6.27 The *greatest common divisor* (*GCD*) of two integers is the largest integer that evenly divides each of the two numbers. Write a method `gcd` that returns the greatest common divisor of two integers. Incorporate the method into an application that reads two values from the user and displays the result.

6.28 Write a method `qualityPoints` that inputs a student's average and returns 4 if the student's average is 90–100, 3 if the average is 80–89, 2 if the average is 70–79, 1 if the average is 60–69 and 0 if the average is lower than 60. Incorporate the method into an application that reads a value from the user and displays the result.

6.29 Write an application that simulates coin tossing. Let the program toss a coin each time the user chooses the "Toss Coin" menu option. Count the number of times each side of the coin appears. Display the results. The program should call a separate method `flip` that takes no arguments and returns `false` for tails and `true` for heads. [*Note*: If the program realistically simulates coin tossing, each side of the coin should appear approximately half the time.]

6.30 Computers are playing an increasing role in education. Write a program that will help an elementary school student learn multiplication. Use a `Random` object to produce two positive one-digit integers. The program should then prompt the user with a question, such as

```
How much is 6 times 7?
```

The student then inputs the answer. Next, the program checks the student's answer. If it is correct, display the message `"Very good!"` and ask another multiplication question. If the answer is wrong, display the message `"No. Please try again."` and let the student try the same question repeatedly until the student finally gets it right. A separate method should be used to generate each new question. This method should be called once when the application begins execution and each time the user answers the question correctly.

6.31 The use of computers in education is referred to as *computer-assisted instruction* (*CAI*). One problem that develops in CAI environments is student fatigue. This problem can be eliminated by varying the computer's responses to hold the student's attention. Modify the program of Exercise 6.30 so that the various comments are displayed for each correct answer and each incorrect answer as follows:
Responses to a correct answer:

```
Very good!
Excellent!
Nice work!
Keep up the good work!
```

Responses to an incorrect answer:

```
No. Please try again.
Wrong. Try once more.
Don't give up!
No. Keep trying.
```

Use random-number generation to choose a number from 1 to 4 that will be used to select an appropriate response to each answer. Use a `switch` statement to issue the responses.

6.32 More sophisticated computer-assisted instruction systems monitor the student's performance over a period of time. The decision to begin a new topic is often based on the student's success with previous topics. Modify the program of Exercise 6.31 to count the number of correct and incorrect responses typed by the student. After the student types 10 answers, your program should calculate the percentage of correct responses. If the percentage is lower than 75%, display `Please ask your instructor for extra help` and reset the program so another student can try it.

6.33 Write an application that plays "guess the number" as follows: Your program chooses the number to be guessed by selecting a random integer in the range 1 to 1000. The application displays the prompt `Guess a number between 1 and 1000`. The player inputs a first guess. If the player's guess is incorrect, your program should display `Too high. Try again.` or `Too low. Try again.` to help the player "zero in" on the correct answer. The program should prompt the user for the next guess. When the user enters the correct answer, display `Congratulations. You guessed the number!`, and allow the user to choose whether to play again. [*Note*: The guessing technique employed in this problem is similar to a binary search, which is discussed in Chapter 16, Searching and Sorting.]

6.34 Modify the program of Exercise 6.33 to count the number of guesses the player makes. If the number is 10 or fewer, display `Either you know the secret or you got lucky!` If the player guesses the number in 10 tries, display `Aha! You know the secret!` If the player makes more than 10 guesses, display `You should be able to do better!` Why should it take no more than 10 guesses? Well, with each "good guess," the player should be able to eliminate half of the numbers. Now show why any number from 1 to 1000 can be guessed in 10 or fewer tries.

6.35 Exercise 6.30 through Exercise 6.32 developed a computer-assisted instruction program to teach an elementary school student multiplication. Perform the following enhancements:

a) Modify the program to allow the user to enter a school grade-level capability. A grade level of 1 means that the program should use only single-digit numbers in the problems, a grade level of 2 means that the program should use numbers as large as two digits, and so on.

b) Modify the program to allow the user to pick the type of arithmetic problems he or she wishes to study. An option of 1 means addition problems only, 2 means subtraction problems only, 3 means multiplication problems only, 4 means division problems only and 5 means a random mixture of problems of all these types.

6.36 Write method `distance` to calculate the distance between two points (*x1*, *y1*) and (*x2*, *y2*). All numbers and return values should be of type `double`. Incorporate this method into an application that enables the user to enter the coordinates of the points.

6.37 Modify the craps program of Fig. 6.9 to allow wagering. Initialize variable `bankBalance` to 1000 dollars. Prompt the player to enter a `wager`. Check that `wager` is less than or equal to `bankBalance`, and if it is not, have the user reenter `wager` until a valid `wager` is entered. After a correct `wager` is entered, run one game of craps. If the player wins, increase `bankBalance` by `wager` and display the new `bankBalance`. If the player loses, decrease `bankBalance` by `wager`, display the new `bankBalance`, check whether `bankBalance` has become zero and, if so, display the message `"Sorry. You busted!"` As the game progresses, display various messages to create some "chatter," such as `"Oh, you're going for broke, huh?"` or `"Aw c'mon, take a chance!"` or `"You're up big. Now's the time to cash in your chips!"`. Implement the "chatter" as a separate method that randomly chooses the string to display.

6.38 Write an application that displays a table of the binary, octal, and hexadecimal equivalents of the decimal numbers in the range 1 through 256. If you are not familiar with these number systems, read Appendix E first.

Arrays

Now go, write it before them in a table, and note it in a book.
—Isaiah 30:8

To go beyond is as wrong as to fall short.
—Confucius

Begin at the beginning, … and go on till you come to the end: then stop.
—Lewis Carroll

OBJECTIVES

In this chapter you will learn:

- What arrays are.
- To use arrays to store data in and retrieve data from lists and tables of values.
- To declare an array, initialize an array and refer to individual elements of an array.
- To use the enhanced **for** statement to iterate through arrays.
- To pass arrays to methods.
- To declare and manipulate multidimensional arrays.
- To write methods that use variable-length argument lists.
- To read command-line arguments into a program.

7.1 Introduction

This chapter introduces the important topic of data structures—collections of related data items. Arrays are data structures consisting of related data items of the same type. Arrays are fixed-length entities—they remain the same length once they are created, although an array variable may be reassigned such that it refers to a new array of a different length.

After discussing how arrays are declared, created and initialized, this chapter presents a series of practical examples that demonstrate several common array manipulations. We also present a case study that examines how arrays can help simulate the shuffling and dealing of playing cards for use in an application that implements a card game. The chapter then introduces Java's enhanced `for` statement, which allows a program to access the data in an array more easily than the counter-controlled `for` statement presented in Section 5.3 does. Two sections of the chapter enhance the case study of class `GradeBook` in Chapters 3–5. In particular, we use arrays to enable the class to maintain a set of grades in memory and analyze student grades from multiple exams in a semester—two capabilities that were absent from previous versions of the class. These and other chapter examples demonstrate the ways in which arrays allow programmers to organize and manipulate data.

7.2 Arrays

An array is a group of variables (called elements or components) containing values that all have the same type. Recall that types are divided into two categories—primitive types and reference types. Arrays are objects, so they are considered reference types. As you will soon see, what we typically think of as an array is actually a reference to an array object in memory. The elements of an array can be either primitive types or reference types (including arrays, as we will see in Section 7.9). To refer to a particular element in an array, we specify the name of the reference to the array and the position number of the element in the array. The position number of the element is called the element's index or subscript.

Figure 7.1 shows a logical representation of an integer array called c. This array contains 12 elements. A program refers to any one of these elements with an **array-access expression** that includes the name of the array followed by the index of the particular element in **square brackets** ([]). The first element in every array has **index zero** and is sometimes called the **zeroth element.** Thus, the elements of array c are c[0], c[1], c[2] and so on. The highest index in array c is 11, which is 1 less than 12—the number of elements in the array. Array names follow the same conventions as other variable names.

An index must be a nonnegative integer. A program can use an expression as an index. For example, if we assume that variable a is 5 and variable b is 6, then the statement

```
c[ a + b ] += 2;
```

adds 2 to array element c[11]. Note that an indexed array name is an array-access expression. Such expressions can be used on the left side of an assignment to place a new value into an array element.

Common Programming Error 7.1

Using a value of type long as an array index results in a compilation error. An index must be an int value or a value of a type that can be promoted to int—namely, byte, short or char, but not long.

Let us examine array c in Fig. 7.1 more closely. The name of the array is c. Every array object knows its own length and maintains this information in a **length** field. The expression c.length accesses array c's length field to determine the length of the array. Note that, even though the length member of an array is public, it cannot be changed because it is a final variable. This array's 12 elements are referred to as c[0], c[1], c[2], ..., c[11]. The value of c[0] is -45, the value of c[1] is 6, the value of c[2] is 0, the value

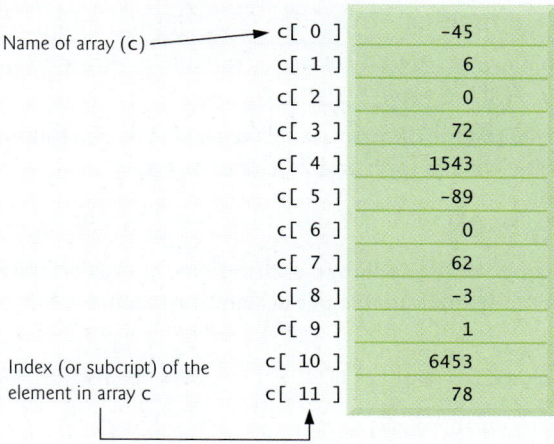

Fig. 7.1 | A 12-element array.

of c[7] is 62 and the value of c[11] is 78. To calculate the sum of the values contained in the first three elements of array c and store the result in variable sum, we would write

```
sum = c[ 0 ] + c[ 1 ] + c[ 2 ];
```

To divide the value of c[6] by 2 and assign the result to the variable x, we would write

```
x = c[ 6 ] / 2;
```

7.3 Declaring and Creating Arrays

Array objects occupy space in memory. Like other objects, arrays are created with keyword new. To create an array object, the programmer specifies the type of the array elements and the number of elements as part of an array-creation expression that uses keyword new. Such an expression returns a reference that can be stored in an array variable. The following declaration and array-creation expression create an array object containing 12 int elements and store the array's reference in variable c:

```
int c[] = new int[ 12 ];
```

This expression can be used to create the array shown in Fig. 7.1. This task also can be performed in two steps as follows:

```
int c[];             // declare the array variable
c = new int[ 12 ];   // create the array; assign to array variable
```

In the declaration, the square brackets following the variable name c indicate that c is a variable that will refer to an array (i.e., the variable will store an array reference). In the assignment statement, the array variable c receives the reference to a new array of 12 int elements. When an array is created, each element of the array receives a default value—zero for the numeric primitive-type elements, false for boolean elements and null for references (any nonprimitive type). As we will soon see, we can provide specific, nondefault initial element values when we create an array.

Common Programming Error 7.2

In an array declaration, specifying the number of elements in the square brackets of the declaration (e.g., int c[12];) is a syntax error.

A program can create several arrays in a single declaration. The following String array declaration reserves 100 elements for b and 27 elements for x:

```
String b[] = new String[ 100 ], x[] = new String[ 27 ];
```

In this case, the class name String applies to each variable in the declaration. For readability, we prefer to declare only one variable per declaration, as in:

```
String b[] = new String[ 100 ]; // create array b
String x[] = new String[ 27 ];  // create array x
```

Good Programming Practice 7.1

For readability, declare only one variable per declaration. Keep each declaration on a separate line, and include a comment describing the variable being declared.

When an array is declared, the type of the array and the square brackets can be combined at the beginning of the declaration to indicate that all the identifiers in the declaration are array variables. For example, the declaration

```
double[] array1, array2;
```

indicates that `array1` and `array2` are "array of `double`" variables. The preceding declaration is equivalent to:

```
double array1[];
double array2[];
```

or

```
double[] array1;
double[] array2;
```

The preceding pairs of declarations are equivalent—when only one variable is declared in each declaration, the square brackets can be placed either after the type or after the array variable name.

Common Programming Error 7.3

Declaring multiple array variables in a single declaration can lead to subtle errors. Consider the declaration `int[] a, b, c;`. If a, b and c should be declared as array variables, then this declaration is correct—placing square brackets directly following the type indicates that all the identifiers in the declaration are array variables. However, if only a is intended to be an array variable, and b and c are intended to be individual `int` variables, then this declaration is incorrect—the declaration `int a[], b, c;` would achieve the desired result.

A program can declare arrays of any type. Every element of a primitive-type array contains a value of the array's declared type. Similarly, in an array of a reference type, every element is a reference to an object of the array's declared type. For example, every element of an `int` array is an `int` value, and every element of a `String` array is a reference to a `String` object.

7.4 Examples Using Arrays

This section presents several examples that demonstrate declaring arrays, creating arrays, initializing arrays and manipulating array elements.

Creating and Initializing an Array

The application of Fig. 7.2 uses keyword `new` to create an array of 10 `int` elements, which are initially zero (the default for `int` variables).

Line 8 declares `array`—a reference capable of referring to an array of `int` elements. Line 10 creates the array object and assigns its reference to variable `array`. Line 12 outputs the column headings. The first column contains the index (0–9) of each array element, and the second column contains the default value (0) of each array element.

The `for` statement in lines 15–16 outputs the index number (represented by `counter`) and value of each array element (represented by `array[ counter ]`). Note that the loop control variable `counter` is initially 0—index values start at 0, so using zero-based counting allows the loop to access every element of the array. The `for`'s loop-continuation condition uses the expression `array.length` (line 15) to determine the length of the array. In this example, the length of the array is 10, so the loop continues executing as long as

```
1   // Fig. 7.2: InitArray.java
2   // Creating an array.
3
4   public class InitArray
5   {
6      public static void main( String args[] )
7      {
8         int array[]; // declare array named array
9
10        array = new int[ 10 ]; // create the space for array
11
12        System.out.printf( "%s%8s\n", "Index", "Value" ); // column headings
13
14        // output each array element's value
15        for ( int counter = 0; counter < array.length; counter++ )
16           System.out.printf( "%5d%8d\n", counter, array[ counter ] );
17     } // end main
18  } // end class InitArray
```

```
Index   Value
   0       0
   1       0
   2       0
   3       0
   4       0
   5       0
   6       0
   7       0
   8       0
   9       0
```

Fig. 7.2 | Initializing the elements of an array to default values of zero.

the value of control variable counter is less than 10. The highest index value of a 10-element array is 9, so using the less-than operator in the loop-continuation condition guarantees that the loop does not attempt to access an element beyond the end of the array (i.e., during the final iteration of the loop, counter is 9). We will soon see what Java does when it encounters such an out-of-range index at execution time.

Using an Array Initializer

A program can create an array and initialize its elements with an **array initializer**, which is a comma-separated list of expressions (called an **initializer list**) enclosed in braces ({ and }). In this case, the array length is determined by the number of elements in the initializer list. For example, the declaration

```
int n[] = { 10, 20, 30, 40, 50 };
```

creates a five-element array with index values 0, 1, 2, 3 and 4. Element n[0] is initialized to 10, n[1] is initialized to 20, and so on. This declaration does not require new to create the array object. When the compiler encounters an array declaration that includes an initializer list, the compiler counts the number of initializers in the list to determine the size of the array, then sets up the appropriate new operation "behind the scenes."

The application in Fig. 7.3 initializes an integer array with 10 values (line 9) and displays the array in tabular format. The code for displaying the array elements (lines 14–15) is identical to that in Fig. 7.2 (lines 15–16).

Calculating a Value to Store in Each Array Element

Some programs calculate the value stored in each array element. The application in Fig. 7.4 creates a 10-element array and assigns to each element one of the even integers from 2 to 20 (2, 4, 6, ..., 20). Then the application displays the array in tabular format. The for statement at lines 12–13 calculates an array element's value by multiplying the current value of the for loop's control variable counter by 2, then adding 2.

Line 8 uses the modifier **final** to declare the **constant variable** ARRAY_LENGTH, whose value is 10. Constant variables (also known as final variables) must be initialized before they are used and cannot be modified thereafter. If an attempt is made to modify a final variable after it is initialized in its declaration (as in line 8), the compiler issues the error message

```
cannot assign a value to final variable variableName
```

```
 1   // Fig. 7.3: InitArray.java
 2   // Initializing the elements of an array with an array initializer.
 3
 4   public class InitArray
 5   {
 6      public static void main( String args[] )
 7      {
 8         // initializer list specifies the value for each element
 9         int array[] = { 32, 27, 64, 18, 95, 14, 90, 70, 60, 37 };
10
11         System.out.printf( "%s%8s\n", "Index", "Value" ); // column headings
12
13         // output each array element's value
14         for ( int counter = 0; counter < array.length; counter++ )
15            System.out.printf( "%5d%8d\n", counter, array[ counter ] );
16      } // end main
17   } // end class InitArray
```

```
Index    Value
    0       32
    1       27
    2       64
    3       18
    4       95
    5       14
    6       90
    7       70
    8       60
    9       37
```

Fig. 7.3 | Initializing the elements of an array with an array initializer.

```
1   // Fig. 7.4: InitArray.java
2   // Calculating values to be placed into elements of an array.
3
4   public class InitArray
5   {
6      public static void main( String args[] )
7      {
8         final int ARRAY_LENGTH = 10; // declare constant
9         int array[] = new int[ ARRAY_LENGTH ]; // create array
10
11        // calculate value for each array element
12        for ( int counter = 0; counter < array.length; counter++ )
13           array[ counter ] = 2 + 2 * counter;
14
15        System.out.printf( "%s%8s\n", "Index", "Value" ); // column headings
16
17        // output each array element's value
18        for ( int counter = 0; counter < array.length; counter++ )
19           System.out.printf( "%5d%8d\n", counter, array[ counter ] );
20     } // end main
21  } // end class InitArray
```

```
Index   Value
   0       2
   1       4
   2       6
   3       8
   4      10
   5      12
   6      14
   7      16
   8      18
   9      20
```

Fig. 7.4 | Calculating values to be placed into elements of an array.

If an attempt is made to access the value of a `final` variable before it is initialized, the compiler issues the error message

> variable *variableName* might not have been initialized

Good Programming Practice 7.2

Constant variables also are called named constants or read-only variables. Such variables often make programs more readable than programs that use literal values (e.g., 10)—a named constant such as ARRAY_LENGTH clearly indicates its purpose, whereas a literal value could have different meanings based on the context in which it is used.

Common Programming Error 7.4

Assigning a value to a constant after the variable has been initialized is a compilation error.

Common Programming Error 7.5

Attempting to use a constant before it is initialized is a compilation error.

Summing the Elements of an Array

Often, the elements of an array represent a series of values to be used in a calculation. For example, if the elements of an array represent exam grades, a professor may wish to total the elements of the array and use that sum to calculate the class average for the exam. The examples using class GradeBook later in the chapter, namely Fig. 7.14 and Fig. 7.18, use this technique.

The application in Fig. 7.5 sums the values contained in a 10-element integer array. The program declares, creates and initializes the array at line 8. The for statement performs the calculations. [*Note:* The values supplied as array initializers are often read into a program rather than specified in an initializer list. For example, an application could input the values from a user or from a file on disk (as discussed in Chapter 14, Files and Streams). Reading the data into a program makes the program more reusable, because it can be used with different sets of data.]

Using Bar Charts to Display Array Data Graphically

Many programs present data to users in a graphical manner. For example, numeric values are often displayed as bars in a bar chart. In such a chart, longer bars represent proportionally larger numeric values. One simple way to display numeric data graphically is with a bar chart that shows each numeric value as a bar of asterisks (*).

Professors often like to examine the distribution of grades on an exam. A professor might graph the number of grades in each of several categories to visualize the grade distribution for the exam. Suppose the grades on an exam were 87, 68, 94, 100, 83, 78, 85, 91, 76 and 87. Note that there was one grade of 100, two grades in the 90s, four grades in the 80s, two grades in the 70s, one grade in the 60s and no grades below 60. Our next applica-

```
1   // Fig. 7.5: SumArray.java
2   // Computing the sum of the elements of an array.
3
4   public class SumArray
5   {
6      public static void main( String args[] )
7      {
8         int array[] = { 87, 68, 94, 100, 83, 78, 85, 91, 76, 87 };
9         int total = 0;
10
11        // add each element's value to total
12        for ( int counter = 0; counter < array.length; counter++ )
13           total += array[ counter ];
14
15        System.out.printf( "Total of array elements: %d\n", total );
16     } // end main
17  } // end class SumArray
```

```
Total of array elements: 849
```

Fig. 7.5 | Computing the sum of the elements of an array.

```
1   // Fig. 7.6: BarChart.java
2   // Bar chart printing program.
3
4   public class BarChart
5   {
6      public static void main( String args[] )
7      {
8         int array[] = { 0, 0, 0, 0, 0, 0, 1, 2, 4, 2, 1 };
9
10        System.out.println( "Grade distribution:" );
11
12        // for each array element, output a bar of the chart
13        for ( int counter = 0; counter < array.length; counter++ )
14        {
15           // output bar label ( "00-09: ", ..., "90-99: ", "100: " )
16           if ( counter == 10 )
17              System.out.printf( "%5d: ", 100 );
18           else
19              System.out.printf( "%02d-%02d: ",
20                 counter * 10, counter * 10 + 9  );
21
22           // print bar of asterisks
23           for ( int stars = 0; stars < array[ counter ]; stars++ )
24              System.out.print( "*" );
25
26           System.out.println(); // start a new line of output
27        } // end outer for
28     } // end main
29  } // end class BarChart
```

```
Grade distribution:
00-09:
10-19:
20-29:
30-39:
40-49:
50-59:
60-69: *
70-79: **
80-89: ****
90-99: **
  100: *
```

Fig. 7.6 | Bar chart printing program.

tion (Fig. 7.6) stores this grade distribution data in an array of 11 elements, each corresponding to a category of grades. For example, array[0] indicates the number of grades in the range 0–9, array[7] indicates the number of grades in the range 70–79 and array[10] indicates the number of 100 grades. The two versions of class GradeBook later in the chapter (Fig. 7.14 and Fig. 7.18) contain code that calculates these grade frequencies based on a set of grades. For now, we manually create the array by looking at the set of grades.

The application reads the numbers from the array and graphs the information as a bar chart. The program displays each grade range followed by a bar of asterisks indicating the number of grades in that range. To label each bar, lines 16–20 output a grade range (e.g., "70-79: ") based on the current value of counter. When counter is 10, line 17 outputs 100 with a field width of 5, followed by a colon and a space, to align the label "100: " with the other bar labels. The nested for statement (lines 23–24) outputs the bars. Note the loop-continuation condition at line 23 (stars < array[counter]). Each time the program reaches the inner for, the loop counts from 0 up to array[counter], thus using a value in array to determine the number of asterisks to display. In this example, array[0]–array[5] contain zeroes because no students received a grade below 60. Thus, the program displays no asterisks next to the first six grade ranges. Note that line 19 uses the format specifier %02d to output the numbers in a grade range. This specifier indicates that an int value should be formatted as a field of two digits. The **0 flag** in the format specifier indicates that values with fewer digits than the field width (2) should begin with a leading 0.

Using the Elements of an Array as Counters
Sometimes, programs use counter variables to summarize data, such as the results of a survey. In Fig. 6.8, we used separate counters in our die-rolling program to track the number of occurrences of each side of a die as the program rolled the die 6000 times. An array version of the application in Fig. 6.8 is shown in Fig. 7.7.

```java
1   // Fig. 7.7: RollDie.java
2   // Roll a six-sided die 6000 times.
3   import java.util.Random;
4
5   public class RollDie
6   {
7      public static void main( String args[] )
8      {
9         Random randomNumbers = new Random(); // random number generator
10        int frequency[] = new int[ 7 ]; // array of frequency counters
11
12        // roll die 6000 times; use die value as frequency index
13        for ( int roll = 1; roll <= 6000; roll++ )
14           ++frequency[ 1 + randomNumbers.nextInt( 6 ) ];
15
16        System.out.printf( "%s%10s\n", "Face", "Frequency" );
17
18        // output each array element's value
19        for ( int face = 1; face < frequency.length; face++ )
20           System.out.printf( "%4d%10d\n", face, frequency[ face ] );
21     } // end main
22  } // end class RollDie
```

```
Face Frequency
   1        988
   2        963
   3       1018
   4       1041
   5        978
   6       1012
```

Fig. 7.7 | Die-rolling program using arrays instead of switch.

Fig. 7.7 uses the array frequency (line 10) to count the occurrences of each side of the die. *The single statement in line 14 of this program replaces lines 23–46 of Fig. 6.8.* Line 14 uses the random value to determine which frequency element to increment during each iteration of the loop. The calculation in line 14 produces random numbers from 1 to 6, so array frequency must be large enough to store six counters. However, we use a seven-element array in which we ignore frequency[0]—it is more logical to have the face value 1 increment frequency[1] than frequency[0]. Thus, each face value is used as an index for array frequency. We also replaced lines 50–52 from Fig. 6.8 by looping through array frequency to output the results (lines 19–20).

Using Arrays to Analyze Survey Results

Our next example uses arrays to summarize the results of data collected in a survey:

> *Forty students were asked to rate the quality of the food in the student cafeteria on a scale of 1 to 10 (where 1 means awful and 10 means excellent). Place the 40 responses in an integer array, and summarize the results of the poll.*

This is a typical array-processing application (see Fig. 7.8). We wish to summarize the number of responses of each type (i.e., 1 through 10). The array responses (lines 9–11) is a 40-element integer array of the students' responses to the survey. We use an 11-element array frequency (line 12) to count the number of occurrences of each response. Each element of the array is used as a counter for one of the survey responses and is initialized to zero by default. As in Fig. 7.7, we ignore frequency[0].

```
1   // Fig. 7.8: StudentPoll.java
2   // Poll analysis program.
3
4   public class StudentPoll
5   {
6      public static void main( String args[] )
7      {
8         // array of survey responses
9         int responses[] = { 1, 2, 6, 4, 8, 5, 9, 7, 8, 10, 1, 6, 3, 8, 6,
10            10, 3, 8, 2, 7, 6, 5, 7, 6, 8, 6, 7, 5, 6, 6, 5, 6, 7, 5, 6,
11            4, 8, 6, 8, 10 };
12         int frequency[] = new int[ 11 ]; // array of frequency counters
13
14         // for each answer, select responses element and use that value
15         // as frequency index to determine element to increment
16         for ( int answer = 0; answer < responses.length; answer++ )
17            ++frequency[ responses[ answer ] ];
18
19         System.out.printf( "%s%10s", "Rating", "Frequency" );
20
21         // output each array element's value
22         for ( int rating = 1; rating < frequency.length; rating++ )
23            System.out.printf( "%d%10d", rating, frequency[ rating ] );
24      } // end main
25   } // end class StudentPoll
```

Fig. 7.8 | Poll analysis program. (Part 1 of 2.)

```
Rating Frequency
  1        2
  2        2
  3        2
  4        2
  5        5
  6       11
  7        5
  8        7
  9        1
 10        3
```

Fig. 7.8 | Poll analysis program. (Part 2 of 2.)

The for loop at lines 16–17 takes the responses one at a time from array responses and increments one of the 10 counters in the frequency array (frequency[1] to frequency[10]). The key statement in the loop is line 17, which increments the appropriate frequency counter, depending on the value of responses[answer].

Let's consider several iterations of the for loop. When control variable answer is 0, the value of responses[answer] is the value of responses[0] (i.e., 1), so the program interprets ++frequency[responses[answer]] as

++frequency[1]

which increments the value in array element 1. To evaluate the expression, start with the value in the innermost set of square brackets (answer). Once you know answer's value (which is the value of the loop control variable in line 16), plug it into the expression and evaluate the next outer set of square brackets (i.e., responses[answer], which is a value selected from the responses array in lines 9–11). Then use the resulting value as the index for the frequency array to specify which counter to increment.

When answer is 1, responses[answer] is the value of responses[1] (2), so the program interprets ++frequency[responses[answer]] as

++frequency[2]

which increments array element 2.

When answer is 2, responses[answer] is the value of responses[2] (6), so the program interprets ++frequency[responses[answer]] as

++frequency[6]

which increments array element 6, and so on. Regardless of the number of responses processed in the survey, the program requires only an 11-element array (ignoring element zero) to summarize the results, because all the response values are between 1 and 10 and the index values for an 11-element array are 0 through 10.

If the data in the responses array had contained invalid values, such as 13, the program would have attempted to add 1 to frequency[13], which is outside the bounds of the array. Java disallows this. When a Java program executes, the JVM checks array indices to ensure that they are valid (i.e., they must be greater than or equal to 0 and less than the length of the array). If a program uses an invalid index, Java generates a so-called exception to indicate that an error occurred in the program at execution time. A control statement can be used to prevent such an "out-of-bounds" error from occurring. For example, the condition in a control statement could determine whether an index is valid before allowing it to be used in an array-access expression.

Error-Prevention Tip 7.1

An exception indicates that an error has occurred in a program. A programmer often can write code to recover from an exception and continue program execution, rather than abnormally terminating the program. When a program attempts to access an element outside the array bounds, an ArrayIndexOutOfBoundsException occurs. Exception handling is discussed in Chapter 13.

Error-Prevention Tip 7.2

When writing code to loop through an array, ensure that the array index is always greater than or equal to 0 and less than the length of the array. The loop-continuation condition should prevent the accessing of elements outside this range.

7.5 Case Study: Card Shuffling and Dealing Simulation

The examples in the chapter thus far have used arrays containing elements of primitive types. Recall from Section 7.2 that the elements of an array can be either primitive types or reference types. This section uses random number generation and an array of reference-type elements, namely objects representing playing cards, to develop a class that simulates card shuffling and dealing. This class can then be used to implement applications that play specific card games. The exercises at the end of the chapter use the classes developed here to build a simple poker application.

We first develop class Card (Fig. 7.9), which represents a playing card that has a face (e.g., "Ace", "Deuce", "Three", ..., "Jack", "Queen", "King") and a suit (e.g., "Hearts", "Diamonds", "Clubs", "Spades"). Next, we develop the DeckOfCards class (Fig. 7.10), which creates a deck of 52 playing cards in which each element is a Card object. We then build a test application (Fig. 7.11) that demonstrates class DeckOfCards's card shuffling and dealing capabilities.

Class Card
Class Card (Fig. 7.9) contains two String instance variables—face and suit—that are used to store references to the face name and suit name for a specific Card. The constructor for the class (lines 10–14) receives two Strings that it uses to initialize face and suit. Method toString (lines 17–20) creates a String consisting of the face of the card, the String " of " and the suit of the card. Recall from Chapter 6 that the + operator can be used to concatenate (i.e., combine) several Strings to form one larger String. Card's toString method can be invoked explicitly to obtain a string representation of a Card object (e.g., "Ace of Spades"). The toString method of an object is called implicitly when the object is used where a String is expected (e.g., when printf outputs the object as a String using the %s format specifier or when the object is concatenated to a String using the + operator). For this behavior to occur, toString must be declared with the header shown in Fig. 7.9.

```
 1   // Fig. 7.9: Card.java
 2   // Card class represents a playing card.
 3
 4   public class Card
 5   {
 6      private String face; // face of card ("Ace", "Deuce", ...)
 7      private String suit; // suit of card ("Hearts", "Diamonds", ...)
 8
 9      // two-argument constructor initializes card's face and suit
10      public Card( String cardFace, String cardSuit )
11      {
12         face = cardFace; // initialize face of card
13         suit = cardSuit; // initialize suit of card
14      } // end two-argument Card constructor
15
16      // return String representation of Card
17      public String toString()
18      {
19         return face + " of " + suit;
20      } // end method toString
21   } // end class Card
```

Fig. 7.9 | Card class represents a playing card.

Class DeckOfCards

Class DeckOfCards (Fig. 7.10) declares an instance variable array named deck of Card objects (line 7). Like primitive-type array declarations, the declaration of an array of objects includes the type of the elements in the array, followed by the name of the array variable and square brackets (e.g., Card deck[]). Class DeckOfCards also declares an integer instance variable currentCard (line 8) representing the next Card to be dealt from the deck array and a named constant NUMBER_OF_CARDS (line 9) indicating the number of Cards in the deck (52).

```
 1   // Fig. 7.10: DeckOfCards.java
 2   // DeckOfCards class represents a deck of playing cards.
 3   import java.util.Random;
 4
 5   public class DeckOfCards
 6   {
 7      private Card deck[]; // array of Card objects
 8      private int currentCard; // index of next Card to be dealt
 9      private final int NUMBER_OF_CARDS = 52; // constant number of Cards
10      private Random randomNumbers; // random number generator
11
12      // constructor fills deck of Cards
13      public DeckOfCards()
14      {
15         String faces[] = { "Ace", "Deuce", "Three", "Four", "Five", "Six",
16            "Seven", "Eight", "Nine", "Ten", "Jack", "Queen", "King" };
17         String suits[] = { "Hearts", "Diamonds", "Clubs", "Spades" };
```

Fig. 7.10 | DeckOfCards class represents a deck of playing cards that can be shuffled and dealt one at a time. (Part 1 of 2.)

```
18
19          deck = new Card[ NUMBER_OF_CARDS ]; // create array of Card objects
20          currentCard = 0; // set currentCard so first Card dealt is deck[ 0 ]
21          randomNumbers = new Random(); // create random number generator
22
23          // populate deck with Card objects
24          for ( int count = 0; count < deck.length; count++ )
25             deck[ count ] =
26                new Card( faces[ count % 13 ], suits[ count / 13 ] );
27       } // end DeckOfCards constructor
28
29       // shuffle deck of Cards with one-pass algorithm
30       public void shuffle()
31       {
32          // after shuffling, dealing should start at deck[ 0 ] again
33          currentCard = 0; // reinitialize currentCard
34
35          // for each Card, pick another random Card and swap them
36          for ( int first = 0; first < deck.length; first++ )
37          {
38             // select a random number between 0 and 51
39             int second =  randomNumbers.nextInt( NUMBER_OF_CARDS );
40
41             // swap current Card with randomly selected Card
42             Card temp = deck[ first ];
43             deck[ first ] = deck[ second ];
44             deck[ second ] = temp;
45          } // end for
46       } // end method shuffle
47
48       // deal one Card
49       public Card dealCard()
50       {
51          // determine whether Cards remain to be dealt
52          if ( currentCard < deck.length )
53             return deck[ currentCard++ ]; // return current Card in array
54          else
55             return null; // return null to indicate that all Cards were dealt
56       } // end method dealCard
57    } // end class DeckOfCards
```

Fig. 7.10 | DeckOfCards class represents a deck of playing cards that can be shuffled and dealt one at a time. (Part 2 of 2.)

The class's constructor instantiates the deck array (line 19) to be of size NUMBER_OF_CARDS. When first created, the elements of the deck array are null by default, so the constructor uses a for statement (lines 24–26) to fill the deck array with Cards. The for statement initializes control variable count to 0 and loops while count is less than deck.length, causing count to take on each integer value from 0 to 51 (the indices of the deck array). Each Card is instantiated and initialized with two Strings—one from the faces array (which contains the Strings "Ace" through "King") and one from the suits array (which contains the Strings "Hearts", "Diamonds", "Clubs" and "Spades"). The calculation count % 13 always results in a value from 0 to 12 (the 13 indices of the faces array in lines 15–16), and the calculation count / 13 always results in a value from 0 to 3 (the four indices of the suits array in line 17). When the deck array is initialized, it contains the Cards with faces "Ace" through "King" in order for each suit.

Method shuffle (lines 30–46) shuffles the Cards in the deck. The method loops through all 52 Cards (array indices 0 to 51). For each Card, a number between 0 and 51 is picked randomly to select another Card. Next, the current Card object and the randomly selected Card object are swapped in the array. This exchange is performed by the three assignments in lines 42–44. The extra variable temp temporarily stores one of the two Card objects being swapped. The swap cannot be performed with only the two statements

```
deck[ first ] = deck[ second ];
deck[ second ] = deck[ first ];
```

If deck[first] is the "Ace" of "Spades" and deck[second] is the "Queen" of "Hearts", after the first assignment, both array elements contain the "Queen" of "Hearts" and the "Ace" of "Spades" is lost—hence, the extra variable temp is needed. After the for loop terminates, the Card objects are randomly ordered. A total of only 52 swaps are made in a single pass of the entire array, and the array of Card objects is shuffled!

Method dealCard (lines 49–56) deals one Card in the array. Recall that currentCard indicates the index of the next Card to be dealt (i.e., the Card at the top of the deck). Thus, line 52 compares currentCard to the length of the deck array. If the deck is not empty (i.e., currentCard is less than 52), line 53 returns the top Card and increments currentCard to prepare for the next call to dealCard—otherwise, null is returned. Recall from Chapter 3 that null represents a "reference to nothing."

Shuffling and Dealing Cards
The application of Fig. 7.11 demonstrates the card dealing and shuffling capabilities of class DeckOfCards (Fig. 7.10). Line 9 creates a DeckOfCards object named myDeckOfCards. Recall that the DeckOfCards constructor creates the deck with the 52 Card objects in order by suit and face. Line 10 invokes myDeckOfCards's shuffle method to rearrange the Card objects. The for statement in lines 13–19 deals all 52 Cards in the deck and prints them in four columns of 13 Cards each. Lines 16–18 deal and print four Card objects, each obtained by invoking myDeckOfCards's dealCard method. When printf outputs a Card with the %-20s format specifier, the Card's toString method (declared in lines 17–20 of Fig. 7.9) is implicitly invoked, and the result is output left justified in a field of width 20.

7.6 Enhanced for Statement
In previous examples, we demonstrated how to use counter-controlled for statements to iterate through the elements in an array. In this section, we introduce a feature new in J2SE 5.0—the enhanced for statement, which iterates through the elements of an array or a collection without using a counter. This section discusses how to use the enhanced for statement to loop through an array. We show how to use the enhanced for statement with collections in Chapter 19, Collections. The syntax of an enhanced for statement is:

```
for ( parameter : arrayName )
    statement
```

```
 1    // Fig. 7.11: DeckOfCardsTest.java
 2    // Card shuffling and dealing application.
 3
 4    public class DeckOfCardsTest
 5    {
 6       // execute application
 7       public static void main( String args[] )
 8       {
 9          DeckOfCards myDeckOfCards = new DeckOfCards();
10          myDeckOfCards.shuffle(); // place Cards in random order
11
12          // print all 52 Cards in the order in which they are dealt
13          for ( int i = 0; i < 13; i++ )
14          {
15             // deal and print 4 Cards
16             System.out.printf( "%-20s%-20s%-20s%-20s\n",
17                myDeckOfCards.dealCard(), myDeckOfCards.dealCard(),
18                myDeckOfCards.dealCard(), myDeckOfCards.dealCard() );
19          } // end for
20       } // end main
21    } // end class DeckOfCardsTest
```

Six of Spades	Eight of Spades	Six of Clubs	Nine of Hearts
Queen of Hearts	Seven of Clubs	Nine of Spades	King of Hearts
Three of Diamonds	Deuce of Clubs	Ace of Hearts	Ten of Spades
Four of Spades	Ace of Clubs	Seven of Diamonds	Four of Hearts
Three of Clubs	Deuce of Hearts	Five of Spades	Jack of Diamonds
King of Clubs	Ten of Hearts	Three of Hearts	Six of Diamonds
Queen of Clubs	Eight of Diamonds	Deuce of Diamonds	Ten of Diamonds
Three of Spades	King of Diamonds	Nine of Clubs	Six of Hearts
Ace of Spades	Four of Diamonds	Seven of Hearts	Eight of Clubs
Deuce of Spades	Eight of Hearts	Five of Hearts	Queen of Spades
Jack of Hearts	Seven of Spades	Four of Clubs	Nine of Diamonds
Ace of Diamonds	Queen of Diamonds	Five of Clubs	King of Spades
Five of Diamonds	Ten of Clubs	Jack of Spades	Jack of Clubs

Fig. 7.11 | Card shuffling and dealing.

where *parameter* has two parts—a type and an identifier (e.g., int number), and *arrayName* is the array through which to iterate. The type of the parameter must match the type of the elements in the array. As the next example illustrates, the identifier represents successive values in the array on successive iterations of the enhanced for statement.

Figure 7.12 uses the enhanced for statement to calculate the sum of the integers in an array of student grades (lines 12–13). The type specified in the parameter to the enhanced for is int, because array is an array containing int values—therefore, the loop will select one int value from the array during each iteration. The enhanced for statement iterates through successive values in the array one-by-one. The enhanced for header can be read concisely as "for each iteration, assign the next element of array to int variable number, then execute the following statement." Thus, for each iteration, identifier number represents an int value in array. Lines 12–13 are equivalent to the following counter-controlled repetition used in lines 12–13 of Fig. 7.5 to total the integers in array:

```
1  // Fig. 7.12: EnhancedForTest.java
2  // Using enhanced for statement to total integers in an array.
3
4  public class EnhancedForTest
5  {
6     public static void main( String args[] )
7     {
8        int array[] = { 87, 68, 94, 100, 83, 78, 85, 91, 76, 87 };
9        int total = 0;
10
11       // add each element's value to total
12       for ( int number : array )
13          total += number;
14
15       System.out.printf( "Total of array elements: %d\n", total );
16    } // end main
17 } // end class EnhancedForTest
```

```
Total of array elements: 849
```

Fig. 7.12 | Using the enhanced for statement to total integers in an array.

```
for ( int counter = 0; counter < array.length; counter++ )
   total += array[ counter ];
```

The enhanced for statement simplifies the code for iterating through an array. Note, however, that the enhanced for statement can be used only to access array elements—it cannot be used to modify elements. If your program needs to modify elements, use the traditional counter-controlled for statement.

The enhanced for statement can be used in place of the counter-controlled for statement whenever code looping through an array does not require access to the counter indicating the index of the current array element. For example, totalling the integers in an array requires access only to the element values—the index of each element is irrelevant. However, if a program must use a counter for some reason other than simply to loop through an array (e.g., to print an index number next to each array element value, as in the examples earlier in this chapter), use the counter-controlled for statement.

7.7 Passing Arrays to Methods

This section demonstrates how to pass arrays and array elements as arguments to methods. At the end of the section, we discuss how all types of arguments are passed to methods. To pass an array argument to a method, specify the name of the array without any brackets. For example, if array hourlyTemperatures is declared as

```
double hourlyTemperatures[] = new double[ 24 ];
```

then the method call

```
modifyArray( hourlyTemperatures );
```

passes the reference of array `hourlyTemperatures` to method `modifyArray`. Every array object "knows" its own length (via its `length` field). Thus, when we pass an array object's reference into a method, we need not pass the array length as an additional argument.

For a method to receive an array reference through a method call, the method's parameter list must specify an array parameter. For example, the method header for method `modifyArray` might be written as

```
void modifyArray( int b[] )
```

indicating that `modifyArray` receives the reference of an integer array in parameter b. The method call passes array `hourlyTemperature`'s reference, so when the called method uses the array variable b, it refers to the same array object as `hourlyTemperatures` in the calling method.

When an argument to a method is an entire array or an individual array element of a reference type, the called method receives a copy of the reference. However, when an argument to a method is an individual array element of a primitive type, the called method receives a copy of the element's value. Such primitive values are called scalars or scalar quantities. To pass an individual array element to a method, use the indexed name of the array as an argument in the method call.

Figure 7.13 demonstrates the difference between passing an entire array and passing a primitive-type array element to a method. The enhanced `for` statement at lines 16–17 outputs the five elements of array (an array of int values). Line 19 invokes method `modifyArray`, passing array as an argument. Method `modifyArray` (lines 36–40) receives a copy of array's reference and uses the reference to multiply each of array's elements by 2. To prove that array's elements were modified, the `for` statement at lines 23–24 outputs the five elements of array again. As the output shows, method `modifyArray` doubled the value of each element.

```
1   // Fig. 7.13: PassArray.java
2   // Passing arrays and individual array elements to methods.
3
4   public class PassArray
5   {
6      // main creates array and calls modifyArray and modifyElement
7      public static void main( String args[] )
8      {
9         int array[] = { 1, 2, 3, 4, 5 };
10
11        System.out.println(
12           "Effects of passing reference to entire array:\n" +
13           "The values of the original array are:" );
14
15        // output original array elements
16        for ( int value : array )
17           System.out.printf( "   %d", value );
18
19        modifyArray( array ); // pass array reference
20        System.out.println( "\n\nThe values of the modified array are:" );
```

Fig. 7.13 | Passing arrays and individual array elements to methods. (Part 1 of 2.)

```
21
22          // output modified array elements
23          for ( int value : array )
24             System.out.printf( "      %d", value );
25
26          System.out.printf(
27             "\n\nEffects of passing array element value:\n" +
28             "array[3] before modifyElement: %d\n", array[ 3 ] );
29
30          modifyElement( array[ 3 ] ); // attempt to modify array[ 3 ]
31          System.out.printf(
32             "array[3] after modifyElement: %d\n", array[ 3 ] );
33       } // end main
34
35       // multiply each element of an array by 2
36       public static void modifyArray( int array2[] )
37       {
38          for ( int counter = 0; counter < array2.length; counter++ )
39             array2[ counter ] *= 2;
40       } // end method modifyArray
41
42       // multiply argument by 2
43       public static void modifyElement( int element )
44       {
45          element *= 2;
46          System.out.printf(
47             "Value of element in modifyElement: %d\n", element );
48       } // end method modifyElement
49    } // end class PassArray
```

```
Effects of passing reference to entire array:
The values of the original array are:
   1   2   3   4   5

The values of the modified array are:
   2   4   6   8   10

Effects of passing array element value:
array[3] before modifyElement: 8
Value of element in modifyElement: 16
array[3] after modifyElement: 8
```

Fig. 7.13 | Passing arrays and individual array elements to methods. (Part 2 of 2.)

Figure 7.13 next demonstrates that when a copy of an individual primitive-type array element is passed to a method, modifying the copy in the called method does not affect the original value of that element in the calling method's array. To show the value of array[3] before invoking method modifyElement, lines 26–28 output the value of array[3] (8). Line 30 calls method modifyElement and passes array[3] as an argument. Remember that array[3] is actually one int value (8) in array. Therefore, the program passes a copy of the value of array[3]. Method modifyElement (lines 43–48) multiplies the value received as an argument by 2, stores the result in its parameter element, then outputs the value of element (16). Since method parameters, like local variables, cease to exist when the method in which they are declared completes execution, the method parameter element is destroyed when method modifyElement terminates. Thus, when the program returns control to main, lines 31–32 output the unmodified value of array[3] (i.e., 8).

Notes on Passing Arguments to Methods

The preceding example demonstrated the different ways that arrays and primitive-type array elements are passed as arguments to methods. We now take a closer look at how arguments in general are passed to methods. Two ways to pass arguments in method calls in many programming languages are pass-by-value and pass-by-reference (also called call-by-value and call-by-reference). When an argument is passed by value, a copy of the argument's value is passed to the called method. The called method works exclusively with the copy. Changes to the called method's copy do not affect the original variable's value in the caller.

When an argument is passed by reference, the called method can access the argument's value in the caller directly and modify that data, if necessary. Pass-by-reference improves performance by eliminating the need to copy possibly large amounts of data.

Unlike some other languages, Java does not allow programmers to choose pass-by-value or pass-by-reference—all arguments are passed by value. A method call can pass two types of values to a method—copies of primitive values (e.g., values of type int and double) and copies of references to objects (including references to arrays). Objects themselves cannot be passed to methods. When a method modifies a primitive-type parameter, changes to the parameter have no effect on the original argument value in the calling method. For example, when line 30 in main of Fig. 7.13 passes array[3] to method modifyElement, the statement in line 45 that doubles the value of parameter element has no effect on the value of array[3] in main. This is also true for reference-type parameters. If you modify a reference-type parameter by assigning it the reference of another object, the parameter refers to the new object, but the reference stored in the caller's variable still refers to the original object.

Although an object's reference is passed by value, a method can still interact with the referenced object by calling its public methods using the copy of the object's reference. Since the reference stored in the parameter is a copy of the reference that was passed as an argument, the parameter in the called method and the argument in the calling method refer to the same object in memory. For example, in Fig. 7.13, both parameter array2 in method modifyArray and variable array in main refer to the same array object in memory. Any changes made using the parameter array2 are carried out on the same object that is referenced by the variable that was passed as an argument in the calling method. In Fig. 7.13, the changes made in modifyArray using array2 affect the contents of the array object referenced by array in main. Thus, with a reference to an object, the called method can manipulate the caller's object directly.

Performance Tip 7.1

Passing arrays by reference makes sense for performance reasons. If arrays were passed by value, a copy of each element would be passed. For large, frequently passed arrays, this would waste time and consume considerable storage for the copies of the arrays.

7.8 Case Study: Class GradeBook Using an Array to Store Grades

This section further evolves class GradeBook, introduced in Chapter 3 and expanded in Chapters 4–5. Recall that this class represents a grade book used by a professor to store and analyze a set of student grades. Previous versions of the class process a set of grades entered by the user, but do not maintain the individual grade values in instance variables of the class. Thus, repeat calculations require the user to reenter the same grades. One way to solve this problem would be to store each grade entered in an individual instance of the class. For example, we could create instance variables grade1, grade2, …, grade10 in class GradeBook to store 10 student grades. However, the code to total the grades and determine the class average would be cumbersome, and the class would not be able to process any more than 10 grades at a time. In this section, we solve this problem by storing grades in an array.

*Storing Student Grades in an Array in Class **GradeBook***
The version of class GradeBook (Fig. 7.14) presented here uses an array of integers to store the grades of several students on a single exam. This eliminates the need to repeatedly input the same set of grades. Array grades is declared as an instance variable in line 7—therefore, each GradeBook object maintains its own set of grades. The class's constructor (lines 10–14) has two parameters—the name of the course and an array of grades. When an application (e.g., class GradeBookTest in Fig. 7.15) creates a GradeBook object, the application passes an existing int array to the constructor, which assigns the array's reference to instance variable grades (line 13). The size of the array grades is determined by the class that passes the array to the constructor. Thus, a GradeBook object can process a variable number of grades. The grade values in the passed array could have been input from a user or read from a file on disk (as discussed in Chapter 14). In our test application, we simply initialize an array with a set of grade values (Fig. 7.15, line 10). Once the grades are stored in instance variable

```
1   // Fig. 7.14: GradeBook.java
2   // Grade book using an array to store test grades.
3
4   public class GradeBook
5   {
6      private String courseName; // name of course this GradeBook represents
7      private int grades[]; // array of student grades
8
9      // two-argument constructor initializes courseName and grades array
10     public GradeBook( String name, int gradesArray[] )
11     {
12        courseName = name; // initialize courseName
13        grades = gradesArray; // store grades
14     } // end two-argument GradeBook constructor
15
16     // method to set the course name
17     public void setCourseName( String name )
18     {
19        courseName = name; // store the course name
20     } // end method setCourseName
```

Fig. 7.14 | GradeBook class using an array to store test grades. (Part I of 4.)

```
21
22       // method to retrieve the course name
23       public String getCourseName()
24       {
25          return courseName;
26       } // end method getCourseName
27
28       // display a welcome message to the GradeBook user
29       public void displayMessage()
30       {
31          // getCourseName gets the name of the course
32          System.out.printf( "Welcome to the grade book for\n%s!\n\n",
33             getCourseName() );
34       } // end method displayMessage
35
36       // perform various operations on the data
37       public void processGrades()
38       {
39          // output grades array
40          outputGrades();
41
42          // call method getAverage to calculate the average grade
43          System.out.printf( "\nClass average is %.2f\n", getAverage() );
44
45          // call methods getMinimum and getMaximum
46          System.out.printf( "Lowest grade is %d\nHighest grade is %d\n\n",
47             getMinimum(), getMaximum() );
48
49          // call outputBarChart to print grade distribution chart
50          outputBarChart();
51       } // end method processGrades
52
53       // find minimum grade
54       public int getMinimum()
55       {
56          int lowGrade = grades[ 0 ]; // assume grades[ 0 ] is smallest
57
58          // loop through grades array
59          for ( int grade : grades )
60          {
61             // if grade lower than lowGrade, assign it to lowGrade
62             if ( grade < lowGrade )
63                lowGrade = grade; // new lowest grade
64          } // end for
65
66          return lowGrade; // return lowest grade
67       } // end method getMinimum
68
69       // find maximum grade
70       public int getMaximum()
71       {
72          int highGrade = grades[ 0 ]; // assume grades[ 0 ] is largest
73
```

Fig. 7.14 | GradeBook class using an array to store test grades. (Part 2 of 4.)

```
74          // loop through grades array
75          for ( int grade : grades )
76          {
77             // if grade greater than highGrade, assign it to highGrade
78             if ( grade > highGrade )
79                highGrade = grade; // new highest grade
80          } // end for
81
82          return highGrade; // return highest grade
83       } // end method getMaximum
84
85       // determine average grade for test
86       public double getAverage()
87       {
88          int total = 0; // initialize total
89
90          // sum grades for one student
91          for ( int grade : grades )
92             total += grade;
93
94          // return average of grades
95          return (double) total / grades.length;
96       } // end method getAverage
97
98       // output bar chart displaying grade distribution
99       public void outputBarChart()
100      {
101         System.out.println( "Grade distribution:" );
102
103         // stores frequency of grades in each range of 10 grades
104         int frequency[] = new int[ 11 ];
105
106         // for each grade, increment the appropriate frequency
107         for ( int grade : grades )
108            ++frequency[ grade / 10 ];
109
110         // for each grade frequency, print bar in chart
111         for ( int count = 0; count < frequency.length; count++ )
112         {
113            // output bar label ( "00-09: ", ..., "90-99: ", "100: " )
114            if ( count == 10 )
115               System.out.printf( "%5d: ", 100 );
116            else
117               System.out.printf( "%02d-%02d: ",
118                  count * 10, count * 10 + 9  );
119
120            // print bar of asterisks
121            for ( int stars = 0; stars < frequency[ count ]; stars++ )
122               System.out.print( "*" );
123
124            System.out.println(); // start a new line of output
125         } // end outer for
126      } // end method outputBarChart
```

Fig. 7.14 | GradeBook class using an array to store test grades. (Part 3 of 4.)

```
127
128     // output the contents of the grades array
129     public void outputGrades()
130     {
131        System.out.println( "The grades are:\n" );
132
133        // output each student's grade
134        for ( int student = 0; student < grades.length; student++ )
135           System.out.printf( "Student %2d: %3d\n",
136              student + 1, grades[ student ] );
137     } // end method outputGrades
138  } // end class GradeBook
```

Fig. 7.14 | GradeBook class using an array to store test grades. (Part 4 of 4.)

grades of class GradeBook, all the class's methods can access the elements of grades as needed to perform various calculations.

Method processGrades (lines 37–51) contains a series of method calls that result in the output of a report summarizing the grades. Line 40 calls method outputGrades to print the contents of the array grades. Lines 134–136 in method outputGrades use a for statement to output each student's grade. A counter-controlled for must be used in this case, because lines 135–136 use counter variable student's value to output each grade next to a particular student number (see Fig. 7.15). Although array indices start at 0, a professor would typically number students starting at 1. Thus, lines 135–136 output student + 1 as the student number to produce grade labels "Student 1: ", "Student 2: ", and so on.

Method processGrades next calls method getAverage (line 43) to obtain the average of the grades in the array. Method getAverage (lines 86–96) uses an enhanced for statement to total the values in array grades before calculating the average. The parameter in the enhanced for's header (e.g., int grade) indicates that for each iteration, the int variable grade takes on a value in the array grades. Note that the averaging calculation in line 95 uses grades.length to determine the number of grades being averaged.

Lines 46–47 in method processGrades calls methods getMinimum and getMaximum to determine the lowest and highest grades of any student on the exam, respectively. Each of these methods uses an enhanced for statement to loop through array grades. Lines 59–64 in method getMinimum loop through the array, and lines 62–63 compare each grade to lowGrade. If a grade is less than lowGrade, lowGrade is set to that grade. When line 66 executes, lowGrade contains the lowest grade in the array. Method getMaximum (lines 70–83) works the same way as method getMinimum.

Finally, line 50 in method processGrades calls method outputBarChart to print a distribution chart of the grade data using a technique similar to that in Fig. 7.6. In that example, we manually calculated the number of grades in each category (i.e., 0–9, 10–19, …, 90–99 and 100) by simply looking at a set of grades. In this example, lines 107–108 use a technique similar to that in Fig. 7.7 and Fig. 7.8 to calculate the frequency of grades in each category. Line 104 declares and creates array frequency of 11 ints to store the frequency of grades in each grade category. For each grade in array grades, lines 107–108 increment the appropriate element of the frequency array. To determine which element to increment, line 108 divides the current grade by 10 using integer division. For example, if grade is 85, line 108 increments frequency[8] to update the count of grades in the range 80–89. Lines 111–125 next print the bar chart (see Fig. 7.15) based on the values in array frequency. Like lines 23–24 of Fig. 7.6, lines 121–122 of Fig. 7.14 use a value in array frequency to determine the number of asterisks to display in each bar.

Class *GradeBookTest* That Demonstrates Class *GradeBook*

The application of Fig. 7.15 creates an object of class GradeBook (Fig. 7.14) using the int array gradesArray (declared and initialized in line 10). Lines 12–13 pass a course name and gradesArray to the GradeBook constructor. Line 14 displays a welcome message, and line 15 invokes the GradeBook object's processGrades method. The output reveals the summary of the 10 grades in myGradeBook.

Software Engineering Observation 7.1

A test harness (or test application) is responsible for creating an object of the class being tested and providing it with data. This data could come from any of several sources. Test data can be placed directly into an array with an array initializer, it can come from the user at the keyboard, it can come from a file (as you will see in Chapter 14), or it can come from a network (as you will see in Chapter 24). After passing this data to the class's constructor to instantiate the object, the test harness should call upon the object to test its methods and manipulate its data. Gathering data in the test harness like this allows the class to manipulate data from several sources.

7.9 Multidimensional Arrays

Multidimensional arrays with two dimensions are often used to represent tables of values consisting of information arranged in rows and columns. To identify a particular table element, we must specify two indices. By convention, the first identifies the element's row and the second its column. Arrays that require two indices to identify a particular element are called two-dimensional arrays. (Multidimensional arrays can have more than two dimensions.) Java does not support multidimensional arrays directly, but it does allow the

```
1   // Fig. 7.15: GradeBookTest.java
2   // Creates GradeBook object using an array of grades.
3
4   public class GradeBookTest
5   {
6      // main method begins program execution
7      public static void main( String args[] )
8      {
9         // array of student grades
10        int gradesArray[] = { 87, 68, 94, 100, 83, 78, 85, 91, 76, 87 };
11
12        GradeBook myGradeBook = new GradeBook(
13           "CS101 Introduction to Java Programming", gradesArray );
14        myGradeBook.displayMessage();
15        myGradeBook.processGrades();
16     } // end main
17  } // end class GradeBookTest
```

Fig. 7.15 | GradeBookTest creates a GradeBook object using an array of grades, then invokes method processGrades to analyze them. (Part 1 of 2.)

```
Welcome to the grade book for
CS101 Introduction to Java Programming!

The grades are:

Student  1:  87
Student  2:  68
Student  3:  94
Student  4: 100
Student  5:  83
Student  6:  78
Student  7:  85
Student  8:  91
Student  9:  76
Student 10:  87

Class average is 84.90
Lowest grade is 68
Highest grade is 100

Grade distribution:
00-09:
10-19:
20-29:
30-39:
40-49:
50-59:
60-69: *
70-79: **
80-89: ****
90-99: **
  100: *
```

Fig. 7.15 | GradeBookTest creates a GradeBook object using an array of grades, then invokes method processGrades to analyze them. (Part 2 of 2.)

programmer to specify one-dimensional arrays whose elements are also one-dimensional arrays, thus achieving the same effect. Figure 7.16 illustrates a two-dimensional array a that contains three rows and four columns (i.e., a three-by-four array). In general, an array with *m* rows and *n* columns is called an *m-by-n array*.

Every element in array a is identified in Fig. 7.16 by an array-access expression of the form a[row][column]; a is the name of the array, and row and column are the indices that uniquely identify each element in array a by row and column number. Note that the names of the elements in row 0 all have a first index of 0, and the names of the elements in column 3 all have a second index of 3.

Arrays of One-Dimensional Arrays

Like one-dimensional arrays, multidimensional arrays can be initialized with array initializers in declarations. A two-dimensional array b with two rows and two columns could be declared and initialized with nested array initializers as follows:

```
int b[][] = { { 1, 2 }, { 3, 4 } };
```

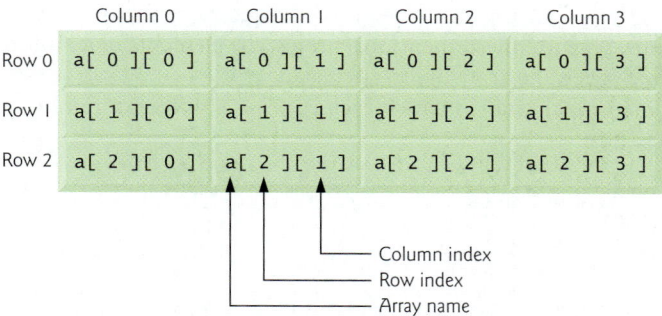

Fig. 7.16 | Two-dimensional array with three rows and four columns.

The initializer values are grouped by row in braces. So 1 and 2 initialize b[0][0] and b[0][1], respectively, and 3 and 4 initialize b[1][0] and b[1][1], respectively. The compiler counts the number of nested array initializers (represented by sets of braces within the outer braces) in the array declaration to determine the number of rows in array b. The compiler counts the initializer values in the nested array initializer for a row to determine the number of columns in that row. As we will see momentarily, this means that rows can have different lengths.

Multidimensional arrays are maintained as arrays of one-dimensional arrays. Therefore array b in the preceding declaration is actually composed of two separate one-dimensional arrays—one containing the values in the first nested initializer list { 1, 2 } and one containing the values in the second nested initializer list { 3, 4 }. Thus, array b itself is an array of two elements, each a one-dimensional array of int values.

Two-Dimensional Arrays with Rows of Different Lengths
The manner in which multidimensional arrays are represented makes them quite flexible. In fact, the lengths of the rows in array b are not required to be the same. For example,

```
int b[][] = { { 1, 2 }, { 3, 4, 5 } };
```

creates integer array b with two elements (determined by the number of nested array initializers) that represent the rows of the two-dimensional array. Each element of b is a reference to a one-dimensional array of int variables. The int array for row 0 is a one-dimensional array with two elements (1 and 2), and the int array for row 1 is a one-dimensional array with three elements (3, 4 and 5).

Creating Two-Dimensional Arrays with Array-Creation Expressions
A multidimensional array with the same number of columns in every row can be created with an array-creation expression. For example, the following lines declare array b and assign it a reference to a three-by-four array:

```
int b[][];
b = new int[ 3 ][ 4 ];
```

In this case, we use the literal values 3 and 4 to specify the number of rows and number of columns, respectively, but this is not required. Programs can also use variables to specify array dimensions. As with one-dimensional arrays, the elements of a multidimensional array are initialized when the array object is created.

A multidimensional array in which each row has a different number of columns can be created as follows:

```java
int b[][];
b = new int[ 2 ][ ];    // create 2 rows
b[ 0 ] = new int[ 5 ]; // create 5 columns for row 0
b[ 1 ] = new int[ 3 ]; // create 3 columns for row 1
```

The preceding statements create a two-dimensional array with two rows. Row 0 has five columns, and row 1 has three columns.

Two-Dimensional Array Example: Displaying Element Values

Figure 7.17 demonstrates initializing two-dimensional arrays with array initializers and using nested for loops to traverse the arrays (i.e., manipulate every element of each array).

```java
 1   // Fig. 7.17: InitArray.java
 2   // Initializing two-dimensional arrays.
 3
 4   public class InitArray
 5   {
 6      // create and output two-dimensional arrays
 7      public static void main( String args[] )
 8      {
 9         int array1[][] = { { 1, 2, 3 }, { 4, 5, 6 } };
10         int array2[][] = { { 1, 2 }, { 3 }, { 4, 5, 6 } };
11
12         System.out.println( "Values in array1 by row are" );
13         outputArray( array1 ); // displays array1 by row
14
15         System.out.println( "\nValues in array2 by row are" );
16         outputArray( array2 ); // displays array2 by row
17      } // end main
18
19      // output rows and columns of a two-dimensional array
20      public static void outputArray( int array[][] )
21      {
22         // loop through array's rows
23         for ( int row = 0; row < array.length; row++ )
24         {
25            // loop through columns of current row
26            for ( int column = 0; column < array[ row ].length; column++ )
27               System.out.printf( "%d  ", array[ row ][ column ] );
28
29            System.out.println(); // start new line of output
30         } // end outer for
31      } // end method outputArray
32   } // end class InitArray
```

Fig. 7.17 | Initializing two-dimensional arrays. (Part 1 of 2.)

```
Values in array1 by row are
1   2   3
4   5   6

Values in array2 by row are
1   2
3
4   5   6
```

Fig. 7.17 | Initializing two-dimensional arrays. (Part 2 of 2.)

Class `InitArray`'s `main` declares two arrays. The declaration of `array1` (line 9) uses nested array initializers to initialize the first row of the array to the values 1, 2 and 3, and the second row to the values 4, 5 and 6. The declaration of `array2` (line 10) uses nested initializers of different lengths. In this case, the first row is initialized to have two elements with values 1 and 2, respectively. The second row is initialized to have one element with value 3. The third row is initialized to have three elements with the values 4, 5 and 6, respectively.

Lines 13 and 16 call method `outputArray` (lines 20–31) to output the elements of `array1` and `array2`, respectively. Method `outputArray` specifies the array parameter as `int array[][]` to indicate that the method receives a two-dimensional array. The `for` statement (lines 23–30) outputs the rows of a two-dimensional array. In the loop-continuation condition of the outer `for` statement, the expression `array.length` determines the number of rows in the array. In the inner `for` statement, the expression `array[ row ].length` determines the number of columns in the current row of the array. This condition enables the loop to determine the exact number of columns in each row.

Common Multidimensional-Array Manipulations Performed with **for** *Statements*
Many common array manipulations use `for` statements. As an example, the following `for` statement sets all the elements in row 2 of array a in Fig. 7.16 to zero:

```
for ( int column = 0; column < a[ 2 ].length; column++)
   a[ 2 ][ column ] = 0;
```

We specified row 2; therefore, we know that the first index is always 2 (0 is the first row, and 1 is the second row). This `for` loop varies only the second index (i.e., the column index). The preceding `for` statement is equivalent to the assignment statements

```
a[ 2 ][ 0 ] = 0;
a[ 2 ][ 1 ] = 0;
a[ 2 ][ 2 ] = 0;
a[ 2 ][ 3 ] = 0;
```

The following nested `for` statement totals the values of all the elements in array a:

```
int total = 0;

for ( int row = 0; row < a.length; row++ )
{
   for ( int column = 0; column < a[ row ].length; column++ )
      total += a[ row ][ column ];
} // end outer for
```

This nested for statements total the array elements one row at a time. The outer for statement begins by setting the row index to 0 so that the first row's elements may be totaled by the inner for statement. The outer for then increments row to 1 so that the second row can be totaled. Then, the outer for increments row to 2 so that the third row can be totaled. The variable total can be displayed when the outer for statement terminates. In the next example, we show how to process a two-dimensional array in a similar manner using nested enhanced for statements.

7.10 Case Study: Class GradeBook Using a Two-Dimensional Array

In Section 7.8, we presented class GradeBook (Fig. 7.14), which used a one-dimensional array to store student grades on a single exam. In most semesters, students take several exams. Professors are likely to want to analyze grades across the entire semester, both for a single student and for the class as a whole.

*Storing Student Grades in a Two-Dimensional Array in Class **GradeBook***
Figure 7.18 contains a version of class GradeBook that uses a two-dimensional array grades to store the grades of a number of students on multiple exams. Each row of the array represents a single student's grades for the entire course, and each column represents a grade on one of the exams the students took during the course. An application such as GradeBookTest (Fig. 7.19) passes the array as an argument to the GradeBook constructor. In this example, we use a ten-by-three array containing ten students' grades on three exams. Five methods perform array manipulations to process the grades. Each method is similar to its counterpart in the earlier one-dimensional array version of class GradeBook (Fig. 7.14). Method getMinimum (lines 52–70) determines the lowest grade of any student for the semester. Method getMaximum (lines 73–91) determines the highest grade of any student for the semester. Method getAverage (lines 94–104) determines a particular student's semester average. Method outputBarChart (lines 107–137) outputs a bar chart of the distribution of all student grades for the semester. Method outputGrades (lines 140–164) outputs the two-dimensional array in a tabular format, along with each student's semester average.

```
1   // Fig. 7.18: GradeBook.java
2   // Grade book using a two-dimensional array to store grades.
3
4   public class GradeBook
5   {
6      private String courseName; // name of course this grade book represents
7      private int grades[][]; // two-dimensional array of student grades
8
9      // two-argument constructor initializes courseName and grades array
10     public GradeBook( String name, int gradesArray[][] )
11     {
12        courseName = name; // initialize courseName
13        grades = gradesArray; // store grades
14     } // end two-argument GradeBook constructor
15
```

Fig. 7.18 | GradeBook class using a two-dimensional array to store grades. (Part 1 of 4.)

```
16    // method to set the course name
17    public void setCourseName( String name )
18    {
19       courseName = name; // store the course name
20    } // end method setCourseName
21
22    // method to retrieve the course name
23    public String getCourseName()
24    {
25       return courseName;
26    } // end method getCourseName
27
28    // display a welcome message to the GradeBook user
29    public void displayMessage()
30    {
31       // getCourseName gets the name of the course
32       System.out.printf( "Welcome to the grade book for\n%s!\n\n",
33          getCourseName() );
34    } // end method displayMessage
35
36    // perform various operations on the data
37    public void processGrades()
38    {
39       // output grades array
40       outputGrades();
41
42       // call methods getMinimum and getMaximum
43       System.out.printf( "\n%s %d\n%s %d\n\n",
44          "Lowest grade in the grade book is", getMinimum(),
45          "Highest grade in the grade book is", getMaximum() );
46
47       // output grade distribution chart of all grades on all tests
48       outputBarChart();
49    } // end method processGrades
50
51    // find minimum grade
52    public int getMinimum()
53    {
54       // assume first element of grades array is smallest
55       int lowGrade = grades[ 0 ][ 0 ];
56
57       // loop through rows of grades array
58       for ( int studentGrades[] : grades )
59       {
60          // loop through columns of current row
61          for ( int grade : studentGrades )
62          {
63             // if grade less than lowGrade, assign it to lowGrade
64             if ( grade < lowGrade )
65                lowGrade = grade;
66          } // end inner for
67       } // end outer for
```

Fig. 7.18 | GradeBook class using a two-dimensional array to store grades. (Part 2 of 4.)

```
68
69        return lowGrade; // return lowest grade
70     } // end method getMinimum
71
72     // find maximum grade
73     public int getMaximum()
74     {
75        // assume first element of grades array is largest
76        int highGrade = grades[ 0 ][ 0 ];
77
78        // loop through rows of grades array
79        for ( int studentGrades[] : grades )
80        {
81           // loop through columns of current row
82           for ( int grade : studentGrades )
83           {
84              // if grade greater than highGrade, assign it to highGrade
85              if ( grade > highGrade )
86                 highGrade = grade;
87           } // end inner for
88        } // end outer for
89
90        return highGrade; // return highest grade
91     } // end method getMaximum
92
93     // determine average grade for particular set of grades
94     public double getAverage( int setOfGrades[] )
95     {
96        int total = 0; // initialize total
97
98        // sum grades for one student
99        for ( int grade : setOfGrades )
100          total += grade;
101
102       // return average of grades
103       return (double) total / setOfGrades.length;
104    } // end method getAverage
105
106    // output bar chart displaying overall grade distribution
107    public void outputBarChart()
108    {
109       System.out.println( "Overall grade distribution:" );
110
111       // stores frequency of grades in each range of 10 grades
112       int frequency[] = new int[ 11 ];
113
114       // for each grade in GradeBook, increment the appropriate frequency
115       for ( int studentGrades[] : grades )
116       {
117          for ( int grade : studentGrades )
118             ++frequency[ grade / 10 ];
119       } // end outer for
```

Fig. 7.18 | GradeBook class using a two-dimensional array to store grades. (Part 3 of 4.)

```
120
121        // for each grade frequency, print bar in chart
122        for ( int count = 0; count < frequency.length; count++ )
123        {
124           // output bar label ( "00-09: ", ..., "90-99: ", "100: " )
125           if ( count == 10 )
126              System.out.printf( "%5d: ", 100 );
127           else
128              System.out.printf( "%02d-%02d: ",
129                 count * 10, count * 10 + 9 );
130
131           // print bar of asterisks
132           for ( int stars = 0; stars < frequency[ count ]; stars++ )
133              System.out.print( "*" );
134
135           System.out.println(); // start a new line of output
136        } // end outer for
137     } // end method outputBarChart
138
139     // output the contents of the grades array
140     public void outputGrades()
141     {
142        System.out.println( "The grades are:\n" );
143        System.out.print( "             " ); // align column heads
144
145        // create a column heading for each of the tests
146        for ( int test = 0; test < grades[ 0 ].length; test++ )
147           System.out.printf( "Test %d  ", test + 1 );
148
149        System.out.println( "Average" ); // student average column heading
150
151        // create rows/columns of text representing array grades
152        for ( int student = 0; student < grades.length; student++ )
153        {
154           System.out.printf( "Student %2d", student + 1 );
155
156           for ( int test : grades[ student ] ) // output student's grades
157              System.out.printf( "%8d", test );
158
159           // call method getAverage to calculate student's average grade;
160           // pass row of grades as the argument to getAverage
161           double average = getAverage( grades[ student ] );
162           System.out.printf( "%9.2f\n", average );
163        } // end outer for
164     } // end method outputGrades
165  } // end class GradeBook
```

Fig. 7.18 | GradeBook class using a two-dimensional array to store grades. (Part 4 of 4.)

Methods getMinimum, getMaximum, outputBarChart and outputGrades each loop through array grades by using nested for statements—for example, the nested enhanced for statement from the declaration of method getMinimum (lines 58–67). The outer enhanced for statement iterates through the two-dimensional array grades, assigning successive rows to parameter studentGrades on successive iterations. The square brackets following the parameter name indicate that studentGrades refers to a one-dimensional int array—namely, a row in array grades containing one student's grades. To find the lowest overall grade, the inner for statement compares the elements of the current one-dimensional array studentGrades to variable lowGrade. For example, on the first iteration of the outer for, row 0 of grades is assigned to parameter studentGrades. The inner enhanced for statement then loops through studentGrades and compares each grade value with lowGrade. If a grade is less than lowGrade, lowGrade is set to that grade. On the second iteration of the outer enhanced for statement, row 1 of grades is assigned to student-Grades, and the elements of this row are compared with variable lowGrade. This repeats until all rows of grades have been traversed. When execution of the nested statement is complete, lowGrade contains the lowest grade in the two-dimensional array. Method get-Maximum works similarly to method getMinimum.

Method outputBarChart in Fig. 7.18 is nearly identical to the one in Fig. 7.14. However, to output the overall grade distribution for a whole semester, the method here uses a nested enhanced for statement (lines 115–119) to create the one-dimensional array frequency based on all the grades in the two-dimensional array. The rest of the code in each of the two outputBarChart methods that displays the chart is identical.

Method outputGrades (lines 140–164) also uses nested for statements to output values of the array grades, in addition to each student's semester average. The output in Fig. 7.19 shows the result, which resembles the tabular format of a professor's physical grade book. Lines 146–147 print the column headings for each test. We use a counter-controlled for statement here so that we can identify each test with a number. Similarly, the for statement in lines 152–163 first outputs a row label using a counter variable to identify each student (line 154). Although array indices start at 0, note that lines 147 and 154 output test + 1 and student + 1, respectively, to produce test and student numbers starting at 1 (see Fig. 7.19). The inner for statement in lines 156–157 uses the outer for statement's counter variable student to loop through a specific row of array grades and output each student's test grade. Note that an enhanced for statement can be nested in a counter-controlled for statement, and vice versa. Finally, line 161 obtains each student's semester average by passing the current row of grades (i.e., grades[student]) to method getAverage.

Method getAverage (lines 94–104) takes one argument—a one-dimensional array of test results for a particular student. When line 161 calls getAverage, the argument is grades[student], which specifies that a particular row of the two-dimensional array grades should be passed to getAverage. For example, based on the array created in Fig. 7.19, the argument grades[1] represents the three values (a one-dimensional array of grades) stored in row 1 of the two-dimensional array grades. Remember that a two-dimensional array is an array whose elements are one-dimensional arrays. Method getAverage calculates the sum of the array elements, divides the total by the number of test results and returns the floating-point result as a double value (line 103).

Class *GradeBookTest* That Demonstrates Class *GradeBook*

The application in Fig. 7.19 creates an object of class GradeBook (Fig. 7.18) using the two-dimensional array of ints named gradesArray (declared and initialized in lines 10–19). Lines 21–22 pass a course name and gradesArray to the GradeBook constructor. Lines 23–24 then invoke myGradeBook's displayMessage and processGrades methods to display a welcome message and obtain a report summarizing the students' grades for the semester, respectively.

```
1   // Fig. 7.19: GradeBookTest.java
2   // Creates GradeBook object using a two-dimensional array of grades.
3
4   public class GradeBookTest
5   {
6      // main method begins program execution
7      public static void main( String args[] )
8      {
9         // two-dimensional array of student grades
10        int gradesArray[][] = { { 87, 96, 70 },
11                                { 68, 87, 90 },
12                                { 94, 100, 90 },
13                                { 100, 81, 82 },
14                                { 83, 65, 85 },
15                                { 78, 87, 65 },
16                                { 85, 75, 83 },
17                                { 91, 94, 100 },
18                                { 76, 72, 84 },
19                                { 87, 93, 73 } };
20
21        GradeBook myGradeBook = new GradeBook(
22           "CS101 Introduction to Java Programming", gradesArray );
23        myGradeBook.displayMessage();
24        myGradeBook.processGrades();
25     } // end main
26  } // end class GradeBookTest
```

```
Welcome to the grade book for
CS101 Introduction to Java Programming!

The grades are:

           Test 1  Test 2  Test 3  Average
Student  1     87      96      70    84.33
Student  2     68      87      90    81.67
Student  3     94     100      90    94.67
Student  4    100      81      82    87.67
Student  5     83      65      85    77.67
Student  6     78      87      65    76.67
Student  7     85      75      83    81.00
Student  8     91      94     100    95.00
Student  9     76      72      84    77.33
Student 10     87      93      73    84.33

Lowest grade in the grade book is 65
Highest grade in the grade book is 100

Overall grade distribution:
00-09:
10-19:
20-29:
```

(continued top of next page...)

Fig. 7.19 | Creates GradeBook object using a two-dimensional array of grades, then invokes method processGrades to analyze them. (Part 1 of 2.)

(continued from previous page...)

```
30-39:
40-49:
50-59:
60-69: ***
70-79: ******
80-89: ***********
90-99: *******
  100: ***
```

Fig. 7.19 | Creates GradeBook object using a two-dimensional array of grades, then invokes method processGrades to analyze them. (Part 2 of 2.)

7.11 Variable-Length Argument Lists

Variable-length argument lists are a new feature in J2SE 5.0. Programmers can create methods that receive an unspecified number of arguments. An argument type followed by an ellipsis (...) in a method's parameter list indicates that the method receives a variable number of arguments of that particular type. This use of the ellipsis can occur only once in a parameter list, and the ellipsis, together with its type, must be placed at the end of the parameter list. While programmers can use method overloading and array passing to accomplish much of what is accomplished with "varargs," or variable-length argument lists, using an ellipsis in a method's parameter list is more concise.

Figure 7.20 demonstrates method average (lines 7–16), which receives a variable-length sequence of doubles. Java treats the variable-length argument list as an array whose elements are all of the same type. Hence, the method body can manipulate the parameter numbers as an array of doubles. Lines 12–13 use the enhanced for loop to walk through the array and calculate the total of the doubles in the array. Line 15 accesses numbers.length to obtain the size of the numbers array for use in the averaging calculation. Lines 29, 31 and 33 in main call method average with two, three and four arguments, respectively. Method average has a variable-length argument list, so it can average as many double arguments as the caller passes. The output reveals that each call to method average returns the correct value.

```java
1  // Fig. 7.20: VarargsTest.java
2  // Using variable-length argument lists.
3
4  public class VarargsTest
5  {
6     // calculate average
7     public static double average( double... numbers )
8     {
9        double total = 0.0; // initialize total
10
11       // calculate total using the enhanced for statement
12       for ( double d : numbers )
13          total += d;
14
```

Fig. 7.20 | Using variable-length argument lists. (Part 1 of 2.)

```
15              return total / numbers.length;
16          } // end method average
17
18          public static void main( String args[] )
19          {
20              double d1 = 10.0;
21              double d2 = 20.0;
22              double d3 = 30.0;
23              double d4 = 40.0;
24
25              System.out.printf( "d1 = %.1f\nd2 = %.1f\nd3 = %.1f\nd4 = %.1f\n\n",
26                  d1, d2, d3, d4 );
27
28              System.out.printf( "Average of d1 and d2 is %.1f\n",
29                  average( d1, d2 ) );
30              System.out.printf( "Average of d1, d2 and d3 is %.1f\n",
31                  average( d1, d2, d3 ) );
32              System.out.printf( "Average of d1, d2, d3 and d4 is %.1f\n",
33                  average( d1, d2, d3, d4 ) );
34          } // end main
35      } // end class VarargsTest
```

```
d1 = 10.0
d2 = 20.0
d3 = 30.0
d4 = 40.0

Average of d1 and d2 is 15.0
Average of d1, d2 and d3 is 20.0
Average of d1, d2, d3 and d4 is 25.0
```

Fig. 7.20 | Using variable-length argument lists. (Part 2 of 2.)

 Common Programming Error 7.6

Placing an ellipsis in the middle of a method parameter list is a syntax error. An ellipsis may be placed only at the end of the parameter list.

7.12 Using Command-Line Arguments

On many systems it is possible to pass arguments from the command line (these are known as command-line arguments) to an application by including a parameter of type String[] (i.e., an array of Strings) in the parameter list of main, exactly as we have done in every application in the book. By convention, this parameter is named args. When an application is executed using the java command, Java passes the command-line arguments that appear after the class name in the java command to the application's main method as Strings in the array args. The number of arguments passed in from the command line is obtained by accessing the array's length attribute. For example, the command "java MyClass a b" passes two command-line arguments to application MyClass. Note that command-line arguments are separated by white space, not commas. When this command executes, MyClass's main method receives the two-element array args (i.e., args.length is 2) in which args[0] contains the String "a" and args[1] contains the

String "b". Common uses of command-line arguments include passing options and file names to applications.

Figure 7.21 uses three command-line arguments to initialize an array. When the program executes, if args.length is not 3, the program prints an error message and terminates (lines 9–12). Otherwise, lines 14–32 initialize and display the array based on the values of the command-line arguments.

The command-line arguments become available to main as Strings in args. Line 16 gets args[0]—a String that specifies the array size—and converts it to an int value that the program uses to create the array in line 17. The **static** method **parseInt** of class **Integer** converts its String argument to an int.

```
 1   // Fig. 7.21: InitArray.java
 2   // Using command-line arguments to initialize an array.
 3
 4   public class InitArray
 5   {
 6      public static void main( String args[] )
 7      {
 8         // check number of command-line arguments
 9         if ( args.length != 3 )
10            System.out.println(
11               "Error: Please re-enter the entire command, including\n" +
12               "an array size, initial value and increment." );
13         else
14         {
15            // get array size from first command-line argument
16            int arrayLength = Integer.parseInt( args[ 0 ] );
17            int array[] = new int[ arrayLength ]; // create array
18
19            // get initial value and increment from command-line argument
20            int initialValue = Integer.parseInt( args[ 1 ] );
21            int increment = Integer.parseInt( args[ 2 ] );
22
23            // calculate value for each array element
24            for ( int counter = 0; counter < array.length; counter++ )
25               array[ counter ] = initialValue + increment * counter;
26
27            System.out.printf( "%s%8s\n", "Index", "Value" );
28
29            // display array index and value
30            for ( int counter = 0; counter < array.length; counter++ )
31               System.out.printf( "%5d%8d\n", counter, array[ counter ] );
32         } // end else
33      } // end main
34   } // end class InitArray
```

```
java InitArray
Error: Please re-enter the entire command, including
an array size, initial value and increment.
```

Fig. 7.21 | Initializing an array using command-line arguments. (Part 1 of 2.)

```
java InitArray 5 0 4
Index   Value
   0       0
   1       4
   2       8
   3      12
   4      16
```

```
java InitArray 10 1 2
Index   Value
   0       1
   1       3
   2       5
   3       7
   4       9
   5      11
   6      13
   7      15
   8      17
   9      19
```

Fig. 7.21 | Initializing an array using command-line arguments. (Part 2 of 2.)

Lines 20–21 convert the args[1] and args[2] command-line arguments to int values and store them in initialValue and increment, respectively. Lines 24–25 calculate the value for each array element.

The output of the first sample execution indicates that the application received an insufficient number of command-line arguments. The second sample execution uses command-line arguments 5, 0 and 4 to specify the size of the array (5), the value of the first element (0) and the increment of each value in the array (4), respectively. The corresponding output indicates that these values create an array containing the integers 0, 4, 8, 12 and 16. The output from the third sample execution illustrates that the command-line arguments 10, 1 and 2 produce an array whose 10 elements are the nonnegative odd integers from 1 to 19.

7.13 (Optional) GUI and Graphics Case Study: Drawing Arcs

Using Java's graphics features, we can create complex drawings that would be more tedious to code line by line. In Fig. 7.22 and Fig. 7.23, we use arrays and repetition statements to draw a rainbow by using Graphics method fillArc. Drawing arcs in Java is similar to drawing ovals—an arc is simply a section of an oval.

```java
1  // Fig. 7.22: DrawRainbow.java
2  // Demonstrates using colors in an array.
3  import java.awt.Color;
4  import java.awt.Graphics;
5  import javax.swing.JPanel;
```

Fig. 7.22 | Drawing a rainbow using arcs and an array of colors. (Part 1 of 2.)

```
6
7    public class DrawRainbow extends JPanel
8    {
9       // Define indigo and violet
10      final Color VIOLET = new Color( 128, 0, 128 );
11      final Color INDIGO = new Color( 75, 0, 130 );
12
13      // colors to use in the rainbow, starting from the innermost
14      // The two white entries result in an empty arc in the center
15      private Color colors[] =
16         { Color.WHITE, Color.WHITE, VIOLET, INDIGO, Color.BLUE,
17           Color.GREEN, Color.YELLOW, Color.ORANGE, Color.RED };
18
19      // constructor
20      public DrawRainbow()
21      {
22         setBackground( Color.WHITE ); // set the background to white
23      } // end DrawRainbow constructor
24
25      // draws a rainbow using concentric circles
26      public void paintComponent( Graphics g )
27      {
28         super.paintComponent( g );
29
30         int radius = 20; // radius of an arch
31
32         // draw the rainbow near the bottom-center
33         int centerX = getWidth() / 2;
34         int centerY = getHeight() - 10;
35
36         // draws filled arcs starting with the outermost
37         for ( int counter = colors.length; counter > 0; counter-- )
38         {
39            // set the color for the current arc
40            g.setColor( colors[ counter - 1 ] );
41
42            // fill the arc from 0 to 180 degrees
43            g.fillArc( centerX - counter * radius,
44               centerY - counter * radius,
45               counter * radius * 2, counter * radius * 2, 0, 180 );
46         } // end for
47      } // end method paintComponent
48   } // end class DrawRainbow
```

Fig. 7.22 | Drawing a rainbow using arcs and an array of colors. (Part 2 of 2.)

Figure 7.22 begins with the usual import statements for creating drawings (lines 3–5). Lines 9–10 declare and create two new colors—VIOLET and INDIGO. As you may know, the colors of a rainbow are red, orange, yellow, green, blue, indigo and violet. Java only has predefined constants for the first five colors. Lines 15–17 initialize an array with the colors of the rainbow, starting with the innermost arcs first. The array begins with two Color.WHITE elements, which, as you will soon see, are for drawing the empty arcs at the center of the rainbow. Note that the instance variables can be initialized when they are

```
1   // Fig. 7.23: DrawRainbowTest.java
2   // Test application to display a rainbow.
3   import javax.swing.JFrame;
4
5   public class DrawRainbowTest
6   {
7      public static void main( String args[] )
8      {
9         DrawRainbow panel = new DrawRainbow();
10        JFrame application = new JFrame();
11
12        application.setDefaultCloseOperation( JFrame.EXIT_ON_CLOSE );
13        application.add( panel );
14        application.setSize( 400, 250 );
15        application.setVisible( true );
16     } // end main
17  } // end class DrawRainbowTest
```

Fig. 7.23 | Creating JFrame to display a rainbow.

declared, as shown in lines 10–17. The constructor (lines 20–23) contains a single statement that calls method **setBackground** (which is inherited from class JPanel) with the parameter Color.WHITE. Method setBackground takes a single Color argument and sets the background of the component to that color.

Line 30 in paintComponent declares local variable radius, which determines the thickness of each arc. Local variables centerX and centerY (lines 33–34) determine the location of the midpoint on the base of the rainbow. The loop at lines 37–46 uses control variable counter to count backwards from the end of the array, drawing the largest arcs first and placing each successive smaller arc on top of the previous one. Line 40 sets the color to draw the current arc from the array. The reason we have Color.WHITE entries at the beginning of the array is to create the empty arc in the center. Otherwise, the center of the rainbow would just be a solid violet semicircle. [*Note:* You can change the individual colors and the number of entries in the array to create new designs.]

The **fillArc** method call at lines 43–45 draws a filled semicircle. Method fillArc requires six parameters. The first four represent the bounding rectangle in which the arc will be drawn. The first two specify the coordinates for the upper-left corner of the bounding rectangle, and the next two specify its width and height. The fifth parameter is the starting angle on the oval, and the sixth specifies the **sweep**, or the amount of arc to cover. The starting angle and sweep are measured in degrees, with zero degrees pointing right. A positive sweep draws the arc counter-clockwise, while a negative sweep draws the arc clockwise. A method similar to `fillArc` is **drawArc**—it requires the same parameters as `fillArc`, but draws the edge of the arc rather than filling it.

Class `DrawRainbowTest` (Fig. 7.23) creates and sets up a `JFrame` to display the rainbow. Once the program makes the `JFrame` visible, the system calls the `paintComponent` method in class `DrawRainbow` to draw the rainbow on the screen.

GUI and Graphics Case Study Exercise

7.1 (*Drawing Spirals*) In this exercise, you will draw spirals with methods `drawLine` and `drawArc`.
  a) Draw a square-shaped spiral (as in the left screen capture of Fig. 7.24), centered on the panel, using method `drawLine`. One technique is to use a loop that increases the line length after drawing every second line. The direction in which to draw the next line should follow a distinct pattern, such as down, left, up, right.
  b) Draw a circular spiral (as in the right screen capture of Fig. 7.24), using method `drawArc` to draw one semicircle at a time. Each successive semicircle should have a larger radius (as specified by the bounding rectangle's width) and should continue drawing where the previous semicircle finished.

7.14 (Optional) Software Engineering Case Study: Collaboration Among Objects

In this section, we concentrate on the collaborations (interactions) among objects. When two objects communicate with each other to accomplish a task, they are said to **collaborate**—objects do this by invoking one another's operations. A **collaboration** consists of an object of one class sending a **message** to an object of another class. Messages are sent in Java via method calls.

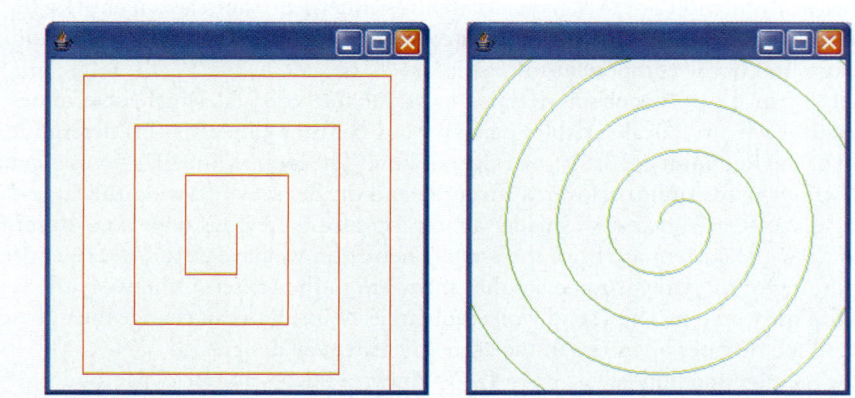

Fig. 7.24 | Drawing a spiral using `drawLine` (left) and `drawArc` (right).

In Section 6.14, we determined many of the operations of the classes in our system. In this section, we concentrate on the messages that invoke these operations. To identify the collaborations in the system, we return to the requirements document in Section 2.9. Recall that this document specifies the range of activities that occur during an ATM session (e.g., authenticating a user, performing transactions). The steps used to describe how the system must perform each of these tasks are our first indication of the collaborations in our system. As we proceed through this and the remaining "Software Engineering Case Study" sections, we may discover additional collaborations.

Identifying the Collaborations in a System

We identify the collaborations in the system by carefully reading the sections of the requirements document that specify what the ATM should do to authenticate a user and to perform each transaction type. For each action or step described in the requirements document, we decide which objects in our system must interact to achieve the desired result. We identify one object as the sending object and another as the receiving object. We then select one of the receiving object's operations (identified in Section 6.14) that must be invoked by the sending object to produce the proper behavior. For example, the ATM displays a welcome message when idle. We know that an object of class Screen displays a message to the user via its displayMessage operation. Thus, we decide that the system can display a welcome message by employing a collaboration between the ATM and the Screen in which the ATM sends a displayMessage message to the Screen by invoking the displayMessage operation of class Screen. [*Note:* To avoid repeating the phrase "an object of class…," we refer to an object by using its class name preceded by an article ("a," "an" or "the")—for example, "the ATM" refers to an object of class ATM.]

Figure 7.25 lists the collaborations that can be derived from the requirements document. For each sending object, we list the collaborations in the order in which they first occur during an ATM session (i.e., the order in which they are discussed in the requirements document). We list each collaboration involving a unique sender, message and recipient only once, even though the collaborations may occur at several different times throughout an ATM session. For example, the first row in Fig. 7.25 indicates that the ATM collaborates with the Screen whenever the ATM needs to display a message to the user.

Let's consider the collaborations in Fig. 7.25. Before allowing a user to perform any transactions, the ATM must prompt the user to enter an account number, then to enter a PIN. It accomplishes each of these tasks by sending a displayMessage message to the Screen. Both of these actions refer to the same collaboration between the ATM and the Screen, which is already listed in Fig. 7.25. The ATM obtains input in response to a prompt by sending a getInput message to the Keypad. Next, the ATM must determine whether the user-specified account number and PIN match those of an account in the database. It does so by sending an authenticateUser message to the BankDatabase. Recall that the BankDatabase cannot authenticate a user directly—only the user's Account (i.e., the Account that contains the account number specified by the user) can access the user's PIN on record to authenticate the user. Figure 7.25 therefore lists a collaboration in which the BankDatabase sends a validatePIN message to an Account.

After the user is authenticated, the ATM displays the main menu by sending a series of displayMessage messages to the Screen and obtains input containing a menu selection

An object of class...	sends the message...	to an object of class...
ATM	displayMessage	Screen
	getInput	Keypad
	authenticateUser	BankDatabase
	execute	BalanceInquiry
	execute	Withdrawal
	execute	Deposit
BalanceInquiry	getAvailableBalance	BankDatabase
	getTotalBalance	BankDatabase
	displayMessage	Screen
Withdrawal	displayMessage	Screen
	getInput	Keypad
	getAvailableBalance	BankDatabase
	isSufficientCashAvailable	CashDispenser
	debit	BankDatabase
	dispenseCash	CashDispenser
Deposit	displayMessage	Screen
	getInput	Keypad
	isEnvelopeReceived	DepositSlot
	credit	BankDatabase
BankDatabase	validatePIN	Account
	getAvailableBalance	Account
	getTotalBalance	Account
	debit	Account
	credit	Account

Fig. 7.25 | Collaborations in the ATM system.

by sending a getInput message to the Keypad. We have already accounted for these collaborations, so we do not add anything to Fig. 7.25. After the user chooses a type of transaction to perform, the ATM executes the transaction by sending an execute message to an object of the appropriate transaction class (i.e., a BalanceInquiry, a Withdrawal or a Deposit). For example, if the user chooses to perform a balance inquiry, the ATM sends an execute message to a BalanceInquiry.

Further examination of the requirements document reveals the collaborations involved in executing each transaction type. A BalanceInquiry retrieves the amount of money available in the user's account by sending a getAvailableBalance message to the BankDatabase, which responds by sending a getAvailableBalance message to the user's Account. Similarly, the BalanceInquiry retrieves the amount of money on deposit by sending a getTotalBalance message to the BankDatabase, which sends the same message to the user's Account. To display both measures of the user's balance at the same time, the BalanceInquiry sends a displayMessage message to the Screen.

A Withdrawal sends a series of displayMessage messages to the Screen to display a menu of standard withdrawal amounts (i.e., $20, $40, $60, $100, $200). The Withdrawal sends a getInput message to the Keypad to obtain the user's menu selection. Next, the Withdrawal determines whether the requested withdrawal amount is less than or equal to the user's account balance. The Withdrawal can obtain the amount of money available in the user's account by sending a getAvailableBalance message to the BankDatabase. The Withdrawal then tests whether the cash dispenser contains enough cash by sending an isSufficientCashAvailable message to the CashDispenser. A Withdrawal sends a debit message to the BankDatabase to decrease the user's account balance. The BankDatabase in turn sends the same message to the appropriate Account. Recall that debiting funds from an Account decreases both the totalBalance and the availableBalance. To dispense the requested amount of cash, the Withdrawal sends a dispenseCash message to the CashDispenser. Finally, the Withdrawal sends a displayMessage message to the Screen, instructing the user to take the cash.

A Deposit responds to an execute message first by sending a displayMessage message to the Screen to prompt the user for a deposit amount. The Deposit sends a getInput message to the Keypad to obtain the user's input. The Deposit then sends a displayMessage message to the Screen to tell the user to insert a deposit envelope. To determine whether the deposit slot received an incoming deposit envelope, the Deposit sends an isEnvelopeReceived message to the DepositSlot. The Deposit updates the user's account by sending a credit message to the BankDatabase, which subsequently sends a credit message to the user's Account. Recall that crediting funds to an Account increases the totalBalance but not the availableBalance.

Interaction Diagrams

Now that we have identified a set of possible collaborations between the objects in our ATM system, let us graphically model these interactions using the UML. The UML provides several types of interaction diagrams that model the behavior of a system by modeling how objects interact. The communication diagram emphasizes which objects participate in collaborations. [*Note:* Communication diagrams were called collaboration diagrams in earlier versions of the UML.] Like the communication diagram, the sequence diagram shows collaborations among objects, but it emphasizes *when* messages are sent between objects *over time*.

Communication Diagrams

Figure 7.26 shows a communication diagram that models the ATM executing a BalanceInquiry. Objects are modeled in the UML as rectangles containing names in the form objectName : ClassName. In this example, which involves only one object of each type, we disregard the object name and list only a colon followed by the class name. [*Note:* Specifying the name of each object in a communication diagram is recommended when modeling multiple objects of the same type.] Communicating objects are connected with solid lines, and messages are passed between objects along these lines in the direction shown by arrows. The name of the message, which appears next to the arrow, is the name of an operation (i.e., a method in Java) belonging to the receiving object—think of the name as a "service" that the receiving object provides to sending objects (its "clients").

The solid filled arrow in Fig. 7.26 represents a message—or synchronous call—in the UML and a method call in Java. This arrow indicates that the flow of control is from the

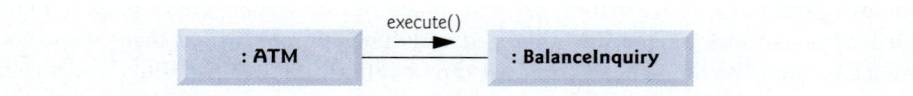

Fig. 7.26 | Communication diagram of the ATM executing a balance inquiry.

sending object (the ATM) to the receiving object (a BalanceInquiry). Since this is a syn-chronous call, the sending object may not send another message, or do anything at all, until the receiving object processes the message and returns control to the sending object. The sender just waits. For example, in Fig. 7.26, the ATM calls method execute of a Bal-anceInquiry and may not send another message until execute has finished and returns control to the ATM. [*Note:* If this were an **asynchronous call**, represented by a stick arrow-head, the sending object would not have to wait for the receiving object to return con-trol—it would continue sending additional messages immediately following the asynchronous call. Asynchronous calls are implemented in Java using a technique called multithreading, which is discussed in Chapter 23, Multithreading.]

Sequence of Messages in a Communication Diagram
Figure 7.27 shows a communication diagram that models the interactions among objects in the system when an object of class BalanceInquiry executes. We assume that the ob-ject's accountNumber attribute contains the account number of the current user. The col-laborations in Fig. 7.27 begin after the ATM sends an execute message to a BalanceInquiry (i.e., the interaction modeled in Fig. 7.26). The number to the left of a message name indicates the order in which the message is passed. The **sequence of mes-sages** in a communication diagram progresses in numerical order from least to greatest. In

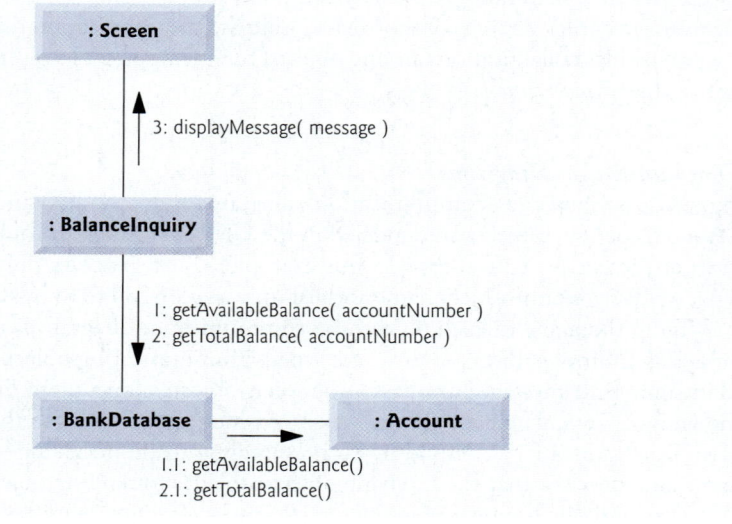

Fig. 7.27 | Communication diagram for executing a balance inquiry.

this diagram, the numbering starts with message 1 and ends with message 3. The Balance-Inquiry first sends a getAvailableBalance message to the BankDatabase (message 1), then sends a getTotalBalance message to the BankDatabase (message 2). Within the parentheses following a message name, we can specify a comma-separated list of the names of the parameters sent with the message (i.e., arguments in a Java method call)—the BalanceInquiry passes attribute accountNumber with its messages to the BankDatabase to indicate which Account's balance information to retrieve. Recall from Fig. 6.22 that operations getAvailableBalance and getTotalBalance of class BankDatabase each require a parameter to identify an account. The BalanceInquiry next displays the availableBalance and the totalBalance to the user by passing a displayMessage message to the Screen (message 3) that includes a parameter indicating the message to be displayed.

Note, however, that Fig. 7.27 models two additional messages passing from the BankDatabase to an Account (message 1.1 and message 2.1). To provide the ATM with the two balances of the user's Account (as requested by messages 1 and 2), the BankDatabase must pass a getAvailableBalance and a getTotalBalance message to the user's Account. Such messages passed within the handling of another message are called **nested messages**. The UML recommends using a decimal numbering scheme to indicate nested messages. For example, message 1.1 is the first message nested in message 1—the BankDatabase passes a getAvailableBalance message during BankDatabase's processing of a message by the same name. [*Note:* If the BankDatabase needed to pass a second nested message while processing message 1, the second message would be numbered 1.2.] A message may be passed only when all the nested messages from the previous message have been passed. For example, the BalanceInquiry passes message 3 only after messages 2 and 2.1 have been passed, in that order.

The nested numbering scheme used in communication diagrams helps clarify precisely when and in what context each message is passed. For example, if we numbered the messages in Fig. 7.27 using a flat numbering scheme (i.e., 1, 2, 3, 4, 5), someone looking at the diagram might not be able to determine that BankDatabase passes the getAvailableBalance message (message 1.1) to an Account *during* the BankDatabase's processing of message 1, as opposed to *after* completing the processing of message 1. The nested decimal numbers make it clear that the second getAvailableBalance message (message 1.1) is passed to an Account within the handling of the first getAvailableBalance message (message 1) by the BankDatabase.

Sequence Diagrams

Communication diagrams emphasize the participants in collaborations, but model their timing a bit awkwardly. A sequence diagram helps model the timing of collaborations more clearly. Figure 7.28 shows a sequence diagram modeling the sequence of interactions that occur when a Withdrawal executes. The dotted line extending down from an object's rectangle is that object's **lifeline**, which represents the progression of time. Actions occur along an object's lifeline in chronological order from top to bottom—an action near the top happens before one near the bottom.

Message passing in sequence diagrams is similar to message passing in communication diagrams. A solid arrow with a filled arrowhead extending from the sending object to the receiving object represents a message between two objects. The arrowhead points to an activation on the receiving object's lifeline. An **activation**, shown as a thin vertical rect-

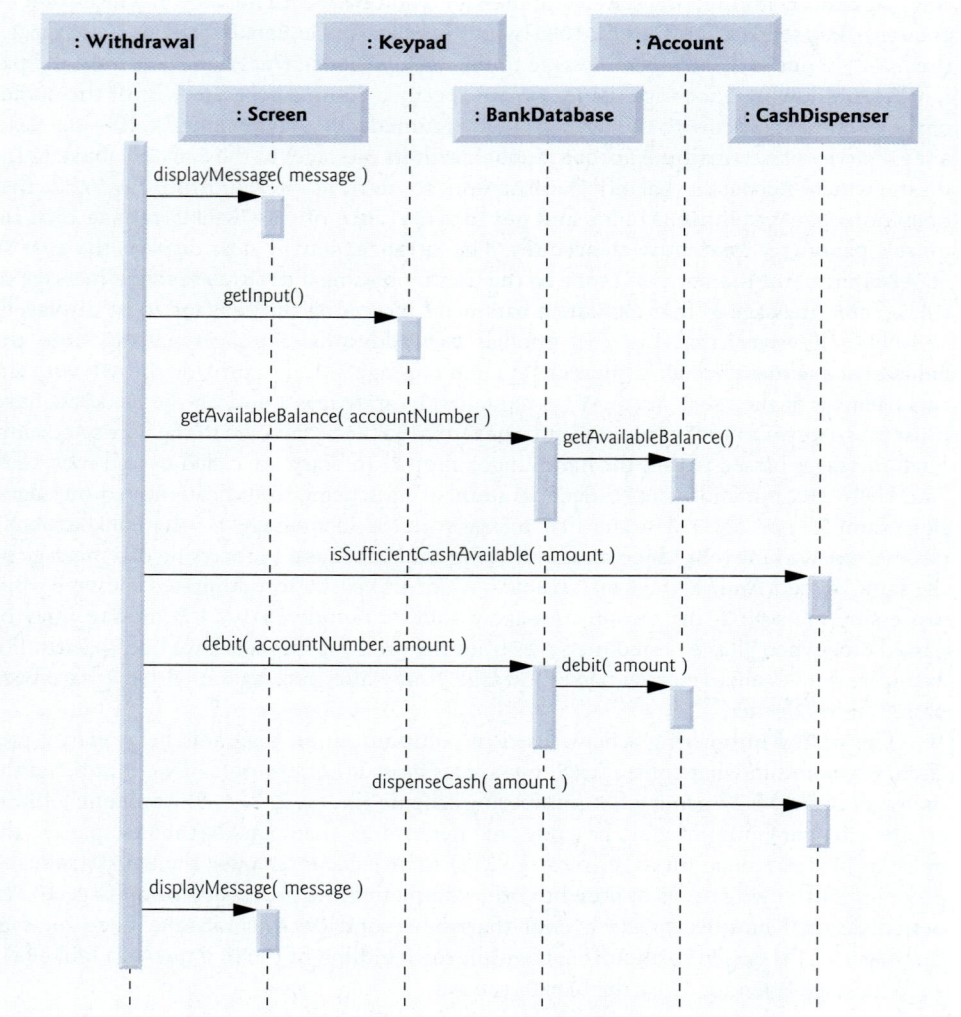

Fig. 7.28 | Sequence diagram that models a `Withdrawal` executing.

angle, indicates that an object is executing. When an object returns control, a return message, represented as a dashed line with a stick arrowhead, extends from the activation of the object returning control to the activation of the object that initially sent the message. To eliminate clutter, we omit the return-message arrows—the UML allows this practice to make diagrams more readable. Like communication diagrams, sequence diagrams can indicate message parameters between the parentheses following a message name.

The sequence of messages in Fig. 7.28 begins when a `Withdrawal` prompts the user to choose a withdrawal amount by sending a `displayMessage` message to the `Screen`. The `Withdrawal` then sends a `getInput` message to the `Keypad`, which obtains input from the user. We have already modeled the control logic involved in a `Withdrawal` in the activity diagram of

Fig. 5.31, so we do not show this logic in the sequence diagram of Fig. 7.28. Instead, we model the best-case scenario in which the balance of the user's account is greater than or equal to the chosen withdrawal amount, and the cash dispenser contains a sufficient amount of cash to satisfy the request. For information on how to model control logic in a sequence diagram, please refer to the Web resources and recommended readings listed at the end of Section 2.9.

After obtaining a withdrawal amount, the `Withdrawal` sends a `getAvailableBalance` message to the `BankDatabase`, which in turn sends a `getAvailableBalance` message to the user's `Account`. Assuming that the user's account has enough money available to permit the transaction, the `Withdrawal` next sends an `isSufficientCashAvailable` message to the `CashDispenser`. Assuming that there is enough cash available, the `Withdrawal` decreases the balance of the user's account (i.e., both the `totalBalance` and the `availableBalance`) by sending a `debit` message to the `BankDatabase`. The `BankDatabase` responds by sending a `debit` message to the user's `Account`. Finally, the `Withdrawal` sends a `dispenseCash` message to the `CashDispenser` and a `displayMessage` message to the `Screen`, telling the user to remove the cash from the machine.

We have identified the collaborations among objects in the ATM system and modeled some of these collaborations using UML interaction diagrams—both communication diagrams and sequence diagrams. In the next "Software Engineering Case Study" section (Section 8.19), we enhance the structure of our model to complete a preliminary object-oriented design, then we begin implementing the ATM system.

Software Engineering Case Study Self-Review Exercises

7.1   A(n) _____ consists of an object of one class sending a message to an object of another class.
    a) association
    b) aggregation
    c) collaboration
    d) composition

7.2   Which form of interaction diagram emphasizes *what* collaborations occur? Which form emphasizes *when* collaborations occur?

7.3   Create a sequence diagram that models the interactions among objects in the ATM system that occur when a `Deposit` executes successfully, and explain the sequence of messages modeled by the diagram.

Answers to Software Engineering Case Study Self-Review Exercises

7.1   c.

7.2   Communication diagrams emphasize *what* collaborations occur. Sequence diagrams emphasize *when* collaborations occur.

7.3   Figure 7.29 presents a sequence diagram that models the interactions between objects in the ATM system that occur when a `Deposit` executes successfully.

Figure 7.29 indicates that a `Deposit` first sends a `displayMessage` message to the `Screen` to ask the user to enter a deposit amount. Next the `Deposit` sends a `getInput` message to the `Keypad` to receive input from the user. The `Deposit` then instructs the user to enter a deposit envelope by sending a `displayMessage` message to the `Screen`. The `Deposit` next sends an `isEnvelopeReceived` message to the `DepositSlot` to confirm that the deposit envelope has been received by the ATM. Finally, the `Deposit` increases the `totalBalance` attribute (but not the `availableBalance` attribute) of the user's `Account` by sending a `credit` message to the `BankDatabase`. The `BankDatabase` responds by sending the same message to the user's `Account`.

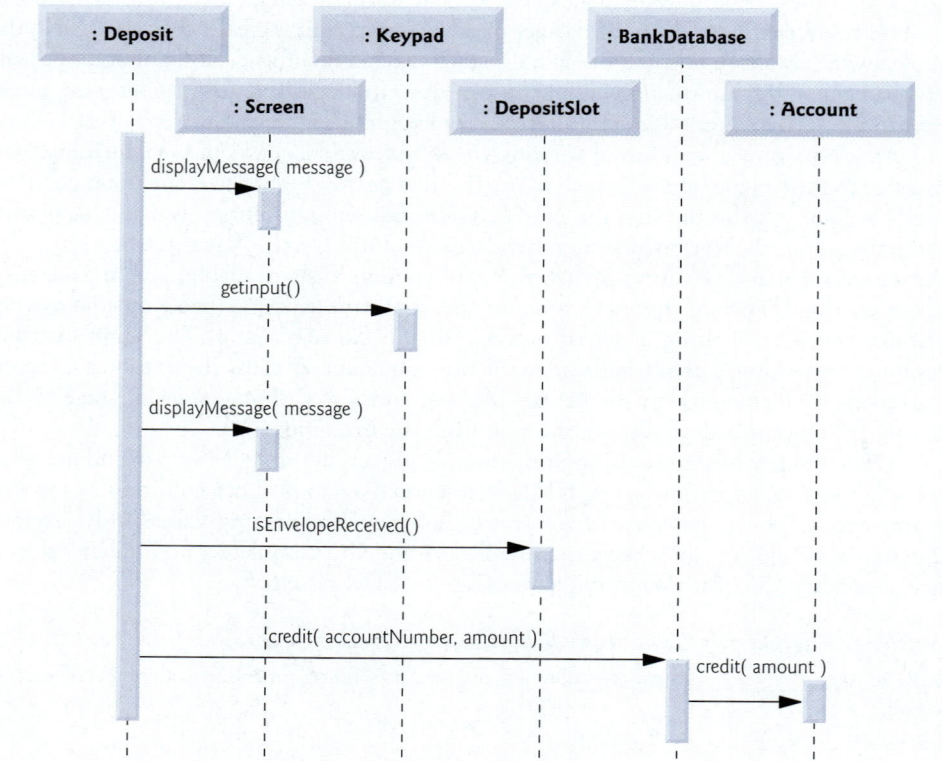

Fig. 7.29 | Sequence diagram that models a `Deposit` executing.

7.15 Wrap-Up

This chapter began our introduction to data structures, exploring the use of arrays to store data in and retrieve data from lists and tables of values. The chapter examples demonstrated how to declare an array, initialize an array and refer to individual elements of an array. The chapter introduced the enhanced `for` statement to iterate through arrays. We also illustrated how to pass arrays to methods and how to declare and manipulate multidimensional arrays. Finally, the chapter showed how to write methods that use variable-length argument lists and how to read arguments passed to a program from the command line.

We continue our coverage of data structures in Chapter 17, Data Structures, which introduces dynamic data structures, such as lists, queues, stacks and trees, that can grow and shrink as programs execute. Chapter 18, Generics, presents one of J2SE 5.0's new features—generics—which provides the means to create general models of methods and classes that can be declared once, but used with many different data types. Chapter 19, Collections, introduces the Java Collections Framework, which uses generics to allow programmers to specify the exact types of objects that a particular data structure will store. Chapter 19 also introduces Java's predefined data structures, which programmers can use instead of building their own. Chapter 19 discusses many data structure classes, including

`Vector` and `ArrayList`, which are array-like data structures that can grow and shrink in response to a program's changing storage requirements. The Collections API also provides class `Arrays`, which contains utility methods for array manipulation. Chapter 19 uses several `static` methods of class `Arrays` to perform such manipulations as sorting and searching the data in an array. You will be able to use some of the `Arrays` methods discussed in Chapter 19 after reading the current chapter, but some of the `Arrays` methods require knowledge of concepts presented later in the book.

We have now introduced the basic concepts of classes, objects, control statements, methods and arrays. In Chapter 8, we take a deeper look at classes and objects.

Summary

- Arrays are data structures consisting of related data items of the same type. Arrays are fixed-length entities—they remain the same length once they are created, although an array variable may be reassigned the reference of a new array of a different length.

- An array is a group of variables (called elements or components) containing values that all have the same type. Arrays are objects, so they are considered reference types. The elements of an array can be either primitive types or reference types (including arrays).

- To refer to a particular element in an array, we specify the name of the reference to the array and the index (subscript) of the element in the array.

- A program refers to any one of an array's elements with an array-access expression that includes the name of the array followed by the index of the particular element in square brackets (`[]`).

- The first element in every array has index zero and is sometimes called the zeroth element.

- An index must be a nonnegative integer. A program can use an expression as an index.

- Every array object knows its own length and maintains this information in a `length` field. The expression *array*.`length` accesses *array*'s `length` field to determine the length of the array.

- To create an array object, the programmer specifies the type of the array elements and the number of elements as part of an array-creation expression that uses keyword `new`. The following array-creation expression creates an array of 100 `int` values:

    ```
    int b[] = new int[ 100 ];
    ```

- When an array is created, each element of the array receives a default value—zero for numeric primitive-type elements, `false` for boolean elements and `null` for references (any nonprimitive type).

- When an array is declared, the type of the array and the square brackets can be combined at the beginning of the declaration to indicate that all the identifiers in the declaration are array variables, as in

    ```
    double[] array1, array2;
    ```

- A program can declare arrays of any type. Every element of a primitive-type array contains a variable of the array's declared type. Similarly, in an array of a reference type, every element is a reference to an object of the array's declared type.

- A program can create an array and initialize its elements with an array initializer (i.e., an initializer list enclosed in braces).

- Constant variables (also called named constants or read-only variables) must be initialized before they are used and cannot be modified thereafter.

- When a Java program executes, the JVM checks array indices to ensure that they are valid (i.e., they must be greater than or equal to 0 and less than the length of the array). If a program uses an invalid index, Java generates a so-called exception to indicate that an error occurred in the program at execution time.

- The enhanced for statement allows programmers to iterate through the elements of an array or a collection without using a counter. The syntax of an enhanced for statement is:

      for (*parameter* : *arrayName*)
          statement

  where *parameter* has two parts—a type and an identifier (e.g., int number), and *arrayName* is the array through which to iterate.

- The enhanced for statement cannot be used to modify elements in an array. If a program needs to modify elements, use the traditional counter-controlled for statement.

- When an argument is passed by value, a copy of the argument's value is made and passed to the called method. The called method works exclusively with the copy.

- When an argument is passed by reference, the called method can access the argument's value in the caller directly and possibly modify it.

- Java does not allow programmers to choose between pass-by-value and pass-by-reference—all arguments are passed by value. A method call can pass two types of values to a method—copies of primitive values (e.g., values of type int and double) and copies of references to objects. Although an object's reference is passed by value, a method can still interact with the referenced object by calling its public methods using the copy of the object's reference.

- To pass an object reference to a method, simply specify in the method call the name of the variable that refers to the object.

- When an argument to a method is an entire array or an individual array element of a reference type, the called method receives a copy of the array or element's reference. When an argument to a method is an individual array element of a primitive type, the called method receives a copy of the element's value.

- To pass an individual array element to a method, use the indexed name of the array as an argument in the method call.

- Multidimensional arrays with two dimensions are often used to represent tables of values consisting of information arranged in rows and columns.

- Arrays that require two indices to identify a particular element are called two-dimensional arrays. An array with *m* rows and *n* columns is called an *m*-by-*n* array. A two-dimensional array can be initialized with an array initializer of the form

      arrayType *arrayName*[][] = { { *row1 initializer* }, { *row2 initializer* }, ... };

- Multidimensional arrays are maintained as arrays of separate one-dimensional arrays. As a result, the lengths of the rows in a two-dimensional array are not required to be the same.

- A multidimensional array with the same number of columns in every row can be created with an array-creation expression of the form

      arrayType *arrayName*[][] = new *arrayType*[*numRows*][*numColumns*];

- An argument type followed by an ellipsis (...) in a method's parameter list indicates that the method receives a variable number of arguments of that particular type. The ellipsis can occur only once in a method's parameter list and it must be at the end of the parameter list.

- A variable-length argument list is treated as an array within the method body. The number of arguments in the array can be obtained using the array's `length` field.
- Passing arguments to `main` in a Java application from the command line is achieved by including a parameter of type `String[]` in the parameter list of `main`. By convention, `main`'s parameter is named `args`.
- Java passes the command-line arguments that appear after the class name in the `java` command to the application's `main` method as `String`s in the array `args`. The number of arguments passed in from the command line is obtained by accessing the array's `length` attribute.
- The `static` method `parseInt` of class `Integer` converts its `String` argument to an `int`.

Terminology

0 flag (in a format specifier)	multidimensional array
a[i]	name of an array
a[i][j]	named constant
array	nested array initializers
array-access expression	off-by-one error
array-creation expression	one-dimensional array
array initializer	parseInt method of class Integer
bounds checking	pass-by-reference
column index	pass-by-value
column of an array	passing arrays to methods
command-line arguments	position number
component of an array	read-only variable
constant variable	row index
data structure	row of an array
declare an array	scalar
element of an array	scalar quantity
ellipsis (...) in a method's parameter list	square brackets, []
enhanced for statement	subscript
final keyword	table of values
index	tabular format
index zero	traverse an array
initialize an array	two-dimensional array
initializer list	value of an element
length field of an array	variable-length argument list
m-by-n array	zeroth element

Self-Review Exercises

7.1 Fill in the blank(s) in each of the following statements:
   a) Lists and tables of values can be stored in _____.
   b) An array is a group of _____ (called elements or components) containing values that all have the same _____.
   c) The _____ allows programmers to iterate through the elements in an array without using a counter.
   d) The number used to refer to a particular element of an array is called the element's _____.
   e) An array that uses two indices is referred to as a(n) _____ array.
   f) Use the enhanced for statement _____ to walk through double array numbers.

g) Command-line arguments are stored in _____.

h) Use the expression _____ to receive the total number of arguments in a command line. Assume that command-line arguments are stored in `String args[]`.

i) Given the command `java MyClass test`, the first command-line argument is _____.

j) A(/n) _____ in the parameter list of a method indicates that the method can receive a variable number of arguments.

7.2 Determine whether each of the following is *true* or *false*. If *false*, explain why.

a) An array can store many different types of values.

b) An array index should normally be of type `float`.

c) An individual array element that is passed to a method and modified in that method will contain the modified value when the called method completes execution.

d) Command-line arguments are separated by commas.

e) Expression `array.length` is used to access the number of arguments of a variable-length argument called `array`.

7.3 Perform the following tasks for an array called `fractions`:

a) Declare a constant `ARRAY_SIZE` that is initialized to 10.

b) Declare an array with `ARRAY_SIZE` elements of type `double`, and initialize the elements to 0.

c) Name the fourth element of the array.

d) Refer to array element 4.

e) Assign the value `1.667` to array element 9.

f) Assign the value `3.333` to the seventh element of the array.

g) Sum all the elements of the array, using a `for` statement. Declare the integer variable x as a control variable for the loop.

7.4 Perform the following tasks for an array called `table`:

a) Declare and create the array as an integer array that has three rows and three columns. Assume that the constant `ARRAY_SIZE` has been declared to be 3.

b) How many elements does the array contain?

c) Use a `for` statement to initialize each element of the array to the sum of its indices. Assume that the integer variables x and y are declared as control variables.

7.5 Find and correct the error in each of the following program segments:

a)
```
final int ARRAY_SIZE = 5;
ARRAY_SIZE = 10;
```

b) Assume `int b[] = new int[ 10 ];`
```
for ( int i = 0; i <= b.length; i++ )
   b[ i ] = 1;
```

c) Assume `int a[][] = { { 1, 2 }, { 3, 4 } };`
```
a[ 1, 1 ] = 5;
```

Answers to Self-Review Exercises

7.1 a) arrays. b) variables, type. c) enhanced for statement. d) index (or subscript or position number). e) two-dimensional. f) for (double d : numbers). g) an array of Strings, usually called args. h) args.length. i) test. j) ellipsis (...).

7.2 a) False. An array can store only values of the same type.

b) False. An array index must be an integer or an integer expression.

c) For individual primitive-type elements of an array: False. A called method receives and manipulates a copy of the value of such an element, so modifications do not affect the original value. If the reference of an array is passed to a method, however, modifications to the array elements made in the called method are indeed reflected in the original. For individual elements of a nonprimitive type: True. A called method receives a copy of the reference of such an element, and changes to the referenced object will be reflected in the original array element.

d) False. Command-line arguments are separated by white space.

e) True.

7.3   a) `final int ARRAY_SIZE = 10;`

b) `double fractions[] = new double[ ARRAY_SIZE ];`

c) `fractions[ 3 ]`

d) `fractions[ 4 ]`

e) `fractions[ 9 ] = 1.667;`

f) `fractions[ 6 ] = 3.333;`

g) `double total = 0.0;`
   `for ( int x = 0; x < fractions.length; x++ )`
   `    total += fractions[ x ];`

7.4   a) `int table[][] = new int[ ARRAY_SIZE ][ ARRAY_SIZE ];`

b) Nine.

c) `for ( int x = 0; x < table.length; x++ )`
   `    for ( int y = 0; y < table[ x ].length; y++ )`
   `        table[ x ][ y ] = x + y;`

7.5   a) Error: Assigning a value to a constant after it has been initialized.
Correction: Assign the correct value to the constant in a `final int ARRAY_SIZE` declaration or declare another variable.

b) Error: Referencing an array element outside the bounds of the array (`b[10]`).
Correction: Change the `<=` operator to `<`.

c) Error: Array indexing is performed incorrectly.
Correction: Change the statement to `a[ 1 ][ 1 ] = 5;`.

Exercises

7.6   Fill in the blanks in each of the following statements:

a) One-dimensional array p contains four elements. The names of those elements are _____, _____, _____ and _____.

b) Naming an array, stating its type and specifying the number of dimensions in the array is called _____ the array.

c) In a two-dimensional array, the first index identifies the _____ of an element and the second index identifies the _____ of an element.

d) An *m*-by-*n* array contains _____ rows, _____ columns and _____ elements.

e) The name of the element in row 3 and column 5 of array d is _____.

7.7   Determine whether each of the following is *true* or *false*. If *false*, explain why.

a) To refer to a particular location or element within an array, we specify the name of the array and the value of the particular element.

b) An array declaration reserves space for the array.

c) To indicate that 100 locations should be reserved for integer array p, the programmer writes the declaration
   `p[ 100 ];`

d) An application that initializes the elements of a 15-element array to zero must contain at least one for statement.

e) An application that totals the elements of a two-dimensional array must contain nested for statements.

7.8 Write Java statements to accomplish each of the following tasks:
a) Display the value of the seventh element of character array f.
b) Initialize each of the five elements of one-dimensional integer array g to 8.
c) Total the 100 elements of floating-point array c.
d) Copy 11-element array a into the first portion of array b, which contains 34 elements.
e) Determine and display the smallest and largest values contained in 99-element floating-point array w.

7.9 Consider a two-by-three integer array t.
a) Write a statement that declares and creates t.
b) How many rows does t have?
c) How many columns does t have?
d) How many elements does t have?
e) Write the names of all the elements in the second row of t.
f) Write the names of all the elements in the third column of t.
g) Write a single statement that sets the element of t in row 1 and column 2 to zero.
h) Write a series of statements that initializes each element of t to zero. Do not use a repetition statement.
i) Write a nested for statement that initializes each element of t to zero.
j) Write a nested for statement that inputs the values for the elements of t from the user.
k) Write a series of statements that determines and displays the smallest value in t.
l) Write a statement that displays the elements of the first row of t.
m) Write a statement that totals the elements of the third column of t.
n) Write a series of statements that displays the contents of t in tabular format. List the column indices as headings across the top, and list the row indices at the left of each row.

7.10 *(Sales Commissions)* Use a one-dimensional array to solve the following problem: A company pays its salespeople on a commission basis. The salespeople receive $200 per week plus 9% of their gross sales for that week. For example, a salesperson who grosses $5000 in sales in a week receives $200 plus 9% of $5000, or a total of $650. Write an application (using an array of counters) that determines how many of the salespeople earned salaries in each of the following ranges (assume that each salesperson's salary is truncated to an integer amount):
a) $200–299
b) $300–399
c) $400–499
d) $500–599
e) $600–699
f) $700–799
g) $800–899
h) $900–999
i) $1000 and over
Summarize the results in tabular format.

7.11 Write statements that perform the following one-dimensional-array operations:
a) Set the 10 elements of integer array counts to zero.
b) Add one to each of the 15 elements of integer array bonus.
c) Display the five values of integer array bestScores in column format.

7.12 *(Duplicate Elimination)* Use a one-dimensional array to solve the following problem: Write an application that inputs five numbers, each of which is between 10 and 100, inclusive. As each number is read, display it only if it is not a duplicate of a number already read. Provide for the "worst case," in which all five numbers are different. Use the smallest possible array to solve this problem. Display the complete set of unique values input after the user inputs each new value.

7.13 Label the elements of three-by-five two-dimensional array `sales` to indicate the order in which they are set to zero by the following program segment:

```
for ( int row = 0; row < sales.length; row++ )
{
    for ( int col = 0; col < sales[ row ].length; col++ )
    {
        sales[ row ][ col ] = 0;
    }
}
```

7.14 Write an application that calculates the product of a series of integers that are passed to method `product` using a variable-length argument list. Test your method with several calls, each with a different number of arguments.

7.15 Rewrite Fig. 7.2 so that the size of the array is specified by the first command-line argument. If no command-line argument is supplied, use 10 as the default size of the array.

7.16 Write an application that uses an enhanced `for` statement to sum the `double` values passed by the command-line arguments. [*Hint:* Use the `static` method `parseDouble` of class `Double` to convert a `String` to a `double` value.]

7.17 *(Dice Rolling)* Write an application to simulate the rolling of two dice. The application should use an object of class `Random` once to roll the first die and again to roll the second die. The sum of the two values should then be calculated. Each die can show an integer value from 1 to 6, so the sum of the values will vary from 2 to 12, with 7 being the most frequent sum and 2 and 12 being the least frequent sums. Figure 7.30 shows the 36 possible combinations of the two dice. Your application should roll the dice 36,000 times. Use a one-dimensional array to tally the number of times each possible sum appears. Display the results in tabular format. Determine whether the totals are reasonable (e.g., there are six ways to roll a 7, so approximately one-sixth of the rolls should be 7).

7.18 *(Game of Craps)* Write an application that runs 1000 games of craps (Fig. 6.9) and answers the following questions:

    a) How many games are won on the first roll, second roll, ..., twentieth roll and after the twentieth roll?

    b) How many games are lost on the first roll, second roll, ..., twentieth roll and after the twentieth roll?

    c) What are the chances of winning at craps? [*Note:* You should discover that craps is one of the fairest casino games. What do you suppose this means?]

    d) What is the average length of a game of craps?

    e) Do the chances of winning improve with the length of the game?

	1	2	3	4	5	6
1	2	3	4	5	6	7
2	3	4	5	6	7	8
3	4	5	6	7	8	9
4	5	6	7	8	9	10
5	6	7	8	9	10	11
6	7	8	9	10	11	12

Fig. 7.30 | The 36 possible sums of two dice.

7.19 (*Airline Reservations System*) A small airline has just purchased a computer for its new automated reservations system. You have been asked to develop the new system. You are to write an application to assign seats on each flight of the airline's only plane (capacity: 10 seats).

Your application should display the following alternatives: Please type 1 for First Class and Please type 2 for Economy. If the user types 1, your application should assign a seat in the first-class section (seats 1–5). If the user types 2, your application should assign a seat in the economy section (seats 6–10). Your application should then display a boarding pass indicating the person's seat number and whether it is in the first-class or economy section of the plane.

Use a one-dimensional array of primitive type boolean to represent the seating chart of the plane. Initialize all the elements of the array to false to indicate that all the seats are empty. As each seat is assigned, set the corresponding elements of the array to true to indicate that the seat is no longer available.

Your application should never assign a seat that has already been assigned. When the economy section is full, your application should ask the person if it is acceptable to be placed in the first-class section (and vice versa). If yes, make the appropriate seat assignment. If no, display the message "Next flight leaves in 3 hours."

7.20 (*Total Sales*) Use a two-dimensional array to solve the following problem: A company has four salespeople (1 to 4) who sell five different products (1 to 5). Once a day, each salesperson passes in a slip for each type of product sold. Each slip contains the following:
a) The salesperson number
b) The product number
c) The total dollar value of that product sold that day

Thus, each salesperson passes in between 0 and 5 sales slips per day. Assume that the information from all the slips for last month is available. Write an application that will read all this information for last month's sales and summarize the total sales by salesperson and by product. All totals should be stored in the two-dimensional array sales. After processing all the information for last month, display the results in tabular format, with each column representing a particular salesperson and each row representing a particular product. Cross-total each row to get the total sales of each product for last month. Cross-total each column to get the total sales by salesperson for last month. Your tabular output should include these cross-totals to the right of the totaled rows and to the bottom of the totaled columns.

7.21 (*Turtle Graphics*) The Logo language made the concept of *turtle graphics* famous. Imagine a mechanical turtle that walks around the room under the control of a Java application. The turtle holds a pen in one of two positions, up or down. While the pen is down, the turtle traces out shapes as it moves, and while the pen is up, the turtle moves about freely without writing anything. In this problem, you will simulate the operation of the turtle and create a computerized sketchpad.

Use a 20-by-20 array floor that is initialized to zeros. Read commands from an array that contains them. Keep track of the current position of the turtle at all times and whether the pen is currently up or down. Assume that the turtle always starts at position (0, 0) of the floor with its pen up. The set of turtle commands your application must process are shown in Fig. 7.31.

Suppose that the turtle is somewhere near the center of the floor. The following "program" would draw and display a 12-by-12 square, leaving the pen in the up position:

```
2
5,12
3
5,12
3
5,12
```

Command	Meaning
1	Pen up
2	Pen down
3	Turn right
4	Turn left
5,10	Move forward 10 spaces (replace 10 for a different number of spaces)
6	Display the 20-by-20 array
9	End of data (sentinel)

Fig. 7.31 | Turtle graphics commands.

```
3
5,12
1
6
9
```

As the turtle moves with the pen down, set the appropriate elements of array floor to 1s. When the 6 command (display the array) is given, wherever there is a 1 in the array, display an asterisk or any character you choose. Wherever there is a 0, display a blank.

Write an application to implement the turtle graphics capabilities discussed here. Write several turtle graphics programs to draw interesting shapes. Add other commands to increase the power of your turtle graphics language.

7.22 (*Knight's Tour*) One of the more interesting puzzlers for chess buffs is the Knight's Tour problem, originally proposed by the mathematician Euler. Can the chess piece called the knight move around an empty chessboard and touch each of the 64 squares once and only once? We study this intriguing problem in depth here.

The knight makes only L-shaped moves (two spaces in one direction and one space in a perpendicular direction). Thus, as shown in Fig. 7.32, from a square near the middle of an empty chessboard, the knight (labeled K) can make eight different moves (numbered 0 through 7).

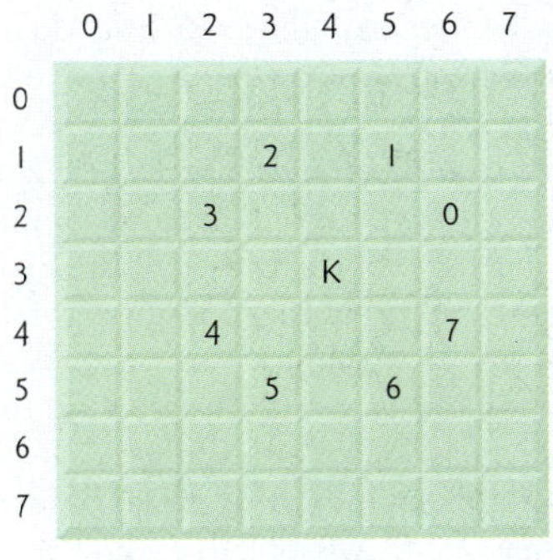

Fig. 7.32 | The eight possible moves of the knight.

a) Draw an eight-by-eight chessboard on a sheet of paper, and attempt a Knight's Tour by hand. Put a 1 in the starting square, a 2 in the second square, a 3 in the third, and so on. Before starting the tour, estimate how far you think you will get, remembering that a full tour consists of 64 moves. How far did you get? Was this close to your estimate?

b) Now let us develop an application that will move the knight around a chessboard. The board is represented by an eight-by-eight two-dimensional array board. Each square is initialized to zero. We describe each of the eight possible moves in terms of their horizontal and vertical components. For example, a move of type 0, as shown in Fig. 7.32, consists of moving two squares horizontally to the right and one square vertically upward. A move of type 2 consists of moving one square horizontally to the left and two squares vertically upward. Horizontal moves to the left and vertical moves upward are indicated with negative numbers. The eight moves may be described by two one-dimensional arrays, horizontal and vertical, as follows:

```
horizontal[ 0 ] = 2        vertical[ 0 ] = -1
horizontal[ 1 ] = 1        vertical[ 1 ] = -2
horizontal[ 2 ] = -1       vertical[ 2 ] = -2
horizontal[ 3 ] = -2       vertical[ 3 ] = -1
horizontal[ 4 ] = -2       vertical[ 4 ] = 1
horizontal[ 5 ] = -1       vertical[ 5 ] = 2
horizontal[ 6 ] = 1        vertical[ 6 ] = 2
horizontal[ 7 ] = 2        vertical[ 7 ] = 1
```

Let the variables currentRow and currentColumn indicate the row and column, respectively, of the knight's current position. To make a move of type moveNumber, where moveNumber is between 0 and 7, your application should use the statements

```
currentRow += vertical[ moveNumber ];
currentColumn += horizontal[ moveNumber ];
```

Write an application to move the knight around the chessboard. Keep a counter that varies from 1 to 64. Record the latest count in each square the knight moves to. Test each potential move to see if the knight has already visited that square. Test every potential move to ensure that the knight does not land off the chessboard. Run the application. How many moves did the knight make?

c) After attempting to write and run a Knight's Tour application, you have probably developed some valuable insights. We will use these insights to develop a *heuristic* (or "rule of thumb") for moving the knight. Heuristics do not guarantee success, but a carefully developed heuristic greatly improves the chance of success. You may have observed that the outer squares are more troublesome than the squares nearer the center of the board. In fact, the most troublesome or inaccessible squares are the four corners.

Intuition may suggest that you should attempt to move the knight to the most troublesome squares first and leave open those that are easiest to get to, so that when the board gets congested near the end of the tour, there will be a greater chance of success.

We could develop an "accessibility heuristic" by classifying each of the squares according to how accessible it is and always moving the knight (using the knight's L-shaped moves) to the most inaccessible square. We label a two-dimensional array accessibility with numbers indicating from how many squares each particular square is accessible. On a blank chessboard, each of the 16 squares nearest the center is rated as 8, each corner square is rated as 2, and the other squares have accessibility numbers of 3, 4 or 6 as follows:

```
2  3  4  4  4  4  3  2
3  4  6  6  6  6  4  3
4  6  8  8  8  8  6  4
4  6  8  8  8  8  6  4
4  6  8  8  8  8  6  4
4  6  8  8  8  8  6  4
3  4  6  6  6  6  4  3
2  3  4  4  4  4  3  2
```

Write a new version of the Knight's Tour, using the accessibility heuristic. The knight should always move to the square with the lowest accessibility number. In case of a tie, the knight may move to any of the tied squares. Therefore, the tour may begin in any of the four corners. [*Note:* As the knight moves around the chessboard, your application should reduce the accessibility numbers as more squares become occupied. In this way, at any given time during the tour, each available square's accessibility number will remain equal to precisely the number of squares from which that square may be reached.] Run this version of your application. Did you get a full tour? Modify the application to run 64 tours, one starting from each square of the chessboard. How many full tours did you get?

d) Write a version of the Knight's Tour application that, when encountering a tie between two or more squares, decides what square to choose by looking ahead to those squares reachable from the "tied" squares. Your application should move to the tied square for which the next move would arrive at a square with the lowest accessibility number.

7.23 (*Knight's Tour: Brute-Force Approaches*) In part (c) of Exercise 7.22, we developed a solution to the Knight's Tour problem. The approach used, called the "accessibility heuristic," generates many solutions and executes efficiently.

As computers continue to increase in power, we will be able to solve more problems with sheer computer power and relatively unsophisticated algorithms. Let us call this approach "brute-force" problem solving.

a) Use random-number generation to enable the knight to walk around the chessboard (in its legitimate L-shaped moves) at random. Your application should run one tour and display the final chessboard. How far did the knight get?

b) Most likely, the application in part (a) produced a relatively short tour. Now modify your application to attempt 1000 tours. Use a one-dimensional array to keep track of the number of tours of each length. When your application finishes attempting the 1000 tours, it should display this information in neat tabular format. What was the best result?

c) Most likely, the application in part (b) gave you some "respectable" tours, but no full tours. Now let your application run until it produces a full tour. (*Caution:* This version of the application could run for hours on a powerful computer.) Once again, keep a table of the number of tours of each length, and display this table when the first full tour is found. How many tours did your application attempt before producing a full tour? How much time did it take?

d) Compare the brute-force version of the Knight's Tour with the accessibility-heuristic version. Which required a more careful study of the problem? Which algorithm was more difficult to develop? Which required more computer power? Could we be certain (in advance) of obtaining a full tour with the accessibility-heuristic approach? Could we be certain (in advance) of obtaining a full tour with the brute-force approach? Argue the pros and cons of brute-force problem solving in general.

7.24 (*Eight Queens*) Another puzzler for chess buffs is the Eight Queens problem, which asks the following: Is it possible to place eight queens on an empty chessboard so that no queen is "attacking" any other (i.e., no two queens are in the same row, in the same column or along the same diagonal)?

Use the thinking developed in Exercise 7.22 to formulate a heuristic for solving the Eight Queens problem. Run your application. (*Hint:* It is possible to assign a value to each square of the chessboard to indicate how many squares of an empty chessboard are "eliminated" if a queen is placed in that square. Each of the corners would be assigned the value 22, as demonstrated by Fig. 7.33. Once these "elimination numbers" are placed in all 64 squares, an appropriate heuristic might be as follows: Place the next queen in the square with the smallest elimination number. Why is this strategy intuitively appealing?

7.25 (*Eight Queens: Brute-Force Approaches*) In this exercise, you will develop several brute-force approaches to solving the Eight Queens problem introduced in Exercise 7.24.

    a) Use the random brute-force technique developed in Exercise 7.23 to solve the Eight Queens problem.

    b) Use an exhaustive technique (i.e., try all possible combinations of eight queens on the chessboard) to solve the Eight Queens problem.

    c) Why might the exhaustive brute-force approach not be appropriate for solving the Knight's Tour problem?

    d) Compare and contrast the random brute-force and exhaustive brute-force approaches.

7.26 (*Knight's Tour: Closed-Tour Test*) In the Knight's Tour (Exercise 7.22), a full tour occurs when the knight makes 64 moves, touching each square of the chessboard once and only once. A closed tour occurs when the 64th move is one move away from the square in which the knight started the tour. Modify the application you wrote in Exercise 7.22 to test for a closed tour if a full tour has occurred.

7.27 (*Sieve of Eratosthenes*) A prime number is any integer greater than one that is evenly divisible only by itself and 1. The Sieve of Eratosthenes is a method of finding prime numbers. It operates as follows:

    a) Create a primitive type `boolean` array with all elements initialized to `true`. Array elements with prime indices will remain `true`. All other array elements will eventually be set to `false`.

    b) Starting with array index 2, determine whether a given element is `true`. If so, loop through the remainder of the array and set to `false` every element whose index is a multiple of the index for the element with value `true`. Then continue the process with the next element with value `true`. For array index 2, all elements beyond element 2 in the array that have indices which are multiples of 2 (indices 4, 6, 8, 10, etc.) will be set to `false`; for array index 3, all elements beyond element 3 in the array that have indices which are multiples of 3 (indices 6, 9, 12, 15, etc.) will be set to `false`; and so on.

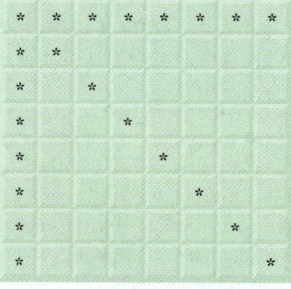

Fig. 7.33 | The 22 squares eliminated by placing a queen in the upper left corner.

When this process completes, the array elements that are still true indicate that the index is a prime number. These indices can be displayed. Write an application that uses an array of 1000 elements to determine and display the prime numbers between 2 and 999. Ignore array elements 0 and 1.

7.28   (*Simulation: The Tortoise and the Hare*) In this problem, you will re-create the classic race of the tortoise and the hare. You will use random-number generation to develop a simulation of this memorable event.

Our contenders begin the race at square 1 of 70 squares. Each square represents a possible position along the race course. The finish line is at square 70. The first contender to reach or pass square 70 is rewarded with a pail of fresh carrots and lettuce. The course weaves its way up the side of a slippery mountain, so occasionally the contenders lose ground.

A clock ticks once per second. With each tick of the clock, your application should adjust the position of the animals according to the rules in Fig. 7.34. Use variables to keep track of the positions of the animals (i.e., position numbers are 1–70). Start each animal at position 1 (the "starting gate"). If an animal slips left before square 1, move it back to square 1.

Generate the percentages in Fig. 7.34 by producing a random integer i in the range $1 \leq i \leq 10$. For the tortoise, perform a "fast plod" when $1 \leq i \leq 5$, a "slip" when $6 \leq i \leq 7$ or a "slow plod" when $8 \leq i \leq 10$. Use a similar technique to move the hare.

Begin the race by displaying

```
BANG !!!!!
AND THEY'RE OFF !!!!!
```

Then, for each tick of the clock (i.e., each repetition of a loop), display a 70-position line showing the letter T in the position of the tortoise and the letter H in the position of the hare. Occasionally, the contenders will land on the same square. In this case, the tortoise bites the hare, and your application should display OUCH!!! beginning at that position. All output positions other than the T, the H or the OUCH!!! (in case of a tie) should be blank.

After each line is displayed, test for whether either animal has reached or passed square 70. If so, display the winner and terminate the simulation. If the tortoise wins, display TORTOISE WINS!!! YAY!!! If the hare wins, display Hare wins. Yuch. If both animals win on the same tick of the clock, you may want to favor the tortoise (the "underdog"), or you may want to display It's a tie. If neither animal wins, perform the loop again to simulate the next tick of the clock. When you are ready to run your application, assemble a group of fans to watch the race. You'll be amazed at how involved your audience gets!

Animal	Move type	Percentage of the time	Actual move
Tortoise	Fast plod	50%	3 squares to the right
	Slip	20%	6 squares to the left
	Slow plod	30%	1 square to the right
Hare	Sleep	20%	No move at all
	Big hop	20%	9 squares to the right
	Big slip	10%	12 squares to the left
	Small hop	30%	1 square to the right
	Small slip	20%	2 squares to the left

Fig. 7.34 | Rules for adjusting the positions of the tortoise and the hare.

Later in the book, we introduce a number of Java capabilities, such as graphics, images, animation, sound and multithreading. As you study those features, you might enjoy enhancing your tortoise-and-hare contest simulation.

7.29 *(Fibonacci Series)* The Fibonacci series

0, 1, 1, 2, 3, 5, 8, 13, 21, …

begins with the terms 0 and 1 and has the property that each succeeding term is the sum of the two preceding terms.

a) Write a method `fibonacci( n )` that calculates the *n*th Fibonacci number. Incorporate this method into an application that enables the user to enter the value of n.

b) Determine the largest Fibonacci number that can be displayed on your system.

c) Modify the application you wrote in part (a) to use `double` instead of `int` to calculate and return Fibonacci numbers, and use this modified application to repeat part (b).

Exercise 7.30–Exercise 7.33 are reasonably challenging. Once you have done these problems, you ought to be able to implement most popular card games easily.

7.30 *(Card Shuffling and Dealing)* Modify the application of Fig. 7.11 to deal a five-card poker hand. Then modify class `DeckOfCards` of Fig. 7.10 to include methods that determine whether a hand contains

a) a pair

b) two pairs

c) three of a kind (e.g., three jacks)

d) four of a kind (e.g., four aces)

e) a flush (i.e., all five cards of the same suit)

f) a straight (i.e., five cards of consecutive face values)

g) a full house (i.e., two cards of one face value and three cards of another face value)

[*Hint:* Add methods `getFace` and `getSuit` to class `Card` of Fig. 7.9.]

7.31 *(Card Shuffling and Dealing)* Use the methods developed in Exercise 7.30 to write an application that deals two five-card poker hands, evaluates each hand and determines which is the better hand.

7.32 *(Card Shuffling and Dealing)* Modify the application developed in Exercise 7.31 so that it can simulate the dealer. The dealer's five-card hand is dealt "face down," so the player cannot see it. The application should then evaluate the dealer's hand, and, based on the quality of the hand, the dealer should draw one, two or three more cards to replace the corresponding number of unneeded cards in the original hand. The application should then reevaluate the dealer's hand. [*Caution:* This is a difficult problem!]

7.33 *(Card Shuffling and Dealing)* Modify the application developed in Exercise 7.32 so that it can handle the dealer's hand automatically, but the player is allowed to decide which cards of the player's hand to replace. The application should then evaluate both hands and determine who wins. Now use this new application to play 20 games against the computer. Who wins more games, you or the computer? Have a friend play 20 games against the computer. Who wins more games? Based on the results of these games, refine your poker-playing application. (This, too, is a difficult problem.) Play 20 more games. Does your modified application play a better game?

Special Section: Building Your Own Computer

In the next several problems, we take a temporary diversion from the world of high-level language programming. To "peel open" a computer and look at its internal structure. We introduce machine-language programming and write several machine-language programs. To make this an especially valuable experience, we then build a computer (through the technique of software-based *simulation*) on which you can execute your machine-language programs.

7.34 (*Machine-Language Programming*) Let us create a computer called the Simpletron. As its name implies, it is a simple, but powerful, machine. The Simpletron runs programs written in the only language it directly understands: Simpletron Machine Language, or SML for short.

The Simpletron contains an *accumulator*—a special register in which information is put before the Simpletron uses that information in calculations or examines it in various ways. All the information in the Simpletron is handled in terms of *words*. A word is a signed four-digit decimal number, such as +3364, -1293, +0007 and -0001. The Simpletron is equipped with a 100-word memory, and these words are referenced by their location numbers 00, 01, ..., 99.

Before running an SML program, we must *load*, or place, the program into memory. The first instruction (or statement) of every SML program is always placed in location 00. The simulator will start executing at this location.

Each instruction written in SML occupies one word of the Simpletron's memory (and hence instructions are signed four-digit decimal numbers). We shall assume that the sign of an SML instruction is always plus, but the sign of a data word may be either plus or minus. Each location in the Simpletron's memory may contain an instruction, a data value used by a program or an unused (and hence undefined) area of memory. The first two digits of each SML instruction are the *operation code* specifying the operation to be performed. SML operation codes are summarized in Fig. 7.35.

Operation code	Meaning
Input/output operations:	
`final int READ = 10;`	Read a word from the keyboard into a specific location in memory.
`final int WRITE = 11;`	Write a word from a specific location in memory to the screen.
Load/store operations:	
`final int LOAD = 20;`	Load a word from a specific location in memory into the accumulator.
`final int STORE = 21;`	Store a word from the accumulator into a specific location in memory.
Arithmetic operations:	
`final int ADD = 30;`	Add a word from a specific location in memory to the word in the accumulator (leave the result in the accumulator).
`final int SUBTRACT = 31;`	Subtract a word from a specific location in memory from the word in the accumulator (leave the result in the accumulator).
`final int DIVIDE = 32;`	Divide a word from a specific location in memory into the word in the accumulator (leave result in the accumulator).
`final int MULTIPLY = 33;`	Multiply a word from a specific location in memory by the word in the accumulator (leave the result in the accumulator).

Fig. 7.35 | Simpletron Machine Language (SML) operation codes. (Part 1 of 2.)

Operation code	Meaning
Transfer of control operations:	
`final int BRANCH = 40;`	Branch to a specific location in memory.
`final int BRANCHNEG = 41;`	Branch to a specific location in memory if the accumulator is negative.
`final int BRANCHZERO = 42;`	Branch to a specific location in memory if the accumulator is zero.
`final int HALT = 43;`	Halt. The program has completed its task.

Fig. 7.35 | Simpletron Machine Language (SML) operation codes. (Part 2 of 2.)

The last two digits of an SML instruction are the *operand*—the address of the memory location containing the word to which the operation applies. Let's consider several simple SML programs.

The first SML program (Fig. 7.36) reads two numbers from the keyboard and computes and displays their sum. The instruction +1007 reads the first number from the keyboard and places it into location 07 (which has been initialized to 0). Then instruction +1008 reads the next number into location 08. The *load* instruction, +2007, puts the first number into the accumulator, and the *add* instruction, +3008, adds the second number to the number in the accumulator. *All SML arithmetic instructions leave their results in the accumulator.* The *store* instruction, +2109, places the result back into memory location 09, from which the *write* instruction, +1109, takes the number and displays it (as a signed four-digit decimal number). The *halt* instruction, +4300, terminates execution.

The second SML program (Fig. 7.37) reads two numbers from the keyboard and determines and displays the larger value. Note the use of the instruction +4107 as a conditional transfer of control, much the same as Java's if statement.

Now write SML programs to accomplish each of the following tasks:

a) Use a sentinel-controlled loop to read 10 positive numbers. Compute and display their sum.

b) Use a counter-controlled loop to read seven numbers, some positive and some negative, and compute and display their average.

c) Read a series of numbers, and determine and display the largest number. The first number read indicates how many numbers should be processed.

7.35 (*Computer Simulator*) In this problem, you are going to build your own computer. No, you will not be soldering components together. Rather, you will use the powerful technique of *software-based simulation* to create an object-oriented *software model* of the Simpletron of Exercise 7.34. Your Simpletron simulator will turn the computer you are using into a Simpletron, and you will actually be able to run, test and debug the SML programs you wrote in Exercise 7.34.

When you run your Simpletron simulator, it should begin by displaying:

```
*** Welcome to Simpletron! ***
*** Please enter your program one instruction ***
*** (or data word) at a time into the input    ***
*** text field. I will display the location    ***
*** number and a question mark (?). You then    ***
*** type the word for that location. Press the ***
*** Done button to stop entering your program. ***
```

Your application should simulate the memory of the Simpletron with a one-dimensional array memory that has 100 elements. Now assume that the simulator is running, and let us examine the dialog as we enter the program of Fig. 7.37 (Exercise 7.34):

Location	Number	Instruction
00	+1007	(Read A)
01	+1008	(Read B)
02	+2007	(Load A)
03	+3008	(Add B)
04	+2109	(Store C)
05	+1109	(Write C)
06	+4300	(Halt)
07	+0000	(Variable A)
08	+0000	(Variable B)
09	+0000	(Result C)

Fig. 7.36 | SML program that reads two integers and computes their sum.

Location	Number	Instruction
00	+1009	(Read A)
01	+1010	(Read B)
02	+2009	(Load A)
03	+3110	(Subtract B)
04	+4107	(Branch negative to 07)
05	+1109	(Write A)
06	+4300	(Halt)
07	+1110	(Write B)
08	+4300	(Halt)
09	+0000	(Variable A)
10	+0000	(Variable B)

Fig. 7.37 | SML program that reads two integers and determines the larger.

```
00 ? +1009
01 ? +1010
02 ? +2009
03 ? +3110
04 ? +4107
05 ? +1109
06 ? +4300
07 ? +1110
08 ? +4300
09 ? +0000
10 ? +0000
11 ? -99999
```

Your program should display the memory location followed by a question mark. Each of the values to the right of a question mark is input by the user. When the sentinel value -99999 is input, the program should display the following:

```
*** Program loading completed ***
*** Program execution begins   ***
```

The SML program has now been placed (or loaded) in array memory. Now the Simpletron executes the SML program. Execution begins with the instruction in location 00 and, as in Java, continues sequentially, unless directed to some other part of the program by a transfer of control.

Use the variable accumulator to represent the accumulator register. Use the variable instructionCounter to keep track of the location in memory that contains the instruction being performed. Use the variable operationCode to indicate the operation currently being performed (i.e., the left two digits of the instruction word). Use the variable operand to indicate the memory location on which the current instruction operates. Thus, operand is the rightmost two digits of the instruction currently being performed. Do not execute instructions directly from memory. Rather, transfer the next instruction to be performed from memory to a variable called instructionRegister. Then "pick off" the left two digits and place them in operationCode, and "pick off" the right two digits and place them in operand. When the Simpletron begins execution, the special registers are all initialized to zero.

Now, let us "walk through" execution of the first SML instruction, +1009 in memory location 00. This procedure is called an *instruction execution cycle*.

The instructionCounter tells us the location of the next instruction to be performed. We *fetch* the contents of that location from memory by using the Java statement

```
instructionRegister = memory[ instructionCounter ];
```

The operation code and the operand are extracted from the instruction register by the statements

```
operationCode = instructionRegister / 100;
operand = instructionRegister % 100;
```

Now the Simpletron must determine that the operation code is actually a *read* (versus a *write*, a *load*, etc.). A switch differentiates among the 12 operations of SML. In the switch statement, the behavior of various SML instructions is simulated as shown in Fig. 7.38. We discuss branch instructions shortly and leave the others to you.

When the SML program completes execution, the name and contents of each register as well as the complete contents of memory should be displayed. Such a printout is often called a computer dump (no, a computer dump is not a place where old computers go). To help you program

Instruction	Description
read:	Display the prompt "Enter an integer", then input the integer and store it in location memory[operand].
load:	accumulator = memory[operand];
add:	accumulator += memory[operand];
halt:	This instruction displays the message *** Simpletron execution terminated ***

Fig. 7.38 | Behavior of several SML instructions in the Simpletron.

your dump method, a sample dump format is shown in Fig. 7.39. Note that a dump after executing a Simpletron program would show the actual values of instructions and data values at the moment execution terminated.

Let us proceed with the execution of our program's first instruction—namely, the +1009 in location 00. As we have indicated, the `switch` statement simulates this task by prompting the user to enter a value, reading the value and storing it in memory location `memory[ operand ]`. The value is then read into location 09.

At this point, simulation of the first instruction is completed. All that remains is to prepare the Simpletron to execute the next instruction. Since the instruction just performed was not a transfer of control, we need merely increment the instruction-counter register as follows:

```
instructionCounter++;
```

This action completes the simulated execution of the first instruction. The entire process (i.e., the instruction execution cycle) begins anew with the fetch of the next instruction to execute.

Now let us consider how the branching instructions—the transfers of control—are simulated. All we need to do is adjust the value in the instruction counter appropriately. Therefore, the unconditional branch instruction (40) is simulated within the `switch` as

```
instructionCounter = operand;
```

The conditional "branch if accumulator is zero" instruction is simulated as

```
if ( accumulator == 0 )
    instructionCounter = operand;
```

At this point, you should implement your Simpletron simulator and run each of the SML programs you wrote in Exercise 7.34. If you desire, you may embellish SML with additional features and provide for these features in your simulator.

Your simulator should check for various types of errors. During the program-loading phase, for example, each number the user types into the Simpletron's `memory` must be in the range -9999

```
REGISTERS:
accumulator            +0000
instructionCounter        00
instructionRegister    +0000
operationCode             00
operand                   00

MEMORY:
         0      1      2      3      4      5      6      7      8      9
 0   +0000  +0000  +0000  +0000  +0000  +0000  +0000  +0000  +0000  +0000
10   +0000  +0000  +0000  +0000  +0000  +0000  +0000  +0000  +0000  +0000
20   +0000  +0000  +0000  +0000  +0000  +0000  +0000  +0000  +0000  +0000
30   +0000  +0000  +0000  +0000  +0000  +0000  +0000  +0000  +0000  +0000
40   +0000  +0000  +0000  +0000  +0000  +0000  +0000  +0000  +0000  +0000
50   +0000  +0000  +0000  +0000  +0000  +0000  +0000  +0000  +0000  +0000
60   +0000  +0000  +0000  +0000  +0000  +0000  +0000  +0000  +0000  +0000
70   +0000  +0000  +0000  +0000  +0000  +0000  +0000  +0000  +0000  +0000
80   +0000  +0000  +0000  +0000  +0000  +0000  +0000  +0000  +0000  +0000
90   +0000  +0000  +0000  +0000  +0000  +0000  +0000  +0000  +0000  +0000
```

Fig. 7.39 | A sample dump.

to +9999. Your simulator should test that each number entered is in this range and, if not, keep prompting the user to reenter the number until the user enters a correct number.

During the execution phase, your simulator should check for various serious errors, such as attempts to divide by zero, attempts to execute invalid operation codes, and accumulator overflows (i.e., arithmetic operations resulting in values larger than +9999 or smaller than –9999). Such serious errors are called *fatal errors*. When a fatal error is detected, your simulator should display an error message, such as

```
*** Attempt to divide by zero ***
*** Simpletron execution abnormally terminated ***
```

and should display a full computer dump in the format we discussed previously. This treatment will help the user locate the error in the program.

7.36   (*Simpletron Simulator Modifications*) In Exercise 7.35, you wrote a software simulation of a computer that executes programs written in Simpletron Machine Language (SML). In this exercise, we propose several modifications and enhancements to the Simpletron Simulator. In Exercise 17.26 and Exercise 17.27, we propose building a compiler that converts programs written in a high-level programming language (a variation of Basic) to Simpletron Machine Language. Some of the following modifications and enhancements may be required to execute the programs produced by the compiler:

a) Extend the Simpletron Simulator's memory to contain 1000 memory locations to enable the Simpletron to handle larger programs.

b) Allow the simulator to perform remainder calculations. This modification requires an additional SML instruction.

c) Allow the simulator to perform exponentiation calculations. This modification requires an additional SML instruction.

d) Modify the simulator to use hexadecimal values rather than integer values to represent SML instructions.

e) Modify the simulator to allow output of a newline. This modification requires an additional SML instruction.

f) Modify the simulator to process floating-point values in addition to integer values.

g) Modify the simulator to handle string input. [*Hint:* Each Simpletron word can be divided into two groups, each holding a two-digit integer. Each two-digit integer represents the ASCII (see Appendix B) decimal equivalent of a character. Add a machine-language instruction that will input a string and store the string, beginning at a specific Simpletron memory location. The first half of the word at that location will be a count of the number of characters in the string (i.e., the length of the string). Each succeeding half-word contains one ASCII character expressed as two decimal digits. The machine-language instruction converts each character into its ASCII equivalent and assigns it to a half-word.]

h) Modify the simulator to handle output of strings stored in the format of part (g). [*Hint:* Add a machine-language instruction that will display a string, beginning at a certain Simpletron memory location. The first half of the word at that location is a count of the number of characters in the string (i.e., the length of the string). Each succeeding half-word contains one ASCII character expressed as two decimal digits. The machine-language instruction checks the length and displays the string by translating each two-digit number into its equivalent character.]

8

Classes and Objects: A Deeper Look

*Instead of this absurd
division into sexes, they
ought to class people as
static and dynamic.*
—Evelyn Waugh

*Is it a world to hide virtues
in?*
—William Shakespeare

*But what, to serve
our private ends,
Forbids the cheating
of our friends?*
—Charles Churchill

*This above all: to thine own
self be true.*
—William Shakespeare

*Don't be "consistent,"
but be simply true.*
—Oliver Wendell Holmes, Jr.

OBJECTIVES

In this chapter you will learn:

- Encapsulation and data hiding.
- The notions of data abstraction and abstract data types (ADTs).
- To use keyword **this**.
- To use **static** variables and methods.
- To import **static** members of a class.
- To use the **enum** type to create sets of constants with unique identifiers.
- How to declare **enum** constants with parameters.

8.1 Introduction

In our discussions of object-oriented programs in the preceding chapters, we introduced many basic concepts and terminology that relate to Java object-oriented programming (OOP). We also discussed our program development methodology: We selected appropriate variables and methods for each program and specified the manner in which an object of our class collaborated with objects of Java API classes to accomplish the program's overall goals.

In this chapter, we take a deeper look at building classes, controlling access to members of a class and creating constructors. We discuss composition—a capability that allows a class to have references to objects of other classes as members. We reexamine the use of *set* and *get* methods and further explore the new J2SE 5.0 class type enum (introduced in Section 6.10) that enables programmers to declare and manipulate sets of unique identifiers that represent constant values. In Section 6.10, we introduced the basic enum type, which appeared within another class and simply declared a set of constants. In this chapter, we discuss the relationship between enum types and classes, demonstrating that an enum, like a class, can be declared in its own file with constructors, methods and fields. The chapter also discusses static class members and final instance variables in detail. We investigate issues such as software reusability, data abstraction and encapsulation. Finally, we explain how to organize classes in packages to help manage large applications and promote reuse, then show a special relationship between classes in the same package.

Chapter 9, Object-Oriented Programming: Inheritance, and Chapter 10, Object-Oriented Programming: Polymorphism, introduce inheritance and polymorphism, respectively—two additional key object-oriented programming technologies.

8.2 Time Class Case Study

Time1 *Class Declaration*

Our first example consists of two classes—Time1 (Fig. 8.1) and Time1Test (Fig. 8.2). Class Time1 represents the time of day. Class Time1Test is an application class in which the main method creates one object of class Time1 and invokes its methods. These classes must be declared in separate files because they are both public classes. The output of this program appears in Fig. 8.2.

Class Time1 contains three private instance variables of type int (Fig. 8.1, lines 6–8)—hour, minute and second—that represent the time in universal-time format (24-hour clock format in which hours are in the range 0–23). Class Time1 contains public methods setTime (lines 12–17), toUniversalString (lines 20–23) and toString (lines 26–31). These methods are also called the **public services** or the **public interface** that the class provides to its clients.

In this example, class Time1 does not declare a constructor, so the class has a default constructor that is supplied by the compiler. Each instance variable implicitly receives the default value 0 for an int. Note that instance variables also can be initialized when they are declared in the class body using the same initialization syntax as with a local variable.

Method setTime (lines 12–17) is a public method that declares three int parameters and uses them to set the time. A conditional expression tests each argument to determine whether the value is in a specified range. For example, the hour value (line 14) must be greater than or equal to 0 and less than 24, because universal-time format represents hours as integers from 0 to 23 (e.g., 1 PM is hour 13 and 11 PM is hour 23; midnight is hour 0 and noon is hour 12). Similarly, both minute and second values (lines 15 and 16) must be greater than or equal to 0 and less than 60. Any values outside these ranges are set to zero to ensure that a Time1 object always contains consistent data—that is, the object's data values are always kept in range, even if the values provided as arguments to method setTime were incorrect. In this example, zero is a consistent value for hour, minute and second.

A value passed to setTime is a correct value if that value is in the allowed range for the member it is initializing. So, any number in the range 0–23 would be a correct value for the hour. A correct value is always a consistent value. However, a consistent value is not necessarily a correct value. If setTime sets hour to 0 because the argument received was out of range, then setTime is taking an incorrect value and making it consistent, so the object remains in a consistent state at all times. In this case, the program might want to indicate that the object is incorrect. In Chapter 13, Exception Handling, you will learn techniques that enable your classes to indicate when incorrect values are received.

Software Engineering Observation 8.1

Methods that modify the values of private variables should verify that the intended new values are proper. If they are not, the set methods should place the private variables into an appropriate consistent state.

```
 1   // Fig. 8.1: Time1.java
 2   // Time1 class declaration maintains the time in 24-hour format.
 3
 4   public class Time1
 5   {
 6      private int hour;   // 0 - 23
 7      private int minute; // 0 - 59
 8      private int second; // 0 - 59
 9
10      // set a new time value using universal time; ensure that
11      // the data remains consistent by setting invalid values to zero
12      public void setTime( int h, int m, int s )
13      {
14         hour = ( ( h >= 0 && h < 24 ) ? h : 0 );    // validate. hour
15         minute = ( ( m >= 0 && m < 60 ) ? m : 0 ); // validate minute
16         second = ( ( s >= 0 && s < 60 ) ? s : 0 ); // validate second
17      } // end method setTime
18
19      // convert to String in universal-time format (HH:MM:SS)
20      public String toUniversalString()
21      {
22         return String.format( "%02d:%02d:%02d", hour, minute, second );
23      } // end method toUniversalString
24
25      // convert to String in standard-time format (H:MM:SS AM or PM)
26      public String toString()
27      {
28         return String.format( "%d:%02d:%02d %s",
29            ( ( hour == 0 || hour == 12 ) ? 12 : hour % 12 ),
30            minute, second, ( hour < 12 ? "AM" : "PM" ) );
31      } // end method toString
32   } // end class Time1
```

Fig. 8.1 | Time1 class declaration maintains the time in 24-hour format.

Method toUniversalString (lines 20–23) takes no arguments and returns a String in universal-time format, consisting of six digits—two for the hour, two for the minute and two for the second. For example, if the time were 1:30:07 PM, method toUniversalString would return 13:30:07. The return statement (line 22) uses static method **format** of class String to return a String containing the formatted hour, minute and second values, each with two digits and possibly a leading 0 (specified with the 0 flag). Method format is similar to method System.out.printf except that format returns a formatted String rather than displaying it in a command window. The formatted String is returned by method toUniversalString.

Method toString (lines 26–31) takes no arguments and returns a String in standard-time format, consisting of the hour, minute and second values separated by colons and followed by an AM or PM indicator (e.g., 1:27:06 PM). Like method toUniversalString, method toString uses static String method format to format the minute and second as two-digit values with leading zeros if necessary. Line 29 uses a conditional operator (?:) to determine the value for hour in the string—if the hour is 0 or 12 (AM or PM), it appears as 12—otherwise, the hour appears as a value from 1 to 11. The conditional operator in line 30 determines whether AM or PM will be returned as part of the String.

Recall from Section 6.4 that all objects in Java have a toString method that returns a String representation of the object. We chose to return a String containing the time in standard-time format. Method toString can be called implicitly whenever a Time1 object appears in the code where a String is needed, such as the value to output with a %s format specifier in a call to System.out.printf.

Using Class *Time1*

As you learned in Chapter 3, each class you declare represents a new type in Java. Therefore, after declaring class Time1, we can use it as a type in declarations such as

```
Time1 sunset; // sunset can hold a reference to a Time1 object
```

The Time1Test application class (Fig. 8.2) uses class Time1. Line 9 declares and creates a Time1 object and assigns it to local variable time. Note that new implicitly invokes class Time1's default constructor, since Time1 does not declare any constructors. Lines 12–16 output the time first in universal-time format (by invoking time's toUniversalString method in line 13), then in standard-time format (by explicitly invoking time's toString method in line 15) to confirm that the Time1 object was initialized properly.

Line 19 invokes method setTime of the time object to change the time. Then lines 20–24 output the time again in both formats to confirm that the time was set correctly.

To illustrate that method setTime maintains the object in a consistent state, line 27 calls method setTime with arguments of 99 for the hour, minute and second. Lines 28–32 output the time again in both formats to confirm that setTime maintained the object's consistent state, then the program terminates. The last two lines of the application's output show that the time is reset to midnight—the initial value of a Time1 object—after an attempt to set the time with three out-of-range values.

Notes on the *Time1* Class Declaration

Consider several issues of class design with respect to class Time1. The instance variables hour, minute and second are each declared private. The actual data representation used within the class is of no concern to the class's clients. For example, it would be perfectly reasonable for Time1 to represent the time internally as the number of seconds since midnight or the number of minutes and seconds since midnight. Clients could use the same public methods and get the same results without being aware of this. (Exercise 8.5 asks you to represent the time in class Time1 as the number of seconds since midnight and show that there is indeed no change visible to the clients of the class.)

Software Engineering Observation 8.2

Classes simplify programming, because the client can use only the public methods exposed by the class. Such methods are usually client oriented rather than implementation oriented. Clients are neither aware of, nor involved in, a class's implementation. Clients generally care about what the class does but not how the class does it.

Software Engineering Observation 8.3

Interfaces change less frequently than implementations. When an implementation changes, implementation-dependent code must change accordingly. Hiding the implementation reduces the possibility that other program parts will become dependent on class-implementation details.

```
 1   // Fig. 8.2: Time1Test.java
 2   // Time1 object used in an application.
 3
 4   public class Time1Test
 5   {
 6      public static void main( String args[] )
 7      {
 8         // create and initialize a Time1 object
 9         Time1 time = new Time1(); // invokes Time1 constructor
10
11         // output string representations of the time
12         System.out.print( "The initial universal time is: " );
13         System.out.println( time.toUniversalString() );
14         System.out.print( "The initial standard time is: " );
15         System.out.println( time.toString() );
16         System.out.println(); // output a blank line
17
18         // change time and output updated time
19         time.setTime( 13, 27, 6 );
20         System.out.print( "Universal time after setTime is: " );
21         System.out.println( time.toUniversalString() );
22         System.out.print( "Standard time after setTime is: " );
23         System.out.println( time.toString() );
24         System.out.println(); // output a blank line
25
26         // set time with invalid values; output updated time
27         time.setTime( 99, 99, 99 );
28         System.out.println( "After attempting invalid settings:" );
29         System.out.print( "Universal time: " );
30         System.out.println( time.toUniversalString() );
31         System.out.print( "Standard time: " );
32         System.out.println( time.toString() );
33      } // end main
34   } // end class Time1Test
```

```
The initial universal time is: 00:00:00
The initial standard time is: 12:00:00 AM

Universal time after setTime is: 13:27:06
Standard time after setTime is: 1:27:06 PM

After attempting invalid settings:
Universal time: 00:00:00
Standard time: 12:00:00 AM
```

Fig. 8.2 | Time1 object used in an application.

8.3 Controlling Access to Members

The access modifiers public and private control access to a class's variables and methods. (In Chapter 9, we will introduce the additional access modifier protected.) As we stated in Section 8.2, the primary purpose of public methods is to present to the class's clients a view of the services the class provides (the class's public interface). Clients of the class need not be concerned with how the class accomplishes its tasks. For this reason, the private variables and private methods of a class (i.e., the class's implementation details) are not directly accessible to the class's clients.

Figure 8.3 demonstrates that private class members are not directly accessible outside the class. Lines 9–11 attempt to access directly the private instance variables hour, minute and second of the Time1 object time. When this program is compiled, the compiler generates error messages stating that these private members are not accessible. [*Note:* This program assumes that the Time1 class from Fig. 8.1 is used.]

Common Programming Error 8.1

An attempt by a method that is not a member of a class to access a private member of that class is a compilation error.

8.4 Referring to the Current Object's Members with the `this` Reference

Every object can access a reference to itself with keyword **this** (sometimes called the **this reference**). When a non-static method is called for a particular object, the method's body implicitly uses keyword this to refer to the object's instance variables and other methods. As you will see in Fig. 8.4, you can also use keyword this explicitly in a non-static meth-

```
 1   // Fig. 8.3: MemberAccessTest.java
 2   // Private members of class Time1 are not accessible.
 3   public class MemberAccessTest
 4   {
 5      public static void main( String args[] )
 6      {
 7         Time1 time = new Time1(); // create and initialize Time1 object
 8
 9         time.hour = 7;     // error: hour has private access in Time1
10         time.minute = 15; // error: minute has private access in Time1
11         time.second = 30; // error: second has private access in Time1
12      } // end main
13   } // end class MemberAccessTest
```

```
MemberAccessTest.java:9: hour has private access in Time1
      time.hour = 7;     // error: hour has private access in Time1
          ^
MemberAccessTest.java:10: minute has private access in Time1
      time.minute = 15; // error: minute has private access in Time1
          ^
MemberAccessTest.java:11: second has private access in Time1
      time.second = 30; // error: second has private access in Time1
          ^
3 errors
```

Fig. 8.3 | Private members of class Time1 are not accessible.

od's body. Section 8.5 shows another interesting use of keyword `this`. Section 8.11 explains why keyword `this` cannot be used in a `static` method.

We now demonstrate implicit and explicit use of the `this` reference to enable class `ThisTest`'s `main` method to display the `private` data of a class `SimpleTime` object (Fig. 8.4). Note that this example is the first in which we declare two classes in one file—class `ThisTest` is declared in lines 4–11, and class `SimpleTime` is declared in lines 14–47. We did this to demonstrate that when you compile a `.java` file that contains more than one class, the compiler produces a separate class file with the `.class` extension for every compiled class. In this case two separate files are produced—one for `SimpleTime` and one for `ThisTest`. When one source-code (`.java`) file contains multiple class declarations, the class files for those classes are placed in the same directory by the compiler. Also, note that only class `ThisTest` is declared `public` in Fig. 8.4. A source-code file can contain only one `public` class—otherwise, a compilation error occurs.

Class `SimpleTime` (lines 14–47) declares three `private` instance variables—hour, minute and second (lines 16–18). The constructor (lines 23–28) receives three int arguments to initialize a `SimpleTime` object. Note that we used parameter names for the constructor (line 23) that are identical to the class's instance variable names (lines 16–18). We don't recommend this practice, but we did it here to shadow (hide) the corresponding instance variables so that we could illustrate explicit use of the `this` reference. If a method

```java
1   // Fig. 8.4: ThisTest.java
2   // this used implicitly and explicitly to refer to members of an object.
3
4   public class ThisTest
5   {
6      public static void main( String args[] )
7      {
8         SimpleTime time = new SimpleTime( 15, 30, 19 );
9         System.out.println( time.buildString() );
10     } // end main
11  } // end class ThisTest
12
13  // class SimpleTime demonstrates the "this" reference
14  class SimpleTime
15  {
16     private int hour;    // 0-23
17     private int minute;  // 0-59
18     private int second;  // 0-59
19
20     // if the constructor uses parameter names identical to
21     // instance variable names the "this" reference is
22     // required to distinguish between names
23     public SimpleTime( int hour, int minute, int second )
24     {
25        this.hour = hour;      // set "this" object's hour
26        this.minute = minute;  // set "this" object's minute
27        this.second = second;  // set "this" object's second
28     } // end SimpleTime constructor
```

Fig. 8.4 | `this` used implicitly and explicitly to refer to members of an object. (Part 1 of 2.)

```
29
30       // use explicit and implicit "this" to call toUniversalString
31       public String buildString()
32       {
33          return String.format( "%24s: %s\n%24s: %s",
34             "this.toUniversalString()", this.toUniversalString(),
35             "toUniversalString()", toUniversalString() );
36       } // end method buildString
37
38       // convert to String in universal-time format (HH:MM:SS)
39       public String toUniversalString()
40       {
41          // "this" is not required here to access instance variables,
42          // because method does not have local variables with same
43          // names as instance variables
44          return String.format( "%02d:%02d:%02d",
45             this.hour, this.minute, this.second );
46       } // end method toUniversalString
47    } // end class SimpleTime
```

```
this.toUniversalString(): 15:30:19
     toUniversalString(): 15:30:19
```

Fig. 8.4 | this used implicitly and explicitly to refer to members of an object. (Part 2 of 2.)

contains a local variable with the same name as a field, that method will refer to the local variable rather than the field. In this case, the local variable shadows the field in the method's scope. However, the method can use the this reference to refer to the shadowed field explicitly, as shown in lines 25–27 for SimpleTime's shadowed instance variables.

Method buildString (lines 31–36) returns a String created by a statement that uses the this reference explicitly and implicitly. Line 34 uses the this reference explicitly to call method toUniversalString. Line 35 uses the this reference implicitly to call the same method. Note that both lines perform the same task. Programmers typically do not use this explicitly to reference other methods within the current object. Also, note that line 45 in method toUniversalString explicitly uses the this reference to access each instance variable. This is not necessary here, because the method does not have any local variables that shadow the instance variables of the class.

Common Programming Error 8.2

It is often a logic error when a method contains a parameter or local variable that has the same name as a field of the class. In this case, use reference this if you wish to access the field of the class—otherwise, the method parameter or local variable will be referenced.

Error-Prevention Tip 8.1

Avoid method parameter names or local variable names that conflict with field names. This helps prevent subtle, hard-to-locate bugs.

Application class ThisTest (lines 4–11) demonstrates class SimpleTime. Line 8 creates an instance of class SimpleTime and invokes its constructor. Line 9 invokes the object's buildString method, then displays the results.

> **Performance Tip 8.1**
>
> *Java conserves storage by maintaining only one copy of each method per class—this method is invoked by every object of the class. Each object, on the other hand, has its own copy of the class's instance variables (i.e., non-static fields). Each method of the class implicitly uses this to determine the specific object of the class to manipulate.*

8.5 Time Class Case Study: Overloaded Constructors

As you know, you can declare your own constructor to specify how objects of a class should be initialized. Next, we demonstrate a class with several overloaded constructors that enable objects of that class to be initialized in different ways. To overload constructors, simply provide multiple constructor declarations with different signatures. Recall from Section 6.12 that the compiler differentiates signatures by the number and types of the parameters in each signature.

Class *Time2 with Overloaded Constructors*

The default constructor for class Time1 (Fig. 8.1) initialized hour, minute and second to their default 0 values (which is midnight in universal time). The default constructor does not enable the class's clients to initialize the time with specific non-zero values. Class Time2 (Fig. 8.5) contains five overloaded constructors that provide convenient ways to initialize objects of the new class Time2. Every object each constructor initializes begins in a consistent state. In this program, four of the constructors invoke a fifth constructor, which, in turn, calls method setTime to ensure that the value supplied for hour is in the range 0 to 23 and that the values for minute and second are each in the range 0 to 59. If a value is out of range, it is set to zero by setTime (once again ensuring that each instance variable remains in a consistent state). The compiler invokes the appropriate constructor by matching the number and types of the arguments specified in the constructor call with the num-

```
1   // Fig. 8.5: Time2.java
2   // Time2 class declaration with overloaded constructors.
3
4   public class Time2
5   {
6      private int hour;   // 0 - 23
7      private int minute; // 0 - 59
8      private int second; // 0 - 59
9
10     // Time2 no-argument constructor: initializes each instance variable
11     // to zero; ensures that Time2 objects start in a consistent state
12     public Time2()
13     {
14        this( 0, 0, 0 ); // invoke Time2 constructor with three arguments
15     } // end Time2 no-argument constructor
16
17     // Time2 constructor: hour supplied, minute and second defaulted to 0
18     public Time2( int h )
19     {
20        this( h, 0, 0 ); // invoke Time2 constructor with three arguments
21     } // end Time2 one-argument constructor
22
```

Fig. 8.5 | Time2 class with overloaded constructors. (Part 1 of 3.)

```
23    // Time2 constructor: hour and minute supplied, second defaulted to 0
24    public Time2( int h, int m )
25    {
26       this( h, m, 0 ); // invoke Time2 constructor with three arguments
27    } // end Time2 two-argument constructor
28
29    // Time2 constructor: hour, minute and second supplied
30    public Time2( int h, int m, int s )
31    {
32       setTime( h, m, s ); // invoke setTime to validate time
33    } // end Time2 three-argument constructor
34
35    // Time2 constructor: another Time2 object supplied
36    public Time2( Time2 time )
37    {
38       // invoke Time2 three-argument constructor
39       this( time.getHour(), time.getMinute(), time.getSecond() );
40    } // end Time2 constructor with a Time2 object argument
41
42    // Set Methods
43    // set a new time value using universal time; ensure that
44    // the data remains consistent by setting invalid values to zero
45    public void setTime( int h, int m, int s )
46    {
47       setHour( h );   // set the hour
48       setMinute( m ); // set the minute
49       setSecond( s ); // set the second
50    } // end method setTime
51
52    // validate and set hour
53    public void setHour( int h )
54    {
55       hour = ( ( h >= 0 && h < 24 ) ? h : 0 );
56    } // end method setHour
57
58    // validate and set minute
59    public void setMinute( int m )
60    {
61       minute = ( ( m >= 0 && m < 60 ) ? m : 0 );
62    } // end method setMinute
63
64    // validate and set second
65    public void setSecond( int s )
66    {
67       second = ( ( s >= 0 && s < 60 ) ? s : 0 );
68    } // end method setSecond
69
70    // Get Methods
71    // get hour value
72    public int getHour()
73    {
74       return hour;
75    } // end method getHour
```

Fig. 8.5 | Time2 class with overloaded constructors. (Part 2 of 3.)

```
76
77      // get minute value
78      public int getMinute()
79      {
80         return minute;
81      } // end method getMinute
82
83      // get second value
84      public int getSecond()
85      {
86         return second;
87      } // end method getSecond
88
89      // convert to String in universal-time format (HH:MM:SS)
90      public String toUniversalString()
91      {
92         return String.format(
93            "%02d:%02d:%02d", getHour(), getMinute(), getSecond() );
94      } // end method toUniversalString
95
96      // convert to String in standard-time format (H:MM:SS AM or PM)
97      public String toString()
98      {
99         return String.format( "%d:%02d:%02d %s",
100           ( (getHour() == 0 || getHour() == 12) ? 12 : getHour() % 12 ),
101           getMinute(), getSecond(), ( getHour() < 12 ? "AM" : "PM" ) );
102     } // end method toString
103 } // end class Time2
```

Fig. 8.5 | Time2 class with overloaded constructors. (Part 3 of 3.)

ber and types of the parameters specified in each constructor declaration. Note that class Time2 also provides *set* and *get* methods for each instance variable.

Class Time2's Constructors

Lines 12–15 declare a so-called **no-argument constructor**—that is, a constructor invoked without arguments. Such a constructor simply initializes the object as specified in the constructor's body. In the body, we introduce a use of the this reference that is allowed only as the first statement in a constructor's body. Line 14 uses this in method-call syntax to invoke the Time2 constructor that takes three arguments (lines 30–33). The no-argument constructor passes values of 0 for the hour, minute and second to the constructor with three parameters. Using the this reference as shown here is a popular way to reuse initialization code provided by another of the class's constructors rather than defining similar code in the no-argument constructor's body. We use this syntax in four of the five Time2 constructors to make the class easier to maintain and modify. If we need to change how objects of class Time2 are initialized, only the constructor that the class's other constructors call would need to be modified. In fact, even that constructor might not need modification in this example. That constructor simply calls the setTime method to perform the actual initialization, so it is possible that the changes the class might require would be localized to the *set* methods.

Common Programming Error 8.3

It is a syntax error when this is used in a constructor's body to call another constructor of the same class if that call is not the first statement in the constructor. It is also a syntax error when a method attempts to invoke a constructor directly via this.

Lines 18–21 declare a Time2 constructor with a single int parameter representing the hour, which is passed with 0 for the minute and second to the constructor at lines 30–33. Lines 24–27 declare a Time2 constructor that receives two int parameters representing the hour and minute, which are passed with 0 for the second to the constructor at lines 30–33. Like the no-argument constructor, each of these constructors invokes the constructor at lines 30–33 to minimize code duplication. Lines 30–33 declare the Time2 constructor that receives three int parameters representing the hour, minute and second. This constructor calls setTime to initialize the instance variables to consistent values.

Common Programming Error 8.4

A constructor can call methods of the class. Be aware that the instance variables might not yet be in a consistent state, because the constructor is in the process of initializing the object. Using instance variables before they have been initialized properly is a logic error.

Lines 36–40 declare a Time2 constructor that receives a Time2 reference to another Time2 object. In this case, the values from the Time2 argument are passed to the three-argument constructor at lines 30–33 to initialize the hour, minute and second. Note that line 39 could have directly accessed the hour, minute and second values of the constructor's argument time with the expressions time.hour, time.minute and time.second—even though hour, minute and second are declared as private variables of class Time2. This is due to a special relationship between objects of the same class.

Software Engineering Observation 8.4

When one object of a class has a reference to another object of the same class, the first object can access all the second object's data and methods (including those that are private).

Notes Regarding Class *Time2's* Set *and* Get *Methods and Constructors*

Note that Time2's *set* and *get* methods are called throughout the body of the class. In particular, method setTime calls methods setHour, setMinute and setSecond in lines 47–49, and methods toUniversalString and toString call methods getHour, getMinute and getSecond in line 93 and lines 100–101, respectively. In each case, these methods could have accessed the class's private data directly without calling the *set* and *get* methods. However, consider changing the representation of the time from three int values (requiring 12 bytes of memory) to a single int value representing the total number of seconds that have elapsed since midnight (requiring only 4 bytes of memory). If we make such a change, only the bodies of the methods that access the private data directly would need to change—in particular, the individual *set* and *get* methods for the hour, minute and second. There would be no need to modify the bodies of methods setTime, toUniversalString or toString because they do not access the data directly. Designing the class in this manner reduces the likelihood of programming errors when altering the class's implementation.

Similarly, each Time2 constructor could be written to include a copy of the appropriate statements from method setTime. Doing so may be slightly more efficient, because the extra constructor call and call to setTime are eliminated. However, duplicating statements in multiple methods or constructors makes changing the class's internal data representation more difficult. Having the Time2 constructors call the constructor with three arguments (or even call setTime directly) requires any changes to the implementation of setTime to be made only once.

Software Engineering Observation 8.5

When implementing a method of a class, use the class's set *and* get *methods to access the class's private data. This simplifies code maintenance and reduces the likelihood of errors.*

Using Class *Time2*'s Overloaded Constructors

Class Time2Test (Fig. 8.6) creates six Time2 objects (lines 8–13) to invoke the overloaded Time2 constructors. Line 8 shows that the no-argument constructor (lines 12–15 of Fig. 8.5) is invoked by placing an empty set of parentheses after the class name when allocating a Time2 object with new. Lines 9–13 of the program demonstrate passing arguments to the other Time2 constructors. Java invokes the appropriate overloaded constructor by matching the number and types of the arguments specified in the constructor call with the number and types of the parameters specified in each constructor declaration. Line 9 invokes the constructor at lines 18–21 of Fig. 8.5. Line 10 invokes the constructor at lines 24–27 of Fig. 8.5. Lines 11–12 invoke the constructor at lines 30–33 of Fig. 8.5. Line 13 invokes the constructor at lines 36–40 of Fig. 8.5. The application displays the String representation of each initialized Time2 object to confirm that it was initialized properly.

```java
1   // Fig. 8.6: Time2Test.java
2   // Overloaded constructors used to initialize Time2 objects.
3
4   public class Time2Test
5   {
6      public static void main( String args[] )
7      {
8         Time2 t1 = new Time2();              // 00:00:00
9         Time2 t2 = new Time2( 2 );           // 02:00:00
10        Time2 t3 = new Time2( 21, 34 );      // 21:34:00
11        Time2 t4 = new Time2( 12, 25, 42 );  // 12:25:42
12        Time2 t5 = new Time2( 27, 74, 99 );  // 00:00:00
13        Time2 t6 = new Time2( t4 );          // 12:25:42
14
15        System.out.println( "Constructed with:" );
16        System.out.println( "t1: all arguments defaulted" );
17        System.out.printf( "   %s\n", t1.toUniversalString() );
18        System.out.printf( "   %s\n", t1.toString() );
19
20        System.out.println(
21           "t2: hour specified; minute and second defaulted" );
22        System.out.printf( "   %s\n", t2.toUniversalString() );
23        System.out.printf( "   %s\n", t2.toString() );
24
```

Fig. 8.6 | Overloaded constructors used to initialize Time2 objects. (Part 1 of 2.)

```
25          System.out.println(
26             "t3: hour and minute specified; second defaulted" );
27          System.out.printf( "   %s\n", t3.toUniversalString() );
28          System.out.printf( "   %s\n", t3.toString() );
29
30          System.out.println( "t4: hour, minute and second specified" );
31          System.out.printf( "   %s\n", t4.toUniversalString() );
32          System.out.printf( "   %s\n", t4.toString() );
33
34          System.out.println( "t5: all invalid values specified" );
35          System.out.printf( "   %s\n", t5.toUniversalString() );
36          System.out.printf( "   %s\n", t5.toString() );
37
38          System.out.println( "t6: Time2 object t4 specified" );
39          System.out.printf( "   %s\n", t6.toUniversalString() );
40          System.out.printf( "   %s\n", t6.toString() );
41       } // end main
42    } // end class Time2Test
```

```
t1: all arguments defaulted
   00:00:00
   12:00:00 AM
t2: hour specified; minute and second defaulted
   02:00:00
   2:00:00 AM
t3: hour and minute specified; second defaulted
   21:34:00
   9:34:00 PM
t4: hour, minute and second specified
   12:25:42
   12:25:42 PM
t5: all invalid values specified
   00:00:00
   12:00:00 AM
t6: Time2 object t4 specified
   12:25:42
   12:25:42 PM
```

Fig. 8.6 | Overloaded constructors used to initialize `Time2` objects. (Part 2 of 2.)

8.6 Default and No-Argument Constructors

Every class must have at least one constructor. As you learned in Section 3.7, if you do not provide any constructors in a class's declaration, the compiler creates a default constructor that takes no arguments when it is invoked. The default constructor initializes the instance variables to the initial values specified in their declarations or to their default values (zero for primitive numeric types, `false` for `boolean` values and `null` for references). In Section 9.4.1, you will learn that the default constructor performs another task in addition to initializing instance variables to their default value.

If your class declares constructors, the compiler will not create a default constructor for your class. In this case, to specify the default initialization for objects of your class, you must declare a no-argument constructor—as in lines 12–15 of Fig. 8.5. Like a default constructor, a no-argument constructor is invoked with empty parentheses. Note that the

`Time2` no-argument constructor explicitly initializes a `Time2` object by passing to the three-argument constructor 0 for each parameter. Since 0 is the default value for `int` instance variables, the no-argument constructor in this example could actually be declared with an empty body. In this case, each instance variable would receive its default value when the no-argument constructor is called. If we omit the no-argument constructor, clients of this class would not be able to create a `Time2` object with the expression `new Time2()`.

Common Programming Error 8.5

If a class has constructors, but none of the `public` constructors are no-argument constructors, and a program attempts to call a no-argument constructor to initialize an object of the class, a compilation error occurs. A constructor can be called with no arguments only if the class does not have any constructors (in which case the default constructor is called) or if the class has a `public` no-argument constructor.

Software Engineering Observation 8.6

Java allows other methods of the class besides its constructors to have the same name as the class and to specify return types. Such methods are not constructors and will not be called when an object of the class is instantiated. Java determines which methods are constructors by locating the methods that have the same name as the class and do not specify a return type.

8.7 Notes on *Set* and *Get* Methods

As you know, a class's `private` fields can be manipulated only by methods of that class. A typical manipulation might be the adjustment of a customer's bank balance (e.g., a `private` instance variable of a class `BankAccount`) by a method `computeInterest`. Classes often provide `public` methods to allow clients of the class to *set* (i.e., assign values to) or *get* (i.e., obtain the values of) `private` instance variables.

As a naming example, a method that sets instance variable `interestRate` would typically be named `setInterestRate` and a method that gets the `interestRate` would typically be called `getInterestRate`. *Set* methods are also commonly called **mutator methods**, because they typically change a value. *Get* methods are also commonly called **accessor methods** or **query methods**.

Set *and* Get *Methods vs.* `public` *Data*

It would seem that providing *set* and *get* capabilities is essentially the same as making the instance variables `public`. This is a subtlety of Java that makes the language so desirable for software engineering. A `public` instance variable can be read or written by any method that has a reference to an object that contains the instance variable. If an instance variable is declared `private`, a `public` *get* method certainly allows other methods to access the variable, but the *get* method can control how the client can access the variable. For example, a *get* method might control the format of the data it returns and thus shield the client code from the actual data representation. A `public` *set* method can—and should—carefully scrutinize attempts to modify the variable's value to ensure that the new value is appropriate for that data item. For example, an attempt to *set* the day of the month to 37 would be rejected, an attempt to *set* a person's weight to a negative value would be rejected, and so on. Thus, although *set* and *get* methods provide access to `private` data, the access is restricted by the programmer's implementation of the methods. This helps promote good software engineering.

Validity Checking in Set *Methods*

The benefits of data integrity are not automatic simply because instance variables are declared `private`—the programmer must provide validity checking. Java enables programmers to design better programs in a convenient manner. A class's *set* methods can return values indicating that attempts were made to assign invalid data to objects of the class. A client of the class can test the return value of a *set* method to determine whether the client's attempt to modify the object was successful and to take appropriate action. In Chapter 13, Exception Handling, we demonstrate how clients of a class can be notified when an attempt is made to modify an object with an inappropriate value.

Software Engineering Observation 8.7

When necessary, provide `public` *methods to change and retrieve the values of* `private` *instance variables. This architecture helps hide the implementation of a class from its clients, which improves program modifiability.*

Software Engineering Observation 8.8

Class designers need not provide set *or* get *methods for each* `private` *field. These capabilities should be provided only when it makes sense.*

Predicate Methods

Another common use for accessor methods is to test whether a condition is true or false—such methods are often called **predicate methods.** An example of a predicate method would be an `isEmpty` method for a **container class**—a class capable of holding many objects, such as a linked list, a stack or a queue. (These data structures are discussed in depth in Chapters 17 and 19.) A program might test `isEmpty` before attempting to read another item from a container object. A program might test `isFull` before attempting to insert another item into a container object.

Using Set *and* Get *Methods to Create a Class That Is Easier to Debug and Maintain*

If only one method performs a particular task, such as setting the hour in a `Time2` object, it is easier to debug and maintain the class. If the `hour` is not being set properly, the code that actually modifies instance variable `hour` is localized to one method's body—`setHour`. Thus, your debugging efforts can be focused on method `setHour`.

8.8 Composition

A class can have references to objects of other classes as members. Such a capability is called **composition** and is sometimes referred to as a *has-a* relationship. For example, an object of class `AlarmClock` needs to know the current time and the time when it is supposed to sound its alarm, so it is reasonable to include two references to `Time` objects as members of the `AlarmClock` object.

Software Engineering Observation 8.9

One form of software reuse is composition, in which a class has as members references to objects of other classes.

Our example of composition contains three classes—`Date` (Fig. 8.7), `Employee` (Fig. 8.8) and `EmployeeTest` (Fig. 8.9). Class `Date` (Fig. 8.7) declares instance variables month, day and year (lines 6–8) to represent a date. The constructor receives three `int`

```java
1   // Fig. 8.7: Date.java
2   // Date class declaration.
3
4   public class Date
5   {
6      private int month; // 1-12
7      private int day;   // 1-31 based on month
8      private int year;  // any year
9
10     // constructor: call checkMonth to confirm proper value for month;
11     // call checkDay to confirm proper value for day
12     public Date( int theMonth, int theDay, int theYear )
13     {
14        month = checkMonth( theMonth ); // validate month
15        year = theYear; // could validate year
16        day = checkDay( theDay ); // validate day
17
18        System.out.printf(
19           "Date object constructor for date %s\n", this );
20     } // end Date constructor
21
22     // utility method to confirm proper month value
23     private int checkMonth( int testMonth )
24     {
25        if ( testMonth > 0 && testMonth <= 12 ) // validate month
26           return testMonth;
27        else // month is invalid
28        {
29           System.out.printf(
30              "Invalid month (%d) set to 1.", testMonth );
31           return 1; // maintain object in consistent state
32        } // end else
33     } // end method checkMonth
34
35     // utility method to confirm proper day value based on month and year
36     private int checkDay( int testDay )
37     {
38        int daysPerMonth[] =
39           { 0, 31, 28, 31, 30, 31, 30, 31, 31, 30, 31, 30, 31 };
40
41        // check if day in range for month
42        if ( testDay > 0 && testDay <= daysPerMonth[ month ] )
43           return testDay;
44
45        // check for leap year
46        if ( month == 2 && testDay == 29 && ( year % 400 == 0 ||
47           ( year % 4 == 0 && year % 100 != 0 ) ) )
48           return testDay;
49
50        System.out.printf( "Invalid day (%d) set to 1.", testDay );
51        return 1;  // maintain object in consistent state
52     } // end method checkDay
53
```

Fig. 8.7 | Date class declaration. (Part 1 of 2.)

```
54       // return a String of the form month/day/year
55       public String toString()
56       {
57          return String.format( "%d/%d/%d", month, day, year );
58       } // end method toString
59    } // end class Date
```

Fig. 8.7 | Date class declaration. (Part 2 of 2.)

parameters. Line 14 invokes utility method checkMonth (lines 23–33) to validate the month—an out-of-range value is set to 1 to maintain a consistent state. Line 15 assumes that the value for year is correct and does not validate it. Line 16 invokes utility method checkDay (lines 36–52) to validate the value for day based on the current month and year. Lines 42–43 determine whether the day is correct based on the number of days in the particular month. If the day is not correct, lines 46–47 determine whether the month is February, the day is 29 and the year is a leap year. If lines 42–48 do not return a correct value for day, line 51 returns 1 to maintain the Date in a consistent state. Note that lines 18–19 in the constructor output the this reference as a String. Since this is a reference to the current Date object, the object's toString method (lines 55–58) is called implicitly to obtain the object's String representation.

Class Employee (Fig. 8.8) has instance variables firstName, lastName, birthDate and hireDate. Members birthDate and hireDate (lines 8–9) are references to Date objects. This demonstrates that a class can have as instance variables references to objects of other classes. The Employee constructor (lines 12–19) takes four parameters—first, last, dateOfBirth and dateOfHire. The objects referenced by the parameters dateOfBirth and dateOfHire are assigned to the Employee object's birthDate and hireDate instance variables, respectively. Note that when class Employee's toString method is called, it returns a String containing the String representations of the two Date objects. Each of these Strings is obtained with an implicit call to the Date class's toString method.

Class EmployeeTest (Fig. 8.9) creates two Date objects (lines 8–9) to represent an Employee's birthday and hire date, respectively. Line 10 creates an Employee and initializes its instance variables by passing to the constructor two Strings (representing the Employee's first and last names) and two Date objects (representing the birthday and hire date). Line 12 implicitly invokes the Employee's toString method to display the values of its instance variables and demonstrate that the object was initialized properly.

```
1    // Fig. 8.8: Employee.java
2    // Employee class with references to other objects.
3
4    public class Employee
5    {
6       private String firstName;
7       private String lastName;
8       private Date birthDate;
9       private Date hireDate;
10
```

Fig. 8.8 | Employee class with references to other objects. (Part 1 of 2.)

```
11      // constructor to initialize name, birth date and hire date
12      public Employee( String first, String last, Date dateOfBirth,
13         Date dateOfHire )
14      {
15         firstName = first;
16         lastName = last;
17         birthDate = dateOfBirth;
18         hireDate = dateOfHire;
19      } // end Employee constructor
20
21      // convert Employee to String format
22      public String toString()
23      {
24         return String.format( "%s, %s  Hired: %s  Birthday: %s",
25            lastName, firstName, hireDate, birthDate );
26      } // end method toString
27   } // end class Employee
```

Fig. 8.8 | `Employee` class with references to other objects. (Part 2 of 2.)

```
1   // Fig. 8.9: EmployeeTest.java
2   // Composition demonstration.
3
4   public class EmployeeTest
5   {
6      public static void main( String args[] )
7      {
8         Date birth = new Date( 7, 24, 1949 );
9         Date hire = new Date( 3, 12, 1988 );
10        Employee employee = new Employee( "Bob", "Blue", birth, hire );
11
12        System.out.println( employee );
13     } // end main
14  } // end class EmployeeTest
```

```
Date object constructor for date 7/24/1949
Date object constructor for date 3/12/1988
Blue, Bob  Hired: 3/12/1988  Birthday: 7/24/1949
```

Fig. 8.9 | Composition demonstration.

8.9 Enumerations

In Fig. 6.9 (`Craps.java`), we introduced the basic enum type which defines a set of constants that are represented as unique identifiers. In that program, the enum constants represented the game's status. In this section, we discuss the relationship between enum types and classes. Like classes, all enum types are reference types, which means that you can refer to an object of an enum type with a reference. An enum type is declared with an **enum declaration**, which is a comma-separated list of enum constants—the declaration may optionally include other components of traditional classes, such as constructors, fields and methods. Each enum declaration declares an enum class with the following restrictions:

1. enum types are implicitly `final`, because they declare constants that should not be modified.

2. enum constants are implicitly `static`.

3. Any attempt to create an object of an enum type with operator new results in a compilation error.

The enum constants can be used anywhere constants can be used, such as in the `case` labels of `switch` statements and to control enhanced `for` statements.

Figure 8.10 illustrates how to declare instance variables, a constructor and methods in an enum type. The enum declaration (lines 5–37) contains two parts—the enum constants and the other members of the enum type. The first part (lines 8–13) declares six enum constants. Each enum constant is optionally followed by arguments which are passed to the enum constructor (lines 20–24). Like the constructors you have seen in classes, an enum constructor can specify any number of parameters and can be overloaded. In this example, the enum constructor has two `String` parameters, hence each enum constant is followed by parentheses containing two `String` arguments. The second part (lines 16–36) declares the other members of the enum type—two instance variables (lines 16–17), a constructor (lines 20–24) and two methods (lines 27–30 and 33–36).

```java
1   // Fig. 8.10: Book.java
2   // Declaring an enum type with constructor and explicit instance fields
3   // and accessors for these field
4
5   public enum Book
6   {
7      // declare constants of enum type
8      JHTP6( "Java How to Program 6e", "2005" ),
9      CHTP4( "C How to Program 4e", "2004" ),
10     IW3HTP3( "Internet & World Wide Web How to Program 3e", "2004" ),
11     CPPHTP4( "C++ How to Program 4e", "2003" ),
12     VBHTP2( "Visual Basic .NET How to Program 2e", "2002" ),
13     CSHARPHTP( "C# How to Program", "2002" );
14
15     // instance fields
16     private final String title; // book title
17     private final String copyrightYear; // copyright year
18
19     // enum constructor
20     Book( String bookTitle, String year )
21     {
22        title = bookTitle;
23        copyrightYear = year;
24     } // end enum Book constructor
25
26     // accessor for field title
27     public String getTitle()
28     {
29        return title;
30     } // end method getTitle
```

Fig. 8.10 | Declaring enum type with instance fields, constructor and methods. (Part 1 of 2.)

```
31
32      // accessor for field copyrightYear
33      public String getCopyrightYear()
34      {
35         return copyrightYear;
36      } // end method getCopyrightYear
37   } // end enum Book
```

Fig. 8.10 | Declaring **enum** type with instance fields, constructor and methods. (Part 2 of 2.)

Lines 16–17 declare the instance variables `title` and `copyrightYear`. Each enum constant in `Book` is actually an object of type `Book` that has its own copy of instance variables `title` and `copyrightYear`. The constructor (lines 20–24) takes two `String` parameters, one that specifies the book title and one that specifies the copyright year of the book. Lines 22–23 assign these parameters to the instance variables. Lines 27–36 declare two methods, which return the book title and copyright year, respectively. Figure 8.11 tests the enum type declared in Fig. 8.10 and illustrates how to iterate through a range of enum constants.

For every enum, the compiler generates a `static` method called **values** (called in line 12) that returns an array of the enum's constants in the order in which they were declared. Recall from Section 7.6 that the enhanced `for` statement can be used to iterate through an array. Lines 12–14 use the enhanced `for` statement to display all the constants declared in the enum `Book`. Line 14 invokes the enum `Book`'s `getTitle` and `getCopyrightYear` methods to get the title and copyright year associated with the constant. Note that when an enum constant is converted to a `String` (e.g., book in line 13), the constant's identifier is used as the `String` representation (e.g., JHTP6 for the first enum constant).

```
1    // Fig. 8.11: EnumTest.java
2    // Testing enum type Book.
3    import java.util.EnumSet;
4
5    public class EnumTest
6    {
7       public static void main( String args[] )
8       {
9          System.out.println( "All books:\n" );
10
11         // print all books in enum Book
12         for ( Book book : Book.values() )
13            System.out.printf( "%-10s%-45s%s\n", book,
14               book.getTitle(), book.getCopyrightYear() );
15
16         System.out.println( "\nDisplay a range of enum constants:\n" );
17
18         // print first four books
19         for ( Book book : EnumSet.range( Book.JHTP6, Book.CPPHTP4 ) )
20            System.out.printf( "%-10s%-45s%s\n", book,
21               book.getTitle(), book.getCopyrightYear() );
22      } // end main
23   } // end class EnumTest
```

Fig. 8.11 | Testing an **enum** type. (Part 1 of 2.)

```
All books:

JHTP6      Java How to Program 6e                        2005
CHTP4      C How to Program 4e                           2004
IW3HTP3    Internet & World Wide Web How to Program 3e   2004
CPPHTP4    C++ How to Program 4e                         2003
VBHTP2     Visual Basic .NET How to Program 2e           2002
CSHARPHTP  C# How to Program                             2002

Display a range of enum constants:

JHTP6      Java How to Program 6e                        2005
CHTP4      C How to Program 4e                           2004
IW3HTP3    Internet & World Wide Web How to Program 3e   2004
CPPHTP4    C++ How to Program 4e                         2003
```

Fig. 8.11 | Testing an enum type. (Part 2 of 2.)

Lines 19–21 use the static method range of class EnumSet (declared in package java.util) to display a range of the enum Book's constants. Method range takes two parameters—the first enum constant in the range and the last enum constant in the range—and returns an EnumSet that contains all the constants between these two constants, inclusive. For example, EnumSet.range(Book.JHTP6, Book.CPPHTP4) returns an EnumSet containing Book.JHTP6, Book.CHTP4, Book.IW3HTP3 and Book.CPPHTP4. The enhanced for statement can be used with an EnumSet just as it can with an array, so lines 19–21 use the enhanced for statement to display the title and copyright year of every book in the EnumSet. Class EnumSet provides several other static methods for creating sets of enum constants from the same enum type. For more details of class EnumSet, visit java.sun.com/j2se/5.0/docs/api/java/util/EnumSet.html.

Common Programming Error 8.6

In an enum declaration, it is a syntax error to declare enum constants after the enum type's constructors, fields and methods in the enum declaration.

8.10 Garbage Collection and Method `finalize`

Every class in Java has the methods of class Object (package java.lang), one of which is the **finalize method**. This method is rarely used. In fact, we searched over 6500 source-code files for the Java API classes and found fewer than 50 declarations of the finalize method. Nevertheless, because this method is part of every class, we discuss it here to help you understand its intended purpose in case you encounter it in your studies or in industry. The complete details of the finalize method are beyond the scope of this book, and most programmers should not use it—you'll soon see why. You will learn more about class Object in Chapter 9, Object-Oriented Programming: Inheritance.

Every object you create uses various system resources, such as memory. We need a disciplined way to give resources back to the system when they are no longer needed to avoid "resource leaks." The Java Virtual Machine (JVM) performs automatic garbage collection to reclaim the memory occupied by objects that are no longer in use. When there are no more references to an object, the object is marked for garbage collection by the JVM. The memory for such an object can be reclaimed when the JVM executes its garbage collector, which is responsible for retrieving the memory of objects that are no longer used so the memory can be used for other objects. Therefore, memory leaks that are common in other languages like C and C++ (because memory is not automatically reclaimed in those languages) are less likely in Java (but some can still happen in subtle ways). Other types of resource leaks can occur. For example, an application could open a file on disk to modify the file's contents. If the application does not close the file, no other application can use the file until the application that opened the file completes.

The `finalize` method is called by the garbage collector to perform termination housekeeping on an object just before the garbage collector reclaims the object's memory. Method `finalize` does not take parameters and has return type `void`. A problem with method `finalize` is that the garbage collector is not guaranteed to execute at a specified time. In fact, the garbage collector may never execute before a program terminates. Thus, it is unclear if, or when, method `finalize` will be called. For this reason, most programmers should avoid method `finalize`. In Section 8.11, we demonstrate a situation in which method `finalize` is called by the garbage collector.

Software Engineering Observation 8.10

A class that uses system resources, such as files on disk, should provide a method to eventually release the resources. Many Java API classes provide `close` or `dispose` methods for this purpose. For example, class Scanner (java.sun.com/j2se/5.0/docs/api/java/util/Scanner.html) has a `close` method.

8.11 `static` Class Members

Every object has its own copy of all the instance variables of the class. In certain cases, only one copy of a particular variable should be shared by all objects of a class. A **static field**—called a class variable—is used in such cases. A `static` variable represents classwide information—all objects of the class share the same piece of data. The declaration of a `static` variable begins with the keyword `static`.

Let's motivate `static` data with an example. Suppose that we have a video game with `Martians` and other space creatures. `Martians` tend to be brave and willing to attack other space creatures when the `Martian` is aware that there are at least four other `Martians` present. If fewer than five `Martians` are present, become cowardly. Thus each `Martian` needs to know the `martianCount`. We could endow class `Martian` with `martianCount` as an instance variable. If we do this, then every `Martian` will have a separate copy of the instance variable, and every time we create a new `Martian`, we will have to update the instance variable `martianCount` in every `Martian`. This wastes space with the redundant copies, wastes time in updating the separate copies and is error prone. Instead, we declare `martianCount` to be `static`, making `martianCount` classwide data. Every `Martian` can see the `martianCount` as if it were an instance variable of class `Martian`, but only one copy of the `static` `martianCount` is maintained. This saves space. We save time by having the `Martian` constructor increment the `static` `martianCount`—there is only one copy, so we do not have to increment separate copies of `martianCount` for each `Martian` object.

Software Engineering Observation 8.11

Use a `static` variable when all objects of a class must use the same copy of the variable.

Static variables have class scope. A class's public static members can be accessed through a reference to any object of the class, or they can be accessed by qualifying the member name with the class name and a dot (.), as in Math.random(). A class's private static class members can be accessed only through methods of the class. Actually, static class members exist even when no objects of the class exist—they are available as soon as the class is loaded into memory at execution time. To access a public static member when no objects of the class exist (and even when they do), prefix the class name and a dot (.) to the static member, as in Math.PI. To access a private static member when no objects of the class exist, a public static method must be provided and the method must be called by qualifying its name with the class name and a dot.

Software Engineering Observation 8.12

Static class variables and methods exist, and can be used, even if no objects of that class have been instantiated.

Our next program declares two classes—Employee (Fig. 8.12) and EmployeeTest (Fig. 8.13). Class Employee declares private static variable count (Fig. 8.12, line 9), and public static method getCount (lines 46–49). The static variable count is initialized to zero in line 9. If a static variable is not initialized, the compiler assigns a default value to the variable—in this case 0, the default value for type int. Variable count maintains a count of the number of objects of class Employee that currently reside in memory. This includes objects that have already been marked for garbage collection by the JVM, but have not yet been reclaimed by the garbage collector.

When Employee objects exist, member count can be used in any method of an Employee object—this example increments count in the constructor (line 18) and decrements it in the finalize method (line 28). When no objects of class Employee exist, member count can still be referenced, but only through a call to public static method getCount (lines 46–49), as in Employee.getCount(), which returns the number of Employee objects currently in memory. When objects exist, method getCount can also be called through any reference to an Employee object, as in the call e1.getCount().

```
I    // Fig. 8.12: Employee.java
2    // Static variable used to maintain a count of the number of
3    // Employee objects in memory.
4
5    public class Employee
6    {
7       private String firstName;
8       private String lastName;
9       private static int count = 0; // number of objects in memory
10
11      // initialize employee, add 1 to static count and
12      // output String indicating that constructor was called
13      public Employee( String first, String last )
14      {
```

Fig. 8.12 | static variable used to maintain a count of the number of Employee objects in memory. (Part 1 of 2.)

```
15          firstName = first;
16          lastName = last;
17
18          count++;  // increment static count of employees
19          System.out.printf( "Employee constructor: %s %s; count = %d\n",
20             firstName, lastName, count );
21       } // end Employee constructor
22
23       // subtract 1 from static count when garbage
24       // collector calls finalize to clean up object;
25       // confirm that finalize was called
26       protected void finalize()
27       {
28          count--; // decrement static count of employees
29          System.out.printf( "Employee finalizer: %s %s; count = %d\n",
30             firstName, lastName, count );
31       } // end method finalize
32
33       // get first name
34       public String getFirstName()
35       {
36          return firstName;
37       } // end method getFirstName
38
39       // get last name
40       public String getLastName()
41       {
42          return lastName;
43       } // end method getLastName
44
45       // static method to get static count value
46       public static int getCount()
47       {
48          return count;
49       } // end method getCount
50    } // end class Employee
```

Fig. 8.12 | `static` variable used to maintain a count of the number of `Employee` objects in memory. (Part 2 of 2.)

```
1    // Fig. 8.13: EmployeeTest.java
2    // Static member demonstration.
3
4    public class EmployeeTest
5    {
6       public static void main( String args[] )
7       {
8          // show that count is 0 before creating Employees
9          System.out.printf( "Employees before instantiation: %d\n",
10            Employee.getCount() );
11
```

Fig. 8.13 | `static` member demonstration. (Part 1 of 2.)

```
12          // create two Employees; count should be 2
13          Employee e1 = new Employee( "Susan", "Baker" );
14          Employee e2 = new Employee( "Bob", "Blue" );
15
16          // show that count is 2 after creating two Employees
17          System.out.println( "\nEmployees after instantiation: " );
18          System.out.printf( "via e1.getCount(): %d\n", e1.getCount() );
19          System.out.printf( "via e2.getCount(): %d\n", e2.getCount() );
20          System.out.printf( "via Employee.getCount(): %d\n",
21             Employee.getCount() );
22
23          // get names of Employees
24          System.out.printf( "\nEmployee 1: %s %s\nEmployee 2: %s %s\n\n",
25             e1.getFirstName(), e1.getLastName(),
26             e2.getFirstName(), e2.getLastName() );
27
28          // in this example, there is only one reference to each Employee,
29          // so the following two statements cause the JVM to mark each
30          // Employee object for garbage collection
31          e1 = null;
32          e2 = null;
33
34          System.gc(); // ask for garbage collection to occur now
35
36          // show Employee count after calling garbage collector; count
37          // displayed may be 0, 1 or 2 based on whether garbage collector
38          // executes immediately and number of Employee objects collected
39          System.out.printf( "\nEmployees after System.gc(): %d\n",
40             Employee.getCount() );
41       } // end main
42    } // end class EmployeeTest
```

```
Employees before instantiation: 0
Employee constructor: Susan Baker; count = 1
Employee constructor: Bob Blue; count = 2

Employees after instantiation:
via e1.getCount(): 2
via e2.getCount(): 2
via Employee.getCount(): 2

Employee 1: Susan Baker
Employee 2: Bob Blue

Employee finalizer: Bob Blue; count = 1
Employee finalizer: Susan Baker; count = 0

Employees after System.gc(): 0
```

Fig. 8.13 | static member demonstration. (Part 2 of 2.)

Good Programming Practice 8.1

Invoke every static method by using the class name and a dot (.) to emphasize that the method being called is a static method.

Note that the `Employee` class has a `finalize` method (lines 26–31). This method is included only to show when the garbage collector executes in this program. Method `finalize` is normally declared `protected`, so it is not part of the `public` services of a class. We will discuss the `protected` member access modifier in detail in Chapter 9.

`EmployeeTest` method `main` (Fig. 8.13) instantiates two `Employee` objects (lines 13–14). When each `Employee` object's constructor is invoked, lines 15–16 of Fig. 8.12 assign the `Employee`'s first name and last name to instance variables `firstName` and `lastName`. Note that these two statements do not make copies of the original `String` arguments. Actually, `String` objects in Java are immutable—they cannot be modified after they are created. Therefore, it is safe to have many references to one `String` object. This is not normally the case for objects of most other classes in Java. If `String` objects are immutable, you might wonder why are we able to use operators + and += to concatenate `String` objects. String concatenation operations actually result in a new `Strings` object containing the concatenated values. The original `String` objects are not modified.

When `main` has finished using the two `Employee` objects, the references `e1` and `e2` are set to `null` at lines 31–32. At this point, references `e1` and `e2` no longer refer to the objects that were instantiated on lines 13–14. This "marks the objects for garbage collection" because there are no more references to the objects in the program.

Eventually, the garbage collector might reclaim the memory for these objects (or the operating system surely will reclaim the memory when the program terminates). The JVM does not guarantee when the garbage collector will execute (or even whether it will execute), so this program explicitly calls the garbage collector in line 34 using `static` method **gc** of class `System` (package `java.lang`) to indicate that the garbage collector should make a best-effort attempt to reclaim objects that are eligible for garbage collection. This is just a best effort—it is possible that no objects or only a subset of the eligible objects will be collected. In Fig. 8.13's sample output, the garbage collector did execute before lines 39–40 displayed current `Employee` count. The last output line indicates that the number of `Employee` objects in memory is 0 after the call to `System.gc()`. The third- and second-to-last lines of the output show that the `Employee` object for Bob Blue was finalized before the `Employee` object for Susan Baker. The output on your system may differ, because the garbage collector is not guaranteed to execute when `System.gc()` is called, nor is it guaranteed to collect objects in a specific order.

[*Note:* A method declared `static` cannot access non-`static` class members, because a `static` method can be called even when no objects of the class have been instantiated. For the same reason, the `this` reference cannot be used in a `static` method—the `this` reference must refer to a specific object of the class, and when a `static` method is called, there might not be any objects of its class in memory. The `this` reference is required to allow a method of a class to access other non-`static` members of the same class.]

Common Programming Error 8.7

A compilation error occurs if a `static` method calls an instance (non-`static`) method in the same class by using only the method name. Similarly, a compilation error occurs if a `static` method attempts to access an instance variable in the same class by using only the variable name.

Common Programming Error 8.8

Referring to this in a `static` method is a syntax error.

8.12 **static** Import

In Section 6.3, you learned about the static fields and methods of class Math. We invoked class Math's static fields and methods by preceding each with the class name Math and a dot (.). A **static import** declaration (a new feature of J2SE 5.0) enables programmers to refer to imported static members as if they were declared in the class that uses them—the class name and a dot (.) are not required to use an imported static member.

A static import declaration has two forms—one that imports a particular static member (which is known as **single static import**) and one that imports all static members of a class (which is known as **static import on demand**). The following syntax imports a particular static member:

       import static *packageName.ClassName.staticMemberName*;

where *packageName* is the package of the class (e.g., java.lang), *ClassName* is the name of the class (e.g., Math) and *staticMemberName* is the name of the static field or method (e.g., PI or abs). The following syntax imports all static members of a class:

       import static *packageName.ClassName.**;

where *packageName* is the package of the class (e.g., java.lang) and *ClassName* is the name of the class (e.g., Math). The asterisk (*) indicates that *all* static members of the specified class should be available for use in the class(es) declared in the file. Note that static import declarations import only static class members. Regular import statements should be used to specify the classes used in a program.

Figure 8.14 demonstrates a static import. Line 3 is a static import declaration, that imports all static fields and methods of class Math from package java.lang. Lines 9–12 access the Math class's static field E (line 11) and the static methods sqrt (line 9), ceil (line 10), log (line 11) and cos (line 12) without preceding the field name or method names with class name Math and a dot.

```
1   // Fig. 8.14: StaticImportTest.java
2   // Using static import to import static methods of class Math.
3   import static java.lang.Math.*;
4
5   public class StaticImportTest
6   {
7      public static void main( String args[] )
8      {
9         System.out.printf( "sqrt( 900.0 ) = %.1f\n", sqrt( 900.0 ) );
10        System.out.printf( "ceil( -9.8 ) = %.1f\n", ceil( -9.8 ) );
11        System.out.printf( "log( E ) = %.1f\n", log( E ) );
12        System.out.printf( "cos( 0.0 ) = %.1f\n", cos( 0.0 ) );
13     } // end main
14  } // end class StaticImportTest
```

```
sqrt( 900.0 ) = 30.0
ceil( -9.8 ) = -9.0
log( E ) = 1.0
cos( 0.0 ) = 1.0
```

Fig. 8.14 | Static import Math methods.

Common Programming Error 8.9

A compilation error occurs if a program attempts to import static methods that have the same signature or static fields that have the same name from two or more classes.

8.13 final Instance Variables

The principle of least privilege is fundamental to good software engineering. In the context of an application, the principle states that code should be granted only the amount of privilege and access that the code needs to accomplish its designated task, but no more. Let us see how this principle applies to instance variables.

Some instance variables need to be modifiable and some do not. You can use the keyword final to specify that a variable is not modifiable (i.e., it is a constant) and that any attempt to modify it is an error. For example,

```
private final int INCREMENT;
```

declares a final (constant) instance variable INCREMENT of type int. Although constants can be initialized when they are declared, this is not required. Constants can be initialized by each of the class's constructors.

Software Engineering Observation 8.13

Declaring an instance variable as final helps enforce the principle of least privilege. If an instance variable should not be modified, declare it to be final to prevent modification.

Our next example contains two classes—class Increment (Fig. 8.15) and class IncrementTest (Fig. 8.16). Class Increment contains a final instance variable of type int named INCREMENT (Fig. 8.15, line 7). Note that the final variable is not initialized in its declaration, so it must be initialized by the class's constructor (lines 9–13). If the class provided multiple constructors, every constructor would be required to initialize the final variable. The constructor receives int parameter incrementValue and assigns its value to INCREMENT (line 12). A final variable cannot be modified by assignment after it is initialized. Application class IncrementTest creates an object of class Increment (Fig. 8.16, line 8) and provides as the argument to the constructor the value 5 to be assigned to the constant INCREMENT.

```java
1   // Fig. 8.15: Increment.java
2   // final instance variable in a class.
3
4   public class Increment
5   {
6      private int total = 0; // total of all increments
7      private final int INCREMENT; // constant variable (uninitialized)
8
9      // constructor initializes final instance variable INCREMENT
10     public Increment( int incrementValue )
11     {
12        INCREMENT = incrementValue; // initialize constant variable (once)
13     } // end Increment constructor
14
```

Fig. 8.15 | final instance variable in a class. (Part 1 of 2.)

```
15        // add INCREMENT to total
16        public void addIncrementToTotal()
17        {
18           total += INCREMENT;
19        } // end method addIncrementToTotal
20
21        // return String representation of an Increment object's data
22        public String toString()
23        {
24           return String.format( "total = %d", total );
25        } // end method toIncrementString
26     } // end class Increment
```

Fig. 8.15 | **final** instance variable in a class. (Part 2 of 2.)

```
1     // Fig. 8.16: IncrementTest.java
2     // final variable initialized with a constructor argument.
3
4     public class IncrementTest
5     {
6        public static void main( String args[] )
7        {
8           Increment value = new Increment( 5 );
9
10          System.out.printf( "Before incrementing: %s\n\n", value );
11
12          for ( int i = 1; i <= 3; i++ )
13          {
14             value.addIncrementToTotal();
15             System.out.printf( "After increment %d: %s\n", i, value );
16          } // end for
17       } // end main
18    } // end class IncrementTest
```

```
Before incrementing: total = 0

After increment 1: total = 5
After increment 2: total = 10
After increment 3: total = 15
```

Fig. 8.16 | **final** variable initialized with a constructor argument.

Common Programming Error 8.10

Attempting to modify a **final** *instance variable after it is initialized is a compilation error.*

Error-Prevention Tip 8.2

Attempts to modify a **final** *instance variable are caught at compilation time rather than causing execution-time errors. It is always preferable to get bugs out at compilation time, if possible, rather than allow them to slip through to execution time (where studies have found that the cost of repair is often many times more expensive).*

Software Engineering Observation 8.14

A final field should also be declared static if it is initialized in its declaration. Once a final field is initialized in its declaration, its value can never change. Therefore, it is not necessary to have a separate copy of the field for every object of the class. Making the field static enables all objects of the class to share the final field.

If a final variable is not initialized, a compilation error occurs. To demonstrate this, we placed line 12 of Fig. 8.15 in a comment and recompiled the class. Fig. 8.17 shows the error message produced by the compiler.

Common Programming Error 8.11

Not initializing a final instance variable in its declaration or in every constructor of the class yields a compilation error indicating that the variable might not have been initialized. The same error occurs if the class initializes the variable in some, but not all, of the class's constructors.

8.14 Software Reusability

Java programmers concentrate on crafting new classes and reusing existing classes. Many class libraries exist, and others are being developed worldwide. Software is then constructed from existing, well-defined, carefully tested, well-documented, portable, widely available components. This kind of software reusability speeds the development of powerful, high-quality software. Rapid application development (RAD) is of great interest today.

Java programmers now have thousands of classes in the Java API from which to choose to help them implement Java programs. Indeed, Java is not just a programming language. It is a framework in which Java developers can work to achieve true reusability and rapid application development. Java programmers can focus on the task at hand when developing their programs and leave the lower-level details to the classes of the Java API. For example, to write a program that draws graphics, a Java programmer does not require knowledge of graphics on every computer platform where the program will execute. Instead, the programmer can concentrate on learning Java's graphics capabilities (which are quite substantial and growing) and write a Java program that draws the graphics, using Java's API classes, such as Graphics. When the program executes on a given computer, it is the job of the JVM to translate Java commands into commands that the local computer can understand.

The Java API classes enable Java programmers to bring new applications to market faster by using preexisting, tested components. Not only does this reduce development time, it also improves the programmer's ability to debug and maintain applications. To take advantage of Java's many capabilities, it is essential that programmers familiarize themselves with the variety of packages and classes in the Java API. There are many Web-based resources at java.sun.com to help you with this task. The primary resource for learning about the Java API is the Java API documentation, which can be found at

> java.sun.com/j2se/5.0/docs/api/index.html

```
Increment.java:13: variable INCREMENT might not have been initialized
   } // end Increment constructor
   ^
1 error
```

Fig. 8.17 | final variable INCREMENT must be initialized.

We overview how to use the documentation in Appendix G, Using the Java API Documentation. You can download the API documentation from

`java.sun.com/j2se/5.0/download.html`

In addition, `java.sun.com` provides many other resources, including tutorials, articles and sites specific to individual Java topics.

Good Programming Practice 8.2

Avoid reinventing the wheel. Study the capabilities of the Java API. If the API contains a class that meets your program's requirements, use that class rather than create your own.

To realize the full potential of software reusability, we need to improve cataloging schemes, licensing schemes, protection mechanisms which ensure that master copies of classes are not corrupted, description schemes that system designers use to determine whether existing objects meet their needs, browsing mechanisms that determine what classes are available and how closely they meet software developer requirements, and the like. Many interesting research and development problems have been solved and many more need to be solved. These problems will likely be solved because the potential value of increased software reuse is enormous.

8.15 Data Abstraction and Encapsulation

Classes normally hide the details of their implementation from their clients. This is called information hiding. As an example, let us consider the stack data structure introduced in Section 6.6. Recall that a stack is a last-in, first-out (LIFO) data structure—the last item pushed (inserted) on the stack is the first item popped (removed) from the stack.

Stacks can be implemented with arrays and with other data structures, such as linked lists. (We discuss stacks and linked lists in Chapter 17, Data Structures, and in Chapter 19, Collections.) A client of a stack class need not be concerned with the stack's implementation. The client knows only that when data items are placed in the stack, they will be recalled in last-in, first-out order. The client cares about what functionality a stack offers, not about how that functionality is implemented. This concept is referred to as data abstraction. Although programmers might know the details of a class's implementation, they should not write code that depends on these details. This enables a particular class (such as one that implements a stack and its operations, *push* and *pop*) to be replaced with another version without affecting the rest of the system. As long as the `public` services of the class do not change (i.e., every original method still has the same name, return type and parameter list in the new class declaration), the rest of the system is not affected.

Most programming languages emphasize actions. In these languages, data exists to support the actions that programs must take. Data is "less interesting" than actions. Data is "crude." Only a few primitive types exist, and it is difficult for programmers to create their own types. Java and the object-oriented style of programming elevate the importance of data. The primary activities of object-oriented programming in Java are the creation of types (e.g., classes) and the expression of the interactions among objects of those types. To create languages that emphasize data, the programming-languages community needed to formalize some notions about data. The formalization we consider here is the notion of abstract data types (ADTs), which improve the program-development process.

Consider primitive type `int`, which most people would associate with an integer in mathematics. Rather, an `int` is an abstract representation of an integer. Unlike mathematical integers, computer `int`s are fixed in size. For example, type `int` in Java is limited to the range −2,147,483,648 to +2,147,483,647. If the result of a calculation falls outside this range, an error occurs, and the computer responds in some machine-dependent manner. It might, for example, "quietly" produce an incorrect result, such as a value too large to fit in an `int` variable (commonly called arithmetic overflow). Mathematical integers do not have this problem. Therefore, the notion of a computer `int` is only an approximation of the notion of a real-world integer. The same is true of `float` and other built-in types.

We have taken the notion of `int` for granted until this point, but we now consider it from a new perspective. Types like `int`, `float`, and `char` are all examples of abstract data types. They are representations of real-world notions to some satisfactory level of precision within a computer system.

An ADT actually captures two notions: A data representation and the operations that can be performed on that data. For example, in Java, an `int` contains an integer value (data) and provides addition, subtraction, multiplication, division and remainder operations—division by zero is undefined. Java programmers use classes to implement abstract data types.

Software Engineering Observation 8.15

Programmers create types through the class mechanism. New types can be designed to be convenient to use as the built-in types. This marks Java as an extensible language. Although the language is easy to extend via new types, the programmer cannot alter the base language itself.

Another abstract data type we discuss is a queue, which is similar to a "waiting line." Computer systems use many queues internally. A queue offers well-understood behavior to its clients: Clients place items in a queue one at a time via an *enqueue* operation, then get them back one at a time via a *dequeue* operation. A queue returns items in first-in, first-out (FIFO) order, which means that the first item inserted in a queue is the first item removed from the queue. Conceptually, a queue can become infinitely long, but real queues are finite.

The queue hides an internal data representation that keeps track of the items currently waiting in line, and it offers operations to its clients (*enqueue* and *dequeue*). The clients are not concerned about the implementation of the queue—they simply depend on the queue to operate "as advertised." When a client enqueues an item, the queue should accept that item and place it in some kind of internal FIFO data structure. Similarly, when the client wants the next item from the front of the queue, the queue should remove the item from its internal representation and deliver it in FIFO order (i.e., the item that has been in the queue the longest should be the next one returned by the next dequeue operation).

The queue ADT guarantees the integrity of its internal data structure. Clients cannot manipulate this data structure directly—only the queue ADT has access to its internal data. Clients are able to perform only allowable operations on the data representation—the ADT rejects operations that its public interface does not provide.

8.16 Time Class Case Study: Creating Packages

We have seen in almost every example in the text that classes from preexisting libraries, such as the Java API, can be imported into a Java program. Each class in the Java API belongs to a package that contains a group of related classes. As applications become more complex, packages help programmers manage the complexity of application components. Packages also facilitate software reuse by enabling programs to import classes from other packages (as we have done in most examples). Another benefit of packages is that they provide a convention for unique class names, which helps prevent class-name conflicts (discussed later in this section). This section introduces how to create your own packages.

Steps for Declaring a Reusable Class

Before a class can be imported into multiple applications, it must be placed in a package to make it reusable. Figure 8.18 shows how to specify the package in which a class should be placed. Figure 8.19 shows how to import our packaged class so that it can be used in an application. The steps for creating a reusable class are:

1. Declare a public class. If the class is not public, it can be used only by other classes in the same package.

2. Choose a package name and add a **package declaration** to the source-code file for the reusable class declaration. There can be only one package declaration in each Java source-code file, and it must precede all other declarations and statements in the file. Note that comments are not statements, so comments can be placed before a package statement in a file.

3. Compile the class so that it is placed in the appropriate package directory structure.

4. Import the reusable class into a program and use the class.

Steps 1 and 2: Creating a **public** Class and Adding the **package** Statement

For *Step 1*, we modify the public class Time1 declared in Fig. 8.1. The new version is shown in Fig. 8.18. No modifications have been made to the implementation of the class, so we will not discuss its implementation details again here.

For *Step 2*, we add a package declaration (line 3) that declares a package named com.deitel.jhtp6.ch08. Placing a package declaration at the beginning of a Java source file indicates that the class declared in the file is part of the specified package. Only package declarations, import declarations and comments can appear outside the braces of a class declaration. A Java source-code file must have the following order:

1. a package declaration (if any),

2. import declarations (if any), then

3. class declarations.

Only one of the class declarations in a particular file can be public. Other classes in the file are placed in the package and can be used only by the other classes in the package. Non-public classes are in a package to support the reusable classes in the package.

In an effort to provide unique names for every package, Sun Microsystems specifies a convention for package naming that all Java programmers should follow. Every package name should start with your Internet domain name in reverse order. For example, our domain name is deitel.com, so our package names begin with com.deitel. For the domain name *yourcollege*.edu, the package name should begin with edu.*yourcollege*. After the domain name is reversed, you can choose any other names you want for your package. If you are part of a company with many divisions or a university with many schools, you

```
1   // Fig. 8.18: Time1.java
2   // Time1 class declaration maintains the time in 24-hour format.
3   package com.deitel.jhtp6.ch08;
4
5   public class Time1
6   {
7      private int hour;    // 0 - 23
8      private int minute;  // 0 - 59
9      private int second;  // 0 - 59
10
11     // set a new time value using universal time; perform
12     // validity checks on the data; set invalid values to zero
13     public void setTime( int h, int m, int s )
14     {
15        hour = ( ( h >= 0 && h < 24 ) ? h : 0 );    // validate hour
16        minute = ( ( m >= 0 && m < 60 ) ? m : 0 );  // validate minute
17        second = ( ( s >= 0 && s < 60 ) ? s : 0 );  // validate second
18     } // end method setTime
19
20     // convert to String in universal-time format (HH:MM:SS)
21     public String toUniversalString()
22     {
23        return String.format( "%02d:%02d:%02d", hour, minute, second );
24     } // end method toUniversalString
25
26     // convert to String in standard-time format (H:MM:SS AM or PM)
27     public String toString()
28     {
29        return String.format( "%d:%02d:%02d %s",
30           ( ( hour == 0 || hour == 12 ) ? 12 : hour % 12 ),
31           minute, second, ( hour < 12 ? "AM" : "PM" ) );
32     } // end method toString
33  } // end class Time1
```

Fig. 8.18 | Packaging class Time1 for reuse.

may want to use the name of your division or school as the next name in the package. We chose to use jhtp6 as the next name in our package name to indicate that this class is from *Java How to Program, Sixth Edition*. The last name in our package name specifies that this package is for Chapter 8 (ch08).

Step 3: Compiling the Packaged Class

Step 3 is to compile the class so that it is stored in the appropriate package. When a Java file containing a package declaration is compiled, the resulting class file is placed in the directory specified by the package declaration. The package declaration in Fig. 8.18 indicates that class Time1 should be placed in the directory

```
com
   deitel
      jhtp6
         ch08
```

The directory names in the package declaration specify the exact location of the classes in the package.

When compiling a class in a package, the javac command-line option **-d** causes the javac compiler to create appropriate directories based on the class's package declaration. The option also specifies where the directories should be stored. For example, in a command window, we used the compilation command

```
javac -d . Time1.java
```

to specify that the first directory in our package name should be placed in the current directory. The period (.) after -d in the preceding command represents the current directory on the Windows, UNIX and Linux operating systems (and several others as well). After executing the compilation command, the current directory contains a directory called com, com contains a directory called deitel, deitel contains a directory called jhtp6 and jhtp6 contains a directory called ch08. In the ch08 directory, you can find the file Time1.class. [*Note:* If you do not use the -d option, then you must copy or move the class file to the appropriate package directory after compiling it.]

The package name is part of the fully qualified class name, so the name of class Time1 is actually com.deitel.jhtp6.ch08.Time1. You can use this fully qualified name in your programs, or you can import the class and use its simple name (the class name by itself—Time1) in the program. If another package also contains a Time1 class, the fully qualified class names can be used to distinguish between the classes in the program and prevent a name conflict (also called a name collision).

Step 4: Importing the Reusable Class
Once the class is compiled and stored in its package, the class can be imported into programs (*Step 4*). In the Time1PackageTest application of Fig. 8.19, line 3 specifies that class Time1 should be imported for use in class Time1PackageTest. Class Time1PackageTest is in the default package because the class's .java file does not contain a package declaration. Since the two classes are in different packages, the import at line 3 is required so that class Time1PackageTest can use class Time1.

Line 3 is known as a single-type-import declaration—that is, the import declaration specifies one class to import. When your program uses multiple classes from the same package, you can import those classes with a single import declaration. For example, the import declaration

```
import java.util.*; // import classes from package java.util
```

uses an asterisk (*) at the end of the import declaration to inform the compiler that all classes from the java.util package are available for use in the program. This is known as a type-import-on-demand declaration. Only the classes from package java.util that are used in the program are loaded by the JVM. The preceding import allows you to use the simple name of any class from the java.util package in the program. Throughout this book, we use single-type-import declarations for clarity.

Common Programming Error 8.12

Using the import declaration import java.; causes a compilation error. You must specify the exact name of the package from which you want to import classes.*

```
1   // Fig. 8.19: Time1PackageTest.java
2   // Time1 object used in an application.
3   import com.deitel.jhtp6.ch08.Time1; // import class Time1
4
5   public class Time1PackageTest
6   {
7      public static void main( String args[] )
8      {
9         // create and initialize a Time1 object
10        Time1 time = new Time1(); // calls Time1 constructor
11
12        // output string representations of the time
13        System.out.print( "The initial universal time is: " );
14        System.out.println( time.toUniversalString() );
15        System.out.print( "The initial standard time is: " );
16        System.out.println( time.toString() );
17        System.out.println(); // output a blank line
18
19        // change time and output updated time
20        time.setTime( 13, 27, 6 );
21        System.out.print( "Universal time after setTime is: " );
22        System.out.println( time.toUniversalString() );
23        System.out.print( "Standard time after setTime is: " );
24        System.out.println( time.toString() );
25        System.out.println(); // output a blank line
26
27        // set time with invalid values; output updated time
28        time.setTime( 99, 99, 99 );
29        System.out.println( "After attempting invalid settings:" );
30        System.out.print( "Universal time: " );
31        System.out.println( time.toUniversalString() );
32        System.out.print( "Standard time: " );
33        System.out.println( time.toString() );
34     } // end main
35  } // end class Time1PackageTest
```

```
The initial universal time is: 00:00:00
The initial standard time is: 12:00:00 AM

Universal time after setTime is: 13:27:06
Standard time after setTime is: 1:27:06 PM

After attempting invalid settings:
Universal time: 00:00:00
Standard time: 12:00:00 AM
```

Fig. 8.19 | Time1 object used in an application.

Specifying the Classpath During Compilation
When compiling Time1PackageTest, javac must locate the .class file for Time1 to en-sure that class Time1PackageTest uses class Time1 correctly. The compiler uses a special object called a **class loader** to locate the classes it needs. The class loader begins by search-

ing the standard Java classes that are bundled with the JDK. Then it searches for optional
packages. Java provides an extension mechanism that enables new (optional) packages to
be added to Java for development and execution purposes. [*Note:* The extension mechanism is beyond the scope of this book. For more information, visit java.sun.com/j2se/
5.0/docs/guide/extensions.] If the class is not found in the standard Java classes or in
the extension classes, the class loader searches the classpath, which contains a list of locations in which classes are stored. The classpath consists of a list of directories or archive
files, each separated by a directory separator—a semicolon (;) on Windows or a colon (:)
on UNIX/Linux/Mac OS X. Archive files are individual files that contain directories of
other files, typically in a compressed format. For example, the standard classes used by
your programs are contained in the archive file rt.jar, which is installed with the JDK.
Archive files normally end with the .jar or .zip file-name extensions. The directories and
archive files specified in the classpath contain the classes you wish to make available to the
Java compiler and the JVM.

By default, the classpath consists only of the current directory. However, the classpath
can be modified by

1. providing the -classpath option to the javac compiler or

2. setting the CLASSPATH environment variable (a special variable that you define
   and the operating system maintains so that applications can search for classes in
   the specified locations).

For more information on the classpath, visit java.sun.com/j2se/5.0/docs/tooldocs/
tools.html. The section entitled "General Information" contains information on setting
the classpath for UNIX/Linux and Windows.

Common Programming Error 8.13

*Specifying an explicit classpath eliminates the current directory from the classpath. This prevents
classes in the current directory (including packages in the current directory) from loading properly. If classes must be loaded from the current directory, include a dot (.) in the classpath to
specify the current directory.*

Software Engineering Observation 8.16

*In general, it is a better practice to use the -classpath option of the compiler, rather than the
CLASSPATH environment variable, to specify the classpath for a program. This enables each
application to have its own classpath.*

Error-Prevention Tip 8.3

*Specifying the classpath with the CLASSPATH environment variable can cause subtle and difficult-
to-locate errors in programs that use different versions of the same package.*

For the example of Fig. 8.18 and Fig. 8.19, we did not specify an explicit classpath.
Thus, to locate the classes in the com.deitel.jhtp6.ch08 package from this example, the
class loader looks in the current directory for the first name in the package—com. Next,
the class loader navigates the directory structure. Directory com contains the subdirectory
deitel. Directory deitel contains the subdirectory jhtp6. Finally, directory jhtp6 contains subdirectory ch08. In the ch08 directory is the file Time1.class, which is loaded by
the class loader to ensure that the class is used properly in our program.

Specifying the Classpath When Executing an Application

When you execute an application, the JVM must be able to locate the classes used in that application. Like the compiler, the `java` command uses a class loader that searches the standard classes and extension classes first, then searches the classpath (the current directory by default). The classpath for the JVM can be specified explicitly by using either of the techniques discussed for the compiler. As with the compiler, it is better to specify an individual program's classpath via command-line options to the JVM. You can specify the classpath in the `java` command via the `-classpath` or `-cp` command-line options, followed by a list of directories or archive files separated by semicolons (;) on Microsoft Windows or by colons (:) on UNIX/Linux/Mac OS X. Again, if classes must be loaded from the current directory, be sure to include a dot (.) in the classpath to specify the current directory.

8.17 Package Access

If no access modifier (public, `protected` or `private`—protected is discussed in Chapter 9) is specified for a method or variable when it is declared in a class, the method or variable is considered to have package access. In a program that consists of one class declaration, this has no specific effect. However, if a program uses multiple classes from the same package (i.e., a group of related classes), these classes can access each other's package-access members directly through references to objects of the appropriate classes.

The application in Fig. 8.20 demonstrates package access. The application contains two classes in one source-code file—the `PackageDataTest` application class (lines 5–21) and the `PackageData` class (lines 24–41). When you compile this program, the compiler produces two separate .class files—`PackageDataTest.class` and `PackageData.class`. The compiler places the two .class files in the same directory, so the classes are considered to be part of the same package. Since they are part of the same package, class `PackageDataTest` is allowed to modify the package-access data of `PackageData` objects.

In the `PackageData` class declaration, lines 26–27 declare the instance variables number and `string` with no access modifiers—therefore, these are package-access instance variables. The `PackageDataTest` application's main method creates an instance of the `PackageData` class (line 9) to demonstrate the ability to modify the `PackageData` instance variables directly (as shown on lines 15–16). The results of the modification can be seen in the output window.

8.18 (Optional) GUI and Graphics Case Study: Using Objects with Graphics

Most of the graphics you have seen to this point did not vary each time you executed the program. However, Exercise 6.2 asked you to create a program that generated shapes and colors at random. In that exercise, the drawing changed every time the system called paintComponent to redraw the panel. To create a more consistent drawing that remains the same each time it is drawn, we must store information about the displayed shapes so that we can reproduce them exactly each time the system calls paintComponent.

```java
1   // Fig. 8.20: PackageDataTest.java
2   // Package-access members of a class are accessible by other classes
3   // in the same package.
4
5   public class PackageDataTest
6   {
7      public static void main( String args[] )
8      {
9         PackageData packageData = new PackageData();
10
11         // output String representation of packageData
12         System.out.printf( "After instantiation:\n%s\n", packageData );
13
14         // change package access data in packageData object
15         packageData.number = 77;
16         packageData.string = "Goodbye";
17
18         // output String representation of packageData
19         System.out.printf( "\nAfter changing values:\n%s\n", packageData );
20      } // end main
21   } // end class PackageDataTest
22
23   // class with package access instance variables
24   class PackageData
25   {
26      int number; // package-access instance variable
27      String string; // package-access instance variable
28
29      // constructor
30      public PackageData()
31      {
32         number = 0;
33         string = "Hello";
34      } // end PackageData constructor
35
36      // return PackageData object String representation
37      public String toString()
38      {
39         return String.format( "number: %d; string: %s", number, string );
40      } // end method toString
41   } // end class PackageData
```

```
After instantiation:
number: 0; string: Hello

After changing values:
number: 77; string: Goodbye
```

Fig. 8.20 | Package-access members of a class are accessible by other classes in the same package.

To do this, we will create a set of shape classes that store information about each shape. We will make these classes "smart" by allowing objects of these classes to draw themselves if provided with a Graphics object. Figure 8.21 declares class MyLine, which has all these capabilities.

Class MyLine imports Color and Graphics (lines 3–4). Lines 8–11 declare instance variables for the coordinates needed to draw a line, and line 12 declares the instance variable that stores the color of the line. The constructor at lines 15–22 takes five parameters, one for each instance variable that it initializes. Method draw at lines 25–29 requires a Graphics object and uses it to draw the line in the proper color and at the proper coordinates.

In Fig. 8.22, we declare class DrawPanel, which will generate random objects of class MyLine. Line 12 declares a MyLine array to store the lines to draw. Inside the constructor (lines 15–37), line 17 sets the background color to Color.WHITE. Line 19 creates the array with a random length between 5 and 9. The loop at lines 22–36 creates a new MyLine for every element in the array. Lines 25–28 generate random coordinates for each line's endpoints, and lines 31–32 generate a random color for the line. Line 35 creates a new MyLine object with the randomly generated values and stores it in the array.

```java
1   // Fig. 8.21: MyLine.java
2   // Declaration of class MyLine.
3   import java.awt.Color;
4   import java.awt.Graphics;
5
6   public class MyLine
7   {
8      private int x1; // x coordinate of first endpoint
9      private int y1; // y coordinate of first endpoint
10     private int x2; // x coordinate of second endpoint
11     private int y2; // y coordinate of second endpoint
12     private Color myColor; // color of this shape
13
14     // constructor with input values
15     public MyLine( int x1, int y1, int x2, int y2, Color color )
16     {
17        this.x1 = x1; // set x coordinate of first endpoint
18        this.y1 = y1; // set y coordinate of first endpoint
19        this.x2 = x2; // set x coordinate of second endpoint
20        this.y2 = y2; // set y coordinate of second endpoint
21        myColor = color; // set the color
22     } // end MyLine constructor
23
24     // Draw the line in the specified color
25     public void draw( Graphics g )
26     {
27        g.setColor( myColor );
28        g.drawLine( x1, y1, x2, y2 );
29     } // end method draw
30  } // end class MyLine
```

Fig. 8.21 | MyLine class represents a line.

```
1   // Fig. 8.22: DrawPanel.java
2   // Program that uses class MyLine
3   // to draw random lines.
4   import java.awt.Color;
5   import java.awt.Graphics;
6   import java.util.Random;
7   import javax.swing.JPanel;
8
9   public class DrawPanel extends JPanel
10  {
11     private Random randomNumbers = new Random();
12     private MyLine lines[]; // array of lines
13
14     // constructor, creates a panel with random shapes
15     public DrawPanel()
16     {
17        setBackground( Color.WHITE );
18
19        lines = new MyLine[ 5 + randomNumbers.nextInt( 5 ) ];
20
21        // create lines
22        for ( int count = 0; count < lines.length; count++ )
23        {
24           // generate random coordinates
25           int x1 = randomNumbers.nextInt( 300 );
26           int y1 = randomNumbers.nextInt( 300 );
27           int x2 = randomNumbers.nextInt( 300 );
28           int y2 = randomNumbers.nextInt( 300 );
29
30           // generate a random color
31           Color color = new Color( randomNumbers.nextInt( 256 ),
32              randomNumbers.nextInt( 256 ), randomNumbers.nextInt( 256 ) );
33
34           // add the line to the list of lines to be displayed
35           lines[ count ] = new MyLine( x1, y1, x2, y2, color );
36        } // end for
37     } // end DrawPanel constructor
38
39     // for each shape array, draw the individual shapes
40     public void paintComponent( Graphics g )
41     {
42        super.paintComponent( g );
43
44        // draw the lines
45        for ( MyLine line : lines )
46           line.draw( g );
47     } // end method paintComponent
48  } // end class DrawPanel
```

Fig. 8.22 | Creating random MyLine objects.

Method paintComponent iterates through the MyLine objects in array lines using an enhanced for statement (lines 45–46). Each iteration calls the draw method of the current

```
1   // Fig. 8.23: TestDraw.java
2   // Test application to display a DrawPanel.
3   import javax.swing.JFrame;
4
5   public class TestDraw
6   {
7      public static void main( String args[] )
8      {
9         DrawPanel panel = new DrawPanel();
10        JFrame application = new JFrame();
11
12        application.setDefaultCloseOperation( JFrame.EXIT_ON_CLOSE );
13        application.add( panel );
14        application.setSize( 300, 300 );
15        application.setVisible( true );
16     } // end main
17  } // end class TestDraw
```

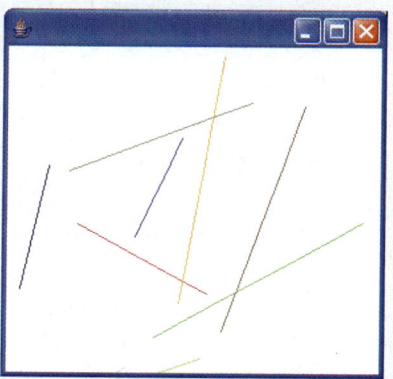

Fig. 8.23 | Creating `JFrame` to display `DrawPanel`.

`MyLine` object and passes it the `Graphics` object for drawing on the panel. Class `TestDraw` in Fig. 8.23 sets up a new window to display our drawing. Since we are setting the coordinates for the lines only once in the constructor, the drawing does not change if `paintComponent` is called to refresh the drawing on the screen.

GUI and Graphics Case Study Exercise

8.1   Extend the program in Fig. 8.21–Fig. 8.23 to randomly draw rectangles and ovals. Create classes `MyRectangle` and `MyOval`. Both of these classes should include *x1*, *y1*, *x2*, *y2* coordinates, a color and a `boolean` flag to determine whether the shape is a filled shape. Declare a constructor in each class with arguments for initializing all the instance variables. To help draw rectangles and ovals, each class should provide methods `getUpperLeftX`, `getUpperLeftY`, `getWidth` and `getHeight` that calculate the upper-left *x*-coordinate, upper-left *y*-coordinate, width and height, respectively. The upper-left *x*-coordinate is the smaller of the two *x*-coordinate values, the upper-left *y*-coordinate is the smaller of the two *y*-coordinate values, the width is the absolute value of the difference between the two *x*-coordinate values, and the height is the absolute value of the difference between the two *y*-coordinate values.

Class `DrawPanel`, which extends `JPanel` and handles the creation of the shapes, should declare three arrays, one for each shape type. The length of each array should be a random number between 1 and 5. The constructor of class `DrawPanel` will fill each of the arrays with shapes of random position, size, color and fill.

In addition, modify all three shape classes to include the following:

a) A constructor with no arguments that sets all the coordinates of the shape to 0, the color of the shape to `Color.BLACK`, and the filled property to `false` (`MyRect` and `MyOval` only).

b) *Set* methods for the instance variables in each class. The methods that set a coordinate value should verify that the argument is greater than or equal to zero before setting the coordinate—if it is not, they should set the coordinate to zero. The constructor should call the *set* methods rather than initialize the local variables directly.

c) *Get* methods for the instance variables in each class. Method `draw` should reference the coordinates by the *get* methods rather than access them directly.

8.19 (Optional) Software Engineering Case Study: Starting to Program the Classes of the ATM System

In the "Software Engineering Case Study" sections in Chapters 1–7, we introduced the fundamentals of object orientation and developed an object-oriented design for our ATM system. Earlier in this chapter, we discussed many of the details of programming with Java classes. We now begin implementing our object-oriented design in Java. At the end of this section, we show how to convert class diagrams to Java code. In the final "Software Engineering Case Study" section (Section 10.9), we modify the code to incorporate the object-oriented concept of inheritance. We present the full Java code implementation in Appendix J.

Visibility

We now apply access modifiers to the members of our classes. In Chapter 3, we introduced access modifiers `public` and `private`. Access modifiers determine the visibility or accessibility of an object's attributes and methods to other objects. Before we can begin implementing our design, we must consider which attributes and methods of our classes should be `public` and which should be `private`.

In Chapter 3, we observed that attributes normally should be `private` and that methods invoked by clients of a given class should be `public`. Methods that are called only by other methods of the class as "utility methods," however, normally should be `private`. The UML employs visibility markers for modeling the visibility of attributes and operations. Public visibility is indicated by placing a plus sign (+) before an operation or an attribute, whereas a minus sign (–) indicates private visibility. Figure 8.24 shows our updated class diagram with visibility markers included. [*Note:* We do not include any operation parameters in Fig. 8.24—this is perfectly normal. Adding visibility markers does not affect the parameters already modeled in the class diagrams of Fig. 6.22–Fig. 6.25.]

Navigability

Before we begin implementing our design in Java, we introduce an additional UML notation. The class diagram in Fig. 8.25 further refines the relationships among classes in the ATM system by adding navigability arrows to the association lines. Navigability arrows (represented as arrows with stick arrowheads in the class diagram) indicate in which direction an association can be traversed. When implementing a system designed using the

Fig. 8.24 | Class diagram with visibility markers.

UML, programmers use navigability arrows to help determine which objects need references to other objects. For example, the navigability arrow pointing from class ATM to class BankDatabase indicates that we can navigate from the former to the latter, thereby enabling the ATM to invoke the BankDatabase's operations. However, since Fig. 8.25 does not contain a navigability arrow pointing from class BankDatabase to class ATM, the BankDatabase cannot access the ATM's operations. Note that associations in a class diagram that have navigability arrows at both ends or do not have navigability arrows at all indicate bidirectional navigability—navigation can proceed in either direction across the association.

Like the class diagram of Fig. 3.24, the class diagram of Fig. 8.25 omits classes BalanceInquiry and Deposit to keep the diagram simple. The navigability of the associations in which these classes participate closely parallels the navigability of class Withdrawal. Recall from Section 3.10 that BalanceInquiry has an association with class Screen. We can navigate from class BalanceInquiry to class Screen along this association, but we cannot navigate from class Screen to class BalanceInquiry. Thus, if we were to model class BalanceInquiry in Fig. 8.25, we would place a navigability arrow at class

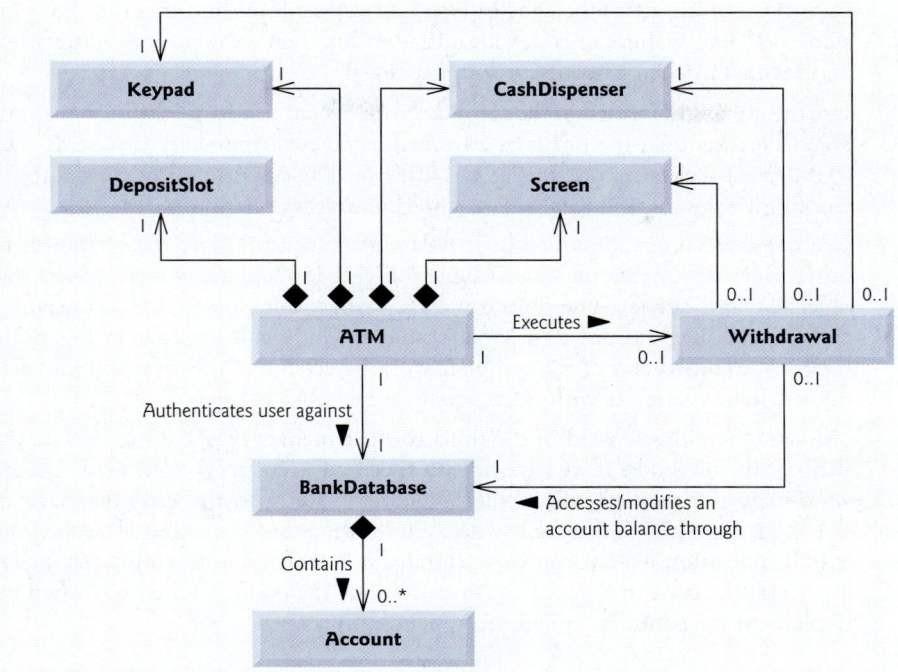

Fig. 8.25 | Class diagram with navigability arrows.

Screen's end of this association. Also recall that class Deposit associates with classes Screen, Keypad and DepositSlot. We can navigate from class Deposit to each of these classes, but not vice versa. We therefore would place navigability arrows at the Screen, Keypad and DepositSlot ends of these associations. [*Note:* We model these additional classes and associations in our final class diagram in Section 10.9, after we have simplified the structure of our system by incorporating the object-oriented concept of inheritance.]

Implementing the ATM System from Its UML Design

We are now ready to begin implementing the ATM system. We first convert the classes in the diagrams of Fig. 8.24 and Fig. 8.25 into Java code. The code will represent the "skeleton" of the system. In Chapter 10, we modify the code to incorporate the object-oriented concept of inheritance. In Appendix J, ATM Case Study Code, we present the complete working Java code for our model.

As an example, we develop the code from our design of class Withdrawal in Fig. 8.24. We use this figure to determine the attributes and operations of the class. We use the UML model in Fig. 8.25 to determine the associations among classes. We follow the following four guidelines for each class:

1. Use the name located in the first compartment to declare the class as a public class with an empty no-argument constructor. We include this constructor simply as a placeholder to remind us that most classes will indeed need constructors. In Appendix J, when we complete a working version of this class, we add any necessary arguments and code the body of the constructor as needed. For example,

class `Withdrawal` yields the code in Fig. 8.26. [*Note:* If we find that the class's instance variables require only default initialization, then we remove the empty no-argument constructor because it is unnecessary.]

2. Use the attributes located in the second compartment to declare the instance variables. For example, the `private` attributes `accountNumber` and `amount` of class `Withdrawal` yield the code in Fig. 8.27. [*Note:* The constructor of the complete working version of this class will assign values to these attributes.]

3. Use the associations described in the class diagram to declare the references to other objects. For example, according to Fig. 8.25, `Withdrawal` can access one object of class `Screen`, one object of class `Keypad`, one object of class `CashDispenser` and one object of class `BankDatabase`. This yields the code in Fig. 8.28. [*Note:* The constructor of the complete working version of this class will initialize these instance variables with references to actual objects.]

4. Use the operations located in the third compartment of Fig. 8.24 to declare the shells of the methods. If we have not yet specified a return type for an operation, we declare the method with return type `void`. Refer to the class diagrams of Fig. 6.22–Fig. 6.25 to declare any necessary parameters. For example, adding the `public` operation `execute` in class `Withdrawal`, which has an empty parameter list, yields the code in Fig. 8.29. [*Note:* We code the bodies of methods when we implement the complete system in Appendix J.]

This concludes our discussion of the basics of generating classes from UML diagrams.

```
1   // Class Withdrawal represents an ATM withdrawal transaction
2   public class Withdrawal
3   {
4      // no-argument constructor
5      public Withdrawal()
6      {
7      } // end no-argument Withdrawal constructor
8   } // end class Withdrawal
```

Fig. 8.26 | Java code for class `Withdrawal` based on Fig. 8.24 and Fig. 8.25.

```
1   // Class Withdrawal represents an ATM withdrawal transaction
2   public class Withdrawal
3   {
4      // attributes
5      private int accountNumber; // account to withdraw funds from
6      private double amount; // amount to withdraw
7
8      // no-argument constructor
9      public Withdrawal()
10     {
11     } // end no-argument Withdrawal constructor
12  } // end class Withdrawal
```

Fig. 8.27 | Java code for class `Withdrawal` based on Fig. 8.24 and Fig. 8.25.

```
1   // Class Withdrawal represents an ATM withdrawal transaction
2   public class Withdrawal
3   {
4      // attributes
5      private int accountNumber; // account to withdraw funds from
6      private double amount; // amount to withdraw
7
8      // references to associated objects
9      private Screen screen; // ATM's screen
10     private Keypad keypad; // ATM's keypad
11     private CashDispenser cashDispenser; // ATM's cash dispenser
12     private BankDatabase bankDatabase; // account info database
13
14     // no-argument constructor
15     public Withdrawal()
16     {
17     } // end no-argument Withdrawal constructor
18  } // end class Withdrawal
```

Fig. 8.28 | Java code for class Withdrawal based on Fig. 8.24 and Fig. 8.25.

```
1   // Class Withdrawal represents an ATM withdrawal transaction
2   public class Withdrawal
3   {
4      // attributes
5      private int accountNumber; // account to withdraw funds from
6      private double amount; // amount to withdraw
7
8      // references to associated objects
9      private Screen screen; // ATM's screen
10     private Keypad keypad; // ATM's keypad
11     private CashDispenser cashDispenser; // ATM's cash dispenser
12     private BankDatabase bankDatabase; // account info database
13
14     // no-argument constructor
15     public Withdrawal()
16     {
17     } // end no-argument Withdrawal constructor
18
19     // operations
20     public void execute()
21     {
22     } // end method execute
23  } // end class Withdrawal
```

Fig. 8.29 | Java code for class Withdrawal based on Fig. 8.24 and Fig. 8.25.

Software Engineering Case Study Self-Review Exercises

8.1   State whether the following statement is *true* or *false*, and if *false*, explain why: If an attribute of a class is marked with a minus sign (-) in a class diagram, the attribute is not directly accessible outside of the class.

8.2 In Fig. 8.25, the association between the ATM and the Screen indicates that:
a) we can navigate from the Screen to the ATM
b) we can navigate from the ATM to the Screen
c) Both a and b; the association is bidirectional
d) None of the above

8.3 Write Java code to begin implementing the design for class Keypad.

Answers to Software Engineering Case Study Self-Review Exercises

8.1 True. The minus sign (–) indicates private visibility.

8.2 b.

8.3 The design for class Keypad yields the code in Fig. 8.30. Recall that class Keypad has no attributes for the moment, but attributes may become apparent as we continue the implementation. Also note that if we were designing a real ATM, method getInput would need to interact with the ATM's keypad hardware. We will actually do input from the keyboard of a personal computer when we write the complete Java code in Appendix J.

8.20 Wrap-Up

In this chapter, we presented additional class concepts. The Time class case study presented a complete class declaration consisting of private data, overloaded public constructors for initialization flexibility, *set* and *get* methods for manipulating the class's data, and methods that returned String representations of a Time object in two different formats. You also learned that every class can declare a toString method that returns a String representation of an object of the class and that method toString can be called implicitly whenever an object of a class appears in the code where a String is expected.

You learned that the this reference is used implicitly in a class's non-static methods to access the class's instance variables and other non-static methods. You also saw explicit uses of the this reference to access the class's members (including shadowed fields) and how to use keyword this in a constructor to call another constructor of the class.

```java
1   // Class Keypad represents an ATM's keypad
2   public class Keypad
3   {
4      // no attributes have been specified yet
5
6      // no-argument constructor
7      public Keypad()
8      {
9      } // end no-argument Keypad constructor
10
11     // operations
12     public int getInput()
13     {
14     } // end method getInput
15  } // end class Keypad
```

Fig. 8.30 | Java code for class Keypad based on Fig. 8.24 and Fig. 8.25.

The chapter discussed the differences between default constructors provided by the compiler and no-argument constructors provided by the programmer. You learned that a class can have references to objects of other classes as members—a concept known as composition. You saw the new enum class type introduced in J2SE 5.0 and learned how it can be used to create a set of constants for use in a program. You learned about Java's garbage collection capability and how it reclaims the memory of objects that are no longer used. The chapter explained the motivation for static fields in a class and demonstrated how to declare and use static fields and methods in your own classes. You also learned how to declare and initialize final variables.

You learned how to package your own classes for reuse and how to import those classes into an application. Finally, you learned that fields declared without an access modifier are given package access by default. You saw the relationship between classes in the same package that allows each class in a package to access the package-access members of other classes in the package.

In the next chapter, you will learn about an important aspect of object-oriented programming in Java—inheritance. You will see that all classes in Java are related directly or indirectly to the class called Object. You will also begin to understand how the relationships between classes enable you to build more powerful applications.

Summary

- Every class you declare represents a new type in Java.
- The public methods of a class are also known as the class's public services or public interface. The primary purpose of public methods is to present to the class's clients a view of the services the class provides. Clients of the class need not be concerned with how the class accomplishes its tasks. For this reason, private class members are not directly accessible to the class's clients.
- An object that contains consistent data has data values that are always kept in range.
- A value passed to a method to modify an instance variable is a correct value if that value is in the instance variable's allowed range. A correct value is always a consistent value, but a consistent value is not correct if a method receives an out-of-range value and sets it to a consistent value to maintain the object in a consistent state.
- String class static method format is similar to method System.out.printf except that format returns a formatted String rather than displaying it in a command window.
- All objects in Java have a toString method that returns a String representation of the object. Method toString is called implicitly when an object appears in code where a String is needed.
- A non-static method of an object implicitly uses keyword this to refer to the object's instance variables and other methods. Keyword this can also be used explicitly.
- The compiler produces a separate file with the .class extension for every compiled class.
- If a method contains a local variable with the same name as one of its class's fields, the local variable shadows the field in the method's scope. The method can use the this reference to refer to the shadowed field explicitly.
- Overloaded constructors enable objects of a class to be initialized in different ways. The compiler differentiates overloaded constructors by their signatures.

- Every class must have at least one constructor. If none are provided, the compiler creates a default constructor that initializes the instance variables to the initial values specified in their declarations or to their default values.

- If a class declares constructors, the compiler will not create a default constructor. To specify the default initialization for objects of a class with multiple constructors, the programmer must declare a no-argument constructor.

- *Set* methods are commonly called mutator methods because they typically change a value. *Get* methods are commonly called accessor methods or query methods. A predicate method tests whether a condition is true or false.

- A class can have references to objects of other classes as members. Such a capability is called composition and is sometimes referred to as a *has-a* relationship.

- All enum types are reference types. An enum type is declared with an enum declaration, which is a comma-separated list of enum constants. The declaration may optionally include other components of traditional classes, such as constructors, fields and methods.

- enum types are implicitly `final`, because they declare constants that should not be modified.

- enum constants are implicitly `static`.

- Any attempt to create an object of an enum type with operator new results in a compilation error.

- enum constants can be used anywhere constants can be used, such as in the `case` labels of `switch` statements and to control enhanced `for` statements.

- Each enum constant in an enum declaration is optionally followed by arguments which are passed to the enum constructor.

- For every enum, the compiler generates a `static` method called `values` that returns an array of the enum's constants in the order in which they were declared.

- `EnumSet` static method `range` takes two parameters—the first enum constant in a range and the last enum constant in a range—and returns an `EnumSet` that contains all the constants between these two constants, inclusive.

- Every class in Java has the methods of class `Object`, one of which is the `finalize` method.

- The Java Virtual Machine (JVM) performs automatic garbage collection to reclaim the memory occupied by objects that are no longer in use. When there are no more references to an object, the object is marked for garbage collection by the JVM. The memory for such an object can be reclaimed when the JVM executes its garbage collector.

- The `finalize` method is called by the garbage collector just before it reclaims the object's memory. Method `finalize` does not take parameters and has return type void.

- The garbage collector may never execute before a program terminates. Thus, it is unclear if, or when, method `finalize` will be called.

- A `static` variable represents classwide information that is shared among all objects of the class.

- Static variables have class scope. A class's `public` `static` members can be accessed through a reference to any object of the class, or they can be accessed by qualifying the member name with the class name and a dot (.). A class's `private` `static` class members can be accessed only through methods of the class.

- `static` class members exist even when no objects of the class exist—they are available as soon as the class is loaded into memory at execution time. To access a `private` `static` member when no objects of the class exist, a `public` `static` method must be provided.

- `System` class `static` method `gc` indicates that the garbage collector should make a best-effort attempt to reclaim objects that are eligible for garbage collection.

- A method declared `static` cannot access non-`static` class members, because a `static` method can be called even when no objects of the class have been instantiated.

- The `this` reference cannot be used in a `static` method.

- A `static` import declaration enables programmers to refer to imported `static` members without the class name and a dot (`.`). A single `static` import declaration imports one `static` member, and a `static` import on demand imports all `static` members of a class.

- In the context of an application, the principle of least privilege states that code should be granted only the amount of privilege and access that the code needs to accomplish its designated task.

- Keyword `final` specifies that a variable is not modifiable—in other words, it is constant. Constants can be initialized when they are declared or by each of a class's constructors. If a `final` variable is not initialized, a compilation error occurs.

- Software is constructed from existing, well-defined, carefully tested, well-documented, portable, widely available components. Software reusability speeds the development of powerful, high-quality software. Rapid application development (RAD) is of great interest today.

- Java programmers now have thousands of classes in the Java API from which to choose to help them implement Java programs. The Java API classes enable Java programmers to bring new applications to market faster by using preexisting, tested components.

- The client of a class cares about the functionality the class offers, but not about how the functionality is implemented. This is referred to as data abstraction. Although programmers may know the details of a class's implementation, they should not write code that depends on these details. This enables a class to be replaced with another version without affecting the rest of the system.

- An abstract data type (ADT) consists of a data representation and the operations that can be performed on that data.

- Each class in the Java API belongs to a package that contains a group of related classes. Packages help manage the complexity of application components and facilitate software reuse.

- Packages provide a convention for unique class names that helps prevent class name conflicts.

- Before a class can be imported into multiple applications, the class must be placed in a package. There can be only one `package` declaration in each Java source-code file, and it must precede all other declarations and statements in the file.

- Every package name should start with your Internet domain name in reverse order. After the domain name is reversed, you can choose any other names you want for your package.

- When compiling a class in a package, the `javac` command-line option `-d` specifies where to store the package and causes the compiler to create the package's directories if they do not exist.

- The `package` name is part of the fully qualified class name. This helps prevent name conflicts.

- A single-type-import declaration specifies one class to import. A type-import-on-demand declaration imports only the classes that the program uses from a particular package.

- The compiler uses a class loader to locate the classes it needs in the classpath. The classpath consists of a list of directories or archive files, each separated by a directory separator.

- The classpath for the compiler and JVM can be specified by providing the `-classpath` option to the `javac` or `java` command, or by setting the `CLASSPATH` environment variable. The classpath for the JVM can also be specified via the `-cp` command-line option. If classes must be loaded from the current directory, include a dot (`.`) in the classpath.

- If no access modifier is specified for a method or variable when it is declared in a class, the method or variable is considered to have package access.

Terminology

abstract data type (ADT)	mutator method
access modifier	name collision
accessor method	name conflict
attribute	no-argument constructor
behavior	optional package
class library	overloaded constructors
class loader	package access
class scope	package declaration
class variable	predicate method
classpath	principle of least privilege
`-classpath` command line argument to `javac`	`private` access modifier
`CLASSPATH` environment variable	`protected` access modifier
composition	`public` access modifier
constant variable	query method
`-d` command line argument to `javac`	range method of `EnumSet`
data abstraction	rapid application development (RAD)
default constructor	resource leak
directory separator	service of a class
enum keyword	simple name of a class, field or method
enum constant	single `static` import
`EnumSet` class	single-type-import declaration
extensible language	static field (class variable)
extensions mechanism	`static` import
`finalize` method	`static` import on demand
`format` method of `String`	termination housekeeping
garbage collector	`this` keyword
`gc` method of `System`	type-import-on-demand declaration
has-a relationship	validity checking
mark an object for garbage collection	`values` method of an enum
memory leak	variable is not modifiable

Self-Review Exercises

8.1 Fill in the blanks in each of the following statements:

a) When compiling a class in a package, the `javac` command-line option _____ specifies where to store the package and causes the compiler to create the package's directories if they do not exist.

b) `String` class `static` method _____ is similar to method `System.out.printf`, but returns a formatted `String` rather than displaying a `String` in a command window.

c) If a method contains a local variable with the same name as one of its class's fields, the local variable _____ the field in that method's scope.

d) The _____ method is called by the garbage collector just before it reclaims an object's memory.

e) A(n) _____ declaration specifies one class to import.

f) If a class declares constructors, the compiler will not create a(n) _____.

g) An object's _____ method is called implicitly when an object appears in code where a `String` is needed.

h) *Get* methods are commonly called _____ or _____.

i) A(n) _____ method tests whether a condition is true or false.

j) For every enum, the compiler generates a `static` method called _____ that returns an array of the enum's constants in the order in which they were declared.

k) Composition is sometimes referred to as a(n) _____ relationship.

l) A(n) _____ declaration contains a comma-separated list of constants.

m) A(n) _____ variable represents classwide information that is shared by all the objects of the class.

n) A(n) _____ declaration imports one `static` member.

o) The _____ states that code should be granted only the amount of privilege and access that the code needs to accomplish its designated task.

p) Keyword _____ specifies that a variable is not modifiable.

q) A(n) _____ consists of a data representation and the operations that can be performed on the data.

r) There can be only one _____ in a Java source-code file, and it must precede all other declarations and statements in the file.

s) A(n) _____ declaration imports only the classes that the program uses from a particular package.

t) The compiler uses a(n) _____ to locate the classes it needs in the classpath.

u) The classpath for the compiler and JVM can be specified with the _____ option to the `javac` or `java` command, or by setting the _____ environment variable.

v) *Set* methods are commonly called _____ because they typically change a value.

w) A(n) _____ imports all `static` members of a class.

x) The `public` methods of a class are also known as the class's _____ or _____.

y) `System` class `static` method _____ indicates that the garbage collector should make a best-effort attempt to reclaim objects that are eligible for garbage collection.

z) An object that contains _____ has data values that are always kept in range.

Answers to Self-Review Exercises

8.1   a) -d. b) format. c) shadows. d) `finalize`. e) single-type-import. f) default constructor. g) `toString`. h) accessor methods, query methods. i) predicate. j) `values`. k) *has-a*. l) enum. m) static. n) single `static` import. o) principle of least privilege. p) `final`. q) abstract data type (ADT). r) package declaration. s) type-import-on-demand. t) class loader. u) `-classpath`, CLASSPATH. v) mutator methods. w) `static` import on demand. x) `public` services, `public` interface. y) `gc`. z) consistent data.

Exercises

8.2   Explain the notion of package access in Java. Explain the negative aspects of package access.

8.3   What happens when a return type, even `void`, is specified for a constructor?

8.4   *(Rectangle Class)* Create a class `Rectangle`. The class has attributes `length` and `width`, each of which defaults to 1. It has methods that calculate the `perimeter` and the `area` of the rectangle. It has *set* and *get* methods for both `length` and `width`. The *set* methods should verify that `length` and `width` are each floating-point numbers larger than 0.0 and less than 20.0. Write a program to test class `Rectangle`.

8.5   *(Modifying the Internal Data Representation of a Class)* It would be perfectly reasonable for the `Time2` class of Fig. 8.5 to represent the time internally as the number of seconds since midnight rather than the three integer values `hour`, `minute` and `second`. Clients could use the same `public` methods and get the same results. Modify the `Time2` class of Fig. 8.5 to implement the `Time2` as the number of seconds since midnight and show that no change is visible to the clients of the class.

8.6   *(Savings Account Class)* Create class SavingsAccount. Use a static variable annualInterestRate to store the annual interest rate for all account holders. Each object of the class contains a private instance variable savingsBalance indicating the amount the saver currently has on deposit. Provide method calculateMonthlyInterest to calculate the monthly interest by multiplying the savingsBalance by annualInterestRate divided by 12—this interest should be added to savingsBalance. Provide a static method modifyInterestRate that sets the annualInterestRate to a new value. Write a program to test class SavingsAccount. Instantiate two savingsAccount objects, saver1 and saver2, with balances of $2000.00 and $3000.00, respectively. Set annualInterestRate to 4%, then calculate the monthly interest and print the new balances for both savers. Then set the annualInterestRate to 5%, calculate the next month's interest and print the new balances for both savers.

8.7   *(Enhancing Class Time2)* Modify class Time2 of Fig. 8.5 to include a tick method that increments the time stored in a Time2 object by one second. Provide method incrementMinute to increment the minute and method incrementHour to increment the hour. The Time2 object should always remain in a consistent state. Write a program that tests the tick method, the incrementMinute method and the incrementHour method to ensure that they work correctly. Be sure to test the following cases:
   a)   incrementing into the next minute,
   b)   incrementing into the next hour and
   c)   incrementing into the next day (i.e., 11:59:59 PM to 12:00:00 AM).

8.8   *(Enhancing Class Date)* Modify class Date of Fig. 8.7 to perform error checking on the initializer values for instance variables month, day and year (currently it validates only the month and day). Provide a method nextDay to increment the day by one. The Date object should always remain in a consistent state. Write a program that tests the nextDay method in a loop that prints the date during each iteration of the loop to illustrate that the nextDay method works correctly. Test the following cases:
   a)   incrementing into the next month and
   b)   incrementing into the next year.

8.9   *(Returning Error Indicators from Methods)* Modify the *set* methods in class Time2 of Fig. 8.5 to return appropriate error values if an attempt is made to set one of the instance variables hour, minute or second of an object of class Time to an invalid value. [*Hint:* Use boolean return types on each method.] Write a program that tests these new *set* methods and outputs error messages when incorrect values are supplied.

8.10   Rewrite Fig. 8.14 to use a separate import declaration for each static member of class Math that is used in the example.

8.11   Write an enum type TrafficLight, whose constants (RED, GREEN, YELLOW) take one parameter—the duration of the light. Write a program to test the TrafficLight enum so that it displays the enum constants and their durations.

8.12   *(Complex Numbers)* Create a class called Complex for performing arithmetic with complex numbers. Complex numbers have the form

   realPart + *imaginaryPart* * *i*

where *i* is

   $\sqrt{-1}$

Write a program to test your class. Use floating-point variables to represent the private data of the class. Provide a constructor that enables an object of this class to be initialized when it is declared.

Provide a no-argument constructor with default values in case no initializers are provided. Provide `public` methods that perform the following operations:

   a) Add two `Complex` numbers: The real parts are added together and the imaginary parts are added together.

   b) Subtract two `Complex` numbers: The real part of the right operand is subtracted from the real part of the left operand, and the imaginary part of the right operand is subtracted from the imaginary part of the left operand.

   c) Print `Complex` numbers in the form (a, b), where a is the real part and b is the imaginary part.

8.13 *(Date and Time Class)* Create class `DateAndTime` that combines the modified `Time2` class of Exercise 8.7 and the modified `Date` class of Exercise 8.8. Modify method `incrementHour` to call method `nextDay` if the time is incremented into the next day. Modify methods `toStandardString` and `toUniversalString` to output the date in addition to the time. Write a program to test the new class `DateAndTime`. Specifically, test incrementing the time to the next day.

8.14 *(Enhanced Rectangle Class)* Create a more sophisticated `Rectangle` class than the one you created in Exercise 8.4. This class stores only the Cartesian coordinates of the four corners of the rectangle. The constructor calls a *set* method that accepts four sets of coordinates and verifies that each of these is in the first quadrant with no single *x*- or *y*-coordinate larger than 20.0. The *set* method also verifies that the supplied coordinates specify a rectangle. Provide methods to calculate the `length`, `width`, `perimeter` and `area`. The length is the larger of the two dimensions. Include a predicate method `isSquare` which determines whether the rectangle is a square. Write a program to test class `Rectangle`.

8.15 *(Set of Integers)* Create class `IntegerSet`. Each `IntegerSet` object can hold integers in the range 0–100. The set is represented by an array of `boolean`s. Array element a[i] is true if integer *i* is in the set. Array element a[j] is false if integer *j* is not in the set. The no-argument constructor initializes the Java array to the "empty set" (i.e., a set whose array representation contains all false values).

Provide the following methods: Method `union` creates a third set that is the set-theoretic union of two existing sets (i.e., an element of the third set's array is set to true if that element is true in either or both of the existing sets—otherwise, the element of the third set is set to false). Method `intersection` creates a third set which is the set-theoretic intersection of two existing sets (i.e., an element of the third set's array is set to false if that element is false in either or both of the existing sets—otherwise, the element of the third set is set to true). Method `insertElement` inserts a new integer *k* into a set (by setting a[k] to true). Method `deleteElement` deletes integer *m* (by setting a[m] to false). Method `toSetString` returns a string containing a set as a list of numbers separated by spaces. Include only those elements that are present in the set. Use --- to represent an empty set. Method `isEqualTo` determines whether two sets are equal. Write a program to test class `IntegerSet`. Instantiate several `IntegerSet` objects. Test that all your methods work properly.

8.16 *(Date Class)* Create class `Date` with the following capabilities:

   a) Output the date in multiple formats, such as

```
MM/DD/YYYY
June 14, 1992
DDD YYYY
```

   b) Use overloaded constructors to create `Date` objects initialized with dates of the formats in part (a). In the first case the constructor should receive three integer values. In the second case it should receive a `String` and two integer values. In the third case it should receive two integer values, the first of which represents the day number in the year. [*Hint:* To convert the string representation of the month to a numeric value, compare strings using the `equals` method. For example, if s1 and s2 are strings, the method call s1.equals(s2) returns true if the strings are identical and otherwise returns false.]

8.17 *(Rational Numbers)* Create a class called Rational for performing arithmetic with fractions. Write a program to test your class. Use integer variables to represent the private instance variables of the class—the numerator and the denominator. Provide a constructor that enables an object of this class to be initialized when it is declared. The constructor should store the fraction in reduced form. The fraction

   2/4

is equivalent to 1/2 and would be stored in the object as 1 in the numerator and 2 in the denominator. Provide a no-argument constructor with default values in case no initializers are provided. Provide public methods that perform each of the following operations:

a) Add two Rational numbers: The result of the addition should be stored in reduced form.

b) Subtract two Rational numbers: The result of the subtraction should be stored in reduced form.

c) Multiply two Rational numbers: The result of the multiplication should be stored in reduced form.

d) Divide two Rational numbers: The result of the division should be stored in reduced form.

e) Print Rational numbers in the form a/b, where a is the numerator and b is the denominator.

f) Print Rational numbers in floating-point format. (Consider providing formatting capabilities that enable the user of the class to specify the number of digits of precision to the right of the decimal point.)

8.18 *(Huge Integer Class)* Create a class HugeInteger which uses a 40-element array of digits to store integers as large as 40 digits each. Provide methods input, output, add and subtract. For comparing HugeInteger objects, provide the following methods: isEqualTo, isNotEqualTo, isGreaterThan, isLessThan, isGreaterThanOrEqualTo and isLessThanOrEqualTo. Each of these is a predicate method that returns true if the relationship holds between the two HugeInteger objects and returns false if the relationship does not hold. Provide a predicate method isZero. If you feel ambitious, also provide methods multiply, divide and remainder. [*Note:* Primitive boolean values can be output as the word "true" or the word "false" with format specifier %b.]

8.19 *(Tic-Tac-Toe)* Create a class TicTacToe that will enable you to write a complete program to play the game of Tic-Tac-Toe. The class contains a private 3-by-3 two-dimensional array of integers. The constructor should initialize the empty board to all zeros. Allow two human players. Wherever the first player moves, place a 1 in the specified square, and place a 2 wherever the second player moves. Each move must be to an empty square. After each move, determine whether the game has been won and whether it is a draw. If you feel ambitious, modify your program so that the computer makes the moves for one of the players. Also, allow the player to specify whether he or she wants to go first or second. If you feel exceptionally ambitious, develop a program that will play three-dimensional Tic-Tac-Toe on a 4-by-4-by-4 board [*Note:* This is a challenging project that could take many weeks of effort!].

9

Object-Oriented Programming: Inheritance

OBJECTIVES

In this chapter you will learn:

- How inheritance promotes software reusability.
- The notions of superclasses and subclasses.
- To use keyword **extends** to create a class that inherits attributes and behaviors from another class.
- To use access modifier **protected** to give subclass methods access to superclass members.
- To access superclass members with **super**.
- How constructors are used in inheritance hierarchies.
- The methods of class **Object**, the direct or indirect superclass of all classes in Java.

9.1 Introduction

This chapter continues our discussion of object-oriented programming (OOP) by introducing one of its primary features—inheritance, which is a form of software reuse in which a new class is created by absorbing an existing class's members and embellishing them with new or modified capabilities. With inheritance, programmers save time during program development by reusing proven and debugged high-quality software. This also increases the likelihood that a system will be implemented effectively.

When creating a class, rather than declaring completely new members, the programmer can designate that the new class should inherit the members of an existing class. The existing class is called the superclass, and the new class is the subclass. (The C++ programming language refers to the superclass as the base class and the subclass as the derived class.) Each subclass can become the superclass for future subclasses.

A subclass normally adds its own fields and methods. Therefore, a subclass is more specific than its superclass and represents a more specialized group of objects. Typically, the subclass exhibits the behaviors of its superclass and additional behaviors that are specific to the subclass.

The direct superclass is the superclass from which the subclass explicitly inherits. An indirect superclass is any class above the direct superclass in the class hierarchy, which defines the inheritance relationships between classes. In Java, the class hierarchy begins with class Object (in package java.lang), which *every* class in Java directly or indirectly extends (or "inherits from"). Section 9.7 lists the methods of class Object, which every other class inherits. In the case of single inheritance, a class is derived from one direct superclass. Java, unlike C++, does not support multiple inheritance (which occurs when a class is derived from more than one direct superclass). In Chapter 10, Object-Oriented Programming: Polymorphism, we explain how Java programmers can use interfaces to realize many of the benefits of multiple inheritance while avoiding the associated problems.

Experience in building software systems indicates that significant amounts of code deal with closely-related special cases. When programmers are preoccupied with special cases, the details can obscure the big picture. With object-oriented programming, programmers focus on the commonalities among objects in the system rather than on the special cases.

We distinguish between the "is-a" relationship and the "has-a" relationship. "Is-a" represents inheritance. In an "is-a" relationship, an object of a subclass can also be treated as an object of its superclass. For example, a car *is a* vehicle. By contrast, "has-a" represents composition (see Chapter 8). In a "has-a" relationship, an object contains one or more object references as members. For example, a car *has a* steering wheel (and a car object has a reference to a steering wheel object).

New classes can inherit from classes in class libraries. Organizations develop their own class libraries and can take advantage of others available worldwide. Some day, most new software likely will be constructed from standardized reusable components, just as automobiles and most computer hardware are constructed today. This will facilitate the development of more powerful, abundant and economical software.

9.2 Superclasses and Subclasses

Often, an object of one class "is an" object of another class as well. For example, in geometry, a rectangle *is a* quadrilateral (as are squares, parallelograms and trapezoids). Thus, in Java, class `Rectangle` can be said to inherit from class `Quadrilateral`. In this context, class `Quadrilateral` is a superclass and class `Rectangle` is a subclass. A rectangle *is a* specific type of quadrilateral, but it is incorrect to claim that every quadrilateral *is a* rectangle—the quadrilateral could be a parallelogram or some other shape. Figure 9.1 lists several simple examples of superclasses and subclasses—note that superclasses tend to be "more general" and subclasses tend to be "more specific."

Because every subclass object "is an" object of its superclass, and one superclass can have many subclasses, the set of objects represented by a superclass is typically larger than the set of objects represented by any of its subclasses. For example, the superclass `Vehicle` represents all vehicles, including cars, trucks, boats, bicycles and so on. By contrast, subclass `Car` represents a smaller, more specific subset of vehicles.

Superclass	Subclasses
Student	GraduateStudent, UndergraduateStudent
Shape	Circle, Triangle, Rectangle
Loan	CarLoan, HomeImprovementLoan, MortgageLoan
Employee	Faculty, Staff
BankAccount	CheckingAccount, SavingsAccount

Fig. 9.1 | Inheritance examples.

Inheritance relationships form tree-like hierarchical structures. A superclass exists in a hierarchical relationship with its subclasses. When classes participate in inheritance relationships, they become "affiliated" with other classes. A class becomes either a superclass, supplying members to other classes, or a subclass, inheriting its members from other classes. In some cases, a class is both a superclass and a subclass.

Let us develop a sample class hierarchy (Fig. 9.2), also called an inheritance hierarchy. A university community has thousands of members, including employees, students and alumni. Employees are either faculty members or staff members. Faculty members are either administrators (such as deans and department chairpersons) or teachers. Note that the hierarchy could contain many other classes. For example, students can be graduate or undergraduate students. Undergraduate students can be freshmen, sophomores, juniors or seniors.

Each arrow in the hierarchy represents an "is-a" relationship. As we follow the arrows in this class hierarchy, we can state, for instance, that "an Employee *is a* CommunityMember" and "a Teacher *is a* Faculty member." CommunityMember is the direct superclass of Employee, Student and Alumnus, and is an indirect superclass of all the other classes in the diagram. Starting from the bottom of the diagram, the reader can follow the arrows and apply the "is-a" relationship up to the topmost superclass. For example, an Administrator *is a* Faculty member, *is an* Employee and *is a* CommunityMember.

Now consider the Shape inheritance hierarchy in Fig. 9.3. This hierarchy begins with superclass Shape, which is extended by subclasses TwoDimensionalShape and ThreeDimensionalShape—Shapes are either TwoDimensionalShapes or ThreeDimensionalShapes. The third level of this hierarchy contains some more specific types of TwoDimensionalShapes and ThreeDimensionalShapes. As in Fig. 9.2, we can follow the arrows from the bottom of the diagram to the topmost superclass in this class hierarchy to identify several "is-a" relationships. For instance, a Triangle *is a* TwoDimensionalShape and *is a* Shape, while a Sphere *is a* ThreeDimensionalShape and *is a* Shape. Note that this hierarchy could contain many other classes. For example, ellipses and trapezoids are TwoDimensionalShapes.

Not every class relationship is an inheritance relationship. In Chapter 8, we discussed the "has-a" relationship, in which classes have members that are references to objects of other classes. Such relationships create classes by composition of existing classes. For

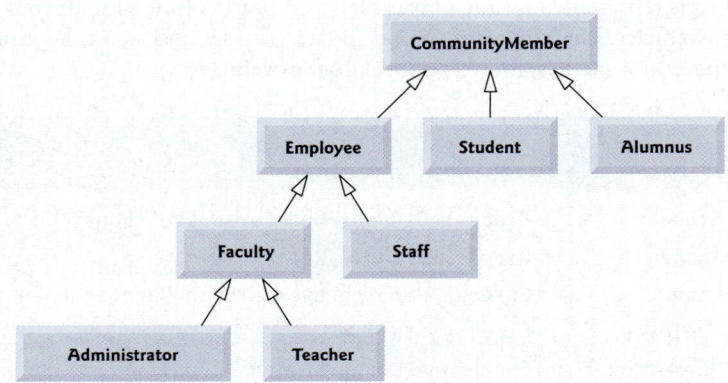

Fig. 9.2 | Inheritance hierarchy for university CommunityMembers.

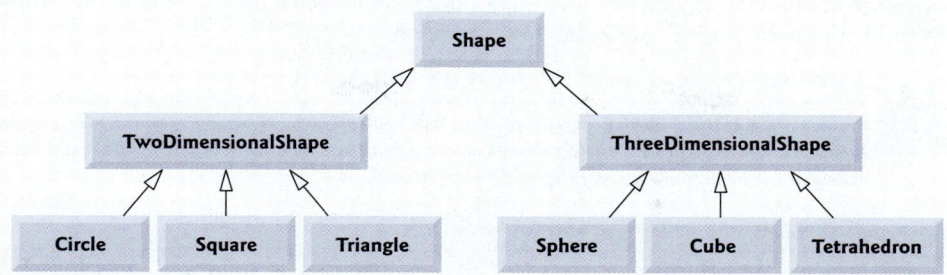

Fig. 9.3 | Inheritance hierarchy for Shapes.

example, given the classes Employee, BirthDate and TelephoneNumber, it is improper to say that an Employee *is a* BirthDate or that an Employee *is a* TelephoneNumber. However, an Employee *has a* BirthDate, and an Employee *has a* TelephoneNumber.

It is possible to treat superclass objects and subclass objects similarly—their commonalities are expressed in the members of the superclass. Objects of all classes that extend a common superclass can be treated as objects of that superclass (i.e., such objects have an "is-a" relationship with the superclass). However, superclass objects cannot be treated as objects of their subclasses. For example, all cars are vehicles, but not all vehicles are cars (the other vehicles could be trucks, planes or bicycles, for example). Later in this chapter and in Chapter 10, Object-Oriented Programming: Polymorphism, we consider many examples that take advantage of the "is-a" relationship.

One problem with inheritance is that a subclass can inherit methods that it does not need or should not have. Even when a superclass method is appropriate for a subclass, that subclass often needs a customized version of the method. In such cases, the subclass can override (redefine) the superclass method with an appropriate implementation, as we will see often in the chapter's code examples.

9.3 protected Members

Chapter 8 discussed access modifiers public and private. A class's public members are accessible wherever the program has a reference to an object of that class or one of its subclasses. A class's private members are accessible only from within the class itself. A superclass's private members are not inherited by its subclasses. In this section, we introduce access modifier **protected**. Using protected access offers an intermediate level of access between public and private. A superclass's protected members can be accessed by members of that superclass, by members of its subclasses and by members of other classes in the same package (i.e., protected members also have package access).

All public and protected superclass members retain their original access modifier when they become members of the subclass (i.e., public members of the superclass become public members of the subclass, and protected members of the superclass become protected members of the subclass).

Subclass methods can refer to public and protected members inherited from the superclass simply by using the member names. When a subclass method overrides a superclass method, the superclass method can be accessed from the subclass by preceding the superclass method name with keyword **super** and a dot (.) separator. We discuss accessing overridden members of the superclass in Section 9.4.

Software Engineering Observation 9.1

Methods of a subclass cannot directly access private members of their superclass. A subclass can change the state of private superclass instance variables only through non-private methods provided in the superclass and inherited by the subclass.

Software Engineering Observation 9.2

Declaring private instance variables helps programmers test, debug and correctly modify systems. If a subclass could access its superclass's private instance variables, classes that inherit from that subclass could access the instance variables as well. This would propagate access to what should be private instance variables, and the benefits of information hiding would be lost.

9.4 Relationship between Superclasses and Subclasses

In this section, we use an inheritance hierarchy containing types of employees in a company's payroll application to discuss the relationship between a superclass and its subclass. In this company, commission employees (who will be represented as objects of a superclass) are paid a percentage of their sales, while base-salaried commission employees (who will be represented as objects of a subclass) receive a base salary plus a percentage of their sales.

We divide our discussion of the relationship between commission employees and base-salaried commission employees into five examples. The first example declares class CommissionEmployee, which directly inherits from class Object and declares as private instance variables a first name, last name, social security number, commission rate and gross (i.e., total) sales amount.

The second example declares class BasePlusCommissionEmployee, which also directly inherits from class Object and declares as private instance variables a first name, last name, social security number, commission rate, gross sales amount and base salary. We create the latter class by writing every line of code the class requires—we will soon see that it is much more efficient to create this class by inheriting from class CommissionEmployee.

The third example declares a separate BasePlusCommissionEmployee2 class that extends class CommissionEmployee (i.e., a BasePlusCommissionEmployee2 *is a* CommissionEmployee who also has a base salary) and attempts to access class CommissionEmployee's private members—this results in compilation errors, because the subclass cannot access the superclass's private instance variables.

The fourth example shows that if CommissionEmployee's instance variables are declared as protected, a BasePlusCommissionEmployee3 class that extends class CommissionEmployee2 can access that data directly. For this purpose, we declare class CommissionEmployee2 with protected instance variables. Both of the BasePlusCommissionEmployee classes contain identical functionality, but we show how the class BasePlusCommissionEmployee3 is easier to create and manage.

After we discuss the convenience of using protected instance variables, we create the fifth example, which sets the CommissionEmployee instance variables back to private in class CommissionEmployee3 to enforce good software engineering. Then we show how a separate BasePlusCommissionEmployee4 class, which extends class CommissionEmployee3, can use CommissionEmployee3's public methods to manipulate CommissionEmployee3's private instance variables.

9.4.1 Creating and Using a CommissionEmployee Class

We begin by declaring class CommissionEmployee (Fig. 9.4). Line 4 begins the class declaration and indicates that class CommissionEmployee extends (i.e., inherits from) class Object (from package java.lang). Java programmers use inheritance to create classes from existing classes. In fact, every class in Java (except Object) extends an existing class. Because class CommissionEmployee extends class Object, class CommissionEmployee inherits the methods of class Object—class Object does not have any fields. In fact, every Java class directly or indirectly inherits Object's methods. If a class does not specify that it extends another class, the new class implicitly extends Object. For this reason, programmers typically do not include "extends Object" in their code—we do so in this example for demonstration purposes.

Software Engineering Observation 9.3

The Java compiler sets the superclass of a class to Object when the class declaration does not explicitly extend a superclass.

```java
 1   // Fig. 9.4: CommissionEmployee.java
 2   // CommissionEmployee class represents a commission employee.
 3
 4   public class CommissionEmployee extends Object
 5   {
 6      private String firstName;
 7      private String lastName;
 8      private String socialSecurityNumber;
 9      private double grossSales; // gross weekly sales
10      private double commissionRate; // commission percentage
11
12      // five-argument constructor
13      public CommissionEmployee( String first, String last, String ssn,
14         double sales, double rate )
15      {
16         // implicit call to Object constructor occurs here
17         firstName = first;
18         lastName = last;
19         socialSecurityNumber = ssn;
20         setGrossSales( sales ); // validate and store gross sales
21         setCommissionRate( rate ); // validate and store commission rate
22      } // end five-argument CommissionEmployee constructor
23
24      // set first name
25      public void setFirstName( String first )
26      {
27         firstName = first;
28      } // end method setFirstName
29
30      // return first name
31      public String getFirstName()
32      {
```

Fig. 9.4 | CommissionEmployee class represents an employee paid a percentage of gross sales. (Part 1 of 3.)

```
33          return firstName;
34       } // end method getFirstName
35
36       // set last name
37       public void setLastName( String last )
38       {
39          lastName = last;
40       } // end method setLastName
41
42       // return last name
43       public String getLastName()
44       {
45          return lastName;
46       } // end method getLastName
47
48       // set social security number
49       public void setSocialSecurityNumber( String ssn )
50       {
51          socialSecurityNumber = ssn; // should validate
52       } // end method setSocialSecurityNumber
53
54       // return social security number
55       public String getSocialSecurityNumber()
56       {
57          return socialSecurityNumber;
58       } // end method getSocialSecurityNumber
59
60       // set gross sales amount
61       public void setGrossSales( double sales )
62       {
63          grossSales = ( sales < 0.0 ) ? 0.0 : sales;
64       } // end method setGrossSales
65
66       // return gross sales amount
67       public double getGrossSales()
68       {
69          return grossSales;
70       } // end method getGrossSales
71
72       // set commission rate
73       public void setCommissionRate( double rate )
74       {
75          commissionRate = ( rate > 0.0 && rate < 1.0 ) ? rate : 0.0;
76       } // end method setCommissionRate
77
78       // return commission rate
79       public double getCommissionRate()
80       {
81          return commissionRate;
82       } // end method getCommissionRate
83
```

Fig. 9.4 | `CommissionEmployee` class represents an employee paid a percentage of gross sales. (Part 2 of 3.)

```
84        // calculate earnings
85        public double earnings()
86        {
87           return commissionRate * grossSales;
88        } // end method earnings
89
90        // return String representation of CommissionEmployee object
91        public String toString()
92        {
93           return String.format( "%s: %s %s\n%s: %s\n%s: %.2f\n%s: %.2f",
94              "commission employee", firstName, lastName,
95              "social security number", socialSecurityNumber,
96              "gross sales", grossSales,
97              "commission rate", commissionRate );
98        } // end method toString
99     } // end class CommissionEmployee
```

Fig. 9.4 | CommissionEmployee class represents an employee paid a percentage of gross sales. (Part 3 of 3.)

The public services of class CommissionEmployee include a constructor (lines 13–22) and methods earnings (lines 85–88) and toString (lines 91–98). Lines 25–82 declare public *get* and *set* methods for manipulating the class's instance variables (declared in lines 6–10) firstName, lastName, socialSecurityNumber, grossSales and commissionRate. Class CommissionEmployee declares each of its instance variables as private, so objects of other classes cannot directly access these variables. Declaring instance variables as private and providing *get* and *set* methods to manipulate and validate the instance variables helps enforce good software engineering. Methods setGrossSales and setCommissionRate, for example, validate their arguments before assigning the values to instance variables gross-Sales and commissionRate, respectively.

Constructors are not inherited, so class CommissionEmployee does not inherit class Object's constructor. However, class CommissionEmployee's constructor calls class Object's constructor implicitly. In fact, the first task of any subclass constructor is to call its direct superclass's constructor, either explicitly or implicitly (if no constructor call is specified), to ensure that the instance variables inherited from the superclass are initialized properly. The syntax for calling a superclass constructor explicitly is discussed in Section 9.4.3. If the code does not include an explicit call to the superclass constructor, Java implicitly calls the superclass's default or no-argument constructor. The comment in line 16 of Fig. 9.4 indicates where the implicit call to the superclass Object's default constructor is made (the programmer does not write the code for this call). Object's default (empty) constructor does nothing. Note that even if a class does not have constructors, the default constructor that the compiler implicitly declares for the class will call the superclass's default or no-argument constructor.

After the implicit call to Object's constructor occurs, lines 17–21 of CommissionEmployee's constructor assign values to the class's instance variables. Note that we do not validate the values of arguments first, last and ssn before assigning them to the corresponding instance variables. While validating data is good software engineering, including extensive validation in this class could add a potentially large amount of code that would obscure the focus of this example. We certainly could validate the first and last names—perhaps by ensuring that they are of a reasonable length. Similarly, a social security number could be validated to ensure that it contains nine digits, with or without dashes (e.g., 123-45-6789 or 123456789).

Method `earnings` (lines 85–88) calculates a `CommissionEmployee`'s earnings. Line 87 multiplies the `commissionRate` by the `grossSales` and returns the result.

Method `toString` (lines 91–98) is special—it is one of the methods that every class inherits directly or indirectly from class `Object`, which is the root of the Java class hierarchy. Section 9.7 summarizes class `Object`'s methods. Method `toString` returns a `String` representing an object. This method is called implicitly by a program whenever an object must be converted to a string representation, such as when an object is output by `printf` or `String` method `format` using the `%s` format specifier. Class `Object`'s `toString` method returns a `String` that includes the name of the object's class. It is primarily a placeholder that can be overridden by a subclass to specify an appropriate string representation of the data in a subclass object. Method `toString` of class `CommissionEmployee` overrides (redefines) class `Object`'s `toString` method. When invoked, `CommissionEmployee`'s `toString` method uses `String` method `format` to return a `String` containing information about the `CommissionEmployee`. We use format specifier `%.2f` to format both the `grossSales` and the `commissionRate` with two digits of precision to the right of the decimal point. To override a superclass method, a subclass must declare a method with the same signature (method name, number of parameters and parameter types) as the superclass method—`Object`'s `toString` method takes no parameters, so `CommissionEmployee` declares `toString` with no parameters.

Common Programming Error 9.1

It is a syntax error to override a method with a more restricted access modifier—a `public` method of the superclass cannot become a `protected` or `private` method in the subclass; a `protected` method of the superclass cannot become a `private` method in the subclass. Doing so would break the "is-a" relationship in which it is required that all subclass objects be able to respond to method calls that are made to `public` methods declared in the superclass. If a `public` method could be overridden as a `protected` or `private` method, the subclass objects would not be able to respond to the same method calls as superclass objects. Once a method is declared `public` in a superclass, the method remains `public` for all that class's direct and indirect subclasses.

Figure 9.5 tests class `CommissionEmployee`. Lines 9–10 instantiate a `CommissionEmployee` object and invoke `CommissionEmployee`'s constructor (lines 13–22 of Fig. 9.4) to

```java
 1   // Fig. 9.5: CommissionEmployeeTest.java
 2   // Testing class CommissionEmployee.
 3
 4   public class CommissionEmployeeTest
 5   {
 6      public static void main( String args[] )
 7      {
 8         // instantiate CommissionEmployee object
 9         CommissionEmployee employee = new CommissionEmployee(
10            "Sue", "Jones", "222-22-2222", 10000, .06 );
11
```

Fig. 9.5 | `CommissionEmployee` class test program. (Part 1 of 2.)

```
12          // get commission employee data
13          System.out.println(
14             "Employee information obtained by get methods: \n" );
15          System.out.printf( "%s %s\n", "First name is",
16             employee.getFirstName() );
17          System.out.printf( "%s %s\n", "Last name is",
18             employee.getLastName() );
19          System.out.printf( "%s %s\n", "Social security number is",
20             employee.getSocialSecurityNumber() );
21          System.out.printf( "%s %.2f\n", "Gross sales is",
22             employee.getGrossSales() );
23          System.out.printf( "%s %.2f\n", "Commission rate is",
24             employee.getCommissionRate() );
25
26          employee.setGrossSales( 500 ); // set gross sales
27          employee.setCommissionRate( .1 ); // set commission rate
28
29          System.out.printf( "\n%s:\n\n%s\n",
30             "Updated employee information obtained by toString", employee );
31       } // end main
32    } // end class CommissionEmployeeTest
```

```
Employee information obtained by get methods:

First name is Sue
Last name is Jones
Social security number is 222-22-2222
Gross sales is 10000.00
Commission rate is 0.06

Updated employee information obtained by toString:

commission employee: Sue Jones
social security number: 222-22-2222
gross sales: 500.00
commission rate: 0.10
```

Fig. 9.5 | CommissionEmployee class test program. (Part 2 of 2.)

initialize it with "Sue" as the first name, "Jones" as the last name, "222-22-2222" as the social security number, 10000 as the gross sales amount and .06 as the commission rate. Lines 15–24 use CommissionEmployee's *get* methods to retrieve the object's instance variable values for output. Lines 26–27 invoke the object's methods setGrossSales and setCommissionRate to change the values of instance variables grossSales and commissionRate. Lines 29–30 output the string representation of the updated CommissionEmployee. Note that when an object is output using the %s format specifier, the object's toString method is invoked implicitly to obtain the object's string representation.

9.4.2 Creating a BasePlusCommissionEmployee Class without Using Inheritance

We now discuss the second part of our introduction to inheritance by declaring and testing (a completely new and independent) class BasePlusCommissionEmployee (Fig. 9.6), which contains a first name, last name, social security number, gross sales amount, commission rate and base salary. Class `BasePlusCommissionEmployee`'s public services include a `BasePlusCommissionEmployee` constructor (lines 15–25) and methods earnings

```java
1   // Fig. 9.6: BasePlusCommissionEmployee.java
2   // BasePlusCommissionEmployee class represents an employee that receives
3   // a base salary in addition to commission.
4
5   public class BasePlusCommissionEmployee
6   {
7      private String firstName;
8      private String lastName;
9      private String socialSecurityNumber;
10     private double grossSales; // gross weekly sales
11     private double commissionRate; // commission percentage
12     private double baseSalary; // base salary per week
13
14     // six-argument constructor
15     public BasePlusCommissionEmployee( String first, String last,
16        String ssn, double sales, double rate, double salary )
17     {
18        // implicit call to Object constructor occurs here
19        firstName = first;
20        lastName = last;
21        socialSecurityNumber = ssn;
22        setGrossSales( sales ); // validate and store gross sales
23        setCommissionRate( rate ); // validate and store commission rate
24        setBaseSalary( salary ); // validate and store base salary
25     } // end six-argument BasePlusCommissionEmployee constructor
26
27     // set first name
28     public void setFirstName( String first )
29     {
30        firstName = first;
31     } // end method setFirstName
32
33     // return first name
34     public String getFirstName()
35     {
36        return firstName;
37     } // end method getFirstName
38
39     // set last name
40     public void setLastName( String last )
41     {
42        lastName = last;
43     } // end method setLastName
44
45     // return last name
46     public String getLastName()
47     {
```

Fig. 9.6 | `BasePlusCommissionEmployee` class represents an employee who receives a base salary in addition to a commission. (Part 1 of 3.)

```
48          return lastName;
49       } // end method getLastName
50
51       // set social security number
52       public void setSocialSecurityNumber( String ssn )
53       {
54          socialSecurityNumber = ssn; // should validate
55       } // end method setSocialSecurityNumber
56
57       // return social security number
58       public String getSocialSecurityNumber()
59       {
60          return socialSecurityNumber;
61       } // end method getSocialSecurityNumber
62
63       // set gross sales amount
64       public void setGrossSales( double sales )
65       {
66          grossSales = ( sales < 0.0 ) ? 0.0 : sales;
67       } // end method setGrossSales
68
69       // return gross sales amount
70       public double getGrossSales()
71       {
72          return grossSales;
73       } // end method getGrossSales
74
75       // set commission rate
76       public void setCommissionRate( double rate )
77       {
78          commissionRate = ( rate > 0.0 && rate < 1.0 ) ? rate : 0.0;
79       } // end method setCommissionRate
80
81       // return commission rate
82       public double getCommissionRate()
83       {
84          return commissionRate;
85       } // end method getCommissionRate
86
87       // set base salary
88       public void setBaseSalary( double salary )
89       {
90          baseSalary = ( salary < 0.0 ) ? 0.0 : salary;
91       } // end method setBaseSalary
92
93       // return base salary
94       public double getBaseSalary()
95       {
96          return baseSalary;
97       } // end method getBaseSalary
98
```

Fig. 9.6 | `BasePlusCommissionEmployee` class represents an employee who receives a base salary in addition to a commission. (Part 2 of 3.)

```
 99      // calculate earnings
100      public double earnings()
101      {
102         return baseSalary + ( commissionRate * grossSales );
103      } // end method earnings
104
105      // return String representation of BasePlusCommissionEmployee
106      public String toString()
107      {
108         return String.format(
109            "%s: %s %s\n%s: %s\n%s: %.2f\n%s: %.2f\n%s: %.2f",
110            "base-salaried commission employee", firstName, lastName,
111            "social security number", socialSecurityNumber,
112            "gross sales", grossSales, "commission rate", commissionRate,
113            "base salary", baseSalary );
114      } // end method toString
115 } // end class BasePlusCommissionEmployee
```

Fig. 9.6 | `BasePlusCommissionEmployee` class represents an employee who receives a base salary in addition to a commission. (Part 3 of 3.)

(lines 100–103) and `toString` (lines 106–114). Lines 28–97 declare public *get* and *set* methods for the class's `private` instance variables (declared in lines 7–12) `firstName`, `lastName`, `socialSecurityNumber`, `grossSales`, `commissionRate` and `baseSalary`. These variables and methods encapsulate all the necessary features of a base-salaried commission employee. Note the similarity between this class and class `CommissionEmployee` (Fig. 9.4)—in this example, we will not yet exploit that similarity.

Note that class `BasePlusCommissionEmployee` does not specify "extends Object" on line 5, so the class implicitly extends `Object`. Also note that, like class `CommissionEmployee`'s constructor (lines 13–22 of Fig. 9.4), class `BasePlusCommissionEmployee`'s constructor invokes class `Object`'s default constructor implicitly, as noted in the comment on line 18.

Class `BasePlusCommissionEmployee`'s earnings method (lines 100–103) computes the earnings of a base-salaried commission employee. Line 102 returns the result of adding the employee's base salary to the product of the commission rate and the employee's gross sales.

Class `BasePlusCommissionEmployee` overrides `Object` method `toString` to return a String containing the `BasePlusCommissionEmployee`'s information. Once again, we use format specifier `%.2f` to format the gross sales, commission rate and base salary with two digits of precision to the right of the decimal point (line 109).

Figure 9.7 tests class `BasePlusCommissionEmployee`. Lines 9–11 instantiate a `BasePlusCommissionEmployee` object and pass "Bob", "Lewis", "333-33-3333", 5000, .04 and 300 to the constructor as the first name, last name, social security number, gross sales, commission rate and base salary, respectively. Lines 16–27 use `BasePlusCommissionEmployee`'s *get* methods to retrieve the values of the object's instance variables for output. Line 29 invokes the object's `setBaseSalary` method to change the base salary. Method `setBaseSalary` (Fig. 9.6, lines 88–91) ensures that instance variable `baseSalary` is not assigned a negative value, because an employee's base salary cannot be negative. Lines 31–33 of Fig. 9.7 invoke the object's `toString` method explicitly to get the object's string representation.

```
1   // Fig. 9.7: BasePlusCommissionEmployeeTest.java
2   // Testing class BasePlusCommissionEmployee.
3
4   public class BasePlusCommissionEmployeeTest
5   {
6      public static void main( String args[] )
7      {
8         // instantiate BasePlusCommissionEmployee object
9         BasePlusCommissionEmployee employee =
10           new BasePlusCommissionEmployee(
11           "Bob", "Lewis", "333-33-3333", 5000, .04, 300 );
12
13        // get base-salaried commission employee data
14        System.out.println(
15           "Employee information obtained by get methods: \n" );
16        System.out.printf( "%s %s\n", "First name is",
17           employee.getFirstName() );
18        System.out.printf( "%s %s\n", "Last name is",
19           employee.getLastName() );
20        System.out.printf( "%s %s\n", "Social security number is",
21           employee.getSocialSecurityNumber() );
22        System.out.printf( "%s %.2f\n", "Gross sales is",
23           employee.getGrossSales() );
24        System.out.printf( "%s %.2f\n", "Commission rate is",
25           employee.getCommissionRate() );
26        System.out.printf( "%s %.2f\n", "Base salary is",
27           employee.getBaseSalary() );
28
29        employee.setBaseSalary( 1000 ); // set base salary
30
31        System.out.printf( "\n%s:\n\n%s\n",
32           "Updated employee information obtained by toString",
33           employee.toString() );
34     } // end main
35  } // end class BasePlusCommissionEmployeeTest
```

```
Employee information obtained by get methods:

First name is Bob
Last name is Lewis
Social security number is 333-33-3333
Gross sales is 5000.00
Commission rate is 0.04
Base salary is 300.00

Updated employee information obtained by toString:

base-salaried commission employee: Bob Lewis
social security number: 333-33-3333
gross sales: 5000.00
commission rate: 0.04
base salary: 1000.00
```

Fig. 9.7 | BasePlusCommissionEmployee test program.

Note that much of the code for class BasePlusCommissionEmployee (Fig. 9.6) is similar, if not identical, to the code for class CommissionEmployee (Fig. 9.4). For example, in class BasePlusCommissionEmployee, private instance variables firstName and lastName and methods setFirstName, getFirstName, setLastName and getLastName are identical to those of class CommissionEmployee. Classes CommissionEmployee and BasePlusCommissionEmployee also both contain private instance variables socialSecurityNumber, commissionRate and grossSales, as well as *get* and *set* methods to manipulate these variables. In addition, the BasePlusCommissionEmployee constructor is almost identical to that of class CommissionEmployee, except that BasePlusCommissionEmployee's constructor also sets the baseSalary. The other additions to class BasePlusCommissionEmployee are private instance variable baseSalary and methods setBaseSalary and getBaseSalary. Class BasePlusCommissionEmployee's toString method is nearly identical to that of class CommissionEmployee except that BasePlusCommissionEmployee's toString also outputs the value of instance variable baseSalary with two digits of precision to the right of the decimal point.

We literally copied code from class CommissionEmployee and pasted it into class BasePlusCommissionEmployee, then modified class BasePlusCommissionEmployee to include a base salary and methods that manipulate the base salary. This "copy-and-paste" approach is often error prone and time consuming. Worse yet, it can spread many physical copies of the same code throughout a system, creating a code-maintenance nightmare. Is there a way to "absorb" the instance variables and methods of one class in a way that makes them part of other classes without duplicating code? In the next several examples, we answer this question, using a more elegant approach to building classes that emphasizes the benefits of inheritance.

Software Engineering Observation 9.4

Copying and pasting code from one class to another can spread errors across multiple source code files. To avoid duplicating code (and possibly errors), use inheritance, rather than the "copy-and-paste" approach, in situations where you want one class to "absorb" the instance variables and methods of another class.

Software Engineering Observation 9.5

With inheritance, the common instance variables and methods of all the classes in the hierarchy are declared in a superclass. When changes are required for these common features, software developers need only to make the changes in the superclass—subclasses then inherit the changes. Without inheritance, changes would need to be made to all the source code files that contain a copy of the code in question.

9.4.3 Creating a CommissionEmployee–BasePlusCommissionEmployee Inheritance Hierarchy

Now we declare class BasePlusCommissionEmployee2 (Fig. 9.8), which extends class CommissionEmployee (Fig. 9.4). A BasePlusCommissionEmployee2 object *is a* CommissionEmployee (because inheritance passes on the capabilities of class CommissionEmployee), but class BasePlusCommissionEmployee2 also has instance variable baseSalary (Fig. 9.8, line 6). Keyword extends in line 4 of the class declaration indicates inheritance. As a subclass, BasePlusCommissionEmployee2 inherits the public and protected instance variables and methods of class CommissionEmployee. The constructor of class CommissionEmployee is not inherited. Thus, the public services of BasePlusCommissionEmployee2 include its constructor (lines 9–16), public methods inherited from class CommissionEmployee, method set-BaseSalary (lines 19–22), method getBaseSalary (lines 25–28), method earnings (lines 31–35) and method toString (lines 38–47).

```
1   // Fig. 9.8: BasePlusCommissionEmployee2.java
2   // BasePlusCommissionEmployee2 inherits from class CommissionEmployee.
3
4   public class BasePlusCommissionEmployee2 extends CommissionEmployee
5   {
6      private double baseSalary; // base salary per week
7
8      // six-argument constructor
9      public BasePlusCommissionEmployee2( String first, String last,
10        String ssn, double sales, double rate, double salary )
11     {
12        // explicit call to superclass CommissionEmployee constructor
13        super( first, last, ssn, sales, rate );
14
15        setBaseSalary( salary ); // validate and store base salary
16     } // end six-argument BasePlusCommissionEmployee2 constructor
17
18     // set base salary
19     public void setBaseSalary( double salary )
20     {
21        baseSalary = ( salary < 0.0 ) ? 0.0 : salary;
22     } // end method setBaseSalary
23
24     // return base salary
25     public double getBaseSalary()
26     {
27        return baseSalary;
28     } // end method getBaseSalary
29
30     // calculate earnings
31     public double earnings()
32     {
33        // not allowed: commissionRate and grossSales private in superclass
34        return baseSalary + ( commissionRate * grossSales );
35     } // end method earnings
36
37     // return String representation of BasePlusCommissionEmployee2
38     public String toString()
39     {
40        // not allowed: attempts to access private superclass members
41        return String.format(
42           "%s: %s %s\n%s: %s\n%s: %.2f\n%s: %.2f\n%s: %.2f",
43           "base-salaried commission employee", firstName, lastName,
44           "social security number", socialSecurityNumber,
45           "gross sales", grossSales, "commission rate", commissionRate,
46           "base salary", baseSalary );
47     } // end method toString
48  } // end class BasePlusCommissionEmployee2
```

Fig. 9.8 | private superclass members cannot be accessed in a subclass. (Part 1 of 2.)

```
BasePlusCommissionEmployee2.java:34: commissionRate has private access in Com-
missionEmployee
      return baseSalary + ( commissionRate * grossSales );
                            ^
BasePlusCommissionEmployee2.java:34: grossSales has private access in
CommissionEmployee
      return baseSalary + ( commissionRate * grossSales );
                                             ^
BasePlusCommissionEmployee2.java:43: firstName has private access in
CommissionEmployee
         "base-salaried commission employee", firstName, lastName,
                                               ^
BasePlusCommissionEmployee2.java:43: lastName has private access in
CommissionEmployee
         "base-salaried commission employee", firstName, lastName,
                                                          ^
BasePlusCommissionEmployee2.java:44: socialSecurityNumber has private access
in CommissionEmployee
         "social security number", socialSecurityNumber,
                                   ^
BasePlusCommissionEmployee2.java:45: grossSales has private access in
CommissionEmployee
         "gross sales", grossSales, "commission rate", commissionRate,
                        ^
BasePlusCommissionEmployee2.java:45: commissionRate has private access in Com-
missionEmployee
         "gross sales", grossSales, "commission rate", commissionRate,
                                                        ^
7 errors
```

Fig. 9.8 | `private` superclass members cannot be accessed in a subclass. (Part 2 of 2.)

Each subclass constructor must implicitly or explicitly call its superclass constructor to ensure that the instance variables inherited from the superclass are initialized properly. BasePlusCommissionEmployee2's six-argument constructor (lines 9–16) explicitly calls class CommissionEmployee's five-argument constructor to initialize the superclass portion of a BasePlusCommissionEmployee2 object (i.e., variables firstName, lastName, social-SecurityNumber, grossSales and commissionRate). Line 13 in BasePlusCommission-Employee2's six-argument constructor invokes the CommissionEmployee's five-argument constructor (declared at lines 13–22 of Fig. 9.4) by using the superclass constructor call syntax—keyword super, followed by a set of parentheses containing the superclass constructor arguments. The arguments first, last, ssn, sales and rate are used to initialize superclass members firstName, lastName, socialSecurityNumber, grossSales and commissionRate, respectively. If BasePlusCommissionEmployee2's constructor did not invoke CommissionEmployee's constructor explicitly, Java would attempt to invoke class CommissionEmployee's no-argument or default constructor—but the class does not have such a constructor, so the compiler would issue an error. The explicit superclass constructor call on line 13 must be the first statement in the subclass constructor's body. Also, when a superclass contains a no-argument constructor, you can use super() to call that constructor explicitly, but this is rarely done.

Common Programming Error 9.2

A compilation error occurs if a subclass constructor calls one of its superclass constructors with arguments that do not match exactly the number and types of parameters specified in one of the superclass constructor declarations.

The compiler generates errors for line 34 of Fig. 9.8 because superclass CommissionEmployee's instance variables commissionRate and grossSales are private—subclass BasePlusCommissionEmployee2's methods are not allowed to access superclass CommissionEmployee's private instance variables. Note that we used red text in Fig. 9.8 to indicate erroneous code. The compiler issues additional errors at lines 43–45 of BasePlusCommissionEmployee2's toString method for the same reason. The errors in BasePlusCommissionEmployee2 could have been prevented by using the *get* methods inherited from class CommissionEmployee. For example, line 34 could have used getCommissionRate and getGrossSales to access CommissionEmployee's private instance variables commissionRate and grossSales, respectively. Lines 43–45 also could have used appropriate *get* methods to retrieve the values of the superclass's instance variables.

9.4.4 CommissionEmployee–BasePlusCommissionEmployee Inheritance Hierarchy Using protected Instance Variables

To enable class BasePlusCommissionEmployee to directly access superclass instance variables firstName, lastName, socialSecurityNumber, grossSales and commissionRate, we can declare those members as protected in the superclass. As we discussed in Section 9.3, a superclass's protected members *are* inherited by all subclasses of that superclass. Class CommissionEmployee2 (Fig. 9.9) is a modification of class CommissionEmployee (Fig. 9.4)

```
 1   // Fig. 9.9: CommissionEmployee2.java
 2   // CommissionEmployee2 class represents a commission employee.
 3
 4   public class CommissionEmployee2
 5   {
 6      protected String firstName;
 7      protected String lastName;
 8      protected String socialSecurityNumber;
 9      protected double grossSales; // gross weekly sales
10      protected double commissionRate; // commission percentage
11
12      // five-argument constructor
13      public CommissionEmployee2( String first, String last, String ssn,
14         double sales, double rate )
15      {
16         // implicit call to Object constructor occurs here
17         firstName = first;
18         lastName = last;
19         socialSecurityNumber = ssn;
20         setGrossSales( sales ); // validate and store gross sales
21         setCommissionRate( rate ); // validate and store commission rate
22      } // end five-argument CommissionEmployee2 constructor
23
```

Fig. 9.9 | CommissionEmployee2 with protected instance variables. (Part 1 of 3.)

```
24      // set first name
25      public void setFirstName( String first )
26      {
27         firstName = first;
28      } // end method setFirstName
29
30      // return first name
31      public String getFirstName()
32      {
33         return firstName;
34      } // end method getFirstName
35
36      // set last name
37      public void setLastName( String last )
38      {
39         lastName = last;
40      } // end method setLastName
41
42      // return last name
43      public String getLastName()
44      {
45         return lastName;
46      } // end method getLastName
47
48      // set social security number
49      public void setSocialSecurityNumber( String ssn )
50      {
51         socialSecurityNumber = ssn; // should validate
52      } // end method setSocialSecurityNumber
53
54      // return social security number
55      public String getSocialSecurityNumber()
56      {
57         return socialSecurityNumber;
58      } // end method getSocialSecurityNumber
59
60      // set gross sales amount
61      public void setGrossSales( double sales )
62      {
63         grossSales = ( sales < 0.0 ) ? 0.0 : sales;
64      } // end method setGrossSales
65
66      // return gross sales amount
67      public double getGrossSales()
68      {
69         return grossSales;
70      } // end method getGrossSales
71
72      // set commission rate
73      public void setCommissionRate( double rate )
74      {
75         commissionRate = ( rate > 0.0 && rate < 1.0 ) ? rate : 0.0;
76      } // end method setCommissionRate
```

Fig. 9.9 | CommissionEmployee2 with protected instance variables. (Part 2 of 3.)

```
77
78      // return commission rate
79      public double getCommissionRate()
80      {
81         return commissionRate;
82      } // end method getCommissionRate
83
84      // calculate earnings
85      public double earnings()
86      {
87         return commissionRate * grossSales;
88      } // end method earnings
89
90      // return String representation of CommissionEmployee2 object
91      public String toString()
92      {
93         return String.format( "%s: %s %s\n%s: %s\n%s: %.2f\n%s: %.2f",
94            "commission employee", firstName, lastName,
95            "social security number", socialSecurityNumber,
96            "gross sales", grossSales,
97            "commission rate", commissionRate );
98      } // end method toString
99   } // end class CommissionEmployee2
```

Fig. 9.9 | CommissionEmployee2 with protected instance variables. (Part 3 of 3.)

that declares instance variables firstName, lastName, socialSecurityNumber, grossSales and commissionRate as protected (Fig. 9.9, lines 6–10) rather than private. Other than the change in the class name (and thus the change in the constructor name) to CommissionEmployee2, the rest of the class declaration in Fig. 9.9 is identical to that of Fig. 9.4.

We could have declared the superclass CommissionEmployee2's instance variables firstName, lastName, socialSecurityNumber, grossSales and commissionRate as public to enable subclass BasePlusCommissionEmployee2 to access the superclass instance variables. However, declaring public instance variables is poor software engineering because it allows unrestricted access to the instance variables, greatly increasing the chance of errors. With protected instance variables, the subclass gets access to the instance variables, but classes that are not subclasses and classes that are not in the same package cannot access these variables directly. Recall that protected class members are also visible to other classes in the same package.

Class BasePlusCommissionEmployee3 (Fig. 9.10) is a modification of class BasePlusCommissionEmployee2 (Fig. 9.8) that extends CommissionEmployee2 (line 5) rather than class CommissionEmployee. Objects of class BasePlusCommissionEmployee3 inherit CommissionEmployee2's protected instance variables firstName, lastName, socialSecurityNumber, grossSales and commissionRate—all these variables are now protected members of BasePlusCommissionEmployee3. As a result, the compiler does not generate errors when compiling line 32 of method earnings and lines 40–42 of method toString. If another class extends BasePlusCommissionEmployee3, the new subclass also inherits the protected members.

```java
 1   // Fig. 9.10: BasePlusCommissionEmployee3.java
 2   // BasePlusCommissionEmployee3 inherits from CommissionEmployee2 and has
 3   // access to CommissionEmployee2's protected members.
 4
 5   public class BasePlusCommissionEmployee3 extends CommissionEmployee2
 6   {
 7      private double baseSalary; // base salary per week
 8
 9      // six-argument constructor
10      public BasePlusCommissionEmployee3( String first, String last,
11         String ssn, double sales, double rate, double salary )
12      {
13         super( first, last, ssn, sales, rate );
14         setBaseSalary( salary ); // validate and store base salary
15      } // end six-argument BasePlusCommissionEmployee3 constructor
16
17      // set base salary
18      public void setBaseSalary( double salary )
19      {
20         baseSalary = ( salary < 0.0 ) ? 0.0 : salary;
21      } // end method setBaseSalary
22
23      // return base salary
24      public double getBaseSalary()
25      {
26         return baseSalary;
27      } // end method getBaseSalary
28
29      // calculate earnings
30      public double earnings()
31      {
32         return baseSalary + ( commissionRate * grossSales );
33      } // end method earnings
34
35      // return String representation of BasePlusCommissionEmployee3
36      public String toString()
37      {
38         return String.format(
39            "%s: %s %s\n%s: %s\n%s: %.2f\n%s: %.2f\n%s: %.2f",
40            "base-salaried commission employee", firstName, lastName,
41            "social security number", socialSecurityNumber,
42            "gross sales", grossSales, "commission rate", commissionRate,
43            "base salary", baseSalary );
44      } // end method toString
45   } // end class BasePlusCommissionEmployee3
```

Fig. 9.10 | BasePlusCommissionEmployee3 inherits protected instance variables from CommissionEmployee2.

Class BasePlusCommissionEmployee3 does not inherit class CommissionEmployee2's constructor. However, class BasePlusCommissionEmployee3's six-argument constructor (lines 10–15) calls class CommissionEmployee2's five-argument constructor explicitly. BasePlusCommissionEmployee3's six-argument constructor must explicitly call the five-argument constructor of class CommissionEmployee2, because CommissionEmployee2 does not provide a no-argument constructor that could be invoked implicitly.

Figure 9.11 uses a BasePlusCommissionEmployee3 object to perform the same tasks that Fig. 9.7 performed on a BasePlusCommissionEmployee object (Fig. 9.6). Note that the outputs of the two programs are identical. Although we declared class BasePlusCommissionEmployee without using inheritance and declared class BasePlusCommissionEmployee3 using inheritance, both classes provide the same functionality. The source code for class BasePlusCommissionEmployee3, which is 45 lines, is considerably shorter than that for class BasePlusCommissionEmployee, which is 115 lines, because class BasePlusCommissionEmployee3 inherits most of its functionality from CommissionEmployee2, whereas class BasePlusCommissionEmployee inherits only class Object's functionality. Also, there is now only one copy of the commission employee functionality

```java
1   // Fig. 9.11: BasePlusCommissionEmployeeTest3.java
2   // Testing class BasePlusCommissionEmployee3.
3
4   public class BasePlusCommissionEmployeeTest3
5   {
6      public static void main( String args[] )
7      {
8         // instantiate BasePlusCommissionEmployee3 object
9         BasePlusCommissionEmployee3 employee =
10           new BasePlusCommissionEmployee3(
11           "Bob", "Lewis", "333-33-3333", 5000, .04, 300 );
12
13        // get base-salaried commission employee data
14        System.out.println(
15           "Employee information obtained by get methods: \n" );
16        System.out.printf( "%s %s\n", "First name is",
17           employee.getFirstName() );
18        System.out.printf( "%s %s\n", "Last name is",
19           employee.getLastName() );
20        System.out.printf( "%s %s\n", "Social security number is",
21           employee.getSocialSecurityNumber() );
22        System.out.printf( "%s %.2f\n", "Gross sales is",
23           employee.getGrossSales() );
24        System.out.printf( "%s %.2f\n", "Commission rate is",
25           employee.getCommissionRate() );
26        System.out.printf( "%s %.2f\n", "Base salary is",
27           employee.getBaseSalary() );
28
29        employee.setBaseSalary( 1000 ); // set base salary
30
31        System.out.printf( "\n%s:\n\n%s\n",
32           "Updated employee information obtained by toString",
33           employee.toString() );
34     } // end main
35   } // end class BasePlusCommissionEmployeeTest3
```

Fig. 9.11 | protected superclass members inherited into subclass BasePlusCommissionEmployee3. (Part 1 of 2.)

```
Employee information obtained by get methods:

First name is Bob
Last name is Lewis
Social security number is 333-33-3333
Gross sales is 5000.00
Commission rate is 0.04
Base salary is 300.00

Updated employee information obtained by toString:

base-salaried commission employee: Bob Lewis
social security number: 333-33-3333
gross sales: 5000.00
commission rate: 0.04
base salary: 1000.00
```

Fig. 9.11 | protected superclass members inherited into subclass
BasePlusCommissionEmployee3. (Part 2 of 2.)

declared in class CommissionEmployee2. This makes the code easier to maintain, modify and debug, because the code related to a commission employee exists only in class CommissionEmployee2.

In this example, we declared superclass instance variables as protected so that subclasses could inherit them. Inheriting protected instance variables slightly increases performance, because we can directly access the variables in the subclass without incurring the overhead of a *set* or *get* method call. In most cases, however, it is better to use private instance variables to encourage proper software engineering, and leave code optimization issues to the compiler. Your code will be easier to maintain, modify and debug.

Using protected instance variables creates several potential problems. First, the subclass object can set an inherited variable's value directly without using a *set* method. Therefore, a subclass object can assign an invalid value to the variable, thus leaving the object in an inconsistent state. For example, if we were to declare CommissionEmployee3's instance variable grossSales as protected, a subclass object (e.g., BasePlusCommissionEmployee) could then assign a negative value to grossSales. The second problem with using protected instance variables is that subclass methods are more likely to be written so that they depend on the superclass's data implementation. In practice, subclasses should depend only on the superclass services (i.e., non-private methods) and not on the superclass data implementation. With protected instance variables in the superclass, we may need to modify all the subclasses of the superclass if the superclass implementation changes. For example, if for some reason we were to change the names of instance variables firstName and lastName to first and last, then we would have to do so for all occurrences in which a subclass directly references superclass instance variables firstName and lastName. In such a case, the software is said to be fragile or brittle, because a small change in the superclass can "break" subclass implementation. The programmer should be able to change the superclass implementation while still providing the same services to the subclasses. (Of course, if the superclass services change, we must reimplement our subclasses.) A third problem is that a class's protected members are visible to all classes in the same package as the class containing the protected members—this is not always desirable.

Software Engineering Observation 9.6

Use the protected *access modifier when a superclass should provide a method only to its subclasses and other classes in the same package, but not to other clients.*

Software Engineering Observation 9.7

Declaring superclass instance variables private *(as opposed to* protected*) enables the superclass implementation of these instance variables to change without affecting subclass implementations.*

Error-Prevention Tip 9.1

When possible, do not include protected *instance variables in a superclass. Instead, include non-private methods that access* private *instance variables. This will ensure that objects of the class maintain consistent states.*

9.4.5 CommissionEmployee–BasePlusCommissionEmployee Inheritance Hierarchy Using private Instance Variables

We now reexamine our hierarchy once more, this time using the best software engineering practices. Class CommissionEmployee3 (Fig. 9.12) declares instance variables firstName, lastName, socialSecurityNumber, grossSales and commissionRate as private (lines 6–10)

```
 1   // Fig. 9.12: CommissionEmployee3.java
 2   // CommissionEmployee3 class represents a commission employee.
 3
 4   public class CommissionEmployee3
 5   {
 6      private String firstName;
 7      private String lastName;
 8      private String socialSecurityNumber;
 9      private double grossSales; // gross weekly sales
10      private double commissionRate; // commission percentage
11
12      // five-argument constructor
13      public CommissionEmployee3( String first, String last, String ssn,
14         double sales, double rate )
15      {
16         // implicit call to Object constructor occurs here
17         firstName = first;
18         lastName = last;
19         socialSecurityNumber = ssn;
20         setGrossSales( sales ); // validate and store gross sales
21         setCommissionRate( rate ); // validate and store commission rate
22      } // end five-argument CommissionEmployee3 constructor
23
24      // set first name
25      public void setFirstName( String first )
26      {
27         firstName = first;
28      } // end method setFirstName
29
```

Fig. 9.12 | CommissionEmployee3 class uses methods to manipulate its private instance variables. (Part 1 of 3.)

```
30        // return first name
31        public String getFirstName()
32        {
33           return firstName;
34        } // end method getFirstName
35
36        // set last name
37        public void setLastName( String last )
38        {
39           lastName = last;
40        } // end method setLastName
41
42        // return last name
43        public String getLastName()
44        {
45           return lastName;
46        } // end method getLastName
47
48        // set social security number
49        public void setSocialSecurityNumber( String ssn )
50        {
51           socialSecurityNumber = ssn; // should validate
52        } // end method setSocialSecurityNumber
53
54        // return social security number
55        public String getSocialSecurityNumber()
56        {
57           return socialSecurityNumber;
58        } // end method getSocialSecurityNumber
59
60        // set gross sales amount
61        public void setGrossSales( double sales )
62        {
63           grossSales = ( sales < 0.0 ) ? 0.0 : sales;
64        } // end method setGrossSales
65
66        // return gross sales amount
67        public double getGrossSales()
68        {
69           return grossSales;
70        } // end method getGrossSales
71
72        // set commission rate
73        public void setCommissionRate( double rate )
74        {
75           commissionRate = ( rate > 0.0 && rate < 1.0 ) ? rate : 0.0;
76        } // end method setCommissionRate
77
78        // return commission rate
79        public double getCommissionRate()
80        {
```

Fig. 9.12 | CommissionEmployee3 class uses methods to manipulate its private instance variables. (Part 2 of 3.)

```
81             return commissionRate;
82       } // end method getCommissionRate
83
84       // calculate earnings
85       public double earnings()
86       {
87             return getCommissionRate() * getGrossSales();
88       } // end method earnings
89
90       // return String representation of CommissionEmployee3 object
91       public String toString()
92       {
93             return String.format( "%s: %s %s\n%s: %s\n%s: %.2f\n%s: %.2f",
94                "commission employee", getFirstName(), getLastName(),
95                "social security number", getSocialSecurityNumber(),
96                "gross sales", getGrossSales(),
97                "commission rate", getCommissionRate() );
98       } // end method toString
99   } // end class CommissionEmployee3
```

Fig. 9.12 | CommissionEmployee3 class uses methods to manipulate its private instance variables. (Part 3 of 3.)

and provides public methods setFirstName, getFirstName, setLastName, getLastName, setSocialSecurityNumber, getSocialSecurityNumber, setGrossSales, getGrossSales, setCommissionRate, getCommissionRate, earnings and toString for manipulating these values. Note that methods earnings (lines 85–88) and toString (lines 91–98) use the class's *get* methods to obtain the values of its instance variables. If we decide to change the instance variable names, the earnings and toString declarations will not require modification—only the bodies of the *get* and *set* methods that directly manipulate the instance variables will need to change. Note that these changes occur solely within the superclass—no changes to the subclass are needed. Localizing the effects of changes like this is a good software engineering practice. Subclass BasePlusCommissionEmployee4 (Fig. 9.13) inherits CommissionEmployee3's non-private methods and can access the private superclass members via those methods.

Class BasePlusCommissionEmployee4 (Fig. 9.13) has several changes to its method implementations that distinguish it from class BasePlusCommissionEmployee3 (Fig. 9.10). Methods earnings (Fig. 9.13, lines 31–34) and toString (lines 37–41) each invoke method getBaseSalary to obtain the base salary value, rather than accessing baseSalary directly. If we decide to rename instance variable baseSalary, only the bodies of method setBaseSalary and getBaseSalary will need to change.

Class BasePlusCommissionEmployee4's earnings method (Fig. 9.13, lines 31–34) overrides class CommissionEmployee3's earnings method (Fig. 9.12, lines 85–88) to calculate the earnings of a base-salaried commission employee. The new version obtains the portion of the employee's earnings based on commission alone by calling CommissionEmployee3's earnings method with the expression super.earnings() (Fig. 9.13, line 33). BasePlusCommissionEmployee4's earnings method then adds the base salary to this value to calculate the total earnings of the employee. Note the syntax used to invoke an overridden superclass method from a subclass—place the keyword super and a dot (.) separator before the superclass method name. This method invocation

```
 1   // Fig. 9.13: BasePlusCommissionEmployee4.java
 2   // BasePlusCommissionEmployee4 class inherits from CommissionEmployee3 and
 3   // accesses CommissionEmployee3's private data via CommissionEmployee3's
 4   // public methods.
 5
 6   public class BasePlusCommissionEmployee4 extends CommissionEmployee3
 7   {
 8      private double baseSalary; // base salary per week
 9
10      // six-argument constructor
11      public BasePlusCommissionEmployee4( String first, String last,
12         String ssn, double sales, double rate, double salary )
13      {
14         super( first, last, ssn, sales, rate );
15         setBaseSalary( salary ); // validate and store base salary
16      } // end six-argument BasePlusCommissionEmployee4 constructor
17
18      // set base salary
19      public void setBaseSalary( double salary )
20      {
21         baseSalary = ( salary < 0.0 ) ? 0.0 : salary;
22      } // end method setBaseSalary
23
24      // return base salary
25      public double getBaseSalary()
26      {
27         return baseSalary;
28      } // end method getBaseSalary
29
30      // calculate earnings
31      public double earnings()
32      {
33         return getBaseSalary() + super.earnings();
34      } // end method earnings
35
36      // return String representation of BasePlusCommissionEmployee4
37      public String toString()
38      {
39         return String.format( "%s %s\n%s: %.2f", "base-salaried",
40            super.toString(), "base salary", getBaseSalary() );
41      } // end method toString
42   } // end class BasePlusCommissionEmployee4
```

Fig. 9.13 | `BasePlusCommissionEmployee4` class extends `CommissionEmployee3`, which provides only private instance variables.

is a good software-engineering practice: Recall from **Software Engineering Observation 8.5** that if a method performs all or some of the actions needed by another method, call that method rather than duplicate its code. By having `BasePlusCommissionEmployee4`'s earnings method invoke `CommissionEmployee3`'s earnings method to calculate part of a `BasePlusCommissionEmployee4` object's earnings, we avoid duplicating the code and reduce code-maintenance problems.

Common Programming Error 9.3

When a superclass method is overridden in a subclass, the subclass version often calls the super-class version to do a portion of the work. Failure to prefix the superclass method name with the keyword super and a dot (.) separator when referencing the superclass's method causes the subclass method to call itself, creating an error called infinite recursion. Recursion, used correctly, is a powerful capability discussed in Chapter 15, Recursion.

Similarly, BasePlusCommissionEmployee4's toString method (Fig. 9.13, lines 37–41) overrides class CommissionEmployee3's toString method (Fig. 9.12, lines 91–98) to return a string representation that is appropriate for a base-salaried commission employee. The new version creates part of a BasePlusCommissionEmployee4 object's string representation (i.e., the string "commission employee" and the values of class CommissionEmployee3's private instance variables) by calling CommissionEmployee3's toString method with the expression super.toString() (Fig. 9.13, line 40). BasePlusCommissionEmployee4's toString method then outputs the remainder of a BasePlusCommissionEmployee4 object's string representation (i.e., the value of class BasePlusCommissionEmployee4's base salary).

Figure 9.14 performs the same manipulations on a BasePlusCommissionEmployee4 object as did Fig. 9.7 and Fig. 9.11 on objects of classes BasePlusCommissionEmployee and BasePlusCommissionEmployee3, respectively. Although each "base-salaried commission employee" class behaves identically, class BasePlusCommissionEmployee4 is the best engineered. By using inheritance and by calling methods that hide the data and ensure consistency, we have efficiently and effectively constructed a well-engineered class.

```java
 1  // Fig. 9.14: BasePlusCommissionEmployeeTest4.java
 2  // Testing class BasePlusCommissionEmployee4.
 3
 4  public class BasePlusCommissionEmployeeTest4
 5  {
 6     public static void main( String args[] )
 7     {
 8        // instantiate BasePlusCommissionEmployee4 object
 9        BasePlusCommissionEmployee4 employee =
10           new BasePlusCommissionEmployee4(
11           "Bob", "Lewis", "333-33-3333", 5000, .04, 300 );
12
13        // get base-salaried commission employee data
14        System.out.println(
15           "Employee information obtained by get methods: \n" );
16        System.out.printf( "%s %s\n", "First name is",
17           employee.getFirstName() );
18        System.out.printf( "%s %s\n", "Last name is",
19           employee.getLastName() );
20        System.out.printf( "%s %s\n", "Social security number is",
21           employee.getSocialSecurityNumber() );
22        System.out.printf( "%s %.2f\n", "Gross sales is",
23           employee.getGrossSales() );
```

Fig. 9.14 | Superclass private instance variables are accessible to a subclass via public or protected methods inherited by the subclass. (Part 1 of 2.)

```
24          System.out.printf( "%s %.2f\n", "Commission rate is",
25              employee.getCommissionRate() );
26          System.out.printf( "%s %.2f\n", "Base salary is",
27              employee.getBaseSalary() );
28
29          employee.setBaseSalary( 1000 ); // set base salary
30
31          System.out.printf( "\n%s:\n\n%s\n",
32              "Updated employee information obtained by toString",
33              employee.toString() );
34      } // end main
35  } // end class BasePlusCommissionEmployeeTest4
```

```
Employee information obtained by get methods:

First name is Bob
Last name is Lewis
Social security number is 333-33-3333
Gross sales is 5000.00
Commission rate is 0.04
Base salary is 300.00

Updated employee information obtained by toString:

base-salaried commission employee: Bob Lewis
social security number: 333-33-3333
gross sales: 5000.00
commission rate: 0.04
base salary: 1000.00
```

Fig. 9.14 | Superclass `private` instance variables are accessible to a subclass via `public` or `protected` methods inherited by the subclass. (Part 2 of 2.)

In this section, you saw an evolutionary set of examples that was carefully designed to teach key capabilities for good software engineering with inheritance. You learned how to use the keyword `extends` to create a subclass using inheritance, how to use `protected` superclass members to enable a subclass to access inherited superclass instance variables and how to override superclass methods to provide versions that are more appropriate for subclass objects. In addition, you learned how to apply software-engineering techniques from Chapter 8 and this chapter to create classes that are easy to maintain, modify and debug.

9.5 Constructors in Subclasses

As we explained in the preceding section, instantiating a subclass object begins a chain of constructor calls in which the subclass constructor, before performing its own tasks, invokes its direct superclass's constructor either explicitly (via the `super` reference) or implicitly (calling the superclass's default constructor or no-argument constructor). Similarly, if the superclass is derived from another class (as is, of course, every class except `Object`), the superclass constructor invokes the constructor of the next class up in the hierarchy, and so on. The last constructor called in the chain is always the constructor for class `Object`. The original subclass constructor's body finishes executing last. Each superclass's constructor manipulates the superclass instance variables that the subclass object inherits. For example, consider again the

CommissionEmployee3–BasePlusCommissionEmployee4 hierarchy from Fig. 9.12 and Fig. 9.13. When a program creates a BasePlusCommissionEmployee4 object, the BasePlus-CommissionEmployee4 constructor is called. That constructor calls CommissionEmployee3's constructor, which in turn calls Object's constructor. Class Object's constructor has an empty body, so it immediately returns control to CommissionEmployee3's constructor, which then initializes the private instance variables of CommissionEmployee3 that are part of the BasePlusCommissionEmployee4 object. When CommissionEmployee3's constructor completes execution, it returns control to BasePlusCommissionEmployee4's constructor, which initializes the BasePlusCommissionEmployee4 object's baseSalary.

Software Engineering Observation 9.8

When a program creates a subclass object, the subclass constructor immediately calls the superclass constructor (explicitly, via super, or implicitly). The superclass constructor's body executes to initialize the superclass's instance variables that are part of the subclass object, then the subclass constructor's body executes to initialize the subclass-only instance variables. Java ensures that even if a constructor does not assign a value to an instance variable, the variable is still initialized to its default value (e.g., 0 for primitive numeric types, false for booleans, null for references).

Our next example revisits the commission employee hierarchy by declaring a CommissionEmployee4 class (Fig. 9.15) and a BasePlusCommissionEmployee5 class (Fig. 9.16). Each class's constructor prints a message when invoked, enabling us to observe the order in which the constructors in the hierarchy execute.

```java
 1   // Fig. 9.15: CommissionEmployee4.java
 2   // CommissionEmployee4 class represents a commission employee.
 3
 4   public class CommissionEmployee4
 5   {
 6      private String firstName;
 7      private String lastName;
 8      private String socialSecurityNumber;
 9      private double grossSales; // gross weekly sales
10      private double commissionRate; // commission percentage
11
12      // five-argument constructor
13      public CommissionEmployee4( String first, String last, String ssn,
14         double sales, double rate )
15      {
16         // implicit call to Object constructor occurs here
17         firstName = first;
18         lastName = last;
19         socialSecurityNumber = ssn;
20         setGrossSales( sales ); // validate and store gross sales
21         setCommissionRate( rate ); // validate and store commission rate
22
23         System.out.printf(
24            "\nCommissionEmployee4 constructor:\n%s\n", this );
25      } // end five-argument CommissionEmployee4 constructor
26
```

Fig. 9.15 | CommissionEmployee4's constructor outputs text. (Part 1 of 3.)

```
27      // set first name
28      public void setFirstName( String first )
29      {
30         firstName = first;
31      } // end method setFirstName
32
33      // return first name
34      public String getFirstName()
35      {
36         return firstName;
37      } // end method getFirstName
38
39      // set last name
40      public void setLastName( String last )
41      {
42         lastName = last;
43      } // end method setLastName
44
45      // return last name
46      public String getLastName()
47      {
48         return lastName;
49      } // end method getLastName
50
51      // set social security number
52      public void setSocialSecurityNumber( String ssn )
53      {
54         socialSecurityNumber = ssn; // should validate
55      } // end method setSocialSecurityNumber
56
57      // return social security number
58      public String getSocialSecurityNumber()
59      {
60         return socialSecurityNumber;
61      } // end method getSocialSecurityNumber
62
63      // set gross sales amount
64      public void setGrossSales( double sales )
65      {
66         grossSales = ( sales < 0.0 ) ? 0.0 : sales;
67      } // end method setGrossSales
68
69      // return gross sales amount
70      public double getGrossSales()
71      {
72         return grossSales;
73      } // end method getGrossSales
74
75      // set commission rate
76      public void setCommissionRate( double rate )
77      {
78         commissionRate = ( rate > 0.0 && rate < 1.0 ) ? rate : 0.0;
79      } // end method setCommissionRate
```

Fig. 9.15 | CommissionEmployee4's constructor outputs text. (Part 2 of 3.)

```
80
81      // return commission rate
82      public double getCommissionRate()
83      {
84          return commissionRate;
85      } // end method getCommissionRate
86
87      // calculate earnings
88      public double earnings()
89      {
90          return getCommissionRate() * getGrossSales();
91      } // end method earnings
92
93      // return String representation of CommissionEmployee4 object
94      public String toString()
95      {
96          return String.format( "%s: %s %s\n%s: %s\n%s: %.2f\n%s: %.2f",
97              "commission employee", getFirstName(), getLastName(),
98              "social security number", getSocialSecurityNumber(),
99              "gross sales", getGrossSales(),
100             "commission rate", getCommissionRate() );
101     } // end method toString
102 } // end class CommissionEmployee4
```

Fig. 9.15 | CommissionEmployee4's constructor outputs text. (Part 3 of 3.)

Class CommissionEmployee4 (Fig. 9.15) contains the same features as the version of the class shown in Fig. 9.4. We modified the constructor (lines 13–25) to output text upon its invocation. Note that outputting this with the %s format specifier (lines 23–24) implicitly invokes the toString method of the object being constructed to obtain the object's string representation.

Class BasePlusCommissionEmployee5 (Fig. 9.16) is almost identical to BasePlus-CommissionEmployee4 (Fig. 9.13), except that BasePlusCommissionEmployee5's constructor also outputs text when invoked. As in CommissionEmployee4 (Fig. 9.15), we output this using the %s format specifier in line 16 to obtain the object's string representation.

```
1    // Fig. 9.16: BasePlusCommissionEmployee5.java
2    // BasePlusCommissionEmployee5 class declaration.
3
4    public class BasePlusCommissionEmployee5 extends CommissionEmployee4
5    {
6        private double baseSalary; // base salary per week
7
8        // six-argument constructor
9        public BasePlusCommissionEmployee5( String first, String last,
10           String ssn, double sales, double rate, double salary )
11       {
12           super( first, last, ssn, sales, rate );
13           setBaseSalary( salary ); // validate and store base salary
14
```

Fig. 9.16 | BasePlusCommissionEmployee5's constructor outputs text. (Part 1 of 2.)

```
15        System.out.printf(
16           "\nBasePlusCommissionEmployee5 constructor:\n%s\n", this );
17     } // end six-argument BasePlusCommissionEmployee5 constructor
18
19     // set base salary
20     public void setBaseSalary( double salary )
21     {
22        baseSalary = ( salary < 0.0 ) ? 0.0 : salary;
23     } // end method setBaseSalary
24
25     // return base salary
26     public double getBaseSalary()
27     {
28        return baseSalary;
29     } // end method getBaseSalary
30
31     // calculate earnings
32     public double earnings()
33     {
34        return getBaseSalary() + super.earnings();
35     } // end method earnings
36
37     // return String representation of BasePlusCommissionEmployee5
38     public String toString()
39     {
40        return String.format( "%s %s\n%s: %.2f", "base-salaried",
41           super.toString(), "base salary", getBaseSalary() );
42     } // end method toString
43  } // end class BasePlusCommissionEmployee5
```

Fig. 9.16 | BasePlusCommissionEmployee5's constructor outputs text. (Part 1 of 2.)

Figure 9.17 demonstrates the order in which constructors are called for objects of classes that are part of an inheritance hierarchy. Method main begins by instantiating CommissionEmployee4 object employee1 (lines 8–9). Next, lines 12–14 instantiate

```
1   // Fig. 9.17: ConstructorTest.java
2   // Display order in which superclass and subclass constructors are called.
3
4   public class ConstructorTest
5   {
6      public static void main( String args[] )
7      {
8         CommissionEmployee4 employee1 = new CommissionEmployee4(
9            "Bob", "Lewis", "333-33-3333", 5000, .04 );
10
11        System.out.println();
12        BasePlusCommissionEmployee5 employee2 =
13           new BasePlusCommissionEmployee5(
14           "Lisa", "Jones", "555-55-5555", 2000, .06, 800 );
15
```

Fig. 9.17 | Constructor call order. (Part 1 of 2.)

```
16          System.out.println();
17          BasePlusCommissionEmployee5 employee3 =
18             new BasePlusCommissionEmployee5(
19             "Mark", "Sands", "888-88-8888", 8000, .15, 2000 );
20       } // end main
21    } // end class ConstructorTest
```

```
CommissionEmployee4 constructor:
commission employee: Bob Lewis
social security number: 333-33-3333
gross sales: 5000.00
commission rate: 0.04


CommissionEmployee4 constructor:
base-salaried commission employee: Lisa Jones
social security number: 555-55-5555
gross sales: 2000.00
commission rate: 0.06
base salary: 0.00

BasePlusCommissionEmployee5 constructor:
base-salaried commission employee: Lisa Jones
social security number: 555-55-5555
gross sales: 2000.00
commission rate: 0.06
base salary: 800.00


CommissionEmployee4 constructor:
base-salaried commission employee: Mark Sands
social security number: 888-88-8888
gross sales: 8000.00
commission rate: 0.15
base salary: 0.00

BasePlusCommissionEmployee5 constructor:
base-salaried commission employee: Mark Sands
social security number: 888-88-8888
gross sales: 8000.00
commission rate: 0.15
base salary: 2000.00
```

Fig. 9.17 | Constructor call order. (Part 2 of 2.)

BasePlusCommissionEmployee5 object employee2. This invokes the CommissionEmployee4 constructor, which prints output with the values passed from the BasePlusCommissionEmployee5 constructor, then performs the output specified in the BasePlusCommissionEmployee5 constructor. Lines 17–19 then instantiate BasePlusCommissionEmployee5 object employee3. Again, the CommissionEmployee4 and BasePlusCommissionEmployee5 constructors are both called. In each case, the body of the CommissionEmployee4 constructor executes before the body of the BasePlusCommissionEmployee5 constructor executes. Note that employee2 is constructed completely before construction of employee3 begins.

9.6 Software Engineering with Inheritance

This section discusses customizing existing software with inheritance. When a new class extends an existing class, the new class inherits the non-`private` members of the existing class. We can customize the new class to meet our needs by including additional members and by overriding superclass members. Doing this does not require the subclass programmer to change the superclass's source code. Java simply requires access to the superclass's `.class` file so it can compile and execute any program that uses or extends the superclass. This powerful capability is attractive to independent software vendors (ISVs), who can develop proprietary classes for sale or license and make them available to users in bytecode format. Users then can derive new classes from these library classes rapidly and without accessing the ISVs' proprietary source code.

Software Engineering Observation 9.9

Despite the fact that inheriting from a class does not require access to the class's source code, developers often insist on seeing the source code to understand how the class is implemented. Developers in industry want to ensure that they are extending a solid class—for example, a class that performs well and is implemented securely.

Sometimes, students have difficulty appreciating the scope of the problems faced by designers who work on large-scale software projects in industry. People experienced with such projects say that effective software reuse improves the software development process. Object-oriented programming facilitates software reuse, potentially shortening development time.

The availability of substantial and useful class libraries delivers the maximum benefits of software reuse through inheritance. Application designers build their applications with these libraries, and library designers are rewarded by having their libraries included with the applications. The standard Java class libraries that are shipped with J2SE 5.0 tend to be rather general purpose. Many special-purpose class libraries exist and more are being created.

Software Engineering Observation 9.10

At the design stage in an object-oriented system, the designer often finds that certain classes are closely related. The designer should "factor out" common instance variables and methods and place them in a superclass. Then the designer should use inheritance to develop subclasses, specializing them with capabilities beyond those inherited from the superclass.

Software Engineering Observation 9.11

Declaring a subclass does not affect its superclass's source code. Inheritance preserves the integrity of the superclass.

Software Engineering Observation 9.12

Just as designers of non-object-oriented systems should avoid method proliferation, designers of object-oriented systems should avoid class proliferation. Such proliferation creates management problems and can hinder software reusability, because in a huge class library it becomes difficult for a client to locate the most appropriate classes. The alternative is to create fewer classes that provide more substantial functionality, but such classes might prove cumbersome.

Performance Tip 9.1

If subclasses are larger than they need to be (i.e., contain too much functionality), memory and processing resources might be wasted. Extend the superclass that contains the functionality that is closest to what is needed.

Reading subclass declarations can be confusing, because inherited members are not declared explicitly in the subclasses, but are nevertheless present in them. A similar problem exists in documenting subclass members.

9.7 Object Class

As we discussed earlier in this chapter, all classes in Java inherit directly or indirectly from the Object class (package java.lang), so its 11 methods are inherited by all other classes. Figure 9.18 summarizes Object's methods.

Method	Description
clone	This **protected** method, which takes no arguments and returns an Object reference, makes a copy of the object on which it is called. When cloning is required for objects of a class, the class should override method clone as a **public** method and should implement interface Cloneable (package java.lang). The default implementation of this method performs a so-called shallow copy—instance variable values in one object are copied into another object of the same type. For reference types, only the references are copied. A typical overridden clone method's implementation would perform a deep copy that creates a new object for each reference type instance variable. There are many subtleties to overriding method clone. You can learn more about cloning in the following article: java.sun.com/developer/JDCTechTips/2001/tt0306.html
equals	This method compares two objects for equality and returns true if they are equal and false otherwise. The method takes any Object as an argument. When objects of a particular class must be compared for equality, the class should override method equals to compare the contents of the two objects. The method's implementation should meet the following requirements: • It should return false if the argument is null. • It should return true if an object is compared to itself, as in object1.equals(object1). • It should return true only if both object1.equals(object2) and object2.equals(object1) would return true. • For three objects, if object1.equals(object2) returns true and object2.equals(object3) returns true, then object1.equals(object3) should also return true. • If equals is called multiple times with the two objects and the objects do not change, the method should consistently return true if the objects are equal and false otherwise. A class that overrides equals should also override hashCode to ensure that equal objects have identical hashcodes. The default equals implementation uses operator == to determine whether two references *refer to the same object* in memory. Section 29.3.3 demonstrates class String's equals method and differentiates between comparing String objects with == and with equals.

Fig. 9.18 | Object methods that are inherited directly or indirectly by all classes. (Part 1 of 2.)

Method	Description
finalize	This **protected** method (introduced in Section 8.10 and Section 8.11) is called by the garbage collector to perform termination housekeeping on an object just before the garbage collector reclaims the object's memory. It is not guaranteed that the garbage collector will reclaim an object, so it cannot be guaranteed that the object's **finalize** method will execute. The method must specify an empty parameter list and must return **void**. The default implementation of this method serves as a placeholder that does nothing.
getClass	Every object in Java knows its own type at execution time. Method **get-Class** (used in Section 10.5 and Section 21.3) returns an object of class **Class** (package **java.lang**) that contains information about the object's type, such as its class name (returned by **Class** method **getName**). You can learn more about class **Class** in the online API documentation at **java.sun.com/j2se/5.0/docs/api/java/lang/Class.html**.
hashCode	A hashtable is a data structure (discussed in Section 19.10) that relates one object, called the key, to another object, called the value. When initially inserting a value into a hashtable, the key's **hashCode** method is called. The hashcode value returned is used by the hashtable to determine the location at which to insert the corresponding value. The key's hashcode is also used by the hashtable to locate the key's corresponding value.
notify, notifyAll, wait	Methods **notify**, **notifyAll** and the three overloaded versions of **wait** are related to multithreading, which is discussed in Chapter 23. In J2SE 5.0, the multithreading model has changed substantially, but these features continue to be supported.
toString	This method (introduced in Section 9.4.1) returns a **String** representation of an object. The default implementation of this method returns the package name and class name of the object's class followed by a hexadecimal representation of the value returned by the object's **hashCode** method.

Fig. 9.18 | **Object** methods that are inherited directly or indirectly by all classes. (Part 2 of 2.)

We discuss several of **Object** methods throughout this book (as indicated in the table). You can learn more about **Object**'s methods in **Object**'s online API documentation and in *The Java Tutorial* at the following sites:

```
java.sun.com/j2se/5.0/docs/api/java/lang/Object.html
java.sun.com/docs/books/tutorial/java/javaOO/objectclass
```

Recall from Chapter 7 that arrays are objects. As a result, like all other objects, an array inherits the members of class **Object**. Note that arrays have an overridden **clone** method that copies the array. However, if the array stores references to objects, the objects are not copied. For more information about the relationship between arrays and class **Object**, please see *Java Language Specification, Chapter 10*, at

```
java.sun.com/docs/books/jls/second_edition/html/arrays.doc.html
```

9.8 (Optional) GUI and Graphics Case Study: Displaying Text and Images Using Labels

Programs often use labels when they need to display information or instructions to the user in a graphical user interface. Labels are a convenient way of keeping the user informed about the current state of a program. In Java, an object of class JLabel (from package javax.swing) can display a single line of text, an image or both. The example in Fig. 9.19 demonstrates several JLabel features.

Lines 3–6 import the classes we need to display JLabels. BorderLayout from package java.awt contains constants that specify where we can place GUI components in the JFrame. Class **ImageIcon** represents an image that can be displayed on a JLabel, and class JFrame represents the window that will contain all the labels.

Line 13 creates a JLabel that displays its constructor argument—the string "North". Line 16 declares local variable labelIcon and assigns it a new ImageIcon. The constructor for ImageIcon receives a String that specifies the path to the image. Since we only specify a file name, Java assumes that it is in the same directory as class LabelDemo. ImageIcon can load images in GIF, JPEG and PNG image formats. Line 19 declares and initializes local variable centerLabel with a JLabel that displays the labelIcon. Line 22 declares and initializes local variable southLabel with a JLabel similar to the one in line 19. However, line 25 calls method **setText** to change the text the label displays. Method setText can be called on any JLabel to change its text. This JLabel displays both the icon and the text.

Line 28 creates the JFrame that displays the JLabels, and line 30 indicates that the program should terminate when the JFrame is closed. We attach the labels to the JFrame in lines 34–36 by calling an overloaded version of method add that takes two parameters. The first parameter is the component we want to attach, and the second is the region in which it should be placed. Each JFrame has an associated layout that helps the JFrame position the GUI components that are attached to it. The default layout for a JFrame is known as a **BorderLayout** and has five regions—NORTH (top), SOUTH (bottom), EAST (right side), WEST (left side) and CENTER. Each of these is declared as a constant in class BorderLayout. When calling method add with one argument, the JFrame places the component in the CENTER automatically. If a position already contains a component, then the new component takes its place. Lines 38 and 39 set the size of the JFrame and make it visible on screen.

```
1   // Fig 9.19: LabelDemo.java
2   // Demonstrates the use of labels.
3   import java.awt.BorderLayout;
4   import javax.swing.ImageIcon;
5   import javax.swing.JLabel;
6   import javax.swing.JFrame;
7
8   public class LabelDemo
9   {
10     public static void main( String args[] )
11     {
12        // Create a label with plain text
13        JLabel northLabel = new JLabel( "North" );
```

Fig. 9.19 | JLabel with text and with images. (Part 1 of 2.)

```
14
15          // create an icon from an image so we can put it on a JLabel
16          ImageIcon labelIcon = new ImageIcon( "GUItip.gif" );
17
18          // create a label with an Icon instead of text
19          JLabel centerLabel = new JLabel( labelIcon );
20
21          // create another label with an Icon
22          JLabel southLabel = new JLabel( labelIcon );
23
24          // set the label to display text (as well as an icon)
25          southLabel.setText( "South" );
26
27          // create a frame to hold the labels
28          JFrame application = new JFrame();
29
30          application.setDefaultCloseOperation( JFrame.EXIT_ON_CLOSE );
31
32          // add the labels to the frame; the second argument specifies
33          // where on the frame to add the label
34          application.add( northLabel, BorderLayout.NORTH );
35          application.add( centerLabel, BorderLayout.CENTER );
36          application.add( southLabel, BorderLayout.SOUTH );
37
38          application.setSize( 300, 300 ); // set the size of the frame
39          application.setVisible( true ); // show the frame
40      } // end main
41  } // end class LabelDemo
```

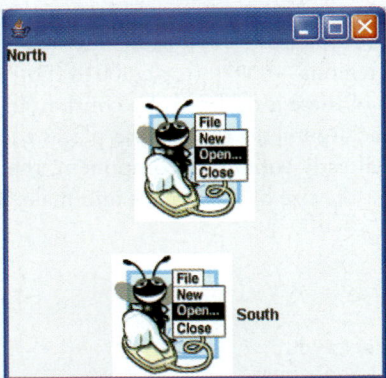

Fig. 9.19 | JLabel with text and with images. (Part 2 of 2.)

GUI and Graphics Case Study Exercise

9.1   Modify Exercise 8.1 to include a JLabel as a status bar that displays counts representing the number of each shape displayed. Class DrawPanel should declare a method that returns a String containing the status text. In main, first create the DrawPanel, then create the JLabel with the status text as an argument to the JLabel's constructor. Attach the JLabel to the SOUTH region of the JFrame, as shown in Fig. 9.20.

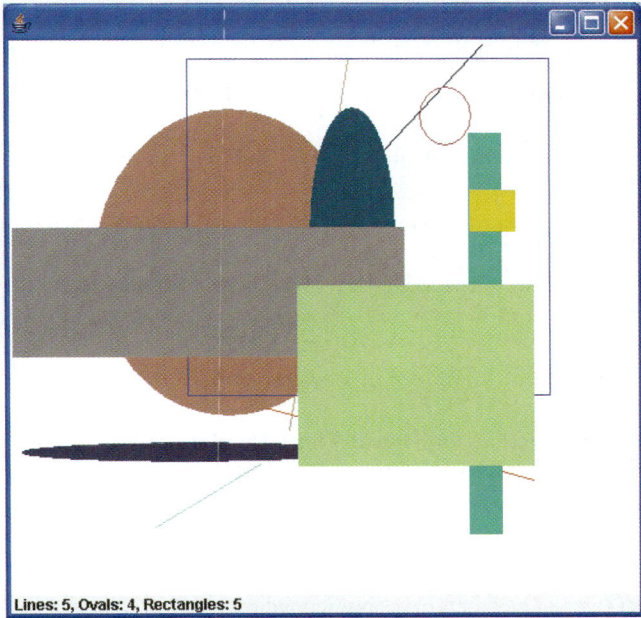

Fig. 9.20 | `JLabel` displaying shape statistics.

9.9 Wrap-Up

This chapter introduced inheritance—the ability to create classes by absorbing an existing class's members and embellishing them with new capabilities. You learned the notions of superclasses and subclasses and used keyword `extends` to create a subclass that inherits members from a superclass. The chapter introduced the access modifier `protected`; subclass methods can access `protected` superclass members. You learned how to access superclass members with `super`. You also saw how constructors are used in inheritance hierarchies. Finally, you learned about the methods of class `Object`, the direct or indirect superclass of all classes in Java.

In Chapter 10, Object-Oriented Programming: Polymorphism, we build on our discussion of inheritance by introducing polymorphism—an object-oriented concept that enables us to write programs that handle, in a more general manner, objects of a wide variety of classes related by inheritance. After studying Chapter 10, you will be familiar with classes, objects, encapsulation, inheritance and polymorphism—the most essential aspects of object-oriented programming.

Summary

- Software reuse reduces program-development time.
- The direct superclass of a subclass (specified by the keyword `extends` in the first line of a class declaration) is the superclass from which the subclass inherits. An indirect superclass of a subclass is two or more levels up the class hierarchy from that subclass.

- In single inheritance, a class is derived from one direct superclass. In multiple inheritance, a class is derived from more than one direct superclass. Java does not support multiple inheritance.
- A subclass is more specific than its superclass and represents a smaller group of objects.
- Every object of a subclass is also an object of that class's superclass. However, a superclass object is not an object of its class's subclasses.
- An "is-a" relationship represents inheritance. In an "is-a" relationship, an object of a subclass also can be treated as an object of its superclass.
- A "has-a" relationship represents composition. In a "has-a" relationship, a class object contains references to objects of other classes.
- A subclass cannot access or inherit the private members of its superclass—allowing this would violate the encapsulation of the superclass. A subclass can, however, inherit the non-private members of its superclass.
- A superclass method can be overridden in a subclass to declare an appropriate implementation for the subclass.
- Single-inheritance relationships form tree-like hierarchical structures—a superclass exists in a hierarchical relationship with its subclasses.
- A superclass's public members are accessible wherever the program has a reference to an object of that superclass or one of its subclasses.
- A superclass's private members are accessible only within the declaration of that superclass.
- A superclass's protected members have an intermediate level of protection between public and private access. They can be accessed by members of the superclass, by members of its subclasses and by members of other classes in the same package.
- The first task of any subclass constructor is to call its direct superclass's constructor, either explicitly or implicitly, to ensure that the instance variables inherited from the superclass are initialized properly.
- A subclass can explicitly invoke a constructor of its superclass by using the superclass constructor call syntax—keyword super, followed by a set of parentheses containing the superclass constructor arguments.
- When a subclass method overrides a superclass method, the superclass method can be accessed from the subclass if the superclass method name is preceded by the keyword super and a dot (.) separator.
- Declaring instance variables private, while providing non-private methods to manipulate and perform validation, helps enforce good software engineering.
- Method toString takes no arguments and returns a String. The Object class's toString method is normally overridden by a subclass.
- When an object is output using the %s format specifier, the object's toString method is called implicitly to obtain its string representation.

Terminology

base class	derived class
brittle software	direct superclass
class hierarchy	equals method of class Object
class library	extends keyword
clone method of class Object	fragile software
composition	getClass method of class Object

"has-a" relationship	`private` superclass member
`hashCode` method of class `Object`	`protected` keyword
hierarchical relationship	`protected` superclass member
hierarchy diagram	`public` superclass member
indirect superclass	single inheritance
inheritance	software reusability
inheritance hierarchy	standardized reusable components
inherited member	subclass
inherited method	subclass constructor
invoke a superclass constructor	`super` keyword
invoke a superclass method	superclass
"is-a" relationship	superclass constructor
`Object` class	superclass constructor call syntax
object of a subclass	superclass no-argument constructor
object of a superclass	`toString` method of class `Object`
override (redefine) a superclass method	

Self-Review Exercises

9.1   Fill in the blanks in each of the following statements:

a) _____ is a form of software reusability in which new classes acquire the members of existing classes and embellish those classes with new capabilities.

b) A superclass's _____ members can be accessed in the superclass declaration and in subclass declarations.

c) In a(n) _____ relationship, an object of a subclass can also be treated as an object of its superclass.

d) In a(n) _____ relationship, a class object has references to objects of other classes as members.

e) In single inheritance, a class exists in a(n) _____ relationship with its subclasses.

f) A superclass's _____ members are accessible anywhere that the program has a reference to an object of that superclass or to an object of one of its subclasses.

g) When an object of a subclass is instantiated, a superclass _____ is called implicitly or explicitly.

h) Subclass constructors can call superclass constructors via the _____ keyword.

9.2   State whether each of the following is *true* or *false*. If a statement is *false*, explain why.

a) Superclass constructors are not inherited by subclasses.

b) A "has-a" relationship is implemented via inheritance.

c) A `Car` class has an "is-a" relationship with the `SteeringWheel` and `Brakes` classes.

d) Inheritance encourages the reuse of proven high-quality software.

e) When a subclass redefines a superclass method by using the same signature, the subclass is said to overload that superclass method.

Answers to Self-Review Exercises

9.1   a) Inheritance. b) `public` or `protected`. c) "is-a" or inheritance. d) "has-a" or composition. e) hierarchical. f) `public`. g) constructor. h) `super`.

9.2   a) True. b) False. A "has-a" relationship is implemented via composition. An "is-a" relationship is implemented via inheritance. c) False. This is an example of a "has-a" relationship. Class `Car` has an "is-a" relationship with class `Vehicle`. d) True. e) False. This is known as overriding, not overloading.

Exercises

9.3   Many programs written with inheritance could be written with composition instead, and vice versa. Rewrite class BasePlusCommissionEmployee4 (Fig. 9.13) of the CommissionEmployee3–BasePlusCommissionEmployee4 hierarchy to use composition rather than inheritance. After you do this, assess the relative merits of the two approaches for the CommissionEmployee3 and BasePlusCommissionEmployee4 problems, as well as for object-oriented programs in general. Which approach is more natural? Why?

9.4   Discuss the ways in which inheritance promotes software reuse, saves time during program development and helps prevent errors.

9.5   Draw an inheritance hierarchy for students at a university similar to the hierarchy shown in Fig. 9.2. Use Student as the superclass of the hierarchy, then extend Student with classes UndergraduateStudent and GraduateStudent. Continue to extend the hierarchy as deep (i.e., as many levels) as possible. For example, Freshman, Sophomore, Junior and Senior might extend UndergraduateStudent, and DoctoralStudent and MastersStudent might be subclasses of GraduateStudent. After drawing the hierarchy, discuss the relationships that exist between the classes. [*Note:* You do not need to write any code for this exercise.]

9.6   The world of shapes is much richer than the shapes included in the inheritance hierarchy of Fig. 9.3. Write down all the shapes you can think of—both two-dimensional and three-dimensional—and form them into a more complete Shape hierarchy with as many levels as possible. Your hierarchy should have class Shape at the top. Class TwoDimensionalShape and class ThreeDimensionalShape should extend Shape. Add additional subclasses, such as Quadrilateral and Sphere, at their correct locations in the hierarchy as necessary.

9.7   Some programmers prefer not to use protected access, because they believe it breaks the encapsulation of the superclass. Discuss the relative merits of using protected access vs. using private access in superclasses.

9.8   Write an inheritance hierarchy for classes Quadrilateral, Trapezoid, Parallelogram, Rectangle and Square. Use Quadrilateral as the superclass of the hierarchy. Make the hierarchy as deep (i.e., as many levels) as possible. Specify the instance variables and methods for each class. The private instance variables of Quadrilateral should be the *x-y* coordinate pairs for the four endpoints of the Quadrilateral. Write a program that instantiates objects of your classes and outputs each object's area (except Quadrilateral).

Object-Oriented Programming: Polymorphism

One Ring to rule them all,
One Ring to find them,
One Ring to bring them all
and in the darkness bind
them.
—John Ronald Reuel Tolkien

General propositions do not
decide concrete cases.
—Oliver Wendell Holmes

A philosopher of imposing
stature doesn't think in a
vacuum. Even his most
abstract ideas are, to some
extent, conditioned by
what is or is not known
in the time when he lives.
—Alfred North Whitehead

Why art thou cast down,
O my soul?
—Psalms 42:5

OBJECTIVES

In this chapter you will learn:

- The concept of polymorphism.
- To use overridden methods to effect polymorphism.
- To distinguish between abstract and concrete classes.
- To declare abstract methods to create abstract classes.
- How polymorphism makes systems extensible and maintainable.
- To determine an object's type at execution time.
- To declare and implement interfaces.

10.1 Introduction

We now continue our study of object-oriented programming by explaining and demonstrating polymorphism with inheritance hierarchies. Polymorphism enables us to "program in the general" rather than "program in the specific." In particular, polymorphism enables us to write programs that process objects that share the same superclass in a class hierarchy as if they are all objects of the superclass.

Consider the following example of polymorphism. Suppose we create a program that simulates the movement of several types of animals for a biological study. Classes Fish, Frog and Bird represent the three types of animals under investigation. Imagine that each of these classes extends superclass Animal, which contains a method move and maintains an animal's current location as *x-y* coordinates. Each subclass implements method move. Our program maintains an array of references to objects of the various Animal subclasses. To simulate the animals' movements, the program sends each object the same message once per second—namely, move. However, each specific type of Animal responds to a move message in a unique way—a Fish might swim three feet, a Frog might jump five feet and a Bird might fly ten feet. The program issues the same message (i.e., move) to each animal object generically, but each object knows how to modify its *x-y* coordinates appropriately for its specific type of movement. Relying on each object to know how to "do the right thing" (i.e., do what is appropriate for that type of object) in response to the same method call is the key concept of polymorphism. The same message (in this case, move) sent to a variety of objects has "many forms" of results—hence the term polymorphism.

With polymorphism, we can design and implement systems that are easily extensible—new classes can be added with little or no modification to the general portions of the program, as long as the new classes are part of the inheritance hierarchy that the program processes generically. The only parts of a program that must be altered to accommodate new classes are those that require direct knowledge of the new classes that the programmer adds to the hierarchy. For example, if we extend class Animal to create class Tortoise (which might respond to a move message by crawling one inch), we need to write only the Tortoise class and the part of the simulation that instantiates a Tortoise object. The portions of the simulation that process each Animal generically can remain the same.

This chapter has several key parts. First, we discuss common examples of polymorphism. We then provide a live-code example demonstrating polymorphic behavior. As you will soon see, you will use superclass references to manipulate both superclass objects and subclass objects polymorphically.

We then present a case study that revisits the employee hierarchy of Section 9.4.5. We develop a simple payroll application that polymorphically calculates the weekly pay of several different types of employees using each employee's earnings method. Though the earnings of each type of employee are calculated in a specific way, polymorphism allows us to process the employees "in the general." In the case study, we enlarge the hierarchy to include two new classes—SalariedEmployee (for people paid a fixed weekly salary) and HourlyEmployee (for people paid an hourly salary and so-called time-and-a-half for overtime). We declare a common set of functionality for all the classes in the updated hierarchy in a so-called abstract class, Employee, from which classes SalariedEmployee, HourlyEmployee and CommissionEmployee inherit directly and class BasePlusCommissionEmployee4 inherits indirectly. As you will soon see, when we invoke each employee's earnings method off a superclass Employee reference, the correct earnings calculation is performed due to Java's polymorphic capabilities.

Occasionally, when performing polymorphic processing, we need to program "in the specific." Our Employee case study demonstrates that a program can determine the type of an object at execution time and act on that object accordingly. In the case study, we use these capabilities to determine whether a particular employee object *is a* BasePlusCommissionEmployee. If so, we increase that employee's base salary by 10%.

The chapter continues with an introduction to Java interfaces. An interface describes a set of methods that can be called on an object, but does not provide concrete implementations for the methods. Programmers can declare classes that **implement** (i.e., provide concrete implementations for the methods of) one or more interfaces. Each interface method must be declared in all the classes that implement the interface. Once a class implements an interface, all objects of that class have an *is-a* relationship with the interface type, and all objects of the class are guaranteed to provide the functionality described by the interface. This is true of all subclasses of that class as well.

Interfaces are particularly useful for assigning common functionality to possibly unrelated classes. This allows objects of unrelated classes to be processed polymorphically—objects of classes that implement the same interface can respond to the same method calls. To demonstrate creating and using interfaces, we modify our payroll application to create a general accounts payable application that can calculate payments due for company employees and invoice amounts to be billed for purchased goods. As you will see, interfaces enable polymorphic capabilities similar to those possible with inheritance.

10.2 Polymorphism Examples

We now consider several additional examples of polymorphism. If class Rectangle is derived from class Quadrilateral, then a Rectangle object is a more specific version of a Quadrilateral object. Any operation (e.g., calculating the perimeter or the area) that can be performed on a Quadrilateral object can also be performed on a Rectangle object. These operations can also be performed on other Quadrilaterals, such as Squares, Parallelograms and Trapezoids. The polymorphism occurs when a program invokes a method through a superclass variable—at execution time, the correct subclass version of the method is called, based on the type of the reference stored in the superclass variable. You will see a simple code example that illustrates this process in Section 10.3.

As another example, suppose we design a video game that manipulates objects of many different types, including objects of classes Martian, Venusian, Plutonian, Space-Ship and LaserBeam. Imagine that each class inherits from the common superclass called SpaceObject, which contains method draw. Each subclass implements this method. A screen-manager program maintains a collection (e.g., a SpaceObject array) of references to objects of the various classes. To refresh the screen, the screen manager periodically sends each object the same message—namely, draw. However, each object responds in a unique way. For example, a Martian object might draw itself in red with the appropriate number of antennae. A SpaceShip object might draw itself as a bright silver flying saucer. A LaserBeam object might draw itself as a bright red beam across the screen. Again, the same message (in this case, draw) sent to a variety of objects has "many forms" of results.

A polymorphic screen manager might use polymorphism to facilitate adding new classes to a system with minimal modifications to the system's code. Suppose that we want to add Mercurian objects to our video game. To do so, we must build a class Mercurian that extends SpaceObject and provides its own draw method implementation. When objects of class Mercurian appear in the SpaceObject collection, the screen manager code invokes method draw, exactly as it does for every other object in the collection, regardless of its type. So the new Mercurian objects simply "plug right in" without any modification of the screen manager code by the programmer. Thus, without modifying the system (other than to build new classes and modify the code that creates new objects), programmers can use polymorphism to include additional types that were not envisioned when the system was created.

With polymorphism, the same method name and signature can be used to cause different actions to occur, depending on the type of object on which the method is invoked. This gives the programmer tremendous expressive capability.

Software Engineering Observation 10.1

Polymorphism enables programmers to deal in generalities and let the execution-time environment handle the specifics. Programmers can command objects to behave in manners appropriate to those objects, without knowing the types of the objects (as long as the objects belong to the same inheritance hierarchy).

Software Engineering Observation 10.2

Polymorphism promotes extensibility: Software that invokes polymorphic behavior is independent of the object types to which messages are sent. New object types that can respond to existing method calls can be incorporated into a system without requiring modification of the base system. Only client code that instantiates new objects must be modified to accommodate new types.

10.3 Demonstrating Polymorphic Behavior

Section 9.4 created a commission employee class hierarchy, in which class BasePlusCommissionEmployee inherited from class CommissionEmployee. The examples in that section manipulated CommissionEmployee and BasePlusCommissionEmployee objects by using references to them to invoke their methods. We aimed superclass references at superclass objects and subclass references at subclass objects. These assignments are natural and straightforward—superclass references are intended to refer to superclass objects, and subclass references are intended to refer to subclass objects. However, as you will soon see, other assignments are possible.

In the next example, we aim a superclass reference at a subclass object. We then show how invoking a method on a subclass object via a superclass reference invokes the subclass functionality—the type of the *actual referenced object*, not the type of the *reference*, determines which method is called. This example demonstrates the key concept that an object of a subclass can be treated as an object of its superclass. This enables various interesting manipulations. A program can create an array of superclass references that refer to objects of many subclass types. This is allowed because each subclass object *is an* object of its superclass. For instance, we can assign the reference of a BasePlusCommissionEmployee object to a superclass CommissionEmployee variable because a BasePlusCommissionEmployee *is a* CommissionEmployee—we can treat a BasePlusCommissionEmployee as a CommissionEmployee.

As you will learn later in the chapter, we cannot treat a superclass object as a subclass object because a superclass object is not an object of any of its subclasses. For example, we cannot assign the reference of a CommissionEmployee object to a subclass BasePlusCommissionEmployee variable because a CommissionEmployee is not a BasePlusCommissionEmployee—a CommissionEmployee does not have a baseSalary instance variable and does not have methods setBaseSalary and getBaseSalary. The *is-a* relationship applies only from a subclass to its direct (and indirect) superclasses, and not vice versa.

It turns out that the Java compiler does allow the assignment of a superclass reference to a subclass variable if we explicitly cast the superclass reference to the subclass type—a technique we discuss in greater detail in Section 10.5. Why would we ever want to perform such an assignment? A superclass reference can be used to invoke only the methods declared in the superclass—attempting to invoke subclass-only methods through a superclass reference results in compilation errors. If a program needs to perform a subclass-specific operation on a subclass object referenced by a superclass variable, the program must first cast the superclass reference to a subclass reference through a technique known as **downcasting**. This enables the program to invoke subclass methods that are not in the superclass. We will show you a concrete example of downcasting in Section 10.5.

The example in Fig. 10.1 demonstrates three ways to use superclass and subclass variables to store references to superclass and subclass objects. The first two are straightforward—as in Section 9.4, we assign a superclass reference to a superclass variable, and we assign a subclass reference to a subclass variable. Then we demonstrate the relationship between subclasses and superclasses (i.e., the *is-a* relationship) by assigning a subclass reference to a superclass variable. [*Note:* This program uses classes `CommissionEmployee3` and `BasePlusCommissionEmployee4` from Fig. 9.12 and Fig. 9.13, respectively.]

```java
 1   // Fig. 10.1: PolymorphismTest.java
 2   // Assigning superclass and subclass references to superclass and
 3   // subclass variables.
 4
 5   public class PolymorphismTest
 6   {
 7      public static void main( String args[] )
 8      {
 9         // assign superclass reference to superclass variable
10         CommissionEmployee3 commissionEmployee = new CommissionEmployee3(
11            "Sue", "Jones", "222-22-2222", 10000, .06 );
12
13         // assign subclass reference to subclass variable
14         BasePlusCommissionEmployee4 basePlusCommissionEmployee =
15            new BasePlusCommissionEmployee4(
16            "Bob", "Lewis", "333-33-3333", 5000, .04, 300 );
17
18         // invoke toString on superclass object using superclass variable
19         System.out.printf( "%s %s:\n\n%s\n\n",
20            "Call CommissionEmployee3's toString with superclass reference ",
21            "to superclass object", commissionEmployee.toString() );
22
23         // invoke toString on subclass object using subclass variable
24         System.out.printf( "%s %s:\n\n%s\n\n",
25            "Call BasePlusCommissionEmployee4's toString with subclass",
26            "reference to subclass object",
27            basePlusCommissionEmployee.toString() );
28
29         // invoke toString on subclass object using superclass variable
30         CommissionEmployee3 commissionEmployee2 =
31            basePlusCommissionEmployee;
32         System.out.printf( "%s %s:\n\n%s\n",
33            "Call BasePlusCommissionEmployee4's toString with superclass",
34            "reference to subclass object", commissionEmployee2.toString() );
35      } // end main
36   } // end class PolymorphismTest
```

Fig. 10.1 | Assigning superclass and subclass references to superclass and subclass variables. (Part 1 of 2.)

```
Call CommissionEmployee3's toString with superclass reference to superclass
object:

commission employee: Sue Jones
social security number: 222-22-2222
gross sales: 10000.00
commission rate: 0.06

Call BasePlusCommissionEmployee4's toString with subclass reference to
subclass object:

base-salaried commission employee: Bob Lewis
social security number: 333-33-3333
gross sales: 5000.00
commission rate: 0.04
base salary: 300.00

Call BasePlusCommissionEmployee4's toString with superclass reference to
subclass object:

base-salaried commission employee: Bob Lewis
social security number: 333-33-3333
gross sales: 5000.00
commission rate: 0.04
base salary: 300.00
```

Fig. 10.1 | Assigning superclass and subclass references to superclass and subclass variables. (Part 2 of 2.)

In Fig. 10.1, lines 10–11 create a CommissionEmployee3 object and assign its reference to a CommissionEmployee3 variable. Lines 14–16 create a BasePlusCommission-Employee4 object and assign its reference to a BasePlusCommissionEmployee4 variable. These assignments are natural—for example, a CommissionEmployee3 variable's primary purpose is to hold a reference to a CommissionEmployee3 object. Lines 19–21 use reference commissionEmployee to invoke toString explicitly. Because commissionEmployee refers to a CommissionEmployee3 object, superclass CommissionEmployee3's version of toString is called. Similarly, lines 24–27 use basePlusCommissionEmployee to invoke toString explicitly on the BasePlusCommissionEmployee4 object. This invokes subclass BasePlus-CommissionEmployee4's version of toString.

Lines 30–31 then assign the reference to subclass object basePlusCommissionEmployee to a superclass CommissionEmployee3 variable, which lines 32–34 use to invoke method toString. A superclass variable that contains a reference to a subclass object and is used to call a method actually calls the subclass version of the method. Hence, commission-Employee2.toString() in line 34 actually calls class BasePlusCommissionEmployee4's toString method. The Java compiler allows this "crossover" because an object of a subclass *is an* object of its superclass (but not vice versa). When the compiler encounters a method call made through a variable, the compiler determines if the method can be called by checking the variable's class type. If that class contains the proper method declaration (or inherits one), the compiler allows the call to be compiled. At execution time, the type of the object to which the variable refers determines the actual method to use.

10.4 **Abstract Classes and Methods**

When we think of a class type, we assume that programs will create objects of that type. In some cases, however, it is useful to declare classes for which the programmer never intends to instantiate objects. Such classes are called abstract classes. Because they are used only as superclasses in inheritance hierarchies, we refer to them as abstract superclasses. These classes cannot be used to instantiate objects, because, as we will soon see, abstract classes are incomplete. Subclasses must declare the "missing pieces." We demonstrate abstract classes in Section 10.5.

The purpose of an abstract class is primarily to provide an appropriate superclass from which other classes can inherit and thus share a common design. In the Shape hierarchy of Fig. 9.3, for example, subclasses inherit the notion of what it means to be a Shape—common attributes such as location, color and borderThickness, and behaviors such as draw, move, resize and changeColor. Classes that can be used to instantiate objects are called concrete classes. Such classes provide implementations of every method they declare (some of the implementations can be inherited). For example, we could derive concrete classes Circle, Square and Triangle from abstract superclass TwoDimensionalShape. Similarly, we could derive concrete classes Sphere, Cube and Tetrahedron from abstract superclass ThreeDimensionalShape. Abstract superclasses are too general to create real objects—they specify only what is common among subclasses. We need to be more specific before we can create objects. For example, if you send the draw message to abstract class TwoDimensionalShape, it knows that two-dimensional shapes should be drawable, but it does not know what specific shape to draw, so it cannot implement a real draw method. Concrete classes provide the specifics that make it reasonable to instantiate objects.

Not all inheritance hierarchies contain abstract classes. However, programmers often write client code that uses only abstract superclass types to reduce client code's dependencies on a range of specific subclass types. For example, a programmer can write a method with a parameter of an abstract superclass type. When called, such a method can be passed an object of any concrete class that directly or indirectly extends the superclass specified as the parameter's type.

Abstract classes sometimes constitute several levels of the hierarchy. For example, the Shape hierarchy of Fig. 9.3 begins with abstract class Shape. On the next level of the hierarchy are two more abstract classes, TwoDimensionalShape and ThreeDimensionalShape. The next level of the hierarchy declares concrete classes for TwoDimensionalShapes (Circle, Square and Triangle) and for ThreeDimensionalShapes (Sphere, Cube and Tetrahedron).

You make a class abstract by declaring it with keyword **abstract**. An abstract class normally contains one or more abstract methods. An abstract method is one with keyword abstract in its declaration, as in

```
public abstract void draw(); // abstract method
```

Abstract methods do not provide implementations. A class that contains any abstract methods must be declared as an abstract class even if that class contains concrete (non-abstract) methods. Each concrete subclass of an abstract superclass also must provide concrete implementations of the superclass's abstract methods. Constructors and static methods cannot be declared abstract. Constructors are not inherited, so an abstract constructor could never be implemented. Similarly, subclasses cannot override static methods, so an abstract static method could never be implemented.

Software Engineering Observation 10.3

An abstract class declares common attributes and behaviors of the various classes in a class hierarchy. An abstract class typically contains one or more abstract methods that subclasses must override if the subclasses are to be concrete. The instance variables and concrete methods of an abstract class are subject to the normal rules of inheritance.

Common Programming Error 10.1

Attempting to instantiate an object of an abstract class is a compilation error.

Common Programming Error 10.2

Failure to implement a superclass's abstract methods in a subclass is a compilation error unless the subclass is also declared `abstract`.

Although we cannot instantiate objects of abstract superclasses, you will soon see that we *can* use abstract superclasses to declare variables that can hold references to objects of any concrete class derived from those abstract classes. Programs typically use such variables to manipulate subclass objects polymorphically. We also can use abstract superclass names to invoke `static` methods declared in those abstract superclasses.

Consider another application of polymorphism. A drawing program needs to display many shapes, including new shape types that the programmer will add to the system after writing the drawing program. The drawing program might need to display shapes, such as `Circles`, `Triangles`, `Rectangles` or others, that derive from abstract superclass `Shape`. The drawing program uses `Shape` variables to manage the objects that are displayed. To draw any object in this inheritance hierarchy, the drawing program uses a superclass `Shape` variable containing a reference to the subclass object to invoke the object's `draw` method. This method is declared `abstract` in superclass `Shape`, so each concrete subclass *must* implement method `draw` in a manner specific to that shape. Each object in the `Shape` inheritance hierarchy knows how to draw itself. The drawing program does not have to worry about the type of each object or whether the drawing program has ever encountered objects of that type.

Polymorphism is particularly effective for implementing so-called layered software systems. In operating systems, for example, each type of physical device could operate quite differently from the others. Even so, commands to read or write data from and to devices may have a certain uniformity. For each device, the operating system uses a piece of software called a device driver to control all communication between the system and the device. The write message sent to a device-driver object needs to be interpreted specifically in the context of that driver and how it manipulates devices of a specific type. However, the write call itself really is no different from the write to any other device in the system: Place some number of bytes from memory onto that device. An object-oriented operating system might use an abstract superclass to provide an "interface" appropriate for all device drivers. Then, through inheritance from that abstract superclass, subclasses are formed that all behave similarly. The device driver methods are declared as abstract methods in the abstract superclass. The implementations of these abstract methods are provided in the subclasses that correspond to the specific types of device drivers. New devices are always being developed, and often long after the operating system has been released. When you buy a new device, it comes with a device driver provided by the device vendor. The device is immediately operational after you connect it to your computer and install the driver. This is another elegant example of how polymorphism makes systems extensible.

It is common in object-oriented programming to declare an *iterator class* that can traverse all the objects in a collection, such as an array (Chapter 7) or an ArrayList (Chapter 19, Collections). For example, a program can print an ArrayList of objects by creating an iterator object and using it to obtain the next list element each time the iterator is called. Iterators often are used in polymorphic programming to traverse a collection that contains references to objects from various levels of a hierarchy. (Chapter 19, presents a thorough treatment of ArrayList, iterators and J2SE 5.0's new "generics" capabilities.) An ArrayList of objects of class TwoDimensionalShape, for example, could contain objects from subclasses Square, Circle, Triangle and so on. Calling method draw for each TwoDimensionalShape object off a TwoDimensionalShape variable would polymorphically draw each object correctly on the screen.

10.5 Case Study: Payroll System Using Polymorphism

This section reexamines the CommissionEmployee-BasePlusCommissionEmployee hierarchy that we explored throughout Section 9.4. Now we use an abstract method and polymorphism to perform payroll calculations based on the type of employee. We create an enhanced employee hierarchy to solve the following problem:

> *A company pays its employees on a weekly basis. The employees are of four types: Salaried employees are paid a fixed weekly salary regardless of the number of hours worked, hourly employees are paid by the hour and receive overtime pay for all hours worked in excess of 40 hours, commission employees are paid a percentage of their sales and salaried-commission employees receive a base salary plus a percentage of their sales. For the current pay period, the company has decided to reward salaried-commission employees by adding 10% to their base salaries. The company wants to implement a Java application that performs its payroll calculations polymorphically.*

We use abstract class Employee to represent the general concept of an employee. The classes that extend Employee are SalariedEmployee, CommissionEmployee and Hourly-Employee. Class BasePlusCommissionEmployee—which extends CommissionEmployee—represents the last employee type. The UML class diagram in Fig. 10.2 shows the inheritance hierarchy for our polymorphic employee-payroll application. Note that abstract class Employee is italicized, as per the convention of the UML.

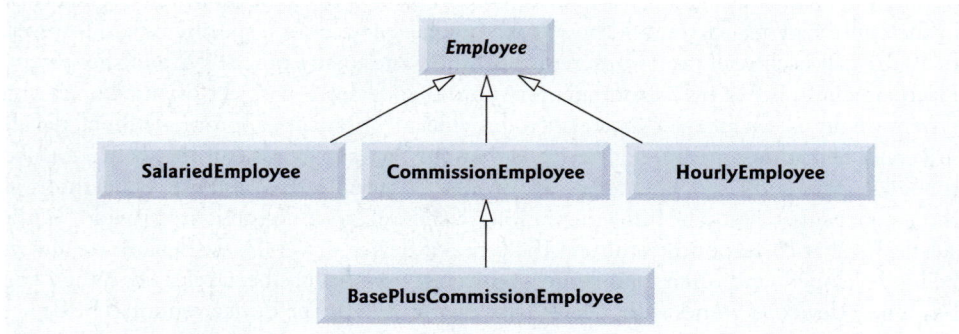

Fig. 10.2 | Employee hierarchy UML class diagram.

Abstract superclass `Employee` declares the "interface" to the hierarchy—that is, the set of methods that a program can invoke on all `Employee` objects. We use the term "interface" here in a general sense to refer to the various ways programs can communicate with objects of any `Employee` subclass. Be careful not to confuse the general notion of an "interface" to something with the formal notion of a Java interface, the subject of Section 10.7. Each employee, regardless of the way his or her earnings are calculated, has a first name, a last name and a social security number, so `private` instance variables `firstName`, `last-Name` and `socialSecurityNumber` appear in abstract superclass `Employee`.

Software Engineering Observation 10.4

A subclass can inherit "interface" or "implementation" from a superclass. Hierarchies designed for implementation inheritance tend to have their functionality high in the hierarchy—each new subclass inherits one or more methods that were implemented in a superclass, and the subclass uses the superclass implementations. Hierarchies designed for interface inheritance tend to have their functionality lower in the hierarchy—a superclass specifies one or more abstract methods that must be declared for each concrete class in the hierarchy, and the individual subclasses override these methods to provide subclass-specific implementations.

The following sections implement the `Employee` class hierarchy. The first four sections each implement one of the concrete classes. The last section implements a test program that builds objects of all these classes and processes those objects polymorphically.

10.5.1 Creating Abstract Superclass `Employee`

Class `Employee` (Fig. 10.4) provides methods `earnings` and `toString`, in addition to the *get* and *set* methods that manipulate `Employee`'s instance variables. An `earnings` method certainly applies generically to all employees. But each earnings calculation depends on the employee's class. So we declare `earnings` as `abstract` in superclass `Employee` because a default implementation does not make sense for that method—there is not enough information to determine what amount `earnings` should return. Each subclass overrides `earnings` with an appropriate implementation. To calculate an employee's earnings, the program assigns a reference to the employee's object to a superclass `Employee` variable, then invokes the `earnings` method on that variable. We maintain an array of `Employee` variables, each of which holds a reference to an `Employee` object (of course, there cannot be `Employee` objects because `Employee` is an abstract class—because of inheritance, however, all objects of all subclasses of `Employee` may nevertheless be thought of as `Employee` objects). The program iterates through the array and calls method `earnings` for each `Employee` object. Java processes these method calls polymorphically. Including `earnings` as an abstract method in `Employee` forces every direct subclass of `Employee` to override `earnings` in order to become a concrete class. This enables the designer of the class hierarchy to demand that each subclass provide an appropriate pay calculation.

Method `toString` in class `Employee` returns a `String` containing the first name, last name and social security number of the employee. As we will see, each subclass of `Employee` overrides method `toString` to create a string representation of an object of that class that contains the employee's type (e.g., `"salaried employee:"`) followed by the rest of the employee's information.

The diagram in Fig. 10.3 shows each of the five classes in the hierarchy down the left side and methods `earnings` and `toString` across the top. For each class, the diagram

	earnings	toString
Employee	abstract	*firstName lastName* social security number: *SSN*
Salaried- Employee	weeklySalary	salaried employee: *firstName lastName* social security number: *SSN* weekly salary: *weeklysalary*

Hourly- Employee	*If hours <= 40*
	    wage * hours
	 If hours > 40
	    40 * wage +
	    (hours - 40) *
	    wage * 1.5
		hourly employee: *firstName lastName*
		 social security number: *SSN*
		 hourly wage: *wage*; hours worked: *hours*

Commission- Employee	commissionRate * grossSales	commission employee: *firstName lastName* social security number: *SSN* gross sales: *grossSales*; commission rate: *commissionRate*
BasePlus- Commission- Employee	(commissionRate * grossSales) + baseSalary	base salaried commission employee: *firstName lastName* social security number: *SSN* gross sales: *grossSales*; commission rate: *commissionRate*; base salary: *baseSalary*

Fig. 10.3 | Polymorphic interface for the Employee hierarchy classes.

shows the desired results of each method. [*Note:* We do not list superclass Employee's *get* and *set* methods because they are not overridden in any of the subclasses—each of these methods is inherited and used "as is" by each of the subclasses.]

Let us consider class Employee's declaration (Fig. 10.4). The class includes a constructor that takes the first name, last name and social security number as arguments (lines 11–16); *get* methods that return the first name, last name and social security number (lines 25–28, 37–40 and 49–52, respectively); *set* methods that set the first name, last name and social security number (lines 19–22, 31–34 and 43–46, respectively); method toString (lines 55–59), which returns the string representation of Employee; and abstract method earnings (line 62), which will be implemented by subclasses. Note that the Employee constructor does not validate the social security number in this example. Normally, such validation should be provided.

Why did we decide to declare earnings as an abstract method? It simply does not make sense to provide an implementation of this method in class Employee. We cannot calculate the earnings for a general Employee—we first must know the specific Employee type to determine the appropriate earnings calculation. By declaring this method abstract, we indicate that each concrete subclass *must* provide an appropriate earnings implementation and that a program will be able to use superclass Employee variables to invoke method earnings polymorphically for any type of Employee.

```
 1   // Fig. 10.4: Employee.java
 2   // Employee abstract superclass.
 3
 4   public abstract class Employee
 5   {
 6      private String firstName;
 7      private String lastName;
 8      private String socialSecurityNumber;
 9
10      // three-argument constructor
11      public Employee( String first, String last, String ssn )
12      {
13         firstName = first;
14         lastName = last;
15         socialSecurityNumber = ssn;
16      } // end three-argument Employee constructor
17
18      // set first name
19      public void setFirstName( String first )
20      {
21         firstName = first;
22      } // end method setFirstName
23
24      // return first name
25      public String getFirstName()
26      {
27         return firstName;
28      } // end method getFirstName
29
30      // set last name
31      public void setLastName( String last )
32      {
33         lastName = last;
34      } // end method setLastName
35
36      // return last name
37      public String getLastName()
38      {
39         return lastName;
40      } // end method getLastName
41
42      // set social security number
43      public void setSocialSecurityNumber( String ssn )
44      {
45         socialSecurityNumber = ssn; // should validate
46      } // end method setSocialSecurityNumber
47
48      // return social security number
49      public String getSocialSecurityNumber()
50      {
51         return socialSecurityNumber;
52      } // end method getSocialSecurityNumber
```

Fig. 10.4 | Employee abstract superclass. (Part 1 of 2.)

```
53
54    // return String representation of Employee object
55    public String toString()
56    {
57       return String.format( "%s %s\nsocial security number: %s",
58          getFirstName(), getLastName(), getSocialSecurityNumber() );
59    } // end method toString
60
61    // abstract method overridden by subclasses
62    public abstract double earnings(); // no implementation here
63 } // end abstract class Employee
```

Fig. 10.4 | Employee abstract superclass. (Part 2 of 2.)

10.5.2 Creating Concrete Subclass SalariedEmployee

Class SalariedEmployee (Fig. 10.5) extends class Employee (line 4) and overrides earnings (lines 29–32), which makes SalariedEmployee a concrete class. The class includes a constructor (lines 9–14) that takes a first name, a last name, a social security number and a weekly salary as arguments; a *set* method to assign a new non-negative value to instance variable weeklySalary (lines 17–20); a *get* method to return weeklySalary's value (lines 23–26); a method earnings (lines 29–32) to calculate a SalariedEmployee's earnings; and a method toString (lines 35–39), which returns a String including the employee's type, namely, "salaried employee: " followed by employee-specific information produced by superclass Employee's toString method and SalariedEmployee's getWeeklySalary method. Class SalariedEmployee's constructor passes the first name, last name and social security number to the Employee constructor (line 12) to initialize the

```
1    // Fig. 10.5: SalariedEmployee.java
2    // SalariedEmployee class extends Employee.
3
4    public class SalariedEmployee extends Employee
5    {
6       private double weeklySalary;
7
8       // four-argument constructor
9       public SalariedEmployee( String first, String last, String ssn,
10         double salary )
11      {
12         super( first, last, ssn ); // pass to Employee constructor
13         setWeeklySalary( salary ); // validate and store salary
14      } // end four-argument SalariedEmployee constructor
15
16      // set salary
17      public void setWeeklySalary( double salary )
18      {
19         weeklySalary = salary < 0.0 ? 0.0 : salary;
20      } // end method setWeeklySalary
21
```

Fig. 10.5 | SalariedEmployee class derived from Employee. (Part I of 2.)

```
22      // return salary
23      public double getWeeklySalary()
24      {
25         return weeklySalary;
26      } // end method getWeeklySalary
27
28      // calculate earnings; override abstract method earnings in Employee
29      public double earnings()
30      {
31         return getWeeklySalary();
32      } // end method earnings
33
34      // return String representation of SalariedEmployee object
35      public String toString()
36      {
37         return String.format( "salaried employee: %s\n%s: $%,.2f",
38            super.toString(), "weekly salary", getWeeklySalary() );
39      } // end method toString
40   } // end class SalariedEmployee
```

Fig. 10.5 | `SalariedEmployee` class derived from `Employee`. (Part 2 of 2.)

`private` instance variables not inherited from the superclass. Method `earnings` overrides abstract method `earnings` in `Employee` to provide a concrete implementation that returns the `SalariedEmployee`'s weekly salary. If we do not implement `earnings`, class `SalariedEmployee` must be declared `abstract`—otherwise, a compilation error occurs (and, of course, we want `SalariedEmployee` here to be a concrete class).

Method `toString` (lines 35–39) of class `SalariedEmployee` overrides `Employee` method `toString`. If class `SalariedEmployee` did not override `toString`, `SalariedEmployee` would have inherited the `Employee` version of `toString`. In that case, `SalariedEmployee`'s `toString` method would simply return the employee's full name and social security number, which does not adequately represent a `SalariedEmployee`. To produce a complete string representation of a `SalariedEmployee`, the subclass's `toString` method returns `"salaried employee: "` followed by the superclass `Employee`-specific information (i.e., first name, last name and social security number) obtained by invoking the superclass's `toString` (line 38)—this is a nice example of code reuse. The string representation of a `SalariedEmployee` also contains the employee's weekly salary obtained by invoking the class's `getWeeklySalary` method.

10.5.3 Creating Concrete Subclass `HourlyEmployee`

Class `HourlyEmployee` (Fig. 10.6) also extends class `Employee` (line 4). The class includes a constructor (lines 10–16) that takes as arguments a first name, a last name, a social security number, an hourly wage and the number of hours worked. Lines 19–22 and 31–35 declare *set* methods that assign new values to instance variables `wage` and `hours`, respectively. Method `setWage` (lines 19–22) ensures that `wage` is non-negative, and method `setHours` (lines 31–35) ensures that `hours` is between 0 and 168 (the total number of hours in a week). Class `HourlyEmployee` also includes *get* methods (lines 25–28 and 38–41) to return the values of `wage` and `hours`, respectively; a method `earnings` (lines 44–50) to calculate an `HourlyEmployee`'s earnings; and a method `toString` (lines 53–58), which returns the employee's type, namely, "hourly employee: " and employee-specific information. Note that the HourlyEmployee constructor, like the SalariedEmployee constructor, passes the first name, last name

```java
1    // Fig. 10.6: HourlyEmployee.java
2    // HourlyEmployee class extends Employee.
3
4    public class HourlyEmployee extends Employee
5    {
6       private double wage; // wage per hour
7       private double hours; // hours worked for week
8
9       // five-argument constructor
10      public HourlyEmployee( String first, String last, String ssn,
11         double hourlyWage, double hoursWorked )
12      {
13         super( first, last, ssn );
14         setWage( hourlyWage ); // validate hourly wage
15         setHours( hoursWorked ); // validate hours worked
16      } // end five-argument HourlyEmployee constructor
17
18      // set wage
19      public void setWage( double hourlyWage )
20      {
21         wage = ( hourlyWage < 0.0 ) ? 0.0 : hourlyWage;
22      } // end method setWage
23
24      // return wage
25      public double getWage()
26      {
27         return wage;
28      } // end method getWage
29
30      // set hours worked
31      public void setHours( double hoursWorked )
32      {
33         hours = ( ( hoursWorked >= 0.0 ) && ( hoursWorked <= 168.0 ) ) ?
34            hoursWorked : 0.0;
35      } // end method setHours
36
37      // return hours worked
38      public double getHours()
39      {
40         return hours;
41      } // end method getHours
42
43      // calculate earnings; override abstract method earnings in Employee
44      public double earnings()
45      {
46         if ( getHours() <= 40 ) // no overtime
47            return getWage() * getHours();
48         else
49            return 40 * getWage() + ( gethours() - 40 ) * getWage() * 1.5;
50      } // end method earnings
```

Fig. 10.6 | HourlyEmployee class derived from Employee. (Part 1 of 2.)

```
51
52        // return String representation of HourlyEmployee object
53        public String toString()
54        {
55           return String.format( "hourly employee: %s\n%s: $%,.2f; %s: %,.2f",
56              super.toString(), "hourly wage", getWage(),
57              "hours worked", getHours() );
58        } // end method toString
59     } // end class HourlyEmployee
```

Fig. 10.6 | `HourlyEmployee` class derived from `Employee`. (Part 2 of 2.)

and social security number to the superclass `Employee` constructor (line 13) to initialize the `private` instance variables. In addition, method `toString` calls superclass method `toString` (line 56) to obtain the `Employee`-specific information (i.e., first name, last name and social security number)—this is another nice example of code reuse.

10.5.4 Creating Concrete Subclass CommissionEmployee

Class `CommissionEmployee` (Fig. 10.7) extends class `Employee` (line 4). The class includes a constructor (lines 10–16) that takes a first name, a last name, a social security number, a sales amount and a commission rate; *set* methods (lines 19–22 and 31–34) to assign new values to instance variables `commissionRate` and `grossSales`, respectively; *get* methods (lines 25–28 and 37–40) that retrieve the values of these instance variables; method earnings (lines 43–46) to calculate a `CommissionEmployee`'s earnings; and method `toString`

```
1     // Fig. 10.7: CommissionEmployee.java
2     // CommissionEmployee class extends Employee.
3
4     public class CommissionEmployee extends Employee
5     {
6        private double grossSales; // gross weekly sales
7        private double commissionRate; // commission percentage
8
9        // five-argument constructor
10       public CommissionEmployee( String first, String last, String ssn,
11          double sales, double rate )
12       {
13          super( first, last, ssn );
14          setGrossSales( sales );
15          setCommissionRate( rate );
16       } // end five-argument CommissionEmployee constructor
17
18       // set commission rate
19       public void setCommissionRate( double rate )
20       {
21          commissionRate = ( rate > 0.0 && rate < 1.0 ) ? rate : 0.0;
22       } // end method setCommissionRate
23
```

Fig. 10.7 | `CommissionEmployee` class derived from `Employee`. (Part 1 of 2.)

```
24      // return commission rate
25      public double getCommissionRate()
26      {
27          return commissionRate;
28      } // end method getCommissionRate
29
30      // set gross sales amount
31      public void setGrossSales( double sales )
32      {
33          grossSales = ( sales < 0.0 ) ? 0.0 : sales;
34      } // end method setGrossSales
35
36      // return gross sales amount
37      public double getGrossSales()
38      {
39          return grossSales;
40      } // end method getGrossSales
41
42      // calculate earnings; override abstract method earnings in Employee
43      public double earnings()
44      {
45          return getCommissionRate() * getGrossSales();
46      } // end method earnings
47
48      // return String representation of CommissionEmployee object
49      public String toString()
50      {
51          return String.format( "%s: %s\n%s: $%,.2f; %s: %.2f",
52              "commission employee", super.toString(),
53              "gross sales", getGrossSales(),
54              "commission rate", getCommissionRate() );
55      } // end method toString
56  } // end class CommissionEmployee
```

Fig. 10.7 | CommissionEmployee class derived from Employee. (Part 2 of 2.)

(lines 49–55), which returns the employee's type, namely, "commission employee: " and employee-specific information. The CommissionEmployee's constructor also passes the first name, last name and social security number to the Employee constructor (line 13) to initialize Employee's private instance variables. Method toString calls superclass method toString (line 52) to obtain the Employee-specific information (i.e., first name, last name and social security number).

10.5.5 Creating Indirect Concrete Subclass BasePlusCommissionEmployee

Class BasePlusCommissionEmployee (Fig. 10.8) extends class CommissionEmployee (line 4) and therefore is an indirect subclass of class Employee. Class BasePlusCommissionEmployee has a constructor (lines 9–14) that takes as arguments a first name, a last name, a social security number, a sales amount, a commission rate and a base salary. It then passes the first name, last name, social security number, sales amount and commission rate to the CommissionEmployee constructor (line 12) to initialize the inherited members. BasePlusCommis-

```
1   // Fig. 10.8: BasePlusCommissionEmployee.java
2   // BasePlusCommissionEmployee class extends CommissionEmployee.
3
4   public class BasePlusCommissionEmployee extends CommissionEmployee
5   {
6      private double baseSalary; // base salary per week
7
8      // six-argument constructor
9      public BasePlusCommissionEmployee( String first, String last,
10        String ssn, double sales, double rate, double salary )
11     {
12        super( first, last, ssn, sales, rate );
13        setBaseSalary( salary ); // validate and store base salary
14     } // end six-argument BasePlusCommissionEmployee constructor
15
16     // set base salary
17     public void setBaseSalary( double salary )
18     {
19        baseSalary = ( salary < 0.0 ) ? 0.0 : salary; // non-negative
20     } // end method setBaseSalary
21
22     // return base salary
23     public double getBaseSalary()
24     {
25        return baseSalary;
26     } // end method getBaseSalary
27
28     // calculate earnings; override method earnings in CommissionEmployee
29     public double earnings()
30     {
31        return getBaseSalary() + super.earnings();
32     } // end method earnings
33
34     // return String representation of BasePlusCommissionEmployee object
35     public String toString()
36     {
37        return String.format( "%s %s; %s: $%,.2f",
38           "base-salaried", super.toString(),
39           "base salary", getBaseSalary() );
40     } // end method toString
41  } // end class BasePlusCommissionEmployee
```

Fig. 10.8 | BasePlusCommissionEmployee class derived from CommissionEmployee.

sionEmployee also contains a *set* method (lines 17–20) to assign a new value to instance variable baseSalary and a *get* method (lines 23–26) to return baseSalary's value. Method earnings (lines 29–32) calculates a BasePlusCommissionEmployee's earnings. Note that line 31 in method earnings calls superclass CommissionEmployee's earnings method to calculate the commission-based portion of the employee's earnings. This is a nice example of code reuse. BasePlusCommissionEmployee's toString method (lines 35–40) creates a string representation of a BasePlusCommissionEmployee that contains "base-salaried", followed by the String obtained by invoking superclass CommissionEmployee's toString method (another example of code reuse), then the base salary. The result is a String beginning with "base-salaried commission employee" followed by the rest of the BasePlus-CommissionEmployee's information. Recall that CommissionEmployee's toString obtains the employee's first name, last name and social security number by invoking the toString method of its superclass (i.e., Employee)—yet another example of code reuse. Note that BasePlusCommissionEmployee's toString initiates a chain of method calls that span all three levels of the Employee hierarchy.

10.5.6 Demonstrating Polymorphic Processing, Operator instanceof and Downcasting

To test our Employee hierarchy, the application in Fig. 10.9 creates an object of each of the four concrete classes SalariedEmployee, HourlyEmployee, CommissionEmployee and BasePlusCommissionEmployee. The program manipulates these objects, first via variables of each object's own type, then polymorphically, using an array of Employee variables. While processing the objects polymorphically, the program increases the base salary of each BasePlusCommissionEmployee by 10% (this, of course, requires determining the object's type at execution time). Finally, the program polymorphically determines and outputs the type of each object in the Employee array. Lines 9–18 create objects of each of the four concrete Employee subclasses. Lines 22–30 output the string representation and earnings of each of these objects. Note that each object's toString method is called implicitly by printf when the object is output as a String with the %s format specifier.

Line 33 declares employees and assigns it an array of four Employee variables. Line 36 assigns to element employees[0] the reference to a SalariedEmployee object. Line 37 assigns to element employees[1] the reference to an HourlyEmployee object. Line 38 assigns to element employees[2] the reference to a CommissionEmployee object. Line 39 assigns to element employee[3] the reference to a BasePlusCommissionEmployee object.

```java
1   // Fig. 10.9: PayrollSystemTest.java
2   // Employee hierarchy test program.
3
4   public class PayrollSystemTest
5   {
6      public static void main( String args[] )
7      {
8         // create subclass objects
9         SalariedEmployee salariedEmployee =
10           new SalariedEmployee( "John", "Smith", "111-11-1111", 800.00 );
11        HourlyEmployee hourlyEmployee =
12           new HourlyEmployee( "Karen", "Price", "222-22-2222", 16.75, 40 );
13        CommissionEmployee commissionEmployee =
14           new CommissionEmployee(
15           "Sue", "Jones", "333-33-3333", 10000, .06 );
16        BasePlusCommissionEmployee basePlusCommissionEmployee =
17           new BasePlusCommissionEmployee(
18           "Bob", "Lewis", "444-44-4444", 5000, .04, 300 );
19
20        System.out.println( "Employees processed individually:\n" );
```

Fig. 10.9 | Employee class hierarchy test program. (Part 1 of 3.)

```
21
22        System.out.printf( "%s\n%s: $%,.2f\n\n",
23           salariedEmployee, "earned", salariedEmployee.earnings() );
24        System.out.printf( "%s\n%s: $%,.2f\n\n",
25           hourlyEmployee, "earned", hourlyEmployee.earnings() );
26        System.out.printf( "%s\n%s: $%,.2f\n\n",
27           commissionEmployee, "earned", commissionEmployee.earnings() );
28        System.out.printf( "%s\n%s: $%,.2f\n\n",
29           basePlusCommissionEmployee,
30           "earned", basePlusCommissionEmployee.earnings() );
31
32        // create four-element Employee array
33        Employee employees[] = new Employee[ 4 ];
34
35        // initialize array with Employees
36        employees[ 0 ] = salariedEmployee;
37        employees[ 1 ] = hourlyEmployee;
38        employees[ 2 ] = commissionEmployee;
39        employees[ 3 ] = basePlusCommissionEmployee;
40
41        System.out.println( "Employees processed polymorphically:\n" );
42
43        // generically process each element in array employees
44        for ( Employee currentEmployee : employees )
45        {
46           System.out.println( currentEmployee ); // invokes toString
47
48           // determine whether element is a BasePlusCommissionEmployee
49           if ( currentEmployee instanceof BasePlusCommissionEmployee )
50           {
51              // downcast Employee reference to
52              // BasePlusCommissionEmployee reference
53              BasePlusCommissionEmployee employee =
54                 ( BasePlusCommissionEmployee ) currentEmployee;
55
56              double oldBaseSalary = employee.getBaseSalary();
57              employee.setBaseSalary( 1.10 * oldBaseSalary );
58              System.out.printf(
59                 "new base salary with 10%% increase is: $%,.2f\n",
60                 employee.getBaseSalary() );
61           } // end if
62
63           System.out.printf(
64              "earned $%,.2f\n\n", currentEmployee.earnings() );
65        } // end for
66
67        // get type name of each object in employees array
68        for ( int j = 0; j < employees.length; j++ )
69           System.out.printf( "Employee %d is a %s\n", j,
70              employees[ j ].getClass().getName() );
71     } // end main
72  } // end class PayrollSystemTest
```

Fig. 10.9 | Employee class hierarchy test program. (Part 2 of 3.)

```
Employees processed individually:

salaried employee: John Smith
social security number: 111-11-1111
weekly salary: $800.00
earned: $800.00

hourly employee: Karen Price
social security number: 222-22-2222
hourly wage: $16.75; hours worked: 40.00
earned: $670.00

commission employee: Sue Jones
social security number: 333-33-3333
gross sales: $10,000.00; commission rate: 0.06
earned: $600.00

base-salaried commission employee: Bob Lewis
social security number: 444-44-4444
gross sales: $5,000.00; commission rate: 0.04; base salary: $300.00
earned: $500.00

Employees processed polymorphically:

salaried employee: John Smith
social security number: 111-11-1111
weekly salary: $800.00
earned $800.00

hourly employee: Karen Price
social security number: 222-22-2222
hourly wage: $16.75; hours worked: 40.00
earned $670.00

commission employee: Sue Jones
social security number: 333-33-3333
gross sales: $10,000.00; commission rate: 0.06
earned $600.00

base-salaried commission employee: Bob Lewis
social security number: 444-44-4444
gross sales: $5,000.00; commission rate: 0.04; base salary: $300.00
new base salary with 10% increase is: $330.00
earned $530.00

Employee 0 is a SalariedEmployee
Employee 1 is a HourlyEmployee
Employee 2 is a CommissionEmployee
Employee 3 is a BasePlusCommissionEmployee
```

Fig. 10.9 | Employee class hierarchy test program. (Part 3 of 3.)

Each assignment is allowed, because a SalariedEmployee *is an* Employee, an HourlyEmployee *is an* Employee, a CommissionEmployee *is an* Employee and a BasePlusCommissionEmployee *is an* Employee. Therefore, we can assign the references of SalariedEmployee,

`HourlyEmployee`, `CommissionEmployee` and `BasePlusCommissionEmployee` objects to superclass `Employee` variables, even though `Employee` is an abstract class.

Lines 44–65 iterate through array `employees` and invoke methods `toString` and `earnings` with `Employee` variable `currentEmployee`, which is assigned the reference to a different `Employee` in the array during each iteration. The output illustrates that the appropriate methods for each class are indeed invoked. All calls to method `toString` and `earnings` are resolved at execution time, based on the type of the object to which `currentEmployee` refers. This process is known as **dynamic binding** or **late binding**. For example, line 46 implicitly invokes method `toString` of the object to which `currentEmployee` refers. As a result of dynamic binding, Java decides which class's `toString` method to call at execution time rather than at compile time. Please note that only the methods of class `Employee` can be called via an `Employee` variable (and `Employee`, of course, includes the methods of class `Object`). (Section 9.7 discusses the set of methods that all classes inherit from class `Object`.) A superclass reference can be used to invoke only methods of the superclass.

We perform special processing on `BasePlusCommissionEmployee` objects—as we encounter these objects, we increase their base salary by 10%. When processing objects polymorphically, we typically do not need to worry about the "specifics," but to adjust the base salary, we do have to determine the specific type of `Employee` object at execution time. Line 49 uses the **instanceof** operator to determine whether a particular `Employee` object's type is `BasePlusCommissionEmployee`. The condition in line 49 is true if the object referenced by `currentEmployee` *is a* `BasePlusCommissionEmployee`. This would also be true for any object of a `BasePlusCommissionEmployee` subclass because of the *is-a* relationship a subclass has with its superclass. Lines 53–54 downcast `currentEmployee` from type `Employee` to type `BasePlusCommissionEmployee`—this cast is allowed only if the object has an *is-a* relationship with `BasePlusCommissionEmployee`. The condition at line 49 ensures that this is the case. This cast is required if we are to invoke subclass `BasePlusCommissionEmployee` methods `getBaseSalary` and `setBaseSalary` on the current `Employee` object—as you will see momentarily, attempting to invoke a subclass-only method directly on a superclass reference is a compilation error.

Common Programming Error 10.3
Assigning a superclass variable to a subclass variable (without an explicit cast) is a compilation error.

Software Engineering Observation 10.5
If at execution time the reference of a subclass object has been assigned to a variable of one of its direct or indirect superclasses, it is acceptable to cast the reference stored in that superclass variable back to a reference of the subclass type. Before performing such a cast, use the `instanceof` operator to ensure that the object is indeed an object of an appropriate subclass type.

Common Programming Error 10.4
When downcasting an object, a `ClassCastException` occurs, if at execution time the object does not have an is-a relationship with the type specified in the cast operator. An object can be cast only to its own type or to the type of one of its superclasses.

If the `instanceof` expression in line 49 is `true`, the `if` statement (lines 49–61) performs the special processing required for the `BasePlusCommissionEmployee` object. Using

BasePlusCommissionEmployee variable employee, lines 56 and 57 invoke subclass-only methods getBaseSalary and setBaseSalary to retrieve and update the employee's base salary with the 10% raise.

Lines 63–64 invoke method earnings on currentEmployee, which calls the appropriate subclass object's earnings method polymorphically. Note that obtaining the earnings of the SalariedEmployee, HourlyEmployee and CommissionEmployee polymorphically in lines 63–64 produces the same result as obtaining these employees' earnings individually in lines 22–27. However, the earnings amount obtained for the BasePlusCommissionEmployee in lines 63–64 is higher than that obtained in lines 28–30, due to the 10% increase in its base salary.

Lines 68–70 display each employee's type as a string. Every object in Java knows its own class and can access this information through method **getClass**, which all classes inherit from class Object. Method getClass returns an object of type **Class** (package java.lang), which contains information about the object's type, including its class name. Line 70 invokes method getClass on the object to get its runtime class (i.e., a Class object that represents the object's type). Then method **getName** is invoked on the object returned by getClass to get the class's name.

In the previous example, we avoid several compilation errors by downcasting an Employee variable to a BasePlusCommissionEmployee variable in lines 53–54. If we remove the cast operator (BasePlusCommissionEmployee) from line 54 and attempt to assign Employee variable currentEmployee directly to BasePlusCommissionEmployee variable employee, we would receive an "incompatible types" compilation error. This error indicates that the attempt to assign the reference of superclass object commissionEmployee to subclass variable basePlusCommissionEmployee is not allowed. The compiler prevents this assignment because a CommissionEmployee is not a BasePlusCommissionEmployee—the *is-a* relationship applies only between the subclass and its superclasses, not vice versa.

Similarly, if lines 56, 57 and 60 used superclass variable currentEmployee, rather than subclass variable employee, to invoke subclass-only methods getBaseSalary and setBaseSalary, we would receive a "cannot find symbol" compilation error on each of these lines. Attempting to invoke subclass-only methods on a superclass reference is not allowed. While lines 56, 57 and 60 execute only if instanceof in line 49 returns true to indicate that currentEmployee has been assigned a reference to a BasePlusCommission-Employee object, we cannot attempt to invoke subclass BasePlusCommissionEmployee methods getBaseSalary and setBaseSalary on superclass Employee reference current-Employee. The compiler would generate errors on lines 56, 57 and 60, because getBas-eSalary and setBaseSalary are not superclass methods and cannot be invoked on a superclass variable. Although the actual method that is called depends on the object's type at execution time, a variable can be used to invoke only those methods that are members of that variable's type, which the compiler verifies. Using a superclass Employee variable, we can invoke only methods found in class Employee—earnings, toString and Employee's *get* and *set* methods.

10.5.7 Summary of the Allowed Assignments Between Superclass and Subclass Variables

Now that you have seen a complete application that processes diverse subclass objects polymorphically, we summarize what you can and cannot do with superclass and subclass objects and variables. Although a subclass object also *is a* superclass object, the two objects are nevertheless different. As discussed previously, subclass objects can be treated as if they are superclass objects. However, the subclass can have additional subclass-only members. For this reason, assigning a superclass reference to a subclass variable is not allowed without an explicit cast—such an assignment would leave the subclass members undefined for the superclass object.

In the current section, in Section 10.3 and in Chapter 9, we have discussed four ways to assign superclass and subclass references to variables of superclass and subclass types:

1. Assigning a superclass reference to a superclass variable is straightforward.

2. Assigning a subclass reference to a subclass variable is straightforward.

3. Assigning a subclass reference to a superclass variable is safe, because the subclass object *is an* object of its superclass. However, this reference can be used to refer only to superclass members. If this code refers to subclass-only members through the superclass variable, the compiler reports errors.

4. Attempting to assign a superclass reference to a subclass variable is a compilation error. To avoid this error, the superclass reference must be cast to a subclass type explicitly. At execution time, if the object to which the reference refers is not a subclass object, an exception will occur. (For more on exception handling, see Chapter 13, Exception Handling.) The instanceof operator can be used to ensure that such a cast is performed only if the object is a subclass object.

10.6 final Methods and Classes

We saw in Section 6.10 that variables can be declared final to indicate that they cannot be modified after they are declared and that they must be initialized when they are declared—such variables represent constant values. It is also possible to declare methods and classes with the final modifier.

A method that is declared final in a superclass cannot be overridden in a subclass. Methods that are declared private are implicitly final, because it is impossible to override them in a subclass (though the subclass can declare a new method with the same signature as the private method in the superclass). Methods that are declared static are also implicitly final, because static methods cannot be overridden either. A final method's declaration can never change, so all subclasses use the same method implementation and calls to final methods are resolved at compile time—this is known as static binding. Since the compiler knows that final methods cannot be overridden, it can optimize programs by removing calls to final methods and replacing them with the expanded code of their declarations at each method call location—a technique known as inlining the code.

Performance Tip 10.1

The compiler can decide to inline a final method call and will do so for small, simple final methods. Inlining does not violate encapsulation or information hiding, but does improve performance because it eliminates the overhead of making a method call.

A class that is declared final cannot be a superclass (i.e., a class cannot extend a final class). All methods in a final class are implicitly final. Class String is an example of a final class. This class cannot be extended, so programs that use Strings can rely on the functionality of String objects as specified in the Java API. Making the class final also prevents programmers from creating subclasses that might bypass security restrictions. For more information on final classes and methods, visit java.sun.com/docs/books/tutorial/java/java00/final.html. This site contains additional insights into using final classes to improve the security of a system.

Common Programming Error 10.5

Attempting to declare a subclass of a final class is a compilation error.

Software Engineering Observation 10.6

In the Java API, the vast majority of classes are not declared final. This enables inheritance and polymorphism—the fundamental capabilities of object-oriented programming. However, in some cases, it is important to declare classes final—typically for security reasons.

10.7 Case Study: Creating and Using Interfaces

Our next example (Fig. 10.11–Fig. 10.13) reexamines the payroll system of Section 10.5. Suppose that the company involved wishes to perform several accounting operations in a single accounts payable application—in addition to calculating the earnings that must be paid to each employee, the company must also calculate the payment due on each of several invoices (i.e., bills for goods purchased). Though applied to unrelated things (i.e., employees and invoices), both operations have to do with obtaining some kind of payment amount. For an employee, the payment refers to the employee's earnings. For an invoice, the payment refers to the total cost of the goods listed on the invoice. Can we calculate such different things as the payments due for employees and invoices in a single application polymorphically? Does Java offer a capability that requires that unrelated classes implement a set of common methods (e.g., a method that calculates a payment amount)? Java interfaces offer exactly this capability.

Interfaces define and standardize the ways in which things such as people and systems can interact with one another. For example, the controls on a radio serve as an interface between radio users and a radio's internal components. The controls allow users to perform only a limited set of operations (e.g., changing the station, adjusting the volume, choosing between AM and FM), and different radios may implement the controls in different ways (e.g., using push buttons, dials, voice commands). The interface specifies *what* operations a radio must permit users to perform but does not specify *how* the operations are performed. Similarly, the interface between a driver and a car with a manual transmission includes the steering wheel, the gear shift, the clutch pedal, the gas pedal and the brake pedal. This same interface is found in nearly all manual transmission cars, enabling someone who knows how to drive one particular manual transmission car to drive just about any manual transmission car. The components of each individual car may look different, but the components' general purpose is the same—to allow people to drive the car.

Software objects also communicate via interfaces. A Java interface describes a set of methods that can be called on an object, to tell the object to perform some task or return some piece of information, for example. The next example introduces an interface named Payable to describe the functionality of any object that must be capable of being paid and thus must offer a method to determine the proper payment amount due. An **interface dec-**

laration begins with the keyword `interface` and contains only constants and `abstract` methods. Unlike classes, all interface members must be `public`, and interfaces may not specify any implementation details, such as concrete method declarations and instance variables. So all methods declared in an interface are implicitly `public abstract` methods and all fields are implicitly `public`, `static` and `final`.

Good Programming Practice 10.1

According to Chapter 9 of the Java Language Specification, *it is proper style to declare an interface's methods without keywords* `public` *and* `abstract` *because they are redundant in interface method declarations. Similarly, constants should be declared without keywords* `public`, `static` *and* `final` *because they, too, are redundant.*

To use an interface, a concrete class must specify that it `implements` the interface and must declare each method in the interface with the signature specified in the interface declaration. A class that does not implement all the methods of the interface is an abstract class and must be declared `abstract`. Implementing an interface is like signing a contract with the compiler that states, "I will declare all the methods specified by the interface or I will declare my class `abstract`."

Common Programming Error 10.6

Failing to implement any method of an interface in a concrete class that `implements` *the interface results in a syntax error indicating that the class must be declared* `abstract`.

An interface is typically used when disparate (i.e., unrelated) classes need to share common methods and constants. This allows objects of unrelated classes to be processed polymorphically—objects of classes that implement the same interface can respond to the same method calls. Programmers can create an interface that describes the desired functionality, then implement this interface in any classes that require that functionality. For example, in the accounts payable application developed in this section, we implement interface `Payable` in any class that must be able to calculate a payment amount (e.g., `Employee`, `Invoice`).

An interface is often used in place of an `abstract` class when there is no default implementation to inherit—that is, no fields and no default method implementations. Like `public abstract` classes, interfaces are typically `public` types, so they are normally declared in files by themselves with the same name as the interface and the `.java` file-name extension.

10.7.1 Developing a `Payable` Hierarchy

To build an application that can determine payments for employees and invoices alike, we first create interface `Payable` (Fig. 10.11). Interface `Payable` contains method `getPaymentAmount` that returns a `double` amount that must be paid for an object of any class that implements the interface. Method `getPaymentAmount` is a general purpose version of method `earnings` of the `Employee` hierarchy—method `earnings` calculates a payment amount specifically for an `Employee`, while `getPaymentAmount` can be applied to a broad range of unrelated objects. After declaring interface `Payable`, we introduce class `Invoice` (Fig. 10.12), which implements interface `Payable`. We then modify class `Employee` such that it also implements interface `Payable`. Finally, we update `Employee` subclass `SalariedEmployee` to "fit" into the `Payable` hierarchy (i.e., rename `SalariedEmployee` method `earnings` as `getPaymentAmount`).

Good Programming Practice 10.2

When declaring a method in an interface, choose a method name that describes the method's purpose in a general manner, because the method may be implemented by a broad range of unrelated classes.

Classes `Invoice` and `Employee` both represent things for which the company must be able to calculate a payment amount. Both classes implement `Payable`, so a program can invoke method `getPaymentAmount` on `Invoice` objects and `Employee` objects alike. As we will soon see, this enables the polymorphic processing of `Invoice`s and `Employee`s required for our company's accounts payable application.

The UML class diagram in Fig. 10.10 shows the hierarchy used in our accounts payable application. The hierarchy begins with interface `Payable`. The UML distinguishes an interface from other classes by placing the word "interface" in guillemets (« and ») above the interface name. The UML expresses the relationship between a class and an interface through a relationship known as a *realization*. A class is said to "realize," or implement, the methods of an interface. A class diagram models a realization as a dashed arrow with a hollow arrowhead pointing from the implementing class to the interface. The diagram in Fig. 10.10 indicates that classes `Invoice` and `Employee` each realize (i.e., implement) interface `Payable`. Note that, as in the class diagram of Fig. 10.2, class `Employee` appears in italics, indicating that it is an abstract class. Concrete class `SalariedEmployee` extends `Employee` and inherits its superclass's realization relationship with interface `Payable`.

10.7.2 Declaring Interface `Payable`

The declaration of interface `Payable` begins in Fig. 10.11 at line 4. Interface `Payable` contains `public abstract` method `getPaymentAmount` (line 6). Note that the method is not explicitly declared `public` or `abstract`. Interface methods must be `public` and `abstract`, so they do not need to be declared as such. Interface `Payable` has only one method—interfaces can have any number of methods. (We will see later in the book the notion of "tagging interfaces"—these actually have *no* methods. In fact, a tagging interface contains no constant values either—it simply contains an empty interface declaration.) In addition, method `getPaymentAmount` has no parameters, but interface methods can have parameters.

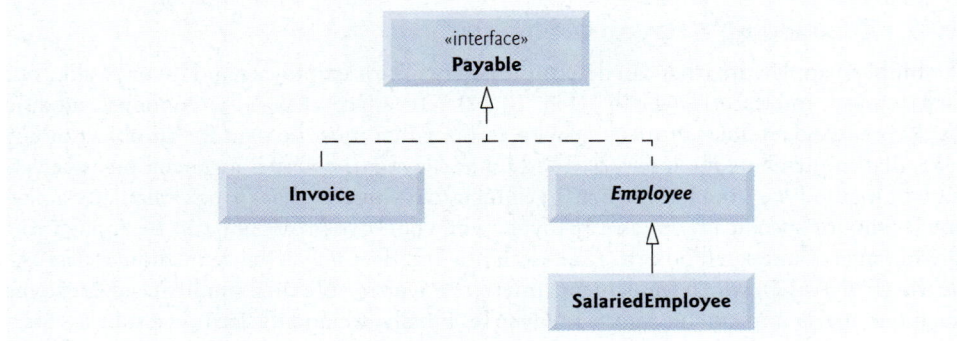

Fig. 10.10 | `Payable` interface hierarchy UML class diagram.

```
1   // Fig. 10.11: Payable.java
2   // Payable interface declaration.
3
4   public interface Payable
5   {
6      double getPaymentAmount(); // calculate payment; no implementation
7   } // end interface Payable
```

Fig. 10.11 | Payable interface declaration.

10.7.3 Creating Class Invoice

We now create class Invoice (Fig. 10.12) to represent a simple invoice that contains billing information for only one kind of part. The class declares private instance variables partNumber, partDescription, quantity and pricePerItem (in lines 6–9) that indicate the part number, a description of the part, the quantity of the part ordered and the price per item. Class Invoice also contains a constructor (lines 12–19), *get* and *set* methods (lines 22–67) that manipulate the class's instance variables and a toString method (lines

```
1   // Fig. 10.12: Invoice.java
2   // Invoice class implements Payable.
3
4   public class Invoice implements Payable
5   {
6      private String partNumber;
7      private String partDescription;
8      private int quantity;
9      private double pricePerItem;
10
11     // four-argument constructor
12     public Invoice( String part, String description, int count,
13        double price )
14     {
15        partNumber = part;
16        partDescription = description;
17        setQuantity( count ); // validate and store quantity
18        setPricePerItem( price ); // validate and store price per item
19     } // end four-argument Invoice constructor
20
21     // set part number
22     public void setPartNumber( String part )
23     {
24        partNumber = part;
25     } // end method setPartNumber
26
27     // get part number
28     public String getPartNumber()
29     {
30        return partNumber;
31     } // end method getPartNumber
```

Fig. 10.12 | Invoice class that implements Payable. (Part 1 of 2.)

```
32
33      // set description
34      public void setPartDescription( String description )
35      {
36          partDescription = description;
37      } // end method setPartDescription
38
39      // get description
40      public String getPartDescription()
41      {
42          return partDescription;
43      } // end method getPartDescription
44
45      // set quantity
46      public void setQuantity( int count )
47      {
48          quantity = ( count < 0 ) ? 0 : count; // quantity cannot be negative
49      } // end method setQuantity
50
51      // get quantity
52      public int getQuantity()
53      {
54          return quantity;
55      } // end method getQuantity
56
57      // set price per item
58      public void setPricePerItem( double price )
59      {
60          pricePerItem = ( price < 0.0 ) ? 0.0 : price; // validate price
61      } // end method setPricePerItem
62
63      // get price per item
64      public double getPricePerItem()
65      {
66          return pricePerItem;
67      } // end method getPricePerItem
68
69      // return String representation of Invoice object
70      public String toString()
71      {
72          return String.format( "%s: \n%s: %s (%s) \n%s: %d \n%s: $%,.2f",
73              "invoice", "part number", getPartNumber(), getPartDescription(),
74              "quantity", getQuantity(), "price per item", getPricePerItem() );
75      } // end method toString
76
77      // method required to carry out contract with interface Payable
78      public double getPaymentAmount()
79      {
80          return getQuantity() * getPricePerItem(); // calculate total cost
81      } // end method getPaymentAmount
82  } // end class Invoice
```

Fig. 10.12 | Invoice class that implements Payable. (Part 2 of 2.)

70–75) that returns a string representation of an `Invoice` object. Note that methods `set-Quantity` (lines 46–49) and `setPricePerItem` (lines 58–61) ensure that `quantity` and `pricePerItem` obtain only non-negative values.

Line 4 of Fig. 10.12 indicates that class `Invoice` implements interface `Payable`. Like all classes, class `Invoice` also implicitly extends `Object`. Java does not allow subclasses to inherit from more than one superclass, but it does allow a class to inherit from a superclass and implement more than one interface. In fact, a class can implement as many interfaces as it needs, in addition to extending another class. To implement more than one interface, use a comma-separated list of interface names after keyword `implements` in the class declaration, as in:

> `public class` *ClassName* `extends` *SuperclassName* `implements` *FirstInterface*,
>   *SecondInterface*, ...

All objects of a class that implement multiple interfaces have the *is-a* relationship with each implemented interface type.

Class `Invoice` implements the one method in interface `Payable`. Method `getPaymentAmount` is declared in lines 78–81. The method calculates the total payment required to pay the invoice. The method multiplies the values of `quantity` and `pricePerItem` (obtained through the appropriate *get* methods) and returns the result (line 80). This method satisfies the implementation requirement for this method in interface `Payable`—we have fulfilled the interface contract with the compiler.

10.7.4 Modifying Class `Employee` to Implement Interface `Payable`

We now modify class `Employee` such that it implements interface `Payable`. Figure 10.13 contains the modified `Employee` class. This class declaration is identical to that of Fig. 10.4 with only two exceptions. First, line 4 of Fig. 10.13 indicates that class `Employee` now implements interface `Payable`. Second, since `Employee` now implements interface `Payable`, we must rename `earnings` to `getPaymentAmount` throughout the `Employee` hierarchy. As with method `earnings` in the version of class `Employee` in Fig. 10.4, however, it does not

```
1   // Fig. 10.13: Employee.java
2   // Employee abstract superclass implements Payable.
3
4   public abstract class Employee implements Payable
5   {
6      private String firstName;
7      private String lastName;
8      private String socialSecurityNumber;
9
10     // three-argument constructor
11     public Employee( String first, String last, String ssn )
12     {
13        firstName = first;
14        lastName = last;
15        socialSecurityNumber = ssn;
16     } // end three-argument Employee constructor
17
```

Fig. 10.13 | `Employee` class that implements `Payable`. (Part 1 of 2.)

```
18      // set first name
19      public void setFirstName( String first )
20      {
21          firstName = first;
22      } // end method setFirstName
23
24      // return first name
25      public String getFirstName()
26      {
27          return firstName;
28      } // end method getFirstName
29
30      // set last name
31      public void setLastName( String last )
32      {
33          lastName = last;
34      } // end method setLastName
35
36      // return last name
37      public String getLastName()
38      {
39          return lastName;
40      } // end method getLastName
41
42      // set social security number
43      public void setSocialSecurityNumber( String ssn )
44      {
45          socialSecurityNumber = ssn; // should validate
46      } // end method setSocialSecurityNumber
47
48      // return social security number
49      public String getSocialSecurityNumber()
50      {
51          return socialSecurityNumber;
52      } // end method getSocialSecurityNumber
53
54      // return String representation of Employee object
55      public String toString()
56      {
57          return String.format( "%s %s\nsocial security number: %s",
58              getFirstName(), getLastName(), getSocialSecurityNumber() );
59      } // end method toString
60
61      // Note: We do not implement Payable method getPaymentAmount here so
62      // this class must be declared abstract to avoid a compilation error.
63  } // end abstract class Employee
```

Fig. 10.13 | `Employee` class that implements `Payable`. (Part 2 of 2.)

make sense to implement method getPaymentAmount in class Employee because we cannot calculate the earnings payment owed to a general Employee—first we must know the specific type of Employee. In Fig. 10.4, we declared method earnings as abstract for this reason, and as a result class Employee had to be declared abstract. This forced each Employee subclass to override earnings with a concrete implementation.

In Fig. 10.13, we handle this situation differently. Recall that when a class implements an interface, the class makes a contract with the compiler stating either that the class will implement each of the methods in the interface or that the class will be declared `abstract`. If the latter option is chosen, we do not need to declare the interface methods as `abstract` in the abstract class—they are already implicitly declared as such in the interface. Any concrete subclass of the abstract class must implement the interface methods to fulfill the superclass's contract with the compiler. If the subclass does not do so, it too must be declared `abstract`. As indicated by the comments in lines 61–62, class `Employee` of Fig. 10.13 does not implement method `getPaymentAmount`, so the class is declared `abstract`. Each direct `Employee` subclass inherits the superclass's contract to implement method `getPaymentAmount` and thus must implement this method to become a concrete class for which objects can be instantiated. A class that extends one of `Employee`'s concrete subclasses will inherit an implementation of `getPaymentAmount` and thus will also be a concrete class.

10.7.5 Modifying Class `SalariedEmployee` for Use in the `Payable` Hierarchy

Figure 10.14 contains a modified version of class `SalariedEmployee` that extends `Employee` and fulfills superclass `Employee`'s contract to implement method `getPaymentAmount` of interface `Payable`. This version of `SalariedEmployee` is identical to that of Fig. 10.5 with the exception that the version here implements method `getPaymentAmount` (lines 30–33) instead of method `earnings`. The two methods contain the same functionality but have different names. Recall that the `Payable` version of the method has a more general name to be applicable to possibly disparate classes. The remaining `Employee` subclasses (e.g., `HourlyEmployee`, `CommissionEmployee` and `BasePlusCommissionEmployee`) also must be modified to contain method `getPaymentAmount` in place of `earnings` to reflect the fact that `Employee` now implements `Payable`. We leave these modifications as an exercise and use only `SalariedEmployee` in our test program in this section.

When a class implements an interface, the same *is-a* relationship provided by inheritance applies. For example, class `Employee` implements `Payable`, so we can say that an `Employee` *is a* `Payable`. In fact, objects of any classes that extend `Employee` are also `Payable` objects. `SalariedEmployee` objects, for instance, are `Payable` objects. As with inheritance relationships, an object of a class that implements an interface may be thought of as an object of the interface class. Objects of any subclasses of the class that implements the interface can also be thought of as objects of the interface class. Thus, just as we can assign the reference of a `SalariedEmployee` object to a superclass `Employee` variable, we can assign the reference of a `SalariedEmployee` object to an interface `Payable` variable. `Invoice` implements `Payable`, so an `Invoice` object also *is a* `Payable` object, and we can assign the reference of an `Invoice` object to a `Payable` variable.

Software Engineering Observation 10.7

Inheritance and interfaces are similar in their implementation of the "is-a" relationship. An object of a class that implements an interface may be thought of as an object of that interface type. An object of any subclasses of a class that implements an interface also can be thought of as an object of the interface type.

```
 1   // Fig. 10.14: SalariedEmployee.java
 2   // SalariedEmployee class extends Employee, which implements Payable.
 3
 4   public class SalariedEmployee extends Employee
 5   {
 6      private double weeklySalary;
 7
 8      // four-argument constructor
 9      public SalariedEmployee( String first, String last, String ssn,
10         double salary )
11      {
12         super( first, last, ssn ); // pass to Employee constructor
13         setWeeklySalary( salary ); // validate and store salary
14      } // end four-argument SalariedEmployee constructor
15
16      // set salary
17      public void setWeeklySalary( double salary )
18      {
19         weeklySalary = salary < 0.0 ? 0.0 : salary;
20      } // end method setWeeklySalary
21
22      // return salary
23      public double getWeeklySalary()
24      {
25         return weeklySalary;
26      } // end method getWeeklySalary
27
28      // calculate earnings; implement interface Payable method that was
29      // abstract in superclass Employee
30      public double getPaymentAmount()
31      {
32         return getWeeklySalary();
33      } // end method getPaymentAmount
34
35      // return String representation of SalariedEmployee object
36      public String toString()
37      {
38         return String.format( "salaried employee: %s\n%s: $%,.2f",
39            super.toString(), "weekly salary", getWeeklySalary() );
40      } // end method toString
41   } // end class SalariedEmployee
```

Fig. 10.14 | `SalariedEmployee` class that implements interface `Payable` method `getPaymentAmount`.

Software Engineering Observation 10.8

The "is-a" relationship that exists between superclasses and subclasses, and between interfaces and the classes that implement them, holds when passing an object to a method. When a method parameter receives a variable of a superclass or interface type, the method processes the object received as an argument polymorphically.

Software Engineering Observation 10.9

Using a superclass reference, we can polymorphically invoke any method specified in the superclass declaration (and in class Object). Using an interface reference, we can polymorphically invoke any method specified in the interface declaration (and in class Object).

10.7.6 Using Interface Payable to Process Invoices and Employees Polymorphically

PayableInterfaceTest (Fig. 10.15) illustrates that interface Payable can be used to process a set of Invoices and Employees polymorphically in a single application. Line 9 declares payableObjects and assigns it an array of four Payable variables. Lines 12–13 assign the references of Invoice objects to the first two elements of payableObjects. Lines 14–17 then assign the references of SalariedEmployee objects to the remaining two elements of payableObjects. These assignments are allowed because an Invoice *is a* Payable, a SalariedEmployee *is an* Employee and an Employee *is a* Payable. Lines 23–29 use the enhanced for statement to polymorphically process each Payable object in payableObjects, printing

```
1   // Fig. 10.15: PayableInterfaceTest.java
2   // Tests interface Payable.
3
4   public class PayableInterfaceTest
5   {
6      public static void main( String args[] )
7      {
8         // create four-element Payable array
9         Payable payableObjects[] = new Payable[ 4 ];
10
11        // populate array with objects that implement Payable
12        payableObjects[ 0 ] = new Invoice( "01234", "seat", 2, 375.00 );
13        payableObjects[ 1 ] = new Invoice( "56789", "tire", 4, 79.95 );
14        payableObjects[ 2 ] =
15           new SalariedEmployee( "John", "Smith", "111-11-1111", 800.00 );
16        payableObjects[ 3 ] =
17           new SalariedEmployee( "Lisa", "Barnes", "888-88-8888", 1200.00 );
18
19        System.out.println(
20           "Invoices and Employees processed polymorphically:\n" );
21
22        // generically process each element in array payableObjects
23        for ( Payable currentPayable : payableObjects )
24        {
25           // output currentPayable and its appropriate payment amount
26           System.out.printf( "%s \n%s: $%,.2f\n\n",
27              currentPayable.toString(),
28              "payment due", currentPayable.getPaymentAmount() );
29        } // end for
30     } // end main
31  } // end class PayableInterfaceTest
```

Fig. 10.15 | Payable interface test program processing Invoices and Employees polymorphically. (Part 1 of 2.)

```
Invoices and Employees processed polymorphically:

invoice:
part number: 01234 (seat)
quantity: 2
price per item: $375.00
payment due: $750.00

invoice:
part number: 56789 (tire)
quantity: 4
price per item: $79.95
payment due: $319.80

salaried employee: John Smith
social security number: 111-11-1111
weekly salary: $800.00
payment due: $800.00

salaried employee: Lisa Barnes
social security number: 888-88-8888
weekly salary: $1,200.00
payment due: $1,200.00
```

Fig. 10.15 | Payable interface test program processing `Invoices` and `Employees` polymorphically. (Part 2 of 2.)

the object as a `String`, along with the payment amount due. Note that line 27 invokes method `toString` off a `Payable` interface reference, even though `toString` is not declared in interface `Payable`—all references (including those of interface types) refer to objects that extend `Object` and therefore have a `toString` method. Line 28 invokes `Payable` method `getPaymentAmount` to obtain the payment amount for each object in `payableObjects`, regardless of the actual type of the object. The output reveals that the method calls in lines 27–28 invoke the appropriate class's implementation of methods `toString` and `getPayment-Amount`. For instance, when `currentEmployee` refers to an `Invoice` during the first iteration of the `for` loop, class `Invoice`'s `toString` and `getPaymentAmount` execute.

Software Engineering Observation 10.10

All methods of class `Object` can be called by using a reference of an interface type. A reference refers to an object, and all objects inherit the methods of class `Object`.

10.7.7 Declaring Constants with Interfaces

As we mentioned in Section 10.7, an interface can declare constants. The constants are implicitly `public`, `static` and `final`—again, these keywords are not required in the interface declaration. One popular use of an interface is to declare a set of constants that can be used in many class declarations. Consider interface `Constants`:

```
public interface Constants
{
   int ONE = 1;
   int TWO = 2;
   int THREE = 3;
}
```

A class can use these constants by importing the interface, then referring to each constant as `Constants.ONE`, `Constants.TWO` and `Constants.THREE`. Note that a class can refer to the imported constants with just their names (i.e., `ONE`, `TWO` and `THREE`) if it uses a `static import` declaration (presented in Section 8.12) to import the interface.

Software Engineering Observation 10.11

As of J2SE 5.0, it is considered a better programming practice to create sets of constants as enumerations with keyword enum. *See Section 6.10 for an introduction to* enum *and Section 8.9 for additional* enum *details.*

10.7.8 Common Interfaces of the Java API

In this section, we overview several common interfaces found in the Java API. The power and flexibility of interfaces is used frequently throughout the Java API. These interfaces are implemented and used in the same manner as the interfaces you create (e.g., interface `Payable` in Section 10.7.2). As you will see throughout this book, the Java API's interfaces enable you to extend many important aspects of Java with your own classes. Figure 10.16 presents a brief overview of a few of the more popular interfaces of the Java API that we use in *Java How to Program, Sixth Edition.*

Interface	Description
`Comparable`	As you learned in Chapter 2, Java contains several comparison operators (e.g., `<`, `<=`, `>`, `>=`, `==`, `!=`) that allow you to compare primitive values. However, these operators cannot be used to compare the contents of objects. Interface `Comparable` is used to allow objects of a class that implements the interface to be compared to one another. The interface contains one method, `compareTo`, that compares the object that calls the method to the object passed as an argument to the method. Classes must implement `compareTo` such that it returns a value indicating whether the object on which it is invoked is less than (negative integer return value), equal to (0 return value) or greater than (positive integer return value) the object passed as an argument, using any criteria specified by the programmer. For example, if class `Employee` implements `Comparable`, its `compareTo` method could compare `Employee` objects by their earnings amounts. Interface `Comparable` is commonly used for ordering objects in a collection such as an array. We use `Comparable` in Chapter 18, Generics, and Chapter 19, Collections.
`Serializable`	A tagging interface used only to identify classes whose objects can be written to (i.e., serialized) or read from (i.e., deserialized) some type of storage (e.g., file on disk, database field) or transmitted across a network. We use `Serializable` in Chapter 14, Files and Streams, and Chapter 24, Networking.

Fig. 10.16 | Common interfaces of the Java API. (Part 1 of 2.)

Interface	Description
Runnable	Implemented by any class for which objects of that class should be able to execute in parallel using a technique called multi-threading (discussed in Chapter 23, Multithreading). The interface contains one method, run, which describes the behavior of an object when executed.
GUI event-listener interfaces	You work with Graphical User Interfaces (GUIs) every day. For example, in your Web browser, you might type in a text field the address of a Web site to visit, or you might click a button to return to the previous site you visited. When you type a Web site address or click a button in the Web browser, the browser must respond to your interaction and perform the desired task for you. Your interaction is known as an event, and the code that the browser uses to respond to an event is known as an event handler. In Chapter 11, GUI Components: Part 1, and Chapter 22, GUI Components: Part 2, you will learn how to build Java GUIs and how to build event handlers to respond to user interactions. The event handlers are declared in classes that implement an appropriate event-listener interface. Each event listener interface specifies one or more methods that must be implemented to respond to user interactions.
SwingConstants	Contains a set of constants used in GUI programming to position GUI elements on the screen. We explore GUI programming in Chapters 11 and 22.

Fig. 10.16 | Common interfaces of the Java API. (Part 2 of 2.)

10.8 (Optional) GUI and Graphics Case Study: Drawing with Polymorphism

You may have noticed in the drawing program created in Exercise 8.1 (and modified in Exercise 9.1) that there are many similarities between the shape classes. Using inheritance, we can "factor out" the common features from all three classes and place them in a single shape superclass. We can then manipulate objects of all three shape types polymorphically using variables of the superclass type. Removing the redundancy in the code will result in a smaller, more flexible program that is easier to maintain.

GUI and Graphics Case Study Exercises

10.1   Modify the MyLine, MyOval and MyRectangle classes of Exercise 8.1 and Exercise 9.1 to create the class hierarchy in Fig. 10.17. Classes of the MyShape hierarchy should be "smart" shape classes that know how to draw themselves (if provided with a Graphics object that tells them where to draw). Once the program creates an object from this hierarchy, it can manipulate it polymorphically for the rest of its lifetime as a MyShape.

In your solution, class MyShape in Fig. 10.17 *must* be abstract. Since MyShape represents any shape in general, you cannot implement a draw method without knowing exactly what shape it is. The data representing the coordinates and color of the shapes in the hierarchy should be declared

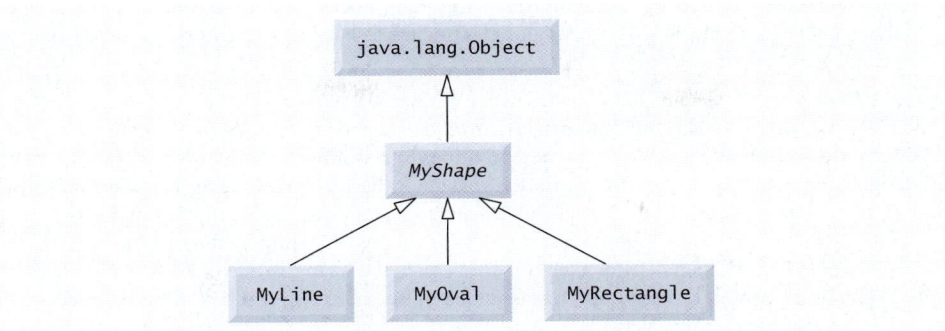

Fig. 10.17 | MyShape hierarchy.

as private members of class MyShape. In addition to the common data, class MyShape should declare the following methods:

a) A no-argument constructor that sets all the coordinates of the shape to 0 and the color to Color.BLACK.

b) A constructor that initializes the coordinates and color to the values of the arguments supplied.

c) *Set* methods for the individual coordinates and color that allow the programmer to set any piece of data independently for a shape in the hierarchy.

d) *Get* methods for the individual coordinates and color that allow the programmer to retrieve any piece of data independently for a shape in the hierarchy.

e) The abstract method

```
public abstract void draw( Graphics g );
```

which will be called from the program's paintComponent method to draw a shape on the screen.

To ensure proper encapsulation, all data in class MyShape must be private. This requires declaring proper *set* and *get* methods to manipulate the data. Class MyLine should provide a no-argument constructor and a constructor with arguments for the coordinates and color. Classes MyOval and MyRect should provide a no-argument constructor and a constructor with arguments for the coordinates, color and determining whether the shape is filled. The no-argument constructor should, in addition to setting the default values, set the shape to be an unfilled shape.

You can draw lines, rectangles and ovals if you know two points in space. Lines require *x1*, *y1*, *x2* and *y2* coordinates. The drawLine method of the Graphics class will connect the two points supplied with a line. If you have the same four coordinate values (*x1*, *y1*, *x2* and *y2*) for ovals and rectangles, you can calculate the four arguments needed to draw them. Each requires an upper-left *x*-coordinate value (the smaller of the two *x*-coordinate values), an upper-left *y*-coordinate value (the smaller of the two *y* coordinate values), a *width* (the absolute value of the difference between the two *x*-coordinate values) and a *height* (the absolute value of the difference between the two *y*-coordinate values). Rectangles and ovals should also have a filled flag that determines whether to draw the shape as a filled shape.

There should be no MyLine, MyOval or MyRectangle variables in the program—only MyShape variables that contain references to MyLine, MyOval and MyRectangle objects. The program should generate random shapes and store them in an array of type MyShape. Method paintComponent should walk through the MyShape array and draw every shape (i.e., polymorphically calling every shape's draw method).

Allow the user to specify (via an input dialog) the number of shapes to generate. The program will then generate and display the shapes along with a status bar that informs the user how many of each shape were created.

10.2 *(Drawing Application Modification)* In Exercise 10.1, you created a MyShape hierarchy in which classes MyLine, MyOval and MyRectangle extend MyShape directly. If your hierarchy was properly designed, you should be able to see the similarities between the MyOval and MyRectangle classes. Redesign and reimplement the code for the MyOval and MyRectangle classes to "factor out" the common features into the abstract class MyBoundedShape to produce the hierarchy in Fig. 10.18.

Class MyBoundedShape should declare two constructors that mimic the constructors of class MyShape, only with an added parameter to set whether the shape is filled. Class MyBoundedShape should also declare *get* and *set* methods for manipulating the filled flag and methods that calculate the upper-left *x*-coordinate, upper-left *y*-coordinate, width and height. Remember, the values needed to draw an oval or a rectangle can be calculated from two *(x, y)* coordinates. If designed properly, the new MyOval and MyRectangle classes should each have two constructors and a draw method.

10.9 (Optional) Software Engineering Case Study: Incorporating Inheritance into the ATM System

We now revisit our ATM system design to see how it might benefit from inheritance. To apply inheritance, we first look for commonality among classes in the system. We create an inheritance hierarchy to model similar (yet not identical) classes in a more elegant and efficient manner. We then modify our class diagram to incorporate the new inheritance relationships. Finally, we demonstrate how our updated design is translated into Java code.

In Section 3.10, we encountered the problem of representing a financial transaction in the system. Rather than create one class to represent all transaction types, we decided to create three individual transaction classes—BalanceInquiry, Withdrawal and Deposit—to represent the transactions that the ATM system can perform. Figure 10.19 shows the attributes and operations of classes BalanceInquiry, Withdrawal and Deposit. Note that these classes have one attribute (accountNumber) and one operation (execute) in common. Each class requires attribute accountNumber to specify the account to which the

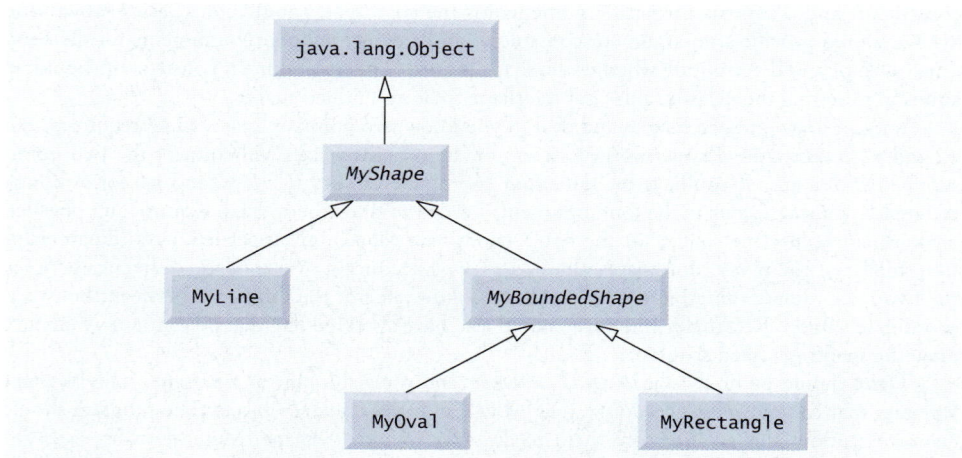

Fig. 10.18 | MyShape hierarchy with MyBoundedShape.

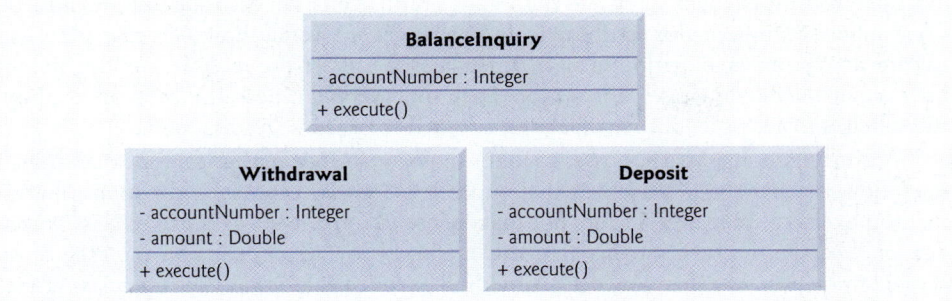

Fig. 10.19 | Attributes and operations of classes `BalanceInquiry`, `Withdrawal` and `Deposit`.

transaction applies. Each class contains operation `execute`, which the ATM invokes to perform a transaction. Clearly, `BalanceInquiry`, `Withdrawal` and `Deposit` represent *types of* transactions. Figure 10.19 reveals commonality among the transaction classes, so using inheritance to factor out the common features seems appropriate for designing classes `BalanceInquiry`, `Withdrawal` and `Deposit`. We place the common functionality in a superclass, `Transaction`, that classes `BalanceInquiry`, `Withdrawal` and `Deposit` extend.

The UML specifies a relationship called a **generalization** to model inheritance. Figure 10.20 is the class diagram that models the generalization of superclass `Transaction` and subclasses `BalanceInquiry`, `Withdrawal` and `Deposit`. The arrows with triangular hollow arrowheads indicate that classes `BalanceInquiry`, `Withdrawal` and `Deposit` extend class `Transaction`. Class `Transaction` is said to be a generalization of classes `BalanceInquiry`, `Withdrawal` and `Deposit`. Class `BalanceInquiry`, `Withdrawal` and `Deposit` are said to be **specializations** of class `Transaction`.

Classes `BalanceInquiry`, `Withdrawal` and `Deposit` share integer attribute `accountNumber`, so we factor out this common attribute and place it in superclass `Transaction`.

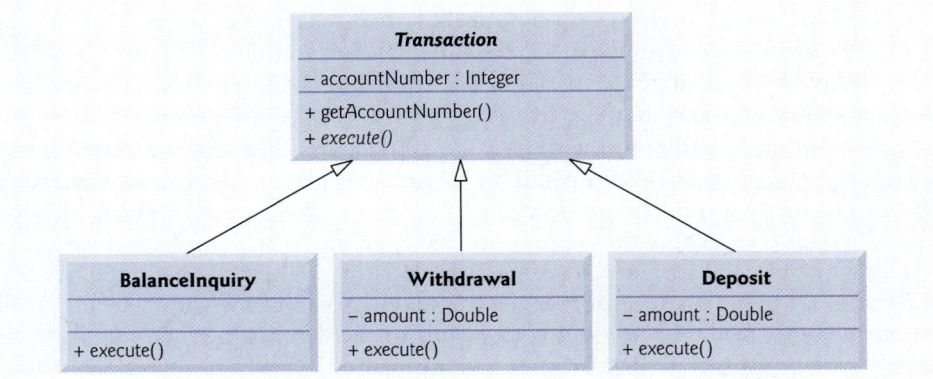

Fig. 10.20 | Class diagram modeling generalization of superclass `Transaction` and subclasses `BalanceInquiry`, `Withdrawal` and `Deposit`. Note that abstract class names (e.g., `Transaction`) and method names (e.g., `execute` in class `Transaction`) appear in italics.

We no longer list `accountNumber` in the second compartment of each subclass, because the three subclasses inherit this attribute from `Transaction`. Recall, however, that subclasses cannot access `private` attributes of a superclass. We therefore include `public` method `getAccountNumber` in class `Transaction`. Each subclass will inherit this method, enabling the subclass to access its `accountNumber` as needed to execute a transaction.

According to Fig. 10.19, classes `BalanceInquiry`, `Withdrawal` and `Deposit` also share operation `execute`, so we decided that superclass `Transaction` should contain `public` method `execute`. However, it does not make sense to implement `execute` in class `Transaction`, because the functionality that this method provides depends on the type of the actual transaction. We therefore declare method `execute` as `abstract` in superclass `Transaction`. Any class that contains at least one abstract method must also be declared `abstract`. This forces any subclass of `Transaction` that must be a concrete class (i.e., `BalanceInquiry`, `Withdrawal` and `Deposit`) to implement method `execute`. The UML requires that we place abstract class names (and abstract methods) in italics, so `Transaction` and its method `execute` appear in italics in Fig. 10.20. Note that method `execute` is not italicized in subclasses `BalanceInquiry`, `Withdrawal` and `Deposit`. Each subclass overrides superclass `Transaction`'s `execute` method with a concrete implementation that performs the steps appropriate for completing that type of transaction. Note that Fig. 10.20 includes operation `execute` in the third compartment of classes `BalanceInquiry`, `Withdrawal` and `Deposit`, because each class has a different concrete implementation of the overridden method.

Incorporating inheritance provides the ATM with an elegant way to execute all transactions "in the general." For example, suppose a user chooses to perform a balance inquiry. The ATM sets a `Transaction` reference to a new object of class `BalanceInquiry`. When the ATM uses its `Transaction` reference to invoke method `execute`, `BalanceInquiry`'s version of `execute` is called.

This polymorphic approach also makes the system easily extensible. Should we wish to create a new transaction type (e.g., funds transfer or bill payment), we would just create an additional `Transaction` subclass that overrides the `execute` method with a version of the method appropriate for executing the new transaction type. We would need to make only minimal changes to the system code to allow users to choose the new transaction type from the main menu and for the ATM to instantiate and execute objects of the new subclass. The ATM could execute transactions of the new type using the current code, because it executes all transactions polymorphically using a general `Transaction` reference.

As you learned earlier in the chapter, an abstract class like `Transaction` is one for which the programmer never intends to instantiate objects. An abstract class simply declares common attributes and behaviors of its subclasses in an inheritance hierarchy. Class `Transaction` defines the concept of what it means to be a transaction that has an account number and executes. You may wonder why we bother to include `abstract` method `execute` in class `Transaction` if it lacks a concrete implementation. Conceptually, we include this method because it corresponds to the defining behavior of all transactions—executing. Technically, we must include method `execute` in superclass `Transaction` so that the ATM (or any other class) can polymorphically invoke each subclass's overridden version of this method through a `Transaction` reference. Also, from a software engineering perspective, including an abstract method in a superclass forces the implementor of the subclasses to override that method with concrete implementations in the subclasses, or else the subclasses, too, will be abstract, preventing objects of those subclasses from being instantiated.

Subclasses BalanceInquiry, Withdrawal and Deposit inherit attribute accountNumber from superclass Transaction, but classes Withdrawal and Deposit contain the additional attribute amount that distinguishes them from class BalanceInquiry. Classes Withdrawal and Deposit require this additional attribute to store the amount of money that the user wishes to withdraw or deposit. Class BalanceInquiry has no need for such an attribute and requires only an account number to execute. Even though two of the three Transaction subclasses share this attribute, we do not place it in superclass Transaction—we place only features common to all the subclasses in the superclass, otherwise subclasses could inherit attributes (and methods) that they do not need and should not have.

Figure 10.21 presents an updated class diagram of our model that incorporates inheritance and introduces class Transaction. We model an association between class ATM and class Transaction to show that the ATM, at any given moment, is either executing a transaction or it is not (i.e., zero or one objects of type Transaction exist in the system at a time). Because a Withdrawal is a type of Transaction, we no longer draw an association line directly between class ATM and class Withdrawal. Subclass Withdrawal inherits superclass Transaction's association with class ATM. Subclasses BalanceInquiry and Deposit

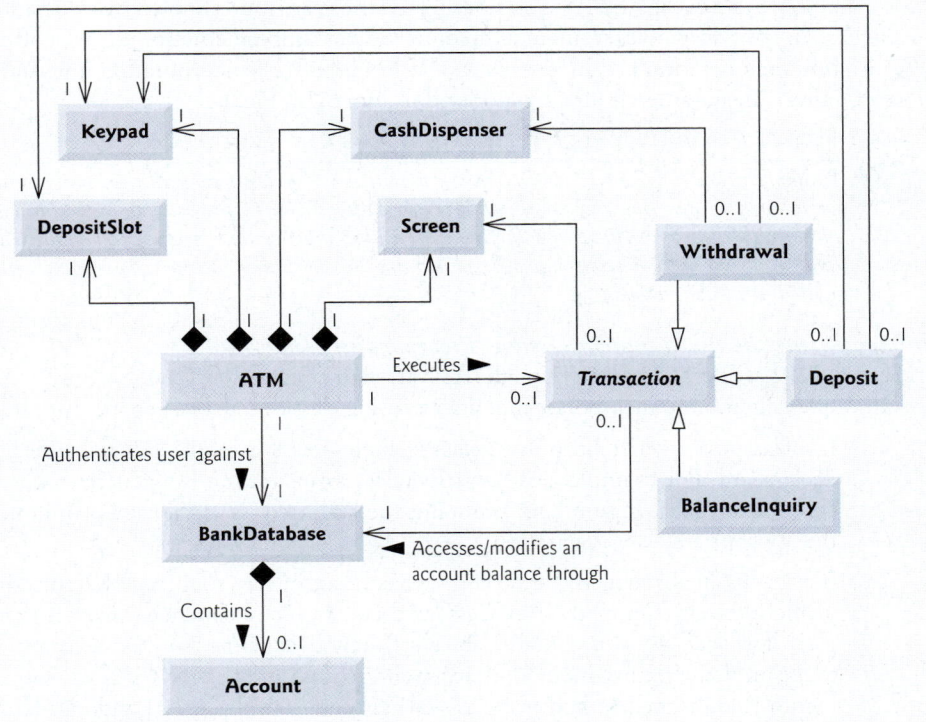

Fig. 10.21 | Class diagram of the ATM system (incorporating inheritance). Note that abstract class names (e.g., Transaction) appear in italics.

inherit this association, too, so the previously omitted associations between ATM and classes BalanceInquiry and Deposit no longer exist either.

We also add an association between class Transaction and the BankDatabase (Fig. 10.21). All Transactions require a reference to the BankDatabase so they can access and modify account information. Because each Transaction subclass inherits this reference, we no longer model the association between class Withdrawal and the BankDatabase. Similarly, the previously omitted associations between the BankDatabase and classes BalanceInquiry and Deposit no longer exist.

We show an association between class Transaction and the Screen. All Transactions display output to the user via the Screen. Thus, we no longer include the association previously modeled between Withdrawal and the Screen, although Withdrawal still participates in associations with the CashDispenser and the Keypad. Our class diagram incorporating inheritance also models Deposit and BalanceInquiry. We show associations between Deposit and both the DepositSlot and the Keypad. Note that class BalanceInquiry takes part in no associations other than those inherited from class Transaction—a BalanceInquiry needs to interact only with the BankDatabase and with the Screen.

The class diagram of Fig. 8.24 showed attributes and operations with visibility markers. Now we present a modified class diagram that incorporates inheritance in Fig. 10.22. This abbreviated diagram does not show inheritance relationships, but instead shows the attributes and methods after we have employed inheritance in our system. To save space, as we did in Fig. 4.24, we do not include those attributes shown by associations in Fig. 10.21—we do, however, include them in the Java implementation in Appendix J. We also omit all operation parameters, as we did in Fig. 8.24—incorporating inheritance does not affect the parameters already modeled in Fig. 6.22–Fig. 6.25.

Software Engineering Observation 10.12

A complete class diagram shows all the associations among classes and all the attributes and operations for each class. When the number of class attributes, methods and associations is substantial (as in Fig. 10.21 and Fig. 10.22), a good practice that promotes readability is to divide this information between two class diagrams—one focusing on associations and the other on attributes and methods.

Implementing the ATM System Design (Incorporating Inheritance)

In Section 8.19, we began implementing the ATM system design in Java code. We now modify our implementation to incorporate inheritance, using class Withdrawal as an example.

1. If a class A is a generalization of class B, then class B extends class A in the class declaration. For example, abstract superclass Transaction is a generalization of class Withdrawal. Figure 10.23 contains the shell of class Withdrawal containing the appropriate class declaration.

2. If class A is an abstract class and class B is a subclass of class A, then class B must implement the abstract methods of class A if class B is to be a concrete class. For example, class Transaction contains abstract method execute, so class Withdrawal must implement this method if we want to instantiate a Withdrawal object. Figure 10.24 is the Java code for class Withdrawal from Fig. 10.21 and Fig. 10.22. Class Withdrawal inherits field accountNumber from superclass Transaction, so Withdrawal does not need to declare this field. Class Withdrawal also inherits references to the Screen and the BankDatabase from its superclass Transaction, so

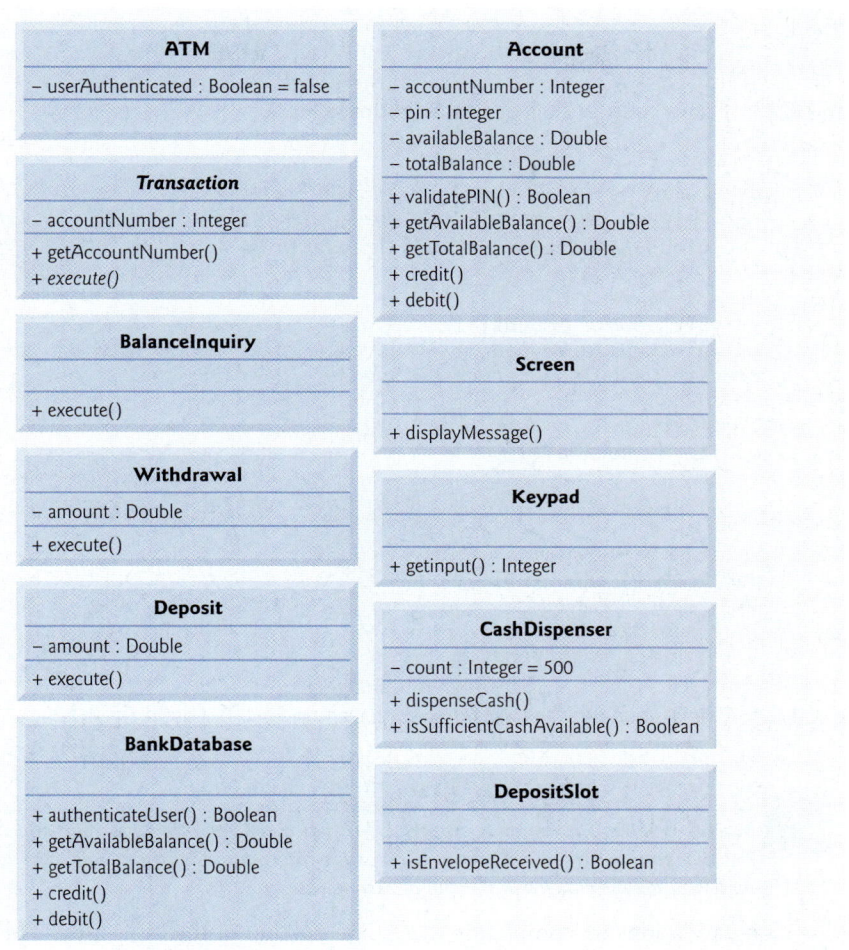

Fig. 10.22 | Class diagram with attributes and operations (incorporating inheritance). Note that abstract class names (e.g., `Transaction`) and method names (e.g., `execute` in class `Transaction`) appear in italics.

we do not include these references in our code. Figure 10.22 specifies attribute `amount` and operation `execute` for class `Withdrawal`. Line 6 of Fig. 10.24 declares a field for attribute `amount`. Lines 16–18 declare the shell of a method for operation `execute`. Recall that subclass `Withdrawal` must provide a concrete implementation of the abstract method `execute` in superclass `Transaction`. The keypad and cashDispenser references (lines 7–8) are fields derived from `Withdrawal`'s associations in Fig. 10.21. [*Note:* The constructor in the complete working version of this class will initialize these references to actual objects.]

```
1    // Class Withdrawal represents an ATM withdrawal transaction
2    public class Withdrawal extends Transaction
3    {
4    } // end class Withdrawal
```

Fig. 10.23 | Java code for shell of class `Withdrawal`.

```
1    // Withdrawal.java
2    // Generated using the class diagrams in Fig. 10.21 and Fig. 10.22
3    public class Withdrawal extends Transaction
4    {
5       // attributes
6       private double amount; // amount to withdraw
7       private Keypad keypad; // reference to keypad
8       private CashDispenser cashDispenser; // reference to cash dispenser
9
10      // no-argument constructor
11      public Withdrawal()
12      {
13      } // end no-argument Withdrawal constructor
14
15      // method overriding execute
16      public void execute()
17      {
18      } // end method execute
19   } // end class Withdrawal
```

Fig. 10.24 | Java code for class `Withdrawal` based on Fig. 10.21 and Fig. 10.22.

Software Engineering Observation 10.13

Several UML modeling tools convert UML-based designs into Java code and can speed the implementation process considerably. For more information on these tools, refer to the Internet and Web Resources listed at the end of Section 2.9.

Congratulations on completing the design portion of the case study! This concludes our object-oriented design of the ATM system. We completely implement the ATM system in 670 lines of Java code in Appendix J. We recommend that you carefully read the code and its description. The code is abundantly commented and precisely follows the design with which you are now familiar. The accompanying description is carefully written to guide your understanding of the implementation based on the UML design. Mastering this code is a wonderful culminating accomplishment after studying Chapters 1–8.

Software Engineering Case Study Self-Review Exercises

10.1   The UML uses an arrow with a _____ to indicate a generalization relationship.
  a) solid filled arrowhead
  b) triangular hollow arrowhead
  c) diamond-shaped hollow arrowhead
  d) stick arrowhead

10.2   State whether the following statement is *true* or *false*, and if *false*, explain why: The UML requires that we underline abstract class names and method names.

10.3   Write Java code to begin implementing the design for class `Transaction` specified in Fig. 10.21 and Fig. 10.22. Be sure to include `private` reference-type attributes based on class `Transaction`'s associations. Also be sure to include `public` *get* methods that provide access to any of these `private` attributes that the subclasses require to perform their tasks.

Answers to Software Engineering Case Study Self-Review Exercises

10.1   b.

10.2   False. The UML requires that we italicize abstract class names and method names.

10.3   The design for class `Transaction` yields the code in Fig. 10.25. The bodies of the class constructor and methods will be completed in Appendix J. When fully implemented, methods `getScreen` and `getBankDatabase` will return superclass `Transaction`'s `private` reference attributes `screen` and `bankDatabase`, respectively. These methods allow the `Transaction` subclasses to access the ATM's screen and interact with the bank's database.

```
1  // Abstract class Transaction represents an ATM transaction
2  public abstract class Transaction
3  {
4     // attributes
5     private int accountNumber; // indicates account involved
6     private Screen screen; // ATM's screen
7     private BankDatabase bankDatabase; // account info database
8
9     // no-argument constructor invoked by subclasses using super()
10    public Transaction()
11    {
12    } // end no-argument Transaction constructor
13
14    // return account number
15    public int getAccountNumber()
16    {
17    } // end method getAccountNumber
18
19    // return reference to screen
20    public Screen getScreen()
21    {
22    } // end method getScreen
23
24    // return reference to bank database
25    public BankDatabase getBankDatabase()
26    {
27    } // end method getBankDatabase
28
29    // abstract method overridden by subclasses
30    public abstract void execute();
31 } // end class Transaction
```

Fig. 10.25 | Java code for class **Transaction** based on Fig. 10.21 and Fig. 10.22.

10.10 Wrap-Up

This chapter introduced polymorphism—the ability to process objects that share the same superclass in a class hierarchy as if they are all objects of the superclass. The chapter discussed how polymorphism makes systems extensible and maintainable, then demonstrated how to use overridden methods to effect polymorphic behavior. We introduced abstract classes, which allow programmers to provide an appropriate superclass from which other classes can inherit. You learned that an abstract class can declare abstract methods that each subclass must implement to become a concrete class and that a program can use variables of an abstract class to invoke subclasses' implementations of abstract methods polymorphically. You also learned how to determine an object's type at execution time. Finally, the chapter discussed declaring and implementing an interface as another way to achieve polymorphic behavior.

You should now be familiar with classes, objects, encapsulation, inheritance, interfaces and polymorphism—the most essential aspects of object-oriented programming. In the next chapter, we take a deeper look at Graphical User Interfaces (GUIs).

Summary

- With polymorphism, it is possible to design and implement systems that are more easily extensible. Programs can be written to process even objects of types that do not exist when the program is under development.
- There are many situations in which it is useful to declare abstract classes for which the programmer never intends to create objects. These are used only as superclasses, so we sometimes refer to them as abstract superclasses. You cannot instantiate objects of an abstract class.
- Classes from which objects can be created are called concrete classes.
- A class must be declared abstract if one or more of its methods are abstract. An abstract method is one with keyword abstract to the left of the return type in its declaration.
- If a class extends a class with an abstract method and does not provide a concrete implementation of that method, then that method remains abstract in the subclass. Consequently, the subclass is also an abstract class and must be declared abstract.
- Java enables polymorphism—the ability for objects of different classes related by inheritance or interface implementation to respond differently to the same method call.
- When a request is made through a superclass reference to a subclass object to use an abstract method, Java executes the implemented version of the method found in the subclass.
- Although we cannot instantiate objects of abstract classes, we can declare variables of abstract-class types. Such variables can be used to reference subclass objects.
- Due to dynamic binding (also called late binding), the specific type of a subclass object need not be known at compile time for a method call off a superclass variable to be compiled. At execution time, the correct subclass version of the method is called, based on the type of the reference stored in the superclass variable.
- Operator instanceof checks the type of the object to which its left operand refers and determines whether this type has an *is-a* relationship with the type specified as its right operand. If the two have an *is-a* relationship, the instanceof expression is true. If not, the instanceof expression is false.
- Every object in Java knows its own class and can access this information through method getClass, which all classes inherit from class Object. Method getClass returns an object of type

Class (package java.lang), which contains information about the object's type that can be accessed using Class's public methods. Class method getName, for example, returns the name of the class.

- An interface declaration begins with the keyword interface and contains a set of public abstract methods. Interfaces may also contain public static final fields.
- To use an interface, a class must specify that it implements the interface and must either declare every method in the interface with the signatures specified in the interface declaration or be declared abstract.
- An interface is typically used when disparate (i.e., unrelated) classes need to provide common functionality (i.e., methods) or use common constants.
- An interface is often used in place of an abstract class when there is no default implementation to inherit.
- When a class implements an interface, it establishes an *is-a* relationship with the interface type, as do all its subclasses.
- To implement more than one interface, simply provide a comma-separated list of interface names after keyword implements in the class declaration.

Terminology

abstract class	implementation inheritance
abstract keyword	implements keyword
abstract method	inlining code
abstract superclass	instanceof operator
Class class	interface declaration
concrete class	interface inheritance
constants declared in an interface	interface keyword
downcasting	iterator class
dynamic binding	late binding
final class	polymorphism
final method	static binding
getClass method of Object	subclass reference
getName method of Class	superclass reference
implement an interface	

Self-Review Exercises

10.1   Fill in the blanks in each of the following statements:
  a) Polymorphism helps eliminate _____ logic.
  b) If a class contains at least one abstract method, it is a(n) _____ class.
  c) Classes from which objects can be instantiated are called _____ classes.
  d) _____ involves using a superclass variable to invoke methods on superclass and subclass objects, enabling you to "program in the general."
  e) Methods that are not interface methods and that do not provide implementations must be declared using keyword _____.
  f) Casting a reference stored in a superclass variable to a subclass type is called _____.

10.2   State whether each of the statements that follows is *true* or *false*. If *false*, explain why.
  a) It is possible to treat superclass objects and subclass objects similarly.
  b) All methods in an abstract class must be declared as abstract methods.

c) It is dangerous to try to invoke a subclass-only method through a subclass variable.
d) If a superclass declares an abstract method, a subclass must implement that method.
e) An object of a class that implements an interface may be thought of as an object of that interface type.

Answers to Self-Review Exercises

10.1   a) switch. b) abstract. c) concrete. d) Polymorphism. e) abstract. f) downcasting.

10.2   a) True. b) False. An abstract class can include methods with implementations and abstract methods. c) False. Trying to invoke a subclass-only method with a superclass variable is dangerous. d) False. Only a concrete subclass must implement the method. e) True.

Exercises

10.3   How does polymorphism enable you to program "in the general" rather than "in the specific"? Discuss the key advantages of programming "in the general."

10.4   A subclass can inherit "interface" or "implementation" from a superclass. How do inheritance hierarchies designed for inheriting interface differ from those designed for inheriting implementation?

10.5   What are abstract methods? Describe the circumstances in which an abstract method would be appropriate.

10.6   How does polymorphism promote extensibility?

10.7   Discuss four ways in which you can assign superclass and subclass references to variables of superclass and subclass types.

10.8   Compare and contrast abstract classes and interfaces. Why would you use an abstract class? Why would you use an interface?

10.9   *(Payroll System Modification)* Modify the payroll system of Fig. 10.4–Fig. 10.9 to include private instance variable birthDate in class Employee. Use class Date of Fig. 8.7 to represent an employee's birthday. Add *get* methods to class Date and replace method toDateString with method toString. Assume that payroll is processed once per month. Create an array of Employee variables to store references to the various employee objects. In a loop, calculate the payroll for each Employee (polymorphically), and add a $100.00 bonus to the person's payroll amount if the current month is the month in which the Employee's birthday occurs.

10.10   *(Shape Hierarchy)* Implement the Shape hierarchy shown in Fig. 9.3. Each TwoDimensionalShape should contain method getArea to calculate the area of the two-dimensional shape. Each ThreeDimensionalShape should have methods getArea and getVolume to calculate the surface area and volume, respectively, of the three-dimensional shape. Create a program that uses an array of Shape references to objects of each concrete class in the hierarchy. The program should print a text description of the object to which each array element refers. Also, in the loop that processes all the shapes in the array, determine whether each shape is a TwoDimensionalShape or a ThreeDimensionalShape. If a shape is a TwoDimensionalShape, display its area. If a shape is a ThreeDimensionalShape, display its area and volume.

10.11   *(Payroll System Modification)* Modify the payroll system of Fig. 10.4–Fig. 10.9 to include an additional Employee subclass PieceWorker that represents an employee whose pay is based on the number of pieces of merchandise produced. Class PieceWorker should contain private instance variables wage (to store the employee's wage per piece) and pieces (to store the number of pieces produced). Provide a concrete implementation of method earnings in class PieceWorker that calculates the employee's earnings by multiplying the number of pieces produced by the wage per piece. Create an array of Employee variables to store references to objects of each concrete class in the new Employee hierarchy. For each Employee, display its string representation and earnings.

10.12 *(Accounts Payable System Modification)* In this exercise, we modify the accounts payable application of Fig. 10.11–Fig. 10.15 to include the complete functionality of the payroll application of Fig. 10.4–Fig. 10.9. The application should still process two Invoice objects, but now should process one object of each of the four Employee subclasses. If the object currently being processed is a BasePlusCommissionEmployee, the application should increase the BasePlusCommissionEmployee's base salary by 10%. Finally, the application should output the payment amount for each object. Complete the following steps to create the new application:

    a)   Modify classes HourlyEmployee (Fig. 10.6) and CommissionEmployee (Fig. 10.7) to place them in the Payable hierarchy as subclasses of the version of Employee (Fig. 10.13) that implements Payable. [*Hint:* Change the name of method earnings to getPayment-Amount in each subclass so that the class satisfies its inherited contract with interface Payable.]

    b)   Modify class BasePlusCommissionEmployee (Fig. 10.8) such that it extends the version of class CommissionEmployee created in Part *a*.

    c)   Modify PayableInterfaceTest (Fig. 10.15) to polymorphically process two Invoices, one SalariedEmployee, one HourlyEmployee, one CommissionEmployee and one BasePlusCommissionEmployee. First output a string representation of each Payable object. Next, if an object is a BasePlusCommissionEmployee, increase its base salary by 10%. Finally, output the payment amount for each Payable object.

GUI Components: Part 1

OBJECTIVES

In this chapter you will learn:

- The design principles of graphical user interfaces (GUIs).

- To build GUIs and handle events generated by user interactions with GUIs.

- To understand the packages containing GUI components, event-handling classes and interfaces.

- To create and manipulate buttons, labels, lists, text fields and panels.

- To handle mouse events and keyboard events.

- To use layout managers to arrange GUI components

11.1 Introduction

A graphical user interface (GUI) presents a user-friendly mechanism for interacting with an application. A GUI (pronounced "GOO-ee") gives an application a distinctive "look" and "feel." Providing different applications with consistent, intuitive user interface components allows users to be somewhat familiar with an application, so that they can learn it more quickly and use it more productively.

Look-and-Feel Observation 11.1

Consistent user interfaces enable a user to learn new applications faster.

As an example of a GUI, Fig. 11.1 contains an Internet Explorer Web-browser window with some of its GUI components labeled. At the top is a title bar that contains the window's title. Below that is a menu bar containing menus (File, Edit, View, etc.).

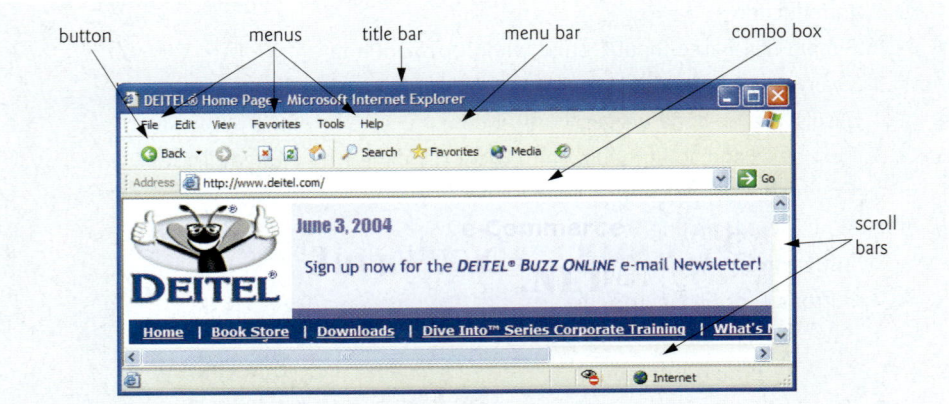

Fig. 11.1 | Internet Explorer window with GUI components.

Below the menu bar is a set of **buttons** that the user can click to perform tasks in Internet Explorer. Below the buttons is a **combo box**; the user can type into it the name of a Web site to visit or can click the down arrow at the right side of the box to select from a list of sites previously visited. The menus, buttons and combo box are part of Internet Explorer's GUI. They enable you to interact with Internet Explorer.

GUIs are built from **GUI components**. These are sometimes called **controls** or **widgets**—short for **window gadgets**—in other languages. A GUI component is an object with which the user interacts via the mouse, the keyboard or another form of input, such as voice recognition. In this chapter and Chapter 22, GUI Components: Part 2, you will learn about many of Java's GUI components. [Note: Several concepts covered in this chapter have already been covered in the optional GUI and Graphics Case Study of Chapters 3–10. So, some material will be repetitive if you read the case study. You do not need to read the case study to understand this chapter.]

11.2 Simple GUI-Based Input/Output with JOptionPane

The applications in Chapters 2–10 display text at the command window and obtain input from the command window. Most applications you use on a daily basis use windows or **dialog boxes** (also called **dialogs**) to interact with the user. For example, e-mail programs allow you to type and read messages in a window provided by the e-mail program. Typically, dialog boxes are windows in which programs display important messages to the user or obtain information from the user. Java's `JOptionPane` class (package `javax.swing`) provides prepackaged dialog boxes for both input and output. These dialogs are displayed by invoking `static JOptionPane` methods. Figure 11.2 presents a simple addition application that uses two **input dialogs** to obtain integers from the user and a **message dialog** to display the sum of the integers the user enters.

Line 3 imports class `JOptionPane` for use in this application. Lines 10–11 declare the local `String` variable `firstNumber` and assign it the result of the call `JOptionPane static` method **`showInputDialog`**. This method displays an input dialog (see the first screen capture in Fig. 11.2), using the method's `String` argument (`"Enter first integer"`) as a prompt to the user.

```
1   // Fig. 11.2: Addition.java
2   // Addition program that uses JOptionPane for input and output.
3   import javax.swing.JOptionPane; // program uses JOptionPane
4
5   public class Addition
6   {
7      public static void main( String args[] )
8      {
9         // obtain user input from JOptionPane input dialogs
10        String firstNumber =
11           JOptionPane.showInputDialog( "Enter first integer" );
12        String secondNumber =
13           JOptionPane.showInputDialog( "Enter second integer" );
14
15        // convert String inputs to int values for use in a calculation
16        int number1 = Integer.parseInt( firstNumber );
17        int number2 = Integer.parseInt( secondNumber );
18
19        int sum = number1 + number2; // add numbers
20
21        // display result in a JOptionPane message dialog
22        JOptionPane.showMessageDialog( null, "The sum is " + sum,
23           "Sum of Two Integers", JOptionPane.PLAIN_MESSAGE );
24     } // end method main
25  } // end class Addition
```

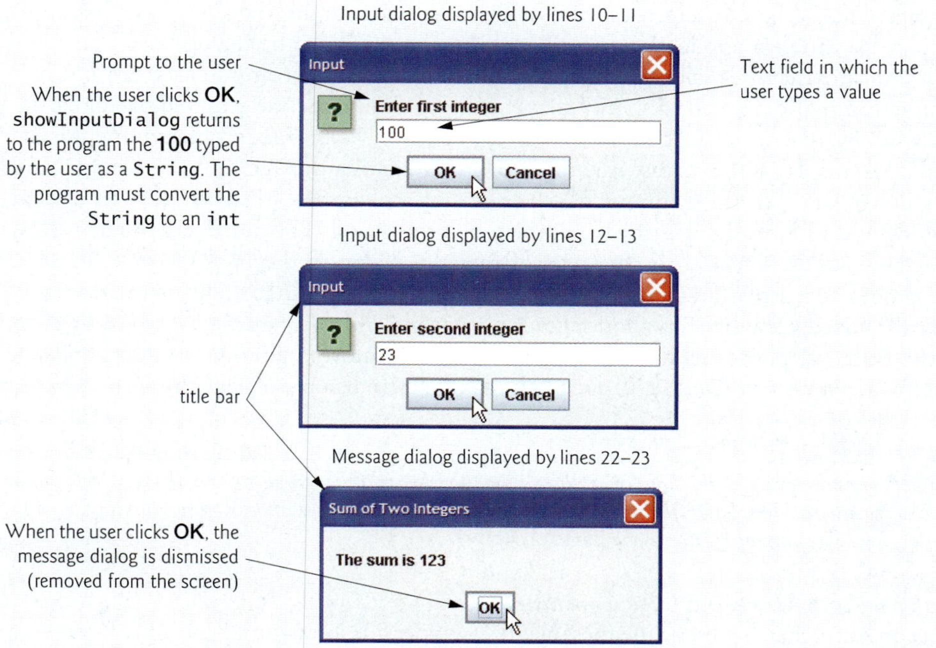

Fig. 11.2 | JOptionPane input and message dialogs used to input values from the user and display results.

Look-and-Feel Observation 11.2

The prompt in an input dialog typically uses sentence-style capitalization—a style that capitalizes only the first letter of the first word in the text unless the word is a proper noun (for example, Deitel).

The user types characters in the text field, then clicks the **OK** button or presses the *Enter* key to submit the `String` to the program. Clicking **OK** also dismisses (hides) the dialog. [*Note:* If you type in the text field and nothing appears, activate the text field by clicking it with the mouse.] Unlike `Scanner`, which can be used to input values of several types from the user at the keyboard, an input dialog can input only input `Strings`. This is typical of most GUI components. Technically, the user can type anything in the input dialog's text field. Our program assumes that the user enters a valid integer value. If the user clicks the **Cancel** button, `showInputDialog` returns `null`. If the user either types a noninteger value or clicks the **Cancel** button in the input dialog, a runtime logic error will occur in this program and it will not operate correctly. Chapter 13, Exception Handling, discusses how to handle such errors. Lines 12–13 display another input dialog that prompts the user to enter the second integer.

To perform the calculation in this application, we must convert the `Strings` that the user entered to `int` values. Recall from Section 7.12 that the `Integer` class's `static` method `parseInt` converts its `String` argument to an `int` value. Lines 16–17 assign the converted values to local variables `number1` and `number2`. Then, line 19 sums these values and assigns the result to local variable `sum`.

Lines 22–23 use `JOptionPane` static method `showMessageDialog` to display a message dialog (the last screen capture of Fig. 11.2) containing the sum. The first argument helps the Java application determine where to position the dialog box. The value `null` indicates that the dialog should appear in the center of the computer screen. The first argument can also be used to specify that the dialog should appear centered over a particular window, which we will demonstrate later in Section 11.8. The second argument is the message to display—in this case, the result of concatenating the `String` `"The sum is "` and the value of `sum`. The third argument—`"Sum of Two Integers"`—represents the string that should appear in the dialog's title bar at the top of the dialog. The fourth argument—`JOptionPane.PLAIN_MESSAGE`—is the type of message dialog to display. A `PLAIN_MESSAGE` dialog does not display an icon to the left of the message. Class `JOptionPane` provides several overloaded versions of methods `showInputDialog` and `showMessageDialog`, as well as methods that display other dialog types. For complete information on class `JOptionPane`, visit `java.sun.com/j2se/1.5.0/docs/api/javax/swing/JOptionPane.html`.

Look-and-Feel Observation 11.3

The title bar of a window typically uses book-title capitalization—a style that capitalizes the first letter of each significant word in the text and does not end with any punctuation (for example, Capitalization in a Book Title).

JOptionPane Message Dialog Constants

The constants that represent the message dialog types are shown in Fig. 11.3. All message dialog types except `PLAIN_MESSAGE` display an icon to the left of the message. These icons provide a visual indication of the message's importance to the user. Note that a `QUESTION_MESSAGE` icon is the default icon for an input dialog box (see Fig. 11.2).

Message dialog type	Icon	Description
ERROR_MESSAGE		A dialog that indicates an error to the user.
INFORMATION_MESSAGE		A dialog with an informational message to the user.
WARNING_MESSAGE		A dialog warning the user of a potential problem.
QUESTION_MESSAGE		A dialog that poses a question to the user. This dialog normally requires a response, such as clicking a **Yes** or a **No** button.
PLAIN_MESSAGE	no icon	A dialog that contains a message, but no icon.

Fig. 11.3 | JOptionPane static constants for message dialogs.

11.3 Overview of Swing Components

Though it is possible to perform input and output using the JOptionPane dialogs presented in Section 11.2, most GUI applications require more elaborate, customized user interfaces. The remainder of this chapter discusses many GUI components that enable application developers to create robust GUIs. Figure 11.4 lists several Swing GUI components from package **javax.swing** that are used to build Java GUIs. Most Swing components are pure Java components—they are written, manipulated and displayed completely in Java. They are part of the Java Foundation Classes (JFC)—Java's libraries for cross-platform GUI development. Visit java.sun.com/products/jfc for more information on JFC.

Component	Description
JLabel	Displays uneditable text or icons.
JTextField	Enables user to enter data from the keyboard. Can also be used to display editable or uneditable text.
JButton	Triggers an event when clicked with the mouse.
JCheckBox	Specifies an option that can be selected or not selected.
JComboBox	Provides a drop-down list of items from which the user can make a selection by clicking an item or possibly by typing into the box.
JList	Provides a list of items from which the user can make a selection by clicking on any item in the list. Multiple elements can be selected.
JPanel	Provides an area in which components can be placed and organized. Can also be used as a drawing area for graphics.

Fig. 11.4 | Some basic GUI components.

Swing vs. AWT

There are actually two sets of GUI components in Java. Before Swing was introduced in J2SE 1.2, Java GUIs were built with components from the Abstract Window Toolkit (AWT) in package `java.awt`. When a Java application with an AWT GUI executes on different Java platforms, the application's GUI components display differently on each platform. Consider an application that displays an object of type `Button` (package `java.awt`). On a computer running the Microsoft Windows operating system, the `Button` will have the same appearance as the buttons in other Windows applications. Similarly, on a computer running the Apple Mac OS X operating system, the `Button` will have the same look and feel as the buttons in other Macintosh applications. Sometimes, the manner in which a user can interact with a particular AWT component differs between platforms.

Together, the appearance and the way in which the user interacts with the application are known as that application's look-and-feel. Swing GUI components allow you to specify a uniform look-and-feel for your application across all platforms or to use each platform's custom look-and-feel. An application can even change the look-and-feel during execution to enable users to choose their own preferred look-and-feel.

Portability Tip 11.1

Swing components are implemented in Java, so they are more portable and flexible than the original Java GUI components from package `java.awt`, which were based on the GUI components of the underlying platform. For this reason, Swing GUI components are generally preferred.

Lightweight vs. Heavyweight GUI Components

Most Swing components are not tied to actual GUI components supported by the underlying platform on which an application executes. Such GUI components are known as lightweight components. AWT components (many of which parallel the Swing components), are tied to the local platform and are called heavyweight components, because they rely on the local platform's windowing system to determine their functionality and their look-and-feel.

Several Swing components are heavyweight components. Like AWT components, heavyweight Swing GUI components require direct interaction with the local windowing system, which may restrict their appearance and functionality. As you will learn, lightweight components provide you with more control over their appearance and functionality.

Look-and-Feel Observation 11.4

The look and feel of a GUI defined with heavyweight GUI components from package `java.awt` may vary across platforms. Because heavyweight components are tied to the local-platform GUI, the look and feel varies from platform to platform.

Superclasses of Swing's Lightweight GUI Components

The UML class diagram of Fig. 11.5 shows an inheritance hierarchy containing classes from which lightweight Swing components inherit their common attributes and behaviors. As discussed in Chapter 9, class `Object` is the superclass of the Java class hierarchy.

Software Engineering Observation 11.1

Study the attributes and behaviors of the classes in the class hierarchy of Fig. 11.5. These classes declare the features that are common to most Swing components.

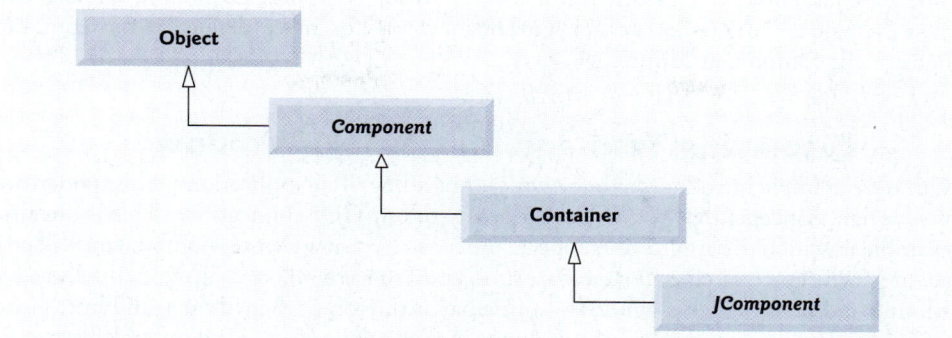

Fig. 11.5 | Common superclasses of many of the Swing components.

Class **Component** (package java.awt) is a subclass of Object that declares many of the attributes and behaviors common to the GUI components in packages java.awt and javax.swing. Most GUI components extend class Component directly or indirectly. Visit java.sun.com/j2se/5.0/docs/api/java/awt/Component.html for a complete list of these common features.

Class **Container** (package java.awt) is a subclass of Component. As you will soon see, Components are attached to Containers (such as windows) so the Components can be organized and displayed on the screen. Any object that *is a* Container can be used to organize other Components in a GUI. Because a Container *is a* Component, you can attach Containers to other Containers to help organize a GUI. Visit java.sun.com/j2se/5.0/docs/api/java/awt/Container.html for a complete list of the Container features that are common to Swing lightweight components.

Class **JComponent** (package javax.swing) is a subclass of Container. JComponent is the superclass of all lightweight Swing components and declares their common attributes and behaviors. Because JComponent is a subclass of Container, all lightweight Swing components are also Containers. Some common lightweight component features supported by JComponent include:

1. A **pluggable look-and-feel** that can be used to customize the appearance of components (e.g., for use on particular platforms). You will see an example of this in Section 22.6.

2. Shortcut keys (called **mnemonics**) for direct access to GUI components through the keyboard. You will see an example of this in Section 22.4.

3. Common event-handling capabilities for cases where several GUI components initiate the same actions in an application.

4. Brief descriptions of a GUI component's purpose (called **tool tips**) that are displayed when the mouse cursor is positioned over the component for a short time. You will see an example of this in the next section.

5. Support for assistive technologies, such as braille screen readers for the visually impaired.

6. Support for user-interface **localization**—that is, customizing the user interface to display in different languages and use local cultural conventions.

These are just some of the many features of the Swing components. Visit `java.sun.com/ j2se/5.0/docs/api/javax/swing/JComponent.html` for more details of the common lightweight component features.

11.4 Displaying Text and Images in a Window

Our next example introduces a framework for building GUI applications. This framework uses several concepts that you will see in many of our GUI applications. This is our first example in which the application appears in its own window. Most windows you will create are an instance of class `JFrame` or a subclass of `JFrame`. `JFrame` provides the basic attributes and behaviors of a window—a title bar at the top of the window, and buttons to minimize, maximize and close the window. Since an application's GUI is typically specific to the application, most of our examples will consist of two classes—a subclass of `JFrame` that helps us demonstrate new GUI concepts and an application class in which `main` creates and displays the application's primary window.

Labeling GUI Components

A typical GUI consists of many components. In a large GUI, it can be difficult to identify the purpose of every component unless the GUI designer provides text instructions or information stating the purpose of each component. Such text is known as a label and is created with class `JLabel`—a subclass of `JComponent`. A `JLabel` displays a single line of read-only text, an image, or both text and an image. Applications rarely change a label's contents after creating it.

Look-and-Feel Observation 11.5

Text in a `JLabel` normally uses sentence-style capitalization.

The application of Fig. 11.6 and Fig. 11.7 demonstrates several `JLabel` features and presents the framework we use in most of our GUI examples. We did not highlight the code in this example since most of it is new. [*Note:* There are many more features for each GUI component than we can cover in our examples. To learn the complete details of each GUI component, visit its page in the online documentation. For class `JLabel`, visit `java.sun.com/j2se/5.0/docs/api/javax/swing/JLabel.html`.]

Class `LabelFrame` (Fig. 11.6) is a subclass of `JFrame`. We will use an instance of class `LabelFrame` to display a window containing three `JLabel`s. Lines 3–8 import the classes used in class `LabelFrame`. The class extends `JFrame` to inherit the features of a window. Lines 12–14 declare the three `JLabel` instance variables, each of which is instantiated in the `LabelFrame` constructor (lines 17–41). Typically, the `JFrame` subclass's constructor builds the GUI that is displayed in the window when the application executes. Line 19 invokes superclass `JFrame`'s constructor with the argument `"Testing JLabel"`. `JFrame`'s constructor uses this `String` to specify the text in the window's title bar.

Specifying the Layout

When building a GUI, each GUI component must be attached to a container, such as a window created with a `JFrame`. Also, you typically must decide where to position each GUI component. This is known as specifying the layout of the GUI components. As you

```
 1   // Fig. 11.6: LabelFrame.java
 2   // Demonstrating the JLabel class.
 3   import java.awt.FlowLayout; // specifies how components are arranged
 4   import javax.swing.JFrame; // provides basic window features
 5   import javax.swing.JLabel; // displays text and images
 6   import javax.swing.SwingConstants; // common constants used with Swing
 7   import javax.swing.Icon; // interface used to manipulate images
 8   import javax.swing.ImageIcon; // loads images
 9
10   public class LabelFrame extends JFrame
11   {
12      private JLabel label1; // JLabel with just text
13      private JLabel label2; // JLabel constructed with text and icon
14      private JLabel label3; // JLabel with added text and icon
15
16      // LabelFrame constructor adds JLabels to JFrame
17      public LabelFrame()
18      {
19         super( "Testing JLabel" );
20         setLayout( new FlowLayout() ); // set frame layout
21
22         // JLabel constructor with a string argument
23         label1 = new JLabel( "Label with text" );
24         label1.setToolTipText( "This is label1" );
25         add( label1 ); // add label1 to JFrame
26
27         // JLabel constructor with string, Icon and alignment arguments
28         Icon bug = new ImageIcon( getClass().getResource( "bug1.gif" ) );
29         label2 = new JLabel( "Label with text and icon", bug,
30            SwingConstants.LEFT );
31         label2.setToolTipText( "This is label2" );
32         add( label2 ); // add label2 to JFrame
33
34         label3 = new JLabel(); // JLabel constructor no arguments
35         label3.setText( "Label with icon and text at bottom" );
36         label3.setIcon( bug ); // add icon to JLabel
37         label3.setHorizontalTextPosition( SwingConstants.CENTER );
38         label3.setVerticalTextPosition( SwingConstants.BOTTOM );
39         label3.setToolTipText( "This is label3" );
40         add( label3 ); // add label3 to JFrame
41      } // end LabelFrame constructor
42   } // end class LabelFrame
```

Fig. 11.6 | JLabels with text and icons.

will learn at the end of this chapter and in Chapter 22, Java provides several layout managers that can help you position components.

Many integrated development environments provide GUI design tools in which you can specify the exact size and location of a component in a visual manner by using the mouse, then the IDE will generate the GUI code for you. Though such IDEs can greatly simplify GUI creation, they are each different in capability.

To ensure that the code in this book can be used with any IDE, we did not use an IDE to create our GUI code. For this reason, we take advantage of Java's various layout

```
1   // Fig. 11.7: LabelTest.java
2   // Testing LabelFrame.
3   import javax.swing.JFrame;
4
5   public class LabelTest
6   {
7      public static void main( String args[] )
8      {
9         LabelFrame labelFrame = new LabelFrame(); // create LabelFrame
10        labelFrame.setDefaultCloseOperation( JFrame.EXIT_ON_CLOSE );
11        labelFrame.setSize( 275, 180 ); // set frame size
12        labelFrame.setVisible( true ); // display frame
13     } // end main
14  } // end class LabelTest
```

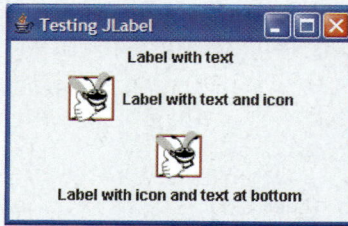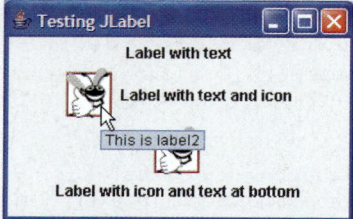

Fig. 11.7 | Test class for `LabelFrame`.

managers in our GUI examples. One such layout manager is **FlowLayout** in which GUI components are placed on a container from left to right in the order in which they are attached to the container by the program. When there is no more room to fit components left to right, components continue to display left to right on the next line. If the container is resized, a FlowLayout reflows (i.e., rearranges) the components to accommodate the new width of the container, possibly with fewer or more rows of GUI components. Line 20 specifies that the layout of the LabelFrame should be a FlowLayout. Method **setLayout** is inherited into class LabelFrame indirectly from class Container. The argument to the method must be an object of a class that implements the LayoutManager interface, such as an object of class FlowLayout. In this case, we create a new FlowLayout object and pass its reference as the argument to setLayout.

Creating and Attaching `label1`

Now that we have specified the layout for the window, we can begin creating and attaching GUI components to the window. Line 23 creates a JLabel object and passes the String "Label with text" to the constructor. The JLabel displays this text when the JLabel appears on the screen as part of the application's GUI. Line 24 uses method **setTool-TipText** (inherited by JLabel from JComponent) to specify the tool tip that is displayed when the user positions the mouse cursor over the JLabel in the GUI. You can see a sample tool tip in the second screen capture of Fig. 11.7. When you execute this application, try positioning the mouse over each JLabel to see its tool tip. Line 25 attaches label1 to the LabelFrame by passing label1 to the **add** method, which is inherited indirectly from class Container.

Common Programming Error 11.1

If you do not explicitly add a GUI component to a container, the GUI component will not be displayed when the container appears on the screen.

Look-and-Feel Observation 11.6

Use tool tips to add descriptive text to your GUI components. This text helps the user determine the GUI component's purpose in the user interface.

Creating and Attaching label2

Icons are a popular way to enhance the look-and-feel of an application and are also commonly used to indicate functionality. For examples, most of today's VCRs and DVD players use the same icon to play a tape or DVD. Several Swing components can display images. An icon is normally specified with an `Icon` argument to a constructor or to the component's `setIcon` method. An Icon is an object of any class that implements interface `Icon` (package `javax.swing`). One such class is `ImageIcon` (package `javax.swing`), which supports several image formats, including **Graphics Interchange Format (GIF)**, **Portable Network Graphics (PNG)** and **Joint Photographic Experts Group (JPEG)**. File names for each of these types end with `.gif`, `.png` or `.jpg` (or `.jpeg`), respectively. We discuss images in more detail in Chapter 21, Multimedia: Applets and Applications.

Line 28 declares an `ImageIcon` object. The file `bug1.gif` contains the image to load and store in the `ImageIcon` object. (This image is included in the directory for this example on the CD that accompanies this book) The `ImageIcon` object is assigned to Icon reference bug. Remember, class `ImageIcon` implements interface `Icon`; an `ImageIcon` *is an* Icon.

In line 28, the expression `getClass().getResource( "bug1.gif" )` invokes method **getClass** (inherited from class `Object`) to retrieve a reference to the `Class` object that represents the `LabelFrame` class declaration. That reference is then used to invoke `Class` method **getResource**, which returns the location of the image as a URL. The `ImageIcon` constructor uses the URL to locate the image then loads it into memory. As we discussed in Chapter 1, the JVM loads class declarations into memory, using a class loader. The class loader knows where each class it loads is located on disk. Method `getResource` uses the `Class` object's class loader to determine the location of a resource, such as an image file. In this example, the image file is stored in the same location as the `LabelFrame.class` file. The techniques described here enable an application to load image files from locations that are relative to `LabelFrame`'s `.class` file on disk.

A `JLabel` can display an Icon. Lines 29–30 use another `JLabel` constructor to create a `JLabel` that displays the text `"Label with text and icon"` and the Icon bug created in line 28. The last constructor argument indicates that the label's contents are left justified, or **left aligned** (i.e., the icon and text are at the left side of the label's area on the screen). Interface **SwingConstants** (package `javax.swing`) declares a set of common integer constants (such as `SwingConstants.LEFT`) that are used with many Swing components. By default, the text appears to the right of the image when a label contains both text and an image. Note that the horizontal and vertical alignments of a `JLabel` can be set with methods **setHorizontalAlignment** and **setVerticalAlignment**, respectively. Line 31 specifies the tool-tip text for label2, and line 32 adds label2 to the `JFrame`.

Creating and Attaching `label3`

Class `JLabel` provides many methods to change a label's appearance after the label has been instantiated. Line 34 creates a `JLabel` and invokes its no-argument constructor. Such a label initially has no text or `Icon`. Line 35 uses `JLabel` method **`setText`** to set the text displayed on the label. The corresponding method **`getText`** retrieves the current text displayed on a label. Line 36 uses `JLabel` method **`setIcon`** to specify the `Icon` to display on the label. The corresponding method **`getIcon`** retrieves the current `Icon` displayed on a label. Lines 37–38 use `JLabel` methods **`setHorizontalTextPosition`** and **`setVerticalTextPosition`** to specify the text position in the label. In this case, the text will be centered horizontally and will appear at the bottom of the label. Thus, the `Icon` will appear above the text. The horizontal-position constants in `SwingConstants` are LEFT, CENTER and RIGHT (Fig. 11.8). The vertical-position constants in `SwingConstants` are TOP, CENTER and BOTTOM (Fig. 11.8). Line 39 sets the tool-tip text for `label3`. Line 40 adds `label3` to the `JFrame`.

Creating and Displaying a **`LabelFrame`** *Window*

Class `LabelTest` (Fig. 11.7) creates an object of class `LabelFrame` (line 9), then specifies the default close operation for the window. By default, closing a window simply hides the window. However, when the user closes the `LabelFrame` window, we would like the application to terminate. Line 10 invokes `LabelFrame`'s **`setDefaultCloseOperation`** method (inherited from class `JFrame`) with constant **`JFrame.EXIT_ON_CLOSE`** as the argument to indicate that the program should terminate when the window is closed by the user. This line is important. Without it the application will not terminate when the user closes the window. Next, line 11 invokes `LabelFrame`'s **`setSize`** method to specify the width and height of the window. Finally, line 12 invokes `LabelFrame`'s **`setVisible`** method with the argument `true` to display the window on the screen. Try resizing the window to see how the `FlowLayout` changes the `JLabel` positions as the window width changes.

11.5 Text Fields and an Introduction to Event Handling with Nested Classes

Normally, a user interacts with an application's GUI to indicate the tasks that the application should perform. For example, when you write an e-mail in an e-mail application,

Constant	Description
Horizontal-position constants	
`SwingConstants.LEFT`	Place text on the left.
`SwingConstants.CENTER`	Place text in the center.
`SwingConstants.RIGHT`	Place text on the right.
Vertical-position constants	
`SwingConstants.TOP`	Place text at the top.
`SwingConstants.CENTER`	Place text in the center.
`SwingConstants.BOTTOM`	Place text at the bottom.

Fig. 11.8 | Some basic GUI components.

clicking the **Send** button tells the application to send the e-mail to the specified e-mail addresses. GUIs are event driven. When the user interacts with a GUI component, the interaction—known as an event—drives the program to perform a task. Some common events (user interactions) that might cause an application to perform a task include clicking a button, typing in a text field, selecting an item from a menu, closing a window and moving the mouse. The code that performs a task in response to an event is called an event handler and the overall process of responding to events is known as event handling.

In this section, we introduce two new GUI components that can generate events—`JTextFields` and `JPasswordFields` (package `javax.swing`). Class `JTextField` extends class `JTextComponent` (package `javax.swing.text`), which provides many features common to Swing's text-based components. Class `JPasswordField` extends `JTextField` and adds several methods that are specific to processing passwords. Each of these components is a single-line area in which the user can enter text via the keyboard. Applications can also display text in a `JTextField` (see the output of Fig. 11.10). A `JPasswordField` shows that characters are being typed as the user enters them, but hides the actual characters with an echo character, assuming that they represent a password that should remain known only to the user.

When the user types data into a `JTextField` or a `JPasswordField`, then presses *Enter*, an event occurs. Our next example demonstrates how a program can perform a task when that event occurs. The techniques shown here are applicable to all GUI components that generate events.

The application of Fig. 11.9 and Fig. 11.10 uses classes `JTextField` and `JPassword-Field` to create and manipulate four text fields. When the user types in one of the text fields, then presses *Enter*, the application displays a message dialog box containing the text the user typed. You can only type in the text field that is "in focus." A component receives the focus when the user clicks the component. This is important because the text field with the focus is the one that generates an event when the user presses *Enter*. In this example, when the user presses *Enter* in the `JPasswordField`, the password is revealed. We begin by discussing the setup of the GUI, then discuss the event-handling code.

Lines 3–9 import the classes and interfaces we use in this example. Class `TextField-Frame` extends `JFrame` and declares three `JTextField` variables and a `JPasswordField` variable (lines 13–16). Each of the corresponding text fields is instantiated and attached to the `TextFieldFrame` in the constructor (lines 19–47).

```
1   // Fig. 11.9: TextFieldFrame.java
2   // Demonstrating the JTextField class.
3   import java.awt.FlowLayout;
4   import java.awt.event.ActionListener;
5   import java.awt.event.ActionEvent;
6   import javax.swing.JFrame;
7   import javax.swing.JTextField;
8   import javax.swing.JPasswordField;
9   import javax.swing.JOptionPane;
10
11  public class TextFieldFrame extends JFrame
12  {
```

Fig. 11.9 | `JTextFields` and `JPasswordFields`. (Part 1 of 3.)

```
13     private JTextField textField1; // text field with set size
14     private JTextField textField2; // text field constructed with text
15     private JTextField textField3; // text field with text and size
16     private JPasswordField passwordField; // password field with text
17
18     // TextFieldFrame constructor adds JTextFields to JFrame
19     public TextFieldFrame()
20     {
21        super( "Testing JTextField and JPasswordField" );
22        setLayout( new FlowLayout() ); // set frame layout
23
24        // construct textfield with 10 columns
25        textField1 = new JTextField( 10 );
26        add( textField1 ); // add textField1 to JFrame
27
28        // construct textfield with default text
29        textField2 = new JTextField( "Enter text here" );
30        add( textField2 ); // add textField2 to JFrame
31
32        // construct textfield with default text and 21 columns
33        textField3 = new JTextField( "Uneditable text field", 21 );
34        textField3.setEditable( false ); // disable editing
35        add( textField3 ); // add textField3 to JFrame
36
37        // construct passwordfield with default text
38        passwordField = new JPasswordField( "Hidden text" );
39        add( passwordField ); // add passwordField to JFrame
40
41        // register event handlers
42        TextFieldHandler handler = new TextFieldHandler();
43        textField1.addActionListener( handler );
44        textField2.addActionListener( handler );
45        textField3.addActionListener( handler );
46        passwordField.addActionListener( handler );
47     } // end TextFieldFrame constructor
48
49     // private inner class for event handling
50     private class TextFieldHandler implements ActionListener
51     {
52        // process text field events
53        public void actionPerformed( ActionEvent event )
54        {
55           String string = ""; // declare string to display
56
57           // user pressed Enter in JTextField textField1
58           if ( event.getSource() == textField1 )
59              string = String.format( "textField1: %s",
60                 event.getActionCommand() );
61
62           // user pressed Enter in JTextField textField2
63           else if ( event.getSource() == textField2 )
64              string = String.format( "textField2: %s",
65                 event.getActionCommand() );
```

Fig. 11.9 | JTextFields and JPasswordFields. (Part 2 of 3.)

```
66
67              // user pressed Enter in JTextField textField3
68           else if ( event.getSource() == textField3 )
69              string = String.format( "textField3: %s",
70                 event.getActionCommand() );
71
72              // user pressed Enter in JTextField passwordField
73           else if ( event.getSource() == passwordField )
74              string = String.format( "passwordField: %s",
75                 new String( passwordField.getPassword() ) );
76
77              // display JTextField content
78           JOptionPane.showMessageDialog( null, string );
79        } // end method actionPerformed
80     } // end private inner class TextFieldHandler
81  } // end class TextFieldFrame
```

Fig. 11.9 | JTextFields and JPasswordFields. (Part 3 of 3.)

```
1   // Fig. 11.10: TextFieldTest.java
2   // Testing TextFieldFrame.
3   import javax.swing.JFrame;
4
5   public class TextFieldTest
6   {
7      public static void main( String args[] )
8      {
9         TextFieldFrame textFieldFrame = new TextFieldFrame();
10        textFieldFrame.setDefaultCloseOperation( JFrame.EXIT_ON_CLOSE );
11        textFieldFrame.setSize( 325, 100 ); // set frame size
12        textFieldFrame.setVisible( true ); // display frame
13     } // end main
14  } // end class TextFieldTest
```

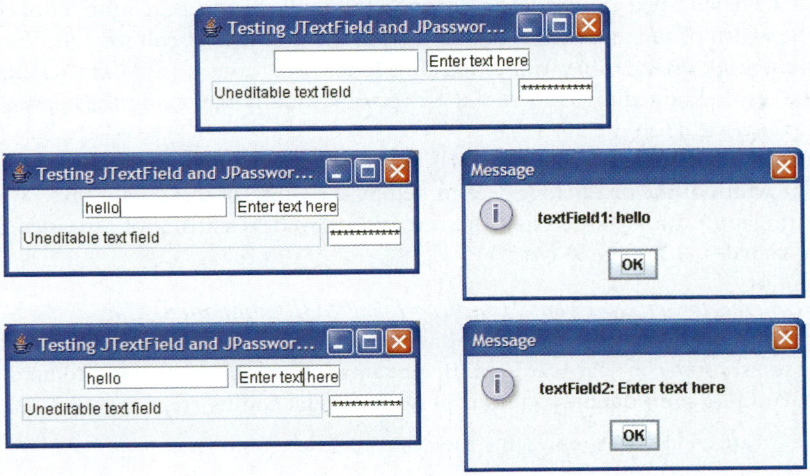

Fig. 11.10 | Test class for TextFieldFrame. (Part 1 of 2.)

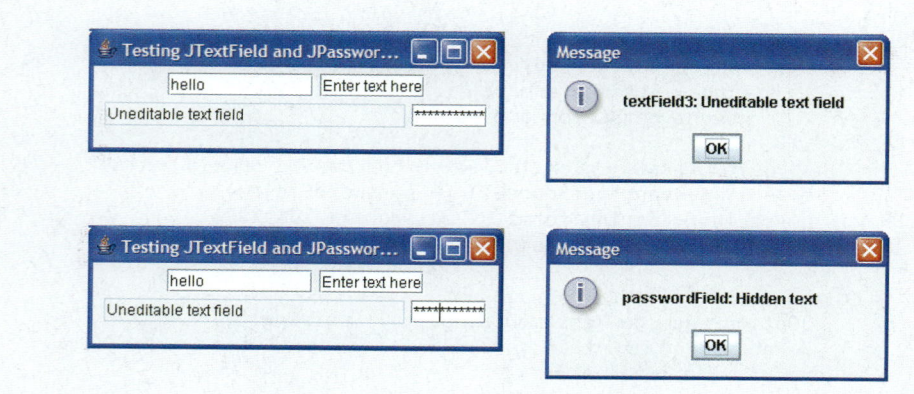

Fig. 11.10 | Test class for `TextFieldFrame`. (Part 2 of 2.)

Creating the GUI

Line 22 sets the layout of the `TextFieldFrame` to `FlowLayout`. Line 25 creates `textField1` with 10 columns of text. The width in pixels of a text column is determined by the average width of a character in the text field's current font. When text is displayed in a text field and the text is wider than the text field itself, a portion of the text at the right side is not visible. If you are typing in a text field and the cursor reaches the right edge of the text field, the text at the left edge is pushed off the left side of the text field and will no longer be visible. Users can use the left and right arrow keys to move through the complete text even though the entire text will not be visible at one time. Line 26 adds `textField1` to the `JFrame`.

Line 29 creates `textField2` with the initial text `"Enter text here"` to display in the text field. The width of the text field is determined by the width of the default text specified in the constructor. Line 30 adds `textField2` to the `JFrame`.

Line 33 creates `textField3` and calls the `JTextField` constructor with two arguments—the default text `"Uneditable text field"` to display and the number of columns (21). The width of the text field is determined by the number of columns specified. Line 34 uses method **setEditable** (inherited by `JTextField` from class `JTextComponent`) to make the text field uneditable—i.e., the user cannot modify the text in the text field. Line 35 adds `textField3` to the `JFrame`.

Line 38 creates `passwordField` with the text `"Hidden text"` to display in the text field. The width of the text field is determined by the width of the default text. When you execute the application, notice that the text is displayed as a string of asterisks. Line 39 adds `passwordField` to the `JFrame`.

Steps Required to Set Up Event Handling for a GUI Component

This example should display a message dialog containing the text from a text field when the user presses *Enter* in that text field. Before an application can respond to an event for a particular GUI component, you must perform several coding steps:

1. Create a class that represents the event handler.

2. Implement an appropriate interface, known as an **event-listener interface**, in the class from *Step 1*.

3. Indicate that an object of the class from *Steps 1* and *2* should be notified when the event occurs. This is known as registering the event handler.

Using a Nested Class to Implement an Event Handler

All the classes discussed so far were so-called top-level classes—that is, the classes were not declared inside another class. Java allows you to declare classes inside other classes—these are called nested classes. Nested classes can be static or non-static. Non-static nested classes are called inner classes and are frequently used for event handling.

Software Engineering Observation 11.2

An inner class is allowed to directly access its top-level class's variables and methods, even if they are private.

Before an object of an inner class can be created, there must first be an object of the top-level class that contains the inner class. This is required because an inner-class object implicitly has a reference to an object of its top-level class. There is also a special relationship between these objects—the inner-class object is allowed to directly access all the instance variables and methods of the outer class. A nested class that is static does not require an object of its top-level class and does not implicitly have a reference to an object of the top-level class. As you will see in Chapter 12, the Java 2D graphics API uses static nested classes extensively.

The event handling in this example is performed by an object of the private inner class TextFieldHandler (lines 50–80). This class is private because it will be used only to create event handlers for the text fields in top-level class TextFieldFrame. As with other members of a class, inner classes can be declared public, protected or private.

GUI components can generate a variety of events in response to user interactions. Each event is represented by a class and can be processed only by the appropriate type of event handler. In most cases, the events a GUI component supports are described in the Java API documentation for that component's class and its superclasses. When the user presses *Enter* in a JTextField or JPasswordField, the GUI component generates an ActionEvent (package java.awt.event). Such an event is processed by an object that implements the interface ActionListener (package java.awt.event). The information discussed here is available in the Java API documentation for classes JTextField and ActionEvent. Since JPasswordField is a subclass of JTextField, JPasswordField supports the same events.

To prepare to handle the events in this example, inner class TextFieldHandler implements interface ActionListener and declares the only method in that interface—action-Performed (lines 53–79). This method specifies the tasks to perform when an ActionEvent occurs. So inner class TextFieldHandler satisfies *Steps 1* and *2* listed earlier in this section. We'll discuss the details of method actionPerformed shortly.

Registering the Event Handler for Each Text Field

In the TextFieldFrame constructor, line 42 creates a TextFieldHandler object and assigns it to variable handler. This object's actionPerformed method will be called automatically when the user presses *Enter* in any of the GUI's text fields. However, before this can occur, the program must register this object as the event handler for each text field.

Lines 43–46 are the event-registration statements that specify handler as the event handler for the three JTextFields and the JPasswordField. The application calls JTextField method **addActionListener** to register the event handler for each component. This method receives as its argument an ActionListener object, which can be an object of any class that implements ActionListener. The object handler *is an* ActionListener, because class TextFieldHandler implements ActionListener. After lines 43–46 execute, the object handler listens for events. Now, when the user presses *Enter* in any of these four text fields, method actionPerformed (line 53–79) in class TextFieldHandler is called to handle the event. If an event handler is not registered for a particular text field, the event that occurs when the user presses *Enter* in that text field is consumed—i.e., it is simply ignored by the application.

Software Engineering Observation 11.3

The event listener for an event must implement the appropriate event-listener interface.

Common Programming Error 11.2

Forgetting to register an event-handler object for a particular GUI component's event type causes events of that type to be ignored.

Details of Class TextFieldHandler*'s* actionPerformed *Method*

In this example, we are using one event-handling object's actionPerformed method (lines 53–79) to handle the events generated by four text fields. Since we'd like to output the name of each text field's instance variable for demonstration purposes, we must determine which text field generated the event each time actionPerformed is called. The GUI component with which the user interacts is the event source. In this example, the event source is one of the text fields or the password field. When the user presses *Enter* while one of these GUI components has the focus, the system creates a unique ActionEvent object that contains information about the event that just occurred, such as the event source and the text in the text field. The system then passes this ActionEvent object in a method call to the event listener's actionPerformed method. In this example, we display some of that information in a message dialog. Line 55 declares the String that will be displayed. The variable is initialized with the empty string—a string containing no characters. The compiler requires this in case none of the branches of the nested if in lines 58–75 executes.

ActionEvent method getSource (called in lines 58, 63, 68 and 73) returns a reference to the event source. The condition in line 58 asks, "Is the event source textField1?" This condition compares the references on either side of the == operator to determine whether they refer to the same object. If they both refer to textField1, then the program knows that the user pressed *Enter* in textField1. In this case, lines 59–60 create a String containing the message that line 78 will display in a message dialog. Line 60 uses ActionEvent method **getActionCommand** to obtain the text the user typed in the text field that generated the event.

If the user interacted with the JPasswordField, lines 74–75 use JPasswordField method **getPassword** to obtain the password and create the String to display. This method returns the password as an array of type char that is used as an argument to a String constructor to create a string containing the characters in the array.

Class *TextFieldTest*

Class `TextFieldTest` (Fig. 11.10) contains the `main` method that executes this application and displays an object of class `TextFieldFrame`. When you execute the application, note that even the uneditable `JTextField` (textField3) can generate an `ActionEvent`. To test this, click the text field to give it the focus, then press *Enter*. Also note that the actual text of the password is displayed when you press *Enter* in the `JPasswordField`. Of course, you would normally not display the password!

This application used a single object of class `TextFieldHandler` as the event listener for four text fields. Starting in Section 11.9, you will see that it is possible to declare several event-listener objects of the same type and register each individual object for a separate GUI component's event. This technique enables us to eliminate the `if...else` logic used in this example's event handler by providing separate event handlers for each component's events.

11.6 **Common GUI Event Types and Listener Interfaces**

In Section 11.5, you learned that information about the event that occurs when the user presses *Enter* in a text field is stored in an `ActionEvent` object. There are many different types of events that can occur when the user interacts with a GUI. The information about any GUI event that occurs is stored in an object of a class that extends `AWTEvent`. Figure 11.11 illustrates a hierarchy containing many event classes from the package `java.awt.event`. Some of these are discussed in this chapter and Chapter 22. These event types are used with both AWT and Swing components. Additional event types that are specific to Swing GUI components are declared in package `javax.swing.event`.

Let's summarize the three parts to the event-handling mechanism that you saw in Section 11.5—the event source, the event object and the event listener. The event source is the particular GUI component with which the user interacts. The event object encapsulates information about the event that occurred, such as a reference to the event source and any event-specific information that may be required by the event listener for it to handle the event. The event listener is an object that is notified by the event source when an event occurs; in effect, it "listens" for an event and one of its methods executes in response to the event. A method of the event listener receives an event object when the event listener is notified of the event. The event listener then uses the event object to respond to the event. The event-handling model described here is known as the delegation event model—an event's processing is delegated to a particular object (the event listener) in the application.

For each event-object type, there is typically a corresponding event-listener interface. An event listener for a GUI event is an object of a class that implements one or more of the event-listener interfaces from packages `java.awt.event` and `javax.swing.event`. Many of the event-listener types are common to both Swing and AWT components. Such types are declared in package `java.awt.event`, and some of them are shown in Fig. 11.12. Additional event-listener types that are specific to Swing components are declared in package `javax.swing.event`.

Each event-listener interface specifies one or more event-handling methods that must be declared in the class that implements the interface. Recall from Section 10.7 that any class which implements an interface must declare all the `abstract` methods of that interface; otherwise, the class is an `abstract` class and cannot be used to create objects.

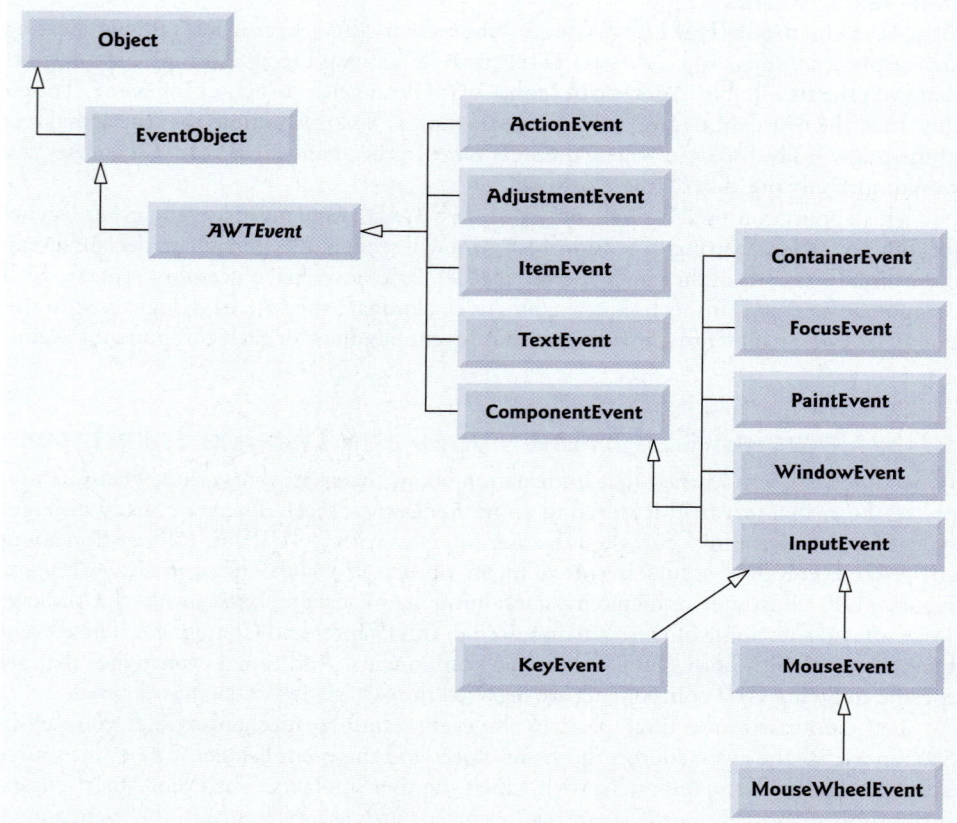

Fig. 11.11 | Some event classes of package `java.awt.event`.

When an event occurs, the GUI component with which the user interacted notifies its registered listeners by calling each listener's appropriate event-handling method. For example, when the user presses the *Enter* key in a JTextField, the registered listener's `actionPerformed` method is called. How did the event handler get registered? How does the GUI component know to call `actionPerformed` rather than another event-handling method? We answer these questions and diagram the interaction in the next section.

11.7 How Event Handling Works

Let us illustrate how the event-handling mechanism works, using `textField1` from the example of Fig. 11.9. We have two remaining open questions from Section 11.5:

1. How did the event handler get registered?

2. How does the GUI component know to call `actionPerformed` rather than some other event-handling method?

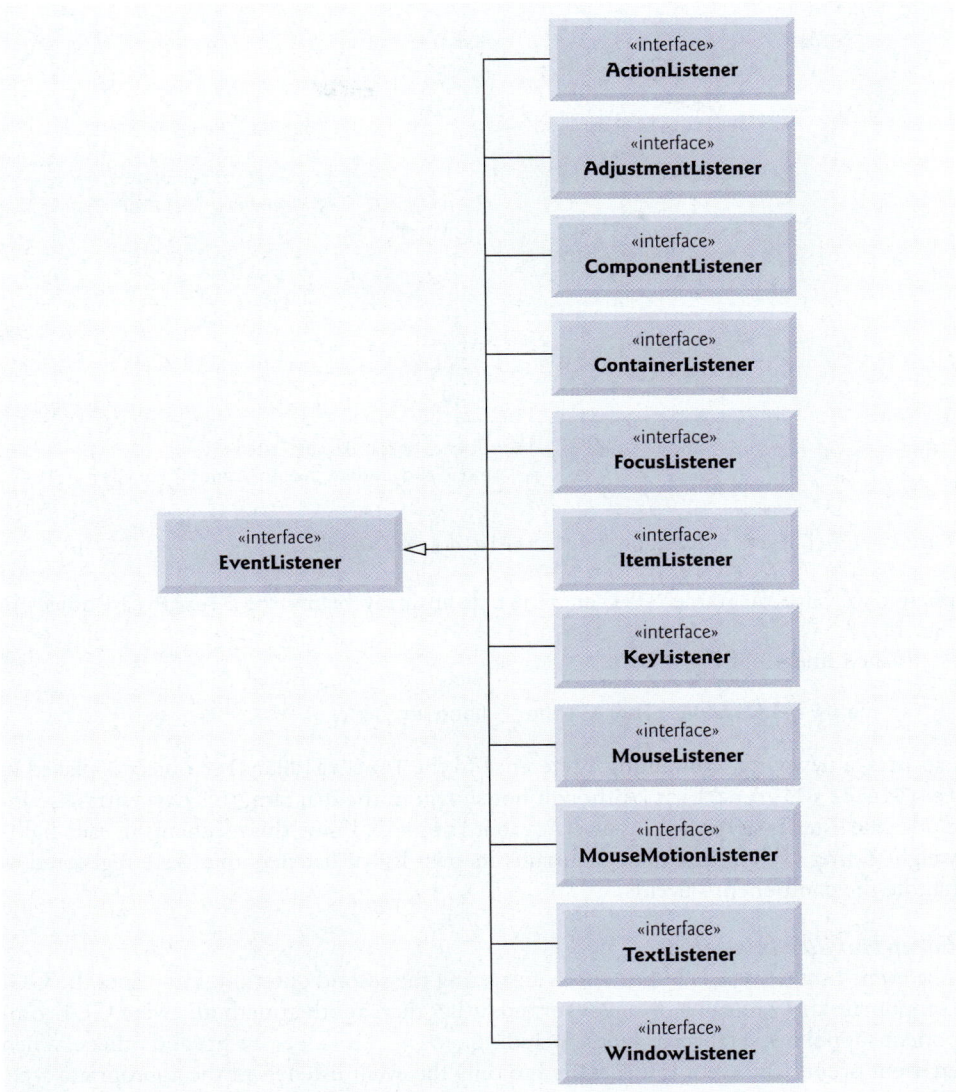

Fig. 11.12 | Some common event-listener interfaces of package `java.awt.event`.

The first question is answered by the event registration performed in lines 43–46 of the application. Figure 11.13 diagrams JTextField variable textField1, TextFieldHandler variable handler and the objects to which they refer.

Registering Events

Every JComponent has an instance variable called **listenerList** that refers to an object of class **EventListenerList** (package javax.swing.event). Each object of a JComponent subclass maintains a references to all its registered listeners in the listenerList. For sim-

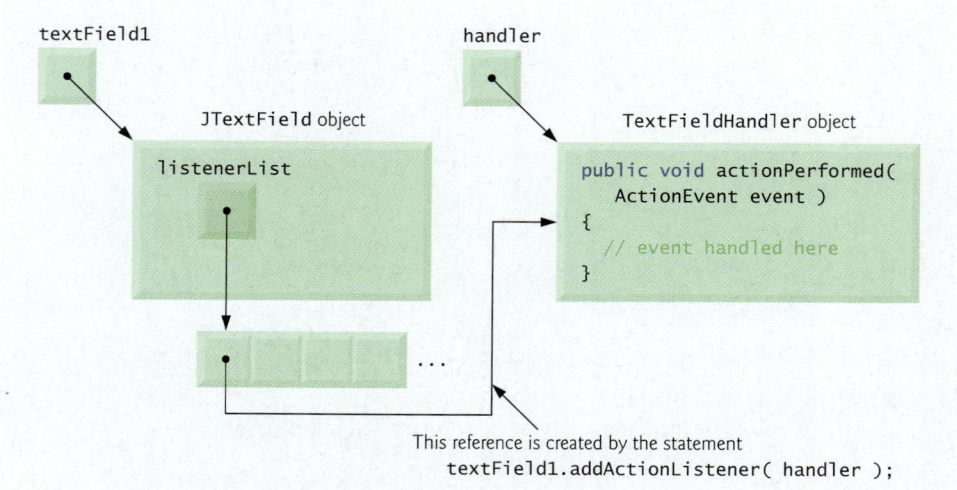

Fig. 11.13 | Event registration for JTextField textField1.

plicity, we have diagramed listenerList as an array below the JTextField object in Fig. 11.13.

When line 43 of Fig. 11.9

```
textField1.addActionListener( handler );
```

executes, a new entry containing a reference to the TextFieldHandler object is placed in textField1's listenerList. Although not shown in the diagram, this new entry also includes the listener's type (in this case, ActionListener). Using this mechanism, each lightweight Swing GUI component maintains its own list of listeners that were registered to handle the component's events.

Event-Handler Invocation

The event-listener type is important in answering the second question: How does the GUI component know to call actionPerformed rather than another method? Every GUI component supports several event types, including mouse events, key events and others. When an event occurs, the event is dispatched to only the event listeners of the appropriate type. Dispatching is simply the process by which the GUI component calls an event-handling method on each of its listeners that are registered for the particular event type that occurred.

Each event type has one or more corresponding event-listener interfaces. For example, ActionEvents are handled by ActionListeners, MouseEvents are handled by MouseListeners and MouseMotionListeners, and KeyEvents are handled by KeyListeners. When an event occurs, the GUI component receives (from the JVM) a unique event ID specifying the event type. The GUI component uses the event ID to decide the listener type to which the event should be dispatched and to decide which method to call on each listener object. For an ActionEvent, the event is dispatched to every registered ActionListener's actionPerformed method (the only method in interface ActionListener). For a Mouse-Event, the event is dispatched to every registered MouseListener or MouseMotionListener, depending on the mouse event that occurs. The MouseEvent's event ID determines which of the several mouse event-handling methods are called. All these decisions are handled for you by the GUI components. All you need to do is register an event handler for the particular event type that your application requires and the GUI component will ensure that the event handler's appropriate method gets called when the event occurs. [*Note:* We discuss other event types and event-listener interfaces as they are needed with each new component we introduce.]

11.8 JButton

A button is a component the user clicks to trigger a specific action. A Java application can use several types of buttons, including command buttons, check boxes, toggle buttons and radio buttons. Figure 11.14 shows the inheritance hierarchy of the Swing buttons we cover in this chapter. As you can see, all the button types are subclasses of AbstractButton (package javax.swing), which declares the common features of Swing buttons. In this section, we concentrate on buttons that are typically used to initiate a command.

> **Look-and-Feel Observation 11.7**
>
> *Buttons typically use book-title capitalization.*

A command button (see output of Fig. 11.15) generates an ActionEvent when the user clicks the button. Command buttons are created with class JButton. The text on the face of a JButton is called a button label. A GUI can have many JButtons, but each button label typically should be unique in the portion of the GUI that is currently displayed.

> **Look-and-Feel Observation 11.8**
>
> *Having more than one JButton with the same label makes the JButtons ambiguous to the user. Provide a unique label for each button.*

The application of Fig. 11.15 and Fig. 11.16 creates two JButtons and demonstrates that JButtons support the display of Icons. Event handling for the buttons is performed by a single instance of inner class ButtonHandler (lines 39–47).

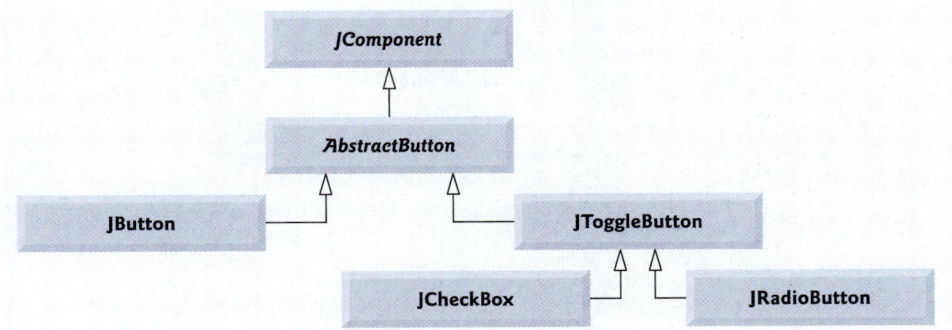

Fig. 11.14 | Swing button hierarchy.

```java
1   // Fig. 11.15: ButtonFrame.java
2   // Creating JButtons.
3   import java.awt.FlowLayout;
4   import java.awt.event.ActionListener;
5   import java.awt.event.ActionEvent;
6   import javax.swing.JFrame;
7   import javax.swing.JButton;
8   import javax.swing.Icon;
9   import javax.swing.ImageIcon;
10  import javax.swing.JOptionPane;
11
12  public class ButtonFrame extends JFrame
13  {
14     private JButton plainJButton; // button with just text
15     private JButton fancyJButton; // button with icons
16
17     // ButtonFrame adds JButtons to JFrame
18     public ButtonFrame()
19     {
20        super( "Testing Buttons" );
21        setLayout( new FlowLayout() ); // set frame layout
22
23        plainJButton = new JButton( "Plain Button" ); // button with text
24        add( plainJButton ); // add plainJButton to JFrame
25
26        Icon bug1 = new ImageIcon( getClass().getResource( "bug1.gif" ) );
27        Icon bug2 = new ImageIcon( getClass().getResource( "bug2.gif" ) );
28        fancyJButton = new JButton( "Fancy Button", bug1 ); // set image
29        fancyJButton.setRolloverIcon( bug2 ); // set rollover image
30        add( fancyJButton ); // add fancyJButton to JFrame
31
32        // create new ButtonHandler for button event handling
33        ButtonHandler handler = new ButtonHandler();
34        fancyJButton.addActionListener( handler );
35        plainJButton.addActionListener( handler );
36     } // end ButtonFrame constructor
37
38     // inner class for button event handling
39     private class ButtonHandler implements ActionListener
40     {
41        // handle button event
42        public void actionPerformed( ActionEvent event )
43        {
44           JOptionPane.showMessageDialog( ButtonFrame.this, String.format(
45              "You pressed: %s", event.getActionCommand() ) );
46        } // end method actionPerformed
47     } // end private inner class ButtonHandler
48  } // end class ButtonFrame
```

Fig. 11.15 | Command buttons and action events.

```
 1    // Fig. 11.16: ButtonTest.java
 2    // Testing ButtonFrame.
 3    import javax.swing.JFrame;
 4
 5    public class ButtonTest
 6    {
 7       public static void main( String args[] )
 8       {
 9          ButtonFrame buttonFrame = new ButtonFrame(); // create ButtonFrame
10          buttonFrame.setDefaultCloseOperation( JFrame.EXIT_ON_CLOSE );
11          buttonFrame.setSize( 275, 110 ); // set frame size
12          buttonFrame.setVisible( true ); // display frame
13       } // end main
14    } // end class ButtonTest
```

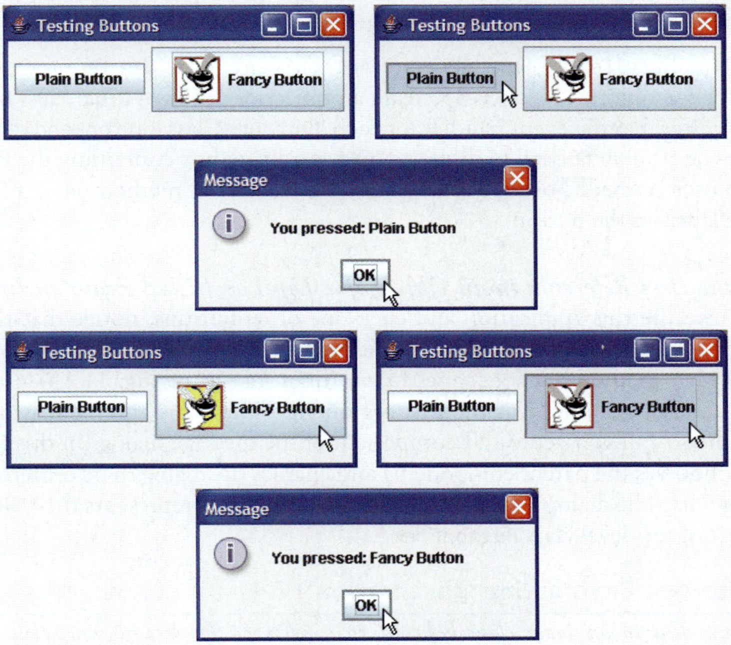

Fig. 11.16 | Test class for `ButtonFrame`.

Lines 14–15 declare `JButton` variables `plainButton` and `fancyButton`. The corresponding objects are instantiated in the constructor. Line 23 creates `plainButton` with the button label `"Plain Button"`. Line 24 adds the button to the `JFrame`.

A `JButton` can display an `Icon`. To provide the user with an extra level of visual interaction with the GUI, a `JButton` can also have a **rollover** `Icon`—an `Icon` that is displayed when the user positions the mouse over the button. The icon on the button changes as the mouse moves in and out of the button's area on the screen. Lines 26–27 create two `Image-Icon` objects that represent the default `Icon` and rollover `Icon` for the `JButton` created at line 28. Both statements assume that the image files are stored in the same directory as the application (which is commonly the case for applications that use images). These image files have been provided for you.

Line 28 creates fancyButton with the text "Fancy Button" and the icon bug1. By default, the text is displayed to the right of the icon. Line 29 uses **setRolloverIcon** (inherited from class AbstractButton) to specify the image displayed on the button when the user positions the mouse over it. Line 30 adds the button to the JFrame.

Look-and-Feel Observation 11.9

Because class AbstractButton supports displaying text and images on a button, all subclasses of AbstractButton also support displaying text and images.

Look-and-Feel Observation 11.10

Using rollover icons for JButtons provides users with visual feedback indicating that when they click the mouse while the cursor is positioned over the button, an action will occur.

JButtons, like JTextFields, generate ActionEvents that can be processed by any ActionListener object. Lines 33–35 create an object of private inner class ButtonHandler and register it as the event handler for each JButton. Class ButtonHandler (lines 39–47) declares actionPerformed to display a message dialog box containing the label for the button the user pressed. For a JButton event, ActionEvent method getActionCommand returns the label on the button.

Accessing the this Reference in an Object of a Top-Level Class From an Inner Class
When you execute this application and click one of its buttons, notice that the message dialog that appears is centered over the application's window. This occurs because the call to JOptionPane method showMessageDialog (lines 44–45 of Fig. 11.15) uses ButtonFrame.this rather than null as the first argument. When this argument is not null, it represents the so-called parent GUI component of the message dialog (in this case the application window is the parent component) and enables the dialog to be centered over that component when the dialog is displayed. ButtonFrame.this represents the this reference of the object of top-level class ButtonFrame.

Software Engineering Observation 11.4

When used in an inner class, keyword this refers to the current inner-class object being manipulated. An inner-class method can use its outer-class object's this by preceding this with the outer-class name and a dot, as in ButtonFrame.this.

11.9 Buttons That Maintain State

The Swing GUI components contain three types of state buttons—JToggleButton, JCheckBox and JRadioButton—that have on/off or true/false values. Classes JCheckBox and JRadioButton are subclasses of JToggleButton (Fig. 11.14). A JRadioButton is different from a JCheckBox in that normally several JRadioButtons are grouped together, and are mutually exclusive—only one in the group can be selected at any time. We first discuss class JCheckBox. The next two subsections also demonstrate that an inner class can access the members of its top-level class.

11.9.1 JCheckBox

The application of Fig. 11.17 and Fig. 11.18 uses two `JCheckBox` objects to select the desired font style of the text displayed in a `JTextField`. When selected, one applies a bold style and the other an italic style. If both are selected, the style of the font is bold and italic. When the application initially executes, neither `JCheckBox` is checked (i.e., they are both `false`), so the font is plain. Class `CheckBoxTest` (Fig. 11.18) contains the `main` method that executes this application.

```java
 1   // Fig. 11.17: CheckBoxFrame.java
 2   // Creating JCheckBox buttons.
 3   import java.awt.FlowLayout;
 4   import java.awt.Font;
 5   import java.awt.event.ItemListener;
 6   import java.awt.event.ItemEvent;
 7   import javax.swing.JFrame;
 8   import javax.swing.JTextField;
 9   import javax.swing.JCheckBox;
10
11   public class CheckBoxFrame extends JFrame
12   {
13      private JTextField textField; // displays text in changing fonts
14      private JCheckBox boldJCheckBox; // to select/deselect bold
15      private JCheckBox italicJCheckBox; // to select/deselect italic
16
17      // CheckBoxFrame constructor adds JCheckBoxes to JFrame
18      public CheckBoxFrame()
19      {
20         super( "JCheckBox Test" );
21         setLayout( new FlowLayout() ); // set frame layout
22
23         // set up JTextField and set its font
24         textField = new JTextField( "Watch the font style change", 20 );
25         textField.setFont( new Font( "Serif", Font.PLAIN, 14 ) );
26         add( textField ); // add textField to JFrame
27
28         boldJCheckBox = new JCheckBox( "Bold" ); // create bold checkbox
29         italicJCheckBox = new JCheckBox( "Italic" ); // create italic
30         add( boldJCheckBox ); // add bold checkbox to JFrame
31         add( italicJCheckBox ); // add italic checkbox to JFrame
32
33         // register listeners for JCheckBoxes
34         CheckBoxHandler handler = new CheckBoxHandler();
35         boldJCheckBox.addItemListener( handler );
36         italicJCheckBox.addItemListener( handler );
37      } // end CheckBoxFrame constructor
38
39      // private inner class for ItemListener event handling
40      private class CheckBoxHandler implements ItemListener
41      {
42         private int valBold = Font.PLAIN; // controls bold font style
43         private int valItalic = Font.PLAIN; // controls italic font style
```

Fig. 11.17 | JCheckBox buttons and item events. (Part 1 of 2.)

```
44
45          // respond to checkbox events
46          public void itemStateChanged( ItemEvent event )
47          {
48             // process bold checkbox events
49             if ( event.getSource() == boldJCheckBox )
50                valBold =
51                   boldJCheckBox.isSelected() ? Font.BOLD : Font.PLAIN;
52
53             // process italic checkbox events
54             if ( event.getSource() == italicJCheckBox )
55                valItalic =
56                   italicJCheckBox.isSelected() ? Font.ITALIC : Font.PLAIN;
57
58             // set text field font
59             textField.setFont(
60                new Font( "Serif", valBold + valItalic, 14 ) );
61          } // end method itemStateChanged
62       } // end private inner class CheckBoxHandler
63    } // end class CheckBoxFrame
```

Fig. 11.17 | JCheckBox buttons and item events. (Part 2 of 2.)

```
1     // Fig. 11.18: CheckBoxTest.java
2     // Testing CheckBoxFrame.
3     import javax.swing.JFrame;
4
5     public class CheckBoxTest
6     {
7        public static void main( String args[] )
8        {
9           CheckBoxFrame checkBoxFrame = new CheckBoxFrame();
10          checkBoxFrame.setDefaultCloseOperation( JFrame.EXIT_ON_CLOSE );
11          checkBoxFrame.setSize( 275, 100 ); // set frame size
12          checkBoxFrame.setVisible( true ); // display frame
13       } // end main
14    } // end class CheckBoxTest
```

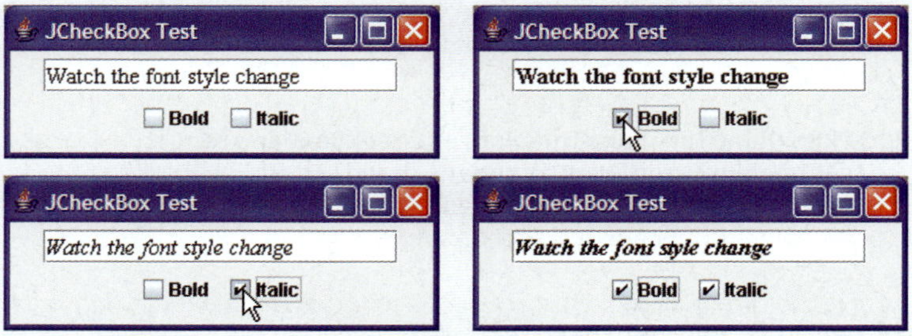

Fig. 11.18 | Test class for CheckBoxFrame.

After the JTextField is created and initialized (Fig. 11.17, line 24), line 25 uses method **setFont** (inherited by JTextField indirectly from class Component) to set the font of the JTextField to a new object of class **Font** (package java.awt). The new Font is initialized with "Serif" (a generic font name representing a font such as Times and is supported on all Java platforms), Font.PLAIN style and 14-point size. Next, lines 28–29 create two JCheckBox objects. The string passed to the JCheckBox constructor is the checkbox label that appears to the right of the JCheckBox by default.

When the user clicks a JCheckBox, an **ItemEvent** occurs. This event can be handled by an **ItemListener** object, which must implement method **itemStateChanged**. In this example, the event handling is performed by an instance of private inner class CheckBox-Handler (lines 40–62). Lines 34–36 create an instance of class CheckBoxHandler and register it with method **addItemListener** as the listener for both the JCheckBox objects.

Lines 42–43 declare instance variables for the inner class CheckBoxHandler. Together, these variables represent the font style for the text displayed in the JTextField. Initially both are Font.PLAIN to indicate that the font is not bold and is not italic. Method item-StateChanged (lines 46–61) is called when the user clicks the bold or the italic JCheckBox. The method uses event.getSource() to determine which JCheckBox the user clicked. If it was the boldJCheckBox, line 51 uses JCheckBox method **isSelected** to determine if the JCheckBox is selected (i.e., it is checked). If the checkbox is selected, local variable valBold is assigned Font.BOLD; otherwise, it is assigned Font.PLAIN. A similar statement executes if the user clicks the italicJCheckBox. If the italicJCheckBox is selected, local variable valItalic is assigned Font.ITALIC; otherwise, it is assigned Font.PLAIN. Lines 59–60 change the font of the JTextField, using the same font name and point size. The sum of valBold and valItalic represents the JTextField's new font style. Each of the Font constants represents a unique value. Font.PLAIN has the value 0, so if both valBold and valItalic are set to Font.PLAIN, the font will have the plain style. If one of the values is Font.BOLD or Font.ITALIC, the font will be bold or italic accordingly. If one is BOLD and the other is ITALIC, the font will be both bold and italic.

Relationship Between an Inner Class and Its Top-Level Class

You may have noticed that class CheckBoxHandler used variables boldJCheckBox (Fig. 11.17, lines 49 and 51), italicJCheckBox (lines 54 and 56) and textField (line 59) even though these variables are not declared in the inner class. An inner class has a special relationship with its top-level class—the inner class is allowed to access directly all the instance variables and methods of the top-level class. Method itemStateChanged (line 46–61) of class CheckBoxHandler uses this relationship to determine which JCheckBox is the event source, to determine the state of a JCheckBox and to set the font on the JTextField. Notice that none of the code in inner class CheckBoxHandler requires a reference to the top-level class object.

11.9.2 JRadioButton

Radio buttons (declared with class **JRadioButton**) are similar to check boxes in that they have two states—selected and not selected (also called deselected). However, radio buttons normally appear as a group in which only one button can be selected at a time (see output of Fig. 11.20). Selecting a different radio button forces all others to be deselected. Radio buttons are used to represent mutually exclusive options (i.e., multiple options in the group cannot be selected at the same time). The logical relationship between radio buttons is maintained by a **ButtonGroup** object (package javax.swing), which itself is not a GUI component. A ButtonGroup object organizes a group of buttons and is not itself displayed in a user interface. Rather, the individual JRadioButton objects from the group are displayed in the GUI.

Common Programming Error 11.3

Adding a ButtonGroup object (or an object of any other class that does not derive from Component) to a container results in a compilation error.

The application of Fig. 11.19 and Fig. 11.20 is similar to that of Fig. 11.17 and Fig. 11.18. The user can alter the font style of a JTextField's text. The application uses radio buttons that permit only a single font style in the group to be selected at a time. Class RadioButtonTest (Fig. 11.20) contains the main method that executes this application.

Lines 35–42 in the constructor (Fig. 11.19) create four JRadioButton objects and add them to the JFrame. Each JRadioButton is created with a constructor call like that in line 35. This constructor specifies the label that appears to the right of the JRadioButton by default and the initial state of the JRadioButton. A true second argument indicates that the JRadioButton should appear selected when it is displayed.

```
1   // Fig. 11.19: RadioButtonFrame.java
2   // Creating radio buttons using ButtonGroup and JRadioButton.
3   import java.awt.FlowLayout;
4   import java.awt.Font;
5   import java.awt.event.ItemListener;
6   import java.awt.event.ItemEvent;
7   import javax.swing.JFrame;
8   import javax.swing.JTextField;
9   import javax.swing.JRadioButton;
10  import javax.swing.ButtonGroup;
11
12  public class RadioButtonFrame extends JFrame
13  {
14     private JTextField textField; // used to display font changes
15     private Font plainFont; // font for plain text
16     private Font boldFont; // font for bold text
17     private Font italicFont; // font for italic text
18     private Font boldItalicFont; // font for bold and italic text
19     private JRadioButton plainJRadioButton; // selects plain text
20     private JRadioButton boldJRadioButton; // selects bold text
21     private JRadioButton italicJRadioButton; // selects italic text
22     private JRadioButton boldItalicJRadioButton; // bold and italic
23     private ButtonGroup radioGroup; // buttongroup to hold radio buttons
24
25     // RadioButtonFrame constructor adds JRadioButtons to JFrame
26     public RadioButtonFrame()
27     {
28        super( "RadioButton Test" );
29        setLayout( new FlowLayout() ); // set frame layout
30
31        textField = new JTextField( "Watch the font style change", 25 );
32        add( textField ); // add textField to JFrame
```

Fig. 11.19 | JRadioButtons and ButtonGroups. (Part 1 of 2.)

```
33
34        // create radio buttons
35        plainJRadioButton = new JRadioButton( "Plain", true );
36        boldJRadioButton = new JRadioButton( "Bold", false );
37        italicJRadioButton = new JRadioButton( "Italic", false );
38        boldItalicJRadioButton = new JRadioButton( "Bold/Italic", false );
39        add( plainJRadioButton ); // add plain button to JFrame
40        add( boldJRadioButton ); // add bold button to JFrame
41        add( italicJRadioButton ); // add italic button to JFrame
42        add( boldItalicJRadioButton ); // add bold and italic button
43
44        // create logical relationship between JRadioButtons
45        radioGroup = new ButtonGroup(); // create ButtonGroup
46        radioGroup.add( plainJRadioButton ); // add plain to group
47        radioGroup.add( boldJRadioButton ); // add bold to group
48        radioGroup.add( italicJRadioButton ); // add italic to group
49        radioGroup.add( boldItalicJRadioButton ); // add bold and italic
50
51        // create font objects
52        plainFont = new Font( "Serif", Font.PLAIN, 14 );
53        boldFont = new Font( "Serif", Font.BOLD, 14 );
54        italicFont = new Font( "Serif", Font.ITALIC, 14 );
55        boldItalicFont = new Font( "Serif", Font.BOLD + Font.ITALIC, 14 );
56        textField.setFont( plainFont ); // set initial font to plain
57
58        // register events for JRadioButtons
59        plainJRadioButton.addItemListener(
60           new RadioButtonHandler( plainFont ) );
61        boldJRadioButton.addItemListener(
62           new RadioButtonHandler( boldFont ) );
63        italicJRadioButton.addItemListener(
64           new RadioButtonHandler( italicFont ) );
65        boldItalicJRadioButton.addItemListener(
66           new RadioButtonHandler( boldItalicFont ) );
67     } // end RadioButtonFrame constructor
68
69     // private inner class to handle radio button events
70     private class RadioButtonHandler implements ItemListener
71     {
72        private Font font; // font associated with this listener
73
74        public RadioButtonHandler( Font f )
75        {
76           font = f; // set the font of this listener
77        } // end constructor RadioButtonHandler
78
79        // handle radio button events
80        public void itemStateChanged( ItemEvent event )
81        {
82           textField.setFont( font ); // set font of textField
83        } // end method itemStateChanged
84     } // end private inner class RadioButtonHandler
85  } // end class RadioButtonFrame
```

Fig. 11.19 | JRadioButtons and ButtonGroups. (Part 2 of 2.)

```
1   // Fig. 11.20: RadioButtonTest.java
2   // Testing RadioButtonFrame.
3   import javax.swing.JFrame;
4
5   public class RadioButtonTest
6   {
7      public static void main( String args[] )
8      {
9         RadioButtonFrame radioButtonFrame = new RadioButtonFrame();
10        radioButtonFrame.setDefaultCloseOperation( JFrame.EXIT_ON_CLOSE );
11        radioButtonFrame.setSize( 300, 100 ); // set frame size
12        radioButtonFrame.setVisible( true ); // display frame
13     } // end main
14  } // end class RadioButtonTest
```

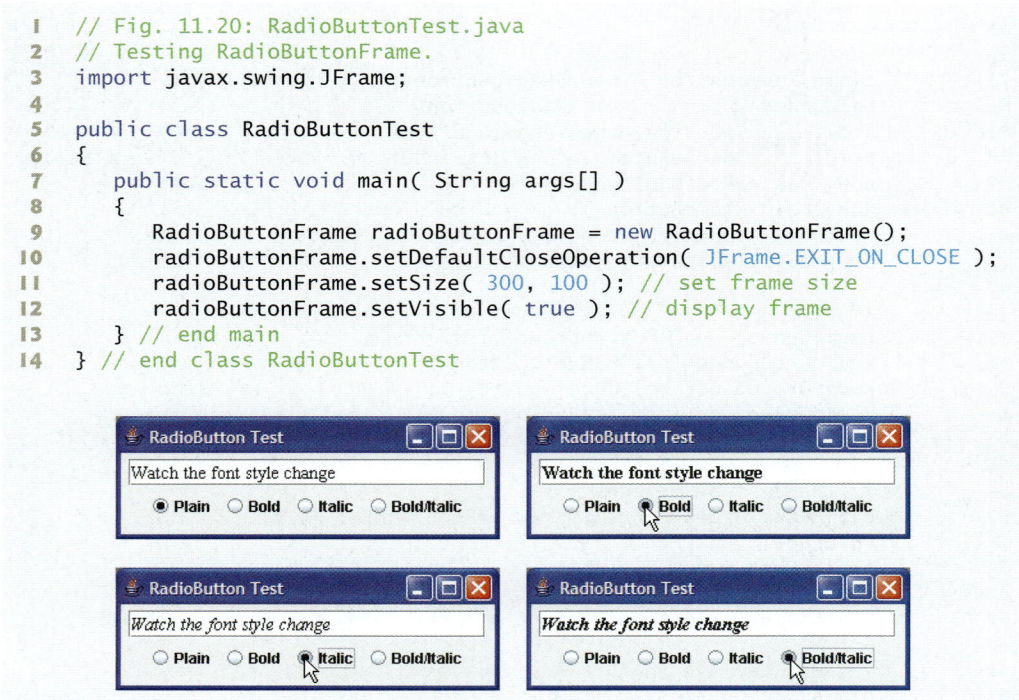

Fig. 11.20 | Test class for `RadioButtonFrame`.

Line 45 instantiates `ButtonGroup` object `radioGroup`. This object is the "glue" that forms the logical relationship between the four `JRadioButton` objects and allows only one of the four to be selected at a time. It is possible that no `JRadioButtons` in a `ButtonGroup` are selected, but this can only occur if no preselected `JRadioButtons` are added to the `But-tonGroup` and the user has not selected a `JRadioButton` yet. Lines 46–49 use `ButtonGroup` method **add** to associate each of the `JRadioButtons` with `radioGroup`. If more than one selected `JRadioButton` object is added to the group, the selected one that was added first will be selected when the GUI is displayed.

`JRadioButtons`, like `JCheckBoxes`, generate `ItemEvents` when they are clicked. Lines 59–66 create four instances of inner class `RadioButtonHandler` (declared at lines 70–84). In this example, each event listener object is registered to handle the `ItemEvent` generated when the user clicks a particular `JRadioButton`. Notice that each `RadioButtonHandler` object is initialized with a particular `Font` object (created in lines 52–55).

Class `RadioButtonHandler` (line 70–84) implements interface `ItemListener` so it can handle `ItemEvents` generated by the `JRadioButtons`. The constructor stores the `Font` object it receives as an argument in the event-listener object's instance variable `font` (declared at line 72). When the user clicks a `JRadioButton`, `radioGroup` turns off the previously selected `JRadioButton` and method `itemStateChanged` (line 80–83) sets the font in the `JTextField` to the `Font` stored in the `JRadioButton`'s corresponding event-listener object. Notice that line 82 of inner class `RadioButtonHandler` uses the top-level class's `textField` instance variable to set the font.

11.10   **JComboBox** and Using an Anonymous Inner Class for Event Handling

A combo box (sometimes called a drop-down list) provides a list of items (Fig. 11.22) from which the user can make a single selection. Combo boxes are implemented with class JComboBox, which extends class JComponent. JComboBoxes generate ItemEvents like JCheckBoxes and JRadioButtons. This example also demonstrates a special form of inner class that is used frequently in event handling.

The application of Fig. 11.21 and Fig. 11.22 uses a JComboBox to provide a list of four image file names from which the user can select one image to display. When the user selects a name, the application displays the corresponding image as an Icon on a JLabel. Class ComboBoxTest (Fig. 11.22) contains the main method that executes this application. The screen captures for this application show the JComboBox list after the selection was made to illustrate which image file name was selected.

Lines 19–23 (Fig. 11.21) declare and initialize array icons with four new ImageIcon objects. String array names (lines 17–18) contains the names of the four image files that are stored in the same directory as the application.

At line 31, the constructor creates a JComboBox object, using the Strings in array names as the elements in the list. Each item in the list has an index. The first item is added at index 0, the next at index 1 and so forth. The first item added to a JComboBox appears as the currently selected item when the JComboBox is displayed. Other items are selected by clicking the JComboBox, which expands into a list from which the user can make a selection.

Line 32 uses JComboBox method setMaximumRowCount to set the maximum number of elements that are displayed when the user clicks the JComboBox. If there are additional items, the JComboBox provides a scrollbar (see the first screen capture) that allows the user to scroll through all the elements in the list. The user can click the scroll arrows at the top and bottom of the scrollbar to move up and down through the list one element at a time, or else drag the scroll box in the middle of the scrollbar up and down. To drag the scroll box, position the mouse cursor on it, hold the mouse button down and move the mouse.

Look-and-Feel Observation 11.11

Set the maximum row count for a JComboBox to a number of rows that prevents the list from expanding outside the bounds of the window in which it is used. This configuration will ensure that the list displays correctly when it is expanded by the user.

Line 48 attaches the JComboBox to the ComboBoxFrame's FlowLayout (set in line 29). Line 49 creates the JLabel that is used to display each ImageIcon and initializes it with the first ImageIcon in array icons. Line 50 attaches the JLabel to the ComboBoxFrame's Flow-Layout.

Using an Anonymous Inner Class for Event Handling

Lines 34–46 are one statement that declares the event listener's class, creates an object of that class and registers that object as the listener for imagesJComboBox's ItemEvents. In this example, the event-listener object is an instance of an anonymous inner class—a special form of inner class that is declared without a name and typically appears inside a method declaration. As with other inner classes, an anonymous inner class can access its top-level class's members. However, an anonymous inner class has limited access to the local

```java
 1   // Fig. 11.21: ComboBoxFrame.java
 2   // Using a JComboBox to select an image to display.
 3   import java.awt.FlowLayout;
 4   import java.awt.event.ItemListener;
 5   import java.awt.event.ItemEvent;
 6   import javax.swing.JFrame;
 7   import javax.swing.JLabel;
 8   import javax.swing.JComboBox;
 9   import javax.swing.Icon;
10   import javax.swing.ImageIcon;
11
12   public class ComboBoxFrame extends JFrame
13   {
14      private JComboBox imagesJComboBox; // combobox to hold names of icons
15      private JLabel label; // label to display selected icon
16
17      private String names[] =
18         { "bug1.gif", "bug2.gif",  "travelbug.gif", "buganim.gif" };
19      private Icon icons[] = {
20         new ImageIcon( getClass().getResource( names[ 0 ] ) ),
21         new ImageIcon( getClass().getResource( names[ 1 ] ) ),
22         new ImageIcon( getClass().getResource( names[ 2 ] ) ),
23         new ImageIcon( getClass().getResource( names[ 3 ] ) ) };
24
25      // ComboBoxFrame constructor adds JComboBox to JFrame
26      public ComboBoxFrame()
27      {
28         super( "Testing JComboBox" );
29         setLayout( new FlowLayout() ); // set frame layout
30
31         imagesJComboBox = new JComboBox( names ); // set up JComboBox
32         imagesJComboBox.setMaximumRowCount( 3 ); // display three rows
33
34         imagesJComboBox.addItemListener(
35            new ItemListener() // anonymous inner class
36            {
37               // handle JComboBox event
38               public void itemStateChanged( ItemEvent event )
39               {
40                  // determine whether check box selected
41                  if ( event.getStateChange() == ItemEvent.SELECTED )
42                     label.setIcon( icons[
43                        imagesJComboBox.getSelectedIndex() ] );
44               } // end method itemStateChanged
45            } // end anonymous inner class
46         ); // end call to addItemListener
47
48         add( imagesJComboBox ); // add combobox to JFrame
49         label = new JLabel( icons[ 0 ] ); // display first icon
50         add( label ); // add label to JFrame
51      } // end ComboBoxFrame constructor
52   } // end class ComboBoxFrame
```

Fig. 11.21 | JComboBox that displays a list of image names.

```
 1   // Fig. 11.22: ComboBoxTest.java
 2   // Testing ComboBoxFrame.
 3   import javax.swing.JFrame;
 4
 5   public class ComboBoxTest
 6   {
 7      public static void main( String args[] )
 8      {
 9         ComboBoxFrame comboBoxFrame = new ComboBoxFrame();
10         comboBoxFrame.setDefaultCloseOperation( JFrame.EXIT_ON_CLOSE );
11         comboBoxFrame.setSize( 350, 150 ); // set frame size
12         comboBoxFrame.setVisible( true ); // display frame
13      } // end main
14   } // end class ComboBoxTest
```

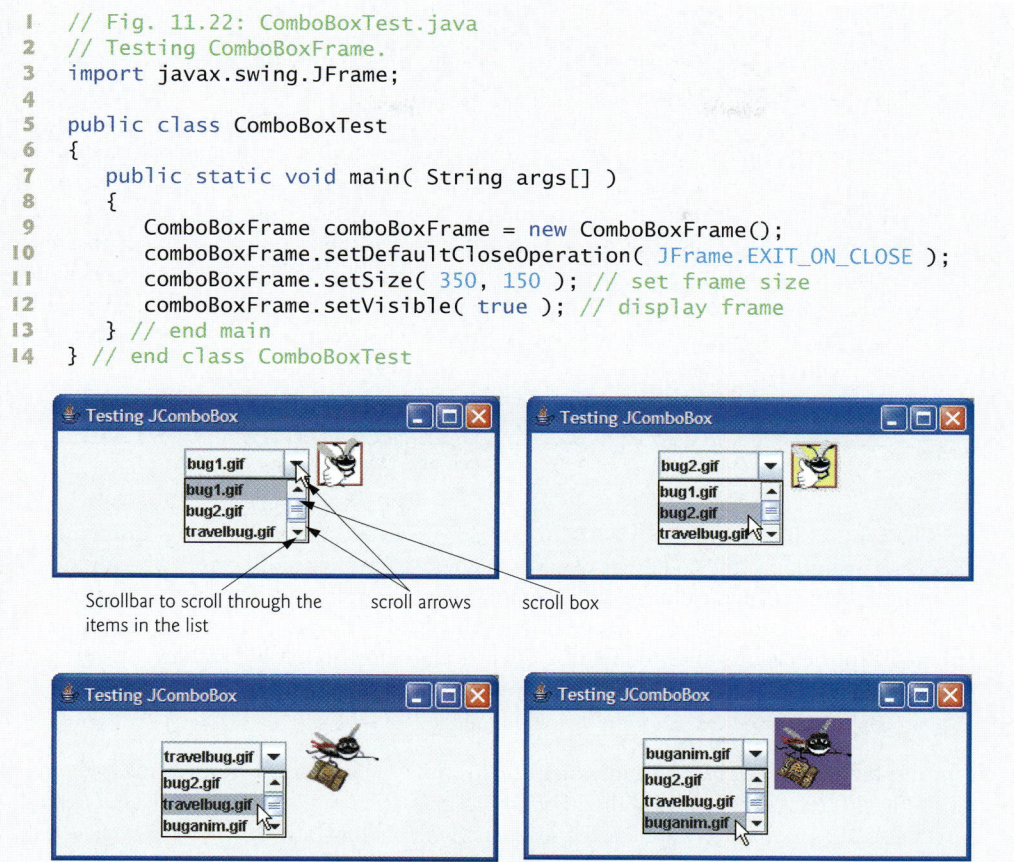

Fig. 11.22 | Test class for `ComboBoxFrame`.

variables of the method in which the anonymous inner class is declared. Since an anonymous inner class has no name, one object of the anonymous inner class must be created at the point where the class is declared.

Software Engineering Observation 11.5

An anonymous inner class declared in a method can access the instance variables and methods of the top-level class object that declared it, as well as the method's `final` local variables, but cannot access the method's non-`final` variables.

Lines 34–46 are a call to `imagesJComboBox`'s `addItemListener` method. The argument to this method must be an object that *is an* `ItemListener` (i.e., any object of a class that implements `ItemListener`). Lines 35–45 are a class-instance creation expression that declares an anonymous inner class and creates one object of that class. A reference to that object is then passed as the argument to `addItemListener`. The syntax `ItemListener()` after `new` begins the declaration of an anonymous inner class that implements interface `ItemListener`. This is similar to beginning a class declaration with

```
public class MyHandler implements ItemListener
```

The parentheses after `ItemListener` indicate a call to the default constructor of the anonymous inner class.

The opening left brace ({) at 36 and the closing right brace (}) at line 45 delimit the body of the anonymous inner class. Lines 38–44 declare the `ItemListener`'s `itemState-Changed` method. When the user makes a selection from `imagesJComboBox`, this method sets `label`'s `Icon`. The `Icon` is selected from array `icons` by determining the index of the selected item in the `JComboBox` with method `getSelectedIndex` in line 43. Note that for each item selected from a `JComboBox`, another item is first deselected—so two `ItemEvents` occur when an item is selected. We wish to display only the icon for the item the user just selected. For this reason, line 41 determines whether `ItemEvent` method `getStateChange` returns `ItemEvent.SELECTED`. If so, lines 42–43 set `label`'s icon.

Software Engineering Observation 11.6

Like any other class, when an anonymous inner class implements an interface, the class must implement every method in the interface.

The syntax shown in lines 35–45 for creating an event handler with an anonymous inner class is similar to the code that would be generated by a Java integrated development environment (IDE). Typically, an IDE enables the programmer to design a GUI visually, then the IDE generates code that implements the GUI. The programmer simply inserts statements in the event-handling methods that declare how to handle each event.

11.11 JList

A *list* displays a series of items from which the user may select one or more items (see output of Fig. 11.23). Lists are created with class `JList`, which directly extends class `JComponent`. Class `JList` supports single-selection lists (which allow only one item to be selected at a time) and multiple-selection lists (which allow any number of items to be selected). In this section, we discuss single-selection lists.

The application of Fig. 11.23 and Fig. 11.24 creates a `JList` containing 13 color names. When a color name is clicked in the `JList`, a `ListSelectionEvent` occurs and the application changes the background color of the application window to the selected color. Class `ListTest` (Fig. 11.24) contains the `main` method that executes this application.

```
1   // Fig. 11.23: ListFrame.java
2   // Selecting colors from a JList.
3   import java.awt.FlowLayout;
4   import java.awt.Color;
5   import javax.swing.JFrame;
6   import javax.swing.JList;
7   import javax.swing.JScrollPane;
8   import javax.swing.event.ListSelectionListener;
9   import javax.swing.event.ListSelectionEvent;
10  import javax.swing.ListSelectionModel;
11
```

Fig. 11.23 | `JList` that displays a list of colors. (Part 1 of 2.)

```
12   public class ListFrame extends JFrame
13   {
14      private JList colorJList; // list to display colors
15      private final String colorNames[] = { "Black", "Blue", "Cyan",
16         "Dark Gray", "Gray", "Green", "Light Gray", "Magenta",
17         "Orange", "Pink", "Red", "White", "Yellow" };
18      private final Color colors[] = { Color.BLACK, Color.BLUE, Color.CYAN,
19         Color.DARK_GRAY, Color.GRAY, Color.GREEN, Color.LIGHT_GRAY,
20         Color.MAGENTA, Color.ORANGE, Color.PINK, Color.RED, Color.WHITE,
21         Color.YELLOW };
22
23      // ListFrame constructor add JScrollPane containing JList to JFrame
24      public ListFrame()
25      {
26         super( "List Test" );
27         setLayout( new FlowLayout() ); // set frame layout
28
29         colorJList = new JList( colorNames ); // create with colorNames
30         colorJList.setVisibleRowCount( 5 ); // display five rows at once
31
32         // do not allow multiple selections
33         colorJList.setSelectionMode( ListSelectionModel.SINGLE_SELECTION );
34
35         // add a JScrollPane containing JList to frame
36         add( new JScrollPane( colorJList ) );
37
38         colorJList.addListSelectionListener(
39            new ListSelectionListener() // anonymous inner class
40            {
41               // handle list selection events
42               public void valueChanged( ListSelectionEvent event )
43               {
44                  getContentPane().setBackground(
45                     colors[ colorJList.getSelectedIndex() ] );
46               } // end method valueChanged
47            } // end anonymous inner class
48         ); // end call to addListSelectionListener
49      } // end ListFrame constructor
50   } // end class ListFrame
```

Fig. 11.23 | JList that displays a list of colors. (Part 2 of 2.)

```
1    // Fig. 11.24: ListTest.java
2    // Selecting colors from a JList.
3    import javax.swing.JFrame;
4
5    public class ListTest
6    {
7       public static void main( String args[] )
8       {
9          ListFrame listFrame = new ListFrame(); // create ListFrame
```

Fig. 11.24 | Test class for ListFrame. (Part 1 of 2.)

```
10          listFrame.setDefaultCloseOperation( JFrame.EXIT_ON_CLOSE );
11          listFrame.setSize( 350, 150 ); // set frame size
12          listFrame.setVisible( true ); // display frame
13      } // end main
14  } // end class ListTest
```

Fig. 11.24 | Test class for `ListFrame`. (Part 2 of 2.)

Line 29 (Fig. 11.23) creates `JList` object `colorList`. The argument to the `JList` constructor is the array of `Objects` (in this case `Strings`) to display in the list. Line 30 uses `JList` method **setVisibleRowCount** to determine the number of items that are visible in the list.

Line 33 uses `JList` method **setSelectionMode** to specify the list's **selection mode**. Class **ListSelectionModel** (of package `javax.swing`) declares three constants that specify a `JList`'s selection mode—**SINGLE_SELECTION** (which allows only one item to be selected at a time), **SINGLE_INTERVAL_SELECTION** (for a multiple-selection list that allows selection of several contiguous items) and **MULTIPLE_INTERVAL_SELECTION** (for a multiple-selection list that does not restrict the items that can be selected).

Unlike a `JComboBox`, a `JList` *does not* provide a scrollbar if there are more items in the list than the number of visible rows. In this case, a **JScrollPane** object is used to provide the scrolling capability. Line 36 adds a new instance of class `JScrollPane` to the `JFrame`. The `JScrollPane` constructor receives as its argument the `JComponent` that needs scrolling functionality (in this case, `colorList`). Notice in the screen captures that a scrollbar created by the `JScrollPane` appears at the right side of the `JList`. By default, the scrollbar appears only when the number of items in the `JList` exceeds the number of visible items.

Lines 38–48 use `JList` method **addListSelectionListener** to register an object that implements **ListSelectionListener** (package `javax.swing.event`) as the listener for the `JList`'s selection events. Once again, we use an instance of an anonymous inner class (lines 39–47) as the listener. In this example, when the user makes a selection from `colorList`, method **valueChanged** (line 42–46) should change the background color of the List-Frame to the selected color. This is accomplished in lines 44–45. Note the use of `JFrame` method **getContentPane** on line 44. Each `JFrame` actually consists of three layers—the background, the content pane and the glass pane. The content pane appears in front of the background and is where the GUI components in the `JFrame` are displayed. The glass pane is used to display tool tips and other items that should appear in front of the GUI components on the screen. The content pane completely hides the background of the `JFrame`; thus, to change the background color behind the GUI components, you must change the content pane's background color. Method `getContentPane` returns a reference to the `JFrame`'s content pane (an object of class `Container`). In line 44, we then use that reference to call method **setBackground**, which sets the content pane's background color to an element in the colors array. The color is selected from the array by using the selected item's index. JList method **getSelectedIndex** returns the selected item's index. As with arrays and JComboBoxes, JList indexing is zero based.

11.12 Multiple-Selection Lists

A multiple-selection list enables the user to select many items from a JList (see output of Fig. 11.26). A SINGLE_INTERVAL_SELECTION list allows selecting a contiguous range of items. To do so, click the first item, then press and hold the *Shift* key while clicking the last item in the range. A MULTIPLE_INTERVAL_SELECTION list allows continuous range selection as described for a SINGLE_INTERVAL_SELECTION list. Such a list allows miscellaneous items to be selected by pressing and holding the *Ctrl* key (sometimes called the *Control* key) while clicking each item to select. To deselect an item, press and hold the *Ctrl* key while clicking the item a second time.

The application of Fig. 11.25 and Fig. 11.26 uses multiple-selection lists to copy items from one JList to another. One list is a MULTIPLE_INTERVAL_SELECTION list and the other is a SINGLE_INTERVAL_SELECTION list. When you execute the application, try using the selection techniques described previously to select items in both lists.

Line 27 of Fig. 11.25 creates JList colorJList and initializes it with the strings in the array colorNames. Line 28 sets the number of visible rows in colorJList to 5. Lines 29–30 specify that colorList is a MULTIPLE_INTERVAL_SELECTION list. Line 31 adds a new

```java
1   // Fig. 11.25: MultipleSelectionFrame.java
2   // Copying items from one List to another.
3   import java.awt.FlowLayout;
4   import java.awt.event.ActionListener;
5   import java.awt.event.ActionEvent;
6   import javax.swing.JFrame;
7   import javax.swing.JList;
8   import javax.swing.JButton;
9   import javax.swing.JScrollPane;
10  import javax.swing.ListSelectionModel;
11
12  public class MultipleSelectionFrame extends JFrame
13  {
14     private JList colorJList; // list to hold color names
15     private JList copyJList; // list to copy color names into
16     private JButton copyJButton; // button to copy selected names
17     private final String colorNames[] = { "Black", "Blue", "Cyan",
18        "Dark Gray", "Gray", "Green", "Light Gray", "Magenta", "Orange",
19        "Pink", "Red", "White", "Yellow" };
20
21     // MultipleSelectionFrame constructor
22     public MultipleSelectionFrame()
23     {
24        super( "Multiple Selection Lists" );
25        setLayout( new FlowLayout() ); // set frame layout
26
```

Fig. 11.25 | JList that allows multiple selections. (Part 1 of 2.)

```
27          colorJList = new JList( colorNames ); // holds names of all colors
28          colorJList.setVisibleRowCount( 5 ); // show five rows
29          colorJList.setSelectionMode(
30             ListSelectionModel.MULTIPLE_INTERVAL_SELECTION );
31          add( new JScrollPane( colorJList ) ); // add list with scrollpane
32
33          copyJButton = new JButton( "Copy >>>" ); // create copy button
34          copyJButton.addActionListener(
35
36             new ActionListener() // anonymous inner class
37             {
38                // handle button event
39                public void actionPerformed( ActionEvent event )
40                {
41                   // place selected values in copyJList
42                   copyJList.setListData( colorJList.getSelectedValues() );
43                } // end method actionPerformed
44             } // end anonymous inner class
45          ); // end call to addActionListener
46
47          add( copyJButton ); // add copy button to JFrame
48
49          copyJList = new JList(); // create list to hold copied color names
50          copyJList.setVisibleRowCount( 5 ); // show 5 rows
51          copyJList.setFixedCellWidth( 100 ); // set width
52          copyJList.setFixedCellHeight( 15 ); // set height
53          copyJList.setSelectionMode(
54             ListSelectionModel.SINGLE_INTERVAL_SELECTION );
55          add( new JScrollPane( copyJList ) ); // add list with scrollpane
56       } // end MultipleSelectionFrame constructor
57 } // end class MultipleSelectionFrame
```

Fig. 11.25 | JList that allows multiple selections. (Part 2 of 2.)

```
1  // Fig. 11.26: MultipleSelectionTest.java
2  // Testing MultipleSelectionFrame.
3  import javax.swing.JFrame;
4
5  public class MultipleSelectionTest
6  {
7     public static void main( String args[] )
8     {
9        MultipleSelectionFrame multipleSelectionFrame =
10          new MultipleSelectionFrame();
11       multipleSelectionFrame.setDefaultCloseOperation(
12          JFrame.EXIT_ON_CLOSE );
13       multipleSelectionFrame.setSize( 350, 140 ); // set frame size
14       multipleSelectionFrame.setVisible( true ); // display frame
15    } // end main
16 } // end class MultipleSelectionTest
```

Fig. 11.26 | Test class for MultipleSelectionFrame. (Part 1 of 2.)

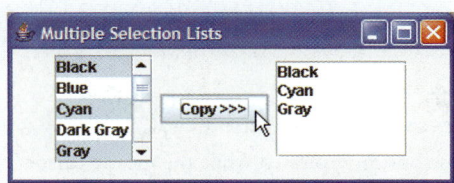

Fig. 11.26 | Test class for `MultipleSelectionFrame`. (Part 2 of 2.)

`JScrollPane` containing `colorJList` to the `JFrame`. Lines 49–55 perform similar tasks for `copyJList`, which is declared as a `SINGLE_INTERVAL_SELECTION` list. Line 51 uses `JList` method `setFixedCellWidth` to set `copyJList`'s width to 100 pixels. Line 52 uses `JList` method `setFixedCellHeight` to set the height of each item in the `JList` to 15 pixels.

There are no events to indicate that a user has made multiple selections in a multiple-selection list. Normally, an event generated by another GUI component (known as an external event) specifies when the multiple selections in a `JList` should be processed. In this example, the user clicks the `JButton` called `copyJButton` to trigger the event that copies the selected items in `colorJList` to `copyJList`.

Lines 39–45 declare, create and register an `ActionListener` for the `copyButton`. When the user clicks `copyJButton`, method `actionPerformed` (lines 39–43) uses `JList` method `setListData` to set the items displayed in `copyJList`. Line 42 calls `colorJList`'s method `getSelectedValues`, which returns an array of `Objects` representing the selected items in `colorJList`. In this example, the returned array is passed as the argument to `copyJList`'s setListData method.

You might be wondering why `copyJList` can be used in line 42 even though the application does not create the object to which it refers until Line 49? Remember that method `actionPerformed` (lines 39–43) does not execute until the user presses the `copy-JButton`, which cannot occur until after the constructor completes execution and the application displays the GUI. At that point in the application's execution, `copyJList` is already initialized with a new `JList` object.

11.13 Mouse Event Handling

This section presents the `MouseListener` and `MouseMotionListener` event-listener interfaces for handling mouse events. Mouse events can be trapped for any GUI component that derives from `java.awt.Component`. The methods of interfaces `MouseListener` and `MouseMotionListener` are summarized in Figure 11.27. Package `javax.swing.event` contains interface `MouseInputListener`, which extends interfaces `MouseListener` and `MouseMotionListener` to create a single interface containing all the `MouseListener` and `MouseMotionListener` methods. The `MouseListener` and `MouseMotionListener` methods are called when the mouse interacts with a `Component` if appropriate event-listener objects are registered for that `Component`.

Each of the mouse event-handling methods takes a `MouseEvent` object as its argument. A `MouseEvent` object contains information about the mouse event that occurred, including the x- and y-coordinates of the location where the event occurred. These coordinates are measured from the upper-left corner of the GUI component on which the

---

MouseListener and MouseMotionListener interface methods

Methods of interface MouseListener

`public void mousePressed( MouseEvent event )`

> Called when a mouse button is pressed while the mouse cursor is on a component.

`public void mouseClicked( MouseEvent event )`

> Called when a mouse button is pressed and released while the mouse cursor remains stationary on a component. This event is always preceded by a call to `mousePressed`.

`public void mouseReleased( MouseEvent event )`

> Called when a mouse button is released after being pressed. This event is always preceded by a call to `mousePressed` and one or more calls to `mouseDragged`.

`public void mouseEntered( MouseEvent event )`

> Called when the mouse cursor enters the bounds of a component.

`public void mouseExited( MouseEvent event )`

> Called when the mouse cursor leaves the bounds of a component.

Methods of interface MouseMotionListener

`public void mouseDragged( MouseEvent event )`

> Called when the mouse button is pressed while the mouse cursor is on a component and the mouse is moved while the mouse button remains pressed. This event is always preceded by a call to `mousePressed`. All drag events are sent to the component on which the user began to drag the mouse.

`public void mouseMoved( MouseEvent event )`

> Called when the mouse is moved when the mouse cursor is on a component. All move events are sent to the component over which the mouse is currently positioned.

Fig. 11.27 | MouseListener and MouseMotionListener interface methods. (Part 1 of 2.)

event occurred. The *x*-coordinates start at 0 and increase from left to right. The *y*-coordinates start at 0 and increase from top to bottom. In addition, the methods and constants of class **InputEvent** (MouseEvent's superclass) enable an application to determine which mouse button the user clicked.

Look-and-Feel Observation 11.12

Method calls to mouseDragged and mouseReleased are sent to the MouseMotionListener for the Component on which a mouse drag operation started. Similarly, the mouseReleased method call at the end of a drag operation is sent to the MouseListener for the Component on which the drag operation started.

Java also provides interface **MouseWheelListener** to enable applications to respond to the rotation of a mouse wheel. This interface declares method **mouseWheelMoved**, which receives a **MouseWheelEvent** as its argument. Class MouseWheelEvent (a subclass of Mouse-Event) contains methods that enable the event handler to obtain information about the amount of wheel rotation.

Tracking Mouse Events on a *JPanel*

The MouseTracker application (Fig. 11.28 and Fig. 11.29) demonstrates the Mouse-Listener and MouseMotionListener interface methods. The application class implements both interfaces so it can listen for its own mouse events. Note that all seven methods from these two interfaces must be declared by the programmer when a class implements both interfaces. Each mouse event in this example displays a string in the JLabel called statusBar at the bottom of the window.

Line 23 in Fig. 11.28 creates JPanel mousePanel. This JPanel's mouse events will be tracked by the application. Line 24 sets mousePanel's background color to white. When the user moves the mouse into the mousePanel, the application will change mousePanel's background color to green. When the user moves the mouse out of the mousePanel, the

```java
1   // Fig. 11.28: MouseTrackerFrame.java
2   // Demonstrating mouse events.
3   import java.awt.Color;
4   import java.awt.BorderLayout;
5   import java.awt.event.MouseListener;
6   import java.awt.event.MouseMotionListener;
7   import java.awt.event.MouseEvent;
8   import javax.swing.JFrame;
9   import javax.swing.JLabel;
10  import javax.swing.JPanel;
11
12  public class MouseTrackerFrame extends JFrame
13  {
14     private JPanel mousePanel; // panel in which mouse events will occur
15     private JLabel statusBar; // label that displays event information
16
17     // MouseTrackerFrame constructor sets up GUI and
18     // registers mouse event handlers
19     public MouseTrackerFrame()
20     {
21        super( "Demonstrating Mouse Events" );
22
23        mousePanel = new JPanel(); // create panel
24        mousePanel.setBackground( Color.WHITE ); // set background color
25        add( mousePanel, BorderLayout.CENTER ); // add panel to JFrame
26
27        statusBar = new JLabel( "Mouse outside JPanel" );
28        add( statusBar, BorderLayout.SOUTH ); // add label to JFrame
29
30        // create and register listener for mouse and mouse motion events
31        MouseHandler handler = new MouseHandler();
32        mousePanel.addMouseListener( handler );
33        mousePanel.addMouseMotionListener( handler );
34     } // end MouseTrackerFrame constructor
35
36     private class MouseHandler implements MouseListener,
37        MouseMotionListener
38     {
```

Fig. 11.28 | Mouse event handling. (Part 1 of 2.)

```
39          // MouseListener event handlers
40          // handle event when mouse released immediately after press
41          public void mouseClicked( MouseEvent event )
42          {
43             statusBar.setText( String.format( "Clicked at [%d, %d]",
44                event.getX(), event.getY() ) );
45          } // end method mouseClicked
46
47          // handle event when mouse pressed
48          public void mousePressed( MouseEvent event )
49          {
50             statusBar.setText( String.format( "Pressed at [%d, %d]",
51                event.getX(), event.getY() ) );
52          } // end method mousePressed
53
54          // handle event when mouse released after dragging
55          public void mouseReleased( MouseEvent event )
56          {
57             statusBar.setText( String.format( "Released at [%d, %d]",
58                event.getX(), event.getY() ) );
59          } // end method mouseReleased
60
61          // handle event when mouse enters area
62          public void mouseEntered( MouseEvent event )
63          {
64             statusBar.setText( String.format( "Mouse entered at [%d, %d]",
65                event.getX(), event.getY() ) );
66             mousePanel.setBackground( Color.GREEN );
67          } // end method mouseEntered
68
69          // handle event when mouse exits area
70          public void mouseExited( MouseEvent event )
71          {
72             statusBar.setText( "Mouse outside JPanel" );
73             mousePanel.setBackground( Color.WHITE );
74          } // end method mouseExited
75
76          // MouseMotionListener event handlers
77          // handle event when user drags mouse with button pressed
78          public void mouseDragged( MouseEvent event )
79          {
80             statusBar.setText( String.format( "Dragged at [%d, %d]",
81                event.getX(), event.getY() ) );
82          } // end method mouseDragged
83
84          // handle event when user moves mouse
85          public void mouseMoved( MouseEvent event )
86          {
87             statusBar.setText( String.format( "Moved at [%d, %d]",
88                event.getX(), event.getY() ) );
89          } // end method mouseMoved
90       } // end inner class MouseHandler
91    } // end class MouseTrackerFrame
```

Fig. 11.28 | Mouse event handling. (Part 2 of 2.)

```
1   // Fig. 11.29: MouseTrackerFrame.java
2   // Testing MouseTrackerFrame.
3   import javax.swing.JFrame;
4
5   public class MouseTracker
6   {
7      public static void main( String args[] )
8      {
9         MouseTrackerFrame mouseTrackerFrame = new MouseTrackerFrame();
10        mouseTrackerFrame.setDefaultCloseOperation( JFrame.EXIT_ON_CLOSE );
11        mouseTrackerFrame.setSize( 300, 100 ); // set frame size
12        mouseTrackerFrame.setVisible( true ); // display frame
13     } // end main
14  } // end class MouseTracker
```

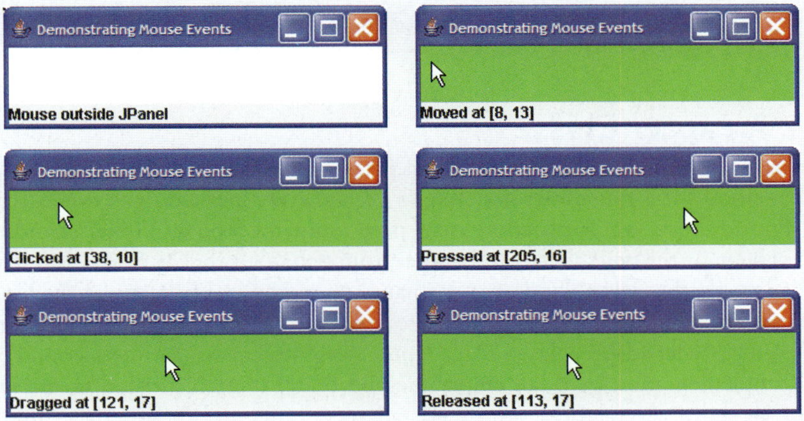

Fig. 11.29 | Test class for `MouseTrackerFrame`.

application will change the background color back to white. Line 25 attaches mousePanel to the JFrame. As you learned in Section 11.4, you typically must specify the layout of the GUI components in a JFrame. In that section, we introduced the layout manager FlowLayout. Here we use the default layout of a JFrame's content pane—**BorderLayout**. This layout manager arranges components into five regions: NORTH, SOUTH, EAST, WEST and CENTER. NORTH corresponds to the top of the container. This example uses the CENTER and SOUTH regions. Line 25 uses a two-argument version of method add to place mousePanel in the CENTER region. The BorderLayout automatically sizes the component in the CENTER to use all the space in the JFrame that is not occupied by components in the other regions. Section 11.17.2 discusses BorderLayout in more detail.

Lines 27–28 in the constructor declare JLabel statusBar and attach it to the JFrame's SOUTH region. This JLabel occupies the width of the JFrame. The region's height is determined by the JLabel.

Line 31 creates an instance of inner class MouseHandler (lines 36–90) called handler that responds to mouse events. Lines 32–33 register handler as the listener for mousePanel's mouse events. Methods **addMouseListener** and **addMouseMotionListener** are inherited indirectly from class Component and can be used to register MouseListeners and

MouseMotionListeners, respectively. A MouseHandler object is both a MouseListener and a MouseMotionListener because the class implements both interfaces. [*Note:* In this example, we chose to implement both interfaces to demonstrate a class that implements more than one interface. However, we also could have implemented interface MouseInputListener here.]

When the mouse enters and exits mousePanel's area, methods mouseEntered (lines 62–67) and mouseExited (lines 70–74) are called, respectively. Method mouseEntered displays a message in the statusBar indicating that the mouse entered the JPanel and changes the background color to green. Method mouseExited displays a message in the statusBar indicating that the mouse is outside the JPanel (see the first sample output window) and changes the background color to white.

When any of the other five events occurs, it displays a message in the statusBar that includes a string containing the event and the coordinates at which it occurred. MouseEvent methods **getX** and **getY** return the *x*- and *y*-coordinates, respectively, of the mouse at the time the event occurred.

11.14 Adapter Classes

Many event-listener interfaces, such as MouseListener and MouseMotionListener, contain multiple methods. It is not always desirable to declare every method in an event-listener interface. For instance, an application may need only the mouseClicked handler from MouseListener or the mouseDragged handler from MouseMotionListener. Interface WindowListener specifies seven window event-handling methods. For many of the listener interfaces that have multiple methods, packages java.awt.event and javax.swing.event provide event-listener adapter classes. An adapter class implements an interface and provides a default implementation (with an empty method body) of each method in the interface. Figure 11.30 shows several java.awt.event adapter classes and the interfaces they implement. You can extend an adapter class to inherit the default implementation of every method and subsequently override only the method(s) you need for event handling.

Software Engineering Observation 11.7

When a class implements an interface, the class has an "is a" relationship with that interface. All direct and indirect subclasses of that class inherit this interface. Thus, an object of a class that extends an event-adapter class is an object of the corresponding event-listener type (e.g., an object of a subclass of MouseAdapter is a MouseListener).

Extending *MouseAdapter*

The application of Fig. 11.31 and Fig. 11.32 demonstrates how to determine the number of mouse clicks (i.e., the click count) and how to distinguish between the different mouse buttons. The event listener in this application is an object of inner class MouseClickHandler (lines 26–46) that extends MouseAdapter, so we can declare just the mouseClicked method we need in this example.

Common Programming Error 11.4

If you extend an adapter class and misspell the name of the method you are overriding, your method simply becomes another method in the class. This is a logic error that is difficult to detect, since the program will call the empty version of the method inherited from the adapter class.

Event-adapter class in `java.awt.event`	Implements interface
ComponentAdapter	ComponentListener
ContainerAdapter	ContainerListener
FocusAdapter	FocusListener
KeyAdapter	KeyListener
MouseAdapter	MouseListener
MouseMotionAdapter	MouseMotionListener
WindowAdapter	WindowListener

Fig. 11.30 | Event-adapter classes and the interfaces they implement in package `java.awt.event`.

```
1   // Fig. 11.31: MouseDetailsFrame.java
2   // Demonstrating mouse clicks and distinguishing between mouse buttons.
3   import java.awt.BorderLayout;
4   import java.awt.Graphics;
5   import java.awt.event.MouseAdapter;
6   import java.awt.event.MouseEvent;
7   import javax.swing.JFrame;
8   import javax.swing.JLabel;
9
10  public class MouseDetailsFrame extends JFrame
11  {
12     private String details; // String representing
13     private JLabel statusBar; // JLabel that appears at bottom of window
14
15     // constructor sets title bar String and register mouse listener
16     public MouseDetailsFrame()
17     {
18        super( "Mouse clicks and buttons" );
19
20        statusBar = new JLabel( "Click the mouse" );
21        add( statusBar, BorderLayout.SOUTH );
22        addMouseListener( new MouseClickHandler() ); // add handler
23     } // end MouseDetailsFrame constructor
24
25     // inner class to handle mouse events
26     private class MouseClickHandler extends MouseAdapter
27     {
28        // handle mouse click event and determine which button was pressed
29        public void mouseClicked( MouseEvent event )
30        {
31           int xPos = event.getX(); // get x position of mouse
32           int yPos = event.getY(); // get y position of mouse
33
34           details = String.format( "Clicked %d time(s)",
35              event.getClickCount() );
```

Fig. 11.31 | Left, center and right mouse-button clicks. (Part 1 of 2.)

```
36
37            if ( event.isMetaDown() ) // right mouse button
38               details += " with right mouse button";
39            else if ( event.isAltDown() ) // middle mouse button
40               details += " with center mouse button";
41            else // left mouse button
42               details += " with left mouse button";
43
44            statusBar.setText( details ); // display message in statusBar
45         } // end method mouseClicked
46      } // end private inner class MouseClickHandler
47   } // end class MouseDetailsFrame
```

Fig. 11.31 | Left, center and right mouse-button clicks. (Part 2 of 2.)

```
1   // Fig. 11.32: MouseDetails.java
2   // Testing MouseDetailsFrame.
3   import javax.swing.JFrame;
4
5   public class MouseDetails
6   {
7      public static void main( String args[] )
8      {
9         MouseDetailsFrame mouseDetailsFrame = new MouseDetailsFrame();
10        mouseDetailsFrame.setDefaultCloseOperation( JFrame.EXIT_ON_CLOSE );
11        mouseDetailsFrame.setSize( 400, 150 ); // set frame size
12        mouseDetailsFrame.setVisible( true ); // display frame
13     } // end main
14  } // end class MouseDetails
```

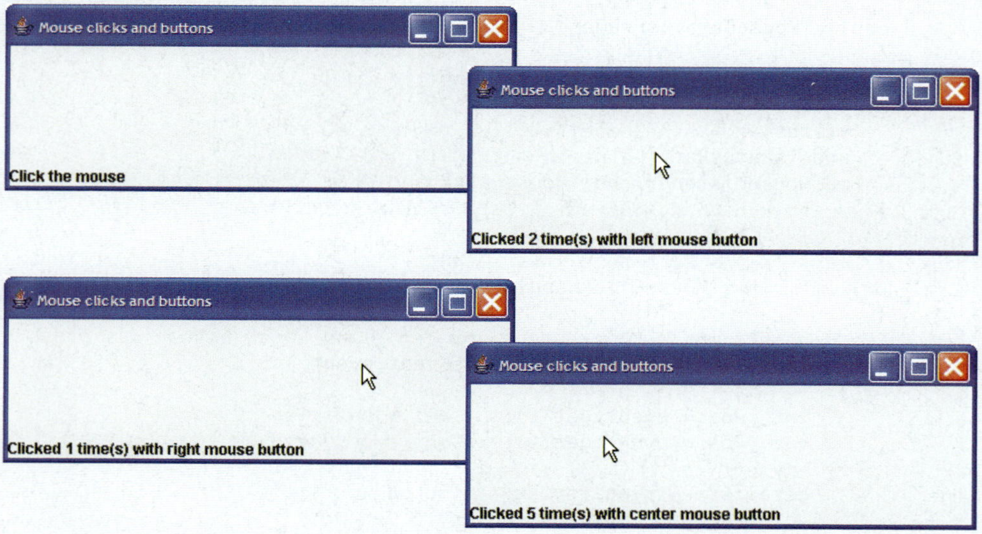

Fig. 11.32 | Test class for MouseDetailsFrame.

A user of a Java application may be on a system with a one-, two- or three-button mouse. Java provides a mechanism to distinguish among mouse buttons. Class Mouse-Event inherits several methods from class InputEvent that can distinguish among mouse buttons on a multibutton mouse or can mimic a multibutton mouse with a combined key-stroke and mouse-button click. Figure 11.33 shows the InputEvent methods used to distinguish among mouse-button clicks. Java assumes that every mouse contains a left mouse button. Thus, it is simple to test for a left-mouse-button click. However, users with a one- or two-button mouse must use a combination of keystrokes and mouse-button clicks at the same time to simulate the missing buttons on the mouse. In the case of a one- or two-button mouse, a Java application assumes that the center mouse button is clicked if the user holds down the *Alt* key and clicks the left mouse button on a two-button mouse or the only mouse button on a one-button mouse. In the case of a one-button mouse, a Java application assumes that the right mouse button is clicked if the user holds down the *Meta* key and clicks the mouse button.

Line 22 of Fig. 11.31 registers a MouseListener for the MouseDetailsFrame. The event listener is an object of class MouseClickHandler, which extends MouseAdapter. This enables us to declare only method mouseClicked (lines 29–45). This method first captures the coordinates where the event occurred and stores them in local variables xPos and yPos (lines 31–32). Lines 34–35 create a String called details containing the number of mouse clicks, which is returned by MouseEvent method **getClickCount** at line 35. Lines 37–42 use methods **isMetaDown** and **isAltDown** to determine which mouse button the user clicked and append an appropriate String to details in each case. The resulting String is displayed in the statusBar. Class MouseDetails (Fig. 11.32) contains the main method that executes the application. Try clicking with each of your mouse's buttons repeatedly to see the click count increment.

11.15 JPanel Subclass for Drawing with the Mouse

Section 11.13 showed how to track mouse events in a JPanel. In this section, we use a JPanel as a dedicated drawing area in which the user can draw by dragging the mouse. In addition, this section demonstrates an event listener that extends an adapter class.

InputEvent method	Description
isMetaDown()	Returns true when the user clicks the right mouse button on a mouse with two or three buttons. To simulate a right-mouse-button click on a one-button mouse, the user can hold down the *Meta* key on the keyboard and click the mouse button.
isAltDown()	Returns true when the user clicks the middle mouse button on a mouse with three buttons. To simulate a middle-mouse-button click on a one- or two-button mouse, the user can press the *Alt* key on the keyboard and click the only- or left-mouse button, respectively.

Fig. 11.33 | InputEvent methods that help distinguish among left-, center- and right-mouse-button clicks.

Method `paintComponent`

Lightweight Swing components that extend class JComponent (such as JPanel) contain method **paintComponent**, which is called when a lightweight Swing component is displayed. By overriding this method, you can specify how to draw shapes using Java's graphics capabilities. When customizing a JPanel for use as a dedicated drawing area, the subclass should override method paintComponent and call the superclass version of paint-Component as the first statement in the body of the overridden method to ensure that the component displays correctly. The reason for this is that subclasses of JComponent support transparency. To display a component correctly, the program must determine whether the component is transparent. The code that determines this is in superclass JComponent's paintComponent implementation. When a component is transparent, paintComponent will not clear its background when the program displays the component. When a component is opaque, paintComponent clears the component's background before the component is displayed. If the superclass version of paintComponent is not called, an opaque GUI component typically will not display correctly on the user interface. Also, if the superclass version is called after performing the customized drawing statements, the results typically will be erased. The transparency of a Swing lightweight component can be set with method **setOpaque** (a `false` argument indicates that the component is transparent).

Look-and-Feel Observation 11.13

Most Swing GUI components can be transparent or opaque. If a Swing GUI component is opaque, its background will be cleared when its `paintComponent` method is called. Only opaque components can display a customized background color. JPanel objects are opaque by default.

Error-Prevention Tip 11.1

In a JComponent subclass's `paintComponent` method, the first statement should always be a call to the superclass's `paintComponent` method to ensure that an object of the subclass displays correctly.

Common Programming Error 11.5

If an overridden `paintComponent` method does not call the superclass's version, the subclass component may not display properly. If an overridden `paintComponent` method calls the superclass's version after other drawing is performed, the drawing will be erased.

Defining the Custom Drawing Area

The Painter application of Fig. 11.34 and Fig. 11.35 demonstrates a customized subclass of JPanel that is used to create a dedicated drawing area. The application uses the mouseDragged event handler to create a simple drawing application. The user can draw pictures by dragging the mouse on the JPanel. This example does not use method mouse-Moved, so our event-listener class (the anonymous inner class at lines 22-34) extends MouseMotionAdapter. Since, this class already declares both mouseMoved and mouse-Dragged, we can simply override mouseDragged to provide the event handling this application requires.

Class PaintPanel (Fig. 11.34) extends JPanel to create the dedicated drawing area. Lines 3–7 import the classes used in class PaintPanel. Class **Point** (package java.awt) represents an *x-y* coordinate. We use objects of this class to store the coordinates of each mouse drag event. Class **Graphics** is used to draw.

```
 1   // Fig. 11.34: PaintPanel.java
 2   // Using class MouseMotionAdapter.
 3   import java.awt.Point;
 4   import java.awt.Graphics;
 5   import java.awt.event.MouseEvent;
 6   import java.awt.event.MouseMotionAdapter;
 7   import javax.swing.JPanel;
 8
 9   public class PaintPanel extends JPanel
10   {
11      private int pointCount = 0; // count number of points
12
13      // array of 10000 java.awt.Point references
14      private Point points[] = new Point[ 10000 ];
15
16      // set up GUI and register mouse event handler
17      public PaintPanel()
18      {
19         // handle frame mouse motion event
20         addMouseMotionListener(
21
22            new MouseMotionAdapter() // anonymous inner class
23            {
24               // store drag coordinates and repaint
25               public void mouseDragged( MouseEvent event )
26               {
27                  if ( pointCount < points.length )
28                  {
29                     points[ pointCount ] = event.getPoint(); // find point
30                     pointCount++; // increment number of points in array
31                     repaint(); // repaint JFrame
32                  } // end if
33               } // end method mouseDragged
34            } // end anonymous inner class
35         ); // end call to addMouseMotionListener
36      } // end PaintPanel constructor
37
38      // draw oval in a 4-by-4 bounding box at specified location on window
39      public void paintComponent( Graphics g )
40      {
41         super.paintComponent( g ); // clears drawing area
42
43         // draw all points in array
44         for ( int i = 0; i < pointCount; i++ )
45            g.fillOval( points[ i ].x, points[ i ].y, 4, 4 );
46      } // end method paintComponent
47   } // end class PaintPanel
```

Fig. 11.34 | Adapter classes used to implement event handlers.

In this example, we use an array of 10000 Points (line 14) to store the location at which each mouse-drag event occurs. As you will see, method paintComponent uses these Points to draw. Instance variable pointCount (line 11) maintains the total number of Points captured from mouse drag events so far.

Lines 20–35 register a `MouseMotionListener` to listen for the `PaintPanel`'s mouse-motion events. Lines 22–34 create an object of an anonymous inner class that extends the adapter class `MouseMotionAdapter`. Recall that `MouseMotionAdapter` implements `Mouse-MotionListener`, so the anonymous inner class object is a `MouseMotionListener`. The anonymous inner class inherits a default implementation of methods `mouseMoved` and `mouseDragged`, so it already satisfies the requirement that all methods of the interface must be implemented. However, the default methods do nothing when they are called. So, we override method `mouseDragged` at lines 25–33 to capture the coordinates of a mouse-dragged event and store them as a `Point` object. Line 27 ensures that we store the event's coordinates only if there are still empty elements in the array. If so, line 29 invokes the `MouseEvent`'s **`getPoint`** method to obtain the `Point` where the event occurred and stores it in the array at index `pointCount`. Line 30 increments the `pointCount`, and line 31 calls method **`repaint`** (inherited indirectly from class `Component`) to indicate that the `Paint-Panel` should be refreshed on the screen as soon as possible with a call to the `PaintPanel`'s `paintComponent` method.

Method `paintComponent` (lines 39–46), which receives a `Graphics` parameter, is called automatically any time the `PaintPanel` needs to be displayed on the screen (such as when the GUI is first displayed) or refreshed on the screen (such as when method `repaint` is called or when the GUI component was hidden by another window on the screen and subsequently becomes visible again).

Look-and-Feel Observation II.I4

Calling `repaint` for a Swing GUI component indicates that the component should be refreshed on the screen as soon as possible. The background of the GUI component is cleared only if the component is opaque. `JComponent` method `setOpaque` can be passed a `boolean` argument indicating whether the component is opaque (`true`) or transparent (`false`).

Line 41 invokes the superclass version of `paintComponent` to clear the `PaintPanel`'s background (`JPanel`s are opaque by default). Lines 44–45 draw an oval at the location specified by each `Point` in the array (up to the `pointCount`). `Graphics` method **`fillOval`** draws a solid oval. The method's four parameters represent a rectangular area (called the **bounding box**) in which the oval is displayed. The first two parameters are the upper-left *x*-coordinate and the upper-left *y*-coordinate of the rectangular area. The last two coordinates represent the rectangular area's width and height. Method `fillOval` draws the oval so it touches the middle of each side of the rectangular area. In line 45, the first two arguments are specified by using class `Point`'s two `public` instance variables—`x` and `y`. The loop terminates either when a `null` reference is encountered in the array or when the end of the array is reached. You will learn more `Graphics` features in Chapter 12.

Look-and-Feel Observation II.I5

Drawing on any GUI component is performed with coordinates that are measured from the upper-left corner (0, 0) of that GUI component, not the upper-left corner of the screen.

*Using the Custom **JPanel** in an Application*

Class `Painter` (Fig. 11.35) contains the main method that executes this application. Line 14 creates a `PaintPanel` object on which the user can drag the mouse to draw. Line 15 attaches the `PaintPanel` to the `JFrame`.

```
1   // Fig. 11.35: Painter.java
2   // Testing PaintPanel.
3   import java.awt.BorderLayout;
4   import javax.swing.JFrame;
5   import javax.swing.JLabel;
6
7   public class Painter
8   {
9      public static void main( String args[] )
10     {
11        // create JFrame
12        JFrame application = new JFrame( "A simple paint program" );
13
14        PaintPanel paintPanel = new PaintPanel(); // create paint panel
15        application.add( paintPanel, BorderLayout.CENTER ); // in center
16
17        // create a label and place it in SOUTH of BorderLayout
18        application.add( new JLabel( "Drag the mouse to draw" ),
19           BorderLayout.SOUTH );
20
21        application.setDefaultCloseOperation( JFrame.EXIT_ON_CLOSE );
22        application.setSize( 400, 200 ); // set frame size
23        application.setVisible( true ); // display frame
24     } // end main
25  } // end class Painter
```

Fig. 11.35 | Test class for `PaintFrame`.

11.16 Key-Event Handling

This section presents the **KeyListener** interface for handling key events. Key events are generated when keys on the keyboard are pressed and released. A class that implements KeyListener must provide declarations for methods **keyPressed**, **keyReleased** and **key-Typed**, each of which receives a **KeyEvent** as its argument. Class KeyEvent is a subclass of InputEvent. Method keyPressed is called in response to pressing any key. Method key-Typed is called in response to pressing any key that is not an **action key**. (The action keys are any arrow key, *Home, End, Page Up, Page Down*, any function key, *Num Lock, Print Screen, Scroll Lock, Caps Lock* and *Pause*.) Method keyReleased is called when the key is released after any keyPressed or keyTyped event.

The application of Fig. 11.36 and Fig. 11.37 demonstrates the `KeyListener` methods. Class `KeyDemo` implements the `KeyListener` interface, so all three methods are declared in the application.

```java
1   // Fig. 11.36: KeyDemoFrame.java
2   // Demonstrating keystroke events.
3   import java.awt.Color;
4   import java.awt.event.KeyListener;
5   import java.awt.event.KeyEvent;
6   import javax.swing.JFrame;
7   import javax.swing.JTextArea;
8
9   public class KeyDemoFrame extends JFrame implements KeyListener
10  {
11     private String line1 = ""; // first line of textarea
12     private String line2 = ""; // second line of textarea
13     private String line3 = ""; // third line of textarea
14     private JTextArea textArea; // textarea to display output
15
16     // KeyDemoFrame constructor
17     public KeyDemoFrame()
18     {
19        super( "Demonstrating Keystroke Events" );
20
21        textArea = new JTextArea( 10, 15 ); // set up JTextArea
22        textArea.setText( "Press any key on the keyboard..." );
23        textArea.setEnabled( false ); // disable textarea
24        textArea.setDisabledTextColor( Color.BLACK ); // set text color
25        add( textArea ); // add textarea to JFrame
26
27        addKeyListener( this ); // allow frame to process key events
28     } // end KeyDemoFrame constructor
29
30     // handle press of any key
31     public void keyPressed( KeyEvent event )
32     {
33        line1 = String.format( "Key pressed: %s",
34           event.getKeyText( event.getKeyCode() ) ); // output pressed key
35        setLines2and3( event ); // set output lines two and three
36     } // end method keyPressed
37
38     // handle release of any key
39     public void keyReleased( KeyEvent event )
40     {
41        line1 = String.format( "Key released: %s",
42           event.getKeyText( event.getKeyCode() ) ); // output released key
43        setLines2and3( event ); // set output lines two and three
44     } // end method keyReleased
45
```

Fig. 11.36 | Key event handling. (Part 1 of 2.)

```
46      // handle press of an action key
47      public void keyTyped( KeyEvent event )
48      {
49         line1 = String.format( "Key typed: %s", event.getKeyChar() );
50         setLines2and3( event ); // set output lines two and three
51      } // end method keyTyped
52
53      // set second and third lines of output
54      private void setLines2and3( KeyEvent event )
55      {
56         line2 = String.format( "This key is %san action key",
57            ( event.isActionKey() ? "" : "not " ) );
58
59         String temp = event.getKeyModifiersText( event.getModifiers() );
60
61         line3 = String.format( "Modifier keys pressed: %s",
62            ( temp.equals( "" ) ? "none" : temp ) ); // output modifiers
63
64         textArea.setText( String.format( "%s\n%s\n%s\n",
65            line1, line2, line3 ) ); // output three lines of text
66      } // end method setLines2and3
67   } // end class KeyDemoFrame
```

Fig. 11.36 | Key event handling. (Part 2 of 2.)

```
 1   // Fig. 11.37: KeyDemo.java
 2   // Testing KeyDemoFrame.
 3   import javax.swing.JFrame;
 4
 5   public class KeyDemo
 6   {
 7      public static void main( String args[] )
 8      {
 9         KeyDemoFrame keyDemoFrame = new KeyDemoFrame();
10         keyDemoFrame.setDefaultCloseOperation( JFrame.EXIT_ON_CLOSE );
11         keyDemoFrame.setSize( 350, 100 ); // set frame size
12         keyDemoFrame.setVisible( true ); // display frame
13      } // end main
14   } // end class KeyDemo
```

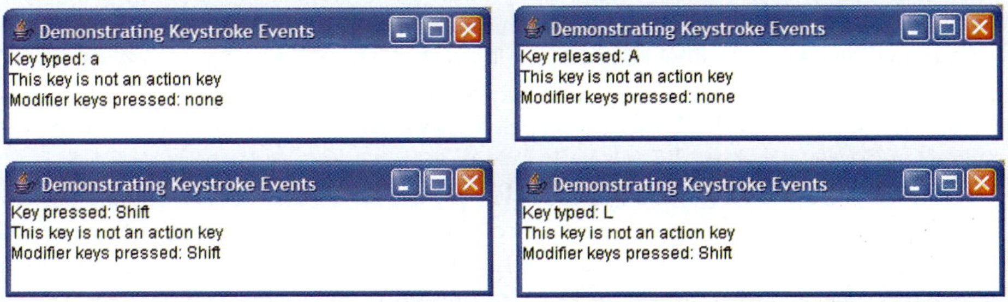

Fig. 11.37 | Test class for KeyDemoFrame. (Part 1 of 2.)

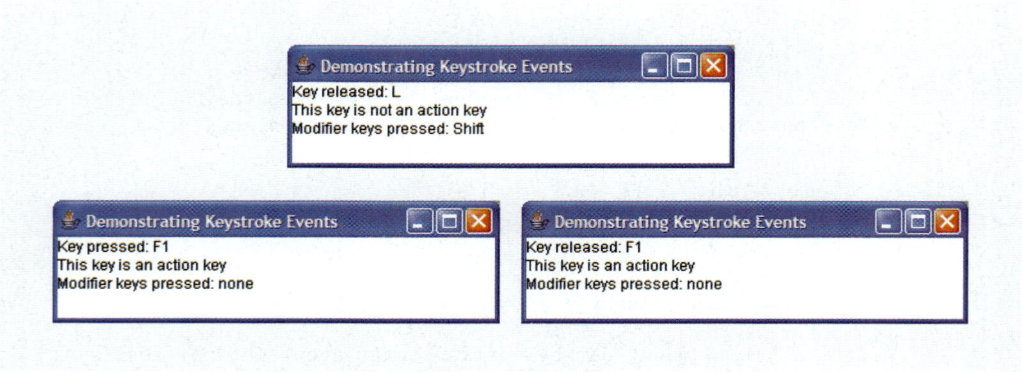

Fig. 11.37 | Test class for `KeyDemoFrame`. (Part 2 of 2.)

The constructor (Fig. 11.36, lines 17–28) registers the application to handle its own key events by using method **addKeyListener** at line 27. Method `addKeyListener` is declared in class `Component`, so every subclass of `Component` can notify `KeyListener` objects of key events for that `Component`.

At line 25, the constructor adds `JTextArea textArea` (where the application's output is displayed) to the `JFrame`. Notice in the screen captures that `textArea` occupies the entire window. This is due to the `JFrame`'s default `BorderLayout` (discussed in Section 11.17.2 and demonstrated in Fig. 11.41). When a single `Component` is added to a `BorderLayout`, the `Component` occupies the entire `Container`. Note that line 24 uses method `setDisabledTextColor` to change the color of the text in the textarea to black.

Methods `keyPressed` (lines 31–36) and `keyReleased` (lines 39–44) use `KeyEvent` method **getKeyCode** to get the virtual key code of the key that was pressed. Class `KeyEvent` maintains a set of constants—the virtual key-code constants—that represents every key on the keyboard. These constants can be compared with the return value of `getKeyCode` to test for individual keys on the keyboard. The value returned by `getKeyCode` is passed to `KeyEvent` method **getKeyText**, which returns a string containing the name of the key that was pressed. For a complete list of virtual key constants, see the on-line documentation for class `KeyEvent` (package `java.awt.event`). Method `keyTyped` (lines 47–51) uses `KeyEvent` method **getKeyChar** to get the Unicode value of the character typed.

All three event-handling methods finish by calling method `setLines2and3` (lines 54–66) and passing it the `KeyEvent` object. This method uses `KeyEvent` method **isActionKey** (line 57) to determine whether the key in the event was an action key. Also, `InputEvent` method **getModifiers** is called (line 59) to determine whether any modifier keys (such as *Shift*, *Alt* and *Ctrl*) were pressed when the key event occurred. The result of this method is passed to `KeyEvent` method **getKeyModifiersText**, which produces a string containing the names of the pressed modifier keys.

[*Note:* If you need to test for a specific key on the keyboard, class `KeyEvent` provides a key constant for every key on the keyboard. These constants can be used from the key event handlers to determine whether a particular key was pressed. Also, to determine whether the *Alt*, *Ctrl*, *Meta* and *Shift* keys are pressed individually, `InputEvent` methods **isAltDown**, **isControlDown**, **isMetaDown** and **isShiftDown** each return a `boolean` indicating if the particular key was pressed during the key event.]

11.17 Layout Managers

Layout managers are provided to arrange GUI components in a container for presentation purposes. Programmers can use the layout managers for basic layout capabilities instead of determining the exact position and size of every GUI component. This functionality enables the programmer to concentrate on the basic look-and-feel and lets the layout managers process most of the layout details. All layout managers implement the interface `LayoutManager` (in package `java.awt`). Class `Container`'s `setLayout` method takes an object that implements the `LayoutManager` interface as an argument. There are basically three ways for you to arrange components in a GUI:

1. Absolute positioning: This provides the greatest level of control over a GUI's appearance. By setting a `Container`'s layout to `null`, you can specify the absolute position of each GUI component with respect to the upper-left corner of the `Container`. If you do this, you also must specify each GUI component's size. Programming a GUI with absolute positioning can be tedious unless you have an integrated development environment (IDE) that can generate the code for you.

2. Layout managers: Using layout managers to position elements can be simpler and faster than creating a GUI with absolute positioning, but you lose some control over the size and the precise positioning of GUI components.

3. Visual programming in an IDE: IDEs provide tools that make it easy to create GUIs. Each IDE typically provides a GUI design tool that allows you to drag and drop GUI components from a tool box onto a design area. You can then position, size and align GUI components as you like. The IDE generates the Java code that creates the GUI. In addition, you can typically add event-handling code for a particular component by double-clicking the component. Some design tools also allow you to use the layout managers described in this chapter and in Chapter 22.

Look-and-Feel Observation 11.16

Most Java programming environments provide GUI design tools that help a programmer graphically design a GUI; the design tools then write the Java code to create the GUI. Such tools often provide greater control over the size, position and alignment of GUI components than do the built-in layout managers.

Look-and-Feel Observation 11.17

It is possible to set a `Container`'s layout to `null`, which indicates that no layout manager should be used. In a `Container` without a layout manager, the programmer must position and size the components in the given container and take care that, on resize events, all components are repositioned as necessary. A component's resize events can be processed by a `ComponentListener`.

Figure 11.38 summarizes the layout managers presented in this chapter. Other layout managers are discussed in Chapter 22.

11.17.1 FlowLayout

`FlowLayout` is the simplest layout manager. GUI components are placed on a container from left to right in the order in which they are added to the container. When the edge of the container is reached, components continue to display on the next line. Class `FlowLayout` allows GUI components to be left aligned, centered (the default) and right aligned.

Layout manager	Description
FlowLayout	Default for `javax.swing.JPanel`. Places components sequentially (left to right) in the order they were added. It is also possible to specify the order of the components by using the `Container` method add, which takes a `Component` and an integer index position as arguments.
BorderLayout	Default for `JFrames` (and other windows). Arranges the components into five areas: NORTH, SOUTH, EAST, WEST and CENTER.
GridLayout	Arranges the components into rows and columns.

Fig. 11.38 | Layout managers.

The application of Fig. 11.39 and Fig. 11.40 creates three `JButton` objects and adds them to the application, using a `FlowLayout` layout manager. The components are center aligned by default. When the user clicks **Left**, the alignment for the layout manager is changed to a left-aligned `FlowLayout`. When the user clicks **Right**, the alignment for the layout manager is changed to a right-aligned `FlowLayout`. When the user clicks **Center**, the alignment for the layout manager is changed to a center-aligned `FlowLayout`. Each button has its own event handler that is declared with an inner class that implements `ActionListener`. The sample output windows show each of the `FlowLayout` alignments. Also, the last sample output window shows the centered alignment after the window has been resized to a smaller width. Notice that the button **Right** flows onto a new line.

As seen previously, a container's layout is set with method `setLayout` of class `Container`. Line 25 sets the layout manager to the `FlowLayout` declared at line 23. Normally, the layout is set before any GUI components are added to a container.

```
1   // Fig. 11.39: FlowLayoutFrame.java
2   // Demonstrating FlowLayout alignments.
3   import java.awt.FlowLayout;
4   import java.awt.Container;
5   import java.awt.event.ActionListener;
6   import java.awt.event.ActionEvent;
7   import javax.swing.JFrame;
8   import javax.swing.JButton;
9
10  public class FlowLayoutFrame extends JFrame
11  {
12     private JButton leftJButton; // button to set alignment left
13     private JButton centerJButton; // button to set alignment center
14     private JButton rightJButton; // button to set alignment right
15     private FlowLayout layout; // layout object
16     private Container container; // container to set layout
17
18     // set up GUI and register button listeners
19     public FlowLayoutFrame()
20     {
21        super( "FlowLayout Demo" );
```

Fig. 11.39 | `FlowLayout` allows components to flow over multiple lines. (Part 1 of 3.)

```java
22      layout = new FlowLayout(); // create FlowLayout
23      container = getContentPane(); // get container to layout
24      setLayout( layout ); // set frame layout
25
26
27      // set up leftJButton and register listener
28      leftJButton = new JButton( "Left" ); // create Left button
29      add( leftJButton ); // add Left button to frame
30      leftJButton.addActionListener(
31
32         new ActionListener() // anonymous inner class
33         {
34            // process leftJButton event
35            public void actionPerformed( ActionEvent event )
36            {
37               layout.setAlignment( FlowLayout.LEFT );
38
39               // realign attached components
40               layout.layoutContainer( container );
41            } // end method actionPerformed
42         } // end anonymous inner class
43      ); // end call to addActionListener
44
45      // set up centerJButton and register listener
46      centerJButton = new JButton( "Center" ); // create Center button
47      add( centerJButton ); // add Center button to frame
48      centerJButton.addActionListener(
49
50         new ActionListener() // anonymous inner class
51         {
52            // process centerJButton event
53            public void actionPerformed( ActionEvent event )
54            {
55               layout.setAlignment( FlowLayout.CENTER );
56
57               // realign attached components
58               layout.layoutContainer( container );
59            } // end method actionPerformed
60         } // end anonymous inner class
61      ); // end call to addActionListener
62
63      // set up rightJButton and register listener
64      rightJButton = new JButton( "Right" ); // create Right button
65      add( rightJButton ); // add Right button to frame
66      rightJButton.addActionListener(
67
68         new ActionListener() // anonymous inner class
69         {
70            // process rightJButton event
71            public void actionPerformed( ActionEvent event )
72            {
73               layout.setAlignment( FlowLayout.RIGHT );
74
```

Fig. 11.39 | FlowLayout allows components to flow over multiple lines. (Part 2 of 3.)

```
75                      // realign attached components
76                      layout.layoutContainer( container );
77                  } // end method actionPerformed
78              } // end anonymous inner class
79          ); // end call to addActionListener
80      } // end FlowLayoutFrame constructor
81  } // end class FlowLayoutFrame
```

Fig. 11.39 | FlowLayout allows components to flow over multiple lines. (Part 3 of 3.)

```
1   // Fig. 11.40: FlowLayoutDemo.java
2   // Testing FlowLayoutFrame.
3   import javax.swing.JFrame;
4
5   public class FlowLayoutDemo
6   {
7      public static void main( String args[] )
8      {
9         FlowLayoutFrame flowLayoutFrame = new FlowLayoutFrame();
10        flowLayoutFrame.setDefaultCloseOperation( JFrame.EXIT_ON_CLOSE );
11        flowLayoutFrame.setSize( 300, 75 ); // set frame size
12        flowLayoutFrame.setVisible( true ); // display frame
13     } // end main
14  } // end class FlowLayoutDemo
```

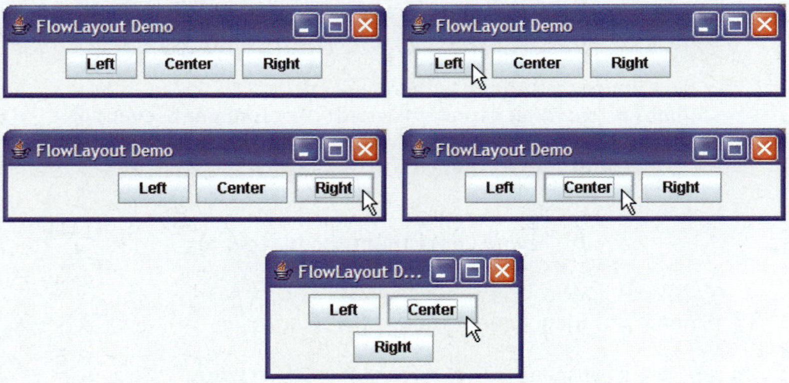

Fig. 11.40 | Test class for FlowLayoutFrame.

Look-and-Feel Observation 11.18

Each container can have only one layout manager. Separate containers in the same application can use different layout managers.

Note in this example that each button's event handler is specified with a separate anonymous inner class object (lines 30–43, 48–61 and 66–71, respectively). Each button's actionPerformed event handler executes two statements. For example, line 37 in method actionPerformed for button left uses FlowLayout method **setAlignment** to change the alignment for the FlowLayout to a left-aligned (FlowLayout.LEFT) FlowLayout. Line 40 uses LayoutManager interface method layoutContainer (which is inherited by all layout managers) to specify that the JFrame should be rearranged based on the adjusted layout. According to which button was clicked, the actionPerformed method for each button sets the FlowLayout's alignment to FlowLayout.LEFT (line 37), FlowLayout.CENTER (line 55) or FlowLayout.RIGHT (line 73).

11.17.2 BorderLayout

The BorderLayout layout manager (the default layout manager for a JFrame) arranges components into five regions: NORTH, SOUTH, EAST, WEST and CENTER. NORTH corresponds to the top of the container. Class BorderLayout extends Object and implements interface LayoutManager2 (a subinterface of LayoutManager that adds several methods for enhanced layout processing).

A BorderLayout limits a Container to containing at most five components—one in each region. The component placed in each region can be a container to which other components are attached. The components placed in the NORTH and SOUTH regions extend horizontally to the sides of the container and are as tall as the components placed in those regions. The EAST and WEST regions expand vertically between the NORTH and SOUTH regions and are as wide as the components placed in those regions. The component placed in the CENTER region expands to fill all remaining space in the layout (which is the reason the JTextArea in Fig. 11.36 occupies the entire window). If all five regions are occupied, the entire container's space is covered by GUI components. If the NORTH or SOUTH region is not occupied, the GUI components in the EAST, CENTER and WEST regions expand vertically to fill the remaining space. If the EAST or WEST region is not occupied, the GUI component in the CENTER region expands horizontally to fill the remaining space. If the CENTER region is not occupied, the area is left empty—the other GUI components do not expand to fill the remaining space. The application of Fig. 11.41 and Fig. 11.42 demonstrates the BorderLayout layout manager by using five JButtons.

Line 21 of Fig. 11.41 creates a BorderLayout. The constructor arguments specify the number of pixels between components that are arranged horizontally (horizontal gap space) and between components that are arranged vertically (vertical gap space), respectively. The default is one pixel of gap space horizontally and vertically. Line 22 uses method setLayout to set the content pane's layout to layout.

We add Components to a BorderLayout with another version of Container method add that takes two arguments—the Component to add and the region in which the Component should appear. For example, line 32 specifies that buttons[0] should appear in the NORTH region. The components can be added in any order, but only one component should be added to each region.

Look-and-Feel Observation 11.19

If no region is specified when adding a Component to a BorderLayout, the layout manager assumes that the Component should be added to region BorderLayout.CENTER.

Common Programming Error 11.6

When more than one component is added to a region in a BorderLayout, only the last component added to that region will be displayed. There is no error that indicates this problem.

```java
1   // Fig. 11.41: BorderLayoutFrame.java
2   // Demonstrating BorderLayout.
3   import java.awt.BorderLayout;
4   import java.awt.event.ActionListener;
5   import java.awt.event.ActionEvent;
6   import javax.swing.JFrame;
7   import javax.swing.JButton;
8
9   public class BorderLayoutFrame extends JFrame implements ActionListener
10  {
11     private JButton buttons[]; // array of buttons to hide portions
12     private final String names[] = { "Hide North", "Hide South",
13        "Hide East", "Hide West", "Hide Center" };
14     private BorderLayout layout; // borderlayout object
15
16     // set up GUI and event handling
17     public BorderLayoutFrame()
18     {
19        super( "BorderLayout Demo" );
20
21        layout = new BorderLayout( 5, 5); // 5 pixel gaps
22        setLayout( layout ); // set frame layout
23        buttons = new JButton[ names.length ]; // set size of array
24
25        // create JButtons and register listeners for them
26        for ( int count = 0; count < names.length; count++ )
27        {
28           buttons[ count ] = new JButton( names[ count ] );
29           buttons[ count ].addActionListener( this );
30        } // end for
31
32        add( buttons[ 0 ], BorderLayout.NORTH ); // add button to north
33        add( buttons[ 1 ], BorderLayout.SOUTH ); // add button to south
34        add( buttons[ 2 ], BorderLayout.EAST ); // add button to east
35        add( buttons[ 3 ], BorderLayout.WEST ); // add button to west
36        add( buttons[ 4 ], BorderLayout.CENTER ); // add button to center
37     } // end BorderLayoutFrame constructor
38
39     // handle button events
40     public void actionPerformed( ActionEvent event )
41     {
42        // check event source and layout content pane correspondingly
43        for ( JButton button : buttons )
44        {
45           if ( event.getSource() == button )
46              button.setVisible( false ); // hide button clicked
47           else
48              button.setVisible( true ); // show other buttons
49        } // end for
50
51        layout.layoutContainer( getContentPane() ); // layout content pane
52     } // end method actionPerformed
53  } // end class BorderLayoutFrame
```

Fig. 11.41 | BorderLayout containing five buttons.

```
 1   // Fig. 11.42: BorderLayoutDemo.java
 2   // Testing BorderLayoutFrame.
 3   import javax.swing.JFrame;
 4
 5   public class BorderLayoutDemo
 6   {
 7      public static void main( String args[] )
 8      {
 9         BorderLayoutFrame borderLayoutFrame = new BorderLayoutFrame();
10         borderLayoutFrame.setDefaultCloseOperation( JFrame.EXIT_ON_CLOSE );
11         borderLayoutFrame.setSize( 300, 200 ); // set frame size
12         borderLayoutFrame.setVisible( true ); // display frame
13      } // end main
14   } // end class BorderLayoutDemo
```

Fig. 11.42 | Test class for `BorderLayoutFrame`.

Note that class `BorderLayoutFrame` implements `ActionListener` directly in this example, so the `BorderLayoutFrame` will handle the events of the `JButtons`. For this reason, line 29 passes the `this` reference to the `addActionListener` method of each `JButton`. When the user clicks a particular `JButton` in the layout, method action-

Performed (lines 40–52) executes. The enhanced for statement at lines 43–49 uses an if...else to hide the particular JButton that generated the event. Method **setVisible** (inherited into JButton from class Component) is called with a false argument (line 46) to hide the JButton. If the current JButton in the array is not the one that generated the event, method setVisible is called with a true argument (line 48) to ensure that the JButton is displayed on the screen. Line 51 uses LayoutManager method layoutContainer to recalculate the layout of the content pane. Notice in the screen captures of Fig. 11.41 that certain regions in the BorderLayout change shape as JButtons are hidden and displayed in other regions. Try resizing the application window to see how the various regions resize based on the window's width and height. For more complex layouts, group components in JPanels, each with a separate layout manager. Place the JPanels on the JFrame using either the default BorderLayout or some other layout.

11.17.3 GridLayout

The **GridLayout** layout manager divides the container into a grid so that components can be placed in rows and columns. Class GridLayout inherits directly from class Object and implements interface LayoutManager. Every Component in a GridLayout has the same width and height. Components are added to a GridLayout starting at the top-left cell of the grid and proceeding left to right until the row is full. Then the process continues left to right on the next row of the grid, and so on. The application of Fig. 11.43 and Fig. 11.44 demonstrates the GridLayout layout manager by using six JButtons.

```
1   // Fig. 11.43: GridLayoutFrame.java
2   // Demonstrating GridLayout.
3   import java.awt.GridLayout;
4   import java.awt.Container;
5   import java.awt.event.ActionListener;
6   import java.awt.event.ActionEvent;
7   import javax.swing.JFrame;
8   import javax.swing.JButton;
9
10  public class GridLayoutFrame extends JFrame implements ActionListener
11  {
12     private JButton buttons[]; // array of buttons
13     private final String names[] =
14        { "one", "two", "three", "four", "five", "six" };
15     private boolean toggle = true; // toggle between two layouts
16     private Container container; // frame container
17     private GridLayout gridLayout1; // first gridlayout
18     private GridLayout gridLayout2; // second gridlayout
19
20     // no-argument constructor
21     public GridLayoutFrame()
22     {
23        super( "GridLayout Demo" );
24        gridLayout1 = new GridLayout( 2, 3, 5, 5 ); // 2 by 3; gaps of 5
25        gridLayout2 = new GridLayout( 3, 2 ); // 3 by 2; no gaps
26        container = getContentPane(); // get content pane
```

Fig. 11.43 | GridLayout containing six buttons. (Part 1 of 2.)

```
27          setLayout( gridLayout1 ); // set JFrame layout
28          buttons = new JButton[ names.length ]; // create array of JButtons
29
30          for ( int count = 0; count < names.length; count++ )
31          {
32             buttons[ count ] = new JButton( names[ count ] );
33             buttons[ count ].addActionListener( this ); // register listener
34             add( buttons[ count ] ); // add button to JFrame
35          } // end for
36       } // end GridLayoutFrame constructor
37
38       // handle button events by toggling between layouts
39       public void actionPerformed( ActionEvent event )
40       {
41          if ( toggle )
42             container.setLayout( gridLayout2 ); // set layout to second
43          else
44             container.setLayout( gridLayout1 ); // set layout to first
45
46          toggle = !toggle; // set toggle to opposite value
47          container.validate(); // re-layout container
48       } // end method actionPerformed
49    } // end class GridLayoutFrame
```

Fig. 11.43 | GridLayout containing six buttons. (Part 2 of 2.)

```
 1   // Fig. 11.44: GridLayoutDemo.java
 2   // Testing GridLayoutFrame.
 3   import javax.swing.JFrame;
 4
 5   public class GridLayoutDemo
 6   {
 7      public static void main( String args[] )
 8      {
 9         GridLayoutFrame gridLayoutFrame = new GridLayoutFrame();
10         gridLayoutFrame.setDefaultCloseOperation( JFrame.EXIT_ON_CLOSE );
11         gridLayoutFrame.setSize( 300, 200 ); // set frame size
12         gridLayoutFrame.setVisible( true ); // display frame
13      } // end main
14   } // end class GridLayoutDemo
```

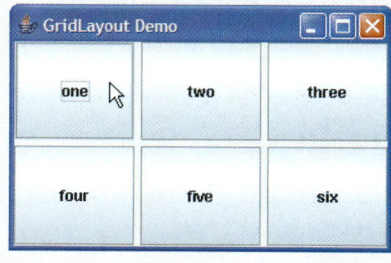 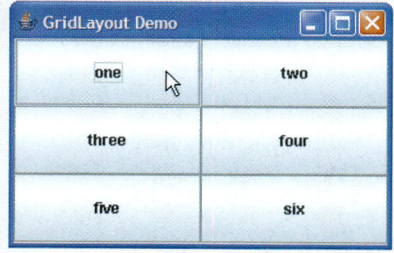

Fig. 11.44 | Test class for GridLayoutFrame.

Lines 24–25 create two `GridLayout` objects (variables `grid1` and `grid2` are declared at lines 17–18). The `GridLayout` constructor used at line 24 specifies a `GridLayout` with 2 rows, 3 columns, 5 pixels of horizontal-gap space between `Components` in the grid and 5 pixels of vertical-gap space between `Components` in the grid. The `GridLayout` constructor used at line 25 specifies a `GridLayout` with 3 rows and 2 columns that uses the default gap space (1 pixel).

The `JButton` objects in this example initially are arranged using `grid1` (set for the content pane at line 27 with method `setLayout`). The first component is added to the first column of the first row. The next component is added to the second column of the first row, and so on. When a `JButton` is pressed, method `actionPerformed` (lines 39–48) is called. Every call to `actionPerformed` toggles the layout between `grid2` and `grid1`, using `boolean` variable `toggle` to determine the next layout to set.

Line 47 illustrates another way to reformat a container for which the layout has changed. `Container` method **validate** recomputes the container's layout based on the current layout manager for the `Container` and the current set of displayed GUI components.

11.18 Using Panels to Manage More Complex Layouts

Complex GUIs (like Fig. 11.1) require that each component be placed in an exact location. They often consist of multiple panels, with each panel's components arranged in a specific layout. Class `JPanel` extends `JComponent` and `JComponent` extends class `Container`, so every `JPanel` is a `Container`. Thus, every `JPanel` may have components, including other panels, attached to it with `Container` method add. The application of Fig. 11.45 and Fig. 11.46 demonstrates how a `JPanel` can be used to create a more complex layout in which several `JButtons` are placed in the SOUTH region of a `BorderLayout`.

```java
1   // Fig. 11.45: PanelFrame.java
2   // Using a JPanel to help lay out components.
3   import java.awt.GridLayout;
4   import java.awt.BorderLayout;
5   import javax.swing.JFrame;
6   import javax.swing.JPanel;
7   import javax.swing.JButton;
8
9   public class PanelFrame extends JFrame
10  {
11     private JPanel buttonJPanel; // panel to hold buttons
12     private JButton buttons[]; // array of buttons
13
14     // no-argument constructor
15     public PanelFrame()
16     {
17        super( "Panel Demo" );
18        buttons = new JButton[ 5 ]; // create buttons array
19        buttonJPanel = new JPanel(); // set up panel
20        buttonJPanel.setLayout( new GridLayout( 1, buttons.length ) );
21
```

Fig. 11.45 | `JPanel` with five `JButtons` in a `GridLayout` attached to the SOUTH region of a `BorderLayout`. (Part 1 of 2.)

```
22          // create and add buttons
23          for ( int count = 0; count < buttons.length; count++ )
24          {
25             buttons[ count ] = new JButton( "Button " + ( count + 1 ) );
26             buttonJPanel.add( buttons[ count ] ); // add button to panel
27          } // end for
28
29          add( buttonJPanel, BorderLayout.SOUTH ); // add panel to JFrame
30       } // end PanelFrame constructor
31    } // end class PanelFrame
```

Fig. 11.45 | JPanel with five JButtons in a GridLayout attached to the SOUTH region of a BorderLayout. (Part 2 of 2.)

```
1    // Fig. 11.46: PanelDemo.java
2    // Testing PanelFrame.
3    import javax.swing.JFrame;
4
5    public class PanelDemo extends JFrame
6    {
7       public static void main( String args[] )
8       {
9          PanelFrame panelFrame = new PanelFrame();
10         panelFrame.setDefaultCloseOperation( JFrame.EXIT_ON_CLOSE );
11         panelFrame.setSize( 450, 200 ); // set frame size
12         panelFrame.setVisible( true ); // display frame
13      } // end main
14   } // end class PanelDemo
```

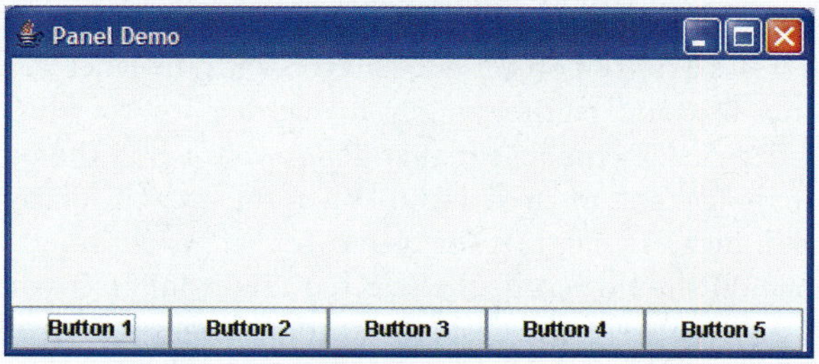

Fig. 11.46 | Test class for PanelFrame.

After JPanel buttonPanel is declared in line 11 and created at line 19, line 20 sets buttonPanel's layout to a GridLayout of one row and five columns (there are five JButtons in array buttons). Lines 23–27 add the five JButtons in array buttons to the JPanel in the loop. Line 26 adds the buttons directly to the JPanel—class JPanel does not have a content pane, unlike a JFrame. Line 29 uses the default BorderLayout to add buttonPanel to the SOUTH region. Note that the SOUTH region is as tall as the buttons on buttonPanel. A JPanel is sized to the components it contains. As more components are added, the JPanel grows (according to the restrictions of its layout manager) to accommodate the components. Resize the window to see how the layout manager affects the size of the JButtons.

11.19 JTextArea

A **JTextArea** provides an area for manipulating multiple lines of text. Like class **JText-Field**, JTextArea is a subclass of JTextComponent, which declares common methods for JTextFields, JTextAreas and several other text-based GUI components.

The application in Fig. 11.47 and Fig. 11.48 demonstrates JTextAreas. One JTextArea displays text that the user can select. The other JTextArea is uneditable and is used to display the text the user selected in the first JTextArea. Unlike JTextFields, JTextAreas do not have action events. As with multiple-selection JLists (Section 11.12), an external event from another GUI component indicates when to process the text in a JTextArea. For example, when typing an e-mail message, you normally click a **Send** button to send the text of the message to the recipient. Similarly, when editing a document in a word processor, you normally save the file by selecting a **Save** or **Save As...** menu item. In this program, the button **Copy >>>** generates the external event that copies the selected text in the left JTextArea and displays it in the right JTextArea.

In the constructor (lines 18–48), line 21 creates a **Box** container (package javax.swing) to organize the GUI components. Box is a subclass of Container that uses a **BoxLayout** layout manager (discussed in detail in Section 22.9) to arrange the GUI components either horizontally or vertically. Box's static method **createHorizontalBox** creates a Box that arranges components from left to right in the order that they are attached.

Lines 26 and 43 create JTextAreas textArea1 and textArea2. Line 26 uses JTextArea's three-argument constructor, which takes a String representing the initial text and two ints specifying that the JTextArea has 10 rows and 15 columns. Line 43 uses JTextArea's two-argument constructor, specifying that the JTextArea has 10 rows and 15 columns. Line 26 specifies that demo should be displayed as the default JTextArea content. A JTextArea does not provide scrollbars if it cannot display its complete contents. So, line 27 creates a **JScrollPane** object, initializes it with textArea1 and attaches it to container box. By default, horizontal and vertical scrollbars will appear as necessary in a JScrollPane.

Lines 29–41 create JButton object copyButton with the label "Copy >>>", add copyButton to container box and register the event handler for copyButton's ActionEvent. This button provides the external event that determines when the program should copy the selected text in textArea1 to textArea2. When the user clicks copyButton, line 38 in actionPerformed indicates that method **getSelectedText** (inherited into JTextArea from JTextComponent) should return the selected text from textArea1. The user selects text by dragging the mouse over the desired text to highlight it. Method setText changes the text in textArea2 to the string returned by getSelectedText.

Lines 43–45 create textArea2, set its editable property to false and add it to container box. Line 47 adds box to the JFrame. Recall from Section 11.17 that the default layout of a JFrame is a BorderLayout and that the add method by default attaches its argument to the CENTER of the BorderLayout.

It is sometimes desirable, when text reaches the right side of a JTextArea, to have the text wrap to the next line. This is referred to as **line wrapping**. By default, JTextArea does not wrap lines.

Look-and-Feel Observation 11.20

To provide line-wrapping functionality for a JTextArea, invoke JTextArea method **setLineWrap** *with a* true *argument.*

```
1   // Fig. 11.47: TextAreaFrame.java
2   // Copying selected text from one textarea to another.
3   import java.awt.event.ActionListener;
4   import java.awt.event.ActionEvent;
5   import javax.swing.Box;
6   import javax.swing.JFrame;
7   import javax.swing.JTextArea;
8   import javax.swing.JButton;
9   import javax.swing.JScrollPane;
10
11  public class TextAreaFrame extends JFrame
12  {
13     private JTextArea textArea1; // displays demo string
14     private JTextArea textArea2; // highlighted text is copied here
15     private JButton copyJButton; // initiates copying of text
16
17     // no-argument constructor
18     public TextAreaFrame()
19     {
20        super( "TextArea Demo" );
21        Box box = Box.createHorizontalBox(); // create box
22        String demo = "This is a demo string to\n" +
23           "illustrate copying text\nfrom one textarea to \n" +
24           "another textarea using an\nexternal event\n";
25
26        textArea1 = new JTextArea( demo, 10, 15 ); // create textarea1
27        box.add( new JScrollPane( textArea1 ) ); // add scrollpane
28
29        copyJButton = new JButton( "Copy >>>" ); // create copy button
30        box.add( copyJButton ); // add copy button to box
31        copyJButton.addActionListener(
32
33           new ActionListener() // anonymous inner class
34           {
35              // set text in textArea2 to selected text from textArea1
36              public void actionPerformed( ActionEvent event )
37              {
38                 textArea2.setText( textArea1.getSelectedText() );
39              } // end method actionPerformed
40           } // end anonymous inner class
41        ); // end call to addActionListener
42
43        textArea2 = new JTextArea( 10, 15 ); // create second textarea
44        textArea2.setEditable( false ); // disable editing
45        box.add( new JScrollPane( textArea2 ) ); // add scrollpane
46
47        add( box ); // add box to frame
48     } // end TextAreaFrame constructor
49  } // end class TextAreaFrame
```

Fig. 11.47 | Copying selected text from one JTextArea to another.

```
1   // Fig. 11.48: TextAreaDemo.java
2   // Copying selected text from one textarea to another.
3   import javax.swing.JFrame;
4
5   public class TextAreaDemo
6   {
7      public static void main( String args[] )
8      {
9         TextAreaFrame textAreaFrame = new TextAreaFrame();
10        textAreaFrame.setDefaultCloseOperation( JFrame.EXIT_ON_CLOSE );
11        textAreaFrame.setSize( 425, 200 ); // set frame size
12        textAreaFrame.setVisible( true ); // display frame
13     } // end main
14  } // end class TextAreaDemo
```

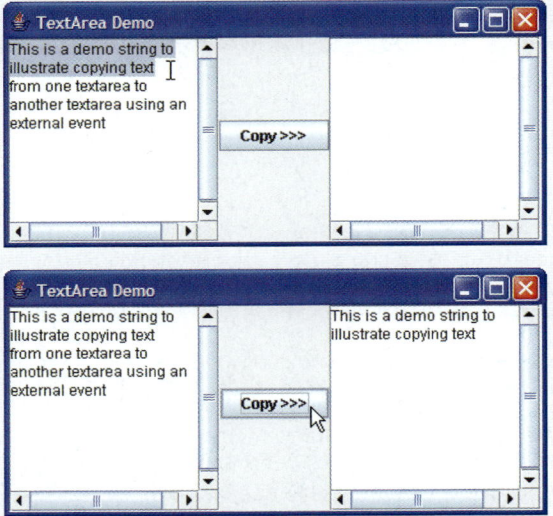

Fig. 11.48 | Test class for `TextAreaFrame`.

JScrollPane Scrollbar Policies

This example uses a `JScrollPane` to provide scrolling for a `JTextArea`. By default, `JScrollPane` displays scrollbars only if they are required. You can set the horizontal and vertical **scrollbar policies** of a `JScrollPane` when it is constructed. If a program has a reference to a `JScrollPane`, the program can use `JScrollPane` methods **set-HorizontalScrollBarPolicy** and **setVerticalScrollBarPolicy** to change the scrollbar policies at any time. Class `JScrollPane` declares the constants

```
JScrollPane.VERTICAL_SCROLLBAR_ALWAYS
JScrollPane.HORIZONTAL_SCROLLBAR_ALWAYS
```

to indicate that a scrollbar should always appear, constants

```
JScrollPane.VERTICAL_SCROLLBAR_AS_NEEDED
JScrollPane.HORIZONTAL_SCROLLBAR_AS_NEEDED
```

to indicate that a scrollbar should appear only if necessary (the defaults) and constants

```
JScrollPane.VERTICAL_SCROLLBAR_NEVER
JScrollPane.HORIZONTAL_SCROLLBAR_NEVER
```

to indicate that a scrollbar should never appear. If the horizontal scrollbar policy is set to `JScrollPane.HORIZONTAL_SCROLLBAR_NEVER`, a `JTextArea` attached to the `JScrollPane` will automatically wrap lines.

11.20 Wrap-Up

In this chapter, you learned many GUI components and how to implement event handling. You also learned about nested classes, inner classes and anonymous inner classes. You saw the special relationship between an inner-class object and an object of its top-level class. You learned how to use `JOptionPane` dialogs to obtain text input from the user and how to display messages to the user. You also learned how to create applications that execute in their own windows. We discussed class `JFrame` and components that enable a user to interact with an application. We also showed you how to display text and images to the user. You learned how to customize `JPanel`s to create custom drawing areas, which you will use extensively in the next chapter. You saw how to organize components on a window using layout managers and how to creating more complex GUIs by using `JPanel`s to organize components. Finally, you learned about the JTextArea component in which a user can enter text and an application can display text. In Chapter 22, GUI Components: Part 2, you will learn about more advanced GUI components, such as sliders, menus and more complex layout managers. In the next chapter, you will learn how to add graphics to your GUI application. Graphics allow you to draw shapes and text with colors and styles.

Summary

- A graphical user interface (GUI) presents a user-friendly mechanism for interacting with an application. A GUI gives an application a distinctive "look" and "feel."

- Providing different applications with consistent, intuitive user interface components allows users to be somewhat familiar with an application, so that they can learn it more quickly.

- GUIs are built from GUI components—sometimes called controls or widgets.

- Most applications use windows or dialog boxes (also called dialogs) to interact with the user.

- Class `JOptionPane` (package `javax.swing`) provides prepackaged dialog boxes for both input and output. `JOptionPane` static method `showInputDialog` displays an input dialog.

- A prompt typically uses sentence-style capitalization—a style that capitalizes only the first letter of the first word in the text unless the word is a proper noun.

- An input dialog can input only input `String`s. This is typical of most GUI components.

- `JOptionPane` static method `showMessageDialog` displays a message dialog.

- Most Swing GUI components are located in package `javax.swing`. They are part of the Java Foundation Classes (JFC)—Java's libraries for cross-platform GUI development.

- Together, the appearance and the way in which the user interacts with the application are known as that application's look-and-feel. Swing GUI components allow you to specify a uniform look-and-feel for your application across all platforms or to use each platform's custom look-and-feel.

- Lightweight Swing components are not tied to actual GUI components supported by the underlying platform on which an application executes.

- Several Swing components are heavyweight components that require direct interaction with the local windowing system, which may restrict their appearance and functionality.
- Class `Component` (package `java.awt`) declares many of the attributes and behaviors common to the GUI components in packages `java.awt` and `javax.swing`.
- Class `Container` (package `java.awt`) is a subclass of `Component`. `Component`s are attached to `Container`s so the `Component`s can be organized and displayed on the screen.
- Class `JComponent` (package `javax.swing`) is a subclass of `Container`. `JComponent` is the superclass of all lightweight Swing components and declares their common attributes and behaviors.
- Some common `JComponent` features include a pluggable look-and-feel, shortcut keys called mnemonics, tool tips, support for assistive technologies and support for user interface localization.
- Most windows are instances of class `JFrame` or a subclass of `JFrame`. `JFrame` provides the basic attributes and behaviors of a window.
- A `JLabel` displays a single line of read-only text, an image, or both text and an image. Text in a `JLabel` normally uses sentence-style capitalization.
- When building a GUI, each GUI component must be attached to a container, such as a window created with a `JFrame`.
- Many IDEs provide GUI design tools in which you can specify the exact size and location of a component by using the mouse, then the IDE will generate the GUI code for you.
- `JComponent` method `setToolTipText` specifies the tool tip that is displayed when the user positions the mouse cursor over a lightweight component.
- `Container` method `add` attaches a GUI component to a `Container`.
- Class `ImageIcon` (package `javax.swing`) supports several image formats, including Graphics Interchange Format (GIF), Portable Network Graphics (PNG) and Joint Photographic Experts Group (JPEG).
- Method `getClass` (of class `Object`) retrieves a reference to the `Class` object that represents the the class declaration for the object on which the method is called.
- `Class` method `getResource` returns the location of its argument as a URL. Method `getResource` uses the `Class` object's class loader to determine the location of the resource.
- Interface `SwingConstants` (package `javax.swing`) declares a set of common integer constants that are used with many Swing components.
- The horizontal and vertical alignments of a `JLabel` can be set with methods `setHorizontalAlignment` and `setVerticalAlignment`, respectively.
- `JLabel` method `setText` sets the text displayed on a label. The corresponding method `getText` retrieves the current text displayed on a label.
- `JLabel` method `setIcon` specifies the `Icon` to display on a label. The corresponding method `getIcon` retrieves the current `Icon` displayed on a label.
- `JLabel` methods `setHorizontalTextPosition` and `setVerticalTextPosition` specify the text position in the label.
- `JFrame` method `setDefaultCloseOperation` with constant `JFrame.EXIT_ON_CLOSE` as the argument indicates that the program should terminate when the window is closed by the user.
- `Component` method `setSize` specifies the width and height of a component.
- `Component` method `setVisible` with the argument `true` displays a `JFrame` on the screen.
- GUIs are event driven—when the user interacts with a GUI component, events drive the program to perform tasks.

- The code that performs a task in response to an event is called an event handler and the overall process of responding to events is known as event handling.

- Class `JTextField` extends class `JTextComponent` (package `javax.swing.text`), which provides many features common to Swing's text-based components. Class `JPasswordField` extends `JTextField` and adds several methods that are specific to processing passwords.

- A `JPasswordField` shows that characters are being typed as the user enters them, but hides the actual characters with echo characters.

- A component receives the focus when the user clicks the component.

- `JTextComponent` method `setEditable` can be used to make a text field uneditable.

- Before an application can respond to an event for a particular GUI component, you must perform several coding steps: 1) Create a class that represents the event handler. 2) Implement an appropriate interface, known as an event-listener interface, in the class from *Step 1*. 3) Indicate that an object of the class from *Steps 1* and *2* should be notified when the event occurs. This is known as registering the event handler.

- Java allows you to declare nested classes inside other classes. Nested classes can be static or non-static. Non-static nested classes are called inner classes and are frequently used for event handling.

- Before an object of an inner class can be created, there must first be an object of the top-level class that contains the inner class, because an inner-class object implicitly has a reference to an object of its top-level class.

- An inner-class object is allowed to directly access all the instance variables and methods of its top-level class.

- A nested class that is `static` does not require an object of its top-level class and does not implicitly have a reference to an object of the top-level class.

- When the user presses *Enter* in a `JTextField` or `JPasswordField`, the GUI component generates an `ActionEvent` (package `java.awt.event`). Such an event is processed by an object that implements the interface `ActionListener` (package `java.awt.event`).

- `JTextField` method `addActionListener` registers the event handler for a component text field. This method receives as its argument an `ActionListener` object.

- The GUI component with which the user interacts is the event source.

- An `ActionEvent` object contains information about the event that just occurred, such as the event source and the text in the text field.

- `ActionEvent` method `getSource` returns a reference to the event source. `ActionEvent` method `getActionCommand` returns the text the user typed in a text field or the label on a `JButton`.

- `JPasswordField` method `getPassword` returns the password the user typed.

- For each event-object type, there is typically a corresponding event-listener interface. Each event-listener interface specifies one or more event-handling methods that must be declared in the class that implements the interface.

- When an event occurs, the GUI component with which the user interacted notifies its registered listeners by calling each listener's appropriate event-handling method.

- Every `JComponent` has an instance variable called `listenerList` that refers to an object of class `EventListenerList` (package `javax.swing.event`). Each object of a `JComponent` subclass maintains a references to all of its registered listeners in the `listenerList`.

- Every GUI component supports several event types, including mouse events, key events and others. When an event occurs, the event is dispatched only to the event listeners of the appropriate type. The GUI component receives a unique event ID specifying the event type, which it uses to decide the listener type to which the event should be dispatched and which method to call on each listener object.

- A button is a component the user clicks to trigger a specific action. All the button types are subclasses of `AbstractButton` (package `javax.swing`), which declares the common features of Swing buttons. Button labels typically use book-title capitalization—a style that capitalizes the first letter of each significant word in the text and does not end with any punctuation.

- Command buttons are created with class `JButton`.

- A `JButton` can display an `Icon`. To provide the user with an extra level of visual interaction with the GUI, a `JButton` can also have a rollover `Icon`—an `Icon` that is displayed when the user positions the mouse over the button.

- Method `setRolloverIcon` (of class `AbstractButton`) specifies the image displayed on a button when the user positions the mouse over it.

- The Swing GUI components contain three types of state buttons—`JToggleButton`, `JCheckBox` and `JRadioButton`.

- Classes `JCheckBox` and `JRadioButton` are subclasses of `JToggleButton`. A `JRadioButton` is different from a `JCheckBox` in that normally several `JRadioButtons` are grouped together, and only one in the group can be selected at any time.

- Method `setFont` (of class `Component`) sets the font of a component to a new object of class `Font` (package `java.awt`).

- When the user clicks a `JCheckBox`, an `ItemEvent` occurs. This event can be handled by an `ItemListener` object, which must implement method `itemStateChanged`. Method `addItemListener` registers the listener for a `JCheckBox` or `JRadioButton` object.

- `JCheckBox` method `isSelected` determines if a `JCheckBox` is selected.

- `JRadioButtons` are similar to `JCheckBoxes` in that they have two states—selected and not selected. However, radio buttons normally appear as a group in which only one button can be selected at a time. Selecting a different radio button forces all others to be deselected.

- `JRadioButtons` are used to represent mutually exclusive options.

- The logical relationship between `JRadioButtons` is maintained by a `ButtonGroup` object (package `javax.swing`).

- `ButtonGroup` method `add` associates each a `JRadioButton` with a `ButtonGroup`. If more than one selected `JRadioButton` object is added to a group, the selected one that was added first will be selected when the GUI is displayed.

- `JRadioButtons` generate `ItemEvents` when they are clicked.

- A `JComboBox` provides a list of items from which the user can make a single selection. `JComboBoxes` generate `ItemEvents`.

- Each item in a `JComboBox` has an index. The first item added to a `JComboBox` appears as the currently selected item when the `JComboBox` is displayed. Other items are selected by clicking the `JComboBox`, which expands into a list from which the user can make a selection.

- `JComboBox` method `setMaximumRowCount` sets the maximum number of elements that are displayed when the user clicks the `JComboBox`. If there are additional items, the `JComboBox` provides a scrollbar that allows the user to scroll through all the elements in the list.

- An anonymous inner class is a special form of inner class that is declared without a name and typically appears inside a method declaration. Since an anonymous inner class has no name, one object of the anonymous inner class must be created at the point where the class is declared.

- `JComboBox` method `getSelectedIndex` returns the index of the selected item.

- A `JList` displays a series of items from which the user may select one or more items. Class `JList` supports single-selection lists and multiple-selection lists.
- When the user clicks an item in a `JList`, a `ListSelectionEvent` occurs. `JList` method `addList-SelectionListener` registers a `ListSelectionListener` for a `JList`'s selection events. A `ListSelectionListener` (package `javax.swing.event`) must implement method `valueChanged`.
- `JList` method `setVisibleRowCount` specifies the number of items that are visible in the list.
- `JList` method `setSelectionMode` specifies a list's selection mode.
- A `JList` does not provide a scrollbar if there are more items in the list than the number of visible rows. In this case, a `JScrollPane` object can be used to provide the scrolling capability.
- `JFrame` method `getContentPane` returns a reference to the `JFrame`'s content pane where GUI components are displayed.
- `JList` method `getSelectedIndex` returns the selected item's index.
- A multiple-selection list enables the user to select many items from a `JList`.
- `JList` method `setFixedCellWidth` sets a `JList`'s width. Method `setFixedCellHeight` sets the height of each item in a `JList`.
- There are no events to indicate that a user has made multiple selections in a multiple-selection list. Normally, an external event generated by another GUI component specifies when the multiple selections in a `JList` should be processed.
- `JList` method `setListData` sets the items displayed in a `JList`. `JList` method `getSelectedValues` returns an array of `Object`s representing the selected items in a `JList`.
- The `MouseListener` and `MouseMotionListener` event-listener interfaces are used to handle mouse events. Mouse events can be trapped for any GUI component that extends `Component`.
- Interface `MouseInputListener` (package `javax.swing.event`) extends interfaces `MouseListener` and `MouseMotionListener` to create a single interface containing all their methods.
- Each of the mouse event-handling methods takes a `MouseEvent` object as its argument. A `MouseEvent` object contains information about the mouse event that occurred, including the x- and y-coordinates of the location where the event occurred. These coordinates are measured from the upper-left corner of the GUI component on which the event occurred.
- The methods and constants of class `InputEvent` (`MouseEvent`'s superclass) enable an application to determine which mouse button the user clicked.
- Interface `MouseWheelListener` enables applications to respond to the rotation of a mouse wheel.
- GUI components inherit methods `addMouseListener` and `addMouseMotionListener` from class `Component`.
- Many event-listener interfaces contain multiple methods. For many of these interfaces, packages `java.awt.event` and `javax.swing.event` provide event-listener adapter classes. An adapter class implements an interface and provides a default implementation of each method in the interface. You can extend an adapter class to inherit the default implementation of every method and subsequently override only the method(s) you need for event handling.
- `MouseEvent` method `getClickCount` returns the number of mouse button clicks. Methods `isMetaDown` and `isAltDown` determine which mouse button the user clicked.
- Lightweight Swing components that extend class `JComponent` contain method `paintComponent`, which is called when a lightweight Swing component is displayed. By overriding this method, you can specify how to draw shapes using Java's graphics capabilities.
- When customizing a `JPanel` for use as a dedicated drawing area, the subclass should override method `paintComponent` and call the superclass version of `paintComponent` as the first statement in the body of the overridden method.

- Subclasses of JComponent support transparency. When a component is opaque, paintComponent clears the component's background before the component is displayed.

- The transparency of a Swing lightweight component can be set with method setOpaque (a false argument indicates that the component is transparent).

- Class Point (package java.awt) represents an *x-y* coordinate.

- Class Graphics is used to draw.

- MouseEvent method getPoint obtains the Point where a mouse event occurred.

- Method repaint (inherited indirectly from class Component) indicates that a component should be refreshed on the screen as soon as possible.

- Method paintComponent receives a Graphics parameter and is called automatically any time a lightweight component needs to be displayed on the screen.

- Graphics method fillOval draws a solid oval. The method's four parameters represent the bounding box in which the oval is displayed. The first two parameters are the upper-left *x*-coordinate and the upper-left *y*-coordinate of the rectangular area. The last two coordinates represent the rectangular area's width and height.

- Interface KeyListener is used to handle key events that are generated when keys on the keyboard are pressed and released. Method addKeyListener of class Component registers a KeyListener for a component.

- KeyEvent method getKeyCode gets the virtual key code of the key that was pressed. Class KeyEvent maintains a set of virtual key-code constants that represent every key on the keyboard.

- KeyEvent method getKeyText returns a string containing the name of the key that was pressed.

- KeyEvent method getKeyChar gets the Unicode value of the character typed.

- KeyEvent method isActionKey determines whether the key in an event was an action key.

- InputEvent method getModifiers determines whether any modifier keys (such as *Shift*, *Alt* and *Ctrl*) were pressed when the key event occurred.

- KeyEvent method getKeyModifiersText produces a string containing the names of the pressed modifier keys.

- Layout managers arrange GUI components in a container for presentation purposes.

- All layout managers implement the interface LayoutManager (package java.awt).

- Container method setLayout specifies the layout of a container.

- FlowLayout is the simplest layout manager. GUI components are placed on a container from left to right in the order in which they are added to the container. When the edge of the container is reached, components continue to display on the next line. Class FlowLayout allows GUI components to be left aligned, centered (the default) and right aligned.

- FlowLayout method setAlignment changes the alignment for a FlowLayout.

- The BorderLayout layout manager (the default for a JFrame) arranges components into five regions: NORTH, SOUTH, EAST, WEST and CENTER. NORTH corresponds to the top of the container.

- A BorderLayout limits a Container to containing at most five components—one in each region.

- The GridLayout layout manager divides the container into a grid so that components can be placed in rows and columns.

- Container method validate recomputes a container's layout based on the current layout manager for the Container and the current set of displayed GUI components.

- A JTextArea provides an area for manipulating multiple lines of text. JTextArea is a subclass of JTextComponent, which declares common methods for JTextFields, JTextAreas and several other text-based GUI components.

- Class Box is a subclass of Container that uses a BoxLayout layout manager to arrange the GUI components either horizontally or vertically.
- Box static method createHorizontalBox creates a Box that arranges components from left to right in the order that they are attached.
- Method getSelectedText (inherited into JTextArea from JTextComponent) returns the selected text from a JTextArea.
- You can set the horizontal and vertical scrollbar policies of a JScrollPane when it is constructed. JScrollPane methods setHorizontalScrollBarPolicy and setVerticalScrollBarPolicy can be used change the scrollbar policies at any time.

Terminology

AbstractButton class
ActionEvent class
ActionListener interface
actionPerformed method of ActionListener
adapter class
add method of class ButtonGroup
add method of Container
addActionListener method of class JTextField
addItemListener method of class
    AbstractButton
addKeyListener method of class Component
addListSelectionListener method of
    class JList
addMouseListener method of class Component
addMouseMotionListener method of class
    Component
addWindowListener method of class JFrame
anonymous inner class
AWTEvent class
book-title capitalization
BorderLayout class
Box class
BoxLayout class
ButtonGroup class
Class class
Component class
Container class
content pane
createHorizontalBox method of class Box
dedicated drawing area
default constructor of an anonymous inner class
delegation event model
dialog box
dispatch an event
event
event driven
event handler
event handling

event listener
event-listener adapter class
event-listener interface
event object
event registration
event source
EventListenerList class
fillOval method of class Graphics
FlowLayout class
focus
Font class
getActionCommand method of ActionEvent
getClass method of Object
getClickCount method of MouseEvent
getContentPane method of JFrame
getIcon method of JLabel
getKeyChar method of KeyEvent
getKeyCode method of KeyEvent
getKeyModifiersText method of KeyEvent
getKeyText method of KeyEvent
getModifiers method of InputEvent
getPassword method of JPasswordField
getPoint method of MouseEvent
getResource method of Class
getSelected Index method of JList
getSelectedIndex method of JComboBox
getSelectedText method of JTextComponent
getSelectedValues method of JList
getSource method of EventObject
getStateChange method of ItemEvent
getText method of JLabel
getX method of MouseEvent
getY method of MouseEvent
graphical user interface (GUI)
Graphics class
GridLayout class
GUI component
heavyweight GUI component

setVerticalAlignment method of JLabel

setVerticalScrollBarPolicy method of JSlider

setVerticalTextPosition method of JLabel

setVisible method of Component

setVisible method of JFrame

setVisibleRowCount method of JList

showInputDialog method of JOptionPane

showMessageDialog method of JOptionPane

static nested class

Swing GUI components

SwingConstants interface

tool tip

top-level class

transparency of a JComponent

typing in a text field

validate method of Container

valueChanged method of ListSelectionListener

WindowAdapter class

windowClosing method of WindowListener

WindowListener interface

Self-Review Exercises

11.1 Fill in the blanks in each of the following statements:

a) Method _____ is called when the mouse is moved with no buttons pressed and an event listener is registered to handle the event.

b) Text that cannot be modified by the user is called _____ text.

c) A(n) _____ arranges GUI components in a Container.

d) The add method for attaching GUI components is a method of class _____.

e) GUI is an acronym for _____.

f) Method _____ is used to specify the layout manager for a container.

g) A mouseDragged method call is preceded by a(n) _____ method call and followed by a(n) _____ method call.

h) Class _____ contains methods that display message dialogs and input dialogs.

i) An input dialog capable of receiving input from the user is displayed with method _____ of class _____.

j) A dialog capable of displaying a message to the user is displayed with method _____ of class _____.

k) Both JTextFields and JTextAreas directly extend class _____.

11.2 Determine whether each statement is *true* or *false*. If *false*, explain why.

a) BorderLayout is the default layout manager for a JFrame's content pane.

b) When the mouse cursor is moved into the bounds of a GUI component, method mouseOver is called.

c) A JPanel cannot be added to another JPanel.

d) In a BorderLayout, two buttons added to the NORTH region will be placed side by side.

e) When one is using BorderLayout, a maximum of five components can be displayed.

f) Inner classes are not allowed to access the members of the enclosing class.

g) A JTextArea's text is always read-only.

h) Class JTextArea is a direct subclass of class Component.

11.3 Find the error(s) in each of the following statements, and explain how to correct it (them):

```
a) buttonName = JButton( "Caption" );
b) JLabel aLabel, JLabel;         // create references
c) txtField = new JTextField( 50, "Default Text" );
d) Container container = getContentPane();
   setLayout( new BorderLayout() );
   button1 = new JButton( "North Star" );
   button2 = new JButton( "South Pole" );
   container.add( button1 );
   container.add( button2 );
```

Answers to Self-Review Exercises

11.1 a) mouseMoved. b) uneditable (read-only). c) layout manager. d) Container. e) graphical user interface. f) setLayout. g) mousePressed, mouseReleased. h) JOptionPane. i) showInputDialog, JOptionPane. j) showMessageDialog, JOptionPane. k) JTextComponent.

11.2 a) True.
b) False. Method mouseEntered is called.
c) False. A JPanel can be added to another JPanel, because JPanel is an indirect subclass of Component. Therefore, a JPanel is a Component. Any Component can be added to a Container.
d) False. Only the last button added will be displayed. Remember that only one component should be added to each region in a BorderLayout.
e) True.
f) False. Inner classes have access to all members of the enclosing class declaration.
g) False. JTextAreas are editable by default.
h) False. JTextArea derives from class JTextComponent.

11.3 a) new is needed to create an object.
b) JLabel is a class name and cannot be used as a variable name.
c) The arguments passed to the constructor are reversed. The String must be passed first.
d) BorderLayout has been set, and components are being added without specifying the region so both are added to the center region. Proper add statements might be
```
container.add( button1, BorderLayout.NORTH );
container.add( button2, BorderLayout.SOUTH );
```

Exercises

11.4 Fill in the blanks in each of the following statements:
a) The JTextField class directly extends class _____.
b) Container method _____ attaches a GUI component to a container.
c) Method _____ is called when a mouse button is released (without moving the mouse).
d) The _____ class is used to create a group of JRadioButtons.

11.5 Determine whether each statement is *true* or *false*. If *false*, explain why.
a) Only one layout manager can be used per Container.
b) GUI components can be added to a Container in any order in a BorderLayout.
c) JRadioButtons provide a series of mutually exclusive options (i.e., only one can be true at a time).
d) Graphics method setFont is used to set the font for text fields.
e) A JList displays a scrollbar if there are more items in the list than can be displayed.
f) A Mouse object has a method called mouseDragged.

11.6 Determine whether each statement is *true* or *false*. If *false*, explain why.
a) A JPanel is a JComponent.
b) A JPanel is a Component.
c) A JLabel is a Container.
d) A JList is a JPanel.
e) An AbstractButton is a JButton.
f) A JTextField is an Object.
g) ButtonGroup is a subclass of JComponent.

11.7   Find any errors in each of the following lines of code, and explain how to correct them.

a) `import javax.swing.JFrame`
b) `panelObject.GridLayout( 8, 8 ); // set GridLayout`
c) `container.setLayout( new FlowLayout( FlowLayout.DEFAULT ) );`
d) `container.add( eastButton, EAST );   // BorderLayout`

11.8   Create the following GUI. You do not have to provide any functionality.

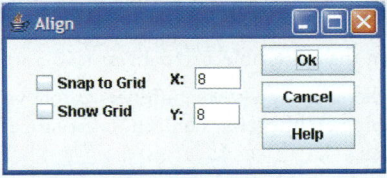

11.9   Create the following GUI. You do not have to provide any functionality.

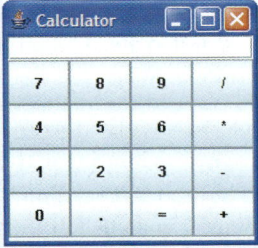

11.10   Create the following GUI. You do not have to provide any functionality.

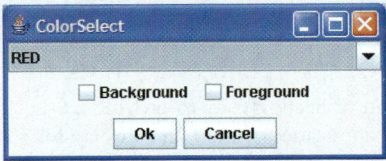

11.11   Create the following GUI. You do not have to provide any functionality.

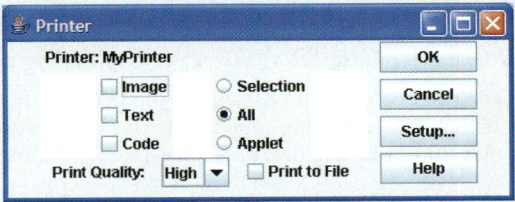

11.12   Write a temperature conversion application that converts from Fahrenheit to Celsius. The Fahrenheit temperature should be entered from the keyboard (via a `JTextField`). A `JLabel` should be used to display the converted temperature. Use the following formula for the conversion:

$$Celsius = \frac{5}{9} \times (\ Fahrenheit\ -\ 32\ )$$

11.13 Enhance the temperature conversion application of Exercise 11.12 by adding the Kelvin temperature scale. The application should also allow the user to make conversions between any two scales. Use the following formula for the conversion between Kelvin and Celsius (in addition to the formula in Exercise 11.12):

```
Kelvin = Celsius + 273.15
```

11.14 Write an application that displays events as they occur in a JTextArea. Provide a JComboBox with a minimum of four items. The user should be able to choose an event to monitor from the JComboBox. When that particular event occurs, display information about the event in the JTextArea. Use method toString on the event object to convert it to a string representation.

11.15 Write an application that plays "guess the number" as follows: Your application chooses the number to be guessed by selecting an integer at random in the range 1–1000. The application then displays the following in a label:

```
I have a number between 1 and 1000. Can you guess my number?
Please enter your first guess.
```

A JTextField should be used to input the guess. As each guess is input, the background color should change to either red or blue. Red indicates that the user is getting "warmer," and blue indicates that the user is getting "colder." A JLabel should display either "Too High" or "Too Low" to help the user zero in on the correct answer. When the user gets the correct answer, "Correct!" should be displayed, and the JTextField used for input should be changed to be uneditable. A JButton should be provided to allow the user to play the game again. When the JButton is clicked, a new random number should be generated and the input JTextField changed to be editable.

11.16 It is often useful to display the events that occur during the execution of an application. This can help you understand when the events occur and how they are generated. Write an application that enables the user to generate and process every event discussed in this chapter. The application should provide methods from the ActionListener, ItemListener, ListSelectionListener, MouseListener, MouseMotionListener and KeyListener interfaces to display messages when the events occur. Use method toString to convert the event objects received in each event handler into a String that can be displayed. Method toString creates a String containing all the information in the event object.

11.17 Modify the application of Section 6.10 to provide a GUI that enables the user to click a JButton to roll the dice. The application should also display four JLabels and four JTextFields, with one JLabel for each JTextField. The JTextFields should be used to display the values of each die and the sum of the dice after each roll. The point should be displayed in the fourth JTextField when the user does not win or lose on the first roll and should continue to be displayed until the game is lost.

(Optional) GUI and Graphics Case Study Exercise: Expanding the Interface

11.18 In this exercise, you will implement a GUI application that uses the MyShape hierarchy from Exercise 10.10 to create an interactive drawing application. You will create two classes for the GUI and provide a test class that launches the application. The classes of the MyShape hierarchy require no additional changes.

The first class to create is a subclass of JPanel called DrawPanel, which represents the area on which the user draws the shapes. Class DrawPanel should have the following instance variables:

a) An array shapes of type MyShape that will store all the shapes the user draws.
b) An integer shapeCount that counts the number of shapes in the array.
c) An integer shapeType that determines the type of shape to draw.
d) A MyShape currentShape that represents the current shape the user is drawing.
e) A Color currentColor that represents the current drawing color.

f) A boolean filledShape that determines whether to draw a filled shape.

g) A JLabel statusLabel that represents the status bar. The status bar will display the co-ordinates of the current mouse position.

Class DrawPanel should also declare the following methods:

a) Overridden method paintComponent that draws the shapes in the array. Use instance variable shapeCount to determine how many shapes to draw. Method paintComponent should also call currentShape's draw method, provided that currentShape is not null.

b) Set methods for the shapeType, currentColor and filledShape.

c) Method clearLastShape should clear the last shape drawn by decrementing instance variable shapeCount. Ensure that shapeCount is never less than zero.

d) Method clearDrawing should remove all the shapes in the current drawing by setting shapeCount to zero.

Methods clearLastShape and clearDrawing should call method repaint (inherited from JPanel) to refresh the drawing on the DrawPanel by indicating that the system should call method paint-Component.

Class DrawPanel should also provide event handling to enable the user to draw with the mouse. Create a single inner class that both extends MouseAdapter and implements MouseMotion-Listener to handle all mouse events in one class.

In the inner class, override method mousePressed so that it assigns currentShape a new shape of the type specified by shapeType and initializes both points to the mouse position. Next, override method mouseReleased to finish drawing the current shape and place it in the array. Set the second point of currentShape to the current mouse position and add currentShape to the array. Instance variable shapeCount determines the insertion index. Set currentShape to null and call method repaint to update the drawing with the new shape.

Override method mouseMoved to set the text of the statusLabel so that it displays the mouse coordinates—this will update the label with the coordinates every time the user moves (but does not drag) the mouse within the DrawPanel. Next, override method mouseDragged so that it sets the second point of the currentShape to the current mouse position and calls method repaint. This will allow the user to see the shape while dragging the mouse. Also, update the JLabel in mouse-Dragged with the current position of the mouse.

Create a constructor for DrawPanel that has a single JLabel parameter. In the constructor, ini-tialize statusLabel with the value passed to the parameter. Also initialize array shapes with 100 entries, shapeCount to 0, shapeType to the value that represents a line, currentShape to null and currentColor to Color.BLACK. The constructor should then set the background color of the Draw-Panel to Color.WHITE and register the MouseListener and MouseMotionLister so the JPanel prop-erly handles mouse events.

Next, create a JFrame subclass called DrawFrame that provides a GUI that enables the user to control various aspects of drawing. For the layout of the DrawFrame, we recommend a BorderLay-out, with the components in the NORTH region, the main drawing panel in the CENTER region, and a status bar in the SOUTH region, as in Fig. 11.49. In the top panel, create the components listed below. Each component's event handler should call the appropriate method in class DrawPanel.

a) A button to undo the last shape drawn.

b) A button to clear all shapes from the drawing.

c) A combo box for selecting the color from the 13 predefined colors.

d) A combo box for selecting the shape to draw.

e) A check box that specifies whether a shape should be filled or unfilled.

Declare and create the interface components in DrawFrame's constructor. You will need to cre-ate the status bar JLabel before you create the DrawPanel, so you can pass the JLabel as an argu-ment to DrawPanel's constructor. Finally, create a test class that initializes and displays the DrawFrame to execute the application.

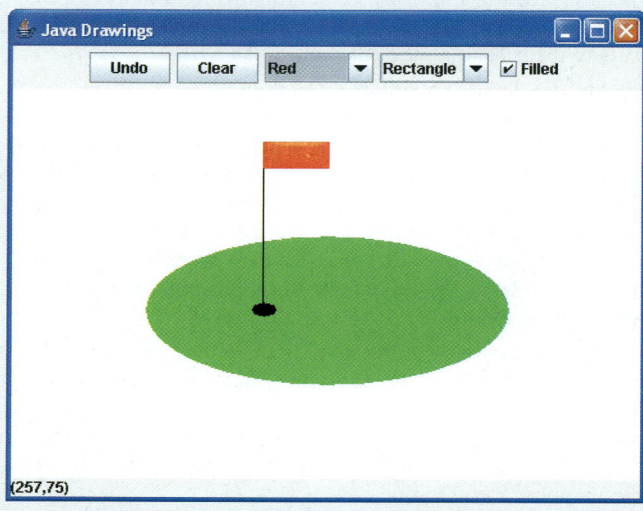

Fig. 11.49 | Interface for drawing shapes.

12

Graphics and Java 2D™

OBJECTIVES

In this chapter you will learn:

- To understand graphics contexts and graphics objects.
- To understand and be able to manipulate colors.
- To understand and be able to manipulate fonts.
- To use methods of class `Graphics` to draw lines, rectangles, rectangles with rounded corners, three-dimensional rectangles, ovals, arcs and polygons.
- To use methods of class `Graphics2D` from the `Java 2D` API to draw lines, rectangles, rectangles with rounded corners, ellipses, arcs and general paths.
- To be able to specify `Paint` and `Stroke` characteristics of shapes displayed with `Graphics2D`.

12.1 Introduction

In this chapter, we overview several of Java's capabilities for drawing two-dimensional shapes, controlling colors and controlling fonts. One of Java's initial appeals was its support for graphics that enabled programmers to visually enhance their applications. Java now contains many more sophisticated drawing capabilities as part of the Java 2D™ API. This chapter begins with an introduction to many of Java's original drawing capabilities. Next we present several of the more powerful Java 2D capabilities, such as controlling the style of lines used to draw shapes and the way shapes are filled with color and patterns. [*Note:* Several concepts covered in this chapter have already been covered in the optional GUI and Graphics Case Study of Chapters 3–10. So, some material will be repetitive if you read the case study. You do not need to read the case study to understand this chapter.]

Figure 12.1 shows a portion of the Java class hierarchy that includes several of the basic graphics classes and Java 2D API classes and interfaces covered in this chapter. Class **Color** contains methods and constants for manipulating colors. Class JComponent contains method paintComponent, which will be used to draw graphics on a component. Class **Font** contains methods and constants for manipulating fonts. Class **FontMetrics** contains methods for obtaining font information. Class Graphics contains methods for drawing strings, lines, rectangles and other shapes. Class **Graphics2D**, which extends class Graphics, is used for drawing with the Java 2D API. Class **Polygon** contains methods for creating polygons. The bottom half of the figure lists several classes and interfaces from the Java 2D API. Class **BasicStroke** helps specify the drawing characteristics of lines. Classes **GradientPaint** and **TexturePaint** help specify the characteristics for filling shapes with colors or patterns. Classes GeneralPath, Line2D, Arc2D, Ellipse2D, Rectangle2D and RoundRectangle2D represent several Java 2D shapes. [*Note:* We begin the chapter by discussion Java's original graphics capabilities, then move on to the Java 2D API. However, it is important to understand that the classes discussed as part of Java's original graphics capabilities are now also considered to be part of the Java 2D API.]

To begin drawing in Java, we must first understand Java's **coordinate system** (Fig. 12.2), which is a scheme for identifying every point on the screen. By default, the upper-left corner of a GUI component (e.g., a window) has the coordinates (0, 0). A coordinate pair is composed of an *x*-coordinate (the **horizontal coordinate**) and a *y*-coordinate (the **vertical coordinate**). The *x*-coordinate is the horizontal distance moving right from the left of the screen. The *y*-

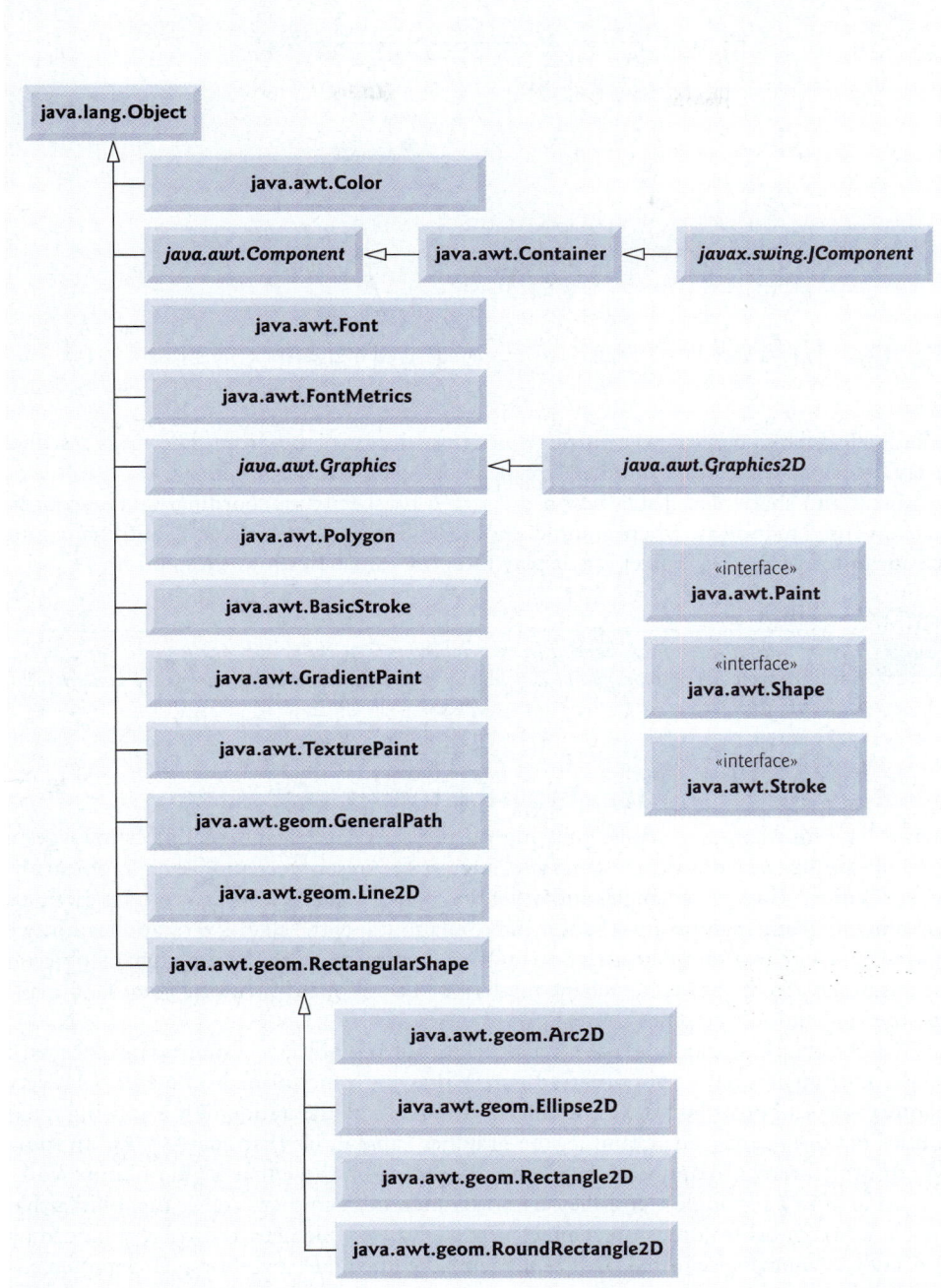

Fig. 12.1 | Classes and interfaces used in this chapter from Java's original graphics capabilities and from the Java 2D API. [*Note:* Class `Object` appears here because it is the superclass of the Java class hierarchy.]

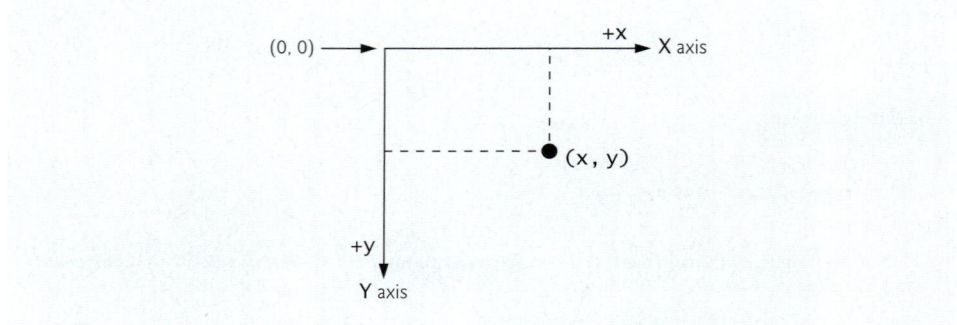

Fig. 12.2 | Java coordinate system. Units are measured in pixels.

coordinate is the vertical distance moving down from the top of the screen. The *x-axis* describes every horizontal coordinate, and the *y-axis* describes every vertical coordinate.

Text and shapes are displayed on the screen by specifying coordinates. The coordinates are used to indicate where graphics should be displayed on a screen. Coordinate units are measured in pixels. A pixel is a display monitor's smallest unit of resolution.

 Portability Tip 12.1

Different display monitors have different resolutions (i.e., the density of the pixels varies). This can cause graphics to appear to be different sizes on different monitors or on the same monitor with different settings.

12.2 Graphics Contexts and Graphics Objects

A Java graphics context enables drawing on the screen. A Graphics object manages a graphics context and draws pixels on the screen that represent text and other graphical object (e.g., lines, ellipses, rectangles and other polygons). Graphics objects contain methods for drawing, font manipulation, color manipulation and the like. Every application we have seen in the text that performs drawing on the screen has used the Graphics object g (the argument to the paintComponent method of a component such as a JPanel) to manage the application's graphics context.

Class Graphics is an abstract class (i.e., Graphics objects cannot be instantiated). This contributes to Java's portability. Because drawing is performed differently on every platform that supports Java, there cannot be just one implementation of the drawing capabilities on all systems. For example, the graphics capabilities that enable a PC running Microsoft Windows to draw a rectangle are different from those that enable a Linux workstation to draw a rectangle—and they are both different from the graphics capabilities that enable a Macintosh to draw a rectangle. When Java is implemented on each platform, a subclass of Graphics is created that implements the drawing capabilities. This implementation is hidden from us by class Graphics, which supplies the interface that enables us to use graphics in a platform-independent manner.

Class Component is the superclass for many of the classes in the java.awt package. (We discussed class Component in Chapter 11.) Class JComponent, which inherits indirectly from class `Component`, contains a `paintComponent` method that can be used to draw graphics. Method `paintComponent` takes a `Graphics` object as an argument. This object is passed to the `paintComponent` method by the system when a lightweight Swing component needs to be repainted. The header for the `paintComponent` method is

```
public void paintComponent( Graphics g )
```

Parameter g receives a reference to an instance of the system-specific subclass that `Graphics` extends. The preceding method header should look familiar to you—it is the same one we used in some of the applications in Chapter 11. Actually, class `JComponent` is a superclass of `JPanel`. Many capabilities of class `JPanel` are inherited from class `JComponent`.

Method `paintComponent` is seldom called directly by the programmer because drawing graphics is an event-driven process. When a GUI application executes, the application container calls method `paintComponent` for each lightweight component as the GUI is displayed. For `paintComponent` to be called again, an event must occur (such as covering and uncovering the component with another window).

If the programmer needs to have `paintComponent` execute (i.e., if the programmer wants to update the graphics drawn on the Swing component), a call is made to method **repaint**, which is inherited by all `JComponents` indirectly from class `Component` (package `java.awt`). Method `repaint` is frequently called by the programmer to request a call to method `paintComponent`. Method `repaint` should not be overridden, because it performs some system-dependent tasks. The header for `repaint` is

```
public void repaint()
```

12.3 Color Control

Class `Color` declares methods and constants for manipulating colors in a Java program. The predeclared color constants are summarized in Fig. 12.3, and several color methods and constructors are summarized in Fig. 12.4. Note that two of the methods in Fig. 12.4 are `Graphics` methods that are specific to colors.

Every color is created from a red, a green and a blue component. Together these components are called **RGB values**. All three RGB components can be integers in the range from 0 to 255, or they can be floating-point values in the range 0.0 to 1.0. The first RGB component specifies the amount of red, the second the amount of green and the third the amount of blue. The larger the RGB value, the greater the amount of that particular color. Java enables the programmer to choose from $256 \times 256 \times 256$ (or approximately 16.7 million) colors. However, not all computers are capable of displaying all these colors. The computer will display the closest color it can.

Two of class `Color`'s constructors are shown in Fig. 12.4—one that takes three `int` arguments and one that takes three `float` arguments, with each argument specifying the amount of red, green and blue. The `int` values must be in the range 0–255 and the `float` values must be in the range 0.0–1.0. The new `Color` object will have the specified amounts of red, green and blue. `Color` methods **getRed**, **getGreen** and **getBlue** return integer values from 0 to 255 representing the amount of red, green and blue, respectively. `Graphics` method **getColor** returns a `Color` object representing the current drawing color. `Graphics` method **setColor** sets the current drawing color.

Color constant	Color	RGB value
public final static Color RED	red	255, 0, 0
public final static Color GREEN	green	0, 255, 0
public final static Color BLUE	blue	0, 0, 255
public final static Color ORANGE	orange	255, 200, 0
public final static Color PINK	pink	255, 175, 175
public final static Color CYAN	cyan	0, 255, 255
public final static Color MAGENTA	magenta	255, 0, 255
public final static Color YELLOW	yellow	255, 255, 0
public final static Color BLACK	black	0, 0, 0
public final static Color WHITE	white	255, 255, 255
public final static Color GRAY	gray	128, 128, 128
public final static Color LIGHT_GRAY	light gray	192, 192, 192
public final static Color DARK_GRAY	dark gray	64, 64, 64

Fig. 12.3 | Color constants and their RGB values.

Method	Description

Color constructors and methods

public Color(int r, int g, int b)

Creates a color based on red, green and blue components expressed as integers from 0 to 255.

public Color(float r, float g, float b)

Creates a color based on red, green and blue components expressed as floating-point values from 0.0 to 1.0.

public int getRed()

Returns a value between 0 and 255 representing the red content.

public int getGreen()

Returns a value between 0 and 255 representing the green content.

public int getBlue()

Returns a value between 0 and 255 representing the blue content.

Graphics *methods for manipulating* Colors

public Color getColor()

Returns Color object representing current color for the graphics context.

public void setColor(Color c)

Sets the current color for drawing with the graphics context.

Fig. 12.4 | Color methods and color-related Graphics methods .

The application of Fig. 12.5–Fig. 12.6 demonstrates several methods from Fig. 12.4 by drawing filled rectangles and strings in several different colors. When the application begins execution, class `ColorJPanel`'s `paintComponent` method (lines 10–37 of Fig. 12.5) is called to paint the window. Line 17 uses `Graphics` method `setColor` to set the current drawing color. Method `setColor` receives a `Color` object. The expression `new Color( 255, 0, 0 )` creates a new `Color` object that represents red (red value 255, and 0 for the green and blue values). Line 18 uses `Graphics` method **`fillRect`** to draw a filled rectangle in the current color. Method `fillRect` draws a rectangle based on its four arguments. The first two integer values represent the upper-left x-coordinate and upper-left y-coordinate, where the `Graphics` object begins drawing the rectangle. The third and fourth arguments are nonnegative inte-

```java
1   // Fig. 12.5: ColorJPanel.java
2   // Demonstrating Colors.
3   import java.awt.Graphics;
4   import java.awt.Color;
5   import javax.swing.JPanel;
6
7   public class ColorJPanel extends JPanel
8   {
9      // draw rectangles and Strings in different colors
10     public void paintComponent( Graphics g )
11     {
12        super.paintComponent( g ); // call superclass's paintComponent
13
14        this.setBackground( Color.WHITE );
15
16        // set new drawing color using integers
17        g.setColor( new Color( 255, 0, 0 ) );
18        g.fillRect( 15, 25, 100, 20 );
19        g.drawString( "Current RGB: " + g.getColor(), 130, 40 );
20
21        // set new drawing color using floats
22        g.setColor( new Color( 0.50f, 0.75f, 0.0f ) );
23        g.fillRect( 15, 50, 100, 20 );
24        g.drawString( "Current RGB: " + g.getColor(), 130, 65 );
25
26        // set new drawing color using static Color objects
27        g.setColor( Color.BLUE );
28        g.fillRect( 15, 75, 100, 20 );
29        g.drawString( "Current RGB: " + g.getColor(), 130, 90 );
30
31        // display individual RGB values
32        Color color = Color.MAGENTA;
33        g.setColor( color );
34        g.fillRect( 15, 100, 100, 20 );
35        g.drawString( "RGB values: " + color.getRed() + ", " +
36           color.getGreen() + ", " + color.getBlue(), 130, 115 );
37     } // end method paintComponent
38  } // end class ColorJPanel
```

Fig. 12.5 | Color changed for drawing.

```
1   // Fig. 12.6: ShowColors.java
2   // Demonstrating Colors.
3   import javax.swing.JFrame;
4
5   public class ShowColors
6   {
7      // execute application
8      public static void main( String args[] )
9      {
10        // create frame for ColorJPanel
11        JFrame frame = new JFrame( "Using colors" );
12        frame.setDefaultCloseOperation( JFrame.EXIT_ON_CLOSE );
13
14        ColorJPanel colorJPanel = new ColorJPanel(); // create ColorJPanel
15        frame.add( colorJPanel ); // add colorJPanel to frame
16        frame.setSize( 400, 180 ); // set frame size
17        frame.setVisible( true ); // displayt frame
18     } // end main
19  } // end class ShowColors
```

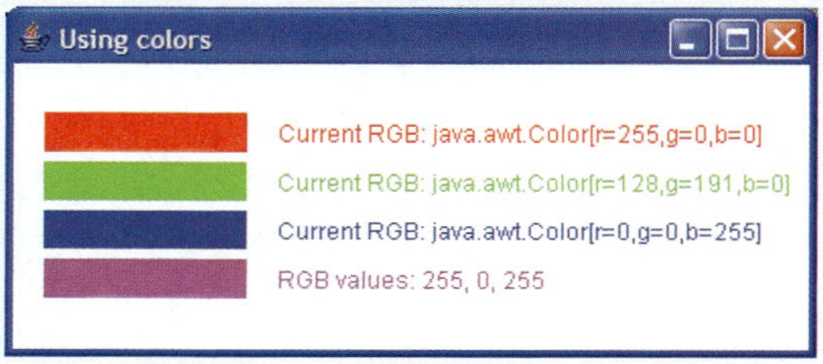

Fig. 12.6 | Creating JFrame to display colors on JPanel.

gers that represent the width and the height of the rectangle in pixels, respectively. A rectangle drawn using method fillRect is filled by the current color of the Graphics object.

Line 19 uses Graphics method **drawString** to draw a String in the current color. The expression g.getColor() retrieves the current color from the Graphics object. The returned Color object is concatenated with string "Current RGB: ", resulting in an implicit call to class Color's toString method. Note that the String representation of the Color object contains the class name and package (java.awt.Color), and the red, green and blue values.

Look-and-Feel Observation 12.1

Everyone perceives colors differently. Choose your colors carefully to ensure that your application is readable. Try to avoid using many different colors in close proximity.

Lines 22–24 and lines 27–29 perform the same tasks again. Line 22 uses the Color constructor with three float arguments to create a dark green color (0.50f for red, 0.75f for green and 0.0f for blue). Note the syntax of the values. The letter f appended to a floating-point literal indicates that the literal should be treated as type float. Recall that by default, floating-point literals are treated as type double.

Line 27 sets the current drawing color to one of the predeclared `Color` constants (`Color.BLUE`). The `Color` constants are `static`, so they are created when class `Color` is loaded into memory at execution time.

The statement in lines 35–36 makes calls to `Color` methods `getRed`, `getGreen` and `getBlue` on the predeclared `Color.MAGENTA` constant. Method `main` of class `ShowColors` (lines 8–18 of Fig. 12.6) creates the `JFrame` that will contain a `ColorJPanel` object where the colors will be displayed.

Software Engineering Observation 12.1

To change the color, you must create a new `Color` object (or use one of the predeclared `Color` constants). Like `String` objects, `Color` objects are immutable (not modifiable).

Package `javax.swing` provides the `JColorChooser` GUI component that enables application users to select colors. The application of Fig. 12.7–Fig. 12.8 demonstrate a `JColorChooser` dialog. When you click the **Change Color** button, a `JColorChooser` dialog appears. When you select a color and press the dialog's **OK** button, the background color of the application window changes.

```java
1   // Fig. 12.7: ShowColors2JFrame.java
2   // Choosing colors with JColorChooser.
3   import java.awt.BorderLayout;
4   import java.awt.Color;
5   import java.awt.event.ActionEvent;
6   import java.awt.event.ActionListener;
7   import javax.swing.JButton;
8   import javax.swing.JFrame;
9   import javax.swing.JColorChooser;
10  import javax.swing.JPanel;
11
12  public class ShowColors2JFrame extends JFrame
13  {
14     private JButton changeColorJButton;
15     private Color color = Color.LIGHT_GRAY;
16     private JPanel colorJPanel;
17
18     // set up GUI
19     public ShowColors2JFrame()
20     {
21        super( "Using JColorChooser" );
22
23        // create JPanel for display color
24        colorJPanel = new JPanel();
25        colorJPanel.setBackground( color );
26
27        // set up changeColorJButton and register its event handler
28        changeColorJButton = new JButton( "Change Color" );
29        changeColorJButton.addActionListener(
30
```

Fig. 12.7 | `JColorChooser` dialog. (Part 1 of 2.)

```
31             new ActionListener() // anonymous inner class
32             {
33                // display JColorChooser when user clicks button
34                public void actionPerformed( ActionEvent event )
35                {
36                   color = JColorChooser.showDialog(
37                      ShowColors2JFrame.this, "Choose a color", color );
38
39                   // set default color, if no color is returned
40                   if ( color == null )
41                      color = Color.LIGHT_GRAY;
42
43                   // change content pane's background color
44                   colorJPanel.setBackground( color );
45                } // end method actionPerformed
46             } // end anonymous inner class
47          ); // end call to addActionListener
48
49          add( colorJPanel, BorderLayout.CENTER ); // add colorJPanel
50          add( changeColorJButton, BorderLayout.SOUTH ); // add button
51
52          setSize( 400, 130 ); // set frame size
53          setVisible( true ); // display frame
54       } // end ShowColor2JFrame constructor
55    } // end class ShowColors2JFrame
```

Fig. 12.7 | JColorChooser dialog. (Part 2 of 2.)

Class JColorChooser provides a static convenience method **showDialog** that creates a JColorChooser object, attaches it to a dialog box and displays the dialog. Lines 36–37 of Fig. 12.7 invoke this method to display the color chooser dialog. Method showDialog returns the selected Color object, or null if the user presses **Cancel** or closes the dialog without pressing **OK**. The method takes three arguments—a reference to its parent Component, a String to display in the title bar of the dialog and the initial selected Color for the dialog. The parent component is a reference to the window from which the dialog is displayed (in this case the JFrame, with the reference name frame). The dialog will be centered

```
1   // Fig. 12.8: ShowColors2.java
2   // Choosing colors with JColorChooser.
3   import javax.swing.JFrame;
4
5   public class ShowColors2
6   {
7      // execute application
8      public static void main( String args[] )
9      {
10        ShowColors2JFrame application = new ShowColors2JFrame();
11        application.setDefaultCloseOperation( JFrame.EXIT_ON_CLOSE );
12     } // end main
13  } // end class ShowColors2
```

Fig. 12.8 | Choosing colors with JColorChooser. (Part 1 of 2.)

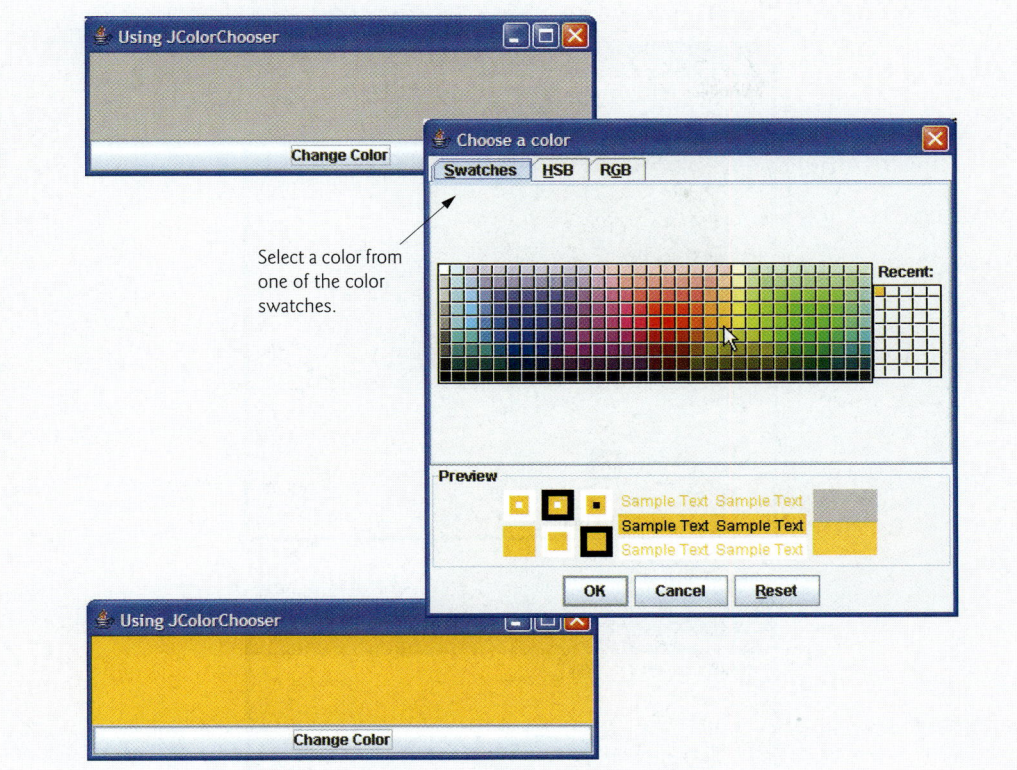

Select a color from one of the color swatches.

Fig. 12.8 | Choosing colors with `JColorChooser`. (Part 2 of 2.)

on the parent. If the parent is `null`, the dialog is centered on the screen. While the color chooser dialog is on the screen, the user cannot interact with the parent component. This type of dialog is called a **modal dialog** (discussed in Chapter 22, GUI Components: Part 2).

After the user selects a color, lines 40–41 determine whether `color` is `null`, and, if so, set `color` to `Color.LIGHT_GRAY`. Line 44 invokes method `setBackground` to change the background color of the `JPanel`. Method `setBackground` is one of the many `Component` methods that can be used on most GUI components. Note that the user can continue to use the **Change Color** button to change the background color of the application. Figure 12.8 contains method `main`, which executes the program.

The second screen capture of Fig. 12.8 demonstrates the default `JColorChooser` dialog that allows the user to select a color from a variety of **color swatches**. Note that there are actually three tabs across the top of the dialog—**Swatches**, **HSB** and **RGB**. These represent three different ways to select a color. The **HSB** tab allows you to select a color based on **hue**, **saturation** and **brightness**—values that are used to define the amount of light in a color. We do not discuss HSB values. For more information on hue, saturation and brightness, visit `whatis.techtarget.com/definition/0,,sid9_gci212262,00.html`. The **RGB** tab allows you to select a color by using sliders to select the red, green and blue components. The **HSB** and **RGB** tabs are shown in Fig. 12.9.

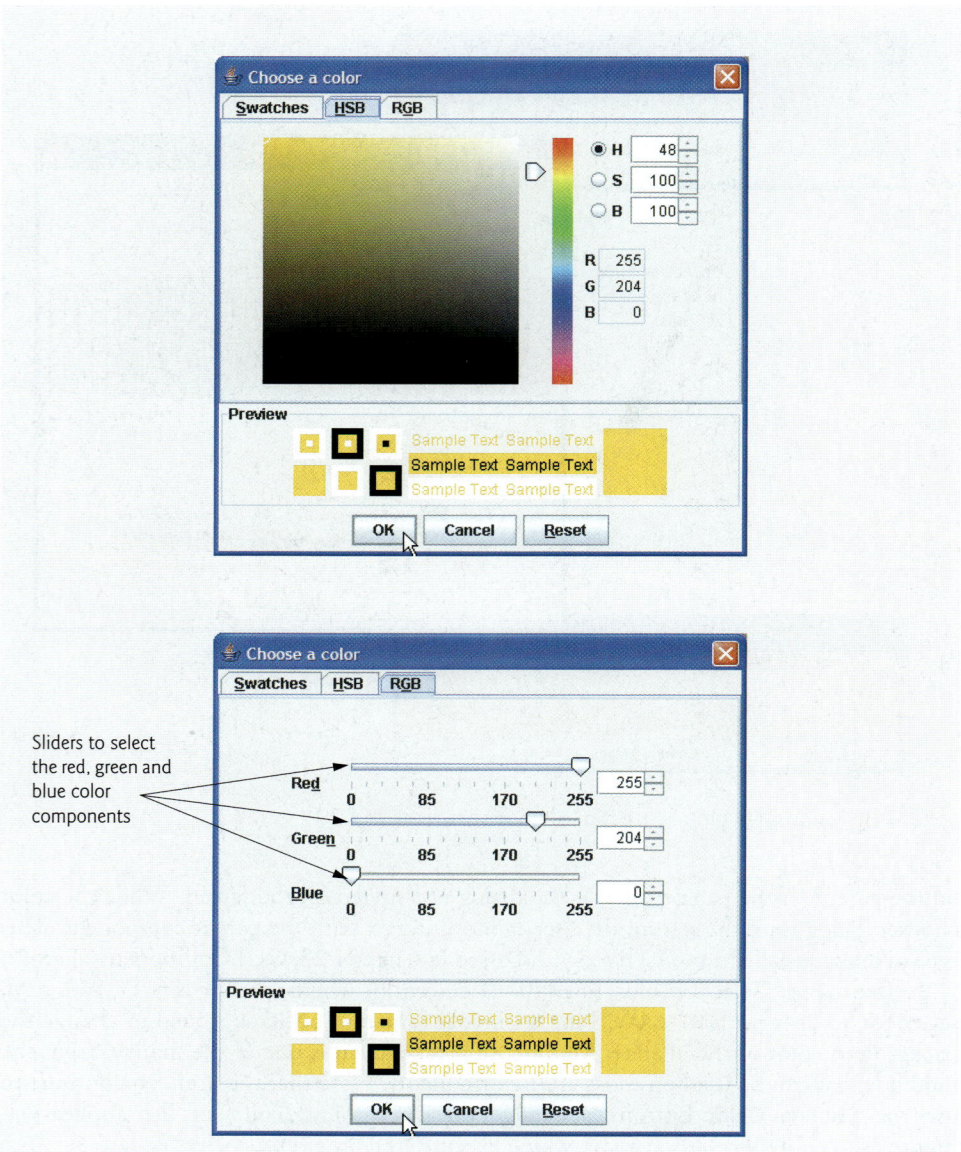

Fig. 12.9 | **HSB** and **RGB** tabs of the JColorChooser dialog.

12.4 Font Control

This section introduces methods and constants for font control. Most font methods and font constants are part of class Font. Some methods of class Font and class Graphics are summarized in Fig. 12.10.

Method or constant	Description

Font constants, constructors and methods

`public final static int PLAIN`

A constant representing a plain font style.

`public final static int BOLD`

A constant representing a bold font style.

`public final static int ITALIC`

A constant representing an italic font style.

`public Font( String name, int style, int size )`

Creates a `Font` object with the specified font name, style and size.

`public int getStyle()`

Returns an integer value indicating the current font style.

`public int getSize()`

Returns an integer value indicating the current font size.

`public String getName()`

Returns the current font name as a string.

`public String getFamily()`

Returns the font's family name as a string.

`public boolean isPlain()`

Returns `true` if the font is plain, else `false`.

`public boolean isBold()`

Returns `true` if the font is bold, else `false`.

`public boolean isItalic()`

Returns `true` if the font is italic, else `false`.

Graphics methods for manipulating Fonts

`public Font getFont()`

Returns a `Font` object reference representing the current font.

`public void setFont( Font f )`

Sets the current font to the font, style and size specified by the `Font` object reference `f`.

Fig. 12.10 | Font-related methods and constants.

Class `Font`'s constructor takes three arguments—the **font name**, **font style** and **font size**. The font name is any font currently supported by the system on which the program is running, such as standard Java fonts `Monospaced`, `SansSerif` and `Serif`. The font style is **Font.PLAIN**, **Font.ITALIC** or **Font.BOLD** (each is a `static` field of class `Font`). Font styles can be used in combination (e.g., `Font.ITALIC + Font.BOLD`). The font size is measured in points. A **point** is 1/72 of an inch. `Graphics` method **setFont** sets the current drawing font—the font in which text will be displayed—to its `Font` argument.

Portability Tip 12.2

The number of fonts varies greatly across systems. Java provides five logical font names—Serif, Monospaced, SansSerif, Dialog and DialogInput—that can be used on all Java platforms. The Java runtime environment (JRE) on each platform maps these logical font names to actual fonts installed on the platform. The actual fonts used may vary by platform.

The application of Fig. 12.11–Fig. 12.12 displays text in four different fonts, with each font in a different size. Figure 12.11 uses the Font constructor to initialize Font objects (in lines 16, 20, 24 and 29) that are each passed to Graphics method setFont to change the drawing font. Each call to the Font constructor passes a font name (Serif, Monospaced or SansSerif) as a string, a font style (Font.PLAIN, Font.ITALIC or Font.BOLD) and a font size. Once Graphics method setFont is invoked, all text displayed following the call will appear in the new font until the font is changed. Each font's information is displayed in lines 17, 21, 25 and 30–31 using method drawString. Note that the coordinate passed to drawString corresponds to the lower-left corner of the baseline of the font. Line 28 changes the drawing color to red, so the next string displayed appears

```java
1  // Fig. 12.11: FontJPanel.java
2  // Display strings in different fonts and colors.
3  import java.awt.Font;
4  import java.awt.Color;
5  import java.awt.Graphics;
6  import javax.swing.JPanel;
7
8  public class FontJPanel extends JPanel
9  {
10    // display Strings in different fonts and colors
11    public void paintComponent( Graphics g )
12    {
13       super.paintComponent( g ); // call superclass's paintConponent
14
15       // set font to Serif (Times), bold, 12pt and draw a string
16       g.setFont( new Font( "Serif", Font.BOLD, 12 ) );
17       g.drawString( "Serif 12 point bold.", 20, 50 );
18
19       // set font to Monospaced (Courier), italic, 24pt and draw a string
20       g.setFont( new Font( "Monospaced", Font.ITALIC, 24 ) );
21       g.drawString( "Monospaced 24 point italic.", 20, 70 );
22
23       // set font to SansSerif (Helvetica), plain, 14pt and draw a string
24       g.setFont( new Font( "SansSerif", Font.PLAIN, 14 ) );
25       g.drawString( "SansSerif 14 point plain.", 20, 90 );
26
27       // set font to Serif (Times), bold/italic, 18pt and draw a string
28       g.setColor( Color.RED );
29       g.setFont( new Font( "Serif", Font.BOLD + Font.ITALIC, 18 ) );
30       g.drawString( g.getFont().getName() + " " + g.getFont().getSize() +
31          " point bold italic.", 20, 110 );
32    } // end method paintComponent
33 } // end class FontJPanel
```

Fig. 12.11 | Graphics method setFont changes the drawing font.

```
 1   // Fig. 12.12: Fonts.java
 2   // Using fonts.
 3   import javax.swing.JFrame;
 4
 5   public class Fonts
 6   {
 7      // execute application
 8      public static void main( String args[] )
 9      {
10         // create frame for FontJPanel
11         JFrame frame = new JFrame( "Using fonts" );
12         frame.setDefaultCloseOperation( JFrame.EXIT_ON_CLOSE );
13
14         FontJPanel fontJPanel = new FontJPanel(); // create FontJPanel
15         frame.add( fontJPanel ); // add fontJPanel to frame
16         frame.setSize( 420, 170 ); // set frame size
17         frame.setVisible( true ); // display frame
18      } // end main
19   } // end class Fonts
```

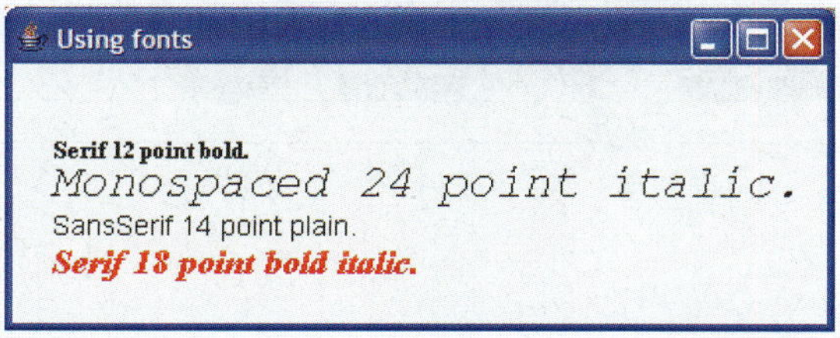

Fig. 12.12 | Creating JFrame to display fonts.

in red. Lines 30–31 display information about the final Font object. Method **getFont** of class Graphics returns a Font object representing the current font. Method **getName** returns the current font name as a string. Method **getSize** returns the font size in points.

Figure 12.12 contains method main, which creates a JFrame. We add a FontJPanel object to this JFrame (line 15), which displays the graphics created in Fig. 12.11.

Software Engineering Observation 12.2

To change the font, you must create a new Font object. Font objects are immutable—class Font has no set *methods to change the characteristics of the current font.*

Font Metrics

Sometimes it is necessary to get information about the current drawing font, such as its name, style and size. Several Font methods used to get font information are summarized in Fig. 12.10. Method **getStyle** returns an integer value representing the current style. The integer value returned is either Font.PLAIN, Font.ITALIC, Font.BOLD or the combination of Font.ITALIC and Font.BOLD. Method **getFamily** returns the name of the font family to which the current font belongs. The name of the font family is platform specific.

Font methods are also available to test the style of the current font, and these too are summarized in Fig. 12.10. Methods **isPlain**, **isBold** and **isItalic** return true if the current font style is plain, bold or italic, respectively.

Sometimes precise information about a font's metrics must be known—such as **height**, **descent** (the amount a character dips below the baseline), **ascent** (the amount a character rises above the baseline) and **leading** (the difference between the descent of one line of text and the ascent of the line of text below it—that is, the interline spacing). Figure 12.13 illustrates some of the common **font metrics**.

Class **FontMetrics** declares several methods for obtaining font metrics. These methods and **Graphics** method **getFontMetrics** are summarized in Fig. 12.14. The application of Fig. 12.15–Fig. 12.16 uses the methods of Fig. 12.14 to obtain font metric information for two fonts.

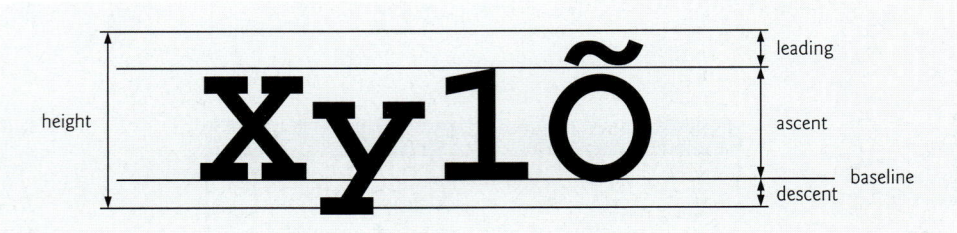

Fig. 12.13 | Font metrics.

Method	Description
FontMetrics methods	
public int getAscent()	
	Returns the ascent of a font in points.
public int getDescent()	
	Returns the descent of a font in points.
public int getLeading()	
	Returns the leading of a font in points.
public int getHeight()	
	Returns the height of a font in points.
Graphics methods for getting a Font's FontMetrics	
public FontMetrics getFontMetrics()	
	Returns the FontMetrics object for the current drawing Font.
public FontMetrics getFontMetrics(Font f)	
	Returns the FontMetrics object for the specified Font argument.

Fig. 12.14 | FontMetrics and Graphics methods for obtaining font metrics.

```
1   // Fig. 12.15: MetricsJPanel.java
2   // FontMetrics and Graphics methods useful for obtaining font metrics.
3   import java.awt.Font;
4   import java.awt.FontMetrics;
5   import java.awt.Graphics;
6   import javax.swing.JPanel;
7
8   public class MetricsJPanel extends JPanel
9   {
10      // display font metrics
11      public void paintComponent( Graphics g )
12      {
13         super.paintComponent( g ); // call superclass's paintComponent
14
15         g.setFont( new Font( "SansSerif", Font.BOLD, 12 ) );
16         FontMetrics metrics = g.getFontMetrics();
17         g.drawString( "Current font: " + g.getFont(), 10, 40 );
18         g.drawString( "Ascent: " + metrics.getAscent(), 10, 55 );
19         g.drawString( "Descent: " + metrics.getDescent(), 10, 70 );
20         g.drawString( "Height: " + metrics.getHeight(), 10, 85 );
21         g.drawString( "Leading: " + metrics.getLeading(), 10, 100 );
22
23         Font font = new Font( "Serif", Font.ITALIC, 14 );
24         metrics = g.getFontMetrics( font );
25         g.setFont( font );
26         g.drawString( "Current font: " + font, 10, 130 );
27         g.drawString( "Ascent: " + metrics.getAscent(), 10, 145 );
28         g.drawString( "Descent: " + metrics.getDescent(), 10, 160 );
29         g.drawString( "Height: " + metrics.getHeight(), 10, 175 );
30         g.drawString( "Leading: " + metrics.getLeading(), 10, 190 );
31      } // end method paintComponent
32   } // end class MetricsJPanel
```

Fig. 12.15 | Font metrics.

Line 15 of Fig. 12.15 creates and sets the current drawing font to a SansSerif, bold, 12-point font. Line 16 uses Graphics method getFontMetrics to obtain the FontMetrics object for the current font. Line 17 outputs the String representation of the Font returned by g.getFont(). Lines 18–21 use FontMetric methods to obtain the ascent, descent, height and leading for the font.

Line 23 creates a new Serif, italic, 14-point font. Line 24 uses a second version of Graphics method getFontMetrics, which accepts a Font argument and returns a corresponding FontMetrics object. Lines 27–30 obtain the ascent, descent, height and leading for the font. Note that the font metrics are slightly different for the two fonts.

12.5 Drawing Lines, Rectangles and Ovals

This section presents Graphics methods for drawing lines, rectangles and ovals. The methods and their parameters are summarized in Fig. 12.17. For each drawing method that requires a width and height parameter, the width and height must be nonnegative values. Otherwise, the shape will not display.

```
 1   // Fig. 12.16: Metrics.java
 2   // Displaying font metrics.
 3   import javax.swing.JFrame;
 4
 5   public class Metrics
 6   {
 7      // execute application
 8      public static void main( String args[] )
 9      {
10         // create frame for MetricsJPanel
11         JFrame frame = new JFrame( "Demonstrating FontMetrics" );
12         frame.setDefaultCloseOperation( JFrame.EXIT_ON_CLOSE );
13
14         MetricsJPanel metricsJPanel = new MetricsJPanel();
15         frame.add( metricsJPanel ); // add metricsJPanel to frame
16         frame.setSize( 510, 250 ); // set frame size
17         frame.setVisible( true ); // display frame
18      } // end main
19   } // end class Metrics
```

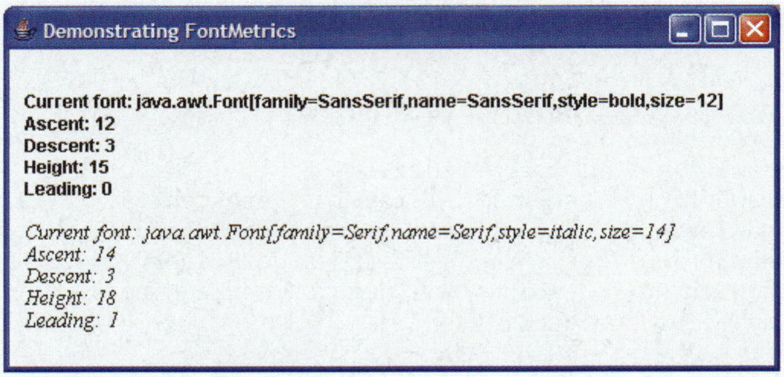

Fig. 12.16 | Creating JFrame to display font metric information.

Method	Description
public void drawLine(int x1, int y1, int x2, int y2)	
	Draws a line between the point (x1, y1) and the point (x2, y2).
public void drawRect(int x, int y, int width, int height)	
	Draws a rectangle of the specified width and height. The top-left corner of the rectangle has the coordinates (x, y). Only the outline of the rectangle is drawn using the Graphics object's color—the body of the rectangle is not filled with this color.
public void fillRect(int x, int y, int width, int height)	
	Draws a filled rectangle with the specified width and height. The top-left corner of the rectangle has the coordinate (x, y). The rectangle is filled with the Graphics object's color.

Fig. 12.17 | Graphics methods that draw lines, rectangles and ovals. (Part 1 of 2.)

Method	Description
public void clearRect(int x, int y, int width, int height)	
	Draws a filled rectangle with the specified width and height in the current background color. The top-left corner of the rectangle has the coordinate (x, y). This method is useful if the programmer wants to remove a portion of an image.
public void drawRoundRect(int x, int y, int width, int height, int arcWidth, int arcHeight)	
	Draws a rectangle with rounded corners in the current color with the specified width and height. The arcWidth and arcHeight determine the rounding of the corners (see Fig. 12.20). Only the outline of the shape is drawn.
public void fillRoundRect(int x, int y, int width, int height, int arcWidth, int arcHeight)	
	Draws a filled rectangle with rounded corners in the current color with the specified width and height. The arcWidth and arcHeight determine the rounding of the corners (see Fig. 12.20).
public void draw3DRect(int x, int y, int width, int height, boolean b)	
	Draws a three-dimensional rectangle in the current color with the specified width and height. The top-left corner of the rectangle has the coordinates (x, y). The rectangle appears raised when b is true and lowered when b is false. Only the outline of the shape is drawn.
public void fill3DRect(int x, int y, int width, int height, boolean b)	
	Draws a filled three-dimensional rectangle in the current color with the specified width and height. The top-left corner of the rectangle has the coordinates (x, y). The rectangle appears raised when b is true and lowered when b is false.
public void drawOval(int x, int y, int width, int height)	
	Draws an oval in the current color with the specified width and height. The bounding rectangle's top-left corner is at the coordinates (v, y). The oval touches all four sides of the bounding rectangle at the center of each side (see Fig. 12.21). Only the outline of the shape is drawn.
public void fillOval(int x, int y, int width, int height)	
	Draws a filled oval in the current color with the specified width and height. The bounding rectangle's top-left corner is at the coordinates (x, y). The oval touches all four sides of the bounding rectangle at the center of each side (see Fig. 12.21).

Fig. 12.17 | Graphics methods that draw lines, rectangles and ovals. (Part 2 of 2.)

The application of Fig. 12.18–Fig. 12.19 demonstrates drawing a variety of lines, rectangles, three-dimensional rectangles, rounded rectangles and ovals.

In Fig. 12.18, line 17 draws a red line, line 20 draws an empty blue rectangle and line 21 draws a filled blue rectangle. Methods fillRoundRect (line 24) and **drawRoundRect**

```
 1    // Fig. 12.18: LinesRectsOvalsJPanel.java
 2    // Drawing lines, rectangles and ovals.
 3    import java.awt.Color;
 4    import java.awt.Graphics;
 5    import javax.swing.JPanel;
 6
 7    public class LinesRectsOvalsJPanel extends JPanel
 8    {
 9       // display various lines, rectangles and ovals
10       public void paintComponent( Graphics g )
11       {
12          super.paintComponent( g ); // call superclass's paint method
13
14          this.setBackground( Color.WHITE );
15
16          g.setColor( Color.RED );
17          g.drawLine( 5, 30, 380, 30 );
18
19          g.setColor( Color.BLUE );
20          g.drawRect( 5, 40, 90, 55 );
21          g.fillRect( 100, 40, 90, 55 );
22
23          g.setColor( Color.CYAN );
24          g.fillRoundRect( 195, 40, 90, 55, 50, 50 );
25          g.drawRoundRect( 290, 40, 90, 55, 20, 20 );
26
27          g.setColor( Color.YELLOW );
28          g.draw3DRect( 5, 100, 90, 55, true );
29          g.fill3DRect( 100, 100, 90, 55, false );
30
31          g.setColor( Color.MAGENTA );
32          g.drawOval( 195, 100, 90, 55 );
33          g.fillOval( 290, 100, 90, 55 );
34       } // end method paintComponent
35    } // end class LinesRectsOvalsJPanel
```

Fig. 12.18 | Drawing lines, rectangles and ovals.

(line 25) draw rectangles with rounded corners. Their first two arguments specify the coordinates of the upper-left corner of the **bounding rectangle**—the area in which the rounded rectangle will be drawn. Note that the upper-left corner coordinates are not the edge of the rounded rectangle, but the coordinates where the edge would be if the rectangle had square corners. The third and fourth arguments specify the width and height of the rectangle. The last two arguments determine the horizontal and vertical diameters of the arc (i.e., the arc width and arc height) used to represent the corners.

Figure 12.20 labels the arc width, arc height, width and height of a rounded rectangle. Using the same value for the arc width and arc height produces a quarter circle at each corner. When the arc width, arc height, width and height have the same values, the result is a circle. If the values for width and height are the same and the values of arcWidth and arcHeight are 0, the result is a square.

```
1    // Fig. 12.19: LinesRectsOvals.java
2    // Drawing lines, rectangles and ovals.
3    import java.awt.Color;
4    import javax.swing.JFrame;
5
6    public class LinesRectsOvals
7    {
8       // execute application
9       public static void main( String args[] )
10      {
11         // create frame for LinesRectsOvalsJPanel
12         JFrame frame =
13            new JFrame( "Drawing lines, rectangles and ovals" );
14         frame.setDefaultCloseOperation( JFrame.EXIT_ON_CLOSE );
15
16         LinesRectsOvalsJPanel linesRectsOvalsJPanel =
17            new LinesRectsOvalsJPanel();
18         linesRectsOvalsJPanel.setBackground( Color.WHITE );
19         frame.add( linesRectsOvalsJPanel ); // add panel to frame
20         frame.setSize( 400, 210 ); // set frame size
21         frame.setVisible( true ); // display frame
22      } // end main
23   } // end class LinesRectsOvals
```

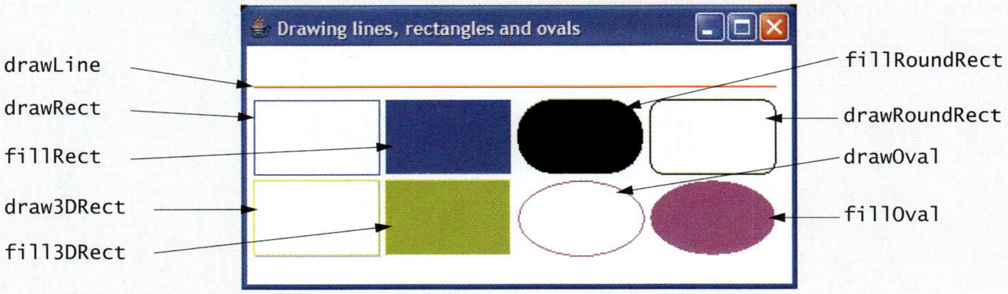

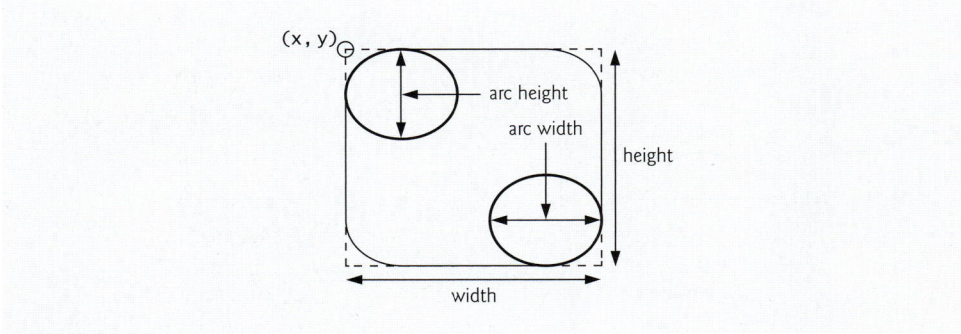

Fig. 12.19 | Creating JFrame to display lines, rectangles and ovals.

Fig. 12.20 | Arc width and arc height for rounded rectangles.

Methods `draw3DRect` (line 28) and `fill3DRect` (line 29) take the same arguments. The first two arguments specify the top-left corner of the rectangle. The next two arguments specify the width and height of the rectangle, respectively. The last argument determines whether the rectangle is raised (`true`) or lowered (`false`). The three-dimensional effect of `draw3DRect` appears as two edges of the rectangle in the original color and two edges in a slightly darker color. The three-dimensional effect of `fill3DRect` appears as two edges of the rectangle in the original drawing color and the fill and other two edges in a slightly darker color. Raised rectangles have the original drawing color edges at the top and left of the rectangle. Lowered rectangles have the original drawing color edges at the bottom and right of the rectangle. The three-dimensional effect is difficult to see in some colors.

Methods `drawOval` and `fillOval` (lines 32–33) take the same four arguments. The first two arguments specify the top-left coordinate of the bounding rectangle that contains the oval. The last two arguments specify the width and height of the bounding rectangle, respectively. Figure 12.21 shows an oval bounded by a rectangle. Note that the oval touches the center of all four sides of the bounding rectangle. (The bounding rectangle is not displayed on the screen.)

12.6 Drawing Arcs

An arc is drawn as a portion of an oval. Arc angles are measured in degrees. Arcs sweep (i.e., move along a curve) from a starting angle by the number of degrees specified by their arc angle. The starting angle indicates in degrees where the arc begins. The arc angle specifies the total number of degrees through which the arc sweeps. Figure 12.22 illustrates

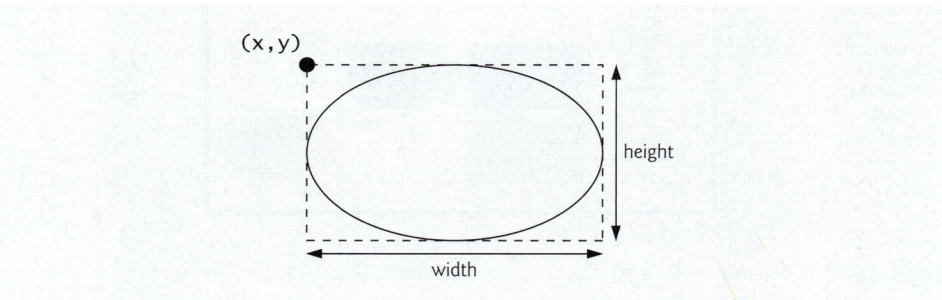

Fig. 12.21 | Oval bounded by a rectangle.

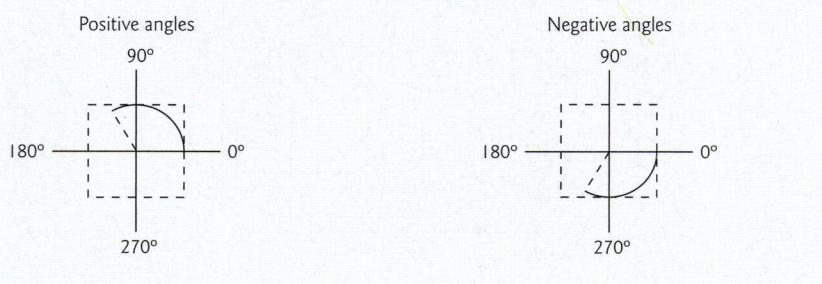

Fig. 12.22 | Positive and negative arc angles.

two arcs. The left set of axes shows an arc sweeping from zero degrees to approximately 110 degrees. Arcs that sweep in a counterclockwise direction are measured in positive degrees. The set of axes on the right shows an arc sweeping from zero degrees to approximately −110 degrees. Arcs that sweep in a clockwise direction are measured in negative degrees. Note the dashed boxes around the arcs in Fig. 12.22. When drawing an arc, we specify a bounding rectangle for an oval. The arc will sweep along part of the oval. Graphics methods drawArc and fillArc for drawing arcs are summarized in Fig. 12.23.

The application of Fig. 12.24–Fig. 12.25 demonstrates the arc methods of Fig. 12.23. The application draws six arcs (three unfilled and three filled). To illustrate the bounding rectangle that helps determine where the arc appears, the first three arcs are displayed inside a red rectangle that has the same x, y, width and height arguments as the arcs.

Method	Description
public void drawArc(int x, int y, int width, int height, int startAngle, int arcAngle)	
	Draws an arc relative to the bounding rectangle's top-left x and y coordinates with the specified width and height. The arc segment is drawn starting at startAngle and sweeps arcAngle degrees.
public void fillArc(int x, int y, int width, int height, int startAngle, int arcAngle)	
	Draws a filled arc (i.e., a sector) relative to the bounding rectangle's top-left x and y coordinates with the specified width and height. The arc segment is drawn starting at startAngle and sweeps arcAngle degrees.

Fig. 12.23 | Graphics methods for drawing arcs.

```
1   // Fig. 12.24: ArcsJPanel.java
2   // Drawing arcs.
3   import java.awt.Color;
4   import java.awt.Graphics;
5   import javax.swing.JPanel;
6
7   public class ArcsJPanel extends JPanel
8   {
9      // draw rectangles and arcs
10     public void paintComponent( Graphics g )
11     {
12        super.paintComponent( g ); // call superclass's paintComponent
13
14        // start at 0 and sweep 360 degrees
15        g.setColor( Color.RED );
16        g.drawRect( 15, 35, 80, 80 );
17        g.setColor( Color.BLACK );
18        g.drawArc( 15, 35, 80, 80, 0, 360 );
19
```

Fig. 12.24 | Arcs displayed with drawArc and fillArc. (Part 1 of 2.)

```
20          // start at 0 and sweep 110 degrees
21          g.setColor( Color.RED );
22          g.drawRect( 100, 35, 80, 80 );
23          g.setColor( Color.BLACK );
24          g.drawArc( 100, 35, 80, 80, 0, 110 );
25
26          // start at 0 and sweep -270 degrees
27          g.setColor( Color.RED );
28          g.drawRect( 185, 35, 80, 80 );
29          g.setColor( Color.BLACK );
30          g.drawArc( 185, 35, 80, 80, 0, -270 );
31
32          // start at 0 and sweep 360 degrees
33          g.fillArc( 15, 120, 80, 40, 0, 360 );
34
35          // start at 270 and sweep -90 degrees
36          g.fillArc( 100, 120, 80, 40, 270, -90 );
37
38          // start at 0 and sweep -270 degrees
39          g.fillArc( 185, 120, 80, 40, 0, -270 );
40       } // end method paintComponent
41    } // end class ArcsJPanel
```

Fig. 12.24 | Arcs displayed with `drawArc` and `fillArc`. (Part 2 of 2.)

12.7 Drawing Polygons and Polylines

Polygons are closed multisided shapes composed of straight line segments. Polylines are sequences of connected points. Figure 12.26 discusses methods for drawing polygons and polylines. Note that some methods require a **Polygon** object (package java.awt). Class Polygon's constructors are also described in Fig. 12.26. The application of Fig. 12.27–Fig. 12.28 draws polygons and polylines.

```
1  // Fig. 12.25: DrawArcs.java
2  // Drawing arcs.
3  import javax.swing.JFrame;
4
5  public class DrawArcs
6  {
7     // execute application
8     public static void main( String args[] )
9     {
10        // create frame for ArcsJPanel
11        JFrame frame = new JFrame( "Drawing Arcs" );
12        frame.setDefaultCloseOperation( JFrame.EXIT_ON_CLOSE );
13
14        ArcsJPanel arcsJPanel = new ArcsJPanel(); // create ArcsJPanel
15        frame.add( arcsJPanel ); // add arcsJPanel to frame
16        frame.setSize( 300, 210 ); // set frame size
17        frame.setVisible( true ); // display frame
18     } // end main
19  } // end class DrawArcs
```

Fig. 12.25 | Creating JFrame to display arcs. (Part 1 of 2.)

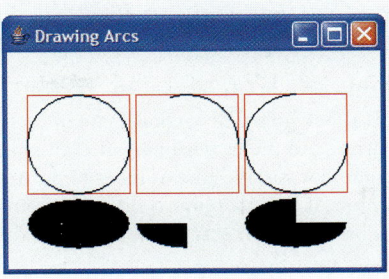

Fig. 12.25 │ Creating `JFrame` to display arcs. (Part 2 of 2.)

Lines 15–16 of Fig. 12.27 create two `int` arrays and use them to specify the points for `Polygon polygon1`. The `Polygon` constructor call in line 17 receives array `xValues`, which contains the *x*-coordinate of each point; array `yValues`, which contains the *y*-coordinate of each point and 6 (the number of points in the polygon). Line 18 displays `polygon1` by passing it as an argument to `Graphics` method **drawPolygon**.

Lines 21–22 create two `int` arrays and use them to specify the points for a series of connected lines. Array `xValues2` contains the *x*-coordinate of each point and array `yValues2` the *y*-coordinate of each point. Line 23 uses `Graphics` method **drawPolyline** to display the series of connected lines specified with the arguments `xValues2`, `yValues2` and 7 (the number of points).

Lines 26–27 create two `int` arrays and use them to specify the points of a polygon. Array `xValues3` contains the *x*-coordinate of each point and array `yValues3` the *y*-coordinate of each point. Line 28 displays a polygon by passing to `Graphics` method **fill-Polygon** the two arrays (`xValues3` and `yValues3`) and the number of points to draw (4).

Method	Description
`Graphics` *methods for drawing polygons*	
`public void drawPolygon( int xPoints[], int yPoints[], int points )`	
	Draws a polygon. The *x*-coordinate of each point is specified in the `xPoints` array, and the *y*-coordinate of each point in the `yPoints` array. The last argument specifies the number of `points`. This method draws a closed polygon. If the last point is different from the first, the polygon is closed by a line that connects the last point to the first.
`public void drawPolyline( int xPoints[], int yPoints[], int points )`	
	Draws a sequence of connected lines. The *x*-coordinate of each point is specified in the `xPoints` array, and the *y*-coordinate of each point in the `yPoints` array. The last argument specifies the number of `points`. If the last point is different from the first, the polyline is not closed.
`public void drawPolygon( Polygon p )`	
	Draws the specified polygon.

Fig. 12.26 │ `Graphics` methods for polygons and class `Polygon` methods. (Part 1 of 2.)

Method	Description

`public void fillPolygon( int xPoints[], int yPoints[], int points )`

Draws a filled polygon. The *x*-coordinate of each point is specified in the xPoints array, and the *y*-coordinate of each point in the yPoints array. The last argument specifies the number of points. This method draws a closed polygon. If the last point is different from the first, the polygon is closed by a line that connects the last point to the first.

`public void fillPolygon( Polygon p )`

Draws the specified filled polygon. The polygon is closed.

Polygon *constructors and methods*

`public Polygon()`

Constructs a new polygon object. The polygon does not contain any points.

`public Polygon( int xValues[], int yValues[], int numberOfPoints )`

Constructs a new polygon object. The polygon has numberOfPoints sides, with each point consisting of an *x*-coordinate from xValues and a *y*-coordinate from yValues.

`public void addPoint( int x, int y )`

Adds pairs of *x*- and *y*-coordinates to the Polygon.

Fig. 12.26 | Graphics methods for polygons and class Polygon methods. (Part 2 of 2.)

```java
1   // Fig. 12.27: PolygonsJPanel.java
2   // Drawing polygons.
3   import java.awt.Graphics;
4   import java.awt.Polygon;
5   import javax.swing.JPanel;
6
7   public class PolygonsJPanel extends JPanel
8   {
9      // draw polygons and polylines
10     public void paintComponent( Graphics g )
11     {
12        super.paintComponent( g ); // call superclass's paintComponent
13
14        // draw polygon with Polygon object
15        int xValues[] = { 20, 40, 50, 30, 20, 15 };
16        int yValues[] = { 50, 50, 60, 80, 80, 60 };
17        Polygon polygon1 = new Polygon( xValues, yValues, 6 );
18        g.drawPolygon( polygon1 );
19
20        // draw polylines with two arrays
21        int xValues2[] = { 70, 90, 100, 80, 70, 65, 60 };
22        int yValues2[] = { 100, 100, 110, 110, 130, 110, 90 };
23        g.drawPolyline( xValues2, yValues2, 7 );
24
```

Fig. 12.27 | Polygons displayed with drawPolygon and fillPolygon. (Part 1 of 2.)

```
25          // fill polygon with two arrays
26          int xValues3[] = { 120, 140, 150, 190 };
27          int yValues3[] = { 40, 70, 80, 60 };
28          g.fillPolygon( xValues3, yValues3, 4 );
29
30          // draw filled polygon with Polygon object
31          Polygon polygon2 = new Polygon();
32          polygon2.addPoint( 165, 135 );
33          polygon2.addPoint( 175, 150 );
34          polygon2.addPoint( 270, 200 );
35          polygon2.addPoint( 200, 220 );
36          polygon2.addPoint( 130, 180 );
37          g.fillPolygon( polygon2 );
38      } // end method paintComponent
39   } // end class PolygonsJPanel
```

Fig. 12.27 | Polygons displayed with `drawPolygon` and `fillPolygon`. (Part 2 of 2.)

```
 1   // Fig. 12.28: DrawPolygons.java
 2   // Drawing polygons.
 3   import javax.swing.JFrame;
 4
 5   public class DrawPolygons
 6   {
 7      // execute application
 8      public static void main( String args[] )
 9      {
10         // create frame for PolygonsJPanel
11         JFrame frame = new JFrame( "Drawing Polygons" );
12         frame.setDefaultCloseOperation( JFrame.EXIT_ON_CLOSE );
13
14         PolygonsJPanel polygonsJPanel = new PolygonsJPanel();
15         frame.add( polygonsJPanel ); // add polygonsJPanel to frame
16         frame.setSize( 280, 270 ); // set frame size
17         frame.setVisible( true ); // display frame
18      } // end main
19   } // end class DrawPolygons
```

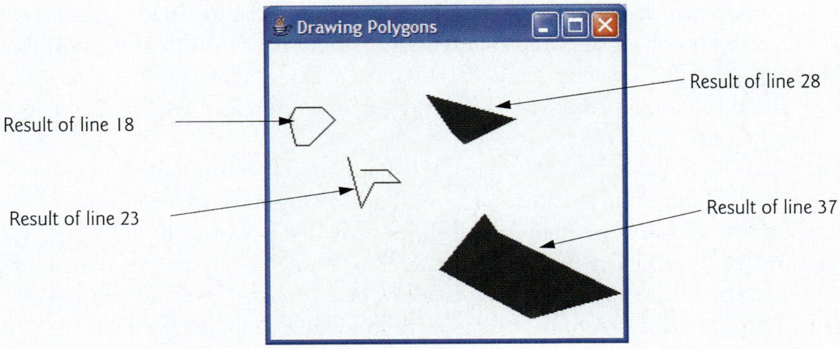

Result of line 28

Result of line 18

Result of line 23

Result of line 37

Fig. 12.28 | Creating `JFrame` to display polygons.

Common Programming Error 12.1

An ArrayIndexOutOfBoundsException is thrown if the number of points specified in the third argument to method drawPolygon or method fillPolygon is greater than the number of elements in the arrays of coordinates that specify the polygon to display.

Line 31 creates Polygon polygon2 with no points. Lines 32–36 use Polygon method **addPoint** to add pairs of *x*- and *y*-coordinates to the Polygon. Line 37 displays Polygon polygon2 by passing it to Graphics method fillPolygon.

12.8 Java 2D API

The Java 2D API provides advanced two-dimensional graphics capabilities for programmers who require detailed and complex graphical manipulations. The API includes features for processing line art, text and images in packages java.awt, java.awt.image, java.awt.color, java.awt.font, java.awt.geom, java.awt.print and java.awt.image.renderable. The capabilities of the API are far too broad to cover in this textbook. For an overview of the capabilities, see the Java 2D demo (discussed in Chapter 20, Introduction to Java Applets) or visit java.sun.com/products/java-media/2D/index.html. In this section, we overview several Java 2D capabilities.

Drawing with the Java 2D API is accomplished with a **Graphics2D** reference (package java.awt). Graphics2D is an abstract subclass of class Graphics, so it has all the graphics capabilities demonstrated earlier in this chapter. In fact, the actual object used to draw in every paintComponent method is an instance of a subclass of Graphics2D that is passed to method paintComponent and accessed via the superclass Graphics. To access Graphics2D capabilities, we must cast the Graphics reference (g) passed to paintComponent into a Graphics2D reference with a statement such as

```
Graphics2D g2d = ( Graphics2D ) g;
```

The next two examples use this technique.

Lines, Rectangles, Round Rectangles, Arcs and Ellipses

The next example demonstrates several Java 2D shapes from package java.awt.geom, including **Line2D.Double**, **Rectangle2D.Double**, **RoundRectangle2D.Double**, **Arc2D.Double** and **Ellipse2D.Double**. Note the syntax of each class name. Each of these classes represents a shape with dimensions specified as double-precision floating-point values. There is a separate version of each represented with single-precision floating-point values (e.g., **Ellipse2D.Float**). In each case, Double is a static nested class of the class specified to the left of the dot (e.g., Ellipse2D). To use the static nested class, we simply qualify its name with the outer class name.

In Fig. 12.29–Fig. 12.30, we draw Java 2D shapes and modify their drawing characteristics, such as changing line thickness, filling shapes with patterns and drawing dashed lines. These are just a few of the many capabilities provided by Java 2D.

Line 25 of Fig. 12.29 casts the Graphics reference received by paintComponent to a Graphics2D reference and assigns it to g2d to allow access to the Java 2D features.

The first shape we draw is an oval filled with gradually changing colors. Lines 28–29 invoke Graphics2D method **setPaint** to set the **Paint** object that determines the color for the shape to display. A Paint object is an object that implements interface java.awt.Paint.

The Paint object can be something as simple as one of the predeclared Color objects introduced in Section 12.3 (class Color implements Paint), or it can be an instance of the Java 2D API's GradientPaint, SystemColor or TexturePaint classes. In this case, we use a GradientPaint object.

```java
1   // Fig. 12.29: ShapesJPanel.java
2   // Demonstrating some Java 2D shapes.
3   import java.awt.Color;
4   import java.awt.Graphics;
5   import java.awt.BasicStroke;
6   import java.awt.GradientPaint;
7   import java.awt.TexturePaint;
8   import java.awt.Rectangle;
9   import java.awt.Graphics2D;
10  import java.awt.geom.Ellipse2D;
11  import java.awt.geom.Rectangle2D;
12  import java.awt.geom.RoundRectangle2D;
13  import java.awt.geom.Arc2D;
14  import java.awt.geom.Line2D;
15  import java.awt.image.BufferedImage;
16  import javax.swing.JPanel;
17
18  public class ShapesJPanel extends JPanel
19  {
20     // draw shapes with Java 2D API
21     public void paintComponent( Graphics g )
22     {
23        super.paintComponent( g ); // call superclass's paintComponent
24
25        Graphics2D g2d = ( Graphics2D ) g; // cast g to Graphics2D
26
27        // draw 2D ellipse filled with a blue-yellow gradient
28        g2d.setPaint( new GradientPaint( 5, 30, Color.BLUE, 35, 100,
29           Color.YELLOW, true ) );
30        g2d.fill( new Ellipse2D.Double( 5, 30, 65, 100 ) );
31
32        // draw 2D rectangle in red
33        g2d.setPaint( Color.RED );
34        g2d.setStroke( new BasicStroke( 10.0f ) );
35        g2d.draw( new Rectangle2D.Double( 80, 30, 65, 100 ) );
36
37        // draw 2D rounded rectangle with a buffered background
38        BufferedImage buffImage = new BufferedImage( 10, 10,
39           BufferedImage.TYPE_INT_RGB );
40
41        // obtain Graphics2D from bufferImage and draw on it
42        Graphics2D gg = buffImage.createGraphics();
43        gg.setColor( Color.YELLOW ); // draw in yellow
44        gg.fillRect( 0, 0, 10, 10 ); // draw a filled rectangle
45        gg.setColor( Color.BLACK );  // draw in black
46        gg.drawRect( 1, 1, 6, 6 ); // draw a rectangle
47        gg.setColor( Color.BLUE ); // draw in blue
```

Fig. 12.29 | Java 2D shapes. (Part 1 of 2.)

```
48        gg.fillRect( 1, 1, 3, 3 ); // draw a filled rectangle
49        gg.setColor( Color.RED ); // draw in red
50        gg.fillRect( 4, 4, 3, 3 ); // draw a filled rectangle
51
52        // paint buffImage onto the JFrame
53        g2d.setPaint( new TexturePaint( buffImage,
54           new Rectangle( 10, 10 ) ) );
55        g2d.fill(
56           new RoundRectangle2D.Double( 155, 30, 75, 100, 50, 50 ) );
57
58        // draw 2D pie-shaped arc in white
59        g2d.setPaint( Color.WHITE );
60        g2d.setStroke( new BasicStroke( 6.0f ) );
61        g2d.draw(
62           new Arc2D.Double( 240, 30, 75, 100, 0, 270, Arc2D.PIE ) );
63
64        // draw 2D lines in green and yellow
65        g2d.setPaint( Color.GREEN );
66        g2d.draw( new Line2D.Double( 395, 30, 320, 150 ) );
67
68        // draw 2D line using stroke
69        float dashes[] = { 10 }; // specify dash pattern
70        g2d.setPaint( Color.YELLOW );
71        g2d.setStroke( new BasicStroke( 4, BasicStroke.CAP_ROUND,
72           BasicStroke.JOIN_ROUND, 10, dashes, 0 ) );
73        g2d.draw( new Line2D.Double( 320, 30, 395, 150 ) );
74     } // end method paintComponent
75  } // end class ShapesJPanel
```

Fig. 12.29 | Java 2D shapes. (Part 2 of 2.)

```
1  // Fig. 12.30: Shapes.java
2  // Demonstrating some Java 2D shapes.
3  import javax.swing.JFrame;
4
5  public class Shapes
6  {
7     // execute application
8     public static void main( String args[] )
9     {
10        // create frame for ShapesJPanel
11        JFrame frame = new JFrame( "Drawing 2D shapes" );
12        frame.setDefaultCloseOperation( JFrame.EXIT_ON_CLOSE );
13
14        // create ShapesJPanel
15        ShapesJPanel shapesJPanel = new ShapesJPanel();
16
17        frame.add( shapesJPanel ); // add shapesJPanel to frame
18        frame.setSize( 425, 200 ); // set frame size
19        frame.setVisible( true ); // display frame
20     } // end main
21  } // end class Shapes
```

Fig. 12.30 | Creating JFrame to display shapes. (Part 1 of 2.)

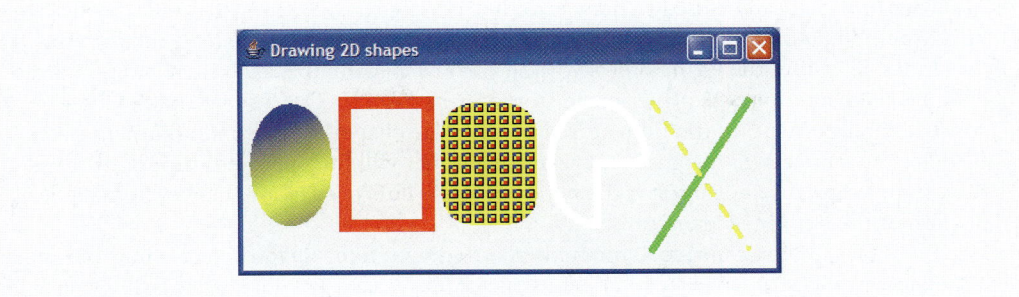

Fig. 12.30 | Creating `JFrame` to display shapes. (Part 2 of 2.)

Class `GradientPaint` helps draw a shape in gradually changing colors—called a gradient. The `GradientPaint` constructor used here requires seven arguments. The first two specify the starting coordinate for the gradient. The third specifies the starting `Color` for the gradient. The fourth and fifth specify the ending coordinate for the gradient. The sixth specifies the ending `Color` for the gradient. The last argument specifies whether the gradient is cyclic (`true`) or acyclic (`false`). The two sets of coordinates determine the direction of the gradient. Because the second coordinate (35, 100) is down and to the right of the first coordinate (5, 30), the gradient goes down and to the right at an angle. Because this gradient is cyclic (`true`), the color starts with blue, gradually becomes yellow, then gradually returns to blue. If the gradient is acyclic, the color transitions from the first color specified (e.g., blue) to the second color (e.g., yellow).

Line 30 uses `Graphics2D` method `fill` to draw a filled **Shape** object—an object that implements interface `Shape` (package `java.awt`). In this case, we display an `Ellipse2D.Double` object. The `Ellipse2D.Double` constructor receives four arguments specifying the bounding rectangle for the ellipse to display.

Next we draw a red rectangle with a thick border. Line 33 invokes `setPaint` to set the `Paint` object to `Color.RED`. Line 34 uses `Graphics2D` method `setStroke` to set the characteristics of the rectangle's border (or the lines for any other shape). Method `setStroke` requires as its argument an object that implements interface **Stroke** (package `java.awt`). In this case, we use an instance of class `BasicStroke`. Class `BasicStroke` provides several constructors to specify the width of the line, how the line ends (called the **end caps**), how lines join together (called **line joins**) and the dash attributes of the line (if it is a dashed line). The constructor here specifies that the line should be 10 pixels wide.

Line 35 uses `Graphics2D` method `draw` to draw a `Shape` object—in this case, a `Rectangle2D.Double`. The `Rectangle2D.Double` constructor receives four arguments specifying the upper-left *x*-coordinate, upper-left *y*-coordinate, width and height of the rectangle.

Next we draw a rounded rectangle filled with a pattern created in a **BufferedImage** (package `java.awt.image`) object. Lines 38–39 create the `BufferedImage` object. Class `BufferedImage` can be used to produce images in color and grayscale. This particular `BufferedImage` is 10 pixels wide and 10 pixels tall (as specified by the first two arguments of the constructor). The third argument `BufferedImage.TYPE_INT_RGB` indicates that the image is stored in color using the RGB color scheme.

To create the fill pattern for the rounded rectangle, we must first draw into the `BufferedImage`. Line 42 creates a `Graphics2D` object (with a call to `BufferedImage` method **cre-**

ateGraphics) that can be used to draw into the BufferedImage. Lines 43–50 use methods setColor, fillRect and drawRect (discussed earlier in this chapter) to create the pattern.

Lines 53–54 set the Paint object to a new TexturePaint (package java.awt) object. A TexturePaint object uses the image stored in its associated BufferedImage (the first constructor argument) as the fill texture for a filled-in shape. The second argument specifies the Rectangle area from the BufferedImage that will be replicated through the texture. In this case, the Rectangle is the same size as the BufferedImage. However, a smaller portion of the BufferedImage can be used.

Lines 55–56 use Graphics2D method fill to draw a filled Shape object—in this case, a RoundRectangle2D.Double. The constructor for class RoundRectangle2D.Double receives six arguments specifying the rectangle dimensions and the arc width and arc height used to determine the rounding of the corners.

Next we draw a pie-shaped arc with a thick white line. Line 59 sets the Paint object to Color.WHITE. Line 60 sets the Stroke object to a new BasicStroke for a line 6 pixels wide. Lines 61–62 use Graphics2D method draw to draw a Shape object—in this case, an Arc2D.Double. The Arc2D.Double constructor's first four arguments specify the upper-left x-coordinate, upper-left y-coordinate, width and height of the bounding rectangle for the arc. The fifth argument specifies the start angle. The sixth argument specifies the arc angle. The last argument specifies how the arc is closed. Constant **Arc2D.PIE** indicates that the arc is closed by drawing two lines—one line from the arc's starting point to the center of the bounding rectangle and one line from the center of the bounding rectangle to the ending point. Class Arc2D provides two other static constants for specifying how the arc is closed. Constant **Arc2D.CHORD** draws a line from the starting point to the ending point. Constant **Arc2D.OPEN** specifies that the arc should not be closed.

Finally, we draw two lines using **Line2D** objects—one solid and one dashed. Line 65 sets the Paint object to Color.GREEN. Line 66 uses Graphics2D method draw to draw a Shape object—in this case, an instance of class Line2D.Double. The Line2D.Double constructor's arguments specify the starting coordinates and ending coordinates of the line.

Line 69 declares a one-element float array containing the value 10. This array will be used to describe the dashes in the dashed line. In this case, each dash will be 10 pixels long. To create dashes of different lengths in a pattern, simply provide the length of each dash as an element in the array. Line 70 sets the Paint object to Color.YELLOW. Lines 71–72 set the Stroke object to a new BasicStroke. The line will be 4 pixels wide and will have rounded ends (**BasicStroke.CAP_ROUND**). If lines join together (as in a rectangle at the corners), their joining will be rounded (**BasicStroke.JOIN_ROUND**). The dashes argument specifies the dash lengths for the line. The last argument indicates the starting index in the dashes array for the first dash in the pattern. Line 73 then draws a line with the current Stroke.

General Paths

Next we present a general path—a shape constructed from straight lines and complex curves. A general path is represented with an object of class **GeneralPath** (package java.awt.geom). The application of Fig. 12.31 and Fig. 12.32 demonstrates drawing a general path in the shape of a five-pointed star.

Lines 18–19 declare two int arrays representing the x- and y-coordinates of the points in the star. Line 22 creates GeneralPath object star. Line 25 uses GeneralPath method moveTo to specify the first point in the star. The for statement in lines 28–29 uses GeneralPath

```
 1   // Fig. 12.31: Shapes2JPanel.java
 2   // Demonstrating a general path.
 3   import java.awt.Color;
 4   import java.awt.Graphics;
 5   import java.awt.Graphics2D;
 6   import java.awt.geom.GeneralPath;
 7   import java.util.Random;
 8   import javax.swing.JPanel;
 9
10   public class Shapes2JPanel extends JPanel
11   {
12      // draw general paths
13      public void paintComponent( Graphics g )
14      {
15         super.paintComponent( g ); // call superclass's paintComponent
16         Random random = new Random(); // get random number generator
17
18         int xPoints[] = { 55, 67, 109, 73, 83, 55, 27, 37, 1, 43 };
19         int yPoints[] = { 0, 36, 36, 54, 96, 72, 96, 54, 36, 36 };
20
21         Graphics2D g2d = ( Graphics2D ) g;
22         GeneralPath star = new GeneralPath(); // create GeneralPath object
23
24         // set the initial coordinate of the General Path
25         star.moveTo( xPoints[ 0 ], yPoints[ 0 ] );
26
27         // create the star--this does not draw the star
28         for ( int count = 1; count < xPoints.length; count++ )
29            star.lineTo( xPoints[ count ], yPoints[ count ] );
30
31         star.closePath(); // close the shape
32
33         g2d.translate( 200, 200 ); // translate the origin to (200, 200)
34
35         // rotate around origin and draw stars in random colors
36         for ( int count = 1; count <= 20; count++ )
37         {
38            g2d.rotate( Math.PI / 10.0 ); // rotate coordinate system
39
40            // set random drawing color
41            g2d.setColor( new Color( random.nextInt( 256 ),
42               random.nextInt( 256 ), random.nextInt( 256 ) ) );
43
44            g2d.fill( star ); // draw filled star
45         } // end for
46      } // end method paintComponent
47   } // end class Shapes2JPanel
```

Fig. 12.31 | Java 2D general paths.

method **lineTo** to draw a line to the next point in the star. Each new call to **lineTo** draws a line from the previous point to the current point. Line 31 uses GeneralPath method **close-Path** to draw a line from the last point to the point specified in the last call to moveTo. This completes the general path.

```
 1   // Fig. 12.32: Shapes2.java
 2   // Demonstrating a general path.
 3   import java.awt.Color;
 4   import javax.swing.JFrame;
 5
 6   public class Shapes2
 7   {
 8      // execute application
 9      public static void main( String args[] )
10      {
11         // create frame for Shapes2JPanel
12         JFrame frame = new JFrame( "Drawing 2D Shapes" );
13         frame.setDefaultCloseOperation( JFrame.EXIT_ON_CLOSE );
14
15         Shapes2JPanel shapes2JPanel = new Shapes2JPanel();
16         frame.add( shapes2JPanel ); // add shapes2JPanel to frame
17         frame.setBackground( Color.WHITE ); // set frame background color
18         frame.setSize( 400, 400 ); // set frame size
19         frame.setVisible( true ); // display frame
20      } // end main
21   } // end class Shapes2
```

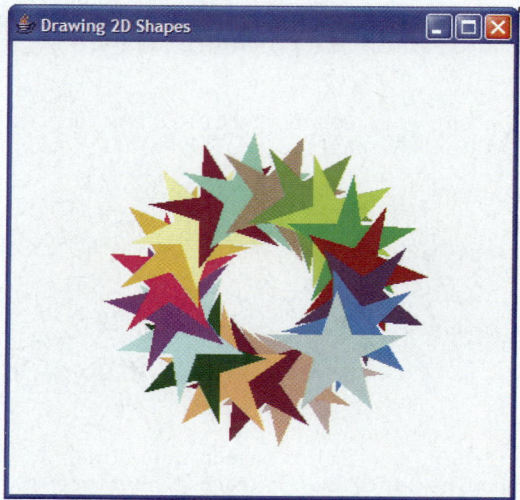

Fig. 12.32 | Creating JFrame to display stars.

Line 33 uses Graphics2D method **translate** to move the drawing origin to location (200, 200). All drawing operations now use location (200, 200) as (0, 0).

The for statement in lines 36–45 draws the star 20 times by rotating it around the new origin point. Line 38 uses Graphics2D method **rotate** to rotate the next displayed shape. The argument specifies the rotation angle in radians (with 360° = 2π radians). Line 44 uses Graphics2D method **fill** to draw a filled version of the star.

12.9 Wrap-Up

In this chapter, you learned how to use Java's graphics capabilities to produce colorful drawings. You learned how to specify the location of an object using Java's coordinate system, and how to draw on a window using the `paintComponent` method. You were introduced to class `Color`, and how to use this class to specify different colors using their RGB components. You used the `JColorChooser` dialog to allow users to select colors in a program. You then learned how to work with fonts when drawing text on a window. You learned how to create a `Font` object from a font name, style and size, as well as how to access the metrics of a font. From there, you learned how to draw various shapes on a window, such as rectangles (regular, rounded and 3D), ovals and polygons, as well as lines and arcs. You then used the Java 2D API to create more complex shapes, and to fill them with gradients or patterns. The chapter concluded with a discussion of general paths, used to construct shapes from straight lines and complex curves. In the next chapter, you will learn about exceptions, useful for handling errors during a program's execution. Handling errors in this way provides for more robust programs.

Summary

- Java's coordinate system is a scheme for identifying every point on the screen.
- A coordinate pair is composed of an *x*-coordinate (the horizontal coordinate) and a *y*-coordinate (the vertical coordinate).
- Text and shapes are displayed on the screen by specifying coordinates. The coordinates are used to indicate where graphics should be displayed on a screen.
- Coordinate units are measured in pixels. A pixel is a display monitor's smallest unit of resolution.
- A Java graphics context enables drawing on the screen.
- Class `Graphics` contains methods for drawing strings, lines, rectangles and other shapes. Methods are also included for font manipulation and color manipulation.
- A `Graphics` object manages a graphics context and draws pixels on the screen that represent text and other graphical object (e.g., lines, ellipses, rectangles and other polygons).
- Class `Graphics` is an abstract class. This contributes to Java's portability—when Java is implemented on a platform, a subclass of `Graphics` is created that implements the drawing capabilities. This implementation is hidden from us by class `Graphics`, which supplies the interface that enables us to use graphics in a platform-independent manner.
- Class `JComponent` contains a `paintComponent` method that can be used to draw graphics in a Swing component.
- Method `paintComponent` takes a `Graphics` object as an argument. This object is passed to the `paintComponent` method by the system when a lightweight Swing component needs to be repainted.
- Method `paintComponent` is seldom called directly by the programmer because drawing graphics is an event-driven process. When an application executes, the application container calls method `paintComponent`. For `paintComponent` to be called again, an event must occur.
- When a `JComponent` is displayed, its `paintComponent` method is called.
- Programmers call method `repaint` to update the graphics drawn on the Swing component.
- Class `Color` declares methods and constants for manipulating colors in a Java program.

- Every color is created from a red, a green and a blue component. Together these components are called RGB values.
- The first RGB component specifies the amount of red, the second the amount of green and the third the amount of blue. The larger the RGB value, the greater the amount of that particular color.
- Color methods getRed, getGreen and getBlue return integer values from 0 to 255 representing the amount of red, green and blue, respectively.
- Graphics method getColor returns a Color object representing the current drawing color.
- Graphics method setColor sets the current drawing color.
- Graphics method fillRect draws a rectangle that is filled by the current color of the Graphics object.
- Graphics method drawString draws a String in the current color.
- The JColorChooser GUI component enables application users to select colors.
- Class JColorChooser provides the static convenience method showDialog that creates a JColorChooser object, attaches it to a dialog box and displays the dialog.
- While the color chooser dialog is on the screen, the user cannot interact with the parent component. This type of dialog is called a modal dialog.
- Class Font contains methods and constants for manipulating fonts.
- Class Font's constructor takes three arguments—the font name, font style and font size.
- A Font's font style can be Font.PLAIN, Font.ITALIC or Font.BOLD (each is a static field of class Font). Font styles can be used in combination (e.g., Font.ITALIC + Font.BOLD).
- The font size is measured in points. A point is 1/72 of an inch.
- Graphics method setFont sets the current drawing font—the font in which text will be displayed.
- Font method getStyle returns an integer value representing the current Font's style.
- Font method getSize returns the font size in points.
- Font method getName returns the current font name as a string.
- Font method getFamily returns the name of the font family to which the current font belongs. The name of the font family is platform specific.
- Class FontMetrics contains methods for obtaining font information.
- Font metrics include height, descent (the amount a character dips below the baseline), ascent (the amount a character rises above the baseline) and leading (the difference between the descent of one line of text and the ascent of the line of text below it—that is, the interline spacing).
- Graphics methods fillRoundRect and drawRoundRect draw rectangles with rounded corners.
- Graphics methods draw3DRect and fill3DRect draw three-dimensional rectangles.
- Graphics methods drawOval and fillOval draw ovals.
- An arc is drawn as a portion of an oval.
- Arcs sweep (i.e., move along a curve) from a starting angle by the number of degrees specified by their arc angle.
- Graphics methods drawArc and fillArc are used for drawing arcs.
- Class Polygon contains methods for creating polygons.
- Polygons are closed multisided shapes composed of straight line segments.
- Polylines are a sequence of connected points.

- `Graphics` method `drawPolyline` displays a series of connected lines.
- `Graphics` methods `drawPolygon` and `fillPolygon` are used to draw polygons.
- `Polygon` method `addPoint` of class `Polygon` adds pairs of *x*- and *y*-coordinates to the `Polygon`.
- The Java 2D API provides advanced two-dimensional graphics capabilities for programmers who require detailed and complex graphical manipulations.
- Class `Graphics2D`, which extends class `Graphics`, is used for drawing with the Java 2D API.
- The Java 2D API contains several classes for drawing shapes, including `Line2D.Double`, `Rectangle2D.Double`, `RoundRectangle2D.Double`, `Arc2D.Double` and `Ellipse2D.Double`.
- Class `GradientPaint` helps draw a shape in gradually changing colors—called a gradient.
- `Graphics2D` method `fill` draws a filled `Shape` object—an object that implements interface `Shape`.
- Class `BasicStroke` helps specify the drawing characteristics of lines.
- `Graphics2D` method `draw` is used to draw a `Shape` object.
- Classes `GradientPaint` and `TexturePaint` help specify the characteristics for filling shapes with colors or patterns.
- A general path is a shape constructed from straight lines and complex curves.
- A general path is represented with an object of class `GeneralPath`.
- `GeneralPath` method `moveTo` specifies the first point in a general path.
- `GeneralPath` method `lineTo` draws a line to the next point in the path. Each new call to `lineTo` draws a line from the previous point to the current point.
- `GeneralPath` method `closePath` draws a line from the last point to the point specified in the last call to `moveTo`. This completes the general path.
- `Graphics2D` method `translate` is used to move the drawing origin to a new location.
- `Graphics2D` method `rotate` is used to rotate the next displayed shape.

Terminology

acyclic gradient
addPoint method of class `Polygon`
arc
arc angle
ascent (font metrics)
baseline (font metrics)
`BasicStroke` class
BOLD constant of class `Font`
bounding rectangle
CAP_ROUND constant of class `BasicStroke`
clearRect method of class `Graphics`
closed polygons
closePath method of class `GeneralPath`
color chooser dialog
`Color` class
color manipulation
color swatches
complex curve
connected lines
coordinate system
createGraphics method of class `BufferedImage`

cyclic gradient
dashed lines
descent (font metrics)
draw method of class `Graphics2D`
draw3DRect method of class `Graphics`
drawArc method of class `Graphics`
drawLine method of class `Graphics`
drawOval method of class `Graphics`
drawPolygon method of class `Graphics`
drawPolyline method of class `Graphics`
drawRect method of class `Graphics`
drawRoundRect method of class `Graphics`
drawString method of class `Graphics`
fill method of class `Graphics2D`
fill pattern
fill texture
fill3DRect method of class `Graphics`
fillArc method of class `Graphics`
fillOval method of class `Graphics`
fillPolygon method of class `Graphics`
fillRect method of class `Graphics`

fillRoundRect method of class Graphics
font
Font class
font metric
FontMetrics class
general path
GeneralPath class
getAscent method of class FontMetrics
getBlue method of class Color
getColor method of class Graphics
getDescent method of class FontMetrics
getFamily method of class Font
getFont method of class Graphics
getFontMetrics method of class Graphics
getGreen method of class Color
getHeight method of class FontMetrics
getLeading method of class FontMetrics
getName method of class Font
getRed method of class Color
getSize method of class Font
getStyle method of class Font
gradient
GradientPaint class
Graphics class
graphics context
Graphics2D class
height (font metrics)
horizontal coordinate
isBold method of class Font
isItalic method of class Font
isPlain method of class Font
ITALIC constant of class Font
Java 2D API
JColorChooser class
JOIN_ROUND constant of class BasicStroke
leading (font metrics)
line join
lineTo method of class GeneralPath
modal dialog

moveTo method of class GeneralPath
oval
oval bounded by a rectangle
Paint object
paintComponent method of class JComponent
pixel ("picture element")
PLAIN constant of class Font
point (font size)
polygon
Polygon class
polylines
raised rectangle
repaint method of class JComponent
RGB value
rotate method of class Graphics2D
rounded rectangle
setBackground method of class Component
setColor method of class Graphics
setFont method of class Graphics
setPaint method of class Graphics2D
setStroke method of class Graphics2D
showDialog method of class JColorChooser
starting angle
Stroke object
sweep
TexturePaint class
three-dimensional rectangle
translate method of class Graphics2D
two-dimensional graphics
two-dimensional shapes
upper-left corner of a GUI component
upper-left x-coordinate
upper-left y-coordinate
vertical coordinate
x axis
x-coordinate
y axis
y-coordinate

Self-Review Exercises

12.1 Fill in the blanks in each of the following statements:

a) In Java 2D, method _____ of class _____ sets the characteristics of a line used to draw a shape.

b) Class _____ helps specify the fill for a shape such that the fill gradually changes from one color to another.

c) The _____ method of class Graphics draws a line between two points.

d) RGB is short for _____, _____ and _____.

e) Font sizes are measured in units called _____.

f) Class _____ helps specify the fill for a shape using a pattern drawn in a BufferedImage.

12.2   State whether each of the following is *true* or *false*. If *false*, explain why.
   a)   The first two arguments of `Graphics` method `drawOval` specify the center coordinate of the oval.
   b)   In the Java coordinate system, *x* values increase from left to right.
   c)   `Graphics` method `fillPolygon` draws a filled polygon in the current color.
   d)   `Graphics` method `drawArc` allows negative angles.
   e)   `Graphics` method `getSize` returns the size of the current font in centimeters.
   f)   Pixel coordinate *(0, 0)* is located at the exact center of the monitor.

12.3   Find the error(s) in each of the following and explain how to correct the error(s). Assume that g is a `Graphics` object.
   a)   `g.setFont( "SansSerif" );`
   b)   `g.erase( x, y, w, h );      // clear rectangle at (x, y)`
   c)   `Font f = new Font( "Serif", Font.BOLDITALIC, 12 );`
   d)   `g.setColor( 255, 255, 0 );  // change color to yellow`

Answers to Self-Review Exercises

12.1   a) `setStroke`, `Graphics2D`. b) `GradientPaint`. c) `drawLine`. d) red, green, blue. e) points. f) `TexturePaint`.

12.2   a)   False. The first two arguments specify the upper-left corner of the bounding rectangle.
   b)   True.
   c)   True.
   d)   True.
   e)   False. Font sizes are measured in points.
   f)   False. The coordinate *(0,0)* corresponds to the upper-left corner of a GUI component on which drawing occurs.

12.3   a)   The `setFont` method takes a `Font` object as an argument—not a `String`.
   b)   The `Graphics` class does not have an `erase` method. The `clearRect` method should be used.
   c)   `Font.BOLDITALIC` is not a valid font style. To get a bold italic font, use `Font.BOLD + Font.ITALIC`.
   d)   Method `setColor` takes a `Color` object as an argument, not three integers.

Exercises

12.4   Fill in the blanks in each of the following statements:
   a)   Class _____ of the Java 2D API is used to draw ovals.
   b)   Methods `draw` and `fill` of class `Graphics2D` require an object of type _____ as their argument.
   c)   The three constants that specify font style are _____, _____ and _____.
   d)   `Graphics2D` method _____ sets the painting color for Java 2D shapes.

12.5   State whether each of the following is *true* or *false*. If *false*, explain why.
   a)   `Graphics` method `drawPolygon` automatically connects the endpoints of the polygon.
   b)   `Graphics` method `drawLine` draws a line between two points.
   c)   `Graphics` method `fillArc` uses degrees to specify the angle.
   d)   In the Java coordinate system, values on the *y*-axis increase from left to right.
   e)   `Graphics` inherits directly from class `Object`.
   f)   `Graphics` is an abstract class.
   g)   The `Font` class inherits directly from class `Graphics`.

12.6 *(Concentric Circles Using Method `drawArc`)* Write an application that draws a series of eight concentric circles. The circles should be separated by 10 pixels. Use `Graphics` method `drawArc`.

12.7 *(Concentric Circles Using Class `Ellipse2D.Double`)* Modify your solution to Exercise 12.6 to draw the ovals by using class `Ellipse2D.Double` and method `draw` of class `Graphics2D`.

12.8 *(Random Lines Using Class `Line2D.Double`)* Modify your solution to Exercise 12.7 to draw random lines, in random colors and random line thicknesses. Use class `Line2D.Double` and method `draw` of class `Graphics2D` to draw the lines.

12.9 *(Random Triangles)* Write an application that displays randomly generated triangles in different colors. Each triangle should be filled with a different color. Use class `GeneralPath` and method `fill` of class `Graphics2D` to draw the triangles.

12.10 *(Random Characters)* Write an application that randomly draws characters in different font sizes and colors.

12.11 *(Grid Using Method `drawLine`)* Write an application that draws an 8-by-8 grid. Use `Graphics` method `drawLine`.

12.12 *(Grid Using Class `Line2D.Double`)* Modify your solution to Exercise 12.11 to draw the grid using instances of class `Line2D.Double` and method `draw` of class `Graphics2D`.

12.13 *(Grid Using Method `drawRect`)* Write an application that draws a 10-by-10 grid. Use the `Graphics` method `drawRect`.

12.14 *(Grid Using Class `Rectangle2D.Double`)* Modify your solution to Exercise 12.13 to draw the grid by using class `Rectangle2D.Double` and method `draw` of class `Graphics2D`.

12.15 *(Drawing Tetrahedrons)* Write an application that draws a tetrahedron (a three-dimensional shape with four triangular faces). Use class `GeneralPath` and method `draw` of class `Graphics2D`.

12.16 *(Drawing Cubes)* Write an application that draws a cube. Use class `GeneralPath` and method `draw` of class `Graphics2D`.

12.17 *(Circles Using Class `Ellipse2D.Double`)* Write an application that asks the user to input the radius of a circle as a floating-point number and draws the circle, as well as the values of the circle's diameter, circumference and area. Use the value 3.14159 for π. [*Note:* You may also use the predefined constant `Math.PI` for the value of π. This constant is more precise than the value 3.14159. Class `Math` is declared in the `java.lang` package, so you do not need to `import` it.] Use the following formulas (*r* is the radius):

$$diameter = 2r$$
$$circumference = 2\pi r$$
$$area = \pi r^2$$

The user should also be prompted for a set of coordinates in addition to the radius. Then draw the circle, and display the circle's diameter, circumference and area, using an `Ellipse2D.Double` object to represent the circle and method `draw` of class `Graphics2D` to display the circle.

12.18 *(Screen Saver)* Write an application that simulates a screen saver. The application should randomly draw lines using method `drawLine` of class `Graphics`. After drawing 100 lines, the application should clear itself and start drawing lines again. To allow the program to draw continuously, place a call to `repaint` as the last line in method `paintComponent`. Do you notice any problems with this on your system?

12.19 *(Screen Saver Using Timer)* Package `javax.swing` contains a class called `Timer` that is capable of calling method `actionPerformed` of interface `ActionListener` at a fixed time interval (specified in milliseconds). Modify your solution to Exercise 12.18 to remove the call to `repaint` from method `paintComponent`. Declare your class to implement `ActionListener`. (The `actionPerformed` method should simply call `repaint`.) Declare an instance variable of type `Timer` called `timer` in your class. In the constructor for your class, write the following statements:

```
timer = new Timer( 1000, this );
timer.start();
```

This creates an instance of class `Timer` that will call `this` object's `actionPerformed` method every 1000 milliseconds (i.e., every second).

12.20 *(Screen Saver for a Random Number of Lines)* Modify your solution to Exercise 12.19 to enable the user to enter the number of random lines that should be drawn before the application clears itself and starts drawing lines again. Use a `JTextField` to obtain the value. The user should be able to type a new number into the `JTextField` at any time during the program's execution. Use an inner class to perform event handling for the `JTextField`.

12.21 *(Screen Saver with Shapes)* Modify your solution to Exercise 12.19 such that it uses random-number generation to choose different shapes to display. Use methods of class `Graphics`.

12.22 *(Screen Saver Using the Java 2D API)* Modify your solution to Exercise 12.21 to use classes and drawing capabilities of the Java 2D API. Draw shapes like rectangles and ellipses, with randomly generated gradients. Use class `GradientPaint` to generate the gradient.

12.23 *(Turtle Graphics)* Modify your solution to Exercise 7.21—*Turtle Graphics*—to add a graphical user interface using `JTextFields` and `JButtons`. Draw lines rather than asterisks (*). When the turtle graphics program specifies a move, translate the number of positions into a number of pixels on the screen by multiplying the number of positions by 10 (or any value you choose). Implement the drawing with Java 2D API features.

12.24 *(Knight's Tour)* Produce a graphical version of the Knight's Tour problem (Exercise 7.22, Exercise 7.23 and Exercise 7.26). As each move is made, the appropriate cell of the chessboard should be updated with the proper move number. If the result of the program is a *full tour* or a *closed tour*, the program should display an appropriate message. If you like, use class `Timer` (see Exercise 12.19) to help animate the Knight's Tour.

12.25 *(Tortoise and Hare)* Produce a graphical version of the *Tortoise and Hare* simulation (Exercise 7.28). Simulate the mountain by drawing an arc that extends from the bottom-left corner of the window to the top-right corner of the window. The tortoise and the hare should race up the mountain. Implement the graphical output to actually print the tortoise and the hare on the arc for every move. [*Note:* Extend the length of the race from 70 to 300 to allow yourself a larger graphics area.]

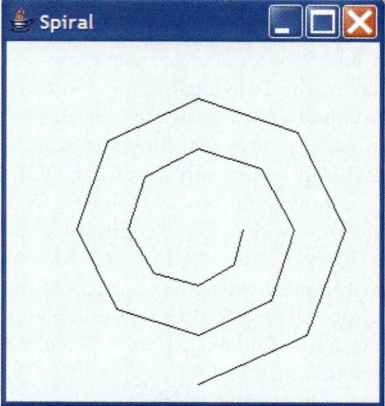

Fig. 12.33 | Spiral drawn using method `drawPolyline`.

12.26 *(Drawing Spirals)* Write an application that uses `Graphics` method `drawPolyline` to draw a spiral similar to the one shown in Fig. 12.33.

12.27 *(Pie Chart)* Write a program that inputs four numbers and graphs them as a pie chart. Use class `Arc2D.Double` and method `fill` of class `Graphics2D` to perform the drawing. Draw each piece of the pie in a separate color.

12.28 *(Selecting Shapes)* Write an application that allows the user to select a shape from a `JComboBox` and draws it 20 times with random locations and dimensions in method `paintComponent`. The first item in the `JComboBox` should be the default shape that is displayed the first time `paintComponent` is called.

12.29 *(Random Colors)* Modify Exercise 12.28 to draw each of the 20 randomly sized shapes in a randomly selected color. Use all 13 predefined `Color` objects in an array of `Colors`.

12.30 *(JColorChooser Dialog)* Modify Exercise 12.28 to allow the user to select the color in which shapes should be drawn from a `JColorChooser` dialog.

(Optional) GUI and Graphics Case Study: Adding Java2D

12.31 Java2D introduces many new capabilities for creating unique and impressive graphics. We will add a small subset of these features to the drawing application you created in Exercise 11.18. In this version of the drawing application, you will enable the user to specify gradients for filling shapes and to change stroke characteristics for drawing lines and outlines of shapes. The user will be able to choose which colors compose the gradient and set the width and dash length of the stroke.

First, you must update the `MyShape` hierarchy to support Java2D functionality. Make the following changes in class `MyShape`:

    a) Change abstract method `draw`'s parameter type from `Graphics` to `Graphics2D`.

    b) Change all variables of type `Color` to type `Paint` to enable support for gradients. [*Note:* Recall that class `Color` implements interface `Paint`.]

    c) Add an instance variable of type `Stroke` in class `MyShape` and a `Stroke` parameter in the constructor to initialize the new instance variable. The default stroke should be an instance of class `BasicStroke`.

Classes `MyLine`, `MyBoundedShape`, `MyOval` and `MyRect` should each add a `Stroke` parameter to their constructors. In the draw methods, each shape should set the `Paint` and the `Stroke` before drawing or filling a shape. Since `Graphics2D` is a subclass of `Graphics`, we can continue to use `Graphics` methods `drawLine`, `drawOval`, `fillOval`, etc. to draw the shapes. When these methods are called, they will draw the appropriate shape using the specified `Paint` and `Stroke` settings.

Next, you will update the `DrawPanel` to handle the Java2D features. Change all `Color` variables to `Paint` variables. Declare an instance variable `currentStroke` of type `Stroke` and provide a *set* method for it. Update the calls to the individual shape constructors to include the `Paint` and `Stroke` arguments. In method `paintComponent`, cast the `Graphics` reference to type `Graphics2D` and use the `Graphics2D` reference in each call to `MyShape` method `draw`.

Next, make the new Java2D features accessible from the GUI. Create a `JPanel` of GUI components for setting the Java2D options. Add these components at the top of the `DrawFrame` below the panel that currently contains the standard shape controls (see Fig. 12.34). These GUI components should include:

    a) A check box to specify whether to paint using a gradient

    b) Two `JButtons` that each show a `JColorChooser` dialog to allow the user to choose the first and second color in the gradient. (These will replace the `JComboBox` used for choosing the color in Exercise 11.18.)

    c) A text field for entering the `Stroke` width

    d) A text field for entering the `Stroke` dash length

    e) A check box for selecting whether to draw a dashed or solid line

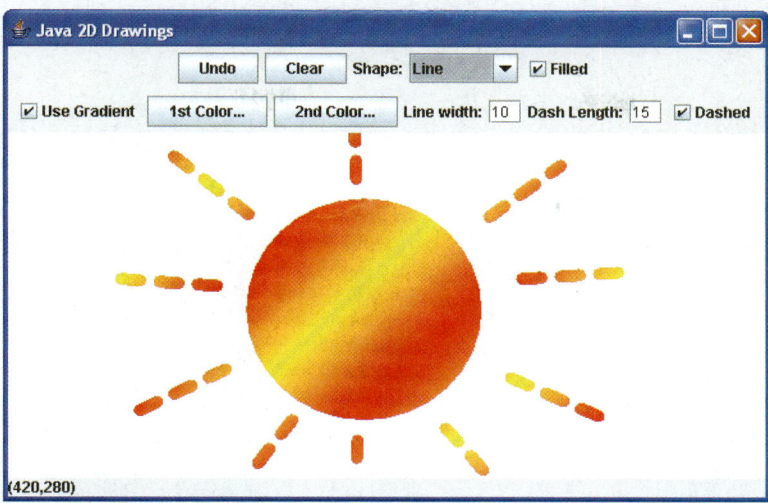

Fig. 12.34 | Drawing with Java2D.

If the user selects to draw with a gradient, set the `Paint` on the `DrawPanel` to be a gradient of the two colors chosen by the user. The expression

```
new GradientPaint( 0, 0, color1, 50, 50, color2, true ) )
```

creates a `GradientPaint` that cycles diagonally from the upper-left to the bottom-right every 50 pixels. Variables `color1` and `color2` represent the colors chosen by the user. If the user does not select to use a gradient, then simply set the `Paint` on the `DrawPanel` to be the first `Color` chosen by the user.

For strokes, if the user chooses a solid line, then create the `Stroke` with the expression

```
new BasicStroke( width, BasicStroke.CAP_ROUND, BasicStroke.JOIN_ROUND )
```

where variable `width` is the width specified by the user in the line-width text field. If the user chooses a dashed line, then create the `Stroke` with the expression

```
new BasicStroke( width, BasicStroke.CAP_ROUND, BasicStroke.JOIN_ROUND,
    10, dashes, 0 )
```

where `width` again is the width in the line-width field, and `dashes` is an array with one element whose value is the length specified in the dash-length field. The `Panel` and `Stroke` objects should be passed to the shape object's constructor when the shape is created in `DrawPanel`.

Exception
Handling

OBJECTIVES

In this chapter you will learn:

- How exception and error handling works.

- To use `try`, `throw` and `catch` to detect, indicate and handle exceptions, respectively.

- To use the `finally` block to release resources.

- How stack unwinding enables exceptions not caught in one scope to be caught in another scope.

- How stack traces help in debugging.

- How exceptions are arranged in an exception class hierarchy.

- To declare new exception classes.

- To create chained exceptions that maintain complete stack trace information.

13.1 Introduction

In this chapter, we introduce exception handling. An exception is an indication of a problem that occurs during a program's execution. The name "exception" implies that the problem occurs infrequently—if the "rule" is that a statement normally executes correctly, then the "exception to the rule" is that a problem occurs. Exception handling enables programmers to create applications that can resolve (or handle) exceptions. In many cases, handling an exception allows a program to continue executing as if no problem had been encountered. A more severe problem could prevent a program from continuing normal execution, instead requiring it to notify the user of the problem before terminating in a controlled manner. The features presented in this chapter enable programmers to write robust and fault-tolerant programs (i.e., programs that are able to deal with problems that may arise and continue executing). The style and details of Java exception handling are based in part on the Andrew Koenig's and Bjarne Stroustrup's paper, "Exception Handling for C++ (revised)."[1]

Error-Prevention Tip 13.1

Exception handling helps improve a program's fault tolerance.

You have already been briefly introduced to exceptions in earlier chapters. In Chapter 7 you learned that an `ArrayIndexOutOfBoundsException` occurs when an attempt is made to access an element past the end of an array. Such a problem may occur if there is an "off by one" error in a `for` statement that manipulates an array. In Chapter 10, we introduced the `ClassCastException`, which occurs when an attempt is made to cast an object that does not have an *is-a* relationship with the type specified in the cast operator. Chapter 11 briefly mentioned the `NullPointerException`, which occurs whenever a `null` reference is used where an object is expected (for example, when an attempt is made to attach a GUI component to

---

1. Koenig, A., and B. Stroustrup. "Exception Handling for C++ (revised)," *Proceedings of the Usenix C++ Conference*, pp. 149–176, San Francisco, April 1990.

a `Container`, but the GUI component has not yet been created). You have also used class `Scanner` throughout this text, which as you will see in this chapter also may cause exceptions.

The chapter begins with an overview of exception-handling concepts, then demonstrates basic exception-handling techniques. We show these techniques in action by handling an exception that occurs when a method attempts to divide an integer by zero. Next, we introduce several classes at the top of Java's class hierarchy for exception handling. As you will see, only classes that extend `Throwable` (package `java.lang`) directly or indirectly can be used with exception handling. We then discuss the chained exception feature that was introduced in J2SE 1.4. This feature allows programmers to wrap information about an exception that occurred in another exception object to provide more detailed information about a problem in a program. Next, we discuss additional exception-handling issues, such as how to handle exceptions that occur in a constructor. We introduce preconditions and postconditions, which users of the classes you create understand conditions that must be true when your methods are called and when those methods return. Finally, we present assertions, which programmers use at development time to help debug their code.

13.2 Exception-Handling Overview

Programs frequently test conditions to determine how program execution should proceed. Consider the following pseudocode:

> *Perform a task*
>
> *If the preceding task did not execute correctly*
> *Perform error processing*
>
> *Perform next task*
>
> *If the preceding task did not execute correctly*
> *Perform error processing*
>
> *...*

In this pseudocode, we begin by performing a task; then we test whether that task executed correctly. If not, we perform error processing. Otherwise, we continue with the next task. Although this form of error handling works, intermixing program logic with error-handling logic can make programs difficult to read, modify, maintain and debug—especially in large applications.

> **Performance Tip 13.1**
>
> *If the potential problems occur infrequently, intermixing program and error-handling logic can degrade a program's performance, because the program must perform (potentially frequent) tests to determine whether the task executed correctly and the next task can be performed.*

Exception handling enables programmers to remove error-handling code from the "main line" of the program's execution, improving program clarity and enhancing modifiability. Programmers can decide to handle any exceptions they choose—all exceptions, all exceptions of a certain type or all exceptions of a group of related types (i.e., exception types that are related through an inheritance hierarchy). Such flexibility reduces the likelihood that errors will be overlooked, thus making programs more robust.

With programming languages that do not support exception handling, programmers often delay writing error-processing code or sometimes forget to include it. This results in less robust software products. Java enables programmers to deal with exception handling easily from the inception of a project.

13.3 Example: Divide By Zero Without Exception Handling

First we demonstrate what happens when errors arise in an application that does not use exception handling. Figure 13.1 prompts the user for two integers and passes them to method quotient, which calculates the quotient and returns an int result. In this example, we will see that exceptions are **thrown** (i.e., the exception occurs) when a method detects a problem and is unable to handle it.

The first of the three sample executions in Fig. 13.1 shows a successful division. In the second sample execution, the user enters the value 0 as the denominator. Notice that several lines of information are displayed in response to this invalid input. This information is known as the **stack trace**, which includes the name of the exception (java.lang.ArithmeticException) in a descriptive message that indicates the problem that occurred and the complete method-call stack (i.e., the call chain) at the time the exception occurred. The stack trace includes the path of execution that led to the exception method by method. This information helps in debugging a program. The first line specifies that an ArithmeticException has occurred. The text after the name of the exception, "/ by zero", indicates that this exception occurred as a result of an attempt to divide by zero. Java does not allow division by zero in integer arithmetic. [*Note:* Java *does* allow division by zero with floating-point values. Such a calculation results in the value infinity, which is represented in Java as a floating-point value (but actually displays as the string Infinity).] When division by zero in integer arithmetic occurs, Java throws an **ArithmeticException**. ArithmeticExceptions can arise from a number of different problems in arithmetic, so the extra data ("/ by zero") gives us more information about this specific exception.

Starting from the last line of the stack trace, we see that the exception was detected in line 22 of method main. Each line of the stack trace contains the class name and method (DivideByZeroNoExceptionHandling.main) followed by the file name and line number (DivideByZeroNoExceptionHandling.java:22). Moving up the stack trace, we see that the exception occurs in line 10, in method quotient. The top row of the call chain indicates the **throw point**—the initial point at which the exception occurs. The throw point of this exception is in line 10 of method quotient.

In the third execution, the user enters the string "hello" as the denominator. Notice again that a stack trace is displayed. This informs us that an InputMismatchException has occurred (package java.util). Our prior examples that read numeric values from the user assumed that the user would input a proper integer value. However, users sometimes make mistakes and input noninteger values. An **InputMismatchException** occurs when Scanner method nextInt receives a string that does not represent a valid integer. Starting from the end of the stack trace, we see that the exception was detected in line 20 of method main. Moving up the stack trace, we see that the exception occurs in method nextInt. Notice that in place of the file name and line number, we are provided with the text Unknown Source. This means that the JVM does not have access to the source code for where the exception occurred.

Notice that in the sample executions of Fig. 13.1 when exceptions occur and stack traces are displayed, the program also exits. This does not always occur in Java—sometimes

```java
 1   // Fig. 13.1: DivideByZeroNoExceptionHandling.java
 2   // An application that attempts to divide by zero.
 3   import java.util.Scanner;
 4
 5   public class DivideByZeroNoExceptionHandling
 6   {
 7      // demonstrates throwing an exception when a divide-by-zero occurs
 8      public static int quotient( int numerator, int denominator )
 9      {
10         return numerator / denominator; // possible division by zero
11      } // end method quotient
12
13      public static void main( String args[] )
14      {
15         Scanner scanner = new Scanner( System.in ); // scanner for input
16
17         System.out.print( "Please enter an integer numerator: " );
18         int numerator = scanner.nextInt();
19         System.out.print( "Please enter an integer denominator: " );
20         int denominator = scanner.nextInt();
21
22         int result = quotient( numerator, denominator );
23         System.out.printf(
24            "\nResult: %d / %d = %d\n", numerator, denominator, result );
25      } // end main
26   } // end class DivideByZeroNoExceptionHandling
```

```
Please enter an integer numerator: 100
Please enter an integer denominator: 7

Result: 100 / 7 = 14
```

```
Please enter an integer numerator: 100
Please enter an integer denominator: 0
Exception in thread "main" java.lang.ArithmeticException: / by zero
        at DivideByZeroNoExceptionHandling.quotient(DivideByZeroNoException-
Handling.java:10)
        at DivideByZeroNoExceptionHandling.main(DivideByZeroNoExceptionHan-
dling.java:22)
```

```
Please enter an integer numerator: 100
Please enter an integer denominator: hello
Exception in thread "main" java.util.InputMismatchException
        at java.util.Scanner.throwFor(Unknown Source)
        at java.util.Scanner.next(Unknown Source)
        at java.util.Scanner.nextInt(Unknown Source)
        at java.util.Scanner.nextInt(Unknown Source)
        at DivideByZeroNoExceptionHandling.main(DivideByZeroNoExceptionHan-
dling.java:20)
```

Fig. 13.1 | Integer division without exception handling.

a program may continue even though an exception has occurred and a stack trace has been printed. In such cases, the application may produce unexpected results. The next section demonstrates how to handle these exceptions and keep the program running successfully.

In Fig. 13.1 both types of exceptions were detected in method `main`. In the next example, we will see how to handle these exceptions to enable the program to run to normal completion.

13.4 Example: Handling ArithmeticExceptions and InputMismatchExceptions

The application in Fig. 13.2, which is based on Fig. 13.1, uses exception handling to process any `ArithmeticExceptions` and `InputMistmatchExceptions` that might arise. The application still prompts the user for two integers and passes them to method `quotient`, which calculates the quotient and returns an `int` result. This version of the application uses exception handling so that if the user makes a mistake, the program catches and handles (i.e., deals with) the exception—in this case, allowing the user to try to enter the input again.

The first sample execution in Fig. 13.2 shows a successful execution that does not encounter any problems. In the second execution, the user enters a zero denominator and an `ArithmeticException` exception occurs. In the third execution, the user enters the string `"hello"` as the denominator, and an `InputMismatchException` occurs. For both exceptions, the user is informed of their mistake and asked to try again, then is prompted for two new integers. In each sample execution, the program runs successfully to completion.

```
1   // Fig. 13.2: DivideByZeroWithExceptionHandling.java
2   // An exception-handling example that checks for divide-by-zero.
3   import java.util.InputMismatchException;
4   import java.util.Scanner;
5
6   public class DivideByZeroWithExceptionHandling
7   {
8      // demonstrates throwing an exception when a divide-by-zero occurs
9      public static int quotient( int numerator, int denominator )
10        throws ArithmeticException
11     {
12        return numerator / denominator; // possible division by zero
13     } // end method quotient
14
15     public static void main( String args[] )
16     {
17        Scanner scanner = new Scanner( System.in ); // scanner for input
18        boolean continueLoop = true; // determines if more input is needed
19
20        do
21        {
22           try // read two numbers and calculate quotient
23           {
24              System.out.print( "Please enter an integer numerator: " );
25              int numerator = scanner.nextInt();
26              System.out.print( "Please enter an integer denominator: " );
```

Fig. 13.2 | Handling `ArithmeticExceptions` and `InputMismatchExceptions`. (Part 1 of 2.)

```
27              int denominator = scanner.nextInt();
28
29              int result = quotient( numerator, denominator );
30              System.out.printf( "\nResult: %d / %d = %d\n", numerator,
31                 denominator, result );
32              continueLoop = false; // input successful; end looping
33           } // end try
34           catch ( InputMismatchException inputMismatchException )
35           {
36              System.err.printf( "\nException: %s\n",
37                 inputMismatchException );
38              scanner.nextLine(); // discard input so user can try again
39              System.out.println(
40                 "You must enter integers. Please try again.\n" );
41           } // end catch
42           catch ( ArithmeticException arithmeticException )
43           {
44              System.err.printf( "\nException: %s\n", arithmeticException );
45              System.out.println(
46                 "Zero is an invalid denominator. Please try again.\n" );
47           } // end catch
48        } while ( continueLoop ); // end do...while
49     } // end main
50  } // end class DivideByZeroWithExceptionHandling
```

```
Please enter an integer numerator: 100
Please enter an integer denominator: 7

Result: 100 / 7 = 14
```

```
Please enter an integer numerator: 100
Please enter an integer denominator: 0

Exception: java.lang.ArithmeticException: / by zero
Zero is an invalid denominator. Please try again.

Please enter an integer numerator: 100
Please enter an integer denominator: 7

Result: 100 / 7 = 14
```

```
Please enter an integer numerator: 100
Please enter an integer denominator: hello

Exception: java.util.InputMismatchException
You must enter integers. Please try again.

Please enter an integer numerator: 100
Please enter an integer denominator: 7

Result: 100 / 7 = 14
```

Fig. 13.2 | Handling ArithmeticExceptions and InputMismatchExceptions. (Part 2 of 2.)

Class `InputMismatchException` is imported in line 3. Class `ArithmeticException` does not need to be imported because it is located in package `java.lang`. Method `main` (lines 15–49) creates a `Scanner` object at line 17. Line 18 creates the `boolean` variable continueLoop, which is true if the user has not yet entered valid input. Lines 20–48 contain a `do...while` statement that repeatedly asks users for input until a valid input is received.

Enclosing Code in a *try Block*

Lines 22–33 contain a **try block**, which encloses the code that might `throw` an exception and the code that should not execute if an exception occurs (i.e., if an exception occurs, the remaining code in the `try` block will be skipped). A `try` block consists of the keyword `try` followed by a block of code enclosed in curly braces ({}). [*Note:* The term "try block" sometimes refers only to the block of code that follows the `try` keyword (not including the `try` keyword itself). For simplicity, we use the term "try block" to refer to the block of code that follows the `try` keyword, as well as the `try` keyword.] The statements that read the integers from the keyboard (lines 25 and 27) each use method `nextInt` to read an `int` value. Method `nextInt` throws an `InputMismatchException` if the value read in is not a valid integer.

The division that can cause an `ArithmeticException` is not performed in the `try` block. Rather, the call to method `quotient` (line 29) invokes the code that attempts the division (line 12); the JVM throws an `ArithmeticException` object when the denominator is zero.

Software Engineering Observation 13.1

Exceptions may surface through explicitly mentioned code in a `try` block, through calls to other methods, through deeply nested method calls initiated by code in a `try` block or from the Java Virtual Machine as it executes Java bytecodes.

Catching Exceptions

The `try` block in this example is followed by two `catch` blocks—one that handles an InputMismatchException (lines 34–41) and one that handles an `ArithmeticException` (lines 42–47). A **catch block** (also called a **catch clause** or **exception handler**) catches (i.e., receives) and handles an exception. A `catch` block begins with the keyword `catch` and is followed by a parameter in parentheses (called the exception parameter, discussed shortly) and a block of code enclosed in curly braces. [*Note:* The term "catch clause" is sometimes used to refer to the keyword `catch` followed by a block of code, where the term "catch block" refers to only the block of code following the `catch` keyword, but not including it. For simplicity, we use the term "catch block" to refer to the block of code following the `catch` keyword, as well as the keyword itself.]

At least one `catch` block or a **finally block** (discussed in Section 13.7) must immediately follow the `try` block. Each `catch` block specifies in parentheses an **exception parameter** that identifies the exception type the handler can process. When an exception occurs in a `try` block, the `catch` block that executes is the one whose type matches the type of the exception that occurred (i.e., the type in the `catch` block matches the thrown exception type exactly or is a superclass of it). The exception parameter's name enables the `catch` block to interact with a caught exception object—e.g., to implicitly invoke the caught exception's `toString` method (as in lines 37 and 44), which displays basic information about the exception. Line 38 of the first `catch` block calls `Scanner` method `nextLine`.

Because an `InputMismatchException` occurred, the call to method `nextInt` never successfully read in the user's data—so we read that input with a call to method `nextLine`. We do not do anything with the input at this point, because we know that it is invalid. Each `catch` block displays an error message and asks the user to try again. After either `catch` block terminates, the user is prompted for input. We will soon take a deeper look at how this flow of control works in exception handling.

Common Programming Error 13.1

It is a syntax error to place code between a try block and its corresponding catch blocks.

Common Programming Error 13.2

Each catch block can have only a single parameter—specifying a comma-separated list of exception parameters is a syntax error.

Common Programming Error 13.3

It is a compilation error to catch the same type in two different catch blocks in a single try statement.

An **uncaught exception** is an exception that occurs for which there are no matching `catch` blocks. You saw uncaught exceptions in the second and third outputs of Fig. 13.1. Recall that when exceptions occurred in that example, the application terminated early (after displaying the exception's stack trace). This does not always occur as a result of uncaught exceptions. As you will learn in Chapter 23, Java uses a multithreaded model of program execution. Each **thread** is a parallel activity. One program can have many threads. If a program has only one thread, an uncaught exception will cause the program to terminate. If a program has multiple threads, an uncaught exception will terminate only the thread where the exception occurred. In such programs, however, certain threads may rely on others and if one thread terminates due to an uncaught exception, there may be adverse effects to the rest of the program.

Termination Model of Exception Handling

If an exception occurs in a `try` block (such as an `InputMismatchException` being thrown as a result of the code at line 25 of Fig. 13.2), the `try` block terminates immediately and program control transfers to the first of the following `catch` blocks in which the exception parameter's type matches the type of the thrown exception. In Fig. 13.2, the first `catch` block catches `InputMismatchExceptions` (which occur if invalid input is entered) and the second `catch` block catches `ArithmeticExceptions` (which occur if an attempt is made to divide by zero). After the exception is handled, program control does not return to the throw point because the `try` block has expired (which also causes any of its local variables to be lost). Rather control resumes after the last `catch` block. This is known as the **termination model of exception handling**. [*Note:* Some languages use the **resumption model of exception handling**, in which, after an exception is handled, control resumes just after the throw point.]

Common Programming Error 13.4

Logic errors can occur if you assume that after an exception is handled, control will return to the first statement after the throw point.

Error-Prevention Tip 13.2

With exception handling, a program can continue executing (rather than terminating) after dealing with a problem. This helps ensure the kind of robust applications that contribute to what is called mission-critical computing or business-critical computing.

Notice that we name our exception parameters (inputMismatchException and arithmeticException) based on their type. Java programmers often simply use the letter e as the name of their exception parameters.

Good Programming Practice 13.1

Using an exception parameter name that reflects the parameter's type promotes clarity by reminding the programmer of the type of exception being handled.

After executing a catch block, this program's flow of control proceeds to the first statement after the last catch block (line 48 in this case). The condition in the do...while statement is true (variable continueLoop contains its initial value of true), so control returns to the beginning of the loop and the user is once again prompted for input. This control statement will loop until valid input is entered. At that point, program control reaches line 32 which assigns false to variable continueLoop. The try block then terminates. If no exceptions are thrown in the try block, the catch blocks are skipped and control continues with the first statement after the catch blocks (or after the finally block, if one is present). Now the condition for the do...while loop is false, and method main ends.

The try block and its corresponding catch and/or finally blocks together form a **try statement**. It is important not to confuse the terms "try block" and "try statement"—the term "try block" refers to the keyword try followed by a block of code, while the term "try statement" includes the try block, as well as the following catch blocks and/or finally block.

As with any other block of code, when a try block terminates, local variables declared in the block go out of scope (and are destroyed). When a catch block terminates, local variables declared within the catch block (including the exception parameter of that catch block) also go out of scope and are destroyed. Any remaining catch blocks in the try statement are ignored and execution resumes at the first line of code after the try...catch sequence—this will be a finally block, if one is present.

*Using the **throws** Clause*

Now let us examine method quotient (lines 9–13). The portion of the method declaration located at line 10 is known as a **throws clause**. A throws clause specifies the exceptions the method throws. This clause appears after the method's parameter list and before the method's body. The clause contains a comma-separated list of the exceptions that the method will throw if a problem occurs. Such exceptions may be thrown by statements in the method's body or by methods called in the body. A method can throw exceptions of the classes listed in its throws clause or of their subclasses. We have added the throws clause to this application to indicate to the rest of the program that this method may throw an ArithmeticException. Clients of method quotient are thus informed that the method may throw an ArithmeticException and that the exception should be caught. You will learn more about the throws clause in Section 13.6.

Error-Prevention Tip 13.3

If you know that a method might throw an exception, include appropriate exception-handling code in your program to make it more robust.

Error-Prevention Tip 13.4

Read the online API documentation for a method before using that method in a program. The documentation specifies the exceptions thrown by the method (if any) and indicates reasons why such exceptions may occur. Then provide for handling those exceptions in your program.

Error-Prevention Tip 13.5

Read the online API documentation for an exception class before writing exception-handling code for that type of exception. The documentation for an exception class typically contains potential reasons that such exceptions occur during program execution.

When line 12 executes, if the `denominator` is zero, the JVM throws an `ArithmeticException` object. This object will be caught by the `catch` block at lines 42–47, which displays basic information about the exception by implicitly invoking the exception's `toString` method, then asks the user to try again.

If the `denominator` is not zero, method `quotient` performs the division and returns the result to the point of invocation of method `quotient` in the `try` block (line 29). Lines 30–31 display the result of the calculation and line 32 sets `continueLoop` to `false`. In this case, the `try` block completes successfully, so the program skips the `catch` blocks, fails the condition at line 48 and method `main` completes execution normally.

Note that when `quotient` throws an `ArithmeticException`, `quotient` terminates and does not return a value, and `quotient`'s local variables go out of scope (and the variables are destroyed). If `quotient` contained local variables that were references to objects and there are no other references to those object, would be marked for garbage collection. Also, when an exception occurs, the `try` block from which `quotient` was called terminates before lines 30–32 can execute. Here, too, if local variables were created in the `try` block prior to the exception being thrown, these variables would go out of scope.

If an `InputMismatchException` is generated by lines 25 or 27, the `try` block terminates and execution continues with the `catch` block at lines 34–41. In this case, method `quotient` is not called. Then method `main` continues after the last `catch` block (line 48).

13.5 When to Use Exception Handling

Exception handling is designed to process synchronous errors, which occur when a statement executes. Common examples we will see throughout the book are out-of-range array indices, arithmetic overflow (i.e., a value outside the representable range of values), division by zero, invalid method parameters, thread interruption and unsuccessful memory allocation (due to lack of memory). Exception handling is not designed to process problems associated with asynchronous events (e.g., disk I/O completions, network message arrivals, mouse clicks and keystrokes), which occur in parallel with, and independent of, the program's flow of control.

Software Engineering Observation 13.2

Incorporate your exception-handling strategy into your system from the design process's inception. Including effective exception handling after a system has been implemented can be difficult.

Software Engineering Observation 13.3

Exception handling provides a single, uniform technique for processing problems. This helps programmers working on large projects understand each other's error-processing code.

Software Engineering Observation 13.4

Avoid using exception handling as an alternate form of flow of control. These "additional" exceptions can "get in the way" of genuine error-type exceptions.

Software Engineering Observation 13.5

Exception handling simplifies combining software components and enables them to work together effectively by enabling predefined components to communicate problems to application-specific components, which can then process the problems in an application-specific manner.

13.6 Java Exception Hierarchy

All Java exception classes inherit, either directly or indirectly, from class `Exception`, forming an inheritance hierarchy. Programmers can extend this hierarchy to create their own exception classes.

Figure 13.3 shows a small portion of the inheritance hierarchy for class `Throwable` (a subclass of `Object`), which is the superclass of class `Exception`. Only `Throwable` objects can be used with the exception-handling mechanism. Class `Throwable` has two subclasses: `Exception` and `Error`. Class `Exception` and its subclasses—for instance, `RuntimeException` (package `java.lang`) and `IOException` (package `java.io`)—represent

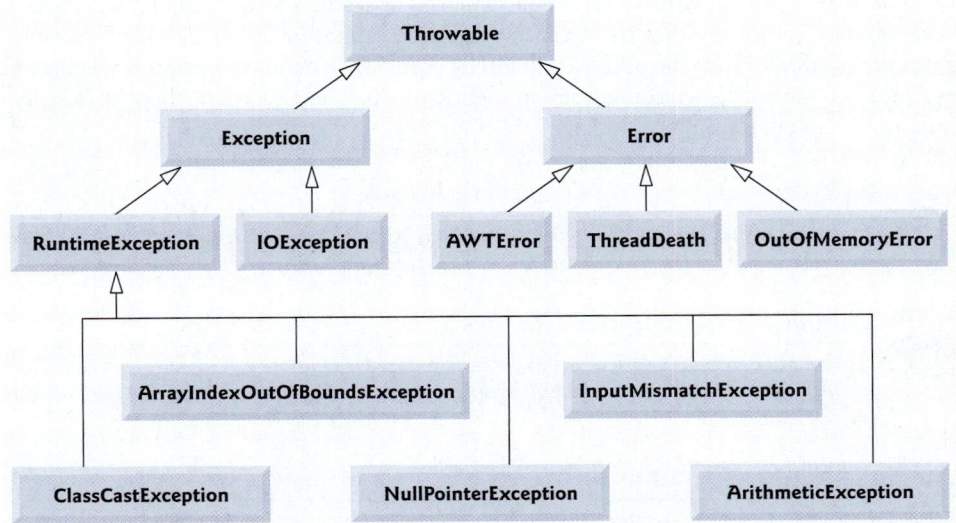

Fig. 13.3 | Portion of class `Throwable`'s inheritance hierarchy.

exceptional situations that can occur in a Java program and that can be caught by the application. Class `Error` and its subclasses (e.g., `OutOfMemoryError`) represent abnormal situations that could happen in the JVM. `Errors` happen infrequently and should not be caught by applications—it is usually not possible for applications to recover from `Errors`. [*Note:* The Java exception hierarchy is enormous, containing hundreds of classes. Information about Java's exception classes can be found throughout the Java API. The documentation for class `Throwable` can be found at `java.sun.com/j2se/5.0/docs/api/java/lang/Throwable.html`. From there, you can look at this class's subclasses to get more information about Java's `Exceptions` and `Errors`.]

Java distinguishes between two categories of exceptions: checked exceptions and unchecked exceptions. This distinction is important, because the Java compiler enforces a catch-or-declare requirement for checked exceptions. An exception's type determines whether the exception is checked or unchecked. All exception types that are direct or indirect subclasses of class `RuntimeException` (package `java.lang`) are unchecked exceptions. This includes exceptions you have seen already, such as `ArrayIndexOutOfBoundsExceptions` and `ArithmeticExceptions` (shown in Fig. 13.3). All classes that inherit from class `Exception` but not class `RuntimeException` are considered to be checked exceptions. Classes that inherit from class `Error` are considered to be unchecked. The compiler *checks* each method call and method declaration to determine whether the method throws checked exceptions. If so, the compiler ensures that the checked exception is caught or is declared in a `throws` clause. Recall from Section 13.4 that the `throws` clause specifies the exceptions a method throws. Such exceptions are not caught in the method's body. To satisfy the *catch* part of the catch-or-declare requirement, the code that generates the exception must be wrapped in a `try` block and must provide a `catch` handler for the checked-exception type (or one of its superclass types). To satisfy the *declare* part of the catch-or-declare requirement, the method containing the code that generates the exception must provide a `throws` clause containing the checked-exception type after its parameter list and before its method body. If the catch-or-declare requirement is not satisfied, the compiler will issue an error message indicating that the exception must be caught or declared. This forces programmers to think about the problems that may occur when a method that throws checked exceptions is called. Exception classes are defined to be checked when they are consider important enough to catch or declare.

Software Engineering Observation 13.6

Programmers are forced to deal with checked exceptions. This results in more robust code than would be created if programmers were able to simply ignore the exceptions.

Common Programming Error 13.5

A compilation error occurs if a method explicitly attempts to throw a checked exception (or calls another method that throws a checked exception) and that exception is not listed in that method's throws *clause.*

Common Programming Error 13.6

If a subclass method overrides a superclass method, it is an error for the subclass method to list more exceptions in its throws *clause than the overridden superclass method does. However, a subclass's* throws *clause can contain a subset of a superclass's* throws *list.*

Software Engineering Observation 13.7

If your method calls other methods that explicitly throw checked exceptions, those exceptions must be caught or declared in your method. If an exception can be handled meaningfully in a method, the method should catch the exception rather than declare it.

Unlike checked exceptions, the Java compiler does not check the code to determine whether an unchecked exception is caught or declared. Unchecked exceptions typically can be prevented by proper coding. For example, the unchecked `ArithmeticException` thrown by method `quotient` (lines 9–13) in Fig. 13.2 can be avoided if the method ensures that the denominator is not zero before attempting to perform the division. Unchecked exceptions are not required to be listed in a method's `throws` clause—even if they are, it is not required that such exceptions be caught by an application.

Software Engineering Observation 13.8

Although the compiler does not enforce the catch-or-declare requirement for unchecked exceptions, provide appropriate exception-handling code when it is known that such exceptions might occur. For example, a program should process the `NumberFormatException` from `Integer` method `parseInt`, even though `NumberFormatException` (a subclass of `RuntimeException`) is an unchecked exception type. This makes your programs more robust.

Various exception classes can be derived from a common superclass. If a `catch` handler is written to catch exception objects of a superclass type, it can also catch all objects of that class's subclasses. This enables a `catch` block to handle related errors with a concise notation and allows for polymorphic processing of related exceptions. One could certainly catch each subclass type individually if those exceptions required different processing. Of course, catching related exceptions in one `catch` block makes sense only if the handling behavior is the same for all subclasses.

If there are multiple `catch` blocks that match a particular exception type, only the first matching `catch` block executes when an exception of that type occurs. We stated earlier that it is a compilation error to catch the same type in two different `catch` blocks associated with a particular `try` block. This occurs when both types are *exactly* the same. However, there may be several `catch` blocks that match an exception—i.e., several `catch` blocks whose types are the same as the exception type or a superclass of that type. For instance, we could follow a `catch` block for type `ArithmeticException` with a `catch` block for type `Exception`—both would match `ArithmeticExceptions`, but only the first matching `catch` block would execute.

Error-Prevention Tip 13.6

Catching subclass types individually is subject to error if you forget to test for one or more of the subclass types explicitly; catching the superclass guarantees that objects of all subclasses will be caught. Positioning a `catch` block for the superclass type after all other subclass `catch` blocks for subclasses of that superclass ensures that all subclass exceptions are eventually caught.

Common Programming Error 13.7

Placing a `catch` block for a superclass exception type before other `catch` blocks that catch subclass exception types prevents those blocks from executing, so a compilation error occurs.

13.7 `finally` block

Programs that obtain certain types of resources must return them to the system explicitly to avoid so-called resource leaks. In programming languages such as C and C++, the most common kind of resource leak is a memory leak. Java performs automatic garbage collection of memory no longer used by programs, thus avoiding most memory leaks. However, other types of resource leaks can occur. For example, files, database connections and network connections that are not closed properly might not be available for use in other programs.

Error-Prevention Tip 13.7

A subtle issue is that Java does not entirely eliminate memory leaks. Java will not garbage collect an object until there are no more references to it. Thus, memory leaks can occur, if programmers erroneously keep references to unwanted objects.

The `finally` block (which consists of the `finally` keyword, followed by code enclosed in curly braces) is optional, and is sometimes referred to as the **`finally` clause**. If it is present, it is placed after the last `catch` block, as in Fig. 13.4:

Java guarantees that a `finally` block (if one is present in a `try` statement) will execute whether or not an exception is thrown in the corresponding `try` block or any of its corresponding `catch` blocks. Java also guarantees that a `finally` block (if one is present) will execute if a `try` block exits by using a `return`, `break` or `continue` statement. The `finally` block will *not* execute if the application exits early from a `try` block by calling method `System.exit`. This method, which we demonstrate in the next chapter, immediately terminates an application.

Because a `finally` block almost always executes, it typically contains resource-release code. Suppose a resource is allocated in a `try` block. If no exception occurs, the `catch` blocks

```
try
{
    statements
    resource-acquisition statements
} // end try
catch ( AKindOfException exception1 )
{
    exception-handling statements
} // end catch
   .
   .
   .
catch ( AnotherKindOfException exception2 )
{
    exception-handling statements
} // end catch
finally
{
    statements
    resource-release statements
} // end finally
```

Fig. 13.4 | Position of the `finally` block after the last `catch` block in a `try` statement.

are skipped and control proceeds to the finally block, which frees the resource. Control then proceeds to the first statement after the finally block. If an exception does occur in the try block, the program skips the rest of the try block. If the program catches the exception in one of the catch blocks, the program processes the exception, then the finally block releases the resource and control proceeds to the first statement after the finally block.

Performance Tip 13.2

Always release each resource explicitly and at the earliest possible moment at which the resource is no longer needed. This makes resources immediately available to be reused by your program or by other programs, thus improving resource utilization. Because the finally block is guaranteed to execute whether or not an exception occurs in the corresponding try block, this block is an ideal place to release resources acquired in a try block.

Error-Prevention Tip 13.8

A finally block typically contains code to release resources acquired in its corresponding try block; this is an effective way to eliminate resource leaks. For example, the finally block should close any files opened in the try block.

If an exception that occurs in a try block cannot be caught by one of that try block's catch handlers, the program skips the rest of the try block and control proceeds to the finally block. Then the program passes the exception to the next outer try block—normally in the calling method—where an associated catch block might catch it. This process can occur through many levels of try blocks.

If a catch block throws an exception, the finally block still executes. Then the exception is passed to the next outer try block—again, normally in the calling method.

The Java application of Fig. 13.5 demonstrates that the finally block executes even if an exception is not thrown in the corresponding try block. The program contains static methods main (lines 7–19), throwException (lines 22–45) and doesNotThrowException (lines 48–65). Methods throwException and doesNotThrowException are declared static, so main can call them directly.

```java
1   // Fig. 13.5: UsingExceptions.java
2   // Demonstration of the try...catch...finally exception handling
3   // mechanism.
4
5   public class UsingExceptions
6   {
7      public static void main( String args[] )
8      {
9         try
10        {
11           throwException(); // call method throwException
12        } // end try
13        catch ( Exception exception ) // exception thrown by throwException
14        {
15           System.err.println( "Exception handled in main" );
16        } // end catch
```

Fig. 13.5 | try...catch...finally exception-handling mechanism. (Part 1 of 3.)

```
17
18          doesNotThrowException();
19      } // end main
20
21      // demonstrate try...catch...finally
22      public static void throwException() throws Exception
23      {
24          try // throw an exception and immediately catch it
25          {
26              System.out.println( "Method throwException" );
27              throw new Exception(); // generate exception
28          } // end try
29          catch ( Exception exception ) // catch exception thrown in try
30          {
31              System.err.println(
32                  "Exception handled in method throwException" );
33              throw exception; // rethrow for further processing
34
35              // any code here would not be reached
36
37          } // end catch
38          finally // executes regardless of what occurs in try...catch
39          {
40              System.err.println( "Finally executed in throwException" );
41          } // end finally
42
43          // any code here would not be reached, exception rethrown in catch
44
45      } // end method throwException
46
47      // demonstrate finally when no exception occurs
48      public static void doesNotThrowException()
49      {
50          try // try block does not throw an exception
51          {
52              System.out.println( "Method doesNotThrowException" );
53          } // end try
54          catch ( Exception exception ) // does not execute
55          {
56              System.err.println( exception );
57          } // end catch
58          finally // executes regardless of what occurs in try...catch
59          {
60              System.err.println(
61                  "Finally executed in doesNotThrowException" );
62          } // end finally
63
64          System.out.println( "End of method doesNotThrowException" );
65      } // end method doesNotThrowException
66  } // end class UsingExceptions
```

Fig. 13.5 | try...catch...finally exception-handling mechanism. (Part 2 of 3.)

```
Method throwException
Exception handled in method throwException
Finally executed in throwException
Exception handled in main
Method doesNotThrowException
Finally executed in doesNotThrowException
End of method doesNotThrowException
```

Fig. 13.5 | try...catch...finally exception-handling mechanism. (Part 3 of 3.)

Before we discuss the flow of control for this example, we would like to point out the use of the System.err to output data (lines 15, 31–32, 40, 56 and 60–61). By default, System.err.println, like System.out.println, displays data to the command prompt.

Both System.out and System.err are streams—a sequence of bytes. While System.out (known as the **standard output stream**) is used to display a program's output, System.err (known as the **standard error stream**) is used to display a program's errors. Output from these streams can be redirected (i.e., sent somewhere other than the command prompt such as a file). Using two different streams enables the programmer to easily separate error messages from other output. For instance, data output from System.err could be sent to a log file, while data output from System.out can be displayed on the screen. For simplicity, this chapter will not redirect output from System.err, but will display such messages to the command prompt. You will learn more about streams in Chapter 14, Files and Streams.

Throwing Exceptions Using the throw *Statement*
Method main (Fig. 13.5) begins executing, enters its try block and immediately calls method throwException (line 11). Method throwException throws an Exception (line 27), catches it (line 29) and rethrows it (line 33). The statement at line 27 is known as a **throw statement**. The throw statement is executed to indicate that an exception has occurred. So far, you have only caught exceptions thrown by called methods. Programmers can throw exceptions by using the throw statement. Just as with exceptions thrown by the Java API's methods, this indicates to client applications that an error has occurred. A throw statement specifies an object to be thrown. The operand of a throw can be of any class derived from class Throwable.

Software Engineering Observation 13.9

When toString is invoked on any Throwable object, its resulting string includes the descriptive string that was supplied to the constructor, or simply the class name if no string was supplied.

Software Engineering Observation 13.10

An object can be thrown without containing information about the problem that occurred. In this case, simple knowledge that an exception of a particular type occurred may provide sufficient information for the handler to process the problem correctly.

Software Engineering Observation 13.11

Exceptions can be thrown from constructors. When an error is detected in a constructor, an exception should be thrown rather than creating an improperly formed object.

Rethrowing Exceptions

Line 33 of Fig. 13.5 rethrows the exception. Exceptions are rethrown when a `catch` block, upon receiving an exception, decides either that it cannot process that exception or that it can only partially process it. Rethrowing an exception defers the exception handling (or perhaps a portion of it) to another `catch` block associated with an outer `try` statement. An exception is rethrown by using the **throw keyword**, followed by a reference to the exception object that was just caught. Note that exceptions cannot be rethrown from a `finally` block, as the exception parameter from the `catch` block has expired.

When a rethrow occurs, the next enclosing `try` block detects the rethrown exception, and that `try` block's `catch` blocks attempt to handle the exception. In this case, the next enclosing `try` block is found at lines 9–12 in method `main`. Before the rethrown exception is handled, however, the `finally` block (lines 38–41) executes. Then method `main` detects the rethrown exception in the `try` block and handles it in the `catch` block (lines 13–16).

Next, `main` calls method `doesNotThrowException` (line 18). No exception is thrown in `doesNotThrowException`'s `try` block (lines 50–53), so the program skips the `catch` block (lines 54–57), but the `finally` block (lines 58–62) nevertheless executes. Control proceeds to the statement after the `finally` block (line 64). Then control returns to `main` and the program terminates.

Common Programming Error 13.8

If an exception has not been caught when control enters a `finally` block and the `finally` block throws an exception that is not caught in the `finally` block, the first exception will be lost and the exception from the `finally` block will be returned to the calling method.

Error-Prevention Tip 13.9

Avoid placing code that can `throw` an exception in a `finally` block. If such code is required, enclose the code in a `try...catch` within the `finally` block.

Common Programming Error 13.9

Assuming that an exception thrown from a `catch` block will be processed by that `catch` block or any other `catch` block associated with the same `try` statement can lead to logic errors.

Good Programming Practice 13.2

Java's exception-handling mechanism is intended to remove error-processing code from the main line of a program's code to improve program clarity. Do not place `try...catch...finally` around every statement that may throw an exception. This makes programs difficult to read. Rather, place one `try` block around a significant portion of your code, follow that `try` block with `catch` blocks that handle each possible exception and follow the `catch` blocks with a single `finally` block (if one is required).

13.8 Stack Unwinding

When an exception is thrown but not caught in a particular scope, the method-call stack is "unwound," and an attempt is made to `catch` the exception in the next outer `try` block. This process is called stack unwinding. Unwinding the method-call stack means that the method in which the exception was not caught terminates, all local variables in that method go out of scope and control returns to the statement that originally invoked that method. If a try block encloses that statement, an attempt is made to catch the exception. If a try block does not enclose that statement, stack unwinding occurs again. If no catch block ever catches this exception and the exception is checked (as in the following example), compiling the program will result in an error. The program of Fig. 13.6 demonstrates stack unwinding.

When method main executes, line 10 in the try block calls method throwException (lines 19–35). In the try block of method throwException (lines 21–25), line 24 throws an Exception. This terminates the try block immediately, and control skips the catch block at line 26, because the type being caught (RuntimeException) is not an exact match

```java
1   // Fig. 13.6: UsingExceptions.java
2   // Demonstration of stack unwinding.
3
4   public class UsingExceptions
5   {
6      public static void main( String args[] )
7      {
8         try // call throwException to demonstrate stack unwinding
9         {
10            throwException();
11         } // end try
12         catch ( Exception exception ) // exception thrown in throwException
13         {
14            System.err.println( "Exception handled in main" );
15         } // end catch
16      } // end main
17
18      // throwException throws exception that is not caught in this method
19      public static void throwException() throws Exception
20      {
21         try // throw an exception and catch it in main
22         {
23            System.out.println( "Method throwException" );
24            throw new Exception(); // generate exception
25         } // end try
26         catch ( RuntimeException runtimeException ) // catch incorrect type
27         {
28            System.err.println(
29               "Exception handled in method throwException" );
30         } // end catch
31         finally // finally block always executes
32         {
33            System.err.println( "Finally is always executed" );
34         } // end finally
35      } // end method throwException
36   } // end class UsingExceptions
```

```
Method throwException
Finally is always executed
Exception handled in main
```

Fig. 13.6 | Stack unwinding.

with the thrown type (Exception) and is not a superclass of it. Method throwException terminates (but not until its finally block executes) and returns control to line 10—the point from which it was called in the program. Line 10 is in an enclosing try block. The exception has not yet been handled, so the try block terminates and an attempt is made to catch the exception at line 12. The type being caught (Exception) does match the thrown type. Consequently, the catch block processes the exception, and the program terminates at the end of main. If there were no matching catch blocks, a compilation error would occur. Remember that this is not always the case—for unchecked exceptions, the application will compile, but run with unexpected results.

13.9 printStackTrace, getStackTrace and getMessage

Recall from Section 13.6 that exceptions derive from class Throwable. Class Throwable offers a **printStackTrace** method that outputs to the standard error stream the stack trace (discussed in Section 13.3). Often, this is helpful in testing and debugging. Class Throwable also provides a **getStackTrace** method that retrieves stack-trace information that might be printed by printStackTrace. Class Throwable's **getMessage** method returns the descriptive string stored in an exception. The example in this section demonstrates these three methods.

Error-Prevention Tip 13.10

An exception that is not caught in an application causes Java's default exception handler to run. This displays the name of the exception, a descriptive message that indicates the problem that occurred and a complete execution stack trace.

Error-Prevention Tip 13.11

Throwable method toString (inherited by all Throwable subclasses) returns a string containing the name of the exception's class and a descriptive message.

Figure 13.7 demonstrates getMessage, printStackTrace and getStackTrace. If we wanted to output the stack-trace information to streams other than the standard error stream, we could use the information returned from getStackTrace, and output this data to another stream. You will learn about sending data to other streams in Chapter 14, Files and Streams.

In main, the try block (lines 8–11) calls method1 (declared at lines 35–38). Next, method1 calls method2 (declared at lines 41–44), which in turn calls method3 (declared at lines 47–50). Line 49 of method3 throws an Exception object—this is the throw point. Because throw statement at line 49 is not enclosed in a try block, stack unwinding occurs—method3 terminates at line 49, then returns control to the statement in method2 that invoked method3 (i.e., line 43). Because no try block encloses line 43, stack unwinding occurs again—method2 terminates at line 43 and returns control to the statement in method1 that invoked method2 (i.e., line 37). Because no try block encloses line 37, stack unwinding occurs one more time—method1 terminates at line 37 and returns control to the statement in main that invoked method1 (i.e., line 10). The try block at lines 8–11 encloses this statement. The exception has not been handled, so the try block terminates and the first matching catch block (lines 12–31) catches and processes the exception.

```java
1   // Fig. 13.7: UsingExceptions.java
2   // Demonstrating getMessage and printStackTrace from class Exception.
3
4   public class UsingExceptions
5   {
6      public static void main( String args[] )
7      {
8         try
9         {
10           method1(); // call method1
11        } // end try
12        catch ( Exception exception ) // catch exception thrown in method1
13        {
14           System.err.printf( "%s\n\n", exception.getMessage() );
15           exception.printStackTrace(); // print exception stack trace
16
17           // obtain the stack-trace information
18           StackTraceElement[] traceElements = exception.getStackTrace();
19
20           System.out.println( "\nStack trace from getStackTrace:" );
21           System.out.println( "Class\t\tFile\t\t\tLine\tMethod" );
22
23           // loop through traceElements to get exception description
24           for ( StackTraceElement element : traceElements )
25           {
26              System.out.printf( "%s\t", element.getClassName() );
27              System.out.printf( "%s\t", element.getFileName() );
28              System.out.printf( "%s\t", element.getLineNumber() );
29              System.out.printf( "%s\n", element.getMethodName() );
30           } // end for
31        } // end catch
32     } // end main
33
34     // call method2; throw exceptions back to main
35     public static void method1() throws Exception
36     {
37        method2();
38     } // end method method1
39
40     // call method3; throw exceptions back to method1
41     public static void method2() throws Exception
42     {
43        method3();
44     } // end method method2
45
46     // throw Exception back to method2
47     public static void method3() throws Exception
48     {
49        throw new Exception( "Exception thrown in method3" );
50     } // end method method3
51  } // end class UsingExceptions
```

Fig. 13.7 | Throwable methods getMessage, getStackTrace and printStackTrace. (Part 1 of 2.)

```
Exception thrown in method3

java.lang.Exception: Exception thrown in method3
        at UsingExceptions.method3(UsingExceptions.java:49)
        at UsingExceptions.method2(UsingExceptions.java:43)
        at UsingExceptions.method1(UsingExceptions.java:37)
        at UsingExceptions.main(UsingExceptions.java:10)

Stack trace from getStackTrace:
Class            File                   Line    Method
UsingExceptions  UsingExceptions.java    49     method3
UsingExceptions  UsingExceptions.java    43     method2
UsingExceptions  UsingExceptions.java    37     method1
UsingExceptions  UsingExceptions.java    10     main
```

Fig. 13.7 | `Throwable` methods `getMessage`, `getStackTrace` and `printStackTrace`. (Part 2 of 2.)

Line 14 invokes the exception's `getMessage` method to get the exception description. Line 15 invokes the exception's `printStackTrace` method to output the stack trace that indicates where the exception occurred. Line 18 invokes the exception's `getStackTrace` method to obtain the stack-trace information as an array of **StackTraceElement** objects. Lines 24–30 get each `StackTraceElement` in the array and invoke its methods **getClassName**, **getFileName**, **getLineNumber** and **getMethodName** to get the class name, file name, line number and method name, respectively, for that `StackTraceElement`. Each `StackTraceElement` represents one method call on the method-call stack.

The output in Fig. 13.7 shows that the stack-trace information printed by `printStackTrace` follows the pattern: *className.methodName(fileName:lineNumber)*, where *className*, *methodName* and *fileName* indicate the names of the class, method and file in which the exception occurred, respectively, and the *lineNumber* indicates where in the file the exception occurred. You saw this in the output for Fig. 13.1. Method `getStackTrace` enables custom processing of the exception information. Compare the output of `printStackTrace` with the output created from the `StackTraceElement`s to see that both contain the same stack-trace information.

Software Engineering Observation 13.12

Never ignore an exception you catch. At least use `printStackTrace` to output an error message. This will inform users that a problem exists, so that they can take appropriate actions.

13.10 Chained Exceptions

Sometimes a `catch` block catches one exception type, then throws a new exception of a different type to indicate that a program-specific exception occurred. In earlier Java versions, there was no mechanism to wrap the original exception information with the new exception's information to provide a complete stack trace showing where the original problem occurred in the program. This made debugging such problems particularly difficult. J2SE 1.4 added chained exceptions to enable an exception object to maintain the complete stack-trace information. Figure 13.8 presents a mechanical example that demonstrates how chained exceptions work.

```
1   // Fig. 13.8: UsingChainedExceptions.java
2   // Demonstrating chained exceptions.
3
4   public class UsingChainedExceptions
5   {
6      public static void main( String args[] )
7      {
8         try
9         {
10           method1(); // call method1
11        } // end try
12        catch ( Exception exception ) // exceptions thrown from method1
13        {
14           exception.printStackTrace();
15        } // end catch
16     } // end main
17
18     // call method2; throw exceptions back to main
19     public static void method1() throws Exception
20     {
21        try
22        {
23           method2(); // call method2
24        } // end try
25        catch ( Exception exception ) // exception thrown from method2
26        {
27           throw new Exception( "Exception thrown in method1", exception );
28        } // end try
29     } // end method method1
30
31     // call method3; throw exceptions back to method1
32     public static void method2() throws Exception
33     {
34        try
35        {
36           method3(); // call method3
37        } // end try
38        catch ( Exception exception ) // exception thrown from method3
39        {
40           throw new Exception( "Exception thrown in method2", exception );
41        } // end catch
42     } // end method method2
43
44     // throw Exception back to method2
45     public static void method3() throws Exception
46     {
47        throw new Exception( "Exception thrown in method3" );
48     } // end method method3
49  } // end class UsingChainedExceptions
```

Fig. 13.8 | Chained exceptions. (Part 1 of 2.)

```
java.lang.Exception: Exception thrown in method1
        at UsingChainedExceptions.method1(UsingChainedExceptions.java:27)
        at UsingChainedExceptions.main(UsingChainedExceptions.java:10)
Caused by: java.lang.Exception: Exception thrown in method2
        at UsingChainedExceptions.method2(UsingChainedExceptions.java:40)
        at UsingChainedExceptions.method1(UsingChainedExceptions.java:23)
        ... 1 more
Caused by: java.lang.Exception: Exception thrown in method3
        at UsingChainedExceptions.method3(UsingChainedExceptions.java:47)
        at UsingChainedExceptions.method2(UsingChainedExceptions.java:36)
        ... 2 more
```

Fig. 13.8 | Chained exceptions. (Part 2 of 2.)

The program consists of four methods—main (lines 6–16), method1 (lines 19–29), method2 (lines 32–42) and method3 (lines 45–48). Line 10 in method main's try block calls method1. Line 23 in method1's try block calls method2. Line 36 in method2's try block calls method3. In method3, line 47 throws a new Exception. Because this statement is not in a try block, method3 terminates, and the exception is returned to the calling method (method2) at line 36. This statement *is* in a try block; therefore, the try block terminates and the exception is caught at lines 38–41. Line 40 in the catch block throws a new exception. In this case, the Exception constructor with two arguments is called. The second argument represents the exception that was the original cause of the problem. In this program, that exception occurred at line 47. Because an exception is thrown from the catch block, method2 terminates and returns the new exception to the calling method (method1) at line 23. Once again, this statement is in a try block, so the try block terminates and the exception is caught at lines 25–28. Line 27 in the catch block throws a new exception and uses the exception that was caught as the second argument to the Exception constructor. Because an exception is thrown from the catch block, method1 terminates and returns the new exception to the calling method (main) at line 10. The try block in main terminates, and the exception is caught at lines 12–15. Line 14 prints a stack trace.

Notice in the program output that the first three lines show the most recent exception that was thrown (i.e., the one from method1 at line 23). The next four lines indicate the exception that was thrown from method2 at line 40. Finally, the last four lines represent the exception that was thrown from method3 at line 47. Also notice that, as you read the output in reverse, it shows how many more chained exceptions remain.

13.11 Declaring New Exception Types

Most Java programmers use existing classes from the Java API, third-party vendors and freely available class libraries (usually downloadable from the Internet) to build Java applications. The methods of those classes typically are declared to throw appropriate exceptions when problems occur. Programmers write code that processes these existing exceptions to make programs more robust.

If you are a programmer who builds classes that other programmers will use in their programs, you might find it useful to declare your own exception classes that are specific to the problems that can occur when another programmer uses your reusable classes.

Software Engineering Observation 13.13

If possible, indicate exceptions from your methods by using existing exception classes, rather than creating new exception classes. The Java API contains many exception classes that might be suitable for the type of problem your method needs to indicate.

A new exception class must extend an existing exception class to ensure that the class can be used with the exception-handling mechanism. Like any other class, an exception class can contains fields and methods. However, a typical new exception class contains only two constructors—one that takes no arguments and passes a default exception message to the superclass constructor, and one that receives a customized exception message as a string and passes it to the superclass constructor.

Good Programming Practice 13.3

Associating each type of serious execution-time malfunction with an appropriately named Exception class improves program clarity.

Software Engineering Observation 13.14

When defining your own exception type, study the existing exception classes in the Java API and try to extend a related exception class. For example, if you are creating a new class to represent when a method attempts a division by zero, you might extend class ArithmeticException because division by zero occurs during arithmetic. If the existing classes are not appropriate superclasses for your new exception class, decide whether your new class should be a checked or an unchecked exception class. The new exception class should be a checked exception (i.e., extend Exception but not RuntimeException) if possible clients should be required to handle the exception. The client application should be able to reasonably recover from such an exception. The new exception class should extend RuntimeException if the client code should be able to ignore the exception (i.e., the exception is an unchecked exception).

In Chapter 17, Data Structures, we provide an example of a custom exception class. We declare a reusable class called List that is capable of storing a list of references to objects. Some operations typically performed on a List are not allowed if the List is empty, such as removing an item from the front or back of the list (i.e., no items can be removed, as the List does not currently contain any items). For this reason, some List methods throw exceptions of exception class EmptyListException.

Good Programming Practice 13.4

By convention, all exception-class names should end with the word Exception.

13.12 Preconditions and Postconditions

Programmers spends significant portions of their time on code maintenance and debugging. To facilitate these tasks and to improve the overall design, programmers generally specify the expected states before and after a method's execution. These states are called preconditions and postconditions, respectively.

A method's **precondition** is a condition that must be true when the method is invoked. Preconditions describe method parameters and any other expectations the method has about the current state of a program. If a user fails to meet the preconditions, then the method's behavior is undefined—it may throw an exception, proceed with an illegal value or attempt to recover from the error. However, you should never rely on or expect consistent behavior if the preconditions are not satisfied.

A method's **postcondition** of a method is a condition that is true after the method successfully returns. Postconditions describe the return value and any other side-effects the method may have. When calling a method, you may assume that a method fulfills all of its postconditions. If you are writing your own method, you should document all postconditions so others know what to expect when they call the method.

As an example, examine `String` method `charAt`, which has one `int` parameter—an index in the `String`. For a precondition, method `charAt` assumes that `index` is greater than or equal to zero and less than the length of the `String`. If the precondition is met, the postcondition states the method will return the character at the position in the `String` specified by the parameter `index`. Otherwise, the method throws an `IndexOutOfBoundsException`. We trust that method `charAt` satisfies its postcondition, provided that we meet the precondition. We do not need to be concerned with the details of how the method actually retrieves the character at the index. This allows the programmer to focus more on the overall design of the program rather than on the implementation details.

Some programmers state the preconditions and postconditions informally as part of the general method specification, while others prefer a more formal approach by explicitly defining them. When designing your own methods, you should state the preconditions and postconditions in a comment before the method declaration in whichever manner you prefer. Stating the preconditions and postconditions before writing a method will also help guide you as you implement the method.

13.13 Assertions

When implementing and debugging a class, it is sometimes useful to state conditions that should be true at a particular point in a method. These conditions, called **assertions**, help ensure a program's validity by catching potential bugs and identifying possible logic errors during development. Preconditions and postconditions are two types of assertions. Preconditions are assertions about a program's state when a method is invoked, and postconditions are assertions about a program's state after a method finishes.

While assertions can be stated as comments to guide the programmer during development, Java includes two versions of the **assert** statement for validating assertions programatically. The `assert` statement evaluates a `boolean` expression and determines whether it is true or false. The first form of the `assert` statement is

```
assert expression;
```

This statement evaluates *expression* and throws an `AssertionError` if the expression is `false`. The second form is

```
assert expression1 : expression2;
```

This statement evaluates *expression1* and throws an `AssertionError` with *expression2* as the error message if *expression1* is `false`.

You can use assertions to programmatically implement preconditions and postconditions or to verify any other intermediate states that help you ensure your code is working correctly. The example in Fig. 13.9 demonstrates the functionality of the `assert` state-

```
 1  // Fig. 13.9: AssertTest.java
 2  // Demonstrates the assert statement
 3  import java.util.Scanner;
 4
 5  public class AssertTest
 6  {
 7     public static void main( String args[] )
 8     {
 9        Scanner input = new Scanner( System.in );
10
11        System.out.print( "Enter a number between 0 and 10: " );
12        int number = input.nextInt();
13
14        // assert that the absolute value is >= 0
15        assert ( number >= 0 && number <= 10 ) : "bad number: " + number;
16
17        System.out.printf( "You entered %d\n", number );
18     } // end main
19  } // end class AssertTest
```

```
Enter a number between 0 and 10: 5
You entered 5
```

```
Enter a number between 0 and 10: 50
Exception in thread "main" java.lang.AssertionError: bad number: 50
        at AssertTest.main(AssertTest.java:15)
```

Fig. 13.9 | Checking with `assert` that a value is within range.

ment. Line 11 prompts the user to enter a number between 0 and 10, then line 12 reads the number from the command line. The `assert` statement on line 15 determines whether the user entered a number within the valid range. If the user entered a number that is out of range, then the program reports an error. Otherwise, the program proceeds normally.

Assertions are primarily used by the programmer for debugging and identifying logic errors in a application. By default, assertions are disabled when executing a program because they reduce performance and are unnecessary for the program's user. To enable assertions at runtime, use the `-ea` command-line option when to the `java` command. To execute the program in Fig. 13.9 with assertions enabled, type

        java -ea AssertTest

You should not encounter any `AssertionError`s through normal execution of a properly written program. Such errors should only indicate bugs in the implementation. As a result, you should never catch an `AssertionError`. Rather, you should allow the program to terminate when the error occurs, so you can see the error message, then you should locate and fix the source of the problem. Since application users can choose not to enable assertions at runtime, you should not use the `assert` statement to indicate runtime problems in production code. Rather, you should use the exception mechanism for this purpose.

13.14 Wrap-Up

In this chapter, you learned how to use exception handling to deal with errors in an application. You learned that exception handling enables programmers to remove error-handling code from the "main line" of the program's execution. You saw exception handling in the context of a divide-by-zero example. You learned how to use try blocks to enclose code that may throw an exception, and how to use catch blocks to deal with exceptions that may arise. You learned about the termination model of exception handling, which dictates that after an exception is handled, program control does not return to the throw point. You learned the difference between checked and unchecked exceptions, and how to specify with the throws clause that exceptions occurring in a method will be thrown by that method to its caller. Next, you learned how to use the finally block to release resources whether or not an exception occurred. In that discussion, you also learned how to throw and rethrow exceptions. You then learned how to obtain information about an exception using methods printStackTrace, getStackTrace and getMessage. The chapter continued with a discussion of chained exceptions, which allow programmers to wrap original exception information with new exception information. Next, we overviewed how to create your own exception classes. We then introduced preconditions and postconditions to help programmers using your methods understand conditions that must be true with the method is called and when it returns. Finally, we discuss the assert statement and how it can be used to help you debug your programs. In the next chapter, you will learn about file processing, including how persistent data is stored and how to manipulate it.

Summary

- An exception is an indication of a problem that occurs during a program's execution.
- Exception handling enables programmers to create applications that can resolve exceptions.
- Exception handling enables programmers to remove error-handling code from the "main line" of the program's execution, improving program clarity and enhancing modifiability.
- Exceptions are thrown when a method detects a problem and is unable to handle it.
- An exception's stack trace includes the name of the exception in a descriptive message that indicates the problem that occurred and the complete method-call stack (i.e., the call chain) at the time the exception occurred.
- The point in the program at which an exception occurs is called the throw point.
- A try block encloses the code that might throw an exception and the code that should not execute if that exception occurs.
- Exceptions may surface through explicitly mentioned code in a try block, through calls to other methods or even through deeply nested method calls initiated by code in the try block.
- A catch block begins with the keyword catch and an exception parameter followed by a block of code that catches (i.e., receives) and handles the exception. This code executes when the try block detects the exception.
- An uncaught exception is an exception that occurs for which there are no matching catch blocks.
- An uncaught exception will cause a program to terminate early if that program contains only one thread. If the program contains more than one thread, only the thread where the exception occurred will terminate. The rest of the program will run, but may yield adverse effects.
- At least one catch block or a finally block must immediately follow the try block.

- Each `catch` block specifies in parentheses an exception parameter that identifies the exception type the handler can process. The exception parameter's name enables the `catch` block to interact with a caught exception object.

- If an exception occurs in a `try` block, the `try` block terminates immediately and program control transfers to the first of the following `catch` blocks whose exception parameter type matches the type of the thrown exception.

- After an exception is handled, program control does not return to the throw point because the `try` block has expired. This is known as the termination model of exception handling.

- If there are multiple matching `catch` blocks when an exception occurs, only the first is executed.

- After executing a `catch` block, this program's flow of control proceeds to the first statement after the last `catch` block.

- A `throws` clause specifies the exceptions the method throws, and appears after the method's parameter list and before the method body.

- The `throws` clause contains a comma-separated list of exceptions that the method will throw if a problem occurs when the method executes.

- Exception handling is designed to process synchronous errors, which occur when a statement executes.

- Exception handling is not designed to process problems associated with asynchronous events, which occur in parallel with, and independent of, the program's flow of control.

- All Java exception classes inherit, either directly or indirectly, from class `Exception`. Because of this fact, Java's exception classes form a hierarchy. Programmers can extend this hierarchy to create their own exception classes.

- Class `Throwable` is the superclass of class `Exception`, and is therefore also the superclass of all exceptions. Only `Throwable` objects can be used with the exception-handling mechanism.

- Class `Throwable` has two subclasses: `Exception` and `Error`.

- Class `Exception` and its subclasses represent exceptional situations that could occur in a Java program and be caught by the application.

- Class `Error` and its subclasses represent exceptional situations that could happen in the Java runtime system. `Error`s happen infrequently, and typically should not be caught by an application.

- Java distinguishes between two categories of exceptions: checked and unchecked.

- Unlike checked exceptions, the Java compiler does not check the code to determine whether an unchecked exception is caught or declared. Unchecked exceptions typically can be prevented by proper coding.

- An exception's type determines whether the exception is checked or unchecked. All exception types that are direct or indirect subclasses of class `RuntimeException` are unchecked exceptions. All exception types that inherit from class `Exception` but not from `RuntimeException` are checked.

- Various exception classes can be derived from a common superclass. If a `catch` block is written to catch exception objects of a superclass type, it can also catch all objects of that class's subclasses. This allows for polymorphic processing of related exceptions.

- Programs that obtain certain types of resources must return them to the system explicitly to avoid so-called resource leaks. Resource-release code typically is placed in a `finally` block.

- The `finally` block is optional. If it is present, it is placed after the last `catch` block.

- Java guarantees that a provided `finally` block will execute whether or not an exception is thrown in the corresponding `try` block or any of its corresponding `catch` blocks. Java also guarantees that a `finally` block executes if a `try` block exits by using a `return`, `break` or `continue` statement.

- If an exception that occurs in the try block cannot be caught by one of that try block's associated catch handlers, the program skips the rest of the try block and control proceeds to the finally block, which releases the resource. Then the program passes to the next outer try block—normally in the calling method.

- If a catch block throws an exception, the finally block still executes. Then the exception is passed to the next outer try block—normally in the calling method.

- Programmers can throw exceptions by using the throw statement.

- A throw statement specifies an object to be thrown. The operand of a throw can be of any class derived from class Throwable.

- Exceptions are rethrown when a catch block, upon receiving an exception, decides either that it cannot process that exception or that it can only partially process it. Rethrowing an exception defers the exception handling (or perhaps a portion of it) to another catch block.

- When a rethrow occurs, the next enclosing try block detects the rethrown exception, and that try block's catch blocks attempt to handle the exception.

- When an exception is thrown but not caught in a particular scope, the method-call stack is unwound, and an attempt is made to catch the exception in the next outer try statement. This process is called stack unwinding.

- Class Throwable offers a printStackTrace method that prints the method-call stack. Often, this is helpful in testing and debugging.

- Class Throwable also provides a getStackTrace method that obtains stack-trace information printed by printStackTrace.

- Class Throwable's getMessage method returns the descriptive string stored in an exception.

- Method getStackTrace obtains the stack-trace information as an array of StackTraceElement objects. Each StackTraceElement represents one method call on the method-call stack.

- StackTraceElement methods getClassName, getFileName, getLineNumber and getMethodName get the class name, file name, line number and method name, respectively.

- Chained exceptions enable an exception object to maintain the complete stack-trace information, including information about previous exceptions that caused the current exception.

- A new exception class must extend an existing exception class to ensure that the class can be used with the exception-handling mechanism.

- A method's precondition is a condition that must be true when the method is invoked.

- A method's postcondition is a condition that is true after the method successfully returns.

- When designing your own methods, you should state the preconditions and postconditions in a comment before the method declaration.

- Within an application, the programmer may state conditions that they assumed to be true at a particular point. These conditions, called assertions, help ensure a program's validity by catching potential bugs and indentifying possible logic errors.

- Java includes two versions of an assert statement for validating assertions programatically.

- To enable assertions at run time, use the -ea switch when running the java command.

Terminology

ArithmeticException class	catch an exception
assert statement	catch block
assertion	catch clause
asynchronous event	catch-or-declare requirement

chained exception	`printStackTrace` method of class `Throwable`
checked exception	release a resource
constructor failure	resource leak
enclosing `try` block	resumption model of exception handling
`Error` class	rethrowing an exception
exception	`RuntimeException` class
`Exception` class	stack trace
exception handler	`StackTraceElement` class
exception handling	stack unwinding
exception parameter	standard error stream
fault-tolerant program	standard output stream
`finally` block	synchronous error
`finally` clause	`System.err` stream
`getClassName` method of class	termination model of exception handling
`StackTraceElement`	throw an exception
`getFileName` method of class	throw keyword
`StackTraceElement`	throw point
`getLineNumber` method of class	throw statement
`StackTraceElement`	`Throwable` class
`getMessage` method of class `Throwable`	throws clause
`getMethodName` method of class	`try` block
`StackTraceElement`	`try` statement
`getStackTrace` method of class `Throwable`	`try...catch...finally` exception-handling
`InputMismatchException` class	mechanism
postcondition	uncaught exception
precondition	unchecked exceptions

Self-Review Exercises

13.1 List five common examples of exceptions.

13.2 Give several reasons why exception-handling techniques should not be used for conventional program control.

13.3 Why are exceptions particularly appropriate for dealing with errors produced by methods of classes in the Java API?

13.4 What is a "resource leak"?

13.5 If no exceptions are thrown in a `try` block, where does control proceed to when the `try` block completes execution?

13.6 Give a key advantage of using `catch( Exception` *exceptionName* `)`.

13.7 Should a conventional application catch `Error` objects? Explain.

13.8 What happens if no catch handler matches the type of a thrown object?

13.9 What happens if several `catch` blocks match the type of the thrown object?

13.10 Why would a programmer specify a superclass type as the type in a `catch` block?

13.11 What is the key reason for using `finally` blocks?

13.12 What happens when a `catch` block throws an `Exception`?

13.13 What does the statement `throw` *exceptionReference* do?

13.14 What happens to a local reference in a `try` block when that block throws an `Exception`?

Answers to Self-Review Exercises

13.1   Memory exhaustion, array index out of bounds, arithmetic overflow, division by zero, invalid method parameters.

13.2   (a) Exception handling is designed to handle infrequently occurring situations that often result in program termination, not situations that arise all the time. (b) Flow of control with conventional control structures is generally clearer and more efficient than with exceptions. (c) The "additional" exceptions can get in the way of genuine error-type exceptions. It becomes more difficult for the programmer to keep track of the larger number of exception cases.

13.3   It is unlikely that methods of classes in the Java API could perform error processing that would meet the unique needs of all users.

13.4   A "resource leak" occurs when an executing program does not properly release a resource when it is no longer needed.

13.5   The catch blocks for that try statement are skipped, and the program resumes execution after the last catch block. If there is a finally block, it is executed first; then the program resumes execution after the finally block.

13.6   The form catch(Exception *exceptionName*) catches any type of exception thrown in a try block. An advantage is that no thrown Exception can slip by without being caught. The programmer can then decide to handle the exception or possibly rethrow it.

13.7   Errors are usually serious problems with the underlying Java system; most programs will not want to catch Errors because the program will not be able to recover from such problems.

13.8   This causes the search for a match to continue in the next enclosing try statement. If there is a finally block, it will be executed before the exception goes to the next enclosing try statement. If there are no enclosing try statements for which there are matching catch blocks, and the exception is *checked*, a compilation error occurs. If there are no enclosing try statements for which there are matching catch blocks and the exception is *unchecked*, a stack trace is printed and the current thread terminates early.

13.9   The first matching catch block after the try block is executed.

13.10   This enables a program to catch related types of exceptions and process them in a uniform manner. However, it is often useful to process the subclass types individually for more precise exception handling.

13.11   The finally block is the preferred means for releasing resources to prevent resource leaks.

13.12   First, control passes to the finally block if there is one. Then the exception will be processed by a catch block (if one exists) associated with an enclosing try block (if one exists).

13.13   It rethrows the exception for processing by an exception handler of an enclosing try statement, after the finally block of the current try statement executes.

13.14   The reference goes out of scope, and the reference count for the object is decremented. If the reference count becomes zero, the object is marked for garbage collection.

Exercises

13.15   List the various exceptional conditions that have occurred in programs throughout this text so far. List as many additional exceptional conditions as you can. For each of these, describe briefly how a program typically would handle the exception by using the exception-handling techniques discussed in this chapter. Some typical exceptions are division by zero, arithmetic overflow, array index out of bounds, etc.

13.16   Until this chapter, we have found that dealing with errors detected by constructors is a bit awkward. Explain why exception handling is an effective means for dealing with constructor failure.

13.17   *(Catching Exceptions with Superclasses)* Use inheritance to create an exception superclass (called ExceptionA) and exception subclasses ExceptionB and ExceptionC, where ExceptionB inherits from ExceptionA and ExceptionC inherits from ExceptionB. Write a program to demonstrate that the catch block for type ExceptionA catches exceptions of types ExceptionB and ExceptionC.

13.18   *(Catching Exceptions Using Class Exception)* Write a program that demonstrates how various exceptions are caught with

    catch (Exception exception)

This time, define classes ExceptionA (which inherits from class Exception) and ExceptionB (which inherits from class ExceptionA). In your program, create try blocks that throw exceptions of types ExceptionA, ExceptionB, NullPointerException and IOException. All exceptions should be caught with catch blocks specifying type Exception.

13.19   *(Order of catch Blocks)* Write a program that shows that the order of catch blocks is important. If you try to catch a superclass exception type before a subclass type, the compiler should generate errors.

13.20   *(Constructor Failure)* Write a program that shows a constructor passing information about constructor failure to an exception handler. Define class SomeException, which throws an Exception in the constructor. You program should try to create an object of type SomeException, and catch the exception that is thrown from the constructor.

13.21   *(Rethrowing Exceptions)* Write a program that illustrates rethrowing an exception. Define methods someMethod and someMethod2. Method someMethod2 should initially throw an exception. Method someMethod should call someMethod2, catch the exception and rethrow it. Call someMethod from method main, and catch the rethrown exception. Print the stack trace of this exception.

13.22   *(Catching Exceptions Using Outer Scopes)* Write a program showing that a method with its own try block does not have to catch every possible error generated within the try. Some exceptions can slip through to, and be handled in, other scopes.

14

Files and Streams

OBJECTIVES

In this chapter you will learn:

- To create, read, write and update files.

- To use class `File` to retrieve information about files and directories.

- The Java input/output stream class hierarchy.

- The differences between text files and binary files.

- Sequential-access and random-access file processing.

- To use classes `Scanner` and `Formatter` to process text files.

- To use the `FileInputStream` and `FileOutputStream` classes.

- To use a `JFileChooser` dialog.

- To use the `ObjectInputStream` and `ObjectOutputStream` classes.

- To use class `RandomAccessFile`.

I can only assume that a "Do Not File" document is filed in a "Do Not File" file.
—Senator Frank Church
Senate Intelligence
Subcommittee Hearing, 1975

Consciousness … does not appear to itself chopped up in bits. … A "river" or a "stream" are the metaphors by which it is most naturally described.
—William James

I read part of it all the way through.
—Samuel Goldwyn

A great memory does not make a philosopher, any more than a dictionary can be called grammar.
—John Henry, Cardinal Newman

14.1 Introduction

Storage of data in variables and arrays is temporary—the data is lost when a local variable goes out of scope or when the program terminates. Computers use files for long-term retention of large amounts of data, even after the programs that created the data terminate. You use files every day for tasks such as writing an essay or creating a spreadsheet. We refer to data maintained in files as persistent data because it exists beyond the duration of program execution. Computers store files on secondary storage devices such as hard disks, optical disks and magnetic tapes. In this chapter, we explain how Java programs create, update and process data files.

File processing is one of the most important capabilities a language must have to support commercial applications, which typically store and process massive amounts of persistent data. In this chapter, we discuss Java's powerful file-processing and stream input/output features. The term "stream" refers to ordered data that is read from or written to a file. We discuss streams in more detail in Section 14.3. File processing is a subset of Java's stream-processing capabilities, which enable a program to read and write data in memory, in files and over network connections. We have two goals in this chapter—to introduce file-processing concepts (making the reader more comfortable with using files programmatically) and to provide the reader with sufficient stream-processing capabilities to support the networking features introduced in Chapter 24, Networking. Java provides substantial stream-processing capabilities—far more than we can cover in one chapter. We discuss three forms of file processing here—text-file processing, object serialization and random-access file processing.

We begin by discussing the hierarchy of data contained in files. We then cover Java's architecture for handling files programmatically by discussing several classes in package `java.io`. Next we explain that data can be stored in two different types of files—text files and binary files—and cover the differences between them. We demonstrate retrieving information about a file or directory using class `File` and then devote several sections to the different mechanisms for writing data to and reading data from files. First we demonstrate creating and manipulating sequential-access text files. Working with text files allows the reader to quickly and easily start manipulating files. As you will learn, however, it is difficult to read data from text files back into object form. Fortunately, many object-oriented languages (including Java) provide ways to write objects to and read objects from files (known as object serialization and deserialization). To demonstrate this, we recreate some of the sequential-access programs that used text files, this time by storing objects in binary files. We then consider random-access files, which enable us to directly and quickly access specific portions of a file. Understanding random-access files provides a foundation for understanding databases, discussed in Chapter 25, Accessing Databases with JDBC.

14.2 Data Hierarchy

Ultimately, a computer processes all data items as combinations of zeros and ones, because it is simple and economical for engineers to build electronic devices that can assume two stable states—one representing 0 and the other representing 1. It is remarkable that the impressive functions performed by computers involve only the most fundamental manipulations of 0s and 1s.

The smallest data item in a computer can assume the value 0 or the value 1. Such a data item is called a bit (short for "binary digit"—a digit that can assume one of two values). Computer circuitry performs various simple bit manipulations, such as examining the value of a bit, setting the value of a bit and reversing the value of a bit (from 1 to 0 or from 0 to 1).

It is cumbersome for programmers to work with data in the low-level form of bits. Instead, programmers prefer to work with data in such forms as decimal digits (0–9), letters (A–Z and a–z), and special symbols (e.g., $, @, %, &, *, (,), –, +, ", :, ? and /). Digits, letters and special symbols are known as characters. The computer's character set is the set of all the characters used to write programs and represent data items. Computers process only 1s and 0s, so a computer's character set represents every character as a pattern of 1s and 0s. Characters in Java are Unicode characters composed of two bytes, each composed of eight bits. Java contains a data type, byte, that can be used to represent byte data. The Unicode character set contains characters for many of the world's languages. See Appendix F for more information on this character set. See Appendix B, ASCII Character Set for more information on the ASCII (American Standard Code for Information Interchange) character set, a subset of the Unicode character set that represents uppercase and lowercase letters, digits and various common special characters.

Just as characters are composed of bits, fields are composed of characters or bytes. A field is a group of characters or bytes that conveys meaning. For example, a field consisting of uppercase and lowercase letters can be used to represent a person's name.

Data items processed by computers form a data hierarchy that becomes larger and more complex in structure as we progress from bits to characters to fields, and so on.

Typically, several fields compose a record (implemented as a `class` in Java). In a payroll system, for example, the record for an employee might consist of the following fields (possible types for these fields are shown in parentheses):

- Employee identification number (`int`)
- Name (`String`)
- Address (`String`)
- Hourly pay rate (`double`)
- Number of exemptions claimed (`int`)
- Year-to-date earnings (`int` or `double`)
- Amount of taxes withheld (`int` or `double`)

Thus, a record is a group of related fields. In the preceding example, all the fields belong to the same employee. Of course, a company might have many employees and thus have a payroll record for each employee. A file is a group of related records. [*Note:* More generally, a file contains arbitrary data in arbitrary formats. In some operating systems, a file is viewed as nothing more than a collection of bytes—any organization of the bytes in a file (e.g., organizing the data into records) is a view created by the applications programmer.] A company's payroll file normally contains one record for each employee. Thus, a payroll file for a small company might contain only 22 records, whereas one for a large company might contain 100,000 records. It is not unusual for a company to have many files, some containing billions, or even trillions, of characters of information. Figure 14.1 illustrates a portion of the data hierarchy.

To facilitate the retrieval of specific records from a file, at least one field in each record is chosen as a record key. A record key identifies a record as belonging to a particular person or entity and is unique to each record. This field typically is used to search and sort records. In the payroll record described previously, the employee identification number normally would be chosen as the record key.

There are many ways to organize records in a file. The most common is called a sequential file, in which records are stored in order by the record-key field. In a payroll file, records are placed in ascending order by employee identification number.

Most businesses store data in many different files. For example, companies might have payroll files, accounts receivable files (listing money due from clients), accounts payable files (listing money due to suppliers), inventory files (listing facts about all the items handled by the business) and many others. Often, a group of related files is called a database. A collection of programs designed to create and manage databases is called a database management system (DBMS). We discuss this topic in Chapter 25, Accessing Databases with JDBC.

14.3 Files and Streams

Java views each file as a sequential stream of bytes (Fig. 14.2). Every operating system provides a mechanism to determine the end of a file, such as an end-of-file marker or a count of the total bytes in the file that is recorded in a system-maintained administrative data

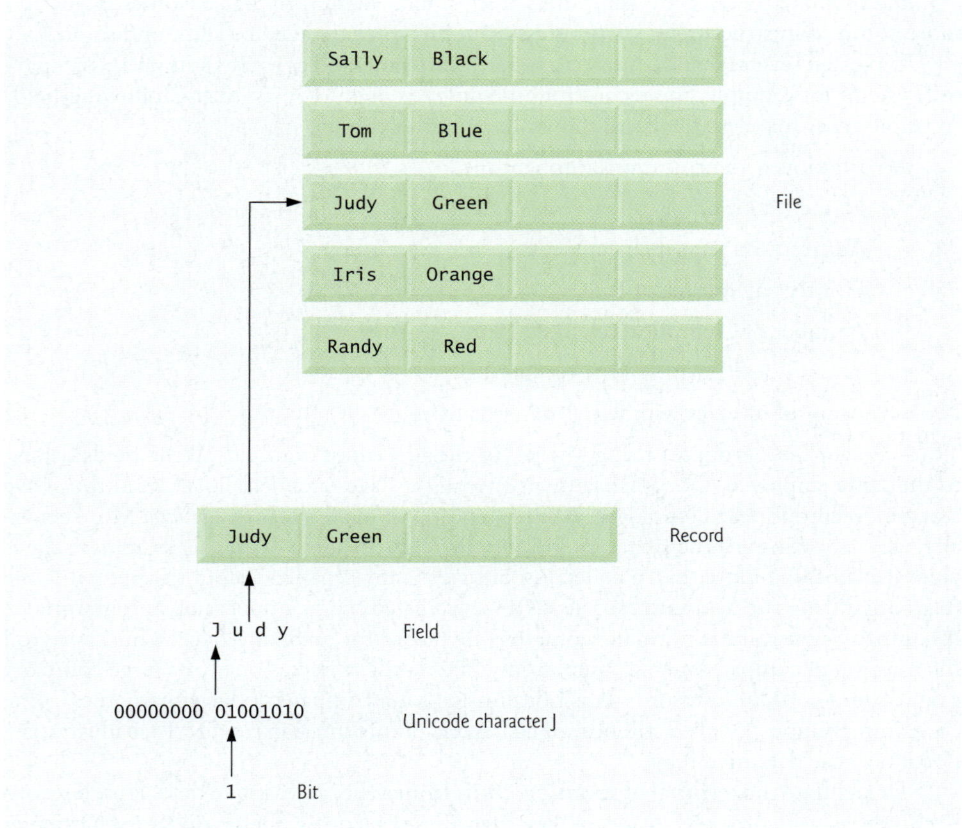

Sally	Black	
Tom	Blue	
Judy	Green		File
Iris	Orange	
Randy	Red	

| Judy | Green | | Record

J u d y   Field

00000000 01001010   Unicode character J

1   Bit

Fig. 14.1 | Data hierarchy.

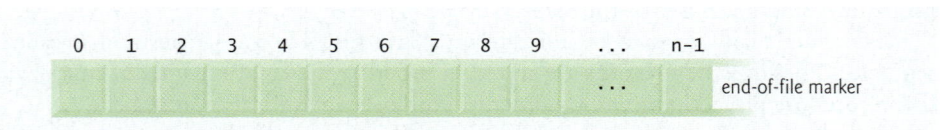

0	1	2	3	4	5	6	7	8	9	...	n–1	
										...		end-of-file marker

Fig. 14.2 | Java's view of a file of n bytes.

structure. A Java program processing a stream of bytes simply receives an indication from the operating system when the program reaches the end of the stream—the program does not need to know how the underlying platform represents files or streams. In some cases, the end-of-file indication occurs as an exception. In other cases, the indication is a return value from a method invoked on a stream-processing object.

File streams can be used to input and output data as either characters or bytes. Streams that input and output bytes to files are known as **byte-based streams**, storing data in its binary format. Streams that input and output characters to files are known as **character-based streams**, storing data as a sequence of characters. For instance, if the value 5 were being stored using a byte-based stream, it would be stored in the binary format of the numeric value 5, or 101. If the value 5 were being stored using a character-based stream, it would be stored in the binary format of the character 5, or 00000000 00110101 (this is the binary for the numeric value 53, which indicates the character 5 in the Unicode character sets). The difference between the numeric value 5 and the character 5 is that the numeric value can be used as an integer, whereas the character 5 is simply a character that can be used in a string of text, as in "Sarah Miller is 15 years old". Files that are created using byte-based streams are referred to as binary files, while files created using character-based streams are referred to as text files. Text files can be read by text editors, while binary files are read by a program that converts the data to a human-readable format.

A Java program opens a file by creating an object and associating a stream of bytes or characters with it. The classes used to create these objects are discussed shortly. Java can also associate streams with different devices. In fact, Java creates three stream objects that are associated with devices when a Java program begins executing—System.in, System.out and System.err. Object System.in (the standard input stream object) normally enables a program to input bytes from the keyboard; object System.out (the standard output stream object) normally enables a program to output data to the screen; and object System.err (the standard error stream object) normally enables a program to output error messages to the screen. Each of these streams can be redirected. For System.in, this capability enables the program to read bytes from a different source. For System.out and System.err, this capability enables the output to be sent to a different location, such as a file on disk. Class System provides methods setIn, setOut and setErr to redirect the standard input, output and error streams, respectively.

Java programs perform file processing by using classes from package java.io. This package includes definitions for stream classes, such as FileInputStream (for byte-based input from a file), FileOutputStream (for byte-based output to a file), FileReader (for character-based input from a file) and FileWriter (for character-based output to a file). Files are opened by creating objects of these stream classes, which inherit from classes InputStream, OutputStream, Reader and Writer, respectively (these classes will be discussed later in this chapter). Thus, the methods of these stream classes can all be applied to file streams as well.

Java contains classes that enable the programmer to perform input and output of objects or variables of primitive data types. The data will still be stored as bytes or characters behind the scenes, allowing the programmer to read or write data in the form of integers, strings, or other data types without having to worry about the details of converting such values to byte-format. To perform such input and output, objects of classes Object-InputStream and ObjectOutputStream can be used together with the byte-based file stream classes FileInputStream and FileOutputStream (these classes will be discussed in more detail shortly). The complete hierarchy of classes in package java.io can be viewed in the online documentation at

> java.sun.com/j2se/5.0/docs/api/java/io/package-tree.html

Each indentation level in the hierarchy indicates that the indented class extends the class under which it is indented. For example, class InputStream is a subclass of Object. Click a class's name in the hierarchy to view the details of the class.

As you can see in the hierarchy, Java offers many classes for performing input/output operations. We use several of these classes in this chapter to implement file-processing programs that create and manipulate sequential-access files and random-access files (discussed in Section 14.7). We also include a detailed example on class `File`, which is useful for obtaining information about files and directories. In Chapter 24, Networking, we use stream classes extensively to implement networking applications. Several other classes in the `java.io` package that we do not use in this chapter are discussed briefly in Section 14.8.

In addition to the classes in this package, character-based input and output can be performed with classes `Scanner` and `Formatter`. Class `Scanner` is used extensively to input data from the keyboard. As we will see, this class can also read data from a file. Class `Formatter` enables formatted data to be output to the screen or to a file in a manner similar to `System.out.printf`. Chapter 28, Formatted Output, presents the details of formatted output with `System.out.printf`. All these features can be used to format text files as well.

14.4 Class `File`

This section presents class `File`, which is particularly useful for retrieving information about files or directories from disk. Objects of class `File` do not open files or provide any file-processing capabilities. However, `File` objects are used frequently with objects of other `java.io` classes to specify files or directories to manipulate.

Creating `File` Objects
Class `File` provides four constructors. The constructor

```
public File( String name )
```

specifies the `name` of a file or directory to associate with the `File` object. The `name` can contain **path information** as well as a file or directory name. A file or directory's path specifies its location on disk. The path includes some or all of the directories leading to the file or directory. An **absolute path** contains all the directories, starting with the **root directory**, that lead to a specific file or directory. Every file or directory on a particular disk drive has the same root directory in its path. A **relative path** normally starts from the directory in which the application began executing, and is therefore a path that is "relative" to the current directory.

The constructor

```
public File( String pathToName, String name )
```

uses argument `pathToName` (an absolute or relative path) to locate the file or directory specified by `name`.

The constructor

```
public File( File directory, String name )
```

uses an existing `File` object `directory` (an absolute or relative path) to locate the file or directory specified by `name`. Figure 14.3 lists some common `File` methods. The complete list can be viewed at `java.sun.com/j2se/5.0/docs/api/java/io/File.html`.

The constructor

```
public File( URI uri )
```

Method	Description
`boolean canRead()`	Returns `true` if a file is readable by the current application; `false` otherwise.
`boolean canWrite()`	Returns `true` if a file is writable by the current application; `false` otherwise.
`boolean exists()`	Returns true if the name specified as the argument to the `File` constructor is a file or directory in the specified path; `false` otherwise.
`boolean isFile()`	Returns true if the name specified as the argument to the `File` constructor is a file; `false` otherwise.
`boolean isDirectory()`	Returns true if the name specified as the argument to the `File` constructor is a directory; `false` otherwise.
`boolean isAbsolute()`	Returns true if the arguments specified to the `File` constructor indicate an absolute path to a file or directory; `false` otherwise.
`String getAbsolutePath()`	Returns a string with the absolute path of the file or directory.
`String getName()`	Returns a string with the name of the file or directory.
`String getPath()`	Returns a string with the path of the file or directory.
`String getParent()`	Returns a string with the parent directory of the file or directory (i.e., the directory in which the file or directory can be found).
`long length()`	Returns the length of the file, in bytes. If the `File` object represents a directory, 0 is returned.
`long lastModified()`	Returns a platform-dependent representation of the time at which the file or directory was last modified. The value returned is useful only for comparison with other values returned by this method.
`String[] list()`	Returns an array of strings representing the contents of a directory. Returns `null` if the `File` object does not represent a directory.

Fig. 14.3 | `File` methods.

uses the given `URI` object to locate the file. A **Uniform Resource Identifier (URI)** is a more general form of the **Uniform Resource Locators (URLs)** that are used to locate Web sites. For example, `http://www.deitel.com/` is the URL for the Deitel & Associates' Web site. URIs for locating files vary across operating systems. On Windows platforms, the URI

```
file:/C:/data.txt
```

identifies the file `data.txt` stored in the root directory of the C: drive. On UNIX/Linux platforms, the URI

```
file:/home/student/data.txt
```

identifies the file `data.txt` stored in the `home` directory of the user `student`.

Error-Prevention Tip 14.1

Use File method isFile to determine whether a File object represents a file (not a directory) before attempting to open the file.

Demonstrating Class **File**

Figure 14.4–Fig. 14.5 demonstrate class File. The application prompts the user to enter a file name or directory name, then outputs information about the file name or directory name input.

```java
1   // Fig. 14.4: FileDemonstration.java
2   // Demonstrating the File class.
3   import java.io.File;
4
5   public class FileDemonstration
6   {
7      // display information about file user specifies
8      public void analyzePath( String path )
9      {
10        // create File object based on user input
11        File name = new File( path );
12
13        if ( name.exists() ) // if name exists, output information about it
14        {
15           // display file (or directory) information
16           System.out.printf(
17              "%s%s\n%s\n%s\n%s\n%s%s\n%s%s\n%s%s\n%s%s\n%s%s",
18              name.getName(), " exists",
19              ( name.isFile() ? "is a file" : "is not a file" ),
20              ( name.isDirectory() ? "is a directory" :
21                 "is not a directory" ),
22              ( name.isAbsolute() ? "is absolute path" :
23                 "is not absolute path" ), "Last modified: ",
24              name.lastModified(), "Length: ", name.length(),
25              "Path: ", name.getPath(), "Absolute path: ",
26              name.getAbsolutePath(), "Parent: ", name.getParent() );
27
28           if ( name.isDirectory() ) // output directory listing
29           {
30              String directory[] = name.list();
31              System.out.println( "\n\nDirectory contents:\n" );
32
33              for ( String directoryName : directory )
34                 System.out.printf( "%s\n", directoryName );
35           } // end if
36        } // end outer if
37        else // not file or directory, output error message
38        {
39           System.out.printf( "%s %s", path, "does not exist." );
40        } // end else
41     } // end method analyzePath
42  } // end class FileDemonstration
```

Fig. 14.4 | File class used to obtain file and directory information.

```
1   // Fig. 14.5: FileDemonstrationTest.java
2   // Testing the FileDemonstration class.
3   import java.util.Scanner;
4
5   public class FileDemonstrationTest
6   {
7      public static void main( String args[] )
8      {
9         Scanner input = new Scanner( System.in );
10        FileDemonstration application = new FileDemonstration();
11
12        System.out.print( "Enter file or directory name here: " );
13        application.analyzePath( input.nextLine() );
14     } // end main
15  } // end class FileDemonstrationTest
```

```
Enter file or directory name here: C:\Program Files\Java\jdk1.5.0\demo\jfc
jfc exists
is not a file
is a directory
is absolute path
Last modified: 1083938776645
Length: 0
Path: C:\Program Files\Java\jdk1.5.0\demo\jfc
Absolute path: C:\Program Files\Java\jdk1.5.0\demo\jfc
Parent: C:\Program Files\Java\jdk1.5.0\demo

Directory contents:

CodePointIM
FileChooserDemo
Font2DTest
Java2D
Metalworks
Notepad
SampleTree
Stylepad
SwingApplet
SwingSet2
TableExample
```

```
Enter file or directory name here:
C:\Program Files\Java\jdk1.5.0\demo\jfc\Java2D\readme.txt
readme.txt exists
is a file
is not a directory
is absolute path
Last modified: 1083938778347
Length: 7501
Path: C:\Program Files\Java\jdk1.5.0\demo\jfc\Java2D\readme.txt
Absolute path: C:\Program Files\Java\jdk1.5.0\demo\jfc\Java2D\readme.txt
Parent: C:\Program Files\Java\jdk1.5.0\demo\jfc\Java2D
```

Fig. 14.5 | Testing class FileDemonstration.

The program begins by prompting the user for a file or directory (line 12 of Fig. 14.5). Line 13 inputs the file name or directory name and passes it to method ana-lyzePath (lines 8–41 of Fig. 14.4). The method creates a new File object (line 11) and assigns its reference to name. Line 13 invokes File method exists to determine whether the name input by the user exists (either as a file or as a directory) on the disk. If the name input by the user does not exist, control proceeds to lines 37–40 and displays a message to the screen containing the name the user typed, followed by "does not exist." Otherwise, the body of the if statement (lines 13–36) executes. The program outputs the name of the file or directory (line 18), followed by the results of testing the File object with isFile (line 19), isDirectory (line 20) and isAbsolute (line 22). Next, the program displays the values returned by lastModified (line 24), length (line 24), getPath (line 25), getAbso-lutePath (line 26) and getParent (line 26). If the File object represents a directory (line 28), the program obtains a list of the directory's contents as an array of Strings by using File method list (line 30) and displays the list on the screen.

The first output of this program demonstrates a File object associated with the jfc directory from the Java 2 Software Development Kit. The second output demonstrates a File object associated with the readme.txt file from the Java 2D example that comes with the Java 2 Software Development Kit. In both cases, we specified an absolute path on our personal computer.

A *separator character* is used to separate directories and files in the path. On a Windows computer, the separator character is a backslash (\) character. On a UNIX workstation, it is a forward slash (/) character. Java processes both characters identically in a path name. For example, if we were to use the path

```
c:\Program Files\Java\jdk1.5.0\demo/jfc
```

which employs each separator character, Java still processes the path properly. When building strings that represent path information, use File.separator to obtain the local computer's proper separator character rather than explicitly using / or \. This constant returns a String consisting of one character—the proper separator for the system.

Common Programming Error 14.1

Using \ as a directory separator rather than \\ in a string literal is a logic error. A single \ indicates that the \ followed by the next character represents an escape sequence. Use \\ to insert a \ in a string literal.

14.5 Sequential-Access Text Files

In this section, we create and manipulate sequential-access files. As mentioned earlier, these are files in which records are stored in order by the record-key field. We first demonstrate sequential-access files using text files, allowing the reader to quickly create and edit human-readable files. In the subsections of this chapter we discuss creating, writing data to, reading data from and updating sequential-access text files. We also include a credit-inquiry program that retrieves specific data from a file.

14.5.1 Creating a Sequential-Access Text File

Java imposes no structure on a file—notions such as a record do not exist as part of the Java language. Therefore, the programmer must structure files to meet the requirements of the intended application. In the following example, we see how to impose a record structure on a file.

The program in Fig. 14.6–Fig. 14.7 and Fig. 14.9 creates a simple sequential-access file that might be used in an accounts receivable system to help keep track of the amounts owed to a company by its credit clients. For each client, the program obtains from the user an account number, the client's name and the client's balance (i.e., the amount the client owes the company for goods and services received). The data obtained for each client constitutes a "record" for that client. The account number is used as the record key in this application—the file will be created and maintained in account number order. The program assumes that the user enters the records in account number order. In a comprehensive accounts receivable system (based on sequential-access files), a sorting capability would be provided so that the user could enter the records in any order. The records would then be sorted and written to the file.

Class `AccountRecord` (Fig. 14.6) encapsulates the client record information (i.e., account, first name, etc.) used by the examples in this chapter. The class `AccountRecord` is declared in package `com.deitel.jhtp6.ch14` (line 3), so that it can be imported into several examples. Class `AccountRecord` contains `private` data members `account`, `firstName`, `lastName` and `balance` (lines 7–10). This class also provides `public` *set* and *get* methods for accessing the `private` fields.

Compile class `AccountRecord` as follows:

```
javac -d c:\examples\ch14 com\deitel\jhtp6\ch14\AccountRecord.java
```

```java
1   // Fig. 14.6: AccountRecord.java
2   // A class that represents one record of information.
3   package com.deitel.jhtp6.ch14; // packaged for reuse
4
5   public class AccountRecord
6   {
7      private int account;
8      private String firstName;
9      private String lastName;
10     private double balance;
11
12     // no-argument constructor calls other constructor with default values
13     public AccountRecord()
14     {
15        this( 0, "", "", 0.0 ); // call four-argument constructor
16     } // end no-argument AccountRecord constructor
17
18     // initialize a record
19     public AccountRecord( int acct, String first, String last, double bal )
20     {
21        setAccount( acct );
22        setFirstName( first );
23        setLastName( last );
24        setBalance( bal );
25     } // end four-argument AccountRecord constructor
26
```

Fig. 14.6 | `AccountRecord` maintains information for one account. (Part 1 of 2.)

```
27      // set account number
28      public void setAccount( int acct )
29      {
30         account = acct;
31      } // end method setAccount
32
33      // get account number
34      public int getAccount()
35      {
36         return account;
37      } // end method getAccount
38
39      // set first name
40      public void setFirstName( String first )
41      {
42         firstName = first;
43      } // end method setFirstName
44
45      // get first name
46      public String getFirstName()
47      {
48         return firstName;
49      } // end method getFirstName
50
51      // set last name
52      public void setLastName( String last )
53      {
54         lastName = last;
55      } // end method setLastName
56
57      // get last name
58      public String getLastName()
59      {
60         return lastName;
61      } // end method getLastName
62
63      // set balance
64      public void setBalance( double bal )
65      {
66         balance = bal;
67      } // end method setBalance
68
69      // get balance
70      public double getBalance()
71      {
72         return balance;
73      } // end method getBalance
74   } // end class AccountRecord
```

Fig. 14.6 | AccountRecord maintains information for one account. (Part 2 of 2.)

This places AccountRecord.class in its package directory structure and places the package in c:\examples\ch14. When you compile class AccountRecord (or any other classes that will be reused in this chapter), you should place them in a common directory (e.g., c:\examples\ch14). When you compile or execute classes that use AccountRecord (e.g., CreateTextFile in Fig. 14.7), you must specify the command-line argument -classpath to both javac and java, as in

```
javac -classpath .;c:\examples\ch14 CreateTextFile.java
java -classpath .;c:\examples\ch14 CreateTextFile
```

Note that the current directory (specified with .) is included in the classpath. This ensures that the compiler can locate other classes in the same directory as the class being compiled. The path separator used in the preceding commands should be the one that is appropriate for your platform—for example, a semicolon (;) on Windows and a colon (:) on UNIX/Linux/Mac OS X.

Now let us examine class CreateTextFile (Fig. 14.7). Line 14 declares Formatter variable output. As discussed in Section 14.3, a Formatter object outputs formatted strings, using the same formatting capabilities as method System.out.printf. A Formatter object can output to various locations, such as the screen or a file, as is done here. The Formatter object is instantiated in line 21 in method openFile (lines 17–34). The constructor used in line 21 takes one argument—a String containing the name of the file, including its path. If a path is not specified, as is the case here, the JVM assumes that the files is in the directory from which the program was executed. For text files, we use the .txt file extension. If the file does not exist, it will be created. If an existing file is opened, the contents of the file are truncated—all the data in the file is discarded. At this point the file is open for writing, and the resulting Formatter object can be used to write data to the file. Lines 23–28 handle the SecurityException, which occurs if the user does not have permission to write data to the file. Lines 29–33 handle the FileNotFoundException, which occurs if the file does not exist and a new file cannot be created. This exception may also occur if there is an error opening the file. Note that in both exception handlers, we call static method System.exit, and pass the value 1. This method terminates the application. An argument of 0 to method exit indicates successful program termination. A nonzero value, such as 1 in this example, normally indicates that an error has occurred. This value is passed to the command window that executed the program. The argument is useful if the program is executed from a batch file on Windows systems or a shell script on UNIX/Linux/Mac OS X systems. Batch files and shell scripts offer a convenient way of executing several programs in sequence. When the first program ends, the next program begins execution. It is possible to use the argument to method exit in a batch file or shell script to determine whether other programs should execute. For more information on batch files or shell scripts, see your operating system's documentation.

Method addRecords (lines 37–91) prompts the user to enter the various fields for each record or to enter the end-of-file key sequence when data entry is complete. Figure 14.8 lists the key combinations for entering end-of-file for various computer systems.

Line 40 creates an AccountRecord object, which will be used to store the values of the current record entered by the user. Line 42 creates a Scanner object to read input from the user at the keyboard. Lines 44–48 and 50–52 prompt the user for input.

Line 54 uses Scanner method hasNext to determine whether the end-of-file key combination has been entered. The loop executes until hasNext encounters the end-of-file indicators.

```java
1   // Fig. 14.7: CreateTextFile.java
2   // Writing data to a text file with class Formatter.
3   import java.io.FileNotFoundException;
4   import java.lang.SecurityException;
5   import java.util.Formatter;
6   import java.util.FormatterClosedException;
7   import java.util.NoSuchElementException;
8   import java.util.Scanner;
9
10  import com.deitel.jhtp6.ch14.AccountRecord;
11
12  public class CreateTextFile
13  {
14     private Formatter output; // object used to output text to file
15
16     // enable user to open file
17     public void openFile()
18     {
19        try
20        {
21           output = new Formatter( "clients.txt" );
22        } // end try
23        catch ( SecurityException securityException )
24        {
25           System.err.println(
26              "You do not have write access to this file." );
27           System.exit( 1 );
28        } // end catch
29        catch ( FileNotFoundException filesNotFoundException )
30        {
31           System.err.println( "Error creating file." );
32           System.exit( 1 );
33        } // end catch
34     } // end method openFile
35
36     // add records to file
37     public void addRecords()
38     {
39        // object to be written to file
40        AccountRecord record = new AccountRecord();
41
42        Scanner input = new Scanner( System.in );
43
44        System.out.printf( "%s\n%s\n%s\n%s\n\n",
45           "To terminate input, type the end-of-file indicator ",
46           "when you are prompted to enter input.",
47           "On UNIX/Linux/Mac OS X type <ctrl> d then press Enter",
48           "On Windows type <ctrl> z then press Enter" );
49
50        System.out.printf( "%s\n%s",
51           "Enter account number (> 0), first name, last name and balance.",
52           "? " );
53
```

Fig. 14.7 | Creating a sequential text file. (Part 1 of 2.)

```
54        while ( input.hasNext() ) // loop until end-of-file indicator
55        {
56            try // output values to file
57            {
58                // retrieve data to be output
59                record.setAccount( input.nextInt() ); // read account number
60                record.setFirstName( input.next() ); // read first name
61                record.setLastName( input.next() ); // read last name
62                record.setBalance( input.nextDouble() ); // read balance
63
64                if ( record.getAccount() > 0 )
65                {
66                    // write new record
67                    output.format( "%d %s %s %.2f\n", record.getAccount(),
68                        record.getFirstName(), record.getLastName(),
69                        record.getBalance() );
70                } // end if
71                else
72                {
73                    System.out.println(
74                        "Account number must be greater than 0." );
75                } // end else
76            } // end try
77            catch ( FormatterClosedException formatterClosedException )
78            {
79                System.err.println( "Error writing to file." );
80                return;
81            } // end catch
82            catch ( NoSuchElementException elementException )
83            {
84                System.err.println( "Invalid input. Please try again." );
85                input.nextLine(); // discard input so user can try again
86            } // end catch
87
88            System.out.printf( "%s %s\n%s", "Enter account number (>0),",
89                "first name, last name and balance.", "? " );
90        } // end while
91    } // end method addRecords
92
93    // close file
94    public void closeFile()
95    {
96        if ( output != null )
97            output.close();
98    } // end method closeFile
99 } // end class CreateTextFile
```

Fig. 14.7 | Creating a sequential text file. (Part 2 of 2.)

Lines 59–62 read data from the user, storing the record information in the AccountRecord object. Each statement throws a NoSuchElementException (handled in lines 82–86) if the data is in the wrong format (e.g., a string when an int is expected) or if there is no more data to input. If the account number is greater than 0 (line 64), the record's information is written to clients.txt (lines 67–69) using method format. This

Operating system	Key combination
UNIX/Linux/Mac OS X	*<return>* *<ctrl>* d
Windows	*<ctrl>* z

Fig. 14.8 | End-of-file key combinations for various popular operating systems.

method can perform identical formatting to the System.out.printf method used extensively in earlier chapters. This method outputs a formatted string to the output destination of the Formatter object, in this case the file clients.txt. The format string "%d %s %s %.2\n" indicates that the current record will be stored as an integer (the account number) followed by a string (the first name), another string (the last name) and a floating-point value (the balance). Each piece of information is separated from the next by a space and the double value (the balance) is output with two digits to the right of the decimal point. The data in the text file can be viewed with a text editor, or retrieved later by a program designed to read the file (Section 14.5.2). When lines 67–69 execute, if the Formatter object is closed, a **FormatterClosedException** will be thrown (handled in lines 77–81). [*Note:* You can also output data to a text file using class **java.io.PrintWriter**, which also provides method format for outputting formatted data.]

Lines 94–98 declare method closeFile, which closes the Formatter and the underlying output file. Line 97 closes the object by simply calling method **close**. If method close is not called explicitly, the operating system normally will close the file when program execution terminates. This is an example of operating system "housekeeping."

Figure 14.9 runs the program. Line 8 creates a CreateTextFile object, which is then used to open, add records to and close the file (lines 10–12). The sample data for this application is shown in Fig. 14.10. In the sample execution for this program, the user enters information for five accounts, then enters end-of-file to signal that data entry is complete. The sample execution does not show how the data records actually appear in the file. In the next section to verify that the file has been created successfully, we present a program that reads the file and prints its contents. Because this is a text file, you can also verify the information by opening the file in a text editor.

14.5.2 Reading Data from a Sequential-Access Text File

Data is stored in files so that it may be retrieved for processing when needed. Section 14.5.1 demonstrated how to create a file for sequential access. This section shows how to read data sequentially from a text file. In this section, we demonstrate how class Scanner can be used to input data from a file rather than the keyboard.

The application in Fig. 14.11 and Fig. 14.12 reads records from the file "clients.txt" created by the application of Section 14.5.1 and displays the record contents. Line 13 of Fig. 14.11 declares a Scanner that will be used to retrieve input from the file.

Method openFile (lines 16–27) opens the file for reading by instantiating a Scanner object in line 20. We pass a File object to the constructor, which specifies that the Scanner object will read from the file "clients.txt" located in the directory from which the application executes. If the file cannot be found, a FileNotFoundException occurs. The exception is handled in lines 22–26.

```
1   // Fig. 14.9: CreateTextFileTest.java
2   // Testing the CreateTextFile class.
3
4   public class CreateTextFileTest
5   {
6      public static void main( String args[] )
7      {
8         CreateTextFile application = new CreateTextFile();
9
10        application.openFile();
11        application.addRecords();
12        application.closeFile();
13     } // end main
14  } // end class CreateTextFileTest
```

```
To terminate input, type the end-of-file indicator
when you are prompted to enter input.
On UNIX/Linux/Mac OS X type <ctrl> d then press Enter
On Windows type <ctrl> z then press Enter

Enter account number (> 0), first name, last name and balance.
? 100 Bob Jones 24.98
Enter account number (> 0), first name, last name and balance.
? 200 Steve Doe -345.67
Enter account number (> 0), first name, last name and balance.
? 300 Pam White 0.00
Enter account number (> 0), first name, last name and balance.
? 400 Sam Stone -42.16
Enter account number (> 0), first name, last name and balance.
? 500 Sue Rich 224.62
Enter account number (> 0), first name, last name and balance.
? ^Z
```

Fig. 14.9 | Testing the CreateTextFile class.

Sample data			
100	Bob	Jones	24.98
200	Steve	Doe	-345.67
300	Pam	White	0.00
400	Sam	Stone	-42.16
500	Sue	Rich	224.62

Fig. 14.10 | Sample data for the program in Fig. 14.7.

Method readRecords (lines 30–64) reads and displays records from the file. Line 33 creates AccountRecord object record to store the current record's information. Lines 35–36 display headers for the columns in the application's output. Lines 40–51 read data from the file until the end-of-file marker is reached (in which case, method hasNext will return false at line 40). Lines 42–45 use Scanner methods nextInt, next and nextDouble to input an integer (the account number), two strings (the first and last names) and a double value (the balance). Each record is one line of data in the file. The values are stored in object record. If the information in the file is not properly formed (e.g., there is a last name where there should be a balance), a NoSuchElementException occurs when the record is input. This exception is handled in lines 53–58. If the Scanner was closed before

```java
1   // Fig. 14.11: ReadTextFile.java
2   // This program reads a text file and displays each record.
3   import java.io.File;
4   import java.io.FileNotFoundException;
5   import java.lang.IllegalStateException;
6   import java.util.NoSuchElementException;
7   import java.util.Scanner;
8
9   import com.deitel.jhtp6.ch14.AccountRecord;
10
11  public class ReadTextFile
12  {
13     private Scanner input;
14
15     // enable user to open file
16     public void openFile()
17     {
18        try
19        {
20           input = new Scanner( new File( "clients.txt" ) );
21        } // end try
22        catch ( FileNotFoundException fileNotFoundException )
23        {
24           System.err.println( "Error opening file." );
25           System.exit( 1 );
26        } // end catch
27     } // end method openFile
28
29     // read record from file
30     public void readRecords()
31     {
32        // object to be written to screen
33        AccountRecord record = new AccountRecord();
34
35        System.out.printf( "%-10s%-12s%-12s%10s\n", "Account",
36           "First Name", "Last Name", "Balance" );
37
38        try // read records from file using Scanner object
39        {
40           while ( input.hasNext() )
41           {
42              record.setAccount( input.nextInt() ); // read account number
43              record.setFirstName( input.next() ); // read first name
44              record.setLastName( input.next() ); // read last name
45              record.setBalance( input.nextDouble() ); // read balance
```

Fig. 14.11 | Sequential file reading using a Scanner. (Part 1 of 2.)

```
46
47                   // display record contents
48               System.out.printf( "%-10d%-12s%-12s%10.2f\n",
49                   record.getAccount(), record.getFirstName(),
50                   record.getLastName(), record.getBalance() );
51            } // end while
52         } // end try
53         catch ( NoSuchElementException elementException )
54         {
55            System.err.println( "File improperly formed." );
56            input.close();
57            System.exit( 1 );
58         } // end catch
59         catch ( IllegalStateException stateException )
60         {
61            System.err.println( "Error reading from file." );
62            System.exit( 1 );
63         } // end catch
64      } // end method readRecords
65
66      // close file and terminate application
67      public void closeFile()
68      {
69         if ( input != null )
70            input.close(); // close file
71      } // end method closeFile
72   } // end class ReadTextFile
```

Fig. 14.11 | Sequential file reading using a Scanner. (Part 2 of 2.)

```
1   // Fig. 14.12: ReadTextFileTest.java
2   // This program test class ReadTextFile.
3
4   public class ReadTextFileTest
5   {
6      public static void main( String args[] )
7      {
8         ReadTextFile application = new ReadTextFile();
9
10        application.openFile();
11        application.readRecords();
12        application.closeFile();
13     } // end main
14  } // end class ReadTextFileTest
```

Account	First Name	Last Name	Balance
100	Bob	Jones	24.98
200	Steve	Doe	-345.67
300	Pam	White	0.00
400	Sam	Stone	-42.16
500	Sue	Rich	224.62

Fig. 14.12 | Testing the ReadTextFile class.

the data was input, an `IllegalStateException` occurs (handled in lines 59–63). If no exceptions occur, the record's information is displayed on the screen (lines 48–50). Note in the format string in line 48 that the account number, first name and last name are left justified, while the balance is right justified and output with two digits of precision. Each iteration of the loop inputs one line of text from the text file, which represents one record.

Lines 67–71 define method `closeFile`, which closes the `Scanner`. Method `main` is defined in Fig. 14.12, in lines 6–13. Line 8 creates a `ReadTextFile` object, which is then used to open, add records to and close the file (lines 10–12).

14.5.3 Case Study: A Credit-Inquiry Program

To retrieve data sequentially from a file, programs normally start reading from the beginning of the file and read all the data consecutively until the desired information is found. It might be necessary to process the file sequentially several times (from the beginning of the file) during the execution of a program. Class `Scanner` does not provide the ability to reposition to the beginning of the file. If it is necessary to read the file again, the program must close the file and reopen it.

The program in Fig. 14.13–Fig. 14.15 allows a credit manager to obtain lists of customers with zero balances (i.e., customers who do not owe any money), customers with credit balances (i.e., customers to whom the company owes money) and customers with debit balances (i.e., customers who owe the company money for goods and services received). A credit balance is a negative amount, and a debit balance is a positive amount.

We begin by creating an `enum` type (Fig. 14.13) to define the different menu options the user will have. The options and their values are listed in lines 7–10. Method `getValue` (lines 19–22) retrieves the value of a specific `enum` constant.

```java
1    // Fig. 14.13: MenuOption.java
2    // Defines an enum type for the credit inquiry program's options.
3
4    public enum MenuOption
5    {
6       // declare contents of enum type
7       ZERO_BALANCE( 1 ),
8       CREDIT_BALANCE( 2 ),
9       DEBIT_BALANCE( 3 ),
10      END( 4 );
11
12      private final int value; // current menu option
13
14      MenuOption( int valueOption )
15      {
16         value = valueOption;
17      } // end MenuOptions enum constructor
18
19      public int getValue()
20      {
21         return value;
22      } // end method getValue
23   } // end enum MenuOption
```

Fig. 14.13 | Enumeration for menu options.

Figure 14.14 contains the functionality for the credit-inquiry program, and Fig. 14.15 contains the main method that executes the program. The program displays a text menu and allows the credit manager to enter one of three options to obtain credit information. Option 1 (ZERO_BALANCE) produces a list of accounts with zero balances. Option 2 (CREDIT_BALANCE) produces a list of accounts with credit balances. Option 3 (DEBIT_BALANCE) produces a list of accounts with debit balances. Option 4 (END) terminates program execution. A sample output is shown in Fig. 14.16.

The record information is collected by reading through the entire file and determining whether each record satisfies the criteria for the account type selected by the credit manager. Method processRequests (lines 116–139 of Fig. 14.14) calls method getRequest to display the menu options (line 119) and stores the result in MenuOption variable

```java
1   // Fig. 14.14: CreditInquiry.java
2   // This program reads a file sequentially and displays the
3   // contents based on the type of account the user requests
4   // (credit balance, debit balance or zero balance).
5   import java.io.File;
6   import java.io.FileNotFoundException;
7   import java.lang.IllegalStateException;
8   import java.util.NoSuchElementException;
9   import java.util.Scanner;
10
11  import com.deitel.jhtp6.ch14.AccountRecord;
12
13  public class CreditInquiry
14  {
15     private MenuOption accountType;
16     private Scanner input;
17     private MenuOption choices[] = { MenuOption.ZERO_BALANCE,
18        MenuOption.CREDIT_BALANCE, MenuOption.DEBIT_BALANCE,
19        MenuOption.END };
20
21     // read records from file and display only records of appropriate type
22     private void readRecords()
23     {
24        // object to be written to file
25        AccountRecord record = new AccountRecord();
26
27        try // read records
28        {
29           // open file to read from beginning
30           input = new Scanner( new File( "clients.txt" ) );
31
32           while ( input.hasNext() ) // input the values from the file
33           {
34              record.setAccount( input.nextInt() ); // read account number
35              record.setFirstName( input.next() ); // read first name
36              record.setLastName( input.next() ); // read last name
37              record.setBalance( input.nextDouble() ); // read balance
38
```

Fig. 14.14 | Credit-inquiry program. (Part 1 of 3.)

```
39                    // if proper acount type, display record
40                    if ( shouldDisplay( record.getBalance() ) )
41                       System.out.printf( "%-10d%-12s%-12s%10.2f\n",
42                          record.getAccount(), record.getFirstName(),
43                          record.getLastName(), record.getBalance() );
44                 } // end while
45              } // end try
46              catch ( NoSuchElementException elementException )
47              {
48                 System.err.println( "File improperly formed." );
49                 input.close();
50                 System.exit( 1 );
51              } // end catch
52              catch ( IllegalStateException stateException )
53              {
54                 System.err.println( "Error reading from file." );
55                 System.exit( 1 );
56              } // end catch
57              catch ( FileNotFoundException fileNotFoundException )
58              {
59                 System.err.println( "File cannot be found." );
60                 System.exit( 1 );
61              } // end catch
62              finally
63              {
64                 if ( input != null )
65                    input.close(); // close the Scanner and the file
66              } // end finally
67           } // end method readRecords
68
69           // use record type to determine if record should be displayed
70           private boolean shouldDisplay( double balance )
71           {
72              if ( ( accountType == MenuOption.CREDIT_BALANCE )
73                 && ( balance < 0 ) )
74                 return true;
75
76              else if ( ( accountType == MenuOption.DEBIT_BALANCE )
77                 && ( balance > 0 ) )
78                 return true;
79
80              else if ( ( accountType == MenuOption.ZERO_BALANCE )
81                 && ( balance == 0 ) )
82                 return true;
83
84              return false;
85           } // end method shouldDisplay
86
87           // obtain request from user
88           private MenuOption getRequest()
89           {
90              Scanner textIn = new Scanner( System.in );
91              int request = 1;
```

Fig. 14.14 | Credit-inquiry program. (Part 2 of 3.)

```
 92
 93          // display request options
 94          System.out.printf( "\n%s\n%s\n%s\n%s\n%s\n",
 95             "Enter request", " 1 - List accounts with zero balances",
 96             " 2 - List accounts with credit balances",
 97             " 3 - List accounts with debit balances", " 4 - End of run" );
 98
 99          try // attempt to input menu choice
100          {
101             do // input user request
102             {
103                System.out.print( "\n? " );
104                request = textIn.nextInt();
105             } while ( ( request < 1 ) || ( request > 4 ) );
106          } // end try
107          catch ( NoSuchElementException elementException )
108          {
109             System.err.println( "Invalid input." );
110             System.exit( 1 );
111          } // end catch
112
113          return choices[ request - 1 ]; // return enum value for option
114       } // end method getRequest
115
116       public void processRequests()
117       {
118          // get user's request (e.g., zero, credit or debit balance)
119          accountType = getRequest();
120
121          while ( accountType != MenuOption.END )
122          {
123             switch ( accountType )
124             {
125                case ZERO_BALANCE:
126                   System.out.println( "\nAccounts with zero balances:\n" );
127                   break;
128                case CREDIT_BALANCE:
129                   System.out.println( "\nAccounts with credit balances:\n" );
130                   break;
131                case DEBIT_BALANCE:
132                   System.out.println( "\nAccounts with debit balances:\n" );
133                   break;
134             } // end switch
135
136             readRecords();
137             accountType = getRequest();
138          } // end while
139       } // end method processRequests
140    } // end class CreditInquiry
```

Fig. 14.14 | Credit-inquiry program. (Part 3 of 3.)

accountType. Note that getRequest translates the number typed by the user into a Menu-
Option by using the number to select a MenuOption from array choices. Lines 121–138

```
 1   // Fig. 14.15: CreditInquiryTest.java
 2   // This program tests class CreditInquiry.
 3
 4   public class CreditInquiryTest
 5   {
 6      public static void main( String args[] )
 7      {
 8         CreditInquiry application = new CreditInquiry();
 9         application.processRequests();
10      } // end main
11   } // end class CreditInquiryTest
```

Fig. 14.15 | Testing the `CreditInquiry` class.

```
Enter request
 1 - List accounts with zero balances
 2 - List accounts with credit balances
 3 - List accounts with debit balances
 4 - End of run

? 1

Accounts with zero balances:

300        Pam          White            0.00

Enter request
 1 - List accounts with zero balances
 2 - List accounts with credit balances
 3 - List accounts with debit balances
 4 - End of run

? 2

Accounts with credit balances:
200        Steve        Doe          -345.67
400        Sam          Stone         -42.16

Enter request
 1 - List accounts with zero balances
 2 - List accounts with credit balances
 3 - List accounts with debit balances
 4 - End of run

? 3

Accounts with debit balances:
100        Bob          Jones          24.98
500        Sue          Rich          224.62

? 4
```

Fig. 14.16 | Sample output of the credit-inquiry program in Fig. 14.15.

loop until the user specifies that the program should terminate. The switch statement in lines 123–134 displays a header for the current set of records to be output to the screen. Line 136 calls method readRecords (lines 22–67), which loops through the file and reads every record.

Line 30 of method readRecords opens the file for reading with a Scanner. Note that the file will be opened for reading with a new Scanner object each time this method is called, so that we can again read from the beginning of the file. Lines 34–37 read a record. Line 40 calls method shouldDisplay (lines 70–85) to determine whether the current record satisfies the account type requested. If shouldDisplay returns true, the program displays the account information. When the end-of-file marker is reached, the loop terminates and line 65 calls the Scanner's close method to close the Scanner and the file. Notice that this occurs in a finally block, which will execute whether or not the file was successfully read. Once all the records have been read, control returns to method process-Requests and getRequest is again called (line 137) to retrieve the user's next menu option. Figure 14.15 contains method main, and calls method processRequests in line 9.

14.5.4 Updating Sequential-Access Files

The data in many sequential files cannot be modified without the risk of destroying other data in the file. For example, if the name "White" needed to be changed to "Worthington," the old name cannot simply be overwritten because the new name requires more space. The record for White was written to the file as

```
300 Pam White 0.00
```

If the record is rewritten beginning at the same location in the file using the new name, the record would be

```
300 Pam Worthington 0.00
```

The new record is larger (has more characters) than the original record. The characters beyond the second "o" in "Worthington" would overwrite the beginning of the next sequential record in the file. The problem here is that fields in a text file—and hence records—can vary in size. For example, 7, 14, –117, 2074 and 27383 are all ints stored in the same number of bytes (4) internally, but they are different-sized fields when displayed on the screen or written to a file as text.

Therefore, records in a sequential-access file are not usually updated in place. Instead, the entire file is usually rewritten. To make the preceding name change, the records before 300 Pam White 0.00 in a sequential-access file would be copied to a new file, the new record (which can be of a different size than the one it replaces) would be written and the records after 300 Pam White 0.00 would be copied to the new file. It is uneconomical just to update one record, but reasonable if a substantial portion of the records needs to be updated.

14.6 Object Serialization

In Section 14.5, we demonstrated how to write the individual fields of an AccountRecord object into a file as text, and how to read those fields from a file and place their values into an AccountRecord object in memory. In the examples, AccountRecord was used to aggregate the information for one record. When the instance variables for an `AccountRecord` were output to a disk file, certain information was lost, such as the type of each value. For instance, if the value "3" were read from a file, there is no way to tell if the value came from an `int`, a `String` or a `double`. We have only data, not type information, on a disk. If the program that is going to read this data "knows" what object type the data corresponds to, then the data is simply read into objects of that type. For example, in Section 14.5.2, we know that we are inputting an `int` (the account number), followed by two `String`s (the first and last name) and a `double` (the balance). We also know that these values are separated by spaces, with only one record on each line. Sometimes we will not know exactly how the data is stored in a file. In such cases, we would like to read or write an entire object from a file. Java provides such a mechanism, called object serialization. A so-called serialized object is an object represented as a sequence of bytes that includes the object's data as well as information about the object's type and the types of data stored in the object. After a serialized object has been written into a file, it can be read from the file and deserialized—that is, the type information and bytes that represent the object and its data can be used to recreate the object in memory.

Classes `ObjectInputStream` and `ObjectOutputStream`, which respectively implement the `ObjectInput` and `ObjectOutput` interfaces, enable entire objects to be read from or written to a stream (possibly a file). To use serialization with files, we initialize `ObjectInputStream` and `ObjectOutputStream` objects with stream objects that read from and write to files—objects of classes `FileInputStream` and `FileOutputStream`, respectively. Initializing stream objects with other stream objects in this manner is sometimes called wrapping—the new stream object being created wraps the stream object specified as a constructor argument. To wrap a `FileInputStream` in an `ObjectInputStream`, for instance, we pass the `FileInputStream` object to the `ObjectInputStream`'s constructor.

The `ObjectOutput` interface contains method `writeObject`, which takes an `Object` that implements interface `Serializable` (discussed shortly) as an argument and writes its information to an `OutputStream`. Correspondingly, the `ObjectInput` interface contains method `readObject`, which reads and returns a reference to an `Object` from an `InputStream`. After an object has been read, its reference can be cast to the object's actual type. As you will see in Chapter 24, Networking, applications that communicate via a network, such as the Internet, can also transmit entire objects across the network.

In this section, we create and manipulate sequential-access files using object serialization. Object serialization is performed with byte-based streams, so the sequential files created and manipulated will be binary files. Recall that binary files cannot be viewed in standard text editors. For this reason, we write a separate application that knows how to read and display serialized objects.

14.6.1 Creating a Sequential-Access File Using Object Serialization

We begin by creating and writing serialized objects to a sequential-access file. In this section, we reuse much of the code from Section 14.5, so we focus only on the new features.

Defining the `AccountRecordSerializable` Class

Let us begin by modifying our `AccountRecord` class so that objects of this class can be serialized. Class `AccountRecordSerializable` (Fig. 14.17) implements interface `Serializable` (line 7), which allows objects of `AccountRecordSerializable` to be serialized and

```
1    // Fig. 14.17: AccountRecordSerializable.java
2    // A class that represents one record of information.
3    package com.deitel.jhtp6.ch14; // packaged for reuse
4
5    import java.io.Serializable;
6
7    public class AccountRecordSerializable implements Serializable
8    {
9       private int account;
10       private String firstName;
11       private String lastName;
12       private double balance;
13
14       // no-argument constructor calls other constructor with default values
15       public AccountRecordSerializable()
16       {
17          this( 0, "", "", 0.0 );
18       } // end no-argument AccountRecordSerializable constructor
19
20       // four-argument constructor initializes a record
21       public AccountRecordSerializable(
22          int acct, String first, String last, double bal )
23       {
24          setAccount( acct );
25          setFirstName( first );
26          setLastName( last );
27          setBalance( bal );
28       } // end four-argument AccountRecordSerializable constructor
29
30       // set account number
31       public void setAccount( int acct )
32       {
33          account = acct;
34       } // end method setAccount
35
36       // get account number
37       public int getAccount()
38       {
39          return account;
40       } // end method getAccount
41
42       // set first name
43       public void setFirstName( String first )
44       {
45          firstName = first;
46       } // end method setFirstName
47
48       // get first name
49       public String getFirstName()
50       {
51          return firstName;
52       } // end method getFirstName
53
```

Fig. 14.17 | AccountRecordSerializable class for serializable objects. (Part 1 of 2.)

```
54        // set last name
55        public void setLastName( String last )
56        {
57           lastName = last;
58        } // end method setLastName
59
60        // get last name
61        public String getLastName()
62        {
63           return lastName;
64        } // end method getLastName
65
66        // set balance
67        public void setBalance( double bal )
68        {
69           balance = bal;
70        } // end method setBalance
71
72        // get balance
73        public double getBalance()
74        {
75           return balance;
76        } // end method getBalance
77     } // end class AccountRecordSerializable
```

Fig. 14.17 | `AccountRecordSerializable` class for serializable objects. (Part 2 of 2.)

deserialized with `ObjectOutputStreams` and `ObjectInputStreams`. Interface `Serializable` is a tagging interface. Such an interface contains no methods. A class that implements `Serializable` is tagged as being a `Serializable` object. This is important because an `ObjectOutputStream` will not output an object unless it *is a* `Serializable` object, which is the case for any object of a class that implements `Serializable`.

In a class that implements `Serializable`, the programmer must ensure that every instance variable of the class is a `Serializable` type. Any instance variable that is not serializable must be declared **transient** to indicate that it is not `Serializable` and should be ignored during the serialization process. By default, all primitive-type variables are serializable. For variables of reference types, you must check the definition of the class (and possibly its superclasses) to ensure that the type is `Serializable`. By default, array objects are serializable. However, if the array contains references to other objects, those objects may or may not be serializable.

Class `AccountRecordSerializable` contains `private` data members account, `firstName`, `lastName` and `balance`. This class also provides `public` *get* and *set* methods for accessing the `private` fields.

Now let us discuss the code that creates the sequential-access file (Fig. 14.18– Fig. 14.19). We concentrate only on new concepts here. As stated in Section 14.3, a program can open a file by creating an object of stream class `FileInputStream` or `FileOutputStream`. In this example, the file is to be opened for output, so the program creates a `FileOutputStream` (line 21 of Fig. 14.18). The string argument that is passed to the `FileOutputStream`'s constructor represents the name and path of the file to be opened. Existing files that are opened for output in this manner are truncated. Note that the .ser file extension is used—we use this file extension for binary files that contain serialized objects.

```java
// Fig. 14.18: CreateSequentialFile.java
// Writing objects sequentially to a file with class ObjectOutputStream.
import java.io.FileOutputStream;
import java.io.IOException;
import java.io.ObjectOutputStream;
import java.util.NoSuchElementException;
import java.util.Scanner;

import com.deitel.jhtp6.ch14.AccountRecordSerializable;

public class CreateSequentialFile
{
   private ObjectOutputStream output; // outputs data to file

   // allow user to specify file name
   public void openFile()
   {
      try // open file
      {
         output = new ObjectOutputStream(
            new FileOutputStream( "clients.ser" ) );
      } // end try
      catch ( IOException ioException )
      {
         System.err.println( "Error opening file." );
      } // end catch
   } // end method openFile

   // add records to file
   public void addRecords()
   {
      AccountRecordSerializable record; // object to be written to file
      int accountNumber = 0; // account number for record object
      String firstName; // first name for record object
      String lastName; // last name for record object
      double balance; // balance for record object

      Scanner input = new Scanner( System.in );

      System.out.printf( "%s\n%s\n%s\n%s\n\n",
         "To terminate input, type the end-of-file indicator ",
         "when you are prompted to enter input.",
         "On UNIX/Linux/Mac OS X type <ctrl> d then press Enter",
         "On Windows type <ctrl> z then press Enter" );

      System.out.printf( "%s\n%s",
         "Enter account number (> 0), first name, last name and balance.",
         "? " );
```

Fig. 14.18 | Sequential file created using ObjectOutputStream. (Part 1 of 2.)

```
50          while ( input.hasNext() ) // loop until end-of-file indicator
51          {
52              try // output values to file
53              {
54                  accountNumber = input.nextInt(); // read account number
55                  firstName = input.next(); // read first name
56                  lastName = input.next(); // read last name
57                  balance = input.nextDouble(); // read balance
58
59                  if ( accountNumber > 0 )
60                  {
61                      // create new record
62                      record = new AccountRecordSerializable( accountNumber,
63                          firstName, lastName, balance );
64                      output.writeObject( record ); // output record
65                  } // end if
66                  else
67                  {
68                      System.out.println(
69                          "Account number must be greater than 0." );
70                  } // end else
71              } // end try
72              catch ( IOException ioException )
73              {
74                  System.err.println( "Error writing to file." );
75                  return;
76              } // end catch
77              catch ( NoSuchElementException elementException )
78              {
79                  System.err.println( "Invalid input. Please try again." );
80                  input.nextLine(); // discard input so user can try again
81              } // end catch
82
83              System.out.printf( "%s %s\n%s", "Enter account number (>0),",
84                  "first name, last name and balance.", "? " );
85          } // end while
86      } // end method addRecords
87
88      // close file and terminate application
89      public void closeFile()
90      {
91          try // close file
92          {
93              if ( output != null )
94                  output.close();
95          } // end try
96          catch ( IOException ioException )
97          {
98              System.err.println( "Error closing file." );
99              System.exit( 1 );
100         } // end catch
101     } // end method closeFile
102 } // end class CreateSequentialFile
```

Fig. 14.18 | Sequential file created using `ObjectOutputStream`. (Part 2 of 2.)

```
 1    // Fig. 14.19: CreateSequentialFileTest.java
 2    // Testing class CreateSequentialFile.
 3
 4    public class CreateSequentialFileTest
 5    {
 6       public static void main( String args[] )
 7       {
 8          CreateSequentialFile application = new CreateSequentialFile();
 9
10          application.openFile();
11          application.addRecords();
12          application.closeFile();
13       } // end main
14    } // end class CreateSequentialFileTest
```

```
To terminate input, type the end-of-file indicator
when you are prompted to enter input.
On UNIX/Linux/Mac OS X type <ctrl> d then press Enter
On Windows type <ctrl> z then press Enter

Enter account number (> 0), first name, last name and balance.
? 100 Bob Jones 24.98
Enter account number (> 0), first name, last name and balance.
? 200 Steve Doe -345.67
Enter account number (> 0), first name, last name and balance.
? 300 Pam White 0.00
Enter account number (> 0), first name, last name and balance.
? 400 Sam Stone -42.16
Enter account number (> 0), first name, last name and balance.
? 500 Sue Rich 224.62
Enter account number (> 0), first name, last name and balance.
? ^Z
```

Fig. 14.19 | Testing class `CreateSequentialFile`.

Common Programming Error 14.2

It is a logic error to open an existing file for output when, in fact, the user wishes to preserve the file.

Class `FileOutputStream` provides methods for writing byte arrays and individual bytes to a file. In this program we wish to write objects to a file—a capability not provided by `FileOutputStream`. For this reason, we wrap a `FileOutputStream` in an `ObjectOutputStream` by passing the new `FileOutputStream` object to the `ObjectOutputStream`'s constructor (lines 20–21). The `ObjectOutputStream` object uses the `FileOutputStream` object to write objects into the file. Lines 20–21 might throw an `IOException` if a problem occurs while opening the file (e.g., when a file is opened for writing on a drive with insufficient space or when a read-only file is opened for writing). If so, the program displays an error message (lines 23–26). If no exception occurs, the file is open and variable `output` can be used to write objects to the file.

This program assumes that data is input correctly and in the proper record-number order. Method `addRecords` (lines 30–86) performs the write operation. Lines 62–63 create an `AccountRecordSerializable` object from the data entered by the user. Line 64 calls `ObjectOutputStream` method `writeObject` to write the `record` object to the output file. Note that only one statement is required to write the entire object.

Method `closeFile` (lines 89–101) closes the file. Method `closeFile` calls `ObjectOutputStream` method **close** on output to close both the `ObjectOutputStream` and its underlying `FileOutputStream` (line 94). Note that the call to method `close` is contained in a `try` block. Method `close` throws an `IOException` if the file cannot be closed properly. In this case, it is important to notify the user that the information in the file might be corrupted. When using wrapped streams, closing the outermost stream also closes the underlying file.

In the sample execution for the program in Fig. 14.19, we entered information for five accounts—the same information shown in Fig. 14.10. The program does not show how the data records actually appear in the file. Remember that now we are using binary files, which are not humanly readable. To verify that the file has been created successfully, the next section presents a program to read the file's contents.

14.6.2 Reading and Deserializing Data from a Sequential-Access File

As discussed in Section 14.5.2, data is stored in files so that it may be retrieved for processing when needed. The preceding section showed how to create a file for sequential access using object serialization. In this section, we discuss how to read serialized data sequentially from a file.

The program in Fig. 14.20–Fig. 14.21 reads records from a file created by the program in Section 14.6.1 and displays the contents. The program opens the file for input by creating a `FileInputStream` object (line 21). The name of the file to open is specified as

```
1   // Fig. 14.20: ReadSequentialFile.java
2   // This program reads a file of objects sequentially
3   // and displays each record.
4   import java.io.EOFException;
5   import java.io.FileInputStream;
6   import java.io.IOException;
7   import java.io.ObjectInputStream;
8
9   import com.deitel.jhtp6.ch14.AccountRecordSerializable;
10
11  public class ReadSequentialFile
12  {
13     private ObjectInputStream input;
14
15     // enable user to select file to open
16     public void openFile()
17     {
18        try // open file
19        {
20           input = new ObjectInputStream(
21              new FileInputStream( "clients.ser" ) );
22        } // end try
23        catch ( IOException ioException )
24        {
```

Fig. 14.20 | Sequential file read using an `ObjectInputStream`. (Part 1 of 2.)

```
25              System.err.println( "Error opening file." );
26           } // end catch
27        } // end method openFile
28
29        // read record from file
30        public void readRecords()
31        {
32           AccountRecordSerializable record;
33           System.out.printf( "%-10s%-12s%-12s%10s\n", "Account",
34              "First Name", "Last Name", "Balance" );
35
36           try // input the values from the file
37           {
38              while ( true )
39              {
40                 record = ( AccountRecordSerializable ) input.readObject();
41
42                 // display record contents
43                 System.out.printf( "%-10d%-12s%-12s%10.2f\n",
44                    record.getAccount(), record.getFirstName(),
45                    record.getLastName(), record.getBalance() );
46              } // end while
47           } // end try
48           catch ( EOFException endOfFileException )
49           {
50              return; // end of file was reached
51           } // end catch
52           catch ( ClassNotFoundException classNotFoundException )
53           {
54              System.err.println( "Unable to create object." );
55           } // end catch
56           catch ( IOException ioException )
57           {
58              System.err.println( "Error during read from file." );
59           } // end catch
60        } // end method readRecords
61
62        // close file and terminate application
63        public void closeFile()
64        {
65           try // close file and exit
66           {
67              if ( input != null )
68                 input.close();
69           } // end try
70           catch ( IOException ioException )
71           {
72              System.err.println( "Error closing file." );
73              System.exit( 1 );
74           } // end catch
75        } // end method closeFile
76     } // end class ReadSequentialFile
```

Fig. 14.20 | Sequential file read using an `ObjectInputStream`. (Part 2 of 2.)

```
 1   // Fig. 14.21: ReadSequentialFileTest.java
 2   // This program test class ReadSequentialFile.
 3
 4   public class ReadSequentialFileTest
 5   {
 6      public static void main( String args[] )
 7      {
 8         ReadSequentialFile application = new ReadSequentialFile();
 9
10         application.openFile();
11         application.readRecords();
12         application.closeFile();
13      } // end main
14   } // end class ReadSequentialFileTest
```

```
Account   First Name   Last Name      Balance
100       Bob          Jones            24.98
200       Steve        Doe            -345.67
300       Pam          White             0.00
400       Sam          Stone           -42.16
500       Sue          Rich            224.62
```

Fig. 14.21 | Testing class `ReadSequentialFile`.

an argument to the `FileInputStream` constructor. In Fig. 14.18, we wrote objects to the file, using an `ObjectOutputStream` object. Data must be read from the file in the same format in which it was written. Therefore, we use an `ObjectInputStream` wrapped around a `FileInputStream` in this program (lines 20–21) If no exceptions occur when opening the file, variable `input` can be used to read objects from the file.

The program reads records from the file in method `readRecords` (lines 30–60). Line 40 calls `ObjectInputStream` method `readObject` to read an `Object` from the file. To use `AccountRecordSerializable`-specific methods, we downcast the returned `Object` to type `AccountRecordSerializable`. Method `readObject` throws an **EOFException** (processed at lines 48–51) if an attempt is made to read beyond the end of the file. Method `readObject` throws a `ClassNotFoundException` if the class for the object being read cannot be located. This might occur if the file is accessed on a computer that does not have the class. Figure 14.21 contains method `main` (lines 6–13), which opens the file, calls method `readRecords` and closes the file.

14.7 Random-Access Files

So far, we have seen how to create and manipulate sequential-access files. Sequential-access files are inappropriate for so-called **instant-access applications**, in which the desired information must be located immediately. Some popular instant-access applications are airline-reservation systems, banking systems, point-of-sale systems, automated teller machines (ATMs) and other kinds of **transaction-processing systems** that require rapid access to specific data. The bank at which you have your account may have hundreds of thousands, or even millions, of other customers, but when you use an ATM, the bank determines in seconds whether your account has sufficient funds for the transaction. This kind of instant access is possible with **random-access files** and with databases (Chapter 25). A program can access individual records of a random-access file directly (and quickly) without searching through other records. Random-access files are sometimes called **direct-access files**.

Recall from Section 14.5 that Java does not impose structure on a file, so an application that wants to use random-access files must specify the format of those files. Several techniques can be used to create random-access files. Perhaps the simplest is to require that all the records in a file be of the same fixed length. Using fixed-length records makes it easy for a program to calculate (as a function of the record size and the record key) the exact location of any record relative to the beginning of the file. We soon see how this capability facilitates direct access to specific records, even in large files.

Figure 14.22 illustrates Java's view of a random-access file composed of fixed-length records. (Each record in this figure is 100 bytes long.) A random-access file is like a railroad train with many cars—some empty, some with contents.

A program can insert data in a random-access file without destroying the other data in the file. Similarly, a program can update or delete data stored previously without rewriting the entire file. In the following sections, we explain how to create a random-access file, enter data, read the data both sequentially and randomly, update the data and delete the data.

14.7.1 Creating a Random-Access File

A `RandomAccessFile` is useful for direct-access applications. With a sequential-access file, each successive input/output request reads or writes the next consecutive set of data in the file. With a random-access file, each successive input/output request could be directed to any part of the file—perhaps a section widely separated from the part referenced in the previous request. Direct-access applications provide rapid access to specific data items in large files, but users often have to wait for answers. In many instances, however, answers must be made available quickly, to prevent people from becoming impatient and taking their business elsewhere.

RandomAccessFile objects have all the capabilities of classes `FileInputStream` and `FileOutputStream`, as well as the capabilities described by interfaces **DataInput** and **DataOutput**. These interfaces provide methods for reading and writing primitive-type values, byte arrays and strings. When a program associates an object of class RandomAccessFile with a file, the program reads or writes data, beginning at the location in the file

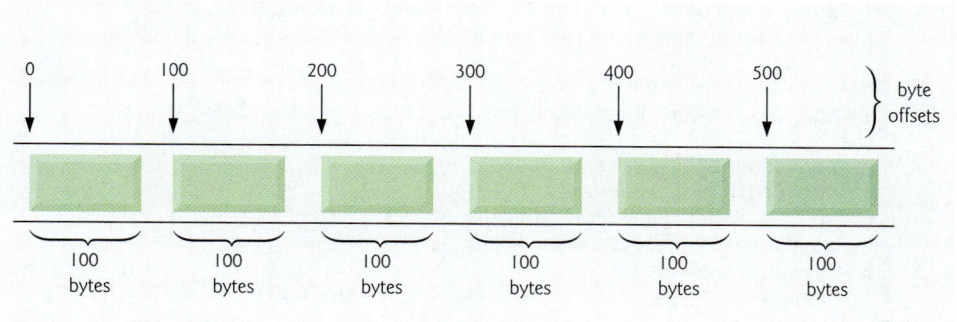

Fig. 14.22 | Java's view of a random-access file.

specified by the **file-position pointer** (the byte number of the next byte in the file to be read or written to), and manipulates all the data as primitive types. When writing an `int` value, four bytes are output to the file. When reading a `double` value, eight bytes are input from the file. The size of the types is guaranteed, because Java has fixed representations and sizes for all primitive types, regardless of the computing platform.

Random-access file-processing programs rarely write a single field to a file. Normally they write one object at a time, as we show in the upcoming examples. Consider the following problem:

> *Create a transaction-processing program capable of storing up to 100 fixed-length records for a company that can have up to 100 customers. Each record should consist of an account number (that will be used as the record key), a last name, a first name and a balance. The program should be able to update an account, insert a new account and delete an account.*

The next several sections introduce the techniques necessary to create this credit-processing program. Figure 14.23 contains the `RandomAccessAccountRecord` class that is used by the next four programs for both reading records from and writing records to a file.

```
 1   // Fig. 14.23: RandomAccessAccountRecord.java
 2   // Subclass of AccountRecord for random-access file programs.
 3   package com.deitel.jhtp6.ch14; // packaged for reuse
 4
 5   import java.io.RandomAccessFile;
 6   import java.io.IOException;
 7
 8   public class RandomAccessAccountRecord extends AccountRecord
 9   {
10      public static final int SIZE = 72;
11
12      // no-argument constructor calls other constructor with default values
13      public RandomAccessAccountRecord()
14      {
15         this( 0, "", "", 0.0 );
16      } // end no-argument RandomAccessAccountRecord constructor
17
18      // initialize a RandomAccessAccountRecord
19      public RandomAccessAccountRecord( int account, String firstName,
20         String lastName, double balance )
21      {
22         super( account, firstName, lastName, balance );
23      } // end four-argument RandomAccessAccountRecord constructor
24
25      // read a record from specified RandomAccessFile
26      public void read( RandomAccessFile file ) throws IOException
27      {
28         setAccount( file.readInt() );
29         setFirstName( readName( file ) );
30         setLastName( readName( file ) );
31         setBalance( file.readDouble() );
32      } // end method read
```

Fig. 14.23 | `RandomAccessAccountRecord` class used in random-access file programs. (Part 1 of 2.)

```
33
34      // ensure that name is proper length
35      private String readName( RandomAccessFile file ) throws IOException
36      {
37         char name[] = new char[ 15 ], temp;
38
39         for ( int count = 0; count < name.length; count++ )
40         {
41            temp = file.readChar();
42            name[ count ] = temp;
43         } // end for
44
45         return new String( name ).replace( '\0', ' ' );
46      } // end method readName
47
48      // write a record to specified RandomAccessFile
49      public void write( RandomAccessFile file ) throws IOException
50      {
51         file.writeInt( getAccount() );
52         writeName( file, getFirstName() );
53         writeName( file, getLastName() );
54         file.writeDouble( getBalance() );
55      } // end method write
56
57      // write a name to file; maximum of 15 characters
58      private void writeName( RandomAccessFile file, String name )
59         throws IOException
60      {
61         StringBuffer buffer = null;
62
63         if ( name != null )
64            buffer = new StringBuffer( name );
65         else
66            buffer = new StringBuffer( 15 );
67
68         buffer.setLength( 15 );
69         file.writeChars( buffer.toString() );
70      } // end method writeName
71   } // end class RandomAccessAccountRecord
```

Fig. 14.23 | RandomAccessAccountRecord class used in random-access file programs. (Part 2 of 2.)

Class `RandomAccessAccountRecord` inherits our `AccountRecord` implementation (Fig. 14.6), which includes private fields—account, lastName, firstName and balance—as well as *set* and *get* methods for each field. We could inherit from either AccountRecord or AccountRecordSerializable. We do not use object serialization when processing random-access files in this chapter, so we inherit from class AccountRecord. Note that the class is in package com.deitel.jhtp6.ch14.

Finally, this example also introduces class **StringBuffer**, a class that allows us to dynamically manipulate strings. Class String provides many capabilities for processing strings. However, `String` objects are immutable—their character contents cannot be changed after they are created. Class `StringBuffer` provides features for creating and manipulating dynamic string information—that is, modifiable strings. Every `String-Buffer` is capable of storing a number of characters specified by its capacity. If the capacity of a `StringBuffer` is exceeded, the capacity is expanded to accommodate the additional characters. We use class `StringBuffer` to specify the size of a person's first or last name. We discuss class `StringBuffer` in more detail in Section 14.8, as well as in Chapter 29, Strings, Characters and Regular Expressions.

Line 10 declares the constant `SIZE` to represent the size, in bytes, of a record. A `Ran-domAccessAccountRecord` contains an `int` (4 bytes), two strings that we restrict to 15 characters each (30 bytes for the first name, 30 bytes for the last name) for this example and a `double` (8 bytes), for a total of 72 bytes.

Method `read` (lines 26–32) reads one record from the `RandomAccessFile` specified as its argument. `RandomAccessFile` methods **`readInt`** (line 28) and **`readDouble`** (line 31) read the `account` and `balance`, respectively. Lines 29–30 call utility method `readName` (lines 35–46) twice to obtain the first and last names. Method `readName` reads 15 characters from the `RandomAccessFile` and returns a `String`. If a name is shorter than 15 characters, the extra characters have the default value `'\0'`—the default for a `char`. Swing GUI components, such as `JTextFields`, cannot display null-byte characters—instead, they display them as rectangles. Line 45 solves this problem by using `String` method **`replace`** to replace null bytes with spaces. Although our program does not use a GUI, we added this capability for those who wish to reuse this class in a GUI program.

Method `write` (lines 49–55) outputs one record to the `RandomAccessFile` specified as its argument. This method uses `RandomAccessFile` method **`writeInt`** to output the integer `account`, method **`writeChars`** (called from utility method `writeName` in line 69) to output the `firstName` and `lastName` character arrays, and method **`writeDouble`** to output the `double balance`. [*Note:* To ensure that all the records in the `RandomAccessFile` are the same size, we write exactly 15 characters for the first name and exactly 15 for the last name.] Method `writeName` (lines 58–70) performs the write operations for the first and last names. Lines 63–66 create a `StringBuffer` that is initialized with either the `name` specified as an argument or with 15 to specify the size of the `StringBuffer` if name is `null`. Line 68 sets the number of characters in the `StringBuffer`. If a name is longer than 15 characters, it will be truncated to 15 characters. If a name is smaller than 15 characters it will be set to have 15 characters, with null characters (`'\0'`) to fill the extra space.

Figure 14.24–Fig. 14.25 illustrates the process of opening a random-access file and writing data to the disk. This program writes 100 blank `RandomAccessAccountRecords`. Each `RandomAccessAccountRecord` object contains 0 for the account number, `null` for the last name, `null` for the first name and `0.0` for the balance. The file is initialized to create the proper amount of "empty" space in which the account data will be stored and to enable us to determine in subsequent programs whether each record is empty or contains data.

Line 19 of Fig. 14.24 attempts to open a `RandomAccessFile` for use in this program. The `RandomAccessFile` constructor accepts two arguments—the file name and the **file-open mode**. The file-open mode for a `RandomAccessFile` is either `"r"` (to open the file for reading) or `"rw"` (to open the file for reading and writing). Once again, we have used a new file extension (`.dat`). We use this file extension for binary files that do not use object serialization.

```java
1   // Fig. 14.24: CreateRandomFile.java
2   // Creates random-access file by writing 100 empty records to disk.
3   import java.io.IOException;
4   import java.io.RandomAccessFile;
5
6   import com.deitel.jhtp6.ch14.RandomAccessAccountRecord;
7
8   public class CreateRandomFile
9   {
10     private static final int NUMBER_RECORDS = 100;
11
12     // enable user to select file to open
13     public void createFile()
14     {
15        RandomAccessFile file = null;
16
17        try // open file for reading and writing
18        {
19           file = new RandomAccessFile( "clients.dat", "rw" );
20
21           RandomAccessAccountRecord blankRecord =
22              new RandomAccessAccountRecord();
23
24           // write 100 blank records
25           for ( int count = 0; count < NUMBER_RECORDS; count++ )
26              blankRecord.write( file );
27
28           // display message that file was created
29           System.out.println( "Created file clients.dat." );
30
31           System.exit( 0 ); // terminate program
32        } // end try
33        catch ( IOException ioException )
34        {
35           System.err.println( "Error processing file." );
36           System.exit( 1 );
37        } // end catch
38        finally
39        {
40           try
41           {
42              if ( file != null )
43                 file.close(); // close file
44           } // end try
45           catch ( IOException ioException )
46           {
47              System.err.println( "Error closing file." );
48              System.exit( 1 );
49           } // end catch
50        } // end finally
51     } // end method createFile
52  } // end class CreateRandomFile
```

Fig. 14.24 | Random-access file created sequentially.

```
1    // Fig. 14.25: CreateRandomFileTest.java
2    // Testing class CreateRandomFile.
3
4    public class CreateRandomFileTest
5    {
6       public static void main( String args[] )
7       {
8          CreateRandomFile application = new CreateRandomFile();
9          application.createFile();
10      } // end main
11   } // end class CreateRandomFileTest
```

```
Created file clients.dat.
```

Fig. 14.25 | Testing class `CreateRandomFile`.

If an `IOException` occurs while opening the file, the program displays a message and terminates. If the file opens properly, lines 25–26 invoke `RandomAccessAccountRecord` method `write` 100 times. This method causes the fields of object `blankRecord` to be written to the file associated with `RandomAccessFile` object `file`. Then line 43 closes the file. The code for closing the file is placed in it's own `try` statement—if an attempt to close the file generates an `IOException`, this exception is caught in lines 45–49. Figure 14.25 begins the execution of the program with method `main` (lines 6–10). Line 8 creates a `CreateRandomFile` object and line 9 calls its `createFile` method to create the file of 100 blank records.

14.7.2 Writing Data Randomly to a Random-Access File

The application in Fig. 14.26–Fig. 14.27 writes data to a file that is opened with the "rw" mode (for reading and writing). It uses `RandomAccessFile` method **seek** to position to the

```
1    // Fig. 14.26: WriteRandomFile.java
2    // This program retrieves information from the user at the
3    // keyboard and writes the information to a random-access file.
4    import java.io.File;
5    import java.io.IOException;
6    import java.io.RandomAccessFile;
7    import java.util.NoSuchElementException;
8    import java.util.Scanner;
9
10   import com.deitel.jhtp6.ch14.RandomAccessAccountRecord;
11
12   public class WriteRandomFile
13   {
14      private RandomAccessFile output;
15
16      private static final int NUMBER_RECORDS = 100;
17
```

Fig. 14.26 | Writing data to a random-access file. (Part 1 of 3.)

```java
18      // enable user to choose file to open
19      public void openFile()
20      {
21          try // open file
22          {
23              output = new RandomAccessFile( "clients.dat", "rw" );
24          } // end try
25          catch ( IOException ioException )
26          {
27              System.err.println( "File does not exist." );
28          } // end catch
29      } // end method openFile
30
31      // close file and terminate application
32      public void closeFile()
33      {
34          try // close file and exit
35          {
36              if ( output != null )
37                  output.close();
38          } // end try
39          catch ( IOException ioException )
40          {
41              System.err.println( "Error closing file." );
42              System.exit( 1 );
43          } // end catch
44      } // end method closeFile
45
46      // add records to file
47      public void addRecords()
48      {
49          // object to be written to file
50          RandomAccessAccountRecord record = new RandomAccessAccountRecord();
51
52          int accountNumber = 0; // account number for AccountRecord object
53          String firstName; // first name for AccountRecord object
54          String lastName; // last name for AccountRecord object
55          double balance; // balance for AccountRecord object
56
57          Scanner input = new Scanner( System.in );
58
59          System.out.printf( "%s\n%s\n%s\n%s\n\n",
60              "To terminate input, type the end-of-file indicator ",
61              "when you are prompted to enter input.",
62              "On UNIX/Linux/Mac OS X type <ctrl> d then press Enter",
63              "On Windows type <ctrl> z then press Enter" );
64
65          System.out.printf( "%s %s\n%s", "Enter account number (1-100),",
66              "first name, last name and balance.", "? " );
67
68          while ( input.hasNext() ) // loop until end-of-file indicator
69          {
```

Fig. 14.26 | Writing data to a random-access file. (Part 2 of 3.)

```
70                  try // output values to file
71                  {
72                      accountNumber = input.nextInt(); // read account number
73                      firstName = input.next(); // read first name
74                      lastName = input.next(); // read last name
75                      balance = input.nextDouble(); // read balance
76
77                      if ( accountNumber > 0 && accountNumber <= NUMBER_RECORDS )
78                      {
79                          record.setAccount( accountNumber );
80                          record.setFirstName( firstName );
81                          record.setLastName( lastName );
82                          record.setBalance( balance );
83
84                          output.seek( ( accountNumber - 1 ) * // position to proper
85                              RandomAccessAccountRecord.SIZE ); // location for file
86                          record.write( output );
87                      } // end if
88                      else
89                          System.out.println( "Account must be between 0 and 100." );
90                  } // end try
91                  catch ( IOException ioException )
92                  {
93                      System.err.println( "Error writing to file." );
94                      return;
95                  } // end catch
96                  catch ( NoSuchElementException elementException )
97                  {
98                      System.err.println( "Invalid input. Please try again." );
99                      input.nextLine(); // discard input so user can try again
100                 } // end catch
101
102                 System.out.printf( "%s %s\n%s", "Enter account number (1-100),",
103                     "first name, last name and balance.", "? " );
104             } // end while
105         } // end method addRecords
106 } // end class WriteRandomFile
```

Fig. 14.26 | Writing data to a random-access file. (Part 3 of 3.)

exact location in the file at which a record of information is stored. Method seek sets the file-position pointer to a specific location in the file relative to the beginning of the file, and RandomAccessAccountRecord method write outputs the data at the current position in the file. The program assumes that the user does not enter duplicate account numbers.

The user enters values for the account number, first name, last name and balance. After each record is entered, the program stores the data in RandomAccessAccountRecord object record (lines 79–82 of Figure 14.26) and calls record's write method to output the data (line 86).

Lines 84–85 call RandomAccessFile method seek to position the file-position pointer for object output to the byte location calculated by (accountNumber - 1) * RandomAccessAccountRecord.SIZE. Account numbers in this program are in the range 1–100. We subtract one from the account number when calculating the byte location of the record.

```
 1   // Fig. 14.27: WriteRandomFileTest.java
 2   // This program tests class WriteRandomFile.
 3
 4   public class WriteRandomFileTest
 5   {
 6      public static void main( String args[] )
 7      {
 8         WriteRandomFile application = new WriteRandomFile();
 9         application.openFile();
10         application.addRecords();
11         application.closeFile();
12      } // end main
13   } // end class WriteRandomFileTest
```

```
To terminate input, type the end-of-file indicator
when you are prompted to enter input.
On UNIX/Linux/Mac OS X type <ctrl> d then press Enter
On Windows type <ctrl> z then press Enter

Enter account number (1-100), first name, last name and balance.
? 37 Doug Barker 0.00
Enter account number (1-100), first name, last name and balance.
? 29 Nancy Brown -24.54
Enter account number (1-100), first name, last name and balance.
? 96 Sam Stone 34.98
Enter account number (1-100), first name, last name and balance.
? 88 Dave Smith 258.34
Enter account number (1-100), first name, last name and balance.
? 33 Stacey Dunn 314.33
Enter account number (1-100), first name, last name and balance.
? ^Z
```

Fig. 14.27 | Testing class `WriteRandomFile`.

Thus, for record one, the file-position pointer is set to byte zero of the file. For record 100, the file-position pointer is set to skip the first 99 records in the file.

14.7.3 Reading Data Sequentially from a Random-Access File

In the preceding sections, we created a random-access file and wrote data to it. In this section, we develop a program (Fig. 14.28–Fig. 14.29) that opens a `RandomAccessFile` for reading with the "r" file-open mode (line 19 of Fig. 14.28), reads through the file sequentially and displays only those records containing data. The program produces an additional benefit. See whether you can determine what it is—we reveal it at the end of this section.

Good Programming Practice 14.1

Open a file with the "r" file-open mode for input if the contents should not be modified. This practice prevents unintentional modification of the file's contents. This is another example of the principle of least privilege.

The program reads records by invoking method `readRecords` (lines 28–59). This method invokes class `RandomAccessAccountRecord`'s read method (line 41) to read one

```java
1   // Fig. 14.28: ReadRandomFile.java
2   // This program reads a random-access file sequentially and
3   // displays the contents one record at a time in text fields.
4   import java.io.EOFException;
5   import java.io.IOException;
6   import java.io.RandomAccessFile;
7
8   import com.deitel.jhtp6.ch14.RandomAccessAccountRecord;
9
10  public class ReadRandomFile
11  {
12      private RandomAccessFile input;
13
14      // enable user to select file to open
15      public void openFile()
16      {
17          try // open file
18          {
19              input = new RandomAccessFile( "clients.dat", "r" );
20          } // end try
21          catch ( IOException ioException )
22          {
23              System.err.println( "File does not exist." );
24          } // end catch
25      } // end method openFile
26
27      // read and display records
28      public void readRecords()
29      {
30          RandomAccessAccountRecord record = new RandomAccessAccountRecord();
31
32          System.out.printf( "%-10s%-15s%-15s%10s\n", "Account",
33              "First Name", "Last Name", "Balance" );
34
35          try // read a record and display
36          {
37              while ( true )
38              {
39                  do
40                  {
41                      record.read( input );
42                  } while ( record.getAccount() == 0 );
43
44                  // display record contents
45                  System.out.printf( "%-10d%-12s%-12s10.2f\n",
46                      record.getAccount(), record.getFirstName(),
47                      record.getLastName(), record.getBalance() );
48              } // end while
49          } // end try
50          catch ( EOFException eofException ) // close file
51          {
```

Fig. 14.28 | Reading data sequentially from a random-access file. (Part 1 of 2.)

```
52          return; // end of file was reached
53       } // end catch
54       catch ( IOException ioException )
55       {
56          System.err.println( "Error reading file." );
57          System.exit( 1 );
58       } // end catch
59    } // end method readRecords
60
61    // close file and terminate application
62    public void closeFile()
63    {
64       try // close file and exit
65       {
66          if ( input != null )
67             input.close();
68       } // end try
69       catch ( IOException ioException )
70       {
71          System.err.println( "Error closing file." );
72          System.exit( 1 );
73       } // end catch
74    } // end method closeFile
75 } // end class ReadRandomFile
```

Fig. 14.28 | Reading data sequentially from a random-access file. (Part 2 of 2.)

```
1  // Fig. 14.29: ReadRandomFileTest.java
2  // Testing class ReadRandomFile.
3
4  public class ReadRandomFileTest
5  {
6     public static void main( String args[] )
7     {
8        ReadRandomFile application = new ReadRandomFile();
9        application.openFile();
10       application.readRecords();
11       application.closeFile();
12    } // end main
13 } // end class ReadRandomFileTest
```

Account	First Name	Last Name	Balance
29	Nancy	Brown	-24.54
33	Stacey	Dunn	314.33
37	Doug	Barker	0.00
88	Dave	Smith	258.34
96	Sam	Stone	34.98

Fig. 14.29 | Testing class `ReadRandomFile`.

record's data into `RandomAccessAccountRecord` object record. Method `readRecords`
reads from the file using two loops. The outer loop, a `while` statement, loops until an attempt is made to read past the end of the file. The inner loop, a `do...while` statement, is

used to read records until one is encountered with a nonzero account number (zero is the account number for empty records). At this point, the record is displayed. When all the records have been read, the file is closed and the program terminates. Figure 14.29 contains method `main` and begins the execution of the program. Lines 9–11 open the file, call method `readRecords` and close the file.

What about that additional benefit we promised? If you examine the output, you will notice that the records are displayed in sorted order (by account number)! This ordering is a simple consequence of the way we stored these records in the file, using direct-access techniques. Sorting with direct-access techniques is blazingly fast. The speed is achieved by making the file large enough to hold every possible record that might be created, which enables the program to insert a record between other records without having to reorganize the file. This configuration, of course, means that the file could be sparsely occupied most of the time, a waste of storage. So this situation is another example of the space/time trade-off. By using large amounts of space, we are able to develop a much faster sorting algorithm.

14.7.4 Case Study: A Transaction-Processing Program

We now present a substantial transaction-processing program (Fig. 14.33–Fig. 14.36), using a random-access file to achieve instant-access processing. The program maintains a bank's account information—it displays existing accounts, updates accounts, adds new accounts and deletes accounts. We assume that the program in Fig. 14.24–Fig. 14.25 has been executed to create a file, and that the program in Fig. 14.26–Fig. 14.27 has been executed to insert initial data. The techniques used in this example were presented in the earlier `RandomAccessFile` examples.

The program has five options. Option 1 displays a list of all the accounts in the file, using the same techniques as in the preceding section. Choosing option 1 displays the information in Fig. 14.30.

Option 2 is used to update an account. The application will only update an existing record, so the function first checks to see whether the record specified by the user is empty. The record is read from the file, then the account number is compared to 0. If it is 0, the record contains no information, and a message is printed stating that the record is empty. Then, the menu choices are displayed. If the record contains information, the record's current information is displayed first. The user is then prompted for a change in the balance (either a charge or a payment), and the updated record is displayed. A typical output for option 2 is shown in Fig. 14.31.

Option 3 is used to add a new account to the file. The user is prompted to enter information for a new record. If the user enters an account number for an existing account, an error message is displayed indicating that the record already contains information, and the

```
Account    First Name    Last Name         Balance
29         Nancy         Brown             -24.54
33         Stacey        Dunn              314.33
37         Doug          Barker              0.00
88         Dave          Smith             258.34
96         Sam           Stone              34.98
```

Fig. 14.30 | Transaction processor displaying records.

```
Enter account to update ( 1 - 100 ): 37
37          Doug           Barker              0.00

Enter charge ( + ) or payment ( - ): +87.99
37          Doug           Barker              87.99
```

Fig. 14.31 | Transaction processor updating a record.

menu choices are printed again. If the account number entered does not correspond to an existing record (and all the data entered is valid), the new record is created and stored in the file. This code for this option uses the same process to add a new account as does the program in Fig. 14.26–Fig. 14.27. A typical output for option 3 is shown in Fig. 14.32.

Option 4 is used to delete a record from the file. Deletion is accomplished by asking the user for the account number and reinitializing the record (i.e., writing a blank record in its place). If the account contains no information, deleteRecord displays an error message stating that the account does not exist. Option 5 terminates program execution. The program is shown in Fig. 14.33–Fig. 14.36. Figure 14.33 defines the enum type for the user's options. The options are listed in lines 7–11.

```
Enter account number, first name, last name and balance.
(Account number must be 1 - 100)
? 22 Sarah Johnston 247.45
```

Fig. 14.32 | Transaction processor inserting a record.

```java
1   // Fig. 14.33: MenuOption.java
2   // Defines an enum type for the credit inquiry program's options.
3
4   public enum MenuOption
5   {
6      // declare contents of enum type
7      PRINT( 1 ),
8      UPDATE( 2 ),
9      NEW( 3 ),
10     DELETE( 4 ),
11     END( 5 );
12
13     private final int value; // current menu option
14
15     MenuOption( int valueOption )
16     {
17        value = valueOption;
18     } // end MenuOptions enum constructor
19
20     public int getValue()
21     {
22        return value;
23     } // end method getValue
24  } // end enum MenuOption
```

Fig. 14.33 | Transaction processor's menu options.

Class `FileEditor` (Fig. 14.34) declares methods for manipulating records in a random-access file. This class uses all the techniques shown in the earlier examples. Method `getRecord` (lines 31–45) reads the record with the given account number and stores its information in a `RandomAccessAccountRecord` object. Method `updateRecord` (lines 48–64) modifies the record with the given account number, as long as the account number corresponds to a non-empty record. Method `newRecord` (lines 67–83) adds a new record to the file using the provided account number, first name, last name and balance. Method `deleteRecord` (lines 86–100) deletes the record with the given account number from the file, provided that the specified account exists. Method `readRecords` (lines 103–136) displays all the currently existing records in the file.

```java
1   // Fig. 14.34: FileEditor.java
2   // This class declares methods that manipulate bank account
3   // records in a random access file.
4   import java.io.EOFException;
5   import java.io.File;
6   import java.io.IOException;
7   import java.io.RandomAccessFile;
8   import java.util.Scanner;
9
10  import com.deitel.jhtp6.ch14.RandomAccessAccountRecord;
11
12  public class FileEditor
13  {
14     RandomAccessFile file; // reference to the file
15     Scanner input = new Scanner( System.in );
16
17     // open the file
18     public FileEditor( String fileName ) throws IOException
19     {
20        file = new RandomAccessFile( fileName, "rw" );
21     } // end FileEditor constructor
22
23     // close the file
24     public void closeFile() throws IOException
25     {
26        if ( file != null )
27           file.close();
28     } // end method closeFile
29
30     // get a record from the file
31     public RandomAccessAccountRecord getRecord( int accountNumber )
32        throws IllegalArgumentException, NumberFormatException, IOException
33     {
34        RandomAccessAccountRecord record = new RandomAccessAccountRecord();
35
36        if ( accountNumber < 1 || accountNumber > 100 )
37           throw new IllegalArgumentException( "Out of range" );
38
```

Fig. 14.34 | `FileEditor` class that encapsulates the file-processing capabilities required in Fig. 14.35. (Part 1 of 3.)

```
39          // seek appropriate record in file
40          file.seek( ( accountNumber - 1 ) * RandomAccessAccountRecord.SIZE );
41
42          record.read( file );
43
44          return record;
45       } // end method getRecord
46
47       // update record in file
48       public void updateRecord( int accountNumber, double transaction )
49          throws IllegalArgumentException, IOException
50       {
51          RandomAccessAccountRecord record = getRecord( accountNumber );
52
53          if ( record.getAccount() == 0 )
54             throw new IllegalArgumentException( "Account does not exist" );
55
56          // seek appropriate record in file
57          file.seek( ( accountNumber - 1 ) * RandomAccessAccountRecord.SIZE );
58
59          record = new RandomAccessAccountRecord(
60             record.getAccount(), record.getFirstName(),
61             record.getLastName(), record.getBalance() + transaction );
62
63          record.write( file ); // write updated record to file
64       } // end method updateRecord
65
66       // add record to file
67       public void newRecord( int accountNumber, String firstName,
68          String lastName, double balance )
69          throws IllegalArgumentException, IOException
70       {
71          RandomAccessAccountRecord record = getRecord( accountNumber );
72
73          if ( record.getAccount() != 0 )
74             throw new IllegalArgumentException( "Account already exists" );
75
76          // seek appropriate record in file
77          file.seek( ( accountNumber - 1 ) * RandomAccessAccountRecord.SIZE );
78
79          record = new RandomAccessAccountRecord( accountNumber,
80             firstName, lastName, balance );
81
82          record.write( file ); // write record to file
83       } // end method newRecord
84
85       // delete record from file
86       public void deleteRecord( int accountNumber )
87          throws IllegalArgumentException, IOException
88       {
```

Fig. 14.34 | FileEditor class that encapsulates the file-processing capabilities required in Fig. 14.35. (Part 2 of 3.)

```
89              RandomAccessAccountRecord record = getRecord( accountNumber );
90
91              if ( record.getAccount() == 0 )
92                 throw new IllegalArgumentException( "Account does not exist" );
93
94              // seek appropriate record in file
95              file.seek( ( accountNumber - 1 ) * RandomAccessAccountRecord.SIZE );
96
97              // create a blank record to write to the file
98              record = new RandomAccessAccountRecord();
99              record.write( file );
100         } // end method deleteRecord
101
102         // read and display records
103         public void readRecords()
104         {
105            RandomAccessAccountRecord record = new RandomAccessAccountRecord();
106
107            System.out.printf( "%-10s%-15s%-15s%10s\n", "Account",
108               "First Name", "Last Name", "Balance" );
109
110            try // read a record and display
111            {
112               file.seek( 0 );
113
114               while ( true )
115               {
116                  do
117                  {
118                     record.read( file );
119                  } while ( record.getAccount() == 0 );
120
121                  // display record contents
122                  System.out.printf( "%-10d%-15s%-15s%10.2f\n",
123                     record.getAccount(), record.getFirstName(),
124                     record.getLastName(), record.getBalance() );
125               } // end while
126            } // end try
127            catch ( EOFException eofException ) // close file
128            {
129               return; // end of file was reached
130            } // end catch
131            catch ( IOException ioException )
132            {
133               System.err.println( "Error reading file." );
134               System.exit( 1 );
135            } // end catch
136         } // end method readRecords
137      } // end class FileEditor
```

Fig. 14.34 | `FileEditor` class that encapsulates the file-processing capabilities required in Fig. 14.35. (Part 3 of 3.)

Class `TransactionProcessor` (Fig. 14.35) displays the menu for the application and manages the interactions with the `FileEditor` object that is created in the `openFile` method (lines 20–34).

```java
1   // Fig. 14.35: TransactionProcessor.java
2   // A transaction processing program using random-access files.
3   import java.io.IOException;
4   import java.util.NoSuchElementException;
5   import java.util.Scanner;
6
7   import com.deitel.jhtp6.ch14.RandomAccessAccountRecord;
8
9   public class TransactionProcessor
10  {
11     private FileEditor dataFile;
12     private RandomAccessAccountRecord record;
13     private MenuOption choices[] = { MenuOption.PRINT,
14        MenuOption.UPDATE, MenuOption.NEW,
15        MenuOption.DELETE, MenuOption.END };
16
17     private Scanner input = new Scanner( System.in );
18
19     // get the file name and open the file
20     private boolean openFile()
21     {
22        try // attempt to open file
23        {
24           // call the helper method to open the file
25           dataFile = new FileEditor( "clients.dat" );
26        } // end try
27        catch ( IOException ioException )
28        {
29           System.err.println( "Error opening file." );
30           return false;
31        } // end catch
32
33        return true;
34     } // end method openFile
35
36     // close file and terminate application
37     private void closeFile()
38     {
39        try // close file
40        {
41           dataFile.closeFile();
42        } // end try
43        catch ( IOException ioException )
44        {
45           System.err.println( "Error closing file." );
46           System.exit( 1 );
47        } // end catch
48     } // end method closeFile
```

Fig. 14.35 | Transaction-processing program. (Part 1 of 4.)

```
49
50        // create, update or delete the record
51        private void performAction( MenuOption action )
52        {
53           int accountNumber = 0; // account number of record
54           String firstName; // first name for account
55           String lastName; // last name for account
56           double balance; // account balance
57           double transaction; // amount to change in balance
58
59           try // attempt to manipulate files based on option selected
60           {
61              switch ( action ) // switch based on option selected
62              {
63                 case PRINT:
64                    System.out.println();
65                    dataFile.readRecords();
66                    break;
67                 case NEW:
68                    System.out.printf( "\n%s%s\n%s\n%s",
69                       "Enter account number,",
70                       " first name, last name and balance.",
71                       "(Account number must be 1 - 100)", "? " );
72
73                    accountNumber = input.nextInt(); // read account number
74                    firstName = input.next(); // read first name
75                    lastName = input.next(); // read last name
76                    balance = input.nextDouble(); // read balance
77
78                    dataFile.newRecord( accountNumber, firstName,
79                       lastName, balance ); // create new record
80                    break;
81                 case UPDATE:
82                    System.out.print(
83                       "\nEnter account to update ( 1 - 100 ): " );
84                    accountNumber = input.nextInt();
85                    record = dataFile.getRecord( accountNumber );
86
87                    if ( record.getAccount() == 0 )
88                       System.out.println( "Account does not exist." );
89                    else
90                    {
91                       // display record contents
92                       System.out.printf( "%-10d%-12s%-12s%10.2f\n\n",
93                          record.getAccount(), record.getFirstName(),
94                          record.getLastName(), record.getBalance() );
95
96                       System.out.print(
97                          "Enter charge ( + ) or payment ( - ): " );
98                       transaction = input.nextDouble();
99                       dataFile.updateRecord( accountNumber, // update record
100                         transaction );
```

Fig. 14.35 | Transaction-processing program. (Part 2 of 4.)

```
101
102                        // retrieve updated record
103                        record = dataFile.getRecord( accountNumber );
104
105                        // display updated record
106                        System.out.printf( "%-10d%-12s%-12s%10.2f\n",
107                           record.getAccount(), record.getFirstName(),
108                           record.getLastName(), record.getBalance() );
109                     } // end else
110                     break;
111                  case DELETE:
112                     System.out.print(
113                        "\nEnter an account to delete (1 - 100): " );
114                     accountNumber = input.nextInt();
115
116                     dataFile.deleteRecord( accountNumber ); // delete record
117                     break;
118                  default:
119                     System.out.println( "Invalid action." );
120                     break;
121               } // end switch
122            } // end try
123            catch ( NumberFormatException format )
124            {
125               System.err.println( "Bad input." );
126            } // end catch
127            catch ( IllegalArgumentException badAccount )
128            {
129               System.err.println( badAccount.getMessage() );
130            } // end catch
131            catch ( IOException ioException )
132            {
133               System.err.println( "Error writing to the file." );
134            } // end catch
135            catch ( NoSuchElementException elementException )
136            {
137               System.err.println( "Invalid input. Please try again." );
138               input.nextLine(); // discard input so user can try again
139            } // end catch
140         } // end method performAction
141
142         // enable user to input menu choice
143         private MenuOption enterChoice()
144         {
145            int menuChoice = 1;
146
147            // display available options
148            System.out.printf( "\n%s\n%s\n%s\n%s\n%s\n%s",
149               "Enter your choice", "1 - List accounts",
150               "2 - Update an account", "3 - Add a new account",
151               "4 - Delete an account", "5 - End program\n? " );
152
```

Fig. 14.35 | Transaction-processing program. (Part 3 of 4.)

```
153        try
154        {
155           menuChoice = input.nextInt();
156        }
157        catch ( NoSuchElementException elementException )
158        {
159           System.err.println( "Invalid input." );
160           System.exit( 1 );
161        } // end catch
162
163        return choices[ menuChoice - 1 ]; // return choice from user
164     } // end enterChoice
165
166     public void processRequests()
167     {
168        openFile();
169
170        // get user's request
171        MenuOption choice = enterChoice();
172
173        while ( choice != MenuOption.END )
174        {
175           performAction( choice );
176           choice = enterChoice();
177        } // end while
178
179        closeFile();
180     } // end method processRequests
181  } // end class TransactionProcessor
```

Fig. 14.35 | Transaction-processing program. (Part 4 of 4.)

Method processRequests (lines 166–180) processes the choices entered by the user. If the user does not enter 5 (which ends the program), method performAction (lines 51–140) is called. This method inputs information from the user and sends it to the appropriate method of class FileEditor (Fig. 14.34), which encapsulates the file-processing operations in this example. The method to call is determined by performAction's MenuOption argument. Each option is handled in the switch statement of lines 61–121.

```
1   // Fig. 14.36: TransactionProcessorTest.java
2   // Testing the transaction processor.
3
4   public class TransactionProcessorTest
5   {
6      public static void main( String args[] )
7      {
8         TransactionProcessor application = new TransactionProcessor();
9         application.processRequests();
10     } // end main
11  } // end class TransactionProcessorTest
```

Fig. 14.36 | Testing class TransactionProcessor.

Method `performAction` also handles any exceptions that might be thrown from File-Editor's methods.

14.8 Additional `java.io` Classes

We now introduce you to other useful classes in the `java.io` package. We overview additional interfaces and classes for byte-based input and output streams, and character-based input and output streams.

Interfaces and Classes for Byte-Based Input and Output

InputStream and **OutputStream** (subclasses of Object) are abstract classes that declare methods for performing byte-based input and output, respectively. We used concrete classes FileInputStream (a subclass of InputStream) and FileOutputStream (a subclass of OutputStream) to manipulate files in this chapter.

Pipes are synchronized communication channels between threads. We discuss threads in Chapter 23, Multithreading. Java provides **PipedOutputStream** (a subclass of Output-Stream) and **PipedInputStream** (a subclass of InputStream) to establish pipes between two threads in a program. One thread sends data to another by writing to a PipedOutput-Stream. The target thread reads information from the pipe via a PipedInputStream.

A **FilterInputStream** filters an InputStream, and a **FilterOutputStream** filters an OutputStream. Filtering means simply that the filter stream provides additional functionality, such as aggregating data bytes into meaningful primitive-type units. FilterInput-Stream and FilterOutputStream are abstract classes, so some of their filtering capabilities are provided by their concrete subclasses.

A **PrintStream** (a subclass of FilterOutputStream) performs text output to the specified stream. Actually, we have been using PrintStream output throughout the text to this point—System.out and System.err are PrintStream objects.

Reading data as raw bytes is fast, but crude. Usually, programs read data as aggregates of bytes that form ints, floats, doubles and so on. Java programs can use several classes to input and output data in aggregate form.

Interface DataInput (discussed in Section 14.7.1) describes methods for reading primitive types from an input stream. Classes **DataInputStream** and RandomAccessFile each implement this interface to read sets of bytes and view them as primitive-type values. Interface DataInput includes methods readLine (for byte arrays), readBoolean, readByte, readChar, readDouble, readFloat, readFully (for byte arrays), readInt, readLong, read-Short, readUnsignedByte, readUnsignedShort, readUTF (for reading Unicode characters encoded by Java—we discuss UTF encoding in Appendix F, Unicode®) and skipBytes.

Interface DataOutput (discussed in Section 14.7.1) describes a set of methods for writing primitive types to an output stream. Classes **DataOutputStream** (a subclass of Fil-terOutputStream) and RandomAccessFile each implement this interface to write primitive-type values as bytes. Interface DataOutput includes overloaded versions of method write (for a byte or for a byte array) and methods writeBoolean, writeByte, write-Bytes, writeChar, writeChars (for Unicode Strings), writeDouble, writeFloat, writeInt, writeLong, writeShort and writeUTF (to output text modified for Unicode).

Buffering is an I/O-performance-enhancement technique. With a **BufferedOutput-Stream** (a subclass of class FilterOutputStream), each output statement does not necessarily result in an actual physical transfer of data to the output device (which is a slow operation compared to processor and main memory speeds). Rather, each output operation is directed to a region in memory called a buffer that is large enough to hold the data of many output operations. Then, actual transfer to the output device is performed in one large **physical output operation** each time the buffer fills. The output operations directed to the output buffer in memory are often called **logical output operations**. With a `BufferedOutputStream`, a partially filled buffer can be forced out to the device at any time by invoking the stream object's `flush` method.

Using buffering can greatly increase the efficiency of an application. Typical I/O operations are extremely slow compared with the speed of accessing computer memory. Buffering reduces the number of I/O operations by first combining smaller outputs together in memory. The number of actual physical I/O operations is small compared with the number of I/O requests issued by the program. Thus, the program that is using buffering is more efficient.

Performance Tip 14.1

Buffered I/O can yield significant performance improvements over unbuffered I/O.

With a `BufferedInputStream` (a subclass of class `FilterInputStream`), many "logical" chunks of data from a file are read as one large **physical input operation** into a memory buffer. As a program requests each new chunk of data, it is taken from the buffer. (This procedure is sometimes referred to as a **logical input operation**.) When the buffer is empty, the next actual physical input operation from the input device is performed to read in the next group of "logical" chunks of data. Thus, the number of actual physical input operations is small compared with the number of read requests issued by the program.

Earlier in the chapter we used class `StringBuffer`, which allows us to dynamically manipulate strings. It is important to note that class `StringBuffer` can be used to buffer output that will be displayed later to the screen or in a `JTextArea`. This increases the efficiency of a program—just as with buffering, it is much faster to first combine all the program's output in a `StringBuffer` object and display the final output to a `JTextArea` or the screen, then to continually add text to a `JTextArea` or the screen. We discuss class `StringBuffer` in more detail in Chapter 29, Strings, Characters and Regular Expressions.

Java stream I/O includes capabilities for inputting from byte arrays in memory and outputting to byte arrays in memory. A `ByteArrayInputStream` (a subclass of `InputStream`) reads from a byte array in memory. A `ByteArrayOutputStream` (a subclass of `OutputStream`) outputs to a byte array in memory. One use of byte-array I/O is data validation. A program can input an entire line at a time from the input stream into a byte array. Then a validation routine can scrutinize the contents of the byte array and correct the data if necessary. Finally, the program can proceed to input from the byte array, "knowing" that the input data is in the proper format. Outputting to a byte array is a nice way to take advantage of the powerful output-formatting capabilities of Java streams. For example, data can be stored in a byte array, using the same formatting that will be displayed at a later time, and the byte array can then be output to a disk file to preserve the screen image.

A `SequenceInputStream` (a subclass of `InputStream`) enables concatenation of several `InputStreams`, which means that the program sees the group as one continuous `InputStream`. When the program reaches the end of an input stream, that stream closes, and the next stream in the sequence opens.

Interfaces and Classes for Character-Based Input and Output

In addition to the byte-based streams, Java provides the **Reader** and **Writer** abstract classes, which are Unicode two-byte, character-based streams. Most of the byte-based streams have corresponding character-based concrete Reader or Writer classes.

Classes **BufferedReader** (a subclass of abstract class Reader) and **BufferedWriter** (a subclass of abstract class Writer) enable buffering for character-based streams. Remember that character-based streams use Unicode characters—such streams can process data in any language that the Unicode character set represents.

Classes **CharArrayReader** and **CharArrayWriter** read and write, respectively, a stream of characters to a character array. A **LineNumberReader** (a subclass of BufferedReader) is a buffered character stream that keeps track of the number of lines read (i.e., a newline, a return or a carriage-return–line-feed combination). Keeping track of line numbers can be useful if the program needs to inform the reader of an error on a specific line.

Class FileReader (a subclass of **InputStreamReader**) and class FileWriter (a subclass of **OutputStreamWriter**) read characters from and write characters to a file, respectively. Class **PipedReader** and class **PipedWriter** implement piped-character streams that can be used to transfer information between threads. Class **StringReader** and **StringWriter** read characters from and write characters to Strings, respectively. A PrintWriter writes characters to a stream.

14.9 Opening Files with `JFileChooser`

We conclude this chapter by introducing class **JFileChooser**. We use this class to display a dialog (known as the **JFileChooser dialog**) that enables users of our program to easily select files. To demonstrate the JFileChooser dialog, we enhance the example in Section 14.4, as shown in Fig. 14.37–Fig. 14.38. The example now contains a graphical user interface, but still displays the same data as before. The constructor calls method analyzePath in line 34. This method then calls method getFile in line 68 to retrieve the File object.

Method getFile is defined in lines 38–62 of Fig. 14.37. Line 41 creates a JFileChooser and assigns its reference to fileChooser. Lines 42–43 call method **setFileSelectionMode** to specify what the user can select from the fileChooser. For this program, we use JFileChooser static constant **FILES_AND_DIRECTORIES** to indicate that files and directories can be selected. Other static constants include **FILES_ONLY** and **DIRECTORIES_ONLY**.

Line 45 calls method **showOpenDialog** to display the JFileChooser dialog titled **Open**. Argument this specifies the JFileChooser dialog's parent window, which determines the position of the dialog on the screen. If null is passed, the dialog is displayed in the center of the screen—otherwise, the dialog is centered over the application window (specified by the argument this). A JFileChooser dialog is a modal dialog that does not allow the user to interact with any other window in the program until the user closes the JFileChooser by clicking the **Open** or **Cancel** button. The user selects the drive, directory or file name, then clicks **Open**. Method showOpenDialog returns an integer specifying which button (**Open** or **Cancel**) the user clicked to close the dialog. Line 48 tests whether the user clicked **Cancel** by comparing the result with static constant **CANCEL_OPTION**. If they are equal, the program terminates. Line 51 retrieves the file the user selected by calling JFileChooser method **getSelectedFile**. The program then displays information about the selected file or directory.

```java
 1   // Fig. 14.37: FileDemonstration.java
 2   // Demonstrating the File class.
 3   import java.awt.BorderLayout;
 4   import java.awt.event.ActionEvent;
 5   import java.awt.event.ActionListener;
 6   import java.io.File;
 7   import javax.swing.JFileChooser;
 8   import javax.swing.JFrame;
 9   import javax.swing.JOptionPane;
10   import javax.swing.JScrollPane;
11   import javax.swing.JTextArea;
12   import javax.swing.JTextField;
13
14   public class FileDemonstration extends JFrame
15   {
16      private JTextArea outputArea; // used for output
17      private JScrollPane scrollPane; // used to provide scrolling to output
18
19      // set up GUI
20      public FileDemonstration()
21      {
22         super( "Testing class File" );
23
24         outputArea = new JTextArea();
25
26         // add outputArea to scrollPane
27         scrollPane = new JScrollPane( outputArea );
28
29         add( scrollPane, BorderLayout.CENTER ); // add scrollPane to GUI
30
31         setSize( 400, 400 ); // set GUI size
32         setVisible( true ); // display GUI
33
34         analyzePath(); // create and analyze File object
35      } // end FileDemonstration constructor
36
37      // allow user to specify file name
38      private File getFile()
39      {
40         // display file dialog, so user can choose file to open
41         JFileChooser fileChooser = new JFileChooser();
42         fileChooser.setFileSelectionMode(
43            JFileChooser.FILES_AND_DIRECTORIES );
44
45         int result = fileChooser.showOpenDialog( this );
46
47         // if user clicked Cancel button on dialog, return
48         if ( result == JFileChooser.CANCEL_OPTION )
49            System.exit( 1 );
50
```

Fig. 14.37 | Demonstrating `JFileChooser`. (Part 1 of 2.)

```
51          File fileName = fileChooser.getSelectedFile(); // get selected file
52
53          // display error if invalid
54          if ( ( fileName == null ) || ( fileName.getName().equals( "" ) ) )
55          {
56             JOptionPane.showMessageDialog( this, "Invalid File Name",
57                "Invalid File Name", JOptionPane.ERROR_MESSAGE );
58             System.exit( 1 );
59          } // end if
60
61          return fileName;
62       } // end method getFile
63
64       // display information about file user specifies
65       public void analyzePath()
66       {
67          // create File object based on user input
68          File name = getFile();
69
70          if ( name.exists() ) // if name exists, output information about it
71          {
72             // display file (or directory) information
73             outputArea.setText( String.format(
74                "%s%s\n%s\n%s\n%s\n%s%s\n%s%s\n%s%s\n%s%s\n%s%s",
75                name.getName(), " exists",
76                ( name.isFile() ? "is a file" : "is not a file" ),
77                ( name.isDirectory() ? "is a directory" :
78                   "is not a directory" ),
79                ( name.isAbsolute() ? "is absolute path" :
80                   "is not absolute path" ), "Last modified: ",
81                name.lastModified(), "Length: ", name.length(),
82                "Path: ", name.getPath(), "Absolute path: ",
83                name.getAbsolutePath(), "Parent: ", name.getParent() ) );
84
85             if ( name.isDirectory() ) // output directory listing
86             {
87                String directory[] = name.list();
88                outputArea.append( "\n\nDirectory contents:\n" );
89
90                for ( String directoryName : directory )
91                   outputArea.append( directoryName + "\n" );
92             } // end else
93          } // end outer if
94          else // not file or directory, output error message
95          {
96             JOptionPane.showMessageDialog( this, name +
97                " does not exist.", "ERROR", JOptionPane.ERROR_MESSAGE );
98          } // end else
99       } // end method analyzePath
100   } // end class FileDemonstration
```

Fig. 14.37 | Demonstrating `JFileChooser`. (Part 2 of 2.)

```
1   // Fig. 14.38: FileDemonstrationTest.java
2   // Testing the FileDmonstration class.
3   import javax.swing.JFrame;
4
5   public class FileDemonstrationTest
6   {
7      public static void main( String args[] )
8      {
9         FileDemonstration application = new FileDemonstration();
10        application.setDefaultCloseOperation( JFrame.EXIT_ON_CLOSE );
11     } // end main
12  } // end class FileDemonstrationTest
```

Select location for file here

Files and directories are displayed here

Click **Open** to submit new file name to program

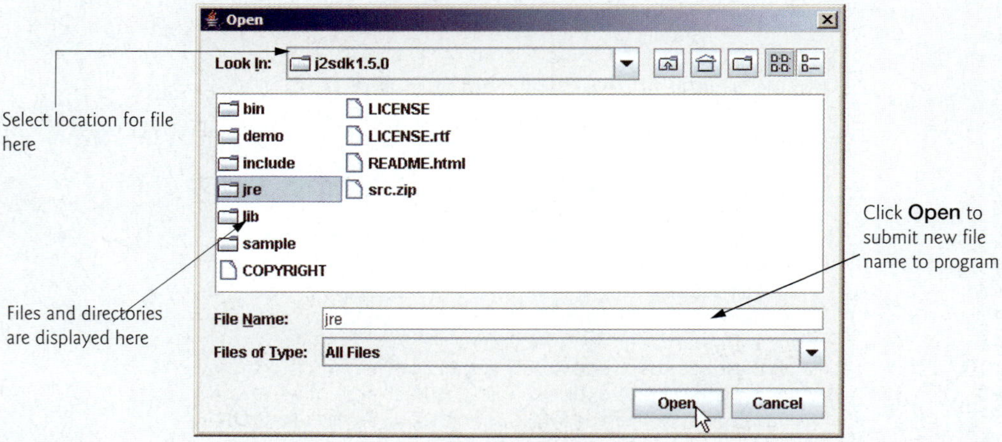

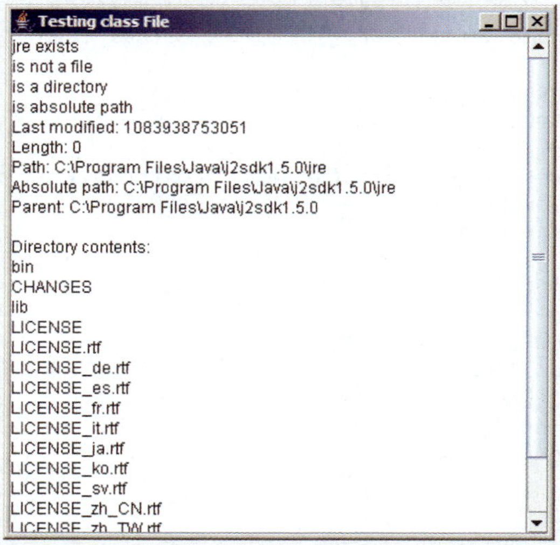

Fig. 14.38 | Testing class `FileDemonstration`.

14.10 Wrap-Up

In this chapter, you learned how to use file processing to manipulate persistent data. You learned that data is stored in computers as 0s and 1s, and that combinations of these values are used to form bytes, fields, records and eventually files. You were given an overview of the differences between character-based and byte-based streams, as well as an introduction to several file-processing classes provided by the `java.io` package. You used class `File` to retrieve information about a file or directory. Next, you learned how to use sequential-access file processing to manipulate records that are stored in order by the record-key field. In that discussion, you learned the differences between text-file processing and object serialization, and used serialization to store and retrieve entire objects. You then learned how to use random-access files to instantly retrieve and manipulate fixed-length records. The chapter concluded with an overview of other classes provided by the `java.io` package, and a small example of using a `JFileChooser` dialog to allow users to easily select files from a GUI. In the next chapter, you will learn the concept of recursion—methods that call themselves. Defining methods in this manner sometimes leads to more intuitive programs.

Summary

- Data stored in variables and arrays is temporary—the data is lost when a local variable goes out of scope or when the program terminates. Computers use files for long-term retention of large amounts of data, even after the programs that created the data terminate.
- Persistent data maintained in files exists beyond the duration of program execution.
- Computers store files on secondary storage devices such as hard disks.
- The smallest data item in a computer can assume the value 0 or the value 1 and is called a bit. Ultimately, a computer processes all data items as combinations of zeros and ones.
- The computer's character set is the set of all characters used to write programs and represent data.
- Characters in Java are Unicode characters composed of two bytes, each composed of eight bits.
- Just as characters are composed of bits, fields are composed of characters or bytes. A field is a group of characters or bytes that conveys meaning.
- Data items processed by computers form a data hierarchy that becomes larger and more complex in structure as we progress from bits to characters to fields, and so on.
- Typically, several fields compose a record (implemented as a `class` in Java).
- A record is a group of related fields.
- A file is a group of related records.
- To facilitate the retrieval of specific records from a file, at least one field in each record is chosen as a record key. A record key identifies a record as belonging to a particular person or entity and is unique to each record.
- There are many ways to organize records in a file. The most common is called a sequential file, in which records are stored in order by the record-key field.
- A group of related files is often called a database. A collection of programs designed to create and manage databases is called a database management system (DBMS).
- Java views each file as a sequential stream of bytes.
- Every operating system provides a mechanism to determine the end of a file, such as an end-of-file marker or a count of the total bytes in the file that is recorded in a system-maintained administrative data structure.

- Byte-based streams represent data in binary format.

- Character-based streams represent data as sequences of characters.

- Files that are created using byte-based streams are binary files. Files created using character-based streams are text files. Text files can be read by text editors, whereas binary files are read by a program that converts the data to a human-readable format.

- Java also can associate streams with different devices. Three stream objects are associated with devices when a Java program begins executing—System.in, System.out and System.err.

- The java.io package includes definitions for stream classes, such as FileInputStream (for byte-based input from a file), FileOutputStream (for byte-based output to a file), FileReader (for character-based input from a file) and FileWriter (for character-based output to a file). Files are opened by creating objects of these stream classes.

- Class File is used to obtain information about files and directories.

- Character-based input and output can be performed with classes Scanner and Formatter.

- Class Formatter enables formatted data to be output to the screen or to a file in a manner similar to System.out.printf.

- A file or directory's path specifies its location on disk.

- An absolute path contains all the directories, starting with the root directory, that lead to a specific file or directory. Every file or directory on a disk drive has the same root directory in its path.

- A relative path normally starts from the directory in which the application began executing.

- A separator character is used to separate directories and files in the path.

- Java imposes no structure on a file—notions such as a record do not exist as part of the Java language. The programmer must structure files to meet an application's requirements.

- To retrieve data sequentially from a file, programs normally start reading from the beginning of the file and read all the data consecutively until the desired information is found.

- Data in many sequential files cannot be modified without the risk of destroying other data in the file. Therefore, records in a sequential-access file are not usually updated in place. Instead, the entire file is usually rewritten.

- Java provides a mechanism called object serialization that enables entire objects to be written to or read from a stream.

- A serialized object is an object represented as a sequence of bytes that includes the object's data as well as information about the object's type and the types of data stored in the object.

- After a serialized object has been written into a file, it can be read from the file and deserialized—that is, the type information and bytes that represent the object and its data can be used to re-create the object in memory.

- Classes ObjectInputStream and ObjectOutputStream, which respectively implement the ObjectInput and ObjectOutput interfaces, enable entire objects to be read from or written to a stream (possibly a file).

- Only classes that implement interface Serializable can be serialized and deserialized with ObjectOutputStreams and ObjectInputStreams.

- The ObjectOutput interface contains method writeObject, which takes an Object that implements interface Serializable as an argument and writes its information to an OutputStream.

- The ObjectInput interface contains method readObject, which reads and returns a reference to an Object from an InputStream. After an object has been read, its reference can be cast to the object's actual type.

- Instant record access is possible with random-access files and with databases. A program can access individual records of a random-access file directly (and quickly) without searching through other records. Random-access files are sometimes called direct-access files.

- Several techniques can be used to create random-access files. Perhaps the simplest is to require that all the records in a file be of the same fixed length.

- Using fixed-length records makes it easy for a program to calculate (as a function of the record size and the record key) the exact location of any record relative to the beginning of the file.

- When a program associates an object of class `RandomAccessFile` with a file, the program reads or writes data, beginning at the location in the file specified by the file-position pointer, and manipulates all the data as primitive types.

- `RandomAccessFile` method `seek` positions to the exact location in the file at which a record of information is stored. Method `seek` sets the file-position pointer to a specific location in the file relative to the beginning of the file.

- Buffering is an I/O-performance-enhancement technique. With a `BufferedOutputStream`, each output statement does not necessarily result in an actual physical transfer of data to the output device. Rather, each output operation is directed to a region in memory called a buffer that is large enough to hold the data of many output operations. Actual transfer to the output device is then performed in one large physical output operation each time the buffer fills.

- With a `BufferedInputStream`, many "logical" chunks of data from a file are read as one large physical input operation into a memory buffer. As a program requests each new chunk of data, it is taken from the buffer. When the buffer is empty, the next actual physical input operation from the input device is performed to read in the next group of "logical" chunks of data.

- Class `JFileChooser` is used to display a dialog that enables users of a program to easily select files from a GUI.

Terminology

absolute path

ASCII (American Standard Code for Information Interchange) character set

batch file

binary file

bit (binary digit)

buffer

byte-based stream

byte data type

`CANCEL_OPTION` constant of class `JFileChooser`

`canRead` method of class `File`

`canWrite` method of class `File`

capacity

character-based stream

character set

`-classpath` command line argument to java

`-classpath` command line argument to javac

data hierarchy

database

database management system (DBMS)

`DataInput` interface

`DataInputStream` class

`DataOutput` interface

`DataOutputStream` class

decimal digit

deserialized object

direct-access application

direct-access files

`DIRECTORIES_ONLY` constant of class `JFileChooser`

directory

directory name

disk

end-of-file marker

`EndOfFileException`

`exists` method of class `File`

`exit` method of class `System`

field

file

`File` class

file-open mode

file-position pointer

file processing

`FileInputStream` class

Self-Review Exercises

14.1 Fill in the blanks in each of the following statements:

a) Ultimately, all data items processed by a computer are reduced to combinations of _____ and _____.

b) The smallest data item a computer can process is called a(n) _____.

c) A(n) _____ can sometimes be viewed as a group of related records.

d) Digits, letters and special symbols are referred to as _____.

e) A group of related files is called a _____.

f) Object _____ normally enables a program to output error messages to the screen.

g) `RandomAccessFile` method _____ reads an integer from the specified stream.

h) `RandomAccessFile` method _____ sets the file-position pointer to a specific location in a file for input or output.

14.2 Determine which of the following statements are *true* and which are *false*. If *false*, explain why.

a) The programmer must explicitly create the stream objects `System.in`, `System.out` and `System.err`.

b) When reading data from a file using class `Scanner`, if the programmer wishes to read data in the file multiple times, the file must be closed and reopened to read from the beginning of the file. This moves the file-position pointer back to the beginning of the file.

c) Method `exists` of class `File` returns `true` if the name specified as the argument to the `File` constructor is a file or directory in the specified path.

d) It is not necessary to search all the records in a random-access file to find a record.

e) Binary files are human readable.

f) An absolute path contains all the directories, starting with the root directory, that lead to a specific file or directory.

g) Class `Formatter` contains method `printf`, which enables formatted data to be output to the screen or to a file.

14.3 Complete the following tasks, assuming that each applies to the same program:

a) Write a statement that opens file `"oldmast.txt"` for input—use `Scanner` variable `inOldMaster`.

b) Write a statement that opens file `"trans.txt"` for input—use `Scanner` variable `inTransaction`.

c) Write a statement that opens file `"newmast.txt"` for output (and creation)—use `Formatter` variable `outNewMaster`.

d) Write the statements needed to read a record from the file `"oldmast.txt"`. The data read should be used to create an object of class `AccountRecord`—use `Scanner` variable `inOldMaster`. Assume that class `AccountRecord` is the same as the `AccountRecord` class in Fig. 14.6.

e) Write the statements needed to read a record from the file `"trans.txt"`. The record is an object of class `TransactionRecord`—use `Scanner` variable `inTransaction`. Assume that class `TransactionRecord` contains method `setAccount` (which takes an `int`) to set the account number and method `setAmount` (which takes a `double`) to set the amount of the transaction.

f) Write a statement that outputs a record to the file `"newmast.txt"`. The record is an object of type `AccountRecord`—use `Formatter` variable `outNewMaster`.

14.4 Complete the following tasks, assuming that each applies to the same program:

a) Write a statement that opens file `"oldmast.ser"` for input—use `ObjectInputStream` variable `inOldMaster` to wrap a `FileInputStream` object.

b) Write a statement that opens file `"trans.ser"` for input—use `ObjectInputStream` variable `inTransaction` to wrap a `FileInputStream` object.

c) Write a statement that opens file `"newmast.ser"` for output (and creation)—use `ObjectOutputStream` variable `outNewMaster` to wrap a `FileOutputStream`.

d) Write a statement that reads a record from the file `"oldmast.ser"`. The record is an object of class `AccountRecordSerializable`—use `ObjectInputStream` variable `inOldMaster`. Assume class `AccountRecordSerializable` is the same as the `AccountRecordSerializable` class in Fig. 14.17

e) Write a statement that reads a record from the file `"trans.ser"`. The record is an object of class `TransactionRecord`—use `ObjectInputStream` variable `inTransaction`.

f) Write a statement that outputs a record to the file `"newmast.ser"`. The record is an object of type `AccountRecordSerializable`—use `ObjectOutputStream` variable `outNewMaster`.

14.5 Find the error in each block of code and show how to correct it.

a) Assume that account, company and amount are declared.

```
ObjectOutputStream outputStream;

outputStream.writeInt( account );
outputStream.writeChars( company );
outputStream.writeDouble( amount );
```

b) The following statements should read a record from the file `"payables.txt"`. The Scanner variable `inPayable` should be used to refer to this file.

```
Scanner inPayable = new Scanner( new File( "payables.txt" ) );
PayablesRecord record = ( PayablesRecord ) inPayable.readObject();
```

Answers to Self-Review Exercises

14.1 a) ones, zeros. b) bit. c) file. d) characters. e) database. f) `System.err`. g) `readInt`. h) seek.

14.2 a) False. These three streams are created for the programmer when a Java application begins executing.
b) True.
c) True.
d) True.
e) False. Text files are human readable.
f) True.
g) False. Class `Formatter` contains method `format`, which enables formatted data to be output to the screen or to a file.

14.3 a) `Scanner inOldMaster = new Scanner( new File ( "oldmast.txt" ) );`
b) `Scanner inTransaction = new Scanner( new File( "trans.txt" ) );`
c) `Formatter outNewMaster = new Formatter( "newmast.txt" );`
d) `AccountRecord account = new AccountRecord();`
`    account.setAccount( inOldMaster.nextInt() );`
`    account.setFirstName( inOldMaster.next() );`
`    account.setLastName( inOldMaster.next() );`
`    account.setBalance( inOldMaster.nextDouble() );`
e) `TransactionRecord transaction = new Transaction();`
`    transaction.setAccount( inTransaction.nextInt() );`
`    transaction.setAmount( inTransaction.nextDouble() );`

f) `outNewMaster.format( "%d %s %s %.2f\n",`
   `account.getAccount(), account.getFirstName(),`
   `account.getLastName(), account.getBalance() );`

14.4 a) `ObjectInputStream inOldMaster = new ObjectInputStream(`
   `new FileInputStream( "oldmast.ser" ) );`

b) `ObjectInputStream inTransaction = new ObjectInputStream(`
   `new FileInputStream( "trans.ser" ) );`

c) `ObjectOutputStream outNewMaster = new ObjectOutputStream(`
   `new FileOutputStream( "newmast.ser" ) );`

d) `accountRecord = ( AccountRecordSerializable ) inOldMaster.readObject();`

e) `transactionRecord = ( TransactionRecord ) inTransaction.readObject();`

f) `outNewMaster.writeObject( newAccountRecord );`

14.5 a) Error: The file has not been opened before the attempt is made to output data to the stream.
   Correction: Open a file for output by creating a new `ObjectOutputStream` object that wraps a `FileOutputStream` object.

b) Error: This example uses text files with a `Scanner`, there is no object serialization. As a result, method `readObject` cannot be used to read that data from the file. Each piece of data must be read separately, then used to create a `PayablesRecord` object.
   Correction: Use methods of `inPayable` to read each piece of the `PayablesRecord` object.

Exercises

14.6 Fill in the blanks in each of the following statements:
a) Computers store large amounts of data on secondary storage devices as _____.
b) A(n) _____ is composed of several fields.
c) To facilitate the retrieval of specific records from a file, one field in each record is chosen as a(n) _____.
d) Files that are created using byte-based streams are referred to as _____ files, while files created using character-based streams are referred to as _____ files.
e) The standard stream objects are _____, _____ and _____.

14.7 Determine which of the following statements are *true* and which are *false*. If *false*, explain why.
a) The impressive functions performed by computers essentially involve the manipulation of zeros and ones.
b) People specify programs and data items as characters. Computers then manipulate and process these characters as groups of zeros and ones.
c) Data items represented in computers form a data hierarchy in which data items become larger and more complex as we progress from fields to characters to bits and so on.
d) A record key identifies a record as belonging to a particular field.
e) Companies store all their information in a single file to facilitate computer processing of the information. When a program creates a file, the file is retained by the computer for future reference.

14.8 *(File Matching)* Self-Review Exercise 14.3 asks the reader to write a series of single statements. Actually, these statements form the core of an important type of file-processing program, namely, a file-matching program. In commercial data processing, it is common to have several files in each application system. In an accounts receivable system, for example, there is generally a master file containing detailed information about each customer, such as the customer's name, address, telephone number, outstanding balance, credit limit, discount terms, contract arrangements and possibly a condensed history of recent purchases and cash payments.

As transactions occur (i.e., sales are made and payments arrive in the mail), information about them is entered into a file. At the end of each business period (a month for some companies, a week for others, and a day in some cases), the file of transactions (called "trans.txt") is applied to the master file (called "oldmast.txt") to update each account's purchase and payment record. During an update, the master file is rewritten as the file "newmast.txt", which is then used at the end of the next business period to begin the updating process again.

File-matching programs must deal with certain problems that do not arise in single-file programs. For example, a match does not always occur. If a customer on the master file has not made any purchases or cash payments in the current business period, no record for this customer will appear on the transaction file. Similarly, a customer who did make some purchases or cash payments could have just moved to this community, and if so, the company may not have had a chance to create a master record for this customer.

Write a complete file-matching accounts receivable program. Use the account number on each file as the record key for matching purposes. Assume that each file is a sequential text file with records stored in increasing account-number order.

a)   Define class TransactionRecord. Objects of this class contain an account number and amount for the transaction. Provide methods to modify and retrieve these values.

b)   Modify class AccountRecord in Fig. 14.6 to include method combine, which takes a TransactionRecord object and combines the balance of the AccountRecord object and the amount value of the TransactionRecord object.

c)   Write a program to create data for testing the program. Use the sample account data in Fig. 14.39 and Fig. 14.40. Run the program to create the files trans.txt and oldmast.txt, to be used by your file-matching program.

d)   Create class FileMatch to perform the file-matching functionality. The class should contain methods that read oldmast.txt and trans.txt. When a match occurs (i.e., records with the same account number appear in both the master file and the transaction file), add the dollar amount in the transaction record to the current balance in the

Master file Account number	Name	Balance
100	Alan Jones	348.17
300	Mary Smith	27.19
500	Sam Sharp	0.00
700	Suzy Green	−14.22

Fig. 14.39 | Sample data for master file.

Transaction file Account number	Transaction amount
100	27.14
300	62.11
400	100.56
900	82.17

Fig. 14.40 | Sample data for transaction file.

master record, and write the "newmast.txt" record. (Assume that purchases are indicated by positive amounts in the transaction file and payments by negative amounts.) When there is a master record for a particular account, but no corresponding transaction record, merely write the master record to "newmast.txt". When there is a transaction record, but no corresponding master record, print to a log file the message "Unmatched transaction record for account number..." (fill in the account number from the transaction record). The log file should be a text file named "log.txt".

14.9 *(File Matching with Multiple Transactions)* It is possible (and actually common) to have several transaction records with the same record key. This situation occurs, for example, when a customer makes several purchases and cash payments during a business period. Rewrite your accounts receivable file-matching program from Exercise 14.8 to provide for the possibility of handling several transaction records with the same record key. Modify the test data of CreateData.java to include the additional transaction records in Fig. 14.41.

14.10 *(File Matching with Object Serialization)* Recreate your solution for Exercise 14.9 using object serialization. Use the statements from Exercise 14.4 as your basis for this program. You may want to create applications to read the data stored in the .ser files—the code in Section 14.7.3 can be modified for this purpose.

14.11 *(Hardware Store Inventory)* You are the owner of a hardware store and need to keep an inventory that can tell you what different tools you stock, how many of each you have on hand and the cost of each one. Write a program that initializes the random-access file "hardware.dat" to 100 empty records and lets you input the data concerning each tool, list all your tools, delete a record for a tool that you no longer have and update *any* information in the file. The tool identification number should be the record number. Use the information in Fig. 14.42 to start your file.

Account number	Dollar amount
300	83.89
700	80.78
700	1.53

Fig. 14.41 | Additional transaction records.

Record number	Tool name	Quantity	Cost
3	Sander	18	35.99
19	Hammer	128	10.00
26	Jigsaw	16	14.25
39	Mower	10	79.50
56	Saw	8	89.99
76	Screwdriver	236	4.99
81	Sledgehammer	32	19.75
88	Wrench	65	6.48

Fig. 14.42 | Data for Exercise 14.11.

14.12 *(Telephone-Number Word Generator)* Standard telephone keypads contain the digits zero through nine. The numbers two through nine each have three letters associated with them (Fig. 14.43). Many people find it difficult to memorize phone numbers, so they use the correspondence between digits and letters to develop seven-letter words that correspond to their phone numbers. For example, a person whose telephone number is 686-2377 might use the correspondence indicated in Fig. 14.43 to develop the seven-letter word "NUMBERS." Every seven-letter word corresponds to exactly one seven-digit telephone number. A restaurant wishing to increase its takeout business could surely do so with the number 825-3688 (i.e., "TAKEOUT").

Every seven-letter phone number corresponds to many different seven-letter words. Unfortunately, most of these words represent unrecognizable juxtapositions of letters. It is possible, however, that the owner of a barbershop would be pleased to know that the shop's telephone number, 424-7288, corresponds to "HAIRCUT." The owner of a liquor store would, no doubt, be delighted to find that the store's number, 233-7226, corresponds to "BEERCAN." A veterinarian with the phone number 738-2273 would be pleased to know that the number corresponds to the letters "PETCARE." An automotive dealership would be pleased to know that the dealership number, 639-2277, corresponds to "NEWCARS."

Write a program that, given a seven-digit number, uses a `PrintStream` object to write to a file every possible seven-letter word combination corresponding to that number. There are 2,187 (3^7) such combinations. Avoid phone numbers with the digits 0 and 1.

14.13 *(Student Poll)* Figure 7.8 contains an array of survey responses that is hard coded into the program. Suppose we wish to process survey results that are stored in a file. This exercise requires two separate programs. First, create an application that prompts the user for survey responses and outputs each response to a file. Use a `Formatter` to create a file called `numbers.txt`. Each integer should be written using method `format`. Then modify the program in Fig. 7.8 to read the survey responses from `numbers.txt`. The responses should be read from the file by using a `Scanner`. Method `nextInt` should be used to input one integer at a time from the file. The program should continue to read responses until it reaches the end of file. The results should be output to the text file `"output.txt"`.

14.14 Modify Exercise 11.18 to allow the user to save a drawing into a file or load a prior drawing from a file using object serialization. Add buttons **Load** (to read objects from a file), **Save** (to write objects to a file) and **Generate Shapes** (to display a random set of shapes on the screen). Use an `ObjectOutputStream` to write to the file and an `ObjectInputStream` to read from the file. Write the array of `MyShape` objects using method `writeObject` (class `ObjectOutputStream`), and read the array

Digit	Letters
2	A B C
3	D E F
4	G H I
5	J K L
6	M N O
7	P R S
8	T U V
9	W X Y

Fig. 14.43 | Telephone keypad digits and letters.

using method readObject (ObjectInputStream). Note that the object-serialization mechanism can read or write entire arrays—it is not necessary to manipulate each element of the array of MyShape objects individually. It is simply required that all the shapes be Serializable. For both the **Load** and **Save** buttons, use a JFileChooser to allow the user to select the file in which the shapes will be stored or from which they will be read. When the user first runs the program, no shapes should be displayed on the screen. The user can display shapes by opening a previously saved file of shapes or by clicking the **Generate Shapes** button. When the **Generate Shapes** button is clicked, the application should generate a random number of shapes up to a total of 15. Once there are shapes on the screen, users can save them to a file using the **Save** button.

15

Recursion

OBJECTIVES

In this chapter you will learn:

- The concept of recursion.

- How to write and use recursive methods.

- How to determine the base case and recursion step in a recursive algorithm.

- How recursive method calls are handled by the system.

- The differences between recursion and iteration, and when it is appropriate to use each.

15.1   Introduction

The programs we have discussed thus far are generally structured as methods that call one another in a disciplined, hierarchical manner. For some problems, however, it is useful to have a method call itself. Such a method is known as a **recursive method**. A recursive method can be called either directly, or indirectly through another method. Recursion is an important topic discussed at length in upper-level computer science courses. In this chapter, we consider recursion conceptually, then present several programs containing recursive methods. Figure 15.1 summarizes the recursion examples and exercises in the book.

15.2   Recursion Concepts

Recursive problem-solving approaches have a number of elements in common. When a recursive method is called to solve a problem, the method actually is capable of solving only the simplest case(s), or **base case(s)**. If the method is called with a base case, the method returns a result. If the method is called with a more complex problem, the method typically divides the problem into two conceptual pieces—a piece that the method knows how to do and a piece that the method does not know how to do. To make recursion feasible, the latter piece must resemble the original problem, but be a slightly simpler or smaller version of it. Because this new problem looks like the original problem, so the method calls a fresh copy of itself to work on the smaller problem—this is referred to as a **recursive call** and is also called the **recursion step**. The recursion step normally includes a return statement, because its result will be combined with the portion of the problem the method knew how to solve to form a result that will be passed back to the original caller. This concept of separating the problem into two smaller portions is a form of the divide-and-conquer approach introduced at the beginning of Chapter 6.

The recursion step executes while the original call to the method is still active (i.e., while it has not finished executing). The recursion step can result in many more recursive calls as the method divides each new subproblem into two conceptual pieces. For the recursion to eventually terminate, each time the method calls itself with a simpler version

Chapter	Recursion examples and exercises in this book
15	Factorial Method (Fig. 15.3 and Fig. 15.4) Fibonacci Method (Fig. 15.5 and Fig. 15.6) String Permutations (Fig. 15.12 and Fig. 15.13) Towers of Hanoi (Fig. 15.15 and Fig. 15.16) Fractals (Fig. 15.23 and Fig. 15.24) What Does This Code Do? (Exercise 15.7, Exercise 15.12 and Exercise 15.13) Find the Error in the Following Code (Exercise 15.8) Raising an Integer to an Integer Power (Exercise 15.9) Visualizing Recursion (Exercise 15.10) Greatest Common Divisor (Exercise 15.11) Determine Whether a String Is a Palindrome (Exercise 15.14) Eight Queens (Exercise 15.15) Print an Array (Exercise 15.16) Print an Array Backward (Exercise 15.17) Minimum Value in an Array (Exercise 15.18) Star Fractal (Exercise 15.19) Maze Traversal Using Recursive Backtracking (Exercise 15.20) Generating Mazes Randomly (Exercise 15.21) Mazes of Any Size (Exercise 15.22) Time Needed to Calculate a Fibonacci Number (Exercise 15.23)
16	Merge Sort (Fig. 16.10 and Fig. 16.11) Linear Search (Exercise 16.8) Binary Search (Exercise 16.9) Quicksort (Exercise 16.10)
17	Binary-Tree Insert (Fig. 17.17) Preorder Traversal of a Binary Tree (Fig. 17.17) Inorder Traversal of a Binary Tree (Fig. 17.17) Postorder Traversal of a Binary Tree (Fig. 17.17) Print a Linked List Backward (Exercise 17.20) Search a Linked List (Exercise 17.21)

Fig. 15.1 | Summary of the 32 recursion examples and exercises in this text.

of the original problem, the sequence of smaller and smaller problems must converge on a base case. At that point, the method recognizes the base case and returns a result to the previous copy of the method. A sequence of returns ensues until the original method call returns the final result to the caller.

A recursive method may call another method, which may in turn make a call back to the recursive method. Such a process is known as an **indirect recursive call** or **indirect recursion**. For example, method A calls method B, which makes a call back to method A. This is still considered recursion, because the second call to method A is made while the first call to method A is active—that is, the first call to method A has not yet finished executing (because it is waiting on method B to return a result to i) and has not returned to method A's original caller.

To better understand the concept of recursion, let us look at an example of recursion that is quite common to computer users—the recursive definition of a directory on a computer. A computer normally stores related files in a directory. A directory can be empty, can contain files and/or can contain other directories (usually referred to as subdirectories). Each of these subdirectories, in turn, may also contain both files and directories. If we wanted to list each file in a directory (including all the files in the directory's subdirectories), we would need to create a method that first lists the initial directory's files, then makes recursive calls to list the files in each of that directory's subdirectories. The base case would occur when a directory is reached that does not contain any subdirectories. At this point, all the files in the original directory have been listed and no further recursive calls need to be made.

15.3 Example Using Recursion: Factorials

Let us write a recursive program to perform a popular mathematical calculation. Consider the factorial of a positive integer n, written $n!$ (and pronounced "n factorial"), which is the product

$$n \cdot (n - 1) \cdot (n - 2) \cdot \ldots \cdot 1$$

with 1! equal to 1 and 0! defined to be 1. For example, 5! is the product $5 \cdot 4 \cdot 3 \cdot 2 \cdot 1$, which is equal to 120.

The factorial of integer number (where number ≥ 0) can be calculated *iteratively* (non-recursively) using a for statement as follows:

```
factorial = 1;

for ( int counter = number; counter >= 1; counter-- )
    factorial *= counter;
```

A recursive declaration of the factorial method is arrived at by observing the following relationship:

$$n! = n \cdot (n - 1)!$$

For example, 5! is clearly equal to $5 \cdot 4!$, as is shown by the following equations:

$$5! = 5 \cdot 4 \cdot 3 \cdot 2 \cdot 1$$
$$5! = 5 \cdot (4 \cdot 3 \cdot 2 \cdot 1)$$
$$5! = 5 \cdot (4!)$$

The evaluation of 5! would proceed as shown in Fig. 15.2. Figure 15.2(a) shows how the succession of recursive calls proceeds until 1! (the base case) is evaluated to be 1, which terminates the recursion. Figure 15.2(b) shows the values returned from each recursive call to its caller until the final value is calculated and returned.

Figure 15.3 uses recursion to calculate and print the factorials of the integers from 0–10. The recursive method factorial (lines 7–13) first tests to determine whether a terminating condition (line 9) is true. If number is less than or equal to 1 (the base case), factorial returns 1, no further recursion is necessary and the method returns. If number is greater than 1, line 12 expresses the problem as the product of number and a recursive call to `factorial` evaluating the factorial of `number - 1`, which is a slightly simpler problem than the original calculation, `factorial( number )`.

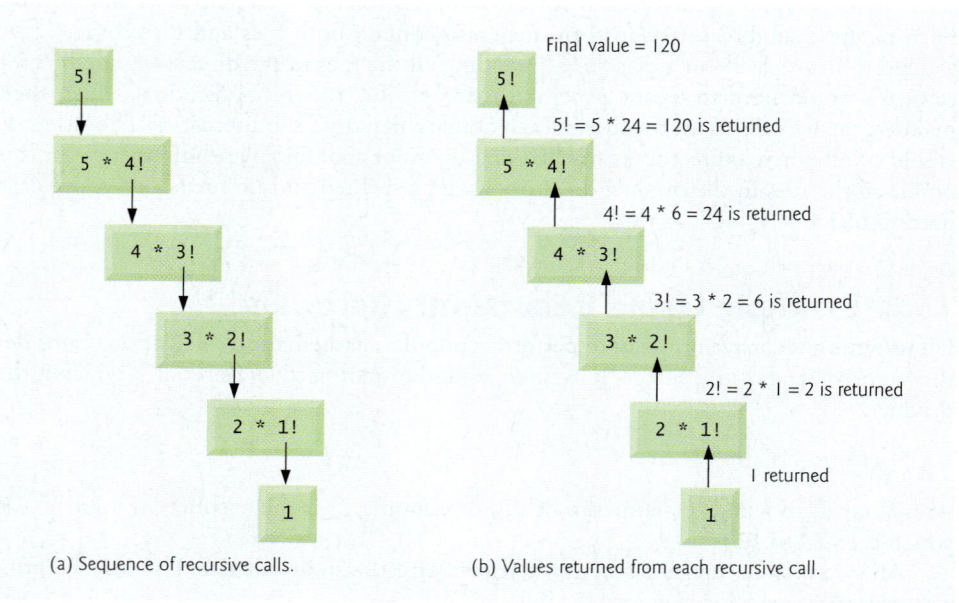

(a) Sequence of recursive calls.

(b) Values returned from each recursive call.

Fig. 15.2 | Recursive evaluation of 5!.

```
1   // Fig. 15.3: FactorialCalculator.java
2   // Recursive factorial method.
3
4   public class FactorialCalculator
5   {
6      // recursive method factorial
7      public long factorial( long number )
8      {
9         if ( number <= 1 ) // test for base case
10           return 1; // base cases: 0! = 1 and 1! = 1
11        else // recursion step
12           return number * factorial( number - 1 );
13     } // end method factorial
14
15     // output factorials for values 0-10
16     public void displayFactorials()
17     {
18        // calculate the factorials of 0 through 10
19        for ( int counter = 0; counter <= 10; counter++ )
20           System.out.printf( "%d! = %d\n", counter, factorial( counter ) );
21     } // end method displayFactorials
22  } // end class FactorialCalculator
```

Fig. 15.3 | Factorial calculations with a recursive method.

Common Programming Error 15.1

Either omitting the base case or writing the recursion step incorrectly so that it does not converge on the base case can cause a logic error known as infinite recursion, where recursive calls are continuously made until memory has been exhausted. This error is analogous to the problem of an infinite loop in an iterative (nonrecursive) solution.

Method displayFactorials (lines 16–21) displays the factorials of 0–10. The call to method factorial occurs in line 20. Method factorial receives a parameter of type long and returns a result of type long. Figure 15.4 tests our factorial and displayFactorials methods by calling displayFactorials (line 10). As can be seen from the output of Fig. 15.4, factorial values become large quickly. We use type long (which can represent relatively large integers) so the program can calculate factorials greater than 12!. Unfortunately, the factorial method produces large values so quickly that factorial values soon exceed the maximum value that can be stored even in a long variable.

Due to the limitations of integral types, float or double variables may ultimately be needed to calculate factorials of larger numbers. This points to a weakness in most programming languages—namely, that the languages are not easily extended to handle the unique application requirements. As we saw in Chapter 9, Java is an extensible language that allows us to create arbitrarily large integers if we wish. In fact, package java.math provides classes BigInteger and BigDecimal explicitly for arbitrary precision mathematical calculations that cannot be performed with primitive types. For more information on these classes visit, java.sun.com/j2se/5.0/docs/api/java/math/BigInteger.html and java.sun.com/j2se/5.0/docs/api/java/math/BigDecimal.html, respectively.

```
1   // Fig. 15.4: FactorialTest.java
2   // Testing the recursive factorial method.
3
4   public class FactorialTest
5   {
6      // calculate factorials of 0-10
7      public static void main( String args[] )
8      {
9         FactorialCalculator factorialCalculator = new FactorialCalculator();
10        factorialCalculator.displayFactorials();
11     } // end main
12  } // end class FactorialTest
```

```
0!  = 1
1!  = 1
2!  = 2
3!  = 6
4!  = 24
5!  = 120
6!  = 720
7!  = 5040
8!  = 40320
9!  = 362880
10! = 3628800
```

Fig. 15.4 | Testing the factorial method.

15.4 Example Using Recursion: Fibonacci Series
The **Fibonacci series**,

$$0, 1, 1, 2, 3, 5, 8, 13, 21, \ldots$$

begins with 0 and 1 and has the property that each subsequent Fibonacci number is the sum of the previous two Fibonacci numbers. This series occurs in nature and, in particular, describes a form of spiral. The ratio of successive Fibonacci numbers converges on a constant value of 1.618..., a number that has been called the **golden ratio** or the **golden mean**. Humans tend to find the golden mean aesthetically pleasing. Architects often design windows, rooms and buildings whose length and width are in the ratio of the golden mean. Postcards are often designed with a golden-mean length-to-width ratio.

The Fibonacci series may be defined recursively as follows:

```
fibonacci(0) = 0
fibonacci(1) = 1
fibonacci(n) = fibonacci(n – 1) + fibonacci(n – 2)
```

Note that there are two base cases for the Fibonacci calculation: fibonacci(0) is defined to be 0, and fibonacci(1) is defined to be 1. The program in Fig. 15.5 calculates the ith Fibonacci number recursively, using method fibonacci (lines 7–13). Method displayFibonacci (lines 15–20) tests fibonacci, displaying the Fibonacci values of 0–10. The variable counter created in the for header in line 17 indicates which Fibonacci number to calculate for each iteration of the for statement. The value of counter is stored in variable number (line 7) for each call to method fibonacci. Fibonacci numbers tend to become large quickly. Therefore, we use type long as the parameter type and the return type of method fibonacci. Figure 15.6 calls method displayFibonacci (line 9) to calculate the Fibonacci values.

```java
1   // Fig. 15.5: FibonacciCalculator.java
2   // Recursive fibonacci method.
3
4   public class FibonacciCalculator
5   {
6      // recursive declaration of method fibonacci
7      public long fibonacci( long number )
8      {
9         if ( ( number == 0 ) || ( number == 1 ) ) // base cases
10           return number;
11        else // recursion step
12           return fibonacci( number - 1 ) + fibonacci( number - 2 );
13     } // end method fibonacci
14
15     public void displayFibonacci()
16     {
17        for ( int counter = 0; counter <= 10; counter++ )
18           System.out.printf( "Fibonacci of %d is: %d\n", counter,
19              fibonacci( counter ) );
20     } // end method displayFibonacci
21  } // end class FibonacciCalculator
```

Fig. 15.5 | Fibonacci numbers generated with a recursive method.

```
1   // Fig. 15.6: FibonacciTest.java
2   // Testing the recursive fibonacci method.
3
4   public class FibonacciTest
5   {
6      public static void main( String args[] )
7      {
8         FibonacciCalculator fibonacciCalculator = new FibonacciCalculator();
9         fibonacciCalculator.displayFibonacci();
10      } // end main
11   } // end class FibonacciTest
```

```
Fibonacci of 0 is: 0
Fibonacci of 1 is: 1
Fibonacci of 2 is: 1
Fibonacci of 3 is: 2
Fibonacci of 4 is: 3
Fibonacci of 5 is: 5
Fibonacci of 6 is: 8
Fibonacci of 7 is: 13
Fibonacci of 8 is: 21
Fibonacci of 9 is: 34
Fibonacci of 10 is: 55
```

Fig. 15.6 | Testing the fibonacci method.

The call to method fibonacci (line 19 of Fig. 15.5) from displayFibonacci is not a recursive call, but all subsequent calls to fibonacci performed from the body of fibonacci (line 12 of Fig. 15.5) are recursive, because at that point the calls are initiated by method fibonacci itself. Each time fibonacci is called, it immediately tests for the base cases—number equal to 0 or number equal to 1 (line 9). If this condition is true, fibonacci simply returns number because fibonacci(0) is 0, and fibonacci(1) is 1. Interestingly, if number is greater than 1, the recursion step generates *two* recursive calls (line 12), each for a slightly simpler problem than the original call to fibonacci.

Figure 15.7 shows how method fibonacci evaluates fibonacci(3). Note that at the bottom of the figure, we are left with the values 1, 0 and 1—the results of evaluating the base cases. The first two return values (from left to right), 1 and 0, are returned as the values for the calls fibonacci(1) and fibonacci(0). The sum 1 plus 0 is returned as the value of fibonacci(2). This is added to the result (1) of the call to fibonacci(1), producing the value 2. This final value is then returned as the value of fibonacci(3).

Figure 15.7 raises some interesting issues about the order in which Java compilers evaluate the operands of operators. This order is different from the order in which operators are applied to their operands—namely, the order dictated by the rules of operator precedence. From Figure 15.7, it appears that while fibonacci(3) is being evaluated, two recursive calls will be made—fibonacci(2) and fibonacci(1). But in what order will these calls be made? The Java language specifies that the order of evaluation of the operands is from left to right. Thus, the call fibonacci(2) is made first and the call fibonacci(1) is made second.

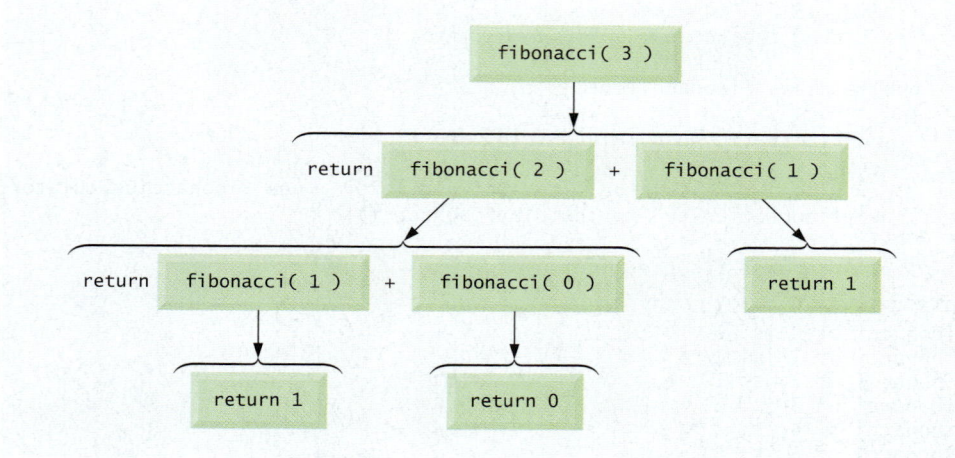

Fig. 15.7 | Set of recursive calls for `fibonacci( 3 )`.

A word of caution is in order about recursive programs like the one we use here to generate Fibonacci numbers. Each invocation of the `fibonacci` method that does not match one of the base cases (0 or 1) results in two more recursive calls to the `fibonacci` method. Hence, this set of recursive calls rapidly gets out of hand. Calculating the Fibonacci value of 20 with the program in Fig. 15.5 requires 21,891 calls to the `fibonacci` method; calculating the Fibonacci value of 30 requires 2,692,537 calls! As you try to calculate larger Fibonacci values, you will notice that each consecutive Fibonacci number you use the application to calculate results in a substantial increase in calculation time and in the number of calls to the `fibonacci` method. For example, the Fibonacci value of 31 requires 4,356,617 calls, and the Fibonacci value of 32 requires 7,049,155 calls! As you can see, the number of calls to `fibonacci` increases quickly—1,664,080 additional calls between Fibonacci values of 30 and 31 and 2,692,538 additional calls between Fibonacci values of 31 and 32! The difference in the number of calls made between Fibonacci values of 31 and 32 is more than 1.5 times the number of calls for Fibonacci values between 30 and 31. Problems of this nature can humble even the world's most powerful computers. [*Note:* In the field of complexity theory, computer scientists study how hard algorithms work to complete their tasks. Complexity issues are discussed in detail in the upper-level computer science curriculum course generally called "Algorithms." We introduce various complexity issues in Chapter 16, Searching and Sorting.] In the exercises, you will be asked to enhance the Fibonacci program of Fig. 15.5 such that it calculates the approximate amount of time required to perform the calculation. For this purpose, you will call `static` `System` method `currentTimeMillis`, which takes no arguments and returns the computer's current time in milliseconds.

Performance Tip 15.1

Avoid Fibonacci-style recursive programs, because they result in an exponential "explosion" of method calls.

15.5 Recursion and the Method Call Stack

In Chapter 6, the stack data structure was introduced in the context of understanding how Java performs method calls. We discussed both the method call stack (also known as the program execution stack) and activation records. In this section, we will use these concepts to demonstrate how the program execution stack handles recursive method calls.

Let us begin by returning to the Fibonacci example—specifically, calling method fibonacci with the value 3, as in Fig. 15.7. To more easily demonstrate in what order the activation records for the method calls are placed on the stack, we have lettered the method calls, as shown in Fig. 15.8.

When the first method call (A) is made, an activation record is pushed onto the program execution stack which contains the value of the local variable number (3, in this case). The program execution stack, including the activation record for method call A, is illustrated in part a of Fig. 15.9. [*Note:* In an actual computer, the program execution stack and its activation records would be more complex than in Fig. 15.9, containing such information as where the method call is to return to when it has completed execution. We use a simplified stack to demonstrate how the program execution stack works.]

Within method call A, method calls B and E are made. The original method call has not yet completed, so its activation record remains on the stack. The first method call to be made from within A is method call B, so the activation record for method call B is pushed onto the stack on top of the activation record for method call A. Method call B must execute and complete before method call E is made. Within method call B, method calls C and D will be made. Method call C is made first, and its activation record is pushed onto the stack (part b of Fig. 15.9). Method call B has not yet finished, and its activation record is still on the method call stack. When method call C executes, it does not make any further method calls, but simply returns the value 1. When this method returns, its activation record is popped off the top of the stack. The method call at the top of the stack is now B, which continues to execute by performing method call D. The activation record for method call D is pushed onto the stack (part c of Fig. 15.9). Method call D completes without making any more method calls, and returns the value 0. The activation record for

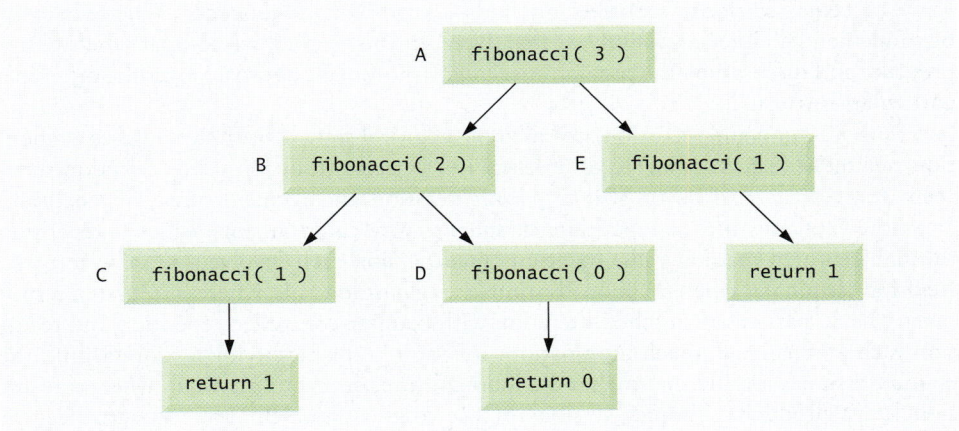

Fig. 15.8 | Method calls made within the call fibonacci(3).

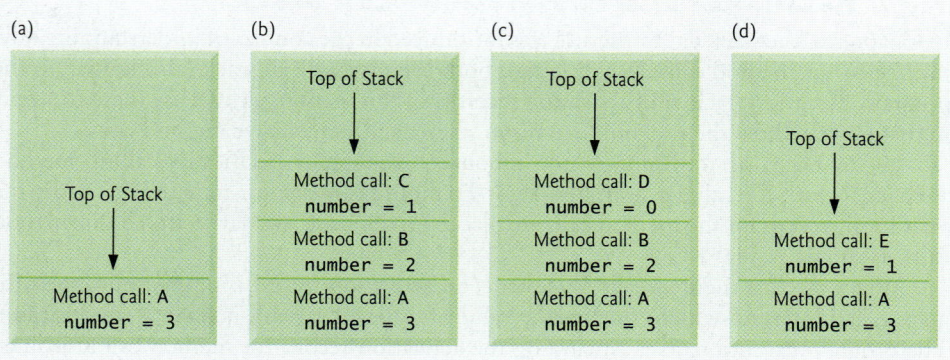

Fig. 15.9 | Method calls on the program execution stack.

this method call is then popped off the stack. Now, both method calls made from within method call B have returned. Method call B continues to execute, returning the value 1. Method call B completes and its activation record is popped off the stack. At this point, the activation record for method call A is at the top of the stack and the method continues its execution. This method makes method call E, whose activation record is now pushed onto the stack (part d of Fig. 15.9). Method call E completes and returns the value 1. The activation record for this method call is popped off the stack, and once again method call A continues to execute. At this point, method call A will not be making any other method calls, and can finish its execution, returning the value 2 to A's caller (Fib(3) = 2). A's activation record is popped off the stack. Note that the current method executing is always the method whose activation record is at the top of the stack, and that the activation record for that method contains the values of the method's local variables.

15.6 Recursion vs. Iteration

In the preceding sections, we studied methods `factorial` and `fibonacci`, which can easily be implemented either recursively or iteratively. In this section, we compare the two approaches and discuss why the programmer might choose one approach over the other in a particular situation.

Both iteration and recursion are based on a control statement: Iteration uses a repetition statement (e.g., `for`, `while` or `do...while`), whereas recursion uses a selection statement (e.g., `if`, `if...else` or `switch`). Both iteration and recursion involve repetition: Iteration explicitly uses a repetition statement, whereas recursion achieves repetition through repeated method calls. Iteration and recursion each involve a termination test: Iteration terminates when the loop-continuation condition fails, whereas recursion terminates when a base case is reached. Iteration with counter-controlled repetition and recursion each gradually approach termination: Iteration keeps modifying a counter until the counter assumes a value that makes the loop-continuation condition fail, whereas recursion keeps producing simpler versions of the original problem until the base case is reached. Both iteration and recursion can occur infinitely: An infinite loop occurs with iteration if the loop-continuation test never becomes false, whereas infinite recursion occurs if the recursion step does not reduce the problem each time in a manner that converges on the base case, or if the base case is not tested.

To illustrate the differences between iteration and recursion, let us examine an iterative solution to the factorial problem (Fig. 15.10–Fig. 15.11). Note that a repetition statement is used (lines 12–13 of Fig. 15.10) rather than the selection statement of the recursive solution (lines 9–12 of Fig. 15.3). Note that both solutions use a termination test. In the recursive solution, line 9 tests for the base case. In the iterative solution, line 12 tests the loop-continuation condition—if the test fails, the loop terminates. Finally, note that instead of producing simpler versions of the original problem, the iterative solution uses a counter that is modified until the loop-continuation condition becomes false.

Recursion has many negatives. It repeatedly invokes the mechanism, and consequently the overhead, of method calls. This repetition can be expensive in terms of both processor time and memory space. Each recursive call causes another copy of the method (actually, only the method's variables, stored in the activation record) to be created—this set of copies can consume considerable memory space. Since iteration occurs within a method, repeated method calls and extra memory assignment are avoided. So why choose recursion?

Software Engineering Observation 15.1

Any problem that can be solved recursively can also be solved iteratively (nonrecursively). A recursive approach is normally preferred over an iterative approach when the recursive approach more naturally mirrors the problem and results in a program that is easier to understand and debug. A recursive approach can often be implemented with fewer lines of code. Another reason to choose a recursive approach is that an iterative one might not be apparent.

```java
// Fig. 15.10: FactorialCalculator.java
// Iterative factorial method.

public class FactorialCalculator
{
   // recursive declaration of method factorial
   public long factorial( long number )
   {
      long result = 1;

      // iterative declaration of method factorial
      for ( long i = number; i >= 1; i-- )
         result *= i;

      return result;
   } // end method factorial

   // output factorials for values 0-10
   public void displayFactorials()
   {
      // calculate the factorials of 0 through 10
      for ( int counter = 0; counter <= 10; counter++ )
         System.out.printf( "%d! = %d\n", counter, factorial( counter ) );
   } // end method displayFactorials
} // end class FactorialCalculator
```

Fig. 15.10 | Iterative factorial solution.

```
 1    // Fig. 15.11: FactorialTest.java
 2    // Testing the iterative factorial method.
 3
 4    public class FactorialTest
 5    {
 6       // calculate factorials of 0-10
 7       public static void main( String args[] )
 8       {
 9          FactorialCalculator factorialCalculator = new FactorialCalculator();
10          factorialCalculator.displayFactorials();
11       } // end main
12    } // end class FactorialTest
```

```
0! = 1
1! = 1
2! = 2
3! = 6
4! = 24
5! = 120
6! = 720
7! = 5040
8! = 40320
9! = 362880
10! = 3628800
```

Fig. 15.11 | Testing the iterative factorial solution.

Performance Tip 15.2

Avoid using recursion in situations requiring high performance. Recursive calls take time and consume additional memory.

Common Programming Error 15.2

Accidentally having a nonrecursive method call itself either directly or indirectly through another method can cause infinite recursion.

15.7 String Permutations

The example in this section provides a more in-depth walkthrough of how to solve a recursive problem, especially one that does not involve a simple mathematical formula. The problem we analyze in this section is creating the **permutations** of a string of text—all the different strings that can be created by rearranging the characters of the original string. Words created from these strings are known as **anagrams**. The permutations for the string "abc" are:

        abc
        acb
        bac
        bca
        cab
        cba

Such a program could come in handy if one wants to unscramble a string of characters, determine all the words that can be created from a string, or determine all the words that can be created from the characters associated with a telephone number.

We have already provided a few recursive solutions in this chapter, but we have not considered the flow of thought that results in a recursive solution. We do this now, in the context of string permutations. To begin, we look for a pattern that can be used to solve the problem. In the preceding list of permutations, note that two of the resulting permutations start with "a" ("abc" and "acb"), two with "b" ("bac" and "bca"), and two with "c" ("cab", "cba"). For each letter, permutations are provided that begin with that letter, followed by permutations of the remaining letters. If we were to begin with the letter "b", for example, we would have two permutations—"bac" and "bca". These are determined by simply looking at the remaining two letters, "a" and "c", and seeing that there are only two permutations using these letters—namely, "ac" and "ca". Note that we have now just determined all the permutations on the smaller string, "ac". To do this, we can use the same thought process as before, namely, determining all the permutations that start with the letter "a" followed by all the permutations that start with the letter "c". If we start with the letter "a", we have only one letter left, the letter "c". For a string with only one character, the string itself is the only permutation.

We now have the permutations of our substrings, but not the final permutations as shown above. To create these, we need to precede the permutations of the substrings with the characters that were removed to create the substring. For example, when determining the permutations of "bac", we divided the string into two strings ("b" and "ac"), and determined the permutations of the second string (in this case, "ac" and "ca"). We need our solution to precede "ac" and "ca" with the character that was removed to create this substring (namely, "b"). Our solution will need a way to keep track of these removed letters.

We have now found a way to break up our problem into two pieces: a single character from the original string, concatenated with all the permutations of the remaining characters—the recursion step calculates all such permutations. The recursion step includes a recursive call for each letter in the string, with a different letter being used as the first letter of the permutation. Each call takes a different character from the string being permuted, and creates a substring of the remaining values, to be passed to the recursive call. For instance, if we are using the example of "abc", the first call to our recursive method results in three recursive calls—one which determines all the permutations that begin with "a" (where the substring is "bc"), one which determines all the permutations that begin with "b" (where the substring is "ac") and one which determines all the permutations that begin with "c" (where the substring is "ab").

We have now discovered the recursion step for our program (determining the permutations of the various substrings) and our base case (a string with one letter will always have only one permutation, the letter itself). The next step is to ensure that the base case will be reached. Because our recursion step always calls with a string that is one character shorter than the string before it, we can be sure that we will always reach a string of one character—the base case. Note that the base case also handles the situation where the user enters an empty string (i.e., one whose length is 0).

Now that we have determined our base case, the recursion step and that the base case will always be reached, we present the code for our solution (Fig. 15.12). Method permuteString (lines 7–38) takes two arguments. The first, beginningString, contains

```
1   // Fig. 15.12: Permutation.java
2   // Recursive method to find all permutations of a String.
3
4   public class Permutation
5   {
6      // recursive declaration of method permuteString
7      private void permuteString(
8         String beginningString, String endingString )
9      {
10        // base case: if string to permute is length less than or equal to
11        // 1, just display this string concatenated with beginningString
12        if ( endingString.length() <= 1 )
13           System.out.println( beginningString + endingString );
14        else // recursion step: permute endingString
15        {
16           // for each character in endingString
17           for ( int i = 0; i < endingString.length(); i++ )
18           {
19              try
20              {
21                 // create new string to permute by eliminating the
22                 // character at index i
23                 String newString = endingString.substring( 0, i ) +
24                    endingString.substring( i + 1 );
25
26                 // recursive call with a new string to permute
27                 // and a beginning string to concatenate, which
28                 // includes the character at index i
29                 permuteString( beginningString +
30                    endingString.charAt( i ), newString );
31              } // end try
32              catch ( StringIndexOutOfBoundsException exception )
33              {
34                 exception.printStackTrace();
35              } // end catch
36           } // end for
37        } // end else
38     } // end method permuteString
39  } // end class Permutation
```

Fig. 15.12 | String permutations generated with a recursive method.

the characters that were removed from the string in previous calls and now need to precede the permutations that are being created. The second argument, endingString, contains the string that needs to be permuted (we call it endingString because for our final results it will be displayed after beginningString). When the method is called with the original string, the first argument will be the empty string, as there are no characters from previous calls that need to be added to the solution. The base case occurs in lines 12–13, when the string being permuted contains only one character. In this case, we simply print the characters from previous calls (beginningString) followed by the character in endingString.

The recursion step occurs in lines 14–37. The for statement makes a recursive call for each of the substrings. The current character being removed is the character returned from endingString.charAt(i). Method **charAt** takes an integer argument and returns the character in the String at that index. As with arrays, the first element of a string is considered to be at position 0. The for statement iterates through each character in ending-String, so that permutations will be created that begin with each letter in endingString.

To create the substring that needs to be permuted, the character at index i needs to be removed from the string that will be passed in the recursive call. To remove a character, we concatenate two substrings—the first substring contains all the characters that occur before the character being removed, and the second substring contains the portion of the string that occurs after the character being removed. For instance, to remove the character "s" from the word "recursion," we create the new string by concatenating the first substring, "recur", with "ion", resulting in "recurion." Lines 23–24 create this substring using String method **substring**. Class String provides two substring methods to return a new String object created by copying part of an existing String object. The call in line 23 passes method substring two integers (0 and i). The first argument specifies the starting index in the original string from which characters are copied. The second argument specifies the index one beyond the last character to be copied (i.e., copy up to, but not including, that index in the string). The substring returned contains copies of the specified range of characters from the original string. Therefore, the method call in line 23 returns all the characters from the beginning of endingString up to, but not including, the character at index i (the character we are trying to remove). If the arguments are outside the bounds of the string, the program generates a StringIndexOutOfBoundsException (handled in lines 32–35).

The method call in line 24 uses the substring method that takes one integer argument (i + 1), which specifies the starting index in the original string from which characters are to be copied. The substring returned contains a copy of the characters from the starting index to the end of the string. Therefore, the method call in line 24 returns all the characters that occur after the character we are trying to remove. If the argument is outside the bounds of the string, the program generates a StringIndexOutOfBoundsException (also handled in lines 32–35).

Lines 29–30 perform the recursive call. The first argument passed is beginning-String concatenated with endingString.charAt(i). This way we combine the characters isolated from previous calls (beginningString) with the character being isolated in this call. The second argument is newString, which is the substring to be permuted.

Figure 15.13 tests our recursive method. Line 9 creates a Scanner object to read a string in from the keyboard. Line 10 creates a Permutation object with which to call method permuteString. The string is read in at line 13 and passed to method permuteString in line 16. Note that this call provides an empty string as the first argument and the string to permute as the second argument. Because we have not yet removed any characters from the string, beginningString (the first argument) should be an empty string. Some programmers may want to define method permuteString as private, and create another public method that takes only the string to permute. This method could then call permuteString with the empty string as the first argument and the string to permute as the second argument. This would ensure that the user does not enter something other than the empty string as the first argument to method permuteString.

The permutations will be printed to the command prompt. Note that if a string is entered with repeated characters (e.g., "hello"), each character is treated on its own,

```
 1   // Fig. 15.13: PermutationTest.java
 2   // Testing the recursive method to permute strings.
 3   import java.util.Scanner;
 4
 5   public class PermutationTest
 6   {
 7      public static void main( String args[] )
 8      {
 9         Scanner scanner = new Scanner( System.in );
10         Permutation permutationObject = new Permutation();
11
12         System.out.print( "Enter a string: " );
13         String input = scanner.nextLine(); // retrieve String to permute
14
15         // permute String
16         permutationObject.permuteString( "", input );
17      } // end main
18   } // end class PermutationTest
```

```
math
maht
mtah
mtha
mhat
mhta
amth
amht
atmh
athm
ahmt
ahtm
tmah
tmha
tamh
tahm
thma
tham
hmat
hmta
hamt
hatm
htma
htam
```

Fig. 15.13 | Testing the recursive method for permutations.

resulting in repeated permutations. One way to handle this problem is to store permutations as they are created—when each new permutation is formed, check the previously created strings and add the new string only if it has not already appeared. Finally, note from the output that there are 24 permutations for the string "math". The number of unique permutations for a string with n unique characters is equal to the factorial of n (i.e., there are four characters in "math", resulting in 4! permutations, or 24 permutations).

15.8 Towers of Hanoi

In the preceding sections of this chapter, we studied methods that can be easily implemented both recursively and iteratively. In this section, we present a problem whose recursive solution demonstrates the elegance of recursion, and whose iterative solution may not be as apparent.

The Towers of Hanoi is one of the most famous classic problems every budding computer scientist must grapple with. Legend has it that in a temple in the Far East, priests are attempting to move a stack of golden disks from one diamond peg to another (Fig. 15.14). The initial stack has 64 disks threaded onto one peg and arranged from bottom to top by decreasing size. The priests are attempting to move the stack from one peg to another under the constraints that exactly one disk is moved at a time and at no time may a larger disk be placed above a smaller disk. Three pegs are provided, one being used for temporarily holding disks. Supposedly, the world will end when the priests complete their task, so there is little incentive for us to facilitate their efforts.

Let us assume that the priests are attempting to move the disks from peg 1 to peg 3. We wish to develop an algorithm that prints the precise sequence of peg-to-peg disk transfers.

If we were to approach this problem with conventional methods, we would rapidly find ourselves hopelessly knotted up in managing the disks. Instead, attacking this problem with recursion in mind allows the steps to be simple. Moving n disks can be viewed in terms of moving only $n - 1$ disks (hence the recursion) as follows:

a) Move $n - 1$ disks from peg 1 to peg 2, using peg 3 as a temporary holding area.
b) Move the last disk (the largest) from peg 1 to peg 3.
c) Move the $n - 1$ disks from peg 2 to peg 3, using peg 1 as a temporary holding area.

The process ends when the last task involves moving $n = 1$ disk (i.e., the base case). This task is accomplished by simply moving the disk, without the need for a temporary holding area.

Figure 15.15 displays the precise instructions it will take to move the disks from the starting peg to the destination peg. In the constructor (lines 9–12), the number of disks to

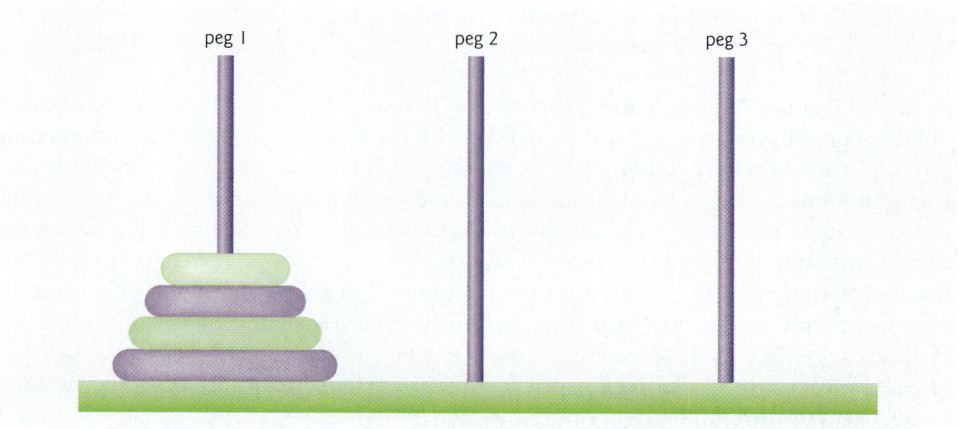

Fig. 15.14 | Towers of Hanoi for the case with four disks.

```
1    // Fig. 15.15: TowersOfHanoi.java
2    // Program solves the towers of Hanoi problem, and
3    // demonstrates recursion.
4
5    public class TowersOfHanoi
6    {
7       int numDisks; // number of disks to move
8
9       public TowersOfHanoi( int disks )
10      {
11         numDisks = disks;
12      } // end TowersOfHanoi constructor
13
14      // recusively move disks through towers
15      public void solveTowers( int disks, int sourcePeg, int destinationPeg,
16         int tempPeg )
17      {
18         // base case -- only one disk to move
19         if ( disks == 1 )
20         {
21            System.out.printf( "\n%d --> %d", sourcePeg, destinationPeg );
22            return;
23         } // end if
24
25         // recursion step -- move disk to tempPeg, then to destinationPeg
26         // move ( disks - 1 ) disks from sourcePeg to tempPeg recursively
27         solveTowers( disks - 1, sourcePeg, tempPeg, destinationPeg );
28
29         // move last disk from sourcePeg to destinationPeg
30         System.out.printf( "\n%d --> %d", sourcePeg, destinationPeg );
31
32         // move ( disks - 1 ) disks from tempPeg to destinationPeg
33         solveTowers( disks - 1, tempPeg, destinationPeg, sourcePeg );
34      } // end method solveTowers
35   } // end class TowersOfHanoi
```

Fig. 15.15 | Towers of Hanoi solution with a recursive method.

be moved (numDisks) is initialized. Method solveTowers (lines 15–34) solves the Towers of Hanoi puzzle given the total number of disks (in this case 3), the starting peg, the ending peg, and the temporary holding peg as parameters. The base case (lines 19–23) occurs when only one disk needs to be moved from the starting peg to the ending peg. In the recursion step (lines 27–33), line 27 moves disks - 1 disks from the first peg (sourcePeg) to the temporary holding peg (tempPeg). When all but one of the disks have been moved to the temporary peg, line 30 records the step to move one disk, the largest one, from the start peg to the destination peg. Line 33 finishes the rest of the moves by calling the method solveTowers to recursively move disks - 1 disks from the temporary peg (tempPeg) back to the destination peg (destinationPeg), this time using the first peg (sourcePeg) as the temporary peg.

Figure 15.16 tests our Towers of Hanoi solution. In the main method (lines 6–16), line 12 creates a TowersOfHanoi object, passing as a parameter the total number of disks

```
I    // Fig. 15.16: TowersOfHanoiTest.java
2    // Test the solution to the Towers of Hanoi problem.
3
4    public class TowersOfHanoiTest
5    {
6       public static void main( String args[] )
7       {
8          int startPeg = 1;    // value 1 used to indicate startPeg in output
9          int endPeg = 3;      // value 3 used to indicate endPeg in output
10         int tempPeg = 2;     // value 2 used to indicate tempPeg in output
11         int totalDisks = 3;  // number of disks
12         TowersOfHanoi towersOfHanoi = new TowersOfHanoi( totalDisks );
13
14         // initial nonrecursive call: move all disks.
15         towersOfHanoi.solveTowers( totalDisks, startPeg, endPeg, tempPeg );
16      } // end main
17   } // end class TowersOfHanoiTest
```

```
1 --> 3
1 --> 2
3 --> 2
1 --> 3
2 --> 1
2 --> 3
1 --> 3
```

Fig. 15.16 | Testing the Towers of Hanoi solution.

to be moved from one peg to another. Line 15 calls the recursive solveTowers method which outputs the steps to the command prompt.

15.9 Fractals

A fractal is a geometric figure that often can be generated from a pattern repeated recursively an infinite number of times (Fig. 15.17). The figure is modified by applying the pattern to each segment of the original figure. Real geometric figures do not have their patterns repeated an infinite number of times, but after several repetitions appear as they would if repeated infinitely. We will look at a few such approximations in this section. [*Note:* We will refer to our geometric figures as fractals, even though they are approximations.] Although these figures had been studied before the 20th century, it was the Polish mathematician Benoit Mandelbrot who introduced the term "fractal" in the 1970s, along with the specifics of how a fractal is created and the practical applications of fractals. Mandelbrot's fractal geometry provides mathematical models for many complex forms found in nature, such as mountains, clouds and coastlines. Fractals have many uses in mathematics and science. Fractals can be used to better understand systems or patterns that appear in nature (e.g., ecosystems), in the human body (e.g., in the folds of the brain), or in the universe (e.g., galaxy clusters). Drawing fractals has become a popular art form. Fractals have a self-similar property—when subdivided into parts, each resembles a reduced-size copy of the whole. Many fractals yield an exact copy of the original when a portion of the original image is magnified—such a fractal is said to be **strictly self similar**. Links are provided in Section 15.12 for various Web sites that discuss and demonstrate fractals.

As an example, let us look at a popular strictly self-similar fractal known as the **Koch Curve** (Fig. 15.17). This fractal is formed by removing the middle third of each line in the drawing and replacing it with two lines that form a point, such that if the middle third of the original line remained, an equilateral triangle would be formed. Formulas for creating fractals often involve removing all or part of the previous fractal image. This pattern has already been determined for this fractal—in this section we focus not on how to determine what formulas are needed for a specific fractal, but how to use those formulas within a recursive solution. Most formulas can be used to create fractals, but not all fractals will resemble objects in nature.

We start with a straight line (Fig. 15.17, Part *a*) and apply the pattern, creating a triangle from the middle third (Fig. 15.17, Part *b*). We then apply the pattern again to each straight line, resulting in Fig. 15.17, Part *c*. Each time the pattern is applied, we say that the fractal is at a new **level**, or **depth** (sometimes the term **order** is also used). Fractals can

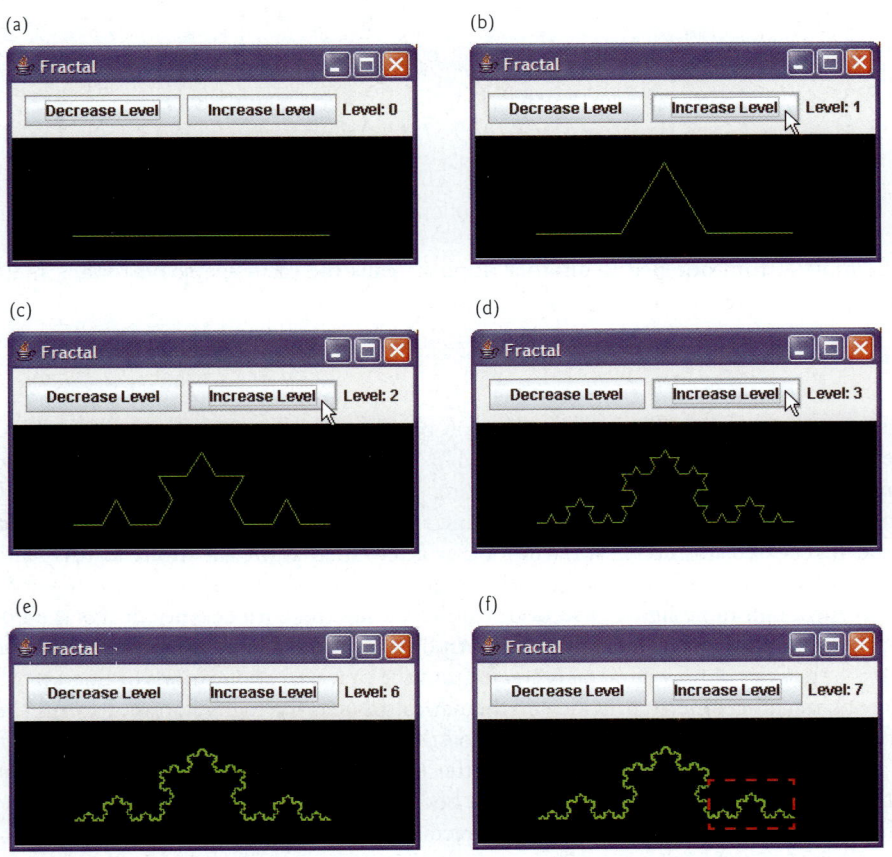

Fig. 15.17 | Koch Curve fractal.

be displayed at many levels—for instance, a fractal at level 3 has had three iterations of the pattern applied (Fig. 15.17, Part *d*). After only a few iterations, this fractal begins to look the same, like a portion of a snowflake (Fig. 15.17, Parts *e* and *f*). The applications of the pattern are now too small for the human eye to see a difference. Since this is a strictly self-similar fractal, each portion of the fractal contains an exact copy of the fractal. In Part *f* of Fig. 15.17, for example, we have highlighted a portion of the fractal with a dashed red box. If the image in this box were increased in size, it would look exactly like the entire fractal of Part *f*.

There is a similar fractal, the Koch Snowflake, which is the same as the Koch Curve but begins with a triangle rather than a line. The same pattern is applied to each side of the triangle, resulting in an image that looks like an enclosed snowflake. We have chosen to focus on the Koch Curve for simplicity. We will be moving on shortly to another fractal, but if the reader wishes to learn more about the Koch Curve and Koch Snowflake, see the links in Section 15.12.

We now demonstrate the use of recursion to draw fractals by writing a program to create a strictly self-similar fractal. We call this the "Lo fractal," named for Sin Han Lo, a Deitel & Associates colleague who created it. The fractal will eventually resemble one-half of a feather (see the outputs in Fig. 15.24). The base case, or fractal level of 0, begins as a line between two points, A and B (Fig. 15.18). To create the next higher level, we find the midpoint (C) of the line. To calculate the location of point C, use the following formula: [*Note:* The x and y to the left of each letter refer to the *x*-coordinate and *y*-coordinate of that point, respectively. For instance, xA refers to the *x*-coordinate of point A, while yC refers to the *y*-coordinate of point C. In our diagrams we denote the point by its letter, followed by two numbers representing the *x*- and *y*-coordinates.]

```
xC = (xA + xB) / 2;

yC = (yA + yB) / 2;
```

To create this fractal, we also must find a point D that lies left of segment AC and creates an isosceles right triangle ADC. To calculate the location of point D, use the following formulas:

```
xD = xA + (xC - xA) / 2 - (yC - yA) / 2;

yD = yA + (yC - yA) / 2 + (xC - xA) / 2;
```

We continue the example in Fig. 15.18 by moving on to the next level (from level 0 to level 1) as follows: First, add points C and D (as in Fig. 15.19). Then, remove the original line and add segments DA, DC and DB. The remaining lines curve at an angle, causing our fractal to look like a feather. For the next level of the fractal, this algorithm is repeated on each of the three lines in level 1. For each line, the formulas above are applied, where the former point D is now considered to be point A, while the other end of each line is considered to be point B. Figure 15.20 contains the line from level 0 (now a dashed line) and the three added lines from level 1. We have changed point D to be point A, and the original points A, C and B to B1, B2 and B3 (the numbers are used to differentiate the various points). The preceding formulas have been used to find the new points C and D on each line. These points are also numbered 1–3 to keep track of which point is associated with each line.

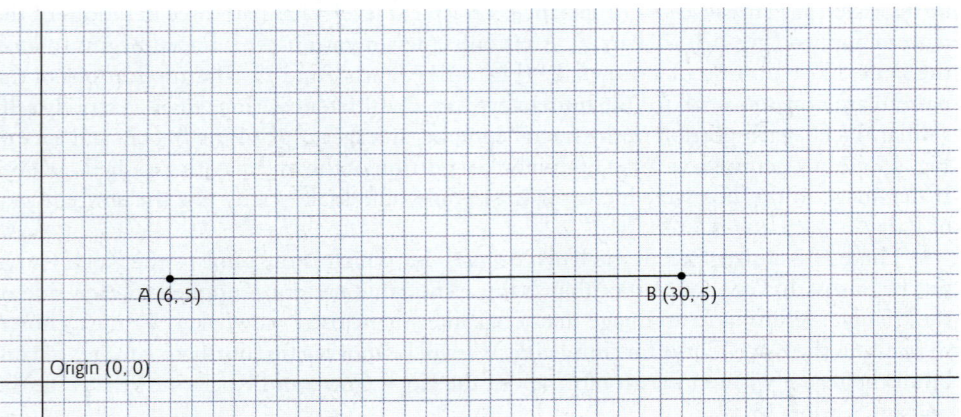

Fig. 15.18 | "Lo fractal" at level 0.

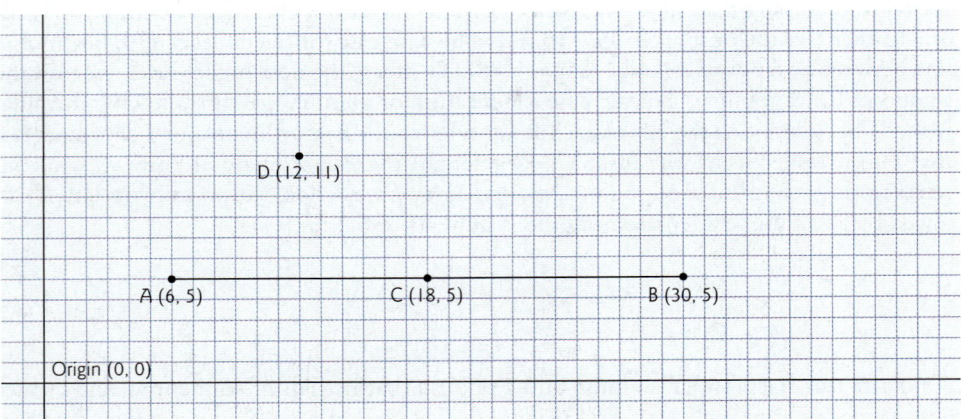

Fig. 15.19 | Determining points C and D for level 1 of "Lo fractal."

The points C1 and D1, for instance, represent points C and D associated with the line formed from points A to B1. To achieve level 2, the three lines in Fig. 15.20 are removed and replaced with new lines from the C and D points just added. Figure 15.21 shows the new lines (the lines from level 2 are shown as dashed lines for your convenience). Figure 15.22 shows level 2 without the dashed lines from level 1. Once this process has been repeated several times, the fractal created will begin to look like one-half of a feather, as shown in the output of Fig. 15.24. We will discuss the code for this application shortly.

The application in Fig. 15.23 defines the user interface for drawing this fractal (shown at the end of Fig. 15.24). The interface consists of three buttons—one for the user to change the color of the fractal, one to increase the level of recursion and one to decrease the level of recursion. A JLabel will keep track of the current level of recursion, which is modified by calling method setLevel, to be discussed shortly. Lines 15–16 specify constants WIDTH and HEIGHT to be 400 and 480 respectively for the size of the JFrame. The default color to draw the fractal will be blue (line 18). The user triggers an ActionEvent

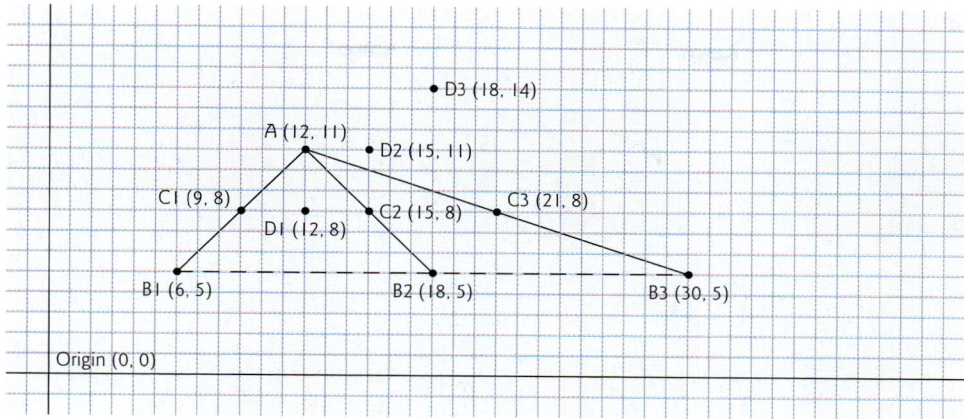

Fig. 15.20 | "Lo fractal" at level 1, with C and D points determined for level 2. *[Note: The fractal at level 0 is included as a dashed line as a reminder of where the line was located in relation to the current fractal.*

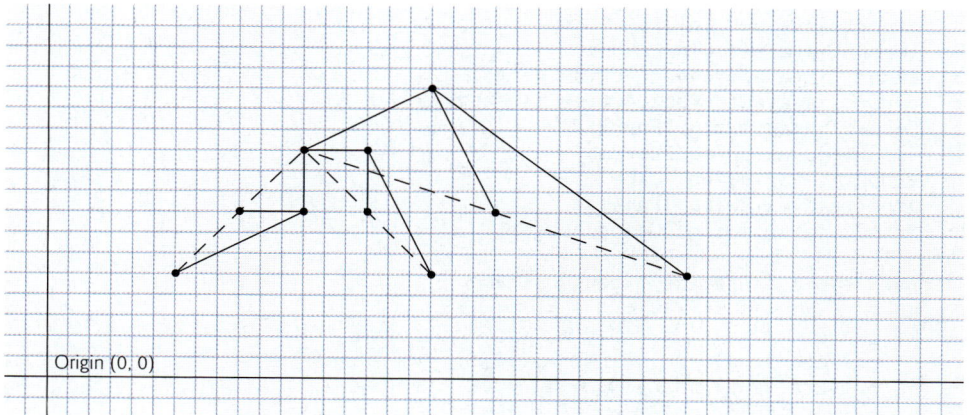

Fig. 15.21 | "Lo fractal" at level 2, with dashed lines from level 1 provided.

by clicking the **Color** button. The event handler for this button is registered in lines 38–54. The method `actionPerformed` displays a `JColorChooser`. This dialog returns the selected `Color` object or blue (if the user presses **Cancel** or closes the dialog without pressing **OK**). Line 51 calls the `setColor` method in class `FractalJPanel` to update the color.

The event handler for the **Decrease Level** button is registered in lines 60–78. In method `actionPerformed`, lines 66–67 retrieve the current level of recursion and decrement it by 1. Line 70 checks to make sure that the level is greater than or equal to 0 (`MIN_LEVEL`). This is because the fractal is not defined for any recursion level lower than 0. The program allows the user to go up to any desired level, but it is important to note that at a certain point (level 10 and higher in this example) the rendering of the fractal becomes increasingly slower, as there is a lot of detail to be drawn. Lines 72–74 reset the

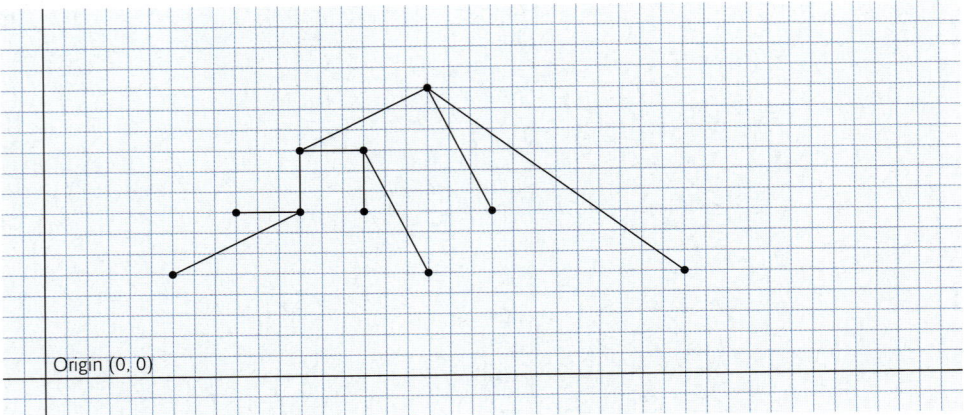

Fig. 15.22 | "Lo fractal" at level 2.

```
1   // Fig. 15.23: Fractal.java
2   // Demonstrates user interface for drawing a fractal.
3   import java.awt.Color;
4   import java.awt.FlowLayout;
5   import java.awt.event.ActionEvent;
6   import java.awt.event.ActionListener;
7   import javax.swing.JFrame;
8   import javax.swing.JButton;
9   import javax.swing.JLabel;
10  import javax.swing.JPanel;
11  import javax.swing.JColorChooser;
12
13  public class Fractal extends JFrame
14  {
15     private final int WIDTH = 400;  // define width of GUI
16     private final int HEIGHT = 480; // define height of GUI
17     private final int MIN_LEVEL = 0;
18     private Color color = Color.BLUE;
19
20     private JButton changeColorJButton, increaseLevelJButton,
21        decreaseLevelJButton;
22     private JLabel levelJLabel;
23     private FractalJPanel drawSpace;
24     private JPanel mainJPanel, controlJPanel;
25
26     // set up GUI
27     public Fractal()
28     {
29        super( "Fractal" );
30
31        // set up control panel
32        controlJPanel = new JPanel();
33        controlJPanel.setLayout( new FlowLayout() );
```

Fig. 15.23 | Demonstrating the fractal user interface. (Part 1 of 3.)

```
34
35          // set up color button and register listener
36          changeColorJButton = new JButton( "Color" );
37          controlJPanel.add( changeColorJButton );
38          changeColorJButton.addActionListener(
39             new ActionListener() // anonymous inner class
40             {
41                // process changeColorJButton event
42                public void actionPerformed( ActionEvent event )
43                {
44                   color = JColorChooser.showDialog(
45                      Fractal.this, "Choose a color", color );
46
47                   // set default color, if no color is returned
48                   if ( color == null )
49                      color = Color.BLUE;
50
51                   drawSpace.setColor( color );
52                } // end method actionPerformed
53             } // end anonymous inner class
54          ); // end addActionListener
55
56          // set up decrease level button to add to control panel and
57          // register listener
58          decreaseLevelJButton = new JButton( "Decrease Level" );
59          controlJPanel.add( decreaseLevelJButton );
60          decreaseLevelJButton.addActionListener(
61             new ActionListener() // anonymous inner class
62             {
63                // process decreaseLevelJButton event
64                public void actionPerformed( ActionEvent event )
65                {
66                   int level = drawSpace.getLevel();
67                   level--; // decrease level by one
68
69                   // modify level if possible
70                   if ( level >= MIN_LEVEL )
71                   {
72                      levelJLabel.setText( "Level: " + level );
73                      drawSpace.setLevel( level );
74                      repaint();
75                   } // end if
76                } // end method actionPerformed
77             } // end anonymous inner class
78          ); // end addActionListener
79
80          // set up increase level button to add to control panel
81          // and register listener
82          increaseLevelJButton = new JButton( "Increase Level" );
83          controlJPanel.add( increaseLevelJButton );
84          increaseLevelJButton.addActionListener(
85             new ActionListener() // anonymous inner class
86             {
```

Fig. 15.23 | Demonstrating the fractal user interface. (Part 2 of 3.)

```
87              // process increaseLevelJButton event
88              public void actionPerformed( ActionEvent event )
89              {
90                 int level = drawSpace.getLevel();
91                 level++; // increase level by one
92
93                 // modify level if possible
94                 if ( level >= MIN_LEVEL )
95                 {
96                    levelJLabel.setText( "Level: " + level );
97                    drawSpace.setLevel( level );
98                    repaint();
99                 } // end if
100             } // end method actionPerformed
101          } // end anonymous inner class
102       ); // end addActionListener
103
104       // set up levelJLabel to add to controlJPanel
105       levelJLabel = new JLabel( "Level: 0" );
106       controlJPanel.add( levelJLabel );
107
108       drawSpace = new FractalJPanel( 0 );
109
110       // create mainJPanel to contain controlJPanel and drawSpace
111       mainJPanel = new JPanel();
112       mainJPanel.add( controlJPanel );
113       mainJPanel.add( drawSpace );
114
115       add( mainJPanel ); // add JPanel to JFrame
116
117       setSize( WIDTH, HEIGHT ); // set size of JFrame
118       setVisible( true ); // display JFrame
119    } // end Fractal constructor
120
121    public static void main( String args[] )
122    {
123       Fractal demo = new Fractal();
124       demo.setDefaultCloseOperation( JFrame.EXIT_ON_CLOSE );
125    } // end main
126 } // end class Fractal
```

Fig. 15.23 | Demonstrating the fractal user interface. (Part 3 of 3.)

level label to reflect the change—the new level is set and the repaint method is called to update the image to show the fractal corresponding to the new level.

The **Increase Level** JButton works the same way as the **Decrease Level** JButton, except that the level is incremented rather than decremented to show more details of the fractal (lines 90–91). When the application is first executed, the level will be set to 0, which will display a blue line between two points that were specified in the FractalJPanel class.

The FractalJPanel class in Fig. 15.24 specifies the dimensions of the drawing JPanel to be 400 by 400 (lines 13–14). The FractalJPanel constructor (lines 18–24) takes the current level as a parameter and assigns it to its instance variable level. Instance variable color is set to the default color blue. Lines 22–23 change the background color of the JPanel to be white (for visibility of the colors used to draw the fractal), and set the new dimensions of the JPanel where the fractal will be drawn.

```java
 1   // Fig. 15.24: FractalJPanel.java
 2   // FractalJPanel demonstrates recursive drawing of a fractal.
 3   import java.awt.Graphics;
 4   import java.awt.Color;
 5   import java.awt.Dimension;
 6   import javax.swing.JPanel;
 7
 8   public class FractalJPanel extends JPanel
 9   {
10      private Color color; // stores color used to draw fractal
11      private int level;   // stores current level of fractal
12
13      private final int WIDTH = 400;  // defines width of JPanel
14      private final int HEIGHT = 400; // defines height of JPanel
15
16      // set the initial fractal level to the value specified
17      // and set up JPanel specifications
18      public FractalJPanel( int currentLevel )
19      {
20         color = Color.BLUE;  // initialize drawing color to blue
21         level = currentLevel; // set initial fractal level
22         setBackground( Color.WHITE );
23         setPreferredSize( new Dimension( WIDTH, HEIGHT ) );
24      } // end FractalJPanel constructor
25
26      // draw fractal recursively
27      public void drawFractal( int level, int xA, int yA, int xB,
28         int yB, Graphics g )
29      {
30         // base case: draw a line connecting two given points
31         if ( level == 0 )
32            g.drawLine( xA, yA, xB, yB );
33         else // recursion step: determine new points, draw next level
34         {
35            // calculate midpoint between (xA, yA) and (xB, yB)
36            int xC = ( xA + xB ) / 2;
37            int yC = ( yA + yB ) / 2;
38
39            // calculate the fourth point (xD, yD) which forms an
40            // isosceles right triangle between (xA, yA) and (xC, yC)
41            // where the right angle is at (xD, yD)
42            int xD = xA + ( xC - xA ) / 2 - ( yC - yA ) / 2;
43            int yD = yA + ( yC - yA ) / 2 + ( xC - xA ) / 2;
44
45            // recursively draw the Fractal
46            drawFractal( level - 1, xD, yD, xA, yA, g );
47            drawFractal( level - 1, xD, yD, xC, yC, g );
48            drawFractal( level - 1, xD, yD, xB, yB, g );
49         } // end else
50      } // end method drawFractal
```

Fig. 15.24 | Drawing "Lo fractal" using recursion. (Part I of 3.)

```
51
52      // start the drawing of fractal
53      public void paintComponent( Graphics g )
54      {
55         super.paintComponent( g );
56
57         // draw fractal pattern
58         g.setColor( color );
59         drawFractal( level, 100, 90, 290, 200, g );
60      } // end method paintComponent
61
62      // set the drawing color to c
63      public void setColor( Color c )
64      {
65         color = c;
66      } // end method setColor
67
68      // set the new level of recursion
69      public void setLevel( int currentLevel )
70      {
71         level = currentLevel;
72      } // end method setLevel
73
74      // returns level of recursion
75      public int getLevel()
76      {
77         return level;
78      } // end method getLevel
79   } // end class FractalJPanel
```

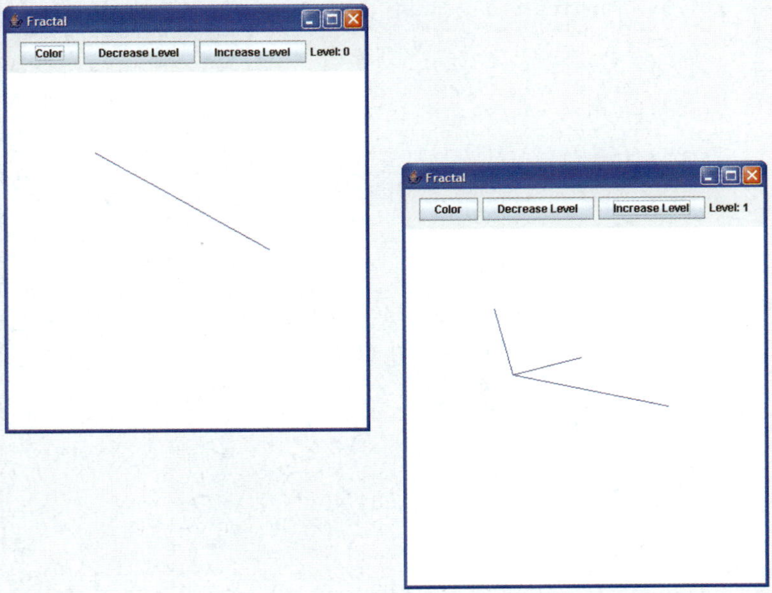

Fig. 15.24 | Drawing "Lo fractal" using recursion. (Part 2 of 3.)

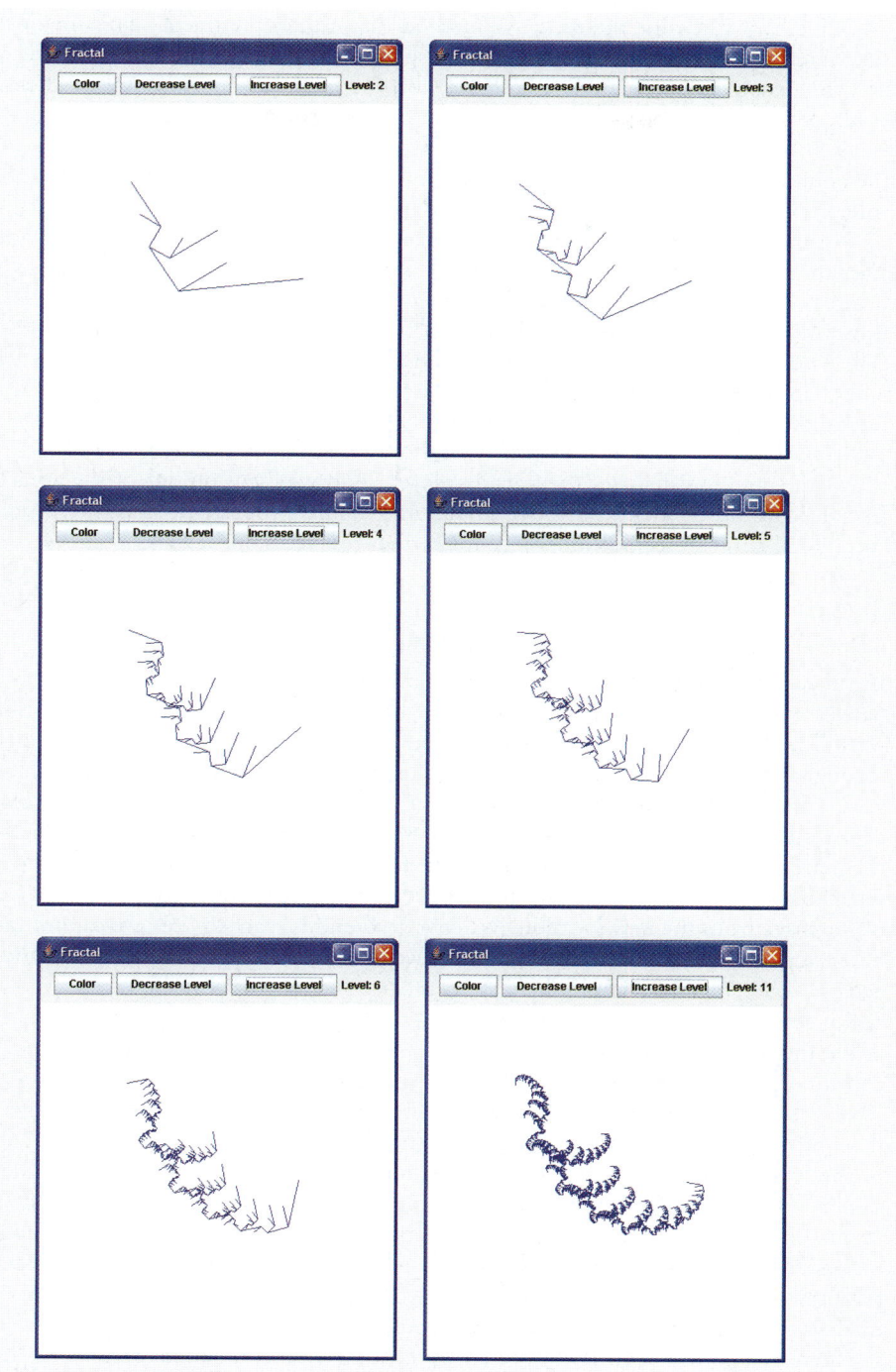

Fig. 15.24 | Drawing "Lo fractal" using recursion. (Part 3 of 3.)

Lines 27–50 define the recursive method that creates the fractal. This method takes six parameters: the level, four integers that specify the *x* and *y* coordinates of two points, and the Graphics object g. The base case for this method (line 31) occurs when level equals 0, at which time a line will be drawn between the two points given as parameters. Lines 36–43 calculate (xC, yC), the midpoint between (xA, yA) and (xB, yB), and (xD, yD), the point that creates a right isosceles triangle with (xA, yA) and (xC, yC). Lines 46–48 make three recursive calls on three different sets of points.

In method paintComponent, line 59 makes the first call to method drawFractal to start the drawing. This method call is not recursive, but all subsequent calls to draw-Fractal performed from the body of drawFractal are. Since the lines will not be drawn until the base case is reached, the distance between two points decreases on each recursive call. As the level of recursion increases, the fractal becomes smoother and more detailed. The shape of this fractal stabilizes as the level approaches 11. Fractals will stabilize at different levels based on the shape and size of the fractal.

Fig. 15.24 shows the development of the fractal from level zero to six. The last image shows the defining shape of the fractal at level 11. If we focus on one of the arms of this fractal, it would be identical to the whole image. This property defines the fractal to be strictly self-similar. See Section 15.12 for further resources on fractals.

15.10 Recursive Backtracking

In this chapter's examples, our recursive methods all have a similar architecture—if the base case is reached, return a result; if not, make one or more recursive calls. In this section we will explore a recursive method that is slightly more complex. This method finds a path through a maze, returning true if there is a possible solution to the maze. The solution involves moving through the maze one step at a time where moves can be made by going down, right, up or left (diagonal moves are not permitted). From the current location in the maze (starting with the entry point), the following steps are taken: A direction is chosen, the move is made in that direction and a recursive call is made to solve the remainder of the maze from the new location. When a dead end is reached (i.e., we cannot take any more steps forward without hitting a wall), we back up to the previous location and try to go in a different direction. If there is no other direction that can be taken, we back up again. This process continues until we find a point in the maze where a move can be made in another direction. Once such a location is found, we move in the new direction and continue with another recursive call to solve the rest of the maze.

To back up to the previous location in the maze, our recursive method simply returns false, moving up the method-call chain to the previous recursive call (which references the previous location in the maze). This process of using recursion to return to an earlier decision point is known as recursive backtracking. If one set of recursive calls does not result in a solution to the problem, the program backs up to the previous decision point and makes a different decision, often resulting in another set of recursive calls. In this example, the previous decision point is the previous location in the maze, and the decision to be made is the direction that the next move should take. One direction has led to a dead end, so the search continues with a different direction. Unlike our other recursive programs, which reached the base case and then returned all the way up the method-call chain to the original method call, the recursive backtracking solution to the maze problem uses recursion to return only part of the way up the method-call chain, then try a different direction. If the backtracking reaches the entry location of the maze and the paths in all directions have been attempted, the maze does not have a solution.

In the chapter exercises you are asked to implement recursive backtracking solutions to the maze problem (Exercise 15.20, Exercise 15.21 and Exercise 15.22) and the Eight Queens problem (Exercise 15.15), which attempts to find a way to place eight queens on an empty chessboard so that no queen is "attacking" any other (i.e., no two queens are in the same row, in the same column or along the same diagonal). See Section 15.12 for links to further information on recursive backtracking.

15.11 Wrap-Up

In this chapter, you learned how to create recursive methods—i.e., methods that call themselves. You learned that recursive methods typically divide a problem into two conceptual pieces—a piece that the method knows how to do (the base case) and a piece that the method does not know how to do (the recursion step). The recursion step is a slightly simpler version of the original problem, and is performed by a recursive method call. You saw some popular recursion examples, including calculating factorials and producing values in the Fibonacci series. You the learned how recursion works "under the hood," including the order in which recursive method calls are pushed on or popped off the program execution stack. Next, you learned the differences between recursive and iterative (non-recursive) methods. In that discussion, you learned that iterative solutions usually use a repetition statement, whereas recursive solutions usually use a selection statement. You learned how to solve more complex problems using recursion, including finding all permutations of a string and displaying fractals. The chapter concluded with an introduction to recursive backtracking, a technique for solving problems that involves backing up through recursive calls to try different possible solutions. In the next chapter, you will learn numerous techniques for sorting lists of data and searching for an item in a list of data, and under what circumstances each searching and sorting technique should be used.

15.12 Internet and Web Resources

Recursion Concepts

chortle.ccsu.ctstateu.edu/cs151/cs151java.html
Provides links to files that discuss recursion in detail, using questions to guide the reader.

en.wikipedia.org/wiki/Recursion
Article from Wikipedia (an online encyclopedia) provides the basics of recursion and several resources for students.

www.cafeaulait.org/javatutorial.html
Provides a nice, brief introduction to recursion in Java, and also covers other Java topics.

Stacks

www.cs.auc.dk/~normark/eciu-recursion/html/recit-slide-implerec.html
Provides slides discussing the implementation of recursion using stacks.

faculty.juniata.edu/kruse/cs2java/recurimpl.htm
Provides a detailed diagram of the program execution stack and discusses how the stack works.

Fractals

`math.rice.edu/~lanius/frac/`
Provides examples of other fractals, such as the Koch Snowflake, the Sierpinski gasket, and Jurassic Park fractals.

`www.lifesmith.com/`
Provides hundreds of colorful fractal images along with detailed explanation about the Mandelbrot and Julia sets, two common sets of fractals.

`www.jracademy.com/~jtucek/math/fractals.html`
Contains two AVI movies created by zooming in continuously on the fractals known as the Mandelbrot and Julia equation sets.

`www.faqs.org/faqs/fractal-faq/`
Provides answers to many questions about fractals.

`spanky.triumf.ca/www/fractint/fractint.html`
Contains links to download Fractint, a freeware program for generating fractals.

`www.42explore.com/fractal.htm`
Lists URLs on fractals and software tools that create fractals.

`www.arcytech.org/java/fractals/koch.shtml`
Provides a detailed introduction to the Koch Curve fractal and provides an applet demonstrating the fractal.

`www.cs.ttu.edu/~denton/fractals/Koch.html`
Introduces the Koch fractals, providing source code in Java.

`library.thinkquest.org/26688/koch.html`
Displays a Koch Curve applet and provides the source code.

Recursive Backtracking

`www.cs.sfu.ca/CourseCentral/201/havens/notes/Lecture14.pdf`
Provides a brief introduction to recursive backtracking, including an example on planning a travel route.

`www.cs.utexas.edu/users/scottm/cs307/handouts/Slides/`
`lec11RecursiveBacktracking-4Up.pdf`
Demonstrates recursive backtracking and walks through several examples.

`math.hws.edu/xJava/PentominosSolver`
Provides a program that uses recursive backtracking to solve a problem known as the Pentominos puzzle (described at the site).

`cte.rockhurst.edu/burgerk/research/scramble/paper.pdf`
Demonstrates using recursive backtracking to solve a scrambled squares puzzle.

Summary

- A recursive method is a method that calls itself directly or indirectly through another method.

- When a recursive method is called to solve a problem, the method actually is capable of solving only the simplest case(s), or base case(s). If the method is called with a base case, the method returns a result.

- If a recursive method is called with a more complex problem than a base case, the method typically divides the problem into two conceptual pieces—a piece that the method knows how to do and a piece that the method does not know how to do.

- To make recursion feasible, the piece that the method does not know how to do must resemble the original problem, but be a slightly simpler or smaller version of it. Because this new problem looks like the original problem, the method calls a fresh copy of itself to work on the smaller problem—this is called the recursion step.

- For recursion to eventually terminate, each time a method calls itself with a simpler version of the original problem, the sequence of smaller and smaller problems must converge on a base case. When, the method recognizes the base case, it returns a result to the previous copy of the method.

- A recursive call may be a call to another method, which in turn makes a call back to the original method. Such a process still results in a recursive call to the original method. This is known as an indirect recursive call or indirect recursion.

- Either omitting the base case or writing the recursion step incorrectly so that it does not converge on the base case can cause infinite recursion, eventually exhausting memory. This error is analogous to the problem of an infinite loop in an iterative (nonrecursive) solution.

- The Fibonacci series begins with 0 and 1 and has the property that each subsequent Fibonacci number is the sum of the preceding two Fibonacci numbers.

- The ratio of successive Fibonacci numbers converges on a constant value of 1.618…, a number that has been called the golden ratio or the golden mean.

- Some recursive solutions, such as Fibonacci (which makes two calls per recursion step), result in an "explosion" of method calls.

- The stack is a data structure whose data objects can be added or removed only at the top of the stack.

- A stack is analogous to a pile of dishes. When a dish is placed on the pile, it is always placed at the top (referred to as pushing the dish onto the stack). Similarly, when a dish is removed from the pile, it is always removed from the top (referred to as popping the dish off the stack).

- Stacks are known as last-in, first-out (LIFO) data structures—the last item pushed (inserted) on the stack is the first item popped (removed) from the stack.

- Stacks have many interesting applications. For example, when a program calls a method, the called method must know how to return to its caller, so the return address of the calling method is pushed onto the program execution stack (sometimes referred to as the method call stack).

- The program execution stack contains the memory for local variables on each invocation of a method during a program's execution. This data, stored as a portion of the program execution stack, is known as the activation record or stack frame of the method call.

- If there are more recursive or nested method calls than can be stored on the program execution stack, an error known as a stack overflow occurs.

- Both iteration and recursion are based on a control statement: Iteration uses a repetition statement, whereas recursion uses a selection statement.

- Both iteration and recursion involve repetition: Iteration explicitly uses a repetition statement, whereas recursion achieves repetition through repeated method calls.

- Iteration and recursion each involve a termination test: Iteration terminates when the loop-continuation condition fails, whereas recursion terminates when a base case is recognized.

- Iteration with counter-controlled repetition and recursion each gradually approach termination: Iteration keeps modifying a counter until the counter assumes a value that makes the loop-continuation condition fail, whereas recursion keeps producing simpler versions of the original problem until the base case is reached.

- Both iteration and recursion can occur infinitely: An infinite loop occurs with iteration if the loop-continuation test never becomes false, whereas infinite recursion occurs if the recursion step does not reduce the problem each time in a manner that converges on the base case.

- Recursion repeatedly invokes the mechanism, and consequently the overhead, of method calls.
- Any problem that can be solved recursively can also be solved iteratively.
- A recursive approach is normally preferred over an iterative approach when the recursive approach more naturally mirrors the problem and results in a program that is easier to understand and debug.
- A recursive approach can often be implemented with few lines of code, but a corresponding iterative approach might take a large amount of code. Another reason to choose a recursive solution is that an iterative solution might not be apparent.
- The permutations of a string are all the different strings that can be created by rearranging the characters of the original string.
- Method charAt of class String takes an integer argument and returns the character in the String at that index. As with arrays, the first element of a string is considered to be at position 0.
- Class String provides two substring methods to enable a new String object to be created by copying part of an existing String object. Each method returns a new String object.
- If method substring is passed two integer arguments, the first argument specifies the starting index from which characters are copied in the original string, and the second argument specifies the index one beyond the last character to be copied.
- If method substring is passed one integer argument, the argument specifies the starting index in the original string from which characters are to be copied. The substring returned contains a copy of the characters from the starting index to the end of the string.
- A fractal is a geometric figure that is generated from a pattern repeated recursively an infinite number of times. The figure grows by adding the pattern at different orientations and scaling to the original.
- Fractals have a self-similar property—when subdivided into parts, each is a reduced-size copy of the whole.
- The process of using recursion to return to an earlier decision point is known as recursive backtracking. If one set of recursive calls does not result in a solution to the problem, the program backs up to the previous decision point and makes a different decision, often resulting in another set of recursive calls.

Terminology

activation record
anagram
backtracking
base case
charAt method of String
complexity theory
converge on a base case
Eight Queens problem
exhaustive recursion
factorial
Fibonacci series
fractal
fractal depth
fractal level
fractal order
golden mean
golden ratio

indirect recursion
infinite recursion
Koch Curve fractal
Koch Snowflake fractal
last-in, first-out (LIFO) data structures
level of a fractal
Maze Traversal problem
method call stack
palindrome
permutation
program execution stack
recursion overhead
recursion step
recursive backtracking
recursive call
recursive evaluation
recursive method

self-similar fractal
stack
stack frame
stack overflow

strictly self-similar fractal
substring method of String
termination test
Towers of Hanoi problem

Self-Review Exercises

15.1 State whether each of the following is *true* or *false*. If *false*, explain why.
a) A method that calls itself indirectly is not an example of recursion.
b) Recursion can be efficient in computation because of reduced memory space usage.
c) When a recursive method is called to solve a problem, the method actually is capable of solving only the simplest case(s), or base case(s).
d) To make recursion feasible, the recursion step in a recursive solution must resemble the original problem, but be a slightly larger version of it.

15.2 A _____ is needed to terminate recursion.
a) recursion step
b) break statement
c) void return type
d) base case

15.3 The first call to invoke a recursive method is _____.
a) not recursive
b) recursive
c) the recursion step
d) none of the above

15.4 Each time a fractal's pattern is applied, the fractal is said to be at a new _____.
a) width
b) height
c) level
d) volume

15.5 Iteration and recursion each involve a _____.
a) repetition statement
b) termination test
c) counter variable
d) None of the above

15.6 Fill in the blanks in each of the following statements:
a) The ratio of successive Fibonacci numbers converges on a constant value of 1.618..., a number that has been called the _____ or the _____.
b) Data can be added or removed only from the _____ of the stack.
c) Stacks are known as _____ data structures—the last item pushed (inserted) on the stack is the first item popped (removed) from the stack.
d) The program execution stack contains the memory for local variables on each invocation of a method during a program's execution. This data, stored as a portion of the program execution stack, is known as the _____ or _____ of the method call.
e) If there are more recursive or nested method calls than can be stored on the program execution stack, an error known as a(n) _____ occurs.
f) Iteration normally uses a repetition statement, whereas recursion normally uses a(n) _____ statement.
g) Fractals have a(n) _____ property—when subdivided into parts, each is a reduced-size copy of the whole.

h) The _____ of a string are all the different strings that can be created by rearranging the characters of the original string.

i) The program execution stack is also referred to as the _____ stack.

Answers to Self-Review Exercises

15.1   a) False. A method that calls itself indirectly is an example of recursion—more specifically, an example of indirect recursion. b) False. Recursion can be inefficient in computation because of multiple method calls and memory space usage. c) True. d) False. To make recursion feasible, the recursion step in a recursive solution must resemble the original problem, but be a slightly *smaller* version of it.

15.2   d

15.3   a

15.4   c

15.5   b

15.6   a) golden ratio, golden mean. b) top. c) last-in, first-out (LIFO). d) activation record, stack frame. e) stack overflow. f) selection. g) self-similar. h) permutations. i) method-call.

Exercises

15.7   What does the following code do?

```
public int mystery( int a, int b )
{
   if ( b == 1 )
      return a;
   else
      return a + mystery( a, b - 1 );
} // end method mystery
```

15.8   Find the error(s) in the following recursive method, and explain how to correct it (them). This method should find the sum of the values from 0 to n.

```
public int sum( int n )
{
   if ( n == 0 )
      return 0;
   else
      return n + sum( n );
} // end method sum
```

15.9   (*Recursive power Method*) Write a recursive method power(base, exponent) that, when called, returns

$$base^{\,exponent}$$

For example, power(3,4) = 3 * 3 * 3 * 3. Assume that exponent is an integer greater than or equal to 1. [*Hint:* The recursion step should use the relationship

$$base^{exponent} = base \cdot base^{exponent - 1}$$

and the terminating condition occurs when exponent is equal to 1, because

$$base^1 = base$$

Incorporate this method into a program that enables the user to enter the base and exponent.]

15.10 (*Visualizing Recursion*) It is interesting to watch recursion "in action." Modify the factorial method in Fig. 15.3 to print its local variable and recursive-call parameter. For each recursive call, display the outputs on a separate line, and add a level of indentation. Do your utmost to make the outputs clear, interesting and meaningful. Your goal here is to design and implement an output format that makes it easier to understand recursion. You may want to add such display capabilities to other recursion examples and exercises throughout the text.

15.11 (*Greatest Common Divisor*) The greatest common divisor of integers x and y is the largest integer that evenly divides into both x and y. Write a recursive method gcd that returns the greatest common divisor of x and y. The gcd of x and y is defined recursively as follows: If y is equal to 0, then gcd(x, y) is x; otherwise, gcd(x, y) is gcd(y, x % y), where % is the remainder operator. Use this method to replace the one you wrote in the application of Exercise 6.27.

15.12 What does the following program do?

```java
// Exercise 15.12 Solution: MysteryClass.java

public class MysteryClass
{
   public int mystery( int array2[], int size )
   {
      if ( size == 1 )
         return array2[ 0 ];
      else
         return array2[ size - 1 ] + mystery( array2, size - 1 );
   } // end method mystery
} // end class MysteryClass
```

```java
// Exercise 15.12 Solution: MysteryTest.java

public class MysteryTest
{
   public static void main( String args[] )
   {
      MysteryClass mysteryObject = new MysteryClass();

      int array[] = { 1, 2, 3, 4, 5, 6, 7, 8, 9, 10 };

      int result = mysteryObject.mystery( array, array.length );

      System.out.printf( "Result is: %d\n", result );
   } // end method main
} // end class MysteryTest
```

15.13 What does the following program do?

```java
// Exercise 15.13 Solution: SomeClass.java

public class SomeClass
{
   public String someMethod(
      int array2[], int x, String output )
   {
      if ( x < array2.length )
         return String.format(
            "%s%d ", someMethod( array2, x + 1 ), array2[ x ] );
      else
         return "";
   } // end method someMethod
} // end class SomeClass
```

```java
// Exercise 15.13 Solution: SomeClassTest.java

public class SomeClassTest
{
   public static void main( String args[] )
   {
      SomeClass someClassObject = new SomeClass();

      int array[] = { 1, 2, 3, 4, 5, 6, 7, 8, 9, 10 };

      String results =
         someClassObject.someMethod( array, 0 );

      System.out.println( results );
   } // end main
} // end class SomeClassTest
```

15.14 (*Palindromes*) A palindrome is a string that is spelled the same way forwards and backwards. Some examples of palindromes are "radar," "able was i ere i saw elba" and (if spaces are ignored) "a man a plan a canal panama." Write a recursive method testPalindrome that returns boolean value true if the string stored in the array is a palindrome and false otherwise. The method should ignore spaces and punctuation in the string.

15.15 (*Eight Queens*) A puzzler for chess buffs is the Eight Queens problem, which asks the following: Is it possible to place eight queens on an empty chessboard so that no queen is "attacking" any other (i.e., no two queens are in the same row, in the same column or along the same diagonal)? For instance, if a queen is placed in the upper-left corner of the board, no other queens could be placed in any of the marked squares shown in Fig. 15.25. Solve the problem recursively. [*Hint:* Your solution should begin with the first column and look for a location in that column where a queen can be placed—initially, place the queen in the first row. The solution should then recursively search the remaining columns. In the first few columns, there will be several locations where a queen may be placed. Take the first available location. If a column is reached with no possible location for a queen, the program should return to the previous column, and move the queen in that column to a new row. This continuous backing up and trying new alternatives is an example of recursive backtracking.]

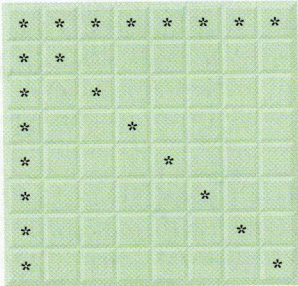

Fig. 15.25 | Squares eliminated by placing a queen in the upper-left corner of a chessboard.

15.16 (*Print an Array*) Write a recursive method printArray that displays all the elements in an array of integers, separated by spaces.

15.17 (*Print an Array Backwards*) Write a recursive method stringReverse that takes a character array containing a string as an argument and prints the string backwards. [*Hint:* Use String method toCharArray, which takes no arguments, to get a char array containing the characters in the String.]

15.18 (*Find the Minimum Value in an Array*) Write a recursive method recursiveMinimum that determines the smallest element in an array of integers. The method should return when it receives an array of one element.

15.19 (*Fractals*) Repeat the fractal pattern in Section 15.9 to form a star. Begin with five lines, instead of one, where each line is a different arm of the star. Apply the "Lo fractal" pattern to each arm of the star.

15.20 (*Maze Traversal Using Recursive Backtracking*) The grid of #s and dots (.) in Fig. 15.26 is a two-dimensional array representation of a maze. The #s represent the walls of the maze, and the dots represent locations in the possible paths through the maze. Moves can be made only to a location in the array that contains a dot.

   Write a recursive method (mazeTraversal) to walk through mazes like the one in Fig. 15.26. The method should receive as arguments a 12-by-12 character array representing the maze and the current location in the maze (the first time this method is called, the current location should be the

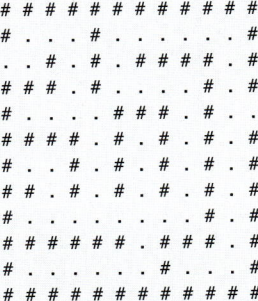

Fig. 15.26 | Two-dimensional array representation of a maze.

entry point of the maze). As mazeTraversal attempts to locate the exit, it should place the character x in each square in the path. There is a simple algorithm for walking through a maze that guarantees finding the exit (assuming there is an exit). If there is no exit, you will arrive at the starting location again. The algorithm for this method is as follows: From the current location in the maze, try to move one space in any of the possible directions (down, right, up or left). If it is possible to move in at least one direction, call mazeTraversal recursively, passing the new spot on the maze as the current spot. If it is not possible to go in any directions, "back up" to a previous location in the maze and try a new direction for that location. Program the method to display the maze after each move so the user can watch as the maze is solved. The final output of the maze should display only the path needed to solve the maze—if going in a particular direction results in a dead end, the x's going in that direction should not be displayed. [*Hint:* To display only the final path, it may be helpful to mark off spots that result in a dead end with another character (such as '0').]

15.21 (*Generating Mazes Randomly*) Write a method mazeGenerator that takes as an argument a two-dimensional 12-by-12 character array and randomly produces a maze. The method should also provide the starting and ending locations of the maze. Test your method mazeTraversal from Exercise 15.20, using several randomly generated mazes.

15.22 (*Mazes of Any Size*) Generalize methods mazeTraversal and mazeGenerator of Exercise 15.20 and Exercise 15.21 to process mazes of any width and height.

15.23 (*Time to Calculate Fibonacci Numbers*) Enhance the Fibonacci program of Fig. 15.5 so that it calculates the approximate amount of time required to perform the calculation and the number of calls made to the recursive method. For this purpose, call static System method currentTimeMillis, which takes no arguments and returns the computer's current time in milliseconds. Call this method twice—once before the call to fibonacci and once after the call to fibonacci. Save each of these values and calculate the difference in the times to determine how many milliseconds were required to perform the calculation. Then, add a variable to the FibonacciCalculator class, and use this variable to determine the number of calls made to method fibonacci. Display your results.

Searching and Sorting

OBJECTIVES

In this chapter you will learn:

- To search for a given value in an array using linear search and binary search.

- To sort arrays using the iterative selection and insertion sort algorithms.

- To sort arrays using the recursive merge sort algorithm.

- To determine the efficiency of searching and sorting algorithms.

16.1 Introduction

Searching data involves determining whether a value (referred to as the search key) is present in the data and, if so, finding the value's location. Two popular search algorithms are the simple linear search and the faster but more complex binary search. Sorting places data in order, typically ascending or descending, based on one or more sort keys. A list of names could be sorted alphabetically, bank accounts could be sorted by account number, employee payroll records could be sorted by social security number, and so on. This chapter introduces two simple sorting algorithms, the selection sort and the insertion sort, along with the more efficient but more complex merge sort. Figure 16.1 summarizes the searching and sorting algorithms discussed in this book.

16.2 Searching Algorithms

Looking up a phone number, accessing a Web site and checking the definition of a word in a dictionary all involve searching large amounts of data. The next two sections discuss two common search algorithms—one that is easy to program yet relatively inefficient and one that is relatively efficient but more complex and difficult to program.

16.2.1 Linear Search

The linear search algorithm searches each element in an array sequentially. If the search key does not match an element in the array, the algorithm tests each element, and when the end of the array is reached, informs the user that the search key is not present. If the search key is in the array, the algorithm tests each element until it finds one that matches the search key and returns the index of that element.

As an example, consider an array containing the following values

    34   56   2   10   77   51   93   30   5   52

and a program that is searching for 51. Using the linear search algorithm, the program first checks whether 34 matches the search key. It does not, so the algorithm checks whether 56 matches the search key. The program continues moving through the array sequentially, testing 2, then 10, then 77. When the program tests 51, which matches the search key, the program returns the index 5, which is the location of 51 in the array. If, after checking

Chapter	Algorithm	Location
Searching Algorithms:		
16	Linear Search	Section 16.2.1
	Binary Search	Section 16.2.2
	Recursive Linear Search	Exercise 16.8
	Recursive Binary Search	Exercise 16.9
17	Linear search of a List	Exercise 17.21
	Binary tree search	Exercise 17.23
19	binarySearch method of class Collections	Fig. 19.14
Sorting Algorithms:		
16	Selection Sort	Section 16.3.1
	Insertion Sort	Section 16.3.2
	Recursive Merge Sort	Section 16.3.3
	Bubble Sort	Exercises 16.3 and 16.4
	Bucket Sort	Exercise 16.7
	Recursive Quicksort	Exercise 16.10
17	Binary tree sort	Section 17.9
19	sort method of class Collections	Fig. 19.8–Fig. 19.11
	SortedSet collection	Fig. 19.19

Fig. 16.1 | Searching and sorting algorithms in this text.

every array element, the program determines that the search key does not match any element in the array, the program returns a sentinel value (e.g. -1).

Figure 16.2 declares the LinearArray class. This class has two private instance variables—an array of ints named data, and a static Random object to fill the array with randomly generated ints. When an object of class LinearArray is instantiated, the constructor (lines 12–19) creates and initializes the array data with random ints in the range 10–99. If there are duplicate values in the array, linear search returns the index of the first element in the array that matches the search key.

Lines 22–30 perform the linear search. The search key is passed to parameter searchKey. Lines 25–27 loop through the elements in the array. Line 26 compares each element in the array with searchKey. If the values are equal, line 27 returns the index of the element. If the loop ends without finding the value, line 29 returns -1. Lines 33–43 declare method toString, which returns a String representation of the array for printing.

Figure 16.3 creates a LinearArray object containing an array of 10 ints (line 16) and allows the user to search the array for specific elements. Lines 20–22 prompt the user for the search key and store it in searchInt. Lines 25–41 then loop until the searchInt is equal to -1. The array holds ints from 10–99 (line 18 of Fig. 16.2). Line 28 calls method linearSearch to determine whether searchInt is in the array. If searchInt is not in the array, linearSearch returns -1 and the program notifies the user (lines 31–32). If

```
1   // Fig 16.2: LinearArray.java
2   // Class that contains an array of random integers and a method
3   // that will search that array sequentially
4   import java.util.Random;
5
6   public class LinearArray
7   {
8      private int[] data; // array of values
9      private static Random generator = new Random();
10
11     // create array of given size and fill with random numbers
12     public LinearArray( int size )
13     {
14        data = new int[ size ]; // create space for array
15
16        // fill array with random ints in range 10-99
17        for ( int i = 0; i < size; i++ )
18           data[ i ] = 10 + generator.nextInt( 90 );
19     } // end LinearArray constructor
20
21     // perform a linear search on the data
22     public int linearSearch( int searchKey )
23     {
24        // loop through array sequentially
25        for ( int index = 0; index < data.length; index++ )
26           if ( data[ index ] == searchKey )
27              return index; // return index of integer
28
29        return -1; // integer was not found
30     } // end method linearSearch
31
32     // method to output values in array
33     public String toString()
34     {
35        StringBuffer temporary = new StringBuffer();
36
37        // iterate through array
38        for ( int element : data )
39           temporary.append( element + " " );
40
41        temporary.append( "\n" ); // add endline character
42        return temporary.toString();
43     } // end method toString
44  } // end class LinearArray
```

Fig. 16.2 | LinearArray class.

searchInt is in the array, linearSearch returns the position of the element, which the program outputs in lines 34–35. Lines 38–40 retrieve the next integer from the user.

Efficiency of Linear Search

Searching algorithms all accomplish the same goal—finding an element that matches a given search key, if such an element does, in fact, exist. There are, however, a number of things that differentiate search algorithms from another. The major difference is the amount of effort they require to complete the search. One way to describe this effort is with **Big O notation**, which indicates the worst-case run time for an algorithm, that is, how hard an algorithm may have to work to solve a problem. For searching and sorting algorithms, this is particularly dependent on how many data elements there are.

Suppose an algorithm is designed to test whether the first element of an array is equal to the second element of the array. If the array has 10 elements, this algorithm requires one comparison. If the array has 1,000 elements, the algorithm still requires one comparison.

```java
1   // Fig 16.3: LinearSearchTest.java
2   // Sequentially search an array for an item.
3   import java.util.Scanner;
4
5   public class LinearSearchTest
6   {
7      public static void main( String args[] )
8      {
9         // create Scanner object to input data
10        Scanner input = new Scanner( System.in );
11
12        int searchInt; // search key
13        int position; // location of search key in array
14
15        // create array and output it
16        LinearArray searchArray = new LinearArray( 10 );
17        System.out.println( searchArray ); // print array
18
19        // get input from user
20        System.out.print(
21           "Please enter an integer value (-1 to quit): " );
22        searchInt = input.nextInt(); // read first int from user
23
24        // repeatedly input an integer; -1 terminates the program
25        while ( searchInt != -1 )
26        {
27           // perform linear search
28           position = searchArray.linearSearch( searchInt );
29
30           if ( position == -1 ) // integer was not found
31              System.out.println( "The integer " + searchInt +
32                 " was not found.\n" );
33           else // integer was found
34              System.out.println( "The integer " + searchInt +
35                 " was found in position " + position + ".\n" );
36
37           // get input from user
38           System.out.print(
39              "Please enter an integer value (-1 to quit): " );
40           searchInt = input.nextInt(); // read next int from user
41        } // end while
42     } // end main
43  } // end class LinearSearchTest
```

Fig. 16.3 | LinearSearchTest class. (Part 1 of 2.)

```
16 35 68 10 48 36 81 60 84 21

Please enter an integer value (-1 to quit): 48
The integer 48 was found in position 4.

Please enter an integer value (-1 to quit): 60
The integer 60 was found in position 7.

Please enter an integer value (-1 to quit): 33
The integer 33 was not found.

Please enter an integer value (-1 to quit): -1
```

Fig. 16.3 | `LinearSearchTest` class. (Part 2 of 2.)

In fact, the algorithm is completely independent of the number of elements in the array. This algorithm is said to have a **constant run time**, which is represented in Big O notation as $O(1)$. An algorithm that is $O(1)$ does not necessarily require only one comparison. $O(1)$ just means that the number of comparisons is *constant*—it does not grow as the size of the array increases. An algorithm that tests whether the first element of an array is equal to any of the next three elements is still $O(1)$ even though it requires three comparisons.

An algorithm that tests whether the first element of an array is equal to *any* of the other elements of the array will require at most $n - 1$ comparisons, where n is the number of elements in the array. If the array has 10 elements, this algorithm requires up to nine comparisons. If the array has 1,000 elements, this algorithm requires up to 999 comparisons. As n grows larger, the n part of the expression "dominates" and subtracting one becomes inconsequential. Big O is designed to highlight these dominant terms and ignore terms that become unimportant as n grows. For this reason, an algorithm that requires a total of $n - 1$ comparisons (such as the one we described earlier) is said to be $O(n)$. An $O(n)$ algorithm is referred to as having a **linear run time**. $O(n)$ is often pronounced "on the order of n" or more simply "order n."

Now suppose you have an algorithm that tests whether *any* element of an array is duplicated elsewhere in the array. The first element must be compared with every other element in the array. The second element must be compared with every other element except the first (it was already compared to the first). The third element must be compared with every other element except the first two. In the end, this algorithm will end up making $(n - 1) + (n - 2) + \ldots + 2 + 1$ or $n^2/2 - n/2$ comparisons. As n increases, the n^2 term dominates and the n term becomes inconsequential. Again, Big O notation highlights the n^2 term, leaving $n^2/2$. But as we will soon see, constant factors are omitted in Big O notation.

Big O is concerned with how an algorithm's run time grows in relation to the number of items processed. Suppose an algorithm requires n^2 comparisons. With four elements, the algorithm will require 16 comparisons; with eight elements, the algorithm will require 64 comparisons. With this algorithm, doubling the number of elements quadruples the number of comparisons. Consider a similar algorithm requiring $n^2/2$ comparisons. With four elements, the algorithm will require eight comparisons; with eight elements, the algorithm will require 32 comparisons. Again, doubling the number of elements quadruples the number of comparisons. Both of these algorithms grow as the square of n, so Big O ignores the constant and both algorithms are considered to be $O(n^2)$, which is referred to as quadratic run time and pronounced "on the order of *n*-squared" or more simply "order *n*-squared."

When *n* is small, $O(n^2)$ algorithms (running on today's billion-operation-per-second personal computers) will not noticeably affect performance. But as *n* grows you will start to notice the performance degradation. An $O(n^2)$ algorithm running on a million-element array would require a trillion "operations" (where each could actually require several machine instructions to execute). This could require a few hours to execute. A billion-element array would require a quintillion operations, a number so large that the algorithm could take decades! $O(n^2)$ algorithms, unfortunately, are easy to write, as you will see in this chapter. You will also see algorithms with more favorable Big O measures. These efficient algorithms often take a bit more cleverness and work to create, but their superior performance can be well worth the extra effort, especially as *n* gets large and as algorithms are compounded into larger programs.

The linear search algorithm runs in $O(n)$ time. The worst case in this algorithm is that every element must be checked to determine whether the search item exists in the array. If the size of the array is doubled, the number of comparisons that the algorithm must perform is also doubled. Note that linear search can provide outstanding performance if the element matching the search key happens to be at or near the front of the array. But we seek algorithms that perform well, on average, across all searches, including those where the element matching the search key is near the end of the array.

Linear search is the easiest search algorithm to program, but it can be slow compared to other search algorithms. If a program needs to perform many searches on large arrays, it may be better to implement a different, more efficient algorithm, such as the binary search which we present in the next section.

Performance Tip 16.1

Sometimes the simplest algorithms perform poorly. Their virtue is that they are easy to program, test and debug. Sometimes more complex algorithms are required to realize maximum performance.

16.2.2 Binary Search

The binary search algorithm is more efficient than the linear search algorithm, but it requires that the array be sorted. The first iteration of this algorithm tests the middle element in the array. If this matches the search key, the algorithm ends. Assuming the array is sorted in ascending order, then if the search key is less than the middle element, the search key cannot match any element in the second half of the array and the algorithm continues with only the first half of the array (i.e., the first element up to, but not including the middle element). If the search key is greater than the middle element, the search key cannot match any element in the first half of the array and the algorithm continues with only the second half of the array (i.e., the element after the middle element through the last element). Each iteration tests the middle value of the remaining portion of the array. If the search key does not match the element, the algorithm eliminates half of the remaining elements. The algorithm ends either by finding an element that matches the search key or reducing the subarray to zero size.

As an example consider the sorted 15-element array

2   3   5   10   27   30   34   51   56   65   77   81   82   93   99

and a search key of 65. A program implementing the binary search algorithm would first check whether 51 is the search key (because 51 is the middle element of the array). The search key (65) is larger than 51, so 51 is discarded along with the first half of the array (all elements smaller than 51.) Next, the algorithm checks whether 81 (the middle element of the remainder of the array) matches the search key. The search key (65) is smaller than 81, so 81 is discarded along with the elements larger than 81. After just two tests, the algorithm has narrowed the number of values to check to three (56, 65 and 77). The algorithm then checks 65 (which indeed matches the search key), and returns the index of the array element containing 65. This algorithm required just three comparisons to determine whether the search key matched an element of the array. Using a linear search algorithm would have required 10 comparisons. [*Note:* In this example, we have chosen to use an array with 15 elements so that there will always be an obvious middle element in the array. With an even number of elements, the middle of the array lies between two elements. We implement the algorithm to chose the lower of those two elements.]

Figure 16.4 declares class BinaryArray. This class is similar to LinearArray—it has two private instance variables, a constructor, a search method (binarySearch), a remainingElements method and a toString method. Lines 13–22 declare the constructor. After

```java
 1   // Fig 16.4: BinaryArray.java
 2   // Class that contains an array of random integers and a method
 3   // that uses binary search to find an integer.
 4   import java.util.Random;
 5   import java.util.Arrays;
 6
 7   public class BinaryArray
 8   {
 9      private int[] data; // array of values
10      private static Random generator = new Random();
11
12      // create array of given size and fill with random integers
13      public BinaryArray( int size )
14      {
15         data = new int[ size ]; // create space for array
16
17         // fill array with random ints in range 10-99
18         for ( int i = 0; i < size; i++ )
19            data[ i ] = 10 + generator.nextInt( 90 );
20
21         Arrays.sort( data );
22      } // end BinaryArray constructor
23
24      // perform a binary search on the data
25      public int binarySearch( int searchElement )
26      {
27         int low = 0; // low end of the search area
28         int high = data.length - 1; // high end of the search area
29         int middle = ( low + high + 1 ) / 2; // middle element
30         int location = -1; // return value; -1 if not found
31
```

Fig. 16.4 | BinaryArray class. (Part 1 of 2.)

```
32          do // loop to search for element
33          {
34              // print remaining elements of array
35              System.out.print( remainingElements( low, high ) );
36
37              // output spaces for alignment
38              for ( int i = 0; i < middle; i++ )
39                  System.out.print( "   " );
40              System.out.println( " * " ); // indicate current middle
41
42              // if the element is found at the middle
43              if ( searchElement == data[ middle ] )
44                  location = middle; // location is the current middle
45
46              // middle element is too high
47              else if ( searchElement < data[ middle ] )
48                  high = middle - 1; // eliminate the higher half
49              else  // middle element is too low
50                  low = middle + 1; // eliminate the lower half
51
52              middle = ( low + high + 1 ) / 2; // recalculate the middle
53          } while ( ( low <= high ) && ( location == -1 ) );
54
55          return location; // return location of search key
56      } // end method binarySearch
57
58      // method to output certain values in array
59      public String remainingElements( int low, int high )
60      {
61          StringBuffer temporary = new StringBuffer();
62
63          // output spaces for alignment
64          for ( int i = 0; i < low; i++ )
65              temporary.append( "   " );
66
67          // output elements left in array
68          for ( int i = low; i <= high; i++ )
69              temporary.append( data[ i ] + " " );
70
71          temporary.append( "\n" );
72          return temporary.toString();
73      } // end method remainingElements
74
75      // method to output values in array
76      public String toString()
77      {
78          return remainingElements( 0, data.length - 1 );
79      } // end method toString
80  } // end class BinaryArray
```

Fig. 16.4 | BinaryArray class. (Part 2 of 2.)

initializing the array with random ints from 10–99 (lines 18–19), line 21 calls the
Arrays.sort method on the array data. Method **sort** is a static method of class Arrays

that sorts the elements in an array in ascending order. Recall that the binary search algorithm will work only on a sorted array.

Lines 25–56 declare method `binarySearch`. The search key is passed into parameter `searchElement` (line 25). Lines 27–29 calculate the `low` end index, `high` end index and `middle` index of the portion of the array that the program is currently searching. At the beginning of the method, the `low` end is 0, the `high` end is the length of the array minus 1 and the `middle` is the average of these two values. Line 30 initializes the `location` of the element to -1—the value that will be returned if the element is not found. Lines 32–53 loop until `low` is greater than `high` (this occurs when the element is not found) or `location` does not equal -1 (indicating that the search key was found). Line 43 tests whether the value in the `middle` element is equal to `searchElement`. If this is `true`, line 44 assigns `middle` to `location`. Then the loop terminates and `location` is returned to the caller. Each iteration of the loop tests a single value (line 43) and eliminates half of the remaining values in the array (line 48 or 50).

Lines 26–44 of Fig. 16.5 loop until the user enters -1. For each other number the user enters, the program performs a binary search on the data to determine whether it matches an element in the array. The first line of output from this program is the array of `int`s, in increasing order. When the user instructs the program to search for 23, the program first

```
1   // Fig 16.5: BinarySearchTest.java
2   // Use binary search to locate an item in an array.
3   import java.util.Scanner;
4
5   public class BinarySearchTest
6   {
7      public static void main( String args[] )
8      {
9         // create Scanner object to input data
10        Scanner input = new Scanner( System.in );
11
12        int searchInt; // search key
13        int position; // location of search key in array
14
15        // create array and output it
16        BinaryArray searchArray = new BinaryArray( 15 );
17        System.out.println( searchArray );
18
19        // get input from user
20        System.out.print(
21           "Please enter an integer value (-1 to quit): " );
22        searchInt = input.nextInt(); // read an int from user
23        System.out.println();
24
25        // repeatedly input an integer; -1 terminates the program
26        while ( searchInt != -1 )
27        {
28           // use binary search to try to find integer
29           position = searchArray.binarySearch( searchInt );
30
```

Fig. 16.5 | BinarySearchTest class. (Part 1 of 2.)

```
31              // return value of -1 indicates integer was not found
32              if ( position == -1 )
33                 System.out.println( "The integer " + searchInt +
34                    " was not found.\n" );
35              else
36                 System.out.println( "The integer " + searchInt +
37                    " was found in position " + position + ".\n" );
38
39              // get input from user
40              System.out.print(
41                 "Please enter an integer value (-1 to quit): " );
42              searchInt = input.nextInt(); // read an int from user
43              System.out.println();
44           } // end while
45        } // end main
46     } // end class BinarySearchTest
```

```
 13 23 24 34 35 36 38 42 47 51 68 74 75 85 97

Please enter an integer value (-1 to quit): 23

13 23 24 34 35 36 38 42 47 51 68 74 75 85 97
                     *
13 23 24 34 35 36 38
            *
13 23 24
      *
The integer 23 was found in position 1.

Please enter an integer value (-1 to quit): 75

13 23 24 34 35 36 38 42 47 51 68 74 75 85 97
                        *
                     47 51 68 74 75 85 97
                              *
                        75 85 97
                              *
                        75
                         *
The integer 75 was found in position 12.

Please enter an integer value (-1 to quit): 52

13 23 24 34 35 36 38 42 47 51 68 74 75 85 97
                        *
                     47 51 68 74 75 85 97
                              *
                     47 51 68
                        *
                        68
                         *
The integer 52 was not found.

Please enter an integer value (-1 to quit): -1
```

Fig. 16.5 | BinarySearchTest class. (Part 2 of 2.)

tests the middle element, which is 42 (as indicated by *). The search key is less than 42, so the program eliminates the second half of the array and tests the middle element from the first half of the array. The search key is smaller than 34, so the program eliminates the second half of the array, leaving only three elements. Finally, the program checks 23 (which matches the search key) and returns the index 1.

Efficiency of Binary Search

In the worst-case scenario, searching a sorted array of 1,023 elements will take only 10 comparisons when using a binary search. Repeatedly dividing 1,023 by 2 (because after each comparison, we are able to eliminate half of the array) and rounding down (because we also remove the middle element) yields the values 511, 255, 127, 63, 31, 15, 7, 3, 1 and 0. The number 1023 ($2^{10} - 1$) is divided by 2 only 10 times to get the value 0, which indicates that there are no more elements to test. Dividing by 2 is equivalent to one comparison in the binary-search algorithm. Thus, an array of 1,048,575 ($2^{20} - 1$) elements takes a maximum of 20 comparisons to find the key, and an array of over one billion elements takes a maximum of 30 comparisons to find the key. This is a tremendous improvement in performance over the linear search. For a one-billion-element array, this is a difference between an average of 500 million comparisons for the linear search and a maximum of only 30 comparisons for the binary search! The maximum number of comparisons needed for the binary search of any sorted array is the exponent of the first power of 2 greater than the number of elements in the array which is represented as $\log_2 n$. All logarithms grow at roughly the same rate, so in big O notation the base can be omitted. This results in a big O of *O(log n)* for a binary search which is also known as logarithmic run time.

16.3 Sorting Algorithms

Sorting data (i.e., placing the data into some particular order, such as ascending or descending) is one of the most important computing applications. A bank sorts all checks by account number so that it can prepare individual bank statements at the end of each month. Telephone companies sort their lists of accounts by last name and, further, by first name to make it easy to find phone numbers. Virtually every organization must sort some data, and often, massive amounts of it. Sorting data is an intriguing, computer-intensive problem that has attracted intense research efforts.

An important item to understand about sorting is that the end result—the sorted array—will be the same no matter which algorithm you use to sort the array. The choice of algorithm affects only the run time and memory use of the program. The rest of the chapter introduces three common sorting algorithms. The first two—selection sort and insertion sort—are simple algorithms to program, but are inefficient. The last algorithm—merge sort—is a much faster algorithm than selection sort and insertion sort, but is harder to program. We focus on sorting arrays of primitive type data, namely ints. It is possible to sort arrays of objects of classes as well. We discuss this in Section 19.6.1.

16.3.1 Selection Sort

Selection sort is a simple, but inefficient, sorting algorithm. The first iteration of the algorithm selects the smallest element in the array and swaps it with the first element. The second iteration selects the second-smallest item (which is the smallest item of the remaining elements) and swaps it with the second element. The algorithm continues until the last iteration selects the second-largest element and swaps it with the second-to-last index, leaving the largest element in the last index. After the ith iteration, the smallest i items of the array will be sorted into increasing order in the first i elements of the array.

As an example, consider the array

> 34   56   4   10   77   51   93   30   5   52

A program that implements selection sort first determines the smallest element (4) of this array which is contained in index 2. The program swaps 4 with 34, resulting in

> 4   56   34   10   77   51   93   30   5   52

The program then determines the smallest value of the remaining elements (all elements except 4), which is 5, contained in index 8. The program swaps 5 with 56, resulting in

> 4   5   34   10   77   51   93   30   56   52

On the third iteration, the program determines the next smallest value (10) and swaps it with 34.

> 4   5   10   34   77   51   93   30   56   52

The process continues until the array is fully sorted.

> 4   5   10   30   34   51   52   56   77   93

Note that after the first iteration, the smallest element is in the first position. After the second iteration, the two smallest elements are in order in the first two positions. After the third iteration, the three smallest elements are in order in the first three positions.

Figure 16.6 declares the SelectionSort class. This class has two private instance variables—an array of ints named data, and a static Random object to generate random integers to fill the array. When an object of class SelectionSort is instantiated, the constructor (lines 12–19) creates and initializes the array data with random ints in the range 10–99.

Lines 22–39 declare the sort method. Line 24 declares the variable smallest, which will store the index of the smallest element in the remaining array. Lines 27–38 loop data.length - 1 times. Line 29 initializes the index of the smallest element to the current item. Lines 32–34 loop over the remaining elements in the array. For each of these elements, line 33 compares its value to the value of the smallest element. If the current element is smaller than the smallest element, line 34 assigns the current element's index to smallest. When this loop finishes, smallest will contain the index of the smallest element in the remaining array. Line 36 calls method swap (lines 42–47) to place the smallest remaining element in the next spot in the array.

Line 9 of Fig. 16.7 creates a SelectionSort object with 10 elements. Line 12 implicitly call method toString to output the unsorted object. Line 14 calls method sort (lines 22–39 of Fig. 16.6), which sorts the elements using selection sort. Then lines 16–17 output the sorted object. The output of this program uses dashes to indicate the portion of the array that is sorted after each pass. An asterisk is placed next to the position of the element that was swapped with the smallest element on that pass. On each pass, the element next to the asterisk and the element above the rightmost set of dashes were the two values that were swapped.

```java
1   // Fig 16.6: SelectionSort.java
2   // Class that creates an array filled with random integers.
3   // Provides a method to sort the array with selection sort.
4   import java.util.Random;
5
6   public class SelectionSort
7   {
8      private int[] data; // array of values
9      private static Random generator = new Random();
10
11     // create array of given size and fill with random integers
12     public SelectionSort( int size )
13     {
14        data = new int[ size ]; // create space for array
15
16        // fill array with random ints in range 10-99
17        for ( int i = 0; i < size; i++ )
18           data[ i ] = 10 + generator.nextInt( 90 );
19     } // end SelectionSort constructor
20
21     // sort array using selection sort
22     public void sort()
23     {
24        int smallest; // index of smallest element
25
26        // loop over data.length - 1 elements
27        for ( int i = 0; i < data.length - 1; i++ )
28        {
29           smallest = i; // first index of remaining array
30
31           // loop to find index of smallest element
32           for ( int index = i + 1; index < data.length; index++ )
33              if ( data[ index ] < data[ smallest ] )
34                 smallest = index;
35
36           swap( i, smallest ); // swap smallest element into position
37           printPass( i + 1, smallest ); // output pass of algorithm
38        } // end outer for
39     } // end method sort
40
41     // helper method to swap values in two elements
42     public void swap( int first, int second )
43     {
44        int temporary = data[ first ]; // store first in temporary
45        data[ first ] = data[ second ]; // replace first with second
46        data[ second ] = temporary; // put temporary in second
47     } // end method swap
48
49     // print a pass of the algorithm
50     public void printPass( int pass, int index )
51     {
52        System.out.print( String.format( "after pass %2d: ", pass ) );
53
```

Fig. 16.6 | SelectionSort class. (Part 1 of 2.)

```
54              // output elements till selected item
55              for ( int i = 0; i < index; i++ )
56                  System.out.print( data[ i ] + "  " );
57
58              System.out.print( data[ index ] + "* " ); // indicate swap
59
60              // finish outputting array
61              for ( int i = index + 1; i < data.length; i++ )
62                  System.out.print( data[ i ] + "  " );
63
64              System.out.print( "\n                    " ); // for alignment
65
66              // indicate amount of array that is sorted
67              for ( int j = 0; j < pass; j++ )
68                  System.out.print( "-- " );
69              System.out.println( "\n" ); // add endline
70          } // end method indicateSelection
71
72          // method to output values in array
73          public String toString()
74          {
75              StringBuffer temporary = new StringBuffer();
76
77              // iterate through array
78              for ( int element : data )
79                  temporary.append( element + "  " );
80
81              temporary.append( "\n" ); // add endline character
82              return temporary.toString();
83          } // end method toString
84      } // end class SelectionSort
```

Fig. 16.6 | SelectionSort class. (Part 2 of 2.)

Efficiency of Selection Sort

The selection sort algorithm runs in $O(n^2)$ time. The sort method in lines 22–39 of Fig. 16.6, which implements the selection sort algorithm, contains two for loops. The outer for loop (lines 27–38) iterates over the first $n - 1$ elements in the array, swapping the smallest remaining item into its sorted position. The inner for loop (lines 32–34) iterates over each item in the remaining array, searching for the smallest element. This loop executes $n - 1$ times during the first iteration of the outer loop, $n - 2$ times during the second iteration, then $n - 3, \ldots, 3, 2, 1$. This inner loop will iterate a total of $n(n-1)/2$ or $(n^2 - n)/2$. In Big O notation, smaller terms drop out and constants are ignored, leaving a final Big O of $O(n^2)$.

```
1   // Fig 16.7: SelectionSortTest.java
2   // Test the selection sort class.
3
4   public class SelectionSortTest
5   {
```

Fig. 16.7 | SelectionSortTest class. (Part 1 of 2.)

```
 6      public static void main( String[] args )
 7      {
 8         // create object to perform selection sort
 9         SelectionSort sortArray = new SelectionSort( 10 );
10
11         System.out.println( "Unsorted array:" );
12         System.out.println( sortArray ); // print unsorted array
13
14         sortArray.sort(); // sort array
15
16         System.out.println( "Sorted array:" );
17         System.out.println( sortArray ); // print sorted array
18      } // end main
19   } // end class SelectionSortTest
```

```
Unsorted array:
61  87  80  58  40  50  20  13  71  45

after pass  1: 13  87  80  58  40  50  20  61* 71  45
               --

after pass  2: 13  20  80  58  40  50  87* 61  71  45
               --  --

after pass  3: 13  20  40  58  80* 50  87  61  71  45
               --  --  --

after pass  4: 13  20  40  45  80  50  87  61  71  58*
               --  --  --  --

after pass  5: 13  20  40  45  50  80* 87  61  71  58
               --  --  --  --  --

after pass  6: 13  20  40  45  50  58  87  61  71  80*
               --  --  --  --  --  --

after pass  7: 13  20  40  45  50  58  61  87* 71  80
               --  --  --  --  --  --  --

after pass  8: 13  20  40  45  50  58  61  71  87* 80
               --  --  --  --  --  --  --  --

after pass  9: 13  20  40  45  50  58  61  71  80  87*
               --  --  --  --  --  --  --  --  --

Sorted array:
13  20  40  45  50  58  61  71  80  87
```

Fig. 16.7 | SelectionSortTest class. (Part 2 of 2.)

16.3.2 Insertion Sort

Insertion sort is another simple, but inefficient, sorting algorithm. The first iteration of this algorithm takes the second element in the array and, if it is less than the first element, swaps it with the first element. The second iteration looks at the third element and inserts it into the correct position with respect to the first two elements, so all three elements are in order. At the *i*th iteration of this algorithm, the first *i* elements in the original array will be sorted.

Consider as an example the following array [*Note:* This array is identical to the array used in the discussions of selection sort and merge sort.]

| 34 | 56 | 4 | 10 | 77 | 51 | 93 | 30 | 5 | 52 |

A program that implements the insertion sort algorithm will first look at the first two elements of the array, 34 and 56. These two elements are already in order, so the program continues (if they were out of order, the program would swap them).

In the next iteration, the program looks at the third value, 4. This value is less than 56, so the program stores 4 in a temporary variable and moves 56 one element to the right. The program then checks and determines that 4 is less than 34, so it moves 34 one element to the right. The program has now reached the beginning of the array, so it places 4 in the zeroth element. The array now is

| 4 | 34 | 56 | 10 | 77 | 51 | 93 | 30 | 5 | 52 |

In the next iteration, the program stores the value 10 in a temporary variable. Then the program compares 10 to 56 and moves 56 one element to the right because it is larger than 10. The program then compares 10 to 34, moving 34 right one element. When the program compares 10 to 4, it observes that 10 is larger than 4 and places 10 in element 1. The array now is

| 4 | 10 | 34 | 56 | 77 | 51 | 93 | 30 | 5 | 52 |

Using this algorithm, at the *i*th iteration, the first *i* elements of the original array are sorted. They may not be in their final locations, however, because smaller values may be located later in the array.

Figure 16.8 declares the InsertionSort class. Lines 22–46 declare the sort method. Line 24 declares the variable insert, which holds the element you are going to insert while you move the other elements. Lines 27–45 loop over data.length - 1 items in the array. In each iteration, line 30 stores in insert the value of the element that will be inserted into the sorted portion of the array. Line 33 declares and initializes the variable moveItem, which keeps track of where to insert the element. Lines 36–41 loop to locate the correct position where the element should be inserted. The loop will terminate either when the program reaches the front of the array or when it reaches an element that is less than the value to be inserted. Line 39 moves an element to the right, and line 40 decrements the position at which to insert the next element. After the loop ends, line 43 inserts the element into place. Figure 16.9 is the same as Fig. 16.7 except that it creates and uses an InsertionSort object. The output of this program uses dashes to indicate the portion of the array that is sorted after each pass. An asterisk is placed next to the element that was inserted into place on that pass.

```
1   // Fig 16.8: InsertionSort.java
2   // Class that creates an array filled with random integers.
3   // Provides a method to sort the array with insertion sort.
4   import java.util.Random;
```

Fig. 16.8 | InsertionSort class. (Part 1 of 3.)

```
5
6    public class InsertionSort
7    {
8       private int[] data; // array of values
9       private static Random generator = new Random();
10
11      // create array of given size and fill with random integers
12      public InsertionSort( int size )
13      {
14         data = new int[ size ]; // create space for array
15
16         // fill array with random ints in range 10-99
17         for ( int i = 0; i < size; i++ )
18            data[ i ] = 10 + generator.nextInt( 90 );
19      } // end InsertionSort constructor
20
21      // sort array using insertion sort
22      public void sort()
23      {
24         int insert; // temporary variable to hold element to insert
25
26         // loop over data.length - 1 elements
27         for ( int next = 1; next < data.length; next++ )
28         {
29            // store value in current element
30            insert = data[ next ];
31
32            // initialize location to place element
33            int moveItem = next;
34
35            // search for place to put current element
36            while ( moveItem > 0 && data[ moveItem - 1 ] > insert )
37            {
38               // shift element right one slot
39               data[ moveItem ] = data[ moveItem - 1 ];
40               moveItem--;
41            } // end while
42
43            data[ moveItem ] = insert; // place inserted element
44            printPass( next, moveItem ); // output pass of algorithm
45         } // end for
46      } // end method sort
47
48      // print a pass of the algorithm
49      public void printPass( int pass, int index )
50      {
51         System.out.print( String.format( "after pass %2d: ", pass ) );
52
53         // output elements till swapped item
54         for ( int i = 0; i < index; i++ )
55            System.out.print( data[ i ] + "   " );
56
```

Fig. 16.8 | InsertionSort class. (Part 2 of 3.)

```
57              System.out.print( data[ index ] + "* " ); // indicate swap
58
59          // finish outputting array
60          for ( int i = index + 1; i < data.length; i++ )
61              System.out.print( data[ i ] + "  " );
62
63          System.out.print( "\n                    " ); // for alignment
64
65          // indicate amount of array that is sorted
66          for( int i = 0; i <= pass; i++ )
67              System.out.print( "-- " );
68          System.out.println( "\n" ); // add endline
69      } // end method printPass
70
71      // method to output values in array
72      public String toString()
73      {
74          StringBuffer temporary = new StringBuffer();
75
76          // iterate through array
77          for ( int element : data )
78              temporary.append( element + "  " );
79
80          temporary.append( "\n" ); // add endline character
81          return temporary.toString();
82      } // end method toString
83  } // end class InsertionSort
```

Fig. 16.8 | InsertionSort class. (Part 3 of 3.)

```
1   // Fig 16.9: InsertionSortTest.java
2   // Test the insertion sort class.
3
4   public class InsertionSortTest
5   {
6       public static void main( String[] args )
7       {
8           // create object to perform selection sort
9           InsertionSort sortArray = new InsertionSort( 10 );
10
11          System.out.println( "Unsorted array:" );
12          System.out.println( sortArray ); // print unsorted array
13
14          sortArray.sort(); // sort array
15
16          System.out.println( "Sorted array:" );
17          System.out.println( sortArray ); // print sorted array
18      } // end main
19  } // end class InsertionSortTest
```

Fig. 16.9 | InsertionSortTest class. (Part 1 of 2.)

```
Unsorted array:
40  17  45  82  62  32  30  44  93  10

after pass  1: 17* 40  45  82  62  32  30  44  93  10
               --  --

after pass  2: 17  40  45* 82  62  32  30  44  93  10
               --  --  --

after pass  3: 17  40  45  82* 62  32  30  44  93  10
               --  --  --  --

after pass  4: 17  40  45  62* 82  32  30  44  93  10
               --  --  --  --  --

after pass  5: 17  32* 40  45  62  82  30  44  93  10
               --  --  --  --  --  --

after pass  6: 17  30* 32  40  45  62  82  44  93  10
               --  --  --  --  --  --  --

after pass  7: 17  30  32  40  44* 45  62  82  93  10
               --  --  --  --  --  --  --  --

after pass  8: 17  30  32  40  44  45  62  82  93* 10
               --  --  --  --  --  --  --  --  --

after pass  9: 10* 17  30  32  40  44  45  62  82  93
               --  --  --  --  --  --  --  --  --  --

Sorted array:
10  17  30  32  40  44  45  62  82  93
```

Fig. 16.9 | `InsertionSortTest` class. (Part 2 of 2.)

Efficiency of Insertion Sort
The insertion sort algorithm also runs in $O(n^2)$ time. Like selection sort, the implementation of insertion sort (lines 22–46 of Fig. 16.8) contains two loops. The `for` loop (lines 27–45) iterates `data.length - 1` times, inserting an element into the appropriate position in the elements sorted so far. For the purposes of this application, `data.length - 1` is equivalent to $n - 1$ (as `data.length` is the size of the array). The `while` loop (lines 36–41) iterates over the preceding elements in the array. In the worst case, this `while` loop will require $n - 1$ comparisons. Each individual loop runs in $O(n)$ time. In Big O notation, nested loops mean that you must multiply the number of comparisons. For each iteration of an outer loop, there will be a certain number of iterations of the inner loop. In this algorithm, for each $O(n)$ iterations of the outer loop, there will be $O(n)$ iterations of the inner loop. Multiplying these values results in a Big O of $O(n^2)$.

16.3.3 Merge Sort

Merge sort is an efficient sorting algorithm, but is conceptually more complex than selection sort and insertion sort. The merge sort algorithm sorts an array by splitting it into two equal-sized subarrays, sorting each subarray and then merging them into one larger array. With an odd number of elements, the algorithm creates the two subarrays such that one has one more element than the other.

The implementation of merge sort in this example is recursive. The base case is an array with one element. A one-element array is, of course, sorted, so merge sort immediately returns when it is called with a one-element array. The recursion step splits an array into two approximately equal pieces, recursively sorts them and then merges the two sorted arrays into one larger, sorted array.

Suppose the algorithm has already merged smaller arrays to create sorted arrays A:

   4   10   34   56   77

and B:

   5   30   51   52   93

Merge sort combines these two arrays into one larger, sorted array. The smallest element in A is 4 (located in the zeroth index of A). The smallest element in B is 5 (located in the zeroth index of B). In order to determine the smallest element in the larger array, the algorithm compares 4 and 5. The value from A is smaller, so 4 becomes the first element in the merged array. The algorithm continues by comparing 10 (the second element in A) to 5 (the first element in B). The value from B is smaller, so 5 becomes the second element in the larger array. The algorithm continues by comparing 10 to 30, with 10 becoming the third element in the array, and so on.

Lines 22–25 of Fig. 16.10 declare the sort method. Line 24 calls method sortArray with 0 and data.length - 1 as the arguments. The arguments correspond to the beginning and ending indices of the array to be sorted. These values tell method sortArray to operate on the entire array.

```
1    // Figure 16.10: MergeSort.java
2    // Class that creates an array filled with random integers.
3    // Provides a method to sort the array with merge sort.
4    import java.util.Random;
5
6    public class MergeSort
7    {
8       private int[] data; // array of values
9       private static Random generator = new Random();
10
11      // create array of given size and fill with random integers
12      public MergeSort( int size )
13      {
14         data = new int[ size ]; // create space for array
15
16         // fill array with random ints in range 10-99
17         for ( int i = 0; i < size; i++ )
18            data[ i ] = 10 + generator.nextInt( 90 );
19      } // end MergeSort constructor
20
```

Fig. 16.10 | MergeSort class. (Part 1 of 3.)

```
21      // calls recursive split method to begin merge sorting
22      public void sort()
23      {
24          sortArray( 0, data.length - 1 ); // split entire array
25      } // end method sort
26
27      // splits array, sorts subarrays and merges subarrays into sorted array
28      private void sortArray( int low, int high )
29      {
30          // test base case; size of array equals 1
31          if ( ( high - low ) >= 1 ) // if not base case
32          {
33              int middle1 = ( low + high ) / 2; // calculate middle of array
34              int middle2 = middle1 + 1; // calculate next element over
35
36              // output split step
37              System.out.println( "split:   " + subarray( low, high ) );
38              System.out.println( "         " + subarray( low, middle1 ) );
39              System.out.println( "         " + subarray( middle2, high ) );
40              System.out.println();
41
42              // split array in half; sort each half (recursive calls)
43              sortArray( low, middle1 ); // first half of array
44              sortArray( middle2, high ); // second half of array
45
46              // merge two sorted arrays after split calls return
47              merge ( low, middle1, middle2, high );
48          } // end if
49      } // end method split
50
51      // merge two sorted subarrays into one sorted subarray
52      private void merge( int left, int middle1, int middle2, int right )
53      {
54          int leftIndex = left; // index into left subarray
55          int rightIndex = middle2; // index into right subarray
56          int combinedIndex = left; // index into temporary working array
57          int[] combined = new int[ data.length ]; // working array
58
59          // output two subarrays before merging
60          System.out.println( "merge:   " + subarray( left, middle1 ) );
61          System.out.println( "         " + subarray( middle2, right ) );
62
63          // merge arrays until reaching end of either
64          while ( leftIndex <= middle1 && rightIndex <= right )
65          {
66              // place smaller of two current elements into result
67              // and move to next space in arrays
68              if ( data[ leftIndex ] <= data[ rightIndex ] )
69                  combined[ combinedIndex++ ] = data[ leftIndex++ ];
70              else
71                  combined[ combinedIndex++ ] = data[ rightIndex++ ];
72          } // end while
73
```

Fig. 16.10 | MergeSort class. (Part 2 of 3.)

```
74          // if left array is empty
75          if ( leftIndex == middle2 )
76             // copy in rest of right array
77             while ( rightIndex <= right )
78                combined[ combinedIndex++ ] = data[ rightIndex++ ];
79          else // right array is empty
80             // copy in rest of left array
81             while ( leftIndex <= middle1 )
82                combined[ combinedIndex++ ] = data[ leftIndex++ ];
83
84          // copy values back into original array
85          for ( int i = left; i <= right; i++ )
86             data[ i ] = combined[ i ];
87
88          // output merged array
89          System.out.println( "          " + subarray( left, right ) );
90          System.out.println();
91       } // end method merge
92
93       // method to output certain values in array
94       public String subarray( int low, int high )
95       {
96          StringBuffer temporary = new StringBuffer();
97
98          // output spaces for alignment
99          for ( int i = 0; i < low; i++ )
100            temporary.append( "     " );
101
102         // output elements left in array
103         for ( int i = low; i <= high; i++ )
104            temporary.append( " " + data[ i ] );
105
106         return temporary.toString();
107      } // end method subarray
108
109      // method to output values in array
110      public String toString()
111      {
112         return subarray( 0, data.length - 1 );
113      } // end method toString
114   } // end class MergeSort
```

Fig. 16.10 | MergeSort class. (Part 3 of 3.)

Method sortArray is declared in lines 28–49. Line 31 tests the base case. If the size of the array is 1, the array is already sorted, so the method simply returns immediately. If the size of the array is greater than 1, the method splits the array in two, recursively calls method sortArray to sort the two subarrays, then merges them. Line 43 recursively calls method sortArray on the first half of the array, and line 44 recursively calls method sortArray on the second half of the array. When these two method calls return, each half of the array has been sorted. Line 47 calls method merge (lines 52–91) on the two halves of the array to combine the two sorted arrays into one larger sorted array.

Lines 64–72 in method `merge` loop until the program reaches the end of either subarray. Line 68 tests which element at the beginning of the arrays is smaller. If the element in the left array is smaller, line 69 places it in position in the combined array. If the element in the right array is smaller, line 71 places it in position in the combined array. When the `while` loop has completed (line 72), one entire subarray is placed in the combined array, but the other subarray still contains data. Line 75 tests whether the left array has reached the end. If so, lines 77–78 fill the combined array with the elements of the right array. If the left array has not reached the end, then the right array must have reached the end, and lines 81–82 fill the combined array with the elements of the left array. Finally, lines 85–86 copy the combined array into the original array. Figure 16.11 creates and uses a `Merge-Sort` object. The output from this program displays the splits and merges performed by merge sort, showing the progress of the sort at each step of the algorithm.

```
 1   // Figure 16.11: MergeSortTest.java
 2   // Test the merge sort class.
 3
 4   public class MergeSortTest
 5   {
 6      public static void main( String[] args )
 7      {
 8         // create object to perform merge sort
 9         MergeSort sortArray = new MergeSort( 10 );
10
11         // print unsorted array
12         System.out.println( "Unsorted:" + sortArray + "\n" );
13
14         sortArray.sort(); // sort array
15
16         // print sorted array
17         System.out.println( "Sorted:   " + sortArray );
18      } // end main
19   } // end class MergeSortTest
```

```
Unsorted: 75 56 85 90 49 26 12 48 40 47

split:    75 56 85 90 49 26 12 48 40 47
          75 56 85 90 49
                         26 12 48 40 47

split:    75 56 85 90 49
          75 56 85
                   90 49

split:    75 56 85
          75 56
                85

split:    75 56
          75
             56
```

Fig. 16.11 | MergeSortTest class. (Part 1 of 2.)

```
merge:     75
               56
           56 75

merge:     56 75
                   85
           56 75 85

split:                 90 49
                       90
                           49

merge:                 90
                           49
                       49 90

merge:     56 75 85
                       49 90
           49 56 75 85 90

split:                 26 12 48 40 47
                       26 12 48
                               40 47

split:                 26 12 48
                       26 12
                             48

split:                 26 12
                       26
                          12

merge:                 26
                          12
                       12 26

merge:                 12 26
                             48
                       12 26 48

split:                     40 47
                           40
                               47

merge:                     40
                               47
                           40 47

merge:                 12 26 48
                           40 47
                       12 26 40 47 48

merge:     49 56 75 85 90

           12 26 40 47 48 49 56 75 85 90

Sorted:    12 26 40 47 48 49 56 75 85 90
```

Fig. 16.11 | MergeSortTest class. (Part 2 of 2.)

Efficiency of Merge Sort

Merge sort is a far more efficient algorithm than either insertion sort or selection sort. Consider the first (nonrecursive) call to method `sortArray`. This results in two recursive calls to method `sortArray` with subarrays each approximately half the size of the original array, and a single call to method `merge`. This call to method `merge` requires, at worst, $n - 1$ comparisons to fill the original array, which is $O(n)$. (Recall that each element in the array can be chosen by comparing one element from each of the subarrays.) The two calls to method `sortArray` result in four more recursive calls to method `sortArray`, each with a subarray approximately a quarter the size of the original array along with two calls to method `merge`. These two calls to method `merge` each require, at worst, $n/2 - 1$ comparisons for a total number of comparisons of $O(n)$. This process continues, each call to `sortArray` generating two additional calls to `sortArray` and a call to `merge`, until the algorithm has split the array into one-element subarrays. At each level, $O(n)$ comparisons are required to merge the s ubarrays. Each level splits the size of the arrays in half, so doubling the size of the array requires one more level. Quadrupling the size of the array requires two more levels. This pattern is logarithmic and results in $\log_2 n$ levels. This results in a total efficiency of $O(n \log n)$. Figure 16.12 summarizes many of the searching and sorting algorithms covered in this book and lists the Big O for each of them. Figure 16.13 lists the Big O values we have covered in this chapter along with a number of values for n to highlight the differences in the growth rates.

16.4 Invariants

After writing an application, a programmer typically tests it thoroughly. Creating an exhaustive set of tests often is quite difficult, and it is always possible that a particular case remains untested. One technique that can help you test your programs thoroughly is to use invariants. An **invariant** is an assertion (see Section 13.13) that is true before and after the a portion of your code executes. Invariants are mathematical in nature and their concepts are more applicable to the theoretical side of computer science.

Algorithm	Location	Big O
Searching Algorithms:		
Linear Search	Section 16.2.1	$O(n)$
Binary Search	Section 16.2.2	$O(\log n)$
Recursive Linear Search	Exercise 16.8	$O(n)$
Recursive Binary Search	Exercise 16.9	$O(\log n)$
Sorting Algorithms:		
Selection Sort	Section 16.3.1	$O(n^2)$
Insertion Sort	Section 16.3.2	$O(n^2)$
Merge Sort	Section 16.3.3	$O(n \log n)$
Bubble Sort	Exercises 16.3 and 16.4	$O(n^2)$

Fig. 16.12 | Searching and sorting algorithms with Big O values.

n =	O(log n)	O(n)	O(n log n)	O(n²)
1	0	1	0	1
2	1	2	2	4
3	1	3	3	9
4	1	4	4	16
5	1	5	5	25
10	1	10	10	100
100	2	100	200	10000
1,000	3	1000	3000	10^6
1,000,000	6	1000000	6000000	10^{12}
1,000,000,000	9	1000000000	9000000000	10^{18}

Fig. 16.13 | Number of comparisons for common Big O notations.

The most common type of invariant is a **loop invariant**. A loop invariant is an assertion that remains true

- before the execution of the loop,
- after every iteration of the loop body, and
- when the loop terminates.

A properly written loop invariant, can help you code a loop correctly. There are four steps to developing a loop from a loop invariant.

1. Set initial values for any loop control variables.

2. Determine the condition that causes the loop to terminate.

3. Modify the control variable(s) so the loop progresses toward termination.

4. Check that the invariant remains true at the end of each iteration.

As an example, we will examine method `linearSearch` from class `LinearArray` in Fig. 16.2. The invariant for the linear search algorithm is:

for all k *such that* 0 <= k *and* k < index
       data[k] != searchKey

For example, suppose `index` equals 3. If we pick any non-negative number less than 3 such as 1 for the value of k, the element in `data` at location k in the array does not equal the `searchKey`. This invariant basically states that the portion of the array, called a subarray, from the start of the array up to but not including the element at `index` does not contain the `searchKey`. A subarray can have no elements, or it can encompass the entire array.

According to *Step 1*, we must first initialize control variable `index`. From the invariant, we see that if we set `index` to 0, then the subarray contains zero elements. Therefore, the invariant is true because a subarray with no elements cannot contain a value that matches the `searchKey`.

The second step is to determine the condition that causes the loop to terminate. The loop should end after searching the entire array—when `index` equals the length of the array. In this case, no element of array `data` matches the `searchKey`. Once the `index` reaches the end of the array, the invariant remains true—no elements in the subarray (which in this case is the entire array) equal the `searchKey`.

For the loop to proceed to the next element, we increment control variable `index`. The last step is to ensure the invariant remains true after each iteration. The `if` statement (lines 26–27 of Fig. 16.2) determines whether `data[ index ]` equals the `searchKey`. If so, the method finishes and returns `index`. Because `index` is the first occurrence of `searchKey` in `data`, the invariant is still true—the subarray up to `index` does not contain the `searchKey`.

16.5 Wrap-up

This chapter introduced searching and sorting data. We discussed two searching algorithms—linear search and binary search—and three sorting algorithms—selection sort, insertion sort and merge sort. We also introduced Big-O notation, which helps you analyze the efficiency of an algorithm. You also learned about loop invariants, which must remain true before the loop begins executing, while the loop executes and when the loop terminates. In the next chapter, you will learn about dynamic data structures that can grow or shrink at execution time.

Summary

- Searching data involves determining whether a search key is present in the data and, if so, finding its location.
- Sorting involves arranging data into order.
- The linear search algorithm searches each element in the array sequentially until it finds the correct element. If the element is not in the array, the algorithm tests each element in the array, and when the end of the array is reached, informs the user that the element is not present. If the element is in the array, linear search tests each item until it finds the correct item.
- A major difference among searching algorithms is the amount of effort they require in order to return a result.
- One way to describe the efficiency of an algorithm is with Big O notation (O), which indicates how hard an algorithm may have to work to solve a problem.
- For searching and sorting algorithms, Big O is often dependent on how many elements are in the data.
- An algorithm that is $O(1)$ does not necessarily require only one comparison. It just means that the number of comparisons does not grow as the size of the array increases.
- An $O(n)$ algorithm is referred to as having a linear run time.
- Big O is designed to highlight dominant factors and ignore terms that become unimportant with high n values.
- Big O notation is concerned with the growth rate of algorithm run times, so constants are ignored.
- The linear search algorithm runs in $O(n)$ time.
- The worst case in linear search is that every element must be checked to determine whether the search item exists. This occurs if the search key is the last element in the array or is not present.

- The binary search algorithm is more efficient than the linear search algorithm, but it requires that the array be sorted.
- The first iteration of binary search tests the middle element in the array. If this is the search key, the algorithm returns its location. If the search key is less than the middle element, binary search continues with the first half of the array. If the search key is greater than the middle element, binary search continues with the second half of the array. Each iteration of binary search tests the middle value of the remaining array and, if the element is not found, eliminates half of the remaining elements.
- Binary search is a more efficient searching algorithm than linear search because binary search with each comparison eliminates from consideration half of the elements in the array.
- Binary search runs in $O(\log n)$ time because each step removes half of the remaining elements.
- If the size of the array is doubled, binary search requires only one extra comparison to complete successfully.
- Selection sort is a simple, but inefficient, sorting algorithm.
- The first iteration of selection sort selects the smallest element in the array and swaps it with the first element. The second iteration of selection sort selects the second-smallest item (which is the smallest remaining item) and swaps it with the second element. Selection sort continues until the last iteration selects the second-largest element and swaps it with the second-to-last index, leaving the largest element in the last index. At the ith iteration of selection sort, the smallest i items of the whole array are sorted into the first i indices.
- The selection sort algorithm runs in $O(n^2)$ time.
- The first iteration of insertion sort takes the second element in the array and, if it is less than the first element, swaps it with the first element. The second iteration of insertion sort looks at the third element and inserts it in the correct position with respect to the first two elements. After the ith iteration of insertion sort, the first i elements in the original array are sorted.
- The insertion sort algorithm runs in $O(n^2)$ time.
- Merge sort is a sorting algorithm that is faster, but more complex to implement, than selection sort and insertion sort.
- The merge sort algorithm sorts an array by splitting the array into two equal-sized subarrays, sorting each subarray recursively and merging the subarrays into one larger array.
- Merge sort's base case is an array with one element. A one-element array is already sorted, so merge sort immediately returns when it is called with a one-element array. The merge part of merge sort takes two sorted arrays (these could be one-element arrays) and combines them into one larger sorted array.
- Merge sort performs the merge by looking at the first element in each array, which is also the smallest element in the array. Merge sort takes the smallest of these and places it in the first element of the larger array. If there are still elements in the subarray, merge sort looks at the second element in that subarray (which is now the smallest element remaining) and compares it to the first element in the other subarray. Merge sort continues this process until the larger array is filled.
- In the worst case, the first call to merge sort has to make $O(n)$ comparisons to fill the n slots in the final array.
- The merging portion of the merge sort algorithm is performed on two subarrays, each of approximately size $n/2$. Creating each of these subarrays requires $n / 2 - 1$ comparisons for each subarray, or $O(n)$ comparisons total. This pattern continues as each level works on twice as many arrays, but each is half the size of the previous array.
- Similar to binary search, this halving results in $\log n$ levels for a total efficiency of $O(n \log n)$.

- An invariant is an assertion that is true before and after the execution of a portion of your code.
- A loop invariant is an assertion that is true before you begin executing the loop, during each iteration of the loop and after the loop terminates.

Terminology

Big O notation	$O(1)$
binary search	$O(\log n)$
constant run time	$O(n \log n)$
insertion sort	$O(n)$
invariant	$O(n^2)$
linear run time	search key
linear search	quadratic run time
logarithmic run time	searching
loop invariant	selection sort
merge sort	sorting

Self-Review Exercises

16.1 Fill in the blanks in each of the following statements:
  a) A selection sort application would take approximately _____ times as long to run on a 128-element array as on a 32-element array.
  b) The efficiency of merge sort is _____.

16.2 What key aspect of both the binary search and the merge sort accounts for the logarithmic portion of their respective Big Os?

16.3 In what sense is the insertion sort superior to the merge sort? In what sense is the merge sort superior to the insertion sort?

16.4 In the text, we say that after the merge sort splits the array into two subarrays, it then sorts these two subarrays and merges them. Why might someone be puzzled by our statement that "it then sorts these two subarrays"?

Answers to Self-Review Exercises

16.1   a) 16, because an $O(n^2)$ algorithm takes 16 times as long to sort four times as much information. b) $O(n \log n)$.

16.2   Both of these algorithms incorporate "halving"—somehow reducing something by half. The binary search eliminates from consideration one half of the array after each comparison. The merge sort splits the array in half each time it is called.

16.3   The insertion sort is easier to understand and to program than the merge sort. The merge sort is far more efficient ($O(n \log n)$) than the insertion sort ($O(n^2)$).

16.4   In a sense, it does not really sort these two subarrays. It simply keeps splitting the original array in half until it provides a one-element subarray, which is, of course, sorted. It then builds up the original two subarrays by merging these one-element arrays to form larger subarrays which are then merged, and so on.

Exercises

16.5 *(Bubble Sort)* Implement bubble sort—another simple yet inefficient sorting technique. It is called bubble sort or sinking sort because smaller values gradually "bubble" their way to the top of the array (i.e., toward the first element) like air bubbles rising in water, while the larger values sink to the bottom (end) of the array. The technique uses nested loops to make several passes through the array. Each pass compares successive pairs of elements. If a pair is in increasing order (or the values are equal), the bubble sort leaves the values as they are. If a pair is in decreasing order, the bubble sort swaps their values in the array.

The first pass compares the first two elements of the array and swaps them if necessary. It then compares the second and third elements in the array. The end of this pass compares the last two elements in the array and swaps them if necessary. After one pass, the largest element will be in the last index. After two passes, the largest two elements will be in the last two indices. Explain why bubble sort is an $O(n^2)$ algorithm.

16.6 *(Enhanced Bubble Sort)* Make the following simple modifications to improve the performance of the bubble sort you developed in Exercise 16.5:

   a) After the first pass, the largest number is guaranteed to be in the highest-numbered element of the array; after the second pass, the two highest numbers are "in place"; and so on. Instead of making nine comparisons on every pass, modify the bubble sort to make eight comparisons on the second pass, seven on the third pass, and so on.

   b) The data in the array may already be in the proper order or near-proper order, so why make nine passes if fewer will suffice? Modify the sort to check at the end of each pass whether any swaps have been made. If none have been made, the data must already be in the proper order, so the program should terminate. If swaps have been made, at least one more pass is needed.

16.7 *(Bucket Sort)* A bucket sort begins with a one-dimensional array of positive integers to be sorted and a two-dimensional array of integers with rows indexed from 0 to 9 and columns indexed from 0 to $n-1$, where n is the number of values to be sorted. Each row of the two-dimensional array is referred to as a *bucket*. Write a class named BucketSort containing a method called sort that operates as follows:

   a) Place each value of the one-dimensional array into a row of the bucket array, based on the value's "ones" (right-most) digit. For example, 97 is placed in row 7, 3 is placed in row 3 and 100 is placed in row 0. This procedure is called a *distribution pass*.

   b) Loop through the bucket array row by row, and copy the values back to the original array. This procedure is called a *gathering pass*. The new order of the preceding values in the one-dimensional array is 100, 3 and 97.

   c) Repeat this process for each subsequent digit position (tens, hundreds, thousands, etc.).
      On the second (tens digit) pass, 100 is placed in row 0, 3 is placed in row 0 (because 3 has no tens digit) and 97 is placed in row 9. After the gathering pass, the order of the values in the one-dimensional array is 100, 3 and 97. On the third (hundreds digit) pass, 100 is placed in row 1, 3 is placed in row 0 and 97 is placed in row 0 (after the 3). After this last gathering pass, the original array is in sorted order.
      Note that the two-dimensional array of buckets is 10 times the length of the integer array being sorted. This sorting technique provides better performance than a bubble sort, but requires much more memory—the bubble sort requires space for only one additional element of data. This comparison is an example of the space–time trade-off: The bucket sort uses more memory than the bubble sort, but performs better. This version of the bucket sort requires copying all the data back to the original array on each pass. Another possibility is to create a second two-dimensional bucket array and repeatedly swap the data between the two bucket arrays.

16.8 *(Recursive Linear Search)* Modify Fig. 16.2 to use recursive method recursiveLinearSearch to perform a linear search of the array. The method should receive the search key and starting index as arguments. If the search key is found, return its index in the array; otherwise, return -1. Each call to the recursive method should check one index in the array.

16.9   (*Recursive Binary Search*) Modify Fig. 16.4 to use recursive method `recursiveBinarySearch` to perform a binary search of the array. The method should receive the search key, starting index and ending index as arguments. If the search key is found, return its index in the array. If the search key is not found, return –1.

16.10   (*Quicksort*) The recursive sorting technique called quicksort uses the following basic algorithm for a one-dimensional array of values:

a) *Partitioning Step*: Take the first element of the unsorted array and determine its final location in the sorted array (i.e., all values to the left of the element in the array are less than the element, and all values to the right of the element in the array are greater than the element—we show how to do this below). We now have one element in its proper location and two unsorted subarrays.

b) *Recursive Step*: Perform *Step 1* on each unsorted subarray. Each time *Step 1* is performed on a subarray, another element is placed in its final location of the sorted array, and two unsorted subarrays are created. When a subarray consists of one element, that element is in its final location (because a one-element array is already sorted).

The basic algorithm seems simple enough, but how do we determine the final position of the first element of each subarray? As an example, consider the following set of values (the element in bold is the partitioning element—it will be placed in its final location in the sorted array):

37 2 6 4 89 8 10 12 68 45

Starting from the right-most element of the array, compare each element with **37** until an element less than **37** is found; then swap **37** and that element. The first element less than **37** is 12, so **37** and 12 are swapped. The new array is

12 2 6 4 89 8 10 *37* 68 45

Element 12 is in italics to indicate that it was just swapped with **37**.

Starting from the left of the array, but beginning with the element after 12, compare each element with **37** until an element greater than **37** is found—then swap **37** and that element. The first element greater than **37** is 89, so **37** and 89 are swapped. The new array is

12 2 6 4 *37* 8 10 *89* 68 45

Starting from the right, but beginning with the element before 89, compare each element with **37** until an element less than **37** is found—then swap **37** and that element. The first element less than **37** is 10, so **37** and 10 are swapped. The new array is

12 2 6 4 *10* 8 *37* 89 68 45

Starting from the left, but beginning with the element after 10, compare each element with **37** until an element greater than **37** is found—then swap **37** and that element. There are no more elements greater than **37**, so when we compare **37** with itself, we know that **37** has been placed in its final location of the sorted array. Every value to the left of **37** is smaller than it, and every value to the right of **37** is larger than it.

Once the partition has been applied on the previous array, there are two unsorted subarrays. The subarray with values less than 37 contains 12, 2, 6, 4, 10 and 8. The subarray with values greater than 37 contains 89, 68 and 45. The sort continues recursively with both subarrays being partitioned in the same manner as the original array.

Based on the preceding discussion, write recursive method `quickSortHelper` to sort a one-dimensional integer array. The method should receive as arguments a starting index and an ending index on the original array being sorted.

Data Structures

Much that I bound, I could not free;
Much that I freed returned to me.
—Lee Wilson Dodd

'Will you walk a little faster?' said a whiting to a snail,
'There's a porpoise close behind us, and he's treading on my tail.'
—Lewis Carroll

There is always room at the top.
—Daniel Webster

Push on—keep moving.
—Thomas Morton

I'll turn over a new leaf.
—Miguel de Cervantes

OBJECTIVES

In this chapter you will learn:

- To form linked data structures using references, self-referential classes and recursion.
- The type-wrapper classes that enable programs to process primitive data values as objects.
- To use autoboxing to convert a primitive value to an object of the corresponding type-wrapper class.
- To use auto-unboxing to convert an object of a type-wrapper class to a primitive value.
- To create and manipulate dynamic data structures, such as linked lists, queues, stacks and binary trees.
- Various important applications of linked data structures.
- How to create reusable data structures with classes, inheritance and composition.

17.1 Introduction

In previous chapters, we have studied fixed-size **data structures** such as one-dimensional and multidimensional arrays. This chapter introduces **dynamic data structures** that grow and shrink at execution time. **Linked lists** are collections of data items "linked up in a chain"—insertions and deletions can be made anywhere in a linked list. **Stacks** are important in compilers and operating systems; insertions and deletions are made only at one end of a stack—its **top**. **Queues** represent waiting lines; insertions are made at the back (also referred to as the **tail**) of a queue and deletions are made from the front (also referred to as the **head**). **Binary trees** facilitate high-speed searching and sorting of data, eliminating duplicate data items efficiently, representing file-system directories, compiling expressions into machine language and many other interesting applications.

We will discuss each of these major types of data structures and implement programs that create and manipulate them. We use classes, inheritance and composition to create and package these data structures for reusability and maintainability. In Chapter 19, Collections, we discuss Java's predefined classes that implement the data structures discussed in this chapter.

The examples presented here are practical programs that can be used in advanced courses and in industrial applications. The exercises include a rich collection of useful applications.

This chapter's examples manipulate primitive values for simplicity. However, most of the data-structure implementations in this chapter store only `Object`s. J2SE 5.0 has added a new feature, called boxing, that allows primitive values to be converted to and from objects for use in cases like this. The objects that represent primitive values are instances of Java's so-called type-wrapper classes in package `java.lang`. We discuss these classes and boxing in the next two sections, so we can use them in this chapter's examples.

We encourage you to attempt the major project described in the special section entitled *Building Your Own Compiler*. You have been using a Java compiler to translate your Java programs to bytecodes so that you could execute these programs on your computer. In this project, you will actually build your own compiler. It will read a file of statements written in a simple, yet powerful high-level language similar to early versions of the popular language BASIC. Your compiler will translate these statements into a file of Simpletron Machine Language (SML) instructions—SML is the language you learned in the Chapter 7 special section, *Building Your Own Computer*. Your Simpletron Simulator program will then execute the SML program produced by your compiler! Implementing this project by using an object-oriented approach will give you a wonderful opportunity to exercise most of what you have learned in this book. The special section carefully walks you through the specifications of the high-level language and describes the algorithms you will need to convert each high-level language statement into machine-language instructions. If you enjoy being challenged, you might attempt the many enhancements to both the compiler and the Simpletron Simulator suggested in the exercises.

17.2 Type-Wrapper Classes for Primitive Types

Each primitive type (listed in Appendix D, Primitive Types) has a corresponding type-wrapper class (in package `java.lang`). These classes are called `Boolean`, `Byte`, `Character`, `Double`, `Float`, `Integer`, `Long` and `Short`. Each type-wrapper class enables you to manipulate primitive-type values as objects. Many of the data structures that we develop or reuse in Chapters 17–19 manipulate and share `Object`s. These classes cannot manipulate variables of primitive types, but they can manipulate objects of the type-wrapper classes, because every class ultimately derives from `Object`.

Each of the numeric type-wrapper classes—`Byte`, `Short`, `Integer`, `Long`, `Float` and `Double`—extends class `Number`. Also, the type-wrapper classes are `final` classes, so you cannot extend them.

Primitive types do not have methods, so the methods related to a primitive type are located in the corresponding type-wrapper class (e.g., method `parseInt`, which converts a `String` to an `int` value, is located in class `Integer`). If you need to manipulate a primitive value in your program, first refer to the documentation for the type-wrapper classes—the method you need might already be declared.

17.3 Autoboxing and Auto-Unboxing

In versions of Java prior to J2SE 5.0, if you wanted to insert a primitive value into a data structure that could store only `Object`s, you had to create a new object of the corresponding type-wrapper class, then insert this object in the collection. Similarly, if you wanted to retrieve an object of a type-wrapper class from a collection and manipulate its primitive value, you had to invoke a method on the object to obtain its corresponding primitive-type value. For example, suppose you want to add an `int` to an array that stores only references to `Integer` objects. Prior to J2SE 5.0, you would be required to "wrap" an `int` value in an `Integer` object before adding the integer to the array and to "unwrap" the `int` value from the `Integer` object to retrieve the value from the array, as in

```
Integer[] integerArray = new Integer[ 5 ]; // create integerArray

// assign Integer 10 to integerArray[ 0 ]
integerArray[ 0 ] = new Integer( 10 );

// get int value of Integer
int value = integerArray[ 0 ].intValue();
```

Notice that the `int` primitive value 10 is used to initialize an `Integer` object. This achieves the desired result but requires extra code and is cumbersome. We then need to invoke method `intValue` of class `Integer` to obtain the `int` value in the `Integer` object.

J2SE 5.0 simplifies converting between primitive-type values and type-wrapper objects, requiring no additional code on the part of the programmer. J2SE 5.0 introduces two new conversions—the boxing conversion and the unboxing conversion. A boxing conversion converts a value of a primitive type to an object of the corresponding type-wrapper class. An unboxing conversion converts an object of a type-wrapper class to a value of the corresponding primitive type. J2SE 5.0 allows these conversions to be performed automatically (called autoboxing and auto-unboxing). For example, the previous statements can be rewritten as

```
Integer[] integerArray = new Integer[ 5 ]; // create integerArray
integerArray[ 0 ] = 10; // assign Integer 10 to integerArray[ 0 ]
int value = integerArray[ 0 ]; // get int value of Integer
```

In this case, autoboxing occurs when assigning an int value (10) to integerArray[0], because integerArray stores references to Integer objects, not int primitive values. Auto-unboxing occurs when assigning integerArray[0] to int variable value, because variable value stores an int value, not a reference to an Integer object. Autoboxing and auto-unboxing also occur in control statements—the condition of a control statement can evaluate to a primitive boolean type or a Boolean reference type. Many of this chapter's examples use these conversions to store primitive values in and retrieve them from data structures that store only references to Objects.

17.4 Self-Referential Classes

A self-referential class contains an instance variable that refers to another object of the same class type. For example, the declaration

```
class Node
{
   private int data;
   private Node nextNode; // reference to next linked node

   public Node( int data )           { /* constructor body */ }
   public void setData( int data )   { /* method body */ }
   public int getData()              { /* method body */ }
   public void setNext( Node next )  { /* method body */ }
   public Node getNext()             { /* method body */ }
} // end class Node
```

declares class Node, which has two private instance variables—integer data and Node reference nextNode. Field nextNode references a Node object, an object of the same class being declared here—hence, the term "self-referential class." Field nextNode is a link—it "links" an object of type Node to another object of the same type. Type Node also has five methods: a constructor that receives an integer to initialize data, a setData method to set the value of data, a getData method to return the value of data, a setNext method to set the value of nextNode and a getNext method to return a reference to the next node.

Programs can link self-referential objects together to form such useful data structures as lists, queues, stacks and trees. Figure 17.1 illustrates two self-referential objects linked together to form a list. A backslash—representing a null reference—is placed in the link member of the second self-referential object to indicate that the link does not refer to

Fig. 17.1 | Self-referential-class objects linked together.

another object. Note the backslash is illustrative; it does not correspond to the backslash character in Java. Normally, a `null` reference indicates the end of a data structure. There are other ways to represent the end of a data structure that are beyond the scope of this text.

17.5 Dynamic Memory Allocation

Creating and maintaining dynamic data structures requires dynamic memory allocation—the ability for a program to obtain more memory space at execution time to hold new nodes and to release space no longer needed. Remember that Java programs do not explicitly release dynamically allocated memory. Rather, Java performs automatic garbage collection of objects that are no longer referenced in a program.

The limit for dynamic memory allocation can be as large as the amount of available physical memory in the computer or the amount of available disk space in a virtual-memory system. Often, the limits are much smaller, because the computer's available memory must be shared among many applications.

The declaration and class-instance creation expression

```
Node nodeToAdd = new Node( 10 ); // 10 is nodeToAdd's data
```

allocates the memory to store a `Node` object and returns a reference to the object, which is assigned to `nodeToAdd`. If insufficient memory is available, the expression throws an `OutOfMemoryError`.

The following sections discuss lists, stacks, queues and trees that all use dynamic memory allocation and self-referential classes to create dynamic data structures.

17.6 Linked Lists

A linked list is a linear collection (i.e., a sequence) of self-referential-class objects, called nodes, connected by reference links—hence, the term "linked" list. Typically, a program accesses a linked list via a reference to the first node in the list. The program accesses each subsequent node via the link reference stored in the previous node. By convention, the link reference in the last node is set to `null` to mark the end of the list. Data is stored in a linked list dynamically—the program creates each node as necessary. A node can contain data of any type, including references to objects of other classes. Stacks and queues are also linear data structures and, as we will see, are constrained versions of linked lists. Trees are non-linear data structures.

Lists of data can be stored in arrays, but linked lists provide several advantages. A linked list is appropriate when the number of data elements to be represented in the data structure is unpredictable. Linked lists are dynamic, so the length of a list can increase or decrease as necessary. The size of a "conventional" Java array, however, cannot be altered, because the array size is fixed at the time the program creates the array. "Conventional" arrays can become full. Linked lists become full only when the system has insufficient memory to satisfy dynamic storage allocation requests. Package `java.util` contains class `LinkedList` for implementing and manipulating linked lists that grow and shrink during program execution. We discuss class `LinkedList` in Chapter 19.

Performance Tip 17.1

An array can be declared to contain more elements than the number of items expected, but this wastes memory. Linked lists provide better memory utilization in these situations. Linked lists allow the program to adapt to storage needs at runtime.

Performance Tip 17.2

Insertion into a linked list is fast—only two references have to be modified (after locating the insertion point). All existing node objects remain at their current locations in memory.

Linked lists can be maintained in sorted order simply by inserting each new element at the proper point in the list. (It does, of course, take time to locate the proper insertion point.) Existing list elements do not need to be moved.

Performance Tip 17.3

Insertion and deletion in a sorted array can be time consuming—all the elements following the inserted or deleted element must be shifted appropriately.

Linked list nodes normally are not stored contiguously in memory. Rather, they are logically contiguous. Figure 17.2 illustrates a linked list with several nodes. This diagram presents a **singly linked list**—each node contains one reference to the next node in the list. Often, linked lists are implemented as doubly linked lists—each node contains a reference to the next node in the list and a reference to the previous node in the list. Java's `LinkedList` class is a doubly linked list implementation.

Performance Tip 17.4

Normally, the elements of an array are contiguous in memory. This allows immediate access to any array element, because its address can be calculated directly as its offset from the beginning of the array. Linked lists do not afford such immediate access to their elements—an element can be accessed only by traversing the list from the front (or from the back in a doubly linked list).

The program of Fig. 17.3–Fig. 17.5 uses an object of our `List` class to manipulate a list of miscellaneous objects. The program consists of four classes—`ListNode` (Fig. 17.3,

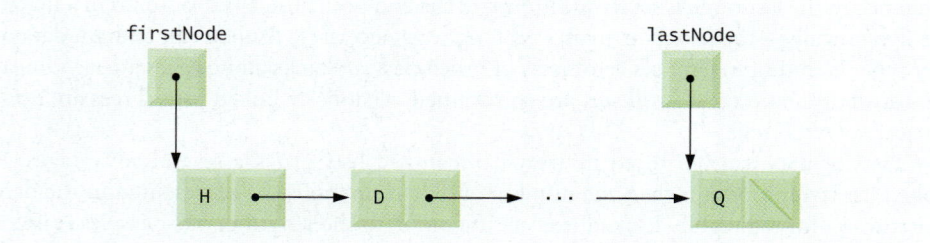

Fig. 17.2 | Linked list graphical representation.

lines 6–37), List (Fig. 17.3, lines 40–147), EmptyListException (Fig. 17.4) and List-Test (Fig. 17.5). The List, ListNode and EmptyListException classes are placed in package com.deitel.jhtp6.ch17, so they can be reused throughout this chapter. Encapsulated in each List object is a linked list of ListNode objects. [*Note:* Many of the classes in this chapter are declared in the package com.deitel.jhtp6.ch17. Each such class should be compiled with the -d command-line option to javac. When compiling the classes that are not in this package and when running the programs, be sure to use the -classpath option to javac and java, respectively.]

Class ListNode (Fig. 17.3, lines 6–37) declares package-access fields data and next-Node. The data field is an Object reference, so it can refer to any object. ListNode member nextNode stores a reference to the next ListNode object in the linked list (or null if the node is the last one in the list).

```java
1   // Fig. 17.3: List.java
2   // ListNode and List class definitions.
3   package com.deitel.jhtp6.ch17;
4
5   // class to represent one node in a list
6   class ListNode
7   {
8      // package access members; List can access these directly
9      Object data;
10     ListNode nextNode;
11
12     // constructor creates a ListNode that refers to object
13     ListNode( Object object )
14     {
15        this( object, null );
16     } // end ListNode one-argument constructor
17
18     // constructor creates ListNode that refers to
19     // Object and to next ListNode
20     ListNode( Object object, ListNode node )
21     {
22        data = object;
23        nextNode = node;
24     } // end ListNode two-argument constructor
25
26     // return reference to data in node
27     Object getObject()
28     {
29        return data; // return Object in this node
30     } // end method getObject
31
32     // return reference to next node in list
33     ListNode getNext()
34     {
35        return nextNode; // get next node
36     } // end method getNext
37  } // end class ListNode
```

Fig. 17.3 | ListNode and List class declarations. (Part 1 of 4.)

```
38
39   // class List definition
40   public class List
41   {
42      private ListNode firstNode;
43      private ListNode lastNode;
44      private String name; // string like "list" used in printing
45
46      // constructor creates empty List with "list" as the name
47      public List()
48      {
49         this( "list" );
50      } // end List no-argument constructor
51
52      // constructor creates an empty List with a name
53      public List( String listName )
54      {
55         name = listName;
56         firstNode = lastNode = null;
57      } // end List one-argument constructor
58
59      // insert Object at front of List
60      public void insertAtFront( Object insertItem )
61      {
62         if ( isEmpty() ) // firstNode and lastNode refer to same object
63            firstNode = lastNode = new ListNode( insertItem );
64         else // firstNode refers to new node
65            firstNode = new ListNode( insertItem, firstNode );
66      } // end method insertAtFront
67
68      // insert Object at end of List
69      public void insertAtBack( Object insertItem )
70      {
71         if ( isEmpty() ) // firstNode and lastNode refer to same Object
72            firstNode = lastNode = new ListNode( insertItem );
73         else // lastNode's nextNode refers to new node
74            lastNode = lastNode.nextNode = new ListNode( insertItem );
75      } // end method insertAtBack
76
77      // remove first node from List
78      public Object removeFromFront() throws EmptyListException
79      {
80         if ( isEmpty() ) // throw exception if List is empty
81            throw new EmptyListException( name );
82
83         Object removedItem = firstNode.data; // retrieve data being removed
84
85         // update references firstNode and lastNode
86         if ( firstNode == lastNode )
87            firstNode = lastNode = null;
88         else
89            firstNode = firstNode.nextNode;
90
```

Fig. 17.3 | ListNode and List class declarations. (Part 2 of 4.)

```
91          return removedItem; // return removed node data
92      } // end method removeFromFront
93
94      // remove last node from List
95      public Object removeFromBack() throws EmptyListException
96      {
97          if ( isEmpty() ) // throw exception if List is empty
98              throw new EmptyListException( name );
99
100         Object removedItem = lastNode.data; // retrieve data being removed
101
102         // update references firstNode and lastNode
103         if ( firstNode == lastNode )
104             firstNode = lastNode = null;
105         else // locate new last node
106         {
107             ListNode current = firstNode;
108
109             // loop while current node does not refer to lastNode
110             while ( current.nextNode != lastNode )
111                 current = current.nextNode;
112
113             lastNode = current; // current is new lastNode
114             current.nextNode = null;
115         } // end else
116
117         return removedItem; // return removed node data
118     } // end method removeFromBack
119
120     // determine whether list is empty
121     public boolean isEmpty()
122     {
123         return firstNode == null; // return true if List is empty
124     } // end method isEmpty
125
126     // output List contents
127     public void print()
128     {
129         if ( isEmpty() )
130         {
131             System.out.printf( "Empty %s\n", name );
132             return;
133         } // end if
134
135         System.out.printf( "The %s is: ", name );
136         ListNode current = firstNode;
137
138         // while not at end of list, output current node's data
139         while ( current != null )
140         {
141             System.out.printf( "%s ", current.data );
142             current = current.nextNode;
143         } // end while
```

Fig. 17.3 | ListNode and List class declarations. (Part 3 of 4.)

```
144
145          System.out.println( "\n" );
146      } // end method print
147  } // end class List
```

Fig. 17.3 | ListNode and List class declarations. (Part 4 of 4.)

Lines 42–43 of class List (Fig. 17.3, lines 40–147) declare references to the first and last ListNodes in a List (firstNode and lastNode, respectively). The constructors (lines 47–50 and 53–57) initialize both references to null. The most important methods of class List are insertAtFront (lines 60–66), insertAtBack (lines 69–75), removeFromFront (lines 78–92) and removeFromBack (lines 95–118). Method isEmpty (lines 121–124) is a *predicate method* that determines whether the list is empty (i.e., the reference to the first node of the list is null). Predicate methods typically test a condition and do not modify the object on which they are called. If the list is empty, method isEmpty returns true; otherwise, it returns false. Method print (lines 127–146) displays the list's contents. A detailed discussion of List's methods follows Fig. 17.5.

Method main of class ListTest (Fig. 17.5) inserts objects at the beginning of the list using method insertAtFront, inserts objects at the end of the list using method insertAtBack, deletes objects from the front of the list using method removeFromFront and deletes objects from the end of the list using method removeFromBack. After each insert and remove operation, ListTest calls List method print to display the current list contents. If an attempt is made to remove an item from an empty list, an Empty-ListException (Fig. 17.4) is thrown, so the method calls to removeFromFront and removeFromBack are placed in a try block that is followed by an appropriate exception handler. Notice in lines 13, 15, 17 and 19 that the applications passes literal primitive int

```
1   // Fig. 17.4: EmptyListException.java
2   // Class EmptyListException definition.
3   package com.deitel.jhtp6.ch17;
4
5   public class EmptyListException extends RuntimeException
6   {
7      // no-argument constructor
8      public EmptyListException()
9      {
10         this( "List" ); // call other EmptyListException constructor
11      } // end EmptyListException no-argument constructor
12
13      // one-argument constructor
14      public EmptyListException( String name )
15      {
16         super( name + " is empty" ); // call superclass constructor
17      } // end EmptyListException one-argument constructor
18  } // end class EmptyListException
```

Fig. 17.4 | EmptyListException class declaration.

values to methods insertAtFront and insertAtBack, even though each of these methods was declared with a parameter of type Object (Fig. 17.3, lines 60 and 69). In this case, the JVM autoboxes each literal value in an Integer object and that object is actually inserted into the list. This, of course, is allowed because Object is an indirect superclass of Integer.

```java
1   // Fig. 17.5: ListTest.java
2   // ListTest class to demonstrate List capabilities.
3   import com.deitel.jhtp6.ch17.List;
4   import com.deitel.jhtp6.ch17.EmptyListException;
5
6   public class ListTest
7   {
8      public static void main( String args[] )
9      {
10        List list = new List(); // create the List container
11
12        // insert integers in list
13        list.insertAtFront( -1 );
14        list.print();
15        list.insertAtFront( 0 );
16        list.print();
17        list.insertAtBack( 1 );
18        list.print();
19        list.insertAtBack( 5 );
20        list.print();
21
22        // remove objects from list; print after each removal
23        try
24        {
25           Object removedObject = list.removeFromFront();
26           System.out.printf( "%s removed\n", removedObject );
27           list.print();
28
29           removedObject = list.removeFromFront();
30           System.out.printf( "%s removed\n", removedObject );
31           list.print();
32
33           removedObject = list.removeFromBack();
34           System.out.printf( "%s removed\n", removedObject );
35           list.print();
36
37           removedObject = list.removeFromBack();
38           System.out.printf( "%s removed\n", removedObject );
39           list.print();
40        } // end try
41        catch ( EmptyListException emptyListException )
42        {
43           emptyListException.printStackTrace();
44        } // end catch
45     } // end main
46  } // end class ListTest
```

Fig. 17.5 | Linked list manipulations. (Part 1 of 2.)

```
The list is: -1

The list is: 0 -1

The list is: 0 -1 1

The list is: 0 -1 1 5

0 removed
The list is: -1 1 5

-1 removed
The list is: 1 5

5 removed
The list is: 1

1 removed
Empty list
```

Fig. 17.5 | Linked list manipulations. (Part 2 of 2.)

Now we discuss each method of class List (Fig. 17.3) in detail and provide diagrams showing the reference manipulations performed by methods insertAtFront, insertAt-Back, removeFromFront and removeFromBack. Method insertAtFront (lines 60–66 of Fig. 17.3) places a new node at the front of the list. The steps are:

1. Call isEmpty to determine whether the list is empty (line 62).

2. If the list is empty, assign firstNode and lastNode to the new ListNode that was initialized with insertItem (line 63). The ListNode constructor at lines 13–16 calls the ListNode constructor at lines 20–24 to set instance variable data to refer to the insertItem passed as an argument and to set reference nextNode to null, because this is the first and last node in the list.

3. If the list is not empty, the new node is "linked" into the list by setting firstNode to a new ListNode object and initializing that object with insertItem and firstNode (line 65). When the ListNode constructor (lines 20–24) executes, it sets instance variable data to refer to the insertItem passed as an argument and performs the insertion by setting the nextNode reference of the new node to the ListNode passed as an argument, which previously was the first node.

In Fig. 17.6, part (a) shows a list and a new node during the insertAtFront operation and before the program links the new node into the list. The dotted arrows in part (b) illustrate *Step 3* of the insertAtFront operation that enables the node containing 12 to become the new first node in the list.

Method insertAtBack (lines 69–75 of Fig. 17.3) places a new node at the back of the list. The steps are:

1. Call isEmpty to determine whether the list is empty (line 71).

2. If the list is empty, assign firstNode and lastNode to the new ListNode that was initialized with insertItem (line 72). The ListNode constructor at lines 13–16 calls the constructor at lines 20–24 to set instance variable data to refer to the insertItem passed as an argument and to set reference nextNode to null.

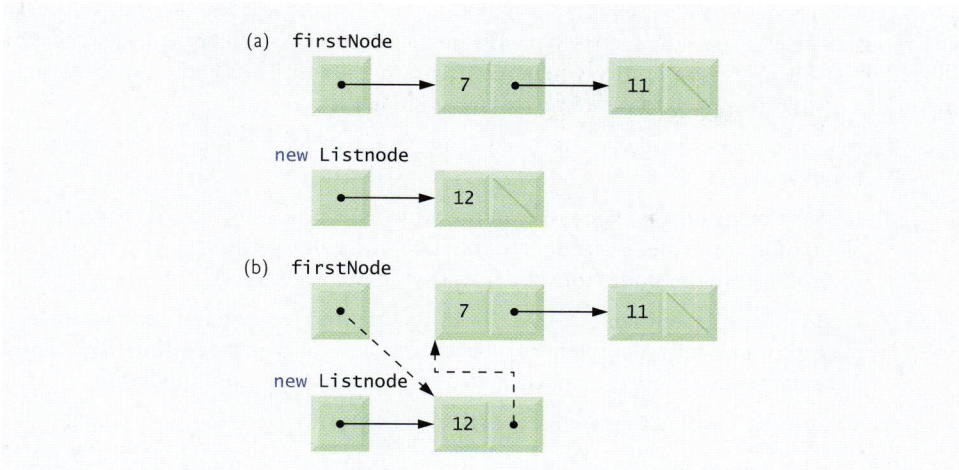

Fig. 17.6 | Graphical representation of operation `insertAtFront`.

3. If the list is not empty, line 74 links the new node into the list by assigning to `lastNode` and `lastNode.nextNode` the reference to the new `ListNode` that was initialized with `insertItem`. `ListNode`'s constructor (lines 13–16), sets instance variable `data` to refer to the `insertItem` passed as an argument and sets reference `nextNode` to `null`, because this is the last node in the list.

In Fig. 17.7, part (a) shows a list and a new node during the `insertAtBack` operation and before the program links the new node into the list. The dotted arrows in part (b) illustrate *Step 3* of method `insertAtBack`, which adds the new node to the end of a list that is not empty.

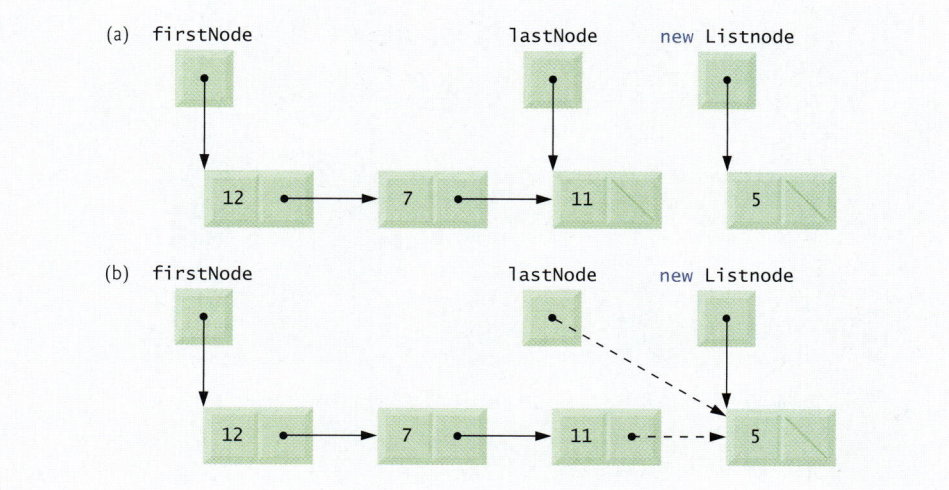

Fig. 17.7 | Graphical representation of operation `insertAtBack`.

Method `removeFromFront` (lines 78–92 of Fig. 17.3) removes the first node of the list and returns a reference to the removed data. The method throws an `EmptyListException` (lines 80–81) if the list is empty when the program calls this method. Otherwise, the method returns a reference to the removed data. The steps are:

1. Assign `firstNode.data` (the data being removed from the list) to reference `removedItem` (line 83).

2. If `firstNode` and `lastNode` refer to the same object (line 86), the list has only one element at this time. So, the method sets `firstNode` and `lastNode` to `null` (line 87) to remove the node from the list (leaving the list empty).

3. If the list has more than one node, then the method leaves reference `lastNode` as is and assigns the value of `firstNode.nextNode` to `firstNode` (line 89). Thus, `firstNode` references the node that was previously the second node in the list.

4. Return the `removedItem` reference (line 91).

In Fig. 17.8, part (a) illustrates the list before the removal operation. The dashed lines and arrows in part (b) show the reference manipulations.

Method `removeFromBack` (lines 95–118 of Fig. 17.3) removes the last node of a list and returns a reference to the removed data. The method throws an `EmptyListException` (lines 97–98) if the list is empty when the program calls this method. The steps are:

1. Assign `lastNode.data` (the data being removed from the list) to `removedItem` (line 100).

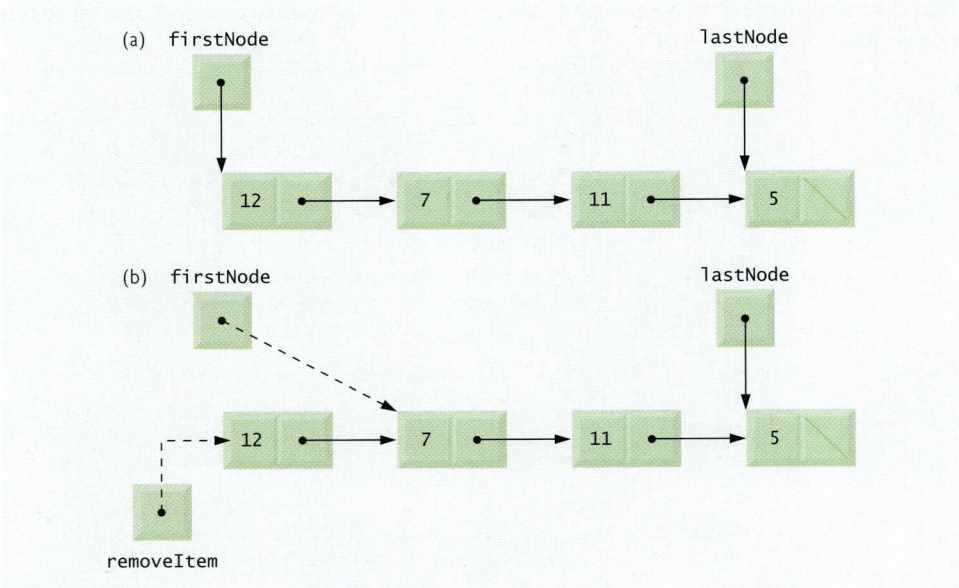

Fig. 17.8 | Graphical representation of operation `removeFromFront`.

2. If the `firstNode` and `lastNode` refer to the same object (line 103), the list has only one element at this time. So, line 104 sets `firstNode` and `lastNode` to `null` to remove that node from the list (leaving the list empty).

3. If the list has more than one node, create the `ListNode` reference `current` and assign it `firstNode` (line 107).

4. Now "walk the list" with `current` until it references the node before the last node. The `while` loop (lines 110–111) assigns `current.nextNode` to `current` as long as `current.nextNode` (the next node in the list) is not `lastNode`.

5. After locating the second-to-last node, assign `current` to `lastNode` (line 113) to update which node is last in the list.

6. Set the `current.nextNode` to `null` (line 114) to remove the last node from the list and terminate the list at the current node.

7. Return the `removedItem` reference (line 117).

In Fig. 17.9, part (a) illustrates the list before the removal operation. The dashed lines and arrows in part (b) show the reference manipulations.

Method `print` (lines 127–146) first determines whether the list is empty (lines 129–133). If so, `print` displays a message indicating that the list is empty and returns control to the calling method. Otherwise, `print` outputs the list's data. Line 136 creates `ListNode` `current` and initializes it with `firstNode`. While `current` is not `null`, there are more items in the list. Therefore, line 141 outputs a string representation of `current.data`. Line 142 moves to the next node in the list by assigning the value of reference `current.next-Node` to `current`. This printing algorithm is identical for linked lists, stacks and queues.

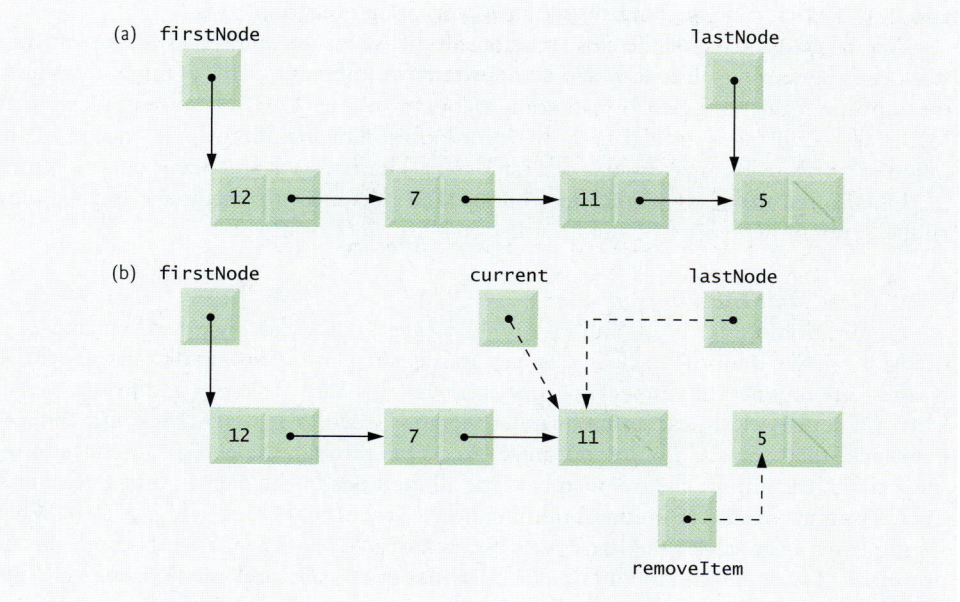

Fig. 17.9 | Graphical representation of operation `removeFromBack`.

17.7 **Stacks**

A stack is a constrained version of a linked list—new nodes can be added to and removed from a stack only at the top. [*Note:* A stack does not have to be implemented using a linked list.] For this reason, a stack is referred to as a last-in, first-out (LIFO) data structure. The link member in the bottom (i.e., last) node of the stack is set to null to indicate the bottom of the stack.

The primary methods for manipulating a stack are **push** and **pop**. Method push adds a new node to the top of the stack. Method pop removes a node from the top of the stack and returns the data from the popped node.

Stacks have many interesting applications. For example, when a program calls a method, the called method must know how to return to its caller, so the return address of the calling method is pushed onto the program execution stack. If a series of method calls occurs, the successive return addresses are pushed onto the stack in last-in, first-out order so that each method can return to its caller. Stacks support recursive method calls in the same manner as they do conventional nonrecursive method calls.

The program execution stack also contains the memory for local variables on each invocation of a method during a program's execution. When the method returns to its caller, the memory for that method's local variables is popped off the stack, and those variables are no longer known to the program. If the local variable is a reference, the reference count for the object to which it referred is decremented by 1. If the reference count becomes zero, the object can be garbage collected.

Compilers use stacks to evaluate arithmetic expressions and generate machine-language code to process the expressions. The exercises in this chapter explore several applications of stacks, including using them to develop a complete working compiler. Also, package java.util contains class Stack (see Chapter 19) for implementing and manipulating stacks that can grow and shrink during program execution.

We take advantage of the close relationship between lists and stacks to implement a stack class by reusing a list class. We demonstrate two different forms of reusability. First, we implement the stack class by extending class List of Fig. 17.3. Then we implement an identically performing stack class through composition by including a reference to a List object as a private instance variable of a stack class. The list, stack and queue data structures in this chapter are implemented to store Object references to encourage further reusability. Thus, any object type can be stored in a list, stack or queue.

Stack Class That Inherits from List

The application of Fig. 17.10 and Fig. 17.11 creates a stack class by extending class List of Fig. 17.3. We want the stack to have methods push, pop, isEmpty and print. Essentially, these are the methods insertAtFront, removeFromFront, isEmpty and print of class List. Of course, class List contains other methods (such as insertAtBack and removeFromBack) that we would rather not make accessible through the public interface to the stack class. It is important to remember that all methods in the public interface of class List class also are public methods of the subclass StackInheritance (Fig. 17.10). When we implement the stack's methods, we have each StackInheritance method call the appropriate List method—method push calls insertAtFront and method pop calls removeFromFront. Clients of class StackInheritance can call methods isEmpty and print because they are inherited from List. Class StackInheritance is declared as part of pack-

```
 1   // Fig. 17.10: StackInheritance.java
 2   // Derived from class List.
 3   package com.deitel.jhtp6.ch17;
 4
 5   public class StackInheritance extends List
 6   {
 7      // no-argument constructor
 8      public StackInheritance()
 9      {
10         super( "stack" );
11      } // end StackInheritance no-argument constructor
12
13      // add object to stack
14      public void push( Object object )
15      {
16         insertAtFront( object );
17      } // end method push
18
19      // remove object from stack
20      public Object pop() throws EmptyListException
21      {
22         return removeFromFront();
23      } // end method pop
24   } // end class StackInheritance
```

Fig. 17.10 | StackInheritance extends class List.

age com.deitel.jhtp6.ch17 for reuse purposes. Note that StackInheritance does not import List, because both classes are in the same package.

Class StackInheritanceTest's method main (Fig. 17.11) creates an object of class StackInheritance called stack (line 10). The program pushes integers onto the stack (lines 13, 15, 17 and 19). Once again, note that autoboxing is used here to insert Integer objects into the data structure. Lines 27–32 pop the objects from the stack in an infinite while loop. If method pop is invoked on an empty stack, the method throws an Empty-ListException. In this case, the program displays the exception's stack trace, which shows the methods on the program execution stack at the time the exception occurred. Note that the program uses method print (inherited from List) to output the contents of the stack.

```
 1   // Fig. 17.11: StackInheritanceTest.java
 2   // Class StackInheritanceTest.
 3   import com.deitel.jhtp6.ch17.StackInheritance;
 4   import com.deitel.jhtp6.ch17.EmptyListException;
 5
 6   public class StackInheritanceTest
 7   {
 8      public static void main( String args[] )
 9      {
10         StackInheritance stack = new StackInheritance();
11
```

Fig. 17.11 | Stack manipulation program. (Part 1 of 2.)

```
12          // use push method
13          stack.push( -1 );
14          stack.print();
15          stack.push( 0 );
16          stack.print();
17          stack.push( 1 );
18          stack.print();
19          stack.push( 5 );
20          stack.print();
21
22          // remove items from stack
23          try
24          {
25             Object removedObject = null;
26
27             while ( true )
28             {
29                removedObject = stack.pop(); // use pop method
30                System.out.printf( "%s popped\n", removedObject );
31                stack.print();
32             } // end while
33          } // end try
34          catch ( EmptyListException emptyListException )
35          {
36             emptyListException.printStackTrace();
37          } // end catch
38       } // end main
39    } // end class StackInheritanceTest
```

```
The stack is: -1

The stack is: 0 -1

The stack is: 1 0 -1

The stack is: 5 1 0 -1

5 popped
The stack is: 1 0 -1

1 popped
The stack is: 0 -1

0 popped
The stack is: -1

-1 popped
Empty stack
com.deitel.jhtp6.ch17.EmptyListException: stack is empty
        at com.deitel.jhtp6.ch17.List.removeFromFront(List.java:81)
        at com.deitel.jhtp6.ch17.StackInheritance.pop(StackInheritance.java:22)
        at StackInheritanceTest.main(StackInheritanceTest.java:29)
```

Fig. 17.11 | Stack manipulation program. (Part 2 of 2.)

Stack Class That Contains a Reference to a `List`

You can also implement a class by reusing a list class through composition. Figure 17.12 uses a `private List` (line 7) in class `StackComposition`'s declaration. Composition enables us to hide the `List` methods that should not be in our stack's `public` interface. We provide `public` interface methods that use only the required `List` methods. Implementing each stack method as a call to a `List` method is called delegation—the stack method invoked delegates the call to the appropriate `List` method. In particular, `StackComposition` delegates calls to `List` methods `insertAtFront`, `removeFromFront`, `isEmpty` and `print`. In this example, we do not show class `StackCompositionTest`, because the only difference is that we change the type of the stack from `StackInheritance` to `StackComposition` (lines 3 and 10 of Fig. 17.11). The output is identical using either version of the stack.

```
 1   // Fig. 17.12: StackComposition.java
 2   // Class StackComposition definition with composed List object.
 3   package com.deitel.jhtp6.ch17;
 4
 5   public class StackComposition
 6   {
 7      private List stackList;
 8
 9      // no-argument constructor
10      public StackComposition()
11      {
12         stackList = new List( "stack" );
13      } // end StackComposition no-argument constructor
14
15      // add object to stack
16      public void push( Object object )
17      {
18         stackList.insertAtFront( object );
19      } // end method push
20
21      // remove object from stack
22      public Object pop() throws EmptyListException
23      {
24         return stackList.removeFromFront();
25      } // end method pop
26
27      // determine if stack is empty
28      public boolean isEmpty()
29      {
30         return stackList.isEmpty();
31      } // end method isEmpty
32
33      // output stack contents
34      public void print()
35      {
36         stackList.print();
37      } // end method print
38   } // end class StackComposition
```

Fig. 17.12 | `StackComposition` uses a composed `List` object.

17.8 Queues

Another commonly used data structure is the queue. A queue is similar to a checkout line in a supermarket—the cashier services the person at the beginning of the line first. Other customers enter the line only at the end and wait for service. Queue nodes are removed only from the head (or front) of the queue and are inserted only at the tail (or end). For this reason, a queue is a **first-in, first-out** (**FIFO**) data structure. The insert and remove operations are known as **enqueue** and **dequeue**.

Queues have many uses in computer systems. Most computers have only a single processor, so only one application at a time can be serviced. Each application requiring processor time is placed in a queue. The application at the front of the queue is the next to receive service. Each application gradually advances to the front as the applications before it receive service.

Queues are also used to support **print spooling**. For example, a single printer might be shared by all users of a network. Many users can send print jobs to the printer, even when the printer is already busy. These print jobs are placed in a queue until the printer becomes available. A program called a **spooler** manages the queue to ensure that, as each print job completes, the next print job is sent to the printer.

Information packets also wait in queues in computer networks. Each time a packet arrives at a network node, it must be routed to the next node along the path to the packet's final destination. The routing node routes one packet at a time, so additional packets are enqueued until the router can route them.

A file server in a computer network handles file-access requests from many clients throughout the network. Servers have a limited capacity to service requests from clients. When that capacity is exceeded, client requests wait in queues.

Figure 17.13 creates a queue class that contains an object of class List (Fig. 17.3). Class Queue (Fig. 17.13) provides methods enqueue, dequeue, isEmpty and print. Class List contains other methods (e.g., insertAtFront and removeFromBack) that we would rather not make accessible through the public interface of class Queue. By using composition, these methods in the public interface of class List are not accessible to clients of class Queue. Each method of class Queue calls an appropriate List method—method enqueue calls List method insertAtBack, method dequeue calls List method removeFromFront,

```
1   // Fig. 17.13: Queue.java
2   // Class Queue.
3   package com.deitel.jhtp6.ch17;
4
5   public class Queue
6   {
7      private List queueList;
8
9      // no-argument constructor
10     public Queue()
11     {
12        queueList = new List( "queue" );
13     } // end Queue no-argument constructor
14
```

Fig. 17.13 | Queue uses class List. (Part 1 of 2.)

```
15        // add object to queue
16        public void enqueue( Object object )
17        {
18           queueList.insertAtBack( object );
19        } // end method enqueue
20
21        // remove object from queue
22        public Object dequeue() throws EmptyListException
23        {
24           return queueList.removeFromFront();
25        } // end method dequeue
26
27        // determine if queue is empty
28        public boolean isEmpty()
29        {
30           return queueList.isEmpty();
31        } // end method isEmpty
32
33        // output queue contents
34        public void print()
35        {
36           queueList.print();
37        } // end method print
38     } // end class Queue
```

Fig. 17.13 | Queue uses class List. (Part 2 of 2.)

method isEmpty calls List method isEmpty and method print calls List method print. For reuse purposes, class Queue is declared in package com.deitel.jhtp6.ch17.

Class QueueTest (Fig. 17.14) method main creates an object of class Queue called queue. Lines 13, 15, 17 and 19 enqueue four integers, taking advantage of autoboxing to insert Integer objects into the queue. Lines 27–32 use an infinite while loop to dequeue the objects in first-in, first-out order. When the queue is empty, method dequeue throws an EmptyListException, and the program displays the exception's stack trace.

```
1    // Fig. 17.14: QueueTest.java
2    // Class QueueTest.
3    import com.deitel.jhtp6.ch17.Queue;
4    import com.deitel.jhtp6.ch17.EmptyListException;
5
6    public class QueueTest
7    {
8       public static void main( String args[] )
9       {
10          Queue queue = new Queue();
11
12          // use enqueue method
13          queue.enqueue( -1 );
14          queue.print();
15          queue.enqueue( 0 );
```

Fig. 17.14 | Queue processing program. (Part 1 of 2.)

```
16          queue.print();
17          queue.enqueue( 1 );
18          queue.print();
19          queue.enqueue( 5 );
20          queue.print();
21
22          // remove objects from queue
23          try
24          {
25              Object removedObject = null;
26
27              while ( true )
28              {
29                  removedObject = queue.dequeue(); // use dequeue method
30                  System.out.printf( "%s dequeued\n", removedObject );
31                  queue.print();
32              } // end while
33          } // end try
34          catch ( EmptyListException emptyListException )
35          {
36              emptyListException.printStackTrace();
37          } // end catch
38      } // end main
39  } // end class QueueTest
```

```
The queue is: -1

The queue is: -1 0

The queue is: -1 0 1

The queue is: -1 0 1 5

-1 dequeued
The queue is: 0 1 5

0 dequeued
The queue is: 1 5

1 dequeued
The queue is: 5

5 dequeued
Empty queue
com.deitel.jhtp6.ch17.EmptyListException: queue is empty
        at com.deitel.jhtp6.ch17.List.removeFromFront(List.java:81)
        at com.deitel.jhtp6.ch17.Queue.dequeue(Queue.java:24)
        at QueueTest.main(QueueTest.java:29)
```

Fig. 17.14 | Queue processing program. (Part 2 of 2.)

17.9 Trees

Linked lists, stacks and queues are linear data structures (i.e., sequences). A tree is a non-linear, two-dimensional data structure with special properties. Tree nodes contain two or more links. This section discusses binary trees (Fig. 17.15)—trees whose nodes each contain two links (one or both of which may be `null`). The root node is the first node in a tree. Each link in the root node refers to a child. The left child is the first node in the left subtree (also known as the root node of the left subtree), and the right child is the first node in the right subtree (also known as the root node of the right subtree). The children of a specific node are called siblings. A node with no children is called a leaf node. Computer scientists normally draw trees from the root node down—exactly the opposite of the way most trees grow in nature.

In our example, we create a special binary tree called a binary search tree. A binary search tree (with no duplicate node values) has the characteristic that the values in any left subtree are less than the value in that subtree's parent node, and the values in any right subtree are greater than the value in that subtree's parent node. Figure 17.16 illustrates a binary search tree with 12 integer values. Note that the shape of the binary search tree that corresponds to a set of data can vary, depending on the order in which the values are inserted into the tree.

The application of Fig. 17.17 and Fig. 17.18 creates a binary search tree of integers and traverses it (i.e., walks through all its nodes) three ways—using recursive inorder, preorder and postorder traversals. The program generates 10 random numbers and inserts each into the tree. Class `Tree` is declared in package `com.deitel.jhtp6.ch17` for reuse purposes.

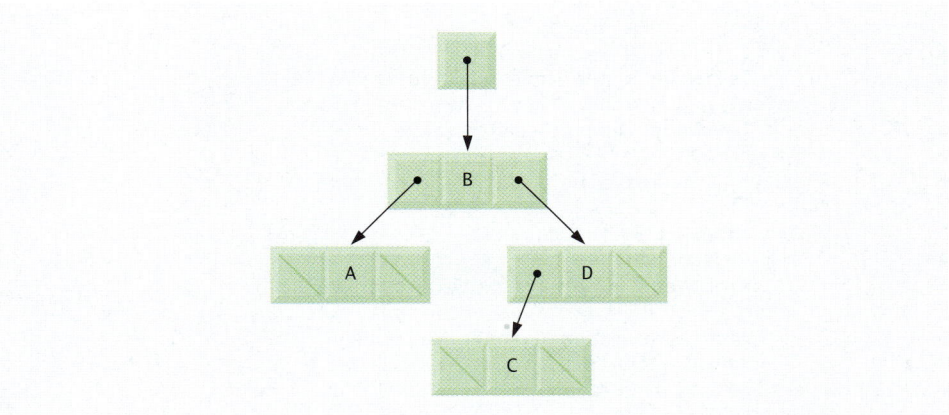

Fig. 17.15 | Binary tree graphical representation.

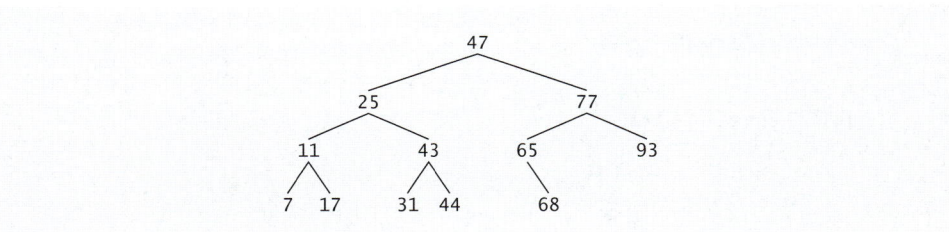

Fig. 17.16 | Binary search tree containing 12 values.

```java
1   // Fig. 17.17: Tree.java
2   // Definition of class TreeNode and class Tree.
3   package com.deitel.jhtp6.ch17;
4
5   // class TreeNode definition
6   class TreeNode
7   {
8      // package access members
9      TreeNode leftNode; // left node
10     int data; // node value
11     TreeNode rightNode; // right node
12
13     // constructor initializes data and makes this a leaf node
14     public TreeNode( int nodeData )
15     {
16        data = nodeData;
17        leftNode = rightNode = null; // node has no children
18     } // end TreeNode no-argument constructor
19
20     // locate insertion point and insert new node; ignore duplicate values
21     public void insert( int insertValue )
22     {
23        // insert in left subtree
24        if ( insertValue < data )
25        {
26           // insert new TreeNode
27           if ( leftNode == null )
28              leftNode = new TreeNode( insertValue );
29           else // continue traversing left subtree
30              leftNode.insert( insertValue );
31        } // end if
32        else if ( insertValue > data ) // insert in right subtree
33        {
34           // insert new TreeNode
35           if ( rightNode == null )
36              rightNode = new TreeNode( insertValue );
37           else // continue traversing right subtree
38              rightNode.insert( insertValue );
39        } // end else if
40     } // end method insert
41  } // end class TreeNode
42
43  // class Tree definition
44  public class Tree
45  {
46     private TreeNode root;
47
48     // constructor initializes an empty Tree of integers
49     public Tree()
50     {
51        root = null;
52     } // end Tree no-argument constructor
```

Fig. 17.17 | TreeNode and Tree class declarations for a binary search tree. (Part 1 of 3.)

```
53
54      // insert a new node in the binary search tree
55      public void insertNode( int insertValue )
56      {
57         if ( root == null )
58            root = new TreeNode( insertValue ); // create the root node here
59         else
60            root.insert( insertValue ); // call the insert method
61      } // end method insertNode
62
63      // begin preorder traversal
64      public void preorderTraversal()
65      {
66         preorderHelper( root );
67      } // end method preorderTraversal
68
69      // recursive method to perform preorder traversal
70      private void preorderHelper( TreeNode node )
71      {
72         if ( node == null )
73            return;
74
75         System.out.printf( "%d ", node.data ); // output node data
76         preorderHelper( node.leftNode );        // traverse left subtree
77         preorderHelper( node.rightNode );       // traverse right subtree
78      } // end method preorderHelper
79
80      // begin inorder traversal
81      public void inorderTraversal()
82      {
83         inorderHelper( root );
84      } // end method inorderTraversal
85
86      // recursive method to perform inorder traversal
87      private void inorderHelper( TreeNode node )
88      {
89         if ( node == null )
90            return;
91
92         inorderHelper( node.leftNode );         // traverse left subtree
93         System.out.printf( "%d ", node.data ); // output node data
94         inorderHelper( node.rightNode );        // traverse right subtree
95      } // end method inorderHelper
96
97      // begin postorder traversal
98      public void postorderTraversal()
99      {
100        postorderHelper( root );
101     } // end method postorderTraversal
102
```

Fig. 17.17 | TreeNode and Tree class declarations for a binary search tree. (Part 2 of 3.)

```
103       // recursive method to perform postorder traversal
104       private void postorderHelper( TreeNode node )
105       {
106          if ( node == null )
107             return;
108
109          postorderHelper( node.leftNode );     // traverse left subtree
110          postorderHelper( node.rightNode );    // traverse right subtree
111          System.out.printf( "%d ", node.data ); // output node data
112       } // end method postorderHelper
113   } // end class Tree
```

Fig. 17.17 | TreeNode and Tree class declarations for a binary search tree. (Part 3 of 3.)

Let us walk through the binary tree program. Method main of class TreeTest (Fig. 17.18) begins by instantiating an empty Tree object and assigning its reference to variable tree (line 10). Lines 17–22 randomly generate 10 integers, each of which is inserted into the binary tree through a call to method insertNode (line 21). The program then performs preorder, inorder and postorder traversals (these will be explained shortly) of tree (lines 25, 28 and 31, respectively).

Class Tree (Fig. 17.17, lines 44–113) has private field root (line 46)—a TreeNode reference to the root node of the tree. Tree's constructor (lines 49–52) initializes root to null to indicate that the tree is empty. The class contains method insertNode (lines 55–61) to insert a new node in the tree and methods preorderTraversal (lines 64–67), inorderTraversal (lines 81–84) and postorderTraversal (lines 98–101) to begin traversals of the tree. Each of these methods calls a recursive utility method to perform the traversal operations on the internal representation of the tree. (Recursion is discussed in Chapter 15.)

Class Tree's method insertNode (lines 55–61) first determines whether the tree is empty. If so, line 58 allocates a new TreeNode, initializes the node with the integer being inserted in the tree and assigns the new node to reference root. If the tree is not empty, line 60 calls TreeNode method insert (lines 21–41). This method uses recursion to determine the location for the new node in the tree and inserts the node at that location. A node can be inserted only as a leaf node in a binary search tree.

TreeNode method insert compares the value to insert with the data value in the root node. If the insert value is less than the root node data (line 24), the program determines if the left subtree is empty (line 27). If so, line 28 allocates a new TreeNode, initializes it with the integer being inserted and assigns the new node to reference leftNode. Otherwise, line 30 recursively calls insert for the left subtree to insert the value into the left subtree. If the insert value is greater than the root node data (line 32), the program determines if the right subtree is empty (line 35). If so, line 36 allocates a new TreeNode, initializes it with the integer being inserted and assigns the new node to reference rightNode. Otherwise, line 38 recursively calls insert for the right subtree to insert the value in the right subtree. If the insertValue is already in the tree, it is simply ignored.

Methods inorderTraversal, preorderTraversal and postorderTraversal call Tree helper methods inorderHelper (lines 87–95), preorderHelper (lines 70–78) and postorderHelper (lines 104–112), respectively, to traverse the tree and print the node values.

```java
 1   // Fig. 17.18: TreeTest.java
 2   // This program tests class Tree.
 3   import java.util.Random;
 4   import com.deitel.jhtp6.ch17.Tree;
 5
 6   public class TreeTest
 7   {
 8      public static void main( String args[] )
 9      {
10         Tree tree = new Tree();
11         int value;
12         Random randomNumber = new Random();
13
14         System.out.println( "Inserting the following values: " );
15
16         // insert 10 random integers from 0-99 in tree
17         for ( int i = 1; i <= 10; i++ )
18         {
19            value = randomNumber.nextInt( 100 );
20            System.out.print( value + " " );
21            tree.insertNode( value );
22         } // end for
23
24         System.out.println ( "\n\nPreorder traversal" );
25         tree.preorderTraversal(); // perform preorder traversal of tree
26
27         System.out.println ( "\n\nInorder traversal" );
28         tree.inorderTraversal(); // perform inorder traversal of tree
29
30         System.out.println ( "\n\nPostorder traversal" );
31         tree.postorderTraversal(); // perform postorder traversal of tree
32         System.out.println();
33      } // end main
34   } // end class TreeTest
```

```
Inserting the following values:
92 73 77 16 30 30 94 89 26 80

Preorder traversal
92 73 16 30 26 77 89 80 94

Inorder traversal
16 26 30 73 77 80 89 92 94

Postorder traversal
26 30 16 80 89 77 73 94 92
```

Fig. 17.18 | Binary tree test program.

The helper methods in class Tree enable the programmer to start a traversal without having to pass the root node to the method. Reference root is an implementation detail that a programmer should not be able to access. Methods inorderTraversal, preorderTraversal and `postorderTraversal` simply take the private `root` reference and pass it to the appropriate helper method to initiate a traversal of the tree. The base case for each helper method determines whether the reference it receives is `null` and, if so, returns immediately.

Method `inorderHelper` (lines 87–95) defines the steps for an inorder traversal:

1. Traverse the left subtree with a call to `inorderHelper` (line 92).

2. Process the value in the node (line 93).

3. Traverse the right subtree with a call to `inorderHelper` (line 94).

The inorder traversal does not process the value in a node until the values in that node's left subtree are processed. The inorder traversal of the tree in Fig. 17.19 is

    6 13 17 27 33 42 48

Note that the inorder traversal of a binary search tree prints the node values in ascending order. The process of creating a binary search tree actually sorts the data; thus, it is called the **binary tree sort**.

Method `preorderHelper` (lines 70–78) defines the steps for a preorder traversal:

1. Process the value in the node (line 75).

2. Traverse the left subtree with a call to `preorderHelper` (line 76).

3. Traverse the right subtree with a call to `preorderHelper` (line 77).

The preorder traversal processes the value in each node as the node is visited. After processing the value in a given node, the preorder traversal processes the values in the left subtree, then the values in the right subtree. The preorder traversal of the tree in Fig. 17.19 is

    27 13 6 17 42 33 48

Method `postorderHelper` (lines 104–112) defines the steps for a postorder traversal:

1. Traverse the left subtree with a call to `postorderHelper` (line 109).

2. Traverse the right subtree with a call to `postorderHelper` (line 110).

3. Process the value in the node (line 111).

The postorder traversal processes the value in each node after the values of all that node's children are processed. The `postorderTraversal` of the tree in Fig. 17.19 is

    6 17 13 33 48 42 27

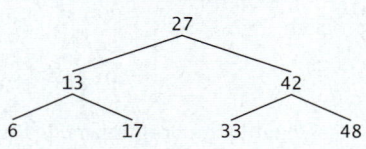

Fig. 17.19 | Binary search tree with seven values.

The binary search tree facilitates duplicate elimination. While building a tree, the insertion operation recognizes attempts to insert a duplicate value, because a duplicate follows the same "go left" or "go right" decisions on each comparison as the original value did. Thus, the insertion operation eventually compares the duplicate with a node containing the same value. At this point, the insertion operation can decide to discard the duplicate value (as we do in this example).

Searching a binary tree for a value that matches a key value is fast, especially for tightly packed (or balanced) trees. In a tightly packed tree, each level contains about twice as many elements as the previous level. Figure 17.19 is a tightly packed binary tree. A tightly packed binary search tree with n elements has $\log_2 n$ levels. Thus, at most $\log_2 n$ comparisons are required either to find a match or to determine that no match exists. Searching a (tightly packed) 1000-element binary search tree requires at most 10 comparisons, because $2^{10} > 1000$. Searching a (tightly packed) 1,000,000-element binary search tree requires at most 20 comparisons, because $2^{20} > 1,000,000$.

The chapter exercises present algorithms for several other binary tree operations, such as deleting an item from a binary tree, printing a binary tree in a two-dimensional tree format and performing a level-order traversal of a binary tree. The level-order traversal visits the nodes of the tree row by row, starting at the root node level. On each level of the tree, a level-order traversal visits the nodes from left to right. Other binary tree exercises include allowing a binary search tree to contain duplicate values, inserting string values in a binary tree and determining how many levels are contained in a binary tree. Chapter 19 continues our discussion of data structures by presenting the data structures in the Java API.

17.10 Wrap-Up

In this chapter, you learned about type-wrapper classes, boxing and dynamic data structures that grow and shrink at execution time. You learned that each primitive type has a corresponding type-wrapper class in package java.lang. You also saw that Java can convert between primitive values and objects of the type-wrapper classes using J2SE 5.0's new feature called boxing.

You learned that linked lists are collections of data items that are "linked up in a chain." You also saw that an application can perform insertions and deletions anywhere in a linked list. You learned that the stack and queue data structures are constrained versions of lists. For stacks, you saw that insertions and deletions are made only at its top. For queues that represent waiting lines, you saw that insertions are made at the tail and deletions are made from the head. You also learned the binary tree data structure. You saw a binary search tree that facilitated high-speed searching and sorting of data and eliminating duplicate data items efficiently. Throughout the chapter, you learned how to create and package these data structures for reusability and maintainability.

In Chapter 18, Generics, we discuss J2SE 5.0's new feature called generics, which provides a mechanism for declaring classes and methods without specific type information so that the classes and methods can be used with many different reference types. Generics are used extensively in Java's built-in set of data structures, known as the Collections API. You will learn about collections in Chapter 19, Collections.

Summary

- Dynamic data structures can grow and shrink at execution time.
- Linked lists are collections of data items "linked up in a chain"—insertions and deletions can be made anywhere in a linked list.
- Stacks are important in compilers and operating systems—insertions and deletions are made only at one end of a stack, its top.
- Queues represent waiting lines; insertions are made at the tail of a queue and deletions are made from the head.
- Binary trees facilitate high-speed searching and sorting of data, eliminating duplicate data items efficiently, representing file-system directories and compiling expressions into machine language.
- Type-wrapper classes (e.g., `Integer`, `Double`, `Boolean`) enable programmers to manipulate primitive-type values as objects. Objects of these classes can be used in collections and data structures that can store only references to objects—not primitive-type values.
- J2SE 5.0 introduces two new conversions, the boxing conversion and the unboxing conversion. A boxing conversion converts a value of a primitive type to an object of the corresponding type-wrapper class. An unboxing conversion converts an object of a type-wrapper class to a value of the corresponding primitive type.
- J2SE 5.0 performs boxing conversions and unboxing conversions automatically (called autoboxing and auto-unboxing).
- A self-referential class contains a reference that refers to another object of the same class type. Self-referential objects can be linked together to form dynamic data structures.
- The limit for dynamic memory allocation can be as large as the available physical memory in the computer or the amount of available disk space in a virtual-memory system. Often, the limits are much smaller because the computer's available memory must be shared among many users.
- If no memory is available, an `OutOfMemoryError` is thrown.
- A linked list is accessed via a reference to the first node of the list. Each subsequent node is accessed via the link-reference member stored in the previous node.
- By convention, the link reference in the last node of a list is set to `null` to mark the end of the list.
- A node can contain data of any type, including objects of other classes.
- A linked list is appropriate when the number of data elements to be stored is unpredictable. Linked lists are dynamic, so the length of a list can increase or decrease as necessary.
- The size of a "conventional" Java array cannot be altered—it is fixed at creation time.
- Linked lists can be maintained in sorted order simply by inserting each new element at the proper point in the list.
- List nodes normally are not stored contiguously in memory. Rather, they are logically contiguous.
- A stack is a last-in, first-out (LIFO) data structure. The primary methods used to manipulate a stack are `push` and `pop`. Method `push` adds a new node to the top of the stack. Method `pop` removes a node from the top of the stack and returns the `data` object from the popped node.
- Stacks have many interesting applications. When a method call is made, the called method must know how to return to its caller, so the return address is pushed onto the program execution stack. If a series of method calls occurs, the successive return values are pushed onto the stack in last-in, first-out order so that each method can return to its caller. The program execution stack contains the space created for local variables on each invocation of a method. When the method returns to its caller, the space for that method's local variables is popped off the stack, and those variables are no longer available to the program.

- Stacks are used by compilers to evaluate arithmetic expressions and generate machine-language code to process the expressions.
- The technique of implementing each stack method as a call to a `List` method is called delegation—the stack method invoked delegates the call to the appropriate `List` method.
- A queue is similar to a checkout line in a supermarket—the first person in line is serviced first, and other customers enter the line only at the end and wait to be serviced.
- Queue nodes are removed only from the head of the queue and are inserted only at the tail. For this reason, a queue is referred to as a first-in, first-out (FIFO) data structure.
- The insert and remove operations for a queue are known as enqueue and dequeue.
- Queues have many uses in computer systems. Most computers have only a single processor, so only one application at a time can be serviced. Entries for the other applications are placed in a queue. The entry at the front of the queue is the next to receive service. Each entry gradually advances to the front of the queue as applications receive service.
- A tree is a nonlinear, two-dimensional data structure. Tree nodes contain two or more links.
- A binary tree is a tree whose nodes all contain two links. The root node is the first node in a tree.
- Each link in the root node refers to a child. The left child is the first node in the left subtree, and the right child is the first node in the right subtree.
- The children of a node are called siblings. A node with no children is called a leaf node.
- A binary search tree (with no duplicate node values) has the characteristic that the values in any left subtree are less than the value in the subtree's parent node, and the values in any right subtree are greater than the value in the subtree's parent node. A node can be inserted only as a leaf node in a binary search tree.
- An inorder traversal of a binary search tree processes the node values in ascending order.
- In a preorder traversal, the value in each node is processed as the node is visited. Then the values in the left subtree are processed, and then the values in the right subtree.
- In a postorder traversal, the value in each node is processed after the values of its children.
- The binary search tree facilitates duplicate elimination. As the tree is created, attempts to insert a duplicate value are recognized, because a duplicate follows the same "go left" or "go right" decisions on each comparison as the original value did. Thus, the duplicate eventually is compared with a node containing the same value. The duplicate value can be discarded at this point.
- Searching a binary tree for a value that matches a key value is also fast, especially for tightly packed trees. In a tightly packed tree, each level contains about twice as many elements as the previous one. So a tightly packed binary search tree with n elements has $\log_2 n$ levels, and thus at most $\log_2 n$ comparisons would have to be made either to find a match or to determine that no match exists. Searching a (tightly packed) 1000-element binary search tree requires at most 10 comparisons, because $2^{10} > 1000$. Searching a (tightly packed) 1,000,000-element binary search tree requires at most 20 comparisons, because $2^{20} > 1,000,000$.

Terminology

dequeue
Double class
duplicate elimination
dynamic data structure
enqueue
FIFO (first-in, first-out)
Float class
head of a queue
inorder traversal of a binary tree
insert a node
Integer class
leaf node
left child
left subtree
level-order traversal of a binary tree
LIFO (last-in, first-out)
linear data structure
linked list
Long class
node
nonlinear data structure
null reference
OutOfMemoryError
packed tree

parent node
pop
postorder traversal of a binary tree
predicate method
preorder traversal of a binary tree
program execution stack
push
queue
recursive tree traversal algorithms
right child
right subtree
root node
self-referential class
Short class
stack
subtree
tail of a queue
top of a stack
traversal
tree
type-wrapper classes
unboxing conversion
visiting a node

Self-Review Exercises

17.1 Fill in the blanks in each of the following statements:

a) A self-_____ class is used to form dynamic data structures that can grow and shrink at execution time.

b) A(n) _____ is a constrained version of a linked list in which nodes can be inserted and deleted only from the start of the list.

c) A method that does not alter a linked list, but simply looks at it to determine whether it is empty, is referred to as a(n) _____ method.

d) A queue is referred to as a(n) _____ data structure because the first nodes inserted are the first ones removed.

e) The reference to the next node in a linked list is referred to as a(n) _____.

f) Automatically reclaiming dynamically allocated memory in Java is called _____.

g) A(n) _____ is a constrained version of a linked list in which nodes can be inserted only at the end of the list and deleted only from the start of the list.

h) A(n) _____ is a nonlinear, two-dimensional data structure that contains nodes with two or more links.

i) A stack is referred to as a(n) _____ data structure because the last node inserted is the first node removed.

j) The nodes of a(n) _____ tree contain two link members.

k) The first node of a tree is the _____ node.

l) Each link in a tree node refers to a(n) _____ or _____ of that node.

m) A tree node that has no children is called a(n) _____ node.

n) The three traversal algorithms we mentioned in the text for binary search trees are _____, _____ and _____.

   o) Assuming that `myArray` contains references to `Double` objects, _____ occurs when the statement `"double number = myArray[ 0 ];"` executes.

   p) Assuming that `myArray` contains references to `Double` objects, _____ occurs when the statement `"myArray[ 0 ] = 1.25;"` executes.

17.2 What are the differences between a linked list and a stack?

17.3 What are the differences between a stack and a queue?

17.4 Perhaps a more appropriate title for this chapter would have been "Reusable Data Structures." Comment on how each of the following entities or concepts contributes to the reusability of data structures:

   a) classes
   b) inheritance
   c) composition

17.5 Manually provide the inorder, preorder and postorder traversals of the binary search tree of Fig. 17.20.

Answers to Self-Review Exercises

17.1 a) referential. b) stack. c) predicate. d) first-in, first-out (FIFO). e) link. f) garbage collection. g) queue. h) tree i) last-in, first-out (LIFO). j) binary. k) root. l) child or subtree. m) leaf. n) inorder, preorder, postorder. o) auto-unboxing. p) autoboxing.

17.2 It is possible to insert a node anywhere in a linked list and remove a node from anywhere in a linked list. Nodes in a stack may be inserted only at the top of the stack and removed only from the top.

17.3 A queue is a FIFO data structure that has references to both its head and its tail, so that nodes may be inserted at the tail and deleted from the head. A stack is a LIFO data structure that has a single reference to the top of the stack, where both insertion and deletion of nodes are performed.

17.4 a) Classes allow us to instantiate as many data structure objects of a certain type (i.e., class) as we wish.

   b) Inheritance enables a subclass to reuse the functionality from a superclass. Public methods of a superclass can be accessed through a subclass to eliminate duplicate logic.

   c) Composition enables a class to reuse code by storing an instance of another class in a field. Public methods of the member class can be called by methods in the composite class.

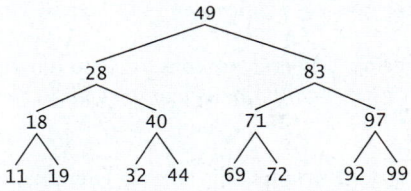

Fig. 17.20 | Binary search tree with 15 nodes.

17.5 The inorder traversal is

     11 18 19 28 32 40 44 49 69 71 72 83 92 97 99

The preorder traversal is

     49 28 18 11 19 40 32 44 83 71 69 72 97 92 99

The postorder traversal is

     11 19 18 32 44 40 28 69 72 71 92 99 97 83 49

Exercises

17.6 Write a program that concatenates two linked-list objects of characters. Class `ListConcat-enate` should include a method `concatenate` that takes references to both list objects as arguments and concatenates the second list to the first list.

17.7 Write a program that merges two ordered-list objects of integers into a single ordered-list object of integers. Method `merge` of class `ListMerge` should receive references to each of the list objects to be merged and return a reference to the merged list object.

17.8 Write a program that inserts 25 random integers from 0 to 100 in order into a linked-list object. The program should calculate the sum of the elements and the floating-point average of the elements.

17.9 Write a program that creates a linked-list object of 10 characters, then creates a second list object containing a copy of the first list, but in reverse order.

17.10 Write a program that inputs a line of text and uses a stack object to print the words of the line in reverse order.

17.11 Write a program that uses a stack to determine whether a string is a palindrome (i.e., the string is spelled identically backward and forward). The program should ignore spaces and punctuation.

17.12 Stacks are used by compilers to help in the process of evaluating expressions and generating machine-language code. In this and the next exercise, we investigate how compilers evaluate arithmetic expressions consisting only of constants, operators and parentheses.

Humans generally write expressions like 3 + 4 and 7 / 9 in which the operator (+ or / here) is written between its operands—this is called *infix notation*. Computers "prefer" *postfix notation*, in which the operator is written to the right of its two operands. The preceding infix expressions would appear in postfix notation as 3 4 + and 7 9 /, respectively.

To evaluate a complex infix expression, a compiler would first convert the expression to postfix notation and evaluate the postfix version. Each of these algorithms requires only a single left-to-right pass of the expression. Each algorithm uses a stack object in support of its operation, but each uses the stack for a different purpose.

In this exercise, you will write a Java version of the infix-to-postfix conversion algorithm. In the next exercise, you will write a Java version of the postfix expression evaluation algorithm. In a later exercise, you will discover that code you write in this exercise can help you implement a complete working compiler.

Write class `InfixToPostfixConverter` to convert an ordinary infix arithmetic expression (assume a valid expression is entered) with single-digit integers such as

    (6 + 2) * 5 - 8 / 4

to a postfix expression. The postfix version of the preceding infix expression is (note that no parentheses are needed)

    6 2 + 5 * 8 4 / -

The program should read the expression into StringBuffer infix and use one of the stack classes implemented in this chapter to help create the postfix expression in StringBuffer postfix. The algorithm for creating a postfix expression is as follows:

a) Push a left parenthesis '(' on the stack.

b) Append a right parenthesis ')' to the end of infix.

c) While the stack is not empty, read infix from left to right and do the following:

If the current character in infix is a digit, append it to postfix.

If the current character in infix is a left parenthesis, push it onto the stack.

If the current character in infix is an operator:

Pop operators (if there are any) at the top of the stack while they have equal or higher precedence than the current operator, and append the popped operators to postfix.

Push the current character in infix onto the stack.

If the current character in infix is a right parenthesis:

Pop operators from the top of the stack and append them to postfix until a left parenthesis is at the top of the stack.

Pop (and discard) the left parenthesis from the stack.

The following arithmetic operations are allowed in an expression:

+   addition

-   subtraction

*   multiplication

/   division

^   exponentiation

%   remainder

The stack should be maintained with stack nodes that each contain an instance variable and a reference to the next stack node. Some of the methods you may want to provide are as follows:

a) Method convertToPostfix, which converts the infix expression to postfix notation.

b) Method isOperator, which determines whether c is an operator.

c) Method precedence, which determines whether the precedence of operator1 (from the infix expression) is less than, equal to or greater than the precedence of operator2 (from the stack). The method returns true if operator1 has lower precedence than operator2. Otherwise, false is returned.

d) Method stackTop (this should be added to the stack class), which returns the top value of the stack without popping the stack.

17.13 Write class PostfixEvaluator, which evaluates a postfix expression such as

6 2 + 5 * 8 4 / -

The program should read a postfix expression consisting of digits and operators into a String-Buffer. Using modified versions of the stack methods implemented earlier in this chapter, the program should scan the expression and evaluate it (assume it is valid). The algorithm is as follows:

a) Append a right parenthesis ')' to the end of the postfix expression. When the right-parenthesis character is encountered, no further processing is necessary.

b) When the right-parenthesis character has not been encountered, read the expression from left to right.

If the current character is a digit, do the following:

Push its integer value on the stack (the integer value of a digit character is its value in the computer's character set minus the value of '0' in Unicode).

Otherwise, if the current character is an *operator*:

Pop the two top elements of the stack into variables x and y.

Calculate y *operator* x.

Push the result of the calculation onto the stack.

c) When the right parenthesis is encountered in the expression, pop the top value of the stack. This is the result of the postfix expression.

[*Note:* In b) above (based on the sample expression at the beginning of this exercise), if the operator is '/', the top of the stack is 2 and the next element in the stack is 8, then pop 2 into x, pop 8 into y, evaluate 8 / 2 and push the result, 4, back on the stack. This note also applies to operator '-'.] The arithmetic operations allowed in an expression are:

+   addition
-    subtraction
*   multiplication
/   division
^   exponentiation
%   remainder

The stack should be maintained with one of the stack classes introduced in this chapter. You may want to provide the following methods:

a) Method `evaluatePostfixExpression`, which evaluates the postfix expression.
b) Method `calculate`, which evaluates the expression op1 operator op2.
c) Method `push`, which pushes a value onto the stack.
d) Method `pop`, which pops a value off the stack.
e) Method `isEmpty`, which determines whether the stack is empty.
f) Method `printStack`, which prints the stack.

17.14 Modify the postfix evaluator program of Exercise 17.13 so that it can process integer operands larger than 9.

17.15 *(Supermarket Simulation)* Write a program that simulates a checkout line at a supermarket. The line is a queue object. Customers (i.e., customer objects) arrive in random integer intervals of from 1 to 4 minutes. Also, each customer is serviced in random integer intervals of from 1 to 4 minutes. Obviously, the rates need to be balanced. If the average arrival rate is larger than the average service rate, the queue will grow infinitely. Even with "balanced" rates, randomness can still cause long lines. Run the supermarket simulation for a 12-hour day (720 minutes), using the following algorithm:

a) Choose a random integer between 1 and 4 to determine the minute at which the first customer arrives.
b) At the first customer's arrival time, do the following:
     Determine customer's service time (random integer from 1 to 4).
     Begin servicing the customer.
     Schedule arrival time of next customer (random integer 1 to 4 added to the current time).
c) For each minute of the day, consider the following:
     If the next customer arrives, proceed as follows:
         Say so.
         Enqueue the customer.
         Schedule the arrival time of the next customer.
     If service was completed for the last customer, do the following:
         Say so.
         Dequeue next customer to be serviced.
         Determine customer's service completion time (random integer from 1 to 4 added to the current time).

Now run your simulation for 720 minutes and answer each of the following:

a) What is the maximum number of customers in the queue at any time?
b) What is the longest wait any one customer experiences?
c) What happens if the arrival interval is changed from 1 to 4 minutes to 1 to 3 minutes?

17.16 Modify Fig. 17.17 and Fig. 17.18 to allow the binary tree to contain duplicates.

17.17 Write a program based on the program of Fig. 17.17 and Fig. 17.18 that inputs a line of text, tokenizes the sentence into separate words (you might want to use the `StreamTokenizer` class from the `java.io` package), inserts the words in a binary search tree and prints the inorder, preorder and postorder traversals of the tree.

17.18 In this chapter, we saw that duplicate elimination is straightforward when creating a binary search tree. Describe how you would perform duplicate elimination when using only a one-dimensional array. Compare the performance of array-based duplicate elimination with the performance of binary-search-tree-based duplicate elimination.

17.19 Write a method `depth` that receives a binary tree and determines how many levels it has.

17.20 (*Recursively Print a List Backward*) Write a method `printListBackward` that recursively outputs the items in a linked list object in reverse order. Write a test program that creates a sorted list of integers and prints the list in reverse order.

17.21 (*Recursively Search a List*) Write a method `searchList` that recursively searches a linked list object for a specified value. Method `searchList` should return a reference to the value if it is found; otherwise, `null` should be returned. Use your method in a test program that creates a list of integers. The program should prompt the user for a value to locate in the list.

17.22 (*Binary Tree Delete*) In this exercise, we discuss deleting items from binary search trees. The deletion algorithm is not as straightforward as the insertion algorithm. Three cases are encountered when deleting an item—the item is contained in a leaf node (i.e., it has no children), the item is contained in a node that has one child or the item is contained in a node that has two children.

If the item to be deleted is contained in a leaf node, the node is deleted and the reference in the parent node is set to null.

If the item to be deleted is contained in a node with one child, the reference in the parent node is set to reference the child node and the node containing the data item is deleted. This causes the child node to take the place of the deleted node in the tree.

The last case is the most difficult. When a node with two children is deleted, another node in the tree must take its place. However, the reference in the parent node cannot simply be assigned to reference one of the children of the node to be deleted. In most cases, the resulting binary search tree would not embody the following characteristic of binary search trees (with no duplicate values): *The values in any left subtree are less than the value in the parent node, and the values in any right subtree are greater than the value in the parent node.*

Which node is used as a *replacement node* to maintain this characteristic? It is either the node containing the largest value in the tree less than the value in the node being deleted, or the node containing the smallest value in the tree greater than the value in the node being deleted. Let us consider the node with the smaller value. In a binary search tree, the largest value less than a parent's value is located in the left subtree of the parent node and is guaranteed to be contained in the rightmost node of the subtree. This node is located by walking down the left subtree to the right until the reference to the right child of the current node is null. We are now referencing the replacement node, which is either a leaf node or a node with one child to its left. If the replacement node is a leaf node, the steps to perform the deletion are as follows:

a) Store the reference to the node to be deleted in a temporary reference variable.

b) Set the reference in the parent of the node being deleted to reference the replacement node.

c) Set the reference in the parent of the replacement node to `null`.

d) Set the reference to the right subtree in the replacement node to reference the right subtree of the node to be deleted.

e) Set the reference to the left subtree in the replacement node to reference the left subtree of the node to be deleted.

The deletion steps for a replacement node with a left child are similar to those for a replacement node with no children, but the algorithm also must move the child into the replacement node's position in the tree. If the replacement node is a node with a left child, the steps to perform the deletion are as follows:

a) Store the reference to the node to be deleted in a temporary reference variable.

b) Set the reference in the parent of the node being deleted to reference the replacement node.

c) Set the reference in the parent of the replacement node reference to the left child of the replacement node.

d) Set the reference to the right subtree in the replacement node reference to the right subtree of the node to be deleted.

e) Set the reference to the left subtree in the replacement node to reference the left subtree of the node to be deleted.

Write method `deleteNode`, which takes as its argument the value to delete. Method `deleteNode` should locate in the tree the node containing the value to delete and use the algorithms discussed here to delete the node. If the value is not found in the tree, the method should print a message that indicates whether the value is deleted. Modify the program of Fig. 17.17 and Fig. 17.18 to use this method. After deleting an item, call the methods `inorderTraversal`, `preorderTraversal` and `postorderTraversal` to confirm that the delete operation was performed correctly.

17.23 (*Binary Tree Search*) Write method `binaryTreeSearch`, which attempts to locate a specified value in a binary search tree object. The method should take as an argument a search key to be located. If the node containing the search key is found, the method should return a reference to that node; otherwise, it should return a null reference.

17.24 (*Level-Order Binary Tree Traversal*) The program of Fig. 17.17 and Fig. 17.18 illustrated three recursive methods of traversing a binary tree—inorder, preorder and postorder traversals. This exercise presents the *level-order traversal* of a binary tree, in which the node values are printed level-by-level, starting at the root node level. The nodes on each level are printed from left to right. The level-order traversal is not a recursive algorithm. It uses a queue object to control the output of the nodes. The algorithm is as follows:

a) Insert the root node in the queue.

b) While there are nodes left in the queue, do the following:

   Get the next node in the queue.

   Print the node's value.

   If the reference to the left child of the node is not null:

      Insert the left child node in the queue.

   If the reference to the right child of the node is not null:

      Insert the right child node in the queue.

Write method `levelOrder` to perform a level-order traversal of a binary tree object. Modify the program of Fig. 17.17 and Fig. 17.18 to use this method. [*Note:* You will also need to use queue-processing methods of Fig. 17.13 in this program.]

17.25 (*Printing Trees*) Write a recursive method `outputTree` to display a binary tree object on the screen. The method should output the tree row by row, with the top of the tree at the left of the screen and the bottom of the tree toward the right of the screen. Each row is output vertically. For example, the binary tree illustrated in Fig. 17.20 is output as shown in Fig. 17.21.

Note that the rightmost leaf node appears at the top of the output in the rightmost column and the root node appears at the left of the output. Each column of output starts five spaces to the right of the preceding column. Method `outputTree` should receive an argument `totalSpaces` representing the number of spaces preceding the value to be output. (This variable should start at zero so that the root node is output at the left of the screen.) The method uses a modified inorder tra-

Fig. 17.21 | Sample output of recursive method `outputTree`.

versal to output the tree—it starts at the rightmost node in the tree and works back to the left. The algorithm is as follows:

> While the reference to the current node is not null, perform the following:
> Recursively call `outputTree` with the right subtree of the current node and
> `totalSpaces + 5`.
> Use a `for` statement to count from 1 to `totalSpaces` and output spaces.
> Output the value in the current node.
> Set the reference to the current node to refer to the left subtree of the current node.
> Increment `totalSpaces` by 5.

Special Section: Building Your Own Compiler

In Exercise 7.34 and Exercise 7.35, we introduced Simpletron Machine Language (SML), and you implemented a Simpletron computer simulator to execute programs written in SML. In this section, we build a compiler that converts programs written in a high-level programming language to SML. This section "ties" together the entire programming process. You will write programs in this new high-level language, compile them on the compiler you build and run them on the simulator you built in Exercise 7.35. You should make every effort to implement your compiler in an object-oriented manner.

17.26 (*The Simple Language*) Before we begin building the compiler, we discuss a simple, yet powerful high-level language similar to early versions of the popular language BASIC. We call the language *Simple*. Every Simple *statement* consists of a *line number* and a Simple *instruction*. Line numbers must appear in ascending order. Each instruction begins with one of the following Simple *commands*: rem, input, let, print, goto, if/goto or end (see Fig. 17.22). All commands except end can be used repeatedly. Simple evaluates only integer expressions using the +, -, * and / operators. These operators have the same precedence as in Java. Parentheses can be used to change the order of evaluation of an expression.

    Our Simple compiler recognizes only lowercase letters. All characters in a Simple file should be lowercase. (Uppercase letters result in a syntax error unless they appear in a rem statement, in which case they are ignored.) A *variable name* is a single letter. Simple does not allow descriptive variable names, so variables should be explained in remarks to indicate their use in a program. Simple uses only integer variables. Simple does not have variable declarations—merely mentioning a variable name in a program causes the variable to be declared and initialized to zero. The syntax of

Command	Example statement	Description
rem	50 rem this is a remark	Any text following the command rem is for documentation purposes only and is ignored by the compiler.
input	30 input x	Display a question mark to prompt the user to enter an integer. Read that integer from the keyboard and store the integer in x.
let	80 let u = 4 * (j - 56)	Assign u the value of 4 * (j - 56). Note that an arbitrarily complex expression can appear to the right of the equal sign.
print	10 print w	Display the value of w.
goto	70 goto 45	Transfer program control to line 45.
if/goto	35 if i == z goto 80	Compare i and z for equality and transfer program control to line 80 if the condition is true; otherwise, continue execution with the next statement.
end	99 end	Terminate program execution.

Fig. 17.22 | Simple commands.

Simple does not allow string manipulation (reading a string, writing a string, comparing strings, etc.). If a string is encountered in a Simple program (after a command other than rem), the compiler generates a syntax error. The first version of our compiler assumes that Simple programs are entered correctly. Exercise 17.29 asks the reader to modify the compiler to perform syntax error checking.

Simple uses the conditional if/goto and unconditional goto statements to alter the flow of control during program execution. If the condition in the if/goto statement is true, control is transferred to a specific line of the program. The following relational and equality operators are valid in an if/goto statement: <, >, <=, >=, == or !=. The precedence of these operators is the same as in Java.

Let us now consider several programs that demonstrate Simple's features. The first program (Fig. 17.23) reads two integers from the keyboard, stores the values in variables a and b and computes and prints their sum (stored in variable c).

The program of Fig. 17.24 determines and prints the larger of two integers. The integers are input from the keyboard and stored in s and t. The if/goto statement tests the condition s >= t. If the condition is true, control is transferred to line 90 and s is output; otherwise, t is output and control is transferred to the end statement in line 99, where the program terminates.

Simple does not provide a repetition statement (such as Java's for, while or do...while). However, Simple can simulate each of Java's repetition statements by using the if/goto and goto statements. Figure 17.25 uses a sentinel-controlled loop to calculate the squares of several integers. Each integer is input from the keyboard and stored in variable j. If the value entered is the sentinel value -9999, control is transferred to line 99, where the program terminates. Otherwise, k is assigned the square of j, k is output to the screen and control is passed to line 20, where the next integer is input.

```
 1    10 rem     determine and print the sum of two integers
 2    15 rem
 3    20 rem     input the two integers
 4    30 input a
 5    40 input b
 6    45 rem
 7    50 rem     add integers and store result in c
 8    60 let c = a + b
 9    65 rem
10    70 rem     print the result
11    80 print c
12    90 rem     terminate program execution
13    99 end
```

Fig. 17.23 | Simple program that determines the sum of two integers.

```
 1    10 rem     determine and print the larger of two integers
 2    20 input s
 3    30 input t
 4    32 rem
 5    35 rem     test if s >= t
 6    40 if s >= t goto 90
 7    45 rem
 8    50 rem     t is greater than s, so print t
 9    60 print t
10    70 goto 99
11    75 rem
12    80 rem     s is greater than or equal to t, so print s
13    90 print s
14    99 end
```

Fig. 17.24 | Simple program that finds the larger of two integers.

```
 1    10 rem     calculate the squares of several integers
 2    20 input j
 3    23 rem
 4    25 rem     test for sentinel value
 5    30 if j == -9999 goto 99
 6    33 rem
 7    35 rem     calculate square of j and assign result to k
 8    40 let k = j * j
 9    50 print k
10    53 rem
11    55 rem     loop to get next j
12    60 goto 20
13    99 end
```

Fig. 17.25 | Calculate the squares of several integers.

Using the sample programs of Fig. 17.23–Fig. 17.25 as your guide, write a Simple program to accomplish each of the following:

    a) Input three integers, determine their average and print the result.

b) Use a sentinel-controlled loop to input 10 integers and compute and print their sum.
c) Use a counter-controlled loop to input 7 integers, some positive and some negative, and compute and print their average.
d) Input a series of integers and determine and print the largest. The first integer input indicates how many numbers should be processed.
e) Input 10 integers and print the smallest.
f) Calculate and print the sum of the even integers from 2 to 30.
g) Calculate and print the product of the odd integers from 1 to 9.

17.27   (*Building A Compiler. Prerequisites: Complete Exercise 7.34, Exercise 7.35, Exercise 17.12, Exercise 17.13 and Exercise 17.26*) Now that the Simple language has been presented (Exercise 17.26), we discuss how to build a Simple compiler. First, we consider the process by which a Simple program is converted to SML and executed by the Simpletron simulator (see Fig. 17.26). A file containing a Simple program is read by the compiler and converted to SML code. The SML code is output to a file on disk, in which SML instructions appear one per line. The SML file is then loaded into the Simpletron simulator, and the results are sent to a file on disk and to the screen. Note that the Simpletron program developed in Exercise 7.35 took its input from the keyboard. It must be modified to read from a file so it can run the programs produced by our compiler.

The Simple compiler performs two *passes* of the Simple program to convert it to SML. The first pass constructs a *symbol table* (object) in which every *line number* (object), *variable name* (object) and *constant* (object) of the Simple program is stored with its type and corresponding location in the final SML code (the symbol table is discussed in detail below). The first pass also produces the corresponding SML instruction object(s) for each of the Simple statements (object, etc.). If the Simple program contains statements that transfer control to a line later in the program, the first pass results in an SML program containing some "unfinished" instructions. The second pass of the compiler locates and completes the unfinished instructions and outputs the SML program to a file.

First Pass

The compiler begins by reading one statement of the Simple program into memory. The line must be separated into its individual *tokens* (i.e., "pieces" of a statement) for processing and compilation. (The StreamTokenizer class from the java.io package can be used.) Recall that every statement begins with a line number followed by a command. As the compiler breaks a statement into tokens, if the token is a line number, a variable or a constant, it is placed in the symbol table. A line number is placed in the symbol table only if it is the first token in a statement. The symbolTable object is an array of tableEntry objects representing each symbol in the program. There is no restriction on the number of symbols that can appear in the program. Therefore, the symbolTable for a particular program could be large. Make it a 100-element array for now. You can increase or decrease its size once the program is working.

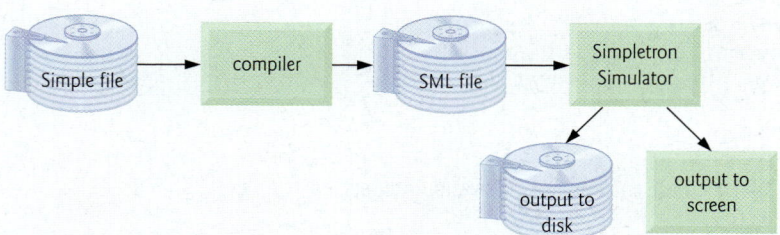

Fig. 17.26 | Writing, compiling and executing a Simple language program.

Each `tableEntry` object contains three fields. Field `symbol` is an integer containing the Unicode representation of a variable (remember that variable names are single characters), a line number or a constant. Field `type` is one of the following characters indicating the symbol's type: `'C'` for constant, `'L'` for line number or `'V'` for variable. Field `location` contains the Simpletron memory location (00 to 99) to which the symbol refers. Simpletron memory is an array of 100 integers in which SML instructions and data are stored. For a line number, the location is the element in the Simpletron memory array at which the SML instructions for the Simple statement begin. For a variable or constant, the location is the element in the Simpletron memory array in which the variable or constant is stored. Variables and constants are allocated from the end of Simpletron's memory backward. The first variable or constant is stored at location 99, the next at location 98, etc.

The symbol table plays an integral part in converting Simple programs to SML. We learned in Chapter 7 that an SML instruction is a four-digit integer comprised of two parts—the *operation code* and the *operand*. The operation code is determined by commands in Simple. For example, the simple command `input` corresponds to SML operation code 10 (read), and the Simple command `print` corresponds to SML operation code 11 (write). The operand is a memory location containing the data on which the operation code performs its task (e.g., operation code 10 reads a value from the keyboard and stores it in the memory location specified by the operand). The compiler searches `symbolTable` to determine the Simpletron memory location for each symbol, so the corresponding location can be used to complete the SML instructions.

The compilation of each Simple statement is based on its command. For example, after the line number in a `rem` statement is inserted in the symbol table, the remainder of the statement is ignored by the compiler, because a remark is for documentation purposes only. The `input`, `print`, `goto` and `end` statements correspond to the SML *read, write, branch* (to a specific location) and *halt* instructions. Statements containing these Simple commands are converted directly to SML. (*Note:* A `goto` statement may contain an unresolved reference if the specified line number refers to a statement further into the Simple program file; this is sometimes called a forward reference.)

When a `goto` statement is compiled with an unresolved reference, the SML instruction must be *flagged* to indicate that the second pass of the compiler must complete the instruction. The flags are stored in a 100-element array `flags` of type `int` in which each element is initialized to -1. If the memory location to which a line number in the Simple program refers is not yet known (i.e., it is not in the symbol table), the line number is stored in array `flags` in the element with the same index as the incomplete instruction. The operand of the incomplete instruction is set to 00 temporarily. For example, an unconditional branch instruction (making a forward reference) is left as +4000 until the second pass of the compiler. The second pass will be described shortly.

Compilation of `if/goto` and `let` statements is more complicated than for other statements— they are the only statements that produce more than one SML instruction. For an `if/goto` statement, the compiler produces code to test the condition and to branch to another line if necessary. The result of the branch could be an unresolved reference. Each of the relational and equality operators can be simulated by using SML's *branch zero* and *branch negative* instructions (or possibly a combination of both).

For a `let` statement, the compiler produces code to evaluate an arbitrarily complex arithmetic expression consisting of integer variables and/or constants. Expressions should separate each operand and operator with spaces. Exercise 17.12 and Exercise 17.13 presented the infix-to-postfix conversion algorithm and the postfix evaluation algorithm used by compilers to evaluate expressions. Before proceeding with your compiler, you should complete each of these exercises. When a compiler encounters an expression, it converts the expression from infix notation to postfix notation, then evaluates the postfix expression.

How is it that the compiler produces the machine language to evaluate an expression containing variables? The postfix evaluation algorithm contains a "hook" where the compiler can generate SML instructions rather than actually evaluating the expression. To enable this "hook" in the compiler, the postfix evaluation algorithm must be modified to search the symbol table for each symbol it encounters (and possibly insert it), determine the symbol's corresponding memory location and *push the memory location (instead of the symbol) onto the stack.* When an operator is encountered in the postfix expression, the two memory locations at the top of the stack are popped, and machine language for effecting the operation is produced by using the memory locations as operands. The result of each subexpression is stored in a temporary location in memory and pushed back onto the stack so the evaluation of the postfix expression can continue. When postfix evaluation is complete, the memory location containing the result is the only location left on the stack. This is popped, and SML instructions are generated to assign the result to the variable at the left of the `let` statement.

Second Pass

The second pass of the compiler performs two tasks: Resolve any unresolved references and output the SML code to a file. Resolution of references occurs as follows:

  a) Search the `flags` array for an unresolved reference (i.e., an element with a value other than `-1`).
  b) Locate the object in array `symbolTable` containing the symbol stored in the `flags` array (be sure that the type of the symbol is `'L'` for line number).
  c) Insert the memory location from field `location` into the instruction with the unresolved reference (remember that an instruction containing an unresolved reference has operand `00`).
  d) Repeat *Steps (a), (b)* and *(c)* until the end of the `flags` array is reached.

After the resolution process is complete, the entire array containing the SML code is output to a disk file with one SML instruction per line. This file can be read by the Simpletron for execution (after the simulator is modified to read its input from a file). Compiling your first Simple program into an SML file and executing that file should give you a real sense of personal accomplishment.

A Complete Example

The following example illustrates the complete conversion of a Simple program to SML as it will be performed by the Simple compiler. Consider a Simple program that inputs an integer and sums the values from 1 to that integer. The program and the SML instructions produced by the first pass of the Simple compiler are illustrated in Fig. 17.27. The symbol table constructed by the first pass is shown in Fig. 17.28.

Most Simple statements convert directly to single SML instructions. The exceptions in this program are remarks, the `if/goto` statement in line 20 and the `let` statements. Remarks do not translate into machine language. However, the line number for a remark is placed in the symbol table in case the line number is referenced in a `goto` statement or an `if/goto` statement. Line 20 of the program specifies that, if the condition `y == x` is true, program control is transferred to line 60. Since line 60 appears later in the program, the first pass of the compiler has not as yet placed 60 in the symbol table. (Statement line numbers are placed in the symbol table only when they appear as the first token in a statement.) Therefore, it is not possible at this time to determine the operand of the SML *branch zero* instruction at location 03 in the array of SML instructions. The compiler places 60 in location 03 of the `flags` array to indicate that the second pass completes this instruction.

We must keep track of the next instruction location in the SML array because there is not a one-to-one correspondence between Simple statements and SML instructions. For example, the `if/goto` statement of line 20 compiles into three SML instructions. Each time an instruction is produced, we must increment the *instruction counter* to the next location in the SML array. Note that the size of Simpletron's memory could present a problem for Simple programs with many statements, variables and constants. It is conceivable that the compiler will run out of memory. To test for this case, your program should contain a *data counter* to keep track of the location at which the

Simple program	SML location and instruction	Description
5 rem sum 1 to x	*none*	rem ignored
10 input x	00 +1099	read x into location 99
15 rem check y == x	*none*	rem ignored
20 if y == x goto 60	01 +2098	load y (98) into accumulator
	02 +3199	sub x (99) from accumulator
	03 +4200	branch zero to unresolved location
25 rem increment y	*none*	rem ignored
30 let y = y + 1	04 +2098	load y into accumulator
	05 +3097	add 1 (97) to accumulator
	06 +2196	store in temporary location 96
	07 +2096	load from temporary location 96
	08 +2198	store accumulator in y
35 rem add y to total	*none*	rem ignored
40 let t = t + y	09 +2095	load t (95) into accumulator
	10 +3098	add y to accumulator
	11 +2194	store in temporary location 94
	12 +2094	load from temporary location 94
	13 +2195	store accumulator in t
45 rem loop y	*none*	rem ignored
50 goto 20	14 +4001	branch to location 01
55 rem output result	*none*	rem ignored
60 print t	15 +1195	output t to screen
99 end	16 +4300	terminate execution

Fig. 17.27 | SML instructions produced after the compiler's first pass.

next variable or constant will be stored in the SML array. If the value of the instruction counter is larger than the value of the data counter, the SML array is full. In this case, the compilation process should terminate, and the compiler should print an error message indicating that it ran out of memory during compilation. This serves to emphasize that, although the programmer is freed from the burdens of managing memory by the compiler, the compiler itself must carefully determine the placement of instructions and data in memory and must check for such errors as memory being exhausted during the compilation process.

A Step-by-Step View of the Compilation Process

Let us now walk through the compilation process for the Simple program in Fig. 17.27. The compiler reads the first line of the program

```
5 rem sum 1 to x
```

Symbol	Type	Location
5	L	00
10	L	00
'x'	V	99
15	L	01
20	L	01
'y'	V	98
25	L	04
30	L	04
1	C	97
35	L	09
40	L	09
't'	V	95
45	L	14
50	L	14
55	L	15
60	L	15
99	L	16

Fig. 17.28 | Symbol table for program of Fig. 17.27.

into memory. The first token in the statement (the line number) is determined using the String-Tokenizer class. (See Chapter 29 for a discussion of this class.) The token returned by the String-Tokenizer is converted to an integer by using static method Integer.parseInt(), so the symbol 5 can be located in the symbol table. If the symbol is not found, it is inserted in the symbol table.

We are at the beginning of the program and this is the first line, and no symbols are in the table yet. Therefore, 5 is inserted into the symbol table as type L (line number) and assigned the first location in the SML array (00). Although this line is a remark, a space in the symbol table is still allocated for the line number (in case it is referenced by a goto or an if/goto). No SML instruction is generated for a rem statement, so the instruction counter is not incremented.

```
10 input x
```

is tokenized next. The line number 10 is placed in the symbol table as type L and assigned the first location in the SML array (00 because a remark began the program, so the instruction counter is currently 00). The command input indicates that the next token is a variable (only a variable can appear in an input statement). input corresponds directly to an SML operation code; therefore, the compiler simply has to determine the location of x in the SML array. Symbol x is not found in the symbol table. So, it is inserted into the symbol table as the Unicode representation of x, given type V and assigned location 99 in the SML array (data storage begins at 99 and is allocated backward). SML code can now be generated for this statement. Operation code 10 (the SML read operation code) is multiplied by 100, and the location of x (as determined in the symbol table) is added to complete the instruction. The instruction is then stored in the SML array at location 00. The instruction counter is incremented by one, because a single SML instruction was produced.

The statement

```
15 rem    check y == x
```

is tokenized next. The symbol table is searched for line number 15 (which is not found). The line number is inserted as type L and assigned the next location in the array, 01. (Remember that rem statements do not produce code, so the instruction counter is not incremented.)

The statement

```
20 if y == x goto 60
```

is tokenized next. Line number 20 is inserted in the symbol table and given type L at the next location in the SML array 01. The command if indicates that a condition is to be evaluated. The variable y is not found in the symbol table, so it is inserted and given the type V and the SML location 98. Next, SML instructions are generated to evaluate the condition. There is no direct equivalent in SML for the if/goto; it must be simulated by performing a calculation using x and y and branching according to the result. If y is equal to x, the result of subtracting x from y is zero, so the *branch zero* instruction can be used with the result of the calculation to simulate the if/goto statement. The first step requires that y be loaded (from SML location 98) into the accumulator. This produces the instruction 01 +2098. Next, x is subtracted from the accumulator. This produces the instruction 02 +3199. The value in the accumulator may be zero, positive or negative. The operator is ==, so we want to *branch zero*. First, the symbol table is searched for the branch location (60 in this case), which is not found. So, 60 is placed in the flags array at location 03, and the instruction 03 +4200 is generated. (We cannot add the branch location because we have not yet assigned a location to line 60 in the SML array.) The instruction counter is incremented to 04.

The compiler proceeds to the statement

```
25 rem    increment y
```

The line number 25 is inserted in the symbol table as type L and assigned SML location 04. The instruction counter is not incremented.

When the statement

```
30 let y = y + 1
```

is tokenized, the line number 30 is inserted in the symbol table as type L and assigned SML location 04. Command let indicates that the line is an assignment statement. First, all the symbols on the line are inserted in the symbol table (if they are not already there). The integer 1 is added to the symbol table as type C and assigned SML location 97. Next, the right side of the assignment is converted from infix to postfix notation. Then the postfix expression (y 1 +) is evaluated. Symbol y is located in the symbol table, and its corresponding memory location is pushed onto the stack. Symbol 1 is also located in the symbol table, and its corresponding memory location is pushed onto the stack. When the operator + is encountered, the postfix evaluator pops the stack into the right operand of the operator and pops the stack again into the left operand of the operator, then produces the SML instructions

```
04 +2098    (load y)
05 +3097    (add 1)
```

The result of the expression is stored in a temporary location in memory (96) with instruction

```
06 +2196    (store temporary)
```

and the temporary location is pushed onto the stack. Now that the expression has been evaluated, the result must be stored in y (i.e., the variable on the left side of =). So, the temporary location is loaded into the accumulator and the accumulator is stored in y with the instructions

```
07 +2096    (load temporary)
08 +2198    (store y)
```

The reader should immediately notice that SML instructions appear to be redundant. We will discuss this issue shortly.

When the statement

```
35 rem   add y to total
```

is tokenized, line number 35 is inserted in the symbol table as type L and assigned location 09.

The statement

```
40 let t = t + y
```

is similar to line 30. The variable t is inserted in the symbol table as type V and assigned SML location 95. The instructions follow the same logic and format as line 30, and the instructions 09 +2095, 10 +3098, 11 +2194, 12 +2094 and 13 +2195 are generated. Note that the result of t + y is assigned to temporary location 94 before being assigned to t (95). Once again, the reader should note that the instructions in memory locations 11 and 12 appear to be redundant. Again, we will discuss this shortly.

The statement

```
45 rem   loop y
```

is a remark, so line 45 is added to the symbol table as type L and assigned SML location 14.

The statement

```
50 goto 20
```

transfers control to line 20. Line number 50 is inserted in the symbol table as type L and assigned SML location 14. The equivalent of goto in SML is the *unconditional branch* (40) instruction that transfers control to a specific SML location. The compiler searches the symbol table for line 20 and finds that it corresponds to SML location 01. The operation code (40) is multiplied by 100, and location 01 is added to it to produce the instruction 14 +4001.

The statement

```
55 rem   output result
```

is a remark, so line 55 is inserted in the symbol table as type L and assigned SML location 15.

The statement

```
60 print t
```

is an output statement. Line number 60 is inserted in the symbol table as type L and assigned SML location 15. The equivalent of print in SML is operation code 11 (*write*). The location of t is determined from the symbol table and added to the result of the operation code multiplied by 100.

The statement

```
99 end
```

is the final line of the program. Line number 99 is stored in the symbol table as type L and assigned SML location 16. The end command produces the SML instruction +4300 (43 is *halt* in SML), which is written as the final instruction in the SML memory array.

This completes the first pass of the compiler. We now consider the second pass. The flags array is searched for values other than -1. Location 03 contains 60, so the compiler knows that instruction 03 is incomplete. The compiler completes the instruction by searching the symbol table for 60, determining its location and adding the location to the incomplete instruction. In this case, the search determines that line 60 corresponds to SML location 15, so the completed instruction 03 +4215 is produced, replacing 03 +4200. The Simple program has now been compiled successfully.

To build the compiler, you will have to perform each of the following tasks:

a) Modify the Simpletron simulator program you wrote in Exercise 7.35 to take its input from a file specified by the user (see Chapter 14). The simulator should output its results to a disk file in the same format as the screen output. Convert the simulator to be an object-oriented program. In particular, make each part of the hardware an object. Arrange the instruction types into a class hierarchy using inheritance. Then execute the program polymorphically simply by telling each instruction to execute itself with an executeInstruction message.

b) Modify the infix-to-postfix evaluation algorithm of Exercise 17.12 to process multidigit integer operands and single-letter variable name operands. [*Hint:* Class StringTokenizer can be used to locate each constant and variable in an expression, and constants can be converted from strings to integers by using Integer class method parseInt.] [*Note:* The data representation of the postfix expression must be altered to support variable names and integer constants.]

c) Modify the postfix evaluation algorithm to process multidigit integer operands and variable name operands. Also, the algorithm should now implement the "hook" discussed earlier so that SML instructions are produced rather than directly evaluating the expression. [*Hint:* Class StringTokenizer can be used to locate each constant and variable in an expression, and constants can be converted from strings to integers by using Integer class method parseInt.] [*Note:* The data representation of the postfix expression must be altered to support variable names and integer constants.]

d) Build the compiler. Incorporate parts b) and c) for evaluating expressions in let statements. Your program should contain a method that performs the first pass of the compiler and a method that performs the second pass of the compiler. Both methods can call other methods to accomplish their tasks. Make your compiler as object oriented as possible.

17.28 (*Optimizing the Simple Compiler*) When a program is compiled and converted into SML, a set of instructions is generated. Certain combinations of instructions often repeat themselves, usually in triplets called *productions*. A production normally consists of three instructions, such as *load*, *add* and *store*. For example, Fig. 17.29 illustrates five of the SML instructions that were produced in the compilation of the program in Fig. 17.27. The first three instructions are the production that adds 1 to y. Note that instructions 06 and 07 store the accumulator value in temporary location 96, then load the value back into the accumulator so instruction 08 can store the value in location 98. Often a production is followed by a load instruction for the same location that was just stored. This code can be *optimized* by eliminating the store instruction and the subsequent load instruction that operate on the same memory location, thus enabling the Simpletron to execute the program faster. Figure 17.30 illustrates the optimized SML for the program of Fig. 17.27. Note that there are four fewer instructions in the optimized code—a memory-space savings of 25%.

17.29 (*Modifications to the Simple Compiler*) Perform the following modifications to the Simple compiler. Some of these modifications might also require modifications to the Simpletron simulator program written in Exercise 7.35.

a) Allow the remainder operator (%) to be used in let statements. Simpletron Machine Language must be modified to include a remainder instruction.

b) Allow exponentiation in a let statement using ^ as the exponentiation operator. Simpletron Machine Language must be modified to include an exponentiation instruction.

1	04	+2098	*(load)*
2	05	+3097	*(add)*
3	06	+2196	*(store)*
4	07	+2096	*(load)*
5	08	+2198	*(store)*

Fig. 17.29 | Unoptimized code from the program of Fig. 19.25.

Simple program	SML location and instruction		Description
5 rem sum 1 to x	*none*		rem ignored
10 input x	00	+1099	read x into location 99
15 rem check y == x	*none*		rem ignored
20 if y == x goto 60	01	+2098	load y (98) into accumulator
	02	+3199	sub x (99) from accumulator
	03	+4211	branch to location 11 if zero
25 rem increment y	*none*		rem ignored
30 let y = y + 1	04	+2098	load y into accumulator
	05	+3097	add 1 (97) to accumulator
	06	+2198	store accumulator in y (98)
35 rem add y to total	*none*		rem ignored
40 let t = t + y	07	+2096	load t from location (96)
	08	+3098	add y (98) accumulator
	09	+2196	store accumulator in t (96)
45 rem loop y	*none*		rem ignored
50 goto 20	10	+4001	branch to location 01
55 rem output result	*none*		rem ignored
60 print t	11	+1196	output t (96) to screen
99 end	12	+4300	terminate execution

Fig. 17.30 | Optimized code for the program of Fig. 17.27.

c) Allow the compiler to recognize uppercase and lowercase letters in Simple statements (e.g., 'A' is equivalent to 'a'). No modifications to the Simpletron simulator are required.

d) Allow input statements to read values for multiple variables such as input x, y. No modifications to the Simpletron simulator are required to perform this enhancement to the Simple compiler.

e) Allow the compiler to output multiple values from a single print statement, such as print a, b, c. No modifications to the Simpletron simulator are required to perform this enhancement.

f) Add syntax-checking capabilities to the compiler so error messages are output when syntax errors are encountered in a Simple program. No modifications to the Simpletron simulator are required.

g) Allow arrays of integers. No modifications to the Simpletron simulator are required to perform this enhancement.

h) Allow subroutines specified by the Simple commands gosub and return. Command gosub passes program control to a subroutine and command return passes control back to the statement after the gosub. This is similar to a method call in Java. The same subroutine can be called from many gosub commands distributed throughout a program. No modifications to the Simpletron simulator are required.

i)   Allow repetition statements of the form

```
for x = 2 to 10 step 2
    Simple statements
next
```

This for statement loops from 2 to 10 with an increment of 2. The next line marks the end of the body of the for line. No modifications to the Simpletron simulator are required.

j)   Allow repetition statements of the form

```
for x = 2 to 10
    Simple statements
next
```

This for statement loops from 2 to 10 with a default increment of 1. No modifications to the Simpletron simulator are required.

k)   Allow the compiler to process string input and output. This requires the Simpletron simulator to be modified to process and store string values. [*Hint:* Each Simpletron word (i.e., memory location) can be divided into two groups, each holding a two-digit integer. Each two-digit integer represents the Unicode decimal equivalent of a character. Add a machine-language instruction that will print a string beginning at a certain Simpletron memory location. The first half of the Simpletron word at that location is a count of the number of characters in the string (i.e., the length of the string). Each succeeding half word contains one Unicode character expressed as two decimal digits. The machine-language instruction checks the length and prints the string by translating each two-digit number into its equivalent character.]

l)   Allow the compiler to process floating-point values in addition to integers. The Simpletron Simulator must also be modified to process floating-point values.

17.30   (*A Simple Interpreter*) An interpreter is a program that reads a high-level language program statement, determines the operation to be performed by the statement and executes the operation immediately. The high-level language program is not converted into machine language first. Interpreters execute more slowly than compilers do, because each statement encountered in the program being interpreted must first be deciphered at execution time. If statements are contained in a loop, the statements are deciphered each time they are encountered in the loop. Early versions of the BASIC programming language were implemented as interpreters. Most Java programs are run interpretively.

Write an interpreter for the Simple language discussed in Exercise 17.26. The program should use the infix-to-postfix converter developed in Exercise 17.12 and the postfix evaluator developed in Exercise 17.13 to evaluate expressions in a let statement. The same restrictions placed on the Simple language in Exercise 17.26 should be adhered to in this program. Test the interpreter with the Simple programs written in Exercise 17.26. Compare the results of running these programs in the interpreter with the results of compiling the Simple programs and running them in the Simpletron simulator built in Exercise 7.35.

17.31   (*Insert/Delete Anywhere in a Linked List*) Our linked-list class allowed insertions and deletions at only the front and the back of the linked list. These capabilities were convenient for us when we used inheritance or composition to produce a stack class and a queue class with a minimal amount of code simply by reusing the list class. Linked lists are normally more general than those we provided. Modify the linked-list class we developed in this chapter to handle insertions and deletions anywhere in the list.

17.32   (*Lists and Queues without Tail References*) Our implementation of a linked list (Fig. 17.3) used both a firstNode and a lastNode. The lastNode was useful for the insertAtBack and remove-

FromBack methods of the List class. The insertAtBack method corresponds to the enqueue method of the Queue class.

Rewrite the List class so that it does not use a lastNode. Thus, any operations on the tail of a list must begin searching the list from the front. Does this affect our implementation of the Queue class (Fig. 17.13)?

17.33   *(Performance of Binary Tree Sorting and Searching)* One problem with the binary tree sort is that the order in which the data is inserted affects the shape of the tree—for the same collection of data, different orderings can yield binary trees of dramatically different shapes. The performance of the binary tree sorting and searching algorithms is sensitive to the shape of the binary tree. What shape would a binary tree have if its data were inserted in increasing order? in decreasing order? What shape should the tree have to achieve maximal searching performance?

17.34   *(Indexed Lists)* As presented in the text, linked lists must be searched sequentially. For large lists, this can result in poor performance. A common technique for improving list-searching performance is to create and maintain an index to the list. An index is a set of references to key places in the list. For example, an application that searches a large list of names could improve performance by creating an index with 26 entries—one for each letter of the alphabet. A search operation for a last name beginning with 'Y' would then first search the index to determine where the 'Y' entries begin, then "jump into" the list at that point and search linearly until the desired name is found. This would be much faster than searching the linked list from the beginning. Use the List class of Fig. 17.3 as the basis of an IndexedList class.

Write a program that demonstrates the operation of indexed lists. Be sure to include methods insertInIndexedList, searchIndexedList and deleteFromIndexedList.

17.35   In Section 17.7, we created a stack class from class List with inheritance (Fig. 17.10) and with composition (Fig. 17.12). In Section 17.8 we created a queue class from class List with composition (Fig. 17.13). Create a queue class by inheriting from class List. What are the differences between this class and the one we created with composition?

Generics

OBJECTIVES

In this chapter you will learn:

- To create generic methods that perform identical tasks on arguments of different types.
- To create a generic **Stack** class that can be used to store objects of any class or interface type.
- To understand how to overload generic methods with non-generic methods or with other generic methods.
- To understand raw types and how they help achieve backwards compatibility.
- To use wildcards when precise type information about a parameter is not required in the method body.
- The relationship between generics and inheritance.

18.1 Introduction

It would be nice if we could write a single sort method that could sort the elements in an Integer array, a String array or an array of any type that supports ordering (i.e., its elements can be compared). It would also be nice if we could write a single Stack class that could be used as a Stack of integers, a Stack of floating-point numbers, a Stack of Strings or a Stack of any other type. It would be even nicer if we could detect type mismatches at compile time—known as compile-time type safety. For example, if a Stack stores only integers, attempting to push a String on to that Stack should issue a compile-time error.

This chapter discusses one of J2SE 5.0's new features—generics—which provides the means to create the general models mentioned above. Generic methods and generic classes enable programmers to specify, with a single method declaration, a set of related methods or, with a single class declaration, a set of related types, respectively. Generics also provide compile-time type safety that allows programmers to catch invalid types at compile time.

We might write a generic method for sorting an array of objects, then invoke the generic method with Integer arrays, Double arrays, String arrays and so on, to sort the array elements. The compiler could perform type checking to ensure that the array passed to the sorting method contains same type elements. We might write a single generic Stack class that manipulates a stack of objects, then instantiate Stack objects for a stack of Integers, a stack of Doubles, a stack of Strings and so on. The compiler could perform type checking to ensure that the Stack stores elements of the same type.

Software Engineering Observation 18.1

Generic methods and classes are among Java's most powerful capabilities for software reuse with compile-time type safety.

This chapter presents generic method and generic class examples. It also considers the relationships between generics and other Java features, such as overloading and inheritance. Chapter 19, Collections, presents an in-depth treatment of the Java Collections Framework's generic methods and classes. A collection is a data structure that maintains references to many objects. The Java Collections Framework uses generics to allow programmers to specify the exact types of objects that a particular collection will store in a program.

18.2 Motivation for Generic Methods

Overloaded methods are often used to perform similar operations on different types of data. To motivate generic methods, let's begin with an example (Fig. 18.1) that contains three overloaded printArray methods (lines 7–14, lines 17–24 and lines 27–34). These methods print the string representations of the elements of an Integer array, a Double array and a Character array, respectively. Note that we could have used arrays of primitive types int, double and char in this example. We chose to use arrays of type Integer, Double and Character to set up our generic method example, because only reference types can be used with generic methods and classes.

```java
1   // Fig. 18.1: OverloadedMethods.java
2   // Using overloaded methods to print array of different types.
3
4   public class OverloadedMethods
5   {
6      // method printArray to print Integer array
7      public static void printArray( Integer[] inputArray )
8      {
9         // display array elements
10        for ( Integer element : inputArray )
11           System.out.printf( "%s ", element );
12
13        System.out.println();
14     } // end method printArray
15
16     // method printArray to print Double array
17     public static void printArray( Double[] inputArray )
18     {
19        // display array elements
20        for ( Double element : inputArray )
21           System.out.printf( "%s ", element );
22
23        System.out.println();
24     } // end method printArray
25
26     // method printArray to print Character array
27     public static void printArray( Character[] inputArray )
28     {
29        // display array elements
30        for ( Character element : inputArray )
31           System.out.printf( "%s ", element );
32
33        System.out.println();
34     } // end method printArray
35
36     public static void main( String args[] )
37     {
38        // create arrays of Integer, Double and Character
39        Integer[] integerArray = { 1, 2, 3, 4, 5, 6 };
40        Double[] doubleArray = { 1.1, 2.2, 3.3, 4.4, 5.5, 6.6, 7.7 };
```

Fig. 18.1 | Printing array elements using overloaded methods. (Part 1 of 2.)

```
41          Character[] characterArray = { 'H', 'E', 'L', 'L', 'O' };
42
43          System.out.println( "Array integerArray contains:" );
44          printArray( integerArray ); // pass an Integer array
45          System.out.println( "\nArray doubleArray contains:" );
46          printArray( doubleArray ); // pass a Double array
47          System.out.println( "\nArray characterArray contains:" );
48          printArray( characterArray ); // pass a Character array
49      } // end main
50  } // end class OverloadedMethods
```

```
Array integerArray contains:
1 2 3 4 5 6

Array doubleArray contains:
1.1 2.2 3.3 4.4 5.5 6.6 7.7

Array characterArray contains:
H E L L O
```

Fig. 18.1 | Printing array elements using overloaded methods. (Part 2 of 2.)

The program begins by declaring and initializing three arrays—six-element Integer array integerArray (line 39), seven-element Double array doubleArray (line 40) and five-element Character array characterArray (line 41). Then, lines 43–48 output the arrays.

When the compiler encounters a method call, it always attempts to locate a method declaration that has the same method name and parameters that match the argument types in the method call. In this example, each printArray call exactly matches one of the printArray method declarations. For example, line 44 calls printArray with integer-Array as its argument. At compile time, the compiler determines argument integer-Array's type (i.e., Integer[]) and attempts to locate a method named printArray that specifies a single Integer[] parameter (lines 7–14) and sets up a call to that method. Similarly, when the compiler encounters the printArray call at line 46, it determines argument doubleArray's type (i.e., Double[]), then attempts to locate a method named printArray that specifies a single Double[] parameter (lines 17–24) and sets up a call to that method. Finally, when the compiler encounters the printArray call at line 48, it determines argument characterArray's type (i.e., Character[]), then attempts to locate a method named printArray that specifies a single Character[] parameter (lines 27–34) and sets up a call to that method.

Study each printArray method. Note that the array element type appears in two locations in each method—the method header (lines 7, 17 and 27) and the for statement header (lines 10, 20 and 30). If we replace the element types in each method with a generic name—by convention we'll use E to represent the "element" type—then all three methods would look like the one in Fig. 18.2. It appears that if we can replace the array element type in each of the three methods with a single generic type, then we should be able to declare one print-Array method that can display the string representations of the elements of any array that contains objects. Note that the format specifier %s can be used to output any object's string representation—the object's toString method will be called implicitly. The method in Fig. 18.2 is similar to the generic printArray method declaration we discuss in Section 18.3.

```
 1   public static void printArray( E[] inputArray )
 2   {
 3      // display array elements
 4      for ( E element : inputArray )
 5         System.out.printf( "%s ", element );
 6
 7      System.out.println();
 8   } // end method printArray
```

Fig. 18.2 | `printArray` method in which actual type names are replaced by convention with the generic name E.

18.3 Generic Methods: Implementation and Compile-Time Translation

If the operations performed by several overloaded methods are identical for each argument type, the overloaded methods can be more compactly and conveniently coded using a generic method. You can write a single generic method declaration that can be called with arguments of different types. Based on the types of the arguments passed to the generic method, the compiler handles each method call appropriately.

Figure 18.3 reimplements the application of Fig. 18.1 using a generic `printArray` method (lines 7–14). Note that the `printArray` method calls in lines 24, 26 and 28 are identical to those of Fig. 18.1 (lines 44, 46 and 48) and that the outputs of the two applications are identical. This dramatically demonstrates the expressive power of generics.

Line 7 begins method `printArray`'s declaration. All generic method declarations have a **type parameter section** delimited by **angle brackets** (< and >) that precedes the method's return type (< E > in this example). Each type parameter section contains one or more **type parameters** (also called **formal type parameters**), separated by commas. A type parameter, also known as a **type variable**, is an identifier that specifies a generic type name. The type parameters can be used to declare the return type, parameter types and local variable types in a generic method declaration, and act as placeholders for the types of the arguments passed to the generic method, which are known as **actual type arguments**. A generic method's body is declared like that of any other method. Note that type parameters can represent only reference types—not primitive types (like int, double and char). Note, too, that the type parameter names throughout the method declaration must match those declared in the type parameter section. For example, line 10 declares `element` as type E, which matches the type parameter (E) declared in line 7. Also, a type parameter can be declared only once in the type parameter section but can appear more than once in the method's parameter list. For example, the type parameter name E appears twice in the following method's parameter list:

```
public static < E > void printTwoArrays( E[] array1, E[] array2 )
```

Type parameter names need not be unique among different generic methods.

Common Programming Error 18.1

When declaring a generic method, failing to place a type parameter section before the return type of a method is a syntax error—the compiler will not understand the type parameter name when it is encountered in the method.

```
1   // Fig. 18.3: GenericMethodTest.java
2   // Using generic methods to print array of different types.
3
4   public class GenericMethodTest
5   {
6      // generic method printArray
7      public static < E > void printArray( E[] inputArray )
8      {
9         // display array elements
10        for ( E element : inputArray )
11           System.out.printf( "%s ", element );
12
13        System.out.println();
14     } // end method printArray
15
16     public static void main( String args[] )
17     {
18        // create arrays of Integer, Double and Character
19        Integer[] intArray = { 1, 2, 3, 4, 5 };
20        Double[] doubleArray = { 1.1, 2.2, 3.3, 4.4, 5.5, 6.6, 7.7 };
21        Character[] charArray = { 'H', 'E', 'L', 'L', 'O' };
22
23        System.out.println( "Array integerArray contains:" );
24        printArray( integerArray ); // pass an Integer array
25        System.out.println( "\nArray doubleArray contains:" );
26        printArray( doubleArray ); // pass a Double array
27        System.out.println( "\nArray characterArray contains:" );
28        printArray( characterArray ); // pass a Character array
29     } // end main
30  } // end class GenericMethodTest
```

```
Array integerArray contains:
1 2 3 4 5 6

Array doubleArray contains:
1.1 2.2 3.3 4.4 5.5 6.6 7.7

Array characterArray contains:
H E L L O
```

Fig. 18.3 | Printing array elements using generic method `printArray`.

Method `printArray`'s type parameter section declares type parameter, `E`, as the placeholder for the array element type that `printArray` will output. Note that `E` appears in the parameter list as the array element type (line 7). The `for` statement header (line 10) also uses `E` as the element type. These are the same two locations where the overloaded `printArray` methods of Fig. 18.1 specified `Integer`, `Double` or `Character` as the array element type. The remainder of `printArray` is identical to the versions presented in Fig. 18.1.

Good Programming Practice 18.1

It is recommended that type parameters be specified as individual capital letters. Typically, a type parameter that represents the type of an element in an array (or other collection) is named `E` for "element."

As in Fig. 18.1, the program begins by declaring and initializing six-element `Integer` array `integerArray` (line 19), seven-element `Double` array `doubleArray` (line 20) and five-element `Character` array `characterArray` (line 21). Then the program outputs each array by calling `printArray` (lines 24, 26 and 28)—once with argument `integerArray`, once with argument `doubleArray` and once with argument `characterArray`.

When the compiler encounters line 24, it first determines argument `integerArray`'s type (i.e., `Integer[]`) and attempts to locate a method named `printArray` that specifies a single `Integer[]` parameter. There is no such method in this example. Next, the compiler determines whether there is a generic method named `printArray` that specifies a single array parameter and uses a type parameter to represent the array element type. The compiler determines that method `printArray` (lines 7–14) is a match and sets up a call to the method. The same process is repeated for the calls to method `printArray` at lines 26 and 28.

Common Programming Error 18.2

If the compiler cannot match a method call to a non-generic or a generic method declaration, a compilation error occurs.

Common Programming Error 18.3

If the compiler does not find a method declaration that matches a method call exactly, but does find two or more generic methods that can satisfy the method call, a compilation error occurs.

In addition to setting up the method calls, the compiler also determines whether the operations in the method body can be applied to elements of the type stored in the array argument. The only operation performed on the array elements in this example is to output the string representation of the elements. Line 11 performs an implicit `toString` call on every `element`. To work with generics, every element of the array must be an object of a class or interface type. Since all objects have a `toString` method, the compiler is satisfied that line 11 performs a valid operation for any object in `printArray`'s array argument. The `toString` methods of classes `Integer`, `Double` and `Character` return the string representation of the underlying `int`, `double` or `char` value, respectively.

When the compiler translates generic method `printArray` into Java bytecodes, it removes the type parameter section and replaces the type parameters with actual types. This process is known as **erasure**. By default all generic types are replaced with type `Object`. So the compiled version of method `printArray` appears as shown in Fig. 18.4—there is only one copy of this code that is used for all `printArray` calls in the example. This is quite different from other, similar mechanisms, such as C++'s templates in which a separate copy of the source code is generated and compiled for every type passed as an argument to the method. As we will discuss in Section 18.4, the translation and compilation of generics is a bit more involved than what we have discussed in this section.

By declaring `printArray` as a generic method in Fig. 18.3, we eliminated the need for the overloaded methods of Fig. 18.1, saving 20 lines of code and creating a reusable method that can output the string representations of the elements in any array that contains objects. However, this particular example could have simply declared the `printArray` method as shown in Fig. 18.4 using an `Object` array as the parameter. This would have yielded the same results because any `Object` can be output as a `String`. In a generic method, the benefits become apparent when the method also uses a type parameter as the method's return type, as we demonstrate in the next section.

```
1   public static void printArray( Object[] inputArray )
2   {
3       // display array elements
4       for ( Object element : inputArray )
5           System.out.printf( "%s ", element );
6
7       System.out.println();
8   } // end method printArray
```

Fig. 18.4 | Generic method `printArray` after erasure is performed by the compiler.

18.4 Additional Compile-Time Translation Issues: Methods That Use a Type Parameter as the Return Type

Let's consider a generic method example in which type parameters are used in the return type and in the parameter list (Fig. 18.5). The application uses a generic method `maximum` to determine and return the largest of its three arguments of the same type. Unfortunately, the relational operator > cannot be used with reference types. However, it is possible to compare two objects of the same class if that class implements the generic interface `Comparable< T >` (package `java.lang`). All the type-wrapper classes for primitive types implement this interface. Like generic classes, generic interfaces enable programmers to specify, with a single interface declaration, a set of related types. `Comparable< T >` objects have a `compareTo` method. For example, if we have two `Integer` objects, `integer1` and `integer2`, they can be compared with the expression:

```
integer1.compareTo( integer2 )
```

It is the responsibility of the programmer who declares a class that implements `Comparable< T >` to declare method `compareTo` such that it compares the contents of two objects of that class and returns the results of the comparison. The method must return 0 if the objects are equal, -1 if `object1` is less than `object2` or 1 if `object1` is greater than `object2`. For example, class `Integer`'s `compareTo` method compares the `int` values stored in two `Integer` objects. A benefit of implementing interface `Comparable< T >` is that `Comparable< T >` objects can be used with the sorting and searching methods of class `Collections` (package `java.util`). We discuss those methods in Chapter 19, Collections. In this example, we'll use method `compareTo` in method `maximum` to help determine the largest value.

Generic method `maximum` (lines 7–18) uses type parameter `T` as the return type of the method (line 7), as the type of method parameters `x`, `y` and `z` (line 7), and as the type of local variable `max` (line 9). The type parameter section specifies that `T` extends `Comparable< T >`—only objects of classes that implement interface `Comparable< T >` can be used with this method. In this case, `Comparable` is known as the upper bound of the type parameter. By default, `Object` is the upper bound. Note that type parameter declarations that bound the parameter always use keyword `extends` regardless of whether the type parameter extends a class or implements an interface. This type parameter is more restrictive than the type parameter specified for `printArray` in Fig. 18.3, which was able to output arrays containing any type of object. The restriction of using `Comparable< T >` objects is important because not all objects can be compared. However, `Comparable< T >` objects are guaranteed to have a `compareTo` method.

```
 1   // Fig. 18.5: MaximumTest.java
 2   // Generic method maximum returns the largest of three objects.
 3
 4   public class MaximumTest
 5   {
 6      // determines the largest of three Comparable objects
 7      public static < T extends Comparable< T > > T maximum( T x, T y, T z )
 8      {
 9         T max = x; // assume x is initially the largest
10
11         if ( y.compareTo( max ) > 0 )
12            max = y; // y is the largest so far
13
14         if ( z.compareTo( max ) > 0 )
15            max = z; // z is the largest
16
17         return max; // returns the largest object
18      } // end method maximum
19
20      public static void main( String args[] )
21      {
22         System.out.printf( "Maximum of %d, %d and %d is %d\n\n", 3, 4, 5,
23            maximum( 3, 4, 5 ) );
24         System.out.printf( "Maximum of %.1f, %.1f and %.1f is %.1f\n\n",
25            6.6, 8.8, 7.7, maximum( 6.6, 8.8, 7.7 ) );
26         System.out.printf( "Maximum of %s, %s and %s is %s\n", "pear",
27            "apple", "orange", maximum( "pear", "apple", "orange" ) );
28      } // end main
29   } // end class MaximumTest
```

```
Maximum of 3, 4 and 5 is 5

Maximum of 6.6, 8.8 and 7.7 is 8.8

Maximum of pear, apple and orange is pear
```

Fig. 18.5 | Generic method maximum with an upper bound on its type parameter.

Method maximum uses the same algorithm that we used in Section 6.4 to determine the largest of its three arguments. The method assumes that its first argument (x) is the largest and assigns it to local variable max (line 9). Next, the if statement at lines 11–12 determines whether y is greater than max. The condition invokes y's compareTo method with the expression y.compareTo(max), which returns -1, 0 or 1, to determine y's relationship to max. If the return value of the compareTo is greater than 0, then y is greater and is assigned to variable max. Similarly, the if statement at lines 14–15 determines whether z is greater than max. If so, line 15 assigns z to max. Then, line 17 returns max to the caller.

In main (lines 20–28), line 23 calls maximum with the integers 3, 4 and 5. When the compiler encounters this call, it first looks for a maximum method that takes three arguments of type int. There is no such method, so the compiler looks for a generic method that can be used and finds generic method maximum. However, recall that the arguments to a generic method must be of a reference type. So the compiler autoboxes the three int values as Integer objects and specifies that the three Integer objects will be passed to maximum. Note that class Integer (package java.lang) implements interface Comparable< Integer > such that method compareTo compares the int values in two Integer objects. Therefore, Integers are valid arguments to method maximum. When the Integer representing the maximum is returned, we attempt to output it with the %d format specifier, which outputs an int primitive type value. So maximum's return value is output as an int value.

A similar process occurs for the three double arguments passed to maximum in line 25. Each double is autoboxed as a Double object and passed to maximum. Again, this is allowed because class Double (package java.lang) implements the Comparable< Double > interface. The Double returned by maximum is output with the format specifier %.1f, which outputs a double primitive type value. So maximum's return value is auto-unboxed and output as a double. The call to maximum in line 27 receives three Strings, which are also Comparable< String > objects. Note that we intentionally placed the largest value in a different position in each method call (lines 23, 25 and 27) to show that the generic method always finds the maximum value, regardless of its position in the argument list.

When the compiler translates generic method maximum into Java bytecodes, it uses erasure (introduced in Section 18.3) to replace the type parameters with actual types. In Fig. 18.3, all generic types were replaced with type Object. Actually, all type parameters are replaced with the upper bound of the type parameter—unless specified otherwise, Object is the default upper bound. The upper bound of a type parameter is specified in the type parameter section. To indicate the upper bound, follow the type parameter's name with the keyword extends and the class or interface name that represents the upper bound. In method maximum's type parameter section (Fig. 18.5), we specified the upper bound as type Comparable< T >. Thus, only Comparable< T > objects can be passed as arguments to maximum—anything that is not Comparable< T > will result in compilation errors. Figure 18.6 simulates the erasure of method maximum's types by showing the method's source code after the type parameter section is removed and type parameter T is replaced with the upper bound, Comparable, throughout the method declaration. Note that the erasure of Comparable< T > is simply Comparable.

After erasure, the compiled version of method maximum specifies that it returns type Comparable. However, the calling method does not expect to receive a Comparable. Rather, the caller expects to receive an object of the same type that was passed to maximum

```
1    public static Comparable maximum(Comparable x, Comparable y, Comparable z)
2    {
3       Comparable max = x; // assume x is initially the largest
4
5       if ( y.compareTo( max ) > 0 )
6          max = y; // y is the largest so far
7
8       if ( z.compareTo( max ) > 0 )
9          max = z; // z is the largest
10
11      return max; // returns the largest object
12   } // end method maximum
```

Fig. 18.6 | Generic method maximum after erasure is performed by the compiler.

an argument—Integer, Double or String in this example. When the compiler replaces the type parameter information with the upper bound type in the method declaration, it also inserts explicit cast operations in front of each method call to ensure that the returned value is of the type expected by the caller. Thus, the call to maximum in line 23 (Fig. 18.5) is preceded by an Integer cast, as in

```
(Integer) maximum( 3, 4, 5 )
```

the call to maximum in line 25 is preceded by a Double cast, as in

```
(Double) maximum( 6.6, 8.8, 7.7 )
```

and the call to maximum in line 27 is preceded by a String cast, as in

```
(String) maximum( "pear", "apple", "orange" )
```

In each case, the type of the cast for the return value is inferred from the types of the method arguments in the particular method call because, according to the method declaration, the return type and the argument types match. Note that you cannot use a method that accepts Objects because class Object provides only an equality comparison. Also note that without generics, programmers are responsible for the casting operation.

18.5 Overloading Generic Methods

A generic method may be overloaded. A class can provide two or more generic methods that specify the same method name but different method parameters. For example, generic method printArray of Fig. 18.3 could be overloaded with another printArray generic method with the additional parameters lowSubscript and highSubscript to specify the portion of the array to output (see Exercise 18.5).

A generic method can also be overloaded by non-generic methods that have the same method name and number of parameters. When the compiler encounters a method call, it searches for the method declaration that most precisely matches the method name and the argument types specified in the call. For example, generic method printArray of Fig. 18.3 could be overloaded with a version that is specific to Strings, which outputs the Strings in neat, tabular format (see Exercise 18.6).

When the compiler encounters a method call, it performs a matching process to determine which method to invoke. The compiler tries to find and use a precise match in which the method names and argument types of the method call match those of a specific method declaration. If there is no such method, the compiler determines whether there is an inexact but applicable matching method.

18.6 Generic Classes

The concept of a data structure, such as a stack, can be understood independently of the element type it manipulates. Generic classes provide a means for describing the concept of a stack (or any other class) in a type-independent manner. We can then instantiate type-specific objects of the generic class. This capability provides a wonderful opportunity for software reusability.

Once you have a generic class, you can use a simple, concise notation to indicate the actual type(s) that should be used in place of the class's type parameter(s). At compilation time, the Java compiler ensures the type safety of your code and uses the erasure techniques described in Section 18.3 and Section 18.4 to enable your client code to interact with the generic class.

One generic `Stack` class, for example, could be the basis for creating many `Stack` classes (e.g., "Stack of `Double`," "Stack of `Integer`," "Stack of `Character`," "Stack of `Employee`," etc.). These classes are known as parameterized classes or parameterized types because they accept one or more parameters. Recall that type parameters represent only reference types, which means the `Stack` generic class cannot be instantiated with primitive types. However, we can instantiate a `Stack` that stores objects of Java's type-wrapper classes and allow Java to use autoboxing to convert the primitive values into objects. Auto-boxing occurs when a value of a primitive type (e.g., `int`) is pushed onto a `Stack` that contains wrapper-class objects (e.g., `Integer`). Auto-unboxing occurs when an object of the wrapper class is popped off the `Stack` and assigned it to a primitive type variable.

Figure 18.7 presents a generic `Stack` class declaration. A generic class declaration looks like a non-generic class declaration, except that the class name is followed by a type parameter section (line 4). In this case, type parameter E represents the element type the `Stack` will manipulate. As with generic methods, the type parameter section of a generic class can have one or more type parameters separated by commas. (You will create a generic class with two type parameters in Exercise 18.8.) Type parameter E is used throughout the `Stack` class declaration to represent the element type. [*Note:* This example implements a `Stack` as an array.]

Class `Stack` declares variable `elements` as an array of type E (line 8). This array will store the `Stack`'s elements. We would like to create an array of type E to store the elements. However, the generics mechanism does not allow type parameters in array-creation expressions because the type parameter (in this case, E) is not available at runtime. To create an array with the appropriate type, line 22 in the one-argument constructor creates the array as an array of type `Object` and casts the reference returned by `new` to type `E[]`. Any object could be stored in an `Object` array, but the compiler's type-checking mechanism ensures that only objects of the array variable's declared type can be assigned to the array via any array-access expression that uses variable `elements`. Yet when this class is compiled using the `-Xlint:unchecked` option, e.g.,

```
javac -Xlint:unchecked Stack.java
```

the compiler issues the following warning message about line 22:

```
Stack.java:22: warning: [unchecked] unchecked cast
found    : java.lang.Object[]
required: E[]
        elements = ( E[] ) new Object[ size ]; // create array
```

The reason for this message is that the compiler cannot ensure with 100% certainty that an array of type `Object` will never contain objects of types other than E. Assume that E represents type `Integer`, so that array elements should store `Integer` objects. It is possible to assign variable `elements` to a variable of type `Object[]`, as in

```
Object[] objectArray = elements;
```

```
1   // Fig. 18.7: Stack.java
2   // Generic class Stack.
3
4   public class Stack< E >
5   {
6      private final int size; // number of elements in the stack
7      private int top; // location of the top element
8      private E[] elements; // array that stores stack elements
9
10     // no-argument constructor creates a stack of the default size
11     public Stack()
12     {
13        this( 10 ); // default stack size
14     } // end no-argument Stack constructor
15
16     // constructor creates a stack of the specified number of elements
17     public Stack( int s )
18     {
19        size = s > 0 ? s : 10; // set size of Stack
20        top = -1; // Stack initially empty
21
22        elements = ( E[] ) new Object[ size ]; // create array
23     } // end Stack constructor
24
25     // push element onto stack; if successful, return true;
26     // otherwise, throw FullStackException
27     public void push( E pushValue )
28     {
29        if ( top == size - 1 ) // if stack is full
30           throw new FullStackException( String.format(
31              "Stack is full, cannot push %s", pushValue ) );
32
33        elements[ ++top ] = pushValue; // place pushValue on Stack
34     } // end method push
35
36     // return the top element if not empty; else throw EmptyStackException
37     public E pop()
38     {
39        if ( top == -1 ) // if stack is empty
40           throw new EmptyStackException( "Stack is empty, cannot pop" );
41
42        return elements[ top-- ]; // remove and return top element of Stack
43     } // end method pop
44  } // end class Stack< E >
```

Fig. 18.7 | Generic class Stack declaration.

Then any object can be placed into the array with an assignment statement like

```
objectArray[ 0 ] = "hello";
```

which places a String in an array that should contain only Integers, which would lead to runtime problems when the Stack is manipulated. As long as you do not perform statements like those shown here, your Stack will contain objects of only the correct element type.

Method push (lines 27–34) first determines whether an attempt is being made to push an element onto a full Stack. If so, lines 30–31 throw a FullStackException. Class Full-StackException is declared in Fig. 18.8. If the Stack is not full, line 33 increments the top counter and places the argument in that location of array elements.

Method pop (lines 37–43) first determines whether an attempt is being made to pop an element from an empty Stack. If so, line 40 throws an EmptyStackException. Class EmptyStackException is declared in Fig. 18.9. Otherwise, line 42 returns the top element of the Stack, then postdecrements the top counter to indicate the position of the next top element.

Classes FullStackException (Fig. 18.8) and EmptyStackException (Fig. 18.9) each provide the conventional no-argument constructor and one-argument constructor of exception classes (as discussed in Section 13.11). The no-argument constructor sets the default error message, and the one-argument constructor sets a custom exception message.

```
1   // Fig. 18.8: FullStackException.java
2   // Indicates a stack is full.
3   public class FullStackException extends RuntimeException
4   {
5      // no-argument constructor
6      public FullStackException()
7      {
8         this( "Stack is full" );
9      } // end no-argument FullStackException constructor
10
11     // one-argument constructor
12     public FullStackException( String exception )
13     {
14        super( exception );
15     } // end one-argument FullStackException constructor
16  } // end class FullStackException
```

Fig. 18.8 | FullStackException class declaration.

```
1   // Fig. 18.9: EmptyStackException.java
2   // Indicates a stack is full.
3   public class EmptyStackException extends RuntimeException
4   {
5      // no-argument constructor
6      public EmptyStackException()
7      {
8         this( "Stack is empty" );
9      } // end no-argument EmptyStackException constructor
10
11     // one-argument constructor
12     public EmptyStackException( String exception )
13     {
14        super( exception );
15     } // end one-argument EmptyStackException constructor
16  } // end class EmptyStackException
```

Fig. 18.9 | EmptyStackException class declaration.

As with generic methods, when a generic class is compiled, the compiler performs erasure on the class's type parameters and replaces them with their upper bounds. For class Stack (Fig. 18.7), no upper bound is specified, so the default upper bound, Object, is used. The scope of a generic class's type parameter is the entire class. However, type parameters cannot be used in a class's static declarations.

Now, let's consider the test application (Fig. 18.10) that uses the Stack generic class. Lines 9–10 declare variables of type Stack< Double > (pronounced "Stack of Double") and Stack< Integer > (pronounced "Stack of Integer"). The types Double and Integer are known as the Stack's type arguments. They are used by the compiler to replace the type parameters so that the compiler can perform type checking and insert cast operations as necessary. We'll discuss the cast operations in more detail shortly. Method testStack (called from main) instantiates objects doubleStack of size 5 (line 15) and integerStack of size 10 (line 16), then calls methods testPushDouble (lines 25–44), testPopDouble (lines 47–67), testPushInteger (lines 70–89) and testPopInteger (lines 92–112) to demonstrate the two Stacks in this example.

Method testPushDouble (lines 25–44) invokes method push to place the double values 1.1, 2.2, 3.3, 4.4 and 5.5 stored in array doubleElements onto doubleStack. The for loop terminates when the test program attempts to push a sixth value onto doubleStack (which is full, because doubleStack can store only five elements). In this case, the method throws a FullStackException (Fig. 18.8) to indicate that the Stack is full. Lines 39–43 catch this exception and print the stack trace information. The stack trace indicates the exception that occurred and shows that Stack method push generated the exception at lines 30–31 of the file Stack.java (Fig. 18.7). The trace also shows that method push was called by StackTest method testPushDouble at line 36 of StackTest.java, that method

```
 1   // Fig. 18.10: StackTest.java
 2   // Stack generic class test program.
 3
 4   public class StackTest
 5   {
 6      private double[] doubleElements = { 1.1, 2.2, 3.3, 4.4, 5.5, 6.6 };
 7      private int[] integerElements = { 1, 2, 3, 4, 5, 6, 7, 8, 9, 10, 11 };
 8
 9      private Stack< Double > doubleStack; // stack stores Double objects
10      private Stack< Integer > integerStack; // stack stores Integer objects
11
12      // test Stack objects
13      public void testStacks()
14      {
15         doubleStack = new Stack< Double >( 5 ); // Stack of Doubles
16         integerStack = new Stack< Integer >( 10 ); // Stack of Integers
17
18         testPushDouble(); // push double onto doubleStack
19         testPopDouble(); // pop from doubleStack
20         testPushInteger(); // push int onto intStack
21         testPopInteger(); // pop from intStack
22      } // end method testStacks
23
```

Fig. 18.10 | Generic class Stack test program. (Part 1 of 4.)

```
24      // test push method with double stack
25      public void testPushDouble()
26      {
27         // push elements onto stack
28         try
29         {
30            System.out.println( "\nPushing elements onto doubleStack" );
31
32            // push elements to Stack
33            for ( double element : doubleElements )
34            {
35               System.out.printf( "%.1f ", element );
36               doubleStack.push( element ); // push onto doubleStack
37            } // end for
38         } // end try
39         catch ( FullStackException fullStackException )
40         {
41            System.err.println();
42            fullStackException.printStackTrace();
43         } // end catch FullStackException
44      } // end method testPushDouble
45
46      // test pop method with double stack
47      public void testPopDouble()
48      {
49         // pop elements from stack
50         try
51         {
52            System.out.println( "\nPopping elements from doubleStack" );
53            double popValue; // store element removed from stack
54
55            // remove all elements from Stack
56            while ( true )
57            {
58               popValue = doubleStack.pop(); // pop from doubleStack
59               System.out.printf( "%.1f ", popValue );
60            } // end while
61         } // end try
62         catch( EmptyStackException emptyStackException )
63         {
64            System.err.println();
65            emptyStackException.printStackTrace();
66         } // end catch EmptyStackException
67      } // end method testPopDouble
68
69      // test push method with integer stack
70      public void testPushInteger()
71      {
72         // push elements to stack
73         try
74         {
75            System.out.println( "\nPushing elements onto intStack" );
76
```

Fig. 18.10 | Generic class Stack test program. (Part 2 of 4.)

```
77            // push elements to Stack
78            for ( int element : integerElements )
79            {
80               System.out.printf( "%d ", element );
81               integerStack.push( element ); // push onto integerStack
82            } // end for
83         } // end try
84         catch ( FullStackException fullStackException )
85         {
86            System.err.println();
87            fullStackException.printStackTrace();
88         } // end catch FullStackException
89      } // end method testPushInteger
90
91      // test pop method with integer stack
92      public void testPopInteger()
93      {
94         // pop elements from stack
95         try
96         {
97            System.out.println( "\nPopping elements from intStack" );
98            int popValue; // store element removed from stack
99
100            // remove all elements from Stack
101            while ( true )
102            {
103               popValue = integerStack.pop(); // pop from intStack
104               System.out.printf( "%d ", popValue );
105            } // end while
106         } // end try
107         catch( EmptyStackException emptyStackException )
108         {
109            System.err.println();
110            emptyStackException.printStackTrace();
111         } // end catch EmptyStackException
112      } // end method testPopInteger
113
114      public static void main( String args[] )
115      {
116         StackTest application = new StackTest();
117         application.testStacks();
118      } // end main
119   } // end class StackTest
```

```
Pushing elements onto doubleStack
1.1 2.2 3.3 4.4 5.5 6.6
FullStackException: Stack is full, cannot push 6.6
        at Stack.push(Stack.java:30)
        at StackTest.testPushDouble(StackTest.java:36)
        at StackTest.testStacks(StackTest.java:18)
        at StackTest.main(StackTest.java:117)
```

(continued at top of next page...)

Fig. 18.10 | Generic class Stack test program. (Part 3 of 4.)

(... continued from previous page)

```
Popping elements from doubleStack
5.5 4.4 3.3 2.2 1.1
EmptyStackException: Stack is empty, cannot pop
        at Stack.pop(Stack.java:40)
        at StackTest.testPopDouble(StackTest.java:58)
        at StackTest.testStacks(StackTest.java:19)
        at StackTest.main(StackTest.java:117)

Pushing elements onto integerStack
1 2 3 4 5 6 7 8 9 10 11
FullStackException: Stack is full, cannot push 11
        at Stack.push(Stack.java:30)
        at StackTest.testPushInteger(StackTest.java:81)
        at StackTest.testStacks(StackTest.java:20)
        at StackTest.main(StackTest.java:117)

Popping elements from integerStack
10 9 8 7 6 5 4 3 2 1
EmptyStackException: Stack is empty, cannot pop
        at Stack.pop(Stack.java:40)
        at StackTest.testPopInteger(StackTest.java:103)
        at StackTest.testStacks(StackTest.java:21)
        at StackTest.main(StackTest.java:117)
```

Fig. 18.10 | Generic class `Stack` test program. (Part 4 of 4.)

`testPushDouble` was called from method `testStacks` at line 18 of `StackTest.java` and that method `testStacks` was called from method `main` at line 117 of `StackTest.java`. This information enables you to determine the methods that were on the method-call stack at the time that the exception occurred. Because the program catches the exception, the Java runtime environment considers the exception to have been handled and the program can continue executing. Note that autoboxing occurs in line 36 when the program tries to push a primitive `double` value onto the `doubleStack`, which stores only `Double` objects.

Method `testPopDouble` (lines 47–67) invokes `Stack` method `pop` in an infinite `while` loop to remove all the values from the stack. Note in the output that the values indeed `pop` off in last-in-first-out order (this, of course, is the defining characteristic of stacks). The `while` loop (lines 57–61) continues until the stack is empty (i.e., until an `Empty-StackException` occurs), which causes the program to proceed to the `catch` block (lines 62–66) and handle the exception, so the program can continue executing. When the test program attempts to `pop` a sixth value, the `doubleStack` is empty, so the `pop` throws an `EmptyStackException`. Auto-unboxing occurs in line 58 when the program assigns the `Double` object popped from the stack to a `double` primitive variable. Recall from Section 18.4 that the compiler inserts cast operations to ensure that the proper types are returned from generic methods. After erasure, `Stack` method `pop` returns type `Object`. However, the client code in method `testPopDouble` expects to receive a `double` when method `pop` returns. So the compiler inserts a `Double` cast, as in

```
popValue = ( Double ) doubleStack.pop();
```

to ensure that a reference of the appropriate type is returned, auto-unboxed and assigned to `popValue`.

Method `testPushInteger` (lines 70–89) invokes Stack method push to place values onto `integerStack` until it is full. Method `testPopInteger` (lines 92–112) invokes Stack method pop to remove values from `integerStack` until it is empty. Once again, note that the values pop off in last-in-first-out order. During the erasure process, the compiler recognizes that the client code in method `testPopInteger` expects to receive an int when method pop returns. So the compiler inserts an Integer cast, as in

```
popValue = ( Integer ) integerStack.pop();
```

to ensure that a reference of the appropriate type is returned, auto-unboxed and assigned to popValue.

Creating Generic Methods to Test Class *Stack< E >*

Note that the code in methods `testPushDouble` and `testPushInteger` is almost identical for pushing values onto a Stack< Double > or a Stack< Integer >, respectively, and the code in methods `testPopDouble` and `testPopInteger` is almost identical for popping values from a Stack< Double > or a Stack< Integer >, respectively. This presents another opportunity to use generic methods. Figure 18.11 declares generic method testPush (lines 26–46) to perform the same tasks as `testPushDouble` and `testPushInteger` in Fig. 18.10—that is, push values onto a Stack< T >. Similarly, generic method testPop (lines 49–69) performs the same tasks as `testPopDouble` and `testPopInteger` in Fig. 18.10—that is, pop values off a Stack< T >. Note that the output of Fig. 18.11 precisely matches the output of Fig. 18.10.

```
1   // Fig. 18.11: StackTest2.java
2   // Stack generic class test program.
3
4   public class StackTest2
5   {
6      private Double[] doubleElements = { 1.1, 2.2, 3.3, 4.4, 5.5, 6.6 };
7      private Integer[] integerElements =
8         { 1, 2, 3, 4, 5, 6, 7, 8, 9, 10, 11 };
9
10     private Stack< Double > doubleStack; // stack stores Double objects
11     private Stack< Integer > integerStack; // stack stores Integer objects
12
13     // test Stack objects
14     public void testStacks()
15     {
16        doubleStack = new Stack< Double >( 5 ); // Stack of Doubles
17        integerStack = new Stack< Integer >( 10 ); // Stack of Integers
18
19        testPush( "doubleStack", doubleStack, doubleElements );
20        testPop( "doubleStack", doubleStack );
21        testPush( "integerStack", integerStack, integerElements );
22        testPop( "integerStack", integerStack );
23     } // end method testStacks
24
```

Fig. 18.11 | Passing a generic type Stack to a generic method. (Part 1 of 3.)

```
25      // generic method testPush pushes elements onto a Stack
26      public < T > void testPush( String name, Stack< T > stack,
27         T[] elements )
28      {
29         // push elements onto stack
30         try
31         {
32            System.out.printf( "\nPushing elements onto %s\n", name );
33
34            // push elements onto Stack
35            for ( T element : elements )
36            {
37               System.out.printf( "%s ", element );
38               stack.push( element ); // push element onto stack
39            }
40         } // end try
41         catch ( FullStackException fullStackException )
42         {
43            System.out.println();
44            fullStackException.printStackTrace();
45         } // end catch FullStackException
46      } // end method testPush
47
48      // generic method testPop pops elements from a Stack
49      public < T > void testPop( String name, Stack< T > stack )
50      {
51         // pop elements from stack
52         try
53         {
54            System.out.printf( "\nPopping elements from %s\n", name );
55            T popValue; // store element removed from stack
56
57            // remove elements from Stack
58            while ( true )
59            {
60               popValue = stack.pop(); // pop from stack
61               System.out.printf( "%s ", popValue );
62            } // end while
63         } // end try
64         catch( EmptyStackException emptyStackException )
65         {
66            System.out.println();
67            emptyStackException.printStackTrace();
68         } // end catch EmptyStackException
69      } // end method testPop
70
71      public static void main( String args[] )
72      {
73         StackTest2 application = new StackTest2();
74         application.testStacks();
75      } // end main
76   } // end class StackTest2
```

Fig. 18.11 | Passing a generic type `Stack` to a generic method. (Part 2 of 3.)

```
Pushing elements onto doubleStack
1.1 2.2 3.3 4.4 5.5 6.6
FullStackException: Stack is full, cannot push 6.6
        at Stack.push(Stack.java:30)
        at StackTest2.testPush(StackTest2.java:38)
        at StackTest2.testStacks(StackTest2.java:19)
        at StackTest2.main(StackTest2.java:74)

Popping elements from doubleStack
5.5 4.4 3.3 2.2 1.1
EmptyStackException: Stack is empty, cannot pop
        at Stack.pop(Stack.java:40)
        at StackTest2.testPop(StackTest2.java:60)
        at StackTest2.testStacks(StackTest2.java:20)
        at StackTest2.main(StackTest2.java:74)

Pushing elements onto integerStack
1 2 3 4 5 6 7 8 9 10 11
FullStackException: Stack is full, cannot push 11
        at Stack.push(Stack.java:30)
        at StackTest2.testPush(StackTest2.java:38)
        at StackTest2.testStacks(StackTest2.java:21)
        at StackTest2.main(StackTest2.java:74)

Popping elements from integerStack
10 9 8 7 6 5 4 3 2 1
EmptyStackException: Stack is empty, cannot pop
        at Stack.pop(Stack.java:40)
        at StackTest2.testPop(StackTest2.java:60)
        at StackTest2.testStacks(StackTest2.java:22)
        at StackTest2.main(StackTest2.java:74)
```

Fig. 18.11 | Passing a generic type Stack to a generic method. (Part 3 of 3.)

The testStacks method (lines 14–23) creates the Stack< Double > (line 16) and Stack< Integer > (line 17) objects. Lines 19–22 invoke generic methods testPush and testPop to test the Stack objects. Recall that type parameters can represent only reference types. Therefore, to be able to pass arrays doubleElements and integerElements to generic method testPush, the arrays declared in lines 6–8 must be declared with the wrapper types Double and Integer. When these arrays are initialized with primitive values, the compiler autoboxes each primitive value.

Generic method testPush (lines 26–46) uses type parameter T (specified at line 26) to represent the data type stored in the Stack< T >. The generic method takes three arguments—a String that represents the name of the Stack< T > object for output purposes, a reference to an object of type Stack< T > and an array of type T—the type of elements that will be pushed onto Stack< T >. Note that the compiler enforces consistency between the type of the Stack and the elements that will be pushed onto the Stack when push is invoked, which is the real value of the generic method call. Generic method testPop (lines 49–69) takes two arguments—a String that represents the name of the Stack< T > object for output purposes and a reference to an object of type Stack< T >.

18.7 Raw Types

The test programs for generic class `Stack` in Section 18.6 instantiate `Stack`s with type arguments `Double` and `Integer`. It is also possible to instantiate generic class `Stack` without specifying a type argument, as follows:

```
Stack objectStack = new Stack( 5 ); // no type argument specified
```

In this case, the `objectStack` is said to have a raw type, which means that the compiler implicitly uses type `Object` throughout the generic class for each type argument. Thus the preceding statement creates a `Stack` that can store objects of any type. This is important for backwards compatibility with prior versions of Java. For example, the data structures of the Java Collections Framework (see Chapter 19, Collections) all stored references to `Object`s, but are now implemented as generic types.

A raw type `Stack` variable can be assigned a `Stack` that specifies a type argument, such as a `Stack< Double >` object, as follows:

```
Stack rawTypeStack2 = new Stack< Double >( 5 );
```

because type `Double` is a subclass of `Object`. This assignment is allowed because the elements in a `Stack< Double >` (i.e., `Double` objects) are certainly objects—class `Double` is an indirect subclass of `Object`.

Similarly, a `Stack` variable that specifies a type argument in its declaration can be assigned a raw type `Stack` object, as in:

```
Stack< Integer > integerStack = new Stack( 10 );
```

Although this assignment is permitted, it is unsafe because a `Stack` of raw type might store types other than `Integer`. In this case, the compiler issues a warning message which indicates the unsafe assignment.

The test program of Fig. 18.12 uses the notion of raw type. Line 14 instantiates generic class `Stack` with raw type, which indicates that `rawTypeStack1` can hold objects of any type. Line 17 assigns a `Stack< Double >` to variable `rawTypeStack2`, which is declared as a `Stack` of raw type. Line 20 assigns a `Stack` of raw type to `Stack< Integer >` variable, which is legal but causes the compiler to issue a warning message (Fig. 18.13) indicating a potentially unsafe assignment—again, this occurs because a `Stack` of raw type might store types other than `Integer`. Also, each of the calls to generic method `testPush` and `testPop` in lines 22–25 results in a compiler warning message (Fig. 18.13). These warnings occur because variables `rawTypeStack1` and `rawTypeStack2` are declared as `Stack`s of raw type, but methods `testPush` and `testPop` each expect a second argument that is a `Stack` with a specific type argument. The warnings indicate that the compiler cannot guarantee that the types manipulated by the stacks are the correct types, because we did not supply a variable declared with a type argument. Methods `testPush` (lines 31–51) and `testPop` (lines 54–74) are the same as in Fig. 18.11.

Figure 18.13 shows the warning messages generated by the compiler (compiled with the `-Xlint:unchecked` option) when the file `RawTypeTest.java` (Fig. 18.12) is compiled. The first warning is generated for line 20, which assigned a raw type `Stack` to a `Stack< Integer >` variable—the compiler cannot ensure that all objects in the `Stack` will be `Integer` objects. The second warning is generated for line 22. Because the second method argument is a raw type Stack variable, the compiler determines the type argument for method testPush from the Double array passed as the third argument. In this case, Double is the type argument, so the compiler expects a Stack< Double > to be passed as the second argument. The warning occurs because the compiler cannot ensure that a raw type Stack contains only Double objects. The warning at line 24 occurs for the same reason, even though the actual Stack that rawTypeStack2 references is a Stack< Double >. The compiler cannot guarantee that the variable will always refer to the same Stack object, so it must use the variable's declared type to perform all type checking. Lines 23 and 25 each generate warnings because method testPop expects as an argument a Stack for which a type argument has been specified. However, in each call to testPop, we pass a raw type Stack variable. Thus, the compiler indicates a warning because it cannot check the types used in the body of the method.

18.8 Wildcards in Methods That Accept Type Parameters

In this section, we introduce a powerful generics concept known as wildcards. For this purpose, we will also introduce a new data structure from package java.util. Chapter 19, Collections, discusses the Java Collections Framework, which provides many generic data structures and algorithms that manipulate the elements of those data structures. Perhaps

```
1   // Fig. 18.12: RawTypeTest.java
2   // Raw type test program.
3
4   public class RawTypeTest
5   {
6      private Double[] doubleElements = { 1.1, 2.2, 3.3, 4.4, 5.5, 6.6 };
7      private Integer[] integerElements =
8         { 1, 2, 3, 4, 5, 6, 7, 8, 9, 10, 11 };
9
10     // method to test Stacks with raw types
11     public void testStacks()
12     {
13        // Stack of raw types assigned to Stack of raw types variable
14        Stack rawTypeStack1 = new Stack( 5 );
15
16        // Stack< Double > assigned to Stack of raw types variable
17        Stack rawTypeStack2 = new Stack< Double >( 5 );
18
19        // Stack of raw types assigned to Stack< Integer > variable
20        Stack< Integer > integerStack = new Stack( 10 );
21
22        testPush( "rawTypeStack1", rawTypeStack1, doubleElements );
23        testPop( "rawTypeStack1", rawTypeStack1 );
24        testPush( "rawTypeStack2", rawTypeStack2, doubleElements );
25        testPop( "rawTypeStack2", rawTypeStack2 );
26        testPush( "integerStack", integerStack, integerElements );
27        testPop( "integerStack", integerStack );
28     } // end method testStacks
```

Fig. 18.12 | Raw type test program. (Part 1 of 3.)

```
29
30      // generic method pushes elements onto stack
31      public < T > void testPush( String name, Stack< T > stack,
32         T[] elements )
33      {
34         // push elements onto stack
35         try
36         {
37            System.out.printf( "\nPushing elements onto %s\n", name );
38
39            // push elements onto Stack
40            for ( T element : elements )
41            {
42               System.out.printf( "%s ", element );
43               stack.push( element ); // push element onto stack
44            } // end for
45         } // end try
46         catch ( FullStackException fullStackException )
47         {
48            System.out.println();
49            fullStackException.printStackTrace();
50         } // end catch FullStackException
51      } // end method testPush
52
53      // generic method testPop pops elements from stack
54      public < T > void testPop( String name, Stack< T > stack )
55      {
56         // pop elements from stack
57         try
58         {
59            System.out.printf( "\nPopping elements from %s\n", name );
60            T popValue; // store element removed from stack
61
62            // remove elements from Stack
63            while ( true )
64            {
65               popValue = stack.pop(); // pop from stack
66               System.out.printf( "%s ", popValue );
67            } // end while
68         } // end try
69         catch( EmptyStackException emptyStackException )
70         {
71            System.out.println();
72            emptyStackException.printStackTrace();
73         } // end catch EmptyStackException
74      } // end method testPop
75
76      public static void main( String args[] )
77      {
78         RawTypeTest application = new RawTypeTest();
79         application.testStacks();
80      } // end main
81   } // end class RawTypeTest
```

Fig. 18.12 | Raw type test program. (Part 2 of 3.)

```
Pushing elements onto rawTypeStack1
1.1 2.2 3.3 4.4 5.5 6.6
FullStackException: Stack is full, cannot push 6.6
        at Stack.push(Stack.java:30)
        at RawTypeTest.testPush(RawTypeTest.java:43)
        at RawTypeTest.testStacks(RawTypeTest.java:22)
        at RawTypeTest.main(RawTypeTest.java:79)

Popping elements from rawTypeStack1
5.5 4.4 3.3 2.2 1.1
EmptyStackException: Stack is empty, cannot pop
        at Stack.pop(Stack.java:40)
        at RawTypeTest.testPop(RawTypeTest.java:65)
        at RawTypeTest.testStacks(RawTypeTest.java:23)
        at RawTypeTest.main(RawTypeTest.java:79)

Pushing elements onto rawTypeStack2
1.1 2.2 3.3 4.4 5.5 6.6
FullStackException: Stack is full, cannot push 6.6
        at Stack.push(Stack.java:30)
        at RawTypeTest.testPush(RawTypeTest.java:43)
        at RawTypeTest.testStacks(RawTypeTest.java:24)
        at RawTypeTest.main(RawTypeTest.java:79)

Popping elements from rawTypeStack2
5.5 4.4 3.3 2.2 1.1
EmptyStackException: Stack is empty, cannot pop
        at Stack.pop(Stack.java:40)
        at RawTypeTest.testPop(RawTypeTest.java:65)
        at RawTypeTest.testStacks(RawTypeTest.java:25)
        at RawTypeTest.main(RawTypeTest.java:79)

Pushing elements onto integerStack
1 2 3 4 5 6 7 8 9 10 11
FullStackException: Stack is full, cannot push 11
        at Stack.push(Stack.java:30)
        at RawTypeTest.testPush(RawTypeTest.java:43)
        at RawTypeTest.testStacks(RawTypeTest.java:26)
        at RawTypeTest.main(RawTypeTest.java:79)

Popping elements from integerStack
10 9 8 7 6 5 4 3 2 1
EmptyStackException: Stack is empty, cannot pop
        at Stack.pop(Stack.java:40)
        at RawTypeTest.testPop(RawTypeTest.java:65)
        at RawTypeTest.testStacks(RawTypeTest.java:27)
        at RawTypeTest.main(RawTypeTest.java:79)
```

Fig. 18.12 | Raw type test program. (Part 3 of 3.)

the simplest of these data structures is class **ArrayList**—a dynamically resizable, array-like data structure. As part of this discussion, you will learn how to create an ArrayList, add elements to it and traverse those elements using an enhanced for statement.

Before we introduce wildcards, let's consider an example that helps us motivate their use. Suppose that you would like to implement a generic method sum that totals the numbers in a collection, such as an ArrayList. You would begin by inserting the numbers in

```
RawTypeTest.java:20: warning: unchecked assignment
found    : Stack
required: Stack<java.lang.Integer>
      Stack< Integer > integerStack = new Stack( 10 );
                                      ^
RawTypeTest.java:22: warning: [unchecked] unchecked method invocation:
<T>testPush(java.lang.String,Stack<T>,T[]) in RawTypeTest is applied to
(java.lang.String,Stack,java.lang.Double[])
      testPush( "rawTypeStack1", rawTypeStack1, doubleElements );
      ^
RawTypeTest.java:23: warning: [unchecked] unchecked method invocation:
<T>testPop(java.lang.String,Stack<T>) in RawTypeTest is applied to
(java.lang.String,Stack)
      testPop( "rawTypeStack1", rawTypeStack1 );
      ^
RawTypeTest.java:24: warning: [unchecked] unchecked method invocation:
<T>testPush(java.lang.String,Stack<T>,T[]) in RawTypeTest is applied to
(java.lang.String,Stack,java.lang.Double[])
      testPush( "rawTypeStack2", rawTypeStack2, doubleElements );
      ^
RawTypeTest.java:25: warning: [unchecked] unchecked method invocation:
<T>testPop(java.lang.String,Stack<T>) in RawTypeTest is applied to
(java.lang.String,Stack)
      testPop( "rawTypeStack2", rawTypeStack2 );
      ^
5 warnings
```

Fig. 18.13 | Warning message from the compiler.

the collection. As you know, generic classes can be used only with class or interface types. So the numbers would be autoboxed as objects of the type-wrapper classes. For example, any int value would be autoboxed as an Integer object, and any double value would be autoboxed as a Double object. We'd like to be able to total all the numbers in the Array-List regardless of their type. For this reason, we'll declare the ArrayList with the type argument Number, which is the superclass of both Integer and Double. In addition, method sum will receive a parameter of type ArrayList< Number > and total its elements. Figure 18.14 demonstrates totaling the elements of an ArrayList of Numbers.

Line 11 declares and initializes an array of Numbers. Because the initializers are primitive values, Java autoboxes each primitive value as an object of its corresponding wrapper type. The int values 1 and 3 are autoboxed as Integer objects, and the double values 2.4 and 4.1 are autoboxed as Double objects. Line 12 declares and creates an ArrayList object that stores Numbers and assigns it to variable numberList. Note that we do not have to specify the size of the ArrayList because it will grow automatically as we insert objects.

Lines 14–15 traverse array numbers and place each element in numberList. Method **add** of class ArrayList appends an element to the end of the collection. Line 17 outputs the contents of the ArrayList as a String. This statement implicitly invokes the Array-List's **toString** method, which returns a string of the form "[*elements*]" in which *elements* is a comma-separated list of the elements' string representations. Lines 18–19 display the sum of the elements that is returned by the call to method sum at line 19.

Method sum (lines 23–32) receives an ArrayList of Numbers and calculates the total of the Numbers in the collection. The method uses double values to perform the calculations

```
 1   // Fig. 18.14: TotalNumbers.java
 2   // Summing the elements of an ArrayList.
 3   import java.util.ArrayList;
 4
 5   public class TotalNumbers
 6   {
 7      public static void main( String args[] )
 8      {
 9         // create, initialize and output ArrayList of Numbers containing
10         // both Integers and Doubles, then display total of the elements
11         Number[] numbers = { 1, 2.4, 3, 4.1 }; // Integers and Doubles
12         ArrayList< Number > numberList = new ArrayList< Number >();
13
14         for ( Number element : numbers )
15            numberList.add( element ); // place each number in numberList
16
17         System.out.printf( "numberList contains: %s\n", numberList );
18         System.out.printf( "Total of the elements in numberList: %.1f\n",
19            sum( numberList ) );
20      } // end main
21
22      // calculate total of ArrayList elements
23      public static double sum( ArrayList< Number > list )
24      {
25         double total = 0; // initialize total
26
27         // calculate sum
28         for ( Number element : list )
29            total += element.doubleValue();
30
31         return total;
32      } // end method sum
33   } // end class TotalNumbers
```

```
numberList contains: [1, 2.4, 3, 4.1]
Total of the elements in numberList: 10.5
```

Fig. 18.14 | Totaling the numbers in an ArrayList< Number >.

and returns the result as a double. Line 25 declares local variable total and initializes it to 0. Lines 28–29 use the enhanced for statement, which is designed to work with both arrays and the collections of the Collections Framework, to total the elements of the ArrayList. The for statement assigns each Number in the ArrayList to variable element, then uses method **doubleValue** of class Number to obtain the Number's underlying primitive value as a double value. The result is added to total. When the loop terminates, the method returns the total.

Implementing Method sum With a Wildcard Type Argument in Its Parameter
Recall that the purpose of method sum in Fig. 18.14 was to total any type of Numbers stored in an ArrayList. We created an ArrayList of Numbers that contained both Integer and Double objects. The output of Fig. 18.14 demonstrates that method sum worked properly.

Given that method sum can total the elements of an ArrayList of Numbers, you might expect that the method would also work for ArrayLists that contain elements of only one numeric type, such as ArrayList< Integer >. So we modified class TotalNumbers to create an ArrayList of Integers and pass it to method sum. When we compile the program, the compiler issues the following error message:

```
sum(java.util.ArrayList<java.lang.Number>) in TotalNumbersErrors
cannot be applied to (java.util.ArrayList<java.lang.Integer>)
```

Although Number is the superclass of Integer, the compiler does not consider the parameterized type ArrayList< Number > to be a supertype of ArrayList< Integer >. If it were, then every operation we could perform on ArrayList< Number > would also work on an ArrayList< Integer >. Consider the fact that you can add a Double object to an ArrayList< Number > because a Double *is a* Number, but you cannot add a Double object to an ArrayList< Integer > because a Double *is not* an Integer. Thus, the subtype relationship does not hold.

How do we create a more flexible version of method sum that can total the elements of any ArrayList that contains elements of any subclass of Number? This is where wildcard type arguments are important. Wildcards enable you to specify method parameters, return values, variables or fields, etc. that act as supertypes of parameterized types. In Fig. 18.15, method sum's parameter is declared in line 50 with the type:

```
ArrayList< ? extends Number >
```

A wildcard type argument is denoted by a question mark (?). A question mark by itself represents an "unknown type." In this case, the wildcard extends class Number, which means that the wildcard has an upper bound of Number. Thus, the unknown type argument must be either Number or a subclass of Number. With the parameter type shown here, method sum can receive an ArrayList argument that contains any type of Number, such as ArrayList< Integer > (line 20), ArrayList< Double > (line 33) or ArrayList< Number > (line 46).

```
1   // Fig. 18.15: WildcardTest.java
2   // Wildcard test program.
3   import java.util.ArrayList;
4
5   public class WildcardTest
6   {
7      public static void main( String args[] )
8      {
9         // create, initialize and output ArrayList of Integers, then
10        // display total of the elements
11        Integer[] integers = { 1, 2, 3, 4, 5 };
12        ArrayList< Integer > integerList = new ArrayList< Integer >();
13
14        // insert elements in integerList
15        for ( Integer element : integers )
16           integerList.add( element );
17
```

Fig. 18.15 | Wildcard test program. (Part 1 of 2.)

```
18          System.out.printf( "integerList contains: %s\n", integerList );
19          System.out.printf( "Total of the elements in integerList: %.0f\n\n",
20             sum( integerList ) );
21
22          // create, initialize and output ArrayList of Doubles, then
23          // display total of the elements
24          Double[] doubles = { 1.1, 3.3, 5.5 };
25          ArrayList< Double > doubleList = new ArrayList< Double >();
26
27          // insert elements in doubleList
28          for ( Double element : doubles )
29             doubleList.add( element );
30
31          System.out.printf( "doubleList contains: %s\n", doubleList );
32          System.out.printf( "Total of the elements in doubleList: %.1f\n\n",
33             sum( doubleList ) );
34
35          // create, initialize and output ArrayList of Numbers containing
36          // both Integers and Doubles, then display total of the elements
37          Number[] numbers = { 1, 2.4, 3, 4.1 }; // Integers and Doubles
38          ArrayList< Number > numberList = new ArrayList< Number >();
39
40          // insert elements in numberList
41          for ( Number element : numbers )
42             numberList.add( element );
43
44          System.out.printf( "numberList contains: %s\n", numberList );
45          System.out.printf( "Total of the elements in numberList: %.1f\n",
46             sum( numberList ) );
47       } // end main
48
49       // calculate total of stack elements
50       public static double sum( ArrayList< ? extends Number > list )
51       {
52          double total = 0; // initialize total
53
54          // calculate sum
55          for ( Number element : list )
56             total += element.doubleValue();
57
58          return total;
59       } // end method sum
60    } // end class WildcardTest
```

```
integerList contains: [1, 2, 3, 4, 5]
Total of the elements in integerList: 15

doubleList contains: [1.1, 3.3, 5.5]
Total of the elements in doubleList: 9.9

numberList contains: [1, 2.4, 3, 4.1]
Total of the elements in numberList: 10.5
```

Fig. 18.15 | Wildcard test program. (Part 2 of 2.)

Lines 11–20 create and initialize an `ArrayList< Integer >` called `integerList`, output its elements and total its elements by calling method `sum` (line 20). Lines 24–33 perform the same operations for an `ArrayList< Double >` called `doubleList`. Lines 37–46 perform the same operations for an `ArrayList< Number >` called `numberList` that contains both `Integers` and `Doubles`.

In method `sum` (lines 50–59), although the `ArrayList` argument's element types are not directly known by the method, they are known to be at least of type `Number` because the wildcard was specified with the upper bound `Number`. For this reason, line 56 is allowed because all `Number` objects have a `doubleValue` method.

Although wildcards provide flexibility when passing parameterized types to a method, they also have some disadvantages. Because the wildcard (?) in the method's header (line 50) does not specify a type parameter name, you cannot use it as a type name throughout the method's body (i.e., you cannot replace `Number` with ? in line 55). If the wildcard is specified without an upper bound, then only the methods of type `Object` can be invoked on values of the wildcard type. Also, methods that use wildcards in their parameter's type arguments cannot be used to add elements to a collection referenced by the parameter.

Common Programming Error 18.4

Using a wildcard in a method's type parameter section or using a wildcard as an explicit type of a variable in the method body is a syntax error.

18.9 Generics and Inheritance: Notes

Generics can be used with inheritance in several ways:

- A generic class can be derived from a non-generic class. For example, the `Object` class is a direct or indirect superclass of every generic class.

- A generic class can be derived from another generic class. For example, generic class `Stack` (in package `java.util`) is a subclass of generic class `Vector` (in package `java.util`). We discuss these classes in Chapter 19, Collections.

- A non-generic class can be derived from a generic class. For example, non-generic class `Properties` (in package `java.util`) is a subclass of generic class `Hashtable` (in package `java.util`). We also discuss these classes in Chapter 19.

- Finally, a generic method in a subclass can override a generic method in a superclass if both methods have the same signatures.

18.10 Wrap-Up

This chapter introduced J2SE 5.0's new generics capability. You learned how to declare generic methods and classes. You learned how J2SE 5.0 achieves backwards compatibility via raw types. You also learned how to use wildcards in a generic method or a generic class. In the next chapter, we demonstrate the interfaces, classes and algorithms of the Java collections framework. As you will see, the collections presented all use the generics capabilties you learned here.

18.11   Internet and Web Resources

`www.jcp.org/aboutJava/communityprocess/review/jsr014/`

Java Community Process download page for the generics specification document *Adding Generics to the Java Programming Language: Public Draft Specification, Version 2.0.*

`java.sun.com/j2se/5.0/pdf/generics-tutorial.pdf`

The tutorial *Generics in the Java Programming Language* by Gilad Bracha (the specification lead for JSR-14 and a reviewer of this book) introduces generics concepts with sample code snippets.

`today.java.net/pub/a/today/2003/12/02/explorations.html`
`today.java.net/pub/a/today/2004/01/15/wildcards.html`

The articles *Explorations: Generics, Erasure, and Bridging* and *Explorations: Wildcards in the Generics Specification*, each by William Grosso, overview generics features and how to use wildcards.

Summary

- Generic methods enable programmers to specify, with a single method declaration, a set of related methods.

- Generic classes enable programmers to specify, with a single class declaration, a set of related types.

- Generic methods and classes are among Java's most powerful capabilities for software reuse with compile-time type safety.

- Overloaded methods are often used to perform similar operations on different types of data.

- When the compiler encounters a method call, it always attempts to locate a method declaration that has the same method name and parameters that match the argument types in the method call.

- If the operations performed by several overloaded methods are identical for each argument type, the overloaded methods can be more compactly and conveniently coded using a generic method. You can write a single generic method declaration, which can be called with arguments of different data types. Based on the types of the arguments passed to the generic method, the compiler handles each method call appropriately.

- All generic method declarations have a type parameter section delimited by angle brackets (< and >) that precedes the method's return type.

- Each type parameter section contains one or more type parameters (also called formal type parameters) separated by commas.

- A type parameter, also known as type variable, is an identifier that specifies a generic type name. The type parameters can be used as the return type, parameter types and local variable types in a generic method declaration, and act as placeholders for the types of the arguments passed to the generic method, which are known as actual type arguments. Type parameters can represent only reference types.

- The names used for type parameters throughout the method declaration must match those declared in the type parameter section. The name of a type parameter can be declared only once in the type parameter section but can appear more than once in the method's parameter list. Type parameter names need not be unique among different generic methods.

- When the compiler encounters a method call, it first determines the argument types and attempts to locate a method with the same name that specifies parameters that match the argument types. If there is no such method, the compiler determines whether there is an inexact but applicable match.

- The relational operator > cannot be used with reference types. However, it is possible to compare two objects of the same class if that class implements the generic interface Comparable (package java.lang).

- Comparable objects have a compareTo method that must return 0 if the objects are equal, -1 if the first object is less than the second or 1 if the first object is greater than the second.
- All the type-wrapper classes for primitive types implement Comparable.
- A benefit of implementing interface Comparable is that Comparable objects can be used with the sorting and searching methods of class Collections (package java.util).
- When the compiler translates a generic method into Java bytecodes, it removes the type parameter section and replaces the type parameters with actual types. This process is known as erasure. By default each type parameter is replaced with its upper bound. By default, the upper bound is type Object unless specified otherwise in the type parameter section.
- When the compiler performs erasure on a method that returns a type variable, it also inserts explicit cast operations in front of each method call to ensure that the returned value is of the type expected by the caller.
- A generic method may be overloaded. A class can provide two or more generic methods that specify the same method name but different method parameters. A generic method can also be overloaded by non-generic methods that have the same method name and number of parameters. When the compiler encounters a method call, it searches for the method declaration that most precisely matches the method name and the argument types specified in the call.
- When the compiler encounters a method call, it performs a matching process to determine which method to call. The compiler tries to find and use a precise match in which the method names and argument types of the method call match those of a specific method declaration. If this fails, the compiler determines whether a generic method is available that provides a precise match of the method name and argument types, and if so, uses that generic method.
- Generic classes provide a means for describing a class in a type-independent manner. We can then instantiate type-specific objects of the generic class.
- A generic class declaration looks like a non-generic class declaration, except that the class name is followed by a type parameter section. As with generic methods, the type parameter section of a generic class can have one or more type parameters separated by commas.
- When a generic class is compiled, the compiler performs erasure on the class's type parameters and replaces them with their upper bounds.
- Type parameters cannot be used in a class's static declarations.
- When instantiating an object of a generic class, the types specified in angle brackets after the class name are known as type arguments. They are used by the compiler to replace the type parameters so that the compiler can perform type checking and insert cast operations as necessary.
- It is possible to instantiate a generic class without specifying a type argument. In this case, the new object of the class is said to have a raw type, which means that the compiler implicitly uses type Object (or the type parameter's upper bound) throughout the generic class for each type argument.
- The Java Collections Framework provides many generic data structures and algorithms that manipulate the elements of those data structures. Perhaps the simplest of the data structures is class ArrayList—a dynamically resizable, array-like data structure.
- Class Number is the superclass of both Integer and Double.
- Method add of class ArrayList appends an element to the end of the collection.
- Method toString of class ArrayList returns a string of the form "[*elements*]" in which *elements* is a comma-separated list of the elements' string representations.
- Method doubleValue of class Number obtains the Number's underlying primitive value as a double value.

- Wildcard type arguments enable you to specify method parameters, return values, variables, etc. that act as supertypes of parameterized types. A wildcard type argument is denoted by the question mark (?), which represents an "unknown type." A wildcard can also have an upper bound.

- Because a wildcard (?) is not a type parameter name, you cannot use it as a type name throughout a method's body.

- If a wildcard is specified without an upper bound, then only the methods of type `Object` can be invoked on values of the wildcard type.

- Methods that use wildcards as type arguments cannot be used to add elements to a collection referenced by the parameter.

- A generic class can be derived from a non-generic class. For example, `Object` is a direct or indirect superclass of every generic class.

- A generic class can be derived from another generic class.

- A non-generic class can be derived from a generic class.

- A generic method in a subclass can override a generic method in a superclass if both methods have the same signatures.

Terminology

? (wildcard type argument)	Java Collections Framework
actual type arguments	`Number` class
add method of `ArrayList`	overloaded a generic method
angle brackets (< and >)	parameterized class
`ArrayList` class	parameterized type
`Comparable<T>` interface	raw type
compareTo method of `Comparable<T>`	scope of a type parameter
default upper bound (`Object`) of a type	`toString` method of `ArrayList`
parameter	type argument
`Double` class	type parameter
doubleValue method of `Number`	type parameter scope
erasure	type parameter section
formal type parameter	type variable
generics	upper bound of a type parameter
generic class	upper bound of a wildcard
generic interface	wildcard (?)
generic method	wildcard as a type argument
`Integer` class	wildcard without an upper bound

Self-Review Exercises

18.1 State whether each of the following is *true* or *false*. If *false*, explain why.

a) A generic method cannot have the same method name as a non-generic method.

b) All generic method declarations have a type parameter section that immediately precedes the method name.

c) A generic method can be overloaded by another generic method with the same method name but different method parameters.

d) A type parameter can be declared only once in the type parameter section but can appear more than once in the method's parameter list.

e) Type parameter names among different generic methods must be unique.

f) The scope of a generic class's type parameter is the entire class except its `static` members.

18.2   Fill in the blanks in each of the following:

a) _____ and _____ enable programmers to specify, with a single method declaration, a set of related methods, or with a single class declaration, a set of related types, respectively.

b) A type parameter section is delimited by _____.

c) The _____ of a generic method can be used to specify the types of the arguments to the method, to specify the return type of the method and to declare variables within the method.

d) The statement "Stack objectStack = new Stack();" indicates that objectStack stores _____.

e) In a generic class declaration, the class name is followed by a(n) _____.

f) The syntax _____ specifies that the upper bound of a wildcard is type E.

Answers to Self-Review Exercises

18.1   a) False. Generic methods and non-generic methods can have same method name. A generic method can overload another generic method with the same method name but different method parameters. A generic method also can be overloaded by providing non-generic methods with the same method name and number of arguments. b) False. All generic method declarations have a type parameter section that immediately precedes the method's return type. c) True. d) True. e) False. Type parameter names among different generic methods need not be unique. f) True.

18.2   a) Generic methods, generic classes. b) angle brackets (< and >). c) type parameters. d) a raw type. e) type parameter section. f) ? extends E.

Exercises

18.3   Explain the use of the following notation in a Java program:

```
public class Array< T > { }
```

18.4   Write a generic method selectionSort based on the sort program of Fig. 16.6 and Fig. 16.7. Write a test program that inputs, sorts and outputs an Integer array and a Float array. [*Hint:* Use < T extends Comparable< T > > in the type parameter section for method selectionSort, so that you can use method compareTo to compare the objects of two generic types T.]

18.5   Overload generic method printArray of Fig. 18.3 so that it takes two additional integer arguments, lowSubscript and highSubscript. A call to this method prints only the designated portion of the array. Validate lowSubscript and highSubscript. If either is out-of-range, or if highSubscript is less than or equal to lowSubscript, the overloaded printArray method should throw an InvalidSubscriptException; otherwise, printArray should return the number of elements printed. Then modify main to exercise both versions of printArray on arrays integerArray, doubleArray and characterArray. Test all capabilities of both versions of printArray.

18.6   Overload generic method printArray of Fig. 18.3 with a non-generic version that specifically prints an array of strings in neat, tabular format, as shown in the sample output that follows:

```
Array stringArray contains:
one      two      three    four
five     six      seven    eight
```

18.7   Write a simple generic version of method isEqualTo that compares its two arguments with the equals method and returns true if they are equal and false otherwise. Use this generic method in a program that calls isEqualTo with a variety of built-in types, such as Object or Integer. What result do you get when you attempt to run this program?

18.8   Write a generic class Pair which has two type parameters—F and S, each represents the type of the first and second element of the pair respectively. Add *get* and *set* methods for the first and second elements of the pair. [*Hint:* The class header should be public class Pair< F, S >.]

18.9   Convert classes TreeNode and Tree from Fig. 17.17 into generic classes. To insert an object in a Tree, the object must be compared to the objects in existing TreeNodes. For this reason, classes TreeNode and Tree should specify Comparable< E > as the upper bound of each class's type parameter. After modifying classes TreeNode and Tree, write a test application that creates three Tree objects—one that stores Integers, one that stores Doubles and one that stores Strings. Insert 10 values into each tree. Then output the preorder, inorder and postorder traversals for each Tree.

18.10   Modify your test program from Exercise 18.9 to use a generic method named testTree to test the three Tree objects. The method should be called three times—once for each Tree object.

18.11   How can generic methods be overloaded?

18.12   The compiler performs a matching process to determine which method to call when a method is invoked. Under what circumstances does an attempt to make a match result in a compile-time error?

18.13   Explain why a Java program might use the statement

```
ArrayList< Employee > workerList = new ArrayList< Employee >();
```

19

Collections

OBJECTIVES

In this chapter you will learn:

- What collections are.
- To use class `Arrays` for array manipulations.
- To use the collections framework (prepackaged data structure) implementations.
- To use collections framework algorithms to manipulate (such as `search`, `sort` and `fill`) collections.
- To use the collections framework interfaces to program with collections polymorphically.
- To use iterators to "walk through" a collection.
- To use persistent hash tables manipulated with objects of class `Properties`.
- To use synchronization and modifiability wrappers.

19.1 Introduction

In Chapter 17, we discussed how to create and manipulate data structures. The discussion was "low level" in the sense that we painstakingly created each element of each data structure dynamically and modified the data structures by directly manipulating their elements and the references to their elements. In this chapter, we consider the Java collections framework, which contains prepackaged data structures, interfaces and algorithms for manipulating those data structures. Some examples of collections are the cards you hold in a card game, your favorite songs stored in your computer, the members of a sports team and the real-estate records in your local registry of deeds (which map book numbers and page numbers to property owners). In this chapter, we also discuss how generics (see Chapter 18) are used in the Java collections framework.

With collections, programmers use existing data structures, without concern for how they are implemented. This is a marvelous example of code reuse. Programmers can code faster and can expect excellent performance, maximizing execution speed and minimizing memory consumption. In this chapter, we discuss the collections framework interfaces that list the capabilities of each collection type, the implementation classes, the algorithms that process the collections, and the so-called *iterators* and enhanced `for` statement syntax that "walk through" collections. This chapter provides an introduction to the collections framework. For complete details, visit `java.sun.com/j2se/5.0/docs/guide/collections`.

The Java collections framework provides ready-to-go, reusable componentry—you do not need to write your own collection classes, but you can if you wish to. The collections are standardized so that applications can share them easily without concern with for details of their implementation. The collections framework encourages further reusability. As new data structures and algorithms are developed that fit this framework, a large base of programmers will already be familiar with the interfaces and algorithms implemented by those data structures.

19.2 Collections Overview

A *collection* is a data structure—actually, an object—that can hold references to other objects. Usually, collections contain references to objects that are all of the same type. The collections framework interfaces declare the operations to be performed generically on various types of collections. Figure 19.1 lists some of the interfaces of the collections framework. Several implementations of these interfaces are provided within the framework. Programmers may also provide implementations specific to their own requirements.

The collections framework provides high-performance, high-quality implementations of common data structures and enables software reuse. These features minimize the amount of coding programmers need to do to create and manipulate collections. The classes and interfaces of the collections framework are members of package `java.util`. In the next section, we begin our discussion by examining the collections framework capabilities for array manipulation.

In earlier versions of Java, the classes in the collections framework stored and manipulated `Object` references. Thus, you could store any object in a collection. One inconvenient aspect of storing `Object` references occurs when retrieving them from a collection. A program normally has the need to process specific types of objects. As a result, the `Object` references obtained from a collection typically need to be cast to an appropriate type to allow the program to process the objects correctly.

In J2SE 5.0, the collections framework has been enhanced with the generics capabilities we introduced in Chapter 18. This means that you can specify the exact type that will

Interface	Description
`Collection`	The root interface in the collections hierarchy from which interfaces `Set`, `Queue` and `List` are derived.
`Set`	A collection that does not contain duplicates.
`List`	An ordered collection that can contain duplicate elements.
`Map`	Associates keys to values and cannot contain duplicate keys.
`Queue`	Typically a first-in, first-out collection that models a waiting line; other orders can be specified.

Fig. 19.1 | Some collection framework interfaces.

be stored in a collection. You also receive the benefits of compile-time type checking—the compiler ensures that you are using appropriate types with your collection and, if not, issues compile-time error messages. Also, once you specify the type stored in a collection, any reference you retrieve from the collection will have the specified type. This eliminates the need for explicit type casts that can throw `ClassCastExceptions` if the referenced object is not of the appropriate type. Programs that were implemented with prior java versions and that use collections can compile properly because the compiler automatically uses raw types when it encounters collections for which type arguments were not specified.

19.3 Class Arrays

Class `Arrays` provides `static` methods for manipulating arrays. In Chapter 7, our discussion of array manipulation was low level in the sense that we wrote the actual code to sort and search arrays. Class Arrays provides high-level methods, such as **sort** for sorting an array, **binarySearch** for searching a sorted array, **equals** for comparing arrays and **fill** for placing values into an array. These methods are overloaded for primitive-type arrays and `Object` arrays. In addition, methods `sort` and `binarySearch` are overloaded with generic versions that allow programmers to sort and search arrays containing objects of any type. Figure 19.2 demonstrates methods `fill`, `sort`, `binarySearch` and `equals`. Method `main` (lines 65–85) creates a `UsingArrays` object and invokes its methods.

Line 17 calls `static` method `fill` of class `Arrays` to populate all 10 elements of `filledIntArray` with 7s. Overloaded versions of `fill` allow the programmer to populate a specific range of elements with the same value.

Line 18 sorts the elements of array `doubleArray`. The `static` method `sort` of class `Arrays` orders the array's elements in ascending order by default. We discuss how to sort in descending order later in the chapter. Overloaded versions of `sort` allow the programmer to sort a specific range of elements.

Lines 21–22 copy array `intArray` into array `intArrayCopy`. The first argument (`intArray`) passed to `System` method **arraycopy** is the array from which elements are to be copied. The second argument (0) is the index that specifies the starting point in the range of elements to copy from the array. This value can be any valid array index. The third argument (`intArrayCopy`) specifies the destination array that will store the copy. The fourth argument (0) specifies the index in the destination array where the first copied element should be stored. The last argument specifies the number of elements to copy from the array in the first argument. In this case, we copy all the elements in the array.

Line 50 calls `static` method `binarySearch` of class `Arrays` to perform a binary search on `intArray`, using `value` as the key. If `value` is found, `binarySearch` returns the index of the element; otherwise, `binarySearch` returns a negative value. The negative value returned is based on the search key's **insertion point**—the index where the key would be inserted in the array if we were performing an insert operation. After `binarySearch` determines the insertion point, it changes its sign to negative and subtracts 1 to obtain the return value. For example, in Fig. 19.2, the insertion point for the value 8763 is the element with index 6 in the array. Method `binarySearch` changes the insertion point to –6, subtracts 1 from it and returns the value –7. Subtracting 1 from the insertion point guarantees that method `binarySearch` returns positive values (>=0) if and only if the key is found. This return value is useful for inserting elements in a sorted array. Chapter 16, Searching and Sorting, discusses binary searching in detail.

```
1   // Fig. 19.2: UsingArrays.java
2   // Using Java arrays.
3   import java.util.Arrays;
4
5   public class UsingArrays
6   {
7      private int intArray[] = { 1, 2, 3, 4, 5, 6 };
8      private double doubleArray[] = { 8.4, 9.3, 0.2, 7.9, 3.4 };
9      private int filledIntArray[], intArrayCopy[];
10
11     // constructor initializes arrays
12     public UsingArrays()
13     {
14        filledIntArray = new int[ 10 ]; // create int array with 10 elements
15        intArrayCopy = new int[ intArray.length ];
16
17        Arrays.fill( filledIntArray, 7 ); // fill with 7s
18        Arrays.sort( doubleArray ); // sort doubleArray ascending
19
20        // copy array intArray into array intArrayCopy
21        System.arraycopy( intArray, 0, intArrayCopy,
22           0, intArray.length );
23     } // end UsingArrays constructor
24
25     // output values in each array
26     public void printArrays()
27     {
28        System.out.print( "doubleArray: " );
29        for ( double doubleValue : doubleArray )
30           System.out.printf( "%.1f ", doubleValue );
31
32        System.out.print( "\nintArray: " );
33        for ( int intValue : intArray )
34           System.out.printf( "%d ", intValue );
35
36        System.out.print( "\nfilledIntArray: " );
37        for ( int intValue : filledIntArray )
38           System.out.printf( "%d ", intValue );
39
40        System.out.print( "\nintArrayCopy: " );
41        for ( int intValue : intArrayCopy )
42           System.out.printf( "%d ", intValue );
43
44        System.out.println( "\n" );
45     } // end method printArrays
46
47     // find value in array intArray
48     public int searchForInt( int value )
49     {
50        return Arrays.binarySearch( intArray, value );
51     } // end method searchForInt
52
```

Fig. 19.2 | Arrays class methods. (Part 1 of 2.)

```
53        // compare array contents
54        public void printEquality()
55        {
56            boolean b = Arrays.equals( intArray, intArrayCopy );
57            System.out.printf( "intArray %s intArrayCopy\n",
58                ( b ? "==" : "!=" ) );
59
60            b = Arrays.equals( intArray, filledIntArray );
61            System.out.printf( "intArray %s filledIntArray\n",
62                ( b ? "==" : "!=" ) );
63        } // end method printEquality
64
65        public static void main( String args[] )
66        {
67            UsingArrays usingArrays = new UsingArrays();
68
69            usingArrays.printArrays();
70            usingArrays.printEquality();
71
72            int location = usingArrays.searchForInt( 5 );
73            if ( location >= 0 )
74                System.out.printf(
75                    "Found 5 at element %d in intArray\n", location );
76            else
77                System.out.println( "5 not found in intArray" );
78
79            location = usingArrays.searchForInt( 8763 );
80            if ( location >= 0 )
81                System.out.printf(
82                    "Found 8763 at element %d in intArray\n", location );
83            else
84                System.out.println( "8763 not found in intArray" );
85        } // end main
86    } // end class UsingArrays
```

```
doubleArray: 0.2 3.4 7.9 8.4 9.3
intArray: 1 2 3 4 5 6
filledIntArray: 7 7 7 7 7 7 7 7 7 7
intArrayCopy: 1 2 3 4 5 6

intArray == intArrayCopy
intArray != filledIntArray
Found 5 at element 4 in intArray
8763 not found in intArray
```

Fig. 19.2 | Arrays class methods. (Part 2 of 2.)

Common Programming Error 19.1

Passing an unsorted array to binarySearch is a logic error—the value returned is undefined.

Lines 56 and 60 call static method equals of class Arrays to determine whether the elements of two arrays are equivalent. If the arrays contain the same elements in the same order, the method returns true; otherwise, it returns false. The equality of each element is compared using `Object` method `equals`. Many classes override method `equals` to perform the comparisons in a manner specific to those classes. For example, class `String` declares `equals` to compare the individual characters in the two `Strings` being compared. If method `equals` is not overridden, the original version of method `equals` inherited from class `Object` is used.

19.4 Interface `Collection` and Class `Collections`

Interface `Collection` is the root interface in the collection hierarchy from which interfaces `Set`, `Queue` and `List` are derived. Interface `Set` defines a collection that does not contain duplicates. Interface `Queue` defines a collection that represents a waiting line—typically, insertions are made at the back of a queue and deletions are made from the front, though other orders can be specified. We discuss `Queue` and `Set` in Section 19.8 and Section 19.9, respectively. Interface `Collection` contains bulk operations (i.e., operations performed on an entire collection) for adding, clearing, comparing and retaining objects (or elements) in a collection. A `Collection` can also be converted to an array. In addition, interface `Collection` provides a method that returns an `Iterator` object, which allows a program to walk through the collection and remove elements from the collection during the iteration. We discuss class `Iterator` in Section 19.5.1. Other methods of interface `Collection` enable a program to determine a collection's size and whether a collection is empty.

Software Engineering Observation 19.1

`Collection` is used commonly as a method parameter type to allow polymorphic processing of all objects that implement interface `Collection`.

Software Engineering Observation 19.2

Most collection implementations provide a constructor that takes a `Collection` argument, thereby allowing a new collection to be constructed containing the elements of the specified collection.

Class `Collections` provides `static` methods that manipulate collections polymorphically. These methods implement algorithms for searching, sorting and so on. Chapter 16, Searching and Sorting, discussed and implemented various searching and sorting algorithms. Section 19.6 discusses more about the algorithms that are available in class `Collections`. We also cover the wrapper methods of class `Collections` that enable you to treat a collection as a synchronized collection (Section 19.12) or an unmodifiable collection (Section 19.13). Unmodifiable collections are useful when a client of a class needs to view the elements of a collection, but should not be allowed to modify the collection by adding and removing elements. Synchronized collections are for use with a powerful capability called multithreading (discussed in Chapter 23). Multithreading enables programs to perform operations in parallel. When two or more threads of a program share a collection, there is the potential for problems to occur. As a brief analogy, consider a traffic intersection. We cannot allow all cars access to one intersection at the same time—if we did, accidents would occur. For this reason, traffic lights are provided at intersections to control access to the intersection. Similarly, we can synchronize access to a collection to ensure that only one thread manipulates the collection at a time. The synchronization wrapper methods of class `collection` return synchronized versions of collections that can be shared among threads in a program.

19.5 Lists

A List (sometimes called a *sequence*) is an ordered Collection that can contain duplicate elements. Like array indices, List indices are zero based (i.e., the first element's index is zero). In addition to the methods inherited from Collection, List provides methods for manipulating elements via their indices, manipulating a specified range of elements, searching for elements and getting a ListIterator to access the elements.

Interface List is implemented by several classes, including classes ArrayList, LinkedList and Vector. Autoboxing occurs when you add primitive-type values to objects of these classes, because they store only references to objects. Class ArrayList and Vector are resizable-array implementations of List. Class LinkedList is a linked-list implementation of interface List.

Class ArrayList's behavior and capabilities are similar to those of class Vector. The primary difference between Vector and ArrayList is that objects of class Vector are synchronized by default, whereas objects of class ArrayList are not. Also, class Vector is from Java 1.0, before the collections framework was added to Java. As such, Vector has several methods that are not part of interface List and are not implemented in class ArrayList, but perform identical tasks. For example, Vector methods addElement and add both append an element to a Vector, but only method add is specified in interface List and implemented by ArrayList. Unsynchronized collections provide better performance than synchronized ones. For this reason, ArrayList is typically preferred over Vector in programs that do not share a collection among threads.

Performance Tip 19.1

ArrayLists behave like Vectors without synchronization and therefore execute faster than Vectors because ArrayLists do not have the overhead of thread synchronization.

Software Engineering Observation 19.3

LinkedLists can be used to create stacks, queues, trees and deques (double-ended queues, pronounced "decks"). The collections framework provides implementations of some of these data structures.

The following three subsections demonstrate the List and Collection capabilities with several examples. Section 19.5.1 focuses on removing elements from an ArrayList with an Iterator. Section 19.5.2 focuses on ListIterator and several List- and LinkedList-specific methods. Section 19.5.3 introduces more List methods and several Vector-specific methods.

19.5.1 ArrayList and Iterator

Figure 19.3 uses an ArrayList to demonstrate several Collection interface capabilities. The program places two Color arrays in ArrayLists and uses an Iterator to remove elements in the second ArrayList collection from the first ArrayList collection.

Lines 10–13 declare and initialize two String array variables, which are declared final, so they always refer to these arrays. Recall that it is good programing practice to declare constants with keywords static and final. Lines 18–19 create ArrayList objects and assign their references to variables list and removeList, respectively. These two lists store String objects. Note that ArrayList is a generic class in J2SE 5.0, so we are able to specify a type argument (String in this case) to indicate the type of the elements in each list. Both list and removeList are collections of Strings. Lines 22–23 populate list with Strings stored in array colors, and lines 26–27 populate removelist with Strings stored in array removeColors using List method **add**. Lines 32–33 output each element of list. Line 32 calls List method **size** to get the number of ArrayList elements. Line 33 uses List method **get** to retrieve individual element values. Lines 32–33 could have used the enhanced for statement. Line 36 calls method removeColors (lines 46–57), passing list and removeList as arguments. Method removeColors deletes Strings specified in removeList from the list collection. Lines 41–42 print list's elements after removeColors removes the String objects specified in removeList from the list.

```java
1   // Fig. 19.3: CollectionTest.java
2   // Using the Collection interface.
3   import java.util.List;
4   import java.util.ArrayList;
5   import java.util.Collection;
6   import java.util.Iterator;
7
8   public class CollectionTest
9   {
10     private static final String[] colors =
11        { "MAGENTA", "RED", "WHITE", "BLUE", "CYAN" };
12     private static final String[] removeColors =
13        { "RED", "WHITE", "BLUE" };
14
15     // create ArrayList, add Colors to it and manipulate it
16     public CollectionTest()
17     {
18        List< String > list = new ArrayList< String >();
19        List< String > removeList = new ArrayList< String >();
20
21        // add elements in colors array to list
22        for ( String color : colors )
23           list.add( color );
24
25        // add elements in removeColors to removeList
26        for ( String color : removeColors )
27           removeList.add( color );
28
29        System.out.println( "ArrayList: " );
30
31        // output list contents
32        for ( int count = 0; count < list.size(); count++ )
33           System.out.printf( "%s ", list.get( count ) );
34
35        // remove colors contained in removeList
36        removeColors( list, removeList );
37
38        System.out.println( "\n\nArrayList after calling removeColors: " );
39
```

Fig. 19.3 | Collection interface demonstrated via an ArrayList object. (Part 1 of 2.)

```
40          // output list contents
41          for ( String color : list )
42             System.out.printf( "%s ", color );
43       } // end CollectionTest constructor
44
45       // remove colors specified in collection2 from collection1
46       private void removeColors(
47          Collection< String > collection1, Collection< String > collection2 )
48       {
49          // get iterator
50          Iterator< String > iterator = collection1.iterator();
51
52          // loop while collection has items
53          while ( iterator.hasNext() )
54
55             if ( collection2.contains( iterator.next() ) )
56                iterator.remove(); // remove current Color
57       } // end method removeColors
58
59       public static void main( String args[] )
60       {
61          new CollectionTest();
62       } // end main
63    } // end class CollectionTest
```

```
ArrayList:
MAGENTA RED WHITE BLUE CYAN

ArrayList after calling removeColors:
MAGENTA CYAN
```

Fig. 19.3 | Collection interface demonstrated via an ArrayList object. (Part 2 of 2.)

Method removeColors declares two Collection parameters (line 47) that allow any Collections containing strings to be passed as arguments to this method. The method accesses the elements of the first Collection (collection1) via an Iterator. Line 50 calls Collection method **iterator** to get an Iterator for the Collection. Note that interfaces Collection and Iterator are generic types. The loop-continuation condition (line 53) calls Iterator method **hasNext** to determine whether the Collection contains more elements. Method hasNext returns true if another element exists and false otherwise.

The if condition in line 55 calls Iterator method **next** to obtain a reference to the next element, then uses method **contains** of the second Collection (collection2) to determine whether collection2 contains the element returned by next. If so, line 56 calls Iterator method **remove** to remove the element from the Collection collection1.

Common Programming Error 19.2

If a collection is modified by one of its methods after an iterator is created for that collection, the iterator immediately becomes invalid—any operations performed with the iterator after this point throw ConcurrentModificationExceptions. For this reason, iterators are said to be "fail fast."

19.5.2 LinkedList

Figure 19.4 demonstrates operations on LinkedLists. The program creates two LinkedLists that contain Strings. The elements of one List are added to the other. Then all the Strings are converted to uppercase, and a range of elements is deleted.

```java
1   // Fig. 19.4: ListTest.java
2   // Using LinkLists.
3   import java.util.List;
4   import java.util.LinkedList;
5   import java.util.ListIterator;
6
7   public class ListTest
8   {
9      private static final String colors[] = { "black", "yellow",
10        "green", "blue", "violet", "silver" };
11     private static final String colors2[] = { "gold", "white",
12        "brown", "blue", "gray", "silver" };
13
14     // set up and manipulate LinkedList objects
15     public ListTest()
16     {
17        List< String > list1 = new LinkedList< String >();
18        List< String > list2 = new LinkedList< String >();
19
20        // add elements to list link
21        for ( String color : colors )
22           list1.add( color );
23
24        // add elements to list link2
25        for ( String color : colors2 )
26           list2.add( color );
27
28        list1.addAll( list2 ); // concatenate lists
29        list2 = null; // release resources
30        printList( list1 ); // print list1 elements
31
32        convertToUppercaseStrings( list1 ); // convert to upper case string
33        printList( list1 ); // print list1 elements
34
35        System.out.print( "\nDeleting elements 4 to 6..." );
36        removeItems( list1, 4, 7 ); // remove items 4-7 from list
37        printList( list1 ); // print list1 elements
38        printReversedList( list1 ); // print list in reverse order
39     } // end ListTest constructor
40
41     // output List contents
42     public void printList( List< String > list )
43     {
44        System.out.println( "\nlist: " );
45
46        for ( String color : list )
47           System.out.printf( "%s ", color );
```

Fig. 19.4 | Lists and ListIterators. (Part 1 of 2.)

```
48
49          System.out.println();
50       } // end method printList
51
52       // locate String objects and convert to uppercase
53       private void convertToUppercaseStrings( List< String > list )
54       {
55          ListIterator< String > iterator = list.listIterator();
56
57          while ( iterator.hasNext() )
58          {
59             String color = iterator.next();   // get item
60             iterator.set( color.toUpperCase() ); // convert to upper case
61          } // end while
62       } // end method convertToUppercaseStrings
63
64       // obtain sublist and use clear method to delete sublist items
65       private void removeItems( List< String > list, int start, int end )
66       {
67          list.subList( start, end ).clear();   // remove items
68       } // end method removeItems
69
70       // print reversed list
71       private void printReversedList( List< String > list )
72       {
73          ListIterator< String > iterator = list.listIterator( list.size() );
74
75          System.out.println( "\nReversed List:" );
76
77          // print list in reverse order
78          while ( iterator.hasPrevious() )
79             System.out.printf( "%s ", iterator.previous() );
80       } // end method printReversedList
81
82       public static void main( String args[] )
83       {
84          new ListTest();
85       } // end main
86    } // end class ListTest
```

```
list:
black yellow green blue violet silver gold white brown blue gray silver

list:
BLACK YELLOW GREEN BLUE VIOLET SILVER GOLD WHITE BROWN BLUE GRAY SILVER

Deleting elements 4 to 6...
list:
BLACK YELLOW GREEN BLUE WHITE BROWN BLUE GRAY SILVER

Reversed List:
SILVER GRAY BLUE BROWN WHITE BLUE GREEN YELLOW BLACK
```

Fig. 19.4 | Lists and ListIterators. (Part 2 of 2.)

Lines 17–18 create LinkedLists list1 and list2 of type String. Note that LinkedList is a generic class that has one type parameter for which we specify the type argument String in this example. Lines 21–26 call List method add to append elements from arrays colors and colors2 to the end of list1 and list2, respectively.

Line 28 calls List method **addAll** to append all elements of list2 to the end of list1. Line 29 sets list2 to null, so the LinkedList to which list2 referred can be garbage collected. Line 30 calls method printList (lines 42–50) to output list list1's contents. Line 32 calls method convertToUppercaseStrings (lines 53–62) to convert each String element to uppercase, then line 33 calls printList again to display the modified Strings. Line 36 calls method removeItems (lines 65–68) to remove the elements starting at index 4 up to, but not including, index 7 of the list. Line 38 calls method printReversedList (lines 71–80) to print the list in reverse order.

Method convertToUppercaseStrings (lines 53–62) changes lowercase String elements in its List argument to uppercase Strings. Line 55 calls List method **listIterator** to get a **bidirectional iterator** (i.e., an iterator that can traverse a List backward or forward) for the List. Note that ListIterator is a generic class. In this example, the ListIterator contains String objects, because method listIterator is called on a List of Strings. The while condition (line 57) calls method hasNext to determine whether the List contains another element. Line 59 gets the next String in the List. Line 60 calls String method **toUpperCase** to get an uppercase version of the String and calls ListIterator method **set** to replace the current String to which iterator refers with the String returned by method toUpperCase. Like method toUpperCase, String method **toLowerCase** returns a lowercase version of the String.

Method removeItems (lines 65–68) removes a range of items from the list. Line 67 calls List method **subList** to obtain a portion of the List (called a **sublist**). The sublist is simply another view into the List on which subList is called. Method subList takes two arguments—the beginning and the ending index for the sublist. The ending index is not part of the range of the sublist. In this example, we pass (in line 36) 4 for the beginning index and 7 for the ending index to subList. The sublist returned is the set of elements with indices 4 through 6. Next, the program calls List method **clear** on the sublist to remove the elements of the sublist from the List. Any changes made to a sublist are also made to the original List.

Method printReversedList (lines 71–80) prints the list backward. Line 73 calls List method listIterator with one argument that specifies the starting position (in our case, the last element in the list) to get a bidirectional iterator for the list. List method **size** returns the number of items in the List. The while condition (line 78) calls method **hasPrevious** to determine whether there are more elements while traversing the list backward. Line 79 gets the previous element from the list and outputs it to the standard output stream.

An important feature of the collections framework is the ability to manipulate the elements of one collection type (such as a set) through a different collection type (such as a list), regardless of the collection's internal implementation. The set of public methods through which collections are manipulated is called a **view**.

Class Arrays provides static method **asList** to view an array as a **List** collection (which encapsulates behavior similar to that of the linked lists created in Chapter 17). A List view allows the programmer to manipulate the array as if it were a list. This is useful for adding the elements in an array to a collection (e.g., a LinkedList) and for sorting array elements. The next example demonstrates how to create a LinkedList with a List view of an array, because we cannot pass the array to a LinkedList constructor. Sorting array elements with a List view is demonstrated in Fig. 19.9. Any modifications made through the List view change the array, and any modifications made to the array change the List view. The only operation permitted on the view returned by asList is *set*, which changes the value of the view and the backing array. Any other attempts to change the view (such as adding or removing elements) result in an **UnsupportedOperationException**.

Figure 19.5 uses method asList to view an array as a List collection and uses method **toArray** of a List to get an array from a LinkedList collection. The program calls method asList to create a List view of an array, which is then used for creating a LinkedList object, adds a series of strings to a LinkedList and calls method toArray to obtain an array containing references to the strings. Notice that the instantiation of LinkedList (line 13) indicates that LinkedList is a generic class that accepts one type argument—String, in this example.

```java
1   // Fig. 19.5: UsingToArray.java
2   // Using method toArray.
3   import java.util.LinkedList;
4   import java.util.Arrays;
5
6   public class UsingToArray
7   {
8      // constructor creates LinkedList, adds elements and converts to array
9      public UsingToArray()
10     {
11        String colors[] = { "black", "blue", "yellow" };
12
13        LinkedList< String > links =
14           new LinkedList< String >( Arrays.asList( colors ) );
15
16        links.addLast( "red" );    // add as last item
17        links.add( "pink" );       // add to the end
18        links.add( 3, "green" );   // add at 3rd index
19        links.addFirst( "cyan" );  // add as first item
20
21        // get LinkedList elements as an array
22        colors = links.toArray( new String[ links.size() ] );
23
24        System.out.println( "colors: " );
25
26        for ( String color : colors )
27           System.out.println( color );
28     } // end UsingToArray constructor
29
30     public static void main( String args[] )
31     {
32        new UsingToArray();
33     } // end main
34  } // end class UsingToArray
```

Fig. 19.5 | List method toArray. (Part 1 of 2.)

```
colors:
cyan
black
blue
yellow
green
red
pink
```

Fig. 19.5 | List method toArray. (Part 2 of 2.)

Lines 13–14 construct a LinkedList of Strings containing the elements of array colors and assigns the LinkedList reference to links. Note the use of Arrays method asList to return a view of the array as a List, then initialize the LinkedList with the List. Line 16 calls LinkedList method **addLast** to add "red" to the end of links. Lines 17–18 call LinkedList method **add** to add "pink" as the last element and "green" as the element at index 3 (i.e., the fourth element). Note that method addLast (line 16) is identical in function to method add (line 17). Line 19 calls LinkedList method **addFirst** to add "cyan" as the new first item in the LinkedList. The add operations are permitted because they operate on the LinkedList object, not the view returned by asList. [*Note:* When "cyan" is added as the first element, "green" becomes the fifth element in the LinkedList.]

Line 22 calls List method toArray to get a String array from links. The array is a copy of the list's elements—modifying the contents of the array does not modify the list. The array passed to method toArray is of the same type that you would like method toArray to return. If the number of elements in the array is greater than or equal to the number of elements in the LinkedList, toArray copies the list's elements into its array argument and returns that array. If the LinkedList has more elements than the number of elements in the array passed to toArray, toArray allocates a new array of the same type it receives as an argument, copies the list's elements into the new array and returns the new array.

Common Programming Error 19.3

Passing an array that contains data to toArray can cause logic errors. If the number of elements in the array is smaller than the number of elements in the list on which toArray is called, a new array is allocated to store the list's elements—without preserving the array argument's elements. If the number of elements in the array is greater than the number of elements in the list, the elements of the array (starting at index zero) are overwritten with the list's elements. Array elements that are not overwritten retain their values.

19.5.3 Vector

Like ArrayList, class Vector provides the capabilities of array-like data structures that can resize themselves dynamically. Recall that class ArrayList's behavior and capabilities are similar to those of class Vector, except that ArrayLists do not provide synchronization by default. We cover class Vector here primarily because it is the superclass of class Stack, which is presented in Section 19.7.

At any time, a Vector contains a number of elements that is less than or equal to its capacity. The capacity is the space that has been reserved for the Vector's elements. If a Vector requires additional capacity, it grows by a capacity increment that you specify or by a default capacity increment. If you do not specify a capacity increment or specify one that is less than or equal to zero, the system will double the size of a Vector each time additional capacity is needed.

Performance Tip 19.2

Inserting an element into a Vector whose current size is less than its capacity is a relatively fast operation.

Performance Tip 19.3

Inserting an element into a Vector that needs to grow larger to accommodate the new element is a relatively slow operation.

Performance Tip 19.4

The default capacity increment doubles the size of the Vector. This may seem a waste of storage, but it is actually an efficient way for many Vectors to grow quickly to be "about the right size." This operation is much more efficient than growing the Vector each time by only as much space as it takes to hold a single element. The disadvantage is that the Vector might occupy more space than it requires. This is a classic example of the space–time trade-off.

Performance Tip 19.5

If storage is at a premium, use Vector method trimToSize to trim a Vector's capacity to the Vector's exact size. This operation optimizes a Vector's use of storage. However, adding another element to the Vector will force the Vector to grow dynamically (again, a relatively slow operation)—trimming leaves no room for growth.

Figure 19.6 demonstrates class Vector and several of its methods. For complete information on class Vector, please visit java.sun.com/j2se/5.0/docs/api/java/util/Vector.html.

The application's constructor creates a Vector (line 13) of type String with an initial capacity of 10 elements and capacity increment of zero (the defaults for a Vector). Note that Vector is a generic class, which takes one argument that specifies the type of the elements stored in the Vector. A capacity increment of zero indicates that this Vector will double in size each time it needs to grow to accommodate more elements. Class Vector

```
1   // Fig. 19.6: VectorTest.java
2   // Using the Vector class.
3   import java.util.Vector;
4   import java.util.NoSuchElementException;
5
6   public class VectorTest
7   {
8      private static final String colors[] = { "red", "white", "blue" };
9
10     public VectorTest()
11     {
12        Vector< String > vector = new Vector< String >();
13        printVector( vector ); // print vector
14
```

Fig. 19.6 | Vector class of package java.util. (Part 1 of 3.)

```
15        // add elements to the vector
16        for ( String color : colors )
17           vector.add( color );
18
19     printVector( vector ); // print vector
20
21        // output the first and last elements
22        try
23        {
24           System.out.printf( "First element: %s\n", vector.firstElement());
25           System.out.printf( "Last element: %s\n", vector.lastElement() );
26        } // end try
27        // catch exception if vector is empty
28        catch ( NoSuchElementException exception )
29        {
30           exception.printStackTrace();
31        } // end catch
32
33        // does vector contain "red"?
34        if ( vector.contains( "red" ) )
35           System.out.printf( "\n\"red\" found at index %d\n\n",
36              vector.indexOf( "red" ) );
37        else
38           System.out.println( "\n\"red\" not found\n" );
39
40        vector.remove( "red" ); // remove the string "red"
41        System.out.println( "\"red\" has been removed" );
42        printVector( vector ); // print vector
43
44        // does vector contain "red" after remove operation?
45        if ( vector.contains( "red" ) )
46           System.out.printf(
47              "\"red\" found at index %d\n", vector.indexOf( "red" ) );
48        else
49           System.out.println( "\"red\" not found" );
50
51        // print the size and capacity of vector
52        System.out.printf( "\nSize: %d\nCapacity: %d\n", vector.size(),
53           vector.capacity() );
54     } // end Vector constructor
55
56     private void printVector( Vector< String > vectorToOutput )
57     {
58        if ( vectorToOutput.isEmpty() )
59           System.out.print( "vector is empty" ); // vectorToOutput is empty
60        else  // iterate through the elements
61        {
62           System.out.print( "vector contains: " );
63
64           // output elements
65           for ( String element : vectorToOutput )
66              System.out.printf( "%s ", element );
67        } // end else
```

Fig. 19.6 | Vector class of package `java.util`. (Part 2 of 3.)

```
68
69          System.out.println( "\n" );
70      } // end method printVector
71
72      public static void main( String args[] )
73      {
74          new VectorTest(); // create object and call its constructor
75      } // end main
76  } // end class VectorTest
```

```
vector is empty

vector contains: red white blue

First element: red
Last element: blue

"red" found at index 0

"red" has been removed
vector contains: white blue

"red" not found

Size: 2
Capacity: 10
```

Fig. 19.6 | Vector class of package `java.util`. (Part 3 of 3.)

provides three other constructors. The constructor that takes one integer argument creates an empty Vector with the initial capacity specified by that argument. The constructor that takes two arguments creates a Vector with the initial capacity specified by the first argument and the capacity increment specified by the second argument. Each time the Vector needs to grow, it will add space for the specified number of elements in the capacity increment. The constructor that takes a Collection creates a copy of a collection's elements and stores them in the Vector.

Line 18 calls Vector method **add** to add objects (Strings in this program) to the end of the Vector. If necessary, the Vector increases its capacity to accommodate the new element. Class Vector also provides a method add that takes two arguments. This method takes an object and an integer and inserts the object at the specified index in the Vector. Method **set** will replace the element at a specified position in the Vector with a specified element. Method **insertElementAt** provides the same functionality as the method add that takes two arguments, except that the order of the parameters is reversed.

Line 25 calls Vector method **firstElement** to return a reference to the first element in the Vector. Line 26 calls Vector method **lastElement** to return a reference to the last element in the Vector. Each of these methods throws a NoSuchElementException if there are no elements in the Vector when the method is called.

Line 35 calls Vector method **contains** to determine whether the Vector contains "red". The method returns true if its argument is in the Vector—otherwise, the method returns `false`. Method `contains` uses `Object` method `equals` to determine whether the search key is equal to one of the `Vector`'s elements. Many classes override method `equals` to perform the comparisons in a manner specific to those classes. For example, class `String` declares `equals` to compare the individual characters in the two `Strings` being compared. If method `equals` is not overridden, the original version of method `equals` inherited from class `Object` is used.

Common Programming Error 19.4

Without overriding method `equals`, the program performs comparisons using operator `==` to determine whether two references refer to the same object in memory.

Line 37 calls `Vector` method **`indexOf`** to determine the index of the first location in the `Vector` that contains the argument. The method returns –1 if the argument is not found in the `Vector`. An overloaded version of this method takes a second argument specifying the index in the `Vector` at which the search should begin.

Performance Tip 19.6

`Vector` methods `contains` and `indexOf` perform linear searches of a `Vector`'s contents. These searches are inefficient for large `Vector`s. If a program frequently searches for elements in a collection, consider using one of the Java Collection API's `Map` implementations (Section 19.10), which provide high-speed searching capabilities.

Line 41 calls `Vector` method **`remove`** to remove the first occurrence of its argument from the `Vector`. The method returns `true` if it finds the element in the `Vector`; otherwise, the method returns `false`. If the element is removed, all elements after that element in the `Vector` shift one position toward the beginning of the `Vector` to fill in the position of the removed element. Class `Vector` also provides method **`removeAllElements`** to remove every element from a `Vector` and method **`removeElementAt`** to remove the element at a specified index.

Lines 53–54 use `Vector` methods **`size`** and **`capacity`** to determine the number of elements currently in the `Vector` and the number of elements that can be stored in the `Vector` without allocating more memory, respectively.

Line 59 calls `Vector` method **`isEmpty`** to determine whether the `Vector` is empty. The method returns `true` if there are no elements in the `Vector`; otherwise, the method returns `false`. Lines 66–67 use the enhanced `for` statement to print out all elements in the vector.

Among the methods introduced in Fig. 19.6, `firstElement`, `lastElement` and `capacity` can be used only with `Vector`. Other methods (e.g., `add`, `contains`, `indexOf`, `remove`, `size` and `isEmpty`) are declared by `List`, which means that they can be used by any class that implements `List`, such as `Vector`.

19.6 Collections Algorithms

The collections framework provides several high-performance algorithms for manipulating collection elements. These algorithms are implemented as `static` methods of class `Collections` (Fig. 19.7). Algorithms `sort`, `binarySearch`, `reverse`, `shuffle`, `fill` and `copy` operate on `List`s. Algorithms `min`, `max`, `addAll`, `frequency` and `disjoint` operate on `Collections`.

Algorithm	Description
sort	Sorts the elements of a List.
binarySearch	Locates an object in a List.
reverse	Reverses the elements of a List.
shuffle	Randomly orders a List's elements.
fill	Sets every List element to refer to a specified object.
copy	Copies references from one List into another.
min	Returns the smallest element in a Collection.
max	Returns the largest element in a Collection.
addAll	Appends all elements in an array to a collection.
frequency	Calculates how many elements in the collection are equal to the specified element.
disjoint	Determines whether two collections have no elements in common.

Fig. 19.7 | Collections algorithms.

Software Engineering Observation 19.4

The collections framework algorithms are polymorphic. That is, each algorithm can operate on objects that implement specific interfaces, regardless of the underlying implementations.

19.6.1 Algorithm sort

Algorithm **sort** sorts the elements of a List, which must implement the **Comparable** interface. The order is determined by the natural order of the elements' type as implemented by its class's compareTo method. Method compareTo is declared in interface Comparable and is sometimes called the natural comparison method. The sort call may specify as a second argument a **Comparator** object that determines an alternative ordering of the elements.

Sorting in Ascending Order
Figure 19.8 uses algorithm sort to order the elements of a List in ascending order (line 20). Recall that List is a generic type and accepts one type argument that specifies the list element type—line 15 declares list as a List of String. Note that lines 18 and 23 each use an implicit call to the list's toString method to output the list contents in the format shown on the second and fourth lines of the output.

Sorting in Descending Order
Figure 19.9 sorts the same list of strings used in Fig. 19.8 in descending order. The example introduces the Comparator interface, which is used for sorting a Collection's elements in a different order. Line 21 calls Collections's method sort to order the List in descending order. The static Collections method **reverseOrder** returns a Comparator object that orders the collection's elements in reverse order.

```
 1   // Fig. 19.8: Sort1.java
 2   // Using algorithm sort.
 3   import java.util.List;
 4   import java.util.Arrays;
 5   import java.util.Collections;
 6
 7   public class Sort1
 8   {
 9      private static final String suits[] =
10         { "Hearts", "Diamonds", "Clubs", "Spades" };
11
12      // display array elements
13      public void printElements()
14      {
15         List< String > list = Arrays.asList( suits ); // create List
16
17         // output list
18         System.out.printf( "Unsorted array elements:\n%s\n", list );
19
20         Collections.sort( list ); // sort ArrayList
21
22         // output list
23         System.out.printf( "Sorted array elements:\n%s\n", list );
24      } // end method printElements
25
26      public static void main( String args[] )
27      {
28         Sort1 sort1 = new Sort1();
29         sort1.printElements();
30      } // end main
31   } // end class Sort1
```

```
Unsorted array elements:
[Hearts, Diamonds, Clubs, Spades]
Sorted array elements:
[Clubs, Diamonds, Hearts, Spades]
```

Fig. 19.8 | Collections method sort.

```
 1   // Fig. 19.9: Sort2.java
 2   // Using a Comparator object with algorithm sort.
 3   import java.util.List;
 4   import java.util.Arrays;
 5   import java.util.Collections;
 6
 7   public class Sort2
 8   {
 9      private static final String suits[] =
10         { "Hearts", "Diamonds", "Clubs", "Spades" };
```

Fig. 19.9 | Collections method sort with a Comparator object. (Part 1 of 2.)

```
11
12       // output List elements
13       public void printElements()
14       {
15          List list = Arrays.asList( suits ); // create List
16
17          // output List elements
18          System.out.printf( "Unsorted array elements:\n%s\n", list );
19
20          // sort in descending order using a comparator
21          Collections.sort( list, Collections.reverseOrder() );
22
23          // output List elements
24          System.out.printf( "Sorted list elements:\n%s\n", list );
25       } // end method printElements
26
27       public static void main( String args[] )
28       {
29          Sort2 sort2 = new Sort2();
30          sort2.printElements();
31       } // end main
32    } // end class Sort2
```

```
Unsorted array elements:
[Hearts, Diamonds, Clubs, Spades]
Sorted list elements:
[Spades, Hearts, Diamonds, Clubs]
```

Fig. 19.9 | `Collections` method `sort` with a `Comparator` object. (Part 2 of 2.)

Sorting with a Comparator

Figure 19.10 creates a custom `Comparator` class, named `TimeComparator`, that implements interface `Comparator` to compare two `Time2` objects. Class `Time2`, declared in Fig. 8.5, represents times with hours, minutes and seconds.

Class `TimeComparator` implements interface `Comparator`, a generic type that takes one argument (in this case `Time2`). Method `compare` (lines 7–26) performs comparisons between `Time2` objects. Line 9 compares the two hours of the `Time2` objects. If the hours are different (line 12), then we return this value. If this value is positive, then the first hour is greater than the second and the first time is greater than the second. If this value is negative, then the first hour is less than the second and the first time is less than the second. If this value is zero, the hours are the same and we must test the minutes (and maybe the seconds) to determine which time is greater.

Figure 19.11 sorts a list using the custom `Comparator` class `TimeComparator`. Line 11 creates an `ArrayList` of `Time2` objects. Recall that both `ArrayList` and `List` are generic types and accept a type argument that specifies the element type of the collection. Lines 13–17 create five `Time2` objects and add them to this list. Line 23 calls method `sort`, passing it an object of our `TimeComparator` class (Fig. 19.10).

```
1   // Fig. 19.10: TimeComparator.java
2   // Custom Comparator class that compares two Time2 objects.
3   import java.util.Comparator;
4
5   public class TimeComparator implements Comparator< Time2 >
6   {
7      public int compare( Time2 time1, Time2 time2 )
8      {
9         int hourCompare = time1.getHour() - time2.getHour(); // compare hour
10
11        // test the hour first
12        if ( hourCompare != 0 )
13           return hourCompare;
14
15        int minuteCompare =
16           time1.getMinute() - time2.getMinute(); // compare minute
17
18        // then test the minute
19        if ( minuteCompare != 0 )
20           return minuteCompare;
21
22        int secondCompare =
23           time1.getSecond() - time2.getSecond(); // compare second
24
25        return secondCompare; // return result of comparing seconds
26     } // end method compare
27  } // end class TimeComparator
```

Fig. 19.10 | Custom Comparator class that compares two Time2 objects.

```
1   // Fig. 19.11: Sort3.java
2   // Sort a list using the custom Comparator class TimeComparator.
3   import java.util.List;
4   import java.util.ArrayList;
5   import java.util.Collections;
6
7   public class Sort3
8   {
9      public void printElements()
10     {
11        List< Time2 > list = new ArrayList< Time2 >(); // create List
12
13        list.add( new Time2(  6, 24, 34 ) );
14        list.add( new Time2( 18, 14, 58 ) );
15        list.add( new Time2(  6, 05, 34 ) );
16        list.add( new Time2( 12, 14, 58 ) );
17        list.add( new Time2(  6, 24, 22 ) );
18
19        // output List elements
20        System.out.printf( "Unsorted array elements:\n%s\n", list );
21
```

Fig. 19.11 | Collections method sort with a custom Comparator object. (Part 1 of 2.)

```
22          // sort in order using a comparator
23          Collections.sort( list, new TimeComparator() );
24
25          // output List elements
26          System.out.printf( "Sorted list elements:\n%s\n", list );
27       } // end method printElements
28
29       public static void main( String args[] )
30       {
31          Sort3 sort3 = new Sort3();
32          sort3.printElements();
33       } // end main
34    } // end class Sort3
```

```
Unsorted array elements:
[6:24:34 AM, 6:14:58 PM, 6:05:34 AM, 12:14:58 PM, 6:24:22 AM]
Sorted list elements:
[6:05:34 AM, 6:24:22 AM, 6:24:34 AM, 12:14:58 PM, 6:14:58 PM]
```

Fig. 19.11 | Collections method sort with a custom Comparator object. (Part 2 of 2.)

19.6.2 Algorithm shuffle

Algorithm **shuffle** randomly orders a List's elements. In Chapter 7, we presented a card shuffling and dealing simulation that used a loop to shuffle a deck of cards. In Fig. 19.12, we use algorithm shuffle to shuffle a deck of Card objects that might be used in a card game simulator.

Class Card (lines 8–41) represents a card in a deck of cards. Each Card has a face and a suit. Lines 10–12 declare two enum types—Face and Suit—which represent the face and the suit of the card, respectively. Method toString (lines 37–40) returns a String containing the face and suit of the Card separated by the string " of ". When an enum constant is converted to a string, the constant's identifier is used as the string representation. Normally we would use all uppercase letters for enum constants. In this example, we chose to use capital letters for only the first letter of each enum constant because we want the card to be displayed with initial capital letters for the face and the suit (e.g., "Ace of Spades").

```
1   // Fig. 19.12: DeckOfCards.java
2   // Using algorithm shuffle.
3   import java.util.List;
4   import java.util.Arrays;
5   import java.util.Collections;
6
7   // class to represent a Card in a deck of cards
8   class Card
9   {
10     public static enum Face { Ace, Deuce, Three, Four, Five, Six,
11        Seven, Eight, Nine, Ten, Jack, Queen, King };
12     public static enum Suit { Clubs, Diamonds, Hearts, Spades };
13
```

Fig. 19.12 | Card shuffling and dealing with Collections method shuffle. (Part 1 of 3.)

```
14       private final Face face; // face of card
15       private final Suit suit; // suit of card
16
17       // two-argument constructor
18       public Card( Face cardFace, Suit cardSuit )
19       {
20          face = cardFace; // initialize face of card
21          suit = cardSuit; // initialize suit of card
22       } // end two-argument Card constructor
23
24       // return face of the card
25       public Face getFace()
26       {
27          return face;
28       } // end method getFace
29
30       // return suit of Card
31       public Suit getSuit()
32       {
33          return suit;
34       } // end method getSuit
35
36       // return String representation of Card
37       public String toString()
38       {
39          return String.format( "%s of %s", face, suit );
40       } // end method toString
41    } // end class Card
42
43    // class DeckOfCards declaration
44    public class DeckOfCards
45    {
46       private List< Card > list; // declare List that will store Cards
47
48       // set up deck of Cards and shuffle
49       public DeckOfCards()
50       {
51          Card[] deck = new Card[ 52 ];
52          int count = 0; // number of cards
53
54          // populate deck with Card objects
55          for ( Card.Suit suit : Card.Suit.values() )
56          {
57             for ( Card.Face face : Card.Face.values() )
58             {
59                deck[ count ] = new Card( face, suit );
60                count++;
61             } // end for
62          } // end for
63
64          list = Arrays.asList( deck ); // get List
65          Collections.shuffle( list );  // shuffle deck
66       } // end DeckOfCards constructor
```

Fig. 19.12 | Card shuffling and dealing with `Collections` method `shuffle`. (Part 2 of 3.)

```
67
68      // output deck
69      public void printCards()
70      {
71          // display 52 cards in two columns
72          for ( int i = 0; i < list.size(); i++ )
73              System.out.printf( "%-20s%s", list.get( i ),
74                  ( ( i + 1 ) % 2 == 0 ) ? "\n" : "\t" );
75      } // end method printCards
76
77      public static void main( String args[] )
78      {
79          DeckOfCards cards = new DeckOfCards();
80          cards.printCards();
81      } // end main
82  } // end class DeckOfCards
```

```
King of Diamonds      Jack of Spades
Four of Diamonds      Six of Clubs
King of Hearts        Nine of Diamonds
Three of Spades       Four of Spades
Four of Hearts        Seven of Spades
Five of Diamonds      Eight of Hearts
Queen of Diamonds     Five of Hearts
Seven of Diamonds     Seven of Hearts
Nine of Hearts        Three of Clubs
Ten of Spades         Deuce of Hearts
Three of Hearts       Ace of Spades
Six of Hearts         Eight of Diamonds
Six of Diamonds       Deuce of Clubs
Ace of Clubs          Ten of Diamonds
Eight of Clubs        Queen of Hearts
Jack of Clubs         Ten of Clubs
Seven of Clubs        Queen of Spades
Five of Clubs         Six of Spades
Nine of Spades        Nine of Clubs
King of Spades        Ace of Diamonds
Ten of Hearts         Ace of Hearts
Queen of Clubs        Deuce of Spades
Three of Diamonds     King of Clubs
Four of Clubs         Jack of Diamonds
Eight of Spades       Five of Spades
Jack of Hearts        Deuce of Diamonds
```

Fig. 19.12 | Card shuffling and dealing with `Collections` method `shuffle`. (Part 3 of 3.)

Lines 55–62 populate the deck array with cards that have unique face and suit combinations. Both `Face` and `Suit` are `public static enum` types of class `Card`. To use these enum types outside of class `Card`, you must qualify each enum's type name with the name of the class in which it resides (i.e., `Card`) and a dot (`.`) separator. Hence, lines 55 and 57 use `Card.Suit` and `Card.Face` to declare the control variables of the `for` statements. Recall that method `values` of an enum type returns an array that contains all the constants of the enum type. Lines 55–62 use enhanced `for` statements to construct 52 new `Card`s.

The shuffling occurs in line 65, which calls static method shuffle of class Collections to shuffle the elements of the array. Method shuffle requires a List argument, so we must obtain a List view of the array before we can shuffle it. Line 64 invokes static method asList of class Arrays to get a List view of the deck array.

Method printCards (lines 69–75) displays the deck of cards in two columns. In each iteration of the loop, lines 73–74 output a card left justified in a 20-character field followed by either a newline or an empty string based on the number of cards output so far. If the number of cards is even, a newline is output; otherwise, a tab is output.

19.6.3 Algorithms reverse, fill, copy, max and min

Class Collections provides algorithms for reversing, filling and copying Lists. Algorithm **reverse** reverses the order of the elements in a List, and algorithm **fill** overwrites elements in a List with a specified value. The fill operation is useful for reinitializing a List. Algorithm **copy** takes two arguments—a destination List and a source List. Each source List element is copied to the destination List. The destination List must be at least as long as the source List; otherwise, an IndexOutOfBoundsException occurs. If the destination List is longer, the elements not overwritten are unchanged.

Each of the algorithms we have seen so far operates on Lists. Algorithms **min** and **max** each operate on any Collection. Algorithm min returns the smallest element in a Collection, and algorithm max returns the largest element in a Collection. Both of these algorithms can be called with a Comparator object as a second argument to perform custom comparisons of objects, such as the TimeComparator in Fig. 19.11. Figure 19.13 demonstrates the use of algorithms reverse, fill, copy, min and max. Note that the generic type List is declared to store Characters.

```
I   // Fig. 19.13: Algorithms1.java
2   // Using algorithms reverse, fill, copy, min and max.
3   import java.util.List;
4   import java.util.Arrays;
5   import java.util.Collections;
6
7   public class Algorithms1
8   {
9      private Character[] letters = { 'P', 'C', 'M' };
10     private Character[] lettersCopy;
11     private List< Character > list;
12     private List< Character > copyList;
13
14     // create a List and manipulate it with methods from Collections
15     public Algorithms1()
16     {
17        list = Arrays.asList( letters ); // get List
18        lettersCopy = new Character[ 3 ];
19        copyList = Arrays.asList( lettersCopy ); // list view of lettersCopy
20
21        System.out.println( "Initial list: " );
22        output( list );
23
```

Fig. 19.13 | Collections methods reverse, fill, copy, max and min. (Part 1 of 2.)

```
24          Collections.reverse( list ); // reverse order
25          System.out.println( "\nAfter calling reverse: " );
26          output( list );
27
28          Collections.copy( copyList, list ); // copy List
29          System.out.println( "\nAfter copying: " );
30          output( copyList );
31
32          Collections.fill( list, 'R' ); // fill list with Rs
33          System.out.println( "\nAfter calling fill: " );
34          output( list );
35       } // end Algorithms1 constructor
36
37       // output List information
38       private void output( List< Character > listRef )
39       {
40          System.out.print( "The list is: " );
41
42          for ( Character element : listRef )
43             System.out.printf( "%s ", element );
44
45          System.out.printf( "\nMax: %s", Collections.max( listRef ) );
46          System.out.printf( "  Min: %s\n", Collections.min( listRef ) );
47       } // end method output
48
49       public static void main( String args[] )
50       {
51          new Algorithms1();
52       } // end main
53    } // end class Algorithms1
```

```
Initial list:
The list is: P C M
Max: P  Min: C

After calling reverse:
The list is: M C P
Max: P  Min: C

After copying:
The list is: M C P
Max: P  Min: C

After calling fill:
The list is: R R R
Max: R  Min: R
```

Fig. 19.13 | `Collections` methods reverse, fill, copy, max and min. (Part 2 of 2.)

Line 24 calls `Collections` method reverse to reverse the order of list. Method reverse takes one `List` argument. In this case, list is a `List` view of array letters. Array letters now has its elements in reverse order. Line 28 copies the elements of list into copyList, using `Collections` method copy. Changes to copyList do not change let-ters, because copyList is a separate `List` that is not a `List` view for letters. Method copy requires two List arguments. Line 32 calls Collections method fill to place the string "R" in each element of list. Because list is a List view of letters, this operation changes each element in letters to "R". Method fill requires a List for the first argument and an Object for the second argument. Lines 45–46 call Collections methods max and min to find the largest and the smallest element of the collection, respectively. Recall that a List is a Collection, so lines 45–46 can pass a List to methods max and min.

19.6.4 Algorithm binarySearch

In Section 16.2.2, we studied the high-speed binary-search algorithm. This algorithm is built into the Java collections framework as a static method of class Collections. The binarySearch algorithm locates an object in a List (i.e., a LinkedList, a Vector or an ArrayList). If the object is found, its index is returned. If the object is not found, binarySearch returns a negative value. Algorithm binarySearch determines this negative value by first calculating the insertion point and making its sign negative. Then, binarySearch subtracts 1 from the insertion point to obtain the return value, which guarantees that method binarySearch returns positive numbers (>=0) if and only if the object is found. If multiple elements in the list match the search key, there is no guarantee which one will be located first. Figure 19.14 uses the binarySearch algorithm to search for a series of strings in an ArrayList.

Recall that both List and ArrayList are generic types (lines 12 and 17). Collections method binarySearch expects the list's elements to be sorted in ascending order, so line 18 in the constructor sorts the list with Collections method sort. If the list's elements are not sorted, the result is undefined. Line 19 outputs the sorted list. Method search (lines 23–31) is called from main to perform the searches. Each search calls method printSearchResults (lines 34–45) to perform the search and output the results. Line 39 calls Collections

```
 1   // Fig. 19.14: BinarySearchTest.java
 2   // Using algorithm binarySearch.
 3   import java.util.List;
 4   import java.util.Arrays;
 5   import java.util.Collections;
 6   import java.util.ArrayList;
 7
 8   public class BinarySearchTest
 9   {
10      private static final String colors[] = { "red", "white",
11         "blue", "black", "yellow", "purple", "tan", "pink" };
12      private List< String > list; // ArrayList reference
13
14      // create, sort and output list
15      public BinarySearchTest()
16      {
17         list = new ArrayList< String >( Arrays.asList( colors ) );
18         Collections.sort( list ); // sort the ArrayList
19         System.out.printf( "Sorted ArrayList: %s\n", list );
20      } // end BinarySearchTest constructor
```

Fig. 19.14 | Collections method binarySearch. (Part 1 of 2.)

```
21
22      // search list for various values
23      private void search()
24      {
25         printSearchResults( colors[ 3 ] ); // first item
26         printSearchResults( colors[ 0 ] ); // middle item
27         printSearchResults( colors[ 7 ] ); // last item
28         printSearchResults( "aqua" ); // below lowest
29         printSearchResults( "gray" ); // does not exist
30         printSearchResults( "teal" ); // does not exist
31      } // end method search
32
33      // perform searches and display search result
34      private void printSearchResults( String key )
35      {
36         int result = 0;
37
38         System.out.printf( "\nSearching for: %s\n", key );
39         result = Collections.binarySearch( list, key );
40
41         if ( result >= 0 )
42            System.out.printf( "Found at index %d\n", result );
43         else
44            System.out.printf( "Not Found (%d)\n",result );
45      } // end method printSearchResults
46
47      public static void main( String args[] )
48      {
49         BinarySearchTest binarySearchTest = new BinarySearchTest();
50         binarySearchTest.search();
51      } // end main
52   } // end class BinarySearchTest
```

```
Sorted ArrayList: [black, blue, pink, purple, red, tan, white, yellow]

Searching for: black
Found at index 0

Searching for: red
Found at index 4

Searching for: pink
Found at index 2

Searching for: aqua
Not Found (-1)

Searching for: gray
Not Found (-3)

Searching for: teal
Not Found (-7)
```

Fig. 19.14 | Collections method binarySearch. (Part 2 of 2.)

method binarySearch to search list for the specified key. Method binarySearch takes a List as the first argument and an Object as the second argument. Lines 41–44 output the results of the search. An overloaded version of binarySearch takes a Comparator object as its third argument, which specifies how binarySearch should compare elements.

19.6.5 Algorithms addAll, frequency and disjoint

Among others, J2SE 5.0 includes three new algorithms in class Collections, namely **addAll**, **frequency** and **disjoint**. Algorithm addAll takes two arguments—a Collection into which to insert the new element(s) and an array that provides elements to be inserted. Algorithm frequency takes two arguments—a Collection to be searched and an Object to be searched for in the collection. Method frequency returns the number of times that the second argument appears in the collection. Algorithm disjoint takes two Collections and returns true if they have no elements in common. Figure 19.15 demonstrates the use of algorithms addAll, frequency and disjoint.

```java
 1  // Fig. 19.15: Algorithms2.java
 2  // Using algorithms addAll, frequency and disjoint.
 3  import java.util.List;
 4  import java.util.Vector;
 5  import java.util.Arrays;
 6  import java.util.Collections;
 7
 8  public class Algorithms2
 9  {
10     private String[] colors = { "red", "white", "yellow", "blue" };
11     private List< String > list;
12     private Vector< String > vector = new Vector< String >();
13
14     // create List and Vector
15     // and manipulate them with methods from Collections
16     public Algorithms2()
17     {
18        // initialize list and vector
19        list = Arrays.asList( colors );
20        vector.add( "black" );
21        vector.add( "red" );
22        vector.add( "green" );
23
24        System.out.println( "Before addAll, vector contains: " );
25
26        // display elements in vector
27        for ( String s : vector )
28           System.out.printf( "%s ", s );
29
30        // add elements in colors to list
31        Collections.addAll( vector, colors );
32
33        System.out.println( "\n\nAfter addAll, vector contains: " );
34
```

Fig. 19.15 | Collections method addAll, frequency and disjoint. (Part 1 of 2.)

```
35          // display elements in vector
36          for ( String s : vector )
37              System.out.printf( "%s ", s );
38
39          // get frequency of "red"
40          int frequency = Collections.frequency( vector, "red" );
41          System.out.printf(
42              "\n\nFrequency of red in vector: %d\n", frequency );
43
44          // check whether list and vector have elements in common
45          boolean disjoint = Collections.disjoint( list, vector );
46
47          System.out.printf( "\nlist and vector %s elements in common\n",
48              ( disjoint ? "do not have" : "have"  ) );
49      } // end Algorithms2 constructor
50
51      public static void main( String args[] )
52      {
53          new Algorithms2();
54      } // end main
55  } // end class Algorithms2
```

```
Before addAll, vector contains:
black red green

After addAll, vector contains:
black red green red white yellow blue

Frequency of red in vector: 2

list and vector have elements in common
```

Fig. 19.15 | Collections method `addAll`, `frequency` and `disjoint`. (Part 2 of 2.)

Line 19 initializes `list` with elements in array `colors`, and lines 20–22 add `Strings` "black", "red" and "green" to `vector`. Line 31 invokes method `addAll` to add elements in array `colors` to `vector`. Line 40 gets the frequency of `String` "red" in `Collection` `vector` using method `frequency`. Note that lines 41–42 use the new `printf` method to print the frequency. Line 45 invokes method `disjoint` to test whether `Collections` `list` and `vector` have elements in common.

19.7 Stack Class of Package `java.util`

In Chapter 17, Data Structures, we learned how to build fundamental data structures, including linked lists, stacks, queues and trees. In a world of software reuse, rather than building data structures as we need them, we can often take advantage of existing data structures. In this section, we investigate class **Stack** in the Java utilities package (`java.util`).

Section 19.5.3 discussed class `Vector`, which implements a dynamically resizable array. Class `Stack` extends class `Vector` to implement a stack data structure. Autoboxing occurs when you add a primitive type to a `Stack`, because class `Stack` stores only references to objects. Figure 19.16 demonstrates several `Stack` methods. For the details of class `Stack`, visit `java.sun.com/j2se/5.0/docs/api/java/util/Stack.html`.

```
 1   // Fig. 19.16: StackTest.java
 2   // Program to test java.util.Stack.
 3   import java.util.Stack;
 4   import java.util.EmptyStackException;
 5
 6   public class StackTest
 7   {
 8      public StackTest()
 9      {
10         Stack< Number > stack = new Stack< Number >();
11
12         // create numbers to store in the stack
13         Long longNumber = 12L;
14         Integer intNumber = 34567;
15         Float floatNumber = 1.0F;
16         Double doubleNumber = 1234.5678;
17
18         // use push method
19         stack.push( longNumber ); // push a long
20         printStack( stack );
21         stack.push( intNumber ); // push an int
22         printStack( stack );
23         stack.push( floatNumber ); // push a float
24         printStack( stack );
25         stack.push( doubleNumber ); // push a double
26         printStack( stack );
27
28         // remove items from stack
29         try
30         {
31            Number removedObject = null;
32
33            // pop elements from stack
34            while ( true )
35            {
36               removedObject = stack.pop(); // use pop method
37               System.out.printf( "%s popped\n", removedObject );
38               printStack( stack );
39            } // end while
40         } // end try
41         catch ( EmptyStackException emptyStackException )
42         {
43            emptyStackException.printStackTrace();
44         } // end catch
45      } // end StackTest constructor
46
47      private void printStack( Stack< Number > stack )
48      {
49         if ( stack.isEmpty() )
50            System.out.print( "stack is empty\n\n" ); // the stack is empty
51         else  // stack is not empty
52         {
53            System.out.print( "stack contains: " );
```

Fig. 19.16 | Stack class of package `java.util`. (Part 1 of 2.)

```
54
55                // iterate through the elements
56                for ( Number number : stack )
57                   System.out.printf( "%s ", number );
58
59                System.out.print( "(top) \n\n" ); // indicates top of the stack
60            } // end else
61      } // end method printStack
62
63      public static void main( String args[] )
64      {
65         new StackTest();
66      } // end main
67   } // end class StackTest
```

```
stack contains: 12 (top)

stack contains: 12 34567 (top)

stack contains: 12 34567 1.0 (top)

stack contains: 12 34567 1.0 1234.5678 (top)

1234.5678 popped
stack contains: 12 34567 1.0 (top)

1.0 popped
stack contains: 12 34567 (top)

34567 popped
stack contains: 12 (top)

12 popped
stack is empty

java.util.EmptyStackException
        at java.util.Stack.peek(Unknown Source)
        at java.util.Stack.pop(Unknown Source)
        at StackTest.<init>(StackTest.java:36)
        at StackTest.main(StackTest.java:65)
```

Fig. 19.16 | Stack class of package `java.util`. (Part 2 of 2.)

Line 10 of the constructor creates an empty `Stack` of type `Number`. Class `Number` (in package `java.lang`) is the superclass of most wrapper classes (e.g., `Integer`, `Double`) for the primitive types. By creating a `Stack` of `Number`, objects of any class that extends the `Number` class can be pushed onto the stack. Lines 19, 21, 23 and 25 each call `Stack` method **push** to add objects to the top of the stack. Note the literals `12L` (line 13) and `1.0F` (line 15). Any integer literal that has the **suffix L** is a `long` value. An integer literal without a suffix is an `int` value. Similarly, any floating-point literal that has the **suffix F** is a `float` value. A floating-point literal without a suffix is a `double` value. You can learn more about numeric literals in the *Java Language Specification* at `java.sun.com/docs/books/jls/ second_edition/html/expressions.doc.html#224125`.

An infinite loop (lines 34–39) calls Stack method **pop** to remove the top element of the stack. The method returns a Number reference to the removed element. If there are no elements in the Stack, method pop throws an **EmptyStackException**, which terminates the loop. Class Stack also declares method **peek**. This method returns the top element of the stack without popping the element off the stack.

Line 49 calls Stack method **isEmpty** (inherited by Stack from class Vector) to determine whether the stack is empty. If it is empty, the method returns true; otherwise, the method returns false.

Method printStack (lines 47–61) uses the enhanced for statement to iterate through the elements in the stack. The current top of the stack (the last value pushed onto the stack) is the first value printed. Because class Stack extends class Vector, the entire public interface of class Vector is available to clients of class Stack.

Error-Prevention Tip 19.1

Because Stack extends Vector, all public Vector methods can be called on Stack objects, even if the methods do not represent conventional stack operations. For example, Vector method add can be used to insert an element anywhere in a stack—an operation that could "corrupt" the stack. When manipulating a Stack, only methods push and pop should be used to add elements to and remove elements from the Stack, respectively.

19.8 Class PriorityQueue and Interface Queue

In Section 17.8, we introduced the queue data structure and created our own implementation of it. In this section we investigate interface **Queue** and class **PriorityQueue** in the Java utilities package (java.util). Queue, a new collection interface introduced in J2SE 5.0, extends interface Collection and provides additional operations for inserting, removing and inspecting elements in a queue. PriorityQueue, one of the classes that implements the Queue interface, orders elements by their natural ordering as specified by Comparable elements' compareTo method or by a Comparator object that is supplied through the constructor.

Class PriorityQueue provides functionality that enables insertions in sorted order into the underlying data structure and deletions from the front of the underlying data structure. When adding elements to a PriorityQueue, the elements are inserted in priority order such that the highest-priority element (i.e., the largest value) will be the first element removed from the PriorityQueue.

The common PriorityQueue operations are **offer** to insert an element at the appropriate location based on priority order, **poll** to remove the highest-priority element of the priority queue (i.e., the head of the queue), **peek** to get a reference to the highest-priority element of the priority queue (without removing that element), **clear** to remove all elements in the priority queue and **size** to get the number of elements in the priority queue. Figure 19.17 demonstrates the PriorityQueue class.

Line 10 creates a PriorityQueue that stores Doubles with an initial capacity of 11 elements and orders the elements according to the object's natural ordering (the defaults for a PriorityQueue). Note that PriorityQueue is a generic class and that line 10 instantiates a PriorityQueue with a type argument Double. Class PriorityQueue provides five additional constructors. One of these takes an int and a Comparator object to create a PriorityQueue with the initial capacity specified by the int and the ordering by the Comparator. Lines 13–15 use method offer to add elements to the priority queue. Method offer throws a NullPointException if the program attempts to add a null

```
1   // Fig. 19.17: PriorityQueueTest.java
2   // Standard library class PriorityQueue test program.
3   import java.util.PriorityQueue;
4
5   public class PriorityQueueTest
6   {
7      public static void main( String args[] )
8      {
9         // queue of capacity 11
10        PriorityQueue< Double > queue = new PriorityQueue< Double >();
11
12        // insert elements to queue
13        queue.offer( 3.2 );
14        queue.offer( 9.8 );
15        queue.offer( 5.4 );
16
17        System.out.print( "Polling from queue: " );
18
19        // display elements in queue
20        while ( queue.size() > 0 )
21        {
22           System.out.printf( "%.1f ", queue.peek() ); // view top element
23           queue.poll(); // remove top element
24        } // end while
25     } // end main
26  } // end class PriorityQueueTest
```

```
Polling from queue: 3.2 5.4 9.8
```

Fig. 19.17 | PriorityQueue test program.

object to the queue. The loop in lines 20–24 use method `size` to determine whether the priority queue is empty (line 20). While there are more elements, line 22 uses Priority-Queue method `peek` to retrieve the highest-priority element in the queue for output (without actually removing the element from the queue). Line 23 removes the highest-priority element in the queue with method `poll`.

19.9 Sets

A **Set** is a `Collection` that contains unique elements (i.e., no duplicate elements). The collections framework contains several `Set` implementations, including **HashSet** and **TreeSet**. HashSet stores its elements in a hash table, and TreeSet stores its elements in a tree. The concept of hash tables is presented in Section 19.10. Figure 19.18 uses a HashSet to remove duplicate strings from a List. Recall that both List and Collection are generic types, so line 18 creates a List that contains String objects, and line 24 passes a Collection of Strings to method printNonDuplicates.

Method `printNonDuplicates` (lines 24–35), which is called from the constructor, takes a Collection argument. Line 27 constructs a HashSet from the Collection argument. Note that both Set and HashSet are generic types. By definition, Sets do not contain any duplicates, so when the HashSet is constructed, it removes any duplicates in the Collection. Lines 31–32 output elements in the Set.

```
 1   // Fig. 19.18: SetTest.java
 2   // Using a HashSet to remove duplicates.
 3   import java.util.List;
 4   import java.util.Arrays;
 5   import java.util.HashSet;
 6   import java.util.Set;
 7   import java.util.Collection;
 8
 9   public class SetTest
10   {
11      private static final String colors[] = { "red", "white", "blue",
12         "green", "gray", "orange", "tan", "white", "cyan",
13         "peach", "gray", "orange" };
14
15      // create and output ArrayList
16      public SetTest()
17      {
18         List< String > list = Arrays.asList( colors );
19         System.out.printf( "ArrayList: %s\n", list );
20         printNonDuplicates( list );
21      } // end SetTest constructor
22
23      // create set from array to eliminate duplicates
24      private void printNonDuplicates( Collection< String > collection )
25      {
26         // create a HashSet
27         Set< String > set = new HashSet< String >( collection );
28
29         System.out.println( "\nNonduplicates are: " );
30
31         for ( String s : set )
32            System.out.printf( "%s ", s );
33
34         System.out.println();
35      } // end method printNonDuplicates
36
37      public static void main( String args[] )
38      {
39         new SetTest();
40      } // end main
41   } // end class SetTest
```

```
ArrayList: [red, white, blue, green, gray, orange, tan, white, cyan, peach,
gray, orange]

Nonduplicates are:
red cyan white tan gray green orange blue peach
```

Fig. 19.18 | HashSet used to remove duplicate values from array of strings.

Sorted Sets

The collections framework also includes interface **SortedSet** (which extends Set) for sets that maintain their elements in sorted order—either the elements' natural order (e.g., numbers are in ascending order) or an order specified by a Comparator. Class TreeSet implements SortedSet. The program in Fig. 19.19 places strings into a TreeSet. The strings are sorted as they are added to the TreeSet. This example also demonstrates range-view methods, which enable a program to view a portion of a collection.

```java
 1  // Fig. 19.19: SortedSetTest.java
 2  // Using TreeSet and SortedSet.
 3  import java.util.Arrays;
 4  import java.util.SortedSet;
 5  import java.util.TreeSet;
 6
 7  public class SortedSetTest
 8  {
 9     private static final String names[] = { "yellow", "green",
10        "black", "tan", "grey", "white", "orange", "red", "green" };
11
12     // create a sorted set with TreeSet, then manipulate it
13     public SortedSetTest()
14     {
15        // create TreeSet
16        SortedSet< String > tree =
17           new TreeSet< String >( Arrays.asList( names ) );
18
19        System.out.println( "sorted set: " );
20        printSet( tree ); // output contents of tree
21
22        // get headSet based on "orange"
23        System.out.print( "\nheadSet (\"orange\"):   " );
24        printSet( tree.headSet( "orange" ) );
25
26        // get tailSet based upon "orange"
27        System.out.print( "tailSet (\"orange\"):   " );
28        printSet( tree.tailSet( "orange" ) );
29
30        // get first and last elements
31        System.out.printf( "first: %s\n", tree.first() );
32        System.out.printf( "last : %s\n", tree.last() );
33     } // end SortedSetTest constructor
34
35     // output set
36     private void printSet( SortedSet< String > set )
37     {
38        for ( String s : set )
39           System.out.printf( "%s ",   s );
40
41        System.out.println();
42     } // end method printSet
43
44     public static void main( String args[] )
45     {
46        new SortedSetTest();
47     } // end main
48  } // end class SortedSetTest
```

Fig. 19.19 | Using SortedSets and TreeSets. (Part I of 2.)

```
sorted set:
black green grey orange red tan white yellow

headSet ("orange"):  black green grey
tailSet ("orange"):  orange red tan white yellow
first: black
last : yellow
```

Fig. 19.19 | Using SortedSets and TreeSets. (Part 2 of 2.)

Lines 16–17 of the constructor create a TreeSet of String that contains the elements of array names and assigns the SortedSet to the reference tree. Both SortedSet and TreeSet are generic types. Line 20 outputs the initial set of strings using method printSet (lines 36–42), which we discuss momentarily. Line 24 calls TreeSet method **headSet** to get a subset of the TreeSet in which every element is less than "orange". The view returned from headSet is then output with printSet. If any changes are made to the subset, they will also be made to the original TreeSet because the subset returned by headSet is a view of the TreeSet.

Line 28 calls TreeSet method **tailSet** to get a subset in which each element is greater than or equal to "orange". The view returned by tailSet is then output. Any changes made through the tailSet view are made to the original TreeSet. Lines 31–32 call SortedSet methods **first** and **last** to get the smallest and largest elements of the set, respectively.

Method printSet (lines 36–42) accepts a SortedSet as an argument and prints it. Lines 38–39 print each element of the SortedSet using the enhanced for statement.

19.10 Maps

Maps associate keys to values and cannot contain duplicate keys (i.e., each key can map to only one value; this is called one-to-one mapping). Maps differ from Sets in that Maps contain keys and values, whereas Sets contain only values. Three of the several classes that implement interface Map are **Hashtable**, **HashMap** and **TreeMap**. Hashtables and HashMaps store elements in hash tables, and TreeMaps store elements in trees. This section discusses hash tables and provides an example that uses a HashMap to store key/value pairs. Interface **SortedMap** extends Map and maintains its keys in sorted order—either the elements' natural order or an order specified by a Comparator. Class TreeMap implements SortedMap.

Map Implementation with Hash Tables

Object-oriented programming languages facilitate creating new types. When a program creates objects of new or existing types, it may need to store and retrieve them efficiently. Storing and retrieving information with arrays is efficient if some aspect of your data directly matches a numerical key value and if the keys are unique and tightly packed. If you have 100 employees with nine-digit Social Security numbers and you want to store and retrieve employee data by using the Social Security number as a key, the task would require an array with one billion elements, because there are one billion unique nine-digit numbers (000,000,000–999,999,999). This is impractical for virtually all applications that use Social Security numbers as keys. A program that had an array that large could achieve high performance for both storing and retrieving employee records by simply using the Social Security number as the array index.

There are numerous applications that have this problem, namely, that either the keys are of the wrong type (e.g., not positive integers that correspond to array subscripts) or they are of the right type, but sparsely spread over a huge range. What is needed is a high-speed scheme for converting keys such as Social Security numbers, inventory part numbers and the like into unique array indices. Then, when an application needs to store something, the scheme could convert the application's key rapidly into an index, and the record of information could be stored at that slot in the array. Retrieval is accomplished the same way: Once the application has a key for which it wants to retrieve a data record, the application simply applies the conversion to the key—this produces the array index where the data is stored and retrieved.

The scheme we describe here is the basis of a technique called hashing. Why the name? When we convert a key into an array index, we literally scramble the bits, forming a kind of "mishmashed," or hashed, number. The number actually has no real significance beyond its usefulness in storing and retrieving a particular data record.

A glitch in the scheme is called a collision—this occurs when two different keys "hash into" the same cell (or element) in the array. We cannot store two values in the same space, so we need to find an alternative home for all values beyond the first that hash to a particular array index. There are many schemes for doing this. One is to "hash again" (i.e., to apply another hashing transformation to the key to provide a next candidate cell in the array). The hashing process is designed to distribute the values throughout the table, so the assumption is that an available cell will be found with just a few hashes.

Another scheme uses one hash to locate the first candidate cell. If that cell is occupied, successive cells are searched in order until an available cell is found. Retrieval works the same way: The key is hashed once to determine the initial location and check whether it contains the desired data. If it does, the search is finished. If it does not, successive cells are searched linearly until the desired data is found.

The most popular solution to hash-table collisions is to have each cell of the table be a hash "bucket," typically a linked list of all the key-value pairs that hash to that cell. This is the solution that Java's `Hashtable` and `HashMap` classes (from package `java.util`) implement. Both `Hashtable` and `HashMap` implement the `Map` interface. The primary differences between them are that `HashMap` is unsynchronized (multiple threads can modify a `HashMap` concurrently), and allows `null` keys and `null` values.

A hash table's load factor affects the performance of hashing schemes. The load factor is the ratio of the number of occupied cells in the hash table to the total number of cells in the hash table. The closer this ratio gets to 1.0, the greater the chance of collisions.

Performance Tip 19.7

The load factor in a hash table is a classic example of a memory-space/execution-time trade-off: By increasing the load factor, we get better memory utilization, but the program runs slower, due to increased hashing collisions. By decreasing the load factor, we get better program speed, because of reduced hashing collisions, but we get poorer memory utilization, because a larger portion of the hash table remains empty.

Hash tables are complex to program. Computer science students study hashing schemes in courses called "Data Structures" and "Algorithms." Java provides classes `Hashtable` and `HashMap` to enable programmers to use hashing without having to implement hash table mechanisms. This concept is profoundly important in our study of object-oriented programming. As discussed in earlier chapters, classes encapsulate and hide complexity (i.e., implementation details) and offer user-friendly interfaces. Properly crafting classes to exhibit such behavior is one of the most valued skills in the field of object-oriented programming. Figure 19.20 uses a HashMap to count the number of occurrences of each word in a string.

```java
1   // Fig. 19.20: WordTypeCount.java
2   // Program counts the number of occurrences of each word in a string
3   import java.util.StringTokenizer;
4   import java.util.Map;
5   import java.util.HashMap;
6   import java.util.Set;
7   import java.util.TreeSet;
8   import java.util.Scanner;
9
10  public class WordTypeCount
11  {
12     private Map< String, Integer > map;
13     private Scanner scanner;
14
15     public WordTypeCount()
16     {
17        map = new HashMap< String, Integer >(); // create HashMap
18        scanner = new Scanner( System.in ); // create scanner
19        createMap(); // create map based on user input
20        displayMap(); // display map content
21     } // end WordTypeCount constructor
22
23     // create map from user input
24     private void createMap()
25     {
26        System.out.println( "Enter a string:" ); // prompt for user input
27        String input = scanner.nextLine();
28
29        // create StringTokenizer for input
30        StringTokenizer tokenizer = new StringTokenizer( input );
31
32        // processing input text
33        while ( tokenizer.hasMoreTokens() ) // while more input
34        {
35           String word = tokenizer.nextToken().toLowerCase(); // get word
36
37           // if the map contains the word
38           if ( map.containsKey( word ) ) // is word in map
39           {
40              int count = map.get( word ); // get current count
41              map.put( word, count + 1 );   // increment count
42           } // end if
43           else
44              map.put( word, 1 ); // add new word with a count of 1 to map
45        } // end while
46     } // end method createMap
```

Fig. 19.20 | HashMaps and Maps. (Part 1 of 2.)

```
47
48        // display map content
49        private void displayMap()
50        {
51            Set< String > keys = map.keySet(); // get keys
52
53            // sort keys
54            TreeSet< String > sortedKeys = new TreeSet< String >( keys );
55
56            System.out.println( "Map contains:\nKey\t\tValue" );
57
58            // generate output for each key in map
59            for ( String key : sortedKeys )
60                System.out.printf( "%-10s%10s\n", key, map.get( key ) );
61
62            System.out.printf(
63                "\nsize:%d\nisEmpty:%b\n", map.size(), map.isEmpty() );
64        } // end method displayMap
65
66        public static void main( String args[] )
67        {
68            new WordTypeCount();
69        } // end main
70    } // end class WordTypeCount
```

```
Enter a string:
To be or not to be: that is the question Whether 'tis nobler to suffer
Map contains:
Key                Value
'tis                   1
be                     1
be:                    1
is                     1
nobler                 1
not                    1
or                     1
question               1
suffer                 1
that                   1
the                    1
to                     3
whether                1

size:13
isEmpty:false
```

Fig. 19.20 | HashMaps and Maps. (Part 2 of 2.)

Line 17 creates an empty HashMap with a default initial capacity (16 elements) and a default load factor (0.75)—these defaults are built into the implementation of HashMap. When the number of occupied slots in the HashMap becomes greater than the capacity times the load factor, the capacity is doubled automatically. Note that HashMap is a generic class that takes two type arguments. The first type argument specifies the type of key (i.e., String), and the second type argument specifies the type of value (i.e., Integer). Recall that the type arguments passed to a generic class must be reference types, hence the second type argument is Integer, not int. Line 18 creates a Scanner that reads user input from the standard input stream. Line 19 calls method createMap (lines 24–46), which uses a map to store the number of occurrences of each word in the sentence. Line 27 invokes method nextLine of scanner to obtain the user input, and line 30 creates a StringTokenizer to breaks the input string into its component individual words. This StringTokenier constructor takes a string argument and creates a StringTokenizer for that string and will use the whitespace to separate the string. The condition in the while statement in lines 33–45 uses StringTokenizer method hasMoreTokens to determine whether there are more tokens in the string being tokenized. If so, line 35 converts the next token to lowercase letters. The next token is obtained with a call to StringTokenizer method nextToken that returns a String. [*Note:* Section 29.6 discusses class StringTokenizer in detail.] Then line 38 calls Map method containsKey to determine whether the word is in the map (and thus has occurred previously in the string). If the Map does not contain a mapping for the word, line 44 uses Map method put to create a new entry in the map, with the word as the key and an Integer object containing 1 as the value. Note that autoboxing occurs when the program passes integer 1 to method put, because the map stores the number of occurrences of the word as Integer. If the word does exist in the map, line 40 uses Map method get to obtain the key's associated value (the count) in the map. Line 41 increments that value and uses put to replace the key's associated value in the map. Method put returns the prior value associated with the key, or null if the key was not in the map.

Method displayMap (lines 49–64) displays all the entries in the map. It uses HashMap method keySet (line 51) to get a set of the keys. The keys have type String in the map, so method keySet returns a generic type Set with type parameter specified to be String. Line 54 creates a TreeSet of the keys, in which the keys are sorted. The loop in lines 59–60 accesses each key and its value in the map. Line 60 displays each key and its value using format specifier %-10s to left justify each key and format specifier %10s to right justify each value. Note that the keys are displayed in ascending order. Line 63 calls Map method size to get the number of key-value pairs in the Map. Line 64 calls isEmpty, which returns a boolean indicating whether the Map is empty.

19.11 Properties Class

A Properties object is a persistent Hashtable that normally stores key-value pairs of strings—assuming that you use methods setProperty and getProperty to manipulate the table rather than inherited Hashtable methods put and get. By "persistent," we mean that the Properties object can be written to an output stream (possibly a file) and read back in through an input stream. In fact, most objects in Java can be output and input with Java's object serialization, presented in Chapter 14. A common use of Properties objects in prior versions of Java was to maintain application-configuration data or user preferences for applications. [*Note:* The Preferences API (package java.util.prefs), introduced in Java 1.4, is meant to replace the use of class Properties, but is beyond the scope of this book. To learn more, visit java.sun.com/j2se/5.0/docs/guide/lang/preferences.html.]

Class Properties extends class Hashtable. Figure 19.21 demonstrates several methods of class Properties.

Line 16 uses the no-argument constructor to create an empty `Properties` table with no default properties. Class `Properties` also provides an overloaded constructor that receives a reference to a `Properties` object containing default property values. Lines 19 and 20 each call `Properties` method `setProperty` to store a value for the specified key. If the key does not exist in the `table`, `setProperty` returns `null`; otherwise, it returns the previous value for that key.

Line 41 calls `Properties` method `getProperty` to locate the value associated with the specified key. If the key is not found in this `Properties` object, `getProperty` returns `null`. An overloaded version of this method receives a second argument that specifies the default value to return if `getProperty` cannot locate the key.

Line 57 calls `Properties` method **store** to save the contents of the `Properties` object to the `OutputStream` object specified as the first argument (in this case, `FileOutputStream`

```java
1   // Fig. 19.21: PropertiesTest.java
2   // Demonstrates class Properties of the java:util package.
3   import java.io.FileOutputStream;
4   import java.io.FileInputStream;
5   import java.io.IOException;
6   import java.util.Properties;
7   import java.util.Set;
8
9   public class PropertiesTest
10  {
11     private Properties table;
12
13     // set up GUI to test Properties table
14     public PropertiesTest()
15     {
16        table = new Properties(); // create Properties table
17
18        // set properties
19        table.setProperty( "color", "blue" );
20        table.setProperty( "width", "200" );
21
22        System.out.println( "After setting properties" );
23        listProperties(); // display property values
24
25        // replace property value
26        table.setProperty( "color", "red" );
27
28        System.out.println( "After replacing properties" );
29        listProperties(); // display property values
30
31        saveProperties(); // save properties
32
33        table.clear(); // empty table
34
35        System.out.println( "After clearing properties" );
36        listProperties(); // display property values
37
```

Fig. 19.21 | `Properties` class of package `java.util`. (Part 1 of 3.)

```
38            loadProperties(); // load properties
39
40            // get value of property color
41            Object value = table.getProperty( "color" );
42
43            // check if value is in table
44            if ( value != null )
45               System.out.printf( "Property color's value is %s\n", value );
46            else
47               System.out.println( "Property color is not in table" );
48         } // end PropertiesTest constructor
49
50         // save properties to a file
51         public void saveProperties()
52         {
53            // save contents of table
54            try
55            {
56               FileOutputStream output = new FileOutputStream( "props.dat" );
57               table.store( output, "Sample Properties" ); // save properties
58               output.close();
59               System.out.println( "After saving properties" );
60               listProperties();
61            } // end try
62            catch ( IOException ioException )
63            {
64               ioException.printStackTrace();
65            } // end catch
66         } // end method saveProperties
67
68         // load properties from a file
69         public void loadProperties()
70         {
71            // load contents of table
72            try
73            {
74               FileInputStream input = new FileInputStream( "props.dat" );
75               table.load( input ); // load properties
76               input.close();
77               System.out.println( "After loading properties" );
78               listProperties(); // display property values
79            } // end try
80            catch ( IOException ioException )
81            {
82               ioException.printStackTrace();
83            } // end catch
84         } // end method loadProperties
85
86         // output property values
87         public void listProperties()
88         {
89            Set< Object > keys = table.keySet(); // get property names
90
```

Fig. 19.21 | Properties class of package java.util. (Part 2 of 3.)

```
91          // output name/value pairs
92          for ( Object key : keys )
93          {
94              System.out.printf(
95                  "%s\t%s\n", key, table.getProperty( ( String ) key ) );
96          } // end for
97
98          System.out.println();
99      } // end method listProperties
100
101     public static void main( String args[] )
102     {
103         new PropertiesTest();
104     } // end main
105 } // end class PropertiesTest
```

```
After setting properties
color    blue
width    200

After replacing properties
color    red
width    200

After saving properties
color    red
width    200

After clearing properties

After loading properties
color    red
width    200

Property color's value is red
```

Fig. 19.21 | `Properties` class of package `java.util`. (Part 3 of 3.)

output). The second argument, a `String`, is a description of the `Properties` object. Class `Properties` also provides method `list`, which takes a `PrintStream` argument. This method is useful for displaying the list of properties.

Line 75 calls `Properties` method `load` to restore the contents of the `Properties` object from the `InputStream` specified as the first argument (in this case, a `FileInput-Stream`). Line 89 calls `Properties` method `keySet` to obtain a `Set` of the property names. Line 94 obtains the value of a property by passing a key to method `getProperty`.

19.12 Synchronized Collections

In Chapter 23, we discuss multithreading. The collections in the collections framework are unsynchronized by default, so they can operate efficiently when multithreading is not required. Because they are unsynchronized, however, concurrent access to a `Collection` by multiple threads could cause indeterminate results or fatal errors. To prevent potential threading problems, synchronization wrappers are used for collections that might be accessed by multiple threads. A **wrapper** object receives method calls, adds thread synchronization (to prevent concurrent access to the collection) and delegates the calls to the wrapped collection object. The `Collections` API provides a set of `static` methods for wrapping collections as synchronized versions. Method headers for the synchronization wrappers are listed in Fig. 19.22. Details about these methods are available at `java.sun.com/j2se/5.0/docs/api/java/util/Collections.html`. All these methods take a generic type and return a synchronized view of the generic type. For example, the following code creates a synchronized `List` (`list2`) that stores `String` objects:

```
List< String > list1 = new ArrayList< String >();
List< String > list2 = Collections.synchronizedList( list1 );
```

19.13 Unmodifiable Collections

The `Collections` API provides a set of `static` methods that create **unmodifiable wrappers** for collections. Unmodifiable wrappers throw `UnsupportedOperationExceptions` if attempts are made to modify the collection. Headers for these methods are listed in Fig. 19.23. Details about these methods are available at `java.sun.com/j2se/5.0/docs/api/java/util/Collections.html`. All these methods take a generic type and return an unmodifiable view of the generic type. For example, the following code creates an unmodifiable `List` (`list2`) that stores `String` objects:

```
List< String > list1 = new ArrayList< String >();
List< String > list2 = Collections.unmodifiableList( list1 );
```

Software Engineering Observation 19.5

You can use an unmodifiable wrapper to create a collection that offers read-only access to others, while allowing read–write access to yourself. You do this simply by giving others a reference to the unmodifiable wrapper while retaining for yourself a reference to the original collection.

19.14 Abstract Implementations

The collections framework provides various abstract implementations of `Collection` interfaces from which the programmer can quickly "flesh out" complete customized imple-

public static method headers
< T > Collection< T > synchronizedCollection(Collection< T > c)
< T > List< T > synchronizedList(List< T > aList)
< T > Set< T > synchronizedSet(Set< T > s)
< T > SortedSet< T > synchronizedSortedSet(SortedSet< T > s)
< K, V > Map< K, V > synchronizedMap(Map< K, V > m)
< K, V > SortedMap< K, V > synchronizedSortedMap(SortedMap< K, V > m)

Fig. 19.22 | Synchronization wrapper methods.

public static method headers
< T > Collection< T > unmodifiableCollection(Collection< T > c)
< T > List< T > unmodifiableList(List< T > aList)
< T > Set< T > unmodifiableSet(Set< T > s)
< T > SortedSet< T > unmodifiableSortedSet(SortedSet< T > s)
< K, V > Map< K, V > unmodifiableMap(Map< K, V > m)
< K, V > SortedMap< K, V > unmodifiableSortedMap(SortedMap< K, V > m)

Fig. 19.23 | Unmodifiable wrapper methods.

mentations. These abstract implementations include a thin Collection implementation called an **AbstractCollection**, a thin List implementation that allows random access to its elements called an **AbstractList**, a thin Map implementation called an **AbstractMap**, a thin List implementation that allows sequential access to its elements called an **Abstract-SequentialList**, a thin Set implementation called an **AbstractSet** and a thin Queue implementation called **AbstractQueue**. You can learn more about these classes at java.sun.com/j2se/5.0/docs/api/java/util/package-summary.html.

To write a custom implementation, you can extend the abstract implementation class that best meets your needs, and implement each of the class's abstract methods. Then, if your collection is to be modifiable, override any concrete methods that prevent modification.

19.15 Wrap-Up

This chapter introduced the Java collections framework. You learned how to use class Arrays to perform array manipulations. You learned the collection hierarchy and how to use the collections framework interfaces to program with collections polymorphically. You also learned several predefined algorithms for manipulating collections. In the next chapter, we introduce Java applets, which are Java programs that typically execute in a Web browser. We start with sample applets that come with the JDK, then show you how to write and execute your own applets.

Summary

- The Java collections framework gives the programmer access to prepackaged data structures as well as to algorithms for manipulating them.
- A collection is an object that can hold references to other objects. The collection interfaces declare the operations that can be performed on each type of collection.
- The classes and interfaces of the collections framework are in package java.util.
- Class Arrays provides static methods for manipulating arrays, including sort for sorting an array, binarySearch for searching a sorted array, equals for comparing arrays and fill for placing items in an array.
- Arrays method asList returns a List view of an array, which enables a program to manipulate the array as if it were a List. Any modifications made through the List view change the array, and any modifications to the array change the List view.

- Method size gets the number of items in a List, and method get returns a List element.
- Interface Collection is the root interface in the collection hierarchy from which interfaces Set and List are derived. Interface Collection contains bulk operations for adding, clearing, comparing and retaining objects in a collection. Interface Collection provides a method iterator for getting an Iterator.
- Class Collections provides static methods for manipulating collections. Many of the methods are implementations of polymorphic algorithms for searching, sorting and so on.
- A List is an ordered Collection that can contain duplicate elements.
- Interface List is implemented by classes ArrayList, LinkedList and Vector. Class ArrayList is a resizable-array implementation of a List. A LinkedList is a linked-list implementation of a List.
- Iterator method hasNext determines whether a Collection contains another element. Method next returns a reference to the next object in the Collection and advances the Iterator.
- Method subList returns a view of a portion of a List. Any changes made to this view are also made to the List.
- Method clear removes elements from a List.
- Method toArray returns the contents of a collection as an array.
- Class Vector manages dynamically resizable arrays. At any time, a Vector contains a number of elements that is less than or equal to its capacity. If a Vector needs to grow, it grows by its capacity increment. If no capacity increment is specified, Java doubles the size of the Vector each time additional capacity is required. The default capacity is 10 elements.
- Vector method add adds its argument to the end of the Vector. Method insertElementAt inserts an element at the specified position. Method set sets the element at a specific position.
- Vector method remove removes the first occurrence of its argument from the Vector. Method removeAllElements removes every element from the Vector. Method removeElementAt removes the element at the specified index.
- Vector method firstElement returns a reference to the first element. Method lastElement returns a reference to the last element.
- Vector method contains determines whether the Vector contains the searchKey specified as an argument. Vector method indexOf gets the index of the first location of its argument. The method returns –1 if the argument is not found in the Vector.
- Vector method isEmpty determines whether the Vector is empty. Methods size and capacity determine the number of elements currently in the Vector and the number of elements that can be stored in the Vector without allocating more memory, respectively.
- Algorithms sort, binarySearch, reverse, shuffle, fill and copy operate on Lists. Algorithms min and max operate on Collections. Algorithm reverse reverses the elements of a List, fill sets every List element to a specified Object, and copy copies elements from one List into another List. Algorithm sort sorts the elements of a List.
- Algorithms addAll appends all the elements in an array to a collection, frequency calculates how many elements in the collection are equal to the specified element, and disjoint determines whether two collections have elements in common.
- Algorithms min and max find the smallest and largest items in a collection.
- The Comparator interface provides a means of sorting a Collection's elements in an order other than their natural order.
- Collections method reverseOrder returns a Comparator object that can be used with sort to sort elements of a collection in reverse order.

- Algorithm shuffle randomly orders the elements of a List.
- Algorithm binarySearch locates an Object in a sorted List.
- Class Stack extends Vector. Stack method push adds its argument to the top of the stack. Method pop removes the top element of the stack. Method peek returns a reference to the top element without removing it. Stack method empty determines whether the stack is empty.
- Queue, a new collection interface introduced in J2SE 5.0, extends interface Collection and provides additional operations for inserting, removing and inspecting elements in a queue.
- PriorityQueue, one of the Queue implementations, orders elements by their natural ordering (i.e., the implementation of the compareTo method) or by a Comparator object that is supplied through the constructor.
- The common PriorityQueue operations are offer to insert an element at the appropriate location based on priority order, poll to remove the highest-priority element of the priority queue (i.e., the head of the queue), peek to get a reference to the highest-priority element of the priority queue, clear to remove all elements in the priority queue and size to get the number of elements in the priority queue.
- A Set is a Collection that contains no duplicate elements. HashSet stores its elements in a hash table. TreeSet stores its elements in a tree.
- Interface SortedSet extends Set and represents a set that maintains its elements in sorted order. Class TreeSet implements SortedSet.
- TreeSet method headSet gets a view of a TreeSet that is less than a specified element. Method tailSet gets a view that is greater than or equal to a specified element. Any changes made to the view are made to the TreeSet.
- Maps map keys to values and cannot contain duplicate keys. Maps differ from Sets in that Maps contain both keys and values, whereas Sets contain only values. HashMaps store elements in a hash table, and TreeMaps store elements in a tree.
- Hashtables and HashMaps store elements in hash tables, and TreeMaps store elements in trees.
- HashMap is a generic class that takes two type arguments. The first type argument specifies the type of key, and the second type argument specifies the type of value.
- HashMap method put adds a key and a value into a HashMap. Method get locates the value associated with the specified key. Method isEmpty determines whether the map is empty.
- HashMap method keySet returns a set of the keys. Map methods size and isEmpty returns the number of key-value pairs in the Map and a boolean indicating whether the Map is empty, respectively.
- Interface SortedMap extends Map and represents a map that maintains its keys in sorted order. Class TreeMap implements SortedMap.
- A Properties object is a persistent Hashtable object. Class Properties extends Hashtable.
- The Properties no-argument constructor creates an empty Properties table with no default properties. There is also an overloaded constructor that is passed a reference to a default Properties object containing default property values.
- Properties method setProperty specifies the value associated with the key argument. Properties method getProperty locates the value of the key specified as an argument. Method store saves the contents of the Properties object to the OutputStream object specified as the first argument. Method load restores the contents of the Properties object from the InputStream object specified as the argument.

- Collections from the collections framework are unsynchronized. Synchronization wrappers are provided for collections that can be accessed by multiple threads.

- The `Collections` API provides a set of `public static` methods for converting collections to unmodifiable versions. Unmodifiable wrappers throw `UnsupportedOperationExceptions` if attempts are made to modify the collection.

- The collections framework provides various abstract implementations of collection interfaces from which the programmer can quickly flesh out complete customized implementations.

Terminology

`AbstractCollection` class	`firstElement` method of `Vector`
`AbstractList` class	`frequency` method of `Collections`
`AbstractMap` class	`get` method of `HashMap`
`AbstractQueue` class	`getProperty` method of class `Properties`
`AbstractSequentialList` class	hashing
`AbstractSet` class	`HashMap` class
`add` method of `List`	`HashSet` class
`add` method of `Vector`	`Hashtable` class
`addAll` method of `Collections`	`hasMoreTokens` method of `StringTokenizer`
`addFirst` method of `List`	`hasNext` method of `Iterator`
`addLast` method of `List`	`hasPrevious` method of `ListIterator`
algorithms in `Collections`	insert an element into a collection
`ArrayList`	`indexOf` method of `Vector`
array	`isEmpty` method of `Map`
arrays as collections	`isEmpty` method of `Vector`
`asList` method of `Arrays`	iterate through container elements
bidirectional iterator	iterator
`binarySearch` method of `Arrays`	`Iterator` interface
`binarySearch` method of `Collections`	key in `HashMap`
capacity increment of a `Vector`	`keySet` method of `HashMap`
`capacity` method of `Vector`	key/value pair
`clear` method of `List`	`lastElement` method of `Vector`
`clear` method of `PriorityQueue`	lexicographical comparison
collection	`LinkedList` class
`Collection` interface	`List` interface
`Collections` class	`ListIterator` interface
collections framework	load factor in hashing
collections placed in arrays	map
collision in hashing	`Map` collection interface
`contains` method of `Vector`	mapping keys to values
`containsKey` method of `HashMap`	mappings
`Comparable` interface	`max` method of `Collections`
`Comparator` interface	`min` method of `Collections`
`compareTo` method of `Comparable`	modifiable collections
`copy` method of `Collections`	natural comparison method
delete an element from a collection	natural ordering
`disjoint` method of `Collections`	`next` method of `Iterator`
duplicate elements	`nextToken` method of `StringTokenizer`
`fill` method of `Arrays`	`NoSuchElementException` class
`fill` method of `Collections`	`offer` method of `PriorityQueue`

one-to-one mapping	shuffle method of `Collections`
ordered collection	size method of `List`
ordering	size method of `PriorityQueue`
peek method of `PriorityQueue`	sort a `List`
peek method of `Stack`	sort method of `Arrays`
poll method of `PriorityQueue`	sort method of `Collections`
pop method of `Stack`	`SortedMap` collection interface
`PriorityQueue` class	`SortedSet` collection interface
`Properties` class	stable sort
put method of `HashMap`	`Stack` class
`Queue` interface	`StringTokenizer` class
range-view methods	synchronization wrappers
`removeAllElements` method of `Vector`	`TreeMap` class
`removeElement` method of `Vector`	`TreeSet` class
`removeElementAt` method of `Vector`	unmodifiable collections
reverse method of `Collections`	view
`reverseOrder` method of `Collections`	view an array as a `List`
sequence	wrapper class
`Set` interface	

Self-Review Exercises

19.1 Fill in the blanks in each of the following statements:

a) A(n) _____ is used to walk through a collection and can remove elements from the collection during the iteration.

b) An element in a `List` can be accessed by using the element's _____.

c) `List`s are sometimes called _____.

d) Java classes _____ and _____ provide the capabilities of array-like data structures that can resize themselves dynamically.

e) If you do not specify a capacity increment, the system will _____ the size of the `Vector` each time additional capacity is needed.

f) You can use a(n) _____ to create a collection that offers only read-only access to others while allowing read–write access to yourself.

g) _____ can be used to create stacks, queues, trees and deques (double-ended queues).

h) Algorithm _____ of `Collections` determines whether two collections have elements in common.

19.2 Determine whether each statement is *true* or *false*. If *false*, explain why.

a) Values of primitive types may be stored directly in a `Vector`.

b) A `Set` can contain duplicate values.

c) A `Map` can contain duplicate keys.

d) A `LinkedList` can contain duplicate values.

e) `Collections` is an `interface`.

f) `Iterator`s can remove elements.

g) With hashing, as the load factor increases, the chance of collisions decreases.

h) A `PriorityQueue` permits `null` elements.

Answers to Self-Review Exercises

19.1 a) `Iterator`. b) index. c) sequences. d) `ArrayList`, `Vector`. e) double. f) unmodifiable wrapper. g) `LinkedList`s. h) `disjoint`.

19.2   a)   False; a `Vector` stores only objects. Autoboxing occurs when adding a primitive type to the `Vector`, which means the primitive type is converted to its corresponding type-wrapper class.

       b)   False. A `Set` cannot contain duplicate values.

       c)   False. A `Map` cannot contain duplicate keys.

       d)   True.

       e)   False. `Collections` is a `class`; `Collection` is an `interface`.

       f)   True.

       g)   False. With hashing, as the load factor increases, there are fewer available slots relative to the total number of slots, so the chance of selecting an occupied slot (a collision) with a hashing operation increases.

       h)   False. A `NullPointerException` is thrown if the program attempts to add `null` to a `PriorityQueue`.

Exercises

19.3   Define each of the following terms:

       a)   `Collection`

       b)   `Collections`

       c)   `Comparator`

       d)   `List`

       e)   load factor

       f)   collision

       g)   space–time trade-off in hashing

       h)   `HashMap`

19.4   Explain briefly the operation of each of the following methods of class `Vector`:

       a)   `add`

       b)   `insertElementAt`

       c)   `set`

       d)   `remove`

       e)   `removeAllElements`

       f)   `removeElementAt`

       g)   `firstElement`

       h)   `lastElement`

       i)   `isEmpty`

       j)   `contains`

       k)   `indexOf`

       l)   `size`

       m)   `capacity`

19.5   Explain why inserting additional elements into a `Vector` object whose current size is less than its capacity is a relatively fast operation and why inserting additional elements into a `Vector` object whose current size is at capacity is a relatively slow operation.

19.6   By extending class `Vector`, Java's designers were able to create class `Stack` quickly. What are the negative aspects of this use of inheritance, particularly for class `Stack`?

19.7   Briefly answer the following questions:

       a)   What is the primary difference between a `Set` and a `Map`?

       b)   Can a two-dimensional array be passed to `Arrays` method `asList`? If yes, how would an individual element be accessed?

       c)   What happens when you add a primitive type (e.g., `double`) value to a collection?

       d)   Can you print all the elements in a collection without using an `Iterator`? If yes, how?

19.8 Explain briefly the operation of each of the following `Iterator`-related methods:
a) `iterator`
b) `hasNext`
c) `next`

19.9 Explain briefly the operation of each of the following methods of class `HashMap`:
a) `put`
b) `get`
c) `isEmpty`
d) `containsKey`
e) `keySet`

19.10 Determine whether each of the following statements is *true* or *false*. If *false*, explain why.
a) Elements in a `Collection` must be sorted in ascending order before a `binarySearch` may be performed.
b) Method `first` gets the first element in a `TreeSet`.
c) A `List` created with `Arrays` method `asList` is resizable.
d) Class `Arrays` provides `static` method `sort` for sorting array elements.

19.11 Explain the operation of each of the following methods of the `Properties` class:
a) `load`
b) `store`
c) `getProperty`
d) `list`

19.12 Rewrite lines 17–26 in Fig. 19.4 to be more concise by using the `asList` method and the `LinkedList` constructor that takes a `Collection` argument.

19.13 Write a program that reads in a series of first names and stores them in a `LinkedList`. Do not store duplicate names. Allow the user to search for a first name.

19.14 Modify the program of Fig. 19.20 to count the number of occurrences of each letter rather than of each word. For example, the string `"HELLO THERE"` contains two Hs, three Es, two Ls, one O, one T and one R. Display the results.

19.15 Use a `HashMap` to create a reusable class for choosing one of the 13 predefined colors in class `Color`. The names of the colors should be used as keys, and the predefined `Color` objects should be used as values. Place this class in a package that can be imported into any Java program. Use your new class in an application that allows the user to select a color and draw a shape in that color.

19.16 Write a program that determines and prints the number of duplicate words in a sentence. Treat uppercase and lowercase letters the same. Ignore punctuation.

19.17 Rewrite your solution to Exercise 17.8 to use a `LinkedList` collection.

19.18 Rewrite your solution to Exercise 17.9 to use a `LinkedList` collection.

19.19 Write a program that takes a whole number input from a user and determines whether it is prime. If the number is not prime, display the unique prime factors of the number. Remember that a prime number's factors are only 1 and the prime number itself. Every number that is not prime has a unique prime factorization. For example, consider the number 54. The prime factors of 54 are 2, 3, 3 and 3. When the values are multiplied together, the result is 54. For the number 54, the prime factors output should be 2 and 3. Use `Set`s as part of your solution.

19.20 Write a program that uses a `StringTokenizer` to tokenize a line of text input by the user and places each token in a `TreeSet`. Print the elements of the `TreeSet`. [*Note:* This should cause the elements to be printed in ascending sorted order.]

19.21 The output of Fig. 19.17 (`PriorityQueueTest`) shows that `PriorityQueue` orders `Double` elements in ascending order. Rewrite Fig. 19.17 so that it orders `Double` elements in descending order (i.e., `9.8` should be the highest-priority element rather than `3.2`).

20

Introduction to Java Applets

OBJECTIVES

In this chapter you will learn:

- To differentiate between applets and applications.
- To observe some of Java's exciting capabilities through the JDK's demonstration applets.
- To write simple applets.
- To write a simple HyperText Markup Language (HTML) document to load an applet into an applet container and execute the applet.
- Five methods that are called automatically by an applet container during an applet's life cycle.

20.1 Introduction

[*Note:* This chapter and its exercises are intentionally small and simple for readers who wish to learn about applets after reading only the first few chapters of the book—possibly just Chapters 2 and 3. We present more complex applets in Chapter 20, Multimedia: Applets and Applications, Chapter 23, Multithreading and Chapter 24, Networking.]

This chapter introduces applets—Java programs that can be embedded in HyperText Markup Language (HTML) documents (i.e., Web pages). When a browser loads a Web page containing an applet, the applet downloads into the Web browser and executes.

The browser that executes an applet is generically known as the applet container. The JDK includes the `appletviewer` applet container for testing applets as you develop them and before you embed them in Web pages. We typically demonstrate applets using the `appletviewer`. If you would like to execute your applets in a Web browser, be aware that some Web browsers do not support J2SE 5.0 by default. You can visit `java.com` and click the **Get It Now** button to install the J2SE Runtime Environment (JRE) 5.0 for your browser. Several popular browsers are supported.

20.2 Sample Applets Provided with the JDK

Let's consider several demonstration applets provided with the JDK. Each sample applet comes with its source code. Some programmers find it interesting to read this source code to learn new and exciting Java features.

The demonstration programs provided with the JDK are located in a directory called demo. For Windows, the default location of the JDK 5.0's demo directory is

```
C:\Program Files\Java\jdk1.5.0\demo
```

On UNIX/Linux/Mac OS X, the default location is the directory in which you install the JDK followed by `jdk1.5.0/demo`—for example,

```
/usr/local/jdk1.5.0/demo
```

For other platforms, there will be a similar directory (or folder) structure. This chapter assumes that the JDK is installed in `C:\Program Files\Java\jdk1.5.0\demo` on Windows or in your home directory in ~/jdk1.5.0 on UNIX/Linux/Max OS X. You may need to update the locations specified here to reflect your chosen installation directory and disk drive, or a different version of the JDK.

If you are using a Java development tool that does not come with the Sun Java demos, you can download the JDK (with the demos) from the Sun Microsystems Java Web site

```
java.sun.com/j2se/5.0/
```

TicTacToe Applet

The TicTacToe demonstration applet allows you to play Tic-Tac-Toe against the computer. To execute this applet, open a command window and change directories to the JDK's demo directory.

The demo directory contains several subdirectories. You can list them by issuing the dir command on Windows or the ls command on UNIX/Linux/Max OS X. We discuss sample programs in the applets and jfc directories. The applets directory contains several demonstration applets. The jfc (Java Foundation Classes) directory contains applets and applications that demonstrate Java's graphics and GUI features.

Change directories to the applets directory and list its contents to see the directory names for the demonstration applets. Figure 20.1 provides a brief description of each sample applet. If your browser supports J2SE 5.0, you can test these applets by opening the site java.sun.com/j2se/5.0/docs/relnotes/demos.html in your browser and clicking the link to each applet. We will demonstrate three of these applets by using the appletviewer command in a command window.

Example	Description
Animator	Performs one of four separate animations.
ArcTest	Demonstrates drawing arcs. You can interact with the applet to change attributes of the arc that is displayed.
BarChart	Draws a simple bar chart.
Blink	Displays blinking text in different colors.
CardTest	Demonstrates several GUI components and layouts.
Clock	Draws a clock with rotating hands, the current date and the current time. The clock updates once per second.
DitherTest	Demonstrates drawing with a graphics technique known as dithering that allows gradual transformation from one color to another.
DrawTest	Allows the user mouse to draw lines and points in different colors by dragging the mouse.
Fractal	Draws a fractal. Fractals typically require complex calculations to determine how they are displayed.
GraphicsTest	Draws shapes to illustrate graphics capabilities.

Fig. 20.1 | The examples from the applets directory. (Part 1 of 2.)

Example	Description
GraphLayout	Draws a graph consisting of many nodes (represented as rectangles) connected by lines. Drag a node to see the other nodes in the graph adjust on the screen and demonstrate complex graphical interactions.
ImageMap	Demonstrates an image with hot spots. Positioning the mouse pointer over certain areas of the image highlights the area and displays a message in the lower-left corner of the applet container window. Position over the mouth in the image to hear the applet say "hi."
JumpingBox	Moves a rectangle randomly around the screen. Try to catch it by clicking it with the mouse!
MoleculeViewer	Presents a three-dimensional view of several chemical molecules. Drag the mouse to view the molecule from different angles.
NervousText	Draws text that jumps around the applet.
SimpleGraph	Draws a complex curve.
SortDemo	Compares three sorting techniques. Sorting (described in Chapter 16) arranges information in order—like alphabetizing words. When you execute this example from a command window, three appletviewer windows appear. When you execute this example in a browser, the three demos appear side-by-side. Click in each demo to start the sort. Note that the sorts all operate at different speeds.
SpreadSheet	Demonstrates a simple spreadsheet of rows and columns.
TicTacToe	Allows the user to play Tic-Tac-Toe against the computer.
WireFrame	Draws a three-dimensional shape as a wire frame. Drag the mouse to view the shape from different angles.

Fig. 20.1 | The examples from the `applets` directory. (Part 2 of 2.)

Change directories to subdirectory TicTacToe, where you will find the HTML document example1.html that is used to execute the applet. In the command window, type the command

```
appletviewer example1.html
```

and press *Enter*. This executes the appletviewer applet container, which loads the HTML document example1.html specified as its command-line argument. The appletviewer determines from the document which applet to load and executes the applet. Figure 20.2 shows several screen captures of playing Tic-Tac-Toe with this applet.

You are player **X**. To interact with the applet, point the mouse at the square where you want to place an **X** and click the mouse button. The applet plays a sound and places an **X** in the square if the square is open. If the square is occupied, this is an invalid move and the applet plays a different sound indicating that you cannot make the specified move. After you make a valid move, the applet responds by making its own move.

To play again, click the appletviewer's **Applet menu** and select the **Reload menu item** (Fig. 20.3). To terminate the appletviewer, click the appletviewer's **Applet** menu and select the **Quit menu item**.

Fig. 20.2 | `TicTacToe` applet sample execution.

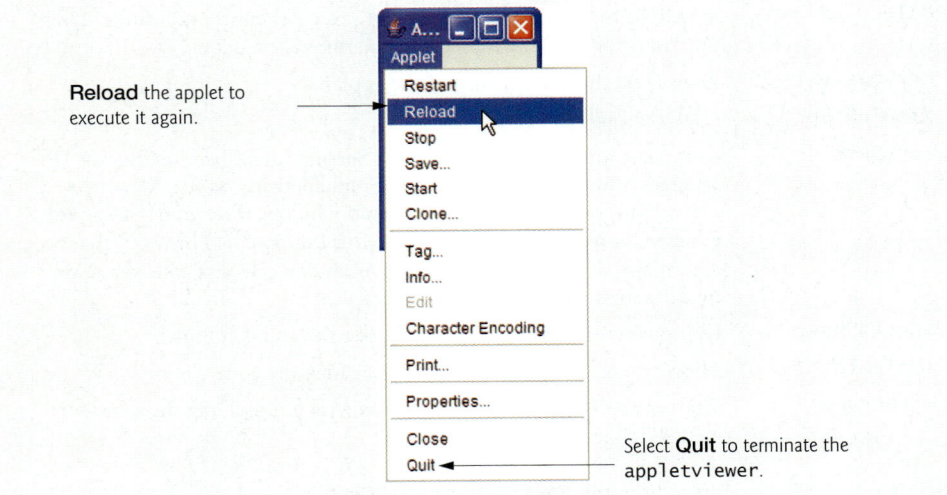

Reload the applet to execute it again.

Select **Quit** to terminate the `appletviewer`.

Fig. 20.3 | **Applet** menu in the `appletviewer`.

DrawTest *Applet*

The `DrawTest` applet allows you to draw lines and points in different colors. In the command window, change directories to directory `applets`, then to subdirectory `DrawTest`. You can move up the directory tree incrementally toward demo by issuing the command "`cd ..`" in the command window. The `DrawTest` directory contains the `example1.html` document that is used to execute the applet. In the command window, type the command

```
appletviewer example1.html
```

and press *Enter*. The `appletviewer` loads `example1.html`, determines from the document which applet to load and executes the applet. Figure 20.4 shows a screen capture after some lines and points have been drawn.

By default the applet allows you to draw black lines by dragging the mouse across the applet. When you drag the mouse, note that the start point of the line always remains in the same place and the end point of the line follows the mouse pointer around the applet. The line is not permanent until you release the mouse button.

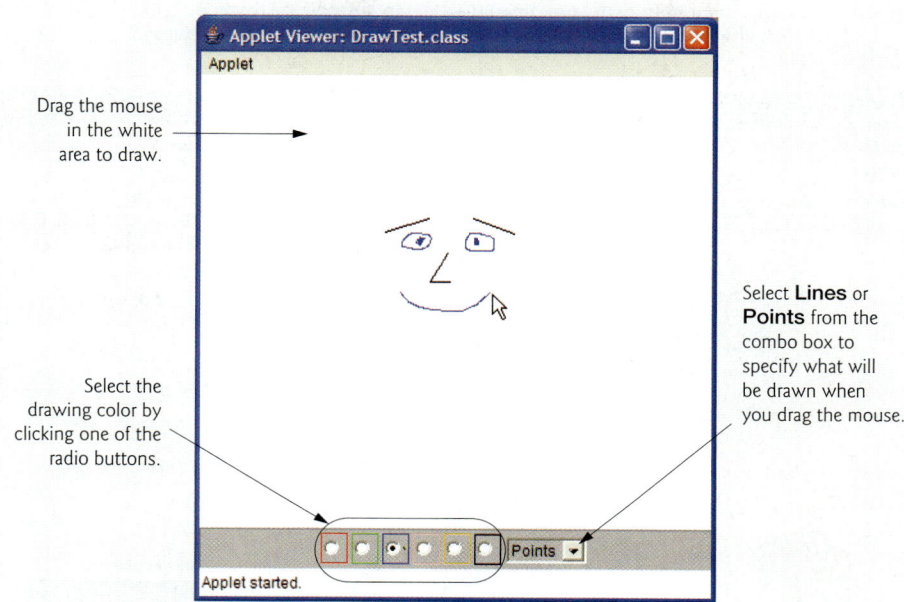

Drag the mouse in the white area to draw.

Select **Lines** or **Points** from the combo box to specify what will be drawn when you drag the mouse.

Select the drawing color by clicking one of the radio buttons.

Fig. 20.4 | `DrawTest` applet sample execution.

Select a color by clicking one of the radio buttons at the bottom of the applet. You can select from red, green, blue, pink, orange and black. Change the shape to draw from **Lines** to **Points** by selecting **Points** from the combo box. To start a new drawing, select **Reload** from the `appletviewer`'s **Applet** menu.

Java2D *Applet*

The `Java2D` applet demonstrates many features of the Java 2D API (which we introduced in Chapter 12). Change directories to the `jfc` directory in the JDK's `demo` directory, then change to the `Java2D` directory. In the command window, type the command

```
appletviewer Java2Demo.html
```

and press *Enter*. The `appletviewer` loads `Java2Demo.html`, determines from the document which applet to load and executes the applet. Figure 20.5 shows a screen capture of one of this applet's many demonstrations of Java's two-dimensional graphics capabilities.

At the top of the applet are tabs that look like file folders in a filing cabinet. This demo provides 12 tabs with Java 2D API features demonstrated on each tab. To change to a different part of the demo, simply click a different tab. Also, try changing the options in the upper-right corner of the applet. Some of these affect the speed with which the applet draws the graphics. For example, click the checkbox to the left of the word **Anti-Aliasing** to turn off anti-aliasing (a graphics technique for producing smoother on-screen graphics in which the edges of the graphic are blurred). When this feature is turned off, the animation speed increases for the animated shapes at the bottom of the demo (Fig. 20.5). This performance increase occurs because shapes that are not anti-aliased are less complex to draw.

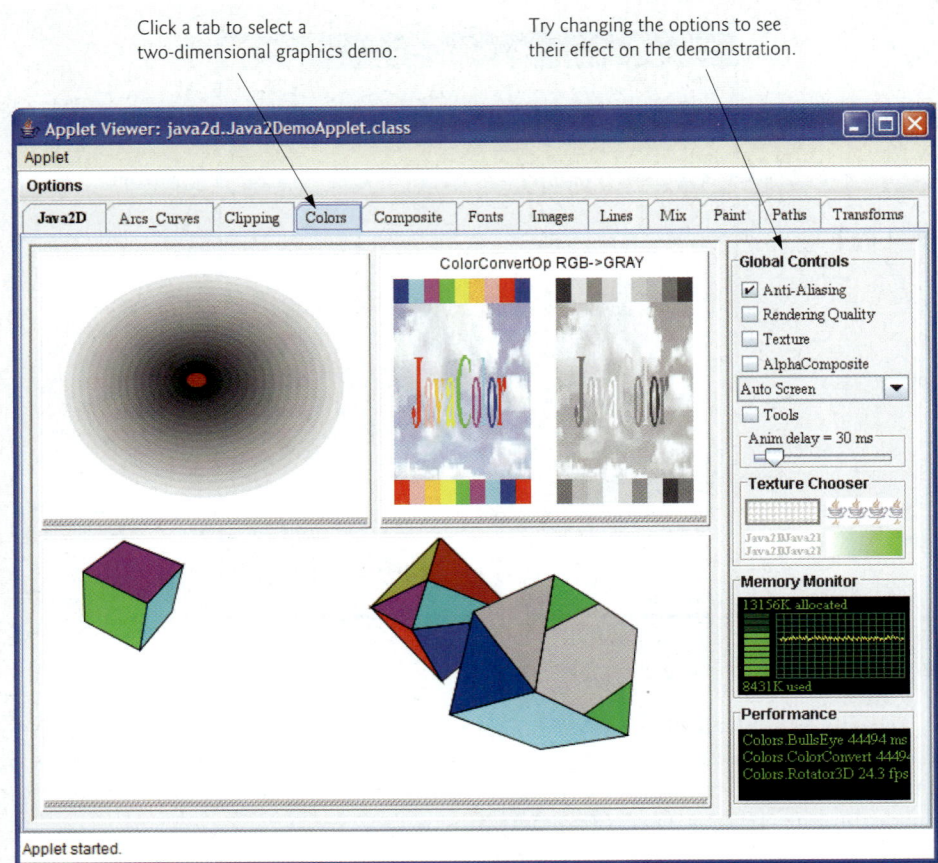

Fig. 20.5 | Java2D applet sample execution.

20.3 Simple Java Applet: Drawing a String

Every Java applet is a graphical user interface on which you can place GUI components using the techniques introduced in Chapter 11 or draw using the techniques demonstrated in Chapter 12. In this chapter, we will demonstrate drawing on an applet. Examples in Chapters 21, 23 and 24 demonstrate building an applet's graphical user interface.

Now let's build an applet of our own. We begin with a simple applet (Fig. 20.6) that draws "Welcome to Java Programming!" on the applet. Figure 20.7 shows this applet executing in two applet containers—the appletviewer and the Microsoft Internet Explorer Web browser. At the end of this section, you will learn how to execute the applet in a Web browser.

Creating the Applet Class

Line 3 imports class Graphics to enable the applet to draw graphics, such as lines, rectangles, ovals and strings of characters. Class **JApplet** (imported at line 4) from package javax.swing is used to create applets. As with applications, every Java applet contains at least

```
 1    // Fig. 20.6: WelcomeApplet.java
 2    // A first applet in Java.
 3    import java.awt.Graphics;    // program uses class Graphics
 4    import javax.swing.JApplet;  // program uses class JApplet
 5
 6    public class WelcomeApplet extends JApplet
 7    {
 8       // draw text on applet's background
 9       public void paint( Graphics g )
10       {
11          // call superclass version of method paint
12          super.paint( g );
13
14          // draw a String at x-coordinate 25 and y-coordinate 25
15          g.drawString( "Welcome to Java Programming!", 25, 25 );
16       } // end method paint
17    } // end class WelcomeApplet
```

Fig. 20.6 | Applet that draws a string.

WelcomeApplet executing in the appletviewer

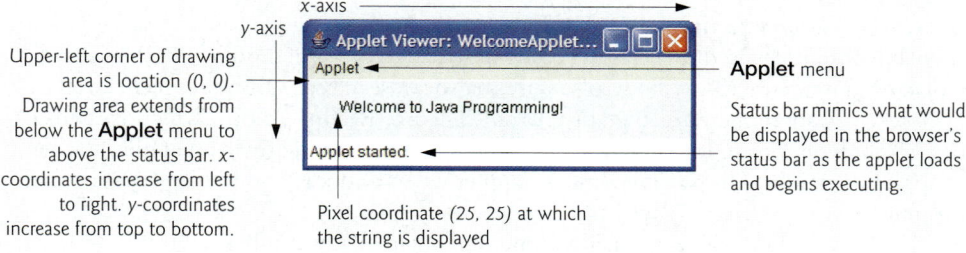

Upper-left corner of drawing area is location *(0, 0)*. Drawing area extends from below the **Applet** menu to above the status bar. x-coordinates increase from left to right. y-coordinates increase from top to bottom.

Applet menu

Status bar mimics what would be displayed in the browser's status bar as the applet loads and begins executing.

Pixel coordinate *(25, 25)* at which the string is displayed

WelcomeApplet executing in Microsoft Internet Explorer

Upper-left corner of drawing area

Pixel coordinate *(25, 25)*

Status bar

Fig. 20.7 | Sample outputs of the WelcomeApplet in Fig. 20.6.

one public class declaration. An applet container can create only objects of classes that are public and extend JApplet (or the Applet class from early versions of Java). For this reason, class WelcomeApplet (lines 6–17) extends JApplet.

An applet container expects every Java applet to have methods named `init`, `start`, `paint`, `stop` and `destroy`, each of which is declared in class JApplet. Each new applet class you create inherits default implementations of these methods from class JApplet. These methods can be overridden (redefined) to perform tasks that are specific to your applet. Section 20.4 discusses each of these methods in more detail.

When an applet container loads class WelcomeApplet, the container creates an object of type WelcomeApplet, then calls three of the applet's methods. In sequence, these three methods are `init`, `start` and `paint`. If you do not declare these methods in your applet, the applet container calls the inherited versions. The superclass methods `init` and `start` have empty bodies, so they do not perform any tasks. The superclass method `paint` does not draw anything on the applet.

You might wonder why it is necessary to inherit methods `init`, `start` and `paint` if their default implementations do not perform tasks. Some applets do not use all three of these methods. However, the applet container does not know that. Thus, it expects every applet to have these methods, so that it can provide a consistent start-up sequence for each applet. This is similar to applications' always starting execution with `main`. Inheriting the "default" versions of these methods guarantees that the applet container can execute each applet uniformly. Also, inheriting default implementations of these methods allows the programmer to concentrate on defining only the methods required for a particular applet.

Overriding Method **paint** for Drawing

To enable our applet to draw, class WelcomeApplet overrides method `paint` (lines 9–16) by placing statements in the body of `paint` that draw a message on the screen. Method `paint` receives a parameter of type Graphics (called g by convention), which is used to draw graphics on the applet. You do not call method `paint` explicitly in an applet. Rather, the applet container calls `paint` to tell the applet when to draw, and the applet container is responsible for passing a Graphics object as an argument.

Line 12 calls the superclass version of method `paint` that was inherited from JApplet. This statement should be the first statement in every applet's `paint` method. Omitting it can cause subtle drawing errors in applets that combine drawing and GUI components.

Line 15 uses Graphics method `drawString` to draw Welcome to Java Programming! on the applet. The method receives as arguments the String to draw and the *x-y* coordinates at which the bottom-left corner of the String should appear in the drawing area. When line 15 executes, it draws the String on the applet at the coordinates 25 and 25.

20.3.1 Executing an Applet in the `appletviewer`

As with application classes, you must compile an applet class before it can execute. After creating class WelcomeApplet and saving it in the file WelcomeApplet.java, open a command window, change to the directory in which you saved the applet class declaration and compile class WelcomeApplet.

Recall that applets are embedded in Web pages for execution in an applet container (appletviewer or a browser). Before you can execute the applet, you must create an HTML (HyperText Markup Language) document that specifies which applet to execute in the applet container. Typically, an HTML document ends with an ".html" or ".htm" file-name extension. Figure 20.8 shows a simple HTML document—WelcomeApplet.html—that loads the applet defined in Fig. 20.6 into an applet container. [*Note:* If

```
1   <html>
2   <applet code = "WelcomeApplet.class" width = "300" height = "45">
3   </applet>
4   </html>
```

Fig. 20.8 | `WelcomeApplet.html` loads `WelcomeApplet` (Fig. 20.6) into an applet container.

you are interested in learning more about HTML, the CD that accompanies this book contains three chapters from our book *Internet and World Wide Web How to Program, Third Edition* that introduce the current version of HTML (known as XHTML) and the Web page formatting capability known as Cascading Style Sheets (CSS).]

Most HTML elements are delimited by pairs of tags. For example, lines 1 and 4 of Fig. 20.8 indicate the beginning and the end, respectively, of the HTML document. All HTML tags begin with a left angle bracket, <, and end with a right angle bracket, >. Lines 2–3 specify an **applet element** that tells the applet container to load a specific applet and defines the size of the applet's display area (its width and height in pixels) in the applet container. Normally, the applet and its corresponding HTML document are stored in the same directory on disk. Typically, a browser loads an HTML document from a computer (other than your own) connected to the Internet. However, HTML documents also can reside on your computer (as you saw in Section 20.2). When an applet container encounters an HTML document that contains an applet, the applet container automatically loads the applet's `.class` file (or files) from the same directory on the computer in which the HTML document resides.

The `applet` element has several **attributes**. The first attribute in line 2, code = "WelcomeApplet.class", indicates that the file `WelcomeApplet.class` contains the compiled applet class. The second and third attributes in line 2 indicate the **width** (300) and the **height** (45) of the applet in pixels. The `</applet>` tag (line 3) terminates the `applet` element that began at line 2. The `</html>` tag (line 4) terminates the HTML document.

Look-and-Feel Observation 20.1

To ensure that it can be viewed properly on most computer screens, an applet should generally be less than 1024 pixels wide and 768 pixels tall—dimensions supported by most computer screens.

Common Programming Error 20.1

Forgetting the ending `</applet>` tag prevents the applet from executing in some applet containers. The `appletviewer` terminates without indicating an error. Some Web browsers simply ignore the incomplete `applet` element.

Error-Prevention Tip 20.1

If you receive a `MissingResourceException` error message when loading an applet into the appletviewer or a browser, check the `<applet>` tag in the HTML document carefully for syntax errors, such as commas (,) between the attributes.

The `appletviewer` understands only the `<applet>` and `</applet>` HTML tags and ignores all other tags in the document. The `appletviewer` is an ideal place to test an applet and ensure that it executes properly. Once the applet's execution is verified, you can add its HTML tags to a Web page that others can view in their Web browsers.

To execute `WelcomeApplet` in the `appletviewer`, open a command window, change to the directory containing your applet and HTML document, then type

```
appletviewer WelcomeApplet.html
```

Error-Prevention Tip 20.2

Test your applets in the `appletviewer` applet container before executing them in a Web browser. Browsers often save a copy of an applet in memory until all the browser's windows are closed. If you change an applet, recompile it, then reload it in your browser, the browser may still execute the original version of the applet. Close all your browser windows to remove the old applet from memory. Open a new browser window and load the applet to see your changes.

Error-Prevention Tip 20.3

Test your applets in every Web browser in which they will execute to ensure that they operate correctly.

20.3.2 Executing an Applet in a Web Browser

The sample program executions in Fig. 20.6 demonstrate `WelcomeApplet` executing in the `appletviewer` and in Microsoft Internet Explorer Web browser. To execute an applet in Internet Explorer, perform the following steps:

1. Select **Open...** from the **File** menu.
2. In the dialog box that appears, click the **Browse...** button.
3. In the dialog box that appears, locate the directory containing the HTML document for the applet you wish to execute.
4. Select the HTML document.
5. Click the **Open** button.
6. Click the **OK** button.

[*Note:* The steps for executing applets in other Web browsers are similar.]

If your applet executes in the `appletviewer`, but does not execute in your Web browser, Java may not be installed and configured for your browser. In this case, visit the Web site `java.com` and click the **Get It Now** button to install Java for your browser. In Internet Explorer, if this does not fix the problem, you might need to manually configure Internet Explorer to use J2SE 5.0. To do so, click the **Tools** menu and select **Internet Options...**, then click the **Advanced** tab in the window that appears. Locate the option "**Use JRE v1.5.0 for <applet> (requires restart)**" and ensure that it is checked, then click **OK**. Close all your browser windows before attempting to execute another applet in the browser.

20.4 Applet Life-Cycle Methods

Now that you have created an applet, let's consider the five applet methods that are called by the applet container from the time the applet is loaded into the browser to the time that the applet is terminated by the browser. These methods correspond to various aspects of an applet's life cycle. Figure 20.9 lists these methods, which are inherited into your applet classes from class `JApplet`. The table specifies when each method gets called and explains

Method	When the method is called and its purpose

`public void init()`

Called once by the applet container when an applet is loaded for execution. This method initializes an applet. Typical actions performed here are initializing fields, creating GUI components, loading sounds to play, loading images to display (see Chapter 20, Multimedia: Applets and Applications) and creating threads (see Chapter 23, Multithreading).

`public void start()`

Called by the applet container after method `init` completes execution. In addition, if the user browses to another Web site and later returns to the applet's HTML page, method `start` is called again. The method performs any tasks that must be completed when the applet is loaded for the first time and that must be performed every time the applet's HTML page is revisited. Actions performed here might include starting an animation (see Chapter 21) or starting other threads of execution (see Chapter 23).

`public void paint( Graphics g )`

Called by the applet container after methods `init` and `start`. Method `paint` is also called when the applet needs to be repainted. For example, if the user covers the applet with another open window on the screen and later uncovers the applet, the `paint` method is called. Typical actions performed here involve drawing with the `Graphics` object g that is passed to the `paint` method by the applet container.

`public void stop()`

This method is called by the applet container when the user leaves the applet's Web page by browsing to another Web page. Since it is possible that the user might return to the Web page containing the applet, method `stop` performs tasks that might be required to suspend the applet's execution, so that the applet does not use computer processing time when it is not displayed on the screen. Typical actions performed here would stop the execution of animations and threads.

`public void destroy()`

This method is called by the applet container when the applet is being removed from memory. This occurs when the user exits the browsing session by closing all the browser windows and may also occur at the browser's discretion when the user has browsed to other Web pages. The method performs any tasks that are required to clean up resources allocated to the applet.

Fig. 20.9 | `JApplet` life cycle methods that are called by an applet container during an applet's execution.

its purpose. Other than method `paint`, these methods have empty bodies by default. If you would like to declare any of these methods in your applets and have the applet container call them, you must use the method headers shown in Fig. 20.9. If you modify the method headers (e.g., by changing the method names or by providing additional parameters), the applet container will not call your methods. Instead, it will call the superclass methods inherited from `JApplet`.

Common Programming Error 20.2

Declaring methods init, start, paint, stop or destroy with method headers that differ from those shown in Figure 20.9 results in methods that will not be called by the applet container. The code specified in your versions of the methods will not execute.

20.5 Initializing an Instance Variable with Method `init`

Our next applet (Fig. 20.10) computes the sum of two values input by the user and displays the result by drawing a String inside a rectangle on the applet. The sum is stored in an instance variable of class AdditionApplet, so it can be used in both method init and method paint. The HTML document to load this applet into the appletviewer is shown in Fig. 20.11.

The applet requests that the user enter two floating-point numbers. Line 9 (Fig. 20.10) declares instance variable sum of type double. The applet contains two methods—init (lines 12–33) and paint (lines 36–46). When an applet container loads

```
1   // Fig. 20.10: AdditionApplet.java
2   // Adding two floating-point numbers.
3   import java.awt.Graphics;      // program uses class Graphics
4   import javax.swing.JApplet;    // program uses class JApplet
5   import javax.swing.JOptionPane; // program uses class JOptionPane
6
7   public class AdditionApplet extends JApplet
8   {
9      private double sum; // sum of values entered by user
10
11     // initialize applet by obtaining values from user
12     public void init()
13     {
14        String firstNumber;  // first string entered by user
15        String secondNumber; // second string entered by user
16
17        double number1; // first number to add
18        double number2; // second number to add
19
20        // obtain first number from user
21        firstNumber = JOptionPane.showInputDialog(
22           "Enter first floating-point value" );
23
24        // obtain second number from user
25        secondNumber = JOptionPane.showInputDialog(
26           "Enter second floating-point value" );
27
28        // convert numbers from type String to type double
29        number1 = Double.parseDouble( firstNumber );
30        number2 = Double.parseDouble( secondNumber );
31
32        sum = number1 + number2; // add numbers
33     } // end method init
34
```

Fig. 20.10 | Adding double values. (Part 1 of 2.)

```
35      // draw results in a rectangle on applet's background
36      public void paint( Graphics g )
37      {
38         super.paint( g ); // call superclass version of method paint
39
40         // draw rectangle starting from (15, 10) that is 270
41         // pixels wide and 20 pixels tall
42         g.drawRect( 15, 10, 270, 20 );
43
44         // draw results as a String at (25, 25)
45         g.drawString( "The sum is " + sum, 25, 25 );
46      } // end method paint
47   } // end class AdditionApplet
```

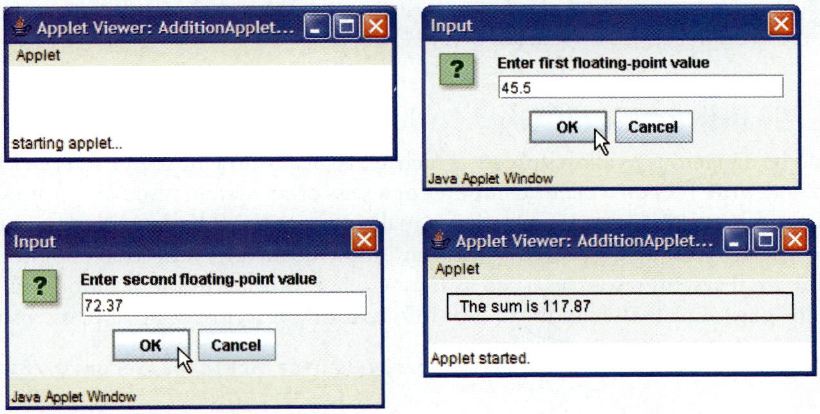

Fig. 20.10 | Adding **double** values. (Part 2 of 2.)

```
1   <html>
2   <applet code = "AdditionApplet.class" width = "300" height = "65">
3   </applet>
4   </html>
```

Fig. 20.11 | `AdditionApplet.html` loads class `AdditionApplet` of Fig. 20.10 into an applet container.

this applet, the container creates an instance of class `AdditionApplet` and calls its `init` method—this occurs only once during an applet's execution. Method `init` normally initializes the applet's fields (if they need to be initialized to values other than their defaults) and performs other tasks that should occur only once when the applet begins execution. The first line of `init` always appears as shown in line 12, which indicates that `init` is a `public` method that receives no arguments and returns no information when it completes.

Lines 14–30 declare variables to store the values entered by the user, obtain the user input and convert the `String`s entered by the user to `double` values by using `Double` method `parseDouble`.

The assignment statement at line 32 sums the values stored in variables `number1` and `number2`, and assigns the result to instance variable `sum`. At this point, the applet's `init` method returns program control to the applet container, which then calls the applet's `start` method. We did not declare `start` in this applet, so the one inherited from class `JApplet` is called here. You will see typical uses of method `start` in Chapters 21 and 23.

Next, the applet container calls the applet's `paint` method. In this example, method `paint` draws a rectangle (line 42) in which the result of the addition will appear. Line 45 calls the `Graphics` object's `drawString` method to display the results. The statement concatenates the value of instance variable `sum` to the `String` `"The sum is "` and displays the concatenated `String`.

Software Engineering Observation 20.1

The only statements that should be placed in an applet's `init` method are those that should execute only once when the applet is initialized.

20.6 Sandbox Security Model

It would be dangerous to allow applets, which are typically downloaded from the Internet, to read and write files on a client computer or access other system resources. For example, what would happen if you downloaded a malicious applet? The Java platform uses the sandbox security model to prevent code that is downloaded to your local computer from accessing local system resources, such as files. Code executing in the "sandbox" is not allowed to "play outside the sandbox." For information on security and applets, visit

```
developer.java.sun.com/developer/technicalArticles/Security/Signed
```

For information on the Java 2 Platform security model, visit

```
java.sun.com/j2se/5.0/docs/guide/security/spec/
security-spec.doc1.html
```

20.7 Internet and Web Resources

If you have access to the Internet, a large number of Java applet resources are available to you. The best place to start is at the source—the Sun Microsystems Java Web site, java.sun.com. The Web page

```
java.sun.com/applets
```

contains several Java applet resources, including free applets that you can use on your own Web site, the demonstration applets from the JDK and other applets (many of which you can download). In a section entitled "Applets at Work," you can read about the uses of applets in industry.

If you do not have Java installed and configured for your browser, you can visit

```
java.com
```

and click the **Get It Now** button to download and install Java in your browser. Instructions are provided for various versions of Windows, Linux, Solaris and Mac OS.

The Sun Microsystems Java Web site

```
java.sun.com
```

includes technical support, discussion forums, technical articles, resources, announcements of new Java features and early access to new Java technologies.

For various free online tutorials, visit the site

```
java.sun.com/learning
```

Another useful Web site is JARS—originally called the Java Applet Rating Service. The JARS site

```
www.jars.com
```

originally was a large Java repository for applets. It rated every applet registered at the site as top 1%, top 5% or top 25%, so you could view the best applets on the Web. Early in the development of the Java language, having your applet rated here was a great way to demonstrate your Java programming abilities. JARS is now an all-around resource for Java programmers.

The resources listed in this section provide hyperlinks to many other Java-related Web sites. If you have Internet access, spend some time browsing these sites, executing applets and reading the source code for the applets when it is available. This will help you to rapidly expand your Java knowledge.

20.8 Wrap-Up

In this chapter, you learned the fundamentals of Java applets. You leaned basic HTML concepts that allowed you to embed an applet in a Web page and execute the applet in an applet container such as the `appletviewer` or a Web browser. In addition, you learned the five methods that are called automatically by the applet container during an applet's life cycle. In the next chapter, you will see several additional applets as we present basic multimedia capabilities. In Chapter 23, Multithreading, you will see an applet with `start` and `stop` methods that are used to control multiple threads of execution. In Chapter 24, Networking, we demonstrate how to customize an applet via parameters that are specified in an `applet` HTML element.

Summary

- Applets are Java programs that can be embedded in HyperText Markup Language (HTML) documents.
- When a browser loads a Web page containing an applet, the applet downloads into the Web browser and executes.
- The browser that executes an applet is generically known as the applet container. The JDK includes the `appletviewer` applet container for testing applets before you embed them in a Web page.
- To reexecute an applet in the `appletviewer`, click the `appletviewer`'s **Applet** menu and select the **Reload** menu item.
- To terminate the `appletviewer`, select **Quit** from the `appletviewer`'s **Applet** menu.

- Every Java applet is a graphical user interface on which you can place GUI components or draw.

- Class JApplet from package javax.swing is used to create applets.

- An applet container can create only objects of classes that are public and extend JApplet (or the Applet class from early versions of Java).

- An applet container expects every Java applet to have methods named init, start, paint, stop and destroy, each of which is declared in class JApplet. Each new applet class you create inherits default implementations of these methods from class JApplet.

- When an applet container loads an applet, the container creates an object of the applet's type, then calls the applet's init, start and paint methods. If you do not declare these methods in your applet, the applet container calls the inherited versions.

- The superclass methods init and start have empty bodies, so they do not perform any tasks. The superclass method paint does not draw anything on the applet.

- To enable an applet to draw, override its method paint. You do not call method paint explicitly in an applet. Rather, the applet container calls paint to tell the applet when to draw, and the applet container is responsible for passing a Graphics object as an argument.

- The first statement in method paint should be a call to the superclass version of method paint. Omitting this can cause subtle drawing errors in applets that combine drawing and GUI components.

- Before you can execute an applet, you must create an HTML (HyperText Markup Language) document that specifies which applet to execute in the applet container. Typically, an HTML document ends with an ".html" or ".htm" file-name extension.

- Most HTML elements are delimited by pairs of tags. All HTML tags begin with a left angle bracket, <, and end with a right angle bracket, >.

- An applet element tells the applet container to load a specific applet and defines the size of the applet's display area (its width and height in pixels) in the applet container.

- Normally, an applet and its corresponding HTML document are stored in the same directory.

- Typically, a browser loads an HTML document from a computer (other than your own) connected to the Internet.

- When an applet container encounters an HTML document that contains an applet, the applet container automatically loads the applet's .class file(s) from the same directory on the computer in which the HTML document resides.

- The appletviewer understands only the <applet> and </applet> HTML tags and ignores all other tags in the document.

- The appletviewer is an ideal place to test an applet and ensure that it executes properly. Once the applet's execution is verified, you can add its HTML tags to a Web page that others can view in their Web browsers.

- There are five applet methods that are called by the applet container from the time the applet is loaded into the browser to the time that the applet is terminated by the browser. These methods correspond to various aspects of an applet's life cycle.

- Method init is called once by the applet container when an applet is loaded for execution. This method initializes the applet.

- Method start is called by the applet container after method init completes execution. In addition, if the user browses to another Web site and later returns to the applet's HTML page, method start is called again.

- Method paint is called by the applet container after methods init and start. Method paint is also called when the applet needs to be repainted.

- Method `stop` is called by the applet container when the user leaves the applet's Web page by browsing to another Web page.
- Method `destroy` is called by the applet container when the applet is being removed from memory. This occurs when the user exits the browsing session by closing all the browser windows and may also occur at the browser's discretion when the user has browsed to other Web pages.

Terminology

applet	`init` method of `JApplet`
applet container	`JApplet` class
`applet` HTML element	left angle bracket (<)
Applet menu in `appletviewer`	`paint` method of `JApplet`
`<applet>` tag	`parseDouble` method of `Double`
`appletviewer`	**Quit** menu item in `appletviewer`
attribute	**Reload** menu item in `appletviewer`
demo directory of the JDK	right angle bracket (>)
`height` of an applet	`start` method of `JApplet`
`.htm` file name extension	`stop` method of `JApplet`
HTML element	tag
`.html` file name extension	`width` of an applet
HyperText Markup Language (HTML)	

Self-Review Exercises

20.1 Fill in the blanks in each of the following:
  a) Java applets begin execution with a series of three method calls: _____, _____ and _____.
  b) The _____ method is invoked for an applet each time the user of a browser leaves an HTML page on which the applet resides.
  c) Every applet should extend class _____.
  d) The _____ or a browser can be used to execute a Java applet.
  e) The _____ method is called each time the user of a browser revisits the HTML page on which an applet resides.
  f) To load an applet into a browser, you must first define a(n) _____ file.
  g) The _____ method is called once when an applet begins execution.
  h) The _____ method is invoked to draw on an applet.
  i) The _____ method is invoked for an applet when the browser removes it from memory.
  j) The _____ and _____ HTML tags specify that an applet should be loaded into an applet container and executed.

Answers to Self-Review Exercises

20.1 a) `init`, `start`, `paint`. b) `stop`. c) `JApplet` (or `Applet`). d) `appletviewer`. e) `start`. f) HTML. g) `init`. h) `paint`. i) `destroy`. j) `<applet>`, `</applet>`.

Exercises

20.2 Write an applet that asks the user to enter two floating-point numbers, obtains the two numbers from the user and draws their sum, product (multiplication), difference and quotient (division). Use the techniques shown in Fig. 20.10.

20.3   Write an applet that asks the user to enter two floating-point numbers, obtains the numbers from the user and displays the two numbers first and then the larger number followed by the words "is larger" as a string on the applet. If the numbers are equal, the applet should print the message "These numbers are equal." Use the techniques shown in Fig. 20.10.

20.4   Write an applet that inputs three floating-point numbers from the user and displays the sum, average, product, smallest and largest of these numbers as strings on the applet. Use the techniques shown in Fig. 20.10.

20.5   Write an applet that asks the user to input the radius of a circle as a floating-point number and draws the circle's diameter, circumference and area. Use the value 3.14159 for π. Use the techniques shown in Fig. 20.10. [*Note:* You may also use the predefined constant Math.PI for the value of π. This constant is more precise than the value 3.14159. Class Math is defined in the java.lang package, so you do not need to import it.] Use the following formulas (*r* is the radius):

$$diameter = 2r$$
$$circumference = 2\pi r$$
$$area = \pi r^2$$

20.6   Write an applet that reads five integers, determines which are the largest and smallest integers in the group and prints them. Use only the programming techniques you learned in this chapter and Chapter 2. Draw the results on the applet.

20.7   Write an applet that draws a checkerboard pattern as follows:

```
* * * * * * * *
 * * * * * * * *
* * * * * * * *
 * * * * * * * *
* * * * * * * *
 * * * * * * * *
* * * * * * * *
 * * * * * * * *
```

20.8   Write an applet that draws rectangles of different sizes and locations.

20.9   Write an applet that allows the user to input values for the arguments required by method drawRect, then draws a rectangle using the four input values.

20.10   Class Graphics contains method drawOval, which takes as arguments the same four arguments as method drawRect. The arguments for method drawOval specify the "bounding box for the oval—the sides of the bounding box are the boundaries of the oval. Write a Java applet that draws an oval and a rectangle with the same four arguments. The oval will touch the rectangle at the center of each side.

20.11   Modify the solution to Exercise 20.10 to output ovals of different shapes and sizes.

20.12   Write an applet that allows the user to input the four arguments required by method drawOval, then draws an oval using the four input values.

Multimedia: Applets and Applications

OBJECTIVES

In this chapter you will learn:

- How to get and display images.
- To create animations from sequences of images.
- To create image maps.
- To get, play, loop and stop sounds, using an `AudioClip`.
- To play video using interface `Player`.

21.1 Introduction

Welcome to what may be the largest revolution in the history of the computer industry. Those who entered the field decades ago were interested in using computers primarily to perform arithmetic calculations at high speed. As the computer field evolved, we began to realize that the data-manipulation capabilities of computers are equally important. The "sizzle" of Java is multimedia—the use of sound, images, graphics and video to make applications "come alive." Although most multimedia in Java applications is two-dimensional, Java programmers already can use the Java 3D API to create substantial 3D graphics applications (Sun provides an online tutorial for the Java 3D API at java.sun.com/developer/onlineTraining/java3d).

Multimedia programming offers many new challenges. The field is already enormous and is growing rapidly. People are rushing to equip their computers for multimedia. Most new computers sold today are "multimedia ready," with CD-RW and DVD drives, audio boards and special video capabilities. Economical desktop and laptop computers are so powerful that they can store and play DVD-quality sound and video, and we expect to see further advances in the kinds of programmable multimedia capabilities available through programming languages. One thing that we have learned is to plan for the "impossible"—in the computer and communications fields, the "impossible" has repeatedly become reality.

Among users who want graphics, many now want three-dimensional, high-resolution, color graphics. True three-dimensional imaging may become available within the next decade. Imagine having high-resolution, "theater-in-the-round," three-dimensional television. Sporting and entertainment events will seem to take place on your living room floor! Medical students worldwide will see operations being performed thousands of miles away, as if they were occurring in the same room. People will be able to learn how to drive with extremely realistic driving simulators in their homes before they get behind the wheel. The possibilities are exciting and endless.

Multimedia demands extraordinary computing power. Until recently, affordable computers with that kind of power were not available. Today's ultrapowerful processors, like the SPARC Ultra 5 from Sun Microsystems, the Pentium and Itanium 2 from Intel, the PowerPC G5 from IBM and Apple, and the processors from MIPS/Silicon Graphics (among others) make effective multimedia possible. The computer and communications industries will be primary beneficiaries of the multimedia revolution. Users will be willing to pay for the faster processors, larger memories and wider communications bandwidths that support demanding multimedia applications. Ironically, users may not have to pay more, because the fierce competition in these industries has historically driven prices down.

We need programming languages that make creating multimedia applications easy. Most programming languages do not incorporate such capabilities. However, Java, through its class libraries, provides extensive multimedia facilities that enable you to start developing powerful multimedia applications immediately.

This chapter presents several examples of interesting multimedia features that you will need to build useful applications, including:

1. the basics of manipulating images.

2. creating smooth animations.

3. playing audio files with the `AudioClip` interface.

4. creating image maps that can sense when the cursor is over them, even without a mouse click.

5. playing video files using the `Player` interface.

The exercises for this chapter suggest dozens of challenging and interesting projects. When we were creating these exercises, the ideas just kept flowing. Multimedia leverages creativity in ways that we did not experience with "conventional" computer capabilities. [*Note:* Java's multimedia capabilities go far beyond those presented in this chapter. They include the Java Media Framework (JMF) API (for adding audio and video media to an application), Java Sound API (for playing, recording and modifying audio), Java 3D API (for creating and modifying 3D graphics), Java Advanced Imaging API (for image-processing capabilities, such as cropping and scaling), Java Speech API (for inputting voice commands from the user or outputting voice commands to the user), Java 2D API (for creating and modifying 2D graphics, covered in Chapter 12) and Java Image I/O API (for reading from and outputting images to files). Section 21.8 provides Web links for each of these APIs.]

21.2 Loading, Displaying and Scaling Images

Java's multimedia capabilities include graphics, images, animations, sounds and video. We begin our discussion with images. We will use a few different images in this chapter. Developers can create such images with any image software, such as Adobe® Photoshop™, Jasc® Paint Shop Pro™ or Microsoft® Paint.

The applet of Fig. 21.1 demonstrates loading an `Image` (package `java.awt`) and loading an `ImageIcon` (package `javax.swing`). Both classes are used to load and display images. The applet displays the `Image` in its original size and scaled to a larger size, using two versions of `Graphics` method **drawImage**. The applet also draws the `ImageIcon`, using the icon's method **paintIcon**. Class `ImageIcon` implements interface `Serializable`, which allows `ImageIcon` objects to be easily written to a file or sent across the Internet. Class `ImageIcon` is also easier to use than `Image`, because its constructor can receive arguments of several different formats, including a `byte` array containing the bytes of an image, an `Image` already loaded in memory, and a `String` or a `URL` object, which both can be used to represent the location of the image. A `URL` object represents a Uniform Resource Locator that serves as a pointer to a resource on the World Wide Web, on your computer or on any networked machine. A URL object is more often used when accessing data over the Internet, while a simple string is more often used when accessing data on the current machine. Using an URL object also enables the programmer to access information from the Web, such as searching for information from a database or through a search engine.

Lines 11 and 12 declare an Image reference and an ImageIcon reference, respectively. Class Image is an abstract class—the applet cannot create an object of class Image directly. Rather, we must call a method that causes the applet container to load and return the Image for use in the program. Class Applet (the direct superclass of JApplet) provides method **getImage** (line 17, in method init) that loads an Image into an applet. This version of getImage takes two arguments—the location of the image file and the file name of the image. In the first argument, Applet method **getDocumentBase** returns a URL representing the location of the image on the Internet (or on your computer if the applet was loaded from your computer). Method getDocumentBase returns the location of the HTML file as an object of class URL. The second argument specifies an image file name.

```
1   // Fig. 21.1: LoadImageAndScale.java
2   // Load an image and display it in its original size and twice its
3   // original size. Load and display the same image as an ImageIcon.
4   import java.awt.Graphics;
5   import java.awt.Image;
6   import javax.swing.ImageIcon;
7   import javax.swing.JApplet;
8
9   public class LoadImageAndScale extends JApplet
10  {
11     private Image image1; // create Image object
12     private ImageIcon image2; // create ImageIcon object
13
14     // load image when applet is loaded
15     public void init()
16     {
17        image1 = getImage( getDocumentBase(), "redflowers.png" );
18        image2 = new ImageIcon( "yellowflowers.png" );
19     } // end method init
20
21     // display image
22     public void paint( Graphics g )
23     {
24        super.paint( g );
25
26        g.drawImage( image1, 0, 0, this ); // draw original image
27
28        // draw image to fit the width and the height less 120 pixels
29        g.drawImage( image1, 0, 120, getWidth(), getHeight() - 120, this );
30
31        // draw icon using its paintIcon method
32        image2.paintIcon( this, g, 180, 0 );
33     } // end method paint
34  } // end class LoadImageAndScale
```

Fig. 21.1 | Loading and displaying an image in an applet. (Part 1 of 2.)

Fig. 21.1 | Loading and displaying an image in an applet. (Part 2 of 2.)

The two arguments together specify the unique name and path of the file being loaded (in this case, the file `redflowers.png` stored in the same directory as the HTML file that invoked the applet). Java supports several image formats, including Graphics Interchange Format (GIF), Joint Photographic Experts Group (JPEG) and Portable Network Graphics (PNG). File names for these types end with `.gif`, `.jpg` (or `.jpeg`) and `.png`, respectively.

Portability Tip 21.1

Class `Image` *is an* `abstract` *class—as a result, programs cannot instantiate class* `Image` *to create objects. To achieve platform independence, the Java implementation on each platform provides its own subclass of* `Image` *to store image information.*

Line 17 begins loading the image from the local computer (or downloading it from the Internet). When the image is required by the program, it is loaded in a separate thread of execution. Remember that a thread is a parallel activity, and that threads will be discussed in detail in Chapter 23, Multithreading. By using a separate thread to load an image, the program can continue execution while the image loads. [*Note:* If the requested file is not available, method `getImage` does not throw an exception. An `Image` object is returned, but when this `Image` is displayed using method `drawImage`, nothing will be displayed.]

Class `ImageIcon` is not an `abstract` class—a program can create an `ImageIcon` object. At line 18, in method `init` creates an `ImageIcon` object that loads `yellowflowers.png`. Class `ImageIcon` provides several constructors that enable programs to initialize `Image-Icon` objects with images from the local computer or stored on the Internet.

The applet's `paint` method (lines 22–33) displays the images. Line 26 uses `Graphics` method `drawImage` to display an `Image`. Method `drawImage` accepts four arguments. The first is a reference to the `Image` object to display (`image1`). The second and third are the *x*- and *y*-coordinates at which to display the image on the applet—the coordinates specify the location of the upper-left corner of the image. The last argument is a reference to an ImageObserver—an interface implemented by class Component. Since class JApplet indirectly extends Component, all JApplets are ImageObservers. This argument is important when displaying large images that require a long time to download from the Internet. It is possible that a program will attempt to display the image before it has downloaded completely. The ImageObserver receives notifications as the Image is loaded and updates the image on the screen if the image was not complete when it was displayed. When executing this applet, watch carefully as pieces of the image display while the image loads. [*Note:* On faster computers, you might not notice this effect.]

Line 29 uses another version of Graphics method drawImage to output a scaled version of the image. The fourth and fifth arguments specify the *width* and *height* of the image for display purposes. Method drawImage scales the image to fit the specified width and height. In this example, the fourth argument indicates that the width of the scaled image should be the width of the applet, and the fifth argument indicates that the height should be 120 pixels less than the height of the applet. The width and height of the applet are determined by calling methods getWidth and getHeight (inherited from class Component).

Line 32 uses ImageIcon method paintIcon to display the image. The method requires four arguments—a reference to the Component on which to display the image, a reference to the Graphics object that will render the image, the *x*-coordinate of the upper-left corner of the image and the *y*-coordinate of the upper-left corner of the image.

21.3 Animating a Series of Images

The next example demonstrates animating a series of images that are stored in an array of ImageIcons. The animation presented in Fig. 21.2–Fig. 21.3 is implemented using a subclass of JPanel called LogoAnimatorJPanel (Fig. 21.2) that can be attached to an application window or a JApplet. Class LogoAnimator (Fig. 21.3) declares a main method (lines 8–20 of Fig. 21.3) to execute the animation as an application. Method main declares an instance of class JFrame and attaches a LogoAnimatorJPasnel object to the JFrame to display the animation.

Class LogoAnimatorJPanel (Fig. 21.2) maintains an array of ImageIcons that are loaded in the constructor (lines 24–36). Lines 29–31 create each ImageIcon object and store the animation's 30 images in array images. The constructor argument uses string concatenation to assemble the file name from the pieces "images/", IMAGE_NAME, count and ".gif". Each image in the animation is in a file called deitel#.gif, where # is a value in the range 0–29 specified by the loop's control variable count. Lines 34–35 determine the width and height of the animation from the size of the first image in array images— we assume that all the images have the same width and height.

After the LogoAnimatorJPanel constructor loads the images, method main of Fig. 21.3 sets up the window in which the animation will appear (lines 12–17), and line 19 calls the LogoAnimatorJPanel's startAnimation method (declared at lines 51–68 of Fig. 21.2). This method starts the program's animation for the first time or restarts the animation that the program stopped previously. [*Note:* This method is called when the program is first run, to begin the animation. Although we provide the functionality for this method to restart the animation if it has been stopped, the example does not call the method for this purpose. We have added the functionality, however, should the reader choose to add GUI components that enable the user to start and stop the animation.] For example, to make an animation "browser friendly" in an applet, the animation should stop when the user switches Web pages. If the user returns to the Web page with the animation, method `startAnimation` can be called to restart the animation. The animation is driven

```java
1   // Fig. 21.2: LogoAnimatorJPanel.java
2   // Animation of a series of images.
3   import java.awt.Dimension;
4   import java.awt.event.ActionEvent;
5   import java.awt.event.ActionListener;
6   import java.awt.Graphics;
7   import javax.swing.ImageIcon;
8   import javax.swing.JPanel;
9   import javax.swing.Timer;
10
11  public class LogoAnimatorJPanel extends JPanel
12  {
13     private final static String IMAGE_NAME = "deitel"; // base image name
14     protected ImageIcon images[]; // array of images
15     private final int TOTAL_IMAGES = 30; // number of images
16     private int currentImage = 0; // current image index
17     private final int ANIMATION_DELAY = 50; // millisecond delay
18     private int width; // image width
19     private int height; // image height
20
21     private Timer animationTimer; // Timer drives animation
22
23     // constructor initializes LogoAnimatorJPanel by loading images
24     public LogoAnimatorJPanel()
25     {
26        images = new ImageIcon[ TOTAL_IMAGES ];
27
28        // load 30 images
29        for ( int count = 0; count < images.length; count++ )
30           images[ count ] = new ImageIcon( getClass().getResource(
31              "images/" + IMAGE_NAME + count + ".gif" ) );
32
33        // this example assumes all images have the same width and height
34        width = images[ 0 ].getIconWidth();   // get icon width
35        height = images[ 0 ].getIconHeight(); // get icon height
36     } // end LogoAnimatorJPanel constructor
37
38     // display current image
39     public void paintComponent( Graphics g )
40     {
41        super.paintComponent( g ); // call superclass paintComponent
42
43        images[ currentImage ].paintIcon( this, g, 0, 0 );
44
45        // set next image to be drawn only if timer is running
46        if ( animationTimer.isRunning() )
47           currentImage = ( currentImage + 1 ) % TOTAL_IMAGES;
48     } // end method paintComponent
```

Fig. 21.2 | Animating a series of images. (Part 1 of 2.)

```
49
50      // start animation, or restart if window is redisplayed
51      public void startAnimation()
52      {
53         if ( animationTimer == null )
54         {
55            currentImage = 0; // display first image
56
57            // create timer
58            animationTimer =
59               new Timer( ANIMATION_DELAY, new TimerHandler() );
60
61            animationTimer.start(); // start timer
62         } // end if
63         else // animationTimer already exists, restart animation
64         {
65            if ( ! animationTimer.isRunning() )
66               animationTimer.restart();
67         } // end else
68      } // end method startAnimation
69
70      // stop animation timer
71      public void stopAnimation()
72      {
73         animationTimer.stop();
74      } // end method stopAnimation
75
76      // return minimum size of animation
77      public Dimension getMinimumSize()
78      {
79         return getPreferredSize();
80      } // end method getMinimumSize
81
82      // return preferred size of animation
83      public Dimension getPreferredSize()
84      {
85         return new Dimension( width, height );
86      } // end method getPreferredSize
87
88      // inner class to handle action events from Timer
89      private class TimerHandler implements ActionListener
90      {
91         // respond to Timer's event
92         public void actionPerformed( ActionEvent actionEvent )
93         {
94            repaint(); // repaint animator
95         } // end method actionPerformed
96      } // end class TimerHandler
97   } // end class LogoAnimatorJPanel
```

Fig. 21.2 | Animating a series of images. (Part 2 of 2.)

by an instance of class Timer (from package javax.swing). A Timer generates Action-
Events at a fixed interval in milliseconds (normally specified as an argument to the Timer's

```
 1   // Fig. 21.3: LogoAnimator.java
 2   // Animation of a series of images.
 3   import javax.swing.JFrame;
 4
 5   public class LogoAnimator
 6   {
 7      // execute animation in a JFrame
 8      public static void main( String args[] )
 9      {
10         LogoAnimatorJPanel animation = new LogoAnimatorJPanel();
11
12         JFrame window = new JFrame( "Animator test" ); // set up window
13         window.setDefaultCloseOperation( JFrame.EXIT_ON_CLOSE );
14         window.add( animation ); // add panel to frame
15
16         window.pack();  // make window just large enough for its GUI
17         window.setVisible( true );   // display window
18
19         animation.startAnimation();  // begin animation
20      } // end main
21   } // end class LogoAnimator
```

Fig. 21.3 | Displaying animated images on a JFrame.

constructor) and notifies all its ActionListeners each time an ActionEvent occurs. Line 53 determines whether the Timer reference animationTimer is null. If it is, method startAnimation is being called for the first time, and a Timer needs to be created so that the animation can begin. Line 55 sets currentImage to 0, which indicates that the animation should begin with the image in the first element of array images. Lines 58–59 assign a new Timer object to animationTimer. The Timer constructor receives two arguments—the delay in milliseconds (ANIMATION_DELAY is 50, as specified in line 17) and the ActionListener that will respond to the Timer's ActionEvents. For the second argument, an object of class TimerHandler is created. This class, which implements ActionListener, is declared in lines 89–96. Line 61 starts the Timer object. Once started, animationTimer will generate an ActionEvent every 50 milliseconds. Each time an ActionEvent is generated, the Timer's event handler actionPerformed (lines 92–95) is called. Line 94 calls LogoAnimatorJPanel's repaint method to schedule a call to LogoAnimatorJPanel's paintComponent method (lines 39–48). Remember that any subclass of JComponent that draws should do so in its paintComponent method. Recall from Chapter 11 that the first statement in any paintComponent method should be a call to the superclass's paintComponent method, to ensure that Swing components are displayed correctly.

If the animation was started earlier, then our Timer has been created and the condition in line 53 will evaluate to false. The program will continue with lines 65–66, which restart the animation that the program stopped previously. The if condition at line 65 uses Timer method isRunning to determine whether the Timer is running (i.e., generating events). If it is not running, line 66 calls Timer method restart to indicate that the Timer should start generating events again. Once this occurs, method actionPerformed (the Timer's event handler) is again called at regular intervals. Each time, a call is made to method repaint (line 94), causing method paintComponent to be called and the next image to be displayed.

Line 43 paints the ImageIcon stored at element currentImage in the array. Lines 46–47 determine whether the animationTimer is running and, if so, prepare for the next image to be displayed by incrementing currentImage by 1. The remainder calculation ensures that the value of currentImage is set to 0 (to repeat the animation sequence) when it is incremented past 29 (the last element index in the array). The if statement ensures that the same image will be displayed if paintComponent is called while the Timer is stopped. This could be useful if a GUI is provided that enables the user to start and stop the animation. For example, if the animation is stopped and the user covers it with another window, then uncovers it, method paintComponent will be called. In this case, we do not want the animation to show the next image (because the animation has been stopped). We simply want the window to display the same image until the animation is restarted.

Method stopAnimation (lines 71–74) stops the animation by calling Timer method stop to indicate that the Timer should stop generating events. This prevents actionPerformed from calling repaint to initiate the painting of the next image in the array. [*Note:* Just as with restarting the animation, this example defines but does not use method stopAnimation. We have provided this method for demonstration purposes, or if the user wishes to modify this example so that it enables the user to stop and restart the animation.]

Software Engineering Observation 21.1

When creating an animation for use in an applet, provide a mechanism for disabling the animation when the user browses a new Web page different from the one on which the animation applet resides.

Remember that by extending class JPanel, we are creating a new GUI component. Thus, we must ensure that our new component works like other components for layout purposes. Layout managers often use a GUI component's **getPreferredSize** method (inherited from class java.awt.Component) to determine the preferred width and height of the component when laying it out as part of a GUI. If a new component has a preferred width and height, it should override method getPreferredSize (lines 83–86) to return that width and height as an object of class **Dimension** (package java.awt). The Dimension class represents the width and height of a GUI component. In this example, the images are 160 pixels wide and 80 pixels tall, so method getPreferredSize returns a Dimension object containing the numbers 160 and 80 (determined at lines 34–35).

Look-and-Feel Observation 21.1

The default size of a JPanel object is 10 pixels wide and 10 pixels tall.

Look-and-Feel Observation 21.2

When subclassing JPanel (or any other JComponent), override method getPreferredSize if the new component is to have a specific preferred width and height.

Lines 77–80 override method **getMinimumSize**. This method determines the minimum width and height of the component. As with method getPreferredSize, new components should override method getMinimumSize (also inherited from class Component). Method getMinimumSize simply calls getPreferredSize (a common programming practice) to indicate that the minimum size and preferred size are the same. Some layout managers ignore the dimensions specified by these methods. For example, a BorderLayout's NORTH and SOUTH regions use only the component's preferred height.

Look-and-Feel Observation 21.3

If a new GUI component has a minimum width and height (i.e., smaller dimensions would render the component ineffective on the display), override method getMinimumSize *to return the minimum width and height as an instance of class* Dimension.

Look-and-Feel Observation 21.4

For many GUI components, method getMinimumSize *is implemented to return the result of a call to the component's* getPreferredSize *method.*

21.4 Image Maps

Image maps are commonly used to create interactive Web pages. An image map is an image with **hot areas** that the user can click to accomplish a task, such as loading a different Web page into a browser. When the user positions the mouse pointer over a hot area, normally a descriptive message appears in the status area of the browser or in a tool tip.

Figure 21.4 loads an image containing several of the programming tip icons used in this book. The program allows the user to position the mouse pointer over an icon to display a descriptive message associated with it. Event handler mouseMoved (lines 39–43) takes the mouse coordinates and passes them to method translateLocation (lines 58–69). Method translateLocation tests the coordinates to determine the icon over which the mouse was positioned when the mouseMoved event occurred—the method then returns a message indicating what the icon represents. This message is displayed in the applet container's status bar using method **showStatus** of class Applet.

Clicking in the applet of Fig. 21.4 will not cause any action. In Chapter 24, Networking, we discuss the techniques required to load another Web page into a browser via URLs and the AppletContext interface. Using those techniques, this applet could associate each icon with a URL that the browser would display when the user clicks the icon.

21.5 Loading and Playing Audio Clips

Java programs can manipulate and play **audio clips**. Users can capture their own audio clips, and many clips are available in software products and over the Internet. Your system needs to be equipped with audio hardware (speakers and a sound card) to be able to play the audio clips.

Java provides several mechanisms for playing sounds in an applet. The two simplest are the Applet's **play** method and the **play** method of the **AudioClip** interface. Additional audio capabilities are available in the Java Media Framework and Java Sound APIs. If you would like to play a sound once in a program, the Applet method play loads the sound and plays it once—the sound is marked for garbage collection after it plays. The Applet method play has two versions:

```
        public void play( URL location, String soundFileName );
        public void play( URL soundURL );
```

The first version loads the audio clip stored in file soundFileName from location and plays the sound. The first argument is normally a call to the applet's getDocumentBase or getCodeBase method. Method getDocumentBase returns the location of the HTML file

```
 1   // Fig. 21.4: ImageMap.java
 2   // Demonstrating an image map.
 3   import java.awt.event.MouseAdapter;
 4   import java.awt.event.MouseEvent;
 5   import java.awt.event.MouseMotionAdapter;
 6   import java.awt.Graphics;
 7   import javax.swing.ImageIcon;
 8   import javax.swing.JApplet;
 9
10   public class ImageMap extends JApplet
11   {
12      private ImageIcon mapImage;
13
14      private static final String captions[] = { "Common Programming Error",
15         "Good Programming Practice", "Graphical User Interface Tip",
16         "Performance Tip", "Portability Tip",
17         "Software Engineering Observation", "Error-Prevention Tip" };
18
19      // sets up mouse listeners
20      public void init()
21      {
22         addMouseListener(
23
24            new MouseAdapter() // anonymous inner class
25            {
26               // indicate when mouse pointer exits applet area
27               public void mouseExited( MouseEvent event )
28               {
29                  showStatus( "Pointer outside applet" );
30               } // end method mouseExited
31            } // end anonymous inner class
32         ); // end call to addMouseListener
33
34         addMouseMotionListener(
35
36            new MouseMotionAdapter() // anonymous inner class
37            {
38               // determine icon over which mouse appears
39               public void mouseMoved( MouseEvent event )
40               {
41                  showStatus( translateLocation(
42                     event.getX(), event.getY() ) );
43               } // end method mouseMoved
44            } // end anonymous inner class
45         ); // end call to addMouseMotionListener
```

Fig. 21.4 | Image map. (Part 1 of 3.)

```
46
47        mapImage = new ImageIcon( "icons.png" ); // get image
48     } // end method init
49
50     // display mapImage
51     public void paint( Graphics g )
52     {
53        super.paint( g );
54        mapImage.paintIcon( this, g, 0, 0 );
55     } // end method paint
56
57     // return tip caption based on mouse coordinates
58     public String translateLocation( int x, int y )
59     {
60        // if coordinates outside image, return immediately
61        if ( x >= mapImage.getIconWidth() || y >= mapImage.getIconHeight() )
62           return "";
63
64        // determine icon number (0 - 6)
65        double iconWidth = ( double ) mapImage.getIconWidth() / 7.0;
66        int iconNumber = ( int )( ( double ) x / iconWidth );
67
68        return captions[ iconNumber ]; // return appropriate icon caption
69     } // end method translateLocation
70  } // end class ImageMap
```

Fig. 21.4 | Image map. (Part 2 of 3.)

Fig. 21.4 | Image map. (Part 3 of 3.)

that loaded the applet. (If the applet is in a package, the method returns the location of the package or the JAR file containing the package.) Method `getCodeBase` indicates the location of the applet's `.class` file. The second version of method `play` takes a URL that contains the location and the file name of the audio clip. The statement

```
play( getDocumentBase(), "hi.au" );
```

loads the audio clip in file `hi.au` and plays the clip once.

The **sound engine** that plays the audio clips supports several audio file formats, including **Sun Audio file format** (**.au** extension), **Windows Wave file format** (**.wav** extension), **Macintosh AIFF file format** (**.aif or .aiff** extensions) and **Musical Instrument Digital Interface (MIDI) file format** (**.mid or .rmi** extensions). The Java Media Framework (JMF) and Java Sound APIs support additional formats.

The program of Fig. 21.5 demonstrates loading and playing an AudioClip (package java.applet). This technique is more flexible than Applet method play. An applet can use an AudioClip to store audio for repeated use throughout a program's execution.

```java
 1   // Fig. 21.5: LoadAudioAndPlay.java
 2   // Load an audio clip and play it.
 3   import java.applet.AudioClip;
 4   import java.awt.event.ItemListener;
 5   import java.awt.event.ItemEvent;
 6   import java.awt.event.ActionListener;
 7   import java.awt.event.ActionEvent;
 8   import java.awt.FlowLayout;
 9   import javax.swing.JApplet;
10   import javax.swing.JButton;
11   import javax.swing.JComboBox;
12
13   public class LoadAudioAndPlay extends JApplet
14   {
15      private AudioClip sound1, sound2, currentSound;
16      private JButton playJButton, loopJButton, stopJButton;
17      private JComboBox soundJComboBox;
18
19      // load the image when the applet begins executing
20      public void init()
21      {
22         setLayout( new FlowLayout() );
23
24         String choices[] = { "Welcome", "Hi" };
25         soundJComboBox = new JComboBox( choices ); // create JComboBox
26
27         soundJComboBox.addItemListener(
28
29            new ItemListener() // anonymous inner class
30            {
31               // stop sound and change to sound to user's selection
32               public void itemStateChanged( ItemEvent e )
33               {
34                  currentSound.stop();
35                  currentSound = soundJComboBox.getSelectedIndex() == 0 ?
36                     sound1 : sound2;
37               } // end method itemStateChanged
38            } // end anonymous inner class
39         ); // end addItemListener method call
40
41         add( soundJComboBox ); // add JComboBox to applet
42
```

Fig. 21.5 | Loading and playing an AudioClip. (Part 1 of 2.)

```
43          // set up button event handler and buttons
44          ButtonHandler handler = new ButtonHandler();
45
46          // create Play JButton
47          playJButton = new JButton( "Play" );
48          playJButton.addActionListener( handler );
49          add( playJButton );
50
51          // create Loop JButton
52          loopJButton = new JButton( "Loop" );
53          loopJButton.addActionListener( handler );
54          add( loopJButton );
55
56          // create Stop JButton
57          stopJButton = new JButton( "Stop" );
58          stopJButton.addActionListener( handler );
59          add( stopJButton );
60
61          // load sounds and set currentSound
62          sound1 = getAudioClip( getDocumentBase(), "welcome.wav" );
63          sound2 = getAudioClip( getDocumentBase(), "hi.au" );
64          currentSound = sound1;
65       } // end method init
66
67       // stop the sound when the user switches Web pages
68       public void stop()
69       {
70          currentSound.stop(); // stop AudioClip
71       } // end method stop
72
73       // private inner class to handle button events
74       private class ButtonHandler implements ActionListener
75       {
76          // process play, loop and stop button events
77          public void actionPerformed( ActionEvent actionEvent )
78          {
79             if ( actionEvent.getSource() == playJButton )
80                currentSound.play(); // play AudioClip once
81             else if ( actionEvent.getSource() == loopJButton )
82                currentSound.loop(); // play AudioClip continuously
83             else if ( actionEvent.getSource() == stopJButton )
84                currentSound.stop(); // stop AudioClip
85          } // end method actionPerformed
86       } // end class ButtonHandler
87    } // end class LoadAudioAndPlay
```

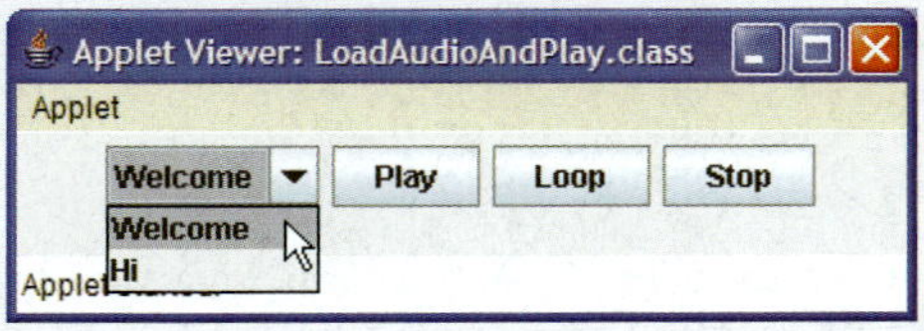

Fig. 21.5 | Loading and playing an `AudioClip`. (Part 2 of 2.)

Applet method `getAudioClip` has two forms that take the same arguments as method `play` described previously. Method `getAudioClip` returns a reference to an `AudioClip`. An `AudioClip` has three methods—`play`, `loop` and `stop`. As mentioned earlier, method `play` plays the audio clip once. Method `loop` continuously loops through the audio clip in the background. Method `stop` terminates an audio clip that is currently playing. In the program, each of these methods is associated with a button on the applet.

Lines 62–63 in the applet's `init` method use `getAudioClip` to load two audio files—a Windows Wave file (`welcome.wav`) and a Sun Audio file (`hi.au`). The user can select which audio clip to play from the `JComboBox soundJComboBox`. Note that the applet's `stop` method is overridden at lines 68–71. When the user switches Web pages, the applet container calls the applet's `stop` method. This enables the applet to stop playing the audio clip. Otherwise, it continues to play in the background—even if the applet is not displayed in the browser. This is not necessarily a problem, but it can be annoying to the user if the audio clip is looping. The `stop` method is provided here as a convenience to the user.

Look-and-Feel Observation 21.5

When playing audio clips in an applet or application, provide a mechanism for the user to disable the audio.

21.6 Playing Video and Other Media with Java Media Framework

A simple video can concisely and effectively convey a great deal of information. Recognizing the value of bringing extensible multimedia capabilities to Java, Sun Microsystems, Intel and Silicon Graphics worked together to produce the multimedia API Java Media Framework (JMF), discussed briefly in Section 21.1. Using the JMF API, programmers can create Java applications that play, edit, stream and capture many popular media types. While the features of JMF are quite extensive, this section briefly introduces some popular media formats and demonstrates playing video using the JMF API.

IBM and Sun developed the latest JMF specification—version 2.0. Sun also provides a reference implementation of the JMF specification—JMF 2.1.1e—that supports media file types such as Microsoft Audio/Video Interleave (`.avi`), Macromedia Flash 2 movies (`.swf`), Future Splash (`.spl`), MPEG Layer 3 Audio (`.mp3`), Musical Instrument Digital Interface (MIDI; `.mid` or `.rmi` extensions), MPEG-1 videos (`.mpeg`, `.mpg`), QuickTime (`.mov`), Sun Audio file format (`.au` extension), and Macintosh AIFF file format (`.aif` or `.aiff` extension). You have already seen some of these files types.

Currently, JMF is available as an extension separate from the Java 2 Software Development Kit. The most recent JMF implementation (2.1.1e) can be downloaded from:

```
http://java.sun.com/products/java-media/jmf/2.1.1/download.html
```

You need to accept the license agreement prior to downloading.

The JMF Web site provides versions of the JMF that take advantage of the performance features of certain platforms. For example, the JMF Windows Performance Pack provides extensive media and device support for Java programs running on Microsoft Windows platforms (Windows 95/98/NT 4.0/2000/XP). JMF's official Web site (`java.sun.com/products/java-media/jmf`) provides continually updated support, information and resources for JMF programmers.

Once the file finishes downloading, open it and follow the on-screen instructions to install the program. Leave all options at their defaults. You may need to restart your computer to finish the installation.

Creating a Simple Media Player

The JMF offers several mechanisms for playing media. The simplest mechanism is using objects that implement interface **Player** declared in package **javax.media**. Package javax.media and its subpackages contain the classes that compose the Java Media Framework. To play a media clip you must first create a URL object that refers to it. Then pass the URL as an argument to static method **createRealizedPlayer** of class Manager to obtain a Player for the media clip. Class **Manager** declares utility methods for accessing system resources to play and to manipulate media. Figure 21.6 declares a JPanel that demonstrates some of these methods.

The constructor (lines 15–51) sets up the JPanel to play the media file specified as a URL parameter to the constructor. MediaPanel uses a BorderLayout (line 17). Line 20 invokes static method **setHint** to set the flag **Manager.LIGHTWEIGHT_RENDER** to true. This instructs the Manager to use a lightweight renderer that is compatible with lightweight Swing components, as opposed to the default heavyweight renderer. Inside the try block (lines 22–38), line 25 invokes static method createRealizedPlayer of class Manager to create and realize a Player that plays the media file. When a Player realizes, it identifies the system resources it needs to play the media. Depending on the file, realizing can be a resource-consuming and time-consuming process. Method createRealized-Player throws three checked exceptions, **NoPlayerException**, **CannotRealizeException** and IOException. A NoPlayerException indicates that the system could not find a player that can play the file format. A CannotRealizeException indicates that the system could not properly identify the resources a media file needs. An IOException indicates that there was an error while reading the file. These exceptions are handled in the catch block in lines 39–50.

Line 28 invokes method **getVisualComponent** of Player to get a Component that displays the visual (generally video) aspect of the media file. Line 29 invokes method **getControlPanelComponent** of Player to get a Component that provides playback and media controls. These components are assigned to local variables video and control, respectively. The if statements in lines 31–32 and lines 34–35 add the video and the controls if they exist. The video Component is added to the CENTER region (line 32), so it fills any available space on the JPanel. The controls Component, which is added to the SOUTH region, typically provides the following controls:

1. A positioning slider to jump to certain points in the media clip.

2. A pause button.

3. A volume button that provides volume control by right clicking and a mute function by left clicking.

4. A media properties button that provides detailed media information by left clicking and frame rate control by right clicking.

Line 37 calls Player method **start** to begin playing the media file. Lines 39–50 handle the various exceptions that createRealizedPlayer throws.

```java
1   // Fig. 21.6: MediaPanel.java
2   // A JPanel the plays media from a URL
3   import java.awt.BorderLayout;
4   import java.awt.Component;
5   import java.io.IOException;
6   import java.net.URL;
7   import javax.media.CannotRealizeException;
8   import javax.media.Manager;
9   import javax.media.NoPlayerException;
10  import javax.media.Player;
11  import javax.swing.JPanel;
12
13  public class MediaPanel extends JPanel
14  {
15     public MediaPanel( URL mediaURL )
16     {
17        setLayout( new BorderLayout() ); // use a BorderLayout
18
19        // Use lightweight components for Swing compatibility
20        Manager.setHint( Manager.LIGHTWEIGHT_RENDERER, true );
21
22        try
23        {
24           // create a player to play the media specified in the URL
25           Player mediaPlayer = Manager.createRealizedPlayer( mediaURL );
26
27           // get the components for the video and the playback controls
28           Component video = mediaPlayer.getVisualComponent();
29           Component controls = mediaPlayer.getControlPanelComponent();
30
31           if ( video != null )
32              add( video, BorderLayout.CENTER ); // add video component
33
34           if ( controls != null )
35              add( controls, BorderLayout.SOUTH ); // add controls
36
37           mediaPlayer.start(); // start playing the media clip
38        } // end try
39        catch ( NoPlayerException noPlayerException )
40        {
41           System.err.println( "No media player found" );
42        } // end catch
43        catch ( CannotRealizeException cannotRealizeException )
44        {
45           System.err.println( "Could not realize media player" );
46        } // end catch
47        catch ( IOException iOException )
48        {
49           System.err.println( "Error reading from the source" );
50        } // end catch
51     } // end MediaPanel constructor
52  } // end class MediaPanel
```

Fig. 21.6 | JPanel that plays a media file from a URL.

The application in Fig. 21.7 displays a JFileChooser dialog for the user to choose a media file. It then creates a MediaPanel that plays the selected file and creates a JFrame to display the MediaPanel.s

```java
1   // Fig. 21.7: MediaTest.java
2   // A simple media player
3   import java.io.File;
4   import java.net.MalformedURLException;
5   import java.net.URL;
6   import javax.swing.JFileChooser;
7   import javax.swing.JFrame;
8
9   public class MediaTest
10  {
11     // launch the application
12     public static void main( String args[] )
13     {
14        // create a file chooser
15        JFileChooser fileChooser = new JFileChooser();
16
17        // show open file dialog
18        int result = fileChooser.showOpenDialog( null );
19
20        if ( result == JFileChooser.APPROVE_OPTION ) // user chose a file
21        {
22           URL mediaURL = null;
23
24           try
25           {
26              // get the file as URL
27              mediaURL = fileChooser.getSelectedFile().toURL();
28           } // end try
29           catch ( MalformedURLException malformedURLException )
30           {
31              System.err.println( "Could not create URL for the file" );
32           } // end catch
33
34           if ( mediaURL != null ) // only display if there is a valid URL
35           {
36              JFrame mediaTest = new JFrame( "Media Tester" );
37              mediaTest.setDefaultCloseOperation( JFrame.EXIT_ON_CLOSE );
38
39              MediaPanel mediaPanel = new MediaPanel( mediaURL );
40              mediaTest.add( mediaPanel );
41
42              mediaTest.setSize( 300, 300 );
43              mediaTest.setVisible( true );
44           } // end inner if
45        } // end outer if
46     } // end main
47  } // end class MediaTest
```

Fig. 21.7 | Test application that creates a MediaPanel from a user-selected file. (Part 1 of 2.)

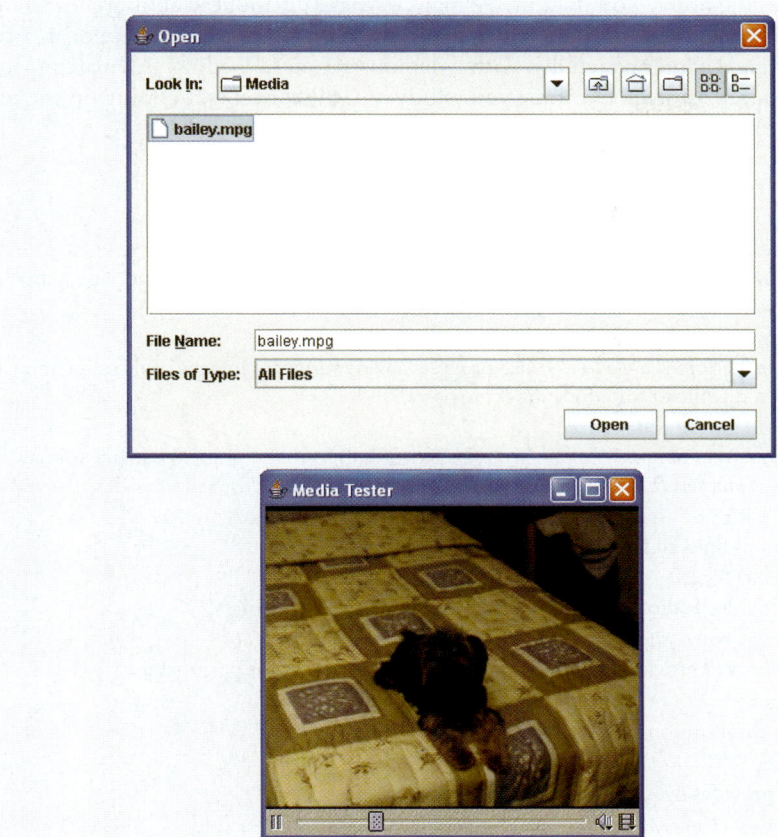

Fig. 21.7 | Test application that creates a MediaPanel from a user-selected file. (Part 2 of 2.)

Method main (lines 12–46) assigns a new JFileChooser to local variable fileChooser (line 15), shows an open file dialog (line 18) and assigns the return value to result. Line 20 checks result to determine whether the user chose a file. To create a Player to play the selected media file, you must convert the File object returned by JFileChooser to a URL object. Method **toURL** of class File returns a URL that points to the File on the system, possibly throwing a MalformedURLException if it cannot create a URL object for the File. The try statement (lines 24–32) creates a URL for the selected file and assigns it to mediaURL. The if statement in lines 34–44 checks that mediaURL is not null and creates the GUI components to play the media.

21.7 Wrap-Up

In this chapter, you learned how to make applications more exciting by including sound, images, graphics and video. We introduced Java's multimedia capabilities, including the Java Media Framework API, Java Sound API and Java 3D API. You used classes Image and ImageIcon to display and manipulate images stored in files, and you learned about the different image formats supported by Java. You created animation by displaying a series of images in a specific order. You used image maps to make an application more interactive. You then learned how to load audio clips, and how to play them either once or in a continuous loop. The chapter concluded with a demonstration of loading and playing video. In the next chapter, you will continue your study of GUI concepts, building on the techniques you learned in Chapter 11.

21.8 Internet and Web Resources

`www.nasa.gov/multimedia/highlights/index.html`
The *NASA Multimedia Gallery* contains a wide variety of images, audio clips and video clips that you can download and use to test your Java multimedia programs.

`sunsite.tus.ac.jp/multimed`
The *Sunsite Japan Multimedia Collection* also provides a wide variety of images, audio clips and video clips that you can download for educational purposes.

`www.anbg.gov.au/anbg/index.html`
The *Australian National Botanic Gardens* Web site provides links to the sounds of many animals. Try, for example, the *Common Birds* link under the "Animals in the Gardens" section.

`www.thefreesite.com`
TheFreeSite.com has links to free sounds and clip art.

`www.soundcentral.com`
SoundCentral provides audio clips in WAV, AU, AIFF and MIDI formats.

`www.animationfactory.com`
The *Animation Factory* provides thousands of free GIF animations for personal use.

`www.clipart.com`
ClipArt.com is a subscription-based service for images and sounds.

`www.pngart.com`
PNGART.com provides over 50,000 free images in PNG format.

`java.sun.com/developer/techDocs/hi/repository`
The *Java look and feel Graphics Repository* provides images designed for use in a Swing GUI, including toolbar button images.

`www.freebyte.com/graphicprograms`
This guide contains links to several free graphics software programs. The software can be used to modify images and draw graphics.

`graphicssoft.about.com/od/pixelbasedfreewin`
This site provides links for free graphics programs designed for use on Windows machines.

Java Multimedia API References

`java.sun.com/products/java-media/jmf`
This is the *Java Media Framework (JMF) API* home page. Here you can download the latest Sun implementation of the JMF. The site also contains the documentation for the JMF.

`java.sun.com/products/java-media/sound`
The *Java Sound API* home page. Java Sound provides capabilities for playing and recording audio.

`java.sun.com/products/java-media/3D`
The *Java 3D API* home page. This API can be used to produce three-dimensional images typical of today's video games.

`java.sun.com/developer/onlineTraining/java3d`
This site provides a *Java 3D API* tutorial.

`java.sun.com/products/java-media/jai`
The *Java Advanced Imaging API* home page. This API provides image-processing capabilities, such as contrast enhancement, cropping, scaling and geometric warping.

`java.sun.com/products/java-media/speech`
The *Java Speech API* enables programs to perform speech synthesis and speech recognition.

`freetts.sourceforge.net/docs/index.php`
FreeTTS is an implementation of the Java Speech API.

`java.sun.com/products/java-media/2D`
This is the *Java 2D API* home page. This API (introduced in Chapter 12) provides complex two-dimensional graphics capabilities.

`java.sun.com/j2se/1.4.2/docs/guide/imageio`
This site contains a guide to the *Java Image I/O API*, which enables programs to load and save images using formats that are not currently supported by the Java APIs.

Summary

- `Applet` method `getImage` loads an `Image`.
- `Applet` method `getDocumentBase` returns the location of the applet's HTML file on the Internet as an object of class `URL`.
- Java supports several image formats, including Graphics Interchange Format (GIF), Joint Photographic Experts Group (JPEG) and Portable Network Graphics (PNG). The file names for these types end with `.gif`, `.jpg` (or `.jpeg`) and `.png`, respectively.
- Class `ImageIcon` provides constructors that allow an `ImageIcon` object to be initialized with an image from the local computer or stored on a Web server on the Internet.
- `Graphics` method `drawImage` accepts four arguments—a reference to the `Image` object in which the image is stored, the *x*- and *y*-coordinates where the image should be displayed and a reference to an `ImageObserver` object.
- Another version of `Graphics` method `drawImage` outputs a scaled image. The fourth and fifth arguments specify the width and height of the image for display purposes.
- Interface `ImageObserver` is implemented by class `Component`. `ImageObserver`s receive notifications as an `Image` is loaded and update the image on the screen if it was not complete when it was displayed.
- `ImageIcon` method `paintIcon` displays the `ImageIcon`'s image. The method requires four arguments—a reference to the `Component` on which the image will be displayed, a reference to the `Graphics` object used to render the image, the *x*-coordinate of the upper-left corner of the image and the *y*-coordinate of the upper-left corner of the image.
- A `URL` object represents a Uniform Resource Locator, which is as a pointer to a resource on the World Wide Web, on your computer or on any networked machine.
- `Timer` objects generate `ActionEvent`s at fixed intervals in milliseconds. The `Timer` constructor receives two arguments—the delay in milliseconds and the `ActionListener`. `Timer` method `start` indicates that the `Timer` should start generating events. `Timer` method `stop` indicates that the `Timer` should stop generating events. `Timer` method `restart` indicates that the `Timer` should start generating events again.
- An image map is an image that has hot areas that the user can click to accomplish a task, such as loading a different Web page into a browser.
- `Applet` method `play` has two forms:

```
public void play( URL location, String soundFileName );
public void play( URL soundURL );
```

One version loads the audio clip stored in file soundFileName from location and plays the sound. The other version takes a URL that contains the location and the file name of the audio clip.

- Applet method getDocumentBase indicates the location of the HTML file that loaded the applet. Method getCodeBase indicates where the .class file for an applet is located.

- The sound engine that plays audio clips supports several audio file formats, including Sun Audio file format (.au extension), Windows Wave file format (.wav extension), Macintosh AIFF file format (.aif or .aiff extension) and Musical Instrument Digital Interface (MIDI) file format (.mid or .rmi extensions). The Java Media Framework (JMF) supports additional formats.

- Applet method getAudioClip has two forms that take the same arguments as the play method. Method getAudioClip returns a reference to an AudioClip. AudioClips have three methods— play, loop and stop. Method play plays the audio clip once. Method loop continuously loops the audio clip. Method stop terminates an audio clip that is currently playing.

- Sun Microsystems, Intel and Silicon Graphics worked together to produce the Java Media Framework (JMF)

- Package javax.media and its subpackages contain the classes that compose the Java Media Framework.

- Class Manager declares utility methods for accessing system resources to play and to manipulate media.

- Method toURL of class File returns a URL that points to the File on the system.

Terminology

.aif file extension
.aiff file extension
.au file extension
audio clip
AudioClip interface
.avi file extension
CannotRealizePlayerException exception
createRealizedPlayer method of class Manager
Dimension class
drawImage method of class Graphics
Future Splash (.spl) files
getAudioClip method of class Applet
getCodeBase method of class Applet
getControlPanelComponent method of interface Player
getDocumentBase method of class Applet
getImage method of class Applet
getMinimumSize method of class Component
getPreferredSize method of class Component
getVisualComponent method of interface Player
.gif file extension
Graphics class
Graphics Interchange Format (GIF)

hot area
Image class
image map
ImageIcon class
ImageObserver interface
Java 3D API
Java Advanced Imaging API
Java Image I/O API
Java Media Framework (JMF) API
Java Sound API
Java Speech API
javax.media package
Joint Photographic Experts Group (JPEG)
.jpeg file extension
.jpg file extension
LIGHTWEIGHT_RENDER constant of class Manager
loop method of interface AudioClip
Macintosh AIFF file format (.aif or .aiff extension)
Macromedia Flash 2 movies (.swf)
Manager class
Microsoft Audio/Video Interleave (.avi) file
.mid file extension
.mov file extension

.mp3 file extension
.mpeg file extension
MPEG Layer 3 Audio (.mp3) files
MPEG-1 videos (.mpeg, .mpg)
.mpg file extension
multimedia
Musical Instrument Digital Interface (MIDI)
    file format (.mid or .rmi extension)
NoPlayerException exception
paintIcon method of class ImageIcon
play method of class Applet
play method of interface AudioClip
Player interface
.png file extension
Portable Network Graphics (PNG)
QuickTime (.mov) files

.rmi file extension
setHint method of class Manager
showStatus method of class Applet
sound
sound engine
.spl file extension
start method of interface Player
stop method of class Timer
stop method of interface AudioClip
Sun Audio file format (.au extension)
.swf file extension
toURL method of class File
URL class
video
.wav file extension
Windows Wave file format (.wav extension)

Self-Review Exercises

21.1 Fill in the blanks in each of the following statements:
    a) Applet method _____ loads an image into an applet.
    b) Graphics method _____ displays an image on an applet.
    c) Java provides two mechanisms for playing sounds in an applet—the Applet's play method and the play method of the _____ interface.
    d) A(n) _____ is an image that has hot areas that the user can click to accomplish a task such as loading a Web page.
    e) Method _____ of class ImageIcon displays the ImageIcon's image.
    f) Java supports several image formats, including _____, _____ and _____.

21.2 Determine whether each of the following statements is *true* or *false*. If *false*, explain why.
    a) A sound is marked for garbage collection after it plays.
    b) Class ImageIcon provides constructors that allow an ImageIcon object to be initialized only with an image from the local computer.
    c) Method play of class AudioClip continuously loops an audio clip.
    d) The Java Image I/O API is used for adding 3D graphics to a Java application.
    e) Applet method getDocumentBase returns, as an object of class URL, the location on the Internet of the HTML file that invoked the applet.

Answers to Self-Review Exercises

21.1 a) getImage. b) drawImage. c) AudioClip. d) image map. e) paintIcon. f) Graphics Interchange Format (GIF), Joint Photographic Experts Group (JPEG), Portable Network Graphics (PNG).

21.2 a) True. b) False. ImageIcon can load images from the Internet as well. c) False. Method play of class AudioClip plays an audio clip once. Method loop of class AudioClip continuously loops an audio clip. d) False. The Java 3D API is used for creating and modifying 3D graphics. The Java Image I/O API is used for reading from and outputting images to files. e) True.

Exercises

21.3 Describe how to make an animation "browser friendly."

21.4 Describe the Java methods for playing and manipulating audio clips.

21.5 Explain how image maps are used. List several examples of their use.

21.6 *(Randomly Erasing an Image)* Suppose an image is displayed in a rectangular screen area. One way to erase the image is simply to set every pixel to the same color immediately, but this is a dull visual effect. Write a Java program that displays an image and then erases it by using random-number generation to select individual pixels to erase. After most of the image is erased, erase all the remaining pixels at once. You can draw individual pixels as a line that starts and ends at the same coordinates. You might try several variants of this problem. For example, you might display lines randomly or display shapes randomly to erase regions of the screen.

21.7 *(Text Flasher)* Create a Java program that repeatedly flashes text on the screen. Do this by alternating the text with a plain background-color image. Allow the user to control the "blink speed" and the background color or pattern. You will need to use methods `getDelay` and `setDelay` of class `Timer`. These methods are used to retrieve and set the interval in milliseconds between Action-Events, respectively

21.8 *(Image Flasher)* Create a Java program that repeatedly flashes an image on the screen. Do this by alternating the image with a plain background-color image.

21.9 *(Digital Clock)* Implement a program that displays a digital clock on the screen.

21.10 *(Calling Attention to an Image)* If you want to emphasize an image, you might place a row of simulated light bulbs around it. You can let the light bulbs flash in unison or fire on and off in sequence one after the other.

21.11 *(Image Zooming)* Create a program that enables you to zoom in on or out from an image.

Special Section: Challenging Multimedia Projects

The preceding exercises are keyed to the text and designed to test the reader's understanding of fundamental multimedia concepts. This section includes a collection of advanced multimedia projects. The reader should find these problems challenging, yet entertaining. The problems vary considerably in difficulty. Some require an hour or two of program writing and implementation. Others are useful for lab assignments that might require two or three weeks of study and implementation. Some are challenging term projects. [*Note to Instructors:* Solutions are not provided for these exercises.].

21.12 *(Animation)* Create a general-purpose Java animation program. It should allow the user to specify the sequence of frames to be displayed, the speed at which the images are displayed, audios to be played while the animation is running and so on.

21.13 *(Limericks)* Modify the limerick-writing program you wrote in Exercise 10.10 to sing the limericks your program creates.

21.14 *(Random Interimage Transition)* This provides a nice visual effect. If you are displaying one image in a given area on the screen and you would like to transition to another image in the same area, store the new screen image in an off-screen buffer and randomly copy pixels from it to the display area, overlaying the pixels already at those locations. When the vast majority of the pixels have been copied, copy the entire new image to the display area to be sure you are displaying the complete new image. To implement this program, you may need to use the `PixelGrabber` and `MemoryImage-Source` classes (see the Java API documentation for descriptions of these classes). You might try several variants of this problem. For example, try selecting all the pixels in a randomly selected straight line or shape in the new image, and overlay them above the corresponding positions of the old image.

21.15 *(Background Audio)* Add background audio to one of your favorite applications by using the `loop` method of class `AudioClip` to play the sound in the background while you interact with your application in the normal way.

21.16 *(Scrolling Marquee Sign)* Create a Java program that scrolls dotted characters from right to left (or from left to right if that is appropriate for your language) across a marquee-like display sign. As an option, display the text in a continuous loop, so that after the text disappears at one end, it reappears at the other.

21.17 *(Scrolling Image Marquee)* Create a Java program that scrolls an image across a marquee screen.

21.18 *(Analog Clock)* Create a Java program that displays an analog clock with hour, minute and second hands that move appropriately as the time changes.

21.19 *(Dynamic Audio and Graphical Kaleidoscope)* Write a kaleidoscope program that displays reflected graphics to simulate the popular children's toy. Incorporate audio effects that "mirror" your program's dynamically changing graphics.

21.20 *(Automatic Jigsaw Puzzle Generator)* Create a Java jigsaw puzzle generator and manipulator. The user specifies an image. Your program loads and displays the image, then breaks it into randomly selected shapes and shuffles them. The user then uses the mouse to move the pieces around to solve the puzzle. Add appropriate audio sounds as the pieces are moved around and snapped back into place. You might keep tabs on each piece and where it really belongs—then use audio effects to help the user get the pieces into the correct positions.

21.21 *(Maze Generator and Walker)* Develop a multimedia-based maze generator and traverser program based on the maze programs you wrote in Exercise 15.20–Exercise 15.22. Let the user customize the maze by specifying the number of rows and columns and by indicating the level of difficulty. Have an animated mouse walk the maze. Use audio to dramatize the movement of your mouse character.

21.22 *(One-Armed Bandit)* Develop a multimedia simulation of a "one-armed bandit." Have three spinning wheels. Place images of various fruits and symbols on each wheel. Use true random-number generation to simulate the spinning of each wheel and the stopping of each wheel on a symbol.

21.23 *(Horse Race)* Create a Java simulation of a horse race. Have multiple contenders. Use audios for a race announcer. Play the appropriate audios to indicate the correct status of each contender throughout the race. Use audios to announce the final results. You might try to simulate the kinds of horse-racing games that are often played at carnivals. The players take turns at the mouse and have to perform some skill-oriented manipulation with it to advance their horses.

21.24 *(Shuffleboard)* Develop a multimedia-based simulation of the game of shuffleboard. Use appropriate audio and visual effects.

21.25 *(Game of Pool)* Create a multimedia-based simulation of the game of pool. Each player takes turns using the mouse to position a pool cue and hit it against the ball at the appropriate angle to try to make other balls fall into the pockets. Your program should keep score.

21.26 *(Artist)* Design a Java art program that will give an artist a great variety of capabilities to draw, use images and use animations to create a dynamic multimedia art display.

21.27 *(Fireworks Designer)* Create a Java program that someone might use to create a fireworks display. Create a variety of fireworks demonstrations. Then orchestrate the firing of the fireworks for maximum effect.

21.28 *(Floor Planner)* Develop a Java program that will help someone arrange furniture in a home. Add features that enable the person to achieve the best possible arrangement.

21.29 *(Crossword)* Crossword puzzles are among the most popular pastimes. Develop a multimedia-based crossword-puzzle program. Your program should enable the player to place and erase words easily. Tie your program to a large computerized dictionary. Your program also should be able to suggest words on which letters have already been filled in. Provide other features that will make the crossword-puzzle enthusiast's job easier.

21.30 *(15 Puzzle)* Write a multimedia-based Java program that enables the user to play the game of 15. The game is played on a 4-by-4 board for a total of 16 slots. One slot is empty, the others are occupied by 15 tiles numbered 1 through 15. Any tile next to the currently empty slot can be moved into that slot by clicking on the tile. Your program should create the board with the tiles out of order. The goal is to arrange the tiles into sequential order, row by row.

21.31 *(Reaction Time/Reaction Precision Tester)* Create a Java program that moves a randomly created shape around the screen. The user moves the mouse to catch and click on the shape. The shape's speed and size can be varied. Keep statistics on how much time the user typically takes to catch a shape of a given size. The user will probably have more difficulty catching faster-moving, smaller shapes.

21.32 *(Calendar/Tickler File)* Using both audio and images, create a general-purpose calendar and "tickler" file. For example, the program should sing "Happy Birthday" when you use it on your birthday. Have the program display images and play audios associated with important events. Also, have the program remind you in advance of these important events. It would be nice, for example, to have the program give you a week's notice so you can pick up an appropriate greeting card for that special person.

21.33 *(Rotating Images)* Create a Java program that lets you rotate an image through some number of degrees (out of a maximum of 360 degrees). The program should let you specify that you want to spin the image continuously. It should let you adjust the spin speed dynamically.

21.34 *(Coloring Black-and-White Photographs and Images)* Create a Java program that lets you paint a black-and-white photograph with color. Provide a color palette for selecting colors. Your program should let you apply different colors to different regions of the image.

21.35 *(Multimedia-Based Simpletron Simulator)* Modify the Simpletron simulator that you developed in the exercises in the previous chapters (Exercise 7.34–Exercise 7.36 and Exercise 17.26–Exercise 17.30) to include multimedia features. Add computer-like sounds to indicate that the Simpletron is executing instructions. Add a breaking-glass sound when a fatal error occurs. Use flashing lights to indicate which cells of memory or which registers are currently being manipulated. Use other multimedia techniques, as appropriate, to make your Simpletron simulator more valuable to its users as an educational tool.

22

GUI Components: Part 2

OBJECTIVES

In this chapter you will learn:

- To create and manipulate sliders, menus, pop-up menus and windows.

- To change the look-and-feel of a GUI, using Swing's pluggable look-and-feel.

- To create a multiple-document interface with **JDesktopPane** and **JInternalFrame**.

- To use additional layout managers.

22.1 Introduction

In this chapter, we continue our study of GUIs. We discuss additional components and layout managers and lay the groundwork for building more complex GUIs.

We begin our discussion with menus that enable the user to effectively perform tasks in the program. The look-and-feel of a Swing GUI can be uniform across all platforms on which a Java program executes, or the GUI can be customized by using Swing's pluggable look-and-feel (PLAF). We provide an example that illustrates how to change between Swing's default metal look-and-feel (which looks and behaves the same across platforms), a look-and-feel that simulates Motif (a popular UNIX look-and-feel) and one that simulates Microsoft's Windows look-and-feel.

Many of today's applications use a multiple-document interface (MDI)—a main window (often called the parent window) containing other windows (often called child windows) to manage several open documents in parallel. For example, many e-mail programs allow you to have several e-mail windows open at the same time so that you can compose or read multiple e-mail messages. We demonstrate Swing's classes for creating multiple-document interfaces. The chapter finishes with a series of examples discussing additional layout managers for organizing graphical user interfaces.

Swing is a large and complex topic. There are many more GUI components and capabilities than can be presented here. Several more Swing GUI components are introduced in the remaining chapters of this book as they are needed. Our book *Advanced Java 2 Platform How to Program* discusses other, more advanced Swing components and capabilities.

22.2 `JSlider`

`JSlider`s enable the user to select from a range of integer values. Class `JSlider` inherits from `JComponent`. Figure 22.1 shows a horizontal `JSlider` with tick marks and the thumb that allows the user to select a value. `JSlider`s can be customized to display major tick marks, minor tick marks and labels for the tick marks. They also support snap-to ticks, which cause the thumb to snap to the closest tick mark when it is positioned between two tick marks.

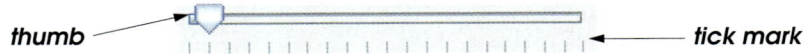

thumb ———— *tick mark*

Fig. 22.1 | JSlider component with horizontal orientation.

Most Swing GUI components support user interactions through the mouse and the keyboard. For example, if a JSlider has the focus (i.e., it is the currently selected GUI component in the user interface), the left arrow key and right arrow key cause the thumb of the JSlider to decrease or increase by 1, respectively. The down arrow key and up arrow key also cause the thumb of the JSlider to decrease or increase by 1 tick, respectively. The *PgDn* (page down) *key* and *PgUp* (page up) *key* cause the thumb of the JSlider to decrease or increase by block increments of one-tenth of the range of values, respectively. The *Home key* moves the thumb to the minimum value of the JSlider, and the *End key* moves the thumb to the maximum value of the JSlider.

JSliders have either a horizontal orientation or a vertical orientation. For a horizontal JSlider, the minimum value is at the left end of the JSlider and the maximum is at the right end. For a vertical JSlider, the minimum value is at the bottom and the maximum is at the top. The minimum and maximum value positions on a JSlider can be reversed by invoking JSlider method **setInverted** with boolean argument true. The relative position of the thumb indicates the current value of the JSlider.

The program in Fig. 22.2, Fig. 22.3 and Fig. 22.4 allows the user to size a circle drawn on a subclass of JPanel called OvalPanel (Fig. 22.2). The user specifies the diameter of the circle with a horizontal JSlider. Class OvalPanel is a subclass of JPanel that knows how to draw a circle on itself, using its own instance variable diameter to determine the diameter of the circle—the diameter is used as the width and height of the bounding box in which the circle is displayed. The diameter value is set when the user interacts with the JSlider. The event handler calls method setDiameter in class OvalPanel to set the diameter and calls repaint to draw the new circle. The repaint call results in a call to OvalPanel's paintComponent method.

Class OvalPanel (Fig. 22.2) contains a paintComponent method (lines 12–17) that draws a filled oval (a circle in this example), a setDiameter method (lines 20–25) that changes the circle's diameter and repaints the OvalPanel, a **getPreferredSize** method (lines 28–31) that returns the preferred width and height of an OvalPanel and a **getMinimumSize** method (lines 34–37) that returns an OvalPanel's minimum width and height.

Look-and-Feel Observation 22.1

If a new GUI component has a minimum width and height (i.e., smaller dimensions would render the component ineffective on the display), override method getMinimumSize to return the minimum width and height as an instance of class Dimension.

Software Engineering Observation 22.1

For many GUI components, method getMinimumSize is implemented to return the result of a call to the component's getPreferredSize method.

Class SliderFrame (Fig. 22.3) creates the JSlider that controls the diameter of the circle. Class SliderFrame's constructor (lines 17–45) creates OvalPanel object myPanel (line 21) and sets its background color (line 22). Lines 25–26 create JSlider object diameterSlider to control the diameter of the circle drawn on the OvalPanel. The JSlider con-

```
1   // Fig. 22.2: OvalPanel.java
2   // A customized JPanel class.
3   import java.awt.Graphics;
4   import java.awt.Dimension;
5   import javax.swing.JPanel;
6
7   public class OvalPanel extends JPanel
8   {
9      private int diameter = 10; // default diameter of 10
10
11     // draw an oval of the specified diameter
12     public void paintComponent( Graphics g )
13     {
14        super.paintComponent( g );
15
16        g.fillOval( 10, 10, diameter, diameter ); // draw circle
17     } // end method paintComponent
18
19     // validate and set diameter, then repaint
20     public void setDiameter( int newDiameter )
21     {
22        // if diameter invalid, default to 10
23        diameter = ( newDiameter >= 0 ? newDiameter : 10 );
24        repaint(); // repaint panel
25     } // end method setDiameter
26
27     // used by layout manager to determine preferred size
28     public Dimension getPreferredSize()
29     {
30        return new Dimension( 200, 200 );
31     } // end method getPreferredSize
32
33     // used by layout manager to determine minimum size
34     public Dimension getMinimumSize()
35     {
36        return getPreferredSize();
37     } // end method getMinimumSize
38  } // end class OvalPanel
```

Fig. 22.2 | JPanel subclass for drawing circles of a specified diameter.

structor takes four arguments. The first argument specifies the orientation of diameterSlider, which is HORIZONTAL (a constant in interface SwingConstants). The second and third arguments indicate the minimum and maximum integer values in the range of values for this JSlider. The last argument indicates that the initial value of the JSlider (i.e., where the thumb is displayed) should be 10.

Lines 27–28 customize the appearance of the JSlider. Method **setMajorTick-Spacing** indicates that each major-tick mark represents 10 values in the range of values supported by the JSlider. Method **setPaintTicks** with a true argument indicates that the tick marks should be displayed (they are not displayed by default). For other methods that are used to customize a JSlider's appearance, see the JSlider on-line documentation (java.sun.com/j2se/5.0/docs/api/javax/swing/JSlider.html).

```
1   // Fig. 22.3: SliderFrame.java
2   // Using JSliders to size an oval.
3   import java.awt.BorderLayout;
4   import java.awt.Color;
5   import javax.swing.JFrame;
6   import javax.swing.JSlider;
7   import javax.swing.SwingConstants;
8   import javax.swing.event.ChangeListener;
9   import javax.swing.event.ChangeEvent;
10
11  public class SliderFrame extends JFrame
12  {
13     private JSlider diameterJSlider; // slider to select diameter
14     private OvalPanel myPanel; // panel to draw circle
15
16     // no-argument constructor
17     public SliderFrame()
18     {
19        super( "Slider Demo" );
20
21        myPanel = new OvalPanel(); // create panel to draw circle
22        myPanel.setBackground( Color.YELLOW ); // set background to yellow
23
24        // set up JSlider to control diameter value
25        diameterJSlider =
26           new JSlider( SwingConstants.HORIZONTAL, 0, 200, 10 );
27        diameterJSlider.setMajorTickSpacing( 10 ); // create tick every 10
28        diameterJSlider.setPaintTicks( true ); // paint ticks on slider
29
30        // register JSlider event listener
31        diameterJSlider.addChangeListener(
32
33           new ChangeListener() // anonymous inner class
34           {
35              // handle change in slider value
36              public void stateChanged( ChangeEvent e )
37              {
38                 myPanel.setDiameter( diameterJSlider.getValue() );
39              } // end method stateChanged
40           } // end anonymous inner class
41        ); // end call to addChangeListener
42
43        add( diameterJSlider, BorderLayout.SOUTH ); // add slider to frame
44        add( myPanel, BorderLayout.CENTER ); // add panel to frame
45     } // end SliderFrame constructor
46  } // end class SliderFrame
```

Fig. 22.3 | JSlider value used to determine the diameter of a circle.

JSliders generate **ChangeEvents** (package javax.swing.event) in response to user interactions. An object of a class that implements interface **ChangeListener** (package javax.swing.event) and declares method **stateChanged** can respond to ChangeEvents. Lines 31–41 register a ChangeListener to handle diameterSlider's events. When

```
 1   // Fig. 22.4: SliderDemo.java
 2   // Testing SliderFrame.
 3   import javax.swing.JFrame;
 4
 5   public class SliderDemo
 6   {
 7      public static void main( String args[] )
 8      {
 9         SliderFrame sliderFrame = new SliderFrame();
10         sliderFrame.setDefaultCloseOperation( JFrame.EXIT_ON_CLOSE );
11         sliderFrame.setSize( 220, 270 ); // set frame size
12         sliderFrame.setVisible( true ); // display frame
13      } // end main
14   } // end class SliderDemo
```

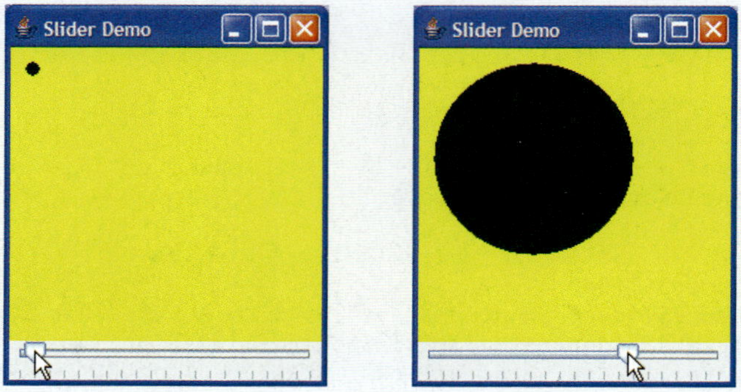

Fig. 22.4 | Test class for `SliderFrame`.

method `stateChanged` (lines 36–39) is called in response to a user interaction, line 38 calls `myPanel`'s `setDiameter` method and passes the current value of the `JSlider` as an argument. `JSlider` method **getValue** returns the current thumb position.

22.3 Windows: Additional Notes

In this section, we discuss several important `JFrame` issues. A `JFrame` is a **window** with a **title bar** and a **border**. Class `JFrame` is a subclass of `java.awt.Frame` (which is a subclass of `java.awt.Window`). As such, `JFrame` is one of the few Swing GUI components that is not a lightweight GUI component. When you display a window from a Java program, the window is provided by the local platform's windowing toolkit, and therefore the window will look like every other window displayed on that platform. When a Java application executes on a Macintosh and displays a window, the window's title bar and borders will look like those of other Macintosh applications. When a Java application executes on a Microsoft Windows system and displays a window, the window's title bar and borders will look like those of other Microsoft Windows applications. And when a Java application executes on a Unix platform and displays a window, the window's title bar and borders will look like other Unix applications on that platform.

Class `JFrame` supports three operations when the user closes the window. By default, a window is hidden (i.e., removed from the screen) when the user closes it. This can be controlled with `JFrame` method **`setDefaultCloseOperation`**. Interface **`WindowConstants`** (package `javax.swing`), which class `JFrame` implements, declares three constants for use with this method—`DISPOSE_ON_CLOSE`, `DO_NOTHING_ON_CLOSE` and `HIDE_ON_CLOSE` (the default). Some platforms allow only a limited number of windows to be displayed on the screen. Thus, a window is a valuable resource that should be given back to the system when it is no longer needed. Class `Window` (an indirect superclass of `JFrame`) declares method **`dispose`** for this purpose. When a `Window` is no longer needed in an application, you should explicitly dispose of it. This can be done by calling the `Window`'s `dispose` method or by calling method `set-DefaultCloseOperation` with the argument `WindowConstants.DISPOSE_ON_CLOSE`. Terminating an application will return window resources to the system. Setting the default close operation to `DO_NOTHING_ON_CLOSE` indicates that the program will determine what to do when the user indicates that the window should be closed.

Good Programming Practice 22.1

Windows are an expensive system resource. Return them to the system when they are no longer needed.

By default, a window is not displayed on the screen until the program invokes the window's `setVisible` method (inherited from class `java.awt.Component`) with a `true` argument. A window's size should be set with a call to method `setSize` (inherited from class `java.awt.Component`). The position of a window when it appears on the screen is specified with method **`setLocation`** (inherited from class `java.awt.Component`).

Common Programming Error 22.1

Forgetting to call method `setVisible` on a window is a runtime logic error—the window is not displayed.

Common Programming Error 22.2

Forgetting to call the `setSize` method on a window is a runtime logic error—only the title bar appears.

When the user manipulates the window, this action generates window events. Event listeners are registered for window events with `Window` method **`addWindowListener`**. Interface **`WindowListener`** provides seven window-event-handling methods—**`windowActivated`** (called when the user makes a window the active window), **`windowClosed`** (called after the window is closed), **`windowClosing`** (called when the user initiates closing of the window), **`windowDeactivated`** (called when the user makes another window the active window), **`windowDeiconified`** (called when the user restores a window from being minimized), **`windowIconified`** (called when the user minimizes a window) and **`windowOpened`** (called when a program first displays a window on the screen).

22.4 Using Menus with Frames

Menus are an integral part of GUIs. Menus allow the user to perform actions without unnecessarily cluttering a GUI with extra components. In Swing GUIs, menus can be attached only to objects of the classes that provide method **`setJMenuBar`**. Two such classes are `JFrame` and `JApplet`. The classes used to declare menus are `JMenuBar`, `JMenu`, `JMenuItem`, `JCheckBoxMenuItem` and class `JRadioButtonMenuItem`.

Look-and-Feel Observation 22.2

Menus simplify GUIs because components can be hidden within them. These components will only be visible when the user looks for them by selecting the menu.

Class **JMenuBar** (a subclass of JComponent) contains the methods necessary to manage a menu bar, which is a container for menus. Class **JMenu** (a subclass of javax.swing.JMenuItem) contains the methods necessary for managing menus. Menus contain menu items and are added to menu bars or to other menus as submenus. When a menu is clicked, it expands to show its list of menu items.

Class **JMenuItem** (a subclass of javax.swing.AbstractButton) contains the methods necessary to manage menu items. A menu item is a GUI component inside a menu that, when selected, causes an action event. A menu item can be used to initiate an action or it can be a submenu that provides more menu items from which the user can select. Submenus are useful for grouping related menu items in a menu.

Class **JCheckBoxMenuItem** (a subclass of javax.swing.JMenuItem) contains the methods necessary to manage menu items that can be toggled on or off. When a JCheckBoxMenuItem is selected, a check appears to the left of the menu item. When the JCheckBoxMenuItem is selected again, the check is removed.

Class **JRadioButtonMenuItem** (a subclass of javax.swing.JMenuItem) contains the methods necessary to manage menu items that can be toggled on or off like JCheckBoxMenuItems. When multiple JRadioButtonMenuItems are maintained as part of a ButtonGroup, only one item in the group can be selected at a given time. When a JRadioButtonMenuItem is selected, a filled circle appears to the left of the menu item. When another JRadioButtonMenuItem is selected, the filled circle of the previously selected menu item is removed.

The application in Fig. 22.5 and Fig. 22.6 demonstrates various menu items. The application also demonstrates how to specify special characters called mnemonics that can

```
1   // Fig. 22.5: MenuFrame.java
2   // Demonstrating menus.
3   import java.awt.Color;
4   import java.awt.Font;
5   import java.awt.BorderLayout;
6   import java.awt.event.ActionListener;
7   import java.awt.event.ActionEvent;
8   import java.awt.event.ItemListener;
9   import java.awt.event.ItemEvent;
10  import javax.swing.JFrame;
11  import javax.swing.JRadioButtonMenuItem;
12  import javax.swing.JCheckBoxMenuItem;
13  import javax.swing.JOptionPane;
14  import javax.swing.JLabel;
15  import javax.swing.SwingConstants;
16  import javax.swing.ButtonGroup;
17  import javax.swing.JMenu;
18  import javax.swing.JMenuItem;
19  import javax.swing.JMenuBar;
```

Fig. 22.5 | JMenus and mnemonics. (Part 1 of 5.)

```
20
21   public class MenuFrame extends JFrame
22   {
23      private final Color colorValues[] =
24         { Color.BLACK, Color.BLUE, Color.RED, Color.GREEN };
25      private JRadioButtonMenuItem colorItems[]; // color menu items
26      private JRadioButtonMenuItem fonts[]; // font menu items
27      private JCheckBoxMenuItem styleItems[]; // font style menu items
28      private JLabel displayJLabel; // displays sample text
29      private ButtonGroup fontButtonGroup; // manages font menu items
30      private ButtonGroup colorButtonGroup; // manages color menu items
31      private int style; // used to create style for font
32
33      // no-argument constructor set up GUI
34      public MenuFrame()
35      {
36         super( "Using JMenus" );
37
38         JMenu fileMenu = new JMenu( "File" ); // create file menu
39         fileMenu.setMnemonic( 'F' ); // set mnemonic to F
40
41         // create About... menu item
42         JMenuItem aboutItem = new JMenuItem( "About..." );
43         aboutItem.setMnemonic( 'A' ); // set mnemonic to A
44         fileMenu.add( aboutItem ); // add about item to file menu
45         aboutItem.addActionListener(
46
47            new ActionListener() // anonymous inner class
48            {
49               // display message dialog when user selects About...
50               public void actionPerformed( ActionEvent event )
51               {
52                  JOptionPane.showMessageDialog( MenuFrame.this,
53                     "This is an example\nof using menus",
54                     "About", JOptionPane.PLAIN_MESSAGE );
55               } // end method actionPerformed
56            } // end anonymous inner class
57         ); // end call to addActionListener
58
59         JMenuItem exitItem = new JMenuItem( "Exit" ); // create exit item
60         exitItem.setMnemonic( 'x' ); // set mnemonic to x
61         fileMenu.add( exitItem ); // add exit item to file menu
62         exitItem.addActionListener(
63
64            new ActionListener() // anonymous inner class
65            {
66               // terminate application when user clicks exitItem
67               public void actionPerformed( ActionEvent event )
68               {
69                  System.exit( 0 ); // exit application
70               } // end method actionPerformed
71            } // end anonymous inner class
72         ); // end call to addActionListener
```

Fig. 22.5 | JMenus and mnemonics. (Part 2 of 5.)

```
73
74      JMenuBar bar = new JMenuBar(); // create menu bar
75      setJMenuBar( bar ); // add menu bar to application
76      bar.add( fileMenu ); // add file menu to menu bar
77
78      JMenu formatMenu = new JMenu( "Format" ); // create format menu
79      formatMenu.setMnemonic( 'r' ); // set mnemonic to r
80
81      // array listing string colors
82      String colors[] = { "Black", "Blue", "Red", "Green" };
83
84      JMenu colorMenu = new JMenu( "Color" ); // create color menu
85      colorMenu.setMnemonic( 'C' ); // set mnemonic to C
86
87      // create radiobutton menu items for colors
88      colorItems = new JRadioButtonMenuItem[ colors.length ];
89      colorButtonGroup = new ButtonGroup(); // manages colors
90      ItemHandler itemHandler = new ItemHandler(); // handler for colors
91
92      // create color radio button menu items
93      for ( int count = 0; count < colors.length; count++ )
94      {
95         colorItems[ count ] =
96            new JRadioButtonMenuItem( colors[ count ] ); // create item
97         colorMenu.add( colorItems[ count ] ); // add item to color menu
98         colorButtonGroup.add( colorItems[ count ] ); // add to group
99         colorItems[ count ].addActionListener( itemHandler );
100     } // end for
101
102     colorItems[ 0 ].setSelected( true ); // select first Color item
103
104     formatMenu.add( colorMenu ); // add color menu to format menu
105     formatMenu.addSeparator(); // add separator in menu
106
107     // array listing font names
108     String fontNames[] = { "Serif", "Monospaced", "SansSerif" };
109     JMenu fontMenu = new JMenu( "Font" ); // create font menu
110     fontMenu.setMnemonic( 'n' ); // set mnemonic to n
111
112     // create radiobutton menu items for font names
113     fonts = new JRadioButtonMenuItem[ fontNames.length ];
114     fontButtonGroup = new ButtonGroup(); // manages font names
115
116     // create Font radio button menu items
117     for ( int count = 0; count < fonts.length; count++ )
118     {
119        fonts[ count ] = new JRadioButtonMenuItem( fontNames[ count ] );
120        fontMenu.add( fonts[ count ] ); // add font to font menu
121        fontButtonGroup.add( fonts[ count ] ); // add to button group
122        fonts[ count ].addActionListener( itemHandler ); // add handler
123     } // end for
124
125     fonts[ 0 ].setSelected( true ); // select first Font menu item
```

Fig. 22.5 | JMenus and mnemonics. (Part 3 of 5.)

```
126        fontMenu.addSeparator(); // add separator bar to font menu
127
128        String styleNames[] = { "Bold", "Italic" }; // names of styles
129        styleItems = new JCheckBoxMenuItem[ styleNames.length ];
130        StyleHandler styleHandler = new StyleHandler(); // style handler
131
132        // create style checkbox menu items
133        for ( int count = 0; count < styleNames.length; count++ )
134        {
135           styleItems[ count ] =
136              new JCheckBoxMenuItem( styleNames[ count ] ); // for style
137           fontMenu.add( styleItems[ count ] ); // add to font menu
138           styleItems[ count ].addItemListener( styleHandler ); // handler
139        } // end for
140
141        formatMenu.add( fontMenu ); // add Font menu to Format menu
142        bar.add( formatMenu ); // add Format menu to menu bar
143
144        // set up label to display text
145        displayJLabel = new JLabel( "Sample Text", SwingConstants.CENTER );
146        displayJLabel.setForeground( colorValues[ 0 ] );
147        displayJLabel.setFont( new Font( "Serif", Font.PLAIN, 72 ) );
148
149        getContentPane().setBackground( Color.CYAN ); // set background
150        add( displayJLabel, BorderLayout.CENTER ); // add displayJLabel
151    } // end MenuFrame constructor
152
153    // inner class to handle action events from menu items
154    private class ItemHandler implements ActionListener
155    {
156        // process color and font selections
157        public void actionPerformed( ActionEvent event )
158        {
159           // process color selection
160           for ( int count = 0; count < colorItems.length; count++ )
161           {
162              if ( colorItems[ count ].isSelected() )
163              {
164                 displayJLabel.setForeground( colorValues[ count ] );
165                 break;
166              } // end if
167           } // end for
168
169           // process font selection
170           for ( int count = 0; count < fonts.length; count++ )
171           {
172              if ( event.getSource() == fonts[ count ] )
173              {
174                 displayJLabel.setFont(
175                    new Font( fonts[ count ].getText(), style, 72 ) );
176              } // end if
177           } // end for
```

Fig. 22.5 | JMenus and mnemonics. (Part 4 of 5.)

```
178
179            repaint(); // redraw application
180         } // end method actionPerformed
181      } // end class ItemHandler
182
183      // inner class to handle item events from check box menu items
184      private class StyleHandler implements ItemListener
185      {
186         // process font style selections
187         public void itemStateChanged( ItemEvent e )
188         {
189            style = 0; // initialize style
190
191            // check for bold selection
192            if ( styleItems[ 0 ].isSelected() )
193               style += Font.BOLD; // add bold to style
194
195            // check for italic selection
196            if ( styleItems[ 1 ].isSelected() )
197               style += Font.ITALIC; // add italic to style
198
199            displayJLabel.setFont(
200               new Font( displayJLabel.getFont().getName(), style, 72 ) );
201            repaint(); // redraw application
202         } // end method itemStateChanged
203      } // end class StyleHandler
204   } // end class MenuFrame
```

Fig. 22.5 | JMenus and mnemonics. (Part 5 of 5.)

provide quick access to a menu or menu item from the keyboard. Mnemonics can be used with all subclasses of javax.swing.AbstractButton.

Class MenuFrame (Fig. 22.5) declares the GUI components and event handling for the menu items. Most of the code in this application appears in the class's constructor (lines 34–151).

Lines 38–76 set up the **File** menu and attach it to the menu bar. The **File** menu contains an **About...** menu item that displays a message dialog when the menu item is selected and an **Exit** menu item that can be selected to terminate the application.

Line 38 creates a JMenu and passes to the constructor the string "File" as the name of the menu. Line 39 uses JMenu method setMnemonic (inherited from class Abstract-Button) to indicate that F is the mnemonic for this menu. Pressing the *Alt* key and the letter *F* opens the menu, just as clicking the menu name with the mouse would. In the GUI, the mnemonic character in the menu's name is displayed with an underline. (See the screen captures in Fig. 22.6.)

 **Look-and-Feel Observation 22.3**

Mnemonics provide quick access to menu commands and button commands through the keyboard.

```
 1   // Fig. 22.6: MenuTest.java
 2   // Testing MenuFrame.
 3   import javax.swing.JFrame;
 4
 5   public class MenuTest
 6   {
 7      public static void main( String args[] )
 8      {
 9         MenuFrame menuFrame = new MenuFrame(); // create MenuFrame
10         menuFrame.setDefaultCloseOperation( JFrame.EXIT_ON_CLOSE );
11         menuFrame.setSize( 500, 200 ); // set frame size
12         menuFrame.setVisible( true ); // display frame
13      } // end main
14   } // end class MenuTest
```

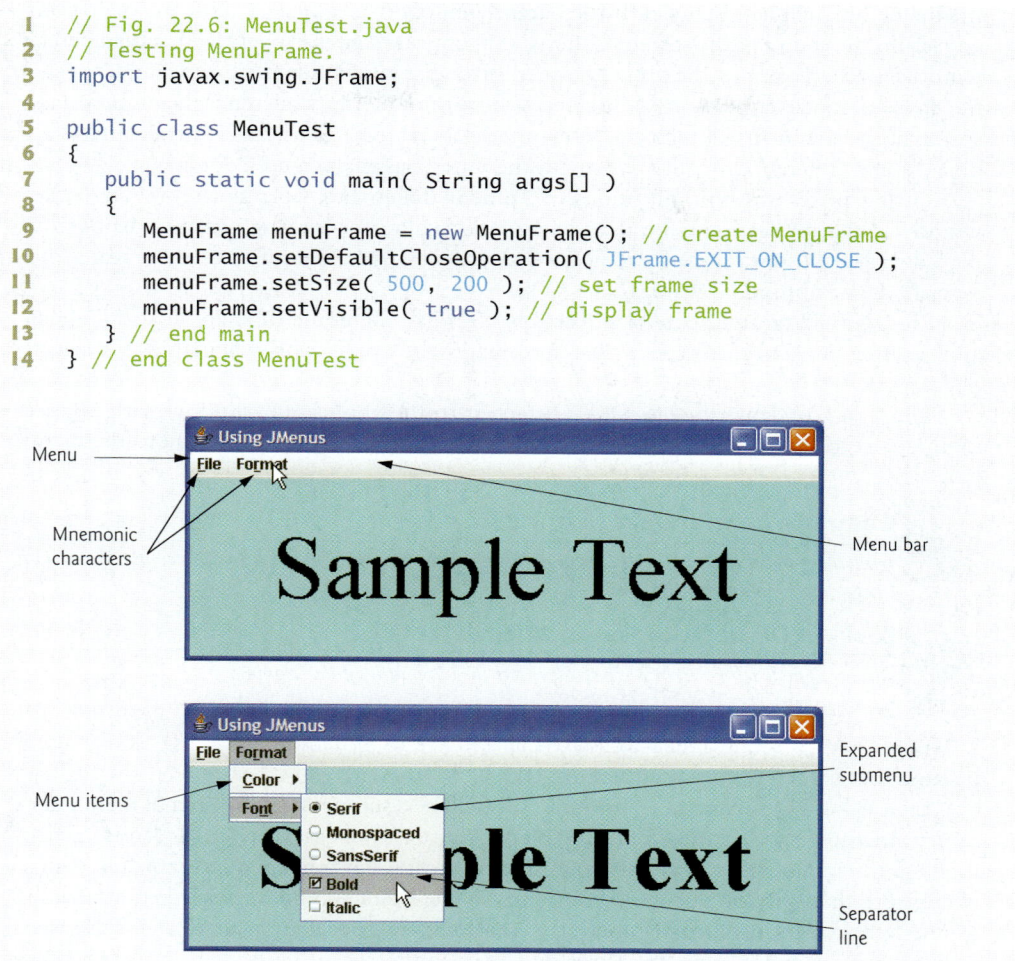

Fig. 22.6 | Test class for `MenuFrame`.

Look-and-Feel Observation 22.4

*Different mnemonics should be used for each button or menu item. Normally, the first letter in the label on the menu item or button is used as the mnemonic. If several buttons or menu items start with the same letter, choose the next most prominent letter in the name (e.g., **x** is commonly chosen for a button or menu item called **Exit**).*

Lines 42–43 create `JMenuItem aboutItem` with the text "About…" and set its mnemonic to the letter A. This menu item is added to `fileMenu` at line 44 with `JMenu` method **add**. To access the **About…** menu item through the keyboard, press the *Alt* key and letter *F* to open the **File** menu, then press *A* to select the **About…** menu item. Lines 47–56 create an `ActionListener` to process `aboutItem`'s action event. Lines 52–54 display a message dialog box. In most prior uses of `showMessageDialog`, the first argument was `null`. The purpose of the first argument is to specify the parent window that helps determine where the dialog box will be displayed. If the parent window is specified as `null`, the dialog box appears in the center of the screen. Otherwise, it appears centered over the specified parent window. In this example, the program specifies the parent window with `MenuTest.this`—the `this` reference of the `MenuTest` object. When using the `this` reference in an inner class, specifying `this` by itself refers to the inner-class object. To reference the outer-class object's `this` reference, qualify `this` with the outer-class name and a dot (`.`).

Dialog boxes are typically modal. A **modal dialog box** does not allow any other window in the application to be accessed until the dialog box is dismissed. The dialogs displayed with class `JOptionPane` are modal dialogs. Class **JDialog** can be used to create your own modal or nonmodal dialogs.

Lines 59–72 create menu item `exitItem`, set its mnemonic to `x`, add it to `fileMenu` and register an `ActionListener` that terminates the application when the user selects `exitItem`.

Lines 74–76 create the `JMenuBar`, attach it to the application window with `JFrame` method `setJMenuBar` and use `JMenuBar` method **add** to attach the `fileMenu` to the menu bar.

Common Programming Error 22.3

Forgetting to set the menu bar with `JFrame` method `setJMenuBar` results in the menu bar not being displayed on the `JFrame`.

Look-and-Feel Observation 22.5

Menus appear left to right in the order that they are added to a `JMenuBar`.

Lines 78–79 create menu `formatMenu` and set its mnemonic to `r`. (F is not used because that is the **File** menu's mnemonic.)

Lines 84–85 create menu `colorMenu` (this will be a submenu in the **Format** menu) and set its mnemonic to `C`. Line 88 creates `JRadioButtonMenuItem` array `colorItems`, which refers to the menu items in `colorMenu`. Line 89 creates `ButtonGroup` `colorGroup`, which will ensure that only one of the menu items in the **Color** submenu is selected at a time. Line 90 creates an instance of inner class `ItemHandler` (declared at lines 154–181) that responds to selections from the **Color** and **Font** submenus (discussed shortly). The `for` statement at lines 93–100 creates each `JRadioButtonMenuItem` in array `colorItems`, adds each menu item to `colorMenu` and to `colorGroup` and registers the `ActionListener` for each menu item.

Line 102 invokes `AbstractButton` method **setSelected** to select the first element in array `colorItems`. Line 104 adds `colorMenu` as a submenu of `formatMenu`. Line 105 invokes `JMenu` method **addSeparator** to add a horizontal **separator** line to the menu.

Look-and-Feel Observation 22.6

A submenu is created by adding a menu as a menu item in another menu. When the mouse is positioned over a submenu (or the submenu's mnemonic is pressed), the submenu expands to show its menu items.

Look-and-Feel Observation 22.7

Separators can be added to a menu to group menu items logically.

Look-and-Feel Observation 22.8

Any lightweight GUI component (i.e., a component that is a subclass of JComponent) can be added to a JMenu or to a JMenuBar.

Lines 108–126 create the **Font** submenu and several JRadioButtonMenuItems and select the first element of JRadioButtonMenuItem array fonts. Line 129 creates a JCheck-BoxMenuItem array to represent the menu items for specifying bold and italic styles for the fonts. Line 130 creates an instance of inner class StyleHandler (declared at lines 184–203) to respond to the JCheckBoxMenuItem events. The for statement at lines 133–139 creates each JCheckBoxMenuItem, adds each menu item to fontMenu and registers the ItemListener for each menu item. Line 141 adds fontMenu as a submenu of formatMenu. Line 142 adds the formatMenu to bar (the menu bar).

Lines 145–147 create a JLabel for which the **Format** menu items control the font, font color and font style. The initial foreground color is set to the first element of array colorValues (Color.BLACK) by invoking JComponent method **setForeground**, and the initial font is set to Serif with PLAIN style and 72-point size. Line 149 sets the background color of the window's content pane to cyan, and line 150 attaches the JLabel to the CENTER of the content pane's BorderLayout.

ItemHandler method actionPerformed (lines 157–180) uses two for statements to determine which font or color menu item generated the event and sets the font or color of the JLabel displayLabel, respectively. The if condition at line 162 uses Abstract-Button method **isSelected** to determine the selected JRadioButtonMenuItem. The if condition at line 172 invokes the event object's getSource method to get a reference to the JRadioButtonMenuItem that generated the event. Line 175 invokes AbstractButton method getText to obtain the name of the font from the menu item.

The program calls StyleHandler method itemStateChanged (lines 187–202) if the user selects a JCheckBoxMenuItem in the fontMenu. Lines 192 and 196 determine whether either or both of the JCheckBoxMenuItems are selected and use their combined state to determine the new style of the font.

22.5 JPopupMenu

Many of today's computer applications provide so-called context-sensitive pop-up menus. In Swing, such menus are created with class **JPopupMenu** (a subclass of JCompo-nent). These menus provide options that are specific to the component for which the pop-up trigger event was generated. On most systems, the pop-up trigger event occurs when the user presses and releases the right mouse button.

Look-and-Feel Observation 22.9

The pop-up trigger event is platform specific. On most platforms that use a mouse with multiple buttons, the pop-up trigger event occurs when the user clicks the right mouse button on a component that supports a pop-up menu.

The application in Figure 22.7 and Fig. 22.8 creates a JPopupMenu that allows the user to select one of three colors and change the background color of the window. When the user clicks the right mouse button on the PopupTest window's background, a JPopupMenu con-taining colors appears. If the user clicks a JRadioButtonMenuItem for a color, ItemHandler method actionPerformed changes the background color of the window's content pane.

```java
1   // Fig. 22.7: PopupFrame.java
2   // Demonstrating JPopupMenus.
3   import java.awt.Color;
4   import java.awt.event.MouseAdapter;
5   import java.awt.event.MouseEvent;
6   import java.awt.event.ActionListener;
7   import java.awt.event.ActionEvent;
8   import javax.swing.JFrame;
9   import javax.swing.JRadioButtonMenuItem;
10  import javax.swing.JPopupMenu;
11  import javax.swing.ButtonGroup;
12
13  public class PopupFrame extends JFrame
14  {
15     private JRadioButtonMenuItem items[]; // holds items for colors
16     private final Color colorValues[] =
17        { Color.BLUE, Color.YELLOW, Color.RED }; // colors to be used
18     private JPopupMenu popupMenu; // allows user to select color
19
20     // no-argument constructor sets up GUI
21     public PopupFrame()
22     {
23        super( "Using JPopupMenus" );
24
25        ItemHandler handler = new ItemHandler(); // handler for menu items
26        String colors[] = { "Blue", "Yellow", "Red" }; // array of colors
27
28        ButtonGroup colorGroup = new ButtonGroup(); // manages color items
29        popupMenu = new JPopupMenu(); // create pop-up menu
30        items = new JRadioButtonMenuItem[ 3 ]; // items for selecting color
31
32        // construct menu item, add to popup menu, enable event handling
33        for ( int count = 0; count < items.length; count++ )
34        {
35           items[ count ] = new JRadioButtonMenuItem( colors[ count ] );
36           popupMenu.add( items[ count ] ); // add item to pop-up menu
37           colorGroup.add( items[ count ] ); // add item to button group
38           items[ count ].addActionListener( handler ); // add handler
39        } // end for
40
41        setBackground( Color.WHITE ); // set background to white
42
43        // declare a MouseListener for the window to display pop-up menu
44        addMouseListener(
45
46           new MouseAdapter() // anonymous inner class
47           {
48              // handle mouse press event
49              public void mousePressed( MouseEvent event )
50              {
51                 checkForTriggerEvent( event ); // check for trigger
52              } // end method mousePressed
```

Fig. 22.7 | JPopupMenu for selecting colors. (Part 1 of 2.)

```
53
54                   // handle mouse release event
55                   public void mouseReleased( MouseEvent event )
56                   {
57                      checkForTriggerEvent( event ); // check for trigger
58                   } // end method mouseReleased
59
60                   // determine whether event should trigger popup menu
61                   private void checkForTriggerEvent( MouseEvent event )
62                   {
63                      if ( event.isPopupTrigger() )
64                         popupMenu.show(
65                            event.getComponent(), event.getX(), event.getY() );
66                   } // end method checkForTriggerEvent
67                } // end anonymous inner class
68             ); // end call to addMouseListener
69          } // end PopupFrame constructor
70
71          // private inner class to handle menu item events
72          private class ItemHandler implements ActionListener
73          {
74             // process menu item selections
75             public void actionPerformed( ActionEvent event )
76             {
77                // determine which menu item was selected
78                for ( int i = 0; i < items.length; i++ )
79                {
80                   if ( event.getSource() == items[ i ] )
81                   {
82                      getContentPane().setBackground( colorValues[ i ] );
83                      return;
84                   } // end if
85                } // end for
86             } // end method actionPerformed
87          } // end private inner class ItemHandler
88       } // end class PopupFrame
```

Fig. 22.7 | JPopupMenu for selecting colors. (Part 2 of 2.)

Line 25 of the PopupFrame constructor (lines 21–69) creates an instance of class Item-Handler (declared in lines 72–87) that will process the item events from the menu items in the pop-up menu. Line 29 creates the JPopupMenu. The for statement (lines 33–39) creates a JRadioButtonMenuItem object (line 35), adds it to popupMenu (line 36), adds it to ButtonGroup colorGroup (line 37) to maintain one selected JRadioButtonMenuItem at a time and registers its ActionListener (line 38). Line 41 sets the initial background to white by invoking method setBackground.

Lines 44–68 register a MouseListener to handle the mouse events of the application window. Methods mousePressed (lines 49–52) and mouseReleased (lines 55–58) check for the pop-up trigger event. Each method calls private utility method checkForTrigger-Event (lines 61–66) to determine whether the pop-up trigger event occurred. If it did, MouseEvent method **isPopupTrigger** returns true, and JPopupMenu method **show** displays the JPopupMenu. The first argument to method show specifies the **origin component**,

```
1   // Fig. 22.8: PopupTest.java
2   // Testing PopupFrame.
3   import javax.swing.JFrame;
4
5   public class PopupTest
6   {
7      public static void main( String args[] )
8      {
9         PopupFrame popupFrame = new PopupFrame(); // create PopupFrame
10        popupFrame.setDefaultCloseOperation( JFrame.EXIT_ON_CLOSE );
11        popupFrame.setSize( 300, 200 ); // set frame size
12        popupFrame.setVisible( true ); // display frame
13     } // end main
14  } // end class PopupTest
```

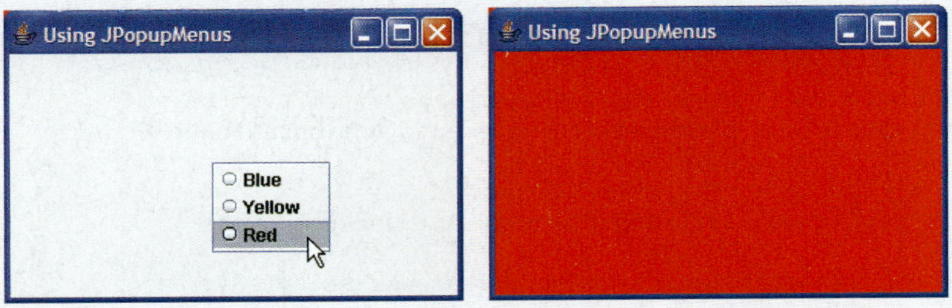

Fig. 22.8 | Test class for `PopupFrame`.

whose position helps determine where the `JPopupMenu` will appear on the screen. The last two arguments are the *x-y* coordinates (measured from the origin component's upper-left corner) at which the `JPopupMenu` is to appear.

Look-and-Feel Observation 22.10

Displaying a `JPopupMenu` for the pop-up trigger event of multiple GUI components requires registering mouse-event handlers for each of those GUI components.

When the user selects a menu item from the pop-up menu, class `ItemHandler`'s method `actionPerformed` (lines 75–86) determines which `JRadioButtonMenuItem` the user selected and sets the background color of the window's content pane.

22.6 Pluggable Look-and-Feel

A program that uses Java's Abstract Window Toolkit GUI components (package `java.awt`) takes on the look-and-feel of the platform on which the program executes. A Java application running on a Macintosh looks like other applications running on a Macintosh. A Java application running on Microsoft Windows looks like other applications running on Microsoft Windows. A Java application running on a UNIX platform looks like other applications running on that UNIX platform. This is sometimes desirable, because it allows users of the application on each platform to use GUI components with which they are already familiar. However, it also introduces interesting portability issues.

Portability Tip 22.1

GUI components look different on different platforms and may require different amounts of space to display. This could change their layout and alignments.

Portability Tip 22.2

GUI components on different platforms have different default functionality (e.g., some platforms allow a button with the focus to be "pressed" with the space bar, and some do not).

Swing's lightweight GUI components eliminate many of these issues by providing uniform functionality across platforms and by defining a uniform cross-platform look-and-feel (known as the metal look-and-feel). Swing also provides the flexibility to customize the look-and-feel to appear as a Microsoft Windows-style look-and-feel (on Window systems), a Motif-style (UNIX) look-and-feel (across all platforms) or a Macintosh look-and-feel (Mac systems).

The application in Fig. 22.9 and Fig. 22.10 demonstrates how to change the look-and-feel of a Swing GUI. The application creates several GUI components, so you can see the change in the look-and-feel of several GUI components at the same time. The first output window shows the standard metal look-and-feel, the second shows the Motif look-and-feel, and the third shows the Windows look-and-feel.

All the GUI components and event handling in this example have been covered before, so we concentrate on the mechanism for changing the look-and-feel in this

```java
1   // Fig. 22.9: LookAndFeelFrame.java
2   // Changing the look and feel.
3   import java.awt.GridLayout;
4   import java.awt.BorderLayout;
5   import java.awt.event.ItemListener;
6   import java.awt.event.ItemEvent;
7   import javax.swing.JFrame;
8   import javax.swing.UIManager;
9   import javax.swing.JRadioButton;
10  import javax.swing.ButtonGroup;
11  import javax.swing.JButton;
12  import javax.swing.JLabel;
13  import javax.swing.JComboBox;
14  import javax.swing.JPanel;
15  import javax.swing.SwingConstants;
16  import javax.swing.SwingUtilities;
17
18  public class LookAndFeelFrame extends JFrame
19  {
20     // string names of look and feels
21     private final String strings[] = { "Metal", "Motif", "Windows" };
22     private UIManager.LookAndFeelInfo looks[]; // look and feels
23     private JRadioButton radio[]; // radiobuttons to select look and feel
24     private ButtonGroup group; // group for radiobuttons
25     private JButton button; // displays look of button
26     private JLabel label; // displays look of label
27     private JComboBox comboBox; // displays look of combo box
```

Fig. 22.9 | Look-and-feel of a Swing-based GUI. (Part 1 of 3.)

```java
28
29      // set up GUI
30      public LookAndFeelFrame()
31      {
32         super( "Look and Feel Demo" );
33
34         JPanel northPanel = new JPanel(); // create north panel
35         northPanel.setLayout( new GridLayout( 3, 1, 0, 5 ) );
36
37         label = new JLabel( "This is a Metal look-and-feel",
38            SwingConstants.CENTER ); // create label
39         northPanel.add( label ); // add label to panel
40
41         button = new JButton( "JButton" ); // create button
42         northPanel.add( button ); // add button to panel
43
44         comboBox = new JComboBox( strings ); // create combobox
45         northPanel.add( comboBox ); // add combobox to panel
46
47         // create array for radio buttons
48         radio = new JRadioButton[ strings.length ];
49
50         JPanel southPanel = new JPanel(); // create south panel
51         southPanel.setLayout( new GridLayout( 1, radio.length ) );
52
53         group = new ButtonGroup(); // button group for look and feels
54         ItemHandler handler = new ItemHandler(); // look and feel handler
55
56         for ( int count = 0; count < radio.length; count++ )
57         {
58            radio[ count ] = new JRadioButton( strings[ count ] );
59            radio[ count ].addItemListener( handler ); // add handler
60            group.add( radio[ count ] ); // add radiobutton to group
61            southPanel.add( radio[ count ] ); // add radiobutton to panel
62         } // end for
63
64         add( northPanel, BorderLayout.NORTH ); // add north panel
65         add( southPanel, BorderLayout.SOUTH ); // add south panel
66
67         // get installed look-and-feel information
68         looks = UIManager.getInstalledLookAndFeels();
69         radio[ 0 ].setSelected( true ); // set default selection
70      } // end LookAndFeelFrame constructor
71
72      // use UIManager to change look-and-feel of GUI
73      private void changeTheLookAndFeel( int value )
74      {
75         try // change look and feel
76         {
77            // set look and feel for this application
78            UIManager.setLookAndFeel( looks[ value ].getClassName() );
79
```

Fig. 22.9 | Look-and-feel of a Swing-based GUI. (Part 2 of 3.)

```
80                // update components in this application
81                SwingUtilities.updateComponentTreeUI( this );
82             } // end try
83             catch ( Exception exception )
84             {
85                exception.printStackTrace();
86             } // end catch
87          } // end method changeTheLookAndFeel
88
89          // private inner class to handle radio button events
90          private class ItemHandler implements ItemListener
91          {
92             // process user's look-and-feel selection
93             public void itemStateChanged( ItemEvent event )
94             {
95                for ( int count = 0; count < radio.length; count++ )
96                {
97                   if ( radio[ count ].isSelected() )
98                   {
99                      label.setText( String.format( "This is a %s look-and-feel",
100                         strings[ count ] ) );
101                      comboBox.setSelectedIndex( count ); // set combobox index
102                      changeTheLookAndFeel( count ); // change look and feel
103                   } // end if
104                } // end for
105             } // end method itemStateChanged
106          } // end private inner class ItemHandler
107       } // end class LookAndFeelFrame
```

Fig. 22.9 | Look-and-feel of a Swing-based GUI. (Part 3 of 3.)

example. Class **UIManager** (package javax.swing) contains nested class **LookAndFeelInfo** (a public static class) that maintains information about a look-and-feel. Line 22 declares an array of type UIManager.LookAndFeelInfo (note the syntax used to identify the inner class LookAndFeelInfo). Line 68 uses UIManager static method **getInstalledLookAnd-Feels** to get the array of UIManager.LookAndFeelInfo objects that describe each look-and-feel available on your system.

> **Performance Tip 22.1**
>
> *Each look-and-feel is represented by a Java class. UIManager method getInstalledLookAnd-Feels does not load each class. Rather, it provides the names of the available look-and-feel classes so that a choice can be made (presumably once at program start-up). This reduces the overhead of having to load all the look-and-feel classes even if the program will not use some of them.*

Our utility method changeTheLookAndFeel (lines 73–87) is called by the event handler for the JRadioButtons at the bottom of the user interface. The event handler (declared in private inner class ItemHandler at lines 90–106) passes an integer representing the element in array looks that should be used to change the look-and-feel. Line 78 invokes static method **setLookAndFeel** of UIManager to change the look-and-feel. Method **get-ClassName** of class UIManager.LookAndFeelInfo determines the name of the look-and-feel class that corresponds to the UIManager.LookAndFeelInfo object. If the look-and-feel

```
1   // Fig. 22.10: LookAndFeelDemo.java
2   // Changing the look and feel.
3   import javax.swing.JFrame;
4
5   public class LookAndFeelDemo
6   {
7      public static void main( String args[] )
8      {
9         LookAndFeelFrame lookAndFeelFrame = new LookAndFeelFrame();
10        lookAndFeelFrame.setDefaultCloseOperation( JFrame.EXIT_ON_CLOSE );
11        lookAndFeelFrame.setSize( 300, 200 ); // set frame size
12        lookAndFeelFrame.setVisible( true ); // display frame
13     } // end main
14  } // end class LookAndFeelDemo
```

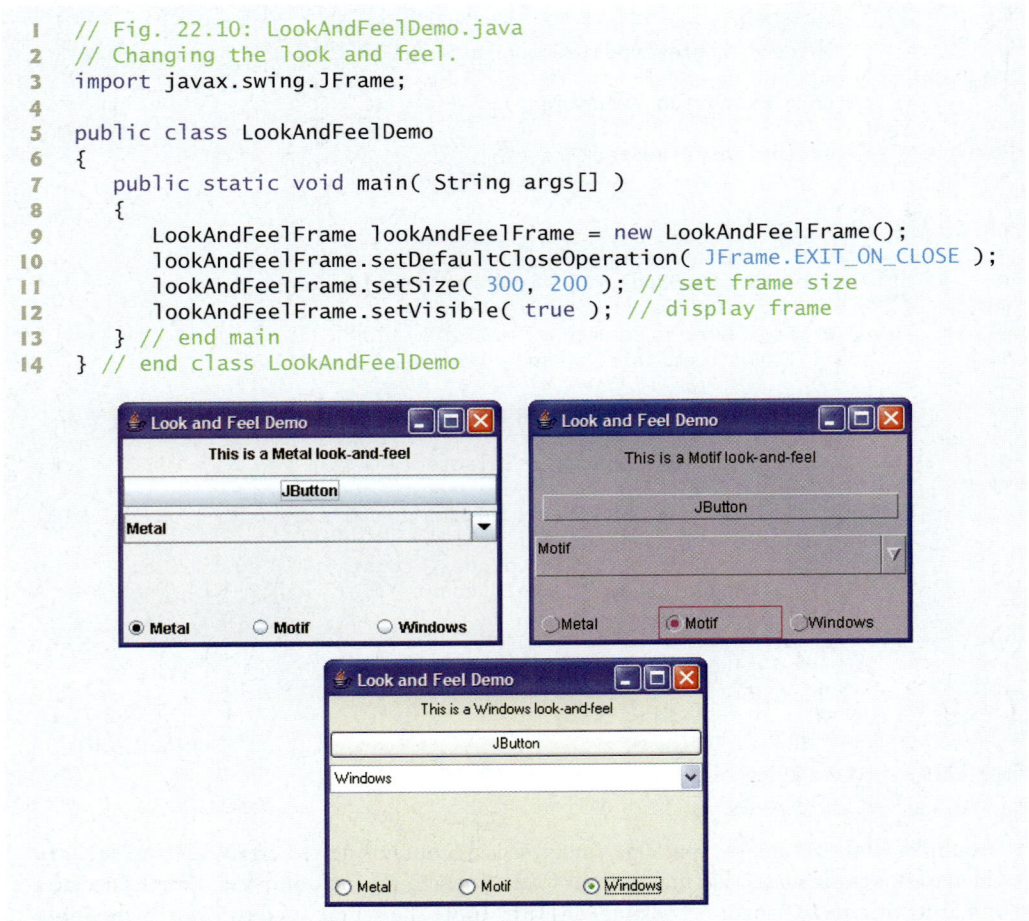

Fig. 22.10 | Test class for `LookAndFeelFrame`.

class is not already loaded, it will be loaded as part of the call to `setLookAndFeel`. Line 81 invokes static method **updateComponentTreeUI** of class **SwingUtilities** (package `javax.swing`) to change the look-and-feel of every GUI component attached to its argument (`this` instance of our application class `LookAndFeelDemo`) to the new look-and-feel.

22.7 JDesktopPane and JInternalFrame

Many of today's applications use a **multiple-document interface (MDI)**—a main window (called the **parent window**) containing other windows (called **child windows**), to manage several open **documents** that are being processed in parallel. For example, many e-mail programs allow you to have several windows open at the same time, thso you can compose or read multiple e-mail messages simultaneously. Similarly, many word processors allow the user to open multiple documents in separate windows, making it possible to switch between them without having to close one to open another. The application in Fig. 22.11

and Fig. 22.12 demonstrates Swing's **JDesktopPane** and **JInternalFrame** classes for implementing multiple-document interfaces.

```java
1   // Fig. 22.11: DesktopFrame.java
2   // Demonstrating JDesktopPane.
3   import java.awt.BorderLayout;
4   import java.awt.Dimension;
5   import java.awt.Graphics;
6   import java.awt.event.ActionListener;
7   import java.awt.event.ActionEvent;
8   import java.util.Random;
9   import javax.swing.JFrame;
10  import javax.swing.JDesktopPane;
11  import javax.swing.JMenuBar;
12  import javax.swing.JMenu;
13  import javax.swing.JMenuItem;
14  import javax.swing.JInternalFrame;
15  import javax.swing.JPanel;
16  import javax.swing.ImageIcon;
17
18  public class DesktopFrame extends JFrame
19  {
20     private JDesktopPane theDesktop;
21
22     // set up GUI
23     public DesktopFrame()
24     {
25        super( "Using a JDesktopPane" );
26
27        JMenuBar bar = new JMenuBar(); // create menu bar
28        JMenu addMenu = new JMenu( "Add" ); // create Add menu
29        JMenuItem newFrame = new JMenuItem( "Internal Frame" );
30
31        addMenu.add( newFrame ); // add new frame item to Add menu
32        bar.add( addMenu ); // add Add menu to menu bar
33        setJMenuBar( bar ); // set menu bar for this application
34
35        theDesktop = new JDesktopPane(); // create desktop pane
36        add( theDesktop ); // add desktop pane to frame
37
38        // set up listener for newFrame menu item
39        newFrame.addActionListener(
40
41           new ActionListener() // anonymous inner class
42           {
43              // display new internal window
44              public void actionPerformed( ActionEvent event )
45              {
46                 // create internal frame
47                 JInternalFrame frame = new JInternalFrame(
48                    "Internal Frame", true, true, true, true );
49
```

Fig. 22.11 | Multiple-document interface. (Part 1 of 2.)

```
50                    MyJPanel panel = new MyJPanel(); // create new panel
51                    frame.add( panel, BorderLayout.CENTER ); // add panel
52                    frame.pack(); // set internal frame to size of contents
53
54                    theDesktop.add( frame ); // attach internal frame
55                    frame.setVisible( true ); // show internal frame
56                } // end method actionPerformed
57             } // end anonymous inner class
58          ); // end call to addActionListener
59       } // end DesktopFrame constructor
60    } // end class DesktopFrame
61
62    // class to display an ImageIcon on a panel
63    class MyJPanel extends JPanel
64    {
65       private static Random generator = new Random();
66       private ImageIcon picture; // image to be displayed
67       private String[] images = { "yellowflowers.png", "purpleflowers.png",
68          "redflowers.png", "redflowers2.png", "lavenderflowers.png" };
69
70       // load image
71       public MyJPanel()
72       {
73          int randomNumber = generator.nextInt( 5 );
74          picture = new ImageIcon( images[ randomNumber ] ); // set icon
75       } // end MyJPanel constructor
76
77       // display imageIcon on panel
78       public void paintComponent( Graphics g )
79       {
80          super.paintComponent( g );
81          picture.paintIcon( this, g, 0, 0 ); // display icon
82       } // end method paintComponent
83
84       // return image dimensions
85       public Dimension getPreferredSize()
86       {
87          return new Dimension( picture.getIconWidth(),
88             picture.getIconHeight() );
89       } // end method getPreferredSize
90    } // end class MyJPanel
```

Fig. 22.11 | Multiple-document interface. (Part 2 of 2.)

Lines 27–33 create a JMenuBar, a JMenu and a JMenuItem, add the JMenuItem to the JMenu, add the JMenu to the JMenuBar and set the JMenuBar for the application window. When the user selects the JMenuItem newFrame, the application creates and displays a new JInternalFrame object containing an image.

Line 35 assigns JDesktopPane (package javax.swing) variable theDesktop a new JDesktopPane object that will be used to manage the JInternalFrame child windows. Line 36 adds the JDesktopPane to the JFrame. By default, the JDesktopPane is added to the center of the content pane's BorderLayout, so the JDesktopPane expands to fill the entire application window.

Lines 39–58 register an `ActionListener` to handle the event when the user selects the `newFrame` menu item. When the event occurs, method `actionPerformed` (lines 44–56) creates a `JInternalFrame` object in lines 47–48. The `JInternalFrame` constructor used here takes five arguments—a string for the title bar of the internal window, a `boolean` indicating whether the internal frame can be resized by the user, a `boolean` indicating whether the internal frame can be closed by the user, a `boolean` indicating whether the internal frame can be maximized by the user and a `boolean` indicating whether the internal frame

```
 1  // Fig. 22.12: DesktopTest.java
 2  // Demonstrating JDesktopPane.
 3  import javax.swing.JFrame;
 4
 5  public class DesktopTest
 6  {
 7     public static void main( String args[] )
 8     {
 9        DesktopFrame desktopFrame = new DesktopFrame();
10        desktopFrame.setDefaultCloseOperation( JFrame.EXIT_ON_CLOSE );
11        desktopFrame.setSize( 600, 480 ); // set frame size
12        desktopFrame.setVisible( true ); // display frame
13     } // end main
14  } // end class DesktopTest
```

Internal Frames   Minimize   Maximize   Close

Minimized internal frames   Position the mouse over any corner of a child window to resize the window (if resizing is allowed).

Fig. 22.12 | Test class for `DeskTopFrame`. (Part I of 2.)

Maximized internal frame

Fig. 22.12 │ Test class for `DeskTopFrame`. (Part 2 of 2.)

can be minimized by the user. For each of the `boolean` arguments, a `true` value indicates that the operation should be allowed (as is the case here).

As with `JFrame`s and `JApplet`s, a `JInternalFrame` has a content pane to which GUI components can be attached. Line 50 creates an instance of our class `MyJPanel` (declared at lines 63–90) that is added to the `JInternalFrame` at line 51.

Line 52 uses `JInternalFrame` method **pack** to set the size of the child window. Method `pack` uses the preferred sizes of the components to determine the window's size. Class `MyJPanel` declares method **getPreferredSize** (lines 85–89) to specify the panel's preferred size for use by the `pack` method. Line 54 adds the `JInternalFrame` to the `JDesktopPane`, and line 55 displays the `JInternalFrame`.

Classes `JInternalFrame` and `JDesktopPane` provide many methods for managing child windows. See the `JInternalFrame` and `JDesktopPane` online API documentation for complete lists of these methods:

```
java.sun.com/j2se/5.0/docs/api/javax/swing/JInternalFrame.html
java.sun.com/j2se/5.0/docs/api/javax/swing/JDesktopPane.html
```

22.8 JTabbedPane

A **JTabbedPane** arranges GUI components into layers in which only one layer is visible at a time. Users access each layer via a tab—similar to folders in a file cabinet. When the user clicks a tab, the appropriate layer is displayed. The tabs appear at the top by default but also can be positioned at the left, right or bottom of the `JTabbedPane`. Any component can be placed on a tab. If the component is a container, such as a panel, it can use any layout manager to lay out several components on the tab. Class JTabbedPane is a subclass of JComponent. The application in Fig. 22.13 and Fig. 22.14 creates one tabbed pane with three tabs. Each tab displays one of the JPanels—panel1, panel2 or panel3.

```java
 1   // Fig. 22.13: JTabbedPaneFrame.java
 2   // Demonstrating JTabbedPane.
 3   import java.awt.BorderLayout;
 4   import java.awt.Color;
 5   import javax.swing.JFrame;
 6   import javax.swing.JTabbedPane;
 7   import javax.swing.JLabel;
 8   import javax.swing.JPanel;
 9   import javax.swing.JButton;
10   import javax.swing.SwingConstants;
11
12   public class JTabbedPaneFrame extends JFrame
13   {
14      // set up GUI
15      public JTabbedPaneFrame()
16      {
17         super( "JTabbedPane Demo " );
18
19         JTabbedPane tabbedPane = new JTabbedPane(); // create JTabbedPane
20
21         // set up panel1 and add it to JTabbedPane
22         JLabel label1 = new JLabel( "panel one", SwingConstants.CENTER );
23         JPanel panel1 = new JPanel(); // create first panel
24         panel1.add( label1 ); // add label to panel
25         tabbedPane.addTab( "Tab One", null, panel1, "First Panel" );
26
27         // set up panel2 and add it to JTabbedPane
28         JLabel label2 = new JLabel( "panel two", SwingConstants.CENTER );
29         JPanel panel2 = new JPanel(); // create second panel
30         panel2.setBackground( Color.YELLOW ); // set background to yellow
31         panel2.add( label2 ); // add label to panel
32         tabbedPane.addTab( "Tab Two", null, panel2, "Second Panel" );
33
34         // set up panel3 and add it to JTabbedPane
35         JLabel label3 = new JLabel( "panel three" );
36         JPanel panel3 = new JPanel(); // create third panel
37         panel3.setLayout( new BorderLayout() ); // use borderlayout
38         panel3.add( new JButton( "North" ), BorderLayout.NORTH );
39         panel3.add( new JButton( "West" ), BorderLayout.WEST );
40         panel3.add( new JButton( "East" ), BorderLayout.EAST );
41         panel3.add( new JButton( "South" ), BorderLayout.SOUTH );
42         panel3.add( label3, BorderLayout.CENTER );
43         tabbedPane.addTab( "Tab Three", null, panel3, "Third Panel" );
44
45         add( tabbedPane ); // add JTabbedPane to frame
46      } // end JTabbedPaneFrame constructor
47   } // end class JTabbedPaneFrame
```

Fig. 22.13 | JTabbedPane used to organize GUI components.

```
1   // Fig. 22.14: JTabbedPaneDemo.java
2   // Demonstrating JTabbedPane.
3   import javax.swing.JFrame;
4
5   public class JTabbedPaneDemo
6   {
7      public static void main( String args[] )
8      {
9         JTabbedPaneFrame tabbedPaneFrame = new JTabbedPaneFrame();
10        tabbedPaneFrame.setDefaultCloseOperation( JFrame.EXIT_ON_CLOSE );
11        tabbedPaneFrame.setSize( 250, 200 ); // set frame size
12        tabbedPaneFrame.setVisible( true ); // display frame
13     } // end main
14  } // end class JTabbedPaneDemo
```

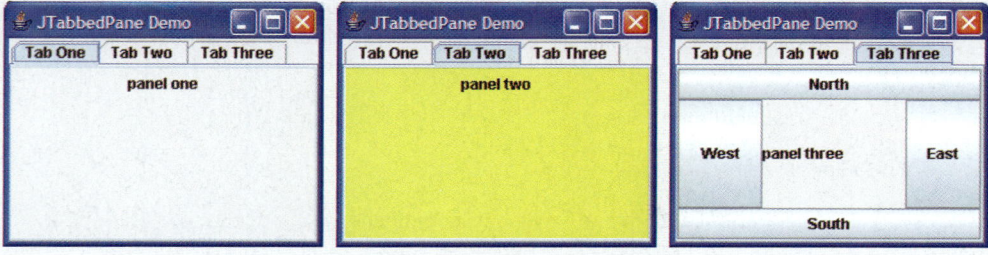

Fig. 22.14 | Test class for `JTabbedPaneFrame`.

The constructor (lines 15–46) builds the GUI. Line 19 creates an empty `JTabbedPane` with default settings—that is, tabs across the top. If the tabs do not fit on one line, they will wrap to form additional lines of tabs. Next the constructor creates the `JPanel`s `panel1`, `panel2` and `panel3` and their GUI components. As we set up each panel, we add it to `tabbedPane`, using `JTabbedPane` method **addTab** with four arguments. The first argument is a string that specifies the title of the tab. The second argument is an `Icon` reference that specifies an icon to display on the tab. If the `Icon` is a `null` reference, no image is displayed. The third argument is a `Component` reference that represents the GUI component to display when the user clicks the tab. The last argument is a string that specifies the tool tip for the tab. For example, line 25 adds `JPanel panel1` to `tabbedPane` with title `"Tab One"` and the tool tip `"First Panel"`. `JPanel`s `panel2` and `panel3` are added to `tabbedPane` at lines 32 and 43. To view a tab, click it with the mouse or use the arrow keys to cycle through the tab=.

22.9 Layout Managers: BoxLayout and GridBagLayout

In Chapter 11, we introduced three layout managers—`FlowLayout`, `BorderLayout` and `GridLayout`. This section presents two additional layout managers (summarized in Fig. 22.15). We discuss these layout managers in the examples that follow.

BoxLayout *Layout Manager*

The `BoxLayout` layout manager (in package `javax.swing`) arranges GUI components horizontally along a container's *x*-axis or vertically along its *y*-axis. The application in

Fig. 22.16 and Fig. 22.17 demonstrates BoxLayout and the container class Box that uses BoxLayout as its default layout manager.

Layout Manager	Description
BoxLayout	A layout manager that allows GUI components to be arranged left-to-right or top-to-bottom in a container. Class Box declares a container with BoxLayout as its default layout manager and provides static methods to create a Box with a horizontal or vertical BoxLayout.
GridBagLayout	A layout manager similar to GridLayout, but unlike it in that components can vary in size and can be added in any order.

Fig. 22.15 | Additional layout managers.

```java
 1  // Fig. 22.16: BoxLayoutFrame.java
 2  // Demonstrating BoxLayout.
 3  import java.awt.Dimension;
 4  import javax.swing.JFrame;
 5  import javax.swing.Box;
 6  import javax.swing.JButton;
 7  import javax.swing.BoxLayout;
 8  import javax.swing.JPanel;
 9  import javax.swing.JTabbedPane;
10
11  public class BoxLayoutFrame extends JFrame
12  {
13     // set up GUI
14     public BoxLayoutFrame()
15     {
16        super( "Demonstrating BoxLayout" );
17
18        // create Box containers with BoxLayout
19        Box horizontal1 = Box.createHorizontalBox();
20        Box vertical1 = Box.createVerticalBox();
21        Box horizontal2 = Box.createHorizontalBox();
22        Box vertical2 = Box.createVerticalBox();
23
24        final int SIZE = 3; // number of buttons on each Box
25
26        // add buttons to Box horizontal1
27        for ( int count = 0; count < SIZE; count++ )
28           horizontal1.add( new JButton( "Button " + count ) );
29
30        // create strut and add buttons to Box vertical1
31        for ( int count = 0; count < SIZE; count++ )
32        {
33           vertical1.add( Box.createVerticalStrut( 25 ) );
34           vertical1.add( new JButton( "Button " + count ) );
35        } // end for
36
```

Fig. 22.16 | BoxLayout layout manager. (Part 1 of 2.)

```
37          // create horizontal glue and add buttons to Box horizontal2
38          for ( int count = 0; count < SIZE; count++ )
39          {
40             horizontal2.add( Box.createHorizontalGlue() );
41             horizontal2.add( new JButton( "Button " + count ) );
42          } // end for
43
44          // create rigid area and add buttons to Box vertical2
45          for ( int count = 0; count < SIZE; count++ )
46          {
47             vertical2.add( Box.createRigidArea( new Dimension( 12, 8 ) ) );
48             vertical2.add( new JButton( "Button " + count ) );
49          } // end for
50
51          // create vertical glue and add buttons to panel
52          JPanel panel = new JPanel();
53          panel.setLayout( new BoxLayout( panel, BoxLayout.Y_AXIS ) );
54
55          for ( int count = 0; count < SIZE; count++ )
56          {
57             panel.add( Box.createGlue() );
58             panel.add( new JButton( "Button " + count ) );
59          } // end for
60
61          // create a JTabbedPane
62          JTabbedPane tabs = new JTabbedPane(
63             JTabbedPane.TOP, JTabbedPane.SCROLL_TAB_LAYOUT );
64
65          // place each container on tabbed pane
66          tabs.addTab( "Horizontal Box", horizontal1 );
67          tabs.addTab( "Vertical Box with Struts", vertical1 );
68          tabs.addTab( "Horizontal Box with Glue", horizontal2 );
69          tabs.addTab( "Vertical Box with Rigid Areas", vertical2 );
70          tabs.addTab( "Vertical Box with Glue", panel );
71
72          add( tabs ); // place tabbed pane on frame
73       } // end BoxLayoutFrame constructor
74   } // end class BoxLayoutFrame
```

Fig. 22.16 | BoxLayout layout manager. (Part 2 of 2.)

Lines 19–22 create Box containers. References horizontal1 and horizontal2 are initialized with static Box method createHorizontalBox, which returns a Box container with a horizontal BoxLayout in which GUI components are arranged left-to-right. Variables vertical1 and vertical2 are initialized with static Box method createVerticalBox, which returns references to Box containers with a vertical BoxLayout in which GUI components are arranged top-to-bottom.

The for statement at lines 27–28 adds three JButtons to horizontal1. The for statement at lines 31–35 adds three JButtons to vertical1. Before adding each button, line 33 adds a vertical strut to the container with static Box method createVerticalStrut. A vertical strut is an invisible GUI component that has a fixed pixel height and is used to guarantee a fixed amount of space between GUI components. The int argument to method createVerticalStrut determines the height of the strut in pixels. When the container is resized, the distance between GUI components separated by struts does not change. Class Box also declares method **createHorizontalStrut** for horizontal BoxLayouts.

The for statement at lines 38–42 adds three JButtons to horizontal2. Before adding each button, line 40 adds horizontal glue to the container with static Box method **createHorizontalGlue**. Horizontal glue is an invisible GUI component that can be used between fixed-size GUI components to occupy additional space. Normally, extra space appears to the right of the last horizontal GUI component or below the last vertical one in a BoxLayout. Glue allows the extra space to be placed between GUI components. When the container is resized, components separated by glue components remain the same size, but the glue stretches or contracts to occupy the space between them. Class Box also declares method **createVerticalGlue** for vertical BoxLayouts.

The for statement at lines 45–49 adds three JButtons to vertical2. Before each button is added, line 47 adds a rigid area to the container with static Box method **createRigidArea**. A rigid area is an invisible GUI component that always has a fixed pixel

```
1    // Fig. 22.17: BoxLayoutDemo.java
2    // Demonstrating BoxLayout.
3    import javax.swing.JFrame;
4
5    public class BoxLayoutDemo
6    {
7       public static void main( String args[] )
8       {
9          BoxLayoutFrame boxLayoutFrame = new BoxLayoutFrame();
10         boxLayoutFrame.setDefaultCloseOperation( JFrame.EXIT_ON_CLOSE );
11         boxLayoutFrame.setSize( 400, 220 ); // set frame size
12         boxLayoutFrame.setVisible( true ); // display frame
13      } // end main
14   } // end class BoxLayoutDemo
```

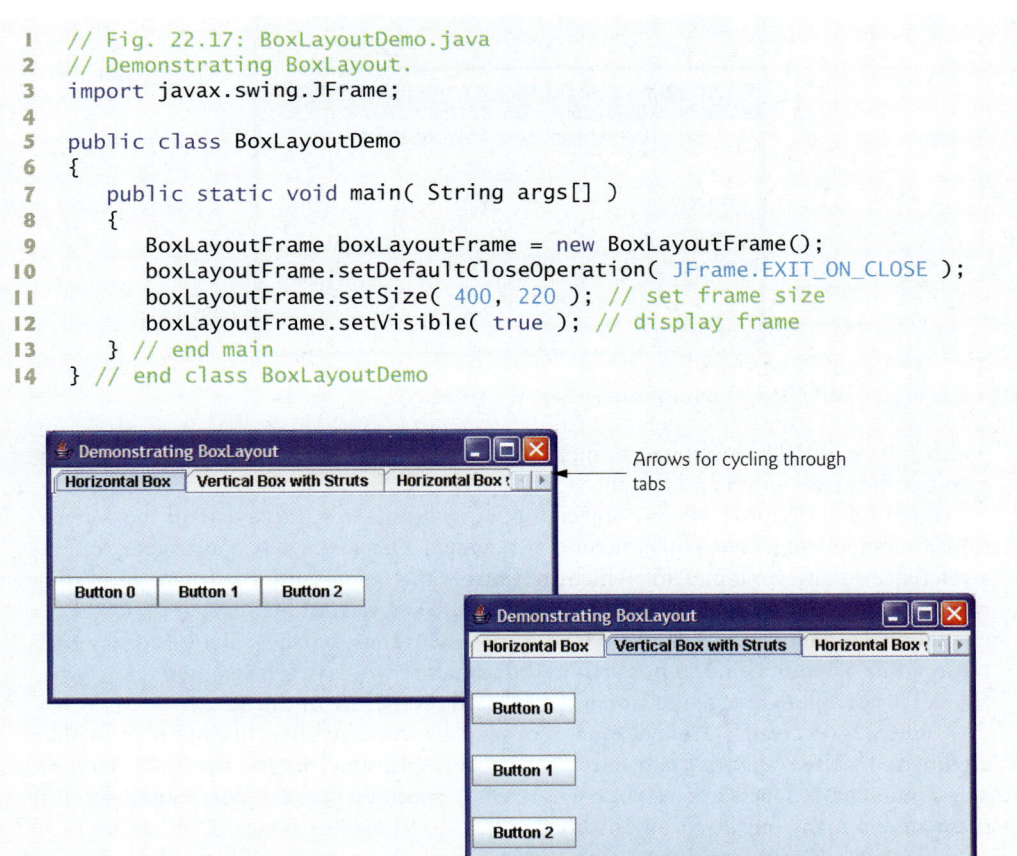

Fig. 22.17 | Test class for BoxLayoutFrame. (Part 1 of 2.)

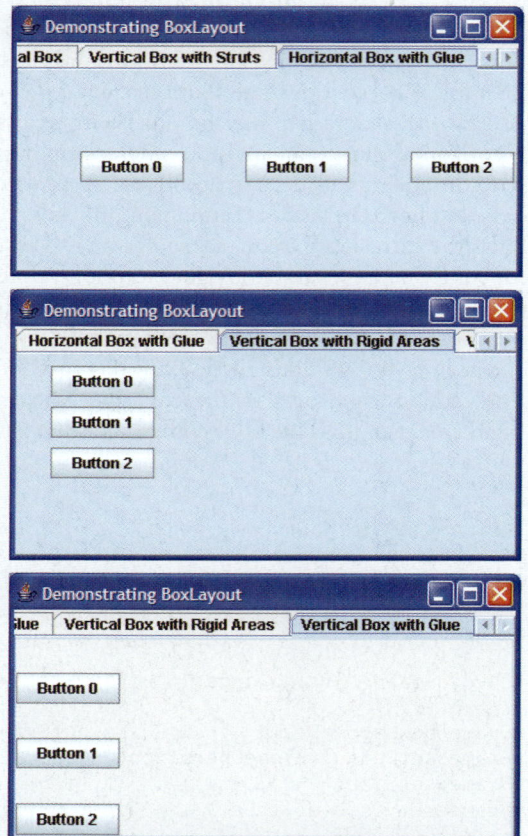

Fig. 22.17 | Test class for `BoxLayoutFrame`. (Part 2 of 2.)

width and height. The argument to method `createRigidArea` is a `Dimension` object that specifies the area's width and height.

Lines 52–53 create a `JPanel` object and set its layout to a `BoxLayout` in the conventional manner, using `Container` method `setLayout`. The `BoxLayout` constructor receives a reference to the container for which it controls the layout and a constant indicating whether the layout is horizontal (`BoxLayout.X_AXIS`) or vertical (`BoxLayout.Y_AXIS`).

The `for` statement at lines 55–59 adds three `JButton`s to `panel`. Before adding each button, line 57 adds a glue component to the container with `static` `Box` method `createGlue`. This component expands or contracts based on the size of the `Box`.

Lines 62–63 create a `JTabbedPane` to display the five containers in this program. The argument `JTabbedPane.TOP` sent to the constructor indicates that the tabs should appear The argument `JTabbedPane.SCROLL_TAB_LAYOUT` specifies that the tabs should scroll if there are too many tabs to fit on one line.

The `Box` containers and the `JPanel` are attached to the `JTabbedPane` at lines 66–70. Try executing the application. When the window appears, resize the window to see how the glue components, strut components and rigid area affect the layout on each tab.

GridBagLayout *Layout Manager*

The most complex and most powerful of the predefined layout managers is GridBagLayout (in package java.awt). This layout is similar to GridLayout in that it arranges components in a grid. However, GridBagLayout is more flexible. The components can vary in size (i.e., they can occupy multiple rows and columns) and can be added in any order.

The first step in using GridBagLayout is determining the appearance of the GUI. For this step you need only a piece of paper. Draw the GUI and then draw a grid over it, dividing the components into rows and columns. The initial row and column numbers should be 0, so that the GridBagLayout layout manager can use the row and column number to properly place the components in the grid. Figure 22.18 demonstrates drawing the lines for the rows and columns over a GUI.

A GridBagConstraints object describes how a component is placed in a GridBagLayout. Several GridBagConstraints fields are summarized in Fig. 22.19.

GridBagConstraints field anchor specifies the relative position of the component in an area that it does not fill. The variable anchor is assigned one of the following GridBagConstraints constants: NORTH, NORTHEAST, EAST, SOUTHEAST, SOUTH, SOUTHWEST, WEST, NORTHWEST or CENTER. The default value is CENTER.

GridBagConstraints field fill defines how the component grows if the area in which it can be displayed is larger than the component. The variable fill is assigned one of the following GridBagConstraints constants: NONE, VERTICAL, HORIZONTAL or BOTH. The default value is NONE, which indicates that the component will not grow in either direction. VERTICAL indicates that it will grow vertically. HORIZONTAL indicates that the component will grow horizontally. BOTH indicates that it will grow in both directions.

Variables gridx and gridy specify where the upper-left corner of the component is placed in the grid. Variable gridx corresponds to the column, and variable gridy corresponds to the row. In Fig. 22.18, the JComboBox (displaying "Iron") has a gridx value of 1 and a gridy value of 2.

Variable gridwidth specifies the number of columns a component occupies. The JComboBox occupies two columns. Variable gridheight specifies the number of rows a component occupies. The JTextArea on the left side of Fig. 22.18 occupies three rows.

Variable weightx specifies how to distribute extra horizontal space to grid slots in a GridBagLayout when the container is resized. A zero value indicates that the grid slot does

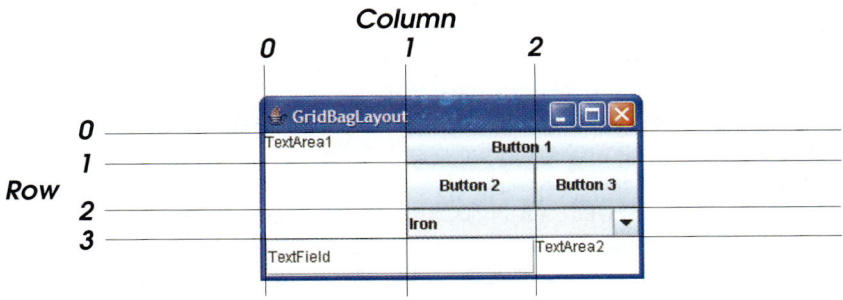

Fig. 22.18 | Designing a GUI that will use GridBagLayout.

GridBagCons-traints field	Description
anchor	Specifies the relative position (NORTH, NORTHEAST, EAST, SOUTHEAST, SOUTH, SOUTHWEST, WEST, NORTHWEST, CENTER) of the component in an area that it does not fill.
fill	Resizes the component in specified direction (NONE, HORIZONTAL, VERTICAL, BOTH) when the display area is larger than the component.
gridx	The column in which the component will be placed.
gridy	The row in which the component will be placed.
gridwidth	The number of columns the component occupies.
gridheight	The number of rows the component occupies.
weightx	The amount of extra space to allocate horizontally. The grid slot can become wider when extra space is available.
weighty	The amount of extra space to allocate vertically. The grid slot can become taller when extra space is available.

Fig. 22.19 | GridBagConstraints fields.

not grow horizontally on its own. However, if the component spans a column containing a component with nonzero weightx value, the component with zero weightx value will grow horizontally in the same proportion as the other component(s) in the same column. This is because each component must be maintained in the same row and column in which it was originally placed.

Variable weighty specifies how to distribute extra vertical space to grid slots in a Grid-BagLayout when the container is resized. A zero value indicates that the grid slot does not grow vertically on its own. However, if the component spans a row containing a component with nonzero weighty value, the component with zero weighty value grows vertically in the same proportion as the other component(s) in the same row.

In Fig. 22.18, the effects of weighty and weightx cannot easily be seen until the container is resized and additional space becomes available. Components with larger weight values occupy more of the additional space than those with smaller weight values.

Components should be given nonzero positive weight values—otherwise they will "huddle" together in the middle of the container. Figure 22.20 shows the GUI of Fig. 22.18 with all weights set to zero.

The application in Fig. 22.21 and Fig. 22.22 uses the GridBagLayout layout manager to arrange the components of the GUI in Fig. 22.18. The application does nothing except demonstrate how to use GridBagLayout.

The GUI consists of three JButtons, two JTextAreas, a JComboBox and a JTextField. The layout manager for the content pane is GridBagLayout. Lines 21–22 create the Grid-BagLayout object and set the layout manager for the JFrame to layout. Line 23 creates the GridBagConstraints object used to determine the location and size of each component in the grid. Lines 26–35 create each GUI component that will be added to the content pane.

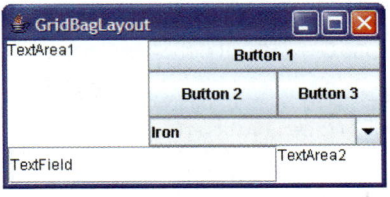

Fig. 22.20 | GridBagLayout with the weights set to zero.

Lines 39–40 configure JTextArea textArea1 and add it to the content pane. The values for weightx and weighty values are not specified in constraints, so each has the value zero by default. Thus, the JTextArea will not resize itself even if space is available.

```java
1   // Fig. 22.21: GridBagFrame.java
2   // Demonstrating GridBagLayout.
3   import java.awt.GridBagLayout;
4   import java.awt.GridBagConstraints;
5   import java.awt.Component;
6   import javax.swing.JFrame;
7   import javax.swing.JTextArea;
8   import javax.swing.JTextField;
9   import javax.swing.JButton;
10  import javax.swing.JComboBox;
11
12  public class GridBagFrame extends JFrame
13  {
14     private GridBagLayout layout; // layout of this frame
15     private GridBagConstraints constraints; // constraints of this layout
16
17     // set up GUI
18     public GridBagFrame()
19     {
20        super( "GridBagLayout" );
21        layout = new GridBagLayout();
22        setLayout( layout ); // set frame layout
23        constraints = new GridBagConstraints(); // instantiate constraints
24
25        // create GUI components
26        JTextArea textArea1 = new JTextArea( "TextArea1", 5, 10 );
27        JTextArea textArea2 = new JTextArea( "TextArea2", 2, 2 );
28
```

Fig. 22.21 | GridBagLayout layout manager. (Part 1 of 2.)

```
29        String names[] = { "Iron", "Steel", "Brass" };
30        JComboBox comboBox = new JComboBox( names );
31
32        JTextField textField = new JTextField( "TextField" );
33        JButton button1 = new JButton( "Button 1" );
34        JButton button2 = new JButton( "Button 2" );
35        JButton button3 = new JButton( "Button 3" );
36
37        // weightx and weighty for textArea1 are both 0: the default
38        // anchor for all components is CENTER: the default
39        constraints.fill = GridBagConstraints.BOTH;
40        addComponent( textArea1, 0, 0, 1, 3 );
41
42        // weightx and weighty for button1 are both 0: the default
43        constraints.fill = GridBagConstraints.HORIZONTAL;
44        addComponent( button1, 0, 1, 2, 1 );
45
46        // weightx and weighty for comboBox are both 0: the default
47        // fill is HORIZONTAL
48        addComponent( comboBox, 2, 1, 2, 1 );
49
50        // button2
51        constraints.weightx = 1000;  // can grow wider
52        constraints.weighty = 1;      // can grow taller
53        constraints.fill = GridBagConstraints.BOTH;
54        addComponent( button2, 1, 1, 1, 1 );
55
56        // fill is BOTH for button3
57        constraints.weightx = 0;
58        constraints.weighty = 0;
59        addComponent( button3, 1, 2, 1, 1 );
60
61        // weightx and weighty for textField are both 0, fill is BOTH
62        addComponent( textField, 3, 0, 2, 1 );
63
64        // weightx and weighty for textArea2 are both 0, fill is BOTH
65        addComponent( textArea2, 3, 2, 1, 1 );
66     } // end GridBagFrame constructor
67
68     // method to set constraints on
69     private void addComponent( Component component,
70        int row, int column, int width, int height )
71     {
72        constraints.gridx = column; // set gridx
73        constraints.gridy = row; // set gridy
74        constraints.gridwidth = width; // set gridwidth
75        constraints.gridheight = height; // set gridheight
76        layout.setConstraints( component, constraints ); // set constraints
77        add( component ); // add component
78     } // end method addComponent
79  } // end class GridBagFrame
```

Fig. 22.21 | GridBagLayout layout manager. (Part 2 of 2.)

```
1   // Fig. 22.22: GridBagDemo.java
2   // Demonstrating GridBagLayout.
3   import javax.swing.JFrame;
4
5   public class GridBagDemo
6   {
7      public static void main( String args[] )
8      {
9         GridBagFrame gridBagFrame = new GridBagFrame();
10        gridBagFrame.setDefaultCloseOperation( JFrame.EXIT_ON_CLOSE );
11        gridBagFrame.setSize( 300, 150 ); // set frame size
12        gridBagFrame.setVisible( true ); // display frame
13     } // end main
14  } // end class GridBagDemo
```

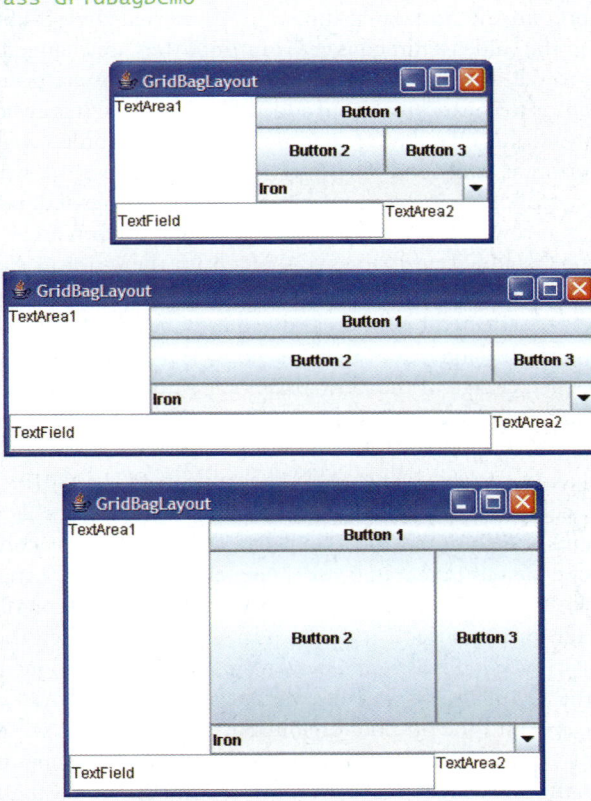

Fig. 22.22 | Test class for GridBagFrame.

However, it spans multiple rows, so the vertical size is subject to the weighty values of JButtons button2 and button3. When either button is resized vertically based on its weighty value, the JTextArea is also resized.

Line 39 sets variable fill in constraints to GridBagConstraints.BOTH, causing the JTextArea to always fill its entire allocated area in the grid. An anchor value is not specified in constraints, so the default CENTER is used. We do not use variable anchor in this application, so all the components will use the default. Line 40 calls our utility method addComponent (declared at lines 69–78). The JTextArea object, the row, the column, the number of columns to span and the number of rows to span are passed as arguments.

JButton button1 is the next component added (lines 43–44). By default, the weightx and weighty values are still zero. The fill variable is set to HORIZONTAL—the component will always fill its area in the horizontal direction. The vertical direction is not filled. The weighty value is zero, so the button will become taller only if another component in the same row has a nonzero weighty value. JButton button1 is located at row 0, column 1. One row and two columns are occupied.

JComboBox comboBox is the next component added (line 48). By default, the weightx and weighty values are zero, and the fill variable is set to HORIZONTAL. The JComboBox button will grow only in the horizontal direction. Note that the weightx, weighty and fill variables retain the values set in constraints until they are changed. The JComboBox button is placed at row 2, column 1. One row and two columns are occupied.

JButton button2 is the next component added (lines 51–54). It is given a weightx value of 1000 and a weighty value of 1. The area occupied by the button is capable of growing in the vertical and horizontal directions. The fill variable is set to BOTH, which specifies that the button will always fill the entire area. When the window is resized, button2 will grow. The button is placed at row 1, column 1. One row and one column are occupied.

JButton button3 is added next (lines 57–59). Both the weightx value and weighty value are set to zero, and the value of fill is BOTH. JButton button3 will grow if the window is resized—it is affected by the weight values of button2. Note that the weightx value for button2 is much larger than that for button3. When resizing occurs, button2 will occupy a larger percentage of the new space. The button is placed at row 1, column 2. One row and one column are occupied.

Both the JTextField textField (line 62) and JTextArea textArea2 (line 65) have a weightx value of 0 and a weighty value of 0. The value of fill is BOTH. The JTextField is placed at row 3, column 0, and the JTextArea at row 3, column 2. The JTextField occupies one row and two columns, the JTextArea one row and one column.

Method addComponent's parameters are a Component reference component and integers row, column, width and height. Lines 72–73 set the GridBagConstraints variables gridx and gridy. The gridx variable is assigned the column in which the Component will be placed, and the gridy value is assigned the row in which the Component will be placed. Lines 74–75 set the GridBagConstraints variables gridwidth and gridheight. The gridwidth variable specifies the number of columns the Component will span in the grid, and the gridheight variable specifies the number of rows the Component will span in the grid. Line 76 sets the GridBagConstraints for a component in the GridBagLayout. Method setConstraints of class GridBagLayout takes a Component argument and a GridBagConstraints argument. Line 77 adds the component to the JFrame.

When you execute this application, try resizing the window to see how the constraints for each GUI component affect its position and size in the window.

GridBagConstraints Constants *RELATIVE* and *REMAINDER*

Instead of gridx and gridy, a variation of GridBagLayout uses GridBagConstraints constants **RELATIVE** and **REMAINDER**. RELATIVE specifies that the next-to-last component in a particular row should be placed to the right of the previous component in the row. RE-MAINDER specifies that a component is the last component in a row. Any component that is not the second-to-last or last component on a row must specify values for GridbagConstraints variables gridwidth and gridheight. The application in Fig. 22.23 and Fig. 22.24 arranges components in GridBagLayout, using these constants.

Lines 21–22 create a GridBagLayout and use it to set the JFrame's layout manager. The components that are placed in GridBagLayout are created in lines 27–38—they are a JComboBox, a JTextField, a JList and five JButtons.

The JTextField is added first (lines 41–45). The weightx and weighty values are set to 1. The fill variable is set to BOTH. Line 44 specifies that the JTextField is the last component on the line. The JTextField is added to the content pane with a call to our utility method addComponent (declared at lines 79–83). Method addComponent takes a Component argument and uses GridBagLayout method setConstraints to set the constraints for the Component. Method add attaches the component to the content pane.

JButton buttons[0] (lines 48–49) has weightx and weighty values of 1. The fill variable is BOTH. Because buttons[0] is not one of the last two components on the row,

```java
1   // Fig. 22.23: GridBagFrame2.java
2   // Demonstrating GridBagLayout constants.
3   import java.awt.GridBagLayout;
4   import java.awt.GridBagConstraints;
5   import java.awt.Component;
6   import javax.swing.JFrame;
7   import javax.swing.JComboBox;
8   import javax.swing.JTextField;
9   import javax.swing.JList;
10  import javax.swing.JButton;
11
12  public class GridBagFrame2 extends JFrame
13  {
14     private GridBagLayout layout; // layout of this frame
15     private GridBagConstraints constraints; // constraints of this layout
16
17     // set up GUI
18     public GridBagFrame2()
19     {
20        super( "GridBagLayout" );
21        layout = new GridBagLayout();
22        setLayout( layout ); // set frame layout
23        constraints = new GridBagConstraints(); // instantiate constraints
24
25        // create GUI components
26        String metals[] = { "Copper", "Aluminum", "Silver" };
27        JComboBox comboBox = new JComboBox( metals );
28
29        JTextField textField = new JTextField( "TextField" );
30
31        String fonts[] = { "Serif", "Monospaced" };T
32        JList list = new JList( fonts );
```

Fig. 22.23 | GridBagConstraints constants RELATIVE and REMAINDER. (Part 1 of 2.)

```
33
34          String names[] = { "zero", "one", "two", "three", "four" };
35          JButton buttons[] = new JButton[ names.length ];
36
37          for ( int count = 0; count < buttons.length; count++ )
38             buttons[ count ] = new JButton( names[ count ] );
39
40          // define GUI component constraints for textField
41          constraints.weightx = 1;
42          constraints.weighty = 1;
43          constraints.fill = GridBagConstraints.BOTH;
44          constraints.gridwidth = GridBagConstraints.REMAINDER;
45          addComponent( textField );
46
47          // buttons[0] -- weightx and weighty are 1: fill is BOTH
48          constraints.gridwidth = 1;
49          addComponent( buttons[ 0 ] );
50
51          // buttons[1] -- weightx and weighty are 1: fill is BOTH
52          constraints.gridwidth = GridBagConstraints.RELATIVE;
53          addComponent( buttons[ 1 ] );
54
55          // buttons[2] -- weightx and weighty are 1: fill is BOTH
56          constraints.gridwidth = GridBagConstraints.REMAINDER;
57          addComponent( buttons[ 2 ] );
58
59          // comboBox -- weightx is 1: fill is BOTH
60          constraints.weighty = 0;
61          constraints.gridwidth = GridBagConstraints.REMAINDER;
62          addComponent( comboBox );
63
64          // buttons[3] -- weightx is 1: fill is BOTH
65          constraints.weighty = 1;
66          constraints.gridwidth = GridBagConstraints.REMAINDER;
67          addComponent( buttons[ 3 ] );
68
69          // buttons[4] -- weightx and weighty are 1: fill is BOTH
70          constraints.gridwidth = GridBagConstraints.RELATIVE;
71          addComponent( buttons[ 4 ] );
72
73          // list -- weightx and weighty are 1: fill is BOTH
74          constraints.gridwidth = GridBagConstraints.REMAINDER;
75          addComponent( list );
76       } // end GridBagFrame2 constructor
77
78       // add a component to the container
79       private void addComponent( Component component )
80       {
81          layout.setConstraints( component, constraints );
82          add( component ); // add component
83       } // end method addComponent
84    } // end class GridBagFrame2
```

Fig. 22.23 | GridBagConstraints constants RELATIVE and REMAINDER. (Part 2 of 2.)

```
1   // Fig. 22.24: GridBagDemo2.java
2   // Demonstrating GridBagLayout constants.
3   import javax.swing.JFrame;
4
5   public class GridBagDemo2
6   {
7      public static void main( String args[] )
8      {
9         GridBagFrame2 gridBagFrame = new GridBagFrame2();
10        gridBagFrame.setDefaultCloseOperation( JFrame.EXIT_ON_CLOSE );
11        gridBagFrame.setSize( 300, 200 ); // set frame size
12        gridBagFrame.setVisible( true ); // display frame
13     } // end main
14  } // end class GridBagDemo2
```

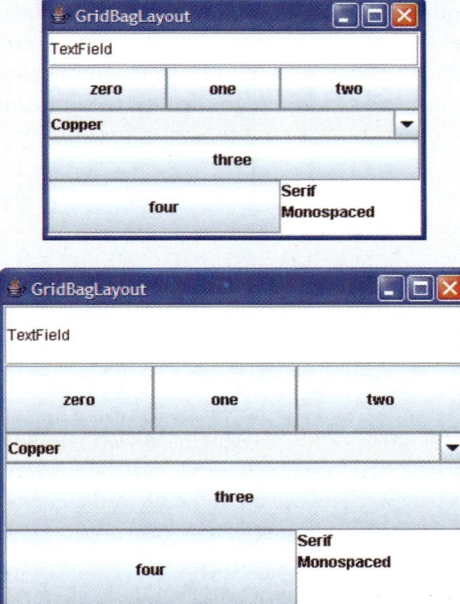

Fig. 22.24 | Test class for `GridBagDemo2`.

it is given a `gridwidth` of 1 and so will occupy one column. The `JButton` is added to the content pane with a call to utility method `addComponent`.

    `JButton buttons[ 1 ]` (lines 52–53) has `weightx` and `weighty` values of 1. The `fill` variable is `BOTH`. Line 52 specifies that the `JButton` is to be placed relative to the previous component. The `Button` is added to the `JFrame` with a call to `addComponent`.

    `JButton buttons[ 2 ]` (lines 56–57) has `weightx` and `weighty` values of 1. The `fill` variable is `BOTH`. This `JButton` is the last component on the line, so `REMAINDER` is used. The `JButton` is added to the content pane with a call to `addComponent`.

The JComboBox (lines 60–62) has a weightx of 1 and a weighty of 0. The JComboBox will not grow in the vertical direction. The JComboBox is the only component on the line, so REMAINDER is used. The JComboBox is added to the content pane with a call to addComponent.

JButton buttons[3] (lines 65–67) has weightx and weighty values of 1. The fill variable is BOTH. This JButton is the only component on the line, so REMAINDER is used. The JButton is added to the content pane with a call to addComponent.

JButton buttons[4] (lines 70–71) has weightx and weighty values of 1. The fill variable is BOTH. This JButton is the next-to-last component on the line, so RELATIVE is used. The JButton is added to the content pane with a call to addComponent.

The JList (lines 74–75) has weightx and weighty values of 1. The fill variable is BOTH. The JList is added to the content pane with a call to addComponent.

22.10 Wrap-Up

This chapter completes our introduction to GUI. In this chapter, you learned about more advanced GUI topics, such as menus, sliders, pop-up menus and the multiple-document interface. All these components can be added to existing applications to make them easier to use and understand. In the next chapter, you will learn about multithreading, a powerful capability that allows applications to use threads to perform multiple tasks at once.

Summary

- JSliders enable the user to select from a range of integer values. JSliders can display major tick marks, minor tick marks and labels for the tick marks. They also support snap-to ticks, where positioning the thumb between two tick marks causes the thumb to snap to the closest tick mark.

- If a JSlider has the focus, the left and right arrow keys cause the thumb of the JSlider to decrease or increase by 1. The down and up arrow keys also cause the thumb of the JSlider to decrease or increase by 1, respectively. The *PgDn* (page down) *key* and *PgUp* (page up) *key* cause the thumb of the JSlider to decrease or increase by block increments of one-tenth of the range of values, respectively. The *Home key* moves the thumb to the minimum value of the JSlider, and the *End key* moves it to the maximum value.

- JSliders have either horizontal or vertical orientation. For a horizontal JSlider, the minimum value is at the extreme left and the maximum value is at the extreme right. For a vertical JSlider, the minimum value is at the extreme bottom and the maximum value is at the extreme top. The position of the thumb indicates the current value of the JSlider. Method getValue of class JSlider returns the current thumb position.

- Method setMajorTickSpacing of class JSlider sets the spacing for tick marks on a JSlider. Method setPaintTicks with a true argument indicates that the tick marks should be displayed.

- JSliders generate ChangeEvents when the user interacts with a JSlider. A ChangeListener declares method stateChanged that can respond to ChangeEvents.

- Every window generates window events when the user manipulates it. Interface WindowListener provides seven window-event-handling methods—windowActivated, windowClosed, windowClosing, windowDeactivated, windowDeiconified, windowIconified and windowOpened.

- Menus are an integral part of GUIs. Menus allow the user to perform actions without unnecessarily cluttering a graphical user interface with extra GUI components. In Swing GUIs, menus can be attached only to objects of classes with method setJMenuBar (e.g., JFrame and JApplet).

- The classes used to declare menus are JMenuBar, JMenuItem, JMenu, JCheckBoxMenuItem and JRadioButtonMenuItem.

- A JMenuBar is a container for menus. A JMenuItem is a GUI component inside a menu that, when selected, causes an action to be performed. A JMenu contains menu items and can be added to a JMenuBar or to other JMenus as submenus.

- When a menu is clicked, it expands to show its list of menu items. JMenu method addSeparator adds a separator line to a menu.

- When a JCheckBoxMenuItem is selected, a check appears to the left of the menu item. When the JCheckBoxMenuItem is selected again, the check is removed.

- When multiple JRadioButtonMenuItems are maintained as part of a ButtonGroup, only one item in the group can be selected at a given time. When an item is selected, a filled circle appears to its left. When another JRadioButtonMenuItem is selected, the filled circle to the left of the previously selected item is removed.

- AbstractButton method setMnemonic specifies the mnemonic for an AbstractButton. Mnemonic characters are normally displayed with an underline.

- A modal dialog box does not allow access to any other window in the application until the dialog is dismissed. The dialogs displayed with class JOptionPane are modal dialogs. Class JDialog can be used to create your own modal or nonmodal dialogs.

- Context-sensitive pop-up menus are created with class JPopupMenu. On most systems, the pop-up trigger event occurs when the user presses and releases the right mouse button. MouseEvent method isPopupTrigger returns true if the pop-up trigger event occurred.

- JPopupMenu method show displays a JPopupMenu. The first argument specifies the origin component, which helps determine where the JPopupMenu will appear. The last two arguments are the coordinates from the origin component's upper-left corner, at which the JPopupMenu appears.

- Class UIManager contains nested class LookAndFeelInfo that maintains information about a look-and-feel.

- UIManager static method getInstalledLookAndFeels gets an array of UIManager.LookAndFeelInfo objects that describe the available look-and-feels.

- UIManager static method setLookAndFeel changes the look-and-feel. SwingUtilities static method updateComponentTreeUI changes the look-and-feel of every component attached to its Component argument to the new look-and-feel.

- Many of today's applications use a multiple-document interface (MDI) to manage several open documents that are being processed in parallel. Swing's JDesktopPane and JInternalFrame classes provide support for creating multiple-document interfaces.

- A JTabbedPane arranges GUI components into layers in which only one layer is visible at a time. Users access each layer via a tab similar to those on folders in a file cabinet. When the user clicks a tab, the appropriate layer is displayed.

- BoxLayout is a layout manager that allows GUI components to be arranged left-to-right or top-to-bottom in a container.

- Class Box declares a container with BoxLayout as its default layout manager and provides static methods to create a Box with a horizontal or vertical BoxLayout.

- GridBagLayout is a layout manager similar to GridLayout. It differs in that each component size can vary, and components can be added in any order.

- A GridBagConstraints object specifies how a component is placed in a GridBagLayout. Method setConstraints of class GridBagLayout takes a Component argument and a GridBagConstraints argument and sets the constraints of the Component.

Terminology

add method of class JMenuBar
addWindowListener method of class Window
anchor field of class GridBagConstraints
border
BOTH constant of class GridBagConstraints
Box class
BoxLayout class
CENTER constant of class GridBagConstraints
ChangeEvent class
ChangeListener interface
child window
context-sensitive pop-up menu
createGlue method of class Box
createHorizontalBox method of class Box
createHorizontalGlue method of class Box
createHorizontalStrut method of class Box
createRigidArea method of class Box
createVerticalBox method of class Box
createVerticalGlue method of class Box
createVerticalStrut method of class Box
Dimension class
dispose method of class Window
document
EAST constant of class GridBagConstraints
getClassName method of class
    UIManager.LookAndFeelInfo
getInstalledLookAndFeels method of class
    UIManager
getPreferredSize method of class Component
getSelectedText method of class
    JTextComponent
getValue method of class JSlider
GridBagConstraints class
GridBagLayout class
gridheight field of class GridBagConstraints
gridwidth field of class GridBagConstraints
gridx field of class GridBagConstraints
gridy field of class GridBagConstraints
HORIZONTAL constant of GridBagConstraints
horizontal glue
isPopupTrigger method of class MouseEvent
isSelected method of class AbstractButton
JCheckBoxMenuItem class
JDesktopPane class
JDialog class
JFrame class
JInternalFrame class
JMenu class
JMenuBar class

JMenuItem class
JRadioButtonMenuItem class
JSlider class
JTabbedPane class
line wrapping
LookAndFeelInfo nested class of class UIManager
menu
menu bar
menu item
metal look-and-feel
minor tick marks of JSlider
mnemonic
modal dialog box
multiple document interface (MDI)
NONE constant of class GridBagConstraints
NORTH constant of class GridBagConstraints
NORTHEAST constant of class
    GridBagConstraints
NORTHWEST constant of class
    GridBagConstraints
opaque
origin component
pack method of class Window
paintComponent method of class JComponent
parent window
parent window for a dialog box
pluggable look and feel (PLAF)
pop-up trigger event
RELATIVE constant of class GridBagConstraints
REMAINDER constant of class
    GridBagConstraints
rigid area
scrollbar policies
selected text
separator line in a menu
setConstraints method of class GridBagLayout
setDefaultCloseOperation method of class
    JFrame
setInverted method of class JSlider
setJMenuBar method of class JFrame
setLocation method of class Component
setLookAndFeel method of class UIManager
setMajorTickSpacing method of class JSlider
setMnemonic method of class AbstractButton
setOpaque method of class JComponent
setPaintTicks method of class JSlider
setSelected method of class AbstractButton
setVerticalScrollBarPolicy method of
    JSlider

Self-Review Exercises

22.1   Fill in the blanks in each of the following statements:

a) The _____ class is used to create a menu object.

b) The _____ method of class `JMenu` places a separator bar in a menu.

c) `JSlider` events are handled by the _____ method of interface _____.

d) The `GridBagConstraints` instance variable _____ is set to CENTER by default.

22.2   State whether each of the following is *true* or *false*. If *false*, explain why.

a) When the programmer creates a `JFrame`, a minimum of one menu must be created and added to the `JFrame`.

b) The variable `fill` belongs to the `GridBagLayout` class.

c) Drawing on a GUI component is performed with respect to the (0, 0) upper-left corner coordinate of the component.

d) The default layout for a Box is `BoxLayout`.

22.3   Find the error(s) in each of the following and explain how to correct the error(s).

a) `JMenubar b;`

b) `mySlider = JSlider( 1000, 222, 100, 450 );`

c) `gbc.fill = GridBagConstraints.NORTHWEST;  // set fill`

d) `// override to paint on a customized Swing component`

```
public void paintcomponent( Graphics g )
{
    g.drawString( "HELLO", 50, 50 );
} // end method paintComponent
```

e) `// create a JFrame and display it`

```
JFrame f = new JFrame( "A Window" );
f.setVisible( true );
```

Answers to Self-Review Exercises

22.1   a) JMenu. b) addSeparator. c) stateChanged, ChangeListener. d) anchor.

22.2   a) False. A JFrame does not require any menus.
b) False. The variable fill belongs to the GridBagConstraints class.
c) True.
d) True.

22.3   a) JMenubar should be JMenuBar.
b) The first argument to the constructor should be either SwingConstants.HORIZONTAL or SwingConstants.VERTICAL, and the keyword new must be used after the = operator.
c) The constant should be either BOTH, HORIZONTAL, VERTICAL or NONE.
d) paintcomponent should be paintComponent, and the method should call super.paintComponent(g) as its first statement.
e) The JFrame's setSize method must also be called to establish the size of the window.

Exercises

22.4   Fill in the blanks in each of the following statements:
a) A JMenuItem that is a JMenu is called a(n) _____
b) Method _____ attaches a JMenuBar to a JFrame.
c) Container class _____ has a default BoxLayout.
d) A(n) _____ manages a set of child windows declared with class JInternalFrame.

22.5   State whether each of the following is *true* or *false*. If *false*, explain why.
a) Menus require a JMenuBar object so they can be attached to a JFrame.
b) BoxLayout is the default layout manager for a JFrame.
c) Method setEditable is a JTextComponent method.
d) Class JFrame directly extends class Container.
e) JApplets can contain menus.

22.6   Find the error(s) in each of the following. Explain how to correct the error(s).
a) x.add(new JMenuItem("Submenu Color")); // create submenu
b) container.setLayout(m = new GridbagLayout());

22.7   Write a program that displays a circle of random size and calculates and displays the area, radius, diameter and circumference. Use the following equations: *diameter = 2 ∞ radius, area = π ∞ radius², circumference = 2 ∞ π ∞ radius*. Use the constant Math.PI for pi (π). All drawing should be done on a subclass of JPanel, and the results of the calculations should be displayed in a read-only JTextArea.

22.8   Enhance the program in Exercise 22.7 by allowing the user to alter the radius with a JSlider. The program should work for all radii in the range from 100 to 200. As the radius changes, the diameter, area and circumference should be updated and displayed. The initial radius should be 150. Use the equations from Exercise 22.7. All drawing should be done on a subclass of JPanel, and the results of the calculations should be displayed in a read-only JTextArea.

22.9   Explore the effects of varying the weightx and weighty values of the program in Fig. 22.21. What happens when a slot has a nonzero weight but is not allowed to fill the whole area (i.e., the fill value is not BOTH)?

22.10   Write a program that uses the paintComponent method to draw the current value of a JSlider on a subclass of JPanel. In addition, provide a JTextField where a specific value can be entered. The JTextField should display the current value of the JSlider at all times. A JLabel should be used to identify the JTextField. The JSlider methods setValue and getValue should be used. [*Note:* The setValue method is a public method that does not return a value and takes one integer argument, the JSlider value, which determines the position of the thumb.]

22.11   Modify the program in Fig. 22.13 by adding a minimum of two new tabs.

22.12   Declare a subclass of JPanel called MyColorChooser that provides three JSlider objects and three JTextField objects. Each JSlider represents the values from 0 to 255 for the red, green and blue parts of a color. Use these values as the arguments to the Color constructor to create a new Color object. Display the current value of each JSlider in the corresponding JTextField. When the user changes the value of the JSlider, the JTextField should be changed accordingly. Use your new GUI component as part of an application that displays the current Color value by drawing a filled rectangle.

22.13   Modify the MyColorChooser class of Exercise 22.12 to allow the user to enter an integer value into a JTextField to set the red, green or blue value. When the user presses *Enter* in the JTextField, the corresponding JSlider should be set to the appropriate value.

22.14   Modify the application in Exercise 22.13 to draw the current color as a rectangle on an instance of a subclass of JPanel which provides its own paintComponent method to draw the rectangle and provides *set* methods to set the red, green and blue values for the current color. When any *set* method is invoked, the drawing panel should automatically repaint itself.

22.15   Modify the application in Exercise 22.14 to allow the user to drag the mouse across the drawing panel (a subclass of JPanel) to draw a shape in the current color. Enable the user to choose what shape to draw.

22.16   Modify the application in Exercise 22.15 to provide the user with the ability to terminate the application by clicking the close box on the window that is displayed and by selecting Exit from a File menu. Use the techniques shown in Fig. 22.5.

22.17   *(Complete Drawing Application)* Using the techniques developed in this chapter and Chapter 11, create a complete drawing application. The program should use the GUI components from Chapter 11 and Chapter 22 to enable the user to select the shape, color and fill characteristics. Each shape should be stored in an array of MyShape objects, where MyShape is the superclass in your hierarchy of shape classes. Use a JDesktopPane and JInternalFrames to allow the user to create multiple separate drawings in separate child windows. Create the user interface as a separate child window containing all the GUI components that allow the user to determine the characteristics of the shape to be drawn. The user can then click in any JInternalFrame to draw the shape.

23

Multithreading

OBJECTIVES

In this chapter you will learn:

- What threads are and why they are useful.
- How threads enable you to manage concurrent activities.
- The life cycle of a thread.
- Thread priorities and scheduling.
- To create and execute `Runnable`s.
- Thread synchronization.
- What producer/consumer relationships are and how they are implemented with multithreading.
- To display output from multiple threads in a Swing GUI.
- About `Callable` and `Future`.

23.1 Introduction

It would be nice if we could perform one action at a time and perform it well, but that is usually difficult to do. The human body performs a great variety of operations in parallel—or, as we will say throughout this chapter, concurrently. Respiration, blood circulation, digestion, thinking and walking, for example, can occur concurrently. All the senses—sight, touch, smell, taste and hearing—can be employed at once. Computers, too, can perform operations concurrently. It is common for personal computers to compile a program, send a file to a printer and receive electronic mail messages over a network concurrently. Only computers that have multiple processors can truly execute operations concurrently. Operating systems on single-processor computers use various techniques to simulate concurrency, but on such computers only a single operation can execute at once.

Most programming languages do not enable programmers to specify concurrent activities. Rather, the languages generally provide control statements that only enable programmers to perform one action at a time, proceeding to the next action after the previous one has finished. Historically, concurrency has been implemented with operating system primitives available only to experienced systems programmers.

The Ada programming language, developed by the United States Department of Defense, made concurrency primitives widely available to defense contractors building military command-and-control systems. However, Ada has not been widely used in academia and commercial industry.

Java makes concurrency available to the applications programmer through its APIs. The programmer specifies that applications contain threads of execution, where each thread designates a portion of a program that may execute concurrently with other threads. This capability, called multithreading, gives the Java programmer powerful capabilities not available in the core C and C++ languages on which Java is based.

Performance Tip 23.1

A problem with single-threaded applications is that lengthy activities must complete before other activities can begin. In a multithreaded application, threads can be distributed across multiple processors (if they are available) so that multiple tasks are performed concurrently and the application can operate more efficiently. Multithreading can also increase performance on single-processor systems that simulate concurrency—when one thread cannot proceed, another can use the processor.

Portability Tip 23.1

Unlike languages that do not have built-in multithreading capabilities (such as C and C++) and must therefore make nonportable calls to operating system multithreading primitives, Java includes multithreading primitives as part of the language itself and as part of its libraries. This facilitates manipulating threads in a portable manner across platforms.

We will discuss many applications of concurrent programming. For example, when programs download large files, such as audio clips or video clips, over the Internet, users may not want to wait until an entire lengthy clip downloads before starting the playback. To solve this problem, we can put multiple threads to work—one thread downloads the clip, and another plays it. These activities proceed concurrently. To avoid choppy playback, we synchronize the threads so that the player thread does not begin until there is a sufficient amount of the clip in memory to keep the player thread busy.

Another example of multithreading is Java's garbage collection. C and C++ require the programmer to reclaim dynamically allocated memory explicitly. Java provides a garbage-collector thread that reclaims memory which is no longer needed.

Writing multithreaded programs can be tricky. Although the human mind can perform functions concurrently, people find it difficult to jump between parallel trains of thought. To see why multithreading can be difficult to program and understand, try the following experiment: Open three books to page 1, and try reading the books concurrently. Read a few words from the first book, then read a few words from the second book, then read a few words from the third book, then loop back and read the next few words from the first book, and so on. After this experiment, you will appreciate the challenges of multithreading—switching between books, reading briefly, remembering your place in each book, moving the book you are reading closer so you can see it and pushing books you are not reading aside—and, amid all this chaos, trying to comprehend the content of the books!

Programming concurrent applications is a difficult and error-prone undertaking. Even some of the simplest concurrent applications are beyond the capability of beginner programmers. If you find that you must use synchronization in a program, you should follow some simple guidelines. First, use existing classes from the Java API (such as the ArrayBlockingQueue class discussed in Section 23.9, Producer/Consumer Relationship: ArrayBlockingQueue) that manage synchronization for you. The classes in the Java API have been fully tested and debugged and help you avoid common traps and pitfalls. Second, if you find that you need more custom functionality than that provided in the Java APIs, you should use the synchronized keyword and Object methods wait, notify and notifyAll (discussed in Section 23.12, Monitors and Monitor Locks). Finally, if you need even more complex capabilities, then you should use the Lock and Condition interfaces that are introduced in Section 23.5, Thread Synchronization).

The Lock and Condition interfaces are advanced tools and should be used only by advanced programmers who are familiar with the common traps and pitfalls of concurrent programming with synchronization. We explain these topics in this chapter for a number of reasons. For one, they provide a solid basis for understanding how concurrent applications synchronize access to shared memory. Even, if an application does not use these tools explicitly, the concepts are still important to understand. We have also discussed these topics to highlight the new concurrency features introduced by J2SE 5.0. Finally, by showing you the complexity involved in using these low-level features, we hope to impress upon you the importance of using prepackaged concurrent capabilities whenever possible.

23.2 Thread States: Life Cycle of a Thread

At any time, a thread is said to be in one of several **thread states** that are illustrated in the UML state diagram in Fig. 23.1. A few of the terms in the diagram are defined in later sections.

A new thread begins its life cycle in the *new* state. It remains in this state until the program starts the thread, which places the thread in the *runnable* state. A thread in this state is considered to be executing its task.

Sometimes a thread transitions to the *waiting* state while the thread waits for another thread to perform a task. Once in this state, a thread transitions back to the *runnable* state only when another thread signals the waiting thread to continue executing.

A *runnable* thread can enter the *timed waiting* state for a specified interval of time. A thread in this state transitions back to the *runnable* state when that time interval expires or when the event it is waiting for occurs. *Timed waiting* threads cannot use a processor, even if one is available. A thread can transition to the *timed waiting* state if it provides an optional wait interval when it is waiting for another thread to perform a task. Such a thread will return to the *runnable* state when it is signaled by another thread or when the timed interval expires—whichever comes first. Another way to place a thread in the *timed waiting* state is to put the thread to sleep. A **sleeping thread** remains in the *timed waiting* state for a designated period of time (called a **sleep interval**) at which point it returns to

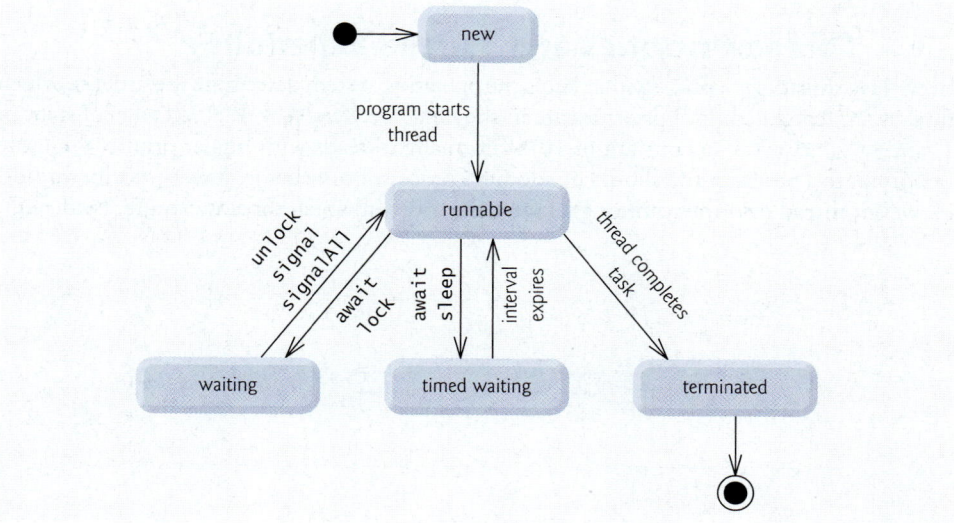

Fig. 23.1 | Thread life-cycle UML state diagram.

the *runnable* state. Threads sleep when they momentarily do not have work to perform. For example, a word processor may contain a thread that periodically writes a copy of the current document to disk for recovery purposes. If the thread did not sleep between successive backups, it would require a loop in which it continually tests whether it should write a copy of the document to disk. This loop would consume processor time without performing productive work, thus reducing system performance. In this case, it is more efficient for the thread to specify a sleep interval (equal to the period between successive backups) and enter the *timed waiting* state. This thread is returned to the *runnable* state when its sleep interval expires, at which point it writes a copy of the document to disk and reenters the *timed waiting* state.

A *runnable* thread enters the *terminated* state when it completes its task or otherwise terminates (perhaps due to an error condition). In the UML state diagram in Fig. 23.1, the *terminated* state is followed by the UML final state (the bull's-eye symbol) to indicate the end of the state transitions.

At the operating-system level, Java's *runnable* state actually encompasses two separate states (Fig. 23.2). The operating system hides these two states from the Java Virtual Machine (JVM), which only sees the *runnable* state. When a thread first transitions to the *runnable* state from the *new* state, the thread is in the *ready* state. A *ready* thread enters the *running* state (i.e., begins executing) when the operating system assigns the thread to a processor—also known as **dispatching the thread**. In most operating systems, each thread is given a small amount of processor time—called a **quantum** or **timeslice**—with which to perform its task. When the thread's quantum expires, the thread returns to the *ready* state and the operating system assigns another thread to the processor (see Section 23.3). Transitions between these states are handled solely by the operating system. The JVM does not "see" these two states—it simply views a thread as being in the *runnable* state and leaves it up to the operating system to transition threads between the *ready* and *running* states. The process that an operating system uses to decide which thread to dispatch is known as **thread scheduling** and is dependent on thread priorities (discussed in the next section).

23.3 Thread Priorities and Thread Scheduling

Every Java thread has a **priority** that helps the operating system determine the order in which threads are scheduled. Java priorities are in the range between `MIN_PRIORITY` (a constant of 1) and `MAX_PRIORITY` (a constant of 10). Informally, threads with higher priority are more important to a program and should be allocated processor time before lower-priority threads. However, thread priorities cannot guarantee the order in which threads execute. By default,

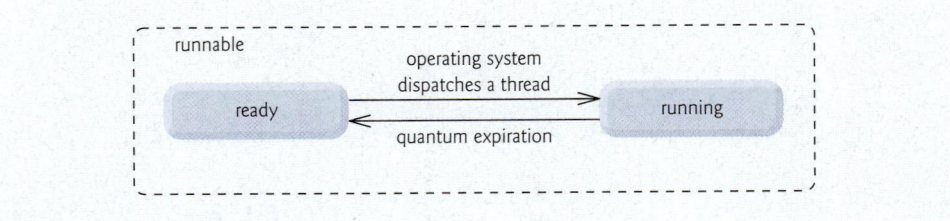

Fig. 23.2 | Operating system's internal view of Java's runnable state.

every thread is given priority NORM_PRIORITY (a constant of 5). Each new thread inherits the priority of the thread that created it.

[*Note:* These constants (MAX_PRIORITY, MIN_PRIORITY and NORM_PRIORITY) are declared in the **Thread** class. It is recommended that you do not explicitly create and use Thread objects to implement concurrency, but rather use the Runnable interface (which is described in Section 23.4). The Thread class does contain some static methods that are useful, as you will see later in this chapter.]

Most Java platforms support timeslicing, which enables threads of equal priority to share a processor. Without timeslicing, each thread in a set of equal-priority threads runs to completion (unless it leaves the *runnable* state and enters the *waiting* or *timed waiting* state, or gets interrupted by a higher-priority thread) before other threads of equal priority get a chance to execute. With timeslicing, even if the thread has not finished executing when the quantum expires, the processor is taken away from that thread and given to the next thread of equal priority, if one is available.

The job of an operating system's **thread scheduler** is to determine which thread runs next. One simple implementation of the thread scheduler keeps the highest-priority thread *running* at all times and, if there is more than one highest-priority thread, ensures that all such threads execute for a quantum each in **round-robin** fashion. Figure 23.3 illustrates a multi-level priority queue for threads. In the figure, assuming a single-processor computer, threads *A* and *B* each execute for a quantum in round-robin fashion until both threads complete execution. This means that *A* gets a quantum of time to run. Then *B* gets a quantum. Then *A* gets another quantum. Then *B* gets another quantum. This continues until one thread completes. The processor then devotes all its power to the thread that remains (unless another thread of that priority becomes ready). Next, thread *C* runs to completion (assuming that no higher-priority threads arrive). Threads *D*, *E* and *F* each execute for a quantum in round-robin fashion until they all complete execution (again assuming that no higher-priority threads arrive). This process continues until all threads run to completion.

Portability Tip 23.2

Thread scheduling is platform dependent—an application that uses multithreading could behave differently on separate Java implementations.

When a higher-priority thread enters the *ready* state, the operating system generally preempts the currently *running* thread (an operation known as **preemptive scheduling**). Depending on the operating system, higher-priority threads could postpone—possibly indefinitely—the execution of lower-priority threads. Such **indefinite postponement** often is referred to more colorfully as **starvation**.

Portability Tip 23.3

When designing applets and applications that use threads, you must consider the threading capabilities of all the platforms on which the applets and applications will execute.

J2SE 5.0 provides higher-level concurrency utilities to hide some complexity and make multithreaded programs less error prone (though they are still certainly complex). Thread priorities are still used behind the scenes to interact with the operating system, but most programmers who use J2SE 5.0 multithreading will not be concerned with setting and adjusting thread priorities. You can learn more about priorities and threading at java.sun.com/j2se/5.0/docs/api/java/lang/Thread.html.

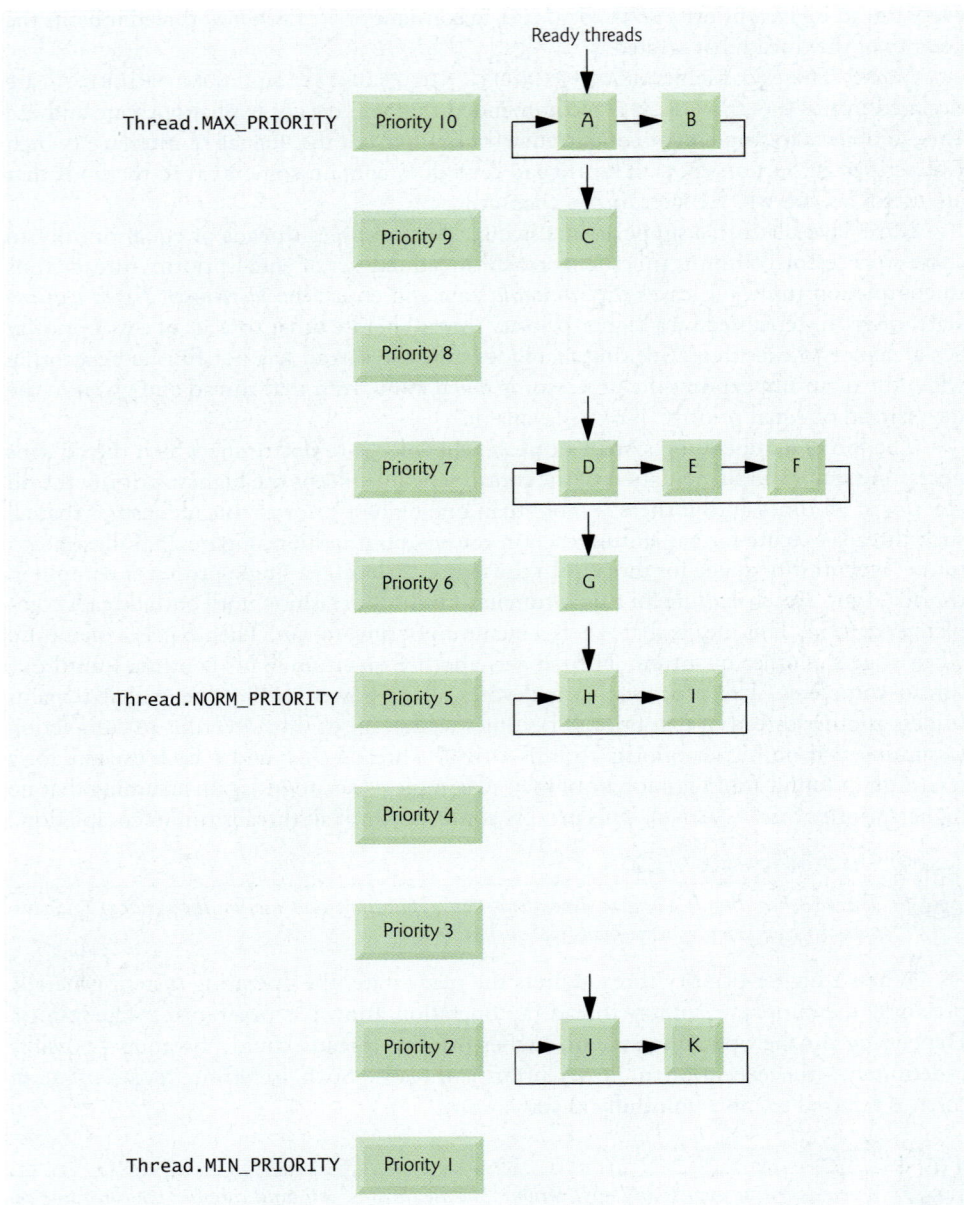

Fig. 23.3 | Thread-priority scheduling.

23.4 Creating and Executing Threads

In J2SE 5.0, the preferred means of creating a multithreaded application is to implement the **Runnable** interface (package java.lang) and use built-in methods and classes to create Threads that execute the Runnables. The Runnable interface declares a single method named `run`. Runnables are executed by an object of a class that implements the `Executor` interface (package `java.util.concurrent`). This interface declares a single method named `execute`. An Executor object typically creates and manages a group of threads called a thread pool. These threads execute the Runnable objects passed to the `execute` method. The Executor assigns each Runnable to one of the available threads in the thread pool. If there are no available threads in the thread pool, the Executor creates a new thread or waits for a thread to become available and assigns that thread the Runnable that was passed to method `execute`. Depending on the Executor type, there may be a limit to the number of threads that can be created. Interface `ExecutorService` (package java.util.concurrent) is a subinterface of Executor that declares a number of other methods for managing the life cycle of the Executor. An object that implements the ExecutorService interface can be created using `static` methods declared in class `Executors` (package java.util.concurrent). We use these interfaces and methods in the next application, which executes three threads.

Class `PrintTask` (Fig. 23.4) implements `Runnable` (line 5), so that each `PrintTask` object can execute concurrently. Variable `sleepTime` (line 7) stores a random integer value (line 17) chosen when the `PrintTask` constructor executes. Each thread running a `PrintTask` object sleeps for the amount of time specified by the corresponding `PrintTask` object's `sleepTime`, then outputs its name.

When a `PrintTask` is assigned to a processor for the first time, its `run` method (lines 21–38) begins execution. Lines 25–26 display a message indicating the name of the currently executing thread and stating that the thread is going to sleep for a certain number of milliseconds. Line 26 uses the `threadName` field which was initialized at line 14 with the `PrintTask` constructor's argument. Line 28 invokes `static` method `sleep` of class Thread to place the thread into the *timed waiting* state. At this point, the thread loses the processor, and the system allows another thread to execute. When the thread awakens, it reenters the *runnable* state. When the `PrintTask` is assigned to a processor again, line 37 outputs the thread's name in a message that indicates the thread is done sleeping—then method `run` terminates. Note that the `catch` at lines 31–34 is required because method `sleep` might throw an `InterruptedException`, which is a checked exception. Such an exception occurs if a sleeping thread's `interrupt` method is called. Most programmers do not directly manipulate Thread objects, so InterruptedExceptions are unlikely to occur.

Figure 23.5 creates three threads of execution using the `PrintTask` class. Method `main` (lines 8–28) creates and names three `PrintTask` objects (lines 11–13). Line 18 creates a new ExecutorService. This line uses the `newFixedThreadPool` method of class Executors, which creates a pool consisting of a fixed number of Threads as indicated by the method's argument (in this case, 3). These Threads are used by threadExecutor to execute the Runnables. If method execute is called and all the threads in the ExecutorService are being used, the Runnable will be placed in a queue and assigned to the first thread that completes its previous task. Executors method `newCachedThreadPool` returns an ExecutorService that creates new threads as they are needed by the application.

Lines 21–23 invoke the ExecutorService's execute method. This method creates a new Thread inside the ExecutorService to run the Runnable passed to it as an argument (in this case a PrintTask) and transitions that Thread from the *new* state to the *runnable* state. Method execute returns immediately from each invocation—the program does not wait for each PrintTask to finish. Line 25 calls ExecutorService method `shutdown`,

```
1    // Fig. 23.4: PrintTask.java
2    // PrintTask class sleeps for a random time from 0 to 5 seconds
3    import java.util.Random;
4
5    class PrintTask implements Runnable
6    {
7       private int sleepTime; // random sleep time for thread
8       private String threadName; // name of thread
9       private static Random generator = new Random();
10
11      // assign name to thread
12      public PrintTask( String name )
13      {
14         threadName = name; // set name of thread
15
16         // pick random sleep time between 0 and 5 seconds
17         sleepTime = generator.nextInt( 5000 );
18      } // end PrintTask constructor
19
20      // method run is the code to be executed by new thread
21      public void run()
22      {
23         try // put thread to sleep for sleepTime amount of time
24         {
25            System.out.printf( "%s going to sleep for %d milliseconds.\n",
26               threadName, sleepTime );
27
28            Thread.sleep( sleepTime ); // put thread to sleep
29         } // end try
30         // if thread interrupted while sleeping, print stack trace
31         catch ( InterruptedException exception )
32         {
33            exception.printStackTrace();
34         } // end catch
35
36         // print thread name
37         System.out.printf( "%s done sleeping\n", threadName );
38      } // end method run
39   } // end class PrintTask
```

Fig. 23.4 | Threads sleeping and awakening.

which will end each Thread in threadExecutor as soon as each finishes executing its Runnable. Line 27 outputs a message indicating that the threads were started. [*Note:* Line 18 creates the ExecutorService using method newFixedThreadPool and the argument 3. This program executes only three Runnables, so a new Thread will be created by the ExecutorService for each Runnable. If the program executed more than three Runnables, additional Threads would not be created, but rather an existing Thread would be reused when it completed the Runnable assigned to it.]

The code in method main executes in the **main thread**. This thread is created by the JVM and executes the main method. The code in the run method of PrintTask (lines 21–38 of Fig. 23.4) executes in the threads created by the ExecutorService. When method

```
 1    // Fig. 23.5: RunnableTester.java
 2    // Multiple threads printing at different intervals.
 3    import java.util.concurrent.Executors;
 4    import java.util.concurrent.ExecutorService;
 5
 6    public class RunnableTester
 7    {
 8       public static void main( String[] args )
 9       {
10          // create and name each runnable
11          PrintTask task1 = new PrintTask( "thread1" );
12          PrintTask task2 = new PrintTask( "thread2" );
13          PrintTask task3 = new PrintTask( "thread3" );
14
15          System.out.println( "Starting threads" );
16
17          // create ExecutorService to manage threads
18          ExecutorService threadExecutor = Executors.newFixedThreadPool( 3 );
19
20          // start threads and place in runnable state
21          threadExecutor.execute( task1 ); // start task1
22          threadExecutor.execute( task2 ); // start task2
23          threadExecutor.execute( task3 ); // start task3
24
25          threadExecutor.shutdown(); // shutdown worker threads
26
27          System.out.println( "Threads started, main ends\n" );
28       } // end main
29    } // end class RunnableTester
```

```
Starting threads
Threads started, main ends

thread1 going to sleep for 1217 milliseconds
thread2 going to sleep for 3989 milliseconds
thread3 going to sleep for 662 milliseconds
thread3 done sleeping
thread1 done sleeping
thread2 done sleeping
```

```
Starting threads
thread1 going to sleep for 314 milliseconds
thread2 going to sleep for 1990 milliseconds
Threads started, main ends

thread3 going to sleep for 3016 milliseconds
thread1 done sleeping
thread2 done sleeping
thread3 done sleeping
```

Fig. 23.5 | Creates three PrintTasks and executes them.

main terminates (line 28), the program itself continues running because there are still threads that are alive (i.e., the threads started by threadExecutor that have not yet reached the *terminated* state). The program will not terminate until its last thread completes execution.

The sample outputs for this program show each thread's name and sleep time as the thread goes to sleep. The thread with the shortest sleep time normally awakens first, indicates that it is done sleeping and terminates. In Section 23.8, we discuss multithreading issues that could prevent the thread with the shortest sleep time from awakening first. In the first output, the main thread terminates before any of the other threads output their names and sleep times. This shows that the main thread runs to completion before any of the other threads get a chance to run. In the second output, the first two threads output their names and sleep times before the main thread terminates. This shows that the operating system allowed other threads to execute before the main thread terminated. This is an example of the round-robin scheduling we discussed in Section 23.3.

23.5 Thread Synchronization

Often, multiple threads of execution manipulate a shared object in memory. When multiple threads share an object and that object is modified by one or more of the threads, indeterminate results may occur (as we will soon see in the chapter examples) unless the shared object is managed properly. If one thread is in the process of updating a shared object and another thread tries to update it too, it is possible that part of the object will reflect the information from one thread while another part of the object reflects information from a different thread. When this happens, the program's behavior cannot be trusted. Sometimes the program will produce the correct results, but other times it will produce incorrect results. In either case there will be no error message to indicate that the shared object was manipulated incorrectly.

The problem can be solved by giving one thread at a time exclusive access to code that manipulates the shared object. During that time, other threads desiring to manipulate the object are kept waiting. When the thread with exclusive access to the object finishes manipulating it, one of the threads that was kept waiting is allowed to proceed. In this fashion, each thread accessing the shared object excludes all other threads from doing so simultaneously. This is called mutual exclusion. Mutual exclusion allows the programmer to perform thread synchronization, which coordinates access to shared data by multiple concurrent threads.

Java uses locks to perform synchronization. Any object can contain an object that implements the **Lock** interface (package `java.util.concurrent.locks`). A thread calls the Lock's `lock` method to obtain the lock. Once a Lock has been obtained by one thread, the Lock object will not allow another thread to obtain the lock until the first thread releases the Lock (by calling the Lock's `unlock` method). If there are several threads trying to call method `lock` on the same Lock object at the same time, only one thread may obtain the lock at a time—all other threads attempting to obtain the Lock contained in the same object are placed in the *waiting* state for that lock. When a thread calls method `unlock`, the lock on the object is released and the highest-priority waiting thread attempting to lock the object proceeds. Class **ReentrantLock** (package `java.util.concurrent.locks`) is a basic implementation of the Lock interface. The constructor for a ReentrantLock takes a `boolean` argument that specifies whether the lock has a fairness policy. If this is set to `true`, the ReentrantLock's fairness policy states that the longest-waiting thread will acquire the lock when it is available. If this is set to `false`, there is no guarantee as to which waiting thread will acquire the lock when it is available.

Performance Tip 23.2

Using a Lock with a fairness policy helps avoid indefinite postponement, but can also dramatically reduce the overall efficiency of a program. Because of the large decrease in performance, fair locks are only necessary in extreme circumstances.

If a thread that owns the lock on an object determines that it cannot continue with its task until some condition is satisfied, the thread can wait on a **condition variable**. This removes the thread from contention for the processor, places it in a wait queue for the condition variable and releases the lock on the object. Condition variables must be associated with a Lock and are created by calling Lock method `newCondition`, which returns an object that implements the `Condition` interface (package java.util.concurrent.locks). To wait on a condition variable, the thread can call the Condition's `await` method. This immediately releases the associated Lock and places the thread in the *waiting* state for that Condition. Other threads can then try to obtain the Lock. When a *runnable* thread completes a task and determines that the *waiting* thread can now continue, the *runnable* thread can call Condition method `signal` to allow a thread in that Condition's *waiting* state to return to the *runnable* state. At this point, the thread that transitioned from the *waiting* state to the *runnable* state can attempt to reacquire the Lock on the object. Even if it is able to reacquire the Lock, the thread still might not be able to perform its task at this time—in which case the thread can call method `await` to release the Lock and reenter the *waiting* state. If multiple threads are in a Condition's *waiting* state when `signal` is called, the default implementation of Condition signals the longest-waiting thread to move to the *runnable* state. If a thread calls Condition method `signalAll`, then all the threads waiting for that condition move to the *runnable* state and become eligible to reacquire the Lock. Only one of those threads can obtain the Lock on the object at a time—other threads that attempt to acquire the same Lock will wait until the Lock becomes available again. If the Lock was created with a fairness policy, the longest-waiting thread will then acquire the Lock. When a thread is finished with a shared object, it must call method `unlock` to release the Lock.

Common Programming Error 23.1

Deadlock occurs when a waiting thread (let us call this thread1) cannot proceed because it is waiting (either directly or indirectly) for another thread (let us call this thread2) to proceed, while simultaneously thread2 cannot proceed because it is waiting (either directly or indirectly) for thread1 to proceed. Two threads are waiting for each other, so the actions that would enable each thread to continue execution never occur.

Error-Prevention Tip 23.1

When multiple threads manipulate a shared object using locks, ensure that if one thread calls method `await` to enter the waiting state for a condition variable, a separate thread eventually will call Condition method `signal` to transition the thread waiting on the condition variable back to the runnable state. If multiple threads may be waiting on the condition variable, a separate thread can call Condition method `signalAll` as a safeguard to ensure that all the waiting threads have another opportunity to perform their tasks. If this is not done, indefinite postponement or deadlock could occur.

Software Engineering Observation 23.1

The locking that occurs with the execution of the `lock` and `unlock` methods could lead to deadlock if the locks are never released. Calls to method `unlock` should be placed in `finally` blocks to ensure that locks are released and avoid these kinds of deadlocks.

Performance Tip 23.3

Synchronization to achieve correctness in multithreaded programs can make programs run more slowly, as a result of thread overhead and the frequent transition of threads between the waiting *and* runnable *states. There is not much to say, however, for highly efficient yet incorrect multithreaded programs!*

Common Programming Error 23.2

It is an error if a thread issues an await, *a* signal, *or a* signalAll *on a condition variable without having acquired the lock for that condition variable. This causes an* IllegalMonitorStateException.

23.6 Producer/Consumer Relationship without Synchronization

In a producer/consumer relationship, the producer portion of an application generates data and stores it in a shared object, and the consumer portion of an application reads data from the shared object. One example of a common producer/consumer relationship is print spooling. A word processor spools data to a buffer (typically a file) and that data is subsequently consumed by the printer as it prints the document. Similarly, an application that copies data onto compact discs places data in a fixed-size buffer that is emptied as the CD-RW drive burns the data onto the compact disc.

In a multithreaded producer/consumer relationship, a producer thread generates data and places it in a shared object called a buffer. A consumer thread reads data from the buffer. If the producer waiting to put the next data into the buffer determines that the consumer has not yet read the previous data from the buffer, the producer thread should call await so that the consumer can read the data before further updates—otherwise the consumer never sees the previous data and that data is lost to the application. When the consumer thread reads the data, it should call signal to allow a waiting producer to store the next value. If a consumer thread finds the buffer empty or finds that the previous data has already been read, the consumer should call await—otherwise the consumer might read old data again from the buffer. When the producer places the next data into the buffer, the producer should call signal to allow the consumer thread to proceed, so that the consumer can read the new data.

Let us consider how logic errors can arise if we do not synchronize access among multiple threads manipulating shared data. Our next example (Fig. 23.6–Fig. 23.10) implements a producer/consumer relationship in which a producer thread writes the numbers 1 through 10 into a shared buffer—a memory location shared between two threads (a single int variable called buffer in line 6 of Fig. 23.9 in this example). The consumer thread reads this data from the shared buffer and displays the data. The program's output shows the values that the producer writes (produces) into the shared buffer and the values that the consumer reads (consumes) from the shared buffer.

Each value the producer thread writes to the shared buffer must be consumed exactly once by the consumer thread. However, the threads in this example are not synchronized. Therefore, data can be lost if the producer places new data into the shared buffer before the consumer consumes the previous data. Also, data can be incorrectly duplicated if the consumer consumes data again before the producer produces the next value. To show these possibilities, the consumer thread in the following example keeps a total of all the values it reads. The producer thread produces values from 1 through 10. If the consumer reads each value produced once and only once, the total will be 55. However, if you execute this program several times, you will see that the total is not always 55 (as shown in the outputs in Fig. 23.10). To emphasize the point, the producer and consumer threads in the example each sleep for random intervals of up to three seconds between performing their tasks. Thus, we do not know exactly when the producer thread will attempt to write a new value, nor do we know when the consumer thread will attempt to read a value.

The program consists of interface `Buffer` (Fig. 23.6) and four classes—`Producer` (Fig. 23.7), `Consumer` (Fig. 23.8), `UnsynchronizedBuffer` (Fig. 23.9) and `SharedBuffer-Test` (Fig. 23.10). Interface `Buffer` declares methods `set` and `get` that a `Buffer` must implement to enable the `Producer` thread to place a value in the `Buffer` and the `Consumer` thread to retrieve a value from the `Buffer`. We will see the implementation of this interface in Fig. 23.9.

Class `Producer` (Fig. 23.7) implements the `Runnable` interface, allowing it to be executed in a separate thread. The constructor (lines 11–14) initializes `Buffer` reference `sharedLocation` with an object created in `main` (line 14 of Fig. 23.10) and passed to the constructor in the parameter `shared`. As we will see, this is an `UnsynchronizedBuffer` object that implements interface `Buffer` without synchronizing access to the shared object. The `Producer` thread in this program executes the tasks specified in method `run` (lines 17–39). Each iteration of the loop (lines 21–35) invokes `Thread` method `sleep` (line 25) to place the `Producer` thread into the *timed waiting* state for a random time interval between 0 and 3 seconds. When the thread awakens, line 26 passes the value of control variable `count` to the `Buffer` object's `set` method to set the shared buffer's value. Line 27 keeps a total of all the values produced so far and line 28 outputs that value. When the loop completes, lines 37–38 display a message indicating that the thread has finished producing data and is terminating. Next, method `run` terminates which indicates that the `Producer` completed its task. It is important to note that any method called from a thread's `run` method (e.g., `Buffer` method `set`) executes as part of that thread of execution. In fact, each thread has its own method call stack. This fact becomes important in Section 23.7 when we add synchronization to the producer/consumer relationship.

Class `Consumer` (Fig. 23.8) also implements interface `Runnable`, allowing the Consumer to be executed concurrently with the `Producer`. The constructor (lines 11–14) initializes `Buffer` reference `sharedLocation` with an object that implements the `Buffer` interface created in `main` (Fig. 23.10) and passed to the constructor as the parameter `shared`. As we will see, this is the same `UnsynchronizedBuffer` object that is used to initialize the `Producer` object—thus, the two threads share the same object. The `Consumer`

```
1   // Fig. 23.6: Buffer.java
2   // Buffer interface specifies methods called by Producer and Consumer.
3
4   public interface Buffer
5   {
6      public void set( int value ); // place int value into Buffer
7      public int get(); // return int value from Buffer
8   } // end interface Buffer
```

Fig. 23.6 | `Buffer` interface used in producer/consumer examples.

```
1    // Fig. 23.7: Producer.java
2    // Producer's run method stores the values 1 to 10 in buffer.
3    import java.util.Random;
4
5    public class Producer implements Runnable
6    {
7        private static Random generator = new Random();
8        private Buffer sharedLocation; // reference to shared object
9
10       // constructor
11       public Producer( Buffer shared )
12       {
13           sharedLocation = shared;
14       } // end Producer constructor
15
16       // store values from 1 to 10 in sharedLocation
17       public void run()
18       {
19           int sum = 0;
20
21           for ( int count = 1; count <= 10; count++ )
22           {
23               try // sleep 0 to 3 seconds, then place value in Buffer
24               {
25                   Thread.sleep( generator.nextInt( 3000 ) ); // sleep thread
26                   sharedLocation.set( count ); // set value in buffer
27                   sum += count; // increment sum of values
28                   System.out.printf( "\t%2d\n", sum );
29               } // end try
30               // if sleeping thread interrupted, print stack trace
31               catch ( InterruptedException exception )
32               {
33                   exception.printStackTrace();
34               } // end catch
35           } // end for
36
37           System.out.printf( "\n%s\n%s\n", "Producer done producing.",
38               "Terminating Producer." );
39       } // end method run
40   } // end class Producer
```

Fig. 23.7 | Producer represents the producer thread in a producer/consumer relationship.

thread in this program performs the tasks specified in method run (lines 17–39). The loop at lines 21–35 loops ten times. Each iteration of the loop invokes Thread method sleep (line 26) to put the Consumer thread into the *timed waiting* state for between 0 and 3 seconds. Next, line 27 uses the Buffer's get method to retrieve the value in the shared buffer, then adds the value to variable sum. Line 28 displays the total of all the values consumed so far. When the loop completes, lines 37–38 display a line indicating the sum of the consumed values. Then method run terminates, which indicates that the Consumer completed its task. Once both threads enter the *terminated* state, the program ends.

```java
 1   // Fig. 23.8: Consumer.java
 2   // Consumer's run method loops ten times reading a value from buffer.
 3   import java.util.Random;
 4
 5   public class Consumer implements Runnable
 6   {
 7      private static Random generator = new Random();
 8      private Buffer sharedLocation; // reference to shared object
 9
10      // constructor
11      public Consumer( Buffer shared )
12      {
13         sharedLocation = shared;
14      } // end Consumer constructor
15
16      // read sharedLocation's value four times and sum the values
17      public void run()
18      {
19         int sum = 0;
20
21         for ( int count = 1; count <= 10; count++ )
22         {
23            // sleep 0 to 3 seconds, read value from buffer and add to sum
24            try
25            {
26               Thread.sleep( generator.nextInt( 3000 ) );
27               sum += sharedLocation.get();
28               System.out.printf( "\t\t\t%2d\n", sum );
29            } // end try
30            // if sleeping thread interrupted, print stack trace
31            catch ( InterruptedException exception )
32            {
33               exception.printStackTrace();
34            } // end catch
35         } // end for
36
37         System.out.printf( "\n%s %d.\n%s\n",
38            "Consumer read values totaling", sum, "Terminating Consumer." );
39      } // end method run
40   } // end class Consumer
```

Fig. 23.8 | Consumer represents the consumer thread in a producer/consumer relationship.

[*Note:* We use method sleep in method run of the Producer and Consumer classes to emphasize the fact that in multithreaded applications, it is unpredictable when each thread will perform its task and for how long it will perform the task when it has a processor. Normally, these thread-scheduling issues are the job of the computer's operating system and therefore beyod the control of the Java developer. In this program, our thread's tasks are quite simple—for the Producer, write the values 1 to 10 to the buffer, and for the Consumer, read 10 values from the buffer and add each value to variable sum. Without the sleep method call, and if the Producer executes first, given today's phenomenally fast processors, the Producer would likely complete its task before the Consumer gets a chance to execute. If the Consumer executes first, it would likely consume –1 ten times, then terminate before the Producer could produce the first real value.]

Class UnsynchronizedBuffer (Fig. 23.9) implements interface Buffer (line 4). An object of this class is shared between the Producer and the Consumer. Line 6 declares instance variable buffer and initializes it with the value –1. This value is used to demonstrate the case in which the Consumer attempts to consume a value before the Producer ever places a value in buffer. Methods set (lines 9–13) and get (lines 16–20) do not synchronize access to field buffer. Method set simply assigns its argument to buffer (line 12), and method get simply returns the value of buffer (line 19).

Class SharedBufferTest contains method main (lines 8–32), which launches the application. Line 11 creates an ExecutorService with two threads—one to execute the Producer and one to execute the Consumer. Line 14 creates an UnsynchronizedBuffer object and assigns its reference to Buffer variable sharedLocation. This object stores the data that will be shared between the Producer and Consumer threads. Lines 23–24 create and execute the Producer and Consumer. Note that the Producer and Consumer constructors are each passed the same Buffer object (sharedLocation), so each object is initialized with a reference to the same Buffer. These lines also implicitly launch the threads and call each Runnable's run method. Finally, line 31 calls method shutdown so that the application can terminate when the Producer and Consumer threads complete their tasks. When method main terminates (line 32), the main thread of execution enters the *terminated* state.

Recall from the overview of this example that we would like the Producer thread to execute first and every value produced by the Producer to be consumed exactly once by the Consumer. However, when we study the first output of Fig. 23.10, we see that the Producer writes a value three times before the Consumer reads its first value (3). Therefore, the

```
1    // Fig. 23.9: UnsynchronizedBuffer.java
2    // UnsynchronizedBuffer represents a single shared integer.
3
4    public class UnsynchronizedBuffer implements Buffer
5    {
6       private int buffer = -1; // shared by producer and consumer threads
7
8       // place value into buffer
9       public void set( int value )
10      {
11         System.out.printf( "Producer writes\t%2d", value );
12         buffer = value;
13      } // end method set
14
15      // return value from buffer
16      public int get()
17      {
18         System.out.printf( "Consumer reads\t%2d", buffer );
19         return buffer;
20      } // end method get
21   } // end class UnsynchronizedBuffer
```

Fig. 23.9 | UnsynchronizedBuffer maintains the shared integer that is accessed by a producer thread and a consumer thread via methods set and get.

values 1 and 2 are lost. Later, the values 5, 6 and 9 are lost, while 7 and 8 are read twice and 10 is read four times. So the first output produced an incorrect total of 77, instead of a correct total of 55. In the second output, note that the Consumer reads before the Producer ever writes a value. Also note that the Consumer has already read five times before the Producer writes the value 2. Meanwhile, the values 5, 7, 8, 9 and 10 are all lost. An incorrect output of 19 is produced. (Lines in the output where the Producer or Consumer has acted out of order are highlighted.) This example clearly demonstrates that access to a shared object by concurrent threads must be controlled carefully, for otherwise a program may produce incorrect results.

To solve the problems of lost and duplicated data, Section 23.7 presents an example in which we use a Lock and Condition methods await and signal to synchronize access to the code that manipulates the shared object, guaranteeing that each and every value will be processed once and only once. When a thread acquires a lock, no other threads can acquire that same lock until the original thread releases it.

```
1   // Fig 23.10: SharedBufferTest.java
2   // Application shows two threads manipulating an unsynchronized buffer.
3   import java.util.concurrent.ExecutorService;
4   import java.util.concurrent.Executors;
5
6   public class SharedBufferTest
7   {
8      public static void main( String[] args )
9      {
10        // create new thread pool with two threads
11        ExecutorService application = Executors.newFixedThreadPool( 2 );
12
13        // create UnsynchronizedBuffer to store ints
14        Buffer sharedLocation = new UnsynchronizedBuffer();
15
16        System.out.println( "Action\t\tValue\tProduced\tConsumed" );
17        System.out.println( "------\t\t-----\t--------\t--------\n" );
18
19        // try to start producer and consumer giving each of them access
20        // to sharedLocation
21        try
22        {
23           application.execute( new Producer( sharedLocation ) );
24           application.execute( new Consumer( sharedLocation ) );
25        } // end try
26        catch ( Exception exception )
27        {
28           exception.printStackTrace();
29        } // end catch
30
31        application.shutdown(); // terminate application when threads end
32     } // end main
33  } // end class SharedBufferTest
```

Fig. 23.10 | SharedBufferTest sets up a producer/consumer application that uses an unsynchronized buffer. (Part 1 of 3.)

```
Action            Value   Produced          Consumed
------            -----   --------          --------

Producer writes   1       1
Producer writes   2       3
Producer writes   3       6
Consumer reads    3                         3
Producer writes   4       10
Consumer reads    4                         7
Producer writes   5       15
Producer writes   6       21
Producer writes   7       28
Consumer reads    7                         14
Consumer reads    7                         21
Producer writes   8       36
Consumer reads    8                         29
Consumer reads    8                         37
Producer writes   9       45
Producer writes  10       55

Producer done producing.
Terminating Producer.
Consumer reads   10                         47
Consumer reads   10                         57
Consumer reads   10                         67
Consumer reads   10                         77

Consumer read values totaling 77.
Terminating Consumer.

Action            Value   Produced          Consumed
------            -----   --------          --------

Consumer reads   -1                         -1
Producer writes   1       1
Consumer reads    1                         0
Consumer reads    1                         1
Consumer reads    1                         2
Consumer reads    1                         3
Consumer reads    1                         4
Producer writes   2       3
Consumer reads    2                         6
Producer writes   3       6
Consumer reads    3                         9
Producer writes   4       10
Consumer reads    4                         13
Producer writes   5       15
Producer writes   6       21
Consumer reads    6                         19

Consumer read values totaling 19.
Terminating Consumer.
Producer writes   7       28
Producer writes   8       36
Producer writes   9       45
Producer writes  10       55
```

Fig. 23.10 | `SharedBufferTest` sets up a producer/consumer application that uses an unsynchronized buffer. (Part 2 of 3.)

```
Producer done producing.
Terminating Producer.
```

Fig. 23.10 | `SharedBufferTest` sets up a producer/consumer application that uses an unsynchronized buffer. (Part 3 of 3.)

23.7 Producer/Consumer Relationship with Synchronization

The application in Fig. 23.11 and Fig. 23.12 demonstrates a producer and a consumer accessing a shared buffer with synchronization. In this case, the consumer correctly consumes only after the producer produces a value, and the producer correctly produces a new

```java
1   // Fig. 23.11: SynchronizedBuffer.java
2   // SynchronizedBuffer synchronizes access to a single shared integer.
3   import java.util.concurrent.locks.Lock;
4   import java.util.concurrent.locks.ReentrantLock;
5   import java.util.concurrent.locks.Condition;
6
7   public class SynchronizedBuffer implements Buffer
8   {
9      // Lock to control synchronization with this buffer
10     private Lock accessLock = new ReentrantLock();
11
12     // conditions to control reading and writing
13     private Condition canWrite = accessLock.newCondition();
14     private Condition canRead = accessLock.newCondition();
15
16     private int buffer = -1; // shared by producer and consumer threads
17     private boolean occupied = false; // whether buffer is occupied
18
19     // place int value into buffer
20     public void set( int value )
21     {
22        accessLock.lock(); // lock this object
23
24        // output thread information and buffer information, then wait
25        try
26        {
27           // while buffer is not empty, place thread in waiting state
28           while ( occupied )
29           {
30              System.out.println( "Producer tries to write." );
31              displayState( "Buffer full. Producer waits." );
32              canWrite.await(); // wait until buffer is empty
33           } // end while
34
35           buffer = value; // set new buffer value
36
```

Fig. 23.11 | `SynchronizedBuffer` synchronizes access to a shared integer. (Part 1 of 3.)

```
37              // indicate producer cannot store another value
38              // until consumer retrieves current buffer value
39              occupied = true;
40
41              displayState( "Producer writes " + buffer );
42
43              // signal thread waiting to read from buffer
44              canRead.signal();
45           } // end try
46           catch ( InterruptedException exception )
47           {
48              exception.printStackTrace();
49           } // end catch
50           finally
51           {
52              accessLock.unlock(); // unlock this object
53           } // end finally
54        } // end method set
55
56        // return value from buffer
57        public int get()
58        {
59           int readValue = 0; // initialize value read from buffer
60           accessLock.lock(); // lock this object
61
62           // output thread information and buffer information, then wait
63           try
64           {
65              // while no data to read, place thread in waiting state
66              while ( !occupied )
67              {
68                 System.out.println( "Consumer tries to read." );
69                 displayState( "Buffer empty. Consumer waits." );
70                 canRead.await(); // wait until buffer is full
71              } // end while
72
73              // indicate that producer can store another value
74              // because consumer just retrieved buffer value
75              occupied = false;
76
77              readValue = buffer; // retrieve value from buffer
78              displayState( "Consumer reads " + readValue );
79
80              // signal thread waiting for buffer to be empty
81              canWrite.signal();
82           } // end try
83           // if waiting thread interrupted, print stack trace
84           catch ( InterruptedException exception )
85           {
86              exception.printStackTrace();
87           } // end catch
88           finally
89           {
```

Fig. 23.11 | SynchronizedBuffer synchronizes access to a shared integer. (Part 2 of 3.)

```
90              accessLock.unlock(); // unlock this object
91          } // end finally
92
93          return readValue;
94      } // end method get
95
96      // display current operation and buffer state
97      public void displayState( String operation )
98      {
99          System.out.printf( "%-40s%d\t\t%b\n\n", operation, buffer,
100             occupied );
101     } // end method displayState
102 } // end class SynchronizedBuffer
```

Fig. 23.11 | `SynchronizedBuffer` synchronizes access to a shared integer. (Part 3 of 3.)

value only after the consumer consumes the previous value produced. We reuse interface Buffer (Fig. 23.6) and use classes Producer (Fig. 23.7 modified to remove line 28) and Consumer (Fig. 23.8 modified to remove line 28) from the example in Section 23.6. This approach enables us to demonstrate that the threads accessing the shared object are unaware that they are being synchronized. The code that performs the synchronization is placed in the set and get methods of class SynchronizedBuffer (Fig. 23.11), which implements interface Buffer (line 7). Thus, the Producer's and Consumer's run methods simply call the shared object's set and get methods, as in the example in Section 23.6.

Class SynchronizedBuffer (Fig. 23.11) contains five fields. Line 10 creates a new object of type ReentrantLock and assigns its reference to Lock variable accessLock. The ReentrantLock is created without the fairness policy because only a single Producer or Consumer will be waiting to acquire the Lock in this example. Lines 13–14 create two Conditions using Lock method newCondition. Condition canWrite contains a queue for threads waiting while the buffer is full (i.e., there is data in the buffer that the Consumer has not read yet). If the buffer is full, the Producer calls method await on this Condition. When the Consumer reads data from a full buffer, it calls method signal on this Condition. Condition canRead contains a queue for threads waiting while the buffer is empty (i.e., there is no data in the buffer for the Consumer to read). If the buffer is empty, the Consumer calls method await on this Condition. When the Producer writes to the empty buffer, it calls method signal on this Condition. The int buffer (line 16) holds the shared data, and the boolean variable occupied (line 17) keeps track of whether the buffer currently holds data (that the Consumer should read) or not.

Line 22 in method set calls the lock method of the SynchronizedBuffer's accessLock. If the lock is available (i.e., no other thread has acquired this lock), method lock will return immediately (this thread now owns the lock) and the thread will continue. If the lock is unavailable (i.e., the lock is held by another thread), this method will wait until the lock is released by the other thread. After the lock is acquired, the try block in lines 25–45 executes. Line 28 tests occupied to determine whether the buffer is full. If it is, lines 30–31 output that the thread will wait. Line 32 calls Condition method await on the canWrite condition variable which will temporarily release the SynchronizedBuffer's lock and wait for a signal from the Consumer that the buffer is available for writing. When the buffer is available for writing, the method proceeds, writing to the buffer (line 35), setting occupied to true (line 39) and outputting that the producer wrote a value. Line 44 calls Condition method signal on condition variable canRead to notify the waiting Consumer that the buffer has new data to be read. Line 52 calls method unlock within a finally block to release the lock and allow the Consumer to proceed.

Common Programming Error 23.3

Place calls to Lock method unlock *in a* finally *block. If an exception is thrown,* unlock *must still be called or deadlock could occur.*

Line 60 of method get (lines 57–94) calls method lock to acquire the lock for this object. This method will wait until the lock is available. Once the lock is acquired, line 66 tests whether occupied is false, indicating that the buffer has no data. If the buffer is empty, line 70 calls method await on condition variable canRead. Recall that method signal is called on variable canRead in the set method (line 44). When the condition variable is signaled, the get method continues. Line 75 sets occupied to false, line 77 stores the value of buffer in readValue and line 78 outputs the readValue. Then line 81 signals the condition variable canWrite. This will awaken the Producer if it is indeed waiting for the buffer to be emptied. Line 90 calls method unlock in a finally block to release the lock, and line 93 returns the value of the buffer to the calling method.

Software Engineering Observation 23.2

Always invoke method await *in a loop that tests an appropriate condition. It is possible that a thread will reenter the* runnable *state before the condition it was waiting on is satisfied. Testing the condition again ensures that the thread will not erroneously execute if it was signaled early.*

Common Programming Error 23.4

Forgetting to signal *a thread that is waiting for a condition is a logic error. The thread will remain in the* waiting *state, which will prevent the thread from doing any further work. Such waiting can lead to indefinite postponement or deadlock.*

Class SharedBufferTest2 (Fig. 23.12) is similar to class SharedBufferTest (Fig. 23.10). SharedBufferTest2 contains method main (lines 8–30), which launches the application. Line 11 creates an ExecutorService with two threads to run the Producer and Consumer. Line 14 creates a SynchronizedBuffer object and assigns its reference to Buffer variable sharedLocation. This object stores the data that will be shared between the Producer and Consumer threads. Lines 16–17 display the column heads for the output. Lines 21–22 execute a Producer and a Consumer. Finally, line 29 calls method shutdown to end the application when the Producer and Consumer complete their tasks. When method main ends (line 30), the main thread of execution terminates.

Study the outputs in Fig. 23.12. Observe that every integer produced is consumed exactly once—no values are lost, and no values are consumed more than once. The synchronization and condition variables ensure that the Producer and Consumer cannot perform their tasks unless it is their turn. The Producer must go first, the Consumer must wait if the Producer has not produced since the Consumer last consumed, and the Producer must wait if the Consumer has not yet consumed the value that the Producer most recently produced. Execute this program several times to confirm that every integer produced is consumed exactly once. In the sample output, note the lines indicating when the Producer and Consumer must wait to perform their respective tasks.

```
 1   // Fig 23.12: SharedBufferTest2.java
 2   // Application shows two threads manipulating a synchronized buffer.
 3   import java.util.concurrent.ExecutorService;
 4   import java.util.concurrent.Executors;
 5
 6   public class SharedBufferTest2
 7   {
 8      public static void main( String[] args )
 9      {
10         // create new thread pool with two threads
11         ExecutorService application = Executors.newFixedThreadPool( 2 );
12
13         // create SynchronizedBuffer to store ints
14         Buffer sharedLocation = new SynchronizedBuffer();
15
16         System.out.printf( "%-40s%s\t\t%s\n%-40s%s\n\n", "Operation",
17            "Buffer", "Occupied", "---------", "------\t\t--------" );
18
19         try // try to start producer and consumer
20         {
21            application.execute( new Producer( sharedLocation ) );
22            application.execute( new Consumer( sharedLocation ) );
23         } // end try
24         catch ( Exception exception )
25         {
26            exception.printStackTrace();
27         } // end catch
28
29         application.shutdown();
30      } // end main
31   } // end class SharedBufferTest2
```

Operation	Buffer	Occupied
Producer writes 1	1	true
Producer tries to write. Buffer full. Producer waits.	1	true
Consumer reads 1	1	false
Producer writes 2	2	true
Producer tries to write. Buffer full. Producer waits.	2	true
Consumer reads 2	2	false
Producer writes 3	3	true
Consumer reads 3	3	false

Fig. 23.12 | SharedBufferTest2 sets up a producer/consumer application that uses a synchronized buffer. (Part 1 of 2.)

Producer writes 4	4	true
Consumer reads 4	4	false
Consumer tries to read. Buffer empty. Consumer waits.	4	false
Producer writes 5	5	true
Consumer reads 5	5	false
Consumer tries to read. Buffer empty. Consumer waits.	5	false
Producer writes 6	6	true
Consumer reads 6	6	false
Producer writes 7	7	true
Consumer reads 7	7	false
Producer writes 8	8	true
Consumer reads 8	8	false
Producer writes 9	9	true
Consumer reads 9	9	false
Producer writes 10	10	true
Producer done producing. Terminating Producer. Consumer reads 10	10	false
Consumer read values totaling 55. Terminating Consumer.		

Fig. 23.12 | `SharedBufferTest2` sets up a producer/consumer application that uses a synchronized buffer. (Part 2 of 2.)

23.8 Producer/Consumer Relationship: Circular Buffer

The program in Section 23.7 uses thread synchronization to guarantee that two threads manipulate data in a shared buffer correctly. However, the application may not perform optimally. If the two threads operate at different speeds, one of the threads will spend more (or most) of its time waiting. For example, in the program in Section 23.7 we shared a single integer variable between the two threads. If the producer thread produces values faster than the consumer can consume them, then the producer thread waits for the consumer, because there are no other locations in memory in which to place the next value. Similarly, if the consumer consumes values faster than the producer produces them, the consumer waits until the producer places the next value in the shared location in memory. Even when we have threads that operate at the same relative speeds, those threads may occasionally become "out of sync" over a period of time, causing one of them to wait for the other. We cannot make assumptions about the relative speeds of concurrent threads—interactions that occur with the operating system, the network, the user and other components can cause the threads to operate at different speeds. When this happens, threads wait. When threads wait excessively, programs become less efficient, user-interactive programs become less responsive and applications suffer longer delays.

To minimize the amount of waiting time for threads that share resources and operate at the same average speeds, we can implement a circular buffer that provides extra buffer space into which the producer can place values and from which the consumer can retrieve those values. Let us assume that the buffer is implemented as an array. The producer and consumer work from the beginning of the array. When either thread reaches the end of the array, it simply returns to the first element of the array to perform its next task. If the producer temporarily produces values faster than the consumer can consume them, the producer can write additional values into the extra buffer space (if any are available). This capability enables the producer to perform its task even though the consumer is not ready to receive the current value being produced. Similarly, if the consumer consumes faster than the producer produces new values, the consumer can read additional values (if there are any) from the buffer. This enables the consumer to keep busy even though the producer is not ready to produce additional values.

Note that the circular buffer would be inappropriate if the producer and the consumer operate consistently at different speeds. If the consumer always executes faster than the producer, then a buffer containing one location is enough. Additional locations would waste memory. If the producer always executes faster, only a buffer with an infinite number of locations would be able to absorb the extra production.

The key to using a circular buffer with a producer and consumer that operate at about the same speed is to provide it with enough locations to handle the anticipated "extra" production. If, over a period of time, we determine that the producer often produces as many as three more values than the consumer can consume, we can provide a buffer of at least three cells to handle the extra production. We do not want the buffer to be too small, because that would cause threads to wait longer. On the other hand, we do not want the buffer to be too large, because that would waste memory.

Performance Tip 23.4

Even when using a circular buffer, it is possible that a producer thread could fill the buffer, which would force the producer thread to wait until a consumer consumes a value to free an element in the buffer. Similarly, if the buffer is empty at any given time, the consumer thread must wait until the producer produces another value. The key to using a circular buffer is to optimize the buffer size to minimize the amount of thread wait time.

The program in Fig. 23.13–Fig. 23.14 demonstrates a producer and a consumer accessing a circular buffer (in this case, a shared array of three cells) with synchronization. In this version of the producer/consumer relationship, the consumer consumes a value only when the array is not empty and the producer produces a value only when the array is not full. The statements that created and started the thread objects in the `main` method of class `SharedBufferTest2` (Fig. 23.12) now appear in class `CircularBufferTest` (Fig. 23.14).

```java
 1    // Fig. 23.13: CircularBuffer.java
 2    // SynchronizedBuffer synchronizes access to a single shared integer.
 3    import java.util.concurrent.locks.Lock;
 4    import java.util.concurrent.locks.ReentrantLock;
 5    import java.util.concurrent.locks.Condition;
 6
 7    public class CircularBuffer implements Buffer
 8    {
 9       // Lock to control synchronization with this buffer
10       private Lock accessLock = new ReentrantLock();
11
12       // conditions to control reading and writing
13       private Condition canWrite = accessLock.newCondition();
14       private Condition canRead = accessLock.newCondition();
15
16       private int[] buffer = { -1, -1, -1 };
17
18       private int occupiedBuffers = 0; // count number of buffers used
19       private int writeIndex = 0; // index to write next value
20       private int readIndex = 0; // index to read next value
21
22       // place value into buffer
23       public void set( int value )
24       {
25          accessLock.lock(); // lock this object
26
27          // output thread information and buffer information, then wait
28          try
29          {
30             // while no empty locations, place thread in waiting state
31             while ( occupiedBuffers == buffer.length )
32             {
33                System.out.printf( "All buffers full. Producer waits.\n" );
34                canWrite.await();// await until a buffer element is free
35             } // end while
36
37             buffer[ writeIndex ] = value; // set new buffer value
38
39             // update circular write index
40             writeIndex = ( writeIndex + 1 ) % buffer.length;
41
42             occupiedBuffers++; // one more buffer element is full
43             displayState( "Producer writes " + buffer[ writeIndex ] );
44             canRead.signal(); // signal threads waiting to read from buffer
45          } // end try
46          catch ( InterruptedException exception )
47          {
48             exception.printStackTrace();
49          } // end catch
50          finally
51          {
```

Fig. 23.13 | CircularBuffer synchronizes access to a circular buffer containing three slots. (Part 1 of 3.)

```
52              accessLock.unlock(); // unlock this object
53          } // end finally
54      } // end method set
55
56      // return value from buffer
57      public int get()
58      {
59          int readValue = 0; // initialize value read from buffer
60          accessLock.lock(); // lock this object
61
62          // wait until buffer has data, then read value
63          try
64          {
65              // while no data to read, place thread in waiting state
66              while ( occupiedBuffers == 0 )
67              {
68                  System.out.printf( "All buffers empty. Consumer waits.\n" );
69                  canRead.await(); // await until a buffer element is filled
70              } // end while
71
72              readValue = buffer[ readIndex ]; // read value from buffer
73
74              // update circular read index
75              readIndex = ( readIndex + 1 ) % buffer.length;
76
77              occupiedBuffers--; // one more buffer element is empty
78              displayState( "Consumer reads " + readValue );
79              canWrite.signal(); // signal threads waiting to write to buffer
80          } // end try
81          // if waiting thread interrupted, print stack trace
82          catch ( InterruptedException exception )
83          {
84              exception.printStackTrace();
85          } // end catch
86          finally
87          {
88              accessLock.unlock(); // unlock this object
89          } // end finally
90
91          return readValue; \
92      } // end method get
93
94      // display current operation and buffer state
95      public void displayState( String operation )
96      {
97          // output operation and number of occupied buffers
98          System.out.printf( "%s%s%d)\n%s", operation,
99              " (buffers occupied: ", occupiedBuffers, "buffers:  " );
100
101         for ( int value : buffer )
102             System.out.printf( " %2d  ", value ); // output values in buffer
```

Fig. 23.13 | CircularBuffer synchronizes access to a circular buffer containing three slots. (Part 2 of 3.)

```
103
104         System.out.print( "\n              " );
105         for ( int i = 0; i < buffer.length; i++ )
106             System.out.print( "---- " );
107
108         System.out.print( "\n              " );
109         for ( int i = 0; i < buffer.length; i++ )
110         {
111             if ( i == writeIndex && i == readIndex )
112                 System.out.print( " WR " ); // both write and read index
113             else if ( i == writeIndex )
114                 System.out.print( " W  " ); // just write index
115             else if ( i == readIndex )
116                 System.out.print( "  R " ); // just read index
117             else
118                 System.out.print( "    " ); // neither index
119         } // end for
120
121         System.out.println( "\n" );
122     } // end method displayState
123 } // end class CircularBuffer
```

Fig. 23.13 | CircularBuffer synchronizes access to a circular buffer containing three slots. (Part 3 of 3.)

The significant changes to the example in Section 23.7 occur in CircularBuffer (Fig. 23.13), which replaces SynchronizedBuffer (Fig. 23.11). Line 10 creates a new ReentrantLock object and assigns its reference to Lock variable accessLock. The ReentrantLock is created without a fairness policy because we have only two threads in this example and only one will ever be waiting. Lines 13–14 create two Conditions using Lock method newCondition. Condition canWrite contains a queue for threads waiting while the buffer is full. If the buffer is full, the Producer calls method await on this Condition—when the Consumer frees space in a full buffer, it calls method signal on this Condition. Condition canRead contains a queue for threads waiting while the buffer is empty. If the buffer is empty, the Consumer calls method await on this Condition—when the Producer writes to the buffer, it calls method signal on this Condition. Array buffer (line 16) is a three-element integer array that represents the circular buffer. Variable occupiedBuffers (line 18) counts the number of elements in buffer that are filled with data available to be read. When occupiedBuffers is 0, there is no data in the circular buffer and the Consumer must wait—when occupiedBuffers is 3 (the size of the circular buffer), the circular buffer is full and the Producer must wait. Variable writeIndex (line 19) indicates the next location in which a value can be placed by a Producer. Variable readIndex (line 20) indicates the position from which the next value can be read by a Consumer.

CircularBuffer method set (lines 23–54) performs the same tasks that it did in Fig. 23.11, with a few modifications. The while loop at lines 31–35 determines whether the Producer must wait (i.e., all buffers are full). If so, line 33 indicates that the Producer is waiting to perform its task. Then line 34 invokes Condition method await to place the Producer thread in the *waiting* state on the canWrite condition variable. When execution eventually continues at line 37 after the while loop, the value written by the Producer is placed in the circular buffer at location writeIndex. Then line 40 updates writeIndex for the next call to CircularBuffer method set. This line is the key to the circularity of the buffer. When writeIndex is incremented past the end of the buffer, this line sets it to 0. Line 42 increments occupiedBuffers, because there is now at least one value in the buffer that the Consumer can read. Next, line 43 invokes method displayState to update the output with the value produced, the number of occupied buffers, the contents of the buffers and the current writeIndex and readIndex. Line 44 invokes Condition method signal to indicate that a Consumer thread waiting on the canRead condition variable (if there is a waiting thread) should transition to the *runnable* state. Line 52 releases access-Lock by calling method unlock inside a finally block.

Method get (lines 57–92) of class CircularBuffer also performs the same tasks as it did in Fig. 23.11, with a few minor modifications. The while loop at lines 66–70 determines whether the Consumer must wait (i.e., all buffers are empty). If the Consumer thread must wait, line 68 updates the output to indicate that the Consumer is waiting to perform its task. Then line 69 invokes Condition method await to place the current thread in the *waiting* state on the canRead condition variable. When execution eventually continues at line 72 after a signal call from the Producer, readValue is assigned the value at location readIndex in the circular buffer. Then line 75 updates readIndex for the next call to CircularBuffer method get. This line and line 40 create the circular effect of the buffer. Line 77 decrements the occupiedBuffers, because there is at least one open position in the buffer in which the Producer thread can place a value. Line 78 invokes method displayState to update the output with the consumed value, the number of occupied buffers, the contents of the buffers and the current writeIndex and readIndex. Line 79 invokes Condition method signal to transition the thread waiting to write into the CircularBuffer object into the *runnable* state. Line 88 releases accessLock inside a finally block to guarantee that the lock is released. Then line 91 returns the consumed value to the calling method.

Method displayState (lines 95–122) outputs the state of the application. Lines 101–102 output the current buffers. Line 102 uses method printf with a %2d format specifier to print the contents of each buffer with a leading space if it is a single digit. Lines 109–119 output the current writeIndex and readIndex with the letters W and R respectively.

Class CircularBufferTest (Fig. 23.14) contains the main method that launches the application. Line 11 creates the ExecutorService with two threads, and line 14 creates a CircularBuffer object and assigns its reference to Buffer variable sharedLocation. Lines

```
 1   // Fig 23.14: CircularBufferTest.java
 2   // Application shows two threads manipulating a circular buffer.
 3   import java.util.concurrent.ExecutorService;
 4   import java.util.concurrent.Executors;
 5
 6   public class CircularBufferTest
 7   {
 8      public static void main( String[] args )
 9      {
10         // create new thread pool with two threads
11         ExecutorService application = Executors.newFixedThreadPool( 2 );
```

Fig. 23.14 | CircularBufferTest sets up a producer/consumer application and instantiates producer and consumer threads. (Part 1 of 4.)

```
12
13          // create CircularBuffer to store ints
14          Buffer sharedLocation = new CircularBuffer();
15
16          try // try to start producer and consumer
17          {
18             application.execute( new Producer( sharedLocation ) );
19             application.execute( new Consumer( sharedLocation ) );
20          } // end try
21          catch ( Exception exception )
22          {
23             exception.printStackTrace();
24          } // end catch
25
26          application.shutdown();
27       } // end main
28    } // end class CircularBufferTest
```

```
Producer writes 1 (buffers occupied: 1)
buffers:    1    -1    -1
           ---- ---- ----
            R    W

Consumer reads 1 (buffers occupied: 0)
buffers:    1    -1    -1
           ---- ---- ----
                WR

All buffers empty. Consumer waits.
Producer writes 2 (buffers occupied: 1)
buffers:    1    2    -1
           ---- ---- ----
                R    W

Consumer reads 2 (buffers occupied: 0)
buffers:    1    2    -1
           ---- ---- ----
                     WR

Producer writes 3 (buffers occupied: 1)
buffers:    1    2    3
           ---- ---- ----
            W              R

Consumer reads 3 (buffers occupied: 0)
buffers:    1    2    3
           ---- ---- ----
            WR

Producer writes 4 (buffers occupied: 1)
buffers:    4    2    3
           ---- ---- ----
                R    W
```

Fig. 23.14 │ `CircularBufferTest` sets up a producer/consumer application and instantiates producer and consumer threads. (Part 2 of 4.)

```
Producer writes 5 (buffers occupied: 2)
buffers:    4    5    3
           ---- ---- ----
            R         W

Consumer reads 4 (buffers occupied: 1)
buffers:    4    5    3
           ---- ---- ----
                 R    W

Producer writes 6 (buffers occupied: 2)
buffers:    4    5    6
           ---- ---- ----
            W         R

Producer writes 7 (buffers occupied: 3)
buffers:    7    5    6
           ---- ---- ----
                 WR

Consumer reads 5 (buffers occupied: 2)
buffers:    7    5    6
           ---- ---- ----
            W         R

Producer writes 8 (buffers occupied: 3)
buffers:    7    8    6
           ---- ---- ----
                      WR

Consumer reads 6 (buffers occupied: 2)
buffers:    7    8    6
           ---- ---- ----
            R         W

Consumer reads 7 (buffers occupied: 1)
buffers:    7    8    6
           ---- ---- ----
                 R    W

Producer writes 9 (buffers occupied: 2)
buffers:    7    8    9
           ---- ---- ----
            W         R

Consumer reads 8 (buffers occupied: 1)
buffers:    7    8    9
           ---- ---- ----
            W         R

Consumer reads 9 (buffers occupied: 0)
buffers:    7    8    9
           ---- ---- ----
            WR
```

Fig. 23.14 | `CircularBufferTest` sets up a producer/consumer application and instantiates producer and consumer threads. (Part 3 of 4.)

```
Producer writes 10 (buffers occupied: 1)
buffers:    10    8    9
            ---- ---- ----
             R    W


Producer done producing.
Terminating Producer.
Consumer reads 10 (buffers occupied: 0)
buffers:    10    8    9
            ---- ---- ----
                 WR


Consumer read values totaling: 55.
Terminating Consumer.
```

Fig. 23.14 | `CircularBufferTest` sets up a producer/consumer application and instantiates producer and consumer threads. (Part 4 of 4.)

18–19 execute the Producer and Consumer. Line 26 calls method shutdown to end the application when the Producer and Consumer complete their tasks.

Each time the Producer writes a value or the Consumer reads a value, the program outputs the action performed (a read or a write) along with the contents of the buffer and the location of the write index and read index. In this output, the Producer first writes the value 1. The buffer then contains the value 1 in the first slot and the value -1 (the default value) in the other two slots. The write index is updated to the second slot, while the read index stays at the first slot. Next, the Consumer reads 1. The buffer contains the same values, but the read index has been updated to the second slot. The Consumer then tries to read again, but the buffer is empty and the Consumer is forced to wait. Note that only once in this execution of the program was it necessary for either thread to wait.

23.9 Producer/Consumer Relationship: ArrayBlockingQueue

J2SE 5.0 includes a fully-implemented circular buffer class named **ArrayBlockingQueue** in package java.util.concurrent, which implements the **BlockingQueue** interface. The BlockingQueue interface implements the Queue interface, discussed in Chapter 19 and declares methods **put** and **take**, the blocking equivalents of Queue methods offer and poll, respectively. This means that method put will place an element at the end of the BlockingQueue, waiting if the queue is full. Method take will remove an element from the head of the BlockingQueue, waiting if the queue is empty. Class ArrayBlockingQueue implements the BlockingQueue interface using an array. This makes the data structure fixed size, meaning that it will not expand to accommodate extra elements. Class ArrayBlockingQueue encapsulates all the functionality of our circular buffer class (Fig. 23.13).

The program in Fig. 23.15–Fig. 23.16 demonstrates a Producer and a Consumer accessing a circular buffer (in this case, an ArrayBlockingQueue) with synchronization. Class BlockingBuffer implements interface Buffer (Fig. 23.15) and contains an ArrayBlockingQueue instance variable that stores Integer objects (line 7). By choosing to

```
1   // Fig. 23.15: BlockingBuffer.java
2   // Class synchronizes access to a blocking buffer.
3   import java.util.concurrent.ArrayBlockingQueue;
4
5   public class BlockingBuffer implements Buffer
6   {
7       private ArrayBlockingQueue<Integer> buffer;
8
9       public BlockingBuffer()
10      {
11          buffer = new ArrayBlockingQueue<Integer>( 3 );
12      } // end BlockingBuffer constructor
13
14      // place value into buffer
15      public void set( int value )
16      {
17          try
18          {
19              buffer.put( value ); // place value in circular buffer
20              System.out.printf( "%s%2d\t%s%d\n", "Producer writes ", value,
21                  "Buffers occupied: ", buffer.size() );
22          } // end try
23          catch ( Exception exception )
24          {
25              exception.printStackTrace();
26          } // end catch
27      } // end method set
28
29      // return value from buffer
30      public int get()
31      {
32          int readValue = 0; // initialize value read from buffer
33
34          try
35          {
36              readValue = buffer.take(); // remove value from circular buffer
37              System.out.printf( "%s %2d\t%s%d\n", "Consumer reads ",
38                  readValue, "Buffers occupied: ", buffer.size() );
39          } // end try
40          catch ( Exception exception )
41          {
42              exception.printStackTrace();
43          } // end catch
44
45          return readValue;
46      } // end method get
47   } // end class BlockingBuffer
```

Fig. 23.15 | BlockingBuffer creates a blocking circular buffer using the ArrayBlockingQueue class.

implement Buffer, our application can reuse the Producer (Fig. 23.7) and Consumer (Fig. 23.8) classes.

Line 19 in method set (lines 15–27) calls method put on the ArrayBlockingQueue. This method call will block until there is room in buffer to place value. Method get (lines 30–46) of class BlockingBuffer calls method take (line 36) on the ArrayBlockingQueue. Again, this method call will block until there is an element in buffer to remove. Note that neither of these methods requires a Lock or Condition object. The ArrayBlockingQueue handles all of the synchronization for you. The amount of code in this program is greatly decreased from the previous circular buffer (from 123 lines to 47 lines) and is much easier to understand. This is an excellent example of encapsulation and software reuse.

Class BlockingBufferTest (Fig. 23.16) contains the main method that launches the application. Line 11 creates the ExecutorService, and line 14 creates a BlockingBuffer object and assigns its reference to Buffer variable sharedLocation. Lines 18–19 execute the Producer and Consumer Runnables. Line 26 calls method shutdown to end the application when the Producer and Consumer finish.

In our prior synchronization examples, the output statements in the Buffer's set and get methods that indicated what the Producer was writing or the Consumer was reading were always executed while the Buffer's lock was held by the thread calling set or get. This guaranteed the order in which the output would be displayed. If the Consumer had the lock, the Producer could not execute the set method—therefore, it was not possible

```
1   // Fig 23.16: BlockingBufferTest.java
2   // Application shows two threads manipulating a blocking buffer.
3   import java.util.concurrent.ExecutorService;
4   import java.util.concurrent.Executors;
5
6   public class BlockingBufferTest
7   {
8      public static void main( String[] args )
9      {
10        // create new thread pool with two threads
11        ExecutorService application = Executors.newFixedThreadPool( 2 );
12
13        // create BlockingBuffer to store ints
14        Buffer sharedLocation = new BlockingBuffer();
15
16        try // try to start producer and consumer
17        {
18           application.execute( new Producer( sharedLocation ) );
19           application.execute( new Consumer( sharedLocation ) );
20        } // end try
21        catch ( Exception exception )
22        {
23           exception.printStackTrace();
24        } // end catch
25
26        application.shutdown();
27     } // end main
28  } // end class BlockingBufferTest
```

Fig. 23.16 | BlockingBufferTest sets up a producer/consumer application using a blocking circular buffer. (Part 1 of 2.)

```
Producer writes  1      Buffers occupied: 1
Consumer reads   1      Buffers occupied: 0
Producer writes  2      Buffers occupied: 1
Consumer reads   2      Buffers occupied: 0
Producer writes  3      Buffers occupied: 1
Consumer reads   3      Buffers occupied: 0
Producer writes  4      Buffers occupied: 1
Consumer reads   4      Buffers occupied: 0
Producer writes  5      Buffers occupied: 1
Consumer reads   5      Buffers occupied: 0
Producer writes  6      Buffers occupied: 1
Consumer reads   6      Buffers occupied: 0
Producer writes  7      Buffers occupied: 1
Producer writes  8      Buffers occupied: 2
Consumer reads   7      Buffers occupied: 1
Producer writes  9      Buffers occupied: 2
Consumer reads   8      Buffers occupied: 1
Producer writes 10      Buffers occupied: 2

Producer done producing.
Terminating Producer.
Consumer reads   9      Buffers occupied: 1
Consumer reads  10      Buffers occupied: 0

Consumer read values totaling 55.
Terminating Consumer.
```

Fig. 23.16 | BlockingBufferTest sets up a producer/consumer application using a blocking circular buffer. (Part 2 of 2.)

for the Producer to output out of turn. The reverse was also true. In Fig. 23.15, methods set and get no longer use locks—all locking is handled by the ArrayBlockingQueue. Because this class is from the Java API, we cannot modify it to perform output from its put and take methods. For these reasons, it is possible that the Producer and Consumer output statements in this example could print out of order. Even though the ArrayBlockingQueue is properly synchronizing access to the data, the output statements are no longer synchronized.

23.10 Multithreading with GUI

This program uses separate threads to modify the content displayed in a Swing GUI. The nature of multithreaded programming prevents the programmer from knowing exactly when a thread will execute. Swing components are not thread safe—if multiple threads manipulate a Swing GUI component, the results may not be correct. All interactions with Swing GUI components should be performed as part of the event-dispatching thread (also known as the event-handling thread). Class SwingUtilities (package javax.swing) provides static method invokeLater to help with this process. Method invokeLater specifies GUI processing statements to execute later as part of the event-dispatching thread. Method invokeLater receives as its argument an object that implements interface Runnable. The method places the Runnable as an event into the event-dispatching thread's queue of events. These events are processed in the order they appear in the queue. Because only one thread handles these events, it can be guaranteed that the GUI will be updated properly.

Our next example (Fig. 23.17) demonstrates this concept. When this program calls invokeLater, the GUI component update will be queued for execution in the event-dispatching thread. The Runnable's run method will then be invoked as part of the event-dispatching thread to perform the output and ensure that the GUI component is updated in a thread-safe manner. This example also demonstrates how to suspend a thread (i.e., temporarily prevent it from executing) and how to resume a suspended thread.

Class RunnableObject (Fig. 23.17) implements interface Runnable's run method (lines 26–74). Line 29 uses static Thread method currentThread to determine the currently executing thread and Thread method getName to return the name of that thread. Every executing thread has a default name that includes the number of the thread (see the output of Fig. 23.18). Lines 31–73 are an infinite loop. [*Note:* In earlier chapters we have said that infinite loops are bad programming because the application will not terminate. In this case, the infinite loop is in a separate thread from the main thread. When the application window is closed in this example, all the threads created by the main thread are closed as well, including threads (such as this one) that are executing infinite loops.] In each iteration of the loop, the thread sleeps for a random interval from 0 to 1 seconds (line 36).

When the thread awakens, line 38 acquires the Lock on this application. Lines 41–44 loop while the boolean variable suspended is true. Line 43 calls method await on Condition suspend to temporarily release the Lock and place this thread into the *waiting* state. When this thread is signaled, it reacquires the Lock, moves back to the *runnable* state and releases the Lock (line 48). When suspended is false, the thread should resume execution. If suspended is still true, the loop executes again.

```java
1   // Fig. 23.17: RunnableObject.java
2   // Runnable that writes a random character to a JLabel
3   import java.util.Random;
4   import java.util.concurrent.locks.Condition;
5   import java.util.concurrent.locks.Lock;
6   import javax.swing.JLabel;
7   import javax.swing.SwingUtilities;
8   import java.awt.Color;
9
10  public class RunnableObject implements Runnable
11  {
12     private static Random generator = new Random(); // for random letters
13     private Lock lockObject; // application lock; passed in to constructor
14     private Condition suspend; // used to suspend and resume thread
15     private boolean suspended = false; // true if thread suspended
16     private JLabel output; // JLabel for output
17
18     public RunnableObject( Lock theLock, JLabel label )
19     {
20        lockObject = theLock; // store the Lock for the application
21        suspend = lockObject.newCondition(); // create new Condition
22        output = label; // store JLabel for outputting character
23     } // end RunnableObject constructor
24
```

Fig. 23.17 | RunnableObject outputs a random uppercase letter on a JLabel. Allows user to suspend and resume execution. (Part 1 of 3.)

```
25          // place random characters in GUI
26          public void run()
27          {
28             // get name of executing thread
29             final String threadName = Thread.currentThread().getName();
30
31             while ( true ) // infinite loop; will be terminated from outside
32             {
33                try
34                {
35                   // sleep for up to 1 second
36                   Thread.sleep( generator.nextInt( 1000 ) );
37
38                   lockObject.lock(); // obtain the lock
39                   try
40                   {
41                      while ( suspended ) // loop until not suspended
42                      {
43                         suspend.await(); // suspend thread execution
44                      } // end while
45                   } // end try
46                   finally
47                   {
48                      lockObject.unlock(); // unlock the lock
49                   } // end finally
50                } // end try
51                // if thread interrupted during wait/sleep
52                catch ( InterruptedException exception )
53                {
54                   exception.printStackTrace(); // print stack trace
55                } // end catch
56
57                // display character on corresponding JLabel
58                SwingUtilities.invokeLater(
59                   new Runnable()
60                   {
61                      // pick random character and display it
62                      public void run()
63                      {
64                         // select random uppercase letter
65                         char displayChar =
66                            ( char ) ( generator.nextInt( 26 ) + 65 );
67
68                         // output character in JLabel
69                         output.setText( threadName + ": " + displayChar );
70                      } // end method run
71                   } // end inner class
72                ); // end call to SwingUtilities.invokeLater
73             } // end while
74          } // end method run
75
```

Fig. 23.17 | RunnableObject outputs a random uppercase letter on a JLabel. Allows user to suspend and resume execution. (Part 2 of 3.)

```
76        // change the suspended/running state
77        public void toggle()
78        {
79           suspended = !suspended; // toggle boolean controlling state
80
81           // change label color on suspend/resume
82           output.setBackground( suspended ? Color.RED : Color.GREEN );
83
84           lockObject.lock(); // obtain lock
85           try
86           {
87              if ( !suspended ) // if thread resumed
88              {
89                 suspend.signal(); // resume thread
90              } // end if
91           } // end try
92           finally
93           {
94              lockObject.unlock(); // release lock
95           } // end finally
96        } // end method toggle
97     } // end class RunnableObject
```

Fig. 23.17 | `RunnableObject` outputs a random uppercase letter on a `JLabel`. Allows user to suspend and resume execution. (Part 3 of 3.)

Lines 58–72 call `SwingUtilities` method `invokeLater`. Lines 59–71 declare an anonymous inner class that implements the `Runnable` interface, and lines 62–70 declare method run. The method call to `invokeLater` places this `Runnable` object in a queue to be executed by the event-dispatching thread. Lines 65–66 create a random uppercase character. Line 69 calls method `setText` on the `JLabel` output to display the thread name and the random character on the `JLabel` in the application window.

When the user clicks the `JCheckBox` to the right of a particular `JLabel`, the corresponding thread should be suspended (temporarily prevented from executing) or resumed (allowed to continue executing). Suspending and resuming of a thread can be implemented by using thread synchronization and `Condition` methods `await` and `signal`. Lines 77–96 declare method `toggle`, which will change the suspended/resumed state of the current thread. Line 79 reverses the value of `boolean` variable `suspended`. Line 82 changes the background color of the `JLabel` by calling method `setBackground`. If the thread is suspended, the background color will be `Color.RED`, whereas if the thread is running, the background color will be `Color.GREEN`. Method `toggle` is called from the event handler in Fig. 23.18, so its tasks will be performed in the event-dispatch thread—thus, there is no need to use `invokeLater` for line 82. Line 84 acquires the `Lock` for this application. Line 87 then tests whether the thread was just resumed. If this is true, line 89 calls method `signal` on `Condition` suspend. This method call will alert a thread that was placed in the *waiting* state by the `await` method call in line 43. Line 94 releases the `Lock` on this application inside a `finally` block.

Note that the `if` statement in line 87 does not have an associated `else`. If this condition fails, it means that the thread has just been suspended. When this happens, a thread executing at line 38 will enter the `while` loop and line 43 will suspend the thread with a call to method `await`.

Class RandomCharacters (Fig. 23.18) displays three JLabels and three JCheckBoxes. A separate thread of execution is associated with each JLabel and JCheckBox pair. Each thread randomly displays letters from the alphabet in its corresponding JLabel object. Line 33 creates a new ExecutorService with method newFixedThreadPool. Lines 36–56 iterate three times. Lines 38–41 create and customize the JLabel. Line 44 creates the JCheckBox, and line 47 adds an ActionListener for each JCheckBox (this will be discussed later.) Lines 51–52 create a new RunnableObject implements the Runnable interface. Line 55 executes the RunnableObject with one of the threads of execution created in runner in line 33.

If the user clicks the **Suspended** checkbox next to a particular JLabel, the program invokes method actionPerformed (lines 65–74) to determine which checkbox generated the event. Lines 68–73 determine which checkbox generated the event. Line 71 checks

```java
 1   // Fig. 23.18: RandomCharacters.java
 2   // Class RandomCharacters demonstrates the Runnable interface
 3   import java.awt.Color;
 4   import java.awt.GridLayout;
 5   import java.awt.event.ActionEvent;
 6   import java.awt.event.ActionListener;
 7   import java.util.concurrent.Executors;
 8   import java.util.concurrent.ExecutorService;
 9   import java.util.concurrent.locks.Condition;
10   import java.util.concurrent.locks.Lock;
11   import java.util.concurrent.locks.ReentrantLock;
12   import javax.swing.JCheckBox;
13   import javax.swing.JFrame;
14   import javax.swing.JLabel;
15
16   public class RandomCharacters extends JFrame implements ActionListener
17   {
18      private final static int SIZE = 3; // number of threads
19      private JCheckBox checkboxes[]; // array of JCheckBoxes
20      private Lock lockObject = new ReentrantLock( true ); // single lock
21
22      // array of RunnableObjects to display random characters
23      private RunnableObject[] randomCharacters =
24         new RunnableObject[ SIZE ];
25
26      // set up GUI and arrays
27      public RandomCharacters()
28      {
29         checkboxes = new JCheckBox[ SIZE ]; // allocate space for array
30         setLayout( new GridLayout( SIZE, 2, 5, 5 ) ); // set layout
31
32         // create new thread pool with SIZE threads
33         ExecutorService runner = Executors.newFixedThreadPool( SIZE );
```

Fig. 23.18 | RandomCharacters creates a JFrame with three RunnableObjects and three JCheckBoxes to allow the user to suspend and resume threads. (Part 1 of 3.)

```
34
35          // loop SIZE times
36          for ( int count = 0; count < SIZE; count++ )
37          {
38              JLabel outputJLabel = new JLabel(); // create JLabel
39              outputJLabel.setBackground( Color.GREEN ); // set color
40              outputJLabel.setOpaque( true ); // set JLabel to be opaque
41              add( outputJLabel ); // add JLabel to JFrame
42
43              // create JCheckBox to control suspend/resume state
44              checkboxes[ count ] = new JCheckBox( "Suspended" );
45
46              // add listener which executes when JCheckBox is clicked
47              checkboxes[ count ].addActionListener( this );
48              add( checkboxes[ count ] ); // add JCheckBox to JFrame
49
50              // create a new RunnableObject
51              randomCharacters[ count ] =
52                  new RunnableObject( lockObject, outputJLabel );
53
54              // execute RunnableObject
55              runner.execute( randomCharacters[ count ] );
56          } // end for
57
58          setSize( 275, 90 ); // set size of window
59          setVisible( true ); // show window
60
61          runner.shutdown(); // shutdown runner when threads finish
62      } // end RandomCharacters constructor
63
64      // handle JCheckBox events
65      public void actionPerformed( ActionEvent event )
66      {
67          // loop over all JCheckBoxes in array
68          for ( int count = 0; count < checkboxes.length; count++ )
69          {
70              // check if this JCheckBox was source of event
71              if ( event.getSource() == checkboxes[ count ] )
72                  randomCharacters[ count ].toggle(); // toggle state
73          } // end for
74      } // end method actionPerformed
75
76      public static void main( String args[] )
77      {
78          // create new RandomCharacters object
79          RandomCharacters application = new RandomCharacters();
80
81          // set application to end when window is closed
82          application.setDefaultCloseOperation( EXIT_ON_CLOSE );
83      } // end main
84  } // end class RandomCharacters
```

Fig. 23.18 | RandomCharacters creates a JFrame with three RunnableObjects and three JCheckBoxes to allow the user to suspend and resume threads. (Part 2 of 3.)

Fig. 23.18 | RandomCharacters creates a JFrame with three RunnableObjects and three JCheckBoxes to allow the user to suspend and resume threads. (Part 3 of 3.)

whether the source of the event is the JCheckBox in the current index. If it is, line 72 calls method toggle (lines 75–92 of Fig. 23.17) on that RunnableObject.

23.11 Other Classes and Interfaces in `java.util.concurrent`

The Runnable interface provides only the most basic functionality for multithreaded programming. In fact, this interface has several limitations. Suppose a Runnable encounters a problem and tries to throw a checked exception. The run method is not declared to throw any exceptions, so the problem must be handled within the Runnable—the exception cannot be passed to the calling thread. Now suppose a Runnable is performing a long calculation and the application wants to retrieve the result of that calculation. The run method cannot return a value, so the application must use shared data to pass the value back to the calling thread. This also involves the overhead of synchronizing access to the data. The developers of the new concurrency APIs in J2SE 5.0 recognized these limitations and created a new interface to fix them. The **Callable** interface (package java.util.concurrent) declares a single method named **call**. This interface is designed to be similar to the Runnable interface—allowing an action to be performed concurrently in a separate thread—but the call method allows the thread to return a value or to throw a checked exception.

An application that creates a Callable likely wants to run the Callable concurrently with other Runnables and Callables. The ExecutorService interface provides method **submit**, which will execute a Callable passed in as its argument. The submit method returns an object of type **Future** (package java.util.concurrent), which is an interface that represents the executing Callable. The Future interface declares method **get** to return the result of the Callable and provides other methods to manage a Callable's execution.

23.12 Monitors and Monitor Locks

Another way to perform synchronization is to use Java's built-in **monitors**. Every object has a monitor. The monitor allows one thread at a time to execute inside a **synchronized statement** on the object. This is accomplished by acquiring a lock on the object when the program enters the synchronized statement. These statements are declared using the **synchronized** keyword with the form

```
synchronized ( object )
{
    statements
} // end synchronized statement
```

where *object* is the object whose monitor lock will be acquired. If there are several syn-chronized statements trying to execute on an object at the same time, only one of them may be active on the object at once—all the other threads attempting to enter a synchro-nized statement on the same object are placed in the *blocked* state.

The *blocked* state is not included in Fig. 23.1, but it transitions to and from the *run-nable* state. When a *runnable* thread must wait to enter a synchronized statement, it tran-sitions to the *blocked* state. When the *blocked* thread enters the synchronized statement, it transitions to the *runnable* state.

When a synchronized statement finishes executing, the monitor lock on the object is released and the highest-priority *blocked* thread attempting to enter a synchronized statement proceeds. Java also allows **synchronized methods**. A synchronized method is equivalent to a synchronized statement enclosing the entire body of a method.

If a thread obtains the monitor lock on an object and then determines that it cannot continue with its task on that object until some condition is satisfied, the thread can call Object method **wait**, releasing the monitor lock on the object. The thread releases the monitor lock on the object and waits in the *waiting* state while the other threads try to enter the object's synchronized statement(s). When a thread executing a synchronized statement completes or satisfies the condition on which another thread may be waiting, it can call Object method **notify** to allow a waiting thread to transition to the *blocked* state again. At this point, the thread that transitioned from the *wait* state to the *blocked* state can attempt to reacquire the monitor lock on the object. Even if the thread is able to reac-quire the monitor lock, it still might not be able to perform its task at this time—in which case the thread will reenter the *waiting* state and release the monitor lock. If a thread calls **notifyAll**, then all the threads waiting for the monitor lock become eligible to reacquire the lock (that is, they all transition to the *blocked* state). Remember that only one thread at a time can obtain the monitor lock on the object—other threads that attempt to acquire the same monitor lock will be *blocked* until the monitor lock becomes available again (i.e., until no other thread is executing in a synchronized statement on that object). Methods wait, notify and notifyAll are inherited by all classes from class Object.

Software Engineering Observation 23.3

The locking that occurs with the execution of synchronized methods could lead to deadlock if the locks are never released. When exceptions occur, Java's exception mechanism coordinates with Java's synchronization mechanism to release locks and avoid these kinds of deadlocks.

Common Programming Error 23.5

It is an error if a thread issues a wait, a notify or a notifyAll on an object without having acquired a lock for it. This causes an IllegalMonitorStateException.

The application in Fig. 23.19 and Fig. 23.20 demonstrates a producer and a con-sumer accessing a shared buffer with synchronization. In this case, the consumer consumes only after the producer produces a value, and the producer produces a new value only after the consumer consumes the value produced previously. In this example, we reuse interface Buffer (Fig. 23.6) and classes Producer (Fig. 23.7) and Consumer (Fig. 23.8) from the example in Section 23.6. The code that performs the synchronization is placed in the set and get methods of class SynchronizedBuffer (Fig. 23.19), which implements interface Buffer (line 4). Thus, the Producer's and Consumer's run methods simply call the shared object's set and get methods, as in the example in Section 23.6.

```
1   // Fig. 23.19: SynchronizedBuffer.java
2   // SynchronizedBuffer synchronizes access to a single shared integer.
3
4   public class SynchronizedBuffer implements Buffer
5   {
6      private int buffer = -1; // shared by producer and consumer threads
7      private boolean occupied = false; // count of occupied buffers
8
9      // place value into buffer
10     public synchronized void set( int value )
11     {
12        // while there are no empty locations, place thread in waiting state
13        while ( occupied )
14        {
15           // output thread information and buffer information, then wait
16           try
17           {
18              System.out.println( "Producer tries to write." );
19              displayState( "Buffer full. Producer waits." );
20              wait();
21           } // end try
22           catch ( InterruptedException exception )
23           {
24              exception.printStackTrace();
25           } // end catch
26        } // end while
27
28        buffer = value; // set new buffer value
29
30        // indicate producer cannot store another value
31        // until consumer retrieves current buffer value
32        occupied = true;
33
34        displayState( "Producer writes " + buffer );
35
36        notify(); // tell waiting thread to enter runnable state
37     } // end method set; releases lock on SynchronizedBuffer
38
39     // return value from buffer
40     public synchronized int get()
41     {
42        // while no data to read, place thread in waiting state
43        while ( !occupied )
44        {
45           // output thread information and buffer information, then wait
46           try
47           {
48              System.out.println( "Consumer tries to read." );
49              displayState( "Buffer empty. Consumer waits." );
50              wait();
51           } // end try
```

Fig. 23.19 | Synchronizes access to shared data using `Object` methods `wait` and `notify`.
(Part 1 of 2.)

```
52              catch ( InterruptedException exception )
53              {
54                 exception.printStackTrace();
55              } // end catch
56           } // end while
57
58           // indicate that producer can store another value
59           // because consumer just retrieved buffer value
60           occupied = false;
61
62           int readValue = buffer; // store value in buffer
63           displayState( "Consumer reads " + readValue );
64
65           notify(); // tell waiting thread to enter runnable state
66
67           return readValue;
68        } // end method get; releases lock on SynchronizedBuffer
69
70        // display current operation and buffer state
71        public void displayState( String operation )
72        {
73           System.out.printf( "%-40s%d\t\t%b\n\n", operation, buffer,
74              occupied );
75        } // end method displayState
76     } // end class SynchronizedBuffer
```

Fig. 23.19 | Synchronizes access to shared data using `Object` methods `wait` and `notify`. (Part 2 of 2.)

Class `SynchronizedBuffer` (Fig. 23.19) contains two fields—`buffer` (line 6) and `occupied` (line 7). Method `set` (lines 10–37) and method `get` (lines 40–68) are declared as `synchronized` methods by adding the `synchronized` keyword between the method modifier and the return type—thus, only one thread can call any of these methods at a time on a particular `SynchronizedBuffer` object. Field `occupied` is used in conditional expressions to determine whether it is the producer's or the consumer's turn to perform a task. If `occupied` is `false`, `buffer` is empty and the producer can call method `set` to place a value into variable `buffer`. This condition also means that the consumer cannot call `SynchronizedBuffer`'s `get` method to read the value of `buffer` because it is empty. If `occupied` is `true`, the consumer can call `SynchronizedBuffer`'s `get` method to read a value from variable `buffer`, because the variable contains new information. This condition also means that the producer cannot call `SynchronizedBuffer`'s `set` method to place a value into `buffer`, because the buffer is currently full.

When the `Producer` thread's `run` method invokes synchronized method `set`, the thread attempts to acquire the monitor lock on the `SynchronizedBuffer` object. If the monitor lock is available, the `Producer` thread acquires the lock. Then the `while` loop at lines 13–26 determines whether `occupied` is `true`. If so, the buffer is full, so line 18 outputs a message indicating that the `Producer` thread is trying to write a value, and line 19 invokes method `displayState` (lines 71–75) to output another message indicating that the buffer is full and that the `Producer` thread is in the *waiting* state. Line 20 invokes method `wait` (inherited from `Object` by `SynchronizedBuffer`) to place the thread that called method set (i.e., the Producer thread) in the *waiting* state for the Synchronized-Buffer object. The call to wait causes the calling thread to release the lock on the Syn-chronizedBuffer object. This is important because the thread cannot currently perform its task and because other threads should be allowed to access the object at this time to allow the condition (occupied) to change. Now another thread can attempt to acquire the SynchronizedBuffer object's lock and invoke the object's set or get method.

The producer thread remains in the *waiting* state until the thread is notified by another thread that it may proceed—at which point the producer thread returns to the *blocked* state and attempts to reacquire the lock on the SynchronizedBuffer object. If the lock is available, the producer thread reacquires the lock, and method set continues executing with the next statement after wait. Because wait is called in a loop (lines 13–26), the loop-continuation condition is tested again to determine whether the thread can proceed with its execution. If not, wait is invoked again—otherwise, method set continues with the next statement after the loop.

Line 28 in method set assigns value to buffer. Line 32 sets occupied to true to indicate that the buffer now contains a value (i.e., a consumer can read the value, and a producer cannot yet put another value there). Line 34 invokes method displayState to output a line to the console window indicating that the producer is writing a new value into the buffer. Line 36 invokes method notify (inherited from Object). If there are any waiting threads, the first one enters the *blocked* state, indicating that the thread can now attempt to acquire the lock again. Method notify returns immediately and method set returns to its caller. Invoking method notify works correctly in this program because only one thread calls method get at any time (the ConsumerThread). In programs that have multiple threads waiting on a condition, it may be more appropriate to use method noti-fyAll or call method wait with an optional timeout. When method set returns, it implicitly releases the lock on the shared memory.

Methods get and set are implemented similarly. When the Consumer thread's run method invokes synchronized method get, the thread attempts to acquire the monitor lock on the SynchronizedBuffer object. If the lock is available, the Consumer thread acquires it. Then the while loop at lines 43–56 determines whether occupied is false. If so, the buffer is empty, so line 48 outputs a message indicating that the Consumer thread is trying to read a value, and line 49 invokes method displayState to output another message indicating that the buffer is empty and that the Consumer thread is waiting. Line 50 invokes method wait to place the thread that called method get (i.e., the Consumer thread) in the *waiting* state for the SynchronizedBuffer object. Again, the call to wait causes the calling thread to release the lock on the SynchronizedBuffer object, so another thread can attempt to acquire the SynchronizedBuffer object's lock and invoke the object's set or get method. If the lock on the SynchronizedBuffer is not available (e.g., if the ProducerThread has not yet returned from method set), the ConsumerThread is blocked until the lock becomes available.

The consumer thread object remains in the *waiting* state until the thread is notified by another thread that it may proceed—at which point the consumer thread returns to the *blocked* state and attempts to reacquire the lock on the SynchronizedBuffer object. If the lock is available, the consumer thread reacquires the lock and method get continues executing with the next statement after wait. Because wait is called in a loop (lines 43–56), the loop-continuation condition is tested again to determine whether the thread can proceed with its execution. If not, `wait` is invoked again—otherwise, method `get` continues with the next statement after the loop. Line 60 sets `occupied` to `false` to indicate that `buffer` is now empty (i.e., a consumer cannot read the value, but a producer can place another value into `buffer`), line 63 calls method `displayState` to indicate that the consumer is reading and line 65 invokes method `notify`. If there are any threads in the *blocked* state for the lock on this `SynchronizedBuffer` object, one of them enters the *runnable* state, indicating that the thread can now attempt to reacquire the lock and continue performing its task. Method `notify` returns immediately, then method `get` returns the value of `buffer` to its caller. Invoking method `notify` works correctly in this program because only one thread calls method set at any time (the `ProducerThread`). Programs that have multiple threads waiting on a condition should invoke `notifyAll` to ensure that multiple threads receive notifications properly. When method `get` returns, the lock on the `SynchronizedBuffer` object is implicitly released.

Class `SharedBufferTest2` (Fig. 23.20) is identical to class `SharedBufferTest` (Fig. 23.12). Study the outputs in Fig. 23.20. Observe that every integer produced is consumed exactly once—no values are lost, and no values are consumed more than once. The

```
1   // Fig 23.20: SharedBufferTest2.java
2   // Application shows two threads manipulating a synchronized buffer.
3   import java.util.concurrent.ExecutorService;
4   import java.util.concurrent.Executors;
5
6   public class SharedBufferTest2
7   {
8      public static void main( String[] args )
9      {
10        // create new thread pool with two threads
11        ExecutorService application = Executors.newFixedThreadPool( 2 );
12
13        // create SynchronizedBuffer to store ints
14        Buffer sharedLocation = new SynchronizedBuffer();
15
16        System.out.printf( "%-40s%s\t\t%s\n%-40s%s\n\n", "Operation",
17           "Buffer", "Occupied", "---------", "------\t\t--------" );
18
19        try // try to start producer and consumer
20        {
21           application.execute( new Producer( sharedLocation ) );
22           application.execute( new Consumer( sharedLocation ) );
23        } // end try
24        catch ( Exception exception )
25        {
26           exception.printStackTrace();
27        } // end catch
28
29        application.shutdown();
30     } // end main
31  } // end class SharedBufferTest2
```

Fig. 23.20 | SharedBufferTest2 sets up a producer/consumer application that uses a synchronized buffer. (Part 1 of 3.)

Operation	Buffer	Occupied
Consumer tries to read. Buffer empty. Consumer waits.	-1	false
Producer writes 1	1	true
Consumer reads 1	1	false
Consumer tries to read. Buffer empty. Consumer waits.	1	false
Producer writes 2	2	true
Consumer reads 2	2	false
Producer writes 3	3	true
Consumer reads 3	3	false
Consumer tries to read. Buffer empty. Consumer waits.	3	false
Producer writes 4	4	true
Consumer reads 4	4	false
Consumer tries to read. Buffer empty. Consumer waits.	4	false
Producer writes 5	5	true
Consumer reads 5	5	false
Producer writes 6	6	true
Consumer reads 6	6	false
Consumer tries to read. Buffer empty. Consumer waits.	6	false
Producer writes 7	7	true
Consumer reads 7	7	false
Consumer tries to read. Buffer empty. Consumer waits.	7	false
Producer writes 8	8	true
Consumer reads 8	8	false
Producer writes 9	9	true

Fig. 23.20 | SharedBufferTest2 sets up a producer/consumer application that uses a synchronized buffer. (Part 2 of 3.)

```
Producer tries to write.
Buffer full. Producer waits.          9              true

Consumer reads 9                      9              false

Producer writes 10                    10             true


Producer done producing.
Terminating Producer.
Consumer reads 10                     10             false


Consumer read values totaling 55.
Terminating Consumer.
```

Fig. 23.20 | `SharedBufferTest2` sets up a producer/consumer application that uses a synchronized buffer. (Part 3 of 3.)

synchronization and condition variable ensure that the producer and consumer cannot perform their tasks unless it is their turn. The producer must go first, the consumer must wait if the producer has not produced since the consumer last consumed, and the producer must wait if the consumer has not yet consumed the value that the producer most recently produced. Execute this program several times to confirm that every integer produced is consumed exactly once. In the sample output, note the lines indicating when the producer and consumer must wait to perform their respective tasks.

23.13 Wrap-Up

This chapter presented Java's new concurrency API and demonstrated the powerful technique of thread synchronization. Multithreading is an advanced topic that is the subject of many books. We use the multithreading techniques introduced here again in Chapter 24, Networking, to help build multithreaded servers that can interact with multiple clients concurrently.

Summary

- Computers perform operations concurrently, such as compiling programs, sending files to a printer and receiving electronic mail messages over a network.

- Programming languages generally provide a set of control statements that only enable programmers to perform one action at a time.

- Historically, concurrency has been implemented as operating-system primitives available only to experienced systems programmers.

- Java makes concurrency available to the applications programmer. The programmer specifies that applications contain threads of execution—each thread designating a portion of a program that may execute concurrently with other threads. This capability is called multithreading.

- A new thread begins its life cycle in the *new* state. It remains in the *new* state until the program starts the thread, which places the thread in the *runnable* state.

- A *runnable* thread enters the *terminated* state when it completes its task or otherwise terminates.

- Sometimes a thread transitions to the *waiting* state while it waits for another thread to perform a task. Once in this state, a thread transitions back to the *runnable* state only when another thread signals the waiting thread to continue executing.

- A *runnable* thread can enter the *timed waiting* state for a specified interval of time. A thread in this state transitions back to the *runnable* state when that time interval expires. A thread can transition to the *timed waiting* state if it provides an optional wait interval when it is waiting for another thread to perform a task. Such a thread will return to the *runnable* state when it is signaled by another thread or when the timed interval expires—whichever comes first. Another way to place a thread in the *timed waiting* state is to put the thread to sleep.

- At the operating system level, the *runnable* state actually encompasses two separate states . When a thread first transitions to the *runnable* state from the *new* state, the thread is in the *ready* state. A *ready* thread enters the *running* state (i.e., begins executing) when the operating system assigns the thread to a processor. When the thread's quantum expires, the thread returns to the *ready* state, and the operating system assigns to the processor another thread.

- Every Java thread has a priority in the range between MIN_PRIORITY (1) and MAX_PRIORITY (10). By default, each thread is given priority NORM_PRIORITY (5).

- Most Java platforms support timeslicing. Without timeslicing, each thread in a set of equal-priority threads runs to completion before other equal priority threads get a chance to execute. With timeslicing, each thread receives a brief burst of processor time, or quantum, during which the thread can execute. When the quantum expires, even if the thread has not finished executing, the processor is taken away from it and given to the next thread of equal priority, if one is available.

- The thread scheduler determines which thread runs next. One simple implementation will keep the highest-priority thread running at all times. If there is more than one highest-priority thread, the scheduler ensures that all such threads execute for a quantum each in round-robin fashion.

- Multithreading in Java is accomplished by implementing the Runnable interface, which declares a single method named run.

- Runnables are executed using a class that implements the Executor interface, which declares a single method named execute.

- Interface ExecutorService is a subinterface of Executor that declares several methods for managing the life cycle of the Executor. An object that implements the ExecutorService interface can be created using static methods declared in class Executors.

- ExecutorService method shutdown ends each thread in an ExecutorService as soon as it finishes executing its Runnable.

- When multiple threads share an object, indeterminate results may occur unless the shared object is synchronization properly. Mutual exclusion allows the programmer to perform such thread synchronization.

- Once a Lock has been obtained by a thread (by calling the lock method), the Lock object will not allow another thread to obtain the lock until the first thread releases the Lock (by calling the unlock method). When a thread calls method unlock, the lock on the object is released and the highest-priority waiting thread attempting to lock the object proceeds.

- Once a thread obtains the lock on an object, if the thread determines that it cannot continue with its task until some condition is satisfied, the thread can wait on a condition variable, thus removing it from contention for the processor and releasing the lock on the object. Condition variables are created by calling Lock method newCondition, which returns a Condition object.

- A thread can call method await on a Condition object to release the associated Lock and place that thread in the *waiting* state while other threads try to obtain the Lock. When another thread satisfies the condition on which the first thread is *waiting*, that thread can call Condition method `signal` to allow the waiting thread to transition to the *runnable* state again. If a thread calls `Condition` method `signalAll`, then all the threads waiting for the lock become eligible to reacquire the lock. Only one of those threads can obtain the lock on the object at a time—other threads that attempt to acquire the same lock will have to wait until the lock becomes available again.

- In a producer/consumer relationship, the producer portion of an application generates data and stores it in a shared object, and the consumer portion of an application reads data from the shared object. In a multithreaded producer/consumer relationship, a producer thread generates data and places it in a shared object called a buffer. A consumer thread reads data from the buffer.

- To minimize the amount of waiting time for threads that share resources and operate at the same average speeds, use a circular buffer that provides extra buffer space into which the producer can place values and from which the consumer can retrieve those values.

- The `BlockingQueue` interface declares methods `put` and `take`, which are the blocking equivalents of `Queue` methods `offer` and `remove`, respectively. This means that method `put` will place an element at the end of the `BlockingQueue`, waiting if the queue is full. Method `take` will remove an element from the head of the `BlockingQueue`, waiting if the queue is empty. Class `ArrayBlockingQueue` implements the `BlockingQueue` interface using an array. This makes the data structure fixed size, meaning that it will not expand to accommodate extra elements.

- Swing components are not thread safe—if multiple threads manipulate a Swing GUI component, the results may not be correct. All interactions with Swing GUI components should be performed in the event-dispatch thread. Class `SwingUtilities` provides `static` method `invokeLater` to help with this process. Method `invokeLater` receives as its argument an object that implements interface `Runnable` and performs the GUI updates.

- The `Callable` interface declares a single method named `call` which allows the user to return a value or throw a checked exception. The `ExecutorService` interface provides method `submit` which will execute a `Callable` passed in as its argument. The `submit` method returns an object of type `Future` which is an interface that represents the executing `Callable`. The `Future` interface declares method `get` to return the result of the `Callable` and provides other methods to manage the execution of the `Callable`.

- An object's monitor allows one thread at a time to execute inside a `synchronized` statement on that object.

- When a *runnable* thread must wait to enter a `synchronized` statement, it transitions to the *blocked* state. When the *blocked* thread enters the `synchronized` statement, it transitions to the *runnable* state.

- Java also allows `synchronized` methods which is equivalent to a `synchronized` statement that encloses the entire body of the method.

- Once a thread obtains the monitor lock on an object, if the thread determines that it cannot continue with its task on that object until some condition is satisfied, the thread can call `Object` method `wait`, releasing the monitor lock on the object.

- When a thread executing a `synchronized` statement completes or satisfies the condition on which another thread may be waiting, the thread can call `Object` method `notify` to allow a waiting thread to transition to the *blocked* state again.

- If a thread calls `notifyAll`, then all threads waiting for the monitor lock become eligible to reacquire the lock (that is, they all transition to the *blocked* state).

Terminology

`ArrayBlockingQueue` class	*blocked* state
`await` method of interface `Condition`	`BlockingQueue` interface

buffer
call method of interface Callable
Callable interface
circular buffer
concurrency
concurrent programming
Condition interface
condition variable
consumer
consumer thread
deadlock
dispatching a thread
event-dispatching thread
execute method of interface Executor
Executor interface
Executors class
ExecutorService interface
fairness policy of a lock
Future interface
garbage collection
garbage-collector thread
get method of interface Future
IllegalMonitorStateException class
indefinite postponement
interrupt method of class Thread
InterruptedException class
invokeLater method of class SwingUtilities
Lock interface
lock method of interface Lock
main thread
memory leak
monitor
multithreading
mutual exclusion
new state
newCachedThreadPool method of class Executors
newCondition method of interface Lock
newFixedThreadPool method of class Executors
obtain the lock
notify method of class Object
notifyAll method of class Object
parallel operations
preemptive scheduling

priority of a thread
producer
producer thread
producer/consumer relationship
put method of interface BlockingQueue
quantum
ready state
ReentrantLock class
resume a thread
round-robin scheduling
run method of interface Runnable
Runnable interface
runnable state
running state
shutdown method of class ExecutorService
signal method of class Condition
signalAll method of class Condition
sleep interval
sleep method of class Thread
sleeping thread
starvation
submit method of class ExecutorService
suspend a thread
SwingUtilities class
synchronization
synchronized keyword
synchronized method
synchronized statement
take method of interface BlockingQueue
terminated state
thread
Thread class
thread pool
thread scheduler
thread scheduling
thread state
thread synchronization
timed waiting state
timeslice
unlock method of interface Lock
wait method of class Object
waiting state

Self-Review Exercises

23.1 Fill in the blanks in each of the following statements:
   a) C and C++ are _____-threaded languages, whereas Java is a(n) _____-threaded language.

b) A thread enters the *terminated* state when _____.

c) To pause for a designated number of milliseconds and resume execution, a thread should call method _____.

d) Method _____ of class `Condition` moves a single thread in an object's *waiting* state to the *runnable* state.

e) Method _____ of class `Condition` moves every thread in an object's *waiting* state to the *runnable* state.

f) A(n) _____ thread enters the _____ state when it completes its task or otherwise terminates.

g) A *runnable* thread can enter the _____ state for a specified interval of time.

h) At the operating-system level, the *runnable* state actually encompasses two separate states, _____ and _____.

i) `Runnables` are executed using a class that implements the _____ interface.

j) `ExecutorService` method _____ ends each thread in an `ExecutorService` as soon as it finishes executing its current `Runnable`, if any.

k) A thread can call method _____ on a `Condition` object to release the associated `Lock` and place that thread in the _____ state.

l) In a(n) _____ relationship, the _____ portion of an application generates data and stores it in a shared object, and the _____ portion of an application reads data from the shared object.

m) To minimize the amount of waiting time for threads that share resources and operate at the same average speeds, use a(n) _____.

n) Class _____ implements the `BlockingQueue` interface using an array.

o) The keyword _____ indicates that only one thread at a time should execute on an object.

23.2 State whether each of the following is *true* or *false*. If *false*, explain why.

a) A thread is not *runnable* if it is dead.

b) In Java, a higher-priority *runnable* thread should preempt threads of lower priority.

c) Some operating systems use timeslicing with threads. Therefore, they can enable threads to preempt threads of the same priority.

d) When the thread's quantum expires, the thread returns to the *running* state as the operating system assigns the thread to a processor.

e) Without timeslicing, each thread in a set of equal-priority threads runs to completion before other threads of equal priority get a chance to execute.

Answers to Self-Review Exercises

23.1 a) single, multi. b) its run method ends. c) `Thread.sleep`. d) `signal`. e) `signalAll`. f) *runnable, terminated*. g) *timed waiting*. h) *ready, running*. i) `Executor`. j) `shutdown`. k) `await`, *waiting*. l) producer/consumer, producer, consumer. m) circular buffer. n) `ArrayBlockingQueue`. o) `synchronized`.

23.2 a) True. b) True. c) False. Timeslicing allows a thread to execute until its timeslice (or quantum) expires. Then other threads of equal priority can execute. d) False. When a thread's quantum expires, the thread returns to the *ready* state and the operating system assigns to the processor another thread. e) True.

Exercises

23.3 State whether each of the following is *true* or *false*. If *false*, explain why.

a) Method `sleep` does not consume processor time while a thread sleeps.

    b) Using a Lock guarantees that deadlock cannot occur.
    c) Once a Lock has been obtained by a thread, the Lock object will not allow another thread to obtain the lock until the first thread releases it.
    d) Swing components are thread safe.

23.4 Define each of the following terms.
    a) thread
    b) multithreading
    c) *runnable* state
    d) *timed waiting* state
    e) preemptive scheduling
    f) Runnable interface
    g) signal method of class Condition
    h) producer/consumer relationship
    i) quantum

23.5 Discuss each of the following terms in the context of Java's threading mechanisms:
    a) Lock
    b) producer
    c) consumer
    d) await
    e) signal
    f) Condition

23.6 Two problems that can occur in systems like Java, that allow threads to wait, are deadlock, in which one or more threads will wait forever for an event that cannot occur, and indefinite postponement, in which one or more threads will be delayed for some unpredictably long time. Give an example of how each of these problems can occur in a multithreaded Java program.

23.7 Discuss the difference between Condition method await with no arguments and Condition method await with a time-interval argument. In particular, what states do threads enter, and how can those threads return to the runnable state?

23.8 Name three threads that are created automatically by the Java virtual machine and discuss the purpose of each thread.

23.9 Write a program that bounces a blue ball inside a JPanel. The ball should begin moving with a mousePressed event. When the ball hits the edge of the JPanel, it should bounce off the edge and continue in the opposite direction. The ball should be updated using a Runnable.

23.10 Modify the program in Exercise 23.9 to add a new ball each time the user clicks the mouse. Provide for a minimum of 20 balls. Randomly choose the color for each new ball.

23.11 Modify the program in Exercise 23.10 to add shadows. As a ball moves, draw a solid black oval at the bottom of the JPanel. You may consider adding a 3-D effect by increasing or decreasing the size of each ball when it hits the edge of the JPanel.

23.12 Modify the program in Exercise 23.10 or Exercise 23.11 to bounce the balls off each other when they collide. A collision should occur between two balls when the distance between the centers of those two balls is less than the sum of the two balls' radii.

Networking

If the presence of electricity can be made visible in any part of a circuit, I see no reason why intelligence may not be transmitted instantaneously by electricity.
—Samuel F. B. Morse

Protocol is everything.
—Francois Giuliani

What networks of railroads, highways and canals were in another age, the networks of telecommunications, information and computerization ... are today.
—Bruno Kreisky

The port is near, the bells I hear, the people all exulting.
—Walt Whitman

OBJECTIVES

In this chapter you will learn:

- To understand Java networking with URLs, sockets and datagrams.

- To implement Java networking applications by using sockets and datagrams.

- To understand how to implement Java clients and servers that communicate with one another.

- To understand how to implement network-based collaborative applications.

- To construct a multithreaded server.

24.1 Introduction

There is much excitement about the Internet and the World Wide Web. The Internet ties the information world together. The World Wide Web makes the Internet easy to use and gives it the flair and sizzle of multimedia. Organizations see the Internet and the Web as crucial to their information-systems strategies. Java provides a number of built-in networking capabilities that make it easy to develop Internet-based and Web-based applications. Java can enable programs to search the world for information and to collaborate with programs running on other computers internationally, nationally or just within an organization. Java can enable applets and applications to communicate with one another (subject to security constraints).

Networking is a massive and complex topic. Computer science and computer engineering students will typically take a full-semester, upper-level course in computer networking and continue with further study at the graduate level. Java is often used as an implementation vehicle in computer networking courses. In *Java How to Program, Sixth Edition*, we introduce a portion of Java's networking concepts and capabilities. We discuss more advanced networking capabilities in our book *Advanced Java 2 Platform How to Program*.

Java's fundamental networking capabilities are declared by classes and interfaces of package **java.net**, through which Java offers stream-based communications that enable applications to view networking as streams of data. The classes and interfaces of package java.net also offer packet-based communications for transmitting individual packets of information—commonly used to transmit audio and video over the Internet. In this chapter, we show how to create and manipulate sockets and how to communicate with packets and streams of data.

Our discussion of networking focuses on both sides of the client-server relationship. The client requests that some action be performed, and the server performs the action and responds to the client. A common implementation of the request-response model is between Web browsers and Web servers. When a user selects a Web site to browse through a browser (the client application), a request is sent to the appropriate Web server (the server application). The server normally responds to the client by sending an appropriate HTML Web page.

We introduce Java's socket-based communications, which enable applications to view networking as if it were file I/O—a program can read from a socket or write to a socket as simply as reading from a file or writing to a file. The socket is simply a software construct that represents one endpoint of a connection. We show how to create and manipulate stream sockets and datagram sockets.

With stream sockets, a process establishes a connection to another process. While the connection is in place, data flows between the processes in continuous streams. Stream sockets are said to provide a connection-oriented service. The protocol used for transmission is the popular TCP (Transmission Control Protocol).

With datagram sockets, individual packets of information are transmitted. This is not appropriate for everyday programmers, because the protocol used—UDP, the User Datagram Protocol—is a connectionless service, and thus does not guarantee that packets arrive in any particular order. With UDP, packets can even be lost or duplicated. Significant extra programming is required on the programmer's part to deal with these problems (if the programmer chooses to do so). UDP is most appropriate for network applications that do not require the error checking and reliability of TCP. Stream sockets and the TCP protocol will be more desirable for the vast majority of Java programmers.

Performance Tip 24.1

Connectionless services generally offer greater performance but less reliability than connection-oriented services.

Portability Tip 24.1

TCP, UDP and related protocols enable a great variety of heterogeneous computer systems (i.e., computer systems with different processors and different operating systems) to intercommunicate.

The chapter includes a case study in which we implement a client/server chat application similar to the instant-messaging services popular on the Web today. The application incorporates many networking techniques introduced in this chapter. It also introduces multicasting, in which a server can publish information and clients can subscribe to that information. Each time the server publishes more information, all subscribers receive it. Throughout the examples of this chapter, we will see that many of the networking details are handled by the Java APIs.

24.2 Manipulating URLs

The Internet offers many protocols. The Hypertext Transfer Protocol (HTTP), which forms the basis of the World Wide Web, uses URIs (Uniform Resource Identifiers) to identify data on the Internet. URIs that specify the locations of documents are called URLs (Uniform Resource Locators). Common URLs refer to files or directories and can reference objects that perform complex tasks, such as database lookups and Internet searches. If you know the HTTP URL of a publicly available HTML document anywhere on the Web, you can access it through HTTP.

Java makes it easy to manipulate URLs. When you use a URL that refers to the exact location of a resource (e.g., a Web page) as an argument to the **showDocument** method of interface `AppletContext`, the browser in which the applet is executing will display that resource. The applet in Fig. 24.1 and Fig. 24.2 demonstrates simple networking capabilities. It enables the user to select a Web page from a `JList` and causes the browser to display the corresponding page. In this example, the networking is performed by the browser.

This applet takes advantage of **applet parameters** specified in the HTML document that invokes the applet. When browsing the World Wide Web, you will often come across applets that are in the public domain—you can use them free of charge on your own Web pages (normally in exchange for crediting the applet's creator). Many applets can be customized via parameters supplied from the HTML file that invokes the applet. For example, Fig. 24.1 contains the HTML that invokes the applet `SiteSelector` in Fig. 24.2.

The HTML document contains eight parameters specified with the **param tag**—these lines must appear between the starting and ending `applet` tags. The applet can read these values and use them to customize itself. Any number of `param` tags can appear between the starting and ending `applet` tags. Each parameter has a **name** and a **value**. `Applet` method **getParameter** retrieves the `value` associated with a specific parameter name and returns it as a string. The argument passed to `getParameter` is a string containing the name of the parameter in the `param` element. In this example, parameters represent the title and location of each Web site the user can select. Parameters specified for this applet are named `title#`, where the value of # starts at 0 and increments by 1 for each new title. Each title should have a corresponding location parameter of the form `location#`, where the value of # starts at 0 and increments by 1 for each new location. The statement

```
String title = getParameter( "title0" );
```

gets the value associated with parameter "title0" and assigns it to reference `title`. If there is no `param` tag containing the specified parameter, `getParameter` returns `null`.

The applet (Fig. 24.2) obtains from the HTML document (Fig. 24.1) the choices that will be displayed in the applet's `JList`. Class `SiteSelector` uses a `HashMap` (package `java.util`) to store the Web site names and URLs. In this example, the *key* is the string in the `JList` that represents the Web site name, and the *value* is a URL object that stores the location of the Web site to display in the browser.

```
1   <html>
2   <title>Site Selector</title>
3   <body>
4      <applet code = "SiteSelector.class" width = "300" height = "75">
5         <param name = "title0" value = "Java Home Page">
6         <param name = "location0" value = "http://java.sun.com/">
7         <param name = "title1" value = "Deitel">
8         <param name = "location1" value = "http://www.deitel.com/">
9         <param name = "title2" value = "JGuru">
10        <param name = "location2" value = "http://www.jGuru.com/">
11        <param name = "title3" value = "JavaWorld">
12        <param name = "location3" value = "http://www.javaworld.com/">
13     </applet>
14  </body>
15  </html>
```

Fig. 24.1 | HTML document to load `SiteSelector` applet.

Class `SiteSelector` also contains an `ArrayList` (package `java.util`) in which the site names are placed so that they can be used to initialize the `JList` (one version of the `JList` constructor receives an array of `Object`s which is returned by `ArrayList`'s `toArray` method). An `ArrayList` is a dynamically resizable array of references. Class `ArrayList` provides method `add` to add a new element to the end of the `ArrayList`. (We provide discussions of classes `ArrayList` and `HashMap` in Chapter 19.)

Lines 25–26 in the applet's `init` method (lines 23–57) create a `HashMap` object and an `ArrayList` object. Line 29 calls our utility method `getSitesFromHTMLParameters` (declared at lines 60–89) to obtain the HTML parameters from the HTML document that invoked the applet.

```java
1   // Fig. 24.2: SiteSelector.java
2   // This program loads a document from a URL.
3   import java.net.MalformedURLException;
4   import java.net.URL;
5   import java.util.HashMap;
6   import java.util.ArrayList;
7   import java.awt.BorderLayout;
8   import java.applet.AppletContext;
9   import javax.swing.JApplet;
10  import javax.swing.JLabel;
11  import javax.swing.JList;
12  import javax.swing.JScrollPane;
13  import javax.swing.event.ListSelectionEvent;
14  import javax.swing.event.ListSelectionListener;
15
16  public class SiteSelector extends JApplet
17  {
18     private HashMap< Object, URL > sites; // site names and URLs
19     private ArrayList< String > siteNames; // site names
20     private JList siteChooser; // list of sites to choose from
21
22     // read HTML parameters and set up GUI
23     public void init()
24     {
25        sites = new HashMap< Object, URL >(); // create HashMap
26        siteNames = new ArrayList< String >(); // create ArrayList
27
28        // obtain parameters from HTML document
29        getSitesFromHTMLParameters();
30
31        // create GUI components and layout interface
32        add( new JLabel( "Choose a site to browse" ), BorderLayout.NORTH );
33
34        siteChooser = new JList( siteNames.toArray() ); // populate JList
35        siteChooser.addListSelectionListener(
36           new ListSelectionListener() // anonymous inner class
37           {
```

Fig. 24.2 | Loading a document from a URL into a browser. (Part 1 of 3.)

```
38              // go to site user selected
39              public void valueChanged( ListSelectionEvent event )
40              {
41                 // get selected site name
42                 Object object = siteChooser.getSelectedValue();
43
44                 // use site name to locate corresponding URL
45                 URL newDocument = sites.get( object );
46
47                 // get applet container
48                 AppletContext browser = getAppletContext();
49
50                 // tell applet container to change pages
51                 browser.showDocument( newDocument );
52              } // end method valueChanged
53           } // end anonymous inner class
54        ); // end call to addListSelectionListener
55
56        add( new JScrollPane( siteChooser ), BorderLayout.CENTER );
57     } // end method init
58
59     // obtain parameters from HTML document
60     private void getSitesFromHTMLParameters()
61     {
62        String title; // site title
63        String location; // location of site
64        URL url; // URL of location
65        int counter = 0; // count number of sites
66
67        title = getParameter( "title" + counter ); // get first site title
68
69        // loop until no more parameters in HTML document
70        while ( title != null )
71        {
72           // obtain site location
73           location = getParameter( "location" + counter );
74
75           try // place title/URL in HashMap and title in ArrayList
76           {
77              url = new URL( location ); // convert location to URL
78              sites.put( title, url ); // put title/URL in HashMap
79              siteNames.add( title ); // put title in ArrayList
80           } // end try
81           catch ( MalformedURLException urlException )
82           {
83              urlException.printStackTrace();
84           } // end catch
85
86           counter++;
87           title = getParameter( "title" + counter ); // get next site title
88        } // end while
89     } // end method getSitesFromHTMLParameters
90  } // end class SiteSelector
```

Fig. 24.2 | Loading a document from a URL into a browser. (Part 2 of 3.)

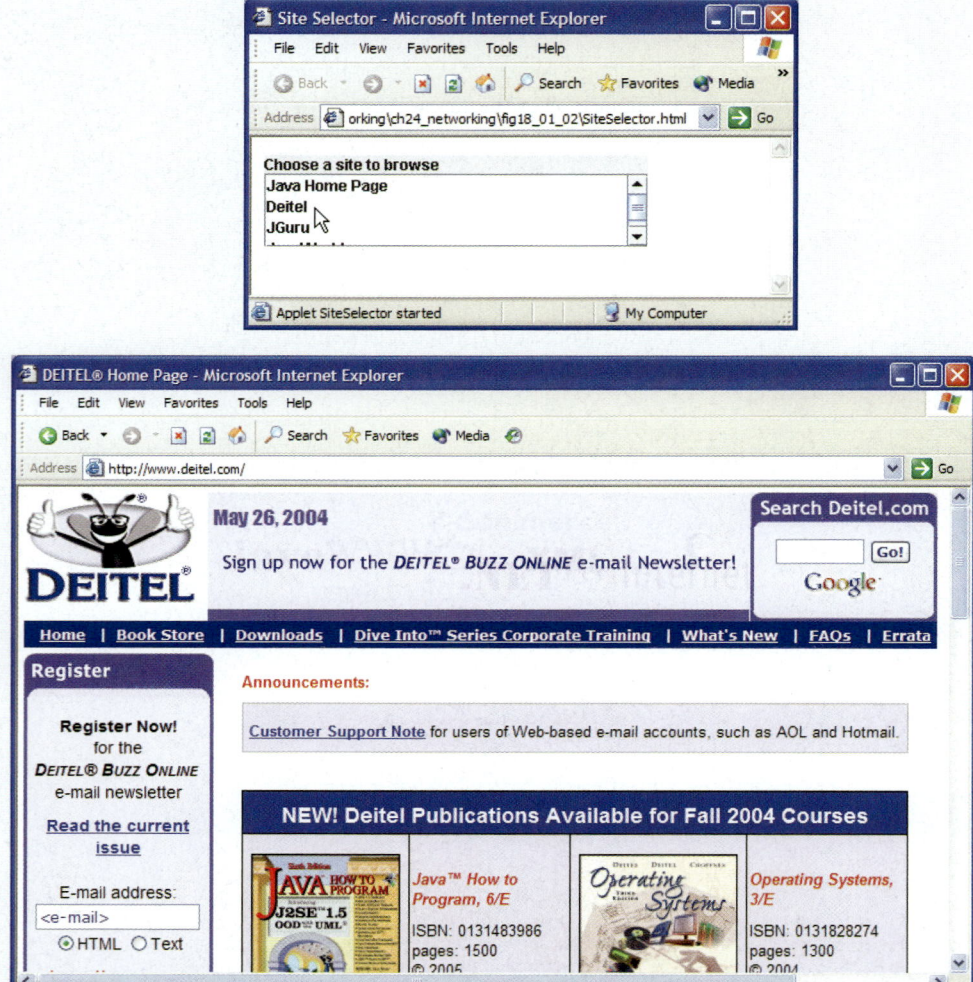

Fig. 24.2 | Loading a document from a URL into a browser. (Part 3 of 3.)

In method getSitesFromHTMLParameters, line 67 uses Applet method getParameter to obtain a Web site title. If the title is not null, the loop at lines 70–88 begins executing. Line 73 uses Applet method getParameter to obtain the Web site location. Line 77 uses the location as the value of a new URL object. The URL constructor determines whether its argument represents a valid URL. If not, the URL constructor throws a **MalformedURLException**. Note that the URL constructor must be called in a try block. If the URL constructor generates a MalformedURLException, the call to printStackTrace (line 83) causes the program to output a stack trace to the Java console. On Windows machines, the Java console can be viewed by right clicking the Java icon in the notification area of the taskbar. Then the program attempts to obtain the next Web site title. The program does not add the site for the invalid URL to the HashMap, so the title will not be displayed in the JList.

For a proper URL, line 78 places the title and URL into the HashMap, and line 79 adds the title to the ArrayList. Line 87 gets the next title from the HTML document. When the call to getParameter at line 87 returns null, the loop terminates.

When method getSitesFromHTMLParameters returns to init, lines 32–56 construct the applet's GUI. Line 32 adds the JLabel "Choose a site to browse" to the NORTH of the JFrame's BorderLayout. Line 34 creates JList siteChooser to allow the user to select a Webpage to view. Lines 35–54 register a ListSelectionListener to handle the siteChooser's events. Line 56 adds siteChooser to the CENTER of the JFrame's Border-Layout.

When the user selects one of the Web sites listed in siteChooser, the program calls method valueChanged (lines 39–52). Line 42 obtains the selected site name from the JList. Line 45 passes the selected site name (the *key*) to HashMap method get, which locates and returns a reference to the corresponding URL object (the *value*) that is assigned to reference newDocument.

Line 48 uses Applet method **getAppletContext** to get a reference to an AppletContext object that represents the applet container. Line 51 uses the AppletContext reference browser to invoke method showDocument, which receives a URL object as an argument and passes it to the AppletContext (i.e., the browser). The browser displays in the current browser window the World Wide Web resource associated with that URL. In this example, all the resources are HTML documents.

For programmers familiar with HTML frames, there is a second version of Applet-Context method showDocument that enables an applet to specify the so-called target frame in which to display the Web resource. This second version takes two arguments—a URL object specifying the resource to display and a string representing the target frame. There are some special target frames that can be used as the second argument. The target frame **_blank** results in a new Web browser window to display the content from the specified URL. The target frame **_self** specifies that the content from the specified URL should be displayed in the same frame as the applet (the applet's HTML page is replaced in this case). The target frame **_top** specifies that the browser should remove the current frames in the browser window, then display the content from the specified URL in the current window. [*Note:* If you are interested in learning more about HTML, the CD that accompanies this book contains three chapters from our book *Internet and World Wide Web How to Program, Third Edition* that introduce the current version of HTML (known as XHTML) and the Web page formatting capability known as Cascading Style Sheets (CSS).]

Error-Prevention Tip 24.1

The applet in Fig. 24.2 must be run from a Web browser, such as Mozilla or Microsoft Internet Explorer, to see the results of displaying another Web page. The appletviewer *is capable only of executing applets—it ignores all other HTML tags. If the Web sites in the program contained Java applets, only those applets would appear in the* appletviewer *when the user selected a Web site. Each applet would execute in a separate* appletviewer *window.*

24.3 Reading a File on a Web Server

Our next example once again hides the networking details from us. The application in Fig. 24.3 uses Swing GUI component **JEditorPane** (from package javax.swing) to display the contents of a file on a Web server. The user inputs a URL in the JTextField at the top of the window, and the application displays the corresponding document (if it exists) in the JEditorPane. Class JEditorPane is able to render both plain text and HTML-formatted text, as illustrated in the two screen captures (Fig. 24.4), so this application acts as a simple Web browser. The application also demonstrates how to process **Hyper-linkEvents** when the user clicks a hyperlink in the HTML document. The techniques shown in this example can also be used in applets. However, an applet is allowed to read files only on the server from which it was downloaded.

```java
 1   // Fig. 24.3: ReadServerFile.java
 2   // Use a JEditorPane to display the contents of a file on a Web server.
 3   import java.awt.BorderLayout;
 4   import java.awt.event.ActionEvent;
 5   import java.awt.event.ActionListener;
 6   import java.io.IOException;
 7   import javax.swing.JEditorPane;
 8   import javax.swing.JFrame;
 9   import javax.swing.JOptionPane;
10   import javax.swing.JScrollPane;
11   import javax.swing.JTextField;
12   import javax.swing.event.HyperlinkEvent;
13   import javax.swing.event.HyperlinkListener;
14
15   public class ReadServerFile extends JFrame
16   {
17      private JTextField enterField; // JTextField to enter site name
18      private JEditorPane contentsArea; // to display Web site
19
20      // set up GUI
21      public ReadServerFile()
22      {
23         super( "Simple Web Browser" );
24
25         // create enterField and register its listener
26         enterField = new JTextField( "Enter file URL here" );
27         enterField.addActionListener(
28            new ActionListener()
29            {
30               // get document specified by user
31               public void actionPerformed( ActionEvent event )
32               {
33                  getThePage( event.getActionCommand() );
34               } // end method actionPerformed
35            } // end inner class
36         ); // end call to addActionListener
37
38         add( enterField, BorderLayout.NORTH );
```

Fig. 24.3 | Reading a file by opening a connection through a URL. (Part 1 of 2.)

```
39
40        contentsArea = new JEditorPane(); // create contentsArea
41        contentsArea.setEditable( false );
42        contentsArea.addHyperlinkListener(
43           new HyperlinkListener()
44           {
45              // if user clicked hyperlink, go to specified page
46              public void hyperlinkUpdate( HyperlinkEvent event )
47              {
48                 if ( event.getEventType() ==
49                    HyperlinkEvent.EventType.ACTIVATED )
50                    getThePage( event.getURL().toString() );
51              } // end method hyperlinkUpdate
52           } // end inner class
53        ); // end call to addHyperlinkListener
54
55        add( new JScrollPane( contentsArea ), BorderLayout.CENTER );
56        setSize( 400, 300 ); // set size of window
57        setVisible( true ); // show window
58     } // end ReadServerFile constructor
59
60     // load document
61     private void getThePage( String location )
62     {
63        try // load document and display location
64        {
65           contentsArea.setPage( location ); // set the page
66           enterField.setText( location ); // set the text
67        } // end try
68        catch ( IOException ioException )
69        {
70           JOptionPane.showMessageDialog( this,
71              "Error retrieving specified URL", "Bad URL",
72              JOptionPane.ERROR_MESSAGE );
73        } // end catch
74     } // end method getThePage
75  } // end class ReadServerFile
```

Fig. 24.3 | Reading a file by opening a connection through a URL. (Part 2 of 2.)

```
1   // Fig. 24.4: ReadServerFileTest.java
2   // Create and start a ReadServerFile.
3   import javax.swing.JFrame;
4
5   public class ReadServerFileTest
6   {
7      public static void main( String args[] )
8      {
9         ReadServerFile application = new ReadServerFile();
10        application.setDefaultCloseOperation( JFrame.EXIT_ON_CLOSE );
11     } // end main
12  } // end class ReadServerFileTest
```

Fig. 24.4 | Test class for ReadServerFile. (Part 1 of 2.)

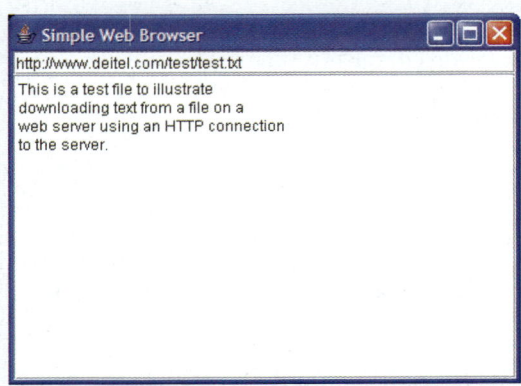

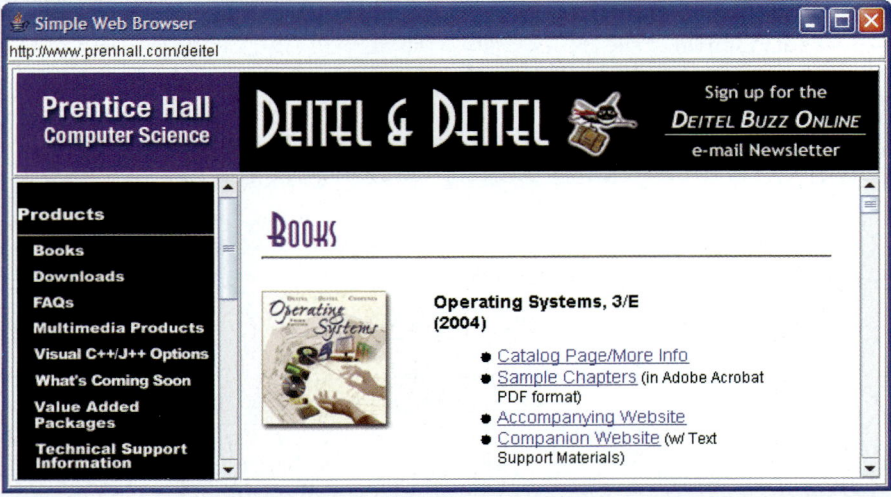

Fig. 24.4 | Test class for `ReadServerFile`. (Part 2 of 2.)

The application class `ReadServerFile` contains `JTextField enterField`, in which the user enters the URL of the file to read and `JEditorPane contentsArea` to display the contents of the file. When the user presses the *Enter* key in `enterField`, the application calls method `actionPerformed` (lines 31–34). Line 33 uses `ActionEvent` method `getActionCommand` to get the string the user input in the `JTextField` and passes the string to utility method `getThePage` (lines 61–74).

Line 65 invokes `JEditorPane` method **setPage** to download the document specified by `location` and display it in the `JEditorPane`. If there is an error downloading the document, method `setPage` throws an `IOException`. Also, if an invalid URL is specified, a `MalformedURLException` (a subclass of `IOException`) occurs. If the document loads successfully, line 66 displays the current location in `enterField`.

Typically, an HTML document contains **hyperlinks**—text, images or GUI components which, when clicked, provide quick access to another document on the Web. If a

JEditorPane contains an HTML document and the user clicks a hyperlink, the JEditor-Pane generates a **HyperlinkEvent** (package javax.swing.event) and notifies all registered **HyperlinkListeners** (package javax.swing.event) of that event. Lines 42–53 register a HyperlinkListener to handle HyperlinkEvents. When a HyperlinkEvent occurs, the program calls method **hyperlinkUpdate** (lines 46–51). Lines 48–49 use HyperlinkEvent method **getEventType** to determine the type of the HyperlinkEvent. Class Hyper-linkEvent contains a public nested class called **EventType** that declares three static EventType objects, which represent the hyperlink event types. **ACTIVATED** indicates that the user clicked a hyperlink to change Web pages, **ENTERED** indicates that the user moved the mouse over a hyperlink and **EXITED** indicates that the user moved the mouse away from a hyperlink. If a hyperlink was ACTIVATED, line 50 uses HyperlinkEvent method **getURL** to obtain the URL represented by the hyperlink. Method toString converts the returned URL to a string that can be passed to utility method getThePage.

> **Look-and-Feel Observation 24.1**
>
> *A JEditorPane generates HyperlinkEvents only if it is uneditable.*

24.4 Establishing a Simple Server Using Stream Sockets

The two examples discussed so far use high-level Java networking capabilities to communicate between applications. In the examples, it was not the Java programmer's responsibility to establish the connection between a client and a server. The first program relied on the Web browser to communicate with a Web server. The second program relied on a JEditorPane to perform the connection. This section begins our discussion of creating your own applications that can communicate with one another.

Establishing a simple server in Java requires five steps. *Step 1* is to create a **Server-Socket** object. A call to the ServerSocket constructor, such as

```
ServerSocket server = new ServerSocket( portNumber, queueLength );
```

registers an available TCP **port number** and specifies a maximum number of clients that can wait to connect to the server (i.e., the **queue length**). The port number is used by clients to locate the server application on the server computer. This is often called the **hand-shake point**. If the queue is full, the server refuses client connections. The constructor establishes the port where the server waits for connections from clients—a process known as **binding the server to the port**. Each client will ask to connect to the server on this **port**. Only one application at a time can be bound to a specific port on the server.

> **Software Engineering Observation 24.1**
>
> *Port numbers can be between 0 and 65,535. Most operating systems reserve port numbers below 1024 for system services (e.g., e-mail and World Wide Web servers). Generally, these ports should not be specified as connection ports in user programs. In fact, some operating systems require special access privileges to bind to port numbers below 1024.*

Programs manage each client connection with a **Socket** object. In *Step 2*, the server listens indefinitely (or **blocks**) for an attempt by a client to connect. To listen for a client connection, the program calls ServerSocket method **accept**, as in

```
Socket connection = server.accept();
```

which returns a Socket when a connection with a client is established. The Socket allows the server to interact with the client. The interactions with the client actually occur at a different server port from the handshake point. This allows the port specified in *Step 1* to be used again in a multithreaded server to accept another client connection. We demonstrate this concept in Section 24.8.

Step 3 is to get the OutputStream and InputStream objects that enable the server to communicate with the client by sending and receiving bytes. The server sends information to the client via an OutputStream and receives information from the client via an Input-Stream. The server invokes method **getOutputStream** on the Socket to get a reference to the Socket's OutputStream and invokes method **getInputStream** on the Socket to get a reference to the Socket's InputStream.

The stream objects can be used to send or receive individual bytes or sequences of bytes with the OutputStream's method write and the InputStream's method read, respectively. Often it is useful to send or receive values of primitive types (e.g., int and double) or Serializable objects (e.g., Strings or other serializable types) rather than sending bytes. In this case, we can use the techniques discussed in Chapter 14 to wrap other stream types (e.g., ObjectOutputStream and ObjectInputStream) around the Out-putStream and InputStream associated with the Socket. For example,

```
ObjectInputStream input =
    new ObjectInputStream( connection.getInputStream() );

ObjectOutputStream output =
    new ObjectOutputStream( connection.getOutputStream() );
```

The beauty of establishing these relationships is that whatever the server writes to the ObjectOutputStream is sent via the OutputStream and is available at the client's InputStream, and whatever the client writes to its OutputStream (with a corresponding ObjectOutputStream) is available via the server's InputStream. The transmission of the data over the network is seamless and is handled completely by Java.

Step 4 is the *processing* phase, in which the server and the client communicate via the OutputStream and InputStream objects. In *Step 5*, when the transmission is complete, the server closes the connection by invoking the **close** method on the streams and on the Socket.

Software Engineering Observation 24.2

With sockets, network I/O appears to Java programs to be similar to sequential file I/O. Sockets hide much of the complexity of network programming from the programmer.

Software Engineering Observation 24.3

With Java's multithreading, we can create multithreaded servers that can manage many simultaneous connections with many clients. This multithreaded-server architecture is precisely what popular network servers use.

Software Engineering Observation 24.4

A multithreaded server can take the Socket returned by each call to accept and create a new thread that manages network I/O across that Socket. Alternatively, a multithreaded server can maintain a pool of threads (a set of already existing threads) ready to manage network I/O across the new Sockets as they are created. See Chapter 23 for more information on multithreading.

Performance Tip 24.2

In high-performance systems in which memory is abundant, a multithreaded server can be implemented to create a pool of threads that can be assigned quickly to handle network I/O across each new Socket as it is created. Thus, when the server receives a connection, it need not incur the overhead of thread creation. When the connection is closed, the thread is returned to the pool for reuse.

24.5 Establishing a Simple Client Using Stream Sockets

Establishing a simple client in Java requires four steps. In *Step 1*, we create a Socket to connect to the server. The Socket constructor establishes the connection to the server. For example, the statement

```
Socket connection = new Socket( serverAddress, port );
```

uses the Socket constructor with two arguments—the server's address (*serverAddress*) and the *port* number. If the connection attempt is successful, this statement returns a Socket. A connection attempt that fails throws an instance of a subclass of IOException, so many programs simply catch IOException. An **UnknownHostException** occurs specifically when the system is unable to resolve the server address specified in the call to the Socket constructor to a corresponding IP address.

In *Step 2*, the client uses Socket methods getInputStream and getOutputStream to obtain references to the Socket's InputStream and OutputStream. As we mentioned in the preceding section, we can use the techniques of Chapter 14 to wrap other stream types around the InputStream and OutputStream associated with the Socket. If the server is sending information in the form of actual types, the client should receive the information in the same format. Thus, if the server sends values with an ObjectOutputStream, the client should read those values with an ObjectInputStream.

Step 3 is the processing phase in which the client and the server communicate via the InputStream and OutputStream objects. In *Step 4*, the client closes the connection when the transmission is complete by invoking the close method on the streams and on the Socket. The client must determine when the server is finished sending information so that it can call close to close the Socket connection. For example, the InputStream method read returns the value –1 when it detects end-of-stream (also called EOF—end-of-file). If an ObjectInputStream is used to read information from the server, an EOFException occurs when the client attempts to read a value from a stream on which end-of-stream is detected.

24.6 Client/Server Interaction with Stream Socket Connections

Figure 24.5 and Fig. 24.7 use stream sockets to demonstrate a simple client/server chat application. The server waits for a client connection attempt. When a client connects to the server, the server application sends the client a String object (recall that Strings are Serializable objects) indicating that the connection was successful. Then the client displays the message. The client and server applications each provide textfields that allow the user to type a message and send it to the other application. When the client or the server sends the string "TERMINATE", the connection terminates. Then the server waits for the next client to connect. The declaration of class Server appears in Fig. 24.5. The declaration of class Client appears in Fig. 24.7. The screen captures showing the execution between the client and the server are shown as part of Fig. 24.7.

Server Class

Server's constructor (lines 30–55) creates the server's GUI, which contains a JTextField and a JTextArea. Server displays its output in the JTextArea. When the main method (lines 7–12 of Fig. 24.6) executes, it creates a Server object, specifies the window's default close operation and calls method runServer (declared at lines 58–87).

```java
1   // Fig. 24.5: Server.java
2   // Set up a Server that will receive a connection from a client, send
3   // a string to the client, and close the connection.
4   import java.io.EOFException;
5   import java.io.IOException;
6   import java.io.ObjectInputStream;
7   import java.io.ObjectOutputStream;
8   import java.net.ServerSocket;
9   import java.net.Socket;
10  import java.awt.BorderLayout;
11  import java.awt.event.ActionEvent;
12  import java.awt.event.ActionListener;
13  import javax.swing.JFrame;
14  import javax.swing.JScrollPane;
15  import javax.swing.JTextArea;
16  import javax.swing.JTextField;
17  import javax.swing.SwingUtilities;
18
19  public class Server extends JFrame
20  {
21     private JTextField enterField; // inputs message from user
22     private JTextArea displayArea; // display information to user
23     private ObjectOutputStream output; // output stream to client
24     private ObjectInputStream input; // input stream from client
25     private ServerSocket server; // server socket
26     private Socket connection; // connection to client
27     private int counter = 1; // counter of number of connections
28
29     // set up GUI
30     public Server()
31     {
32        super( "Server" );
33
34        enterField = new JTextField(); // create enterField
35        enterField.setEditable( false );
36        enterField.addActionListener(
37           new ActionListener()
38           {
39              // send message to client
40              public void actionPerformed( ActionEvent event )
41              {
```

Fig. 24.5 | Server portion of a client/server stream-socket connection. (Part 1 of 4.)

```
42                        sendData( event.getActionCommand() );
43                        enterField.setText( "" );
44                     } // end method actionPerformed
45                  } // end anonymous inner class
46               ); // end call to addActionListener
47
48               add( enterField, BorderLayout.NORTH );
49
50               displayArea = new JTextArea(); // create displayArea
51               add( new JScrollPane( displayArea ), BorderLayout.CENTER );
52
53               setSize( 300, 150 ); // set size of window
54               setVisible( true ); // show window
55            } // end Server constructor
56
57            // set up and run server
58            public void runServer()
59            {
60               try // set up server to receive connections; process connections
61               {
62                  server = new ServerSocket( 12345, 100 ); // create ServerSocket
63
64                  while ( true )
65                  {
66                     try
67                     {
68                        waitForConnection(); // wait for a connection
69                        getStreams(); // get input & output streams
70                        processConnection(); // process connection
71                     } // end try
72                     catch ( EOFException eofException )
73                     {
74                        displayMessage( "\nServer terminated connection" );
75                     } // end catch
76                     finally
77                     {
78                        closeConnection(); // close connection
79                        counter++;
80                     } // end finally
81                  } // end while
82               } // end try
83               catch ( IOException ioException )
84               {
85                  ioException.printStackTrace();
86               } // end catch
87            } // end method runServer
88
89            // wait for connection to arrive, then display connection info
90            private void waitForConnection() throws IOException
91            {
92               displayMessage( "Waiting for connection\n" );
93               connection = server.accept(); // allow server to accept connection
```

Fig. 24.5 | Server portion of a client/server stream-socket connection. (Part 2 of 4.)

```
94      displayMessage( "Connection " + counter + " received from: " +
95         connection.getInetAddress().getHostName() );
96   } // end method waitForConnection
97
98   // get streams to send and receive data
99   private void getStreams() throws IOException
100  {
101     // set up output stream for objects
102     output = new ObjectOutputStream( connection.getOutputStream() );
103     output.flush(); // flush output buffer to send header information
104
105     // set up input stream for objects
106     input = new ObjectInputStream( connection.getInputStream() );
107
108     displayMessage( "\nGot I/O streams\n" );
109  } // end method getStreams
110
111  // process connection with client
112  private void processConnection() throws IOException
113  {
114     String message = "Connection successful";
115     sendData( message ); // send connection successful message
116
117     // enable enterField so server user can send messages
118     setTextFieldEditable( true );
119
120     do // process messages sent from client
121     {
122        try // read message and display it
123        {
124           message = ( String ) input.readObject(); // read new message
125           displayMessage( "\n" + message ); // display message
126        } // end try
127        catch ( ClassNotFoundException classNotFoundException )
128        {
129           displayMessage( "\nUnknown object type received" );
130        } // end catch
131
132     } while ( !message.equals( "CLIENT>>> TERMINATE" ) );
133  } // end method processConnection
134
135  // close streams and socket
136  private void closeConnection()
137  {
138     displayMessage( "\nTerminating connection\n" );
139     setTextFieldEditable( false ); // disable enterField
140
141     try
142     {
143        output.close(); // close output stream
144        input.close(); // close input stream
145        connection.close(); // close socket
146     } // end try
```

Fig. 24.5 | Server portion of a client/server stream-socket connection. (Part 3 of 4.)

```
147          catch ( IOException ioException )
148          {
149             ioException.printStackTrace();
150          } // end catch
151       } // end method closeConnection
152
153       // send message to client
154       private void sendData( String message )
155       {
156          try // send object to client
157          {
158             output.writeObject( "SERVER>>> " + message );
159             output.flush(); // flush output to client
160             displayMessage( "\nSERVER>>> " + message );
161          } // end try
162          catch ( IOException ioException )
163          {
164             displayArea.append( "\nError writing object" );
165          } // end catch
166       } // end method sendData
167
168       // manipulates displayArea in the event-dispatch thread
169       private void displayMessage( final String messageToDisplay )
170       {
171          SwingUtilities.invokeLater(
172             new Runnable()
173             {
174                public void run() // updates displayArea
175                {
176                   displayArea.append( messageToDisplay ); // append message
177                } // end method run
178             } // end anonymous inner class
179          ); // end call to SwingUtilities.invokeLater
180       } // end method displayMessage
181
182       // manipulates enterField in the event-dispatch thread
183       private void setTextFieldEditable( final boolean editable )
184       {
185          SwingUtilities.invokeLater(
186             new Runnable()
187             {
188                public void run() // sets enterField's editability
189                {
190                   enterField.setEditable( editable );
191                } // end method run
192             } // end inner class
193          ); // end call to SwingUtilities.invokeLater
194       } // end method setTextFieldEditable
195    } // end class Server
```

Fig. 24.5 | Server portion of a client/server stream-socket connection. (Part 4 of 4.)

Method `runServer` sets up the server to receive a connection and processes one connection at a time. Line 62 creates a `ServerSocket` called `server` to wait for connections.

```
 1   // Fig. 24.6: ServerTest.java
 2   // Test the Server application.
 3   import javax.swing.JFrame;
 4
 5   public class ServerTest
 6   {
 7      public static void main( String args[] )
 8      {
 9         Server application = new Server(); // create server
10         application.setDefaultCloseOperation( JFrame.EXIT_ON_CLOSE );
11         application.runServer(); // run server application
12      } // end main
13   } // end class ServerTest
```

Fig. 24.6 | Test class for `Server`.

The `ServerSocket` listens for a connection from a client at port `12345`. The second argument to the constructor is the number of connections that can wait in a queue to connect to the server (100 in this example). If the queue is full when a client attempts to connect, the server refuses the connection.

Common Programming Error 24.1

Specifying a port that is already in use or specifying an invalid port number when creating a `ServerSocket` results in a `BindException`.

Line 68 calls method `waitForConnection` (declared at lines 90–96) to wait for a client connection. After the connection is established, line 69 calls method `getStreams` (declared at lines 99–109) to obtain references to the streams for the connection. Line 70 calls method `processConnection` (declared at lines 112–133) to send the initial connection message to the client and to process all messages received from the client. The `finally` block (lines 76–80) terminates the client connection by calling method `closeConnection` (lines 136–151) even if an exception occurs. Method `displayMessage` (lines 169–180) is called from these methods to use the event-dispatch thread to display messages in the application's `JTextArea`.

In method `waitForConnection` (lines 90–96), line 93 uses `ServerSocket` method `accept` to wait for a connection from a client. When a connection occurs, the resulting `Socket` is assigned to `connection`. Method `accept` blocks until a connection is received (i.e., the thread in which `accept` is called stops executing until a client connects). Lines 94–95 output the host name of the computer that made the connection. `Socket` method `getInetAddress` returns an `InetAddress` (package `java.net`) containing information about the client computer. `InetAddress` method `getHostName` returns the host name of the client computer. For example, there is a special IP address (`127.0.0.1`) and host name (`localhost`) that is useful for testing networking applications on your local computer (this is also known as the loopback address). If `getHostName` is called on an `InetAddress` containing `127.0.0.1`, the corresponding host name returned by the method would be `localhost`.

Method `getStreams` (lines 99–109) obtains references to the `Socket`'s streams and uses them to initialize an `ObjectOutputStream` (line 102) and an `ObjectInputStream` (line 106), respectively. Note the call to `ObjectOutputStream` method `flush` at line 103. This statement causes the `ObjectOutputStream` on the server to send a stream header to the corresponding client's `ObjectInputStream`. The stream header contains such information as the version of object serialization being used to send objects. This information is required by the `ObjectInputStream` so that it can prepare to receive those objects correctly.

Software Engineering Observation 24.5

When using an `ObjectOutputStream` and `ObjectInputStream` to send and receive data over a network connection, always create the `ObjectOutputStream` first and flush the stream so that the client's `ObjectInputStream` can prepare to receive the data. This is required only for networking applications that communicate using `ObjectOutputStream` and `ObjectInputStream`.

Performance Tip 24.3

A computer's input and output components are typically much slower than its memory. Output buffers typically are used to increase the efficiency of an application by sending larger amounts of data fewer times, thus reducing the number of times an application accesses the computer's input and output components.

Line 114 of method `processConnection` (lines 112–133) calls method `sendData` to send "SERVER>>> Connection successful" as a string to the client. The loop at lines 120–132 executes until the server receives the message "CLIENT>>> TERMINATE". Line 124 uses `ObjectInputStream` method `readObject` to read a `String` from the client. Line 125 invokes method `displayMessage` to append the message to the `JTextArea`.

When the transmission is complete, method `processConnection` returns, and the program calls method `closeConnection` (lines 136–151) to close the streams associated with the `Socket` and close the `Socket`. Then the server waits for the next connection attempt from a client by continuing with line 68 at the beginning of the `while` loop.

When the user of the server application enters a string in the textfield and presses the *Enter* key, the program calls method `actionPerformed` (lines 40–44), which reads the string from the textfield and calls utility method `sendData` (lines 154–166) to send the string to the client. Method `sendData` writes the object, flushes the output buffer and appends the same string to the textarea in the server window. It is not necessary to invoke `displayMessage` to modify the textarea here, because method `sendData` is called from an event handler—thus, `sendData` executes as part of the event-dispatch thread.

Note that `Server` receives a connection, processes it, closes it and waits for the next connection. A more likely scenario would be a `Server` that receives a connection, sets it up to be processed as a separate thread of execution, then immediately waits for new connections. The separate threads that process existing connections can continue to execute while the `Server` concentrates on new connection requests. This makes the server more efficient, because multiple client requests can be processed concurrently. We demonstrate a multithreaded server in Section 24.8.

Client Class

Like class `Server`, class `Client`'s (Fig. 24.7) constructor (lines 29–56) creates the GUI of the application (a `JTextField` and a `JTextArea`). `Client` displays its output in the textarea. When method `main` (lines 7–19 of Fig. 24.8) executes, it creates an instance of class `Client`, specifies the window's default close operation and calls method `runClient` (declared at lines 59–79). In this example, you can execute the client from any computer on the Internet and specify the IP address or host name of the server computer as a command-line argument to the program. For example, the command

```
java Client 192.168.1.15
```

attempts to connect to the `Server` on the computer with IP address `192.168.1.15`.

`Client` method `runClient` (lines 59–79) sets up the connection to the server, processes messages received from the server and closes the connection when communication is complete. Line 63 calls method `connectToServer` (declared at lines 82–92) to perform the connection. After connecting, line 64 calls method `getStreams` (declared at lines 95–105) to obtain references to the `Socket`'s stream objects. Then line 65 calls method `processConnection` (declared at lines 108–126) to receive and display messages sent from the server. The `finally` block (lines 75–78) calls `closeConnection` (lines 129–144) to close the streams and the `Socket` even if an exception has occurred. Method `displayMessage` (lines 162–173) is called from these methods to use the event-dispatch thread to display messages in the application's textarea.

```java
1   // Fig. 24.7: Client.java
2   // Client that reads and displays information sent from a Server.
3   import java.io.EOFException;
4   import java.io.IOException;
5   import java.io.ObjectInputStream;
6   import java.io.ObjectOutputStream;
7   import java.net.InetAddress;
8   import java.net.Socket;
9   import java.awt.BorderLayout;
10  import java.awt.event.ActionEvent;
11  import java.awt.event.ActionListener;
12  import javax.swing.JFrame;
13  import javax.swing.JScrollPane;
14  import javax.swing.JTextArea;
15  import javax.swing.JTextField;
16  import javax.swing.SwingUtilities;
17
18  public class Client extends JFrame
19  {
20     private JTextField enterField; // enters information from user
21     private JTextArea displayArea; // display information to user
22     private ObjectOutputStream output; // output stream to server
23     private ObjectInputStream input; // input stream from server
24     private String message = ""; // message from server
25     private String chatServer; // host server for this application
26     private Socket client; // socket to communicate with server
27
28     // initialize chatServer and set up GUI
29     public Client( String host )
30     {
31        super( "Client" );
32
33        chatServer = host; // set server to which this client connects
```

Fig. 24.7 | Client portion of a stream-socket connection between client and server. (Part 1 of 4.)

```
34
35          enterField = new JTextField(); // create enterField
36          enterField.setEditable( false );
37          enterField.addActionListener(
38             new ActionListener()
39             {
40                // send message to server
41                public void actionPerformed( ActionEvent event )
42                {
43                   sendData( event.getActionCommand() );
44                   enterField.setText( "" );
45                } // end method actionPerformed
46             } // end anonymous inner class
47          ); // end call to addActionListener
48
49          add( enterField, BorderLayout.NORTH );
50
51          displayArea = new JTextArea(); // create displayArea
52          add( new JScrollPane( displayArea ), BorderLayout.CENTER );
53
54          setSize( 300, 150 ); // set size of window
55          setVisible( true ); // show window
56       } // end Client constructor
57
58       // connect to server and process messages from server
59       public void runClient()
60       {
61          try // connect to server, get streams, process connection
62          {
63             connectToServer(); // create a Socket to make connection
64             getStreams(); // get the input and output streams
65             processConnection(); // process connection
66          } // end try
67          catch ( EOFException eofException )
68          {
69             displayMessage( "\nClient terminated connection" );
70          } // end catch
71          catch ( IOException ioException )
72          {
73             ioException.printStackTrace();
74          } // end catch
75          finally
76          {
77             closeConnection(); // close connection
78          } // end finally
79       } // end method runClient
80
81       // connect to server
82       private void connectToServer() throws IOException
83       {
84          displayMessage( "Attempting connection\n" );
85
```

Fig. 24.7 | Client portion of a stream-socket connection between client and server. (Part 2 of 4.)

```
86            // create Socket to make connection to server
87            client = new Socket( InetAddress.getByName( chatServer ), 12345 );
88
89            // display connection information
90            displayMessage( "Connected to: " +
91               client.getInetAddress().getHostName() );
92         } // end method connectToServer
93
94         // get streams to send and receive data
95         private void getStreams() throws IOException
96         {
97            // set up output stream for objects
98            output = new ObjectOutputStream( client.getOutputStream() );
99            output.flush(); // flush output buffer to send header information
100
101           // set up input stream for objects
102           input = new ObjectInputStream( client.getInputStream() );
103
104           displayMessage( "\nGot I/O streams\n" );
105        } // end method getStreams
106
107        // process connection with server
108        private void processConnection() throws IOException
109        {
110           // enable enterField so client user can send messages
111           setTextFieldEditable( true );
112
113           do // process messages sent from server
114           {
115              try // read message and display it
116              {
117                 message = ( String ) input.readObject(); // read new message
118                 displayMessage( "\n" + message ); // display message
119              } // end try
120              catch ( ClassNotFoundException classNotFoundException )
121              {
122                 displayMessage( "\nUnknown object type received" );
123              } // end catch
124
125           } while ( !message.equals( "SERVER>>> TERMINATE" ) );
126        } // end method processConnection
127
128        // close streams and socket
129        private void closeConnection()
130        {
131           displayMessage( "\nClosing connection" );
132           setTextFieldEditable( false ); // disable enterField
133
134           try
135           {
136              output.close(); // close output stream
137              input.close(); // close input stream   1
```

Fig. 24.7 | Client portion of a stream-socket connection between client and server. (Part 3 of 4.)

```
138            client.close(); // close socket
139         } // end try
140         catch ( IOException ioException )
141         {
142            ioException.printStackTrace();
143         } // end catch
144      } // end method closeConnection
145
146      // send message to server
147      private void sendData( String message )
148      {
149         try // send object to server
150         {
151            output.writeObject( "CLIENT>>> " + message );
152            output.flush(); // flush data to output
153            displayMessage( "\nCLIENT>>> " + message );
154         } // end try
155         catch ( IOException ioException )
156         {
157            displayArea.append( "\nError writing object" );
158         } // end catch
159      } // end method sendData
160
161      // manipulates displayArea in the event-dispatch thread
162      private void displayMessage( final String messageToDisplay )
163      {
164         SwingUtilities.invokeLater(
165            new Runnable()
166            {
167               public void run() // updates displayArea
168               {
169                  displayArea.append( messageToDisplay );
170               } // end method run
171            }  // end anonymous inner class
172         ); // end call to SwingUtilities.invokeLater
173      } // end method displayMessage
174
175      // manipulates enterField in the event-dispatch thread
176      private void setTextFieldEditable( final boolean editable )
177      {
178         SwingUtilities.invokeLater(
179            new Runnable()
180            {
181               public void run() // sets enterField's editability
182               {
183                  enterField.setEditable( editable );
184               } // end method run
185            } // end anonymous inner class
186         ); // end call to SwingUtilities.invokeLater
187      } // end method setTextFieldEditable
188   } // end class Client
```

Fig. 24.7 | Client portion of a stream-socket connection between client and server. (Part 4 of 4.)

Method `connectToServer` (lines 82–92) creates a `Socket` called `client` (line 87) to establish a connection. The method passes two arguments to the `Socket` constructor—the IP address of the server computer and the port number (12345) where the server application is awaiting client connections. In the first argument, `InetAddress` static method **getByName** returns an `InetAddress` object containing the IP address specified as a command-line argument to the application (or `127.0.0.1` if no command-line arguments are specified). Method `getByName` can receive a string containing either the actual IP address or the host name of the server. The first argument also could have been written other ways. For the localhost address 127.0.0.1, the first argument could be

```
InetAddress.getByName( "localhost" )
```

or

```
InetAddress.getLocalHost()
```

Also, there are versions of the `Socket` constructor that receive a string for the IP address or host name. The first argument could have been specified as "127.0.0.1" or "localhost". We chose to demonstrate the client/server relationship by connecting between applications executing on the same computer (`localhost`). Normally, this first argument would be the IP address of another computer. The `InetAddress` object for another computer can be obtained by specifying the computer's IP address or host name as the argument to `InetAddress` method `getByName`. The `Socket` constructor's second argument is the server port number. This must match the port number at which the server is waiting for connections (called the handshake point). Once the connection is made, lines 90–91 display a message in the text area indicating the name of the server computer to which the client has connected.

The `Client` uses an `ObjectOutputStream` to send data to the server and an `ObjectInputStream` to receive data from the server. Method `getStreams` (lines 95–105) creates

```java
 1   // Fig. 24.8: ClientTest.java
 2   // Test the Client class.
 3   import javax.swing.JFrame;
 4
 5   public class ClientTest
 6   {
 7      public static void main( String args[] )
 8      {
 9         Client application; // declare client application
10
11         // if no command line args
12         if ( args.length == 0 )
13            application = new Client( "127.0.0.1" ); // connect to localhost
14         else
15            application = new Client( args[ 0 ] ); // use args to connect
16
17         application.setDefaultCloseOperation( JFrame.EXIT_ON_CLOSE );
18         application.runClient(); // run client application
19      } // end main
20   } // end class ClientTest
```

Fig. 24.8 | Class that tests the `Client`. (Part 1 of 2.)

Fig. 24.8 | Class that tests the Client. (Part 2 of 2.)

the ObjectOutputStream and ObjectInputStream objects that use the streams associated with the client socket.

Method processConnection (lines 108–126) contains a loop that executes until the client receives the message "SERVER>>> TERMINATE". Line 117 reads a String object from the server. Line 118 invokes displayMessage to append the message to the textarea.

When the transmission is complete, method closeConnection (lines 129–144) closes the streams and the Socket.

When the user of the client application enters a string in the textfield and presses the *Enter* key, the program calls method actionPerformed (lines 41–45) to read the string and invoke utility method sendData (147–159) to send the string to the server. Method send-Data writes the object, flushes the output buffer and appends the same string to the JText-Area in the client window. Once again, it is not necessary to invoke utility method `displayMessage` to modify the textarea here, because method `sendData` is called from an event handler.

24.7 Connectionless Client/Server Interaction with Datagrams

We have been discussing connection-oriented, streams-based transmission. Now we consider connectionless transmission with datagrams.

Connection-oriented transmission is like the telephone system in which you dial and are given a connection to the telephone of the person with whom you wish to communicate. The connection is maintained for the duration of your phone call, even when you are not talking.

Connectionless transmission with datagrams is more like the way mail is carried via the postal service. If a large message will not fit in one envelope, you break it into separate message pieces that you place in separate, sequentially numbered envelopes. Each of the letters is then mailed at the same time. The letters could arrive in order, out of order or not at all (the last case is rare, but it does happen). The person at the receiving end reassembles the message pieces into sequential order before attempting to make sense of the message. If your message is small enough to fit in one envelope, you need not worry about the "out-of-sequence" problem, but it is still possible that your message might not arrive. One difference between datagrams and postal mail is that duplicates of datagrams can arrive at the receiving computer.

Figure 24.9–Fig. 24.12 use datagrams to send packets of information via the User Datagram Protocol (UDP) between a client application and a server application. In the

```java
1   // Fig. 24.9: Server.java
2   // Server that receives and sends packets from/to a client.
3   import java.io.IOException;
4   import java.net.DatagramPacket;
5   import java.net.DatagramSocket;
6   import java.net.SocketException;
7   import java.awt.BorderLayout;
8   import javax.swing.JFrame;
9   import javax.swing.JScrollPane;
10  import javax.swing.JTextArea;
11  import javax.swing.SwingUtilities;
12
13  public class Server extends JFrame
14  {
15     private JTextArea displayArea; // displays packets received
16     private DatagramSocket socket; // socket to connect to client
17
18     // set up GUI and DatagramSocket
19     public Server()
20     {
21        super( "Server" );
22
```

Fig. 24.9 | Server side of connectionless client/server computing with datagrams. (Part 1 of 3.)

```
23          displayArea = new JTextArea(); // create displayArea
24          add( new JScrollPane( displayArea ), BorderLayout.CENTER );
25          setSize( 400, 300 ); // set size of window
26          setVisible( true ); // show window
27
28          try // create DatagramSocket for sending and receiving packets
29          {
30             socket = new DatagramSocket( 5000 );
31          } // end try
32          catch ( SocketException socketException )
33          {
34             socketException.printStackTrace();
35             System.exit( 1 );
36          } // end catch
37       } // end Server constructor
38
39       // wait for packets to arrive, display data and echo packet to client
40       public void waitForPackets()
41       {
42          while ( true )
43          {
44             try // receive packet, display contents, return copy to client
45             {
46                byte data[] = new byte[ 100 ]; // set up packet
47                DatagramPacket receivePacket =
48                   new DatagramPacket( data, data.length );
49
50                socket.receive( receivePacket ); // wait to receive packet
51
52                // display information from received packet
53                displayMessage( "\nPacket received:" +
54                   "\nFrom host: " + receivePacket.getAddress() +
55                   "\nHost port: " + receivePacket.getPort() +
56                   "\nLength: " + receivePacket.getLength() +
57                   "\nContaining:\n\t" + new String( receivePacket.getData(),
58                      0, receivePacket.getLength() ) ) );
59
60                sendPacketToClient( receivePacket ); // send packet to client
61             } // end try
62             catch ( IOException ioException )
63             {
64                displayMessage( ioException.toString() + "\n" );
65                ioException.printStackTrace();
66             } // end catch
67          } // end while
68       } // end method waitForPackets
69
70       // echo packet to client
71       private void sendPacketToClient( DatagramPacket receivePacket )
72          throws IOException
73       {
74          displayMessage( "\n\nEcho data to client..." );
75
```

Fig. 24.9 | Server side of connectionless client/server computing with datagrams. (Part 2 of 3.)

```
76          // create packet to send
77          DatagramPacket sendPacket = new DatagramPacket(
78             receivePacket.getData(), receivePacket.getLength(),
79             receivePacket.getAddress(), receivePacket.getPort() );
80
81          socket.send( sendPacket ); // send packet to client
82          displayMessage( "Packet sent\n" );
83       } // end method sendPacketToClient
84
85       // manipulates displayArea in the event-dispatch thread
86       private void displayMessage( final String messageToDisplay )
87       {
88          SwingUtilities.invokeLater(
89             new Runnable()
90             {
91                public void run() // updates displayArea
92                {
93                   displayArea.append( messageToDisplay ); // display message
94                } // end method run
95             } // end anonymous inner class
96          ); // end call to SwingUtilities.invokeLater
97       } // end method displayMessage
98    } // end class Server
```

Fig. 24.9 | Server side of connectionless client/server computing with datagrams. (Part 3 of 3.)

Client application (Fig. 24.11), the user types a message into a textfield and presses *Enter*. The program converts the message into a byte array and places it in a datagram packet that is sent to the server. The Server (Fig. 24.9) receives the packet and displays the information in it, then **echoes** the packet back to the client. Upon receiving the packet, the client displays the information it contains.

Server Class
Class Server (Fig. 24.9) declares two **DatagramPackets** that the server uses to send and receive information and one **DatagramSocket** that sends and receives the packets. The

```
1    // Fig. 24.10: ServerTest.java
2    // Tests the Server class.
3    import javax.swing.JFrame;
4
5    public class ServerTest
6    {
7       public static void main( String args[] )
8       {
9          Server application = new Server(); // create server
10         application.setDefaultCloseOperation( JFrame.EXIT_ON_CLOSE );
11         application.waitForPackets(); // run server application
12      } // end main
13   } // end class ServerTest
```

Fig. 24.10 | Class that tests the Server. (Part 1 of 2.)

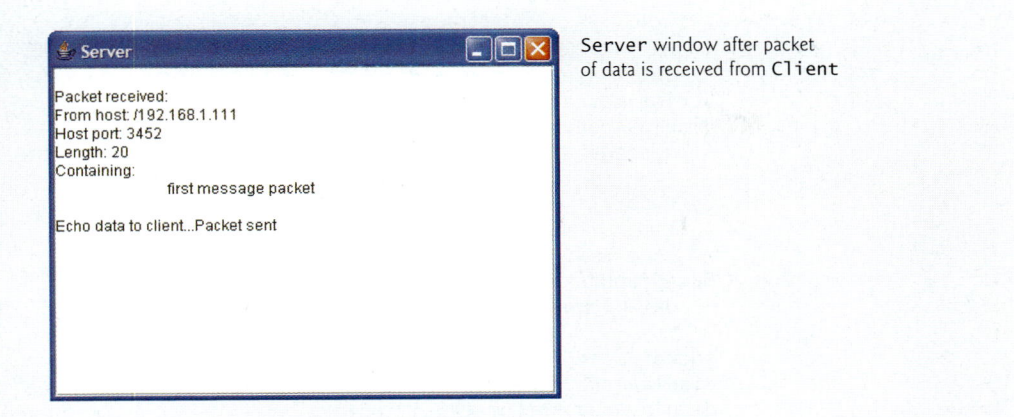

Server window after packet of data is received from `Client`

Fig. 24.10 | Class that tests the `Server`. (Part 2 of 2.)

```java
1   // Fig. 24.11: Client.java
2   // Client that sends and receives packets to/from a server.
3   import java.io.IOException;
4   import java.net.DatagramPacket;
5   import java.net.DatagramSocket;
6   import java.net.InetAddress;
7   import java.net.SocketException;
8   import java.awt.BorderLayout;
9   import java.awt.event.ActionEvent;
10  import java.awt.event.ActionListener;
11  import javax.swing.JFrame;
12  import javax.swing.JScrollPane;
13  import javax.swing.JTextArea;
14  import javax.swing.JTextField;
15  import javax.swing.SwingUtilities;
16
17  public class Client extends JFrame
18  {
19     private JTextField enterField; // for entering messages
20     private JTextArea displayArea; // for displaying messages
21     private DatagramSocket socket; // socket to connect to server
22
23     // set up GUI and DatagramSocket
24     public Client()
25     {
26        super( "Client" );
27
28        enterField = new JTextField( "Type message here" );
29        enterField.addActionListener(
30           new ActionListener()
31           {
32              public void actionPerformed( ActionEvent event )
33              {
```

Fig. 24.11 | Client side of connectionless client/server computing with datagrams. (Part 1 of 3.)

```
34              try // create and send packet
35              {
36                  // get message from textfield
37                  String message = event.getActionCommand();
38                  displayArea.append( "\nSending packet containing: " +
39                      message + "\n" );
40
41                  byte data[] = message.getBytes(); // convert to bytes
42
43                  // create sendPacket
44                  DatagramPacket sendPacket = new DatagramPacket( data,
45                      data.length, InetAddress.getLocalHost(), 5000 );
46
47                  socket.send( sendPacket ); // send packet
48                  displayArea.append( "Packet sent\n" );
49                  displayArea.setCaretPosition(
50                      displayArea.getText().length() );
51              } // end try
52              catch ( IOException ioException )
53              {
54                  displayMessage( ioException.toString() + "\n" );
55                  ioException.printStackTrace();
56              } // end catch
57          } // end actionPerformed
58      } // end inner class
59  ); // end call to addActionListener
60
61  add( enterField, BorderLayout.NORTH );
62
63  displayArea = new JTextArea();
64  add( new JScrollPane( displayArea ), BorderLayout.CENTER );
65
66  setSize( 400, 300 ); // set window size
67  setVisible( true ); // show window
68
69  try // create DatagramSocket for sending and receiving packets
70  {
71      socket = new DatagramSocket();
72  } // end try
73  catch ( SocketException socketException )
74  {
75      socketException.printStackTrace();
76      System.exit( 1 );
77  } // end catch
78  } // end Client constructor
79
80  // wait for packets to arrive from Server, display packet contents
81  public void waitForPackets()
82  {
83      while ( true )
84      {
85          try // receive packet and display contents
86          {
```

Fig. 24.11 | Client side of connectionless client/server computing with datagrams. (Part 2 of 3.)

```
87          byte data[] = new byte[ 100 ]; // set up packet
88          DatagramPacket receivePacket = new DatagramPacket(
89             data, data.length );
90
91          socket.receive( receivePacket ); // wait for packet
92
93          // display packet contents
94          displayMessage( "\nPacket received:" +
95             "\nFrom host: " + receivePacket.getAddress() +
96             "\nHost port: " + receivePacket.getPort() +
97             "\nLength: " + receivePacket.getLength() +
98             "\nContaining:\n\t" + new String( receivePacket.getData(),
99                0, receivePacket.getLength() ) );
100         } // end try
101         catch ( IOException exception )
102         {
103            displayMessage( exception.toString() + "\n" );
104            exception.printStackTrace();
105         } // end catch
106      } // end while
107   } // end method waitForPackets
108
109   // manipulates displayArea in the event-dispatch thread
110   private void displayMessage( final String messageToDisplay )
111   {
112      SwingUtilities.invokeLater(
113         new Runnable()
114         {
115            public void run() // updates displayArea
116            {
117               displayArea.append( messageToDisplay );
118            } // end method run
119         } // end inner class
120      ); // end call to SwingUtilities.invokeLater
121   } // end method displayMessage
122 } // end class Client
```

Fig. 24.11 | Client side of connectionless client/server computing with datagrams. (Part 3 of 3.)

```
1  // Fig. 24.12: ClientTest.java
2  // Tests the Client class.
3  import javax.swing.JFrame;
4
5  public class ClientTest
6  {
7     public static void main( String args[] )
8     {
9        Client application = new Client(); // create client
10       application.setDefaultCloseOperation( JFrame.EXIT_ON_CLOSE );
11       application.waitForPackets(); // run client application
12    } // end main
13 } // end class ClientTest
```

Fig. 24.12 | Class that tests the Client. (Part 1 of 2.)

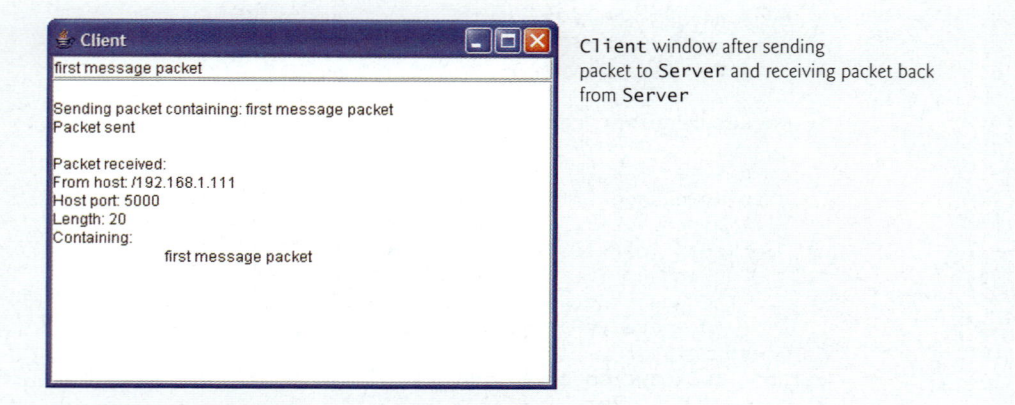

Client window after sending packet to Server and receiving packet back from Server

Fig. 24.12 | Class that tests the Client. (Part 2 of 2.)

Server constructor (lines 19–37) creates the graphical user interface in which the packets of information will be displayed. Line 30 creates the DatagramSocket in a try block. Line 30 uses the DatagramSocket constructor that takes an integer port number argument (5000 in this example) to bind the server to a port where it can receive packets from clients. Clients sending packets to this Server specify the same port number in the packets they send. A **SocketException** is thrown if the DatagramSocket constructor fails to bind the DatagramSocket to the specified port.

Common Programming Error 24.2

Specifying a port that is already in use or specifying an invalid port number when creating a DatagramSocket results in a SocketException.

Server method waitForPackets (lines 40–68) uses an infinite loop to wait for packets to arrive at the Server. Lines 47–48 create a DatagramPacket in which a received packet of information can be stored. The DatagramPacket constructor for this purpose receives two arguments—a byte array in which the data will be stored and the length of the array. Line 50 uses DatagramSocket method **receive** to wait for a packet to arrive at the Server. Method receive blocks until a packet arrives, then stores the packet in its DatagramPacket argument. The method throws an IOException if an error occurs while receiving a packet.

When a packet arrives, lines 53–58 call method displayMessage (declared at lines 86–97) to append the packet's contents to the textarea. DatagramPacket method **getAddress** (line 54) returns an InetAddress object containing the host name of the computer from which the packet was sent. Method **getPort** (line 55) returns an integer specifying the port number through which the host computer sent the packet. Method **getLength** (line 56) returns an integer representing the number of bytes of data sent. Method **getData** (line 57) returns a byte array containing the data. Lines 57–58 initialize a String object using a three-argument constructor that takes a byte array, the offset and the length. This String is then appended to the text to display.

After displaying a packet, line 60 calls method sendPacketToClient (declared at lines 71–83) to create a new packet and send it to the client. Lines 77–79 create a Datagram-

Packet and pass four arguments to its constructor. The first argument specifies the byte array to send. The second argument specifies the number of bytes to send. The third argument specifies the client computer's Internet address, to which the packet will be sent. The fourth argument specifies the port where the client is waiting to receive packets. Line 81 sends the packet over the network. Method **send** of DatagramSocket throws an IOException if an error occurs while sending a packet.

Client Class

Class Client (Fig. 24.11) works similarly to class Server, except that the Client sends packets only when the user types a message in a textfield and presses the *Enter* key. When this occurs, the program calls method actionPerformed (lines 32–57), which converts the string the user entered into a byte array (line 41). Lines 44–45 create a DatagramPacket and initialize it with the byte array, the length of the string that was entered by the user, the IP address to which the packet is to be sent (InetAddress.getLocalHost() in this example) and the port number at which the Server is waiting for packets (5000 in this example). Line 47 sends the packet. Note that the client in this example must know that the server is receiving packets at port 5000—otherwise, the server will not receive the packets.

Note that the DatagramSocket constructor call (line 71) in this application does not specify any arguments. This no-argument constructor allows the computer to select the next available port number for the DatagramSocket. The client does not need a specific port number, because the server receives the client's port number as part of each DatagramPacket sent by the client. Thus, the server can send packets back to the same computer and port number from which it receives a packet of information.

Client method waitForPackets (lines 81–107) uses an infinite loop to wait for packets from the server. Line 91 blocks until a packet arrives. This does not prevent the user from sending a packet, because the GUI events are handled in the event-dispatch thread. It only prevents the while loop from continuing until a packet arrives at the Client. When a packet arrives, line 91 stores it in receivePacket, and lines 94–99 call method displayMessage (declared at lines 110–121) to display the packet's contents in the textarea.

24.8 Client/Server Tic-Tac-Toe Using a Multithreaded Server

In this section, we present the popular game Tic-Tac-Toe implemented by using client/server techniques with stream sockets. The program consists of a TicTacToeServer application (Fig. 24.13–Fig. 24.14) that allows two TicTacToeClient applications (Fig. 24.15–Fig. 24.16) to connect to the server and play Tic-Tac-Toe. Sample outputs are shown in Fig. 24.17.

TicTacToeServer Class

As the TicTacToeServer receives each client connection, it creates an instance of inner-class Player (lines 182–301 of Fig. 24.13) to process the client in a separate thread. These threads enable the clients to play the game independently. The first client to connect to the server is player X and the second is player O. Player X makes the first move. The server maintains the information about the board so it can determine whether a player's move is valid or invalid.

```
1   // Fig. 24.13: TicTacToeServer.java
2   // This class maintains a game of Tic-Tac-Toe for two clients.
3   import java.awt.BorderLayout;
4   import java.net.ServerSocket;
5   import java.net.Socket;
6   import java.io.IOException;
7   import java.util.Formatter;
8   import java.util.Scanner;
9   import java.util.concurrent.ExecutorService;
10  import java.util.concurrent.Executors;
11  import java.util.concurrent.locks.Lock;
12  import java.util.concurrent.locks.ReentrantLock;
13  import java.util.concurrent.locks.Condition;
14  import javax.swing.JFrame;
15  import javax.swing.JTextArea;
16  import javax.swing.SwingUtilities;
17
18  public class TicTacToeServer extends JFrame
19  {
20     private String[] board = new String[ 9 ]; // tic-tac-toe board
21     private JTextArea outputArea; // for outputting moves
22     private Player[] players; // array of Players
23     private ServerSocket server; // server socket to connect with clients
24     private int currentPlayer; // keeps track of player with current move
25     private final static int PLAYER_X = 0; // constant for first player
26     private final static int PLAYER_O = 1; // constant for second player
27     private final static String[] MARKS = { "X", "O" }; // array of marks
28     private ExecutorService runGame; // will run players
29     private Lock gameLock; // to lock game for synchronization
30     private Condition otherPlayerConnected; // to wait for other player
31     private Condition otherPlayerTurn; // to wait for other player's turn
32
33     // set up tic-tac-toe server and GUI that displays messages
34     public TicTacToeServer()
35     {
36        super( "Tic-Tac-Toe Server" ); // set title of window
37
38        // create ExecutorService with a thread for each player
39        runGame = Executors.newFixedThreadPool( 2 );
40        gameLock = new ReentrantLock(); // create lock for game
41
42        // condition variable for both players being connected
43        otherPlayerConnected = gameLock.newCondition();
44
45        // condition variable for the other player's turn
46        otherPlayerTurn = gameLock.newCondition();
47
48        for ( int i = 0; i < 9; i++ )
49           board[ i ] = new String( "" ); // create tic-tac-toe board
50        players = new Player[ 2 ]; // create array of players
51        currentPlayer = PLAYER_X; // set current player to first player
52
```

Fig. 24.13 | Server side of client/server Tic-Tac-Toe program. (Part 1 of 6.)

```
53          try
54          {
55             server = new ServerSocket( 12345, 2 ); // set up ServerSocket
56          } // end try
57          catch ( IOException ioException )
58          {
59             ioException.printStackTrace();
60             System.exit( 1 );
61          } // end catch
62
63          outputArea = new JTextArea(); // create JTextArea for output
64          add( outputArea, BorderLayout.CENTER );
65          outputArea.setText( "Server awaiting connections\n" );
66
67          setSize( 300, 300 ); // set size of window
68          setVisible( true ); // show window
69       } // end TicTacToeServer constructor
70
71       // wait for two connections so game can be played
72       public void execute()
73       {
74          // wait for each client to connect
75          for ( int i = 0; i < players.length; i++ )
76          {
77             try // wait for connection, create Player, start runnable
78             {
79                players[ i ] = new Player( server.accept(), i );
80                runGame.execute( players[ i ] ); // execute player runnable
81             } // end try
82             catch ( IOException ioException )
83             {
84                ioException.printStackTrace();
85                System.exit( 1 );
86             } // end catch
87          } // end for
88
89          gameLock.lock(); // lock game to signal player X's thread
90
91          try
92          {
93             players[ PLAYER_X ].setSuspended( false ); // resume player X
94             otherPlayerConnected.signal(); // wake up player X's thread
95          } // end try
96          finally
97          {
98             gameLock.unlock(); // unlock game after signalling player X
99          } // end finally
100      } // end method execute
101
102      // display message in outputArea
103      private void displayMessage( final String messageToDisplay )
104      {
```

Fig. 24.13 | Server side of client/server Tic-Tac-Toe program. (Part 2 of 6.)

```
105          // display message from event-dispatch thread of execution
106          SwingUtilities.invokeLater(
107             new Runnable()
108             {
109                public void run() // updates outputArea
110                {
111                   outputArea.append( messageToDisplay ); // add message
112                } // end  method run
113             } // end inner class
114          ); // end call to SwingUtilities.invokeLater
115      } // end method displayMessage
116
117      // determine if move is valid
118      public boolean validateAndMove( int location, int player )
119      {
120         // while not current player, must wait for turn
121         while ( player != currentPlayer )
122         {
123            gameLock.lock(); // lock game to wait for other player to go
124
125            try
126            {
127               otherPlayerTurn.await(); // wait for player's turn
128            } // end try
129            catch ( InterruptedException exception )
130            {
131               exception.printStackTrace();
132            } // end catch
133            finally
134            {
135               gameLock.unlock(); // unlock game after waiting
136            } // end finally
137         } // end while
138
139         // if location not occupied, make move
140         if ( !isOccupied( location ) )
141         {
142            board[ location ] = MARKS[ currentPlayer ]; // set move on board
143            currentPlayer = ( currentPlayer + 1 ) % 2; // change player
144
145            // let new current player know that move occurred
146            players[ currentPlayer ].otherPlayerMoved( location );
147
148            gameLock.lock(); // lock game to signal other player to go
149
150            try
151            {
152               otherPlayerTurn.signal(); // signal other player to continue
153            } // end try
154            finally
155            {
156               gameLock.unlock(); // unlock game after signaling
157            } // end finally
```

Fig. 24.13 | Server side of client/server Tic-Tac-Toe program. (Part 3 of 6.)

```
158
159           return true; // notify player that move was valid
160        } // end if
161        else // move was not valid
162           return false; // notify player that move was invalid
163     } // end method validateAndMove
164
165     // determine whether location is occupied
166     public boolean isOccupied( int location )
167     {
168        if ( board[ location ].equals( MARKS[ PLAYER_X ] ) ||
169           board [ location ].equals( MARKS[ PLAYER_O ] ) )
170           return true; // location is occupied
171        else
172           return false; // location is not occupied
173     } // end method isOccupied
174
175     // place code in this method to determine whether game over
176     public boolean isGameOver()
177     {
178        return false; // this is left as an exercise
179     } // end method isGameOver
180
181     // private inner class Player manages each Player as a runnable
182     private class Player implements Runnable
183     {
184        private Socket connection; // connection to client
185        private Scanner input; // input from client
186        private Formatter output; // output to client
187        private int playerNumber; // tracks which player this is
188        private String mark; // mark for this player
189        private boolean suspended = true; // whether thread is suspended
190
191        // set up Player thread
192        public Player( Socket socket, int number )
193        {
194           playerNumber = number; // store this player's number
195           mark = MARKS[ playerNumber ]; // specify player's mark
196           connection = socket; // store socket for client
197
198           try // obtain streams from Socket
199           {
200              input = new Scanner( connection.getInputStream() );
201              output = new Formatter( connection.getOutputStream() );
202           } // end try
203           catch ( IOException ioException )
204           {
205              ioException.printStackTrace();
206              System.exit( 1 );
207           } // end catch
208        } // end Player constructor
209
```

Fig. 24.13 | Server side of client/server Tic-Tac-Toe program. (Part 4 of 6.)

```
210    // send message that other player moved
211    public void otherPlayerMoved( int location )
212    {
213        output.format( "Opponent moved\n" );
214        output.format( "%d\n", location ); // send location of move
215        output.flush(); // flush output
216    } // end method otherPlayerMoved
217
218    // control thread's execution
219    public void run()
220    {
221        // send client its mark (X or O), process messages from client
222        try
223        {
224            displayMessage( "Player " + mark + " connected\n" );
225            output.format( "%s\n", mark ); // send player's mark
226            output.flush(); // flush output
227
228            // if player X, wait for another player to arrive
229            if ( playerNumber == PLAYER_X )
230            {
231                output.format( "%s\n%s", "Player X connected",
232                    "Waiting for another player\n" );
233                output.flush(); // flush output
234
235                gameLock.lock(); // lock game to  wait for second player
236
237                try
238                {
239                    while( suspended )
240                    {
241                        otherPlayerConnected.await(); // wait for player O
242                    } // end while
243                } // end try
244                catch ( InterruptedException exception )
245                {
246                    exception.printStackTrace();
247                } // end catch
248                finally
249                {
250                    gameLock.unlock(); // unlock game after second player
251                } // end finally
252
253                // send message that other player connected
254                output.format( "Other player connected. Your move.\n" );
255                output.flush(); // flush output
256            } // end if
257            else
258            {
259                output.format( "Player O connected, please wait\n" );
260                output.flush(); // flush output
261            } // end else
262
```

Fig. 24.13 | Server side of client/server Tic-Tac-Toe program. (Part 5 of 6.)

```
263                    // while game not over
264                    while ( !isGameOver() )
265                    {
266                       int location = 0; // initialize move location
267
268                       if ( input.hasNext() )
269                          location = input.nextInt(); // get move location
270
271                       // check for valid move
272                       if ( validateAndMove( location, playerNumber ) )
273                       {
274                          displayMessage( "\nlocation: " + location );
275                          output.format( "Valid move.\n" ); // notify client
276                          output.flush(); // flush output
277                       } // end if
278                       else // move was invalid
279                       {
280                          output.format( "Invalid move, try again\n" );
281                          output.flush(); // flush output
282                       } // end else
283                    } // end while
284                 } // end try
285                 finally
286                 {
287                    try
288                    {
289                       connection.close(); // close connection to client
290                    } // end try
291                    catch ( IOException ioException )
292                    {
293                       ioException.printStackTrace();
294                       System.exit( 1 );
295                    } // end catch
296                 } // end finally
297              } // end method run
298
299              // set whether or not thread is suspended
300              public void setSuspended( boolean status )
301              {
302                 suspended = status; // set value of suspended
303              } // end method setSuspended
304           } // end class Player
305        } // end class TicTacToeServer
```

Fig. 24.13 | Server side of client/server Tic-Tac-Toe program. (Part 6 of 6.)

We begin with a discussion of the server side of the Tic-Tac-Toe game. When the Tic-TacToeServer application executes, the main method (lines 7–12 of Fig. 24.14) creates a TicTacToeServer object called application. The constructor (lines 34–69 of Fig. 24.13) attempts to set up a ServerSocket. If successful, the program displays the server window, then main invokes the TicTacToeServer method execute (lines 72–100). Method execute loops twice, blocking at line 79 each time while waiting for a client connection. When

```
 1   // Fig. 24.14: TicTacToeServerTest.java
 2   // Tests the TicTacToeServer.
 3   import javax.swing.JFrame;
 4
 5   public class TicTacToeServerTest
 6   {
 7      public static void main( String args[] )
 8      {
 9         TicTacToeServer application = new TicTacToeServer();
10         application.setDefaultCloseOperation( JFrame.EXIT_ON_CLOSE );
11         application.execute();
12      } // end main
13   } // end class TicTacToeServerTest
```

Fig. 24.14 | Class that tests Tic-Tac-Toe server.

a client connects, line 79 creates a new Player object to manage the connection as a separate thread, and line 80 executes the Player in the runGame thread pool.

When the TicTacToeServer creates a Player, the Player constructor (lines 192–208) receives the Socket object representing the connection to the client and gets the associated input and output streams. Line 201 creates a Formatter (see Chapter 28) by wrapping it around the output stream of the socket. The Player's run method (lines 219–297) controls the information that is sent to and received from the client. First, it passes to the client the character that the client will place on the board when a move is made (line 225). Line 226 calls Formatter method **flush** to force this output to the client. Line 241 suspends player X's thread as it starts executing, because player X can move only after player O connects.

After player O connects, the game can be played, and the run method begins executing its while statement (lines 264–283). Each iteration of this loop reads an integer (line 269) representing the location where the client wants to place a mark, and line 272 invokes the TicTacToeServer method validateAndMove (declared at lines 118–163) to check the move. If the move is valid, line 275 sends a message to the client to this effect. If not, line 280 sends a message indicating that the move was invalid. The program maintains board locations as numbers from 0 to 8 (0 through 2 for the first row, 3 through 5 for the second row and 6 through 8 for the third row).

Method validateAndMove (lines 118–163 in class TicTacToeServer) allows only one player at a time to move, thereby preventing them from modifying the state information of the game simultaneously. If the Player attempting to validate a move is not the current player (i.e., the one allowed to make a move), it is placed in a *wait* state until its turn to move. If the position for the move being validated is already occupied on the board, validMove returns false. Otherwise, the server places a mark for the player in its local representation of the board (line 142), notifies the other Player object (line 146) that a move has been made (so that the client can be sent a message), invokes method signal (line 152) so that the waiting Player (if there is one) can validate a move and returns true (line 159) to indicate that the move is valid.

TicTacToeClient *Class*

Each TicTacToeClient application (Fig. 24.15) maintains its own GUI version of the Tic-Tac-Toe board on which it displays the state of the game. The clients can place a mark only in an empty square on the board. Inner class Square (lines 205–262 of Fig. 24.15) implements each of the nine squares on the board. When a TicTacToeClient begins execution, it creates a JTextArea in which messages from the server and a representation of the board using nine Square objects are displayed. The startClient method (lines 80–100) opens a connection to the server and gets the associated input and output streams from the Socket object. Lines 85–86 make a connection to the server. Class TicTacToeClient implements interface Runnable so that a separate thread can read messages from the server. This approach enables the user to interact with the board (in the event-dispatch thread) while waiting for messages from the server. After establishing the connection to the server, line 99 executes the client with the worker ExecutorService. The run method (lines 103–124) controls the separate thread of execution. The method first reads the mark character (X or O) from the server (line 105), then loops continuously (lines 121–125) and reads messages from the server (line 124). Each message is passed to the processMessage method (lines 129–156) for processing.

```
1   // Fig. 24.15: TicTacToeClient.java
2   // Client that let a user play Tic-Tac-Toe with another across a network.
3   import java.awt.BorderLayout;
4   import java.awt.Dimension;
5   import java.awt.Graphics;
6   import java.awt.GridLayout;
7   import java.awt.event.MouseAdapter;
8   import java.awt.event.MouseEvent;
9   import java.net.Socket;
10  import java.net.InetAddress;
11  import java.io.IOException;
12  import javax.swing.JFrame;
13  import javax.swing.JPanel;
14  import javax.swing.JScrollPane;
15  import javax.swing.JTextArea;
16  import javax.swing.JTextField;
17  import javax.swing.SwingUtilities;
18  import java.util.Formatter;
```

Fig. 24.15 | Client side of client/server Tic-Tac-Toe program. (Part 1 of 6.)

```
19    import java.util.Scanner;
20    import java.util.concurrent.Executors;
21    import java.util.concurrent.ExecutorService;
22
23    public class TicTacToeClient extends JFrame implements Runnable
24    {
25       private JTextField idField; // textfield to display player's mark
26       private JTextArea displayArea; // JTextArea to display output
27       private JPanel boardPanel; // panel for tic-tac-toe board
28       private JPanel panel2; // panel to hold board
29       private Square board[][]; // tic-tac-toe board
30       private Square currentSquare; // current square
31       private Socket connection; // connection to server
32       private Scanner input; // input from server
33       private Formatter output; // output to server
34       private String ticTacToeHost; // host name for server
35       private String myMark; // this client's mark
36       private boolean myTurn; // determines which client's turn it is
37       private final String X_MARK = "X"; // mark for first client
38       private final String O_MARK = "O"; // mark for second client
39
40       // set up user-interface and board
41       public TicTacToeClient( String host )
42       {
43          ticTacToeHost = host; // set name of server
44          displayArea = new JTextArea( 4, 30 ); // set up JTextArea
45          displayArea.setEditable( false );
46          add( new JScrollPane( displayArea ), BorderLayout.SOUTH );
47
48          boardPanel = new JPanel(); // set up panel for squares in board
49          boardPanel.setLayout( new GridLayout( 3, 3, 0, 0 ) );
50
51          board = new Square[ 3 ][ 3 ]; // create board
52
53          // loop over the rows in the board
54          for ( int row = 0; row < board.length; row++ )
55          {
56             // loop over the columns in the board
57             for ( int column = 0; column < board[ row ].length; column++ )
58             {
59                // create square
60                board[ row ][ column ] = new Square( ' ', row * 3 + column );
61                boardPanel.add( board[ row ][ column ] ); // add square
62             } // end inner for
63          } // end outer for
64
65          idField = new JTextField(); // set up textfield
66          idField.setEditable( false );
67          add( idField, BorderLayout.NORTH );
68
69          panel2 = new JPanel(); // set up panel to contain boardPanel
70          panel2.add( boardPanel, BorderLayout.CENTER ); // add board panel
```

Fig. 24.15 | Client side of client/server Tic-Tac-Toe program. (Part 2 of 6.)

```
71            add( panel2, BorderLayout.CENTER ); // add container panel
72
73            setSize( 300, 225 ); // set size of window
74            setVisible( true ); // show window
75
76            startClient();
77        } // end TicTacToeClient constructor
78
79        // start the client thread
80        public void startClient()
81        {
82            try // connect to server, get streams and start outputThread
83            {
84                // make connection to server
85                connection = new Socket(
86                    InetAddress.getByName( ticTacToeHost ), 12345 );
87
88                // get streams for input and output
89                input = new Scanner( connection.getInputStream() );
90                output = new Formatter( connection.getOutputStream() );
91            } // end try
92            catch ( IOException ioException )
93            {
94                ioException.printStackTrace();
95            } // end catch
96
97            // create and start worker thread for this client
98            ExecutorService worker = Executors.newFixedThreadPool( 1 );
99            worker.execute( this ); // execute client
100       } // end method startClient
101
102       // control thread that allows continuous update of displayArea
103       public void run()
104       {
105           myMark = input.nextLine(); // get player's mark (X or O)
106
107           SwingUtilities.invokeLater(
108               new Runnable()
109               {
110                   public void run()
111                   {
112                       // display player's mark
113                       idField.setText( "You are player \"" + myMark + "\"" );
114                   } // end method run
115               } // end anonymous inner class
116           ); // end call to SwingUtilities.invokeLater
117
118           myTurn = ( myMark.equals( X_MARK ) ); // determine if client's turn
119
120           // receive messages sent to client and output them
121           while ( true )
122           {
```

Fig. 24.15 | Client side of client/server Tic-Tac-Toe program. (Part 3 of 6.)

```
123              if ( input.hasNextLine() )
124                  processMessage( input.nextLine() );
125          } // end while
126      } // end method run
127
128      // process messages received by client
129      private void processMessage( String message )
130      {
131          // valid move occurred
132          if ( message.equals( "Valid move." ) )
133          {
134              displayMessage( "Valid move, please wait.\n" );
135              setMark( currentSquare, myMark ); // set mark in square
136          } // end if
137          else if ( message.equals( "Invalid move, try again" ) )
138          {
139              displayMessage( message + "\n" ); // display invalid move
140              myTurn = true; // still this client's turn
141          } // end else if
142          else if ( message.equals( "Opponent moved" ) )
143          {
144              int location = input.nextInt(); // get move location
145              input.nextLine(); // skip newline after int location
146              int row = location / 3; // calculate row
147              int column = location % 3; // calculate column
148
149              setMark( board[ row ][ column ],
150                  ( myMark.equals( X_MARK ) ? O_MARK : X_MARK ) ); // mark move
151              displayMessage( "Opponent moved. Your turn.\n" );
152              myTurn = true; // now this client's turn
153          } // end else if
154          else
155              displayMessage( message + "\n" ); // display the message
156      } // end method processMessage
157
158      // manipulate outputArea in event-dispatch thread
159      private void displayMessage( final String messageToDisplay )
160      {
161          SwingUtilities.invokeLater(
162              new Runnable()
163              {
164                  public void run()
165                  {
166                      displayArea.append( messageToDisplay ); // updates output
167                  } // end method run
168              } // end inner class
169          ); // end call to SwingUtilities.invokeLater
170      } // end method displayMessage
171
172      // utility method to set mark on board in event-dispatch thread
173      private void setMark( final Square squareToMark, final String mark )
174      {
```

Fig. 24.15 | Client side of client/server Tic-Tac-Toe program. (Part 4 of 6.)

```java
175             SwingUtilities.invokeLater(
176                new Runnable()
177                {
178                   public void run()
179                   {
180                      squareToMark.setMark( mark ); // set mark in square
181                   } // end method run
182                } // end anonymous inner class
183             ); // end call to SwingUtilities.invokeLater
184          } // end method setMark
185
186          // send message to server indicating clicked square
187          public void sendClickedSquare( int location )
188          {
189             // if it is my turn
190             if ( myTurn )
191             {
192                output.format( "%d\n", location ); // send location to server
193                output.flush();
194                myTurn = false; // not my turn anymore
195             } // end if
196          } // end method sendClickedSquare
197
198          // set current Square
199          public void setCurrentSquare( Square square )
200          {
201             currentSquare = square; // set current square to argument
202          } // end method setCurrentSquare
203
204          // private inner class for the squares on the board
205          private class Square extends JPanel
206          {
207             private String mark; // mark to be drawn in this square
208             private int location; // location of square
209
210             public Square( String squareMark, int squareLocation )
211             {
212                mark = squareMark; // set mark for this square
213                location = squareLocation; // set location of this square
214
215                addMouseListener(
216                   new MouseAdapter()
217                   {
218                      public void mouseReleased( MouseEvent e )
219                      {
220                         setCurrentSquare( Square.this ); // set current square
221
222                         // send location of this square
223                         sendClickedSquare( getSquareLocation() );
224                      } // end method mouseReleased
225                   } // end anonymous inner class
226                ); // end call to addMouseListener
227             } // end Square constructor
```

Fig. 24.15 | Client side of client/server Tic-Tac-Toe program. (Part 5 of 6.)

```
228
229        // return preferred size of Square
230        public Dimension getPreferredSize()
231        {
232            return new Dimension( 30, 30 ); // return preferred size
233        } // end method getPreferredSize
234
235        // return minimum size of Square
236        public Dimension getMinimumSize()
237        {
238            return getPreferredSize(); // return preferred size
239        } // end method getMinimumSize
240
241        // set mark for Square
242        public void setMark( String newMark )
243        {
244            mark = newMark; // set mark of square
245            repaint(); // repaint square
246        } // end method setMark
247
248        // return Square location
249        public int getSquareLocation()
250        {
251            return location; // return location of square
252        } // end method getSquareLocation
253
254        // draw Square
255        public void paintComponent( Graphics g )
256        {
257            super.paintComponent( g );
258
259            g.drawRect( 0, 0, 29, 29 ); // draw square
260            g.drawString( mark, 11, 20 ); // draw mark
261        } // end method paintComponent
262    } // end inner-class Square
263 } // end class TicTacToeClient
```

Fig. 24.15 | Client side of client/server Tic-Tac-Toe program. (Part 6 of 6.)

If the message received is "Valid move.", lines 134–135 display the message "Valid move, please wait." and call method setMark (lines 173–184) to set the client's mark in the current square (the one in which the user clicked) using SwingUtilities method invokeLater to ensure that the GUI updates occur in the event-dispatch thread. If the message received is "Invalid move, try again.", line 139 displays the message so that the user can click a different square. If the message received is "Opponent moved.", line 145 reads an integer from the server indicating where the opponent moved, and lines 149–150 place a mark in that square of the board (again using SwingUtilities method invoke-Later to ensure that the GUI updates occur in the event-dispatch thread). If any other message is received, line 155 simply displays the message. Figure 24.17 shows sample screen captures of two applications interacting via the TicTacToeServer.

```
 1   // Fig. 24.16: TicTacToeClientTest.java
 2   // Tests the TicTacToeClient class.
 3   import javax.swing.JFrame;
 4
 5   public class TicTacToeClientTest
 6   {
 7      public static void main( String args[] )
 8      {
 9         TicTacToeClient application; // declare client application
10
11         // if no command line args
12         if ( args.length == 0 )
13            application = new TicTacToeClient( "127.0.0.1" ); // localhost
14         else
15            application = new TicTacToeClient( args[ 0 ] ); // use args
16
17         application.setDefaultCloseOperation( JFrame.EXIT_ON_CLOSE );
18      } // end main
19   } // end class TicTacToeClientTest
```

Fig. 24.16 | Test class for Tic-Tac-Toe client.

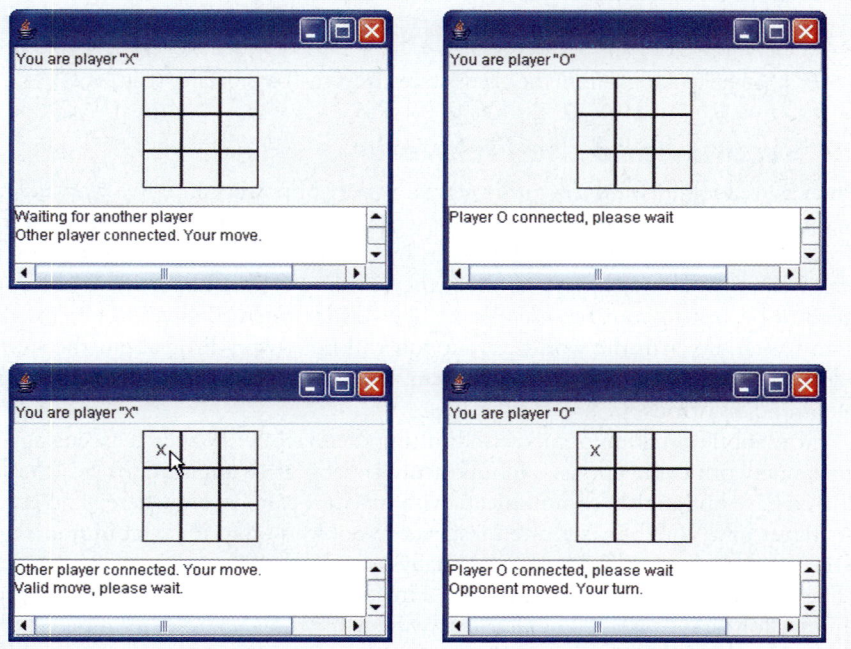

Fig. 24.17 | Sample outputs from the client/server Tic-Tac-Toe program. (Part 1 of 2.)

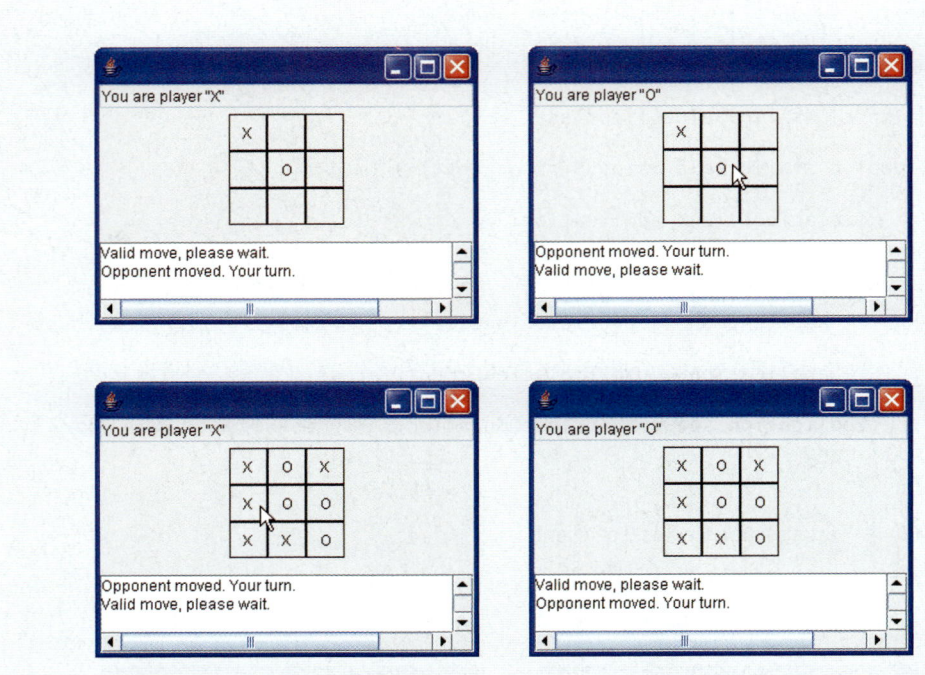

Fig. 24.17 | Sample outputs from the client/server Tic-Tac-Toe program. (Part 2 of 2.)

24.9 Security and the Network

As much as we look forward to writing a great variety of powerful network-based applications, our efforts may be limited because of security concerns. Many Web browsers, such as Mozilla and Microsoft Internet Explorer, by default prohibit Java applets from doing file processing on the machines on which they execute. Think about it. A Java applet is designed to be sent to your browser via an HTML document that could be downloaded from any Web server in the world. Often you will know very little about the sources of Java applets that will execute on your system. To allow these applets free rein with your files could be disastrous.

A more subtle situation occurs with limiting the machines to which executing applets can make network connections. To build truly collaborative applications, we would ideally like to have our applets communicate with machines almost anywhere. The Java security manager in a Web browser often restricts an applet so that it can communicate only with the machine from which it was originally downloaded.

These restrictions may seem too strict. However, the Java Security API now provides capabilities for digitally signed applets that will enable browsers to determine whether an applet is downloaded from a **trusted source**. A trusted applet can be given additional access to the computer on which it is executing. The features of the Java Security API and additional networking capabilities are discussed in our text *Advanced Java 2 Platform How to Program*.

24.10 Case Study: DeitelMessenger Server and Client

Chat rooms have become common on the Internet. They provide a central location where users can chat with each other via short text messages. Each participant can see all messages that the other users post, and each user can post messages. This section presents our capstone networking case study, which integrates many of the Java networking, multithreading and Swing GUI features we have learned thus far to build an online chat system. We also introduce **multicasting**, which enables an application to send DatagramPackets to groups of clients. After reading this section, you will be able to build more significant networking applications.

24.10.1 DeitelMessengerServer and Supporting Classes

DeitelMessengerServer (Fig. 24.18) is the heart of the online chat system. This class appears in package com.deitel.messenger.sockets.server. Chat clients can participate in a chat by connecting to the DeitelMessengerServer. Method startServer (lines 20–53) launches DeitelMessengerServer. Lines 28–29 create a ServerSocket to accept incoming network connections. Recall that the ServerSocket constructor takes as its first argument the port on which the server should listen for incoming connections. Interface SocketMessengerConstants (Fig. 24.20) declares the port number as the constant SERVER_PORT to ensure that the server and the clients use the correct port number.

Lines 35–47 listen continuously for new client connections. Line 38 invokes Server-Socket method accept to wait for and accept a new client connection. Lines 41–42 create and start a new MessageReceiver for the client. Class MessageReceiver (Fig. 24.22) of package com.deitel.messenger.sockets.server implements Runnable and listens for incoming messages from a client. The first argument to the MessageReceiver constructor is a MessageListener (Fig. 24.21), to which messages from the client should be delivered. Class DeitelMessengerServer implements interface MessageListener (line 15) of package com.deitel.messenger and therefore can pass the this reference to the MessageReceiver constructor.

When each MessageReceiver receives a new message from a client, the MessageReceiver passes the message to a MessageListener through method messageReceived (lines 56–64). Line 59 concatenates the from string with the separator >>> and the message

```
 1   // Fig. 24.18: DeitelMessengerServer.java
 2   // DeitelMessengerServer is a multi-threaded, socket- and
 3   // packet-based chat server.
 4   package com.deitel.messenger.sockets.server;
 5
 6   import java.net.ServerSocket;
 7   import java.net.Socket;
 8   import java.io.IOException;
 9   import java.util.concurrent.Executors;
10   import java.util.concurrent.ExecutorService;
11
12   import com.deitel.messenger.MessageListener;
13   import static com.deitel.messenger.sockets.SocketMessengerConstants.*;
```

Fig. 24.18 | DeitelMessengerServer for managing a chat room. (Part 1 of 2.)

```
14
15    public class DeitelMessengerServer implements MessageListener
16    {
17        private ExecutorService serverExecutor; // executor for server
18
19        // start chat server
20        public void startServer()
21        {
22            // create executor for server runnables
23            serverExecutor = Executors.newCachedThreadPool();
24
25            try // create server and manage new clients
26            {
27                // create ServerSocket for incoming connections
28                ServerSocket serverSocket =
29                    new ServerSocket( SERVER_PORT, 100 );
30
31                System.out.printf( "%s%d%s", "Server listening on port ",
32                    SERVER_PORT, " ..." );
33
34                // listen for clients constantly
35                while ( true )
36                {
37                    // accept new client connection
38                    Socket clientSocket = serverSocket.accept();
39
40                    // create MessageReceiver for receiving messages from client
41                    serverExecutor.execute(
42                        new MessageReceiver( this, clientSocket ) );
43
44                    // print connection information
45                    System.out.println( "Connection received from: " +
46                        clientSocket.getInetAddress() );
47                } // end while
48            } // end try
49            catch ( IOException ioException )
50            {
51                ioException.printStackTrace();
52            } // end catch
53        } // end method startServer
54
55        // when new message is received, broadcast message to clients
56        public void messageReceived( String from, String message )
57        {
58            // create String containing entire message
59            String completeMessage = from + MESSAGE_SEPARATOR + message;
60
61            // create and start MulticastSender to broadcast messages
62            serverExecutor.execute(
63                new MulticastSender( completeMessage.getBytes() ) );
64        } // end method messageReceived
65    } // end class DeitelMessengerServer
```

Fig. 24.18 | DeitelMessengerServer for managing a chat room. (Part 2 of 2.)

```
1    // Fig. 24.19: DeitelMessengerServerTest.java
2    // Test the DeitelMessengerServer class.
3    package com.deitel.messenger.sockets.server;
4
5    public class DeitelMessengerServerTest
6    {
7       public static void main ( String args[] )
8       {
9          DeitelMessengerServer application = new DeitelMessengerServer();
10         application.startServer(); // start server
11      } // end main
12   } // end class DeitelMessengerServerTest
```

```
Server listening on port 12345 ...
Connection received from: /127.0.0.1
Connection received from: /127.0.0.1
Connection received from: /127.0.0.1
```

Fig. 24.19 | Test class for `DeitelMessengerServer`.

body. Lines 62–63 create and start a new `MulticastSender` to deliver `completeMessage` to all clients. Class `MulticastSender` (Fig. 24.23) of package `com.deitel.messenger.sockets.server` uses multicasting as an efficient mechanism for sending one message to multiple clients. We discuss the details of multicasting shortly. Method `main` (lines 7–11 of Fig. 24.19) creates a new `DeitelMessengerServer` instance and starts the server.

Interface `SocketMessengerConstants` (Fig. 24.20) declares constants for use in the various classes that make up the Deitel messenger system. Classes can access these `static` constants by using a static `import` as shown in Fig. 24.22.

```
1    // Fig. 24.20: SocketMessengerConstants.java
2    // SocketMessengerConstants defines constants for the port numbers
3    // and multicast address in DeitelMessenger
4    package com.deitel.messenger.sockets;
5
6    public interface SocketMessengerConstants
7    {
8       // address for multicast datagrams
9       public static final String MULTICAST_ADDRESS = "239.0.0.1";
10
11      // port for listening for multicast datagrams
12      public static final int MULTICAST_LISTENING_PORT = 5555;
13
14      // port for sending multicast datagrams
15      public static final int MULTICAST_SENDING_PORT = 5554;
16
17      // port for Socket connections to DeitelMessengerServer
18      public static final int SERVER_PORT = 12345;
19
```

Fig. 24.20 | `SocketMessengerConstants` declares constants for use in the `DeitelMessengerServer` and `DeitelMessenger`. (Part I of 2.)

```
20      // String that indicates disconnect
21      public static final String DISCONNECT_STRING = "DISCONNECT";
22
23      // String that separates the user name from the message body
24      public static final String MESSAGE_SEPARATOR = ">>>";
25
26      // message size (in bytes)
27      public static final int MESSAGE_SIZE = 512;
28   } // end interface SocketMessengerConstants
```

Fig. 24.20 | SocketMessengerConstants declares constants for use in the DeitelMessengerServer and DeitelMessenger. (Part 2 of 2.)

Line 9 declares the String constant MULTICAST_ADDRESS, which contains the address to which a MulticastSender (Fig. 24.23) should send messages. This address is one of the addresses reserved for multicast, which we describe in the discussion of Fig. 24.23. Line 12 declares the integer constant MULTICAST_LISTENING_PORT—the port on which clients should listen for new messages. Line 15 declares the integer constant MULTICAST_SENDING_PORT—the port to which a MulticastSender should post new messages at the MULTICAST_ADDRESS. Line 18 declares the integer constant SERVER_PORT—the port on which DeitelMessengerServer listens for incoming client connections. Line 21 declares String constant DISCONNECT_STRING, which is the String that a client sends to DeitelMessengerServer when the user wishes to leave the chat room. Line 24 declares String constant MESSAGE_SEPARATOR, which separates the user name from the message body. Line 27 specifies the maximum message size in bytes.

Many different classes in the Deitel messenger system receive messages. For example, DeitelMessengerServer receives messages from clients and delivers them to all chat room participants. As we will see, the user interface for each client also receives messages and displays them to the users. Each class that receives messages implements interface MessageListener (Fig. 24.21). The interface (from package com.deitel.messenger) declares method messageReceived, which allows an implementing class to receive chat messages. Method messageReceived takes two string arguments representing the name of the sender and the message body, respectively.

DeitelMessengerServer uses instances of class MessageReceiver (Fig. 24.22) from package com.deitel.messenger.sockets.server to listen for new messages from each

```
1    // Fig. 24.21: MessageListener.java
2    // MessageListener is an interface for classes that wish to
3    // receive new chat messages.
4    package com.deitel.messenger;
5
6    public interface MessageListener
7    {
8       // receive new chat message
9       public void messageReceived( String from, String message );
10   } // end interface MessageListener
```

Fig. 24.21 | MessageListener interface that declares method messageReceived for receiving new chat messages.

```
1   // Fig. 24.22: MessageReceiver.java
2   // MessageReceiver is a Runnable that listens for messages from a
3   // particular client and delivers messages to a MessageListener.
4   package com.deitel.messenger.sockets.server;
5
6   import java.io.BufferedReader;
7   import java.io.IOException;
8   import java.io.InputStreamReader;
9   import java.net.Socket;
10  import java.net.SocketTimeoutException;
11  import java.util.StringTokenizer;
12
13  import com.deitel.messenger.MessageListener;
14  import static com.deitel.messenger.sockets.SocketMessengerConstants.*;
15
16  public class MessageReceiver implements Runnable
17  {
18     private BufferedReader input; // input stream
19     private MessageListener messageListener; // message listener
20     private boolean keepListening = true; // when false, ends runnable
21
22     // MessageReceiver constructor
23     public MessageReceiver( MessageListener listener, Socket clientSocket )
24     {
25        // set listener to which new messages should be sent
26        messageListener = listener;
27
28        try
29        {
30           // set timeout for reading from client
31           clientSocket.setSoTimeout( 5000 ); // five seconds
32
33           // create BufferedReader for reading incoming messages
34           input = new BufferedReader( new InputStreamReader(
35              clientSocket.getInputStream() ) );
36        } // end try
37        catch ( IOException ioException )
38        {
39           ioException.printStackTrace();
40        } // end catch
41     } // end MessageReceiver constructor
42
43     // listen for new messages and deliver them to MessageListener
44     public void run()
45     {
46        String message; // String for incoming messages
47
48        // listen for messages until stopped
49        while ( keepListening )
50        {
```

Fig. 24.22 | MessageReceiver for listening for new messages from
DeitelMessengerServer clients in separate threads. (Part 1 of 3.)

```
51          try
52          {
53             message = input.readLine(); // read message from client
54          } // end try
55          catch ( SocketTimeoutException socketTimeoutException )
56          {
57             continue; // continue to next iteration to keep listening
58          } // end catch
59          catch ( IOException ioException )
60          {
61             ioException.printStackTrace();
62             break;
63          } // end catch
64
65          // ensure non-null message
66          if ( message != null )
67          {
68             // tokenize message to retrieve user name and message body
69             StringTokenizer tokenizer = new StringTokenizer(
70                message, MESSAGE_SEPARATOR );
71
72             // ignore messages that do not contain a user
73             // name and message body
74             if ( tokenizer.countTokens() == 2 )
75             {
76                // send message to MessageListener
77                messageListener.messageReceived(
78                   tokenizer.nextToken(), // user name
79                   tokenizer.nextToken() ); // message body
80             } // end if
81             else
82             {
83                // if disconnect message received, stop listening
84                if ( message.equalsIgnoreCase(
85                   MESSAGE_SEPARATOR + DISCONNECT_STRING ) )
86                   stopListening();
87             } // end else
88          } // end if
89       } // end while
90
91       try
92       {
93          input.close(); // close BufferedReader (also closes Socket)
94       } // end try
95       catch ( IOException ioException )
96       {
97          ioException.printStackTrace();
98       } // end catch
99    } // end method run
100
```

Fig. 24.22 | `MessageReceiver` for listening for new messages from
`DeitelMessengerServer` clients in separate threads. (Part 2 of 3.)

```
101        // stop listening for incoming messages
102        public void stopListening()
103        {
104           keepListening = false;
105        } // end method stopListening
106  } // end class MessageReceiver
```

Fig. 24.22 | `MessageReceiver` for listening for new messages from `DeitelMessengerServer` clients in separate threads. (Part 3 of 3.)

client. Class `MessageReceiver` implements interface `Runnable`. This enables `Deitel-MessengerServer` to create an object of class `MessageReceiver` to run in a separate thread for each client, so that messages from multiple clients can be handled concurrently. When `DeitelMessengerServer` receives a new client connection, `DeitelMessengerServer` creates a new `MessageReceiver` for the client, then continues listening for new client connections. The `MessageReceiver` listens for messages from a single client and passes them back to the `DeitelMessengerServer` through method `messageReceived`.

The `MessageReceiver` constructor (lines 23–41) takes a `MessageListener` as its first argument. The `MessageReceiver` will deliver new messages to this listener by invoking its `messageReceived` method. The `MessageReceiver` constructor's `Socket` argument is the connection to a particular client. Line 26 sets the `MessageListener` to which the `MessageReceiver` should deliver new messages. Line 31 invokes `Socket` method **setSoTimeout** with an integer argument of 5000 milliseconds. Reading data from a `Socket` is a blocking call—the current thread does not execute until the read operation completes. Method `setSoTimeout` specifies that if no data is received in the given number of milliseconds, the `Socket` should issue a `SocketTimeoutException`, which the current thread can catch, then continue executing. This technique prevents the current thread from deadlocking if no more data is available from the `Socket`. Lines 34–35 create a new `BufferedReader` for the `clientSocket`'s `InputStream`. The `MessageReceiver` uses this `BufferedReader` to read new messages from the client.

Method `run` (lines 44–99) listens continuously for new messages from the client. Lines 49–89 loop as long as the `boolean` variable `keepListening` is `true`. Line 53 invokes `BufferedReader` method `readLine` to read a line of text from the client. If more than 5000 milliseconds pass without any data being read, method `readLine` throws an `InterruptedIOException`, which indicates that the time-out set on line 31 has expired. Line 57 uses a `continue` statement to go to the next iteration of the `while` loop to continue listening for messages. Lines 59–63 catch an `IOException`, which indicates a more severe problem from method `readLine`. In this case, line 61 prints a stack trace to aid in debugging the application, and line 62 uses keyword `break` to terminate the loop.

When sending a message to the server, the client separates the user's name from the message body with `MESSAGE_SEPARATOR` declared in interface `SocketMessengerConstants`. If no exceptions are thrown when reading data from the client and the message is not null (line 66), lines 69–70 create a new `StringTokenizer` that uses delimiter `MESSAGE_SEPARATOR` to separate each message into two tokens—the sender's user name and the message. Line 74 checks for the proper number of tokens (using `StringTokenizer` method **countTokens**), and lines 77–79 invoke method `messageReceived` of interface `MessageListener` to deliver the new message to the registered `MessageListener`. If the

StringTokenizer does not produce two tokens, lines 84–85 check the message to see whether it matches the constant DISCONNECT_STRING, which would indicate that the user wishes to leave the chat room. Line 84 uses String method **equalsIgnoreCase** to test whether the input String equals the disconnect string. This method is equivalent to String method equals, but it does not consider the case of the letters. This allows the user to type DISCONNECT, disconnect or even dIscoNNEcT to terminate the connection. If the strings match, line 86 invokes MessageReceiver method stopListening to terminate the MessageReceiver.

Method stopListening (lines 102–105) sets boolean variable keepListening to false. This causes the while loop condition that starts at line 49 to fail and causes the MessageReceiver to close the client Socket (line 93). Then method run returns, which terminates the MessageReceiver's execution.

MulticastSender (Fig. 24.23) delivers DatagramPackets containing chat messages to a group of clients. Multicast is an efficient way to send data to many clients without the overhead of broadcasting it to every host on the Internet. To understand multicast, let us look at a real-world analogy—the relationship between a magazine's publisher and its subscribers. The publisher produces a magazine and provides it to a distributor. Customers obtain a subscription and begin receiving the magazine in the mail from the distributor. This communication is quite different from a television broadcast. When a television station produces a television show, the station broadcasts the show throughout a geographical region or perhaps throughout the world by using satellites. Broadcasting a show for 1,000,000 viewers costs no more than broadcasting one for 100 viewers—the signal carrying the broadcast reaches a wide area. However, printing and delivering a magazine to 1,000,000 readers would be much more expensive than for 100 readers. Most publishers could not stay in business if they had to broadcast their magazines to everyone, so they multicast them to a group of subscribers instead.

```java
 1   // Fig. 24.23: MulticastSender.java
 2   // MulticastSender broadcasts a chat message using a multicast datagram.
 3   package com.deitel.messenger.sockets.server;
 4
 5   import java.io.IOException;
 6   import java.net.DatagramPacket;
 7   import java.net.DatagramSocket;
 8   import java.net.InetAddress;
 9
10   import static com.deitel.messenger.sockets.SocketMessengerConstants.*;
11
12   public class MulticastSender implements Runnable
13   {
14      private byte[] messageBytes; // message data
15
16      public MulticastSender( byte[] bytes )
17      {
18         messageBytes = bytes; // create the message
19      } // end MulticastSender constructor
```

Fig. 24.23 | MulticastSender for delivering outgoing messages to a multicast group via DatagramPackets. (Part I of 2.)

```
20
21      // deliver message to MULTICAST_ADDRESS over DatagramSocket
22      public void run()
23      {
24         try // deliver message
25         {
26            // create DatagramSocket for sending message
27            DatagramSocket socket =
28               new DatagramSocket( MULTICAST_SENDING_PORT );
29
30            // use InetAddress reserved for multicast group
31            InetAddress group = InetAddress.getByName( MULTICAST_ADDRESS );
32
33            // create DatagramPacket containing message
34            DatagramPacket packet = new DatagramPacket( messageBytes,
35               messageBytes.length, group, MULTICAST_LISTENING_PORT );
36
37            socket.send( packet ); // send packet to multicast group
38            socket.close(); // close socket
39         } // end try
40         catch ( IOException ioException )
41         {
42            ioException.printStackTrace();
43         } // end catch
44      } // end method run
45   } // end class MulticastSender
```

Fig. 24.23 | `MulticastSender` for delivering outgoing messages to a multicast group via `DatagramPackets`. (Part 2 of 2.)

Using multicast, an application can "publish" `DatagramPackets` to "subscriber" applications by sending them to a **multicast address**, which is an IP address reserved for multicast. Multicast addresses are in the range from 224.0.0.0 to 239.255.255.255. Addresses starting with 239 are reserved for intranets, so we use one of these (239.0.0.1) in our case study. Clients that wish to receive these `DatagramPackets` can connect to the appropriate multicast address to join the group of subscribers—the **multicast group**. When an application sends a `DatagramPacket` to the multicast address, each client in the group receives it. Multicast `DatagramPackets`, like unicast `DatagramPackets` (Fig. 24.7), are not reliable—packets are not guaranteed to reach any destination or arrive in any particular order.

Class `MulticastSender` implements interface `Runnable` to enable `Deitel-MessengerServer` to send multicast messages in a separate thread. The `Deitel-MessengerServer` creates a `MulticastSender` with the contents of the message and starts the thread. The `MulticastSender` constructor (lines 16–19) takes as an argument an array of bytes containing the message.

Method run (lines 22–44) delivers the message to the multicast address. Lines 27–28 create a new `DatagramSocket`. Recall from Section 24.7 that we use `DatagramSockets` to send **unicast** `DatagramPackets`—packets sent from one host directly to another host. Multicast `DatagramPackets` are sent the same way, except that the address to which they are sent is a multicast address. Line 31 create an `InetAddress` object for the multicast address, which is declared as a constant in interface `SocketMessengerConstants`. Lines 34–35 create the DatagramPacket containing the message. The first argument to the Datagram-Packet constructor is the byte array containing the message. The second argument is the length of the byte array. The third argument specifies the InetAddress to which the packet should be sent, and the last specifies the port number at which the packet should be delivered to the multicast address. Line 37 sends the packet with DatagramSocket method send. All clients listening to the multicast address on the proper port will receive this DatagramPacket. Line 38 closes the DatagramSocket, and the run method returns, terminating the MulticastSender.

Executing the *DeitelMessengerServerTest*

To execute the DeitelMessengerServerTest, open a **Command Prompt** window and change directories to the location in which package com.deitel.messenger.sock-ets.server resides (i.e., the directory in which com is located). Then type

```
java com.deitel.messenger.sockets.server.DeitelMessengerServerTest
```

to execute the server.

24.10.2 DeitelMessenger Client and Supporting Classes

The client for the DeitelMessengerServer has several components. A class that implements interface MessageManager (Fig. 24.24) manages communication with the server. A Runnable subclass listens for messages at DeitelMessengerServer's multicast address. Another Runnable subclass sends messages from the client to the server. A JFrame subclass provides the client's GUI.

Interface MessageManager (Fig. 24.24) declares methods for managing communication with DeitelMessengerServer. We declare this interface to abstract the base functionality a client needs to interact with a chat server from the underlying communication

```
1   // Fig. 24.24: MessageManager.java
2   // MessageManger is an interface for objects capable of managing
3   // communications with a message server.
4   package com.deitel.messenger;
5
6   public interface MessageManager
7   {
8      // connect to message server and route incoming messages
9      // to given MessageListener
10     public void connect( MessageListener listener );
11
12     // disconnect from message server and stop routing
13     // incoming messages to given MessageListener
14     public void disconnect( MessageListener listener );
15
16     // send message to message server
17     public void sendMessage( String from, String message );
18  } // end interface MessageManager
```

Fig. 24.24 | MessageManager interface that declares methods for communicating with a DeitelMessengerServer.

mechanism. This abstraction enables us to provide `MessageManager` implementations that use other network protocols to implement the communication details. For example, if we wanted to connect to a different chat server that did not use multicast `DatagramPackets`, we could implement the `MessageManager` interface with the appropriate network protocols for this alternative messaging server. We would not need to modify any other code in the client, because the client's other components refer only to interface `MessageManager`, not a particular `MessageManager` implementation. Similarly, `MessageManager` methods refer to other components of the client only through interface `MessageListener`, so other client components can change without requiring changes in the `MessageManager` or its implementations. Method `connect` (line 10) connects a `MessageManager` to `DeitelMessengerServer` and routes incoming messages to the appropriate `MessageListener`. Method `disconnect` (line 14) disconnects a `MessageManager` from the `DeitelMessengerServer` and stops delivering messages to the given `MessageListener`. Method `sendMessage` (line 17) sends a new message to `DeitelMessengerServer`.

Class `SocketMessageManager` (Fig. 24.25) implements `MessageManager` (line 18), using `Sockets` and `MulticastSockets` to communicate with `DeitelMessengerServer` and

```
1   // Fig. 24.25: SocketMessageManager.java
2   // SocketMessageManager communicates with a DeitelMessengerServer using
3   // Sockets and MulticastSockets.
4   package com.deitel.messenger.sockets.client;
5
6   import java.net.InetAddress;
7   import java.net.Socket;
8   import java.io.IOException;
9   import java.util.concurrent.Executors;
10  import java.util.concurrent.ExecutorService;
11  import java.util.concurrent.ExecutionException;
12  import java.util.concurrent.Future;
13
14  import com.deitel.messenger.MessageListener;
15  import com.deitel.messenger.MessageManager;
16  import static com.deitel.messenger.sockets.SocketMessengerConstants.*;
17
18  public class SocketMessageManager implements MessageManager
19  {
20     private Socket clientSocket; // Socket for outgoing messages
21     private String serverAddress; // DeitelMessengerServer address
22     private PacketReceiver receiver; // receives multicast messages
23     private boolean connected = false; // connection status
24     private ExecutorService serverExecutor; // executor for server
25
26     public SocketMessageManager( String address )
27     {
28        serverAddress = address; // store server address
29        serverExecutor = Executors.newCachedThreadPool();
30     } // end SocketMessageManager constructor
31
```

Fig. 24.25 | `SocketMessageManager` implementation of interface `MessageManager` for communicating via `Sockets` and multicast `DatagramPackets`. (Part 1 of 3.)

```
32    // connect to server and send messages to given MessageListener
33    public void connect( MessageListener listener )
34    {
35       if ( connected )
36          return; // if already connected, return immediately
37
38       try // open Socket connection to DeitelMessengerServer
39       {
40          clientSocket = new Socket(
41             InetAddress.getByName( serverAddress ), SERVER_PORT );
42
43          // create runnable for receiving incoming messages
44          receiver = new PacketReceiver( listener );
45          serverExecutor.execute( receiver ); // execute runnable
46          connected = true; // update connected flag
47       } // end try
48       catch ( IOException ioException )
49       {
50          ioException.printStackTrace();
51       } // end catch
52    } // end method connect
53
54    // disconnect from server and unregister given MessageListener
55    public void disconnect( MessageListener listener )
56    {
57       if ( !connected )
58          return; // if not connected, return immediately
59
60       try // stop listener and disconnect from server
61       {
62          // notify server that client is disconnecting
63          Runnable disconnecter = new MessageSender( clientSocket, "",
64             DISCONNECT_STRING );
65          Future disconnecting = serverExecutor.submit( disconnecter );
66          disconnecting.get(); // wait for disconnect message to be sent
67          receiver.stopListening(); // stop receiver
68          clientSocket.close(); // close outgoing Socket
69       } // end try
70       catch ( ExecutionException exception )
71       {
72          exception.printStackTrace();
73       } // end catch
74       catch ( InterruptedException exception )
75       {
76          exception.printStackTrace();
77       } // end catch
78       catch ( IOException ioException )
79       {
80          ioException.printStackTrace();
81       } // end catch
82
```

Fig. 24.25 | SocketMessageManager implementation of interface MessageManager for communicating via Sockets and multicast DatagramPackets. (Part 2 of 3.)

```
83              connected = false; // update connected flag
84          } // end method disconnect
85
86          // send message to server
87          public void sendMessage( String from, String message )
88          {
89              if ( !connected )
90                  return; // if not connected, return immediately
91
92              // create and start new MessageSender to deliver message
93              serverExecutor.execute(
94                  new MessageSender( clientSocket, from, message) );
95          } // end method sendMessage
96      } // end method SocketMessageManager
```

Fig. 24.25 | SocketMessageManager implementation of interface MessageManager for communicating via Sockets and multicast DatagramPackets. (Part 3 of 3.)

receive incoming messages. Line 20 declares the Socket used to connect to and send messages to DeitelMessengerServer. Line 22 declares a PacketReceiver (Fig. 24.27) that listens for new incoming messages. The connected flag (line 23) indicates whether the SocketMessageManager is currently connected to DeitelMessengerServer.

The SocketMessageManager constructor (lines 26–30) receives the address of the DeitelMessengerServer to which SocketMessageManager should connect. Method connect (lines 33–52) connects SocketMessageManager to DeitelMessengerServer. If it was connected previously, line 36 returns from method connect. Lines 40–41 create a new Socket to communicate with the server. Line 41 creates an InetAddress object for the server's address and uses the constant SERVER_PORT to specify the port on which the client should connect. Line 44 creates a new PacketReceiver, which listens for incoming multicast messages from the server, and line 45 executes the Runnable. Line 46 updates boolean variable connected to indicate that SocketMessageManager is connected to the server.

Method disconnect (lines 55–84) terminates the SocketMessageManager's connection to the server. If SocketMessageManager is not connected, line 58 returns from method disconnect. Lines 63–64 create a new MessageSender (Fig. 24.26) to send DISCONNECT_STRING to DeitelMessengerServer. Class MessageSender delivers a message to DeitelMessengerServer over the SocketMessageManager's Socket connection. Line 65 starts the MessageSender to deliver the message using method **submit** of the ExecutorService. This method returns a Future which represents the executing Runnable. Line 66 invokes Future method get to wait for the disconnect message to be delivered and the Runnable to terminate. Once the disconnect message has been delivered, line 67 invokes PacketReceiver method stopListening to stop receiving incoming chat messages. Line 68 closes the Socket connection to DeitelMessengerServer.

Method sendMessage (lines 87–95) sends an outgoing message to the server. If SocketMessageManager is not connected, line 90 returns from method sendMessage. Lines 93–94 create and start a new MessageSender (Fig. 24.26) to deliver the new message in a separate thread of execution.

Class `MessageSender` (Fig. 24.26), which implements `Runnable`, delivers outgoing messages to the server in a separate thread of execution. `MessageSender`'s constructor (lines 16–22) takes as arguments the `Socket` over which to send the message, the `userName` from whom the message came and the message. Line 21 concatenates these arguments to build `messageToSend`. Constant `MESSAGE_SEPARATOR` enables the message recipient to parse the message into two parts—the sending user's name and the message body—by using a `StringTokenizer`.

Method `run` (lines 25–38) delivers the complete message to the server, using the `Socket` provided to the `MessageSender` constructor. Lines 29–30 create a new `Formatter` for the `clientSocket`'s `OutputStream`. Line 31 invokes `Formatter` method `format` to send

```java
1   // Fig. 24.26: MessageSender.java
2   // Sends a message to the chat server in a separate runnable.
3   package com.deitel.messenger.sockets.client;
4
5   import java.io.IOException;
6   import java.util.Formatter;
7   import java.net.Socket;
8
9   import static com.deitel.messenger.sockets.SocketMessengerConstants.*;
10
11  public class MessageSender implements Runnable
12  {
13     private Socket clientSocket; // Socket over which to send message
14     private String messageToSend; // message to send
15
16     public MessageSender( Socket socket, String userName, String message )
17     {
18        clientSocket = socket; // store socket for client
19
20        // build message to be sent
21        messageToSend = userName + MESSAGE_SEPARATOR + message;
22     } // end MessageSender constructor
23
24     // send message and end
25     public void run()
26     {
27        try // send message and flush PrintWriter
28        {
29           Formatter output =
30              new Formatter( clientSocket.getOutputStream() );
31           output.format( "%s\n", messageToSend ); // send message
32           output.flush(); // flush output
33        } // end try
34        catch ( IOException ioException )
35        {
36           ioException.printStackTrace();
37        } // end catch
38     } // end method run
39  } // end class MessageSender
```

Fig. 24.26 | `MessageSender` for delivering outgoing messages to `DeitelMessengerServer`.

the message. Line 32 invokes method `flush` of class `Formatter` to ensure that the message is sent immediately. Note that class `MessageSender` does not close the `clientSocket`. Class `SocketMessageManager` uses a new object of class `MessageSender` for each message the client sends, so the `clientSocket` must remain open until the user disconnects from `DeitelMessengerServer`.

Class `PacketReceiver` (Fig. 24.27) implements interface `Runnable` to enable `Socket-MessageManager` to listen for incoming messages in a separate thread of execution. Line 18 declares the `MessageListener` to which `PacketReceiver` will deliver incoming messages. Line 19 declares a `MulticastSocket` for receiving multicast `DatagramPackets`. Line 20 declares an `InetAddress` reference for the multicast address to which `Deitel-MessengerServer` posts new chat messages. The `MulticastSocket` connects to this `InetAddress` to listen for incoming chat messages.

The `PacketReceiver` constructor (lines 23–46) takes as an argument the `Message-Listener` to which the `PacketReceiver` is to deliver incoming messages. Recall that interface `MessageListener` declares method `messageReceived`. When the `PacketReceiver`

```java
 1   // Fig. 24.27: PacketReceiver.java
 2   // PacketReceiver listens for DatagramPackets containing
 3   // messages from a DeitelMessengerServer.
 4   package com.deitel.messenger.sockets.client;
 5
 6   import java.io.IOException;
 7   import java.net.InetAddress;
 8   import java.net.MulticastSocket;
 9   import java.net.DatagramPacket;
10   import java.net.SocketTimeoutException;
11   import java.util.StringTokenizer;
12
13   import com.deitel.messenger.MessageListener;
14   import static com.deitel.messenger.sockets.SocketMessengerConstants.*;
15
16   public class PacketReceiver implements Runnable
17   {
18      private MessageListener messageListener; // receives messages
19      private MulticastSocket multicastSocket; // receive broadcast messages
20      private InetAddress multicastGroup; // InetAddress of multicast group
21      private boolean keepListening = true; // terminates PacketReceiver
22
23      public PacketReceiver( MessageListener listener )
24      {
25         messageListener = listener; // set MessageListener
26
27         try // connect MulticastSocket to multicast address and port
28         {
29            // create new MulticastSocket
30            multicastSocket = new MulticastSocket(
31               MULTICAST_LISTENING_PORT );
32
```

Fig. 24.27 | `PacketReceiver` for listening for new multicast messages from `DeitelMessengerServer` in a separate thread. (Part 1 of 3.)

```
33              // use InetAddress to get multicast group
34              multicastGroup = InetAddress.getByName( MULTICAST_ADDRESS );
35
36              // join multicast group to receive messages
37              multicastSocket.joinGroup( multicastGroup );
38
39              // set 5 second timeout when waiting for new packets
40              multicastSocket.setSoTimeout( 5000 );
41           } // end try
42           catch ( IOException ioException )
43           {
44              ioException.printStackTrace();
45           } // end catch
46        } // end PacketReceiver constructor
47
48        // listen for messages from multicast group
49        public void run()
50        {
51           // listen for messages until stopped
52           while ( keepListening )
53           {
54              // create buffer for incoming message
55              byte[] buffer = new byte[ MESSAGE_SIZE ];
56
57              // create DatagramPacket for incoming message
58              DatagramPacket packet = new DatagramPacket( buffer,
59                 MESSAGE_SIZE );
60
61              try // receive new DatagramPacket (blocking call)
62              {
63                 multicastSocket.receive( packet );
64              } // end try
65              catch ( SocketTimeoutException socketTimeoutException )
66              {
67                 continue; // continue to next iteration to keep listening
68              } // end catch
69              catch ( IOException ioException )
70              {
71                 ioException.printStackTrace();
72                 break;
73              } // end catch
74
75              // put message data in a String
76              String message = new String( packet.getData() );
77
78              message = message.trim(); // trim whitespace from message
79
80              // tokenize message to retrieve user name and message body
81              StringTokenizer tokenizer = new StringTokenizer(
82                 message, MESSAGE_SEPARATOR );
83
```

Fig. 24.27 | `PacketReceiver` for listening for new multicast messages from `DeitelMessengerServer` in a separate thread. (Part 2 of 3.)

```
84              // ignore messages that do not contain a user
85              // name and message body
86              if ( tokenizer.countTokens() == 2 )
87              {
88                  // send message to MessageListener
89                  messageListener.messageReceived(
90                      tokenizer.nextToken(), // user name
91                      tokenizer.nextToken() ); // message body
92              } // end if
93          } // end while
94
95          try
96          {
97              multicastSocket.leaveGroup( multicastGroup ); // leave group
98              multicastSocket.close(); // close MulticastSocket
99          } // end try
100         catch ( IOException ioException )
101         {
102             ioException.printStackTrace();
103         } // end catch
104     } // end method run
105
106     // stop listening for new messages
107     public void stopListening()
108     {
109         keepListening = false;
110     } // end method stopListening
111 } // end class PacketReceiver
```

Fig. 24.27 | `PacketReceiver` for listening for new multicast messages from `DeitelMessengerServer` in a separate thread. (Part 3 of 3.)

receives a new chat message over the MulticastSocket, PacketReceiver invokes messageReceived to deliver the new message to the MessageListener.

Lines 30–31 create a new MulticastSocket and pass to the MulticastSocket constructor the constant MULTICAST_LISTENING_PORT from interface SocketMessengerConstants. This argument specifies the port on which the MulticastSocket will listen for incoming chat messages. Line 34 creates an InetAddress object for the MULTICAST_ADDRESS, to which DeitelMessengerServer multicasts new chat messages. Line 37 invokes MulticastSocket method **joinGroup** to register the MulticastSocket to receive messages sent to MULTICAST_ADDRESS. Line 40 invokes MulticastSocket method **setSoTimeout** to specify that if no data is received in 5000 milliseconds, the MulticastSocket should issue an InterruptedIOException, which the current thread can catch, then continue executing. This approach prevents PacketReceiver from blocking indefinitely when waiting for incoming data. Also, if the MulticastSocket never timed out, the while loop would not be able to check the keepListening variable and would therefore prevent PacketReceiver from stopping if keepListening were set to false.

Method run (lines 49–104) listens for incoming multicast messages. Lines 58–59 create a DatagramPacket to store the incoming message. Line 63 invokes MulticastSocket method receive to read an incoming packet from the multicast address. If 5000 milliseconds pass without receipt of a packet, method `receive` throws an `Interrupted-IOException`, because we previously set a 5000-millisecond time-out (line 40). Line 67 uses `continue` to proceed to the next loop iteration to listen for incoming messages. For other `IOExceptions`, line 72 breaks the `while` loop to terminate the `PacketReceiver`.

Line 76 invokes `DatagramPacket` method `getData` to retrieve the message data. Line 78 invokes method `trim` of class `String` to remove extra white space from the end of the message. Recall that `DatagramPackets` are of a fixed size—512 bytes in this example—so, if the message is shorter than 512 bytes, there will be extra white space after it. Lines 81–82 create a `StringTokenizer` to separate the message body from the name of the user who sent the message. Line 86 checks for the correct number of tokens. Lines 89–91 invoke method `messageReceived` of interface `MessageListener` to deliver the incoming message to the `PacketReceiver`'s `MessageListener`.

If the program invokes method `stopListening` (lines 107–110), the `while` loop in method `run` (lines 49–104) terminates. Line 97 invokes `MulticastSocket` method `leave-Group` to stop receiving messages from the multicast address. Line 98 invokes `Multicast-Socket` method `close` to close the `MulticastSocket`. When method `run` completes execution, the `PacketReceiver` terminates.

Class `ClientGUI` (Fig. 24.28) extends class `JFrame` to create a GUI for a user to send and receive chat messages. The GUI consists of a `JTextArea` for displaying incoming messages

```
1   // Fig. 24.28: ClientGUI.java
2   // ClientGUI provides a user interface for sending and receiving
3   // messages to and from the DeitelMessengerServer.
4   package com.deitel.messenger;
5
6   import java.awt.BorderLayout;
7   import java.awt.event.ActionEvent;
8   import java.awt.event.ActionListener;
9   import java.awt.event.WindowAdapter;
10  import java.awt.event.WindowEvent;
11  import javax.swing.Box;
12  import javax.swing.BoxLayout;
13  import javax.swing.Icon;
14  import javax.swing.ImageIcon;
15  import javax.swing.JButton;
16  import javax.swing.JFrame;
17  import javax.swing.JLabel;
18  import javax.swing.JMenu;
19  import javax.swing.JMenuBar;
20  import javax.swing.JMenuItem;
21  import javax.swing.JOptionPane;
22  import javax.swing.JPanel;
23  import javax.swing.JScrollPane;
24  import javax.swing.JTextArea;
25  import javax.swing.SwingUtilities;
26  import javax.swing.border.BevelBorder;
27
```

Fig. 24.28 | `ClientGUI` subclass of `JFrame` for presenting a GUI for viewing and sending chat messages. (Part 1 of 6.)

```
28   public class ClientGUI extends JFrame
29   {
30      private JMenu serverMenu; // for connecting/disconnecting server
31      private JTextArea messageArea; // displays messages
32      private JTextArea inputArea; // inputs messages
33      private JButton connectButton; // button for connecting
34      private JMenuItem connectMenuItem; // menu item for connecting
35      private JButton disconnectButton; // button for disconnecting
36      private JMenuItem disconnectMenuItem; // menu item for disconnecting
37      private JButton sendButton; // sends messages
38      private JLabel statusBar; // label for connection status
39      private String userName; // userName to add to outgoing messages
40      private MessageManager messageManager; // communicates with server
41      private MessageListener messageListener; // receives incoming messages
42
43      // ClientGUI constructor
44      public ClientGUI( MessageManager manager )
45      {
46         super( "Deitel Messenger" );
47
48         messageManager = manager; // set the MessageManager
49
50         // create MyMessageListener for receiving messages
51         messageListener = new MyMessageListener();
52
53         serverMenu = new JMenu ( "Server" ); // create Server JMenu
54         serverMenu.setMnemonic( 'S' ); // set mnemonic for server menu
55         JMenuBar menuBar = new JMenuBar(); // create JMenuBar
56         menuBar.add( serverMenu ); // add server menu to menu bar
57         setJMenuBar( menuBar ); // add JMenuBar to application
58
59         // create ImageIcon for connect buttons
60         Icon connectIcon = new ImageIcon(
61            lus().getResource( "images/Connect.gif" ) );
62
63         // create connectButton and connectMenuItem
64         connectButton = new JButton( "Connect", connectIcon );
65         connectMenuItem = new JMenuItem( "Connect", connectIcon );
66         connectMenuItem.setMnemonic( 'C' );
67
68         // create ConnectListener for connect buttons
69         ActionListener connectListener = new ConnectListener();
70         connectButton.addActionListener( connectListener );
71         connectMenuItem.addActionListener( connectListener );
72
73         // create ImageIcon for disconnect buttons
74         Icon disconnectIcon = new ImageIcon(
75            getClass().getResource( "images/Disconnect.gif" ) );
76
77         // create disconnectButton and disconnectMenuItem
78         disconnectButton = new JButton( "Disconnect", disconnectIcon );
```

Fig. 24.28 | ClientGUI subclass of JFrame for presenting a GUI for viewing and sending chat messages. (Part 2 of 6.)

```
79    disconnectMenuItem = new JMenuItem( "Disconnect", disconnectIcon );
80    disconnectMenuItem.setMnemonic( 'D' );
81
82    // disable disconnect button and menu item
83    disconnectButton.setEnabled( false );
84    disconnectMenuItem.setEnabled( false );
85
86    // create DisconnectListener for disconnect buttons
87    ActionListener disconnectListener = new DisconnectListener();
88    disconnectButton.addActionListener( disconnectListener );
89    disconnectMenuItem.addActionListener( disconnectListener );
90
91    // add connect and disconnect JMenuItems to fileMenu
92    serverMenu.add( connectMenuItem );
93    serverMenu.add( disconnectMenuItem );
94
95    // add connect and disconnect JButtons to buttonPanel
96    JPanel buttonPanel = new JPanel();
97    buttonPanel.add( connectButton );
98    buttonPanel.add( disconnectButton );
99
100   messageArea = new JTextArea(); // displays messages
101   messageArea.setEditable( false ); // disable editing
102   messageArea.setWrapStyleWord( true ); // set wrap style to word
103   messageArea.setLineWrap( true ); // enable line wrapping
104
105   // put messageArea in JScrollPane to enable scrolling
106   JPanel messagePanel = new JPanel();
107   messagePanel.setLayout( new BorderLayout( 10, 10 ) );
108   messagePanel.add( new JScrollPane( messageArea ),
109      BorderLayout.CENTER );
110
111   inputArea = new JTextArea( 4, 20 ); // for entering new messages
112   inputArea.setWrapStyleWord( true ); // set wrap style to word
113   inputArea.setLineWrap( true ); // enable line wrapping
114   inputArea.setEditable( false ); // disable editing
115
116   // create Icon for sendButton
117   Icon sendIcon = new ImageIcon(
118      getClass().getResource( "images/Send.gif" ) );
119
120   sendButton = new JButton( "Send", sendIcon ); // create send button
121   sendButton.setEnabled( false ); // disable send button
122   sendButton.addActionListener(
123      new ActionListener()
124      {
125         // send new message when user activates sendButton
126         public void actionPerformed( ActionEvent event )
127         {
128            messageManager.sendMessage( userName,
129               inputArea.getText() ); // send message
```

Fig. 24.28 | ClientGUI subclass of JFrame for presenting a GUI for viewing and sending chat messages. (Part 3 of 6.)

```
130                 inputArea.setText( "" ); // clear inputArea
131             } // end method actionPerformed
132         } // end anonymous inner class
133      ); // end call to addActionListener
134
135      Box box = new Box( BoxLayout.X_AXIS ); // create new box for layout
136      box.add( new JScrollPane( inputArea ) ); // add input area to box
137      box.add( sendButton ); // add send button to box
138      messagePanel.add( box, BorderLayout.SOUTH ); // add box to panel
139
140      // create JLabel for statusBar with a recessed border
141      statusBar = new JLabel( "Not Connected" );
142      statusBar.setBorder( new BevelBorder( BevelBorder.LOWERED ) );
143
144      add( buttonPanel, BorderLayout.NORTH ); // add button panel
145      add( messagePanel, BorderLayout.CENTER ); // add message panel
146      add( statusBar, BorderLayout.SOUTH ); // add status bar
147
148      // add WindowListener to disconnect when user quits
149      addWindowListener (
150          new WindowAdapter ()
151          {
152              // disconnect from server and exit application
153              public void windowClosing ( WindowEvent event )
154              {
155                  messageManager.disconnect( messageListener );
156                  System.exit( 0 );
157              } // end method windowClosing
158          } // end anonymous inner class
159      ); // end call to addWindowListener
160   } // end ClientGUI constructor
161
162   // ConnectListener listens for user requests to connect to server
163   private class ConnectListener implements ActionListener
164   {
165      // connect to server and enable/disable GUI components
166      public void actionPerformed( ActionEvent event )
167      {
168          // connect to server and route messages to messageListener
169          messageManager.connect( messageListener );
170
171          // prompt for userName
172          userName = JOptionPane.showInputDialog(
173              ClientGUI.this, "Enter user name:" );
174
175          messageArea.setText( "" ); // clear messageArea
176          connectButton.setEnabled( false ); // disable connect
177          connectMenuItem.setEnabled( false ); // disable connect
178          disconnectButton.setEnabled( true ); // enable disconnect
179          disconnectMenuItem.setEnabled( true ); // enable disconnect
180          sendButton.setEnabled( true ); // enable send button
```

Fig. 24.28 | ClientGUI subclass of JFrame for presenting a GUI for viewing and sending chat messages. (Part 4 of 6.)

```
181            inputArea.setEditable( true ); // enable editing for input area
182            inputArea.requestFocus(); // set focus to input area
183            statusBar.setText( "Connected: " + userName ); // set text
184         } // end method actionPerformed
185      } // end ConnectListener inner class
186
187      // DisconnectListener listens for user requests to disconnect
188      // from DeitelMessengerServer
189      private class DisconnectListener implements ActionListener
190      {
191         // disconnect from server and enable/disable GUI components
192         public void actionPerformed( ActionEvent event )
193         {
194            // disconnect from server and stop routing messages
195            messageManager.disconnect( messageListener );
196            sendButton.setEnabled( false ); // disable send button
197            disconnectButton.setEnabled( false ); // disable disconnect
198            disconnectMenuItem.setEnabled( false ); // disable disconnect
199            inputArea.setEditable( false ); // disable editing
200            connectButton.setEnabled( true ); // enable connect
201            connectMenuItem.setEnabled( true ); // enable connect
202            statusBar.setText( "Not Connected" ); // set status bar text
203         } // end method actionPerformed
204      } // end DisconnectListener inner class
205
206      // MyMessageListener listens for new messages from MessageManager and
207      // displays messages in messageArea using MessageDisplayer.
208      private class MyMessageListener implements MessageListener
209      {
210         // when received, display new messages in messageArea
211         public void messageReceived( String from, String message )
212         {
213            // append message using MessageDisplayer
214            SwingUtilities.invokeLater(
215               new MessageDisplayer( from, message ) );
216         } // end method messageReceived
217      } // end MyMessageListener inner class
218
219      // Displays new message by appending message to JTextArea.  Should
220      // be executed only in Event thread; modifies live Swing component
221      private class MessageDisplayer implements Runnable
222      {
223         private String fromUser; // user from which message came
224         private String messageBody; // body of message
225
226         // MessageDisplayer constructor
227         public MessageDisplayer( String from, String body )
228         {
229            fromUser = from; // store originating user
230            messageBody = body; // store message body
231         } // end MessageDisplayer constructor
```

Fig. 24.28 | ClientGUI subclass of JFrame for presenting a GUI for viewing and sending chat messages. (Part 5 of 6.)

```
232
233        // display new message in messageArea
234        public void run()
235        {
236            // append new message
237            messageArea.append( "\n" + fromUser + "> " + messageBody );
238        } // end method run
239     } // end MessageDisplayer inner class
240 } // end class ClientGUI
```

Fig. 24.28 | `ClientGUI` subclass of `JFrame` for presenting a GUI for viewing and sending chat messages. (Part 6 of 6.)

(line 31), a `JTextArea` for entering new messages (line 32), `JButtons` and `JMenuItems` for connecting to and disconnecting from the server (lines 33–36) and a `JButton` for sending messages (line 37). The GUI also contains a `JLabel` that displays whether the client is connected or disconnected (line 38).

ClientGUI uses a `MessageManager` (line 40) to handle all communication with the chat server. Recall that `MessageManager` is an interface that enables `ClientGUI` to use any `MessageManager` implementation. Class `ClientGUI` also uses a `MessageListener` (line 41) to receive incoming messages from the `MessageManager`.

The `ClientGUI` constructor (lines 44–160) takes as an argument the `MessageManager` for communicating with `DeitelMessengerServer`. Line 48 sets the `ClientGUI`'s `Message-Manager`. Line 51 creates an instance of `MyMessageListener`, which implements interface `MessageListener`. Lines 53–57 create a **Server** menu that contains `JMenuItems` for connecting to and disconnecting from the chat server. Lines 60–61 create an `ImageIcon` for `connectButton` and `connectMenuItem`.

Lines 64–65 create `connectButton` and `connectMenuItem`, each with the label "Connect" and the `Icon` `connectIcon`. Line 66 invokes method `setMnemonic` to set the mnemonic character for keyboard access to `connectMenuItem`. Line 69 creates an instance of inner class `ConnectListener` (declared at lines 163–185), which implements interface `ActionListener` to handle `ActionEvents` from `connectButton` and `connectMenuItem`. Lines 70–71 add `connectListener` as an `ActionListener` for `connectButton` and `connectMenuItem`.

Lines 74–75 create an `ImageIcon` for the `disconnectButton` and `disconnectMenu-Item` components. Lines 78–79 create `disconnectButton` and `disconnectMenuItem`, each with the label "Disconnect" and the `Icon` `disconnectIcon`. Line 80 invokes method `set-Mnemonic` to enable keyboard access to `disconnectMenuItem`. Lines 83–84 invoke method `setEnabled` with a `false` argument on `disconnectButton` and `disconnectMenuItem` to disable these components. This prevents the user from attempting to disconnect from the server because the client is not yet connected. Line 87 creates an instance of inner class `DisconnectListener` (declared at lines 189–204), which implements interface `Action-Listener` to handle `ActionEvents` from `disconnectButton` and `disconnectMenuItem`. Lines 88–89 add `disconnectListener` as an `ActionListener` for `disconnectButton` and `disconnectMenuItem`.

Lines 92–93 add `connectMenuItem` and `disconnectMenuItem` to menu **Server**. Lines 96–98 create a `JPanel` and add `connectButton` and `disconnectButton` to it. Line 100 creates the textarea `messageArea`, in which the client displays incoming messages. Line 101 invokes method `setEditable` with a `false` argument, to disable editing. Lines 102–103 invoke `JTextArea` methods `setWrapStyleWord` and `setLineWrap` to enable word wrapping in `messageArea`. If a message is longer than `messageArea`'s width, the `messageArea` will wrap the text after the last word that fits on each line, making longer messages easier to read. Lines 106–109 create a `JPanel` for the `messageArea` and add the `messageArea` to the `JPanel` in a `JScrollPane`.

Line 111 creates the `inputArea` `JTextArea` for entering new messages. Lines 112–113 enable word and line wrapping, and line 114 disables editing the `inputArea`. When the client connects to the chat server, `ConnectListener` enables the `inputArea` to allow the user to type new messages.

Lines 117–118 create an `ImageIcon` for `sendButton`. Line 120 creates `sendButton`, which the user can click to send a message. Line 121 disables `sendButton`—the `ConnectListener` enables the `sendButton` when the client connects to the chat server. Lines 122–133 add an `ActionListener` to `sendButton`. Lines 128–129 invoke method `sendMessage` of interface `MessageManager` with the `userName` and `inputArea` text as arguments. This statement sends the user's name and message as a new chat message to `DeitelMessengerServer`. Line 130 clears the `inputArea` for the next message.

Lines 135–138 use a horizontal `Box` container to arrange components `inputArea` and `sendButton`. Line 136 places `inputArea` in a `JScrollPane` to enable scrolling of long messages. Line 138 adds the `Box` containing `inputArea` and `sendButton` to the `SOUTH` region of `messagePanel`. Line 141 creates the `statusBar` `JLabel`. This label displays whether the client is connected to or disconnected from the chat server. Line 142 invokes method **setBorder** of class `JLabel` and creates a new **BevelBorder** of type **BevelBorder.LOWERED**. This **border** makes the label appear recessed, as is common with status bars in many applications. Lines 144–146 add `buttonPanel`, `messagePanel` and `statusBar` to the `ClientGUI`.

Lines 149–159 add a `WindowListener` to the `ClientGUI`. Line 155 invokes method `disconnect` of interface `MessageManager` to disconnect from the chat server in case the user quits while still connected. Then line 156 terminates the application.

Inner class `ConnectListener` (lines 163–185) handles events from `connectButton` and `connectMenuItem`. Line 169 invokes `MessageManager` method `connect` to connect to the chat server. Line 169 passes as an argument to method `connect` the `MessageListener` to which new messages should be delivered. Lines 172–173 prompt the user for a user name, and line 175 clears the `messageArea`. Lines 176–181 enable the components for disconnecting from the server and for sending messages and disable the components for connecting to the server. Line 182 invokes `inputArea`'s **requestFocus** method (inherited from class `Component`) to place the text-input cursor in the `inputArea` so that the user can immediately begin typing a message.

Inner class `DisconnectListener` (lines 189–204) handles events from `disconnectButton` and `disconnectMenuItem`. Line 195 invokes `MessageManager` method `disconnect` to disconnect from the chat server. Lines 196–201 disable the components for sending messages and the components for disconnecting, then enable the components for connecting to the chat server.

Inner class `MyMessageListener` (lines 208–217) implements interface `MessageListener` to receive incoming messages from the `MessageManager`. When a new message is received, the MessageManager invokes method messageReceived (lines 211–216) with the user name of the sender and the message body. Lines 214–215 invoke SwingUtilities method invokeLater with a MessageDisplayer object that appends the new message to messageArea. Recall, from Chapter 23, that Swing components should be accessed only from the event-dispatch thread. Method messageReceived is invoked by the PacketReceiver in class SocketMessageManager and therefore cannot append the message text to messageArea directly, as this would occur in PacketReceiver, not the event-dispatch thread.

Inner class MessageDisplayer (lines 221–239) implements interface Runnable to provide a thread-safe way to append text to the messageArea. The MessageDisplayer constructor (lines 227–231) takes as arguments the user name and the message to send. Method run (lines 234–238) appends the user name, "> " and messageBody to messageArea.

Class DeitelMessenger (Fig. 24.29) launches the client for the DeitelMessengerServer. Lines 15–20 create a new SocketMessageManager to connect to the DeitelMessengerServer with the IP address specified as a command-line argument to the application (or localhost, if no address is provided). Lines 23–26 create a ClientGUI for the MessageManager, set the ClientGUI size and make the ClientGUI visible.

```java
1   // Fig. 24.29: DeitelMessenger.java
2   // DeitelMessenger is a chat application that uses a ClientGUI
3   // and SocketMessageManager to communicate with DeitelMessengerServer.
4   package com.deitel.messenger.sockets.client;
5
6   import com.deitel.messenger.MessageManager;
7   import com.deitel.messenger.ClientGUI;
8
9   public class DeitelMessenger
10  {
11     public static void main( String args[] )
12     {
13        MessageManager messageManager; // declare MessageManager
14
15        if ( args.length == 0 )
16           // connect to localhost
17           messageManager = new SocketMessageManager( "localhost" );
18        else
19           // connect using command-line arg
20           messageManager = new SocketMessageManager( args[ 0 ] );
21
22        // create GUI for SocketMessageManager
23        ClientGUI clientGUI = new ClientGUI( messageManager );
24        clientGUI.setSize( 300, 400 ); // set window size
25        clientGUI.setResizable( false ); // disable resizing
26        clientGUI.setVisible( true ); // show window
27     } // end main
28  } // end class DeitelMessenger
```

Fig. 24.29 | DeitelMessenger application for participating in a DeitelMessengerServer chat session. (Part 1 of 2.)

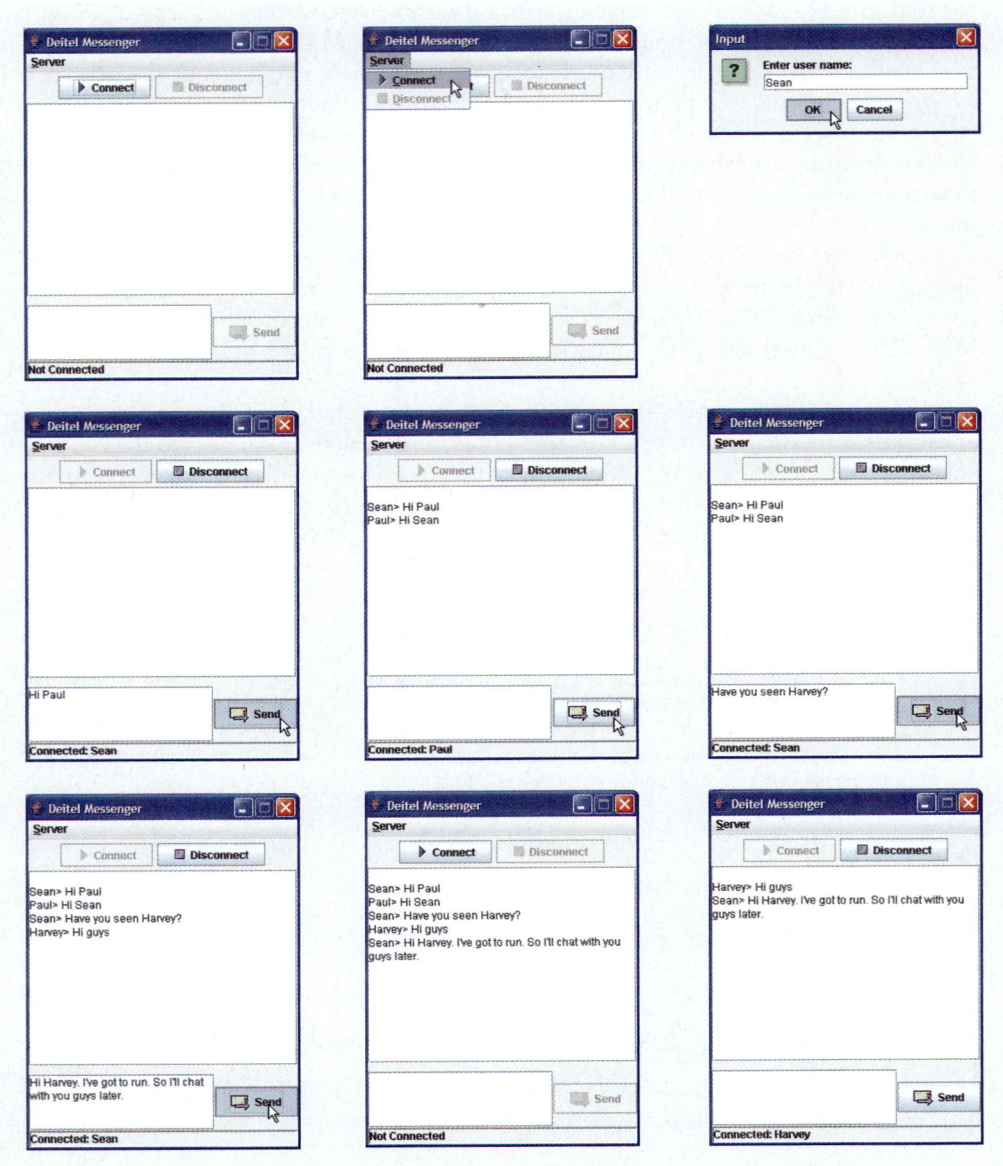

Fig. 24.29 | DeitelMessenger application for participating in a DeitelMessengerServer chat session. (Part 2 of 2.)

Executing the *DeitelMessenger Client Application*

To execute the DeitelMessenger client, open a command window and change directories to the location in which package com.deitel.messenger.sockets.client resides (i.e., the directory in which com is located). Then type

```
java com.deitel.messenger.sockets.client.DeitelMessenger
```

to execute the client and connect to the `DeitelMessengerServer` running on your local computer. If the server resides on another computer, follow the preceding command with the hostname or IP address of that computer. The preceding command is equivalent to

```
java com.deitel.messenger.sockets.client.DeitelMessenger localhost
```

or

```
java com.deitel.messenger.sockets.client.DeitelMessenger 127.0.0.1
```

Deitel Messenger Case Study Summary

The Deitel messenger case study is a significant application that uses many intermediate Java features, such as networking with `Sockets`, `DatagramPackets` and `MulticastSockets`, multithreading and Swing GUI. The case study also demonstrates good software engineering practices by separating interface from implementation, enabling developers to build `MessageManagers` for different network protocols and `MessageListeners` that provide different user interfaces. You should now be able to apply these techniques to your own, more complex, Java projects.

24.11 Wrap-Up

In this chapter, you have learned the basics of network programming in Java. You learned two different methods of sending data over a network: streams-based networking using TCP/IP and datagrams-based networking using UDP. You also learned about multicasting, which allows you to send data to multiple clients with a single command. In the next chapter, you will learn basic database concepts, how to interact with data in a database using SQL and how to use JDBC to allow Java applications to manipulate database data.

Summary

- Java provides stream sockets and datagram sockets. With stream sockets, a process establishes a connection to another process. While the connection is in place, data flows between the processes in streams. Stream sockets are said to provide a connection-oriented service. The protocol used for transmission is the popular TCP (Transmission Control Protocol).

- With datagram sockets, individual packets of information are transmitted. UDP (User Datagram Protocol) is a connectionless service that does not guarantee that packets will not can be lost, duplicated or arrive out of sequence. Extra programming is required on the programmer's part to deal with these problems.

- The HTTP protocol (Hypertext Transfer Protocol) that forms the basis of the Web uses URIs (Uniform Resource Identifiers) to locate data on the Internet. Common URIs represent files or directories and can represent complex tasks such as database lookups and Internet searches. A URI that represents a document is called a URL (Uniform Resource Locator).

- Web browsers often restrict an applet so that it can communicate only with the machine from which it was originally downloaded.

- Applet method `getAppletContext` returns a reference to an `AppletContext` object that represents the applet's environment (i.e., the browser in which the applet is executing). `AppletContext` method `showDocument` receives a URL as an argument and passes it to the `AppletContext` (i.e., the browser), which displays the Web resource associated with that URL. A second version of show-Document enables an applet to specify the target frame in which to display a Web resource. Special target frames include _blank (display in a new Web browser window), _self (display in the same frame as the applet) and _top (remove the current frames, then display in the current window).

- JEditorPane method setPage downloads the document specified by its argument and displays it in the JEditorPane.

- Typically, an HTML document contains hyperlinks—text, images or GUI components that, when clicked, link to another document on the Web. If an HTML document is displayed in a JEditorPane and the user clicks a hyperlink, the JEditorPane generates a HyperlinkEvent and notifies all registered HyperlinkListeners of the event.

- HyperlinkEvent method getEventType determines the event type. HyperlinkEvent contains nested class EventType, which declares three hyperlink event types: ACTIVATED (hyperlink clicked), ENTERED (mouse over a hyperlink) and EXITED (mouse moved away from a hyperlink). HyperlinkEvent method getURL obtains the URL represented by the hyperlink.

- Stream-based connections are managed with Socket objects.

- A ServerSocket object establishes the port where a server waits for connections from clients. The second argument to the ServerSocket constructor is the number of connections that can wait in a queue to connect to the server. If the queue of clients is full, client connections are refused. The ServerSocket method accept waits indefinitely (i.e., blocks) for a connection from a client and returns a Socket object when a connection is established.

- Socket methods getOutputStream and getInputStream get references to a Socket's Output-Stream and InputStream, respectively. Socket method close terminates a connection.

- A server name and port number are specified when creating a Socket object to enable it to connect a client to the server. A failed connection attempt throws an IOException.

- InetAddress method getByName returns an InetAddress object containing the host name of the computer for which the host name or IP address is specified as an argument. InetAddress method getLocalHost returns an InetAddress object containing the host name of the local computer executing the program.

- Connection-oriented transmission is like the telephone system—you dial and are given a connection to the telephone of the person with whom you wish to communicate. The connection is maintained for the duration of your phone call, even when you are not talking.

- Connectionless transmission with datagrams is similar to mail carried via the postal service. A large message that will not fit in one envelope can be broken into separate message pieces that are placed in separate, sequentially numbered envelopes. All the letters are then mailed at once. They could arrive in order, out of order or not at all.

- DatagramPacket objects store packets of data that are to be sent or that are received by an application. DatagramSockets send and receive DatagramPackets.

- The DatagramSocket constructor that takes no arguments binds the application to a port chosen by the computer on which the program executes. The DatagramSocket constructor that takes an integer port number argument binds the application to the specified port. If a DatagramSocket constructor fails to bind the application to a port, a SocketException occurs. DatagramSocket method receive blocks (waits) until a packet arrives, then stores the packet in its argument.

- DatagramPacket method getAddress returns an InetAddress object containing information about the host computer from which the packet was sent. Method getPort returns an integer specifying the port number through which the host computer sent the DatagramPacket. Method getLength returns an integer representing the number of bytes of data in a DatagramPacket. Method getData returns a byte array containing the data in a DatagramPacket.

- The DatagramPacket constructor for a packet to be sent takes four arguments—the byte array to be sent, the number of bytes to be sent, the client address to which the packet will be sent and the port number where the client is waiting to receive packets.

- DatagramSocket method send sends a DatagramPacket out over the network.

- If an error occurs when receiving or sending a DatagramPacket, an IOException occurs.

- Reading data from a Socket is a blocking call—the current thread is put in the blocked state while it waits for the read operation to complete. Method setSoTimeout specifies that if no data is received in the given number of milliseconds, the Socket is to issue an Interrupted-IOException, which the current thread can catch, then continue executing. This prevents the current thread from blocking indefinitely if no more data is available from the Socket.

- Multicast is an efficient way to send data to many clients without the overhead of broadcasting it to every host on the Internet. Using multicast, an application can "publish" DatagramPackets to be delivered to subscriber applications. An application multicasts DatagramPackets by sending them to a multicast address—an IP address in the range from 224.0.0.0 to 239.255.255.255, reserved for multicast.

- Clients that wish to receive DatagramPackets can join the multicast group that will receive the DatagramPackets published to the multicast address.

- Multicast DatagramPackets are not reliable—packets are not guaranteed to reach any destination or to arrive in any particular order.

- The MulticastSocket constructor takes as an argument the port to which the MulticastSocket connects to receive incoming DatagramPackets.

- Method joinGroup of class MulticastSocket takes as an argument the InetAddress of the multicast group to join. Method receive of class MulticastSocket reads an incoming Datagram-Packet from a multicast address.

Terminology

accept method of class ServerSocket
ACTIVATED constant of nested class EventType
applet parameter
AppletContext interface
BevelBorder class
binding the server to the port
_blank target frame
block
border of a GUI component
class loader
client
client-server relationship
client/server chat
close method of class MulticastSocket
close method of class Socket
connection
connection-oriented service
connection-oriented, streams-based
    transmission
connectionless service
connectionless transmission
datagram packet

datagram socket
DatagramPacket class
DatagramSocket class
echoes a packet back to the client
ENTERED constant of nested class EventType
EventType nested class of HyperlinkEvent
EXITED constant of nested class EventType
getAddress method of class DatagramPacket
getAppletContext method of class Applet
getByName method of class InetAddress
getData method of class DatagramPacket
getEventType method of class HyperlinkEvent
getHostName method of class InetAddress
getInetAddress method of class Socket
getInputStream method of class Socket
getLength method of class DatagramPacket
getLocalHost method of class InetAddress
getOutputStream method of class Socket
getParameter method of class Applet
getPort method of class DatagramPacket
getResource method of class Class
getURL method of class HyperlinkEvent

handshake point
HTML frame
hyperlink
`HyperlinkEvent` class
`HyperlinkListener` interface
`hyperlinkUpdate` method of interface
    `HyperlinkListener`
HyperText Transfer Protocol (HTTP)
`InetAddress` class
`java.net` package
`JEditorPane` class
`joinGroup` method of class `MulticastSocket`
`leaveGroup` method of class `MulticastSocket`
loopback address
`LOWERED` constant of class `BevelBorder`
`MalformedURLException` class
multicast
multicast address
multicast group
`MulticastSocket` class
packet
packet-based communications
param tag
port
port number
publish
queue length
`receive` method of class `DatagramSocket`
`receive` method of class `MulticastSocket`
register a port
`_self` target frame

`send` method of class `DatagramSocket`
server
`ServerSocket` class
`setBorder` method of class `JComponent`
`setPage` method of class `JEditorPane`
`setSoTimeout` method of class `MulticastSocket`
`setSoTimeOut` method of class `Socket`
`setWrapStyleWord` method of class `JTextArea`
`showDocument` method of class `AppletContext`
socket
socket-based communication
`Socket` class
`SocketException` class
stream header
stream socket
stream-based communications
streams
streams-based transmission
`submit` method of interface `ExecutorService`
subscribe
target frame
TCP (Transmission Control Protocol)
`_top` target frame
trusted source
UDP (User Datagram Protocol)
unicast
Uniform Resource Identifier (URI)
`UnknownHostException` class
User Datagram Protocol (UDP)
World Wide Web Consortium (W3C)

Self-Review Exercises

24.1 Fill in the blanks in each of the following statements:

a) Exception _____ occurs when an input/output error occurs when closing a socket.

b) Exception _____ occurs when a host name indicated by a client cannot be resolved to an address.

c) If a `DatagramSocket` constructor fails to set up a `DatagramSocket` properly, an exception of type _____ occurs.

d) Many of Java's networking classes are contained in package _____.

e) Class _____ binds the application to a port for datagram transmission.

f) An object of class _____ contains an IP address.

g) The two types of sockets we discussed in this chapter are _____ and _____.

h) The acronym URL stands for _____.

i) The acronym URI stands for _____.

j) The key protocol that forms the basis of the World Wide Web is _____.

k) `AppletContext` method _____ receives a `URL` object as an argument and displays in a browser the World Wide Web resource associated with that URL.

l) Method `getLocalHost` returns a(n) _____ object containing the local host name of the computer on which the program is executing.

m) `MulticastSocket` method _____ subscribes a `MulticastSocket` to a multicast group.

n) The `URL` constructor determines whether its string argument is a valid URL. If so, the `URL` object is initialized with that location. If not, a(n) _____ exception occurs.

24.2 State whether each of the following is *true or false*. If *false*, explain why.

a) Multicast broadcasts `DatagramPackets` to every host on the Internet.

b) UDP is a connection-oriented protocol.

c) With stream sockets a process establishes a connection to another process.

d) A server waits at a port for connections from a client.

e) Datagram packet transmission over a network is reliable—packets are guaranteed to arrive in sequence.

f) For security reasons, many Web browsers, such as Mozilla, allow Java applets to do file processing only on the machines on which they execute.

g) Web browsers often restrict an applet so that it can only communicate with the machine from which it was originally downloaded.

h) IP addresses from 224.0.0.0 to 239.255.255.255 are reserved for multicast.

Answers to Self-Review Exercises

24.1 a) `IOException`.   b) `UnknownHostException`.   c) `SocketException`.   d) `java.net`.
e) `DatagramSocket`. f) `InetAddress`. g) stream sockets, datagram sockets. h) Uniform Resource Locator.   i) Uniform Resource Identifier.   j) HTTP.   k) `showDocument`.   l) `InetAddress`.
m) `joinGroup`. n) `MalformedURLException`.

24.2 a) False; multicast sends `DatagramPackets` only to hosts that have joined the multicast group. b) False; UDP is a connectionless protocol and TCP is a connection-oriented protocol.
c) True. d) True. e) False; packets can be lost, arrive out of order or be duplicated. f) False; most browsers prevent applets from doing file processing on the client machine. g) True. h) True.

Exercises

24.3 Distinguish between connection-oriented and connectionless network services.

24.4 How does a client determine the host name of the client computer?

24.5 Under what circumstances would a `SocketException` be thrown?

24.6 How can a client get a line of text from a server?

24.7 Describe how a client connects to a server.

24.8 Describe how a server sends data to a client.

24.9 Describe how to prepare a server to receive a stream-based connection request from a single client.

24.10 How does a server listen for streams-based socket connections at a port?

24.11 What determines how many connect requests from clients can wait in a queue to connect to a server?

24.12 As described in the text, what reasons might cause a server to refuse a connection request from a client?

24.13 Use a socket connection to allow a client to specify a file name and have the server send the contents of the file or indicate that the file does not exist.

24.14 Modify Exercise 24.13 to allow the client to modify the contents of the file and send the file back to the server for storage. The user can edit the file in a JTextArea, then click a *save changes* button to send the file back to the server.

24.15 Modify the program in Fig. 24.2 to allow users to add their own sites to the list and remove sites from the list.

24.16 Multithreaded servers are quite popular today, especially because of the increasing use of multiprocessing servers. Modify the simple server application presented in Section 24.6 to be a multithreaded server. Then use several client applications and have each of them connect to the server simultaneously. Use an ArrayList to store the client threads. ArrayList provides several methods of use in this exercise. Method size determines the number of elements in an ArrayList. Method get returns the element in the location specified by its argument. Method add places its argument at the end of the ArrayList. Method remove deletes its argument from the ArrayList.

24.17 (*Checkers Game*) In the text, we presented a Tic-Tac-Toe program controlled by a multithreaded server. Develop a checkers program modeled after the Tic-Tac-Toe program. The two users should alternate making moves. Your program should mediate the players' moves, determining whose turn it is and allowing only valid moves. The players themselves will determine when the game is over.

24.18 (*Chess Game*) Develop a chess-playing program modeled after the checkers program in the Exercise 24.17.

24.19 (*Blackjack Game*) Develop a blackjack card game program in which the server application deals cards to each of the client applets. The server should deal additional cards (as per the rules of the game) to each player as requested.

24.20 (*Poker Game*) Develop a poker card game in which the server application deals cards to each of the client applets. The server should deal additional cards (as per the rules of the game) to each player as requested.

24.21 (*Modifications to the Multithreaded Tic-Tac-Toe Program*) The programs in Fig. 24.13 and Fig. 24.15 implemented a multithreaded, client/server version of the game of Tic-Tac-Toe. Our goal in developing this game was to demonstrate a multithreaded server that could process multiple connections from clients at the same time. The server in the example is really a mediator between the two client applets—it makes sure that each move is valid and that each client moves in the proper order. The server does not determine who won or lost or whether there was a draw. Also, there is no capability to allow a new game to be played or to terminate an existing game.

The following is a list of suggested modifications to Fig. 24.13 and Fig. 24.15:

a) Modify the TicTacToeServer class to test for a win, loss or draw on each move in the game. Send a message to each client applet that indicates the result of the game when the game is over.

b) Modify the TicTacToeClient class to display a button that when clicked allows the client to play another game. The button should be enabled only when a game completes. Note that both class TicTacToeClient and class TicTacToeServer must be modified to reset the board and all state information. Also, the other TicTacToeClient should be notified that a new game is about to begin so that its board and state can be reset.

c) Modify the TicTacToeClient class to provide a button that allows a client to terminate the program at any time. When the user clicks the button, the server and the other client should be notified. The server should then wait for a connection from another client so that a new game can begin.

d) Modify the TicTacToeClient class and the TicTacToeServer class so that the winner of a game can choose game piece X or O for the next game. Remember: X always goes first.

e) If you would like to be ambitious, allow a client to play against the server while the server waits for a connection from another client.

24.22 *(3-D Multithreaded Tic-Tac-Toe)* Modify the multithreaded, client/server Tic-Tac-Toe program to implement a three-dimensional 4-by-4-by-4 version of the game. Implement the server application to mediate between the two clients. Display the three-dimensional board as four boards containing four rows and four columns each. If you would like to be ambitious, try the following modifications:

a) Draw the board in a three-dimensional manner.

b) Allow the server to test for a win, loss or draw. Beware! There are many possible ways to win on a 4-by-4-by-4 board!

24.23 *(Networked Morse Code)* Perhaps the most famous of all coding schemes is the Morse code, developed by Samuel Morse in 1832 for use with the telegraph system. The Morse code assigns a series of dots and dashes to each letter of the alphabet, each digit, and a few special characters (e.g., period, comma, colon and semicolon). In sound-oriented systems, the dot represents a short sound and the dash represents a long sound. Other representations of dots and dashes are used with light-oriented systems and signal-flag systems. Separation between words is indicated by a space or, simply, the absence of a dot or dash. In a sound-oriented system, a space is indicated by a short time during which no sound is transmitted. The international version of the Morse code appears in Fig. 24.30.

Character	Code	Character	Code
A	. -	T	-
B	- . . .	U	. . -
C	- . - .	V	. . . -
D	- . .	W	. - -
E	.	X	- . . -
F	. . - .	Y	- . - -
G	- - .	Z	- - . .
H	. . . .		
I	. .	*Digits*	
J	. - - -	1	. - - - -
K	- . -	2	. . - - -
L	. - . .	3	. . . - -
M	- -	4	. . . . -
N	- .	5	. . . . .
O	- - -	6	- . . . .
P	. - - .	7	- - . . .
Q	- - . -	8	- - - . .
R	. - .	9	- - - - .
S	. . .	0	- - - - -

Fig. 24.30 | The letters of the alphabet as expressed in international Morse code.

Write a client/server application in which two clients can send Morse code messages to each other through a multithreaded server application. The client application should allow the user to type English-language phrases in a JTextArea. When the user sends the message, the client application encodes the text into Morse code and sends the coded message through the server to the other client. Use one blank between each Morse-coded letter and three blanks between each Morse-coded word. When messages are received, they should be decoded and displayed as normal characters and as Morse code. The client should have one JTextField for typing and one JTextArea for displaying the other client's messages.

Accessing Databases with JDBC

It is a capital mistake to theorize before one has data.
—Arthur Conan Doyle

Now go, write it before them in a table, and note it in a book, that it may be for the time to come for ever and ever.
—The Holy Bible, Isaiah 30:8

Get your facts first, and then you can distort them as much as you please.
—Mark Twain

I like two kinds of men: domestic and foreign.
—Mae West

OBJECTIVES

In this chapter you will learn:

- Relational database concepts.
- To use Structured Query Language (SQL) to retrieve data from and manipulate data in a database.
- To use the JDBC™ API of package `java.sql` to access databases.

25.1 Introduction

A **database** is an organized collection of data. There are many different strategies for organizing data to facilitate easy access and manipulation. A **database management system** (**DBMS**) provides mechanisms for storing, organizing, retrieving and modifying data for many users. Database management systems allow for the access and storage of data without concern for the internal representation of data.

Today's most popular database systems are **relational databases**. A language called **SQL**—pronounced "sequel," or as its individual letters—is the international standard language used almost universally with relational databases to perform **queries** (i.e., to request information that satisfies given criteria) and to manipulate data. [*Note:* As you learn about SQL, you will see some authors writing "a SQL statement" (which assumes the pronunciation "sequel") and others writing "an SQL statement" (which assumes that the individual letters are pronounced). In this book we pronounce SQL as "sequel." Thus the article preceding SQL is "a," as in "a SQL statement."]

Some popular **relational database management systems** (**RDBMSs**) are Microsoft SQL Server, Oracle, Sybase, IBM DB2, Informix, PostgreSQL and MySQL. In this chapter, we present examples using MySQL, which is located on the CD that accompanies this book and can also be downloaded from `dev.mysql.com/downloads/mysql/`

4.0.html. MySQL is open source and is available for both Windows and Linux. [*Note:* We discuss basic MySQL features required to execute the examples in this chapter. Please refer to the detailed MySQL documentation for complete information on using MySQL.]

Java programs communicate with databases and manipulate their data using the **JDBC™ API**. A **JDBC driver** enables Java applications to connect to a database in a particular DBMS and allows programmers to manipulate that database using the JDBC API. JDBC is almost always used with a relational database. However, it can be used with any table-based data source.

Software Engineering Observation 25.1

The separation of the JDBC API from particular database drivers enables developers to change the underlying database without modifying the Java code that accesses the database.

Most popular database management systems now provide JDBC drivers. There are also many third-party JDBC drivers available. In this chapter, we introduce JDBC and use it to manipulate a MySQL database. The techniques demonstrated here can also be used to manipulate other databases that have JDBC drivers. Check your system's documentation to determine whether your DBMS comes with a JDBC driver. If not, many third-party vendors provide JDBC drivers for a wide variety of databases.

For more information on JDBC, visit

```
java.sun.com/products/jdbc
```

This site contains information concerning JDBC, including the JDBC specification, JDBC FAQs, a learning resource center and software downloads. For a list of available JDBC drivers, visit

```
servlet.java.sun.com/products/jdbc/drivers/
```

This site provides a search engine to help you locate drivers appropriate to your DBMS.

25.2 Relational Databases

A **relational database** is a logical representation of data that allows the data to be accessed without consideration of its physical structure. A relational database stores data in **tables**. Figure 25.1 illustrates a sample table that might be used in a personnel system. The table name is Employee, and its primary purpose is to store the attributes of an employee. Tables are composed of **rows**, and rows are composed of **columns** in which values are stored. This table consists of six rows. The Number column of each row in this table is the table's **primary key**—a column (or group of columns) in a table with a unique value that cannot be duplicated in other rows. This guarantees that each row can be identified by its primary key. Good examples of primary key columns are a Social Security number, an employee ID number and a part number in an inventory system, as values in each of these columns are guaranteed to be unique. The rows in Fig. 25.1 are displayed in order by primary key. In this case, the rows are listed in increasing order, but we could also use decreasing order. Rows in tables are not guaranteed to be stored in any particular order. As we will demonstrate in an upcoming example, programs can specify ordering criteria when requesting data from a database.

Fig. 25.1 | Employee table sample data.

Each column represents a different data attribute. Rows are normally unique (by primary key) within a table, but particular column values may be duplicated between rows. For example, three different rows in the Employee table's Department column contain number 413.

Different users of a database are often interested in different data and different relationships among the data. Most users require only subsets of the rows and columns. To obtain these subsets, we use queries to specify which data to select from a table. Programmers use SQL to define complex queries that select data from a table. For example, we might select data from the Employee table to create a result that shows where each department is located. This result is shown in Fig. 25.2. SQL queries are discussed in Section 25.4.

25.3 Relational Database Overview: The books Database

This section overviews relational databases in the context of a sample books database we created for this chapter. Before we discuss SQL, we overview the tables of the books database. We use this database to introduce various database concepts, including how to use SQL to obtain information from the database and to manipulate the data. We provide a script to create the database. You can find the script in the examples directory for this chapter on the CD that accompanies this book. Section 25.5 explains how to use this script.

The database consists of four tables: authors, publishers, authorISBN and titles. The authors table (described in Fig. 25.3) consists of three columns that maintain each author's unique ID number, first name and last name. Figure 25.4 contains sample data from the authors table of the books database.

Department	Location
413	New Jersey
611	Orlando
642	Los Angeles

Fig. 25.2 | Result of selecting distinct Department and Location data from table Employee.

Column	Description
authorID	Author's ID number in the database. In the books database, this integer column is defined as **autoincremented**. For each row inserted in this table, the authorID value is increased by 1 automatically to ensure that each row has a unique authorID. This column represents the table's primary key.
firstName	Author's first name (a string).
lastName	Author's last name (a string).

Fig. 25.3 | authors table from books.

authorID	firstName	lastName
1	Harvey	Deitel
2	Paul	Deitel
3	Tem	Nieto
4	Sean	Santry

Fig. 25.4 | Sample data from the authors table.

The publishers table (described in Fig. 25.5) consists of two columns representing each publisher's unique ID and name. Figure 25.6 contains the data from the publishers table of the books database. The titles table (described in Fig. 25.7) consists of seven columns that maintain general information about each book in the database, including the ISBN, title, edition number, copyright year, publisher's ID number, name of a file containing an image of the book cover and price. The publisherID column is a **foreign key**— a column in this table that matches the primary key column in another table (i.e., publisherID in the publishers table). Foreign keys are specified when creating a table. The foreign key helps maintain the **Rule of Referential Integrity**: Every foreign key value must

Column	Description
publisherID	The publisher's ID number in the database. This autoincremented integer is the table's primary key.
publisherName	The name of the publisher (a string).

Fig. 25.5 | publishers table from books.

publisherID	publisherName
1	Prentice Hall
2	Prentice Hall PTG

Fig. 25.6 | Data from the publishers table.

Column	Description
`isbn`	ISBN of the book (a string). The table's primary key. ISBN is an abbreviation for "International Standard Book Number"—a numbering scheme that publishers worldwide use to give every book a unique identification number.
`title`	Title of the book (a string).
`editionNumber`	Edition number of the book (an integer).
`copyright`	Copyright year of the book (a string).
`publisherID`	Publisher's ID number (an integer). A foreign key that relates this table to the `publishers` table.
`imageFile`	Name of the file containing the book's cover image (a string).
`price`	Suggested retail price of the book (a real number). [*Note:* The prices shown in Fig. 25.8 are for example purposes only.]

Fig. 25.7 | `titles` table from `books`.

appear as another table's primary key value. This enables the DBMS to determine whether the `publisherID` value for a particular book is valid. Foreign keys also allow related data in multiple tables to be selected from those tables for analytic purposes—this is known as joining the data. There is a one-to-many relationship between a primary key and a corresponding foreign key (e.g., one publisher can publish many books). This means that a foreign key can appear many times in its own table, but can only appear once (as the primary key) in another table. Figure 25.8 contains sample data from the `titles` table.

The `authorISBN` table (described in Fig. 25.9) consists of two columns that maintain each ISBN and the corresponding author's ID number. This table associates authors with their books. Both columns are foreign keys that represent the relationship between the tables `authors` and `titles`—one row in table `authors` may be associated with many rows in table `titles`, and vice versa. Figure 25.10 contains sample data from the `authorISBN` table of the `books` database. [*Note:* To save space, we have split the contents of this table into two columns, each containing the `authorID` and `isbn` columns.]

Figure 25.11 is an **entity-relationship** (**ER**) **diagram** for the `books` database. This diagram shows the tables in the database and the relationships among them. The first compartment in each box contains the table's name. The names in green are primary keys. A table's primary key uniquely identifies each row in the table. Every row must have a value in the primary key, and the value of the key must be unique in the table. This is known as the **Rule of Entity Integrity**.

Common Programming Error 25.1

Not providing a value for every column in a primary key breaks the Rule of Entity Integrity and causes the DBMS to report an error.

Common Programming Error 25.2

Providing the same value for the primary key in multiple rows causes the DBMS to report an error.

isbn	title	edition Number	copy- right	publisher ID	image File	price
013142 6443	C How to Program	4	2004	1	chtp4 .jpg	85.00
013038 4747	C++ How to Program	4	2003	1	cppht p4.jp g	85.00
013046 1342	Java Web Services for Experienced Programmers	1	2003	1	jwsfe p1.jp g	54.99
013148 3986	Java How to Program	6	2005	1	jhtp6 .jpg	85.00
013100 252X	The Complete C++ Training Course	4	2003	2	cppct c4.jp g	109.99
013089 5601	Advanced Java 2 Platform How to Program	1	2002	1	advjh tp1.j pg	69.95

Fig. 25.8 | Sample data from the titles table of books .

Column	Description
authorID	The author's ID number, a foreign key to the authors table.
isbn	The ISBN for a book, a foreign key to the titles table.

Fig. 25.9 | authorISBN table from books.

authorID	isbn	authorID	isbn
1	0130895725	2	0139163050
2	0130895725	3	0130829293
2	0132261197	3	0130284173
2	0130895717	3	0130284181
2	0135289106	4	0130895601

Fig. 25.10 | Sample data from the authorISBN table of books.

The lines connecting the tables in Fig. 25.11 represent the relationships between the tables. Consider the line between the publishers and titles tables. On the publishers end of the line, there is a 1, and on the titles end, there is an infinity symbol (∞), indicating a **one-to-many relationship** in which every publisher in the publishers table can have an arbitrary number of books in the titles table. Note that the relationship line links the publisherID column in the table publishers (i.e., its primary key) to the publisherID column in table titles (i.e., its foreign key). The publisherID column in the titles table is a foreign key.

> ### Common Programming Error 25.3
> *Providing a foreign-key value that does not appear as a primary-key value in another table breaks the Rule of Referential Integrity and causes the DBMS to report an error.*

The line between the authorISBN and authors tables indicates that for each author in the authors table, there can be an arbitrary number of ISBNs for books written by that author in the authorISBN table. The authorID column in the authorISBN table is a foreign key matching the authorID column (the primary key) of the authors table. Note again that the line between the tables links the foreign key in table authorISBN to the corresponding primary key in table authors. The authorISBN table associates rows in the titles and authors tables.

Finally, the line between the titles and authorISBN tables illustrates a one-to-many relationship; a title can be written by any number of authors. In fact, the sole purpose of the authorISBN table is to provide a many-to-many relationship between the authors and titles tables—an author can write any number of books and a book can have any number of authors.

25.4 SQL

We now provide an overview of SQL in the context of our books sample database. You will be able to use the SQL discussed here in the examples later in the chapter.

The SQL keywords listed in Fig. 25.12 are discussed in the context of complete SQL queries and statements in the next several subsections. Other SQL keywords are beyond the scope of this text. To learn other keywords, you could refer to the SQL reference guide supplied by the vendor of the RDBMS you are using. [*Note:* For more information on SQL, please refer to the Internet and Web resources in Section 25.12 and the Recommended Readings at the end of this chapter.]

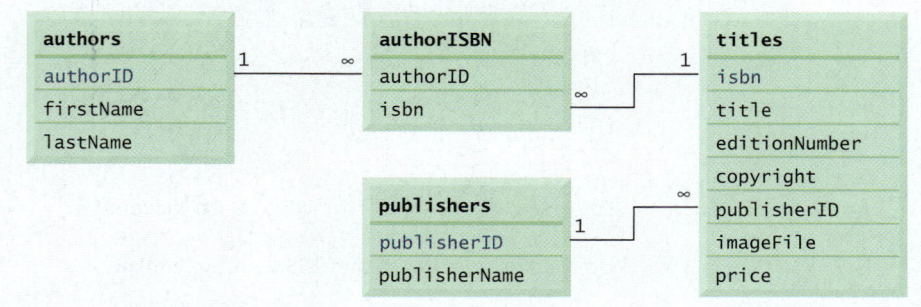

Fig. 25.11 | Table relationships in books.

SQL keyword	Description
SELECT	Retrieves data from one or more tables.
FROM	Tables involved in the query. Required in every SELECT.
WHERE	Criteria for selection that determine the rows to be retrieved, deleted or updated. Optional in a SQL query or a SQL statement.
GROUP BY	Criteria for grouping rows. Optional in a SELECT query.
ORDER BY	Criteria for ordering rows. Optional in a SELECT query.
INNER JOIN	Merge rows from multiple tables.
INSERT	Insert rows into a specified table.
UPDATE	Update rows in a specified table.
DELETE	Delete rows from a specified table.

Fig. 25.12 | SQL query keywords.

25.4.1 Basic SELECT Query

Let us consider several SQL queries that extract information from database books. A SQL query "selects" rows and columns from one or more tables in a database. Such selections are performed by queries with the **SELECT** keyword. The basic form of a SELECT query is

SELECT * FROM *tableName*

in which the asterisk (*) indicates that all columns from the *tableName* table should be retrieved. For example, to retrieve all the data in the authors table, use

SELECT * FROM authors

Most programs do not require all the data in a table. To retrieve only specific columns from a table, replace the asterisk (*) with a comma-separated list of the column names. For example, to retrieve only the columns authorID and lastName for all rows in the authors table, use the query

SELECT authorID, lastName FROM authors

This query returns the data listed in Fig. 25.13.

Software Engineering Observation 25.2

For most queries, the asterisk (*) should not be used to specify column names. In general, programmers process results by knowing in advance the order of the columns in the result—for example selecting authorID and lastName from table authors ensures that the columns will appear in the result with authorID as the first column and lastName as the second column. Programs typically process result columns by specifying the column number in the result (starting from number 1 for the first column). Selecting columns by name also avoids returning unneeded columns and protects against changes in the actual order of the columns in the table(s).

authorID	lastName
1	Deitel
2	Deitel
3	Nieto
4	Santry

Fig. 25.13 | Sample `authorID` and `lastName` data from the `authors` table.

 Common Programming Error 25.4

If a programmer assumes that the columns are always returned in the same order from a query that uses the asterisk (*), the program may process the result incorrectly. If the column order in the table(s) changes or if additional columns are added at a later time, the order of the columns in the result would change accordingly.

25.4.2 WHERE Clause

In most cases, it is necessary to locate rows in a database that satisfy certain **selection criteria**. Only rows that satisfy the selection criteria (formally called **predicates**) are selected. SQL uses the optional **WHERE clause** in a query to specify the selection criteria for the query. The basic form of a query with selection criteria is

SELECT *columnName1*, *columnName2*, … FROM *tableName* WHERE *criteria*

For example, to select the `title`, `editionNumber` and `copyright` columns from table `titles` for which the `copyright` date is greater than 2002, use the query

```
SELECT title, editionNumber, copyright
   FROM titles
   WHERE copyright > 2002
```

Figure 25.14 shows the result of the preceding query. The WHERE clause criteria can contain the operators <, >, <=, >=, =, <> and LIKE. Operator **LIKE** is used for **pattern matching** with wildcard characters **percent (%)** and **underscore (_)**. Pattern matching allows SQL to search for strings that match a given pattern.

title	editionNumber	copyright
The Complete C++ Training Course	4	2003
Java How to Program	5	2003
C How to Program	4	2004
Internet and World Wide Web How to Program	3	2004
Java How to Program	6	2005
C# How to Program	1	2003

Fig. 25.14 | Sampling of titles with copyrights after 2002 from table `titles`.

A pattern that contains a percent character (%) searches for strings that have zero or more characters at the percent character's position in the pattern. For example, the following query locates the rows of all the authors whose last name starts with the letter D:

```
SELECT authorID, firstName, lastName
    FROM authors
    WHERE lastName LIKE 'D%'
```

The preceding query selects the two rows shown in Fig. 25.15, because two of the four authors in our database have a last name starting with the letter D (followed by zero or more characters). The % in the WHERE clause's LIKE pattern indicates that any number of characters can appear after the letter D in the lastName column. Note that the pattern string is surrounded by single-quote characters.

Portability Tip 25.1

See the documentation for your database system to determine whether SQL is case sensitive on your system and to determine the syntax for SQL keywords (i.e., should they be all uppercase letters, all lowercase letters or some combination of the two?).

Portability Tip 25.2

Read your database system's documentation carefully to determine whether your system supports the LIKE operator.

Portability Tip 25.3

*Some databases use the * character in place of the % character in a pattern.*

An underscore (_) in the pattern string indicates a single wildcard character at that position in the pattern. For example, the following query locates the rows of all the authors whose last names start with any character (specified by _), followed by the letter i, followed by any number of additional characters (specified by %):

```
SELECT authorID, firstName, lastName
    FROM authors
    WHERE lastName LIKE '_i%'
```

The preceding query produces the row shown in Fig. 25.16, because only one author in our database has a last name that contains the letter i as its second letter.

Portability Tip 25.4

Some database systems use the ? character in place of the _ character in a pattern.

authorID	firstName	lastName
1	Harvey	Deitel
2	Paul	Deitel

Fig. 25.15 | Authors whose last name starts with D from the authors table.

authorID	firstName	lastName
3	Tem	Nieto

Fig. 25.16 | The only author from the `authors` table whose last name contains i as the second letter.

25.4.3 ORDER BY Clause

The rows in the result of a query can be sorted into ascending or descending order by using the optional ORDER BY clause. The basic form of a query with an ORDER BY clause is

```
SELECT columnName1, columnName2, ... FROM tableName ORDER BY column ASC
SELECT columnName1, columnName2, ... FROM tableName ORDER BY column DESC
```

where ASC specifies ascending order (lowest to highest), DESC specifies descending order (highest to lowest) and *column* specifies the column on which the sort is based. For example, to obtain the list of authors in ascending order by last name (Fig. 25.17), use the query

```
SELECT authorID, firstName, lastName
    FROM authors
    ORDER BY lastName ASC
```

Note that the default sorting order is ascending, so ASC is optional. To obtain the same list of authors in descending order by last name (Fig. 25.18), use the query

```
SELECT authorID, firstName, lastName
    FROM authors
    ORDER BY lastName DESC
```

authorID	firstName	lastName
1	Harvey	Deitel
2	Paul	Deitel
3	Tem	Nieto
4	Sean	Santry

Fig. 25.17 | Sample data from table `authors` in ascending order by `lastName`.

authorID	firstName	lastName
4	Sean	Santry
3	Tem	Nieto
1	Harvey	Deitel
2	Paul	Deitel

Fig. 25.18 | Sample data from table `authors` in descending order by `lastName`.

Multiple columns can be used for sorting with an ORDER BY clause of the form

> ORDER BY *column1 sortingOrder*, *column2 sortingOrder*, ...

where *sortingOrder* is either ASC or DESC. Note that the *sortingOrder* does not have to be identical for each column. The query

```
SELECT authorID, firstName, lastName
    FROM authors
    ORDER BY lastName, firstName
```

sorts all the rows in ascending order by last name, then by first name. If any rows have the same last name value, they are returned sorted by first name (Fig. 25.19).

The WHERE and ORDER BY clauses can be combined in one query. For example, the query

```
SELECT isbn, title, editionNumber, copyright, price
    FROM titles
    WHERE title LIKE '%How to Program'
    ORDER BY title ASC
```

returns the isbn, title, editionNumber, copyright and price of each book in the titles table that has a title ending with "How to Program" and sorts them in ascending order by title. A portion of the query results are shown in Fig. 25.20.

25.4.4 Merging Data from Multiple Tables: INNER JOIN

Database designers often split related data into separate tables to ensure that a database does not store data redundantly. For example, the books database has tables authors and titles. We use an authorISBN table to store the relationship data between authors and their corresponding titles. If we did not separate this information into individual tables, we would need to include author information with each entry in the titles table. This would result in the database storing duplicate author information for authors who wrote multiple books. Often, it is necessary to merge data from multiple tables into a single result. Referred to as joining the tables, this is specified by an INNER JOIN operator in the query. An INNER JOIN merges rows from two tables by matching values in columns that are common to the tables. The basic form of an INNER JOIN is:

```
SELECT columnName1, columnName2, ...
FROM table1
INNER JOIN table2
    ON table1.columnName = table2.columnName
```

authorID	firstName	lastName
1	Harvey	Deitel
2	Paul	Deitel
3	Tem	Nieto
4	Sean	Santry

Fig. 25.19 | Sample data from authors in ascending order by lastName and firstName.

isbn	title	edition-Number	copy-right	price
0130895601	Advanced Java 2 Platform How to Program	1	2002	69.95
0131426443	C How to Program	4	2004	85.00
0130384747	C++ How to Program	4	2003	85.00
013028419x	e-Business and e-Commerce How to Program	1	2001	69.95
0131450913	Internet and World Wide Web How to Program	3	2004	85.00
0130284181	Perl How to Program	1	2001	69.95
0134569555	Visual Basic 6 How to Program	1	1999	69.95
0130284173	XML How to Program	1	2001	69.95

Fig. 25.20 | Sampling of books from table `titles` whose titles end with `How to Program` in ascending order by `title`.

The **ON clause** of the INNER JOIN specifies the columns from each table that are compared to determine which rows are merged. For example, the following query produces a list of authors accompanied by the ISBNs for books written by each author:

```
SELECT firstName, lastName, isbn
FROM authors
INNER JOIN authorISBN
    ON authors.authorID = authorISBN.authorID
ORDER BY lastName, firstName
```

The query merges data from the `firstName` and `lastName` columns from table `authors` with the `isbn` column from table `authorISBN`, sorting the result in ascending order by `lastName` and `firstName`. Note the use of the syntax *tableName.columnName* in the ON clause. This syntax (called a **qualified name**) specifies the columns from each table that should be compared to join the tables. The "*tableName.*" syntax is required if the columns have the same name in both tables. The same syntax can be used in any query to distinguish columns in different tables that have the same name. In some systems, table names qualified with the database name can be used to perform cross-database queries.

Software Engineering Observation 25.3

If a SQL statement includes columns from multiple tables that have the same name, the statement must precede those column names with their table names and a dot (e.g., `authors.authorID`).

Common Programming Error 25.5

In a query, failure to qualify names for columns that have the same name in two or more tables is an error.

As always, the query can contain an ORDER BY clause. Figure 25.21 depicts a portion of the results of the preceding query, ordered by lastName and firstName. [*Note:* To save space, we split the result of the query into two columns, each containing the firstName, lastName and isbn columns.]

25.4.5 INSERT Statement

The **INSERT** statement inserts a row into a table. The basic form of this statement is

```
INSERT INTO tableName ( columnName1, columnName2, ..., columnNameN )
    VALUES ( value1, value2, ..., valueN )
```

where *tableName* is the table in which to insert the row. The *tableName* is followed by a comma-separated list of column names in parentheses (this list is not required if the INSERT operation specifies a value for every column of the table in the correct order). The list of column names is followed by the SQL keyword **VALUES** and a comma-separated list of values in parentheses. The values specified here must match the columns specified after the table name in both order and type (se.g., if *columnName1* is supposed to be the first-Name column, then *value1* should be a string in single quotes representing the first name). Always explicitly list the columns when inserting rows. If the order of the columns changes in the table, using only VALUES may cause an error. The INSERT statement

```
INSERT INTO authors ( firstName, lastName )
    VALUES ( 'Sue', 'Smith' )
```

inserts a row into the authors table. The statement indicates that values are provided for the firstName and lastName columns. The corresponding values are 'Sue' and 'Smith'. We do not specify an authorID in this example because authorID is an **autoincremented**

firstName	lastName	isbn	firstName	lastName	isbn
Harvey	Deitel	0130895601	Paul	Deitel	0130895717
Harvey	Deitel	0130284181	Paul	Deitel	0132261197
Harvey	Deitel	0134569555	Paul	Deitel	0130895725
Harvey	Deitel	0139163050	Paul	Deitel	0130829293
Harvey	Deitel	0135289106	Paul	Deitel	0134569555
Harvey	Deitel	0130895717	Paul	Deitel	0130829277
Harvey	Deitel	0130284173	Tem	Nieto	0130161438
Harvey	Deitel	0130829293	Tem	Nieto	013028419x
Paul	Deitel	0130852473	Sean	Santry	0130895601

Fig. 25.21 | Sampling of authors and ISBNs for the books they have written in ascending order by lastName and firstName.

column in the `authors` table. For every row added to this table, MySQL assigns a unique `authorID` value that is the next value in the autoincremented sequence (i.e., 1, 2, 3 and so on). In this case, Sue Smith would be assigned `authorID` number 5. Figure 25.22 shows the `authors` table after the `INSERT` operation. [*Note:* Not every database management system supports autoincremented columns. Check the documentation for your DBMS for alternatives to autoincremented columns.]

Common Programming Error 25.6

It is an error to specify a value for an autoincrement column.

Common Programming Error 25.7

SQL uses the single-quote (**'** *) character as a delimiter for strings. To specify a string containing a single quote (e.g., O'Malley) in a SQL statement, the string must have two single quotes in the position where the single-quote character appears in the string (e.g.,* `'O''Malley'`*). The first of the two single-quote characters acts as an escape character for the second. Not escaping single-quote characters in a string that is part of a SQL statement is a SQL syntax error.*

25.4.6 UPDATE Statement

An **UPDATE** statement modifies data in a table. The basic form of the `UPDATE` statement is

```
UPDATE tableName
   SET columnName1 = value1, columnName2 = value2, …, columnNameN = valueN
   WHERE criteria
```

where *tableName* is the table to update. The *tableName* is followed by keyword **SET** and a comma-separated list of column name-value pairs in the format *columnName = value*. The optional `WHERE` clause provides criteria that determine which rows to update. Though not required, the `WHERE` clause is typically used, unless a change is to be made to every row. The `UPDATE` statement

```
UPDATE authors
   SET lastName = 'Jones'
   WHERE lastName = 'Smith' AND firstName = 'Sue'
```

updates a row in the `authors` table. The statement indicates that `lastName` will be assigned the value `Jones` for the row in which `lastName` is equal to `Smith` and `firstName` is equal

authorID	firstName	lastName
1	Harvey	Deitel
2	Paul	Deitel
3	Tem	Nieto
4	Sean	Santry
5	Sue	Smith

Fig. 25.22 | Sample data from table `Authors` after an `INSERT` operation.

to Sue. [*Note:* If there are multiple rows with the first name "Sue" and the last name "Smith," this statement will modify all such rows to have the last name "Jones."] If we know the authorID in advance of the UPDATE operation (possibly because we searched for it previously), the WHERE clause could be simplified as follows:

```
WHERE AuthorID = 5
```

Figure 25.23 shows the authors table after the UPDATE operation has taken place.

25.4.7 DELETE Statement

A SQL DELETE statement removes rows from a table. The basic form of a DELETE statement is

```
DELETE FROM tableName WHERE criteria
```

where *tableName* is the table from which to delete. The optional WHERE clause specifies the criteria used to determine which rows to delete. The DELETE statement

```
DELETE FROM authors
    WHERE lastName = 'Jones' AND firstName = 'Sue'
```

deletes the row for Sue Jones in the authors table. If we know the authorID in advance of the DELETE operation, the WHERE clause can be simplified as follows:

```
WHERE authorID = 5
```

Figure 25.24 shows the authors table after the DELETE operation has taken place.

authorID	firstName	lastName
1	Harvey	Deitel
2	Paul	Deitel
3	Tem	Nieto
4	Sean	Santry
5	Sue	Jones

Fig. 25.23 | Sample data from table authors after an UPDATE operation.

authorID	firstName	lastName
1	Harvey	Deitel
2	Paul	Deitel
3	Tem	Nieto
4	Sean	Santry

Fig. 25.24 | Sample data from table authors after a DELETE operation.

25.5 Instructions to install MySQL and MySQL Connector/J

The CD that accompanies this book includes MySQL 4.0.20—an open-source database management system. MySQL executes on many platforms, including Windows, Solaris, Linux, and Macintosh. Complete information about MySQL is available from

> www.mysql.com/products/mysql/

To install MySQL:

1. Insert the CD into the CD drive (the `D:` drive on our system), and change directories to `D:\software\MySQL\mysql-4.0.20c-win`.

2. Double click `SETUP.EXE` to start the MySQL installer. Follow the instructions to install MySQL in the `C:\mysql` directory, which is the default directory.

Instructions for installing MySQL can also be found in Chapter 2 of the *MySQL Manual* at `dev.mysql.com/doc/mysql/en/index.html`.

To use MySQL with JDBC, you also need to install MySQL Connector/J—a JDBC driver that allows programs to access MySQL databases via JDBC. MySQL Connector/J is on the CD that accompanies this book and can also be downloaded from

> www.mysql.com/products/connector/j/

At the time of this writing, the current stable release of MySQL Connector/J is 3.0.14. To install MySQL Connector/J:

1. Copy `mysql-connector-java-3.0.14-production.zip` to your hard disk.

2. Open `mysql-connector-java-3.0.14-production.zip` with a file extractor, such as WinZip, which can be downloaded from www.winzip.com. Extract its content to the `C:\` drive. This will create a directory named `mysql-connector-java-3.0.14-production`. The documentation for MySQL Connector/J is in `connector-j-en.pdf` in the docs subdirectory of `mysql-connector-java-3.0.14-production`, or you can view it online at `dev.mysql.com/doc/connector/j/en/index.html`.

25.6 Instructions on Setting MySQL User Account

For the examples in the book to execute correctly, you need to set up a user account that allows users to create, delete and modify a database. After MySQL is installed, follow the steps below to set up a user account (these steps assume MySQL is installed in its default installation directory):

1. Open a **Command Prompt** and start the database server by executing the `C:\mysql\bin\mysqld` script.

2. Open another **Command Prompt** and change to the `C:\mysql\bin` directory. To start the MySQL monitor so you can set up a user account, execute the command

> `C:\mysql\bin>mysql -h localhost -u root`

3. For our examples, we set up a user account on the local computer (localhost) with the username set "jhtp6" and the password "jhtp6". To do this, execute the following commands in the **Command Prompt** created in Step 2:

```
mysql> USE mysql;
mysql> INSERT INTO user SET Host='localhost', User='jhtp6',
       Password=PASSWORD('jhtp6'), Select_priv='Y',
       Insert_priv='Y', Update_priv='Y', Delete_priv='Y',
       Create_priv='Y', Drop_priv='Y', References_priv='Y',
       Execute_priv='Y';
mysql> FLUSH PRIVILEGES;
mysql> exit;
```

25.7 Creating Database books in MySQL

For each MySQL database we discuss in this book, we provide a SQL script that will set up the database and its tables. These scripts can be executed with a command-line tool called mysql that is part of the MySQL installation. In the examples directory for this chapter on the CD that accompanies this book, you will find the SQL script books.sql.

To create the books database:

1. Open a **Command Prompt** and change to the C:\mysql\bin directory. [*Note:* If you installed MySQL on a directory other than C:\mysql, replace C:\mysql with your MySQL installation directory.]

2. Start the database server by executing the command

    C:\mysql\bin>mysqld

3. Copy the SQL script books.sql to the C:\mysql\bin directory. [*Note:* If you installed MySQL on a directory other than C:\mysql, replace C:\mysql with your MySQL installation directory.]

4. Open a new **Command Prompt** and change to the C:\mysql\bin directory. [*Note:* If you installed MySQL on a directory other than C:\mysql, replace C:\mysql with your MySQL installation directory.]

5. Create the books database by executing the command

    C:\mysql\bin>mysql -h localhost -u jhtp6 -p < books.sql

When the above command is executed, you are prompted for entering the password, which is jhtp6. After completing this task, a new directory named books will be created in the C:\mysql\data directory. This new directory contains the books database. You are now ready to proceed to the first JDBC example.

25.8 Manipulating Databases with JDBC

In this section, we present two examples. The first example introduces how to connect to a database and query the database. The second example demonstrates how to display the result of the query in a JTable.

25.8.1 Connecting to and Querying a Database

The example of Fig. 25.25 performs a simple query on the books database that retrieves the entire authors table and displays the data. The program illustrates connecting to the database, querying the database and processing the result. The following discussion presents the key JDBC aspects of the program. [*Note:* Section 25.5 demonstrates how to start the MySQL server, how to prepare the MySQL database and how to create the books database. The steps in Section 25.5 must be performed before executing the program of Fig. 25.25.]

Lines 3–8 import the JDBC interfaces and classes from package java.sql used in this program. Line 13 declares a String constant that contains the MySQL JDBC driver's class name. The program will use this value to load the proper driver into memory. Line 14 declares a string constant for the database URL. This identifies the name of the database to connect to, as well as information about the protocol used by the JDBC driver (discussed shortly). Method main (lines 17–76) connects to the books database, queries the database, displays the result of the query and closes the database connection.

```java
1   // Fig. 25.25: DisplayAuthors.java
2   // Displaying the contents of the authors table.
3   import java.sql.Connection;
4   import java.sql.Statement;
5   import java.sql.DriverManager;
6   import java.sql.ResultSet;
7   import java.sql.ResultSetMetaData;
8   import java.sql.SQLException;
9
10  public class DisplayAuthors
11  {
12     // JDBC driver name and database URL
13     static final String JDBC_DRIVER = "com.mysql.jdbc.Driver";
14     static final String DATABASE_URL = "jdbc:mysql://localhost/books";
15
16     // launch the application
17     public static void main( String args[] )
18     {
19        Connection connection = null; // manages connection
20        Statement statement = null; // query statement
21
22        // connect to database books and query database
23        try
24        {
25           Class.forName( JDBC_DRIVER ); // load database driver class
26
27           // establish connection to database
28           connection =
29              DriverManager.getConnection( DATABASE_URL, "jhtp6", "jhtp6" );
30
31           // create Statement for querying database
32           statement = connection.createStatement();
33
```

Fig. 25.25 | Displaying the authors table from the books database (Part 1 of 2.).

```
34              // query database
35              ResultSet resultSet = statement.executeQuery(
36                 "SELECT authorID, firstName, lastName FROM authors" );
37
38              // process query results
39              ResultSetMetaData metaData = resultSet.getMetaData();
40              int numberOfColumns = metaData.getColumnCount();
41              System.out.println( "Authors Table of Books Database:" );
42
43              for ( int i = 1; i <= numberOfColumns; i++ )
44                 System.out.printf( "%-8s\t", metaData.getColumnName( i ) );
45              System.out.println();
46
47              while ( resultSet.next() )
48              {
49                 for ( int i = 1; i <= numberOfColumns; i++ )
50                    System.out.printf( "%-8s\t", resultSet.getObject( i ) );
51                 System.out.println();
52              } // end while
53           }  // end try
54        catch ( SQLException sqlException )
55        {
56           sqlException.printStackTrace();
57           System.exit( 1 );
58        } // end catch
59        catch ( ClassNotFoundException classNotFound )
60        {
61           classNotFound.printStackTrace();
62           System.exit( 1 );
63        } // end catch
64        finally // ensure statement and connection are closed properly
65        {
66           try
67           {
68              statement.close();
69              connection.close();
70           } // end try
71           catch ( Exception exception )
72           {
73              exception.printStackTrace();
74              System.exit( 1 );
75           } // end catch
76        } // end finally
77     } // end main
78  } // end class DisplayAuthors
```

```
Authors Table of Books Database:
authorID        firstName       lastName
1               Harvey          Deitel
2               Paul            Deitel
3               Tem             Nieto
4               Sean            Santry
```

Fig. 25.25 | Displaying the authors table from the books database (Part 2 of 2.).

The program must load the database driver before connecting to the database. Line 25 uses static method **forName** of class Class to load the class for the database driver. This line throws a checked exception of type **java.lang.ClassNotFoundException** if the class loader cannot locate the driver class. To avoid this exception, you need to include the mysql-connector-java-3.0.14-production-bin.jar (in the C:\mysql-connector-java-3.0.14-production directory) in your program's classpath when you execute the program, as in:

```
java -classpath c:\mysql-connector-java-3.0.14-production\mysql-con-
nector-java-3.0.14-production-bin.jar;. DisplayAuthors
```

In the above command, notice the period (.) before DisplayAuthors. If this period is missing, the JVM will not find the DisplayAuthors class file. You may also copy the mysql-connector-java-3.0.14-production-bin.jar file to the JRE's lib\ext directory, e.g., C:\Program Files\Java\jdk1.5.0\jre\lib\ext. After doing so, you could run the application simply using the command java DisplayAuthors.

JDBC supports four categories of drivers: **JDBC-to-ODBC bridge driver** (Type 1), **Native-API, partly Java driver** (Type 2), **Pure Java client to server driver** (Type 3) and **Pure Java driver** (Type 4). A description of each driver type is shown in Fig. 25.26. The MySQL driver com.mysql.jdbc.Driver is a Type-4 driver.

Type	Description
1	The JDBC-to-ODBC bridge driver connects Java programs to Microsoft ODBC (Open Database Connectivity) data sources. The Java 2 Software Development Kit from Sun Microsystems, Inc. includes the JDBC-to-ODBC Bridge driver (sun.jdbc.odbc.JdbcOdbcDriver). This driver typically requires the ODBC driver on the client computer and normally requires configuration of ODBC data sources. The Bridge driver was introduced primarily for development purposes, before other types of drivers were available, and should not be used for production applications.
2	Native-API, partly Java drivers enable JDBC programs to use database-specific APIs (normally written in C or C++) that allow client programs to access databases via the Java Native Interface (JNI). JNI is a bridge between a JVM and code written and compiled in a platform-specific language such as C or C++. Such code is known as native code. JNI enables Java applications to interact with native code. A Type 2 driver translates JDBC into database-specific calls. Type 2 drivers were introduced for reasons similar to the Type 1 ODBC bridge driver.
3	Pure Java client to server drivers take JDBC requests and translate them into a network protocol that is not database specific. These requests are sent to a server, which translates the database requests into a database-specific protocol.
4	Pure Java drivers implement database-specific network protocols, so that Java programs can connect directly to a database.

Fig. 25.26 | JDBC driver types.

Software Engineering Observation 25.4

Most major database vendors provide their own JDBC database drivers, and many third-party vendors provide JDBC drivers as well. For more information on JDBC drivers, visit the Sun Microsystems JDBC Web site, `servlet.java.sun.com/products/jdbc/drivers`.

Software Engineering Observation 25.5

On the Microsoft Windows platform, most databases support access via Open Database Connectivity (ODBC). ODBC is a technology developed by Microsoft to allow generic access to disparate database systems on the Windows platform (and some UNIX platforms). The JDBC-to-ODBC Bridge *allows any Java program to access any ODBC data source. The driver is class* `JdbcOdbcDriver` *in package* `sun.jdbc.odbc`.

Lines 28–29 of Fig. 25.25 creates a **Connection** object (package `java.sql`) referenced by `connection`. An object that implements interface `Connection` manages the connection between the Java program and the database. `Connection` objects enable programs to create SQL statements that access databases. The program initializes `connection` with the result of a call to `static` method **getConnection** of class **DriverManager** (package `java.sql`), which attempts to connect to the database specified by its URL. Method `getConnection` takes three arguments—a `String` that specifies the database URL, a `String` that specifies the username and a `String` that specifies the password. The username and password are set in Section 25.6. If you used different username and password, you need to replace the username (second argument) and password (third argument) passed to method `getConnection` in line 29. The URL locates the database (possibly on a network or in the local file system of the computer). The URL `jdbc:mysql://localhost/books` specifies the protocol for communication (`jdbc`), the **subprotocol** for communication (`mysql`) and the location of the database (`//localhost/books`, where `localhost` is the name of the MySQL server host and `books` is the database name). The subprotocol `mysql` indicates that the program uses a MySQL-specific subprotocol to connect to the MySQL database. If the `DriverManager` cannot connect to the database, method `getConnection` throws a **SQLException** (package `java.sql`). Figure 25.27 lists the JDBC driver names and database URL formats of several popular RDBMSs.

RDBMS	JDBC driver name	Database URL format
MySQL	`com.mysql.jdbc.Driver`	`jdbc:mysql://`*hostname*`/`*database-Name*
ORA-CLE	`oracle.jdbc.driver.OracleDriver`	`jdbc:oracle:thin:@`*hostname*`:`*port Number*`:`*databaseName*
DB2	`COM.ibm.db2.jdbc.net.DB2Driver`	`jdbc:db2:`*hostname*`:`*portnumber*`/`*data baseName*
Sybase	`com.sybase.jdbc.SybDriver`	`jdbc:sybase:Tds:`*hostname*`:`*portnum-ber*`/`*databaseName*

Fig. 25.27 | Popular JDBC driver names and database URL.

Software Engineering Observation 25.6

Most database management systems require the user to log in before accessing the database contents. DriverManager *method* getConnection *is overloaded with versions that enable the program to supply the user name and password to gain access.*

Line 32 invokes Connection method **createStatement** to obtain an object that implements interface Statement (package java.sql). The program uses the **Statement** object to submit SQL to the database.

Lines 35–36 use the Statement object's **executeQuery** method to submit a query that selects all the author information from table authors. This method returns an object that implements interface **ResultSet** and contains the result of the query. The ResultSet methods enable the program to manipulate the query result.

Lines 39–52 process the ResultSet. Line 39 obtains the metadata for the ResultSet as a **ResultSetMetaData** (package java.sql) object. The metadata describes the ResultSet's contents. Programs can use metadata programmatically to obtain information about the ResultSet's column names and types. Line 40 uses ResultSetMetaData method **getColumnCount** to retrieve the number of columns in the ResultSet. Lines 42–43 display the column names.

Software Engineering Observation 25.7

Metadata enables programs to process ResultSet *contents dynamically when detailed information about the* ResultSet *is not known in advance.*

Lines 47–52 display the data in each ResultSet row. Before processing the ResultSet, the program positions the ResultSet cursor to the first row in the ResultSet with method **next** (line 47). The cursor points to the current row. Method next returns boolean value true if it is able to position to the next row; otherwise the method returns false.

Common Programming Error 25.8

Initially, a ResultSet *cursor is positioned before the first row. Attempting to access a* ResultSet's *contents before positioning the* ResultSet *cursor to the first row with method* next *causes a* SQLException.

If there are rows in the ResultSet, line 50 extracts the contents of one column in the current row. When processing a ResultSet, it is possible to extract each column of the ResultSet as a specific Java type. In fact, ResultSetMetaData method **getColumnType** returns a constant integer from class **Types** (package java.sql) indicating the type of a specified column. Programs can use these values in a switch statement to invoke ResultSet methods that return the column values as appropriate Java types. If the type of a column is Types.INT, ResultSet method **getInt** returns the column value as an int. ResultSet *get* methods typically receive as an argument either a *column number* (as an int) or a *column name* (as a String) indicating which column's value to obtain. Visit

```
java.sun.com/j2se/5.0/docs/guide/jdbc/getstart/
    GettingStartedTOC.fm.html
```

for detailed mappings of SQL data types to Java types and to determine the appropriate ResultSet method to call for each SQL data type.

Performance Tip 25.1

If a query specifies the exact columns to select from the database, the ResultSet contains the columns in the specified order. In this case, using the column number to obtain the column's value is more efficient than using the column name. The column number provides direct access to the specified column. Using the column name requires a linear search of the column names to locate the appropriate column.

For simplicity, this example treats each value as an Object. The program retrieves each column value with ResultSet method **getObject** (line 50) and prints the String representation of the Object. Note that, unlike array indices, which start at 0, ResultSet column numbers start at 1. The finally block (lines 64–76) closes the Statement (line 68) and the database Connection (line 69).

Common Programming Error 25.9

Specifying column number 0 when obtaining values from a ResultSet causes a SQLException.

Common Programming Error 25.10

Attempting to manipulate a ResultSet after closing the Statement that created the ResultSet causes a SQLException. The program discards the ResultSet when the corresponding Statement is closed.

Software Engineering Observation 25.8

Each Statement object can open only one ResultSet object at a time. When a Statement returns a new ResultSet, the Statement closes the prior ResultSet. To use multiple ResultSets in parallel, separate Statement objects must return the ResultSets.

25.8.2 Querying the books Database

The next example (Fig. 25.28 and Fig. 25.31) allows the user to enter any query into the program. The example displays the result of a query in a **JTable**, using a **TableModel** object to provide the ResultSet data to the JTable. Class ResultSetTableModel (Fig. 25.28) performs the connection to the database and maintains the ResultSet. Class DisplayQueryResults (Fig. 25.31) creates the GUI and specifies an instance of class ResultSetTableModel to provide data for the JTable.

Class ResultSetTableModel (Fig. 25.28) extends class **AbstractTableModel** (package javax.swing.table), which implements interface TableModel. Class ResultSetTableModel overrides TableModel methods **getColumnClass**, **getColumnCount**, **getColumnName**, **getRowCount** and **getValueAt**. The default implementations of TableModel methods isCellEditable and setValueAt (provided by AbstractTableModel) are not overridden, because this example does not support editing the JTable cells. The default implementations of TableModel methods **addTableModelListener** and **removeTableModelListener** (provided by AbstractTableModel) are not overridden, because the implementations of these methods in AbstractTableModel properly add and remove event listeners.

The ResultSetTableModel constructor (lines 30–50) accepts five String arguments—the driver class name, the URL of the database, the username, the password and the default query to perform. The constructor throws any exceptions that occur in its body back to the application that created the ResultSetTableModel object, so that the application can determine how to handle the exception (e.g., report an error and terminate the

```
1   // Fig. 25.28: ResultSetTableModel.java
2   // A TableModel that supplies ResultSet data to a JTable.
3   import java.sql.Connection;
4   import java.sql.Statement;
5   import java.sql.DriverManager;
6   import java.sql.ResultSet;
7   import java.sql.ResultSetMetaData;
8   import java.sql.SQLException;
9   import javax.swing.table.AbstractTableModel;
10
11  // ResultSet rows and columns are counted from 1 and JTable
12  // rows and columns are counted from 0. When processing
13  // ResultSet rows or columns for use in a JTable, it is
14  // necessary to add 1 to the row or column number to manipulate
15  // the appropriate ResultSet column (i.e., JTable column 0 is
16  // ResultSet column 1 and JTable row 0 is ResultSet row 1).
17  public class ResultSetTableModel extends AbstractTableModel
18  {
19     private Connection connection;
20     private Statement statement;
21     private ResultSet resultSet;
22     private ResultSetMetaData metaData;
23     private int numberOfRows;
24
25     // keep track of database connection status
26     private boolean connectedToDatabase = false;
27
28     // constructor initializes resultSet and obtains its meta data object;
29     // determines number of rows
30     public ResultSetTableModel( String driver, String url,
31        String username, String password, String query )
32        throws SQLException, ClassNotFoundException
33     {
34        // load database driver class
35        Class.forName( driver );
36
37        // connect to database
38        connection = DriverManager.getConnection( url, username, password );
39
40        // create Statement to query database
41        statement = connection.createStatement(
42           ResultSet.TYPE_SCROLL_INSENSITIVE,
43           ResultSet.CONCUR_READ_ONLY );
44
45        // update database connection status
46        connectedToDatabase = true;
47
48        // set query and execute it
49        setQuery( query );
50     } // end constructor ResultSetTableModel
51
```

Fig. 25.28 | ResultSetTableModel enables a JTable to display the contents of a ResultSet. (Part 1 of 4.)

```
52    // get class that represents column type
53    public Class getColumnClass( int column ) throws IllegalStateException
54    {
55       // ensure database connection is available
56       if ( !connectedToDatabase )
57          throw new IllegalStateException( "Not Connected to Database" );
58
59       // determine Java class of column
60       try
61       {
62          String className = metaData.getColumnClassName( column + 1 );
63
64          // return Class object that represents className
65          return Class.forName( className );
66       } // end try
67       catch ( Exception exception )
68       {
69          exception.printStackTrace();
70       } // end catch
71
72       return Object.class; // if problems occur above, assume type Object
73    } // end method getColumnClass
74
75    // get number of columns in ResultSet
76    public int getColumnCount() throws IllegalStateException
77    {
78       // ensure database connection is available
79       if ( !connectedToDatabase )
80          throw new IllegalStateException( "Not Connected to Database" );
81
82       // determine number of columns
83       try
84       {
85          return metaData.getColumnCount();
86       } // end try
87       catch ( SQLException sqlException )
88       {
89          sqlException.printStackTrace();
90       } // end catch
91
92       return 0; // if problems occur above, return 0 for number of columns
93    } // end method getColumnCount
94
95    // get name of a particular column in ResultSet
96    public String getColumnName( int column ) throws IllegalStateException
97    {
98       // ensure database connection is available
99       if ( !connectedToDatabase )
100         throw new IllegalStateException( "Not Connected to Database" );
101
```

Fig. 25.28 | ResultSetTableModel enables a JTable to display the contents of a ResultSet. (Part 2 of 4.)

```
102          // determine column name
103          try
104          {
105              return metaData.getColumnName( column + 1 );
106          } // end try
107          catch ( SQLException sqlException )
108          {
109              sqlException.printStackTrace();
110          } // end catch
111
112          return ""; // if problems, return empty string for column name
113      } // end method getColumnName
114
115      // return number of rows in ResultSet
116      public int getRowCount() throws IllegalStateException
117      {
118          // ensure database connection is available
119          if ( !connectedToDatabase )
120              throw new IllegalStateException( "Not Connected to Database" );
121
122          return numberOfRows;
123      } // end method getRowCount
124
125      // obtain value in particular row and column
126      public Object getValueAt( int row, int column )
127          throws IllegalStateException
128      {
129          // ensure database connection is available
130          if ( !connectedToDatabase )
131              throw new IllegalStateException( "Not Connected to Database" );
132
133          // obtain a value at specified ResultSet row and column
134          try
135          {
136              resultSet.absolute( row + 1 );
137              return resultSet.getObject( column + 1 );
138          } // end try
139          catch ( SQLException sqlException )
140          {
141              sqlException.printStackTrace();
142          } // end catch
143
144          return ""; // if problems, return empty string object
145      } // end method getValueAt
146
147      // set new database query string
148      public void setQuery( String query )
149          throws SQLException, IllegalStateException
150      {
151          // ensure database connection is available
152          if ( !connectedToDatabase )
153              throw new IllegalStateException( "Not Connected to Database" );
```

Fig. 25.28 | ResultSetTableModel enables a JTable to display the contents of a ResultSet. (Part 3 of 4.)

```
154
155        // specify query and execute it
156        resultSet = statement.executeQuery( query );
157
158        // obtain meta data for ResultSet
159        metaData = resultSet.getMetaData();
160
161        // determine number of rows in ResultSet
162        resultSet.last();                     // move to last row
163        numberOfRows = resultSet.getRow();    // get row number
164
165        // notify JTable that model has changed
166        fireTableStructureChanged();
167     } // end method setQuery
168
169     // close Statement and Connection
170     public void disconnectFromDatabase()
171     {
172        if ( !connectedToDatabase )
173           return;
174
175        // close Statement and Connection
176        try
177        {
178           statement.close();
179           connection.close();
180        } // end try
181        catch ( SQLException sqlException )
182        {
183           sqlException.printStackTrace();
184        } // end catch
185        finally  // update database connection status
186        {
187           connectedToDatabase = false;
188        } // end finally
189     } // end method disconnectFromDatabase
190  }  // end class ResultSetTableModel
```

Fig. 25.28 | `ResultSetTableModel` enables a `JTable` to display the contents of a `ResultSet`. (Part 4 of 4.)

application). Line 35 loads the database driver. Line 38 establishes a connection to the database. Lines 41–43 invoke `Connection` method `createStatement` to create a `Statement` object. This example uses a version of method `createStatement` that takes two arguments—the **result set type** and the **result set concurrency**. The result set type (Fig. 25.29) specifies whether the `ResultSet`'s cursor is able to scroll in both directions or forward only and whether the `ResultSet` is sensitive to changes. `ResultSets` that are sensitive to changes reflect those changes immediately after they are made with methods of interface `ResultSet`. If a `ResultSet` is insensitive to changes, the query that produced the `ResultSet` must be executed again to reflect any changes made. The result set concurrency (Fig. 25.30) specifies whether the `ResultSet` can be updated with `ResultSet`'s update methods. This example uses a `ResultSet` that is scrollable, insensitive to changes and read only. Line 49 invokes `ResultSetTableModel` method `setQuery` (lines 148–167) to perform the default query.

Portability Tip 25.5

Some JDBC drivers do not support scrollable `ResultSet`s. In such cases, the driver typically returns a `ResultSet` in which the cursor can move only forward. For more information, see your database driver documentation.

Portability Tip 25.6

Some JDBC drivers do not support updatable `ResultSet`s. In such cases, the driver typically returns a read-only `ResultSet`. For more information, see your database driver documentation.

Common Programming Error 25.11

Attempting to update a `ResultSet` when the database driver does not support updatable `ResultSet`s causes `SQLException`s.

ResultSet static type constant	Description
TYPE_FORWARD_ONLY	Specifies that a `ResultSet`'s cursor can move only in the forward direction (i.e., from the first row to the last row in the `ResultSet`).
TYPE_SCROLL_INSENSITIVE	Specifies that a `ResultSet`'s cursor can scroll in either direction and that the changes made to the `ResultSet` during `ResultSet` processing are not reflected in the `ResultSet` unless the program queries the database again.
TYPE_SCROLL_SENSITIVE	Specifies that a `ResultSet`'s cursor can scroll in either direction and that the changes made to the `ResultSet` during `ResultSet` processing are reflected immediately in the `ResultSet`.

Fig. 25.29 | `ResultSet` constants for specifying `ResultSet` type .

ResultSet static concurrency constant	Description
CONCUR_READ_ONLY	Specifies that a `ResultSet` cannot be updated (i.e., changes to the `ResultSet` contents cannot be reflected in the database with `ResultSet`'s *update* methods).
CONCUR_UPDATABLE	Specifies that a `ResultSet` can be updated (i.e., changes to the `ResultSet` contents can be reflected in the database with `ResultSet`'s *update* methods).

Fig. 25.30 | `ResultSet` constants for specifying result properties.

Common Programming Error 25.12

Attempting to move the cursor backwards through a ResultSet *when the database driver does not support backwards scrolling causes a* SQLException.

Method getColumnClass (lines 53–73) returns a Class object that represents the superclass of all objects in a particular column. The JTable uses this information to configure the default cell renderer and cell editor for that column in the JTable. Line 62 uses ResultSetMetaData method **getColumnClassName** to obtain the fully qualified class name for the specified column. Line 65 loads the class and returns the corresponding Class object. If an exception occurs, the catch in lines 67–70 prints a stack trace and line 72 returns Object.class—the Class instance that represents class Object—as the default type. [*Note:* Line 62 uses the argument column + 1. Like arrays, JTable row and column numbers are counted from 0. However, ResultSet row and column numbers are counted from 1. Thus, when processing ResultSet rows or columns for use in a JTable, it is necessary to add 1 to the row or column number to manipulate the appropriate ResultSet row or column.]

Method getColumnCount (lines 76–93) returns the number of columns in the model's underlying ResultSet. Line 85 uses ResultSetMetaData method getColumnCount to obtain the number of columns in the ResultSet. If an exception occurs, the catch in lines 87–90 prints a stack trace and line 92 returns 0 as the default number of columns.

Method getColumnName (lines 96–113) returns the name of the column in the model's underlying ResultSet. Line 105 uses ResultSetMetaData method **getColumn-Name** to obtain the column name from the ResultSet. If an exception occurs, the catch in lines 107–110 prints a stack trace and line 112 returns the empty string as the default column name.

Method getRowCount (lines 116–123) returns the number of rows in the model's underlying ResultSet. When method setQuery (lines 148–167) performs a query, it stores the number of rows in variable numberOfRows.

Method getValueAt (lines 126–145) returns the Object in a particular row and column of the model's underlying ResultSet. Line 136 uses ResultSet method **absolute** to position the ResultSet cursor at a specific row. Line 137 uses ResultSet method get-Object to obtain the Object in a specific column of the current row. If an exception occurs, the catch in lines 139–142 prints a stack trace and line 144 returns an empty string as the default value.

Method setQuery (lines 148–167) executes the query it receives as an argument to obtain a new ResultSet (line 156). Line 159 gets the ResultSetMetaData for the new ResultSet. Line 162 uses ResultSet method **last** to position the ResultSet cursor at the last row in the ResultSet. Line 163 uses ResultSet method **getRow** to obtain the row number for the current row in the ResultSet. Line 166 invokes method **fireTable-StructureChanged** (inherited from class AbstractTableModel) to notify any JTable using this ResultSetTableModel object as its model that the structure of the model has changed. This causes the JTable to repopulate its rows and columns with the new ResultSet data. Method setQuery throws any exceptions that occur in its body back to the application that invoked setQuery.

Method disconnectFromDatabase (lines 170–189) implements an appropriate termination method for class ResultSetTableModel. A class designer should provide a public method that clients of the class must invoke explicitly to free resources that an object has used. In this case, method `disconnectFromDatabase` closes the database statement and connection (lines 178–179), which are considered limited resources. Clients of the `Result-SetTableModel` class should always invoke this method when the instance of this class is no longer needed. Before releasing resources, line 172 verifies whether the connection is already terminated. If so, the method simply returns. In addition, note that each other method in the class throws an `IllegalStateException` if the boolean field `connectedTo-Database` is `false`. Method `disconnectFromDatabase` sets `connectedToDatabase` to `false` (line 184) to ensure that clients do not use an instance of `ResultSetTableModel` after that instance has already been terminated. `IllegalStateException` is an exception from the Java libraries that is appropriate for indicating this error condition.

The `DisplayQueryResults` (Fig. 25.31) constructor (lines 34–140) creates a `Result-SetTableModel` object and the GUI for the application. Lines 22–25 and 28 declare the database driver class name, database URL, username, password and default query that are

```
 1   // Fig. 25.31: DisplayQueryResults.java
 2   // Display the contents of the Authors table in the
 3   // Books database.
 4   import java.awt.BorderLayout;
 5   import java.awt.event.ActionListener;
 6   import java.awt.event.ActionEvent;
 7   import java.awt.event.WindowAdapter;
 8   import java.awt.event.WindowEvent;
 9   import java.sql.SQLException;
10   import javax.swing.JFrame;
11   import javax.swing.JTextArea;
12   import javax.swing.JScrollPane;
13   import javax.swing.ScrollPaneConstants;
14   import javax.swing.JTable;
15   import javax.swing.JOptionPane;
16   import javax.swing.JButton;
17   import javax.swing.Box;
18
19   public class DisplayQueryResults extends JFrame
20   {
21      // JDBC driver and database URL
22      static final String JDBC_DRIVER = "com.mysql.jdbc.Driver";
23      static final String DATABASE_URL = "jdbc:mysql://localhost/books";
24      static final String USERNAME= "jhtp6";
25      static final String PASSWORD= "jhtp6";
26
27      // default query selects all rows from authors table
28      static final String DEFAULT_QUERY = "SELECT * FROM authors";
29
30      private ResultSetTableModel tableModel;
31      private JTextArea queryArea;
32
33      // create ResultSetTableModel and GUI
34      public DisplayQueryResults()
35      {
```

Fig. 25.31 | `DisplayQueryResults` for querying database **books**. (Part 1 of 4.)

```
36          super( "Displaying Query Results" );
37
38          // create ResultSetTableModel and display database table
39          try
40          {
41             // create TableModel for results of query SELECT * FROM authors
42             tableModel = new ResultSetTableModel( JDBC_DRIVER, DATABASE_URL,
43                USERNAME, PASSWORD, DEFAULT_QUERY );
44
45             // set up JTextArea in which user types queries
46             queryArea = new JTextArea( DEFAULT_QUERY, 3, 100 );
47             queryArea.setWrapStyleWord( true );
48             queryArea.setLineWrap( true );
49
50             JScrollPane scrollPane = new JScrollPane( queryArea,
51                ScrollPaneConstants.VERTICAL_SCROLLBAR_AS_NEEDED,
52                ScrollPaneConstants.HORIZONTAL_SCROLLBAR_NEVER );
53
54             // set up JButton for submitting queries
55             JButton submitButton = new JButton( "Submit Query" );
56
57             // create Box to manage placement of queryArea and
58             // submitButton in GUI
59             Box box = Box.createHorizontalBox();
60             box.add( scrollPane );
61             box.add( submitButton );
62
63             // create JTable delegate for tableModel
64             JTable resultTable = new JTable( tableModel );
65
66             // place GUI components on content pane
67             add( box, BorderLayout.NORTH );
68             add( new JScrollPane( resultTable ), BorderLayout.CENTER );
69
70             // create event listener for submitButton
71             submitButton.addActionListener(
72
73                new ActionListener()
74                {
75                   // pass query to table model
76                   public void actionPerformed( ActionEvent event )
77                   {
78                      // perform a new query
79                      try
80                      {
81                         tableModel.setQuery( queryArea.getText() );
82                      } // end try
83                      catch ( SQLException sqlException )
84                      {
85                         JOptionPane.showMessageDialog( null,
86                            sqlException.getMessage(), "Database error",
87                            JOptionPane.ERROR_MESSAGE );
88
```

Fig. 25.31 | DisplayQueryResults for querying database books. (Part 2 of 4.)

```
89                        // try to recover from invalid user query
90                        // by executing default query
91                        try
92                        {
93                           tableModel.setQuery( DEFAULT_QUERY );
94                           queryArea.setText( DEFAULT_QUERY );
95                        } // end try
96                        catch ( SQLException sqlException2 )
97                        {
98                           JOptionPane.showMessageDialog( null,
99                              sqlException2.getMessage(), "Database error",
100                             JOptionPane.ERROR_MESSAGE );
101
102                          // ensure database connection is closed
103                          tableModel.disconnectFromDatabase();
104
105                          System.exit( 1 ); // terminate application
106                       } // end inner catch
107                    } // end outer catch
108                 } // end actionPerformed
109              } // end ActionListener inner class
110           ); // end call to addActionListener
111
112        setSize( 500, 250 ); // set window size
113        setVisible( true ); // display window
114     } // end try
115     catch ( ClassNotFoundException classNotFound )
116     {
117        JOptionPane.showMessageDialog( null,
118           "MySQL driver not found", "Driver not found",
119           JOptionPane.ERROR_MESSAGE );
120
121        System.exit( 1 ); // terminate application
122     } // end catch
123     catch ( SQLException sqlException )
124     {
125        JOptionPane.showMessageDialog( null, sqlException.getMessage(),
126           "Database error", JOptionPane.ERROR_MESSAGE );
127
128        // ensure database connection is closed
129        tableModel.disconnectFromDatabase();
130
131        System.exit( 1 );   // terminate application
132     } // end catch
133
134     // dispose of window when user quits application (this overrides
135     // the default of HIDE_ON_CLOSE)
136     setDefaultCloseOperation( DISPOSE_ON_CLOSE );
137
138     // ensure database connection is closed when user quits application
139     addWindowListener(
140
```

Fig. 25.31 | DisplayQueryResults for querying database books. (Part 3 of 4.)

```
141                new WindowAdapter()
142                {
143                   // disconnect from database and exit when window has closed
144                   public void windowClosed( WindowEvent event )
145                   {
146                      tableModel.disconnectFromDatabase();
147                      System.exit( 0 );
148                   } // end method windowClosed
149                } // end WindowAdapter inner class
150             ); // end call to addWindowListener
151          } // end DisplayQueryResults constructor
152
153          // execute application
154          public static void main( String args[] )
155          {
156             new DisplayQueryResults();
157          } // end main
158       } // end class DisplayQueryResults
```

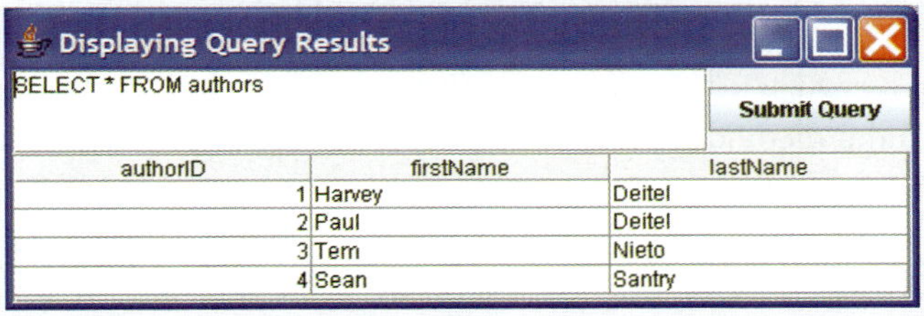

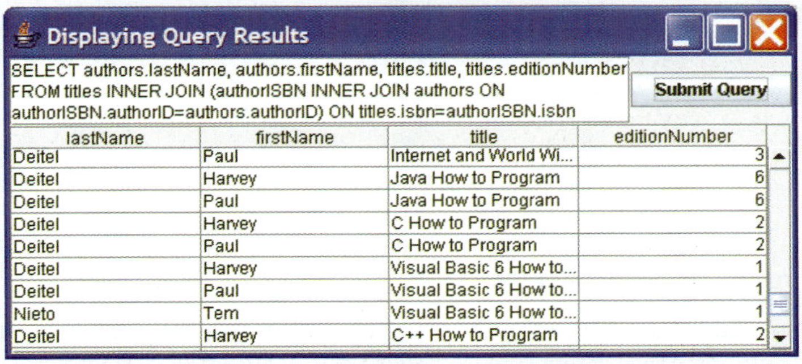

Fig. 25.31 | `DisplayQueryResults` for querying database `books`. (Part 4 of 4.)

passed to the `ResultSetTableModel` constructor to make the initial connection to the database and perform the default query. Line 64 creates the `JTable` object and passes a `ResultSetTableModel` object to the `JTable` constructor, which then registers the `JTable` as a listener for `TableModelEvents` generated by the `ResultSetTableModel`. Lines 71–110 register an event handler for the `submitButton` that the user clicks to submit a query to the database. When the user clicks the button, method `actionPerformed` (lines 76–108) invokes `ResultSetTableModel` method `setQuery` to execute the new query. If the user's query fails (e.g., because of a syntax error in the user's input), lines 93–94 execute the default query. If the default query also fails, there could be a more serious error, so line 103 ensures that the database connection is closed and line 105 exits the program. The screen captures in Fig. 25.31 show the results of two queries. The first screen capture shows the default query that retrieves all the data from table authors of database books. The second screen capture shows a query that selects each author's first name and last name from the authors table and combines that information with the title and edition number from the titles table. Try entering your own queries in the text area and clicking the **Submit Query** button to execute the query.

25.9 Stored Procedures

Many database management systems can store individual SQL statements or sets of SQL statements in a database, so that programs accessing that database can invoke them. Such named collections of SQL are called stored procedures. JDBC enables programs to invoke stored procedures using objects that implement interface **CallableStatement**. Callable-Statements can receive arguments specified with the methods inherited from interface **PreparedStatement**. In addition, CallableStatements can specify output parameters in which a stored procedure can place return values. Interface CallableStatement includes methods to specify which parameters in a stored procedure are output parameters. The interface also includes methods to obtain the values of output parameters returned from a stored procedure.

Portability Tip 25.7

Although the syntax for creating stored procedures differs across database management systems, interface CallableStatement provides a uniform interface for specifying input and output parameters for stored procedures and for invoking stored procedures.

Portability Tip 25.8

According to the Java API documentation for interface CallableStatement, for maximum portability between database systems, programs should process the update counts or ResultSets returned from a CallableStatement before obtaining the values of any output parameters.

25.10 RowSet Interface

In the previous examples, you learned how to query a database by explicitly establishing a Connection to the database, preparing a Statement for querying the database and executing the query. In this section, we demonstrate the **RowSet** interface, which configures the database connection and prepares query statements automatically. Interface RowSet provides several *set* methods that allow the programmer to specify the properties needed to establish a connection (such as the database URL, user name and password of the database) and create a Statement (such as a query). Interface RowSet also provides several *get* methods that return these properties.

RowSet is part of the **javax.sql** package. Although part of Java 2 Standard Edition, the classes and interfaces of package javax.sql are most frequently used in the context of the Java 2 Platform Enterprise Edition (J2EE). J2EE is used in industry to build substantial distributed applications that often process database data. J2EE is beyond the scope of this book. You can learn more about J2EE by visiting java.sun.com/j2ee/.

There are two types of RowSet objects—connected and disconnected. A **connected RowSet** object connects to the database once and remains connected until the application terminates. A **disconnected RowSet** object connects to the database, executes a query to retrieve the data from the database and then closes the connection. A program may change the data in a disconnected RowSet while it is disconnected. Modified data can be updated in the database after a disconnected RowSet reestablishes the connection with the database.

J2SE 5.0 package **javax.sql.rowset** contains two subinterfaces of RowSet—Jdbc-RowSet and CachedRowSet. **JdbcRowSet**, a connected RowSet, acts as a wrapper around a ResultSet object, and allows programmers to scroll through and update the rows in the ResultSet. Recall that by default, a ResultSet object is non-scrollable and read only—you must explicitly set the result-set type constant to TYPE_SCROLL_INSENSITIVE and set the result-set concurrency constant to CONCUR_UPDATABLE to make a ResultSet object scrollable and updatable. A JdbcRowSet object is scrollable and updatable by default. **CachedRowSet**, a disconnected RowSet, caches the data of a ResultSet in memory and disconnects from the database. Like JdbcRowSet, a CachedRowSet object is scrollable and updatable by default. A CachedRowSet object is also serializable, so it can be passed between Java applications through a network, such as the Internet. However, Cached-RowSet has a limitation—the amount of data that can be stored in memory is limited. Besides JdbcRowSet and CachedRowSet, package javax.sql.rowset contains three other subinterfaces of RowSet. For details of these interfaces, visit java.sun.com/j2se/5.0/docs/guide/jdbc/getstart/rowsetImpl.html.

Figure 25.32 reimplements the example of Fig. 25.25 using a RowSet. Rather than establish the connection and create a Statement explicitly, Fig. 25.32 uses a JdbcRowSet object to create a Connection and a Statement automatically.

```java
1   // Fig. 25.32: JdbcRowSetTest.java
2   // Displaying the contents of the authors table using JdbcRowSet.
3   import java.sql.ResultSetMetaData;
4   import java.sql.SQLException;
5   import javax.sql.rowset.JdbcRowSet;
6   import com.sun.rowset.JdbcRowSetImpl; // Sun's JdbcRowSet implementation
7
8   public class JdbcRowSetTest
9   {
10     // JDBC driver name and database URL
11     static final String JDBC_DRIVER = "com.mysql.jdbc.Driver";
12     static final String DATABASE_URL = "jdbc:mysql://localhost/books";
13     static final String USERNAME = "jhtp6";
14     static final String PASSWORD = "jhtp6";
15
16     // constructor connects to database, queries database, processes
17     // results and displays results in window
18     public JdbcRowSetTest()
19     {
20       // connect to database books and query database
21       try
22       {
23         Class.forName( JDBC_DRIVER ); // load database driver class
```

Fig. 25.32 | Displaying the authors table using JdbcRowSet. (Part 1 of 2.)

```
24
25              // specify properties of JdbcRowSet
26              JdbcRowSet rowSet = new JdbcRowSetImpl();
27              rowSet.setUrl( DATABASE_URL ); // set database URL
28              rowSet.setUsername( USERNAME ); // set username
29              rowSet.setPassword( PASSWORD ); // set password
30              rowSet.setCommand( "SELECT * FROM authors" ); // set query
31              rowSet.execute(); // execute query
32
33              // process query results
34              ResultSetMetaData metaData = rowSet.getMetaData();
35              int numberOfColumns = metaData.getColumnCount();
36              System.out.println( "Authors Table of Books Database:" );
37
38              // display rowset header
39              for ( int i = 1; i <= numberOfColumns; i++ )
40                 System.out.printf( "%-8s\t", metaData.getColumnName( i ) );
41              System.out.println();
42
43              // display each row
44              while ( rowSet.next() )
45              {
46                 for ( int i = 1; i <= numberOfColumns; i++ )
47                    System.out.printf( "%-8s\t", rowSet.getObject( i ) );
48                 System.out.println();
49              } // end while
50           } // end try
51           catch ( SQLException sqlException )
52           {
53              sqlException.printStackTrace();
54              System.exit( 1 );
55           } // end catch
56           catch ( ClassNotFoundException classNotFound )
57           {
58              classNotFound.printStackTrace();
59              System.exit( 1 );
60           } // end catch
61        } // end DisplayAuthors constructor
62
63        // launch the application
64        public static void main( String args[] )
65        {
66           JdbcRowSetTest window = new JdbcRowSetTest();
67        } // end main
68     } // end class JdbcRowSetTest
```

```
Authors Table of Books Database:
authorID         firstName        lastName
1                Harvey           Deitel
2                Paul             Deitel
3                Tem              Nieto
4                Sean             Santry
```

Fig. 25.32 | Displaying the authors table using JdbcRowSet. (Part 2 of 2.)

Line 26 uses Sun's reference implementation of the JdbcRowSet interface, **Jdbc-RowSetImpl** from package **com.sun.rowset**, to create a JdbcRowSet object. Package com.sun.rowset provides implementations of the interfaces in package javax.sql.rowset. We used class JdbcRowSetImpl here to demonstrate the capability of the JdbcRowSet interface. Some databases may provide their own RowSet implementations.

Line 27 invokes JdbcRowSet method **setUrl** to specify the database URL, which is then used by the DriverManager to establish a connection. Line 28 invokes JdbcRowSet method **setUsername** to specify the username, which is then used by the DriverManagger to establish a connection. Line 29 invokes JdbcRowSet method **setPassword** to specify the password, which is then used by the DriverManager to establish a connection. Line 30 invokes JdbcRowSet method **setCommand** to specify the SQL query. Line 31 invokes Jdbc-RowSet method **execute** to execute the SQL query. Method execute performs four actions—it establishes a Connection, prepares the query Statement, executes the query and stores the ResultSet returned by query. The Connection, Statement and ResultSet are encapsulated in the JdbcRowSet object. The remaining code is almost identical to Fig. 25.25, except that line 34 obtains a ResultSetMetaData object from the JdbcRowSet, line 44 uses the JdbcRowSet's next method to get the next row of the result, and line 47uses the JdbcRowSet's getObject method to obtain a column's value. Note that the output of this application is exactly the same as that of Fig. 25.25.

In this chapter, you learned basic database concepts, how to interact with data in a database using SQL and how to use JDBC to allow Java applications to manipulate database data. You learned the explicit steps for obtaining a Connection to the database, creating a Statement to interact with the database's data, executing the statement and processing the results. Finally you saw how to use a RowSet to simplify the process of connecting to a database and creating statements. In the next chapter, you will learn about servlets, which are Java programs that enhance a Web Server's capabilities. Servlets sometimes use JDBC to interact with databases on behalf of users who make requests via Web browsers.

25.11 Wrap-Up

This chapter introduced the SQL and the JDBC API. You learned basic SQL to retrieve data from and update data in a database. You examined the contents of a sample database and learned how to set it up for use with the MySQL database management system. You also learned how to access and manipulate the MySQL database via the JDBC API. Then, you learned the new RowSet interface introduced in J2SE 5.0. In the next chapter, we demonstrate how to build Web applications using Java servlets. We also introduce the concept of a three-tier application, in which an application is divided into three pieces that can reside on the same computer or can be distributed among separate computers across a network, such as the Internet.

25.12 Internet and Web Resources

java.sun.com/products/jdbc
Sun Microsystems, Inc.'s JDBC home page.

java.sun.com/docs/books/tutorial/jdbc/index.html
The Java Tutorial's JDBC track.

industry.java.sun.com/products/jdbc/drivers
Sun Microsystems search engine for locating JDBC drivers.

www.sql.org
This SQL portal provides links to many resources, including SQL syntax, tips, tutorials, books, magazines, discussion groups, companies with SQL services, SQL consultants and free software.

java.sun.com/j2se/5.0/docs/guide/jdbc/index.html
Sun Microsystems JDBC API documentation.

java.sun.com/products/jdbc/faq.html
Sun Microsystems FAQs on JDBC.

www.jguru.com/faq/JDBC
The JGuru JDBC FAQs.

www.mysql.com
This site is the MySQL database home page. You can download the latest versions of MySQL and MySQL Connector/J and access their online documentation.

www.mysql.com/products/mysql
Introduction to the MySQL database server and links to its documentation and download sites.

dev.mysql.com/doc/mysql/en/index.html
MySQL reference manual.

dev.mysql.com/doc/connector/j/en/index.html
MySQL Connector/J documentation, including the installation instructions and examples.

java.sun.com/j2se/5.0/docs/guide/jdbc/getstart/rowsetImpl.html
Overviews the RowSet interface and its subinterfaces. This site also discusses the reference implementations of these interfaces from Sun and their usage.

developer.java.sun.com/developer/Books/JDBCTutorial/chapter5.html
Chapter 5 (RowSet Tutorial) of the book *The JDBC 2.0 API Tutorial and Reference, Second Edition*.

Recommended Readings

Ashmore, D. C. "Best Practices for JDBC Programming." *Java Developers Journal*, 5: no. 4 (2000): 42–54.

Blaha, M. R., W. J. Premerlani and J. E. Rumbaugh. "Relational Database Design Using an Object-Oriented Methodology." *Communications of the ACM*, 31: no. 4 (1988): 414–427.

Brunner, R. J. "The Evolution of Connecting." *Java Developers Journal*, 5: no. 10 (2000): 24–26.

Brunner, R. J. "After the Connection." *Java Developers Journal*, 5: no. 11 (2000): 42–46.

Callahan, T. "So You Want a Stand-Alone Database for Java." *Java Developers Journal*, 3: no. 12 (1998): 28–36.

Codd, E. F. "A Relational Model of Data for Large Shared Data Banks." *Communications of the ACM*, June 1970.

Codd, E. F. "Further Normalization of the Data Base Relational Model." *Courant Computer Science Symposia*, Vol. 6, *Data Base Systems*. Upper Saddle River, NJ: Prentice Hall, 1972.

Codd, E. F. "Fatal Flaws in SQL." *Datamation*, 34: no. 16 (1988): 45–48.

Cooper, J. W. "Making Databases Easier for Your Users." *Java Pro*, 4: no. 10 (2000): 47–54.

Date, C. J. *An Introduction to Database Systems, 8/e*. Reading, MA: Pearson Education, 2003.

Deitel, H. M., P. J. Deitel, and D. R. Choffnes. *Operating Systems, Third Edition*. Upper Saddle River, NJ: Prentice Hall, 2004.

Duguay, C. "Electronic Mail Merge." *Java Pro*, Winter 1999/2000, 22–32.

Ergul, S. "Transaction Processing with Java." *Java Report*, January 2001, 30–36.

Fisher, M. "JDBC Database Access," (a trail in *The Java Tutorial*), `<java.sun.com/docs/books/tutorial/jdbc/index.html>`.

Harrison, G., "Browsing the JDBC API." *Java Developers Journal*, 3: no. 2 (1998): 44–52.

Jasnowski, M. "Persistence Frameworks." *Java Developers Journal*, 5: no. 11 (2000): 82–86.

"JDBC API Documentation." `<java.sun.com/j2se/5.0/docs/guide/jdbc/index.html>`.

Jordan, D. "An Overview of Sun's Java Data Objects Specification." *Java Pro*, 4: no. 6 (2000): 102–108.

Khanna, P. "Managing Object Persistence with JDBC." *Java Pro*, 4: no. 5 (2000): 28–33.

Reese, G. *Database Programming with JDBC and Java, Second Edition*. Cambridge, MA: O'Reilly, 2001.

Spell, B. "Create Enterprise Applications with JDBC 2.0." *Java Pro*, 4: no. 4 (2000): 40–44.

Stonebraker, M. "Operating System Support for Database Management." *Communications of the ACM*, 24: no. 7 (1981): 412–418.

Taylor, A. *JDBC Developer's Resource: Database Programming on the Internet*. Upper Saddle River, NJ: Prentice Hall, 1999.

Thilmany, C. "Applying Patterns to JDBC Development." *Java Developers Journal*, 5: no. 6 (2000): 80–90.

Venugopal, S. 2000. "Cross-Database Portability with JDBC." *Java Developers Journal*, 5: no. 1 (2000): 58–62.

White, S., M. Fisher, R. Cattell, G. Hamilton and M. Hapner. *JDBC API Tutorial and Reference, Second Edition*. Boston, MA: Addison Wesley, 1999.

Winston, A. "A Distributed Database Primer." *UNIX World*, April 1988, 54–63.

Summary

- A database is an integrated collection of data. A database management system (DBMS) provides mechanisms for storing, organizing, retrieving and modifying data for many users.
- Today's most popular database management systems are relational database systems.
- SQL is the international standard language used almost universally with relational database systems to perform queries and manipulate data.
- Programs connect to, and interact with, relational databases via an interface—software that facilitates communications between a database management system and a program.
- Java programmers communicate with databases and manipulate their data using the JDBC API. A JDBC driver enables Java applications to connect to a database in a particular DBMS and allows programmers to retrieve and manipulate database data.
- A relational database stores data in tables. Tables are composed of rows and rows are composed of columns in which values are stored.
- A primary key provides a unique value that cannot be duplicated in other rows of the same table.
- Each column of a table represents a different attribute.
- The primary key can be composed of more than one column.
- SQL provides a rich set of language constructs that enable programmers to define complex queries to retrieve data from a database.
- Every column in a primary key must have a value, and the value of the primary key must be unique. This is known as the Rule of Entity Integrity.

- A one-to-many relationship between tables indicates that a row in one table can have many related rows in a separate table.
- A foreign key is a column in a table that matches the primary key column in another table.
- The foreign key helps maintain the Rule of Referential Integrity: Every foreign key value must appear as another table's primary key value. Foreign keys enable information from multiple tables to be joined together. There is a one-to-many relationship between a primary key and its corresponding foreign key.
- The basic form of a query is

        SELECT * FROM *tableName*

  where the asterisk (*) indicates that all columns from *tableName* should be selected, and *tableName* specifies the table in the database from which rows will be retrieved.
- To retrieve specific columns from a table, replace the asterisk (*) with a comma-separated list of column names.
- Programmers process query results by knowing in advance the order of the columns in the result. Specifying columns explicitly guarantees that they are always returned in the specified order, even if the actual order in the table(s) is different.
- The optional WHERE clause in a query specifies the selection criteria for the query. The basic form of a query with selection criteria is

        SELECT *columnName1*, *columnName2*, … FROM *tableName* WHERE *criteria*

- The WHERE clause can contain operators <, >, <=, >=, =, <> and LIKE. Operator LIKE is used for string pattern matching with wildcard characters percent (%) and underscore (_).
- A percent character (%) in a pattern indicates that a string matching the pattern can have zero or more characters at the percent character's location in the pattern.
- An underscore (_) in the pattern string indicates a single character at that position in the pattern.
- The result of a query can be sorted in ascending or descending order using the optional ORDER BY clause. The simplest form of an ORDER BY clause is

        SELECT *columnName1*, *columnName2*, … FROM *tableName* ORDER BY *column* ASC
        SELECT *columnName1*, *columnName2*, … FROM *tableName* ORDER BY *column* DESC

  where ASC specifies ascending order, DESC specifies descending order and *column* specifies the column on which the sort is based. The default sorting order is ascending, so ASC is optional.
- Multiple columns can be used for ordering purposes with an ORDER BY clause of the form

        ORDER BY *column1* *sortingOrder*, *column2* *sortingOrder*, …

- The WHERE and ORDER BY clauses can be combined in one query. If used, ORDER BY must be the last clause in the query.
- An INNER JOIN merges rows from two tables by matching values in columns that are common to the tables. The basic form for the INNER JOIN operator is:

        SELECT *columnName1, columnName2, …*
        FROM *table1*
        INNER JOIN *table2*
          ON *table1.columnName* = *table2.columnName*

  The ON clause specifies the columns from each table that are compared to determine which rows are joined. If a SQL statement uses columns with the same name from multiple tables, the column names must be fully qualified by prefixing them with their table names and a dot (.).

- An INSERT statement inserts a new row into a table. The basic form of this statement is

  INSERT INTO *tableName* (*columnName1*, *columnName2*, ..., *columnNameN*)
     VALUES (*value1*, *value2*, ..., *valueN*)

  where *tableName* is the table in which to insert the row. The *tableName* is followed by a comma-separated list of column names in parentheses. The list of column names is followed by the SQL keyword VALUES and a comma-separated list of values in parentheses.

- SQL uses single quotes (') as the delimiter for strings. To specify a string containing a single quote in SQL, the single quote must be escaped with another single quote.

- An UPDATE statement modifies data in a table. The basic form of an UPDATE statement is

  UPDATE *tableName*
     SET *columnName1* = *value1*, *columnName2* = *value2*, ..., *columnNameN* = *valueN*
     WHERE *criteria*

  where *tableName* is the table in which to update data. The *tableName* is followed by keyword SET and a comma-separated list of column name/value pairs in the format *columnName* = *value*. The optional WHERE clause *criteria* determines which rows to update.

- A DELETE statement removes rows from a table. The simplest form for a DELETE statement is

  DELETE FROM *tableName* WHERE *criteria*

  where *tableName* is the table from which to delete a row (or rows). The optional WHERE *criteria* determines which rows to delete.

- Package java.sql contains classes and interfaces for accessing relational databases in Java.

- A program must load a JDBC driver class before the program can connect to a database.

- JDBC supports four categories of drivers: JDBC-to-ODBC bridge driver (Type 1), Native-API, partly Java driver (Type 2), Pure Java client to server driver (Type 3) and Pure Java driver (Type 4).

- An object that implements interface Connection manages the connection between a Java program and a database. Connection objects enable programs to create SQL statements that access data.

- Method getConnection of class DriverManager attempts to connect to a database specified by its URL argument. The URL helps the program locate the database. The URL includes the protocol for communication, the subprotocol for communication and the name of the database.

- Connection method createStatement creates an object of type Statement. The program uses the Statement object to submit SQL statements to the database.

- Statement method executeQuery executes a query and returns an object that implements interface ResultSet containing the query result. ResultSet methods enable a program to manipulate query results.

- A ResultSetMetaData object describes a ResultSet's contents. Programs can use metadata programmatically to obtain information about the ResultSet column names and types.

- ResultSetMetaData method getColumnCount retrieves the number of ResultSet columns.

- ResultSet method next positions the ResultSet cursor to the next row in the ResultSet. The cursor points to the current row. Method next returns boolean value true if it is able to position to the next row; otherwise, the method returns false. This method must be called to begin processing a ResultSet.

- When processing ResultSets, it is possible to extract each column of the ResultSet as a specific Java type. ResultSetMetaData method getColumnType returns a constant integer from class Types (package java.sql) indicating the type of the data for a specific column.

- ResultSet *get* methods typically receive as an argument either a column number (as an int) or a column name (as a String) indicating which column's value to obtain.

- `ResultSet` row and column numbers start at 1.
- Each `Statement` object can open only one `ResultSet` object at a time. When a `Statement` returns a new `ResultSet`, the `Statement` closes the prior `ResultSet`.
- `Connection` method `createStatement` has an overloaded version that takes two arguments: the result type and the result concurrency. The result type specifies whether the `ResultSet`'s cursor is able to scroll in both directions or forward only and whether the `ResultSet` is sensitive to changes. The result concurrency specifies whether the `ResultSet` can be updated with `Result-Set`'s update methods.
- Some JDBC drivers do not support scrollable or updatable `ResultSets`.
- `TableModel` method `getColumnClass` returns a `Class` object that represents the superclass of all objects in a particular column. `JTable` uses this information to set up the default cell renderer and cell editor for that column in a `JTable`.
- `ResultSetMetaData` method `getColumnClassName` obtains the fully qualified class name of the specified column.
- `TableModel` method `getColumnCount` returns the number of columns in the model's underlying `ResultSet`.
- `TableModel` method `getColumnName` returns the name of the column in the model's underlying `ResultSet`.
- `ResultSetMetaData` method `getColumnName` obtains the column name from the `ResultSet`.
- `TableModel` method `getRowCount` returns the number of rows in the model's underlying `ResultSet`.
- `TableModel` method `getValueAt` returns the `Object` at a particular row and column of the model's underlying `ResultSet`.
- `ResultSet` method `absolute` positions the `ResultSet` cursor at a specific row.
- `AbstractTableModel` method `fireTableStructureChanged` notifies any `JTable` using a particular `TableModel` object as its model that the data in the model has changed.
- JDBC enables programs to invoke stored procedures using objects that implement interface `CallableStatement`.
- `CallableStatement` can specify input parameters, like `PreparedStatement`. In addition, `CallableStatement` can specify output parameters in which a stored procedure can place return values.
- Interface `RowSet` configures the database connection and executes the query automatically.
- There are two types of `RowSets`—connected and disconnected.
- A connected `RowSet` connects to the database once and remains connected until the application terminates.
- A disconnected `RowSet` connects to the database, executes a query to retrieve the data from the database and then closes the connection.
- `JdbcRowSet`, a connected `RowSet`, acts as a wrapper for a `ResultSet` object, and allows programmers to scroll and update the rows in the `ResultSet`. Unlike a `ResultSet` object, a `JdbcRowSet` object is scrollable and updatable by default.
- `CachedRowSet`, a disconnected `RowSet`, caches the data of a `ResultSet` in memory. Like `Jdbc-RowSet`, a `CachedRowSet` object is scrollable and updatable. A `CachedRowSet` object is also serializable, so it can be passed between Java applications through a network, such as the Internet.

Terminology

% SQL wildcard character	`AbstractTableModel` class
_ SQL wildcard character	`addTableModelListener` method of `TableModel`
absolute method of `ResultSet`	`CachedRowSet` interface

CallableStatement interface
close method of Connection
close method of Statement
com.mysql.jdbc.Driver
column
connect to a database
connected RowSet
Connection interface
createStatement method of Connection
database
DELETE SQL statement
deleteRow method of ResultSet
disconnected RowSet
DriverManager class
execute method of JdbcRowSet
execute method of Statement
executeQuery method of Statement
executeUpdate method of Statement
fireTableStructureChanged method of
     AbstractTableModel
foreign key
getColumnClass method of TableModel
getColumnClassName method of
     ResultSetMetaData
getColumnCount method of ResultSetMetaData
getColumnCount method of TableModel
getColumnName method of ResultSetMetaData
getColumnName method of TableModel
getColumnType method of ResultSetMetaData
getConnection method of DriverManager
getMetaData method of ResultSet
getMoreResults method of Statement
getObject method of ResultSet
getResultSet method of Statement
getRow method of ResultSet
getRowCount method of TableModel
getUpdateCount method of Statement
getValueAt method of TableModel
INNER JOIN SQL operator
INSERT SQL statement
insertRow method of ResultSet
java.sql package
javax.sql package
javax.sql.rowset package
javax.swing.table package
Java Native Interface (JNI)
JDBC
JDBC driver
JdbcRowSet interface
JdbcRowSetImpl class

join
last method of ResultSet
metadata
moveToCurrentRow method of ResultSet
moveToInsertRow method of ResultSet
MySQL Connector/J
MySQL database
native code
next method of ResultSet
ON clause
one-to-many relationship
ORDER BY clause
ordering rows
output parameter
pattern matching
primary key
query a database
relational database
removeTableModelListener method
result
ResultSet interface
ResultSetMetaData interface
row
Rule of Entity Integrity
Rule of Referential Integrity
SELECT SQL keyword
selection criteria
setCommand method of JdbcRowSet
setPassword method of JdbcRowSet
setString method of PreparedStatement
setUsername method of JdbcRowSet
setUrl method of JdbcRowSet
SQL (Structured Query Language)
SQL script
SQLException class
Statement interface
stored procedure
sun.jdbc.odbc.JdbcOdbcDriver
TableModel interface
TableModelEvent class
table
Type 1 (JDBC-to-ODBC bridge) driver
Type 2 (Native-API, partly Java) driver
Type 3 (Pure Java client to server) driver
Type 4 (Pure Java) driver
Types class
updatable ResultSet
UPDATE SQL statement
updateRow method of ResultSet
WHERE clause of a SQL statement

Self-Review Exercises

25.1 Fill in the blanks in each of the following statements:
a) The international standard database language is _____.
b) A table in a database consists of _____ and _____.
c) Statement objects return SQL query results as _____ objects.
d) The _____ uniquely identifies each row in a table.
e) SQL keyword _____ is followed by the selection criteria that specify the rows to select in a query.
f) SQL keywords _____ specify the order in which rows are sorted in a query.
g) Merging rows from multiple database tables is called _____ the tables.
h) A(n) _____ is an organized collection of data.
i) A(n) _____ is a set of columns whose values match the primary key values of another table.
j) A(n) _____ object is used to obtain a Connection to a database.
k) Interface _____ helps manage the connection between a Java program and a database.
l) A(n) _____ object is used to submit a query to a database.
m) Unlike a ResultSet object, _____ and _____ objects are scrollable and updatable by default.
n) _____, a disconnected RowSet, caches the data of a ResultSet in memory.

Answers to Self-Review Exercises

25.1 a) SQL. b) rows, columns. c) ResultSet. d) primary key. e) WHERE. f) ORDER BY. g) joining. h) database. i) foreign key. j) DriverManager. k) Connection. l) Statement. m) JdbcRowSet, CachedRowSet n) CachedRowSet.

Exercises

25.2 Using the techniques shown in this chapter, define a complete query application for the books database. Provide the following predefined queries:
a) Select all authors from the authors table.
b) Select all publishers from the publishers table.
c) Select a specific author and list all books for that author. Include the title, year and ISBN. Order the information alphabetically by the author's last name and first name.
d) Select a specific publisher and list all books published by that publisher. Include the title, year and ISBN. Order the information alphabetically by title.
e) Provide any other queries you feel are appropriate.

Display a JComboBox with appropriate names for each predefined query. Also allow users to supply their own queries.

25.3 Define a complete data manipulation application for the books database. The user should be able to edit existing data and add new data to the database (obeying referential and entity integrity constraints). Allow the user to edit the database in the following ways:
a) Add a new author.
b) Edit the existing information for an author.
c) Add a new title for an author. (Remember that the book must have an entry in the authorISBN table.) Be sure to specify the publisher of the title.
d) Add a new publisher.
e) Edit the existing information for a publisher.
f) Add a new entry in the authorISBN table to link authors with titles.

25.4   In Section 10.7, we introduced an employee-payroll hierarchy to calculate each employee's payroll. In this exercise, we provide a database of employees that corresponds to the employee payroll hierarchy. (A SQL script to create the `employees` database is provided with the examples for this chapter on the CD that accompanies this text and on our Web site, www.deitel.com.) Write an application that allows the user to:

    a) Add employees to the Employee table.

    b) Add payroll information to the appropriate table for each new employee. For example, for a salaried employee add the payroll information to the `salariedEmployees` table.

Figure 25.33 is the entity-relationship diagram for the `employees` database.

25.5   Modify Exercise 25.4 to provide a `JComboBox` and a `JTextArea` to allow the user to perform a query that is either selected from the `JComboBox` or defined in the `JTextArea`. Sample predefined queries are:

    a) Select all employees working in Department SALES.

    b) Select hourly employees working over 30 hours.

    c) Select all commission employees in descending order of the commission rate.

25.6   Modify Exercise 25.5 to perform the following tasks:

    a) Increase base salary by 10% for all base plus commission employees.

    b) If the employee's birthday is in the current month, add a $100 bonus.

    c) For all commission employees with gross sales over $10,000, add a $100 bonus.

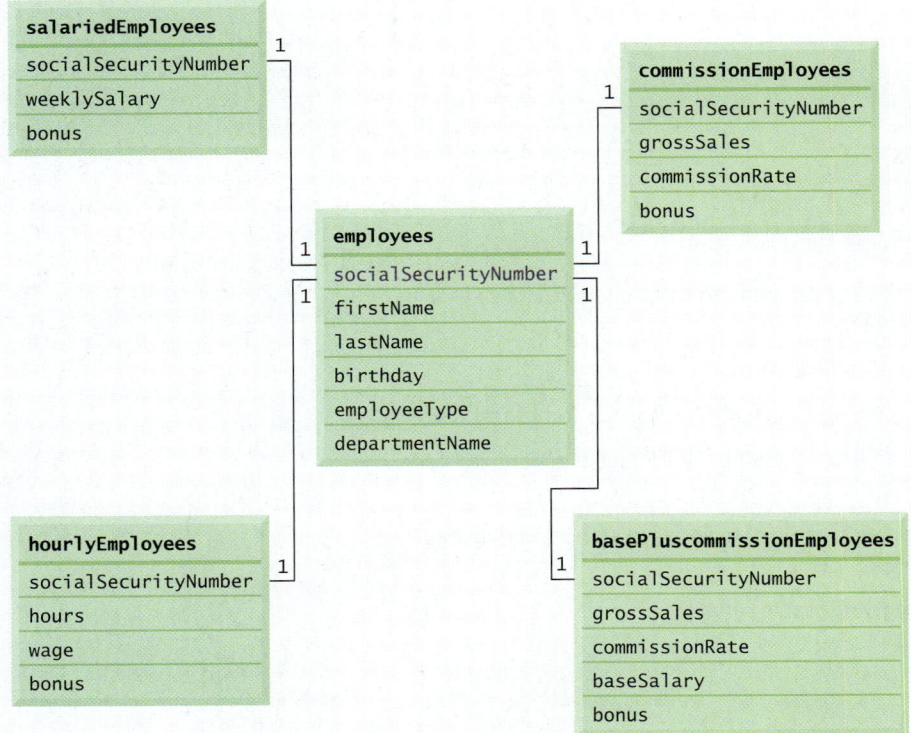

Fig. 25.33 | Table relationships in `employees`.

26

Servlets

OBJECTIVES

In this chapter you will learn:

- How servlets can be used to extend a Web server's functionality.
- The servlet life cycle.
- To execute servlets with the Apache Tomcat server.
- To be able to respond to HTTP requests from an `HttpServlet`.
- To be able to redirect requests to static and dynamic Web resources.
- To use JDBC from a servlet.

26.1 Introduction

Chapter 24 presented Java's fundamental networking capabilities from package `java.net`, which offers both socket- and packet-based communication. Higher-level views of networking are provided by classes and interfaces in the **`java.rmi`** packages (five packages) for **Remote Method Invocation (RMI)** and the **`org.omg`** packages (seven packages) for **Common Object Request Broker Architecture (CORBA)**. The RMI packages allow Java objects running on separate JVMs (normally on separate computers) to communicate via remote method calls. Such calls appear to invoke methods on an object in the same program, but actually have built-in networking (based on the capabilities of package `java.net`) that communicates the method calls to another object on a separate computer. The CORBA packages provide functionality similar to that of the RMI packages. A key difference between RMI and CORBA is that RMI can only be used between Java objects, whereas CORBA can be used between any two applications that understand CORBA—including applications written in other programming languages. [*Note:* **Remote Method Invocation over the Internet Inter-Orb Protocol (RMI-IIOP)** enables the integration of Java with non-Java distributed objects by using CORBA IIOP.] In Chapter 13 of our book *Advanced Java 2 Platform How to Program*, we present Java's RMI capabilities. Chapters 26–27 of *Advanced Java 2 Platform How to Program* discuss the basic CORBA concepts and present a case study that implements a distributed system in CORBA.

Client-Server Relationship

Our discussion in this chapter continues the focus in Chapter 24—the client-server relationship. The client requests that some action be performed and the server performs the action and responds to the client. This request-response model of communication is the foundation for the highest-level views of networking in Java—**servlets** and **JavaServer**

Pages (JSP). A servlet extends the functionality of a server, such as a Web server that serves Web pages to a user's browser using the HTTP protocol. Packages `javax.servlet` and `javax.servlet.http` provide the classes and interfaces to define servlets. Packages `javax.servlet.jsp` and `javax.servlet.jsp.tagext` provide the classes and interfaces that extend the servlet capabilities for JavaServer Pages. Using special syntax, JSP allows Web-page implementors to create pages that encapsulate Java functionality and even to write scriptlets of actual Java code directly in the page.

A common implementation of the request-response model is between Web browsers and Web servers. When a user selects a Web site to browse through the browser (the client application), a request is sent to the appropriate Web server (the server application). The server normally responds to the client by sending the appropriate XHTML Web page. [*Note:* If you are not familiar with XHTML and CSS, refer to the PDF documents Introduction to XHTML: Part 1, Introduction to XHTML: Part 2 and Cascading Style Sheets (CSS) on the CD that accompanies this book. For the purposes of this chapter and Chapter 27, JavaServer Pages (JSP), we assume you already know XHTML.] Servlets are effective for developing Web-based solutions that help provide secure access to a Web site, interact with databases on behalf of a client, dynamically generate custom XHTML documents to be displayed by browsers and maintain unique session information for each client.

This chapter continues our networking discussions by discussing servlets that enhance the functionality of Web servers—the most common form of servlet. Chapter 27, JavaServer Pages (JSP), discusses JSPs, which are translated into servlets. JSPs are a convenient and powerful way to implement the request-response mechanism of the Web without getting into the lower-level details of servlets. Together, servlets and JSPs form the Web components of the Java 2 Enterprise Edition (J2EE) that run on a J2EE server.

Thin Clients

Many developers feel that servlets are the right solution for database-intensive applications that communicate with so-called thin clients—applications that provide presentation but do not process data, thus requiring fewer computing resources. The server is responsible for database access. Clients connect to the server using standard protocols available on most client platforms. Thus, the presentation-logic code for generating dynamic content can be written once and reside on the server for access by clients, to allow programmers to create efficient thin clients.

In this chapter, our servlet examples demonstrate the Web's request-response mechanism (primarily with get and post requests), redirecting requests to other resources and interacting with databases through JDBC. We placed this chapter after our discussion of JDBC and databases intentionally, so that we can build multitier, client-server applications that access databases.

Apache Jakarta Project and the Tomcat Server

Sun Microsystems, through the Java Community Process, is responsible for the development of the servlet and JavaServer Pages specifications. The reference implementation of both these standards is developed by the Apache Software Foundation (www.apache.org) as part of the Jakarta Project (jakarta.apache.org). As stated on the Jakarta Project's home page, "The goal of the Jakarta Project is to provide commercial-quality server solutions based on the Java Platform that are developed in an open and cooperative fashion."

There are many subprojects under the Jakarta project to help commercial server-side developers. The servlet and JSP part of the Jakarta Project is called Tomcat. This is the official reference implementation of the JSP and servlet standards. We use Tomcat to demonstrate the servlets in this chapter. The most recent implementation of Tomcat at the time of this writing was version 5.0.25. For your convenience, Tomcat 5.0.25 is included on the CD that accompanies this book. However, the most recent version always can be downloaded from the Apache Group's Web site. To execute the servlets in this chapter, you must install Tomcat or an equivalent servlet and JavaServer Pages implementation. We discuss the setup and configuration of Tomcat in Section 26.3 and Section 26.4.1, after we introduce our first example.

In our directions for testing each of the examples in this chapter, we indicate that you should copy files into specific Tomcat directories. All the example files for this chapter are located on the CD that accompanies this book and on our Web site, www.deitel.com. At the end of Section 26.11, we provide a list of Internet specifications (as discussed in the Servlet 2.4 Specification) for technologies related to servlet development. Each is listed with its RFC (Request for Comments) number. An RFC is a document that describes standard protocols, mechanisms and procedures for Internet development. We provide the URL of a Web site that allows you to locate each specification for your review.

26.2 Servlet Overview and Architecture

This section overviews Java servlet technology, discussing at a high level the servlet-related classes, methods and exceptions. The next several sections present examples in which we build multitier client-server systems using servlet and JDBC technology.

The Internet offers many protocols. The HTTP (Hypertext Transfer Protocol) that forms the basis of the World Wide Web uses URLs (Uniform Resource Locators) to locate resources on the Internet. Common URLs represent files or directories and can represent complex tasks such as database lookups and Internet searches. For more information on URL formats, visit www.w3.org/Addressing. For more information on the HTTP protocol, visit www.w3.org/Protocols/HTTP. For information on a variety of World Wide Web topics, visit the World Wide Web Consortium's Web site—www.w3.org.

JavaServer Pages technology, an extension of servlet technology, simplifies the process of creating pages by separating presentation from content. Normally, JSPs are used when most of the content sent to the client is static text and markup, and only a small portion of the content is generated dynamically with Java code. Servlets commonly are used when a small portion of the content sent to the client is static text or markup. In fact, some servlets do not produce content. Rather, they perform a task on behalf of the client, then invoke other servlets or JSPs to provide a response. Note that in most cases servlet and JSP technologies are interchangeable. The server that executes a servlet is referred to as the servlet container or servlet engine.

Servlets and JavaServer Pages have become so popular that they are now supported directly or with third-party plug-ins by most major Web servers and application servers—servers that execute applications to generate dynamic Web pages in response to requests. Several popular Web servers and application servers include the Sun Java System Application Server (wwws.sun.com/software/products/appsrvr/home_appsrvr.html), Microsoft's Internet Information Services (IIS) (www.microsoft.com/iis), the Apache HTTP Server (httpd.apache.org/), BEA's WebLogic application server (www.bea.com/products/ weblogic/server/index.shtml), IBM's WebSphere application server (www-3.ibm.com/ software/webservers/appserv/) and the World Wide Web Consortium's Jigsaw Web server (www.w3.org/Jigsaw/).

The servlets in this chapter demonstrate communication between clients and servers via the HTTP protocol (Fig. 26.1). A client sends an HTTP request to the server. The servlet container receives the request and directs it to be processed by the appropriate servlet. The servlet does its processing, which may include interacting with a database or other server-side components, such as other servlets or JSPs. The servlet returns its results to the client—normally in the form of an HTML, XHTML or XML (Extensible Markup Language, which is used to exchange structured data on the Web) document to display in a browser. Other data formats, such as images and binary data, can also be returned.

26.2.1 Interface `Servlet` and the Servlet Life Cycle

Architecturally, all servlets must implement the **`Servlet`** interface of package `javax.serv-let`. The methods of interface `Servlet` are invoked by the servlet container. This interface declares five methods described in Fig. 26.2. You can view the details of the `Servlet` interface online at `java.sun.com/j2ee/1.4/docs/api/javax/servlet/Servlet.html`.

Software Engineering Observation 26.1

Servlets implement the `Servlet` interface of package `javax.servlet`.

A servlet's life cycle begins when the servlet container loads it into memory—normally, in response to the first request for the servlet. Before the servlet can handle that request, the container invokes the servlet's **`init`** method. After `init` completes execution, the servlet can respond to its first request. All requests are handled by a servlet's **`service`** method, which receives the request, processes it and sends a response to the client. During a servlet's life cycle, method `service` is called once per request. Each new request is typically handled in a separate thread of execution (managed by the servlet container) in which method `service` executes. When the servlet container terminates the servlet (e.g., when

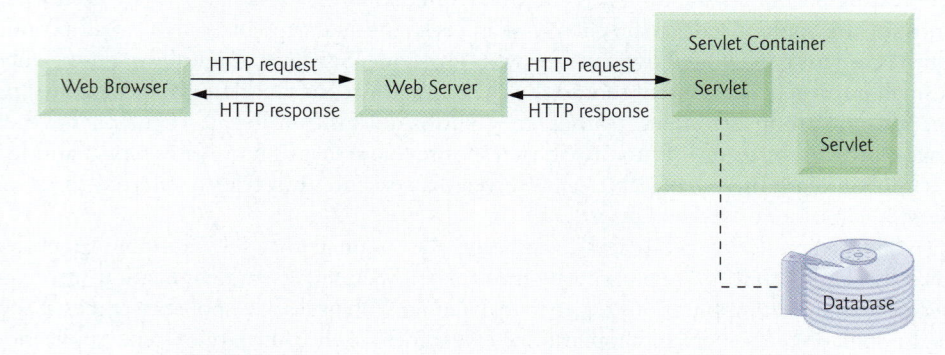

Fig. 26.1 | Servlet architecture.

Method	Description
`void init( ServletConfig config )`	
	The servlet container calls this method once during a servlet's execution cycle to initialize the servlet. The `ServletConfig` argument is supplied by the servlet container that executes the servlet.
`ServletConfig getServletConfig()`	
	This method returns a reference to an object that implements interface `ServletConfig`. This object provides access to the servlet's configuration information, such as its initialization parameters and `ServletContext`, which provides the servlet with access to its environment (i.e., the servlet container in which the servlet executes).
`String getServletInfo()`	
	This method is defined by a servlet programmer to return a string containing servlet information, such as the servlet's author and version.
`void service( ServletRequest request, ServletResponse response )`	
	The servlet container calls this method to respond to a client request to the servlet.
`void destroy()`	
	This "cleanup" method is called when a servlet is terminated by its servlet container. Resources used by the servlet, such as open files or open database connections, should be deallocated here.

Fig. 26.2 | `Servlet` interface methods.

the servlet container needs more memory or when it is shut down), the servlet's `destroy` method is called to release servlet resources.

The servlet packages define two `abstract` classes that implement interface `Servlet`—class **GenericServlet** (from the package `javax.servlet`) and class **HttpServlet** (from the package `javax.servlet.http`). These classes provide default implementations of some `Servlet` methods. Most servlets extend either `GenericServlet` or `HttpServlet` and override some or all of their methods. The `GenericServlet` is a protocol-independent servlet, while the `HTTPServlet` uses the HTTP protocol to exchange the information between the server and the client. `HTTPServlet` is used on the Web. If your servlets need to implement protocols other than HTTP, they may extend `GenericServlet`. To extend `GenericServlet`, the servlet must override the `abstract` method `service`. To extend `HttpServlet`, the servlet must override at least one method declared in class `HttpServlet`.

The examples in this chapter all extend class `HttpServlet`, which defines enhanced processing capabilities for servlets that extend a Web server's functionality. The key method in every servlet is `service`, which accepts both a **ServletRequest** object and a **ServletResponse** object. These objects provide access to input and output streams that allow the servlet to read data from and send data to the client. These streams can be either byte based or character based. If problems occur during the execution of a servlet, either `ServletExceptions` or `IOExceptions` are thrown to indicate the problem.

26.2.2 HttpServlet Class

Servlets typically extend class HttpServlet, which overrides method service to distinguish between the typical requests received from a client Web browser. The two most common **HTTP request types** (also known as **request methods**) are **get** and **post**. A get request gets (or retrieves) information from a server. Such requests often retrieve an HTML document or an image. A post request posts (or sends) data to a server, such as authentication information or data from a form that gathers user input. Usually, post requests are used to post a message to a news group or a discussion forum, pass user input to a data-handling process and store or update the data on a server.

Class HttpServlet defines methods **doGet** and **doPost** to respond to get and post requests from a client, respectively. These methods are called by method service, which is called by the servlet container when a request arrives at the server. Method service first determines the request type, then calls the appropriate method for handling such a request. Methods of class HttpServlet that respond to the other request types are shown in Fig. 26.3. For more details about these methods, visit java.sun.com/j2ee/1.4/docs/api/javax/servlet/http/HttpServlet.html. Each method accepts parameters of type HttpServletRequest and HttpServletResponse and returns void. These methods are not frequently used.

Method	Description
doDelete	Called in response to an HTTP **delete** request. Such a request is normally used to delete a file from a server. This may not be available on some servers because of its inherent security risks (e.g., the client could delete a file that is critical to the execution of the server or an application).
doHead	Called in response to an HTTP **head** request. Such a request is normally used when the client wants only the response's headers, such as its content type and content length. By overriding this method, the servlet does not compute the response body, thus improving performance.
doOptions	Called in response to an HTTP **options** request. This returns information to the client indicating the HTTP options supported by the server, such as the HTTP version (1.0 or 1.1) and the request methods the server supports.
doPut	Called in response to an HTTP **put** request. Such a request is normally used to store a file on the server. This may not be available on some servers because of its inherent security risks (e.g., the client could place an executable application on the server, which, if executed, could damage the server—perhaps by deleting critical files or occupying resources).
doTrace	Called in response to an HTTP **trace** request. Such a request is normally used for debugging. The implementation of this method automatically returns an HTML document to the client containing the request header information (data sent by the browser as part of the request).

Fig. 26.3 | HttpServlet class's other methods.

> ### Software Engineering Observation 26.2
>
> *Do not override method* `service` *in an* `HttpServlet` *subclass. Doing so prevents the servlet from distinguishing between request types.*

Methods `doGet` and `doPost` accept as arguments an `HttpServletRequest` object and an `HttpServletResponse` object that enable interaction between the client and the server. The methods of `HttpServletRequest` allow access to the data supplied as part of the request. The `HttpServletResponse` methods make it easy to return the servlet's results to the Web client. Interfaces `HttpServletRequest` and `HttpServletResponse` are discussed in the next two sections.

26.2.3 HttpServletRequest Interface

Every call to `doGet` or `doPost` for an `HttpServlet` receives an object that implements interface `HttpServletRequest`. The servlet container creates an `HttpServletRequest` object and passes it to the servlet's `service` method (which, in turn, passes it to `doGet` or `doPost`). This object contains the client's request and provides methods that enable the servlet to process the request. Some methods are from interface **ServletRequest**—the interface that `HttpServletRequest` extends. A few key methods used in this chapter are presented in Fig. 26.4. You can view a complete list of `HttpServletRequest` methods online at java.sun.com/j2ee/1.4/docs/api/javax/servlet/http/HttpServletRequest.html. You can also install Tomcat (discussed in Section 26.3) and view the documentation on your local computer.

26.2.4 HttpServletResponse Interface

Every call to `doGet` or `doPost` for an `HttpServlet` receives an object that implements interface `HttpServletResponse`. The servlet container creates an `HttpServletResponse` object and passes it to the servlet's `service` method (which, in turn, passes it to `doGet` or `doPost`). This object provides methods that enable the servlet to formulate the response to the client. Some of these are from interface *ServletResponse*—the interface that `HttpServletResponse` extends. A few key methods used in this chapter are presented in Fig. 26.5. You can view a complete list of `HttpServletResponse` methods online at java.sun.com/j2ee/1.4/docs/api/javax/servlet/http/HttpServletResponse.html. You can also view the documentation on your local computer through Tomcat.

26.3 Setting Up the Apache Tomcat Server

Tomcat is a fully functional implementation of servlets and JavaServer Pages (JSP). It includes a Web server, so it can be used as a standalone test container for servlets and JSPs. Tomcat can also be specified as the handler for JSP and servlet requests received by popular Web servers such as the Apache Software Foundation's Apache HTTP server or Microsoft's Internet Information Services (IIS). Tomcat is also integrated into the Java 2 Enterprise Edition reference implementation from Sun Microsystems.

The most recent release of Tomcat at the time of printing (version 5.0.25) can be downloaded from

```
apache.towardex.com/jakarta/tomcat-5/v5.0.25/bin/
```

Method	Description
`String getParameter( String name )`	
	Obtains the value of a parameter sent to the servlet as part of a `get` or `post` request. The `name` argument represents the parameter name.
`Enumeration getParameterNames()`	
	Returns the names of all the parameters sent to the servlet as part of a `post` request.
`String[] getParameterValues( String name )`	
	For a parameter with multiple values, this method returns an array of strings containing the values for a specified servlet parameter.
`Cookie[] getCookies()`	
	Returns an array of `Cookie` objects stored on the client by the server. `Cookie` objects can be used to uniquely identify clients to the servlet.
`HttpSession getSession( boolean create )`	
	Returns an `HttpSession` object associated with the client's current browsing session. This method can create an `HttpSession` object (`true` argument) if one does not already exist for the client. `HttpSession` objects and `Cookies` are used in similar ways for uniquely identifying clients.
`String getLocalName()`	
	Gets the host name on which the request was received.
`String getLocalAddr()`	
	Gets the Internet Protocol (IP) address on which the request was received.
`int getLocalPort()`	
	Gets the Internet Protocol (IP) port number on which the request was received.

Fig. 26.4 | `HttpServletRequest` methods.

where there are several archive files. The complete Tomcat implementation is contained in the files that begin with the name `jakarta-tomcat-5.0.25`. Apache provides zip, `exe`, tar and compressed `tar` files.

Following the steps below to install Tomcat:

1. Download `jakarta-tomcat-5.0.25.zip` (or the version appropriate for your system) to your hard disk.

2. Use a file extractor tool (such as WinZip, available at `www.winzip.com`) to extract the content of `jakarta-tomcat-5.0.25.zip` to the `C:\` drive. This will create a directory named `jakarta-tomcat-5.0.25`.

For Tomcat to work correctly, you must define environment variables JAVA_HOME and CATALINA_HOME. JAVA_HOME should point to the directory containing your Java installation

Method	Description
`void addCookie( Cookie cookie )`	
	Used to add a `Cookie` to the header of the response to the client. The `Cookie`'s maximum age and whether `Cookies` are enabled on the client determine whether `Cookies` are stored on the client.
`ServletOutputStream getOutputStream()`	
	Obtains a byte-based output stream for sending binary data to the client.
`PrintWriter getWriter()`	
	Obtains a character-based output stream for sending text data (usually HTML formatted text) to the client.
`void setContentType( String type )`	
	Specifies the content type of the response to the browser. The content type helps the browser determine how to display the data (or possibly what other application to execute to process the data). The content type is also known as MIME (Multipurpose Internet Mail Extension) type of the data. For examples, content type `"text/html"` indicates that the response is an HTML document, so the browser displays the HTML page; content type `"image/gif"` indicates that the response is an image, so the browser displays the image. For a complete list of content types, visit `www.isi.edu/in-notes/iana/assignments/media-types/media-types`.
`String getContentType()`	
	Gets the content type of the response.

Fig. 26.5 | `HttpServletResponse` methods.

(ours is `C:\Program Files\Java\jdk1.5.0`), and `CATALINA_HOME` should point to the directory that contains Tomcat (ours is `C:\jakarta-tomcat-5.0.25`). To define these variables on Windows,

1. Right click on the **My Computer** icon on your desktop and select **Properties** from the menu. The **System Properties** dialog appears.

2. Select the **Advanced** tab at the top of the System Properties dialog. Click the **Environment Variables** button to display the **Environment Variables** dialog.

3. Click the **New** button under the **User variables** box. This will cause the **Edit User Variable** dialog to appear.

4. Enter `JAVA_HOME` for **Variable name** and `C:\Program Files\Java\jdk1.5.0` for **Variable value**. Click the **OK** button to complete the setting of the `JAVA_HOME` variable. This will return to the **Environment Variables** dialog.

5. Click the **New** button under the **User variables** box. This will cause the **Edit User Variable** dialog to appear.

6. Enter CATALINA_HOME for **Variable name** and C:\jakarta-tomcat-5.0.25 for **Variable value**. Click the **OK** button to complete the setting of the CATALINA_HOME variable. This will return to the **Environment Variables** dialog.

7. Click the **OK** buttons to close the **Environment Variables** and **System Properties** dialogs.

Error-Prevention Tip 26.1

On some platforms you may need to restart your computer for the new environment variables to take effect.

After setting the environment variables, you can start the Tomcat server. In a command prompt (or shell), change to the bin directory in jakarta-tomcat-5.0.25. In this directory are the files **startup.bat**, **shutdown.bat**, **startup.sh** and **shutdown.sh**, for starting and stopping the Tomcat server on Windows and UNIX/Linux/Mac OS X, respectively. To start the server, type

```
startup
```

This launches the Tomcat server, which executes on TCP port 8080 to prevent conflicts with standard Web servers that typically execute on TCP port 80. [*Note:* If port 8080 is already in use by another application, you can change the port number for Tomcat by modifying the file server.xml, which is located in the Tomcat installation directory's conf directory. To do so, edit line 92 of server.xml (which contains the text <Connector port="8080") and replace "8080" with the port number you want to use.] To verify that Tomcat is executing and can respond to requests, open your Web browser and enter the URL

```
http://localhost:8080/
```

[*Note*: If you changed the port number, use the new port number you specified.] This should display the Tomcat documentation home page (Fig. 26.6). The host localhost indicates to the Web browser that it should request the home page from the Tomcat server on the local computer.

Error-Prevention Tip 26.2

If the host name localhost does not work on your computer, substitute the IP address 127.0.0.1 instead.

To shut down the Tomcat server, issue the command

```
shutdown
```

from the command prompt (or shell) that starts the Tomcat server.

26.4 Handling HTTP get Requests

The primary purpose of an HTTP get request is to retrieve the content of a specified URL—normally an HTML or XHTML document. The servlet in Fig. 26.7 and the XHTML document in Fig. 26.8 demonstrate a servlet that handles HTTP get requests. When the user clicks the **Get HTML Document** button (Fig. 26.8), a get request is sent to the servlet WelcomeServlet (Fig. 26.7). The servlet responds to the request by dynamically generating

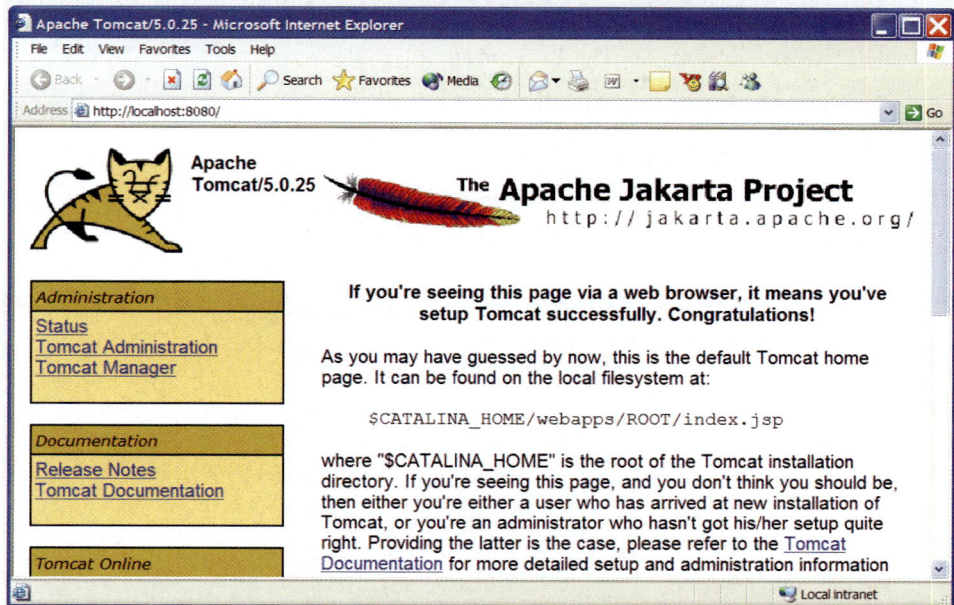

Fig. 26.6 | Tomcat documentation home page. Copyright © 2000-2004 The Apache Software Foundation (`http://www.apache.org/`). All rights reserved.

an XHTML document for the client that displays "Welcome to Servlets!". Figure 26.7 shows the WelcomeServlet source code. Figure 26.8 shows the XHTML document the client loads to access the servlet and shows screen captures of the client's browser window before and after the servlet interaction. [*Note:* Section 26.3 discusses how to set up and configure Tomcat to execute this example.]

Lines 3–6 import various classes in the javax.servlet and javax.servlet.http packages. We use several data types from these packages in the example. Package javax.servlet.http provides superclass HttpServlet for servlets that handle HTTP get requests and HTTP post requests. This class implements interface javax.servlet.Servlet and adds methods that support HTTP protocol requests. Class WelcomeServlet extends HttpServlet (line 10) for this reason.

Superclass HttpServlet provides method doGet to respond to get requests. Its default functionality is to indicate a "Method not supported" error. Typically, this error is indicated in Internet Explorer and in Netscape with a Web page that states "HTTP status 405." Lines 13–44 override method doGet to provide custom get request processing. Method doGet accepts two arguments—an HttpServletRequest object and an HttpServletResponse object (both from package javax.servlet.http). The HttpServletRequest object represents the client's request, and the HttpServletResponse object represents the server's response to the client. If method doGet is unable to handle a client's request, it throws an exception of type **javax.servlet.ServletException**. If doGet encounters an error during stream processing (reading from the client or writing to the client), it throws a java.io.IOException.

```
1    // Fig. 26.7: WelcomeServlet.java
2    // A simple servlet to process get requests.
3    import javax.servlet.ServletException;
4    import javax.servlet.http.HttpServlet;
5    import javax.servlet.http.HttpServletRequest;
6    import javax.servlet.http.HttpServletResponse;
7    import java.io.IOException;
8    import java.io.PrintWriter;
9
10   public class WelcomeServlet extends HttpServlet
11   {
12      // process "get" requests from clients
13      protected void doGet( HttpServletRequest request,
14         HttpServletResponse response )
15            throws ServletException, IOException
16      {
17         response.setContentType( "text/html" );
18         PrintWriter out = response.getWriter();
19
20         // send XHTML page to client
21
22         // start XHTML document
23         out.println( "<?xml version = \"1.0\"?>" );
24
25         out.printf( "%s%s%s", "<!DOCTYPE html PUBLIC",
26            " \"-//W3C//DTD XHTML 1.0 Strict//EN\"",
27            " \"http://www.w3.org/TR/xhtml1/DTD/xhtml1-strict.dtd\">\n" );
28
29         out.println( "<html xmlns = \"http://www.w3.org/1999/xhtml\">" );
30
31         // head section of document
32         out.println( "<head>" );
33         out.println( "<title>A Simple Servlet Example</title>" );
34         out.println( "</head>" );
35
36         // body section of document
37         out.println( "<body>" );
38         out.println( "<h1>Welcome to Servlets!</h1>" );
39         out.println( "</body>" );
40
41         // end XHTML document
42         out.println( "</html>" );
43         out.close();  // close stream to complete the page
44      } // end method doGet
45   } // end class WelcomeServlet
```

Fig. 26.7 | WelcomeServlet that responds to a simple HTTP get request.

To demonstrate a response to a get request, our servlet creates an XHTML document containing the text "Welcome to Servlets!" The text of the XHTML document is the response to the client. The response is sent to the client through the PrintWriter object obtained from the HttpServletResponse object.

Line 17 uses the response object's setContentType method to specify the content type of the data to be sent as the response to the client. This enables the client browser to understand and handle the content. The content type is also known as the MIME (Multipurpose Internet Mail Extension) type of the data. In this example, the content type is text/html to indicate to the browser that the response is an XHTML document. The browser knows that it must read the XHTML tags, format the document accordingly and display it in the browser window.

Line 18 uses the response object's getWriter method to obtain a reference to the PrintWriter object that enables the servlet to send content to the client. [*Note:* If the response is binary data, such as an image, method getOutputStream is used to obtain a reference to a ServletOutputStream object.]

Lines 23–42 create the XHTML document by writing strings with the out object's println method. This method outputs a newline character after its String argument. When rendering the Web page, the browser does not use the newline character. Rather, the newline character appears in the XHTML source that you can see by selecting **Source** from the **View** menu in Internet Explorer or **Page Source** from the **View** menu in Netscape. Line 43 closes the output stream, flushes the output buffer and sends the information to the client.

The XHTML document in Fig. 26.8 provides a form that invokes the servlet defined in Fig. 26.7. The form's action attribute (/jhtp6/welcome1) specifies the URL path that invokes the servlet, and the form's method attribute indicates that the browser sends a get request to the server, which results in a call to the servlet's doGet method. The URL specified as the action in this example is discussed in detail in Section 26.4.1 after we show how to set up and configure the Apache Tomcat server to execute the servlet in Fig. 26.7.

Note that the sample screen captures show a URL containing the server name localhost—a well-known server host name on most computers that support TCP/IP-based networking protocols such as HTTP. We often use localhost to demonstrate networking programs on the local computer, so that readers without a network connection can still learn network programming concepts. In this example, localhost indicates that the server on which the servlet is installed is running on the local machine. The server host name is followed by :8080, specifying the TCP port number at which the Tomcat server listens for requests from clients. Web browsers assume TCP port 80 by default as the server port at which clients make requests, but the Tomcat server listens for client requests at TCP port 8080. This allows Tomcat to execute on the same computer as a standard Web server application without affecting the Web server's ability to handle requests. If we do not explicitly specify the port number in the URL, the servlet will not receive our request and an error message will be displayed in the browser.

Software Engineering Observation 26.3

The Tomcat documentation specifies how to integrate Tomcat with popular Web server applications such as the Apache HTTP Server and Microsoft's IIS.

Ports in this case are not physical hardware ports to which you attach cables—they are logical locations named with integer values that allow clients to request different services on the same server. The port number specifies the logical location where a server waits for and receives connections from clients—this is also called the handshake point. A client connecting to a server to request a service must specify the port number for that service; otherwise, the request cannot be processed. Port numbers are positive integers with values up to 65,535, and there are separate sets of these numbers for both the TCP and UDP

```
 1   <?xml version = "1.0"?>
 2   <!DOCTYPE html PUBLIC "-//W3C//DTD XHTML 1.0 Strict//EN"
 3      "http://www.w3.org/TR/xhtml1/DTD/xhtml1-strict.dtd">
 4
 5   <!-- Fig. 26.7: WelcomeServlet.html -->
 6
 7   <html xmlns = "http://www.w3.org/1999/xhtml">
 8   <head>
 9      <title>Handling an HTTP Get Request</title>
10   </head>
11
12   <body>
13      <form action = "/jhtp6/welcome1" method = "get">
14         <p><label>Click the button to invoke the servlet
15            <input type = "submit" value = "Get HTML Document" />
16         </label></p>
17      </form>
18   </body>
19   </html>
```

Fig. 26.8 | HTML document in which the form's `action` invokes `WelcomeServlet` through the alias `welcome1` specified in `web.xml`.

protocols. Many operating systems reserve port numbers below 1024 for system services (such as e-mail and World Wide Web servers). Generally, these ports should not be specified as connection ports in your own server programs. In fact, some operating systems require special access privileges to use port numbers below 1024.

With so many ports from which to choose, how does a client know which port to use when requesting a service? The term well-known port number is often used when describing popular services on the Internet, such as Web servers and e-mail servers. All Web browsers know 80 as the well-known port on a Web server where requests for HTML documents are made. So when you type a URL into a Web browser, the browser by default connects to port 80 on the server. Because, the Tomcat server uses port 8080 as its port number, requests to Tomcat for Web pages or to invoke servlets and JavaServer Pages must specify that the Tomcat server listens on port 8080.

The client can access the servlet only if it is installed on a server that can respond to servlet requests. In some cases, servlet support is built directly into the Web server, and no special configuration is required to handle servlet requests. In other cases, it is necessary to integrate a servlet container with a Web server (as can be done with Tomcat and the Apache or IIS Web servers). Web servers that support servlets normally have an installation procedure for servlets. If you intend to execute your servlet as part of a Web server, please refer to your server's documentation on how to install a servlet. For our examples, we demonstrate servlets with the Apache Tomcat server. Section 26.3 discusses the setup and configuration of Tomcat for use with this chapter. Section 26.4.1 discusses the deployment of the servlet in Fig. 26.7.

26.4.1 Deploying a Web Application

JSPs, servlets and their supporting files are deployed as part of Web applications. Normally, Web applications are deployed in the webapps subdirectory of jakarta-tomcat-5.0.25. A Web application has a well-known directory structure in which all the files that are part of the application reside. This structure can be created by the server administrator in the webapps directory, or the entire directory structure can be archived in a Web application archive file. Such an archive is known as a WAR file and ends with the .war file extension. Such files are typically placed in the webapps directory. When the Tomcat server begins execution, it extracts the WAR file's contents into the appropriate webapps subdirectory structure. For simplicity as we teach servlets and JavaServer Pages, we create the already expanded directory structure for all the examples in this chapter.

The Web application directory structure contains a context root—the top-level directory for an entire Web application—and several subdirectories. These are described in Fig. 26.9.

Common Programming Error 26.1

Using "servlet" or "servlets" as a context root may prevent a servlet from working correctly on some servers. x

Configuring the context root for a Web application in Tomcat requires creating a subdirectory in the webapps directory. When Tomcat begins execution, it creates a context root for each subdirectory of webapps, using each subdirectory's name as a context root name. To test the examples in this chapter, create the directory jhtp6 in Tomcat's webapps directory.

After configuring the context root, we must configure our Web application to handle the requests. This configuration occurs in a deployment descriptor, which is stored in a file called web.xml. This specifies various configuration parameters, such as the name used to invoke the servlet (i.e., its alias), a description of the servlet, the servlet's fully qualified class name and a servlet mapping (i.e., the path or paths that cause the servlet container to invoke the servlet). You must create the web.xml file for this example. Many Java Web application deployment tools create the web.xml file for you. The one for the first example in this chapter is shown in Fig. 26.10. We will enhance this file as we add other servlets to the Web application throughout this chapter.

Directory	Description
context root	This is the root directory for the Web application. All the JSPs, HTML documents, servlets and supporting files such as images and class files reside in this directory or its subdirectories. The name of this directory is specified by the Web application creator. To provide structure in a Web application, subdirectories can be placed in the context root. For example, if your application uses many images, you might place an `images` subdirectory in this directory. The examples of this chapter use `jhtp6` as the context root.
WEB-INF	This directory contains the Web application deployment descriptor (`web.xml`).
WEB-INF/classes	This directory contains the servlet class files and other supporting class files used in a Web application. If the classes are part of a package, the complete package directory structure would begin here.
WEB-INF/lib	This directory contains Java archive (JAR) files. The JAR files can contain servlet class files and other supporting class files used in a Web application.

Fig. 26.9 | Web application standard directories.

Element **web-app** (lines 1–37) defines the configuration of each servlet in the Web application and the servlet mapping for each servlet. Element **display-name** (lines 8–11) specifies a name that can be displayed to the administrator of the server on which the Web application is installed. Element **description** (lines 13–16) specifies a description of the Web application that might be displayed to the server administrator.

Element **servlet** (lines 19–29) describes a servlet. Element **servlet-name** (line 20) is the name we chose for the servlet (welcome1). Element description (lines 22–24) specifies a description for this particular servlet. Again, this can be displayed to the server administrator. Element **servlet-class** (lines 26–28) specifies the compiled servlet's fully qualified class name. Thus, the servlet welcome1 is defined by class WelcomeServlet.

Element **servlet-mapping** (lines 32–35) specifies servlet-name and **url-pattern** elements. The URL pattern helps the server determine which requests are sent to the servlet (welcome1). Our Web application will be installed as part of the jhtp6 context root discussed in Section 26.4.1. Thus, the relative URL we supply to the browser to invoke the servlet in this example is

```
/jhtp6/welcome1
```

where /jhtp6 specifies the context root that helps the server determine which Web application handles the request and /welcome1 specifies the URL pattern that is mapped to servlet welcome1 to handle the request. Note that the server on which the servlet resides is not specified here, although this can be done as follows:

```
http://localhost:8080/jhtp6/welcome1
```

```
 1   <web-app xmlns="http://java.sun.com/xml/ns/j2ee"
 2      xmlns:xsi="http://www.w3.org/2001/XMLSchema-instance"
 3      xsi:schemaLocation="http://java.sun.com/xml/ns/j2ee
 4         http://java.sun.com/xml/ns/j2ee/web-app_2_4.xsd"
 5      version="2.4">
 6
 7      <!-- General description of your Web application -->
 8      <display-name>
 9         Java How to Program JSP
10         and Servlet Chapter Examples
11      </display-name>
12
13      <description>
14         This is the Web application in which we
15         demonstrate our JSP and Servlet examples.
16      </description>
17
18      <!-- Servlet definitions -->
19      <servlet>
20         <servlet-name>welcome1</servlet-name>
21
22         <description>
23            A simple servlet that handles an HTTP get request.
24         </description>
25
26         <servlet-class>
27            WelcomeServlet
28         </servlet-class>
29      </servlet>
30
31      <!-- Servlet mappings -->
32      <servlet-mapping>
33         <servlet-name>welcome1</servlet-name>
34         <url-pattern>/welcome1</url-pattern>
35      </servlet-mapping>
36
37   </web-app>
```

Fig. 26.10 | Deployment descriptor (`web.xml`) for the `jhtp6` Web application.

If the explicit server and port number are not specified as part of the URL, the browser assumes that the form handler (i.e., the value of the `action` attribute of the `form` element in HTML) resides at the same server and port number from which the browser downloaded the Web page containing the `form`.

There are several URL pattern formats that can be used. The `/welcome1` URL pattern requires an exact match of the pattern. You can also specify path mappings, extension mappings and a default servlet for a Web application. A path mapping begins with a / and ends with a /*. For example, the URL pattern

```
/jhtp6/example/*
```

indicates that any URL path beginning with /jhtp6/example/ will be sent to the servlet that has the preceding URL pattern. An extension mapping begins with *. and ends with a file-name extension. For example, the URL pattern

```
*.jsp
```

indicates that any request for a file with extension .jsp will be sent to the servlet that handles JSP requests. In fact, servers with JSP containers have an implicit mapping of the .jsp extension to a servlet that handles JSP requests. The URL pattern / represents the default servlet for the Web application. This is similar to the default document of a Web server. For example, if you type the URL www.deitel.com into your Web browser, the document you receive from our Web server is the default document index.html. If the URL pattern matches the default servlet for a Web application, that servlet is invoked to return a default response to the client. This can be useful for personalizing Web content to specific users. To compile your servlet, you will need to use javac's -classpath option to specify the name and location of the file servlet-api.jar, which is located in Tomcat's common\libs directory. Finally, we are ready to place our files into the appropriate directories to complete the deployment of our first servlet for testing. We have three files to place— WelcomeServlet.html, WelcomeServlet.class and web.xml. In your jakarta-tomcat-5.0.25\webapps\jhtp6 directory—the context root for our Web application—create subdirectories named servlets and WEB-INF. We place our HTML files for this servlets chapter in the servlets directory. Copy the WelcomeServlet.html file into the servlets directory. In the WEB-INF directory, create the subdirectory classes, then copy the web.xml file into the WEB-INF directory, and copy the WelcomeServlet.class file into the classes directory. Thus, the directory and file structure under the webapps directory should be as shown in Fig. 26.11 (file names are in italics).After the files are placed in the proper directories, start the Tomcat server, open your browser and type the following URL

```
http://localhost:8080/jhtp6/servlets/WelcomeServlet.html
```

to load WelcomeServlet.html into the Web browser. Then click the **Get HTML Document** button to invoke the servlet. You should see the results shown in Fig. 26.8. You can try this servlet from several different Web browsers to demonstrate that the results are the same across Web browsers.

WelcomeServlet Web application directory and file structure

```
jhtp6
   servlets
      WelcomeServlet.html
   WEB-INF
      web.xml
      classes
         WelcomeServlet.class
```

Fig. 26.11 | Web application directory and file structure for WelcomeServlet.

Common Programming Error 26.2

Not placing a servlet or other class files in the appropriate directory structure prevents the server from locating those classes properly. This results in an error response to the client Web browser.

Actually, the HTML file in Fig. 26.8 was not necessary to invoke this servlet. A get request can be sent to a server simply by typing the URL in a browser—exactly as you do when you request a Web page in the browser. In this example, you can type

```
http://localhost:8080/jhtp6/welcome1
```

in the **Address** or **Location** field of your browser to invoke the servlet directly.

Error-Prevention Tip 26.3

*You can test a servlet that handles HTTP get requests by typing the URL that invokes the servlet directly into your browser's **Address** or **Location** field because get is the default HTTP method when browsing.*

26.5 Handling HTTP get Requests Containing Data

When requesting a document or resource from a Web server, it is possible to supply data as part of the request. The servlet WelcomeServlet2 in Fig. 26.12 responds to an HTTP get request that contains a name supplied by the user. The servlet uses the name as part of the response to the client.

Parameters are passed as name-value pairs in a get request. Line 17 demonstrates how to obtain information that was passed to the servlet as part of the client request. The request object's getParameter method accepts the parameter name as an argument and returns the corresponding String value, or null if the parameter is not part of the request. Note that parameter names are case sensitive and must match exactly. Line 41 uses the result of line 17 as part of the response to the client.

The WelcomeServlet2.html document (Fig. 26.13) provides a form in which the user can input a name in the text input element firstname (line 16) and click the **Submit** button to invoke WelcomeServlet2. When the user presses the **Submit** button, the values of the input elements are placed in name-value pairs as part of the request to the server. In the second screen capture in Fig. 26.13, note that the browser appended

```
?firstname=Jon
```

to the end of the action URL. The ? separates the query string (i.e., the data passed as part of the get request) from the rest of the URL in a get request. The name-value pairs are passed with the name and the value separated by =. If there is more than one name-value pair, each pair is separated by &.

Once again, we use our jhtp6 context root to demonstrate the servlet of Fig. 26.12. Place WelcomeServlet2.html in the servlets directory created in Section 26.4.1. Place WelcomeServlet2.class in the classes subdirectory of WEB-INF in the jhtp6 context root. Remember that classes in a package must be placed in the appropriate package directory structure. Then edit the web.xml deployment descriptor in the WEB-INF directory to include the information specified in Fig. 26.14. This table contains the information for the servlet and servlet-mapping elements that you will add to the web.xml deployment

```
 1   // Fig. 26.12: WelcomeServlet2.java
 2   // Processing HTTP get requests containing data.
 3   import javax.servlet.ServletException;
 4   import javax.servlet.http.HttpServlet;
 5   import javax.servlet.http.HttpServletRequest;
 6   import javax.servlet.http.HttpServletResponse;
 7   import java.io.IOException;
 8   import java.io.PrintWriter;
 9
10   public class WelcomeServlet2 extends HttpServlet
11   {
12      // process "get" request from client
13      protected void doGet( HttpServletRequest request,
14         HttpServletResponse response )
15            throws ServletException, IOException
16      {
17         String firstName = request.getParameter( "firstname" );
18
19         response.setContentType( "text/html" );
20         PrintWriter out = response.getWriter();
21
22         // send XHTML document to client
23
24         // start XHTML document
25         out.println( "<?xml version = \"1.0\"?>" );
26
27         out.printf( "%s%s%s", "<!DOCTYPE html PUBLIC",
28            " \"-//W3C//DTD XHTML 1.0 Strict//EN\"",
29            " \"http://www.w3.org/TR/xhtml1/DTD/xhtml1-strict.dtd\">\n" );
30
31         out.println( "<html xmlns = \"http://www.w3.org/1999/xhtml\">" );
32
33         // head section of document
34         out.println( "<head>" );
35         out.println(
36            "<title>Processing get requests with data</title>" );
37         out.println( "</head>" );
38
39         // body section of document
40         out.println( "<body>" );
41         out.println( "<h1>Hello " + firstName + ",<br />" );
42         out.println( "Welcome to Servlets!</h1>" );
43         out.println( "</body>" );
44
45         // end XHTML document
46         out.println( "</html>" );
47         out.close();   // close stream to complete the page
48      } // end method doGet
49   } // end class WelcomeServlet2
```

Fig. 26.12 | WelcomeServlet2 responds to a get request containing data.

descriptor. You should not type the italic text into the deployment descriptor. Restart Tomcat and type the following URL in your Web browser:

```
 1   <?xml version = "1.0"?>
 2   <!DOCTYPE html PUBLIC "-//W3C//DTD XHTML 1.0 Strict//EN"
 3      "http://www.w3.org/TR/xhtml1/DTD/xhtml1-strict.dtd">
 4
 5   <!-- Fig. 26.13: WelcomeServlet2.html -->
 6
 7   <html xmlns = "http://www.w3.org/1999/xhtml">
 8   <head>
 9      <title>Processing get requests with data</title>
10   </head>
11
12   <body>
13      <form action = "/jhtp6/welcome2" method = "get">
14         <p><label>
15            Type your first name and press the Submit button
16            <br /><input type = "text" name = "firstname" />
17            <input type = "submit" value = "Submit" />
18         </p></label>
19      </form>
20   </body>
21   </html>
```

form data specified in URL's query string as part of a get request

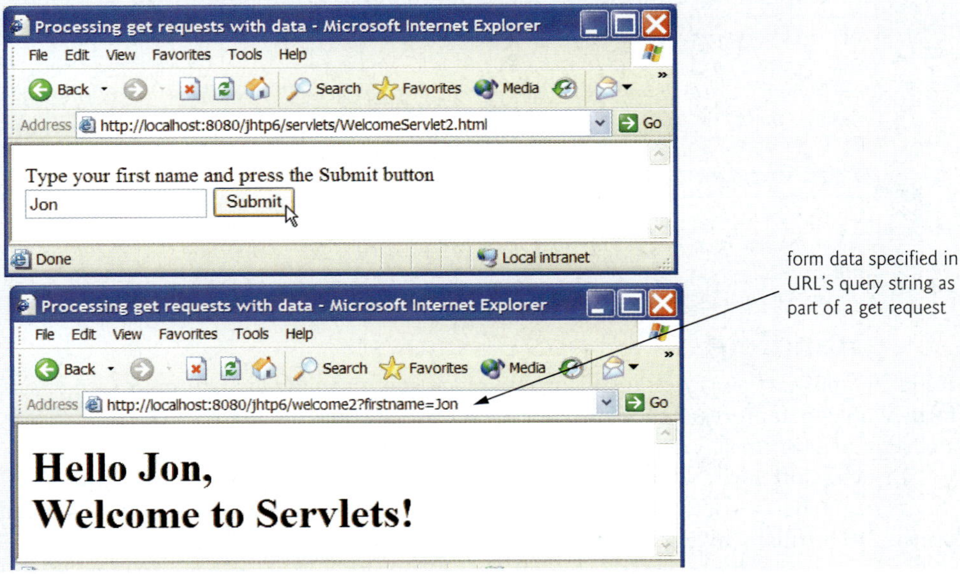

Fig. 26.13 | HTML document in which the form's **action** invokes **WelcomeServlet2** through the alias **welcome2** specified in **web.xml**.

```
http://localhost:8080/jhtp6/servlets/WelcomeServlet2.html
```

Type your name in the text field of the Web page, then click **Submit** to invoke the servlet.

Once again, note that the **get** request could have been typed directly into the browser's **Address** or **Location** field as follows:

```
http://localhost:8080/jhtp6/welcome2?firstname=Jon
```

Descriptor element	Value
servlet element	
servlet-name	welcome2
description	Handling HTTP get requests with data.
servlet-class	WelcomeServlet2
servlet-mapping element	
servlet-name	welcome2
url-pattern	/welcome2

Fig. 26.14 | Deployment descriptor information for servlet WelcomeServlet2.

Error-Prevention Tip 26.4

If an error occurs during the servlet invocation, the log files in the logs directory of the Tomcat installation can help you determine the error and debug the problem.

Software Engineering Observation 26.4

A get request is limited to standard characters, which means that you cannot submit any special characters via a get request. The length of the URL in a get request is limited. For example, the maximum URL length in Internet Explorer is 2,083 characters. Some Web servers might restrict this even more.

Good Programming Practice 26.1

A get request should not be used for sending sensitive data (e.g., a password) because the form data is placed in a query string that is appended to the request URL as plain text and can be intercepted.

26.6 Handling HTTP post Requests

An HTTP post request is frequently used to send data from an HTML form to a server-side form handler that processes the data. For example, when you respond to a Web-based survey, a post request normally supplies the information you type in the form to the Web server.

Browsers often cache (save on disk) Web pages so they can quickly reload them. If there are no changes between the last version stored in the cache and the current version on the Web, this helps speed up your browsing experience. The browser first asks the server whether the document has changed or expired since the date the file was cached. If not, the browser loads the document from the cache. Thus, the browser minimizes the amount of data that must be downloaded for you to view a Web page. Browsers typically do not cache the server's response to a post request, because the next post might not return the same result. For example, in a survey, many users could visit the same Web page and respond to a question. The survey results could then be displayed for the user. Each new response changes the overall results of the survey.

When you use a Web-based search engine, the browser normally supplies the information you specify in an HTML form to the search engine with a get request. The search engine performs the search, then returns the results to you as a Web page. Such pages are often cached by the browser in case you perform the same search again. As with post requests, get requests can supply parameters as part of the request to the Web server.

The WelcomeServlet3 servlet in Fig. 26.15 is identical to the servlet in Fig. 26.12, except that it defines a doPost method (lines 13–48) rather than a doGet method to respond to post requests. The default functionality of doPost is to indicate a "Method not supported" error. We override this method to provide custom post request processing. Method doPost accepts the same two arguments as doGet—an object that implements interface HttpServletRequest to represent the client's request and an object that implements interface HttpServletResponse to represent the servlet's response. As with doGet, method doPost throws a ServletException if it is unable to handle a client's request and throws an IOException if a problem occurs during stream processing.

```java
1   // Fig. 26.15: WelcomeServlet3.java
2   // Processing post requests containing data.
3   import javax.servlet.ServletException;
4   import javax.servlet.http.HttpServlet;
5   import javax.servlet.http.HttpServletRequest;
6   import javax.servlet.http.HttpServletResponse;
7   import java.io.IOException;
8   import java.io.PrintWriter;
9
10  public class WelcomeServlet3 extends HttpServlet
11  {
12     // process "post" request from client
13     protected void doPost( HttpServletRequest request,
14        HttpServletResponse response )
15           throws ServletException, IOException
16     {
17        String firstName = request.getParameter( "firstname" );
18
19        response.setContentType( "text/html" );
20        PrintWriter out = response.getWriter();
21
22        // send XHTML page to client
23
24        // start XHTML document
25        out.println( "<?xml version = \"1.0\"?>" );
26
27        out.printf( "%s%s%s", "<!DOCTYPE html PUBLIC",
28           " \"-//W3C//DTD XHTML 1.0 Strict//EN\"",
29           " \"http://www.w3.org/TR/xhtml1/DTD/xhtml1-strict.dtd\">\n" );
30
31        out.println( "<html xmlns = \"http://www.w3.org/1999/xhtml\">" );
32
33        // head section of document
34        out.println( "<head>" );
35        out.println(
36           "<title>Processing post requests with data</title>" );
37        out.println( "</head>" );
38
```

Fig. 26.15 | WelcomeServlet3 responds to a post request containing data. (Part 1 of 2.)

```
39        // body section of document
40        out.println( "<body>" );
41        out.println( "<h1>Hello " + firstName + ",<br />" );
42        out.println( "Welcome to Servlets!</h1>" );
43        out.println( "</body>" );
44
45        // end XHTML document
46        out.println( "</html>" );
47        out.close(); // close stream to complete the page
48      } // end method doPost
49   } // end class WelcomeServlet3
```

Fig. 26.15 | WelcomeServlet3 responds to a post request containing data. (Part 2 of 2.)

WelcomeServlet3.html (Fig. 26.16) provides a form (lines 13–19) in which the user can input a name in the text input element firstname (line 16), then click the **Submit** button to invoke WelcomeServlet3. When the user presses the **Submit** button, the values of the input elements are sent to the server as part of the request. However, note that the values are not appended to the request URL. The form's method in this example is post, but note that a post request cannot be typed into the browser's **Address** or **Location** field, and users cannot bookmark post requests in their browsers.

We use our jhtp6 context root to demonstrate the servlet in Fig. 26.15. Place WelcomeServlet3.html in the servlets directory created in Section 26.4.1. Place WelcomeServlet3.class in the classes subdirectory of WEB-INF in the jhtp6 context root. Then, using the information specified in Fig. 26.17, edit the web.xml deployment

```
1    <?xml version = "1.0"?>
2    <!DOCTYPE html PUBLIC "-//W3C//DTD XHTML 1.0 Strict//EN"
3        "http://www.w3.org/TR/xhtml1/DTD/xhtml1-strict.dtd">
4
5    <!-- Fig. 26.16: WelcomeServlet3.html -->
6
7    <html xmlns = "http://www.w3.org/1999/xhtml">
8    <head>
9       <title>Handling an HTTP Post Request with Data</title>
10   </head>
11
12   <body>
13      <form action = "/jhtp6/welcome3" method = "post">
14         <p><label>
15            Type your first name and press the Submit button
16            <br /><input type = "text" name = "firstname" />
17            <input type = "submit" value = "Submit" />
18         </label></p>
19      </form>
20   </body>
21   </html>
```

Fig. 26.16 | HTML document in which the form's action invokes WelcomeServlet3 through the alias welcome3 specified in web.xml. (Part 1 of 2.)

Fig. 26.16 | HTML document in which the form's `action` invokes `WelcomeServlet3` through the alias `welcome3` specified in `web.xml`. (Part 2 of 2.)

Descriptor element	Value
servlet element	
servlet-name	welcome3
description	Handling HTTP post requests with data.
servlet-class	WelcomeServlet3
servlet-mapping element	
servlet-name	welcome3
url-pattern	/welcome3

Fig. 26.17 | Deployment descriptor information for servlet `WelcomeServlet3`.

descriptor in the `WEB-INF` directory. Restart Tomcat and type the following URL in your Web browser:

```
http://localhost:8080/jhtp6/servlets/WelcomeServlet3.html
```

Type your name in the text field of the Web page, then click **Submit** to invoke the servlet.

26.7 Redirecting Requests to Other Resources

Sometimes it is useful to redirect a request to a different resource. For example, a servlet could determine the type of the client browser and redirect the request to a Web page that was designed specifically for that browser. This technique is also used to redirect browsers to an error page when handling a request fails. The `RedirectServlet` in Fig. 26.18 receives a page parameter as part of a `get` request, then uses that parameter to redirect the request to a different resource.

Line 17 obtains the `page` parameter from the request. If the value returned is not `null`, the nested `if...else if` statement at lines 21–24 determines whether the value is either

```java
1   // Fig. 26.18: RedirectServlet.java
2   // Redirecting a user to a different Web page.
3   import javax.servlet.ServletException;
4   import javax.servlet.http.HttpServlet;
5   import javax.servlet.http.HttpServletRequest;
6   import javax.servlet.http.HttpServletResponse;
7   import java.io.IOException;
8   import java.io.PrintWriter;
9
10  public class RedirectServlet extends HttpServlet
11  {
12     // process "get" request from client
13     protected void doGet( HttpServletRequest request,
14        HttpServletResponse response )
15           throws ServletException, IOException
16     {
17        String location = request.getParameter( "page" );
18
19        if ( location != null )
20        {
21           if ( location.equals( "deitel" ) )
22              response.sendRedirect( "http://www.deitel.com" );
23           else if ( location.equals( "welcome1" ) )
24              response.sendRedirect( "welcome1" );
25        } // end if
26
27        // code that executes only if this servlet
28        // does not redirect the user to another page
29        response.setContentType( "text/html" );
30        PrintWriter out = response.getWriter();
31
32        // start XHTML document
33        out.println( "<?xml version = \"1.0\"?>" );
34
35        out.printf( "%s%s%s", "<!DOCTYPE html PUBLIC",
36           " \"-//W3C//DTD XHTML 1.0 Strict//EN\"",
37           " \"http://www.w3.org/TR/xhtml1/DTD/xhtml1-strict.dtd\">\n" );
38
39        out.println(
40           "<html xmlns = \"http://www.w3.org/1999/xhtml\">" );
41
42        // head section of document
43        out.println( "<head>" );
44        out.println( "<title>Invalid page</title>" );
45        out.println( "</head>" );
```

Fig. 26.18 | Redirecting requests to other resources. (Part 1 of 2.)

```
46
47          // body section of document
48          out.println( "<body>" );
49          out.println( "<h1>Invalid page requested</h1>" );
50          out.println( "<p><a href = " +
51             "\"servlets/RedirectServlet.html\">" );
52          out.println( "Click here to choose again</a></p>" );
53          out.println( "</body>" );
54
55          // end XHTML document
56          out.println( "</html>" );
57          out.close();  // close stream to complete the page
58       } // end method doGet
59  } // end class RedirectServlet
```

Fig. 26.18 | Redirecting requests to other resources. (Part 2 of 2.)

"deitel" or "welcome1". If the value is "deitel," the response object's **sendRedirect** method (line 22) redirects the request to www.deitel.com. If the value is "welcome1," line 24 redirects the request to the servlet of Fig. 26.7. Note that line 24 does not explicitly specify the jhtp6 context root for our Web application. When a servlet uses a relative path to reference another static or dynamic resource, the servlet assumes the same base URL and context root as the one that invoked the servlet—unless a complete URL is specified for the resource. So line 24 actually is requesting the resource located at

> http://localhost:8080/jhtp6/welcome1

Similarly, line 51 is actually requesting the resource located at

> http://localhost:8080/jhtp6/servlets/RedirectServlet.html

Software Engineering Observation 26.5

Using relative paths to reference resources in the same context root makes your Web application more flexible. For example, you can change the context root without making changes to the static and dynamic resources in the application.

Once method sendRedirect executes, processing of the original request by the RedirectServlet terminates. If method sendRedirect is not called, the remainder of method doGet outputs a Web page indicating that an invalid request was made. The page allows the user to try again by returning to the XHTML document of Fig. 26.19. Note that one of the redirects is sent to a static XHTML Web page and the other is sent to a servlet.

RedirectServlet.html (Fig. 26.19) provides two links (lines 15–16 and 17–18) that allow the user to invoke the servlet RedirectServlet. Each link specifies a page parameter as part of the URL. To demonstrate passing an invalid page, you can type the URL into your browser with no value for the page parameter.

We use our jhtp6 context root to demonstrate the servlet of Fig. 26.18. Place RedirectServlet.html in the servlets directory created in Section 26.4.1. Place RedirectServlet.class in the classes subdirectory of WEB-INF in the jhtp6 context root. Then,

```
 1   <?xml version = "1.0"?>
 2   <!DOCTYPE html PUBLIC "-//W3C//DTD XHTML 1.0 Strict//EN"
 3      "http://www.w3.org/TR/xhtml1/DTD/xhtml1-strict.dtd">
 4
 5   <!-- Fig. 26.19: RedirectServlet.html -->
 6
 7   <html xmlns = "http://www.w3.org/1999/xhtml">
 8   <head>
 9      <title>Redirecting a Request to Another Site</title>
10   </head>
11
12   <body>
13      <p>Click a link to be redirected to the appropriate page</p>
14      <p>
15      <a href = "/jhtp6/redirect?page=deitel">
16         www.deitel.com</a><br />
17      <a href = "/jhtp6/redirect?page=welcome1">
18         Welcome servlet</a>
19      </p>
20   </body>
21   </html>
```

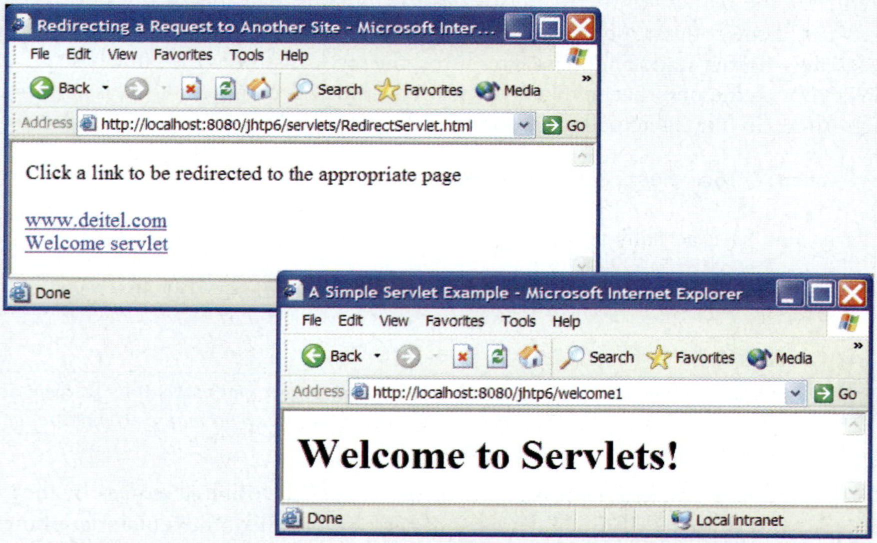

Fig. 26.19 | `RedirectServlet.html` document to demonstrate redirecting requests to other resources.

edit the web.xml deployment descriptor in the WEB-INF directory to include the information specified in Fig. 26.20. Restart Tomcat, and type the following URL in your Web browser:

```
http://localhost:8080/jhtp6/servlets/RedirectServlet.html
```

Click a link in the Web page to invoke the servlet.

Descriptor element	Value
servlet element	
servlet-name	redirect
description	Redirecting to static Web pages and other servlets.
servlet-class	RedirectServlet
servlet-mapping element	
servlet-name	redirect
url-pattern	/redirect

Fig. 26.20 | Deployment descriptor information for servlet RedirectServlet.

When redirecting requests, the request parameters from the original request are passed as parameters to the new request. Additional request parameters can also be passed. For example, the URL passed to sendRedirect could contain name-value pairs. New parameters are added to the existing parameters. A new parameter with the same name as an existing parameter takes precedence over the original value. However, all the values are still passed. In this case, the complete set of values for a given parameter name can be obtained by calling method getParameterValues from interface HttpServletRequest. This method accepts the parameter name as an argument and returns an array of strings containing the parameter values in most-recent-to-least-recent-order.

26.8 Multitier Applications: Using JDBC from a Servlet

Servlets can communicate with databases via JDBC (Chapter 25). Many of today's applications are three-tier distributed applications, consisting of a user interface, business logic and a database. The user interface in such an application is often created using HTML or XHTML (as shown in this chapter). HTML and XHTML are preferred in systems where portability is a concern. Using the networking provided by the browser, the user interface can communicate with the middle-tier business logic. The middle tier can then access the database to manipulate the data. The three tiers can reside on separate computers that are connected to a network.

In multitier architectures, Web servers often are used in the middle tier. Server-side components, such as servlets, execute in an application server alongside the Web server. These components provide the business logic that manipulates data from databases and communicates with client Web browsers. Servlets, through JDBC, can interact with popular database systems. Developers use SQL for queries, and JDBC drivers handle the specifics of interacting with each database system.

The SurveyServlet in Fig. 26.21 and the Survey.html document in Fig. 26.22 implement portions of a three-tier distributed application. The middle tier is Survey-Servlet, which handles requests from the client browser and provides access to the third tier—a MySQL database accessed via JDBC. The servlet in this example allows users to vote for their favorite animals. When the servlet receives a post request from the Web browser, the servlet uses JDBC to update the total number of votes for that animal in the database and returns a dynamically generated XHTML document containing the survey results to the client.

Lines 21 and 22 begin by declaring a Connection to manage the database connection and a Statement for updating the vote count for an animal, totaling all the votes and obtaining the complete survey results.

```java
1   // Fig. 26.21: SurveyServlet.java
2   // A Web-based survey that uses JDBC from a servlet.
3   package com.deitel.jhtp6.servlets;
4
5   import java.io.PrintWriter;
6   import java.io.IOException;
7   import java.sql.Connection;
8   import java.sql.DriverManager;
9   import java.sql.Statement;
10  import java.sql.ResultSet;
11  import java.sql.SQLException;
12  import javax.servlet.ServletConfig;
13  import javax.servlet.ServletException;
14  import javax.servlet.UnavailableException;
15  import javax.servlet.http.HttpServlet;
16  import javax.servlet.http.HttpServletRequest;
17  import javax.servlet.http.HttpServletResponse;
18
19  public class SurveyServlet extends HttpServlet
20  {
21     private Connection connection;
22     private Statement statement;
23
24     // set up database connection and create SQL statement
25     public void init( ServletConfig config ) throws ServletException
26     {
27        // attempt database connection and create Statements
28        try
29        {
30           Class.forName( config.getInitParameter( "databaseDriver" ) );
31           connection = DriverManager.getConnection(
32              config.getInitParameter( "databaseName" ) );
33              config.getInitParameter( "username" ),
34              config.getInitParameter( "password" ) );
35
36           // create Statement to query database
37           statement = connection.createStatement();
38        } // end try
39        // for any exception throw an UnavailableException to
40        // indicate that the servlet is not currently available
41        catch ( Exception exception )
42        {
43           exception.printStackTrace();
44           throw new UnavailableException(exception.getMessage());
45        } // end catch
46     } // end method init
```

Fig. 26.21 | Multitier Web-based survey using XHTML, servlets and JDBC. (Part 1 of 3.)

```
47
48      // process survey response
49      protected void doPost( HttpServletRequest request,
50         HttpServletResponse response )
51            throws ServletException, IOException
52      {
53         // set up response to client
54         response.setContentType( "text/html" );
55         PrintWriter out = response.getWriter();
56
57         // start XHTML document
58         out.println( "<?xml version = \"1.0\"?>" );
59
60         out.printf( "%s%s%s", "<!DOCTYPE html PUBLIC",
61            " \"-//W3C//DTD XHTML 1.0 Strict//EN\"",
62            " \"http://www.w3.org/TR/xhtml1/DTD/xhtml1-strict.dtd\">\n" );
63
64         out.println(
65            "<html xmlns = \"http://www.w3.org/1999/xhtml\">" );
66
67         // head section of document
68         out.println( "<head>" );
69
70         // read current survey response
71         int value =
72            Integer.parseInt( request.getParameter( "animal" ) );
73         String sql;
74
75         // attempt to process a vote and display current results
76         try
77         {
78            // update total for current survey response
79            sql = "UPDATE surveyresults SET votes = votes + 1 " +
80               "WHERE id = " + value;
81            statement.executeUpdate( sql );
82
83            // get total of all survey responses
84            sql = "SELECT sum( votes ) FROM surveyresults";
85            ResultSet totalRS = statement.executeQuery( sql );
86            totalRS.next(); // position to first record
87            int total = totalRS.getInt( 1 );
88
89            // get results
90            sql = "SELECT surveyoption, votes, id FROM surveyresults " +
91               "ORDER BY id";
92            ResultSet resultsRS = statement.executeQuery( sql );
93            out.println( "<title>Thank you!</title>" );
94            out.println( "</head>" );
95
96            out.println( "<body>" );
97            out.println( "<p>Thank you for participating." );
98            out.println( "<br />Results:</p><pre>" );
99
```

Fig. 26.21 | Multitier Web-based survey using XHTML, servlets and JDBC. (Part 2 of 3.)

```
100            // process results
101            int votes;
102
103            while ( resultsRS.next() )
104            {
105               out.print( resultsRS.getString( 1 ) );
106               out.print( ": " );
107               votes = resultsRS.getInt( 2 );
108               out.printf( "%.2f", ( double ) votes / total * 100 );
109               out.print( "% responses: " );
110               out.println( votes );
111            } // end while
112
113            resultsRS.close();
114
115            out.print( "Total responses: " );
116            out.print( total );
117
118            // end XHTML document
119            out.println( "</pre></body></html>" );
120            out.close();
121         } // end try
122         // if database exception occurs, return error page
123         catch ( SQLException sqlException )
124         {
125            sqlException.printStackTrace();
126            out.println( "<title>Error</title>" );
127            out.println( "</head>" );
128            out.println( "<body><p>Database error occurred. " );
129            out.println( "Try again later.</p></body></html>" );
130            out.close();
131         } // end catch
132      } // end method doPost
133
134      // close SQL statements and database when servlet terminates
135      public void destroy()
136      {
137         // attempt to close statements and database connection
138         try
139         {
140            statement.close();
141            connection.close();
142         } // end try
143         // handle database exceptions by returning error to client
144         catch ( SQLException sqlException )
145         {
146            sqlException.printStackTrace();
147         } // end catch
148      } // end method destroy
149 } // end class SurveyServlet
```

Fig. 26.21 | Multitier Web-based survey using XHTML, servlets and JDBC. (Part 3 of 3.)

Servlets are initialized by method `init`, which we override in `SurveyServlet` (lines 25–46). Method `init` is called exactly once in a servlet's life cycle, before any client requests are accepted. The method takes `ServletConfig` argument and throws a `Servlet-Exception`. The argument provides the servlet with information about its initialization parameters (i.e., parameters not associated with a request, but passed to the servlet for initializing the servlet). These parameters are specified in the `web.xml` deployment descriptor file as part of a `servlet` element. Each parameter appears in an init-param element of the following form:

```
<init-param>
    <param-name>parameter name</param-name>
    <param-value>parameter value</param-value>
</init-param>
```

Servlets can obtain initialization parameter values by invoking `ServletConfig` method `getInitParameter`, which receives a string representing the param-name of the parameter and returns the param-value as a string.

In this example, the servlet's `init` method (lines 25–46) performs the connection to the MySQL database. Line 30 loads the driver (`com.mysql.jdbc.Driver`, which is specified in the initialization parameter `"databaseDriver"`). Lines 31–34 attempt to open a connection to the `animalsurvey` database. The database name, username and password are specified in the initialization parameters `"databaseName"`, `"username"` and `"password"`, respectively. The database contains one table (`surveyresults`) that consists of three fields—a unique integer to identify each record (`id`), a string representing the survey option (`surveyoption`) and an integer representing the number of votes for a survey option (`votes`). [*Note:* The examples folder for this chapter contains the SQL script `animalsurvey.sql` with which you can create the `animalsurvey` database for this example. For information on executing the SQL script, please refer to Chapter 25.]

When a user submits a survey response, method `doPost` (lines 49–132) handles the request. Lines 71–72 obtain the survey response, then lines 76–121 attempt to process it. Lines 79–80 specify an update statement to increment the `votes` value for the record with the specified ID and update the database. Lines 85–87 execute the query specified in line 84 to retrieve the total number of votes received using SQL's built-in `sum` function to total all the votes in the `surveyresults` table. Then lines 92–120 execute the query specified in lines 90–91 to obtain the data in the table and process the `ResultSet` to create the survey summary for the client. When the servlet container terminates the servlet, method `destroy` (lines 135–148) closes the `Statement`, then closes the database connection. Figure 26.22 shows `survey.html`, which invokes `SurveyServlet` through alias `animal-survey` when the user submits the form.

We use our `jhtp6` context root to demonstrate the servlet of Fig. 26.21. Place `Survey.html` in the `servlets` directory created previously. Place `SurveyServlet.class` (with the complete package structure) in the `classes` subdirectory of `WEB-INF` in the `jhtp6` context root. Then, edit the `web.xml` deployment descriptor in the `WEB-INF` directory to include the information specified in Fig. 26.23. This program cannot execute in Tomcat unless the Web application has access to the JAR file that contains the MySQL database driver and its supporting classes. This JAR file (`mysql-connector-java-3.0.14-production-bin.jar`) can be found in your MySQL Connector's installation directory.

Place a *copy* of this file in the WEB-INF subdirectory lib to make its contents available to the Web application. Please refer to Chapter 25 for more information on how to configure MySQL.

After copying these files, type the following URL in your Web browser:

```
http://localhost:8080/jhtp6/servlets/Survey.html
```

Select an animal and press the **Submit** button to invoke the servlet. [*Note:* The MySQL database server should be running when the servlet is invoked.]

26.9 Welcome Files

Web application developers can specify an ordered list of welcome files to be loaded when the request URL is not mapped to a servlet. These files are typically HTML or JSP documents. Welcome files are defined using the **welcome-file-list** element in the deployment descriptor. Element welcome-file-list contains one or more **welcome-file** elements. Each welcome-file element specifies the partial URL of a welcome file without a leading or trailing /. For example, the following welcome-file-list element indicates that index.html and index.htm are the welcome files.

```
<welcome-file-list>
    <welcome-file>index.html</welcome-file>
    <welcome-file>index.htm</welcome-file>
</welcome-file-list>
```

```
1   <?xml version = "1.0"?>
2   <!DOCTYPE html PUBLIC "-//W3C//DTD XHTML 1.0 Strict//EN"
3       "http://www.w3.org/TR/xhtml1/DTD/xhtml1-strict.dtd">
4
5   <!-- Fig. 26.22: Survey.html -->
6
7   <html xmlns = "http://www.w3.org/1999/xhtml">
8   <head>
9       <title>Survey</title>
10  </head>
11
12  <body>
13  <form method = "post" action = "/jhtp6/animalsurvey">
14      <p>What is your favorite pet?</p>
15      <p>
16          <input type = "radio" name = "animal"
17              value = "1" />Dog<br />
18          <input type = "radio" name = "animal"
19              value = "2" />Cat<br />
20          <input type = "radio" name = "animal"
21              value = "3" />Bird<br />
22          <input type = "radio" name = "animal"
23              value = "4" />Snake<br />
```

Fig. 26.22 | Survey.html document that allows users to submit survey responses to SurveyServlet. (Part 1 of 2.)

```
24              <input type = "radio" name = "animal"
25                 value = "5" checked = "checked" />None
26         </p>
27         <p><input type = "submit" value = "Submit" /></p>
28      </form>
29      </body>
30      </html>
```

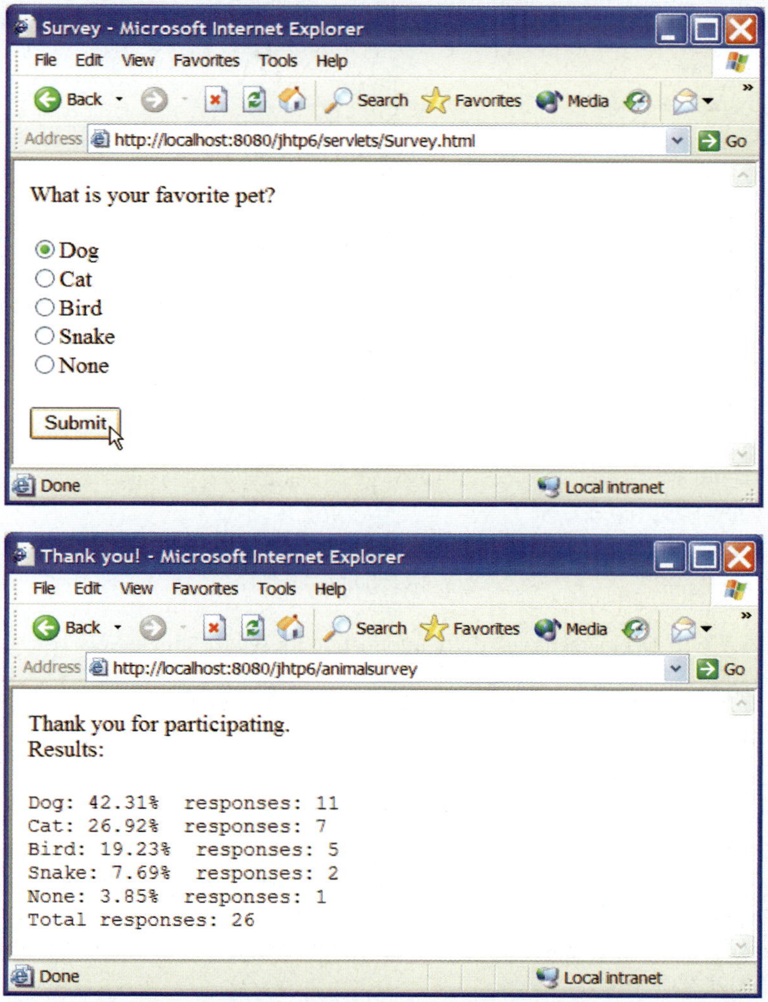

Fig. 26.22 | `Survey.html` document that allows users to submit survey responses to `SurveyServlet`. (Part 2 of 2.)

To specify the welcome files for the `jhtp6` context root, insert the preceding `welcome-file-list` element after the last `servlet-mapping` element in the `web.xml` deployment descriptor. When the URL `http://localhost:8080/jhtp6/` is requested, the Web server

Descriptor element	Value
servlet element	
servlet-name	animalsurvey
description	Connecting to a database from a serv-let.
servlet-class	com.deitel.jhtp6.servlets.SurveyServlet
init-param	
param-name	databaseDriver
param-value	com.mysql.jdbc.Driver
init-param	
param-name	databaseName
param-value	jdbc:mysql://localhost/animalsurvey
init-param	
param-name	username
param-value	jhtp6
init-param	
param-name	password
param-value	jhtp6
servlet-mapping element	
servlet-name	animalsurvey
url-pattern	/animalsurvey

Fig. 26.23 | Deployment descriptor information for servlet `SurveyServlet`.

appends each welcome file in the order specified in the deployment descriptor to the request URL, such as

```
http://localhost:8080/jhtp6/index.html
http://localhost:8080/jhtp6/index.htm
```

and checks whether the resource is valid. The servlet container sends the request to the first matching welcome file. For example, if `index.html` exists in the `jhtp6` directory, the servlet container sends the request to the `http://localhost:8080/jhtp6/index.html`. If no matching welcome file is found, the servlet container returns a response indicating that the resource is not available.

Figure 26.24 is the `index.html` that provides links (lines 15–24) to test all the examples demonstrated in this chapter. Copy this file to `C:\jakarta-tomcat-5.0.25\webapps\jhtp6` and restart the Tomcat server. To test the welcome file, type the following URL in your Web browser:

```
http://localhost:8080/jhtp6/
```

The `index.html` page is loaded. Click a link to test the corresponding servlet example.

```
 1   <?xml version = "1.0"?>
 2   <!DOCTYPE html PUBLIC "-//W3C//DTD XHTML 1.0 Strict//EN"
 3      "http://www.w3.org/TR/xhtml1/DTD/xhtml1-strict.dtd">
 4
 5   <!-- Fig. 26.24: index.html -->
 6
 7   <html xmlns = "http://www.w3.org/1999/xhtml">
 8   <head>
 9      <title>Welcome File</title>
10   </head>
11
12   <body>
13      <p>Click a link to test each example demonstrated in this chapter</p>
14      <p>
15      <a href = "/jhtp6/servlets/WelcomeServlet.html">
16         WelcomeServlet</a><br />
17      <a href = "/jhtp6/servlets/WelcomeServlet2.html">
18         WelcomeServlet2</a><br />
19      <a href = "/jhtp6/servlets/WelcomeServlet3.html">
20         WelcomeServlet3</a><br />
21      <a href = "/jhtp6/servlets/RedirectServlet.html">
22         RedirectServlet</a><br />
23      <a href = "/jhtp6/servlets/Survey.html">
24         SurveyServlet</a><br />
25      </p>
26   </body>
27   </html>
```

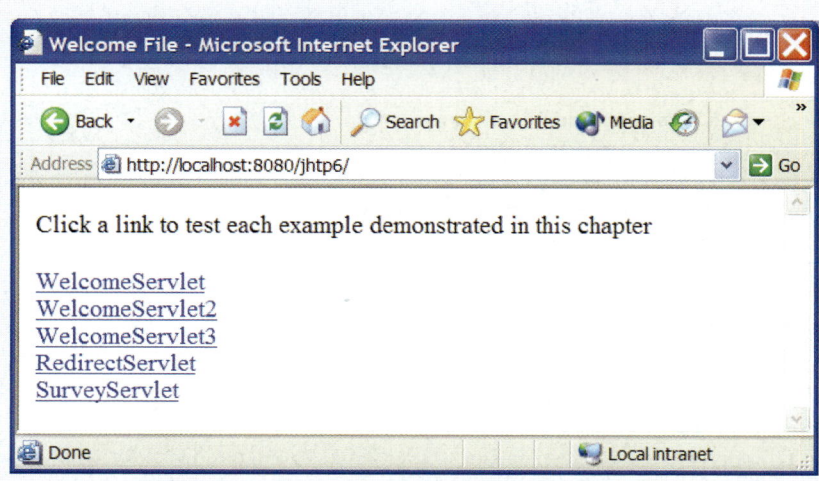

Fig. 26.24 | Welcome file `index.html`.

26.10 Wrap-Up

This chapter continued our networking discussions by presenting servlets that enhance the functionality of Web servers. You learned the architecture and life cycle of servlets. You learned how to respond to HTTP requests by using an `HttpServlet`. You also learned how to redirect requests to a static or dynamic Web resource. You executed the sample servlets with the Apache Tomcat server. You then built a multitier Web application that uses JDBC to access and manipulate a database from a servlet. In the next chapter, we introduce JavaServer Pages—an extension of servlet technology. We demonstrate several JSP components—implicit objects, scripting elements, standard actions and directives. We also discuss how to use `CachedRowSet`s to access a MySQL database from a JavaBean object, then access the JavaBean object from a JSP page.

26.11 Internet and Web Resources

This section lists a variety of servlet resources available on the Internet and provides a brief description of each.

`java.sun.com/products/servlet/index.html`
The servlet page at the Sun Microsystems, Java Web site provides access to the latest servlet information and servlet resources.

`jakarta.apache.org`
This is the Apache Project's home page for the *Jakarta Project*.

`jakarta.apache.org/tomcat/index.html`
Home page for the Tomcat servlets and JavaServer Pages reference implementation.

`www.servlets.com`
This Web site provides news, tools and documents for servlets and JSP technologies. It also links to the book *Java Servlet Programming* published by O'Reilly.

`theserverside.com`
TheServerSide.com is dedicated to information and resources for J2EE.

`www.javacorporate.com/expresso/frame.jsp`
Home of the open-source *Expresso Framework*, which includes a library of extensible servlet components to help speed Web application development.

`www.servlet.com/srvdev.jhtml`
ServletInc's Servlet Developers Forum provides resources for server-side Java developers and information about Web servers that support servlet technologies.

`www.coolservlets.com`
Provides free open-source Java servlets.

`www.cetus-links.org/oo_java_servlets.html`
Provides a list of links to resources on servlets and other technologies.

`www.javaskyline.com`
Java Skyline is an online magazine for servlet developers.

`www.rfc-editor.org`
The RFC Editor provides a search engine for RFCs (Requests for Comments). Many of these RFCs provide details of Web-related technologies. RFCs of interest to servlet developers include *URI in WWW* (RFC 1630), *URI: generic syntax* (RFC 2396), *HTTP State Management Mechanism* (RFC 2109), *Use and Interpretation of HTTP Version Numbers* (RFC 2145), *Hyper Text Coffee Pot Control Protocol* (RFC 2324), HTTP/1.1 (RFC 2616) and *HTTP Authentication: Basic and Digest Authentication* (RFC 2617).

Summary

- The classes and interfaces used to define servlets are found in packages `javax.servlet` and `javax.servlet.http`.
- URLs represent files or directories and can represent complex tasks, such as database lookups and Internet searches.
- JavaServer Pages technology, an extension of servlet technology, simplifies the process of creating pages by separating presentation from content.
- Servlets are normally executed by the servlet container component of a Web application server.
- All servlets must implement the `Servlet` interface. The methods of interface `Servlet` are invoked automatically by the servlet container.
- A servlet's life cycle begins when the servlet container loads the servlet into memory—normally in response to the first request to that servlet. Before the servlet can handle the first request, the servlet container invokes the servlet's `init` method. After `init` completes execution, the servlet can respond to its first request. All requests are handled by a servlet's `service` method, which may be called many times during the servlet's life cycle. When the servlet container terminates the servlet, the servlet's `destroy` method is called to release servlet resources.
- The key method in every servlet is method `service`, which receives both a `ServletRequest` object and a `ServletResponse` object. These objects provide access to input and output streams that allow the servlet to read data from and send data to the client. Commonly, this method should not be overridden.
- Servlets typically extend class `HttpServlet`, which overrides method `service` to distinguish between the typical requests received from a client Web browser. The two most common HTTP request types (also known as request methods) are `get` and `post`.
- Class `HttpServlet` defines methods `doGet` and `doPost` to respond to `get` and `post` requests from a client, respectively.
- Methods `doGet` and `doPost` receive as arguments an `HttpServletRequest` object and an `HttpServletResponse` object that enable interaction between the client and the server.
- A response is sent to the client through a `PrintWriter` object returned by the `getWriter` method of the `HttpServletResponse` object.
- The `HttpServletResponse` object's `setContentType` method specifies the content type of the response to the client. This enables the client browser to understand and handle the content.
- The server `localhost` (IP address `127.0.0.1`) is a well-known host name on computers that support TCP/IP-based networking protocols such as HTTP. This host name can be used to test TCP/IP applications on the local computer.
- The Tomcat server awaits requests from clients on port 8080. This port number must be specified as part of the URL to request a servlet running in Tomcat.
- Tomcat is a fully functional implementation of the JSP and servlet standards. It includes a Web server, so it can be used as a standalone test container for JSPs and servlets.
- JSPs, servlets and their supporting files are deployed as part of Web applications. In Tomcat, Web applications are deployed in the `webapps` subdirectory of the Tomcat installation.
- A Web application has a well-known directory structure in which all the files that are part of the application reside. This directory structure can be set up by the Tomcat server administrator in the `webapps` directory, or the entire directory structure can be archived in a Web application archive file (i.e., `.war` file).
- WAR files are typically placed in the `webapps` directory. When the Tomcat server begins execution, it extracts the contents of the WAR file into the appropriate `webapps` subdirectory structure.

- The Web application directory structure is separated into a context root—the top-level directory for an entire Web application—and several subdirectories. The context root is the root directory for the Web application.

- All the JSPs, HTML documents, servlets and supporting files such as images and class files reside in the root directory or its subdirectories.

- The WEB-INF directory contains the Web application deployment descriptor (web.xml), which is required to deploy a Web application.

- The WEB-INF/classes directory contains the servlet class files and other supporting class files used in a Web application.

- The WEB-INF/lib directory contains Java archive (JAR) files that may include servlet class files and other supporting class files used in a Web application.

- Tomcat uses the directory names in the webapps subdirectory as the context names.

- HTTP get requests can be typed directly into your browser's Address or Location field.

- Parameters are passed as name-value pairs in a get request. A ? sepasrates the URL from the data passed as part of a get request. Name-value pairs are passed with the name and the value separated by =. Two or more name-value pairs are separated by &.

- Method getParameter of HttpServletRequest receives the parameter name as an argument and returns the corresponding String value, or null if the parameter is not part of the request.

- An HTTP post request is often used to post data from a Web-page form to a server-side form handler that processes the data. HTTP post requests are commonly used for passing sensitive data.

- Method doPost receives the same two arguments as doGet—an object that implements interface HttpServletRequest to represent the client's request and an object that implements interface HttpServletResponse to represent the servlet's response.

- Method sendRedirect of HttpServletResponse redirects a request to the specified URL.

- When a servlet uses a relative path to reference another static or dynamic resource, the servlet assumes the same context root unless a complete URL is specified for the resource.

- Once method sendRedirect executes, processing of the request by the servlet that called sendRedirect terminates.

- When redirecting requests, the request parameters from the original request are passed as parameters to the new request. Additional request parameters can also be passed. New parameters are added to the existing request parameters. If a new parameter has the same name as an existing parameter, the new parameter value takes precedence over the original value. However, all the values are still passed.

- The complete set of values for a given request-parameter name can be obtained by calling method getParameterValues of HttpServletRequest, which receives the parameter name as an argument and returns an array of Strings containing the parameter values in order from the most recently to the least recently added.

- Many of today's applications are three-tier distributed applications, consisting of a user interface, business logic and database access.

- In multitier architectures, Web servers are often used in the middle tier. Server-side components, such as servlets, execute in an application server alongside the Web server. These components provide the business logic that manipulates data from databases and communicates with client Web browsers.

- Servlet method init takes a ServletConfig argument, which provides the servlet with information about its initialization parameters specified in a servlet element in the deployment descriptor. Each parameter appears in an init-param element with child elements param-name and param-value.

- Web application developers can specify an ordered list of welcome files to be loaded when the request URL is not mapped to a servlet. These files are typically HTML or JSP documents.
- Welcome files are defined using the `welcome-file-list` element in the deployment descriptor.
- Element `welcome-file-list` contains one or more `welcome-file` elements. Each welcome-file element specifies the partial URL of a welcome file without a leading or trailing /.

Terminology

Apache Tomcat server
business logic
cache a Web page
`CATALINA_HOME` environment variable
context root
deploy a Web application
deployment descriptor
destroy method of `Servlet`
doGet method of `HttpServlet`
doPost method of `HttpServlet`
`GenericServlet` class from `javax.servlet`
get request
getCookies method of `HttpServletRequest`
getOutputStream method of `HTTPServletRe-`
    sponse
getParameter method of `HttpServletRequest`
getParameterNames method of `HttpServletRe-`
    quest
getParameterValues method of `HttpServle-`
    tRequest
getWriter method of `HTTPServletResponse`
host name
HTTP header
HTTP (Hypertext Transfer Protocol)
HTTP request
`HttpServlet` interface
`HttpServletRequest` interface
`HttpServletResponse` interface
init method of `Servlet`
initialization parameter
Jakarta project
`JAVA_HOME` environment variable
`javax.servlet` package
`javax.servlet.http` package
localhost (127.0.0.1)
MIME type

port
post request
put request
redirect a request
request method
request parameter
sendRedirect method of `HttpServletResponse`
service method of `Servlet`
servlet
servlet container
`Servlet` interface
servlet life cycle
servlet mapping
`ServletException` class
`ServletOutputStream` class
`ServletRequest` interface
`ServletResponse` interface
setContentType method of `HttpServletRe-`
    sponse
text/html MIME type
thin client
three-tier distributed application
trace request
URL pattern
WAR (Web application archive) file
Web application
Web application deployment descriptor
    (`web.xml`)
webapps directory
`WEB-INF` directory
`WEB-INF/classes` directory
`WEB-INF/lib` directory
welcome file
`welcome-file` element
`welcome-file-list` element
well-known port number

Self-Review Exercises

26.1 Fill in the blanks in each of the following statements:
    a) Classes `HttpServlet` and `GenericServlet` implement the _____ interface.
    b) Class `HttpServlet` defines the methods _____ and _____ to respond to get and post requests from a client.

    c) `HttpServletResponse` method _____ obtains a character-based output stream that enables text data to be sent to the client.

    d) The `form` attribute _____ specifies the server-side form handler, i.e., the program that handles the request.

    e) _____ is the well-known host name that refers to your own computer.

26.2 State whether each of the following is *true* or *false*. If *false*, explain why.

    a) Servlets usually are used on the client side of a networking application.

    b) Servlet methods are executed by the servlet container.

    c) The two most common HTTP requests are `get` and `put`.

    d) The well-known port number on a Web server where requests for HTML documents are made is 8080.

Answers to Self-Review Exercises

26.1 a) `Servlet`. b) `doGet`, `doPost`. c) `getWriter`. d) `action`. e) `localhost`.

26.2 a) False. Servlets are usually used on the server side.

    b) True.

    c) False. The two most common HTTP request types are `get` and `post`. The `put` request type is often not allowed for security reasons.

    d) False. The well-known port number on a Web server where requests for HTML documents are made is 80. Port 8080 is the Tomcat servlet container's default port.

Exercises

26.3 Create a servlet that displays the current date and time.

26.4 Create a HTML form with three input fields: first name, last name and e-mail. Use the `get` method to pass these values to a servlet. Notice how data is attached to the URL. In the servlet, verify all input fields are non-`null` and display them back to the client.

26.5 Create a Web application for dynamic FAQs. The application should obtain the information to create the dynamic FAQ Web page from a database that consists of a `topics` table and an `faq` table. The `topics` table has two fields—a unique integer ID for each topic (`topicID`) and a name for each topic (`topicName`). The `faq` table has three fields—the `topicID` (a foreign key), a string representing the question (`question`) and the answer to the question (`answer`). When the servlet is invoked, it should read the data from the database and return a dynamically created Web page containing each question and answer, sorted by topic. [*Note:* The `examples` folder for this chapter contains the SQL script `faq.sql` with which you can create the `faq` database for this example. For information on executing the SQL script, please refer to Chapter 25.] In the servlet's `init` method, create a `CachedRowSet` and set the database URL for the `CachedRowSet`. Sun's reference implementation of `CachedRowSet` is named `CachedRowSetImpl` and is located in the package `com.sun.rowset`.

26.6 Modify the Web application in Exercise 26.5 so that the initial request to the servlet returns a Web page of topics in the FAQ database. Then, the user can link to another servlet that returns only the frequently asked questions for a particular topic.

26.7 Modify the Web application in Fig. 26.21 to allow the user to see the survey results without responding to the survey.

26.8 Recall that the Web application in Fig. 26.21 implements a Web-based survey. Write a Web application that can be used generically with any survey of the appropriate form—i.e., a question followed by a set of possible answers. Your Web application should have three servlets. The first is called to dynamically generate a list of survey names. When the user selects a survey, the second servlet should dynamically generate a `form` containing the survey options. When the user chooses an option, the third servlet should update the database and return the survey results. The survey database for this exercise has two tables—surveyCategory and surveyResult. Table surveyCategory has three fields—a unique integer ID for each survey category (id), a string representing the survey name (name) and a string representing the survey question (question). Table surveyResult has three fields—an integer ID (a foreign key) that identifies the survey category (id), a string representing the survey option (surveyOption) and an integer representing the total votes that option has received so far (voteCount). [*Note:* The examples folder for this chapter contains the SQL script survey.sql with which you can create the survey database for this example. For information on executing the SQL script, refer to Chapter 25. The sample database contains sample data for three surveys—Animals, Fruits and Sports.]

26.9 Write a Web application that consists of a servlet (DirectoryServlet) and several Web documents. Document index.html should be the first document the user sees. In it, you should have a series of links for other Web pages in your site. When clicked, each link should invoke the servlet with a get request that contains a page parameter. The servlet should obtain parameter page and redirect the request to the appropriate document.

JavaServer Pages (JSP)

OBJECTIVES

In this chapter you will learn:

- What JSPs are.
- The differences between servlets and JSPs.
- To create and deploy JavaServer Pages.
- To use JSP's implicit objects and scriptlets to create dynamic Web pages.
- To specify global JSP information with directives.
- To use actions to manipulate JavaBeans in a JSP, to include resources dynamically and to forward requests to other JSPs.

27.1 Introduction

In Chapter 26, you learned how to generate dynamic Web pages with servlets. You probably have already noticed in our examples that most of the code in our servlets generated output that consisted of the HTML elements that composed the response to the client. Only a small portion of the code dealt with the business logic. Generating responses from servlets requires that Web application developers be familiar with Java. However, many people involved in Web application development, such as Web site designers, do not know Java. It is difficult for people who are not Java programmers to implement, maintain and extend a Web application that consists of primarily of servlets. The solution to this problem is JavaServer Pages (JSP)—an extension of servlet technology that separates the presentation from the business logic. This lets Java programmers and Web-site designers focus on their strengths—writing Java code and designing Web pages, respectively.

JavaServer Pages simplify the delivery of dynamic Web content. They enable Web application programmers to create dynamic content by reusing predefined components and by interacting with components using server-side scripting. JavaServer Page programmers can use special software components called JavaBeans and custom tag libraries that encapsulate complex, dynamic functionality. A JavaBean is a reusable component that follows certain conventions for class design that are discussed in the JavaBeans specification, which is available at `java.sun.com/products/javabeans/glasgow/index.html`. Custom-tag libraries are a powerful feature of JSP that allows Java developers to hide complex code for database access and other useful services for dynamic Web pages in custom tags. Web sites use these custom tags like any other Web page element to take advantage of the more complex functionality hidden by the tag. Thus, Web-page designers who are not familiar with Java can enhance Web pages with powerful dynamic content and processing capabilities.

The classes and interfaces that are specific to JavaServer Pages programming are located in packages `javax.servlet.jsp` and `javax.servlet.jsp.tagext`. We discuss many of these classes and interfaces throughout this chapter as we present JSP fundamentals. For complete JSP details, see the JavaServer Pages 2.0 specification, which can be downloaded from `java.sun.com/products/jsp/download.html`. We also include other JSP resources in Section 27.10.

27.2 JavaServer Pages Overview

There are four key components to JSPs—directives, actions, scripting elements and tag libraries. **Directives** are messages to the **JSP container**—the server component that executes JSPs—that enable the programmer to specify page settings, to include content from other resources and to specify custom tag libraries for use in a JSP. **Actions** encapsulate functionality in predefined tags that programmers can embed in a JSP. Actions often are performed based on the information sent to the server as part of a particular client request. They also can create Java objects for use in JSP scriptlets. **Scripting elements** enable programmers to insert Java code that interacts with components in a JSP (and possibly other Web application components) to perform request processing. **Scriptlets**, one kind of scripting element, contain code fragments that describe the action to be performed in response to a user request. **Tag libraries** are part of the **tag extension mechanism** that enables programmers to create custom tags. Such tags enable Web page designers to manipulate JSP content without prior Java knowledge. These JSP component types are discussed in detail in subsequent sections.

In some ways, JavaServer Pages look like standard XHTML or XML documents. In fact, JSPs normally include XHTML or XML markup. Such markup is known as **fixed-template data** or **fixed-template text**. Fixed-template data often helps a programmer decide whether to use a servlet or a JSP. Programmers tend to use JSPs when most of the content sent to the client is fixed-template data and little or none of the content is generated dynamically with Java code. Programmers typically use servlets when only a small portion of the content sent to the client is fixed-template data. In fact, some servlets do not produce content. Rather, they perform a task on behalf of the client, then invoke other servlets or JSPs to provide a response. Note that in most cases servlet and JSP technologies are interchangeable. As with servlets, JSPs normally execute as part of a Web server.

Software Engineering Observation 27.1

Literal text in a JSP becomes string literals in the servlet that represents the translated JSP.

When a JSP-enabled server receives the first request for a JSP, the JSP container translates the JSP into a Java servlet that handles the current request and future requests to the JSP. Literal text in a JSP becomes string literals in the servlet that represents the translated JSP. Any errors that occur in compiling the new servlet result in **translation-time errors**. The JSP container places the Java statements that implement the JSP's response in method `_jspService` at translation time. If the new servlet compiles properly, the JSP container invokes method _jspService to process the request. The JSP may respond directly or may invoke other Web application components to assist in processing the request. Any errors that occur during request processing are known as request-time errors.

Performance Tip 27.1

Some JSP containers translate JSPs to servlets at installation time. This eliminates the translation overhead for the first client that requests each JSP.

Overall, the request-response mechanism and the JSP life cycle are the same as those of a servlet. JSPs can override methods jspInit and jspDestroy (similar to servlet methods init and destroy), which the JSP container invokes when initializing and terminating a JSP, respectively. JSP programmers can define these methods using JSP declarations—part of the JSP scripting mechanism.

27.3 First JSP Example

We begin our introduction to JavaServer Pages with a simple example, clock.jsp (Fig. 27.1), in which the current date and time are inserted into a Web page using a JSP expression.

```
1   <?xml version = "1.0"?>
2   <!DOCTYPE html PUBLIC "-//W3C//DTD XHTML 1.0 Strict//EN"
3      "http://www.w3.org/TR/xhtml1/DTD/xhtml1-strict.dtd">
4
5   <!-- Fig. 27.1: clock.jsp -->
6
7   <html xmlns = "http://www.w3.org/1999/xhtml">
8      <head>
9         <meta http-equiv = "refresh" content = "60" />
10         <title>A Simple JSP Example</title>
11         <style type = "text/css">
12            .big { font-family: helvetica, arial, sans-serif;
13                   font-weight: bold;
14                   font-size: 2em; }
15         </style>
16      </head>
17      <body>
18         <p class = "big">Simple JSP Example</p>
19         <table style = "border: 6px outset;">
20            <tr>
21               <td style = "background-color: black;">
22                  <p class = "big" style = "color: cyan;">
23                     <!-- JSP expression to insert date/time -->
24                     <%= new java.util.Date() %>
25                  </p>
26               </td>
27            </tr>
28         </table>
29      </body>
30   </html>
```

Fig. 27.1 | JSP expression inserting the date and time into a Web page. (Part 1 of 2.)

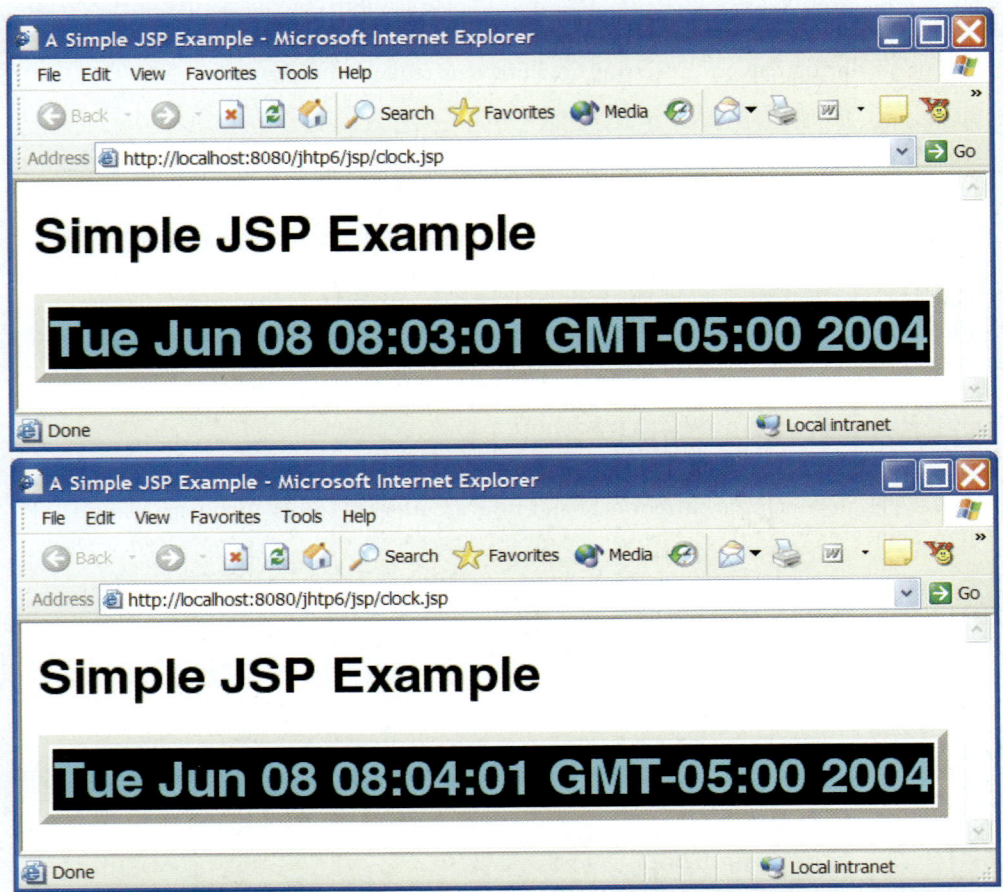

Fig. 27.1 | JSP expression inserting the date and time into a Web page. (Part 2 of 2.)

As you can see, most of clock.jsp consists of XHTML markup. [*Note:* We assume that the reader already knows XHTML and Cascading Style Sheets (CSS). For those who are not familiar with XHTML and CSS, we have included three chapters from our book *Internet & World Wide Web How to Program, Third Edition* as PDF documents on the CD that accompanies this book—Introduction to XHTML: Part 1, Introduction to XHTML: Part 2 and Cascading Style Sheets (CSS).] In cases like this, JSPs are easier to implement than servlets. In a servlet that performs the same task as this JSP, each line of XHTML markup typically is a separate Java statement that outputs the string representing the markup as part of the response to the client. Writing code to output markup can often lead to errors. Most JSP editors provide syntax coloring to help programmers check that their markup follows proper syntax.

Software Engineering Observation 27.2

JavaServer Pages are easier to implement than servlets when the response to a client request consists primarily of markup that remains constant between requests.

The JSP in Fig. 27.1 generates an XHTML document that displays the current date and time. The key line in this JSP (line 24) is the expression

```
<%= new java.util.Date() %>
```

JSP expressions are delimited by `<%=` and `%>`. The preceding expression creates a new instance of class `Date` (package `java.util`). By default, a `Date` object is initialized with the current date and time. When the client requests this JSP, the preceding expression inserts the `String` representation of the date and time in the response to the client. [*Note:* Because the client of a JSP could be anywhere in the world, the JSP should return the date in the client locale's format. However, the JSP executes on the server, so the server's locale determines the `String` representation of the `Date`. In Fig. 27.10, `clock2.jsp` determines the client's locale, then uses a `DateFormat` (package `java.text`) object to format the date using that locale.]

> **Software Engineering Observation 27.3**
>
> *The JSP container converts the result of every JSP expression into a string that is output as part of the response to the client.*

We use the XHTML **meta element** in line 9 to set a **refresh interval** of 60 seconds for the document. This causes the browser to request `clock.jsp` every 60 seconds. For each request to `clock.jsp`, the JSP container reevaluates the expression in line 24, creating a new `Date` object with the server's current date and time.

As in Chapter 26, we use Apache Tomcat to test our JSPs in the `jhtp6` Web application we created previously. For details on creating and configuring the `jhtp6` Web application, review Section 26.3 and Section 26.4.1. To test `clock.jsp`, create a new directory called `jsp` in the `jhtp6` subdirectory of Tomcat's `webapps` directory. Next, copy `clock.jsp` into the `jsp` directory. Open your Web browser and enter the following URL to test `clock.jsp`:

```
http://localhost:8080/jhtp6/jsp/clock.jsp
```

When you first invoke the JSP, you may notice a brief delay as Tomcat translates the JSP into a servlet and invokes the servlet to respond to your request. [*Note:* It is not necessary to create a directory named `jsp` in a Web application. We use this directory to separate the examples in this chapter from the servlet examples in Chapter 26.]

27.4 Implicit Objects

Implicit objects provide access to many servlet capabilities in the context of a JavaServer Page. Implicit objects have four scopes: application, page, request and session. The JSP container owns objects with **application scope**. Any JSP can manipulate such objects. Objects with **page scope** exist only in the page that defines them. Each page has its own instances of the page-scope implicit objects. Objects with **request scope** exist for the duration of the request. For example, a JSP can partially process a request, then forward it to a servlet or another JSP for further processing. Request-scope objects go out of scope when request processing completes with a response to the client. Objects with **session scope** exist for the client's entire browsing session. Figure 27.2 describes the JSP implicit objects and their scopes. This chapter demonstrates several of these objects.

Implicit object	Description
Application Scope	
application	A `javax.servlet.ServletContext` object that represents the container in which the JSP executes.
Page Scope	
config	A `javax.servlet.ServletConfig` object that represents the JSP configuration options. As with servlets, configuration options can be specified in a Web application descriptor.
exception	A `java.lang.Throwable` object that represents an exception that is passed to a JSP error page. This object is available only in a JSP error page.
out	A `javax.servlet.jsp.JspWriter` object that writes text as part of the response to a request. This object is used implicitly with JSP expressions and actions that insert string content in a response.
page	An `Object` that represents the `this` reference for the current JSP instance.
pageContext	A `javax.servlet.jsp.PageContext` object that provides JSP programmers with access to the implicit objects discussed in this table.
response	An object that represents the response to the client and is normally an instance of a class that implements `HttpServletResponse` (package `javax.servlet.http`). If a protocol other than HTTP is used, this object is an instance of a class that implements `javax.servlet.ServletResponse`.
Request Scope	
request	An object that represents the client request and is normally an instance of a class that implements `HttpServletRequest` (package `javax.servlet.http`). If a protocol other than HTTP is used, this object is an instance of a subclass of `javax.servlet.ServletRequest`.
Session Scope	
session	A `javax.servlet.http.HttpSession` object that represents the client session information if such a session has been created. This object is available only in pages that participate in a session.

Fig. 27.2 | JSP implicit objects.

Note that many of the implicit objects extend classes or implement interfaces discussed in Chapter 26. Thus, JSPs can use the same methods that servlets use to interact with such objects, as described in Chapter 26. Most of the examples in this chapter use one or more of the implicit objects in Fig. 27.2.

27.5 Scripting

JavaServer Pages often present dynamically generated content as part of an XHTML document that is sent to the client in response to a request. In some cases, the content is static but is output only if certain conditions are met during a request (e.g., providing values in a form that submits a request). JSP programmers can insert Java code and logic in a JSP using scripting.

27.5.1 Scripting Components

The JSP scripting components include scriptlets, comments, expressions, declarations and escape sequences. This section describes each of these scripting components. Many of these are demonstrated in Fig. 27.4 at the end of Section 27.5.2.

Scriptlets are blocks of code delimited by `<%` and `%>`. They contain Java statements that the container places in method `_jspService` at translation time.

JSPs support three comment styles: JSP comments, XHTML comments and scripting-language comments. JSP comments are delimited by `<%--` and `--%>`. These can be placed throughout a JSP, but not inside scriptlets. XHTML comments are delimited with `<!--` and `-->`. These, too, can be placed throughout a JSP, but not inside scriptlets. Scripting language comments are currently Java comments, because Java currently is the only JSP scripting language. Scriptlets can use Java's end-of-line `//` comments and traditional comments (delimited by `/*` and `*/`). JSP comments and scripting-language comments are ignored and do not appear in the response to a client. When clients view the source code of a JSP response, they will see only the XHTML comments in the source code. The different comment styles are useful for separating comments that the user should be able to see from those that document logic processed on the server.

Common Programming Error 27.1

Placing a JSP comment or XHTML comment inside a scriptlet is a translation-time syntax error that prevents the JSP from being translated properly.

As we discussed in Section 27.3, JSP expressions are delimited by `<%=` and `%>` and contain a Java expression that is evaluated when a client requests the JSP containing the expression. The container converts the result of a JSP expression to a `String` object, then outputs the `String` as part of the response to the client.

Declarations, delimited by `<%!` and `%>`, enable a JSP programmer to define variables and methods for use in a JSP. Variables become instance variables of the servlet class that represents the translated JSP. Similarly, methods become members of the class that represents the translated JSP. Declarations of variables and methods in a JSP use Java syntax. Thus, a variable declaration must end with a semicolon, as in

```
<%! int counter = 0; %>
```

Software Engineering Observation 27.4

JSPs should not store client state information in instance variables. Rather, they should use the JSP implicit `session` object. For more information on how to use the `session` object, visit Sun's J2EE tutorial at `java.sun.com/j2ee/1.4/docs/tutorial/doc/index.html`.

Special characters or character sequences that the JSP container normally uses to delimit JSP code can be included in a JSP as literal characters in scripting elements, fixed template data and attribute values using escape sequences. Figure 27.3 shows the literal character or characters and the corresponding escape sequences and discusses where to use the escape sequences.

Literal	Escape sequence	Description
<%	<\%	The character sequence <% normally indicates the beginning of a scriptlet. The <\% escape sequence places the literal characters <% in the response to the client.
%>	%\>	The character sequence %> normally indicates the end of a scriptlet. The %\> escape sequence places the literal characters %> in the response to the client.
' " \	\' \" \\	As with string literals in a Java program, the escape sequences for characters ', " and \ allow these characters to appear in attribute values. Remember that the literal text in a JSP becomes string literals in the servlet that represents the translated JSP.

Fig. 27.3 | JSP escape sequences.

27.5.2 Scripting Example

Figure 27.4 demonstrates responding to get requests with basic scripting capabilities. The JSP enables the user to input a first name, then outputs that name in the response. Using scripting, the JSP determines whether a firstName parameter was passed as part of the request. If not, the JSP returns an XHTML document containing a form through which the user can input a first name. Otherwise, the JSP obtains the firstName value and uses it as part of an XHTML document that welcomes the user to JavaServer Pages.

Note that most of the code in Fig. 27.4 is XHTML markup (i.e., fixed-template data). Throughout the body element (lines 16–50) are several scriptlets (lines 17–23, 30–35 and 45–49) and a JSP expression (line 26). Note that three JSP comment styles appear in this JSP (at line 5, line17 and line 23).

The scriptlets define an if...else statement that determines whether the JSP received a value for the first name as part of the request. Line 19 uses method getParameter of JSP implicit object request (an HttpServletRequest object) to obtain the value for parameter firstName and assigns the result to variable name. Line 21 determines whether or not name is null. If it is not null, a value for the first name was passed to the JSP as part of the request. If this condition is true, the scriptlet terminates temporarily so that the fixed-template data at lines 25–28 can be output. The JSP expression in line 26 outputs the value of variable name (i.e., the first name passed to the JSP as a request parameter). The scriptlet continues at lines 30–35 with the closing brace of the if statement's body and the beginning of the else part of the if...else statement. If the condition at line 21 is false, lines 25–28 are not output. Instead, lines 37–43 output a form element. The user can type a first name in the form and press the **Submit** button to request the JSP again and execute the if statement's body (lines 25–28).

Software Engineering Observation 27.5

Scriptlets, expressions and fixed-template data can be intermixed in a JSP to create different responses based on the information in a request.

```
1    <?xml version = "1.0"?>
2    <!DOCTYPE html PUBLIC "-//W3C//DTD XHTML 1.0 Strict//EN"
3       "http://www.w3.org/TR/xhtml1/DTD/xhtml1-strict.dtd">
4
5    <!-- Fig. 27.4: welcome.jsp -->
6    <!-- JSP that processes a "get" request containing data. -->
7
8    <html xmlns = "http://www.w3.org/1999/xhtml">
9
10      <!-- head section of document -->
11      <head>
12         <title>Processing "get" requests with data</title>
13      </head>
14
15      <!-- body section of document -->
16      <body>
17         <% // begin scriptlet
18
19            String name = request.getParameter( "firstName" );
20
21            if ( name != null )
22            {
23         %> <%-- end scriptlet to insert fixed template data --%>
24
25               <h1>
26                  Hello <%= name %>, <br />
27                  Welcome to JavaServer Pages!
28               </h1>
29
30         <% // continue scriptlet
31
32            } // end if
33            else {
34
35         %> <%-- end scriptlet to insert fixed template data --%>
36
37               <form action = "welcome.jsp" method = "get">
38                  <p>Type your first name and press Submit</p>
39
40                  <p><input type = "text" name = "firstName" />
41                     <input type = "submit" value = "Submit" />
42                  </p>
43               </form>
44
45         <% // continue scriptlet
46
47            } // end else
48
49         %> <%-- end scriptlet --%>
50      </body>
51
52   </html>  <!-- end XHTML document -->
```

Fig. 27.4 | Scripting a JavaServer Page—`welcome.jsp`. (Part 1 of 2.)

Fig. 27.4 | Scripting a JavaServer Page—`welcome.jsp`. (Part 2 of 2.)

Error-Prevention Tip 27.1

It is sometimes difficult to debug errors in a JSP, because the line numbers reported by a JSP container normally refer to the servlet that represents the translated JSP, not the original JSP line numbers. Program development environments enable JSPs to be compiled in the environment, so you can see syntax error messages. These messages include the statement in the servlet that represents the translated JSP, which can be helpful in determining the error.

Error-Prevention Tip 27.2

Many JSP containers store the source code for the servlets that represent the translated JSPs. For example, the Tomcat installation directory contains a subdirectory called work *in which you can find the source code for the servlets translated by Tomcat. Recall from Chapter 26 that the log files located in the* logs *subdirectory of the Tomcat installation directory are also helpful for determining the errors.*

Error-Prevention Tip 27.3

Always put the closing brace for the if *statement and the* else *statement in the same scriptlet.*

To test Fig. 27.4 in Tomcat, copy `welcome.jsp` into the `jsp` directory created in Section 27.3. Then, open your Web browser and enter the following URL:

```
http://localhost:8080/jhtp6/jsp/welcome.jsp
```

When you first execute the JSP, it displays the `form` in which you can enter your first name, because the preceding URL does not pass a `firstName` parameter to the JSP. After you submit your first name, your browser should appear as shown in the second screen capture of Fig. 27.4. [*Note:* As with servlets, it is possible to pass `get` request arguments as part of the URL. The following URL supplies the `firstName` parameter to `welcome.jsp`.]

```
http://localhost:8080/jhtp6/jsp/welcome.jsp?firstName=Paul
```

27.6 Standard Actions

We continue our JSP discussion with the JSP standard actions (Fig. 27.5). These actions provide JSP implementors with access to several of the most common tasks performed in a JSP, such as including content from other resources, forwarding requests to other resources and interacting with JavaBean software components. JSP containers process actions at request time. Actions are delimited by `<jsp:`*action*`>` and `</jsp:`*action*`>`, where *action* is the standard action name. In cases where nothing appears between the starting and ending tags, the XML empty element syntax `<jsp:`*action* `/>` can be used. Figure 27.5 summarizes the JSP standard actions, which we use in the next several subsections.

Action	Description
`<jsp:include>`	Dynamically includes another resource in a JSP. As the JSP executes, the referenced resource is included and processed.
`<jsp:forward>`	Forwards request processing to another JSP, servlet or static page. This action terminates the current JSP's execution.
`<jsp:plugin>`	Allows a plug-in component to be added to a page in the form of a browser-specific `object` or `embed` HTML element. In the case of a Java applet, this action enables the browser to download and install the Java Plug-in, if it is not already installed on the client computer.
`<jsp:param>`	Used with the `include`, `forward` and `plugin` actions to specify additional name-value pairs of information for use by these actions.
JavaBean Manipulation	
`<jsp:useBean>`	Specifies that the JSP uses a JavaBean instance (i.e., an object of the class that declares the JavaBean). This action specifies the scope of the object and assigns it an ID (i.e., a variable name) that scripting components can use to manipulate the bean.
`<jsp:setProperty>`	Sets a property in the specified JavaBean instance. A special feature of this action is automatic matching of request parameters to bean properties of the same name.
`<jsp:getProperty>`	Gets a property in the specified JavaBean instance and converts the result to a string for output in the response.

Fig. 27.5 | JSP standard actions.

27.6.1 `<jsp:include>` Action

JavaServer Pages support two include mechanisms—the `<jsp:include>` action and the `include directive`. Action `<jsp:include>` enables dynamic content to be included in a JavaServer Page at request time. If the included resource changes between requests, the next request to the JSP containing the `<jsp:include>` action includes the resource's new content. On the other hand, the `include` directive copies the content into the JSP once, at JSP translation time. If the included resource changes, the new content will not be reflected in the JSP that used the `include` directive, unless that JSP is recompiled, which normally would occur only if a new version of the JSP is installed. Figure 27.6 describes the attributes of action `<jsp:include>`.

Software Engineering Observation 27.6

According to the JavaServer Pages 2.0 specification, a JSP container is allowed to determine whether a resource included with the `include` directive has changed. If so, the container can recompile the JSP that included the resource. However, the specification does not provide a mechanism to indicate a change in an included resource to the container.

Performance Tip 27.2

The `<jsp:include>` action is more flexible than the `include` directive, but requires more overhead when page contents change frequently. Use the `<jsp:include>` action only when dynamic content is necessary.

Common Programming Error 27.2

Specifying in a `<jsp:include>` action a page that is not part of the same Web application is a request-time error—the `<jsp:include>` action will not include any content.

The next example demonstrates action `<jsp:include>` using four XHTML and JSP resources that represent both static and dynamic content. JavaServer Page `include.jsp` (Fig. 27.7) includes three other resources: `banner.html` (Fig. 27.8), `toc.html` (Fig. 27.9) and `clock2.jsp` (Fig. 27.10). JavaServer Page `include.jsp` creates an XHTML document containing a `table` in which `banner.html` spans two columns across the top of the table, `toc.html` is the left column of the second row and `clock2.jsp` is the right column of the second row. Figure 27.7 uses three `<jsp:include>` actions (lines 38–39, 45 and 49–50) as the content in `td` elements of the `table`. Using two XHTML documents and a JSP in Fig. 27.7 demonstrates that JSPs can include both static and dynamic content. The output window in Fig. 27.7 demonstrates the result of one request to `include.jsp`.

Attribute	Description
`page`	Specifies the relative URI path of the resource to include. The resource must be part of the same Web application.
`flush`	Specifies whether the implicit object `out` should be flushed before the `include` is performed. If `true`, the `JspWriter out` is flushed prior to the inclusion, hence you could no longer forward to another page later on. The default value is `false`.

Fig. 27.6 | Action `<jsp:include>` attributes.

Figure 27.10 (`clock2.jsp`) demonstrates how to determine the client's **Locale** (package `java.util`) and uses that `Locale` to format a `Date` with a **DateFormat** (package `java.text`) object. Line 14 invokes the `request` object's **getLocale** method, which returns the client's `Locale`. Lines 17–20 invoke `DateFormat` static method `getDateTimeInstance` to obtain a `DateFormat` object. The first two arguments indicate that the date and time formats should each be `LONG` format (other options are `FULL`, `MEDIUM`, `SHORT` and `DEFAULT`, see `java.sun.com/j2se/5.0/docs/api/java/text/DateFormat.html` for details of these formats). The third argument specifies the `Locale` for which the `Date-Format` object should format the date. Line 25 invokes the `DateFormat` object's `format` method to produce a `String` representation of the `Date`. The `DateFormat` object formats this `String` for the `Locale` specified in line 20. [*Note:* This example works for Western languages that use the ISO-8859-1 character set. For other languages, the JSP must specify the proper character set using the JSP page directive (Section 27.7.1). At the site `java.sun.com/j2se/5.0/docs/guide/intl/encoding.doc.html`, Sun provides a list of

```
 1   <?xml version = "1.0"?>
 2   <!DOCTYPE html PUBLIC "-//W3C//DTD XHTML 1.0 Strict//EN"
 3      "http://www.w3.org/TR/xhtml1/DTD/xhtml1-strict.dtd">
 4
 5   <!-- Fig. 27.7: include.jsp -->
 6
 7   <html xmlns = "http://www.w3.org/1999/xhtml">
 8
 9      <head>
10         <title>Using jsp:include</title>
11
12         <style type = "text/css">
13            body
14            {
15               font-family: tahoma, helvetica, arial, sans-serif;
16            }
17
18            table, tr, td
19            {
20               font-size: .9em;
21               border: 3px groove;
22               padding: 5px;
23               background-color: #dddddd;
24            }
25         </style>
26      </head>
27
28      <body>
29         <table>
30            <tr>
31               <td style = "width: 160px; text-align: center">
32                  <img src = "images/logotiny.png"
33                     width = "140" height = "93"
34                     alt = "Deitel & Associates, Inc. Logo" />
35               </td>
```

Fig. 27.7 | JSP `include.jsp` includes resources with `<jsp:include>`. (Part 1 of 2.)

```
36              <td>
37                  <%-- include banner.html in this JSP --%>
38                  <jsp:include page = "banner.html"
39                      flush = "true" />
40              </td>
41          </tr>
42          <tr>
43              <td style = "width: 160px">
44                  <%-- include toc.html in this JSP --%>
45                  <jsp:include page = "toc.html" flush = "true" />
46              </td>
47              <td style = "vertical-align: top">
48                  <%-- include clock2.jsp in this JSP --%>
49                  <jsp:include page = "clock2.jsp"
50                      flush = "true" />
51              </td>
52          </tr>
53      </table>
54  </body>
55 </html>
```

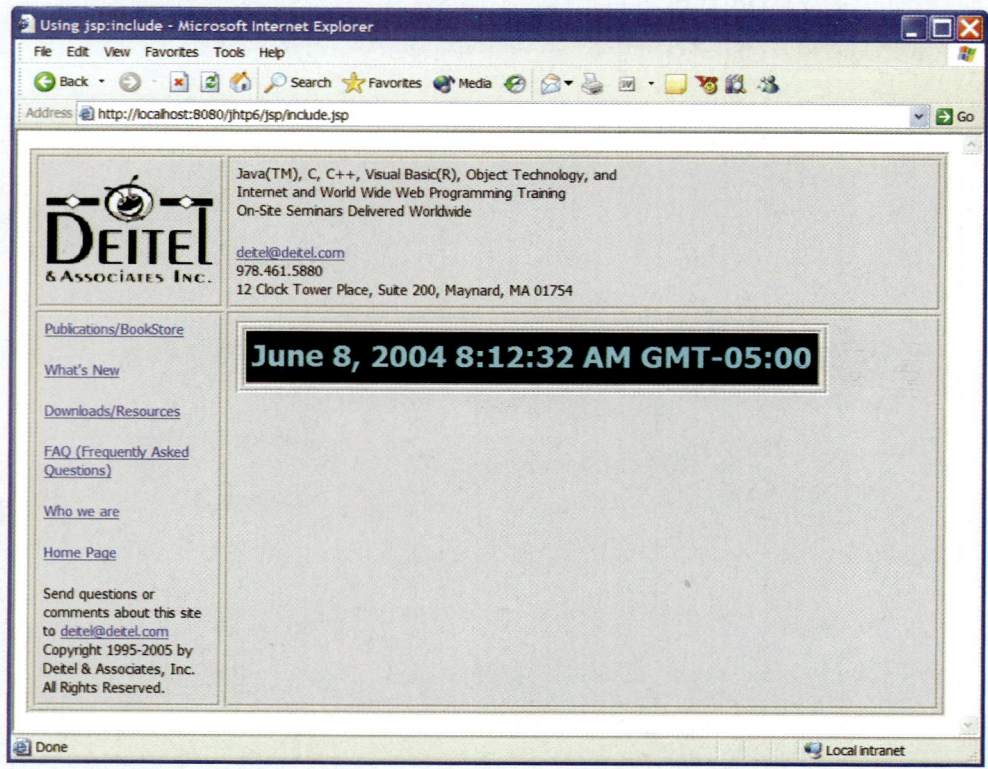

Fig. 27.7 | JSP `include.jsp` includes resources with `<jsp:include>`. (Part 2 of 2.)

```
1   <!-- Fig. 27.8: banner.html                    -->
2   <!-- banner to include in another document -->
3   <div style = "width: 580px">
4      <p>
5         Java(TM), C, C++, Visual Basic(R),
6         Object Technology, and <br /> Internet and
7         World Wide Web Programming Training <br />
8         On-Site Seminars Delivered Worldwide
9      </p>
10     <p>
11        <a href = "mailto:deitel@deitel.com">deitel@deitel.com</a>
12        <br />978.461.5880<br />12 Clock Tower Place, Suite 200,
13        Maynard, MA 01754
14     </p>
15  </div>
```

Fig. 27.8 | Banner (`banner.html`) to include across the top of the XHTML document created by Fig. 27.7 .

```
1   <!-- Fig. 27.9: toc.html                      -->
2   <!-- contents to include in another document -->
3
4   <p><a href = "http://www.deitel.com/books/index.html">
5      Publications/BookStore
6   </a></p>
7
8   <p><a href = "http://www.deitel.com/whatsnew.html">
9      What's New
10  </a></p>
11
12  <p><a href = "http://www.deitel.com/books/downloads.html">
13     Downloads/Resources
14  </a></p>
15
16  <p><a href = "http://www.deitel.com/faq/index.html">
17     FAQ (Frequently Asked Questions)
18  </a></p>
19
20  <p><a href = "http://www.deitel.com/intro.html">
21     Who we are
22  </a></p>
23
24  <p><a href = "http://www.deitel.com/index.html">
25     Home Page
26  </a></p>
27
```

Fig. 27.9 | Table of contents (`toc.html`) to include down the left side of the XHTML document created by Fig. 27.7. (Part 1 of 2.)

```
28    <p>Send questions or comments about this site to
29       <a href = "mailto:deitel@deitel.com">
30          deitel@deitel.com
31       </a><br />
32       Copyright 1995-2005 by Deitel &amp; Associates, Inc.
33       All Rights Reserved.
34    </p>
```

Fig. 27.9 | Table of contents (`toc.html`) to include down the left side of the XHTML document created by Fig. 27.7. (Part 2 of 2.)

```
 1    <!-- Fig. 27.10: clock2.jsp                         -->
 2    <!-- date and time to include in another document -->
 3
 4    <table>
 5       <tr>
 6          <td style = "background-color: black;">
 7             <p class = "big" style = "color: cyan; font-size: 3em;
 8                font-weight: bold;">
 9
10                <%-- script to determine client local and --%>
11                <%-- format date accordingly              --%>
12                <%
13                   // get client locale
14                   java.util.Locale locale = request.getLocale();
15
16                   // get DateFormat for client's Locale
17                   java.text.DateFormat dateFormat =
18                      java.text.DateFormat.getDateTimeInstance(
19                         java.text.DateFormat.LONG,
20                         java.text.DateFormat.LONG, locale );
21
22                %>  <%-- end script --%>
23
24                <%-- output date --%>
25                <%= dateFormat.format( new java.util.Date() ) %>
26             </p>
27          </td>
28       </tr>
29    </table>
```

Fig. 27.10 | JSP `clock2.jsp` to include as the main content in the XHTML document created by Fig. 27.7.

character encodings. The response's content type defines the character set to use in the response. The content type has the form "*mimeType*;charset=*encoding*" (e.g., "text/html;charset=ISO-8859-1".]

To test Fig. 27.7 in Tomcat, copy banner.html, toc.html, clock2.jsp, include.jsp and the images directory into the jsp directory created in Section 27.3. Open your Web browser and enter the following URL:

```
http://localhost:8080/jhtp6/jsp/include.jsp
```

27.6.2 <jsp:forward> Action

Action `<jsp:forward>` enables a JSP to forward request processing to a different resource, such as an error page. Request processing by the original JSP terminates as soon as the JSP forwards the request. Action `<jsp:forward>` has only a `page` attribute that specifies the relative URL of the resource (in the same Web application) to which the request should be forwarded.

> **Software Engineering Observation 27.7**
>
> *When using the `<jsp:forward>` action, the resource to which the request will be forwarded must be in the same context (Web application) as the JSP that originally received the request.*

JavaServer Page `forward1.jsp` (Fig. 27.11) is a modified version of `welcome.jsp` (Fig. 27.4). The primary difference is in lines 20–23, in which JavaServer Page `forward1.jsp` forwards the request to JavaServer Page `forward2.jsp` (Fig. 27.12). Note the `<jsp:param>` action in lines 21–22. This action adds a request parameter representing the date and time at which the initial request was received to the request object that is forwarded to `forward2.jsp`.

```
1   <?xml version = "1.0"?>
2   <!DOCTYPE html PUBLIC "-//W3C//DTD XHTML 1.0 Strict//EN"
3      "http://www.w3.org/TR/xhtml1/DTD/xhtml1-strict.dtd">
4
5   <!-- Fig. 27.11: forward1.jsp -->t
6
7   <html xmlns = "http://www.w3.org/1999/xhtml">
8   <head>
9      <title>Forward request to another JSP</title>
10  </head>
11  <body>
12      <% // begin scriptlet
13
14         String name = request.getParameter( "firstName" );
15
16         if ( name != null )
17         {
18      %> <%-- end scriptlet to insert fixed template data --%>
19
20            <jsp:forward page = "forward2.jsp">
21               <jsp:param name = "date"
22                  value = "<%= new java.util.Date() %>" />
23            </jsp:forward>
24
25      <% // continue scriptlet
26
27         } // end if
28         else
29         {
30      %> <%-- end scriptlet to insert fixed template data --%>
31
```

Fig. 27.11 | JSP `forward1.jsp` receives a `firstName` parameter, adds a date to the request parameters and forwards the request to `forward2.jsp` for further processing. (Part 1 of 2.)

```
32              <form action = "forward1.jsp" method = "get">
33                 <p>Type your first name and press Submit</p>
34
35                 <p><input type = "text" name = "firstName" />
36                     <input type = "submit" value = "Submit" />
37                 </p>
38              </form>
39
40        <%  // continue scriptlet
41
42           } // end else
43
44        %> <%-- end scriptlet --%>
45    </body>
46    </html>  <!-- end XHTML document -->
```

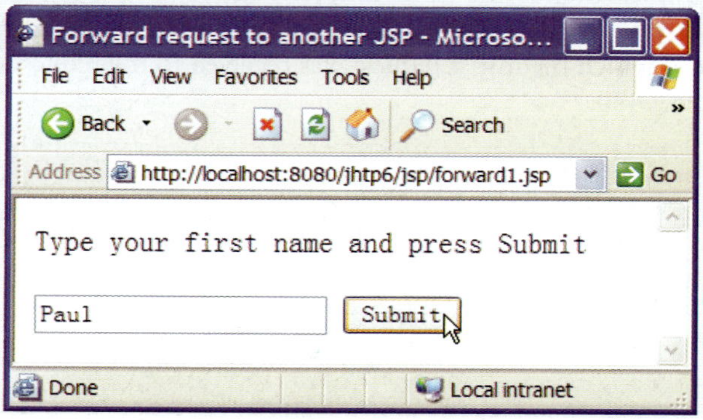

Fig. 27.11 | JSP forward1.jsp receives a firstName parameter, adds a date to the request parameters and forwards the request to forward2.jsp for further processing. (Part 2 of 2.)

```
1    <?xml version = "1.0"?>
2    <!DOCTYPE html PUBLIC "-//W3C//DTD XHTML 1.0 Strict//EN"
3        "http://www.w3.org/TR/xhtml1/DTD/xhtml1-strict.dtd">
4
5    <!-- Fig. 27.12: forward2.jsp -->
6
7    <html xmlns = "http://www.w3.org/1999/xhtml">
8    <head>
9       <title>Processing a forwarded request</title>
10      <style type = "text/css">
11         .big
12         {
13            font-family: tahoma, helvetica, arial, sans-serif;
14            font-weight: bold;
15            font-size: 2em;
16         }
17      </style>
18   </head>
```

Fig. 27.12 | JSP forward2.jsp receives a request (from forward1.jsp in this example) and uses the request parameters as part of the response to the client. (Part 1 of 2.)

```
19    <body>
20       <p class = "big">
21          Hello <%= request.getParameter( "firstName" ) %>, <br />
22          Your request was received <br /> and forwarded at
23       </p>
24       <table style = "border: 6px outset;">
25          <tr>
26             <td style = "background-color: black;">
27                <p class = "big" style = "color: cyan;">
28                   <%= request.getParameter( "date" ) %>
29                </p>
30             </td>
31          </tr>
32       </table>
33    </body>
34    </html>
```

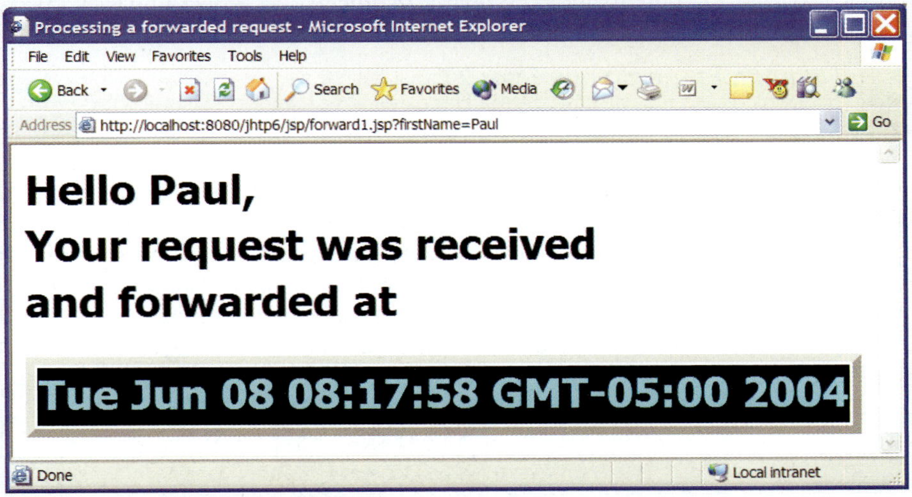

Fig. 27.12 | JSP forward2.jsp receives a request (from forward1.jsp in this example) and uses the request parameters as part of the response to the client. (Part 2 of 2.)

The `<jsp:param>` action specifies name-value pairs of information that are passed to the `<jsp:include>`, `<jsp:forward>` and `<jsp:plugin>` actions. Every `<jsp:param>` action has two required attributes—name and value. If a `<jsp:param>` action specifies a parameter that already exists in the request, the new value for the parameter takes precedence over the original one. All the values for that parameter can be obtained by using the JSP implicit object request's getParameterValues method, which returns an array of Strings.

JSP forward2.jsp uses the name specified in the `<jsp:param>` action ("date") to obtain the date and time. It also uses the firstName parameter originally passed to forward1.jsp to obtain the user's first name. The JSP expressions in Fig. 27.12 (lines 21 and 28) insert the request parameter values in the response to the client. The screen capture in Fig. 27.11 shows the initial interaction with the client. The screen capture in Fig. 27.12 shows the results returned to the client after the request was forwarded to forward2.jsp.

To test Fig. 27.11 and Fig. 27.12 in Tomcat, copy `forward1.jsp` and `forward2.jsp` into the `jsp` directory created in Section 27.3. Open your Web browser and enter the following URL to test `forward1.jsp`:

```
http://localhost:8080/jhtp6/jsp/forward1.jsp
```

27.6.3 `<jsp:useBean>` Action

Action `<jsp:useBean>` enables a JSP to manipulate a Java object. This action creates a Java object or locates an existing object for use in the JSP. Figure 27.13 summarizes action `<jsp:useBean>`'s attributes. If attributes `class` and `beanName` are not specified, the JSP container attempts to locate an existing object of the type specified in attribute `type`. Like JSP implicit objects, objects specified with action `<jsp:useBean>` have a scope—`page`, `request`, `session` or `application`—that indicates where they can be used in a Web application. Objects with `page` scope are accessible only by the page in which they are defined. Multiple JSP pages can potentially access objects in other scopes. For example, all JSPs that process a single request can access an object in `request` scope.

 Common Programming Error 27.3

One or both of the `<jsp:useBean>` attributes `class` and `type` must be specified—otherwise, a translation-time error occurs.

Many Web sites place rotating advertisements on their Web pages. Each visit to one of these pages typically results in a different advertisement being displayed in the user's Web browser. Typically, clicking an advertisement takes you to the Web site of the company that placed the advertisement. Our first example of `<jsp:useBean>` demonstrates a simple advertisement rotator bean that cycles through a list of five advertisements. In this example, the advertisements are covers for some of our books. Clicking a cover takes you to the Amazon.com Web site, where you can read about and possibly order the book.

Attribute	Description
`id`	The name used to manipulate the Java object with actions `<jsp:set-Property>` and `<jsp:getProperty>`. A variable of this name is also declared for use in JSP scripting elements. The name specified here is case sensitive.
`scope`	The scope in which the Java object is accessible—`page`, `request`, `session` or `application`. The default scope is `page`.
`class`	The fully qualified class name of the Java object.
`beanName`	The name of a JavaBean that can be used with method `instantiate` of class `java.beans.Beans` to load a JavaBean into memory.
`type`	The type of the JavaBean. This can be the same type as the `class` attribute, a superclass of that type or an interface implemented by that type. The default value is the same as for attribute `class`. A `ClassCastException` occurs if the Java object is not of the type specified with attribute `type`.

Fig. 27.13 | Attributes of the `<jsp:useBean>` action.

The Rotator bean (Fig. 27.14) has three methods: getImage, getLink and nextAd. Method getImage returns the image file name for the book-cover image. Method getLink returns the hyperlink to the book at Amazon.com. Method nextAd updates the Rotator so that the next calls to getImage and getLink will return information for a different advertisement. Methods getImage and getLink each represent a read-only JavaBean property—image and link, respectively. These are read-only properties because no *set* methods

```
1   // Fig. 27.14: Rotator.java
2   // A JavaBean that rotates advertisements.
3   package com.deitel.jhtp6.jsp.beans;
4
5   public class Rotator
6   {
7      private String images[] = { "images/advjHTP1.jpg",
8         "images/cppHTP4.jpg", "images/iw3HTP2.jpg",
9         "images/jwsFEP1.jpg", "images/vbnetHTP2.jpg" };
10
11     private String links[] = {
12        "http://www.amazon.com/exec/obidos/ASIN/0130895601/" +
13           "deitelassociatin",
14        "http://www.amazon.com/exec/obidos/ASIN/0130384747/" +
15           "deitelassociatin",
16        "http://www.amazon.com/exec/obidos/ASIN/0130308978/" +
17           "deitelassociatin",
18        "http://www.amazon.com/exec/obidos/ASIN/0130461342/" +
19           "deitelassociatin",
20        "http://www.amazon.com/exec/obidos/ASIN/0130293636/" +
21           "deitelassociatin" };
22
23     private int selectedIndex = 0;
24
25     // returns image file name for current ad
26     public String getImage()
27     {
28        return images[ selectedIndex ];
29     } // end method getImage
30
31     // returns the URL for ad's corresponding Web site
32     public String getLink()
33     {
34        return links[ selectedIndex ];
35     } // end method getLink
36
37     // update selectedIndex so next calls to getImage and
38     // getLink return a different advertisement
39     public void nextAd()
40     {
41        selectedIndex = ( selectedIndex + 1 ) % images.length;
42     } // end method nextAd
43  } // end class Rotator
```

Fig. 27.14 | Rotator bean that maintains a set of advertisements.

are provided to change their values. `Rotator` keeps track of the current advertisement with its `selectedIndex` variable, which is updated by invoking method `nextAd`.

JavaBeans were originally intended to be manipulated visually in **visual development environments** (often called **builder tools** or IDEs). Builder tools that support beans provide programmers with tremendous flexibility by allowing them to reuse and integrate existing disparate components that, in many cases, were never intended to be used together. These components can be linked together to create applets, applications or even new beans for reuse by others.

When used in an IDE, JavaBeans usually adhere to the following coding conventions:

1. implement the `Serializable` interface

2. provide a `public` no-argument constructor

3. provide *get* and/or *set* methods for properties (which are normally implemented as fields).

When used on the server side, such as within a JSP or a servlet, JavaBeans are less restricted. For example, the `Rotator` bean does not implement the `Serializable` interface because there is no need to save and load the `Rotator` bean as a file. Recall that by default, if the programmer does not explicitly add constructors to a class, a `public` no-argument constructor is generated automatically. Also note that in the Rotator bean, properties `image` and `link` are read only because they provide only *get* methods.

Lines 7–8 of JavaServer Page `adrotator.jsp` (Fig. 27.15) obtain a reference to an instance of class `Rotator`. The `id` for the bean is `rotator`. The JSP uses this name to manipulate the bean. The scope of the object is `session`, so that every client will see the

```
1   <?xml version = "1.0"?>
2   <!DOCTYPE html PUBLIC "-//W3C//DTD XHTML 1.0 Strict//EN"
3       "http://www.w3.org/TR/xhtml1/DTD/xhtml1-strict.dtd">
4
5   <!-- Fig. 27.15: adrotator.jsp -->
6
7   <jsp:useBean id = "rotator" scope = "session"
8       class = "com.deitel.jhtp6.jsp.beans.Rotator" />
9
10  <html xmlns = "http://www.w3.org/1999/xhtml">
11      <head>
12          <title>AdRotator Example</title>
13          <style type = "text/css">
14              .big { font-family: helvetica, arial, sans-serif;
15                  font-weight: bold;
16                  font-size: 2em }
17          </style>
18          <%-- update advertisement --%>
19          <% rotator.nextAd(); %>
20      </head>
21      <body>
22          <p class = "big">AdRotator Example</p>
```

Fig. 27.15 | JSP `adrotator.jsp` uses a Rotator bean to display a different advertisement on each request for the page. (Part 1 of 2.)

```
23          <p>
24              <a href = "<jsp:getProperty name = "rotator"
25                  property = "link" />">
26
27                  <img src = "<jsp:getProperty name = "rotator"
28                      property = "image" />" alt = "advertisement" />
29              </a>
30          </p>
31      </body>
32  </html>
```

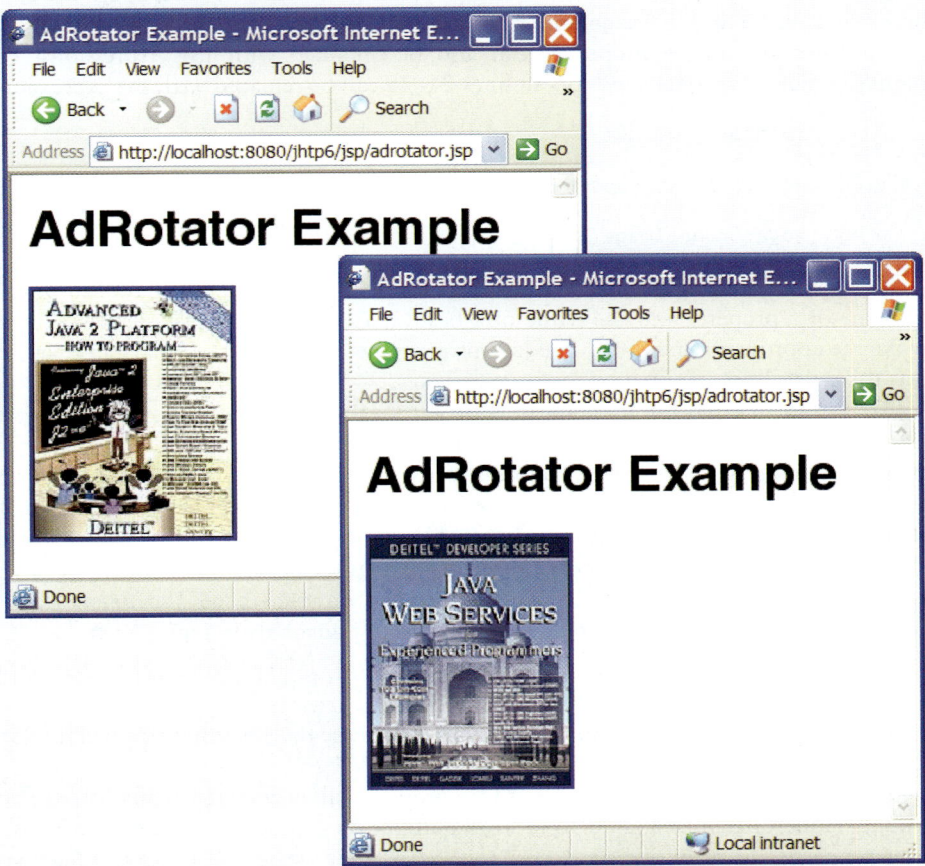

Fig. 27.15 | JSP adrotator.jsp uses a Rotator bean to display a different advertisement on each request for the page. (Part 2 of 2.)

same sequence of ads during their browsing sessions. When adrotator.jsp receives a request from a new client, the JSP container creates the bean and stores it in that client's session (an HttpSession object). In each request to this JSP, line 19 uses the rotator reference created in line 7 to invoke the Rotator bean's nextAd method. Thus, each request will receive the next advertisement selected by the Rotator bean. Lines 24–29 define a hyperlink to the Amazon.com site for a particular book. Lines 24–25 introduce action `<jsp:getProperty>` to obtain the value of the Rotator bean's `link` property. Action `<jsp:getProperty>` has two attributes—`name` and `property`—that specify the bean object to manipulate and the property to get. If the JavaBean object uses standard JavaBean naming conventions, the method used to obtain the `link` property value from the bean should be `getLink`. Action `<jsp:getProperty>` invokes `getLink` on the bean referenced with `rotator`, converts the return value into a `String` and outputs the `String` as part of the response to the client. The `link` property becomes the value of the hyperlink's `href` attribute. The hyperlink is represented in the resulting Web page as the book cover image. Lines 27–28 create an `img` element and use another `<jsp:getProperty>` action to obtain the Rotator bean's `image` property value.

The link and image properties can also be obtained with JSP expressions. For example, action `<jsp:getProperty>` in lines 24–25 can be replaced with the expression

```
<%= rotator.getLink() %>
```

Similarly, action `<jsp:getProperty>` in lines 27–28 can be replaced with the expression

```
<%= rotator.getImage() %>
```

The benefit of using actions is that someone who is unfamiliar with Java can be told the name of a property and the name of a bean, and it is the action's responsibility to invoke the appropriate methods. The Java programmer's job is to create a bean that supports the capabilities required by the page designer.

To test `adrotator.jsp` in Tomcat, copy `adrotator.jsp` into the `jsp` directory created in Section 27.3. You should have copied the `images` directory into the `jsp` directory when you tested Fig. 27.7. If not, you must copy the `images` directory there now. Copy `Rotator.class` into the `jhtp6` Web application's `WEB-INF\classes\com\deitel\jhtp6\jsp\beans` directory in Tomcat. [*Note:* This example will work only if the proper package directory structure for `Rotator` is defined in the `classes` directory. `Rotator` is declared in package `com.deitel.jhtp6.jsp.beans`.] Open your Web browser and enter the following URL to test `adrotator.jsp`:

```
http://localhost:8080/jhtp6/jsp/adrotator.jsp
```

Try reloading this JSP several times in your browser to see the advertisement change with each request.

Action `<jsp:setProperty>` sets JavaBean property values and is particularly useful for mapping request parameter values to JavaBean properties. Request parameters can be used to set properties of primitive types `boolean`, `byte`, `char`, `short`, `int`, `long`, `float` and `double` and `java.lang` types `String`, `Boolean`, `Byte`, `Character`, `Short`, `Integer`, `Long`, `Float` and `Double`. Figure 27.16 summarizes the `<jsp:setProperty>` attributes.

Software Engineering Observation 27.8

Action `<jsp:setProperty>` can use request-parameter values to set JavaBean properties of the following types: `Strings`, primitive types (`boolean`, `byte`, `char`, `short`, `int`, `long`, `float` and `double`) and type-wrapper classes (`Boolean`, `Byte`, `Character`, `Short`, `Integer`, `Long`, `Float` and `Double`). See Fig. 27.22 for an example.

Attribute	Description
name	The ID of the JavaBean for which a property (or properties) will be set.
property	The name of the property to set. Specifying "*" for this attribute specifies that the JSP should match the request parameters to the properties of the bean. For each request parameter that matches (i.e., the name of the request parameter is identical to the bean's property name), the corresponding property in the bean is set to the value of the parameter. If the value of the request parameter is "", the property value in the bean remains unchanged.
param	If request parameter names do not match bean property names, this attribute can be used to specify which request parameter should be used to obtain the value for a specific bean property. This attribute is optional. If this attribute is omitted, the request parameter names must match the bean property names.
value	The value to assign to a bean property. The value typically is the result of a JSP expression. This attribute is particularly useful for setting bean properties that cannot be set using request parameters. This attribute is optional. If this attribute is omitted, the JavaBean property must be of a type that can be set using request parameters.

Fig. 27.16 | Attributes of the `<jsp:setProperty>` action.

Common Programming Error 27.4

Conversion errors occur if you use action `<jsp:setProperty>`'s `value` attribute to set JavaBean property types that cannot be set with request parameters.

27.7 Directives

Directives are messages to the JSP container that enable the programmer to specify page settings (e.g., the error page to invoke if an error occurs), to include content from other resources and to specify custom-tag libraries for use in a JSP. Directives (delimited by `<%@` and `%>`) are processed at translation time. Thus, directives do not produce any immediate output, because they are processed before the JSP accepts any requests. Figure 27.17 summarizes the three directive types. These directives are discussed in the next several subsections.

27.7.1 page Directive

The **page directive** specifies global settings for the JSP in the JSP container. There can be many **page** directives, provided that there is only one occurrence of each attribute. The only exception is the `import` attribute, which can be used repeatedly to import Java packages used in the JSP. Figure 27.18 summarizes the attributes of the **page** directive.

Common Programming Error 27.5

Providing multiple page directives with one or more repeated attributes in common is a JSP translation-time error, unless the values for all repeated attributes are identical. Also, providing a page directive with an attribute or value that is not recognized is a JSP translation-time error.

Directive	Description
`page`	Defines page settings for the JSP container to process.
`include`	Causes the JSP container to perform a translation-time insertion of another resource's content. As the JSP is translated into a servlet and compiled, the referenced file replaces the `include` directive and is translated as if it were originally part of the JSP.
`taglib`	Allows programmers to use new tags from tag libraries that encapsulate more complex functionality and simplify the coding of a JSP.

Fig. 27.17 | JSP directives.

Software Engineering Observation 27.9

According to the JSP specification, section 1.10.1, the `extends` attribute "should not be used without careful consideration as it restricts the ability of the JSP container to provide specialized superclasses that may improve on the quality of rendered service." Remember that a Java class can extend exactly one other class. If your JSP specifies an explicit superclass, the JSP container cannot translate your JSP into a subclass of one of the container application's own enhanced servlet classes.

Attribute	Description
`language`	The scripting language used in the JSP. Currently, the only valid value for this attribute is `java`.
`extends`	Specifies the class from which the translated JSP can inherit. This attribute must be a fully qualified class name.
`import`	Specifies a comma-separated list of fully qualified type names and/or packages that will be used in the current JSP. When the scripting language is `java`, the default import list is `java.lang.*`, `javax.servlet.*`, `javax.servlet.jsp.*` and `javax.servlet.http.*`. If multiple `import` properties are specified, the package names are placed in a list by the container.
`session`	Specifies whether the page participates in a session. The values for this attribute are `true` (participates in a session—the default) or `false` (does not participate in a session). When the page is part of a session, implicit object `session` is available for use in the page. Otherwise, `session` is not available, and using `session` in the scripting code results in a translation-time error.
`buffer`	Specifies the size of the output buffer used with the implicit object `out`. The value of this attribute can be `none` for no buffering or a value such as `8kb` (the default buffer size). The JSP specification indicates that the buffer used must be at least the size specified.

Fig. 27.18 | Attributes of the `page` directive. (Part 1 of 2.)

Attribute	Description
autoFlush	When set to true (the default), this attribute indicates that the output buffer used with implicit object out should be flushed automatically when the buffer fills. If set to false, an exception occurs if the buffer overflows. This attribute's value must be true if the buffer attribute is set to none.
isThreadSafe	Specifies whether the page is thread safe. If true (the default), the page is considered to be thread safe, and it can process multiple requests at the same time. If false, the servlet that represents the page implements interface java.lang.SingleThreadModel and only one request can be processed by that JSP at a time. The JSP standard allows multiple instances of a JSP to exist for JSPs that are not thread safe. This enables the container to handle requests more efficiently. However, this does not guarantee that resources shared across JSP instances are accessed in a thread-safe manner.
info	Specifies an information string that describes the page. This string is returned by the getServletInfo method of the servlet that represents the translated JSP. This method can be invoked through the JSP's implicit page object.
errorPage	Any exceptions in the current page that are not caught are sent to the error page for processing. The error-page implicit object exception references the original exception.
isErrorPage	Specifies whether the current page is an error page that will be invoked in response to an error on another page. If the attribute value is true, the implicit object exception is created and references the original exception that occurred. If false (the default), any use of the exception object in the page results in a translation-time error.
contentType	Specifies the MIME type of the data in the response to the client. The default type is text/html.
pageEncoding	Specifies the character encoding of the JSP page. The default value is ISO-8859-1.
isELIgnored	Specifies whether JSP container should evaluate expressions that use the Expression Language (EL)—a new feature in JSP 2.0 that allows JSP authors to create scriptless JSP pages. EL is typically used with JSP tag libraries, which are beyond the scope of this book. An EL expression has the form ${*exp*}. If the attribute value is true, the EL expressions are ignored, which means that the JSP container does not evaluate the expressions at translation time. If false, the EL expressions are evaluated by the JSP container. For more information on EL, visit java.sun.com/developer/EJTechTips/2004/tt0126.html

Fig. 27.18 | Attributes of the page directive. (Part 2 of 2.)

Common Programming Error 27.6

Using JSP implicit object session in a JSP that does not have its page directive attribute session set to true is a translation-time error.

27.7.2 include Directive

The **include directive** includes the content of another resource once, at JSP translation time. The include directive has only one attribute—file—that specifies the URL of the resource to include. The difference between directive include and action <jsp:include> is noticeable only if the included content changes. For example, if the definition of an XHTML document changes after it is included with directive include, future invocations of the JSP will show the original content of the XHTML document, not the new content. In contrast, action <jsp:include> is processed in each request to the JSP. Therefore, changes to included content would be apparent in the next request to the JSP that uses action <jsp:include>.

JSP includeDirective.jsp (Fig. 27.19) reimplements include.jsp (Fig. 27.7) using include directives. To test includeDirective.jsp in Tomcat, copy it into the jsp directory created in Section 27.3. Open your Web browser and enter the following URL

```
http://localhost:8080/jhtp6/jsp/includeDirective.jsp
```

```
1   <?xml version = "1.0"?>
2   <!DOCTYPE html PUBLIC "-//W3C//DTD XHTML 1.0 Strict//EN"
3      "http://www.w3.org/TR/xhtml1/DTD/xhtml1-strict.dtd">
4
5   <!-- Fig. 27.19: includeDirective.jsp -->
6
7   <html xmlns = "http://www.w3.org/1999/xhtml">
8      <head>
9         <title>Using the include directive</title>
10        <style type = "text/css">
11           body
12           {
13              font-family: tahoma, helvetica, arial, sans-serif;
14           }
15           table, tr, td
16           {
17              font-size: .9em;
18              border: 3px groove;
19              padding: 5px;
20              background-color: #dddddd;
21           }
22        </style>
23     </head>
24     <body>
25        <table>
26           <tr>
27              <td style = "width: 160px; text-align: center">
28                 <img src = "images/logotiny.png"
29                    width = "140" height = "93"
30                    alt = "Deitel & Associates, Inc. Logo" />
31              </td>
32              <td>
33                 <%-- include banner.html in this JSP --%>
```

Fig. 27.19 | JSP includeDirective.jsp demonstrates including content at translation time with directive include. (Part 1 of 2.)

```
34                       <%@ include file = "banner.html" %>
35                  </td>
36              </tr>
37              <tr>
38                  <td style = "width: 160px">
39                      <%-- include toc.html in this JSP --%>
40                      <%@ include file = "toc.html" %>
41                  </td>
42                  <td style = "vertical-align: top">
43                      <%-- include clock2.jsp in this JSP --%>
44                      <%@ include file = "clock2.jsp" %>
45                  </td>
46              </tr>
47          </table>
48      </body>
49  </html>
```

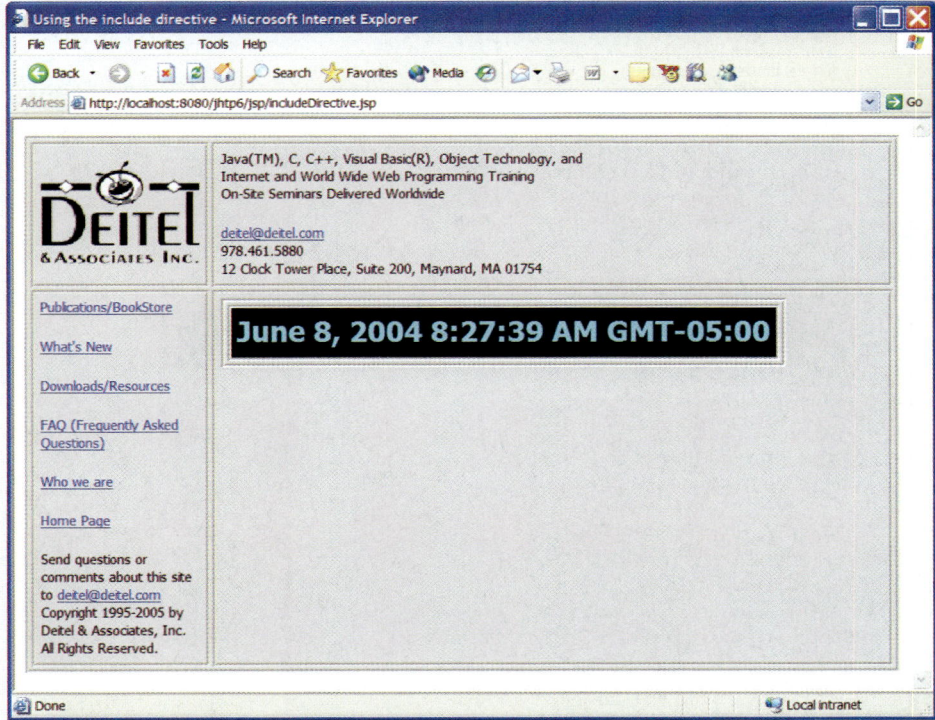

Fig. 27.19 | JSP `includeDirective.jsp` demonstrates including content at translation time with directive `include`. (Part 2 of 2.)

27.8 Case Study: Guest Book

Our next example is a guest book that enables users to place their first name, last name and e-mail address into a guest-book database. After submitting their information, users see a Web page containing all the users in the guest book. Each e-mail address is displayed as a hyperlink that makes it possible to send an e-mail message to the person whose address it is. The example demonstrates action `<jsp:setProperty>`, the JSP page directive, JSP error pages, and using JDBC from a JSP.

The guest-book example consists of JavaBeans `GuestBean` (Fig. 27.20) and `GuestDataBean` (Fig. 27.21), and JSPs `guestBookLogin.jsp` (Fig. 27.22), `guestBookView.jsp`

```java
1   // Fig. 27.20: GuestBean.java
2   // JavaBean to store data for a guest in the guest book.
3   package com.deitel.jhtp6.jsp.beans;
4
5   public class GuestBean
6   {
7      private String firstName;
8      private String lastName;
9      private String email;
10
11     // set the guest's first name
12     public void setFirstName( String name )
13     {
14        firstName = name;
15     } // end method setFirstName
16
17     // get the guest's first name
18     public String getFirstName()
19     {
20        return firstName;
21     } // end method getFirstName
22
23     // set the guest's last name
24     public void setLastName( String name )
25     {
26        lastName = name;
27     } // end method setLastName
28
29     // get the guest's last name
30     public String getLastName()
31     {
32        return lastName;
33     } // end method getLastName
34
35     // set the guest's email address
36     public void setEmail( String address )
37     {
38        email = address;
39     } // end method setEmail
40
41     // get the guest's email address
42     public String getEmail()
43     {
44        return email;
45     } // end method getEmail
46  } // end class GuestBean
```

Fig. 27.20 | `GuestBean` stores information for one guest.

```
1   // Fig. 27.21: GuestDataBean.java
2   // Class GuestDataBean makes a database connection and supports
3   // inserting and retrieving data from the database.
4   package com.deitel.jhtp6.jsp.beans;
5
6   import java.sql.SQLException;
7   import javax.sql.rowset.CachedRowSet;
8   import java.util.ArrayList;
9   import com.sun.rowset.CachedRowSetImpl; // CachedRowSet implementation
10
11  public class GuestDataBean
12  {
13     private CachedRowSet rowSet;
14
15     // construct GuestDataBean object
16     public GuestDataBean() throws Exception
17     {
18        // load the MySQL driver
19        Class.forName( "com.mysql.jdbc.Driver" );
20
21        // specify properties of CachedRowSet
22        rowSet = new CachedRowSetImpl();
23        rowSet.setUrl( "jdbc:mysql://localhost/guestbook" );
24        rowSet.setUsername( "jhtp6" );
25        rowSet.setPassword( "jhtp6" );
26
27        // obtain list of titles
28        rowSet.setCommand(
29           "SELECT firstName, lastName, email FROM guests" );
30        rowSet.execute();
31     } // end GuestDataBean constructor
32
33     // return an ArrayList of GuestBeans
34     public ArrayList< GuestBean > getGuestList() throws SQLException
35     {
36        ArrayList< GuestBean > guestList = new ArrayList< GuestBean >();
37
38        rowSet.beforeFirst(); // move cursor before the first row
39
40        // get row data
41        while ( rowSet.next() )
42        {
43           GuestBean guest = new GuestBean();
44
45           guest.setFirstName( rowSet.getString( 1 ) );
46           guest.setLastName( rowSet.getString( 2 ) );
47           guest.setEmail( rowSet.getString( 3 ) );
48
49           guestList.add( guest );
50        } // end while
51
```

Fig. 27.21 | GuestDataBean performs database access on behalf of guestBookLogin.jsp. (Part 1 of 2.)

```
52          return guestList;
53       } // end method getGuestList
54
55       // insert a guest in guestbook database
56       public void addGuest( GuestBean guest ) throws SQLException
57       {
58          rowSet.moveToInsertRow(); // move cursor to the insert row
59
60          // update the three columns of the insert row
61          rowSet.updateString( 1, guest.getFirstName() );
62          rowSet.updateString( 2, guest.getLastName() );
63          rowSet.updateString( 3, guest.getEmail() );
64          rowSet.insertRow(); // insert row to rowSet
65          rowSet.moveToCurrentRow(); // move cursor to the current row
66          rowSet.acceptChanges(); // propagate changes to database
67       } // end method addGuest
68    } // end class GuestDataBean
```

Fig. 27.21 | GuestDataBean performs database access on behalf of guestBookLogin.jsp. (Part 2 of 2.)

(Fig. 27.23) and guestBookErrorPage.jsp (Fig. 27.24). Sample outputs from this example are shown in Fig. 27.25. JavaBean GuestBean (Fig. 27.20) defines three guest properties—firstName, lastName and email. Each property has *set* and *get* methods to manipulate the property.

JavaBean GuestDataBean (Fig. 27.21) connects to the guestbook database and provides methods getGuestList and addGuest to manipulate the database. The guestbook database has a single table (guests) containing three columns (firstName, lastName and email). Each column stores String values. We provide a SQL script (guestbook.sql) with this example that can be used with the MySQL DBMS to create the guestbook database. For further details on creating a database with MySQL, refer back to Section 25.7.

GuestDataBean constructor (lines 16–29) loads the MySQL database driver, creates a CachedRowSet object using Sun's reference implementation CachedRowSetImpl and sets the properties of the CachedRowSet. Recall that CachedRowSet objects are disconnected rowsets, hence the database connection is automatically closed after the query is executed. Line 23 invokes method **setUrl** (from interface RowSet) to set the CachedRowSet's database URL property. Line 24 invokes method **setUsername** (from interface RowSet) to set the CachedRowSet's database username property. Line 25 invokes method **setPassword** (from interface RowSet) to set the CachedRowSet's database password property. Lines 28–29 invoke method **setCommand** (from interface RowSet) to set the CachedRowSet's command property. Line 30 invokes method **execute** (from interface RowSet) to execute the query specified by the command property.

GuestDataBean method getGuestList (lines 34–53) returns an ArrayList of GuestBean objects representing the guests in the database. Line 38 invokes method **beforeFirst** (from interface ResultSet) to move the CachedRowSet's cursor before the first row. Lines 41–50 create the GuestBean objects for each row in the CachedRowSet.

GuestDataBean method addGuest (lines 56–67) receives a GuestBean as an argument and uses the GuestBean's properties as the arguments to insert a row to the CachedRowSet, which in turn propagates the changes to the underlying database. Recall from Chapter 25 that a CachedRowSet is scrollable and updatable by default. Line 58 invokes the Cached-RowSet's **moveToInsertRow** method to remember the current row position and move the cursor to the insert row—a special row in an updatable result set that allows programmers to insert new rows to the result set. Lines 61–63 invoke the CachedRowSet's **updateString** method to update the column values. Method updateString takes two arguments—an int that specifies the column index and a String that specifies the column value. Line 64 invokes the CachedRowSet's **insertRow** method to insert the row into the rowset. Line 65 invokes the CachedRowSet's **moveToCurrentRow** method to move the cursor back to the current row—the position before method moveToInsertRow was called. Line 66 invokes the CachedRowSet's **acceptChanges** method to propagates the changes in the rowset to the underlying database.

Note that the GuestDataBean's constructor, getGuestList method and addGuest method do not process potential exceptions. In the constructor, line 19 can throw a ClassNotFoundException, and the other statements can throw SQLExceptions. Similarly, SQLExceptions can be thrown from the bodies of methods getGuestList and addGuest. In this example, we purposely let any exceptions that occur get passed back to the JSP that invokes the GuestDataBean's constructor or methods. This enables us to demonstrate JSP error pages. A JSP can include scriptlets that catch potential exceptions and process them. Exceptions that are not caught can be forwarded to a JSP error page for handling.

JavaServer Page guestBookLogin.jsp (Fig. 27.22) is a modified version of forward1.jsp (Fig. 27.11) that displays a form in which users can enter their first name, last name and e-mail address. When the user submits the form, guestBookLogin.jsp is requested again, so it can ensure that all the data values were entered. If they were not, the guestBookLogin.jsp responds with the form again, so the user can fill in missing field(s). If the user supplies all three pieces of information, guestBookLogin.jsp forwards the request to guestBookView.jsp, which displays the guest-book contents.

Line 8 of guestBookLogin.jsp uses the page directive, which defines information that is globally available in a JSP. In this case, the page directive's **errorPage** attribute is set to guestBookErrorPage.jsp (Fig. 27.24), indicating that all uncaught exceptions are forwarded to guestBookErrorPage.jsp for processing.

```
1   <?xml version = "1.0"?>
2   <!DOCTYPE html PUBLIC "-//W3C//DTD XHTML 1.0 Strict//EN"
3       "http://www.w3.org/TR/xhtml1/DTD/xhtml1-strict.dtd">
4
5   <!-- Fig. 27.22: guestBookLogin.jsp -->
6
7   <%-- page settings --%>
8   <%@ page errorPage = "guestBookErrorPage.jsp" %>
9
10  <%-- beans used in this JSP --%>
11  <jsp:useBean id = "guest" scope = "page"
12     class = "com.deitel.jhtp6.jsp.beans.GuestBean" />
13  <jsp:useBean id = "guestData" scope = "request"
14     class = "com.deitel.jhtp6.jsp.beans.GuestDataBean" />
```

Fig. 27.22 | JSP guestBookLogin.jsp enables the user to submit a first name, a last name and an e-mail address to be placed in the guest book. (Part 1 of 3.)

```
15
16   <html xmlns = "http://www.w3.org/1999/xhtml">
17   <head>
18      <title>Guest Book Login</title>
19      <style type = "text/css">
20         body
21         {
22            font-family: tahoma, helvetica, arial, sans-serif;
23         }
24         table, tr, td
25         {
26            font-size: .9em;
27            border: 3px groove;
28            padding: 5px;
29            background-color: #dddddd;
30         }
31      </style>
32   </head>
33   <body>
34      <jsp:setProperty name = "guest" property = "*" />
35      <% // start scriptlet
36         if ( guest.getFirstName() == null ||
37            guest.getLastName() == null ||
38            guest.getEmail() == null )
39         {
40      %> <%-- end scriptlet to insert fixed template data --%>
41            <form method = "post" action = "guestBookLogin.jsp">
42               <p>Enter your first name, last name and email
43                  address to register in our guest book.</p>
44               <table>
45                  <tr>
46                     <td>First name</td>
47                     <td>
48                        <input type = "text" name = "firstName" />
49                     </td>
50                  </tr>
51                  <tr>
52                     <td>Last name</td>
53                     <td>
54                        <input type = "text" name = "lastName" />
55                     </td>
56                  </tr>
57                  <tr>
58                     <td>Email</td>
59                     <td>
60                        <input type = "text" name = "email" />
61                     </td>
62                  </tr>
63                  <tr>
64                     <td colspan = "2">
65                        <input type = "submit" value = "Submit" />
```

Fig. 27.22 | JSP guestBookLogin.jsp enables the user to submit a first name, a last name and an e-mail address to be placed in the guest book. (Part 2 of 3.)

```
66                         </td>
67                     </tr>
68                 </table>
69              </form>
70      <% // continue scriptlet
71         } // end if
72         else
73         {
74             guestData.addGuest( guest );
75      %> <%-- end scriptlet to insert jsp:forward action --%>
76             <%-- forward to display guest book contents --%>
77             <jsp:forward page = "guestBookView.jsp" />
78      <% // continue scriptlet
79         } // end else
80      %> <%-- end scriptlet --%>
81  </body>
82  </html>
```

Fig. 27.22 | JSP `guestBookLogin.jsp` enables the user to submit a first name, a last name and an e-mail address to be placed in the guest book. (Part 3 of 3.)

Lines 11–14 define two `<jsp:useBean>` actions. Lines 11–12 create an instance of `GuestBean` called `guest`. This bean has `page` scope—it exists for use only in this page. Lines 13–14 create an instance of `GuestDataBean` called `guestData`. This bean has `request` scope—it exists for use in this page and any other page that helps process a single client request. Thus, when `guestBookLogin.jsp` forwards a request to `guestBook-View.jsp`, the same `GuestDataBean` instance is still available for use in `guestBook-View.jsp`.

Line 34 demonstrates setting a property of the `GuestBean` called `guest` with a request parameter value. The `input` elements in lines 48, 54 and 60 have the same names as the `GuestBean` properties. So we use action `<jsp:setProperty>`'s ability to match request parameters to properties by specifying `"*"` for attribute `property`. You can set the properties individually by replacing line 34 with the following lines:

```
<jsp:setProperty name = "guest" property = "firstName"
   param = "firstName" />

<jsp:setProperty name = "guest" property = "lastName"
   param = "lastName" />

<jsp:setProperty name = "guest" property = "email"
   param = "email" />
```

If the request parameters had names that differed from `GuestBean`'s properties, the `param` attribute in each of the preceding `<jsp:setProperty>` actions could be changed to the appropriate request parameter name. Or you could make a call to the *set* method directly, like this:

```
<% guest.setFirstName( request.getparameter( "firstName" ) ); %>
```

JavaServer Page `guestBookView.jsp` (Fig. 27.23) outputs an XHTML document containing the guest-book entries in tabular format. Lines 8–10 define three `page` directives. Line 8 specifies that the error page for this JSP is `guestBookErrorPage.jsp`. Line 9 indicates

```
1   <?xml version = "1.0"?>
2   <!DOCTYPE html PUBLIC "-//W3C//DTD XHTML 1.0 Strict//EN"
3       "http://www.w3.org/TR/xhtml1/DTD/xhtml1-strict.dtd">
4
5   <!-- Fig. 27.23: guestBookView.jsp -->
6
7   <%-- page settings --%>
8   <%@ page errorPage = "guestBookErrorPage.jsp" %>
9   <%@ page import = "java.util.*" %>
10  <%@ page import = "com.deitel.jhtp6.jsp.beans.*" %>
11
12  <%-- GuestDataBean to obtain guest list --%>
13  <jsp:useBean id = "guestData" scope = "request"
14     class = "com.deitel.jhtp6.jsp.beans.GuestDataBean" />
15
16  <html xmlns = "http://www.w3.org/1999/xhtml">
17     <head>
18        <title>Guest List</title>
19        <style type = "text/css">
20           body
21           {
22              font-family: tahoma, helvetica, arial, sans-serif;
23           }
24           table, tr, td, th
25           {
26              text-align: center;
27              font-size: .9em;
28              border: 3px groove;
29              padding: 5px;
30              background-color: #dddddd;
31           }
32        </style>
33     </head>
34     <body>
35        <p style = "font-size: 2em;">Guest List</p>
36        <table>
37           <thead>
38              <tr>
39                 <th style = "width: 100px;">Last name</th>
40                 <th style = "width: 100px;">First name</th>
41                 <th style = "width: 200px;">Email</th>
42              </tr>
43           </thead>
44           <tbody>
45              <% // start scriptlet
46                 List guestList = guestData.getGuestList();
47                 Iterator guestListIterator = guestList.iterator();
48                 GuestBean guest;
49
50                 while ( guestListIterator.hasNext() )
51                 {
52                    guest = ( GuestBean ) guestListIterator.next();
53              %> <%-- end scriptlet; insert fixed template data --%>
```

Fig. 27.23 | JSP guestBookView.jsp displays the contents of the guest book. (Part 1 of 2.)

```
54                      <tr>
55                          <td><%= guest.getLastName() %></td>
56                          <td><%= guest.getFirstName() %></td>
57                          <td>
58                              <a href = "mailto:<%= guest.getEmail() %>">
59                                  <%= guest.getEmail() %></a>
60                          </td>
61                      </tr>
62                  <% // continue scriptlet
63                      } // end while
64                  %> <%-- end scriptlet --%>
65              </tbody>
66          </table>
67      </body>
68  </html>
```

Fig. 27.23 | JSP guestBookView.jsp displays the contents of the guest book. (Part 2 of 2.)

that classes from package java.util are used in this JSP, and line 10 indicates that classes from our package com.deitel.jhtp6.jsp.beans are also used.

Lines 13–14 specify a <jsp:useBean> action that declares a reference to a Guest-DataBean object. If a GuestDataBean object already exists, the action returns a reference to the existing object. Otherwise, the action creates a GuestDataBean for use in this JSP. Lines 45–53 define a scriptlet that gets the guest list from the GuestDataBean and begins a loop to output the entries. Lines 54–61 combine fixed template text with JSP expressions to create rows in the table of guest-book data that will be displayed on the client. The scriptlet at lines 62–64 terminates the loop that begins at line 50.

JavaServer Page guestBookErrorPage.jsp (Fig. 27.24) outputs an XHTML document containing an error message based on the type of exception that causes this error page to be invoked. Lines 8–10 define several page directives. Line 8 sets page directive attribute **isErrorPage**. Setting this attribute to true makes the JSP an error page and enables access to the JSP implicit object exception that refers to an exception object indicating the problem that occurred.

```
1   <?xml version = "1.0"?>
2   <!DOCTYPE html PUBLIC "-//W3C//DTD XHTML 1.0 Strict//EN"
3       "http://www.w3.org/TR/xhtml1/DTD/xhtml1-strict.dtd">
4
5   <!-- Fig. 27.24: guestBookErrorPage.jsp -->
6
7   <%-- page settings --%>
8   <%@ page isErrorPage = "true" %>
9   <%@ page import = "java.util.*" %>
10  <%@ page import = "java.sql.*" %>
11
12  <html xmlns = "http://www.w3.org/1999/xhtml">
13      <head>
```

Fig. 27.24 | JSP guestBookErrorPage.jsp responds to exceptions in guestBookLogin.jsp and guestBookView.jsp. (Part 1 of 2.)

```
14          <title>Error!</title>
15          <style type = "text/css">
16             .bigRed
17             {
18                font-size: 2em;
19                color: red;
20                font-weight: bold;
21             }
22          </style>
23       </head>
24       <body>
25          <p class = "bigRed">
26          <% // scriptlet to determine exception type
27             // and output beginning of error message
28             if ( exception instanceof SQLException )
29             {
30          %>

32                A SQLException

34          <%
35             } // end if
36             else if ( exception instanceof ClassNotFoundException )
37             {
38          %>

40                A ClassNotFoundException

42          <%
43             } // end else if
44             else
45             {
46          %>

48                An exception

50          <%
51             } // end else
52          %>
53          <%-- end scriptlet to insert fixed template data --%>

55             <%-- continue error message output --%>
56             occurred while interacting with the guestbook database.
57          </p>
58          <p class = "bigRed">
59             The error message was:<br />
60             <%= exception.getMessage() %>
61          </p>
62          <p class = "bigRed">Please try again later</p>
63       </body>
64    </html>
```

Fig. 27.24 | JSP guestBookErrorPage.jsp responds to exceptions in guestBookLogin.jsp and guestBookView.jsp. (Part 2 of 2.)

Lines 26–52 define scriptlets that determine the type of exception that occurred and begin outputting an appropriate error message with fixed template data. The actual error message from the exception is output at line 60.

Figure 27.25 shows sample interactions between the user and the JSPs in the guest book example. In the first two rows of output, separate users entered their first name, last

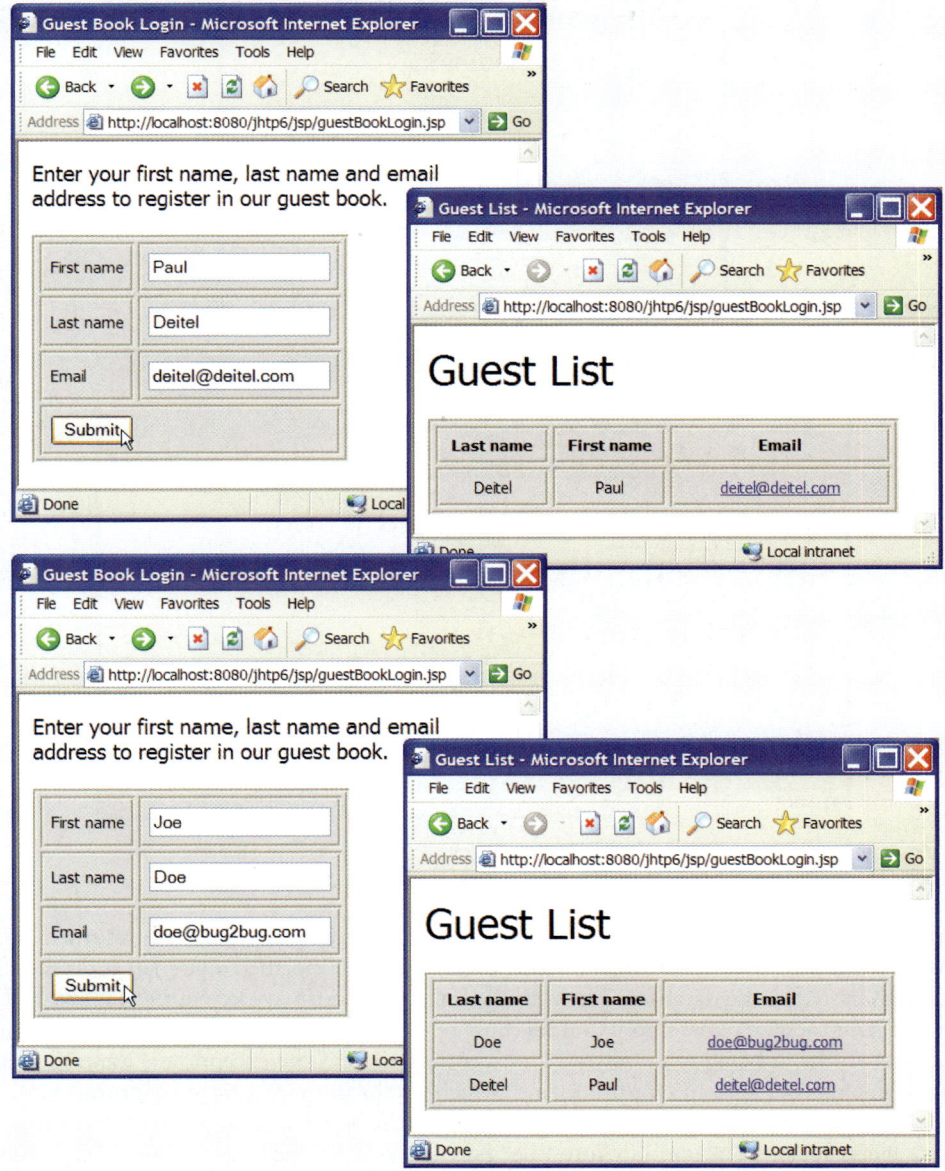

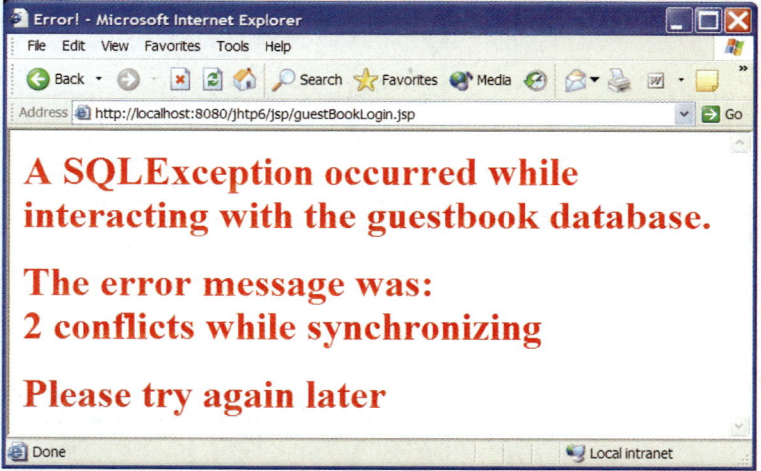

Fig. 27.25 | JSP guest book sample output windows. (Part 2 of 2.)

name and e-mail. In each case, the current contents of the guest book are returned and displayed for the user. In the final interaction, a third user specified an e-mail address that already existed in the database. The e-mail address is the primary key in the guests table of the guestbook database, so its values must be unique. Thus, the database prevents the new record from being inserted, and an exception occurs. The exception is forwarded to guestBookErrorPage.jsp for processing, which results in the last screen capture.

To test the guest book in Tomcat, copy guestBookLogin.jsp, guestBookView.jsp and guestBookErrorPage.jsp into the jsp directory created in Section 27.3. Copy GuestBean.class and GuestDataBean.class into the jhtp6 Web application's WEB-INF\classes\com\deitel\jhtp6\beans directory in Tomcat. [*Note:* This example will work only if the proper package directory structure for GuestBean and GuestDataBean is defined in the classes directory. These classes are declared in package com.deitel.jhtp6.jsp.beans.] Create the database by running the guestbook.sql script included with this example on the CD that accompanies this book. For further details on creating a database with MySQL, refer back to Section 25.7. Open your Web browser and enter the following URL to test guestBookLogin.jsp:

```
http://localhost:8080/jhtp6/jsp/guestBookLogin.jsp
```

27.9 Wrap-Up

In this chapter, you learned several JSP components—implicit objects, scripting elements, standard actions and directives. You saw JSP examples that use these components to separate presentation from business logic and learned that logic can be placed in a JSP via scripting elements. You also learned how to use the CachedRowSet to manipulate a MySQL database in a JavaBean object, then access the JavaBean object in a JSP page. In the next chapter, we summarize how to display formatted output with various format characters and flags. We also demonstrate how to format output with class Formatter.

27.10 Internet and Web Resources

java.sun.com/products/jsp
The home page for information about JavaServer Pages at the Sun Microsystems Java site.

java.sun.com/products/servlet
The home page for information about servlets at the Sun Microsystems Java site.

java.sun.com/j2ee
The home page for the Java 2 Enterprise Edition at the Sun Microsystems Java site.

www.w3.org
The World Wide Web Consortium home page. This site provides information about current and developing Internet and Web standards, such as XHTML, XML and CSS.

jsptags.com
This site includes tutorials, tag libraries, software and other resources for JSP programmers.

jspinsider.com
This Web programming site concentrates on resources for JSP programmers. It includes software, tutorials, articles, sample code, references and links to other JSP and Web programming resources.

Summary

- JavaServer Pages (JSPs) are an extension of servlet technology.
- JSPs enable Web application programmers to create dynamic content by reusing predefined components and by interacting with components using server-side scripting.
- JSP programmers can create custom tag libraries that enable Web page designers who are not familiar with Java to enhance their Web pages with powerful dynamic content and processing capabilities.
- Classes and interfaces specific to JavaServer Pages programming are located in packages javax.servlet.jsp and javax.servlet.jsp.tagext.
- There are four key components to JSPs—directives, actions, scriptlets and tag libraries.
- Directives specify global information that is not associated with a particular JSP request.

- Actions encapsulate functionality in predefined tags that programmers can embed in a JSP.

- Scriptlets enable programmers to insert Java code that interacts with components in a JSP (and possibly other Web application components) to perform request processing.

- Tag libraries are part of the tag extension mechanism that enables programmers to create new tags that encapsulate complex Java functionality.

- JSPs normally include XHTML or XML markup. Such markup is known as fixed-template data or fixed-template text.

- Programmers tend to use JSPs when most of the content sent to the client is fixed-template data and only a small portion of the content is generated dynamically with Java code.

- Programmers use servlets when a small portion of the content is fixed-template data.

- The request/response mechanism and life cycle of a JSP are the same as those of a servlet.

- JSPs can define methods `jspInit` and `jspDestroy` that are invoked when the container initializes a JSP and when the container terminates a JSP, respectively.

- Implicit objects provide programmers with servlet capabilities in the context of a JavaServer Page.

- Implicit objects have four scopes—application, page, request and session.

- Objects with application scope are part of the JSP and servlet container application. Objects with page scope exist only as part of the page in which they are used. Each page has its own instances of the page-scope implicit objects. Objects in request scope exist for the duration of the request. Request-scope objects go out of scope when request processing completes with a response to the client. Objects in session scope exist for the client's entire browsing session.

- JSP scripting components include scriptlets, comments, expressions, declarations and escape sequences.

- JSP comments are delimited by `<%--` and `--%>`.

- XHTML comments are delimited by `<!--` and `-->`.

- Java's end-of-line comments (`//`) and traditional comments (delimited by `/*` and `*/`) can be used inside scriptlets.

- JSP comments and scripting-language comments are ignored and do not appear in a response.

- A JSP expression, delimited by `<%=` and `%>`, contains a Java expression that is evaluated when a client requests the JSP containing the expression. The container converts the result of a JSP expression to a `String` object, then outputs the `String` as part of the response to the client.

- Declarations, delimited by `<%!` and `%>`, enable a JSP programmer to declare variables and methods. Variables become instance variables of the class that represents the translated JSP. Similarly, methods become members of the class that represents the translated JSP.

- Special characters or character sequences that the JSP container normally uses to delimit JSP code can be included in a JSP as literal characters in scripting elements, fixed-template data and attribute values by using escape sequences.

- JavaServer Pages support two include mechanisms—the `<jsp:include>` action and the `include` directive.

- Action `<jsp:include>` enables dynamic content to be included in a JSP. If the included resource changes between requests, the next request to that JSP includes the new content of the included resource.

- The `include` directive is processed once, at JSP translation time, and causes the content to be copied into the JSP. If the included resource changes, the new content will not be reflected in the JSP that used the include directive unless that JSP is recompiled.

- Action `<jsp:forward>` enables a JSP to forward the processing of a request to a different resource. Processing of the request by the original JSP terminates as soon as the request is forwarded.

- Action `<jsp:param>` specifies name-value pairs of information that are passed to the `include`, `forward` and `plugin` actions. Every `<jsp:param>` action has two required attributes—`name` and `value`. If a param action specifies a parameter that already exists in the request, the new value for the parameter takes precedence over the original value. All the values for that parameter can be obtained with the JSP implicit object `request`'s `getParameterValues` method, which returns an array of `Strings`.

- Action `<jsp:useBean>` enables a JSP to manipulate a Java object. This action can be used to create a Java object for use in the JSP or to locate an existing object.

- Like JSP implicit objects, objects specified with action `<jsp:useBean>` have page, request, session or application scope that indicates where they can be used in a Web application.

- Action `<jsp:getProperty>` obtains the value of a JavaBean's property. Action `<jsp:getProperty>` has two attributes—`name` and `property`—that specify the bean object to manipulate and the property to get.

- JavaBean property values can be set with action `<jsp:setProperty>`. Request parameters can be used to set properties of primitive types `boolean`, `byte`, `char`, `short`, `int`, `long`, `float` and `double` and java.lang types `String`, `Boolean`, `Byte`, `Character`, `Short`, `Integer`, `Long`, `Float` and `Double`.

- The page directive defines information that is globally available in a JSP. Directives are delimited by `<%@` and `%>`. The page directive's `errorPage` attribute indicates where all uncaught exceptions are forwarded for processing.

- Action `<jsp:setProperty>` has the ability to match request parameters to properties of the same name in a bean by specifying "`*`" for attribute `property`.

- Attribute `import` of the page directive enables programmers to specify Java classes and packages that are used in the context of a JSP.

- If the attribute `isErrorPage` of the page directive is set to `true`, the JSP is an error page. This condition enables access to the JSP implicit object `exception` that refers to an exception object indicating the problem that occurred.

- Directives are messages to the JSP container that enable the programmer to specify page settings (e.g., the error page), to include content from other resources and to specify custom tag libraries that can be used in a JSP. Directives are processed at the time a JSP is translated into a servlet and compiled. Thus, they do not produce any immediate output.

- The page directive specifies global settings for a JSP in the JSP container. There can be many page directives, provided that there is only one occurrence of each attribute. The exception to this rule is the import attribute, which can be used repeatedly to import Java packages.

Terminology

`%\>` escape sequence for `%>`
`<!--` and `-->` XHTML comment delimiters
`<%--` and `--%>` JSP comment delimiters
`<%` and `%>` scriptlet delimiters
`<%!` and `%>` declaration delimiters
`<%=` and `%>` JSP expression delimiters
`<%@` and `%>` directive delimiters
`<\%` escape sequence for `<%`
`${`*exp*`}`
`acceptChanges` method of `CachedRowSet`

`autoFlush` attribute of page directive
`beanName` attribute of `<jsp:useBean>` action
`beforeFirst` method of `CachedRowSet`
`buffer` attribute of page directive
`class` attribute of `<jsp:useBean>` action
comment
`config` implicit object
`contentType` attribute of page directive
directive
dynamic content

Self-Review Exercises

27.1 Fill in the blanks in each of the following statements:

a) Action _____ has the ability to match request parameters to properties of the same name in a bean by specifying "*" for attribute property.

b) There are four key components to JSPs: _____, _____, _____ and _____.

c) The implicit objects have four scopes: _____, _____, _____ and _____.

d) The _____ directive is processed once at JSP translation time and causes content to be copied into the JSP.

e) Classes and interfaces specific to JavaServer Pages programming are located in packages _____ and _____.

    f) JSPs normally execute as part of a Web server that is referred to as the _____.

    g) JSP scripting components include _____, _____, _____, _____ and _____.

27.2 State whether each of the following is *true* or *false*. If *false*, explain why.

    a) An object with page scope exists in every JSP of a particular Web application.

    b) Directives specify global information that is not associated with a particular JSP request.

    c) Action <jsp:include> is evaluated once at page translation time.

    d) Like XHTML comments, JSP comments and script-language comments appear in the response to the client.

    e) Objects with application scope are part of a particular Web application.

    f) Each page has its own instances of the page-scope implicit objects.

    g) Action <jsp:setProperty> has the ability to match request parameters to properties of the same name in a bean by specifying "*" for attribute property.

    h) Objects with session scope exist for the client's entire browsing session.

Answers to Self-Review Exercises

27.1 a) <jsp:setProperty>. b) directives, actions, scripting elements, tag libraries. c) application, page, request, session. d) include. e) javax.servlet.jsp, javax.servlet.jsp.tagext. f) JSP container. g) scriptlets, comments, expressions, declarations, escape sequences.

27.2 a) False. Objects with page scope exist only as part of the page in which they are used. b) True. c) False. Action <jsp:include> enables dynamic content to be included in a JavaServer Page. d) False. JSP comments and script-language comments are ignored and do not appear in the response. e) False. Objects with application scope are part of the JSP container application. f) True. g) True. h) True.

Exercises

27.3 Write a JSP page to output the string "Hello world!" ten times.

27.4 Modify Exercise 26.6 to run as a JSP page.

27.5 Rewrite Figure 27.15 to provide a form that allow users to select a book title and view the book's cover. Use a JSP expression instead of the getProperty JSP tag.

27.6 Create a JSP- and JDBC-based address book. Use the guest-book example of Fig. 27.20 through Fig. 27.24 as a guide. Your address book should allow the user to insert entries and search for entries. [*Note:* If you are not familiar with XHTML and CSS, refer to the chapters from our book *Internet & World Wide Web HTP, 3/e*—Introduction to XHTML: Part 1, Introduction to XHTML: Part 2 and Cascading Style Sheets (CSS), which are included as PDF documents on the CD that accompanies this book.]

27.7 Reimplement the Web application of Fig. 26.21 (favorite animal survey) using JSPs. [*Note:* If you are not familiar with XHTML and CSS, refer to the chapters from our book *Internet & World Wide Web HTP, 3/e*—Introduction to XHTML: Part 1, Introduction to XHTML: Part 2 and Cascading Style Sheets (CSS), which are included as PDF documents on the CD that accompanies this book.]

27.8 Modify your solution to Exercise 27.7 to allow the user to see the survey results without responding to the survey. [*Note:* If you are not familiar with XHTML and CSS, refer to the chapters from our book *Internet & World Wide Web HTP, 3/e*—Introduction to XHTML: Part 1, Introduction to XHTML: Part 2 and Cascading Style Sheets (CSS), which are included as PDF documents on the CD that accompanies this book.]

Formatted Output

OBJECTIVES

In this chapter you will learn:

■ To understand input and output streams.

■ To use `printf` formatting.

■ To print with field widths and precisions.

■ To use formatting flags in the `printf` format string.

■ To print with an argument index.

■ To output literals and escape sequences.

■ To format output with class `Formatter`.

28.1 Introduction

An important part of the solution to any problem is the presentation of the results. In this chapter, we discuss the formatting features of method `printf` and class `Formatter` (package `java.util`). Method `printf` formats and outputs data to the standard output stream—System.out. Class `Formatter` formats and outputs data to a specified destination, such as a string or a file output stream.

Many features of `printf` were discussed earlier in the text. This chapter summarizes those features and introduces others, such as displaying date and time data in various formats, reordering output based on the index of the argument and displaying numbers and strings with various flags.

28.2 Streams

Input and output are usually performed with streams, which are sequences of bytes. In input operations, the bytes flow from a device (e.g., a keyboard, a disk drive, a network connection) to main memory. In output operations, bytes flow from main memory to a device (e.g., a display screen, a printer, a disk drive, a network connection, etc.).

When program execution begins, three streams are connected to the program automatically. Normally, the standard input stream is connected to the keyboard, and the standard output stream is connected to the screen. A third stream, the standard error stream (System.err), is typically connected to the screen and is used to output error messages to the screen so they can be viewed immediately—even when the standard output stream is writing into a file. Operating systems typically allow these streams to be redirected to other devices. Streams are discussed in detail in Chapter 14, Files and Streams, and Chapter 24, Networking.

28.3 Formatting Output with printf

Precise output formatting is accomplished with printf. [*Note:* J2SE 5.0 borrowed this feature from the C programming language.] Method printf can perform the following formatting capabilities, each of which is discussed in this chapter:

1. Rounding floating-point values to an indicated number of decimal places.

2. Aligning a column of numbers with decimal points appearing one above the other.

3. Right justification and left justification of outputs.

4. Inserting literal characters at precise locations in a line of output.

5. Representing floating-point numbers in exponential format.

6. Representing integers in octal and hexadecimal format. (See Appendix E, Number Systems, for more information on octal and hexadecimal values.)

7. Displaying all types of data with fixed-size field widths and precisions.

8. Displaying dates and times in various formats.

Every call to printf supplies as the first argument a format string that describes the output format. The format string may consist of fixed text and format specifiers. Fixed text is output by printf just as it would be output by System.out methods print or println. Each format specifier is a placeholder for a value and specifies the type of data to output. Format specifiers also may include optional formatting information.

In the simplest form, each format specifier begins with a percent sign (%) and is followed by a conversion character that represents the data type of the value to output. For example, the format specifier %s is a placeholder for a string, and the format specifier %d is a placeholder for an int value. The optional formatting information is specified between the percent sign and the conversion character. The optional formatting information includes an argument index, flags, field width and precision. We define each of these and show examples of them throughout this chapter.

28.4 Printing Integers

An integer is a whole number, such as 776, 0 or –52, that contains no decimal point. Integer values are displayed in one of several formats. Figure 28.1 describes the integral conversion characters.

Figure 28.2 prints an integer using each of the integral conversions. In lines 9–10, note that the plus sign is not displayed by default, but the minus sign is. Later in this chapter (Fig. 28.14) we will see how to force plus signs to print.

Conversion character	Description
d	Display a decimal (base 10) integer.
o	Display an octal (base 8) integer.
x or X	Display a hexadecimal (base 16) integer. X causes the digits 0–9 and the letters A–F to be displayed and x causes the digits 0–9 and a–f to be displayed.

Fig. 28.1 | Integer conversion characters.

```
 1   // Fig. 28.2: IntegerConversionTest.java
 2   // Using the integral conversion characters.
 3
 4   public class IntegerConversionTest
 5   {
 6      public static void main( String args[] )
 7      {
 8         System.out.printf( "%d\n", 26 );
 9         System.out.printf( "%d\n", +26 );
10         System.out.printf( "%d\n", -26 );
11         System.out.printf( "%o\n", 26 );
12         System.out.printf( "%x\n", 26 );
13         System.out.printf( "%X\n", 26 );
14      } // end main
15   } // end class IntegerConversionTest
```

```
26
26
-26
32
1a
1A
```

Fig. 28.2 | Using integer conversion characters.

The printf method has the form

> printf(*format-string*, *argument-list*);

where *format-string* describes the output format, and *argument-list* contains the values that correspond to each format specifier in *format-string*. There can be many format specifiers in one format string.

Each format string in lines 8–10 specifies that printf should output a decimal integer (%d) followed by a newline character. At the format specifier's position, printf substitutes the value of the first argument after the format string. If the format string contained multiple format specifiers, at each subsequent format specifier's position, printf would substitute the value of the next argument in the argument list. The %o format specifier in line 11 outputs the integer in octal format. The %x format specifier in line 12 outputs the integer in hexadecimal format. The %X format specifier in line 13 outputs the integer in hexadecimal format with capital letters.

28.5 Printing Floating-Point Numbers

A floating-point value contains a decimal point, as in 33.5, 0.0 or -657.983. Floating-point values are displayed in one of several formats. Figure 28.3 describes the floating-point conversions. The **conversion character e** and **E** displays floating-point values in **computerized scientific notation** (also called **exponential notation**). Exponential notation is the computer equivalent of the scientific notation used in mathematics. For example, the value 150.4582 is represented in scientific notation in mathematics as

$$1.504582 \times 10^2$$

and is represented in exponential notation as

> 1.504582e+02

in Java. This notation indicates that 1.504582 is multiplied by 10 raised to the second power (e+02). The e stands for "exponent."

Values printed with the conversion characters e, E and f are output with six digits of precision to the right of the decimal point by default (e.g., 1.045921)—other precisions must be specified explicitly. For values printed with the conversion character g, the precision represents the total number of digits displayed, excluding the exponent. The default is six digits (e.g., 12345678.9 is displayed as 1.23457e+07). **Conversion character f** always prints at least one digit to the left of the decimal point. Conversion character e and E print lowercase e and uppercase E preceding the exponent and always print exactly one digit to the left of the decimal point. Rounding occurs if the value being formatted has more significant digits than the precision.

Conversion character g (or G) prints in either e (E) or f format, depending on the floating-point value. For example, the values 0.0000875, 87500000.0, 8.75, 87.50 and 875.0 are printed as 8.750000e-05, 8.750000e+07, 8.750000, 87.500000 and 875.000000 with the conversion character g. The value 0.0000875 uses e notation because the magnitude is less than 10-3. The value 87500000.0 uses e notation because the magnitude is greater than 107. Figure 28.4 demonstrates each of the floating-point conversion characters.

28.6 Printing Strings and Characters

The c and s conversion characters are used to print individual characters and strings, respectively. Conversion character s can also print objects with the results of implicit calls to method toString. **Conversion character c** and C requires a char argument. **Conversion character s** and S can take a String or any Object (this includes all subclasses of Object) as an argument. When an object is passed to the conversion character s, the program

Conversion character	Description
e or E	Display a floating-point value in exponential notation. When conversion character E is used, the output is displayed in uppercase letters.
f	Display a floating-point value in decimal format.
g or G	Display a floating-point value in either the floating-point format f or the exponential format e based on the magnitude of the value. If the magnitude is less than 10^{-3}, or greater than or equal to 10^7, the floating-point value is printed with e (or E). Otherwise, the value is printed in format f. When conversion character G is used, the output is displayed in uppercase letters.
a or A	Display a floating-point number in hexadecimal format. When conversion character A is used, the output is displayed in uppercase letters.

Fig. 28.3 | Floating-point conversion characters.

```
 1   // Fig. 28.4: FloatingNumberTest.java
 2   // Using floating-point conversion characters.
 3
 4   public class FloatingNumberTest
 5   {
 6      public static void main( String args[] )
 7      {
 8         System.out.printf( "%e\n", 12345678.9 );
 9         System.out.printf( "%e\n", +12345678.9 );
10         System.out.printf( "%e\n", -12345678.9 );
11         System.out.printf( "%E\n", 12345678.9 );
12         System.out.printf( "%f\n", 12345678.9 );
13         System.out.printf( "%g\n", 12345678.9 );
14         System.out.printf( "%G\n", 12345678.9 );
15      } // end main
16   } // end class FloatingNumberTest
```

```
1.234568e+07
1.234568e+07
-1.234568e+07
1.234568E+07
12345678.900000
1.23457e+07
1.23457E+07
```

Fig. 28.4 | Using floating-point conversion characters.

implicitly uses the object's toString method to obtain the String representation of the object. When conversion characters C and S are used, the output is displayed in uppercase letters. The program shown in Fig. 28.5 displays characters, strings and objects with conversion characters c and s. Note that autoboxing occurs at line 10 when an int constant is assigned to an Integer object. Line 15 associates an Integer object argument to the conversion character s, which implicitly invokes the toString method to get the integer value. Note that you can also output an Integer object using the %d format specifier. In this case, the int value in the Integer object will be unboxed and output.

Common Programming Error 28.1

Using %c to print a string causes an IllegalFormatConversionException—a string cannot be converted to a character.

28.7 Printing Dates and Times

With the **conversion character t** or **T**, we can print dates and times in various formats. Conversion character t or T is always followed by a **conversion suffix character** that specifies the date and/or time format. When conversion character T is used, the output is displayed in uppercase letters. Figure 28.6 lists the common conversion suffix characters for formatting **date and time compositions** that display both the date and the time. Figure 28.7 lists the common conversion suffix characters for formatting dates. Figure 28.8 lists the common conversion suffix characters for formatting times. To view the complete list of conversion suffix characters, visit the Web site java.sun.com/j2se/5.0/docs/api/java/util/Formatter.html.

```
 1    // Fig. 28.5: CharStringConversion.java
 2    // Using character and string conversion characters.
 3
 4    public class CharStringConversion
 5    {
 6       public static void main( String args[] )
 7       {
 8          char character = 'A';  // initialize char
 9          String string = "This is also a string";  // String object
10          Integer integer = 1234;  // initialize integer (autoboxing)
11
12          System.out.printf( "%c\n", character );
13          System.out.printf( "%s\n", "This is a string" );
14          System.out.printf( "%s\n", string );
15          System.out.printf( "%S\n", string );
16          System.out.printf( "%s\n", integer ); // implicit call to toString
17       } // end main
18    } // end class CharStringConversion
```

```
A
This is a string
This is also a string
THIS IS ALSO A STRING
1234
```

Fig. 28.5 | Using character and string conversion characters.

Conversion suffix character	Description
c	Display date and time formatted as day month date hour:minute:second time-zone year with three characters for day and month, two digits for date, hour, minute and second and four digits for year—for example, Wed Mar 03 16:30:25 GMT-05:00 2004. The 24-hour clock is used. In this example, GMT-05:00 is the time zone.
F	Display date formatted as year-month-date with four digits for the year and two digits each for the month and the date (e.g., 2004-05-04).
D	Display date formatted as month/day/year with two digits each for the month, day and year (e.g., 03/03/04).
r	Display time formatted as hour:minute:second AM|PM with two digits each for the hour, minute and second (e.g., 04:30:25 PM). The 12-hour clock is used.
R	Display time formatted as hour:minute with two digits each for the hour and minute (e.g., 16:30). The 24-hour clock is used.
T	Display time formatted as hour:minute:second with two digits for the hour, minute and second (e.g., 16:30:25). The 24-hour clock is used.

Fig. 28.6 | Date and time composition conversion suffix characters.

Conversion suffix character	Description
A	Display full name of the day of the week (e.g., `Wednesday`).
a	Display the three-character short name of the day of the week (e.g., `Wed`).
B	Display full name of the month (e.g., `March`).
b	Display the three-character short name of the month (e.g., `Mar`).
d	Display the day of the month with two digits, padding with leading zeros as necessary (e.g., `03`).
m	Display the month with two digits, padding with leading zeros as necessary (e.g., `07`).
e	Display the day of month without leading zeros (e.g., `3`).
Y	Display the year with four digits (e.g., `2004`).
y	Display the last two digits of the year with leading zeros as necessary (e.g., `04`).
j	Display the day of the year with three digits, padding with leading zeros as necessary (e.g., `016`).

Fig. 28.7 | Date formatting conversion suffix characters.

Conversion suffix character	Description
H	Display hour in 24-hour clock with a leading zero as necessary (e.g., `16`).
I	Display hour in 12-hour clock with a leading zero as necessary (e.g., `04`).
k	Display hour in 24-hour clock without leading zeros (e.g., `16`).
l	Display hour in 12-hour clock without leading zeros (e.g., `4`).
M	Display minute with a leading zero as necessary (e.g., `06`).
S	Display second with a leading zero as necessary (e.g., `05`).
Z	Display the abbreviation for the time zone (e.g., `GMT-05:00`, stands for Eastern Standard Time, which is 5 hours behind Greenwich Mean Time).
P	Display morning or afternoon marker in lower case (e.g., `pm`).
p	Display morning or afternoon marker in upper case (e.g., `PM`).

Fig. 28.8 | Time formatting conversion suffix characters.

Figure 28.9 uses the conversion character t together with the conversion suffix characters to display dates and times in various formats. Conversion character t requires the corresponding argument to be of type `long`, `Long`, `Calendar` or `Date` (both in package `java.util`)—objects of each of these classes can represent dates and times. Class `Calendar` is the preferred class for this purpose because some constructors and methods in class Date are replaced by those in class Calendar. Line 10 invokes static method **getInstance** of Calendar to obtain a calendar with the current date and time. Lines 13–17, 20–22 and 25–26 use this Calendar object in printf statements as the value to be formatted with conversion character t. Note that lines 20–22 and 25–26 use the optional **argument index** ("1$") to indicate that all format specifiers in the format string use the first argument after the format string in the argument list. You will learn more about argument indices in Section 28.11. Using the argument index eliminates the need to repeatedly list the same argument.

```
1   // Fig. 28.9: DateTimeTest.java
2   // Formatting dates and times with conversion character t and T.
3   import java.util.Calendar;
4
5   public class DateTimeTest
6   {
7      public static void main( String args[] )
8      {
9         // get current date and time
10        Calendar dateTime = Calendar.getInstance();
11
12        // printing with conversion characters for date/time compositions
13        System.out.printf( "%tc\n", dateTime );
14        System.out.printf( "%tF\n", dateTime );
15        System.out.printf( "%tD\n", dateTime );
16        System.out.printf( "%tr\n", dateTime );
17        System.out.printf( "%tT\n", dateTime );
18
19        // printing with conversion characters for date
20        System.out.printf( "%1$tA, %1$tB %1$td, %1$tY\n", dateTime );
21        System.out.printf( "%1$TA, %1$TB %1$Td, %1$TY\n", dateTime );
22        System.out.printf( "%1$ta, %1$tb %1$te, %1$ty\n", dateTime );
23
24        // printing with conversion characters for time
25        System.out.printf( "%1$tH:%1$tM:%1$tS\n", dateTime );
26        System.out.printf( "%1$tZ %1$tI:%1$tM:%1$tS %tP", dateTime );
27     } // end main
28  } // end class DateTimeTest
```

```
Tue Jun 29 11:17:21 GMT-05:00 2004
2004-06-29
06/29/04
11:17:21 AM
11:17:21
Tuesday, June 29, 2004
TUESDAY, JUNE 29, 2004
Tue, Jun 29, 04
11:17:21
GMT-05:00 11:17:21 AM
```

Fig. 28.9 | Formatting dates and times with conversion character t.

28.8 Other Conversion Characters

The remaining conversion characters are b, B, h, H, % and n. These are described in Fig. 28.10.

Lines 9–10 of Fig. 28.11 use %b to print the value of boolean values false and true. Line 11 associates a String to %b, which returns true because it is not null. Line 12 associates a null object to %B, which displays FALSE because test is null. Lines 13–14 use %h to print the string representations of the hash code values for strings "hello" and "Hello". These values could be used to store or locate the strings in a Hashtable or HashMap (both discussed in Chapter 19, Collections). Note that the hash code values for these two strings differ because one string starts with a lowercase letter and the other starts with an uppercase letter. Line 15 uses %H to print null in uppercase letters. The last two printf statements (lines 16–17) use %% to print the % character in a string and %n to print a platform-specific line separator.

Common Programming Error 28.2

Trying to print a literal percent character using % rather than %% in the format string might cause a difficult-to-detect logic error. When % appears in a format string, it must be followed by a conversion character in the string. The single percent could accidentally be followed by a legitimate conversion character, thus causing a logic error.

28.9 Printing with Field Widths and Precisions

The exact size of a field in which data is printed is specified by a field width. If the field width is larger than the data being printed, the data will be right justified within that field by default. (We demonstrate left justification in Section 28.10.) The programmer inserts an integer representing the field width between the percent sign (%) and the conversion character (e.g., %4d) in the format specifier. Figure 28.12 prints two groups of five numbers each, right justifying those numbers that contain fewer digits than the field width.

Conversion character	Description
b or B	Print "true" or "false" for the value of a boolean or Boolean. These conversion characters can also format the value of any reference. If the reference is non-null, "true" is output; otherwise, "false" is output. When conversion character B is used, the output is displayed in uppercase letters.
h or H	Print the string representation of an object's hash code value in hexadecimal format. If the corresponding argument is a null reference, "null" is printed. When conversion character H is used, the output is displayed in uppercase letters.
%	Print the percent character.
n	Print the platform-specific line separator (e.g., \r\n on Windows or \n on UNIX/LINUX).

Fig. 28.10 | Other conversion specifiers.

```
1   // Fig. 28.11: OtherConversion.java
2   // Using the b, B, h, H, % and n conversion characters.
3
4   public class OtherConversion
5   {
6      public static void main( String args[] )
7      {
8         Object test = null;
9         System.out.printf( "%b\n", false );
10        System.out.printf( "%b\n", true );
11        System.out.printf( "%b\n", "Test" );
12        System.out.printf( "%B\n", test );
13        System.out.printf( "Hashcode of \"hello\" is %h\n", "hello" );
14        System.out.printf( "Hashcode of \"Hello\" is %h\n", "Hello" );
15        System.out.printf( "Hashcode of null is %H\n", test );
16        System.out.printf( "Printing a %% in a format string\n" );
17        System.out.printf( "Printing a new line %nnext line starts here" );
18     } // end main
19  } // end class OtherConversion
```

```
false
true
true
FALSE
Hashcode of "hello" is 5e918d2
Hashcode of "Hello" is 42628b2
Hashcode of null is NULL
Printing a % in a format string
Printing a new line
next line starts here
```

Fig. 28.11 | Using the b, B, h, H, % and n conversion characters.

Note that the field width is increased to print values wider than the field and that the minus sign for a negative value uses one character position in the field. Also, if no field width is specified, the data prints in exactly as many positions as it needs. Field widths can be used with all format specifiers except the line separator (%n).

Common Programming Error 28.3

Not providing a sufficiently large field width to handle a value to be printed can offset other data being printed and produce confusing outputs. Know your data!

Method `printf` also provides the ability to specify the precision with which data is printed. Precision has different meanings for different types. When used with floating-point conversion characters e and f, the precision is the number of digits that appear after the decimal point. When used with conversion character g, the precision is the maximum number of significant digits to be printed. When used with conversion character s, the precision is the maximum number of characters to be written from the string. To use precision, place between the percent sign and the conversion specifier a decimal point (.) followed by an integer representing the precision. Figure 28.13 demonstrates the use of precision in format strings. Note that when a floating-point value is printed with a precision smaller

```
1   // Fig. 28.12: FieldWidthTest.java
2   // Right justifying integers in fields.
3
4   public class FieldWidthTest
5   {
6      public static void main( String args[] )
7      {
8         System.out.printf( "%4d\n", 1 );
9         System.out.printf( "%4d\n", 12 );
10        System.out.printf( "%4d\n", 123 );
11        System.out.printf( "%4d\n", 1234 );
12        System.out.printf( "%4d\n\n", 12345 ); // data too large
13
14        System.out.printf( "%4d\n", -1 );
15        System.out.printf( "%4d\n", -12 );
16        System.out.printf( "%4d\n", -123 );
17        System.out.printf( "%4d\n", -1234 ); // data too large
18        System.out.printf( "%4d\n", -12345 ); // data too large
19     } // end main
20  } // end class RightJustifyTest
```

```
   1
  12
 123
1234
12345

  -1
 -12
-123
-1234
-12345
```

Fig. 28.12 | Right justifying integers in fields.

than the original number of decimal places in the value, the value is rounded. Also note that the format specifier %.3g indicates that the total number of digits used to display the floating-point value is 3. Because the value has three digits to the left of the decimal point, the value is rounded to the ones position.

The field width and the precision can be combined by placing the field width, followed by a decimal point, followed by a precision between the percent sign and the conversion character, as in the statement

```
printf( "%9.3f", 123.456789 );
```

which displays 123.457 with three digits to the right of the decimal point right justified in a nine-digit field—this number will be preceded in its field by two blanks.

28.10 Using Flags in the printf Format String

Various flags may be used with method printf to supplement its output formatting capabilities. Seven flags are available for use in format strings (Fig. 28.14).

```
 1    // Fig. 28.13: PrecisionTest.java
 2    // Using precision for floating-point numbers and strings.
 3    public class PrecisionTest
 4    {
 5       public static void main( String args[] )
 6       {
 7          double f = 123.94536;
 8          String s = "Happy Birthday";
 9
10          System.out.printf( "Using precision for floating-point numbers\n" );
11          System.out.printf( "\t%.3f\n\t%.3e\n\t%.3g\n\n", f, f, f );
12
13          System.out.printf( "Using precision for strings\n" );
14          System.out.printf( "\t%.11s\n", s );
15       } // end main
16    } // end class PrecisionTest
```

```
Using precision for floating-point numbers
        123.945
        1.239e+02
        124

Using precision for strings
        Happy Birth
```

Fig. 28.13 | Using precision for floating-point numbers and strings..

Flag	Description
– (minus sign)	Left justify the output within the specified field.
+ (plus sign)	Display a plus sign preceding positive values and a minus sign preceding negative values.
space	Print a space before a positive value not printed with the + flag.
#	Prefix 0 to the output value when used with the octal conversion character o.
	Prefix 0x to the output value when used with the hexadecimal conversion character x.
0 (zero)	Pad a field with leading zeros.
, (comma)	Use the locale-specific thousands separator (i.e., ',' for U.S. locale) to display decimal and floating-point numbers.
(	Enclose negative numbers in parentheses.

Fig. 28.14 | Format string flags.

To use a flag in a format string, place the flag immediately to the right of the percent sign. Several flags may be used in the same format specifier. Figure 28.15 demonstrates right justification and left justification of a string, an integer, a character and a floating-point number. Note that line 9 serves as a counting mechanism for the screen output.

```
 1   // Fig. 28.15: MinusFlagTest.java
 2   // Right justifying and left justifying values.
 3
 4   public class MinusFlagTest
 5   {
 6      public static void main( String args[] )
 7      {
 8         System.out.println( "Columns:" );
 9         System.out.println( "012345678901234567890123456789\n" );
10         System.out.printf( "%10s%10d%10c%10f\n\n", "hello", 7, 'a', 1.23 );
11         System.out.printf(
12            "%-10s%-10d%-10c%-10f\n", "hello", 7, 'a', 1.23 );
13      } // end main
14   } // end class MinusFlagTest
```

```
Columns:
012345678901234567890123456789

     hello         7         a  1.230000

hello     7         a         1.230000
```

Fig. 28.15 | Right justifying and left justifying values.

Figure 28.16 prints a positive number and a negative number, each with and without the + flag. Note that the minus sign is displayed in both cases, but the plus sign is displayed only when the + flag is used.

Figure 28.17 prefixes a space to the positive number with the space flag. This is useful for aligning positive and negative numbers with the same number of digits. Note that the value -547 is not preceded by a space in the output because of its minus sign. Figure 28.18 uses the # flag to prefix 0 to the octal value and 0x to the hexadecimal value.

```
 1   // Fig. 28.16: PlusFlagTest.java
 2   // Printing numbers with and without the + flag.
 3
 4   public class PlusFlagTest
 5   {
 6      public static void main( String args[] )
 7      {
 8         System.out.printf( "%d\t%d\n", 786, -786 );
 9         System.out.printf( "%+d\t%+d\n", 786, -786 );
10      } // end main
11   } // end class PlusFlagTest
```

```
786     -786
+786    -786
```

Fig. 28.16 | Printing numbers with and without the + flag.

```
1   // Fig. 28.17: SpaceFlagTest.java
2   // Printing a space before non-negative values.
3
4   public class SpaceFlagTest
5   {
6      public static void main( String args[] )
7      {
8         System.out.printf( "% d\n% d\n", 547, -547 );
9      } // end main
10  } // end class SpaceFlagTest
```

```
 547
-547
```

Fig. 28.17 | Using the space flag to print a space before non-negative values.

```
1   // Fig. 28.18: PoundFlagTest.java
2   // Using the # flag with conversion characters o and x.
3
4   public class PoundFlagTest
5   {
6      public static void main( String args[] )
7      {
8         int c = 31;       // initialize c
9
10        System.out.printf( "%#o\n", c );
11        System.out.printf( "%#x\n", c );
12     } // end main
13  } // end class PoundFlagTest
```

```
037
0x1f
```

Fig. 28.18 | Using the # flag with conversion characters o and x.

Figure 28.19 combines the + flag, the **0 flag** and the space flag to print 452 in a field of width 9 with a + sign and leading zeros, next prints 452 in a field of width 9 using only the 0 flag, then prints 452 in a field of width 9 using only the space flag.

Figure 28.20 use the comma (,) flag to display a decimal and a floating-point number with the thousands separator. Figure 28.21 encloses negative numbers in parentheses using the (flag. Note that the value 50 is not enclosed in parentheses in the output because it is a positive number.

```
1   // Fig. 28.19: ZeroFlagTest.java
2   // Printing with the 0 (zero) flag fills in leading zeros.
3
4   public class ZeroFlagTest
5   {
```

Fig. 28.19 | Printing with the 0 (zero) flag fills in leading zeros. (Part 1 of 2.)

```
 6        public static void main( String args[] )
 7        {
 8           System.out.printf( "%+09d\n", 452 );
 9           System.out.printf( "%09d\n", 452 );
10           System.out.printf( "% 9d\n", 452 );
11        } // end main
12     } // end class ZeroFlagTest
```

```
+00000452
000000452
      452
```

Fig. 28.19 | Printing with the 0 (zero) flag fills in leading zeros. (Part 2 of 2.)

```
 1     // Fig. 28.20: CommaFlagTest.java
 2     // Using the comma (,) flag to display numbers with thousands separator.
 3
 4     public class CommaFlagTest
 5     {
 6        public static void main( String args[] )
 7        {
 8           System.out.printf( "%,d\n", 58625 );
 9           System.out.printf( "%,.2f", 58625.21 );
10           System.out.printf( "%,.2f", 12345678.9 );
11        } // end main
12     } // end class CommaFlagTest
```

```
58,625
58,625.21
12,345,678.90
```

Fig. 28.20 | Using the comma (,) flag to display number with thousands separator.

```
 1     // Fig. 28.21: ParenthesesFlagTest.java
 2     // Using the ( flag to place parentheses around negative numbers.
 3
 4     public class ParenthesesFlagTest
 5     {
 6        public static void main( String args[] )
 7        {
 8           System.out.printf( "%(d\n", 50 );
 9           System.out.printf( "%(d\n", -50 );
10           System.out.printf( "%(.1e\n", -50.0 );
11        } // end main
12     } // end class ParenthesesFlagTest
```

```
50
(50)
(5.0e+01)
```

Fig. 28.21 | Using the (flag to place parentheses around negative numbers.

28.11 Printing with Argument Indices

An argument index is an optional decimal integer followed by a $ sign that indicates the position of the argument in the argument list. For example, lines 20–21 and 24–25 in Fig. 28.9 use argument index "1$" to indicate that all format specifiers use the first argument in the argument list. Argument indices enable programmers to reorder the output so that the arguments in the argument list are not necessarily in the order of their corresponding format specifiers. Argument indices also help avoid duplicating arguments. Figure 28.22 demonstrates how to print arguments in the argument list in reverse order using the argument index.

28.12 Printing Literals and Escape Sequences

Most literal characters to be printed in a `printf` statement can simply be included in the format string. However, there are several "problem" characters, such as the quotation mark (") that delimits the format string itself. Various control characters, such as newline and tab, must be represented by escape sequences. An escape sequence is represented by a backslash (\), followed by an escape character. Figure 28.23 lists the escape sequences and the actions they cause.

Common Programming Error 28.4

Attempting to print as literal data in a `printf` statement a double quote or backslash character without preceding that character with a backslash to form a proper escape sequence might result in a syntax error.

28.13 Formatting Output with Class Formatter

So far, we have discussed displaying formatted output to the standard output stream. What should we do if we want to send formatted outputs to other output streams or devices, such

```
1   // Fig. 28.22: ArgumentIndexTest
2   // Reordering output with argument indices.
3
4   public class ArgumentIndexTest
5   {
6      public static void main( String args[] )
7      {
8         System.out.printf(
9            "Parameter list without reordering: %s %s %s %s\n",
10           "first", "second", "third", "fourth" );
11        System.out.printf(
12           "Parameter list after reordering: %4$s %3$s %2$s %1$s\n",
13           "first", "second", "third", "fourth" );
14     } // end main
15  } // end class ArgumentIndexTest
```

```
Parameter list without reordering: first second third fourth
Parameter list after reordering: fourth third second first
```

Fig. 28.22 | Reordering output with argument indices.

Escape sequence	Description
\' (single quote)	Output the single quote (') character.
\" (double quote)	Output the double quote (") character.
\\ (backslash)	Output the backslash (\) character.
\b (backspace)	Move the cursor back one position on the current line.
\f (new page or form feed)	Move the cursor to the start of the next logical page.
\n (newline)	Move the cursor to the beginning of the next line.
\r (carriage return)	Move the cursor to the beginning of the current line.
\t (horizontal tab)	Move the cursor to the next horizontal tab position.

Fig. 28.23 | Escape sequences.

as a JTextArea or a file? The solution relies on class **Formatter** (in package java.util), which provides the same formatting capabilities as printf. Formatter is a utility class that enables programmers to output formatted data to a specified destination, such as a file on disk. By default, a Formatter creates a string in memory. Figure 28.24 demonstrates how to use a Formatter to build a formatted string, which is then displayed in a message dialog.

Line 11 creates a Formatter object using the default constructor, so this object will build a string in memory. Other constructors are provided to allow you to specify the destination

```
1   // Fig. Fig. 28.24: FormatterTest.java
2   // Format string with class Formatter.
3   import java.util.Formatter;
4   import javax.swing.JOptionPane;
5
6   public class FormatterTest
7   {
8      public static void main( String args[] )
9      {
10        // create Formatter and format output
11        Formatter formatter = new Formatter();
12        formatter.format( "%d = %#o = %#X", 10, 10, 10 );
13
14        // display output in JOptionPane
15        JOptionPane.showMessageDialog( null, formatter.toString() );
16     } // end main
17  } // end class FormatterTest
```

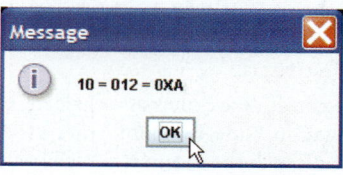

Fig. 28.24 | Formatting output with class Formatter.

to which the formatted data should be output. For details, see java.sun.com/j2se/5.0/docs/api/java/util/Formatter.html.

Line 12 invokes method **format** to format the output. Like printf, method format takes a format string and an argument list. The difference is that printf sends the formatted output directly to the standard output stream, while format sends the formatted output to the destination specified by its constructor (a string in memory in this program). Line 15 invokes the Formatter's toString method to get the formatted data as a string, which is then displayed in a message dialog.

String static *Method* format

Note that class String also provides a static convenience method named format that enables you to create a string in memory without the need to first create a Formatter object. Lines 11–12 and line 15 in Fig. 28.24 could have been replaced by

```
String s = String.format( "%d = %#o = %#^x", 10, 10, 10 );
JOptionPane.showMessageDialog( null, s );
```

28.14 Wrap-Up

This chapter summarized how to display formatted output with various format characters and flags. We displayed decimal numbers using format characters d, o, x and X. We displayed floating-point numbers using format characters e, E, f, g and G. We displayed date and time in various format using format characters t and T and their conversion suffix characters. You learned how to display output with field widths and precisions. We introduced the flags +, -, space, #, 0, comma and (that are used together with the format characters to produce output. We also demonstrated how to format output with class Formatter. In the next chapter, we discuss the String class's methods for manipulating strings. We also introduce regular expressions and demonstrate how to validate user input with regular expressions.

Summary

- Input and output are usually performed with streams, which are sequences of bytes. In input operations, the bytes flow from a device to main memory. In output operations, bytes flow from main memory to a device.

- Normally, the standard input stream is connected to the keyboard, and the standard output stream is connected to the computer screen.

- The printf format string describes the formats in which the output values appear. The format specifier consists of argument index, flags, field widths, precisions and conversion characters.

- Integers are printed with the conversion characters d for decimal integers, o for integers in octal form and x (or X) for integers in hexadecimal form. When the conversion character X is used, the output is displayed in uppercase letters.

- Floating-point values are printed with the conversion characters e (or E) for exponential notation, f for regular floating-point notation, and g (or G) for either e (or E) notation or f notation. When the g conversion specifier is indicated, the e conversion character is used if the value is less than 10^{-3} or greater than or equal to 10^7; otherwise, the f conversion character is used. When the conversion characters E and G are used, the output is displayed in uppercase letters.

- The conversion character c prints a character.
- The conversion character s (or S) prints a string of characters. When the conversion character S is used, the output is displayed in uppercase letters.
- The conversion character t (or T) followed by a conversion suffix character prints the date and time in various forms. When the conversion character T is used, the output is displayed in uppercase letters.
- Conversion character t (or T) requires the argument to be of type long, Long, Calendar or Date.
- Conversion character b (or B) outputs the string representation of a boolean or Boolean. These conversion characters also output "true" for non-null references and "false" for null references. When conversion character B is used, the output is displayed in uppercase letters.
- Conversion character h (or H) returns null for a null reference and a String representation of the hash code value (in base 16) of the object. Hash codes are used to store and retrieve objects in Hashtables and HashMaps. When conversion character H is used, the output is displayed in uppercase letters.
- The conversion character n prints the platform-specific line separator.
- The conversion character % is used to display a literal %.
- If the field width is larger than the object being printed, the object is right justified in the field by default.
- Field widths can be used with all conversion characters except the line-separator conversion.
- Precision used with floating-point conversion characters e and f indicates the number of digits that appear after the decimal point. Precision used with floating-point conversion character g indicates the number of significant digits to appear.
- Precision used with conversion character s indicates the number of characters to be printed.
- The field width and the precision can be combined by placing the field width, followed by a decimal point, followed by the precision between the percent sign and the conversion character.
- The - flag left justifies its argument in a field.
- The + flag prints a plus sign for positive values and a minus sign for negative values.
- The space flag prints a space preceding a positive value. The space flag and the + flag cannot be used together in an integral conversion character.
- The # flag prefixes 0 to octal values and 0x to hexadecimal values.
- The 0 flag prints leading zeros for a value that does not occupy its entire field.
- The comma (,) flag uses the locale-specific thousands separator (i.e., ',' for U.S. locale) to display integer and floating-point numbers.
- The (flag encloses a negative number in parentheses.
- An argument index is an optional decimal integer followed by a $ sign that indicates the position of the argument in the argument list.
- Argument indices enable programmers to reorder the output so that the arguments in the argument list are not necessarily in the order of their corresponding format specifiers. Argument indices also help avoid duplicating arguments.
- Class Formatter (in package java.util) provides the same formatting capabilities as printf. Formatter is a utility class that enables programmers to print formatted output to various destinations, including GUI components, files and other output streams.
- Class Formatter's method format outputs formatted data to the destination specified by the Formatter constructor.
- The static method format of class String formats data and returns the formatted data as a String.

Terminology

# flag	H conversion suffix character
% conversion character	hexadecimal format
(flag	I conversion suffix character
+ (plus) flag	integer conversion
– (minus) flag	j conversion suffix character
, (comma) flag	K conversion suffix character
0 (zero) flag	left justification
A conversion suffix character	m conversion suffix character
a conversion suffix character	M conversion suffix character
alignment	n conversion character
argument index	o conversion character
b conversion character	octal format
B conversion character	P conversion suffix character
B conversion suffix character	p conversion suffix character
b conversion suffix character	precision
c conversion character	printf method
C conversion suffix character	r conversion suffix character
conversion character	redirect a stream
d conversion character	right justification
D conversion suffix character	rounding
e conversion character	s conversion character
E conversion character	S conversion character
e conversion suffix character	S conversion suffix character
exponential floating-point format	scientific notation
f conversion character	space flag
F conversion suffix character	standard error stream
field width	standard input stream
flag	standard output stream
floating-point	stream
floating-point number conversion	StringBuilder class
format method of Formatter	t conversion character
format method of String	T conversion character
format specifier	T conversion suffix character
format string	toString method of Formatter
Formatter class	x conversion character
g conversion character	Y conversion suffix character
G conversion character	y conversion suffix character
h conversion character	Z conversion suffix character
H conversion character	

Self-Review Exercises

28.1 Fill in the blanks in each of the following:

   a) All input and output is dealt with in the form of _____.

   b) The _____ stream is normally connected to the keyboard.

   c) The _____ stream is normally connected to the computer screen.

   d) `System.out`'s _____ method can be used to format text that is displayed on the standard output.

   e) The conversion character _____ may be used to output a decimal integer.

f) The conversion characters _____ and _____ are used to display integers in octal and hexadecimal form, respectively.

g) The conversion character _____ is used to display a floating-point value in exponential notation.

h) The conversion characters e and f are displayed with _____ digits of precision to the right of the decimal point if no precision is specified.

i) The conversion characters _____ and _____ are used to print strings and characters, respectively.

j) The conversion character _____ and conversion suffix character _____ are used to print time for the 24-hour clock as hour:minute:second.

k) The _____ flag causes output to be left justified in a field.

l) The _____ flag causes values to be displayed with either a plus sign or a minus sign.

m) The argument index _____ corresponds to the second argument in the argument list.

n) Class _____ has the same capability as `printf`, but allows programmers to print formatted output to various destinations besides the standard output stream.

28.2 Find the error in each of the following and explain how it can be corrected.

a) The following statement should print the character `'c'`.
   `System.out.printf( "%c\n", "c" );`

b) The following statement should print `9.375%`.
   `System.out.printf( "%.3f%", 9.375 );`

c) The following statement should print the third argument in the argument list.
   `System.out.printf( "%2$s\n", "Mon", "Tue", "Wed", "Thu", "Fri" );`

d) `System.out.printf( ""A string in quotes"" );`

e) `System.out.printf( %d %d, 12, 20 );`

f) `System.out.printf( "%s\n", 'Richard' );`

28.3 Write a statement for each of the following:

a) Print 1234 right justified in a 10 digit field.

b) Print 123.456789 in exponential notation with a sign (+ or -) and 3 digits of precision.

c) Print 100 in octal form preceded by 0.

d) Given a `Calendar` object `calendar`, print a date formatted as month/day/year (each with two digits).

e) Given a `Calendar` object `calendar`, print a time for the 24-hour clock as hour:minute:second (each with two digits) using argument index and conversion suffix characters for formatting time.

f) Print 3.333333 with a sign (+ or -) in a field of 20 characters with a precision of 3.

Answers to Self-Review Exercises

28.1 a) Streams. b) Standard input. c) Standard output. d) `printf`. e) d. f) o, x or X. g) e or E. h) 6. i) s or S, c or C. j) t, T. k) - (minus). l) + (plus). m) 2$. n) `Formatter`.

28.2 a) Error: Conversion character c expects an argument of primitive type char.
   Correction: To print the character `'c'`, change `"c"` to `'c'`.

b) Error: Trying to print the literal character % without using the format specifier %%.
   Correction: Use %% to print a literal % character.

c) Error: Argument index does not start with 0, e.g., the first argument is 1$.
   Correction: To print the third argument use 3$.

d) Error: Trying to print the literal character " without using the \" escape sequence.
   Correction: Replace each quote in the inner set of quotes with \".

e) Error: The format string is not enclosed in double quotes.
   Correction: Enclose %d %d in double quotes.

f) Error: The string to be printed is enclosed in single quotes.
   Correction: Use double quotes instead of single quotes to represent a string.

28.3 a) `System.out.printf( "%10d\n", 1234 );`

b) `System.out.printf( "%+.3e\n", 123.456789 );`

c) `System.out.printf( "%#o\n", 100 );`

d) `System.out.printf( "%tD\n", calendar );`

e) `System.out.printf( "%1$tH:%1$tM:%1$tS\n", calendar );`

f) `System.out.printf( "%+20.3f\n", 3.333333 );`

Exercises

28.4 Write statement(s) for each of the following:

a) Print integer 40000 right justified in a 15-digit field.

b) Print 200 with and without a sign.

c) Print 100 in hexadecimal form preceded by 0x.

d) Print 1.234 with three digits of precision in a nine-digit field with preceding zeros.

28.5 Show what is printed by each of the following statements. If a statement is incorrect, indicate why.

a) `System.out.printf( "%-10d\n", 10000 );`

b) `System.out.printf( "%c\n", "This is a string" );`

c) `System.out.printf( "%8.3f\n", 1024.987654 );`

d) `System.out.printf( "%#o\n%#X\n", 17, 17 );`

e) `System.out.printf( "% d\n%+d\n", 1000000, 1000000 );`

f) `System.out.printf( "%10.2e\n", 444.93738 );`

g) `System.out.printf( "%d\n", 10.987 );`

28.6 Find the error(s) in each of the following program segments. Show the corrected statement.

a) `System.out.printf( "%s\n", 'Happy Birthday' );`

b) `System.out.printf( "%c\n", 'Hello' );`

c) `System.out.printf( "%c\n", "This is a string" );`

d) The following statement should print "Bon Voyage" with the double quotes:
   `System.out.printf( ""%s"", "Bon Voyage" );`

e) The following statement should print "Today is Friday":
   `System.out.printf( "Today is %s\n", "Monday", "Friday" );`

f) `System.out.printf( 'Enter your name: ' );`

g) `System.out.printf( %f, 123.456 );`

h) The following statement should print the current time in the format "hh:mm:ss":
   `Calendar dateTime = Calendar.getInstance();`
   `System.out.printf( "%1$tk:1$%tl:%1$tS\n", dateTime );`

28.7 *(Printing Dates and Times)* Write a program that prints dates and times in the following forms:

```
GMT-05:00 04/30/04 09:55:09 AM
GMT-05:00 April 30 2004 09:55:09
2004-04-30 day-of-the-month:30
2004-04-30 day-of-the-year:121
Fri Apr 30 09:55:09 GMT-05:00 2004
```

[*Note:* Depending on your location, you may get the time zone other than GMT-05:00.]

28.8   Write a program to test the results of printing the integer value 12345 and the floating-point value 1.2345 in various size fields.

28.9   *(Rounding Numbers)* Write a program that prints the value 100.453627 rounded to the nearest digit, tenth, hundredth, thousandth and ten thousandth.

28.10   Write a program that inputs a word from the keyboard and determines the length of the word. Print the word using twice the length as the field width.

28.11   *(Converting Fahrenheit Temperature to Celsius)* Write a program that converts integer Fahrenheit temperatures from 0 to 212 degrees to floating-point Celsius temperatures with three digits of precision. Use the formula

```
celsius = 5.0 / 9.0 * ( fahrenheit - 32 );
```

to perform the calculation. The output should be printed in two right-justified columns of 10 characters each, and the Celsius temperatures should be preceded by a sign for both positive and negative values.

28.12   Write a program to test all the escape sequences in Fig. 28.23. For the escape sequences that move the cursor, print a character before and after the escape sequence so that it is clear where the cursor has moved.

28.13   Write a program that uses the conversion character g to output the value 9876.12345. Print the value with precisions ranging from 1 to 9.

29

Strings, Characters and Regular Expressions

OBJECTIVES

In this chapter you will learn:

- To create and manipulate immutable character string objects of class `String`.

- To create and manipulates mutable character string objects of class `StringBuffer`.

- To create and manipulate objects of class `Character`.

- To use a `StringTokenizer` object to break a `String` object into tokens.

- To use regular expressions to validate `String` data entered into an application.

The chief defect of Henry King
Was chewing little bits of string.
—Hilaire Belloc

Vigorous writing is concise.
A sentence should contain no
unnecessary words, a
paragraph no unnecessary
sentences.
—William Strunk, Jr.

I have made this letter longer
than usual, because I lack
the time to make it short.
—Blaise Pascal

Outline

29.1 Introduction

This chapter introduces Java's string- and character-processing capabilities. The techniques discussed here are appropriate for validating program input, displaying information to users and other text-based manipulations. The techniques are also appropriate for developing text editors, word processors, page-layout software, computerized typesetting systems and other kinds of text-processing software. We have already presented several string-processing capabilities in earlier chapters. This chapter discusses in detail the capabilities of class `String`, class `StringBuffer` and class `Character` from the `java.lang` package and class `StringTokenizer` from the `java.util` package. These classes provide the foundation for string and character manipulation in Java.

The chapter also discusses regular expressions that provide applications with the capability to validate input. The functionality is located in the `String` class along with classes `Matcher` and `Pattern` located in the `java.util.regex` package.

29.2 Fundamentals of Characters and Strings

Characters are the fundamental building blocks of Java source programs. Every program is composed of a sequence of characters that—when grouped together meaningfully—are interpreted by the computer as a series of instructions used to accomplish a task. A program may contain character literals. A character literal is an integer value represented as a character in single quotes. For example, `'z'` represents the integer value of z, and `'\n'` represents the integer value of newline. The value of a character literal is the integer value of the character in the Unicode character set. Appendix B presents the integer equivalents of the characters in the ASCII character set, which is a subset of Unicode (discussed in Appendix F). For detailed information on Unicode, visit `www.unicode.org`.

Recall from Section 2.2 that a string is a sequence of characters treated as a single unit. A string may include letters, digits and various special characters, such as +, -, *, / and $. A string is an object of class `String`. String literals (stored in memory as `String` objects) are written as a sequence of characters in double quotation marks, as in:

```
"John Q. Doe"            (a name)
"9999 Main Street"       (a street address)
"Waltham, Massachusetts" (a city and state)
"(201) 555-1212"         (a telephone number)
```

A string may be assigned to a `String` reference. The declaration

```
String color = "blue";
```

initializes `String` reference `color` to refer to a `String` object that contains the string `"blue"`.

Performance Tip 29.1

Java treats all string literals with the same contents as a single `String` object that has many references to it. This conserves memory.

29.3 Class String

Class `String` is used to represent strings in Java. The next several subsections cover many of class `String`'s capabilities.

29.3.1 String Constructors

Class `String` provides constructors for initializing `String` objects in a variety of ways. Four of the constructors are demonstrated in the `main` method of Fig. 29.1.

Line 12 instantiates a new `String` object using class `String`'s no-argument constructor and assigns its reference to `s1`. The new `String` object contains no characters (the empty string) and has a length of 0.

Line 13 instantiates a new `String` object using class `String`'s constructor that takes a `String` object as an argument and assigns its reference to `s2`. The new `String` object contains the same sequence of characters as the `String` object `s` that is passed as an argument to the constructor.

Software Engineering Observation 29.1

It is not necessary to copy an existing `String` object. `String` objects are immutable—their character contents cannot be changed after they are created, because class `String` does not provide any methods that allow the contents of a `String` object to be modified.

```
1   // Fig. 29.1: StringConstructors.java
2   // String class constructors.
3
4   public class StringConstructors
5   {
6      public static void main( String args[] )
7      {
8         char charArray[] = { 'b', 'i', 'r', 't', 'h', ' ', 'd', 'a', 'y' };
9         String s = new String( "hello" );
10
11        // use String constructors
12        String s1 = new String();
13        String s2 = new String( s );
14        String s3 = new String( charArray );
15        String s4 = new String( charArray, 6, 3 );
16
17        System.out.printf(
18           "s1 = %s\ns2 = %s\ns3 = %s\ns4 = %s\n",
19           s1, s2, s3, s4 ); // display strings
20     } // end main
21  } // end class StringConstructors
```

```
s1 =
s2 = hello
s3 = birth day
s4 = day
```

Fig. 29.1 | String class constructors.

Line 14 instantiates a new String object and assigns its reference to s3 using class String's constructor that takes a char array as an argument. The new String object contains a copy of the characters in the array.

Line 15 instantiates a new String object and assigns its reference to s4 using class String's constructor that takes a char array and two integers as arguments. The second argument specifies the starting position (the offset) from which characters in the array are accessed. Remember that the first character is at position 0. The third argument specifies the number of characters (the count) to access in the array. The new String object contains a string formed from the accessed characters. If the offset or the count specified as an argument results in accessing an element outside the bounds of the character array, a String-IndexOutOfBoundsException is thrown. We discussed exceptions in detail in Chapter 13.

 Common Programming Error 29.1

Attempting to access a character that is outside the bounds of a string (i.e., an index less than 0 or an index greater than or equal to the string's length) results in a StringIndexOutOfBounds-Exception.

29.3.2 String Methods length, charAt and getChars

String methods **length**, charAt and **getChars** return the length of a string, obtain the character at a specific location in a string and retrieve a set of characters from a string as a char array, respectively. The application in Fig. 29.2 demonstrates each of these methods.

```
1    // Fig. 29.2: StringMiscellaneous.java
2    // This application demonstrates the length, charAt and getChars
3    // methods of the String class.
4
5    public class StringMiscellaneous
6    {
7       public static void main( String args[] )
8       {
9          String s1 = "hello there";
10         char charArray[] = new char[ 5 ];
11
12         System.out.printf( "s1: %s", s1 );
13
14         // test length method
15         System.out.printf( "\nLength of s1: %d", s1.length() );
16
17         // loop through characters in s1 with charAt and display reversed
18         System.out.print( "\nThe string reversed is: " );
19
20         for ( int count = s1.length() - 1; count >= 0; count-- )
21            System.out.printf( "%s ", s1.charAt( count ) );
22
23         // copy characters from string into charArray
24         s1.getChars( 0, 5, charArray, 0 );
25         System.out.print( "\nThe character array is: " );
26
27         for ( char character : charArray )
28            System.out.print( character );
29
30         System.out.println();
31      } // end main
32   } // end class StringMiscellaneous
```

```
s1: hello there
Length of s1: 11
The string reversed is: e r e h t   o l l e h
The character array is: hello
```

Fig. 29.2 | String class character-manipulation methods.

Line 15 uses String method length to determine the number of characters in string s1. Like arrays, strings always know their own length. However, unlike arrays, you cannot access a String's length via a length field—instead you must call the String's length method.

The for statement at lines 20–21 print the characters of the string s1 in reverse order (and separated by spaces). String method charAt (line 21) returns the character at a specific position in the string. Method charAt receives an integer argument that is used as the index and returns the character at that position. Like arrays, the first element of a string is at position 0.

Line 24 uses `String` method `getChars` to copy the characters of a string into a char-acter array. The first argument is the starting index in the string from which characters are to be copied. The second argument is the index that is one past the last character to be copied from the string. The third argument is the character array into which the characters are to be copied. The last argument is the starting index where the copied characters are placed in the target character array. Next, line 28 prints the char array contents one character at a time.

29.3.3 Comparing Strings

Chapter 7 discussed sorting and searching arrays. Frequently, the information being sorted or searched consists of strings that must be compared to place them into the proper order or to determine whether a string appears in an array (or other collection). Class `String` provides several methods for comparing strings—these are demonstrated in the next two examples.

To understand what it means for one string to be greater than or less than another string, consider the process of alphabetizing a series of last names. You would, no doubt, place "Jones" before "Smith" because the first letter of "Jones" comes before the first letter of "Smith" in the alphabet. But the alphabet is more than just a list of 26 letters—it is an ordered set of characters. Each letter occurs in a specific position within the set. Z is more than just a letter of the alphabet—it is specifically the twenty-sixth letter of the alphabet.

How does the computer know that one letter comes before another? All characters are represented in the computer as numeric codes (see Appendix B). When the computer compares two strings, it actually compares the numeric codes of the characters in the strings.

Figure 29.3 demonstrates `String` methods `equals`, `equalsIgnoreCase`, `compareTo` and `regionMatches` and using the equality operator `==` to compare `String` objects.

The condition at line 17 uses method `equals` to compare string `s1` and the string literal `"hello"` for equality. Method `equals` (a method of class `Object` overridden in `String`) tests any two objects for equality—the strings contained in the two objects are identical. The method returns `true` if the contents of the objects are equal, and `false` otherwise. The preceding condition is `true` because string `s1` was initialized with the string literal `"hello"`. Method `equals` uses a lexicographical comparison—it compares the integer Unicode values (see Appendix F, Unicode, for more information) that represent each character in each string. Thus, if the string `"hello"` is compared with the string `"HELLO"`, the result is `false`, because the integer representation of a lowercase letter is different from that of the corresponding uppercase letter.

The condition at line 23 uses the equality operator `==` to compare string `s1` for equality with the string literal `"hello"`. Operator `==` has different functionality when it is used to compare references than when it is used to compare values of primitive types. When primitive-type values are compared with `==`, the result is `true` if both values are identical. When references are compared with `==`, the result is `true` if both references refer to the same object in memory. To compare the actual contents (or state information) of objects for equality, a method must be invoked. In the case of `String`s, that method is `equals`. The preceding condition evaluates to `false` at line 23 because the reference `s1` was initialized with the statement

```
s1 = new String( "hello" );
```

```
1   // Fig. 29.3: StringCompare.java
2   // String methods equals, equalsIgnoreCase, compareTo and regionMatches.
3
4   public class StringCompare
5   {
6      public static void main( String args[] )
7      {
8         String s1 = new String( "hello" ); // s1 is a copy of "hello"
9         String s2 = "goodbye";
10        String s3 = "Happy Birthday";
11        String s4 = "happy birthday";
12
13        System.out.printf(
14           "s1 = %s\ns2 = %s\ns3 = %s\ns4 = %s\n\n", s1, s2, s3, s4 );
15
16        // test for equality
17        if ( s1.equals( "hello" ) )  // true
18           System.out.println( "s1 equals \"hello\"" );
19        else
20           System.out.println( "s1 does not equal \"hello\"" );
21
22        // test for equality with ==
23        if ( s1 == "hello" )  // false; they are not the same object
24           System.out.println( "s1 is the same object as \"hello\"" );
25        else
26           System.out.println( "s1 is not the same object as \"hello\"" );
27
28        // test for equality (ignore case)
29        if ( s3.equalsIgnoreCase( s4 ) )  // true
30           System.out.printf( "%s equals %s with case ignored\n", s3, s4 );
31        else
32           System.out.println( "s3 does not equal s4" );
33
34        // test compareTo
35        System.out.printf(
36           "\ns1.compareTo( s2 ) is %d", s1.compareTo( s2 ) );
37        System.out.printf(
38           "\ns2.compareTo( s1 ) is %d", s2.compareTo( s1 ) );
39        System.out.printf(
40           "\ns1.compareTo( s1 ) is %d", s1.compareTo( s1 ) );
41        System.out.printf(
42           "\ns3.compareTo( s4 ) is %d", s3.compareTo( s4 ) );
43        System.out.printf(
44           "\ns4.compareTo( s3 ) is %d\n\n", s4.compareTo( s3 ) );
45
46        // test regionMatches (case sensitive)
47        if ( s3.regionMatches( 0, s4, 0, 5 ) )
48           System.out.println( "First 5 characters of s3 and s4 match" );
49        else
50           System.out.println(
51              "First 5 characters of s3 and s4 do not match" );
52
```

Fig. 29.3 | String comparisons. (Part I of 2.)

```
53            // test regionMatches (ignore case)
54            if ( s3.regionMatches( true, 0, s4, 0, 5 ) )
55                System.out.println( "First 5 characters of s3 and s4 match" );
56            else
57                System.out.println(
58                    "First 5 characters of s3 and s4 do not match" );
59        } // end main
60    } // end class StringCompare
```

```
s1 = hello
s2 = goodbye
s3 = Happy Birthday
s4 = happy birthday

s1 equals "hello"
s1 is not the same object as "hello"
Happy Birthday equals happy birthday with case ignored

s1.compareTo( s2 ) is 1
s2.compareTo( s1 ) is -1
s1.compareTo( s1 ) is 0
s3.compareTo( s4 ) is -32
s4.compareTo( s3 ) is 32

First 5 characters of s3 and s4 do not match
First 5 characters of s3 and s4 match
```

Fig. 29.3 | String comparisons. (Part 2 of 2.)

which creates a new String object with a copy of string literal "hello" and assigns the new object to variable s1. If s1 had been initialized with the statement

```
s1 = "hello";
```

which directly assigns the string literal "hello" to variable s1, the condition would be true. Remember that Java treats all string literal objects with the same contents as one String object to which there can be many references. Thus, lines 8, 17 and 23 all refer to the same String object "hello" in memory.

Common Programming Error 29.2

Comparing references with == can lead to logic errors, because == compares the references to determine whether they refer to the same object, not whether two objects have the same contents. When two identical (but separate) objects are compared with ==, the result will be false. When comparing objects to determine whether they have the same contents, use method equals.

If you are sorting Strings, you may compare them for equality with method equals-IgnoreCase, which ignores whether the letters in each string are uppercase or lowercase when performing the comparison. Thus, the string "hello" and the string "HELLO" compare as equal. Line 29 uses String method equalsIgnoreCase to compare string s3—Happy Birthday—for equality with string s4—happy birthday. The result of this comparison is true because the comparison ignores case sensitivity.

Lines 35–44 use method compareTo to compare strings. Method compareTo is declared in the Comparable interface and implemented in the String class. Line 36 compares string s1 to string s2. Method compareTo returns 0 if the strings are equal, a negative number if the string that invokes compareTo is less than the string that is passed as an argument and a positive number if the string that invokes compareTo is greater than the string that is passed as an argument. Method compareTo uses a lexicographical comparison—it compares the numeric values of corresponding characters in each string. (For more information on the exact value returned by the compareTo method, see java.sun.com/j2se/5.0/docs/api/java/lang/String.html.)

The condition at line 47 uses String method regionMatches to compare portions of two strings for equality. The first argument is the starting index in the string that invokes the method. The second argument is a comparison string. The third argument is the starting index in the comparison string. The last argument is the number of characters to compare between the two strings. The method returns true only if the specified number of characters are lexicographically equal.

Finally, the condition at line 54 uses a five-argument version of String method regionMatches to compare portions of two strings for equality. When the first argument is true, the method ignores the case of the characters being compared. The remaining arguments are identical to those described for the four-argument regionMatches method.

The second example in this section (Fig. 29.4) demonstrates String methods **startsWith** and **endsWith**. Method main creates array strings containing the strings "started", "starting", "ended" and "ending". The remainder of method main consists of three for statements that test the elements of the array to determine whether they start with or end with a particular set of characters.

The first for statement (lines 11–15) uses the version of method startsWith that takes a String argument. The condition in the if statement (line 13) determines whether each String in the array starts with the characters "st". If so, the method returns true and the application prints that String. Otherwise, the method returns false and nothing happens.

The second for statement (lines 20–25) uses the startsWith method that takes a String and an integer as arguments. The integer specifies the index at which the comparison should begin in the string. The condition in the if statement (line 22) determines whether each String in the array has the characters "art" beginning with the third character in each string. If so, the method returns true and the application prints the String.

The third for statement (lines 30–34) uses method endsWith, which takes a String argument. The condition at line 32 determines whether each String in the array ends with the characters "ed". If so, the method returns true and the application prints the String.

29.3.4 Locating Characters and Substrings in Strings

Often it is useful to search for a character or set of characters in a string. For example, if you are creating your own word processor, you might want to provide a capability for searching through documents. Figure 29.5 demonstrates the many versions of String methods **indexOf** and **lastIndexOf** that search for a specified character or substring in a string. All the searches in this example are performed on the string letters (initialized with "abcdefghijklmabcdefghijklm") in method main. Lines 11–16 use method indexOf to locate the first occurrence of a character in a string. If method indexOf finds the character, it returns the character's index in the string—otherwise, indexOf returns –1. There are two versions of indexOf that search for characters in a string. The expression in line 12 uses the version of method indexOf that takes an integer representation of the character to find. The expres-

```
 1   // Fig. 29.4: StringStartEnd.java
 2   // String methods startsWith and endsWith.
 3
 4   public class StringStartEnd
 5   {
 6      public static void main( String args[] )
 7      {
 8         String strings[] = { "started", "starting", "ended", "ending" };
 9
10         // test method startsWith
11         for ( String string : strings )
12         {
13            if ( string.startsWith( "st" ) )
14               System.out.printf( "\"%s\" starts with \"st\"\n", string );
15         } // end for
16
17         System.out.println();
18
19         // test method startsWith starting from position 2 of string
20         for ( String string : strings )
21         {
22            if ( string.startsWith( "art", 2 ) )
23               System.out.printf(
24                  "\"%s\" starts with \"art\" at position 2\n", string );
25         } // end for
26
27         System.out.println();
28
29         // test method endsWith
30         for ( String string : strings )
31         {
32            if ( string.endsWith( "ed" ) )
33               System.out.printf( "\"%s\" ends with \"ed\"\n", string );
34         } // end for
35      } // end main
36   } // end class StringStartEnd
```

```
"started" starts with "st"
"starting" starts with "st"

"started" starts with "art" at position 2
"starting" starts with "art" at position 2

"started" ends with "ed"
"ended" ends with "ed"
```

Fig. 29.4 | String class startsWith and endsWith methods.

sion at line 14 uses another version of method indexOf, which takes two integer arguments—the character and the starting index at which the search of the string should begin.

The statements at lines 19–24 use method lastIndexOf to locate the last occurrence
of a character in a string. Method lastIndexOf performs the search from the end of the

string toward the beginning of the string. If method `lastIndexOf` finds the character, it returns the index of the character in the string—otherwise, `lastIndexOf` returns −1. There are two versions of `lastIndexOf` that search for characters in a string. The expression at line 20 uses the version of method `lastIndexOf` that takes the integer representation of the character. The expression at line 22 uses the version of method `lastIndexOf` that takes two integer arguments—the integer representation of the character and the index from which to begin searching backward.

```java
1   // Fig. 29.5: StringIndexMethods.java
2   // String searching methods indexOf and lastIndexOf.
3
4   public class StringIndexMethods
5   {
6      public static void main( String args[] )
7      {
8         String letters = "abcdefghijklmabcdefghijklm";
9
10        // test indexOf to locate a character in a string
11        System.out.printf(
12           "'c' is located at index %d\n", letters.indexOf( 'c' ) );
13        System.out.printf(
14           "'a' is located at index %d\n", letters.indexOf( 'a', 1 ) );
15        System.out.printf(
16           "'$' is located at index %d\n\n", letters.indexOf( '$' ) );
17
18        // test lastIndexOf to find a character in a string
19        System.out.printf( "Last 'c' is located at index %d\n",
20           letters.lastIndexOf( 'c' ) );
21        System.out.printf( "Last 'a' is located at index %d\n",
22           letters.lastIndexOf( 'a', 25 ) );
23        System.out.printf( "Last '$' is located at index %d\n\n",
24           letters.lastIndexOf( '$' ) );
25
26        // test indexOf to locate a substring in a string
27        System.out.printf( "\"def\" is located at index %d\n",
28           letters.indexOf( "def" ) );
29        System.out.printf( "\"def\" is located at index %d\n",
30           letters.indexOf( "def", 7 ) );
31        System.out.printf( "\"hello\" is located at index %d\n\n",
32           letters.indexOf( "hello" ) );
33
34        // test lastIndexOf to find a substring in a string
35        System.out.printf( "Last \"def\" is located at index %d\n",
36           letters.lastIndexOf( "def" ) );
37        System.out.printf( "Last \"def\" is located at index %d\n",
38           letters.lastIndexOf( "def", 25 ) );
39        System.out.printf( "Last \"hello\" is located at index %d\n",
40           letters.lastIndexOf( "hello" ) );
41     } // end main
42  } // end class StringIndexMethods
```

Fig. 29.5 | `String` class searching methods. (Part 1 of 2.)

```
'c' is located at index 2
'a' is located at index 13
'$' is located at index -1

Last 'c' is located at index 15
Last 'a' is located at index 13
Last '$' is located at index -1

"def" is located at index 3
"def" is located at index 16
"hello" is located at index -1

Last "def" is located at index 16
Last "def" is located at index 16
Last "hello" is located at index -1
```

Fig. 29.5 | String class searching methods. (Part 2 of 2.)

Lines 27–40 demonstrate versions of methods indexOf and lastIndexOf that each take a String as the first argument. These versions of the methods perform identically to those described earlier except that they search for sequences of characters (or substrings) that are specified by their String arguments. If the substring is found, these methods return the index in the string of the first character in the substring.

29.3.5 Extracting Substrings from Strings

Class String provides two substring methods to enable a new String object to be created by copying part of an existing String object. Each method returns a new String object. Both methods are demonstrated in Fig. 29.6.

```java
 1   // Fig. 29.6: SubString.java
 2   // String class substring methods.
 3
 4   public class SubString
 5   {
 6      public static void main( String args[] )
 7      {
 8         String letters = "abcdefghijklmabcdefghijklm";
 9
10         // test substring methods
11         System.out.printf( "Substring from index 20 to end is \"%s\"\n",
12            letters.substring( 20 ) );
13         System.out.printf( "%s \"%s\"\n",
14            "Substring from index 3 up to, but not including 6 is",
15            letters.substring( 3, 6 ) );
16      } // end main
17   } // end class SubString
```

```
Substring from index 20 to end is "hijklm"
Substring from index 3 up to, but not including 6 is "def"
```

Fig. 29.6 | String class substring methods.

The expression `letters.substring( 20 )` at line 12 uses the `substring` method that takes one integer argument. The argument specifies the starting index in the original string `letters` from which characters are to be copied. The substring returned contains a copy of the characters from the starting index to the end of the string. Specifying an index outside the bounds of the string causes a `StringIndexOutOfBoundsException`.

The expression `letters.substring( 3, 6 )` at line 15 uses the `substring` method that takes two integer arguments. The first argument specifies the starting index from which characters are copied in the original string. The second argument specifies the index one beyond the last character to be copied (i.e., copy up to, but not including, that index in the string). The substring returned contains a copy of the specified characters from the original string. Specifying an index outside the bounds of the string causes a `StringIndexOutOfBoundsException`.

29.3.6 Concatenating Strings

String method **concat** (Fig. 29.7) concatenates two `String` objects and returns a new `String` object containing the characters from both original strings. The expression `s1.concat( s2 )` at line 13 forms a string by appending the characters in string `s2` to the characters in string `s1`. The original `String`s to which `s1` and `s2` refer are not modified.

29.3.7 Miscellaneous String Methods

Class `String` provides several methods that return modified copies of strings or that return character arrays. These methods are demonstrated in the application in Fig. 29.8.

Line 16 uses `String` method `replace` to return a new `String` object in which every occurrence in string `s1` of character `'l'` (lowercase el) is replaced with character `'L'`.

```java
1   // Fig. 29.7: StringConcatenation.java
2   // String concat method.
3
4   public class StringConcatenation
5   {
6      public static void main( String args[] )
7      {
8         String s1 = new String( "Happy " );
9         String s2 = new String( "Birthday" );
10
11         System.out.printf( "s1 = %s\ns2 = %s\n\n",s1, s2 );
12         System.out.printf(
13            "Result of s1.concat( s2 ) = %s\n", s1.concat( s2 ) );
14         System.out.printf( "s1 after concatenation = %s\n", s1 );
15      } // end main
16   } // end class StringConcatenation
```

```
s1 = Happy
s2 = Birthday

Result of s1.concat( s2 ) = Happy Birthday
s1 after concatenation = Happy
```

Fig. 29.7 | String method `concat`.

Method `replace` leaves the original string unchanged. If there are no occurrences of the first argument in the string, method `replace` returns the original string.

```java
1   // Fig. 29.8: StringMiscellaneous2.java
2   // String methods replace, toLowerCase, toUpperCase, trim and toCharArray.
3
4   public class StringMiscellaneous2
5   {
6      public static void main( String args[] )
7      {
8         String s1 = new String( "hello" );
9         String s2 = new String( "GOODBYE" );
10        String s3 = new String( "   spaces   " );
11
12        System.out.printf( "s1 = %s\ns2 = %s\ns3 = %s\n\n", s1, s2, s3 );
13
14        // test method replace
15        System.out.printf(
16           "Replace 'l' with 'L' in s1: %s\n\n", s1.replace( 'l', 'L' ) );
17
18        // test toLowerCase and toUpperCase
19        System.out.printf( "s1.toUpperCase() = %s\n", s1.toUpperCase() );
20        System.out.printf( "s2.toLowerCase() = %s\n\n", s2.toLowerCase() );
21
22        // test trim method
23        System.out.printf( "s3 after trim = \"%s\"\n\n", s3.trim() );
24
25        // test toCharArray method
26        char charArray[] = s1.toCharArray();
27        System.out.print( "s1 as a character array = " );
28
29        for ( char character : charArray )
30           System.out.print( character );
31
32        System.out.println();
33     } // end main
34  } // end class StringMiscellaneous2
```

```
s1 = hello
s2 = GOODBYE
s3 =    spaces

Replace 'l' with 'L' in s1: heLLo

s1.toUpperCase() = HELLO
s2.toLowerCase() = goodbye

s3 after trim = "spaces"

s1 as a character array = hello
```

Fig. 29.8 | String methods `replace`, `toLowerCase`, `toUpperCase`, `trim` and `toCharArray`.

Line 19 uses String method toUpperCase to generate a new String object with upper-case letters where corresponding lowercase letters exist in s1. The method returns a new String object containing the converted string and leaves the original string unchanged. If there are no characters to convert, method toUpperCase returns the original string.

Line 20 uses String method toLowerCase to return a new String object with lower-case letters where corresponding uppercase letters exist in s2. The original string remains unchanged. If there are no characters in the original string to convert, toLowerCase returns the original string.

Line 23 uses String method trim to generate a new String object that removes all whitespace characters that appear at the beginning or end of the string on which trim operates. The method returns a new String object containing the string without leading or trailing white space. The original string remains unchanged.

Line 26 uses String method toCharArray to create a new character array containing a copy of the characters in string s1. Lines 29–30 output each char in the array.

29.3.8 String Method valueOf

As we have seen, every object in Java has a toString method that enables a program to obtain the object's string representation. Unfortunately, this technique cannot be used with primitive types because they do not have methods. Class String provides static methods that take an argument of any type and convert the argument to a String object. Figure 29.9 demonstrates the String class valueOf methods.

The expression String.valueOf(charArray) at line 18 uses the character array charArray to create a new String object. The expression String.valueOf(charArray, 3, 3) at line 20 uses a portion of the character array charArray to create a new String object. The second argument specifies the starting index from which the characters are used. The third argument specifies the number of characters to be used.

There are seven other versions of method valueOf, which take arguments of type boolean, char, int, long, float, double and Object, respectively. These are demonstrated in lines 21–30. Note that the version of valueOf that takes an Object as an argument can do so because all Objects can be converted to Strings with method toString.

[*Note:* Lines 12–13 use literal values 10000000000L and 2.5f as the initial values of long variable longValue and float variable floatValue, respectively. By default, Java treats integer literals as type int and floating-point literals as type double. Appending the letter L to the literal 10000000000 and appending letter f to the literal 2.5 indicates to the compiler that 10000000000 should be treated as a long and that 2.5 should be treated as a float. An uppercase L or lowercase l can be used to denote a variable of type long and an uppercase F or lowercase f can be used to denote a variable of type float.]

29.4 Class StringBuffer

Once a String object is created, its contents can never change. We now discuss the features of class StringBuffer for creating and manipulating dynamic string information—that is, modifiable strings. Every StringBuffer is capable of storing a number of characters specified by its capacity. If the capacity of a StringBuffer is exceeded, the capacity is automatically expanded to accommodate the additional characters. Class StringBuffer is also used to implement operators + and += for String concatenation.

```
 1    // Fig. 29.9: StringValueOf.java
 2    // String valueOf methods.
 3
 4    public class StringValueOf
 5    {
 6       public static void main( String args[] )
 7       {
 8          char charArray[] = { 'a', 'b', 'c', 'd', 'e', 'f' };
 9          boolean booleanValue = true;
10          char characterValue = 'Z';
11          int integerValue = 7;
12          long longValue = 10000000000L; // L suffix indicates long
13          float floatValue = 2.5f; // f indicates that 2.5 is a float
14          double doubleValue = 33.333; // no suffix, double is default
15          Object objectRef = "hello"; // assign string to an Object reference
16
17          System.out.printf(
18             "char array = %s\n", String.valueOf( charArray ) );
19          System.out.printf( "part of char array = %s\n",
20             String.valueOf( charArray, 3, 3 ) );
21          System.out.printf(
22             "boolean = %s\n", String.valueOf( booleanValue ) );
23          System.out.printf(
24             "char = %s\n", String.valueOf( characterValue ) );
25          System.out.printf( "int = %s\n", String.valueOf( integerValue ) );
26          System.out.printf( "long = %s\n", String.valueOf( longValue ) );
27          System.out.printf( "float = %s\n", String.valueOf( floatValue ) );
28          System.out.printf(
29             "double = %s\n", String.valueOf( doubleValue ) );
30          System.out.printf( "Object = %s", String.valueOf( objectRef ) );
31       } // end main
32    } // end class StringValueOf
```

```
char array = abcdef
part of char array = def
boolean = true
char = Z
int = 7
long = 10000000000
float = 2.5
double = 33.333
Object = hello
```

Fig. 29.9 | String class valueOf methods.

Performance Tip 29.2

Java can perform certain optimizations involving String objects (such as sharing one String object among multiple references) because it knows these objects will not change. Strings (not StringBuffers) should be used if the data will not change.

Performance Tip 29.3

In programs that frequently perform string concatenation, or other string modifications, it is more efficient to implement the modifications with class StringBuffer (covered in Section 29.4).

29.4.1 StringBuffer Constructors

Class StringBuffer provides four constructors. Three of these constructors are demonstrated in Fig. 29.10. Line 8 uses the no-argument StringBuffer constructor to create a StringBuffer with no characters in it and an initial capacity of 16 characters (the default for a StringBuffer). Line 9 uses the StringBuffer constructor that takes an integer argument to create a StringBuffer with no characters in it and the initial capacity specified by the integer argument (i.e., 10). Line 10 uses the StringBuffer constructor that takes a String argument (in this case, a string literal) to create a StringBuffer containing the characters in the String argument. The initial capacity is the number of characters in the String argument plus 16.

The statements on lines 12–14 uses StringBuffer method toString to output the StringBuffers with the printf method. In Section 29.4.4, we discuss how Java uses StringBuffer objects to implement the + and += operators for string concatenation.

29.4.2 StringBuffer Methods length, capacity, setLength and ensureCapacity

Class StringBuffer provides methods **length** and **capacity** to return the number of characters currently in a StringBuffer and the number of characters that can be stored in a StringBuffer without allocating more memory, respectively. Method **ensureCapacity** guarantees that a StringBuffer has at least the specified capacity. Method setLength increases or decreases the length of a StringBuffer. The application in Fig. 29.11 demonstrates these methods.

The application contains one StringBuffer called buffer. Line 8 uses the StringBuffer constructor that takes a String argument to initialize the StringBuffer with "Hello, how are you?". Lines 10–11 print the contents, length and capacity of the

```
1   // Fig. 29.10: StringBufferConstructors.java
2   // StringBuffer constructors.
3
4   public class StringBufferConstructors
5   {
6      public static void main( String args[] )
7      {
8         StringBuffer buffer1 = new StringBuffer();
9         StringBuffer buffer2 = new StringBuffer( 10 );
10        StringBuffer buffer3 = new StringBuffer( "hello" );
11
12        System.out.printf( "buffer1 = \"%s\"\n", buffer1.toString() );
13        System.out.printf( "buffer2 = \"%s\"\n", buffer2.toString() );
14        System.out.printf( "buffer3 = \"%s\"\n", buffer3.toString() );
15     } // end main
16  } // end class StringBufferConstructors
```

```
buffer1 = ""
buffer2 = ""
buffer3 = "hello"
```

Fig. 29.10 | StringBuffer class constructors.

```
 1   // Fig. 29.11: StringBufferCapLen.java
 2   // StringBuffer length, setLength, capacity and ensureCapacity methods.
 3
 4   public class StringBufferCapLen
 5   {
 6      public static void main( String args[] )
 7      {
 8         StringBuffer buffer = new StringBuffer( "Hello, how are you?" );
 9
10         System.out.printf( "buffer = %s\nlength = %d\ncapacity = %d\n\n",
11            buffer.toString(), buffer.length(), buffer.capacity() );
12
13         buffer.ensureCapacity( 75 );
14         System.out.printf( "New capacity = %d\n\n", buffer.capacity() );
15
16         buffer.setLength( 10 );
17         System.out.printf( "New length = %d\nbuf = %s\n",
18            buffer.length(), buffer.toString() );
19      } // end main
20   } // end class StringBufferCapLen
```

```
buffer = Hello, how are you?
length = 19
capacity = 35

New capacity = 75

New length = 10
buf = Hello, how
```

Fig. 29.11 | StringBuffer methods length and capacity.

StringBuffer. Note in the output window that the capacity of the StringBuffer is initially 35. Recall that the StringBuffer constructor that takes a String argument initializes the capacity to the length of the string passed as an argument plus 16.

Line 13 uses method ensureCapacity to expand the capacity of the StringBuffer to a minimum of 75 characters. Actually, if the original capacity is less than the argument, the method ensures a capacity that is the greater of the number specified as an argument and twice the original capacity plus 2. The StringBuffer's current capacity remains unchanged if it is more than the specified capacity.

Performance Tip 29.4

Dynamically increasing the capacity of a StringBuffer can take a relatively long time. Executing a large number of these operations can degrade the performance of an application. If a StringBuffer is going to increase greatly in size, possibly multiple times, setting its capacity high at the beginning will increase performance.

Line 16 uses method setLength to set the length of the StringBuffer to 10. If the specified length is less than the current number of characters in the StringBuffer, the buffer is truncated to the specified length (i.e., the characters in the StringBuffer after the specified length are discarded). If the specified length is greater than the number of characters currently in the `StringBuffer`, `null` characters (characters with the numeric representation 0) are appended to the `StringBuffer` until the total number of characters in the `StringBuffer` is equal to the specified length. See Section 14.7.1 for more details.

29.4.3 StringBuffer Methods charAt, setCharAt, getChars and reverse

Class `StringBuffer` provides methods **charAt**, **setCharAt**, **getChars** and **reverse** to manipulate the characters in a `StringBuffer`. Each of these methods is demonstrated in Fig. 29.12.

```
1   // Fig. 29.12: StringBufferChars.java
2   // StringBuffer methods charAt, setCharAt, getChars and reverse.
3
4   public class StringBufferChars
5   {
6      public static void main( String args[] )
7      {
8         StringBuffer buffer = new StringBuffer( "hello there" );
9
10        System.out.printf( "buffer = %s\n", buffer.toString() );
11        System.out.printf( "Character at 0: %s\nCharacter at 4: %s\n\n",
12           buffer.charAt( 0 ), buffer.charAt( 4 ) );
13
14        char charArray[] = new char[ buffer.length() ];
15        buffer.getChars( 0, buffer.length(), charArray, 0 );
16        System.out.print( "The characters are: " );
17
18        for ( char character : charArray )
19           System.out.print( character );
20
21        buffer.setCharAt( 0, 'H' );
22        buffer.setCharAt( 6, 'T' );
23        System.out.printf( "\n\nbuf = %s", buffer.toString() );
24
25        buffer.reverse();
26        System.out.printf( "\n\nbuf = %s\n", buffer.toString() );
27     } // end main
28  } // end class StringBufferChars
```

```
buffer = hello there
Character at 0: h
Character at 4: o

The characters are: hello there

buf = Hello There

buf = erehT olleH
```

Fig. 29.12 | `StringBuffer` class character-manipulation methods.

Method charAt (line 12) takes an integer argument and returns the character in the StringBuffer at that index. Method getChars (line 15) copies characters from a String-Buffer into the character array passed as an argument. This method takes four arguments—the starting index from which characters should be copied in the StringBuffer, the index one past the last character to be copied from the StringBuffer, the character array into which the characters are to be copied and the starting location in the character array where the first character should be placed. Method setCharAt (lines 21 and 22) takes an integer and a character argument and sets the character at the specified position in the StringBuffer to the character argument. Method reverse (line 25) reverses the contents of the StringBuffer.

Common Programming Error 29.3

Attempting to access a character that is outside the bounds of a StringBuffer (i.e., with an index less than 0 or greater than or equal to the StringBuffer's length) results in a StringIndexOutOfBoundsException.

29.4.4 StringBuffer append Methods

Class StringBuffer provides overloaded **append** methods to allow values of various types to be appended to the end of a StringBuffer. Versions are provided for each of the primitive types and for character arrays, Strings, Objects, StringBuffers and CharSequences. (Remember that method toString produces a string representation of any Object.) Each of the methods takes its argument, converts it to a string and appends it to the String-Buffer. The append methods are demonstrated in Fig. 29.13.

Actually, StringBuffers and the append methods are used by the compiler to implement the + and += operators for String concatenation. For example, assuming the declarations

```
String string1 = "hello";
String string2 = "BC";
int value = 22;
```

the statement

```
String s = string1 + string2 + value;
```

concatenates "hello", "BC" and 22. The concatenation is performed as follows:

```
new StringBuffer().append( "hello" ).append( "BC" ).append(
   22 ).toString();
```

First, Java creates an empty StringBuffer, then appends to the StringBuffer the string "hello", the string "BC" and the integer 22. Next, StringBuffer's method toString converts the StringBuffer to a String object to be assigned to String s. The statement

```
s += "!";
```

is performed as follows:

```
s = new StringBuffer().append( s ).append( "!" ).toString();
```

First, Java creates an empty `StringBuffer`, then appends to the `StringBuffer` the current contents of s followed by "!". Next, `StringBuffer`'s method `toString` converts the `StringBuffer` to a string representation and the result is assigned to s.

```java
1   // Fig. 29.13: StringBufferAppend.java
2   // StringBuffer append methods.
3
4   public class StringBufferAppend
5   {
6      public static void main( String args[] )
7      {
8         Object objectRef = "hello";
9         String string = "goodbye";
10        char charArray[] = { 'a', 'b', 'c', 'd', 'e', 'f' };
11        boolean booleanValue = true;
12        char characterValue = 'Z';
13        int integerValue = 7;
14        long longValue = 10000000000L;
15        float floatValue = 2.5f; // f suffix indicates 2.5 is a float
16        double doubleValue = 33.333;
17
18        StringBuffer lastBuffer = new StringBuffer( "last StringBuffer" );
19        StringBuffer buffer = new StringBuffer();
20
21        buffer.append( objectRef );
22        buffer.append( "\n" ); // each of these contains new line
23        buffer.append( string );
24        buffer.append( "\n" );
25        buffer.append( charArray );
26        buffer.append( "\n" );
27        buffer.append( charArray, 0, 3 );
28        buffer.append( "\n" );
29        buffer.append( booleanValue );
30        buffer.append( "\n" );
31        buffer.append( characterValue );
32        buffer.append( "\n" );
33        buffer.append( integerValue );
34        buffer.append( "\n" );
35        buffer.append( longValue );
36        buffer.append( "\n" );
37        buffer.append( floatValue );
38        buffer.append( "\n" );
39        buffer.append( doubleValue );
40        buffer.append( "\n" );
41        buffer.append( lastBuffer );
42
43        System.out.printf( "buffer contains %s\n", buffer.toString() );
44     } // end main
45  } // end StringBufferAppend
```

Fig. 29.13 | `StringBuffer` class `append` methods. (Part 1 of 2.)

```
buffer contains hello
goodbye
abcdef
abc
true
Z
7
10000000000
2.5
33.333
last StringBuffer
```

Fig. 29.13 | StringBuffer class append methods. (Part 2 of 2.)

29.4.5 StringBuffer Insertion and Deletion Methods

Class StringBuffer provides overloaded **insert** methods to allow values of various types to be inserted at any position in a StringBuffer. Versions are provided for each of the primitive types and for character arrays, Strings, Objects and CharSequences. Each of the methods takes its second argument, converts it to a string and inserts it immediately preceding the index specified by the first argument. The index specified by the first argument must be greater than or equal to 0 and less than the length of the StringBuffer—otherwise, a StringIndexOutOfBoundsException occurs. Class StringBuffer also provides methods **delete** and **deleteCharAt** for deleting characters at any position in a String-Buffer. Method delete takes two arguments—the starting index and the index one past the end of the characters to delete. All characters beginning at the starting index up to but not including the ending index are deleted. Method deleteCharAt takes one argument—the index of the character to delete. Invalid indices cause both methods to throw a String-IndexOutOfBoundsException. Methods insert, delete and deleteCharAt are demonstrated in Fig. 29.14.

```
1   // Fig. 29.14: StringBufferInsert.java
2   // StringBuffer methods insert, delete and deleteCharAt.
3
4   public class StringBufferInsert
5   {
6      public static void main( String args[] )
7      {
8         Object objectRef = "hello";
9         String string = "goodbye";
10        char charArray[] = { 'a', 'b', 'c', 'd', 'e', 'f' };
11        boolean booleanValue = true;
12        char characterValue = 'K';
13        int integerValue = 7;
14        long longValue = 10000000;
15        float floatValue = 2.5f; // f suffix indicates that 2.5 is a float
16        double doubleValue = 33.333;
17
```

Fig. 29.14 | StringBuffer methods insert and delete. (Part 1 of 2.)

```
18          StringBuffer buffer = new StringBuffer();
19
20          buffer.insert( 0, objectRef );
21          buffer.insert( 0, "  " ); // each of these contains two spaces
22          buffer.insert( 0, string );
23          buffer.insert( 0, "  " );
24          buffer.insert( 0, charArray );
25          buffer.insert( 0, "  " );
26          buffer.insert( 0, charArray, 3, 3 );
27          buffer.insert( 0, "  " );
28          buffer.insert( 0, booleanValue );
29          buffer.insert( 0, "  " );
30          buffer.insert( 0, characterValue );
31          buffer.insert( 0, "  " );
32          buffer.insert( 0, integerValue );
33          buffer.insert( 0, "  " );
34          buffer.insert( 0, longValue );
35          buffer.insert( 0, "  " );
36          buffer.insert( 0, floatValue );
37          buffer.insert( 0, "  " );
38          buffer.insert( 0, doubleValue );
39
40          System.out.printf(
41             "buffer after inserts:\n%s\n\n", buffer.toString() );
42
43          buffer.deleteCharAt( 10 ); // delete 5 in 2.5
44          buffer.delete( 2, 6 ); // delete .333 in 33.333
45
46          System.out.printf(
47             "buffer after deletes:\n%s\n", buffer.toString() );
48       } // end main
49    } // end class StringBufferInsert
```

```
buffer after inserts:
33.333  2.5  10000000  7  K  true  def  abcdef  goodbye  hello

buffer after deletes:
33  2.  10000000  7  K  true  def  abcdef  goodbye  hello
```

Fig. 29.14 | StringBuffer methods insert and delete. (Part 2 of 2.)

29.5 Class Character

Recall from Chapter 17 that Java provides eight type-wrapper classes—Boolean, Character, Double, Float, Byte, Short, Integer and Long—that enable primitive-type values to be treated as objects. In this section, we present class Character—the type-wrapper class for primitive type char.

Most Character methods are static methods designed to be convenience methods for processing individual char values. These methods take at least a character argument and perform either a test or a manipulation of the character. Class Character also contains a constructor that receives a char argument to initialize a Character object. Most of the methods of class Character are presented in the next three examples. For more information on class Character (and all the type-wrapper classes), see the java.lang package in the Java API documentation.

Figure 29.15 demonstrates some static methods that test characters to determine whether they are a specific character type and the static methods that perform case conversions on characters. You can enter any character and apply the methods to the character.

Line 15 uses Character method **isDefined** to determine whether character c is defined in the Unicode character set. If so, the method returns true, and otherwise, it returns false. Line 16 uses Character method **isDigit** to determine whether character c is a defined Unicode digit. If so, the method returns true, and otherwise, it returns false.

Line 18 uses Character method **isJavaIdentifierStart** to determine whether c is a character that can be the first character of an identifier in Java—that is, a letter, an underscore (_) or a dollar sign ($). If so, the method returns true, and otherwise, it returns false. Line 20 uses Character method **isJavaIdentifierPart** to determine whether character c is a character that can be used in an identifier in Java—that is, a digit, a letter,

```java
1   // Fig. 29.15: StaticCharMethods.java
2   // Static Character testing methods and case conversion methods.
3   import java.util.Scanner;
4
5   public class StaticCharMethods
6   {
7      public static void main( String args[] )
8      {
9         Scanner scanner = new Scanner( System.in ); // create scanner
10        System.out.println( "Enter a character and press Enter" );
11        String input = scanner.next();
12        char c = input.charAt( 0 ); // get input character
13
14        // display character info
15        System.out.printf( "is defined: %b\n", Character.isDefined( c ) );
16        System.out.printf( "is digit: %b\n", Character.isDigit( c ) );
17        System.out.printf( "is first character in a Java identifier: %b\n",
18           Character.isJavaIdentifierStart( c ) );
19        System.out.printf( "is part of a Java identifier: %b\n",
20           Character.isJavaIdentifierPart( c ) );
21        System.out.printf( "is letter: %b\n", Character.isLetter( c ) );
22        System.out.printf(
23           "is letter or digit: %b\n", Character.isLetterOrDigit( c ) );
24        System.out.printf(
25           "is lower case: %b\n", Character.isLowerCase( c ) );
26        System.out.printf(
27           "is upper case: %b\n", Character.isUpperCase( c ) );
28        System.out.printf(
29           "to upper case: %s\n", Character.toUpperCase( c ) );
30        System.out.printf(
31           "to lower case: %s\n", Character.toLowerCase( c ) );
32     } // end main
33  } // end class StaticCharMethods
```

Fig. 29.15 | Character class static methods for testing characters and converting character case. (Part 1 of 2.)

```
Enter a character and press Enter
A
is defined: true
is digit: false
is first character in a Java identifier: true
is part of a Java identifier: true
is letter: true
is letter or digit: true
is lower case: false
is upper case: true
to upper case: A
to lower case: a
```

```
Enter a character and press Enter
8
is defined: true
is digit: true
is first character in a Java identifier: false
is part of a Java identifier: true
is letter: false
is letter or digit: true
is lower case: false
is upper case: false
to upper case: 8
to lower case: 8
```

```
Enter a character and press Enter
$
is defined: true
is digit: false
is first character in a Java identifier: true
is part of a Java identifier: true
is letter: false
is letter or digit: false
is lower case: false
is upper case: false
to upper case: $
to lower case: $
```

Fig. 29.15 | `Character` class `static` methods for testing characters and converting character case. (Part 2 of 2.)

an underscore (_) or a dollar sign ($). If so, the method returns `true`, and otherwise, it returns `false`.

Line 21 uses `Character` method **`isLetter`** to determine whether character c is a letter. If so, the method returns `true`, and otherwise, it returns `false`. Line 23 uses `Character` method **`isLetterOrDigit`** to determine whether character c is a letter or a digit. If so, the method returns `true`, and otherwise, it returns `false`.

Line 25 uses `Character` method **`isLowerCase`** to determine whether character c is a lowercase letter. If so, the method returns `true`, and otherwise, it returns `false`. Line 27 uses `Character` method **isUpperCase** to determine whether character c is an uppercase letter. If so, the method returns `true`, and otherwise, it returns `false`.

Line 29 uses `Character` method **toUpperCase** to convert the character c to its uppercase equivalent. The method returns the converted character if the character has an uppercase equivalent, and otherwise, the method returns its original argument. Line 31 uses `Character` method **toLowerCase** to convert the character c to its lowercase equivalent. The method returns the converted character if the character has a lowercase equivalent, and otherwise, the method returns its original argument.

Figure 29.16 demonstrates static `Character` methods **digit** and **forDigit**, which convert characters to digits and digits to characters, respectively, in different number systems. Common number systems include decimal (base 10), octal (base 8), hexadecimal (base 16) and binary (base 2). The base of a number is also known as its **radix**. For more information on conversions between number systems, see Appendix E.

Line 28 uses method `forDigit` to convert the integer `digit` into a character in the number system specified by the integer `radix` (the base of the number). For example, the decimal integer 13 in base 16 (the `radix`) has the character value `'d'`. Note that lowercase letters represent the same value as uppercase letters in number systems. Line 35 uses method `digit` to convert the character c into an integer in the number system specified by the integer `radix` (the base of the number). For example, the character `'A'` is the base

```java
 1   // Fig. 29.16: StaticCharMethods2.java
 2   // Static Character conversion methods.
 3   import java.util.Scanner;
 4
 5   public class StaticCharMethods2
 6   {
 7      // create StaticCharMethods2 object execute application
 8      public static void main( String args[] )
 9      {
10         Scanner scanner = new Scanner( System.in );
11
12         // get radix
13         System.out.println( "Please enter a radix:" );
14         int radix = scanner.nextInt();
15
16         // get user choice
17         System.out.printf( "Please choose one:\n1 -- %s\n2 -- %s\n",
18            "Convert digit to character", "Convert character to digit" );
19         int choice = scanner.nextInt();
20
21         // process request
22         switch ( choice )
23         {
24            case 1: // convert digit to character
25               System.out.println( "Enter a digit:" );
26               int digit = scanner.nextInt();
27               System.out.printf( "Convert digit to character: %s\n",
28                  Character.forDigit( digit, radix ) );
29               break;
```

Fig. 29.16 | `Character` class `static` conversion methods. (Part 1 of 2.)

```
30
31            case 2: // convert character to digit
32               System.out.println( "Enter a character:" );
33               char character = scanner.next().charAt( 0 );
34               System.out.printf( "Convert character to digit: %s\n",
35                  Character.digit( character, radix ) );
36               break;
37         } // end switch
38      } // end main
39   } // end class StaticCharMethods2
```

```
Please enter a radix:
16
Please choose one:
1 -- Convert digit to character
2 -- Convert character to digit
2
Enter a character:
A
Convert character to digit: 10
```

```
Please enter a radix:
16
Please choose one:
1 -- Convert digit to character
2 -- Convert character to digit
1
Enter a digit:
13
Convert digit to character: d
```

Fig. 29.16 | Character class static conversion methods. (Part 2 of 2.)

16 (the radix) representation of the base 10 value 10. The radix must be between 2 and 36, inclusive.

The application in Fig. 29.17 demonstrates the constructor and several non-static methods of class Character—charValue, toString and equals. Lines 8–9 instantiate two Character objects by autoboxing the character constants 'A' and 'a', respectively. Line 12 uses Character method charValue to return the char value stored in Character object c1. Line 12 returns a string representation of Character object c2 using method toString. The condition in the if...else statement at lines 14–17 uses method equals to determine whether the object c1 has the same contents as the object c2 (i.e., the characters inside each object are equal).

29.6 Class StringTokenizer

When you read a sentence, your mind breaks the sentence into tokens—individual words and punctuation marks, each of which conveys meaning to you. Compilers also perform tokenization. They break up statements into individual pieces like keywords, identifiers, operators and other elements of a programming language. In this section, we study Java's

```
 1    // Fig. 29.17: OtherCharMethods.java
 2    // Non-static Character methods.
 3
 4    public class OtherCharMethods
 5    {
 6       public static void main( String args[] )
 7       {
 8          Character c1 = 'A';
 9          Character c2 = 'a';
10
11          System.out.printf(
12             "c1 = %s\nc2 = %s\n\n", c1.charValue(), c2.toString() );
13
14          if ( c1.equals( c2 ) )
15             System.out.println( "c1 and c2 are equal\n" );
16          else
17             System.out.println( "c1 and c2 are not equal\n" );
18       } // end main
19    } // end class OtherCharMethods
```

```
c1 = A
c2 = a

c1 and c2 are not equal
```

Fig. 29.17 | Character class non-static methods.

StringTokenizer class (from package java.util), which breaks a string into its component tokens. Tokens are separated from one another by **delimiters**, typically whitespace characters such as space, tab, newline and carriage return. Other characters can also be used as delimiters to separate tokens. The application in Fig. 29.18 demonstrates class StringTokenizer.

When the user presses the *Enter* key, the input sentence is stored in String variable sentence. Line 17 creates an instance of class StringTokenizer using String sentence. This StringTokenizer constructor takes a string argument and creates a StringTokenizer for it, and will use the default delimiter string " \t\n\r\f" consisting of a space, a tab, a carriage return and a newline for tokenization. There are two other constructors for class StringTokenizer. In the version that takes two String arguments, the second String is the delimiter string. In the version that takes three arguments, the second String is the delimiter string and the third argument (a boolean) determines whether the delimiters are also returned as tokens (only if the argument is true). This is useful if you need to know what the delimiters are.

Line 19 uses StringTokenizer method countTokens to determine the number of tokens in the string to be tokenized. The condition in the while statement at lines 21–22 uses StringTokenizer method **hasMoreTokens** to determine whether there are more tokens in the string being tokenized. If so, line 22 prints the next token in the String. The next token is obtained with a call to StringTokenizer method **nextToken**, which returns a String. The token is output using println, so subsequent tokens appear on separate lines.

```
1   // Fig. 29.18: TokenTest.java
2   // StringTokenizer class.
3   import java.util.Scanner;
4   import java.util.StringTokenizer;
5
6   public class TokenTest
7   {
8      // execute application
9      public static void main( String args[] )
10     {
11        // get sentence
12        Scanner scanner = new Scanner( System.in );
13        System.out.println( "Enter a sentence and press Enter" );
14        String sentence = scanner.nextLine();
15
16        // process user sentence
17        StringTokenizer tokens = new StringTokenizer( sentence );
18        System.out.printf( "Number of elements: %d\nThe tokens are:\n",
19           tokens.countTokens() );
20
21        while ( tokens.hasMoreTokens() )
22           System.out.println( tokens.nextToken() );
23     } // end main
24  } // end class TokenTest
```

```
Enter a sentence and press Enter
This is a sentence with seven tokens
Number of elements: 7
The tokens are:
This
is
a
sentence
with
seven
tokens
```

Fig. 29.18 | StringTokenizer object used to tokenize strings.

If you would like to change the delimiter string while tokenizing a string, you may do so by specifying a new delimiter string in a nextToken call as follows:

```
tokens.nextToken( newDelimiterString );
```

This feature is not demonstrated in Fig. 29.18.

29.7 Regular Expressions, Class Pattern and Class Matcher

Regular expressions are sequences of characters and symbols that define a set of strings. They are useful for validating input and ensuring that data is in a particular format. For example, a ZIP code must consist of five digits, and a last name must contain only letters, spaces, apostrophes and hyphens. One application of regular expressions is to facilitate the construction of a compiler. Often, a large and complex regular expression is used to validate the syntax of a program. If the program code does not match the regular expression, the compiler knows that there is a syntax error within the code.

Class String provides several methods for performing regular-expression operations, the simplest of which is the matching operation. String method **matches** receives a string that specifies the regular expression and matches the contents of the String object on which it is called to the regular expression. The method returns a boolean indicating whether the match succeeded.

A regular expression consists of literal characters and special symbols. Figure 29.19 specifies some predefined character classes that can be used with regular expressions. A character class is an escape sequence that represents a group of characters. A digit is any numeric character. A word character is any letter (uppercase or lowercase), any digit or the underscore character. A whitespace character is a space, a tab, a carriage return, a newline or a form feed. Each character class matches a single character in the string we are attempting to match with the regular expression.

Regular expressions are not limited to these predefined character classes. The expressions employ various operators and other forms of notation to match complex patterns. We examine several of these techniques in the application in Fig. 29.20 and Fig. 29.21 which validates user input via regular expressions. [*Note:* This application is not designed to match all possible valid user input.]

Figure 29.20 validates user input. Line 9 validates the first name. To match a set of characters that does not have a predefined character class, use square brackets, []. For example, the pattern "[aeiou]" matches a single character that is a vowel. Ranges of characters can be represented by placing a dash (-) between two characters. In the example, "[A-Z]" matches a single uppercase letter. If the first character in the brackets is "^", the expression accepts any character other than those indicated. However, it is important to note that "[^Z]" is not the same as "[A-Y]", which matches uppercase letters A–Y— "[^Z]" matches any character other than capital Z, including lowercase letters and non-letters such as the newline character. Ranges in character classes are determined by the letters' integer values. In this example, "[A-Za-z]" matches all uppercase and lowercase letters. The range "[A-z]" matches all letters and also matches those characters (such as % and 6) with an integer value between uppercase Z and lowercase a (for more information on integer values of characters see Appendix B, ASCII Character Set). Like predefined character classes, character classes delimited by square brackets match a single character in the search object.

Character	Matches	Character	Matches
\d	any digit	\D	any non-digit
\w	any word character	\W	any non-word character
\s	any whitespace	\S	any non-whitespace

Fig. 29.19 | Predefined character classes.

```
1   // Fig. 29.20: ValidateInput.java
2   // Validate user information using regular expressions.
3
4   public class ValidateInput
5   {
6      // validate first name
7      public static boolean validateFirstName( String firstName )
8      {
9         return firstName.matches( "[A-Z][a-zA-Z]*" );
10     } // end method validateFirstName
11
12     // validate last name
13     public static boolean validateLastName( String lastName )
14     {
15        return lastName.matches( "[a-zA-z]+([ '-][a-zA-Z]+)*" );
16     } // end method validateLastName
17
18     // validate address
19     public static boolean validateAddress( String address )
20     {
21        return address.matches(
22           "\\d+\\s+([a-zA-Z]+|[a-zA-Z]+\\s[a-zA-Z]+)" );
23     } // end method validateAddress
24
25     // validate city
26     public static boolean validateCity( String city )
27     {
28        return city.matches( "([a-zA-Z]+|[a-zA-Z]+\\s[a-zA-Z]+)" );
29     } // end method validateCity
30
31     // validate state
32     public static boolean validateState( String state )
33     {
34        return state.matches( "([a-zA-Z]+|[a-zA-Z]+\\s[a-zA-Z]+)" ) ;
35     } // end method validateState
36
37     // validate zip
38     public static boolean validateZip( String zip )
39     {
40        return zip.matches( "\\d{5}" );
41     } // end method validateZip
42
43     // validate phone
44     public static boolean validatePhone( String phone )
45     {
46        return phone.matches( "[1-9]\\d{2}-[1-9]\\d{2}-\\d{4}" );
47     } // end method validatePhone
48   } // end class ValidateInput
```

Fig. 29.20 | Validating user information using regular expressions.

In line 9, the asterisk after the second character class indicates that any number of letters can be matched. In general, when the regular-expression operator "*" appears in a regular expression, the application attempts to match zero or more occurrences of the subexpression immediately preceding the "*". Operator "+" attempts to match one or more occurrences of the subexpression immediately preceding "+". So both "A*" and "A+" will match "AAA", but only "A*" will match an empty string.

```java
 1   // Fig. 29.21: Validate.java
 2   // Validate user information using regular expressions.
 3   import java.util.Scanner;
 4
 5   public class Validate
 6   {
 7      public static void main( String[] args )
 8      {
 9         // get user input
10         Scanner scanner = new Scanner( System.in );
11         System.out.println( "Please enter first name:" );
12         String firstName = scanner.nextLine();
13         System.out.println( "Please enter last name:" );
14         String lastName = scanner.nextLine();
15         System.out.println( "Please enter address:" );
16         String address = scanner.nextLine();
17         System.out.println( "Please enter city:" );
18         String city = scanner.nextLine();
19         System.out.println( "Please enter state:" );
20         String state = scanner.nextLine();
21         System.out.println( "Please enter zip:" );
22         String zip = scanner.nextLine();
23         System.out.println( "Please enter phone:" );
24         String phone = scanner.nextLine();
25
26         // validate user input and display error message
27         System.out.println( "\nValidate Result:" );
28
29         if ( !ValidateInput.validateFirstName( firstName ) )
30            System.out.println( "Invalid first name" );
31         else if ( !ValidateInput.validateLastName( lastName ) )
32            System.out.println( "Invalid last name" );
33         else if ( !ValidateInput.validateAddress( address ) )
34            System.out.println( "Invalid address" );
35         else if ( !ValidateInput.validateCity( city ) )
36            System.out.println( "Invalid city" );
37         else if ( !ValidateInput.validateState( state ) )
38            System.out.println( "Invalid state" );
39         else if ( !ValidateInput.validateZip( zip ) )
40            System.out.println( "Invalid zip code" );
41         else if ( !ValidateInput.validatePhone( phone ) )
42            System.out.println( "Invalid phone number" );
43         else
44            System.out.println( "Valid input.  Thank you." );
45      } // end main
46   } // end class Validate
```

Fig. 29.21 | Inputs and validates data from user using the ValidateInput class. (Part 1 of 2.)

```
Please enter first name:
Jane
Please enter last name:
Doe
Please enter address:
123 Some Street
Please enter city:
Some City
Please enter state:
SS
Please enter zip:
123
Please enter phone:
123-456-7890

Validate Result:
Invalid zip code
```

```
Please enter first name:
Jane
Please enter last name:
Doe
Please enter address:
123 Some Street
Please enter city:
Some City
Please enter state:
SS
Please enter zip:
12345
Please enter phone:
123-456-7890

Validate Result:
Valid input.  Thank you.
```

Fig. 29.21 | Inputs and validates data from user using the `ValidateInput` class. (Part 2 of 2.)

If method `validateFirstName` returns `true` (line 29), the application attempts to validate the last name (line 31) by calling `validateLastName` (lines 13–16 of Fig. 29.20). The regular expression to validate the last name matches any number of letters split by spaces, apostrophes or hyphens.

Line 33 validates the address by calling method `validateAddress` (lines 19–23 of Fig. 29.20). The first character class matches any digit one or more times (\\d+). Note that two \ characters are used because \ normally starts an escape sequences in a string. So \\d in a Java string represents the regular expression pattern \d. Then we match one or more whitespace characters (\\s+). The character "|" allows a match of the expression to its left or to its right. For example, "Hi (John|Jane)" matches both "Hi John" and "Hi Jane". The parentheses are used to group parts of the regular expression. In this example, the left side of | matches a single word, and the right side matches two words separated by any amount of white space. So the address must contain a number followed by one or two words. Therefore, "10 Broadway" and "10 Main Street" are both valid addresses in this example. The city (line 26–29 of Fig. 29.20) and state (line 32–35 of Fig. 29.20) methods also match any word of at least one character or, alternatively, any two words of at least one character if the words are separated by a single space. This means both Waltham and West Newton would match.

The asterisk (*) and plus (+) are formally called **quantifiers**. Figure 29.22 lists all the quantifiers. We have already discussed how the asterisk (*) and plus (+) quantifiers work. All quantifiers affect only the subexpression immediately preceding the quantifier. Quantifier question mark (?) matches zero or one occurrences of the expression that it quantifies. A set of braces containing one number ({n}) matches exactly n occurrences of the expression it quantifies. We demonstrate this quantifier to validate the zip code in Fig. 29.20 at line 40. Including a comma after the number enclosed in braces matches at least n occurrences of the quantified expression. The set of braces containing two numbers ({n,m}), matches between n and m occurrences of the expression that it qualifies. Quantifiers may be applied to patterns enclosed in parentheses to create more complex regular expressions.

All of the quantifiers are **greedy**. This means that they will match as many occurrences as they can as long as the match is still successful. However, if any of these quantifiers is followed by a question mark (?), the quantifier becomes **reluctant** (sometimes called **lazy**). It then will match as few occurrences as possible as long as the match is still successful.

The zip code (line 40 in Fig. 29.20) matches a digit five times. This regular expression uses the digit character class and a quantifier with the digit 5 between braces. The phone number (line 46 in Fig. 29.20) matches three digits (the first one cannot be zero) followed by a dash followed by three more digits (again the first one cannot be zero) followed by four more digits.

String Method matches checks whether an entire string conforms to a regular expression. For example, we want to accept "Smith" as a last name, but not "9@Smith#". If only a substring matches the regular expression, method matches returns false.

Replacing Substrings and Splitting Strings

Sometimes it is useful to replace parts of a string or to split a string into pieces. For this purpose, class String provides methods **replaceAll**, **replaceFirst** and **split**. These methods are demonstrated in Fig. 29.23.

Quantifier	Matches
*	Matches zero or more occurrences of the pattern.
+	Matches one or more occurrences of the pattern.
?	Matches zero or one occurrences of the pattern.
{n}	Matches exactly n occurrences.
{$n,$}	Matches at least n occurrences.
{n,m}	Matches between n and m (inclusive) occurrences.

Fig. 29.22 | Quantifiers used in regular expressions.

Method `replaceAll` replaces text in a string with new text (the second argument) wherever the original string matches a regular expression (the first argument). Line 14 replaces every instance of "*" in `firstString` with "∧". Note that the regular expression ("*") precedes character * with two backslashes, \. Normally, * is a quantifier indicating

```
 1   // Fig. 29.23: RegexSubstitution.java
 2   // Using methods replaceFirst, replaceAll and split.
 3
 4   public class RegexSubstitution
 5   {
 6      public static void main( String args[] )
 7      {
 8         String firstString = "This sentence ends in 5 stars *****";
 9         String secondString = "1, 2, 3, 4, 5, 6, 7, 8";
10
11         System.out.printf( "Original String 1: %s\n", firstString );
12
13         // replace '*' with '∧'
14         firstString = firstString.replaceAll( "\\*", "∧" );
15
16         System.out.printf( "∧ substituted for *: %s\n", firstString );
17
18         // replace 'stars' with 'carets'
19         firstString = firstString.replaceAll( "stars", "carets" );
20
21         System.out.printf(
22            "\"carets\" substituted for \"stars\": %s\n", firstString );
23
24         // replace words with 'word'
25         System.out.printf( "Every word replaced by \"word\": %s\n\n",
26            firstString.replaceAll( "\\w+", "word" ) );
27
28         System.out.printf( "Original String 2: %s\n", secondString );
29
30         // replace first three digits with 'digit'
31         for ( int i = 0; i < 3; i++ )
32            secondString = secondString.replaceFirst( "\\d", "digit" );
33
34         System.out.printf(
35            "First 3 digits replaced by \"digit\" : %s\n", secondString );
36         String output = "String split at commas: [";
37
38         String[] results = secondString.split( ",\\s*" ); // split on commas
39
40         for ( String string : results )
41            output += "\"" + string + "\", "; // output results
42
43         // remove the extra comma and add a bracket
44         output = output.substring( 0, output.length() - 2 ) + "]";
45         System.out.println( output );
46      } // end main
47   } // end class RegexSubstitution
```

Fig. 29.23 | Methods `replaceFirst`, `replaceAll` and `split`. (Part 1 of 2.)

```
Original String 1: This sentence ends in 5 stars *****
^ substituted for *: This sentence ends in 5 stars ^^^^^
"carets" substituted for "stars": This sentence ends in 5 carets ^^^^^
Every word replaced by "word": word word word word word word ^^^^^

Original String 2: 1, 2, 3, 4, 5, 6, 7, 8
First 3 digits replaced by "digit" : digit, digit, digit, 4, 5, 6, 7, 8
String split at commas: ["digit", "digit", "digit", "4", "5", "6", "7", "8"]
```

Fig. 29.23 | Methods `replaceFirst`, `replaceAll` and `split`. (Part 2 of 2.)

that a regular expression should match any number of occurrences of a preceding pattern. However, in line 14, we want to find all occurrences of the literal character *—to do this, we must escape character * with character \. By escaping a special regular-expression character with a \, we instruct the regular-expression matching engine to find the actual character, as opposed to what it represents in a regular expression. Since the expression is stored in a Java string and \ is a special character in Java strings, we must include an additional \. So the Java string "*" represents the regular-expression pattern * which matches a single * character in the search string. In line 19, every match for the regular expression "stars" in firstString is replaced with "carets".

Method replaceFirst (line 32) replaces the first occurrence of a pattern match. Java Strings are immutable, therefore method replaceFirst returns a new string in which the appropriate characters have been replaced. This line takes the original string and replaces it with the string returned by replaceFirst. By iterating three times we replace the first three instances of a digit (\d) in secondString with the text "digit".

Method split divides a string into several substrings. The original string is broken in any location that matches a specified regular expression. Method split returns an array of strings containing the substrings between matches for the regular expression. In line 38, we use method split to tokenize a string of comma-separated integers. The argument is the regular expression that locates the delimiter. In this case, we use the regular expression ",\\s*" to separate the substrings wherever a comma occurs. By matching any whitespace characters, we eliminate extra spaces from the resulting substrings. Note that the commas and whitespace are not returned as part of the substrings. Again, note that the Java string ",\\s*" represents the regular expression ,\s*.

Classes *Pattern and Matcher*
In addition to the regular-expression capabilities of class String, Java provides other classes in package java.util.regex that help developers manipulate regular expressions. Class **Pattern** represents a regular expression. Class **Matcher** contains both a regular-expression pattern and a CharSequence in which to search for the pattern.

CharSequence is an interface that allows read access to a sequence of characters. The interface requires that the methods charAt, length, subSequence and toString be declared. Both String and StringBuffer implement interface CharSequence, so an instance of either of these classes can be used with class Matcher.

Common Programming Error 29.4
A regular expression can be tested against an object of any class that implements interface CharSequence, but the regular expression must be a String. Attempting to create a regular expression as a StringBuffer is an error.

If a regular expression will be used only once, static Pattern method `matches` can be used. This method takes a string that specifies the regular expression and a CharSequence on which to perform the match. This method returns a boolean indicating whether the search object (the second argument) matches the regular expression.

If a regular expression will be used more than once, it is more efficient to use static Pattern method `compile` to create a specific Pattern object for that regular expression. This method receives a string representing the pattern and returns a new Pattern object, which can then be used to call method `matcher`. This method receives a CharSequence to search and returns a Matcher object.

Matcher provides method `matches`, which performs the same task as Pattern method matches, but receives no arguments—the search pattern and search object are encapsulated in the Matcher object. Class Matcher provides other methods, including `find`, `lookingAt`, `replaceFirst` and `replaceAll`.

Figure 29.24 presents a simple example that employs regular expressions. This program matches birthdays against a regular expression. The expression only matches birthdays that do not occur in April and that belong to people whose names begin with "J".

Lines 11–12 create a Pattern by invoking static Pattern method compile. The dot character "." in the regular expression (line 12) matches any single character except a newline character.

```java
1   // Fig. 29.24: RegexMatches.java
2   // Demonstrating Classes Pattern and Matcher.
3   import java.util.regex.Matcher;
4   import java.util.regex.Pattern;
5
6   public class RegexMatches
7   {
8      public static void main( String args[] )
9      {
10        // create regular expression
11        Pattern expression =
12           Pattern.compile( "J.*\\d[0-35-9]-\\d\\d-\\d\\d" );
13
14        String string1 = "Jane's Birthday is 05-12-75\n" +
15           "Dave's Birthday is 11-04-68\n" +
16           "John's Birthday is 04-28-73\n" +
17           "Joe's Birthday is 12-17-77";
18
19        // match regular expression to string and print matches
20        Matcher matcher = expression.matcher( string1 );
21
22        while ( matcher.find() )
23           System.out.println( matcher.group() );
24     } // end main
25  } // end class RegexMatches
```

```
Jane's Birthday is 05-12-75
Joe's Birthday is 12-17-77
```

Fig. 29.24 | Regular expressions checking birthdays.

Line 20 creates the `Matcher` object for the compiled regular expression and the matching sequence (`string1`). Lines 22–23 use a `while` loop to iterate through the string. Line 22 uses `Matcher` method `find` to attempt to match a piece of the search object to the search pattern. Each call to this method starts at the point where the last call ended, so multiple matches can be found. `Matcher` method `lookingAt` performs the same way, except that it always starts from the beginning of the search object and will always find the first match if there is one.

Common Programming Error 29.5

Method `matches` (from class `String`, `Pattern` or `Matcher`) will return `true` only if the entire search object matches the regular expression. Methods `find` and `lookingAt` (from class `Matcher`) will return `true` if a portion of the search object matches the regular expression.

Line 23 uses `Matcher` method **group**, which returns the string from the search object that matches the search pattern. The string that is returned is the one that was last matched by a call to `find` or `lookingAt`. The output in Fig. 29.24 shows the two matches that were found in `string1`.

Regular Expression Web Resources

This section presents several of Java's regular-expression capabilities. The following Web sites provide more information on regular expressions.

`developer.java.sun.com/developer/technicalArticles/releases/1.4regex`
Thoroughly describes Java's regular-expression capabilities.

`java.sun.com/docs/books/tutorial/extra/regex/index.html`
This tutorial explains how to use Java's regular-expression API.

`java.sun.com/j2se/5.0/docs/api/java/util/regex/package-summary.html`
This page is the javadoc overview of package `java.util.regex`.

29.8 Wrap-Up

In this chapter, you learned about more `String` methods for selecting portions of `Strings` and manipulating `Strings`. You also learned about the `Character` class and some of the methods it declares to handle `chars`. The chapter also discussed the capabilities of the `StringBuffer` class for creating `Strings`. The end of the chapter discussed regular expressions which provide a powerful capability to search and match portions of `Strings` that fit a particular pattern.

Summary

- A character literal's value is its integer value in the Unicode character set. Strings can include letters, digits and special characters such as +, -, *, / and $. A string in Java is an object of class `String`. `String` literals are often referred to as `String` objects and are written in double quotes in a program.

- `String` objects are immutable—their character contents cannot be changed after they are created.

- `String` method `length` returns the number of characters in a `String`.

- `String` method `charAt` returns the character at a specific position.

- `String` method `equals` tests any two objects for equality. The method returns `true` if the contents of the `Strings` are equal, `false` otherwise. Method `equals` uses a lexicographical comparison for `Strings`.

- When primitive-type values are compared with ==, the result is true if both values are identical. When references are compared with ==, the result is true if both references refer to the same object in memory.

- Java treats all string literals with the same contents as a single String object.

- String method equalsIgnoreCase performs a case-insensitive string comparison.

- String method compareTo uses a lexicographical comparison and returns 0 if the strings it is comparing are equal, a negative number if the string compareTo is invoked on is less than the String that is passed as an argument and a positive number if the string that compareTo is invoked on is greater than the string that is passed as an argument.

- String method regionMatches compares portions of two strings for equality.

- String method startsWith determines whether a string starts with the characters specified as an argument. String method endsWith determines whether a string ends with the characters specified as an argument.

- String method indexOf locates the first occurrence of a character or a substring in a string. String method lastIndexOf locates the last occurrence of a character or a substring in a string.

- String method substring copies and returns part of an existing string object.

- String method concat concatenates two string objects and returns a new string object containing the characters from both original strings.

- String method replace returns a new string object that replaces every occurrence in a String of its first character argument with its second character argument.

- String method toUpperCase returns a new string with uppercase letters in the positions where the original string had lowercase letters. String method toLowerCase returns a new string with lowercase letters in the positions where the original string had uppercase letters.

- String method trim returns a new string object in which all whitespace characters (e.g., spaces, newlines and tabs) have been removed from the beginning and end of a string.

- String method toCharArray returns a char array containing a copy of the string's characters.

- String class static method valueOf returns its argument converted to a string.

- Class StringBuffer provides constructors that enable StringBuffers to be initialized with no characters and an initial capacity of 16 characters, with no characters and an initial capacity specified in the integer argument, or with a copy of the characters of the String argument and an initial capacity that is the number of characters in the String argument plus 16.

- StringBuffer method length returns the number of characters currently stored in a StringBuffer. StringBuffer method capacity returns the number of characters that can be stored in a StringBuffer without allocating more memory.

- StringBuffer method ensureCapacity ensures that a StringBuffer has at least the specified capacity. StringBuffer method setLength increases or decreases the length of a StringBuffer.

- StringBuffer method charAt returns the character at the specified index. StringBuffer method setCharAt sets the character at the specified position. StringBuffer method getChars copies characters in the StringBuffer into the character array passed as an argument.

- Class StringBuffer provides overloaded append methods to add primitive-type, character array, String, Object and CharSequence values to the end of a StringBuffer. StringBuffers and the append methods are used by the Java compiler to implement the + and += concatenation operators.

- Class StringBuffer provides overloaded insert methods to insert primitive-type, character array, String, Object and CharSequence values at any position in a StringBuffer.

- Class Character provides a constructor that takes a char argument.

- `Character` method `isDefined` determines whether a character is defined in the Unicode character set. If so, the method returns `true`—otherwise, it returns `false`.

- `Character` method `isDigit` determines whether a character is a defined Unicode digit. If so, the method returns `true`—otherwise, it returns `false`.

- `Character` method `isJavaIdentifierStart` determines whether a character can be used as the first character of an identifier in Java [i.e., a letter, an underscore (_) or a dollar sign ($)]. If so, the method returns `true`—otherwise, it returns `false`.

- `Character` method `isJavaIdentifierPart` determines whether a character can be used in an identifier in Java [i.e., a digit, a letter, an underscore (_) or a dollar sign ($)]. `Character` method `isLetter` determines whether a character is a letter. `Character` method `isLetterOrDigit` determines whether a character is a letter or a digit. In each case, if so, the method returns `true`—otherwise, it returns `false`.

- `Character` method `isLowerCase` determines whether a character is a lowercase letter. `Character` method `isUpperCase` determines whether a character is an uppercase letter. In both cases, if so, the method returns `true`—otherwise, `false`.

- `Character` method `toUpperCase` converts a character to its uppercase equivalent. `Character` method `toLowerCase` converts a character to its lowercase equivalent.

- `Character` method `digit` converts its character argument into an integer in the number system specified by its integer argument `radix`. `Character` method `forDigit` converts its integer argument `digit` into a character in the number system specified by its integer argument `radix`.

- `Character` method `charValue` returns the `char` stored in a `Character` object. `Character` method `toString` returns a `String` representation of a `Character`.

- `StringTokenizer`'s default constructor creates a `StringTokenizer` for its string argument that will use the default delimiter string " \t\n\r\f", consisting of a space, a tab, a newline and a carriage return for tokenization.

- `StringTokenizer` method `countTokens` returns the number of tokens in a string to be tokenized.

- `StringTokenizer` method `hasMoreTokens` determines whether there are more tokens in the string being tokenized.

- `StringTokenizer` method `nextToken` returns a `String` with the next token.

- Regular expressions are sequences of characters and symbols that define a set of strings. They are useful for validating input and ensuring that data is in a particular format.

- `String` method `matches` receives a string that specifies the regular expression and matches the contents of the `String` object on which it is called to the regular expression. The method returns a `boolean` indicating whether the match succeeded.

- A character class is an escape sequence that represents a group of characters. Each character class matches a single character in the string we are attempting to match with the regular expression.

- A word character (\w) is any letter (uppercase or lowercase), any digit or the underscorecharacter.

- A whitespace character (\s) is a space, a tab, a carriage return, a newline or a form feed.

- A digit (\d) is any numeric character.

- To match a set of characters that does not have a predefined character class, use square brackets, []. Ranges of characters can be represented by placing a dash (-) between two characters. If the first character in the brackets is "^", the expression accepts any character other than those indicated.

- When the regular expression operator "*" appears in a regular expression, the program attempts to match zero or more occurrences of the subexpression immediately preceding the "*".

- Operator "+" attempts to match one or more occurrences of the subexpression preceding it.
- The character "|" allows a match of the expression to its left or to its right.
- The parentheses ( ) are used to group parts of the regular expression.
- The asterisk (*) and plus (+) are formally called quantifiers.
- All quantifiers affect only the subexpression immediately preceding the quantifier.
- Quantifier question mark (?) matches zero or one occurrences of the expression that it quantifies.
- A set of braces containing one number ({n}) matches exactly n occurrences of the expression it quantifies.
- Including a comma after the number enclosed in braces matches at least n occurrences of the quantified expression.
- A set of braces containing two numbers ({n,m}) matches between n and m occurrences of the expression that it qualifies.
- All of the quantifiers are greedy, which means that they will match as many occurrences as they can as long as the match is successful.
- If any of these quantifiers is followed by a question mark (?), the quantifier becomes reluctant, matching as few occurrences as possible as long as the match is successful.
- String method replaceAll replaces text in a string with new text (the second argument) wherever the original string matches a regular expression (the first argument).
- Escaping a special regular-expression character with a \ instructs the regular-expression matching engine to find the actual character, as opposed to what it represents in a regular expression.
- String method replaceFirst replaces the first occurrence of a pattern match. Java Strings are immutable, therefore method replaceFirst returns a new string in which the appropriate characters have been replaced.
- String method split divides a string into several substrings. The original string is broken in any location that matches a specified regular expression. Method split returns an array of strings containing the substrings between matches for the regular expression.
- Class Pattern represents a regular expression.
- Class Matcher contains both a regular-expression pattern and a CharSequence in which to search for the pattern.
- CharSequence is an interface that allows read access to a sequence of characters. Both String and StringBuffer implement interface CharSequence, so an instance of either of these classes can be used with class Matcher.
- If a regular expression will be used only once, static Pattern method matches takes a string that specifies the regular expression and a CharSequence on which to perform the match. This method returns a boolean indicating whether the search object matches the regular expression.
- If a regular expression will be used more than once, it is more efficient to use static Pattern method compile to create a specific Pattern object for that regular expression. This method receives a string representing the pattern and returns a new Pattern object.
- Pattern method matcher receives a CharSequence to search and returns a Matcher object.
- Matcher method matches performs the same task as Pattern method matches, but receives no arguments.
- Matcher method find attempts to match a piece of the search object to the search pattern. Each call to this method starts at the point where the last call ended, so multiple matches can be found.
- Matcher method lookingAt performs the same as find, except that it always starts from the beginning of the search object and will always find the first match if there is one.

- `Matcher` method group returns the string from the search object that matches the search pattern. The string that is returned is the one that was last matched by a call to `find` or `lookingAt`.

Terminology

append method of class `StringBuffer`
capacity method of class `StringBuffer`
character literal
charAt method of class `StringBuffer`
`CharSequence` interface
charValue method of class `Character`
concat method of class `String`
delete method of class `StringBuffer`
deleteCharAt method of class `String`
delimiter for tokens
digit method of class `Character`
empty string
endsWith method of class `String`
ensureCapacity method of class `StringBuffer`
find method of class `Matcher`
forDigit method of class `Character`
getChars method of class `String`
getChars method of class `StringBuffer`
greedy quantifier
hasMoreTokens method of class `StringTokenizer`
immutable
indexOf method of class `String`
isDefined method of class `Character`
isDigit method of class `Character`
isJavaIdentifierPart method of class `Character`
isJavaIdentifierStart method of class `Character`
isLetter method of class `Character`
isLetterOrDigit method of class `Character`
isLowerCase method of class `Character`
isUpperCase method of class `Character`
lastIndexOf method of class `String`
lazy quantifier

length method of class `String`
length method of class `StringBuffer`
lexicographical comparison
lookingAt method of class `Matcher`
`Matcher` class
matcher method of class `Pattern`
matches method of class `Matcher`
matches method of class `Pattern`
matches method of class `String`
nextToken method of class `StringTokenizer`
`Pattern` class
predefined character class
quantifier for regular expression
radix
regionMatches method of class `String`
regular expressions
reluctant quantifier
replaceAll method of class `String`
replaceFirst method of class `String`
reverse method of class `StringBuffer`
setCharAt method of class `StringBuffer`
special character
split method of class `String`
startsWith method of class `String`
string literal
`StringIndexOutOfBoundsException` class
token of a `String`
toLowerCase method of class `Character`
toUpperCase method of class `Character`
trim method of class `StringBuffer`
Unicode character set
valueOf method of class `String`
word character

Self-Review Exercises

29.1 State whether each of the following is *true* or *false*. If *false*, explain why.
- a) When `String` objects are compared using `==`, the result is true if the `Strings` contain the same values.
- b) A `String` can be modified after it is created.

29.2 For each of the following, write a single statement that performs the indicated task:
- a) Compare the string in `s1` to the string in `s2` for equality of contents.
- b) Append the string `s2` to the string `s1`, using `+=`.
- c) Determine the length of the string in `s1`.

Answers to Self-Review Exercises

29.1   a) False. `String` objects that are compared using operator `==` are compared to determine whether they are the same object in memory.

   b) False. `String` objects are immutable and cannot be modified after they are created. `StringBuffer` objects can be modified after they are created.

29.2   a) `s1.equals( s2 )`

   b) `s1 += s2;`

   c) `s1.length()`

Exercises

29.3   Write an application that uses `String` method `compareTo` to compare two strings input by the user. Output whether the first string is less than, equal to or greater than the second.

29.4   Write an application that uses `String` method `regionMatches` to compare two strings input by the user. The application should input the number of characters to be compared and the starting index of the comparison. The application should state whether the strings are equal. Ignore the case of the characters when performing the comparison.

29.5   Write an application that uses random-number generation to create sentences. Use four arrays of strings called `article`, `noun`, `verb` and `preposition`. Create a sentence by selecting a word at random from each array in the following order: `article`, `noun`, `verb`, `preposition`, `article` and `noun`. As each word is picked, concatenate it to the previous words in the sentence. The words should be separated by spaces. When the final sentence is output, it should start with a capital letter and end with a period. The application should generate 20 sentences and output them to a text area.

The article array should contain the articles `"the"`, `"a"`, `"one"`, `"some"` and `"any"`; the noun array should contain the nouns `"boy"`, `"girl"`, `"dog"`, `"town"` and `"car"`; the verb array should contain the verbs `"drove"`, `"jumped"`, `"ran"`, `"walked"` and `"skipped"`; the preposition array should contain the prepositions `"to"`, `"from"`, `"over"`, `"under"` and `"on"`.

After the preceding application is written, modify it to produce a short story consisting of several of these sentences. (How about the possibility of a random term-paper writer?)

29.6   *(Limericks)* A limerick is a humorous five-line verse in which the first and second lines rhyme with the fifth, and the third line rhymes with the fourth. Using techniques similar to those developed in Exercise 29.5, write a Java application that produces random limericks. Polishing this application to produce good limericks is a challenging problem, but the result will be worth the effort!

29.7   *(Pig Latin)* Write an application that encodes English-language phrases into pig Latin. Pig Latin is a form of coded language. There are many different ways to form pig Latin phrases. For simplicity, use the following algorithm:

To form a pig Latin phrase from an English-language phrase, tokenize the phrase into words with an object of class `StringTokenizer`. To translate each English word into a pig Latin word, place the first letter of the English word at the end of the word and add the letters "ay." Thus, the word "jump" becomes "umpjay," the word "the" becomes "hetay," and the word "computer" becomes "omputercay." Blanks between words remain as blanks. Assume the following: The English phrase consists of words separated by blanks, there are no punctuation marks and all words have two or more letters. Method `printLatinWord` should display each word. Each token returned from `nextToken` is passed to method `printLatinWord` to print the pig Latin word. Enable the user to input the sentence. Keep a running display of all the converted sentences in a text area.

29.8   Write an application that inputs a telephone number as a string in the form (555) 555-5555. The application should use an object of class `StringTokenizer` to extract the area code as a token, the first three digits of the phone number as a token and the last four digits of the phone number as a token. The seven digits of the phone number should be concatenated into one string. Both the area code and the phone number should be printed. Remember that you will have to change delimiter characters during the tokenization process.

29.9 Write an application that inputs a line of text, tokenizes the line with an object of class `StringTokenizer` and outputs the tokens in reverse order. Use space characters as delimiters.

29.10 Use the string-comparison methods discussed in this chapter and the techniques for sorting arrays developed in Chapter 16 to write an application that alphabetizes a list of strings. Allow the user to enter the strings in a text field. Display the results in a text area.

29.11 Write an application that inputs a line of text and outputs the text twice—once in all uppercase letters and once in all lowercase letters.

29.12 Write an application that inputs a line of text and a search character and uses `String` method `indexOf` to determine the number of occurrences of the character in the text.

29.13 Write an application based on the application in Exercise 29.12 that inputs a line of text and uses `String` method `indexOf` to determine the total number of occurrences of each letter of the alphabet in the text. Uppercase and lowercase letters should be counted together. Store the totals for each letter in an array, and print the values in tabular format after the totals have been determined.

29.14 Write an application that reads a line of text, tokenizes the line using space characters as delimiters and outputs only those words beginning with the letter "b."

29.15 Write an application that reads a line of text, tokenizes it using space characters as delimiters and outputs only those words ending with the letters "ED."

29.16 Write an application that inputs an integer code for a character and displays the corresponding character. Modify this application so that it generates all possible three-digit codes in the range from 000 to 255 and attempts to print the corresponding characters.

29.17 Write your own versions of `String` search methods `indexOf` and `lastIndexOf`.

29.18 Write an application that reads a five-letter word from the user and produces every possible three-letter string that can be derived from the letters of the five-letter word. For example, the three-letter words produced from the word "bathe" include "ate," "bat," "bet," "tab," "hat," "the" and "tea."

Special Section: Advanced String-Manipulation Exercises

The preceding exercises are keyed to the text and designed to test your understanding of fundamental string-manipulation concepts. This section includes a collection of intermediate and advanced string-manipulation exercises. You should find these problems challenging, yet entertaining. The problems vary considerably in difficulty. Some require an hour or two of application writing and implementation. Others are useful for lab assignments that might require two or three weeks of study and implementation. Some are challenging term projects.

29.19 *(Text Analysis)* The availability of computers with string-manipulation capabilities has resulted in some rather interesting approaches to analyzing the writings of great authors. Much attention has been focused on whether William Shakespeare ever lived. Some scholars believe there is substantial evidence indicating that Christopher Marlowe actually penned the masterpieces attributed to Shakespeare. Researchers have used computers to find similarities in the writings of these two authors. This exercise examines three methods for analyzing texts with a computer.

    a) Write an application that reads a line of text from the keyboard and prints a table indicating the number of occurrences of each letter of the alphabet in the text. For example, the phrase

```
To be, or not to be: that is the question:
```

        contains one "a," two "b's," no "c's," and so on.

b) Write an application that reads a line of text and prints a table indicating the number of one-letter words, two-letter words, three-letter words, and so on, appearing in the text. For example, Fig. 29.25 shows the counts for the phrase

```
Whether 'tis nobler in the mind to suffer
```

c) Write an application that reads a line of text and prints a table indicating the number of occurrences of each different word in the text. The first version of your application should include the words in the table in the same order in which they appear in the text. For example, the lines

```
To be, or not to be: that is the question:
Whether 'tis nobler in the mind to suffer
```

contain the word "to" three times, the word "be" two times, the word "or" once, and so on. A more interesting (and useful) printout should then be attempted in which the words are sorted alphabetically.

29.20 *(Printing Dates in Various Formats)* Dates are printed in several common formats. Two of the more common formats are

```
04/25/1955 and April 25, 1955
```

Write an application that reads a date in the first format and prints it in the second format.

29.21 *(Check Protection)* Computers are frequently employed in check-writing systems, such as payroll and accounts payable applications. There are many strange stories about weekly paychecks being printed (by mistake) for amounts in excess of $1 million. Incorrect amounts are printed by computerized check-writing systems because of human error or machine failure. Systems designers build controls into their systems to prevent such erroneous checks from being issued.

Another serious problem is the intentional alteration of a check amount by someone who plans to cash a check fraudulently. To prevent a dollar amount from being altered, some computerized check-writing systems employ a technique called check protection. Checks designed for imprinting by computer contain a fixed number of spaces in which the computer may print an amount. Suppose a paycheck contains eight blank spaces in which the computer is supposed to print the amount of a weekly paycheck. If the amount is large, then all eight of the spaces will be filled. For example,

Word length	Occurrences
1	0
2	2
3	1
4	2 (including 'tis)
5	0
6	2
7	1

Fig. 29.25 | Word-length counts for the string
`"Whether 'tis nobler in the mind to suffer"`.

```
1,230.60  (check amount)
--------
12345678  (position numbers)
```

On the other hand, if the amount is less than $1000, then several of the spaces would ordinarily be left blank. For example,

```
   99.87
--------
12345678
```

contains three blank spaces. If a check is printed with blank spaces, it is easier for someone to alter the amount of the check. To prevent a check from being altered, many check-writing systems insert *leading asterisks* to protect the amount as follows:

```
***99.87
--------
12345678
```

Write an application that inputs a dollar amount to be printed on a check, then prints the amount in check-protected format with leading asterisks if necessary. Assume that nine spaces are available for printing the amount.

29.22 *(Writing the Word Equivalent of a Check Amount)* Continuing the discussion in Exercise 29.21, we reiterate the importance of designing check-writing systems to prevent alteration of check amounts. One common security method requires that the check amount be written in numbers and spelled out in words as well. Even if someone is able to alter the numerical amount of the check, it is extremely difficult to change the amount in words. Write an application that inputs a numeric check amount and writes the word equivalent of the amount. For example, the amount 112.43 should be written as

```
ONE hundred TWELVE and 43/100
```

29.23 *(Morse Code)* Perhaps the most famous of all coding schemes is the Morse code, developed by Samuel Morse in 1832 for use with the telegraph system. The Morse code assigns a series of dots and dashes to each letter of the alphabet, each digit, and a few special characters (e.g., period, comma, colon, semicolon). In sound-oriented systems, the dot represents a short sound and the dash represents a long sound. Other representations of dots and dashes are used with light-oriented systems and signal-flag systems. Separation between words is indicated by a space or, simply, the absence of a dot or dash. In a sound-oriented system, a space is indicated by a short time during which no sound is transmitted. The international version of the Morse code appears in Fig. 29.26.

Write an application that reads an English-language phrase and encodes it into Morse code. Also write an application that reads a phrase in Morse code and converts it into the English-language equivalent. Use one blank between each Morse-coded letter and three blanks between each Morse-coded word.

29.24 *(Metric Conversion Application)* Write an application that will assist the user with metric conversions. Your application should allow the user to specify the names of the units as strings (i.e., centimeters, liters, grams, etc., for the metric system and inches, quarts, pounds, etc., for the English system) and should respond to simple questions, such as

```
"How many inches are in 2 meters?"
"How many liters are in 10 quarts?"
```

Your application should recognize invalid conversions. For example, the question

```
"How many feet are in 5 kilograms?"
```

is not meaningful because "feet" is a unit of length, whereas "kilograms" is a unit of mass.

Character	Code	Character	Code
A	.-	T	-
B	-...	U	..-
C	-.-.	V	...-
D	-..	W	.--
E	.	X	-..-
F	..-.	Y	-.--
G	--.	Z	--..
H	....		
I	..	*Digits*	
J	.---	1	.----
K	-.-	2	..---
L	.-..	3	...--
M	--	4	....-
N	-.	5	.....
O	---	6	-....
P	.--.	7	--...
Q	--.-	8	---..
R	.-.	9	----.
S	...	0	-----

Fig. 29.26 | The letters of the alphabet as expressed in international Morse code.

Special Section: Challenging String-Manipulation Projects

29.25 (*Project: A Spelling Checker*) Many popular word-processing software packages have built-in spell checkers. In this project, you are asked to develop your own spell-checker utility. We make suggestions to help get you started. You should then consider adding more capabilities. Use a computerized dictionary (if you have access to one) as a source of words.

Why do we type so many words with incorrect spellings? In some cases, it is because we simply do not know the correct spelling, so we make a best guess. In some cases, it is because we transpose two letters (e.g., "defualt" instead of "default"). Sometimes we double-type a letter accidentally (e.g., "hanndy" instead of "handy"). Sometimes we type a nearby key instead of the one we intended (e.g., "biryhday" instead of "birthday"), and so on.

Design and implement a spell-checker application in Java. Your application should maintain an array wordList of strings. Enable the user to enter these strings. [*Note:* In Chapter 14, we have introduced file processing. With this capability, you can obtain the words for the spell checker from a computerized dictionary stored in a file.]

Your application should ask a user to enter a word. The application should then look up that word in the wordList array. If the word is in the array, your application should print "Word is spelled correctly." If the word is not in the array, your application should print "word is not spelled correctly." Then your application should try to locate other words in wordList that might be the word the user intended to type. For example, you can try all possible single transpositions of adjacent letters to discover that the word "default" is a direct match to a word in wordList. Of course, this implies that your application will check all other single transpositions, such as "edfault," "dfeault," "deafult," "defalut" and "defautl." When you find a new word that matches one in wordList, print it in a message, such as

```
Did you mean "default"?
```

Implement other tests, such as replacing each double letter with a single letter, and any other tests you can develop to improve the value of your spell checker.

29.26 *(Project: A Crossword Puzzle Generator)* Most people have worked a crossword puzzle, but few have ever attempted to generate one. Generating a crossword puzzle is suggested here as a string-manipulation project requiring substantial sophistication and effort.

There are many issues the programmer must resolve to get even the simplest crossword-puzzle-generator application working. For example, how do you represent the grid of a crossword puzzle inside the computer? Should you use a series of strings or two-dimensional arrays?

The programmer needs a source of words (i.e., a computerized dictionary) that can be directly referenced by the application. In what form should these words be stored to facilitate the complex manipulations required by the application?

If you are really ambitious, you will want to generate the clues portion of the puzzle, in which the brief hints for each across word and each down word are printed. Merely printing a version of the blank puzzle itself is not a simple problem.

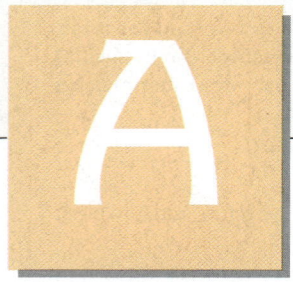

Operator Precedence Chart

A.1 Operator Precedence

Operators are shown in decreasing order of precedence from top to bottom (Fig. A.1).

Operator	Description	Associativity
++ --	unary postfix increment unary postfix decrement	right to left
++ -- + - ! ~ (*type*)	unary prefix increment unary prefix decrement unary plus unary minus unary logical negation unary bitwise complement unary cast	right to left
* / %	multiplication division remainder	left to right
+ -	addition or string concatenation subtraction	left to right
<< >> >>>	left shift signed right shift unsigned right shift	left to right

Fig. A.1 | Operator precedence chart. (Part 1 of 2.)

Operator	Description	Associativity
 <= > >= `instanceof`	less than less than or equal to greater than greater than or equal to type comparison	left to right
== !=	is equal to is not equal to	left to right
&	bitwise AND boolean logical AND	left to right
^	bitwise exclusive OR boolean logical exclusive OR	left to right
|	bitwise inclusive OR boolean logical inclusive OR	left to right
&&	conditional AND	left to right
||	conditional OR	left to right
?:	conditional	right to left
= += -= *= /= %= &= ^= |= <<= >>= >>>=	assignment addition assignment subtraction assignment multiplication assignment division assignment remainder assignment bitwise AND assignment bitwise exclusive OR assignment bitwise inclusive OR assignment bitwise left shift assignment bitwise signed-right-shift assignment bitwise unsigned-right-shift assignment	right to left

Fig. A.1 | Operator precedence chart. (Part 2 of 2.)

B

ASCII Character Set

	0	1	2	3	4	5	6	7	8	9
0	nul	soh	stx	etx	eot	enq	ack	bel	bs	ht
1	nl	vt	ff	cr	so	si	dle	dc1	dc2	dc3
2	dc4	nak	syn	etb	can	em	sub	esc	fs	gs
3	rs	us	sp	!	"	#	$	%	&	'
4	(	)	*	+	,	-	.	/	0	1
5	2	3	4	5	6	7	8	9	:	;
6	<	=	>	?	@	A	B	C	D	E
7	F	G	H	I	J	K	L	M	N	O
8	P	Q	R	S	T	U	V	W	X	Y
9	Z	[	\	]	^	_	'	a	b	c
10	d	e	f	g	h	i	j	k	l	m
11	n	o	p	q	r	s	t	u	v	w
12	x	y	z	{	|	}	~	del		

Fig. B.1 | ASCII Character Set.

The digits at the left of the table are the left digits of the decimal equivalent (0–127) of the character code, and the digits at the top of the table are the right digits of the character code. For example, the character code for "F" is 70, and the character code for "&" is 38.

Most users of this book are interested in the ASCII character set used to represent English characters on many computers. The ASCII character set is a subset of the Unicode character set used by Java to represent characters from most of the world's languages. For more information on the Unicode character set, see Appendix F.

Keywords and Reserved Words

Java Keywords				
abstract	assert	boolean	break	byte
case	catch	char	class	continue
default	do	double	else	enum
extends	final	finally	float	for
if	implements	import	instanceof	int
interface	long	native	new	package
private	protected	public	return	short
static	strictfp	super	switch	synchronized
this	throw	throws	transient	try
void	volatile	while		

Keywords that are not currently used

const	goto			

Fig. C.1 | Java keywords.

Java also contains the reserved words `true` and `false`, which are `boolean` literals, and `null`, which is the literal that represents a reference to nothing. Like keywords, these reserved words cannot be used as identifiers.

Primitive Types

Type	Size in bits	Values	Standard
boolean		true or false	
[*Note:* A boolean's representation is specific to the Java Virtual Machine on each platform.]			
char	16	`'\u0000'` to `'\uFFFF'` (0 to 65535)	(ISO Unicode character set)
byte	8	-128 to $+127$ (-2^7 to $2^7 - 1$)	
short	16	$-32,768$ to $+32,767$ (-2^{15} to $2^{15} - 1$)	
int	32	$-2,147,483,648$ to $+2,147,483,647$ (-2^{31} to $2^{31} - 1$)	
long	64	$-9,223,372,036,854,775,808$ to $+9,223,372,036,854,775,807$ (-2^{63} to $2^{63} - 1$)	
float	32	*Negative range:* $-3.4028234663852886\text{E}+38$ to $-1.40129846432481707\text{e}-45$ *Positive range:* $1.40129846432481707\text{e}-45$ to $3.4028234663852886\text{E}+38$	(IEEE 754 floating point)
double	64	*Negative range:* $-1.7976931348623157\text{E}+308$ to $-4.94065645841246544\text{e}-324$ *Positive range:* $4.94065645841246544\text{e}-324$ to $1.7976931348623157\text{E}+308$	(IEEE 754 floating point)

Fig. D.1 | Java primitive types.

For more information on IEEE 754 visit `grouper.ieee.org/groups/754/`. For more information on Unicode, see Appendix F, Unicode®.

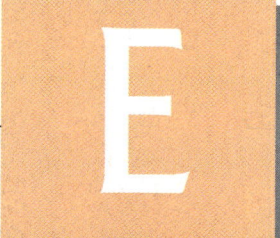

(On CD)
Number Systems

Appendix E (pages 1403–1415) is located on the CD that accompanies this book in printable Adobe® Acrobat PDF format. You can download Adobe® Reader® from

www.adobe.com/products/acrobat/readstep2.html

In the index, page references for all the CD appendices appear in red. Defining occurrences of terms in the CD appendices appear in **bold red**.]

(On CD) Unicode®

Appendix F (pages 1416–1426) is located on the CD that accompanies this book in printable Adobe® Acrobat PDF format. You can download Adobe® Reader® from

`www.adobe.com/products/acrobat/readstep2.html`

In the index, page references for all the CD appendices appear in red. Defining occurrences of terms in the CD appendices appear in **bold red**.]

Using the Java API Documentation

G.1 Introduction

The Java class library contains thousands of predefined classes and interfaces that programmers can use to write their own applications. These classes are grouped into packages based on their functionality. For example, the classes and interfaces used for file processing are grouped into the `java.io` package, and the classes and interfaces for networking applications are grouped into the `java.net` package. The Java API documentation lists the public and protected members of each class and the public members of each interface in the Java class library. The documentation overviews all the classes and interfaces, summarizes their members (i.e., the fields, constructors and methods of classes, and the fields and methods of interfaces) and provides detailed descriptions of each member. Most Java programmers rely on this documentation when writing programs. Normally, programmers would search the API to find the following:

1. The package that contains a particular class or interface.

2. Relationships between a particular class or interface and other classes and interfaces.

3. Class or interface constants—normally declared as public static final fields.

4. Constructors to determine how an object of the class can be initialized.

5. The methods of a class to determine whether they are static or non-static, the number and types of the arguments you need to pass, the return types and any exceptions that might be thrown from the method.

In addition, programmers often rely on the documentation to discover classes and interfaces that they have not used before. For this reason, we demonstrate the documentation with classes you know and classes you may not have studied yet. We show how to use the documentation to locate the information you need to use a class or interface effectively.

[*Note:* Sun Microsystems has renamed the Java 2 Platform, Standard Edition version 1.5.0 to Java 2 Platform, Standard Edition version 5.0. However, they decided not to replace the occurrences of 1.5.0 with 5.0 in the documentation. Although the URLs that represent the documentation on Sun's Java Web site work with 5.0 in the URL, these URLs are redirected to ones that replace the 5.0 with 1.5.0. For this reason, all URLs in this appendix are listed with 1.5.0 in the URL.]

G.2 Navigating the Java API

The Java API documentation can be downloaded to your local hard disk or viewed on line. To download the Java API documentation, go to `java.sun.com/j2se/5.0/download.jsp` and locate the **DOWNLOAD** link in the **J2SE v 1.5.0 Documentation** section. You will be asked to accept a license agreement. To do this, click **Accept**, then click **Continue**. Click the **Java(TM) 2 SDK, Standard Edition Documentation 1.5.0, English** link to begin the download. After downloading the file, you can use a ZIP file-extraction program, such as Win-Zip (`www.winzip.com`), to extract the files. If you are using Windows, extract the contents to your `jdk1.5.0` directory or the directory where you installed Java. (See the *Before You Begin* section of this book for information on installing Java.) To view the API documentation on your local hard disk in Microsoft Windows, open `C:\Program Files\Java\jdk1.5.0\docs\api\index.html` page in your browser. To view the API documentation on line, go to `java.sun.com/j2se/1.5.0/docs/api/index.html` (Fig. G.1).

Upper-left frame lists all packages in alphabetical order.

Tree link displays the hierarchy of all packages and classes.

Deprecated link lists portions of the API that should no longer be used.

Index link lists fields, methods, classes and interfaces.

Help link describes how the API is organized.

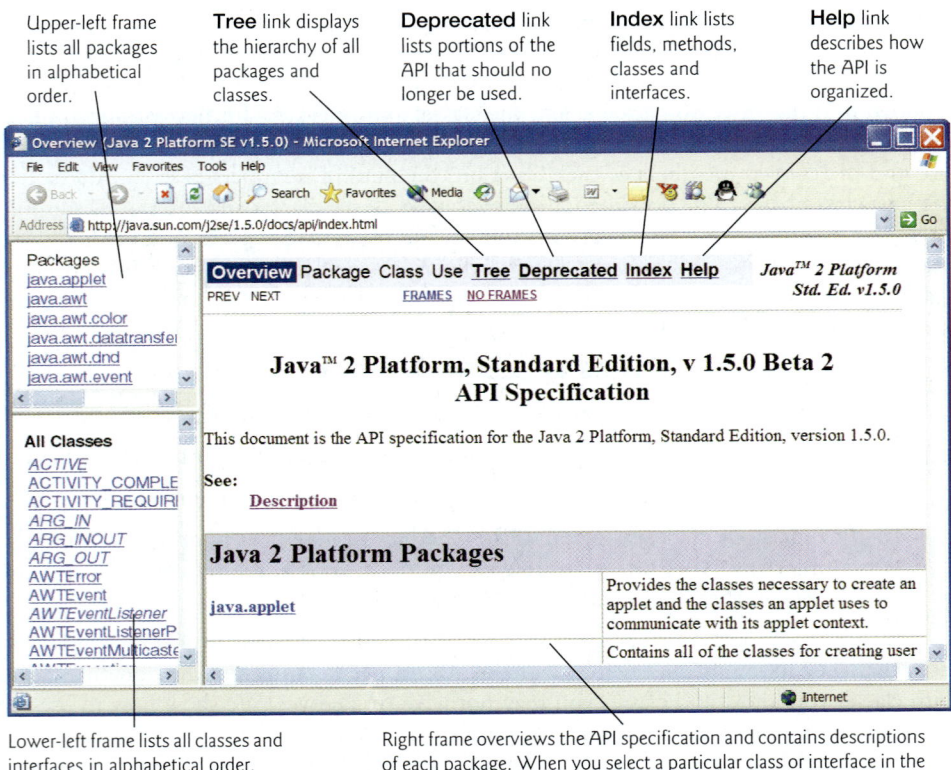

Lower-left frame lists all classes and interfaces in alphabetical order. Interfaces are displayed in italics.

Right frame overviews the API specification and contains descriptions of each package. When you select a particular class or interface in the lower-left frame, its information will be displayed here.

Fig. G.1 | Java API overview. (Courtesy of Sun Microsystems, Inc.)

Frames in the API Documentation's `index.html` Page

The API documentation is divided into three frames (see Fig. G.1). The upper-left frame lists all of the Java API's packages in alphabetical order. The lower-left frame initially lists the Java API's classes and interfaces in alphabetical order. Interface names are displayed in italic. When you click a specific package in the upper-left frame, the lower-left frame lists the classes and interfaces of the selected package. The right frame initially provides a brief description of each package of the Java API specification—read this overview to become familiar wth the general capabilities of the Java APIs. If you select a class or interface in the lower-left frame, the right frame displays information about that class or interface.

Important Links in the `index.html` Page

At the top of the right frame (Fig. G.1), there are four links—**Tree**, **Deprecated**, **Index** and **Help**. The **Tree** link displays the hierarchy of all packages, classes and interfaces in a tree structure. The **Deprecated** link displays interfaces, classes, exceptions, fields, constructors and methods that should no longer be used. The **Index** link displays classes, interfaces, fields, constructors and methods in alphabetical order. The **Help** link describes how the API documentation is organized. You should probably begin by reading the **Help** page.

Viewing the Index Page

If you do not know the name of the class you are looking for, but you do know the name of a method or field, you can use the documentation's index to locate the class. The **Index** link is located near the upper-right corner of the right frame. The index page (Fig. G.2)

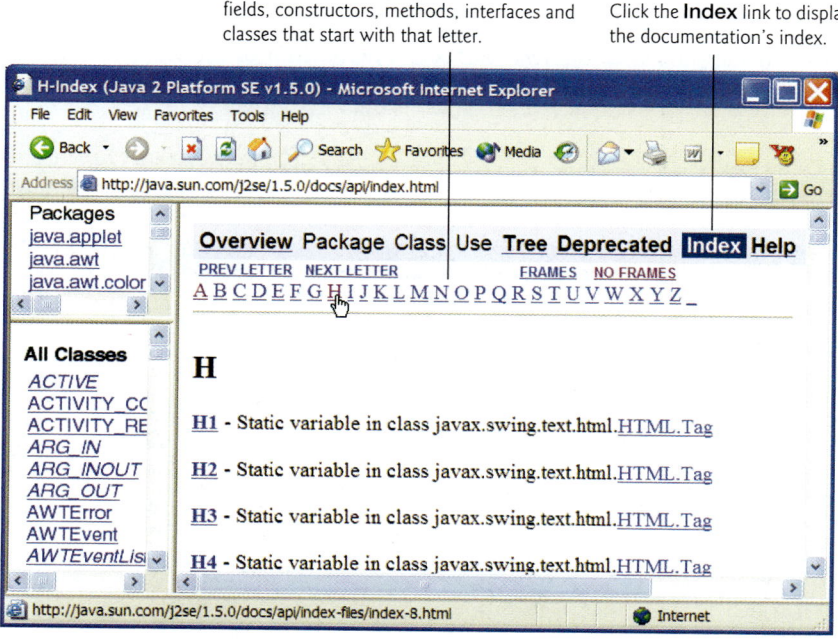

Fig. G.2 | Viewing the **Index** page. (Courtesy of Sun Microsystems, Inc.)

displays fields, constructors, methods, interfaces and classes in alphabetical order. For example, if you are looking for Scanner method hasNextInt, but do not know the class name, you can click the **H** link to go to the alphabetical listing of all items in the Java API that begin with "h". Scroll to method hasNextInt (Fig. G.3). Once there, each method named hasNextInt is listed with the package name and class to which the method belongs. From there, you can click the class name to view the class's complete details, or you can click the method name to view the method's details.

Viewing a Specific Package

When you click the package name in the upper-left frame, all classes and interfaces from that package are displayed in the lower-left frame and are divided into five subsections—**Interfaces, Classes, Enums, Exceptions** and **Errors**—each listed alphabetically. For example, when you click javax.swing in the upper-left frame, the contents of package javax.swing are displayed in the lower-left frame (Fig. G.4). You can click the package name in the lower-left frame to get an overview of the package. If you think that a package contains several classes that could be useful in your application, the package overview can be especially helpful.

Viewing the Details of a Class

When you click a class name or interface name in the lower-left frame, the right frame displays the details of that class or interface. First you will see the class's package name followed by a hierarchy that shows the class's relationship to other classes. You will also see a list of the interfaces implemented by the class and the class's known subclasses. Figure G.5 shows the beginning of the documentation page for class JButton from the javax.swing package. The page first shows the package name in which the class appears. This is followed by the class hierarchy that leads to class JButton, the interfaces class JButton implements and the subclasses of class JButton. The bottom of the right frame shows the beginning of class JButton's description. Note that when you look at the documentation

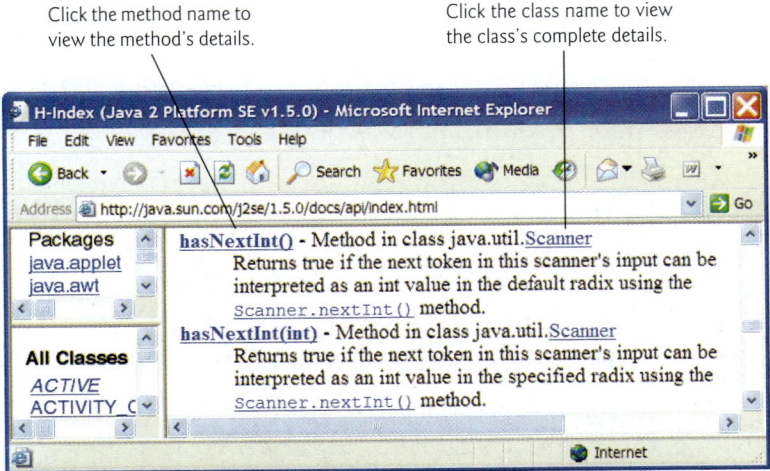

Fig. G.3 | Scroll to method hasNextInt. (Courtesy of Sun Microsystems, Inc.)

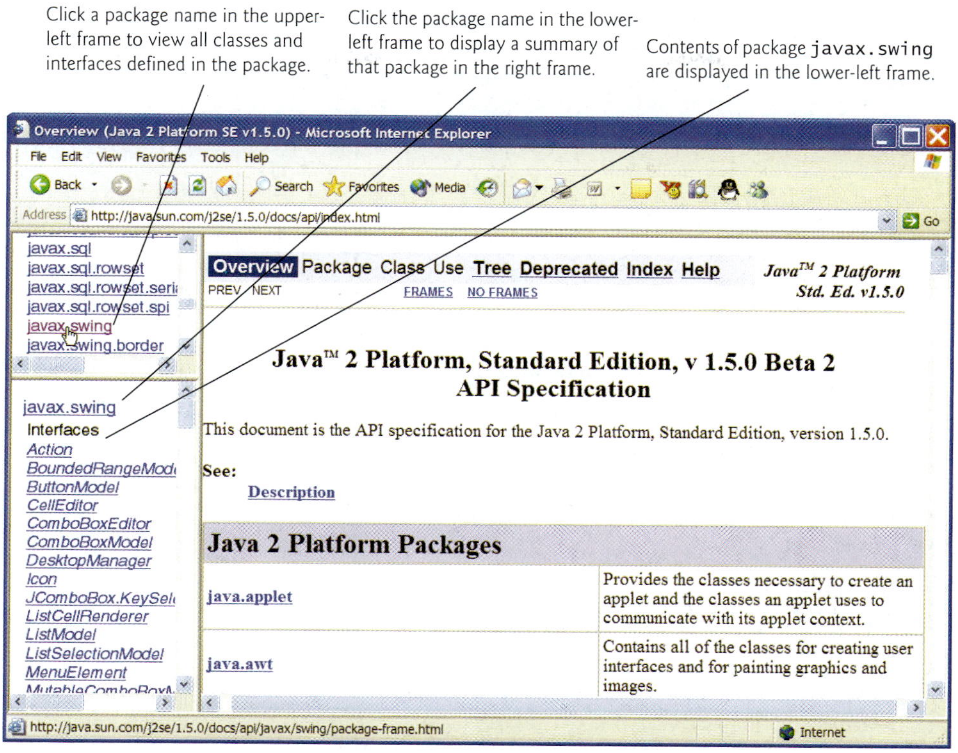

Click a package name in the upper-left frame to view all classes and interfaces defined in the package.

Click the package name in the lower-left frame to display a summary of that package in the right frame.

Contents of package `javax.swing` are displayed in the lower-left frame.

Fig. G.4 | Clicking a package name in the upper-left frame to view all classes and interfaces declared in this package. (Courtesy of Sun Microsystems, Inc.)

for an interface, the right frame does not display a hierarchy for that interface. Instead, the right frame lists the interface's superinterfaces, known subinterfaces and known implementing classes.

Summary Sections in a Class's Documentation Page

Other parts of each API page are listed below. Each part is presented only if the class contains or inherits the items specified. Class members shown in the summary sections are `public` unless they are explicitly marked as `protected`. A class's `private` members are not shown in the documentation, because they cannot be used directly in your programs.

1. The **Nested Class Summary** section summarizes the class's `public` and `protected` nested classes—i.e., classes that are defined inside the class. Unless explicitly specified, these classes are `public` and non-`static`.

2. The **Field Summary** section summarizes the class's `public` and `protected` fields. Unless explicitly specified, these fields are `public` and non-`static`. Figure G.6 shows the **Field Summary** section of class `Color`.

Click the class name to view detailed information about the class.

Detailed information about the class is displayed in the right frame.

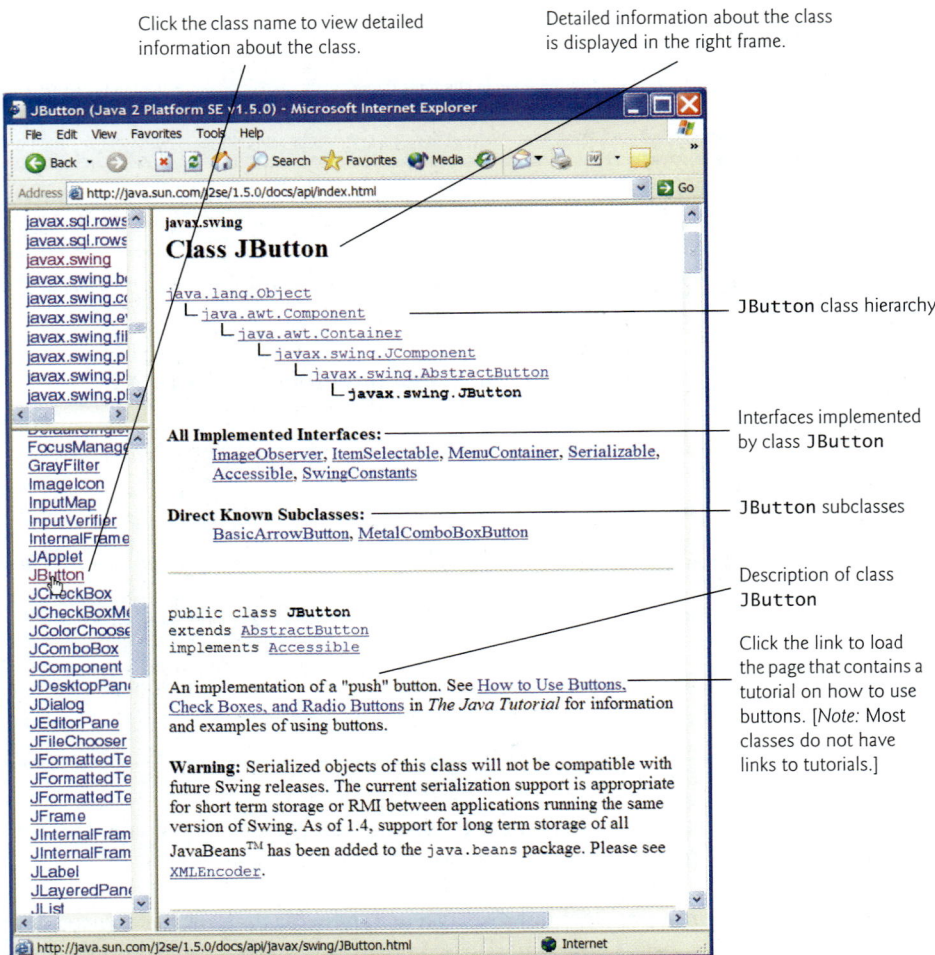

Fig. G.5 | Clicking a class name to view detailed information about the class. (Courtesy of Sun Microsystems, Inc.)

3. The **Constructor Summary** section summarizes the class's constructors. Constructors are not inherited, so this section appears in the documentation for a class only if the class declares one or more constructors. Figure G.7 shows the **Constructor Summary** section of class JButton.

4. The **Method Summary** section summarizes the class's public and protected methods. Unless explicitly specified, these methods are public and non-static. Figure G.8 shows the **Method Summary** section of class BufferedInputStream.

Note that the summary sections typically provide only a one-sentence description of a class member. Additional details are presented in the detail sections discussed next.

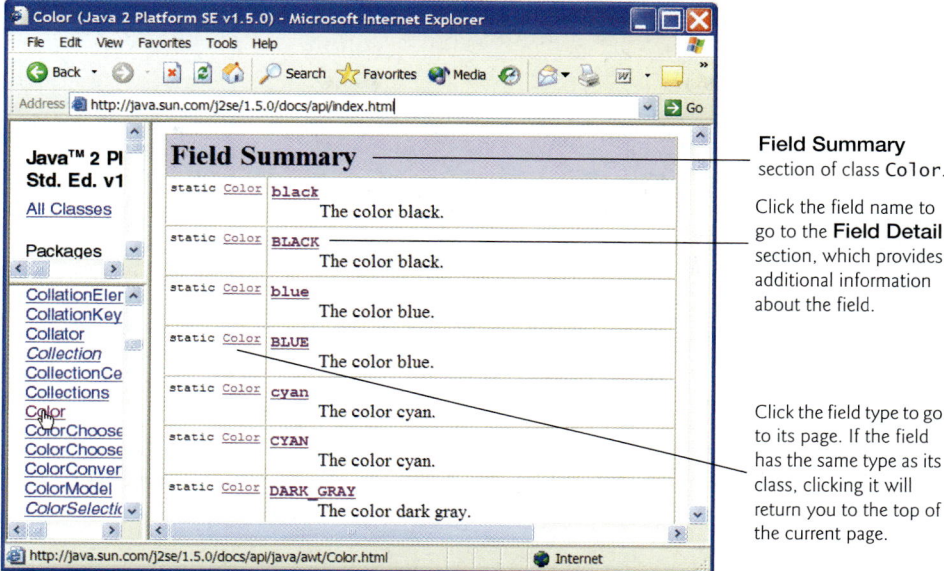

Fig. G.6 | **Field Summary** section of class `Color`. (Courtesy of Sun Microsystems, Inc.)

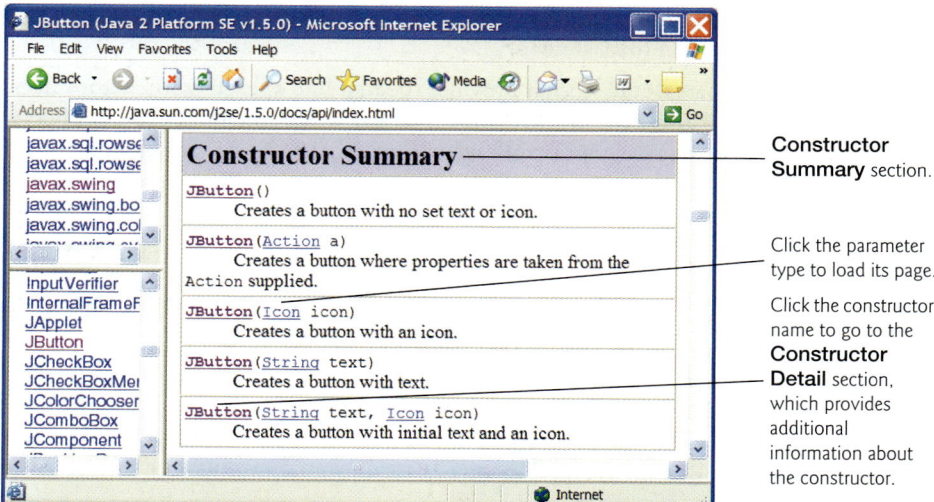

Fig. G.7 | **Constructor Summary** section of class `JButton`. (Courtesy of Sun Microsystems, Inc.)

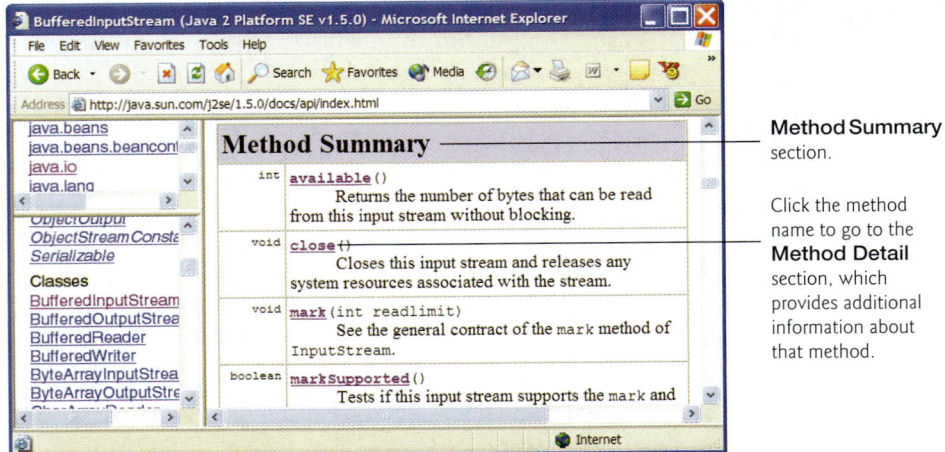

Fig. G.8 | **Method Summary** section of class `BufferedInputStream`. (Courtesy of Sun Microsystems, Inc.)

Detail Sections in a Class's Documentation Page

After the summary sections are detail sections that normally provide more discussion of particular class members. There is not a detail section for nested classes. When you click the link in the **Nested Class Summary** for a particular nested class, a documentation page describing that nested class is displayed. The detail sections are described below.

1. The **Field Detail** section provides the declaration of each field. It also discusses each field, including the field's modifiers and meaning. Figure G.9 shows the **Field Detail** section of class `Color`.

2. The **Constructor Detail** section provides the first line of each constructor's declaration and discusses the constructors. The discussion includes the modifiers of each constructor, a description of each constructor, each constructor's parameters and any exceptions thrown by each constructor. Figure G.10 shows the **Constructor Detail** section of class `JButton`.

3. The **Method Detail** section provides the first line of each method. The discussion of each method includes its modifiers, a more complete method description, the method's parameters, the method's return type and any exceptions thrown by the method. Figure G.11 shows the **Method Detail** section of class `Buffered-InputStream`. The method details show you other methods that might be of interest (labeled as **See Also**). If the method overrides a method of the superclass, the name of the superclass method and the name of the superclass are provided so you can link to the method or superclass for more information.

As you look through the documentation, you will notice that there are often links to other fields, methods, nested-classes and top-level classes. These links enable you to jump from the class you are looking at to another relevant portion of the documentation.

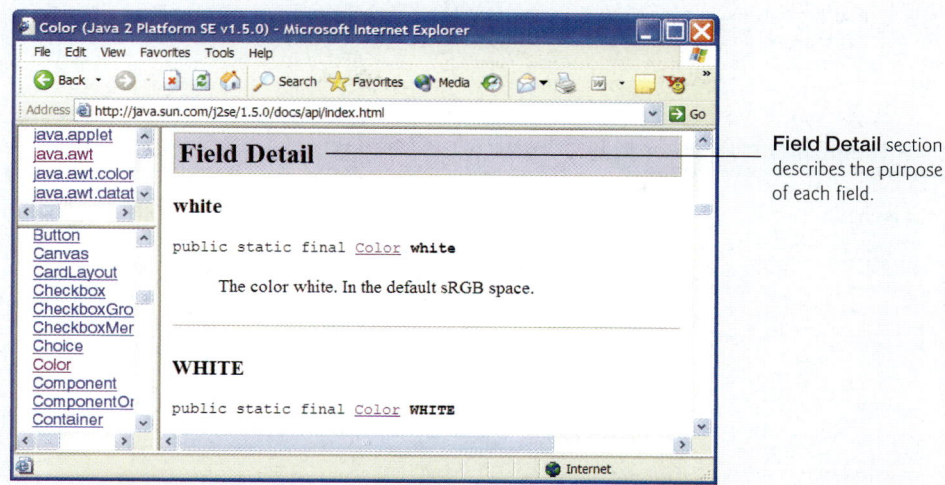

Field Detail section describes the purpose of each field.

Fig. G.9 | **Field Detail** section of class `Color`. (Courtesy of Sun Microsystems, Inc.)

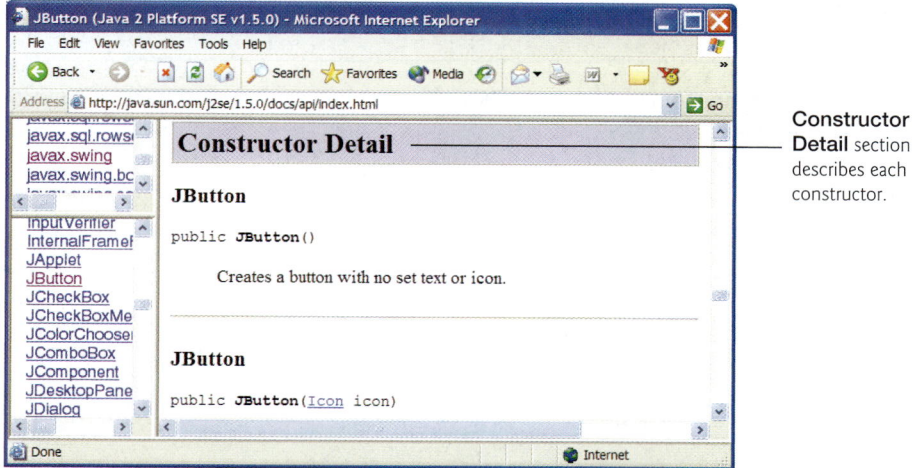

Constructor Detail section describes each constructor.

Fig. G.10 | **Constructor Detail** section of class `JButton`. (Courtesy of Sun Microsystems, Inc.)

Method **read** throws **IOException**. Click **IOException** to load the **IOException** class information page and learn more about the exception type (e.g., why such an exception might be thrown).

Method **read** overrides the **read** method in **FilterInputStream**. Click the name of the overridden method to view detailed information about the superclass's version of that method.

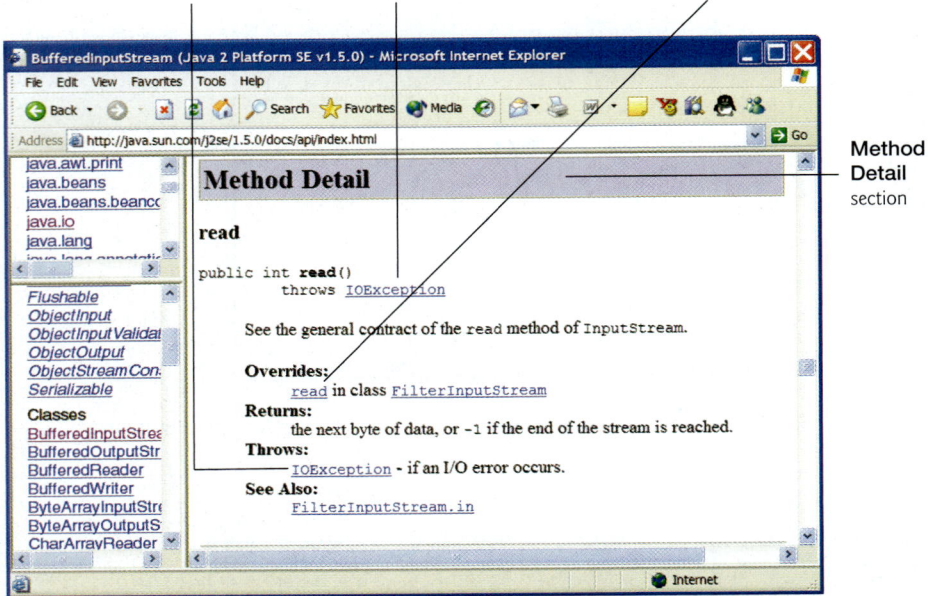

Method Detail section

Fig. G.11 | **Method Detail** section of class **BufferedInputStream**. (Courtesy of Sun Microsystems, Inc.)

(On CD)
Creating Documentation with javadoc

Appendix H (pages 1437–1448) is located on the CD that accompanies this book in printable Adobe® Acrobat PDF format. You can download Adobe® Reader® from

> www.adobe.com/products/acrobat/readstep2.html

In the index, page references for all the CD appendices appear in red. Defining occurrences of terms in the CD appendices appear in **bold red**.]

I

(On CD) Bit Manipulation

Appendix I (pages 1449–1463) is located on the CD that accompanies this book in printable Adobe® Acrobat PDF format. You can download Adobe® Reader® from

www.adobe.com/products/acrobat/readstep2.html

In the index, page references for all the CD appendices appear in red. Defining occurrences of terms in the CD appendices appear in **bold red**.]

(On CD) ATM Case Study Code

Appendix J (pages 1464–1488) is located on the CD that accompanies this book in printable Adobe® Acrobat PDF format. You can download Adobe® Reader® from

    www.adobe.com/products/acrobat/readstep2.html

In the index, page references for all the CD appendices appear in red. Defining occurrences of terms in the CD appendices appear in **bold red**.]

(On CD)
Labeled **break** and `continue` Statements

Appendix K (pages 1489–1491) is located on the CD that accompanies this book in printable Adobe® Acrobat PDF format. You can download Adobe® Reader® from

> www.adobe.com/products/acrobat/readstep2.html

In the index, page references for all the CD appendices appear in red. Defining occurrences of terms in the CD appendices appear in **bold red**.]

(On CD)
UML 2: Additional Diagram Types

Appendix L (pages 1492–1493) is located on the CD that accompanies this book in printable Adobe® Acrobat PDF format. You can download Adobe® Reader® from

      `www.adobe.com/products/acrobat/readstep2.html`

In the index, page references for all the CD appendices appear in red. Defining occurrences of terms in the CD appendices appear in **bold red**.]

(On CD) Design Patterns

Appendix M (pages 1494–1514) is located on the CD that accompanies this book in printable Adobe® Acrobat PDF format. You can download Adobe® Reader® from

www.adobe.com/products/acrobat/readstep2.html

In the index, page references for all the CD appendices appear in red. Defining occurrences of terms in the CD appendices appear in **bold red**.]

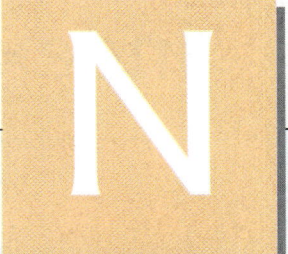

(On CD)
Using the
Debugger

Appendix N (pages 1515–1531) is located on the CD that accompanies this book in printable Adobe® Acrobat PDF format. You can download Adobe® Reader® from

`www.adobe.com/products/acrobat/readstep2.html`

In the index, page references for all the CD appendices appear in red. Defining occurrences of terms in the CD appendices appear in **bold red**.]

Index

[*Note:* Page references for defining occurrences of terms appear in bold blue. Page references for index entries in the appendices on CD appear in red. Defining occurrences of terms in those appendices appear in bold red.]

End User License Agreements

Prentice Hall License Agreement and Limited Warranty

READ THE FOLLOWING TERMS AND CONDITIONS CAREFULLY BEFORE OPENING THIS SOFTWARE PACKAGE. THIS LEGAL DOCUMENT IS AN AGREEMENT BETWEEN YOU AND PRENTICE-HALL, INC. (THE "COMPANY"). BY OPENING THIS SEALED SOFTWARE PACKAGE, YOU ARE AGREEING TO BE BOUND BY THESE TERMS AND CONDITIONS. IF YOU DO NOT AGREE WITH THESE TERMS AND CONDITIONS, DO NOT OPEN THE SOFTWARE PACKAGE. PROMPTLY RETURN THE UNOPENED SOFTWARE PACKAGE AND ALL ACCOMPANYING ITEMS TO THE PLACE YOU OBTAINED THEM FOR A FULL REFUND OF ANY SUMS YOU HAVE PAID.

1.GRANT OF LICENSE: In consideration of your purchase of this book, and your agreement to abide by the terms and conditions of this Agreement, the Company grants to you a nonexclusive right to use and display the copy of the enclosed software program (hereinafter the "SOFTWARE") on a single computer (i.e., with a single CPU) at a single location so long as you comply with the terms of this Agreement. The Company reserves all rights not expressly granted to you under this Agreement.

2.OWNERSHIP OF SOFTWARE: You own only the magnetic or physical media (the enclosed media) on which the SOFTWARE is recorded or fixed, but the Company and the software developers retain all the rights, title, and ownership to the SOFTWARE recorded on the original media copy(ies) and all subsequent copies of the SOFTWARE, regardless of the form or media on which the original or other copies may exist. This license is not a sale of the original SOFTWARE or any copy to you.

3.COPY RESTRICTIONS: This SOFTWARE and the accompanying printed materials and user manual (the "Documentation") are the subject of copyright. The individual programs on the media are copyrighted by the authors of each program. Some of the programs on the media include separate licensing agreements. If you intend to use one of these programs, you must read and follow its accompanying license agreement. You may not copy the Documentation or the SOFTWARE, except that you may make a single copy of the SOFTWARE for backup or archival purposes only. You may be held legally responsible for any copying or copyright infringement which is caused or encouraged by your failure to abide by the terms of this restriction.

4.USE RESTRICTIONS: You may not network the SOFTWARE or otherwise use it on more than one computer or computer terminal at the same time. You may physically transfer the SOFTWARE from one computer to another provided that the SOFTWARE is used on only one computer at a time. You may not distribute copies of the SOFTWARE or Documentation to others. You may not reverse engineer, disassemble, decompile, modify, adapt, translate, or create derivative works based on the SOFTWARE or the Documentation without the prior written consent of the Company.

5. TRANSFER RESTRICTIONS: The enclosed SOFTWARE is licensed only to you and may not be transferred to any one else without the prior written consent of the Company. Any unauthorized transfer of the SOFTWARE shall result in the immediate termination of this Agreement.

6. TERMINATION: This license is effective until terminated. This license will terminate automatically without notice from the Company and become null and void if you fail to comply with any provisions or limitations of this license. Upon termination, you shall destroy the Documentation and all copies of the SOFTWARE. All provisions of this Agreement as to warranties, limitation of liability, remedies or damages, and our ownership rights shall survive termination.

7. MISCELLANEOUS: This Agreement shall be construed in accordance with the laws of the United States of America and the State of New York and shall benefit the Company, its affiliates, and assignees.

8.LIMITED WARRANTY AND DISCLAIMER OF WARRANTY: The Company warrants that the SOFTWARE, when properly used in accordance with the Documentation, will operate in substantial conformity with the description of the SOFTWARE set forth in the Documentation. The Company does not warrant that the SOFTWARE will meet your requirements or that the operation of the SOFTWARE will be uninterrupted or error-free. The Company warrants that the media on which the SOFTWARE is delivered shall be free from defects in materials and workmanship under normal use for a period of thirty

(30) days from the date of your purchase. Your only remedy and the Company's only obligation under these limited warranties is, at the Company's option, return of the warranted item for a refund of any amounts paid by you or replacement of the item. Any replacement of SOFTWARE or media under the warranties shall not extend the original warranty period. The limited warranty set forth above shall not apply to any SOFTWARE which the Company determines in good faith has been subject to misuse, neglect, improper installation, repair, alteration, or damage by you. EXCEPT FOR THE EXPRESSED WARRANTIES SET FORTH ABOVE, THE COMPANY DISCLAIMS ALL WARRANTIES, EXPRESS OR IMPLIED, INCLUDING WITHOUT LIMITATION, THE IMPLIED WARRAN- TIES OF MERCHANTABILITY AND FITNESS FOR A PARTICULAR PURPOSE. EXCEPT FOR THE EXPRESS WARRANTY SET FORTH ABOVE, THE COMPANY DOES NOT WARRANT, GUARANTEE, OR MAKE ANY REPRESENTATION REGARDING THE USE OR THE RESULTS OF THE USE OF THE SOFTWARE IN TERMS OF ITS CORRECTNESS, ACCU- RACY, RELIABILITY, CURRENTNESS, OR OTHERWISE.

IN NO EVENT, SHALL THE COMPANY OR ITS EMPLOYEES, AGENTS, SUPPLIERS, OR CONTRACTORS BE LIABLE FOR ANY INCIDENTAL, INDIRECT, SPECIAL, OR CONSE- QUENTIAL DAMAGES ARISING OUT OF OR IN CONNECTION WITH THE LICENSE GRANTED UNDER THIS AGREEMENT, OR FOR LOSS OF USE, LOSS OF DATA, LOSS OF INCOME OR PROFIT, OR OTHER LOSSES, SUSTAINED AS A RESULT OF INJURY TO ANY PERSON, OR LOSS OF OR DAMAGE TO PROPERTY, OR CLAIMS OF THIRD PARTIES, EVEN IF THE COMPANY OR AN AUTHORIZED REPRESENTATIVE OF THE COMPANY HAS BEEN ADVISED OF THE POSSIBILITY OF SUCH DAMAGES. IN NO EVENT SHALL LIABILITY OF THE COMPANY FOR DAMAGES WITH RESPECT TO THE SOFTWARE EXCEED THE AMOUNTS ACTUALLY PAID BY YOU, IF ANY, FOR THE SOFTWARE.

SOME JURISDICTIONS DO NOT ALLOW THE LIMITATION OF IMPLIED WARRAN- TIES OR LIABILITY FOR INCIDENTAL, INDIRECT, SPECIAL, OR CONSEQUENTIAL DAM- AGES, SO THE ABOVE LIMITATIONS MAY NOT ALWAYS APPLY. THE WARRANTIES IN THIS AGREEMENT GIVE YOU SPECIFIC LEGAL RIGHTS AND YOU MAY ALSO HAVE OTHER RIGHTS WHICH VARY IN ACCORDANCE WITH LOCAL LAW.

ACKNOWLEDGMENT

YOU ACKNOWLEDGE THAT YOU HAVE READ THIS AGREEMENT, UNDERSTAND IT, AND AGREE TO BE BOUND BY ITS TERMS AND CONDITIONS. YOU ALSO AGREE THAT THIS AGREEMENT IS THE COMPLETE AND EXCLUSIVE STATEMENT OF THE AGREEMENT BETWEEN YOU AND THE COMPANY AND SUPERSEDES ALL PROPOSALS OR PRIOR AGREEMENTS, ORAL, OR WRITTEN, AND ANY OTHER COMMUNICATIONS BETWEEN YOU AND THE COMPANY OR ANY REPRESENTATIVE OF THE COMPANY RELATING TO THE SUBJECT MATTER OF THIS AGREEMENT.

Should you have any questions concerning this Agreement or if you wish to contact the Company for any reason, please contact in writing at the address below.

Robin Short
Prentice Hall PTR
One Lake Street
Upper Saddle River, New Jersey 07458

Apache Tomcat License Agreement

Version 2.0, January 2004
http://www.apache.org/licenses/

TERMS AND CONDITIONS FOR USE, REPRODUCTION, AND DISTRIBUTION
1. Definitions.

"License" shall mean the terms and conditions for use, reproduction, and distribution as defined by Sections 1 through 9 of this document.

"Licensor" shall mean the copyright owner or entity authorized by the copyright owner that is granting the License.

"Legal Entity" shall mean the union of the acting entity and all other entities that control, are con- trolled by, or are under common control with that entity. For the purposes of this definition, "control" means (i) the power, direct or indirect, to cause the direction or management of such entity, whether by contract or otherwise, or (ii) ownership of fifty percent (50%) or more of the outstanding shares, or (iii) beneficial ownership of such entity.

"You" (or "Your") shall mean an individual or Legal Entity exercising permissions granted by this License.

"Source" form shall mean the preferred form for making modifications, including but not limited to software source code, documentation source, and configuration files.

"Object" form shall mean any form resulting from mechanical transformation or translation of a Source form, including but not limited to compiled object code, generated documentation, and conversions to other media types.

"Work" shall mean the work of authorship, whether in Source or Object form, made available under the License, as indicated by a copyright notice that is included in or attached to the work (an example is provided in the Appendix below).

"Derivative Works" shall mean any work, whether in Source or Object form, that is based on (or derived from) the Work and for which the editorial revisions, annotations, elaborations, or other modifications represent, as a whole, an original work of authorship. For the purposes of this License, Derivative Works shall not include works that remain separable from, or merely link (or bind by name) to the interfaces of, the Work and Derivative Works thereof.

"Contribution" shall mean any work of authorship, including the original version of the Work and any modifications or additions to that Work or Derivative Works thereof, that is intentionally submitted to Licensor for inclusion in the Work by the copyright owner or by an individual or Legal Entity authorized to submit on behalf of the copyright owner. For the purposes of this definition, "submitted" means any form of electronic, verbal, or written communication sent to the Licensor or its representatives, including but not limited to communication on electronic mailing lists, source code control systems, and issue tracking systems that are managed by, or on behalf of, the Licensor for the purpose of discussing and improving the Work, but excluding communication that is conspicuously marked or otherwise designated in writing by the copyright owner as "Not a Contribution."

"Contributor" shall mean Licensor and any individual or Legal Entity on behalf of whom a Contribution has been received by Licensor and subsequently incorporated within the Work.

2. Grant of Copyright License.

Subject to the terms and conditions of this License, each Contributor hereby grants to You a perpetual, worldwide, non-exclusive, no-charge, royalty-free, irrevocable copyright license to reproduce, prepare Derivative Works of, publicly display, publicly perform, sublicense, and distribute the Work and such Derivative Works in Source or Object form.

3. Grant of Patent License.

Subject to the terms and conditions of this License, each Contributor hereby grants to You a perpetual, worldwide, non-exclusive, no-charge, royalty-free, irrevocable (except as stated in this section) patent license to make, have made, use, offer to sell, sell, import, and otherwise transfer the Work, where such license applies only to those patent claims licensable by such Contributor that are necessarily infringed by their Contribution(s) alone or by combination of their Contribution(s) with the Work to which such Contribution(s) was submitted. If You institute patent litigation against any entity (including a cross-claim or counterclaim in a lawsuit) alleging that the Work or a Contribution incorporated within the Work constitutes direct or contributory patent infringement, then any patent licenses granted to You under this License for that Work shall terminate as of the date such litigation is filed.

4. Redistribution

You may reproduce and distribute copies of the Work or Derivative Works thereof in any medium, with or without modifications, and in Source or Object form, provided that You meet the following conditions:

a. You must give any other recipients of the Work or Derivative Works a copy of this License; and

b. You must cause any modified files to carry prominent notices stating that You changed the files; and

c. You must retain, in the Source form of any Derivative Works that You distribute, all copyright, patent, trademark, and attribution notices from the Source form of the Work, excluding those notices that do not pertain to any part of the Derivative Works; and

d. If the Work includes a "NOTICE" text file as part of its distribution, then any Derivative Works that You distribute must include a readable copy of the attribution notices contained within such NOTICE file, excluding those notices that do not pertain to any part of the Derivative Works, in at least one of the following places: within a NOTICE text file distributed as part of the Derivative Works; within the Source form or documentation, if provided along with the Derivative Works; or, within a display generated by the Derivative Works, if and wherever such third-party notices normally appear. The contentsof the NOTICE file are for informational purposes only and do not modify the License. You may add Your own attribution notices within Derivative Works that You distribute, alongside or as an addendum to the NOTICE text from the Work, provided that such additional attribution notices cannot be construed as modifying the License.

You may add Your own copyright statement to Your modifications and may provide additional or different license terms and conditions for use, reproduction, or distribution of Your modifications, or for any such Derivative Works as a whole, provided Your use, reproduction, and distribution of the Work otherwise complies with the conditions stated in this License.

5. Submission of Contributions

Unless You explicitly state otherwise, any Contribution intentionally submitted for inclusion in the Work by You to the Licensor shall be under the terms and conditions of this License, without any additional terms or conditions. Notwithstanding the above, nothing herein shall supersede or modify the terms of any separate license agreement you may have executed with Licensor regarding such Contributions.

6. Trademarks

This License does not grant permission to use the trade names, trademarks, service marks, or product names of the Licensor, except as required for reasonable and customary use in describing the origin of the Work and reproducing the content of the NOTICE file.

7. Disclaimer of Warranty

Unless required by applicable law or agreed to in writing, Licensor provides the Work (and each Contributor provides its Contributions) on an "AS IS" BASIS, WITHOUT WARRANTIES OR CONDITIONS OF ANY KIND, either express or implied, including, without limitation, any warranties or conditions of TITLE, NON-INFRINGEMENT, MERCHANTABILITY, or FITNESS FOR A PARTICULAR PURPOSE. You are solely responsible for determining the appropriateness of using or redistributing the Work and assume any risks associated with Your exercise of permissions under this License.

8. Limitation of Liability.

In no event and under no legal theory, whether in tort (including negligence), contract, or otherwise, unless required by applicable law (such as deliberate and grossly negligent acts) or agreed to in writing, shall any Contributor be liable to You for damages, including any direct, indirect, special, incidental, or consequential damages of any character arising as a result of this License or out of the use or inability to use the Work (including but not limited to damages for loss of goodwill, work stoppage, computer failure or malfunction, or any and all other commercial damages or losses), even if such Contributor has been advised of the possibility of such damages.

9. Accepting Warranty or Additional Liability.

While redistributing the Work or Derivative Works thereof, You may choose to offer, and charge a fee for, acceptance of support, warranty, indemnity, or other liability obligations and/or rights consistent with this License. However, in accepting such obligations, You may act only on Your own behalf and on Your sole responsibility, not on behalf of any other Contributor, and only if You agree to indemnify, defend, and hold each Contributor harmless for any liability incurred by, or claims asserted against, such Contributor by reason of your accepting any such warranty or additional liability.

END OF TERMS AND CONDITIONS

APPENDIX: How to apply the Apache License to your work

To apply the Apache License to your work, attach the following boilerplate notice, with the fields enclosed by brackets "[]" replaced with your own identifying information. (Don't include the brackets!) The text should be enclosed in the appropriate comment syntax for the file format. We also recommend that a file or class name and description of purpose be included on the same "printed page" as the copyright notice for easier identification within third-party archives.

Copyright [yyyy] [name of copyright owner]
Licensed under the Apache License, Version 2.0 (the "License"); you may not use this file except in compliance with the License.
You may obtain a copy of the License at http://www.apache.org/licenses/LICENSE-2.0
Unless required by applicable law or agreed to in writing, software distributed under the License is distributed on an "AS IS" BASIS, WITHOUT WARRANTIES OR CONDITIONS OF ANY KIND, either express or implied.
See the License for the specific language governing permissions and limitations under the License.

JCreator™ License Agreement

END-USER LICENSE AGREEMENT FOR JCREATOR NOTICE TO ALL USERS:CAREFULLY READ THE FOLLOWING LEGAL AGREEMENT, FOR THE LICENSE OF SPECIFIED SOFTWARE BY XINOX SOFTWARE. BY INSTALLING THE SOFTWARE, YOU (EITHER AN INDIVIDUAL OR A SINGLE ENTITY) CONSENT TO BE BOUND BY AND BECOME A PARTY TO THIS AGREEMENT. IF YOU DO NOT AGREE TO ALL OF THE TERMS OF THIS AGREEMENT, CLICK THE BUTTON THAT INDICATES THAT YOU DO NOT ACCEPT THE TERMS OF THIS AGREEMENT AND DO NOT INSTALL THE SOFTWARE.

1. DEFINITIONS
    (a) "the Software" means the JCreator software program supplied by Xinox Software herewith, which may also include documentation, associated media, printed materials, and online and electronic documentation.

    (b) "User" means an individual end-user of the Software, being either faculty, staff, or an enrolled student in the case of a university or full-time staff in the case of a public institution or industrial firm.

    (c) "Licensee" is a User who has paid the license fee in full and who has been registered with Xinox Software.

    (d) "Xinox Software" or "Company" means Xinox Software and its suppliers and licensors, if any.

    (e) "Evaluation Period" means a version of the Software, so identified, to be used to review and evaluate the Software, only. See section 4.1 for more details.

    (f) "Private/Academic Version" means a version of the Software, so identified, for private(home) use or use by students and faculty of educational institutions, only. Private/Academic Versions may not be used for, or distributed to any party for, any commercial purpose. See section 4.2 for more details.

2. GENERAL
This End-User License Agreement ("EULA") is a legal agreement between you and Xinox Software for the Xinox Software products identified above, which may include computer software and associated media, electronic documentation and printed materials ("The Software"). By installing, copying, distributing or otherwise using The Software you agree to be bound by the terms of this EULA. If you do not agree to the terms of this EULA, you must not install, use or distribute The Software, and you must destroy all copies of The Software that you have. The Software is protected by copyright laws and international copyright treaties, as well as other intellectual property laws and treaties. The Software is licensed, not sold and always remains the property of Xinox Software.

    Xinox Software will supply the Licensee with a single copy of the Software and Documents in electronic format, using a distribution mechanism decided on by Xinox Software. Xinox Software also will additionally supply the Licensee with a serial number and registration key. The Licensee agrees to restrict distribution of the registration key only to staff members with a need to know for purposes of configuring the Software or recording registration information for the usual business records of the Licensee, and will make all reasonable efforts to prevent duplication and any form of publication of the registration material.

    If you have not paid the registration fee for the Software, you are hereby granted an evaluation license to use the Software as described in section 4.1.

3. LICENSE GRANT
Subject to the payment of the applicable license fees, and subject to the terms and conditions of this Agreement, Xinox Software hereby grants to you a non-exclusive, non-transferable right to use the Software and the accompanying documentation (the "Documentation"). Except as set forth below, you may only install one copy of the Software on one computer, workstation or other electronic device for which the Software was designed (each, a "Client Device"). If the Software is licensed as a suite or bundle with more than one specified Software product, this license applies to all such specified Software products, subject to any restrictions or usage terms specified on the applicable price list or product packaging that apply to any of such Software products individually.

    (a) Use. The Software is licensed as a single product; more than one user may not use it on more than one Client Device or at a time, except as set forth in this Section 3. The Software is "in use" on a Client Device when it is loaded into the temporary memory (i.e., random-access memory or RAM) or installed into the permanent memory (e.g., hard disk, CD-ROM, or other storage device) of that Client Device. This license authorizes you to make one copy of the Software solely for backup or archival purposes, provided that the copy you make contains all of the Software's proprietary notices.

    (b) Multiple Client Devices. A licensed user is also granted a license to install the Software on more than one Client Device, for the sole use of that user.

    (c) Server-Mode. You may use the Software on a Client Device as a server ("Server") within a multiuser or networked environment, on a single physical site, ("Server-Mode") only if such use is permitted in the applicable price list or product packaging for the Software. A separate license is required for each Client Device or "seat" that may connect to the Server at any time, regardless of whether such licensed Client Devices or seats are concurrently connected to, accessing or using the Software. Use of software or hardware that reduces the number of Client Devices or seats directly accessing or utilizing the Software (e.g., "multiplexing" or "pooling" software or hardware) does not reduce the number of licenses required (i.e., the required number of licenses would equal the number of distinct inputs to the multiplexing or pooling software or hardware "front end"). If the number of Client Devices or seats that can connect to the Software can exceed the number of licenses you have obtained, and then you must have a reasonable mechanism in place to ensure that your use of the Software does not exceed the use limits specified for the licenses you have obtained. This license authorizes you to make or download one copy of the Documentation for each Client Device or seat that is licensed, provided that each such copy contains all of the Documentation's proprietary notices.

(d) Volume Licenses. If the Software is licensed with volume license terms specified in the applicable price list or product packaging for the Software, you may make, use and install as many additional copies of the Software on the number of Client Devices as the volume license authorizes. You must have a reasonable mechanism in place to ensure that the number of Client Devices on which the Software has been installed does not exceed the number of licenses you have obtained. This license authorizes you to make or download one copy of the Documentation for each additional copy authorized by the volume license, provided that each such copy contains all of the Documentation's proprietary notices.

(e) Site Licenses. If the Software is licensed with site license terms, you may make, use and install unlimited copies of the Software within the organization site. This excludes Client Devices outside the organization, such as the home-computers of the students and staff members. This license authorizes you to make or download one copy of the Documentation for each copy authorized by the site license, provided that each such copy contains all of the Documentation's proprietary notices.

4. LICENSE RESTRICTIONS

(a) Sublicense, sell, assign, transfer, pledge, distribute, rent or remove any proprietary notices on the Software except as expressly permitted in this Agreement.

(b) Use, copy, adapt, disassemble, decompile, reverse engineer or modify the Software, in whole or in part, except as expressly permitted in this Agreement.

(c) Take any action designed to unlock or bypass any Company-implemented restrictions on usage, access to, or number of installations of the Software; or.

(d) Use the Software if you fail to pay any license fee due and the Company notifies you that your license is terminated.

(e) Disclose to third parties, or publish your registration details via electronic or other means.
IF YOU DO ANY OF THE FOREGOING, YOUR RIGHTS UNDER THIS LICENSE WILL AUTOMATICALLY TERMINATE. SUCH TERMINATION SHALL BE IN ADDITION TO AND NOT IN LIEU OF ANY CRIMINAL, CIVIL OR OTHER REMEDIES AVAILABLE TO XINOX SOFTWARE.

4.1 RESTRICTED USE DURING EVALUATION PERIOD

You have a nonexclusive, nontransferable license to load and execute the unregistered copy of the Software for a period of thirty (30) days. (the "Evaluation Period"). The unregistered copy of the Software may be used for evaluation and testing purposes only and not for general commercial use. Customer must pay a license fee for the Software to obtain the right to use the Software for general commercial use and(or) for unlimited period. The unregistered copy of Software contains a feature that will automatically disable the Software in thirty (30) days. If you agree to this License Agreement and pay the license fee, Xinox Software will deactivate this feature. Xinox Software will have no liability to you if the Software is disabled by this feature. You may not disable, destroy, or remove this feature of the Software, and any attempt to do so will terminate your license and rights under this Agreement.

4.2 RESTRICTED USE PRIVATE/ACADEMIC LICENSE

Subject to the terms of this EULA, use the Software for non-commercial purposes only including conducting academic research or providing educational services. You certify that use is directly related to teaching, private non-commercial development or that use is strictly for non-commercial research by students or and faculty members, where the results of such research or development are not intended primarily for the benefit of a third party. (The private/academic version contains the same methodology as the Professional Edition; the only difference is the license.)

5. UPDATES

You are entitled to download revisions and upgrades (maintenance releases) to the Software as and when Xinox Software publishes it via its web site or through other online services. Xinox Software may charge an upgrade fee for new releases which contain significant enhancements.

6. DISTRIBUTION

You are hereby licensed to make as many copies of the installation package for The Software as you wish; give exact copies of the original installation package for The Software to anyone; and distribute the original installation package for The Software in its unmodified form via electronic or other means. The Software must be clearly identified as a freeware or shareware version where described. You are specifically prohibited from charging, or requesting donations, for any such copies, however made; and from distributing The Software including documentation with other products (commercial or otherwise) without prior written permission from Xinox Software. You are also prohibited from distributing components of The Software other than the complete original installation package.

7. OWNERSHIP

The foregoing license gives you limited license to use the Software. Xinox Software and its suppliers retain all right, title and interest, including all copyrights, in and to the Software and all copies thereof. All rights not specifically granted in this EULA, including Federal and International Copyrights, are reserved by

Xinox Software and its suppliers. All title, including but not limited to copyrights, in and to The Software and any copies thereof are owned by Xinox Software. All title and intellectual property rights in and to the content which may be accessed through use of The Software is the property of the respective content owner and may be protected by applicable copyright or other intellectual property laws and treaties. This EULA grants you no rights to use such content. All rights not expressly granted are reserved by Xinox Software.

8. WARRANTY AND DISCLAIMER

LIMITED WARRANTY TO THE MAXIMUM EXTENT PERMITTED BY APPLICABLE LAW, XINOX SOFTWARE DISCLAIMS ALL WARRANTIES AND CONDITIONS, EITHER EXPRESS OR IMPLIED, INCLUDING, BUT NOT LIMITED TO, IMPLIED WARRANTIES OF MER-CHANTABILITY, FITNESS FOR A PARTICULAR PURPOSE, TITLE, AND NON-INFRINGE-MENT, WITH REGARD TO THE SOFTWARE, AND THE PROVISION OF OR FAILURE TO PROVIDE SUPPORT SERVICES.XINOX SOFTWARE DOES NOT WARRANT THAT THE SOFTWARE WILL MEET YOUR REQUIREMENTS OR THAT THE OPERATION OF THE SOFTWARE WILL BE UNINTERRUPTED OR ERROR FREE.THE ENTIRE RISK AS TO SAT-ISFACTORY QUALITY, PERFORMANCE, ACCURACY, AND EFFORT IS WITH YOU, THE USER.

9. LIMITATION OF LIABILITY

LIMITATIONS OF REMEDIES AND LIABILITY TO THE MAXIMUM EXTENT PERMITTED BY APPLICABLE LAW, IN NO EVENT SHALL XINOX SOFTWARE BE LIABLE FOR ANY SPE-CIAL, INCIDENTAL, INDIRECT, CONSEQUENTIAL OR OTHER DAMAGES WHATSOEV-ER (INCLUDING, WITHOUT LIMITATION, DAMAGES FOR LOSS OF PROFITS, BUSINESS INTERRUPTION, LOSS OF INFORMATION, OR ANY OTHER PECUNIARY LOSS) ARISING OUT OF THE USE OF OR INABILITY TO USE THE SOFTWARE PRODUCT OR THE PRO-VISION OF OR FAILURE TO PROVIDE SUPPORT SERVICES, EVEN IF XINOX SOFTWARE HAS BEEN ADVISED OF THE POSSIBILITY OF SUCH DAMAGES. SOME STATES AND JU-RISDICTIONS DO NOT ALLOW THE EXCLUSION OR LIMITATION OF LIABILITY, THE ABOVE LIMITATION MAY NOT APPLY TO YOU.

10. HIGH RISK ACTIVITIES

The Software is not fault-tolerant and is not designed, manufactured or intended for use or resale as on-line control equipment in hazardous environments requiring fail-safe performance, such as in the opera-tion of nuclear facilities, aircraft navigation or communication systems, air traffic control, direct life sup-port machines, or weapons systems, in which the failure of the Software could lead directly to death, personal injury, or severe physical or environmental damage ("High Risk Activities"). Accordingly, Xinox Software and its suppliers and licensors specifically disclaim any express or implied warranty of fitness for High Risk Activities. You agree that Xinox Software and its suppliers and licensors will not be liable for any claims or damages arising from the use of the Software in such applications.

11. TERMINATION

Without prejudice to any other rights, Xinox Software may terminate this EULA if you fail to comply with the terms and conditions of this EULA. In such event, you must destroy all copies of The Software.

12. MISCELLANEOUS

This license is governed by Dutch Law and is subject to exclusive jurisdiction of the Dutch courts. This license constitutes the complete and exclusive statement of our agreement with you and supercedes all proposals, representations, understandings and prior agreements whether oral or written and all commu-nications with you relating thereto.

jEdit License Agreement

jEdit is released under the terms of the GNU General Public License, and developed by Slava Pestov and others.

GNU GENERAL PUBLIC LICENSE
Version 2, June 1991
Copyright (C) 1989, 1991 Free Software Foundation, Inc.
59 Temple Place - Suite 330, Boston, MA 02111-1307, USA
Everyone is permitted to copy and distribute verbatim copies
of this license document, but changing it is not allowed.

Preamble

The licenses for most software are designed to take away your freedom to share and change it. By contrast, the GNU General Public License is intended to guarantee your freedom to share and change free software--to make sure the software is free for all its users. This General Public License applies to most of the Free Software Foundation's software and to any other program whose authors commit to using it. (Some other Free Software Foundation software is covered by the GNU Library General Public License instead.) You can apply it to your programs, too.

When we speak of free software, we are referring to freedom, not price. Our General Public Licenses are designed to make sure that you have the freedom to distribute copies of free software (and charge for this service if you wish), that you receive source code or can get it if you want it, that you can change the software or use pieces of it in new free programs; and that you know you can do these things.

To protect your rights, we need to make restrictions that forbid anyone to deny you these rights or to ask you to surrender the rights. These restrictions translate to certain responsibilities for you if you distribute copies of the software, or if you modify it.

For example, if you distribute copies of such a program, whether gratis or for a fee, you must give the recipients all the rights that you have. You must make sure that they, too, receive or can get the source code. And you must show them these terms so they know their rights.

We protect your rights with two steps: (1) copyright the software, and (2) offer you this license which gives you legal permission to copy, distribute and/or modify the software.

Also, for each author's protection and ours, we want to make certain that everyone understands that there is no warranty for this free software. If the software is modified by someone else and passed on, we want its recipients to know that what they have is not the original, so that any problems introduced by others will not reflect on the original authors' reputations.

Finally, any free program is threatened constantly by software patents. We wish to avoid the danger that redistributors of a free program will individually obtain patent licenses, in effect making the program proprietary. To prevent this, we have made it clear that any patent must be licensed for everyone's free use or not licensed at all.

The precise terms and conditions for copying, distribution and modification follow. **TERMS AND CONDITIONS FOR COPYING, DISTRIBUTION AND MODIFICATION**

0. This License applies to any program or other work which contains a notice placed by the copyright holder saying it may be distributed under the terms of this General Public License. The "Program", below, refers to any such program or work, and a "work based on the Program" means either the Program or any derivative work under copyright law: that is to say, a work containing the Program or a portion of it, either verbatim or with modifications and/or translated into another language. (Hereinafter, translation is included without limitation in the term "modification".) Each licensee is addressed as "you".

Activities other than copying, distribution and modification are not covered by this License; they are outside its scope. The act of running the Program is not restricted, and the output from the Program is covered only if its contents constitute a work based on the Program (independent of having been made by running the Program). Whether that is true depends on what the Program does.

1. You may copy and distribute verbatim copies of the Program's source code as you receive it, in any medium, provided that you conspicuously and appropriately publish on each copy an appropriate copyright notice and disclaimer of warranty; keep intact all the notices that refer to this License and to the absence of any warranty; and give any other recipients of the Program a copy of this License along with the Program.

You may charge a fee for the physical act of transferring a copy, and you may at your option offer warranty protection in exchange for a fee.

2. You may modify your copy or copies of the Program or any portion of it, thus forming a work based on the Program, and copy and distribute such modifications or work under the terms of Section 1 above, provided that you also meet all of these conditions:

a) You must cause the modified files to carry prominent notices stating that you changed the files and the date of any change.

b) You must cause any work that you distribute or publish, that in whole or in part contains or is derived from the Program or any part thereof, to be licensed as a whole at no charge to all third parties under the terms of this License.

c) If the modified program normally reads commands interactively when run, you must cause it, when started running for such interactive use in the most ordinary way, to print or display an announcement including an appropriate copyright notice and a notice that there is no warranty (or else, saying that you provide a warranty) and that users may redistribute the program under these conditions, and telling the user how to view a copy of this License. (Exception: if the Program itself is interactive but does not normally print such an announcement, your work based on the Program is not required to print an announcement.)

These requirements apply to the modified work as a whole. If identifiable sections of that work are not derived from the Program, and can be reasonably considered independent and separate works in themselves, then this License, and its terms, do not apply to those sections when you distribute them as separate works. But when you distribute the same sections as part of a whole which is a work based on the Program, the distribution of the whole must be on the terms of this License, whose permissions for other licensees extend to the entire whole, and thus to each and every part regardless of who wrote it.

Thus, it is not the intent of this section to claim rights or contest your rights to work written entirely by you; rather, the intent is to exercise the right to control the distribution of derivative or collective works based on the Program.

In addition, mere aggregation of another work not based on the Program with the Program (or with a work based on the Program) on a volume of a storage or distribution medium does not bring the other work under the scope of this License.

3. You may copy and distribute the Program (or a work based on it, under Section 2) in object code or executable form under the terms of Sections 1 and 2 above provided that you also do one of the following:

a) Accompany it with the complete corresponding machine-readable source code, which must be distributed under the terms of Sections 1 and 2 above on a medium customarily used for software interchange; or,

b) Accompany it with a written offer, valid for at least three years, to give any third party, for a charge no more than your cost of physically performing source distribution, a complete machine-readable copy of the corresponding source code, to be distributed under the terms of Sections 1 and 2 above on a medium customarily used for software interchange; or,

c) Accompany it with the information you received as to the offer to distribute corresponding source code. (This alternative is allowed only for noncommercial distribution and only if you received the program in object code or executable form with such an offer, in accord with Subsection b above.)

The source code for a work means the preferred form of the work for making modifications to it. For an executable work, complete source code means all the source code for all modules it contains, plus any associated interface definition files, plus the scripts used to control compilation and installation of the executable. However, as a special exception, the source code distributed need not include anything that is normally distributed (in either source or binary form) with the major components (compiler, kernel, and so on) of the operating system on which the executable runs, unless that component itself accompanies the executable.

If distribution of executable or object code is made by offering access to copy from a designated place, then offering equivalent access to copy the source code from the same place counts as distribution of the source code, even though third parties are not compelled to copy the source along with the object code.

4. You may not copy, modify, sublicense, or distribute the Program except as expressly provided under this License. Any attempt otherwise to copy, modify, sublicense or distribute the Program is void, and will automatically terminate your rights under this License. However, parties who have received copies, or rights, from you under this License will not have their licenses terminated so long as such parties remain in full compliance.

5. You are not required to accept this License, since you have not signed it. However, nothing else grants you permission to modify or distribute the Program or its derivative works. These actions are prohibited by law if you do not accept this License. Therefore, by modifying or distributing the Program (or any work based on the Program), you indicate your acceptance of this License to do so, and all its terms and conditions for copying, distributing or modifying the Program or works based on it.

6. Each time you redistribute the Program (or any work based on the Program), the recipient automatically receives a license from the original licensor to copy, distribute or modify the Program subject to these terms and conditions. You may not impose any further restrictions on the recipients' exercise of the rights granted herein. You are not responsible for enforcing compliance by third parties to this License.

7. If, as a consequence of a court judgment or allegation of patent infringement or for any other reason (not limited to patent issues), conditions are imposed on you (whether by court order, agreement or otherwise) that contradict the conditions of this License, they do not excuse you from the conditions of this License. If you cannot distribute so as to satisfy simultaneously your obligations under this License and any other pertinent obligations, then as a consequence you may not distribute the Program at all. For example, if a patent license would not permit royalty-free redistribution of the Program by all those who receive copies directly or indirectly through you, then the only way you could satisfy both it and this License would be to refrain entirely from distribution of the Program.

If any portion of this section is held invalid or unenforceable under any particular circumstance, the balance of the section is intended to apply and the section as a whole is intended to apply in other circumstances.

It is not the purpose of this section to induce you to infringe any patents or other property right claims or to contest validity of any such claims; this section has the sole purpose of protecting the integrity of the free software distribution system, which is implemented by public license practices. Many people have made generous contributions to the wide range of software distributed through that system in reliance on consistent application of that system; it is up to the author/donor to decide if he or she is willing to distribute software through any other system and a licensee cannot impose that choice.

This section is intended to make thoroughly clear what is believed to be a consequence of the rest of this License.

8. If the distribution and/or use of the Program is restricted in certain countries either by patents or by copyrighted interfaces, the original copyright holder who places the Program under this License may add an explicit geographical distribution limitation excluding those countries, so that distribution is permitted only in or among countries not thus excluded. In such case, this License incorporates the limitation as if written in the body of this License.

9. The Free Software Foundation may publish revised and/or new versions of the General Public License from time to time. Such new versions will be similar in spirit to the present version, but may differ in detail to address new problems or concerns.

Each version is given a distinguishing version number. If the Program specifies a version number of this License which applies to it and "any later version", you have the option of following the terms and conditions either of that version or of any later version published by the Free Software Foundation. If the Program does not specify a version number of this License, you may choose any version ever published by the Free Software Foundation.

10. If you wish to incorporate parts of the Program into other free programs whose distribution conditions are different, write to the author to ask for permission. For software which is copyrighted by the Free Software Foundation, write to the Free Software Foundation; we sometimes make exceptions for this. Our decision will be guided by the two goals of preserving the free status of all derivatives of our free software and of promoting the sharing and reuse of software generally.

NO WARRANTY

11. BECAUSE THE PROGRAM IS LICENSED FREE OF CHARGE, THERE IS NO WARRANTY FOR THE PROGRAM, TO THE EXTENT PERMITTED BY APPLICABLE LAW. EXCEPT WHEN OTHERWISE STATED IN WRITING THE COPYRIGHT HOLDERS AND/OR OTHER PARTIES PROVIDE THE PROGRAM "AS IS" WITHOUT WARRANTY OF ANY KIND, EITHER EXPRESSED OR IMPLIED, INCLUDING, BUT NOT LIMITED TO, THE IMPLIED WARRANTIES OF MERCHANTABILITY AND FITNESS FOR A PARTICULAR PURPOSE. THE ENTIRE RISK AS TO THE QUALITY AND PERFORMANCE OF THE PROGRAM IS WITH YOU. SHOULD THE PROGRAM PROVE DEFECTIVE, YOU ASSUME THE COST OF ALL NECESSARY SERVICING, REPAIR OR CORRECTION.

12. IN NO EVENT UNLESS REQUIRED BY APPLICABLE LAW OR AGREED TO IN WRITING WILL ANY COPYRIGHT HOLDER, OR ANY OTHER PARTY WHO MAY MODIFY AND/OR REDISTRIBUTE THE PROGRAM AS PERMITTED ABOVE, BE LIABLE TO YOU FOR DAMAGES, INCLUDING ANY GENERAL, SPECIAL, INCIDENTAL OR CONSEQUENTIAL DAMAGES ARISING OUT OF THE USE OR INABILITY TO USE THE PROGRAM (INCLUDING BUT NOT LIMITED TO LOSS OF DATA OR DATA BEING RENDERED INACCURATE OR LOSSES SUSTAINED BY YOU OR THIRD PARTIES OR A FAILURE OF THE PROGRAM TO OPERATE WITH ANY OTHER PROGRAMS), EVEN IF SUCH HOLDER OR OTHER PARTY HAS BEEN ADVISED OF THE POSSIBILITY OF SUCH DAMAGES.

END OF TERMS AND CONDITIONS

How to Apply These Terms to Your New Programs

If you develop a new program, and you want it to be of the greatest possible use to the public, the best way to achieve this is to make it free software which everyone can redistribute and change under these terms.

To do so, attach the following notices to the program. It is safest to attach them to the start of each source file to most effectively convey the exclusion of warranty; and each file should have at least the "copyright" line and a pointer to where the full notice is found.

> *one line to give the program's name and an idea of what it does.*
> *Copyright (C) yyyy name of author*

> This program is free software; you can redistribute it and/or
> modify it under the terms of the GNU General Public License
> as published by the Free Software Foundation; either version 2
> of the License, or (at your option) any later version.

> This program is distributed in the hope that it will be useful,
> but WITHOUT ANY WARRANTY; without even the implied warranty of

MERCHANTABILITY or FITNESS FOR A PARTICULAR PURPOSE.
See the GNU General Public License for more details.

You should have received a copy of the GNU General Public License
along with this program; if not, write to the Free Software
Foundation, Inc., 59 Temple Place - Suite 330, Boston, MA 02111-1307, USA.

Also add information on how to contact you by electronic and paper mail.

If the program is interactive, make it output a short notice like this when it starts in an interactive mode:

Gnomovision version 69, Copyright (C) year name of author
Gnomovision comes with ABSOLUTELY NO WARRANTY; for details
type `show w'. This is free software, and you are welcome
to redistribute it under certain conditions; type `show c'
for details.

The hypothetical commands `show w' and `show c' should show the appropriate parts of the General Public License. Of course, the commands you use may be called something other than `show w' and `show c'; they could even be mouse-clicks or menu items--whatever suits your program.

You should also get your employer (if you work as a programmer) or your school, if any, to sign a "copyright disclaimer" for the program, if necessary. Here is a sample; alter the names:

Yoyodyne, Inc., hereby disclaims all copyright
interest in the program `Gnomovision'
(which makes passes at compilers) written
by James Hacker.

signature of Ty Coon, 1 April 1989
Ty Coon, President of Vice

This General Public License does not permit incorporating your program into proprietary programs. If your program is a subroutine library, you may consider it more useful to permit linking proprietary applications with the library. If this is what you want to do, use the GNU Library General Public License instead of this License.

jGRASP™ License Agreement

Software License for jGRASP Version 1.7.0
Copyright 1999-2004 Auburn University

Section 1. License Grant.
Auburn University grants to you a non-exclusive and non-transferable license to use jGRASP and the associated documentation provided in jgrasp/help, collectively "jGRASP". jGRASP may be installed for use on a single computer or on a local area network. The "wedge" source code provided in the jgrasp/src directory is free of license restrictions. It may be used or modified for any purpose. jGRASP is a Trademark of Auburn University.

Section 2. Restrictions
Distribution of jGRASP is not permitted without written permission (see Supplements), except that it may be distributed internally within a single organization. Distribution of components of jGRASP separately from the whole is not permitted, except that the complete associated documentation provided in jgrasp/help may be distributed separately. Reverse engineering of jGRASP is not permitted. Any use of image files, icons, or executable components of jGRASP separately from the whole is prohibited.

Section 3. Disclaimer of Warranty
jGRASP is licensed "as is". There are no express or implied warranties, including, but not limited to, the implied warranties of merchantability and fitness for a particular purpose. Auburn University makes no warranty with respect to the accuracy or completeness of information obtained through the use of this program. Auburn University does not warrant that jGRASP will meet all of your requirements or that its

operation will be uninterrupted or error free or that any defect within jGRASP will be corrected. No oral or written information, representation, or advice given by Auburn University or an authorized representative of Auburn University shall create a warranty. Auburn University and its agents shall in no event be held liable to the user for any damages, including direct, indirect, incidental, or consequential damages, lost profits, lost savings, or other such damages arising out of the installation, use, improper use, or inability to use jGRASP, even if Auburn University has been advised of the possibility of such damages, or any claim by any other person or entity related thereto.

Supplements

Distribution for Educational Purposes - Publishers may distribute the jGRASP software and the jGRASP Handbook (Tutorials and Reference) on CDs that accompany their textbooks provided that (1) the title "jGRASP(TM) 1.7.0 copyright 1999-2004 Auburn University" is included on each CD label, (2) descriptions of the CD indicate that jGRASP is included on the CD, and (3) a list of the textbooks that include jGRASP is provided to Auburn University (crossATengDOTauburnDOTedu). Permission to distribute jGRASP for educational purposes covers all CDs created prior to December 31, 2004 for inclusion in textbooks. While it is anticipated that distribution of jGRASP for educational purposes will remain royalty free, this supplement of the jGRASP license will be re-evaluated on an annual basis.

For additional information, contact James H. Cross II, Computer Science and Software Engineering, 107 Dunstan Hall, Auburn University, AL 36849 (334-844-6315, crossATengDOTauburnDOTedu).

NetBeans™ License Agreement

Netbeans IDE and Netbeans Platform are based on software from netbeans.org, developed under Sun Public License (SPL). For more information visit www.netbeans.org.

SUN PUBLIC LICENSE
SUN PUBLIC LICENSE Version 1.0

1.0.1. "Commercial Use" means distribution or otherwise making the Covered Code available to a third party.

1.1. "Contributor" means each entity that creates or contributes to the creation of Modifications.

1.2. "Contributor Version" means the combination of the Original Code, prior Modifications used by a Contributor, and the Modifications made by that particular Contributor.

1.3. "Covered Code" means the Original Code or Modifications or the combination of the Original Code and Modifications, in each case including portions thereof and corresponding documentation released with the source code.

1.4. "Electronic Distribution Mechanism" means a mechanism generally accepted in the software development community for the electronic transfer of data.

1.5. "Executable" means Covered Code in any form other than Source Code.

1.6. "Initial Developer" means the individual or entity identified as the Initial Developer in the Source Code notice required by Exhibit A.

1.7. "Larger Work" means a work which combines Covered Code or portions thereof with code not governed by the terms of this License.

1.8. "License" means this document.

1.8.1. "Licensable" means having the right to grant, to the maximum extent possible, whether at the time of the initial grant or subsequently acquired, any and all of the rights conveyed herein.

1.9. "Modifications" means any addition to or deletion from the substance or structure of either the Original Code or any previous Modifications. When Covered Code is released as a series of files, a Modification is:

A. Any addition to or deletion from the contents of a file containing Original Code or previous Modifications.

B. Any new file that contains any part of the Original Code or previous Modifications.

1.10. "Original Code" means Source Code of computer software code which is described in the Source Code notice required by Exhibit A as Original Code, and which, at the time of its release under this License is not already Covered Code governed by this License.

1.10.1. "Patent Claims" means any patent claim(s), now owned or hereafter acquired, including without limitation, method, process, and apparatus claims, in any patent Licensable by grantor.

1.11. "Source Code" means the preferred form of the Covered Code for making modifications to it, including all modules it contains, plus any associated documentation, interface definition files, scripts used to control compilation and installation of an Executable, or source code differential comparisons against either the Original Code or another well known, available Covered Code of the Contributor's choice. The Source Code can be in a compressed or archival form, provided the appropriate decompression or de-archiving software is widely available for no charge.

1.12. "You" (or "Your") means an individual or a legal entity exercising rights under, and complying with all of the terms of, this License or a future version of this License issued under Section 6.1. For legal entities, "You" includes any entity which controls, is controlled by, or is under common control with You. For purposes of this definition, "control" means (a) the power, direct or indirect, to cause the direction or management of such entity, whether by contract or otherwise, or (b) ownership of more than fifty percent (50%) of the outstanding shares or beneficial ownership of such entity.

2. Source Code License.

2.1 The Initial Developer Grant.

The Initial Developer hereby grants You a world-wide, royalty-free, non-exclusive license, subject to third party intellectual property claims:

(a) under intellectual property rights (other than patent or trademark) Licensable by Initial Developer to use, reproduce, modify, display, perform, sublicense and distribute the Original Code (or portions thereof) with or without Modifications, and/or as part of a Larger Work; and

(b) under Patent Claims infringed by the making, using or selling of Original Code, to make, have made, use, practice, sell, and offer for sale, and/or otherwise dispose of the Original Code (or portions thereof).

(c) the licenses granted in this Section 2.1(a) and (b) are effective on the date Initial Developer first distributes Original Code under the terms of this License.

(d) Notwithstanding Section 2.1(b) above, no patent license is granted: 1) for code that You delete from the Original Code; 2) separate from the Original Code; or 3) for infringements caused by: i) the modification of the Original Code or ii) the combination of the Original Code with other software or devices.

2.2. Contributor Grant.

Subject to third party intellectual property claims, each Contributor hereby grants You a world-wide, royalty-free, non-exclusive license

(a) under intellectual property rights (other than patent or trademark) Licensable by Contributor, to use, reproduce, modify, display, perform, sublicense and distribute the Modifications created by such Contributor (or portions thereof) either on an unmodified basis, with other Modifications, as Covered Code and/or as part of a Larger Work; and

(b) under Patent Claims infringed by the making, using, or selling of Modifications made by that Contributor either alone and/or in combination with its Contributor Version (or portions of such combination), to make, use, sell, offer for sale, have made, and/or otherwise dispose of: 1) Modifications made by that Contributor (or portions thereof); and 2) the combination of Modifications made by that Contributor with its Contributor Version (or portions of such combination).

(c) the licenses granted in Sections 2.2(a) and 2.2(b) are effective on the date Contributor first makes Commercial Use of the Covered Code.

(d) notwithstanding Section 2.2(b) above, no patent license is granted: 1) for any code that Contributor has deleted from the Contributor Version; 2) separate from the Contributor Version; 3) for infringements caused by: i) third party modifications of Contributor Version or ii) the combination of Modifications made by that Contributor with other software (except as part of the Contributor Version) or other devices; or 4) under Patent Claims infringed by Covered Code in the absence of Modifications made by that Contributor.

3. Distribution Obligations.

3.1. Application of License.

The Modifications which You create or to which You contribute are governed by the terms of this License, including without limitation Section 2.2. The Source Code version of Covered Code may be distributed only under the terms of this License or a future version of this License released under Section 6.1, and You must include a copy of this License with every copy of the Source Code You distribute. You may not offer or impose any terms on any Source Code version that alters or restricts the applicable version of this License or the recipients' rights hereunder. However, You may include an additional document offering the additional rights described in Section 3.5.

3.2. Availability of Source Code.

Any Modification which You create or to which You contribute must be made available in Source Code form under the terms of this License either on the same media as an Executable version or via an accepted Electronic Distribution Mechanism to anyone to whom you made an Executable version available; and if made available via Electronic Distribution Mechanism, must remain available for at least twelve (12) months after the date it initially became available, or at least six (6) months after a subsequent version of that particular Modification has been made available to such recipients. You are responsible for ensuring that the Source Code version remains available even if the Electronic Distribution Mechanism is maintained by a third party.

3.3. Description of Modifications.

You must cause all Covered Code to which You contribute to contain a file documenting the changes You made to create that Covered Code and the date of any change. You must include a prominent statement that the Modification is derived, directly or indirectly, from Original Code provided by the Initial Developer and including the name of the Initial Developer in (a) the Source Code, and (b) in any notice in an Executable version or related documentation in which You describe the origin or ownership of the Covered Code.

3.4. Intellectual Property Matters.

(a) Third Party Claims.

If Contributor has knowledge that a license under a third party's intellectual property rights is required to exercise the rights granted by such Contributor under Sections 2.1 or 2.2, Contributor must include a text file with the Source Code distribution titled "LEGAL" which describes the claim and the party making the claim in sufficient detail that a recipient will know whom to contact. If Contributor obtains such knowledge after the Modification is made available as described in Section 3.2, Contributor shall promptly modify the LEGAL file in all copies Contributor makes available thereafter and shall take other steps (such as notifying appropriate mailing lists or newsgroups) reasonably calculated to inform those who received the Covered Code that new knowledge has been obtained.

(b) Contributor APIs.

If Contributor's Modifications include an application programming interface ("API") and Contributor has knowledge of patent licenses which are reasonably necessary to implement that API, Contributor must also include this information in the LEGAL file.

(c) Representations.

Contributor represents that, except as disclosed pursuant to Section 3.4(a) above, Contributor believes that Contributor's Modifications are Contributor's original creation(s) and/or Contributor has sufficient rights to grant the rights conveyed by this License.

3.5. Required Notices.

You must duplicate the notice in Exhibit A in each file of the Source Code. If it is not possible to put such notice in a particular Source Code file due to its structure, then You must include such notice in a location (such as a relevant directory) where a user would be likely to look for such a notice. If You created one or more Modification(s) You may add your name as a Contributor to the notice described in Exhibit A. You must also duplicate this License in any documentation for the Source Code where You describe recipients' rights or ownership rights relating to Covered Code. You may choose to offer, and to charge a fee for, warranty, support, indemnity or liability obligations to one or more recipients of Covered Code. However, You may do so only on Your own behalf, and not on behalf of the Initial Developer or any Contributor. You must make it absolutely clear than any such warranty, support, indemnity or liability obligation is offered by You alone, and You hereby agree to indemnify the Initial Developer and every Contributor for any liability incurred by the Initial Developer or such Contributor as a result of warranty, support, indemnity or liability terms You offer.

3.6. Distribution of Executable Versions.

You may distribute Covered Code in Executable form only if therequirements of Section 3.1-3.5 have been met for that Covered Code,and if You include a notice stating that the Source Code version ofthe Covered Code is available under the terms of this License,including a description of how and where You have fulfilled theobligations of Section 3.2. The notice must be conspicuously includedin any notice in an Executable version, related documentation orcollateral in which You describe recipients' rights relating to theCovered Code. You may distribute the Executable version of CoveredCode or ownership rights under a license of Your choice, which maycontain terms different from this License, provided that You are incompliance with the terms of this License and that the license for theExecutable version does not attempt to limit or alter the recipient'srights in the Source Code version from the rights set forth in thisLicense. If You distribute the Executable version under a differentlicense You must make it absolutely clear that any terms which differfrom this License are offered by You alone, not by the InitialDeveloper or any Contributor. You hereby agree to indemnify theInitial Developer and every Contributor for any liability incurred bythe Initial Developer or such Contributor as a result of any suchterms You offer.

3.7. Larger Works.

You may create a Larger Work by combining Covered Code with other codenot governed by the terms of this License and distribute the LargerWork as a single product. In such a case, You must make sure therequirements of this License are fulfilled for the Covered Code.

4. Inability to Comply Due to Statute or Regulation.

If it is impossible for You to comply with any of the terms of thisLicense with respect to some or all of the Covered Code due tostatute, judicial order, or regulation then You must: (a) comply withthe terms of this License to the maximum extent possible; and (b)describe the limitations and the code they affect. Such descriptionmust be included in the LEGAL file described in Section 3.4 and mustbe included with all distributions of the Source Code. Except to theextent prohibited by statute or regulation, such description must besufficiently detailed for a recipient of ordinary skill to be able tounderstand it.

5. Application of this License.

This License applies to code to which the Initial Developer has attached the notice in Exhibit A and to related Covered Code.

6. Versions of the License.

6.1. New Versions.

Sun Microsystems, Inc. ("Sun") may publish revised and/or new versionsof the License from time to time. Each version will be given adistinguishing version number.

6.2. Effect of New Versions.

Once Covered Code has been published under a particular version of theLicense, You may always continue to use it under the terms of thatversion. You may also choose to use such Covered Code under the termsof any subsequent version of the License published by Sun. No oneother than Sun has the right to modify the terms applicable to CoveredCode created under this License.

6.3. Derivative Works.

If You create or use a modified version of this License (which you mayonly do in order to apply it to code which is not already Covered Codegoverned by this License), You must: (a) rename Your license so thatthe phrases "Sun," "Sun Public License," or "SPL" or any confusinglysimilar phrase do not appear in your license (except to note that yourlicense differs from this License) and (b) otherwise make it clearthat Your version of the license contains terms which differ from theSun Public License. (Filling in the name of the Initial Developer,Original Code or Contributor in the notice described in Exhibit Ashall not of themselves be deemed to be modifications of thisLicense.)

7. DISCLAIMER OF WARRANTY.

COVERED CODE IS PROVIDED UNDER THIS LICENSE ON AN "AS IS" BASIS,WITHOUT WARRANTY OF ANY KIND, EITHER EXPRESSED OR IMPLIED, INCLUDING,WITHOUT LIMITATION, WARRANTIES THAT THE COVERED CODE IS FREE OFDEFECTS, MER-CHANTABLE, FIT FOR A PARTICULAR PURPOSE OR NON-INFRINGING.THE ENTIRE RISK AS TO THE QUALITY AND PERFORMANCE OF THE COVERED CODEIS WITH YOU. SHOULD ANY COVERED CODE PROVE DEFECTIVE IN ANY RESPECT,YOU (NOT THE INITIAL DEVELOPER OR ANY OTHER CONTRIBUTOR) ASSUME THECOST OF ANY NECESSARY SERVICING, REPAIR OR CORRECTION. THIS DISCLAIMEROF WARRANTY CONSTITUTES AN ESSENTIAL PART OF THIS LICENSE. NO USE OFANY COVERED CODE IS AUTHORIZED HEREUNDER EXCEPT UNDER THIS DISCLAIMER.

8. TERMINATION.

8.1. This License and the rights granted hereunder will terminateautomatically if You fail to comply with terms herein and fail to curesuch breach within 30 days of becoming aware of the breach. Allsubli-censes to the Covered Code which are properly granted shallsurvive any termination of this License. Pro-visions which, by theirnature, must remain in effect beyond the termination of this Licenseshall survive.

8.2. If You initiate litigation by asserting a patent infringementclaim (excluding declaratory judg-ment actions) against Initial Developeror a Contributor (the Initial Developer or Contributor against whomYou file such action is referred to as "Participant") alleging that:

(a) such Participant's Contributor Version directly or indirectlyinfringes any patent, then any and all rights granted by suchParticipant to You under Sections 2.1 and/or 2.2 of this Licenseshall, upon 60 days notice from Participant terminate prospectively,unless if within 60 days after receipt of notice You either: (i)agree in writing to pay Participant a mutually agreeable reasonableroyalty for Your past and future use of Modifications made by suchParticipant, or (ii) withdraw Your litigation claim with respect tothe Contributor Version against such Participant. If within 60 daysof notice, a reasonable royalty and payment arrangement are notmutually agreed upon in writing by the parties or the litigation claimis not withdrawn, the rights granted by Participant to You underSections 2.1 and/or 2.2 automatically terminate at the expiration ofthe 60 day notice period specified above.

(b) any software, hardware, or device, other than such Participant'sContributor Version, directly or indirectly infringes any patent, thenany rights granted to You by such Participant under Sections 2.1(b)and 2.2(b) are revoked effective as of the date You first made, used,sold, distributed, or had made, Modifications made by thatParticipant.

8.3. If You assert a patent infringement claim against Participantalleging that such Participant's Contributor Version directly orindirectly infringes any patent where such claim is resolved (such asby license or settlement) prior to the initiation of patentinfringement litigation, then the reasonable value of the licensesgranted by such Participant under Sections 2.1 or 2.2 shall be takeninto account in determining the amount or value of any payment orlicense.

8.4. In the event of termination under Sections 8.1 or 8.2 above, allend user license agreements (excluding distributors and resellers)which have been validly granted by You or any distributor hereunderprior to termination shall survive termination.

9. LIMITATION OF LIABILITY.

UNDER NO CIRCUMSTANCES AND UNDER NO LEGAL THEORY, WHETHER TORT(INCLUDING NEGLIGENCE), CONTRACT, OR OTHERWISE, SHALL YOU, THE INITIALDEVELOPER, ANY OTHER CONTRIBUTOR, OR ANY DISTRIBUTOR OF COVERED CODE,OR ANY SUPPLIER OF ANY OF SUCH PARTIES, BE LIABLE TO ANY PERSON FORANY INDIRECT, SPECIAL, INCIDENTAL, OR CONSEQUENTIAL DAMAGES OF ANYCHARACTER INCLUDING, WITHOUT LIMITATION, DAMAGES FOR LOSS OF GOODWILL,WORK STOPPAGE, COMPUTER FAILURE OR MALFUNCTION, OR ANY AND ALL OTHERCOMMERCIAL DAMAGES OR LOSSES, EVEN IF SUCH PARTY SHALL HAVE BEENINFORMED OF THE POSSIBILITY OF SUCH DAMAGES. THIS LIMITATION OFLIABILITY SHALL NOT APPLY TO LIABILITY FOR DEATH OR PERSONAL INJURYRESULTING FROM SUCH PARTY'S NEGLIGENCE TO THE EXTENT APPLICABLE LAWPROHIBITS SUCH LIMITATION. SOME JURISDICTIONS DO NOT ALLOW THEEXCLUSION OR LIMITATION OF INCIDENTAL OR CONSEQUENTIAL DAMAGES, SOTHIS EXCLUSION AND LIMITATION MAY NOT APPLY TO YOU.

10. U.S. GOVERNMENT END USERS.

The Covered Code is a "commercial item," as that term is defined in 48C.F.R. 2.101 (Oct. 1995), consisting of "commercial computer software"and "commercial computer software documentation," as such terms areused in 48 C.F.R. 12.212 (Sept. 1995). Consistent with 48 C.F.R.12.212 and 48 C.F.R. 227.7202-1 through 227.7202-4 (June 1995), allU.S. Government End Users acquire Covered Code with only those rightsset forth herein.

11. MISCELLANEOUS.

This License represents the complete agreement concerning subjectmatter hereof. If any provision of this License is held to beunenforceable, such provision shall be reformed only to the extentnecessary to make it enforceable. This License shall be governed byCalifornia law provisions (except to the extent applicable law, ifany, provides otherwise), excluding its conflict-of-law provisions.With respect to disputes in which at least one party is a citizen of,or an entity chartered or registered to do business in the UnitedStates of America, any litigation relating to this License shall besubject to the jurisdiction of the Federal Courts of the NorthernDistrict of California, with venue lying in Santa Clara County,California, with the losing party responsible for costs, includingwithout limitation, court costs and reasonable attorneys' fees andexpenses. The application of the United Nations Convention onContracts for the International Sale of Goods is expressly excluded.Any law or regulation which provides that the language of a contractshall be construed against the drafter shall not apply to thisLicense.

12. RESPONSIBILITY FOR CLAIMS.

As between Initial Developer and the Contributors, each party isresponsible for claims and damages arising, directly or indirectly,out of its utilization of rights under this License and You agree towork with Initial Developer and Contributors to distribute suchresponsibility on an equitable basis. Nothing herein is intended orshall be deemed to constitute any admission of liability.

13. MULTIPLE-LICENSED CODE.

Initial Developer may designate portions of the Covered Code as"Multiple-Licensed". "Multiple-Licensed" means that the InitialDeveloper permits you to utilize portions of the Covered Code underYour choice of the alternative licenses, if any, specified by theInitial Developer in the file described in Exhibit A.

Exhibit A -Sun Public License Notice.
The contents of this file are subject to the Sun Public LicenseVersion 1.0 (the "License"); you may not use this file except incompliance with the License. A copy of the License is available athttp://www.sun.com/
The Original Code is _____. The Initial Developer of theOriginal Code is _____.
Portions created by _____ are Copyright(C)_____. All Rights Reserved.
Contributor(s): _____.
Alternatively, the contents of this file may be used under the termsof the _____ license (the "[___] License"), in which case theprovisions of [_____] License are applicable instead of those above.If you wish to allow use of your version of this file only under theterms of the [_____] License and not to allow others to use yourversion of this file under the SPL, indicate your decision by deletingthe provisions above and replace them with the notice and otherprovisions required by the [___] License. If you do not delete theprovisions above, a recipient may use your version of this file undereither the SPL or the [___] License."
[NOTE: The text of this Exhibit A may differ slightly from the text ofthe notices in the Source Code files of the Original Code. You shoulduse the text of this Exhibit A rather than the text found in theOriginal Code Source Code for Your Modifications.]

MySQL® Open Source License

Our software is 100% GPL (General Public License); if yours is 100% GPL compliant, then you have no obligation to pay us for the licenses. This is a great opportunity for the open source community and those of you who are developing open source software.
   The formal terms of the GPL license can be found in the GNU General Public License section of the MySQL Reference Manual. Please note that the General Public License can be restrictive, so if it doesn't meet your needs, you are better served by our Commercial License.
   Specifically:
   • MySQL is free use for those who are 100% GPL. If your application is licensed under GPL or compatible OSI license approved by MySQL AB, you are free to ship any GPL software of MySQL AB with your application ('application' means any type of software application, system, tool or utility). You do not need a separate signed agreement with MySQL AB, because the GPL license is sufficient. We do, however, recommend you contact us as there usually are good opportunities for partnership and co-marketing.
   • Under the Open Source License, you must release the complete source code for the application that is built on MySQL. You do not need to release the source code for components that are generally installed on the operating system on which your application runs, such as system header files or libraries.
   • Free use for those who never copy, modify or distribute. As long as you never distribute (internally or externally) the MySQL Software in any way, you are free to use it for powering your application, irrespective of whether your application is under GPL license or not.
   • You are allowed to modify MySQL Software source code any way you like as long as the distributed derivative work is licensed under the GPL as well.
   • You are allowed to copy MySQL binaries and source code, but when you do so, the copies will fall under the GPL license.
   • Optional GPL License Exception for PHP. As a special exception, MySQL AB gives permission to distribute derivative works that are formed with GPL-licensed MySQL software and with software licensed under version 3.0 of the PHP license. You must obey the GNU General Public License in all respects for all of the code used other than code licensed under version 3.0 of the PHP license.
   • FOSS Exception. We have created a which enables Free and Open Source software ("FOSS") to be able to include the GPL-licensed MySQL client libraries despite the fact that not all open source licenses are compatible with the GPL.

Non-Profits, Academic Institutions, and Private Individuals
If you represent a non-profit organization or an academic institution, we recommend you publish your application as an open source / free software project using the GPL license. Thereby, you are free to use MySQL software free of charge under the GPL license. We believe that if you have strong reasons to not publish your application in accordance with the GPL, you should purchase commercial licenses. Note that non-profits can apply for free commercial licenses, which will be liberally granted.

If you are a private individual you are free to use MySQL software for your personal applications as long as you do not distribute them. If you distribute them, you must make a decision between the Commercial License and the GPL.

Please note that even if you ship a free demo version of your own application, the above rules apply.

Recommendations

Please note that MySQL AB can only give advice on which license is right for you. The final judgment, of course can be made only by a court of law. With that said, we recommend the commercial license to all commercial and government organizations. This frees you from the broad and strict requirements of the GPL license.

To all free software enthusiasts we recommend our products under the GPL license. We believe that MySQL AB is one of the world's largest companies that offers all its software under the GPL license.

To anyone in doubt, we recommend the commercial license. It is never wrong. Thanks to our cost-effective way of producing software, we are able to sell our commercial licenses at prices well under the industry average.

Older Versions

Note that some older versions of the MySQL database server (prior to 3.23.19) are using the . See the documentation for the specific version for more information.

When in Doubt

If you have any questions on MySQL licensing, feel free to contact us:
USA and Canada: + 1-425-743-5635 or
Germany, Austria, and Switzerland: +49-(0)7022-9256-30 or
Scandinavia (Sweden, Norway, and Denmark): +46 730 234 111
France: +33 (0)1.43.077.099 or
Finland: +358 (0)9 2517 5553
Spain, Portugal, and Latin America: +1 (425) 373-3434 or

OSI = Open Source Initiative,
 GPL = GNU General Public License,
Version 4.1, 12 March 2004

G GNU General Public License

Version 2, June 1991
Copyright © 1989, 1991 Free Software Foundation, Inc.
59 Temple Place - Suite 330, Boston, MA 02111-1307, USA

Everyone is permitted to copy and distribute verbatim copies of this license document, but changing it is not allowed.

23.4 PreambleThe licenses for most software are designed to take away your freedom to share and change it. By contrast, the GNU General Public License is intended to guarantee your freedom to share and change free software--to make sure the software is free for all its users. This General Public License applies to most of the Free Software Foundation's software and to any other program whose authors commit to using it. (Some other Free Software Foundation software is covered by the GNU Library General Public License instead.) You can apply it to your programs, too.

When we speak of free software, we are referring to freedom, not price. Our General Public Licenses are designed to make sure that you have the freedom to distribute copies of free software (and charge for this service if you wish), that you receive source code or can get it if you want it, that you can change the software or use pieces of it in new free programs; and that you know you can do these things.

To protect your rights, we need to make restrictions that forbid anyone to deny you these rights or to ask you to surrender the rights. These restrictions translate to certain responsibilities for you if you distribute copies of the software, or if you modify it.

For example, if you distribute copies of such a program, whether gratis or for a fee, you must give the recipients all the rights that you have. You must make sure that they, too, receive or can get the source code. And you must show them these terms so they know their rights.

We protect your rights with two steps: (1) copyright the software, and (2) offer you this license which gives you legal permission to copy, distribute and/or modify the software.

Also, for each author's protection and ours, we want to make certain that everyone understands that there is no warranty for this free software. If the software is modified by someone else and passed on, we want its recipients to know that what they have is not the original, so that any problems introduced by others will not reflect on the original authors' reputations.

Finally, any free program is threatened constantly by software patents. We wish to avoid the danger that redistributors of a free program will individually obtain patent licenses, in effect making the program proprietary. To prevent this, we have made it clear that any patent must be licensed for everyone's free use or not licensed at all.

The precise terms and conditions for copying, distribution and modification follow.

23.5 TERMS AND CONDITIONS FOR COPYING, DISTRIBUTION AND MODIFICATION

1. This License applies to any program or other work which contains a notice placed by the copyright holder saying it may be distributed under the terms of this General Public License. The ``Program'', below, refers to any such program or work, and a ``work based on the Program'' means either the Program or any derivative work under copyright law: that is to say, a work containing the Program or a portion of it, either verbatim or with modifications and/or translated into another language. (Hereinafter, translation is included without limitation in the term ``modification''.) Each licensee is addressed as ``you''. Activities other than copying, distribution and modification are not covered by this License; they are outside its scope. The act of running the Program is not restricted, and the output from the Program is covered only if its contents constitute a work based on the Program (independent of having been made by running the Program). Whether that is true depends on what the Program does.

2. You may copy and distribute verbatim copies of the Program's source code as you receive it, in any medium, provided that you conspicuously and appropriately publish on each copy an appropriate copyright notice and disclaimer of warranty; keep intact all the notices that refer to this License and to the absence of any warranty; and give any other recipients of the Program a copy of this License along with the Program. You may charge a fee for the physical act of transferring a copy, and you may at your option offer warranty protection in exchange for a fee.

3. You may modify your copy or copies of the Program or any portion of it, thus forming a work based on the Program, and copy and distribute such modifications or work under the terms of Section 1 above, provided that you also meet all of these conditions:

1. You must cause the modified files to carry prominent notices stating that you changed the files and the date of any change.

2. You must cause any work that you distribute or publish, that in whole or in part contains or is derived from the Program or any part thereof, to be licensed as a whole at no charge to all third parties under the terms of this License.

3. If the modified program normally reads commands interactively when run, you must cause it, when started running for such interactive use in the most ordinary way, to print or display an announcement including an appropriate copyright notice and a notice that there is no warranty (or else, saying that you provide a warranty) and that users may redistribute the program under these conditions, and telling the user how to view a copy of this License. (Exception: if the Program itself is interactive but does not normally print such an announcement, your work based on the Program is not required to print an announcement.)

These requirements apply to the modified work as a whole. If identifiable sections of that work are not derived from the Program, and can be reasonably considered independent and separate works in themselves, then this License, and its terms, do not apply to those sections when you distribute them as separate works. But when you distribute the same sections as part of a whole which is a work based on the Program, the distribution of the whole must be on the terms of this License, whose permissions for other licensees extend to the entire whole, and thus to each and every part regardless of who wrote it. Thus, it is not the intent of this section to claim rights or contest your rights to work written entirely by you; rather, the intent is to exercise the right to control the distribution of derivative or collective works based on the Program. In addition, mere aggregation of another work not based on the Program with the Program (or with a work based on the Program) on a volume of a storage or distribution medium does not bring the other work under the scope of this License.

4. You may copy and distribute the Program (or a work based on it, under Section 2) in object code or executable form under the terms of Sections 1 and 2 above provided that you also do one of the following:

1. Accompany it with the complete corresponding machine-readable source code, which must be distributed under the terms of Sections 1 and 2 above on a medium customarily used for software interchange; or,

2. Accompany it with a written offer, valid for at least three years, to give any third-party, for a charge no more than your cost of physically performing source distribution, a complete machine-readable copy of the corresponding source code, to be distributed under the terms of Sections 1 and 2 above on a medium customarily used for software interchange; or,

3.   Accompany it with the information you received as to the offer to distribute corresponding source code. (This alternative is allowed only for noncommercial distribution and only if you received the program in object code or executable form with such an offer, in accord with Subsection b above.)

The source code for a work means the preferred form of the work for making modifications to it. For an executable work, complete source code means all the source code for all modules it contains, plus any associated interface definition files, plus the scripts used to control compilation and installation of the executable. However, as a special exception, the source code distributed need not include anything that is normally distributed (in either source or binary form) with the major components (compiler, kernel, and so on) of the operating system on which the executable runs, unless that component itself accompanies the executable. If distribution of executable or object code is made by offering access to copy from a designated place, then offering equivalent access to copy the source code from the same place counts as distribution of the source code, even though third parties are not compelled to copy the source along with the object code.

5.   You may not copy, modify, sublicense, or distribute the Program except as expressly provided under this License. Any attempt otherwise to copy, modify, sublicense or distribute the Program is void, and will automatically terminate your rights under this License. However, parties who have received copies, or rights, from you under this License will not have their licenses terminated so long as such parties remain in full compliance.

6.   You are not required to accept this License, since you have not signed it. However, nothing else grants you permission to modify or distribute the Program or its derivative works. These actions are prohibited by law if you do not accept this License. Therefore, by modifying or distributing the Program (or any work based on the Program), you indicate your acceptance of this License to do so, and all its terms and conditions for copying, distributing or modifying the Program or works based on it.

7.   Each time you redistribute the Program (or any work based on the Program), the recipient automatically receives a license from the original licensor to copy, distribute or modify the Program subject to these terms and conditions. You may not impose any further restrictions on the recipients' exercise of the rights granted herein. You are not responsible for enforcing compliance by third parties to this License.

8.   If, as a consequence of a court judgment or allegation of patent infringement or for any other reason (not limited to patent issues), conditions are imposed on you (whether by court order, agreement or otherwise) that contradict the conditions of this License, they do not excuse you from the conditions of this License. If you cannot distribute so as to satisfy simultaneously your obligations under this License and any other pertinent obligations, then as a consequence you may not distribute the Program at all. For example, if a patent license would not permit royalty-free redistribution of the Program by all those who receive copies directly or indirectly through you, then the only way you could satisfy both it and this License would be to refrain entirely from distribution of the Program. If any portion of this section is held invalid or unenforceable under any particular circumstance, the balance of the section is intended to apply and the section as a whole is intended to apply in other circumstances. It is not the purpose of this section to induce you to infringe any patents or other property right claims or to contest validity of any such claims; this section has the sole purpose of protecting the integrity of the free software distribution system, which is implemented by public license practices. Many people have made generous contributions to the wide range of software distributed through that system in reliance on consistent application of that system; it is up to the author/donor to decide if he or she is willing to distribute software through any other system and a licensee cannot impose that choice. This section is intended to make thoroughly clear what is believed to be a consequence of the rest of this License.

9.   If the distribution and/or use of the Program is restricted in certain countries either by patents or by copyrighted interfaces, the original copyright holder who places the Program under this License may add an explicit geographical distribution limitation excluding those countries, so that distribution is permitted only in or among countries not thus excluded. In such case, this License incorporates the limitation as if written in the body of this License.

10.   The Free Software Foundation may publish revised and/or new versions of the General Public License from time to time. Such new versions will be similar in spirit to the present version, but may differ in detail to address new problems or concerns. Each version is given a distinguishing version number. If the Program specifies a version number of this License which applies to it and ``any later version'', you have the option of following the terms and conditions either of that version or of any later version published by the Free Software Foundation. If the Program does not specify a version number of this License, you may choose any version ever published by the Free Software Foundation.

11.   If you wish to incorporate parts of the Program into other free programs whose distribution conditions are different, write to the author to ask for permission. For software which is copyrighted by the Free Software Foundation, write to the Free Software Foundation; we sometimes make exceptions for this. Our decision will be guided by the two goals of preserving the free status of all derivatives of our free software and of promoting the sharing and reuse of software generally.

23.6 NO WARRANTY

12.   BECAUSE THE PROGRAM IS LICENSED FREE OF CHARGE, THERE IS NO WAR-RANTY FOR THE PROGRAM, TO THE EXTENT PERMITTED BY APPLICABLE LAW. EXCEPT WHEN OTHERWISE STATED IN WRITING THE COPYRIGHT HOLDERS AND/OR OTHER PARTIES PROVIDE THE PROGRAM ``AS IS'' WITHOUT WARRANTY OF ANY KIND, EITHER EXPRESSED OR IMPLIED, INCLUDING, BUT NOT LIMITED TO, THE IMPLIED WARRANTIES OF MERCHANTABILITY AND FITNESS FOR A PARTICULAR PUR-POSE. THE ENTIRE RISK AS TO THE QUALITY AND PERFORMANCE OF THE PROGRAM IS WITH YOU. SHOULD THE PROGRAM PROVE DEFECTIVE, YOU ASSUME THE COST OF ALL NECESSARY SERVICING, REPAIR OR CORRECTION.

13.   IN NO EVENT UNLESS REQUIRED BY APPLICABLE LAW OR AGREED TO IN WRITING WILL ANY COPYRIGHT HOLDER, OR ANY OTHER PARTY WHO MAY MODIFY AND/OR REDISTRIBUTE THE PROGRAM AS PERMITTED ABOVE, BE LIABLE TO YOU FOR DAMAGES, INCLUDING ANY GENERAL, SPECIAL, INCIDENTAL OR CONSEQUEN-TIAL DAMAGES ARISING OUT OF THE USE OR INABILITY TO USE THE PROGRAM (INCLUDING BUT NOT LIMITED TO LOSS OF DATA OR DATA BEING RENDERED INAC-CURATE OR LOSSES SUSTAINED BY YOU OR THIRD PARTIES OR A FAILURE OF THE PROGRAM TO OPERATE WITH ANY OTHER PROGRAMS), EVEN IF SUCH HOLDER OR OTHER PARTY HAS BEEN ADVISED OF THE POSSIBILITY OF SUCH DAMAGES.

23.7 END OF TERMS AND CONDITIONS

23.8 How to Apply These Terms to Your New Programs

If you develop a new program, and you want it to be of the greatest possible use to the public, the best way to achieve this is to make it free software which everyone can redistribute and change under these terms.

To do so, attach the following notices to the program. It is safest to attach them to the start of each source file to most effectively convey the exclusion of warranty; and each file should have at least the ``copyright'' line and a pointer to where the full notice is found.

one line to give the program's name and a brief idea of what it does.
Copyright (C) yyyy   name of author

This program is free software; you can redistribute it and/or modify
it under the terms of the GNU General Public License as published by
the Free Software Foundation; either version 2 of the License, or
(at your option) any later version.

This program is distributed in the hope that it will be useful,
but WITHOUT ANY WARRANTY; without even the implied warranty of
MERCHANTABILITY or FITNESS FOR A PARTICULAR PURPOSE. See the
GNU General Public License for more details.

You should have received a copy of the GNU General Public License
along with this program; if not, write to the Free Software
Foundation, Inc., 59 Temple Place - Suite 330, Boston, MA 02111-1307, USA.

Also add information on how to contact you by electronic and paper mail.
If the program is interactive, make it output a short notice like this when it starts in an interactive mode:

Gnomovision version 69, Copyright (C) 19 yy name of author
Gnomovision comes with ABSOLUTELY NO WARRANTY; for details type `show w'.
This is free software, and you are welcome to redistribute it
under certain conditions; type `show c' for details.

The hypothetical commands `show w' and `show c' should show the appropriate parts of the General Public License. Of course, the commands you use may be called something other than `show w' and `show c'; they could even be mouse-clicks or menu items--whatever suits your program.

You should also get your employer (if you work as a programmer) or your school, if any, to sign a ``copyright disclaimer'' for the program, if necessary. Here is a sample; alter the names:

Yoyodyne, Inc., hereby disclaims all copyright interest in the program

`Gnomovision' (which makes passes at compilers) written by James Hacker.

signature of Ty Coon , 1 April 1989
Ty Coon, President of Vice

This General Public License does not permit incorporating your program into proprietary programs. If your program is a subroutine library, you may consider it more useful to permit linking proprietary applications with the library. If this is what you want to do, use the GNU Library General Public License instead of this License.

The DEITEL® Suite of Products...

HOW TO PROGRAM BOOKS

C++ How to Program Fourth Edition

BOOK / CD-ROM

©2003, 1400 pp., paper
(0-13-038474-7)

Designed for beginning through intermediate courses, this comprehensive, practical introduction to C++ includes hundreds of hands-on exercises, and uses 267 *LIVE-CODE* programs to demonstrate C++'s powerful capabilities. This edition includes a new chapter—Web Programming with CGI—that provides everything readers need to begin developing their own Web-based applications that will run on the Internet! The book provides a carefully designed sequence of examples that introduces inheritance and polymorphism and helps students understand the motivation and implementation of these key object-oriented programming concepts. In addition, the OOD/UML case study has been upgraded to UML 1.4 and all flowcharts and inheritance diagrams in the text have been converted to UML diagrams. The book presents an early introduction to strings and arrays as objects using standard C++ classes **string** and **vector**. The book also covers key concepts and techniques standard C++ developers need to master, including control statements, functions, arrays, pointers and strings, classes and data abstraction, operator overloading, inheritance, virtual functions, polymorphism, I/O, templates, exception handling, file processing, data structures and more.

📖 **Also available:** *C++ in the Lab, Fourth Edition,* a lab manual designed to accompany this book. Use ISBN 0-13-038478-X to order. A Student Solutions Manual is available for use with this text. Use ISBN 0-13-142578-1 to order.

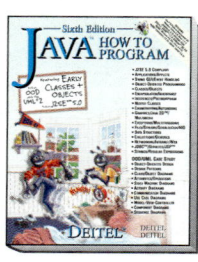

Java™ How to Program Sixth Edition

BOOK / CD-ROM

©2005, 1500 pp., paper
(0-13-148398-6)

The complete authoritative DEITEL® *LIVE-CODE* introduction to programming with the new Java™ 2 Platform Standard Edition 5.0! New early classes and early objects approach. *Java How to Program, Sixth Edition* is up-to-date with J2SE™ 5.0 and includes comprehensive coverage of the fundamentals of object-oriented programming in Java; a new interior design including new colors, new fonts, new design elements and more; and a new optional automated teller machine (ATM) case study that teaches the fundamentals of software engineering and object oriented design with the UML in Chapters 1-8 and 10. Additional integrated case studies appear throughout the text, including GUI and graphics (Chapters 3-12), the **Time** class (Chapter 8), the **Employee** class (Chapters 9 and 10) and the **GradeBook** class in Chapters 3-8. New J2SE 5.0 topics covered included input/output, enhanced **for** loop, autoboxing, generics, new collections APIs and more.

📖 **Also available:** *Java in the Lab, Sixth Edition,* a lab manual designed to accompany this book. Use ISBN 0-13-149497-X. A Student Solutions Manual is available for this text. Use ISBN 0-13-149500-3 to order.

Small Java™ How to Program, Sixth Edition

BOOK / CD-ROM

©2005, 700 pp., paper
(0-13-148660-8)

Based on chapters 1-10 of *Java™ How to Program, Sixth Edition*, *Small Java* is up-to-date with J2SE™ 5.0, features a new early classes and early objects approach and comprehensive coverage of the fundamentals of object-oriented programming in Java. Key topics include applications, variables, data types, control statements, methods, arrays, object-based programming, inheritance and polymorphism.

📖 **Also available:** A *Student Solutions Manual* for use with this book. Use ISBN 0-13-148661-6 to order.

C How to Program
Fourth Edition

BOOK / CD-ROM

©2004, 1255 pp., paper
(0-13-142644-3)

C How to Program, Fourth Edition—the world's best-selling C text—is designed for introductory through intermediate courses as well as programming languages survey courses. This comprehensive text is aimed at readers with little or no programming experience through intermediate audiences. Highly practical in approach, it introduces fundamental notions of structured programming and software engineering and gets up to speed quickly.

A Student Solutions Manual is also available is for use with this text. Use ISBN 0-13-145245-2 to order.

Getting Started with Microsoft® Visual C++™ 6 with an Introduction to MFC

BOOK / CD-ROM

©2000, 163 pp., paper
(0-13-016147-0)

Visual C++ .NET®
How To Program

BOOK / CD-ROM

©2004, 1400 pp., paper
(0-13-437377-4)

Written by the authors of the world's best-selling introductory/intermediate C and C++ textbooks, this comprehensive book thoroughly examines Visual C++® .NET. *Visual C++® .NET How to Program* begins with a strong foundation in the introductory and intermediate programming principles students will need in industry, including fundamental topics such as arrays, functions and control statements. Readers learn the concepts of object-oriented programming. The text then explores such essential topics as networking, databases, XML and multimedia. Graphical user interfaces are also extensively covered, giving students the tools to build compelling and fully interactive programs using the "drag-and-drop" techniques provided by Visual Studio .NET 2003.

Advanced Java™ 2 Platform How to Program

BOOK / CD-ROM

©2002, 1811 pp., paper
(0-13-089560-1)

Expanding on the world's best-selling Java textbook—*Java™ How to Program*—*Advanced Java™ 2 Platform How To Program* presents advanced Java topics for developing sophisticated, user-friendly GUIs; significant, scalable enterprise applications; wireless applications and distributed systems. Primarily based on Java 2 Enterprise Edition (J2EE), this textbook integrates technologies such as XML, JavaBeans, security, JDBC™, JavaServer Pages (JSP™), servlets, Remote Method Invocation (RMI), Enterprise JavaBeans™ (EJB), design patterns, Swing, J2ME™, Java 2D and 3D, XML, design patterns, CORBA, Jini™, JavaSpaces™, Jiro™, Java Management Extensions (JMX) and Peer-to-Peer networking with an introduction to JXTA.

C# How to Program

BOOK / CD-ROM

©2002, 1568 pp., paper
(0-13-062221-4)

C# How to Program provides a comprehensive introduction to Microsoft's C# object-oriented language. C# enables students to create powerful Web applications and components—ranging from XML-based Web services on Microsoft's .NET platform to middle-tier business objects and system-level applications. *C# How to Program* begins with a strong foundation in the introductory- and intermediate-programming principles students will need in industry. It then explores such essential topics as object-oriented programming and exception handling. Graphical user interfaces are extensively covered, giving readers the tools to build compelling and fully interactive programs. Internet technologies such as XML, ADO .NET and Web services are covered as well as topics including regular expressions, multithreading, networking, databases, files and data structures.

Visual Basic® .NET How to Program
Second Edition

BOOK / CD-ROM

©2002, 1400 pp., paper
(0-13-029363-6)

Learn Visual Basic .NET programming from the ground up! This book provides a comprehensive introduction to Visual Basic .NET—featuring extensive updates and increased functionality. *Visual Basic .NET How to Program, Second Edition* covers introductory programming techniques as well as more advanced topics, featuring enhanced treatment of developing Web-based applications. Other topics discussed include XML and wireless applications, databases, SQL and ADO .NET, Web forms, Web services and ASP .NET.

Internet & World Wide Web How to Program
Third Edition

BOOK / CD-ROM

©2004, 1250 pp., paper
(0-13-145091-3)

This book introduces students with little or no programming experience to the exciting world of Web-based applications. This text provides in-depth coverage of introductory programming principles, various markup languages (XHTML, Dynamic HTML and XML), several scripting languages (JavaScript, JScript .NET, ColdFusion, Flash ActionScript, Perl, PHP, VBScript and Python), Web servers (IIS and Apache) and relational databases (MySQL)—all the skills and tools needed to create dynamic Web-based applications. The text contains a comprehensive introduction to ASP .NET and the Microsoft .NET Framework. A case study illustrating how to build an online message board using ASP .NET and XML is also included. New in this edition are chapters on Macromedia ColdFusion, Macromedia Dreamweaver and a much enhanced treatment of Flash, including a case study on building a video game in Flash. After mastering the material in this book, students will be well prepared to build real-world, industrial-strength, Web-based applications.

Wireless Internet & Mobile Business How to Program

©2002, 1292 pp., paper
(0-13-062226-5)

This book offers a thorough treatment of both the management and technical aspects of this growing area, including coverage of current practices and future trends. The first half explores the business issues surrounding wireless technology and mobile business. The book then turns to programming for the wireless Internet, exploring topics such as WAP (including 2.0), WML, WMLScript, XML, XHTML™, wireless Java programming (J2ME™) and more. Other topics covered include career resources, wireless marketing, accessibility, Palm™, PocketPC, Windows CE, i-mode, Bluetooth, MIDP, MIDlets, ASP, Microsoft .NET Mobile Framework, BREW™, multimedia, Flash™ and VBScript.

Python How to Program

BOOK / CD-ROM

©2002, 1376 pp., paper
(0-13-092361-3)

This exciting textbook provides a comprehensive introduction to Python—a powerful object-oriented programming language with clear syntax and the ability to bring together various technologies quickly and easily. This book covers introductory-programming techniques and more advanced topics such as graphical user interfaces, databases, wireless Internet programming, networking, security, process management, multithreading, XHTML, CSS, PSP and multimedia. Readers will learn principles that are applicable to both systems development and Web programming.

e-Business & e-Commerce for Managers

©2001, 794 pp., cloth
(0-13-032364-0)

This comprehensive overview of building and managing e-businesses explores topics such as the decision to bring a business online, choosing a business model, accepting payments, marketing strategies and security, as well as many other important issues (such as career resources). The book features Web resources and online demonstrations that supplement the text and direct readers to additional materials. The book also includes an appendix that develops a complete Web-based shopping-cart application using HTML, JavaScript, VBScript, Active Server Pages, ADO, SQL, HTTP, XML and XSL. Plus, company-specific sections provide "real-world" examples of the concepts presented in the book.

XML How to Program

BOOK / CD-ROM

©2001, 934 pp., paper (0-13-028417-3)

This book is a comprehensive guide to programming in XML. It teaches how to use XML to create customized tags and includes chapters that address markup languages for science and technology, multimedia, commerce and many other fields. Concise introductions to Java, JavaServer Pages, VBScript, Active Server Pages and Perl/CGI provide readers with the essentials of these programming languages and server-side development technologies to enable them to work effectively with XML. The book also covers topics such as XSL, DOM™, SAX, a real-world e-commerce case study and a complete chapter on Web accessibility that addresses Voice XML. Other topics covered include XHTML, CSS, DTD, schema, parsers, XPath, XLink, namespaces, XBase, XInclude, XPointer, XSLT, XSL Formatting Objects, JavaServer Pages, XForms, topic maps, X3D, MathML, OpenMath, CML, BML, CDF, RDF, SVG, Cocoon, WML, XBRL and BizTalk™ and SOAP™ Web resources.

Perl How to Program

BOOK / CD-ROM

©2001, 1057 pp., paper (0-13-028418-1)

This comprehensive guide to Perl programming emphasizes the use of the Common Gateway Interface (CGI) with Perl to create powerful, dynamic multi-tier Web-based client/server applications. The book begins with a clear and careful introduction to programming concepts at a level suitable for beginners, and proceeds through advanced topics such as references and complex data structures. Key Perl topics such as regular expressions and string manipulation are covered in detail. The authors address important and topical issues such as object-oriented programming, the Perl database interface (DBI), graphics and security. Also included is a treatment of XML, a bonus chapter introducing the Python programming language, supplemental material on career resources and a complete chapter on Web accessibility.

e-Business & e-Commerce How to Program

BOOK / CD-ROM

©2001, 1254 pp., paper (0-13-028419-X)

This book explores programming technologies for developing Web-based e-business and e-commerce solutions, and covers e-business and e-commerce models and business issues. Readers learn a full range of options, from "build-your-own" to turnkey solutions. The book examines scores of the top e-businesses (examples include Amazon, eBay, Priceline, Travelocity, etc.), explaining the technical details of building successful e-business and e-commerce sites and their underlying business premises. Learn how to implement the dominant e-commerce models—shopping carts, auctions, name-your-own-price, comparison shopping and bots/intelligent agents—by using markup languages (HTML, Dynamic HTML and XML), scripting languages (JavaScript, VBScript and Perl), server-side technologies (Active Server Pages and Perl/CGI) and database (SQL and ADO), security and online payment technologies.

Visual Basic® 6 How to Program

BOOK / CD-ROM

©1999, 1015 pp., paper (0-13-456955-5)

www·deitel·com   www·prenhall·com/deitel

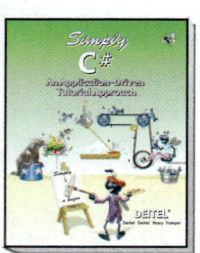

The DEITEL® DEVELOPER SERIES!

Deitel & Associates is recognized worldwide for its best-selling *How to Program Series* of books for college and university students and its signature *LIVE-CODE Approach* to teaching programming languages. Now, for the first time, Deitel & Associates brings its proven teaching methods to a series of books specifically designed for professionals.

THREE TYPES OF BOOKS FOR THREE DISTINCT AUDIENCES

> A Technical Introduction

A Technical Introduction books provide programmers, technical managers, project managers and other technical professionals with introductions to broad new technology areas.

> A Programmer's Introduction

A Programmer's Introduction books offer focused treatments of programming fundamentals for practicing programmers. These books are also appropriate for novices.

> For Experienced Programmers

For Experienced Programmers books are for experienced programmers who want a detailed treatment of a programming language or technology. These books contain condensed introductions to programming language fundamentals and provide extensive intermediate level coverage of high-end topics.

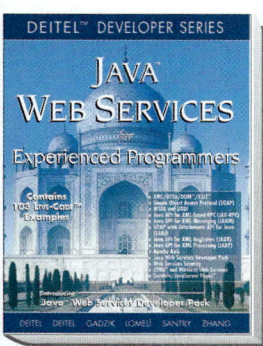

Java™ Web Services for Experienced Programmers

©2003, 700 pp., paper (0-13-046134-2)

Java™ Web Services for Experienced Programmers covers industry standards including XML, SOAP, WSDL and UDDI. Learn how to build and integrate Web services using the Java API for XML RPC, the Java API for XML Messaging, Apache Axis and the Java Web Services Developer Pack. Develop and deploy Web services on several major Web services platforms. Register and discover Web services through public registries and the Java API for XML Registries. Build Web services clients for several platforms, including J2ME. Significant Web services case studies also are included.

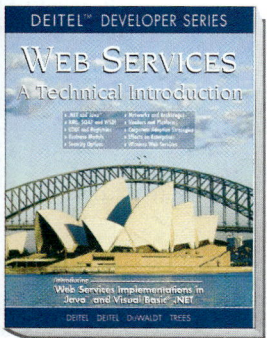

Web Services: A Technical Introduction

©2003, 400 pp., paper (0-13-046135-0)

Web Services: A Technical Introduction familiarizes programmers, technical managers and project managers with key Web services concepts, including what Web services are and why they are revolutionary. The book covers the business case for Web services—the underlying technologies, ways in which Web services can provide competitive advantages and opportunities for Web services-related lines of business. Readers learn the latest Web-services standards, including XML, SOAP, WSDL and UDDI; learn about Web services implementations in .NET and Java; benefit from an extensive comparison of Web services products and vendors; and read about Web services security options. Although this is not a programming book, the appendices show .NET and Java code examples to demonstrate the structure of Web services applications and documents. In addition, the book includes numerous case studies describing ways in which organizations are implementing Web services to increase efficiency, simplify business processes, create new revenue streams and interact better with partners and customers.

Convenience. Simplicity. Success.

Powered by CourseCompass, Blackboard and WebCT.

OneKey is Prentice Hall's exclusive new resource for instructors and students. OneKey gives you access to the best online teaching and learning tools—all available 24 hours a day, 7 days a week. OneKey means all your resources are in one place for maximum convenience, simplicity and success.

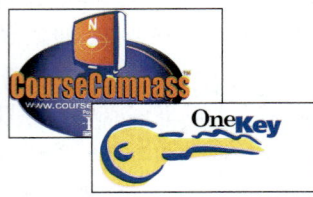 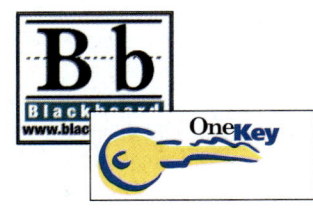 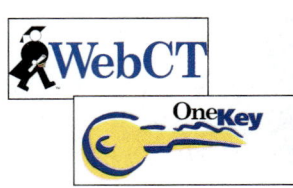

Convenience—Prepare more effectively, present more dramatically and assess more easily. All our best online resources have been combined into one easy-to-use site. Also, an abundance of searchable presentation material together with practice activities and test questions—all organized by chapter or topic—make course preparation easy.

Simplicity—With OneKey there is no longer any need for instructors or students to go to multiple Web sites to find the resources they need. All of our best resources can be accessed with one simple login.

Success—Thousands of test questions—in multiple formats—let instructors create and assign tests for automatic grading. More review and assessment tools let students practice, explore on their own or create study programs to fit their own personal learning style. OneKey is all you and your students need to succeed.

Additional features of CourseCompass, Blackboard and WebCT

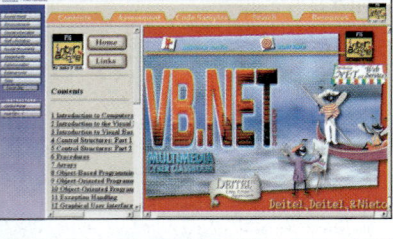

Intuitive Browser-Based Interface

Your students will love our browser-based interface, designed to be user-friendly and easily accessible.

Our use of full-text searching and hyperlinking makes it easy to navigate.

Further Enhancements to the DEITEL® Signature LIVE-CODE Approach

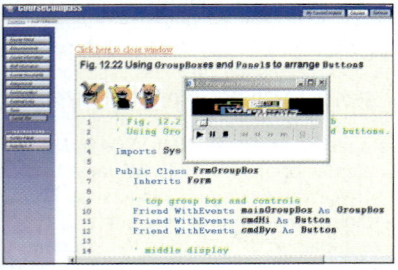

Coming in Spring 2005! New full-feature OneKey course for Java How to Program, 6/e.

Hours of detailed, expert audio descriptions of thousands of lines of code help reinforce concepts. OneKey includes an innovative learning environment for your introductory programming students called CodeKey. CodeKey allows your students to run and modify the programming projects at the end of each chapter, and provides them with meaningful feedback about the structure and function of their programs. Additionally, you can use CodeKey for submission of programming projects for course credit within the OneKey environment.

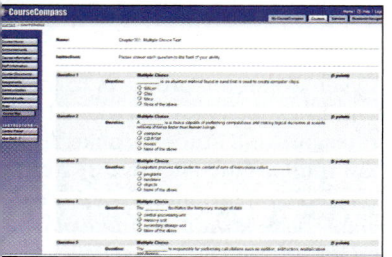
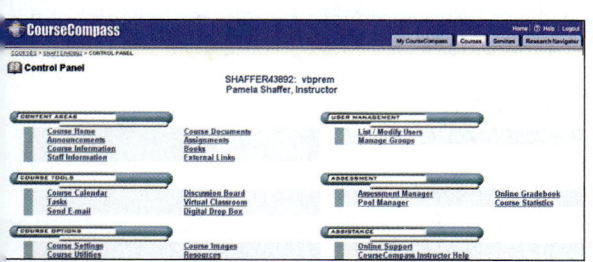

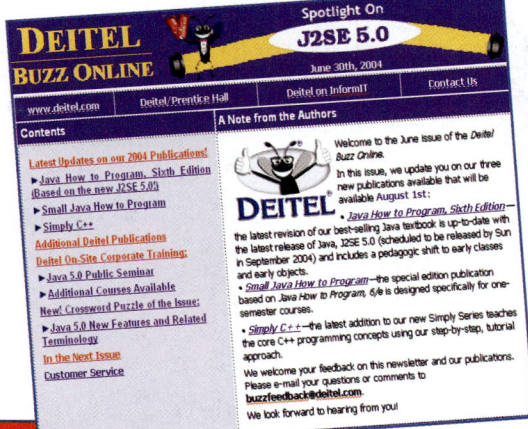
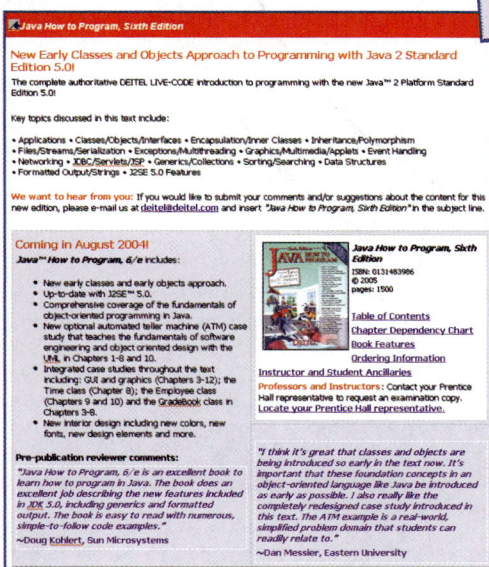

Deitel & Associates, Inc. provides intensive, lecture-and-laboratory courses to organizations worldwide. The programming courses use our signature *Live-Code Approach*, presenting complete working programs.

Deitel & Associates, Inc. has trained over one million students and professionals worldwide through Dive Into Series™ corporate training courses, public seminars, university teaching, *How to Program Series* textbooks, *Deitel® Developer Series* books, *Simply Series* textbooks, *Cyber Classroom Series* multimedia packages, *Complete Training Course Series* textbook and multimedia packages, broadcast-satellite courses and Web-based training.

Educational Consulting

Deitel & Associates, Inc. offers complete educational consulting services for corporate training programs and professional schools including:

- Curriculum design and development
- Preparation of Instructor Guides
- Customized courses and course materials
- Design and implementation of professional training certificate programs
- Instructor certification
- Train-the-trainers programs
- Delivery of software-related corporate training programs

Visit our Web site for more information on our Dive Into™ Series corporate training curriculum and to purchase our training products.

www.deitel.com/training

Would you like to review upcoming publications?

If you are a professor or senior industry professional interested in being a reviewer of our forthcoming publications, please contact us by email at **deitel@deitel.com**. Insert "Content Reviewer" in the subject heading.

Are you interested in a career in computer education, publishing and training?

We offer a limited number of full-time positions available for college graduates in computer science, information systems, information technology and management information systems. Please check our Web site for the latest job postings or contact us by email at **deitel@deitel. com**. Insert "Full-time Job" in the subject heading.

Are you a Boston-area college student looking for an internship?

We have a limited number of competitive summer positions and 20-hr./week school-year opportunities for computer science, IT/IS and MIS majors. Students work at our worldwide headquarters west of Boston. We also offer full-time internships for students taking a semester off from school. This is an excellent opportunity for students looking to gain industry experience and earn money to pay for school. Please contact us by email at **deitel@deitel.com**. Insert "Internship" in the subject heading.

Would you like to explore contract training opportunities with us?

Deitel & Associates, Inc. is looking for contract instructors to teach software-related topics at our clients' sites in the United States and worldwide. Applicants should be experienced professional trainers or college professors. For more information, please visit **www.deitel.com** and send your resume to Abbey Deitel at **abbey.deitel@deitel.com**.

Are you a training company in need of quality course materials?

Corporate training companies worldwide use our *How to Program Series* textbooks, *Complete Training Course Series* book and multimedia packages, *Simply Series* textbooks and our *Deitel® Developer Series* books in their classes. We have extensive ancillary instructor materials for many of our products. For more details, please visit **www.deitel.com** or contact us by email at **deitel@deitel.com**.

License Agreement and Limited Warranty

Using the CD-ROM

The interface to the contents of this CD is designed to start automatically through the **AUTORUN.EXE** file. If a startup screen does not pop up automatically when you insert the CD into your computer, double click on the welcome.htm file to launch the Student CD or refer to the file **readme.txt** on the CD.

Contents of the CD-ROM

- Java™ 2 Platform Development Kit, Standard Edition Version 5.0
- BlueJ Version 1.3.5
- JCreator™ LE Version 3.10 (Windows Only)
- jEdit Version 4.1
- jGRASP Version 1.7.0
- NetBeans™ IDE Version 3.6
- Live code examples from the book *Small Java™ How to Program, 6th Edition*
- Web Resources -- Links to internet sites mentioned in the book *Small Java™ How to Program, 6th Edition*
- MySQL® Version 4.0.20
- MySQL® Connector/J Version 3.0.14
- Apache Tomcat Version 5.0.25
- Additional material (in the Abobe® Acrobat® PDF format) not included in the book

Software and Hardware System Requirements

- 500 MHz (minimum) Pentium III or faster processor
- Microsoft® Windows® XP (with Service Pack 2), Windows XP Home, Windows 2000 Professional (with Service Pack 4), Windows 98 (1st and 2nd Editions), Windows ME, Windows Server 2003, or
- One of the following Linux distributions: Red Hat 9.0, SuSE 8.2, or TurboLinux 8.0
- 256 MB of RAM (minimum), 512 MB of RAM (recommended)
- CD-ROM drive
- Internet connection
- Web browser, Adobe® Acrobat® Reader® and a Zip decompression utility